The complete guide, thoroughly up-to-date

Packed with details that will make your trip

The must-see sights, off and on the beaten path

What to see, what to skip

Mix-and-match vacation itineraries

City strolls, countryside adventures

Smart lodging and dining options

Essential local do's and taboos

Transportation tips, distances and directions

Key contacts, savvy travel tips

When to go, what to pack

Clear, accurate, easy-to-use maps

Fodor's Travel Publications, Inc.
New York • Toronto • London • Sydney • Auckland
www.fodors.com

Fodor's US[illegible]

[illegible] chrane, An- d[illegible] ngin, Anas- t[illegible] editor)
[illegible]
[illegible] Bob Blake, *m[illegible]*
Design: Fabrizio La Rocca, *creative director*; Guido Caroti, *associate art director*; Jolie Novak, *photo editor*
Production/Manufacturing: Mike Costa
Cover Photograph: Richard Nowitz

Copyright

ISBN 0-679-00145-X

Special Sales

Fodor's Travel Publications are available at special discounts for bulk purchases for sales promotions or premiums. Special editions, including personalized covers, excerpts of existing guides, and corporate imprints, can be created in large quantities for special needs. For more information, contact your local bookseller or write to Special Markets, Fodor's Travel Publications, 201 East 50th Street, New York, NY 10022. Inquiries from Canada should be directed to your local Canadian bookseller or sent to Random House of Canada, Ltd., Marketing Department, 2775 Matheson Boulevard East, Mississauga, Ontario L4W 4P7. Inquiries from the United Kingdom should be sent to Fodor's Travel Publications, 20 Vauxhall Bridge Road, London SW1V 2SA, England.

PRINTED IN THE UNITED STATES OF AMERICA

10 9 8 7 6 5 4 3 2 1

CONTENTS

Italic entries are maps.

4 The Middle Atlantic States 195

5 The Southeast 319

6 The Mississippi Valley 445

ON THE ROAD WITH FODOR'S

WHEN I PLAN A VACATION, the first thing I do is cast around among my friends to find someone who's just been where I'm going. Unfortunately, such friends are few and far between. So it's nice to know that there's *Fodor's USA '99*, a book that's written and updated by people you would hit up for travel tips if you knew them. In addition to sound advice, *Fodor's USA '99* includes a full-color map from Rand McNally, the world's largest commercial mapmaker. Just tear out the map, and join us on the road through the USA.

Connections

We're pleased that the American Society of Travel Agents continues to endorse Fodor's as its guidebook of choice. ASTA is the world's largest and most influential travel trade association, operating in more than 170 countries, with 27,000 members pledged to adhere to a strict code of ethics reflecting the Society's motto, "Integrity in Travel." ASTA shares Fodor's devotion to providing smart, honest travel information and advice to travelers, and we've long recommended that our readers—even those who have guidebooks and traveling friends—consult ASTA member agents for the experience and professionalism they bring to your vacation planning.

On Fodor's Web site (www.fodors.com), check out the Resource Center, an online companion to the Gold Guide section of this book, complete with hot links to related sites. In our forums, you get advice from other travelers and tips from Fodor's experts worldwide.

FODOR'S CHOICE

We hope you'll have a chance to experience Fodor's choices yourself while traveling in the U.S. For detailed information about each entry, refer to the appropriate chapters in this guidebook.

Natural Wonders

Northeast

Niagara Falls (NY)

Mid-Atlantic

Delaware Water Gap (PA/NJ)

Natural Bridge (Natural Bridge, VA)

Southeast

Everglades (FL)

Okefenokee (GA)

Mississippi Valley

Buffalo National River (AR)

Mammoth Cave (KY)

Bayou Teche (Acadiana, LA)

Midwest

Pictured Rocks National Lakeshore (Munising, MI)

Boundary Waters Canoe Area Wilderness (MN)

Apostle Islands National Lakeshore (WI)

Great Plains

Badlands (ND/SD)

Southwest

Grand Canyon (AZ)

Palo Duro Canyon (TX)

Rockies

Bryce and Zion canyons (UT)

Glacier National Park (MT)

Old Faithful Geyser (Yellowstone, WY)

West Coast

El Capitan and Half Dome (Yosemite National Park, CA)

Joshua Tree National Park (CA)

Muir Woods (Mill Valley, CA)

Crater Lake (OR)

Hoh Rain Forest (Olympic Peninsula, WA)

Pacific

Mt. McKinley (AK)

Kilauea Volcano (The Big Island, HI)

Historic Buildings and Sites

Northeast

African Meeting House (Boston, MA)

Bunker Hill (Boston, MA)

Old North Church (Boston, MA)

Historic Deerfield (Deerfield, MA)

Plimoth Plantation (Plymouth, MA)

Ellis Island (New York, NY)

Statue of Liberty (New York, NY)

Hunter House (Newport, RI)

Mid-Atlantic

Antietam National Battlefield (Sharpsburg, MD)

Washington Crossing State Park (Titusville, NJ)

Independence National Historical Park (Philadelphia, PA)

Gettysburg National Military Park (Gettysburg, PA)

Monticello (Charlottesville, VA)

Washington Monument (Washington, DC)

Frederick Douglass National Historic Site (Washington, DC)

Vietnam Memorial (Washington, DC)

The White House (Washington, DC)

Harper's Ferry National Park (Harper's Ferry, WV)

Southeast

Civil Rights Memorial (Montgomery, AL)

Birmingham Civil Rights Institute (Birmingham, AL)

Art Deco District (Miami Beach, FL)

Andersonville National Historic Site (Andersonville, GA)

Johnston-Hay House (Macon, GA)

Old Salem (Winston-Salem, NC)

Wright Brothers National Memorial (Kill Devil Hills, NC)

Biltmore House (Asheville, NC)

Ft. Sumter National Monument (Charleston, SC)

Drayton Hall (Charleston, SC)

Mississippi Valley

Old State House (Little Rock, AR)

Old Washington Historic State Park (Washington, AR)

Shaker Village of Pleasant Hill (Harrodsburg, KY)

Old Ursuline Convent (New Orleans, LA)

Rosalie (Natchez, MS)

Midwest

Sears Tower (Chicago, IL)

Pabst Mansion (Milwaukee, WI)

George Rogers Clark National Historical Park (Vincennes, IN)

Great Plains

George Washington Carver National Monument (MO)

Liberty Memorial (Kansas City, MO)

Mt. Rushmore National Memorial (SD)

Southwest

Mission Ysleta (near El Paso, TX)

The Alamo (San Antonio, TX)

Palace of the Governors (Santa Fe, NM)

Rockies

Little Bighorn Battlefield National Monument (MT)

Mesa Verde National Park (CO)

Salt Lake Mormon Tabernacle and Temple (Salt Lake City, UT)

West Coast

Olvera Street (Los Angeles, CA)

Fort Clatsop National Memorial (Astoria, OR)

Hearst Castle (San Simeon, CA)

Sutter's Mill (Coloma, CA)

Pacific

'Iolani Palace (Honolulu, HI)

The Pacific Ketchikan Totem Parks (Ketchikan, AK)

Museums

Northeast

Wadsworth Atheneum (Hartford, CT)

Museum of Fine Arts (Boston, MA)

Isabella Stewart Gardner Museum (Boston, MA)

Hood Museum of Art (Hanover, NH)

Frick Collection (New York, NY)

Metropolitan Museum of Art (New York, NY)

Museum of Modern Art (New York, NY)

Mid-Atlantic

B&O Railroad Museum (Baltimore, MD)

Walters Art Gallery (Baltimore, MD)

Chesapeake Bay Maritime Museum (St. Michaels, MD)

Barnes Foundation (Philadelphia, PA)

Smithsonian Institution (Washington, DC)

Phillips Collection (Washington, DC)

Southeast

Ringling Museum of Art (Sarasota, FL)

Wolfsonian FIO Gallery (Miami Beach, FL)

Morris Museum of Art (Augusta, GA)

Museum of Early Southern Decorative Arts (Winston-Salem, NC)

Mississippi Valley

Louisville Slugger Museum (Louisville, KY)

Midwest
Walker Art Center (Minneapolis, MN)
Art Institute of Chicago (Chicago, IL)
Milwaukee Public Museum (Milwaukee, WI)

Great Plains
Mark Twain Home and Museum (Hannibal, MO)
Nelson-Atkins Museum of Art (Kansas City, MO)
Kansas City Jazz Museum (Kansas City, MO)

Southwest
Heard Museum (Phoenix, AZ)
Museum of International Folk Art (Santa Fe, NM)
Kimbell Art Museum (Fort Worth, TX)

Rockies
Buffalo Bill Historical Center (Cody, WY)
Museum of the Rockies (Bozeman, MT)

West Coast
San Francisco Museum of Modern Art (CA)
Los Angeles County Museum of Art (CA)
Seattle Art Museum (Seattle, WA)

Pacific
Alaska State Museum (Juneau, AK)

Neighborhoods

Northeast
Beacon Hill (Boston, MA)
Brooklyn Heights (New York, NY)

Mid-Atlantic
Fells Point (Baltimore, MD)
Victorian Cape May (Cape May, NJ)
Society Hill (Philadelphia, PA)
Old Town (Alexandria, VA)
Georgetown (Washington, DC)

Southeast
Coconut Grove (Miami Beach, FL)
South Beach (Miami Beach, FL)
Buckhead and Druid Hills (Atlanta, GA)

Mississippi Valley
Old Louisville (Louisville, KY)
French Quarter (New Orleans, LA)
Hodges Gardens (Many, LA)

Midwest
Lincoln Park (Chicago, IL)
Summit Avenue/Ramsey Hill (St. Paul, MN)
German Village (Columbus, OH)

Southwest
Plaza (Santa Fe, NM)
Deep Ellum (Dallas, TX)

West Coast
North Beach (San Francisco, CA)
Rodeo Drive (Beverly Hills, CA)
Nob Hill (Portland, OR)
Pioneer Square (Seattle, WA)

Parks and Gardens

Northeast
Acadia National Park (Bar Harbor, ME)
Public Garden (Boston, MA)
Central Park (New York, NY)

Mid-Atlantic
Winterthur Gardens (Winterthur, DE)
Sherwood Gardens (Baltimore, MD)
Longwood Gardens (Brandywine Valley, PA)
Dumbarton Oaks (Washington, DC)

Southeast
Bellingrath Gardens and Home (Mobile, AL)
Town squares (Savannah, GA)
Biltmore Estate Gardens (Asheville, NC)
Magnolia Plantation (Charleston, SC)
Middleton Place (Charleston, SC)

Mississippi Valley
Cheekwood–Tennessee Botanical Gardens and Museum of Art (Nashville, TN)

Midwest
Lincoln Park (Chicago, IL)

Great Plains
International Peace Garden (ND)
International Friendship Forest (Atchison, KS)

Southwest
Arizona–Sonora Desert Museum (Tucson, AZ)
Water Gardens Park (Fort Worth, TX)
Fair Park (Dallas, TX)
National Wildflower Research Center (Austin, TX)

West Coast
Golden Gate Park (San Francisco, CA)
Huntington Library, Art Collections, and Botanical Gardens (San Marino, CA)
Balboa Park (San Diego, CA)
Washington Park International Rose Test Garden and Japanese Gardens (Portland, OR)

Beaches

Northeast
Cape Cod National Seashore (MA)
Jones Beach (Long Island, NY)
Mansion Beach (Block Island, RI)

Mid-Atlantic
Assateague Island (MD/VA)
Island Beach State Park (NJ)

Southeast
Gulf State Park (AL)
Crandon Park (Miami, FL)
Grayton Beach State Recreation Area (Seaside, FL)
Cumberland Island National Seashore (GA)
Cape Hatteras National Seashore (NC)
Hilton Head Island (SC)

Mississippi Valley
Gulf Islands National Seashore (Ocean Springs, MS)

Midwest
Indiana Dunes National Lakeshore (IN)

Great Plains
Lake McConaughy State Recreation Area (NE)

Southwest
Lake Powell (AZ/UT)
Padre Island National Seashore (TX)

West Coast
Point Reyes National Seashore (CA)
Corona del Mar (CA)
Pismo State Beach (CA)
Cannon Beach (OR)

Pacific
Kauanoa Beach (The Big Island, HI)
Wailea's five crescent beaches (Maui, HI)

Theme Parks

Northeast
Coney Island (NY)

Mid-Atlantic
Adventure World (Mitchellville, MD)
Six Flags Great Adventure (Jackson, NJ)
Sesame Place (Langhorne, PA)

Southeast
Walt Disney World (Orlando, FL)

Mississippi Valley
Dollyland (Pigeon Forge, TN)

Midwest
Cedar Point Amusement Park (Sandusky, OH)

Great Plains
Silver Dollar City (Branson, MO)
Worlds of Fun (Kansas City, MO)

Southwest
Astroworld/Waterworld (Houston, TX)

West Coast
Disneyland (Anaheim, CA)
Universal Studios (Universal City, CA)

Pacific
Alaskaland Park (Fairbanks, AK)

Restaurants

Northeast
Hurricane (Ogunquit, ME; $$–$$$)
Lespinasse (New York, NY; $$$$)
Al Forno (Providence, RI; $$$)

Mid-Atlantic
Tio Pepe (Baltimore, MD; $$$–$$$$)
Le Bec-Fin (Philadelphia, PA; $$$$)
Meskerem (Washington, DC; $–$$)
Red Fox (Snowshoe, WV; $$$–$$$$)

Southeast
Highlands Bar & Grill (Birmingham, AL; $$–$$$)
Norman's (Coral Gables, FL; $$$–$$$$)
Louie's Back Yard (Key West, FL; $$$$)
Bacchanalia (Atlanta, GA; $$$–$$$$)
Elizabeth on 37th (Savannah, GA; $$$)

Mississippi Valley
Lilly's (Louisville, KY; $$–$$$)
Commander's Palace (New Orleans, LA; $$$$)
Nola (New Orleans, LA; $$–$$$)

Midwest
Charlie Trotter's (Chicago, IL; $$$$)
Lelli's Inn (Detroit, MI; $$)
Grenadier's (Milwaukee, WI; $$$)

Great Plains
Stroud's (Kansas City, MO; $$)
Mandan Drug (Mandan, ND; $)
Cattlemen's Steak House (Oklahoma City, OK; $$)

Southwest
Star Canyon (Dallas, TX; $$$–$$$$)
Cafe Annie (Houston, TX; $$$–$$$$)
Christopher's (Phoenix, AZ; $$$)

Rockies
Glitretind (Park City, UT; $$$$)
Strings (Denver, CO; $$–$$$)

West Coast
Postrio (San Francisco, CA; $$$-$$$$)
Campanile (Los Angeles, CA; $$$–$$$)

Pacific

The Double Musky (Anchorage, AK; $$$–$$$$)

A Pacific Café (Kaua'i, HI; $$$)

Hotels

Northeast

Fairmont Copley Plaza (Boston, MA; $$$$)

Charlotte Inn (Edgartown, MA; $$$$)

The Carlyle (New York, NY; $$$$)

The Mark (New York, NY; $$$$)

Castle Hill Inn and Resort (Newport, RI; $$$–$$$$)

Mid-Atlantic

Harbor Court (Baltimore, MD; $$$$)

The Homestead (Hot Springs, VA; $$$–$$$$)

Hay-Adams Hotel (Washington, DC; $$$$)

The Greenbrier (White Sulphur Springs, WV; $$$$)

Southeast

Delano Hotel (Miami Beach, FL; $$$$)

Ritz-Carlton, Buckhead (Atlanta, GA; $$$$)

Grove Park Inn (Asheville, NC; $$$–$$$$)

John Rutledge House Inn (Charleston, SC; $$$$)

Mississippi Valley

The Seelbach (Louisville, KY; $$–$$$)

Windsor Court Hotel (New Orleans, LA; $$$$)

Midwest

The Drake (Chicago, IL; $$$$)

Pfister Hotel (Milwaukee, WI; $$$–$$$$)

Great Plains

Island Guest Ranch (Ames, OK; $$$)

Southwest

The Boulders (Carefree, AZ; $$$$)

Menger Hotel (San Antonio, TX; $$$)

The Mansion on Turtle Creek (Dallas, TX; $$$$)

Rockies

Cliff Lodge at Snowbird Resort (Snowbird, UT; $$$–$$$$)

Oxford (Denver, CO; $$$–$$$$)

Old Faithful Inn (Yellowstone, WY; $–$$$$)

West Coast

Sherman House (San Francisco, CA; $$$$)

Ritz-Carlton Laguna Niguel (Dana Point, CA; $$$$)

Stephanie Inn (Cannon Beach, OR; $$$–$$$$)

The Heathman (Portland, OR; $$$$)

Pacific

Camp Denali (Denali National Park, AK; $$$$)

Princeville Hotel (Kaua'i, HI; $$$$)

How to Use This Book

Organization

Up front is the **Gold Guide,** an easy-to-use section arranged alphabetically by topic. Under each listing you'll find tips and information that will help you accomplish what you need to throughout the USA. You'll also find addresses and telephone numbers of organizations and companies that provide destination-related services and detailed information and publications.

The next chapter, **Special-Interest Vacations,** tells you the best places in the country to pursue your favorite hobby or sport. The **10 regional chapters** that follow begin with the Northeast and zigzag across the country to the Pacific. Each chapter introduction includes a list of that region's best festivals and seasonal events. Within each region, states are listed alphabetically; within each state are sections on the major cities, the popular tourist areas, and worthwhile but less-known destinations grouped together under the heading "Elsewhere in [state name]."

Icons and Symbols

★ Our special recommendations
✕ Restaurant
🏨 Lodging establishment
✕🏨 Lodging establishment whose restaurant warrants a special trip
⛺ Campgrounds
🦆 Good for kids (rubber duck)
☞ Sends you to another section of the guide for more information
✉ Address
☎ Telephone number
⏲ Opening and closing times
🎟 Admission prices (those we give apply to adults; substantially reduced fees are almost always available for children, students, and senior citizens)

Dining and Lodging

The restaurants and lodgings we list are the cream of the crop in each price range. Price categories are as follows:

For restaurants:

CHART 1	(A)	(B)
CATEGORY	MAJOR CITY OR RESORT*	OTHER AREAS*
$$$$	over $50	over $30
$$$	$30–$50	$20–$30
$$	$15–$30	$10–$20
$	under $15	under $10

**Rates are per person for a 3-course meal excluding drinks, tips, and taxes.*

For each region in this book, we specify which dining chart, A or B, applies. The B chart (Other Areas) has been used for all destinations listed under the heading "Elsewhere in [state name]."

For hotels:

CHART 2	(A)	(B)
CATEGORY	MAJOR CITY OR RESORT*	OTHER AREAS*
$$$$	over $200	over $100
$$$	$125–$200	$75–$100
$$	$75–$125	$50–$75
$	under $75	under $50

**Rates are for a standard double room for two, excluding tax and service charges.*

For each region in this book, we specify which lodging chart, A or B, applies. The B chart (Other Areas) has been used for all destinations listed under the heading "Elsewhere in [state name]."

We always list the facilities that are available—but we don't specify whether they cost extra: When pricing accommodations, always ask what's included.

Assume that hotels operate on the **European Plan** (EP, with no meals) unless we note that they use the **Full American Plan** (FAP, with all meals), the **Modified American Plan** (MAP, with breakfast and dinner daily), or the **Continental Plan** (CP, with a Continental breakfast daily), or that they serve a **Full breakfast.**

Hotel Facilities

We always list the facilities that are available—but we don't specify whether you'll be charged extra to use them: When pricing accommodations, always ask what's included. When you book a room, be sure to mention if you have a disability or are traveling with children, if you prefer a private bath or a certain type of bed, or if you have specific dietary needs or other concerns. Assume that all rooms have private baths unless noted otherwise.

Restaurant Reservations and Dress Codes

Reservations are always a good idea; we mention them only when they're essential or are not accepted. Book as far ahead as you can, and reconfirm as soon as you arrive. Unless otherwise noted, the restaurants listed are open daily for lunch and dinner. We mention dress only when men are required to wear a jacket or a jacket and tie. Look for an overview of local dining-out habits in the Gold Guide.

Credit Cards

The following abbreviations are used: **AE,** American Express; **D,** Discover; **DC,** Diners Club; **MC,** MasterCard; and **V,** Visa.

Don't Forget to Write

You can use this book in the confidence that all prices and opening times are based on information supplied to us at press time; Fodor's cannot accept responsibility for any errors. Time inevitably brings changes, so always confirm information when it matters—especially if you're making a detour to visit a specific place.

Were the restaurants we recommended as described? Did you find a museum we recommended a waste of time? Keeping a travel guide up-to-date is a big job, and we welcome your feedback. If you have complaints, we'll look into them and revise our entries when the facts warrant it. If you've discovered a special place that we haven't included, we'll pass the information along to our correspondents and have them check it out. So send us your thoughts via e-mail at editors@fodors.com (specifying the name of the book on the subject line) or on paper in care of the USA editors at Fodor's, 201 East 50th Street, New York, New York 10022. In the meantime, have a wonderful trip!

Karen Cure
Editorial Director

The United States

ONTARIO
CANADA
QUÉBEC
NEW BRUNSWICK
Fredericton
Québec
MAINE
Augusta
Montréal
Ottawa
Montpelier
VT.
Concord
N.H.
Boston
MASS.
R.I.
Providence
Albany
Hartford
CONN.
New York
N.J.
Trenton
Philadelphia
Dover
DEL.
MD.
Baltimore
Annapolis
Washington, D.C.
Richmond
Norfolk
VIRGINIA
WEST VIRGINIA
Charleston
NEW YORK
Hudson R.
PENNSYLVANIA
Harrisburg
Pittsburgh
Buffalo
Lake Ontario
Toronto
Lake Erie
Cleveland
Lake Huron
Lake Superior
Lake Michigan
MINNESOTA
Duluth
WISCONSIN
St. Paul
Minneapolis
Green Bay
Milwaukee
Lansing
Madison
Detroit
Chicago
IOWA
Des Moines
Omaha
ILLINOIS
Springfield
INDIANA
Indianapolis
OHIO
Columbus
Cincinnati
Frankfort
Louisville
St. Louis
Mississippi R.
Ohio R.
Topeka
Kansas City
Jefferson City
MISSOURI
KENTUCKY
Nashville
TENNESSEE
Tulsa
ARKANSAS
Memphis
Chattanooga
Little Rock
Tennessee R.
NORTH CAROLINA
Raleigh
Wilmington
Columbia
SOUTH CAROLINA
Savannah R.
Birmingham
Atlanta
GEORGIA
Savannah
MISSISSIPPI
Montgomery
ALABAMA
Jackson
Jacksonville
Mobile
Tallahassee
Baton Rouge
New Orleans
FLORIDA
Orlando
Houston
LOUISIANA
Tampa/ St. Petersburg
Miami
Bahama Islands
Nassau
ATLANTIC OCEAN
Gulf of Mexico
N
0
500 miles
0
800 km

Amtrak Rail Passenger System

CANADA
MAINE
MINNESOTA
Detroit Lakes
St. Cloud
WISCONSIN
neapolis/ St. Paul
Red Wing
Winona
Montréal
St. Albans
Burlington-Essex Junction
Montpelier
Rouses Point
Plattsburgh
Fort Edward/Glens Falls
VT.
N.H.
Brattleboro
Boston
MASS.
Providence
R.I.
New London
CONN.
NEW YORK
Syracuse
Schenectady
Rochester
Springfield
Albany
Hartford
New Haven
Buffalo
Port Huron
Grand Rapids
Detroit
Milwaukee
Battle Creek
Toledo
Cleveland
PENNSYLVANIA
New York City
Harrisburg
Philadelphia
N.J.
Atlantic City
Wilmington
Johnstown
IOWA
Chicago
Omaha
Ottumwa
Galesburg
Burlington
South Bend
Pittsburgh
OHIO
Cumberland
MD
Baltimore
DEL.
Washington, D.C.
ILLINOIS
Springfield
Quincy
Indianapolis
INDIANA
Cincinnati
W. VA.
Charleston
Staunton
Charlottesville
Richmond
Newport News
VA.
Topeka
St. Louis
Kansas City
Jefferson City
Maysville
Huntington
White Sulphur Springs
Petersburg
Lynchburg
Danville
Centralia
Carbondale
KENTUCKY
Greensboro
Durham
Raleigh
Selma
ton
MISSOURI
Poplar Bluff
Salisbury
TENNESSEE
Charlotte
NORTH CAROLINA
Dyersburg
Spartanburg
Greenville
Florence
MA
ARKANSAS
Memphis
Columbia
Little Rock
Gainesville
SOUTH CAROLINA
Charleston
Birmingham
Atlanta
Anniston
ATLANTIC OCEAN
Greenwood
Texarkana
MISSISSIPPI
Tuscaloosa
GEORGIA
Dallas
Meridian
Savannah
Jackson
ALABAMA
Jessup
Laurel
Jacksonville
McComb
Mobile
Tallahassee
Hammond
Pensacola
Ocala
DeLand
Beaumont
Lafayette
FLORIDA
Orlando
Lake Charles
New Orleans
Walt Disney World
Houston
LOUISIANA
Tampa
Okeechobee
St. Petersburg
West Palm Beach
Fort Lauderdale
Miami
Gulf of Mexico
N
0
500 miles
0
800 km

Mileages Between Major U.S. Cities

	Albuquerque	Atlanta	Boston	Chicago	Cincinnati	Cleveland	Dallas	Denver	Houston	Kansas City	Los An
Albuquerque	—	1409	2225	1343	1402	1608	666	446	876	818	790
Atlanta	1409	—	1105	703	466	715	791	1404	800	801	2199
Boston	2225	1105	—	1018	861	657	1765	2006	1857	1414	3007
Chicago	1343	703	1018	—	296	365	940	1013	1107	511	2014
Cincinnati	1402	466	861	296	—	249	943	1195	1079	592	2192
Cleveland	1608	715	657	365	249	—	1193	1354	1328	797	2355
Dallas	666	791	1765	940	943	1193	—	825	241	523	1440
Denver	446	1404	2006	1013	1195	1354	825	—	1075	606	1004
Houston	876	800	1857	1107	1079	1328	241	1075	—	764	1545
Kansas City	818	801	1414	511	592	797	523	606	764	—	1610
Los Angeles	790	2199	3007	2014	2192	2355	1440	1004	1545	1610	—
Memphis	1004	401	1309	533	487	736	456	1113	592	474	1798
Miami	2009	695	1524	1388	1149	1251	1342	2088	1215	1485	2759
Minneapolis	1255	1121	1435	417	713	782	962	916	1202	437	1889
New Orleans	1178	473	1529	928	818	1067	511	1273	350	842	1894
New York	2002	878	226	814	634	463	1538	1802	1630	1192	2803
Orlando	1770	446	1314	1149	912	1041	1104	1850	976	1247	2521
Philadelphia	1949	779	326	798	581	437	1462	1742	1554	1139	2738
Phoenix	463	1859	2687	1805	1865	2071	1068	832	1173	1280	372
Portland, OR	1411	2599	3046	2126	2370	2466	2009	1241	2205	1796	963
St. Louis	1050	555	1175	293	352	558	647	852	819	249	1840
Salt Lake	646	1876	2396	1403	1647	1743	1290	518	1500	1073	689
San Francisco	1095	2505	3125	2132	2376	2472	1761	1247	1923	1802	381
Seattle	1463	2651	3085	2067	2328	2432	2117	1293	2274	1848	1136
Washington, DC	1875	641	462	733	488	377	1323	1649	1415	1045	2665

Memphis	Miami	Minneapolis	New Orleans	New York	Orlando	Philadelphia	Phoenix	Portland, OR	St. Louis	Salt Lake	San Francisco	Seattle	Washington, DC
1008	2009	1255	1178	2002	1770	1949	463	1411	1050	646	1095	1463	1875
401	685	1121	473	878	446	779	1859	2599	555	1876	2505	2651	641
1309	1524	1435	1529	226	1314	326	2687	3046	1175	2396	3125	3085	462
533	1388	417	928	814	1149	798	1805	2126	293	1403	2132	2067	733
487	1149	713	818	634	912	581	1865	2370	352	1647	2376	2328	488
736	1251	782	1067	453	1041	437	2071	2466	558	1743	2472	2432	377
456	1342	962	511	1538	1104	1462	1068	2009	647	1290	1761	2177	1323
1113	2088	916	1273	1802	1850	1742	832	1241	852	518	1247	1293	1649
592	1215	1202	350	1630	976	1554	1173	2205	819	1500	1923	2274	1415
474	1485	437	842	1192	1247	1139	1280	1796	249	1073	1802	1848	1045
1798	2759	1889	1894	2803	2521	2738	372	963	1840	689	381	1136	2665
—	1045	848	398	1082	807	1006	1471	2276	286	1553	2104	2328	867
1045	—	1805	887	1298	245	1203	2387	3284	1239	2561	3137	3336	1066
848	1805	—	1243	1231	1567	1215	1718	1737	575	1264	1994	1651	1150
398	887	1243	—	1302	649	1226	1512	2505	681	1802	2272	2574	1087
1082	1298	1231	1302	—	1088	95	2465	2915	952	2192	2921	2881	237
807	245	1567	649	1088	—	994	2149	3046	1061	2322	2899	3098	856
1006	1203	1215	1226	95	994	—	2412	2899	899	2176	2905	2751	142
1471	2387	1718	1512	2465	2149	2412	—	1333	1513	673	750	1489	2337
2276	3284	1737	2505	2915	3046	2899	1333	—	2048	765	634	173	2835
286	1239	575	681	952	1061	899	1513	2048	—	1324	2054	2100	806
1553	2561	1264	1802	2192	2322	2176	673	765	1324	—	735	817	2111
2104	3137	1994	2272	2921	2899	2905	750	634	2054	735	—	807	2841
2328	3336	1651	2574	2881	3098	2751	1489	173	2100	817	807	—	2800
867	1066	1150	1087	237	856	142	2337	2835	806	2111	2841	2800	—

1 The Gold Guide

Smart Travel Tips A to Z

Basic Information on Traveling in the United States, Savvy Tips to Make Your Trip a Breeze, and Companies and Organizations to Contact

SMART TRAVEL TIPS A TO Z

AIR TRAVEL

BOOKING YOUR FLIGHT

Price is just one factor to consider when booking a flight: frequency of service and even a carrier's safety record are often just as important. Major airlines offer the greatest number of departures. Smaller airlines—including regional and no-frills airlines—usually have a limited number of flights daily. On the other hand, so-called low-cost airlines usually are cheaper, and their fares impose fewer restrictions, such as advance-purchase requirements. Safety-wise, low-cost carriers as a group have a good history—about equal to that of major carriers.

When you book, **look for nonstop flights** and **remember that "direct" flights stop at least once.** Try to **avoid connecting flights,** which require a change of plane. Two airlines may jointly operate a connecting flight, so ask if your airline operates every segment—you may find that your preferred carrier flies you only part of the way.

Ask your airline if it offers electronic ticketing, which eliminates all paperwork. There's no ticket to pick up or misplace. You go directly to the gate and give the agent your confirmation number—a blessing if you've lost your ticket or made last-minute changes in travel plans. There's no worry about waiting on line at the airport while precious minutes tick by.

CARRIERS

➤ MAJOR AIRLINES: **Air Canada** (☎ 800/776–3000). **Alaska** (☎ 800/426–0333). **American** (☎ 800/433–7300). **America West** (☎ 800/235–9292). **Continental** (☎ 800/525–0280). **Delta** (☎ 800/221–1212). **Northwest** (☎ 800/225–2525). **TWA** (☎ 800/221–2000). **United** (☎ 800/241–6522). **US Airways** (☎ 800/428–4322).

➤ SMALLER CARRIERS: **Aloha** (☎ 800/367–5250). **Hawaiian** (☎ 800/367–5320). **IslandAir** (☎ 800/323–3345). **Mesa** (☎ 800/637–2247). **Pan American** (☎ 800/359–7262). **SkyWest** (☎ 800/453–9417). **Southwest** (☎ 800/435–9792). **Tower Air** (☎ 800/348–6937).

➤ FROM THE U.K.: **American** (☎ 0345/789–789). **British Airways** (☎ 0345/222–111). **Continental** (☎ 0800/776–464 toll-free or 01293/776–464). **Delta** (☎ 0800/414–767). **Northwest** (☎ 0990/561–000). **TWA** (☎ 0800/222–222). **United** (☎ 0800/888–555). **Virgin Atlantic** (☎ 01293/747–747). Most serve at least the New York area plus their own U.S. hubs. British Airways serves the largest number of U.S. cities—an impressive 17 destinations, including Atlanta, Boston, Charlotte, Chicago, Dallas, Detroit, Houston, Los Angeles, Miami, New York, Orlando, Philadelphia, Pittsburgh, San Francisco, Seattle, and Washington, DC. A few cities not served by British Airways can be reached by connections with other major carriers.

➤ FROM AUSTRALIA: **Air New Zealand** (☎ 1800/221–111). **Continental** (☎ 02/9249–0111 in Sydney, 03/9602–4899 in Melbourne).

CONSOLIDATORS

Consolidators buy tickets for scheduled international flights at reduced rates from the airlines, then sell them at prices that beat the best fare available directly from the airlines, usually without restrictions. Sometimes you can even get your money back if you need to return the ticket. Carefully read the fine print detailing penalties for changes and cancellations, and **confirm your consolidator reservation with the airline.**

➤ CONSOLIDATORS: **Cheap Tickets** (☎ 800/377–1000). **Up & Away Travel** (☎ 212/889–2345). **Discount Travel Network** (☎ 800/576–1600). **Unitravel** (☎ 800/325–2222). **World Travel Network** (☎ 800/409–6753).

COURIERS

When you fly as a courier, you trade your checked-luggage space for a ticket deeply subsidized by a courier service. It's all perfectly legitimate, but there are restrictions: You can usually book your flight only a week or two in advance, your length of stay may be set for a certain number of days, and you probably won't be able to book a companion on the same flight. Courier companies in the United States deal only with travel from the United States round-trip to international destinations. Each country has its own laws governing the regulation of courier travel to the United States. The best bet for foreign readers of this guide is to check a local phone directory, contact a local travel agent, and search budget-travel magazines for information on courier flights to the United States.

➤ COURIER CONTACTS: **Discount Travel International** (☎ 212/431–1616).

CUTTING COSTS

The least-expensive airfares to the United States are priced for round-trip travel and usually must be purchased in advance. It's smart to **call a number of airlines, and when you are quoted a good price, book it on the spot**—the same fare may not be available the next day. Airlines generally allow you to change your return date for a fee. If you don't use your ticket, you can apply the cost toward the purchase of a new ticket, again for a small charge. However, most low-fare tickets are nonrefundable. To get the lowest airfare, **check different routings.** Compare prices of flights to and from different airports if your destination or home city has more than one gateway. Also price off-peak flights, which may be significantly less expensive.

When flying within the U.S., **plan to stay over a Saturday night** and **travel during the middle of the week** to get the lowest fare. These low fares are usually priced for round-trip travel and are nonrefundable. You can, however, change your return date for a fee ($75 on most major airlines).

Travel agents, especially those who specialize in finding the lowest fares (☞ Discounts & Deals, *below*), can be especially helpful when booking a plane ticket. When you're quoted a price, **ask your agent if the price is likely to get any lower.** Good agents know the seasonal fluctuations of airfares and can usually anticipate a sale or fare war. However, waiting can be risky: The fare could go *up* as seats become scarce, and you may wait so long that your preferred flight sells out. A wait-and-see strategy works best if your plans are flexible. If you must arrive and depart on certain dates, don't delay.

DISCOUNT PASSES

On flights within the United States, most airlines offer non-U.S. residents discounted Visit USA fares, with savings of 25%–30%, provided the arrangements are made outside the United States. Many airlines, including America West, American, Delta, Hawaiian, Northwest, TWA, and United, also have air-pass programs that give you a fixed number of domestic flights for a flat fee (these also must be booked before you come to America). Check details with the airline or a travel agent.

CHECK IN & BOARDING

Airlines routinely overbook planes, assuming that not everyone with a ticket will show up, but sometimes everyone does. When that happens, airlines ask for volunteers to give up their seats. In return these volunteers usually get a certificate for a free flight and are rebooked on the next flight out. If there are not enough volunteers, the airline must choose who will be denied boarding. The first to get bumped are passengers who checked in late and those flying on discounted tickets, so **get to the gate and check in as early as possible,** especially during peak periods.

Although the trend on international flights is to drop reconfirmation requirements, many airlines still ask you to reconfirm each leg of your international itinerary. Failure to do so may result in your reservation being canceled.

Always **bring a government-issued photo ID to the airport.** You may be asked to show it before you are allowed to check in.

ENJOYING THE FLIGHT

For better service, **fly smaller or regional carriers,** which often have higher passenger-satisfaction ratings. Sometimes you'll find leather seats, more legroom, and better food.

For more legroom, **request an emergency-aisle seat.** Don't sit in the row in front of the emergency aisle or in front of a bulkhead, where seats may not recline.

If you don't like airline food, **ask for special meals when booking.** These can be vegetarian, low-cholesterol, or kosher, for example.

FLYING TIMES

Flying time from London is 7 hours to New York; 8 hours, 40 minutes to Chicago; 9 hours, 45 minutes to Miami; and 11 hours to Los Angeles.

Flying time from Sydney is 21–22 hours to New York; and 13 hours, 25 minutes to Los Angeles on a direct flight. Flights from Melbourne add about 3 hours of flying time.

Flying time from Toronto is 1½ hours to New York and 4½ hours to Los Angeles. Flying time from Vancouver is 2½ hours to Los Angeles, 4 hours to Chicago.

HOW TO COMPLAIN

If your baggage goes astray or your flight goes awry, complain right away. Most carriers require that you **file a claim immediately.**

➤ AIRLINE COMPLAINTS: U.S. Department of Transportation **Aviation Consumer Protection Division** (✉ C-75, Room 4107, Washington, DC 20590, ☏ 202/366–2220). **Federal Aviation Administration Consumer Hotline** (☏ 800/322–7873).

AIRPORTS

The major gateways to the U.S. include New York, Miami, Chicago, and Los Angeles.

➤ AIRPORT INFORMATION: *See* Arriving and Departing by Plane *in* New York City (New York *in* Chapter 3), Miami (Florida *in* Chapter 5), Chicago (Illinois *in* Chapter 7), and Los Angeles (California *in* Chapter 11) for specific information about airports in these cities, or the appropriate Arriving and Departing by Plane section under whatever city or region you are planning to fly into.

BIKE TRAVEL

See Sports and the Outdoors *in* Special-Interest Vacations.

BIKES IN FLIGHT

Most airlines will accommodate bikes as luggage, provided they are dismantled and put into a box. Call to see if your airline sells bike boxes (about $5; bike bags are at least $100) although you can often pick them up free at bike shops. International travelers can sometimes substitute a bike for a piece of checked luggage for free; otherwise, it will cost about $100. Domestic and Canadian airlines charge a $25–$50 fee.

BUS TRAVEL

Aside from the two coasts and the major cities, long-distance buses (motor coaches) serve more of the United States than trains do. Various regional bus companies serve their areas of the country; the most extensive long-haul service is provided by Greyhound Lines. Generally no reservations are needed—**buy your tickets before boarding** (allow 15 minutes in advance in small towns, up to 45 minutes in larger cities). Long-distance buses often have reclining seats, individually controlled reading lights, rest rooms, and air-conditioning and heating.

➤ BUS LINES: **Greyhound Lines** (☏ 800/231–2222, TDD 800/345–3109).

BUS PASSES

Visitors from overseas receive substantial savings on Greyhound by purchasing the International Ameripass through their travel agent prior to arriving in the United States. The cost is $119 for a 4-day pass, $139 for 5 days, $179 for 7 days, $269 for 15 days, $369 for 30 days, and $539 for 60 days. In the United States, the pass can be obtained only in New York City, from Greyhound International; you must show a valid non-U.S. passport. U.S. citizens can also buy Greyhound's Ameripass for unlimited travel; the cost is $199 for 7 days, $299 for 15 days, $409 for 30 days, $599 for 60 days.

The budget and backpacking crowd from abroad and the United States can take advantage of AmeriCan Adventure's new Us Bus pass. Eight routes nationwide are served by 15-passenger vans and sometimes even full-size coaches that make stops at Hostel

International (HI) accredited youth hostels. Like Eurail train passes, these bus passes are offered for a specific number of days within a certain period. The 15-day Us Bus pass, valid for 5 days of travel within the 15-day period, costs $159; the 25-day pass is valid for 10 days of travel and costs $279; the 40-day pass is valid for 15 days of travel and costs $369; the 60-day pass is valid for 30 days of travel and costs $559; and the 90-day pass is valid for 45 days of travel and costs $699. Bus passes can be purchased from overseas and U.S. travel agencies or from AmeriCan Adventures/Road Runner at 800/873–5872.

➤ DISCOUNT PASSES: The **International Ameripass** is available through certain travel agents or, in New York City, from Greyhound International (✉ 625 8th Ave., New York, NY 10018, ☎ 212/971–0492 or 800/246–8572). U.S. citizens can buy Greyhound's **Ameripass** (☎ 800/231–2222).

CHILDREN

On Greyhound buses, one child under age 2 travels free on an adult's lap, and children 2–11 accompanied by an adult pay 50% of the adult fare. Again, call ahead for specifics, as special fares have restrictions.

SENIOR CITIZENS

Greyhound offers a 10% discount on regular fares for passengers 62 and older; there are restrictions, so be sure to call local numbers for specific information.

TRAVELERS WITH DISABILITIES

Greyhound offers no special fares or facilities for passengers with disabilities, but an attendant is entitled to ride for free. If you will be traveling alone and need special assistance, call Greyhound (☎ 800/752–4841) at least 48 hours before departure .

BUSINESS HOURS

Banks are generally open weekdays from 9 AM until 3 PM, post offices weekdays between 8 AM and 5 PM; many branches operate Saturday morning hours. Business hours tend to be weekdays from 9 to 5, a little later on the East Coast and earlier the farther west you go. Many stores may not open until 10 or 11, but they remain open until 6 or 7; most carry on brisk business on Saturday as well. Large suburban shopping malls, the focus of most Americans' shopping activity, are generally open seven days a week, with evening hours every day except Sunday. All across the country, so-called convenience stores sell food and sundries until about 11 PM. Along the highways and in major cities you can usually find all-night diners, supermarkets, drugstores, and convenience stores.

CAMERAS & COMPUTERS

EQUIPMENT PRECAUTIONS

Always **keep your film, tape, or computer disks out of the sun.** Carry an extra supply of batteries, and **be prepared to turn on your camera, camcorder, or laptop** to prove to security personnel that the device is real. Always **ask for hand inspection of film,** which becomes clouded after successive exposure to airport X-ray machines, and **keep videotapes and computer disks away from metal detectors.**

ON LINE ON THE ROAD

Checking your e-mail or surfing the World Wide Web can sometimes be done in the business centers of major hotels, which usually charge an hourly rate. Web access is also available at many fax and copy centers, many of which are open 24 hours and on weekends. In major cities look for cyber cafés, where tabletop computers allow you to log on while sipping coffee or listening to live jazz. *Cyber Cafe: A Worldwide Guide for Travelers,* published by Wandering Traveler, Inc., is a valuable resource with 350 cyber cafés in 65 countries.

Do check out the World Wide Web when you're planning. You'll find everything from up-to-date weather forecasts to virtual tours of famous cities. Fodor's Web site, www.fodors.com, is a great place to start your on-line travels.

➤ PHOTO HELP: **Kodak Information Center** (☎ 800/242–2424). ***Kodak Guide to Shooting Great Travel Pictures,*** available in bookstores or from Fodor's Travel Publications (☎ 800/533–6478; $16.50 plus $4 shipping).

CAR RENTAL

➤ MAJOR AGENCIES: **Alamo** (☎ 800/327–9633, 0800/272–2000 in the U.K.). **Avis** (☎ 800/331–1212, 800/879–2847 in Canada, 008/225–533 in Australia). **Budget** (☎ 800/527–0700, 0800/181181 in the U.K.). **Dollar** (☎ 800/800–4000; 0990/565656 in the U.K., where it is known as Eurodollar). **Hertz** (☎ 800/654–3131, 800/263–0600 in Canada, 0345/555888 in the U.K., 03/9222–2523 in Australia, 03/358–6777 in New Zealand). **National InterRent** (☎ 800/227–7368; 0345/222525 in the U.K., where it is known as Europcar InterRent).

➤ OTHER ALTERNATIVES: **Rent-A-Wreck** (☎ 800/535–1391). **Sears** (☎ 800/527–0770). **Thrifty** (☎ 800/367–2277). **Ugly Duckling** (☎ 800/843–3825).

CUTTING COSTS

To get the best deal, **book through a travel agent who is willing to shop around.** When pricing cars, **ask about the location of the rental lot.** Some off-airport locations offer lower rates, and their lots are only minutes from the terminal via complimentary shuttle. You also may want to **price local car-rental companies,** whose rates may be lower still, although their service and maintenance may not be as good as those of a name-brand agency. Remember to ask about required deposits, cancellation penalties, and drop-off charges if you're planning to pick up the car in one city and leave it in another.

Also **ask your travel agent about a company's customer-service record.** How has the company responded to late plane arrivals and vehicle mishaps? Are there often lines at the rental counter? If you're traveling during a holiday period, does a confirmed reservation guarantee you a car?

Be sure to **look into wholesalers,** companies that do not own fleets but rent in bulk from those that do and often offer better rates than traditional car-rental operations. Prices are best during off-peak periods.

INSURANCE

When driving a rented car you are generally responsible for any damage to or loss of the vehicle. You also are liable for any property damage or personal injury that you may cause while driving. Before you rent, **see what coverage you already have** under the terms of your personal auto-insurance policy and credit cards.

For about $15 to $20 per day, rental companies sell protection, known as a collision- or loss-damage waiver (CDW or LDW), that eliminates your liability for damage to the car; it's always optional and should never be automatically added to your bill. Some states, including California and Nevada, have capped the price of the CDW and LDW. New York and Illinois have outlawed the sale of the CDW and LDW altogether. In New York you pay only for the first $100 of damage to the rental car. In Illinois you pay only for the first $200 of damage to the rental car.

In most states you don't need a CDW if you have personal auto insurance or other liability insurance. In Arizona, Maryland, Massachusetts, and Utah, the car-rental company must pay for damage to third parties up to a preset legal limit. Once that limit is reached, your personal auto or other liability insurance kicks in. However, **make sure you have enough coverage to pay for the car.** If you do not have auto insurance or an umbrella policy that covers damage to third parties, purchasing liability insurance and a CDW or LDW is highly recommended.

REQUIREMENTS

You must be 21 to rent a car, and rates may be higher if you're under 25. (In New York you must be 18.) You'll pay extra for child seats (about $3 per day), which are compulsory for children under five, and for additional drivers (about $2 per day). Non-U.S. residents will need a reservation voucher, a passport, a driver's license, and a travel policy that covers each driver, in order to pick up a car.

SURCHARGES

Before you pick up a car in one city and leave it in another, **ask about**

drop-off charges or one-way service fees, which can be substantial. Note, too, that some rental agencies charge extra if you return the car before the time specified in your contract. To avoid a hefty refueling fee, **fill the tank just before you turn in the car,** but be aware that gas stations near the rental outlet may overcharge.

CAR TRAVEL

AUTO CLUBS

Consider joining the American Automobile Association (AAA), a federation of state auto clubs that offers maps, route planning, and emergency road service to its members; members of Britain's Automobile Association (AA) are granted reciprocal privileges. Check local phone directories under AAA for the nearest club or contact the national organization.

➤ IN AUSTRALIA: **Australian Automobile Association** (☎ 06/247–7311).

➤ IN CANADA: **Canadian Automobile Association** (CAA, ☎ 613/247–0117).

➤ IN NEW ZEALAND: **New Zealand Automobile Association** (☎ 09/377–4660).

➤ IN THE U.K.: **Automobile Association** (AA, ☎ 0990/500–600), **Royal Automobile Club** (RAC, ☎ 0990/722–722 for membership, 0345/121–345 for insurance).

➤ IN THE U.S.: **American Automobile Association** (☎ 800/564–6222).

EMERGENCY SERVICES

In most communities, **dial 911** in an emergency to reach the police, fire, or ambulance services. If your car breaks down on an interstate highway, try to pull over onto the shoulder of the road and either wait for the state police to find you or, if you have other passengers who can wait in the car, walk to the nearest emergency roadside phone and call the state police. If you carry a cellular or car telephone, *55 is the emergency number to call. When calling for help, note your location according to the small green mileage markers posted along the highway. Other highways are also patrolled but may not have emergency phones or mileage markers. If you are a member of the AAA auto club (☞ Driving, *above*), look in a local phone book for the AAA emergency road-service number.

GASOLINE

Gasoline is relatively inexpensive in the United States, though of course the price varies from region to region and fluctuates over time. At press time the price of gas was about $1.25 in Los Angeles, $1.05 in New Jersey, 95¢ in Alabama, and $1.01 in Philadelphia.

In many parts of the United States, long stretches of road present challenges to unwary drivers. Be sure to stock up on gasoline whenever you have the chance. Most gas stations are open late, and many large highways and big cities have 24-hour stations. However, many stations close early on Sunday night.

HIGHWAYS

The fastest routes are usually the interstate highways, each numbered with a prefix "I–". Even numbers (I–80, I–40, and so on) are east–west roads; odd numbers (I–91, I–55, and so on) run north–south. These are fully signposted, limited-access highways, with at least two lanes in each direction. In some cases they are toll roads (the Pennsylvania Turnpike is I–76; the Massachusetts Turnpike is I–90). Near large cities, interstates usually intersect with a circumferential loop highway (I–295, and so on) that carries traffic around the city.

Another highway system is the U.S. highway (designated U.S. 1, and so on); they are not necessarily limited access, but well paved and usually multilane. State highways are also well paved and often have more than one lane in each direction. Large cities usually have a number of limited-access expressways, freeways, and parkways, referred to by names rather than numbers (the Merritt Parkway, the Kennedy Expressway, the Santa Monica Freeway).

ROAD CONDITIONS

Road and highway conditions vary from state to state, depending on the climate and budget allocations of a given area. In general, interstates and parkways are well maintained through revenue generated from tolls charged to all motorists. These can be collected at periodic tollbooths along the road or where you exit, depending on the distance traveled. Large highways also have the advantage of well-spaced roadside stops with public rest rooms and stores selling fast food, maps, and other sundries. Major interstates are frequented by state police and tow trucks, whose drivers can lend assistance in the event of an accident or breakdown.

ROAD MAPS

Maps can usually be purchased at gas stations, convenience stores, and rest stops for about $3. If you plan to cover an entire region within the United States, consider a detailed road atlas; these generally cost about $10 and can be purchased in the same locations mentioned above, as well as in bookstores.

RULES OF THE ROAD

Driving in the U.S. is done on the right side of the road. Speed limits vary and are sign-posted along roads and highways. **Adhere to speed limits.** Recent federal legislation allows each state to set individual speed limits; they may range from 55 miles per hour to unlimited speeds in the Great Plains states. Watch for lower speed limits on back roads. Except for limited-access roads, highways usually post a lower speed limit in towns, so slow down when houses and buildings start to appear. Most states require front-seat passengers to wear seat belts, and in all states **children under age 4 must ride in approved child-safety seats.**

In some communities, it is permissible to make a right turn at a red light once the car has come to a full stop and there is no oncoming traffic. When in doubt about local laws, however, wait for the green light.

Beware of weekday rush-hour traffic—anywhere from 7 AM to 10 AM and 4 PM to 7 PM—around major cities. To encourage car sharing, some crowded expressways may reserve an express lane for cars carrying more than one passenger. In downtown areas, watch signs carefully—there are lots of one-way streets, "no-left-turn" intersections, and blocks closed to car traffic, all in the name of easing congestion.

CHILDREN & TRAVEL

CHILDREN IN THE UNITED STATES

Be sure to plan ahead and **involve your youngsters** as you outline your trip. When packing, include things to keep them busy en route. On sightseeing days try to schedule activities of special interest to your children. If you are renting a car don't forget to **arrange for a car seat** when you reserve. Most hotels in the U.S. allow children under a certain age to stay in their parents' room at no extra charge, but others charge them as extra adults; be sure to **ask about the cutoff age for children's discounts.**

FLYING

If your children are two or older, **ask about children's airfares.** As a general rule, infants under two not occupying a seat fly at greatly reduced fares or even for free.

In general the adult baggage allowance applies to children paying half or more of the adult fare.

Experts agree that it's a good idea to use safety seats aloft for children weighing less than 40 pounds. Airlines, however, can set their own policies: U.S. carriers allow FAA-approved models but usually require that you buy a ticket, even if your child would otherwise ride free, since the seats must be strapped into regular seats. Airline rules vary, so it's important to **check your airline's policy about using safety seats during takeoff and landing.** Safety seats must not obstruct the movement of other passengers in the row, so get an appropriate seat assignment as early as possible.

When making your reservation, **request children's meals or a free-standing bassinet** if you need them; the latter are available only to those seated at the bulkhead, where there's enough legroom. Remember, however, that bulkhead seats may not have their own overhead bins, and there's no storage space in front of you—a major inconvenience.

GROUP TRAVEL

When planning to take your kids on a tour, look for companies that specialize in family travel.

➤ Family-Friendly Tour Operators: **Grandtravel** (✉ 6900 Wisconsin Ave., Suite 706, Chevy Chase, MD 20815, ☎ 301/986–0790 or 800/247–7651) for people traveling with grandchildren ages 7–17. **Families Welcome!** (✉ 92 N. Main St., Ashland, OR 97520, ☎ 541/482–6121 or 800/326–0724, FAX 541/482–0660). **Rascals in Paradise** (✉ 650 5th St., Suite 505, San Francisco, CA 94107, ☎ 415/978–9800 or 800/872–7225, FAX 415/442–0289).

CONSUMER PROTECTION

Whenever possible, **pay with a major credit card** so you can cancel payment or get reimbursed if there's a problem, provided that you have the necessary documentation. This is the best way to pay, whether you're buying travel arrangements before your trip or shopping at your destination.

If you're doing business with a particular company for the first time, **contact your local Better Business Bureau and the attorney general's offices** in your state and the company's home state, as well. Have any complaints been filed?

Finally, if you're buying a package or tour, always **consider travel insurance** that includes default coverage (☞ Insurance, *below*).

➤ Local BBBs: **Council of Better Business Bureaus** (✉ 4200 Wilson Blvd., Suite 800, Arlington, VA 22203, ☎ 703/276–0100, FAX 703/525–8277).

CUSTOMS & DUTIES

When shopping, **keep receipts** for all of your purchases. Upon reentering the country, **be ready to show customs officials what you've bought.** If you feel a duty is incorrect, appeal the assessment. If you object to the way your clearance was handled, get the inspector's badge number. In either case, first ask to see a supervisor, then write to the appropriate authorities, beginning with the port director at your point of entry.

IN AUSTRALIA

Australia residents who are 18 or older may bring back $A400 worth of souvenirs and gifts (including jewelry), 250 cigarettes or 250 grams of tobacco, and 1,125 ml of alcohol (including wine, beer, and spirits). Residents under 18 may bring back $A200 worth of goods.

➤ Information: **Australian Customs Service** (Regional Director, ✉ Box 8, Sydney, NSW 2001, ☎ 02/9213–2000, FAX 02/9213–4000).

IN CANADA

Canadian residents who have been out of Canada for at least 7 days may bring in C$500 worth of goods duty-free. If you've been away less than 7 days but more than 48 hours, the duty-free allowance drops to C$200; if your trip lasts 24–48 hours, the allowance is C$50. You may not pool allowances with family members. Goods claimed under the C$500 exemption may follow you by mail; those claimed under the lesser exemptions must accompany you. Alcohol and tobacco products may be included in the 7-day and 48-hour exemptions but not in the 24-hour exemption. If you meet the age requirements of the province or territory through which you reenter Canada, you may bring in, duty-free, 1.14 liters (40 imperial ounces) of wine or liquor *or* 24 12-ounce cans or bottles of beer or ale. If you are 16 or older you may bring in, duty-free, 200 cigarettes and 50 cigars.

You may send an unlimited number of gifts worth up to C$60 each duty-free to Canada. Label the package UNSOLICITED GIFT—VALUE UNDER $60. Alcohol and tobacco are excluded.

➤ Information: **Revenue Canada** (✉ 2265 St. Laurent Blvd. S, Ottawa, Ontario K1G 4K3, ☎ 613/993–0534, 800/461–9999 in Canada).

IN NEW ZEALAND

Although greeted with a "Haere Mai" ("Welcome to New Zealand"), homeward-bound residents with goods to declare must present themselves for inspection. If you're 17 or older, you may bring back $700 worth of souvenirs and gifts. Your duty-free allowance also includes 4.5 liters of wine or beer; one 1,125-ml bottle of spirits; and either 200 cigarettes, 250 grams of tobacco, 50 cigars, or a combination of all three up to 250 grams.

➤ INFORMATION: **New Zealand Customs** (✉ Custom House, ✉ 50 Anzac Ave., Box 29, Auckland, New Zealand, ☎ 09/359–6655, ☎ 09/309–2978).

IN THE U.K.

From countries outside the EU, including the United States, you may import, duty-free, 200 cigarettes or 50 cigars; 1 liter of spirits or 2 liters of fortified or sparkling wine or liqueurs; 2 liters of still table wine; 60 milliliters of perfume; 250 milliliters of toilet water; plus £136 worth of other goods, including gifts and souvenirs.

➤ INFORMATION: **HM Customs and Excise** (✉ Dorset House, ✉ Stamford St., London SE1 9NG, ☎ 0171/202–4227).

IN THE U.S.

Non-U.S. residents ages 21 and older may import into the United States 200 cigarettes or 50 cigars or 2 kilograms of tobacco, 1 liter of alcohol, and gifts worth $100. Prohibited items include meat products, seeds, plants, and fruits.

➤ INFORMATION: **U.S. Customs Service** (Inquiries, ✉ Box 7407, Washington, DC 20044, ☎ 202/927–6724; complaints, Office of Regulations and Rulings, ✉ 1301 Constitution Ave. NW, Washington, DC 20229; registration of equipment, Resource Management, ✉ 1301 Constitution Ave. NW, Washington DC 20229, ☎ 202/927–0540).

DINING

MEALTIMES

Breakfast is served anywhere from 6 to 11, lunch 11 to 2, dinner from 5 until late. Like business hours in general, mealtimes tend to become earlier when you leave the cities and as you go farther west.

DISABILITIES & ACCESSIBILITY

MAKING RESERVATIONS

When discussing accessibility with an operator or reservations agent, **ask hard questions.** Are there any stairs, inside *or* out? Are there grab bars next to the toilet *and* in the shower/tub? How wide is the doorway to the room? To the bathroom? For the most extensive facilities meeting the latest legal specifications, **opt for newer accommodations,** which are more likely to have been designed with access in mind. Older buildings or ships may have more limited facilities. Be sure to **discuss your needs before booking.**

TRANSPORTATION

➤ COMPLAINTS: **Disability Rights Section** (✉ U.S. Department of Justice, Civil Rights Division, ✉ Box 66738, Washington, DC 20035–6738, ☎ 202/514–0301 or 800/514–0301, TTY 202/514–0383 or 800/514–0383, FAX 202/307–1198) for general complaints. **Aviation Consumer Protection Division** (☞ Air Travel, *above*) for airline-related problems. **Civil Rights Office** (✉ U.S. Department of Transportation, Departmental Office of Civil Rights, S-30, ✉ 400 7th St. SW, Room 10215, Washington, DC, 20590, ☎ 202/366–4648, FAX 202/366–9371) for problems with surface transportation.

TRAVEL AGENCIES & TOUR OPERATORS

As a whole, the travel industry has become more aware of the needs of travelers with disabilities. In the U.S., the Americans with Disabilities Act requires that travel firms serve the needs of all travelers. Note, though, that some agencies and operators specialize in making travel arrangements for individuals and groups with disabilities.

➤ TRAVELERS WITH MOBILITY PROBLEMS: **Access Adventures** (✉ 206 Chestnut Ridge Rd., Rochester, NY 14624, ☎ 716/889–9096), run by a former physical-rehabilitation counselor. **Accessible Journeys** (✉ 35 W. Sellers Ave., Ridley Park, PA 19078, ☎ 610/521–0339 or 800/846–4537, FAX 610/521–6959), for escorted tours exclusively for travelers with mobility impairments. **CareVacations** (✉ 5019 49th Ave., Suite 102, Leduc, Alberta T9E 6T5, ☎ 403/986–6404, 800/648–1116 in Canada) has group tours and is especially helpful with cruise vacations. **Flying Wheels Travel** (✉ 143 W. Bridge St., Box 382, Owatonna, MN 55060, ☎ 507/451–5005 or 800/535–6790, FAX 507/451–1685), a travel agency specializing in customized tours and itineraries worldwide. **Hinsdale Travel Service** (✉ 201 E. Ogden Ave., Suite 100, Hinsdale, IL 60521, ☎ 630/325–1335), a travel agency that benefits from the advice of wheelchair traveler Janice Perkins.

➤ Travelers with Developmental Disabilities: **New Directions** (✉ 5276 Hollister Ave., Suite 207, Santa Barbara, CA 93111, ☎ 805/967–2841 or 888/967–2841, FAX 805/964–7344). **Sprout** (✉ 893 Amsterdam Ave., New York, NY 10025, ☎ 212/222–9575 or 888/222–9575, FAX 212/222–9768).

DISCOUNTS & DEALS

Be a smart shopper and **compare all your options** before making any choice. A plane ticket bought with a promotional coupon may not be cheaper than the least expensive fare from a discount ticket agency. For high-price travel purchases, such as packages or tours, keep in mind that what you get is just as important as what you save. Just because something is cheap doesn't mean it's a bargain.

CLUBS & COUPONS

Many companies sell discounts in the form of travel clubs and coupon books, but these cost money. You must use participating advertisers to get a deal, and only after you recoup the initial membership cost or book price do you begin to save. If you plan to use the club or coupons frequently, you may save considerably. Before signing up, find out what discounts you get for free.

➤ Discount Clubs: **Entertainment Travel Editions** (✉ 2125 Butterfield Rd., Troy, MI 48084, ☎ 800/445–4137; $20–$51, depending on destination). **Great American Traveler** (✉ Box 27965, Salt Lake City, UT 84127, ☎ 801/974–3033 or 800/548–2812; $49.95 per year). **Moment's Notice Discount Travel Club** (✉ 7301 New Utrecht Ave., Brooklyn, NY 11204, ☎ 718/234–6295; $25 per year, single or family). **Privilege Card International** (✉ 237 E. Front St., Youngstown, OH 44503, ☎ 330/746–5211 or 800/236–9732; $74.95 per year). **Sears's Mature Outlook** (✉ Box 9390, Des Moines, IA 50306, ☎ 800/336–6330; $19.95 per year). **Travelers Advantage** (✉ CUC Travel Service, ✉ 3033 S. Parker Rd., Suite 1000, Aurora, CO 80014, ☎ 800/548–1116 or 800/648–4037; $59.95 per year, single or family). **Worldwide Discount Travel Club** (✉ 1674 Meridian Ave., Miami Beach, FL 33139, ☎ 305/534–2082; $50 per year family, $40 single).

CREDIT-CARD BENEFITS

When you use your credit card to make travel purchases you may get free travel-accident insurance, collision-damage insurance, and medical or legal assistance, depending on the card and the bank that issued it. American Express, MasterCard, and Visa provide one or more of these services, so **get a copy of your credit card's travel-benefits policy.** If you are a member of an auto club, always **ask hotel and car-rental reservations agents about auto-club discounts.** Some clubs offer additional discounts on tours, cruises, and admission to attractions.

DISCOUNT RESERVATIONS

To save money, **look into discount-reservations services** with toll-free numbers, which use their buying power to get a better price on hotels, airline tickets, even car rentals. When booking a room, always **call the hotel's local toll-free number** (if one is available) rather than the central reservations number—you'll often get a better price. Always ask about special packages or corporate rates.

➤ Airline Tickets: **☎ 800/FLY–4–LESS. ☎ 800/FLY–ASAP.**

➤ Hotel Rooms: **Accommodations Express** (☎ 800/444–7666). **Hotel Reservations Network** (☎ 800/964–6835). **Players Express Vacations** (☎ 800/458–6161). **Quickbook** (☎ 800/789–9887). **Room Finders USA** (☎ 800/473–7829). **RMC Travel** (☎ 800/245–5738). **Steigenberger Reservation Service** (☎ 800/223–5652).

PACKAGE DEALS

Packages and guided tours can save you money, but don't confuse the two. When you buy a package, your travel remains independent, just as though you had planned and booked the trip yourself. Fly/drive packages, which combine airfare and car rental, are often a good deal.

ELECTRICITY

Overseas visitors will need to bring adapters to convert their personal appliances to the U.S. standard: AC, 110 volts/60 cycles, with a plug of two flat pins set parallel to one another.

EMBASSIES

In addition to their principal headquarters, most embassies have offices in Washington, DC.

➤ AUSTRALIA: **Australian Embassy** (✉ 1601 Massachussetts Ave. NW, Washington, DC 20036, ☎ 202/797–3000, FAX 202/797–3040).

➤ CANADA: **Canadian Embassy** (✉ 501 Pennsylvania Ave. NW, Washington, DC 20001, ☎ 202/682–1740, FAX 202/682–7726).

➤ NEW ZEALAND: **New Zealand Embassy** (✉ 37 Observatory Circle, NW, Washington, DC 20008, ☎ 202/328–4800, FAX 202/667–5227).

➤ UNITED KINGDOM: **British Embassy** (✉ 3100 Massachussetts Ave., NW, Washington, DC 20008, ☎ 202/588–7800, FAX 202/588–7850).

EMERGENCIES

In most communities, **dial 911** in an emergency for police, fire, or ambulance services. In some outlying areas the quickest way to get help in an emergency is to dial 0 for an operator.

FAX MACHINES

You can usually make hotel reservations via fax, and you can probably send a fax on the hotel's machine while staying there, especially if the hotel caters to business travelers. If your hotel isn't helpful or charges exorbitantly for this service, look for fax service at local photocopying stores; the charge may be as much as $2–$3 a page, more for overseas.

GAY & LESBIAN TRAVEL

➤ GAY- AND LESBIAN-FRIENDLY TOUR OPERATORS: **R.S.V.P. Travel Productions** (✉ 2800 University Ave. SE, Minneapolis, MN 55414, ☎ 612/379–4697 or 800/328–7787, FAX 612/379–0484), for cruises and resort vacations for gays. **Hanns Ebensten Travel** (✉ 513 Fleming St., Key West, FL 33040, ☎ 305/294–8174, FAX 305/292–9665), one of the oldest operators in the gay market. **Toto Tours** (✉ 1326 W. Albion Ave., Suite 3W, Chicago, IL 60626, ☎ 773/274–8686 or 800/565–1241, FAX 773/274–8695), for groups.

➤ GAY- AND LESBIAN-FRIENDLY TRAVEL AGENCIES: **Corniche Travel** (✉ 8721 Sunset Blvd., Suite 200, West Hollywood, CA 90069, ☎ 310/854–6000 or 800/429–8747, FAX 310/659–7441). **Islanders Kennedy Travel** (✉ 183 W. 10th St., New York, NY 10014, ☎ 212/242–3222 or 800/988–1181, FAX 212/929–8530). **Now Voyager** (✉ 4406 18th St., San Francisco, CA 94114, ☎ 415/626–1169 or 800/255–6951, FAX 415/626–8626). **Yellowbrick Road** (✉ 1500 W. Balmoral Ave., Chicago, IL 60640, ☎ 773/561–1800 or 800/642–2488, FAX 773/561–4497). **Skylink Travel and Tour** (✉ 3577 Moorland Ave., Santa Rosa, CA 95407, ☎ 707/585–8355 or 800/225–5759, FAX 707/584–5637), serving lesbian travelers.

➤ GAY TRAVEL ASSOCIATIONS: You can also contact the **International Gay Travel Association** (✉ 4331 N. Federal Hwy., Ste. 304, Ft. Lauderdale, FL 33308, ☎ 800/448–8550), which has more than 1,500 travel-industry members. Upon request they will provide a listing of gay-friendly travel agents and tour operators for any specified region. There is no fee for this service.

➤ PUBLICATION: ***Fodor's Gay Guide to the USA,*** ($20) available in bookstores or from Fodor's Travel Publications (☎ 800/533–6478).

HOLIDAYS

Major national holidays include: New Year's Day (Jan. 1); Martin Luther King, Jr. Day (third Mon. in Jan.); President's Day (third Mon. in Feb.); Memorial Day (last Mon. in May);

Independence Day (July 4); Labor Day (first Mon. in Sept.); Thanksgiving Day (fourth Thurs. in Nov.); Christmas Eve and Day (Dec. 24–25); and New Year's Eve (Dec. 31).

INSURANCE

Travel insurance is the best way to **protect yourself against financial loss.** The most useful plan is a comprehensive policy that includes coverage for trip cancellation and interruption, default, trip delay, and medical expenses (with a waiver for preexisting conditions).

Without insurance, you will lose all or most of your money if you cancel your trip, regardless of the reason. Default insurance covers you if your tour operator, airline, or cruise line goes out of business. Trip-delay covers unforeseen expenses that you may incur due to bad weather or mechanical delays. It's important to compare the fine print regarding trip-delay coverage when comparing policies.

For overseas travel, one of the most important components of travel insurance is its medical coverage. Supplemental health insurance will pick up the cost of your medical bills should you get sick or injured while traveling. Residents of the United Kingdom can buy an annual travel-insurance policy valid for most vacations taken during the year in which the coverage is purchased. If you are pregnant or have a pre-existing condition, make sure you're covered. British citizens should buy extra medical coverage when traveling overseas, according to the Association of British Insurers. Australian travelers should buy travel insurance, including extra medical coverage, whenever they go abroad, according to the Insurance Council of Australia.

Always **buy travel insurance directly from the insurance company**; if you buy it from a cruise line, airline, or tour operator that goes out of business you probably will not be covered for the agency or operator's default, a major risk. Before you make any purchase, **review your existing health and home-owner's policies** to find out whether they cover expenses incurred while traveling.

➤ TRAVEL INSURERS: In the U.S., **Access America** (✉ 6600 W. Broad St., Richmond, VA 23230, ☎ 804/285–3300 or 800/284–8300). **Travel Guard International** (✉ 1145 Clark St., Stevens Point, WI 54481, ☎ 715/345–0505 or 800/826–1300). In Canada, **Mutual of Omaha** (✉ Travel Division, ✉ 500 University Ave., Toronto, Ontario M5G 1V8, ☎ 416/598–4083, 800/268–8825 in Canada).

➤ INSURANCE INFORMATION: In the U.K., **Association of British Insurers** (✉ 51 Gresham St., London EC2V 7HQ, ☎ 0171/600–3333). In Australia, the **Insurance Council of Australia** (☎ 613/9614–1077, FAX 613/9614–7924).

LIQUOR LAWS

Liquor laws vary from state to state, affecting such matters as bar and liquor-store opening times and whether restaurants can sell liquor by the glass or only by the bottle. A few states—mostly in the South or Midwest—allow each county to choose its own policy, resulting in so-called dry counties, where no alcoholic beverages are sold, next to counties where the bars do a roaring business.

The drinking age is 21 in all states, and you should **be prepared to show identification** in order to be served. Restaurants must obtain a license to sell alcoholic beverages on the premises, so some inexpensive establishments, or places that have recently opened, may not sell drinks at all or may sell only beer or wine. In many of these restaurants, however, you can bring your own beer or wine to drink with your meal.

Local laws against driving while intoxicated are growing stricter. Many bars now serve nonalcoholic drinks for the "designated driver," so at least one person in a group is sober enough to drive everyone else safely home.

LODGING

A wide variety of lodging facilities is available in the U.S., from gilded suites with marble bathrooms and sweeping views to bare-bones rooms with concrete walls and plastic furniture. An ultralavish hotel or resort room can easily run $500-plus a night, while a spartan roadside motel in a small town could cost $20–$30 per night. Prices vary dramatically depending on location and level of luxury. Whether you're looking for the best, the cheapest, or something in between, there are ample accommodation options to choose from.

Motels are geared to motorists, with locations close to highways and convenient parking. **Airport hotels,** within a few minutes' drive of major airports, are geared to plane travelers in transit, with a strong business-travel clientele; noise may be a problem, although the best ones are soundproofed. **Convention hotels** have hundreds of guest rooms, warrens of meeting rooms (usually on separate floors), and big ballrooms used for exhibits and banquets; when a large convention is staying at one, other guests sometimes feel overwhelmed. Other **downtown hotels** cater more to individual guests and may offer more in the way of health facilities and à la carte restaurants. **Suburban hotels** in many cities attract travelers who want to be close to the circumferential highway and to suburban office parks, shopping malls, or theme parks; they may be larger and more upscale than motels, offering more restaurants, health facilities, and other amenities. **Resorts** tend to be destinations in and of themselves—complete with golf courses, tennis courts, beaches, several restaurants, on-site entertainment, and so on. The setting usually emphasizes a particular outdoor activity, whether skiing, water sports, or golf. One variation on this is the **dude ranch,** where paying guests sample horseback riding, hiking, lake fishing, cookouts, and such western-style activities as rodeos. **Country inns and bed-and-breakfasts** are generally charming older properties that, unlike European B&Bs, tend to be pricey and upscale. They may not have private bathrooms, an in-room phone, or TVs, and as they are frequently meticulously furnished with antiques, they may not be the best place to take young children. There is often an inviting common room where guests can gather for quiet conversation in front of a roaring fireplace or nestle in the folds of a big, soft chair with a good book. Breakfast is usually included in the room rate, but verify this when you make a reservation. For recommendations, see *Fodor's Best Bed & Breakfasts* books for various regions of the country. At the budget end of the scale, **YMCAs and youth hostels** offer somewhat more spartan accommodations, often dormitory style, with limited amenities.

APARTMENT & VILLA RENTALS

If you want a home base that's roomy enough for a family and comes with cooking facilities, **consider a furnished rental.** These can save you money, especially if you're traveling with a large group of people. Home-exchange directories list rentals (often second homes owned by prospective house swappers), and some services search for a house or apartment for you (even a castle if that's your fancy) and handle the paperwork. Some send an illustrated catalog; others send photographs only of specific properties, sometimes at a charge. Up-front registration fees may apply.

➤ RENTAL AGENTS: **Europa-Let/Tropical Inn-Let** (✉ 92 N. Main St., Ashland, OR 97520, ☎ 541/482–5806 or 800/462–4486, FAX 541/482–0660). **Hometours International** (✉ Box 11503, Knoxville, TN 37939, ☎ 423/690–8484 or 800/367–4668). **Rent-a-Home International** (✉ 7200 34th Ave. NW, Seattle, WA 98117, ☎ 206/789–9377 or 800/488–7368, FAX 206/789–9379). **Vacation Home Rentals Worldwide** (✉ 235 Kensington Ave., Norwood, NJ 07648, ☎ 201/767–9393 or 800/633–3284, FAX 201/767–5510).

B&BS

A quaint and often inexpensive option for those interested in getting to know the people as well as the local flavor of a town is to check into a bed-and-breakfast inn. These are often run by individuals or families who open up their homes to paying visitors. Accommodations range from modest to museumlike but often entail shared bathrooms and a limited number of bedrooms.

There are many books on the market and Web sites on the internet that give specific information on B&Bs,

but the fastest way to learn about current availability in a specific town or city is to call the local chamber of commerce for a list of the names and phone numbers of B&Bs in the area. If you have already reached your destination, check the local newspaper: some B&Bs advertise locally.

CAMPING

Some of the most reasonably priced campgrounds with the most compelling sites operate under the auspices of the National Park system (☞ National Parks, *below*). If, however, you opt for private commercial operations, your best source for nationwide information on both public and private parks is the National Association of RV Parks and Campgrounds.

An overnight stay at a commercial campground can cost from $15 to $30, depending on three factors: the amenities, location, and time of year. Tent camping, of course, is the least expensive form of accommodation; if you want water, electric, and sewage hook-ups, you move into the higher end of the price range.

Many private campgrounds are not open year-round, so it's important to **call ahead.** You can make reservations over the phone, and, customarily, a one-night deposit is required. The peak summer months of June, July, and August are very busy at the more desirable locations; the sooner you book, the more you can count on being awarded an attractive site.

➤ INFORMATION: **National Association of RV Parks and Campgrounds** (✉ 8605 Westwood Center Dr., Suite 201, Vienna, VA 22182, ☎ 703/734–3000).

➤ PUBLICATIONS: In ***Woodall's 1998 North American Edition: Campground Directory*** ($21.95; at your local bookstore), all private parks in the United States and Canada are listed, quality inspected, and rated. Look for the annually updated directories published by the **American Automobile Association** for similar assessments. **Fodor's** (☎ 800/533–6478) publishes two guides that provide in-depth coverage of campgrounds around the country: *National Parks of the West* ($17.50) and *National Parks and Seashores of the East* ($17); both are available in bookstores.

HOME EXCHANGES

If you would like to exchange your home for someone else's, **join a home-exchange organization,** which will send you its updated listings of available exchanges for a year and will include your own listing in at least one of them. It's up to you to make specific arrangements.

➤ EXCHANGE CLUBS: **HomeLink International** (✉ Box 650, Key West, FL 33041, ☎ 305/294–7766 or 800/638–3841, FAX 305/294–1148; $83 per year).

HOSTELS

No matter what your age, you can **save on lodging costs by staying at hostels.** In some 5,000 locations in more than 70 countries around the world, Hostelling International (HI), the umbrella group for a number of national youth hostel associations, has single-sex, dorm-style beds and, at many hostels, "couples" rooms and family accommodations. Membership in any HI national hostel association, open to travelers of all ages, allows you to stay in HI-affiliated hostels at member rates (one-year membership is about $25 for adults; hostels run about $10–$25 per night). Members have priority if the hostel is full and are also eligible for discounts around the world, even on rail and bus travel in some countries.

➤ HOSTEL ORGANIZATIONS: **Hostelling International—American Youth Hostels** (✉ 733 15th St. NW, Suite 840, Washington, DC 20005, ☎ 202/783–6161, FAX 202/783–6171). **Hostelling International—Canada** (✉ 400-205 Catherine St., Ottawa, Ontario K2P 1C3, ☎ 613/237–7884, FAX 613/237–7868). **Youth Hostel Association of England and Wales** (✉ Trevelyan House, ✉ 8 St. Stephen's Hill, St. Albans, Hertfordshire AL1 2DY, ☎ 01727/855215 or 01727/845047, FAX 01727/844126); membership in the U.S. $25, in Canada C$26.75, in the U.K. £9.30).

HOTELS

Hotel chains dominate the lodging landscape in the United States. Some of the large chains, such as Holiday Inn, Hilton, Hyatt, Marriott, and Ramada, are even further subdivided into chains of budget properties, all-suite properties, downtown hotels, or luxury resorts, each with a different name. Though some chain hotels may have a standardized look to them, this "cookie-cutter" approach also means that you can rely on the same level of comfort and efficiency at all properties in a well-managed chain, and at a chain's premier properties—its so-called flagship hotels—decor and services may be outstanding.

Most hotels will hold your reservation until 6 PM; **call ahead if you plan to arrive late.** Hotels will be more willing to hold a late reservation for you if you reserve with a credit-card number.

When you call to make a reservation, **ask all the necessary questions up front.** If you are arriving with a car, ask if the hotel has a parking lot or covered garage and whether there is an extra fee for parking. If you like to eat your meals in, ask if the hotel has a restaurant or whether it has room service (most do, but not necessarily 24 hours a day—and be forewarned that it can be expensive). Most hotels have in-room telephones, but double-check this at inexpensive properties and bed-and-breakfasts. Most hotels and motels have in-room TVs, often with cable movies (usually pay-per-view), but verify this if you like to watch TV. If you want an in-room crib for your child, there will probably be an additional charge.

➤ TOLL-FREE NUMBERS: **Adam's Mark** (☏ 800/444–2326). **Best Western** (☏ 800/528–1234). **Budgetel Inns** (☏ 800/301–0400). **Choice** (☏ 800/221–2222). **Clarion** (☏ 800/252–7466). **Colony** (☏ 800/777–1700). **Comfort** (☏ 800/228–5150). **Days Inn** (☏ 800/325–2525). **Doubletree and Red Lion Hotels** (☏ 800/528–0444). **Embassy Suites** (☏ 800/362–2779). **Fairfield Inn** (☏ 800/228–2800). **Forte** (☏ 800/225–5843). **Four Seasons** (☏ 800/332–3442). **Hilton** (☏ 800/445–8667). **Holiday Inn** (☏ 800/465–4329). **Howard Johnson** (☏ 800/654–4656). **Hyatt Hotels & Resorts** (☏ 800/233–1234). **Inter-Continental** (☏ 800/327–0200). **La Quinta** (☏ 800/531–5900). **Marriott** (☏ 800/228–9290). **Le Meridien** (☏ 800/543–4300). **Nikko Hotels International** (☏ 800/645–5687). **Omni** (☏ 800/843–6664). **Quality Inn** (☏ 800/228–5151). **Radisson** (☏ 800/333–3333). **Ramada** (☏ 800/228–2828). **Renaissance Hotels & Resorts** (☏ 800/468–3571). **Ritz-Carlton** (☏ 800/241–3333). **ITT Sheraton** (☏ 800/325–3535). **Sleep Inn** (☏ 800/221–2222). **Westin Hotels & Resorts** (☏ 800/228–3000). **Wyndham Hotels & Resorts** (☏ 800/822–4200).

MOTELS

➤ TOLL-FREE NUMBERS: **Budget Hosts Inns** (☏ 800/283–4678). **Econo Lodge** (☏ 800/553–2666). **Friendship Inns** (☏ 800/453–4511). **Motel 6** (☏ 800/466–8356). **Rodeway** (☏ 800/228–2000). **Super 8** (☏ 800/848–8888).

MAIL

Every address in the United States belongs to a specific zip-code district, and each zip code has five digits. Some addresses include a second sequence of four numbers following the first five numbers, but although this speeds mail delivery for large organizations, it is not necessary to use it. Each zip-code district has at least one post office, where you can buy stamps and aerograms, send parcels, or conduct other postal business. Occasionally you may find small stamp-dispensing machines in airports, train stations, bus terminals, large office buildings, hotel lobbies, drugstores, or grocery stores, but don't count on it. Most Americans go to the post office to buy their stamps, and the lines can be long.

Official mailboxes are either the stout, royal blue steel bins on city sidewalks or mail chutes on the walls of post offices or in large office buildings. A schedule posted on mailboxes and mail slots should indicate when the mail is picked up.

POSTAL RATES

First-class letters weighing up to 1 ounce can be sent anywhere within the United States with a 32¢ stamp;

each additional ounce costs 23¢. Postcards need a 20¢ stamp. A half-ounce airmail letter overseas takes 60¢, an airmail postcard 50¢, and a surface-rate postcard 35¢. For Canada, you'll need a 46¢ stamp for a 1-ounce letter, 40¢ for a postcard. For Mexico, you'll need 40¢ for a half-ounce letter, 35¢ for a postcard. For 50¢, you can buy an aerogram—a single sheet of lightweight blue paper that folds into its own envelope, already stamped for overseas airmail delivery.

RECEIVING MAIL

If you wish to receive mail while traveling in the USA, **have it sent c/o General Delivery** at the city's main post office (be sure to use the right zip code). It should be held there for up to 30 days. You must pick it up in person, and bring identification with you. American Express offices in the United States do not hold mail.

MONEY

CREDIT & DEBIT CARDS

Should you use a credit card or a debit card when traveling? Both have benefits. A credit card allows you to delay payment and gives you certain rights as a consumer (☞ Consumer Protection, *above*). A debit card, also known as a check card, deducts funds directly from your checking account and helps you stay within your budget. When you want to rent a car, though, you may still need an old-fashioned credit card. Although you can always *pay* for your car with a debit card, some agencies will not allow you to *reserve* a car with a debit card.

Otherwise, the two types of plastic are virtually the same. Both will get you cash advances at ATMs worldwide if your card is properly programmed with your personal identification number (PIN). Both offer excellent, wholesale exchange rates. And both protect you against unauthorized use if the card is lost or stolen. Your liability is limited to $50, as long as you report the card missing.

➤ ATM LOCATIONS: **Cirrus** (☎ 800/424–7787). **Plus** (☎ 800/843–7587) for locations in the U.S. and Canada, or visit your local bank.

➤ REPORTING LOST CARDS: To report lost or stolen credit cards, use the following toll-free numbers: **American Express** (☎ 800/327–2177), **Discover Card** (☎ 800/347–2683), **Diners Club** (☎ 800/234–6377), **Master Card** (☎ 800/307–7309), or **Visa** (☎ 800/847–2911).

BANKS

In general, U.S. banks will not cash a personal check for you unless you have an account at that bank (it doesn't have to be at that branch). Only in major cities are large bank branches equipped to exchange foreign currencies. Therefore, it's best to rely on credit cards, cash machines, and traveler's checks to handle expenses while you're traveling.

CURRENCY

The basic unit of U.S. currency is the dollar, which is subdivided into 100 cents. Coins are the copper penny (1¢) and four silver coins: the nickel (5¢), the dime (10¢), the quarter (25¢), and the half-dollar (50¢). Silver $1 coins are rarely seen in circulation. Paper money comes in denominations of $1, $5, $10, $20, $50, and $100. All these bills are the same size and green in color; they are distinguishable only by the dollar amount indicated on them and by pictures of various famous American people and monuments.

At press time (October 1998), the exchange rate was $1.64 to the pound sterling, 69¢ to the Canadian dollar, and 59¢ to the Australian dollar.

EXCHANGING MONEY

In the United States, it is not as easy to find places to exchange currency as it is in European cities. In major international cities, such as New York and Los Angeles, currency may be exchanged at some bank branches, as well as at currency-exchange booths in airports and at foreign-currency offices such as American Express Travel Service and Thomas Cook (check local directories for addresses and phone numbers). The best strategy is to **buy traveler's checks in U.S. dollars** before you come to the United States; although the rates may not be as good abroad, the time saved by not having to search constantly for exchange facilities far outweighs any financial loss.

For the most favorable rates, **change money through banks.** Although fees charged for ATM transactions may be higher abroad than at home, Cirrus and Plus exchange rates are excellent, because they are based on wholesale rates offered only by major banks. You won't do as well at exchange booths in airports or rail and bus stations, in hotels, in restaurants, or in stores, although you may find their hours more convenient. To avoid lines at airport exchange booths, **get a bit of local currency before you leave home.**

➤ EXCHANGE SERVICES: **Chase *Currency To Go*** (☎ 800/935–9935; 935–9935 in NY, NJ, and CT). **International Currency Express** (☎ 888/842–0880 on the East Coast, 888/278–6628 on the West Coast). **Thomas Cook Currency Services** (☎ 800/287–7362 for telephone orders and retail locations).

MONEY ORDERS, FUNDS TRANSFERS

Any U.S. bank is equipped to accept transfers of funds from foreign banks. It helps if you can plan dates to pick up money at specific bank branches. Your home bank can supply you with a list of its correspondent banks in the United States.

If you have more time, and you have a U.S. address where you can receive mail, you can have someone send you a certified check, which you can cash at any bank, or a postal money order (for as much as $700, obtained for a fee of up to 85¢ at any U.S. post office and redeemable at any other post office). From overseas, you can have someone go to a bank to send you an international money order (also called a bank draft), which will cost a $15–$20 commission plus airmail postage. Always bring two valid pieces of identification, preferably with photos, to claim your money.

TRAVELER'S CHECKS

Do you need traveler's checks? It depends on where you're headed. If you're going to rural areas and small towns, go with cash; traveler's checks are best used in cities. Lost or stolen checks can usually be replaced within 24 hours. To ensure a speedy refund, buy your own traveler's checks—don't let someone else pay for them, as this can cause delays. The person who bought the checks should make the call to request a refund.

NATIONAL PARKS

Look into discount passes to **save money on park entrance fees.** The Golden Eagle Pass ($50) gets you and your companions free admission to all parks for one year. (Camping and parking are extra). Both the Golden Age Passport ($10), for those 62 and older, and the Golden Access Passport (free), for travelers with disabilities, entitle holders to free entry to all national parks, plus 50% off fees for the use of many park facilities and services. You must show proof of age and of U.S. citizenship or permanent residency (such as a U.S. passport, driver's license, or birth certificate) and, if requesting Golden Access, proof of disability. All three passes are available at all national park entrances where entrance fees are charged. Golden Eagle and Golden Access passes are also available by mail.

➤ PASSES BY MAIL: **National Park Service** (✉ National Capitol Area Office, ✉ 1100 Ohio Dr. SW, Washington, DC 20242).

PACKING

LUGGAGE

How many carry-on bags you can bring with you is up to the airline. Most allow two, but the limit is often reduced to one on certain flights. Gate agents will take excess baggage—including bags they deem oversize—from you as you board and add it to checked luggage. To avoid this situation, make sure that everything you carry aboard will fit under your seat. Also, get to the gate early, and request a seat at the back of the plane; you'll probably board first, while the overhead bins are still empty. Since big, bulky baggage attracts the attention of gate agents and flight attendants on a busy flight, make sure your carry-on is really a carry-on. Finally, a carry-on that's long and narrow is more likely to remain unnoticed than one that's wide and bulky.

If you are flying internationally, note that baggage allowances may be determined not by piece but by weight—generally 88 pounds (40 kilograms) in first class, 66 pounds (30 kilograms) in business class, and 44 pounds (20 kilograms) in economy.

Airline liability for baggage is limited to $1,250 per person on flights within the United States. On international flights it amounts to $9.07 per pound or $20 per kilogram for checked baggage (roughly $640 per 70-pound bag) and $400 per passenger for unchecked baggage. You can buy additional coverage at check-in for about $10 per $1,000 of coverage, but it excludes a rather extensive list of items, shown on your airline ticket.

Before departure, **itemize your bags' contents** and their worth, and label the bags with your name, address, and phone number. (If you use your home address, cover it so that potential thieves can't see it readily.) Inside each bag, **pack a copy of your itinerary.** At check-in, **make sure that each bag is correctly tagged** with the destination airport's three-letter code. If your bags arrive damaged or fail to arrive at all, file a written report with the airline before leaving the airport.

PACKING LIST

The American lifestyle is generally casual: Women may wear slacks and men may go without a jacket and tie virtually anywhere, except expensive restaurants in larger cities. If you prefer to dress up for dinner or the theater, though, go right ahead. As a rule, people in the Northeast dress more formally, while people in such places as Florida, Texas, and southern California are relatively informal. In beach towns, many hotels and restaurants post signs announcing that they will not serve customers who are shoeless, shirtless, or dressed in bathing suits or other skimpy attire, so tote along some shoes and cover-ups.

The United States has a wide range of climates. When deciding what weather to dress for, **read the "When to Go" sections in chapter introductions** for each region you'll be visiting. One caveat: Even in warm destinations, you may want an extra layer of clothing to compensate for overactive air-conditioning or to protect against brisk ocean breezes. Although you can count on all modern buildings being well heated in winter, historic inns and hunting lodges in rugged climates—New England, the Great Lakes states, the Rockies, or the Pacific Northwest—may be poorly insulated, drafty, or heated only by wood-burning fireplaces. Pack accordingly.

If you'll be sightseeing in historic cities, you'll spend a lot of time walking, so **bring sturdy, well-fitting, flat-heeled shoes.** Don't forget deck shoes if you want to go sailing and sandals for walking across the burning-hot sand of southern beaches. If you plan to hike in the country, pack shoes or boots with strong flexible soles and wear long pants to protect your legs from brambles and insect bites.

Bring sunscreen lotion if you expect to be out in the sun, because prices may be high at beachside stores. These days most upscale hotels provide a basket of toiletries—soaps, shampoo, conditioner, bath gel—but if you prefer using a certain brand, bring your own. Hand-held hair dryers are sometimes provided, but don't rely on this. You can generally request an iron and ironing board from the front desk.

In your carry-on luggage **bring an extra pair of eyeglasses or contact lenses** and **enough of any medication you take** to last the entire trip. You may also want your doctor to write a spare prescription using the drug's generic name, since brand names may vary from country to country. **Never put prescription drugs or valuables in luggage to be checked.** To avoid customs delays, carry medications in their original packaging. And don't forget to copy down and carry addresses of offices that handle refunds of lost traveler's checks.

PASSPORTS & VISAS

When traveling internationally, **carry a passport even if you don't need one** (it's always the best form of I.D.), and make **two photocopies of the data page** (one for someone at home and another for you, carried separately from your passport). If you lose your passport, promptly call the nearest embassy or consulate and the local police.

➤ U.K. CITIZENS: **U.S. Embassy Visa Information Line** (☎ 01891/200–290; calls cost 49p per minute, 39p per minute cheap rate), for U.S. visa information. **U.S. Embassy Visa Branch** (✉ 5 Upper Grosvenor St., London W1A 2JB), for U.S. visa information; send a self-addressed, stamped envelope. Write the **U.S. Consulate General** (✉ Queen's House, ✉ Queen St., Belfast BTI 6EO) if you live in Northern Ireland.

PASSPORT OFFICES

The best time to apply for a passport or to renew is during the fall and winter. Before any trip, be sure to check your passport's expiration date and, if necessary, renew it as soon as possible. (Some countries won't allow you to enter on a passport that's due to expire in six months or less.)

➤ AUSTRALIAN CITIZENS: **Australian Passport Office** (☎ 131–232).

➤ NEW ZEALAND CITIZENS: **New Zealand Passport Office** (☎ 04/494–0700 for information on how to apply, 0800/727–776 for information on applications already submitted).

➤ U.K. CITIZENS: **London Passport Office** (☎ 0990/21010), for fees and documentation requirements and to request an emergency passport.

SENIOR-CITIZEN TRAVEL

To qualify for age-related discounts, **mention your senior-citizen status up front** when booking hotel reservations (not when checking out) and before you're seated in restaurants (not when paying the bill). Note that discounts may be limited to certain menus, days, or hours. When renting a car, **ask about promotional car-rental discounts,** which can be cheaper than senior-citizen rates.

➤ EDUCATIONAL PROGRAMS: **Elderhostel** (✉ 75 Federal St., 3rd floor, Boston, MA 02110, ☎ 617/426–8056).

STUDENT TRAVEL

TRAVEL AGENCIES

➤ STUDENT I.D.S & SERVICES: **Council on International Educational Exchange** (✉ CIEE, ✉ 205 E. 42nd St., 14th floor, New York, NY 10017, ☎ 212/822–2600 or 888/268–6245, FAX 212/822–2699), for mail orders only, in the United States. **Travel Cuts** (✉ 187 College St., Toronto, Ontario M5T 1P7, ☎ 416/979–2406 or 800/667–2887) in Canada.

➤ STUDENT TOURS: **Contiki Holidays** (✉ 300 Plaza Alicante, Suite 900, Garden Grove, CA 92840, ☎ 714/740–0808 or 800/266–8454, FAX 714/740–2034).

TAXES

HOTEL

Many states and cities levy hotel taxes, usually as a percentage of the room rate. For example, in New York City, which already has an 8¼% sales tax, the progressive hotel tax can raise the tariff as much as 13% more, to 21¼%; in New York City there's also a $2 per-room, per-night occupancy tax. When you make room reservations **ask how much tax will be added to the basic rate.**

SALES

There is no U.S. value-added tax, but sales taxes are set by most individual states, and they can range anywhere from 3% to 8¼%. In some states, localities are permitted to add their own sales taxes as well. Exactly what is taxable, however, varies from place to place. In some areas, food and other essentials are not taxable, although you might pay tax for restaurant food. Luxury items such as cigarettes and alcohol are sometimes subject to an extra tax (known colloquially as a "sin tax"), as is gasoline, on the theory that car users should provide funds used to improve local roads.

TELEPHONES

All U.S. telephone numbers consist of 10 digits—the three-digit area code, followed by a seven-digit local number. If you're calling a number from another area-code region, dial "1" then all 10 digits. If you're calling from a distance but within the same area code, dial "1" then the last seven digits. For calls within the same local calling area, just dial the seven-digit number. A map of U.S. area codes is printed in the front of most local telephone directories; throughout this book, we have listed each phone number in full, including its area code.

Four special prefixes, "800," "888," "877," and "900," are not area codes but indicators of particular kinds of service. "800," "888," and "877" numbers can be dialed free from anywhere in the country—usually they are prepaid commercial lines that make it easier for consumers to obtain information, products, or services. The "900" numbers charge you for making the call and generally offer some kind of entertainment, such as horoscope readings, sports scores, or sexually suggestive conversations. These services can be very expensive, so **know what you're getting into before you dial a "900" number.**

COUNTRY CODES

The country code for the United States is 1.

CREDIT-CARD CALLS

U.S. telephone credit cards are not like the magnetic cards used in some European countries, which pay for calls in advance; they simply represent an account that lets you charge a call to your home or business phone. On any phone, you can make a credit-card call by punching in your individual account number or by telling the operator that number. Certain specially marked pay phones (usually found in airports, hotel lobbies, and so on) can be used only for credit-card calls. To get a credit card, contact your long-distance telephone carrier, such as AT&T, MCI, or Sprint.

DIRECTORY & OPERATOR INFORMATION

For assistance from an operator, dial "0". To find out a telephone number, call directory assistance, 555–1212 in every locality. These calls are free even from a pay phone. If you want to charge a long-distance call to the person you're calling, you can call collect by dialing "0" instead of "1" before the 10-digit number, and an operator will come on the line to assist you (the party you're calling, however, has the right to refuse the call).

INTERNATIONAL CALLS

International calls can be direct-dialed from most phones; dial "011," followed by the country code and then the local number (the front pages of many local telephone directories include a list of overseas country codes). To have an operator assist you, dial "0" and ask for the overseas operator. The country code for Australia is 61; New Zealand, 64; and the United Kingdom, 44. To reach Canada, dial 1 + area code + number.

LONG-DISTANCE CALLS

Competitive long-distance carriers make calling within the United States relatively convenient and let you avoid hotel surcharges. By dialing an 800 number, you can get connected to the long-distance company of your choice.

➤ LONG-DISTANCE CARRIERS: **AT&T** (☎ 800/225–5288). **MCI** (☎ 800/888–8000). **Sprint** (☎ 800/366–2255).

PUBLIC PHONES

Instructions for pay telephones should be posted on the phone, but generally you insert your coins—anywhere from 10¢ to 35¢ for a local call—in a slot and wait for the steady hum of a dial tone before dialing the number you wish to reach. If you dial a long-distance number, the operator will come on the line and tell you how much more money you must insert for your call to go through.

TIPPING

Tipping is a way of life in the United States, and some individuals may even be rude if you don't give them the amount of tip they expect. At restaurants, a 15% tip is standard for waiters; up to 20% may be expected at more expensive establishments. The same goes for taxi drivers, bartenders, and hairdressers. Coat-check facilities usually expect $1; bellhops and porters should get about 50¢ per bag; hotel maids in upscale hotels should get about $1 per day of your stay. On package tours, conductors and drivers usually get about $2–$3 per day from each group member; check whether this has already been figured into your cost. For local sightseeing tours, you may individually tip the driver-guide $1 if he or she has been helpful or informative. Ushers in theaters do not expect tips.

TOUR OPERATORS

Buying a prepackaged tour or independent vacation can make your trip less expensive and more hassle-free. Because everything is prearranged, you'll spend less time planning.

Operators that handle several hundred thousand travelers per year can use their purchasing power to give you a good price. Their high volume may also indicate financial stability. But some small companies provide more personalized service; because they tend to specialize, they may also be more knowledgeable about a given area.

BOOKING WITH AN AGENT

Travel agents are excellent resources. In fact, large operators accept bookings made only through travel agents. But it's a good idea to **collect brochures from several agencies,** because some agents' suggestions may be influenced by relationships with tour and package firms that reward them for volume sales. If you have a special interest, **find an agent with expertise in that area**; ASTA (☞ Travel Agencies, *below*) has a database of specialists worldwide.

Make sure your travel agent knows the accommodations and other services. Ask about the hotel's location, room size, beds, and whether it has a pool, room service, or programs for children, if you care about these. Has your agent been there in person or sent others you can contact?

Do some homework on your own, too: Local tourism boards can provide information about lesser-known and small-niche operators, some of which may sell only direct.

BUYER BEWARE

Each year consumers are stranded or lose their money when tour operators—even very large ones with excellent reputations—go out of business. So **check out the operator.** Find out how long the company has been in business, and ask several travel agents about its reputation. If the package or tour you are considering is priced lower than in your wildest dreams, **be skeptical.** Try to **book with a company that has a consumer-protection program.** If the operator has such a program, you'll find information about it in the company's brochure. If the operator you are considering does not offer some kind of consumer protection, then ask for references from satisfied customers.

In the U.S., members of the National Tour Association and United States Tour Operators Association are required to set aside funds to cover your payments and travel arrangements in case the company defaults. It's also a good idea to choose a company that participates in the American Society of Travel Agent's Tour Operator Program (TOP). This gives you a forum if there are any disputes between you and your tour operator; ASTA will act as mediator.

➤ TOUR-OPERATOR RECOMMENDATIONS: **American Society of Travel Agents** (☞ Travel Agencies, *below*). **National Tour Association** (✉ NTA, ✉ 546 E. Main St., Lexington, KY 40508, ☎ 606/226–4444 or 800/755–8687). **United States Tour Operators Association** (✉ USTOA, ✉ 342 Madison Ave., Suite 1522, New York, NY 10173, ☎ 212/599–6599 or 800/468–7862, FAX 212/599–6744).

COSTS

The more your package or tour includes, the better you can predict the ultimate cost of your vacation. Make sure you know exactly what is covered, and **beware of hidden costs.** Are taxes, tips, and service charges included? Transfers and baggage handling? Entertainment and excursions? These can add up.

Prices for packages and tours are usually quoted per person, based on two sharing a room. If traveling solo, you may be required to pay the full double-occupancy rate. Some operators eliminate this surcharge if you agree to be matched with a roommate of the same sex, even if one is not found by departure time.

GROUP TOURS

Among companies that sell tours to the U.S., the following are nationally known, have a proven reputation, and offer plenty of options. The classifications used below represent different price categories, and you'll probably encounter these terms when talking to a travel agent or tour operator. The key difference is usually in accommodations, which run from budget to better, and better-yet to best.

➤ DELUXE: **Globus** (✉ 5301 S. Federal Circle, Littleton, CO 80123-2980, ☎ 303/797–2800 or 800/221–0090, FAX 303/347–2080). **Maupintour** (✉ 1515 St. Andrews Dr., Lawrence, KS 66047, ☎ 913/843–1211 or 800/255–4266, FAX 913/843–8351). **Tauck Tours** (✉ Box 5027, 276 Post Rd. W, Westport, CT 06881-5027, ☎ 203/226–6911 or 800/468–2825, FAX 203/221–6866).

➤ FIRST-CLASS: **Brendan Tours** (✉ 15137 Califa St., Van Nuys, CA 91411, ☎ 818/785–9696 or 800/421–8446, FAX 818/902–9876). **Caravan Tours** (✉ 401 N. Michigan Ave., Chicago, IL 60611, ☎ 312/321–9800 or 800/340–, FAX 312/321–9845). **Collette Tours** (✉ 162 Middle St., Pawtucket, RI 02860, ☎ 401/728–3805 or 800/340–5158, FAX 401/728–4745). **Gadabout Tours** (✉ 700 E. Tahquitz Canyon Way, Palm Springs, CA 92262-6767, ☎ 619/325–5556 or 800/952–5068). **Mayflower Tours** (✉ Box 490, 1225 Warren Ave., Downers Grove, IL 60515, ☎ 630/960–3430 or 800/323–7604, FAX 630/960–3575). **Trafalgar Tours** (✉ 11 E. 26th St., New York, NY 10010, ☎ 212/689–8977 or 800/854–0103, FAX 800/457–6644).

➤ BUDGET: **Cosmos** (☞ Globus, *above*). **Trafalgar** (☞ *above*).

PACKAGES

Like group tours, independent vacation packages are available from major tour operators and airlines. The companies listed below offer vacation packages in a broad price range.

➤ AIR/HOTEL/CAR: **American Airlines Vacations** (☎ 800/321–2121). **Continental Vacations** (☎ 800/634–5555). **Delta Vacations** (☎ 800/872–7786). **United Vacations** (☎ 800/328–6877). **US Airways Vacations** (☎ 800/455–0123).

➤ AIR/HOTEL: **American Airlines Vacations** (☎ 800/321–2121). **Continental Vacations** (☎ 800/634–5555). **Delta Vacations** (☎ 800/872–7786). **TWA Getaway Vacations** (☎ 800/438–2929). **United Vacations** (☎ 800/328–6877). **US Airways Vacations** (☎ 800/455–0123).

➤ HOTEL ONLY: **SuperCities** (✉ 139 Main St., Cambridge, MA 02142, ☎ 800/333–1234).

➤ CUSTOM PACKAGES: **Amtrak Vacations** (☎ 800/321–8684).

➤ FROM THE U.K.: **Trailfinders** (✉ 42–50 Earls Court Rd., London W8 6EJ, ☎ 0171/937–5400; ✉ 58 Deansgate, Manchester M3 2FF, ☎ 0161/839–6969). **Travel Cuts** (✉ 295A Regent St., London W1R 7YA, ☎ 0171/255–2191); ☞ Student Travel, *above*. **Flight Express Travel** (✉ 77 New Bond St., London W1Y 9DB, ☎ 0171/409–3311).

THEME TRIPS

For a complete list of operators, *see* Chapter 2, Special-Interest Vacations.

TRAIN TRAVEL

Amtrak is the national passenger rail service. It runs a limited number of routes; the northeast coast from Boston down to Washington, D.C., is generally well served. Chicago is a major rail terminus as well.

Some trains travel overnight, and you can sleep in your seat or book a couchette at additional cost. Most trains have diner cars with acceptable food, but you may prefer to bring your own. Excursion fares, when available, may save you nearly half the round-trip fare.

➤ RESERVATIONS: **Amtrak** (☎ 800/ 872–7245, ☎ TDD 800/523–6590).

CHILDREN

Children under 2 ride free (one child per adult) if they don't occupy a seat; children 2–15 accompanied by a fare-paying adult pay half-price (two children per adult); children 15 and over pay the full adult fare.

SENIOR CITIZENS

Senior citizens (over 62) are entitled to a 15% discount on the lowest available fares.

TRAVELERS WITH DISABILITIES

Amtrak requests 48 hours' advance notice to provide redcap service, special seats, or wheelchair assistance at stations equipped to provide these services.

Passengers with disabilities receive 15% off an adult one-way fare.

DISCOUNT PASSES

The USA Railpass allows overseas visitors 15 or 30 days of unlimited nationwide travel for $425 or $535 (peak season, June–September 7) and $285–$375 (off peak, September 8–May 31), respectively. Fifteen- and 30-day regional rail passes can be purchased by non-U.S. citizens for the Far West ($240/$310, peak season; $185/$240, off peak), Western ($315/$395, peak; $195/$260, off-peak), Eastern ($250/$310, peak; $205/$255 off-peak), and Northeast ($195/$230, peak; $175/$215 off-peak) areas of the United States; 30-day passes are also offered for rail travel along the East Coast and West Coast (each is $275, peak; $225, off-peak) regions of the country. You can purchase these rail passes in the United States at any Amtrak station, but to qualify you must show a valid non-U.S. passport. If you're a student, ask about student discounts that may apply to certain passes.

TIMETABLES

Train schedules can be obtained at ticket counters or special displays in train terminals. Automated schedule and fare information is often available 24 hours a day on local or toll-free numbers.

TRAVEL AGENCIES

A good travel agent puts your needs first. Look for an agency that has been in business at least five years, emphasizes customer service, and has someone on staff who specializes in your destination. In addition, **make sure the agency belongs to a professional trade organization,** such as ASTA in the United States. If your travel agency is also acting as your tour operator, *see* Buyer Beware in Tour Operators, *above*).

➤ LOCAL AGENT REFERRALS: **American Society of Travel Agents** (ASTA, ☎ 800/965–2782 24-hr hot line, FAX 703/684–8319). **Association of Canadian Travel Agents** (✉ Suite 201, 1729 Bank St., Ottawa, Ontario K1V 7Z5, ☎ 613/521–0474, FAX 613/ 521–0805). **Association of British Travel Agents** (✉ 55–57 Newman St., London W1P 4AH, ☎ 0171/ 637–2444, FAX 0171/637–0713). **Australian Federation of Travel Agents** (☎ 02/9264–3299). **Travel Agents' Association of New Zealand** (☎ 04/499–0104).

TRAVEL GEAR

Travel catalogs specialize in useful items, such as compact alarm clocks and travel irons, that can **save space when packing.**

➤ CATALOGS: **Magellan's** (☎ 800/ 962–4943, FAX 805/568–5406). **Orvis Travel** (☎ 800/541–3541, FAX 540/ 343–7053). **TravelSmith** (☎ 800/ 950–1600, FAX 800/950–1656).

VISITOR INFORMATION

TOURIST INFORMATION

State tourism offices, city tourist bureaus, and local chambers of commerce, which are usually the best sources of information about their communities, are listed throughout this book at the beginning of each state, city, or regional section.

➤ IN CANADA: **Travel USA** (☎ 905/890–5662 or 800/268–3482 in Ontario).

➤ IN THE U.K.: There is no single tourist organization for the United States; U.S. states have their own agencies. Call **Visit USA** (☎ 0891/600–530) for contact addresses and telephone numbers; calls cost 50p per minute peak times, 45p per minute all other times.

U.S. GOVERNMENT

Government agencies can be an excellent source of inexpensive travel information. When planning your trip, **find out what government materials are available.**

➤ PAMPHLETS: **Consumer Information Center** (✉ Consumer Information Catalogue, Pueblo, CO 81009, ☎ 719/948–3334 or 888/878–3256) for a free catalog that includes travel titles.

WHEN TO GO

Although there is no country-wide tourist "season," various regions may have high and low seasons that are reflected in airfares and hotel rates. Unless the weather is a real drawback (as in Alaska in the winter or Miami in August), **visit areas during their off-season to save money and avoid crowds.**

CLIMATE

For climate information in specific regions of the country, **read the "When to Go" sections in chapter introductions.**

➤ FORECASTS: **Weather Channel Connection** (☎ 900/932–8437), 95¢ per minute from a Touch-Tone phone.

2 Special-Interest Vacations

Sports and the Outdoors

Spiritual and Physical Fitness Vacations

Education and Culture

YOU CAN SEE THE UNITED STATES in many ways, but you'll have the most fun seeing it in the company of like-minded travelers while doing what you like to do best. The following pages suggest what's available; contact state tourism departments for other ideas.

By Karen Cure

Updated by Heidi Spangler Sarna

Group Trips

Want a vacation-immersion in archeobotany? How about studying the natural history of New York's Finger Lakes? Have you always wanted someone to teach you kayaking, tennis, or golf? How about learning to cook Indian or Chinese food? Whatever your interest, you'll find a program or an organization sponsoring group trips in the field.

How to Choose

Either pick a destination, or determine the special type of travel you are interested in and let the destination choose you. Then gather names of outfitters or resorts in your area of interest and contact them. For trips, ask about group size and composition (singles, couples, families, and so on), daily schedules, required gear, and any specifics of the activity. When looking into resorts, consider size, facilities, activities, and style. For courses and workshops, also find out about lodging arrangements, instructors' qualifications, and diversions for nonparticipating traveling companions. In every case, inquire about costs—what's included (meals, equipment), what's extra, how you pay, and how you get a refund if necessary. Check references.

Shaw Guides (✉ Box 1295, New York, NY 10023, ☎ 212/799/6464 or 800/247-6553, www.shawguides.com) publishes special-interest guides on academic tours and adult education, photography, cooking, arts and crafts, and sports. Check their Web site for the most up-to-date information.

Sports and the Outdoors

Monuments and museums aside, the nation's deep forests, mighty waters, and wide-open spaces are some of its most distinctive assets. Whether by bicycle or boat, on horseback or skis, or with your own two feet, a sports- or outdoors-oriented vacation will undoubtedly give you a new appreciation of the country's natural wonders.

Group Trips

Knowledgeable leaders make group trips the safest way to experience the wilderness. Because you overnight in campgrounds or simple accommodations, costs are often modest. Some trips are organized for their members by conservation-minded nonprofit groups, such as the **Appalachian Mountain Club** (✉ 5 Joy St., Boston, MA 02108, ☎ 617/523-0636, FAX 617/523-0722) and the **Sierra Club** (✉ 85 Second St., 2nd floor, San Francisco, CA 94105, ☎ 415/977-5522). On Sierra Club trips, members volunteer as leaders, participants do camp chores, and costs stay low. Trips sponsored by the **National Audubon Society** (✉ Nature Odysseys, 700 Broadway, New York, NY 10003, ☎ 212/979-3066, FAX 212/353-0190) focus on birds and other wildlife.

Private firms leading outdoors-oriented trips include **American Wilderness Experience** (✉ Box 1486, Boulder, CO 80306, ☎ 800/444-0099, FAX 303/444-3999), adventure-travel pioneer **Mountain Travel Sobek** (✉ 6420 Fairmount Ave., El Cerrito, CA 94530-3606, ☎ 800/227-2384, FAX 510/525-7710), and for the Southeast, **Nantahala Outdoor Center** (✉ 13077 Hwy. 19W, Bryson City, NC 28713, ☎ 704/488-6737, FAX 704/488-0301).

Bookings and Information

Pat Dickerman, in business since 1949, matches travelers with congenial operators in her books ***Adventure Travel North America***, last updated in 1994; and ***Farm, Ranch, and Country Vacations in America***, last updated in 1995 ($10 each, plus $3 postage, from **Adventure Guides, Inc.** ⊠ 7550 E. McDonald Dr., Scottsdale, AZ 85250, ☏ 800/252–7899). Fodor's publishes **Great American Sports and Adventure Vacations** ($17.50; available in bookstores, or call ☏ 800/533–6478), covering 30 activities with details on more than 500 schools, workshops, and tours throughout the United States. The twice-yearly **Specialty Travel Index** (⊠ 305 San Anselmo Ave., Suite 313, San Anselmo, CA 94960, ☏ 800/442–4922, FAX 415/459–4974), $10 annually, has ads for everything from fishing and mountain-bike trips to gambling and shopping trips. Specialty magazines available on newsstands are full of ideas; the following sections suggest other resources.

Bicycling

Biking the nation's byways, you'll discover farms and factories, forests and strip malls, antique mansions and trailer parks.

DISTINCTIVELY AMERICAN CYCLING

Clapboard houses, salty seacoasts, and pine-and-hardwood forests beckon cyclists to **New England.** Particularly noteworthy are the Maine coast; Vermont's green and bucolic Northeast Kingdom; the forests and farms along the banks of New Hampshire's Connecticut River; Massachusetts's beach-ringed Martha's Vineyard and moor-covered Nantucket Island; northwestern Connecticut's hilly terrain, dotted with old houses and charming inns; mansion-laden Newport, Rhode Island; and the mountains and country roads of New York state's Catskills and Adirondack mountain regions.

The flat to mildly rolling landscape yields a bounty of scenic nooks and crannies in corners of the **mid-Atlantic states,** such as Pennsylvania's Lancaster County, full of peaceful byroads and Amish farms; the manicured emerald lawns of northern Virginia's horse country; Maryland's Eastern Shore, with its long Atlantic beaches and marshy backwaters; and the woods-edged towpath of the old C&O Canal, near Washington, D.C.

In the **Rockies** cyclists are mad for rugged, fat-tired mountain bikes—common sights in the rugged, piney high country, near Durango, Colorado, and on the sandstone cliff top that is the Slickrock Trail, near Moab, Utah, where the landscape is the color of sunset.

In **California** the pedaling is good on the roads through the vineyards of the Napa Valley and on the rock-bound Monterey Peninsula; Highway 1, which teeters on the cliff tops above the Pacific, is the trip of a lifetime. Traveling by bike is also a great way to experience the diverse landscape of **Hawaii's** Big Island.

More than 18,000 mi of abandoned railroad beds nationwide are slated to become bike trails; contact **Rails to Trails Conservancy** (⊠ 1100 17th St. NW, 10th fl., Washington, DC 20036, ☏ 202/331–9696, FAX 202/331–9680) for information.

MOUNTAIN BIKING

Climbing steep inclines, fording streams, and darting over dirt trails are all part of the exhilaration of mountain biking, now a subculture all its own. Look for designated trail systems in city, county, and state parks; in addition, many ski resorts open their slopes, trails, and chairlifts to mountain bikers during the off-season. *See* Resources, *below,* for organized tours.

WITH A GROUP

Bicycle-tour packages include lodging and often meals, along with escorts, "sag wagons" to carry luggage and weary pedalers, and optional rental bikes and helmets. Maps pinpoint routes between overnights so you can pedal at your own pace.

A good source is **Adventure Cycling** (✉ Box 8308, Missoula, MT 59807, ☎ 406/721–1776 or 800/721–8719, FAX 406/721–8754), the country's largest nonprofit recreational-cycling organization.

RESOURCES

Adventure Cycling(☞ *above*) has helpful trip-planning information for members ($30 annually). *Bicycling* magazine (☎ 800/666–2806) lists specialist operators, such as the active **Backroads** (✉ 801 Cedar St., Berkeley, CA 94710, ☎ 510/527–1555 or 800/462–2848, FAX 510/527–1444); **Brooks Country Cycling Tours** (✉ 140 W. 83rd St., New York, NY 10024, ☎ 212/874–5151 or 800/284–8954, FAX 212/874–5286), which roams up and down the East Coast and packages trips with transportation to and from Manhattan; **Timberline Bicycle Tours** (✉ 7975 E. Harvard St., No. J, Denver, CO 80231, ☎ 303/759–3804 or 800/417–2453, FAX 303/368–1651), which concentrates on the West; and **Vermont Bicycle Touring** (✉ Box 711-AN, Bristol, VT 05433, ☎ 800/245–3868), which has won many fans with its trips over country roads and overnight stops at local inns. For organized mountain-biking tours in the national parks of the West, contact **Backcountry Tours** (✉ Box 4029, Bozeman, MT 59772, ☎ 800/575–1540 or 406/586–4288).

Canoeing and Kayaking

Paddling along the ocean's edge, across freshwater lakes, or down free-flowing streams gives you a view of the wilderness that's hard to come by any other way. Moving almost soundlessly, canoes and kayaks seldom disturb wildlife feeding at the water's edge, and paddlers encounter birds and animals, practically eye to eye. The choice of craft is up to you: Canoes are more comfortable and give you more room to carry gear (and easier access to it); kayaks are more stable—important when you're maneuvering among boulders on white water.

DISTINCTIVELY AMERICAN CANOEING

You don't have to be an expert to tackle America's most beautiful paddling waters. Many are within the skills of beginners—though wind, heavy rainfall, or spring runoff can present challenges.

In the East canoeists head for **Maine's wild Allagash River** and the adjacent stream- and portage-connected lakes; or to the island-flecked lakes in **New York's Adirondack Mountains,** where log lean-tos shelter campers on the mainland and on pristine islands. Lush hardwood forests edge white-water torrents in **West Virginia.** In the South the still waters of **Florida's Everglades National Park** and **Georgia's Okefenokee National Wildlife Refuge** access water-based "prairies" and mangrove swamps. The water in parts of the Okefenokee—stained black by leachings from vegetation—mirrors the verdant foliage overhead.

In the Midwest, Voyageurs National Park and the Superior National Forest and its Boundary Waters Canoe Area Wilderness showcase the woods of **northern Minnesota,** crossed by rivers and streams and scattered with lakes; in some areas no motorized vehicles are permitted, and it's possible to explore for months without backtracking. **Missouri's Ozark National Scenic Riverways** and **Arkansas's Buffalo National River**—bluff-edged blends of rapids, fast water, and still pools—are just two of six National Rivers administered by the **National Park Service** (✉ Box 37127, Washington, DC 20013-7127, ☎ 202/208–4747); the service also administers nine National Wild and Scenic Rivers.

RESOURCES

The century-old **American Canoe Association** (✉ 7432 Alban Station Blvd., Suite B226, Springfield, VA 22150, ☎ 703/451–0141, FAX 703/451–2245) has lists of canoeing clubs, schools, books, and trips ($25 annually). Consult *Canoe and Kayak* (☎ 425/827–6363) and *Paddler* (☎ 703/451–0141) magazines for other ideas.

Climbing and Mountaineering

Every year scores of hardy hikers visit the nation's highest peaks and leave invigorated by the view and exhilarated by their accomplishment. Rock-climbing skills put just that many more summits within reach on longer mountaineering expeditions.

DISTINCTIVELY AMERICAN CLIMBS

Routes on Colorado's 14,255-ft **Longs Peak,** Maine's 5,267-ft **Mt. Katahdin,** New Hampshire's 6,288-ft **Mt. Washington,** and New York's 5,344-ft **Mt. Marcy** are within the abilities of well-conditioned hikers. Many other peaks require rock-climbing skills—or expert guiding. In the West the most famous of these may be 20,320-ft **Mt. McKinley,** the Great One, in Alaska's Denali National Park; but the 13,770-ft hunk of granite known as the **Grand Teton,** in Wyoming's eponymous national park, and the granite walls and domes of California's **Yosemite** have comparable charisma. Easterners find challenges in New York's **Adirondacks** and **Shawangunks.**

SCHOOLS AND GUIDED ASCENTS

For extra excitement in national parks and forests, try a day at the **Colorado Mountain School** (✉ Box 2062, Estes Park, CO 80517, ☎ 970/586–5758, FAX 970/586–5798), bordering Rocky Mountain National Park; **Exum Mountain Guides** (✉ Box 56, Moose, WY 83012, ☎ 307/733–2297, FAX 307/733–9613), in the Tetons; and **Yosemite Mountaineering School** (✉ Yosemite National Park, Yosemite, CA 95389, ☎ 209/372–1244 or 209/372–1335 in summer). Offering a good mix of guided climbs and lessons at beginner-to-advanced levels are the **American Alpine Institute** (✉ 1515 12th St., Bellingham, WA 98225, ☎ 360/671–1505, FAX 360/734–8890); **Fantasy Ridge Mountain Guides** (✉ Box 1679, Telluride, CO 81435, ☎ 970/728–3546); **Sierra Wilderness Seminars** (✉ 369-B 3rd St., Suite 347, San Raphael, CA 94901, ☎ 415/455–9358, FAX 415/455–9359); and in the East, **Adirondack Alpine Adventures** (✉ Box 179, Keene, NY 12942, ☎ 518/576–9881, FAX 518/576–9574); the southern Appalachians' **Nantahala Outdoor Center** (✉ 13077 Hwy. 19W, Bryson City, NC 28713, ☎ 704/488–6737, FAX 704/488–0301); the White Mountains' **Eastern Mountain Sports** (✉ Main St., Box 514, North Conway, NH 03860, ☎ 603/356–5433 or 800/310–4504); and the Shawangunks' **Mountain Skills Climbing School** (✉ 595 Peak Rd., Stone Ridge, NY 12484, ☎ 914/687–9643).

RESOURCES

Send $1 and a SASE to the **American Mountain Guides Association** (✉ 710 10th St., Suite 101, Golden, CO 80401, ☎ no phone) for a list of more than 100 qualified guides and services. Contact the **American Alpine Club** (✉ 710 10th St., Suite 100, Golden, CO 80401, ☎ 303/384–0110, FAX 303/384–0111) for information on all facets of climbing.

Fishing

The challenge of filling up a stringer isn't the only reason angling is the country's single most popular sport. There's also the prospect of a fresh-fish dinner. And the quiet hours spent by the water are their own reward.

DISTINCTIVELY AMERICAN ANGLING

Surf casting on Atlantic-pounded beaches and jetties yields good sport from Cape Cod to southern Florida. **Deep-sea fishing** gives you a good dose of the local culture. You can charter anything from a creaky wooden boat to a state-of-the-art yacht or join the often rough-and-ready crowd aboard party boats, where anglers pay by the head. Ocean City, Maryland, thinks of itself as the world's white-marlin capital, but marlin is prime quarry in Hawaii, too, where a whole fleet of boats leaves Kona every morning. There are huge sportfishing fleets in the Florida Panhandle, at small towns such as Destin and Fort Walton Beach; and in the Florida Keys, particularly Islamorada, Marathon, and Key West, where you might catch a long, gleaming needle-nose tarpon. **Fishing for snook,** a wily, scrappy, bony fish, is great sport—the Florida west-coast town of Naples is a hotbed—as is **casting for bonefish** in shallow saltwater flats.

In fresh water **trout fishing** is a whole angling subculture on such celebrated streams as Vermont's Battenkill, New York's Beaverkill, Arkansas's White River, and many rivers in Michigan and the northern Rockies. In Missouri **river fishing** is for bass in clear, slow, bluff- and forest-edged streams; in Idaho it's for steelhead and chinook in rivers like the Salmon, Snake, and Clearwater; and in Oregon it's for steelhead, with huge runs in winter.

Other anglers prefer **lake fishing** and take motorboats or canoes in search of their quarry: lake trout and landlocked salmon in deep waters such as Maine's Moosehead and New Hampshire's Winnepesaukee; crappie and largemouth bass on such man-made lakes in the South and Midwest as Kentucky's Lake Barkley and Kentucky Lake and South Carolina's Lakes Marion and Moultrie. Northern Minnesota woodlands are as famous for yielding creels of scrappy walleye and northern pike and large- and smallmouth bass as for canoeing.

In a class by itself, **fishing in Alaska** is legendary: in the southeast panhandle for salmon (including sockeye, humpback, calico, king, and coho) and in the Interior and South Central regions for grayling. Good fishing is often right beside a highway; but fly-in trips to remote lakes and streams are common.

To plan a trip, decide what kind of fishing you want to do, then pick a destination. A letter to appropriate state fish and wildlife departments and a follow-up phone call are the first steps to a good creel. Or choose a fishing lodge in an area you want to visit, and let the pros find the fish. Bait-and-tackle shops or sporting goods stores, thriving wherever there are waters to fish, will know what's biting where and sell necessary licenses (usually required only by states and necessary only for freshwater fishing).

SCHOOLS

To hone your fishing skills, spend time at the **Wulff School of Fly Fishing** (✉ Box 948, Livingston Manor, NY 12758, ☎ 914/439–5020, FAX 914/439–8055) or **Bud Lilly's Trout Shop** (✉ Box 530, 39 Madison Ave., West Yellowstone, MT 59758, ☎ 406/646–7801), both founded by veteran anglers, or at **Orvis Fly Fishing Schools** (✉ Historic Rte. 7A, Manchester, VT 05254, ☎ 802/362–3622), sponsored by the noted equipment maker.

RESOURCES

Fishing lodges designed specifically for anglers advertise in the magazines *Field & Stream* (☎ 212/779–5000), *North American Fisherman* (☎ 800/843–6232), and *Fly Fisherman* (☎ 717/657–9555).

Golf

Although most top courses are at private clubs, U.S. resorts present challenges for itinerant players, not to mention the chance to enjoy some of the country's lushest scenery.

DISTINCTIVELY AMERICAN GOLFING

The Masters Tournament, held annually at the Augusta National Golf Club in Augusta, Georgia, has made the Southeast famous among golfers. Although that course is not open to the public, golfers can enjoy southern graciousness along with equally verdant, beautifully tended layouts at another American golf center—Pinehurst, North Carolina, home of the **Pinehurst Hotel** (✉ Box 4000, Pinehurst, NC 28374, ☎ 800/487–4653) and no fewer than eight golf courses.

Two southeastern old-line mountain resorts are equally appealing: the **Homestead** (✉ U.S. 220, Main St., Box 2000, Hot Springs, VA 24445, ☎ 540/839–1766 or 800/838–1766) and the **Greenbrier Hotel** (✉ 300 W. Main St., White Sulphur Springs, WV 24986, ☎ 304/536–1110 or 800/624–6070, FAX 304/536–7854). On Hilton Head Island, South Carolina, the beach scene meets the golf culture, and the hybrid attracts golfers from all over the country.

Flung along the ragged edge of the rocky Monterey Peninsula is the world-class **Pebble Beach Golf Links** (✉ 17-Mile Dr., Pebble Beach, CA 93953, ☎ 408/624–3811 or 800/654–9300). For sheer numbers, however, golf enthusiasts look south to San Diego, home of six dozen courses. Courses like the Gold, at the posh **Wigwam Resort** (✉ 300 Wigwam Blvd., Litchfield Park, AZ 85340, ☎ 602/935–3811 or 800/327–0396), have brought Arizona the fame once reserved for California. Elegant Hawaii resorts such as **Mauna Kea** (✉ 62-100 Mauna Kea Beach Dr., Kamuela, HI 96743, ☎ 808/882–7222), **Mauna Lani Bay Hotel and Bungalows** (✉ 68–1310 Mauna Lani Dr., Kohala Coast, HI 96743, ☎ 808/885–6655), and **Princeville Hotel** (✉ Box 3069, Princeville, HI 96722, ☎ 808/826–9644) mix challenges with verdant coastline scenery.

GOLF CLINICS

Most resort pros also teach. Then there are golf clinics, where golfers spend whole vacations working on their swing: the **Golf Digest** Instruction Schools (✉ 5520 Park Ave., Box 395, Trumbull, CT 06611-0395, ☎ 203/373–7130 or 800/243–6121), with programs year-round at resorts nationwide, and the **Craft-Zavichas Golf School** (✉ 600 Dittmer Ave., Pueblo, CO 81005, ☎ 719/564–4449 or 800/858–9633).

RESOURCES

The **Guide to Golf Schools & Camps** (Shaw Guides Publishers, ✉ Box 1295, New York, NY 10023, ☎ 212/799–6464 or 800/247–6553) was last published in 1993 ($16.95 plus $3 shipping), but their Web site (www.shawguides.com) is updated constantly.

Hiking and Backpacking

The United States has enough forests and trails to wear out a lifetime of hiking boots. If you've graduated from short walks in local parks, you're ready to tackle the wide-open spaces of national parks and forests.

DISTINCTIVELY AMERICAN BACKPACKING

The Rockies showcase snowcapped mountains, high-country lakes, and mixed conifer-hardwood forests. Key destinations include national forests such as the huge, wild, and varied **Nez Perce** (✉ Rte. 2, Box 475, Grangeville, ID 83530, ☎ 208/983–1950) and trail-crossed national parks such as Colorado's **Rocky Mountain National Park** (✉ Estes Park, CO 80517, ☎ 970/586–1206), northern Wyoming's **Grand Teton**

National Park (✉ Drawer 170, Moose, WY 83012, ☎ 307/739–3300), and **Yellowstone National Park** (✉ Box 168, Yellowstone National Park, WY 82190, ☎ 307/344–7381) to the north. For a unique experience in **Glacier National Park** (✉ Box 128, West Glacier, MT 59936, ☎ 406/888–7800), book a night in one of its spartan World War I–era chalets, accessible only by trail. You can experience the granite peaks, lichen-splotched granite boulders, and pine and fir forests of the Sierras by staying in one of **Yosemite National Park**'s five High Sierra Camps. Cabins cost $95 per person per night (✉ Yosemite Park Reservations, 5410 E. Home Ave., Fresno, CA 93727, ☎ 209/252–4848).

In the East backpackers tramp the Appalachians, ancient mountains with rounded summits, hardwood forests, and many a killer grade. In the Appalachians' bare, windswept **White Mountains' Presidential Range,** the Appalachian Mountain Club runs no-frills hikers' huts, which cost $55 nightly for members and $62 for nonmembers by reservation through the AMC (✉ Box 298, Gorham, NH 03581, ☎ 603/466–2727, FAX 603/466–3871). The **Great Smoky Mountains National Park** (✉ Gatlinburg, TN 37738, ☎ 423/436–1200), which preserves another range of the Appalachians and is crossed by some 800 mi of trails, shows off a gentler side of these old mountains, splendid in spring when the dogwood is in bloom and in fall when foliage is at its peak.

Backpacking is less common in some areas in the middle of the country, except in Arkansas reserves such as the **Ouachita National Forest** (✉ Box 1270, Hot Springs, AR 71902, ☎ 501/321–5202, FAX 501/321–5353) and the **Ozark–St. Francis National Forest** (✉ 605 W. Main St., Russellville, AR 72801, ☎ 501/968–2354). For hikers in **northern Michigan and Minnesota,** the draw is often the superior fishing in waters accessible only on foot. Try **Isle Royale National Park** (✉ 800 E. Lakeshore Dr., Houghton, MI 49931, ☎ 906/482–0984) and **Superior National Forest** (✉ 8901 Grand Ave. Place, Duluth, MN 55808, ☎ 218/626–4300).

LONG TRAILS

Veteran hikers aspire to walk the length of the 2,147-mi Maine-to-Georgia **Appalachian Trail** (✉ Appalachian Trail Conference, Box 807, Harpers Ferry, WV 25425, ☎ 304/535–6331), Vermont's 265-mi **Long Trail** (✉ Green Mountain Club, R.R. 1, Rte. 100, Box 650, Waterbury Center, VT 05677, ☎ 802/244–7037, FAX 802/244–5867), the 2,700-mi **Continental Divide Trail** (✉ Box 30002, Bethesda, MD 20824, ☎ no phone), and the 2,638-mi **Pacific Crest Trail Association** (✉ 5325 Elk Horn Blvd., No. 256, Sacramento, CA 95842, ☎ 916/349–2109, FAX 916/349–1268).

OFFBEAT GUIDED TRIPS

If you don't have the experience to tackle a long backpacking trip on your own, go with a group. In the West you have the option of llama treks, where the sturdy, gentle animals carry gear. In the East inn-to-inn trips put country comfort at trail's end—and innkeepers transport your gear between stops. Contact **Country Inns Along the Trail** (✉ R.D. 3, Box 3265, Brandon, VT 05733, ☎ 802/247–3300) or **Knapsack Tours** (✉ 5961 Zinn Dr., Oakland, CA 94611, ☎ 510/944–9435, , FAX 510/472–0536). **Vermont Walking Tours** (✉ Box 31, Craftsbury Common, VT 05827, ☎ 802/586–7767, FAX 802/586–7768) specializes in back-roads walks in the Green Mountain State's unspoiled Northeast Kingdom.

RESOURCES

Magazines such as *Outside* (☎ 505/989–7100) and *Walking* (☎ 617/266–3322) list many group trips.

Horseback: Pack Trips and Dude Ranches

Seeing the country from the back of a horse has many advantages. You can cover more ground than you would on foot yet still penetrate deep into the wilderness. Best of all, you don't have to carry your gear.

PACK TRIPS

The horse fancier's version of guided backpacking trips, pack trips mix days of traveling between base camps and layover days filled with hiking, fishing, loafing, and eating. Western hospitality prevails, and experience is seldom required. Some outfitters schedule trips in advance; others do custom trips; daily cost is $85–$175. When choosing, ask about the ratio of traveling to layover days, daily distances covered, and the extent of horse care you're expected to provide. For names of tour specialists, consult state tourism offices or Pat Dickerman's ***Adventure Travel North America*** (☞ Bookings and Information, *above*).

INN-TO-INN RIDES

Eastern horse lovers relish the inn-to-inn rides of **Kedron Valley Stables** (✉ Box 368, South Woodstock, VT 05071, ☎ 802/457–1480 or 800/225–6301, FAX 802/457–3029) and **Vermont Icelandic Horse Farm** (✉ Box 577, Waitsfield, VT 05673, ☎ 802/496–7141, FAX 802/496–5390).

DUDE RANCHES

Some are spiffy, upscale resorts, such as **Rancho de los Caballeros** (✉ 1551 S. Vulture Mine Rd., Wickenburg, AZ 85390, ☎ 520/684–5484, FAX 520/684–2267), where riding is combined with top-notch tennis and golf. Others, such as **Lone Mountain** (✉ Box 69, Big Sky, MT 59716, ☎ 406/995–4644), also lead rafting trips, fishing excursions, and other outdoor activities. At working cattle ranches like **G Bar M** (✉ Box 29, Clyde Park, MT 59018, ☎ 406/686–4687), pitching in is part of the fun. All involve a healthy dose of horse-related activities, such as pack trips, breakfast cookout rides, and horseback picnics. Rates range from $800 weekly to more than twice that.

Pat Dickerman's ***Farm, Ranch, and Country Vacations*** (☞ Bookings and Information, *above*) is a good source; for other listings contact the **Colorado Dude and Guest Ranch Association** (✉ Box 300, Tabernash, CO 80478, ☎ 970/887–9248), the **Dude Ranchers Association** (✉ Box 471, LaPorte, CO 80535, ☎ 970/223–8440, FAX 970/223–0201), which provides a free directory of 101 dude ranches, and **Old West Dude Ranch Vacations** (✉ c/o American Wilderness Experiences, Box 1486, Boulder, CO 80306, ☎ 800/444–3833, FAX 303/444–3999), as well as state tourism offices. Gene Kilgore's *Ranch Vacations* (✉ Box 629000, El Dorado Hills, CA 95762, ☎ 800/637–8100) lists 240 ranches in the United States and western Canada ($22.95 plus $7.95 shipping).

Nature and Wildlife Education

Spotting moose and seals and focusing your binoculars on trumpeter swans are among the pleasures of outdoor activities. Specialized programs and tours help you understand what you see.

NATURE CAMPS

Naturalists on hikes, in classrooms, and around evening campfires provide insights into nature and its interdependencies at several summer programs. The half-century-old **Audubon Ecology Camps** (✉ 613 Riversville Rd., Greenwich, CT 06831, ☎ 203/869–2017, FAX 203/869–4437) attract people of all ages to one-week summer sessions held in Wyoming's Wind River Range; on a 300-acre Maine island; and at a Greenwich, Connecticut, nature sanctuary. Accommodations are simple but comfortable. These are almost as well known among outdoors lovers as those offered by the **Sierra Club National Outings Program**

(✉ 85 2nd St., San Francisco, CA 94105, ☎ 415/977–5522), including wilderness camps in the Sierras, the Rockies, the Smokies, and other wild places, where club members spend a week or two among similarly conservation-minded vacationers, day-hiking into the surrounding countryside, helping with camp tasks under staff supervision, and paying relatively modest fees. Also look into **National Wildlife Federation Conservation Summits** (✉ 8925 Leesburg Pike, Vienna, VA 22184, ☎ 703/790–4363, FAX 703/790–4468), which mix nature, outdoor skills, and folk culture; and the **Chewonki Foundation** (✉ 485 Chewonki Neck Rd., Wiscasset, ME 04578, ☎ 207/882–7323, FAX 207/882–4074), an environmentally oriented group with the twin objectives of nature education and personal growth.

IN THE NATIONAL PARKS

Participants learn about the environment through lectures, field courses, and photography and writing workshops at **Canyonlands Field Institute** (✉ Box 68, Moab, UT 84532, ☎ 801/259–7750, FAX 801/259–2335), in Canyonlands National Park; the **Glacier Institute** (✉ Box 7457, Kalispell, MT 59904, ☎ 406/755–1211); the **Olympic Park Institute** (✉ 111 Barnes Point Rd., Port Angeles, WA 98363, ☎ 360/928–3720, FAX 360/928–3046); **Point Reyes Field Seminars** (✉ Point Reyes National Seashore, Point Reyes Station, CA 94956, ☎ 415/663–1200), at the Point Reyes National Seashore; and the **Yellowstone Institute** (✉ Box 117, Yellowstone National Park, WY 82190, ☎ 307/344–2294).

NATURALIST-LED TOURS AND CRUISES

Guided by university professors, botanists, or zoologists, wildlife tours reveal dimensions of the American landscape that most vacationers never even suspect. Hiking and camping may be involved, but accommodations are often comfortable or even luxurious, and travel is by small cruise boat or van. Whale-watching is often part of the experience. Contact **Nature Expeditions International** (✉ 6400 E. El Dorado Circle, Suite 210, Tucson, AZ 85715, ☎ 520/721–6712 or 800/869–0639, FAX 520/721–6719).

WILDERNESS SKILLS PROGRAMS

You might learn winter camping, sea kayaking, rock climbing, minimum-impact camping, or river rafting; but it's the personal growth from mastering something new that attracts participants to the rigorous mental and physical challenges of **Outward Bound** (✉ Rte. 9D, R2, Box 280, Garrison, NY 10524-9757, ☎ 914/424–4000 or 800/243–8520), or the **National Outdoor Leadership School** (✉ 288 Main St., Lander, WY 82520, ☎ 307/332–6973, FAX 307/332–1220).

River Rafting

The spray soaks your clothes and stings your face, the roar drowns out your screams—nothing reveals nature's power like white water. By comparison, the quiet stretches are all the more peaceful, the campfires more glowing. It's no wonder river rafting is so popular.

DISTINCTIVELY AMERICAN RAFTING

Rafting the **Colorado** through the Grand Canyon may be the ultimate American river experience, with its hundred-odd devilishly named rapids and glowing canyon scenery. However, it gets a run for its money from the river's demanding **Cataract Canyon** section, in Utah's Canyonlands National Park; Idaho's **Salmon** (both the Main Fork, the stream that Lewis and Clark called the River of No Return, and its Middle Fork, with 80 stretches of white water); and Idaho's sometimes-hellish **Selway.** Long, smooth stretches between rapids make Oregon's **Rogue,** a National Wild and Scenic River, especially good for families.

In the East the most famous white-water rafting stream may be Georgia's **Chattooga,** where *Deliverance* was filmed. But river rats know West Virginia as the country's most concentrated area of challenging and diverse white water. A case in point is the powerhouse **New River** (actually the oldest river on the continent), which roars through a gorge so deep it's known as the Grand Canyon of the East.

RAFT TRIPS

Commercial outfitters make even the rowdiest white water accessible to the inexperienced. They also supply gear, food, and appropriate permits—all you have to do is show up (and hold on!). Some outfitters use motorized rafts, some only oar power; some request paddling help, whereas others prohibit it. Find out what's expected before you book.

RESOURCES

State tourism offices and **America Outdoors** (✉ Box 10847, Knoxville, TN 37939, ☎ 423/558–3597, FAX 423/558–3598), a trade organization, have names of outfitters. **OARS** (Outdoor Adventure River Specialists; ✉ Box 67, Angels Camp, CA 95222, ☎ 209/736–4677 or 800/346–6277, FAX 209/736–2902), established in 1972, and the nonprofit **American River Touring Association** (✉ 24000 Casa Loma Rd., Groveland, CA 95321, ☎ 800/323–2782, FAX 209/962–4819) have extensive programs, as does **Dvoák Kayak & Rafting Expeditions** (✉ 17921 U.S. 285, Nathrop, CO 81236, ☎ 719/539–6851 or 800/824–3795, FAX 719/539–3378). *Paddler* magazine (☎ 703/451–0141) covers guided trips and paddling schools.

Sailing

The mighty U.S. coastline ranks among the nation's most stirring sights, and although roads provide access to much of it, seeing the coast from the water gives an undeniably better view.

DISTINCTIVELY AMERICAN SAILING

Nothing says United States quite like **Maine's rocky coast,** known to sailors all over the world for its scenery, good moorings, and abundant facilities. But there's comparable variety among the islands, coves, and shoreside towns of the **Chesapeake Bay** and **Long Island Sound.** The waters off **Newport, Rhode Island,** home of the Museum of Yachting, are light-years away from landlubber gridlock; the crowd is well heeled and tony. In the **Florida Keys** the winds are good, the waters teeming with marine life, and the shoreside life laid-back. In the Midwest sailors relish the challenging **Great Lakes,** which are inland seas. **California** is sail-crazed; Sausalito, near San Francisco Bay, and Marina del Rey and Newport Beach, in the south, are boating centers. In northwestern Washington state the **San Juan Islands** are a maze of coves and beaches teeming with birds and animals. For the adventurous side of the sport, consider **Alaska**—extraordinary with its fjords, shoreline peaks and waterfalls, good fishing, and abundant wildlife.

CHARTERS

You can book craft either crewed (staffed to handle cooking and navigation) or bareboat (for experienced sailors only). Contact state visitor centers for lists of charter operators.

SCHOOLS

The nation's two principal sailing programs are the **Annapolis Sailing School** (✉ Box 3334, Annapolis, MD 21403, ☎ 410/267–7205 or 800/638–9192, FAX 410/268–3114), which has a branch in the U.S. Virgin Islands, and the **Offshore Sailing School** (✉ 16731 McGregor Blvd., Suite 110, Fort Myers, FL 33908, ☎ 941/454–1700 or 800/221–4326, FAX 941/454–1191), founded by former Olympian Steve Colgate and now running programs on Florida's Captiva Island; in Newport, Rhode Island; in Stamford, Connecticut; and in Jersey City, New Jersey.

RESOURCES

Ads and information on charter operators can be found in the magazines *Sail* (☎ 617/964–3030), *Cruising World* (☎ 401/847–1588), and *Yachting* (☎ 212/779–5300).

WINDJAMMER CRUISES

The beating of sails in the wind, the smell of the sea, and the excitement of calling at scenic ports create an unbeatable camaraderie on cruises aboard the nation's fleet of tall ships—restorations or reconstructions of 19th-century craft that accommodate fewer than 30 passengers. Per-person fares are about $100 a day, much lower than those for larger cruise ships, and most people don't mind the cold showers (or absence thereof), since it's easy to clean up at local marinas.

In the East, Rockland, Camden, and Rockport, Maine, are the bases for a dozen ships, mostly members of the **Maine Windjammer Association** (✉ Box 1144, Blue Hill, ME 04614, ☎ 800/807–9463). Also contact Maine's state tourism office. In the Midwest look into the **Traverse Tall Ship Company** (✉ 13390 S.W. Bay Shore Dr., Traverse City, MI 49684, ☎ 616/941–2000 or 800/678–8800 for brochures).

Skiing

Ski areas can be found even in such unlikely states as Indiana, but some of the best skiing in the world is in the Rockies. True, the typical ski area in the Alps has a greater vertical drop (as skiers call the difference in altitude between lift base and the highest lift-served point). But no other ski areas have comparable snow quality. Not only is snowfall (usually) abundant, but it is also dry and featherlight, and snow quality is consistent from top to bottom—a rarity in Europe. To enjoy it all, you don't have to be a hotdog mogul skier or one of the manic daredevils dubbed "extreme skiers": U.S. mountains have slopes appropriate for all levels of skiers.

DISTINCTIVELY AMERICAN SKIING

In the Rockies you'll find affluent crowds in **Sun Valley,** Idaho; **Aspen,** Colorado; faux-alpine **Vail** not far away; and perhaps **Deer Valley,** Utah. For mellow western charm and abundant facilities, it's hard to beat **Breckenridge, Copper Mountain, Keystone,** and **Steamboat,** Colorado, or even **Park City,** Utah. Friendly, low-key spots like **Big Mountain,** near Whitefish, Montana, are practically unknown outside the West. The same can't be said of New Mexico's challenging **Taos;** Wyoming's one-of-a-kind **Jackson Hole;** Utah's cozy, rustic **Alta,** the sine qua non among powder skiers; and its mod cousin, **Snowbird**—though none of these measure up to the big Colorado resorts in terms of sheer fame.

Elsewhere in the West, California's Sierras get massive amounts of snow, and skiers come by the thousands to the resorts around crystal-clear Lake Tahoe, including **Squaw, Heavenly, Northstar,** and **Kirkwood.**

In the East, narrow trails and icy conditions magnify the challenges, although slope grooming and snowmaking ease the sting at Vermont's **Stowe** and its Vermont cousins closer to the big cities: huge **Killington** and **Mt. Snow,** genteel **Stratton** and **Sugarbush.** New Hampshire resorts, such as **Waterville Valley,** are even more relaxed.

To choose, consider the area's personality, terrain, and convenience. Are there slope-side accommodations or do you need a car? Can you find the lodgings you want (motel, inn, B&B, dorm, or resort) at a price you can afford? Are there programs for kids? Families appreciate areas with centralized lift layouts, which make it easy to rendezvous for lunch or at day's end.

SKI SCHOOLS AND PACKAGES

Most ski areas provide instruction and packages. Some offer deals on multiday lift tickets; others add lessons, lodging, or meals. The best deals are midweek, particularly in areas with heavy weekend traffic.

RESOURCES

Ski (☎ 212/779–5000), *Ski Tripper* (☎ 703/772–7644), *Skiing* (☎ 212/779–5000), *Snow Country* (☎ 203/373–7000), and *Powder* (☎ 714/496–5922) magazines cover the field.

Ski Touring

Heavy snows that otherwise make the nation's meadows and forests inaccessible are no problem for those who can cross-country ski.

DISTINCTIVELY AMERICAN SKI TOURING

National and state park and forest trails are sometimes suitable for cross-country skiing, although rental equipment is not always available. At downhill ski areas, valleys at the base and high ridges and plateaus are preferred.

Yellowstone National Park is a sight to behold in winter, when waterfalls freeze into bizarre sculptures, steam billowing from the thermal features turns trees into hoary ghosts, and icicles glitter everywhere. Lodging, equipment, and instruction are available.

Elsewhere in the West there's abundant ski touring at several areas in and around Wyoming's **Grand Teton National Park** and California's **Yosemite National Park.** Idaho's **Sun Valley** has hundreds of skiable acres, and you can even helicopter up to the high country. Communities of cross-country fanatics flourish in Colorado at **Steamboat Springs** and **Vail,** and the trail system in **Aspen** is one of the nation's most extensive. Minnesota's **Superior National Forest** enjoys abundant snowfall and hundreds of miles of trails.

In the East prime areas include Massachusetts's **Berkshire Mountains,** full of parks, forests, and inns; New Hampshire's **Mt. Washington Valley;** and Vermont's **Stowe,** where dozens of miles of trails link restaurants, inns, and shops.

GROUP TRIPS

Rock-climbing schools (☞ Climbing and Mountaineering, *above*) often have cross-country skiing programs. For inn-to-inn tours, contact **Country Inns Along the Trail** (✉ R.D. 3, Box 3265, Brandon, VT 05733, ☎ 802/247–3300). Rugged hut-to-hut tours of Colorado's spectacular Tenth Mountain Trail are offered by **Paragon Guides** (✉ Box 130, Vail, CO 81658, ☎ 970/926–5299, FAX 970/926–5298).

RESOURCES

The **Cross Country Ski Areas Association** (✉ 259 Bolton Rd., Winchester, NH 03470, ☎ 603/239–4341) publishes a book ($3) detailing more than 200 cross-country areas. Also read *Cross Country Skier* magazine (☎ 612/377–0312).

Tennis

If you have nonplaying companions, consider a full-scale resort with a heavy tennis program; otherwise consider sites where tennis is the only activity: tennis camps or clinics. Rather than trying to remake your game, most build on what you already have in order to send you home a better player.

CAMPS AND CLINICS

Staged year-round at resorts nationwide and at private schools in summer, these provide the most intense tennis experience, with up to five hours of play every day. Established in 1968, **Tennis Camps, Ltd.** (✉ 444 E. 82nd St., Ste. 31-D, New York, NY 10028, ☎ 212/879–0225 or 800/223–2442, FAX 212/452–0816) is a major player. The **Nick Bollettieri Tennis Academy** (✉ 5500 34th St. W, Bradenton, FL 34210, ☎ 941/755–1000 or 800/872–6425, FAX 941/756–6891) and **Harry Hopman/Saddlebrook International Tennis** (✉ 5700 Saddlebrook Way, Wesley Chapel, FL 33543, ☎ 813/973–1111 or 800/729–8383, FAX 813/973–4504) are both famed for turning prodigies into pros. For off-court luxury, the last word is **John Gardiner's**—both the exclusive California ranch (✉ Box 228, Carmel Valley, CA 93924, ☎ 408/659–2207, FAX 408/659–2492) and its even posher desert cousin (✉ 5700 E. McDonald Dr., Scottsdale, AZ 85253, ☎ 602/948–2100, FAX 602/483–7314). Former top players mastermind the friendly **John Newcombe's Tennis Ranch** (✉ Box 310–469, New Braunfels, TX 78131, ☎ 830/625–9105 or 800/444–6204, FAX 830/625–2004), the **Van Der Meer Tennis University** (✉ Box 5902, Hilton Head Island, SC 29938, ☎ 803/785–8388 or 800/845–6138, FAX 803/785–7030), and the high-tech **Vic Braden Tennis College** (✉ 23395 Via Alondra, Coto de Caza, CA 92679, ☎ 714/581–2990 or 800/422–6878, FAX 714/858–0174).

RESORTS

Planned resort developments almost always have extensive facilities. At **Hilton Head Island, South Carolina,** two resorts alone have more than five dozen courts—**Sea Pines Plantation** (✉ Box 7000, Hilton Head Island, SC 29928, ☎ 800/845–6131, FAX 803/842–1475) and **Palmetto Dunes** (✉ Box 5606, Hilton Head Island, SC 29938, ☎ 803/785–7300 or 800/845–6130, FAX 803/842–4482). Ski resorts usually have extensive tennis programs—among them are Bolton Valley, Killington, Stratton, and Sugarbush—and so do large resort hotels. A special case is the elegant Gulf Coast **Colony Beach & Tennis Resort** (✉ 1620 Gulf of Mexico Dr., Longboat Key, FL 34228, ☎ 914/383–6464 or 800/237–9443, FAX 914/383–7549), devoted exclusively to tennis.

To choose, ask the pro shop about court fees, reservations procedures and availability, game-matching services, night play, guest tourneys, court-time limits, instruction, and the resort's court-to-room ratio (1 to 10 is fine; half that if there are many other activities).

RESOURCES

See *Tennis* magazine (☎ 212/789–3000) for listings of tennis resorts, camps, and clinics. The Shaw Guides (www.shawguides.com) constantly update their extensive Tennis Schools & Camps Web directory.

Spiritual and Physical Fitness Vacations

Providing meaningful recreation for both mind and body is the objective of hundreds of establishments across the United States. *Fodor's Healthy Escapes* ($17; new edition to pub January, 1999) lists more than 200 health-and-fitness–oriented camps, resorts, and programs throughout the United States, Canada, Mexico, and the Caribbean.

Holistic Centers

The verdant Catskills' **New Age Health Spa** (✉ Rte. 55, Neversink, NY 12765, ☎ 914/985–7601 or 800/682–4348, FAX 914/985–2467) helps guests balance body, soul, and mind via programs ranging from astrological consultations and aerobics to Zen meditation. Flotation tanks and massages supplement nutrition and counseling at old-timers such as the **Omega Institute** (✉ 260 Lake Dr., Rhinebeck, NY 12572, ☎ 914/

266–4301 or 800/944–1001, FAX 914/266–4828). Tucked into California's scenic coastline, the **Esalen Institute** (✉ Big Sur, CA 93920, ☎ 408/667–3000, FAX 408/667–2724) has a broad curriculum of workshops on topics as diverse as hypnosis, dream analysis, cooking, and massage. The **Ojai Foundation** (✉ 9739 Ojai-Santa Paula Rd., Ojai, CA 93023, ☎ 805/646–8343, FAX 805/646–2456) occupies 40 acres of wilderness north of Los Angeles, with programs designed to help guests deepen their personal relationships and reconnect with the earth.

Spas for Luxury and Pampering

To those who say, "No pain, no gain," others reply, "No frills, no thrills" and seek out deluxe establishments for regimens of body wraps, saunas, Swiss showers, massages, manicures, and maybe a yoga class or two. On the cutting edge is **Canyon Ranch** (✉ 8600 E. Rockcliff Rd., Tucson, AZ 85750, ☎ 520/749–9000 or 800/742–9000, FAX 520/749–7755; ✉ 165 Kemble St., Lenox, MA 01240, ☎ 413/637–4100 or 800/742–9000, FAX 413/637–0057), where treatments are combined with outdoor activities such as hiking, biking, and tennis, as well as sophisticated spa cuisine. The women-only **Greenhouse** (✉ Box 1144, Arlington, TX 76004, ☎ 817/640–4000) is a study in elegant southern hospitality. Many luxury spas take the more active approach of the **Golden Door** (✉ Box 463077, Escondido, CA 92046, ☎ 760/744–5777or 800/424–0777, FAX 760/471–2393), where individually planned programs include 6 AM hikes and exercise classes. **La Costa Resort & Spa** (✉ 2100 Costa del Mar Rd., Carlsbad, CA 92009, ☎ 760/438–9111 or 800/854–5000, FAX 760/931–7585) is the megaresort of the breed. The **Spa at Doral** (✉ 8755 N.W. 36th St., Miami, FL 33178, ☎ 305/593–6030 or 800/331–7768, FAX 305/591–9268) fuses a typically American program involving exercise and stress-management training with European treatments, such as warm mud packs for muscular problems.

Weight Management and Preventive Medicine Centers

Medical supervision is the goal at the **Duke University Diet and Fitness Center** (✉ 804 W. Trinity Ave., Durham, NC 27701, ☎ 919/684–6331 or 800/362–8446, FAX 919/684–6176); the **Cooper Institute for Aerobics Fitness** (✉ 12230 Preston Rd., Dallas, TX 75230, ☎ 972/341–3200 or 800/635–7050, FAX 972/991–4626), inspired by aerobics pioneer Dr. Kenneth H. Cooper; and the **Pritikin Longevity Centers** (✉ 1910 Ocean Front Walk, Santa Monica, CA 90405, ☎ 310/450–5433 or 800/421–9911, FAX 310/829–6440; ✉ 5875 Collins Ave., Miami Beach, FL 33140, ☎ 305/866–2237 or 800/327–4914, FAX 305/866–1872), which focus on the late Nathan Pritikin's belief that diet can reverse atherosclerosis.

Education and Culture

All travel stretches the observant voyager's mind. A number of programs—university-sponsored tours and continuing-education courses, as well as workshops in the arts—formalize this process. Equally educational are volunteer programs such as archaeological research or trail building. Although vacations organized around volunteer activities may not send you back home with a tan, they *are* likely to benefit you as well as many others.

Academic Tours and Programs

Once upon a time, **Chautauqua Institution** (✉ 1 Ames Ave., Box 28, Chautauqua, NY 14722, ☎ 716/357–6200, FAX 716/357–9014) was unique among travel destinations because it offered language, history, crafts, hobbies, and music and other arts programs. Established in 1874, it now crams more than 300 courses into the nine-week July–August program on its lakeside campus.

VACATIONS ON COLLEGE CAMPUSES

In the company of university professors and other inquisitive spirits, you can expand your intellectual horizons at summer colleges sponsored by major colleges and universities. Typically, these programs require no tests, give no grades, admit nonalumni as well as alumni, keep costs low with simple dormitory lodging and cafeteria meals, and explore themes such as Victorian England or capitalism in China. They also fill up fast.

Summer schools for adults are available in the East at **Cornell** (✉ 626 Thurston Ave., Ithaca, NY 14850, ☎ 607/255–6260); **Dartmouth** (✉ 308 Blunt Alumni Center, Hanover, NH 03755, ☎ 603/646–2454); **Johns Hopkins** (✉ 3400 N. Charles St., Baltimore, MD 21218, ☎ 410/516–7187, FAX 410/872–1251); and **Penn State** (✉ 315 Keller Bldg., University Park, PA 16802, ☎ 814/863–3781, FAX 814/865–0128). Comparable programs are run in the South at the **University of North Carolina at Chapel Hill** (✉ Vacation College Humanities Program, Campus Box 3425, 3 Bolin Heights, Chapel Hill, NC 27599-3425, ☎ 919/962–1544, FAX 919/962–4318) and **Washington and Lee University** (✉ Office of Special Programs, Lexington, VA 24450, ☎ 540/463–8723, FAX 540/463–8478), and in the Midwest at **Indiana University** (✉ Mini University, Indiana Memorial Union, Suite 400, Bloomington, IN 47405, ☎ 800/824–3044.) Programs come and go, however, so it's best to pick a university you'd like to attend, then call its alumni office or its continuing education or adult education department to inquire about what's available.

ACADEMIC AND OTHER CULTURAL TOURS

Major U.S. museums sponsor dozens of study tours every year, most escorted by museum personnel, university professors, and other experts. Another option is the programs of independent operators; for extensive listings consult the *Guide to Academic Travel* (Shaw Guides Publishers, ✉ Box 1295, New York, NY 10023, ☎ 212/799–6464 or 800/247–6553), last published in 1992 ($16.95 plus $3 shipping).

HISTORY TOURS

American architecture, social history, and culture are emphasized on tours led by the **National Trust for Historic Preservation** (✉ 1785 Massachusetts Ave. NW, Washington, DC 20036, ☎ 202/588–6300 or 800/944–6847). Four- to 30-day trips have explored Virginia's grand houses and plantations, the heritage of the Maine coast, and Route 66. Four- to six-day history seminar tours are the specialty of **Smithsonian Study Tours and Seminars** (✉ 1100 Jefferson Dr. SW, Washington, DC 20560, ☎ 202/357–4700, FAX 202/633–9250), whose expert leaders will help you explore the Civil War, Native American culture, and jazz music, among other topics.

Cooking Schools

Those who love to cook, eat well, and enjoy fine wines have few better travel options than signing up for an intensive multiday cooking course at a hotel or cooking school. When choosing, be sure to find out the demonstration-to-participation ratio.

INTENSIVE COURSES AT COOKING SCHOOLS

Two- to five-day programs are widely available. Some are through professional schools such as the **Culinary Institute of America** (✉ 433 Albany Post Rd., Hyde Park, NY 12538, ☎ 914/452–2230 or 800/888–7850, FAX 914/451–1066), the nation's major professional school, and the **California Culinary Academy** (✉ 625 Polk St., San Francisco, CA 94102, ☎ 415/771–3536, FAX 415/775–5129).

Well-known chefs and cookbook authors sponsor other programs, notably **Julie Sahni's Indian Cooking** (✉ 101 Clark St., Brooklyn Heights, NY 11201, ☎ 718/625–3958, FAX 718/625–3456) and **Karen Lee Chinese Cooking Classes** (✉ 142 West End Ave., New York, NY 10023, ☎ 212/787–2227, FAX 212/496–8178). Other options are at vineyards such as the **Robert Mondavi Winery** (✉ Box 106, Oakville, CA 94562, ☎ 707/944–2866, FAX 707/944–8517).

PROGRAMS AT HOTELS, INNS, AND RESORTS

If your traveling companions would rather play golf or tennis than slave over a hot stove, look into short programs at such grand resorts as the **Greenbrier Hotel** (✉ 300 W. Main St., White Sulphur Springs, WV 24986, ☎ 304/536–1110 or 800/624–6070, FAX 304/536–7854), where La Varenne's Anne Willan directs.

RESOURCES

Consult the *Guide to Cooking Schools* (Shaw Guides Publishers, ✉ Box 1295, New York, NY, 10023, ☎ 212/799–6464 or 800/247–6553) for extensive listings of both short- and long-term programs, as well as information on gourmet and wine tours ($19.95 plus $3 shipping).

Crafts Workshops

Short workshops in fine arts and crafts are staged by major museums and at national parks such as Glacier, Yosemite, and Olympic. More extensive programs—lasting from one to several weeks and focusing on a range of crafts from metal, wood, and ceramics to indigenous regional and Native American crafts—are held at colleges, crafts centers, and individual studios.

INTERDISCIPLINARY CRAFTS CENTERS

Dozens of weekend and weeklong courses in basketry, bookmaking, ceramics, woodworking, and other topics draw pros as well as beginners and intermediates to crafts centers such as **Anderson Ranch Arts Center** (✉ Box 5598, Snowmass Village, CO 81615, ☎ 970/923–3181, FAX 970/923–3871), in the Rocky Mountains near Aspen; the **Arrowmont School of Arts and Crafts** (✉ Box 567, Gatlinburg, TN 37738, ☎ 423/436–5860, FAX 423/430–4101), founded in 1945 on 70 acres just a mile from the Great Smoky Mountains National Park; and the **Haystack Mountain School of Crafts** (✉ Box 518, Deer Isle, ME 04627-0518, ☎ 207/348–2306, FAX 207/348–2307), occupying a shingled, Atlantic-view studio complex on a Maine island. Several focus on traditional folk crafts; the oldest and most active are the **John C. Campbell Folk School** (✉ 1 Folk School Rd., Brasstown, NC 28902, ☎ 704/837–2775), whose campus is a National Historic District, and the **Penland School of Crafts** (✉ Penland Rd., Penland, NC 28765, ☎ 704/765–2359, FAX 704/765–7389), on 500 acres in the Blue Ridge Mountains.

SPECIALIZED PROGRAMS

You can study everything from basketry and boatbuilding to papermaking, couture sewing, and weaving. For extensive listings of what's available, consult the *Guide to Art & Craft Workshops* (Shaw Guides Publishers, ✉ Box 1295, New York, NY 10023, ☎ 212/799–6464 or 800/247–6553), last printed in 1991 ($16.95 plus $3 shipping).

Painting and Fine-Arts Workshops

Amateurs can get professional tutelage at intensive programs at inns, resorts, museums, fine-arts centers, and even crafts schools nationwide (☞ Crafts Workshops, *above*).

VARIED PROGRAMS

Diverse programs that embrace disciplines ranging from printmaking and watercolors to painting styles such as portraiture, still life, and landscape are available at schools such as the **Art Institute of Boston** (✉ Continuing Education, 700 Beacon St., Boston, MA 02215, ☎ 617/262–1223) and **Dillman's Sand Lake Lodge** (✉ Box 98, Lac du Flambeau, WI 54538, ☎ 715/588–3143), an old family-style summer resort in northern Wisconsin. Programs abound in Maine, among them the **Maine Coast Art Workshops** (✉ c/o Merle Donovan, Box 236, Port Clyde, ME 04855, ☎ 207/372–8200).

SPECIALIZED PROGRAMS

Some workshops concentrate on a specific medium, such as pastels or watercolors, or a specific style or theme—realism, western motifs, or seasapes, for instance. A comprehensive listing is in the *Guide to Art & Craft Workshops* (☞ Crafts Workshops, *above*).

RESOURCES

American Artist (☎ 212/764–7300) magazine lists many summer programs, such as those in its March issue.

Photography Workshops and Tours

Throughout the year amateurs and professionals sign up for workshops and tours designed both to polish their techniques and to take them to photogenic spots at the best possible times.

WORKSHOPS

Each workshop has a distinctive focus. Some cover theory and practice through fieldwork and seminars in both black-and-white and color photography; these look at the field as both a fine and an applied art that ranges from fashion shots to photojournalism. Established in 1971, the well-respected **Maine Photographic Workshops** (✉ 2 Central St., Rockport, ME 04856, ☎ 207/236–8581, FAX 207/236–2558), explores most aspects of photography, as do the well-respected if less picturesquely situated **International Center of Photography** (✉ 1130 5th Ave., New York, NY 10128, ☎ 212/860–1776, FAX 212/360–6490) and the **Visual Studies Workshop** (✉ 31 Prince St., Rochester, NY 14607, ☎ 716/442–8676, FAX 716/442–1992). The **Friends of Photography Workshops** (✉ 250 4th St., San Francisco, CA 94103, ☎ 415/495–7000, FAX 415/495–8517) carries on the tradition of and now manages the venerable Ansel Adams Workshop, founded in 1940.

GUIDED PHOTOGRAPHY TOURS

Specialized tours, accompanied by professional photographers and scheduled to catch photogenic spots at optimal times, are offered by many organizations, including **Close-Up Expeditions** (✉ 858 56th St., Oakland, CA 94608, ☎ 510/654–1548 or 800/457–9553, FAX 510/654–3043), the official Photographic Society of America tour operator; and **Photo Adventure Tours** (✉ 2035 Park St., Atlantic Beach, NY 11509, ☎ 516/371–0067 or 800/821–1221, FAX 516/371–1352).

RESOURCES

American Photo (☎ 212/767–6273) and *Popular Photography* (☎ 212/767–6000) magazines advertise tours and workshops. The *Guide to Photography Workshops & Schools* (✉ Shaw Guides Publishers, Box 1295, New York, NY 10023, ☎ 212/799–6464 or 800/247–6553), last published in 1995, has extensive listings of programs ($19.95 plus $3 shipping).

Volunteer Vacations

Although fees for the nation's hundreds of vacation volunteer programs may be partly tax deductible, their allure has less to do with money than with the satisfaction that comes from giving something back to society, the excitement of an entirely new activity, and the intensity of the group experience.

When choosing a program, be sure to ask about insurance, the number of participants and staff, and the standards by which project and leader were chosen.

FIELD RESEARCH

How about tagging dolphins or collecting subtropical plants? Scientists in need of enthusiastic, inexpensive labor for projects like these are happy to enlist help from vacationers, who pay a stipend to cover their own expenses and defray expedition costs. Organizations that match up scientists and vacationers include **Earthwatch** (✉ Box 9104, 680 Mount Auburn St., Watertown, MA 02272, ☎ 617/926–8200 or 800/776–0188, FAX 617/926–8532), the oldest in the field; **Smithsonian Research Expeditions Program** (✉ 490 L'Enfant Plaza SW, Room 4210, Washington, DC 20560, ☎ 202/287–3210); and the **University Research Expeditions Program** (UREP; ✉ c/o University of California, 2223 Fulton St., Berkeley, CA 94720-7050, ☎ 510/642–6586, FAX 510/642–6791), led by University of California scientists.

ARCHAEOLOGICAL RESEARCH

It's hot, dirty, and strenuous—but you don't have to be an archaeologist to catch the excitement. Earthwatch and UREP (☞ Field Research, *above*) often list digs among their fieldwork opportunities. Boston University's 100-plus-year-old **Archaeological Institute of America** (✉ 656 Beacon St., Boston, MA 02215, ☎ 617/353–9361), also known as AIA, publishes newsletters, catalogs and magazines as well as the *Fieldwork Opportunities Bulletin* ($11; Kendall Hunt Publishing Co., ✉ Order Dept., Box 1840, Dubuque, IA 52004-1840, ☎ 800/228–0810, FAX 800/772–9165). Organizations such as the **Four Corners School** (✉ Box 1029, Monticello, UT 84535, ☎ 801/587–2156, FAX 801/587–2193) have hands-on programs where participants can get involved in mapping and surveying sites as well as drawing and photographing geographical features and artifacts.

TRAIL BUILDING AND MAINTENANCE

Helping state and national parks and forests maintain old trails, build new ones, and clean up and replant campgrounds is the mission of several private groups that welcome volunteers—among them the active **Sierra Club** (☞ Sports and Outdoors Group Trips, *above*) and the **Appalachian Mountain Club** (✉ Volunteer Trail Program, Box 298, Gorham, NH 03581, ☎ 603/466–2721, FAX 603/466–2822). Many state parks or conservation departments use volunteers, as do the National Park Service, U.S. Fish and Wildlife Service, and U.S. Forest Service.

SOCIAL SERVICE

Building community centers, repairing churches, setting up youth programs, and serving in group homes are just a few activities of volunteer work camps. Contact clearinghouses such as the **Volunteers for Peace** (✉ 43 Tiffany Rd., Belmont, VT 05730, ☎ 802/259–2759, FAX 802/259–2922) and the **Council on International Educational Exchange** (✉ 205 E. 42nd St., New York, NY 10017, ☎ 212/822–2600 or 800/268–6245).

RESOURCES

The **Points of Light Foundation** (✉ 1737 H St. NW, Washington, DC 20006, ☎ 202/223–9186) and **Volunteers for Peace** (☞ Social Service, *above*) have listings of other volunteer opportunities.

3 The Northeast

Connecticut, Maine, Massachusetts, New Hampshire, New York, Rhode Island, Vermont

THE TWO MAJOR METROPOLITAN AREAS of the Northeast—New York and Boston—offer the best of modern city life, the hurly-burly and intensity that come with so many ambitious citizens pursuing their dreams. New York City—one of the world's leading financial and cultural capitals—belongs to the world as much as to the country. Boston, the nation's oldest (and still leading) college town, has redefined itself as a hub of service and high-tech industries. As distinguished as each metropolis is, neither entirely defines the region: Captured in a single wide-angle lens, the six states of New England and massive New York State are decidedly unurban, with a wider variety of landscapes and outdoor diversions per square mile than any other part of the country.

Beyond the glitz and grime of New York City, the Northeast fans out in waves of increasingly soothing vistas, from the placid charms of the Connecticut River valley through the forests of Vermont and New Hampshire's Green and White mountains to the pristine hinterland of Maine's remote Allagash Wilderness Waterway. Similarly, the "wilderness" of upstate New York begins within an hour's drive of the Bronx: The Hudson River valley lures frazzled urban dwellers northward past the Catskill resorts to 6.2-million-acre Adirondack Park. At the western end of the state, the wonders of Niagara Falls continue to attract photo-snapping tourists from around the world.

The region was historically defined by the coastline, where the Pilgrims first established a toehold in the New World. Until it veers inland north of Yarmouth, Maine, I–95 skirts the inlets and harbors that sheltered the whaling and trading vessels of 17th- to 19th-century settlers—Mystic, Connecticut; Providence, Rhode Island; Cape Cod, Nantucket, and Plymouth, Massachusetts; and Portland, Maine. Beyond the interstate's exits, in between the museums and tourist centers, lies a region with a wealth of diversions—cerebral, spiritual, athletic. Every season brings its own recreations—fishing in New York and in Vermont's Lake Champlain, skiing in the White Mountains, camping on the Appalachian Trail, biking along Maine's rocky coast, sailing on Long Island Sound, applauding world-class musicians in the Berkshires, watching whales cavort off Cape Cod.

The Northeast

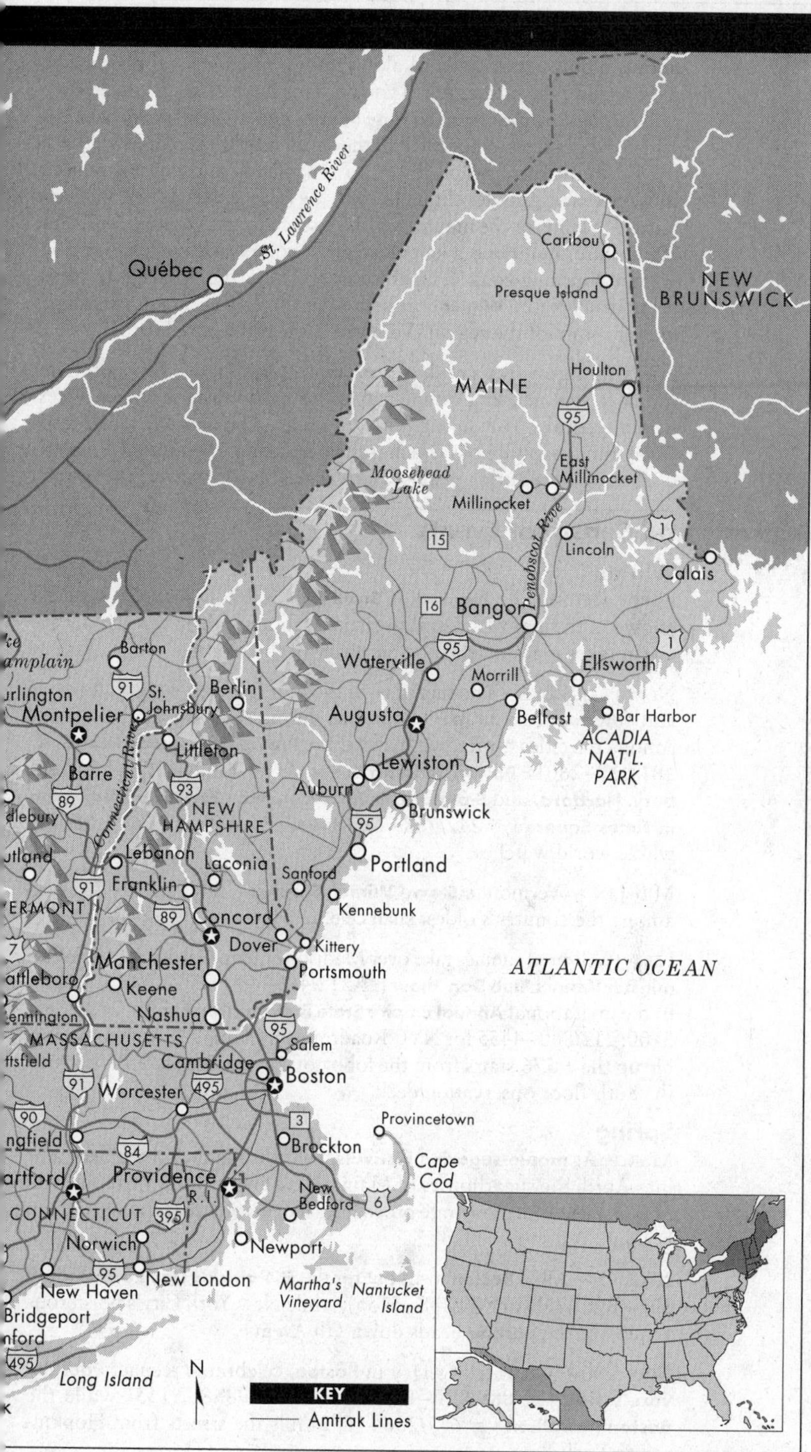
St. Lawrence River
Québec
Caribou
Presque Island
NEW BRUNSWICK
MAINE
Houlton
95
Moosehead Lake
East Millinocket
Millinocket
Penobscot River
1
15
Lincoln
Calais
16
Bangor
95
1
Barton
91
St. Johnsbury
Berlin
Waterville
Morrill
Ellsworth
Montpelier
Augusta
Belfast
Bar Harbor
ACADIA NAT'L. PARK
Littleton
Barre
Lewiston
1
Connecticut River
93
Auburn
Brunswick
89
NEW HAMPSHIRE
95
Lebanon
Laconia
Sanford
Portland
91
Franklin
Kennebunk
89
Concord
Dover
Kittery
Manchester
Portsmouth
ATLANTIC OCEAN
Keene
Nashua
95
MASSACHUSETTS
Salem
Cambridge
Boston
91
Worcester
495
90
3
Provincetown
84
Brockton
Cape Cod
Providence
R.I.
New Bedford
6
CONNECTICUT
395
Norwich
Newport
95
New London
New Haven
Martha's Vineyard
Nantucket Island
Bridgeport
495
Long Island
N
KEY
Amtrak Lines

When to Go

Spring blooms start in April along the southern coastal regions, beginning later the farther north you go. This tends to be the quietest period throughout the region because of rains and melting snows. **Summer,** which ranges from a hot 85°F in the southern region to a low 59°F in the north, attracts beach lovers to the islands and coastal regions; those preferring cooler climes head to the lakes in New York State, the mists of Maine, or the mountains of Massachusetts, Vermont, and New Hampshire. **Autumn** is a kaleidoscope of colors as leaves change from green to burning gold. Temperatures remain around 55°F into October in many places. **Winter** brings snow and skiers to the mountain slopes in every state of the region (Vermont is the most popular).

Prices during an area's peak season climb accordingly—Newport hotel rooms in summer, for example, go for nearly double the winter prices. Room rates also rise during festivals, such as the outdoor music festival at Tanglewood, in Massachusetts's Berkshire mountains. Reservations for hotels during peak seasons should be made well ahead.

Festivals and Seasonal Events

Winter

EARLY DEC.➢ The **Nantucket Stroll** (☎ 508/228—1700), the best known of the many Christmas-season celebrations held throughout the Cape, takes place on the first Saturday of the month.

NEW YEAR'S EVE➢ The final day of the year is observed with festivals and entertainment in many locations during **First Night** celebrations. Among the cities hosting such events are **Providence, Rhode Island** (☎ 401/227–2601); **Boston, Massachusetts** (☎ 617/542–1399); and **Danbury, Hartford,** and **Stamford, Connecticut. New York City**'s **Ball Drop in Times Square** (☎ 212/768–1560) is the New Year's Eve party the whole world watches.

MID-JAN.➢ Vermont's **Stowe Winter Carnival** (☎ 802/253–7321) is among the country's oldest such celebrations.

FEB.➢ Well-bred canines take over Madison Square Garden for the **Westminster Kennel Club Dog Show** (☎ 212/465–6000 or 212/465–6741). In the invitational **Annual Empire State Building Run-Up** (☎ 212/736–3100; 212/860–4455 for NYC Roadrunners Club), 125 runners scramble up the 1,576 stairs from the lobby of the Empire State Building to the 86th-floor observation deck.

Spring

MAR.➢ At **maple-sugaring festivals,** held throughout the month and into April, the sugarhouses of Maine, New Hampshire, Vermont, and Massachusetts demonstrate procedures like maple-tree tapping and sap boiling.

MAR. 17➢ All of **Boston** turns out for the **St. Patrick's Day Parade** (888/SEE–BOSTON or 800/888–5155), while New York City's boisterous version of the **parade** heads down 5th Avenue.

MID-APR.➢ On Patriot's Day in **Boston,** celebrants reenact **Paul Revere's ride** (☎ 888/SEE–BOSTON or 800/888–5155) while the **Boston Marathon** (☎ 617/236–1652) fills the streets from Hopkinton to Back Bay.

LATE APR.➢ **Nantucket**'s four-day **Daffodil Festival** (☎ 508/228–1700) celebrates spring with a flower show, shop-window displays, and a procession of antique cars that ends with tailgate picnics at Siasconset.

EARLY MAY➢ New York's **Cherry Blossom Festival** (☎ 718/622–4433) is held at the Brooklyn Botanic Garden.

Summer

JUNE➢ Lincoln Center hosts the **Annual American Crafts Festival** (☎ 973/746–0091) on a couple of weekends during the month.

EARLY JUNE➢ The **Belmont Stakes** (☎ 718/641–4700, ext. 732), Thoroughbred racing's final Triple Crown event, takes place at Belmont Park, in **Elmont, New York.**

MID-JUNE➢ The **Festival of Historic Houses** (☎ 401/831–7440) celebrates the Colonial, Greek Revival, and Victorian homes of **Providence, Rhode Island.**

LATE JUNE➢ **Lesbian and Gay Pride Week** (☎ 212/807–7433) in New York City includes the world's largest lesbian and gay pride parade. The **Texaco New York Jazz Festival** (☎ 212/219–3006) showcases more than 200 groups spread in venues all over town. Besides classic acts, you'll find acid, Latin, and avant-garde jazz.

LATE JUNE–EARLY JULY➢ **Boston**'s weeklong Fourth of July celebration, **Harborfest** (☎ 617/227–1528), includes a concert synchronized to fireworks over the harbor.

LATE JUNE–AUG.➢ The **Jacob's Pillow Dance Festival** (☎ 413/243–0745), at **Becket, Massachusetts,** in the Berkshires, hosts performers from various dance traditions.

JULY–AUG.➢ The **Mid-Summer Night Swing** (☎ 212/875–5400) fills the Fountain Plaza of New York City's Lincoln Center with swinging couples and live music; swing lessons are given before the dance. The **Tanglewood Music Festival** (☎ 413/637–1600 or 617/638–9235), at **Lenox, Massachusetts,** the summer home of the Boston Symphony Orchestra, schedules top performers.

JULY 4➢ The **Fourth of July Parade** (☎ 401/245–0750) in **Bristol, Rhode Island,** is the oldest Independence Day parade in the country, attracting thousands of visitors and an array of bands and military units.

MID-JULY➢ Held in the picturesque village of **Wickford, Rhode Island,** the **Wickford Art Festival** (☎ 401/295–5566) is one of the oldest, largest, and most diversified art festivals on the East Coast. Rhode Island's **Newport Music Festival** (☎ 401/846–1133) brings together celebrated musicians for two weeks of concerts in **Newport** mansions.

LATE JULY➢ Forty wineries take part in the **Finger Lakes Wine Festival** (☎ 607/535–2481), which also brings hay rides, arts and crafts, food, and jazz, blues, and bluegrass music to **Watkins Glen, New York.**

EARLY AUG.➢ The **Maine Lobster Festival** (☎ 207/596–0376) is a public feast held on the first weekend of the month in **Rockland. Ben & Jerry's Folk Festival** (☎ 401/847–3700), held in Fort Adams State Park in **Newport, Rhode Island,** books top names like the Indigo Girls and Joan Baez.

MID-AUG.➢ **Newport**'s Fort Adams State Park is also host to the **JVC Jazz Festival** (☎ 401/847–3700), formerly the Newport Jazz Festival, one of the nation's premier jazz events.

LATE AUG.➢ The **Cajun & Bluegrass Music and Dance Festival** (☎ 401/351–6312), at the Stepping Stone Ranch in **West Greenwich, Rhode Island,** attracts Cajun music fans from all over.

LATE AUG.–EARLY SEPT.➢ The **U.S. Open Tennis Tournament** (☎ 718/760–6200), in Flushing Meadow–Corona Park, Queens, is one of **New York City**'s premier sport events.

Autumn

EARLY SEPT.➢ Labor Day fairs in the region include the **Vermont State Fair,** in **Rutland,** and Rhode Island's **Providence Waterfront Festival.** The **Common Ground Country Fair,** in **Windsor, Maine,** is an organic farmer's delight.

EARLY OCT.➢ The **Columbus Day Parade** (800/888–5515) in **Boston** moves from East Boston to the North End, while south of Boston on the same weekend, the **Massachusetts Cranberry Harvest Festival** (☎ 508/295–5799 May–Oct.) takes place in both **Plymouth** and neighboring **South Carver**'s Edaville Cranberry Bog.

OCT.➢ The **Nantucket Cranberry Harvest** (☎ 508/228–1700) is a three-day celebration that includes bog and inn tours and a crafts fair.

EARLY NOV.➢ The **New York City Marathon** (☎ 212/860–4455) is the world's largest; it winds through all five boroughs of the city and finishes at Tavern on the Green in Central Park.

LATE NOV.➢ The **Macy's Thanksgiving Day Parade** (☎ 212/494–5432) is a **New York City** tradition; huge balloons float down Central Park West at 77th Street to Broadway and Herald Square. You can also see the balloons being inflated the night before.

Getting Around the Northeast

By Boat

In Rhode Island the **Block Island Ferry** (☎ 401/783–4613) has service from Providence, Newport, and Point Judith to Block Island. **Prince of Fundy Cruises** (☎ 800/341–7540) runs ferries between Yarmouth, Nova Scotia, and Portland, Maine, from May to October. **Casco Bay Lines** (☎ 207/774–7871) has ferries from Portland to the islands of Casco Bay. **Maine State Ferry Service** (☎ 207/596–2203) runs from Rockland to Vinalhaven and Northhaven, Lincolnville to Isleboro, and Bath Harbor to Swan's Island. For information about ferry service to Martha's Vineyard and Nantucket, *see* Massachusetts. The **Bridgeport and Port Jefferson Steamboat Company** (☎ 516/473–0286 or 888/443–3779) has ferries connecting the north shore of New York's Long Island to Bridgeport, Connecticut. **Cross Sound Ferry** (☎ 860/443–5281) connects New London, Connecticut, with Orient Point, New York, in northeastern Long Island.

By Bus

The major bus lines are **Greyhound Lines** (☎ 800/231–2222) and **Bonanza** (☎ 800/556–3815). **Peter Pan** (☎ 413/781–3320 or 800/237–8747) serves western Massachusetts and Connecticut.

By Car

The chief interstate through New England is I–95, which travels out of New York and along the Connecticut coast to Providence, Rhode Island, and into Boston, Massachusetts, before continuing up through New Hampshire and along the coast of Maine. From Boston I–89 goes through southern New Hampshire to central and northwestern Vermont and on into Canada. The New York State Thruway connects New York City to Albany and then veers northwest to Buffalo. I–87 runs between Albany and Montréal, Canada, and passes by Lake Champlain. Crossing the eastern region between Albany and Boston is the Massachusetts Turnpike (I–90). I–84 runs from Pennsylvania to Massachusetts and connects with I–684, which runs north from the New York metropolitan area, near the Connecticut border. Passing through Hartford is I–91, which links coastal Connecticut with New Hampshire and eastern Vermont.

By Plane

New York City has three major airports served by major domestic and international airlines: **John F. Kennedy International Airport** (☎ 718/244–4444), **LaGuardia Airport** (☎ 718/533–3400), and **Newark Airport** (☎ 973/961–6000). Upper New York State has the **Albany-Schenectady County Airport** (☎ 518/869–3021 or 518/869–9611), which is served by most major airlines. Connecticut's **Bradley International Airport** (☎ 860/292–2000), outside Hartford, is also served by most major U.S. carriers. All the major domestic air carriers fly into Boston's **Logan International Airport** (☎ 617/561–1800 or 800/235–6426), as do several international carriers. Vermont's main airport is **Burlington International Airport** (☎ 802/863–2874), served by several major airlines. For New Hampshire and southern Maine the major airport is **Portland International Airport** (☎ 207/774–7301or 207/775–5809), also served by several major U.S. airlines. Maine's other key airport is **Bangor International Airport** (☎ 207/947–0384), served by several major U.S. airlines.

By Train

Amtrak (☎ 800/872–7245) is the major long-distance train service for the region. Frequent trains make the run between New York, Stamford, New Haven, New London, Providence, and Boston. Fewer trains run between New York and Hartford. From Boston the *Lakeshore Limited* travels west, stopping in Springfield and the Berkshires before continuing west to Chicago. The *Vermonter* starts in Washington, D.C., and ends in St. Albans, Vermont. The *Ethan Allen* accommodates winter skiers between New York and Rutland, Vermont.

Local trains of the region: **Metro North** (☎ 212/532–4900; 800/638–7646 outside New York City) connects New York City and New Haven with stops along the coast. The **Massachusetts Bay Transportation Authority** (☎ 617/722–3200) connects Boston with the north and south shores. The **Long Island Railroad** (☎ 516/822–5477) runs from New York City to Montauk on its south-fork route and to Greenport on its north fork.

CONNECTICUT

Updated by Michelle Bodak Acri

Capital	Hartford
Population	3,270,000
Motto	He Who Transplanted Still Sustains
State Bird	American robin
State Flower	Mountain laurel
Postal Abbreviation	CT

Statewide Visitor Information

Department of Tourism (✉ 505 Hudson St., Hartford 06106, ☎ 800/282–6863 for brochure).

Scenic Drives

The narrow roads that wind through the **Litchfield Hills** in northwestern Connecticut offer scenic delights, especially in the spring and autumn. Each road bridge crossing the beautiful and historic **Merritt Parkway** (Route 15) between **Greenwich** and **Stratford** has its own architecturally significant design. The roads (Routes 57 to 53 to 107 to 302) that connect Exit 42 of the Merritt Parkway in **Westport** to Exit 10 of I–84 in **Newtown** take you by Colonial homesteads, over steep ridges, and alongside the **Saugatuck Reservoir.** In northeastern Connecticut, Route 169 from **Norwich** to **North Woodstock** has been designated a National Scenic Byway.

National and State Parks

National Park

Dapper, wooded Wilton is home to **Weir Farm National Historic Site,** dedicated to painter J. Alden Weir. The 60 acres here include hiking paths, picnic areas, and restored rose and perennial gardens. Tours of Weir's studio and sculptor Mahonri Young's studio are conducted, and you can take a self-guided tour of Weir's painting sites. ✉ *735 Nod Hill Rd.,* ☎ *203/834–1896.* *Free.* *Grounds daily dawn–dusk, visitor center Wed.–Sun. 8:30–5.*

State Parks

Connecticut has nearly 100 state parks, among them the 4,000-acre **White Memorial Foundation** (✉ Rte. 202, Litchfield 06759, ☎ 860/567–0857). For information on state parks contact the **State Parks Division, Bureau of Outdoor Recreation** (✉ 79 Elm St., Hartford 06106, ☎ 860/424–3200).

COASTAL CONNECTICUT

The state's 253-mi coastline connects a series of bedroom communities serving New York City with smaller towns linked to Connecticut's major cities of Stamford, Bridgeport, New Haven, and New London. Along with its Colonial heritage and 20th-century urban sprawl, the region has nature centers and wilderness preserves for hiking and bird-watching, as well as restored 18th- and 19th-century townships and marine and other museums dedicated to bringing Connecticut's past alive.

Visitor Information

Southeastern Connecticut: Connecticut's Mystic and More (✉ Box 89, New London 06320, ☎ 860/444–2206 or 800/863–6569). **South-**

western Connecticut: Coastal Fairfield County Convention and Visitors Bureau (✉ 297 West Ave., The Gate Lodge–Mathews Park, Norwalk 06850, ☎ 203/899–2799 or 800/866–7925). **New Haven:** Greater New Haven Convention and Visitors District (✉ 1 Long Wharf Dr., Suite 7, New Haven 06511, ☎ 203/777–8550 or 800/332–7829).

Arriving and Departing

By Bus

Greyhound Lines (☎ 800/231–2222) provides bus service from throughout the U.S. **Bonanza Bus Lines** (☎ 800/556–3815) provides service from various points in New England. **Connecticut Transit** (☎ 203/327–7433) provides bus service in the Stamford, Hartford, and New Haven areas. **Southeast Area Transit** (☎ 860/886–2631) serves Norwich, New London, Mystic, and Niantic.

By Car

The Merritt Parkway and I–95 are the principal coastal highways between New York and New Haven. I–95 continues beyond New Haven into Rhode Island. From Hartford, I–91 goes south to New Haven.

By Ferry

The **Bridgeport and Port Jefferson Steamboat Company** (☎ 888/443–3779 or 516/473–0286) has ferries connecting Bridgeport with the north shore of New York's Long Island. **Cross Sound Ferry** (☎ 860/443–5281) connects New London with northeastern Long Island's Orient Point.

By Plane

The state's chief airport is **Bradley International Airport** (✉ Rte. 20, Exit 40 off I–91, ☎ 860/627–3000), 12 mi north of Hartford, with daily flights by most major U.S. airlines. Along the coast, **Igor Sikorsky Memorial Airport** (✉ 1000 Great Meadow Rd., Exit 30 off I–95, Stratford, ☎ 203/576–7498), 4 mi south of Stratford, is served by US Airways Express. US Airways Express and Continental Express fly into **Tweed/New Haven Airport** (✉ Burr St. off I–95, ☎ 203/946–8283), 5 mi southeast of New Haven.

By Train

Amtrak (☎ 800/872–7245) stops at Stamford, Bridgeport, New Haven, Hartford, New London, and Mystic. **Metro North** (☎ 212/532–4900 or 800/638–7646) runs between New York City and New Haven, with stops at a few inland stations and many towns along the coast.

Exploring Coastal Connecticut

Greenwich, which borders New York state, is the epitome of affluent Fairfield County, with gourmet restaurants and chic boutiques. The **Bruce Museum** (✉ 1 Museum Dr., ☎ 203/869–0376; 🎟 $3.50), closed Monday, has a mineral collection, a small but worthwhile collection of American Impressionist paintings, and a 16th-century-era woodland diorama. The 485-acre **Audubon Center** (✉ 613 Riversville Rd., ☎ 203/869–5272; 🎟 $3) has exhibits on the local environment and 8 mi of secluded hiking trails. The small barn-red **Putnam Cottage** was built about 1690 and was operated as Knapp's Tavern during the Revolutionary War. Inside are Colonial-era furnishings; outside is a lush herb garden. ✉ *243 E. Putnam Ave., Rte. 1,* ☎ *203/869–9697.* 🎟 *$2. Closed Mon.–Tues., Thurs., and Sat.*

Cos Cob is a village within the township of Greenwich. The **Bush-Holley House,** built circa 1732, has paintings by Hassam and Twachtman, sculptures by John Rogers, and pottery by Leon Volkmar. ✉ *39 Strick-*

land Rd., ☎ *203/869–6899.* 🎟 *$6. Closed Jan.–March, Mon.–Tues., Thurs.–Fri.; April–Dec., Mon.–Tues.*

Stamford's shoreline is given over primarily to industry and commerce, but to the north some beautiful nature areas remain. The 118-acre **Stamford Museum and Nature Center** (✉ 39 Scofieldtown Rd., ☎ 203/322–1646; 🎟 $5) has five galleries with changing exhibits on natural history, art, and Americana, a working New England farm, and a permanent exhibit on local Native American history. Shows are offered at the center's observatory and planetarium. In the Champion International Corporation building, downtown, is the **Whitney Museum of American Art at Champion.** Exhibits of primarily 20th-century American painting and photography often include works from the Whitney's collection in New York City. ✉ *Atlantic St. and Tresser Blvd.,* ☎ *203/358–7630.* 🎟 *Free. Closed Sun.–Mon.*

South Norwalk, affectionately dubbed SoNo, is off I–95's Exit 15. Steps away from an avenue of restored art galleries, restaurants, and boutiques is the **Maritime Aquarium at Norwalk,** which has a huge aquarium, marine vessels, and an IMAX theater. ✉ *10 N. Water St.,* ☎ *203/852–0700.* 🎟 *Aquarium $7.75, IMAX $6.50.*

Wilton, a well-preserved community with a wooded countryside and good antiques shopping, is a brief detour from the coast, up Routes 7 and 33 from Norwalk. Wilton has Connecticut's first national park, **Weir Farm National Historical Site** (☞ National and State Parks, *above*). **Ridgefield,** with its sweeping lawns and stately mansions, is where you'll find northwestern Connecticut atmosphere within an hour of Manhattan. Ridgefield is home to the **Aldrich Museum of Contemporary Art,** which has changing exhibits of cutting-edge works and one of the finest sculpture gardens in the Northeast. ✉ *258 Main St.,* ☎ *203/438–4519.* 🎟 *$5. Closed Mon.*

Westport has long been an artistic and literary community and now is also a trendy hub of shops and eateries. In summer visitors flock to **Sherwood Island State Park** (✉ I–95 Exit 18, ☎ 203/226–6983) for its 1½-mi sweep of sandy beach and two water's-edge picnic groves.

The exclusive Colonial village of **Southport** is on the Pequot River. To get there from Sherwood Island, head east along Greens Farms Road, which continues into **Fairfield,** the town almost destroyed in a raid by the British in 1779—four houses survived the attack and still stand on Beach Road. In the northern part of town, the **Connecticut Audubon Society** (✉ 2325 Burr St., ☎ 203/259–6305; 🎟 $2) maintains a 160-acre wildlife sanctuary.

Bridgeport, a city that has fallen on hard times, is unsafe at night and unappealing during the day. It is, however, hard at work at revitalization. **Beardsley Park and Zoological Gardens** (✉ 1875 Noble Ave., ☎ 203/394–6565; 🎟 $5) is Connecticut's only zoo. Here you'll find more than 350 animals as well as a South American rain forest and a carousel. The **Barnum Museum,** associated with onetime mayor P. T. Barnum, has exhibits depicting the great showman's career and a scaled-down model of his famous creation, the five-ring circus. ✉ *820 Main St.,* ☎ *203/331–1104.* 🎟 *$5. Closed Mon.*

New Haven is a city of extremes: Although it's prosperous in the area around the green—encompassing the Yale University campus and the numerous shops, museums, and restaurants of Chapel Street—20% of the city's residents live below the poverty level. Stay near the campus

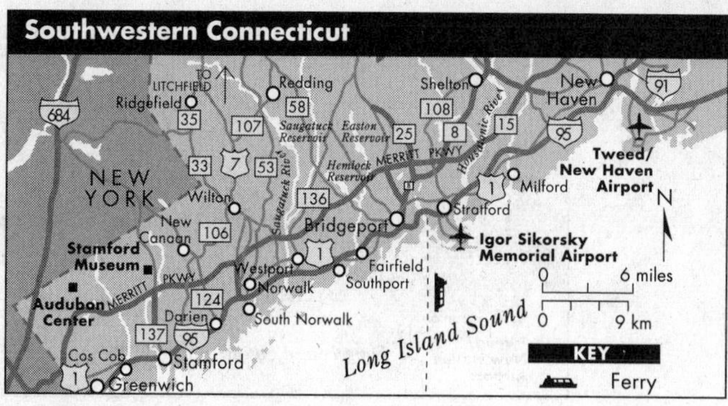

and city common, especially at night, and get a good street map. Knowledgeable guides give one-hour walking tours of the **Yale University campus** (⊠ 149 Elm St., ☎ 203/432–2300; 🎟 free). The **Yale University Art Gallery** (⊠ 1111 Chapel St., ☎ 203/432–0600; 🎟 free), closed Monday, has a collection that spans the centuries and the continents. Closed for most of 1998 for renovation, the **Yale Center for British Art** (⊠ 1080 Chapel St., ☎ 203/432–2800; 🎟 free) is slated to reopen by 1999. The museum, closed Monday, has the most extensive collection of British artwork and rare books outside the United Kingdom. The **Peabody Museum of Natural History** (⊠ 170 Whitney Ave., ☎ 203/432–5050; 🎟 $5) is the largest of its kind in New England.

The urban buildup that characterizes the Connecticut coast west of New Haven dissipates as you drive east on I–95 toward New London. **Old Saybrook** was once a lively shipbuilding and fishing town; today the bustle comes mostly from its many summer vacationers. On the other side of the Connecticut River from Old Saybrook is **Old Lyme.** The **Florence Griswold Museum** (⊠ 96 Lyme St., ☎ 860/434–5542; 🎟 $4) once housed an art colony that included Childe Hassam. The museum displays the colonists' works, along with 19th-century furnishings and decorative items. The **Lyme Academy of Fine Arts** (⊠ 84 Lyme St., ☎ 860/434–5232; 🎟 donation suggested) shows works by students and other contemporary artists.

The seagoing community of **New London** is the home of the **U.S. Coast Guard Academy,** whose 100-acre cluster of traditional redbrick buildings includes a museum. The three-masted training bark *Eagle* may be boarded when in port. ⊠ *15 Mohegan Ave.,* ☎ *860/444–8270.* 🎟 *Free.*

In **Groton,** across the Thames River from New London, is a U.S. submarine base. The world's first nuclear-powered submarine, the *Historic Ship Nautilus,* was launched here in 1954 and is now permanently berthed here and open to visitors. Next to the base is the **Submarine Force Museum,** which contains memorabilia, artifacts, and displays, including working periscopes and controls. ⊠ *Crystal Lake Rd.,* ☎ *860/449–3174 or 860/449–3558.* 🎟 *Free. Closed Tues. late Oct.–early May.*

Mystic, the celebrated whaling seaport, is a few miles east of Groton. **Mystic Seaport** (⊠ 75 Greenmanville Ave., ☎ 860/572–0711; 🎟 $16)—the nation's largest maritime museum, on 17 riverfront acres—has 19th-century sailing vessels you can board, a maritime village with historic homes, seasonal steamboat cruises and small-boat rentals, and craftspeople who give demonstrations. At the **Mystic Marinelife Aquar-**

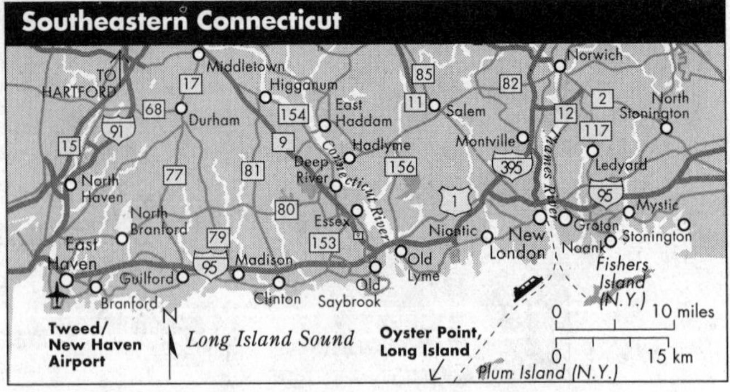

ium (✉ Off I–95 on Coogan Blvd., ☎ 860/536–3323; 🎫 $13) you can see more than 6,000 specimens and 50 live exhibits of sea life.

Stonington is a quiet fishing community clustered around white-spired churches. Past the historic buildings that surround the town green is the **Old Lighthouse Museum,** where you'll find shipping, whaling, and other displays. Climb to the top of the granite tower for a view of Long Island Sound and three states. ✉ *7 Water St.,* ☎ *860/535–1440.* 🎫 *$4. Closed Mon. May–June, Sept.–Oct; Nov.–Apr.*

Dining and Lodging

The **Covered Bridge B&B Reservation Service** (☎ 860/542–5944) and **Nutmeg B&B Agency** (☎ 860/236–6698) are reliable statewide services for B&Bs and small inns. **B&B, Ltd.** (☎ 203/469–3260) is a service for small B&Bs, inns, and rooms rented in private homes. Rooms are costliest in summer and autumn. A 12% lodging tax is added to each bill. For price ranges *see* Charts 1 (B) and 2 (B) *in* On the Road with Fodor's.

Greenwich

$$$$ ★ ✕ **Restaurant Jean-Louis.** Roses, Villeroy & Boch china, and crisp, white tablecloths with lace underskirts complement extraordinary food, carefully served. Specialties include quail-and-vegetable ragout with foie gras sauce and, for dessert, lemon-and-pear gratin. ✉ *61 Lewis St.,* ☎ *203/622–8450. Jacket required. AE, D, DC, MC, V. Closed Sun. No lunch Sat.–Thurs.*

$$$$ ✕🏨 **Homestead Inn.** Each bedroom in this Italianate mansion is decorated with antiques and reproductions. The restaurant (jacket required) serves up-to-the-minute French cuisine. ✉ *420 Field Point Rd., 06830,* ☎ FAX *203/869–7500. 23 rooms. Restaurant. AE, DC, MC, V.*

Mystic

$$$$ ✕🏨 **Inn at Mystic.** The highlight of this inn, which sprawls over 15 hilltop acres and overlooks Pequotsepos Cove, is the five-bedroom Georgian Colonial mansion in which Lauren Bacall and Humphrey Bogart honeymooned. Almost as impressive are the four-bedroom gatehouse and the unusually attractive motor lodge. The sun-filled Floodtide Restaurant serves traditional New England fare. ✉ *Rtes. 1 and 27, 06355,* ☎ *860/536–9604 or 800/237–2415,* FAX *860/572–1635. 68 rooms. Restaurant, pool. AE, D, DC, MC, V.*

$$$$ 🏨 **Whaler's Inn and Motor Court.** A perfect compromise between a chain motel and a country inn, this complex is one block from the Mystic River and downtown. The rooms are decorated in a Victorian style with quilts and reproduction four-poster beds. ✉ *20 E. Main St., 06355,* ☎ *860/536–1506 or 800/243–2588 outside CT,* FAX *860/572–1250. 41 rooms. 3 restaurants. AE, MC, V.*

New Haven

$ ✕ **Frank Pepe's.** The big ovens on the back wall of this New Haven institution bake pizzas that are served by smart-mouthed waitresses. On weekend evenings the wait for a table can be more than an hour, but the pizza—the sole item on the menu—is worth it. ✉ *157 Wooster St.,* ☎ *203/865–5762. Reservations not accepted. No credit cards. Closed Tues. No lunch Mon. and Wed.–Thurs.*

$$$$ ★ **Three Chimneys Inn.** This 1870 Victorian mansion is one of the most polished small inns in the state. Rooms have posh Georgian furnishings: mahogany four-poster beds, oversize armoires, and Chippendale desks. Three rooms have fireplaces. ✉ *1201 Chapel St., 06511,* ☎ *203/789–1201,* FAX *203/776–7363. 10 rooms. Full breakfast. AE, MC, V.*

North Stonington

$$$$ ★ ✕ **Randall's Ordinary.** Famed for its open-hearth cooking of authentic Colonial dishes, the Ordinary serves extraordinary lunches and three-course fixed-price dinners (reservations essential), served by staff in period costume. Accommodations are available in the 17th-century John Randall House, where rooms are simply furnished with antiques, or in the converted barn. ✉ *Rte. 2, Box 243, 06359,* ☎ *860/599–4540,* FAX *860/599–3308. 15 rooms. Restaurant. CP. AE, MC, V.*

Norwalk

$$$$ ★ ✕ **Meson Galicia.** The inventive tapas served in this restored trolley barn electrify the taste buds. Ingredients include sweetbreads, capers, asparagus, chorizo . . . the list goes on. Come with an empty stomach and an open mind, and let the enthusiastic staff spoil you. ✉ *10 Wall St.,,* ☎ *203/866–8800. AE, D, DC, MC, V. No lunch weekends. Closed Mon.*

Norwich

$$$$ **Norwich Inn & Spa.** This luxurious Georgian-style inn is set on 40 acres high on a bluff a few hundred yards from the Thames River. Top-notch treatments and fitness classes are offered in the newly renovated facility. The American spa cuisine served at the inn goes well beyond carrot and celery sticks. ✉ *607 W. Thames St. (Rte. 32), 06360,* ☎ *860/886–2401 or 800/275–4772,* FAX *860/886–4492. 135 rooms. Restaurant, indoor pool, health club. AE, DC, MC, V.*

Old Lyme

$$$–$$$$ ★ ✕ **Bee & Thistle Inn.** This two-story 1756 Colonial is appointed with period antiques and warm touches. Most rooms have canopy or four-poster beds. Fireplaces and candlelight create a romantic atmosphere in the restaurant (closed on Tuesday and the first three weeks in January), where classic American cuisine is served with style. ✉ *100 Lyme St., 06371,* ☎ *860/434–1667 or 800/622–4946 outside CT,* FAX *860/434–3402. 12 rooms. Restaurant. AE, DC, MC, V.*

Old Saybrook

$$$–$$$$ ★ ✕ **Aleia's** is as light, bright, and bountiful as the Italian countryside. Raffia, silk flowers, and hand-painted plates from Capri decorate the walls, and trompe l'oeil fruits, vegetables, and herbs adorn the tabletops. Chef-owner Kimberly Snow takes a contemporary approach to Italian cuisine by applying nouvelle touches to her mother's tried-and-true recipes. ✉ *1687 Boston Post Rd.,* ☎ *860/399–5050. AE, MC, V. Closed Mon. No lunch.*

Stamford

$$$$ ✕ **Amadeus.** One of a dozen great restaurants along its stretch of Summer Street, Amadeus leads the pack. The fare—like the decor—is Continental with a Viennese flair. Try the Mediterranean fish and shellfish soup, followed by the trademark Vienna schnitzel, served

with golden panfried potatoes. ⊠ *201 Summer St.,* ☎ *203/348–7775. AE, D, DC, MC, V. No lunch weekends.*

Westbrook

$$$$ 🏨 **Water's Edge Inn & Resort.** With a spectacular setting on Long Island Sound and its own beach, this weathered gray-shingle compound is one of the Connecticut shore's premier resorts. Rooms in the main building, though not as large as the suites in surrounding outbuildings, have better views and nicer furnishings. ⊠ *1525 Boston Post Rd., 06498,* ☎ *860/399–5901 or 800/222–5901,* FAX *860/399–6172. 100 rooms. Restaurant, indoor and outdoor pools, health club, spa. AE, D, DC, MC, V.*

Westport

$$$–$$$$ ✕ **Café Christina.** Faux columns and other trompe l'oeil touches enliven the decor at this café in a former library. The outstanding variations on American-Mediterranean cuisine include appetizers like risotto fritters with arugula and portobello mushrooms. The sesame seared yellowfin stars among the entrées, which change every few weeks. ⊠ *1 Main St.,* ☎ *203/221–7950. Reservations essential on weekends. AE, DC, MC, V.*

$$$$ ★ ✕🏨 **Inn at National Hall.** The inn's redbrick building on the downtown banks of the Saugatuck River belies its whimsical, exotic interior. Each room is a study in innovative restoration. Outstanding Continental dishes are served in the lushly decorated restaurant (reservations essential). ⊠ *2 Post Rd. W, 06880,* ☎ *203/221–1351 or 800/628–4255,* FAX *203/221–0276. 15 rooms. Restaurant. CP. AE, DC, MC, V.*

Campgrounds

⛺ **Riverdale Farm Campsite** (⊠ 111 River Rd., Clinton, ☎ 860/669–5388). ⛺ **Hammonasset Beach State Park** (⊠ I–95 Exit 62, Madison, ☎ 203/245–1817).

Nightlife and the Arts

Nightlife

Bars and clubs are sprinkled throughout southern Connecticut. The best of them are concentrated in **Westport, South Norwalk, New Haven's** Chapel West area, and along **New London's** Bank Street.

Foxwoods (☎ 860/885–3000), a gambling and entertainment complex on the Mashantucket Pequots Reservation off Route 2 near Ledyard (8 mi north of Groton), is the world's largest casino, with 5,500 slot machines, a high-stakes bingo parlor, poker rooms, a smoke-free gaming area, and more. The new **Mohegan Sun** casino (☎ 860/848–5682), in Uncasville, offers similar facilities on a smaller scale.

The Arts

The Connecticut coast's wealth of successful repertory and Broadway-style theaters includes the **Long Wharf Theatre** (⊠ New Haven, ☎ 203/787–4282), known for its revivals of neglected classics and imaginative productions of new work. The **Shubert Performing Arts Center** (⊠ New Haven, ☎ 203/562–5666) presents an array of full-scale productions. **Stamford Center for the Arts** (☎ 203/325–4466) offers everything from one-act plays to musicals to film festivals. In summer the **Westport Playhouse** (☎ 203/227–4177) presents first-rate plays. The **Yale Repertory Theatre** (⊠ New Haven, ☎ 203/432–1234) is known for its fresh interpretations of classics.

Most coastal towns have outdoor summer concerts and music festivals, and some have smaller regional theaters. Call tourist offices for details (☞ Visitor Information, *above*).

Outdoor Activities and Sports

Fishing

Saltwater fishing is best from June through October; bass, bluefish, and flounder are popular catches. Boats are available from **Hel-Cat Dock** (✉ Groton, ☎ 860/445–5991), **Sea Sprite Charters** (✉ Old Saybrook, ☎ 860/669–9613), **Burr's Yacht Haven** (✉ New London, ☎ 860/443–8457), and **Captain John's Dock** (✉ Waterford, ☎ 860/443–7259).

Golf

Danbury's 18-hole **Richter Park Golf Course** (✉ 100 Aunt Hack Rd., ☎ 203/792–2550) is one of the top public courses in the nation. Three other 18-hole courses are the **H. Smith Richardson Golf Course** (✉ 2425 Morehouse Hwy., Fairfield, ☎ 203/255–7300) and the courses designed by Robert Trent Jones and Gary Player at the **Lyman Orchards Golf Club** (✉ Rte. 147, Middlefield, ☎ 860/349–8055).

Water Sports

Dodson Boat Yard (✉ 194 Water St., Stonington, ☎ 860/535–1507), **Longshore Sailing School** (✉ Longshore Club Park, Westport, ☎ 203/226–4646), and **Shaffer's Boat Livery** (✉ 106 Mason's Island Rd., Mystic, ☎ 203/536–8713) rent sailboats or motorboats.

Shopping

Southwestern Connecticut

Route 7, which runs through **Wilton** and **Ridgefield,** has dozens of antiques sheds and boutiques. Of particular note is **Cannondale Village** (✉ Off Rte. 7, Wilton, ☎ 203/762–2233), a pre–Civil War farm village turned shopping complex. Washington Street in **South Norwalk** (SoNo) has galleries and crafts dealers. The **Stamford Town Center** (✉ 100 Greyrock Pl., ☎ 203/356–9700) houses 130 mostly upscale shops. Main Street in **Westport** is like an outdoor mall, with J. Crew, Ann Taylor, Coach, and dozens of other fashionable shops. **New Canaan, Darien,** and **Greenwich** are also renowned for their swank stores and boutiques.

Southeastern Connecticut

The New Haven and New London areas have typical concentrations of shopping centers. **Clinton Crossing Premium Outlets** (✉ I–95 Exit 63, Clinton, ☎ 860/664–0700) has 70 upscale shops. **Westbrook Factory Stores** (✉ I–95 Exit 65, Westbrook, ☎ 860/399–8656) has 65 outlets. Downtown **Mystic** has an interesting collection of boutiques and galleries. **Olde Mistick Village** (✉ I–95 Exit 90, Mystic, ☎ 860/536–1641), a re-created Colonial village, has crafts and souvenir shops. The **Tradewinds Gallery** (✉ 20 W. Main St., Mystic, ☎ 860/536–0119) specializes in antique prints and maps. The **Essex–Saybrook Antiques Village** (✉ 345 Middlesex Turnpike, Old Saybrook, ☎ 860/388–0689) has more than 120 dealers. **Old Lyme, Guilford,** and **Stonington** are also strong on antiques.

THE LITCHFIELD HILLS

Here, in the foothills of the Berkshires, is some of the most unspoiled scenery in the state. Grand old inns are plentiful, as are surprisingly sophisticated eateries. Rolling farmlands abut thick forests, and engaging trails traverse state parks. Two rivers, Housatonic and Farmington, attract anglers and canoeing enthusiasts, and there are three sizeable lakes, Waramaug, Bantam, and Twin Lakes. Most towns are anchored by sweeping greens and stately homes and offer a glimpse of New England life as it existed two centuries ago.

Visitor Information

Litchfield Hills Travel Council (✉ Box 968, Litchfield 06759, ☎ 860/567–4506).

Exploring the Litchfield Hills

The mountainous northern towns of **Sharon, Lakeville, Salisbury,** and **Norfolk** are crisscrossed by scenic winding roads. From late April to mid-October auto racing fans come to **Lime Rock Park** (✉ Rte. 112, Lakeville, ☎ 860/435–2571), home to the Northeast's best road racing.

The crossroads village of **New Preston** is packed with antiques shops. North of downtown is Lake Waramaug. The scenic drive around the lake (8 mi) will take you past stately homes and beautiful old inns, many of which serve outstanding Continental cuisine. **Kent,** to the northwest, is home to the area's greatest concentration of art galleries, some of them nationally recognized. **Bull's Bridge** (✉ Off Rte. 7) is one of the state's three remaining covered bridges. Within **Kent Falls State Park** (✉ Rte. 7, ☎ 860/927–3238) is one of the state's most impressive waterfalls.

Everything seems on a larger scale in **Litchfield** than in neighboring towns: Great white Colonials line broad streets shaded by majestic elms, and serene Litchfield Green is surrounded by lovely shops and restaurants. Near the green is the **Tapping Reeve House** (✉ 82 South St., ☎ 860/567–4501; $5), America's first law school, which was founded in 1773. It's closed on Monday and mid-October–mid-May. The **Litchfield Historical Society Museum** (✉ Rtes. 63 and 118, ☎ 860/567–4501; 🎫 $5), closed on Monday and mid-November–mid-April, has galleries, a reference library, and information on the town's historic buildings. Admission to the Tapping Reeve House is good for same-day entrance to the historical society museum. **White Flower Farm** (✉ Rte. 63, ☎ 860/567–8789), where much of America shops in person or by mail for perennials and bulbs, is a restful stop.

To the south, the villages of **Washington, Roxbury,** and **Bridgewater** offer a gentler landscape, in which numerous actors and writers seek refuge from the din of Manhattan and Hollywood. You can buy the ingredients for a gourmet picnic lunch—try the **Pantry** (✉ Washington, ☎ 860/868–0258)—then laze on the shores of sparkling Lake Waramaug or enjoy a leisurely drive along precipitous ridges, passing gracious farmsteads and meadows alive with wildflowers.

In Bristol are two amusements for the child in everyone. The **Carousel Museum of New England** (✉ 95 Riverside Ave., ☎ 860/585–5411; 🎫 $4) displays carousel art. **Lake Compounce** (✉ Rte. 229 N., I–84, Exit 31, ☎ 860/583–3631; 🎫 $4.95 general admission, $19.95 with rides) is the country's oldest continually operating amusement park. Highlights of the 325-acre park include an antique carousel, a classic wooden roller coaster, a new water playground, and a lake with a beach.

Dining and Lodging

Litchfield

$$$–$$$$ ✕ **West Street Grill.** This stylish dining room on Litchfield's historic green is the favorite of local glitterati, but all are warmly welcomed. Imaginative grilled fish, steak, poultry, and lamb dishes are served with fresh vegetables and pasta or risotto. The grilled Parmesan aioli bread is superb. ✉ *43 West St. (Rte. 202),* ☎ *860/567–3885. AE, MC, V.*

New Preston

$$$$ ★ ✕🏨 **Boulders Inn.** This is the most idyllic and prestigious of the inns along Lake Waramaug's uneven shoreline. The Boulders opened in 1940 but still looks like the private home it was at the turn of the century. Apart from the main house, a carriage house and several guest houses command panoramic views of the countryside and the lake. Rooms contain Victorian antiques and wood-burning fireplaces; four have double whirlpool baths. The exquisite menu at the Boulders' window-lined, stone-wall dining room changes seasonally. ✉ *E. Shore Rd. (Rte. 45), 06777,* ☎ *860/868–0541 or 800/552–6853,* FAX *860/868–1925. 17 rooms. Restaurant. MAP. AE, MC, V.*

Norfolk

$$$$ ★ 🏨 **Greenwoods Gate.** The cheerful George Shumaker, a former Hilton executive with a penchant for playing cupid, runs Connecticut's foremost romantic hideaway. Every room holds countless amenities, from chocolates and cognac to soaps, fresh flowers, and powders to board games with titles like "Romantic Liaisons"; champagne or a deep massage are available with notice. George prepares a huge breakfast—a spread of muffins and fresh fruit followed by a hearty hot meal—and lays out snacks and afternoon wine and cheese. ✉ *105 Greenwoods Rd. E (Rte. 44), 06058,* ☎ *860/542–5439,* FAX *860/542–5897. 4 suites. Full breakfast. No credit cards.*

Washington

$$–$$$ ✕ **G. W. Tavern.** The walls of G. W. Tavern are covered with a mural depicting the town and surrounding countryside as it used to be. The cuisine—hearty meat loaf, chicken pot pie, roast beef with Yorkshire pudding—is also reminiscent of once upon a time. A stone terrace for warm-weather dining overlooks the Shepaug River. ✉ *20 Bee Brook Rd.,* ☎ *860/868–6633. AE, D, DC, MC, V. Closed Mon. No lunch weekends.*

$$$$ ✕🏨 **Mayflower Inn.** Though some suites at this inn will set you back $580 a night, the place is always booked well ahead—with good reason. The Mayflower is impeccably decorated: Guest rooms have fine 18th- and 19th-century antiques and four-poster canopy beds; oversized baths have mahogany wainscotting and marble throughout. Streams and trails crisscross the 28-acre grounds. The mouthwatering cuisine includes roast Muscovy duck breast. ✉ *118 Woodbury Rd. (Rte. 47), 06793,* ☎ *860/868–9466,* FAX *860/868–1497. 25 rooms. Restaurant, pool, health club. AE, MC, V.*

Woodbury

$$$–$$$$ ★ ✕ **Good News Café.** The emphasis is on healthful, innovative fare: venison filet mignon with a horseradish crust on grilled onions and snow peas with a cherry-cabernet sauce is a tasty example. Or you can bounce in for cappuccino and munchies—there's a separate room just for this purpose, decorated with a fascinating collection of vintage radios. ✉ *694 Main St. S,* ☎ *203/266–4663. AE, MC, V. Closed Tues.*

Nightlife and the Arts

World-renowned artists and ensembles perform Friday and Saturday evening June–August at the **Norfolk Chamber Music Festival** (☎ 860/542–3000), at the Music Shed on the Ellen Battell Stoeckel Estate at the northwest corner of the Norfolk green. Students from the **Yale School of Music** perform Thursday evening and Saturday morning.

Outdoor Activities and Sports

Canoeing

Clarke Outdoors (⊠ West Cornwall, ☎ 860/672–6365) offers canoe and kayak rentals as well as 10-mi trips from Falls Village to Housatonic Meadows State Park.

Hiking

The Litchfield Hills area has terrific hiking terrain, with **Haystack Mountain and Dennis Hill** (⊠ Rte. 272, Norfolk), and the 758-acre **Sharon Audubon Center** (⊠ Cornwall Bridge Rd., ☎ 860/364–0520) offering the region's best opportunities.

Ski Areas

Mohawk Mountain (⊠ Cornwall, ☎ 860/672–6100). **Ski Sundown** (⊠ New Hartford, ☎ 860/379–9851). **Woodbury Ski Area** (⊠ Woodbury, ☎ 203/263–2203).

Shopping

The best antiques and crafts shopping is along Route 6 in **Woodbury** and **Southbury,** Route 45 in **New Preston,** U.S. 7 in **Kent,** Route 128 in **West Cornwall,** and U.S. 202 in **Bantam.**

ELSEWHERE IN CONNECTICUT

The Connecticut River and Hartford

Arriving and Departing

Amtrak, Greyhound, and **Bonanza** provide service to the Hartford area (☞ Coastal Connecticut, *above*). By car take I–91 north from New Haven or I–84, which cuts diagonally southwest–northeast through the state. Head north along Route 9 from Old Saybrook for a scenic drive through this historic area.

What to See and Do

The Connecticut River valley meanders through rolling hills, offering a taste of Colonial history as well as sophisticated inns. Call the **Connecticut River Valley and Shoreline Visitors Council** (⊠ 393 Main St., Middletown 06457, ☎ 860/347–0028 or 800/486–3346) for information. Also try the **Greater Hartford Tourism District** (⊠ 234 Murphy Rd., Hartford 06114, ☎ 860/244–8181 or 800/793–4480).

Essex, on the west bank of the Connecticut River, is where the first submarine, the *American Turtle,* was built. A full-size reproduction is at the **Connecticut River Museum** (⊠ Steamboat Dock, ☎ 860/767–8269; 🎫 $4). In **East Haddam** is the region's leading oddity: a 24-room oak-and-fieldstone hilltop castle that is part of **Gillette Castle State Park** (⊠ 67 River Rd., off Rte. 82, ☎ 860/526–2336; 🎫 $4). East Haddam is also the home of the **Goodspeed Opera House** (⊠ Rte. 82, ☎ 860/873–8668). The upper floors of this elaborate structure have served as a venue for theatrical performances for more than a century.

Hartford, known as the insurance capital of America, is also the state capital. The Federal **Old State House** (⊠ 800 Main St., ☎ 860/522–6766; 🎫 free) was designed by Charles Bulfinch, architect of the U.S. Capitol. **Mark Twain** made his home here in an extravagant Victorian mansion (⊠ 351 Farmington Ave., ☎ 860/493–6411; 🎫 $7.50). The ★ 50,000 artworks and artifacts at the **Wadsworth Atheneum** (⊠ 600 Main St., ☎ 860/278–2670; 🎫 $7), the nation's first public art museum, span 5,000 years and include paintings from the Hudson River School, the Impressionists, and 20th-century painters.

Dining and Lodging

$$$$ ✕ **Restaurant du Village.** A black wrought-iron gate beckons you away from the tony antiquaries of Chester's quaint Main Street to this Colonial storefront, painted in Newport blue and adorned with flower boxes. Sample classic French cuisine—escargots in puff pastry, filet mignon—while recapping the day's shopping coups. ✉ *59 Main St., Chester,* ☎ *860/526–5301. AE, MC, V. Closed Mon., and Tues. No lunch.*

$$$–$$$$ ✕ **Max Downtown.** Upscale Max Downtown serves cuisine from around the world—miso-saki glazed Chilean sea bass, Portobello mushroom napoleons, aged New York strip steaks, and grilled veal loin chops. A separate cigar bar serves classic port and single-malt liquor. ✉ *185 Asylum St., CityPlace, Hartford,* ☎ *860/522–2530. Reservations essential. AE, DC, MC, V. No lunch weekends.*

$$$$ ✕🏨 **Copper Beech Inn.** A magnificent copper beech tree shades the imposing main building of this Victorian inn, which is furnished in period pieces. Each of the main house's four guest rooms has an old-fashioned tub; the nine rooms in the carriage house are more modern and have decks. Seven acres of wooded grounds and terraced gardens create an atmosphere of privileged seclusion. The country French menu in the romantic dining rooms (reservations essential; jacket and tie) changes seasonally. ✉ *46 Main St., Ivoryton 06442,* ☎ *860/767–0330,* FAX *860/767–7840. 13 rooms. Restaurant. CP. AE, DC, MC, V.*

$$$ ✕🏨 **Griswold Inn.** The decor at what's billed as America's oldest inn is kaleidoscopic—some Colonial, a touch of Federal, a little Victorian, and just as much modern—air-conditioning, phones, but no in-room TVs—as is necessary to meet present-day expectations. The chefs at the restaurant ($$–$$$) prepare country-style and gourmet dishes—try the famous 1776 sausages, which come with sauerkraut and German potato salad, or the risotto croquettes. ✉ *36 Main St., Essex 06426,* ☎ *860/767–1776,* FAX *860/767–0481. 30 rooms. Restaurant. CP. AE, MC, V.*

$$$$ ★ 🏨 **Goodwin Hotel.** Considering this grand city hotel's stately exterior, rooms are not as opulent as one might expect, though they're large and have Italian marble baths. The clubby, mahogany-panel Pierpont's Restaurant serves commendable new American fare. ✉ *1 Haynes St., Hartford 06103,* ☎ *860/246–7500 or 800/922–5006,* FAX *860/247–4576. 135 rooms. Restaurant, exercise room. AE, D, DC, MC, V.*

MAINE

By Ed and Roon Frost

Updated by Hilary M. Nangle

Capital	Augusta
Population	1,242,000
Motto	I Direct
State Bird	Chickadee
State Flower	White pinecone and tassel
Postal Abbreviation	ME

Statewide Visitor Information

Maine Publicity Bureau (✉ 325B Water St., Box 2300, Hallowell 04347, ☎ 207/623–0363 or 800/533–9595 outside ME, FAX 207/623–0388). **Maine Innkeepers Association** (✉ 305 Commercial St., Portland 04101, ☎ 207/773–7670).

Scenic Drives

See Exploring sections, *below,* for recommended coastal routes. For a leisurely inland excursion, try **Routes 37** and **35** from Bridgton north through the Waterfords to Bethel, continuing north on **Route 26** past the Sunday River ski resort to Grafton Notch State Park and into northern New Hampshire.

National and State Parks

National Park

★ **Acadia National Park** (✉ Box 177, Bar Harbor 04609, ☎ 207/288–3338; $5 per car or free, depending on where and when you enter), with fine stretches of shoreline and the highest mountains along the East Coast, offers camping, hiking, biking, and boating.

State Parks

More than two dozen state parks offer outdoor recreation along the coast and in less-traveled interior sections. For information contact the **Bureau of Parks and Lands** (✉ State House Station 22, Augusta 04333, ☎ 207/287–3821).

THE SOUTHERN COAST

Maine's southern coast has sandy beaches, historic towns, fine restaurants, and factory-outlet malls within an easy day's trip of many points in New England. Maine's largest city, Portland, is small enough to be seen in a day or two. Near Portland are Freeport, a mecca for shoppers, and Boothbay Harbor, the state's boating capital.

Visitor Information

Boothbay Harbor Region: Chamber of Commerce (✉ Box 356, Boothbay Harbor 04538, ☎ 207/633–2353). **Freeport:** Merchants Association (✉ Box 452, 04032, ☎ 207/865–1212). **Kennebunk-Kennebunkport:** Chamber of Commerce (✉ 171 Port Rd., Kennebunk 04043, ☎ 207/967–0857). **Portland:** Greater Portland Chamber of Commerce (✉ 145 Middle St., Portland, ☎ 207/772–2811). Additional information is available at the **Maine Publicity Bureau** (✉ Rte. 1 [Exit 17 off I–95], Yarmouth, ☎ 207/846–0833; ✉ Rte. 1 and I–95, Kittery, ☎ 207/439–1319).

Arriving and Departing

By Bus

Vermont Transit (☎ 207/772–6587), part of Greyhound Lines, links Portsmouth, New Hampshire, with Portland, Maine. **Concord Trailways** (☎ 800/639–3317) has daily service between Boston and Bangor (via Portland); a coastal route connects towns between Brunswick and Searsport.

By Car

From Boston take U.S. 1 north to I–95, passing through the short New Hampshire seacoast to Kittery, the first town in Maine. I–95 continues past Portland (I–295 gives access to the city) and Freeport (Exit 20 for the outlet stores). Pick up U.S. 1 in Brunswick to reach the coastal communities of Down East.

By Plane

Portland International Jetport (☎ 207/774–7301), 3 mi from Portland, has scheduled daily flights by major U.S. carriers.

Exploring the Coast from Kittery to Pemaquid Point

York County, and Kittery in particular, is probably better known for its outlet shopping than for its beaches. But those who crave the scenic coastline will appreciate the maritime scenery of Routes 103 and 1A.

Route 1A passes through fashionable York Harbor and the chockablock summer cottages of **York Beach. Ogunquit,** a few miles north of the Yorks, is famed for its long white-sand beach and galleries, shops, restaurants, and homes. The old-fashioned pinball machines and hand-cranked moving pictures at the **Wells Auto Museum** (✉ U.S. 1, Wells, ☎ 207/646–9064; 🎟 $3.50) fascinate kids.

★ Summer tourists flock to **Kennebunkport** to soak up salt air, seafood, and sunshine. Dock Square is the busy town center, lined with shops and galleries. **Ocean Avenue** follows the Kennebunk River to the sea, then winds around Cape Arundel.

Trolley rides are the order of the day at the **Seashore Trolley Museum** (✉ Log Cabin Rd., Kennebunkport, ☎ 207/967–2800; 🎟 $8). **Portland** is a thriving seaport whose restaurants, coffee houses, and shops evoke a romantic mood. On Congress Square, the **Portland Museum of Art** (✉ 7 Congress Sq., ☎ 207/775–6148 or 207/773–2787; 🎟 $6; free Fri. evenings 5–9), which is closed on Monday, has works by Winslow Homer, John Marin, Andrew Wyeth, and others. At the **Children's Museum of Maine** (✉ 142 Free St., ☎ 207/828–1234; 🎟 $4), little ones can pretend they are lobster catchers, shopkeepers, or computer experts.

★ Portland's **Old Port Exchange,** built following the Great Fire of 1866, was revitalized in the 1960s by artists and craftspeople. Now it is the city's shopping and dining hub. Allow a couple of hours to stroll on Market, Exchange, Middle, and Fore streets. Try to sample **Casco Bay** on a sunny day aboard a ferry.

Freeport, 17 mi north of Portland, is the home of L. L. Bean, which attracts 3.5 million shoppers a year. Nearby, like seedlings under a mighty spruce, more than 100 other outlets have sprouted (☞ Shopping, *below*).

Bath is farther up the coast. The **Maine Maritime Museum and Shipyard** has a collection to stir the nautical dreams of old salts and young. You can watch boatbuilders wield their tools on classic Maine vessels

Southern Maine Coast

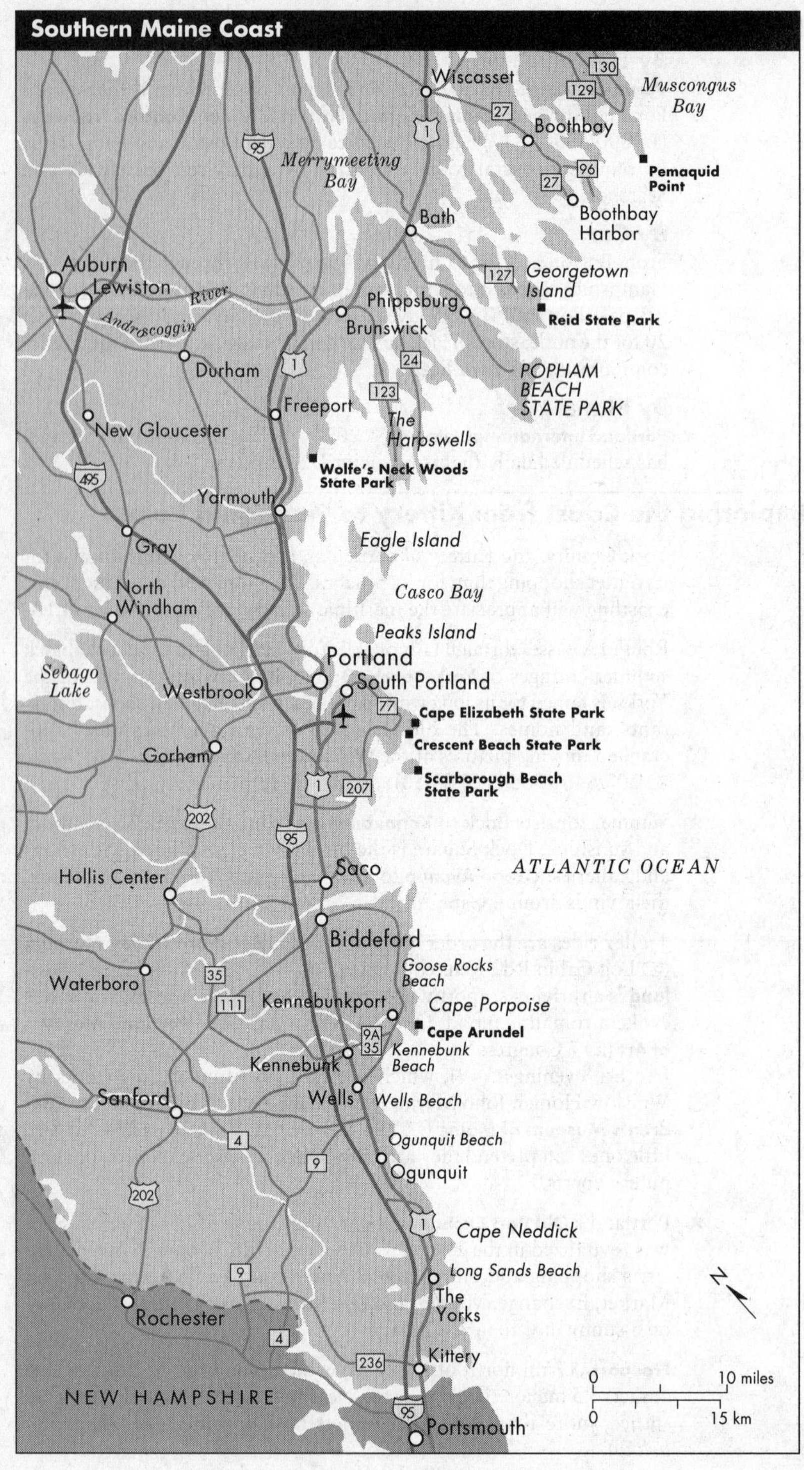
Wiscasset
Muscongus Bay
Boothbay
Merrymeeting Bay
Pemaquid Point
Boothbay Harbor
Bath
Auburn
Lewiston
Georgetown Island
Androscoggin River
Phippsburg
Reid State Park
Brunswick
Durham
POPHAM BEACH STATE PARK
Freeport
New Gloucester
The Harpswells
Wolfe's Neck Woods State Park
Yarmouth
Gray
Eagle Island
North Windham
Casco Bay
Peaks Island
Sebago Lake
Portland
Westbrook
South Portland
Cape Elizabeth State Park
Crescent Beach State Park
Gorham
Scarborough Beach State Park
ATLANTIC OCEAN
Hollis Center
Saco
Biddeford
Goose Rocks Beach
Waterboro
Kennebunkport
Cape Porpoise
Cape Arundel
Kennebunk
Kennebunk Beach
Sanford
Wells
Wells Beach
Ogunquit Beach
Ogunquit
Cape Neddick
Long Sands Beach
The Yorks
Rochester
Kittery
NEW HAMPSHIRE
Portsmouth
0 10 miles
0 15 km
N

at the restored shipyard. ✉ *243 Washington St.,* ☎ *207/443–1316.* 🎟 *$7.75.* ⏲ *Daily 9:30–5.*

Wiscasset bills itself as "Maine's prettiest village" and lives up to it with historic homes, antiques shops, and museums overlooking the Sheepscot River.

Boothbay Harbor swells in summer with visitors and seasonal residents. ★ Wander the shops and waterfront or ride an excursion boat to **Monhegan Island.** At **Pemaquid Point** be sure your camera stand is at the ready for a shot of a much-photographed lighthouse. At **Colonial Pemaquid Restoration,** view the excavations that have turned up thousands of artifacts of a 17th-century English settlement and of earlier Native American life. ✉ *Rte. 130,* ☎ *207/677–2423.* 🎟 *$2. Closed Labor Day–Memorial Day.*

Dining and Lodging

For most visitors Maine means lobster, and this delectable crustacean is served at most Maine restaurants. Aficionados prefer to eat them "in the rough" at classic lobster pounds, where you choose your lobster from a poolful and enjoy it at a picnic table. B&Bs and Victorian inns have joined the family-oriented motels in the coastal towns. For price ranges *see* Charts 1 (B) and 2 (B) *in* On the Road with Fodor's.

Bath

$$–$$$$ ★ ✕ **Robinhood Free Meetinghouse.** Chef Michael Gagne serves multiethnic cuisine in an 1855 Greek Revival meetinghouse. Begin with the artichoke strudel, move on to a classic veal saltimbocca or a confit of duck, and finish up with Gagne's signature, Obsession in Three Chocolates. ✉ *Robinhood Rd., Georgetown,* ☎ *207/371–2188. D, MC, V. Call ahead in winter.*

$$ ✕ **Kristina's Restaurant & Bakery.** This frame house turned restaurant bakes some of the finest pies, pastries, and cakes on the coast. Satisfying dinners are mainly new American cuisine. ✉ *160 Centre St.,* ☎ *207/442–8577. D, MC, V. No dinner Sun., closed Jan., call ahead in winter.*

Boothbay Harbor

$$–$$$ ✕ **Christopher's 1820 House.** This restaurant in quiet East Boothbay serves breakfast, lunch, and dinner in an oceanfront dining room. Choose from appetizers such as pan-seared Maine crab cakes or lobster and cheese quesadilla; then move on to entrées such as Asian-flavored duck confit or Christopher's award-winning lobster succotash. ✉ *Rte. 96, East Boothbay,* ☎ *207/633–6565,* FAX *207/633-6178. MC, V. Closed Nov.–Memorial Day weekend.*

$ ✕ **Lobstermen's Co-op.** Lobster lovers and landlubbers alike will find something at this dockside lobster pound. Seafood, steamers, hot dogs, hamburgers, sandwiches, and desserts are on the menu. Eat indoors or outside while watching the lobstermen at work. ✉ *Atlantic Ave., Boothbay Harbor,* ☎ *207/633–4900. Closed mid-Oct.–mid-May.*

$–$$$ 🏨 **Admiral's Quarters Inn.** This renovated 1830 sea captain's house is ideally situated for exploring Boothbay Harbor by foot, a good thing since in-town parking is limited and expensive. Rooms have private decks, many overlooking the harbor, and on rainy days you can relax by the woodstove in the solarium. ✉ *Commercial St., 04538,* ☎ *207/633–2474,* FAX *207/633–5904. 2 rooms, 4 suites. Full breakfast. D, MC, V.*

Brunswick

$-$$ ✕ **Great Impasta.** At this storefront restaurant, try the seafood lasagna or match your favorite pasta and sauce. ✉ *42 Maine St.,* ☎ *207/729–5858. Reservations not accepted. D, DC, MC, V.*

$-$$$$ 🏨 **Harpswell Inn.** Spacious lawns and neatly pruned shrubs surround this stately white-clapboard, dormered inn. Half the rooms have water views. ✉ *141 Lookout Point Rd., Harpswell 04079,* ☎ *207/833–5509 or 800/843–5509. 14 rooms. No smoking. MC, V.*

Freeport

$ ✕ **Harraseeket Lunch & Lobster Co.** At this bare-bones lobster pound beside the town landing, fried-seafood baskets and lobster dinners, eaten in the dining room or at picnic tables, are what it's all about. ✉ *Main St., South Freeport,* ☎ *207/865–4888. Reservations not accepted. No credit cards. Closed mid-Oct.–Apr.*

$$$$ 🏨 **Harraseeket Inn.** Despite modern appointments such as elevators and whirlpool baths, this 1850 Greek Revival home retains an old-fashioned country-inn feel. Afternoon tea is served in the mahogany drawing room, and guest rooms have reproductions of Federal canopy beds. ✉ *162 Main St., 04032,* ☎ *207/865–9377 or 800/342–6423. 82 rooms. Restaurant, indoor pool. AE, D, DC, MC, V.*

Kennebunkport

$$$$ ★ ✕🏨 **White Barn Inn.** Known for its attentive service, this 19th-century inn has meticulously appointed rooms decorated with hand-painted pieces and period furniture; some have fireplaces and whirlpool baths. The rustic but elegant dining room (jacket required for dinner) serves updated New England cuisine like steamed Maine lobster on fresh fettuccine with carrots, ginger, snow peas, and a cognac-butter sauce. ✉ *Box 560C, 37 Beach St., 04046,* ☎ *207/967–2321,* FAX *207/967–1100. 25 rooms. Restaurant, pool. CP. AE, MC, V.*

$$$$ 🏨 **Captain Lord Mansion.** This sumptuously appointed 1812 Federal-style mansion—with a suspended elliptical staircase, a widow's walk, gas fireplaces in 14 rooms, and near-museum quality decor—has a formal but not stuffy atmosphere. ✉ *Box 800, Pleasant and Green Sts., 04046,* ☎ *207/967–3141,* FAX *207/967–3172. 20 rooms. Full breakfast. D, MC, V.*

Newcastle

$$-$$$$ ✕🏨 **Newcastle Inn.** This classic country inn overlooks the Damariscotta River. Guests spread out in the cozy pub, comfortable living room, and spacious sunporch overlooking the river; some rooms have fireplaces and whirlpools. The dining room (reservations essential) emphasizes Maine seafood such as Pemaquid oysters, lobster, and Atlantic salmon. Choose from three- or five-course dinners. ✉ *River Rd., Newcastle 04553,* ☎ *207/563–5685 or 800/832–8669,* FAX *207/563–6877. 15 rooms. 2 dining rooms. Full breakfast. MAP available. AE, MC, V. Dining room closed Mon. in summer, Mon.–Wed. in winter.*

Ogunquit

$$-$$$ ★ ✕ **Hurricane.** Don't let its weather-beaten exterior deter you—this comfortable bar-and-grill offers first-rate cooking and spectacular views of the crashing surf. Start with lobster chowder, or the house salad (assorted greens with pistachio nuts and roasted shallots). Entrées include lobster cioppino, rack of lamb, and grilled venison loin. Be sure to save room for the crème brûlée. ✉ *Perkins Cove,* ☎ *207/646–6348. AE, D, DC, MC, V.*

Portland

$$-$$$ ★ ✕ **Fore Street.** Two of Maine's best chefs opened this restaurant in an old warehouse. Every table in the two-level main dining room has a view

of the huge brick oven and hearth and the open kitchen, where entrées such as applewood-grilled Atlantic swordfish loin and roasted lobster are prepared. ✉ *288 Fore St.,* ☎ *207/775-2717. AE, D, MC, V.*

$$–$$$ ★ ✕ **Street and Co.** At what may be the best seafood restaurant in Maine, you enter through the kitchen, with all its wonderful aromas, and dine at a copper-topped table amid dried herbs and shelves of grocery staples. ✉ *33 Wharf St.,* ☎ *207/775–0887. AE, MC, V. No lunch.*

$$$$ ✕🏨 **Inn by the Sea.** On Greater Portland's most prime real estate, this all-suites inn is set back from the shoreline and has views of the ocean. The architecture is typical New England; the dining room ($$–$$$$), open to nonguests, serves seafood and other regional cuisine. ✉ *40 Bowery Beach Rd., Cape Elizabeth (7 mi south of Portland) 04107,* ☎ *207/799–3134 or 800/888–4287,* FAX *207/799–4779. 25 suites, 18 cottage condominiums. Restaurant, pool, tennis. AE, D, MC, V.*

$$$$ 🏨 **Portland Regency Hotel.** The only major hotel in the center of the Old Port Exchange, the Regency building was Portland's armory in the late 19th century. Rooms have tall standing mirrors, floral curtains, and love seats; many have four-poster beds. ✉ *20 Milk St., 04101,* ☎ *207/774–4200 or 800/727–3436,* FAX *207/775–2150. 103 rooms. Restaurant, health club. AE, D, DC, MC, V.*

Scarborough

$$$$ 🏨 **Black Point Inn.** At the tip of a peninsula 12 mi south of Portland stands a stylish, tastefully updated old-time resort with views up and down the coast. On the grounds are beaches, a bird sanctuary, hiking trails, and sports facilities. The dining room menu is strong in seafood. ✉ *510 Black Point Rd., 04074,* ☎ *207/883–4126 or 800/258–0003,* FAX *207/883–9976. 94 rooms. Restaurant, indoor and outdoor pools, golf, tennis. MAP. AE, D, MC, V. Closed Dec.–Apr.*

The Yorks

$$–$$$$ ★ ✕🏨 **York Harbor Inn.** A mid-17th-century fishing cabin with dark timbers and a fieldstone fireplace forms the heart of this inn, to which various wings and outbuildings have been added. Rooms are furnished with antiques and country pieces; many have decks overlooking the water, and a few have whirlpool tubs or fireplaces. The dining room has country charm and great ocean views. Try the lobster-stuffed chicken breast or the angel-hair pasta with shrimp and scallops. ✉ *Box 573, Rte. 1A, York Harbor 03911,* ☎ *207/363–5119 or 800/343–3869,* FAX *207/963–7151. 35 rooms, 1 suite. CP. AE, MC, V. No lunch off-season.*

Nightlife and the Arts

Nightlife

Café Club (✉ 38 Wharf St., ☎ 207/772–6976) is a wine and espresso bar with a light menu and desserts. Fine ales are brewed at **Gritty McDuff's Brew Pub** (✉ 396 Fore St., Portland, ☎ 207/772–2739). **Three Dollar Dewey's** (✉ 446 Fore St., Portland, ☎ 207/772–3310), long a popular nightspot, is an English-style alehouse.

The Arts

Bowdoin Summer Music Festival (✉ Bowdoin College, ☎ 207/725–3322 for information; 207/725–3895 for tickets) is a six-week concert series featuring performances by students, faculty, and prestigious guest artists. **Cumberland County Civic Center** (✉ 1 Civic Center Sq., Portland, ☎ 207/775–3458) is a 9,000-seat auditorium which hosts concerts, family shows, and sporting events. **Maine State Music Theater** (✉ Pickard Theater, Bowdoin College, ☎ 207/725–8769) stages musicals from mid-June through August. **Ogunquit Playhouse** (✉ Rte. 1, ☎ 207/646–5511) mounts plays and musicals from late June to Labor

Day. **Portland Performing Arts Center** (✉ 25A Forest Ave., ☎ 207/744–0465) hosts music, dance, and theater.

Outdoor Activities and Sports

Boat Trips

From Perkins Cove in Ogunquit, **Finestkind** (☎ 207/646–5227) runs boats to Nubble Light and schedules lobstering trips. In Portland, for tours of the harbor, Casco Bay, and the islands, try **Bay View Cruises** (☎ 207/761–0496), **Casco Bay Lines** (☎ 207/774–7871), or **Old Port Mariner Fleet** (☎ 207/775–0727). In Boothbay Harbor, ***Balmy Days II*** (☎ 207/633–2284 or 800/298–2284) makes day trips to Monhegan Island, and **Cap'n Fish's Boat Trips** (☎ 207/633–3244) offers sightseeing cruises throughout the region. From New Harbor, **Hardy Boat Cruises** (☎ 800/278–3346 or 207/677–2026) offers lighthouse and seal cruises and sails daily to Monhegan Island.

Canoeing

The **Maine Audubon Society** (☎ 207/781–2330 or 207/883–4100 mid-June–Labor Day) leads daily guided canoe trips in Scarborough Marsh (✉ Rte. 9, Scarborough), the largest salt marsh in Maine.

Deep-Sea Fishing

Cape Arundel Cruises (✉ Kennebunkport, ☎ 207/967–5595) operates half- and full-day fishing trips.

Beaches

Kennebunk Beach is actually three beaches, with cottages and Victorian boardinghouses nearby; for parking permits go to the Kennebunk Town Office (✉ 1 Summer St., ☎ 207/985–2102). **Goose Rocks,** north of Kennebunkport, is the largest area beach and a favorite of families with small children; the Kennebunkport Town Office (✉ Elm St., ☎ 207/967–4244) sells parking permits.

Ogunquit Beach, a fine stretch at the mouth of the river, is protected from the surf. Families gravitate to the ends, while gay visitors camp at the beach's middle.

Old Orchard Beach, with an amusement park reminiscent of Coney Island, is only a few miles north of Biddeford on Route 9.

At the end of Route 209 south of Bath, **Popham Beach State Park** (Phippsburg, ☎ 207/389–1335) has a good sand beach and picnic tables. **Reid State Park** (☎ 207/371–2303), on Georgetown Island off Route 127, has three beaches, bathhouses, picnic tables, and a snack bar.

Shopping

More than 100 **factory outlets** along U.S. 1 around Kittery sell clothing, shoes, glassware, and other products from top manufacturers. **Freeport** is a shopper's mecca. Across from its main store (✉ Rte. 1, ☎ 800/341–4341), an **L. L. Bean** factory outlet has seconds and discontinued merchandise at discount prices. Many of the 100 other in-town outlets are found in the **Fashion Outlet Mall** (✉ 2 Depot St.). More outlets crowd **Main Street** and **Bow Street.** The **Freeport Visitors Guide** (✉ Freeport Merchants Association, Box 452, 04032, ☎ 207/865–1212) has a complete listing of outlets; it's free.

Portland also has shopping. In the Old Port Exchange the better shops are concentrated along Fore and Exchange streets.

Wiscasset offers plenty of antiques shops. Just south of town on Route 1 in Woolwich is the **Montsweag Flea Market,** a trash-and-treasure trove open Wednesday and Friday–Sunday.

PENOBSCOT BAY AND ACADIA

Purists hold that the Maine coast begins at Penobscot Bay, where water vistas are wider and bluer, with the shore a jumble of broken granite boulders, cobblestones, and gravel. East of Penobscot Bay, Acadia is the informal name for Mount Desert (pronounced *dessert*) Island and environs. Mount Desert, Maine's largest island, encompasses most of Acadia National Park, the state's principal tourist attraction. Camden, on Penobscot Bay, and Bar Harbor, on Mount Desert, offer accommodations and restaurants.

Visitor Information

Bar Harbor: Chamber of Commerce (✉ 93 Cottage St., Box 158, 04609, ☎ 207/288–3393, 207/288–5103, or 800/288–5103). **Rockport, Camden, and Lincolnville:** Chamber of Commerce (✉ Public Landing, Box 919, Camden 04843, ☎ 207/236–4404 or 800/223–5459).

Arriving and Departing

By Car

U.S. 1 follows the west coast of Penobscot Bay, linking Rockland, Camden, and Ellsworth. From Ellsworth, Route 3 will take you onto Mount Desert Island.

By Plane

Bangor International Airport (☎ 207/947–0384), 30 mi north of Penobscot Bay, has daily flights by major U.S. carriers. **Knox County Regional Airport** (☎ 207/594–4131), 3 mi south of Rockland, has frequent flights to Boston. **Hancock County Airport** (☎ 207/667–7329), 8 mi northwest of Bar Harbor, is served by Colgan Air/Continental Connection.

Exploring Penobscot Bay and Acadia

Tenants Harbor is a quintessential Maine fishing town. Port Clyde, south of Tenants Harbor, is the point of departure for the mail boat that serves tiny, remote **Monhegan Island.** Known to Basque, Portuguese, and Breton fishermen well before Columbus "discovered" America, it was discovered again by some of America's finest painters, including Rockwell Kent, Robert Henri, A. J. Hammond, and Edward Hopper, who sailed out to paint its meadows, savage cliffs, wild ocean views, and fishermen's shacks. Tourists followed, and Monhegan is now overrun with visitors in summer.

Rockland, home of the Seafood Festival (a.k.a. the Lobster Festival), ranks as the coast's commercial hub, with fishing boats moored alongside a growing flotilla of windjammers. The **Farnsworth Art Museum** specializes in American art, with a focus on Maine-related works. A new gallery and a study center are devoted to the Wyeth family. ✉ *356 Main St.,* ☎ *207/596–6457.* *$9. Closed Mon. Oct.–May.*

★ In **Camden** mountains tower over the harbor, and the fashionable waterfront is home to the nation's largest windjammer fleet; such cruises are a superb way to explore the ports and islands of Penobscot Bay. The 5,500-acre **Camden Hills State Park** (☎ 207/236–3109), 2 mi north of Camden on U.S. 1, contains 20 mi of trails. Hike or take the toll road up Mt. Battie for a magnificent view over the bay.

Kelmscott Farm is a rare-breed animal farm with a nature trail, children's activities, heirloom gardens, and special events most weekends. ✉ *Rte. 52, Lincolnville,* ☎ *207/763–4088.* *$5.* *Memorial Day–Labor Day, Thurs.–Sun., 11–4.*

Searsport claims to be the antiques capital of Maine, with shops and a seasonal weekend flea market. Historic **Castine,** over which French, British, Dutch, and Americans fought, has two museums and the ruins of a British fort. But the finest thing about Castine is the town itself: the lively, welcoming town landing; the serene Federal and Greek Revival houses; and the town common.

Ellsworth has an array of outlets including an L. L. Bean store. It's also the gateway to Bar Harbor and Acadia, where you pick up Route 3 to Mount Desert Island. Although most of **Bar Harbor**'s grand mansions were destroyed in a 1947 fire, this busy resort town on Frenchman Bay has retained its beauty. Shops, restaurants, and hotels are clustered along Main, Mount Desert, and Cottage streets.

★ The Hulls Cove approach to **Acadia National Park** (☞ National and State Parks, *above, and* Hiking, *below*) is northwest of Bar Harbor on Route 3. Though often clogged with traffic, the 27-mi Park Loop Road provides the best introduction to the park. The visitor center shows a free 15-minute film and has trail maps. The Ocean Trail is an easily accessible walk with some of Maine's most spectacular scenery. For a mountaintop experience without the effort of hiking, drive to the summit of **Cadillac Mountain,** the highest point on the eastern coast. The view from the bald summit is spectacular, especially at sunset. **Acadia Zoo** has wild and domesticated animals. ✉ *Rte. 3, Trenton, north of Bar Harbor,* ☎ *207/667–3244.* *$6.* *May–Dec., daily 9:30–dusk.*

Dining and Lodging

For price ranges *see* Charts 1 (B) and 2 (B) *in* On the Road with Fodor's.

Bar Harbor

$$–$$$ ✕ **Porcupine Grill.** Named for a cluster of islets in Frenchman Bay, the Porcupine serves starters such as citrus barbecued quail and main courses such as grilled lobster and twin Portobello filets. Soft green walls, antique furnishings, and Villeroy & Boch porcelain create an ambience that complements the cuisine. At the **Thrumcap** wine bar you can unwind by the fire, choose from 20 wines by the glass, and order from a lighter menu. ✉ *123 Cottage St.,* ☎ *207/288–3884. AE, DC, MC, V. Closed Mon.–Thurs. Nov.–June. No lunch.*

$$ ✕ **Jordan Pond House.** Popovers and tea are a century-old tradition at this rustic restaurant in Acadia National Park, where you can sit on the terrace and admire the views. ✉ *Park Loop Rd.,* ☎ *207/276–3316. AE, D, MC, V. Closed late Oct.–May.*

$$$–$$$$ **Inn at Canoe Point.** Seclusion and privacy are bywords of this snug 100-year-old Tudor-style house at Hulls Cove, 2 mi from Bar Harbor. The large living room has huge windows on the water, a granite fireplace, and a waterfront deck where a full breakfast is served in summer. ✉ *Box 216, Rte. 3, 04609,* ☎ *207/288–9511. 5 rooms. Full breakfast. D, MC, V. Closed winter.*

$–$$ **Bass Cottage in the Field.** Anna Jean Turner began welcoming guests to this 19th-century summer estate in 1928. Her niece now helps her operate the inn, which offers a step back in time in decor and price. Although the guest rooms could use a face-lift, most likely you'll spend your time on the expansive, glassed-in wraparound porch. ✉ *In the Field, Bar Harbor 04609,* ☎ *207/288–3705,* FAX *207/288–2005. 10 rooms, 6 with private baths. No credit cards. Closed mid-Oct.–late May.*

Camden

$$–$$$ ✕ **Waterfront Restaurant.** Come for a ringside seat on Camden Harbor; the best view is from the outdoor deck, open in warm weather. The fare is primarily seafood. ✉ *Bay View St.,* ☎ *207/236–3747. Reservations not accepted. AE, MC, V.*

$$$–$$$$ ✕🏨 **Whitehall Inn.** Camden's best-known inn, a white-clapboard ship-captain's home with a wide porch, was constructed in 1843. Rooms are small and sparsely furnished, with dark-wood bedsteads and claw-foot bathtubs; some have ocean views. The dining room, open to nonguests for dinner and breakfast, serves traditional and creative American cuisine. ✉ *52 High St., Box 558, 04843,* ☎ *207/236–3391,* FAX *207/236–4427. 44 rooms. Tennis. MAP or B&B available. AE, MC, V. Closed mid-Oct.–mid-May.*

$$$$ 🏨 **Samoset Resort.** On the Rockland–Rockport town line, next to the breakwater, this oceanside resort has excellent facilities. Ask about special packages. ✉ *220 Warrenton St., Rockport 04856,* ☎ *207/594–2511; 800/341–1650 outside ME,* FAX *207/594–0722. 150 rooms. Restaurant, indoor and outdoor pools, golf, tennis, exercise room. AE, D, DC, MC, V.*

Castine

$$–$$$ ✕🏨 **Castine Inn.** Upholstered easy chairs and fine prints and paintings are typical appointments in the light, airy guest rooms. The third floor has the best views: the harbor over the formal gardens on one side, the village on the other. The dining room serves New England staples as well as creative cuisine. ✉ *Main St. (Box 41), 04421,* ☎ *207/326–4365,* FAX *207/326–4570. 20 rooms. Restaurant. MC, V. Closed Nov.–Apr.*

Hancock

$$$$ ✕🏨 **Le Domaine** Owner-chef Nicole L. Purslow whips up classic haute cuisine. Le Domaine is known primarily for its food, but its small French-country-style guest rooms are also inviting. Ask for a room in the rear, overlooking the lawns and gardens and away from the noise of Route 1. ✉ *Box 496, Rte. 1, 04640,* ☎ *207/422–3395 or 800/554–8495,* FAX *207/422–2316. 7 rooms. Restaurant. Full breakfast; MAP available. AE, D, MC, V. Closed late Oct.–mid-May.*

Southwest Harbor

$$$–$$$$ ✕🏨 **Claremont Hotel.** Built in 1884, the yellow-clapboard Claremont commands a view of Somes Sound; croquet is played on the lawn, and cocktails and lunch are served at the Boat House in midsummer. The menu changes weekly in the large old-style dining room ($$, reservations essential, jacket required for dinner), open to the public for breakfast and dinner. ✉ *Box 137; off Clark Point Rd., 04679,* ☎ *207/244–5036 or 800/244–5036,* FAX *207/244–3512. 30 rooms, 12 cottages. Restaurant, tennis court. MAP. No credit cards. Hotel closed mid-Oct.–mid-June, cottages closed Nov.–late May.*

$$ 🏨 **Island House.** This sweet B&B on the island's quiet side has simply decorated bedrooms in the main house and a carriage house suite, complete with sleeping loft and kitchenette. ✉ *Box 1006, 04679,* ☎ *207/244–5180. 4 rooms share 3 baths, 1 suite. Full breakfast. MC, V.*

Tenants Harbor

$$–$$$$ ✕🏨 **East Wind Inn & Meeting House.** On a knob of land overlooking the harbor and the islands, the East Wind offers unadorned but comfortable guest rooms, suites, and efficiencies in three buildings. The restaurant, which welcomes nonguests, serves breakfast, dinner, and Sunday brunch. ✉ *Box 149, Rte. 131 (10 mi off Rte. 1), 04860,* ☎ *800/241–8439 or 207/372–6366,* FAX *207/372–6320. 26 rooms, 4 apartments/efficiencies. Restaurant. CP. AE, D, MC, V. Closed Dec.–Apr.*

Campgrounds

The two campgrounds in Acadia National Park—**Blackwoods** (☏ 800/365–2267) and **Seawall** (☏ 207/244–3600)—fill up quickly in summer. Nearby **Lamoine State Park** (☏ 207/667–4778) has a great location on Frenchman Bay.

The Arts

Bay Chamber Concerts (✉ Rockport Opera House, ☏ 207/236–2823) presents chamber music on Thursday and sometimes Friday in July and August. **Arcady Music Festival** (☏ 207/288–3151) offers concerts on Mount Desert Island from late July through August. **Bar Harbor Music Festival** (✉ 59 Cottage St., ☏ 207/288–5744) has concerts from early July to early August.

Outdoor Activities and Sports

Biking

The carriage paths that wind through **Acadia National Park** are ideal for biking; pick up a map from the Hulls Cove visitor center. Bikes can be rented in Bar Harbor from **Acadia Bike & Canoe** (✉ 48 Cottage St., ☏ 207/288–9605) and **Bar Harbor Bicycle Shop** (✉ 141 Cottage St., ☏ 207/288–3886).

Boat Trips

Port Clyde is the point of departure for the ***Laura B.*** (☏ 207/372–8848 for schedules), the mail boat that serves Monhegan Island. From Bar Harbor, the ***Acadian Whale Watcher*** (☏ 207/288–9794 or 800/421–3307) runs whale-watching cruises, and the 65-ft ***Chippewa*** (☏ 207/288–4585) cruises past islands and lighthouses three times a day in summer. The ***Natalie Todd*** (☏ 207/288–4585) offers weekend windjammer cruises. Camden and Rockland are the East Coast **windjammer** headquarters (contact ✉ Maine Windjammer Assoc., Box 1144, Blue Hill 04614, ☏ 800/807–9463; ✉ North End Shipyard Schooners, Box 482, Rockland 04841, ☏ 800/648–4544; ✉ Vessels of Windjammer Wharf, Box 1050, Rockland 04841). In Southwest Harbor, **Manset Yacht Service** (✉ Shore Rd., ☏ 207/244–4040) rents sailboats.

Hiking

Acadia National Park maintains nearly 200 mi of paths. Among the more rewarding hikes are the Precipice Trail to Champlain Mountain, the Great Head Loop, the Gorham Mountain Trail, and the path around Eagle Lake.

Shopping

In Camden, the best shopping streets are Main and Bayview. Antiques shops (abundant in **Searsport**) are scattered around the outskirts of villages; yard sales abound in summer. Galleries and boutiques can be found in **Blue Hill** and **Deer Isle. Bar Harbor** is a good place to browse for gifts. For bargains head for the outlets along Route 3 in **Ellsworth.**

WESTERN LAKES AND MOUNTAINS

Less than 20 mi northwest of Portland, the lakes and mountains of western Maine stretch along the New Hampshire border to Quebec. The Sebago–Long Lake region has antiques stores and lake cruises on a 42-mi waterway. Kezar Lake, in a fold of the White Mountains, is a hideaway of the wealthy. Bethel is a classic New England town, while the less-developed Rangeley Lakes area is a fishing paradise; both become ski country in winter.

Visitor Information

Bethel Area: Chamber of Commerce (✉ Box 439, Bethel 04217, ☎ 207/824–2282 or 800/442–5526). **Bridgton–Lakes Region:** Chamber of Commerce (✉ Box 236, Bridgton 04009, ☎ 207/647–3472). **Rangeley Lakes Region:** Chamber of Commerce (✉ Box 317, Rangeley 04970, ☎ 207/864–5571 or 800/685–2537).

Arriving and Departing

By Car

U.S. 302 provides access to the region from I–95. U.S. 2, which runs east–west, links Bangor to Bethel.

Exploring the Western Lakes and Mountains

Sebago Lake State Park (☎ 207/693–6613 mid-June–Sept.; 207/693–6231 Oct.–mid-June) offers opportunities for swimming, picnicking, camping, boating, and fishing. To the north is **Naples,** with cruises and boat rentals on Long Lake. **Songo Lock** connects the northern tip of Sebago Lake with Long Lake. The ***Songo River Queen II***, a 92-ft stern-wheeler, takes passengers on hour-long cruises on Long Lake and longer voyages down the Songo River and through Songo Lock. ✉ *Rte. 302, Naples Causeway,* ☎ *207/693–6861.* *Songo River ride $10, Long Lake cruise $7.* *July–Labor Day, 5 trips daily; June and Sept., weekends.*

Bridgton, near Highland Lake, has antiques shops in and around town. U.S. 302/Route 5 through Lovell and Route 37 through the Waterfords are scenic routes to **Bethel,** a town with white-clapboard houses, antiques stores, and a mountain vista at the end of every street. Keep this route in mind for your leaf-peeping days—and remember that Maine's forests are usually effulgent the first and second week of October.

The area from Bethel to **Rangeley Lake** is beautiful, too, particularly in autumn. In **Grafton Notch State Park** (☎ 207/824–2912) you can hike to stunning gorges and waterfalls and into the Baldpate Mountains. For a century, **Rangeley** has lured people who fish and hunt to its more than 40 lakes and ponds. **Rangeley Lake State Park** (☎ 207/864–3858) has superb scenery, swimming, picnicking, and boating. Campsites are set well apart. In the shadow of Sugarloaf Mountain, **Kingfield** is prime ski country—a classic New England town with a general store, historic inns, and a white-clapboard church. **Sandy River & Rangeley Lakes Railroad** has a century-old train that traverses the woods. ✉ *Bridge Hill Rd., Phillips (20 mi southeast of Rangeley),* ☎ *207/639–3352.* *$3.* *June–Oct., 1st and 3rd Sun. each month; rides at 11, 1, and 3.*

Dining and Lodging

Bethel has the largest concentration of inns and B&Bs, and its chamber of commerce has a **lodging reservations service** (☎ 207/824–3585). For price ranges *see* Charts 1 (B) and 2 (B) *in* On the Road with Fodor's.

Bethel

$$–$$$ ✕ **Mother's Restaurant.** This gingerbread house furnished with woodstoves and bookshelves is a cozy place to enjoy Maine crab cakes, steaks, and a variety of pastas. There's outside dining in summer. ✉ *Upper Main St.,* ☎ *207/824–2589. MC, V.*

$$$$ ✕ 🏨 **Bethel Inn and Country Club.** Choice rooms in the old-fashioned hotel, sparsely furnished with colonial reproductions, have fireplaces and face the golf course and the mountains beyond. Condos on the fairway are a bit sterile. The dining room serves roast duck and prime rib. ✉ *Box 49, Village Common, 04217,* ☎ *207/824–2175 or 800/654–0125,* FAX *207/824–2233. 97 rooms. Restaurant, pool, tennis, golf, health club. MAP. AE, D, DC, MC, V.*

Kingfield

$$$$ 🏨 **Sugarloaf Mountain Hotel.** This six-story brick structure at the base of the Sugarloaf lifts combines a New England ambience with European-style service. Oak and redwood paneling in the main rooms is enhanced by contemporary furnishings. Valet parking, ski tuning, lockers, and mountain guides are available through the concierge. ✉ *R.R. 1, Box 2299, Carrabassett Valley 04947,* ☎ *207/237–2222 or 800/527–9879,* FAX *207/237–2874. 119 rooms. Restaurant, spa. AE, D, DC, MC, V.*

Rangeley

$$ ✕ 🏨 **Country Club Inn.** This retreat, built in the 1920s on the Mingo Springs Golf Course, enjoys a secluded hilltop location and sweeping lake and mountain views. Rooms in the main building and in the 1950s motel-style wing are cheerfully if minimally decorated. The glassed-in dining room—open to nonguests by reservation only—has linen-draped tables set well apart. The menu includes roast duck, fresh fish, and filet mignon. ✉ *Box 680, Mingo Loop Rd., 04970,* ☎ *207/864–3831. 19 rooms. Restaurant, pool. MAP, B&B available. AE, MC, V. Closed Apr.–mid-May and mid-Oct.–Dec. 25.*

Waterford

$$–$$$$ 🏨 **Bear Mountain Inn.** After a swim at the private beach on Bear Lake or a hike up Bear Mountain across the street, it's nice to return to this rambling farmhouse inn, meticulously decorated with a woodsy theme by the owner, a former interior decorator. ✉ *Rt. 35, South Waterford 04081,* ☎ *207/583–4404. 7 rooms. Full breakfast. MC, V.*

Outdoor Activities and Sports

Canoeing

The **Saco River** and **Rangeley** and **Mooselookmeguntic lakes** are favorites. For rentals try **Canal Bridge Canoes** (✉ Rte. 302, Fryeburg Village, ☎ 207/935–2605), **Oquossoc Cove Marina** (✉ Oquossoc, ☎ 207/864–3463), **Dockside Sports Center** (✉ Town Cove, Rangeley, ☎ 207/864–2424), or **River's Edge Sports** (✉ Rte. 4, Oquossoc, ☎ 207/864–5582).

Fishing

Fishing licenses (required) can be obtained at many sporting goods and hardware stores and at town halls. The **Department of Inland Fisheries and Wildlife** (✉ 284 State St., Augusta 04333, ☎ 207/287–2871) has further information.

Water Sports

Sebago, Long, Rangeley, and Mooselookmeguntic are the most popular lakes for boating. Contact tourist offices for rentals.

Ski Areas

Sugarloaf/USA (✉ Kingfield 04947, ☎ 207/237–2000) has both downhill and cross-country trails. **Sunday River** (✉ Box 450, Bethel 04217, ☎ 207/824–3000) has downhill trails.

ELSEWHERE IN MAINE

The North Woods

Visitor Information

Moosehead Lake Region Chamber of Commerce (✉ Rtes. 6 and 15, Box 581, Greenville 04441, ☎ 207/695–2702).

Arriving and Departing

Charter planes can be arranged from Bangor. Route 6 wends its way from I–95 to Greenville; Route 11 provides access from I–95 to Millinocket.

What to See and Do

Moosehead Lake, Maine's largest, offers rustic camps, restaurants, guides, and outfitters. Its 420 mi of shorefront are virtually uninhabited and mostly accessible only by floatplane or boat. **Greenville** is the locus for canoe rentals, outfitters, and basic lodging. Dam-controlled flows ensure good white-water rafting from May through September on the Kennebec, Dead, and Penobscot rivers. For information contact **Raft Maine** (☎ 800/723–8633).

Baxter State Park (✉ 64 Balsam Dr., Millinocket 04462, ☎ 207/723–5140) is a 200,000-acre wooded wilderness. There are 46 mountains in the park, including **Katahdin,** Maine's highest. They're all accessible from a 150-mi trail network.

Even more remote is the **Allagash Wilderness Waterway,** a 92-mi corridor of lakes and rivers. **Ripogenus Dam,** 30 mi northwest of Millinocket on lumbering roads, is the most popular jumping-off point for Allagash trips. The **Maine Department of Conservation, Bureau of Parks and Lands** (✉ State House Station 22, Augusta 04333, ☎ 207/289–3821) has information on camping and canoeing.

Dining and Lodging

$–$$ ✕ **Road Kill Cafe.** The motto here is "Where the food used to speak for itself." If you don't mind a menu with items such as Bye-Bye Bambi Burgers, Brake and Scrape sandwiches, and Mooseballs, this fun-loving spot is for you. ✉ *Rte. 15, Greenville Junction,* ☎ *207/695–2230. D, MC, V.*

$$$–$$$$ ✕🏨 **Greenville Inn.** Built more than a century ago, this rambling lumber baron's mansion is a block from town, on a rise over Moosehead Lake. The ornate cherry and mahogany paneling, Oriental rugs, and leaded glass create an aura of masculine ease. Cottages have mountain and lake views, and some have decks. The restaurant ($$; reservations essential; no lunch) has water views. The menu, revised daily, reflects the owners' Austrian background: shrimp with mustard-dill sauce, salmon marinated in olive oil and basil, a veal cutlet with a mushroom cream sauce. ✉ *Box 1194, Norris St., Greenville 04441,* ☎ FAX *207/695–2206 or* ☎ *888/695–6000. 6 rooms, 6 cottages. Restaurant. Full breakfast. D, MC, V.*

$$$$ ★ 🏨 **Lodge at Moosehead Lake.** All rooms in this luxurious mansion have a whirlpool, fireplace, and hand-carved four-poster bed; most have lake views. The dining room has a spectacular view of the lake. ✉ *Lily Bay Rd., Greenville 04441,* ☎ *207/695–4400,* FAX *207/695–2281. 8 rooms. Full breakfast. D, MC, V.*

$–$$ 🏨 **Birches Resort.** The living room in the main lodge of this family-oriented resort is dominated by a fieldstone fireplace. Log-cabin cottages have wood-burning stoves or fireplaces and sleep from two to 15 guests. ✉ *Box 41, off Rtes. 6/15, on Moosehead Lake, Rockwood 04478,* ☎ *207/534–7305 or 800/825–9453,* FAX *207/534–8835. 4 lodge rooms, 15 cottages. AE, D, MC, V.*

MASSACHUSETTS

Capital	Boston
Population	6,118,000
Motto	By the Sword We Seek Peace, But Peace Only Under Liberty
State Bird	Chickadee
State Flower	Mayflower
Postal Abbreviation	MA

Statewide Visitor Information

Massachusetts Office of Travel and Tourism (✉ 100 Cambridge St., Boston 02202, ☎ 617/727–3201 or 800/447–6277).

Scenic Drives

Much of Cape Cod's **Route 6A,** from Sandwich to Orleans, is a National Historic District preserving traditional New England seacoast towns. **Routes 133 and 1A** on the North Shore, from Gloucester to Newburyport, cover some of the earliest settlements in the United States, established in the 1630s. In the Berkshires, the **Mohawk Trail,** running 63 mi along Route 2 between Greenfield and North Adams, is famous for its fall foliage, which peaks in late September and early October. In the southwest, **Route 23** from Great Barrington to Westfield travels through wooded hills and rural towns.

National and State Parks

National Park

★ **Cape Cod National Seashore** (☞ Cape Cod and the Islands, *below*), a 30-mi stretch of dune-backed beach between Eastham and Provincetown, has excellent swimming, bike riding, bird-watching, and nature walks.

State Parks

The **Executive Office of Environmental Affairs** (✉ Division of Forests and Parks, 100 Cambridge St., Boston 02202, ☎ 617/727–3159) has information on all state parks, including the Heritage state parks, which have exhibits on the state's industrial history.

Mt. Greylock State Reservation (✉ Rockwell Rd. off Rte. 7, Lanesborough, ☎ 413/499–4262) has the state's highest peak. **Nickerson State Park** (✉ Rte. 6A, Brewster, ☎ 508/896–3491), on Cape Cod, has nearly 2,000 acres of forest with walking trails, trout-stocked ponds, and campsites. **Tolland State Forest** (✉ Rte. 8, Otis, ☎ 413/269–6002), in the Berkshires, has camping facilities and hiking trails.

BOSTON

New England's largest and most important city, and the cradle of American independence, Boston is more than 360 years old. Its most famous buildings are not merely civic landmarks but national icons; its greatest citizens—John Hancock, Paul Revere, and the Adamses—live at the crossroads of history and myth.

Boston is also New England's center of high finance and higher technology, a place of granite-and-glass towers rising along what were once rutted village lanes. Its enormous population of students, academics, artists, and young professionals makes the town a haven for the arts, international cinema, late-night bookstores, alternative music, and unconventional local politics.

Visitor Information

For general information and brochures, contact the **Greater Boston Convention and Visitors Bureau** (⊠ 2 Copley Pl., Suite 105, Boston 02116, ☎ 617/536–4100 or 800/888–5515), which runs a visitor center (closed weekends) near the Park Street station on the T Line. The **Boston Welcome Center** (⊠ 140 Tremont St., Boston 02111, ☎ 617/451–2227) also has general information.

Boston magazine (on newsstands) and *Where: Boston* (free in hotels and visitor centers) list arts and entertainment events. The *Boston Travel Planner,* available from the Greater Boston Convention and Visitors Bureau, contains a calendar of events, sports and regional activities, and information on hotel weekend packages.

Arriving and Departing

By Bus

Bonanza (☎ 800/556–3815), **Greyhound** (☎ 800/231–2222), **Peter Pan Bus Lines** (☎ 617/426–7838), and **Plymouth & Brockton Buses** (☎ 508/746–0378) serve Massachusetts. The depot in Boston for these bus companies is **South Station** (⊠ Atlantic Ave. and Summer St., ☎ 617/345–7451).

By Car

Boston is the traffic hub of New England: I–95 (which is the same as Route 128 in parts) skirts the city along the coast, while I–90 heads west. I–93 connects Boston to the north and New Hampshire; the highway runs through the city as the Fitzgerald Expressway. This section of I–93 is scheduled to be turned into an underground highway as part of the massive Central Artery Project; expect construction and delays here well into 2000.

By Plane

Logan International Airport (☎ 617/561–1800 or 800/235–6426) has scheduled flights by most major domestic and foreign carriers. Cab fare to downtown is about $20 including tip. For 24-hour information on parking, bicycle access, and bus, subway, and water-shuttle transportation, call Logan's **Ground Transportation Desk** (☎ 800/235–6426). The **Massachusetts Bay Transportation Authority** (MBTA) Blue Line subway from the Airport station (85¢) goes downtown; free shuttle buses connect the station with airline terminals and run every 8–12 minutes from 5:30 AM to 1 AM.

By Train

Amtrak (☎ 800/872–7245) serves Boston. All trains stop at South Station; some stop at Back Bay station.

Getting Around Boston

Boston is meant for walking; a majority of its historic and architectural attractions are found in compact areas.

By Car

Boston is not an easy city to drive in. Parking is a tricky business. Some neighborhoods have residents-only rules, with just a handful of two-hour visitor's spaces; others have meters (25¢ for 15 minutes, one or two hours maximum). Major public lots are at Government Center and Quincy Market, beneath Boston Common (entrance on Charles Street), beneath Post Office Square, at the Prudential Center, at Copley Place, and off Clarendon Street near the John Hancock Tower. Smaller lots are scattered throughout downtown. Most are expensive; the few city garages are a bargain at about $6 to $10 per day.

By Public Transportation

The **MBTA** (☎ 617/722–3200 or 800/392–6100; TTY 617/722–5146), known as the T, operates subways, elevated trains, and trolleys along four connecting lines—Red, Blue, Green, and Orange. Trains run from 5:30 AM to about 12:30 AM daily; adult base fare is 85¢. Tourist passes are available for $5 for one day, $9 for three days, and $18 for seven days.

By Taxi

Cabs are not easily hailed; if you're in a hurry, try a hotel taxi stand or telephone for a cab. Fares run about $1.90 per mi, with a pickup fee of $1.50. Companies offering 24-hour service include **Cambridge Taxi** (☎ 617/547–3000), **Checker** (☎ 617/536–7000), **ITOA** (☎ 617/426–8700), and **Yellow** (☎ 617/547–3000).

Orientation Tours

By Boat

Boston Harbor Cruises (✉ 1 Long Wharf, ☎ 617/227–4321) operates five cruises departing from Long Wharf, plus a whale-watching cruise from mid-April to October.

By Bus and Trolley

Brush Hill/Gray Line (☎ 617/236–2148) buses pick up passengers from several suburban and downtown hotels for tours of Boston and neighboring towns like Lexington, Concord, Plymouth, and Salem.

Old Town Trolley (✉ 329 W. 2nd St., South Boston, 02127, ☎ 617/269–7010) runs every 10 minutes 9–4:30, for $20; summer only, tours are also available through Cambridge.

Walking Tours

The 2½-mi **Freedom Trail** (☎ 617/242–5642) tour, which is marked on the sidewalk by a red line, winds past 16 of Boston's most important historic sites, beginning at the visitor center at Boston Common, where you'll find maps and other brochures. The **Black Heritage Trail** (☎ 617/742–5415), which begins on the Boston Common, winds through the Beacon Hill neighborhood, with maps available at the African Meeting House on Joy Street.

Exploring Boston

Boston Common and Beacon Hill

★ **Boston Common,** the oldest public park in the United States and the site of festivals, political rallies, First Night New Year's activities, and family outings, is the heart of Boston. At the Congregationalist **Park Street Church** (✉ 1 Park St., ☎ 617/523–3383), finished in 1810, Samuel Smith's hymn "America" was first sung in 1831. Next to the church is the **Old Granary Burial Ground,** where Revolutionary heroes Samuel Adams, John Hancock, and Paul Revere lie.

At the summit of Beacon Hill is Charles Bulfinch's magnificent neo-★ classical **State House,** its dome both sheathed in copper from Paul Revere's foundry and gilded after the Civil War. Tours are given on weekdays. ✉ *Beacon St. between Hancock and Bowdoin Sts.,* ☎ *617/727–3676.* 🎫 *Free. Closed weekends.*

With its brick row houses, most built between 1800 and 1850, the classic face of **Beacon Hill** is in a style never far from the early Federal norm. Here you'll find **Chestnut and Mt. Vernon streets,** distinguished not only for their individual houses but also for their general atmosphere and character. Henry James lived on Mt. Vernon, which opens out on **Louisburg Square,** the heart of Beacon Hill. Once the home address of William Dean Howells and Louisa May Alcott, the square was an 1840s model for town house development.

★

On the north slope of Beacon Hill is the 1806 **African Meeting House** (✉ 8 Smith Ct., ☎ 617/742–1854), the oldest African American church building in the United States and where the New England Anti-Slavery Society was formed in 1832. The site marks the end of the Black Heritage Trail.

The North End and Charlestown

In the 17th century the **North End** *was* Boston, as much of the rest of the peninsula was still under water. During most of the 20th century the North End has been Italian Boston, full of restaurants, groceries, bakeries, churches, social clubs, cafés, and festivals honoring saints and food.

Off Hanover Street, the North End's main thoroughfare is North Square. The **Paul Revere House,** the oldest home in Boston, was built nearly a century before its illustrious tenant's midnight ride. Colonial-era furniture decorates the rooms. ✉ *19 North Sq.,* ☎ *617/523–1676 or 617/523–2338.* 🎫 *$2.50. Closed Mon., Jan.–Mar.*

Past North Square on Hanover Street is **St. Stephen's,** the only Charles Bulfinch–designed church still standing in Boston. The steeple of Christ Church, more commonly known as the **Old North Church** (✉ 193 Salem St., ☎ 617/523–6676)—where Paul Revere hung the two lanterns to signal Cambridge residents on the night of April 18, 1775—can be seen on Tileston Street. The oldest church building in Boston, it was designed by William Price from a study of Christopher Wren's London churches.

★

Cross the Charlestown Bridge to reach the **USS *Constitution*,** nicknamed "Old Ironsides" for the strength of its oaken hull, which seemed to repel cannon fire. Launched in 1797, it is the oldest commissioned ship in the U.S. Navy and is moored at the Charlestown Navy Yard. During its service against the Barbary pirates and in the War of 1812, the ship never lost an engagement. Nearby is the Constitution Museum which tells the story of the ship with artifacts, maps, photos and videos. ✉ *Constitution Wharf,* ☎ *617/242–5670 or 617/426–1812 for the museum.* 🎫 *Constitution free, museum $4.*

The Battle of Bunker Hill was actually fought on Breed's Hill, and this is where Solomon Willard's **Bunker Hill Monument**—a 221-ft shaft of Quincy granite—stands. It rises from the spot where on June 17, 1775, a citizens' militia—reputedly commanded not to fire "until you see the whites of their eyes"—inflicted more than 1,100 casualties on British regulars (who eventually did seize the hill). The views from the top are worth the 294-step ascent. ✉ *Main St. to Monument St., then straight uphill;* ☎ *617/242–5641.* 🎫 *Free.*

★

Downtown Boston

Downtown is east of the Boston Common. There is little logic to the streets here because they were once village lanes; they are now lined with 40-story office towers. The granite **King's Chapel** (✉ 58 Tremont St., at School St.), built in 1754, houses Paul Revere's largest and—in his own judgment—sweetest-sounding bell.

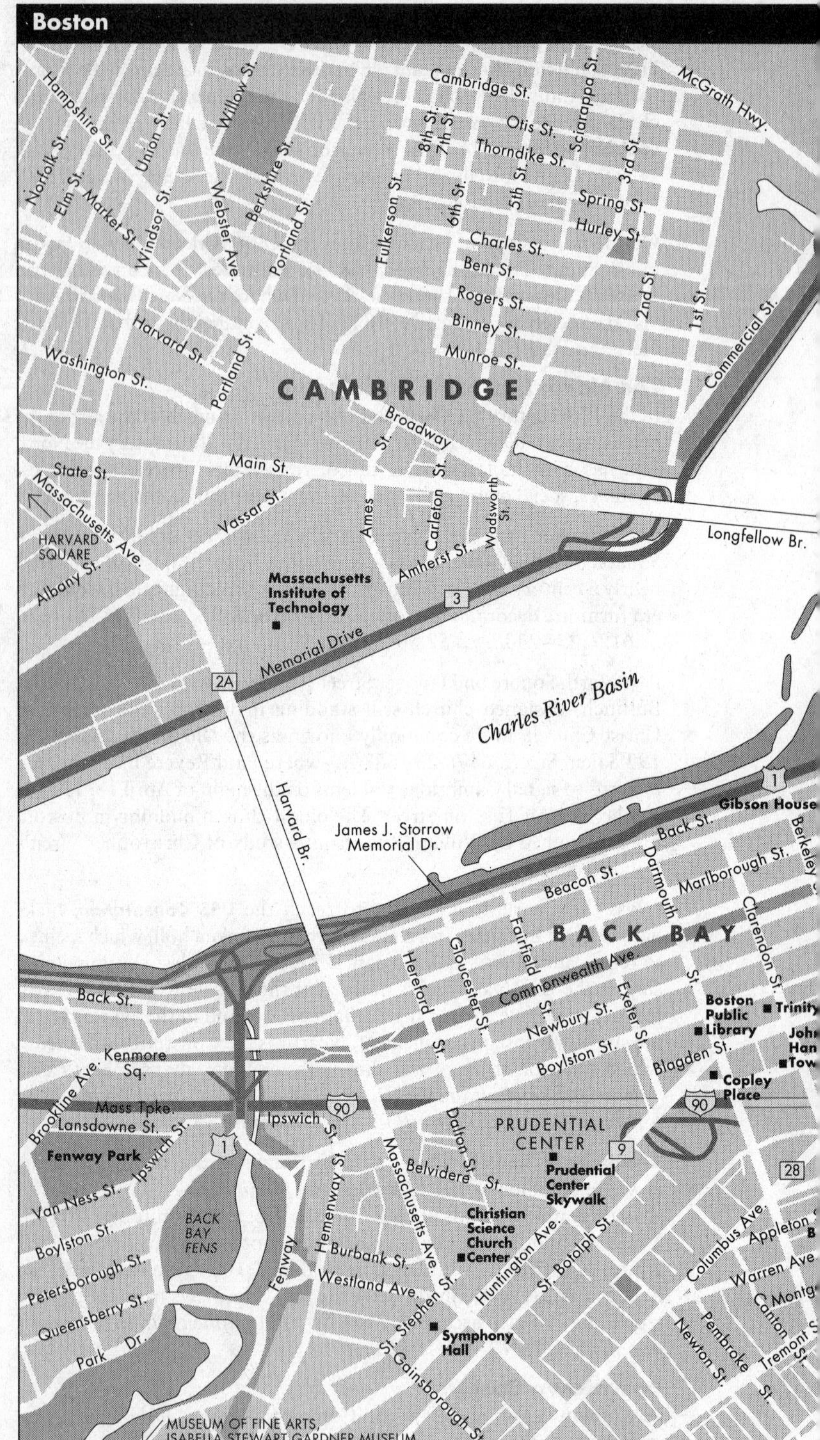
CAMBRIDGE
BACK BAY
Hampshire St.
Norfolk St.
Elm St.
Market St.
Union St.
Windsor St.
Willow St.
Webster Ave.
Berkshire St.
Portland St.
Harvard St.
Washington St.
Cambridge St.
8th St.
7th St.
Otis St.
Thorndike St.
Sciarappa St.
3rd St.
Fulkerson St.
6th St.
5th St.
Spring St.
Hurley St.
Charles St.
Bent St.
Rogers St.
Binney St.
Munroe St.
2nd St.
1st St.
Commercial St.
McGrath Hwy.
Broadway
Main St.
State St.
Massachusetts Ave.
HARVARD SQUARE
Albany St.
Vassar St.
Ames St.
Carleton St.
Wadsworth St.
Amherst St.
Longfellow Br.
Massachusetts Institute of Technology
Memorial Drive
3
2A
Charles River Basin
Harvard Br.
James J. Storrow Memorial Dr.
1
Gibson House
Back St.
Berkeley
Marlborough St.
Beacon St.
Dartmouth
Clarendon St.
Fairfield St.
Gloucester St.
Hereford St.
Commonwealth Ave.
Newbury St.
Exeter St.
Boston Public Library
Trinity
John Han
Tow
Boylston St.
Blagden St.
Copley Place
Kenmore Sq.
Brookline Ave.
Mass Tpke.
Lansdowne St.
Ipswich St.
90
Dalton St.
PRUDENTIAL CENTER
9
Prudential Center Skywalk
28
Fenway Park
Van Ness St.
Boylston St.
Petersborough St.
Queensberry St.
Park Dr.
BACK BAY FENS
Fenway
Hemenway St.
Massachusetts Ave.
Belvidere St.
Burbank St.
Westland Ave.
Christian Science Church Center
Huntington Ave.
St. Botolph St.
Columbus Ave.
Appleton
Warren Ave
Montg
Canton St.
Tremont St.
Pembroke St.
Newton St.
St. Stephen St.
Symphony Hall
Gainsborough St.
MUSEUM OF FINE ARTS, ISABELLA STEWART GARDNER MUSEUM

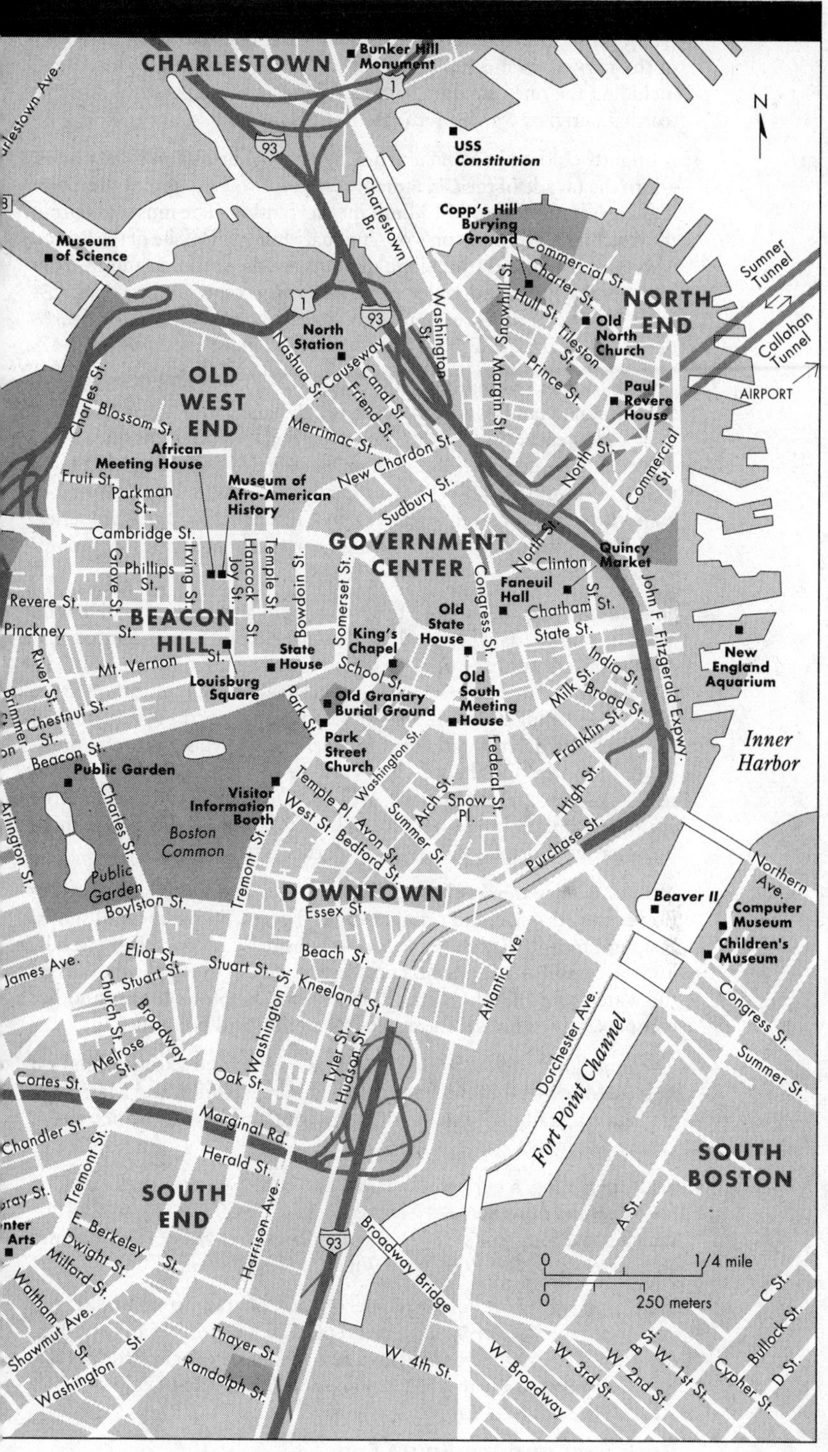
CHARLESTOWN
Bunker Hill Monument
USS Constitution
Museum of Science
Charlestown Br.
Copp's Hill Burying Ground
Commercial St.
Charter St.
Hull St.
Snowhill St.
NORTH END
Old North Church
Tileston St.
Prince St.
Sumner Tunnel
Callahan Tunnel
AIRPORT
Paul Revere House
North Station
Nashua St.
Causeway
Canal St.
Friend St.
Washington St.
Margin St.
OLD WEST END
Charles St.
Blossom St.
Merrimac St.
New Chardon St.
African Meeting House
Museum of Afro-American History
Fruit St.
Parkman St.
Sudbury St.
North St.
Commercial St.
Cambridge St.
GOVERNMENT CENTER
Quincy Market
Clinton
Faneuil Hall
Chatham St.
John F. Fitzgerald Expwy.
Grove St.
Phillips St.
Irving St.
Hancock St.
Joy St.
Temple St.
Bowdoin St.
Somerset St.
Congress St.
Revere St.
Pinckney St.
BEACON HILL
Old State House
King's Chapel
State St.
New England Aquarium
Mt. Vernon St.
State House
School St.
India St.
Louisburg Square
River St.
Brimmer St.
Chestnut St.
Old Granary Burial Ground
Old South Meeting House
Milk St.
Broad St.
Beacon St.
Park St.
Park Street Church
Washington St.
Federal St.
Franklin St.
Inner Harbor
Public Garden
Visitor Information Booth
Temple Pl.
West St.
Arch St.
Snow Pl.
High St.
Boston Common
Tremont St.
Avon St.
Summer St.
Bedford St.
Purchase St.
Arlington St.
Charles St.
Public Garden
Northern Ave.
DOWNTOWN
Boylston St.
Essex St.
Beaver II
Computer Museum
Children's Museum
Beach St.
Eliot St.
James Ave.
Stuart St.
Kneeland St.
Atlantic Ave.
Church St.
Broadway
Washington St.
Tyler St.
Hudson St.
Dorchester Ave.
Congress St.
Melrose St.
Fort Point Channel
Summer St.
Cortes St.
Oak St.
Chandler St.
Marginal Rd.
Herald St.
SOUTH BOSTON
Tremont St.
SOUTH END
Harrison Ave.
E. Berkeley St.
Dwight St.
Milford St.
Broadway Bridge
A St.
0 1/4 mile
0 250 meters
Waltham St.
Shawmut Ave.
Washington St.
Thayer St.
Randolph St.
W. 4th St.
W. Broadway
W. 3rd St.
W. 2nd St.
B St.
W. 1st St.
Cypher St.
C St.
Bullock St.
D St.

The **Old South Meeting House** (✉ 310 Washington St., ☎ 617/482–6439; 💳 $3), built in 1729, is Boston's second-oldest church. Many of the fiery town meetings that led to the Revolution were held here, including the one called by Samuel Adams concerning some dutiable tea that activists wanted returned to England.

A brightly colored lion and unicorn, symbols of British imperial power, adorn the facade of the **Old State House.** This was the seat of the Colonial government from 1713 until the Revolution. The museum within the structure surveys Boston's revolutionary history. The site of the Boston Massacre is marked by a circle of stones in the traffic island in front of the building. A **National Park Service visitor center** is directly across from the Old State House on State Street. ✉ *206 Washington St.,* ☎ *617/720–3290; 617/242–5642 for the National Park Service.* 💳 *$3.*

The **Children's Museum** (✉ 300 Congress St., ☎ 617/426–6500; 💳 $7) contains hands-on exhibits, many designed to help children understand science, cultural diversity, their bodies, and the nature of disabilities. Next door is the **Computer Museum** (✉ 300 Congress St., ☎ 617/426–2800 or 617/413–6758; 💳 $7), which has a two-story walk-through computer, celebrity robot R2D2 of the *Star Wars* series, and a software gallery where families can test out the latest computer games.

★ **Faneuil Hall,** erected in 1742 to serve as both a town meeting hall and a public market, is where in 1772 Samuel Adams first suggested that Massachusetts and the other colonies organize a Committee of Correspondence to maintain semiclandestine lines of communication in the face of hardening British repression. In national election years the hall usually hosts debates among contenders in the Massachusetts presidential primary. On the top floors are the headquarters and museum of the Ancient and Honorable Artillery Company of Massachusetts, the oldest militia in the nation (1638). Its status is now ceremonial, but it proudly displays its arms, uniforms, and other artifacts.

Nearby **Quincy Market** has served as a retail and wholesale distribution center for meat and produce for 150 years. It houses retail shops, restaurants, and offices. Some people consider it all hopelessly trendy, but the 50,000 visitors who come here each day seem to enjoy it. At the waterfront end of Quincy Market is **Marketplace Center,** another complex, which houses more shops, eateries, and boutiques.

The most glittering addition to Boston's waterfront can be found on **Rowes Wharf**—a 15-story redbrick Skidmore, Owings, and Merrill extravaganza, gaily adorned with white trim and home to chic restaurants and shops.

Seals, penguins, a variety of sharks, and other sea creatures reside at **New England Aquarium** (✉ Central Wharf, ☎ 617/973–5200; 💳 $11), which has a four-story, 187,000-gallon coral reef tank. The glass and steel exterior of the 1998 West Wing mimics fish scales.

When you cross Fort Point Channel on the Congress Street Bridge, you encounter the ***Beaver II,*** a faithful replica of a Boston Tea Party ship, like the ones forcibly boarded and unloaded on the night Boston Harbor itself became a teapot. ✉ *Congress St. Bridge,* ☎ *617/338–1773.* 💳 *$7. Closed Dec.–Feb.*

Back Bay and the South End

Southwest of Boston Common is **Back Bay,** once a tidal flat that formed the south bank of a distended Charles River until it was filled as far as the Fens in the 19th century. Back Bay is a living museum of urban Victorian residential architecture. One of the first Back Bay residences (1859), the **Gibson House** (✉ 137 Beacon St., ☎ 617/267–6338; 🎫 $5) has been preserved with all its Victorian fixtures and furniture intact; a Gibson scion lived here until the 1950s and left things as they had always been.

Newbury Street, Boston's poshest shopping district, is lined with sidewalk cafés and dozens of upscale specialty shops offering clothing, china, antiques, and art.

From the 60th-floor observatory of the tallest building in New England, the 62-story **John Hancock Tower,** you'll have one of the best vantage points in the city. ✉ *Observatory ticket office, Trinity Pl. and St. James Ave.,* ☎ *617/247–1977.* 🎫 *$4.25.*

One of the three monumental buildings that dominate **Copley Square** is the stately, bowfront Copley Plaza Hotel. **Trinity Church** is Henry Hobson Richardson's Romanesque Revival masterwork of 1877. And the **Boston Public Library** (☎ 617/536–5400) confirmed the status of McKim, Mead, and White as apostles of Renaissance Revival in 1895. The modern complex **Copley Place** comprises two major hotels (the Westin and the Marriott), dozens of shops and restaurants, and a cinema grouped on several levels around bright, open indoor spaces.

The headquarters of the **Christian Science Church Center** (✉ 175 Huntington Ave., at Massachusetts Ave., ☎ 617/450–3790) is a striking mixture of old and new architecture. Mary Baker Eddy's original granite First Church of Christ, Scientist (1894) and the domed Renaissance basilica added to the site in 1906 are now surrounded by the offices of the *Christian Science Monitor* and by I. M. Pei's 1973 complex of church administration buildings with its distinctive reflecting pool. Overlooking the Christian Science Church, the **Prudential Center Skywalk** (✉ 800 Boylston St., ☎ 617/859–0648; 🎫 $4) is a 50th-floor observatory with great views of the city and suburbs.

Symphony Hall (✉ 301 Massachusetts Ave., ☎ 617/266–1492), since 1900 the home of the Boston Symphony Orchestra, is another contribution of McKim, Mead, and White, though the acoustics rather than exterior design make this a special place.

The **South End,** eclipsed by the Back Bay more than a century ago, has now been gentrified, with galleries and restaurants catering to young professionals, including a large concentration of Boston's gay population. The houses here continue the pattern established on Beacon Hill (in a uniformly bowfront style) but have more florid decoration.

The South End also has a strong African American presence, particularly along Columbus Avenue and Massachusetts Avenue, which marks the beginning of the neighborhood of Roxbury. The early integration of the South End set the stage for its eventual transformation into a remarkably polyglot population. At the northeastern extreme of the South End, Harrison Avenue and Washington Street connect the area with Chinatown.

On Tremont Street you'll find blocks of trendy restaurants and the **Boston Center for the Arts** (✉ 539 Tremont St., ☎ 617/426–5000; 🎫 free), which has a gallery, several small theaters, and the "Cyclorama," a large space now devoted to antiques shows, exhibits, and other events.

The Fens

After all the work that had gone into filling in the bay, it would have been little extra trouble to march row houses straight through to Brookline. Happily, planners hired Frederick Law Olmsted to make the Fens into a park instead. Today's park consists of still, irregular, and reed-bound pools surrounded by broad meadows, trees, and flower gardens.

★ The **Museum of Fine Arts,** between Huntington Avenue and the Fenway, has holdings of American art surpassing those of all but two or three other U.S. museums; an extensive collection of Asian art; and European artwork from the 11th through the 20th centuries. Count on staying a while to have *any* hope of seeing even a smidgen of what is here. The museum has two restaurants and a cafeteria, plus a popular gift shop. ✉ *465 Huntington Ave.,* ☎ *617/267–9300.* 🎫 *$10.*

★ The **Isabella Stewart Gardner Museum** is a monument to one woman's taste. The emphasis among the 2,000 spectacular paintings, sculptures, furniture, and textiles is on Italian Renaissance and 17th-century Dutch masters. Friend to John Singer Sargent, Edith Wharton, and Henry James, Gardner shocked proper Bostonians with the flamboyance of her Venetian-style palazzo. The highlight of the collection—and according to some scholars, the greatest painting in America—is Titian's *Rape of Europa.* At the center of the building is a soaring courtyard planted with flowers. ✉ *280 The Fenway,* ☎ *617/566–1401.* 🎫 *$10. Closed Mon.*

The Boston shrine known as **Fenway Park** (✉ 4 Yawkey Way) is one of the smallest and oldest baseball parks in the major leagues. Built in 1912, it still has real grass on the field. **Kenmore Square** (✉ Commonwealth Ave., Brookline Ave., and Beacon St. intersection) is home to fast-food parlors, alternative rock clubs, an abundance of students from nearby Boston University, and the enormous neon CITGO sign, an area landmark.

Cambridge

In 1636 the country's first college was established in Cambridge, across the Charles River from Boston. Two years later it was named in honor of John Harvard, a young Charlestown clergyman who had recently died, leaving the college his entire library and half his estate. **Harvard** remained the only college in the American colonies until 1693. The information office, in **Holyoke Center** (✉ 1350 Massachusetts Ave., ☎ 617/495–1573), offers area maps and a free hour-long walking tour of Harvard Yard most days. North of Cambridge Common is **Radcliffe College,** founded in 1897; since 1975 Radcliffe students have shared classes and degrees with Harvard students.

Harvard University has three celebrated art museums, each a treasure in itself. The most famous is the **Fogg Art Museum.** Founded in 1895, it now owns 80,000 works of art from every major period and from every corner of the world. Its focus is primarily on European and American art, and it has notable collections of 19th-century French Impressionist and medieval Italian paintings. ✉ *32 Quincy St.,* ☎ *617/495–9400.* 🎫 *$5.*

A ticket to the Fogg also gains you admission to Harvard's **Busch-Reisinger Museum** (☎ 617/495–9400), in Werner Otto Hall, which is entered through the Fogg. The collection specializes in Germanic and Central and Northern European art.

Fogg admission also gets you into the **Arthur M. Sackler Museum** (☎ 617/495–9400) across the street, which concentrates on ancient Greek and Roman, Egyptian, Islamic, Chinese, and other Eastern art.

The **Massachusetts Institute of Technology,** which borders the Charles River south of Harvard Square, boasts distinctive architecture by I. M. Pei and Eero Saarinen. Among the museums on campus is the **MIT Museum** (🎫 $3), where art and science meet. The **Information Center** (✉

77 Massachusetts Ave., Bldg. 7, ☏ 617/253–4795) offers free tours of the campus weekdays at 10 and 2.

Parks, Gardens, and Zoos

★ The **Boston Public Garden,** next to Boston Common, is the oldest botanical garden in the United States. Its pond has been famous since 1877 for its Swan Boats, which offer leisurely cruises during the warm months of the year. The **Franklin Park Zoo** (✉ 1 Franklin Park Rd., ☏ 617/442–2002 or 617/442–4896; 🎟 $6) recently added lions and cheetahs to its roster of exotic animals.

The **Dr. Paul Dudley White Bikeway,** approximately 18 mi long, runs along both sides of the Charles River. The river's banks are also popular with joggers.

Dining

For price ranges *see* Chart 1 (A) *in* On the Road with Fodor's. Addresses below include a neighborhood reference.

$$$$ ★ ✕ **L'Espalier.** An elegantly modernized Victorian Back Bay town house is the setting for what some critics consider Boston's best restaurant. Chef-owner Frank McClelland creates an intoxicating blend of new French and newer American cuisine. ✉ *30 Gloucester St., Back Bay,* ☏ *617/262–3023. Reservations essential. Jacket and tie. AE, D, DC, MC, V. Closed Sun. No lunch.*

$$$–$$$$ ★ ✕ **Biba.** The menu at Boston's best restaurant encourages inventive combinations, unusual cuts and produce, haute comfort food, and big postmodern desserts. Take your time, and don't settle for the "classic lobster pizza" if something like "crusted ocean perch" is available. The wine list is an adventure. ✉ *272 Boylston St., Back Bay,* ☏ *617/426–7878. Reservations essential. D, DC, MC, V.*

$$$ ★ ✕ **East Coast Grill.** Owner-chef-author Chris Schlesinger built his national reputation on grilling and red-hot condiments, but is now angling to make his establishment one of the top fish restaurants in town. Spices and condiments are more restrained. Brunch is served on Sunday. ✉ *1271 Cambridge St., Cambridge,* ☏ *617/491–6568. AE, D, MC, V. No lunch.*

$$$ ★ ✕ **Hamersley's Bistro.** Gordon Hamersley has earned national renown for dishes like his grilled mushroom-and-garlic sandwich and a cassoulet of duck confit, pork, and garlic sausage. His place has a full bar, a café area with 10 tables for walk-ins, and a larger dining room that's a little more formal and decorative than the bar and café. ✉ *553 Tremont St.,* ☏ *617/423–2700. D, MC, V.*

$$$ ★ ✕ **Lala Rokh.** The food at this western Asian restaurant includes exotically flavored Persian specialties and dishes as familiar (but superb here) as eggplant puree, pilaf, kabobs, *fesanjoon* (the classic pomegranate-walnut sauce), and lamb stews. ✉ *97 Mount Vernon St., Beacon Hill,* ☏ *617/720–5511. AE, DC, MC, V. No lunch.*

$$$ ★ ✕ **Union Square Bistro.** Chef David Smoke McCluskey's "native nouvelle" cuisine emphasizes American foodstuffs and game, prepared with a nod to his Native American heritage. Recent dishes have included venison with pemmican sauce made of black cherries and venison jerky. Brunch is served on Sunday. ✉ *16 Bow St., Union Sq., Somerville,* ☏ *617/628–3344. Reservations essential. AE, D, DC, MC, V.*

$$–$$$ ★ ✕ **Legal Sea Foods.** The hallmark here is top-quality seafood; dishes come to the table in whatever order they leave the kitchen, since freshness is of uppermost importance. The smoked bluefish pâté is one of the finest appetizers anywhere, and don't miss the chowder. ✉ *35 Columbus Ave., Park Sq.,* ☏ *617/426–4444.* ✉ *Cambridge: 5 Cambridge*

Center, Kendall Sq., ☎ 617/864-3400. ✉ Logan Airport: Terminal C, ☎ 617/569-4622. Reservations not accepted. AE, D, DC, MC, V.

$$-$$$ ★ ✕ **Les Zygomates.** This restaurant serves up classic French bistro fare that dares to be simple and simply delicious. Prix-fixe menus are offered for both lunch and dinner. Pan-seared catfish with house vinaigrette and roasted rabbit leg stuffed with vegetables typify the taste. ✉ *129 South St.,* ☎ *617/542-5108. Reservations essential. AE, DC, MC, V. No lunch weekends.*

$$-$$$ ✕ **Sonsie.** The restaurant, which opens at 7 AM, is famous for breakfasts that extend well into the afternoon. During warm weather months, the entire front of Sonsie becomes an open-air café looking out on upper Newbury Street. The dishes on the menu are basic bistro with an American twist, such as pan-seared fish sandwich with spicy tartar sauce. ✉ *327 Newbury St., Back Bay,* ☎ *617/351-2500. AE, MC, V.*

$$ ✕ **Brew Moon.** Instead of the usual industrial decor of a brew pub, the flagship of this minichain looks like a California Zen health-food palace and has rather flashy food, although with an emphasis on the salty and peppery morsels that call out for beer. Save room for serious desserts. Also in Harvard Square, Cambridge. ✉ *115 Stuart St.,* ☎ *617/742-5225;* ✉ *Cambridge: 50 Church St., Harvard Square,* ☎ *617/499-2739. AE, DC, MC, V.*

$$ ★ ✕ **Pomodoro.** The dishes at this tiny gem of a trattoria, where there's often a wait, include white beans with various pastas, roasted vegetables, and a fine salad of field greens. The walls are decorated with lacquered cutlery, and the wine list is exceptional. The best choice could well be the clam and tomato stew with herbed flat bread. ✉ *319 Hanover St., North End,* ☎ *617/367-4348. No credit cards.*

$-$$ ★ ✕ **Chau Chow.** Seafood is the speciality at this Chinese restaurant: Try the clams in black bean sauce, steamed sea bass, gray sole with its fried fins, or any dish with their famous ginger sauce. Chau Chow has expanded to a larger storefront called Grand Chau Chow across the street. Seating at old Chau Chow is very tight. ✉ *50 Beach St.,* ☎ *617/426-6266. No credit cards.*

Lodging

Many of the city's most costly lodgings offer attractively priced weekend packages. Consult the *Boston Travel Planner* (☞ Visitor Information, *above*) for current rates. At many hotels children may stay free in their parents' room, or breakfast may be included in the rate.

Although Boston does not have a large number of B&Bs, there are several with daily rates between $55 and $120 per room. Reservations may be made through **Bed and Breakfast Associates Bay Colony** (✉ Box 57166, Babson Park Branch, Boston 02157, ☎ 617/449-5302 or 800/347-5088, FAX 617/449-5302).

For price ranges *see* Chart 2 (A) *in* On the Road with Fodor's.

$$$$ ★ 🏨 **Boston Harbor Hotel at Rowes Wharf.** Everything here is done on a grand scale, starting with the dramatic entrance through an 80-ft archway. Guest rooms—decorated in shades of mauve, green, and cream—have either city or water views, and some have balconies. ✉ *70 Rowes Wharf, 02110,* ☎ *617/439-7000 or 800/752-7077,* FAX *617/345-6799. 256 rooms. 2 restaurants, outdoor café, indoor lap pool, health club. AE, D, DC, MC, V.*

$$$$ ★ 🏨 **Fairmont Copley Plaza.** The public spaces of this landmark, built in 1912, recall an era long gone, with high gilded and painted ceilings, mosaic floors, marble pillars, and crystal chandeliers; the guest rooms have custom furniture from Italy, elegant marble bathrooms, and fax machines. ✉ *138 St. James Ave., 02116,* ☎ *617/267-5300 or 800/*

527–4727, FAX 617/247–6681. 430 rooms. 2 restaurants, 2 bars, exercise room. AE, D, DC, MC, V.

$$$$ ★ **Four Seasons.** The Four Seasons is famed for luxurious personal service of the sort demanded by celebrities and heads of state. It has huge rooms with king-size beds, HBO, and 24-hour concierge and room service. The Bristol Lounge serves high tea daily at 3 PM. ✉ *200 Boylston St., 02116,* ☎ *617/338–4400 or 800/332–3442,* FAX *617/423–0154. 288 rooms. 2 restaurants, indoor pool, health club. AE, D, DC, MC, V.*

$$$$ ★ **Ritz-Carlton.** Suites in the older section have parlors with working fireplaces and wonderful views of the Public Garden. The three top floors cost extra but have butler service and a private club with complimentary food and drinks, newspapers, and games. Public rooms include the elegant café, the sedate bar, and The Lounge. ✉ *Arlington and Newbury Sts., 02117,* ☎ *617/536–5700 or 800/241–3333,* FAX *617/536–1335. 278 rooms. Restaurant, exercise room. AE, D, DC, MC, V.*

$$$–$$$$ ★ **Eliot Hotel.** The luxurious suites at the Eliot have Italian marble bathrooms, two cable-equipped televisions, and tasteful pastel-hued decor. The airy restaurant, Clio, has been garnering rave reviews for its serene ambience and contemporary French-American cuisine. The Eliot is steps from Newbury Street and a short walk to Kenmore Square. ✉ *370 Commonwealth Ave., 02215,* ☎ *617/267–1607 or 800/443–5468,* FAX *617/536–9114. 95 suites. Restaurant. AE, D, DC, MC, V.*

$$$–$$$$ ★ **Lenox Hotel.** The soundproof guest rooms at the Lenox have custom-made traditional furnishings, spacious walk-in closets, and marble baths; some of the corner rooms have working fireplaces. The Samuel Adams Brew House and the popular bistro Anago are both worthy stops. ✉ *710 Boylston St., 02116,* ☎ *617/536–5300 or 800/225–7676,* FAX *617/236–0351. 212 rooms. 2 restaurants, exercise room. AE, D, DC, MC, V.*

$$–$$$$ **Cambridge House Bed and Breakfast.** This Greek Revival Cambridge House home is on busy Massachusetts Avenue but set well back from the road. The B&B is a haven of peace and otherworldliness, with richly carved cherry paneling, a grand mahogany fireplace, elegant Victorian antiques, and polished wood floors overlaid with Oriental rugs. Harvard Square is a distant walk, but public transportation is nearby. ✉ *2218 Massachusetts Ave., Cambridge, 02140,* ☎ *617/491–6300 or 800/232–9989,* FAX *617/868–2848. 16 rooms (4 share baths). Full breakfast. MC, V. No pets. No smoking.*

$$ **Chandler Inn.** Economical rates and a friendly staff make this cozy little hotel one of the best bargains in the city. Located an overpass away from the Back Bay, at the end of one of the South End's prettiest streets, it's an easy walk to the T, the Amtrak station, Newbury Street's boutiques, or any of Tremont Street's trendy restaurants. Rooms are small but comfortable. ✉ *26 Chandler St., 02115,* ☎ *617/482–3450,* FAX *617/542–3428. 56 rooms. Restaurant (Sat., Sun. only), bar. AE, D, DC, MC, V.*

$$ **Hotel Buckminster.** An economical and tastefully decorated European-style inn two blocks from Fenway Park, the Buckminster has maids but no bellhops, and breakfast is by room service only. ✉ *645 Beacon St., 02215,* ☎ *617/236–7050 or 800/727–2825,* FAX *617/236–0068. 120 rooms. AE, D, DC, MC, V.*

$$ ★ **John Jeffries House.** This turn-of-the-century house across from Massachusetts General Hospital has rooms with French country decor. Triple-glazed windows block virtually all noise from busy Charles Circle. Most rooms have kitchenettes and many have views of the Charles River. At the foot of Beacon Hill, the inn is an easy walk from public transportation and most of downtown. ✉ *14 Embankment Rd., 02114,* ☎ *617/367–1866,* FAX *617/742–0313. 23 rooms, 23 suites. No-smoking floors, parking (fee). CP. AE, D, DC, MC, V.*

Motels

🏨 **Holiday Inn Logan Airport** (✉ 225 McClellan Hwy., East Boston, 02128, ☎ 617/569–5250 or 800/798–5849, FAX 617/569–5159), 351 rooms, restaurant, pool, exercise room; *$$$*. 🏨 **Susse Chalet Inn** (✉ 211 Concord Turnpike, 02140, ☎ 617/661–7800 or 800/524–2538, FAX 617/868–8153), 78 rooms, CP; *$–$$*.

Nightlife and the Arts

Thursday's *Boston Globe* calendar and the weekly *Boston Phoenix* provide contemporary listings of events for the coming week.

Nightlife

Quincy Market, Copley Square, and **Kenmore Square** in Boston and **Harvard Square** in Cambridge are centers of nightlife.

BARS AND LOUNGES

Boston Beer Works (✉ 61 Brookline Ave., ☎ 617/536–2337) brews up regular and seasonal brews for a youngish crowd. **Bull & Finch Pub** (✉ 84 Beacon St., at Hampshire House, ☎ 617/227–9605) was the inspiration for the TV series *Cheers.* **Top of the Hub** (✉ Prudential Center, ☎ 617/536–1775) has a wonderful view of the entire city, which along with the sounds of hip jazz makes the drinks at the 52nd-floor lounge worth the steep prices.

CAFÉS AND COFFEEHOUSES

Caffé Vittoria (✉ 296 Hanover St., ☎ 617/227–7606) is the biggest and the best of the North End cafés. **Roasters** (✉ 85 Newbury St., ☎ 617/867–9967) has outdoor seating for sunny days. A huge bay window allows maximum people-watching while you sip coffee roasted on the premises.

COMEDY

Comedy Connection (✉ Faneuil Hall Marketplace, ☎ 617/248–9700) books local and nationally known acts. **Nick's Comedy Stop** (✉ 100 Warrenton St., ☎ 617/482–0930) presents local comics every night except Monday.

DANCE CLUBS

Axis (✉ 13 Lansdowne St., ☎ 617/262–2424), near Kenmore Square, has high-energy disco and a giant dance floor. Some nights are gay, some are straight, some are 18, some are over-21 only. **Buzz** (✉ 67 Stuart St., ☎ 617/267–8969), one of the city's trendiest gay clubs, stands where the South End gives way to the Theater District. **International** (✉ 184 High St., ☎ 617/542–4747) is a multifaceted club in the Financial District. **Roxy** (✉ 279 Tremont St., Theater District, ☎ 617/338–7699) is the biggest nightclub in Boston. On Thursday night, the club caters to an upscale African American crowd, and on Friday, international students take it over. Saturday night is popular with sports stars and celebrities.

MUSIC

Avalon (✉ 15 Lansdowne St., ☎ 617/262–2424) hosts concerts by alternative, rock, and dance acts, then turns into a dance club. Concert show times vary. **Club Passim** (✉ 47 Palmer St., ☎ 617/492–7679) hosts folk music. **House of Blues** (✉ 96 Winthrop St., Cambridge, ☎ 617/491–2583) gets going around 10 PM; on Sunday there's a gospel brunch. **Marketplace Café** (✉ 300 Faneuil Hall, ☎ 617/227–9660) is a "no cover" treasure. It has a blues/jazz format. **The Paradise** (✉ 967 Commonwealth Ave., ☎ 617/254–3939) hosts national and local rock, jazz, folk, blues, alternative, and country acts. **Regattabar** (✉ Charles Hotel, Bennett and Eliot Sts., Cambridge, ☎ 617/864–1200,

617/876–7777 for tickets) headlines top names in jazz. It's closed on Sunday and Monday.

The Arts

BosTix (✉ Faneuil Hall Marketplace and Copley Sq., ☎ 617/723–5181) sells half-price tickets for same-day performances and full-price advance tickets. With major credit cards, you can charge tickets for many events over the phone by calling **Ticketmaster** (☎ 617/931–2000).

DANCE

Boston Ballet (✉ 19 Clarendon St., ☎ 617/695–6950), the city's premier dance company. **Dance Umbrella** (✉ 380 Green St., Cambridge, ☎ 617/492–7578) presents contemporary dance.

MUSIC

Berklee Performance Center (✉ 136 Massachusetts Ave., ☎ 617/266–1400 or 617/266–7455 for recorded information) is best known for its jazz programs. **Jordan Hall at the New England Conservatory** (✉ 30 Gainsborough St., ☎ 617/536–2412) is home to the Boston Philharmonic. **Symphony Hall** (✉ 301 Massachusetts Ave., ☎ 617/266–1492 or 800/274–8499), renowned for its acoustics, is home to the Boston Symphony Orchestra and the Boston Pops.

OPERA

The **Boston Lyric Opera Company** (✉ 114 State St., ☎ 617/542–6772) presents three productions each season.

THEATER

The **Boston Center for the Arts** (✉ 539 Tremont St., ☎ 617/426–7700) houses more than a dozen quirky low-budget troupes in four spaces. The **Loeb Drama Center** (✉ 64 Brattle St., ☎ 617/495–2668) has two theaters, the main one an experimental stage. This is the home of the American Repertory Theater, which produces classic and experimental works. **Emerson Majestic Theatre** (✉ 219 Tremont St., ☎ 617/578–8727) is a 1903 Beaux Arts building that hosts everything from avant-garde dance to drama to classical concerts. The **Huntington Theatre Company** (✉ 264 Huntington Ave., ☎ 617/266–0800), under the auspices of Boston University, is Boston's largest professional resident theater company, performing five plays annually, a mix of established 20th-century plays and classics.

Spectator Sports

Baseball: Boston Red Sox (✉ Fenway Park, 4 Yawkey Way, ☎ 617/267–1700). **Basketball: Boston Celtics** (✉ FleetCenter, Causeway St. at Haverhill St, ☎ 617/624–1000, 617/931–2000 for tickets). **Football: New England Patriots** (✉ Foxboro Stadium, 45 min south of Boston, Foxboro, ☎ 800/543–1776). **Hockey: Boston Bruins** (✉ FleetCenter, ☎ 617/624–1000, 617/931–2000 for tickets).

Shopping

Antiques, clothing, recorded music, and books keep cash registers ringing in Boston. Most Boston stores are in the area bounded by Quincy Market, the Back Bay, downtown, and Copley Square. There are few outlet stores but plenty of bargains, particularly in Filene's Basement and Chinatown's fabric district. Boston's two daily newspapers, the *Globe* and the *Herald,* are the best places to learn about sales.

Shopping Districts

Copley Place, an indoor shopping mall connecting two hotels, has 87 stores, restaurants, and cinemas that blend the elegant, the glitzy, and the overpriced. **Downtown Crossing,** between Summer and Washington streets, is a pedestrian mall with outdoor food and merchandise kiosks, street performers, and benches for people-watchers. **Faneuil Hall Marketplace** has crowds, small shops, and kiosks of every description. The busy food court of **Quincy Market** is also here. **Newbury Street** is where the funky and the trendy give way to the chic and the expensive. **Charles Street** on Beacon Hill is a mecca for antiques lovers from all over the country.

Harvard Square, in Cambridge, has more than 150 stores within a few blocks; it is a book lover's paradise. **CambridgeSide Galleria,** between Kendall Square and the Museum of Science in Cambridge, has about 100 shops.

Department Stores

Filene's (✉ 426 Washington St., ☎ 617/357–2100; ✉ CambridgeSide Galleria, Cambridge, ☎ 617/621–3800) carries name-brand men's and women's clothing. **Filene's Basement** (✉ 426 Washington St., ☎ 617/542–2011), now an entity all its own, pioneered the idea of discounting; it reduces prices according to the number of days items have been on the rack.

Specialty Stores

Louis, Boston (✉ 234 Berkeley St., ☎ 617/262–6100) is Boston's signature clothier, carrying elegantly tailored designs and subtly updated classics in everything from linen to tweeds. **Shreve, Crump & Low** (✉ 330 Boylston St., ☎ 617/267–9100) is an old, well-respected store that carries the finest in jewelry, china, crystal, and silver.

Side Trip to Lexington and Concord

The events of April 19, 1775—the first military encounters of the American War of Independence—are very much a part of present-day Lexington and Concord. These two quintessential New England towns are also rich in literary history: Concord, for example, is the site of Walden Pond, immortalized by Thoreau. Several historic houses have been preserved and can be visited.

Visitor Information

Lexington visitor center (✉ 1875 Massachusetts Ave., 02173, ☎ 781/862–1450). **Minute Man National Historical Park Visitors Center** (✉ Off Rte. 2A, ☎ 781/862–7753).

Arriving and Departing

To reach Lexington and Concord by car from Boston, take Route 2A (Massachusetts Avenue) west from Cambridge or I–95/Route 128 north to the Lexington exit. Route 2A west will take you on to Concord. Both towns are about a half-hour drive from the metropolitan Boston area. The MBTA (☞ Getting Around Boston, *above*) operates buses to Lexington.

What to See and Do

Minuteman captain John Parker assembled his men on **Battle Green,** a 2-acre triangular piece of land, to await the arrival of the British, who were marching from Boston toward Concord to "teach rebels a lesson." Parker's role is commemorated in Henry Hudson Kitson's renowned sculpture, the ***Minuteman* statue.**

Buckman Tavern, built in 1690, is where the minutemen gathered the morning of April 19, 1775. ✉ *1 Bedford St.,* ☎ *781/862–5598.* 🎫 *$3. Closed Nov.–mid-Apr.*

★ The **Museum of Our National Heritage** is a small but dynamic institution that does a superb job not only in displaying items and artifacts from all facets of American life but also in putting them in a social and political context. ✉ *33 Marrett Rd.,* ☎ *781/861–6559.* 🎫 *Free.*

At the **Old North Bridge,** half a mile from Concord's center, the tables were turned on the British on the morning of April 19, 1775, by the Concord minutemen. Daniel Chester French's famous statue of The Minuteman (1875) honors the country's first freedom fighters.

Minute Man National Historical Park Visitor Center is part of the 800-acre Minute Man National Historical Park that extends into Lexington, Concord, and Lincoln. The center's exhibits and film focus on the Revolutionary War. ✉ *Rte. 2A, ½ mi west of Rte. 128,* ☎ *781/862–7753.*

The 19th-century essayist and poet Ralph Waldo Emerson lived in the **Ralph Waldo Emerson House.** ✉ *28 Cambridge Turnpike, on Rte. 2A,* ☎ *978/369–2236.* 🎫 *$4.50. Closed Nov.–mid-Apr.*

The **Concord Museum** has Emerson and Thoreau artifacts and one of the two lanterns hung at the Old North Church the night of April 18, 1775. ✉ *200 Lexington Rd. (Route 2A),* ☎ *978/369–9763.* 🎫 *$6.*

Louisa May Alcott's family home, **Orchard House,** is where the author wrote *Little Women.* ✉ *399 Lexington Rd.,* ☎ *978/369–4118.* 🎫 *$5.50. Closed Jan. 1–15.*

Nathaniel Hawthorne and Ralph Waldo Emerson both lived at the **Old Manse** but at different times. ✉ *Monument St.,* ☎ *978/369–3909.* 🎫 *$5. Closed Nov.–mid-Apr.*

Nathaniel Hawthorne also lived at **the Wayside.** ✉ *455 Lexington Rd. (Rte. 2A),* ☎ *508/369–6975.* 🎫 *$4. Closed Nov.–mid-Apr.*

Walden Pond is Henry David Thoreau's most famous residence. Thoreau published *Walden* (1854), a collection of essays on observations he made while living at this cabin in the woods. The site of that first cabin is staked out in stone. An authentically furnished full-size replica stands about a half mile from the original site, near the parking lot for the Walden Pond State Reservation. You can swim and hike here. ✉ *Rte. 126,* ☎ *508/369–3254.* 🎫 *Free; parking across from pond is $2 per vehicle.*

Side Trip to the South Shore

Southeastern Massachusetts between Boston and the Cape is a region with strong historical associations.

Arriving and Departing

The most direct way to Fall River and New Bedford (themselves connected by I–195) is via Route 24, about a 45-minute drive; I–93 and Route 3 connect Boston with Plymouth, which is about an hour's drive. From Boston **MBTA** buses (☎ 617/722–3200) serve both Quincy and Braintree. **American Eagle** (☎ 508/993–5040) serves New Bedford. **Bonanza** (☎ 617/720–4110) serves Fall River. **Plymouth & Brockton Street Railway** buses (☎ 508/746–0378) call at Plymouth en route to Cape Cod.

What to See and Do

★ The **Plimoth Plantation** living history museum (✉ Warren Ave./Rte. 3A, ☎ 508/746–1622; 🎫 $18.50 [includes entry to Mayflower II]; Plantation only: $15) re-creates the Pilgrims' 1627 village; it's closed December–March. At the waterfront is the ***Mayflower II,*** (☎ 508/746–1622; 🎫 $5.75 or as part of Plimoth Plantation fee) a replica of the ship that brought the Pilgrims from England. Nearby is **Plymouth Rock,** believed to be the very spot on which the Pilgrims first set foot in 1620 after unsuccessfully scouting the Provincetown area as a potential settlement.

Side Trip to the North Shore

The beautiful North Shore extends from the northern suburbs to the Cape Ann region and beyond to the New Hampshire border.

Visitor Information

North of Boston Visitors and Convention Bureau (✉ Box 642, 248 Cabot St., Beverly 01915, ☏ 978/921–4990 or 800/742–5306).

Arriving and Departing

It's about 40 mi from Boston to Gloucester. The primary link between Boston and the North Shore is I–93 north to Route 128E, which then follows the line of the coast as far north as Gloucester. The more scenic route is along coastal Route 1A (which leaves Boston via the Callahan Tunnel) to Route 127.

What to See and Do

Picture-perfect **Marblehead** saunters along the coast, decorated with ancient clapboard houses lined up along narrow, winding streets, impressing neighbors and visitors with their annual window-box competition. **Salem** thrives on a history of witches, millionaires, and maritime trade. **Rockport** brims with crafts shops, galleries and artists' studios. **Gloucester** is the oldest seaport in America. **Newburyport** has a gorgeous redbrick center and rows of clapboard Federal mansions. **Crane Beach** (✉ 290 Argilla Rd., Ipswich, ☏ 978/356–4354) and **Parker River Wildlife Refuge** (✉ Plum Island, Newburyport, ☏ 978/465–5753) are two undeveloped beach sanctuaries. **Newburyport Whale Watch** (☏ 978/465–9885 or 800/848–1111) takes to the high seas. **Cape Ann Whale Watch** (✉ 415 Main St., Gloucester, ☏ 978/283–5110 or 800/877–5110) is another option. The ***Thomas E. Lannon*** (☏ 978/281–6634) schooner takes guests for ocean sails. The **Essex River Cruises** (✉ 35 Dodge St., Essex Marina, ☏ 978/768–6981 or 800/748–3706) heads for tamer waters.

CAPE COD AND THE ISLANDS

Separated from the mainland by the 17½-mi-long Cape Cod Canal, the Cape curves 70 mi from end to end. Every summer crowds are attracted to its charming villages of weathered-shingle houses and white-steepled churches and to its natural beauty of pinewoods, grassy marshes, and beaches backed by rolling dunes. To the south, Martha's Vineyard and Nantucket are resort islands ringed with beautiful sandy beaches; Nantucket preserves a near-pristine whaling-era town.

Visitor Information

Cape Cod: Chamber of Commerce (✉ Rtes. 6 and 132, Hyannis 02601, ☏ 508/362–3225 or 800/332–2732). **Martha's Vineyard:** Chamber of Commerce (✉ Box 1698, Beach Rd., Vineyard Haven 02568, ☏ 508/693–0085). **Nantucket:** Chamber of Commerce (✉ Pacific Club, 48 Main St., Nantucket 02554, ☏ 508/228–1700).

Arriving and Departing

By Bus

Bonanza Bus Lines (☏ 508/548–7588 or 800/556–3815) operates direct service to Bourne, Falmouth, and Woods Hole from Boston and Providence. **Plymouth & Brockton Street Railway** (☏ 508/775–5524 or 508/746–0378) travels to Provincetown from Boston and Logan Airport.

By Car

From Boston take I–93 to Route 3 to the Sagamore Bridge. From New York take I–95 to Providence; change to I–195 and follow signs to the Cape.

By Ferry

Ferries connect Martha's Vineyard and Nantucket to the mainland from Woods Hole, Hyannis, Falmouth, and New Bedford. The **Steamship Authority** (☎ 508/477–8600), **Hy-Line Cruises** (☎ 508/778–2600), and the ***Island Queen*** (☎ 508/548–4800), serve Martha's Vineyard; the **Steamship Authority** and **Hy-Line** serve Nantucket.

By Plane

Hyannis's **Barnstable Municipal Airport** is Cape Cod's air gateway, with flights from **Business Express/Delta Connection** (☎ 800/345–3400), **Cape Air** (☎ 800/352–0714), **Nantucket Airlines** (☎ 508/228–6252 or 800/635–8787 in MA), and **Northwest Airlink** (☎ 800/225–2525). **Provincetown Municipal Airport** is served by **Cape Air.**

Exploring Cape Cod and the Islands

U.S. 6 traverses the relatively unpopulated center of the Cape. Paralleling U.S. 6 but following the north coast is Route 6A, which passes through some of the Cape's old but well-preserved New England towns. The south shore, encompassing Falmouth, Hyannis, and Chatham and traced by Route 28, is heavily populated and the major center for tourism. The sparse outer portion of the Cape, from Orleans to Provincetown, is edged with white-sand beaches and nature preserves. At the Cape's southwestern corner is **Woods Hole,** an international center for marine research. The **Woods Hole Oceanographic Institute Exhibit Center** (✉ 15 School St., ☎ 508/289–2663; 🎫 $2) is a good place ★ to learn about oceans and oceanography. The 16 tanks at the **National Marine Fisheries Service Aquarium** (✉ Albatross and Water Sts., ☎ 508/495–2267; 🎫 free) contain regional fish and shellfish. The aquarium is closed on weekends from mid-September to late June.

The village green in **Falmouth** was a military training field in the 18th century and is today flanked by Colonial homes, fine inns, and an 1856 Congregational church with a bell made by Paul Revere. The **Falmouth Historical Society** (✉ Palmer Ave. at the Village Green, ☎ 508/548–4857; 🎫 $3) maintains two museums (open only on weekday summer afternoons) and conducts free walking tours in season.

Quietly wealthy **Hyannis Port** is the site of the Kennedy family compound. **Hyannis** is the Cape's year-round commercial hub. The **John F. Kennedy Memorial Museum** (☎ 508/775–2201; 🎫 $3) has photographs and videos from the presidential years focusing on John F. Kennedy's ties to the Cape. It's in the Old Town Hall on busy Main Street.

At the southeastern tip of Cape Cod, **Chatham** is a seaside town relatively free of the development and commercialism found elsewhere, though it offers a downtown of traditional shops and fine inns. The view from **Chatham Lighthouse** is spectacular. Off the coast is **Monomoy National Wildlife Refuge** (Headquarters: ✉ Morris Island, Chatham, ☎ 508/945–0594), a 2,750-acre preserve including Monomoy Island, which provides nesting grounds for 285 species of birds and waterfowl.

Sandwich, the oldest town on the Cape, was founded in 1637. Centered by a pond with a waterwheel-powered gristmill, this picturesque town remains famous for the colored glass produced here in the 19th century.

Cape Cod

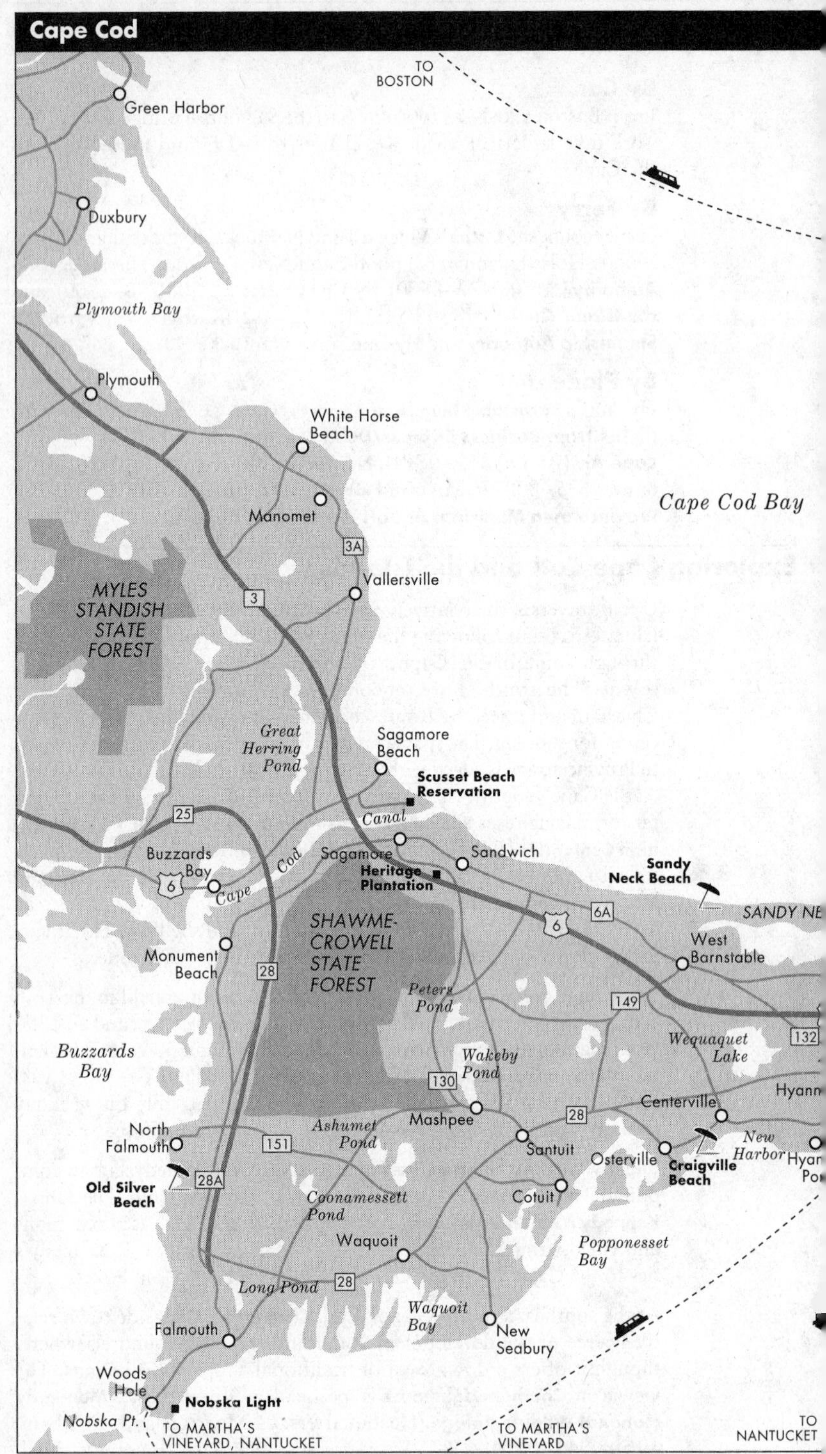
TO BOSTON
Green Harbor
Duxbury
Plymouth Bay
Plymouth
White Horse Beach
Manomet
3A
Cape Cod Bay
Vallersville
3
MYLES STANDISH STATE FOREST
Great Herring Pond
Sagamore Beach
Scusset Beach Reservation
25
Canal
Buzzards Bay
6
Cape
Cod
Sagamore
Heritage Plantation
Sandwich
Sandy Neck Beach
SANDY NE
6A
SHAWME-CROWELL STATE FOREST
Monument Beach
28
West Barnstable
Peters Pond
149
Wequaquet Lake
132
Buzzards Bay
Wakeby Pond
130
Hyann
Centerville
28
Mashpee
North Falmouth
151
Ashumet Pond
Santuit
Osterville
New Harbor
Hyan
Po
Craigville Beach
Old Silver Beach
28A
Coonamessett Pond
Cotuit
Popponesset Bay
Waquoit
Long Pond
28
Waquoit Bay
New Seabury
Falmouth
Woods Hole
Nobska Light
Nobska Pt.
TO MARTHA'S VINEYARD, NANTUCKET
TO MARTHA'S VINEYARD
TO NANTUCKET

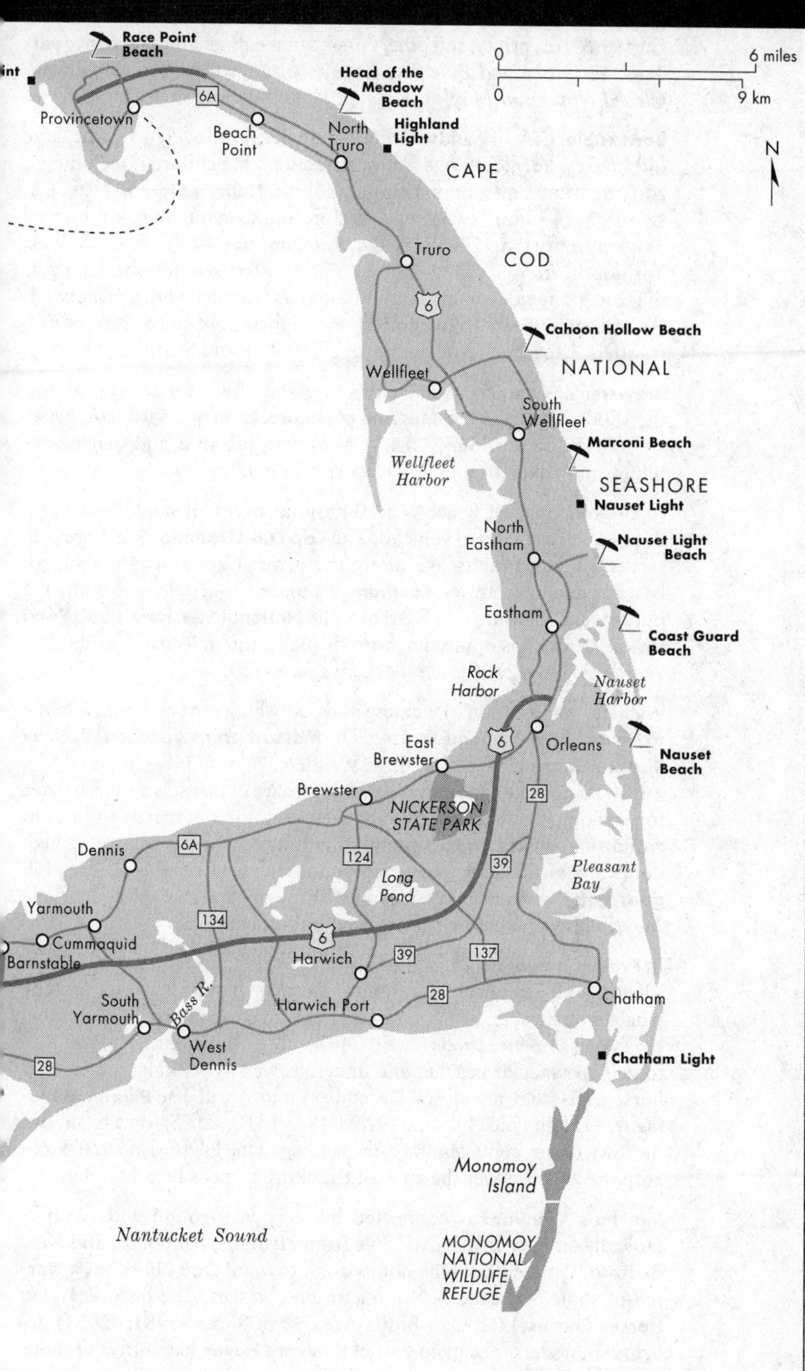

Race Point Beach
int
Provincetown
6A
Beach Point
Head of the Meadow Beach
North Truro
Highland Light
CAPE
COD
NATIONAL
SEASHORE
Truro
6
Cahoon Hollow Beach
Wellfleet
South Wellfleet
Marconi Beach
Wellfleet Harbor
Nauset Light
North Eastham
Nauset Light Beach
Eastham
Coast Guard Beach
Rock Harbor
Nauset Harbor
Orleans
Nauset Beach
East Brewster
Brewster
NICKERSON STATE PARK
28
Dennis
124
39
Pleasant Bay
Long Pond
Yarmouth
Cummaquid
Barnstable
134
137
Harwich
Harwich Port
Chatham
South Yarmouth
Bass R.
West Dennis
Chatham Light
Monomoy Island
Nantucket Sound
MONOMOY NATIONAL WILDLIFE REFUGE
0
6 miles
9 km
N

Off Route 130 is **Heritage Plantation,** a complex of museum buildings displaying classic and historic cars, antique military-related items, Currier & Ives prints, and other Americana—all set amid extensive gardens. ✉ *Grove and Pine Sts., Sandwich,* ☎ *508/888–3300.* *$8. Closed Nov.–mid-May.*

Barnstable, east of Sandwich on Route 6A, is a lovely town of large old houses. **Yarmouth** has a few attractions for children, including a zoo-aquarium and a miniature golf course. **Hallet's Store** (✉ Rte. 6A, ☎ 508/362–3362), a working drugstore and soda fountain, is preserved as it was more than 100 years ago. **ZooQuarium** (✉ 674 Rte. 28, West Yarmouth, ☎ 508/775–8883; $7.50) offers sea lion shows, a petting zoo, pony rides, and aquariums. **Dennis** is a town with a great beach (West Dennis Beach). **Scargo Hill,** the highest spot in the area at 160 ft, offers a spectacular view of Cape Cod Bay and Scargo Lake.

Brewster has numerous mansions originally built for sea captains in the 1800s. The **Cape Cod Museum of Natural History** (✉ Rte. 6A, Brewster, ☎ 508/896–3867; $5) has environmental and marine exhibits, and trails through 80 acres rich in wildlife.

In **Orleans,** Nauset Beach is a 10-mi-long sweep of sandy beach and ★ dunes open to off-road vehicles. The **Cape Cod National Seashore** preserves 30 mi of landscape along the lower Cape, including superb beaches and lighthouses. **Eastham** is a place for people who enjoy the outdoors. Off Route 6 in Eastham, the **National Seashore's Salt Pond Visitor Center** has a museum with displays, tours, lectures, and films. ☎ *508/255–3421. Closed weekdays Jan.–Feb.*

Wellfleet was a Colonial whaling and codfishing port and is now home ★ to fishermen, artists, and artisans. The **Massachusetts Audubon Wellfleet Bay Sanctuary** (✉ Off Rte. 6., S. Wellfleet, ☎ 508/349–2615; $3), a 1,000-acre haven for more than 250 species of birds, is a superb place for walking, birding, and looking west over the salt marsh and bay at wondrous sunsets. **Truro** is popular with writers and artists for its high dunes and virtual lack of development. At the National Seashore's **Pilgrim Heights Area,** trails meander through terrain explored by the *Mayflower* crew before they moved on to Plymouth.

In **Provincetown,** which is filled with first-rate shops and galleries, Portuguese and American fishermen mix with painters, poets, writers, whale-watchers, and a large gay and lesbian community. The National Seashore's **Province Lands** (☎ 508/487–1256) allow access to Provincetown's spectacular beaches and dunes, as well as walking, biking, and horse trails; they are closed December–mid-April. The **Pilgrim Monument** (✉ High Pole Hill Rd., ☎ 508/487–1310; $5), on a hill above the town center, commemorates the landing of the Pilgrims in 1620. From atop the 252-ft tower the view of the entire Cape is breathtaking.

Martha's Vineyard is connected by ferry year-round with Wood's Hole; in summer boats also leave from Hyannis, Falmouth, and New Bedford. On the island the honky-tonk town of **Oak Bluffs** has a warren of some 300 candy-color Victorian cottages. The historic **Flying Horses Carousel** (✉ Oak Bluffs Ave., ☎ 508/693–9481; $1) delights youngsters. The main port of **Vineyard Haven** has a street of shops and a backstreet preserved to reflect the way it appeared in whaling days. Tidy **Edgartown** has upscale boutiques, elegant sea-captains' houses, and beautiful flower gardens. **Chappaquiddick Island,** laced with nature preserves, is accessible by ferry from Edgartown. The dramatically striated red-clay **Gay Head Cliffs,** a major tourist sight, stand in a Wampanoag Indian township on the island's western tip.

Nantucket, 30 mi out in the open Atlantic Ocean, is accessible by ferry from Hyannis. Most of the 42-square-mi island is covered with moors that are scented with bayberry, wild roses, and cranberries; ringing it are miles of clean, white-sand beaches. **Nantucket town,** an exquisitely preserved National Historic District, encapsulates the island's whaling past in more than a dozen historical museums along its cobblestone streets. The beach community of **Siasconset** began as an actors' colony and today offers an unhurried lifestyle in beautiful surroundings; tiny rose-covered cottages and white-clamshell drives abound.

Dining and Lodging

On Martha's Vineyard only Edgartown and Oak Bluffs allow the sale of liquor. For summer, lodgings should be booked as far in advance as possible. **DestINNations** (☎ 508/428–5600 or 800/333–4667) and **Martha's Vineyard and Nantucket Reservations** (☎ 508/693–7200, 800/649–5671 in Massachusetts) are two reservations services.

For price ranges *see* Charts 1 (A) and 2 (A) *in* On the Road with Fodor's.

Brewster

$$$$ ★ ✕ **Chillingsworth.** This crown jewel of Cape restaurants is extremely formal, terribly pricey, and outstanding in every upscale way. The classic French menu and wine cellar continue to win award after award. Recent favorites have been a super-rich risotto, roast lobster, and grilled venison. At dinner, a more modest bistro menu is served in the Garden Room. ✉ *2449 Main St., Rte. 6A,* ☎ *508/896–3640. Reservations essential. AE, DC, MC, V. Closed Mon. mid-June–Thanksgiving; closed some weekdays Memorial Day–mid-June and mid-Oct.–Thanksgiving; closed entirely Thanksgiving–Memorial Day.*

$$$–$$$$ ★ 🏨 **Captain Freeman Inn.** The opulent details at this 1866 Victorian include a marble fireplace, herringbone-inlay flooring, ornate Italian ceiling medallions, and 12-ft ceilings. Guest rooms have hardwood floors, antiques, and eyelet spreads. ✉ *15 Breakwater Rd., 02631,* ☎ *508/896–7481 or 800/843–4664,* FAX *508/896–5618. 12 rooms, 9 with bath. Pool. Full breakfast. AE, MC, V. No smoking.*

Chatham

$$–$$$ ★ ✕ **Vining's Bistro.** The wood grill, where the chef employs zesty spices from all over the globe, is the center of attention here. Spit-roasted Jamaican chicken and the Portobello mushroom sandwich are the restaurant's signature dishes. ✉ *595 Main St.,* ☎ *508/945–5033. Reservations not accepted. AE, D, MC, V. Closed mid-Jan.–Apr.*

$$ ★ ✕ **Chatham Squire.** What was a bar scene and not much more has evolved into an excellent dining experience. The fish is as good as it gets, and the kitchen continues to innovate without forgetting its Cape roots. ✉ *487 Main St.,* ☎ *508/945–0945. Reservations not accepted. AE, D. MC, V.*

$$$–$$$$ ★ 🏨 **Captain's House Inn.** Fine architectural details, superb taste in decorating, opulent home-baked goods, and a feeling of quiet comfort are part of what makes this inn one of the Cape's finest. Rooms in the four buildings have their own personalities—some are lacy and feminine, others refined and elegant. ✉ *371 Old Harbor Rd., 02633,* ☎ *508/945–0127,* FAX *508/945–0866. 19 rooms. Full breakfast. AE, MC, V. No smoking.*

Falmouth

$$$ ★ 🏨 **Mostly Hall.** Set in a landscaped yard, this imposing 1849 house has a wraparound porch and a cupola. Corner rooms have leafy views, reading areas, antique pieces, and reproduction canopy beds. ✉ *27 Main*

St., 02540, ☎ 508/548–3786 or 800/682–0565. 6 rooms. Full breakfast. AE, D, MC, V. Closed Jan.

Hyannis

$$–$$$ ★ ✕ **Roadhouse Café.** Candlelight flickers off the white linen tablecloths and dark wood wainscoting at this stylish café. The calamari appetizer is a chef's favorite, the codfish chowder a hit with locals. In the more casual bistro and the handsome mahogany bar, you can order from a lighter menu of pizzas and sandwiches. ✉ *488 South St., ☎ 508/775–2386. Reservations essential. AE, D, MC, V. No lunch.*

$$ ★ **Sea Breeze Inn.** The rooms at this cedar-shingle seaside B&B have antique or canopied beds and are decorated with well-chosen antiques. The nicest of the three detached cottages is the three-bedroom Rose Garden, which has two baths, a TV room, a fireplace, and a washer and dryer. ✉ *397 Sea St., 02601, ☎ 508/771–7213, FAX 508/862–0663. 14 rooms, 3 cottages. CP. AE, D, MC, V.*

Martha's Vineyard

$$$ ✕ **Black Dog Tavern.** This island landmark (widely known for its T-shirts and other merchandise) serves basic chowders, pastas, fish, and steak, as well as more elaborate dishes. Waiting for a table is something of a tradition. Locals love an early breakfast on the glassed-in porch overlooking the harbor. ✉ *Beach St. Ext., Vineyard Haven, ☎ 508/693–9223. Reservations not accepted. AE, D, MC, V. BYOB.*

$$$$ ★ ✕ **Charlotte Inn.** Come to this tasteful inn for an Edwardian fantasy, an escape in one of the luxurious suites in the Carriage or Coach houses, an utterly tranquil winter holiday with the island nearly to yourself, or a sumptuous prix-fixe meal at L'étoile. ✉ *27 S. Summer St., Edgartown, 02539, ☎ 508/627–4751, FAX 508/627–4652. 25 rooms. Restaurant. CP. AE, MC, V.*

$$$ ✕ **Inn at Blueberry Hill.** The restaurant at this secluded property on 56 acres is relaxed and elegant, and the chefs prepare fresh, innovative, healthful dishes. Shaker-inspired island-made furniture, handmade mattresses with all-cotton sheets and duvets, and fresh flowers decorate the rooms, which have a sparse but tasteful ambience. Some of the less expensive ones are on the small side. ✉ *R.R. 1, Box 309, 74 North Rd., Chilmark, 02535, ☎ 508/645–3322 or 800/356–3322, FAX 508/645–3799. 25 rooms, 1- to 3-room suites available. Pool, tennis court, exercise room. BP. AE, MC, V. Closed Dec.–Apr.*

$$–$$$ ✕ **Lambert's Cove Country Inn.** Rooms in the 1790 farmhouse of this secluded inn have light floral wallpapers and a sweet country feel. Rooms in outbuildings have screened porches or decks. The soft candlelight and excellent Continental cooking make the restaurant (reservations essential; BYOB) a destination for a special occasion. Especially good are the crisp-baked soft-shell crab appetizer and the grilled Muscovy duck breast on caramelized onions. ✉ *Off Lambert's Cove Rd., W. Tisbury;* ✉ *mailing address R.R. 1, Box 422, Vineyard Haven 02568, ☎ 508/693–2298, FAX 508/693–7890. 16 rooms. Restaurant, tennis court. Full breakfast. AE, MC, V.*

Nantucket

$$$$ ✕ **Chanticleer.** For more than 20 years, Anne and Jean-Charles Berruet have been serving superb French food in a formal country setting, complete with gorgeous clematis cascading down the weathered shingles. The food is unimpeachable and the desserts are profoundly rich. ✉ 9 *New St., Siasconset, ☎ 508/257–6231. Jacket. AE, MC, V. Closed Mon.*

$$$$ ✕ **Wauwinet.** Eight miles from town, this deluxe establishment has rooms decorated in country style with pine antiques and fine furnishings; some have rooms spectacular views of the ocean. The sophisti-

cated restaurant specializes in fresh seafood. ✉ *Box 2580, Wauwinet Rd., 02584,* ☎ *508/228–0145 or 800/426–8718,* FAX *508/228–7135. 25 rooms, 5 cottages. Restaurant, 2 tennis courts. Full breakfast. AE, DC, MC, V. Closed Nov.–Apr.*

$$$–$$$$ ★ ✕🏨 **Harbor House.** This family-oriented complex, a sibling to the fancy White Elephant, prides itself on its service. Standard rooms are done in English-country style, with bright floral fabrics and queen-size beds. All rooms have phones and TVs. The hotel's restaurant serves simple New England fare—there's a three-course early-bird "sunset special" between 5 and 6:30—and hosts a lavish Sunday brunch buffet (reservations essential). ✉ *Box 1139, S. Beach St., Nantucket Town, 02554,* ☎ *508/228–1500, 800/475–2637 for reservations;* FAX *508/228–7197. 113 rooms. Restaurant. AE, D, DC, MC, V. Closed mid-Dec.–mid-Apr.*

Provincetown

$$–$$$ ★ ✕ **Bubala's by the Bay.** Personality abounds at this restaurant inside a building painted bright yellow and adorned with campy carved birds. The kitchen serves three meals, with many vegetarian offerings and lots of local seafood. The wine list is priced practically at retail. The bar scene picks up in the evening. ✉ *183 Commercial St.,* ☎ *508/487–0773. AE, D, MC, V. Closed Nov.–Mar.*

$$–$$$ ★ ✕ **Café Edwige.** Delicious contemporary cuisine, friendly service, a homey setting—Café Edwige delivers night after night. Begin with a Maine crab cake or warm goat cheese on crostini, try lobster and Wellfleet scallops over pasta with a wild mushroom and tomato broth. Don't pass on the wonderful desserts. ✉ *333 Commercial St.,* ☎ *508/487–2008. AE, MC, V. Closed Nov.–May.*

$ ★ ✕ **Mojo's.** At Provincetown's fast-food institution, the tiniest of kitchens turns out everything from fresh-cut french fries to fried clams, tacos, and tofu burgers. How they crank it out so fast and so good is anybody's guess. ✉ *5 Ryder St. Ext.,* ☎ *508/487–3140. Reservations not accepted. No credit cards. Closed at some times mid-Oct.–early May.*

$$$–$$$$ ★ 🏨 **Hargood House.** This apartment complex on the water, ½ mi from the town center, is a great option for longer stays. Many of the units have decks and large water-view windows; all have full kitchens, modern baths, and phones. Rentals are mostly by the week in season; there's a two-night minimum in the off season. ✉ *493 Commercial St., 02657–2413,* ☎ FAX *508/487–9133. 19 apartments. AE, MC, V.*

$$–$$$$ 🏨 **The Masthead.** Hidden away in the quiet west end of Commercial Street, the Masthead is a charming cluster of shingled houses that overlook a lush lawn, a 450-ft-long boardwalk, and a private beach. Rooms, efficiencies, apartments, and cottages are among the lodging options. The cottages sleep seven. ✉ *Box 577, 31–41 Commercial St., 02657,* ☎ *508/487–0523 or 800/395–5095,* FAX *508/487–9251. 7 apartments, 3 cottages, 2 efficiencies, 9 rooms. AE, D, DC, MC, V.*

$–$$ 🏨 **The Meadows.** At the far west end of Bradford Street between the town center and the beach, the Meadows is a good value, especially for families. The property is well maintained and nicely landscaped. Rooms are bright and comfortable. ✉ *Bradford St. Ext., 02657,* ☎ *508/487–0880. 20 rooms. MC, V.*

Campgrounds

⛺ **Nickerson State Park** (✉ Rte. 6A, Brewster 02631, ☎ 508/896–3491 or 508/896–4615 for camping reservations), 418 sites, boating, biking, cross-country skiing (☞ National and State Parks, *above*). ⛺ **Shawme–Crowell State Forest** (✉ Rte. 130, Sandwich 02563, ☎ 508/888–0351), 280 sites, beach.

Nightlife and the Arts

Nightlife

Hyannis has many nightclubs and bars featuring live rock and jazz (☎ 508/394–5277 Jazz Hot Line). Circuit Avenue in **Oak Bluffs** has rowdy bars and a year-round dance club. **Nantucket town** offers rock clubs, as well as restaurants with sedate piano bars.

The Arts

The **Cape Playhouse** (⊠ Rte. 6A, Dennis, ☎ 508/385–3911) and the **Wellfleet Harbor Actors Theater** (⊠ W.H.A.T. box office: Main St., Wellfleet, ☎ 508/349–6835) present summer stock. The **Vineyard Playhouse** (⊠ 10 Church St., Vineyard Haven, ☎ 508/693–6450) hosts Equity productions and community theater year-round. **Actor's Theatre of Nantucket** (⊠ Methodist Church, Centre and Main Sts., ☎ 508/228–6325) presents several Broadway-style plays each summer.

Outdoor Activities and Sports

Biking

Cape Cod Rail Trail, a 20-mi paved railroad right-of-way from Dennis to Wellfleet, is the Cape's premier bike path. On either side of the **Cape Cod Canal** is an easy 7-mi straight trail. The **Cape Cod National Seashore and Nickerson State Park** also maintain bicycle trails. On **Martha's Vineyard,** scenic well-paved paths follow the coast from Oak Bluffs to Edgartown and inland from Vineyard Haven to South Beach; some connect with rougher trails that weave through the state forest. **Nantucket** has several miles-long bike paths that meander through the moorland. The more difficult, hilly trails have strategically placed benches and water fountains; an easier trail leads to Surfside Beach.

Fishing

Tuna, mako and blue sharks, bluefish, and bass are the main ocean catches. The necessary license to fish the Cape's freshwater ponds is available at tackle shops, such as **Eastman's Sport & Tackle** (⊠ 150 Main St., Falmouth, ☎ 508/548–6900) and **Truman's** (⊠ Rte. 28, West Yarmouth, ☎ 508/771–3470), which also rent gear. **Dick's Bait & Tackle** (⊠ New York Ave., Oak Bluffs, ☎ 508/693–7669), on Martha's Vineyard, and **Barry Thurston's Fishing Tackle** (⊠ Harbor Sq., ☎ 508/228–9595), on Nantucket, rent equipment and can point out the best fishing spots. Rental boats are available from **Cape Cod Boats** (⊠ Rte. 28 at Bass River Bridge, West Dennis, ☎ 508/394–9268), **Vineyard Boat Rentals** (⊠ Dockside Marketplace, Oak Bluffs Harbor, ☎ 508/693–8476), and **Nantucket Boat Rentals** (⊠ Slip 1, ☎ 508/325–1001).

Deep-sea fishing trips are operated by **Cap'n Bill & Cee Jay** (⊠ Macmillan Wharf, Provincetown, ☎ 508/487–4330 or 800/675–6723), **Hy-Line** (⊠ Ocean St. Dock, Hyannis, ☎ 508/790–0696), and **Patriot Party Boats** (⊠ Falmouth Harbor, ☎ 508/548–2626). On **Martha's Vineyard** the party boat ***Skipper*** (☎ 508/693–1238) leaves from Oak Bluffs Harbor. On **Nantucket** charters sail out of Straight Wharf.

Horseback Riding

To ride horseback try **Deer Meadow Riding Stables** (⊠ Rte. 137, East Harwich, ☎ 508/432–6580), **Haland Stables** (⊠ Rte. 28A, West Falmouth, ☎ 508/540–2552), **Nelson's Riding Stable** (⊠ 43 Race Pt. Rd., Provincetown, ☎ 508/487–1112), **Misty Meadows Horse Farm** (⊠ Old County Rd., West Tisbury, Martha's Vineyard, ☎ 508/693–1870), or **South Shore Stable** (⊠ Across from airport off Edgartown Rd., West Tisbury, Martha's Vineyard, ☎ 508/693–3770).

Water Sports

Arey's Pond Boat Yard (✉ Off Rte. 28, Orleans, ☎ 508/255–0994) has a sailing school. **Cape Water Sports** (☎ 508/432–7079) has locations on several beaches for sailboat, canoe, and other rentals and lessons. Lessons and rentals are also available at **Wind's Up!** (✉ Beach Rd., Vineyard Haven, ☎ 508/693–4252), on Martha's Vineyard, and at **Force 5 Water Sports** (✉ Jetties Beach, ☎ 508/228–5358; ✉ 37 Main St., ☎ 508/228–0700), on Nantucket.

Whale-Watching

The proximity of the Cape to the whales' feeding grounds at Stellwagen Bank (about 6 mi off the tip of Provincetown) affords the rare opportunity of spotting several species of whales, including minke, humpbacks, finbacks, and, occasionally, the endangered white whale. **Hyannis Whale Watcher Cruises** (✉ Millway, Barnstable, ☎ 508/362–6088 or 800/287–0374), ***Dolphin Fleet*** (✉ Macmillian Wharf, Provincetown, ☎ 508/349–1900 or 800/826–9300), and ***Ranger V*** (Ticket office: ✉ Bradford St., Provincetown, ☎ 508/487–3322 or 800/992–9333) operate whale-watching excursions. Naturalists accompany the two boats out of Provincetown.

Beaches

Beaches fronting on **Cape Cod Bay** generally have cold water and gentle waves. South-side beaches, on **Nantucket Sound,** have rolling surf ★ and are warmer. Open-ocean beaches on the **Cape Cod National Seashore** are cold, with serious surf. These beaches, backed by high dunes, are contiguous and have lifeguards and rest rooms. In summer parking lots can be full by 10 AM.

Shopping

Provincetown has many fine galleries. **Wellfleet** has emerged as a vibrant center for arts and crafts. There's a giant **flea market** (✉ U.S. 6, Eastham–Wellfleet town line, ☎ 508/349–2520) on weekends and Monday holidays from April to October, plus Wednesday and Thursday in July and August. **Cape Cod Mall** (✉ Rtes. 132 and 28, Hyannis, ☎ 508/771–0200) holds 90 shops.

On **Martha's Vineyard** there's only one department store, which is in Edgartown. **Edgartown,** the Vineyard's chief shopping town, has the best selection of antiques and crafts shops. The **West Tisbury Farmer's Market** (✉ State Rd., West Tisbury), open on Wednesday and Saturday in summer, is the largest in Massachusetts. **Nantucket**'s specialty is lightship baskets—expensive woven baskets, often decorated with scrimshaw or rosewood.

THE PIONEER VALLEY

The Pioneer Valley, a string of historic settlements along the Connecticut River from Springfield in the south up to the Vermont border, formed the western frontier of New England from the early 1600s until the late 18th century. The northern regions of the Pioneer Valley remain rural and tranquil; farms and small towns have typical New England architecture. Farther south, the cities of Holyoke and Springfield are more industrial. Educational pioneers came to this region as well—to form major colleges and some well-known prep schools.

Visitor Information

The **Greater Springfield Convention and Visitors Bureau** (✉ 34 Boland Way, Springfield 01103, ☎ 413/787–1548).

Arriving and Departing

I–91 runs north–south the entire length of the Pioneer Valley, from Greenfield to Springfield; I–90 links Springfield to Boston; and Route 2 connects Boston with Greenfield in the north. Amtrak stops in Springfield on routes from Boston and New York.

What to See and Do

Four museums have set up shop near downtown Springfield at the **museum quadrangle** (✉ State and Chestnut Sts.). There's a Dr. Seuss exhibit at the **Connecticut Valley Historical Museum** (☎ 413/263–6895), which surveys the history of the Pioneer Valley. The **George Walter Vincent Smith Art Museum** (☎ 413/263–6894) contains Japanese armor, ceramics, and textiles and a gallery of American paintings. The **Museum of Fine Arts** (☎ 413/263–6800) has paintings by Gauguin, Renoir, Degas, and Monet, as well as 18th-century American paintings and contemporary works. The **Springfield Science Museum** (☎ 413/263–6875) has an "Exploration Center" of touchable displays, a planetarium, and dinosaur exhibits. *$4 pass valid for all museums. Wed.–Sun. noon–4.*

The large **Riverside Park,** outside Springfield, has a giant roller coaster and picnic facilities. The admission price—$16.99 for kids under 4 ft tall—includes entry to a new water theme park. *✉ 1623 Main St., Agawam, ☎ 413/786–9300 or 800/370–7488. $24.99. Closed Nov.–Apr. and weekdays Apr.–Memorial Day and Labor Day–Oct.*

Deerfield in the north has many historic buildings and is the site of the
★ prestigious Deerfield Academy. **The Street** (✉ Rte. 5, ☎ 413/774–5581; $10 pass for all houses, $5 for single house) is a tree-lined avenue of 18th- and 19th-century Deerfield homes maintained as a museum site; 14 of the preserved buildings are open to the public year-round. In **Amherst** are three of the valley's five major colleges—the University of Massachusetts, Amherst College, and Hampshire College. The **Emily Dickinson Homestead** (✉ 280 Main St., ☎ 413/542–8161; $3) is also here (house viewed by tour only); the homestead is closed from mid-December to March. **Northampton,** the site of Smith College, was home to the 30th U.S. president, Calvin Coolidge. The village of **South Hadley** is best known for Mount Holyoke, founded in 1837 as the country's first women's college.

★ East of the southern end of the valley is **Old Sturbridge Village,** a living, working model of an early 1800s New England town, with more than 40 buildings on a 200-acre site. *✉ 1 Old Sturbridge Village Rd., Sturbridge, ☎ 508/347–3362. $15.*

Dining and Lodging

Amherst

$$$ ✕ **Lord Jeffery Inn.** Many bedrooms at this gabled brick inn have a light floral decor; others have stencils and pastel woodwork. The formal dining room, where traditional dishes are served, is collegiate and colonial, with old wood panels, heavy drapery, and a large fireplace. Burgers, salads, and the like are served at Boltwood's Tavern, which has a small bar and a wraparound porch. *✉ 30 Boltwood Ave., 01002,*

☎ *413/253–2576,* FAX *413/256–6152. 40 rooms, 8 suites. Restaurant. AE, DC, MC, V.*

$$–$$$$ ★ **Allen House.** Busy, colorful wall coverings reach to the high ceilings of this restored inn. Antiques include a burled walnut bedhead and dresser set, wicker "steamship" chairs, screens, and carved golden-oak beds. Lace curtains grace the windows in the rooms, whose supremely comfortable beds have goose down comforters. Allen House is a short walk from the center of Amherst. ✉ *599 Main St., 01002,* ☎ *413/253–5000. 7 rooms. Full breakfast. AE, MC, V.*

Deerfield

$$$–$$$$ ★ ✕ **Sienna.** The atmosphere at Sienna is soothing and the service well mannered, but the food is what really shines. Choices from the ever-changing menu might include an appetizer of smoked-salmon samosas on a champagne beurre and entrées like tuna loin on a light stir-fry of zucchini, fennel, and gnocchi with a mustard sauce. ✉ *6 Elm St., S. Deerfield,* ☎ *413/665–0215. Reservations essential. MC, V. Closed Mon.–Tues. No lunch.*

$$$–$$$$ ★ ✕ **Deerfield Inn.** Period wallpapers decorate the rooms in the main inn, which was built in 1884; the rooms in an outbuilding have identical papers but are newer (1981) and closer to the parking lot. All rooms have antiques and replicas, sofas, and bureaus. Venison and rack of lamb with Dijon mustard and garlic are among the dishes served in the sunny dining room. ✉ *81 Old Main St., 01342,* ☎ *413/774–5587, 800/926–3865 outside MA;* FAX *413/773–8712. 23 rooms. Restaurant, coffee shop. Full breakfast. AE, DC, MC, V. No smoking.*

$$ ✕ **Whately Inn.** Antiques and four-poster beds slope gently on old-wood floors at the Whately. The two rooms over the restaurant (no lunch) can be noisy, so avoid them. Cajun shrimp, baked lobster with shrimp stuffing, rack of lamb, and other entrées come with salad, appetizer, and dessert. ✉ *Chestnut Plain Rd., Whately Center 01093,* ☎ *413/665–3044 or 800/942–8359. 4 rooms. Restaurant. AE, D, DC, MC, V.*

Northfield

$$ ★ **Northfield Country House.** Truly remote, this big English manor house is amid thick woodlands on 16 acres. Rooms are decorated with antiques; several have brass beds. ✉ *181 School St., 01360,* ☎ *413/498–2692 or 800/498–2692. 7 rooms. Pool. Full breakfast. MC, V.*

Northampton

$$ ✕ **Paul and Elizabeth's.** Plants fill this high-ceiling natural-foods restaurant. Among the seasonal specials are butternut-squash soup, home-baked corn muffins and Indian pudding, a large salad platter, Japanese tempura, and innovative fish entrées. ✉ *150 Main St.,* ☎ *413/584–4832. AE, MC, V.*

THE BERKSHIRES

Though only about a 2½-hour drive west from Boston or north from New York City, the Berkshires live up to storybook images of rural New England, with wooded hills, narrow winding roads, and compact charming villages. Summer offers a variety of cultural events, not the least of which is the Tanglewood festival of classical music, in Lenox. Fall brings a blaze of brilliant foliage. In winter the Berkshires are a popular ski area. Springtime visitors can enjoy maple-sugaring. The region can be crowded any weekend.

Visitor Information

Mohawk Trail Association (✉ Box 722, Charlemont 01339, ☎ 413/664–6256). **Berkshire Visitors Bureau** (✉ Berkshire Common Plaza,

Pittsfield 01201, ☎ 413/443–9186 or 800/237–5747). **Lenox Chamber of Commerce** (✉ Lenox Academy Bldg., 75 Main St., 01240, ☎ 413/637–3646).

Arriving and Departing

By Bus

Peter Pan Bus Lines (☎ 413/442–4451 or 800/237–8747) serves Lee and Pittsfield from Boston and Albany. **Bonanza Bus Lines** (☎ 800/556–3815) connects the Berkshires with Albany, New York City, and Providence.

By Car

The Massachusetts Turnpike (I–90) connects Boston with Lee and Stockbridge. The scenic Mohawk Trail (Route 2) parallels the northern border of Massachusetts. To reach the Berkshires from New York City, take either the New York Thruway (I–87) or the Taconic State Parkway. Within the Berkshires the main north–south road is Route 7.

By Plane

The closest airports are in Boston (☞ *above*), Albany, and New York City (☞ New York), and Hartford (☞ Connecticut). Small airports in Pittsfield and Great Barrington serve private planes.

Exploring the Berkshires

Williamstown is the northernmost Berkshires town, at the junction of Route 2 and U.S. 7. **Williams College** opened here in 1793, and the town still revolves around it. Gracious campus buildings lining the wide main street are open to visitors.

The **Sterling and Francine Clark Art Institute** is an outstanding small museum, with paintings by Renoir, Monet, and Degas. ✉ *225 South St., Williamstown,* ☎ *413/458–9545.* 🎟 *Free. Closed Mon.*

The **Mohawk Trail,** a scenic 7-mi stretch of Route 2, follows a former Native American path east from Williamstown. **Mt. Greylock,** south of Williamstown off Route 7, is, at 3,491 ft, the highest point in the state. **Pittsfield,** county seat and geographic center of the region, has a lively small-town atmosphere. **Hancock Shaker Village,** 5 mi west of Pittsfield on Route 20, was founded in the 1790s as the third Shaker community in America. The religious community closed in 1960, and the site, complete with living quarters, round stone barn, and working crafts shops, is now a museum. ☎ *413/443–0188.* 🎟 *$10. Closed Dec.–Mar.*

The village of **Lenox,** 5 mi south of Pittsfield on Route 7, epitomizes the Berkshires for many visitors. In the thick of the summer-cottage region, it's rich with old inns and majestic mansions. Novelist Edith Wharton's mansion, the **Mount,** is a perfect example of a turn-of-the-century classical American mansion. ✉ *Plunkett St.,* ☎ *413/637–1899.* 🎟 *$6. Closed Nov.–late May.*

★ **Tanglewood** is summer headquarters of the Boston Symphony. Thousands flock to the 200-acre estate every summer weekend to picnic on the lawns as musicians perform on the open-air stage. (☞ The Arts *in* Nightlife and the Arts, *below*).

The touristy, archetypal New England small town of **Stockbridge** has a history of literary and artistic inhabitants, including painter Norman Rockwell and writers Norman Mailer and Robert Sherwood. The **Norman Rockwell Museum** (✉ Rte. 183, ☎ 413/298–4100; 🎟 $8) holds the world's largest collection of his original paintings.

Chesterwood was for 33 years the summer home of the sculptor Daniel Chester French, who created the Minute Man in Concord and the Lincoln Memorial in Washington, D.C. Tours are given of the house, which is maintained in the style of the 1920s, and of the studio, where one can see the casts and models French used to create the Lincoln Memorial. ✉ *Williamsville Rd. off Rte. 183,* ☎ *413/298–3579.* 🎫 *$6.50. Closed Oct.–May.*

Great Barrington is the largest town in the southern Berkshires and a mecca for antiques hunters. **Bartholomew's Cobble** (✉ Rte. 7A, ☎ 413/229–8600; 🎫 $3.50), south of Great Barrington, is a natural rock garden beside the Housatonic River (the Native American name means "river beyond the mountains"). The 277-acre site is filled with trees, ferns, wildflowers, and hiking trails. The visitor center has a museum.

Mt. Washington State Forest (✉ Rte. 23, ☎ 413/528–0330) is 16 mi southwest of Great Barrington on the New York State border. The free primitive camping area is open year-round, but there's a catch—you have to hike 1½ mi from the parking lot. The forest's Bash Bish Brook (say that 10 times, fast) flows through a gorge and over a 50-ft waterfall into a clear natural pool.

Dining and Lodging

Lodging rates may include full or Continental breakfast. For price ranges *see* Charts 1 (B) and 2 (B) *in* On the Road with Fodor's.

Lenox

$$–$$$ ✕ **Church St. Café.** Original art covers the walls, the tables are surrounded by ficus trees, and classical music wafts through the air at this café. The menu, which changes with the seasons, might include roast duck with thyme and Madeira sauce, rack of pork with wild mushrooms, and crab cakes. ✉ *69 Church St.,* ☎ *413/637–2745. MC, V. Closed Sun.–Mon., Nov.–Apr.*

$$$$ ★ 🏨 **Blantyre.** Modeled after a castle in Scotland, Blantyre is truly awe-inspiring, with massive public rooms and 88 acres of beautifully maintained grounds, including a croquet lawn where professional tournaments take place. Huge and lavishly decorated, the rooms in the main house have hand-carved four-poster beds, overstuffed chaise longues, chintz chairs, boudoirs, walk-in closets, and Victorian bathrooms. The rooms in the carriage house are well appointed but can't compete with the formal grandeur of the main house. ✉ *16 Blantyre Rd. off Rte. 20, 01240,* ☎ *413/298–3806,* FAX *413/637–4282. 23 rooms. Restaurant, pool, hot tub, sauna, tennis courts. CP. AE, DC, MC, V. Closed Nov.–May.*

$$ 🏨 **Eastover.** This resort was opened by an ex–circus roustabout. Noisy fun and informality reign. Accommodations include dormitory and motel-style rooms. There are loads of activities planned along with special weekends for couples, singles, and families. The resort is all-inclusive; many guests never leave the vast grounds. ✉ *Box 2160, 430 East St., off Rtes. 20 and 7, 01240,* ☎ *413/637–0625,* FAX *413/637–4939. 195 rooms. Dining room, indoor and outdoor pools, sauna, driving range, tennis courts, exercise room. AP. AE, D, DC, MC, V.*

South Egremont

$$$–$$$$ ✕🏨 **Egremont Inn.** The public rooms in this 1780 inn are enormous, and each has a fireplace. The bedrooms are on the small side, but have four-poster beds, claw-foot baths, and, like the rest of the inn, unpretentious furnishings that'll inspire you to kick back and relax. Windows sweep around two sides of the stylish restaurant (reservations essential weekends in season). The menu changes frequently, but always includes salmon or another fresh fish, a homemade pasta, and a hearty meat dish like rib-eye steak with caramelized onions. ✉ *Box 418, Old Sheffield Rd., 01258,* ☎ *413/528–2111,* FAX *413/528–3284. 19 rooms, 1 suite. Restaurant, pool, tennis courts. CP. AE, D, MC, V. 2-night minimum in season.*

Stockbridge Area

$$$–$$$$ ✕ 🏨 **Red Lion Inn.** An inn since 1773, the Red Lion has a large main building and seven annexes. The rooms in the annex houses tend to be more appealing. All the rooms are furnished with antiques and reproductions and hung with Rockwell prints; some have Oriental rugs. The same menu is served in both dining rooms and (in season) in the garden. New England specialties include clam chowder; broiled scallops prepared with sherry, lemon, and paprika; and steamed or stuffed lobster. ✉ *Main St., 02162,* ☎ *413/298–5545,* FAX *413/298–5130. 122 rooms with bath, 15 rooms share 5 baths. 2 restaurants, pool, exercise room. AE, D, DC, MC, V.*

$$$–$$$$ ★ 🏨 **Historic Merrell Inn.** Meticulously maintained, the inn has an unfussy yet authentic style, with polished wide-board floors, painted walls, and wood antiques. ✉ *1565 Pleasant St./Rte. 102, South Lee 01260,* ☎ *413/243–1794 or 800/243–1794,* FAX *413/243–2669. 9 rooms, 1 suite. Full breakfast. MC, V.*

Williamstown

$$$ ✕ **Mezze Bistro.** Veal sweetbreads with artichoke hearts and radicchio, sautéed pork with roasted shallots, prosciutto over soft polenta, and oven-roasted fennel gazpacho are among the zesty offerings at this hip and happening place that hops late into the evening. ✉ *84 Water St.,* ☎ *413/458–0123. AE, MC, V. Closed Mon. Sept.–May. No lunch.*

$$$$ ★ 🏨 **Field Farm Guest House.** Built in 1948 on 296 acres, this house, which resembles a modern museum, was donated as part of a land trust by the former owners and is now run as a B&B by a nonprofit organization. Three rooms have private decks; two have working fireplaces with tiles depicting animals, birds, and butterflies. ✉ *554 Sloan Rd. (off Rte. 43), 01267,* ☎ *413/458–3135. 5 rooms. Dining room, pool, tennis courts. D, MC, V.*

Nightlife and the Arts

Listings appear daily in the *Berkshire Eagle* from June to Columbus Day. *Berkshires Week* is the summer bible for events listings. Weekly listings appear in the *Williamstown Advocate.* Major concerts are listed in the Thursday *Boston Globe.*

Nightlife

The most popular local nightspot is the **Lion's Den** (☎ 413/298–5545), at the Red Lion Inn in Stockbridge (☞ Dining and Lodging, *above*), with nightly folk music and some contemporary local bands.

The Arts

DANCE

Jacob's Pillow Dance Festival (✉ George Cantor Rd. at Rte. 20, Becket, ☎ 413/637–1322, 413/243–0745 for box office in summer) happens over 10 weeks each summer. The participants range from well-known classical ballet companies to Native American dance groups.

MUSIC

The **Berkshire Performing Arts Theater** (✉ 40 Kemble St., Lenox, ☎ 413/637–4718) attracts top-name artists in jazz, folk, rock, and blues each summer. The season at **Tanglewood** (☎ 617/266–1200 for a schedule; ☞ Exploring the Berkshires, *above*), where the Boston Symphony Orchestra (BSO) performs, runs from June to August.

THEATER

The **Berkshire Theatre Festival** (✉ Rte. 102, Box 797, Stockbridge 01262, ☎ 413/298–5536) stages nightly performances in summer at a century-old theater. The **Williamstown Theatre Festival** (✉ Adams Memorial Theatre, 1000 Main St., Box 517, Williamstown 01267, ☎ 413/597–3400) presents classics and contemporary works each summer.

Outdoor Activities and Sports

Biking

The back roads of Berkshire County can be hilly, but the views and the countryside are incomparable. **Main Street Sports and Leisure** (✉ 48 Main St., Lenox, ☎ 413/637–4407) rents mountain and road bikes and provides maps and route suggestions.

Boating

The **Housatonic River** flows south from Pittsfield between the Berkshire Hills and the Taconic Range toward Connecticut. **Main Street Sports and Leisure** (✉ 48 Main St., Lenox, ☎ 413/637–4407) rents canoes and leads canoe trips on the Housatonic and other local lakes.

Fishing

The area's rivers, lakes, and streams abound with bass, pike, perch, and trout. **Points North Fishing and Hunting Outfitters** (✉ Rte. 8, Adams, ☎ 413/743–4030) organizes summer fly-fishing schools.

Golf

Waubeeka Golf Links (✉ Rte. 7, Williamstown, ☎ 413/458–5869) and the **Cranwell Resort and Hotel** (✉ 55 Lee Rd., 02140, ☎ 413/637–1364 or 800/272–6935) have 18-hole courses open to the public.

Hiking

The **Appalachian Trail** goes through Berkshire County. Hiking is particularly rewarding in the higher elevations of **Mt. Greylock State Reservation** (☞ National and State Parks, *above*).

Ski Areas

Cross-Country

Brodie (✉ Rte. 7, New Ashford 01237, ☎ 413/443–4752). **Butternut Basin** (✉ Rte. 23, Great Barrington 01230, ☎ 413/528–2000).

Downhill

Berkshire East (✉ Box 727, S. River Rd., Charlemont 01339, ☎ 413/339–6617). **Bousquet Ski Area** (✉ Dan Fox Dr., Pittsfield 01201, ☎ 413/442–8316 or 413/442–2436). **Brodie** (☞ Cross-Country, *above*). **Butternut Basin** (☞ Cross-Country, *above*). **Jiminy Peak** (✉ Corey Rd., 01237, ☎ 413/738–5500; 413/738–7325 for snow conditions). **Otis Ridge Ski Area** (✉ Rte. 23, Otis, ☎ 413/269–4446).

Shopping

Antiques

There are antiques stores throughout the Berkshires, but the greatest concentration is around Great Barrington, South Egremont, and Sheffield. For a list of storekeepers who belong to the **Berkshire County Antiques Dealers Association** and guarantee the authenticity of their merchandise, send a self-addressed, stamped envelope to R.D. 1, Box 1, Sheffield 01257.

Outlet Stores

Along Route 7 north of Lenox are two factory-outlet malls, **Lenox House Country Shops** and **Brushwood Farms.**

NEW HAMPSHIRE

By Ed and Roon Frost

Updated by Paula J. Flanders

Capital	Concord
Population	1,173,000
Motto	Live Free or Die
State Bird	Purple finch
State Flower	Purple lilac
Postal Abbreviation	NH

Statewide Visitor Information

New Hampshire Office of Travel and Tourism Development (✉ Box 1856, Concord 03302, ☎ 603/271–2343 or 800/386–4664). **Ski/Foliage hot line** (☎ 800/258–3608).

Scenic Drives

The **Kancamagus Highway** (Route 112) rolls through 35 mi of the White Mountains between Lincoln and Conway. The 32-mi stretch of **Route 113** between Holderness and South Tamworth is full of hills and curves, and winds between mountains and plains. **Routes 12A and 12** parallel the Connecticut River along the Vermont border between Lebanon and Keene, with views of the river and the picturesque towns along the way.

National and State Parks

National Forest

The **White Mountain National Forest** (✉ U.S. Forest Service, 719 N. Main St., Laconia 03246, ☎ 603/528–8721; 🎫 $5 day-use fee, good for 7 consecutive days) occupies 790,000 acres of northern New Hampshire (☞ The White Mountains, *below*).

State Parks

The **Division of Parks and Recreation** (✉ Box 1856, Concord 03302, ☎ 603/271–3556) maintains about 70 state parks, beaches, and historic sites. Surrounded by privately held forests, **Monadnock State Park** (✉ Box 181, Jaffrey 03452, ☎ 603/532–8862) seems larger than its 5,000 acres.

THE SEACOAST

The southern end of New Hampshire's 18-mi coastline is dominated by Hampton Beach—5 mi of sand, sunbathers, motels, arcades, carryouts, and a boardwalk. At the northern end is Portsmouth, with its beautifully restored historic area, one-of-a-kind restaurants, and the state's only working port. In between are dunes, beaches, salt marshes, and state parks where you can picnic, hike, swim, boat, and fish.

Visitor Information

Greater Portsmouth Chamber of Commerce (✉ 500 Market St. Ext., Portsmouth 03801, ☎ 603/436–1118). **Hampton Beach Area Chamber of Commerce** (✉ 836 Lafayette Rd., Hampton 03842, ☎ 603/926–8717).

Arriving and Departing

By Bus

C&J (☎ 603/431–2424). **Concord Trailways** (☎ 800/639–3317). **Vermont Transit** (☎ 603/436–0163 or 800/451–3292).

By Car

I–95 provides access to the Hamptons (Exit 2), central Portsmouth (Exits 3–6), and Portsmouth harbor and historic district (Exit 7).

Exploring the Seacoast

The Atlantic is rarely out of sight from Route 1A, and there are plenty of spots for pulling over. In **North Hampton,** factory outlets coexist with mansions. Take a leisurely drive past what the wealthy refer to as cottages, on **Millionaire's Row.** In summer, stop to see the 2,000 rosebushes at **Fuller Gardens** (✉ 10 Willow Ave., ☎ 603/964–5414; 🎫 $4).

Rye has great beaches. **Odiorne Point State Park** (✉ Rte. 1A, ☎ 603/436–7406; 🎫 $2.50) has more than 350 acres of tidal pools and footpaths. The **Seacoast Science Center** (☎ 603/436–8043; 🎫 $1), in the park, has exhibits and an aquarium. From Rye Harbor inlet, **New Hampshire Seacoast Cruises** (☎ 603/964–5545 or 800/734–6488) makes whale-watching trips and trips to the Isles of Shoals, a Colonial fishing settlement.

★ Walkable **Portsmouth,** a city with a working port, is an easy day trip from Boston. The **Portsmouth Historical Society** (✉ 43 Middle St., ☎ 603/436–8420), housed in the **John Paul Jones House,** is one stop on a self-guided walking tour that includes six historic houses that are open to the public in summer.

Showcasing Portsmouth's architectural diversity is **Strawbery Banke,** a 10-acre village-museum whose 40 buildings date from 1695 to 1820. The gardens are splendid. ✉ *Marcy St.,* ☎ *603/433–1100 or 603/433–1101;* 🎫 *$12. Closed Nov.–mid-Apr., except Thanksgiving weekend and 1st 2 weekends in Dec.*

Historic **Prescott Park** has a formal garden and lively fountains. The **Sheafe Warehouse Museum** (☎ 603/433–1100; 🎫 free), within Prescott Park, is used by Strawbery Banke for demonstrations on shipbuilding and such. Kids will want to start with Portsmouth's lively hands-on **Children's Museum** (✉ 280 Marcy St., ☎ 603/436–3853; 🎫 $4). The **USS Albacore** (✉ 600 Market St., ☎ 603/436–3680; 🎫 $4), a vintage submarine, is another attraction that appeals to youngsters.

Dining and Lodging

Portsmouth shines in warm weather, when restaurants along Bow and Ceres streets open their decks for sea breezes and harbor views. Make summer lodging reservations well in advance. For price ranges *see* Charts 1 (A) and 2 (A) *in* On the Road with Fodor's.

Hampton

$$ **Victoria Inn.** Built as a carriage house in 1875, this romantic B&B is done in the style Victorians loved best: wicker, chandeliers, and lace. One room is completely lilac; the honeymoon suite has white eyelet coverlets and a private sunroom. ✉ *430 High St. (½ mi from Hampton Beach), 03842,* ☎ *603/929–1437. 6 rooms, 3 with bath. Full breakfast. MC, V.*

Hampton Beach

$$–$$$$ ✕ **Ron's Landing at Rocky Point.** This casually elegant restaurant serving fresh seafood and pasta has a second-floor porch that affords a sweeping ocean view. Try the filet mignon topped with fresh horseradish sauce, served with crab legs. ✉ *379 Ocean Blvd.,* ☎ *603/929–2122. AE, D, DC, MC, V.*

$$$ ✕🏨 **Ashworth by the Sea.** At this centrally located favorite of generations of beach goers, most rooms have decks. Some rooms have queen-size four-poster beds and glowing cherry-wood furnishings. ✉ *295 Ocean Blvd., 03842,* ☎ *603/926–6762 or 800/345–6736,* FAX *603/926–2002. 105 rooms. 3 restaurants, pool. AE, D, DC, MC, V.*

$$–$$$ ★ 🏨 **Oceanside Inn.** Inside this plain, square-front building is a hidden treasure. Carefully selected antiques and collectibles and individually decorated rooms with many amenities give the Oceanside the feel of a turn-of-the-century home. And should the nearby boardwalk's crush of people and noise become overwhelming, you'll appreciate the soundproofing that makes this B&B seem like a calm port in a storm. Off-street parking is a plus. ✉ *365 Ocean Blvd., 03842,* ☎ *603/926–3542,* FAX *603/926–3549. 10 rooms. AE, D, MC, V. Closed mid-Oct.–mid-May.*

Portsmouth

$$$ ✕ **Dunfey's Aboard the John Wanamaker.** Portsmouth's only floating restaurant, aboard an elegantly restored tugboat, offers such delicacies as shiitake-encrusted halibut with wild mushroom ravioli. The upper-level deck is a favorite on starry summer nights for light meals, a glass of wine, or dessert and cappuccino. ✉ *1 Harbour Pl., Suite 10,* ☎ *603/433–3111. AE, MC, V.*

$$–$$$ ★ ✕ **Porto Bello Ristorante Italiano.** In this second-story dining room overlooking the harbor, enjoy daily antipasti specials like grilled Portobello mushrooms and entrées such as spinach gnocchi and veal *carciofi*—a cutlet served with artichokes. ✉ *67 Bow St., 2nd floor,* ☎ *603/431–2989. AE, D, MC, V. Closed Mon.–Tues.*

$$ ✕ **Blue Mermaid World Grill.** The stately exterior of this 1810 house belies the hot Jamaican-style dishes that come from the wood-burning grill. The grilled Maine lobster with mango butter is a favorite. ✉ *The Hill,* ☎ *603/427–2583. AE, D, DC, MC, V.*

$$$ ✕🏨 **Sheraton Harborside Hotel.** Portsmouth's only luxury hotel has a nice harbor view and a central location. The main restaurant serves fresh seafood and American cuisine. The Krewe Orleans restaurant prepares Cajun specialties. ✉ *250 Market St., 03801,* ☎ *603/431–2300 or 800/325–3535,* FAX *603/433–5649. 181 rooms. 2 restaurants, bar, indoor pool, spa, exercise room. AE, D, DC, MC, V.*

$$–$$$ ★ 🏨 **Sise Inn.** This Queen Anne town house, full of chintz and gleaming armoires, is convenient for waterfront strolls. No two rooms are alike; some have whirlpool baths. ✉ *40 Court St., 03801,* ☎ FAX *603/433–1200,* ☎ *800/267–0525. 34 rooms. CP. AE, DC, MC, V.*

Nightlife and the Arts

Summer concerts draw crowds at the **Hampton Beach Casino Ballroom** (✉ 169 Ocean Beach Blvd., ☎ 603/926–4541). The 1878 **Music Hall** (✉ 28 Chestnut St., Portsmouth, ☎ 603/436–2400) hosts touring events and an ongoing film series. Catch jazz, folk, or blues at the **Press Room** (✉ 77 Daniel St., Portsmouth, ☎ 603/431–5186). The **Prescott Park Arts Festival** (✉ 105 Marcy St., ☎ 603/436–2848) kicks off with an Independence Day Pops concert and continues through Labor Day with music, dance, theater, and a showcase for regional artists.

Outdoor Activities and Sports

Boating and Fishing

Rentals and charters are available from **Atlantic Fishing Fleet** in Rye Harbor (☎ 603/964–5220). **Al Gauron Deep Sea Fishing** (☎ 603/926–2469) and **Smith & Gilmore** (☎ 603/926–3503) are in Hampton Beach.

Shopping

Portsmouth is chockablock with crafts shops, galleries, and clothing boutiques. Stop at the **North Hampton Factory Outlet Center** (✉ Rte. 1, ☎ 603/964–9050) for bargains.

THE LAKES REGION

The eastern half of central New Hampshire is scattered with beautifully preserved 18th- and 19th-century villages nestled among sparkling lakes—Winnipesaukee (Smile of the Great Spirit) is the largest—that echo with squeals and splashes all summer long.

Visitor Information

Greater Laconia Chamber of Commerce (✉ 11 Veterans Sq., Laconia 03246, ☎ 603/524–5531 or 800/531–2347). **Lakes Region Association** (✉ Box 589, Center Harbor 03226, ☎ 603/253–8555 or 800/605–2537). **Squam Lakes Area Chamber of Commerce** (✉ Box 65, Ashland 03217, ☎ 603/968–4494). **Wolfeboro Chamber of Commerce** (✉ Railroad Ave., Box 547-WT7, Wolfeboro 03894, ☎ 603/569–2200 or 800/516–5324).

Arriving and Departing

By Bus

Concord Trailways (☎ 603/228–3300, 800/639–3317 in New England) serves Laconia, Meredith, Center Harbor, and Moultonborough.

By Car

I–93 is the principal north–south artery. From the coast, Route 11 goes to southern Lake Winnipesaukee; en route to the White Mountains, north–south Route 16 accesses spurs to the lakes.

Exploring the Lakes Region

Alton Bay, at Winnipesaukee's southernmost tip, has the lake's cruise-boat docks and a Victorian bandstand. In affluent Colonial **Gilford** there's a large state beach. The **Gunstock Recreation Area** (✉ Rte. 11A, ☎ 603/293–4341 or 800/486–7862) has swimming, hiking, mountain biking, and camping. In honky-tonk **Weirs Beach,** fireworks light up summer nights. Here you can board **lake cruisers** (☎ 603/366–5531). The **Winnipesaukee Railroad** (☎ 603/279–5253; 🎫 $7.50 and up) carries passengers alongside the lake. **Amusement centers** like Funspot (☎ 603/366–4377), Surf Coaster (☎ 603/366–4991), and Water Slide (☎ 603/366–5161) line Route 3.

Commercial **Meredith,** on the north shore, has restaurants and shops. Kids will like the **Children's Museum and Shop** (✉ 28 Lang St., ☎ 603/279–1007; 🎫 $5). **Moultonborough** has a country store and several miles of lakeside shoreline. The 5,000-acre **Castle in the Clouds** estate (✉ Rte. 171, ☎ 603/476–2352 or 800/729–2468; 🎫 $10) is anchored by an odd and elaborate stone mansion built by an eccentric millionaire. At the **Loon Center** (✉ Lees Mills Rd., ☎ 603/476–5666; 🎫 free), run by the Audubon Society, you can learn about the popular black-and-white birds whose calls haunt New Hampshire's lakes. Holderness's **Science Center of New Hampshire** (✉ Rtes. 113 and 25, ☎ 603/968–7194; 🎫 $8) has lots of hands-on activities, nature trails, and indigenous animals.

Contrasting with the busy southern Winnipesaukee towns are three lakeside villages where you can do lots of antiquing. **Center Sandwich** is

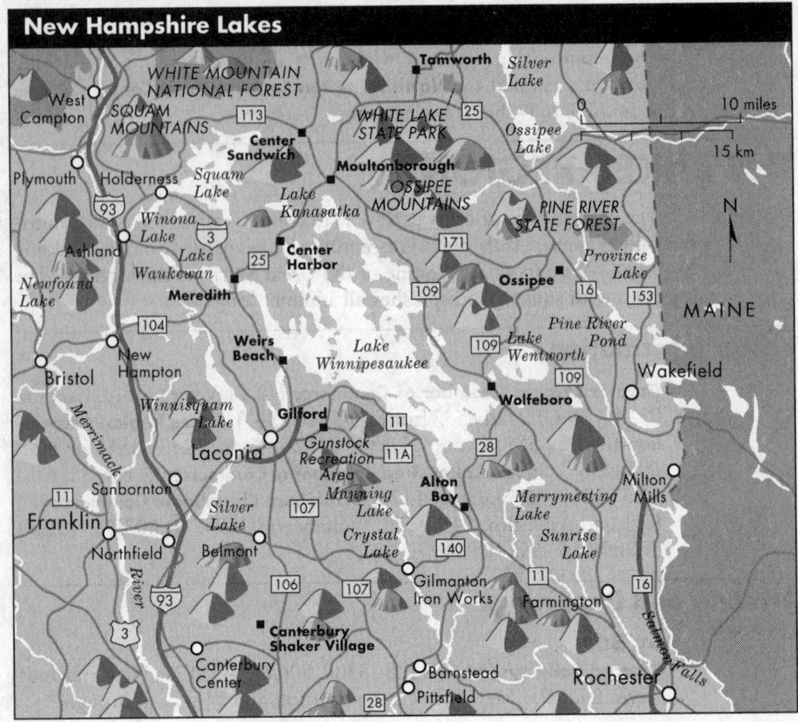

pristine and historic. **Tamworth**'s birch-edged Chocorua Lake has been photographed so often that you may feel you've seen it before. **Ossipee,** divided into three villages, is known for its eponymous lake, which is great for fishing and swimming.

Scenic, lake-hugging Route 109 leads from Moultonborough to **Wolfeboro,** an old-line resort.Uniforms, vehicles, and other artifacts at the **Wright Museum** (✉ 77 Center St., ☎ 603/569–1212; 🎫 $5) illustrate the contributions of those on the home front to America's World War II effort.

At **Canterbury Shaker Village** (✉ Canterbury, ☎ 603/783–9511; 🎫 $9 for 2 consecutive days), southwest of Winnipesaukee, guided tours and crafts demonstrations illuminate 19th-century Shaker life.

Dining and Lodging

This is steak-and-prime-rib country, though there are exceptions. Reserve ahead in most any season for both meals and rooms because summer and fall are crowded, and many businesses close in winter. For price ranges *see* Charts 1 (B) and 2 (B) *in* On the Road with Fodor's.

Center Harbor

$$$$ ✕🏨 **Red Hill Inn.** Furnished with Victorian pieces and country furniture, many rooms in this B&B have fireplaces; one has a mural of nursery-rhyme characters. For dinner ($$–$$$$), try the rack of Vermont lamb served with a feta cheese, Dijon mustard, and bread-crumb stuffing. ✉ *Route 25B (R.D. 1, Box 99M), 03226,* ☎ *603/279–7001 or 800/573–3445,* FAX *603/279–7003. 24 rooms. Restaurant, bar, outdoor hot tub. AE, D, DC, MC, V.*

Holderness

$$$$ ★ ✕▣ **Manor on Golden Pond.** This dignified inn has a dock on Squam Lake, the setting for the movie *On Golden Pond.* Guests can stay in the main inn, carriage-house suites, or a housekeeping cottage. The five-course prix-fixe dinner may include such specialties as rack of lamb, filet mignon, and nonpareil apple pie. ✉ *Rte. 3, 03245,* ☎ *603/968–3348 or 800/545–2141,* FAX *603/968–2116. 17 rooms in main house, 4 carriage house rooms, 4 2-bedroom cottages. Restaurant, pub, pool, beach. AE, MC, V.*

Sanbornton

$$$ ▣ **Ferry Point House.** Built in the 1800s as a summer retreat for the Pillsbury family, this red Victorian farmhouse B&B has superb views of Lake Winnisquam and a gazebo by the water's edge. The pretty rooms have Oriental-style rugs and antique Victorian furniture. ✉ *100 Lower Bay Rd., Sanbornton, 03269,* ☎ *603/524–0087. 6 rooms. Swimming, boating, fishing. No credit cards. Closed Nov.–Apr.*

Tamworth

$$$$ ★ ✕▣ **Tamworth Inn.** Every guest room at this friendly B&B has 19th-century American pieces and handmade quilts. Among the menu highlights in the dining room ($$–$$$; closed Sunday and Monday in summer, Sunday–Tuesday in winter) are the provolone-and-pesto terrine and the pork tenderloin with apple-walnut corn bread stuffing and apple-cider sauce. ✉ *Main St., 03886,* ☎ *603/323–7721 or 800/642–7352,* FAX *603/323–2026. 16 rooms. Restaurant, pub, pool. MC, V.*

Wolfeboro

$$$$ ★ ✕▣ **Wolfeboro Inn.** This landmark waterfront resort, partly dating from the 19th century, has polished cherry and pine pieces and is abloom with flowered chintz. ✉ *90 N. Main St. (Box 1270), 03894,* ☎ *603/569–3016 or 800/451–2389,* FAX *603/569–5375. 45 rooms. 2 restaurants, bar, beach, boating. AE, D, MC, V.*

Campgrounds

Gunstock Campground (✉ Gilford, ☎ 603/293–4341 or 800/486–7862). **Yogi Bear's Jellystone Park** (✉ Ashland, ☎ 603/968–9000, FAX 603/968–7349). **White Lake State Park** (✉ Tamworth, ☎ 603/323–7350 or 603/271–3627 for reservations).

Nightlife and the Arts

The **Belknap Mill Society** (✉ Mill Plaza, Laconia, ☎ 603/524–8813) has year-round concerts in an early 19th-century brick mill building. **Barnstormers** (✉ Main St., Tamworth, ☎ 603/323–8500), New Hampshire's oldest professional theater company, performs in July and August. The ***M/S Mount Washington*** (✉ Weirs Beach, ☎ 603/366–5531) has moonlight cruises with dinner and dancing; it docks in Weirs Beach, Alton Bay, and Wolfeboro.

Outdoor Activities and Sports

Biking

Not too hilly, the Lakes Region is fun for even inexperienced bikers—though summer's heavy traffic can be a bit much. Lake's-edge roads make for pleasant pedaling.

Boating

Rent at **Thurston's,** in Weirs Beach (☎ 603/366–4811), or the **Meredith Marina and Boating Center** (☎ 603/279–7921) or **Wild Meadow Canoes and Kayaks** (☎ 603/253–7536 or 800/427–7536), both in Meredith.

Fishing

Local waters yield trout; Winnipesaukee also has salmon. Hardy anglers fish from "ice bob" huts in winter. The **New Hampshire Department of Fish and Game**'s local office (✉ New Hampton, ☎ 603/744–5470) can tell you where the action is.

Beaches

Most are private, so it's good to know about **Ellacoya State Beach,** in Gilford, a smallish beach that's the area's major public strand. **Wentworth State Beach** is at Wolfeboro.

Shopping

Summer folk prowl area galleries and boutiques like the **Burlwood Antique Center** (✉ Rte. 3, Meredith, ☎ 603/279–6387), a 170-dealer shop, and **Mill Falls Marketplace** (✉ Rte. 3, Meredith, ☎ 603/279–7006). The **League of New Hampshire Craftsmen** runs a shop stocked with one-of-a-kind items in Meredith (✉ Rte. 3, ☎ 603/279–7920). The **Old Country Store** in Moultonborough (✉ Rte. 25, ☎ 603/476–5750) has been purveying pickles and penny candy since 1781. Look for **antiques** in Wolfeboro, the Ossipees, and Center Sandwich as well.

THE WHITE MOUNTAINS

Northern New Hampshire is the home of New England's highest mountains and the 790,000-acre White Mountain National Forest. Rivers are born here, gorges slash the forests, and hikers, climbers, and Sunday drivers marvel at it all. Meanwhile, shoppers hunt bargains in valley towns. Summers are busy, but foliage season draws the biggest crowds.

Visitor Information

Mt. Washington Valley Visitors' Bureau (✉ Box 2300, North Conway 03860, ☎ 603/356–5701 or 800/367–3364).

Arriving and Departing

By Bus

Concord Trailways (☎ 603/228–3300 or 800/639–3317 in New England) serves Littleton, Jackson, Berlin, Conway, Plymouth, and other towns.

By Car

North–south routes include I–93 and Route 3 in the west, and Route 16 in the east. The Kancamagus Highway (Route 112) and Route 302 are the main east–west thoroughfares.

Exploring the White Mountains

One-street **North Conway** overflows with shops, restaurants, and inns. Trails from **Echo Lake State Park** (✉ Off Rte. 302, North Conway, ☎ 603/356–2672 in summer; 🎫 $2.50), in North Conway, lead up to White Horse and Cathedral ledges, both 1,000-ft cliffs overlooking the town. The mountain lakes are good for swimming and the park road for woodland scenery; the picnicking is great. Youngsters love the antique steam- and diesel-powered **Conway Scenic Railroad** (✉ Rtes. 16/302, North Conway, ☎ 603/356–5251 or 800/232–5251; 🎫 $8.50–$42).

Glen is home to two family-oriented attractions. **Story Land** (☎ 603/383–4186; 🎫 $17) has life-size nursery-rhyme characters and themed rides. **Heritage New Hampshire** (☎ 603/383–9776; 🎟 $10) takes a simulated trip into New England history.

Mountain-rimmed **Jackson** has retained its storybook New England character. Dramatic **Pinkham Notch** is the departure point for hikes to the top of the Northeast's highest mountain, 6,288-ft **Mt. Washington** (be sure to carry warm clothing in case of sudden, nasty storms). In summer and fall, weather permitting, you can corkscrew up via the **Mt. Washington Auto Road** (✉ Rte. 16, Glen House, ☎ 603/466–3988; 🎟 $15 per car and driver and $6 per passenger), either in your own car or by guided van tour.

Crawford Notch State Park (✉ Rte. 302 at Twin Mountain, ☎ 603/374–2272; 🎟 $2.50) is good for a picnic and a hike to a waterfall.
★ The steam-powered **Mt. Washington Cog Railway** has been running since 1869 (✉ Off Rte. 302, Bretton Woods, ☎ 603/846–5404 or 800/922–8825; 🎟 $39); reserve ahead.

Many famous writers have stopped by **Franconia.** You can visit poet **Robert Frost's home** (✉ Ridge Rd., ☎ 603/823–5510; 🎟 $3). **Franconia Notch State Park** (☎ 603/745–8391; 🎟 $6 for flume) is known for the Old Man of the Mountains, a rock formation that looks like a human profile, and the 800-ft-long natural chasm known as the Flume.

The **Kancamagus Highway,** 32 mi of mountain scenery to the south (with bumper-to-bumper traffic during foliage season), starts in the resort town of Lincoln and passes campgrounds, scenic overlooks, and trailheads en route to Conway.

Lincoln, on the western end of the Kancamagus Highway, is home to the **Whale's Tale** (✉ Rte. 3, ☎ 603/745–8810; 🎟 $16.50), site of watersliding fun for the whole family.

Dining and Lodging

Reservations are essential in fall and during winter vacations. For price ranges *see* Charts 1 (B) and 2 (B) *in* On the Road with Fodor's.

Bretton Woods

$$$$ ✕🏨 **Mount Washington Hotel.** The 1902 construction of this leviathan was one of the most ambitious projects of its day. The Mount Washington quickly became one of the nation's favorite grand resorts, noted for its 900-ft-long veranda, which affords a full view of the Presidential Range. This jewel of Bretton Woods retains a turn-of-the-century formality; jacket and tie are required in the dining room. ✉ *Rte. 302, 03575,* ☎ *603/278–1000 or 800/258–0330,* FAX *603/278–8838. 200 rooms. 2 restaurants, indoor and outdoor pools, sauna, golf, tennis. MAP. AE, MC, V. Closed mid-Oct.–mid-May.*

Dixville Notch

$$$$ ★ ✕🏨 **Balsams Grand Resort Hotel.** This turn-of-the-century resort on 15,000 acres is a real Victorian, built in 1866. Accommodations are bright and homey, with floral-print wallpaper and lace curtains, and the array of activities, including downhill and cross-country skiing, gives you no reason to leave the grounds. In the restaurant (reservations essential, jacket and tie), the summer buffet lunch is heaped upon a 100-ft-long table. ✉ *Rte. 26, 03576,* ☎ *603/255–3400 or 800/255–0600,* FAX *603/255–4221. 212 rooms. Restaurant, pool, golf, tennis. AE, D, MC, V. Closed Apr.–mid-May, mid-Oct.–mid-Dec.*

Franconia

$$$–$$$$ ✕🏨 **Franconia Inn.** Play tennis, ride horseback, ski, swim, or hike at this family resort. Rooms have designer chintzes, canopy beds, and country furnishings; some have whirlpool baths or fireplaces. At the restaurant ($$–$$$), children choose from a separate menu, while adults savor medallions of veal with apple-mustard sauce or filet mignon with green-chili butter and Madeira sauce. ✉ *1300 Easton Rd., 03580,* ☎ *603/823–5542 or 800/473–5299,* FAX *603/823–8078. 34 rooms. Restaurant, pool, hot tub, tennis. AE, MC, V. Closed Apr.–mid-May.*

Jackson

$$$$ ★ ✕🏨 **Inn at Thorn Hill.** Dark wood furniture and rose-motif wallpaper patterns recall the inn's origins as a home designed by Stanford White. Yet the comforts are strictly up-to-date, and the restaurant ($$$–$$$$), closed midweek in April, is one of the area's best. ✉ *Thorn Hill Rd. (Box A), 03846,* ☎ *603/383–4242 or 800/289–8990,* FAX *603/383–8062. 19 rooms. Restaurant, pub, pool, hot tub. MAP. AE, D, DC, MC, V.*

North Conway

$$–$$$ ✕ **Scottish Lion.** Scotch is the specialty at this restaurant-pub—you can choose from 60 varieties. In the tartan-carpeted dining rooms, scones and Devonshire cream are served at breakfast, and Scottish Highland game pie at lunch and dinner. The "rumbledethump" potatoes are deservedly famous. ✉ *Rte. 16,* ☎ *603/356–6381. AE, D, DC, MC, V.*

$$$–$$$$ ★ ✕🏨 **Snowvillage Inn.** To complement the inn's tome-jammed bookshelves, guest rooms are named for famous authors. The nicest, with 12 windows overlooking the Presidential Range, honors native son Robert Frost. The candlelit dining room (reservations required) serves specialties like roasted rack of lamb with *herbes de Provence.* ✉ *Box 68, Stuart Rd., 03849,* ☎ *603/447–2818 or 800/447–4345,* FAX *603/447–4345. 18 rooms. Restaurant, sauna. MAP available. AE, D, DC, MC, V.*

Nightlife and the Arts

Look into the **Mt. Washington Valley Theater Company** (✉ Main St., North Conway, ☎ 603/356–5776). Catch some music or theater at the **North Country Center for the Performing Arts** (✉ Mill at Loon Mountain, Lincoln, ☎ 603/745–6032). Or sample the bars. The **Red Parka Pub** (✉ Rte. 302, Glen, ☎ 603/383–4344) is favored by under-30s. The **Wildcat Inn & Tavern** (✉ Rte. 16A, Jackson, ☎ 603/383–4245) has live music and is popular with skiers.

Outdoor Activities and Sports

Biking

Great Glen Trails (✉ Rte. 16, Pinkham Notch, ☎ 603/466–2333), rents mountain bikes by the day and half day for use on their extensive network of trails at the base of Mt. Washington.

Fishing

Clear White Mountain streams yield trout and salmon; lakes and ponds have trout and bass. The **New Hampshire Fish and Game Department**'s regional office (☎ 603/788–3164) has the latest information.

Hiking

The White Mountains are crisscrossed with footpaths. The Maine-to-Georgia **Appalachian Trail** crosses the state. The **Appalachian Mountain Club** (✉ Box 298, Gorham 03851, ☎ 603/466–2727 for reservations or a free guide to huts; 603/466–2725 for trail information) operates hikers' huts and suggests routes. The **White Mountains National Forest Office** (☎ 603/528–8721 or 800/283–2267) is a good source of hiking information and the place to obtain the recreation permit needed to park in national forest areas. **New England Hiking Holidays–White Mountains** (✉ Box 1648, North Conway 03860, ☎ 603/356–9696 or 800/869–0949) organizes guided inn-to-inn hikes.

Ski Areas

New Hampshire's best skiing is in the White Mountains. For the latest conditions statewide, call **SKI New Hampshire** (☎ 800/887–5464, FAX 603/745–3002).

Cross-Country

In Jackson nearly 100 mi of trails maintained by the **Jackson Ski Touring Foundation** (☎ 800/927–6697) string together inns, restaurants, and woodlands and connect to another 40 mi of trails maintained by the Appalachian Mountain Club (☞ Hiking *in* Outdoor Activities and Sports, *above*). The **Balsams Grand Resort Hotel** (☞ Dining and Lodging, *above*). **Bear Notch Ski Touring Center** (✉ Rte. 302, Bartlett, ☎ 603/374–2277). **Bretton Woods** (✉ Rte. 302, ☎ 603/278–5000). **Franconia Village Cross-Country Center** (✉ Easton Rd., Franconia, ☎ 603/823–5542). **Great Glen Trails** (☞ Biking *in* Outdoor Activities and Sports, *above*). **Waterville Valley** (✉ Rte. 49, Waterville Valley, ☎ 603/236–8311 or 603/236–4144 for conditions).

Downhill

For New Hampshire's largest ski areas, the 90s have been a decade of growth. But plenty of smaller, low-key areas still offer a pleasant counterpoint. **Waterville Valley** (☞ Cross-Country, *above*). **Loon Mountain** (✉ Kancamagus Hwy., Lincoln, ☎ 603/745–8111 or 603/745–8100 for conditions). **Black Mountain** (✉ Rte. 16B, Jackson, ☎ 603/383–4490). **Attitash Bear Peak** (✉ Rte. 302, Bartlett, ☎ 603/374–2368 or 603/374–0946 for conditions). **Mt. Cranmore** (✉ Snowmobile Rd., North Conway, ☎ 603/356–5543 or 603/356–8516 for conditions). **Wildcat** (✉ Rte. 16, Pinkham Notch, ☎ 603/466–3326 or 800/643–4521 for conditions). **Cannon** (✉ Franconia, ☎ 603/823–5563 or 603/823–7771 for conditions). **Balsams/Wilderness** and **Bretton Woods** (☞ Cross-Country, *above*) are small areas at grand old resort hotels.

Shopping

More than 150 outlets and shops line **Route 16** north of Conway. **Lincoln** offers factory outlets as well. Galleries throughout the region display local artisans' work.

WESTERN NEW HAMPSHIRE

The countryside east of the Connecticut River between the Massachusetts border and the White Mountains' foothills is a land of covered bridges, calendar-page villages, hardwood forests, jewel-like lakes, and lonely mountains. Cultural centers enliven workaday urban centers such as Manchester, Nashua, and the capital, Concord.

Visitor Information

Lake Sunapee Business Association (✉ Box 400, Sunapee 03782, ☎ 603/763–2495 or 800/258–3530 in New England). **Monadnock Travel Council** (✉ 8 Central Sq., Keene 03431, ☎ 603/352–1308). **Concord Chamber of Commerce** (✉ 244 N. Main St., 03301, ☎ 603/224–2508). **Hanover Chamber of Commerce** (✉ Box A-105, 03755, ☎ 603/643–3115). **Manchester Chamber of Commerce** (✉ 889 Elm St., 03101, ☎

603/666–6600). **Peterborough Chamber of Commerce** (✉ Box 401, 03458, ☎ 603/924–7234).

Arriving and Departing

By Bus

Concord Trailways (☎ 800/639–3317) operates within the state and **Advance Transit** (☎ 802/295–1824) within the area.

By Car

I–89 cuts southeast–northwest into Vermont. North–south, I–93 provides scenic travel while I–91 follows the Connecticut River on its Vermont shore; in New Hampshire, Routes 12 and 12A are slow but beautiful. Route 4 winds between Lebanon and the coast.

Exploring Western New Hampshire

Concord, New Hampshire's capital, is undergoing an awakening. The Concord on Foot walking trail covers the historic district and includes the **Pierce Manse** (✉ 14 Penacook St., ☎ 603/224–9620 or 603/224–7668; 🎫 $3), closed September–mid-June, once home to Franklin Pierce, the nation's 14th president. Reserve seats for shows at Concord's high-tech **Christa McAuliffe Planetarium** (✉ 3 Institute Dr., ☎ 603/271–7827; 🎫 $6).

Visit the **Museum of New Hampshire History** (✉ 6 Eagle Sq., ☎ 603/226–3189; 🎫 $5) to see (except on Monday) exhibits spanning the days of the Abenaki Indians to the present.

Three governors were born in **Warner.** Now the quiet town is home to the **Kearsarge Indian Museum,** where you'll find exhibits on Native American crafts. ✉ *Kearsarge Mountain Rd.,* ☎ *603/456–2600.* 🎫 *$6. Closed mid-Dec.–Apr..*

Mountains and parks set off bright, clear **Lake Sunapee.** You can cruise it on the ***M/V Mt. Sunapee II*** (✉ Sunapee Harbor, ☎ 603/763–4030). Or you can rise above it on a chairlift or picnic on a beach at quiet, woodsy **Mt. Sunapee State Park** (✉ Rte. 103, Newbury, ☎ 603/763–2356; 🎫 $2.50).

Tiny Enfield is home to the **Enfield Shaker Museum,** which displays and explains Shaker artifacts and crafts. ✉ *2 Lower Shaker Village Rd.,* ☎ *603/632–4346.* 🎫 *$5. Closed weekdays mid-Oct–May.*

Dartmouth College, in Hanover, is an Ivy League archetype of redbrick and white clapboard around a village green. On Wheelock Street, its ★ **Hood Museum of Art** (☎ 603/646–2808; 🎫 free) houses works from Africa, Asia, Europe, and America. The modern **Hopkins Center** (☎ 603/646–2422) is a focal point for the local arts scene.

In modest **Cornish,** to the south of Hanover via Route 12A, you can cross four covered bridges. The **Saint-Gaudens National Historic Site** displays some of the sculptor's heroic, sensitive work. ✉ *Off Rte. 12A,* ☎ *603/675–2175.* 🎫 *$2. Closed Oct.–late May.*

In **Charlestown** is the **Fort at No. 4,** a frontier outpost in Colonial times; today costumed guides demonstrate crafts. ✉ *Rte. 11,* ☎ *603/826–5700.* 🎫 *$6. Closed late Oct.–late May.*

In **Monadnock State Park** (✉ Off Rte. 124, Jaffrey, ☎ 603/532–8862; 🎫 $2.50) 20 trails ascend to the bald summit of 3,165-ft Mt. Monadnock, one of the world's most-climbed mountains. Near **Dublin,** where proper Bostonians summer and locals publish the *Old Farmer's Almanac,* you can exit Monadnock State Park onto Route 101. **Peterborough,** the model for Thornton Wilder's *Our Town*, is now a computer magazine–publishing center.

Beautifully preserved **Fitzwilliam,** spreading from the edges of an oval common, warrants a detour. Acres of wild rhododendrons burst into bloom in mid-July at **Rhododendron State Park** (✉ Off Rte. 12, 2½ mi northwest of the common, ☎ 603/532–8862; 🎫 $2.50 weekends and holidays, free at other times).

The four villages that make up **Hillsborough** include Hillsborough Center, where 18th-century houses surround a picture-perfect town green. The Hillsborough Historical Society operates the **Pierce Homestead,** where fourteenth President Franklin Pierce was reared. ✉ *Rte. 31 (Box 896), 03244,* ☎ *603/478–3165.* 🎫 *$3. Closed mid-Oct.–May.*

Dining and Lodging

For price ranges *see* Charts 1 (B) and 2 (B) *in* On the Road with Fodor's.

Bedford

$$$$ ✕🏨 **Bedford Village Inn.** Minutes from Manchester, this luxury inn has antique four-poster beds and Italian marble whirlpool baths; some rooms have fireplaces. ✉ *2 Village Inn La., 03110,* ☎ *603/472–2001 or 800/852–1166,* FAX *603/472–2379. 12 suites, 2 apartments. Restaurant. AE, DC, MC, V.*

Chesterfield

$$$$ ★ ✕🏨 **Chesterfield Inn.** Rooms in this B&B, which is surrounded by gardens, are spacious and tastefully decorated with antiques and period-style fabrics. Favorites from the dining room include crab cakes with *rémoulade* (a sauce made with olive oil, mustard, scallions, and spices) and salmon with mustard mango glaze. ✉ *Rte. 9 (Box 155), 03443,* ☎ *603/256–3211 or 800/365–5515,* FAX *603/256–6131. 13 rooms. Restaurant. AE, D, DC, MC, V.*

Concord

$$–$$$ ✕ **Endicott Grill.** Chef Graham Gifford changes the menus monthly, but a typical meal might include smoked salmon Napoleons, roasted free-range half chicken with pecan wild rice and mushroom-wine sauce, and raspberry chocolate pecan cheesecake. ✉ *6 Pleasant St. Ext.,* ☎ *603/224–0582. Reservations advised. MC, V. Closed Sun.–Mon.*

$–$$$ ✕ **Hermanos Cocina Mexicana.** The food at this popular two-level restaurant is standard Mexican, but with fresher ingredients and more subtle sauces than one might expect. ✉ *11 Hills Ave.,* ☎ *603/224–5669. Reservations not accepted. MC, V.*

$$$$ ✕🏨 **Centennial Inn.** Each room in this charming brick and stone structure, built for widows of Civil War veterans in 1896, is individually decorated with antiques and reproductions. In the Franklin Pierce dining room ($$$–$$$$), where the menu changes seasonally, try the shredded duck pizza or the roast medallions of venison. ✉ *96 Pleasant St., 03301,* ☎ *603/225-7102 or 800/267–0525,* FAX *603/225–5031. 32 rooms. Restaurant. AE, D, DC, MC, V.*

Cornish

$$$–$$$$ ★ 🏨 **Chase House Bed & Breakfast Inn.** This is the birthplace of Salmon P. Chase, who was Abraham Lincoln's secretary of the treasury, a chief justice of the United States, and a founder of the Republican Party. It's been gracefully restored with Colonial furnishings and Waverly fabrics. Ask for a room with a view of the Connecticut River valley and Mt. Ascutney. ✉ *Rte. 12A (1½ mi south of the Cornish-Windsor covered bridge), R.R. 2, Box 909, 03745,* ☎ *603/675–5391 or 800/401–*

9455, ℻ *603/675–5010. 8 rooms. Exercise room. MC, V. No smoking. No children under 12.*

Fitzwilliam

$$$–$$$$ ★ **Hannah Davis House.** The original beehive oven still sits in the kitchen of this 1820 Federal-style B&B, and one suite has two Count Rumford fireplaces. The inn is just off the village green—your host has the scoop on area antiquing. ✉ *186 Depot Rd., 03447,* ☎ *603/585–3344. 6 rooms. Full breakfast. D, MC, V.*

Hanover

$$$$ ★ ✕ **Hanover Inn.** Three stories of white-trimmed brick, this embodiment of American traditional architecture, owned by Dartmouth College, is handsomely furnished with 19th-century antiques and reproductions. You can get regional cuisine in the Daniel Webster Room ($$$–$$$$), and lighter bites in the Ivy Grill. ✉ *Box 151, The Green 03755,* ☎ *603/643–4300 or 800/443–7024,* ℻ *603/646–3744. 92 rooms. 2 restaurants. AE, D, DC, MC, V.*

Nightlife and the Arts

The arts flourish at the **Capitol Center for the Arts** (✉ 46 S. Main St., Concord, ☎ 603/225–1111). The **Colonial Theater** (✉ 95 Main St., Keene, ☎ 603/352–2033) has folk, rock, jazz, and movies. **Monadnock Music** (✉ Box 255, Peterborough 03458, ☎ 603/924–7610) has concerts in July and August. Nashua is home to the state's largest professional theater, the **American Stage Festival** (✉ 14 Court St., ☎ 603/886–7000).

Outdoor Activities and Sports

Biking

Try **Route 10** along the Ashuelot River south of Keene; spurs lead to covered bridges. Contact the **Granite State Wheelmen** (✉ 16 Clinton St., Salem 03079, ☎ no phone) for group rides.

Boating

The Connecticut River, while usually safe after June 15, is not for beginners. Rent gear at **Northstar Canoe Livery** (✉ Rte. 12A, Balloch's Crossing, ☎ 603/542–5802).

Fishing

To find out where the action is on the area's 200 lakes and ponds, call the **Department of Fish and Game**'s regional office in Keene (☎ 603/352–9669).

Hiking

Networks of trails can be found in many state parks and forests, among them the **Mt. Sunapee** (✉ Newbury, ☎ 603/763–2356) and rugged **Pillsbury** (✉ Washington, ☎ 603/863–2860) state parks and **Fox State Forest** (✉ Hillsborough, ☎ 603/464–3453).

Shopping

Look for church fairs and artisans' studios marked by blue New Hampshire state signs. Antiques dealers sell "by chance or by appointment"; keep an eye peeled along Route 119 west of Fitzwilliam and along Route 101 east of Marlborough. Keene has malls and **Colony Mill Marketplace** (✉ 222 West St., ☎ 603/357–1240). You can buy outdoor gear at **Eastern Mountain Sports** (✉ Vose Farm Rd., ☎ 603/924–7231).

NEW YORK

Updated by P. Bernstein, J. Donohue, R. Knapp, R. Miller, M. Mittelbach, and T. Steele

Capital	Albany
Population	18,138,000
Motto	Excelsior
State Bird	Bluebird
State Flower	Rose
Postal Abbreviation	NY

Statewide Visitor Information

New York State Division of Tourism (✉ 1 Commerce Plaza, Albany 12245, ☎ 518/474–4116 or 800/225–5697).

Scenic Drives

The **Taconic Parkway,** particularly the stretch from Hopewell Junction to East Chatham, passes through rolling hills, orchards, woods, and pastures reminiscent of the English countryside. To make a dramatic loop around the Adirondacks' **High Peaks** region, pick up Route 73 off the Northway (I–87) at Exit 30, drive northwest through Lake Placid, proceed on Route 86 through Saranac Lake, then head southwest on Route 3 to Tupper Lake, due south on Route 30 to Long Lake, and east on Route 28N to North Creek. For information on the dozen officially designated scenic drives, call 800/225–5697.

National and State Parks

National Parks

The **Gateway National Recreation Area** (✉ Floyd Bennett Field, Bldg. 69, Brooklyn 11234, ☎ 718/338–3338) extends through Brooklyn, Queens, Staten Island, and into New Jersey. It includes the **Jamaica Bay Wildlife Refuge,** a good spot to see migrating birds; **Jacob Riis Park,** where a boardwalk stretches along the surfy Atlantic; plus various beaches, parklands, and facilities for outdoor and indoor festivals. **Fire Island National Seashore** (✉ 120 Laurel St., Patchogue 11772, ☎ 516/289–4810) offers Atlantic surf and beaches on a barrier island.

State Parks

New York has 150 state parks. The **Empire State Passport,** permitting unlimited entrance to the parks for a year (April–March), is available for $30 at most parks; you can also contact the **State Office of Parks and Recreation** (☎ 518/474–0456) or write for an application (✉ Passport, State Parks, Albany 12238).

NEW YORK CITY

Whatever you're looking for in a big-city vacation, you'll find it in New York. The city has a rich history, from early Dutch settlers and the swearing in of George Washington as the first U.S. president to the arrival of millions of immigrants in the late 19th and early 20th centuries. Today's New York City is known around the world for its distinctive skyline, its first-rate museums and performing arts companies, and its status as the capital of finance, fashion, art, publishing, broadcasting, theater, and advertising. And, of course, New Yorkers themselves are world famous—if not always for their charm, at least for their panache, ethnic diversity, street smarts, and accents.

Beyond the list of must-see sights, from the Statue of Liberty to Times Square, from Central Park to the Metropolitan Museum of Art, New York has an indefinable aura all its own. It's a special intensity that comes from being in the big league, where everybody's chasing a dream and still keeping score. To paraphrase a slogan originally coined for the Plaza Hotel, you get the feeling that "nothing unimportant ever happens in New York."

Visitor Information

Convention and Visitors Bureau (✉ 810 7th Ave., 3rd floor, 10019, ☎ 212/397–8222 or 212/484–1200, FAX 212/484–1280).

Arriving and Departing

By Bus

The **Port Authority Terminal** (✉ 40th to 42nd Sts., between 8th and 9th Aves., ☎ 212/564–8484) handles all long-haul and commuter bus lines. Among the bus lines serving New York are **Greyhound Lines** (☎ 212/971–6404 or 800/231–2222), **Bonanza Bus Lines** (☎ 800/556–3815, for travel from New England), **Martz Trailways** (☎ 800/233–8604, from northeastern Pennsylvania), and **New Jersey Transit** (☎ 973/762–5100 New Jersey).

By Car

A complex network of **bridges and tunnels** provides access to Manhattan. I–95 enters via the George Washington Bridge. I–495 enters from Long Island via the Midtown Tunnel. From upstate the city is accessible via the New York (Dewey) Thruway (I–87), which is known as the Major Deegan Expressway within New York City.

By Plane

Virtually every major U.S. and foreign airline serves one or more of New York's three airports. **La Guardia** (☎ 718/533–3400) and **John F. Kennedy International** (☎ 718/244–4444) airports are in Queens. **Newark International Airport** (☎ 973/961–6000) is in New Jersey. Cab fare to midtown Manhattan runs $17–$29 plus tolls and tip from LaGuardia, $30 plus tolls and tip from JFK, and $34–$38 plus tolls and tip from Newark. **Carey Transportation** (☎ 718/632–0509, 800/456–1012, or 800/284–0909) runs buses to midtown every 20–30 minutes from LaGuardia and every 20–30 minutes from JFK. The **Gray Line Airport Shuttle** (☎ 212/315–3006 or 800/451–0455) connects LaGuardia and JFK to Manhattan. **NJ Transit Airport Express** (☎ 973/762–5100) runs between Newark Airport and Manhattan's Port Authority Terminal. By public transportation, the **A train (subway)** to Howard Beach connects with a free airport shuttle bus to JFK.

By Train

MTA Metro-North Railroad (☎ 212/532–4900 or 800/638–7646).

Getting Around New York City

New York is a city of neighborhoods best explored at a leisurely pace, up close, and on foot. Extensive public transportation easily bridges gaps between areas of interest.

By Car

If you're traveling by car, don't plan to use it much in Manhattan. Driving in the city can be a nightmare of gridlocked streets and aggressive fellow motorists. Free parking is almost nonexistent in midtown, and parking lots everywhere are exorbitant ($20 for three hours is not unusual in midtown).

By Public Transportation

The 714-mi **subway** system, the fastest and cheapest way to get around the city, serves Manhattan, Brooklyn, Queens, and the Bronx and operates 24 hours a day. Tokens cost $1.50 each, with reduced fares for people with disabilities and for senior citizens, and are sold in subway stations. MetroCards, purchased for a specific amount, are also available at all subway stations; to use one, swipe it through a reader at the turnstile; the fare is automatically deducted from the card's value. When you purchase a MetroCard for $15 or more you get one fare free. Transfers among subway lines are free at designated interchanges. Most **buses** follow easy-to-understand routes along the Manhattan grid, and some run 24 hours. Routes go up or down the north–south avenues, east and west on the major two-way crosstown streets: 96th, 86th, 79th, 72nd, 57th, 42nd, 34th, 23rd, and 14th. New bus stop signs were introduced in 1996; look for a light blue sign (or green for an express bus) on a green pole. Bus fare is $1.50 in exact coins (no pennies or bills) or a subway token; a MetroCard can also be used on all city buses. If you need one, request a transfer—they're free—to a connecting bus line when paying the fare. Transfers between buses and subways are also free if you use a MetroCard.For **24-hour bus and subway information** call 718/330–1234. For subway or bus **maps** ask at token booths or write to the New York City Transit Authority (✉ Customer Assistance, 370 Jay St., Room 702, Brooklyn 11201).

By Taxi

Taxis (official, licensed ones are yellow) are usually easy to hail on the street, in front of major hotels, and by bus and train stations. The fare is $2 for the first ⅕ mi, 30¢ for each ⅕ mi thereafter, and 25¢ for each 75 seconds not in motion. A 50¢ surcharge is added to rides begun between 8 PM and 6 AM. Bridge and tunnel tolls are extra, and drivers expect a 15% tip. Barring performance above and beyond the call of duty, don't feel obliged to give more.

Orientation Tours

Boat Tour

From March to late December **Circle Line Cruises** (✉ Pier 83, west end of 42nd St., ☎ 212/563–3200) offers a three-hour, 35-mi circumnavigation of Manhattan. Semi-Circle tours are run mid-December through March.

Bus Tours

Gray Line New York Tours (✉ 1740 Broadway, ☎ 212/397–2620) offers a number of standard city bus tours in several languages, trolley tours, and day trips to Atlantic City. **New York Doubledecker Tours** (✉ Empire State Bldg., 350 5th Ave., Room 4503, ☎ 212/967–6008) covers the major attractions and allows you to hop on and off.

Walking Tours

Heritage Trails New York (☎ 212/269–1500) is a self-guided walking tour through the downtown area. **New York City Cultural Walking Tours** (☎ 212/979–2388) focuses on the city's architecture, landmarks, memorials, and outdoor art. The **Municipal Art Society** (☎ 212/935–3960) operates a series of bus and walking tours.

Exploring Manhattan

Midtown is the heart of New York City, so it makes sense to start your exploration here, then move on to the museum-rich Upper West and Upper East sides, then downtown to Chelsea, Greenwich Village, SoHo, Little Italy, and Chinatown, and finally to Lower Manhattan, the city's financial center.

Midtown

★ Many think the heart of midtown is **Rockefeller Center,** a complex of 19 buildings occupying nearly 22 acres of prime real estate between 5th and 7th avenues and 47th and 52nd streets. The outdoor ice rink, on the Lower Plaza between 49th and 50th streets, is the center's trademark. The ice rink becomes an open-air café in warm weather. In December the plaza is decorated with a huge Christmas tree.

The backdrop for the Lower Plaza is Rockefeller Center's tallest tower, the 70-story **GE Building.** The 6,000-seat Art Deco **Radio City Music Hall** (✉ 6th Ave. at 50th St., ☎ 212/247–4777; 🎫 tour $13.75), is America's largest indoor theater. Originally a movie theater, which also presented live entertainment, Radio City produces major concerts, Christmas and Easter extravaganzas, awards presentations, and other special events, and is home of the fabled Rockettes chorus line.

The stretch of **5th Avenue** between Rockefeller Center and 59th Street glitters with world-famous shops, including Saks Fifth Avenue, F.A.O. Schwarz, Prada, and Tiffany & Co. Gothic-style **St. Patrick's** (✉ 5th Ave. at 50th St., ☎ 212/753–2261), the Roman Catholic cathedral of New York, is dedicated to the patron saint of the Irish. The stone structure was begun in 1858, consecrated in 1879, and completed in 1906.

The **Museum of Television and Radio,** in a limestone building designed by Philip Johnson and John Burgee, has three galleries of photographs and artifacts documenting the history of broadcasting. The collection contains more than 60,000 television shows and radio programs, as well as several thousand commercials; you can watch your selections at individual consoles. *✉ 25 W. 52nd St., ☎ 212/621–6600, 212/621–6800 for recorded general information and daily events. 🎫 Donations suggested. Closed Mon.*

★ The **Museum of Modern Art** (MoMA) is the city's—and the world's—foremost showcase for art of the 20th century, in an airy four-story structure built around a secluded sculpture garden. All the greatest modern artists, from van Gogh to Picasso, Matisse to Warhol, are represented. Photography, prints, architecture, and design all have their own galleries. Afternoon and evening film showings are free with the price of admission. *✉ 11 W. 53rd St., ☎ 212/708–9480. 🎫 $9.50; donations suggested Fri. 4:30–8:30. Closed Wed.*

One of New York's principal energy centers, **Times Square** is southwest of the Museum of Modern Art. It's one of many New York City "squares" that are actually triangles formed by the angle of Broadway slashing across a major avenue—in this case it crosses 7th Avenue at 42nd Street. Known as the Crossroads of the World, the Great White Way, and the New Year's Eve Capital of America, it is perhaps best known as the Broadway Theater District. Most theaters considered Broadway theaters are actually on streets west of Broadway. Redevelopment on and around 42nd Street, long in the works, is dramatically transforming the area, especially 42nd Street between 7th and 8th avenues. The Walt Disney Company opened a store and renovated the historic **New Amsterdam Theater** (✉ 214 W. 42nd St., ☎ 212/282–2900), where the acclaimed stage version of *The Lion King* draws crowds nightly. Across from the New Amsterdam, another renovated theatrical jewel, the historic **New Victory Theater** (✉ 209 W. 42nd St., ☎ 212/239–6255) stages productions by and for children. Next door the new **Ford Center for the Performing Arts** (✉ 213–215 42nd St., ☎ 212/307–4100) opened in 1998 with a production of E. L. Doctorow's novel *Ragtime*. Construction on the same block will continue well into the year 2001; coming attractions include a Madame Tussaud's exhibit and E Walk, a huge $300 million hotel, retail, and entertainment complex with 13 movie theaters. Two crouching marble lions guard the entrance to the **New York Public Library**'s (☎ 212/930–0800; 🎫 free) central research facility, between 40th and 42nd streets on 5th Avenue. This 1911 Beaux Arts masterpiece has frequent exhibits; its majestic **main reading room** is slated to reopen in February 1999 after a year-plus ★ renovation. Behind the library, **Bryant Park** has a sunny lawn strewn with hundreds of green café chairs in summer.

The headquarters of the **United Nations** (☎ 212/963–7713; 🎫 tour $7.50) is on a lushly landscaped riverside tract along 1st Avenue between 42nd and 48th streets, several blocks east of the main public library. A line of flagpoles with banners representing the current roster of 185 member nations stands before the striking 505-ft-high slab of the Secretariat Building. Tours depart from the General Assembly lobby.

At the southern end of midtown, the **Morgan Library** is a small, patrician museum whose core is the famous banker's red-damask-lined study and his majestic personal library, with tiers of handsomely bound rare books, letters, and illuminated manuscripts; both rooms were completed in 1905. Rotating exhibitions from the permanent collection showcase drawings, prints, manuscripts, and books. ✉ *29 E. 36th St., at Madison Ave.,* ☎ *212/685–0008.* 🎫 *Donations suggested. Closed Mon.*

★ The **Empire State Building,** just two blocks southwest of the Morgan Library, is no longer the world's tallest building, but it is one of the world's best-loved skyscrapers. The Art Deco structure opened in 1931. Go to the concourse level to buy a ticket for the 86th- and 102nd-floor observation decks. ✉ *5th Ave. and 34th St.,* ☎ *212/736–3100.* 🎫 *$6.*

Upper West Side

One of New York's most desirable neighborhoods, the **Upper West Side** has boutiques and cafés lining Columbus Avenue and renovated brownstones standing proudly on the side streets. **Lincoln Center,** which spearheaded the revitalization of the Upper West Side, is today the area's cultural anchor. Flanking the central fountain are three major concert halls: **Avery Fisher Hall,** where the New York Philharmonic Orchestra performs; the glass-fronted **Metropolitan Opera House,** home of the Metropolitan Opera and the American Ballet Theatre; and the **New York State Theater,** home of the New York City Ballet and the New York City Opera. The **Vivian Beaumont Theater,** behind Lincoln Center's three main megabuildings, is a major New York dramatic venue. **Alice Tully Hall,** an acoustically near-perfect small concert hall, and the **Walter Reade Theater,** the city's poshest house for arty and obscure films, are both at Broadway and 65th Street. ✉ *W. 62nd to 66th Sts. between Broadway and Amsterdam Ave.,* ☎ *212/546–2656 for general information, 212/875–5350 for tour schedule and reservations.* 🎫 *Tour $8.25.*

The **American Museum of Natural History,** with more than 36 million artifacts and specimens, is the largest and most important museum of natural history in the world. Forty-two exhibition halls display an awe-inspiring collection of dinosaur skeletons, a 94-ft replica of a blue whale,

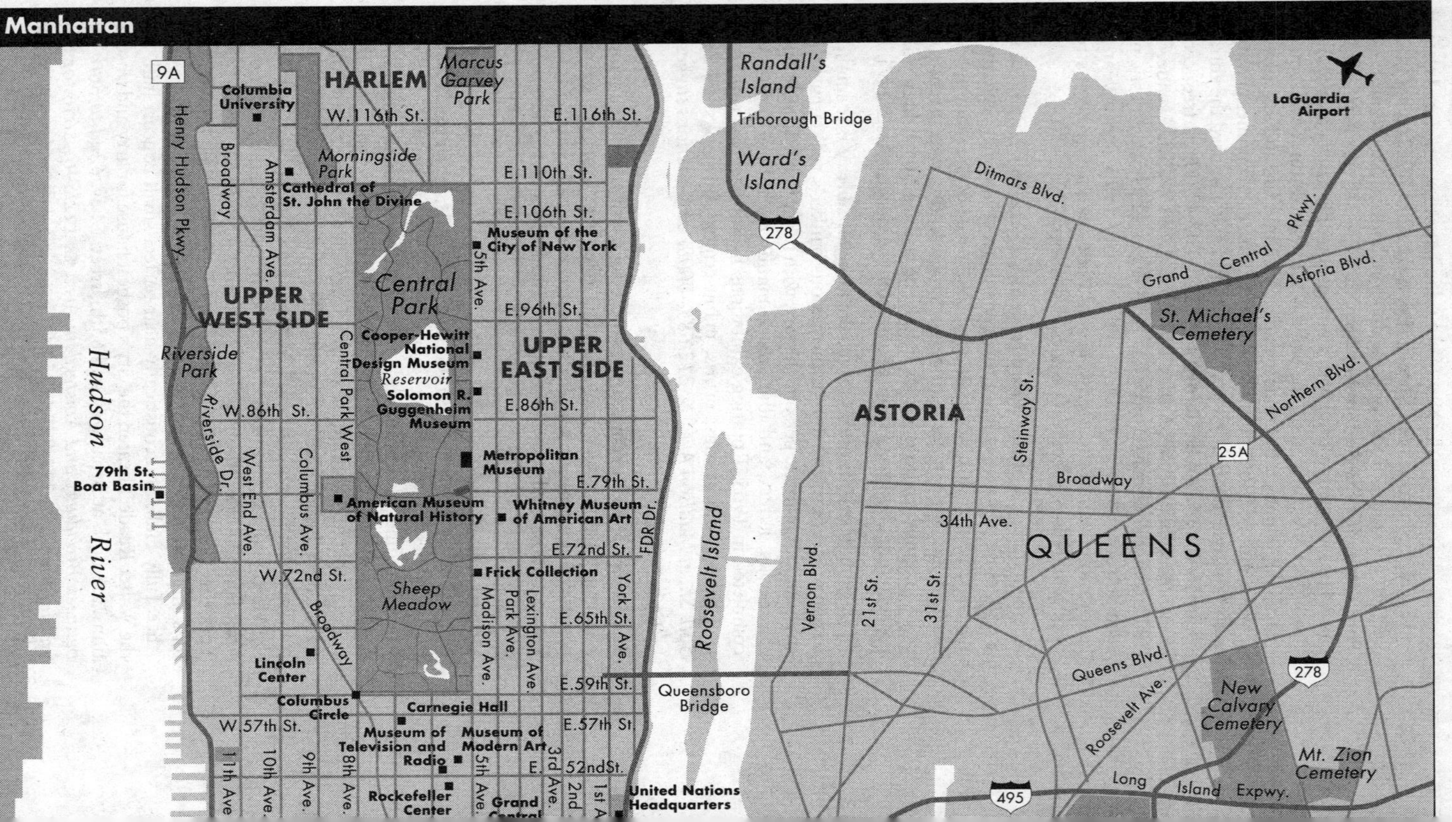
Manhattan
9A
HARLEM
Marcus Garvey Park
Columbia University
W. 116th St.
E. 116th St.
Randall's Island
Triborough Bridge
Ward's Island
LaGuardia Airport
Henry Hudson Pkwy.
Broadway
Amsterdam Ave.
Morningside Park
Cathedral of St. John the Divine
E. 110th St.
E. 106th St.
Museum of the City of New York
278
Ditmars Blvd.
Grand Central Pkwy.
Astoria Blvd.
5th Ave.
Central Park
UPPER WEST SIDE
E. 96th St.
St. Michael's Cemetery
Cooper-Hewitt National Design Museum
Reservoir
Solomon R. Guggenheim Museum
UPPER EAST SIDE
Riverside Park
Riverside Dr.
W. 86th St.
Central Park West
E. 86th St.
Hudson River
ASTORIA
Steinway St.
Northern Blvd.
25A
Metropolitan Museum
E. 79th St.
79th St. Boat Basin
West End Ave.
Columbus Ave.
American Museum of Natural History
Whitney Museum of American Art
FDR Dr.
Broadway
34th Ave.
Roosevelt Island
QUEENS
E. 72nd St.
W. 72nd St.
Frick Collection
Sheep Meadow
Madison Ave.
Park Ave.
Lexington Ave.
York Ave.
E. 65th St.
Vernon Blvd.
21st St.
31st St.
Lincoln Center
Queens Blvd.
Roosevelt Ave.
New Calvary Cemetery
E. 59th St.
Queensboro Bridge
Columbus Circle
Carnegie Hall
W. 57th St.
E. 57th St.
Museum of Television and Radio
Museum of Modern Art
Mt. Zion Cemetery
11th Ave.
10th Ave.
9th Ave.
8th Ave.
Rockefeller Center
Grand Central
3rd Ave.
2nd
1st A
E. 52nd St.
United Nations Headquarters
Long Island Expwy.
495

Bus Terminal
Javits Convention Center
W.34th St.
MIDTOWN
Public Library
Morgan Library
Empire State Building
Madison Square Garden/ Pennsylvania Station
Newtown Creek
Cemetery
Grand Ave.
Humboldt Ave.
Expwy.
2nd Ave.
7th Ave.
Ave. of the Americas
Broadway
Madison Square
W.23rd St.
E.23rd St.
Gramercy Park
CHELSEA
GRAMERCY
East River
Union Square
W.14th St.
E.14th St.
Grace Church
GREENWICH VILLAGE
EAST VILLAGE
Washington Square
Lafayette St.
FDR Dr.
Brooklyn-Queens
Flushing Ave.
West Side Hwy.
Hudson St.
Sheridan Square
New York University
E. 4th St.
E. Houston St.
W. Houston St.
Williamsburg Bridge
NEW JERSEY
SOHO
LITTLE ITALY
Delancy St.
Bushwick Ave.
Holland Tunnel
Canal St.
E. Broadway
Myrtle Ave.
Broadway
TRIBECA
CHINA-TOWN
Bowery
Lafayette Ave.
Hudson River
West St.
Manhattan Bridge
Chambers St.
BATTERY PARK CITY
W.
Brooklyn Bridge
World Financial Center
World Trade Center
Fulton St.
South Street Seaport
Bedford Ave.
N
Trinity Church
Wall St.
Brooklyn Heights Promenade
BROOKLYN HEIGHTS
BROOKLYN
NY Stock Exchange
LOWER MANHATTAN
0 880 yards
0 800 meters
National Museum of the American Indian
Flatbush Ave.
Fulton St.
Battery Park
Staten Island Ferry Terminal
Montague St.
Statue of Liberty
Ellis Island
Brooklyn-Battery Tunnel
Atlantic Ave.

the 563-carat Star of India sapphire, and the 4½-billion-year-old *Ahnighito,* the largest meteorite ever retrieved from the Earth's surface. An **IMAX Theater** screens films about nature; the adjacent **Hayden Planetarium** is undergoing an extensive renovation and is slated to reopen in 2000 as the Center for Earth and Space. ✉ *Central Park W at W. 79th St.,* ☎ *212/769–5200 for museum tickets and programs, 212/769–5100 for museum general information, 212/769–5034 for IMAX Theater show times.* 🎫 *Museum: donations suggested; IMAX Theater: $15; combination tickets available. Closed Mon.*

Founded in 1754, **Columbia University** (☎ 212/854–3574) is a wealthy, private university that is New York City's only Ivy League school. Bounded by 114th and 120th streets, Broadway, and Amsterdam Avenue, the campus is so effectively walled off from the city by buildings that it's easy to believe you're in a more rustic setting. Enter at 116th Street and Broadway for a look around. Close to Columbia University is the **Cathedral of St. John the Divine,** an immense limestone-and-granite church that, when finished, will be the largest Gothic structure in the world. Until then, you can have a rare, fascinating look at a cathedral in progress. ✉ *1047 Amsterdam Ave., at 112th St.,* ☎ *212/316–7540, 212/932–7347 to arrange tours.* 🎫 *Tours: donations suggested.*

Harlem

Harlem has been the mecca for African-American culture for nearly a century. In the 1920s, during an astonishing confluence of talent known as the Harlem Renaissance, black novelists, playwrights, musicians, and artists gathered here. By the 1960s crowded housing, poverty, and crime had turned the neighborhood into a simmering ghetto. Today Harlem is on the way to restoring itself. Mixed in with some seedy remains of the past are old jewels like the refurbished **Apollo Theatre** (✉ 253 W. 125th St., ☎ 212/749–5838), where such music greats as Ella Fitzgerald and Duke Ellington brought black musicians into the limelight. **Schomburg Center for Research in Black Culture** contains more than 5 million items in its collection, including rare manuscripts, art and artifacts, motion pictures, records, and videotapes. Regular exhibits, performing arts programs, and lectures at the center contribute to Harlem's culture. ✉ *515 Lenox Ave., at 135th St.,* ☎ *212/491–2200.* 🎫 *Free.*

Upper East Side

The **Upper East Side,** east of Central Park between 59th and 96th streets, epitomizes the high-style, high-society way of life most people associate with the Big Apple. The neighborhood includes singles bars and high-rise apartment buildings on 1st Avenue, sedate town houses in the east 60s, and an outstanding concentration of art museums and galleries. Along the **Madison Mile,** Madison Avenue between 59th and 79th streets, are patrician art galleries, unique specialty stores, and the boutiques of many of the world's major fashion designers. **Museum Mile** is a strip of cultural institutions, representing a broad spectrum of subjects and styles, on or near 5th Avenue between 70th and 104th streets.

★ The **Frick Collection,** housed in a Beaux Arts–style palace built by Pittsburgh coke and steel baron Henry Clay Frick, is the city's finest small art museum. Specializing in European works from the late 13th to the late 19th centuries, it has masterpieces by Rembrandt, Fragonard, Bellini, Turner, and Vermeer, among others. ✉ *1 E. 70th St., at 5th Ave.,* ☎ *212/288–0700.* 🎫 *$5. Closed Mon.*

The **Whitney Museum of American Art,** a gray granite vault with cantilevering and startling trapezoidal windows that project outward, is devoted exclusively to 20th-century American works, from naturalism and impressionism to pop art, abstractionism, and whatever comes next. ✉ *945 Madison Ave., at 75th St.,* ☎ *212/570–3676.* *$8; free Thurs. 6–8. Closed Mon.–Tues.*

★ The **Metropolitan Museum of Art,** on the edge of Central Park, is the largest art museum in the western hemisphere. Major displays cover prehistoric to modern times and all areas of the world, including impressive Greek and Egyptian collections and an entire wing devoted to tribal arts. The museum has the world's most comprehensive collection of American art, and its holdings of European art are unequaled outside Europe. Also here are the Temple of Dendur, an entire Roman temple (circa 15 BC), and galleries devoted to musical instruments and arms and armor. Walking tours and lectures are free with admission. The separate **Cloisters** (☎ 212/923–3700) building, transported stone by stone from France, overlooks the Hudson River in Fort Tryon Park at the top of Manhattan; it houses the museum's medieval collection. ✉ *5th Ave. at 82nd St.,* ☎ *212/879–5500.* *Donations suggested. Closed Mon.*

★ The **Solomon R. Guggenheim Museum,** designed by Frank Lloyd Wright and expanded and restored in 1992, is a six-story spiral rotunda that winds down past fine exemplars of modern art. Exhibits alternate between new artists and modern masters; the permanent collection includes more than 20 Picassos. ✉ *1071 5th Ave., at 88th St.,* ☎ *212/423–3500.* *$10; donations suggested Fri. 6–8. Closed Thurs.*

The **Cooper-Hewitt National Design Museum,** a branch of the Smithsonian Institution, was once the residence of industrialist and philanthropist Andrew Carnegie. Changing exhibitions focus on various aspects of contemporary or historical design. Major holdings include drawings and prints, textiles, wall coverings, applied arts and industrial design, and contemporary design. ✉ *2 E. 91st St.,* ☎ *212/860–6868.* *$3; free Tues. 5–9. Closed Mon.*

The **Museum of the City of New York** brings the history of the Big Apple to life from its seafaring beginnings to yesterday's headlines, with period rooms, a video, clever displays of memorabilia, and a dollhouse collection. ✉ *5th Ave. at 103rd St.,* ☎ *212/534–1672.* *Donations suggested. Closed Mon.–Tues.*

Chelsea, Greenwich Village, and the East Village

Like its London namesake, **Chelsea** maintains a villagelike personality, with a number of quiet streets graced by lovingly renovated town houses. The neighborhood stretches from 5th Avenue west to the Hudson River and from 14th to 29th streets and is now home to an active gay community that frequents the lively stores and restaurants on 8th and 7th avenues. In recent years the area has witnessed an economic boost with the opening of 6th Avenue superstores and the Chelsea Piers Sports and Entertainment Complex on the Hudson. Galleries have set up shop west of 10th Avenue from 20th to 29th streets.

★ With its narrow tree-lined streets, brick town houses, tiny green parks, and hidden courtyards, **Greenwich Village** is the closest thing to a small town in Manhattan. The Village is ideal for strolling, window-shopping, and café hopping; it extends from 14th Street south to Houston Street and from the Hudson River piers to 5th Avenue.

For generations the preferred haunt of writers, artists, musicians, and bohemians, the Village is known for the scores of famous Americans who lived and worked here and the cultural movements they defined. Perhaps those most synonymous with Greenwich Village are the avant-garde artists of this century, including abstract expressionist painters like Franz Kline and Mark Rothko, Beat writers and poets such as Jack Kerouac and Allen Ginsberg, and folk musicians and poets, notably Bob Dylan and Peter, Paul, and Mary.

You'll encounter all kinds of **historical buildings** in a walk through the Village. At different times Edna St. Vincent Millay and John Barrymore each lived at 75½ Bedford Street—at 9½ ft wide, New York's narrowest house. Theodore Dreiser wrote *An American Tragedy* at 16 St. Luke's Place. The houses at 127 and 129 MacDougal Street were built in 1829 for Aaron Burr, who held much of the land now part of the Village.

Washington Square, at the foot of 5th Avenue, is the best place to begin a walking tour of the Village. In the center of the square is the gleaming white Washington Arch, designed by Stanford White and built in 1889 to commemorate the 100th anniversary of George Washington's inauguration. Most buildings bordering the square belong to New York University. The surrounding area, around the intersection of Bleecker and MacDougal streets, attracts a young crowd to its shops, bars, jazz clubs, Off-Broadway theaters, cabarets, coffeehouses, fast-food stands, cafés, and unpretentious restaurants.

To the northwest, at **Sheridan Square,** is Christopher Street, another hub of New York's gay community and the location of many intriguing boutiques. West of 7th Avenue South, the Village turns into a picture-book warren of twisting tree-lined streets, quaint houses, and tiny restaurants. The stretch of West 4th Street is particularly pleasant.

The **East Village,** east of 4th Avenue (Lafayette Street), has over the centuries housed Jewish, Ukrainian, and Puerto Rican immigrants; beatniks; hippies; punk rockers; artists of various stripes; and most recently, affluent young professionals. Soak up the eclectic atmosphere along St. Marks Place between 2nd Avenue and Avenue B and 9th Street between 2nd Avenue and Avenue A, with their veggie restaurants, alternative clothing boutiques, cafés, and offbeat shops.

SoHo, Little Italy, and Chinatown

SoHo (so named because it is the district *So*uth of *Ho*uston [pronounced *How*-ston] Street, bounded by Broadway, Canal Street, and 6th Avenue) is synonymous with a gritty urban elegance—an amalgam of black-clad artists, hip young Wall Streeters, track-lighted loft apartments, art galleries, and restaurants with a minimalist approach to both food and decor.

West Broadway (paralleling Broadway four blocks to the west) is SoHo's main drag, with many shops and galleries. On Saturday, the big day for gallery hopping, it can be crowded but still great for people-watching. **At 28–30 and 72–76 Greene Street** you'll find two fine examples of cast-iron architecture, of which SoHo has one of the world's greatest concentrations.

Walk one block east to Grand and Mulberry streets to enter **Little Italy,** an ever-shrinking enclave of Italian life. Mulberry Street, lined with tenement buildings, has long been the heart of Little Italy; now it's virtually the entire body. Between Broome and Canal streets, Mulberry consists entirely of restaurants, cafés, bakeries, food shops, and souvenir stores. Each September the Feast of San Gennaro turns the streets of Little Italy into a bright and turbulent Italian kitchen.

In recent years **Chinatown** has expanded beyond its traditional borders into Little Italy to the north and the Lower East Side, once a neighborhood of Jewish immigrants, to the south and east. Canal and Grand streets abound with crowded markets bursting with mounds of fresh seafood and strangely shaped vegetables in extraterrestrial shades of green. Food shops proudly display their wares, from almond cookies to roasted ducks.

Mott Street is Chinatown's principal business street. Narrow and twisting, crammed with souvenir shops and restaurants in funky pagoda-style buildings, and crowded with pedestrians at all hours of the day or night—Mott Street looks the way you'd expect Chinatown to look. Within a few dense blocks, hundreds of restaurants serve every imaginable type of Chinese cuisine, from simple fast-food noodles or dumplings to sumptuous Hunan, Szechuan, Cantonese, Mandarin, and Shanghai feasts.

Lower Manhattan

Lower Manhattan is compact and packed with attractions: narrow streets and immense skyscrapers, Wall Street and Colonial-era houses, South Street Seaport and Battery Park City. The city did not really expand beyond these precincts until the middle of the 19th century. Today Wall Street in many ways dominates Lower Manhattan; the thoroughfare is both an actual street and a shorthand name for the vast, powerful financial community that clusters around the New York and American stock exchanges.

Outside the **Staten Island Ferry Terminal,** at the southernmost tip of Manhattan, is a good place to start your exploration of Lower Manhattan. For great harbor views of the Statue of Liberty, Ellis Island, and the Lower Manhattan skyline, consider the free ferry ride to Staten Island. **Battery Park,** a verdant landfill loaded with monuments and sculpture and the point of embarkation for visits to the Statue of Liberty and Ellis Island, is a short walk up the Battery Park waterfront from the Staten Island Ferry Terminal. Buy your ticket for the ferry ride to the Statue of Liberty or Ellis Island at Castle Clinton National Monument (☎ 212/269–5755; 🎫 ferry: $7 round-trip), inside the park; arrive early and be prepared to wait.

★ The **Statue of Liberty** (☎ 212/363–3200; 🎫 free) has enjoyed a remarkable resurgence of popularity following its centennial restoration in 1986. Once on Liberty Island you may have to wait three hours to take the elevator 10 stories to the top of the pedestal. The strong of heart and limb can climb another 12 stories to the crown.

★ **Ellis Island,** which reopened in 1990 after a $140 million restoration, was once the main East Coast federal immigration facility. Between 1892 and 1954, 17 million men, women, and children—the ancestors of more than 40% of the Americans living today—were processed here. *☎ 212/363–3200. 🎫 Free.*

The **National Museum of the American Indian,** in a stunning Beaux Arts–style building, opened in 1995, is the first national museum dedicated solely to Native American culture, and its exhibits of fascinating objects from around the Americas are accompanied with good documentation. *✉ 1 Bowling Green, ☎ 212/668–6624. 🎫 Free.*

Fraunces Tavern is a combination restaurant, bar, and museum occupying a Colonial house built in 1719 and restored in 1907. Best remembered as the site of George Washington's farewell address to his officers, which celebrated the British evacuation of New York in 1783, it contains two fully furnished period rooms and other displays on 18th- and 19th-century American history. *✉ Broad and Pearl Sts., ☎ 212/425–1778. 🎫 Museum $2.50.*

The **World Trade Center,** a 16-acre complex, contains New York's two tallest buildings (each 1,350 ft). Elevators to the observation deck on the 107th floor of 2 World Trade Center glide a quarter of a mile into the sky in only 58 seconds. *Ticket booth: 2 World Trade Center, mezzanine level,* ☎ *212/323–2340.* 💳 *$10.*

The rock and soil excavated in order to construct the World Trade Center begat **Battery Park City,** 100 new acres of Manhattan on the Hudson River. It includes office buildings, high-rise apartment houses, town houses, a selection of shops, and the **World Financial Center,** a mammoth granite-and-glass complex designed by Cesar Pelli.

Wall Street's principal facility, the **New York Stock Exchange** has its august Corinthian main entrance around the corner from Wall Street, on Broad Street. A self-guided tour, a multimedia presentation, and staff members may help you interpret the chaos that seems to reign on the trading floor. Free tour tickets are distributed beginning at 8:45 AM; come before 1 PM to assure entrance. ✉ *20 Broad St.,* ☎ *212/656–5168.* 💳 *Free. Closed weekends.*

A regal **statue of George Washington** on Wall Street stands at the spot where he was sworn in as the first U.S. president in 1789. After the capital moved to Philadelphia in 1790, the original Federal Hall became New York's city hall but was demolished in 1812. The current **Federal Hall National Memorial** (✉ 26 Wall St., ☎ 212/825–6888; 💳 free), built in 1842, is a stately period structure that contains exhibits on New York and Wall Street; it is closed weekends. **Trinity Church** (✉ Broadway and Wall St., ☎ 212/602–0872) was New York's first Anglican parish (1646). The graves of Alexander Hamilton and Robert Fulton are in the churchyard. The present structure (1846) ranked as the city's tallest building for most of the last half of the 19th century.

South Street Seaport is an 11-block historic district on the East River that encompasses a museum, shopping, historic ships, cruise boats, a multimedia presentation, and innumerable places to eat and drink. You can view the historic ships from Pier 16, which is the departure point for the one-hour Seaport Liberty Cruise (☎ 212/630–8888).

★ The **Brooklyn Bridge,** New York's oldest and best-known span, is just north of the South Street Seaport. When completed in 1883, it was the world's longest suspension bridge and the tallest structure in the city. Walking across the Brooklyn Bridge is a peak New York experience.

Parks, Gardens, and Zoos

★ **Central Park** was designed by landscape architects Frederick Law Olmsted and Calvert Vaux for 843 acres of land acquired by the city in 1856. Bounded by 59th and 110th streets, 5th Avenue, and Central Park West, the park contains grassy meadows, wooded groves, and formal gardens; paths for jogging, strolling, horseback riding, and biking; playing fields; a small zoo; an ice-skating rink; a carousel; an outdoor theater; and numerous fountains and sculptures.

★ The **Bronx Zoo** is the nation's largest urban zoo, with more than 4,000 animals on 265 acres of woods, ponds, streams, and parkland. ✉ *Bronx River Pkwy. and Fordham Rd.,* ☎ *718/367–1010,* 💳 *Apr.–Oct., Thurs.–Tues. $6.75; Nov.–Mar., Thurs.–Tues. $3; free Wed.; Children's Zoo, $2.*

New York's **Aquarium for Wildlife Conservation,** just off the Coney Island Boardwalk, has more than 20,000 creatures on display, with dolphins and sea lions performing in periodic exhibitions. ✉ *W. 8th St. and Surf Ave., Coney Island, Brooklyn,* ☎ *718/265–3474.* 💳 *$7.75.*

The **New York Botanical Garden,** a 250-acre botanical treasury around the dramatic gorge of the Bronx River, is within Bronx Park. Its 40-

acre forest, conservatory, museum, and outdoor gardens draw nature enthusiasts from around the world. ✉ *200th St. and Kazimiroff Blvd.,* ☎ *718/817–8700.* 💵 *Nov.–Mar. $1.50, Apr.–Oct. $3; free Sat. 10–noon and Wed.; Enid A. Haupt Conservatory $3.50; parking $4.*

Dining

New York restaurants don't have to be expensive; savvy diners know how to keep costs within reason. Go for lunch or brunch instead of dinner: Order prix fixe instead of à la carte: Share several appetizers—skipping higher-priced main courses. Or go ethnic: New York has restaurants specializing in almost any cuisine you can name (try Little India on 6th Street between 1st and 2nd avenues, Little Korea on West 32nd Street between 5th and 6th avenues, one of the ubiquitous storefront pasta parlors on the Upper East Side, or Chinatown, for starters). Be sure to make reservations on weekends. For price ranges *see* Chart 1 (A) *in* On the Road with Fodor's.

$$$$ ★ ✕ **Daniel.** At Daniel Boulud's celebrity-frequented restaurant, flower arrangements and antique mirrors adorn the main dining room. The cuisine (combining the contemporary with the classic) is among the best in New York. At press time, the restaurant announced that it would open as a more informal place, Café Boulud. A new Restaurant Daniel will open at 60 East 65th Street in early 1999. ✉ *20 E. 76th St.,* ☎ *212/288–0033. Reservations essential. Jacket required. AE, D, DC, MC, V. Closed Sun. No lunch Mon.*

$$$$ ★ ✕ **Jean-Georges.** Floor-to-ceiling windows, leather banquettes, white marble and terrazzo mosaics, and three silver-leaf screens that frame the exhibition kitchen all contribute to the understated luxury. You might search the culinary universe in vain to discover a more ethereal dish than sea scallops in a caper-raisin emulsion with caramelized cauliflower. ✉ *1 Central Park W,* ☎ *212/299–3900. Reservations essential. Jacket and tie. AE, DC, MC, V. Closed Sun.*

$$$$ ★ ✕ **Le Cirque 2000.** Begin by enjoying the whimsical, wonderful decor of the bar over bargain-priced fresh caviar. There are two main dining rooms, both housed in the historic Villard House, with its breathtaking ceiling. Don't miss the Thursday special, *Bollito Misto,* an aromatic mix of meats, sausage, brains, root vegetables, contrasting condiments, and coarse salt. ✉ *455 Madison Ave.,* ☎ *212/794–9292. Reservations essential. Jacket and tie. AE, DC, MC, V. Closed Sun.*

$$$$ ★ ✕ **Nobu.** A curved wall of river-worn black pebbles, a 12-seat onyx-faced sushi bar (perfect for single diners), birch trees, and a hand-painted beech floor create drama as well as conversation. The hip clientele is as interesting as the kitchen, which is ruled by chef Nobu Matsuhisa. Rock-shrimp tempura, black cod with miso, and sashimi—all are tours de force. ✉ *105 Hudson St., off Franklin St.,* ☎ *212/219–0500 or 212/219–8095 for same-day reservations. Reservations essential. AE, DC, MC, V. Closed Sun. No lunch.*

$$$$ ✕ **Rainbow Room.** This dinner-and-dancing room on the 65th floor of 30 Rock has been a monument to glamour and fantasy, with walls that frame panoramic 50-mi views through floor-to-ceiling windows. At press time, plans for 1999 called for making the restaurant open to the public at only limited times, though a bar would serve food. The Rainbow and Stars cabaret will become a restaurant. ✉ *30 Rockefeller Plaza,* ☎ *212/632–5000 or 212/632–5100. Reservations essential. Jacket and tie. AE, DC, MC, V. Closed Mon.*

$$$$ ★ ✕ **"21" Club.** This four-story brownstone landmark, a former speakeasy, first opened on December 31, 1929. Here is one of the world's great wine cellars, with some 50,000 bottles. The Grill Room is *the* place to

be, with its banquettes, red-checked tablecloths, and a ceiling hung with toys; it serves such standbys as the signature "21" burger and a host of more exciting dishes such as the Asian-style seared tuna. ✉ *21 W. 52nd St.,* ☎ *212/582–7200. Reservations essential. Jacket and tie. AE, DC, MC, V. Closed Sun. No lunch Sat.*

$$$–$$$$ ★ ✕ **Barbetta.** New York's oldest restaurant (opened in 1906) still operated by its founding family was one of the first to produce northern Italian food in America. This island of civility in two distinguished, antiques-furnished town houses has an enchanting garden, verdant with century-old trees. The *carne cruda* (hand-chopped raw veal with lemon juice and olive oil) and handmade *agnolotti* (pasta cut into small round pieces, stuffed with meat or vegetables, and folded in half like turnovers) are superb. ✉ *321 W. 46th St.,* ☎ *212/246–9171. Reservations essential. AE, DC, MC, V. Closed Sun. No lunch Mon.*

$$$–$$$$ ★ ✕ **Ben Benson's.** The expected steaks, chops, and accompaniments are first-rate, but there's a serious chef in this kitchen. Witness such contemporary steak-house fare as cold lobster cocktail and Maryland crab cakes. Don't miss the horseradish-mashed potatoes or the excellent home fries. This convivial spot has a masculine interior—brass plaques inscribed with names of celebrities, framed pictures of animals and game birds. ✉ *123 W. 52nd St.,* ☎ *212/581–8888. Reservations essential. AE, DC, MC, V. No lunch weekends.*

$$$–$$$$ ★ ✕ **Bouterin.** Baskets of apples and copper pans adorn the walls, adding a warm touch to the home of chef-owner Antoine Bouterin. The mix-and-match feel of the decor arises from Bouterin's interest in antiques collecting. The short menu of unpretentious dishes specializes in the cuisine of Provence and includes an old-fashioned lamb stew, cooked for seven hours and best eaten with a spoon. ✉ *420 E. 59th St.,* ☎ *212/758–0323. Reservations essential. Jacket required. AE, DC, MC, V. Closed Sun. No lunch.*

$$$–$$$$ ★ ✕ **Gramercy Tavern.** A 91-ft-long mural of fruit and vegetables wraps around the bar, and although the look is reminiscent of an English tavern, the food is decidedly new American. The section called the Tavern, off the main dining room, offers some terrific plates from the wood-burning grill (hanger steak sandwich, for one). An appealing selection of cheese and a stellar wine list are offered here and in the main room. ✉ *42 E. 20th St.,* ☎ *212/477–0777. Reservations essential for main dining room. AE, DC, MC, V. No lunch Sun.*

$$$–$$$$ ★ ✕ **L'Absinthe.** At this wonderful art nouveau bistro, chef-owner Jean-Michel Bergougnoux beautifully presents shellfish and cheese. Menu highlights include a fine foie gras terrine, slow-braised beef with carrots, poached free-range chicken in truffle broth, and for dessert, a thin, crisp apple tart or warm chocolate cake. ✉ *227 E. 67th St.,* ☎ *212/794–4950. Reservations essential. AE, MC, V.*

$$$–$$$$ ✕ **Water Club.** This glass-enclosed barge in the East River is decidedly dramatic, with its long wood-paneled bar, blazing fireplace, appetizing shellfish display, and panoramic water views. Food is ingeniously presented. The chef shows a fine hand with sautéed red snapper fillet with lobster dumplings, fennel, and saffron bouillon. ✉ *500 E. 30th St.,* ☎ *212/683–3333. Reservations essential. AE, DC, MC, V.*

$$$–$$$$ ★ ✕ **Windows on the World.** This monumental restaurant serving fine contemporary cuisine on the World Trade Center's 107th floor reopened a few years back after a $25 million makeover. The complex now includes the Greatest Bar on Earth, with a full multiethnic menu and dancing after 10 PM; the adjacent Skybox, a cigar-smoking oasis; and the intimate 60-seat Cellar in the Sky, where a seven-course dinner is served, accompanied by five wines. ✉ *1 World Trade Center, 107th floor,* ☎ *212/524–7011, 212/938–0030 for Cellar in the Sky. Reservations essential. Jacket required. AE, DC, MC, V.*

$$$–$$$$ ✕ **Zoë.** This colorful, high-ceiling SoHo eatery with a terra-cotta floor and an open kitchen produces impressive food such as grilled yellowfin tuna on wok-charred vegetables. Zoë also has an exceptionally well-organized wine list. This is one of the better places in Manhattan for weekend brunch. ✉ *90 Prince St., between Broadway and Mercer St.,* ☎ *212/966–6722. Reservations essential. AE, DC, MC, V.*

$$$ ★ ✕ **Balthazar.** Owned by Keith McNally (who also has hypertrendy Pravda and Odeon in his stable) and one of the most difficult reservations to score in town, Balthazar is a hot scene. The vintage French ambience is straight out of movie-set Paris. The Tuesday night special of *choucroute garni* is a delectable mix of several varieties of sausages (including veal and garlic) smoked meats, sauerkraut, and spices, all simmered in white Alsatian wine. ✉ *80 Spring St., between Broadway and Lafayette St.,* ☎ *212/965–1414. Reservations essential. AE, DC, MC, V. No lunch Mon.*

$$–$$$ ★ ✕ **Blue Water Grill.** Housed in what was once a bank, this popular spot retains the original 1904 marble and molded ceiling. The menu is strong on seafood, served neat (chilled whole lobster); in au courant "global" style (Moroccan-spiced red snapper); or in simple preparations from a wood-burning oven. ✉ *31 Union Sq. W,* ☎ *212/675–9500. Reservations essential. AE, DC, MC, V.*

$$–$$$ ✕ **Carmine's.** It's worth lining up for these cavernous family-style eateries that serve up home-style meals at low prices. Dishes like rigatoni in broccoli, sausage, and white-bean sauce are so gargantuan you'll have leftovers. ✉ *2450 Broadway,* ☎ *212/362–2200;* ✉ *200 W. 44th St.,* ☎ *212/221–3800. Reservations not accepted. AE. No lunch.*

$$–$$$ ✕ **Duane Park Café.** This quiet TriBeCa restaurant can spoil you with its comfortable seating, excellent service, serious but fairly priced wines, and international menu. Look for marinated duck and arugula salad and crispy skate with the Japanese-inspired *ponzu* sauce. ✉ *157 Duane St., between W. Broadway and Hudson St.,* ☎ *212/732–5555. AE, D, DC, MC, V. Closed Sun. No lunch Sat.*

$$–$$$ ★ ✕ **Hi-Life Restaurant and Lounge.** Young hip eaters sit down at one of the spacious half-moon-shaped booths at this bi-level Art Deco café. The draw? Soothing prices, huge portions, and great martinis. Polish off sushi or something from the raw bar before you proceed to the filet mignon served with potato salad or heaping bowls of *pad thai* (noodles with chicken or shrimp). ✉ *1340 1st Ave.,* ☎ *212/249–3600;* ✉ *477 Amsterdam Ave.,* ☎ *212/787–7199. AE, DC, MC, V.*

$$–$$$ ✕ **Ipanema.** Sample Brazil's exotic cuisine at this snug, modern restaurant with white- and peach-color walls covered with vivid oil paintings of Rio and Bahia. *Feijoada*—black beans with smoked meats, collard greens, oranges, chili peppers, and a comforting grain called *farofa*—is good here. ✉ *13 W. 46th St.,* ☎ *212/730–5848. AE, DC, MC, V.*

$$–$$$ ★ ✕ **Turkish Kitchen.** This multilevel spot has Turkish carpets on the floors and walls. Order anise-flavored *raki* as an aperitif with such *meze* (appetizers) as fried calamari with garlic sauce. Among entrées, try the succulent *doner* (vertically grilled lamb, sliced paper-thin). ✉ *386 3rd Ave.,* ☎ *212/679–1810. AE, DC, MC, V. No lunch weekends.*

$$ ★ ✕ **Amarone.** Named for a lush variety of Italian red wine, this unpretentious trattoria is arguably the best Italian eatery in Hell's Kitchen. Inquire about such delectable specials as the chef's grandmother's country-style *caviatelli* with sausage, carrots, and potatoes, or the excellent rabbit cacciatore. ✉ *686 Ninth Ave.,* ☎ *212/245–6060. AE, MC, V.*

$$ ★ ✕ **Grange Hall.** Emphasizing American-farm cuisine, this affordable eatery is in a former speakeasy on one of Greenwich Village's most charming tree-lined streets. The menu offers a variety of small plates (potato pancakes with chive–sour cream for example). The well prepared entrées—including the delicious, center-cut cranberry-glazed pork chops—may be ordered by themselves or with a choice of soup or field salad for a couple of bucks more. ✉ *50 Commerce St., at Barrow St.,* ☎ *212/924–5246. Reservations essential. AE.*

$$ ★ ✕ **Joe's Shanghai.** At this modern, clean, and unadorned Chinese dining spot, the specialty is bun (a tasty dumpling containing ground pork or crab and piping-hot broth). Also try Shanghai-fried flat noodles—long, winding doughy miracles in an intense brown sauce with stewed pork balls. ✉ *9 Pell St., between Bowery and Mott St.,* ☎ *212/233–8888. No credit cards.*

$$ ✕ **Mavalli Palace.** Service may be a bit slow, but the gentle prices and marvelous dishes more than compensate at this pretty Indian restaurant with exposed brick walls. Magnificent crepes made with lentils and rice flour are wrapped around potatoes and a fiery chutney. ✉ *46 E. 29th St.,* ☎ *212/679–5535. AE, DC, MC, V. Closed Mon.*

$–$$ ★ ✕ **Boca Chica.** This raffish East Village restaurant has live music, dancing, and assertive food from several Latin American nations. Try the soupy Puerto Rican chicken-and-rice stew known as *asopao,* the Cuban sandwiches, or the Bolivian corn topped with chicken. ✉ *13 1st Ave.,* ☎ *212/473–0108. Reservations not accepted. AE, DC, MC, V.*

$–$$ ✕ **French Roast.** This casual, around-the-clock spot with a Left Bank ambience charges bargain prices for some very good bistro dishes such as poached beef marrow finished with bread crumbs. The *croque monsieur* (melted cheese sandwich, done in the style of French toast) is first-rate. Or just stop for coffee and dessert. A sister spot is on the Upper West Side (✉ 2340 Broadway, at 85th St., ☎ 212/799–1533). ✉ *458 6th Ave.,* ☎ *212/533–2233. AE, MC, V.*

$–$$ ✕ **Ngone.** At this pleasant Senegalese dining spot, colorful African-pattern cloths cover the tables, and the walls display tapestries and painted scenes of the countryside. Among the appealingly hot dishes are traditional *boulettes* (appetizers of boneless fish, seasoned with parsley and spices), chicken *yassa* (cooked with lemon, ginger, carrots, and potatoes), and lamb in a creamy peanut sauce. ✉ *823 6th Ave.,* ☎ *212/967–7899. No credit cards. BYOB. Closed Sun.*

$–$$ ✕ **Republic.** Downtown epicureans on the run flock to this innovative Asian noodle emporium. At one of the two bluestone bars, you can dine and enjoy the spectacle of chefs scurrying amid clouds of steam in the open kitchen. The large dining space also has sleek birch tables. The menu chiefly contains dishes of rice or noodles, stir-fried or served in savory broths. ✉ *37A Union Sq. W,* ☎ *212/627–7172. AE, DC, MC, V.*

$–$$ ★ ✕ **Uncle Nick's.** At this inexpensive taverna you dine in a long room, with a navy blue pipe-lined tin ceiling, an exposed kitchen, and a wood floor. Uncle Nick's owners, Tony and Mike Vanatakis, prepare each fish selection with simplicity and care. Be sure to try as many of the excellent appetizers as your tummy can handle, including crispy fried smelts, tender grilled baby octopus, and giant lima beans with tomatoes and herbs. ✉ *747 9th Ave.,* ☎ *212/245–7992. MC, V.*

$–$$ ✕ **Virgil's.** This massive barbecue roadhouse in the Theater District has clever neon-and-Formica decor. Start with stuffed jalapeños or buttermilk onion rings with blue-cheese dip. Then go for the Pig Out: a rack of pork ribs, Texas hot links, pulled pork, rack of lamb, chicken, and more. Wash it all down with beer from a good list. ✉ *152 W. 44th St.,* ☎ *212/921–9494. Reservations essential. AE, MC, V.*

Lodging

A sustained boom in tourism has resulted in a constant demand for hotel rooms in New York City, allowing hoteliers to jack up their rates to all-time highs: $200 per night is the average rate predicted by 1999. We have scoured the city for good-value hotels and budget properties, but even our $$ category includes hotels that run as high as $125 for one night's stay, double-occupancy room.

Hundreds of **bed-and-breakfast rooms** are available in Manhattan and the outer boroughs, principally Brooklyn, and often cost less than $100 a night. Reservations services include **A Hospitality Co.** (✉ 580 Broadway, 10012, ☎ 212/965–1102 or 800/987–1235, FAX 212/965–1149); **Bed and Breakfast Network of New York** (✉ 134 W. 32nd St., Suite 602, 10001, ☎ 212/645–8134 or 800/900–8134); **Manhattan Home Stays** (✉ Box 20684, Cherokee Station, 10021, ☎ 212/737–3868, FAX 212/265–3561); and **New York Habitat** (✉ 307 7th Ave., Suite 306, 10001, ☎ 212/647–9365, FAX 212/627–1416). For price ranges *see* Chart 2 (A) *in* On the Road with Fodor's.

$$$$ ★ **The Carlyle.** European tradition and Manhattan swank shake hands at this elegant baby grand on Madison Avenue, just steps from Central Park. Everything here suggests refinement, from the Mark Hampton–designed rooms, with their fine antique furniture and artfully framed Audubons and botanicals, to the first-rate service. ✉ *35 E. 76th St., 10021,* ☎ *212/744–1600 or 800/227–5737,* FAX *212/717–4682. 190 rooms. Restaurant, health club. AE, DC, MC, V.*

$$$$ **Essex House.** The lobby of this stately Central Park South property is an Art Deco masterpiece fit for Fred and Ginger. The talented Christian Delouvrier oversees the cuisine, both in the informal Café Botanica and in the acclaimed Les Célébrités, where art painted by luminaries covers the walls. Guest rooms, all with large, marble bathrooms, are outfitted with British Chippendale or French Louis XIV antiques. ✉ *160 Central Park S, 10019,* ☎ *212/247–0300,* FAX *212/315–1839. 597 rooms. 2 restaurants, health club. AE, D, DC, MC, V.*

$$$$ **New York Hilton.** You could easily spend a week in New York without setting foot outside this vast midtown hotel, whose myriad business facilities, eating establishments, and shops are designed for convenience. Considering the size of this property, guest rooms are surprisingly well maintained, and all have coffeemakers, hair dryers, and ironing boards. ✉ *1335 6th Ave., 10019,* ☎ *212/586–7000 or 800/445–8667,* FAX *212/261–5902. 2,081 rooms. 2 restaurants, health club. AE, D, DC, MC, V.*

$$$$ **Waldorf-Astoria.** This Art Deco masterpiece built in 1931 is a hub of city life; the lobby, with its original murals and mosaics, is a meeting place for the rich and powerful. Guest rooms, each individually decorated, are all traditional and elegant. ✉ *301 Park Ave., 10022,* ☎ *212/355–3000 or 800/925–3673,* FAX *212/872–7272. 1,452 rooms. 4 restaurants, health club. AE, D, DC, MC, V.*

$$$$ ★ **The Warwick.** Built by William Randolph Hearst in 1927, the Warwick remains a midtown favorite, catercorner from the New York Hilton and well placed for theater and points west. Its handsome, Regency-style rooms have soft pastel color schemes, mahogany armoires, and nice marble bathrooms. ✉ *65 W. 54th St., 10019,* ☎ *212/247–2700,* FAX *212/489–3926. 416 rooms. Restaurant. AE, DC, MC, V.*

$$$ **Chelsea Savoy Hotel.** Affordable rates and a friendly though often harried young staff make this hip, young Chelsea newcomer a sensible choice. Rooms are small and basic, with jade-green carpets, butterscotch-colored wood furniture, and perhaps a framed van Gogh print. A café was in the works at press time. ✉ *204 W. 23rd St., 10011,* ☎ *212/929–9353,* FAX *212/741–6309. 90 rooms. AE, MC, V.*

$$$ ★ **Hotel Beacon.** The Upper West Side's best affordable buy is a short walk from both Central Park and Lincoln Center. All rooms and suites have kitchenettes with coffeemakers, full-size refrigerators, and stoves; some even have microwaves and stoves. What's more, the closets are huge, and the bathrooms come complete with Hollywood dressing room–style mirrors. ✉ *2130 Broadway, at 75th St., 10023,* ☎ *212/787–1100 or 800/572–4969,* FAX *212/724–0839. 210 rooms. AE, D, DC, MC, V.*

$$$ 🏨 **The Lucerne.** In a handsome brownstone building on a quiet, Upper West Side side street, this bargain newcomer enjoys a constant buzz of activity, thanks to the publike Wilson's Bar & Grill next door. The multihued-marble lobby, with its earth-tone walls and comfy olive-green couches, has more pizzazz than the predictable guest rooms. ✉ *201 W. 79th St., 10024,* ☎ *212/875–1000,* FAX *212/362–7251. 180 rooms. Restaurant, exercise room. AE, D, DC, MC, V.*

$$$ 🏨 **Quality Hotel East Side.** The least antiseptic of Manhattan's three Apple Core hotels, this East-sider on a pleasant residential block has sunny, simple rooms done in primary colors, with framed Americana prints. In the basement are a small exercise room and a tiny business center with a fax, photocopier, and computer. ✉ *161 Lexington Ave., at 30th St., 10016,* ☎ *212/532–2255 or 800/567–7720,* FAX *212/481–7270. 176 rooms. Exercise room. AE, D, DC, MC, V.*

$$$ ★ 🏨 **The Wyndham.** This bargain sleeper has three major trump cards: a plum location catercorner to Central Park South; enormous rooms and suites; and a brilliant collection of art, all of it framed and dramatically lit, filling all the rooms and public areas. Every one of the well-worn rooms is different, but count on a walk-in closet, a few choice paintings, and a handful of books stacked in shelves. ✉ *42 W. 58th St., 10019,* ☎ *212/753–3500 or 800/257–1111,* FAX *212/754–5638. 212 rooms. Restaurant. AE, D, MC, V.*

$$ 🏨 **Herald Square Hotel.** Vintage magazine covers adorning the hallways inside lend character to this historic hotel, housed in the former *Life* magazine building. Rooms are basic and clean, with deep-green carpets and floral-print bedspreads; all have TVs, phones with voice mail, and in-room safes. ✉ *19 W. 31st St., 10001,* ☎ *212/279–4017 or 800/727–1888,* FAX *212/643–9208. 120 rooms. AE, D, MC, V.*

$$ 🏨 **Hotel Edison.** This offbeat old hotel is a popular budget stop for tour groups from here and abroad. The loan-shark murder scene in *The Godfather* was shot in what is now Sophia's restaurant, and the pink-plaster coffee shop is a hot place to eavesdrop on show-business gossip. Guest rooms are clean and fresh; bathrooms are miniscule. ✉ *228 W. 47th St., 10036,* ☎ *212/840–5000 or 800/637–7070,* FAX *212/596–6850. 800 rooms. Restaurant. AE, D, DC, MC, V.*

$$ ★ 🏨 **Larchmont Hotel.** You might miss the entrance to this Beaux Arts brownstone, whose geranium boxes and lanterns blend right in with the old New York feel of West 11th Street. If you don't mind shared bathrooms and no room service or concierge, the residential-style accommodations are all anyone could ask for at this price (doubles are just under $100). ✉ *27 W. 11th St., 10011,* ☎ *212/989–9333,* FAX *212/989–9496. 77 rooms without bath. AE, D, DC, MC, V. CP.*

$$ 🏨 **Washington Square Hotel.** This cozy Greenwich Village hotel has a true European feel and style, from the wrought iron and gleaming brass in the small, elegant lobby to the personal service. Rooms are simple but pleasant and well maintained; request one with a window. There's also a good, reasonably priced restaurant, C3. ✉ *103 Waverly Pl., 10011,* ☎ *212/777–9515 or 800/222–0418,* FAX *212/979–8373. 150 rooms. Restaurant, exercise room. AE, MC, V. CP.*

$–$$ 🏨 **The Gershwin.** Young, foreign travelers flock to this hip budget hotel-cum-hostel, housed in a 13-story Greek Revival. Enter, and be visually assaulted by a giant primary-colored cartoony sculpture, one of many works by house artist Brad Howe. Dormitories have four or eight beds and a remarkable $22 rate. ✉ *7 E. 27th St., 10016,* ☎ *212/545–8000,* FAX *212/684–5546. 120 rooms, 15 dorm rooms. Restaurant. MC, V.*

$–$$ **Pickwick Arms Hotel.** This convenient East Side establishment charges $110 a night for standard doubles and has older singles with shared baths for as little as $65; it's routinely booked solid by bargain hunters. Privations you endure to save a buck start and end with the Lilliputian size of some rooms, which have cheap-looking furnishings. ✉ *230 E. 51st St., 10022,* ☎ *212/355–0300 or 800/742–5945,* FAX *212/755–5029. 350 rooms, 175 with bath. AE, DC, MC, V.*

$ **Malibu Studios Hotel.** This hip, young, budget crash pad could very well pass for a college dorm, especially given its proximity to the Columbia University campus. Though it's farther north than some would care to venture, the neighborhood is lively and safe. Clean, modern double-occupancy rooms with private bath start at $79, and those with shared bath start at $45. Every room has a TV, a desk with a writing lamp, and black-and-white prints of New York. ✉ *2688 Broadway, at 103rd St., 10025,* ☎ *212/222–2954 or 800/647–2227,* FAX *212/678–6842. 150 rooms, 110 with bath. No credit cards. CP.*

Nightlife and the Arts

Full listings of entertainment and cultural events appear in the weekly magazines *New York* and *Time Out New York*; they include capsule summaries of plays and concerts, performance times, and ticket prices. The Arts & Leisure section of the Sunday *New York Times* also lists and describes events, though in somewhat less detail. The Theater Directory in the daily *New York Times* advertises ticket information for Broadway and Off-Broadway shows. Listings of events also appear weekly in *The New Yorker* and the *Village Voice,* a free weekly newspaper that has more nightclub ads than any other rag in the world.

BAR-LOUNGES

Divine Bar (✉ 244 E. 51st St., ☎ 212/319–9463) is an uptown spot with a SoHo feel, with its zebra-striped bar chairs, cigar area, and cozy, velvet couches upstairs. **Pravda** (✉ 281 Lafayette St., ☎ 212/226–4696), a Russian-theme trendy bar, has more than 70 brands of vodka and nearly as many types of martinis. The **Screening Room** (✉ 54 Varick St., ☎ 212/334–2100) offers good food, drinks, and movies all in one congenial TriBeCa space. **Spy** (✉ 101 Greene St., ☎ 212/343–9000) provides a baroque parlor setting with plush couches and pretty people. **Wax** (✉ 113 Mercer St., ☎ 212/226–6082) has bare wooden floors, rather uncomfortable settees, and candles creating a soft glow on the tables.

CABARET

The **Oak Room** at the Algonquin Hotel (✉ 59 W. 44th St., ☎ 212/840–6800) still offers yesteryear's charms. Just head straight for the long, narrow club–cum–watering hole; you might find the hopelessly romantic singer Andrea Marcovicci.

COMEDY CLUBS

Caroline's Comedy Club (✉ 1626 Broadway, ☎ 212/757–4100), a high-gloss venue, features established names as well as comedians on the edge of stardom. **Original Improvisation** (✉ 433 W. 34th St., ☎ 212/279–3446), one of New York's oldest comedy showcases, is where many big-name yucksters got their start.

DANCE CLUBS

Nell's (✉ 246 W. 14th St., ☎ 212/675–1567) has an upstairs live-music jazz salon; downstairs is for dancing to music spun by a DJ. **Roseland** (✉ 239 W. 52nd St., ☎ 212/247–0200) has ballroom dancing Sunday (music by a live orchestra as well as a DJ). **Webster Hall** (✉ 125 E. 11th St., ☎ 212/353–1600), a fave among NYU students and similar species, boasts four floors and five eras of music.

JAZZ CLUBS

Many consider the **Blue Note** (✉ 131 W. 3rd St., ☎ 212/475–8592) the jazz capital of the world. **Michael's Pub** (✉ 57 E. 54th St., ☎ 212/758–2272) is where you can find Woody Allen moonlighting on the clarinet most Monday nights when he performs with his New Orleans Jazz Band. The **Village Vanguard** (✉ 178 7th Ave. S, ☎ 212/255–4037) is a basement joint that has ridden the crest of every new wave in jazz for decades.

POP, ROCK, BLUES, AND COUNTRY

The **Bitter End** (✉ 147 Bleecker St., ☎ 212/673–7030) has been giving a break to folk, rock, jazz, and country acts for more than 25 years. The **Bottom Line** (✉ 15 W. 4th St., ☎ 212/228–7880), an intimate sit-down space, features folk and rock headliners. **Manny's Car Wash** (✉ 1558 3rd Ave., ☎ 212/369–2583) has live blues every night, including powerhouse blues jams on Sunday. **Rodeo Bar** (✉ 375 3rd Ave., ☎ 212/683–6500), a full-scale Texas roadhouse, never charges a cover for its country, rock, rockabilly, and blues bands. **Tramps** (✉ 45 W. 21st St., ☎ 212/727–7788) has delivered bands like NRBQ, George Clinton, and Sponge for more then 25 years.

FOR SINGLES (UNDER 30)

At the **Ear Inn** (✉ 326 Spring St., ☎ 212/226–9060) it's the artsy crowd that makes the place: The regular poetry readings are called Lunch for the Ear. **Hi-Life** (✉ 477 Amsterdam Ave., ☎ 212/787–7199) is big with the Upper West Side's bon vivants. Make your way to **Merc Bar** (✉ 151 Mercer St., ☎ 212/966–2727), in the heart of trendy SoHo. At **Telephone Bar** (✉ 149 2nd Ave., ☎ 212/529–5000) you'll find imported English telephone booths and a polite, handsome crowd.

FOR SINGLES (OVER 30)

Pete's Tavern (✉ 129 E. 18th St., ☎ 212/473–7676) is a crowded, friendly saloon renowned as the place where O. Henry wrote "The Gift of the Magi." The **White Horse Tavern** (✉ 567 Hudson St., ☎ 212/989–3956), famous with the literati, was patronized by Dylan Thomas.

GAY AND LESBIAN BARS AND CLUBS

For advice on the bar scene, health issues, and other assorted quandaries, call the **Gay and Lesbian Switchboard** (☎ 212/777–1800) or stop by the **Lesbian and Gay Community Services Center** (✉ 208 W. 13th St., ☎ 212/620–7310). **g** (✉ 223 W. 19th St., ☎ 212/929–1085), an up-to-the-minute Chelsea favorite, draws an upscale, mostly male crowd to its huge circular bar and two airy, relaxed rooms lined with leather settees. At the **Works** (✉ 428 Columbus Ave., ☎ 212/799–7365), local J. Crew–clad Upper West Siders cruise and mingle. The lesbian-frequented **Henrietta Hudson** (✉ 438 Hudson St., ☎ 212/924–3347) has a pool table. **Julie's** (✉ 204 E. 58th St., ☎ 212/688–1294) is popular with a sophisticated upper-crust female crowd.

The Arts

DANCE

The **American Ballet Theatre** (☎ 212/362–6000) in Lincoln Center is the resident dance company of the Metropolitan Opera House. The **New York City Ballet** (☎ 212/870–5570) performs at Lincoln Center's New York State Theater; it reached world-class prominence under the direction of the late George Balanchine; Peter Martins is now ballet master-in-chief. **City Center** (✉ 131 W. 55th St., ☎ 212/581–1212) hosts innovative dance companies. The **Joyce Theater** (✉ 8th Ave. at 19th St., ☎ 212/242–0800), home to the avant-garde Ballet Tech (founded as Feld Ballet/NY), also schedules a potpourri of international dance troupes.

FILM

On any day of the year visitors to **New York movie theaters** will find all the major new releases, renowned classics, unusual foreign offerings, and experimental works. For information on schedules and theaters dial 212/777–FILM, the MovieFone, sponsored by WNEW 102.7 FM and the *New York Times,* or check the local newspapers. *New York, The New Yorker,* and *Time Out New York* magazines publish programs and reviews. The vast majority of Manhattan theaters are first-run houses.

MUSIC

Lincoln Center (☞ Upper West Side *in* Exploring New York City, *above*) has magnificent concert halls and theaters showcasing much of New York's serious music scene. Its Avery Fisher Hall (☎ 212/875–5030) is home to the New York Philharmonic Orchestra, the Mostly Mozart Festival, and visiting orchestras and soloists. **Carnegie Hall** (✉ 154 W. 57th St., ☎ 212/247–7800), the city's most famous classical-music palace, is more than 100 years old.

OPERA

The **Metropolitan Opera House** (☎ 212/362–6000), at Lincoln Center, is a sublime setting for mostly classic operas performed by world-class stars. The **New York City Opera** (☎ 212/870–5570), at Lincoln Center's State Theater, offers a diverse repertoire consisting of adventurous and rarely seen works as well as classic opera favorites.

THEATER

New York boasts nearly 40 Broadway theaters, three dozen Off-Broadway theaters, and 200 Off-Off-Broadway houses. Nearly all Broadway theaters are in the Theater District, most of which lies between Broadway and 8th Avenue, from 40th to 53nd streets. (The Vivian Beaumont Theatre is at Lincoln Center, Broadway at 65th Street.) Off- and Off-Off-Broadway theaters are scattered all over town.

The **TKTS booths** in Duffy Square (✉ 47th St. and Broadway, ☎ 212/768–1818) and in the Wall Street area (✉ 2 World Trade Center mezzanine, ☎ 212/768–1818) are New York's best-known discount source. TKTS sells day-of-performance tickets for Broadway and some Off-Broadway plays at discounts of 25% or 50% (plus $2.50 surcharge per ticket), depending on a show's popularity. The Broadway booth opens at 10 AM, the World Trade Center booth at 11 AM. TKTS accepts only cash or traveler's checks—no credit cards.

Spectator Sports

Baseball: New York Mets (✉ Shea Stadium, Roosevelt Ave. off Grand Central Pkwy., Flushing, Queens, ☎ 718/507–8499). **New York Yankees** (✉ Yankee Stadium, 161st St., The Bronx, ☎ 212/293–6000). **Basketball: New York Knicks** (✉ Madison Square Garden, 7th Ave. between 31st and 33rd Sts., ☎ 212/465–6741 or 212/465–5867 for Knicks Hot Line). **New York Liberty** (✉ Madison Square Garden, 7th Ave. between 31st and 33rd Sts., ☎ 212/465–6741 or 212/564–9622). **Football: New York Giants** (✉ Continental Airlines Sports Arena, Rte. 3, East Rutherford, NJ, ☎ 201/935–8111 or 201/935–3900). **New York Jets** (✉ Continental Airlines Sports Arena, Rte. 3,

East Rutherford, NJ, ☎ 516/560–8100 or 201/935–3900). **Hockey: New York Rangers** (✉ Madison Square Garden, 7th Ave. between 31st and 33rd Sts., ☎ 212/465–6741 or 212/308–6977 for Rangers Hot Line). **Tennis:** The annual **U.S. Open,** one of the four grand-slam events of tennis, is held in late August and early September at the USTA National Tennis Center in Flushing Meadows–Corona Park, Queens (☎ 800/524–8440).

Shopping

You can buy almost anything you might want or need at almost any time of day or night somewhere in New York City, but in general, major department stores and other shops are open every day and keep late hours on Thursday. Many of the upper-crust shops along upper 5th Avenue and Madison Avenue close on Sunday. The bargain shops along Orchard Street on the Lower East Side are closed on Saturday, mobbed on Sunday. For specialty stores with several branches in the city we have listed the locations in the busier shopping neighborhoods. Sales take place late June and July (for summer merchandise) and late December and January (for winter wares).

Shopping Neighborhoods

Fifth Avenue from 50th to 58th streets contains many of the world's most famous—and expensive—stores, including several excellent jewelers and department stores. **57th Street** between Park and 5th Avenues is still settling down from the building frenzy of 1997; now the ultra-exclusive (Chanel) are joined by more accessible retail blockbusters (Warner Bros. Studio Store). **Madison Avenue** between 59th and 79th streets has scads of couture flagship stores from the best American and international designers. **SoHo**'s galleries, clothing boutiques, and avant-garde housewares shops stretch along West Broadway and radiate off Prince Street. The superstores along SoHo's lower Broadway and in **Chelsea** provide some great bargains; there's also a healthy mix of funky shops and galleries. **Nolita,** a few blocks east of SoHo, has pocket-size housewares and clothing boutiques coming out of the woodwork. Nolita's parallel spines are Elizabeth, Mott, and Mulberry streets, between Houston and Spring. **Columbus Avenue,** between 66th and 86th streets, is a sturdy stretch of familiar chain stores dotted with a few interesting adults' and kids' clothing boutiques. The **Lower East Side** is the place for clothing bargains. The **East Village** offers eclectic designer boutiques and shops.

Department Stores

Though it closed its original flagship Chelsea store in late 1997, **Barneys** (✉ 660 Madison Ave., ☎ 212/826–8900) is still selling chichi designers and home furnishings from its deluxe Madison Avenue store. **Bergdorf Goodman** (✉ 754 5th Ave., ☎ 212/753–7300) is where devastating elegance reigns in a *vieux riches* setting; the men's store is across the street. **Bloomingdale's** (✉ 59th St. and Lexington Ave., ☎ 212/355–5900) is a New York institution, with a stupefying maze of cosmetic counters, mirrors, and black walls on the main floor and a good, dependable selection throughout. **Century 21** (✉ 22 Cortlandt St., between Broadway and Church St., ☎ 212/227–9092) is the mother lode of discount shopping; three large floors are crammed with everything from designer T-shirts to high-quality bedding. **Macy's** (✉ 34th St. and Broadway, ☎ 212/695–4400) has huge housewares and gourmet-foods departments, as well as not-too-fancy designer clothes. **Saks Fifth Avenue** (✉ 611 5th Ave., ☎ 212/753–4000) is a fashion-only department store, with rack after rack of conservative and voguish designer clothes. **Shanghai Tang** (✉ 667 Madison Ave., ☎ 212/

888–0111) is filled with electric colors, shimmering silks, and irreverent takes on Chinese cultural symbols.

Specialty Stores

ANTIQUES

At **Florian Papp** (✉ 962 Madison Ave., ☎ 212/288–6770) the shine of gilt lures knowledgeable collectors. **Israel Sack** (✉ 730 5th Ave., ☎ 212/399–6562) is widely considered one of the very best places in the country for 18th-century American furniture. At **Manhattan Art & Antiques Center** (✉ 1050 2nd Ave., ☎ 212/355–4400) more than 100 dealers stock three floors with antiques from around the world.

BOOKS

All the big national **chain bookstores** are here, with branches all over town—Barnes & Noble, Borders, and Waldenbooks, but New York is the perfect place to rediscover the intimate touch of the independent bookseller. **Crawford Doyle Booksellers** (✉ 1082 Madison Ave., ☎ 212/288–6300) has a thoughtful selection of fiction, nonfiction, biographies, etc., plus some rare books on the tight-fit upstairs balcony. **Gotham Book Mart** (✉ 41 W. 47th St., ☎ 212/719–4448) emphasizes literature and the performing arts in books and magazines. **Rizzoli Bookstore** (✉ 31 W. 57th St., ☎ 212/759–2424; ✉ World Financial Center, ☎ 212/385–1400; ✉ 1334 York Ave., at 72nd St., ☎ 212/606–7434) is a hushed environment with a rich book selection. The downtown branch (✉ 454 West Broadway, ☎ 212/674–1616) has a quirky boutique section and espresso bar. **Shakespeare & Co.** (✉ 939 Lexington Ave., between 68th and 69th Sts., ☎ 212/570–0201; ✉ 716 Broadway at Washington Pl., ☎ 212/529–1330) stocks the latest in just about every field. The somewhat scruffy **Strand** (✉ 828 Broadway, at 12th St., ☎ 212/473–1452; ✉ 95 Fulton St., ☎ 212/732–6070), North America's largest used-book store, offers more than 2 million volumes. **Three Lives & Co.** (✉ 154 W. 10th St., at Waverly Pl., ☎ 212/741–2069), perched on a picture-perfect West Village corner, has one of the city's most impeccable selection of books.

FOOD

Chelsea Market (✉ 75 Ninth Ave/88 Tenth Ave., between 15th and 16th Sts.) is a square block of foodie heaven. Walking through the main corridor, you can watch bakers and butchers at work, pick up a bottle of wine, or devour a whimsically decorated cookie. Those who never venture north of 14th Street head for **Dean & DeLuca** (✉ 560 Broadway, at Prince St., ☎ 212/431–1691), the SoHo trendsetter with a gleaming white space and an encyclopedic selection of gourmet produce and prepared foods, plus shining cookware in back. **Zabar's** (✉ 2245 Broadway, at 80th St., ☎ 212/787–2000) has long been a favorite with New York gourmands, with everything from jams, cheeses, spices, and smoked fish to a superb selection of kitchen wares, all reasonably priced.

JEWELRY

Bulgari (✉ 730 5th Ave., ☎ 212/315–9000; ✉ 783 Madison Ave., ☎ 212/717–2300; ✉ 2 E. 61st St., in the Hotel Pierre, ☎ 212/486–0326) has beautiful, weighty pieces, some encircled with the Bulgari name. Having recently passed the 150-year mark, **Cartier** (✉ 653 5th Ave., ☎ 212/753–0111) still dazzles with extravagant gems. Every store is a jewelry shop in the **Diamond District** (✉ 47th St. between 5th and 6th Aves.); be ready to haggle. At legendary **Tiffany & Co.** (✉ 727 5th Ave., ☎ 212/755–8000) prices can be extravagant, but there's always a selection of lower-price gift items, not to mention some of the most creative display windows on 5th Avenue.

MEN'S AND WOMEN'S WEAR

Calvin Klein (✉ 654 Madison Ave., ☎ 212/292–9000) has a huge, stark store showcasing the luxe end of the designer's clothing line, plus housewares, accessories, and yes, the underwear. In **Dolce & Gabbana** (✉ 825 Madison Ave., ☎ 212/249–4100) it's easy to feel like an Italian movie star amid the extravagant (in every sense) clothes. **Gianni Versace** (✉ 647 5th Ave., ☎ 212/317–0224; ✉ 815 Madison Ave., ☎ 212/744–6868) carries clothes with exuberant designs and colors that are never boring. **Giorgio Armani** (✉ 760 Madison Ave., ☎ 212/988–9191) displays stunning cuts of clothes in a museumlike space. **Gucci** (✉ 685 5th Ave., ☎ 212/826–2600) designer Tom Ford continues to sharpen the line's sexy image. Legendary discounter **Loehmann's** (✉ 101 7th Ave., ☎ 212/352–0856) can produce impressive savings on American and European designers. **Prada** (✉ 841 Madison Ave., ☎ 212/327–4200; ✉ 724 5th Ave., no phone; ✉ 45 E. 57th St., ☎ 212/308–2332) gossamer silks, slick black technofabric suits, and ultraluxe shoes and leather goods are one of the last great fashion coups of the millennium.

MUSIC STORES

Bleecker Bob's Golden Oldies (✉ 118 W. 3rd St., ☎ 212/475–9677) is a Greenwich Village spot with all that good old rock on vinyl. **Kim's Video & Music** (✉ 6 St. Mark's Pl., ☎ 212/598–9985; ✉ 144 Bleeker St., between Thompson St. and LaGuardia Pl., ☎ 212/260–1010; ✉ 350 Bleecker St., at W. 10th St., ☎ 212/675–8996), a scruffy and eclectic spot, is a compact crystallization of the downtown music scene. **Virgin Megastore Times Square** (✉ 1540 Broadway, ☎ 212/921–1020), reportedly the largest music and entertainment store in the world, has a gigantic space with a café, movie theater, bookstore, and laser disc and video section—besides the rows and rows of CDs. At press time a new Megastore was about to open on Union Square.

Side Trips to Other Boroughs

The Bronx

The 250-acre **New York Botanical Garden,** built around the dramatic gorge of the Bronx River, is considered one of the leading botany centers of the world. Less than a mile from the botanical garden is the world-class **Bronx Zoo** For both, (☞ Parks, Gardens, and Zoos, *above*).

ARRIVING AND DEPARTING

For the zoo, take Metro-North to the New York Botanical Garden, or take Subway D or 4 to Bedford Park Boulevard. For the botanical garden, take Subway 2 to Pelham Parkway and walk three blocks west to the zoo or take the Liberty Line BxM-11 express bus from Manhattan (☎ 718/652–8400 for bus schedules, locations of stops, and fares).

Brooklyn

★ **Brooklyn Heights** was New York's first suburb, linked to the city first by ferry and later by the Brooklyn Bridge. In the 1940s and 1950s the Heights was an alternative to the bohemian haven of Greenwich Village—home to writers including Carson McCullers, W. H. Auden, Alfred Kazin, and Norman Mailer. In the late 1960s the neighborhood was designated as New York's first historic district. Some 600 buildings more than 100 years old, representing a wide range of American building styles, are lovingly preserved today. The **Plymouth Church of the Pilgrims** (✉ Orange St., between Henry and Hicks Sts., ☎ 718/624–4743) was the center of abolitionist sentiment in the years before the Civil War, thanks to the oratory of the eminent theologian Henry Ward Beecher. **Willow Street,** between Clark and Pierrepont streets, is one of Brooklyn Heights' prettiest and most architecturally varied blocks. Pierrepont Street ends at the **Brooklyn Heights Promenade,** a quiet sliver of park lined with benches offering a dramatic vista of the Manhattan skyline. Just off the promenade's south end, **Montague Street,** the commercial spine of the Heights, offers a flurry of shops, cafés, and restaurants of every ethnicity.

ARRIVING AND DEPARTING

Walk across the Brooklyn Bridge from lower Manhattan near city hall and return on Subway 2 or 3 from the Clark Street station, a few blocks southwest of the walkway terminus.

Queens

Astoria, in Queens, is one of New York's most vital ethnic neighborhoods; once German, then Italian, it is now heavily Greek and is filled with shops and restaurants reflecting the community. Astoria is the site ★ of the **American Museum of the Moving Image,** where a theater features clips from the works of leading Hollywood cinematographers; galleries offer interactive exhibits on filmmaking techniques; and the collection of movie memorabilia contains costumes worn by everyone from Marlene Dietrich to Robin Williams. ✉ *35th Ave. at 36th St.,* ☎ *718/784–0077.* 🎫 *$8. Closed Mon.*

ARRIVING AND DEPARTING

Take the N train from Manhattan to the Broadway stop. For the Museum of the Moving Image, walk five blocks along Broadway to 36th Street; turn right and walk two blocks to 35th Avenue.

LONG ISLAND

Long Island is not only the largest island on America's East Coast—1,682 square mi—but the most varied. From west to east, Long Island encompasses two Manhattan boroughs (Brooklyn and Queens), congested commuter towns, the farmland of the North Fork, and the world-famous villages of the Hamptons. It has arguably the nation's finest stretch of white-sand beach, as well as the notoriously clogged Long Island Expressway (LIE).

Visitor Information

Long Island Convention and Visitors Bureau (✉ 350 Vanderbilt Motor Pkwy., Suite 103, Hauppauge 11788, ☎ 516/951–3440 or 800/441–4601). **Visitor centers,** open late spring–early fall (✉ Southern State Pkwy., between Exits 13 and 14, Valley Stream; LIE between Exits 52 and 53, Dix Hills–Deer Park; and ✉ Rte. 24, Flanders). **Fire Island Tourism Bureau** (✉ 49 N. Main St., Sayville 11782, ☎ 516/563–8448) is open Memorial Day through Labor Day.

Arriving and Departing

Although mass transit makes Long Island very accessible, a car is necessary to explore the island's nooks and crannies.

By Bus

Hampton Jitney (☎ 516/283–4600 or 800/936–0440 in New York City) links Manhattan and area airports with towns on the southeastern end of Long Island.

By Car

The **Midtown Tunnel** (I–495), **Queensborough Bridge** (Northern Boulevard, Rte. 25A), and the **Triborough Bridge** (I–278) connect Long Island with Manhattan. The **Throgs Neck Bridge** (I–295) and the **Whitestone Bridge** (I–678) provide access from the Bronx and New England.

By Ferry

There are several ferries that service Fire Island: The **Sayville Ferry Service** (☎ 516/589–8980) shuttles from Sayville to Cherry Grove, Fire Island Pines, and Sailor's Haven. **Fire Island Ferries, Inc.** (☎ 516/665–2115) runs from Bayshore to several Fire Island communities.

By Plane

In addition to **John F. Kennedy** and **LaGuardia** airports, in Queens (☞ Arriving and Departing *in* New York City), Long Island is served by **Long Island MacArthur Airport,** in Islip (☎ 516/467–3210).

By Train

The **Long Island Railroad** (☎ 516/822–5477) has frequent service from Penn Station in Manhattan to major towns on Long Island.

Exploring Long Island

The best way to get a feel for Long Island and explore its museums, stately mansions, nature preserves, and coastal villages is to avoid the traffic-choked LIE and take the more leisurely roads that parallel the coasts. On the North Shore your best bet is Route 25A and, on the North Fork, Rte. 25; on the South Shore, Route 27 (Sunrise Highway).

The stretch of wealthy suburbs just outside New York City on the **North Shore** is known as the Gold Coast. Families like the Vanderbilts, Whitneys, and Roosevelts built mansions here in the late 19th and early 20th centuries, making this area on Long Island Sound a fashionable playground for the rich. It wasn't until after World War II that vast numbers of the middle class moved out to Long Island. However, some communities such as Oyster Bay still maintain their elite status.

The **Nassau County Museum of Art** is housed in the former country residence of Henry Clay Frick and displays changing exhibits from Botticelli to Frida Kahlo. Outdoor sculptures dot the 145 acres of formal gardens and rolling fields. ✉ *1 Museum Dr., at Northern Blvd. (Rte. 25A), Roslyn Harbor,* ☎ *516/484–9337. Closed Mon.*

The quaint town of **Oyster Bay** sits on an inlet of the Long Island Sound. The **Planting Fields Arboretum State Historic Park** (✉ Planting Fields Rd., off Oyster Bay–Glen Cove Rd., ☎ 516/922–9200; 🎫 $4 per vehicle) is yet another stunning Gold Coast estate. The British-born marine-insurance magnate William Robertson Coe bought the place in 1913 and worked with landscape artist James Dawson, of the famed Olmsted Brothers' firm, to plan grand allées of trees, azalea walks, and a rhododendron park on the 150 acres surrounding his mansion, Coe Hall. You can tour President Theodore Roosevelt's Victorian summer White House at **Sagamore Hill National Historic Site** (✉ Cove Neck Rd., 1 mi north of Rte. 25A, ☎ 516/922–4447; 🎫 $5).

Cold Spring Harbor, one of the Gold Coast's most enchanting towns, is just east of Oyster Bay. During its heyday in the mid-1800s, this town was home port to a fleet of whaling vessels. Take some time to browse Main Street, which is lined with shops and restaurants.

The **North Fork,** the upper part of Long Island's eastern tail, is bucolic farm country, with a thriving wine-growing business concentrated in Cutchogue and Peconic. Make a stop at **Hargrave Vineyard,** the pioneer winery in the region, for a tour or tasting. ✉ *South side of Rte. 48, Cutchogue,* ☎ *516/734–5158. Closed Jan.–Mar.*

Beautiful and historic **Shelter Island,** in Gardiners Bay nestled between the North and South forks, was among the first parts of Long Island to be settled by the British and is now primarily a summer resort and

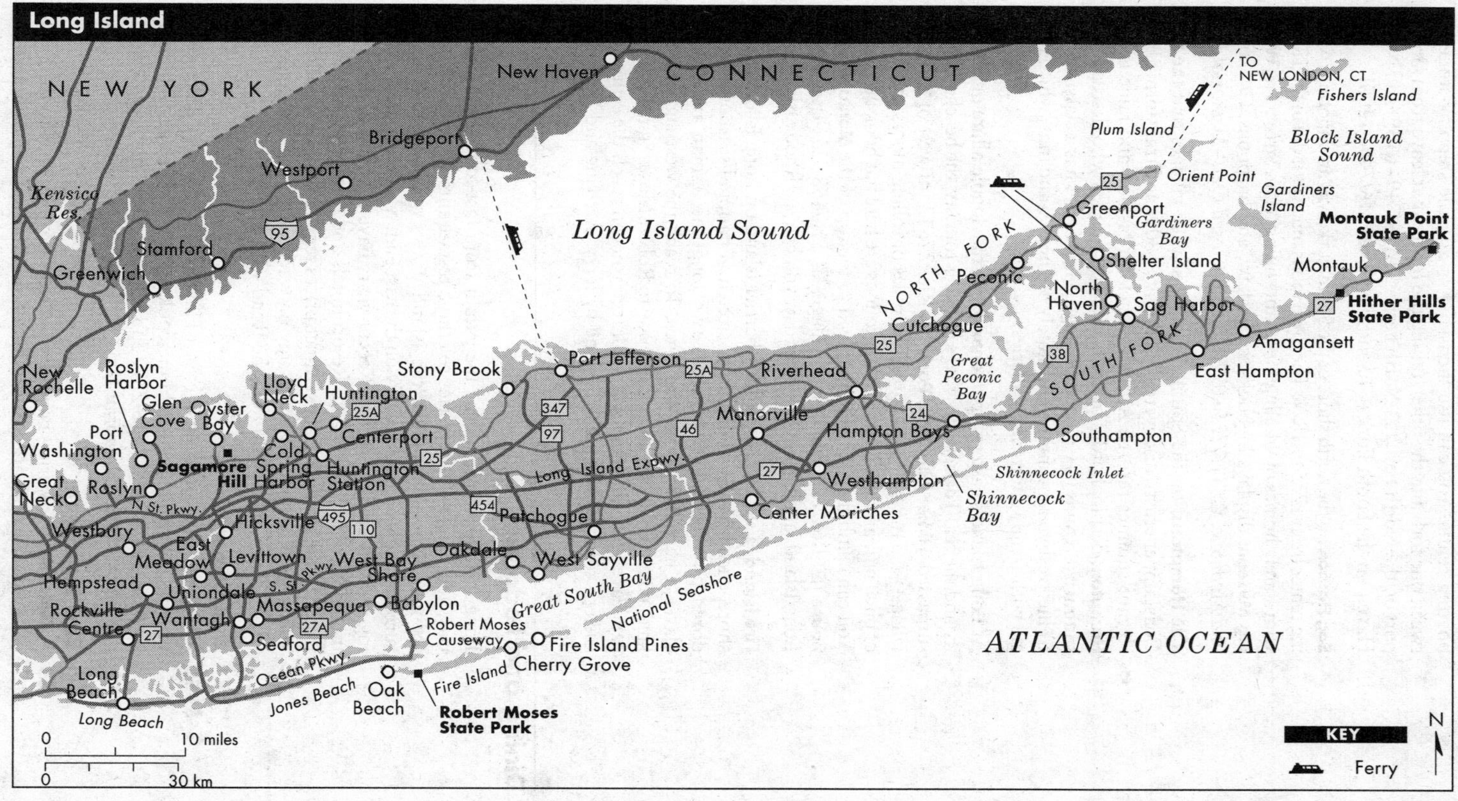

Long Island
NEW YORK
CONNECTICUT
New Haven
TO NEW LONDON, CT
Fishers Island
Plum Island
Block Island Sound
Bridgeport
Westport
Orient Point
Gardiners Island
Kensico Res.
Long Island Sound
Greenport
Gardiners Bay
Montauk Point State Park
Stamford
Greenwich
NORTH FORK
Shelter Island
Peconic
North Haven
Sag Harbor
Montauk
Hither Hills State Park
Cutchogue
Amagansett
SOUTH FORK
East Hampton
Great Peconic Bay
New Rochelle
Roslyn Harbor
Glen Cove
Oyster Bay
Lloyd Neck
Huntington
Stony Brook
Port Jefferson
Riverhead
Manorville
Hampton Bays
Southampton
Port Washington
Centerport
Cold Spring Harbor
Sagamore Hill
Huntington Station
Long Island Expwy.
Westhampton
Shinnecock Inlet
Shinnecock Bay
Great Neck
Roslyn
N St. Pkwy.
Hicksville
Patchogue
Center Moriches
Westbury
East Meadow
Levittown
West Bay Shore
Oakdale
West Sayville
S. St. Pkwy.
Hempstead
Uniondale
Massapequa
Babylon
Great South Bay
National Seashore
Rockville Centre
Wantagh
Seaford
Robert Moses Causeway
Fire Island Pines
Cherry Grove
Fire Island
ATLANTIC OCEAN
Ocean Pkwy.
Long Beach
Jones Beach
Oak Beach
Robert Moses State Park
95
25
25A
27
27A
24
38
46
97
110
347
454
495
0
10 miles
30 km
KEY
Ferry
N

boating center. You can use the island as a scenic stepping-stone between one fork and the other, taking the ferries that leave from Greenport on the North Fork (✉ North Ferry, ☎ 516/749–0139) and North Haven on the South Fork (✉ South Ferry, ☎ 516/749–1200).

Sag Harbor, on the north shore of the South Fork, was an important whaling center from 1775 to 1871. The town looks much as it did in the 1870s, with stately homes of whaling merchants lining Main Street. The **Whaling Museum** displays logbooks, scrimshaw, and harpoons. ✉ *Garden and Main Sts.,* ☎ *516/725–0770.* 🎫 *$3. Closed Oct.–Memorial Day.*

★ The **Hamptons,** on the South Fork, are seaside villages that the East Coast upper crust "discovered" in the late 1800s and transformed into elegant summer resorts. At the pinnacle of fashion and fame is **East Hampton**; despite hordes of celebrities and tourists who descend each summer, it retains its Colonial heritage. Main Street has a classic white-frame Presbyterian church and stately old homes and inns, which mingle with trendy shops and galleries.

At Long Island's eastern tip, **Montauk** has the double allure of extremity and the sea. Though the village is rather touristy, the beaches are unsurpassed. **Hither Hills State Park** (✉ Rte. 27, 12 mi west of Montauk village, ☎ 516/668–2461) preserves miles of rolling moors and forests of pitch pine and scrub oak. Campgrounds are here but book up quickly. You can climb the 137 steps that lead to the top of the **Montauk Lighthouse** (✉ Rte. 27, 6 mi east of village, ☎ 516/668–2544), a famous Long Island landmark. On a clear day, you can see Rhode Island.

Fire Island, a slender 32-mi-long barrier island on Long Island's south shore, encompasses an unspoiled stretch of national seashore. Its half dozen tiny communities include two longtime lesbian and gay enclaves, Cherry Grove and the Pines. To reach the west end of the island, take the Robert Moses Causeway to Robert Moses State Park—you can leave your car here for a small fee. You can reach the central and eastern communities on Fire Island by ferry (Arriving and Departing, *above*).

Dining and Lodging

Long Island restaurants run the gamut from fast-food chains, pizzerias, and family-style eateries to ethnic restaurants and elegant country inns. Not surprisingly, the island draws on the bounty of the surrounding waters, especially on the east end, where commercial fishing remains a vital industry. Recent years have brought all the major motel chains to Long Island. Resort hotels and small inns are concentrated in the Hamptons. In summer prices tend to double, if not triple, and there is often a minimum stay on weekends. For price ranges *see* Charts 1 (A) and 2 (A) *in* On the Road with Fodor's.

Amagansett

$–$$ ✕ **Honest Diner.** Just outside East Hampton, this trendy diner serves up large portions of good home cooking in a 1950s atmosphere. ✉ *74 Montauk Hwy.,* ☎ *516/267–3535. Reservations not accepted. AE. Closed late Oct.–Memorial Day.*

East Hampton

$$ ✕ **Babette's.** Towering banana trees give a tropical feel to the bright yellow, blue, and orange interior of this funky café. Although it's crowded in summer (especially for breakfast), the innovative fare here is worth the wait. There's a large selection of vegetarian dishes; try the smoked tempeh fajitas. ✉ *66 Newtown La.,* ☎ *516/329–5377. AE, MC, V. Closed Mon.–Thurs. Jan.–Mar.*

$$$–$$$$ ★ **Maidstone Arms.** Dating to 1740, this inn is the coziest and most comfortable in town. It also has one of the best locations—right across from a pond and a pristine park, surrounded by East Hampton's oldest streets and most beautiful houses. Beach parking permits are available for guests. An East Hampton mainstay, the inn's always-busy restaurant serves new American cuisine. A breakfast of delicious baked goods is included with the room. ✉ *207 Main St., 11937,* ☎ *516/324–5006,* FAX *516/324–5037. 16 rooms, 3 cottages. Restaurant. AE, MC, V. Full breakfast.*

$$$$ **J. Harper Poor Cottage.** Gary and Rita Reiswig have created the *definitive* East Hampton retreat, where you will be coddled as you should be in the Hamptons. More mansion than cottage, the inn dates back to the 1600s and has been expanded and renovated several times. Today, exquisite William Morris papers cover the walls, and plush overstuffed furniture graces the sitting rooms, which are filled with fresh flowers and a good collection of books. ✉ *181 Main St., 11937,* ☎ *516/324–4081,* FAX *516/329–5931. 5 rooms. AE, MC, V. Full breakfast.*

Greenport

$$–$$$ **Claudio's.** This family-run classic seafood restaurant has been around for more than 125 years. Forget fancy culinary creations: Go for the clams casino, fresh mussels, or fried calamari for starters, and the shrimp scampi or grilled swordfish as a main dish. You can also dine alfresco; the clam bar has tables overlooking Peconic Bay. ✉ *111 Main St.,* ☎ *516/477–0627. MC, V. Closed Jan.–mid-Apr.*

Montauk

$$–$$$ **Gosman's Dock.** This huge, touristy fish restaurant is jam-packed in the summer. It offers a spectacular location—at the entrance to Montauk Harbor—and the freshest possible fish, served indoors or out. You may have a long wait in peak season. ✉ *500 W. Lake Dr.,* ☎ *516/668–5330. Reservations not accepted. MC, V. Closed mid-Oct.–Apr.*

$$$$ **Gurney's Inn Resort and Spa.** Long popular for its fabulous location, on a bluff overlooking 1,000 ft of private ocean beach, Gurney's has become even more famous in recent years for its European-style health-and-beauty spa. The large, luxurious rooms all have ocean views. ✉ *290 Old Montauk Hwy. 11954,* ☎ *516/668–2345,* FAX *516/668–3576. 125 rooms. 2 restaurants, bar, indoor saltwater pool, health club. AE, D, DC, MC, V. MAP.*

Sag Harbor

$$$$ ★ **The American Hotel.** If you can't get a room at this small hotel, at least try to have lunch or dinner at its well-known restaurant (lunch is not served weekdays) where the kitchen puts out such tasty New American dishes as quail-terrine foie gras, and pecan-crusted chicken breast. The bar is the sort where you'd want to sip brandy and light up a cigar. ✉ *25 Main St., 11963,* ☎ *516/725–3535,* FAX *516/725–3573. 8 rooms. Restaurant, bar. AE, D, DC, MC, V. CP.*

Shelter Island

$$–$$$$ ★ **Ram's Head Inn.** This 1929 center-hall Colonial-style island retreat makes for the perfect romantic getaway—far from the Hamptons' crowds. The inn overlooks 800 ft of beachfront, and sailboats and kayaks are available for guests' use, as are tennis courts. The dining room is regarded as one of the best on eastern Long Island. ✉ *108 Ram Island Dr., Shelter Island 11965,* ☎ *516/749–0811,* FAX *516/749–0059. 17 rooms. Restaurant. AE, MC, V. CP.*

Motels

Drake Motor Inn (✉ 16 Penny La., Hampton Bays 11946, ☎ 516/728–1592, FAX 516/728–8770), 15 rooms, pool; *$$–$$$$.* **Ra-**

mada Inn East End (✉ 1830 Rte. 25, Riverhead 11901, ☎ 516/369–2200, FAX 516/369–1202), 100 rooms, restaurant, pool; *$$$.*

Campground

⛺ **Hither Hills State Park** (☞ Exploring Long Island, *above*) has both tent and RV sites.

Nightlife and the Arts

Check the Friday edition of *Newsday,* the Long Island newspaper, which has a weekend supplement containing information about Long Island arts and entertainment, as well as the magazine *Long Island Monthly.*

Nightlife

The Long Island scene is lively, especially in the Hamptons. You can hear live music every night at **Stephen Talkhouse** (✉ Main St., Amagansett, ☎ 516/267–3117), a fashionable hangout. **Oak Beach Inn** (✉ Ocean Pkwy., Oak Beach, ☎ 516/587–0097) has a sing-along upstairs and a DJ on weekends. In Southampton, nightclubbers head to **Jet East** (✉ North Sea Rd., ☎ 516/283–0808), but beware: lots of hype has made this place a scene.

The Arts

Jones Beach Marine Theatre (✉ Jones Beach, Wantagh, ☎ 516/221–1000) hosts major outdoor concerts by contemporary pop artists May–September. **Nassau Veteran's Memorial Coliseum** (✉ 1255 Hempstead Turnpike, Uniondale, ☎ 516/794–9300) has major rock and pop concerts year-round. **Westbury Music Fair** (✉ 590 Brush Hollow Rd., Westbury, ☎ 516/334–0800) presents live concerts, shows, and theater. Rainy days are a good time to catch a flick at the **East Hampton Cinema** (✉ 30 Main St., ☎ 516/324–0448); however, everyone else usually thinks of this, too, so buy your tickets in advance.

Outdoor Activities and Sports

Participant Sports

BOATING

Oyster Bay Sailing School (✉ Box 447, West End Ave., Oyster Bay 11771, ☎ 516/624–7900) offers classes and three- to five-day vacation packages from April through October.

Spectator Sports

Hockey: New York Islanders (✉ Nassau Coliseum, Hempstead Turnpike, Uniondale, ☎ 516/794–4100). **Horse Racing: Belmont Park Race Track** (✉ Hempstead Turnpike, Elmont, ☎ 718/641–4700) is home to the third jewel in horse racing's triple crown, the Belmont Stakes, held in early June.

Beaches

★ **Jones Beach State Park** (✉ Wantagh Pkwy., Wantagh, ☎ 516/785–1600), a wide, sandy stretch of ocean beach, is the most crowded but also the biggest and most fully equipped of Long Island's beaches, with a restaurant, concession stands, changing rooms, a boardwalk, a theater, and sports facilities. The **Robert Moses State Park** (✉ Robert Moses Causeway, Babylon, ☎ 516/669–0449), on Fire Island, is an uncrowded, beautiful, sandy ocean beach. Parking at many of the Hamptons' beaches is difficult; a town permit is usually required.

Shopping

Long Island is known for its shopping malls. The **Roosevelt Field Mall** (✉ Meadowbrook Pkwy., ☎ 516/742–8000), in Garden City, is the largest, with more than 200 stores. **Manhasset's Miracle Mile,** along Route 25A, has department stores and designer boutiques such as Giorgio Armani.

THE HUDSON VALLEY

The landscape along the Hudson River for the 140 mi from Westchester County to Albany, the state capital, is among the loveliest in America. Indeed, this natural beauty—dramatic palisades, pine forests, cool mountain lakes and streams—inspired an entire art movement: the Hudson River School, which originated in the 19th century. Still a rich agricultural region, the valley has scores of orchards, vineyards, and farm markets along country roads. Proximity to Manhattan makes this a viable destination for day trips, but the numerous country inns, B&Bs, and resorts make more leisurely journeys especially attractive.

Visitor Information

Albany County: Convention and Visitors Bureau (✉ 52 S. Pearl St., Albany 12204, ☎ 518/434–1217 or 800/258–3582). **Columbia County:** Chamber of Commerce (✉ 507 Warren St., Hudson 12534, ☎ 518/828–4417). **Dutchess County:** Tourism Promotion Agency (✉ 3 Neptune Rd., Poughkeepsie 12601, ☎ 914/463–4000 or 800/445–3131). **Hudson River Valley:** Hudson Valley Tourism (✉ Box 355, Salt Point 12578, ☎ 800/232–4782).

Arriving and Departing

By Boat

New York Waterways (☎ 800/533–3779) offers boat tours up the Hudson from Manhattan; one includes a stop at Kykuit (☞ Exploring the Hudson Valley, *below*).

By Bus

Adirondack Trailways (☎ 800/225–6815) has daily service between New York's Port Authority Bus Terminal and New Paltz, Kingston, Albany, and other Hudson Valley towns.

By Car

From New York City pick up the New York State Thruway (I–87), which parallels the west bank of the Hudson River, or the more scenic Taconic Parkway, which parallels the east bank. I–84 provides access to the region from southern New England and northeastern Pennsylvania.

By Plane

LaGuardia, John F. Kennedy, and **Newark** airports (☞ Arriving and Departing *in* New York City, *above*) are manageable distances from the Hudson Valley. In the Hudson Valley area itself, **Stewart International Airport** (☎ 914/564–2100), in Newburgh, is served by major airlines. Most major airlines fly into the **Albany County Airport** (☎ 518/869–3021), in Colonie.

By Train

Amtrak (☎ 800/872–7245) provides service to Hudson, Rhinecliff, Rensselaer (Albany), and points west and north of Poughkeepsie. **Metro-North** (☎ 212/532–4900 or 800/638–7646) offers sightseeing packages that include admission to the Hudson Valley's historic sites.

Exploring the Hudson Valley

U.S. 9 hugs the east bank of the Hudson, passing through many picturesque towns, including Tarrytown, Hyde Park, Rhinebeck, and Hudson. U.S. 9W hugs the west bank from Newburgh to Catskill.

Sunnyside, just minutes off the Tappan Zee Bridge, was the romantic estate of Washington Irving, author of *The Legend of Sleepy Hollow.* Guides in Victorian dress give tours regularly; the 17 rooms include Irving's library and many of his original furnishings. ✉ *W. Sunnyside La., off U.S. 9, Tarrytown,* ☎ *914/591–8763.* 🎫 *$7. Closed Jan.–Feb., weekdays Mar., Tues. Apr.–Dec.*

Just north of Sunnyside is **Lyndhurst,** one of America's finest examples of Gothic Revival architecture. The mansion, designed in 1838, has been occupied by three noteworthy New Yorkers and their families: former New York City mayor William Paulding, merchant George Merritt, and railroad magnate Jay Gould. ✉ *635 S. Broadway, off U.S. 9, Tarrytown,* ☎ *914/631–4481.* 🎫 *$9. Closed Mon. late Apr.–Oct., weekdays Nov.–mid-Apr.*

★ If you make reservations early enough (months in advance), you can visit **Kykuit,** the country house of the great American philanthropist John D. Rockefeller and his son John D. Rockefeller, Jr. Two-hour tours of the house, art gallery, and gardens begin at the nearby **Philipsburg Manor,** an 18th-century farm and gristmill. ✉ *U.S. 9, North Tarrytown,* ☎ *914/631–9491.* 🎫 *$18. Closed Nov.–late Apr.*

Harriman and Bear Mountain state parks (✉ Off Palisades Pkwy., ☎ 914/786–2701) are the most famous parks of the vast Palisades interstate system. Outdoor activities include boating, swimming, hiking, fishing, and cross-country skiing on the parks' 54,000 acres.

West Point (✉ U.S. 9W, 5 mi north of Bear Mountain State Park, West Point, ☎ 914/938–2638), America's oldest and most distinguished military academy, is on bluffs overlooking the Hudson River. Stop in the visitor center near the Thayer Gate entrance for a map of the grounds. Just next door in Olmstead Hall is the **West Point Museum,** which houses one of the world's foremost military collections.

Across the river from West Point, the small village of **Cold Spring-on-Hudson,** once one of the largest iron foundries in the United States, was founded in the 19th century. Take time to stroll its quiet streets lined with antiques and crafts shops. **Boscobel,** in Garrison, is a restored Federal-style mansion surrounded by beautiful gardens that afford a breathtaking view of the Hudson River. ✉ *Rte. 9D,* ☎ *914/265–3638.* 🎫 *$7. Closed Jan.–Feb., Tues. Mar.–Dec.*

The country's most respected cooking school, the **Culinary Institute of America** (✉ U.S. 9, Hyde Park, ☎ 914/471–6608), is housed in a former Jesuit seminary on grounds overlooking the Hudson. Founded in 1946, the institute has 2,000 students enrolled in 21-month programs on either culinary arts or baking and pastry arts. Facilities include 36 kitchens and bakeshops, plus eight instructional dining rooms, of which four are student-staffed restaurants open to the public.

Up the Hudson River north of Poughkeepsie at Hyde Park are the **Franklin Delano Roosevelt National Historic Site** (✉ U.S. 9, Hyde Park, ☎ 914/229–2501; 🎫 $10) and nearby Val-kill, the cottage where Eleanor Roosevelt lived from 1945 to 1962. The large Roosevelt family home contains original furnishings and a museum displaying personal documents. At **Val-kill** (✉ Rte. 9G, Hyde Park, ☎ 914/229–9422;

Hudson Valley and the Catskills

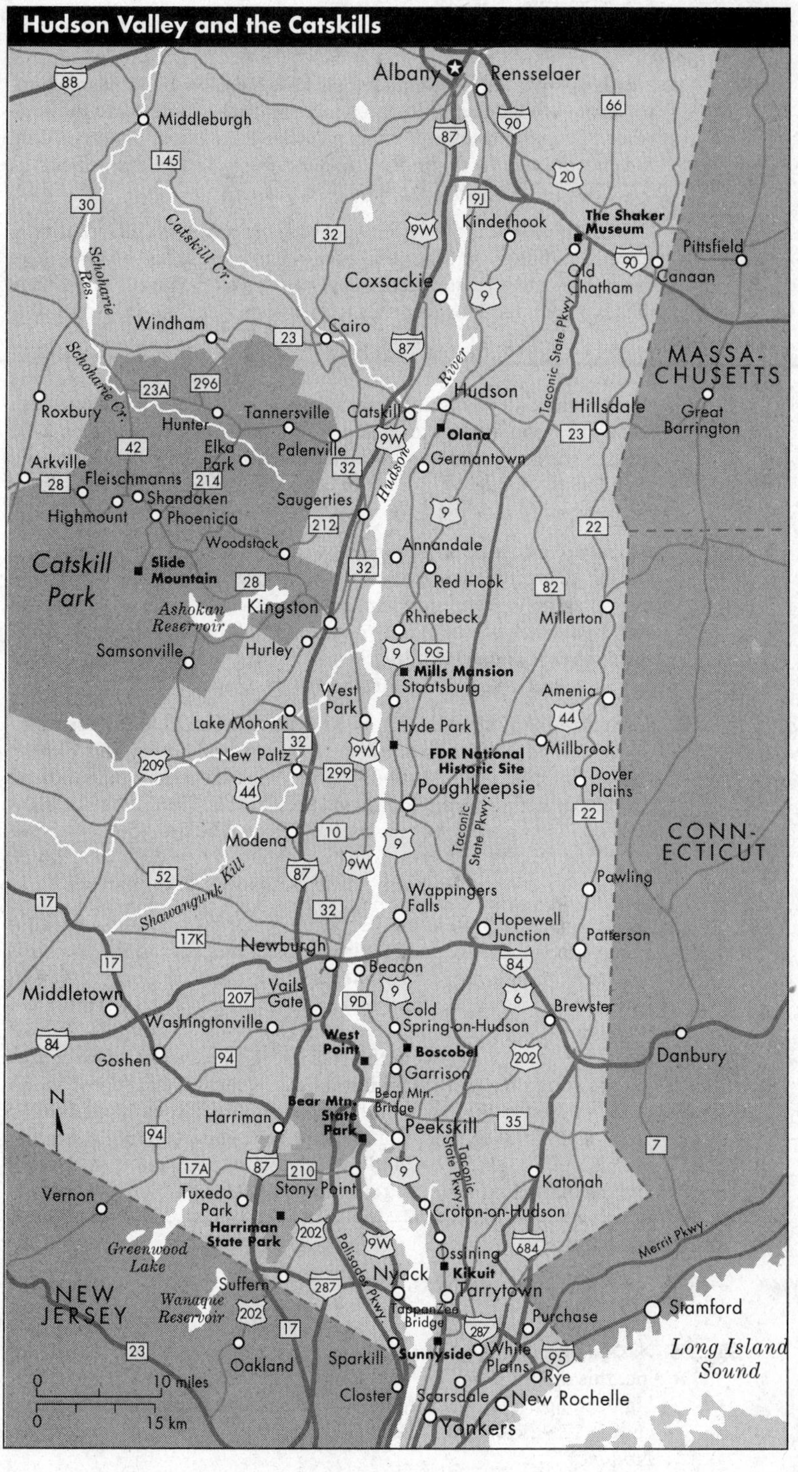

$5) set on 188 wooded acres, the tour includes the film biography *First Lady of the World.*

North of Hyde Park in Staatsburg is **Mills Mansion,** the opulent country estate of Ogden and Ruth Livingston Mills. You can see the interior by guided tour only. Hiking, picnicking, and cross-country skiing are encouraged. ✉ *Old Post Rd., Staatsburg,* ☎ *914/889–8851.* *$3. Closed Oct.–mid-Apr., Mon.–Tues. late Apr.–Sept.*

Quaint **Rhinebeck** is the perfect spot to spend an afternoon—charming storefronts line the streets, beckoning you to come in and browse; there are several galleries and restaurants worth a stop as well. The village makes a great base for day trips to mansions along the Hudson.

Frederic Church, the leading artist of the Hudson River School, built **Olana,** a 37-room Moorish-style castle, on a hilltop with panoramic vistas of the valley. Persian carpets, decorative arts, and paintings, even some of his own works, are on display. The house is open only for guided tours made by reservation; the grounds surrounding Olana are open year-round. ✉ *Rte. 9G, Hudson,* ☎ *518/828–0135.* *$3. Closed Nov.–Mar., Mon.–Tues. Apr.–Oct.*

As you drive north from Hudson towards the villages of Chatham and Old Chatham, the landscape becomes more open and rolling, with sweeping vistas of verdant sheep meadows dotted with large patches of woods; the area is remarkably reminiscent of the English countryside. **The Shaker Museum** (☎ 518/794–9100), in Old Chatham, houses the largest collection of Shaker artifacts in the United States.

A trip to Albany should start in the **Albany Urban Cultural Park Visitor Center** (✉ 25 Quackenbush Sq., corner of Broadway and Clinton Ave., 12207, ☎ 518/434–0405), which has two permanent hands-on exhibits depicting Albany's past and present. The **Henry Hudson Planetarium** here presents star shows and a free orientation film about Albany. The center has a great brochure about its CityWalk tour, which will guide you knowledgeably through Albany's historic streets.

Albany's **Empire State Plaza** (☎ 518/474–2418) is a ¼-mi-long concourse with modern art and sculpture and a mix of government, business, and cultural buildings. The plaza includes the **Corning Tower,** with a free observation deck on the 42nd floor. The **New York State Museum** (✉ Empire State Plaza, ☎ 518/474–5877; free), one of the oldest state museums in the country, has life-size exhibits depicting the state's natural and cultural history, including a reproduction of an Iroquois village with a full-size longhouse. It took more than 30 years (1867–99) to complete the **New York State Capitol** (✉ Empire State Plaza, ☎ 518/474–2418), which incorporates many interesting architectural elements. Free tours are conducted daily on the hour.

Dining and Lodging

For price ranges *see* Charts 1 (A) and 2 (A) *in* On the Road with Fodor's.

Albany

$$–$$$ ★ ✕ **Ogden's.** On the ground floor of a 1903 brick-and-limestone building, this dining room has two-story arched windows built into 30-ft-high ceilings. The menu focuses on Continental and new American cuisine. ✉ *42 Howard St.,* ☎ *518/463–6605. AE, MC, V. Closed Sun. No lunch Sat.*

$$–$$$ ✕ **Mansion Hill Inn.** Standard-issue rooms are eclipsed by the real draw here—the intimate dozen-table restaurant (which doesn't serve lunch). The dinner menu has an imaginative new American flair. If you stay at the inn, breakfast might include items such as blueberry pan-

cakes or frittatas. ✉ *115 Philip St., 12202,* ☎ *518/465–2038,* FAX *518/434–2313. 8 rooms. Restaurant. AE, D, DC, MC, V. Full breakfast.*

$$$–$$$$ ★ **State House.** During the day sunlight pours through the windows of this late-19th-century town house on Washington Park. Mahogany architectural accents complement the interior's hand-glazed walls, high ceilings, fireplaces, and such touches as down comforters. Innkeeper Charles Kuhtic charmingly oversees things. ✉ *393 State St., 12210,* ☎ *518/427–6063,* FAX *518/465–8079. 4 rooms. D, MC, V. Full breakfast.*

Bear Mountain

$$ **Bear Mountain Inn.** For more than 50 years this chalet-style resort has been known for both its bucolic location (in Bear Mountain State Park on the shores of Hessian Lake) and its warm hospitality. Rooms are divided among a main inn and five lodges across the lake. In winter the lobby fireplaces make the lodges cozy; in summer there are great spots nearby for picnicking. Activities abound here, from ice-skating to boating and hiking. ✉ *U.S. 9W, 10911,* ☎ *914/786–2731,* FAX *914/786–2543. 61 rooms. Restaurant, pool. AE, D, MC, V.*

Cold Spring

$ ✕ **Marika's.** Duck into this tiny café for a sweet or savory treat—from freshly baked bread pudding to spinach in puff pastry and Middle Eastern lamb pie. ✉ *137 Main St.,* ☎ *914/265–4375. No credit cards.*

$$–$$$ ✕ **Hudson House.** Clean and simple, this historic clapboard inn has an Early American country feel with Shaker-style furnishings and wide-plank floorboards. Tasty traditional American fare is served in the dining room. The inn is within walking distance of many antiques shops and nearly sits on the Hudson River. ✉ *2 Main St., 10516,* ☎ *914/265–9355. 12 rooms. Restaurant. AE, MC, V.*

Dover Plains

$$$–$$$$ ★ ✕ **Old Drover's Inn.** Although there are only four rooms here guests are pampered as if at a luxury hotel. The employees also run the award-winning restaurant, where you might sample such signature dishes as cheddar cheese soup or seared mahimahi. This early 18th-century inn is one of the state's most romantic hideaways. ✉ *Off Rte. 22, 12522,* ☎ *914/832–9311,* FAX *914/832–6356. 4 rooms. Restaurant. D, MC, V. MAP weekends, CP weekdays.*

Hopewell Junction

$$$–$$$$ ✕ **Le Chambord.** Owner Roy Benich has brought his finely tuned aesthetic sense and prodigious energies to every aspect of this 1863 Georgian-style inn and restaurant. Nine guest rooms are in the main house; 16 newer rooms are in Tara, an adjacent building. Chef Leonard Mott's classic and contemporary French cuisine is served under antique Waterford crystal chandeliers. ✉ *2075 Rte. 52, 12533,* ☎ FAX *914/221–1941 or 800/274–1941. 25 rooms. Restaurant. AE, DC, MC, V. CP.*

Hyde Park

$$–$$$ ✕ **Culinary Institute of America.** The institute (☞ Exploring the Hudson Valley, *above*) has four public restaurants. **Escoffier** features classic French cuisine. **American Bounty** offers American regional fare. **Caterina de Medici** focuses on nouvelle Italian cooking; a four-course prix-fixe menu is offered. **St. Andrew's Cafe** serves low-fat contemporary American health food, from pizza to vegetarian dishes. Reserve months in advance. ✉ *433 Albany Post Rd., U.S. 9,* ☎ *914/471–6608. AE, DC, MC, V. Closed Sun., last 2 wks of July.*

New Paltz

$$$$ **Mohonk Mountain House.** On a 20,000-acre preserve, this awe-inspiring Victorian-era hotel, with its stone-and-shingled terraces, quiet parlors, and red-tiled turrets, perches on the edge of a quiet lake; extensive hiking trails surround the hotel. You'll find plenty to do here, from golf and tennis to croquet and boccie ball. Rates include three hearty yet sadly uninspired meals in the large, bustling dining room as well as afternoon tea. ✉ *1000 Mountain Rest Rd. [Exit 18 off I–87], Lake Mohonk 12561,* ☎ *914/255–1000 or 800/772–6646,* FAX *914/256–2161. 276 rooms. 3 dining rooms. AE, DC, MC, V. FAP.*

Old Chatham

$$$–$$$$ ★ ✕🏨 **Old Chatham Sheepherding Company Inn.** As you approach, you'll probably hear a faint "baaaa" coming from the pastoral fields of this working sheep farm. In 1994, Tom and Nancy Clark purchased the 500-acre farm, and soon after opened the property's 1790 Georgian Manor House as an inn. Rooms are in the main house and two neighboring buildings. You can buy the farm's delicious cheeses—try the Sheep Milk's Camembert—at the company store. The restaurant serves innovative fare, with what else as the specialty—lamb. ✉ *99 Shaker Museum Rd. 12136,* ☎ *518/794–9774,* FAX *518/794–9779. 8 rooms. AE, MC, V. Full breakfast.*

Rhinebeck

$$–$$$ ★ ✕🏨 **Beekman Arms.** In all, 10 buildings make up this inn in the village center: the original 1766 building, with its smallish though cheery and comfortable Colonial-style rooms (with modern baths); a motel-like building, behind the main inn; and, a block away, the mid-19th-century Delamater House, with primarily Victorian-style rooms. The inn's restaurant, Larry Forgione's **Beekman 1766 Tavern,** which incorporates the old taproom, serves American regional fare. ✉ *4 Mill St. (U.S. 9), 12572,* ☎ FAX *914/876–7077,* ☎ *914/871–1766 for restaurant. 59 rooms. AE, DC, MC, V.*

West Point

$$–$$$ 🏨 **Hotel Thayer.** On the grounds of the academy, this stately brick hotel, steeped in history and tradition, has been welcoming military and civilian guests for more than 60 years. Many guest rooms have views of the river and the West Point grounds. ✉ *U.S. 9W, 10996,* ☎ *914/446–4731 or 800/247–5047,* FAX *914/446–0338. 183 rooms. Restaurant, lounge. AE, D, DC, MC, V.*

Motels

🏨 **Sheraton Civic Center Hotel** (✉ 40 Civic Center Plaza, Poughkeepsie 12601, ☎ 914/485–5300 or 800/325–3535, FAX 914/485–4720), 200 rooms, café, health club; *$$.* 🏨 **Roosevelt Inn** (✉ 616 Albany Post Rd., Hyde Park 12538, ☎ 914/229–2443, FAX 914/229–0026), 25 rooms. *$.*

Nightlife and the Arts

The **Empire Center at the Egg** (✉ Madison Ave. and S. Swan St., Albany, ☎ 518/473–1845) has music, dance, and theater performances. The **Palace Theater** (✉ 19 Clinton Ave., Albany, ☎ 518/465–4663) is home to the Albany Symphony Orchestra.

Outdoor Activities and Sports

Fishing

The Hudson River estuary contains a remarkable variety of fish, most notably American shad, black bass, smallmouth and largemouth bass, and sturgeon. For information on licenses (required in fresh waters) and restrictions, as well as fishing hot spots and charts, contact the **New York State Department of Environmental Conservation** (✉ 21 S. Putt Corners Rd., New Paltz 12561, ☎ 914/256–3000; ✉ 50 Wolf Rd., Albany 12233, ☎ 518/457–3521).

Golf

Beekman Country Club (✉ 11 Country Club Rd., Hopewell Junction, ☎ 914/226–7700) has 27 holes. **Dinsmore Golf Course** (✉ U.S. 9, Staatsburg, ☎ 914/889–4082) has 18 holes.

Ski Areas

Cross-Country

Bear Mountain State Park (✉ Bear Mountain, 10911, ☎ 914/786–2701) has 5 mi of trails. **Mills-Norrie State Park** (✉ Old Post Rd., Staatsburg 12580, ☎ 914/889–4100) has 6 mi of trails with views of the Hudson River. **Olana State Historic Site** (✉ Rte. 9G, Hudson 12534, ☎ 518/828–0135) has 7 mi of trails. **Rockefeller State Park** (✉ Rte. 117, North Tarrytown 10591, ☎ 914/631–1470) has about 18 mi of trails.

THE CATSKILLS

The Catskill Mountains have a beauty and variety disproportionate to their modest size. Fringing the western side of the upper Hudson Valley and just a few hours by car from New York City, the area offers streams for fly-fishing, paths for hiking, cliffs for rock climbing, slopes for skiing, and back roads for leisurely driving. Once known as the Borscht Belt for the resort complexes that catered to Jewish families, the region now also attracts wilderness lovers and craftspeople.

Visitor Information

Catskill: Association for Tourism Services (CATS; ✉ Box 449, Catskill 12414, ☎ 518/943–3223 or 800/882–2287). **Delaware County:** Chamber of Commerce (✉ 97 Main St., Delhi 13753, ☎ 800/642–4443). **Greene County:** Promotion Department (✉ Box 527, Catskill 12414, ☎ 518/943–3223 or 800/355–2287). **Sullivan County:** Office of Public Information (✉ 100 North St., Box 5012, Monticello 12701, ☎ 914/794–3000, ext. 5010, or 800/882–2287).

Arriving and Departing

By Bus

Adirondack Trailways (☎ 800/225–6815) offers regular service from New York City and Albany to several Catskill communities, including Kingston, New Paltz, Hunter, and Fleischmanns. **Shortline** (☎ 800/631–8405) connects New York City with a half dozen Sullivan County communities, including Bloomingburg and Wurtsboro.

By Car

The northern Catskills can be reached from I–87 from Catskill (Routes 23 and 23A) and Kingston (Route 28). The western edge of the resort region is also accessible via Route 17 north, reached from either I–87 at Harriman or from I–84 at Middletown.

By Plane

Albany County Airport (☞ Arriving and Departing by Plane *in* the Hudson Valley, *above*) is an hour's drive from the heart of the Catskills. **Oneonta Municipal Airport** (☎ 607/431–1076) is in the northwest corner of the Catskills region.

Exploring the Catskills

In the northeastern section of the Catskills is the actual village of **Catskill,** which has its share of museums and quaint buildings. The **Catskill Game Farm,** in Catskill, is home to 2,000 birds and animals, including a large collection of rare hooved species, and has a petting zoo and a playground. ✉ *400 Game Farm Rd. (off Rte. 32),* ☎ *518/678–9595. Closed Dec.–Apr.*

The nearby **Ponderosa Ranch Fun Park** (✉ 4620 Rte. 32, ☎ 518/678–9206) has the region's largest go-cart track, as well as miniature golf, bumper boats, and rodeos every Saturday night in summer. Beginning by the Hudson River in **Kingston,** a former industrial port city now known for its three historic districts brimming with fine shops and restaurants, head west on Route 28 to reach the heart of the Catskills. At Rte. 375, consider a brief detour to **Woodstock,** which became a rock music legend after the 1969 concert (actually held 50 mi away, in Bethel). Today the town is a fun place for crafts shopping and people-watching. ★ Back on Rte. 28, if you're the least bit hungry, stop by the **Bread Alone bakery** (✉ Rte. 28, Boiceville, ☎ 914/657–3328), where you can sample and purchase some organic hearth-baked breads, from currant buns to *pain levain* (European-style sourdough bread). In the area known as the **High Peaks** from Phoenicia north to the ski resort town of Hunter, Route 214 winds through **Stoney Clove,** a spectacular mountain cleft that has inspired countless tales of the supernatural. Another scenic route out of Phoenicia is across the Esopus River and south up through lovely Woodland Valley to the well-marked trail to Slide Mountain, the highest peak in the Catskills.

Delaware County, newly discovered by big-city vacationers and second-home buyers, has gentler terrain than the High Peaks region, which is to its east. Fishers prize the east and west branches of the Delaware River, and the county's more than 500 farms offer honey, eggs, cider, and maple syrup at numerous roadside stands. **Roxbury,** on Route 30, has the kind of picture-perfect Main Street Norman Rockwell would have loved.

South of Roxbury in Arkville, the **Delaware & Ulster Rail Ride** (✉ Rte. 28, ☎ 607/652–2821), runs a one-hour scenic route between Arkville and Fleischmanns; this steam-powered line was once a major route in the Catskills. It's closed November–April.

Dining and Lodging

The Catskills are best known for mammoth resort hotels, but there are plenty of B&Bs and country inns providing a personal touch, as well as ski-center condos and cabins in the woods. For price ranges *see* Charts 1 (A) and 2 (A) *in* On the Road with Fodor's.

Catskill

$$–$$$ ✕ **La Conca D'Oro.** In 1984 chef-owner Alfonso Acampora brought his Italian culinary skills to the town of Catskill. Fare includes elk, boar, and pheasant prepared with a northern Italian accent. ✉ *440 Main St.,* ☎ *518/943–3549. D, MC, V. Closed Tues. No lunch weekends.*

Elka Park

$$–$$$ ✕🏨 **Redcoat's Return.** Up a twisting mountain road, you'll encounter a bit of the spirit of England in the eastern Catskills. Tom (the Redcoat) and Peg Wright have owned Redcoat's since 1973; mementos from their trips abroad decorate the inn. The dining room (closed Monday–Thursday), with views of surrounding mountains, serves up British-influenced Continental dishes. ✉ *Dale La., 12427,* ☎ FAX *518/589–6379. 14 rooms. Restaurant. AE, MC, V. Full breakfast.*

Kingston

$$–$$$ ★ ✕ **Schneller's.** Schnitzels and wursts are served at this authentic German tavern in Kingston's Uptown Stockade historic district. After your meal you may want to stop in the meat market next door for some imported cheeses or hickory-smoked bacon to take home. The outdoor beer garden is splendid in summer. ✉ *61 John St.,* ☎ *914/331–9800. AE, DC, MC, V. No dinner Mon.–Tues.*

Lewbeach

$$$$ 🏨 **Beaverkill Valley Inn.** Owned and developed by Laurance Rockefeller and managed by able innkeeper Christina Jurgens, the inn caters to those who cherish privacy. Its surrounding forests and nearby fields, preserved as "forever wild," are protected from development. Fly-fishing is definitely the draw here. But those not hooked on angling can head for the croquet court, game room, help-yourself ice-cream parlor, or the wide front porch lined with rockers. ✉ *Beaverkill Rd., off Rte. 151/Rte. 152, Box 13612753,* ☎ *914/439–4844,* FAX *914/439–3884. 20 rooms. Restaurant, pool. AE, MC, V . FAP.*

Shandaken

$$–$$$ ✕ **Auberge des 4 Saisons.** Best known for its first-rate French cuisine, this restaurant is also an inn; the rooms are very basic, with minimum furnishings. The food, however, is superb. ✉ *Rte. 42, about 1 mi from Rte. 28,* ☎ *914/688–2223. AE, D, MC, V.*

Tannersville

$$–$$$ ✕🏨 **Deer Mountain Inn.** This circa-1900 mansion on a 15-acre wooded enclave is lushly packed with items that create a mountain ambience: moose heads, boar heads, bearskin rugs, paintings of European mountain villages, and heavy overstuffed furniture. The dining room (closed Tuesday, no lunch), bracketed by two huge stone fireplaces, serves American fare—trout, veal, and seafood—with a European accent. ✉ *Rte. 25 (Box 443), 12485,* ☎ FAX *518/589–6268. 7 rooms. Restaurant. AE, MC, V. Full breakfast.*

Windham

$$$–$$$$ ✕ **La Griglia.** Elegant country dining here features northern Italian cuisine. A house specialty is the penne *pepperata* (with sautéed sundried tomatoes, sweet red peppers, basil, and a touch of cream). ✉ *Rte. 296,* ☎ *518/734–4499. AE, DC, MC, V. No lunch weekdays.*

$$–$$$$ 🏨 **Albergo Allegria.** This gingerbread Victorian mansion in the northern Catskills is midway between Ski Windham and the White Birches cross-country trails. This B&B is extremely cozy and has spacious rooms with interesting details, from stained-glass windows and fireplaces to cathedral ceilings and chestnut moldings. There's also a Carriage House annex with five private-entrance suites. ✉ *Rte. 296, 12496,* ☎ *518/734–5560. 21 rooms. Swimming pond. D, DC, MC, V. Full breakfast.*

Motel

🏨 **Hunter Inn** (✉ Rte. 23A, Hunter 12442, ☎ 518/263–3777, FAX 518/263–3981), 40 rooms, restaurant, pool, exercise room; *$$$–$$$$.*

Nightlife and the Arts

Contact the regional visitor centers for schedules of the area's performing arts events. Hunter has some lively nightspots during ski season and summer. The large resorts, such as the **Concord** (✉ Kiamesha Lake, ☎ 914/794–4000), present dancing and big-name acts.

Outdoor Activities and Sports

Canoeing

The 79-mi Upper Delaware Scenic and Recreational River is one of the finest streams for paddling in the region. For a list of trip planners and rental firms, contact the **Sullivan County Office of Public Information** (☞ Visitor Information, *above*).

Fishing

Trout are abundant in Catskill streams; smallmouth bass, walleye, and pickerel can be found in many lakes and in six reservoirs. For the "Catskill Fishing" brochure and map, write to **CATS** (☞ Visitor Information, *above*).

Golf

The region has nearly 50 golf courses, many of which are at the big resorts. For the "Golf Catskills" brochure, write to **CATS** (☞ Visitor Information, *above*).

Hiking

The **New York State Department of Environmental Conservation** (✉ 50 Wolf Rd., Albany 12233, ☎ 518/457–7433) puts out several brochures on Catskill Forest Preserve hiking trails.

Tubing

Town Tinker (✉ Bridge St., Phoenicia, ☎ 914/688–5553) rents tubes for beginner and advanced routes along the Esopus River between Shandaken and Mount Pleasant.

Spectator Sports

Horse Racing: You can see harness racing year-round at **Monticello Raceway** (✉ Rtes. 17 and 17B, Monticello, ☎ 914/794–4100).

Ski Areas

For information on area slopes and trails, contact **Ski the Catskills** (✉ Box 135, Arkville 12406, ☎ 914/586–1944).

Cross-Country

Belleayre Mountain (☞ Downhill, *below*) has 5 mi of trails. **Mountain Trails Cross-Country Ski Center at Hyer Meadows** (✉ Box 198, Rte. 23A, 12485, ☎ 518/589–5361) in Tannersville has 20 mi of groomed trails; rentals and lessons are available.

Downhill

Downhill ski areas in the Catskills have snowmaking capabilities. **Belleayre Mountain** (✉ Box 313, off Rte. 28, Highmount 12441, ☎ 914/254–5600), with 33 runs, 9 lifts, and a 1,404-ft vertical drop, is the only state-run ski facility in the Catskills. **Hunter Mountain** (✉ Box 295, Rte. 23A, Hunter 12442, ☎ 518/263–4223) has 48 runs, 13 lifts, and a 1,600-ft drop. **Ski Windham** (✉ C. D. Lane Rd., Windham 12496, ☎ 518/734–4300) has 33 runs, 7 lifts, and a 1,600-ft drop.

Shopping

Shopping is a major diversion in the Catskills, with a scattering of factory outlets, shopping villages, auctions, flea markets, crafts fairs, antiques shops, and galleries. **Woodbury Common Factory Outlets** (✉ Rte. 32, Exit 16 off I–87, Harriman, ☎ 914/928–6840) has more than 150 discount stores, including Gucci and Barneys.

SARATOGA SPRINGS AND THE NORTH COUNTRY

Saratoga Springs, about 30 mi north of Albany, is one of American high society's oldest summer playgrounds. The six-week Thoroughbred-racing season, starting in mid-July, is the high point of the year. Northwest of Saratoga, and in stark contrast, are the rugged mountains, immense forests, and abundant lakes and streams of Adirondack Park, the largest park expanse in the continental United States. The North

Country—anchored by the resort towns of Lake Placid and Lake George—hums year-round. Hikers descend in the summer, autumn brings leaf peepers, and with the snow come many winter-sports enthusiasts.

Visitor Information

Greater Saratoga: Chamber of Commerce (✉ 494 Broadway, Saratoga Springs 12866, ☎ 518/584–3255). **Lake Placid:** Visitors Bureau (✉ 216 Main St., Olympic Center 12946, ☎ 518/523–2445 or 800/447–5224). **Saranac Lake:** Chamber of Commerce (✉ 30 Main St., 12983, ☎ 518/891–1990 or 800/347–1992).

Arriving and Departing

By Bus

Adirondack Trailways (☎ 914/339–4230 or 800/225–6815) provides bus service to Saratoga Springs, Lake Placid, Lake George, Chestertown, Bolton Landing (summer only), and many other area towns.

By Car

The primary route through the region is the Northway (I–87), which links Albany and Montréal.

By Plane

The principal airports are in New York City (207 mi south of Lake George) and Montréal (177 mi north of Lake George). Other airports serving the region are in Albany, Syracuse, and Burlington, Vermont.

By Train

Amtrak (☎ 800/872–7245) operates the *Adirondack,* a daily train between New York and Montréal, with many North Country stops.

Exploring Saratoga Springs and the North Country

People have been frequenting **Saratoga Springs** for its medicinal properties since the late 18th century. In the late 19th century it emerged as one of North America's principal resorts, both for its spa waters and its gambling casino. It also became a horse-racing center in the 1890s, and August still brings crowds for the race meet and yearling sale.

You can still see mineral-water springs bubbling from the ground—22 are currently visible—at **Saratoga Spa State Park.** Listed on the National Register of Historic Places, this 2,000-acre park has walking paths to the springs. Mineral baths and massages are available at the Roosevelt and Lincoln Park bathhouses. Tennis courts, swimming pools, and golf courses are available as well. ✉ *Between U.S. 9 and Rte. 50, 19 Roosevelt Dr., Saratoga Springs 12866,* ☎ *518/584–2000.*

Across from the Saratoga Race Course (☞ Spectator Sports, *below*), site of the renowned horse races, is the **National Museum of Racing.** Its centerpiece is the Hall of Fame, which has video clips of races featuring the horses and jockeys enshrined here. ✉ *Union Ave.,* ☎ *518/584–0400.* 🎫 *$3*

Yaddo (✉ Union Ave., ☎ 518/587–4886), once a private home, is now a highly regarded retreat for artists and writers. The 400-acre grounds and rose garden are open to the public.

The **National Museum of Dance** features rotating exhibits on the history and development of the art form, as well as the Hall of Fame, which honors dance luminaries. The studios allow visitors to watch or participate in a dance class. ✉ *99 S. Broadway,* ☎ *518/584–2225.* 🎫 *$4. Closed Mon. Labor Day–Memorial Day.*

The **Historical Society of Saratoga Springs** is housed in Canfield Casino—an 1870s Italianate building that was a gambling casino. The museum is devoted to the town's colorful history as a gambling center, and changing exhibits are displayed in a contemporary art gallery. ✉ *Congress Park, Broadway and Circular St.,* ☎ *518/584–6920. Closed Mon.–Tues. Oct.–Apr.*

In the Adirondack Mountain range, the 6-million-acre **Adirondack Park** encompasses 1,000 mi of rivers and more than 2,500 lakes and ponds. The southern sections are more developed, while the High Peaks region, in the north-central sector, offers the greatest variety of wilderness activities. *Visitor Interpretive Centers:* ✉ *Paul Smiths (north of Saranac Lake), Rte. 30, 1 mi north of Rte. 86 intersection,* ☎ *518/327–3000;* ✉ *Newcomb, Rte. 28N,* ☎ *518/582–2000.*

Lake George, 40 mi north of Saratoga, is a kitschy tourist town catering to families, with amusement parks, souvenir shops, and miniature golf. Cruises from the town dock are extremely popular from May through October; contact **Lake George Shoreline Cruises** (☎ 518/668–4644) and the **Lake George Steamboat Company** (☎ 518/668–5777).

Just south of town is **Great Escape Fun Park,** the North Country's largest amusement park. ✉ *U.S. 9,* ☎ *518/792–3500. Closed Labor Day–Memorial Day.*

Kids will love the caves and gorge at **Natural Stone Bridge and Caves** (✉ Exit 26 off I–87, near Pottersville, ☎ 518/494–2283; $7.50). Those not big on hiking can sample the beauty of the Adirondack region at **Ausable Chasm** (✉ U.S. 9 just north of Keeseville, ☎ 518/834–7454; $12.95), where you can see massive stone formations.

Another natural attraction, **High Falls Gorge,** has three dramatic waterfalls and a self-guided tour on steel bridges and paths along the Ausable River. ✉ *Off Rte. 86 near Wilmington,* ☎ *518/946–2278. $4. Closed Labor Day–Memorial Day.*

Lake Placid is the hub of the northern Adirondacks. This mountain town is probably best known for its **1932 and 1980 winter Olympics facilities.** The Ice Arena and speed-skating oval are in the center of town; the ski jump is 2 mi out; Whiteface Mountain (scene of the downhill competitions) is a 10-minute drive away, on Route 86; and the bobsled run at Mt. Van Hoevenberg, on Route 73, is 15 minutes away. Call 518/523–1655 or 800/462–6236 for more information.

Self-guided tours can be made of the **John Brown Farm,** home and burial place of the famed abolitionist, who operated the farm for free blacks. ✉ *Off Rte. 73 by the Olympic ski jumps,* ☎ *518/523–3900. Free. Closed Mon.–Tues. and Nov.–Apr.*

The serenity and mountain air of **Saranac Lake** (elevation: 1,600 ft) made it a health resort for the tubercular in the late 19th century. Ten miles west of Lake Placid, it is today the jumping-off point for canoe trips (☞ Outdoor Activities and Sports, *below*). Much of the lake is part of the **St. Regis Canoe Area,** which is off-limits to powerboats.

★ Overlooking Blue Mountain Lake, the open-air **Adirondack Museum** has a day's worth of exhibits on the history, culture, and crafts of the region. The *New York Times* calls it "the best museum of its kind in the world." ✉ *Rte. 30,* ☎ *518/352–7311. $10. Closed mid-Oct.–Memorial Day.*

Dining and Lodging

Saratoga is indisputably the North Country's culinary champion in quality and variety, with Lake Placid a distant second. Elsewhere expect large portions, home cooking, and a rustic atmosphere. Lodging runs the gamut from roadside motels to resorts. For information on B&Bs contact the **Adirondacks Bed and Breakfast Association** (☎ 518/623–2524). For price ranges *see* Charts 1 (A) and 2 (A) *in* On the Road with Fodor's.

Bolton Landing

$$$$ ✕🏨 **Sagamore Resort.** The large public rooms and gracious style of this grand resort on an island in Lake George will take you back to another era. The rooms are spread among the main hotel and lakeside lodges. Each of the six dining rooms has its own atmosphere and cuisine, ranging from the formal, slightly nouvelle touches of Trillium (reservations essential, jacket required, no lunch) to the hearty burgers and steaks of Mr. Brown's Pub. You'll find plenty of opportunity for activity here, including boating, tennis, and golf. ✉ *110 Sagamore Rd., 12814,* ☎ *518/644–9400,* FAX *518/644–2626. 350 rooms. 6 restaurants, pools, health club. AE, D, DC, MC, V.*

Chestertown

$$–$$$$ ★ ✕🏨 **Friends Lake Inn.** Most of the inn's cozy guest rooms have mountain or lake views. There's plenty to do in the area—cross-country skiing, hiking, swimming, or just relaxing in a big Adirondack-style chair on the inn's spacious lawn. The inn's regionally acclaimed restaurant serves new American cuisine. ✉ *Friends Lake Rd., 12817,* ☎ *518/494–4751,* FAX *518/494–4616. 16 rooms. Restaurant. MC, V. MAP.*

Keene Valley

$ ✕ **Noon Mark Diner.** This classic small-town diner is the perfect spot for lunch, and if you've already eaten, at least stop in for some homemade pie. The food here is better than your average greasy spoon, and you'll get a good sense for the local scene. ✉ *Rte. 73,* ☎ *518/576–4499. MC, V.*

Lake Placid

$–$$ ✕ **Cottage Cafe.** You sink your teeth into a Stuffed Shirt, Drunken Kraut, or Brazilian Bombshell sandwich at this always-crowded café overlooking Mirror Lake. When the weather's good, the open-air deck is the perfect place for cocktails. Lunch and dinner fare include salads and sandwiches. ✉ *1 Main St., across from the Mirror Lake Inn,* ☎ *518/523-9845. AE, D, DC, MC, V.*

$ ★ ✕ **Tail o' the Pup.** Conveniently located halfway between Lake Placid and Saranac Lake, this classic roadside restaurant specializes in savory barbecued items like chicken, ribs, and pork. You can dine inside, at the outdoor picnic tables, or in your car—honk twice for service. ✉ *Rte. 86, Ray Brook,* ☎ *518/891–5092. MC, V.*

$$$$ ★ ✕🏨 **Lake Placid Lodge.** Originally a rustic lodge built before the turn of the century, this small hotel embodies the spirit of Lake Placid's past *and* cossets guests with the comforts of luxurious amenities. Rooms are furnished with twig and birch-bark furniture and Adirondack antiques; amenities include featherbeds, terry-cloth robes, and soaking tubs. All but five have granite fireplaces. If seeking privacy, ask about the cabins that sit right on the shores of the lake. The dining room's new American menu changes seasonally. ✉ *Whiteface Inn Rd. (Box 550), 12946,* ☎ *518/523–2700,* FAX *518/523–1124. 22 rooms, 16 cabins. Restaurant, bar. AE, MC, V. Full breakfast.*

$$–$$$$ ✕🏨 **Mirror Lake Inn.** On the shores of Mirror Lake, this stately Adirondack inn is within walking distance of downtown Lake Placid. The atmosphere here is truly genteel. The elegant interior includes an antiques-filled library and a living room with stone fireplaces and walnut floors. The rooms are spread among several buildings; those on the lake have private balconies. ✉ *5 Mirror Lake Dr., 12946,* ☎ *518/523–2544,* FAX *518/523–2871. 128 rooms. 2 restaurants, indoor and outdoor pools, tennis court, spa, beach, boating, fishing, cross-country skiing, meeting rooms. AE, D, DC, MC, V.*

$$–$$$ 🏨 **Lake Placid Resort Holiday Inn.** This friendly resort high on a hill above Lake Placid's Main Street is by no means your typical Holiday Inn: The service is personal, original art decorates public spaces, and amenities range from coffeemakers and microwaves in every room to a Scottish-style links golf course. The lobby's floor-to-ceiling windows overlook Mirror Lake and the mountains beyond. ✉ *1 Olympic Dr., Lake Placid 12946,* ☎ *518/523–2556,* FAX *518/523–9410. 210 rooms. 4 restaurants, indoor pool, health club. AE, D, DC, MC, V.*

Saranac Lake

$$$$ ★ 🏨 **The Point.** Onetime home of William Avery Rockefeller, this all-inclusive elegantly rustic inn is the Adirondacks' and one of the country's most exclusive retreats. You pay in advance—that way, you feel more like a guest for the weekend: You can fix yourself a drink from one of several bars, you can take out one the speedboats for waterskiing, you can borrow snowshoes and trek around the property, and you can even have a seven-course dinner served in your room, all without having to take out your wallet, even upon checkout. There are no signs pointing here; you have to book a room in order to get the address. ✉ *HCR 1 (Box 65), 12983,* ☎ *518/891–5678 or 800/255–3530,* FAX *518/891–1152. 11 rooms. Dining room, bar. AE. FAP.*

Saratoga Springs

$$$ ✕ **43 Phila Bistro.** The innovative offerings at this Saratoga hot spot may include Thai-spiced lobster and pineapple skewers or pan-seared duck breast with apricot-almond risotto. ✉ *43 Phila St.,* ☎ *518/584–2720. Reservations essential. MC, V. Closed Sun.*

$$–$$$ ★ ✕ **Eartha's Kitchen.** This small bistro is a local favorite, especially for the mesquite-grilled seafood and meat dishes that come from Eartha, the wood-fired grill. The ever-changing, eclectic menu incorporates the freshest ingredients available. ✉ *60 Court St.,* ☎ *518/583–0602. Reservations essential. DC, MC, V. Closed Mon.–Tues. Sept.–May. No lunch.*

$$–$$$$ 🏨 **Adelphi Hotel.** This downtown Saratoga showplace is extravagant and fun. The opulent lobby with slowly rotating fans is done in a style so reminiscent of La Belle Epoque that one could picture the Divine Sarah Bernhardt holding court amid its splendor. No two rooms are the same: furnishings are eclectic—and recherché. ✉ *365 Broadway, 12866,* ☎ *518/587–4688. 38 rooms. AE, MC, V. Closed Nov.–Apr.*

Motel

🏨 **Days Inn of Lake George** (✉ 1454 U.S. 9, Suite 1, Lake George 12845, ☎ 518/793–3196 or 800/325–2525), 110 rooms, restaurant, indoor pool ; *$$–$$$.* 🏨 **Wildwood on the Lake** (✉ 88 Saranac Ave., Lake Placid, 12946, ☎ 518/523–2624, FAX 518/523–3248), 35 rooms. 2 pools; *$–$$*

Campgrounds

Adirondak Loj Wilderness Campground (✉ Off Rte. 73, Box 867, Lake Placid 12946, ☎ 518/523–3441) provides information about camping throughout the High Peaks region and operates a campground on Heart Lake, with 34 tent sites and 15 lean-tos, water, no gas or electric, picnic tables, seasonal showers, and toilets.

The Arts

Adirondack Lakes Center for the Arts (✉ Rte. 28, Blue Mountain Lake, ☎ 518/352–7715) is a multipurpose arts center that presents art exhibits and concerts and has coffeehouses and workshops. The **Saratoga Performing Arts Center** (☎ 518/587–3330) hosts the New York City Opera, the New York City Ballet, the Philadelphia Orchestra, and the Newport Jazz Festival–Saratoga, as well as big-name pop stars, from June to September.

Outdoor Activities and Sports

Middle Earth Expeditions (✉ HCR 1, Box 37, Rte. 73, Lake Placid 12946, ☎ 518/523–9572) leads tours and provides guides for individuals or groups in canoeing, white-water rafting, fishing, and backpacking. **Jones Outfitters Ltd.** (✉ 37 Main St., Lake Placid, ☎ 518/523–3468), on Mirror Lake, rents canoes and kayaks. The friendly folks at **McDonald's Adirondack Challenge** (✉ Rte. 30, Lake Clear, ☎ 518/891–1176) sell and rent gear for canoeing, cross-country skiing, snowshoeing, and hiking.

Biking

Roadside signs mark several bike routes, most quite hilly, that wind through the North Country. For a map of routes in the area, contact the **Saranac Lake Chamber of Commerce** (☞ Visitor Information, *above*).

Canoeing

The 170-mi **Raquette River** and the **St. Regis Canoe Area,** east of Saranac Lake, are among the best and most popular canoe routes in the North Country.

Fishing

Brook and lake trout are taken year-round on the lakes and streams of the North Country. Licenses can be obtained at town or county clerk offices, sporting goods stores, and outfitters.

Golf

Among the more challenging courses are those at the **Whiteface Club** (✉ Whiteface Inn Rd., Lake Placid, ☎ 518/523–2551), 18 holes; the **Sagamore Resort** (✉ 110 Sagamore Rd., Bolton Landing, ☎ 518/644–9400), 18 holes; and the **Lake Placid Resort** (✉ Mirror Lake Dr., Lake Placid, ☎ 518/523–4460); 44 holes.

Hiking

The most popular area for hiking is the High Peaks region, accessible from the Lake Placid area in the north, Keene and Keene Valley in the east, and Newcomb in the south. For more information contact the **Adirondack Mountain Club** (✉ ADK, Box 867, Lake Placid 12946, ☎ 518/523–3441).

Rafting

Hudson River Rafting Company (✉ 1 Main St., North Creek, ☎ 800/888–7238) offers day trips on the Hudson, the Sacandaga, and the Black River from April to October.

Spectator Sports

Lake Placid summer and winter athletic competitions: Contact the **Olympic Authority** (☎ 518/523–1655 or 800/462–6236). Events include concerts, ski jumping, and figure-skating shows. **Horse Racing:** The six-week Thoroughbred-racing season starts in mid-July at **Saratoga Race Course** (✉ Union Ave., Saratoga Springs, ☎ 518/584–6200).

Ski Areas

Cross-Country

Mt. Van Hoevenberg, on Route 73, has 30 mi of groomed tracks, which connect with the **Jackrabbit Trail,** a 33-mi network of ski trails through the High Peaks region connecting Lake Placid, Saranac Lake, and Paul Smiths. For information and conditions contact **Adirondack Ski Touring Council** (☒ Box 843, Lake Placid 12946, ☎ 518/523–1365).

Downhill

Whiteface Mountain Ski Center (☒ Wilmington 12997, 8 mi east of Lake Placid, ☎ 518/946–2223) has 65 runs, 10 lifts, a 3,251-ft vertical drop, and snowmaking.

Shopping

The region's maple syrup and sharp cheddar cheese make great gifts. **Blue Mountain Lake** and **Lake Placid** are good bets for crafts hunting. Look for baskets, pottery, and an array of jewelry, leather work, and quilting. The **Adirondack Crafts Center** (☒ Lake Placid Center for the Arts, 93 Saranac Ave., Lake Placid, ☎ 518/523–2062) is a year-round facility where more than 275 local artisans show their wares.

LEATHERSTOCKING COUNTRY AND THE FINGER LAKES

Visitor Information

Cooperstown: Chamber of Commerce (☒ 31 Chestnut St., 13326, ☎ 607/547–9983). **Leatherstocking Country:** (☒ 327 N. Main St., Herkimer 13350, ☎ 315/866–1500 or 800/233–8778). **Finger Lakes Association:** (☒ 309 Lake St., Penn Yan 14527, ☎ 315/536–7488 or 800/548–4386). **Clearly Cayuga:** (☒ 904 E. Shore Dr., Ithaca 14850, ☎ 877/422–9842). **Greater Rochester Visitors Association:** (☒ 126 Andrews St., 14604, ☎ 800/677–7282).

Arriving and Departing

The Leatherstocking region is 200–300 mi from New York City via the New York State Thruway (I–87) and, from Kingston, Route 28. I–90, at this point known also called the New York State Thruway, runs east–west through both Leatherstocking Country and the Finger Lakes, connecting Albany with Buffalo. I–88 runs northeast–southwest, leading from Binghamton to just northwest of Albany.

Exploring Leatherstocking Country and the Finger Lakes

The early Yankees in their leather leggings gave the region its nickname; it is quintessential rural America, with gently rolling countryside, community chicken barbecues, and tree-shaded small towns. Cooperstown ★ is home to the **National Baseball Hall of Fame,** where displays and paintings honor the heroes, recall great moments, and trace the history of the game. ☒ *Main St.,* ☎ *607/547–7200.* *$9.50.*

Binghamton has the **Roberson Museum and Science Center,** comprising a restored 1910 historic house, a complex of museums, a planetarium, and a theater. ☒ *30 Front St.,* ☎ *607/772–0660.* *$4.*

Kids are especially fond of Binghamton's wooded **Ross Park Zoo** (☒ 185 Park Ave., ☎ 607/724–5461; $3.50), where animals (including tigers and a timber wolf pack) live in natural environments.

The 11 parallel **Finger Lakes,** from Conesus Lake, south of Rochester, to Otisco Lake, southwest of Syracuse, stretch north to south like long, narrow fingers through the rolling countryside of western New York. The region's diverse terrain—waterfalls, gorges, rocky hillsides, lush forests—is the perfect backdrop for the area's many vineyards and wineries. The two largest lakes, Seneca and Cayuga, have wine trails; the visitor center has brochures that map them out.

About 5 mi west of the north end of Cayuga Lake is **Seneca Falls,** where on July 18, 1848, 300 people attended America's first women's rights convention, held at the Wesleyan Methodist Chapel on 126 Falls Street. The **Women's Rights National Historical Park Visitor Center** (✉ 136 Falls St., ☎ 315/568–2991), next door, has informative exhibits.

The design studios and factory of the **MacKenzie-Childs, Ltd.** empire are housed in an old country house and barn on the eastern shore of Cayuga Lake. You can see artisans creating the company's signature majolica pottery, glassware, and trimmings on weekdays at 9:30 AM. ✉ *Rte. 90, Aurora,* ☎ *315/364–7123. Closed Sun.*

Ithaca, at the tip of Cayuga Lake, is the home of both Cornell University and Ithaca College. The town is more spectacular than most others in the Finger Lakes because of the deep gorges and more than 100 waterfalls that lace it.

Geneva, at the northern tip of Seneca Lake, seems like a town preserved in time. Its South Main Street, overlooking the lake, is lined with 19th-century houses and century-old trees. The picturesque campuses of Hobart and William Smith colleges are here, too.

The village of Watkins Glen is at the southern end of Seneca Lake adjoining the 669-acre **Watkins Glen State Park.** The 1½-mi gorge here is highlighted by rock formations and 18 waterfalls. It's a great spot for hiking. ✉ *Rte. 14,* ☎ *607/535–4511. Closed Nov.–May.*

Rochester is the headquarters of the Eastman Kodak Company. The George Eastman House, onetime home of the company founder and photographic innovator, now houses the **International Museum of Photography,** the world's largest museum devoted to photographic art and technology. ✉ *900 East Ave.,* ☎ *716/271–3361.* 🎫 *$6.50. Closed Mon.*

It was in Rochester at **Susan B. Anthony's house** that the 19th-century women's rights advocate wrote *The History of Woman Suffrage.* The house is furnished in the style of the mid-1800s. ✉ *17 Madison St.,* ☎ *716/235–6124.* 🎫 *$5. Closed Mon.–Wed.*

In Corning the **Corning Museum of Glass** contains a world-class collection of glass, as well as a time-line exhibit describing 3,500 years of glassmaking, a library covering everything ever written about glass, and a self-guided tour of the Steuben glass factory. ✉ *1 Museum Way, off Rte. 17,* ☎ *607/937–5371.* 🎫 *$6.*

Dining and Lodging

For price ranges *see* Charts 1 (B) and 2 (B) *in* On the Road with Fodor's.

Geneva

$$$$ ✕🏨 **Geneva on the Lake.** Built in 1910, this impressive Renaissance-style palazzo was modeled after the Villa Lancelotti in Frascati, Rome. Originally a private residence, it has served as a monastery and an apartment complex. Now part of a resort, the rooms here are spacious, some have fireplaces, and almost all have a view of the lake and formal gardens. ✉ *1001 Lochland Rd., Rte. 14S, 14456,* ☎ *315/789–7190,* FAX *315/789–0322. 30 suites. Restaurant, pool. AE, D, MC, V. CP.*

BUFFALO, CHAUTAUQUA, AND NIAGARA FALLS

Visitor Information

Greater Buffalo: Convention and Visitors Bureau (✉ 107 Delaware Ave., 14202, ☎ 716/852–0511 or 800/283–3256). **Niagara Falls:** Official Information Center (✉ 4th and Niagara Sts., 14301, ☎ 716/284–2000 or 800/338–7890).

Arriving and Departing

By Bus

Greyhound Lines, Inc. (☎ 800/231–2222) and **New York Trailways, Inc.** (☎ 716/856–8885) serve Buffalo's bus station (✉ 181 Ellicott St. at N. Division St., Buffalo).

By Car

Access to both Buffalo and Chautauqua County is primarily via I–90, the New York State Thruway. From Buffalo, I–190 leads to Niagara Falls.

By Plane

The Buffalo-Niagara area is served by **Buffalo International Airport** (✉ Genessee St., Cheektowaga, ☎ 716/632–3115). Flying time from New York City to Buffalo is one hour

Exploring Buffalo, Chautauqua, and Niagara Falls

Buffalo is a city of Victorian elegance, with many churches and strongly ethnic neighborhoods. Walk along downtown Buffalo's **Elmwood Street** for a taste of the city's eclectic mix of shops and restaurants. **Chippewa Street** (or the Chippewa District), known for its nightclubs and jazz bars, is another lively area in the heart of the city.Just north of downtown Buffalo is the **Albright-Knox Art Gallery** (✉ 1285 Elmwood Ave., ☎ 716/882–8700). The modern art collection here, including works by Mondrian, Miró, and van Gogh, is superb.The Albright-Knox Gallery is on the western side of **Delaware Park** (✉ Parkside and Elmwood Ave., ☎ 716/851–5806), a 350-acre park designed by Frederick Law Olmsted (the creator of New York City's Central Park). More than 23 acres of the park are dedicated to one of the oldest zoos in the country, the **Buffalo Zoological Gardens** (✉ 300 Parkside Ave., ☎ 716/837–3900; 🎫 $6).

Niagara Falls, the most accessible and famous waterfall in the world, is actually three cataracts: the **American** and **Bridal Veil** falls, in New York, and **Horseshoe Falls,** in Ontario, Canada. More than 750,000 gallons of water flow each second in the summer.

For a good orientation to the falls, stop at the Niagara Visitor Center in the **Niagara Reservation State Park** (✉ Prospect Park, Niagara Falls 14303, ☎ 716/278–1701), the oldest state park in the nation. **Goat Island** provides the closest view of the American Falls; cross to the Canadian side for the best view of Horseshoe Falls. The famous ***Maid of the Mist*** boat ride lets you view the falls from the water.

Dining and Lodging

Buffalo

$$$–$$$$ ★ ✕ **The Hourglass.** This spot has been open for business for over 30 years, and continues to maintain it reputation as one of greater Buffalo's best restaurants. All the Continental classics are available here—lamb chops, duck breast, sweetbreads—but the kitchen is especially proud of the seafood it turns out; try the Cape scallops or soft-shell crabs when they're available. ✉ *981 Kenmore Ave., Kenmore,* ☎ *716/877–8788. AE, MC, V. Closed Sun.–Mon. No lunch.*

$$ ✕ **Just Pasta.** This popular Buffalo eatery is the perfect spot for a casual dinner. You'll find good simple pastas here: spinach-and-egg spaghetti with prosciutto, peas, and cream, and gorgonzola ravioli with ricotta and tomato sauce. ✉ *307 Bryant St.,* ☎ *716/881–1888. AE, D, MC, V. Closed Sun.*

$$$–$$$$ 🏨 **Hyatt Regency Buffalo.** This 16-floor hotel is housed in a historic office building, erected in 1923; the building was converted to a hotel 1983. ✉ *2 Fountain Plaza, 14202,* ☎ *716/856–1234,* FAX *716/852–6157. 395 rooms. 3 restaurants. AE, D, MC, V.*

Niagara Falls

$$$–$$$$ 🏨 **Clarion Hotel Niagara Falls.** You can't beat the location of this hotel, only 1,600 ft from the falls. This is Niagara's largest hotel, with plenty of amenites including a Jacuzzi, saunas, and convention and business services. ✉ *3rd and Old Falls Sts., Niagara Falls 14303,* ☎ *716/285–3361,* FAX *716/285–3900. 400 rooms. 2 restaurants, bar, indoor pool, health club. AE, D, DC, MC, V.*

$$$–$$$$ ✕🏨 **Red Coach Inn.**This 1923 inn has an Old England atmosphere. One- and two-bedroom suites are luxurious with gas-burning fireplaces and kitchenettes; all but one of the rooms have a spectacular view of the upper rapids. The restaurant's specialties include prime rib, Boston scrod, and seafood-sausage Mornay—the outdoor patio is splendid for summer dining. ✉ *2 Buffalo Ave., Niagara Falls, 14303,* ☎ *716/282–1459. 10 rooms. Restaurant, bar. AE, D, DC, MC, V.*

Nightlife and the Arts

Shea's Performing Arts Center (✉ 646 Main St. , Buffalo, ☎ 716/847–1410) presents concerts, opera, dance, and touring theater performances, which have included shows like *Stomp* and *Rent.* For information on the Buffalo Chamber Music Society and the Buffalo Philharmonic Orchestra, contact **Kleinhans Music Hall Box Office** (✉ 71 Symphony Circle, Buffalo, ☎ 716/885–5000).

Outdoor Activities and Sports

Spectator Sports

There's always a sports event to see in Buffalo. Check out one of city's local teams: The **Buffalo Bills Football Team** (✉ Rich Stadium, One Bills Dr., Orchard Park, ☎ 716/649–0015); **Buffalo Sabres Hockey** (✉ Marine Midland Arena, One Main St., Buffalo, ☎ 716/855–4100); or the minor league **Buffalo Bisons Baseball Team** (✉ North AMeriCare Park, 275 Washington St., Buffalo, ☎ 716/846–2000).

RHODE ISLAND

Updated by K. D. Weaver

Capital	Providence
Population	987,000
Motto	Hope
State Bird	Rhode Island red hen
State Flower	Violet
Postal Abbreviation	RI

Statewide Visitor Information

Rhode Island Tourism Division (✉ 1 W. Exchange St., Providence 02903, ☎ 800/556–2484).

Scenic Drives

Routes 1 and 1A from Watch Hill to Narragansett travel through the varied landscape of the southern coast. Two bridges on **Route 138** link Newport to Narragansett; this drive affords unbeatable views of Narragansett Bay. **Route 77** runs through the idyllic towns of Tiverton and Little Compton. And nothing compares with the grand mansions along **Newport's Bellevue Avenue.**

State Parks

Rhode Island's 37 state parks and recreational grounds encompass beaches, tidal marshes, swamp lands, woodlands, and bay shores. **Burlingame State Park, Charlestown Breachway, Fishermen's Memorial State Park, George Washington Camping Area,** and the **Ninigret Conservation Area** allow camping. For state parks information contact the Rhode Island Tourism Division (☞ Statewide Visitor Information, *above*).

THE SOUTH COAST

Visitor Information

South County: Tourism Council (✉ 4808 Tower Hill Rd., Wakefield 02879, ☎ 401/789–4422 or 800/548–4662).

Arriving and Departing

By Bus

RIPTA (Rhode Island Public Transportation Authority; ☎ 401/781–9400, 800/244–0444 in RI) provides service from Providence and Warwick to Kingston, Wakefield, Narragansett, and Galilee.

By Car

I–95 passes 10 mi north of Westerly before heading inland toward Providence. Routes 1 and 1A follow the coastline along Narragansett Bay and are the primary routes through the South County resort towns.

By Train

Amtrak (☎ 800/872–7245) stops at Westerly and Kingston.

Exploring the South Coast

The best beaches along the southern coast of Rhode Island are at **Westerly, Charlestown, South Kingstown,** and **Narragansett.**

Watch Hill is a Victorian-era resort village with miles of beautiful beaches and a lighthouse. **Napatree Point** is one of the best long beach walks in Rhode Island. A walk to the end of Bay Street and a left onto Fort Road will lead you to the beach.The **Flying Horse Carousel** (✉ Bay St.; 🎟 50¢), which operates from mid-June to Labor Day, is the oldest merry-go-round in America.

The draws of the town of **South Kingstown** include crafts shops, galleries, and Matunuck Beach. At the **Washington County Jail,** built in 1792, you can tour jail cells, Colonial-period rooms, and a Colonial garden. ✉ *1348 Kingstown Rd.,* ☎ *401/783–1328.* 🎟 *Free. Closed Mon., Wed., Fri., Sun., and Nov.–Apr.*

Narragansett, which includes the maritime village of Galilee and the Point Judith Lighthouse, is a top summer destination for its beaches, bay vistas, and restaurants. **The Towers** (✉ Ocean Rd., Narragansett Pier) are all that remains of the casino that was once the centerpiece of the beachside village known as Narragansett Pier. **South County Museum** houses 20,000 artifacts dating from 1800. ✉ *Anne Hoxie La. off Rte. 1A,* ☎ *401/783–5400.* 🎟 *$3.50. Closed Mon.–Tues. and Nov.–Apr.*

The fishing port of **Galilee** is the departure point for the ferry to Block Island and charter fishing trips. The **Frances Fleet** (✉ 2 State St., ☎ 401/783–4988 or 800/662–2824) conducts whale-watching excursions ($30) between June and September. On Ocean Road are public beaches and, at land's end, the **Point Judith Lighthouse** (☎ 401/789–0444).

Dining and Lodging

The regional fare prepared in Rhode Island includes johnnycakes, a corn-cake–like affair cooked on a griddle, and the native clam, the quahog (pronounced *ko*-hog). "Shore dinners" consist of clam chowder, steamers, clam cakes, sausage, corn-on-the-cob, lobster, watermelon, and Indian pudding (a steamed pudding made with cornmeal and molasses). Along the south shore and in North Kingstown are many small motels and B&Bs.

Narragansett

$$$ ✕ **Coast Guard House.** This restaurant, which dates from 1888 and was a lifesaving station for 50 years, displays interesting photos of Narragansett Pier and the Casino. Candles light the tables and picture windows on three sides allow views of the ocean. The fare is American—seafood, pasta, veal, steak, and lamb. ✉ *40 Ocean Rd.,* ☎ *401/789–0700. AE, D, DC, MC, V.*

$$–$$$ ★ ✕ **Basil's.** Intimate Basil's serves French and Continental cuisine. The specialty is veal topped with a light cream and mushroom sauce; other dishes include fish and duck à l'orange. ✉ *22 Kingstown Rd.,* ☎ *401/789–3743. AE, DC, MC, V. Closed Mon.–Tues. and Oct.–June. No lunch.*

$$$$ 🏨 **Stone Lea.** In the Millionaire's Mile section of private homes, this B&B is replete with rotundas, bay windows, carved-wood paneling, and other accents (like the grand-piano staircase that rises from the parquet floor of the foyer). The Block Island room and the three other large rooms are worth the extra cost. ✉ *40 Newton Ave., 02882,* ☎ *401/783–8237,* FAX *401/792–8237. 7 rooms. Full breakfast. AE, MC, V.*

$$$ 🏨 **The Richards.** Imposing and magnificent, this English manor–style mansion has a broodingly Gothic mystique. Some rooms have 19th-century English antiques, floral-upholstered furniture, and fireplaces. ✉ *144 Gibson Ave., 02882,* ☎ *401/789–7746. 5 rooms, 2 with shared bath. Full breakfast. No credit cards.*

Shopping

The **Fantastic Umbrella Factory** (✉ 4920 Old Post Rd., off Rte. 1, ☎ 401/364–6616) comprises four rustic shops and a barn built around a wild garden where peacocks, pheasants, and chickens parade. For sale in the backyard bazaar are hardy perennials and unusual daylilies, greeting cards, kites, crafts, tapestries, incense, and blown-glass jewelry.

NEWPORT

Newport is one of the great sailing cities of the world and the host to world-class jazz, blues, folk, and classical music festivals. More than 200 Colonial homes and shops still stand from the city's first period of prosperity, the 18th-century Golden Age. In the 19th century during what became known as the Gilded Age, Newport was a summer playground for America's wealthiest families.

Visitor Information

Newport County: The Gateway Center (✉ 23 America's Cup Ave., Newport 02840, ☎ 401/849–8048 or 800/326–6030) provides long-term parking and superlative visitors' resources.

Arriving and Departing

By Bus

Bonanza Bus Lines (☎ 401/751–8800 or 800/556–3815) runs from Boston. **RIPTA** (☎ 401/781–9400; 401/847–0209 in Newport) serves Newport from Providence and elsewhere.

By Car

From Providence take I–95 east into Massachusetts and head south on Route 24. From South County take Route 1 north to Route 138 east. From Boston take I–93 south to Route 24 south.

By Ferry

Interstate Navigation (☎ 401/783–4613) operates daily summer service from Providence and Block Island. **Jamestown and Newport Ferry Company** (☎ 401/423–9900) runs frequently from Jamestown.

By Plane

Newport State Airport (☎ 401/848–7086) is 3 mi northeast of Newport. Charter companies fly from here to T. F. Green State Airport in Warwick. **Cozy Cab** (☎ 401/846–2500) runs a shuttle service ($15) between the airport and Newport's visitors bureau.

Exploring Newport

★ The French admiral de Ternay used 1748 **Hunter House** as his Revolutionary War headquarters. The elliptical arch in the central hall is a typical Newport detail. ✉ *54 Washington St.,* ☎ *401/847–7516. Closed Nov.–Mar., weekdays Apr. and Oct.*

The **Brick Market** (✉ Thames St.) served as Newport's trading center for more than a century. Later used as a theater and a town hall, the building now houses the **Museum of Newport History** (☎ 401/841–8770; 🎟 $5). **Colony House** faces the Brick Market on Washington Square. Built in 1739, it was the government's headquarters—from its balcony the Declaration of Independence was read to Newporters. Courtroom scenes from the film *Amistad* were shot here.

The **Friends Meeting House** (✉ 29 Farewell St., ☎ 401/846–0813; 🎟 $5) was built in 1699 and is the oldest Quaker meetinghouse in Amer-

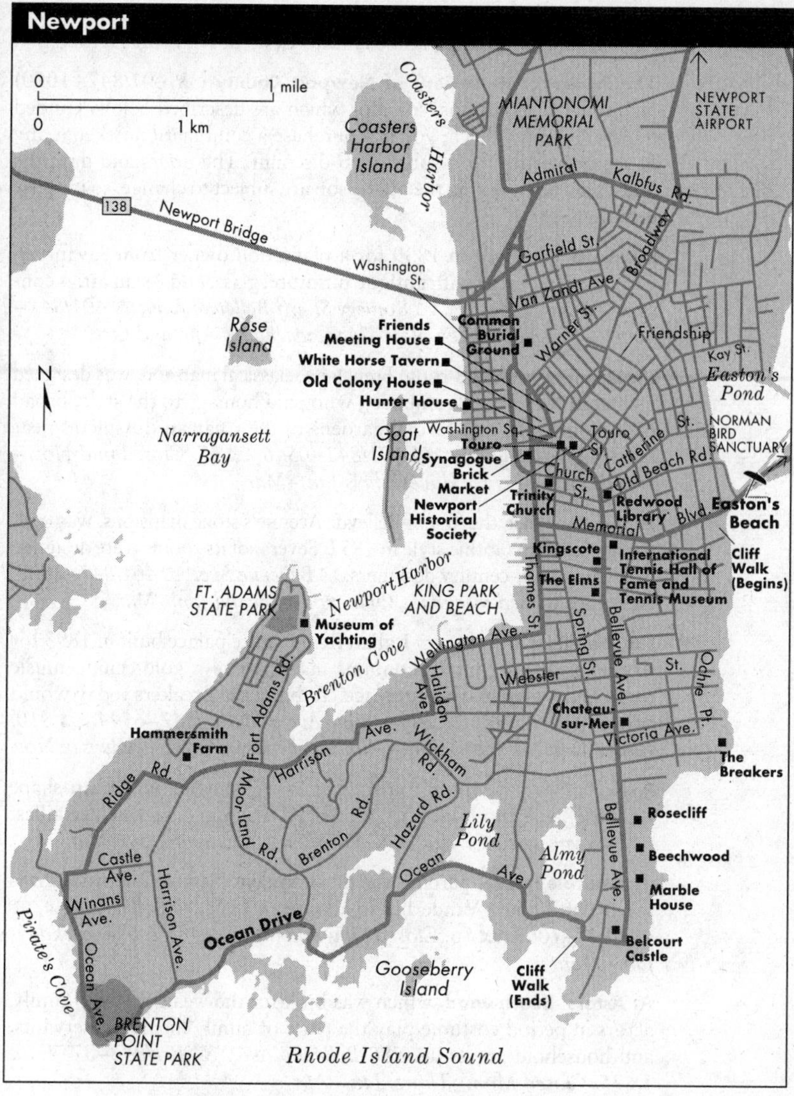

ica; tours are by appointment. Austere from the outside but elaborate within, the **Touro Synagogue** (✉ 85 Touro St., ☎ 401/847–4794), dedicated in 1763, is the oldest synagogue in the country.

Within the headquarters of the **Newport Historical Society** is a small museum with memorabilia, furniture, and maritime items. Walking tours of Newport depart from the society. ✉ *82 Touro St.*, ☎ *401/846–0813.* *Free. Closed Sat.–Mon.*

Trinity Church (✉ Queen Anne Sq., ☎ 401/846–0660), built in 1724, has a three-tier wine-glass pulpit. The 1748 **Redwood Library** (✉ 50 Bellevue Ave., ☎ 401/847–0292), the country's oldest library in continuous use, houses paintings by early American artists. The **Newport Art Museum and Art Association** (✉ 76 Bellevue Ave., ☎ 401/848–8200; $4) exhibits contemporary works by New England artists.

Easton's Beach (✉ Memorial Blvd.), also known as First Beach, is popular for its expansive beach, children's aquarium, and other amusements.

A small, sheltered beach at **Fort Adams State Park** (✉ Ocean Dr.) has a picnic area, lifeguards, and beautiful views of Newport Harbor.

The **Preservation Society of Newport County** (☎ 401/847–1000) maintains 12 mansions, some of which are described below. Guided tours are given of each; you can purchase a combination ticket at any of the properties for a substantial discount. The hours and days the houses are open during the off-season are subject to change, so it's wise to call ahead.

Kingscote was built in 1839 for a plantation owner from Savannah, Georgia. Decorated with antique furniture, glass, and Asian art, it contains Tiffany windows. ✉ *Bowery St. off Bellevue Ave.,* ☎ *401/847–1000.* 🎫 *$6.50. Closed Nov.–Mar.; weekdays Apr. and Oct.*

The Elms, a graceful 48-room French neoclassical mansion, was designed by architect Horace Trumbauer, who paid homage to the style, broad lawn, fountains, and formal gardens of the Château d'Asnières near Paris. ✉ *Bellevue Ave.,* ☎ *401/842–0546.* 🎫 *$7. Closed mid-Nov.–Thanksgiving Day and weekdays Jan.–Mar.*

Chateau-sur-Mer, the first of Bellevue Avenue's stone mansions, was built in the Victorian Gothic style in 1852. Several of its rooms were designed by leading 19th-century designers. ✉ *Bellevue Ave.,* ☎ *401/847–1000.* 🎫 *$6.50. Closed weekdays Oct.–mid-Nov and Jan.–Mar.*

★ **The Breakers,** a four-story Italian Renaissance palace built in 1893 for Cornelius Vanderbilt II, contains marvels like a gold-ceiling music room and a blue marble fireplace. To build the Breakers today would cost $400 million. ✉ *Ochre Point Ave.,* ☎ *401/847–6544.* 🎫 *$10. Closed Dec. (most yrs), Jan.–Mar., weekends in Apr., weekdays in Nov.*

Rosecliff, Newport's most romantic mansion (complete with heart-shape staircase), was modeled after the Grand Trianon palace at Versailles. ✉ *Bellevue Ave.,* ☎ *401/847–5793.* 🎫 *$6. Closed Nov.–Mar.*

The **Marble House,** perhaps the most opulent Newport mansion, was the gift of William Vanderbilt to his wife in 1892. ✉ *Bellevue Ave.,* ☎ *401/847–1000.* 🎫 *$6. Closed Nov. and (most yrs) Dec. and weekdays Jan.–Mar.*

At **Astors' Beechwood,** which was built for the wealthy Astor family, actors in period costume play the parts of family members, servants, and household guests. ✉ *580 Bellevue Ave.,* ☎ *401/846–3777.* 🎫 *$8.75. Closed Mon.–Thurs. Jan.–Apr.*

Belcourt Castle is so filled with European and Asian treasures that locals have dubbed it the Metropolitan Museum of Newport. Sip tea and admire the stained glass and carved wood, and don't miss the Golden Coronation Coach. ✉ *Bellevue Ave.,* ☎ *401/846–0669 or 401/849–1566.* 🎫 *$6.50. Closed Jan.–Feb. and weekdays in Mar.*

★ **Hammersmith Farm** was the childhood summer home of Jacqueline Bouvier Kennedy Onassis, the site of her wedding to John F. Kennedy, and a summer White House during the Kennedy Administration. The elaborate gardens, with breathtaking views of Narragansett Bay, were designed by Frederick Law Olmsted. ✉ *Ocean Dr. near Fort Adams,* ☎ *401/846–7346.* 🎫 *$8.50. Closed mid-Nov.–Feb., with special openings during Christmastime.*

The **International Tennis Hall of Fame and Tennis Museum** (✉ 194 Bellevue Ave., ☎ 401/849–3990; 🎫 $8) is in the magnificent Newport Casino. The **Museum of Yachting** (✉ Fort Adams Park, Ocean Dr., ☎

401/847–1018; 🎟 $3), open from May to October, has four galleries of sailing exhibits.

Old Colony & Newport Railway (✉ 19 America's Cup Ave., ☎ 401/624–6951; 🎟 $6), a vintage diesel train, follows an 8-mi route along Narragansett Bay from Newport to the Green Animals Topiary Gardens in Portsmouth.

Just north of Second Beach, the **Norman Bird Sanctuary** (✉ 583 3rd Beach Rd., Middletown, ☎ 401/846–2577; 🎟 $4) is a 450-acre nature preserve with hiking trails, guided tours, and a small natural history museum.

Dining and Lodging

Entering Newport from the direction of Providence, you will find more than a dozen motels whose room rates are considerably lower than those downtown. For price ranges *see* Charts 1 (A) and 2 (A) *in* On the Road with Fodor's

$$$ ✕ **Asterix & Obelix.** Danish chef John Bach-Sorensen makes fine dining as fun and colorful as the madcap French cartoon strip after which this eatery was named. Asian twists enliven Mediterranean fare with strong French influences. ✉ *599 Thames St.,* ☎ *401/841–8833. AE, D, DC, MC, V.*

$$$ ✕ **Black Pearl.** Tourists and yachters flock to this dignified converted dock shanty, where award-winning clam chowder is sold by the quart. Dining is in the casual tavern or the formal Commodore's Room, where the French and American entrées include swordfish with Dutch pepper butter. ✉ *Bannister's Wharf,* ☎ *401/846–5264. Reservations essential. Jacket. AE, DC, MC, V.*

$$–$$$ ★ ✕ **Scales & Shells.** This busy restaurant serves as many as 15 types of superbly fresh wood-grilled fish. The dining is more formal upstairs at Upscales. ✉ *527 Thames St.,* ☎ *401/848–9378. Reservations not accepted. No credit cards.*

$$ ✕ **Puerini's.** The aroma of garlic and basil greets you as soon as you enter this laid-back neighborhood restaurant. The intriguing menu includes green noodles with chicken in marsala wine sauce and tortellini with seafood. ✉ *24 Memorial Blvd.,* ☎ *401/847–5506. Reservations not accepted. No credit cards. Closed Mon. in winter. No lunch.*

$$$–$$$$ ✕🏨 **Vanderbilt Hall.** A former YMCA building donated to Newport by the Vanderbilt family in 1909 has been converted into the city's most sophisticated inn and restaurant. All the rooms have bathrobes and are individually decorated with antiques. The butler serves canapés and cocktails in the common room while patrons peruse the options for dinner: classic Continental cuisine served on Wedgwood china at tables set with silver. A fire crackles in the somber dining room ($$$$), where a veteran and meticulous waitstaff tends to your needs. ✉ *41 Mary St., 02840,* ☎ *401/846–6200,* FAX *401/846–0701. 40 rooms. Dining room, pool, spa. CP available. AE, DC, MC, V.*

$$$–$$$$ ★ 🏨 **Castle Hill Inn and Resort.** Much of the furniture at this inn is original to the structure, a summer home built in 1874 on a cliff at the mouth of the Narragansett Bay. The inn, 3 mi from the center of Newport, is famous for its Sunday brunches. ✉ *Ocean Dr., 02840,* ☎ *401/849–3800. 18 rooms with bath, 3 share bath. Restaurant. Full breakfast. AE, D, MC, V. Restaurant closed Nov.–Mar.*

$$$–$$$$ ★ 🏨 **Francis Malbone House.** This 1760 structure was tastefully doubled in size in the mid-1990s; the new rooms have whirlpool tubs and fireplaces. The rooms in the main house are all in corners (with two windows) and look out over the courtyard, which has a fountain, or across the street to the harbor. Fifteen rooms have working fireplaces. ✉ *392*

Thames St., 02840, ☎ *401/846–0392 or 800/846–0392. 18 rooms. Full breakfast. AE, MC, V.*

$$$ ★ **Ivy Lodge.** This grand (though small by Newport's standards) Victorian B&B with large and lovely rooms has gables and a turret. The defining feature is a Gothic-style 33-ft-high oak entryway with a three-story turned baluster staircase and a dangling wrought-iron chandelier. Summer guests congregate on the wraparound front porch, which has wicker chairs. ✉ *12 Clay St., 02840,* ☎ *401/849–6865. 8 rooms. Full breakfast. AE, MC, V.*

$ **Harbor Base Pineapple Inn.** All the rooms at this basic motel a five-minute drive from downtown contain two double beds; some also have kitchenettes. Renovations planned for 1999 will likely lead to a rate increase. ✉ *372 Coddington Hwy., 02840,* ☎ *401/847–2600. 48 rooms. AE, D, DC, MC, V.*

Nightlife

Thames Street is the nexus of Newport's lively nightlife. **Newport Blues Café** (✉ 286 Thames St., ☎ 401/841–5510) hosts great blues performers. **One Pelham East** (✉ 270 Thames St., ☎ 401/847–9460) draws a young crowd for progressive rock, reggae, and R&B. **Thames Street Station** (✉ 337 America's Cup Ave., ☎ 401/849–9480) plays high-energy dance music and videos and books rock bands from Thursday to Monday in summer.

Outdoor Activities and Sports

Adventure Sports Rentals (✉ The Inn at Long Wharf, America's Cup Ave., ☎ 401/849–4820) rents waverunners, sailboats, kayaks, and canoes. **Old Port Marine Services** (✉ Sayer's Wharf, ☎ 401/847–9109) operates harbor tours and crewed yacht charters. **Sail Newport** (✉ Fort Adams State Park, ☎ 401/846–1983) rents sailboats by the hour. **Ten Speed Spokes** (✉ 18 Elm St., ☎ 401/847–5609) rents bikes.

Shopping

Many of Newport's arts and antiques shops are on Thames Street; others are on Spring Street, Franklin Street, and at Bowen's and Bannister's wharves. The **Brick Market** area—between Thames Street and America's Cup Avenue—has more than 40 shops that carry crafts, clothing, antiques, and toys. Stores at **Bannister's Wharf** stock clothing and gift shops with a nautical theme.

Side Trip to Block Island

Visitor Information

Block Island Chamber of Commerce (✉ Drawer D, Water St., 02807, ☎ 401/466–2982).

Arriving and Departing

BY FERRY

Interstate Navigation Co. (✉ Galilee State Pier, Narragansett, ☎ 401/783–4613; 🎫 $8.40 from Galilee, $8.25 from Newport) has ferry service from Galilee to Block Island; from Memorial Day to October a passenger boat runs daily from Providence to Block Island via Newport. **Nelesco Navigation Co.** (✉ 2 Ferry St., New London, CT, ☎ 860/442–7891; 🎫 $15) operates car and passenger ferry service from New London to Block Island daily from June to September.

BY PLANE

Block Island State Airport (☒ Center Rd., ☎ 401/466–5511) is served by **New England Airlines** (☎ 401/596–2460 or 800/243–2460) from Westerly.

What to See and Do

Approaching Block Island by sea from New London, Newport, or Point Judith, you'll see the **Old Harbor** area. Here in the island's only village are most of the inns, shops, and restaurants. Three docks, two hotels, and four restaurants huddled in the southeast corner of the Great Salt Pond make up the **New Harbor** commercial area, where two ferries ★ dock. Hiking paths at **Rodman's Hollow,** a fine example of a glacial outwash basin, lead to pristine beaches.

PROVIDENCE

Roger Williams founded Providence in October 1635 as a refuge for freethinkers and religious dissenters. Providence remains a community that embraces independent thinking in business, the arts, and academia—Brown University, Rhode Island School of Design, are among the major schools here. Walking-tour maps of the city's historic areas are available at the Visitor Information Center (☞ *below*).

Visitor Information

Providence Visitor Information Center (☒ Waterplace Park, Clock Tower Building, ☎ 401/751–5069 or 800/556–2484). **Greater Providence:** Convention and Visitors Bureau (☒ 30 Exchange Terr., 02903, ☎ 401/274–1636 or 800/233–1636).

Arriving and Departing

By Bus

Greyhound Lines (☎ 800/231–2222). **Bonanza Bus Lines** (☎ 800/556–3815). **RIPTA** (☎ 401/781–9400 or 401/784–9500) provides local transportation in Providence and service to other parts of the state.

By Car

I–95 cuts diagonally across the state and is the fastest route to Providence from Boston, coastal Connecticut, and New York City. I–195 links Providence with New Bedford and Cape Cod. U.S. 1 follows the coast east from Connecticut before turning north to Providence.

By Plane

T. F. Green State Airport (☒ Rte. 1, Warwick, ☎ 401/737–4000), 10 mi south of Providence, is served by major U.S. airlines and regional carriers. **Airport Van Shuttle** (☎ 888/736–1900) provides service to downtown Providence and elsewhere.

By Train

Amtrak (☎ 800/872–7245) trains stop at **Providence Station** (☒ 100 Gaspee St., ☎ 401/727–7388).

Exploring Providence

The **Providence Athenaeum,** established in 1753 and one of the oldest lending libraries in the world, displays Rhode Island art and artifacts, as well as an original set of the folio *Birds of America* prints by John J. Audubon. ☒ *251 Benefit St.,* ☎ *401/421–6970.* 🎫 *Free. Closed Sun.*

The small but comprehensive **Rhode Island School of Design Museum of Art** contains textiles, Japanese prints, Paul Revere silver, 18th-cen-

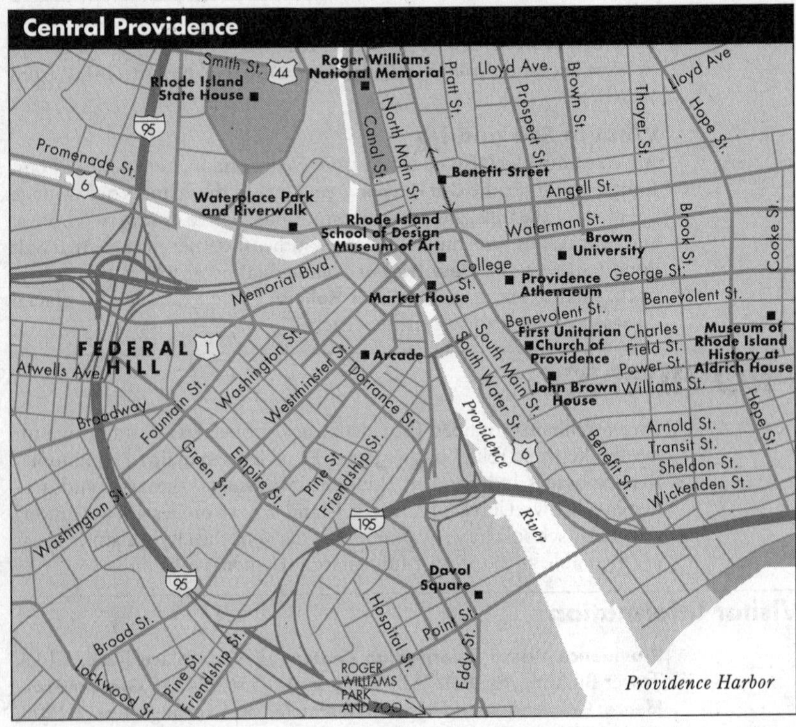

tury porcelain, French Impressionist paintings, and a mummy dating from circa 300 BC. ✉ *224 Benefit St.,* ☎ *401/454–6100.* *$5; free Sat. Closed Mon.*

Also on **Benefit Street**—known as the Mile of History—is a long row of Revolutionary War–era candy-color houses crammed shoulder to shoulder on a steep hill overlooking downtown Providence. The **Providence Preservation Society** (✉ 21 Meeting St., at Benefit St., ☎ 401/831–7440) conducts guided tours from Memorial Day to Labor Day and has maps and pamphlets with self-guided tours.

The **Arcade** (✉ 65 Weybosset St., ☎ 401/598–1199), America's first shopping mall, was built in 1828. A National Historic Landmark, this graceful Greek Revival building, which is closed on Sunday, has three tiers of shops and restaurants.

The **First Unitarian Church of Providence,** built in 1816, houses the largest bell ever cast in Paul Revere's foundry—a 2,500 pounder. ✉ *1 Benevolent St.,* ☎ *401/421–7970.* *Free.*

The awe-inspiring **Rhode Island State House** was built in 1900. Its dome, one of the world's largest, was modeled after St. Peter's Basilica in Rome. On display is the original parchment charter granted by King Charles to the colony of Rhode Island in 1663. ✉ *82 Smith St.,* ☎ *401/222–2357. Closed weekends.*

Roger Williams contributed so significantly to the concepts leading to the Declaration of Independence and the Constitution that the National Park Service dedicated the 4.5-acre **Roger Williams National Memorial** to his memory. Displays offer a quick course in the life and times of Rhode Island's founder. ✉ *282 N. Main St.,* ☎ *401/785–9450.* *Free.*

Waterplace Park and Riverwalk was completed in 1997. The 4-acre tract with Venetian-style footbridges, cobblestone walkways, and an amphitheater encircling a tidal pond on the Providence River has won many design awards. ✉ *Boat House Clock Tower, 2 American Express Way,* ☎ *401/751–1177.*

The 1786 **John Brown House,** one of America's first mansions, is named for a China trader famous for his Revolutionary-era role in the burning of the British customs ship *Gaspee.* The three-story Georgian mansion has elaborate woodwork and furniture, silver, linens, Chinese porcelain, and an antique doll collection. ✉ *52 Power St.,* ☎ *401/331–8575.* *$6. Closed weekdays Jan.–Feb.*

The **Museum of Rhode Island History at Aldrich House,** inside a Federal-style structure built in 1822, presents rotating exhibits about the state's history. ✉ *110 Benevolent St.,* ☎ *401/331–8575.* *$2. Closed Mon.*

Roger Williams Park and Zoo (✉ Elmwood Ave., ☎ 401/785–3510; $3.50) is a beautiful 430-acre Victorian park. The zoo is home to more than 900 animals and 150 different species; in the park you can have a picnic, feed the ducks in the lakes, ride a pony, or rent a paddleboat.

Dining and Lodging

$$$–$$$$ ★ ✕ **The Gatehouse.** Views of the Seekonk River and the classy decor complement the New Orleans–influenced New England cuisine served here. Dishes might include slow-roasted duck with sautéed vegetables, served with spiced pumpkin gravy. ✉ *4 Richmond Sq.,* ☎ *401/521–9229. Reservations essential on weekends. AE, DC, MC, V. No lunch Sat. Brunch served Sun.*

$$–$$$$ ✕ **Camille's.** A classic Italian eatery, Camille's serves traditional fare like veal scallopini and shrimp scampi. Black-tie service and reproductions of early Renaissance murals in the massive dining room impart an air of sophistication. ✉ *71 Bradford St.,* ☎ *401/751–4812. AE, DC, MC, V. Closed Sun. July–Aug.*

$$$ ★ ✕ **Al Forno.** Roasted clams and spicy sausage served in a tomato broth and charcoal-seared tournedos of beef with mashed potatoes are among the entrées at this regionally renowned contemporary eatery. Made-to-order desserts include crepes with apricot puree and crème anglaise. ✉ *577 S. Main St.,* ☎ *401/273–9760. Reservations not accepted. AE, DC, MC, V. Closed Sun.–Mon. No lunch.*

$$–$$$ ★ ✕ **Pot au Feu.** For a quarter century Pot au Feu has worked to perfect the basics, like pâté du foie gras, beef bourguignon, and potatoes au gratin. The dining experience is more casual at the downstairs Bistro than at the upstairs Salon. ✉ *44 Custom House St.,* ☎ *401/273–8953. AE, DC, MC, V. Salon closed Sun.–Mon.*

$–$$ ✕ **India.** Mango chicken curry and swordfish kabobs are two of the inexpensive entrées at this downtown restaurant known for its freshly made breads. ✉ *123 Dorrance St.,* ☎ *401/278–2000. AE, MC, V.*

$$$ **C. C. Ledbetter's.** The unmarked somber green exterior of innkeeper C. C. Ledbetter's mansard-roof 1770 home gives few hints of the vibrancy within—lively art, photographs, quilts, and a shrewd blend of contemporary furnishings and antiques fill the place. ✉ *326 Benefit St., 02903,* ☎ FAX *401/351–4699. 5 rooms; some share bath. CP. AE, V.*

$$$ ★ **Providence Biltmore.** The Biltmore, completed in 1922, has a sleek Art Deco exterior, an external glass elevator with delightful views of Providence, a grand ballroom, and an interesting history. The attentiveness of its staff, the downtown location, and modern amenities make this hotel one of the city's best. ✉ *Kennedy Plaza, Dorrance and*

Washington Sts., 02903, ☎ 401/421–0700, FAX 401/421–0210. 238 rooms. Restaurant. AE, DC, MC, V.

$$–$$$ **Days Hotel on the Harbor.** Half the rooms at this plain but comfortable hotel have harbor views; the other half overlook I–95. ✉ *220 India St., 02903, ☎ 401/272–5577, FAX 401/272–5577. 136 rooms. Restaurant, hot tub, exercise room. AE, D, DC, MC, V.*

$$–$$$ **Marriott Hotel.** Tones of peach and green grace the good-size rooms at this hotel that has all the modern conveniences. The Blue Fin Grille restaurant specializes in local seafood prepared with a French flair. ✉ *Charles and Orms Sts. near Exit 23 off I–95, 02904, ☎ 401/272–2400 or 800/937–7768, FAX 401/273–2686. 351 rooms. Restaurant, indoor and outdoor pools, health club. AE, D, DC, MC, V.*

Nightlife and the Arts

The **Hot Club** (✉ 575 S. Water St., ☎ 401/861–9007) is a fashionable waterside bar. **Lupo's Heartbreak Hotel** (✉ 239 Westminster St., ☎ 401/272–5876), a nightclub, books local and international musical talents. The **Providence Performing Arts Center** (✉ 220 Weybosset St., ☎ 401/421–2787) hosts touring Broadway shows, concerts, and other events. **Snookers** (✉ 145 Clifford St., ☎ 401/351–7665) is a stylish billiard hall in the Jewelry District. **Veterans Memorial Auditorium** (✉ 69 Brownell St., ☎ 401/222–3150) hosts concerts, children's theater, and ballet.

Outdoor Activities and Sports

Biking

For trail information call **Rhode Island Tourism** (☎ 800/556–2484). The **East Bay Bicycle Path** is a 14½-mi paved trail linking Providence's India Point Park to Bristol.

Shopping

Antiques stores and art galleries line **Wickenden Street.** The **Cat's Pajamas** (✉ 227 Wickenden St., ☎ 401/751–8440) specializes in 1920s–60s jewelry, linens, housewares, accessories, and small furnishings. **CAV** (✉ 14 Imperial Pl., ☎ 401/751–9164) is a restaurant, bar, and coffeehouse in a revamped factory space where fine rugs, tapestries, prints, portraits, and antiques are sold. **Tilden-Thurber** (✉ 292 Westminster St., ☎ 401/272–3200) carries high-end Colonial- and Victorian-era furniture, antiques, and estate jewelry.

VERMONT

Updated by Anne Peracca Bijur

Capital	Montpelier
Population	589,000
Motto	Freedom and Unity
State Bird	Hermit thrush
State Flower	Red clover
Postal Abbreviation	VT

Statewide Visitor Information

Vermont Travel Division (☒ 134 State St., Montpelier 05602, ☎ 802/828–3237 or 800/837–6668). **Vermont Chamber of Commerce** (☒ Box 37, Montpelier 05602, ☎ 802/223–3443).

Scenic Drives

Route 100 passes through the eastern edge of Green Mountain National Forest, the Mad River Valley, and the town of Stowe, then continues on to Canada.

National and State Parks

National Park

The 355,000-acre **Green Mountain National Forest** (☒ 231 N. Main St., Rutland 05701, ☎ 802/747–6700) runs through the center of the state, from Bristol south to the Massachusetts border.

State Parks

The 40 parks maintained by the **Department of Forests, Parks, and Recreation** (☒ Waterbury 05671, ☎ 802/241–3655) offer nature and hiking trails, campsites, swimming, boating facilities, and fishing. Especially popular are the **Champlain Islands** sites: Burton Island, Kill Kare, and Sand Bar.

SOUTHERN VERMONT

Many of the Southern Vermont towns with village greens and white-spired churches were founded in the early 18th century as frontier outposts and later became trading centers. In the western region the Green Mountain Boys fought off both the British and land-hungry New Yorkers. The influx of new residents in the past 20 years means the quaintness often comes with a patina of sophistication or funk; shoppers can find not only antiques but New Age crystals, Vermont-made salsa, and the highest-tech ski gear.

Visitor Information

Bennington: Chamber of Commerce (☒ Veterans Memorial Dr., 05201, ☎ 802/447–3311). **Brattleboro:** Chamber of Commerce (☒ 180 Main St., 05301, ☎ 802/254–4565). **Manchester and the mountains:** Chamber of Commerce (☒ 2 Main St., R.R. 2, Box 3451, 05255, ☎ 802/362–2100). **Rutland:** Chamber of Commerce, Convention and Visitors Division (☒ 256 N. Main St., 05701, ☎ 802/773–2747). **Woodstock:** Chamber of Commerce (☒ 4 Central St., Box 486, 05091, ☎ 802/457–3555 or 888/496–6378).

Arriving and Departing

By Bus

Vermont Transit (☎ 802/864–6811 or 800/552–8737). **Bonanza Bus Lines** (☎ 800/556–3815).

By Car

I–91 runs north–south along the eastern edge of Vermont. U.S. 7 goes north–south through western Vermont, and Route 9 runs east–west across the state through Bennington and Brattleboro.

By Train

Amtrak (☎ 800/872–7245) stops at Brattleboro, Bellows Falls, Rutland, and White River Junction.

Exploring Southern Vermont

It was at **Bennington** that Ethan Allen formed the Green Mountain Boys, who helped capture Fort Ticonderoga in 1775. The **Bennington Battle Monument** (✉ 15 Monument Ave., ☎ 802/447–0550; 🎟 $1.50), a 306-ft stone obelisk, commemorates General John Stark's defeat of the British in their attempt to capture Bennington's stockpile of supplies. It is closed from late October to mid-April. The artifacts at the **Bennington Museum** (✉ W. Main St. [Rte. 9], ☎ 802/447–1571; 🎟 $5) include the largest public collection of the work of Grandma Moses, who lived and painted in the area; the only surviving automobile of Bennington's Martin Company; and one of the oldest Stars and Stripes in existence.

The tree-shaded marble sidewalks and stately houses of **Manchester** reflect the luxurious summer-resort lifestyle of a century ago, while upscale factory-outlet stores appeal to the ski crowd. **Hildene** (✉ Rte. 7A, 2 mi south of intersection with Rtes. 11 and 30, ☎ 802/362–1788; 🎟 $7) was the summer home of Abraham Lincoln's son Robert. Noteworthy features in the the 24-room mansion include its Georgian Revival symmetry, formal gardens, grand curved staircase, and 1,000-pipe organ. The house is closed from November to mid-May.

The **American Museum of Fly Fishing** displays the tackle of such noted anglers as Jimmy Carter, Winslow Homer, and Bing Crosby. ✉ *Rte. 7A,* ☎ *802/362–3300.* 🎟 *$3.*

The steep 5-mi drive to the top of **Mt. Equinox** brings you to the Saddle, where the views are outstanding. ✉ *Rte. 7A,* ☎ *802/362–1114.* 🎟 *$6 car and driver, $2 each additional adult. Closed Nov.–Apr.*

In **Rutland** there are strips of shopping centers and a seemingly endless row of traffic lights. The **Chaffee Center for the Visual Arts** (✉ 16 Main St., ☎ 802/775–0356) houses the work of more than 200 Vermont artists. At the **Vermont Marble Exhibit,** northwest of Rutland, visitors can watch the transformation of rough stone into slabs, blocks, and gift items. ✉ *Off Rte. 3, Proctor,* ☎ *802/459–3311 or 800/427–1396.* 🎟 *$5. Closed Nov.–late May.*

Woodstock is the quintessential quiet New England town, on the eastern side of Vermont on U.S. 4. Exquisitely preserved Federal houses surround the tree-lined village green. The **Vermont Institute of Natural Science's Raptor Center** has nature trails and 23 living species of birds of prey. ✉ *Church Hill Rd.,* ☎ *802/457–2779.* 🎟 *$6. Closed Sun. Nov.–Apr.*

A half mile north of the center of Woodstock, the reconstructed farmhouse, school, and general store at the **Billings Farm and Museum**

Vermont

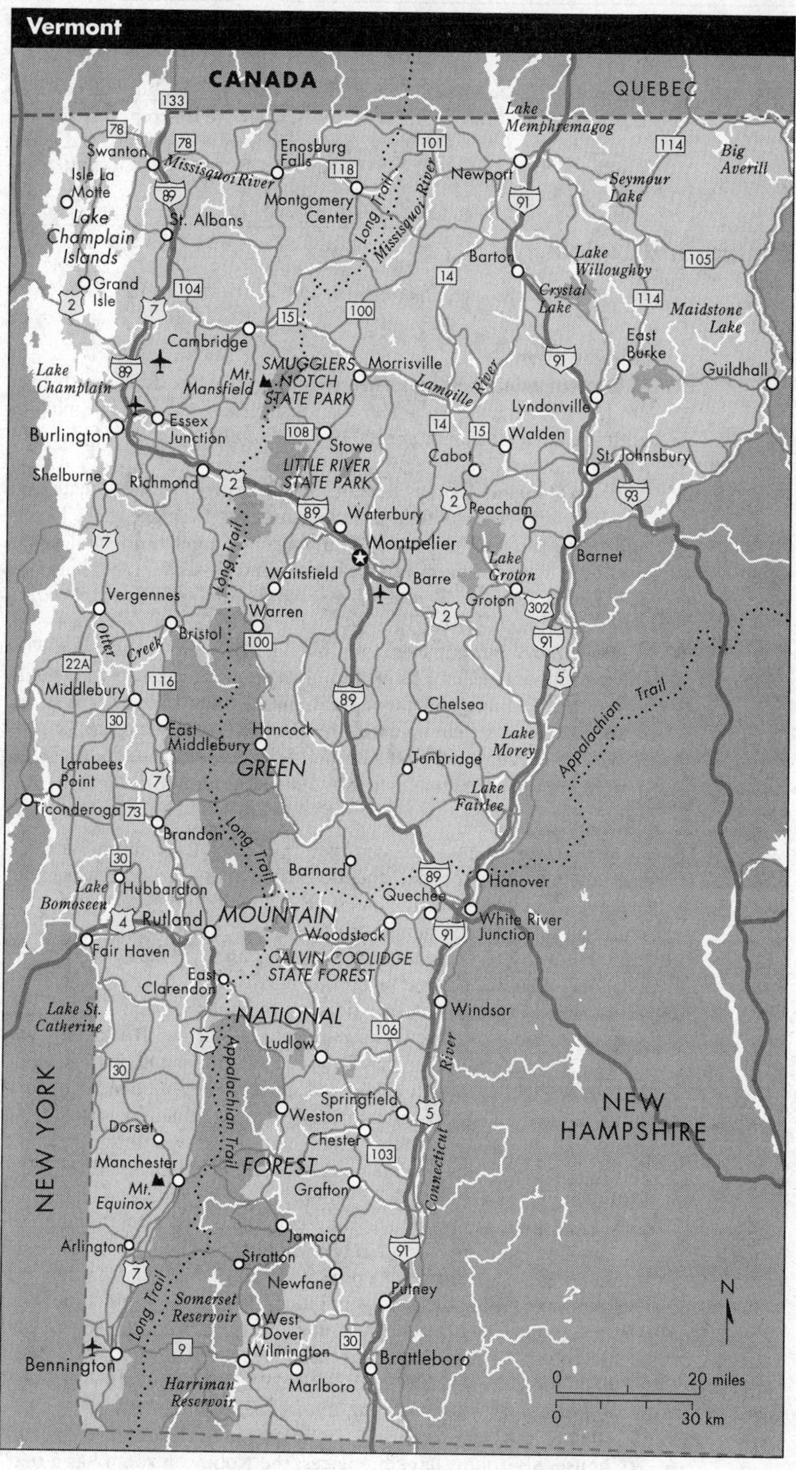
CANADA
QUEBEC
Lake Memphremagog
Swanton
Missisquoi River
Enosburg Falls
Isle La Motte
Lake Champlain Islands
St. Albans
Montgomery Center
Long Trail
Missisquoi River
Newport
Big Averill
Seymour Lake
Barton
Lake Willoughby
Crystal Lake
Maidstone Lake
Grand Isle
Cambridge
Morrisville
SMUGGLERS NOTCH STATE PARK
Mt. Mansfield
East Burke
Guildhall
Lake Champlain
Lamoille River
Lyndonville
Essex Junction
Burlington
Stowe
Walden
LITTLE RIVER STATE PARK
Cabot
St. Johnsbury
Shelburne
Richmond
Peacham
Waterbury
Montpelier
Barnet
Waitsfield
Barre
Lake Groton
Groton
Vergennes
Warren
Bristol
Otter Creek
Middlebury
Chelsea
East Middlebury
Hancock
Lake Morey
Tunbridge
Larabees Point
GREEN
Appalachian Trail
Ticonderoga
Lake Fairlee
Brandon
Long Trail
Barnard
Hanover
Lake Bomoseen
Hubbardton
Quechee
Rutland
MOUNTAIN
White River Junction
Woodstock
Fair Haven
CALVIN COOLIDGE STATE FOREST
East Clarendon
Windsor
Lake St. Catherine
NATIONAL
Ludlow
River
NEW YORK
Appalachian Trail
Springfield
Weston
NEW HAMPSHIRE
Dorset
Chester
Manchester
FOREST
Connecticut
Mt. Equinox
Grafton
Jamaica
Arlington
Stratton
Newfane
Putney
N
Long Trail
Somerset Reservoir
West Dover
Wilmington
Brattleboro
Bennington
Marlboro
Harriman Reservoir
0
20 miles
0
30 km

demonstrate the daily activities of early Vermonters. ✉ *Rte. 12,* ☎ *802/457–2355.* 🎫 *$7. Closed Jan.–May and weekdays Nov.–Dec.*

The mile-long **Quechee Gorge** is visible from U.S. 4, but you can also scramble down one of several descents. **Quechee** is perched astride the Ottauquechee River. On weekdays you can watch potters and glass-blowers at **Simon Pearce** (✉ Main St., ☎ 802/295–2711 or 800/774–5277; 🎫 free).

Dining and Lodging

For price ranges *see* Charts 1 (B) and 2 (B) *in* On the Road with Fodor's.

Bennington

$$ ✕ **The Brasserie.** Chefs create hearty and creative fare using mostly local produce and organic foods. The decor is as clean-lined as the Bennington pottery sold in the same complex. ✉ *324 County St.,* ☎ *802/447–7922. MC, V. Closed Tues.*

$$–$$$ 🏨 **South Shire Inn.** Canopy beds in plushly carpeted rooms, ornate plaster molding on the ceilings, and the mahogany fireplace in the library add up to turn-of-the-century grandeur in a quiet residential neighborhood. Most rooms have fireplaces; some have whirlpool baths. ✉ *124 Elm St., 05201,* ☎ *802/447–3839,* FAX *802/442–3547. 9 rooms. Full breakfast. AE, MC, V.*

$$ ★ 🏨 **Molly Stark Inn.** This gem of a B&B makes you feel as if you were staying with old friends. Blue-plaid wallpaper, gleaming hardwood floors, antique furnishings, and a woodstove in the brick alcove of the sitting room give a country charm to this 1860 Queen Anne Victorian. ✉ *1067 E. Main St. (Rte. 9), 05201,* ☎ *802/442–9631 or 800/356–3076,* FAX *802/442–5224. 7 rooms. Full breakfast. AE, D, MC, V.*

Manchester

$$–$$$ ✕ **Bistro Henry's.** Just outside town, this spacious restaurant attracts a devoted clientele for its authentic French bistro fare, extensive wine list, and attention to detail. Popular items are merlot-braised lamb shank with balsamic glazed onions and an eggplant, mushroom, and fontina terrine Provençal. ✉ *Rte. 11/30, Manchester,* ☎ *802/362–4982. AE, DC, MC, V. Closed Mon.*

$$ ✕ **Quality Restaurant.** Gentrification has reached the down-home neighborhood place that was the model for Norman Rockwell's *War News* painting. The Quality has Provençal wallpaper and polished wood booths, and the sturdy New England standbys of grilled meat loaf and hot roast beef or turkey sandwiches have been joined by tortellini Alfredo with shrimp and smoked salmon, and grilled swordfish with lemon butter. The breakfasts here are popular. ✉ *Main St.,* ☎ *802/362–9839. AE, MC, V.*

$$$–$$$$ ✕🏨 **The Equinox.** This grand white-columned resort was a landmark on Vermont's tourism scene even before Abraham Lincoln's family began summering here. Rooms have pine furnishings, and the front porch is perfect for watching the passing parade. There's a medically supervised spa program, falconry school, tennis courts, golf course, sauna, and steam room. ✉ *Rte. 7A, Manchester Village 05254,* ☎ *802/362–4700 or 800/362–4747,* FAX *802/362–1595. 155 rooms, 10 3-bedroom town houses. 2 restaurants, bar, pools. AE, D, DC, MC, V.*

$$$ ★ 🏨 **1811 House.** Staying here is like staying at an elegant English country house. Six rooms have fireplaces; the Robinson room has a marble-enclosed tub. The pub-style bar serves 58 single-malt scotches. ✉ *Rte. 7A, Box 39, 05254,* ☎ *802/362–1811 or 800/432–1811. 14 rooms. Bar. Full breakfast. No smoking. AE, D, MC, V.*

$$ **Barnstead Innstead.** This 1830s barn was transformed in 1968 into a handful of rooms that combine exposed beams and barn-board walls with modern plumbing and cheerful wallpaper. ✉ *Rte. 30, 05255,* ☎ *802/362–1619 or 800/331–1619,* FAX *802/362–1619. 14 rooms. Pool. AE, MC, V.*

Rutland

$$ ★ ✕ **Back Home Cafe.** Wood booths, black-and-white linoleum tile, and exposed brick lend atmosphere at this second-story café where dinner might be chicken breast stuffed with roasted red peppers and goat cheese. There is often weekend entertainment. ✉ *21 Center St.,* ☎ *802/775–9313. AE, MC, V.*

$$ **Comfort Inn.** Rooms at this chain hotel are a cut above the standard, with upholstered wing chairs and blond-wood furnishings. ✉ *19 Allen St., 05701,* ☎ *802/775–2200 or 800/432–6788,* FAX *802/775–2694. 104 rooms. Restaurant, indoor pool, hot tub, sauna. CP. AE, D, DC, MC, V.*

$–$$ **Inn at Rutland.** In this Victorian mansion an ornate oak staircase leads to rooms with such turn-of-the-century touches as botanical prints, elaborate ceiling moldings, and frosted glass. ✉ *70 N. Main St., 05701,* ☎ *802/773–0575 or 800/808–0575,* FAX *802/775–3506. 12 rooms. Hot tub. Full breakfast. D, DC, MC, V.*

Woodstock

$$$ ★ ✕ **Prince and the Pauper.** Nouvelle French dishes with a Vermont accent are served in a romantically candlelit Colonial setting. ✉ *24 Elm St.,* ☎ *802/457–1818. AE, D, MC, V. No lunch.*

$$ ✕ **Bentleys.** Antique silk-fringed lamp shades and long lace curtains lend a tongue-in-cheek Victorian air to burgers, chili, homemade soups, and entrées like roasted Maple Leaf Farm duckling with sweet mango sauce. ✉ *3 Elm St.,* ☎ *802/457–3232. AE, DC, MC, V.*

$$$–$$$$ ✕ **Kedron Valley Inn.** One of the state's oldest hotels—built in the 1840s—has rooms decorated with family quilts and antiques. The motel units in back have exposed log walls. The pond with a beach is a great place to spend a summer afternoon. The dining room prepares dishes using classic French technique on Vermont ingredients. ✉ *Rte. 106, 05071,* ☎ *802/457–1473 or 800/836–1193,* FAX *802/457–4469. 26 rooms. Restaurant, lounge. MAP. AE, D, MC, V. Closed Apr. and 10 days before Thanksgiving.*

$$$–$$$$ ✕ **Woodstock Inn and Resort.** Patchwork quilts and landscape paintings enliven the standard modern ash furnishings at this inn owned by the Rockefeller family. The dining room (jacket and tie) serves nouvelle New England fare. Many activities are available including golf, tennis, croquet, and cross-country and downhill skiing. ✉ *U.S. 4, 05091,* ☎ *802/457–1100 or 800/448–7900,* FAX *802/457–6699. 146 rooms. 2 restaurants, bar, indoor and outdoor pools, health club. AE, MC, V.*

$$ ★ **Winslow House.** An unpretentious place with great cross-country skiing and golf nearby, this farmhouse built in 1872 has a small common area but two spacious upstairs quarters with separate sitting rooms. ✉ *38 Rte. 4, 05091,* ☎ *802/457–1820,* FAX *802/457–1820. 4 rooms. Full breakfast. D, DC, MC, V.*

Motels

Aspen Motel (✉ Box 548, Manchester Center 05255, ☎ 802/362–2450, FAX 802/362–1348), 24 rooms, pool; *$$.* **Pond Ridge Motel** (✉ U.S. 4, Woodstock 05091, ☎ 802/457–1667, FAX 802/457–1667), 21 rooms; *$$.* **Harwood Hill Motel** (✉ Rte. 7A, Bennington 05201, ☎ 802/442–6278), 16 rooms, 3 cottages; *$.*

Campgrounds

The state park system runs nearly 40 campgrounds with more than 2,000 campsites. Contact the **Department of Forests, Parks, and Recreation** (✉ 103 S. Main St., Waterbury 05671, ☎ 802/244–8711) for a copy of the Vermont Campground Guide. The official state map also lists private campgrounds.

At **Green Mountain National Forest** (✉ 231 N. Main St., Rutland, 05701, ☎ 802/747–6700), you can reserve one campsite area in advance; the remaining areas are first-come, first-served.

Nightlife and the Arts

Most nightlife is concentrated at and around the ski resorts or in the larger towns and cities. The **Marlboro Music Festival** (✉ Marlboro Music Center, ☎ 802/254–2394 or 215/569–4690 Sept.–June) presents chamber music in weekend concerts in July and August. **New England Bach Festival** (✉ Brattleboro Music Center, ☎ 802/257–4523) held in October, is a popular classical music festival.

Outdoor Activities and Sports

Biking

Vermont Bicycle Touring (✉ Box 711, Bristol 05443, ☎ 802/453–4811 or 800/245–3868) conducts guided tours throughout Vermont.

Canoeing

The **Connecticut River** and the **Battenkill** offer easygoing canoe outings. Rentals are available from **Battenkill Canoe** (✉ Rte. 7A, Arlington, ☎ 802/362–2800 or 800/421–5268).

Fishing

The **Battenkill River** is famous for trout. **Orvis** (✉ Rte. 7A, Manchester, ☎ 802/362–3900 or 800/235–9763) runs a fly-fishing school. The necessary fishing license is available through tackle shops, or call the **Department of Fish and Wildlife** (☎ 802/241–3700).

Hiking and Backpacking

The southern half of the **Long Trail** is part of the **Appalachian Trail** and runs from just east of Rutland to Vermont's southern boundary. The **Green Mountain Club** (✉ Rte. 100, R.R. 1, Box 650, Waterbury Center 05677, ☎ 802/244–7037) maintains the trail, staffs its huts in summer, and maps hiking elsewhere in Vermont.

Ski Areas

For up-to-date snow conditions in the state, call 802/828–3239. All listed downhill ski areas have snowmaking equipment.

Cross-Country

Mt. Snow/Haystack (✉ 400 Mountain Rd., Mt. Snow 05356, ☎ 802/464–3333), 62 mi of trails. **Stratton** (✉ Stratton Mountain 05155, ☎ 802/297–2200 or 800/843–6867), 20 mi of trails.

Downhill

Bromley (✉ Box 1130, Manchester Center 05255, ☎ 802/824–5522), 41 runs, 9 lifts, 1,334-ft vertical drop. **Killington/Pico** (✉ 400 Killington Rd., Killington 05751, ☎ 802/422–3333 or 800/621–6867), 212 runs, 3 gondolas, 30 lifts, 3,150-ft drop. **Mt. Snow/Haystack** (✉ 400 Mountain Rd., Mt. Snow 05356, ☎ 802/422–3333), 133 trails, 26 lifts, 1,700-ft drop. **Stratton** (✉ Stratton Mountain 05155, ☎ 802/297–2200 or 800/843–6867), 90 slopes, gondola, 11 lifts, 2,000-ft drop.

Shopping

Antiques and traditional and contemporary crafts are everywhere. Particularly good is **U.S. 7** north of Manchester to Danby. The **Vermont Country Store** (✉ Rte. 100, Weston, ☎ 802/824–3184) carries such forgotten items as Monkey Brand black tooth powder, Flexible Flyer sleds, and pickles in a barrel. **East Meets West** (✉ Rte. 7, north of Rutland, ☎ 802/443–2242 or 800/443–2242) stocks international arts and crafts. The **Bennington Potters Yard** (✉ 324 County St., ☎ 802/447–7531 or 800/205–8033) carries firsts and seconds. **Manchester** has many designer and factory outlets.

NORTHERN VERMONT

Northwestern Vermont is more mountainous than the southern part of the state and has the closest thing Vermont has to a seacoast, Lake Champlain; the nation's smallest state capital, Montpelier; and Burlington, Vermont's largest and most cosmopolitan city. The region's recorded history dates from 1609, when Samuel de Champlain explored the lake now named for him. Northeastern Vermont, known as the Northeast Kingdom, is the least populated part of the state. A great pleasure here is driving through pastoral scenery and discovering charming small towns such as Peacham, Barton, and Craftsbury Common.

Visitor Information

Central Vermont: Chamber of Commerce (✉ Box 336, Barre 05641, ☎ 802/229–5711). **Lake Champlain:** Chamber of Commerce (✉ 60 Main St., Suite 100, Burlington 05401, ☎ 802/863–3489). **Smugglers' Notch:** Chamber of Commerce (✉ Box 364, Jeffersonville 05464, ☎ 802/644–2239). **St. Johnsbury Chamber of Commerce** (✉ 30 Western Ave., 05819, ☎ 802/748–3678 or 800/639–6379). **Stowe:** Area Association (✉ Main St., Box 1320, Stowe 05672, ☎ 802/253–7321 or 800/247–8693).

Arriving and Departing

By Bus

Vermont Transit (☎ 802/864–6811 or 800/552–8737).

By Car

I–89 runs from White River Junction to Vermont's northwestern corner at the Canadian border. To get to the eastern part of the state, drive up I–91.

By Plane

Burlington Airport (✉ South Burlington, ☎ 802/863–2874) is 4½ mi east of town off Route 2 and is served by major airlines. Private planes land at **E. F. Knapp Airport** (☎ 802/223–2221), between Barre and Montpelier.

By Train

Amtrak (☎ 800/872–7245) stops at Montpelier, Waterbury, Essex Junction, and St. Albans.

Exploring Northern Vermont

Middlebury is Robert Frost country; Vermont's former poet laureate spent 23 summers at a farm near here. The **Robert Frost Wayside Trail,** east of Middlebury on Route 125, winds through quiet woodland and has Frost quotations posted along the way.

The University of Vermont's **Morgan Horse Farm** offers tours of its stables and paddocks. ✉ *Follow signs off Rte. 23, 2½ mi from Middlebury,* ☎ *802/388–2011.* 🎫 *$4. Closed Nov.–Apr.*

Shelburne, a town on the banks of Lake Champlain, is known for two ★ attractions. The 37 buildings of the 100-acre **Shelburne Museum** (✉ U.S. 7, 5 mi south of Burlington, ☎ 802/985–3346; 🎫 $17.50 for 2 consecutive days, $7 for 1 day in winter) contain one of the largest Americana collections in the nation. Exhibits include 18th- and 19th-century houses and furniture, fine and folk art, farm tools, carriages and sleighs, and an old side-wheel steamship. At the 1,400-acre **Shelburne Farms** (✉ East of U.S. 7, 6 mi south of Burlington, ☎ 802/985–8686; 🎫 day pass $5, tour is additional $4) visitors can see a working dairy farm, attend nature lectures, visit farm animals at the Children's Farmyard, or stroll along a stretch of Lake Champlain's waterfront. The landscaping, designed by Frederick Law Olmsted, creator of New York's Central Park, gently channels the eye to expansive vistas.

Burlington is enlivened by the 20,000 students of the University of Vermont. **Church Street Marketplace**—with its down-to-earth shops, chic boutiques, and appealing menagerie of sidewalk cafés, food and crafts vendors, and street performers—is an animated downtown focal point. There are narrated tours during the day—and **evening dinner-and-dance cruises**—on the *Spirit of Ethan Allen,* a replica of the paddle wheeler that once plied Lake Champlain. ✉ *Burlington Boat House, College St. at Battery St.,* ☎ *802/862–9685.* 🎫 *$8. Closed mid-Oct.–May.*

Smugglers' Notch is the scenic, bouldered pass over Mt. Mansfield said to have given shelter to 18th-century outlaws. There are roadside picnic tables and a spectacular waterfall. Take Route 15 to Jeffersonville; then go south on narrow, twisting Route 108.

Stowe is best known as a venerable ski center. In summer you can take the 4½-mi toll road from Stowe to the top of Vermont's highest peak, **Mt. Mansfield.** At the road's end is a short and beautiful walk. ✉ *Entrance on Mountain Rd., 8 mi from Rte. 100,* ☎ *802/253–3000.* 🎫 *$12.* ⏲ *Late May–late Oct., daily 10–5.*Another way to ascend Mt. Mansfield is in the **gondola** that shuttles from the base of the ski area up 4,393 ft to the section known as the Chin, where there are scenic views and a restaurant. ✉ *Entrance on Mountain Rd., 8 mi from Rte. 100,* ☎ *802/253–3000.* 🎫 *$9.* ⏲ *June–late Oct., daily 10–5; Dec.–Apr., daily 8:30–4 for skiers; Oct. and May, weekends 10–5.*

Just south of Stowe is the mecca, the nirvana, the veritable Valhalla for ice cream lovers: **Ben & Jerry's Ice Cream Factory.** ✉ *Rte. 100, 1 mi north of I–89,* ☎ *802/244–8687.* 🎫 *$2.*

Montpelier, which has 10,000 residents, is the nation's least populated state capital. The impressive **Vermont State House** has a gleaming gold dome and columns 6 ft in diameter fashioned from granite from neighboring Barre. ✉ *State St.,* ☎ *802/828–2228.* 🎫 *Free. Closed Sun. and late Oct.–June.*

The **Vermont Museum,** on the ground floor of the Vermont Historical Society offices, has intriguing informative exhibits; its docents can answer New England trivia questions such as "Why does the area have covered bridges?" ✉ *109 State St.,* ☎ *802/828–2291.* 🎫 *$3. Closed Mon.*

The chief city of the Northeast Kingdom is **St. Johnsbury.** The **Fairbanks Museum and Planetarium** (✉ Main and Prospect Sts., ☎ 802/748–2372; 🎫 $4) engrosses visitors with its eclectic collections of plants, animals, and Vermontiana and a 50-seat planetarium. The **St. Johns-**

bury Athenaeum is an architectural gem, with dark paneling, polished Victorian woodwork, and ornate circular staircases that rise to a gallery displaying painter Albert Bierstadt's *Domes of Yosemite.* ✉ *30 Main St.,* ☎ *802/748–8291.* 🎫 *Free. Closed Tues., Sun.*

Dining and Lodging

For price ranges *see* Charts 1 (B) and 2 (B) *in* On the Road with Fodor's.

Burlington

$$ ★ ✕ **Isabel's.** Inspired American cuisine artfully presented is the hallmark here. The menu changes weekly and has included Thai seafood pasta and vegetable Wellington. Weekend brunch is popular. ✉ *112 Lake St.,* ☎ *802/865–2522. AE, D, DC, MC, V.*

$–$$ ★ ✕ **Sweet Tomatoes.** The Italian countryside turns up at this boisterous trattoria, which has a wood-fired oven, hand-painted ceramic pitchers, and crusty bread that comes with a bowl of oil and garlic for dunking. The menu includes caponata, farfalle with sweet sausage and roasted red peppers, and pizza. ✉ *83 Church St.,* ☎ *802/660–9533. AE, MC, V.*

$$–$$$$ ★ ✕🏨 **Inn at Shelburne Farms.** Built at the turn of the century, this Tudor-style inn overlooks Lake Champlain, the distant Adirondacks, and the sea of pastures on this 1,400-acre working farm. Each guest room is different, from the wallpaper to the period antiques. The seasonal contemporary menu makes clever use of local ingredients. Guests can play tennis and fish or boat on the property. ✉ *Harbor Rd., Shelburne 05482,* ☎ *802/985–8498. 24 rooms. Restaurant. AE, DC, MC, V. Closed mid-Oct.–mid-May.*

$$–$$$ 🏨 **Willard Street Inn.** Perched high in the historic hill section, this grand house with an exterior marble staircase and English gardens incorporates elements of Queen Anne and Colonial–Georgian Revival styles. Guest rooms are individually decorated and have down comforters and phones; some have lake views and canopy beds. ✉ *349 S. Willard St., 05401,* ☎ *802/651–8710 or 800/577–8712,* FAX *802/651–8714. 15 rooms, 5 with shared bath. Full breakfast. Afternoon tea. AE, D, DC, MC, V.*

Middlebury

$$$ ★ ✕ **Woody's.** In addition to cool jazz, diner-deco light fixtures, and abstract paintings, Woody's has a view of Otter Creek just below. The menu has nightly specials that might include Vermont lamb or a vegetarian grill. ✉ *5 Bakery La.,* ☎ *802/388–4182. AE, DC, MC, V.*

$$$ ✕🏨 **Swift House Inn.** The main building at Swift House, the Georgian home of a 19th-century governor, contains white-panel wainscoting, elaborately carved mahogany and marble fireplaces, and cherry paneling in the dining room. The rooms—each with Oriental rugs and nine with fireplaces—have canopy beds, curtains with swags, and claw-foot tubs. Rooms in the gatehouse suffer from street noise but are charming; a carriage house holds six luxury rooms. One unusual menu item is creamy risotto with seasonal vegetables and maple syrup. ✉ *25 Stewart La., 05753,* ☎ *802/388–9925,* FAX *802/388–9927. 21 rooms. Restaurant, pub, sauna, steam room. CP. AE, D, DC, MC, V.*

Montpelier

$$$ ✕ **Chef's Table** and the **Main Street Bar and Grill.** The staff at these sister restaurants are students at the New England Culinary Institute. At the Chef's Table, upstairs, the menu changes daily but always offers well-prepared, inventive dishes such as swordfish with spinach and cherry tomatoes. Downstairs at the Grill the atmosphere is more ca-

sual but the food no less delicious. ✉ *118 Main St.,* ☎ *802/229–9202, 802/223–3188 for the Grill. AE, D, MC, V. Chef's Table closed Sun.*

$$ ✕ **Horn of the Moon.** The bowls of honey and the bulletin board plastered with political notices hint at Vermont's prominent progressive contingent. This vegetarian restaurant's cuisine includes a little Mexican, a little Thai, a lot of flavor, and not too much tofu. ✉ *8 Langdon St.,* ☎ *802/223–2895. No credit cards. Closed Mon.*

$$$ **Inn at Montpelier.** This spacious early 1800s house has antique four-posters, tapestry-upholstered wing chairs, and classical guitar on the stereo. The sitting room has a Federal feel to it, and the wide wraparound Colonial Revival porch is perfect for reading or watching the townsfolk stroll by. ✉ *147 Main St., 05602,* ☎ *802/223–2727,* FAX *802/223–0722. 19 rooms. CP. AE, D, DC, MC, V.*

St. Johnsbury

$$$–$$$$ ✕ **Rabbit Hill Inn.** Rooms at this formal inn are as stylistically different as they are consistently indulgent: Some have canopy beds, whirlpool baths, mountain views, and fireplaces. Eclectic, regional cuisine is served in the low-ceiling dining room. Meat and fish are smoked on the premises, and the herbs and vegetables often come from gardens out back. ✉ *Rte. 18, Lower Waterford 05848,* ☎ *802/748–5168 or 800/762–8669,* FAX *802/748–8342. 21 rooms. Restaurant, pub, canoeing, cross-country skiing. MAP. Afternoon tea. AE, MC, V. Closed 1st 3 wks in Apr., 1st 2 wks in Nov.*

$$–$$$ ★ ✕ **Wildflower Inn.** Guest rooms in the restored Federal-style main house, as well as in the carriage houses, are decorated simply with reproductions and contemporary furnishings; nearly all have incredible views of the property's 500 acres. Meals feature hearty country-style food, with homemade breads and vegetables from the garden. The many activities available include tennis, fishing, ice-skating, cross-country skiing, and sleigh rides. ✉ *North of St. Johnsbury on Darling Hill Rd., Lyndonville 05851,* ☎ *802/626–8310 or 800/627–8310,* FAX *802/626–3039. 22 rooms. Restaurant, pool, hot tub, sauna, recreation room. Full breakfast. Afternoon snacks. MC, V. Closed Apr. and Nov.*

Stowe

$$–$$$ ★ ✕ **Villa Tragara.** Romance reigns in this farmhouse that has been carved into intimate dining nooks. Among the menu highlights are woodland mushrooms sautéed with garlic, shallots, brandy, and cream served over grilled Italian bread, and risotto with baby shrimp, mussels, scallops, clams, and squid. ✉ *Rte. 100, 6 mi south of Stowe,* ☎ *802/244–5288. AE, MC, V.*

$$$$ ✕ **Topnotch at Stowe Resort and Spa.** The lobby of this resort, one of the state's poshest, has floor-to-ceiling windows, a freestanding circular stone fireplace, and cathedral ceilings. Rooms have thick carpeting, a small shelf of books, and accents like painted barn-board walls or Italian prints. Golf, tennis, aerobics, horseback riding, cross-country skiing, and sleigh rides are among the many available activities. ✉ *Mountain Rd., Stowe 05672,* ☎ *802/253–8585 or 800/451–8686. 100 rooms, 20 1- and 3-bedroom town houses. Restaurant, lounge, pools, health club. AE, D, DC, MC, V.*

$$ **Inn at the Brass Lantern.** Home-baked cookies in the afternoon, a basket of logs by your fireplace, and stenciled hearts along the wainscoting reflect the care taken in turning this 18th-century farmhouse into a place of welcome. All rooms in this B&B have country antiques and locally made quilts; most are oversize and some have fireplaces and whirlpool tubs. ✉ *Rte. 100, 1 mi north of Stowe, 05672,* ☎ *802/253–2229. 9 rooms. Full breakfast. AE, MC, V.*

Motels

☎ **Econo Lodge** (✉ 101 Northfield St., Montpelier 05602, ☎ 802/223–5258, FAX 802/223–0716), 54 rooms, restaurant, CP; $$. ☎ **Greystone Motel** (✉ U.S. 7, Middlebury 05753, ☎ 802/388–4935), 11 rooms; $$.

Nightlife and the Arts

Nightlife

Burlington's nightlife caters to its college-age population, with pubs and a few dance spots. Touring and local musicians come to **Club Toast** (✉ 165 Church St., ☎ 802/660–2088). **Comedy Zone** (✉ Radisson Hotel, 60 Battery St., Burlington, ☎ 802/658–6500) provides the laughs in town on weekends. **The Metronome** (✉ 188 Main St., Burlington, ☎ 802/865–4563) entertains with an eclectic mix of live music almost every night. **Nectar's** (✉ 188 Main St., Burlington, ☎ 802/658–4771) is always jumping to the sounds of local bands and never charges a cover. The **Vermont Pub and Brewery** (✉ College and St. Paul Sts., Burlington, ☎ 802/865–0500) makes its own beers and seltzers.

The Arts

Burlington has the **Vermont Mozart Festival** (☎ 802/862–7352 or 800/639–9097) and the **Flynn Theater for the Performing Arts** (☎ 802/863–8778), which schedules the Vermont Symphony Orchestra, theater, dance, big-name musicians, and lectures. Stowe has a summer **performing arts festival** (☎ 802/253–7792).

Outdoor Activities and Sports

Biking

In addition to the numerous back roads in the Champlain Valley, Stowe has a recreational path, and Burlington has a 9-mi path along its waterfront. Several operators offer guided tours through the state, among them **Vermont Bicycle Touring** (✉ Box 711, Bristol 05443, ☎ 802/453–4811 or 800/245–3868) and **P.O.M.G. Bike Tours of Vermont** (✉ Box 1080, Richmond 05477, ☎ 802/434–2270 or 888/635–2453).

Boating

Lake Champlain has marinas with rentals and charters in or near Vergennes and Burlington. The **North Beaches** border the northern edge of Burlington and are popular for swimming and sailboarding. **Burlington Community Boathouse** (✉ Foot of College St., Burlington Harbor, ☎ 802/865–3377) has sailboard and boat rentals. **True North Kayak Tours** (✉ Burlington, ☎ 802/860–1910) gives guided tours of Lake Champlain.

Fishing

Lake Champlain contains salmon, lake trout, bass, pike, and more. Marina services are offered by **Malletts Bay Marina** (✉ 228 Lakeshore Dr., Colchester, ☎ 802/862–4072) and **Point Bay Marina** (✉ 1401 Thompson's Point Rd., Charlotte, ☎ 802/425–2431).

Golf

Public courses include **Ralph Myhre's** 18 holes, run by Middlebury College (✉ Rte. 30, Middlebury, ☎ 802/443–5125), and the 9 holes at **Montpelier Country Club** (✉ U.S. 2 just south of U.S. 302, Montpelier, ☎ 802/223–7457).

Hiking and Backpacking

Aside from the **Long Trail** (The Green Mountain Club, ✉ Rte. 100, R.R. 1, Box 650, Waterbury Center 05677, ☎ 802/244–7037), day hikes in northern Vermont include the **Little River** area in Mt. Mansfield State Forest, near Stowe, and **Stowe Pinnacle.**

Ski Areas

For statewide snow conditions call 802/828–3239. All downhill areas listed have snowmaking.

Cross-Country

Alpine resorts that have cross-country trails include **Bolton Valley,** 62 mi; **Burke Mountain,** 37 mi; **Jay Peak,** 25 mi; **Smugglers' Notch,** 23 mi; **Stowe,** 18 mi of groomed trails, 12 mi of back-country trails; and **Sugarbush,** 15 mi.

Downhill

Bolton in Vermont (✉ Bolton Access Rd., Bolton 05477, ☎ 802/434–3444 or 888/593–2586), 52 trails, 6 lifts, 1,625-ft vertical drop. **Burke Mountain** (✉ Box 247, East Burke 05832, ☎ 802/626–3305 or 800/541–5480), 31 trails, 4 lifts, 2,000-ft vertical drop. **Jay Peak** (✉ Rte. 242, Jay 05859, ☎ 802/988–2611 or 800/451–4449), 64 trails, 7 lifts, 2,153-ft vertical drop. **Mad River Glen** (✉ Rte. 17, Waitsfield 05673, ☎ 802/496–3551), 44 runs, 4 lifts, 2,037-ft drop. **Smugglers' Notch** (✉ Smugglers' Notch 05464, ☎ 802/644–8851 or 800/451–8752), 60 runs, 8 lifts, 2,610-ft drop. **Stowe** (✉ 5781 Mountain Rd., Stowe 05672, ☎ 802/253–3000 or 800/253–4754 for lodging), 47 trails, 11 lifts, 2,360-ft drop. **Sugarbush** (✉ R.R. 1, Box 350, Warren 05674, ☎ 802/583–2381 or 800/537–8427 for lodging), 112 trails, 18 lifts, 2,400- and 2,600-ft drops.

Shopping

Church Street Marketplace is a pedestrian thoroughfare lined with boutiques. The **Vermont State Craft Center** (✉ Church St., ☎ 802/863–6458) is a display of the work of more than 200 Vermont artisans. Burlington's revitalized waterfront is home to the funky **Wing Building,** which houses many boutiques, a café, and an art gallery.

4 The Middle Atlantic States

Delaware, Maryland, New Jersey, Pennsylvania, Virginia, Washington, D.C., West Virginia

By Conrad Paulus

IN THE CLOSING DECADES of the 18th century, the major action in the New World was here, in five of the original 13 colonies. General George Washington's audacious crossing of the Delaware River made possible the colonists' victory in the Battle of Trenton; Virginia saw the war's final battles and surrender; the Constitution was hammered out in Philadelphia; Delaware ratified the Constitution and became the first state; and Maryland ceded land for the District of Columbia. Today the people of these states remember the past, proudly tending their historic monuments and welcoming visitors.

The Middle Atlantic countryside of rolling farmland and woods, ancient, soft-edged mountains, broad rivers, and green valleys is a livable land in a manageable climate—a land much walked through and fought over. Besides the Revolution, the region suffered many of the battles of the Civil War and today commemorates their sites. On its eastern edge (part of the densely populated urban corridor that runs from Boston to Richmond), you'll find the cities and most of the history. The international, multiracial population produces every possible cuisine, and you can buy anything on earth in the upscale boutiques, department stores, and antiques shops.

Beyond the smog on the New Jersey Turnpike are long beaches, casino-filled Atlantic City, and Victorian Cape May to the east; horse country, ski resorts, and Philadelphia to the west. The Eastern Shore's Delaware and Maryland beaches are sedate or swinging; Virginia Beach is both. And the seafood anywhere near the Chesapeake Bay is superb. Baltimore combines historic buildings with new restaurants and shops; Annapolis and Oxford are ports for boaters gunkholing around the Chesapeake. Washington, D.C., the seat of government, is a wonderful showplace for visitors, with myriad treasures set off by cherry trees. Alexandria's historic district, in Virginia, and Georgetown's splendid town houses recall the capital's early years. In Williamsburg you'll hear echoes of the Revolution and sample 18th-century life.

West of the Tidewater, or the coastal region, the towns are smaller and farther apart. Continuing on a circuit past Richmond, with its glorious capitol, you'll come to Charlottesville, Thomas Jefferson's hometown; farther west rise the Blue Ridge Mountains and West Virginia's Appalachians, sprinkled with palatial 19th-century resorts. At the

The Middle Atlantic States

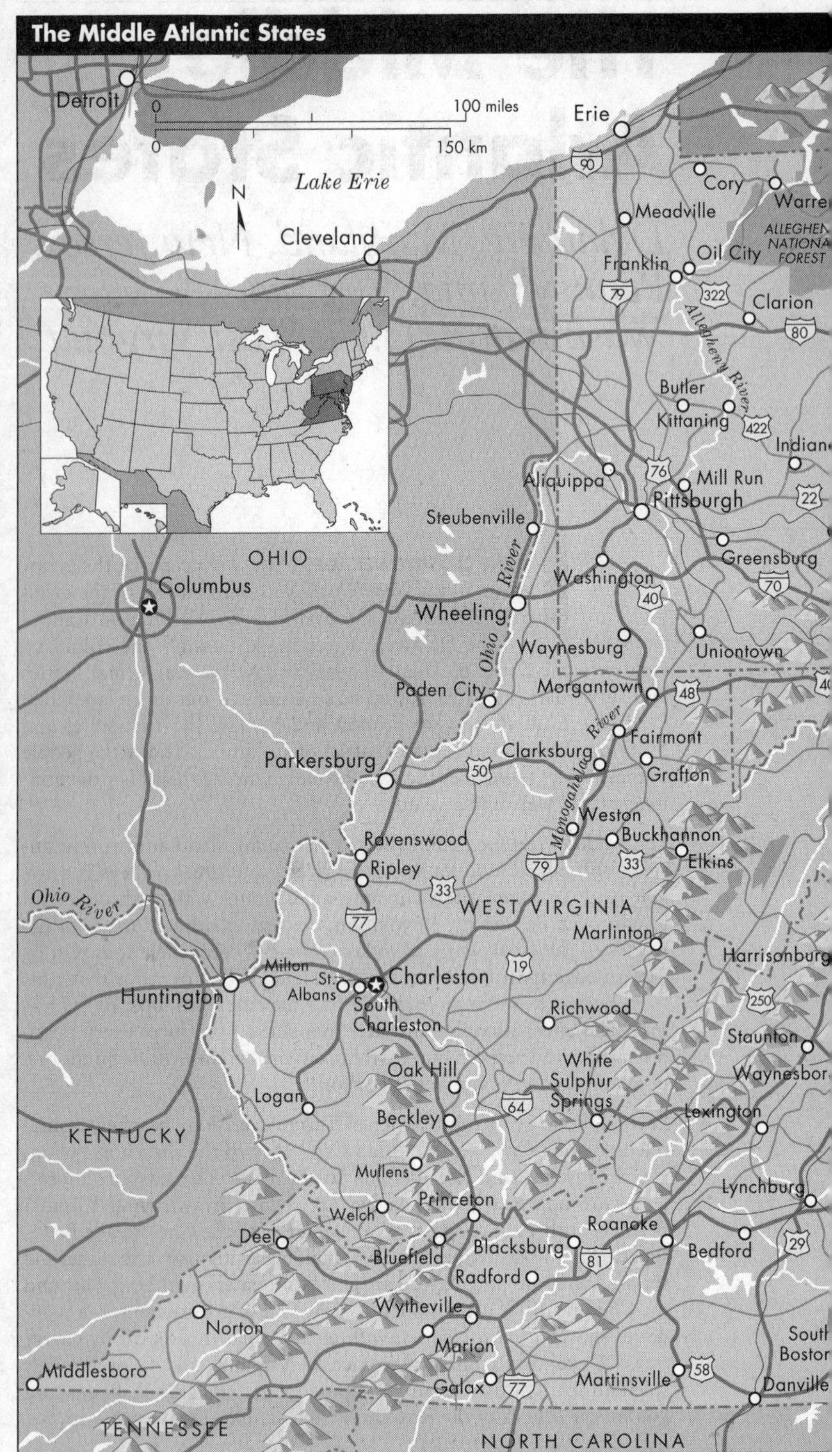

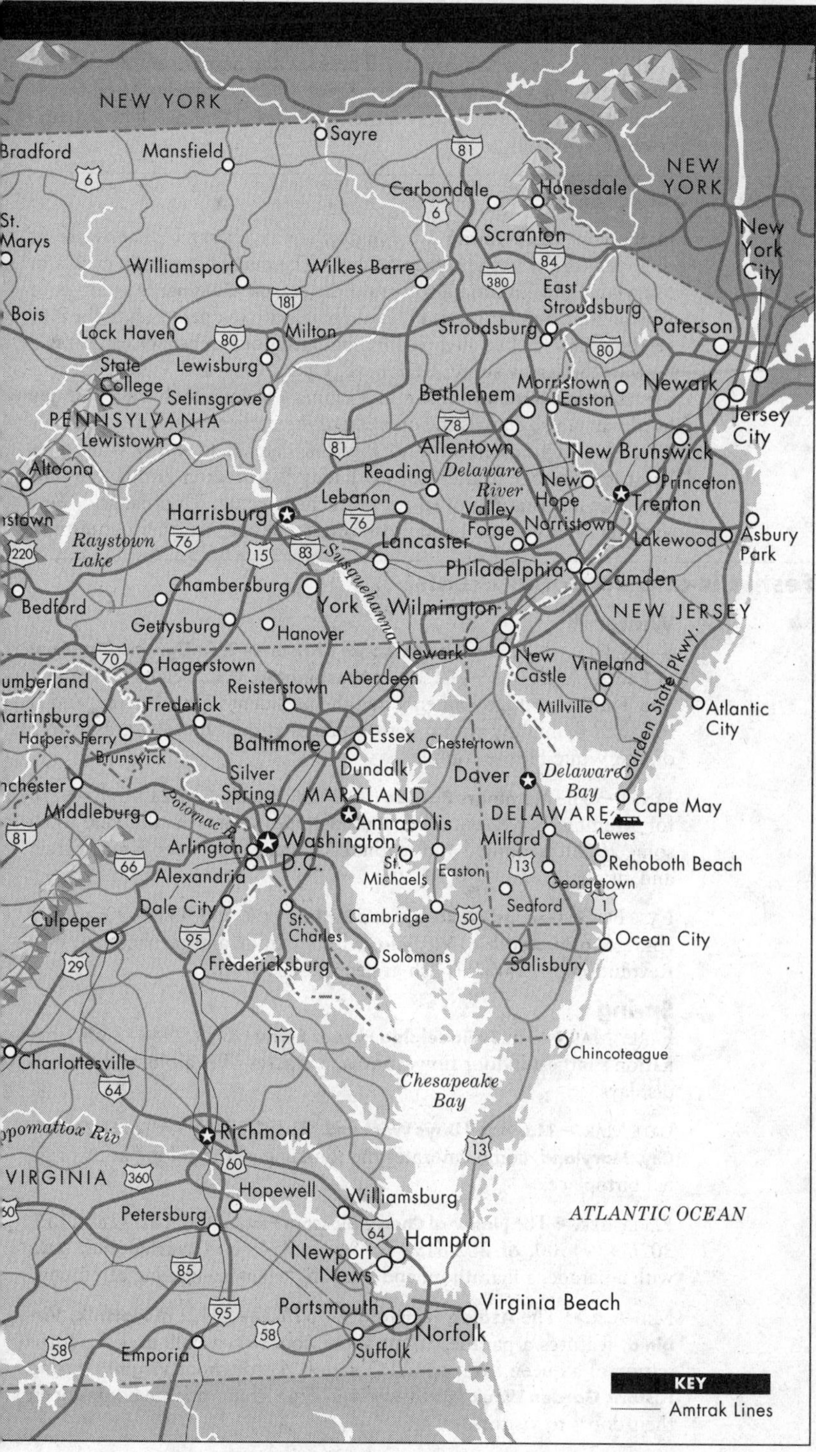
NEW YORK
Sayre
Bradford
Mansfield
Carbondale
Honesdale
NEW YORK
St. Marys
Scranton
New York City
Williamsport
Wilkes Barre
East Stroudsburg
Bois
Lock Haven
Milton
Stroudsburg
Paterson
State College
Lewisburg
Selinsgrove
Morristown
Newark
Bethlehem
Easton
Jersey City
PENNSYLVANIA
Lewistown
Allentown
New Brunswick
Altoona
Reading
Delaware River
New Hope
Princeton
Lebanon
Valley Forge
Trenton
Harrisburg
Norristown
Raystown Lake
Lancaster
Lakewood
Asbury Park
Susquehanna
Philadelphia
Camden
Chambersburg
York
Wilmington
NEW JERSEY
Bedford
Gettysburg
Hanover
Newark
New Castle
Vineland
Hagerstown
Aberdeen
Garden State Pkwy.
Reisterstown
Millville
Atlantic City
Frederick
Harpers Ferry
Essex
Chestertown
Brunswick
Baltimore
Dundalk
Daver
Delaware Bay
Silver Spring
MARYLAND
Cape May
Middleburg
Potomac R.
Annapolis
DELAWARE
Milford
Lewes
Arlington
Washington D.C.
St. Michaels
Easton
Rehoboth Beach
Alexandria
Georgetown
Dale City
Seaford
Culpeper
St. Charles
Cambridge
Ocean City
Fredericksburg
Solomons
Salisbury
Charlottesville
Chincoteague
Chesapeake Bay
Richmond
VIRGINIA
Hopewell
Williamsburg
Petersburg
ATLANTIC OCEAN
Hampton
Newport News
Virginia Beach
Portsmouth
Norfolk
Suffolk
Emporia
KEY
Amtrak Lines

stunning confluence of the Shenandoah and Potomac rivers sits Harpers Ferry, where John Brown met his fate; and back in Pennsylvania are Gettysburg and Amish country. These are the habitats of the country auction, the wonderful local restaurant, and the farmhouse bed-and-breakfast—the secret places off the beaten track that you'll love to discover for yourself.

When to Go

In the cool early **spring** Washington's pink cherry blossoms are at their peak for a few spectacular days. The many equestrian events in Maryland and Virginia also herald the season. **Summer** is swampy in Washington, Baltimore, and Philadelphia, with temperatures in the 80s, yet thousands flock to all three for monuments or baseball. Ocean bathers head to the Jersey shore, Rehoboth, Ocean City, and Virginia Beach. The dazzling **autumn** foliage in Virginia's Shenandoah Valley draws hordes and also signals the opening of the orchestra, theater, and ballet seasons in the cities, most notably Philadelphia. In **winter,** when temperatures average in the 40s, workaday Washington grinds to a halt after just a sprinkling of snow, but Pennsylvania, Virginia, and West Virginia offer downhill and cross-country skiing, weather permitting.

Festivals and Seasonal Events

Winter

EARLY DEC.–JAN. 1➢ The **National Christmas Tree Lighting/Pageant of Peace** (☎ 202/619–7222), in **Washington, D.C.,** begins on the second Thursday in December, when the president lights the tree, and is followed by nightly choral performances at the Ellipse, a grassy area on the White House complex.

JAN. 1➢ The **Mummers Parade** (☎ 215/636–1666 or 215/336–3050 for Mummer's Museum), in **Philadelphia,** ushers in the year with some 20,000 sequined and feathered marchers between Broad Street and city hall.

LATE FEB.➢ **George Washington's Birthday** (☎ 703/838–4200) is celebrated in **Alexandria, Virginia,** with a parade and reenactment of a Revolutionary War skirmish at nearby Fort Ward.

Spring

EARLY MAR.➢ The **Philadelphia Flower Show** (☎ 215/988–8800), the nation's largest indoor flower show, has acres of exhibits and themed displays.

LATE MAR.➢ **Maryland Days Weekend** (☎ 301/862–0990) of **St. Mary's City, Maryland,** commemorates the founding of the colony at its original birthplace.

EARLY APR.➢ The **National Cherry Blossom Festival** (☎ 202/728–1137, 202/547–1500, or 202/619–7275) takes place in **Washington, D.C.,** with a parade, a marathon, and a Japanese lantern-lighting ceremony.

MID-APR.➢ The **Azalea Festival** (☎ 757/622–2312) in **Norfolk, Virginia,** features a parade, an air show, concerts, a ball, and the coronation of a queen from a NATO nation. Throughout **Virginia** during **Historic Garden Week** (☎ 804/644–7776), grand private homes open their doors to visitors.

LATE APR.–EARLY MAY➢ The **Philadelphia Festival of World Cinema** (☎ 800/969–7392) presents more than 100 features, documentaries, and short films from more than 30 countries at venues throughout the city.

EARLY MAY➢ **Old Dover Days** (☏ 302/734–1736) celebrates Delaware's capital city with a parade, dancing, and tours of Colonial homes and gardens. For more than 20 years, the **Point-to-Point Races** (☏ 302/888–4600 or 800/448–3883) at Winterthur outside **Wilmington, Delaware,** have featured steeplechase and pony races and an annual tailgate picnic competition.

LATE MAY➢ The **Preakness** (☏ 410/542–9400), held in **Baltimore, Maryland,** is the second event of horse racing's Triple Crown, after the Kentucky Derby and before the Belmont Stakes. The **Blue and Grey Reunion** (☏ 304/457–4265), in **Philippi, West Virginia,** is four days of music, food, crafts, and a costumed reenactment of the Civil War's first land battle.

Summer

JUNE➢ **Philadelphia**'s **CoreStates U.S. Pro Cycling Championship** (☏ 215/636–1666) the country's premier bicycle race, attracts the world's top cyclists to its 156-mi course; a two-week celebration leads up to the event.

LATE JUNE➢ The **Hampton Jazz Festival** (☏ 757/838–4203), in **Hampton, Virginia,** brings together top performers in various styles of jazz.

LATE JUNE–EARLY JULY➢ The **Festival of American Folklife** (☏ 202/357–2700), held on the Mall in **Washington, D.C.,** celebrates music, arts, crafts, and foods of regional cultures.

EARLY JULY➢ The **Philadelphia Freedom Festival** (☏ 215/636–1666 or 800/537–7676) includes parades, hot-air balloon races, ceremonies at Independence Hall, a restaurant festival, and July 4 fireworks.

JULY 4➢ **Independence Day** celebrations in **Baltimore** (☏ 410/837–4636) culminate in a major show of fireworks over the Inner Harbor. Celebrations in **Washington, D.C.** (☏ 202/619–7222), include a grand parade, a National Symphony Orchestra performance on the steps of the Capitol, and fireworks over the Washington Monument.

EARLY AUG.➢ The **Virginia Highlands Festival** (☏ 540/623–5266 or 540/676–2282), in **Abingdon,** offers crafts and farm animals on exhibit, antiques for sale, painting and writing workshops, hot-air balloon rides, and a variety of musicians in concert.

LATE AUG.➢ The **Wine Festival** (☏ 410/267–6711) in **The Plains, Virginia,** features tastings of vintages from 40 Virginia wineries, plus grape stomping and musical entertainment. The **Philadelphia Folk Festival** (☏ 215/242–0150) is America's oldest (1962) continuous folk festival; performers at the three-day event range from young crooners to folk superstars.

Autumn

LABOR DAY WEEKEND➢ At the **Crafts Festival** (☏ 302/888–4600 or 800/448–3883), at **Winterthur, Delaware,** 200 high-quality craftspeople sell contemporary and traditional work.

EARLY–MID-OCT.➢ **Victorian Week** (609/884–5404 or 800/275–4278) is a 10-day celebration of **Cape May, New Jersey**'s Victorian heritage; historic house tours and craft and antiques shows are a highlight. **United States Sailboat and Powerboat Shows** (☏ 410/268–8828), the world's largest events of their kind, take place in **Annapolis, Maryland.**

MID-OCT.➢ The **Taste of DC Festival** (☏ 202/789–7000) presents dishes from a variety of **Washington, D.C.,** eateries. In **Harpers Ferry, West Virginia,** the park service stages **Election Day 1860** (☏ 304/535–6299), when people portraying the presidential candidates on the ballot in that region come once again to debate the hot topics of their day: states' rights versus a strong federal union.

LATE OCT.➢ **Fiddler's and Sea Witch Weekend Festival** (☎ 302/227–2233), in **Rehoboth Beach, Delaware,** is a madcap Halloween spectacular that welcomes visitors with fiddler's contests, music, parades, hayrides, and the antics of masked marauders.

LATE OCT.–EARLY NOV.➢ New Hollywood and independent movies are screened at the **Virginia Film Festival** (☎ 804/982–5277), in **Charlottesville, Virginia,** fast becoming a major event in the film biz.

EARLY NOV.➢ Backyard inventors test their pumpkin-throwing contraptions at the **Punkin Chunkin** (☎ 800/515–9095), in **Lewes, Delaware;** the current record, set by a gourd-hurling, homemade pneumatic cannon, is a whopping 3,718 ft.

NOV.–DEC.➢ **Yuletide at Winterthur** (☎ 302/888–4600 or 800/448–3883) is a Christmas-theme tour of the treasure-filled rooms at this vast museum near **Wilmington, Delaware.**

Getting Around the Middle Atlantic States

By Bus

Greyhound Lines (☎ 800/231–2222) serves all these states. **NJ Transit** (☎ 201/762–5100 or 800/772–2222 for northern NJ; 215/569–3752 or 800/582–5946 for southern NJ) provides bus service to many areas of the Garden State.

By Car

I–95, the major East Coast artery, runs through all of these states except West Virginia. The New Jersey Turnpike, a toll road, fills in for I–95 in the Garden State. The 470-mi Pennsylvania Turnpike, also a toll road, runs from the Ohio border to Valley Forge, just outside Philadelphia. I–64 runs east–west, intersecting I–95 at Richmond, Virginia. At Staunton, Virginia, I–64 intersects I–81, which runs north–south through the Shenandoah Valley, toward West Virginia and Tennessee.

By Plane

American, Continental, Delta, Northwest, TWA, United, and US Airways, among others, serve **Philadelphia International Airport** (☎ 215/937–6937), **Greater Pittsburgh International Airport** (☎ 412/472–3525), **Baltimore–Washington International Airport** (☎ 410/859–7111 or 800/435–9294), **Ronald Reagan National Airport** (also known as Metropolitan Washington Airport, ☎ 703/572–2700), and **Washington Dulles International Airport** (☎ 703/572–2700).

By Train

Amtrak (☎ 800/872–7245) serves the region both north–south and east–west, with major lines along the coast and inland lines through Pennsylvania, Virginia, and West Virginia. **NJ Transit** (☎ 201/762–5100 or 800/772–2222 for northern NJ; 215/569–3752 or 800/582–5946 for southern NJ), **Southeastern Pennsylvania Transportation Authority** (SEPTA; ☎ 215/580–7800), and **Maryland Area Rail Commuter** (MARC; ☎ 800/325–7245) provide service within their states.

DELAWARE

Updated by Valerie Helmbreck

Capital	Dover
Population	732,000
Motto	Liberty and Independence
State Bird	Blue hen
State Flower	Peach blossom
Postal Abbreviation	DE

Statewide Visitor Information

Delaware State Visitors Center (✉ 406 Federal St., Dover 19901, ☎ 302/739–4266). **Delaware Tourism Office** (✉ 99 Kings Hwy., Box 1401, Dover 19903, ☎ 302/739–4271 or 800/441–8846). **Visitor centers:** I–95, between Routes 896 and 273 (☎ 302/737–4059); at Delaware Memorial Bridge (☎ 302/571–6340); and north of Smyrna, on Route 13 North (☎ 302/653–8910).

Scenic Drives

From Wilmington's western edge, a **30-mi loop** follows winding Route 100 past well-screened estates, a state park, and the meandering Brandywine Creek; and then into Pennsylvania on a section of U.S. 1W, which takes you past several historical attractions; and finally back into Delaware, where you'll travel on Route 52 (locally called Château Country) to villages lined with antiques shops, to horse farms, and to Winterthur, a major du Pont estate turned museum. A drive south along **Route 9** from New Castle to Dover slides past tidal marshes and across creeks on one-lane bridges; side roads veer into bird sanctuaries or out to points of land with a view of Delaware Bay.

National and State Parks

National Parks

Bombay Hook National Wildlife Refuge (✉ Rte. 9 east of Smyrna; R.D. 1, Box 147, Smyrna 19977, ☎ 302/653–6872) is more than 15,000 acres of ponds and fields filled between April and November with both resident and migrating waterfowl. **Prime Hook National Wildlife Refuge** (✉ Country Rd. 236, just off Rte. 16; R.D. 3, Box 195, Milton 19968, ☎ 302/684–8419) is a smaller, well-developed preserve with boat ramps, canoe trails, and a boardwalk trail through marshes.

State Parks

A dozen parks run by the **Delaware Division of Parks and Recreation** (✉ 89 Kings Hwy., Richardson and Robbins Bldg., Box 1401, Dover 19903, ☎ 302/739–4702) are set up for hiking, fishing, and picnicking. The chief inland parks, with freshwater ponds, add seasonal boat rentals to basic amenities. All parks are free from November through April and charge $2.50 per Delaware car or $5 per out-of-state car on weekends between April and November and daily from Memorial Day through Labor Day.

Brandywine Creek State Park (✉ Intersection of Rtes. 92 and 100, Box 3782, Greenville 19807, ☎ 302/577–3534), about 5 mi from Wilmington, is the state's best picnic park, with 800-plus acres of open fields and wooded grounds, a nature center, 12 mi of hiking trails, and perfect sledding slopes in winter. **Cape Henlopen** (✉ 42 Henlopen Dr., Lewes 19958, ☎ 302/645–8983; ✉ Seaside Nature Center, ☎ 302/654–6852), east of Lewes, has more than 150 campsites in pinelands.

Delaware Seashore (✉ 850 Inlet, Rehoboth Beach 19971, ☎ 302/227–2800; ✉ Marina, ☎ 302/227–3071) has both ocean surf and calm bay waters, large bathhouses with showers, and nearly 300 campsites with hookups. **Lums Pond State Park** (✉ Rtes. 301 and 71 south of Newark; 1068 Howell School Rd., Bear 19701, ☎ 302/368–6989) has more than 70 campsites. **Trap Pond** (✉ Off Rte. 24 east of Laurel; R.D. 2, Box 331, Laurel 19956, ☎ 302/875–5153) includes part of the Great Cypress Swamp and has more than 140 rustic sites under a canopy of loblolly pines.

WILMINGTON

Wilmington, the state's commercial hub and largest city, was founded in 1638 as a Swedish settlement and successively taken over by the Dutch and the English. More recently it has been populated by employees of DuPont's company headquarters, credit-card banks, and nearby poultry ranches. Now the city's—and the state's—long-standing pro-business policies have enticed corporations whose towers of granite and glass reflect (literally) the colonial stonework next door. These multinationals have imported many of their employees; the city is now home to more newcomers than natives.

Two nearby towns—Newark, home of the University of Delaware, and New Castle, the state's beautifully restored colonial capital—are linked to Wilmington by a few miles of neighborhoods and strip malls. The wide ribbon of I–95, which crosses the state, connects Wilmington at the eastern edge to Newark at the western border. This nondescript, 20-minute drive is all many travelers ever see of the First State.

Visitor Information

Greater Wilmington: Convention and Visitors Bureau (✉ 100 W. 10th St., 19801–1661, ☎ 302/652–4088 or 800/422–1181).

Arriving and Departing

By Bus

Greyhound Lines (✉ 318 N. Market St., ☎ 302/652–7391 or 800/231–2222).

By Car

Situated between Baltimore and Philadelphia, Wilmington is bisected by I–95 north–south and linked to small-town Pennsylvania by U.S. 202 and Routes 52 and 41.

By Plane

Philadelphia International Airport (☎ 215/937–6937), about 30 mi north of downtown Wilmington, is served by all major U.S. and international airlines. **Taxi** fare is about $25 to Wilmington. Door-to-door shuttle buses to the center of the city—**Airport Super Shuttle** (☎ 302/655–8878) or **Delaware Express Shuttle** (☎ 302/454–7634 or 800/648–5466)—cost $21 and $23 respectively and require reservations.

By Train

Wilmington Train Station (✉ Martin Luther King Blvd. and French St., ☎ 302/429–6523) has **Amtrak** (☎ 800/872–7245) service, as well as **SEPTA** (☎ 215/580–7800) commuter service to Philadelphia.

Getting Around Wilmington

Downtown is compact enough to stroll, but visits to New Castle, Newark, or the museums and parks ringing Wilmington require a car.

Downtown parking is moderately priced in garages and impossible to find on the streets in the jam-packed office district. Buses are geared to commuters, not explorers.

Exploring Wilmington

The four-block **Market Street Mall** marks the city center. The **Grand Opera House** (✉ 818 Market St. Mall, ☎ 302/658–7897) is a working theater. Built by the Masonic Order in 1871 and restored in 1971, the four-story Grand's facade is cast iron painted white in French Second Empire style to mimic the old Paris Opera.

The **Old Town Hall Museum** (✉ 512 Market St., ☎ 302/655–7161; 🎫 Free) is a two-story Georgian-style building with changing exhibits and restored jail cells to tour. The hall and museum shop were restored as headquarters for the Historical Society of Delaware. The **Delaware History Museum** (✉ 504 Market St., ☎ 302/656–0637; 🎫 Free), in a restored 1940s Woolworth's building, has three galleries and a changing exhibit of Delaware history.

The **Hercules Building** (✉ 1313 N. Market St., ☎ 302/594–5000), north of the mall, was built in the 1980s with ziggurat walls and a 20-ft-diameter clock. The core of the building is a 14-story atrium, with ground-level shops and a jungle of plants.

East of the mall and surrounded by some of the city's poorest neighborhoods, a monument to the 1638 landing of a Swedish expedition marks the first permanent settlement in the Delaware Valley. At the **Kalmar Nyckel Shipyard/Museum** volunteers have built a replica of the first vessel to land on these shores. *✉ 1124 E. 7th St., ☎ 302/429–7447. 🎫 $8.*

Two 17th-century structures are worth a visit: **Old Swedes Church,** built in 1698, retains its original hipped roof and high wooden pulpit and is still used regularly for religious services. The **Hendrickson House Museum,** a farmhouse built in 1690 by Swedish settlers, is furnished with period pieces. *Both: ✉ 606 Church St., ☎ 302/652–5629. 🎫 Free. Closed Tues., Thurs., Sun.*

★ Children who visit the **Delaware Museum of Natural History** (✉ Rte. 52 N, ☎ 302/658–9111), 5 mi northwest of Wilmington, can explore the mysteries of Australia's Great Barrier Reef and examine an African water hole and a 500-pound clam. The museum's hands-on, interactive discovery room allows children to use all their senses.

The **Delaware Art Museum,** a few miles west of the city center and I–95, houses a major collection of post-1840 American paintings and illustrations, including works by major figures such as Homer, Eakins, Hopper, Wyeth, Sloan, and illustrator Howard Pyle, as well as the foremost assemblage of English pre-Raphaelite paintings and decorative arts in the United States. *✉ 2301 Kentmere Pkwy., ☎ 302/571–9590. 🎫 $5; free Wed. 4–9 PM and Sat. 10 AM–1 PM. Closed Mon.*

Nemours Mansion and Gardens shows the Alfred du Pont family's preference for fine automobiles, European antiques, Louis XVI–style architecture, and formal French gardens. The estate is adjacent to the renowned A. I. du Pont Hospital for Children. *✉ 1600 Rockland Rd., ☎ 302/651–6912. 🎫 $10 (reservations essential). Closed Mon.–Fri.*

The **Hagley Museum and Library,** one of three former du Pont family properties on the northwest edges of Wilmington, recalls the DuPont company's beginnings in 1802 as an explosives manufacturer. You can tour gunpowder mills, a 19th-century machine shop, and the family

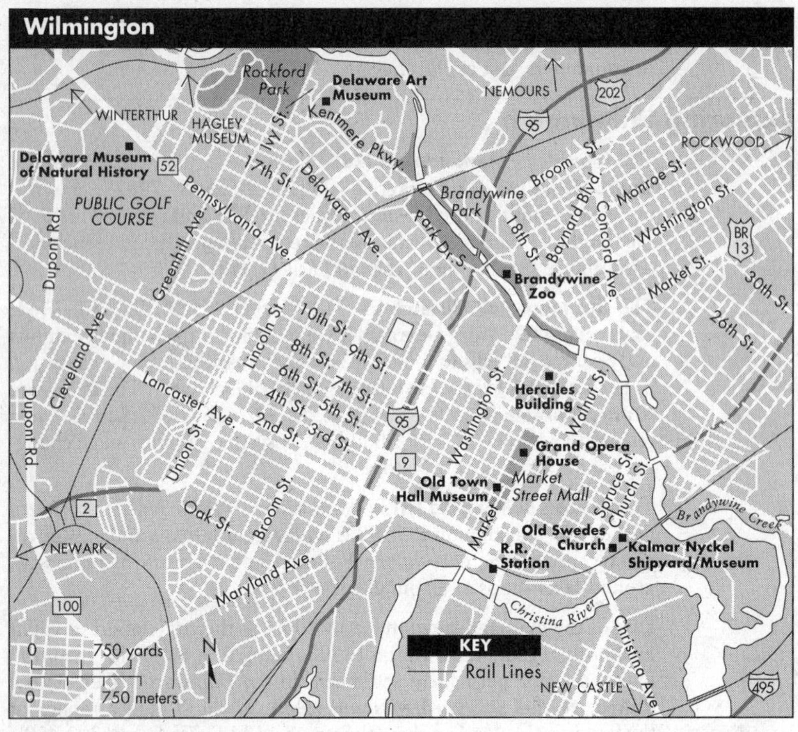

home and gardens, all set on 230 acres. ✉ *Rte. 141,* ☎ *302/658–2400.* *$9.75.*

Outside Wilmington

New Castle, 5 mi south of Wilmington on Route 9, is a barely commercialized gem of a town with restored colonial houses, cobblestone streets, and historic sites along the Delaware River. William Penn's first landing in North America is noted in **Battery Park.** Two blocks west of the waterfront, the **New Castle Courthouse,** Delaware's colonial capital until 1777, is a pristine museum of state history, with three brick wings and a white cupola and spire. ✉ *211 Delaware St.,* ☎ *302/323–4453.* *Free. Closed Mon.*

New Castle's **George Read II House** was built in 1801 in Federal style by a signer of both the Declaration of Independence and the Constitution. Twelve rooms of the big brick house are open, including three furnished in period style. ✉ *42 The Strand,* ☎ *302/322–8411.* *$4. Closed Mon., weekdays Jan.–Feb.*

★ **Winterthur Museum, Garden and Library** focuses on Henry Francis du Pont's passion for collecting furniture and decorative arts made or used in America from 1640 to 1860. The nine-story, 175-room hillside stucco mansion and museum wing shelter a world-class collection in period settings. There are three exhibition galleries and an elegant pavilion that houses the museum shop and glass-enclosed restaurant. The naturalistic gardens showcase native and exotic plants. ✉ *Rte. 52, Winterthur,* ☎ *302/888–4600 or 800/448–3883.* *Price varies depending on tour and seaon.*

Odessa is a tiny, mostly residential village set on the banks of the Appoquinimink River, about 23 mi south of Wilmington off Route 13. Originally a grain-shipping port, it stopped growing in the mid-19th century when disease attacked its peach crops and the railroad passed it by. Today this tiny community is a living-history lesson—until a few years ago, muskrat still topped the menu at the town's one-and-only restaurant. A branch of the Winterthur Museum includes two 18th- and 19th-century Quaker mansions, the **Corbitt Sharp House** and the **Wilson Warner House.** Also open to visitors is the **Brick Hotel Gallery,** which houses rotating exhibits of American furniture and decorative arts. ☎ *302/378–4069.* *$8 ticket admits visitors to all 3 buildings. Closed Jan.–Feb.*

Parks, Gardens, and Zoos

In **Brandywine Creek State Park** (☞ National and State Parks, *above*), shady paths pass colonial stone walls and a tiny brick church that was built in 1740 and used for British wounded during the Revolutionary War. Lush Brandywine Creek and a millrace attract fishermen and splash-happy children. Wilmington's **Brandywine Zoo** tucks outdoor exhibits into cliffs along Brandywine Creek. ✉ *1001 N. Park Dr.,* ☎ *302/571–7747.* *$3 Apr.–Oct; free Nov.–Mar. Exotic-animal house closed Nov.–Mar.*

Rockwood Museum, a 19th-century country estate with a Gothic manor house, displays unusual specimen plants on 6 acres of landscaped grounds and 62 acres of woodlands. ✉ *610 Shipley Rd.,* ☎ *302/761–4340.* *$6. Closed Mon.*

Dining

During the '80s boom Wilmington's kitchens multiplied as new companies' globe-circling employees pushed for diversity. The most established restaurants are Italian and Asian. For price ranges *see* Chart 1 (A) *in* On the Road with Fodor's.

$$$$ ★ ✕ **Green Room.** French cuisine is served in a dramatic, wood-paneled setting of 19th-century opulence. Lunch is served from Monday through Saturday; dinner is only on Saturday. The hotel's clubby **Brandywine Room,** with its original Wyeth paintings and Continental cuisine, is open for dinner Sunday through Thursday. ✉ *Hotel du Pont, 11th and Market Sts.,* ☎ *302/594–3154. Reservations essential. Jacket and tie for dinner. AE, D, DC, MC, V.*

$$–$$$ ✕ **Eclipse.** Chef Patrick D'Amico, known to locals from his cooking at Positano, has opened this new restaurant at the edge of Wilmington's "Little Italy." The innovative seasonal menu, which has featured pan-roasted lamb loin with black-trumpet mushrooms, lingonberries, and a pinot-noir reduction sauce (and a nine-inch chocolate tower for dessert) have made this a Wilmington favorite. ✉ *1020B N. Union St.,* ☎ *302/658–1588. AE, MC, V.*

$$–$$$ ★ ✕ **Harry's Savoy Grill.** Friendly service, great food, and a warm atmosphere have made Harry's one of Delaware's best restaurants. Their Portobello mushroom pizza is a top seller; and in soft-shell crab season nobody does the little critters better. ✉ *2020 Naamans Rd.,* ☎ *302/475–3000. AE, DC, MC, V.*

$$–$$$ ✕ **Jessop's Tavern & Colonial Restaurant.** In a tiny space just steps from the town's waterfront park, Chef Jim Berman presents a menu inspired by the English, Dutch, and Swedish founders of the region. The rich oyster chowder, double-crusted chicken pot pie, and crusty flat bread can be topped off with Berman's signature dessert, an English bread pudding. ✉ *114 Delaware St., New Castle,* ☎ *302/322–6111. MC, V.*

$$–$$$ ✕ **Tavola Toscana.** Chef-owner Dan Butler has built a devoted following in the past five years. The room's centerpiece is an antipasti station with shiny copper dishes hanging from an original iron sculpture overhead.

Don't miss Butler's Milanese-style saffron-scented risotto or his superwide *pappardelle* (ribbed, flat noodles) with rabbit and thyme. ✉ *1412 N. du Pont St.,* ☎ *302/654–8001. AE, DC, MC, V.*

$–$$$ ✕ **Di Nardo's.** More plastic than rustic, with Formica tables and unpadded chairs, this crowded, casual tavern specializes in seafood. The catch of the day is always fresh, and the spicy hard-shell crabs are famous. ✉ *405 N. Lincoln St.,* ☎ *302/656–3685. AE, D, DC, MC, V.*

$$ ✕ **Mirage.** In a colorful, contemporary space, young servers deliver such regional specialties as shrimp, duck, and roasted salmon. Chef Lisa Scolero's sauces, which include a maple glaze and a blue-cheese-and-honey concoction, change daily. This is the only fine-dining option in Newark and lures Wilmington visitors south. ✉ *100 Elkton Rd., Newark,* ☎ *302/453–1711. AE, D, MC, V. Closed Sun. No lunch Sat.*

$–$$ ★ ✕ **Saigon Vietnam.** This authentic, well-run Vietnamese eatery is in a spacious, beautifully decorated space in a revived shopping center at the end of Newark's Main Street. Don't miss their crispy spring rolls, sweet-yet-spicy lemongrass chicken, or clay-cooked specialties. ✉ *207 Main St.,* ☎ *302/737–1590. AE, D, DC, MC, V. Closed Mon.*

Lodging

Most Wilmington-area hotels are mainly business–oriented. For variety there are restored colonial inns (not modern adaptations) and a few bed-and-breakfasts. Two reservation services—**Bed & Breakfast of Delaware, Inc.** (✉ 701 Landon Dr., Suite 200, Wilmington 19810, ☎ 302/479–9500) and **Guesthouses, Inc.** (✉ Box 2137, West Chester, PA 19380, ☎ 800/950–9130)—help locate moderately priced lodgings. For price ranges *see* Chart 2 (A) *in* On the Road with Fodor's.

$$$–$$$$ ★ 🏨 **Inn at Montchanin Village.** These painstakingly restored 19th-century buildings once housed DuPont powder mill workers. Each elegant guest unit is unique, with antique reproduction furniture and luxurious linens. The village is only five minutes from the Winterthur Museum and Gardens, in the heart of Château Country. At the excellent restaurant, Krazy Kat's, guests are treated to breakfast. ✉ *U.S. Rte. 100 and Kirk Road, Montchanin 19710,* ☎ *302/888–2133 or 800/369-2473,* FAX *302/888–0389. 37 rooms. Restaurant. Full breakfast. AE, D, DC, MC, V.*

$$$ ★ 🏨 **Brandywine Guest Suites.** This former store, tucked into a nondescript downtown block, has dramatic contemporary architecture, suites with rich traditional furnishings, and a popular lounge. ✉ *707 King St., 19801,* ☎ *302/656–9300,* FAX *302/656–2459. 49 suites. Restaurant. AE, DC, MC, V.*

$$$ 🏨 **Christiana Hilton Inn.** This modern high-rise southwest of Wilmington is convenient to I–95. Rooms are pleasant and traditional, and the restaurant, Ashley's, is notable. ✉ *100 Continental Dr., Newark 19713,* ☎ *302/454–1500,* FAX *302/454–0233. 266 rooms. 2 restaurants, pool. AE, D, DC, MC, V.*

$$$ 🏨 **Hotel du Pont.** This posh and popular downtown hotel has large rooms with living areas set off by mahogany dividers. The furnishings are 18th-century reproductions. ✉ *11th and Market Sts., 19801,* ☎ *302/594–3100 or 800/441–9019,* FAX *302/594–3108. 217 rooms. 3 restaurants, health club. AE, D, DC, MC, V.*

$$ 🏨 **Boulevard Bed & Breakfast.** This red tile–roofed B&B in the Triangle section of Wilmington is a citified, fancy, but reasonably priced six-bedroom dwelling. Outside, neo-Georgian elements and eccentric, fluted columns adorn the facade; inside, don't miss the Mueller tiles around the library fireplace. Proprietors Charles and Judy Powell serve a full breakfast on an enclosed side porch. ✉ *1909 Baynard Blvd., 19802,* ☎ *302/656–9700. 6 rooms. Full breakfast. AE, MC, V.*

$–$$ **Marriott Courtyard.** Centrally located in downtown Wilmington, this affordable hotel has a Brandywine Valley ambience—lots of hunter green and cranberry red along with Wyeth reproductions. Many businesspeople stay here (there are two meeting rooms), but the Courtyard also specializes in wedding parties and family reunions. ✉ *1102 West St., 19801,* ☎ *302/429–7600 or 800/321–2211,* FAX *302/429–9167. 125 rooms. Restaurant, exercise room. AE, D, DC, MC, V.*

$ **Fairfield Inn.** Close to the University of Delaware and about 9 mi west of Wilmington, this Marriott-owned inn is spartan but convenient. ✉ *65 Geoffrey Dr., Newark 19713,* ☎ *302/292–1500. 135 rooms. Pool. AE, D, DC, MC, V.*

$ **Rodeway Inn.** No-smoking rooms and proximity to historic New Castle are two advantages of this simple motor inn. ✉ *111 S. DuPont Hwy., New Castle 19702,* ☎ *302/328–6246 or 800/321–6246,* FAX *302/328–9493. 40 rooms. AE, D, DC, MC, V.*

Shopping

The **Greenville Shopping Center** (✉ Rte. 52 near the Rte. 141 interchange) has tony dress, shoe, and jewelry stores where merchants cater to the Château Country crowd. Newark's **Christiana Mall** (✉ Rte. 7 at I–95 Exit 4S, ☎ 302/731–9815) has 130 stores, including Macy's and Strawbridge & Clothier. **Concord Mall** (✉ 4737 Concord Pike, ☎ 302/478–9271) has 95 stores and two department store biggies: Strawbridge & Clothier and Boscov's.

THE ATLANTIC COAST

Whether you have a day, a weekend, or the whole summer, a visit to Delaware's beaches will likely be a highlight of a trip to the First State. From Cape Henlopen State Park at the northern end to Fenwick Island at the southern border are 23 mi of Atlantic shoreline. The main route south gets you to shore points the fastest, but if you have time, drive scenic Route 9 (it runs from New Castle to Dover) between farm fields and stands of 10-ft-high grasses. The most scenic stretch of shoreline is south of Dewey Beach, where sand dunes and wide, white Atlantic beaches are just an arm's reach from Route 1.

Visitor Information

Bethany-Fenwick: Chamber of Commerce and Information Center (✉ Rte. 1N, Fenwick Island; Box 1450, Bethany Beach 19930, ☎ 302/539–2100 or 800/962–7873). **Lewes:** Chamber of Commerce and Visitors Bureau (✉ Savannah Rd. and Kings Hwy., Box 1, 19958, ☎ 302/645–8073). **Milton:** Chamber of Commerce (✉ 104 Federal St., 19968, ☎ 302/684–1101). **Rehoboth Beach–Dewey Beach:** Chamber of Commerce (✉ 501 Rehoboth Ave., Box 216, Rehoboth Beach 19971, ☎ 302/227–2233 or 800/441–1329).

Delaware Today magazine (☎ 302/656–1809 or 800/285–0400), published monthly, covers events and region-wide restaurants.

Arriving and Departing

By Bus

Greyhound Lines (☎ 800/231–2222) links Rehoboth Beach with Wilmington, New Castle, and Dover.

By Car

From the north exit I–95 to U.S. 13S at Wilmington. Take U.S. 113 at Dover and Route 1 at Milford. From the south the scenic route to

Delaware's northern shores crosses Chesapeake Bay at Annapolis and continues east via U.S. 301/50; follows U.S. 50 to Route 404 at Wye Mills, Maryland; then crosses Delaware on Routes 404, 18, and 9 to Route 1 at Lewes.

By Ferry

Cape May–Lewes Ferry (☎ 302/645–6346 or 302/645–6313) is a 70-minute ride from Cape May, New Jersey, to Lewes, Delaware.

Exploring the Atlantic Coast

There is ample public access to the Atlantic surf and to the 23 mi of sand, though crowds pour in from Washington, D.C., and points west on holidays and summer weekends. The Broadkill River, Rehoboth Bay, Indian River Bay, and Little Assawoman Bay have sheltered coves.

Just west of the beaches are some of the state's historic villages and scenic bay-side parks (☞ National and State Parks, *above*). In **Milton,** once a major shipbuilding center at the head of the Broadkill River, the whole downtown area is a historic district of 18th- and 19th-century architecture, including old cypress-shingle houses. **Lewes,** a 1631 Dutch settlement at the mouth of Delaware Bay, cherishes its seafaring past with a marine museum and draws visitors with good restaurants, shops, and lodging away from the hectic beach resorts.

Coastal towns include **Rehoboth Beach,** the largest, with a busy boardwalk for strolling and shopping. Next door is **Dewey Beach,** popular with young singles. Adjacent **Bethany Beach, South Bethany,** and **Fenwick Island** (founded as a church camp and known for its fishing), south of the Indian River inlet, are quieter resorts.

Dining and Lodging

Once upon a time this sleepy resort area was full of of basic motels and guest houses with restaurants that served up undistinguished fried seafood and burgers. No more. Downscale tourist businesses have been replaced by swank hotels and restaurants that cater to sophisticated visitors from nearby Washington, D.C., Baltimore, and Philadelphia. The dining renaissance has brought a cadre of talented young chefs and dozens of exciting restaurants to the region. Rehoboth Beach is the center of the culinary boom, which has spread as far north as Milford and southward to the state line at Fenwick Island. For price ranges *see* Charts 1 (B) and 2 (B) *in* On the Road with Fodor's.

Bethany Beach

$$$ ✕ **Sedona.** Among the showstoppers at this southwestern establishment are wild boar rubbed with Thai spices and served with a side dish of tumbleweed onions and West Texas crab cakes with Santa Fe salsa. The casual aesthetic is more reminiscent of Santa Fe or Albuquerque than Bethany or Dewey Beach. ✉ *26 Pennsylvania Ave.,* ☎ *302/539–1200. AE, D, DC, MC, V. Closed Jan.–Mar.*

Dewey Beach

$$–$$$$ ✕ **Rusty Rudder.** In this barnlike, nautical–themed space overlooking Rehoboth Bay, the specialties are down-home service and local seafood, such as crab imperial. A land-and-sea buffet of seafood and chicken specialties is served every Friday year-round and several times weekly during summer months. There's also a Sunday brunch. ✉ *113 Dickinson St., on the bay,* ☎ *302/227–3888. AE, D, DC, MC, V.*

Lewes

$$ ✕ **Lazy Susan's.** For the fattest, sweetest, steamed blue-shell crabs, this simple roadside eatery is the place. Eating inside can be stifling, and the outside deck overlooks the highway, so takeout may be your best bet. Call ahead to make sure the crabs are fresh that day. ✉ *Hwy. 1 at Tenley Court, Lewes,* ☎ *302/645–5115. MC, V.*

$$$–$$$$ **Inn at Canal Square.** Valued for its waterfront location, this inn has conventional rooms as well as the *Legend of Lewes,* a houseboat that floats peacefully at dockside and is equipped with a modern galley, two bedrooms, and two baths. ✉ *122 Market St., 19958,* ☎ *302/645–8499 or 800/222–7902,* FAX *302/645–7083. 18 rooms, 1 houseboat. Continental breakfast. AE, D, DC, MC, V.*

$–$$$$ ★ **New Devon Inn.** The inn was built in 1926 and is listed in the National Register of Historic Places. The lobby and parlor are treasuries of Early Americana. Ask about the self-guided biking inn-to-inn package. ✉ *2nd and Market Sts., Box 516, 19958,* ☎ *302/645–6466 or 800/824–8754,* FAX *302/645–7196. 26 rooms. Restaurant. CP. AE, D, DC, MC, V.*

Milford

$$$ ★ ✕ **Banking House Inn.** The country-French cooking in this restored Victorian bank building uses a lighter approach than traditional French cuisine. Upstairs from the vivid Victoriana of the restaurant, the guest rooms—some with fireplaces—are traditionally decorated. ✉ *112 N.W. Front St., 19963,* ☎ *302/422–5708. 3 rooms. Restaurant. Full breakfast. DC, MC, V.*

$ **Traveler's Inn Motel.** Rooms in this two-story, balconied motel are plain, with two double beds and minimal furnishings (a hanging rack, no closet). ✉ *1036 N. Walnut St., 19963,* ☎ *302/422–8089. 38 rooms. AE, MC, V.*

Rehoboth Beach

$$$$ ✕ **Blue Moon.** Open since 1980, the Blue Moon is Rehoboth's oldest chic restaurant, and still one of the best. The charming old house has a sunny front porch. Chef Peter McMahon specializes in Pacific Rim–influenced cuisine. Seafood lasagne and baked salmon stuffed with scallops and leek typify the entrées. The restaurant is adjacent to the town's main gay bar. ✉ *35 Baltimore Ave.,* ☎ *302/227–6515. AE, DC, MC, V.*

$$$–$$$$ ★ ✕ **La La Land.** In a tiny beach house, this magical restaurant serves eclectic French-cum-Southwest-meets-Pacific Rim cuisine. Try the mignon of roasted eggplant or tenderloin with jalapeño-laced polenta. For a special treat ask to be seated in the bamboo-enclosed terrace. ✉ *22 Wilmington Ave.,* ☎ *302/227–3887. AE, DC, MC, V.*

$$$ ✕ **Sydney's Blues and Jazz.** New Orleans–influenced American cooking issues from the kitchen with such specialties as oysters Rockefeller, authentic gumbo and jambalaya, and a Cajun surf and turf. Wine-flight tastings—samples of three wines served in small portions—are also offered. The innovative grazing menu is great for light eaters or those who like to sample several choices. ✉ *25 Christian St.,* ☎ *302/227–1339. AE, D, DC, MC, V.*

$$–$$$ ★ ✕ **Dogfish Head Brewery.** Delaware's first brew pub, Dogfish Head is owned by two young entrepreneurs who keep their clientele happy with a changing menu of in-house brews, pizzas, and musical performers. ✉ *320 Rehoboth Ave.,* ☎ *302/226–2739. AE, MC, V.*

$$ ✕ **Woody's Bar & Grill.** Casual but stylish, Woody's is part of the Dinner Bell Inn, a Rehoboth institution. Baked crab and artichoke dip, grilled pork chops with applejack-brandy sauce and bread from the on-site bakery are crowd pleasers. ✉ *2 Christian St.,* ☎ *302/227–2561. AE, D, MC, V.*

$ ✕ **Nicola's Pizza.** Home of the original Nic-O-Boli, this family-run pizzeria ships its trademarked neo-stromboli all over the world to demanding fans. The bustling shop is packed until the wee hours of the morning. ✉ *8 N. 1st. St.,* ☎ *302/226–2654. MC, V.*

$ ✕ **Pierre's Pantry.** Pierre's does a fast takeout business and has tables for sit-down dining. The attractions are breakfast sandwiches (served all day), kosher items, Brooklyn bagels, fresh salads, and Cajun chicken or seven-vegetable sandwiches. ✉ *146 Rehoboth Ave.,* ☏ *302/227–7537. AE, MC, V.*

$$$–$$$$ ▣ **Boardwalk Plaza Hotel.** The most deluxe hotel on the boardwalk has grand Victorian trappings. Rooms for guests with disabilities are available; breakfast is served on the terrace right on the boardwalk. ✉ *2 Olive Ave., 19971,* ☏ *302/227–7169 or 800/332–3224. 84 rooms. Restaurant, pool, exercise room. AE, D, MC, V.*

$$–$$$$ ▣ **Brighton Suites.** Each suite has a bedroom with king-size bed and a living room with refrigerator and wet bar. Free parking is another perk. ✉ *34 Wilmington Ave., 19971,* ☏ *302/227–5780 or 800/227–5788. 66 suites. Pool. AE, D, DC, MC, V.*

$–$$$$ ▣ **Best Western Gold Leaf.** A half block from the beach and across the street from the bay, this Best Western has traditionally styled guest rooms, some with water views. ✉ *1400 Hwy. 1, 19971,* ☏ *302/226–1100 or 800/422–8566,* FAX *302/226–9785. 75 rooms. Pool. AE, D, DC, MC, V.*

$ ▣ **Atlantic Budget Inn.** Rooms in this two-story brick inn are crowded, with double or king-size beds and hanging clothes racks (no closets). ✉ *4353 Hwy. 1, 19971,* ☏ *302/227–0401 or 800/245–2112. 74 rooms. AE, DC, MC, V.*

Outdoor Activities and Sports

Fishing

Charter boats for either deep-sea or bay (trout, bluefish) fishing can be booked for either day or half-day trips, including all the gear. Book through your hotel or try **Fisherman's Wharf** (☏ 302/645–8862 or 302/645–8541), in Lewes, or **Delaware Seashore State Park Marina** (☏ 302/422–8940), at the Indian River inlet.

Water Sports

Marinas on Rehoboth Bay and Delaware Bay (at Lewes) rent sailboards, sailboats, and motorboats. Catamarans are for rent at **Fenwick Island State Park** (✉ ½ mi north of Fenwick Island on Rte. 1, ☏ 302/539–9060), among others.

Shopping

On the Atlantic coast bargain hunters scour the shops at **Ocean Outlets** (✉ Hwy. 1, Rehoboth Beach, ☏ 302/226–9223), a manufacturers' outlet center touting 110 stores that sprawl along both sides of the busy, four-lane highway. Farther north, on the southbound side of the highway, the same owner operates the 35-unit **Rehoboth Outlet Center,** which is anchored by an L. L. Bean factory store. Just north of Lewes is the **Lighthouse Outlet** (✉ 753 Hwy. 1., Lewes, ☏ 302/645–1207), which sells discounted fixtures and ceiling fans.

ELSEWHERE IN DELAWARE

Dover

Arriving and Departing

The north and south approaches to Dover are on U.S. 13; Route 10 links it with Goldsboro, Maryland; Route 1 heads toward Dover from the coast towns. **Blue Diamond Lines** (☏ 800/400–3800), a statewide public bus system, serves Wilmington, Newark, Middletown, Dover, and the Atlantic beaches, with various intermediate points.

What to See and Do

An oasis of colonial preservation in a busy government center, the **capitol complex** historic area is on a square laid out in 1722 according to William Penn's 1683 plan. Information about Delaware's historic sites and attractions is available at the **Delaware State Visitors Center** (☒ 406 Federal St., 19901, ☎ 302/739–4266); the Sewell C. Biggs Museum of American Decorative Arts (free) occupies the building's upper floors. The **Dover Air Force Base,** southeast of town, and its C-5 Galaxies are visible from U.S. 113. The **Air Mobility Command Museum** (☎ 302/677–5938; free) is housed in a 20,000-square-ft hangar that's filled with planes and airlift memorabilia, including a Medal of Honor hall of fame. The hangar itself served as a rocket test center during World War II. The museum is closed Sunday.

The **John Dickinson Plantation** (☒ 340 Kitts Hummock Rd., ☎ 302/739–3277) gives visitors a glimpse of 18th-century plantation life in Kent County, Delaware. A horse-drawn wagon, a crop duster, threshers, a corn house, and a privy are only part of the fascinating collection of tools and structures exhibited at the **Delaware Agricultural Museum and Village** (☒ 866 N. DuPont Hwy., ☎ 302/734–1618). A re-created 1890s village and farmstead, the operation is devoted to Delaware's rich agrarian past and present (agriculture is still the state's number-one industry).

Had enough culture? Then head straight for **Dover Downs International Speedway** (☒ North of Dover on Rte. 13, ☎ 302/674–4600 or 800/441–7223), where the grandstands can handle up to 5,000 spectators for stock car and harness racing; there's also a casino.

Dining and Lodging

$$ ✕ **Where Pigs Fly.** With family-style food that's a notch above most, this is a kid-friendly place that's easy on the wallet. ☒ *617 Loockerman St., at U.S. 13,* ☎ *302/678–0586. AE, D, DC, MC, V.*

$$$ **Sheraton Dover Hotel.** Convenient, comfortable, and well appointed, the Sheraton features spacious meeting rooms and a conference center. ☒ *1570 N. DuPont Hwy., 19901,* ☎ *302/678–8500 or 800/325–3535,* FAX *302/678–9073. 153 rooms. Restaurant, pool. AE, D, DC, MC, V.*

MARYLAND

By Francis X. Rocca

Updated by Gregory Tasker

Capital	Annapolis
Population	5,094,000
Motto	Manly Deeds, Womanly Words
State Bird	Baltimore oriole
State Flower	Black-eyed Susan
Postal Abbreviation	MD

Statewide Visitor Information

The **Maryland Office of Tourism** (✉ 217 E. Redwood St., Baltimore 21202, ☎ 410/767–3400 or 800/543–1036) provides free publications and runs seven information centers.

Scenic Drives

Alternate U.S. Route 40, between Frederick and Hagerstown, rolls gently through farmlands and picturesque towns. In summer many farm stands offer fresh fruit and produce. The area is especially attractive in early autumn, when the leaves begin to change. **I–68,** between Hancock and Cumberland in western Maryland, passes through a spectacular cut in the rocky crest of a mountain and then opens to sweeping views of the Appalachians. **U.S. 50/301,** at the eastern end of Kent Island on Maryland's Eastern Shore, traverses an elevated bridge with spectacular views of the inlet and the fishing boats, pleasure craft, and sailboats below.

National and State Parks

National Parks

National Park Service attractions include **Antietam National Battlefield** ★ **Site** (☎ 301/432–5124; $2 per person, $5 per family), **Assateague Island National Seashore** (☎ 410/641–1441; $5 per vehicle, $2 per pedestrian), **Blackwater National Wildlife Refuge** (☎ 410/228–2677; $3 per vehicle; $1 per pedestrian), **Catoctin Mountain Park** (☎ 301/663–9330; free), **Chesapeake and Ohio Canal National Historic Park** (☎ 301/739–4200; free), **Fort McHenry National Monument and Historic Shrine** (☎ 410/962–4290; $5), and **Fort Washington Park** (☎ 301/763–4600; $4, free weekdays Nov.–Apr.).

State Parks

Maryland has 47 parks and forests on more than 280,000 acres of land. The Office of Tourism (☞ Statewide Visitor Information, *above*) has information about each of the parks. **Swallow Falls State Park** (☎ 301/334–9180), along the north-flowing Youghiogheny River in extreme western Maryland, is the site of the scenic 63-ft Muddy Creek Falls. North of Baltimore, **Gunpowder Falls State Park** (☎ 410/592–2897), a 13,020-acre park in the picturesque Gunpowder River valley, has more than 100 mi of hiking and biking trails. **Sandy Point State Park** (☎ 410/974–2149) is an expanse of sandy beaches on the western shore of the Chesapeake Bay, great for picnicking, fishing, and bird-watching. The **Department of Natural Resources** (☎ 410/260–8367) organizes numerous programs, including guided canoe trips, hiking, backpacking, wildflower walks, forest walks, and guided mountain-bike trips.

BALTIMORE

Two decades ago Baltimore transformed itself and its once-dormant waterfront into a bustling tourist attraction, with shopping, restaurants, and the acclaimed National Aquarium. In the process the city became a model for urban redevelopment across the country. Celebrating its bicentennial in 1997, Baltimore found itself in the midst of another renaissance. A new stadium was scheduled to open in early autumn 1998, next to Camden Yards, for the city's new NFL franchise, the aptly named Baltimore Ravens. On the other side of Inner Harbor, the old Power Plant is being transformed into an entertainment complex. And Port Discovery, a children's museum being designed by the Walt Disney Co., is slated for a late 1998 debut. Away from its thriving harbor, Baltimore remains a city of historic neighborhoods, including Mount Vernon and Fells Point. It is a city steeped in history, too. Babe Ruth, Edgar Allen Poe, and H. L. Mencken and the "Star-Spangled Banner" are as synonymous with Baltimore as the Orioles and blue crabs.

Visitor Information

Baltimore Area Visitors Center (✉ 301 E. Pratt St., 21202, ☎ 410/837–4636 or 800/282–6632). **Office of Promotion** (✉ 200 W. Lombard St., 21201, ☎ 410/752–8632).

Arriving and Departing

By Bus

Greyhound Lines (✉ 210 W. Fayette St., ☎ 800/231–2222).

By Car

Baltimore is on I–95, the major East Coast artery.

By Plane

Baltimore-Washington International (BWI) Airport (☎ 410/859–7111), 10 mi south of town, is a destination for most major domestic and foreign carriers. Taxi fare to downtown is roughly $19. **Amtrak** (☞ By Train, *below*) and **Maryland Area Rail Commuter** (MARC; ☎ 800/325–7245) trains run between the airport station (10 minutes from the terminal via free shuttle bus) and Penn Station, about 20 minutes away. **BWI Super Shuttle** (☎ 410/724–0009) has van service to downtown and to most suburban hotels.

By Train

Amtrak serves Baltimore's Penn Station (✉ Charles St. at Mt. Royal Ave., ☎ 800/872–7245). **Central Light Rail Line** (☎ 410/539–5000) provides service from Hunt Valley, north of the city, through downtown and south to Glen Burnie and BWI Airport.

Getting Around Baltimore

Most attractions are a walk or a short trolley ride (☞ Orientation Tours, *below*) from the Inner Harbor. **Water taxis** (☎ 410/563–3901) stop at Fells Point and at Inner Harbor locations. Beyond that a car is useful; the metro line is limited, and bus riding often requires transfers. Call **Mass Transit Administration** (☎ 410/539–5000) for information.

Orientation Tours

From spring through fall **Baltimore Trolley Tours** (☎ 410/563–3901) runs 90-minute narrated tours of Baltimore's downtown attractions for $7. The tours also stop at all downtown hotels. You can get off and on the trolley several times throughout one day for one price. Tours are offered daily May through October.

Exploring Baltimore

The city fans out northward from the Inner Harbor, with newer attractions such as the National Aquarium and Oriole Park concentrated at the center and more historic neighborhoods and sites toward the edges. The major northbound artery is Charles Street; cross streets are labeled "East" or "West" relative to it.

Charles Street

Head north on Charles Street from Baltimore Street toward the impossible-to-miss Washington Monument. Restaurants and art galleries lend an urbane tone to this neighborhood, with its mix of 19th-century brownstones and modern office buildings. A block west of Charles Street is the **Basilica of the Assumption** (✉ Mulberry St. at Cathedral St., ☎ 410/727–3564; 🎫 free), which was built in 1812 and is the oldest Catholic cathedral in the United States. Pope John Paul II visited this national shrine during a trip to Baltimore in October 1995.

★ At the **Walters Art Gallery** (✉ 600 N. Charles St., ☎ 410/547–2787; 🎫 $6), 30,000 objects from antiquity through the 19th century—encompassing Egyptology exhibits, medieval armor and artifacts, decorative arts and paintings—are housed in an Italianate palace. The adjacent Hackerman House has a magnificent gallery of Asian art.

The **Washington Monument** (✉ Mt. Vernon Pl., ☎ 410/396–0929; 🎫 $1), built in 1829, is a 178-ft marble column topped by a 16-ft statue of the first president. A 228-step spiral staircase within leads to a unique view of the city.

Surrounding Washington Monument is **Mt. Vernon Square,** flanked by four block-long parks. Note the bronze sculptures in the parks and the elegant brownstones along East Mt. Vernon Place. The **Peabody Library** (✉ 17 E. Mt. Vernon Pl., ☎ 410/659–8179; 🎫 free) has a handsome reading room with a skylight in its five-story-high ceiling. At the **Maryland Historical Society** (✉ 201 W. Monument St., ☎ 410/685–3750; 🎫 $4), the eclectic display of state memorabilia includes the original manuscript of the "Star-Spangled Banner."

The **Baltimore Museum of Art** (✉ 10 Art Museum Dr., ☎ 410/396–7101; 🎫 $6, free Thursday) displays works by Rodin, Matisse, Picasso, Cézanne, Renoir, and Gauguin. There's also a wing containing 20th-century art, including 19 Andy Warhol paintings. The 140-acre campus of **Johns Hopkins University** (✉ Charles and 34th Sts.), is next door to the museum. The main attraction on campus is **Homewood,**(☎ 410/516–5589; 🎫 $6) once the estate of Charles Carroll Jr., son of Charles Carroll of Carrollton, a signer of the Declaration of Independence. It has been restored to its 1800 appearance and is open to the public.

Inner Harbor and Environs

The **American Visionary Art Museum** (✉ 800 Key Hwy., at Covington St., ☎ 410/244–1900; 🎫 $6), housed in a former whiskey distillery near Federal Hill, showcases the works of self-trained and self-taught artists. Its revolving exhibits include paintings, sculpture, reliefs, drawings, photographs, and a host of other objects created by farmers, housewives, people with disabilities, and other "outsider" artists.

Harborplace (✉ 200 E. Pratt St., ☎ 410/332–4191; 🎫 free) comprises two glass-enclosed shopping malls with more than 100 specialty shops and gourmet markets. The Rouse Company's multilevel **Gallery,** across

Pratt Street from Harborplace, has upscale shopping and dining. Other waterfront attractions are nearby. At the **Maryland Science Center** (✉ 601 Light St., ☎ 410/685–5225; 🎟 $9), the biggest draw is an IMAX movie theater with a five-story-high screen. There is also a planetarium. The **World Trade Center** (✉ 401 Pratt St., ☎ 410/837–4515; 🎟 $3) is the world's tallest pentagonal building (30 stories); its 27th-floor observation deck—the **Top of the World**—offers a terrific view of the city. The World War II submarine **USS *Torsk*** and the lightship ***Chesapeake*** make up the **Baltimore Maritime Museum** (✉ Piers 3 and 4, Pratt St., ☎ 410/396–5528; 🎟 $4.50).

Power Plant (✉ 601 E. Pratt St.) a 35,000-square-ft sports, entertainment, and dining complex, opened in summer 1998 in the city's former power plant. Designed by the Walt Disney Company and ESPN, the two-level, stadiumlike complex has a 10,000-square-ft arena where sports fans can play actual and virtual games. Occasionally, ESPN is expected to broadcast live from the Zone.

The **National Aquarium in Baltimore** (✉ Pier 3, ☎ 410/576–3800; 🎟 $11.95) is home to more than 5,000 species of marine life, including sharks, dolphins, beluga whales, and puffins. Escalators whisk visitors past a tank (which you can later walk through) with a coral reef and then to the rooftop "rain forest." On Pier 4 the **Marine Mammal Pavilion** has themed exhibit areas and performances by Atlantic bottle-nosed dolphins.

East of Inner Harbor is the **Star-Spangled Banner Flag House** (✉ 844 E. Pratt St., ☎ 410/837–1793; 🎟 $4), where the flag that inspired the national anthem was woven.

Although temporarily closed, the complex of buildings around a Lombard Street courtyard between Front and Albemarle streets offer a fascinating glimpse of Baltimore's history. This complex is known as the **City Life Museums** (✉ 800 E. Lombard St., ☎ 410/396–3523; 🎟 $6). Within the complex, the **Morton K. Blaustein City Life Exhibition Center** chronicles Baltimore's urban and cultural history with a display of everyday objects, such as white vinyl reclining chairs from the 1950s and black gas stoves from the 1930s. Other highlights include a row house where actors perform short plays set in 1840 and the elegant town house of Charles Carroll, who was the last signer of the Declaration of Independence to die. Also part of the complex is the **Phoenix Shot Tower,** at East Fayette and Front streets, where shot was made until the Civil War. At press time, City Life Museums was temporarily closed, so call before you visit.

Port Discovery, The Children's Museum in Baltimore (✉ 34 Market Pl., ☎ 410/727–8120; 🎟 admission not set at press time) is an interactive, hands-on museum expected to be open by 1999 in the city's old fish market. Designed by the Walt Disney Co., the museum is packed with exhibits that will make learning fun for kids, including a recreated Egypt, complete with the Nile River, pyramids, and mazes.

North of Inner Harbor on Holliday Street is the golden-domed **Baltimore City Hall,** built in 1875 and completely supported by ironwork. Near city hall is the **Peale Museum** (✉ 225 N. Holliday St., ☎ 410/396–1149; 🎟 $2), which shows paintings by Charles Willson Peale and his family and has been open since 1814, making it the oldest museum in the United States. Unfortunately, the Peale Museum is affiliated with City Life Museums (☞ *above*) and has been temporarily closed; call to confirm its reopening before you visit.

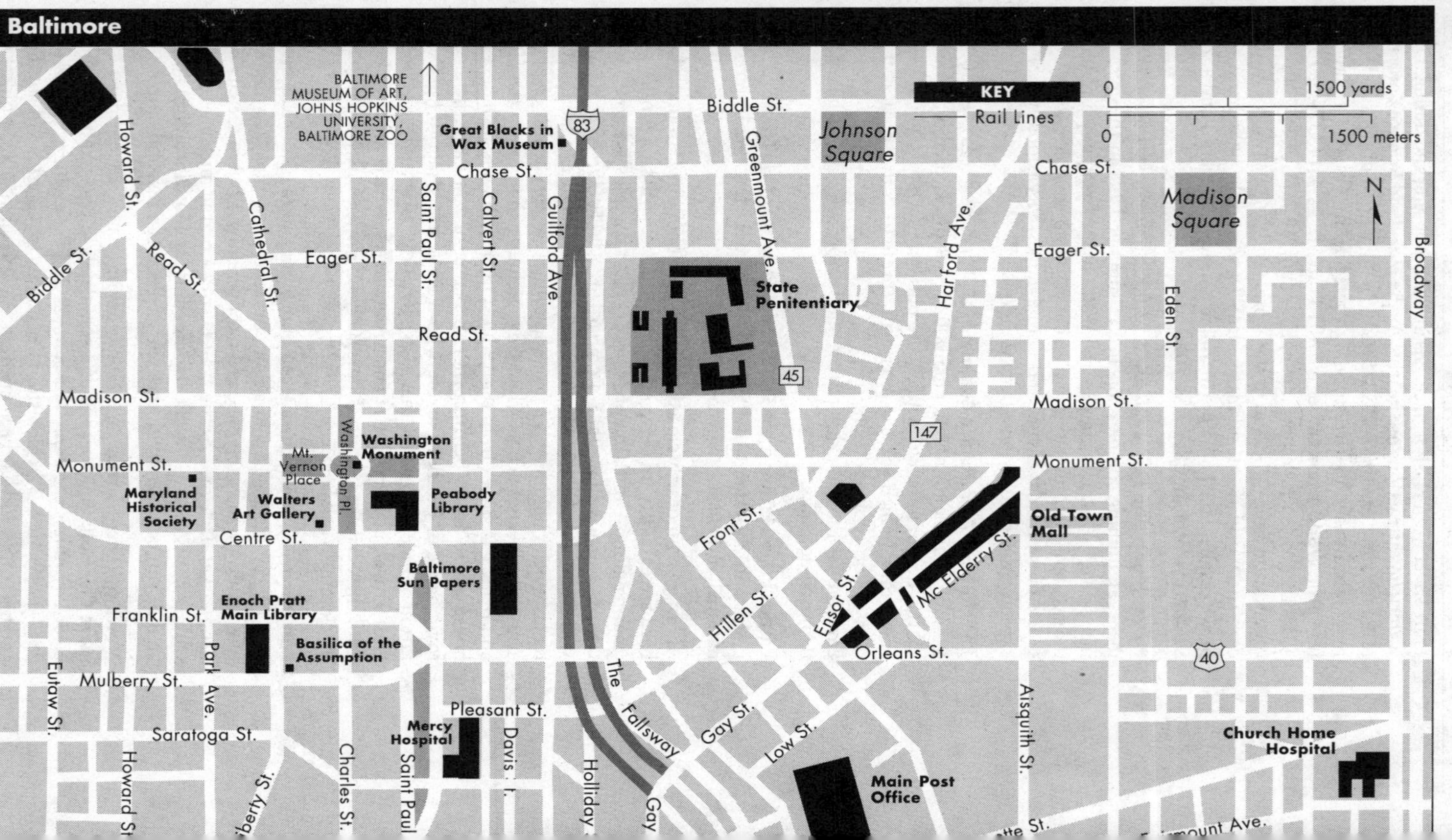
Baltimore
BALTIMORE MUSEUM OF ART, JOHNS HOPKINS UNIVERSITY, BALTIMORE ZOO
Great Blacks in Wax Museum
83
Biddle St.
Johnson Square
KEY
Rail Lines
0
1500 yards
0
1500 meters
Chase St.
Chase St.
Madison Square
N
Howard St.
Cathedral St.
Saint Paul St.
Calvert St.
Guilford Ave.
Greenmount Ave.
Harford Ave.
Eagar St.
Eager St.
Eden St.
Broadway
Biddle St.
Read St.
State Penitentiary
Read St.
45
Madison St.
Madison St.
147
Washington Monument
Mt. Vernon Place
Washington Pl.
Monument St.
Monument St.
Maryland Historical Society
Walters Art Gallery
Peabody Library
Old Town Mall
Front St.
Centre St.
Baltimore Sun Papers
Mc Elderry St.
Enoch Pratt Main Library
Franklin St.
Hillen St.
Ensor St.
Basilica of the Assumption
Orleans St.
40
Eutaw St.
Park Ave.
Mulberry St.
The Fallsway
Pleasant St.
Mercy Hospital
Saratoga St.
Davis St.
Gay St.
Low St.
Aisquith St.
Church Home Hospital
Howard St.
Liberty St.
Charles St.
Saint Paul
Holliday
Gay
Main Post Office
Fayette St.
Fairmount Ave.

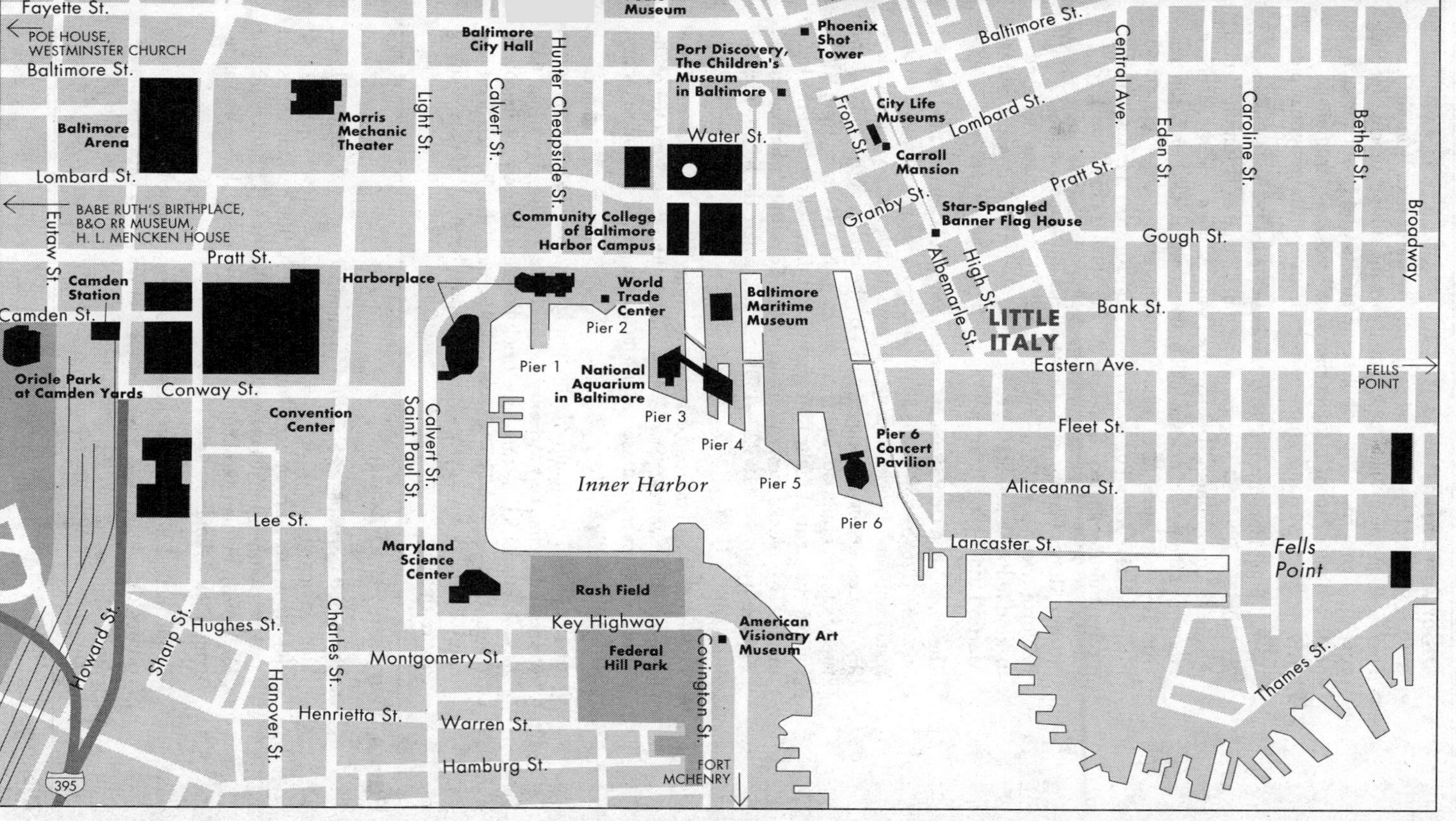
Fayette St.
POE HOUSE, WESTMINSTER CHURCH
Baltimore St.
Baltimore Arena
Morris Mechanic Theater
Baltimore City Hall
Light St.
Calvert St.
Hunter Cheapside St.
Museum
Phoenix Shot Tower
Port Discovery, The Children's Museum in Baltimore
Baltimore St.
City Life Museums
Front St.
Lombard St.
Carroll Mansion
Central Ave.
Eden St.
Caroline St.
Bethel St.
Broadway
Water St.
Lombard St.
BABE RUTH'S BIRTHPLACE, B&O RR MUSEUM, H. L. MENCKEN HOUSE
Eutaw St.
Community College of Baltimore Harbor Campus
Granby St.
Pratt St.
Star-Spangled Banner Flag House
Gough St.
Pratt St.
Camden Station
Camden St.
Harborplace
World Trade Center
Pier 2
Baltimore Maritime Museum
Albemarle St.
High St.
LITTLE ITALY
Bank St.
Eastern Ave.
FELLS POINT
Oriole Park at Camden Yards
Conway St.
Pier 1
National Aquarium in Baltimore
Pier 3
Pier 4
Convention Center
Saint Paul St.
Calvert St.
Pier 6 Concert Pavilion
Fleet St.
Inner Harbor
Pier 5
Aliceanna St.
Pier 6
Lee St.
Lancaster St.
Fells Point
Maryland Science Center
Rash Field
Key Highway
American Visionary Art Museum
Hughes St.
Sharp St.
Howard St.
Charles St.
Montgomery St.
Federal Hill Park
Covington St.
Thames St.
Hanover St.
Henrietta St.
Warren St.
Hamburg St.
FORT MCHENRY
395

Other Attractions

A 10-minute trolley ride (or 12 minutes by water taxi) from the Inner ★ Harbor takes you to **Fells Point,** once a thriving shipbuilding center and now a neighborhood of cobblestone streets and historic redbrick houses, many of them antiques shops, galleries, restaurants, and taverns. At Broadway and Thames streets is an operating tugboat pier.

West of Inner Harbor is the **H. L. Mencken House** (✉ 1524 Hollins St., ☎ 410/396–7997; 🎫 $2), from which the "Sage of Baltimore" ruled American letters from the 1920s to the 1940s. At press time, the Mencken House was temporarily closed; call to confirm that it's open before you visit. The **Poe House** (✉ 203 N. Amity St., ☎ 410/396–7932; 🎫 $3) is where Edgar Allan Poe wrote his first horror story. He lies buried at the Westminster Church Grave (✉ W. Fayette and Greene Sts.).

North of Inner Harbor is the **Great Blacks in Wax Museum** (✉ 1601 E. North Ave., ☎ 410/563–6415; 🎫 $5.75), the first and only one of its kind in the United States. Rosa Parks, Frederick Douglass, and Dr. Martin Luther King Jr. are among the figures you'll see.

The 50,000-seat **Oriole Park at Camden Yards** (✉ Camden and Howard Sts., ☎ 410/685–9800), has a 700-square-ft video scoreboard, several restaurants, and a cocktail lounge. Its brick facade and asymmetric playing field evoke the big-league parks of the early 1900s. Built on the site of a former railroad depot, it is served by MARC trains from Washington, the Central Light Rail trains from the suburbs, and the local metro. Two blocks west of Oriole Park is **Babe Ruth's birthplace** (✉ 216 Emory St., ☎ 410/727–1539; 🎫 $5), where the baseball legend was born in 1895.

★ Locomotives and railroad cars are on display at the **B&O Railroad Museum** (✉ 901 W. Pratt St., ☎ 410/752–2490; 🎫 $6.50). One of the world's largest train museums, it sits on the site of the country's first railroad station.

At the end of the peninsula bounding the Patapsco River's northwestern branch is **Fort McHenry** (✉ Fort Ave. off Key Hwy.), ☎ 410/962–4290; 🎫 $5) a star-shape brick building famous for its role in the national anthem. The "star-spangled banner" that Francis Scott Key saw "by the dawn's early light" on September 14, 1814, was flying above this fort.

Parks, Gardens, and Zoos

★ **Sherwood Gardens** (✉ Stratford Rd. and Greenway, 3 mi from Inner Harbor east of St. Paul St., ☎ 410/323–7982; 🎫 free) is worth a special trip in late April or early May to see its 80,000 peaking tulips and azaleas. South of Inner Harbor is **Federal Hill Park** (✉ Battery St. and Key Hwy.), with an excellent view of the downtown skyline and a jogging track in adjacent **Rash Field.**

More than 1,200 animals, including polar bears, elephants, and penguins occupy the 150 acres of the **Baltimore Zoo** (✉ Druid Park Lake Dr., I-83 to Exit 7, ☎ 410/366–5466; 🎫 $7.50), a year-round child pleaser. The Maryland Wilderness exhibit is home to animals native to the state.

Dining

Seafood, especially Chesapeake Bay blue crab (steamed in the shell, fried in a crab cake, or baked with a white-cream-and-wine sauce), is the specialty here, but every major cuisine is available, especially in Baltimore's Greek and Italian neighborhoods. For price ranges *see* Chart 1 (A) *in* On the Road with Fodor's.

$$$–$$$$ ★ ✕ **Prime Rib.** The bustling but intimate dining room just north of Mount Vernon Square is consistently ranked among the city's best. The traditional menu is headed by sterling prime rib and an even better filet mignon. The jumbo lump crab cakes are highly recommended. ✉ *1101 N. Calvert St.,* ☎ *410/539–1804. Reservations essential. Jacket required. AE, DC, MC, V.*

$$$–$$$$ ★ ✕ **Tio Pepe.** Paella à la Valenciana (chicken, sausage, shrimp, clams, mussels, and saffron rice) is a specialty at this candlelit cellar dining room, as is the lesser-known Basque red snapper—with clams, mussels, asparagus, and boiled egg. ✉ *10 E. Franklin St.,* ☎ *410/539–4675. Reservations essential. Jacket required. AE, D, DC, MC, V.*

$$$ ★ ✕ **Joy America Cafe.** Chef Peter Zimmer presides over Baltimore's most creative kitchen in the unusual American Visionary Art Museum. In a spare, open dining room overlooking the harbor, Zimmer offers museum goers an appropriately unconventional seasonal menu that draws on the flavors of many countries, including dishes such as tropical fruit–barbecued halibut served with fresh peaches, bitter chocolate, and tomato-and-watermelon salsa. ✉ *American Visionary Art Museum, 800 Key Hwy.,* ☎ *410/244–6500. AE, DC, MC, V.*

$$–$$$ ✕ **Bertha's.** Mussels are the specialty here, served steamed (with a choice of eight butter-based sauces) or as a Turkish appetizer (stuffed with sweet-and-spicy rice). The decor is nautical. ✉ *734 S. Broadway,* ☎ *410/327–5795. MC, V.*

$–$$$ ✕ **Haussner's.** Since its opening in 1926 this has been one of Baltimore's favorite special-occasion spots. German dishes are the specialty, but there is something to please everyone—particularly in the dessert department. The walls are adorned with hundreds of original paintings, including pieces by Gainsborough, Rembrandt, Bierstadt, Van Dyck, and Whistler. ✉ *3244 Eastern Ave.,* ☎ *410/327–8365. Reservations not accepted at dinner on Sat. AE, D, DC, MC, V. Closed Sun.–Mon.*

$$ ✕ **O'Brycki's Crab House.** East of Inner Harbor, this 50-year-old Baltimore institution has a homey dining room with brick archways and early-1900s city scenes. Chesapeake Bay fare—steamed crabs and crab cakes—are the specialty, but there's also fresh seafood, steak, and chicken. ✉ *1727 E. Pratt St.,* ☎ *410/732–6399. AE, D, DC, MC, V. Closed Jan.–Feb.*

$–$$ ✕ **Burke's Cafe and Comedy Club.** Just a block from the Inner Harbor, convention center, and Baltimore Arena, Burke's has long been one of downtown's favorite casual dining spots. Though steak and seafood are on the menu, Burke's specialty is pub grub—frosty mugs, giant burgers, and platters of huge onion rings. It's a hit with the after-the-game crowd, tourists, and conventioneers. ✉ *36 Light St., at Lombard St.,* ☎ *410/752–4189. AE, MC, V.*

$–$$ ✕ **Donna's.** A good bet for both fresh-baked morning scones and after-theater espresso—it's open until 1 AM on Friday and Saturday—this Italian coffee bar also serves a variety of pastas, salads, and innovative sandwiches from midday on. ✉ *1 Mt. Vernon Sq. (2 W. Madison St., at Charles St.),* ☎ *410/385–0180. AE, DC, MC, V.*

$ ✕ **City Markets.** These are great for a stand-up or counter-side breakfast or lunch. Each offers different local favorites, including fresh Chesapeake Bay seafood, grilled wursts, homemade soups and salads, sushi, and Philadelphia cheese steaks (☞ Shopping, *below*).

Lodging

Staying around Inner Harbor means ready access to the major attractions. Away from the water, as far north as Mt. Vernon, are reminders of an older Baltimore and some relative bargains in accommodations. For price ranges *see* Chart 2 (A) *in* On the Road with Fodor's.

$$$$ ★ **Harbor Court.** This redbrick tower with an ersatz English-country-house interior has been Baltimore's most prestigious hotel since 1986. The priciest rooms have a harbor view. ✉ *550 Light St., 21202,* ☎ *410/234–0550 or 800/824–0076,* FAX *410/659–5925. 205 rooms. 2 restaurants, pool, exercise room. AE, D, DC, MC, V.*

$$$$ **Renaissance Harborplace Hotel.** Across from the Inner Harbor shopping pavilions and many waterfront tourist sights, the Renaissance Harborplace is the most conveniently located hotel in the city. Rooms with a harbor view are in demand. ✉ *202 E. Pratt St., 21202,* ☎ *410/547–1200,* FAX *410/539–5780. 622 rooms. Restaurant, pool, exercise room. AE, D, DC, MC, V.*

$$$–$$$$ **Sheraton Inner Harbor.** Just two blocks from Harborplace and Oriole Park, the Sheraton is the official hotel of the Baltimore Orioles. It's also within walking distance of most of the city's attractions and has the only Orthodox Union–certified kosher hotel kitchen in town. ✉ *300 S. Charles St., 21201,* ☎ *410/962–8300,* FAX *410/962–8211. 357 rooms. 2 restaurants, pool, exercise room. AE, D, DC, MC, V.*

$$$ **Celie's Waterfront Bed & Breakfast.** The spectacular setting—on Baltimore's historic waterfront in Fells Point—is matched by thoughtful details such as terry-cloth robes and clock radios that play ocean waves to soothe you to sleep. Two front rooms overlook the harbor and have fireplaces and whirlpool tubs. Guests have access to a garden and a rooftop deck. ✉ *1714 Thames St., 21231,* ☎ *410/522–2323,* FAX *410/522–2324. 7 rooms. AE, D, MC, V.*

$$$ **Tremont Hotel.** This small hostelry on a quiet downtown block has a level of service unsurpassed locally: The concierge will arrange free local transportation, and the staff will do guests' personal shopping. All rooms are suites with kitchens. ✉ *8 E. Pleasant St., 21202,* ☎ *410/576–1200 or 800/873–6668,* FAX *410/244–1154. 58 suites. Restaurant, exercise room. AE, D, DC, MC, V.*

$$$ ★ **Tremont Plaza Hotel.** This plain, gray, 37-story tower has suites done in gentle earth tones. All units have kitchens, and those numbered "06" have the best views. ✉ *222 St. Paul Pl., 21202,* ☎ *410/727–2222 or 800/873–6668,* FAX *410/685–4215. 231 suites. Restaurant, pool, exercise room. AE, D, DC, MC, V.*

$$–$$$ **Clarion Hotel.** Formerly the Latham Hotel, this Baltimore landmark retains its original dark wood–paneled lobby; upstairs, a food court includes Pizzeria Uno, Healthy Choice, and Nestlé Tollhouse Cafe. Rooms with views of Mt. Vernon Place and the Washington Monument are coveted. Some rooms have kitchenettes. ✉ *612 Cathedral St., 21201,* ☎ *410/727–7101 or 800/292-5500,* FAX *410/789–3312. 103 rooms. AE, D, DC, MC, V.*

$$–$$$ ★ **Mr. Mole Bed & Breakfast.** Near Baltimore's cultural center, this 1870 brick row house has five tasteful suites with various themes, from English country to whimsical scenes of nature. There's a breakfast spread of coffee cakes, pies, and Amish meats and cheeses. ✉ *1601 Bolton St., 21217,* ☎ *410/728–1179,* FAX *410/728–3379. 5 suites. AE, D, DC, MC, V.*

Motels

Days Inn Inner Harbor (✉ 100 Hopkins Pl., 21201, ☎ 410/576–1000, FAX 410/576–9437), 250 rooms, restaurant, pool; *$$–$$$.*

Hampton Inn Hunt Valley (✉ 11200 York Rd., Hunt Valley 21031, ☎ 410/527–1500, FAX 410/771–0819), 120 rooms, CP; *$–$$.*

Nightlife and the Arts

Events listings appear in the Thursday *Baltimore Sun*, the monthly *Baltimore* magazine, and *City Paper*, a free weekly distributed in shops and from street-corner machines.

Nightlife

The harborside **Explorer's Lounge** (✉ Harbor Court Hotel, ☎ 410/234–0550) serves up jazz and remarkable views. For blues and rock, **8 x 10** (✉ 8 E. Cross St., ☎ 410/625–2000) is the spot. Move to the latest dance mixes at the **Baja Beach Club** (✉ 55 Market Pl., ☎ 410/727–0468). Laughter is the predominant sound at **Winchester's Comedy Club** (✉ Light and Water Sts., ☎ 410/576–8558). The talk is all sports at **DSX** (✉ 200 W. Pratt St., ☎ 410/659–5844). The **Orioles Sports Bar** (✉ Sheraton Inner Harbor Hotel, 300 S. Charles St., ☎ 410/962–8300) celebrates baseball and other sports with autographed baseballs, jerseys, and other memorabilia.

The **Fells Point** area is Baltimore's answer to D.C.'s Georgetown. Nightclubs, restaurants, pubs, coffeehouses, and small theaters line cobblestone streets around the foot of Broadway.

The Arts

Center Stage (✉ 700 N. Calvert St., ☎ 410/332–0033) is the state theater of Maryland. Other venues include **Friedberg Hall** (✉ Peabody Conservatory, E. Mt. Vernon Pl. and Charles St., ☎ 410/659–8124), **Lyric Opera House** (✉ Mt. Royal Ave. and Cathedral St., ☎ 410/685–5086), **Meyerhoff Symphony Hall** (✉ 1212 Cathedral St., ☎ 410/783–8000), **Morris A. Mechanic Theater** (✉ Baltimore and Charles Sts., ☎ 410/625–4230), and **Pier Six Concert Pavilion** (✉ Pier 6 at Pratt St., ☎ 410/752–8632). There are also numerous dinner theaters in the Baltimore suburbs; check newspapers for details.

Spectator Sports

Baseball: Orioles (✉ Oriole Park at Camden Yards, Camden and Howard Sts., ☎ 410/685–9800). **Football: Ravens** (✉ 200 St. Paul Pl., Suite 2400, Baltimore 21202, ☎ 410/261–7283 or 888/919–9797).

Shopping

The city's most diverse and colorful shopping areas are the **malls of Harborplace** and the **shops of Fells Point** (☞ Exploring Baltimore, *above*). There are more than three dozen first-rate **antiques shops** on **Antique Row** (✉ 700 and 800 blocks, N. Howard St.; ✉ 200 block, W. Read St.). At **Kelmscott Bookshop** (✉ 32 W. 25th St., ☎ 410/235–6810) you can browse among the enormous stock of rare books in a converted town house. The city of Baltimore owns and leases space to a number of **indoor food markets:** At least 100 years old are Belair Market (✉ Gay and Fayette Sts.), Broadway Market (✉ Broadway and Fleet Sts.), Cross Street Market (✉ Light and Cross Sts.), Hollins Market (✉ Hollins and Arlington Sts.), Lexington Market (✉ Lexington and Eutaw Sts.), and Northeast Market (✉ Monument and Chester Sts.).

MARYLAND'S CHESAPEAKE

Maryland encompasses the top half of the Chesapeake Bay, where the attractions are, naturally, water-oriented: Annapolis is a world yachting capital, the Eastern Shore is a major duck-hunting ground, and Ocean City is a busy Atlantic resort. Yet the bay-side towns are also rich in history, with many well-preserved 18th-century buildings.

Visitor Information

Annapolis and Anne Arundel County: Convention & Visitors Association (✉ 26 West St., Annapolis 21401, ☎ 410/268–8687). **Calvert County:** Department of Economic Development (✉ County Courthouse, 175 Main St., Prince Frederick 20678, ☎ 410/535–4583 or 800/331–9771). **Caroline County:** County Government (✉ 109 Market St., Room 109, Denton 21629, ☎ 410/479–0660). **Cecil County:** Chamber of Commerce (✉ 135 E. Main St., Elkton 21921, ☎ 410/392–3833 or 800/232–4595). **Charles County:** Tourism Office (✉ 8190 Port Tobacco Rd., Port Tobacco 20677, ☎ 800/766–3386). **Dorchester County:** Department of Tourism (✉ 203 Sunburst Hwy., Cambridge 21613, ☎ 410/228–1000 or 800/522–8687). **Kent County:** Chamber of Commerce and Office of Tourism Development (✉ 400 S. Cross St., Chestertown 21620, ☎ 410/778–0416). **Ocean City:** Convention and Visitors Bureau (✉ Box 158, Ocean City 21842, ☎ 410/289–2800 or 800/626–2326). **Queen Anne's County:** Office of Tourism (✉ 3100 E. Main St., Grasonville 21638, ☎ 410/827–4810). **St. Mary's County:** Division of Tourism (✉ 23115 Leonard Hall Dr., Leonardtown 20650, ☎ 301/475–4411 or 800/327–9023). **St. Michaels:** Talbot County Chamber of Commerce (✉ 210 Marlboro, Suite 300, Easton 21601, ☎ 410/822–4606). **Somerset County:** Tourism Office (✉ Box 243, Princess Anne 21853, ☎ 410/651–2968 or 800/521–9189). **Wicomico County:** Convention and Visitors Bureau (✉ 8480 Ocean Hwy., Delmar 21875, ☎ 410/548–4914). **Worcester County:** Tourism Office (✉ 105 Pearl St., Snow Hill 21863, ☎ 410/632–3617).

Arriving and Departing

By Bus

Baltimore Mass Transit (☎ 410/539–5000) provides service—express on weekdays, local on weekends—between Annapolis and Baltimore. **Carolina Trailways** (☎ 410/727–5014) links Annapolis to Ocean City and intermediate points on the Eastern Shore.

By Car

To Annapolis: From Baltimore follow Route 3/97 to U.S. 50 (Rowe Blvd. exit). **To Southern Maryland:** From Annapolis take Route 2 south, which becomes Route 4 in Calvert County. **To the Eastern Shore:** From Baltimore or Annapolis cross the Bay Bridge (toll charged) northeast of Annapolis and stay on U.S. 50/301.

Exploring Maryland's Chesapeake

Annapolis

Start on the waterfront. Sailboats dock right at the edge of **Market Square,** where there is a visitor information booth. At **City Dock** look for the sidewalk plaque commemorating the arrival of Kunta Kinte, the African slave immortalized in Alex Haley's *Roots.*

At the **Museum Store and Historic Annapolis Foundation** (✉ 77 Main St., ☎ 410/268–5576) you can rent an audiocassette and let narrator Walter Cronkite be your guide on a walking tour of the Historic District.

On the riverside campus of the **United States Naval Academy** (✉ Gate 1, off King George St., ☎ 410/293–1000; 🎟 free, tours $5), known to West Pointers as the "country club on the Severn," the most prominent structure is the bronze-domed **U.S. Naval Chapel,** burial place of the Revolutionary War hero John Paul ("I have not yet begun to fight!") Jones. Outdoors, full-dress parades of midshipmen are a stirring sight.

Once briefly the capital of the United States, Annapolis has one of the finest collections of 18th- and 19th-century buildings in the country, including more than 50 pre-Revolutionary structures. Many of its stately brick buildings are still in use as homes, inns, shops, and restaurants. The three-story redbrick **Hammond-Harwood House** (✉ 19 Maryland Ave., ☎ 410/269–1714; 🎫 $4) is the only verified full-scale example of the work of William Buckland, colonial America's most prominent architect. Across the street the grand Georgian **Chase-Lloyd House** (✉ 22 Maryland Ave., ☎ 410/263–2723; 🎫 $2) was built by Samuel Chase, a signer of the Declaration of Independence. The 37-room redbrick 1765 **William Paca House and Gardens** (✉ 186 Prince George St., ☎ 410/263–5553; 🎫 $5 house only; $4 gardens only; $7 house and gardens combined) was built by another signer of the Declaration of Independence and a governor of Maryland. **St. John's College** (✉ 60 College Ave., ☎ 410/263–2371) is the third-oldest college in the country and alma mater of Francis Scott Key, lyricist of *The Star Spangled Banner.*

★ The **Maryland State House** (✉ State Circle, ☎ 410/974–3400; 🎫 free) is the oldest state capitol in continuous legislative use and the only one that has housed the U.S. Congress. Charles Willson Peale's painting *Washington at the Battle of Yorktown* hangs inside. Free 30-minute tours take place seven days a week at 11 and 3.

Southern Maryland

Calvert County has plenty of striking bay-side scenery. One standout sight is the imposing **Calvert Cliffs,** some 100 ft high, and several miles of surrounding beaches famous for the Miocene-period fossils that can be found along the water's edge. To see the cliffs and beaches, stop at **Calvert Cliffs State Park** (✉ Rte. 2/4, Lusby, ☎ 301/872–5688; 🎫 $2). The fossil sites are about a 2-mi walk from the park entrance. For a glimpse of the Eastern Shore on a clear day, try the observation deck at the **Calvert Cliffs Nuclear Power Plant** (☎ 410/495–4600; 🎫 free) next door. The **Battle Creek Cypress Swamp Sanctuary** (✉ Rte. 2/4 to Rte. 506, ☎ 410/535–5327; 🎫 free) is home to the northernmost naturally occurring stand of the ancient bald cypress tree in the United States.

Down at the tip of the peninsula is **Solomons,** a still-tranquil but increasingly fashionable sailing town. At Solomons' **Calvert Marine Museum** (✉ Rte. 2/4 at Solomons Island Rd., ☎ 410/326–2042; 🎫 $5), boats from various epochs and a 19th-century screw-pile lighthouse are on display.

Vintage aircraft are parked outside the **Patuxent River Naval Air Museum** (✉ Rte. 235 and Shangri-la Dr., ☎ 301/863–7418; 🎫 free) in Lexington Park, south of Solomons. Indoors you'll find failed contraptions on display, including the improbable Goodyear Inflatoplane.

Across the Patuxent in St. Mary's County is **Historic St. Mary's City** (✉ Rte. 5, ☎ 301/862–0990 or 800/762–1634; 🎫 $7.50), where the first colonists dispatched by Lord Baltimore under a grant by Charles I settled in 1634. Until 1694 this was the capital of Maryland. Reconstructions of 17th-century buildings and of the supply ship that accompanied the settlers are on view at this less spectacular but more peaceful version of Virginia's Colonial Williamsburg. At the **Godiah Spray Plantation** (✉ Rosecroft Rd., St. Mary's City, ☎ 301/862–0990; 🎫 $7.50) you'll see authentic demonstrations of activities common to 17th-century plantation life, including planting, cooking, and building. The **Sotterley Plantation** (✉ Rte. 235, ☎ 301/373–2280; 🎫 $7.50) is a fine example of Early American architecture, with the earliest known posted-beam structure in the United States: In place of a foundation, cedar timbers have been driven straight into the ground to support the house.

The Eastern Shore

The William Preston Lane Jr. Memorial Bridge links Annapolis to the Eastern Shore, passing along the way through **Kent Island,** the bay's largest island. This is the site of the first English settlement in Maryland: Agents of Virginia's governor set up a trading post here in 1631. Route 50 continues south past historic towns near the bay and then leads east to the Atlantic.

In the town of **Wye Mills,** on Route 662, stands the state tree—the 400-year-old, 95-ft-tall Wye Oak—and a working 17th-century gristmill that once ground grain for Washington's troops at Valley Forge. The affluent town of **Easton** has a 17th-century Quaker meetinghouse and an 18th-century courthouse.

On the Miles River is **St. Michaels** (on Route 33), once a shipbuilding ★ center and now a fashionable yachting destination. The **Chesapeake Bay Maritime Museum** (✉ Navy Point, ☎ 410/745–2916; 🎫 $7.50) traces the history of the bay and its traditions in boatbuilding, commercial fishing, navigation, and waterfowling.

The **Oxford-Bellevue Ferry** has been running since 1683. Today it takes cars and pedestrians across the Tred Avon River from a spot 7 mi south of St. Michaels to the 17th-century town of Oxford. Few of the surviving buildings in **Oxford** date before the mid-1800s, but the bigger (and less charming) town of Cambridge, 15 mi to the southeast, has several from the 1700s. The area is well suited to cycling; many roads have special bike lanes.

Southwest of Cambridge is the **Blackwater National Wildlife Refuge** (✉ 2145 Key Wallace Dr. , ☎ 410/228–2677; 🎫 car $3, pedestrian or cyclist $1), with more than 22,000 acres of marshland, woodlands, and open fields inhabited by Canada geese, ospreys, and bald eagles. Visitors can travel by car, bicycle, or on foot. The Blackwater Refuge is a favorite of serious nature photographers.

On the Atlantic side of the peninsula is **Ocean City,** with 10 mi of white-sand beach and a flashy 27-block boardwalk. The Coastal Highway, with blocks of high-rise condos, runs down the center of town. More than 4 million vacationers flock here every summer. **Trimper's Amusement Park** (✉ Boardwalk and S. 1st St., ☎ 410/289–8617), with a huge roller coaster and other rides, celebrated its centennial in 1990.

Dining and Lodging

Restaurants in Annapolis and less-expensive southern Maryland, though reliable for seafood, do not warrant a special trip. Across the bay are innovative kitchens and classic crab houses. Lodging reservations are necessary up to a year in advance of the Annapolis sailboat and powerboat shows in October, the Naval Academy commencement in May, and Easton's Waterfowl Festival in November. For price ranges *see* Charts 1 (B) and 2 (B) *in* On the Road with Fodor's.

Annapolis

$$$$ ✕ **The Corinthian.** With cushioned armchairs, oil-lamp lighting, and a courtyard view, this hotel restaurant is the most formal in town, with the elegant feel of an old Maryland home. The distinctive crab cakes have an angel hair–pasta binder, and the New York strip has been aged three weeks. ✉ *Loews Annapolis Hotel, 126 West St.,* ☎ *410/263–7777. AE, D, DC, MC, V.*

$$–$$$$ ★ ✕ **McGarvey's Saloon and Oyster Bar.** This casual saloon and restaurant is a popular hangout with locals, tourists, and sailors. The kitchen serves standard American fare—burgers, steaks, seafood, and fun fin-

ger foods. ✉ *8 Market Space, at northeast corner of Market House, ☎ 410/263–5700. AE, MC, V.*

$$–$$$ ★ ✕ **Middleton's Tavern.** This waterfront building has served as a tavern since 1750. Wooden tables bear blue-and-white-check tablecloths at night, and in winter fireplaces blaze in all four dining rooms. In the warmer months three dozen tables out front allow diners to watch the lively stream of pedestrian traffic at City Dock. The chef has perfected his own rich version of crab imperial, called crab Middleton. His Cuban black bean soup is a rare treat. ✉ *2 Market Space, ☎ 410/263–3323. AE, D, MC, V.*

$$$$ **Annapolis Marriott Waterfront.** Amenities such as bathroom phones typify the pastel-and-floral-theme rooms, all of which face the water, the historic district, or—from private balconies—City Dock. Pusser's Landing is a casual restaurant with a Caribbean flair, Jamaican and English fare, and a waterside setting. ✉ *80 Compromise St., 21401, ☎ 410/268–7555, FAX 410/269–5864. 150 rooms. Restaurant. AE, D, DC, MC, V.*

$$–$$$$ **Gibson's Lodgings.** Three detached houses—two of them historic—stand together across the street from the United States Naval Academy. The inn has the character of a bed-and-breakfast; all rooms have brass or wood beds. Free parking in the courtyard is an advantage in the heart of a small city with heavy traffic. Continental breakfast is served in the formal dining room of the 200-year-old Patterson House. ✉ *110–114 Prince George St., 21401, ☎ 410/268–5555, FAX 410/268–2775 (call first). 21 rooms. Dining room. CP. AE, MC, V.*

Calvert County

$$–$$$$ ✕ **CD Café.** Overlooking the Patuxent River and the main road into Solomons, this cozy café describes itself as a coffeehouse with a bistro flair; the menu is limited but inventive. A favorite is the pan-seared chicken breast with pecans, apples, onions, and deglazed schnapps. The homemade desserts are spectacular. ✉ *14350 Solomons Island Rd., Solomons, ☎ 410/326–3877. MC, V. No dinner Mon.*

$$$$ **Back Creek Inn.** Rooms in this 19th-century wood-frame house have brass beds with colorful quilts and views of the water, a garden, or a quiet street. Guests have use of an outdoor hot tub. ✉ *Calvert and Alexander Sts., Solomons 20688, ☎ 410/326–2022. 6 rooms, cottage. AE, MC, V.*

Ocean City

$$–$$$$ ✕ **The Hobbit.** Murals and carved lamps portray J. R. R. Tolkien characters in this dining room with a two-angled view of Assawoman Bay. Veal with pistachios and the sautéed catch of the day stand out on the menu. ✉ *101 81st St., ☎ 410/524–8100. MC, V.*

$$ ✕ **Lombardi's.** Cozy wooden booths and tables and walls decorated with photos provide the setting for thin-crust pizza, cheese steaks, and cold-cut sandwiches. ✉ *9203 Coastal Hwy., ☎ 410/524–1961. Reservations not accepted. MC, V. Closed Wed.*

$$$ ✕ **Hotels at Fager's Island.** Ocean City's most prestigious guest address is actually two hotels linked by walkways over the street. The Lighthouse Club and the Coconut Mallory have rooms with bedside Jacuzzis and balconies overlooking Assawoman Bay; some rooms also have fireplaces. Guests can dine in the hotels' restaurant, which has one of the state's most extensive wine lists. ✉ *201 60th St., Ocean City 21842, ☎ 410/723–6100 or 800/767–6060. 108 suites. Restaurant, pool, exercise room. AE, DC, MC, V.*

St. Mary's County

$$–$$$ ✕ **Evans Seafood.** Ask for a water view, then order lobster stuffed with crab imperial or the spicy hard-shell crab made from a secret recipe.

⊠ *Rte. 249, Piney Point,* ☎ *301/994–2299. MC, V. Closed Mon. No lunch weekdays Apr.–August and Fri.–Sat., Sept.–March.*

$$–$$$ **Potomac View Farm.** Simple oak furniture and quilts fill this 19th-century wood-frame farmhouse. A mile away is an affiliated marina with a restaurant, bar, pool, and beach. ⊠ *Rte. 249, Tall Timbers 20690,* ☎ *301/994–2311. 5 rooms, 1 cottage. Full breakfast. AE, D, MC, V.*

St. Michaels

$$$$ ★ ✕ **208 Talbot.** An antiques-filled late-19th-century house is the setting for regional cuisine. Maryland's rockfish is sautéed with wild mushrooms in an oyster-cream sauce, and fresh bay oysters are served with a champagne-cream sauce, prosciutto, and pistachio nuts. Look for softshell crab in season. ⊠ *208 N. Talbot St.,* ☎ *410/745–3838. D, MC, V.*

$$ ✕ **Crab Claw.** Bang-them-yourself steamed blue crabs are first-rate at this harborside eatery. Spicy deep-fried hard crab is worth a try, too, as is the vegetable crab soup. ⊠ *Navy Point,* ☎ *410/745–2900. No credit cards. Closed Dec.–Feb.*

$$$$ ★ ✕ **Inn at Perry Cabin.** This early 19th-century farmhouse resembles an English country house, with antiques and Laura Ashley in the bedrooms, a cozy library, spectacular gardens, and a formal dining room. Menu standouts are honey-and-tarragon-glazed lamb shank and marinated salmon on wilted arugula with pickled-onion sauce. ⊠ *308 Watkins La., 21663,* ☎ *410/745–2200 or 800/722–2949,* FAX *410/745–3348. 41 rooms. Restaurant, pool. Full breakfast. AE, DC, MC, V.*

$$–$$$ ✕ **Robert Morris Inn.** Conveniently located near the Bellevue-Oxford Ferry terminal, this friendly inn has efficiencies, river cottages, and simple bedrooms—some with bay windows, others with porches. The inn also is known for its excellent food, especially its crab cakes. ⊠ *314 N. Morris St., Box 70, Oxford 21654,* ☎ *410/226–5111,* FAX *410/226–5744. 35 rooms. CP. AE, MC, V. Restaurant closed Jan.–Mar.*

Motels

Dunes Motel (⊠ 2700 Baltimore Ave., Ocean City 21842, ☎ 410/289–4414), 103 rooms, pool; closed Dec.–mid-Feb.; *$$$.* **Holiday Inn Select Conference Center and Marina** (⊠ 155 Holiday Dr., Box 1099, Solomons 20688, ☎ 410/326–6311 or 800/356–2009, FAX 410/326–1069), 326 rooms, restaurant, pool, tennis, exercise room; *$$$.* **Best Western St. Michaels Motor Inn** (⊠ Rte. 33 and Peaneck Rd., St. Michaels 21663, ☎ 410/745–3333, FAX 410/745–2906), 93 rooms, pools; *$$$–$$$$.*

Nightlife and the Arts

Nightlife

Ocean City has plenty of places for dancing to rock—whether live or recorded; there is even an under-21 club, **Night Light** (⊠ Boardwalk at Worcester St., ☎ 410/289–6313), for those too young to drink. Bars in Annapolis, Solomons, and St. Michaels are favored by the more subdued, and usually, middle-aged, crowds.

The Arts

In summer the **U.S. Naval Academy Band** performs at Annapolis's City Dock on Tuesday evenings. **Ocean City** sponsors free boardwalk concerts; call the convention and visitors bureau (☎ 410/289–2800 or 800/626–2326) for schedules. When the **Colonial Players** (⊠ 108 East St., Annapolis, ☎ 410/268–7373) go on vacation the **Annapolis Summer Garden Theater** (⊠ Compromise and Main Sts., ☎ 410/268–0809) takes over.

Outdoor Activities and Sports

Biking

Viewtrail 100 is a 100-mi circuit in Worcester County, between Berlin and Pocomoke City. In **Ocean City** the right-hand lanes of Coastal Highway are for buses and bikes. Several boardwalk shops rent bikes.

Fishing

The principal catches are black drum, channel bass, flounder, bluefish, white perch, weakfish, croaker, trout, and largemouth bass. One-week **licenses** are sold at many sporting-goods stores; one-year licenses are available from the Department of Natural Resources (⊠ Box 1869, Annapolis 21404, ☎ 410/260–8367). Bay **charters** are available through Bunky's Charter Boats (⊠ Solomons Island Rd., Solomons, ☎ 410/326–3241), the Fishing Center (⊠ Shantytown Rd., West Ocean City, ☎ 410/213–1121), and Bahia Marina (⊠ 22nd St. and the bay, Ocean City, ☎ 410/289–7438).

Golf

Eisenhower Golf Course (⊠ Generals Hwy., Crownsville, northwest of Annapolis, ☎ 410/222–7922) and the **Bay Club** (⊠ 9122 Libertytown Rd., Berlin, west of Ocean City, ☎ 410/641–4081) each have 18 holes. **Ocean City Golf and Yacht Club** (⊠ 11401 Country Club Dr., Berlin, ☎ 410/641–1779) has 36 holes.

Sailing

Annapolis Sailing School (⊠ 601 6th St., ☎ 410/267–7205 or 800/638–9192) offers outfitting and instruction. **Schooner Woodwind** (⊠ 80 Compromise St., Annapolis, ☎ 410/263–8619) runs chartered cruises on a 74-ft yacht and rents sailboats. **Sailing, Etc.** (⊠ 46th St., Bayside, Ocean City, ☎ 410/723–1144) has a wide range of sailboats for rent.

Beaches

Southern Maryland beaches are mainly for strolling and looking. Twelve miles east of Annapolis, **Sandy Point State Park** (⊠ Rte. 50, 12 mi east of Annapolis) is a good area for fishing, swimming, or launching boats. There are no Chesapeake Bay beaches of any consequence on the **Eastern Shore.** South of Ocean City, the northern portion of **Assateague Island National Seashore**(☞ National and State Parks, *above*) is pristine.

ELSEWHERE IN MARYLAND

Western Maryland

Visitor Information

Frederick: visitor center (⊠ 19 E. Church St., 21701, ☎ 301/663–8687 or 800/999–3613).

Arriving and Departing

From Baltimore I–70 runs westward through Frederick and up to the state's narrowest point, pinched between West Virginia and Pennsylvania. U.S. 40 passes through the Narrows into the Panhandle. From Hancock, I–68—the new National Highway—is the quickest route to Cumberland, Deep Creek Lake, and several state parks and forests.

What to See and Do

According to legend and poetry, an old woman defied Stonewall Jackson by waving the Stars and Stripes from the **Barbara Fritchie House and Museum** (⊠ 154 W. Patrick St., ☎ 301/698–0630; 🎫 $2), which is closed from January through March.

Monocacy National Battlefield (✉ 4801 Urbana Pike, ☎ 301/662–3515; 🎟 free) was the site of a little-known confrontation between 18,000 Confederates and 5,800 Union troops on July 9, 1864. The Union victory routed a Confederate invasion of Washington, D.C.

Mount Olivet Cemetery (✉ 515 S. Market St., ☎ 301/662–1164; 🎟 free) is the final resting place of some of Maryland's most famous citizens, including Barbara Fritchie and Francis Scott Key, author of the "Star-Spangled Banner."

The **National Museum of Civil War Medicine** (✉ 48 E. Patrick St., ☎ 301/695–1864; 🎟 $2.50) is a repository of more than 3,000 medical artifacts, including the only known surviving Civil War surgeon's tent. The museum, still being developed, also is the starting point for a walking tour of Frederick's Civil War history during spring, summer, and fall.

★ Near Sharpsburg is **Antietam National Battlefield** (✉ Rte. 65, ☎ 301/432–5124; 🎟 $2), where Union troops repelled Lee's invasion in 1862. This day of fighting was the bloodiest confrontation of the Civil War, fought on a road now known as Bloody Lane. **Hagerstown** (✉ Hagerstown/Washington County Convention and Visitors Bureau, 16 Public Sq., Hagerstown, 21740, ☎ 301/791–3130) was a frontier town founded by Germans in the early 18th century; several buildings from that period have been preserved, including the frontier home-fortress of Jonathan Hager, the town's founder.

The rolling, pastoral farmland west of Hagerstown gives way to rugged stretches of mountains—a landscape reminiscent of the more famous Blue Ridge chain to the south. In **Allegany County** (✉ Visitors Center, Western Maryland Station, Cumberland 21502, ☎ 301/777–5905), the rugged Narrows provides an opening for U.S. 40, formerly called the National Road and taken by westward-bound settlers in the early years of the republic. This is one of western Maryland's most outdoorsy areas. **Garrett County** (✉ Promotion Council, 200 S. 3rd St., Oakland 21550, ☎ 301/334–1948) draws outdoors enthusiasts of all stripes, including skiers.

Dining and Lodging

For price ranges *see* Charts 1 (B) and 2 (B) *in* On the Road with Fodor's.

$$$ ✕ **Brown Pelican.** Pelicans are an unusual theme for a restaurant an hour or so from Chesapeake Bay, but this dark, romantic rathskeller, with tablecloths and candlelight, has one of the finest menus in Frederick. Specialties are veal, seafood, and beef. ✉ *5 E. Church St., Frederick,* ☎ *301/695–5833. AE, D, DC, MC, V.*

$$$$ ★ ✕🏨 **Stone Manor.** Secluded among rolling farmland outside Frederick, this 18th-century majestic stone home with 10 working fireplaces is an elegant retreat and still part of a 114-acre working farm. Diners choose from a chef-selected five-course or four-course menu; featured dishes include wild game and fowl, seafood, and beef. Brunch is served Tuesday through Saturday. ✉ *5820 Carroll Boyer Rd., Middletown 21769,* ☎ *301/473–5454. 6 suites. Full breakfast. AE, D, MC, V.*

$$$–$$$$ ✕🏨 **Turning Point Inn.** This Edwardian-era home was once the residence of a prominent doctor. Today it's a country-style inn that will make you feel right at home with extras such as a bowl of fresh fruit in your room. Highlights on the menu, overseen by Chef William Erlenbach, include grilled pork chops and rack of lamb, prepared with local produce and herbs. ✉ *8406 Urbana Pike, Frederick 21701,* ☎ *301/874–2421. 5 rooms, 2 guest houses. Restaurant. D, DC, MC, V. No lunch Mon. and Sat.*

NEW JERSEY

Updated by Jill Sue Schensul

Capital	Trenton
Population	8,053,000
Motto	Liberty and Prosperity
State Bird	Eastern goldfinch
State Flower	Purple violet
Postal Abbreviation	NJ

Statewide Visitor Information

New Jersey Department of Commerce and Economic Development (✉ Division of Travel and Tourism, Box 826, Trenton 08625-0826, ☎ 609/292–2470 or 800/537–7397, FAX 609/633–7418). There are seven visitor information centers at major destinations around the state. For information on state parks contact the **Department of Environmental Protection, Division of Parks and Forestry** (✉ Box 404, Trenton 08625, ☎ 609/292–2797 or 800/843–6420).

Scenic Drives

For Hudson River views take the **Palisades Interstate Parkway** north from the George Washington Bridge to the state line or take **River Road** from Weehawken north to Fort Lee. Both **Route 23,** northwest from Newfoundland through High Point State Park, and **Route 15,** northwest from I–80, gives you glimpses of lakes, rural estates, and higher-elevation vistas. The back roads off **Routes 202** and **206** in central New Jersey pass by horse farms, antiques shops, and historic sites. Along the southern shore, **Ocean Drive** is a causeway that links barrier islands.

National and State Parks

National Parks

Sandy Hook Unit of Gateway National Recreation Area (✉ Box 530, Highlands 07732, ☎ 732/872–0115) preserves sandbar ecology and fortifications built to protect New York Harbor. On the Delaware River boundary between New Jersey and Pennsylvania is the **Delaware Water Gap National Recreation Area** (✉ Visitor Center, Kittatinny Point, off I–80; Bushkill, PA 18324, ☎ 908/496–4458 or 717/588–2451), the largest national recreation area in the Northeast. The 40,000-acre **Edwin B. Forsythe National Wildlife Refuge's Brigantine Division** (✉ Box 72, Great Creek Rd., Oceanville 08231, ☎ 609/652–1665) has an 8-mi wildlife drive, mainly through diverse coastal habitat, and two short, circular nature trails that are especially worthwhile during spring and fall bird migrations.

State Parks

New Jersey has the third-largest state park system in the nation, with 36 parks, 11 forests, 4 recreation areas, 42 natural areas, 23 historic sites, 4 marinas, and 1 golf course. **Wharton State Forest** (✉ Rte. 542, Hammonton 08037, ☎ 609/561–3262), New Jersey's largest, contains the Batsto State Historic Site (✉ Rte. 542), a restored late 18th- and 19th-century Pinelands ironworking village, where traditional crafts are still demonstrated. **High Point State Park** is named after the state's tallest peak. Many of New Jersey's 19 **lighthouses** are preserved in state parks, including Barnegat Lighthouse, Cape May Point Lighthouse, and Sandy Hook Lighthouse (☞ Exploring the Jersey Shore, *below*).

THE JERSEY SHORE

The Jersey Shore is 127 mi of public beachfront stretching like a pointing finger along the Atlantic Ocean from the Sandy Hook Peninsula in the north to Cape May at the southern tip. There is no one description of what it's like "down the shore." Things change town by town and sometimes season by season—winter storms have a habit of rearranging beaches and boardwalks. Activities along the shore include saltwater fishing from pier, bridge, dock, or boat (licenses not required); all kinds of water sports; bird-, whale-, and dolphin-watching; and bicycling or strolling on the ubiquitous wood-plank or concrete boardwalks. In Atlantic City are the famed gambling casinos; in Cape May, Victorian bed-and-breakfasts; and in between—in Seaside Heights, Point Pleasant, and Wildwood—quintessential seaside amusements.

Visitor Information

Atlantic City: Convention & Visitors Authority (✉ 2314 Pacific Ave., 08401, ☎ 609/348–7100 or 800/262–7395, FAX 609/347–6577). **Cape May:** Chamber of Commerce of Greater Cape May (✉ 609 Lafayette St., Box 556, 08204, ☎ 609/884–5508); Mid-Atlantic Center for the Arts (✉ Box 340, 08204, ☎ 609/884–5404). **Cape May County:** Chamber of Commerce (✉ Box 74, Cape May Court House 08210, ☎ 609/465–7181, FAX 609/465–5017); Department of Tourism and Economic Development (✉ Box 365, Cape May Court House 08210, ☎ 609/886–0901). **Monmouth County:** Department of Promotion and Tourism (✉ 25 E. Main St., Freehold 07728, ☎ 732/431–7476 or 800/523–2587, FAX 908/732–3696). **Ocean County:** Tourism Advisory Council (✉ Box 2191, Toms River 08754, ☎ 732/929–2138 or 800/365–6933, FAX 732/506–5000). **Wildwoods:** Information Center (✉ Box 609, Wildwood 08260, ☎ 609/522–1407 or 800/992–9732).

Arriving and Departing

By Bus

New Jersey Transit (☞ By Train, *below*) provides bus service to most Jersey Shore towns. **Academy Lines** (☎ 732/291–1300) also runs buses between New York City and shore points. **Greyhound Lines** (☎ 609/345–6617 or 800/231–2222) serves Atlantic City. Ask Atlantic City casino hotels about direct service to their properties.

By Car

The main road serving the Jersey Shore is the Garden State Parkway, a north–south toll road that ends in Cape May. From New York City I–80 and the New Jersey Turnpike (toll) connect with the Garden State. From Philadelphia and southern New Jersey suburbs, take the Atlantic City Expressway (toll). From the south take the Delaware Memorial Bridge and continue north on the New Jersey Turnpike. Toms River, Barnegat, and Tuckerton are linked by U.S. 9.

By Ferry

The **Cape May–Lewes Ferry** is a year-round 70-minute car ferry (800 passengers, 100 cars per ferry) across the Delaware Bay(☞ Delaware). *☎ 609/886–1725 or 800/643–3779, 800/717–7245 for reservations.*

By Plane

Philadelphia International (☞ Pennsylvania) **Newark International** (☎ 973/961–6000), and the **New York City airports**(☞ New York) are closest to Atlantic City and shore points. **Atlantic City International** (☎ 609/645–7895 or 888/235–9229) serves the southern shore.

By Train

Amtrak (✉ 1 Atlantic City Expressway, near Kirkman Blvd., ☎ 800/872–7245) serves Atlantic City. **New Jersey Transit** (☎ 973/762–5100 for northern NJ or 800/772–2222 in NJ; 215/569–3752 for southern NJ or 800/582–5946 in NJ) operates local commuter service to Atlantic City from Philadelphia and to the shore towns in Monmouth and Ocean counties from New York City.

Exploring the Jersey Shore

The **New Jersey Coastal Heritage Trail** (☎ 609/447–0103), under joint development by the National Park Service, the state of New Jersey, and other organizations, connects significant natural and cultural resources along the shore. A network of routes (primarily vehicular) stretches from Perth Amboy south along the Atlantic coast to Cape May and then north along the Delaware Bay coast to the Delaware Memorial Bridge in Deepwater. Five theme routes—historic settlements, relaxation and inspiration, wildlife migration, maritime history, and coastal habitats—highlight particular areas and communities.

At the shore's north end the **Sandy Hook Lighthouse,** the oldest continuously operating lighthouse in the country (built in 1764), stands in the **Sandy Hook Unit of Gateway National Recreation Area** (☞ National Parks, *above*), 4 mi east of Atlantic Highlands on Route 36. On this peninsula of barrier beach you can splash in the usually gentle, shallow surf; explore sleepy **Fort Hancock,** established in 1895; and glimpse the New York City skyline, 19 mi across the harbor from North Beach.

Just south on Route 36, **Long Branch** was founded in the 18th century as one of America's first resorts; over the years it has hosted seven presidents, from Grant to Wilson.

A century ago **Asbury Park** was the shore's toniest resort, but efforts to revive that glory have so far been disappointing. Nowadays it is known for its place in rock history; the young Bruce Springsteen performed here in the 1960s. By contrast, neighboring **Ocean Grove** was established in 1859 by Methodists as a camp meeting area and still retains that purpose. The dignified tone is echoed in its Victorian hotels and inns; relatively quiet beaches; a short, gameless boardwalk; and shops and cafés. Ocean Grove is also one of two shore towns that do not sell alcohol—the other is **Ocean City,** another Methodist town patterned after it. The imposing **Great Auditorium** (✉ Pilgrim Pathway, ☎ 732/775–0035 or 800/388–4768) presents a summer schedule of concerts—everything from big bands to country and jazz, with some '50s and '60s oldies to boot.

In **Belmar** the **Municipal Marina** (✉ Rte. 35, ☎ 732/681–2266), on the Shark River, has party and charter boats that head for the ocean daily in search of blackfish, blues, fluke, tuna, and shark. Neighboring **Spring Lake** has an uncommercialized boardwalk, three spring-fed lakes with swans, a small town center, and a handful of romantic B&Bs. At the family-oriented **Point Pleasant Beach, Jenkinson's Aquarium** (✉ Ocean Ave., ☎ 732/899–1659; 🎟 $6.50), on the boardwalk at the Broadway Beach area, is a nice rainy-day diversion.

★ **Six Flags Great Adventure,** inland from Spring Lake, comprises both an amusement park with a multitude of rides and a drive-through safari park. ✉ *Rte. 537, I–195 Exit 16, Jackson,* ☎ *732/928–2000 or 732/928–1821 for recording.* 🎟 *$35; safari only $15; safari–theme park combination $38.02. Closed late Oct.–mid-Apr.*

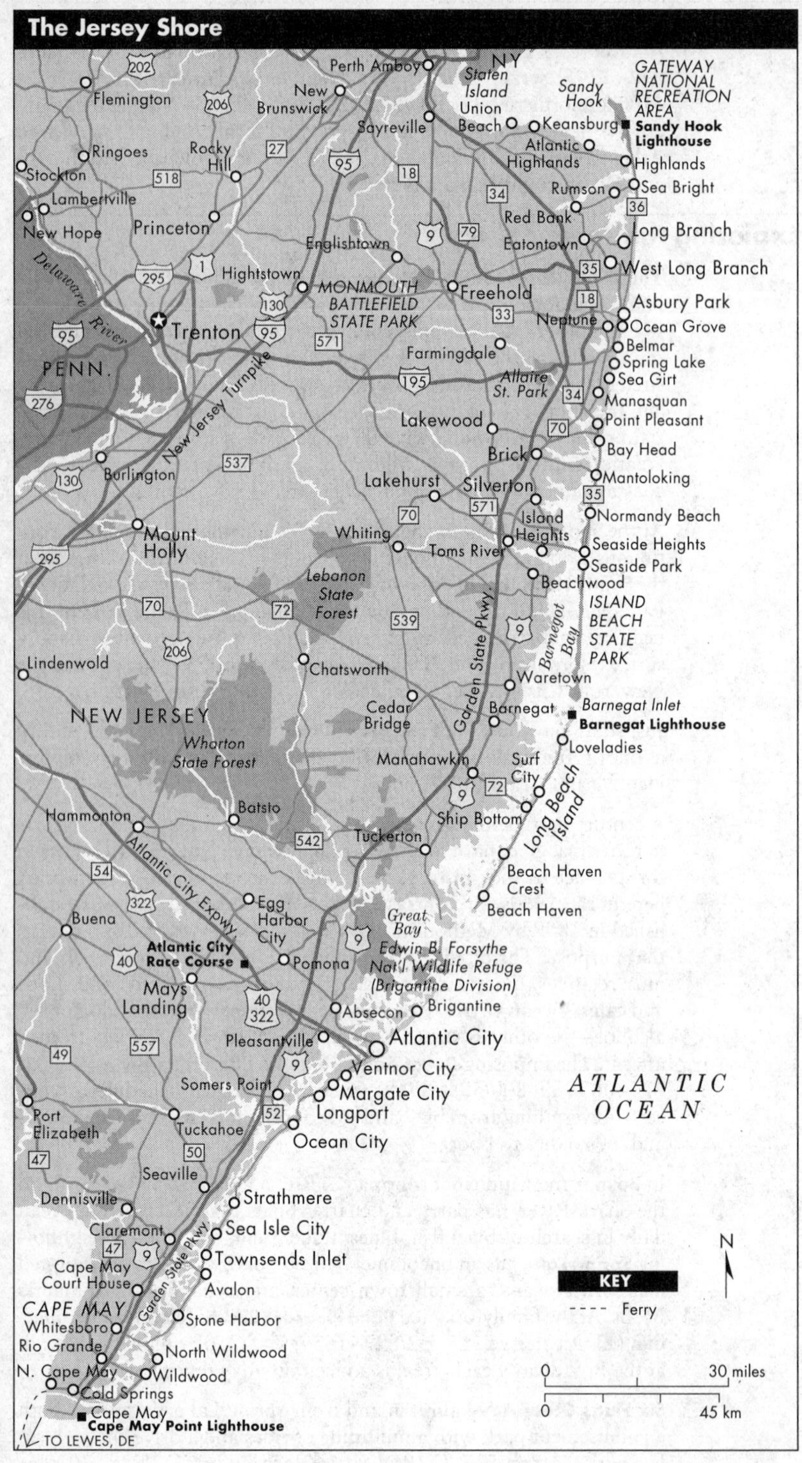
The Jersey Shore
Perth Amboy
NY
Staten Island
Union Beach
Keansburg
Sandy Hook
GATEWAY NATIONAL RECREATION AREA
Sandy Hook Lighthouse
Atlantic Highlands
Highlands
Sea Bright
Rumson
Red Bank
Long Branch
Eatontown
West Long Branch
Asbury Park
Ocean Grove
Neptune
Belmar
Spring Lake
Sea Girt
Manasquan
Point Pleasant
Bay Head
Mantoloking
Normandy Beach
Seaside Heights
Seaside Park
Beachwood
ISLAND BEACH STATE PARK
Barnegat Bay
Waretown
Barnegat Inlet
Barnegat Lighthouse
Barnegat
Loveladies
Surf City
Ship Bottom
Long Beach Island
Beach Haven Crest
Beach Haven
Flemington
New Brunswick
Sayreville
Ringoes
Rocky Hill
Stockton
Lambertville
New Hope
Princeton
Englishtown
Hightstown
MONMOUTH BATTLEFIELD STATE PARK
Freehold
Delaware River
Trenton
PENN.
New Jersey Turnpike
Farmingdale
Allaire St. Park
Lakewood
Brick
Burlington
Lakehurst
Silverton
Island Heights
Whiting
Toms River
Mount Holly
Lebanon State Forest
Garden State Pkwy.
Lindenwold
Chatsworth
NEW JERSEY
Cedar Bridge
Whorton State Forest
Manahawkin
Hammonton
Batsto
Tuckerton
Atlantic City Expwy.
Egg Harbor City
Great Bay
Edwin B. Forsythe Nat'l Wildlife Refuge (Brigantine Division)
Buena
Atlantic City Race Course
Pomona
Mays Landing
Absecon
Brigantine
Pleasantville
Atlantic City
Ventnor City
Margate City
Longport
Somers Point
Ocean City
ATLANTIC OCEAN
Port Elizabeth
Tuckahoe
Seaville
Strathmere
Dennisville
Claremont
Sea Isle City
Townsends Inlet
Cape May Court House
Avalon
CAPE MAY
Whitesboro
Stone Harbor
Rio Grande
North Wildwood
N. Cape May
Wildwood
Cold Springs
Cape May
Cape May Point Lighthouse
TO LEWES, DE
KEY
Ferry
N
0
30 miles
0
45 km
202
206
27
95
18
518
34
79
9
1
295
130
36
35
33
571
195
276
537
70
72
539
206
542
54
322
40
557
49
52
50
47

On Barnegat Peninsula, the side-by-side resorts of **Seaside Heights** and **Seaside Park** have two major amusement piers plus water rides. Don't miss a turn on the antique Dentzel-Looff carousel. Just south but seemingly a world away is narrow **Island Beach State Park** (☎ 732/793–0506; Labor Day–Memorial Day: $4; Memorial Day–Labor Day: $6 weekdays, $7 weekends), 10 mi of ocean and bay beaches with almost no evidence of human habitation.

Return inland over Barnegat Bay to Toms River, once a pirate and privateering port, and today the center of a booming region of retirement communities. The **Ocean County Museum** (✉ 26 Hadley Ave., ☎ 732/341–1880; donations accepted) contains Victorian artifacts and exhibits on the dirigibles that flew from the Lakehurst Naval Air Station, site of the 1937 *Hindenburg* tragedy.

Head south on U.S. 9 and east on Route 72 over Barnegat Bay to **Long Beach Island. Barnegat Lighthouse** (☎ 609/494–2016), known locally as Old Barney and completed in 1858, is at the northern tip of the island. To the south is **Beach Haven,** the island's commercial center, with Victorian houses set around the town square. In one of these houses you'll find the **Long Beach Island Museum** (✉ Engleside and Beach Aves., ☎ 609/492–0700), which conducts walking tours of the historic district from late June to early September.

Back on the mainland, the Garden State Parkway and U.S. 9 lead to **Atlantic City,** the east coast's gambling capital (bettors drop about $8 million daily). Monopoly fans will find the streets that made the board game famous, including the **Boardwalk,** the nation's first elevated wood walkway (1870), where saltwater taffy is still sold. The resort's earlier 19th-century stone hotels have been replaced by 13 **casino** hotels—outrageous in design and entertainment, from the Mardi Gras festivity of the Showboat to the onion-shape domes of the Taj Mahal. Be alert outside at night—the city has a high crime rate.

Some of Atlantic City's famous ocean **amusement piers** can still be seen, but only the **Central Pier** (✉ St. James Pl. and Tennessee Ave.), on the boardwalk, retains its original 1884 appearance. The **Garden Pier** (✉ New Jersey Ave. and the Boardwalk) has been converted to an art center. **The Steel Pier** is now an amusement pier and arcade; Donald Trump, who owns the pier (part of the Taj Mahal casino), plans to convert it into a retail, casino, and entertainment complex. The annual **Miss America Pageant** (☎ 609/345–7571) has moved its headquarters to the new, $268-million **Convention Center**, but the pageant itself will remain at the old boardwalk convention hall (✉ 2301 Boardwalk, ☎ 609/348–7100), which is slated for a major renovation. The new convention center, which opened in May 1997, has Miss America–related memorabilia, as well as a theme lounge.

In Margate **Lucy the Elephant** (✉ Atlantic and Decatur Aves., ☎ 609/823–6473; $3), an elephant-shape building six stories high and a National Historic Landmark, has been drawing the curious of all ages since 1881. It is closed from November through March.

Farther south is **Ocean City,** across Great Egg Harbor. Its **boardwalk** and boardwalk parades are family oriented, and summer-evening concerts at the **Music Pier** (✉ Moorlyn Terr.) are a tradition.

Strathmere Beach is a great place for a quiet walk. Take time out to explore the **Wetlands Institute** (☎ 609/368–1211; $5), in Stone Harbor, a research and education center on coastal ecology; the institute is closed Sunday and Monday between October 15 and May 15. The

Wings 'n Water Festival is held here and in neighboring towns the third weekend of September.

Ocean Drive leads to the little boroughs known as the **Wildwoods.** The best known, loudest, kitschiest, and wildest is **Wildwood** itself. Its 2-mi **boardwalk** has the greatest concentration of outdoor amusement rides on the shore, including seven amusement piers.

★ At the southern tip of the shore, the re-created world of Victorian **Cape May** offers a dramatic change of pace and scenery. The state's oldest ocean resort, it was named for the Dutch captain, Mey, who sighted it in 1620. Cape May today has plenty of bed-and-breakfasts, many in elaborate gingerbread–style Victorian houses. **Victorian Week** (☞ Festivals and Seasonal Events in the Mid-Atlantic introduction) combines madcap frivolity with house tours, dinners, and lectures (make reservations well in advance). The July 4 celebration is vintage Americana, while Christmastime has Dickensian flair, with trolley, candlelight, and walking tours of houses decorated in traditional Victorian finery.

The Cape May area also attracts flocks of birds and bird-watchers, especially during the spring and fall migrations. A favorite birding locale is **Cape May Point State Park** (⊠ Lighthouse Ave., ☎ 609/884–2159), site of the **Cape May Point Lighthouse** (☎ 609/884–5404 or 800/275–4278), built in 1859, which marks the end of the Jersey Shore. Another popular activity is whale-watching; several boats ply the Atlantic spring through fall, often coming upon pods of dolphins as well as whales. Not far from the lighthouse, **Sunset Beach** (⊠ Sunset Blvd., Cape May Point) is the place to collect "Cape May diamonds," pebbles of pure quartz that wash up on the beach; and to watch the sun set over Delaware Bay.

Dining and Lodging

Although the restaurant fare ranges from cheap snacks to pricey haute cuisine, seafood is the Jersey Shore's biggest deal, with local catches featured on most menus. Ocean City and Ocean Grove do not allow the sale of liquor. For price ranges *see* Chart 1(A) *in* On the Road with Fodor's.

Lodgings should be booked far in advance in summer. Beachfront rooms are more expensive. Rooms in Atlantic City casino hotels are the most popular, the most costly, and the most difficult to reserve, especially on weekends from mid-June to Labor Day. Chambers of commerce (☞ Visitor Information, *above*) can provide assistance.

Bed & Breakfast Adventures (⊠ 2310 Central Ave., Suite 132, North Wildwood 08260, ☎ 609/522–4000 or 800/992–2632, FAX 609/522–6125) handles inns and private homes statewide. Also try the **Bed & Breakfast Innkeepers Association of New Jersey** (☎ 732/449–3535). For price ranges *see* Chart 2(A) *in* On the Road with Fodor's.

Atlantic City

$$$–$$$$ ★ ✕ **Le Palais.** Favorites such as shellfish-vegetable mélange Olga, rack of lamb with rosemary and pine nuts, and individual dessert soufflés (order these at the start of the meal) are elegantly served in this lavish mirrored dining room hung with art. ⊠ *Merv Griffin's Resorts Casino Hotel, N. Carolina Ave. and Boardwalk,* ☎ *609/344–6000 or 800/438–7424. AE, D, DC, MC, V. Closed Mon.–Tues.*

$$–$$$ ✕ **Dock's Oyster House.** Owned and operated by the Dougherty family since 1897, the city's oldest restaurant serves seafood in a setting of wood and stained glass engraved with nautical scenes. ⊠ *2405 Atlantic Ave.,* ☎ *609/345–0092. AE, DC, MC, V. Closed Dec.–Feb.*

$$ ★ ✕ **Angelo's Fairmount Tavern.** Locals flock here for lots of good Italian fare served up by the Mancuso family, the owners since 1935. ✉ *2300 Fairmount Ave.,* ☎ *609/344–2439. AE, MC, V.*

$–$$ ✕ **Los Amigos.** South-of-the-border specialties such as Mexican pizza, burritos, and margaritas, served in the dimly lighted back room, are a good bet at this small bar and restaurant two blocks from the boardwalk casinos. ✉ *1926 Atlantic Ave.,* ☎ *609/344–2293. AE, DC, MC, V.*

$ ✕ **White House Sub Shop.** It claims to have sold more than 17 million overstuffed sandwiches since 1946. Apparently, celebrities love them, as witnessed by the photos on the walls. ✉ *Mississippi and Arctic Aves.,* ☎ *609/345–1564 or 609/345–8599. Reservations not accepted. No credit cards.*

$$$–$$$$ ★ **Bally's Park Place Casino Hotel & Tower.** Guests can stay in the art deco–style rooms of the historic Dennis Hotel, built in 1860, or in the newer 37-story tower, whose spacious, angular rooms have picture windows even in the marble-tile bathrooms. The spa facilities are exceptional. ✉ *Park Pl. at Boardwalk, 08401,* ☎ *609/340–2000 or 800/225–5977,* FAX *609/340–4713. 1,268 rooms. 8 restaurants, pool, exercise room. AE, D, DC, MC, V.*

$$$ **Sheraton Atlantic City Convention Center Hotel.** The new art deco–style, 15-story hotel, connected to the convention center by an enclosed walkway, showcases Miss America Pageant memorabilia in outside display windows. Inside, a grand circular staircase leads to the Miss America–theme Shoe Bar, restaurant, and meeting rooms. There are coffeemakers and Starbucks coffee in every room. *(✉ 2000 Kirkman Blvd., 08401,* ☎ *609/344–3535 or 800/325–3535,* FAX *609/348–4336. 502 rooms. 2 restaurants, tennis, health club. AE, D, MC, V.*

$$–$$$ ★ **Quality Inn Atlantic City.** A half block from the boardwalk, one of Atlantic City's best values has a 17-story modern guest wing set atop a Federal-style base. Rooms are outfitted with handsome Colonial reproductions. Merv Griffin's casino is next door. ✉ *S. Carolina and Pacific Aves., 08401,* ☎ *609/345–7070 or 800/356–6044,* FAX *609/345–0633. 203 rooms. Restaurant. AE, D, DC, MC, V.*

$$–$$$ **Trump Marina Hotel Casino.** Blandly modern on the outside, this bayside marina is away from some of the boardwalk glitz. Service is first-rate. ✉ *Huron Ave. and Brigantine Blvd., 08401,* ☎ *609/441–2000 or 800/777–8477,* FAX *609/345–7604. 728 rooms. 8 restaurants, pool, tennis, health club. AE, D, DC, MC, V.*

$ **Flagship Resort.** This pleasant, modern, salmon-color condo hotel is across from the boardwalk (facing Brigantine and the Absecon Inlet), away from the casino action. Every room has a private terrace with a view. ✉ *60 N. Main Ave., 08401,* ☎ *609/343–7447 or 800/647–7890,* FAX *609/343–1608. 300 suites. Restaurant, pool, health club. AE, D, DC, MC, V.*

Cape May

$$$–$$$$ ✕ **Mad Batter.** Eclectic contemporary American cuisine is served in the skylighted Victorian dining room or outside on the porch or the garden terrace. Breakfasts are particularly imaginative and elaborate, albeit pricey. Try the orange-and-almond French toast with strawberry dipping sauce. At lunch the menu might include house-smoked maple chicken on a bed of mesclun greens and, at dinner, crab *mappatello* (crabmeat, spinach, ricotta, and onions in a puff pastry). Upstairs is Carroll Villa, a 22-room B&B. ✉ *19 Jackson St.,* ☎ *609/884–5970. AE, MC, V. Closed Jan.*

$$$–$$$$ **Captain Mey's Inn.** A wraparound veranda and a small, walled courtyard and tulip garden bring charm to this 1890 house close to the Washington Mall and the beach. The Victorian antiques include a

collection of delft china. ✉ *202 Ocean St., 08204,* ☎ *609/884–7793 or 609/884–9637. 8 rooms. Full breakfast. AE, MC, V. Closed Jan.*

$$$–$$$$ **Queen Victoria B & B** and the **Queen's Hotel.** In the center of the historic district, three restored Victorian houses (two devoted to the B&B, the other to the hotel) pay homage to the queen and the period named for her. Rooms, though full of antiques, also have modern touches, including mini-refrigerators, some whirlpool baths, and TVs in the suites. ✉ *102 Ocean St.(B&B), 601 Columbia Ave. (hotel), 08204,* ☎ *609/884–8702 and 609/884–1613 (hotel). 21 rooms (B&B), 11 rooms (hotel). CP (B&B only). AE, MC, V.*

$$$–$$$$ **The Virginia Hotel.** With turndown and room service, a morning newspaper, and privileges at local golf clubs, the Virginia is a full-service hotel on an intimate scale. Rooms, which vary in size, have cherry and poplar furnishings with Victorian lines. Grilled seafood and meats and rich desserts are served at the Ebbit Room Restaurant. ✉ *25 Jackson St., 08204,* ☎ *609/884–5700 or 800/732–4236,* FAX *609/884–1236. 24 rooms. Restaurant. CP. AE, D, DC, MC, V.*

$$$ ★ **The Mainstay Inn.** This 1872 men's gambling club reincarnated as a B&B captures the feel of another era with 14-ft ceilings, stenciling and historic wallpapers, and harmoniously arranged antiques. Across the street is a suites-only sister property in another restored building. ✉ *635 Columbia Ave., 08204,* ☎ *609/884–8690. 16 rooms. CP and full breakfast, depending on season and building. No credit cards.*

$$–$$$ **Chalfonte.** Despite simple original furnishings, this authentic Victorian summer hotel attracts a loyal blue-blooded following. Special programs include evening entertainment; work weeks, during which students and other volunteers stay free at the hotel in return for help in upkeep; and a supervised children's dining room, where youngsters eat from a special menu while parents dine on the famous, mostly southern, home-style cooking. ✉ *301 Howard St., 08204,* ☎ *609/884–8409,* FAX *609/884–4588. 78 rooms, 2 cottages. Restaurant. MAP. MC, V. Closed Columbus Day–Memorial Day weekend.*

$$–$$$ **Manor House.** On a quiet, tree-lined street two blocks from the beach, this 1905 guest house mixes antiques, stained glass, art, and dashes of whimsy such as an old-fashioned barber's chair. Innkeepers Tom and Nancy McDonald prepare the four-course breakfasts from scratch. ✉ *612 Hughes St., 08204,* ☎ *609/884–4710. 10 rooms. Full breakfast. D, MC, V. Closed Jan.*

Spring Lake

$$$–$$$$ **Normandy Inn.** This huge 1888 Italianate mansion has been a guest house since 1909. Owners Michael and Susan Ingino have filled it with museum-quality American Victorian antiques. The Tower Room, with windows on four sides, has views to the ocean, which is a two-minute walk away. ✉ *21 Tuttle Ave., 07762,* ☎ *732/449–7172,* FAX *732/449–1070. 19 rooms. Full breakfast. AE, D, DC, MC, V.*

$$$–$$$$ **Seacrest by the Sea.** This 1885 Queen Anne Victorian is one of many in town. Eight rooms have gas-log fireplaces, and seven have ocean views; all have feather beds and luxurious fabrics. Buttermilk scones are a breakfast standard; there's also daily afternoon tea. ✉ *19 Tuttle Ave., 07762,* ☎ *732/449–9031 or 800/803–9031,* FAX *732/974–0403. 12 rooms. Full breakfast. AE, MC, V.*

$$–$$$ **Hollycroft.** Looking over Lake Como at the northern edge of town, Hollycroft is a mountain-style lodge, only it's by the shore. A 16-ft ironstone fireplace, walls of knotty pine, and stencilled walls in guest rooms make it a charming getaway. ✉ *North Blvd. (Box 448), 07762,* ☎ *732/681–2254. 8 rooms. Full breakfast. AE.*

Toms River

$$–$$$ ✕ **Old Time Tavern.** Italian dishes, steak, seafood, and sandwiches are the lures at this restaurant and tap room, and if you're an early bird, you can get soup-to-dessert meals at bargain prices. ✉ *N. Main St., Rte. 166 off Rte. 37,* ☎ *732/349–8778. AE, DC, MC, V.*

Motels

Ascot Motel (✉ Iowa and Pacific Aves., Box 1824, Atlantic City 08404, ☎ 609/344–5163 or 800/225–1476), 80 rooms, pool; *$$*. **Best Western Bayside Resort at Golf & Tennis World** (✉ 8029 Black Horse Pike, W. Atlantic City 08232, ☎ 609/641–3546 or 800/999–9466, FAX 609/641–4329), 110 rooms, restaurant, pools, tennis, health club; *$$*. **Midtown–Bala Motor Inn** (✉ Indiana and Pacific Aves., Atlantic City 08401, ☎ 609/348–3031 or 800/932–0534, FAX 609/347–6043), 300 rooms, restaurant, pools; *$$*. **Sandpiper** (✉ Boulevard at 10th St., Ship Bottom 08008, ☎ 609/494–6909), 20 rooms, pool; closed Nov.–Apr.; *$–$$*.

Nightlife and the Arts

PNC Bank Arts Center (✉ Garden State Pkwy., Exit 116, Holmdel, ☎ 732/335–0400) has a summer roster of performing arts groups, star acts, and ethnic festivals. Between the gambling action and the nationally famous nightclub acts, nightlife is fierce at the **Atlantic City casino hotels**; call the casino box offices for show reservations.

Outdoor Activities and Sports

Biking

Boardwalks are grand for biking if you don't mind dodging weekend walkers and joggers. The road around **Cape May Point** takes you past Cape May Point State Park and its lighthouse.

Canoeing

Try the many freshwater creeks, streams, and tributaries in the 1.1-million-acre **Pinelands National Reserve** (☎ 609/894–9342), the country's first national reserve, near Chatsworth.

Fishing

Monmouth County has more charter and party boats than any other area along the shore; most popular is the **Belmar Marina** (☞ Exploring the Jersey Shore, *above*). In Ocean County numerous party and charter boats sail from Point Pleasant and Long Beach Island. Fishing boats sail from state marinas in **Leonardo** (☎ 732/291–1333) and **Atlantic City** (☎ 609/441–8482).

Spectator Sports

Horse Racing: Before Atlantic City began staging big-name boxing events, horse racing was the shore's most popular spectator sport. **Monmouth Park Racetrack** (✉ Rte. 36 and Oceanport Ave., Oceanport, ☎ 732/222–5100) is the area's best-known track, with Thoroughbred races from Memorial Day through Labor Day. The **Atlantic City Racetrack** (✉ 4501 Black Horse Pike, Mays Landing, ☎ 609/641–2190) has Thoroughbred racing from June through mid-August and simulcasting year-round. There's harness racing at **Freehold Raceway** (✉ U.S. 9 and Rte. 33, Freehold, ☎ 732/462–3800) from mid-August through May.

Beaches

From Memorial Day to Labor Day the **Water Information Hotline** (☎ 800/648–7263) supplies information about the shore's water quality and beach conditions. ★ **Island Beach State Park** (☞ Exploring the Jersey Shore, *above*) is the most scenic natural beach on the Jersey Shore. Beaches usually charge a fee from Memorial Day or mid-June to Labor Day. Windsurfing is especially good in the calm waters of the open bays. Sailing, rowing, and powerboating are superb on sheltered Barnegat Bay in Ocean County.

Shopping

The **Englishtown Auction** (✉ 90 Wilson Ave., ☎ 732/446–9644), a giant flea market held on weekends between March and January plus selected holidays, covers 50 acres. Arrive at sunrise for the best buys.

ELSEWHERE IN NEW JERSEY

The Northwest Corner

Arriving and Departing

There's easy access from northwestern New Jersey to Manhattan via I–80 and Routes 23 and 15.

What to See and Do

This sparsely developed region of small lakes and low mountains attracts skiers in winter, while the rest of the year brings outdoorsy types who come to enjoy water sports on the Delaware River and Lake Hopatcong, scenic roads, hikes on the Appalachian Trail, and historical sites from the 1700s and 1800s.

The state's highest elevation (1,803 ft) is in **High Point State Park** (☞ State Parks, *above*), 7 mi northwest of Sussex. Hugging the river from ★ I–80 to the northern tip of the state is the **Delaware Water Gap National Recreation Area** (☞ National Parks, *above*). **Waterloo Village** (✉ Waterloo Rd., Stanhope, ☎ 973/347–0900) is a restored Revolutionary War–era canal town. Staff members in period costume greet visitors and demonstrate traditional crafts. Children's activities, such as face painting and storytelling, are ongoing. Its summer concert series attracts renowned jazz, classical, rock, and country performers.

The most popular ski areas, clustered around the nondescript town of **McAfee,** are outfitted with artificial snowmaking equipment, have both day and evening skiing, are family oriented, and provide a mix of all-ability ski terrain. **Vernon Valley/Great Gorge** (✉ Rte. 94, Vernon, ☎ 973/827–2000) is the largest (14 chairlifts, 3 rope tows, 52 trails), with slopes on three mountains. **Hidden Valley** (✉ Rte. 515, Vernon, ☎ 973/764–4200) is a lively alternative, with 3 chairlifts and 12 trails. **Craigmeur Ski Area** (✉ Rte. 513, Rockaway, ☎ 973/697–4500)—small (1 chairlift, 1 rope tow, 1 T-bar, 4 trails) and friendly—is best for beginners or families with younger children.

Dining and Lodging

MILFORD

$$–$$$ ✕ **Ship Inn.** New Jersey's first brew pub serves a half dozen home brews and more than a dozen British draught ales. The fare includes burgers, pub grub, and British specialties such as shepherd's pie, fish-and-chips, and roast beef with Yorkshire pudding. ✉ *61 Bridge St.,* ☎ *908/995–7007 or 800/651–2537. AE, MC, V.*

$$$–$$$$ 🏨 **Chestnut Hill on the Delaware.** There are beautiful views from the rocker-lined veranda of this 1860-vintage B&B. Rooms have some Victorian trappings. There's also a country cottage with carousel horses as well as modern conveniences and absolute privacy. ✉ *63 Church St. (Box N), 08848,* ☎ FAX *908/995–9761. 5 rooms, 1 cottage. Full breakfast. No credit cards.*

STANHOPE

$$$–$$$$ **Whistling Swan Inn.** Tiger-oak woodwork and an octagonal tower room with a conical ceiling are among the fine original features of this 1904 house, now a lovely Victorian B&B. In a tiny village in New Jersey's highlands, the inn is close to winter skiing and ice skating, summer water sports on the lakes, and cultural activities in Waterloo Village; the Delaware River is a 25-minute drive away. ✉ *110 Main St., 07874,* ☎ *201/347–6369,* FAX *201/347–3391. 10 rooms. Full breakfast. AE, D, MC, V.*

WALPACK CENTER

$$–$$$ ✕ **Walpack Inn.** The only restaurant within the boundaries of the Delaware Water Gap National Recreation Area has been here since 1949. Lobster comes solo (two tails) or with steak. The Swedish brown bread is so popular it's sold by the loaf; the fresh fruit pie is the most asked-for dessert. Deer occasionally prance by in the field beyond the skylit greenhouse dining room, which faces the Kittatinny Ridge. The rustic piano bar, with a fieldstone fireplace and mounted moose, bear, and deer heads, is itself worth the trip. ✉ *Rte. 615, 4 mi due south of Walpack Center Historic District,* ☎ *973/948–9849 or 973/948–6505. MC, V. Closed Mon.–Thurs. No lunch.*

Along the Delaware

Arriving and Departing

From Manhattan the New Jersey Turnpike skirts the area, and U.S. 1 and I–195 are key access roads. From Philadelphia I–95 runs up the Pennsylvania side of the river, crossing north of Trenton, while I–295 and the New Jersey Turnpike parallel it on the Jersey side.

What to See and Do

Forming New Jersey's "other shore" (its border with Pennsylvania), the Delaware slowly changes from a relatively small, often rock-studded river in the north to a mighty, navigable river as it flows past Philadelphia and empties into Delaware Bay. The towns that line it change as well. Part of the way down the state, quaint towns like **Milford, Frenchtown, Stockton,** and, the largest of these, **Lambertville** hug the river below ridges and rolling hills beyond. Gracing the pastoral scenery are 18th-century buildings, galleries, antiques and crafts stores, excellent restaurants, and B&Bs and inns. Across the bridge from Lambertville is the artsy town of **New Hope,** in Bucks County (☞ Pennsylvania). Inland a bit, **Flemington** is known for shopping of a different kind, thanks to a huge number of outlet stores. Flemington's **Liberty Village** (✉ 1 Church St., ☎ 908/782–8550) has more than 60 factory and designer outlets.

Follow the river south of Lambertville to find an area where George Washington actually did sleep for 10 critical days in 1776–77 (in fact, Washington and the Continental Army spent about one-third of the ★ war in New Jersey). **Washington Crossing State Park** (✉ Rte. 546, Titusville, ☎ 609/737–0623) is the site of Washington's Christmas night 1776 crossing (reenacted each Christmas Day). Follow Washington's trail south to the state capital, **Trenton,** previously a colonial pottery and manufacturing center, today a small city struggling with a quiet rebirth. One of Trenton's gems is **Chambersburg,** also known as the Burg, a residential neighborhood with dozens of superb Italian restaurants. Washington surprised the sleeping Hessians in the **Old Barracks** (✉ Barrack St., ☎ 609/396–1776; 🎫 $2), now a museum. He followed his victory in Trenton with one in **Princeton,** just to the north. The two battles were the first major victories for the Continental Army. Princeton is now a pretty university town, with upscale shops and the governor's mansion, **Drumthwacket** (✉ 354 Stockton St., ☎

609/683–0057; free); it is open Wednesday from noon to 2 PM, but closed January, February, and August.

South of Trenton, the aging industrial town of **Camden** is enjoying some degree of revitalization along its waterfront. Central to the project is the **Thomas H. Kean New Jersey State Aquarium** (1 Riverside Dr., 609/365–3300; $10.95), built in 1992 and updated in 1995 with the award-winning **Ocean Base Atlantic exhibit,** which features interactive displays and an artful underwater effect extending beyond the tanks of more than 4,000 fish. Within walking distance along the waterfront is the $56 million **Blockbuster–Sony Music Entertainment Centre** (1 Harbour Blvd., 609/365–1300). The state-of-the-art amphitheater accommodates 25,000 people, including 18,000 on the lawn; it is the first such venue to be converted to a year-round indoor theater. Camden also boasts **Walt Whitman's house** (328–330 Mickle Blvd., 609/964–5383; free) and his **tomb** in the Harleigh Cemetery (Vesper and Haddon Aves.); the house is closed on Monday and Tuesday.

Dining and Lodging

FRENCHTOWN

$$$$ **Frenchtown Inn.** This circa-1805 former tavern and boardinghouse is one of the state's most romantic restaurants. Top-notch, modern, French-influenced cuisine is served in three beautiful dining rooms. Among the favorites is the Maine salmon in a sesame-seed crust served with red pepper chutney. The restaurant offers special wine and cigar nights. *5 Bridge St. 08825, 908/996–3300.*

$$$–$$$$ **Hunterdon House.** This 1864 Italianate Victorian mansion, in a landscaped garden overlooking this charming river town, has high ceilings, tall shuttered windows, and period antiques. Guest rooms are dominated by huge, carved Victorian bedroom sets. *12 Bridge St., 08825 908/996–3632 or 800/382–0942, FAX 908/996–2921 (call first). 7 rooms. Full breakfast. AE, MC, V.*

$$–$$$ **National Hotel.** Established in 1851 and renovated in 1985, the National is a major presence in town. Lunch and dinner are served in two lovely old-fashioned dining rooms; an aviation theme enlivens the lounge. The service is friendly; the atmosphere relaxed. *31 Race St., 08825, 908/996–4871, FAX 908/996–3642. 8 rooms. Restaurant. AE, D, DC, MC, V.*

LAMBERTVILLE

$$$$ **Inn at Lambertville Station.** This well-run small hotel overlooks the Delaware River. *11 Bridge St., 08530. 609/397–8300 or 800/524–1091, FAX 609/397–9744. 45 rooms. AE, MC, V.*

STOCKTON

$$–$$$$ **The Stockton Inn.** In 1934 Richard Rodgers and Lorenz Hart escaped from Manhattan to this inn, which inspired their musical *On Your Toes* and its song "There's a Small Hotel with a Wishing Well." The wishing well still stands in the terraced garden. Built as a private home in 1710, the inn became a stagecoach stop in 1796 and a hotel in 1832 (it now comprises five houses). Historic touches remain—eight bedrooms and the five dining rooms have working fireplaces. The restaurant serves contemporary American and Continental fare. *1 Main St., Box C, 08559, 609/397–1250. 11 rooms. Restaurant. CP. AE, DC, MC, V.*

North Jersey

Arriving and Departing

From Manhattan take either the Lincoln Tunnel or the George Washington Bridge, and you're in North Jersey. I–80, to the north, and I–78, through Jersey City and Newark, connect with the New Jersey

Turnpike, the Garden State Parkway, and I–287, which all run northeast–southwest through the region.

What to See and Do

Although Newark International Airport is all some travelers may experience of this part of the state, a wealth of activities is available for those who care to linger. Among the suburban bedroom communities of Manhattan-bound commuters are parks, performing arts venues, museums, great shopping, and some of the state's finest restaurants and accommodations.

Jersey City, at first glance merely gritty and urban, is nonetheless worth a visit—most obviously for its superb views of the broad Hudson River and the Manhattan skyline. It is the site of **Liberty State Park** (✉ New Jersey Turnpike Exit 14B, ☎ 201/915–3400), where ferries leave for the Statue of Liberty and the Ellis Island Immigration Museum on the site of the restored century-old former immigration facility, less than 2,000 ft offshore. Within Liberty State Park is the **Liberty Science Center** (✉ 251 Phillip St., ☎ 201/200–1000; 🎫 $9.50), with three floors of hands-on and interactive exhibits plus an Omnimax theater (a domed screen 88 ft across and 125 ft high), as well as the restored, open-sided 1889 **Central Railroad of New Jersey Terminal,** now used for special events and exhibits. Or stroll along **Liberty Walk,** a promenade along the waterfront.

The "mile-square" city of **Hoboken,** has several claims to fame. It was the setting for the movie *On the Waterfront*; the birthplace of baseball, first played on Elysian Fields (at the site of the now-defunct Maxwell House plant) in 1846; and the hometown of Frank Sinatra. Though its relationship with Old Blue Eyes has been a love-hate one—Sinatra spurned his hometown after being pelted with fruits at a concert there in 1952—his presence can be felt everywhere. A plaque marks **Sinatra's birthplace** (✉ 415 Monroe St.), destroyed by fire in 1967. **Frank Sinatra Way,** hugging the bank of the Hudson River, commands some of the best views in town. Most of the long-standing businesses in town display faded photos of the singer. Music is also part of the draw for a new generation; yuppified **Washington Street** is the thoroughfare for the trendy and boisterous who drop in on its many music venues. **Maxwell's** (✉ 1039 Washington St., ☎ 201/798–4064) is the granddaddy, featuring live, mostly alternative music every night. Hoboken has always been a big artist community; many artists open their studios for an annual tour in October. Washington Street is a suitably arty mix of boutiques, antiques shops, hole-in-the-wall restaurants and liquor stores, and fast-food chain restaurants. Parking is Manhattan-style impossible, especially on weekends.

Newark, the state's largest city, is making a valiant effort to emerge from many years of economic stagnation and urban decay. The new **New Jersey Performing Arts Center** (✉ 1 Newark Ctr., between Military Park and the waterfront, ☎ 973/648–8989) debuted in the fall of 1997, with the 2,750-seat Prudential Hall, 500-seat Victoria Theater, two restaurants, parking facilities, and a landscaped plaza. The $180 million center is the new home to the New Jersey Symphony Orchestra. The **Newark Museum** (✉ 49 Washington St., ☎ 973/596–6550; 🎫 free) has outstanding fine arts, science, and industry collections; its restored Ballantine House, a National Historic Landmark, has two floors of Victorian period rooms and decorative arts. It's closed Monday and Tuesday.

★ The **Edison National Historic Site** (✉ Main and Lakeside Ave., West Orange, ☎ 973/736–0550; 🎫 $2), on the site of Thomas Alva Edison's former home, includes his main laboratory, machine shop and library, and replicas of many of his inventions.

In Millburn, the **Paper Mill Playhouse** (✉ Brookside Dr., ☎ 973/376–4343) has long been regarded as one of the finest off-Broadway theaters, with a constantly changing slate of plays and musicals. In winter the New Jersey Ballet Company performs the *Nutcracker.*

To the west, outside suburban Morristown, is the **Morristown National Historical Park/Jockey Hollow** (✉ Washington Pl., ☎ 973/539–2085; 🎟 $4), where George Washington and his Continental Army camped during the winter of 1779–80. The park includes the elegant Ford Mansion, once Washington's quarters, and the soldiers' log huts. From Morristown U.S. 202 leads south past antiques shops and farm stands. This is horse country, with estates and meadows edged with wood fencing, especially around **Bedminster.** Many horse farms are off U.S. 202 on Route 523. At the headquarters of the **U.S. Equestrian Team** (✉ Rtes. 512 and 206, Gladstone, ☎ 908/234–1251; 🎟 free), you can see the stables and the trophy room, which displays the team's Olympic medals, old photos, and other mementos. Competitions, including a major festival in June, are held throughout the year; the complex is closed weekends. **Far Hills** is the home of the U.S. Golf Association and its museum, Golf House (✉ Rte. 512E, ☎ 908/234–2300; 🎟 free).

The **Great Swamp National Wildlife Refuge** (✉ Basking Ridge, ☎ 973/425–1222; 🎟 free) encompasses a surprisingly large 7,300 acres of wildlife sanctuary, crossed with 8½ mi of trails, blinds, and boardwalks.

For wildlife of a different sort, the **Meadowlands Racetrack,** at the Meadowlands Sports Complex (✉ Rte. 3 and NJ Turnpike, East Rutherford, ☎ 201/935–8500), has Thoroughbred racing in the fall, with harness racing and simulcasts from other tracks the rest of the year. Check local newspapers for gate times. Pegasus (✉ 600 Meadowlands Pkwy., Secaucus, ☎ 201/867–1677) is the most upscale of the four restaurants on site. South of the track, in **Secaucus,** are acres and acres of **outlet shops** that put this otherwise unremarkable city on the map.

Dining and Lodging

BERGENFIELD

$$$$ ✕ **Chez Madeline.** Tables at this romantic French restaurant are small and candlelighted; the mood is elegantly cozy. The menu changes often, but you might start with a napoleon puff pastry with wild mushrooms and asparagus and move on to chicken *à la niçoise* (with tomatoes, black olives, garlic, and anchovies). Save room for the special dessert: five sinful offerings on one platter. Bring your own wine. ✉ *Bedford Ave.,* ☎ *201/384–7637. Reservations required. DC, MC, V. Closed Sun.–Mon.*

EAST RUTHERFORD

$$$–$$$$ ✕ **Park & Orchard.** Vegetarians appreciate the many meatless dishes, including meat-and-dairy-free lasagna and vegetarian stuffed peppers, at this cavernous, noisy, always busy spot. Non–red meat entrées such as boneless chicken breast and blackened tuna steak are also served. The 1,900-bottle wine list has won many awards; the house wines are usually terrific choices. Save room for the peanut-butter pie. ✉ *240 Hackensack St.,* ☎ *201/939–9292. Reservations not accepted, but call ahead for waiting list. AE, D, DC, MC, V.*

SHORT HILLS

$$$$ ★ ✕🏨 **Hilton at Short Hills.** This is one of the state's finest hotels. Its gourmet restaurant, the Dining Room, receives raves for its Continental cuisine. Solace, the hotel's beautiful spa, is reason enough for a visit.

The nearby Mall at Short Hills is great for tony shopping. ✉ *41 JFK Pkwy., 07078,* ☎ *973/379–0100 or 800/445–8667,* FAX *973/379–6870. 300 rooms. 2 restaurants, pool, health club. AE, D, MC, V.*

TENAFLY

$$$$ **Clinton Inn Hotel.** Tucked into a pretty suburban neighborhood, the inn is especially popular for weddings and other special occasions. Good food and personalized service are two hallmarks. ✉ *145 Dean Dr.,* ☎ *201/871–3200 or 800/275–4411,* FAX *201/871–3435. 112 rooms. Restaurant, exercise room. AE, DC, MC, V.*

WEST ORANGE

$$$–$$$$ ✕ **The Manor.** Thousands of northern New Jersey youngsters have celebrated one or another occasion with their parents at this local institution, which offers American and Continental cuisine. Among the highlights are the paella, stir-fries, and the seafood buffet. There's live piano music in the Terrace Lounge and dancing weekends in Le Dome nightclub. ✉ *111 Prospect Ave.,* ☎ *973/731–2360. Jacket and tie. Reservations required. AE, DC, MC, V. Closed Mon.*

PENNSYLVANIA

Updated by Robert DiGiacomo and Gerry Wingenbach

Capital	Harrisburg
Population	12,020,000
Motto	Virtue, Liberty, and Independence
State Bird	Ruffed grouse
State Flower	Mountain laurel
Postal Abbreviation	PA

Statewide Visitor Information

Pennsylvania Department of Commerce, Office of Travel and Tourism (✉ 453 Forum Bldg., Harrisburg 17120, ☎ 717/787–5453 or 800/847–4872). **Welcome centers** are on major highways around the state.

Scenic Drives

In Bucks County **River Road** wends 40 mi along the Delaware River, offering views of 18th- and 19th-century stone farmhouses, tucked-away villages, and fall foliage along wooded hills. In the Poconos **Route 209,** from Stroudsburg to Milford, passes untouched forests and natural waterfalls. The Lancaster County countryside, with its Amish farms and roadside stands, can best be seen along the side roads between **Routes 23** and **340.**

National and State Parks

National Parks

Pennsylvania has 17 national parks, historic sites, and monuments overseen by the **National Park Service** (✉ 200 Chestnut St., Philadelphia 19106, ☎ 215/597–7013), a few of which have camping. The **Delaware Water Gap National Recreation Area** (✉ Bushkill 18324, ☎ 717/588–2451), a 40-mi-long preserve in the northeast corner of the state, has camping, fishing, river rafting, and tubing. The 500,000-acre **Allegheny National Forest** (✉ Box 847, Warren 16365, ☎ 814/723–5150), in the northwestern part of the state, has hiking and cross-country skiing trails, three rivers suitable for canoeing, and outstanding stream fishing.

State Parks

Pennsylvania's 116 state parks have more than 7,000 campsites. The **Bureau of State Parks** (✉ Rachel Carson State Bldg., Box 8551, Harrisburg 17105, ☎ 717/772–0239 or 888/727–2757) provides information and campsite reservations. In the Poconos the heavily wooded 15,480-acre **Hickory Run State Park** (✉ R.D. 1, Box 81, White Haven 18661, ☎ 717/443–0400) offers fishing, camping, and Boulder Field, an area covered in rock formations dating to the Ice Age. The 19,140-acre **Ohiopyle State Park** (✉ Box 105, Ohiopyle 15470, ☎ 412/329–8591) has camping, cross-country skiing, and a 27-mi hiking and biking trail along the Youghiogheny River. **Presque Isle State Park** (✉ Rte. 832, Erie 16505, ☎ 814/833–7424), a 3,200-acre sandy peninsula that extends 7 mi into Lake Erie, is popular for fishing, swimming, boating, and picnicking.

PHILADELPHIA

Almost a century after English Quaker William Penn founded Philadelphia in 1682, the city became the birthplace of the nation and the home of its first government. Today, for visitors and natives alike, Philadelphia is synonymous with Independence Hall, the Liberty Bell, cheese steaks and hoagies, ethnic neighborhoods, theaters, buoyant classical music—and city streets teeming with life. With about 1.5 million people, Penn's "City of Brotherly Love" is the fifth-largest city in the country yet maintains the feel of a friendly small town.

Visitor Information

The **Philadelphia Visitors Center** (✉ 16th St. and John F. Kennedy Blvd., 19102, ☎ 215/636–1666 or 800/321–9563) is a good first stop for brochures, maps, discount coupons for tourist sites, and hotel and restaurant information.

Arriving and Departing

By Bus

Greyhound Lines (✉ 10th and Filbert Sts., ☎ 800/231–2222). **Peter Pan Trailways** (✉ 11th St. between Filbert and Arch Sts., ☎ 800/343–9999).

By Car

The main north–south highway through Philadelphia is I–95; to reach Center City, as the downtown area is called, take the Vine Street exit off I–95S or the Broad Street exit off I–95N. From the west the Schuylkill Expressway (I–76) has several exits to Center City. From the east the New Jersey Turnpike and I–295 provide access to either U.S. 30/I–676, which enters the city via the Benjamin Franklin Bridge, or New Jersey Route 42 and the Walt Whitman Bridge.

By Plane

Philadelphia International Airport (☎ 215/937–6937), 8 mi southwest of downtown, has scheduled flights on most major domestic and foreign carriers. A **SEPTA** (☞ Getting Around Philadelphia, *below*) rail line connects the airport with Center City stations; the trip takes 20 minutes and costs $5. Airport shuttle services, such as **U.S.A. Limousine** (☎ 215/782–8818) and **SuperShuttle** (☎ 215/551–6600), charge about $10 per person. Taxis cost about $20, plus tip.

By Train

Amtrak serves 30th Street Station (✉ 30th and Market Sts., ☎ 800/872–7245). **New Jersey Transit** (✉ 10th and Filbert Sts., ☎ 215/569–3752) trains connect with SEPTA (☞ Getting Around Philadelphia, *below*) trains at Trenton.

Getting Around Philadelphia

The traditional heart of the city is the intersection of Broad and Market streets, where city hall now stands. Market Street divides the city north and south. North–south streets are numbered, starting at the Delaware River with Front (1st) Street and increasing to the west. Most historical and cultural attractions are easy walks from the midtown area, which is safe during the day. After dark ask hotel personnel about the safety of places you're interested in visiting, but in general, cabs are safer than walking.

By Car

The city's narrow streets were designed for Colonial traffic of the four-legged kind, and driving can be difficult. On-street parking is often forbidden during rush hours (parking facilities include those at 41 N. 6th Street; 16th and Arch streets; and 10th and Locust streets). During rush hours avoid the major arteries leading into and out of the city, particularly I–95, U.S. 1, and the Schuylkill Expressway.

By Public Transportation

SEPTA (☎ 215/580–7800) operates an extensive network of buses, trolleys, subways, and commuter trains; the fare is $1.60, transfers 40¢, and exact change is required. Certain lines run 24 hours a day. SEPTA's Day Pass, good for a day's unlimited riding, can be purchased at the visitor center (☞ Visitor Information, *above*) for $5. Bus Route 76 connects the zoo in western Fairmount Park with Penn's Landing at the Delaware River. The purple **Phlash** buses do the downtown loop.

By Taxi

Cabs are plentiful during the day—especially along Broad Street and near hotels and train stations. At night and outside Center City, taxis are scarce, and you may have to call for service. Fares start at $1.80 and increase by 30¢ for every subsequent mile. The main companies are **Quaker City Cab** (☎ 215/728–8000), **United Cab** (☎ 215/425–7000), and **Yellow Cab** (☎ 215/922–8400).

Orientation Tours

Gray Line Tours (☎ 215/569–3666) offers a three-hour tour of historic and cultural areas April through October only. To combine lunch or dinner with a sightseeing cruise on the Delaware River, climb aboard the ***Spirit of Philadelphia*** (☞ *below*).

Boat Tours

The ***Spirit of Philadelphia*** (☎ 215/923–1419) and the ***Liberty Belle*** (☎ 215/629–1131) offer lunch, dinner, and moonlight cruises along the Delaware River. Both dock at Penn's Landing at the foot of Lombard Street.

Carriage Tours

Philadelphia Carriage Co. (☎ 215/922–6840), **'76 Carriage Co.** (☎ 215/923–8516), and **Society Hill Carriage Co.** (☎ 215/627–6128) offer tours of the historic area in antique horse-drawn carriages, narrated by costumed drivers.

Walking Tours

Audio Walk and Tour (⊠ Norman Rockwell Museum, 6th and Sansom Sts., ☎ 215/925–1234 or 215/922–4345; 🎫 $9) provides a cassette player and map for a city historic tour. From May through October **Centipede Tours** (☎ 215/735–3123) gives guided candlelight strolls through Old Philadelphia. The **Foundation for Architecture** (☎ 215/569–3187), which offers tours April through November, specializes in both theme and neighborhood tours.

Exploring Philadelphia

The *Calendar of Events* at the visitor center (☞ Visitor Information, *above*) lists Philadelphia's myriad free events and attractions.

Historic District

Even if you're not a history buff, it's hard not to get excited by the "most ★ historic square mile in America"—**Independence National Historical Park** (☎ 215/597–8974; 🎫 free).

The **visitor center** (⊠ 3rd and Chestnut Sts., ☎ 215/597–8974) has park rangers staffing the information desk and a shop with books and gifts related to Colonial times and the Revolutionary War. Across the street from the visitor center stands the 1797 **First Bank of the United States** (⊠ 120 S. 3rd St.), the oldest bank building in the country. Note

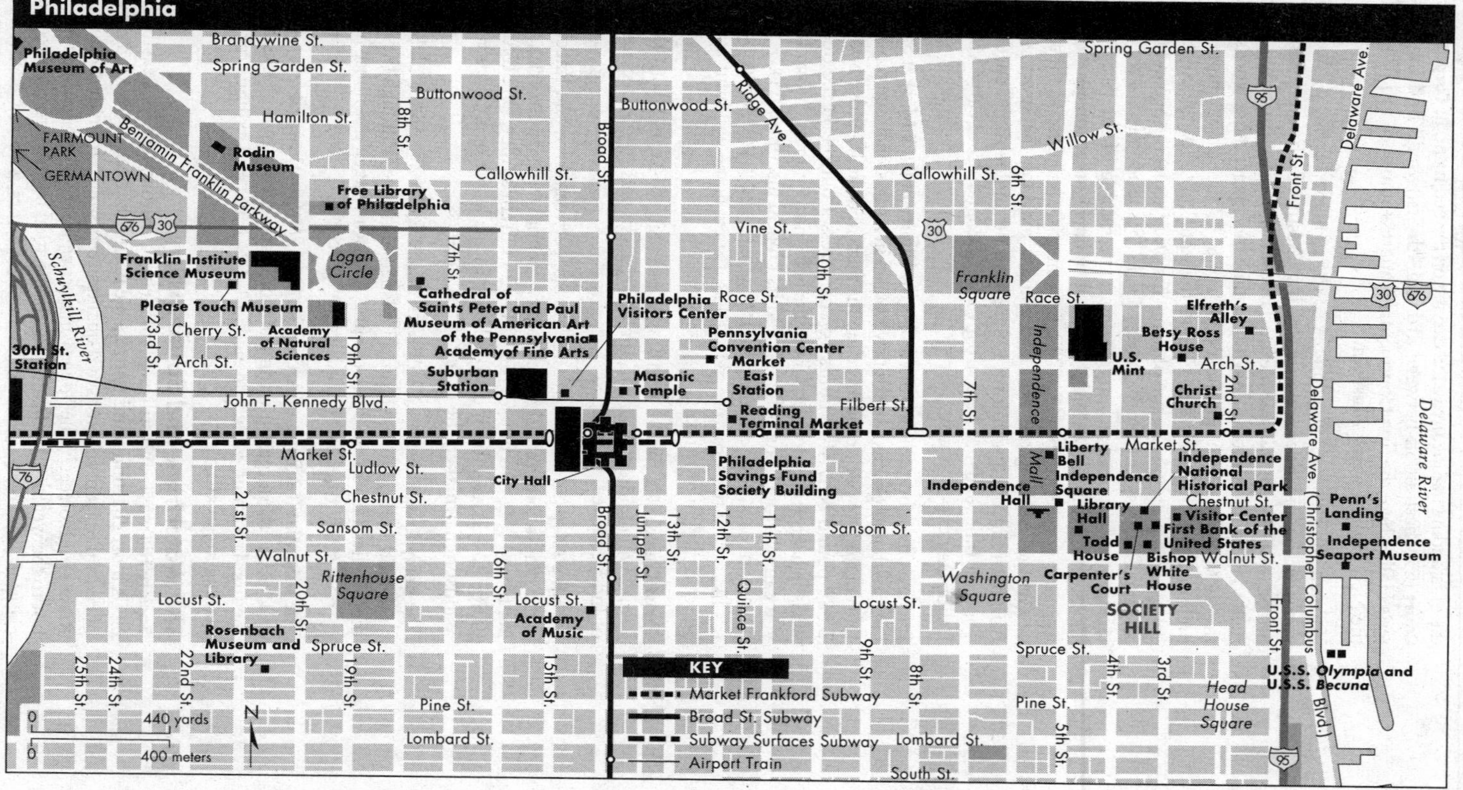
Philadelphia
Philadelphia Museum of Art
Brandywine St.
Spring Garden St.
Buttonwood St.
Hamilton St.
18th St.
FAIRMOUNT PARK
GERMANTOWN
Benjamin Franklin Parkway
Rodin Museum
Callowhill St.
Free Library of Philadelphia
Broad St.
Ridge Ave.
Willow St.
6th St.
Front St.
Delaware Ave.
Schuylkill River
Franklin Institute Science Museum
Logan Circle
17th St.
Vine St.
10th St.
Franklin Square
Cathedral of Saints Peter and Paul
Museum of American Art of the Pennsylvania Academyof Fine Arts
Please Touch Museum
23rd St.
Cherry St.
Academy of Natural Sciences
19th St.
30th St. Station
Arch St.
Philadelphia Visitors Center
Race St.
Pennsylvania Convention Center
Market East Station
Independence
Elfreth's Alley
Betsy Ross House
U.S. Mint
Arch St.
Christ Church
2nd St.
Suburban Station
Masonic Temple
John F. Kennedy Blvd.
Reading Terminal Market
Filbert St.
7th St.
Market St.
Ludlow St.
City Hall
Philadelphia Savings Fund Society Building
Liberty Bell
Independence Square
Mall
Independence Hall
Library Hall
Independence National Historical Park
Chestnut St.
Visitor Center
First Bank of the United States
Todd House
Bishop White House
Walnut St.
Carpenter's Court
Delaware Ave. (Christopher Columbus Blvd.)
Delaware River
Penn's Landing
Independence Seaport Museum
21st St.
Sansom St.
Walnut St.
Rittenhouse Square
20th St.
16th St.
Juniper St.
13th St.
12th St.
11th St.
Quince St.
Washington Square
Locust St.
Academy of Music
SOCIETY HILL
Rosenbach Museum and Library
Spruce St.
22nd St.
24th St.
25th St.
15th St.
9th St.
8th St.
4th St.
3rd St.
Head House Square
U.S.S. Olympia and U.S.S. Becuna
KEY
Market Frankford Subway
Broad St. Subway
Subway Surfaces Subway
Airport Train
Pine St.
Lombard St.
South St.
5th St.
0
440 yards
400 meters
N
30
676
95
76

the outstanding mahogany wood carving on the pediment. In **Carpenter's Court** (✉ Chestnut St. between 3rd and 4th Sts.) you'll find **Carpenter's Hall,** where the first Continental Congress convened in 1774, and the **New Hall Military Museum.**

★ You can almost hear "When in the course of human events . . ." when you stand behind **Independence Hall** (✉ Chestnut St. between 5th and 6th Sts.) on the spot where the Declaration of Independence was first read to the public, and it's easy to imagine the impact those words and this setting had on the colonists on July 8, 1776. Still an impressive building, the hall opened in 1732 as the state house for the colony of Pennsylvania. It was the site of many historic events: the Second Continental Congress, convened on May 10, 1775; the adoption of the Declaration of Independence a year later; the signing of the Articles of Confederation in 1778; and the formal signing of the Constitution by its framers on September 17, 1787. In front of the hall, next to the **statue of George Washington,** note the plaques marking the spots where Abraham Lincoln and John F. Kennedy stood and delivered speeches. Tours of Independence Hall are given year-round; from early May to Labor Day expect a wait.

Philadelphia's best-known symbol is the **Liberty Bell** (✉ Market St. between 5th and 6th Sts.), currently housed in a glass-enclosed pavilion. During the day park rangers relate the facts and the legends about the 2,080-pound bell. After hours you can press a button on the outside walls to hear a recorded account of the bell's history. In its current home you can still touch the bell and read its biblical inscription: PROCLAIM LIBERTY THROUGHOUT ALL THE LAND UNTO ALL THE INHABITANTS THEREOF. It's likely that the structure planned as its new home will limit access. So touch it while you can!

Christ Church (✉ 2nd St. north of Market St., ☎ 215/922–1695; 🎫 free) is where noted colonists, including 15 signers of the Declaration of Independence, worshiped.

Elfreth's Alley (✉ Off Front and 2nd Sts. between Arch and Race Sts.) is the oldest continuously occupied residential street in America, dating from 1702; two houses (✉ 124–126 Elfreth's Alley, ☎ 215/574–0560; 🎫 $2) have been restored, one as the home of a Colonial-era Windsor chairmaker, the other of a seamstress.

The **Betsy Ross House** (✉ 239 Arch St., ☎ 215/627–5343; 🎫 $1) is a splendid example of a Colonial Philadelphia home, although the story that she lived here and sewed the first American flag in this house hangs by only a few threads of historical evidence.

The **U.S. Mint** (✉ 5th and Arch Sts., ☎ 215/408–0114; 🎫 free), built in 1969, is the largest mint in the world and stands two blocks from the first U.S. mint, which opened in 1792. Tours and exhibits on coin making are available.

The Waterfront and Society Hill

★ **Society Hill** was—and still is—Philadelphia's showplace. It is easily the city's most charming and photogenic neighborhood. A treasure trove of Federal brick row houses and quaint streets stretch from the Delaware River to 6th Street. (The *Society* in the neighborhood's moniker refers not to the wealthy Anglicans who first settled here but to the Free Society of Traders, a group of business investors who moved here on William Penn's advice.) Many homes have been lovingly restored by modern pioneers who have kept touches like chimney pots and brass door knockers.

At Society Hill's eastern edge, the spot where William Penn stepped ashore in 1682 is today a 37-acre park known as **Penn's Landing** (✉ Delaware Riverfront from Lombard to Market St., ☎ 215/922–2386), with festivals and concerts from spring to fall and an **ice-skating rink** (☎ 215/925–7465) in winter.

★ The **Independence Seaport Museum** has nautical artifacts, ship displays, and kid-pleasing interactive exhibits. ✉ *211 S. Columbus Blvd.,* ☎ *215/925–5439.* *$5 museum only; $7.50 museum with admission to the* Olympia *and* Becuna.

Docked together are the handsomely restored **USS *Olympia,*** Commodore George Dewey's flagship in the Spanish-American War, and the **U.S.S. *Becuna,*** a World War II submarine, whose guides are sub veterans. ✉ *Penn's Landing at Spruce St.,* ☎ *215/922–1898.* *$5.*

The ***Gazela of Philadelphia,*** built in 1883, is the last of a Portuguese fleet of cod-fishing ships and the oldest wooden square-rigger still sailing. ✉ *Penn's Landing between Walnut and Spruce Sts.,* ☎ *215/923–9030. Closed Oct.–May.*

You can take a 10-minute ride on the **Riverlink Ferry** (✉ Penn's Landing at Walnut St., ☎ 215/922–2386; $5) across the Delaware River to Camden (☞ New Jersey).

The **Bishop White House** (✉ 309 Walnut St.), built in 1786 as the home of the rector of Christ Church, has been restored to Colonial elegance. The simply furnished **Todd House** (✉ 4th and Walnut Sts., ☎ 215/597–8974) has been restored to its appearance in the 1790s, when its best-known resident, Dolley Payne Todd (later Mrs. James Madison), lived here.

Head House Square (✉ 2nd and Pine Sts., ☎ 215/790–0782) was once an open-air Colonial marketplace. Today it is the site of crafts fairs, festivals, and other activities on weekends Memorial Day through the end of September.

City Hall and Environs

★ At the geographic center of Penn's original city stands **city hall**—the largest city hall in the country (it has 642 rooms) and the tallest masonry-bearing building in the world. For a tour of the interior and a 360° view of the city from the William Penn statue, go to Room 121 via the northeast corner of the courtyard and ride the elevator to the top of the 548-ft tower. ✉ *Broad and Market Sts.,* ☎ *215/686–1776 or 215/686–2840 for tour information.* *Free. Closed weekends.*

Philadelphia is the mother city of American Freemasonry, and the **Masonic Temple** is home to the Grand Lodge of Free and Accepted Masons of Pennsylvania. The seven lodge halls, each decorated according to a different architectural theme, make for a fun 45-minute tour. ✉ *1 N. Broad St.,* ☎ *215/988–1917.* *Free.*

The **Academy of Music** (✉ Broad and Locust Sts., ☎ 215/893–1900 or 215/893–1999 for tickets), modeled on Milan's La Scala opera house, is home to the Philadelphia Orchestra and the Opera Company of Philadelphia. The **Philadelphia Savings Fund Society Building** (✉ 12th and Market Sts.), built in 1930 and known locally as the PSFS Building, was one of the city's first skyscrapers and influential in the design of other American high-rises; it is slated to reopen as a Loews hotel in 1999.

The **Pennsylvania Convention Center** (✉ 12th and Arch Sts., ☎ 215/418–4700 or 215/418–4989 for events) includes the restored **Reading Train Shed.** You can tour the complex (free) on Tuesday and Thursday. It sits atop the not-to-be-missed **Reading Terminal Market** (☞ Dining, *below*), food heaven for locals and visitors alike.

★ The city's most elegant park, **Rittenhouse Square** (✉ Walnut St. between 18th and 19th Sts.) resembles a Parisian park and frequently hosts art festivals. The **Rosenbach Museum and Library** (✉ 2010 Delancey Pl., ☎ 215/732–1600; 🎫 $3.50) offers a one-hour tour of its sumptuous collection of antiques, paintings, rare books (including the original manuscript of James Joyce's *Ulysses*), and objets d'art.

Museum District

The **Benjamin Franklin Parkway** angles across the grid of city streets from city hall to Fairmount Park. Lined with distinguished museums, hotels, and apartment buildings, this 250-ft-wide boulevard inspired by the Champs-Elysées was built in the 1920s. Off the parkway you'll find the **Free Library of Philadelphia** (✉ 19th St., ☎ 215/686–5322), with more than 1 million volumes. The **Academy of Natural Sciences** (✉ 19th St., ☎ 215/299–1020; 🎫 $7.75), America's first museum of natural history, has a "Discovering Dinosaurs" exhibit and stuffed animals from around the world displayed in 35 natural settings. The **Please Touch Museum** (✉ 210 N. 21st St., ☎ 215/963–0667; 🎫 $6.95), designed for children ages seven and younger, encourages hands-on participation. The **Rodin Museum** (✉ 22nd St., ☎ 215/763–8100; 🎫 free) has the largest collection of Auguste Rodin's works outside France, including masterworks like *The Kiss, The Thinker,* and *The Burghers of Calais.* The **Franklin Institute Science Museum** (✉ 20th St., ☎ 215/448–1200; 🎫 $9.50) is as clever as its namesake; it includes many dazzling hands-on exhibits, a planetarium, and an Omniverse theater that shows science and nature documentaries with a 79-ft domed screen and 56-speaker high-tech sound system.

★ The crown jewel of the parkway is the **Philadelphia Museum of Art.** Modeled on a larger-scale version of ancient Greek temples, the 200 galleries house more than 300,000 works. The collections include paintings by Renoir, Picasso, Matisse, and Marcel Duchamp; Early American furniture; Amish and Shaker crafts; and reconstructions, including a 12th-century French cloister and a 16th-century Indian temple. ✉ *26th St. and Benjamin Franklin Pkwy.,* ☎ *215/763–8100.* 🎫 *$8; free Sun. 10–1. Closed Mon.*

Along both banks of the Schuylkill River is **Fairmount Park** (✉ Accesses from Kelly Dr., West River Dr., and Belmont Ave., ☎ 215/685–0000), one of the largest city parks in the world, with woodlands, meadows, and rolling hills. Within its 4,500 acres you'll find tennis courts, ball fields, playgrounds, trails, an exercise course, the **Ellen Phillips Samuel Memorial Sculpture Garden,** and some fine Early American country houses (**Laurel Hill, Strawberry Mansion,** and others). **Boathouse Row,** 11 architecturally varied 19th-century buildings on the banks of the Schuylkill that are home to 13 rowing clubs, is best viewed from the West River Drive. In the northwest section of the park is the **Wissahickon,** a 5½-mi-long forested gorge carved out by Wissahickon Creek. At **Valley Green Inn** (☎ 215/247–1730), a restaurant halfway up the valley, you can dine on the porch and watch the ducks swimming in the creek.

★ The **Museum of American Art of the Pennsylvania Academy of the Fine Arts,** in one of the finest extant buildings by eccentric Philadelphia architect Frank Furness, is the oldest art institution in the United States (founded 1804). Its collection ranges from Winslow Homer and Benjamin West to Andrew Wyeth and Red Grooms. ✉ *Broad and Cherry Sts.,* ☎ *215/972–7600.* 🎫 *$5.95; free Sun. 3–5.*

The Italian Renaissance–style **Cathedral of Saints Peter and Paul** (✉ 18th and Race Sts., ☎ 215/561–1313), built between 1846 and 1864, is the basilica of the Roman Catholic archdiocese of Philadelphia.

Germantown

In 1683 Francis Pastorius led 13 Mennonite families out of Germany to seek religious freedom in the New World; they settled 6 mi northwest of Philadelphia in what is now **Germantown,** and many became Quakers. **Cliveden** (✉ 6401 Germantown Ave., ☎ 215/848–1777; 🎫 $6), an elaborate country house built in 1763, was occupied by the British during the Revolution. On October 4, 1777, George Washington's attempt to dislodge them resulted in the Yankees' defeat in the Battle of Germantown. During the yellow fever epidemic of 1793–94, Washington lived in the **Deshler-Morris House** (✉ 5442 Germantown Ave., ☎ 215/596–1748; 🎫 $1) to avoid the unhealthy air of sea-level Philadelphia. Contact the **Germantown Historical Society** (✉ 5501 Germantown Ave., ☎ 215/844–1683) for information on all noteworthy sites in Germantown.

Other Attractions

The **University of Pennsylvania Museum** (✉ 33rd and Spruce Sts., ☎ 215/898–4000; 🎫 $5) is one of the finest archaeology-anthropology museums in the world. The **Mutter Museum** (✉ 19 S. 22nd St., ☎ 215/563–3737; 🎫 $8), a medical museum with a plethora of anatomical and pathological specimens, is best visited on an empty stomach! One of the world's great collections of Impressionist and Postimpressionist art—175 Renoirs, 66 Cézannes, 65 Matisses, plus masterpieces by ★ van Gogh, Degas, Picasso, and others—is at the **Barnes Foundation,** 8 mi west of Center City. ✉ *300 Latches La., Merion,* ☎ *610/667–0290.* 🎫 *$5. Closed Mon.–Thurs.*

★ 🐤 **Sesame Place,** a 45-minute drive north of the city, is an amusement park for children ages 3–13, based on the popular public-television show. ✉ *100 Sesame Rd., Langhorne,* ☎ *215/757–1100.* 🎫 *$22.95.*

Parks, Gardens, and Zoos

Fairmount Park (☞ Exploring Philadelphia, *above*) is the city's largest, encompassing varied terrains as well as many cultural sites. The University of Pennsylvania's **Morris Arboretum** (✉ Hillcrest Ave. between Germantown and Stenton Aves., Chestnut Hill, ☎ 215/247–5777; 🎫 $4) is 166 acres of romantically landscaped seclusion. America's first 🐤 zoo, the **Philadelphia Zoological Gardens** (✉ 34th St. and Girard Ave., ☎ 215/243–1100; 🎫 $8.50) is home to 1,700 animals on 42 acres.

Dining

Once known mainly for hoagies and snapper soup, Philadelphia has become a first-rate restaurant town, with pricey dazzlers and simpler treasures. French food set the pace for years, but star chefs from Italy and China are a vital presence; distinctive ethnic eateries and excellent seafood and steak houses round out the dining scene. For price ranges *see* Chart 1 (A) *in* On the Road with Fodor's.

$$$$ ★ ✕ **The Fountain.** Nestled in the lavish yet dignified lobby of the Four Seasons, with grand windows overlooking Logan Circle's Swann Fountain, this oasis offers predominantly local and American entrées, such as sautéed venison medallions in homemade pasta with fried leeks and juniper sauce. ✉ *1 Logan Sq.,* ☎ *215/963–1500. Reservations essential. Jacket and tie.* AE, D, DC, MC, V.

$$$$ ★ ✕ **Le Bec-Fin.** The Fine Beak (or more loosely, "the Fine Palate") is arguably the best restaurant in Philadelphia. Louis XV furniture, apricot silk walls, and crystal chandeliers create a luxurious mise-en-scène. Owner-chef Georges Perrier oversees every detail of the excellent European service and the haute French five-course prix-fixe menu ($118). The $36 three-course lunch is a relative bargain. ✉ *1523 Walnut St.,* ☎ *215/567–1000. Reservations essential. Jacket and tie. AE, D, DC, MC, V. Closed Sun.*

$$$–$$$$ ★ ✕ **Striped Bass Restaurant and Bar.** The opening of this all-seafood restaurant in the early '90s caused the biggest splash on Philadelphia's dining scene in more than a decade. The visually stunning room with 28-ft ceilings and soaring marble pillars is the setting for such Pacific Rim–influenced dishes as Chilean sea bass with jasmine rice, garlic spinach and ginger teriyaki, as well as a raw bar and chef's table. ✉ *1500 Walnut St.,* ☎ *215/732–4444. Reservations essential. AE, MC, V.*

$$$ ★ ✕ **Susanna Foo.** The handsome renovated dining room sets the tone for the city's most expensive Chinese food. Favorites include Hundred-Corner Crab Cakes and spicy Mongolian lamb; the exotic specials always merit a try. The Sunday brunch of ethereal dim sum is a recent addition. A pastry chef prepares an array of fine French and Asian desserts. ✉ *1512 Walnut St.,* ☎ *215/545–2666. Reservations essential. Jacket and tie. AE, DC, MC, V.*

$$ ✕ **Dock Street Brewery & Restaurant.** Olivier de St. Martin, a chef from the north of France, presides over this large brewery-brasserie. The menu emphasizes the dishes of his native Alsace—hearty favorites like cassoulet—although steaks, fish, and burgers are also served. Several flavors of the house-specialty boutique beer are available on a daily basis. ✉ *2 Logan Sq.,* ☎ *215/496–0413. AE, MC, V.*

$$ ✕ **Friday, Saturday, Sunday.** Locals have been filling the cheek-by-jowl tables at this neighborhood spot since its opening 20 years ago. Fabrics are draped from the ceiling; mirrors and pin lights line the walls. Daily blackboard-listed specials augment the printed menu; popular entrées include duck, salmon, and striped bass. Crème brûlée and coconut cream pie are dessert favorites. ✉ *261 S. 21st St.,* ☎ *215/546–4232. AE, D, DC, MC, V.*

$$ ✕ **Villa di Roma.** This South Philadelphia classic in a central Italian Market location is long-beloved for its basic southern Italian food. Daily specials such as delicious breaded asparagus spark the extensive regular menu. A must for dessert is the *tartufo* (a ball of chocolate ice cream rolled in cocoa). ✉ *936 S. 9th St.,* ☎ *215/592–1295. No credit cards.*

$–$$ ✕ **Joy Tsin Lau.** Chinese symbols, including golden medallions, dragons, and the like, line the walls and the ceiling at this popular Chinatown spot. Lunchtime is a direct re-creation of a Hong Kong teahouse atmosphere, with carts of dim sum being wheeled from table to table. ✉ *1026–1028 Race St.,* ☎ *215/592–7228. AE, D, DC, MC, V.*

$–$$ ✕ **Pamplona.** Decorated with a huge faux-Picasso mural that overlooks the lively, always crowded dining room, this casual, chic restaurant serves fresh interpretations of classic Spanish tapas. Grilled squid and garlicky shrimp are standouts. ✉ *225 S. 12th St.,* ☎ *215/627–9059. No smoking. AE, D, MC, V. No lunch.*

$ ✕ **Jim's Steaks.** A Philadelphia phenomenon, a cheese steak is shaved slices of beef, fried onions, and melted cheese loaded onto an untoasted roll, all dripping with oil and juices. Add some greasy fries topped with more melted cheese and a Tastycake for dessert, and you have a unique Philadelphia dining experience. ✉ *400 South St.,* ☎ *215/928–1911. No credit cards.*

$ ★ ✕ **Reading Terminal Market.** A Philadelphia treasure, this potpourri of 80 stalls, shops, and lunch counters offers a smorgasbord of cuisines, including Chinese, Greek, Mexican, Japanese, soul food, Middle Eastern, and Pennsylvania Dutch. Arrive early to beat the daily lunch rush. ✉ *12th and Arch Sts.,* ☎ *215/922–2317. Closed Sun. No dinner.*

$ ✕ **Restaurant School.** Managed and staffed entirely by students, this restaurant offers Italian and American bistro menus in a restored 1860 Victorian mansion. A fixed price of $15 buys an appetizer and an entrée; desserts and coffee are extra. Meals are occasionally extraordinary (especially for the price), but vary depending on the level of training of the current kitchen staff. ✉ *4207 Walnut St.,* ☎ *215/222–4200. AE, D, DC, MC, V. Closed Sun.–Mon.*

Lodging

With the exception of the Army-Navy football game (around Thanksgiving), and when big conventions are in town, it's easy to find a hotel room. Most bed-and-breakfasts operate under the auspices of booking agencies, such as **Bed and Breakfast, Center City** (✉ 1804 Pine St., 19103, ☎ 215/735–1137 or 800/354–8401), and **Bed and Breakfast Connections** (✉ Box 21, Devon 19333, ☎ 610/687–3565 or 800/448–3619). For price ranges *see* Chart 2 (A) *in* On the Road with Fodor's.

$$$$ ★ **Four Seasons.** Built in 1983 and refurbished in 1996, this eight-story hotel is the city's classiest and most expensive. Rooms are furnished in a classic style with contemporary touches, and the best have romantic views overlooking the fountains in Logan Circle. Six of the floors are no-smoking. ✉ *1 Logan Sq., 19103,* ☎ *215/963–1500 or 800/332–3442,* FAX *215/963–9506. 365 rooms. 2 restaurants, pool, exercise room. AE, D, DC, MC, V.*

$$$$ ★ **The Rittenhouse.** This small luxury hotel, which contains condominium residences on other floors of the building, takes full advantage of its Rittenhouse Square location: Many of the rooms and both restaurants overlook the city's classiest park. Each room has two TVs, three telephones, an entertainment center in an armoire, a fully stocked minibar, and a king-size bed. ✉ *210 W. Rittenhouse Sq., 19103,* ☎ *215/546–9000 or 800/635–1042,* FAX *215/732–3364. 98 rooms. 2 restaurants, pool, health club. AE, D, DC, MC, V.*

$$$–$$$$ **Adam's Mark.** Guest rooms are small here, with a contemporary motif; request one on an upper floor facing south toward Fairmount Park and the downtown skyline. The hotel's big attraction is the nighttime activity at its nightclub, sports bar, and fine restaurant, the Marker. Parking is free. ✉ *City Ave. and Monument Rd., 19131,* ☎ *215/581–5000 or 800/444–2326,* FAX *215/581–5089. 515 rooms. 2 restaurants, pools, health club. AE, D, DC, MC, V.*

$$$–$$$$ **Philadelphia Marriott.** This 23-story full-service convention hotel—the biggest in Pennsylvania—takes up an entire city block. The spacious guest rooms have large windows and traditional cherry furniture. Despite its impersonality, the Marriott tries to meet special needs (iron and ironing board in each room, 24-hour workout room) and offers some of the lowest rates in its price category. ✉ *1201 Market St., 19107,* ☎ *215/625–2900 or 800/228–9290,* FAX *215/625–6000. 1,200 rooms. 4 restaurants, pool, health club. AE, D, DC, MC, V.*

$$$–$$$$ **The Warwick.** First opened in 1924, this 23-story hotel underwent a thorough renovation in 1997, which added a new restaurant and 344 guest rooms from former apartments. The lobby, brightened by gilded mirrors and 18-ft Palladian windows, is always busy. Capriccio, a European-style café, serves desserts and espresso daily until late at night. You can use a nearby health club at no additional charge. ✉ *1701 Locust St., 19103,* ☎ *215/735–6000 or 800/523–4210,* FAX *215/790–7766. 544 rooms. 2 restaurants. AE, DC, MC, V.*

$$–$$$$ **Latham.** At this small, elegant hotel with a European accent and an emphasis on personal service, guest rooms have marble-top bureaus and French writing desks; most have minibars. The entire hotel was renovated in 1997. ✉ *135 S. 17th St., 19103,* ☎ *215/563–7474 or 800/528–4261,* FAX *215/568–0110. 139 rooms. Restaurant, exercise room. AE, D, DC, MC, V.*

$$–$$$ **Clarion Suites.** This eight-story 1892 building, the former Bentwood Rocker Factory, is in Chinatown and within walking distance of the Pennsylvania Convention Center, Reading Terminal Market, and Independence Mall. The suites have a full-size kitchen, dining area, and two televisions; many have exposed brick and wood beams. ✉ *1010 Race St., 19107,* ☎ *215/922–1730 or 800/628–8932,* FAX *215/922–6258. 96 suites. Exercise room. CP. AE, D, DC, MC, V.*

$$–$$$ ★ **Penn's View Inn.** In a refurbished 19th-century commercial building, this cosmopolitan little hotel is on the fringe of the city's oldest warehouse district. Deluxe rooms, done in somber tapestry, have whirlpool baths and windows overlooking the Delaware River. Accommodations are comfortable and rather European, if not strictly stylish, though street noise can be a concern. ✉ *14 N. Front St.,* ✉ *19106,* ☎ *215/922–7600 or 800/331–7634,* FAX *215/922–7642. 28 rooms. Restaurant. CP. AE, DC, MC, V.*

$$ ★ **Thomas Bond House.** Spend the night in the heart of the Old City, the way Philadelphians did more than two centuries ago. Built in 1769, this four-story house has rooms with marble fireplaces and four-poster Thomasville beds—and 20th-century whirlpool baths. ✉ *129 S. 2nd St., 19106,* ☎ *215/923–8523 or 800/845–2663,* FAX *215/923–8504. 12 rooms. CP weekdays; full breakfast weekends. AE, D, DC, MC, V.*

$ **Bank Street Hostel.** On the cusp of Old City and Society Hill, this clean, well-run establishment offers a dormitory arrangement that is a downtown Philly lodging bargain. ✉ *32 S. Bank St., 19106,* ☎ *215/922–0222 or 800/392–4678,* FAX *215/922–4082. 70 beds. No credit cards.*

Nightlife and the Arts

Philadelphia magazine (at newsstands), *Calendar of Events* (free at the visitor center), the *Philadelphia Weekly* and the *City Paper* (weeklies available free from news boxes in Center City), and the *Inquirer* and the *Daily News* (the city's daily papers) list arts and entertainment events. Tickets, often at a discount, for more than 75 performing and cultural organizations can be obtained at **UpStages** (✉ 1412 Chestnut St., ☎ 215/569–9700).

Nightlife

South Street from Front to 7th Street still attracts nighttime crowds, but the big noise is the **Delaware Waterfront** entertainment boom, with more than a dozen clubs opening in the past few years. In the northwestern part of the city, **Main Street** in **Manayunk** has joined **Germantown Avenue** in **Chestnut Hill** as an area in which to dine, shop, and stroll. On Wednesday night downtown shops and some museums stay open late; outside, street bands entertain smiling crowds. On the **First Friday** of every month 25 art galleries in Old City stay open late. Call **Electric Factory Concerts** (☎ 215/568–3222) to learn what's happening around town.

BARS, LOUNGES, AND CABARETS

Egypt (✉ 520 N. Delaware Ave., ☎ 215/922–6500), one of Philly's hottest clubs, has dancing to music ranging from disco and pop to progressive. A loud, young crowd packs **Maui** (✉ Pier 53 N., 1143 N. Columbus Blvd., ☎ 215/423–8116), a large-capacity indoor/outdoor club/disco, every night until 2. **Dirty Frank's** (✉ 347 S. 13th St., ☎

215/732–5010) *is* dirty and attracts a motley crowd of writers, artists, students, and Philly characters. **Woody's** (✉ 202 S. 13th St., ☎ 215/545–1893) is the city's most popular gay bar. The music and decor of the '70s take center stage at **Polly Esther's** (✉ 1201 Race St., ☎ 215/851–0776), which has a *Saturday Night Fever*–style disco floor. Head for **Zanzibar Blue** (✉ Downstairs at the Bellevue, Broad and Walnut Sts., ☎ 215/732–5200) for top local and national names in jazz.

COMEDY

David Brenner's Laugh House (✉ 221 South St., ☎ 215/440–4242) showcases local and national acts Friday through Sunday.

MISCELLANEOUS

By day **Painted Bride Art Center** (✉ 230 Vine St., ☎ 215/925–9914) is an art gallery, by night a stage featuring performance art, readings, dance, and theater. Since 1975 the **Cherry Tree Music Co-op** (✉ 3916 Locust Walk, ☎ 215/386–1640) has staged Sunday-night folk concerts.

The Arts

CONCERTS

The **Philadelphia Orchestra** performs at the Academy of Music (✉ Broad and Locust Sts., ☎ 215/893–1900) in winter and at the Mann Music Center (✉ W. Fairmount Park, ☎ 215/878–7707) in summer. The **Philly Pops** (☎ 215/735–7506), conducted by Peter Nero, performs at the Academy of Music.

DANCE

The **Pennsylvania Ballet** (☎ 215/551–7000) dances at the Academy of Music from October to June. The **Philadelphia Dance Company** (☎ 215/387–8200) performs modern and jazz dance and ballet at the University of Pennsylvania's Annenberg Theater in spring and fall.

OPERA

The **Opera Company of Philadelphia** (☎ 215/928–2100) performs at the Academy of Music from October to May.

THEATER

Performances by touring companies and pre-Broadway productions can be seen at the **Merriam Theater** (✉ 250 S. Broad St., ☎ 215/732–5446), the **Forrest Theater** (✉ 1114 Walnut St., ☎ 215/923–1515), and the **Walnut Street Theater** (✉ 9th and Walnut Sts., ☎ 215/574–3550). The **Arden Theatre Company** (✉ 422 N. 2nd St., ☎ 215/922–8900) and the **Wilma Theater** (✉ Broad and Spruce Sts., ☎ 215/546–7824) have gained a reputation for innovative work with American and European drama and musicals. **Freedom Theater** (✉ 1346 N. Broad St., ☎ 215/765–2793) is the oldest and most active black theater in Philadelphia.

Outdoor Activities and Sports

Golf

Of the six 18-hole courses in Philadelphia open to the public, **Cobbs Creek and Karakung** (✉ 7200 Lansdowne Ave., ☎ 215/877–8707) are the most challenging.

Ice-Skating

Skate outdoors with the Delaware River and Ben Franklin Bridge as a backdrop at the **Blue Cross RiverRink** (✉ Penn's Landing between Market and Chestnut Sts., ☎ 215/925–7465), open daily November to March.

Jogging and Running

Philly runners' favorite workout is the **river loop**—an 8.2-mi circuit starting at the Art Museum and heading up Kelly Drive along the

Schuylkill River, then across Falls Bridge and back down West River Drive.

Spectator Sports

Baseball: Philadelphia Phillies (✉ Veterans Stadium, Broad St. and Pattison Ave., ☎ 215/463–1000). **Basketball: Philadelphia 76ers** (✉ CoreStates Center, Broad St. and Pattison Ave., ☎ 215/336–3600). **Football: Philadelphia Eagles** (✉ Veterans Stadium, ☎ 215/463–5500). **Hockey: Philadelphia Flyers** (✉ CoreStates Center, ☎ 215/336–3600). **Horse Racing: Philadelphia Park** (✉ Street Rd., Bensalem, ☎ 215/639–9000) has Thoroughbred racing year-round. For offtrack betting, try the **Turf Club Center City** (✉ 1635 Market St., ☎ 215/246–1556).

Shopping

There is no sales tax on clothing, medicine, or food bought in stores. Otherwise, Pennsylvania has a 6% sales tax, 7% in Philadelphia.

Shopping Districts

Walnut Street between Broad Street and Rittenhouse Square (now a.k.a. Rittenhouse Row) and the intersecting streets just north and south are filled with upscale boutiques and galleries. At 16th and Chestnut streets, the **Shops at Liberty Place** offer more than 70 stores and restaurants under a 90-ft glass-roof atrium. **Jewelers' Row,** centered on Sansom Street between 7th and 8th streets, is one of the world's oldest and largest markets of precious stones. Pine Street from 9th to 12th streets is **Antiques Row.** Along **South Street** are more than 300 unusual stores selling everything from New Age books and health food to avant-garde art. For local color visit the outdoor stalls and indoor stores of the **Italian Market,** on 9th Street between Christian and Washington streets.

Department Stores

Philadelphia's premier department store, John Wanamaker, was bought by the May Company in 1995, but Philadelphians still rendezvous at the eagle statue in the grand court of what is now **Lord & Taylor** (✉ 13th and Market Sts., ☎ 215/241–9000). **Strawbridge's** (✉ 8th and Market Sts., ☎ 215/629–6000) is the anchor store for the Gallery at Market East (☎ 215/925–7162).

Specialty Stores

AIA Bookstore (✉ 117 S. 17th St., ☎ 215/569–3188) specializes in books on architecture, interior design, and furnishings and carries posters and unusual gifts. **Architectural Antiques Exchange** (✉ 715 N. 2nd St., ☎ 215/922–3669) handles everything from embellishments of Victorian saloons and apothecary shops to stained and beveled glass. **Boyd's** (✉ 1818 Chestnut St., ☎ 215/564–9000), the largest, single-store men's clothier in the country, also has a small women's department. **J. E. Caldwell** (✉ Juniper and Chestnut Sts., ☎ 215/864–7800), since 1839 a local landmark for jewelry, is adorned with antique handblown crystal chandeliers by Baccarat. **Kitchen Kapers** (✉ 213 S. 17th St., ☎ 215/546–8059) is a good source for fine cookware, French copper, cutlery, coffees, and teas. **Urban Outfitters** (✉ 1801 Walnut St., ☎ 215/569–3131) opened its first store in this downtown Beaux Arts mansion.

Side Trip to the Brandywine Valley

Arriving and Departing

Take U.S. 1S from Philadelphia about 25 mi to the valley.

What to See and Do

The Brandywine River valley has inspired generations of Wyeths and du Ponts—the Wyeths to capture its peaceful harmony on canvas, the du Ponts to recontour the landscape with grand gardens, mansions, and mills. The **Brandywine River Museum** (⊠ U.S. 1 and Rte. 100, Chadds Ford, ☎ 610/388–7601; 🎫 $5), in a preserved 19th-century gristmill, celebrates the Brandywine school of artists. ★ **Longwood Gardens** (⊠ U.S. 1, Kennett Square, ☎ 610/388–6741; 🎫 $12), Pierre-Samuel du Pont's 350 acres of ultimate estate gardens, has an international reputation. The **Brandywine Battlefield State Park** (⊠ U.S. 1, Chadds Ford, ☎ 610/459–3342; 🎫 $3.50 for buildings, park free) is near the site of the British defeat of Washington and his troops on September 11, 1777. The region is dotted with antiques shops and cozy inns. The **Brandywine Valley Tourist Information Center** (⊠ 300 Greenwood Rd., Kennett Square 19348, ☎ 610/388–2900 or 800/228–9933) has information.

Side Trip to Bucks County

Arriving and Departing

From Philadelphia follow I–95 north to the Yardley exit, then go north on Route 32 toward New Hope. The trip takes one hour.

What to See and Do

Bucks County is known for antiques, covered bridges, and country inns. **New Hope** is a hodgepodge of art galleries, old stone houses, and shops along crooked little streets. William Penn's reconstructed Georgian-style mansion, **Pennsbury Manor** (⊠ 400 Pennsbury Memorial Rd., Tyburn Rd. E off U.S. 13, between Morrisville and Bristol, ☎ 215/946–0400; 🎫 $5) presents living history demonstrations of 17th-century life. **Washington Crossing Historic Park** (⊠ Rtes. 532 and 32, ☎ 215/493–4076) is where George Washington and his troops crossed the river on Christmas night 1776. Contact the **Bucks County Conference and Visitors Bureau** (⊠ 152 Swamp Rd., Doylestown 18901, ☎ 215/345–4552 or 800/836–28257) or the **New Hope Information Center** (⊠ 1 W. Mechanic St., at Main St., 18938, ☎ 215/862–5880 or 215/862–5030) for more information.

Side Trip to Valley Forge

Arriving and Departing

By car take the Schuylkill Expressway (I–76) west from Philadelphia to Exit 25; then take Route 363 to North Gulph Road and follow the signs to Valley Forge National Historical Park, 18 mi from the city. By bus take SEPTA Route 125 from 16th Street and John F. Kennedy Boulevard.

What to See and Do

The monuments, huts, and headquarters on the 3,500 acres of rolling hills of the **Valley Forge National Historical Park** (⊠ Rte. 23 and N. Gulph Rd., Valley Forge, ☎ 610/783–1077; 🎫 $2 Washington's Headquarters, Apr.–Nov.) preserve the moment in American history when George Washington's Continental Army endured the bitter winter of 1777–78. The former home of John James Audubon, **Mill Grove** (⊠ Audubon and Pauling Rds., Audubon, ☎ 610/666–5593; 🎫 donations accepted) is now a museum displaying the naturalist's work. ★ The **Wharton Esherick Museum** (⊠ Horseshoe Trail, Paoli, ☎ 610/644–5822; 🎫 $6) has more than 200 examples of this eccentric artist's paintings, furniture, and sculpture. With more than 450 stores, including nine department stores, the **Court and the Plaza** (⊠ Rte. 202 and N. Gulph Rd., King of Prussia, ☎ 610/265–5727) is the nation's second-largest shopping complex. For more information contact the **Valley Forge Convention and Visitors Bureau** (⊠ 600 W. Germantown Pike, Suite 130, Plymouth Meeting 19462, ☎ 610/834–1550 or 800/441–3549).

PENNSYLVANIA DUTCH COUNTRY

First of all, the Pennsylvania Dutch aren't Dutch; the name comes from *Deutsch* (German). In the 18th century this rolling farmland 65 mi west of Philadelphia became home to the Amish, the Mennonites, and other German and Swiss immigrants escaping religious persecution. Today their descendants continue to turn their backs on the modern world—and in doing so attract the world's attention. In summer buses jam Route 30, the main thoroughfare. But there is still charm on the back roads, where you will discover Amish farms, hand-painted signs advertising quilts, fields worked with mules, and horse-drawn buggies.

Visitor Information

Pennsylvania Dutch Convention and Visitors Bureau (✉ 501 Greenfield Rd., Lancaster 17601, ☎ 717/299–8901 or 800/PA–DUTCH). **Mennonite Information Center** (✉ 2209 Millstream Rd., Lancaster 17602, ☎ 717/299–0954).

Getting There

By Bus

Greyhound Lines (☎ 800/231–2222) has three runs daily from Philadelphia to Lancaster.

By Car

From Philadelphia (65 mi away) take the Schuylkill Expressway (I–76) west to the Pennsylvania Turnpike, exiting at Exit 20, 21, or 22.

By Train

Amtrak (☎ 800/872–7245) has service from Philadelphia to Lancaster.

Exploring Pennsylvania Dutch Country

Lancaster, a charming Colonial city, is the heart of Pennsylvania Dutch Country. The **Historic Lancaster Walking Tour** (☎ 717/392–1776), a two-hour stroll through the city, is conducted by guides who impart lively anecdotes about local architecture and history. **Central Market** (✉ Penn Sq., ☎ 717/291–4723), one of the oldest covered markets in the country and now housed in an 1889 Romanesque structure, is where the locals shop for fresh produce, meats, and baked goods. The old city hall, reborn as the **Heritage Center of Lancaster County** (✉ King and Queen St., ☎ 717/299–6440; 🎟 free), shows the work of Lancaster County artisans and craftspeople from the past.

Several furnished farmhouses offer simulated up-close looks at how the Amish live, including the **Amish Farm and House** (✉ 2395 Lincoln Hwy. E, ☎ 717/394–6185; 🎟 $5.75). Abe, of **Abe's Buggy Rides** (✉ Rte. 340, Bird-in-Hand, ☎ 717/392–1794; 🎟 $10), chats about the Amish during a 2-mi spin down country roads in an Amish family carriage. **Wheatland** (✉ 1120 Marietta Ave. [Rte. 23], 1½ mi west of Lancaster, ☎ 717/392–8721; 🎟 $5.50), a restored 1828 Federal mansion, was the home of the only president from Pennsylvania, James Buchanan.

Strasburg has a half dozen museums and sights devoted to trains. The **Strasburg Railroad** (✉ Rte. 741 E., ☎ 717/687–7522; 🎟 $8) is a scenic 9-mi round-trip excursion on a wooden coach pulled by a steam locomotive. The **Railroad Museum of Pennsylvania** (✉ Rte. 741, ☎ 717/687–8628; 🎟 $6) displays colossal engines, railcars, and memorabilia documenting railroading in the state.

In **Ephrata** the 18th-century Protestants of the **Ephrata Cloister** (✉ Rtes. 272 and 322, ☎ 717/733–6600; 🎟 $5) led an ascetic life, living examples of William Penn's "holy experiment." Guides now give tours of the restored medieval-style German buildings.

Lititz was founded by Moravians who settled in Pennsylvania to do missionary work among Native Americans. It's a lovely town with a tree-shaded main street of 18th-century cottages and shops. At the **General Sutter Inn** (✉ 14 E. Main St., ☎ 717/626–2115) pick up the Historical Foundation's brochure that details a walking tour of the town.

Dining and Lodging

Like the German cuisine from which it derives, Pennsylvania Dutch cooking is hearty. To sample such regional fare as ham, buttered noodles, chowchow, and shoofly pie, eat at one of the bustling family-style restaurants where diners share tables and the food is passed around. For price ranges *see* Charts 1 (B) and 2 (B) *in* On the Road with Fodor's.

Bird-in-Hand

$–$$ ✕ **Bird-in-Hand Family Restaurant.** This family-owned spot specializes in hearty Pennsylvania Dutch home cooking, served buffet-style for $9.75 or à la carte. ✉ *Rte. 340 just west of N. Ronks Rd.,* ☎ *717/768–8266. MC, V. Closed Sun.*

Ephrata

$$–$$$$ ★ ✕ **The Restaurant at Doneckers.** Classic and country-French cuisine is served downstairs amid Colonial antiques and upstairs in a country garden. A lower-priced bistro menu is also available. ✉ *333 N. State St.,* ☎ *717/738–9501. AE, D, DC, MC, V. No smoking. Closed Wed. and Sun.*

Lancaster

$$$–$$$$ ✕ **Market Fare.** The cuisine is American, and steaks, seafood, and veal are served in a cozy dining room with upholstered armchairs and 19th-century paintings, drawings, and photographs. Homemade soups and breads highlight the diverse menu. The café upstairs offers a light breakfast, quick lunch, and takeout. ✉ *Market and Grant Sts.,* ☎ *717/299–7090. AE, D, DC, MC, V.*

$–$$ ✕ **Center City Grill.** This casual but elegant bar and restaurant serves a varied international menu—anything from Thai chicken in peanut-and-ginger sauce to gourmet pizzas to quiche Lorraine. Most nights there is dancing to DJ-spun tunes. ✉ *10 S. Prince St.,* ☎ *717/299–3456. AE, D, DC, MC, V.*

$$$–$$$$ 🏨 **Best Western Eden Resort Inn.** Spacious contemporary rooms and attractive grounds contribute to the pleasant atmosphere. The suites have kitchens and fireplaces. ✉ *222 Eden Rd. (U.S. 30 and Rte. 272), 17601,* ☎ *717/569–6444,* FAX *717/569–4208. 315 rooms. 2 restaurants, pools, tennis, exercise room. AE, D, DC, MC, V.*

Lititz

$$$ ★ 🏨 **General Sutter Inn.** Built in 1764, the oldest continuously run inn in the state is a Victoriana lover's delight. Furnishings range from Pennsylvania folk art to Louis XIV sofas and marble-top tables. At the crossroads of town, the inn is within easy walking distance of the historic district. ✉ *14 E. Main St. , 17543,* ☎ *717/626–2115,* FAX *717/626–0992. 12 rooms, Restaurant. AE, D, MC, V.*

Mount Joy

$$–$$$ ✕ **Groff's Farm.** Hearty Mennonite farm fare, including chicken, relishes, and cracker pudding, is served family-style in a restored 1756 farmhouse decorated with country fabrics and fresh flowers. ✉ *650 Pinkerton Rd., ☎ 717/653–2048. Reservations essential. AE, D, DC, MC, V*

$$$$ ✕🏨 **Cameron Estate Inn.** Rooms in this sprawling Federal redbrick mansion on 15 wooded acres have Oriental rugs, antique and reproduction furniture, and canopy beds; eight have working fireplaces. Guests have access to a nearby pool and tennis courts. ✉ *1855 Mansion La., 17552, ☎ 717/653–1773, FAX 717/653–8334. 17 rooms. Full breakfast. AE, D, DC, MC, V.*

Strasburg

$$–$$$$ ★ ✕🏨 **Historic Strasburg Inn.** This Colonial-style inn is set on 58 peaceful acres overlooking farmland. ✉ *1 Historic Dr., 17579, ☎ 717/687–7691 or 800/872–0201, FAX 717/687–6098. 101 rooms. 2 restaurants, pool, exercise room. Full breakfast. AE, D, DC, MC, V.*

Campgrounds

The Convention and Visitors Bureau (☞ Visitor Information, *above*) has a list of area campgrounds. Two of the best are ⛺ **Mill Bridge Village and Campresort** (✉ ½ mi south of U.S. 30 on S. Ronks Rd.; Box 86, Strasburg 17579, ☎ 717/687–8181), both attached to a restored 18th-century village, and ⛺ **Spring Gulch Resort Campground** (✉ Rte. 897; 475 Lynch Rd., New Holland 17557, ☎ 717/354–3100).

Nightlife and the Arts

The **American Music Theatre** (✉ 2425 Lincoln Highway E, ☎ 717/397–7700 or 800/648–4102) is a new 1,500-seat facility presenting twice-daily shows that celebrate American music. Plays and concerts, as well as performances by the Lancaster Symphony Orchestra and the Lancaster Opera, are presented at the **Fulton Opera House** (✉ 12 N. Prince St., Lancaster, ☎ 717/394–7133), a restored 19th-century Victorian theater.

Outdoor Activities and Sports

Hot-Air Ballooning

Great Adventure Balloon Club (☎ 717/397–3623) offers a bird's-eye view of Pennsylvania Dutch Country.

Shopping

Antiques

Antiques malls are on Route 272 between Adamstown and Denver, 2 mi east of Pennsylvania Turnpike Exit 21; **Barr's Auctions** (☎ 717/336–2861), **Renninger's Antique and Collector's Market** (☎ 717/336–2177), and **Stoudt's Black Angus** (☎ 717/484–4385) all feature indoor and outdoor sales.

Crafts

Places to see fine local crafts include the **Weathervane Shop** at the Landis Valley Museum (✉ 2451 Kissel Hill Rd., Lancaster, ☎ 717/569–9312), the **Tin Bin** (✉ 20 Valley Rd. off Rte. 501, Neffsville, ☎ 717/569–6210), and the 30-shop **Kitchen Kettle Village** (✉ Rte. 340, Intercourse, ☎ 717/768–8261). International crafts, ideal for Christmas gifts and stocking stuffers, can be found at the **Ten Thousand Villages** (✉ 240 N. Reading Rd., Ephrata, ☎ 717/721–8400), owned and operated by the Mennonite Central Committee.

Farmers Markets

In addition to Lancaster's **Central Market** (☞ Exploring Pennsylvania Dutch Country, *above*), the **Green Dragon Farmers Market and Auction** (✉ 955 N. State St., just off Rte. 272, Ephrata, ☎ 717/738–1117) is an old, traditional agricultural market with a country-carnival atmosphere, open Friday year-round.

Side Trip to Gettysburg

Arriving and Departing

From Lancaster take U.S. 30 east to Gettysburg (about 1½ hours).

What to See and Do

The battle of Gettysburg, fought in July 1863, was, along with Ulysses S. Grant's successful Vicksburg campaign, the turning point of the Civil ★ War. At the **Gettysburg National Military Park** (✉ Visitor Center, 97 Taneytown Rd., ☎ 717/334–1124) you can follow the course of the fighting on a 750-square-ft electronic map or obtain brochures that will guide you along roads through the battleground. The **Gettysburg Convention and Visitors Travel Bureau** (✉ 35 Carlisle St., 17325, ☎ 717/334–6274) provides information on the region.

Side Trip to Hershey

Arriving and Departing

Take I–76 to Exit 20 and follow the signs—it's about 45 minutes from Lancaster.

What to See and Do

The streets have names like Cocoa Avenue, and the streetlights look like Hershey's Kisses at **Hersheypark** (✉ U.S. 422, ☎ 717/534–3090; 🎫 $29.95; $16.95 ages 3–8; ages 2 and under free), a family-oriented amusement park. At **Chocolate World** (✉ Park Blvd., ☎ 717/534–4900; 🎫 free) you can take a 12-minute ride through the process of chocolate making. Contact the **Hershey Information Center** (✉ Hershey 17033, ☎ 800/437–7439).

Side Trip to Reading

Arriving and Departing

From Exit 22 off the Pennsylvania Turnpike take I–276 north and U.S. 422 west into downtown Reading, about an hour from Lancaster.

What to See and Do

Reading, a 19th-century industrial city, today promotes itself as the "outlet capital of the world." **Skyline Drive** is a meandering road with miles of unspoiled vistas and an expansive view of the city. The **Daniel Boone Homestead** (✉ Daniel Boone Rd., off U.S. 422, Birdsboro, ☎ 610/582–4900; 🎫 $4) is a renovation of the frontiersman's home. For information contact **Reading and Berks County Visitors Bureau** (✉ VF Factory Outlet Complex, Park Rd. and Hill Ave., Box 6677, Wyomissing 19610, ☎ 610/375–4085 or 800/443–6610).

PITTSBURGH

At the point where the Monongahela and Allegheny rivers meet to form the Ohio River is a natural fortress first named Ft. Pitt and later Pittsburgh. Prosperity in coal, iron, and steel made the city a giant in the industrial age—and earned it its nickname of Smoky City. Today the smoke has cleared, and Pittsburgh has been recast into an artful blend of turn-of-the-century architectural masterpieces and modern skyscrapers.

Visitor Information

Greater Pittsburgh: Convention and Visitors Bureau (✉ 4 Gateway Center, 15222, ☎ 800/366–0093). The same phone number connects to every **Visitor Information Center:** Downtown (✉ Gateway Center), Oakland (✉ Forbes Ave.), Mount Washington (✉ Grandview Ave.), and Airport (✉ Lower level near baggage claim). The Greater Pittsburgh Convention and Visitors Bureau operates a 24-hour Activities Line (☎ 800/366–0093), which lets you in on the events of the week.

Arriving and Departing

By Bus

Greyhound Lines (✉ 11th St. and Liberty Ave., ☎ 800/231–2222).

By Car

From the north or south take I–79 to I–279, which leads into downtown. From the east or west take the Pennsylvania Turnpike (I–76), then I–376 to the Grant Street exit.

By Plane

Greater Pittsburgh International Airport (☎ 412/472–3525), served by most major airlines, is 14 mi west of downtown; a cab ride there is about $30. **Airlines Transportation Co.** (☎ 412/471–8900) provides motor-coach or van service to the major downtown hotels for $12 one-way and $20 round-trip. **Port Authoriity Transit** (☎ 412/231–5707) operates daily bus service (No. 28X) from 5:30 AM to 12:30 AM between the airport and downtown and Oakland ($1.95).

By Train

Amtrak (✉ Liberty and Grant Sts., ☎ 800/872–7245).

Getting Around Pittsburgh

Port Authority Transit (☎ 412/231–5707) operates daily bus and trolley service. Within the central business district, the subway, called the T, is always free, and buses are free during the day. Two **cable cars**—the *Duquesne Incline,* from West Carson Street west on the Ohio River to the restaurant area of Grandview Avenue, and the *Monongahela Incline,* from Station Square on the Monongahela to Grandview Avenue—carry passengers from river level to the hilly south side of the city.

Exploring Pittsburgh

Downtown, an area framed by the three rivers and called the Golden Triangle, contains **Point State Park** (☞ Parks and Gardens, *below*) and major hotels, restaurants, and theaters. **PPG Place** (✉ Stanwix St. and 4th Ave., ☎ 412/434–3131), with its spires and towers evocative of a medieval castle, exemplifies the Pittsburgh renaissance. Several beautifully restored or maintained commercial and public buildings date from Pittsburgh's early boom days. The interior of the Flemish-Gothic **Two Mellon Bank Center** (✉ 5th Ave. and Grant St., ☎ 412/234–5000), formerly the Union Trust Building, has a glass rotunda. Daniel Burnham's Union Station is now the **Pennsylvanian** (✉ Grant St. and Liberty Ave., ☎ 412/391–6730); the **Oliver Building** (✉ 6th Ave. and Smithfield St., ☎ 412/281–8070) is also notable. H. H. Richardson's **Allegheny County Courthouse and Jail** (✉ 5th Ave. and Grant St., ☎ 412/350–5313), built in 1884, is one of the country's outstanding Romanesque buildings. **Station Square** (☎ 412/261–2811), on the Monongahela across the Smithfield Bridge, is a restored redbrick turn-of-the-century rail station with boutiques, restaurants (☞ Dining, *below*), and nightclubs.

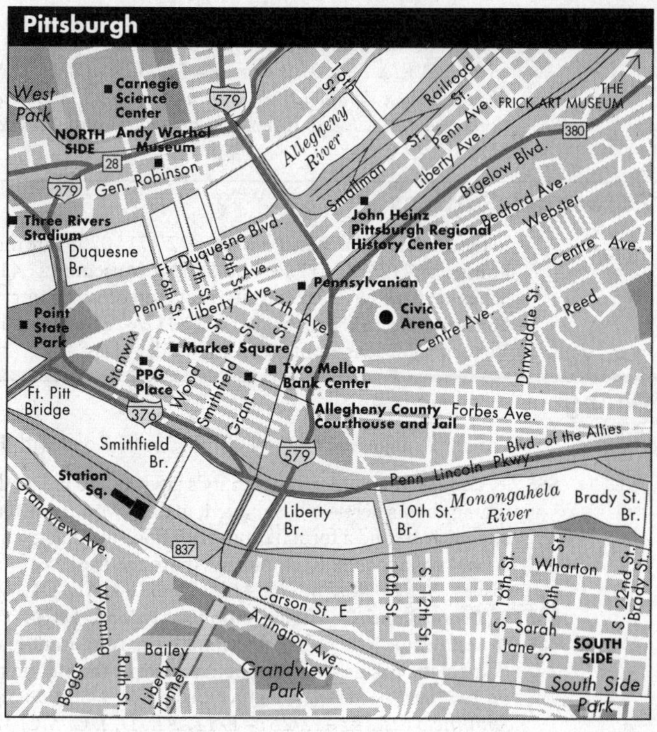

East of downtown, **Oakland** is the headquarters of many of the city's ★ cultural, educational, and medical landmarks. The **Carnegie** is an opulent cultural center, with the **Museum of Art,** the **Museum of Natural History,** the **Music Hall,** and the **Carnegie Library** all under one Beaux Arts roof. Don't miss the 19th-century French and American paintings; the Hall of Architecture, which re-creates in plaster some of the world's architectural masterpieces; the dinosaur collection; and the extravagant Music Hall lobby. ✉ *4400 Forbes Ave.,* ☎ *412/622–3131 or 412/622–3289 for tours.* 🎫 *$6.*

The **Frick Art and Historical Center** (✉ 7227 Reynolds St., ☎ 412/371–0606 or 412/371–0600; 🎫 $6) consists of **Clayton,** the turn-of-the-century home of Henry Clay Frick, which preserves the original furnishings and art; a **carriage museum;** and the **Frick Art Museum,** which possesses a small but choice collection of Old Master works. The **Andy Warhol Museum** (✉ 117 Sandusky St., ☎ 412/237–8300; 🎫 $6) devotes seven floors to the work of the native Pittsburgher and pop art icon. The **John Heinz Pittsburgh Regional History Center** (✉ 1212 Smallman St., ☎ 412/454–6000; 🎫 $6) focuses on western Pennsylvania history; a long-term exhibit explores glassmaking in the region.

The huge **Three Rivers Stadium** commands the north side of the Allegheny River. The **Carnegie Science Center** (✉ Allegheny Center, ☎ 412/237–3300; 🎫 $6.50) has a planetarium, an aquarium, hands-on science exhibits, and a four-story Omnimax theater.

Outside Pittsburgh

Northeast of Pittsburgh the **Laurel Highlands** region has Revolutionary War–era forts and battlefields, restored inns and taverns, and lush mountain scenery. The region is noted for white-water rafting, hiking, and skiing. Contact **Laurel Highlands Visitors Bureau** (✉ Ligonier Town Hall, 120 E. Main St., Ligonier, ☎ 412/238–5661 or 800/925–

★ 7669). **Fallingwater** is Frank Lloyd Wright's residential masterwork—a stone, concrete, and glass house dramatically cantilevered over a waterfall. ✉ *Rte. 381, Mill Run,* ☎ *412/329–8501.* *$12 weekends, $8 weekdays; detailed tour: $30 weekdays, $35 weekends. Reservations essential. Closed Mon. Apr.–mid-Nov. and weekdays mid-Nov.–Mar.*

Parks and Gardens

In the 36-acre **Point State Park** (☎ 412/471–0235) are the **Ft. Pitt Blockhouse** (☎ 412/471–1764) and **Ft. Pitt Museum** (☎ 412/281–9284). Schenley Park has a lake, trails, golf, and cross-country skiing. **Phipps Conservatory** (✉ Schenley Park, ☎ 412/622–6914) is Henry Phipps's Victorian gardens—outdoors and under glass.

Dining

For price ranges *see* Chart 1 (B) *in* On the Road with Fodor's.

$$$ ✕ **Common Plea.** Many of the city's lawyers and judges dine in the three dining rooms here—one subdued, in dark wood; one flashy, with glass and mirrors; and a formal room with floor-to-ceiling wine cabinets and crystal chandeliers. Recommended are the fresh seafood and the veal dishes. ✉ *310 Ross St.,* ☎ *412/281–5140. AE, DC, MC, V.*

$$$ ★ ✕ **Grand Concourse/Gandy Dancer Saloon.** Set in a dazzlingly restored Beaux Arts railroad terminal, the restaurant features seafood, homemade pastas, and gracious service. In the Saloon the emphasis is on raw-bar platters and lighter dishes. ✉ *1 Station Sq., Carson and Smithfield Sts.,* ☎ *412/261–1717. AE, D, DC, MC, V.*

$$ ✕ **Georgetowne Inn.** Wraparound windows offer a majestic view from the Colonial-style dining rooms. The quality of the American food is exceptional; the low-key atmosphere makes this a good place for family dining. ✉ *1230 Grandview Ave.,* ☎ *412/481–4424. AE, D, DC, MC, V. No lunch Sun.*

$ ✕ **Primanti Brothers.** What started out in 1933 as a working-class bar is now a Pittsburgh favorite with eight locations. The cheese steak comes with fries, coleslaw, and tomato—all *in* the sandwich. ✉ *46 18th St.,* ☎ *412/263–2142;* ✉ *11 Cherry Way,* ☎ *412/566–8051;* ✉ *Market Square,* ☎ *412/261–1599. No credit cards.*

Lodging

Choice hotels are limited in downtown Pittsburgh—and most are pricey. Nationally affiliated hotels are in Oakland and outlying suburban areas. For price ranges *see* Chart 2 (B) *in* On the Road with Fodor's.

$$$ ★ **Clubhouse Inn Pittsburgh.** At this garden-style hotel 9 mi from the airport, guest rooms overlook a courtyard. Airport shuttle service is available. ✉ *5311 Campbells Run Rd., 15205,* ☎ *412/788–8400 or 800/258–2466,* FAX *412/788–2577. 152 rooms. Pool, exercise room. Full breakfast. AE, D, DC, MC, V.*

$$$ **Doubletree Hotel Pittsburgh.** The dramatically designed lobby leads to a 21-story tower housing rooms with contemporary decor. ✉ *1000 Penn Ave., 15222,* ☎ *412/281–3700 or 800/367–8478,* FAX *412/227–4500. 616 rooms. Restaurant, pool, exercise room. AE, D, DC, MC, V.*

$$$ ★ **Westin William Penn.** Pittsburgh's grand hotel has a sumptuous lobby with a coffered ceiling, intricate plasterwork, and crystal chandeliers, where people relax over drinks or afternoon tea. The guest rooms are filled with light, and many are large enough for a couch and a wing chair. ✉ *530 William Penn Pl., Mellon Sq., 15230,* ☎ *412/281–7100*

or 800/228–3000, ℻ *412/553–5252. 595 rooms. 2 restaurants, exercise room. AE, D, DC, MC, V.*

$$ 🏨 **Best Western Hotel University Center.** This modern nine-story hotel in the heart of Oakland provides easy access to the university and the museum district. ✉ *3401 Blvd. of the Allies, 15213,* ☎ *412/683–6100 or 800/528–1234,* ℻ *412/682–6115. 119 rooms. Restaurant, pool. AE, D, DC, MC, V.*

$$ ★ 🏨 **The Priory.** This European-style hotel is furnished with antiques and reproductions. ✉ *614 Pressley St., 15212,* ☎ *412/231–3338,* ℻ *412/231–4838. 24 rooms. CP. AE, D, DC, MC, V.*

$$ 🏨 **Ramada Plaza Suites and Conference Center.** In the Golden Triangle, across from the Civic Arena and adjacent to the Steel Plaza subway station, the Ramada is a convenient, mid-price all-suite hotel whose spacious rooms have conventional hotel furnishings. Both full kitchens and kitchenettes are available. ✉ *1 Bigelow Sq., 15219,* ☎ *412/281–5800 or 800/225–5858,* ℻ *412/281–8467. 311 suites. Restaurant, pool, health club. CP. AE, D, DC, MC, V.*

Nightlife and the Arts

Nightlife

Station Square (✉ Carson at Smithfield St.) has **Chauncy's** (☎ 412/232–0601) for dining and dancing, the **FunnyBone Comedy Club** (☎ 412/281–3130), and **Jellyrolls** (☎ 412/391–7464), a piano bar.

The Arts

The **Pittsburgh Symphony Orchestra** appears at the Heinz Hall for the Performing Arts (✉ 600 Penn Ave., ☎ 412/392–4800). The **Pittsburgh Opera** (☎ 412/281–0912) and the **Pittsburgh Ballet** (☎ 412/281–0360) are at the Benedum Center for the Performing Arts (✉ 719 Liberty Ave., ☎ 412/456–6666). The **Point Park College Playhouse** (✉ 222 Craft Ave., ☎ 412/621–4445) presents dance and theater, including shows for children.

Outdoor Activities and Sports

Jogging

Point State Park (☎ 412/471–0235) has an upper and a lower path, each forming a circuit of about a mile in length, with views of the skyline and the city's three rivers.

Golf

The **North Park Golf Course** (✉ Kummer Rd., North Park, ☎ 412/935–1967) is one of the more than 50 courses within a 30-minute drive of downtown, all of which are open to the public.

Spectator Sports

Baseball: Pittsburgh Pirates (✉ Three Rivers Stadium, 400 Stadium Circle, ☎ 412/321–2827). **Football: Pittsburgh Steelers** (✉ Three Rivers Stadium, ☎ 412/323–1200). **Hockey: Pittsburgh Penguins** (✉ Civic Arena, Center Ave. and Auditorium Pl., ☎ 412/642–7367).

Shopping

Pittsburgh's best downtown department stores, **Saks Fifth Avenue** (✉ 513 Smithfield St., ☎ 412/263–4800) and **Kaufmann's** (✉ 5th Ave. and Smithfield St., ☎ 412/232–2000), are the two leading department stores. Nearby are the shopping complexes **Fifth Avenue Place, 1 Oxford Centre,** and **PPG Place.** In the **Strip District** (✉ Between Liberty and Penn Aves. and 16th and 22nd Sts.) are streets lined with farmers' market stalls and sellers of imported food and dry goods. Antiques shops and art galleries are along Carson Street East on the **South Side.**

The Shops at Station Square (☞ Exploring Pittsburgh, *above*) has 70 shops and restaurants.

ELSEWHERE IN PENNSYLVANIA

The Poconos

Getting There

I–80 leads to the Delaware Water Gap, I–84 to Milford. From the south U.S. 611 skirts the Delaware River and takes you into Stroudsburg, which is 98 mi from Philadelphia, 135 mi from Harrisburg, and 318 mi from Pittsburgh.

What to See and Do

The Poconos, in the northeastern corner of the state, encompass 2,400 square mi of mountainous wilderness bordering the Delaware River, with lakes, streams, waterfalls, resorts, and enchanting country inns. A back-roads drive will turn up quaint villages such as **Jim Thorpe** (✉ Rte. 209), a late-Victorian mountain-resort town that has first-rate antiques shops and galleries. Winter brings downhill and cross-country skiing, skating, and snowmobiling; summer offers golf, boating, horseback riding, and hiking. The **Pocono Mountains Vacation Bureau** (✉ 1004 Main St., Stroudsburg 18360, ☎ 717/424–6050 or 800/762–6667) provides information.

Lodging

$$$$ **French Manor.** Forget the heart-shape bathtubs and other honeymoon hokeyness this area is known for—the French Manor is *the* most romantic spot in the Poconos. The chateau-style mansion, secluded on the top of a mountain, offers panoramic views, luxurious amenities, and excellent French cuisine. ✉ *Huckleberry Rd., South Sterling 18460,* ☎ *717/676–3244 or 800/523–8200,* FAX *717/676–9786. 9 rooms. Restaurant. AE, D, DC, MC, V.*

$$$$ **Sterling Inn.** Built in 1857 on an historic Indian site, the clapboard main house and cluster of cottages, including 10 new suites with fireplaces and Jacuzzis, have a bright country ambience. ✉ *Rte. 191, South Sterling 18460,* ☎ *717/676–3311 or 800/523–8200,* FAX *717/676–9786. 65 rooms. Restaurant, pool. AE, D, DC, MC, V.*

VIRGINIA

By Francis X. Rocca

Updated by Bruce Walker

Capital	Richmond
Population	6,676,000
Motto	Thus Always to Tyrants
State Bird	Cardinal
State Flower	Dogwood
Postal Abbreviation	VA

Statewide Visitor Information

Virginia Division of Tourism (✉ 901 E. Byrd St., Richmond 23219, ☎ 804/786–2051 or 800/932–5827) can mail travel brochures and travel information to you. Call **Visit Virginia** (☎ 800/847–4882) for visitor information and a free state map. **Welcome centers** are in Bracey (on I–85), Bristol (I–81), Clearbrook (I–81), Covington (I–64), Fredericksburg (I–95), Lambsburg (I–77), Manassas (I–66), New Church (U.S. 13), Rocky Gap (I–77), and Skippers (I–95).

Scenic Drives

Skyline Drive, the **Blue Ridge Parkway,** and **Goshen Pass** wind through spectacular mountain scenery (☞ Charlottesville and the Shenandoah Valley, *below*). A 25-mi drive north along **Route 20** from Charlottesville to Orange takes you through gently rolling green countryside, past horse farms and vineyards. For a stirring panorama of the famous buildings and monuments of Washington, D.C., drive north from Alexandria on the **George Washington Memorial Parkway.** Between Virginia Beach and the Eastern Shore stretches the 17½-mi **Chesapeake Bay Bridge-Tunnel,** where you are surrounded by sea without leaving your car; there are an observation pier and a restaurant along the way.

National and State Parks

National Parks

Shenandoah National Park (✉ 3655 U.S. 211 E, Luray 22835, ☎ 540/999–3500)—195,000 acres with a vertical change in elevation of 3,500 ft—offers hiking, horseback riding, and fishing. The 2.2-million-acre **George Washington and Jefferson National Forests** (✉ 5162 Valleypointe Pkwy., Roanoke 24019, ☎ 540/265–5100) offer camping, boating, hiking, fishing, swimming, and horseback riding. **Mt. Rogers National Recreation Area** (✉ 3714 Rte. 16, Marion 24354, ☎ 540/783–5196) is a 116,000-acre expanse, including the state's highest point—5,729 ft above sea level.

State Parks

The **Department of Conservation and Recreation** (✉ 203 Governor St., Richmond 23219, ☎ 804/786–1712) has information on Virginia's 28 state parks, which range in size from 500 to 4,500 acres. Two of the most popular are **Douthat State Park** (✉ Rte. 629, Box 212, Millboro 24460, ☎ 540/862–8100) and **First Landing/Seashore State Park** (✉ 2500 Shore Dr., Virginia Beach 23451, ☎ 757/481–2131).

CHARLOTTESVILLE AND THE SHENANDOAH VALLEY

Residents of Charlottesville, in the Piedmont region of rolling plains, call it "Mr. Jefferson's Country." They speak of the Sage of Monticello as if he were still writing, building, and governing. Yet aware as it is of its past, Charlottesville is anything but backward. Home to the state university and a fashionable retreat for tycoons and movie stars, it is one of America's most sophisticated small cities, often called the Santa Fe of the East.

In and along the Shenandoah Valley are small towns that were once frontier outposts; well-traveled driving routes with turnouts overlooking breathtaking scenery; many opportunities for outdoor recreation, on water and solid ground; and accommodations and restaurants to suit all tastes.

Visitor Information

Bath County: Chamber of Commerce (✉ U.S. 220, Box 718, Hot Springs 24445, ☎ 540/839–5409). **Roanoke Valley:** Convention and Visitors Bureau (✉ 114 Market St., Roanoke 24011, ☎ 540/342–6025 or 800/635–5535). **Shenandoah Valley:** Travel Association (✉ Box 1040, New Market 22844, ☎ 540/740–3132). **Charlottesville:** Charlottesville-Albemarle Convention and Visitors Bureau (✉ Box 178, 22902, ☎ 804/977–1783). **Lexington:** Visitor Center (✉ 106 E. Washington St., 24450, ☎ 540/463–3777). **Winchester:** Chamber of Commerce (✉ 1360 S. Pleasant Valley Rd., 22601, ☎ 540/662–4135 or 800/662–1360).

Arriving and Departing

By Bus

Greyhound Lines (☎ 800/231–2222) serves Charlottesville (✉ 310 W. Main St.), Lexington (✉ Classic Creations, 130 S. Rudolph St.), Roanoke (✉ 26 Salem Ave.), and Staunton (✉ 1143 Richmond Rd.).

By Car

Charlottesville is where U.S. 29 (north–south) meets I–64. I–81 and U.S. 11 run north–south the length of the Shenandoah Valley and continue south into Tennessee. I–66 meets I–81 and U.S. 11 at the northern end of the valley; I–64 connects I–81 and U.S. 11 with Charlottesville. Route 39 runs through Bath County and connects with I–81/I–64, just north of Lexington.

By Plane

Charlottesville-Albemarle Airport (☎ 804/973–8341) is 8 mi north of town on U.S. 29. **Roanoke Regional Airport** (☎ 540/362–1999) is 6 mi north of town on I–581.

By Train

Amtrak (☎ 800/872–7245) has service to Charlottesville's Union Station (✉ 810 W. Main St.), to Clifton Forge (✉ 400 Ridgeway St.)—for the Homestead resort in Bath County—and to Staunton (✉ 1 Middlebrook Ave.).

Exploring Charlottesville and the Shenandoah Valley

Charlottesville

★ Jefferson built his beloved **Monticello** (✉ Rte. 53, ☎ 804/984–9800; 🎫 $9) on a "little mountain" over a period of 40 years, from 1769 to 1809. In details and overall conception Monticello was a revolutionary structure, a neoclassical repudiation of the Colonial style with all its political connotations. Throughout the house are Jefferson's inventions, including a seven-day clock and a two-pen contraption for copying letters as he wrote them.

The cozy rooms of **Ash Lawn–Highland** (✉ Rte. 795, southwest of Rte. 53, ☎ 804/293–9539; 🎫 $7), James Monroe's modest presidential residence, evoke the fifth president—our first to spring from the middle class. Outside, sheep and peacocks roam the grounds of this working plantation.

Historic Michie Tavern (✉ Rte. 53, ☎ 804/977–1234; 🎫 $6) is an 18th-century building moved here in the 1920s from a neighboring location. The period rooms are a bit too tidy but otherwise convincing.

There is little to see in downtown Charlottesville besides a pedestrian shopping mall that takes up six brick-paved blocks of Main Street. At the **Virginia Discovery Museum** (✉ 524 E. Main St., ☎ 804/977–1025; 🎫 $4) children can step inside a giant kaleidoscope or an authentic log cabin. At the west end of town is the **University of Virginia** (☎ 804/924–1019; 🎫 free), founded and designed by Thomas Jefferson and still widely acclaimed as the "proudest achievement in American architecture." Pavilions flank the lawn as it flows down from the Rotunda, a half-scale replica of Rome's Pantheon. Behind the pavilions, gardens and landscaping are laced with serpentine walls.

The Shenandoah Valley

At the top of the valley, and almost at the northernmost tip of the state, is **Winchester.** The town hosts parades and a beauty pageant during the Shenandoah Apple Blossom Festival every May (☎ 540/662–3863). September is apple time at pick-your-own orchards throughout the surrounding countryside. Because of its strategic location, Winchester has drawn more than its share of military action over the years. A young Colonel George Washington spent more than a year here during the French and Indian Wars; the log cabin in which he worked is now **George Washington's Office Museum** (✉ 32 W. Cork St., ☎ 540/662–4412; 🎫 $3.50). **Stonewall Jackson's headquarters** (✉ 415 N. Braddock St., ☎ 540/667–3242; 🎫 $3.50) is where the Confederate general planned the First Battle of Winchester (there were eventually three).

Belle Grove (✉ U.S. 11, ☎ 540/869–2028; 🎫 $6), just south of Middletown, is a grand 1790s limestone mansion designed with the help of Thomas Jefferson. It served as headquarters for the victorious Union general Philip Sheridan during the Battle of Cedar Creek (1864) and is today a working farm. Call ahead if you plan to visit—it sometimes closes for part of the winter.

Shenandoah National Park (☞ National and State Parks, *above*), encompassing some 60 peaks, runs more than 80 mi along the Blue Ridge, south from Front Royal to Waynesboro. Mountain meadows open up to gorgeous views of the range. Hiking, camping, fishing, and horseback riding are all available. For information on seasonal activities pick up the free *Shenandoah Overlook* when you enter the park.

★ **Skyline Drive** winds 105 mi over the mountains of the park, affording panoramas of the valley to the west and the rolling country of the Piedmont to the east. On holidays and weekends in spring and fall, crowds slow down traffic to much less than the maximum of 35 mph. Many lodges, campsites, and eating places, and sometimes stretches of the drive itself, are closed from November through April.

Luray Caverns (✉ U.S. 211, Luray, ☎ 540/743–6551; 🎫 $13), the largest caves in the state, are just west of Skyline Drive. Water seepage over millions of years has created striking rock and mineral formations. Tours begin every 20 minutes.

At **New Market** (✉ I–81 Exit 264, ☎ 540/740–3102; 🎟 $5), the site of a costly Confederate victory late in the Civil War, the **New Market Battlefield Historical Park** has exhibits on the battle and the war.

In Staunton (pronounced *Stan*-ton) the **Woodrow Wilson Birthplace and Museum** (✉ 24 N. Coalter St., ☎ 540/885–0897; 🎟 $6.50) has been restored to its appearance in 1856, when the 28th U.S. president was born here. The **Museum of American Frontier Culture** (✉ 1250 Richmond Rd., ☎ 540/332–7850; 🎟 $8), just outside Staunton, is an outdoor living museum that re-creates early American agrarian life on four genuine 18th-century farmsteads, right down to the animals and crops.

The 470-mi **Blue Ridge Parkway,** a continuation of Skyline Drive, runs south through the **George Washington National Forest** (☞ National and State Parks, *above*) to Great Smoky Mountains National Park in North Carolina and Tennessee. Less pristine than the drive, the parkway offers better, higher views—and free admission. At the **Peaks of Otter Recreation Area,** just off the Blue Ridge Parkway northeast of Roanoke, there's a 360-degree panorama.

In Lexington, the sixth-oldest college in the country, **Washington and Lee University** is named for the first U.S. president (an early benefactor) and the Confederate commander Robert E. Lee, who served as college president after the Civil War. Among the campus's white-columned redbrick buildings is the **Lee Memorial Chapel and Museum** (☎ 540/463–8768; 🎟 free), where a saintly statue of the general shown recumbent behind the altar marks his tomb.

Next door to Washington and Lee University are the imposing neo-Gothic buildings of the **Virginia Military Institute,** since its founding in 1839 an all-male institution; a 1996 Supreme Court decision required it either to admit women or lose state funding. Here the **George C. Marshall Museum** (☎ 540/463–7103; 🎟 free) preserves the memory of the general, secretary of state, and Nobel Peace Prize winner. On display at the **Institute Museum** (☎ 540/464–7232; 🎟 free) is Stonewall Jackson's horse, stuffed and mounted. Near the Virginia Military Institute, the **Stonewall Jackson House** offers a glimpse of Jackson's private life (✉ 8 E. Washington St., ☎ 540/463–2552; 🎟 $5).

About 30 mi from Lexington, **Bath County** is the site of thermal springs once used for medical treatments and is still a popular resort area. Between Lexington and Bath County runs **Goshen Pass,** a stunning 3-mi stretch of Route 39 that follows the Maury River as it winds its way through the Alleghenies. The countryside is lush with rhododendrons in May.

★ **Natural Bridge** (✉ I–81, Exit 175 or 180A, ☎ 540/291–2121 or 800/533–1410; 🎟 free), south of Lexington, is a 215-ft-high, 90-ft-long arch that was created as the creek below gradually carved out the limestone. It really *is* a bridge, supporting U.S. 11. It's also part of a 150-acre park.

Roanoke is a quiet and cheerful railroad hub. A restored downtown warehouse called **Center in the Square** (✉ Market Sq., ☎ 540/342–5700) houses a theater, a local historical museum, an art gallery, and the **Science Museum of Western Virginia** (☎ 540/342–5710; 🎟 $5), with interactive exhibits including computer games that entertain and inform youngsters on topics such as energy resources, oceanography, geology, and meteorology. The **Virginia Museum of Transportation** (✉ 303 Norfolk Ave., ☎ 540/342–5670; 🎟 $5) houses dozens of original train cars and engines.

A restored plantation southeast of Roanoke, **Booker T. Washington National Monument** (✉ Rte. 122, ☎ 540/721–2094; free) is the birthplace of the great black educator and a living museum of life under slavery.

About two hours east of Roanoke and less than two hours south of Charlottesville is **Appomattox Courthouse National Historical Park** (✉ Rte. 24, Appomattox, ☎ 804/352–8987; $2), a village of about 30 buildings restored to their appearance on April 9, 1865, when Lee surrendered to Grant in the parlor of the McLean House here. A slide show supplements a self-guided tour, and costumed interpreters answer questions in summer.

Dining and Lodging

Bed-and-breakfast reservations in the region can be made through **Blue Ridge Bed & Breakfast** (✉ Rte. 2, Box 3895, Berryville 22611, ☎ 540/955–1246 or 800/296–1246, FAX 540/955–4240) and **Guesthouses** (✉ Box 5737, Charlottesville 22905, ☎ 804/979–7264). For price ranges *see* Charts 1 (B) and 2 (B) *in* On the Road with Fodor's.

Bath County

$$$–$$$$ ★ **The Homestead.** Famous since 1766 for its mineral waters, this is one of the country's most luxurious resorts. The elegant, spacious guest rooms have traditional Southern decor. The 15,000-acre property includes 100 mi of riding trails, nine ski slopes, and 4 mi of streams stocked with rainbow trout. The formal dining room has nightly live dance music. ✉ *U.S. 220, Hot Springs 24445,* ☎ *540/839–1766 or 800/838–1766,* FAX *540/839–7670. 517 rooms. 10 restaurants, pool, tennis, health club. MAP. AE, D, DC, MC, V.*

$$$–$$$$ **Inn at Gristmill Square.** These five buildings (gristmill, miller's house, country store, blacksmith's house, and hardware store) are a State Historic Landmark; a walk-in wine cellar is set among the gears of the original waterwheel. Entrées may include breast of chicken stuffed with wild rice, sausage, apple, and pecans. Guest rooms have a rustic Colonial Virginia motif. ✉ *Rte. 645, Box 359, Warm Springs 24484,* ☎ *540/839–2231,* FAX *540/839–5770. 16 rooms, 1 apartment. Restaurant, pool, tennis. D, MC, V.*

Blue Ridge Parkway

$$$$ **Doe Run Lodge.** The location on the crest of the Blue Ridge guarantees grand vistas of the Piedmont and proximity to golf, skiing, and hunting. Each chalet or villa has a fireplace and floor-to-ceiling windows. Some rooms have Jacuzzis or hot tubs. ✉ *Milepost 189, Blue Ridge Pkwy., Fancy Gap 24328,* ☎ *540/398–2212 or 800/325–6189,* FAX *540/398–2833. 48 units. Restaurant, pool, tennis. AE, MC, V.*

$$$$ **Wintergreen.** From December through March guests at this 11,000-acre resort are sometimes able to ski and golf on the same day; and there are plenty of sports options all year long. Accommodations range from studio mountain condos to six- and seven-bedroom houses, all-wood buildings that blend in with the leafy surroundings. ✉ *Rte. 664 Box 706, Wintergreen 22958,* ☎ *804/325–2200 or 800/266–2444,* FAX *804/325–8003. 315 units. 6 restaurants, pools, golf, tennis. AE, MC, V.*

$$ **Rocky Knob Cabins.** These log cabins, hidden away in the woods near the spectacular Rock Castle Gorge, have kitchens but no bathtubs or phones. ✉ *Milepost 174, Box 5, Meadows of Dan 24120,* ☎ *540/593–3503. 7 cabins. DC, MC, V. Closed Labor Day–Memorial Day.*

Charlottesville

$$$–$$$$ **Eastern Standard.** Specialties served in the casual but subdued upstairs dining room include kumquat basil–glazed duck breast and

Vietnamese curried vegetarian stew. The lively downstairs bistro serves pastas and light fare. ✉ *West end of Downtown Mall,* ☎ *804/295–8668. AE, D, MC, V. Upstairs closed Sun.–Tues. No lunch.*

$$–$$$$ ✕ **C&O Restaurant.** A boarded-up storefront hung with an illuminated Pepsi sign conceals this formal dining room. Try the terrine *de campagne* (pâté of veal, venison, and pork). When available on the changing menu, the *coquilles* St. Jacques are stellar. ✉ *515 E. Water St.,* ☎ *804/971–7044. AE, MC, V. No lunch Sun.*

$–$$ ✕ **Crozet Pizza.** There are up to 35 toppings from which to choose, including snow peas and asparagus spears in season. The hardwood booths are always full, and on weekends take-out must be ordered hours in advance. ✉ *Rte. 240, Crozet, west of Charlottesville,* ☎ *804/823–2132. No credit cards. Closed Sun.–Mon.*

$$$–$$$$ ✕ **Boar's Head Inn.** Built around a restored early 19th-century gristmill set on two small lakes, the Boar's Head has simple but elegant guest rooms with Victorian antiques. Some suites have fireplaces. In the Old Mill Room restaurant, the costumed staff serves bison carpaccio, cider-marinated pork loin, and the like. ✉ *U.S. 250W (Box 5307), 22905,* ☎ *804/296–2181 or 800/476–1988,* FAX *804/972–6024. 184 rooms. 2 restaurants, pools, golf, tennis courts, exercise room. AE, D, DC, MC, V.*

$$$–$$$$ ✕ **Silver Thatch Inn.** This 18th-century farmhouse has a Colonial America theme, and every guest room is unique. In the restaurant, provisioned by three organic farms, the fish is always fresh and the rabbits and chickens are often locally raised. The wine cellar wins national awards. ✉ *3001 Hollymead Dr., 22911,* ☎ *804/978–4686,* FAX *804/973–6156. 7 rooms. Restaurant, pool. Full breakfast. AE, DC, MC, V.*

$$ **English Inn.** Guests here are treated to the amenities of a fine hotel and the charm of a country inn. Guest rooms are modern; suites have sitting rooms. Guests have free access to a health club about a mile away. ✉ *2000 Morton Dr., 22903,* ☎ *804/971–9900 or 800/786–5400,* FAX *804/977–8008. 88 rooms. Pool, exercise room. CP. AE, DC, MC, V.*

Lexington

$$$–$$$$ ✕ **Maple Hall.** In this mid-19th-century plantation house on 56 acres, guest rooms have period antiques and modern amenities. The main dining room has a large decorative fireplace. Notable entrées include beef fillet with green-peppercorn sauce. ✉ *3111 N. Lee Hwy., 24450 (7 mi north of Lexington on U.S. 11,* ☎ *540/463–6693,* FAX *540/463–7262. 21 rooms. Restaurant, pool, tennis. D, MC, V.*

Roanoke

$ ✕ **Texas Tavern.** The sign says, WE SERVE A THOUSAND, TEN AT A TIME. The tavern is often packed, especially at night, so you may have to wait for one of the 10 stools; but the tough-looking guys behind the counter will fill your order quickly. Chili is the specialty. No liquor is served. ✉ *114 Church Ave.,* ☎ *540/342–4825. Reservations not accepted. No credit cards.*

Staunton

$–$$ ✕ **Rowe's Family Restaurant.** This bright, booth-filled dining room has been operated by the same family since 1947. Specialties include Virginia ham, steak, chicken, and homemade pies (try the mincemeat). ✉ *I–81 Exit 222,* ☎ *540/886–1833. D, MC, V.*

$$$–$$$$ ✕ **Belle Grae Inn.** Dining rooms in this restored Victorian house have brass wall sconces and Oriental rugs; the menu is Continental with a Southern twist. Canopy beds, antiques, and rocking chairs give the guest rooms a turn-of-the-century mood. ✉ *515 W. Frederick St., 24401,* ☎ *540/886–5151,* FAX *540/886–6641. 16 rooms. Restaurant. Full breakfast. AE, MC, V.*

$$$–$$$$ **Frederick House.** Three restored town houses dating from 1810 make up this antiques-filled inn in the center of the historic district. ✉ *28 N. New St., 24401,* ☎ *540/885–4220 or 800/334-5575. 14 rooms. Full breakfast. AE, D, DC, MC, V.*

Motels

Quality Inn Civic Center (✉ 501 Orange Ave., Roanoke 24016, ☎ 540/342–8961, FAX 540/342–3813), 152 rooms, restaurant, pool; *$$.*

Roseloe Motel (✉ Rte. 2, Box 590, Hot Springs 24445, ☎ 540/839–5373), 14 rooms; *$.*

Campgrounds

In Shenandoah National Park (☞ National and State Parks, *above*) the **Big Meadows Campground** (☎ 540/999–3500 or 800/365–2267) accepts reservations. Other campsites in the park are available on a first-come, first-served basis; for information contact the park.

Nightlife and the Arts

Nightlife

In Charlottesville the large and comfortable **Miller's** (✉ 109 W. Main St., Downtown Mall, ☎ 804/971–8511) hosts blues and jazz musicians. At the **Homestead** in Hot Springs (☞ Dining and Lodging, *above*) there's nightly dancing to live music.

The Arts

CHARLOTTESVILLE

For details on performances at the University of Virginia, check the *Cavalier Daily.* **McGuffey Art Center** (✉ 201 2nd St. NW, ☎ 804/295–7973), which houses the studios of painters and sculptors and the contemporary Second Street Gallery, also hosts concerts and performance pieces.

SHENANDOAH VALLEY

Garth Newel Music Center (✉ Hot Springs, ☎ 540/839–5018) hosts chamber music concerts on summer weekends. The **Theater at Lime Kiln** (✉ Lexington, ☎ 540/463–3074) is an outdoor rock-wall pit (the ruins of a lime kiln) where plays and concerts—folk, bluegrass, classical, and other nonrock music—take place throughout the summer. **Roanoke Ballet Theatre** (☎ 540/345–6099) performs in spring and fall.

Outdoor Activities and Sports

Canoeing

Front Royal Canoe (✉ U.S. 340, ☎ 540/635–5440) and **Downriver Canoe** (✉ Rte. 613, ☎ 540/635–5526) are both near Front Royal. **Shenandoah River Outfitters** (✉ Rte. 684, ☎ 540/743–4159) is near Luray.

Fishing

To take advantage of the abundance of trout in some 50 streams of **Shenandoah National Park,** get a five-day Virginia fishing license, available in season (early April–mid-October) at concession stands along Skyline Drive.

Golf

Caverns Country Club Resort (✉ U.S. 211 , Luray, ☎ 540/743–6551). **Greene Hills Club** (✉ Rte. 619, Stanardsville, ☎ 804/985–7328). The **Homestead** (✉ U.S. 220, Hot Springs, ☎ 540/839–1766 or 800/838–1766). **Wintergreen Resort** (✉ Rte. 664, Wintergreen, ☎ 804/325–2200 or 800/325–2200).

Hiking

The stretch of the **Appalachian Trail** running through Shenandoah National Park takes hikers along the Blue Ridge Skyline, taking in stunning views of the Piedmont and the Shenandoah Valley in the distance; white-tailed deer often appear at arm's length. The main pathway's proximity to Skyline Drive and frequent parking lots make hike lengths flexible. For deep-wilderness hikes, 500 mi of marked side trails lead into the backcountry.

Tennis

Caverns Country Club Resort, the **Homestead,** and **Wintergreen Resort** (☞ Golf, *above*) offer tennis.

Spectator Sports

Equestrian events: The **Virginia Horse Center** (✉ Lexington, ☎ 540/463–2194) stages show jumping, hunter trials, and multibreed shows year-round. **Football, soccer, basketball, golf, tennis, and field hockey:** The **University of Virginia** (☎ 804/924–8821) is nationally ranked in several varsity sports. The *Cavalier Daily* has listings.

Ski Areas

The **Homestead** (☞ Golf, *above*) has cross-country, downhill, and night skiing. **Massanutten Resort** (✉ Rte. 644 off U.S. 33, McGaheysville, ☎ 540/289–9441) has rentals and snowmaking facilities. **Wintergreen Resort** (☞ Golf, *above*) maintains 17 slopes and trails.

Shopping

Lewis Glaser Quill Pens (✉ 1700 Sourwood Pl., Charlottesville, ☎ 804/973–7783 or 800/446–6732) sells feather pens and pewter inkwells of the kind it has made for the U.S. Supreme Court and the British royal family. **Court Square Antiques** (✉ 4th and Jefferson Sts., Charlottesville, ☎ 804/295–6244) carries a selection of quilts, furniture, and collectibles.

NORTHERN VIRGINIA

The affluent and cosmopolitan residents of this region look more to neighboring Washington, D.C., than to the rest of the state for direction. Yet they take pride in being Virginians and in protecting the historic treasures they hold in trust for the rest of the nation. Here are some of America's most precious acreage, including Mount Vernon and the Civil War battlefield of Manassas (Bull Run). The enormous Potomac Mills Mall, in Prince William, is Virginia's most visited site. The gracious Old South lives on in the fox hunting and steeplechases of Loudoun County. On the nearby Northern Neck visitors can combine historic sightseeing with fishing and water sports.

Visitor Information

Fairfax County: Convention and Visitors Bureau (✉ 8300 Boone Blvd., Suite 450, Vienna 22182, ☎ 703/790–3329). **Loudoun County:** Tourism Council (✉ 108D South St. SE, Leesburg 20175, ☎ 703/771–2170 or 800/752–6118). **Northern Neck:** Visitor Information Service (✉ Box 312, Reedville 22539, ☎ 800/453–6167). **Alexandria:** Convention and Visitors Association (✉ 221 King St., 22314, ☎ 703/838–4200). **Fredericksburg:** Visitor Center (✉ 706 Caroline St., 22401, ☎ 540/373–1776 or 800/678–4748).

Arriving and Departing

By Bus

Greyhound Lines (☏ 800/231–2222) serves Fairfax (✉ 4103 Rust St.), Arlington (✉ 3860 S. Four Mile Run Dr.), Fredericksburg (✉ 1400 Jefferson Davis Hwy.), and Springfield (✉ 6583 Backlick Rd.).

By Car

I–95 runs north–south along the eastern side of the region. I–66 runs east–west. Fredericksburg is 50 mi south of Washington, D.C., on I–95. Route 3 runs the length of the Northern Neck.

By Plane

Two major airports serve both northern Virginia and the Washington, D.C., area. The busy **Washington National Airport** (☏ 703/419–8000), in Arlington, has scheduled daily flights by all major U.S. carriers. **Dulles International Airport** (☏ 703/419–8000), in Loudoun County 26 mi west of Washington, is a modern facility served by major U.S. airlines and many international carriers.

By Train

Amtrak (☏ 800/872–7245) stops in Alexandria (✉ 110 Callahan Dr.) and Fredericksburg (✉ Caroline St. and Lafayette Blvd.); some travelers find it easiest to arrive in the capital's Union Station (☞ Washington, D.C.).

Exploring Northern Virginia

★ George Washington's **Mount Vernon** (✉ Rte. 235 and George Washington Memorial Pkwy., ☏ 703/780–2000; 🎟 $8) is the most visited house museum in the country. The elegant, porticoed farmhouse, built beginning in 1754 from Washington's own plans, has been restored to its appearance during the years when the first president lived here (1759–75, 1783–89, and 1797–99). Washington and his wife, Martha, are buried here.

Washington's nephew Lawrence Lewis lived at **Woodlawn** (✉ U.S. 1, ☏ 703/780–4000; 🎟 $6 [$10 includes admission to Pope-Leighey House]), designed by the architect of the Capitol, William Thornton, and begun in 1800. The formal gardens include a large collection of rare old-fashioned roses. Also on the grounds is the small **Pope-Leighey House,** designed by Frank Lloyd Wright and built in 1946.

South of Mount Vernon is the relatively unvisited but meticulously restored **Gunston Hall** (✉ Gunston Rd., ☏ 703/550–9220; 🎟 $5), the circa-1755 Georgian-style plantation home of George Mason, one of the framers of the Constitution.

North of Mount Vernon, on the Potomac, is **Alexandria,** a suburb of Washington, D.C., with an identity based on more than two centuries of history. **Old Town** is a neighborhood of 18th- and 19th-century town houses, most of them redbrick. Its major sights can be seen on foot within 20 blocks or so, and the area has scores of shops and restaurants. Parking is usually scarce, but the **Convention and Visitors Association** (☞ Visitor Information, *above*) provides a free 24-hour pass that allows free parking at two-hour meters.

This visitor center—the best place to start a tour—is in the town's oldest structure, **Ramsay House** (✉ 221 King St., ☏ 703/838–4200), believed to have been built around 1724 in Dumfries (25 mi south) and moved here in 1749. The 1752 **Carlyle House** (✉ 121 N. Fairfax St., ☏ 703/549–2997; 🎟 $4), built by Scottish merchant John Carlyle, is still the grandest house in town. The **Old Presbyterian Meeting House**

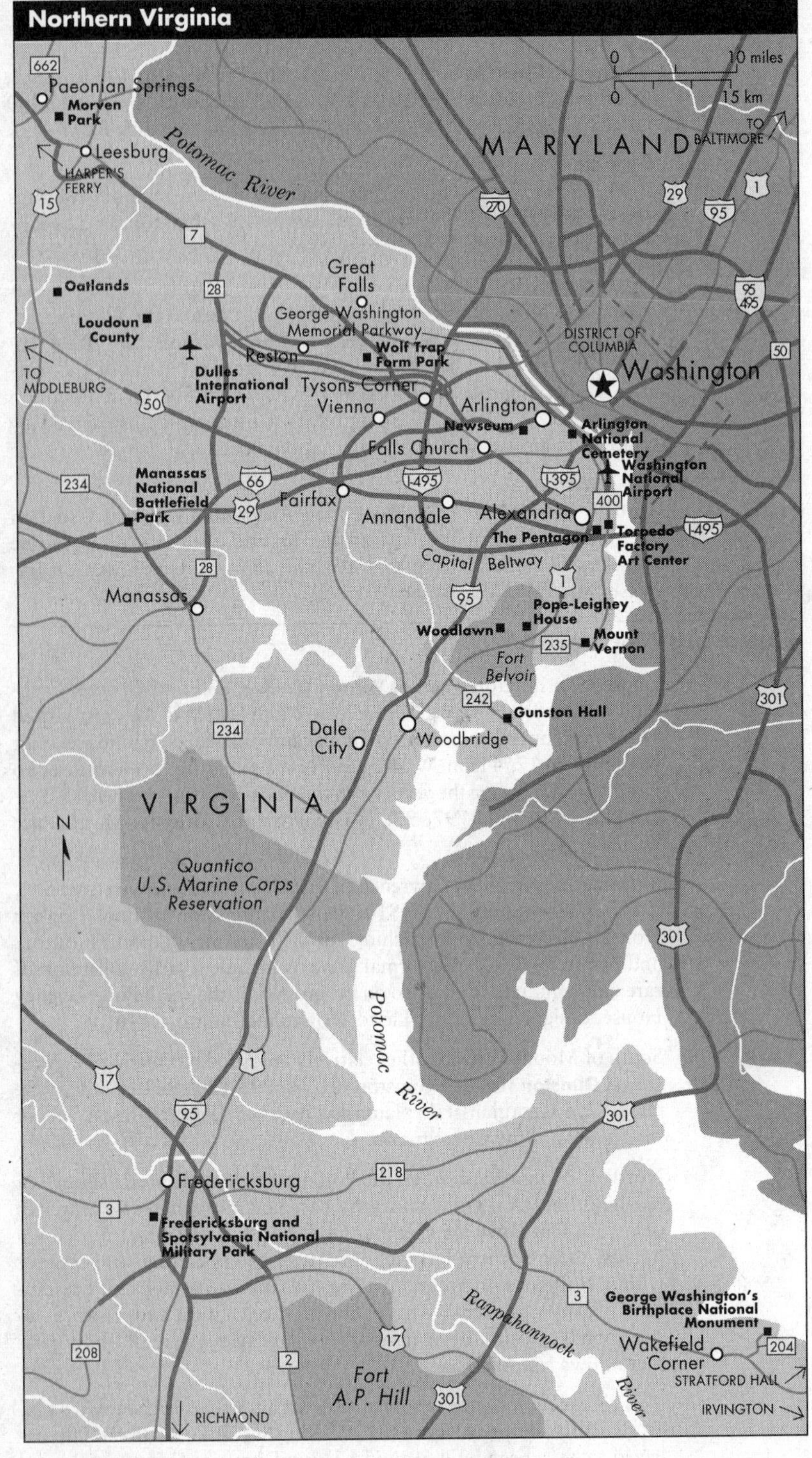
Northern Virginia
0 10 miles
0 15 km
MARYLAND
TO BALTIMORE
VIRGINIA
DISTRICT OF COLUMBIA
Washington
Paeonian Springs
Morven Park
Leesburg
HARPER'S FERRY
Potomac River
Oatlands
Loudoun County
Great Falls
George Washington Memorial Parkway
Reston
Wolf Trap Farm Park
TO MIDDLEBURG
Dulles International Airport
Tysons Corner
Vienna
Arlington
Newseum
Arlington National Cemetery
Falls Church
Washington National Airport
Manassas National Battlefield Park
Fairfax
Annandale
Alexandria
The Pentagon
Torpedo Factory Art Center
Capital Beltway
Manassas
Pope-Leighey House
Woodlawn
Mount Vernon
Fort Belvoir
Gunston Hall
Dale City
Woodbridge
N
Quantico U.S. Marine Corps Reservation
Potomac River
Fredericksburg
Fredericksburg and Spotsylvania National Military Park
Rappahannock River
George Washington's Birthplace National Monument
Wakefield Corner
STRATFORD HALL
IRVINGTON
Fort A.P. Hill
RICHMOND
662
15
7
28
50
234
66
29
28
234
270
29
95
1
95 495
50
I-495
I-395
400
I-495
1
95
235
242
301
301
301
17
1
95
218
3
3
17
208
2
301
204

(✉ 321 S. Fairfax St., ☎ 703/549–6670; 🎫 free) is another fine 18th-century reminder of the town's Scottish heritage.

George Washington frequented the **Stabler-Leadbeater Apothecary Museum** (✉ 105–107 S. Fairfax St., ☎ 703/836–3713; 🎫 $2.50), **Gadsby's Tavern Museum** (✉ 134 N. Royal St., ☎ 703/838–4242; 🎫 $4), and **Christ Church** (✉ 118 N. Washington St., ☎ 703/549–1450; 🎫 free). Another member of Christ Church was Robert E. Lee; the **boyhood home of Robert E. Lee** (✉ 607 Oronoco St., ☎ 703/548–8454; 🎫 $4) is about three blocks from Christ Church.

The homes of less-famous residents help to fill out a picture of 18th- and 19th-century life. The block of Prince Street between Fairfax and Lee, lined by imposing three-story houses, is called **Gentry Row.** The cobblestone block of humbler residences between Lee and Union is called **Captain's Row.**

Alexandria's cultural heritage is honored at the **Lyceum** (✉ 201 S. Washington St., ☎ 703/838–4994), with displays of decorative arts and exhibits on local history. Works by local and national artists are shown at the **Athaeneum** (✉ 201 Prince St., ☎ 703/548–0035). At the **Torpedo Factory Art Center** (✉ 105 N. Union St., ☎ 703/838–4565), a renovated waterfront building where torpedoes were made during both world wars, more than 180 artists and craftspeople make and sell their wares. All three sites have free admission.

Farther away but visible from a distance is the 333-ft-high **George Washington Masonic National Memorial** (✉ 101 Callahan Dr., ☎ 703/683–2007; 🎫 free). Here you'll see relics of the first president and exhibits on the Masonic Order and to go to the top, where there's a spectacular view of Alexandria and nearby Washington, D.C.

★ The **Newseum** (✉ 1101 Wilson Blvd., Arlington, ☎ 703/284–3700 or 888/639–7386; 🎫 free), the world's only museum dedicated exclusively to news, features a 126-ft-long wall of video monitors showing dozens of satellite news feeds from around the world and exhibits tracing the history of news gathering. The museum is closed Monday and Tuesday. Adjacent to the museum is Freedom Park, which honors journalists who have died in the line of duty.

For information on **Arlington National Cemetery** and the **Pentagon,** *see* Washington, D.C., *below*.

Fredericksburg, about an hour south of Washington, D.C., rivals Alexandria and Mount Vernon for associations with the Washington family. From ages 6–16 the future first president lived at Ferry Farm across the Rappahannock River. His sister Betty and her husband lived at **Kenmore** (✉ 1201 Washington Ave., ☎ 540/373–3381; 🎫 $6), a house whose plain facade belies a lavish interior. The home of Charles Washington, George's brother, later became the **Rising Sun Tavern** (✉ 1306 Caroline St., ☎ 540/371–1494; 🎫 $3), a watering hole for such revolutionaries as Patrick Henry and Thomas Jefferson. The **Mary Washington House** (✉ Charles and Lewis Sts., ☎ 540/373–1569; 🎫 $3) is a modest house George bought for his mother during her last years.

The future fifth president lived in Fredericksburg, and the **James Monroe Museum and Memorial Library** (✉ 908 Charles St., ☎ 540/654–1043; 🎫 $3) is in the tiny one-story building where he practiced law from 1787 to 1789.

At the **Hugh Mercer Apothecary Shop** (✉ Caroline and Amelia Sts., ☎ 540/373–3362; 🎫 $3), the guide's explicit descriptions of amputations, cataract operations, and tooth extractions can make latter-day visitors wince.

Four Civil War battlefields—Fredericksburg, Chancellorsville, the Wilderness, and the Spotsylvania Courthouse—make up the **Fredericksburg and Spotsylvania National Military Park.** All are within 17 mi of Fredericksburg, where a **visitor center** (✉ 1013 Lafayette Blvd. [U.S. Bus. 1], ☎ 540/371–0802; 🎫 $3) has an introductory slide show and exhibits.

Route 3 east of Fredericksburg takes you into the **Northern Neck,** a strip of land bounded by the Potomac and the Rappahannock rivers. At the top of the Neck is Westmoreland County, which produced both the Father of Our Country and one of the greatest tragic heroes of the Civil War, Robert E. Lee.

George Washington's Birthplace National Monument (✉ Rte. 204, ☎ 804/224–1732; 🎫 $2), in Oak Grove, preserves the memory of the first president with a working farm and a reproduction of the original early 18th-century plantation house (the original burned down on Christmas Day 1779). Washington's family members are buried on the property.

Stratford Hall (✉ Rte. 214, Stratford, ☎ 804/493–8038; 🎫 $7), the birthplace of Robert E. Lee, is an elegant original from the 1730s, built in the shape of an *H,* with brick and timber produced on the site. Farmers still cultivate 1,600 of the original acres, and their yield, a variety of cereals, is for sale. Lunch is served in a log cabin from April through October.

At the far end of the Northern Neck is a jewel of Tidewater architecture: Irvington's **Christ Church** (✉ Junction of Rtes. 646 and 709, ☎ 804/438–6855; 🎫 free), a redbrick sanctuary of cruciform design, built in 1732.

Twenty-six miles west of Washington is the monumentally important **Manassas National Battlefield Park,** or Bull Run (✉ Rte. 234 off I–66, ☎ 703/361–1339), where the Confederacy won two major victories and Stonewall Jackson earned his nickname.

About an hour west of Washington is horse country. In **Loudoun County**'s fashionable towns of **Leesburg** and **Middleburg,** residents (many of them Yankee transplants) keep up the local traditions of fox hunts and steeplechases. The county visitor center in Leesburg (☞ Visitor Information, *above*) can suggest scenic drives.

Oatlands (✉ Rte. 15, 6 mi south of Leesburg, ☎ 703/777–3174; 🎫 $7) is a restored Greek Revival plantation house whose manicured fields host public and private equestrian events from spring through fall. The Greek Revival mansion at **Morven Park** (✉ Old Waterford Rd., 1 mi north of Leesburg, ☎ 703/777–2414; 🎫 $6), a White House look-alike, contains two museums: one of horse-drawn carriages, the other of hounds and hunting.

Dining and Lodging

Old Town Alexandria's restaurants are many and varied, but they are also pricey and, on weekend nights, crowded. Arlington's Little Saigon, on and around Wilson Boulevard, has many excellent and affordable Vietnamese restaurants.

Lodging prices are high, but so are the standards of comfort and luxury. Bed-and-breakfasts tend to be more elegant here because many serve as romantic weekend hideaways for regular customers from Washington.

For listings try **Bed & Breakfast Accommodations Ltd. of Washington, D.C.** (✉ Box 12011, Washington, DC 20005, ☎ 202/328–3510, FAX 202/332–3885). **Princely Bed & Breakfast** (✉ 2822 Avenham Ave., Roanoke 24014, ☎ 800/470–5588) lists accommodations in historic Old Town homes.

For price ranges *see* Charts 1 (A) and 2 (A) *in* On the Road with Fodor's.

Alexandria

$$–$$$ ✕ **Le Gaulois.** At this quiet country bistro whose white walls are hung with scenes of southern France, specialties include *pot-au-feu gaulois* (a beef-and-chicken stew with whole vegetables) and *cassoulet* (a rich bean casserole with sausage and beef). ✉ *1106 King St.,* ☎ *703/739–9494. AE, D, DC, MC, V. Closed Sun.*

$$–$$$ ✕ **Santa Fe East.** A re-creation of old Santa Fe, with enclosed courtyards, exposed brick, and wood planking, Santa Fe East serves up neosouthwestern items such as shrimp empanadas; smoked duck quesadillas; and chile rellenos stuffed with goat cheese, rolled in blue cornmeal, and deep fried. ✉ *110 S. Pitt St.,* ☎ *703/548–6900. AE, DC, MC, V.*

$$ ★ ✕ **Taverna Cretekou.** Inside, surrounded by whitewashed stucco walls and brightly colored macramé tapestries, or outside in the canopied garden, diners enjoy such dishes as lamb *Exohikon* (baked in a pastry shell). All the wines are Greek. ✉ *818 King St.,* ☎ *703/548–8688. AE, MC, V. Closed Mon.*

$ ✕ **Hard Times Café.** Recorded country-and-western music and framed photographs of Depression-era Oklahoma set the tone at this casual, always crowded hangout. Three kinds of chili are served—Texas (spicy), Cincinnati (mild), and vegetarian. ✉ *1404 King St.,* ☎ *703/683–5340. AE, MC, V.*

$$$ 🏨 **Holiday Inn Select Old Town.** The mahogany-paneled lobby and hunting prints in the guest rooms suggest a men's club. Marble bathtubs, modem-ready phones, and extraordinary service—an exercise bike will be brought to your room on request—make this an exceptional member of the chain. Free shuttle service to the airport and the Metro is provided. ✉ *480 King St., 22314,* ☎ *703/549–6080 or 800/368–5047,* FAX *703/684–6508. 227 rooms. Restaurant, pool, exercise room. AE, D, DC, MC, V.*

$$$ ★ 🏨 **Morrison House.** Butlers unpack for guests in rooms with four-poster beds, and tea is served every afternoon at this convincing Federal-style house (built in 1985). ✉ *116 S. Alfred St., 22314,* ☎ *703/838–8000 or 800/367–0800,* FAX *703/684–6283. 45 rooms. 2 restaurants. CP. AE, DC, MC, V.*

Arlington

$ ★ ✕ **Queen Bee.** Arlington's Little Saigon area has many good Vietnamese restaurants, but this is one of the best. Moist and delicately flavored spring rolls and the Saigon pancake—accented with a mix of crab, pork, and shrimp—are two reasons that diners are willing to wait in line for a table. ✉ *3181 Wilson Blvd.,* ☎ *703/527–3444. AE, MC, V.*

$$$–$$$$ 🏨 **Marriott Crystal Gateway.** White marble, blond wood, and lots of greenery distinguish this hotel for big-budget business travelers and tourists who want to be pampered. ✉ *1700 Jefferson Davis Hwy., 22202,* ☎ *703/920–3230 or 800/228–9290,* FAX *703/271–5212. 697 rooms. 2 restaurants, pools, exercise room. AE, D, DC, MC, V.*

$$$–$$$$ 🏨 **Ritz-Carlton Pentagon City.** This soundproofed enclave of luxury five minutes from the airport has Persian carpets in the lobby and silk wallpaper in the reproduction Federal bedrooms. All rooms have an overstuffed chair and ottoman, Chippendale-style furniture, and silk bed coverings. Many rooms have a view of the monuments across the river

in Washington. ✉ *1250 S. Hayes St., 22202,* ☎ *703/415–5000,* FAX *703/415–5060. 345 rooms. Restaurant, pool, exercise room. AE, D, DC, MC, V.*

$$ **Best Western Arlington.** The attraction here is convenience: easy access to I–395 and a free shuttle to the airport. The rooms are unexceptional and modern. ✉ *2480 S. Glebe Rd., 22206,* ☎ *703/979–4400 or 800/426–6886,* FAX *703/685–0051. 325 rooms. Restaurant, pool, exercise room. AE, D, DC, MC, V.*

Fairfax

$$$ **Bailiwick Inn.** Guest rooms in this 1812 house is take their themes from famous Virginians; all have featherbeds and antiques or period reproductions. Some rooms have fireplaces; the bridal suite has a four-poster bed and whirlpool bath. ✉ *4023 Chain Bridge Rd., 22030,* ☎ *703/691–2266 or 800/366–7666,* FAX *703/934–2112. 14 rooms. Full breakfast. AE, MC, V.*

Fredericksburg

$$–$$$$ ✕ **Le Lafayette.** In this pre-Revolutionary Georgian house guests enjoy what could be called "Virginia French" food: smoked salmon, duckling with raspberry sauce, and other novelties. ✉ *623 Caroline St.,* ☎ *540/373–6895. AE, D, DC, MC, V. Closed Mon.*

$$–$$$$ ✕ **Ristorante Renato.** This candlelighted Italian restaurant, an unusual find in the midst of a Colonial town, specializes in "Romeo and Juliet" (veal and chicken topped with mozzarella in a white-wine sauce) and shrimp scampi Napoli with lemon-butter sauce. ✉ *422 Williams St.,* ☎ *540/371–8228. AE, MC, V.*

$$$–$$$$ **Richard Johnston Inn.** This three-story row house across from the visitor center has parking in the rear under magnolia trees. Guest rooms have 18th- and 19th-century antique reproductions; the suites open onto a courtyard. ✉ *711 Caroline St., 22401,* ☎ *540/899–7606. 8 rooms. AE, MC, V.*

$ **Johnny Appleseed Inn.** This generic two-story, family-oriented motel is five minutes from the battlefields. The most pleasant views are of the pool. ✉ *543 Warrenton Rd., off U.S. 17 or I–95, 22406,* ☎ *540/373–0000 or 800/633–6443,* FAX *540/373–5676. 88 rooms. Restaurant, pool. AE, D, DC, MC, V.*

Great Falls

$$$ ★ ✕ **L'Auberge Chez François.** White stucco, dark exposed beams, and a garden just outside create a country-inn ambience 20 minutes from Tysons Corner. The Alsatian cuisine includes salmon soufflé with salmon-and-scallop mousse and lobster sauce. ✉ *332 Springvale Rd., Rte. 674,* ☎ *703/759–3800. Reservations essential 4 wks in advance. Jacket required. AE, D, DC, MC, V. Closed Mon. No lunch.*

Northern Neck

$$$ **Tides Inn.** At this 500-acre waterfront resort on a Rappahannock tributary, all the rooms have water views. For an even closer look, guests can take a dinner or luncheon cruise on one of the inn's two yachts. Guests have access to a nearby fitness center. ✉ *480 King Carter Dr., Irvington 22480,* ☎ *804/438–5000 or 800/843–3746,* FAX *804/438–5222. 194 rooms. 6 restaurants, pools, tennis. AE, D, DC, MC, V.*

Tysons Corner

$$ ✕ **Clyde's.** Quality is high, service is attentive, and the tone's always lively in these art deco–style dining rooms. The long, eclectic menu includes fresh fish, often in such preparations as trout Parmesan. ✉ *8332 Leesburg Pike,* ☎ *703/734–1900. AE, D, DC, MC, V.*

Motel

Hampton Inn (✉ 2310 William St., Fredericksburg 22401, ☎ 540/371–0330 or 800/426–7866, FAX 540/371–1753), 166 rooms, pool; *$$*.

Nightlife and the Arts

Nightlife

The **Birchmere** (✉ 3701 Mount Vernon Ave., Alexandria, ☎ 703/549–7500) has everything from rockabilly to bluegrass. **Murphy's Irish Pub** (✉ 713 King St., Alexandria, ☎ 703/548–1717) hosts Irish and folk performers. **Two Nineteen** (✉ 219 King St., Alexandria, ☎ 703/549–1141) has jazz upstairs and a sports bar in the basement. **Clyde's** (✉ 8332 Leesburg Pike, Tysons Corner, ☎ 703/734–1900) attracts unattached professionals.

The Arts

The **Arts Council of Fairfax County** (☎ 703/642–0862) acts as a clearinghouse for information about performances and exhibitions throughout northern Virginia. **Wolf Trap Farm Park** (✉ 1551 Trap Rd., Vienna, ☎ 703/255–1860 or 703/938–2404), one of the major performing arts venues in the greater Washington area, presents top musical and dance performers in a grand outdoor pavilion during the warmer months and in 18th-century farm buildings the rest of the year. The facility also hosts many children's activities, including mime, puppet, and animal shows.

Outdoor Activities and Sports

Biking

The 19-mi **Mount Vernon Bicycle Trail** (☎ 703/285–2598) runs along the Potomac, from Rosslyn to Mount Vernon and through Alexandria. The 4-mi **Burke Lake Park Bicycle Trail** (☎ 703/323–6601), in Fairfax County, circles the lake. The Arlington Parks and Recreation Bureau (☎ 703/228–4747) provides a free map of the **county Bikeway System.**

Golf

Algonkian Park (✉ 47001 Fairway Dr., Sterling, ☎ 703/450–4655) and **Burke Lake Park** (✉ Fairfax Station, ☎ 703/323–1641) have public courses. The **Tides Inn** (☎ 804/438–5501; ☞ Dining and Lodging, *above*) has 9- and 18-hole courses.

Water Sports

The Northern Neck gives sailors, water-skiers, and windsurfers access to two rivers and the Chesapeake Bay. For information contact the **Northern Neck Travel Council** (☞ Visitor Information, *above*).

Shopping

Potomac Mills Mall (✉ 2700 Potomac Mills Circle, I–95, Dale City) is the state's most visited attraction; Swedish furniture giant IKEA is one of 220 outlets. **Tysons Corner Center** (✉ 1961 Chain Bridge Rd., junction of Rtes. 7 and 123 and I–495) houses 240 retailers, including Bloomingdale's and Nordstrom. **Galleria at Tysons II** (✉ 2001 International Dr.) has 125 retailers, including Saks Fifth Avenue and Neiman Marcus. **Tiffany & Co.** (✉ 8045 Leesburg Pike, ☎ 703/893–7700) is a few minutes away from the Galleria at Tysons.

The old towns of Alexandria and Fredericksburg are dense with **antiques** shops, many quite expensive, that are particularly strong on the Federal and Victorian periods. The town visitor centers (☞ Visitor Information, *above*) have maps and lists of the stores.

RICHMOND AND TIDEWATER

Strictly speaking, Tidewater Virginia is the region east of the fall line of the rivers flowing into the Chesapeake Bay; but "Tidewater" has also come to stand for the so-called genteel Old South. Richmond, on the fall line of the James, straddles both the Tidewater region and the Piedmont region, with its rolling plains; so, too, it bridges Virginia past and present, with remnants of the Confederacy preserved amid the cultural and commercial bustle of a modern state capital. An hour southeast are two former capitals: Colonial Williamsburg, a restored 18th-century town; and Jamestown, Virginia's original capital, long deserted and all the more stirring for it. With Yorktown, where the Colonies won their independence, these pre-Revolutionary towns form the Historic Triangle.

Visitor Information

Metro Richmond: Visitors Center (✉ 1710 Robin Hood Rd. [Exit 78 off I-95/I-64], 23220, ☎ 804/358-5511); for mailed information, write to 6th St. Marketplace, 5500 E. Marshall St., 22319, ☎ 804/782-2777 or 800/365-7272. **Petersburg:** Visitors Center (✉ 425 Cockade Alley, 23803, ☎ 804/733-2400 or 800/368-3595). **Williamsburg:** Convention and Visitors Bureau (✉ Box 3585, 23187, ☎ 757/253-0192 or 800/368-6511); Colonial Williamsburg (✉ 201 Penniman Rd., ☎ 800/447-8679). **Yorktown:** Colonial National Historical Park (✉ Box 210, 23690, ☎ 757/898-3400).

Arriving and Departing

By Bus

Greyhound Lines (☎ 800/231-2222) serves Richmond (✉ 2910 N. Boulevard) and Williamsburg (✉ 468 N. Boundary St.).

By Car

Richmond is at the intersection of I-95 and I-64; U.S. 1 runs north-south by the city. Petersburg is 20 mi south of Richmond on I-95. Williamsburg is 51 mi east of Richmond via I-64; the Colonial Parkway joins it with Jamestown and Yorktown.

By Plane

Richmond International Airport (☎ 804/226-3000) is served by most major airlines. **Newport News-Williamsburg International Airport** (☎ 757/877-0924), in Newport News, and **Norfolk International Airport** (☎ 757/857-3351) also serve the region.

By Train

Amtrak (☎ 800/872-7245) serves Richmond (✉ 7519 Staples Mill Rd.) and Williamsburg (✉ 468 N. Boundary St.).

Exploring Richmond and Tidewater

Richmond

Most of Richmond's historic attractions lie north of the James River, which bisects the city in a sweeping curve. West of downtown are such gracious residential neighborhoods as Monument Avenue, with its statues of Civil War heroes. Streets fan out southwesterly from Park Avenue to form the gaslighted **Fan District,** a hip neighborhood of restored turn-of-the-century town houses.

The heart of old Richmond is the **Court End District,** which contains seven National Historic Landmarks, three museums, and 11 more buildings on the National Register of Historic Places—all within eight

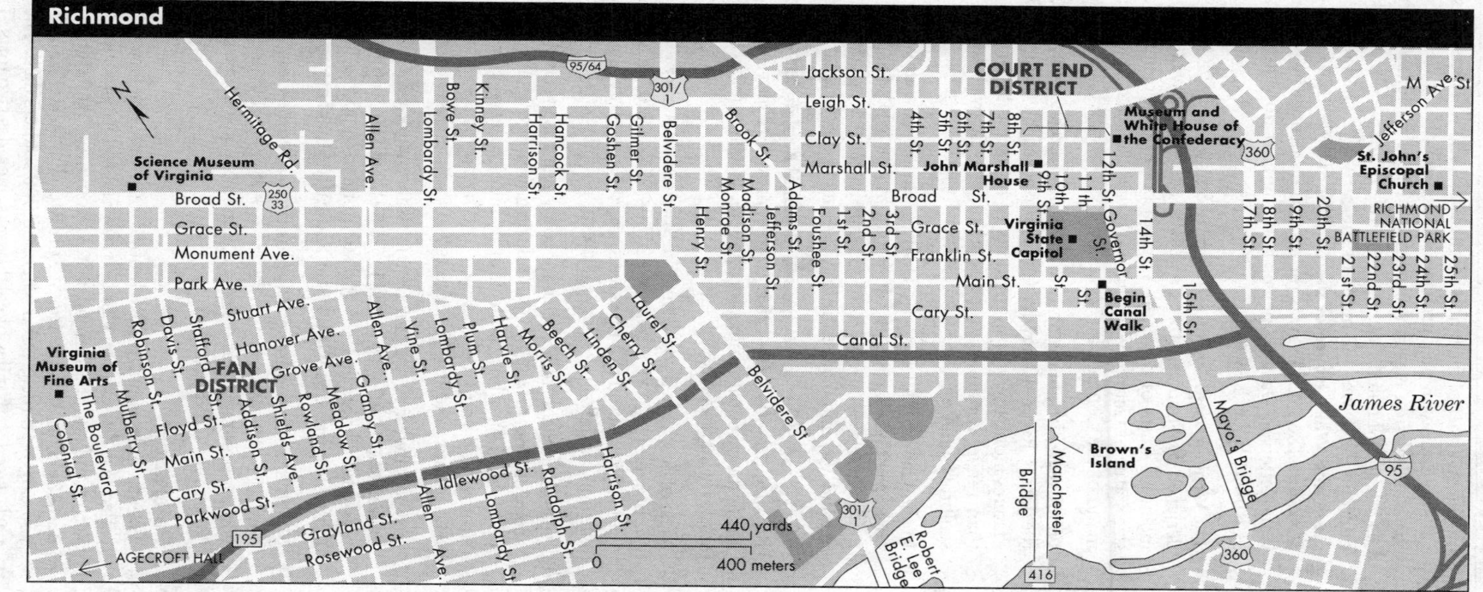

Richmond
COURT END DISTRICT
FAN DISTRICT
Museum and White House of the Confederacy
St. John's Episcopal Church
RICHMOND NATIONAL BATTLEFIELD PARK
John Marshall House
Virginia State Capitol
Begin Canal Walk
Brown's Island
Science Museum of Virginia
Virginia Museum of Fine Arts
AGECROFT HALL
James River
Mayo's Bridge
Manchester Bridge
Robert E. Lee Bridge
Jefferson Ave.
M St.
25th St.
24th St.
23rd. St.
22nd St.
21st St.
20th St.
19th St.
18th St.
17th St.
15th St.
14th St.
12th St.
11th St.
10th St.
9th St.
8th St.
7th St.
6th St.
5th St.
4th St.
3rd St.
2nd St.
1st St.
Governor St.
Jackson St.
Leigh St.
Clay St.
Marshall St.
Broad St.
Grace St.
Franklin St.
Main St.
Cary St.
Canal St.
Foushee St.
Adams St.
Jefferson St.
Madison St.
Monroe St.
Henry St.
Brook St.
Belvidere St.
Gilmer St.
Goshen St.
Hancock St.
Harrison St.
Kinney St.
Bowe St.
Lombardy St.
Allen Ave.
Hermitage Rd.
Monument Ave.
Park Ave.
Stuart Ave.
Hanover Ave.
Grove Ave.
Laurel St.
Cherry St.
Linden St.
Beech St.
Morris St.
Harvie St.
Plum St.
Vine St.
Granby St.
Meadow St.
Rowland St.
Shields Ave.
Addison St.
Stafford St.
Davis St.
Robinson St.
Floyd St.
Mulberry St.
The Boulevard
Colonial St.
Idlewood St.
Randolph St.
Grayland St.
Rosewood St.
Parkwood St.
0
440 yards
0
400 meters
N
95/64
301/1
250/33
360
95
416
195

blocks. At either of the following museums you will receive a self-guided walking tour with the purchase of a discount block ticket ($15), good for all admission fees in this district. The 1790 **John Marshall House** (✉ 9th and Marshall Sts., ☎ 804/648–7998; 🎫 $3), one of the Court End museums, was the home of the early U.S. chief justice. The **Museum and White House of the Confederacy** (✉ 1201 E. Clay St., ☎ 804/649–1861; 🎫 $8) was the official residence of Confederate president Jefferson Davis; a newer building next door houses such relics as Robert E. Lee's sword.

★ The **Virginia State Capitol** (✉ Capitol Sq., ☎ 804/698–1788; 🎫 free), designed by Thomas Jefferson in 1785, contains a wealth of sculpture, including busts of the eight Virginia-born U.S. presidents and a life-size statue of George Washington. It was here that Lee accepted command of the Confederate forces.

Canal Walk, beginning at 12th and Main streets, follows the locks of the James River–Kanawha Canal proposed by George Washington. Plaques along the way note points of historic interest. The walk (less than a mile) continues over a footbridge to **Brown's Island,** the site of sculptures and outdoor concerts.

In the Church Hill Historic District, east of downtown, is **St. John's Episcopal Church** (✉ 2401 E. Broad St., ☎ 804/648–5015; 🎫 free). It was here on March 23, 1775, that Patrick Henry demanded of the Second Virginia Convention: "Give me liberty or give me death!"

The visitor center for **Richmond National Battlefield Park** (✉ 3215 E. Broad St., ☎ 804/226–1981; 🎫 free) provides a movie and a slide show about the three campaigns fought here, as well as maps for a self-guided tour; the park is free.

West of downtown you'll find the **Science Museum of Virginia** (✉ 2500 W. Broad St., ☎ 804/367–6552, 804/367–1080, or 800/659–1727; 🎫 $7.50), housed in a massive, domed former train station. The planetarium, with its huge curved screen, doubles as a movie theater.

★ Aptly situated at the base of the artsy Fan District is the **Virginia Museum of Fine Arts** (✉ The Boulevard and Grove Ave., ☎ 804/367–0844; 🎫 $4), whose collection includes paintings by Goya, Renoir, Monet, and van Gogh, as well as African masks, Roman statuaries, Asian icons, and five Fabergé eggs.

Just southwest of the Fan District stands **Agecroft Hall** (✉ 4305 Sulgrave Rd., ☎ 804/353–4241; 🎫 $4), a 15th-century English house reassembled here in 1925 and surrounded by formal gardens and extensively furnished with Tudor and early Stuart art and furniture.

North of Richmond, the 100-plus rides at **Paramount's Kings Dominion** (✉ I–95 Doswell exit 98, ☎ 804/876–5000) include simulated white-water rafting and seven roller coasters. The park is closed from November to March.

Petersburg

Twenty miles south of Richmond on I–95 lies **Petersburg,** the so-called last ditch of the Confederacy: Its fall in 1865 led to the fall of Richmond and the surrender at Appomattox. At **Petersburg National Battlefield** (✉ Washington St., off Rte. 36, ☎ 804/732–3531; 🎫 $4) you can tread the ground where 60,000 soldiers died. The 1,500-acre park, laced with miles of earthworks, includes two forts. ★ The **Pamplin Park Civil War Site** (✉ 6523 Duncan Rd., Petersburg, ☎ 804/861–2408; 🎫 $3), where Union troops successfully penetrated General Robert E. Lee's defense line, includes an interpretive center and museum, a mile-long battle trail, 8-ft-high earthen fortifications, reconstructed soldier huts, and an 1812 plantation home.

In Old Town Petersburg the Civil War is examined from a local perspective at the **Siege Museum** (✉ 15 W. Bank St., ☎ 804/733–2404; 🎫 $3). Outstanding relics of antebellum Petersburg include the eccentric **Trapezium House** (✉ 244 N. Market St., ☎ 804/733–2404; 🎫 $3), built with no right angles. A 3-yard-long grand piano is among the antiques in the 1823 **Centre Hill Mansion** (✉ Centre Hill Ct., ☎ 804/733–2401; 🎫 $3), remodeled in Victorian style at the turn of this century. The pre-Revolutionary **Old Blanford Church** (✉ 319 S. Crater Rd., ☎ 804/733–2396; 🎫 $3) is today a Confederate shrine surrounded by the graves of 30,000 Southern dead. The Memorial Day tradition is said to have begun in this cemetery.

The James River Plantations

Southeast of Richmond on Route 5, along the north bank of the James River, lie four historical plantations. **Shirley** (✉ Rte. 608, ☎ 804/829–5121; 🎫 $7.50), the oldest in Virginia, has belonged to the same family, the Carters, for 10 generations. Robert E. Lee's mother was born here. The 1723 house is filled with family silver, ancestral portraits, and rare books. The hall staircase rises three stories with no visible supports.

Virginians say that the first Thanksgiving was celebrated not in Massachusetts but at the **Berkeley** (✉ Rte. 5, ☎ 804/829–6018; 🎫 $8.50) plantation, on December 4, 1619. Benjamin Harrison, a signer of the Declaration of Independence, and William Henry Harrison, the short-termed ninth president, were born here. The 1726 Georgian brick house has been restored and furnished with period antiques, and the boxwood gardens are well tended. In addition to a restaurant, there are outdoor tables for picnickers.

Westover (✉ Rte. 5, ☎ 804/829–2882; 🎫 $6 house, $2 gardens) was home to the flamboyant colonel William Byrd II, member of the Colonial legislature and author of one of the region's first travel books (as well as a notorious secret diary). The 1735 house, celebrated for its moldings and carvings, is open only during April Garden Week, but the grounds and gardens can be visited all year.

At 300 ft, **Sherwood Forest** (✉ Rte. 5, ☎ 804/829–5377; 🎫 $7.50) may be the longest frame house in the country. Built in 1720, it was the retirement home of John Tyler, the 10th U.S. president, and remains in his family. The house, furnished with heirloom antiques, and the five outbuildings are open daily.

The Historic Triangle

★ **Colonial Williamsburg** (✉ I–64 Exit 238, ☎ 757/220–7645 or 800/447–8679; 🎫 $25) is a marvel: an improbably sanitary but otherwise convincing re-creation of the city that was the capital of Virginia from 1699 until 1780. The restoration project, financed by John D. Rockefeller Jr., began in 1926; the work of archaeologists and historians of the Colonial Williamsburg Foundation continues to this day. An extensive packet of information is available (☞ Visitor Information, *above*).

On Colonial Williamsburg's 173 acres, 88 original 18th- and early 19th-century structures, such as the **courthouse**, have been meticulously restored; another 50, including the **capitol** and the **governor's palace**, were reconstructed on their original sites. In all, 225 period rooms have been furnished from the foundation's collection of more than 100,000 pieces of furniture, pottery, china, glass, silver, pewter, textiles, tools, and carpeting. Period authenticity also governs the landscaping of the 90 acres of gardens and public greens.

All year hundreds of costumed interpreters, wearing bonnets or three-cornered hats, rove and ride through the cobblestone streets. Dozens of costumed craftspeople, such as the boot maker and gunsmith, demonstrate and explain their trades inside their workshops; their wares are for sale nearby. Three taverns serve fare approximating that of 200 years ago. The restored area must be toured on foot, as all vehicles are banned between 8 AM and 6 PM. Free shuttle buses (available to ticket holders only) run continually to and from the visitor center and around the edge of the restored area. Vehicles for visitors with disabilities are permitted by prior arrangement.

East of Williamsburg is **Busch Gardens Williamsburg** (✉ U.S. 60, ☎ 757/253–3350). Rides include an especially fast and steep roller coaster. Nine re-creations of European hamlets present the cuisine and entertainment of different countries. The park is closed from November to March.

Jamestown Island (✉ Colonial Pkwy., ☎ 757/229–1733; $5), site of the first permanent English settlement in North America (1607) and the capital of Virginia until 1699, is now uninhabited. Foundation walls show the layout of the settlement, and push-button audio stations narrate the local history. The only standing structure is the ruin of a 1639 church tower. A 5-mi nature drive ringing the island is posted with historical markers.

Adjacent to Jamestown Island is **Jamestown Settlement** (✉ Rte. 31 off Colonial Pkwy., ☎ 757/229–1607; $9.75), a living-history museum, with a reconstructed fort staffed by docents dressed as colonists and an "Indian Village" inhabited by buckskin-clad interpreters. At the pier are reproductions of the *Godspeed,* the *Discovery,* and the *Susan Constant,* the ships that carried the settlers to the New World.

In 1781, American and French forces surrounded British troops and forced an end to the American War of Independence at **Yorktown Battlefield** (✉ Colonial Pkwy., ☎ 757/898–3400; $4 [museum only]). Today the museum here displays George Washington's original field tent; dioramas, illuminated maps, and a short movie tell the story. After a look from the observation deck, you can rent the taped audio tour and explore the battlefield (which is free) by car or join a free ranger-led walking tour.

The **Yorktown Victory Center** (✉ Rte. 238 off Colonial Pkwy., ☎ 757/887–1776; $6.75), next door to the Yorktown Battlefield, consists of a Continental Army encampment, with tents, a covered wagon, and interpreters—costumed as soldiers or female auxiliaries—who speak to visitors in the regional dialects of the time. Also on site are a small working tobacco farm and a museum focusing on the experience of ordinary people during the Revolution.

Unlike Jamestown, **Yorktown** remains a living community, albeit a small one. Its Main Street is lined with preserved 18th-century buildings on a bluff overlooking the York River. The elegant **Nelson House** was the residence of a Virginia governor and signer of the Declaration of Independence. Along the Battlefield Tour Road is **Moore House,** where the terms of surrender were negotiated. Nelson and Moore houses are both open for tours in summer (☎ 757/898–3400; $4). On adjacent Church Street, Grace Church, built in 1697, remains an active Episcopal congregation; its walls are made of marl (a mixture of clay, sand, and limestone containing fragments of seashells).

Dining and Lodging

The established upmarket dining rooms of Richmond are dependable, but keep an eye out for intriguing new bistros, often short-lived, in the Fan District. In Williamsburg, dining rooms within walking distance of the restored area are often crowded, and reservations are advised. Richmond's hotel rates are fair for its size, but standards of service lag behind those of many smaller communities. Williamsburg has a greater range of lodging choices for the money, but vacancies are scarce in summer. For price ranges *see* Charts 1 (A) and 2 (A) *in* On the Road with Fodor's.

Richmond

$$$ ✕ **La Petite France.** The emerald-green walls are hung with English landscapes and portraits. Tuxedoed waiters serve lobster simmered in a vegetable fricassee and Dover sole amandine, among other specialties. ✉ *2108 Maywill St.,* ☎ *804/353–8729. AE, DC, MC, V. Closed Sun.–Mon.*

$ ✕ **Joe's Inn.** The specialty at this Fan District hangout is Greek spaghetti, with feta and provolone baked on top; all the sandwiches are oversize. Regulars make newcomers feel right at home. ✉ *205 N. Shields Ave.,* ☎ *804/355–2282. AE, MC, V.*

$$–$$$ ★ ✕🏨 **Mr. Patrick Henry's.** Two houses circa 1858 were restored and joined to create this restaurant and inn. The three suites each have a fireplace. Antiques and fireplaces in the dining room contribute to the Colonial ambience, an English pub is in the basement, and there's a garden café. Menu favorites include crab cakes and crisp roast duck with bing cherry sauce. Breakfast is included for inn guests. ✉ *2300 E. Broad St.,* ☎ *804/644–1322 or 800/932–2654. 3 suites. Restaurant. AE, D, DC, MC, V. Closed Sun. No lunch Sat.*

$$$–$$$$ ★ 🏨 **Jefferson Hotel.** This 1895 National Historic Landmark has a grand lobby, with a tall staircase straight out of *Gone With the Wind.* The rather small guest rooms have reproduction 19th-century furnishings. ✉ *Franklin and Adams Sts., 23220,* ☎ *804/788–8000 or 800/424–8014,* FAX *804/225–0334. 275 rooms. 2 restaurants, health club. AE, D, DC, MC, V.*

$$$ 🏨 **Omni Richmond.** Guest rooms in this luxury hotel have a contemporary look, but the marble lobby, with its equestrian statues and Romanesque vases, calls to mind a Venetian foyer. ✉ *100 S. 12th St., 23219,* ☎ *804/344–7000,* FAX *804/648–6704. 364 rooms. 3 restaurants, pools, sauna, exercise room. AE, D, DC, MC, V.*

$$ 🏨 **Crowne Plaza Hotel.** Triangular suites at the point of this wedge-shape hotel have views of the skyline and the river. The hotel is in the historic district. ✉ *555 E. Canal St., 23219,* ☎ *804/788–0900 or 800/333–3333,* FAX *804/788–7087. 301 rooms. Restaurant, pool, health club. AE, D, DC, MC, V.*

$ 🏨 **Massad House Hotel.** This modest Tudor-style hotel is five blocks from the capitol in the business district, a quiet area after 6 PM. Guest rooms are small, with stucco walls, and are well maintained. ✉ *11 N. 4th St., 23219,* ☎ *804/648–2893,* FAX *804/780–0647. 64 rooms. Restaurant. MC, V.*

Williamsburg

$$–$$$ ✕ **Le Yaca.** The country-French dining room is done in soft pastels with hardwood floors, candlelight, and a central open fireplace where leg of lamb roasts nightly on a spit. ✉ *1915 Pocahontas Trail,* ☎ *757/220–3616. AE, DC, MC, V. Closed Sun. and early Jan.*

$$–$$$ ✕ **The Trellis.** Hardwood floors, ceramic tiles, and green plants evoke Napa Valley, setting the mood for world-class American cuisine. Save

room for Death by Chocolate: seven layers of chocolate topped with cream sauce. ✉ *Merchants Sq.,* ☎ *757/229–8610. AE, MC, V.*

$–$$ ✕ **The Cascades.** Bare polished-wood tables are piled with all-American fare: cheddar cheese soup, sugar-cured ham, fried chicken, and pecan pie. The daily Hunt Breakfast buffet includes fried chicken and oysters in season. ✉ *104 Visitor Center Dr.,* ☎ *757/229–1000. AE, MC, V.*

$$$–$$$$ ★ ✕🏨 **Williamsburg Inn.** This is the grandest local hotel, built in 1937 and decorated in English Regency style. The surrounding Colonial houses, equipped with modern kitchens and baths, are also part of the inn. At the hotel's esteemed Regency Room restaurant, crystal chandeliers, Asian silk-screen prints, and full silver service set the tone. Chateaubriand is carved tableside; other specialties are lobster bisque and rich ice-cream desserts. Reservations for the restaurant are essential; jacket and tie are required for dinner. ✉ *136 E. Francis St., Box 1776, 23187,* ☎ *757/229–1000 or 800/447–8679,* FAX *757/565–8797. 235 rooms. Restaurant, pool, golf, tennis, health club. AE, D, DC, MC, V.*

$$$ 🏨 **Embassy Suites.** All rooms here are two-room suites, complete with two TVs, a minirefrigerator, and a microwave. A cooked-to-order breakfast is included. ✉ *152 Kingsgate Pkwy., 23185,* ☎ *757/229–6800,* FAX *757/220–3486. 168 suites. Pool, exercise room. Full breakfast. AE, D, DC, MC, V.*

$$–$$$ 🏨 **Williamsburg Hospitality House.** This four-story redbrick building, constructed in 1972, faces the College of William and Mary. Guest rooms have antique reproductions; some face a brick-and-tile courtyard. ✉ *415 Richmond Rd., 23185,* ☎ *757/229–4020 or 800/932–9192,* FAX *757/220–1560. 295 rooms. Restaurant, pool. AE, D, DC, MC, V.*

$ 🏨 **Heritage Inn Motel.** Though some rooms open directly onto the parking lot, this is still an unusually quiet, leafy site, and the pool is set in a garden. ✉ *1324 Richmond Rd., 23185,* ☎ *757/229–6220 or 800/782–3800,* FAX *757/229–2774. 54 rooms. Pool. AE, D, DC, MC, V.*

Yorktown

$$ ✕ **Nick's Seafood Pavilion.** Atlantic seafood with a distinctly Mediterranean flavor, including such house specialties as lobster *dien bien* and seafood shish kebab, is served in ample portions at this riverside restaurant. ✉ *Water St.,* ☎ *757/887–5269. Reservations not accepted. AE, DC, MC, V.*

Motels

🏨 **The Woodlands** (✉ 102 Visitor Center Dr., Williamsburg 23185, ☎ 757/229–1000 or 800/447–8679, FAX 757/565–8942), 315 rooms, restaurant, pools, golf, tennis; *$$.* 🏨 **Days Inn North** (✉ 1600 Robin Hood Rd., Richmond 23220, ☎ 804/353–1287, FAX 804/355–2659), 99 rooms, restaurant, pool; *$.* 🏨 **Duke of York Motel** (✉ 508 Water St., Yorktown 23690, ☎ 757/898–3232, FAX 757/898–5922), 57 rooms, restaurant, pool; *$.* 🏨 **Governor Spottswood Motel** (✉ 1508 Richmond Rd., Williamsburg 23185, ☎ 757/229–6444 or 800/368–1244, FAX 757/253–2410), 78 rooms, pool; *$.*

Nightlife and the Arts

Nightlife

Bogart's (✉ 203 N. Lombardy St., Richmond, ☎ 804/353–9280) is a cozy jazz club. **Chowning's Tavern** (✉ Duke of Gloucester St., Williamsburg, ☎ 757/229–1000 or 800/447–8679) has lively "gambols," or Colonial games, with music and other entertainment, daily from 9 PM to 1 AM; a family version is offered from 7 PM to 9 PM.

The Arts

Barksdale Theatre (✉ 1601 Willow Lawn Dr., Richmond, ☎ 804/282–2620), founded in 1953, was the first dinner theater in the country. They now offer theater-in-the-round. **Swift Creek Mill Playhouse** (17401 Jefferson Davis Hwy., Richmond, ☎ 804/748–5203), another dinner theater, is housed in a 17th-century gristmill. **TheatreVirginia** (✉ 2800 Grove Ave., Richmond, ☎ 804/353–6161), an Equity theater maintained by the Virginia Museum of Fine Arts, has a strong repertory. The **Richmond Symphony** (☎ 804/788–1212) often features internationally known soloists. The **Richmond Ballet** (✉ 614 N. Lombardy St., ☎ 804/359–0906) is the city's classical ballet company. The **Virginia Company** (Colonial Williamsburg, ☎ 757/220–7645 or 800/447–8679) presents rollicking 18th-century plays.

Outdoor Activities and Sports

Open to the public in Richmond—for free or at a nominal charge—are more than 150 tennis courts, 11 swimming pools, a golf driving range, and about 7 mi of fitness trails. The **Department of Parks, Recreation, and Community Facilities** (☎ 804/780–5944) has listings.

Biking

In Colonial Williamsburg ticket holders can rent bicycles at the **lodge** on South England Street. Also try **Bikesmith** (✉ 515 York St., ☎ 757/229–9858).

Golf

The **Crossings** (✉ Junction of I–95 and I–295, Glen Allen, ☎ 804/266–2254), north of Richmond, has an 18-hole course open to the public. **Colonial Williamsburg** (☎ 757/220–7696) operates three courses. **Kingsmill Resort** (☎ 757/253–3906), east of Williamsburg near Busch Gardens, has one 9-hole and three 18-hole courses. The PGA's Michelob Championship is held here each October.

Rafting

From March through November **Richmond Raft** (☎ 757/222–7238) offers guided white-water rafting through the heart of the city (Class 3 and 4 rapids) and float trips upriver.

Tennis

Colonial Williamsburg (☎ 757/220–7794) has 10 tennis courts; **Kingsmill** (☎ 757/253–3945) has 15 courts open to the public; additional public courts in Williamsburg are at **Kiwanis Park,** on Long Hill Road, and **Quarterpath Park,** on Pocahontas Street.

Shopping

Fresh produce is for sale at Richmond's **Farmers' Market** (✉ 17th and Main Sts.); art galleries, boutiques, and antiques shops are nearby. The **Colonial Williamsburg Craft House** (✉ Merchants Sq., ☎ 757/220–7747) and the **Craft House Inn** (✉ S. England St., ☎ 757/220–7749) sell approved reproductions of the antiques on display in the houses.

ELSEWHERE IN VIRGINIA

Hampton Roads, Virginia Beach, and the Eastern Shore

Visitor Information

Virginia Beach Visitor Information Center (✉ 2100 Parks Ave., 23451, ☎ 757/437–4888 or 800/446–8038). **Chincoteague Chamber of Commerce** (✉ Box 258, 23336, ☎ 757/336–6161). **Eastern Shore of**

Virginia Chamber of Commerce (✉ Box 460, Melfa 23410, ☎ 757/787–2460).

Arriving and Departing

Norfolk International and **Newport News–Williamsburg International airports** (☞ Richmond and Tidewater, *above*) are served by most major airlines. I–64 connects Richmond with Hampton Roads. U.S. 58 and Route 44 connect I–64 with Virginia Beach; U.S. 13 runs between Virginia Beach and the Eastern Shore via the Chesapeake Bay Bridge-Tunnel. **Greyhound Lines** (☎ 800/231–2222) serves Virginia Beach (✉ 1017 Laskin Rd.) and various locations along U.S. 13 on the Eastern Shore.

What to See and Do

The cities of Newport News and Hampton on the north and Norfolk on the south flank the enormous port of **Hampton Roads,** where the James empties into the Chesapeake. In Newport News the **Mariner's Museum** (✉ I–64 Exit 258A, ☎ 757/595–0368; 🎫 $5) displays tiny hand-carved models of ancient vessels and full-size specimens of more recent ones, including a gondola and a Chinese sampan. The very latest in transportation can be viewed in Hampton at the **Virginia Air and Space Center** (✉ 600 Settlers Landing Rd., ☎ 757/727–0800; 🎫 $6); exhibits include a lunar rock and an *Apollo* capsule. At Hampton's **Fort Monroe** (✉ U.S. 258), the **Casemate Museum** (✉ Casemate 20 Bernard Rd., ☎ 757/727–3391; 🎫 free) tells the Civil War history of this moat-enclosed Union stronghold, which was the object of the battle between the *Monitor* and the *Merrimac* and later where President Jefferson Davis was imprisoned after the Confederacy's defeat.

Norfolk is best known for the **U.S. Naval Base** (✉ Hampton Blvd., ☎ 757/444–7955 or 757/444–1577; 🎫 $5), home to about 115 ships of the Atlantic and Mediterranean fleets, including the nuclear-powered USS *Theodore Roosevelt*—the world's second-largest warship. The sights are gentler at the **Norfolk Botanical Gardens** (✉ I–64 airport exit 279, ☎ 757/441–5831; 🎫 $3.50), with 155 acres of azaleas, camellias, and roses—plus a lone palm tree. The arts are preserved at the **Hermitage Foundation Museum** (✉ 7637 North Shore Rd., ☎ 757/423–2052; 🎫 $4), a reconstructed Tudor mansion with a large collection of Asian art. ★ The collections at the **Chrysler Museum** (✉ 245 W. Olney Rd., ☎ 757/664–6200; 🎫 $4), one of America's major art museums, range from Gainsborough to Roy Lichtenstein. Of historical interest is the elegant **Moses Myers House** (✉ 331 Bank St., ☎ 757/664–6200; 🎫 $3), built in 1792 by Norfolk's first Jewish resident. The **General Douglas MacArthur Memorial** (✉ Bank St. and City Hall Ave., ☎ 757/441–2965; 🎫 free), in the restored former city hall, is the burial place of the controversial war hero.

The heart of **Virginia Beach,** 6 mi of crowded public beach and a raucous 40-block boardwalk, has been a popular summer gathering place for many years. One advantage of the commercialism is easy access to sailing, surfing, and scuba renting. Almost 2 mi inland, at the southern end of Virginia Beach, is one of the state's most visited museums, the **Virginia Marine Science Museum** (✉ 717 General Booth Blvd., ☎ 757/425–3474; 🎫 $7.95), where visitors can use computers to predict the weather and bird-watch in a salt marsh. Also inland from the bay shore, and a throwback to much quieter times, is the 1680 **Adam Thoroughgood House** (✉ 1636 Parish Rd., ☎ 757/664–6200; 🎫 $3), said to be the oldest non-Spanish brick house in the country.

On the Eastern Shore U.S. 13 takes you past historic 17th- to 19th-century towns such as **Eastville,** with its 250-year-old courthouse.

Onancock has a working general store established in 1842 and a wharf where you just might be able to witness a sunset over the bay.

Assateague Island is a 37-mi-long wildlife refuge and recreational area that extends north into Maryland (☞ Maryland). Despite invasive tourism and overdevelopment, ★ **Chincoteague Island** has had at least one tradition survive from a simpler time: Every July the wild ponies from Assateague are driven across the channel and placed at auction here; those unsold swim back home. All year long the fine beaches and natural beauty justify a visit to Chincoteague. On nearby Wallops Island is NASA's **Wallops Flight Facility** (✉ Rte. 175, ☎ 757/824–2298; free), where a museum tells the story of the space program on the site of early rocket launchings.

Dining and Lodging

For price ranges *see* Charts 1 (B) and 2 (B) *in* On the Road with Fodor's.

$$$–$$$$ ✕ **Coastal Grill.** Chef-owner Jerry Bryan prepares American classics with an innovative twist. Spinach salad is paired with sautéed chicken livers and balsamic vinaigrette, New York strip steak comes with melted onions and horseradish cream, and the fresh seafood dishes are sublime. ✉ *1427 Great Neck Rd., Virginia Beach,* ☎ *757/496–3348. Reservations not accepted. AE, D, MC, V. No lunch.*

$$$–$$$$ ✕ **Grate Steak.** Farm implements and unfinished pine walls decorate the four dining rooms. Diners may step up to a common barbecue pit and grill for themselves the steak, shrimp, or chicken of their choosing. The menu also includes fried shrimp, grilled tuna, and baby back pork ribs. ✉ *1934 Coliseum Dr., Hampton,* ☎ *757/827–1886. AE, D, DC, MC, V. No lunch.*

$$–$$$$ ✕ **Duck Inn.** This family seafood restaurant is near the water and within sight of the bridge-tunnel. The specialty of the house, a milk-based fisherman's chowder, contains shrimp, crabmeat, and mushrooms. Crab cakes are popular here, as is the nightly buffet. ✉ *3324 Shore Dr., Virginia Beach,* ☎ *757/481–0201. Reservations not accepted. AE, D, DC, MC, V.*

$$–$$$ ★ ✕ **La Galleria.** In just a few years this restaurant has earned a reputation as one of the best in Norfolk. The decor includes large urns imported from Italy, Corinthian columns, and a long sculpted wall adorned with frames and half frames. Menu choices include a variety of excellent pastas. ✉ *120 College Pl., Norfolk,* ☎ *757/623–3939. AE, MC, V.*

$$–$$$ ✕ **Landmark Crab House.** The servings here are as generous as the view of the water. A creamy crab imperial, baked in a terrine, is the touted specialty; the crab cakes are a slightly drier alternative. Beef dishes, well represented on the regular menu, often appear as specials. A children's menu that includes hamburgers makes this a spot for family dining. ✉ *N. Main St., Chincoteague,* ☎ *757/336–5552. AE, D, DC, MC, V.*

$$$$ **Norfolk Waterside Marriott.** This modern hotel next door to the convention center is connected by a walkway to the Waterside; it opened in late 1991. ✉ *235 E. Main St., 23510,* ☎ *757/627–4200 or 800/228–9290, FAX 757/628–6466. 404 rooms. 2 restaurants, pool, health club. AE, D, DC, MC, V.*

$$$$ **Omni Waterside Hotel.** The Omni is adjacent to the Waterside Festival Market Place, with views of the harbor from about half its rooms. The financial district is only a block away. Guests have access to a nearby health club. ✉ *777 Waterside Dr., 23510,* ☎ *757/622–6664, FAX 757/625–8271. 446 rooms. Restaurant, pool. AE, D, DC, MC, V.*

WASHINGTON, D.C.

By John F. Kelly
Updated by Bruce Walker

Population	529,000
Official Bird	Wood thrush
Official Flower	American Beauty rose

Washington, the District of Columbia, was founded in 1791 as the world's first planned national capital. It's a city of architectural splendors and unforgettable memorials, where the striking image of the Washington Monument is never far from sight and the stirring memories of a young democratic republic are never far from mind. Of course, the capital's attractions are more than monumental and governmental. Washington's museums, arts scene, parks, and gardens make it an American showcase, its arms open to the world.

Visitor Information

Washington, D.C., Convention and Visitors Association information center (✉ 1212 New York Ave. NW, 6th floor, 20005, ☎ 202/789–7000, FAX 202/789–7037). **Dial-A-Park** (☎ 202/619–7275), a recording of events at National Park Service attractions. The **White House Visitor Center** (✉ 1450 Pennsylvania Ave. NW, 20230, ☎ 202/208–1631).

Arriving and Departing

By Bus

Greyhound Lines (✉ 1005 1st St. NE, ☎ 800/231–2222) and **Peter Pan Trailways** (✉ 1000 1st St. NE, ☎ 800/343–9999).

By Car

I–95 approaches Washington from the north and south, skirting east of the city as part of the Capital Beltway. I–495 is the western loop of the Beltway. I–395 connects DC with the Beltway to the south. Connecticut Avenue is the best approach from the north, dropping down from the Beltway in Maryland.

By Plane

Ronald Reagan Washington National Airport (☎ 703/419–8000), in Virginia 4 mi south of downtown Washington, has scheduled flights by most major domestic carriers. It's often cramped and crowded, but it's a convenient 20-minute Metro (short for Metrorail) ride from the city center ($1.10 or $1.40, depending on the time of day). Cab fare to downtown averages $13, including tip. Many transcontinental and international flights arrive at **Dulles International Airport** (☎ 703/419–8000), a modern facility 26 mi west of Washington in Virginia. **Baltimore–Washington International (BWI) Airport** (☎ 410/859–7100) is in Maryland, about 25 mi northeast of DC.

Bus service is provided to National and Dulles airports by the **Washington Flyer** (☎ 703/685–1400) and to National and BWI by the **SuperShuttle** (☎ 800/258–3826).

By Train

Amtrak trains pull into Union Station (✉ 50 Massachusetts Ave. NE, ☎ 800/872–7245).

Getting Around Washington, D.C.

Washington's best-known sights are a short walk—or a short Metro ride—from one another.

By Car

A car can be a drawback in DC. Traffic is horrendous, especially at rush hours (6:30 AM–9:30 AM and 3:30 PM–7 PM). One-way and diagonal streets can make the city seem like a maze, and parking is an adventure. There's free, three-hour parking around the Mall on Jefferson Drive and Madison Drive, but good luck grabbing a spot! You can also park for free—in some spots all day—in areas south of the Lincoln Memorial, on Ohio and West Basin drives in West Potomac Park. Private lots are expensive (up to $4 an hour and $13 a day).

By Public Transportation

The **Washington Metropolitan Area Transit Authority** (☎ 202/637–7000, TTY 202/638–3780) provides Metrorail and Metrobus service in DC and the Maryland and Virginia suburbs. The base rail fare is $1.10. The final fare depends on the time of day and the distance you travel. All bus rides within DC are $1.10; a $5 **Metro Tourist Pass** entitles you to one day of unlimited subway travel weekdays from 9:30 AM to midnight or all day any weekend or holiday (except July 4).

By Taxi

Taxis in DC operate on a zone system, with a one-zone fare of $4. Ask the driver for the total fare before you depart. Two major companies are **Capitol Cab** (☎ 202/546–2400) and **Diamond Cab** (☎ 202/387–6200). Maryland and Virginia taxis are metered and cannot take you between points within DC.

Orientation Tours

Buses from **Old Town Trolley Tours** (☎ 301/985–3021) and **Tourmobile** (☎ 202/554–7950 or 202/554–5100) ply routes around the city's major attractions, allowing you to get on and off as often as you like. **Gray Line Tours** (☎ 301/386–8300) offers a four-hour motor-coach tour of Washington, Embassy Row, and Arlington National Cemetery; four-hour tours of Mount Vernon and Alexandria; and a combination of both.

Walking Tour

Not a specific walking route but groups of sites within historic neighborhoods, the **Black History National Recreation Trail** (brochure available from National Park Service: ✉ 1100 Ohio Dr. SW, 20242, ☎ 202/619–7222) illustrates aspects of African-American history in Washington, from slavery days to the New Deal.

Exploring Washington, D.C.

The major museums and galleries of the Smithsonian Institution surround the Mall. The U.S. Capitol is at the east end, the city's major monuments are to the west, and the White House is just a stone's throw away from the Mall and the monuments. Start your visit here to see Washington the capital; then venture farther afield for Washington the city. Since virtually every major sight in Washington is appropriate to visit with children, child-friendly attractions are not specifically noted.

The Mall

The first museum built by the Smithsonian was architect James Renwick's Norman-style **Castle.** Today it's home to the **Smithsonian Information Center.** An orientation film inside provides an overview of the various Smithsonian offerings, and television monitors announce the day's special events. All museums and monuments on the Mall are free. ✉ *1000 Jefferson Dr. SW,* ☎ *202/357–2700 for all Smithsonian museums, TTY 202/357–1729.*

Washington, D.C.

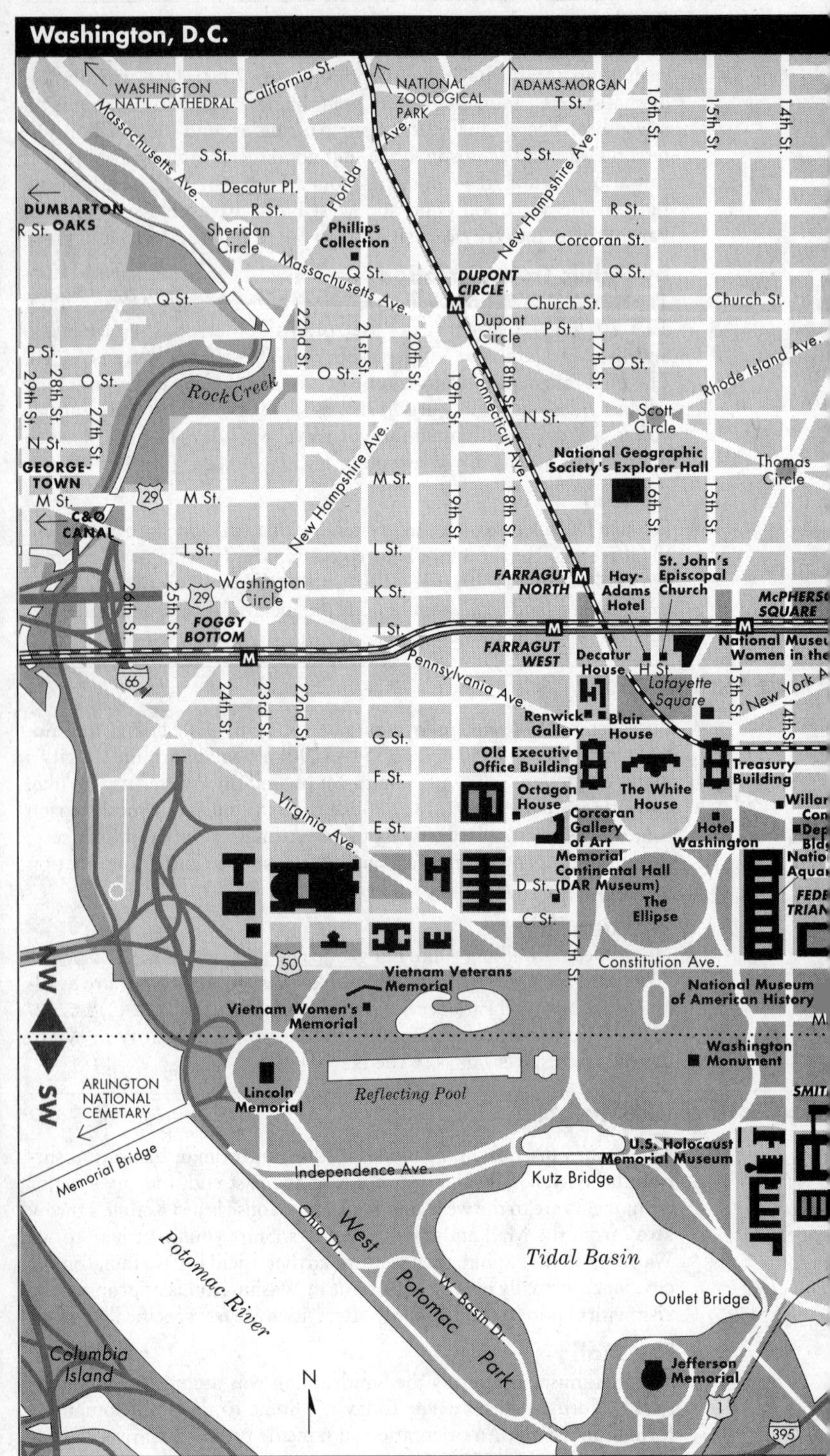

NW
NE
SW
SE
SHAW/HOWARD U.
T St.
S St.
R St.
Q St.
P St.
O St.
N St.
M St.
L St.
I St.
H St.
G St.
F St.
E St.
D St.
C St.
E St.
G St.
Vermont Ave.
Rhode Island Ave.
Florida Ave.
New Jersey Ave.
Lincoln Rd.
NATIONAL ARBORETUM
12th St.
11th St.
10th St.
9th St.
8th St.
7th St.
6th St.
5th St.
4th St.
3rd St.
2nd St.
1st St.
New York Ave.
North Capitol St.
chusetts Ave.
Massachusetts Ave.
Mt. Vernon Square
MT. VERNON
National Portrait Gallery, Museum of American Art
GALLERY PLACE
Pension Building (Nat'l Building Museum)
JUDICIARY SQUARE
UNION STATION
Ford's Theatre
CHINA-TOWN
J. Edgar Hoover FBI Building
Navy Memorial
ARCHIVES / NAVY MEMORIAL
Columbus Memorial Fountain
Louisiana Ave.
Pennsylvania Ave.
National Archives
National Museum of Natural History
National Gallery of Art
U.S. Capitol
Supreme Court
Castle/ Information Center
THE MALL
National Air and Space Museum
Jefferson Dr.
E. Capitol St.
Library of Congress (Jefferson Bldg)
Maryland Ave.
U.S. Botanic Garden
Independence Ave.
Hirshhorn Museum
Arthur M. Sackler Gallery
Arts and Industries Bldg.
Museum of African Art
Freer Gallery of Art
Canal St.
Folger Shakespeare Library
L'ENFANT PLAZA
FEDERAL CENTER S.W.
CAPITOL SOUTH
Dep't of Trans.
Southwest Fwy.
Virginia Ave.
FRED. DOUGLASS NAT'L. HIST. SITE
PENTAGON
Washington Navy Yard
0
500 yards
0
500 meters

A clutch of Smithsonian museums surrounds the Castle. The **Freer Gallery of Art** (✉ 12th St. and Jefferson Dr. SW) is a repository of Asian works that's also known for James McNeill Whistler's stunning painting *Peacock Room.* The **Arthur M. Sackler Gallery** (✉ 1050 Independence Ave. SW) houses a collection including works from China, the Indian subcontinent, Persia, Thailand, and Indonesia. It's connected to the Freer Gallery by an underground tunnel. The **National Museum of African Art** (✉ 950 Independence Ave. SW) is dedicated to the collection, exhibition, and study of the traditional arts of sub-Saharan Africa. The **Arts and Industries Building** (✉ 900 Jefferson Dr. SW), just east of the Castle, is a treasure trove of Victoriana.

Walking counterclockwise around the Mall from the Castle, you'll come first to the cylindrical **Hirshhorn Museum and Sculpture Garden** (✉ 7th St. and Independence Ave. SW), which exhibits modern art both indoors and in its outdoor sculpture garden.

★ The **National Air and Space Museum** is the most visited museum in the world. Twenty-three galleries tell the story of aviation, from our earliest attempts at flight to travels beyond this solar system. Sensational IMAX films are shown on the five-story screen of the museum's Langley Theater (admission charged), while images of celestial bodies are projected on a domed ceiling in the Albert Einstein Planetarium. ✉ *Jefferson Dr. at 6th St. SW.*

★ The two **National Gallery of Art** buildings stand on the north side of the Mall. In its hundred-odd galleries, architect John Russell Pope's elegant, domed **West Building** presents masterworks of Western art from the 13th to the 20th centuries. I. M. Pei's angular **East Building,** with its stunning interior spaces, generally shows modern works. ✉ *Madison Dr. and 4th St. NW,* ☎ *202/737–4215, TTY 202/842–6176.*

The **National Museum of Natural History** is filled with bones, fossils, stuffed animals, and other natural delights, including the popular Dinosaur Hall, the Hope Diamond, and a sea-life display featuring a living coral reef. ✉ *Madison Dr. between 9th and 12th Sts. NW.*

Exhibits on the three floors of the **National Museum of American History** trace the social, political, and technological history of the United States. You'll find a 280-ton steam locomotive, a collection of first ladies' inaugural gowns, and a perennially popular pendulum. ✉ *Madison Ave. between 12th and 14th Sts. NW.*

Alongside the city's many museums celebrating the best of humanity's accomplishments is one that illustrates what humans at their worst are ★ capable of. The **United States Holocaust Memorial Museum** tells the story of the 11 million Jews, Gypsies, homosexuals, political prisoners, and others killed by the Nazis between 1933 and 1945. Arrive early (by 9 AM to be safe) to get free, same-day, timed-entry tickets. Advance tickets are available through Protix (☎ 703/218–6500 or 800/400–9373) for a service charge ($1.75 per ticket plus a $1 charge per phone order). ✉ *100 Raoul Wallenberg Pl. SW (15th St. and Independence Ave. SW),* ☎ *202/488–0400.*

The Monuments

Washington is a city of monuments. Those dedicated to the most famous Americans are west of the Mall on filled-in former marshy flats on the Potomac. Entrance to all monuments is free.

The tallest, of course, is the **Washington Monument,** toward the Mall's west end. Construction of the 555-ft obelisk was started in 1848, interrupted by the Civil War—the reason for the color change about a third of the way up—and completed in 1884. Pick up free timed-tickets at the kiosk on 15th Street for the elevator ride to the monument's top, where the view is unequaled. Unfortunately, the view *of* the monument won't be as stunning: For the next two years its exterior will be covered with scaffolding while its mortar is inspected and repaired. ✉ *Constitution Ave. at 15th St. NW,* ☎ *202/426–6840.*

The exquisitely classical **Jefferson Memorial,** honoring America's third president, rests on the south bank of the **Tidal Basin.** One of the best views of the White House can be seen from the top steps of the memorial, John Russell Pope's reinterpretation of the Pantheon in Rome. ☎ *202/426–6821.*

Cherry trees, beautiful in their early April blossoms, ring the approach ★ to the **Lincoln Memorial,** at the west end of the Mall. Henry Bacon's monument is considered by many to be the most moving spot in the city, its mood set by Daniel Chester French's somber statue of the seated president gazing over the **Reflecting Pool.** Visit this memorial at night for best effect. ☎ *202/426–6895.*

★ In Constitution Gardens, the **Vietnam Veterans Memorial**—a black granite *V* designed by Maya Lin, with sculpture by Frederick Hart—is another landmark that encourages introspection. The names of more than 58,000 Americans who died in Vietnam are etched on the face of the wall in the order of their deaths. The **Vietnam Women's Memorial** was dedicated on Veterans Day 1993 and sits southeast of the Vietnam Veterans Memorial. ✉ *23rd St. and Constitution Ave. NW,* ☎ *202/634–1568.*

The President's Neighborhood

★ The **White House,** one of the world's most famous residences, has pride of place on Pennsylvania Avenue. The building was designed by Irishman James Hoban, who drew upon the Georgian design of Leinster Hall, near Dublin, and other Irish country houses. For a glimpse of some of the public rooms—including the East Room and the State Dining Room—get a ticket (one per person) at the White House Visitor Center (☞ Visitor Information, *above*); arrive by 8 AM to be safe. ✉ *1600 Pennsylvania Ave. NW,* ☎ *202/619–7222 or 202/456–7041 for recorded information.* 🎫 *Free. Closed Sun.–Mon.*

Lafayette Square (also known as Lafayette Park) is an intimate oasis in the midst of downtown Washington. It served as a campsite for soldiers of both the 1812 and Civil wars—in full view of presidents Madison and Lincoln across the way in the White House. At the top of the square, golden-domed **St. John's Episcopal Church** (✉ 16th and H Sts. NW, ☎ 202/347–8766) is known as the Church of the Presidents.. The opulent **Hay-Adams Hotel**(☞ Lodging, *below*), across 16th Street from St. John's, is a favorite with Washington insiders and visiting notables.

The first floor of the Federal-style redbrick **Decatur House** (✉ 748 Jackson Pl. NW, ☎ 202/842–0920; 🎫 $4) is decorated as it was when occupied by naval hero Stephen Decatur in 1819. The green canopy at 1651 Pennsylvania Avenue marks the entrance to **Blair House,** the residence used by visiting heads of state. Flags from their respective countries fly from the outside lampposts when these dignitaries are in town to see the president. The busy, monumental, French Empire–style **Old Executive Office Building** (✉ 17th St. and Pennsylvania Ave. NW) houses many executive branch employees. Former vice president Dan Quayle had his office in here. The current second-in-command, Albert Gore Jr., is a little closer to the action—in the West Wing of the White House, just down the hall from the president.

While most of the Smithsonian museums are on the Mall, the **Renwick Gallery,** devoted to American decorative arts, is downtown. ✉ *Pennsylvania Ave. and 17th St. NW.* 🎫 *Free.*

One of the few large museums in Washington that's not part of the Smithsonian family is the **Corcoran Gallery of Art.** Its collection ranges from works by early-American artists to late-19th- and early 20th-century paintings from Europe. A highlight is the entire 18th-century Grand Salon from the Hôtel d'Orsay in Paris. ✉ *17th St. and New York Ave. NW,* ☎ *202/639–1700.* 🎫 *Donation accepted. Closed Tues.*

Despite its name, the **Octagon,** built in 1801, has six sides. The Treaty of Ghent, ending the War of 1812, was signed in an upstairs study. The building now houses the museum of the American Architectural Foundation, with exhibits relating to architecture, decorative arts, and Washington history. ✉ *1799 New York Ave. NW,* ☎ *202/638–3105.* 🎫 *$3. Closed Mon.*

Memorial Continental Hall is the headquarters of the Daughters of the American Revolution. The 50,000-item collection of the **DAR Museum** includes fine examples of Colonial and Federal silver, china, porcelain, stoneware, earthenware, and glass. ✉ *1776 D St. NW,* ☎ *202/879–3241.* 🎫 *Free. Closed Sat.*

Another building with an excellent aerial view of the downtown area around the White House is the venerable **Hotel Washington.** The view from the rooftop Sky Top Lounge, which is open April–October, is one of the best in the city. ✉ *515 15th St. NW,* ☎ *202/638–5900.*

The huge Greek Revival **Treasury Building** is in fact home to the Department of the Treasury. Tours lead past the Andrew Johnson suite, which he used as the executive office while Mrs. Lincoln moved out of the White House, and the two-story marble cash room. ✉ *15th St. and Pennsylvania Ave. NW.* ☎ *202/622–0896* 🎫 *Free.*

The magazine comes to life at the **National Geographic Society's Explorers Hall.** Interactive exhibits encourage you to learn about the world. The centerpiece is a hand-painted globe, 11 ft in diameter, that floats and spins on a cushion of air, showing off different features of the planet. ✉ *17th and M Sts. NW,* ☎ *202/857–7588.* 🎫 *Free.*

Capitol Hill

Pierre L'Enfant, the French designer of Washington, called Capitol Hill (then known as Jenkins Hill) "a pedestal waiting for a monument." ★ That monument is the **U.S. Capitol,** the gleaming white-dome building in which elected officials toil. George Washington laid the cornerstone on September 18, 1793, and in November 1800 Congress moved down from Philadelphia. The Capitol has grown over the years and today contains some of the city's most inspiring art, from Constantino Brumidi's *Apotheosis of Washington,* the fresco at the center of the dome, to the splendid Statuary Hall. There are also live attractions: senators and representatives speechifying in their respective chambers. If you want to test your architectural eyes, spend a minute or two looking at the dome from afar: Does it fit or is it a bit too large? ✉ *East end of the Mall,* ☎ *202/224–3121 or 202/225–6827.*

East of the Capitol are the three buildings that make up the **Library of Congress,** which contains 108 million items, of which only a quarter are books. The remainder includes manuscripts, prints, films, photographs, sheet music, and the largest collection of maps in the world. The **Jefferson Building** (✉ 1st St. and Independence Ave. SE, ☎ 202/707–8000), with its grand octagonal Main Reading Room and mahogany readers' tables, is the centerpiece of the system. The **Adams Build-**

ing, on Second Street behind the Jefferson, was added in 1939. The **James Madison Building** opened in 1980; it's just south of the Jefferson Building, between Independence Avenue and C Street.

The **Folger Shakespeare Library** is home to a world-class collection of Shakespeareana. Inside are a reproduction of an inn-yard theater and a gallery—designed in the manner of an Elizabethan great hall—that hosts exhibits from the library's collection of works by and about the Bard. ⊠ *201 E. Capitol St. SE,* ☏ *202/544–4600.* *Free. Closed Sun.*

After being shunted around several locations, including a spell in a tavern, the **Supreme Court** got its own building in 1935. The impressive colonnaded white-marble temple was designed by Cass Gilbert. ⊠ *1st and E. Capitol Sts. NE,* ☏ *202/479–3000.* *Free. Closed weekends.*

Union Station is now a shopping center as well as a train terminal and subway station. The Beaux Arts building's wonderful main waiting room is a perfect setting for the inaugural ball that's held here every four years. ⊠ *50 Massachusetts Ave. NE.*

Old Downtown and Federal Triangle

Before the glass office blocks around 16th and K streets NW became the business center of town, Washington's mercantile hub was farther east. The open-air markets are gone, but some of the 19th-century character of Washington's east end remains. In the 1930s the humongous **Federal Triangle** complex was built to accommodate the expanding federal bureaucracy.

The massive redbrick **Pension Building** went up in the 1880s to house workers who processed the pension claims of veterans and their survivors. It's currently home to the **National Building Museum** (⊠ F St. between 4th and 5th Sts. NW, ☏ 202/272–2448; free), devoted to architecture and related arts.

Judiciary Square is Washington's legal core, with local and district court buildings arrayed around it. At the center is the **National Law Enforcement Officers Memorial,** a 3-ft-high wall bearing the names of more than 15,000 American police officers killed in the line of duty since 1794. Washington's compact **Chinatown** is bordered roughly by G, H, 6th, and 8th streets NW.

Two Smithsonian museums share the Greek Revival **Old Patent Office Building.** The **National Portrait Gallery,** on the south side, contains paintings and photographs of presidents and other notable Americans. The north side's **National Museum of American Art** has a collection with items from Colonial times to the present. ⊠ *8th and G Sts. NW.*

Ford's Theatre (⊠ 511 10th St. NW, ☏ 202/426–6924; free), where Abraham Lincoln was assassinated by John Wilkes Booth on April 14, 1865, now houses a museum (in the basement) that displays items connected with Lincoln's life and untimely death.

The Beaux Arts **Willard Hotel** (⊠ 14th St. and Pennsylvania Ave. NW) is one of the most luxurious in Washington. As the story goes, its lobby is the origin of the term "lobbyist": President U. S. Grant would occasionally escape from the White House to have a brandy and cigar in the Willard's lobby, where interested parties would descend on him, trying to bend his ear.

The **Commerce Department Building** forms the base of Federal Triangle. Inside Commerce is the **National Aquarium,** the country's oldest public aquarium, featuring tropical and freshwater fish, moray eels, frogs, turtles, piranhas, even sharks. ⊠ *14th St. and Pennsylvania Ave. NW,* ☏ *202/482–2825.* *$2.*

The tour of the hulking **J. Edgar Hoover Federal Bureau of Investigation Building** outlines the work of the FBI and ends with a live-ammo firearms demonstration. From the end of March through June the wait to get inside may be as long as three hours. ✉ *10th St. and Pennsylvania Ave. NW (tour entrance on E St. NW),* ☎ *202/324–3447.* 🎫 *Free. No tours weekends.*

The Declaration of Independence, the Constitution, and the Bill of Rights are on display in the rotunda of the **National Archives.** ✉ *Constitution Ave. between 7th and 9th Sts. NW,* ☎ *202/501–5000.* 🎫 *Free.*

The statue of a lone sailor staring out over the largest map in the world marks the site of the **Navy Memorial** (✉ 7th St. and Pennsylvania Ave. NW). In summer the memorial's concert stage (☎ 202/737–2300) is the site of military-band performances.

The **National Museum of Women in the Arts** displays the works of prominent female artists from the Renaissance to the present, including Georgia O'Keeffe, Mary Cassatt, Elisabeth Vigée-Lebrun, and Judy Chicago. ✉ *1250 New York Ave. NW,* ☎ *202/783–5000.* 🎫 *Donation accepted.*

Georgetown

At one time a tobacco port, this poshest of Washington neighborhoods is home to some of its wealthiest and best-known citizens. It's also the nucleus of the district's nightlife scene, with dozens of hot spots dotting Wisconsin Avenue and M Street, Georgetown's crossroads.

Downhill from the main bustle of G-town, the **Chesapeake & Ohio Canal** allows for a scenic getaway from the streets. Dug in the 19th century as an alternative to the rough and rocky Potomac, it was used to transport lumber, coal, iron, and flour into northwest Maryland. Runners now tread its scenic towpath, and in summer mule-drawn barges ply its placid waters; tickets are available at the Foundry Mall (✉ 1057 Thomas Jefferson St. NW, ☎ 202/653–5190).

The Shops at Georgetown Park (✉ 3222 M St. NW, ☎ 202/298–5577), home to such high-ticket stores as F. A. O. Schwarz, Williams-Sonoma, and Polo–Ralph Lauren, is a multilevel shopping extravaganza that answers the question "If the Victorians had invented shopping malls, what would they look like?"

Georgetown University, the oldest Jesuit school in the country, has its campus at the western edge of the neighborhood. When seen from the Potomac or from Washington's high ground, the Gothic spires of the university's older buildings give it an almost medieval look.

Dumbarton Oaks, an estate comprising two museums—one of Byzantine works, the other of pre-Columbian art—is surrounded by 10 acres of stunning formal gardens designed by landscape architect Beatrix Farrand. *Art collections:* ✉ *1703 32nd St. NW,* ☎ *202/339–6401.* 🎫 *Donation accepted. Closed Mon. Gardens:* ✉ *31st and R Sts. NW.* 🎫 *$4 Apr.–Oct.*

Other Attractions

The **Bureau of Engraving and Printing** is the birthplace of all paper currency in the United States. Although there are no free samples, the 30-minute guided tour—which takes you past presses that turn out $450 million worth of currency a day—is one of the city's most popular. ✉ *14th and C Sts. SW,* ☎ *202/874–3019. Closed weekends.*

★ The **Frederick Douglass National Historic Site** is at Cedar Hill, the Washington home of the noted abolitionist. The house displays mementos from Douglass's life and has a wonderful view of the Federal City, across the Anacostia River. ✉ *1411 W St. SE,* ☎ *202/426–5961.* 🎫 *$3.*

The **Phillips Collection** was the first permanent museum of modern art in the country. Holdings include works by Braque, Cézanne, Klee, Matisse, Renoir, and John Henry Twachtman. ✉ *1600 21st St. NW,* ☎ *202/387–2151.* 🎫 *$6.50 ($5 Thurs. evening. Closed Mon.*

It took 83 years to complete the Gothic Revival **Washington National Cathedral,** the sixth-largest cathedral in the world. Besides flying buttresses, a nave, transepts, and rib vaults that were built stone by stone, it is adorned with fanciful gargoyles created by skilled stone carvers. ✉ *Wisconsin and Massachusetts Aves. NW,* ☎ *202/537–6200.*

The **Washington Navy Yard** is the navy's oldest shore establishment. A former shipyard and ordnance facility, the yard today is home to the **Navy Museum** and the **Marine Corps Museum,** which outline the history of those two services from their inception to the present. ✉ *9th and M Sts. SE,* ☎ *202/433–4882.* 🎫 *Free.*

Arlington, Virginia

Though the attractions here are across the Potomac, it's well worth making them a part of your visit to the nation's capital.(For more suburban Virginia sights, including Mount Vernon and Old Town Alexandria, *see* Virginia.)

At **Arlington National Cemetery,** you can trace America's history through the aftermath of its battles. Dominating the cemetery is the Greek Revival **Arlington House,** onetime home of Robert E. Lee, which offers a breathtaking view across the Potomac to the Lincoln Memorial and the Mall. On a hillside below are the **Kennedy graves.** John Fitzgerald Kennedy is buried under an eternal flame. Jacqueline Bouvier Kennedy Onassis lies next to him. Robert Francis Kennedy is buried nearby, his grave marked by a simple white cross. The **Tomb of the Unknowns** is also in the cemetery. ✉ *West end of Memorial Bridge,* ☎ *703/607–8052.*

Just north of Arlington Cemetery is the **United States Marine Corps War Memorial,** honoring Marines who have given their lives since the corps was formed in 1775. The memorial statue, sculpted by Felix W. de Weldon, is based on Joe Rosenthal's Pulitzer Prize–winning photograph of six soldiers raising a flag atop Iwo Jima's Mt. Suribachi on February 19, 1945.

The **Pentagon,** headquarters of the Department of Defense, is an exercise in immensity: 23,000 military and civilian employees work here; it's as wide as three Washington Monuments laid end to end; and inside it contains 691 drinking fountains, 7,754 windows, and 17½ mi of corridors. You can take a 75-minute tour on weekdays every half hour 9:30–3:30. A photo ID is required. ✉ *Off I–395,* ☎ *703/695–1776.* 🎫 *Free.*

Parks, Gardens, and Zoos

The 444-acre **National Arboretum** blooms with all manner of plants, with clematis, peonies, rhododendrons, and azaleas among its showier inhabitants. The National Bonsai Collection, National Herb Garden, and an odd and striking hilltop construction of old marble columns from the U.S. Capitol are also well worth seeing. ✉ *3501 New York Ave. NE,* ☎ *202/245–2726.* 🎫 *Free.*

The 160-acre **National Zoological Park,** part of the Smithsonian Institution, is one of the foremost zoos in the world. Innovative compounds show animals in naturalistic settings, and the ambitious Amazonia re-creates the ecosystem of a South American rain forest. ✉ *3001 Connecticut Ave. NW,* ☏ *202/673–4800.* *Free.*

Rock Creek Park is a cool tongue of green jutting down into the center of Washington. Its 1,800 acres include picnic sites and biking, hiking, and equestrian trails that wend through groves of dogwood, beech, oak, and cedar. ✉ *Park starts roughly at P St. on edge of Georgetown and runs along both sides of creek all the way to Montgomery County, MD.* ☏ *202/426–6829.*

The **United States Botanic Garden,** just below the Capitol, is a peaceful plant-filled conservatory that includes a cactus house, a fern house, and a subtropical house filled with orchids. Note that the garden is closed until the year 2000 while it undergoes renovations. ✉ *1st St. and Maryland Ave. SW,* ☏ *202/225–8333.* *Free.*

Dining

Washington's restaurants aren't exactly innovators, but neither are they blind to fashion. That means trends that started elsewhere—nouvelle cuisine, new American, southwestern—quickly show up in the capital. Good ethnic meals can be found in Adams-Morgan (lots of Ethiopian), Georgetown (Afghani to Indonesian), and Chinatown. For price ranges *see* Chart 1 (A) *in* On the Road with Fodor's.

$$$$ ★ ✕ **Citronelle.** The essence of California chic, Citronelle's glass-front kitchen lets you see all the action as chefs scurry to and fro. Appetizers include a tart of thinly sliced grilled scallops on puff pastry surrounded by a tomato vinaigrette. Loin of venison is served with an endive tart and garnished with dried apples. ✉ *3000 M St. NW,* ☏ *202/625–2150. AE, DC, MC, V.*

$$$ ★ ✕ **i Ricchi.** At this airy Tuscan restaurant, the spring-summer menu includes such offerings as rolled pork and rabbit roasted in wine and fresh herbs, while the fall-winter list brings grilled lamb chops and sautéed beef fillet. ✉ *1220 19th St. NW,* ☏ *202/835–0459. AE, DC, MC, V. Closed Sun. No lunch Sat.*

$$$ ★ ✕ **La Colline.** The menu here, at one of the city's best French restaurants, emphasizes seafood, with offerings that range from simple grilled preparations to fricassees and food served au gratin with imaginative sauces. Other items include duck with orange sauce and veal with chanterelle mushrooms. ✉ *400 N. Capitol St. NW,* ☏ *202/737–0400. AE, DC, MC, V. Closed Sun. No lunch Sat.*

$$$ ✕ **Sam and Harry's.** The surroundings at this quintessential steak house are understated and genteel, with five private dining rooms available. The main attractions are porterhouse steak and filet mignon. ✉ *1200 19th St. NW,* ☏ *202/296–4333. AE, D, DC, MC, V. Closed Sun. No lunch Sat.*

$$–$$$ ★ ✕ **Bombay Club.** One block from the White House, the Bombay tries to re-create a private club for 19th-century British colonials in India. The menu includes unusual seafood specialties and a large number of vegetarian dishes, but the real standouts are the breads and the seafood appetizers. ✉ *815 Connecticut Ave. NW,* ☏ *202/659–3727. AE, DC, MC, V. No lunch Sat.*

$$–$$$ ✕ **Café Japone.** Café Japone's dark interior has an alternative-scene edge. Some nights you'll find karaoke; other nights there's a live jazz band. The sushi is not a rave, but it's good. Crispy fried *age dofu* (tofu in a soy broth) is a tasty appetizer. ✉ *2032 P St. NW,* ☏ *202/223–1573. AE, DC, MC, V. No lunch.*

$$–$$$ ★ ✕ **Hibiscus Café.** African masks and neon accents hang from the ceiling of the modish restaurant, where weekend crowds are drawn by spicy jerk chicken, such blackened fish as grouper, shrimp curry, and flavorful soups (try the butternut-ginger bisque). ✉ *3401 K St. NW,* ☎ *202/965–7170. AE, D, MC, V. Closed Mon. No lunch.*

$$–$$$ ✕ **Occidental Grill.** Part of the stately Willard Hotel complex, this popular restaurant offers innovative dishes, attentive service, and lots of photos of politicians and other power brokers past and present. The menu changes frequently, but you can count on grilled poultry, fish, and steak, as well as salads and sandwiches. ✉ *1475 Pennsylvania Ave. NW,* ☎ *202/783–1475. AE, MC, V.*

$$ ★ ✕ **The Islander.** Addie Green's tangy and spicy soup made with vegetables and marinated fish, her delicious *accras* (salt-cod fritters), nine varieties of *roti* (turnovers filled with curried meat, chicken, vegetables, and the like), and tropical herb-and-spice marinated calypso chicken will make you wish that this authentic Trinidadian roost were just around the corner from home. ✉ *1762 Columbia Rd. NW, 2nd floor,* ☎ *202/234–4955. Closed Mon.*

$$ ★ ✕ **Jaleo.** A lively Spanish bistro, Jaleo features a long list of hot and cold tapas, although such entrées as grilled fish and paella—which comes in four different versions—are just as tasty. For dessert, don't miss the crisp and buttery apple charlotte. ✉ *480 7th St. NW,* ☎ *202/628–7949. AE, D, DC, MC, V.*

$$ ✕ **Old Glory.** Always teeming with visiting Texans, Georgetown students, and closet Elvis fans, Old Glory sticks to barbecued basics: sandwiches and platters of pulled and sliced pork, beef brisket, and smoked and pulled ribs and chicken. ✉ *3139 M St. NW,* ☎ *202/337–3406. AE, D, DC, MC, V.*

$$ ✕ **Peyote Café/Roxanne Restaurant.** Mexican influences on traditional southern food define the menus at these two connected restaurants, where you can order from both menus. Grilled rib-eye steak, grilled salmon, and Sweat Hot Fire Shrimp are specialties. ✉ *2319 18th St. NW,* ☎ *202/462–8330. AE, DC, MC, V. No lunch Mon.–Sat.*

$–$$ ✕ **Aditi.** Aditi's two-story dining room seems too elegant for a moderately priced Indian restaurant. Tandoori and curry dishes are expertly prepared and not aggressively spiced; if you want your food spicy, request it. Rice *biryani* (cooked with meats and vegetables) entrées are good for lighter appetites. ✉ *3299 M St. NW,* ☎ *202/625–6825. AE, D, MC, V.*

$–$$ ★ ✕ **Burma.** Batter-fried eggplant and squash are deliciously paired with complex, peppery sauces at this exquisite jewel in Chinatown. Green-tea-leaf and other salads leave the tongue with a pleasant tingle. Such entrées as mango pork, tamarind fish, and Kokang chicken are equally satisfying. ✉ *740 6th St. NW,* ☎ *202/638–1280. AE, D, DC, MC, V. No lunch weekends.*

$–$$ ★ ✕ **City Lights of China.** This restaurant always makes critics' lists. The traditional Chinese fare is excellent. Less common specialties, such as lamb in a tangy peppery sauce and shark's fin soup, are deftly cooked as well. Jumbo shrimp with spicy salt are baked in their shells, then stir-fried with ginger and spices. ✉ *1731 Connecticut Ave. NW,* ☎ *202/265–6688. AE, D, DC, MC, V.*

$–$$ ★ ✕ **Meskerem.** Among Adams-Morgan's many Ethiopian restaurants, Meskerem is distinctive for a balcony where you can eat Ethiopian style: seated on leather floor cushions with large woven baskets for tables. Stews served with *injera* (spongy flat bread) are made with teff, a grain grown only in Ethiopia and Idaho that imparts a distinctive sourness. ✉ *2434 18th St. NW,* ☎ *202/462–4100. AE, DC, MC, V.*

$ ✕ **Sholl's Colonial Cafeteria.** Suited federal workers line up with tourists to grab a bite at this Washington institution, where favorites include chopped steak, liver and onions, and baked chicken and fish. Sholl's is famous for its apple, blueberry, and other fruit pies. ✉ *1990 K St. NW,* ☎ *202/296–3065. No credit cards.*

Lodging

Many Washington hotels, particularly those downtown, offer special **reduced rates** and package deals on weekends, and some are available midweek; be sure to ask about them at the hotel of your choice. **Capitol Reservations** (☎ 202/452–1270 or 800/847–4832 from 9 to 6 weekdays) books rooms at more than 70 better hotels in good locations at rates 20%–40% off; it also offers group packages with tours and meals. **Washington D.C. Accommodations** (☎ 202/289–2220 or 800/554–2220 from 8:30 to 5:30 weekdays) will book rooms at any hotel in town, with discounts of 20%–40% available at about 90 locations.

To find reasonably priced accommodations in small guest houses and private homes, contact **Bed & Breakfast Accommodations Ltd. of Washington, D.C.** (✉ Box 12011, 20005, ☎ 202/328–3510, FAX 202/332–3885) or **Bed & Breakfast League, Ltd./Sweet Dreams & Toast** (✉ Box 9490, 20016-9490, ☎ 202/363–7767, FAX 202/363–8396).

For price ranges *see* Chart 2 (A) *in* On the Road with Fodor's.

$$$$ ★ **Four Seasons Hotel.** This contemporary hotel, conveniently situated between Georgetown and Foggy Bottom, is a gathering place for Washington's elite. Guest rooms are traditionally furnished in light colors. The quieter rooms face the courtyard; others have a view of the C&O Canal. ✉ *2800 Pennsylvania Ave. NW, 20007,* ☎ *202/342–0444,* FAX *202/944–2076. 196 rooms. Restaurant, pool, health club. AE, D, DC, MC, V.*

$$$$ ★ **Hay-Adams Hotel.** The dignified reputation of this White House neighbor has little need to call attention to itself, and it remains a choice for state policy-making meetings. Its elegance extends to guest rooms, where you might feel like you're in a mansion in disguise. ✉ *1 Lafayette Sq., 20006,* ☎ *202/638–6600 or 800/424–5054,* FAX *202/638–2716. 143 rooms. Restaurant. AE, D, DC, MC, V.*

$$$$ ★ **Hotel Washington.** Washingtonians bring visitors to the rooftop bar here for cocktails and a renowned panorama that includes the White House grounds and Washington Monument. Some rooms look directly onto the White House lawn. ✉ *515 15th St. NW, 20004,* ☎ *202/638–5900 or 800/424–9540,* FAX *202/638–1594. 350 rooms. Restaurant, exercise room. AE, D, DC, MC, V.*

$$$$ **Hyatt Regency on Capitol Hill.** Close to Union Station and the Mall, the elegant 11-story Hyatt Regency features a spectacular garden atrium. Suites on the south side have a view of the Capitol dome just a few blocks away, as does the rooftop Capitol View Club restaurant. ✉ *400 New Jersey Ave. NW, 20001,* ☎ *202/737–1234 ,* FAX *202/737–5773. 834 rooms. 2 restaurants, pool, health club . AE, DC, MC, V.*

$$$$ ★ **Sheraton Luxury Collection.** Formerly a Ritz-Carlton property, this hotel near Dupont Circle is still exclusive and intimate, with an English hunt-club theme. Rooms have views of Embassy Row or Georgetown. ✉ *2100 Massachusetts Ave. NW, 20008,* ☎ *202/293–2100,* FAX *202/835–2196. 206 rooms. Restaurant, exercise room. AE, DC, MC, V.*

$$$$ ★ **Washington Hilton and Towers.** One of the city's busiest convention hotels, this high-rise also attracts travelers who like to be where the action is. The light-filled but compact guest rooms are furnished in standard modern hotel style and have marble bathrooms. ✉ *1919 Connecticut Ave. NW, 20009,* ☎ *202/483–3000,* FAX *202/232–0438. 1,122 rooms. 3 restaurants, pool, tennis, health club. AE, D, DC, MC, V.*

$$$$ ★ **Willard Inter-Continental.** The Willard is an opulent Beaux Arts feast to the eye, as the main lobby with its great columns, huge chandeliers, and elaborately carved ceilings attests. The hotel's formal restaurant has won nationwide acclaim. ✉ *1401 Pennsylvania Ave. NW, 20004,* ☎ *202/628–9100,* FAX *202/637–7326. 341 rooms. 2 restaurants, health club. AE, D, DC, MC, V.*

$$$–$$$$ **Phoenix Park Hotel.** Just steps from Union Station and four blocks from the Capitol, this high-rise has a wood-panel-and-brass Irishmen's-club theme and is the home of the Dubliner (☞ Nightlife and the Arts, *below*). Guest rooms are bright, traditionally furnished, and quiet. The wing that was completed in 1997 gave this establishment 61 more rooms and suites, meeting rooms, and a ballroom. ✉ *520 N. Capitol St. NW, 20001,* ☎ *202/638–6900 or 800/824–5419,* FAX *202/393–3236. 149 rooms. Restaurant, health club. AE, D, DC, MC, V.*

$$$ **Holiday Inn Capitol Hill.** For clean, comfortable, low-price rooms with high-price views, this is the place. They offer the same magnificent vistas of the Capitol as the pricier Hyatt. Children under age 18 stay free. ✉ *415 New Jersey Ave. NW, 20001,* ☎ *202/638–1616 or 800/638–1116,* FAX *202/638–0707. 342 rooms. Restaurant, pool. CP. AE, D, DC, MC, V.*

$$$ **Latham Hotel.** A small hotel in the city's liveliest neighborhood, this redbrick neocolonial is popular with Europeans, sports figures, and devotees of Georgetown. Rooms are sleek and contemporary. Some are underground; others have views of the C&O Canal or busy M Street. The restaurant here, Citronelle(☞ Dining, *above*), is considered one of Washington's best. ✉ *3000 M St. NW, 20007,* ☎ *202/726–5000,* FAX *202/337–4250. 143 rooms. Restaurant, pool. CP. AE, D, DC, MC, V.*

$$–$$$ **Hotel Tabard Inn.** Three Victorian town houses near Dupont Circle were linked in the 1920s to form this inn (which is oldest continuously running hotel in Washington). Furnishings are broken-in Victorian and American Empire antiques; a Victorian-inspired carpet cushions the labyrinthine hallways. ✉ *1739 N St. NW, 20036,* ☎ *202/785–1277,* FAX *202/785–6173. 42 rooms, 14 share bath. Restaurant. CP. AE, DC, MC, V.*

$$–$$$ **Lincoln Suites.** A good value, this small hotel has a courteous staff, offers the basics in the midst of the K and L streets business district, and is close to the White House. Some rooms have a full kitchen; king-size, queen-size, or extra-long double beds are available. ✉ *1823 L St. NW, 20036,* ☎ *202/223–4320 or 800/424–2970,* FAX *202/223–8546. 99 rooms. Restaurant. AE, D, DC, MC, V.*

$$–$$$ ★ **Washington Courtyard by Marriott.** One of the city's best values for budget travelers, Marriott's Washington Courtyard hotel is a good alternative for international tourists and businesspeople who can't find rooms at the Washington Hilton. Guest rooms on the west and south have good views. ✉ *1900 Connecticut Ave. NW, 20009,* ☎ *202/332–9300 or 800/842–4211,* FAX *202/328–7039. 147 rooms. Restaurant, pool, health club. AE, D, DC, MC, V.*

$–$$$ ★ **Normandy Inn.** A small European-style hotel on a quiet street in the exclusive embassy area of Connecticut Avenue, the Normandy is near restaurants and some of the most expensive residential real estate in Washington. Rooms are standard, functional, and comfortable; all have refrigerators. ✉ *2118 Wyoming Ave. NW, 20008,* ☎ *202/483–1350 or 800/424–3729,* FAX *202/387–8241. 75 rooms. CP. AE, D, DC, MC, V.*

$ **Washington International AYH-Hostel.** Eight- to 14-person dormitories and family rooms are available. In summer reservations are highly recommended; only groups need to reserve off-season. There's a common kitchen. Maximum stay is 29 days. ✉ *1009 11th St. NW, 20001,* ☎ *202/737–2333,* FAX *202/737–1508. 250 beds. MC, V.*

Nightlife and the Arts

Area arts and entertainment events are listed in the Weekend section of Friday's *Washington Post*, in the free *City Paper*, in *Washingtonian* magazine (on newsstands), and in *Where: Washington* (free in hotels).

Nightlife

Georgetown, Adams-Morgan, Dupont Circle, and **Capitol Hill** are the main nightlife centers in DC.

BARS

The **Brickskeller** (☒ 1523 22nd St. NW, ☎ 202/293–1885) sells more than 500 brands of beer—from Central American lagers to U.S.-microbrewed ales. The **Dubliner** (☒ Phoenix Park Hotel, 520 N. Capitol St. NW, ☎ 202/737–3773) features snug paneled rooms, thick and tasty Guinness, and nightly live Irish entertainment.

CABARET

The **Capitol Steps,** (☎ 202/298–8222 or 703/683–8330) performs political song and satire regularly in Georgetown; performance locations vary, so call for details.

JAZZ

Blues Alley (☒ Rear 1073 Wisconsin Ave. NW, ☎ 202/337–4141) books some of the biggest names in jazz.

ROCK

The **Bayou** (☒ 3135 K St. NW, ☎ 202/333–2897), in Georgetown, features live rock. The **9:30 Club** (☒ 815 V St. NW, ☎ 202/393–0930) books an eclectic mix of local, national, and international artists, mostly playing so-called alternative rock.

The Arts

TicketPlace (☒ Lisner Auditorium, 730 21st St. NW, ☎ 202/842–5387) sells half-price day-of-performance tickets; it's closed Sunday and Monday. **Ticketmaster** (☎ 202/432–7328 or 800/551–7328) takes phone charges for events around the city. All manner of cultural events, from ballet to classical music, are offered at the **John F. Kennedy Center for the Performing Arts** (☒ New Hampshire Ave. and Rock Creek Pkwy. NW, ☎ 202/467–4600 or 800/444–1324).

DANCE

Dance Place (☒ 3225 8th St. NE, ☎ 202/269–1600) hosts a wide array of modern and ethnic dance. The **Washington Ballet** (☎ 202/362–3606) performs at the Kennedy Center and the Warner Theatre (13th and E Sts. NW).

MUSIC

The **National Symphony Orchestra** (☎ 202/416–8100) performs at the Kennedy Center from September through June and during the summer at Wolf Trap Farm Park (☎ 703/255–1900); (☞ Virginia).

The **Armed Forces Concert Series** (☎ 202/767–5658 Air Force, 703/696–3718 Army, 202/433–4011 Marines, 202/433–2525 Navy) offers free military-band performances from June through August, nightly except Wednesday and Saturday, on the West Terrace of the Capitol and at the Sylvan Theater on the Washington Monument grounds.

OPERA

The **Washington Opera** (☎ 202/416–7800 or 800/876–7372) presents seven operas each season in the Kennedy Center's Opera House and in the Kennedy Center's Eisenhower Theater.

THEATER

Arena Stage (✉ 6th St. and Maine Ave. SW, ☏ 202/488–3300) has three theaters and is the city's most respected resident company. The historic **Ford's Theatre** (✉ 511 10th St. NW, ☏ 202/347–4833) is host mainly to musicals. The **National Theatre** (✉ 1321 Pennsylvania Ave. NW, ☏ 202/628–6161) presents tryouts and national touring companies of Broadway shows. The **Shakespeare Theatre** (✉ 450 7th St. NW, ☏ 202/393–2700) presents classics by the Bard. Many scrappy smaller companies—including the Source, the Studio, and the Woolly Mammoth—are clustered near 14th and P streets NW.

Spectator Sports

Basketball: Wizards (✉ MCI Center, 7th and F Sts. NW, ☏ 202/432–7328 or 800/551–7328 for tickets, 301/622–3865 for schedule). **Football:** The **Redskins** have a new stadium in nearby Landover, Maryland (✉ Jack Kent Cooke Stadium, ☏ 301/276–6050), with about 20,000 more seats than their old home at RFK Stadium, but all tickets are held by season-ticket holders. If you're willing to pay dearly, you can get tickets from brokers who advertise in the *Washington Post.* **Hockey: Capitals** (✉ MCI Center, ☏ 202/432–7328, 800/551–7328 for tickets, 301/336–2277 for schedule).

Shopping

Shopping Districts

Georgetown (centered on Wisconsin Ave. and M St. NW) is probably Washington's densest shopping area, with specialty shops selling everything from antiques to designer fashions. In **Adams-Morgan** (around 18th St. and Columbia Rd. NW) you'll find used-book stores, vintage clothing shops, and a bohemian atmosphere.

The **Shops at National Place** (✉ 13th and F Sts. NW, ☏ 202/783–9090) is a glittering three-story collection of stores, including a Sharper Image outlet store and clothing stores such as Powers & Goode and Oaktree. **Union Station** (✉ 50 Massachusetts Ave. NE, ☏ 202/371–9441) has clothing boutiques and special-interest shops. **Mazza Gallerie** (✉ 5300 Wisconsin Ave. NW, ☏ 202/966–6114) is an upscale mall that straddles the Maryland border and is anchored by the ritzy Neiman Marcus and a Filene's Basement.

Department Stores

Hecht's (✉ 12th and G Sts. NW, ☏ 202/628–6661) is downtown Washington's sole remaining department store, as its former neighbors—Garfinckel's, Woodward & Lothrop, Lansburgh's—have all pulled up stakes in the last decade. It's near the Metro Center subway stop.

Specialty Stores

Every museum in Washington has a gift shop, and in each the range of items reflects the museum's collection and extends far beyond the mere souvenir. The largest is probably in the **National Museum of American History** (☞ Exploring Washington, D.C., *above*). The **Indian Craft Shop,** in the Department of the Interior (✉ 1849 C St. NW, ☏ 202/208–4056), sells a variety of handicrafts from more than 35 Native American tribes.

WEST VIRGINIA

Updated by Therese S. Cox

Capital	Charleston
Population	1,816,000
Motto	Mountaineers Are Always Free
State Bird	Cardinal
State Flower	Rhododendron maximum
Postal Abbreviation	WV

Statewide Visitor Information

West Virginia Division of Tourism (✉ 2101 Washington St. E, Charleston 25305, ☎ 304/558–2200 or 800/225–5982, FAX 304/558–0108).

Scenic Drives

In the eastern mountains a **National Scenic Byway** (W.Va. 39/55 and connecting W.Va. 150) roams between Richwood and U.S. 219/W.Va. 55 north of Edray, in the Monongahela National Forest. The **Midland Trail** follows historic U.S. 60, running east–west for 120 mi between White Sulphur Springs and Charleston, tracing the 200-year-old path through the Appalachians first used by Native Americans. The **Coal Heritage Trail** leads from Beckley into the coalfields of Wyoming, McDowell, and Mercer counties along W.Va. 16 and U.S. 52.

National and State Parks

National Parks

Harpers Ferry National Historical Park (✉ Box 65, Harpers Ferry 25425, ☎ 304/535–6223; 🎫 $2 per person per day, 7-day pass $5) is situated at the picturesque confluence of the Potomac and Shenandoah rivers. The **New River Gorge National River** (✉ Box 246, Glen Jean 25846, ☎ 304/465–0508), a 53-mi section of the New River, contains a wide variety of some of America's best white-water recreation. The **Monongahela National Forest** (✉ 200 Sycamore St., Elkins 26241, ☎ 304/636–1800) and **George Washington National Forest** (✉ Lee Ranger District, Rte. 4, Box 515, Edinburg, VA 22824, ☎ 540/984–4101) encompass 900,000 and 100,000 acres, respectively, near the Virginia border.

State Parks

Eight of West Virginia's 35 state parks have fine lodges with restaurants and resort amenities, such as downhill skiing or championship golf courses. Most have cottages, cabins, and campsites with full hookups. **Cacapon Resort State Park** (✉ Rte. 1, Box 304, Berkeley Springs 25411, ☎ 304/258–1022 or 800/225–5982) is noted for its Robert Trent Jones golf course; amenities include 30 cottages and a 49-room lodge with restaurant. At **Canaan Valley Resort State Park** (✉ Rte. 1, Box 330, Davis 26260, ☎ 304/866–4121 or 800/225–5982) the 250-room lodge, 23 deluxe cabins, restaurant, and lounge are bustling year-round; the park has an alpine-skiing area, an 18-hole golf course, and outdoor and indoor pools and fitness center. **Pipestem Resort State Park** (✉ Box 150, Pipestem 25979, ☎ 304/466–1800 or 800/225–5982), southeast of Beckley, has two lodges (143 rooms) with restaurants, 25 deluxe cottages, and 82 campsites, as well as golf, tennis, horseback riding, indoor and outdoor pools, an aerial tramway, cross-country skiing, and tobogganing.

EASTERN WEST VIRGINIA

West Virginia's easternmost counties are replete with captivating, yet largely unsung, Colonial and Civil War history. The towns of Harpers Ferry, Berkeley Springs, Charles Town, Martinsburg, and Shepherdstown predate the Revolutionary War, bear the scars of the Civil War, and have remained largely untouched architecturally in the past 50 years. To the west the scene changes to one of rugged splendor in a swath of mountain land blessed with Canadian weather patterns—and the ski industry to prove it. In the spring the focus shifts to white-water rafting on some of the nation's most exciting rivers.

Visitor Information

Potomac Highlands: Jefferson County Visitor and Convention Bureau (☒ Box A, Harpers Ferry 25425, ☎ 304/535–2627 or 800/848–8687, FAX 304/535–2131); Martinsburg/Berkeley County Convention and Visitors Bureau (☒ 208 S. Queen St., Martinsburg 25401, ☎ 304/264–8801 or 800/498–2386). **Southern West Virginia:** Convention and Visitors Bureau (☒ Box 1799, Beckley 25802, ☎ 304/252–2244, FAX 304/252–2252); Travel Berkeley Springs (☒ 304 Fairfax St., Berkeley Springs 25411, ☎ 304/258–9147 or 800/447–8797).

Arriving and Departing

By Bus

Greyhound Lines (☎ 800/231–2222) serves major towns.

By Car

Three interstates traverse the region: I–64, between White Sulphur Springs and Beckley; I–77, Princeton to Charleston; and I–81, in the eastern panhandle. U.S. 340 enters Harpers Ferry from the east. From the west U.S. 50, I–79, and I–64 provide the best access.

By Plane

The region is served by Beckley's **Raleigh County Memorial Airport** (☎ 304/255–0476), Chantilly's **Dulles International Airport** (☎ 703/419–8000), Hagerstown's **Washington County Regional Airport** (☎ 301/791–3333), Lewisburg's **Greenbrier's Valley Airport** (☎ 304/645–3961), and Winchester's **Winchester Regional Airport** (☎ 540/662–5786).

By Train

Amtrak (☎ 800/872–7245) has stations in Harpers Ferry and Martinsburg.

Exploring Eastern West Virginia

Old and new mingle here in surprising harmony. In the eastern panhandle you can explore pre-Revolutionary buildings, shop for the latest in fashions, and relax in a Roman bath, all in the same day. To the west and south the mountain roads are scenic but sometimes narrow and limited to 40 mph. Do your driving in the daytime to enjoy the many overlooks and small towns reminiscent of the 1950s.

★ At the Panhandle's southeastern tip is **Harpers Ferry National Historical Park** (☞ National and State Parks, *above*), where the Shenandoah and Potomac rivers join. Hand-carved stone steps lead to the overlook where Thomas Jefferson proclaimed the view "worth a trip across the Atlantic." The township of Harpers Ferry grew around a U.S. armory built in 1740, and many buildings have been preserved. Lining the cobblestone streets are shops and museums, where park employees in period costume demonstrate Early American skills and interpret the evolution of American firearms. Each second Saturday in October the park service stages Election Day 1860 (☞ Festivals and Seasonal Events *in* the Mid-Atlantic introduction). Within the park, the **John Brown Wax Museum** depicts the abolitionist's raid on the town. ☎ *304/535–6342.* *$2.50. Closed weekdays Dec.–Mar.*

Charles Town, named for George Washington's brother, who was an early resident, is irrevocably linked with Harpers Ferry, for it is where John Brown was hanged for treason. The Jefferson County Courthouse here houses a museum that includes among its artifacts the wagon that delivered Brown to his fate on the courthouse square.

In **Martinsburg** two pre–Civil War roundhouses (circular buildings for housing and repairing locomotives) at the foot of Martin Street attract railroad buffs, though they're in poor condition. Downtown, pre–Civil War structures of Federal and Greek Revival style can be seen on John, Race, and North Spring streets.

Shepherdstown, on the Potomac River northwest of Harpers Ferry, is one of the region's oldest towns, established in 1730 as Mechlenberg. Today its quaint wooden storefronts and tree-lined brick streets form the framework for a collection of specialty shops, small inns, and restaurants that lure city folk from the Washington-Baltimore area.

Berkeley Springs was officially chartered in 1776 as the Town of Bath by George Washington and speculating friends, who envisioned the site of the ancient healing springs as a spa. The buoyant warm waters still flow freely, attracting a thriving community of massage therapists, practitioners of homeopathy, and artists. A variety of small inns, antiques shops, spa retreats, and services make it a year-round haven for relaxation. **Berkeley Springs State Park** (✉ 121 S. Washington St., Berkeley Springs 25411, ☎ 304/258–2711 or 800/225–5982) offers heated Roman baths and massages.

Potomac Eagle Scenic Rail Excursions (✉ 1 mi north of Romney of W.Va. 28, ☎ 800/223–2453; $18–$44, depending on type of car and time of year) takes passengers in vintage railcars into the wilderness of the South Branch of the Potomac River, where bald eagle sightings are common.

A southwesterly route leads through the Potomac Highlands, an area ★ with boundless opportunity for outdoor recreation, to the **National Radio Astronomy Observatory,** in Green Bank, where huge radio telescopes listen for life in outer space. Bus tours and a slide presentation are available. ✉ *Rte. 28/92,* ☎ *304/456–2011.* *Free. Closed weekdays Sept.–Oct. No tours Nov.–mid-May.*

Cass Scenic Railroad State Park encompasses an authentic turn-of-the-century lumber-company town and offers visitors a tow up to the second-highest peak in West Virginia in open railcars once used to haul logs off the mountain. Trains are drawn by geared Shay steam locomotives, built at the turn of the century to negotiate steep terrain. ✉ *Rte. 66, Cass,* ☎ *304/456–4300 or 800/225–5982.* *$10 weekdays, $12 weekends. Closed Nov.–mid-May.*

The **Youth Museum of Southern West Virginia** (✉ New River Park, Beckley, ☎ 304/252–3730; $2) offers a permanent village of reconstructed or relocated log structures that depict agricultural life in the area before the advent of mining. The **Beckley Exhibition Coal Mine** (✉ New River Park, Drawer A.J., Beckley 25802, ☎ 304/256–1747; $7) has 1,500 ft of restored passages open for guided tours; it's closed from November through Easter.

The **Lewisburg National Historic District** (✉ U.S. 219, ☎ 304/645–1000 or 800/833–2068) encompasses 236 acres and more than 60 18th-century buildings, many of native limestone or brick. At night gas lamps flicker on quaint storefronts and signs, and no overhead power lines spoil the image of a bygone era.

The mammoth **State Fair of West Virginia** (✉ 3 mi south of I–64 on Rte. 219, Lewisburg, ☎ 304/645–1090; 🎟 $6) each day offers livestock shows, harness racing, crafts, and famous entertainers. Each summer some of the foremost folk artists in the United States teach 90 weeklong classes—like old-time fiddle playing, log-house construction, and white-oak rib basketry—at the **Augusta Heritage Workshops** (✉ 300 Sycamore St., Elkins 26241, ☎ 304/636–1800) at Davis & Elkins College. The engineering marvel of the **New River Gorge Bridge,** the world's longest steel arch span, is celebrated annually the third Saturday in October near Fayetteville. More than 200 food and crafts vendors sell their wares while festival goers watch parachutists leap hundreds of feet above the New River Gorge.

Dining and Lodging

Real West Virginia cooking is hearty, simple, and usually homemade from local ingredients—buckwheat cakes for breakfast, beef stew for lunch, brook trout or game for dinner—but more urbane fare is often available. Accommodations range from the Ritz to motels where "the light's always left on for you," but local bed-and-breakfasts (☎ 800/225–5982 for B&B listings and booklet) afford the best access to the state's greatest treasure: its people. For price ranges *see* Charts 1 (B) and 2 (B) *in* On the Road with Fodor's.

Berkeley Springs

$$–$$$ ✕ **Country Inn.** This restaurant's atmosphere suits its name—lots of natural wood and old prints. The best menu choices are crab cakes or lamb. ✉ *207 S. Washington St.,* ☎ *304/258–2210 or 800/822–6630. AE, D, DC, MC, V.*

$$$$ ★ 🏨 **Coolfont Resort & Spectrum Spa.** Accommodations are in modern chalets, rustic cabins, or lodge rooms. Special programs for losing weight, reducing stress, and quitting smoking are offered. The soup-salad-bread bar is exceptional, as are the daily buffet and the fresh brook trout. ✉ *1777 Cold Run Valley Rd., 25411,* ☎ *304/258–4500 or 800/296–8768,* FAX *304/258–5499. 82 units. Restaurant, pool, tennis, health club. MAP. AE, D, DC, MC, V.*

$$ ★ 🏨 **Cacapon Resort State Park.** Locally crafted heavy oak pieces furnish the main lodge's rooms and woodsy dining room, which overlook the golf course or Cacapon Ridge. Rustic cabins are tucked into the surrounding woods. ✉ *Off 522, Rte. 1 (Box 304), 25411,* ☎ *304/258–1022,* FAX *304/258–5323. 49 rooms, 30 cabins. Restaurant, tennis. AE, MC, V.*

Davis

$$–$$$ ✕ **Blackwater Falls State Park.** The stone-pillared dining room, furnished in handmade red oak, perches on the rim of the Blackwater Canyon. Diners' favorites are the breakfast bar, charbroiled chicken breast, and prime rib. ✉ *Rte. 32 to Blackwater Falls State Park Rd.,* ☎ *304/259–5216,* FAX *304/259–5881. AE, MC, V.*

$$$ 🏨 **Canaan Valley Resort State Park.** The rooms here are motel style but spacious, and the resort's wooded setting is superb. Golf, downhill skiing, and ice-skating are popular activities. ✉ *Rte. 1, Box 330, 26260,* ☎ *304/866–4121 or 800/622–4121,* FAX *304/866–2172. 250 rooms, 23 cabins. Restaurant, pools. D, DC, MC, V.*

Durbin

$$$–$$$$ ★ ✕🏨 **Cheat Mountain Club.** Originally an exclusive men's sports hideaway, this 100-year-old hand-hewn-spruce log cabin is surrounded by the 901,000-acre Monongahela National Forest and close to skiing, hiking, mountain biking, and hunting. The pine-paneled guest rooms on the lodge's second floor are immaculately kept. Hearty homemade fare is on the restaurant's three daily menus. Prime rib and lemon-pepper pasta with lemon zest, olive oil, and garlic are typical dinner entrées. ✉ *Rte. 250 (Box 28), Durbin 26264,* ☎ *304/456–4627,* FAX *304/456–3192. 9 rooms and 5-bed dormitory. FAP. MC, V.*

Shepherdstown

$$–$$$$ ✕🏨 **Bavarian Inn and Lodge.** In four alpine chalets overlooking the Potomac River, the Bavarian has luxurious rooms with canopy beds, fireplaces, and whirlpool tubs. The dining areas are decorated with antiques and fine china. The German and American cuisine includes wild pheasant, venison, and boar. ✉ *Rte. 1 (Box 30), 25443,* ☎ *304/876–2551,* FAX *304/876–9355. 42 units. Restaurant, pool, tennis courts. AE, DC, MC, V.*

Snowshoe/Slatyfork

$$$–$$$$ ★ ✕ **Red Fox Restaurant.** A cozy tavern room, plush seating, and greenhouse windows distinguish this restaurant, as do its extensive menu and exceptional service. The chefs use local meats, fish, herbs, and cheeses for such specialties as wild game pâtés or roast quail cooked with apples, country ham, sausages, and applejack brandy. ✉ *Snowshoe Mountain Resort, off U.S. 219,* ☎ *304/572–1111,* FAX *304/572–2222. AE, D, MC, V.*

$$ ★ 🏨 **Snowshoe/Silver Creek Mountain Resort.** This resort can accommodate up to 9,000 guests; lodging varies from motel-style rooms to luxury condos. Snowshoe has an assortment of natural-wood structures in the forest fringing the ski slopes, and Silver Creek has lodgings in a high-rise. ✉ *Off U.S. 219; 10 Snowshoe Rd., 26209,* ☎ *304/572–1000, ext. 268. 1,250 houses and condos, 302 lodge rooms. 22 restaurants, pools, tennis, exercise room. AE, MC, V.*

White Sulphur Springs

$$$$ ★ 🏨 **The Greenbrier.** One of the leading resorts in the country, this 6,500-acre spa is done in grand turn-of-the-century style. Massive white columns rise six stories against a white facade, while inside nine lobbies offer vast, chandeliered common areas. Every guest room is different, decorated in Dorothy Draper pastel prints. Gourmet cuisine features such dishes as farm-raised striped bass and rack of lamb. Horseback riding and three golf courses are among the extensive leisure facilities. ✉ *300 W. Main St., White Sulphur Springs 24986,* ☎ *304/536–1110 or 800/624–6070,* FAX *304/536–7854. 640 units. 4 dining rooms, pool, tennis, health club. AE, DC, MC, V.*

Motel

🏨 **Holiday Inn** (✉ 301 Foxcroft Ave., Martinsburg 25401, ☎ 304/267–5500 or 800/862–6282), 120 rooms; restaurant, pools, health club; *$$$.*

Campgrounds

State park camping facilities and more than 100 commercial campgrounds are listed in a camping booklet; contact the West Virginia Division of Tourism (☞ Statewide Visitor Information, *above*).

Nightlife and the Arts

At Grandview State Park's **Theatre West Virginia** (☎ 304/256–6800 or 800/666–9142), you'll find the state's premier outdoor theatrical productions: *Honey in the Rock,* a Civil War story; *Hatfields and McCoys,* depicting the famous feud; and a different musical each season.

Outdoor Activities and Sports

Biking

Rentals, instruction, and tours are available from **Blackwater Bikes** (✉ Davis, ☎ 304/259–5286), the **Elk River Touring Center** (✉ Slatyfork, ☎ 304/572–3771), and **Snowshoe Mountain Biking Centers** (✉ Snowshoe, ☎ 304/572–1000).

Canoeing

The **Greenbrier River** is one of the country's best paddling rivers. Area outfitters can put you on this and other waterways; for a list of operators contact the West Virginia Division of Tourism (☞ Statewide Visitor Information, *above*).

Fishing

Trout are abundant in faster streams, while bass, crappie, and walleye lurk in big rivers and lakes. Licenses are available at sporting and convenience stores. Most rafting companies organize fishing trips. **Elk Mountain Outfitters** (✉ Corner Rte. 66 and Rte. 219; Box 8, Slatyfork 26291, ☎ 304/572–3000) offers fly-fishing schools and guided trout expeditions.

Golf

Cacapon and **Canaan Valley Resort state parks** (☞ National and State Parks, *above*) offer 18 holes each; the **Greenbrier,** in White Sulphur Springs (☞ Dining and Lodging, *above*), 54 holes; **Locust Hill** (☎ 304/728–7300), in Charles Town, 18 holes; **Pipestem Resort State Park** (☞ National and State Parks, *above*), 27 holes; **Stonebridge** (☎ 304/263–4653 or 800/490–3470), in Martinsburg, 18 holes; the **Woods** (☎ 304/754–7977 or 800/248–2222), in Hedgesville, 27 holes.

Hiking

State and national parks have extensive trail systems. The **Appalachian Trail** (✉ Harpers Ferry 25425, ☎ 304/535–6331) and the **Big Blue Trail** (✉ Potomac Appalachian Trail Club, 118 Park St. SE, Vienna, VA 22180, ☎ 703/242–0965) run through this region.

Horseback Riding

Horseback riding along trails is available in most state parks. Stables at **Glade Springs Resort & Conference Center** (✉ 3000 Lake Dr., Daniels 25832, ☎ 800/634–5233) offer a variety of activities, from short rides to overnight expeditions and wagon rides. **Swift Level** (✉ Rte. 2, Box 269-A, Lewisburg 24901, ☎ 304/645–1155) is a horse farm offering multiday long-distance treks for experienced equestrians.

Rafting

The **New, Gauley,** and **Cheat** are West Virginia's most heavily traveled rivers, followed by the **Tygart** and **Shenandoah.** First-timers can tackle all but the Gauley. For information on more than 30 commercial outfitters that run white-water excursions, contact the West Virginia Division of Tourism (☞ Statewide Visitor Information, *above*).

Ski Areas

Cross-Country

Elk River Touring Center (☞ Biking *in* Outdoor Activities and Sports, *above*) and the **White Grass Ski Touring Center** (✉ Rte. 1, Box 299, Davis 26260, ☎ 304/866–4114) offers rentals, instruction, and tours.

Downhill

Call 800/225–5982 for snow conditions at these ski areas: **Canaan Valley Resort State Park** (☒ Davis), 34 slopes and trails, 3 chairlifts, vertical drop 850 ft, 1¼-mi run; **Snowshoe/Silver Creek** (☒ Snowshoe), 53 trails, 11 chairlifts, vertical drop 1,500 ft, 1½-mi run; **Timberline** (☒ Davis), 35 trails, 3 chairlifts, vertical drop 1,000 ft, 2-mi run, 200-ft half-pipe for snowboarders; and **Winterplace** (☒ Flat Top), 27 trails, 5 chairlifts, vertical drop 603 ft, 1¼-mi run.

Shopping

Fairs and festivals are plentiful and are perfect places to shop for mountain handicrafts; check with the state visitor center for a calendar of events. The wares of 1,500 artists and craftspeople whose works have passed muster with a state jury are sold at **Tamarack** (☒ 1 Tamarack Park, ☎ 304/256–6843), a sprawling center just off I–77. **Berkeley Springs** is home to two large antiques consortiums and several independent dealers in glass, collectibles, and political memorabilia. **Harpers Ferry's Bolivar District** houses wall-to-wall antiques and specialty shops. **Martinsburg** offers antiques stores and several outlet malls, including the Blue Ridge Outlet Center (☒ Stephen and Queen Sts., ☎ 304/263–7467 or 800/445–3993), which houses 60 select manufacturers and designers of quality goods.

WESTERN WEST VIRGINIA

The Charleston-Huntington area is a center of commerce and culture quite different from the mountain wilderness to the east and the farmland to the north. Skilled craftspeople, such as those who supplied the Kennedy White House with glassware, make their homes in this area in the central Ohio River valley. Its northern panhandle suffers from steel-industry troubles, but its fine old mansions and Victorian architecture are reminders of better times. Wheeling's Oglebay Resort and Conference Center is a cultural jewel and one of the finest municipal parks in the nation.

Visitor Information

Charleston: Convention and Visitors Bureau (☒ 200 Civic Center Dr., 25301, ☎ 304/344–5075 or 800/733–5469, FAX 304/344–1241). **Huntington:** Cabell-Huntington Convention and Visitors Bureau (☒ Box 347, 25708, ☎ 304/525–7333 or 800/635–6329). **Wheeling:** Convention and Visitors Bureau (☒ 1233 Main St., Suite 1000, 26003, ☎ 304/233–7709 or 800/828–3097, FAX 304/233–1320). **Northern West Virginia:** Convention and Visitors Bureau (☒ 709 Beechurst Ave., Morgantown 26505, ☎ 304/292–5081 or 800/458–7373, FAX 304/291–1354).

Arriving and Departing

By Car

Major routes covering the region are I–64W; I–77 north–south; I–79 north–south; U.S. 50 between Clarksburg and Parkersburg; and I–70 crossing the northern panhandle at Wheeling.

By Plane

The region is served by Charleston's **Yeager Airport** (☎ 304/344–8033 or 800/241–6522), Huntington's **Tri-State Airport** (☎ 304/453–6165), Parkersburg's **Wood County Airport** (☎ 304/464–5115), Clarksburg/Fairmont's **Benedum Airport** (☎ 304/842–3400), and the **Morgantown Municipal Airport/Hart Field** (☎ 304/291–7461).

By Train

Amtrak (☎ 800/872–7245) provides service from White Sulphur Springs through Charleston to Huntington.

Exploring Western West Virginia

This area is heavily influenced by the early history and commerce of the Ohio River. Charleston, Parkersburg, and Huntington set an urban tone with museums, shopping malls, and cultural and entertainment centers, but the hustle is balanced by lazy days on the river. Moving north through valley farmland, you can watch glassblowers and other craftspeople at work. The boom of the 1890s is reflected throughout the area in grand mansions and nicely preserved Victorian architecture.

Charleston, first settled in 1794, has been the state capital since 1885 and is the hub of the Great Kanawha Valley. The Italian Renaissance **capitol,** designed by Cass Gilbert in 1932, is considered one of America's most beautiful state capitols. From the massive gilt dome, which rises 300 ft above the street, hangs a 2-ton chandelier of hand-cut crystal. ✉ *1900 Kanawha Blvd. E,* ☎ *304/558–3809.* *Free. Closed Sun. Labor Day–Memorial Day; no guided tours on weekends.*

Within the capitol complex is the **Cultural Center** (✉ Greenbrier and Washington Sts., ☎ 304/558–0220; free), with its marble **Great Hall** and the **State Museum,** which traces West Virginia history. **Mountain Stage,** a live contemporary-music radio show, is taped here before an audience 6–8 most Sunday evenings; each show has a different emphasis, from world beat to jazz, blues, folk and rock. Prices vary. ☎ *800/723–4687 for information, 304/342–5757 for tickets.*

Overlooking the capitol is **Sunrise Museum,** comprising two historic mansions that house art galleries, a hands-on science center, and a planetarium. Outside are 16 acres of wooded grounds with gardens and trails. ✉ *746 Myrtle Rd.,* ☎ *304/344–8035.* *$3.50. Closed Mon.–Tues.*

Downtown are a large civic center and the pleasant **Charleston Town Center** shopping area (☞ Shopping, *below*). Eight styles of 19th-century architecture are represented in the **East End Historic District,** bordered by Bradford, Quarrier, and Michigan streets and Kanawha Boulevard.

Charleston takes pride in downtown **Haddad Riverfront Park,** which bustles the week before Labor Day during the annual Sternwheeler Regatta. The paddle wheeler **P. A. Denny** (☎ 304/348–0709 or 304/348–6419) offers cruises year-round.

It takes an hour by I–64 to reach metropolitan **Huntington,** the state's second-largest city, a river and rail town whose meticulously laid out streets are lined with stately turn-of-the-century houses. In the **9th Street West Historic District** the streets are brick, the houses Victorian frame bordered with wrought-iron fences. The **Huntington Museum of Art,** the state's largest museum, covers 52 acres and houses the Junior Art Museum, a celestial observatory, and an amphitheater. ✉ *2033 McCay Rd.,* ☎ *304/529–2701.* *Donations accepted. Closed Mon.*

Near Huntington, at Milton, is the **Blenko Glass Visitor Center and Factory Outlet,** one of more than a dozen handblown-glass factories between Huntington and Parkersburg. ✉ *Exit 28 off I–64 to U.S. 60,* ☎ *304/743–9081. No glassblowing weekends.*

Another thriving Ohio River town, Parkersburg has many restored turn-of-the-century houses, but its main attraction is **Blennerhassett Island**

Charleston, West Virginia

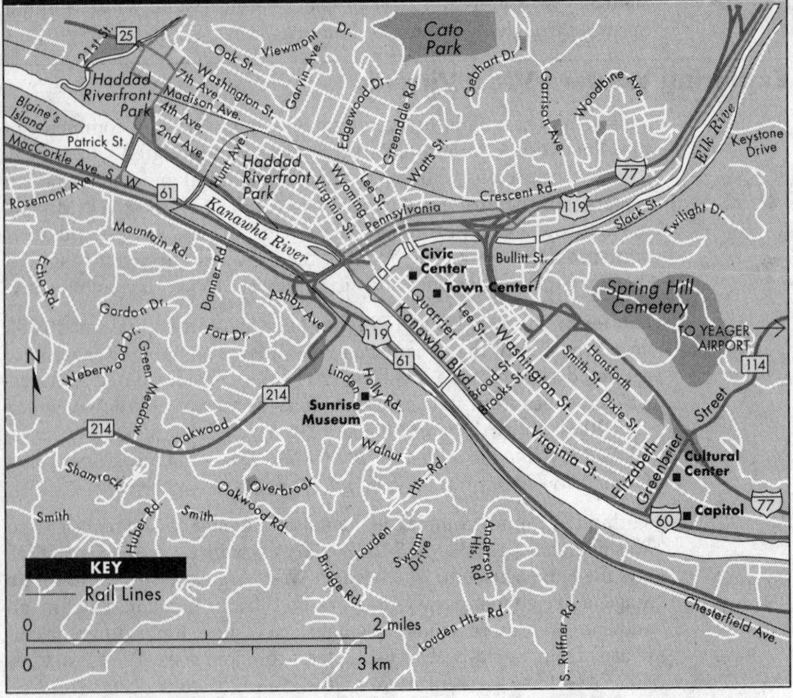

Historical State Park. In 1800 Harman Blennerhassett's magnificent island estate was the talk of the Northwest Territory, but he was later arrested with Aaron Burr for treason. Besides the Palladian-style mansion, you can visit a crafts village and take horse-drawn-wagon tours of the island, which is reached aboard a stern-wheeler. ✉ *Blennerhassett Museum of Regional History, 2nd and Juliana Sts.,* ☎ *304/420–4800 or 800/225–5982.* 🎫 *$6. Island closed Nov.–Apr.*

In the heart of the state is the Mountain Lakes region, dotted with prime fishing areas and a number of Civil War landmarks, such as **Carnifex Ferry Battlefield State Park.** The battle here dashed the South's hopes of controlling the Kanawha Valley. Within the park, the **Patterson House,** which marked the line between Union and Confederate forces, has been restored as a museum. ✉ *Rte. 2, Summersville at Carniflex Ferry Battlefield,* ☎ *304/872–0825.* 🎫 *Free. Museum closed Labor Day–Memorial Day.*

North of Clarksburg is **Morgantown,** an industrial and educational center known internationally for its glass. It is home of **West Virginia University,** where the world's first fully automated transportation system carries students between campuses. There's all the bustle of a college town here, plus the 1,700-acre **Cheat Lake,** which is served by three marinas (**Blosser's,** ☎ 304/594–2541; **Edgewater,** ☎ 304/594–2630; and **Sunset Harbor,** ☎ 304/594–1100).

In the northern panhandle, **Wheeling** was once the gateway to the West. Parks, museums, riverboat rides, and a wealth of restored Victorian houses—for instance, the **Design Co./Eckhart House** (☎ 304/232–5439; 🎫 tour $3) and **Victorian Wheeling Landmarks Foundation** (☎ 304/233–1600; 🎫 tours $4 per house; $12 for 4-house tour)—are reminders

of the old days. **Oglebay Resort and Conference Center** (☎ 304/243–4000 or 800/624–6988) is a 1,500-acre municipal park–resort with a hotel (☞ Dining and Lodging, *below*), a 65-acre petting zoo, planetarium, museum, indoor and outdoor swimming pools, naturalist programs for all ages, and two championship golf courses; prices for activities vary. From early November through late January both the park and downtown Wheeling explode into gigantic thematic displays for the premier **Winter Festival of Lights.**

Dining and Lodging

For price ranges *see* Charts 1 (B) and 2 (B) *in* On the Road with Fodor's.

Charleston

$$–$$$$ ✕🏨 **Embassy Suites.** Opened in December, 1997, in the Downtown area, this comfortable all-suite hotel is ½ block from the Civic Center and across from the Town Center Mall. Rooms have standard but well-kept furnishings. The Athletic Club Sports Bar & Grill serves hearty soups, salads, sandwiches, and pasta dishes for lunch and dinner. ✉ *300 Court St.,* ☎ *304/347–8700 or 800/362–2779,* FAX *304/347–8737. 253 suites. Restaurant, pool, exercise room. Full breakfast. AE, D, DC, MC, V.*

Morgantown

$$–$$$$ ★ ✕🏨 **Lakeview Resort and Conference Center.** This country club turned resort sits on a dramatic cliff overlooking Cheat Lake. Comfortable motel-style rooms are accessed by a warren of halls and stairways. Restaurants have lake or golf course views, and the popular lounge features live entertainment on the weekend. Two golf courses and a $2-million fitness center boost the convention trade. Prime rib and poached salmon are the main attractions in the Reflections on the Lake Restaurant. The Grill Restaurant serves a light, healthy fare. ✉ *Rte. 6 (Box 88A), 26505,* ☎ *304/594–1111 or 800/624–8300,* FAX *304/594–9472. 187 rooms. 2 restaurants, pools, tennis, exercise room. AE, D, DC, MC, V.*

Wheeling

$$–$$$$ ★ ✕🏨 **Stratford Springs.** This historic inn, composed of two turn-of-the-century houses, is on 30 wooded, secluded acres. The rooms are Colonial style, with cherry-wood or Amish furniture. Among the restaurants, which cater mainly to nonguests, the formal Stratford Room (jacket and tie) serves such dishes as stuffed strip steak and baby coho salmon. ✉ *355 Oglebay Dr., 26003,* ☎ *304/233–5100 or 800/521–8435,* FAX *304/232–6447. 3 rooms. Restaurant, pool, exercise room. AE, MC, V.*

$$–$$$$ 🏨 **Oglebay Resort and Conference Center.** Connected to the rustic lodge, which has a huge stone-floor lobby and a stone fireplace, are motel-style rooms and once-detached chalets. Nearby cabins sleeping 12 to 20 are rustic outside and ultramodern inside. ✉ *Rte. 88N,* ☎ *304/243–4000 or 800/624–6988,* FAX *304/243–4070. 204 lodge rooms, 16 suites, 50 deluxe cabins. Restaurant, pools, tennis. AE, D, DC, MC, V.*

Motel

🏨 **Charleston Marriott** (✉ 200 Lee St. E, Charleston 25301, ☎ 304/345–6500 or 800/228–9290, FAX 304/353–3722), 354 rooms, 2 restaurants, indoor pool, health club; *$$.*

Campgrounds

The West Virginia Division of Tourism (☞ Statewide Visitor Information, *above*) has listings of commercial campgrounds as well as facilities in more than a dozen state parks.

Nightlife and the Arts

Wheeling's **Capitol Music Hall** (✉ 1015 Main St., ☎ 800/624–5456), home of WWVA radio's *Jamboree USA,* has live performances by country music greats and two big-name jamborees in July and August.

Outdoor Activities and Sports

Canoeing

The area's many **lakes** are ideal for canoeing; contact the Army Corps of Engineers (☎ 304/529–5211).

Fishing

Native trout are abundant in the faster streams and rivers, while bass, crappie, and walleye lurk in the lakes. Licenses are available at sporting and convenience stores. Rafting companies organize fishing trips. **Sutton Lake** (✉ Sutton, ☎ 304/765–2705) and **Stonewall Jackson Lake** (✉ Weston, ☎ 304/269–0523) are prime areas.

Golf

Coonskin Golf Course (✉ 2000 Coonskin Dr., Charleston, ☎ 304/341–8013), 18 holes. **Lakeview Resort's Lakeview and Mountainview courses** (✉ 1 Lakeview Dr., Morgantown, ☎ 304/594–1111 or 800/624–8300), 36 holes. **Oglebay Park's Crispin and Speidel courses** (✉ Oglebay, Rte. 88N, Wheeling, ☎ 304/243–4000 or 800/624–6988), 36 holes. **Twin Falls Resort State Park Golf Course** (✉ Rte. 97, Mullens, ☎ 304/294–4000 or 800/225–5982), 18 holes. **Worthington Golf Club** (✉ 3414 Roseland Ave., Parkersburg, ☎ 304/428–4297), 18 holes.

Hiking and Backpacking

The **Allegheny Trail** (✉ 633 West Virginia Ave., Morgantown 26505, ☎ 304/296–5158) and the **Kanawha Trace** (✉ 733 7th Ave., Huntington 25701, ☎ 304/523–3408) pass through state and national forests and wilderness areas with rocky overlooks and thickets of rhododendron and mountain laurel.

Rafting

The white waters of the **Cheat** and **Tygart** rivers flow through this region. Call 800/225–5982 for brochures on guided trips and a list of more than 50 licensed outfitters.

Shopping

Antiques and local crafts, particularly handblown glass, are abundant; venues vary from roadside shops to outdoor fairs to sprawling glass-factory outlets (☞ Exploring Western West Virginia, *above*). The largest showcase of West Virginia wares is displayed during July 4th week at the **Mountain State Art & Craft Fair** (☎ 800/225–5982; 🎟 $5), in Ripley. In downtown Charleston, the **Charleston Town Center** (✉ Quarrier and Lee Sts., ☎ 304/345–9525) has 165 shops adjacent to the Charleston Marriott Town Center.

5 The Southeast

Alabama, Florida, Georgia, North Carolina, South Carolina

By Conrad Paulus

Updated by Jane F. Garvey

FROM PINE TO PALM, lapped by the Atlantic Ocean and the Gulf of Mexico, stretch North and South Carolina, Georgia, Florida, and Alabama. Celluloid stereotypes portray southerners as dreaming life away on the veranda, julep in hand, among the magnolias and Spanish moss. Certainly, there are verandas. Magnolias still bloom. Spanish moss drapes trees growing along coastal lowlands. And certainly, too, the Southeast retains its taste for history, especially its own, but nowadays the Southeast is clearly dealing in the present and planning for tomorrow as it vigorously competes with the rest of the country and, indeed, the world for business and economic development.

With the exception of Florida, all these states have both mountains (with resorts and sports) and seashore (with beaches and boating); in Florida the coast is never more than 50 mi away. It's a good thing, too, because the region's temperatures and humidity are fierce, although air-conditioning has transformed the summers. Southerners, chiefly wealthy ones, often sought refuge from the region's legendary heat in the highlands and piney woods of the Carolinas and northern Georgia. Today these areas are highly regarded resort destinations.

It's commonly held that following the Civil War the South entered a period of economic decay from which it has only recently emerged. In fact, huge fortunes—consider Coca-Cola—were made in the South after the war. It was the Great Depression that brought much economic disruption to the region. Post-depression poverty prevented much of the tearing down and rebuilding common in the rest of the East and forced people to make do with that outmoded old Empire and Victorian furniture they had hoped to replace with the new machine-made marvels. It also caused many of the classic homes to suffer decay and, sometimes, to be demolished. But much has been retained and restored. Today dozens of Greek Revival and Victorian mansions containing their original furnishings are open during special festival times to visitors, while others have become house museums open to the public on a regular basis. White-columned houses, some in advanced states of disrepair, have been rescued and restored, often converted into bed-and-breakfast inns, so that travelers may today sleep in those tall mahogany and walnut beds in which wealthy 19th-century plantation owners once slumbered.

The Southeast

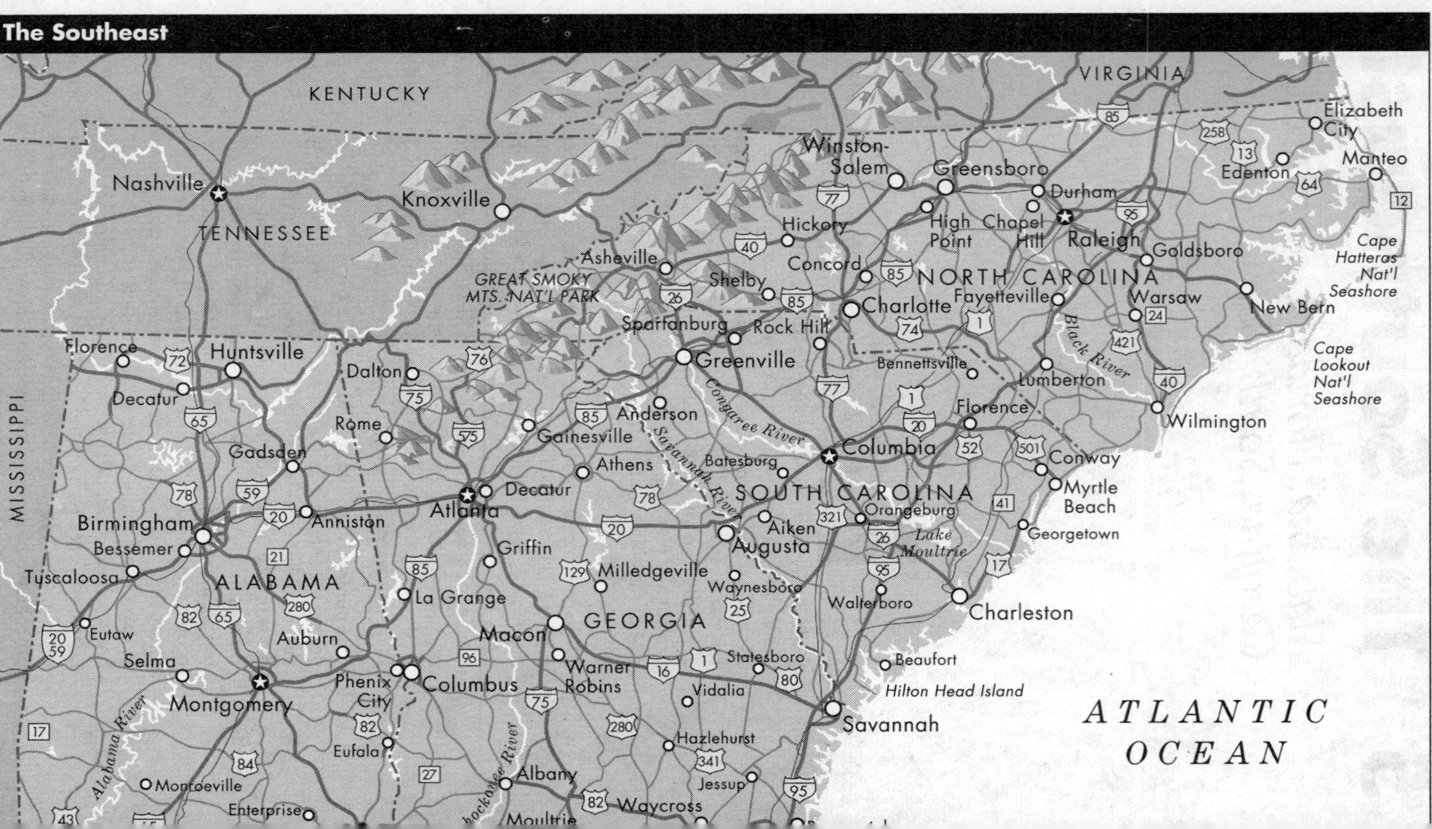

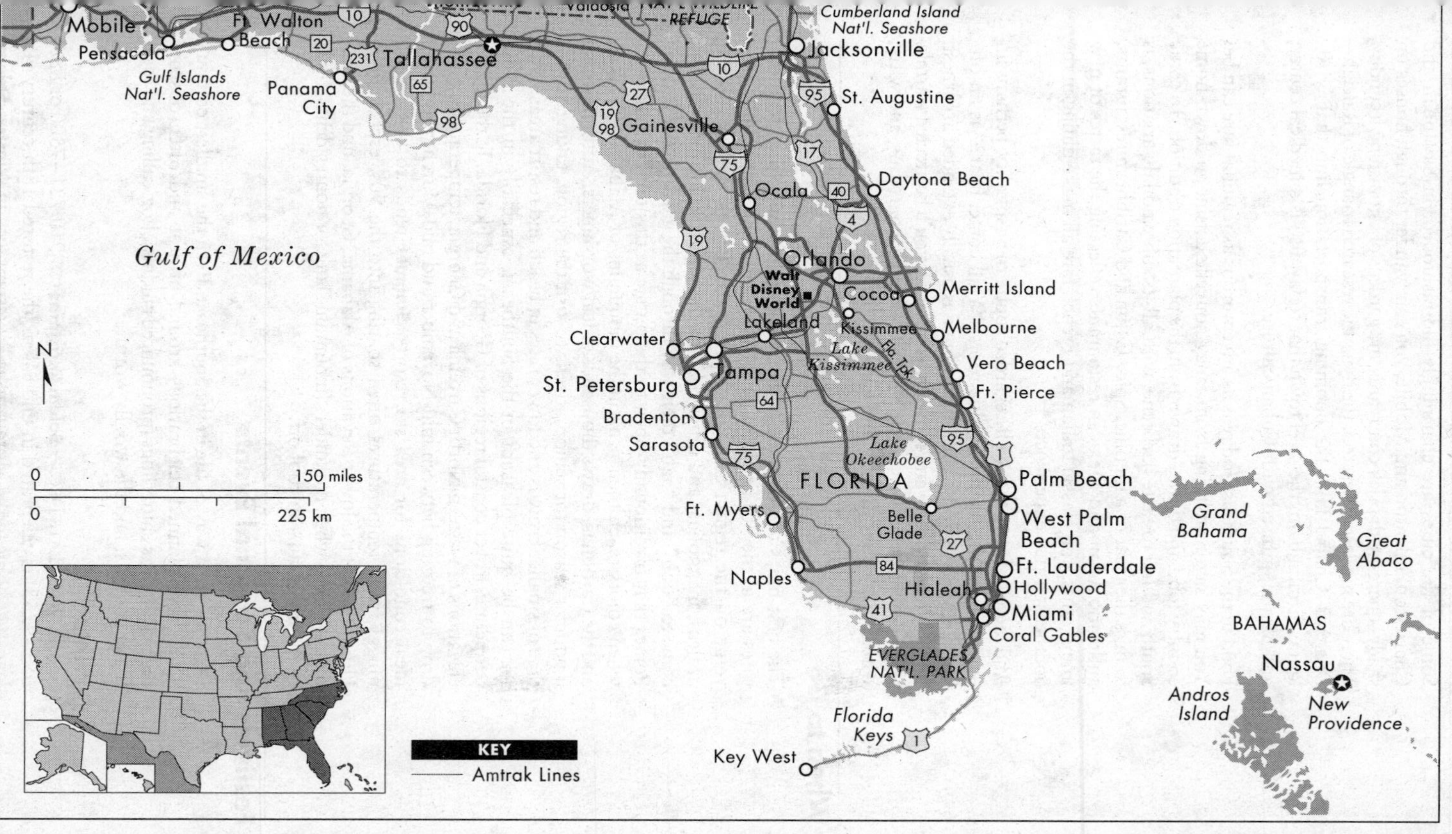

Mobile
Pensacola
Gulf Islands Nat'l. Seashore
Ft. Walton Beach
Panama City
Tallahassee
REFUGE
Cumberland Island Nat'l. Seashore
Jacksonville
St. Augustine
Gainesville
Daytona Beach
Ocala
Gulf of Mexico
Orlando
Walt Disney World
Cocoa
Merritt Island
Lakeland
Kissimmee
Melbourne
Clearwater
Lake Kissimmee
Fla. Tpk.
Vero Beach
Tampa
St. Petersburg
Ft. Pierce
Bradenton
Sarasota
Lake Okeechobee
FLORIDA
Palm Beach
N
0 150 miles
0 225 km
Ft. Myers
Belle Glade
West Palm Beach
Grand Bahama
Great Abaco
Ft. Lauderdale
Naples
Hialeah
Hollywood
Miami
Coral Gables
BAHAMAS
EVERGLADES NAT'L. PARK
Nassau
Andros Island
New Providence
Florida Keys
KEY
Amtrak Lines
Key West

Some of the cities are charmingly old-fashioned; in Savannah and Charleston, Edenton and Mobile, you can wander through houses on shady squares with brick courtyards and gardens of astonishing fecundity. There are modern cities, too: the dynamic research triangle of Raleigh–Durham–Chapel Hill; the booming transportation hub that is Atlanta; Birmingham, the steel town that today also is a medical center; and Miami, infused with Cuban culture.

Food in the Southeast today is as adventurous as regional fare can be: You may savor anything from fancy nouvelle cuisine to down-home country food and dishes drawn from the plantation tradition. To come South and fail to taste barbecue, with all its subregional variations, is to miss the treat of a lifetime. Spicy Cajun and Caribbean restaurants, authentic Asian and Mexican restaurants reflecting the tastes of new immigrants, and classic Italian and French fare all make dining in the Southeast a rich experience.

And there's always that well-regarded southern hospitality, perhaps inherited from the region's Celtic roots. "Y'all come, hear?" is an oft-heard, and oft-parodied, invitation, but it is usually extended in earnest. If you take it seriously and show up, you can bet you'll be greeted warmly. Southerners are an easygoing bunch—talkative, courteous, and witty, with a talent for laughing and enjoying life.

When to Go

The best times to visit the South are **spring** and **fall,** when temperatures are in the 70s and 80s. That's when golf and tennis buffs converge on the region en masse. Spring also brings the magnificent azaleas, magnolias, and other flora of the region to life, and visitors come to "ooh" and "aah" their way through the gardens and historic homes that traditionally open to the public at this time of year. Fall, when colors reach their peak in the mountains of Alabama, Georgia, and the Carolinas, draws thousands of leaf worshipers. Autumn is also a popular season for senior citizens to visit the region, taking advantage of smaller crowds and lower rates in beach and resort areas. **Winter** can be quite pleasant in the Southeast, especially in the more temperate, lower coastal regions of Georgia and Florida. In the higher elevations of western North Carolina and Georgia, temperatures often drop to freezing between mid-November and mid-March, producing ideal conditions for area ski resorts. **Summer** tends to be hot and muggy, with temperatures often soaring into the 90s, especially in Florida and at the lower elevations of Alabama, Georgia, and the Carolinas. That's when flatlanders (mountain slang for nonresidents) flock to the mountains to cool off.

Festivals and Seasonal Events

Festivals are a way of life in the Southeast. Even the smallest communities have planned celebrations around offbeat and often obscure themes, such as chitterlings (pronounced chitlins), hog-calling and -hollering contests, and the woolly worm.

Winter

EARLY NOV.–LATE DEC.➢ **Salem Christmas** (☏ 910/721–7300 or 888/653–7253) is celebrated in Old Salem, the restored 18th-century village once home to the Moravians, a Protestant sect, in **Winston-Salem, North Carolina.**

LATE NOV.–DEC.➢ **Christmas at Biltmore** (☏ 800/543–2961) brings six weeks of festive decorations, musical concerts, and candlelighted tours to this **North Carolina** estate.

EARLY DEC.➢ The **Atlanta Festival of Trees** (☏ 404/264–9348) celebrates the Christmas season with a parade and exhibit of elaborately decorated trees and wreaths.

MID-JAN.➢ **Art Deco Weekend** (☏ 305/539–3000) spotlights **Miami Beach**'s historic district with a street fair, a gala, and live entertainment.

LATE JAN.–EARLY FEB.➢ For more than 15 years, the **Cloister Food and Wine Classic** (☏ 912/638–3611 or 800/732–4752) has enjoyed an international reputation for quality classes, seminars, tastings, and dinners matching food and wine. **Gasparilla Pirate Fest** (☏ 813/223–1111), in **Tampa, Florida,** celebrates Tampa's Hispanic heritage with a parade and other street festivities.

FEB.➢ **Black History Month** is observed throughout the South, with special events at many bookstores, universities, and other cultural venues, including Tuskegee University (☏ 334/727–8837), in **Tuskegee, Alabama**; Southern University (☏ 504/771–3260), in **Baton Rouge, Louisiana**; and in **Atlanta, Georgia,** at the **Martin Luther King Jr. Center for Nonviolent Social Change**(☏ 404/526–1956).

MID-FEB.➢ **Mardi Gras** in **Mobile, Alabama** (☏ 334/434–7304 or 800/252–3862), is an uproarious, pre-Lenten celebration similar to its more famous cousin in New Orleans. The **Miami Film Festival** (☏ 305/377–3456) screens 10 days of international, U.S., and local films. The **Florida Manatee Festival** (☏ 352/795–3149), in **Crystal River,** focuses on both the river and the endangered manatee.

FEB.–MAR.➢ The **Winter Equestrian Festival** (☏ 407/798–7000), at the Palm Beach Polo and Country Club in **West Palm Beach, Florida,** includes more than 1,000 horses and three grand prix equestrian events.

Spring

EARLY MAR.➢ The **Annual Sanibel Shell Fair** (☏ 813/472–2155), which runs for four days starting the first Thursday of the month, is the largest event of the year on **Sanibel Island, Florida.**

MID-MAR.➢ In **South Carolina,** the **Aiken Triple Crown** (☏ 803/641–1111), featuring Thoroughbred trials, harness races, and steeplechases, draws thousands of equestrian enthusiasts. **Macon, Georgia**'s annual **Cherry Blossom Festival** (☏ 912/751–7429) celebrates the city's more than 200,000 cherry trees with tours of classic antebellum and Victorian homes, concerts, art exhibitions and assorted special events.

MID-MAR.–EARLY MAY➢ **Springtime Tallahassee** (☏ 904/224–5012) is a major cultural, sporting, and culinary event in Florida's capital.

MAR. 17➢ The **St. Patrick's Day Celebration** in **Savannah, Georgia** (☏ 800/444–2427), is one of the country's largest honoring Ireland's patron saint.

EARLY APR.➢ The **Masters Golf Tournament** (☏ 706/721–3276), in **Augusta, Georgia,** attracts top golf pros and spectators to this tournament of tournaments. Atlanta's springtime launches with the **Atlanta Steeplechase** (☏ 404/237–7436), a benefit for the Atlanta Speech School. It's held at Kingston Downs, near **Cartersville, Georgia,** just north of Atlanta (advance tickets only).

LATE APR.–EARLY MAY➢ Florida's **Daytona Beach Music Festival** (☏ 800/881–2473), held over four consecutive weekends, includes concerts by marching, jazz, and stage bands, choirs, and orchestras.

MID-MAY–EARLY JUNE➢ **Spoleto Festival USA** (☏ 803/722–2764), a festival featuring world-renowned performers and artists, in **Charleston, South Carolina,** gets global attention.

LATE MAY➢ In **Beaufort, South Carolina,** the annual **Gullah Festival** (☎ 803/525–0628) highlights the fine arts, customs, language, and dress of Lowcountry African-Americans. Over Memorial Day weekend **Greenville, South Carolina,** celebrates **Freedom Weekend Aloft** (☎ 864/232–3700), the second-largest balloon rally in the country.

Summer

EARLY JUNE➢ The **Sun Fun Festival** (☎ 800/356–3016), in **Myrtle Beach, South Carolina,** features beauty-queen contests, sand sculpting, and other activities.

MID-JUNE➢ The **Arts Festival of Atlanta** (☎ 404/589–8777), held over nine days, is the largest arts-and-crafts festival in the Southeast.

MID-JULY➢ The **Annual Highland Games and Gathering of the Scottish Clans** (☎ 704/733–1333 or 800/468–7325), held in the high meadows of **Grandfather Mountain** in **North Carolina,** is one of the largest Scottish celebrations in the world.

MID–LATE JULY➢ The **Hemingway Days Festival** (☎ 305/294–1136) holds look-alike contests as well as first-novel and short-story competitions in **Key West, Florida.**

LATE JULY➢ The **Folkmoot USA➢ North Carolina International Folk Festival** (☎ 704/452–2997), held in **Haywood County** and surrounding areas over a two-week period, spotlights dancers and singers from around the globe.

EARLY–MID-AUG.➢ The **Georgia Mountain Fair** (☎ 706/896–4191) a mountain craft and music extravaganza, is held near **Hiawasee, Georgia.**

Autumn

MID-SEPT.➢ At **Tuscumbia, Alabama**'s Music Hall of Fame, the annual **Harvest Jam** (☎ 205/381–4417 or 800/239–2643) draws top country musicians on the second Saturday of the month.

EARLY OCT.➢ The annual **Indian Key Festival** (☎ 305/664–4815), in **Florida,** celebrates the Key's history the first weekend of the month.

MID-OCT.➢ **Alabama's National Shrimp Festival** (☎ 800/745–7263), held in **Gulf Shores,** celebrates with seafood, arts and crafts, music, sky divers, and hot-air balloons. **Big Pig Jig** (☎ 912/268–8275), in **Vienna, Georgia,** attracts more than 100 entrants to compete for championships in several barbecue categories (ribs, shoulders, whole hog), plus hollering competitions, a beauty pageant, a parade, and music.

MID-NOV.➢ The annual **Miami Book Fair International** (☎ 305/237–3258), the largest book fair in the United States, is held on the Miami-Dade Community College Wolfson Campus.

Getting Around

By Boat

Traveling by boat along the Southeast's extensive waterways and rivers is a popular (and in some cases essential) mode of transportation. The **Intracoastal Waterway,** which extends from New England around Florida to the Gulf of Mexico, is filled with north–south traffic, and many of the region's major rivers are navigable. Ferries connect major islands and the mainlands of Alabama, the Carolinas, Georgia, and Florida. For more information on waterways and ferry schedules, contact the highway departments of individual states.

By Bus

The major intercity carrier is **Greyhound Lines** (☏ 800/231–2222).

By Car

More than a dozen interstate highways, including I–10, I–16, I–20, I–26, I–40, I–59, I–65, I–75, I–77, I–85, and I–95, crisscross the Southeast, linking major cities and providing easy access to other parts of the country. In some cases interstates and federal highways, such as U.S. 1 along the Florida Keys, link the region's many islands to the mainland. In other cases ferries(☞ By Boat, *above*) are the only means of transport. Scenic highways include South Carolina's Foothills Parkway and the Blue Ridge Parkway, the latter traversing the Virginia and North Carolina mountains. Interstate and federal highways are usually well maintained; some secondary roads are narrow, a few unpaved, and in mountain sections roads are often very curvy. Scenic routes connect small towns and offer a glimpse of the region's soul; one such road is U.S. 441, which runs north–south from near Knoxville, Tennessee, through middle Georgia, to central Florida, where it merges with U.S. 27 and continues on to Miami.

By Plane

The region is served by most major domestic airlines, including American, Continental, Delta, Northwest, Southwest, TWA, United, US Airways, and several foreign carriers. Some of the busiest airports in the nation and the world are in the Southeast, including Atlanta's **Hartsfield International Airport** (☏ 404/530–6600), **Miami International Airport** (☏ 305/876–7000), and **Orlando International Airport** (☏ 407/825–2352). Other major airports in the region are **Birmingham International Airport** (☏ 205/595–0533), in Alabama; **Charleston International Airport** (☏ 803/767–1100), in South Carolina; and **Charlotte–Douglas International Airport** (☏ 704/359–4000), in North Carolina.

By Train

Amtrak (☏ 800/872–7245) provides service to major southern cities including Charlotte, North Carolina; Charleston and Columbia, South Carolina; Atlanta and Savannah, Georgia; Miami and Orlando, Florida; and Birmingham and Mobile, Alabama.

ALABAMA

Updated by Lynn Grisard Fullman

Capital	Montgomery
Population	4,319,000
Motto	We Dare Defend Our Rights
State Bird	Yellowhammer
State Flower	Camellia
Postal Abbreviation	AL

State Visitor Information

Alabama Bureau of Tourism and Travel (✉ 401 Adams Ave., Box 4927, Montgomery 36103, ☎ 334/242–4169 or 800/252–2262). **Welcome centers:** I–59 near Valley Head, I–59 at Cuba, I–65 at Elkmont, I–10 north of Seminole, I–10 at Grand Bay, I–20 east of Heflin, I–85 at Lanett, U.S. 231 south of Dothan.

Scenic Drives

Lookout Mountain Parkway is a 100-mi scenic stretch in northeastern Alabama encompassing Routes 117, 89, and 176; markers indicate routes for side trips to Little River Canyon, DeSoto Falls, and Yellow Creek Falls. Maps are available at the welcome center off I–59 near the Georgia state line (☎ 205/635–6522). In and around Mobile, the **Azalea Trail** twines for 27 mi; flowering time is March and April.

State Parks

Alabama's 24 state parks include a wide variety of recreational activities and lodging accommodations. Visitors have the choice of resort lodges, hotels, campgrounds, chalets, and cabins, both modern and rustic. Several parks have marinas, golf courses, and tennis facilities. **DeSoto State Park,** in northern Alabama, has the spectacular Little River Canyon and falls. **Lake Guntersville State Park,** also in the northern part of the state, is home of the annual Eagle Awareness programs. **Gulf State Park,** near Gulf Shores, has one of the most popular beach areas along the Alabama coast. Contact **Alabama State Parks** (✉ 64 N. Union St., Folsom Administrative Bldg., Suite 547, Montgomery 36130, ☎ 800/252–7275) for reservations or information on state parks.

CENTRAL ALABAMA

This region encompasses the hilly Highlands around Birmingham, the state's largest city, and the state capital, Montgomery, with its antebellum history, 90 mi south of Birmingham.

Visitor Information

Birmingham: Convention and Visitors Bureau (✉ 2200 9th Ave. N, 35203-1100, ☎ 205/458–8000 or 800/458–8085). **Montgomery:** Area Chamber of Commerce and Visitor Center (✉ 401 Madison Ave., 36104, ☎ 334/240–9455 or 800/240–9452).

Arriving and Departing

By Bus

Greyhound Lines (✉ 618 N. 19th St., Birmingham; ✉ 950 W. South Blvd., Montgomery; ☎ 800/231–2222) serves major towns.

By Car

I–59 runs northeast from Birmingham into Georgia and Tennessee and southwest into Mississippi. I–20 runs east–west through Birmingham. I–65 is the north–south route connecting Birmingham with Montgomery. I–85 leads southwest from Atlanta to Montgomery.

By Plane

Major airlines serve **Birmingham International Airport** (☎ 205/599–0500). Montgomery's **Dannelly Field** (☎ 334/281–5040) is served by many carriers.

By Train

Amtrak (☎ 800/872–7245) serves Birmingham and Mobile.

Exploring Central Alabama

Birmingham blossomed with the development of coal mines and the iron industry in the 19th century. Today its largest employer is the University of Alabama at Birmingham, home to one of the country's largest medical centers. The city has restored many of its 19th-century buildings and is a hospitable, attractive metropolis.

The **Birmingham Museum of Art,** the Southeast's largest municipal museum, has some 18,000 works, from Italian Early Renaissance to contemporary American. With a multilevel sculpture garden, the museum houses the Southeast's largest collection of Asian art and has the finest collection of Wedgwood outside England. ✉ *8th Ave. and 21st St. N,* ☎ *205/254–2565.* 🎟 *Free. Closed Mon.*

The **Alabama Sports Hall of Fame Museum** (✉ Corner of 22nd St. N and Civic Center Blvd., ☎ 205/323–6665; 🎟 $5), adjacent to the Civic Center, displays memorabilia of such Alabama athletic heroes as coach Bear Bryant, Jesse Owens, Willie Mays, and Hank Aaron.

The Kelly Ingram Park area, southwest of the Civic Center, contains the **16th Street Baptist Church,** a civil rights landmark. Here numerous protests were staged during the 1960s and four black children lost their lives when a bomb planted by white supremacists exploded in 1963; there is a plaque in their memory. ✉ *16th St. and 6th Ave. N,* ☎ *205/251–9402.* 🎟 *Free. No tours Sat.–Mon.*

★ The **Birmingham Civil Rights Institute** uses exhibits, multimedia presentations, music, and oral histories to document the civil rights movement from the 1920s to the present. ✉ *6th Ave. and 16th St. N,* ☎ *205/328–9696;* 🎟 *$3. Closed Mon.*

The **Alabama Jazz Hall of Fame,** two blocks from the Civil Rights Institute, has photos and memorabilia of the state's jazz greats, including Erskine Hawkins, Cleveland Eaton, and Frank Adams. ✉ *4th Ave. and 17th St. N,* ☎ *205/254–2720.* 🎟 *Free. Closed Mon.*

The **Sloss Furnaces,** a massive ironworks, used ore dug from the hills around Birmingham when it was in operation between 1882 and 1971. Guided tours of this National Historic Landmark are given weekends. ✉ *1st Ave. N and 32nd St.,* ☎ *205/324–1911.* 🎟 *Free. Closed Mon.*

The **Red Mountain Museum** (✉ 2230 22nd St. S, ☎ 205/933–4153; 🎟 free), south on U.S. 31, displays samples of rocks, fossils, and minerals found in the area. Sitting atop Red Mountain is ***Vulcan*** (✉ Valley Ave., at U.S. 31S, ☎ 205/328–6198; 🎟 $1), the world's tallest cast-iron statue. The enclosed observation deck has wonderful views of Birmingham.

The **Birmingham Zoo** (✉ 2630 Cahaba Rd., ☎ 205/879–0408; 🎫 $5) is one of the Southeast's largest zoos, with 800 animals. Birmingham's **McWane Center** (✉ 200 19th St. N, ☎ 205/558–2000; 🎫 $6.50 museum, $6.50 IMAX, $9.50 for both) is a hands-on science museum with an IMAX theater.

★ **DeSoto Caverns,** 40 mi from Birmingham (head southeast on U.S. 280 to Childersburg, then east on Route 76), is a network of onyx caves used as a Native American burial ground 2,000 years ago. Rediscovered by Spanish explorer Hernando de Soto in 1540, the caverns later served as a Confederate gunpowder mining center and a Prohibition speakeasy. Tours begin with a sound, water, and laser-light show in the 12-story Great Onyx Cathedral. This is one *big* cave. ☎ *205/378–7252 or 800/933–2283.* 🎫 *$10.95.*

More than 300 Confederate veterans and their wives are buried in **Confederate Memorial Park,** southwest of Childersburg, off U.S. 31 near Mountain Creek. ✉ *437 County Rd. 63, Marbury,* ☎ *205/755–1990.* 🎫 *Free.*

Montgomery, 90 mi south of Birmingham via I–65, is a city steeped in antebellum history. Today many of its old houses have been restored, and the city has become known as a cultural capital of the South. The **visitor center**(☞ Visitor Information, *above*) presents a brief video. You can park your car at the center and see many attractions on foot.

The handsome **state capitol** (✉ Bainbridge St. at Dexter Ave., ☎ 334/242–3184), built in 1851, served as the first capitol for the Confederate States of America. The **Dexter Avenue King Memorial Baptist Church** (✉ 454 Dexter Ave., ☎ 334/263–3970) is where Dr. Martin Luther King, Jr., began his career as a minister in 1954; a basement mural depicts people and events associated with the civil rights movement. The first **White House of the Confederacy** (☎ 334/242–1861; 🎫 free) stands at the corner of Washington Avenue and Union Street. Built in 1835, it contains many items that belonged to Jefferson Davis, the Confederate president, as well as Civil War artifacts.

★ The **Civil Rights Memorial** (✉ 400 Washington Ave., ☎ 334/264–0286)—created by Maya Lin, designer of the Vietnam Veterans' Memorial, in Washington, D.C.—has a plaza and a pool from which water flows over a 40-ft black-granite wall. Inscribed on the wall are excerpts from Martin Luther King, Jr.'s, "I have a dream . . ." speech. Adjacent are the names of many who gave their lives to the civil rights movement.

Dining and Lodging

Throughout Alabama, Old South dishes—fried chicken, barbecue, roast beef, country-fried steak—prevail, though in recent years a number of upscale restaurants with more varied fare have opened in Birmingham and Montgomery. In Birmingham, hotels and motels offer weekend specials but are often crowded during football season; the same holds true in Montgomery, which can be busy when the state legislature is in session. For price ranges *see* Charts 1 (B) and 2 (B) *in* On the Road with Fodor's.

Birmingham

$$–$$$$ ★ ✕ **Highlands Bar and Grill.** Grand gourmet feasts prepared by owner-chef Frank Stitt are served in a sophisticated setting accented with vintage French posters. Delicacies include hickory-grilled Destin grouper with white beans and wild mushrooms or roasted lamb loin with gar-

lic-bread pudding and parsnips. ✉ *2011 11th Ave. S,* ☎ *205/939–1400. Reservations essential. AE, MC, V. Closed Sun.–Mon.*

$–$$ ✕ **Nabeel's Cafe.** Greek-born John Krontiras, his Italian-born wife, Ottavia, and their son, Anthony, serve food prepared with artistry, whether it's an eggplant casserole, spinach-and-feta croissant, or spinach pie. The adjacent gourmet market has most everything you can find in the Mediterranean, and at modest prices. ✉ *1706 Oxmoor Rd., Homewood,* ☎ *205/879–9292. AE, MC, V. Closed Sun.*

$–$$ ✕ **Silvertron Cafe.** Since 1986 owner Alan Potts has been creating great dishes with chicken, Black Angus beef, orange roughy, and pasta; his fresh sauces are notable. Tin ceilings, fresh flowers, and framed photos of early Birmingham set the mood. Save room for a Bailey's Brownie. ✉ *3813 Clairmont Ave.,* ☎ *205/591–3707. AE, MC, V.*

$$$$ ★ 🏨 **Tutwiler.** This National Historic Landmark, with a European ambience, was built in 1913 as a luxury apartment building and was converted in 1986 into a hotel. The elegant lobby has marble floors, chandeliers, antiques, and lots of flowers; guest rooms are furnished with reproductions of antiques. ✉ *Park Pl. at 21st St. N, 35203,* ☎ *205/322–2100 or 800/845–1787,* FAX *205/325–1183. 148 rooms. Restaurant. AE, D, DC, MC, V.*

$$$–$$$$ 🏨 **Wynfrey Hotel.** Rising 15 stories above the Riverchase Galleria mall, this deluxe hotel has an elegant lobby with an Italian marble floor, Chippendale-style furniture, an Oriental rug, an enormous floral arrangement, and a brass escalator. Rooms are done in English and French traditional styles. ✉ *1000 Riverchase Galleria (U.S. 31S), 35244,* ☎ *205/987–1600 or 800/996–3739,* FAX *205/987–9552. 329 rooms. Restaurant, pool, health club. AE, D, DC, MC, V.*

$$–$$$ 🏨 **Mountain Brook Inn.** This eight-story glass-exterior hotel at the foot of Red Mountain has a marble-floor lobby and bi-level suites with spiral staircases. ✉ *2800 U.S. 280, 35223,* ☎ *205/870–3100 or 800/523–7771,* FAX *205/414–2128. 170 rooms. Restaurant, pool. AE, D, DC, MC, V.*

Montgomery

$$–$$$ ✕ **Jubilee Seafood Company.** In this small café setting you'll find some of the finest and freshest seafood in town. ✉ *1057 Woodley Rd., Cloverdale Plaza,* ☎ *334/262–6224. Reservations not accepted. AE, DC, MC, V. Closed Sun.–Mon.*

$$–$$$ ★ ✕ **Sahara Restaurant.** At one of the city's finest restaurants, proprietors Joe and Mike Deep carry on a family tradition of friendly service. Broiled snapper, scampi, and charbroiled steaks are prepared to perfection. ✉ *511 E. Edgemont Ave.,* ☎ *334/262–1215. AE, D, DC, MC, V. Closed Sun.*

$ ✕ **Chris' Hot Dog Stand.** A Montgomery tradition for more than 80 years, this small eatery is always busy at lunchtime. Chris's famous sauce contains chili peppers, onions, and a variety of herbs that give his hot dogs a one-of-a-kind flavor. ✉ *138 Dexter Ave.,* ☎ *334/265–6850. Reservations not accepted. No credit cards. Closed Sun.*

$$ 🏨 **Red Bluff Cottage.** In this delightful cottage in the heart of downtown, guests can eat breakfast in the dining room or on a veranda overlooking the Alabama River plain. Rooms have ceiling fans and are furnished with antiques. A sitting room with fireplace and a music room–library are good places to relax. ✉ *551 Clay St., 36104,* ☎ *334/264–0056. 4 rooms. Full breakfast. AE, D, MC, V.*

Motels

🏨 **Hampton Inn** (✉ 1401 East Blvd., Montgomery 36117, ☎ 334/277–2400), 106 rooms, pool; *$.* 🏨 **Motel Birmingham** (✉ 7905 Crestwood Blvd., Birmingham 35210, ☎ 205/956–4440 or 800/338–9275, FAX 205/956–3011), 242 rooms, pool; *$.*

The Arts

In Montgomery at the world-class **Alabama Shakespeare Festival** (⊠ Eastern Bypass Exit off I–85, ☏ 334/271–5353 or 800/841–4273), Shakespearean plays, contemporary dramas and comedies, and musicals are performed on two stages.

Shopping

Birmingham's **Riverchase Galleria** (☏ 205/985–3039), at the intersection of I–459 and U.S. 31S, is one of the Southeast's largest malls, with more than 200 stores. **Boaz,** about 60 mi north of Birmingham, has more than 200 outlet and specialty stores (☏ 800/746–7262).

MOBILE AND THE GULF COAST

In Mobile, a busy port and one of the oldest cities in Alabama, antebellum buildings survive as a bridge to the past, and azaleas bloom in profusion each spring. The country's first Mardi Gras was held here, and today the city still glories in its pre-Lenten parades and merrymaking. South of Mobile, across the bay, the area around Gulf Shores has 32 mi of white-sand beaches, including those on Pleasure and Dauphin islands. On the atmospheric eastern shore of Mobile Bay, live oaks are laced with Spanish moss, and sprawling clapboard houses with wide porches overlook the bay.

Visitor Information

Alabama Gulf Coast area–Gulf Shores/Orange Beach: Convention and Visitors Bureau (⊠ Drawer 457, Gulf Shores 36542; ⊠ 3150 Gulf Shores Pkwy., Gulf Shores 36547; ⊠ 23685 Perdido Beach Blvd., Orange Beach 36561; ☏ 800/745–7263). **Eastern Shore:** Eastern Shore Chamber of Commerce (⊠ 327 Fairhope Ave., Fairhope 36532, ☏ 334/928–6387). **Mobile:** Department of Tourism (⊠ 150 S. Royal St., 36602, ☏ 800/252–3862).

Arriving and Departing

By Bus

Greyhound Lines (☏ 800/231–2222) has stations in Mobile (⊠ 2545 Government Blvd.) and Pensacola, Florida (⊠ 505 W. Burgess Rd.).

By Car

I–10 leads west from Florida to Mobile and continues into Mississippi. I–65 leads south from Birmingham and Montgomery and ends at Mobile. Twenty miles east of Mobile, along Baldwin County's eastern shore of Mobile Bay, the communities of Fairhope and Point Clear are accessible via U.S. 98 and Alternate U.S. 98A. Gulf Shores is connected with Mobile via I–10 and Route 59; Routes 180 and 182 are the main beach routes.

By Plane

Mobile Regional Airport (☏ 334/633–0313) is served by a number of major domestic carriers. Florida's **Pensacola Regional Airport** (☏ 904/435–1746), about 40 mi east of Gulf Shores/Orange Beach, has service from many carriers.

By Train

Amtrak (☏ 800/872–7245) connects Mobile with the east and west coasts.

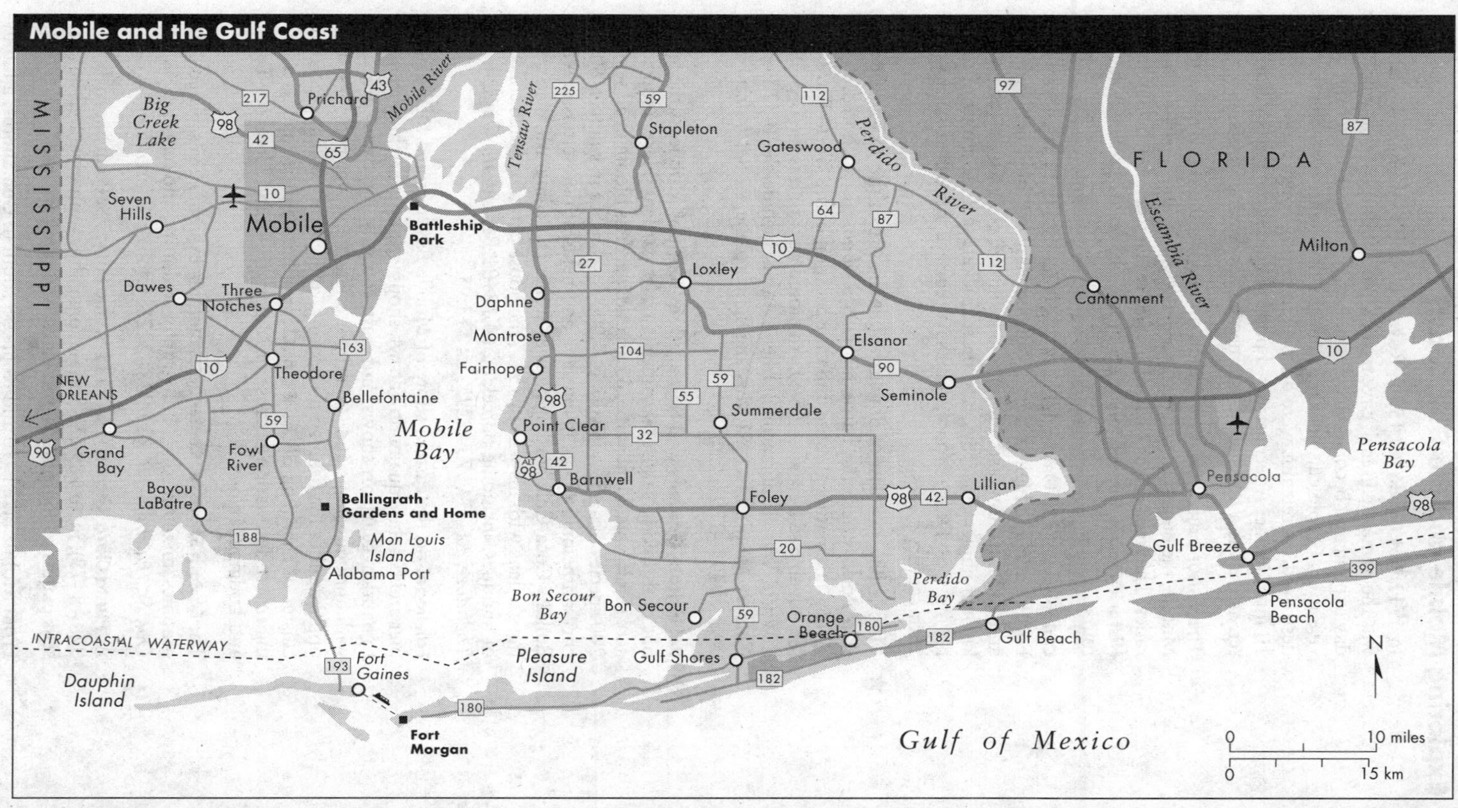

Mobile and the Gulf Coast
MISSISSIPPI
FLORIDA
Big Creek Lake
Prichard
Mobile River
Tensaw River
Stapleton
Gateswood
Perdido River
Escambia River
Milton
Seven Hills
Mobile
Battleship Park
Loxley
Cantonment
Dawes
Three Notches
Daphne
Montrose
Fairhope
Elsanor
Seminole
Theodore
Bellefontaine
NEW ORLEANS
Summerdale
Mobile Bay
Point Clear
Grand Bay
Fowl River
Barnwell
Foley
Lillian
Pensacola
Pensacola Bay
Bayou LaBatre
Bellingrath Gardens and Home
Mon Louis Island
Alabama Port
Gulf Breeze
Perdido Bay
Pensacola Beach
Bon Secour Bay
Bon Secour
Orange Beach
Gulf Beach
INTRACOASTAL WATERWAY
Fort Gaines
Pleasure Island
Gulf Shores
Dauphin Island
Fort Morgan
Gulf of Mexico
N
0 10 miles
0 15 km
217
43
225
59
112
97
87
98
42
65
10
64
87
27
112
163
104
90
59
55
32
42
90
59
98
188
20
180
399
182
193
180

Exploring Mobile and the Gulf Coast

In 1711 **Fort Condé** (✉ 150 S. Royal St., ☎ 334/434–7304; 🎫 free) was the name the French gave to the Colonial outpost that would one day expand and become Mobile. Indeed, the city's French origins survive in its Creole cuisine. One hundred fifty years after the fort was destroyed, its remains were discovered during construction of the I–10 interchange. A reconstructed portion houses the city's **visitor center,** as well as a museum. Costumed guides conduct tours.

The visitor center has information on major annual events hosted by Mobile, the biggest of which is **Mardi Gras,** with balls, parties, and parades. The **Azalea Trail Festival** is held the last weekend of March. The **Historic Mobile Homes Tour,** also in March, opens private homes for tours.

Oakleigh (✉ 350 Oakleigh Pl., ☎ 334/432–1281; 🎫 $5), 1½ mi from Fort Condé, is a high-ceiling, columned mansion, built between 1833 and 1838. It showcases fine period furniture, portraits, silver, jewelry, kitchen implements, toys, and more. Tickets include a tour of neighboring **Cox-Deasy House,** an 1850s cottage furnished with simple 19th-century pieces.

★ Mobile Bay, just east of downtown, is the site of the 155-acre **Battleship Park,** where the battleship USS *Alabama* is anchored. A tour gives a fascinating glimpse into the operation of the World War II vessel, which had a crew of 2,500. Anchored next to it is the USS *Drum,* a World War II submarine. Other exhibits include the B-52 bomber *Calamity Jane* and a P-51 Mustang fighter plane. ✉ *Battleship Pkwy.,* ☎ *334/433–2703;* 🎫 *$8.*

★ **Bellingrath Gardens and Home,** 20 mi south of Mobile, is the site of one of the world's most magnificent azalea gardens. Here, amid a 905-acre semitropical landscape, 65 acres of gardens bloom in all seasons: 200 species of azaleas in spring, 3,000 rosebushes in summer, 60,000 chrysanthemum plants in autumn, and fields of poinsettias in winter. Built by Coca-Cola bottling pioneer Walter D. Bellingrath, who started the gardens with his wife in 1917, the house contains a fine collection of antiques, including porcelain. ✉ *12401 Bellingrath Gardens Rd., Theodore,* ☎ *334/973–2217.* 🎫 *$13.95.*

Fairhope, on the eastern shore of Mobile Bay, is noted for its public pier and beaches, quaint downtown shops (selling everything from toys to nautical gear), art shows, and crafts festivals. A growing art colony with antiques shops and several potteries, the village provides ample opportunities for fishing and boating, and visitors will appreciate its cluster of charming B&Bs. **Point Clear,** a bend in the road, is a leading resort destination because of Marriott's Grand Hotel (☞ Dining and Lodging, *below*).

The **Eastern Shore Art Center** hosts monthly exhibits of oils, watercolors, graphics, mixed-media, photography, sculpture, and ceramics. ✉ *401 Oak St., Fairhope,* ☎ *334/928–2228.* 🎫 *Free. Closed Sun.*

At **Punta Clara Kitchen** (✉ 17111 Scenic Hwy. 98, Point Clear, ☎ 334/928–8477), in an 1897 Victorian home, the family-operated business sells exquisite confections, preserves, and other treats.

From Mobile take I–10 and Route 59 south to **Gulf Shores,** a family-oriented beach area with hotels, restaurants, and attractions. There's ample free parking along the white-as-snow beach, though the traffic is bumper to bumper at peak times. Star-shaped **Fort Morgan** (✉ Mobile Point, ☎ 334/540–7125) sits at the western tip of Pleasure Island,

20 mi west of Gulf Shores at the end of Route 180. The fort was built in the early 1800s to guard the entrance to Mobile Bay. In 1864 after Confederate torpedoes sank the ironclad *Tecumseh,* Union admiral David Farragut shouted, "Damn the torpedoes! Full speed ahead!" The rest of Farragut's fleet forced its way to the bay, and after the Civil War the fort's defenses were improved. The museum at the site tells the story.

Dining and Lodging

In Mobile and throughout the Gulf area, the specialty is fresh seafood, often prepared Creole-style, with peppery spices, crabmeat dressing, and sometimes a tomato-based sauce. The area's hotels and motels are comfortable and varied, offering the particular hospitality of the region alongside the amenities of nationwide chain hotels. For price ranges *see* Charts 1 (B) and 2 (B) *in* On the Road with Fodor's.

Gulf Shores

$$–$$$ ★ ✕ **Original Oyster House.** Dining at this plant-filled restaurant overlooking the bayou has become a local tradition. Oysters, plucked fresh from nearby Perdido Bay, are the specialty of the house. The Cajun-style gumbo—with crab claws, shrimp, amberjack, grouper, redfish, okra and other vegetables, and Cajun spices—has won 20 culinary awards. ✉ *Bayou Village Shopping Center, Rte. 59 ,* ☎ *334/948–2445. Reservations not accepted. AE, D, DC, MC, V.*

$$–$$$$ 🏨 **Gulf Shores Plantation.** This 320-acre family resort, 8 mi east of Fort Morgan on the Gulf, offers condominiums with fully equipped kitchens in high-rises overlooking the beach. Abundant recreational activities are available. ✉ *Rte. 180W (Box 1299), 36547,* ☎ *334/540–5000 or 800/554–0344,* FAX *334/540–6055. 524 units. Indoor and outdoor pools, 8 tennis courts. AE, MC, V.*

Mobile

$–$$$$ ✕ **Roussos.** Just across the street from Fort Condé, this is one of the most popular seafood restaurants in the Mobile area. The outstanding service, family-friendly atmosphere, and excellent seafood—fried, broiled, or Greek style—make Roussos a fun place. ✉ *166 S. Royal St.,* ☎ *334/433–3322. AE, D, DC, MC, V. Closed Sun.*

$$ ★ ✕ **La Louisiana.**Fresh seafood is prepared masterfully at this family-owned Creole-style restaurant in an old, antiques-filled house. The seafood gumbo is a specialty. ✉ *2400 Airport Blvd.,* ☎ *334/476–8130. AE, D, DC, MC, V. Closed Sun. No lunch.*

$$$–$$$$ 🏨 **Radisson Admiral Semmes Hotel.** This hotel is popular with local politicians. Merrymakers appreciate its excellent location on the Mardi Gras parade route. Rooms are furnished in Queen Anne and Chippendale styles. ✉ *251 Government St., 36602,* ☎ *334/432–8000,* FAX *334/405–5942. 170 rooms. Restaurant, pool. AE, D, DC, MC, V.*

$$ 🏨 **Malaga Inn.** A delightful, romantic getaway, the Malaga has a lobby furnished with 19th-century antiques, which opens onto a tropically landscaped central courtyard with a fountain. The large, airy rooms have massive antiques. ✉ *359 Church St., 36602,* ☎ *334/438–4701 or 800/235–1586,* FAX *334/438–4701. 39 rooms. Restaurant, pool. AE, D, MC, V.*

Orange Beach

$$–$$$ ✕ **Bayside Grill.** The nautical decor here blends smartly with the marina view. Fresh seafood is the speciality, along with pastas, steaks, salads, and chicken. A New Orleans–born chef creates such down-home fare as coconut shrimp, black bean soup, Cajun-style gumbo, and bananas Foster strudel. Sunday brunch is bountiful. ✉ *27842 Canal Rd.,* ☎ *334/981–4899. AE, D, DC, MC, V.*

$$–$$$ ✕ **Franco's.** If you're homesick for Italian fare, try this popular restaurant whose specialties include stuffed mushrooms, veal and steak, and seafood fettuccine—all prepared with the freshest ingredients. ✉ *26651 Perdido Beach Blvd.,* ☎ *334/981–9800. Reservations not accepted. AE, D, DC, MC, V.*

$$–$$$ ★ ✕ **Hazel's Family Restaurant.** This plain family-style restaurant with a full menu serves a hearty breakfast (with great biscuits and a popular omelet bar), soup-and-salad lunches, and buffet dinners with such seafood dishes as flounder Florentine. A self-service bar has soft ice cream. ✉ *Gulf View Square Shopping Center, Rte. 182 ,* ☎ *334/981–4628. Reservations not accepted. AE, D, DC, MC, V.*

$$–$$$ ✕ **The Outrigger.** Perched at the tip of Alabama Point on Perdido Pass, this clean, contemporary restaurant has panoramic views of the water. The fried seafood (served with hush puppies) is hard to pass up, but fish also comes broiled or blackened. Hickory-smoked barbecued ribs and other meats are the specialty. ✉ *27500 Perdido Beach Blvd.,* ☎ *334/981–6700. Reservations not accepted. AE, D, DC, MC, V.*

$$$–$$$$ ★ **Original Romar House.** This unassuming beach cottage is full of surprises—from the Caribbean-style upstairs sitting area to the Purple Parrot Bar to the luxurious art deco–style guest rooms. In the evening wine and cheese are served. A guest cottage also is available. ✉ *23500 Perdido Beach Blvd., 36561,* ☎ *334/981–6156 or 800/487–6627,* FAX *334/974–1163. 6 rooms. Full breakfast. AE, MC, V.*

$$$–$$$$ **Perdido Beach Resort.** The exteriors of these Mediterranean-style eight- and nine-story hotel towers are stucco and red tile; the lobby is tiled in terra-cotta and has mosaics by Venetian artists. Luxurious rooms have beach views and balconies. ✉ *27200 Perdido Beach Blvd. (Box 400), 36561,* ☎ *334/981–9811 or 800/634–8001,* FAX *334/981–5670. 345 rooms. Restaurant, indoor-outdoor pool, 4 tennis courts, exercise room. AE, D, DC, MC, V.*

Point Clear

$$$–$$$$ ★ ✕ **Marriott's Grand Hotel.** Set within 550 acres of beautifully landscaped grounds on Mobile Bay, the Grand has been cherished since 1847. Extensively refurbished by Marriott, it has spacious rooms and cottages that are traditionally furnished. The food here is prepared and served elegantly; especially fine is the seafood in the Bay View Restaurant. ✉ *1 Grand Blvd., Box 639, Point Clear 36564,* ☎ *334/928–9201 or 800/544–9933,* FAX *334/928–1149. 306 rooms. 3 restaurants, pool, 8 tennis courts. AE, D, DC, MC, V.*

Outdoor Activities and Sports

Biking

Gulf State Park Resort (☎ 334/948–7275 or 800/252–7275), in Gulf Shores, rents bikes, but you must use them on site.

Canoeing

Sunshine Canoe Rentals (☎ 334/344–8664) runs canoe trips at Escatawpa River, 15 mi west of Mobile. The river has no rapids, so you travel at a leisurely pace past lots of white sandbars.

Fishing

Fishing here is excellent. You can obtain a fishing license from most bait shops. For information contact the **Department of Conservation and Natural Resources** (☎ 334/242–3829). In Gulf Shores, **Gulf State Park** (☞ State Parks, *above*) has fishing from an 825-ft pier; you can also rent flat-bottom boats for lake fishing. Deep-sea fishing from charter boats is very popular; Orange Beach has the ***Moreno Queen*** (☎ 334/981–8499), which offers four- and six-hour fishing trips. Orange Beach has more than 100 charter boats from which to choose.

Golf

In recent years, coastal Alabama has developed into one of the nicest golfing destinations in the Southeast. With winter temperatures averaging in the 60°F range and pleasant breezes, the area has become a true year-round spot. Prices range from about $32 to $70 for greens fees and cart rental. The **Robert Trent Jones Golf Trail** (☎ 800/949–4444 for reservations and information) includes 18 challenging, scenic courses in seven locations around the state, including Mobile.

The spectacular **Kiva Dunes** course, adjacent to Gulf Shores Plantation Resort (✉ 12 mi west of Gulf Shores on Rte. 180, ☎ 334/540–7000), designed by Jerry Pate, combines oceanfront dunes golf with Scottish-style links golf. The **Craft Farms** complex (✉ Rte. 59 just north of Gulf Shores, ☎ 334/968–7500) has 36 holes on two Arnold Palmer–designed courses at **Cotton Creek** and another 18 on the **Woodlands course** designed by Larry Nelson. About 12 mi north of Gulf Shores in Foley, the **Dunes at Glenlakes** (✉ 9530 Clubhouse Dr., ☎ 334/943–8000), a course designed by Bruce Devlin, has 18 challenging holes that play over 7,000 yards and another nine holes stretching 3,100 yards. The course at **Gulf State Park** (✉ 20115 Rte. 135, ☎ 334/948–7275) in Gulf Shores isn't quite as new and challenging as others in the area, but it is one of the most scenic along the coast.

Water Sports

In Orange Beach **Fun Marina** (☎ 334/980–5122) rents Jet Skis, pontoon boats, and 16-ft bay-fishing boats. In Gulf Shores **Island Recreation Services** (☎ 334/948–7334) rents Jet Skis, bikes, body boards, surfboards, and sailboats.

ELSEWHERE IN ALABAMA

Huntsville

Arriving and Departing

Huntsville is 100 mi north of Birmingham via I–65 and U.S. 72E.

Visitor Information

Huntsville/Madison County Convention and Visitors Bureau (✉ 700 Monroe St., Huntsville 35801, ☎ 256/533–5723 or 800/722–2348).

What to See and Do

Huntsville has a clutch of attractions that include golf courses as well as historic homes and a variety of museums. The **U.S. Space and Rocket Center** (✉ 1 Tranquility Base, ☎ 205/837–3400 or 800/637–7223; 🎫 $14) is home to the **U.S. Space Camp and Space Academy.** The center offers a bus tour of the NASA labs and shuttle test sites, hands-on exhibits in the museum, and an outdoor park filled with spacecraft.

Alabama Constitution Village is the site of Alabama's Constitutional Convention of 1819. Demonstrations of such skills as woodworking, printing, cooking, and weaving are performed by craftspeople in period dress. Opening in late 1998, the **Center for Early Southern Life** provides a hands-on history experience in the EarlyWorks Galleries. The **Historic Huntsville Depot** offers a glimpse of railroad life in the early 19th century; it's a few blocks from the village. ✉ *109 Gates Ave.,* ☎ *205/535–6565 or 800/678–1819.* 🎫 *$6. Closed Jan.–Feb.*

Dining and Lodging

$$–$$$ ✕ **Cafe Berlin.** Paintings and photographs of European café scenes adorn the walls, and taped music ensures that the German theme is not forgotten. Schnitzel and wurst are prepared a number of ways; other choices

are fish, chicken, and steak dishes, and enormous salads. ✉ *505 Airport Rd.,* ☎ *205/880–9920. AE, D, MC, V.*

$$–$$$$ **Huntsville Hilton.** Claiming the prize location in town, the Hilton is within walking distance of the historic district and museums, and many rooms overlook either Big Spring Park and Lake or the Von Braun Civic Center. The spacious rooms have irons, hair dryers, and coffeemakers. ✉ *401 Williams Ave., 35801,* ☎ *205/533–1400,* FAX *205/534–7787. 268 rooms, 9 suites. Restaurant, pool, exercise room. AE, D, DC, MC, V.*

Tuscumbia

Arriving and Departing

Tuscumbia is 120 mi northwest of Birmingham via I–65 and U.S. Alternate 72. Take Exit 310 off I–65 at Cullman.

Visitor Information

Colbert County Tourism and Convention Bureau (✉ U.S. 72, Tuscumbia 35674, ☎ 256/383–0783 or 800/344–0783).

What to See and Do

Tuscumbia and the adjoining towns of Florence, Sheffield, and Muscle Shoals form a quad-city area known throughout Alabama simply as the Shoals. Spreading out on both sides of the Tennessee River basin, this is an area rich in culture and history.

Ivy Green is the birthplace of author and lecturer Helen Keller, who was left unable to hear or see at the age of 19 months. With the help of her teacher, Annie Sullivan, she graduated from Radcliffe with honors in 1904 and became a champion for all those with similar disabilities. Tours are year-round. *The Miracle Worker,* the play about Keller's childhood, is performed outdoors from late June through late July. ✉ *300 W. North Commons,* ☎ *205/383–4066.* *$3*

The **Alabama Music Hall of Fame and Museum,** celebrates the history of Alabama's musical heritage and holds the original contracts of Elvis Presley's deal with Sun Records, the actual touring bus of the band Alabama, and exhibits on the likes of Hank Williams, Lionel Richie, and Nat "King" Cole. September's annual **Harvest Jam** draws performers and fans from across the country. ✉ *U.S. 72,* ☎ *205/381–4417 or 800/239–2643.* *$6.*

Lodging

$$ **Key West Inn.** This is a clean, comfortable, and affordable motel; rooms have microwaves and small refrigerators. ✉ *1800 U.S. 72, Tuscumbia 35674,* ☎ *205/383–0700. 41 rooms. AE, D, DC, MC, V.*

FLORIDA

Updated by Pam Acheson, Alan Macher, Gary McKechnie, Diane Marshall, Val Meyer, Nancy Orr, and Rowland Stitler

Capital	Tallahassee
Population	14,654,000
Motto	In God We Trust
State Bird	Mockingbird
State Flower	Orange blossom
Postal Abbreviation	FL

Statewide Visitor Information

Florida Division of Tourism (✉ 126 Van Buren St., Tallahassee 32301, ☎ 904/487–1462). **Information centers:** on U.S. 301 at Hilliard, U.S. 231 near Graceville, I–75 near Jennings, I–10 at Pensacola, I–95 near Yulee, and in the lobby of the capitol in Tallahassee.

Scenic Drives

In **Everglades National Park** the 38-mi drive from the Main Visitor Center to Flamingo reveals a patchwork of ecosystems, including mangrove and cypress forests and saw-grass marshes. Although traffic jams abound during the winter tourist season, the **Overseas Highway** (U.S. 1) from Key Largo to Key West affords spectacular vistas of the Atlantic, Florida Bay, the Gulf of Mexico, and the myriad islands of the Keys. **Route 789,** along the Gulf Coast south from Holmes Beach in Bradenton to Lido Beach in Sarasota and from Casey Key south of Osprey to Nokomis Beach, passes over several picturesque barrier islands. Along the Atlantic coast, north of Jacksonville, the **Buccaneer Trail** (A1A) from Mayport to the old seaport town of Fernandina Beach passes through marshlands and along pristine beaches. **U.S. 98** winds east from historic Pensacola through the lush coastal landscape of the Panhandle.

National and State Parks

National Parks

Everglades and Biscayne national parks (☞ Elsewhere in Florida, *below*) are in Homestead, just south of Miami. In southwestern Florida **Big Cypress National Preserve** (✉ 20 mi east of Ochopee on U.S. 41; HCR 61, Box 110, Ochopee 33943, ☎ 941/695–2000 or 941/262–1066), noted for the bald and dwarf cypress trees that line its marshlands, is a sanctuary for alligators, bald eagles, and the endangered Florida panther.

Florida has three national forests. The 556,500-acre **Apalachicola National Forest** (✉ Rte. 65; Edward Ball Wakulla Spring State Park, Wakulla Spring Rd., Wakulla 32305, ☎ 904/653–9419) is great for canoeing and hiking and has a recreational facility designed for people with disabilities. **Ocala National Forest** (✉ Forest Visitor Center, 10863 E. Rte. 40, Silver Springs 34488, ☎ 904/625–7470) has lakes, springs, hiking trails, campgrounds, and historic sites. **Osceola National Forest** (✉ Osceola Ranger District, Box 70, 10090 Rte. 90, Olustee 32072, ☎ 904/752–2577) is dotted with cypress swamps and offers good fishing and hunting. In addition, the state has five national monuments, two national seashores, and eight national wildlife refuges.

State Parks

The state administers hundreds of parks, nature preserves, and historic sites. Among these are **Blackwater River State Park** (✉ Rte. 1, Box 57C, Holt 32564, ☎ 850/623–2363), 40 mi northeast of Pensacola on I–10, popular with canoeists; **Delnor-Wiggins Pass State Recreation Area** (✉ 1100 Gulfshore Dr. N, Naples 33963, ☎ 941/597–6196), with miles of beaches, picnic areas, and fishing spots; **Florida Caverns State Park** (✉ 3345 Caverns Rd., Mariana 32446, ☎ 850/482–9598), two hours north of Panama City on Route 167, comprising 1,783 acres of caves and nature trails; **Ft. Clinch State Park** (☞ Elsewhere in Florida, *below*); and the **St. Andrews State Recreation Area** (✉ 4415 Thomas Dr., Panama City Beach 32408, ☎ 850/233–5140), in the Panhandle, encompassing 1,038 acres of beaches, pinewoods, and marshes for swimming, pier fishing, and dune hiking. For more information contact the **Florida Department of Natural Resources** (✉ Marjory Stoneman Douglas Bldg., MS 525, 3900 Commonwealth Blvd., Tallahassee 32399, ☎ 904/488–9872).

MIAMI

Running with the energy and passion of Rio, Monte Carlo and Hemingway's Paris, Miami is arguably the most exotic city that Americans can visit without a passport. More than half of its population is Hispanic in origin, and Miami is sometimes called the capital of Latin America. Indeed, Miami is a city of superlatives. This ever-growing metropolis has one of the busiest airports and cruise-ship ports in the world; more than 150 companies base their international operations here; four professional sports teams attract the faithful; and fashion models are photographed for a worldwide audience. Add Miami's architectural treasures, exotic foods, and outdoor recreation, and you have America's favorite sun-drenched tropical playground.

Visitor Information

Greater Miami: Convention and Visitors Bureau (✉ 701 Brickell Ave., Suite 2700, 33131, ☎ 305/539–3063 or 800/283–2707). **Miami Beach:** Chamber of Commerce (✉ 1920 Meridian Ave., 33139, ☎ 305/672–1270, FAX 305/538–4336). **South Dade County:** Visitors Information Center (✉ 160 U.S. 1, Florida City 33034, ☎ 305/245–9180 or 800/388–9669, FAX 305/247–4335).

Arriving and Departing

By Bus

Greyhound Lines (☎ 800/231–2222) stops at four terminals in Greater Miami, including a terminal at the airport.

By Car

I–95, which runs north–south along Florida's east coast, flows into the heart of Miami. From the northwest I–75 leads to the city. Route 836 (also called East–West Expressway or Dolphin Expressway), connecting the airport to downtown (toll eastbound only, 25¢), continues across I–395 and the MacArthur Causeway to lower Miami Beach and the Art Deco District. Route 112 (Airport Expressway) connects the airport with midtown (toll eastbound only, 25¢) and continues across I–195 and the Julia Tuttle Causeway to mid–Miami Beach.

By Plane

Miami International Airport (MIA; ☎ 305/876–7000), 6 mi west of downtown via Route 836, is served by most major carriers and many minor ones. Cab fare to downtown or Miami Beach's Art Deco district is approximately $22–$29 plus tip. **SuperShuttle** (☎ 305/871–2000) vans transport passengers 24 hours a day between MIA and local hotels, the Port of Miami, and even individual residences. The cost to downtown hotels runs $8–$11. **Bus service** is available from Miami-Dade County's updated **Metrobus** (☎ 305/638–6700) and still costs $1.25 (transfer 25¢; exact change required). Look for them in the lower-level lanes in the center of the airport.

By Train

Amtrak (✉ 8303 N.W. 37th Ave., ☎ 305/835–1223 or 800/872–7245).

Getting Around Miami

Greater Miami resembles Los Angeles in its urban sprawl and traffic congestion. You'll need a car to get from one area of the city to another. **Metromover** (☞ *below*), a light-rail mass-transit system, circles the heart of the city on twin elevated loops; use it to tour the downtown area. The Art Deco District in Miami Beach and the heart of Coconut Grove are best explored on foot.

By Car

Miami is laid out in quadrants: northwest, northeast, southwest, southeast. These meet at Miami Avenue, which separates east from west, and Flagler Street, which separates north from south. Avenues and courts run north–south; streets, terraces, and ways run east–west. Roads run diagonally, northwest–southeast. In Miami Beach avenues run north–south; streets, east–west. Streets in Coral Gables have names, not numbers. In other words, be prepared to ask directions early and often.

By Public Transportation

The **Metro–Dade Transit Agency** (☎ 305/638–6700) runs the Metrorail, Metromover, and Metrobus, and provides free maps, schedules, and a "First-Time Riders Kit." **Metrorail** (fare $1.25) runs from downtown Miami north to Hialeah and south along U.S. 1 to Dadeland. **Metromover** (fare 25¢), a separate system, has two loops that circle downtown Miami, linking major hotels, office buildings, and shopping areas. **Metrobus** (fare $1.25) stops are marked by blue-and-green signs with a bus logo and route information. Frequency of service varies widely.

By Taxi

Be on your guard when traveling by cab in Miami. Some drivers are rude and unhelpful and may take advantage of visitors unfamiliar with their destinations. To avoid this, connect with a consortium of drivers who have banded together to provide good service: This nameless group can be reached through its **dispatch service** (☎ 305/888–4444). If you have to use another company, try to be familiar with your route and destination. Major cab companies include **Diamond Cab Company** and **Yellow Cab Company** (☎ 305/444–4444). Fares are set at $1.50 for the first quarter-mile, and 25¢ every eighth-mile after that—a fee that balances out to $3 per first mile and $2 every mile after. The fare includes luggage, tolls, and up to five passengers.

Orientation Tours

Boat Tours

Island Queen, Island Lady, and ***Pink Lady*** (☎ 305/379–5119) lead 90-minute narrated water tours of the Port of Miami and Millionaires' Row, departing from Bayside Marketplace.

Walking Tours

The **Miami Design Preservation League** (☎ 305/672–2014) runs several tours of various districts. The most popular walking tour covers the Art Deco District and departs at 10:30 AM Saturday and 6:30 PM Thursday, leaving from the Ocean Front Auditorium (☒ 1001 Ocean Dr.). Self-guided, tape-narrated tours are also available. Metro-Dade Community College history professor **Paul George** (☎ 305/858–6021) leads fact-filled walking tours through downtown and other historic districts.

Exploring Miami

Downtown

★ Begin your tour of downtown Miami at the **Metro-Dade Cultural Center** (☒ 101 W. Flagler St.), a 3.3-acre postmodern Mediterranean-style complex designed by architect Philip Johnson. An elevated plaza provides a serene haven from the city's commotion. Within the complex are several arts venues, including the **Miami Art Museum** (MAM; ☎ 305/375–1700; 🎟 $5). In the tradition of the European Kunsthalle (exhibition gallery), this art museum has no permanent collection; throughout the year it organizes and borrows temporary exhibitions on diverse themes. The **Historical Museum of Southern Florida** (☎ 305/375–1492; 🎟 $4), also in the cultural center, has artifacts including Tequesta and Seminole ceramics, a 1920s streetcar, cigar and citrus labels, and a railroad exhibit—pure Floridiana. Another cultural center tenant, the **Main Public Library** (☎ 305/375–2665) has nearly 4 million holdings and art exhibits in its auditorium and second-floor lobby.

Between Biscayne Boulevard and Biscayne Bay is the **Mildred and Claude Pepper Bayfront Park** (🎟 free), which Japanese sculptor Isamu Noguchi redesigned just before his death in 1989. It now includes a memorial to the *Challenger* astronauts, two amphitheaters, and a fountain honoring the late Florida congressman Claude Pepper and his wife.

Bayside Marketplace (☎ 305/577–3344; 🎟 free), between Bayfront Park and the entrance to the Port of Miami, is a massive waterside entertainment and shopping center that includes shops, outdoor cafés, and a food court. Street performers entertain throughout the day and evening, and free concerts, typically calypso, jazz, Latin, reggae, and rock, take place every day of the year.

At the **Freedom Tower** (☒ 600 Biscayne Blvd.), the Cuban Refugee Center processed more than 500,000 immigrating Cubans in the 1960s. Built in 1925 as the headquarters of *Miami Daily News,* it was restored to its original grandeur in 1988. This imposing Spanish Baroque–style structure was inspired by the Giralda, an 800-year-old bell tower in Seville, Spain.

South of downtown proper, several architecturally interesting condominiums rise between Brickell Avenue and Biscayne Bay. Israeli artist Yacov Agram painted the rainbow-hued exterior of **Villa Regina** (☒ 1581 Brickell Ave.). Arquitectonica, a nationally prominent architectural firm based in Miami, designed three buildings on Brickell Avenue: **the Palace** (☒ 1541 Brickell Ave.), **the Imperial** (☒ 1627 Brickell Ave.), and **the Atlantis** (☒ 2025 Brickell Ave.).

Miami Beach

Made up of 17 islands in Biscayne Bay, Miami Beach is a separate city from Miami. In recent years this so-called "American Riviera" has revived its fortunes by renewing its ★ **South Beach** area. Today South Beach revels in renewed world glory as a lure for models and millionaires. The hub of South Beach is the 1-square-mi **Art Deco District,** which stretches along Ocean Drive and is the most talked-about beachfront in America. About 800 significant buildings in the district are listed on the National Register of Historic Places—it's the nation's first 20th-century district to be honored as such.

Begin your tour of the Art Deco District at the **Art Deco District Welcome Center** (✉ 1001 Ocean Dr., ☎ 305/531–3484). Proceed north past pastel-hued Art Deco hotels (outlined in brilliant neon at night) on your left, and the palm-fringed beach on your right. You'll also pass the magnificently restored **Amsterdam Palace** (✉ 1114 Ocean Dr.), home of the late fashion designer Gianni Versace, who was murdered outside the front gate in July 1997. The neighborhood's two main commercial streets are **Collins Avenue,** one block west of Ocean Drive, and, one block farther west, **Washington Avenue.** The latter is a colorful mix of Jewish, Cuban, Haitian, and more familiar American cultures, containing delicatessens, avant-garde stores, produce markets, shops selling religious artifacts, and many of the city's best restaurants and nightclubs. Just off Washington, **Espanola Way** is a quaint avenue with a youth hostel, clubs, restaurants, and ethnic shops—a late-afternoon flea market is held here each Sunday. Three blocks north is the **Lincoln Road Mall,** a chic pedestrian shopping street with upscale restaurants, eclectic shops, and great people-watching.

The **Holocaust Memorial** (✉ 1933–1945 Meridian Ave., ☎ 305/538–1663; 🎟 free), across from the Miami Beach Convention Center, is a chilling monumental sculpture and a graphic record in memory of 6 million Jewish victims. The **Jackie Gleason Theater of the Performing Arts** (✉ 1700 Washington Ave., ☎ 305/673–7300) is where Gleason's television show originated. A short drive north, the **Bass Museum of Art** (✉ 2121 Park Ave., ☎ 305/673–7530; 🎟 $5) has a diverse collection of European works. A 70,000-plus-item collection of modern design and "propaganda arts" lies within the **Wolfsonian-FIU (Florida International University) Gallery** (✉ 1001 Washington Ave., ☎ 305/531–1001; 🎟 $5), an elegantly renovated 1927 storage facility. A research center is also on premises. The gallery is closed Monday.

The striking triumphal archway that looms on Collins Avenue is a mural of illusionary art by Richard Haas that depicts the **Fontainebleau Hilton Resort and Towers** (✉ 4441 Collins Ave., ☎ 305/538–2000), which actually sits behind it. The grandiose 1,200-room hotel preserves the "bigger is better" attitude of the 1950s.

Little Havana

Nearly 40 years ago the tidal wave of Cubans fleeing the Castro regime flooded an older neighborhood just west of downtown with refugees. The area became known as **Little Havana,** although today more than half a million Cubans live throughout the greater Miami area. **Calle Ocho** (✉ S.W. 8th St.) is Little Havana's main commercial thoroughfare.

At the **Plaza de la Cubanidad** (✉ S.W. 17th Ave.; 🎟 free), on the southwest corner of Flagler Street and Teddy Roosevelt Avenue, redbrick sidewalks surround a fountain and monument inscribed with words from José Martí, a leader in Cuba's struggle for independence from Spain: LAS PALMAS SON NOVIAS QUE ESPERAN (The palm trees are girlfriends who will wait).

Visit **Versailles** (✉ 3555 S.W. 8th St., ☎ 305/445–7614), a Cuban restaurant whose menu and decor will immerse you in Cuban-American popular culture. The **Brigade 2506 Memorial** (✉ S.W. 13th Ave.), which stands at Calle Ocho and Memorial Boulevard, commemorates the victims of the unsuccessful 1961 Bay of Pigs invasion of Cuba by an exile force. **El Credito** (✉ 1106 S.W. 8th St., ☎ 305/858–4162 or 800/726–9481) is a cigar shop seemingly transported from the Cuban capital

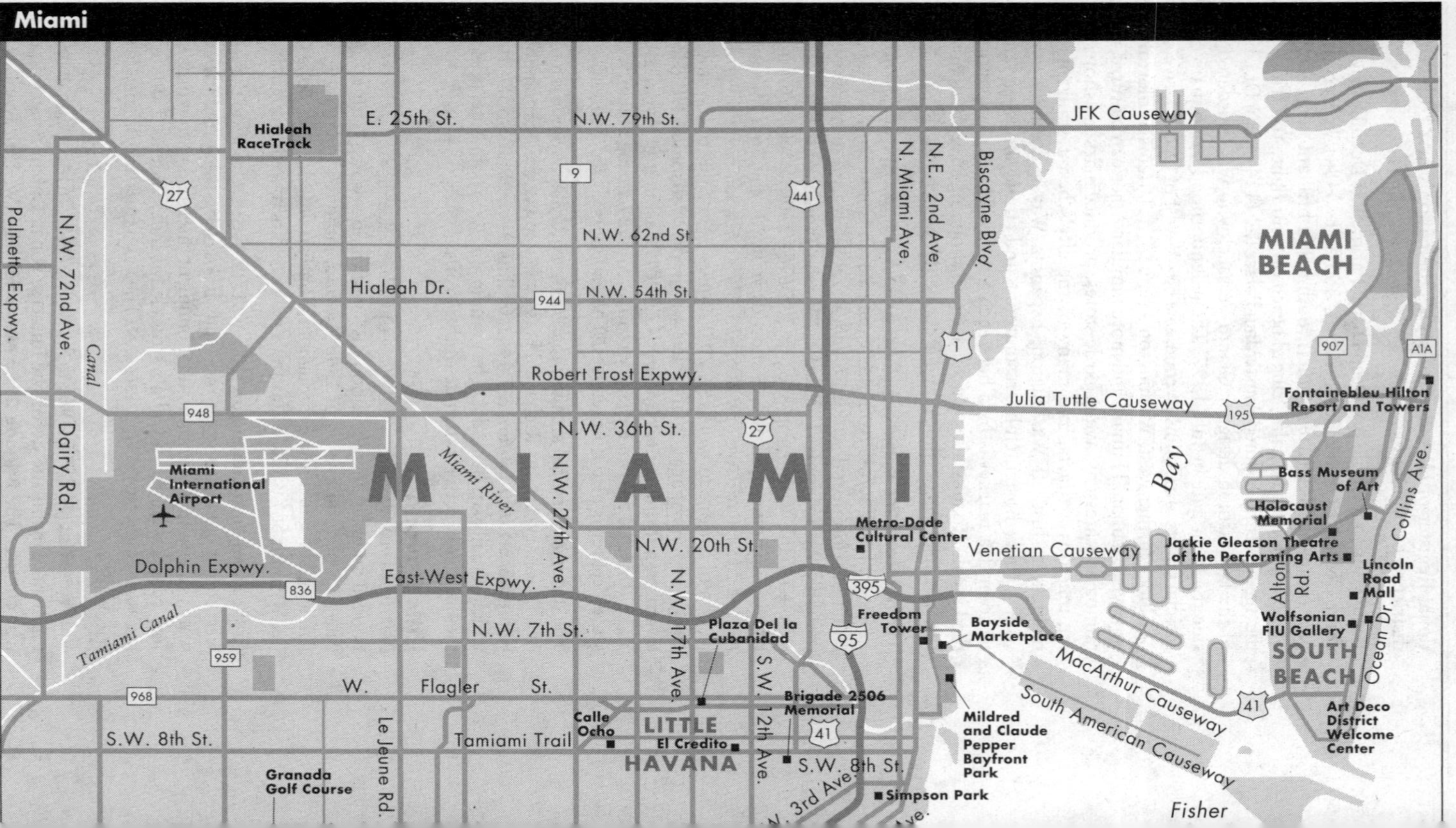
Miami
Hialeah RaceTrack
E. 25th St.
N.W. 79th St.
JFK Causeway
9
27
441
N. Miami Ave.
N.E. 2nd Ave.
Biscayne Blvd.
MIAMI BEACH
Palmetto Expwy.
N.W. 72nd Ave.
Canal
N.W. 62nd St.
Hialeah Dr.
944
N.W. 54th St.
1
907
A1A
Robert Frost Expwy.
Julia Tuttle Causeway
195
Fontainebleu Hilton Resort and Towers
948
N.W. 36th St.
27
Dairy Rd.
MIAMI
Miami River
N.W. 27th Ave.
Miami International Airport
Bay
Bass Museum of Art
Holocaust Memorial
Collins Ave.
Metro-Dade Cultural Center
N.W. 20th St.
Venetian Causeway
Jackie Gleason Theatre of the Performing Arts
Lincoln Road Mall
Alton Rd.
Dolphin Expwy.
East-West Expwy.
836
395
Freedom Tower
N.W. 17th Ave.
Tamiami Canal
N.W. 7th St.
Plaza Del la Cubanidad
95
Bayside Marketplace
Wolfsonian FIU Gallery
Ocean Dr.
SOUTH BEACH
959
MacArthur Causeway
W. Flagler St.
968
Brigade 2506 Memorial
S.W. 12th Ave.
41
South American Causeway
Art Deco District Welcome Center
Calle Ocho
LITTLE HAVANA
S.W. 8th St.
Tamiami Trail
El Credito
Mildred and Claude Pepper Bayfront Park
Le Jeune Rd.
Granada Golf Course
S.W. 8th St.
S.W. 3rd Ave.
Simpson Park
Fisher

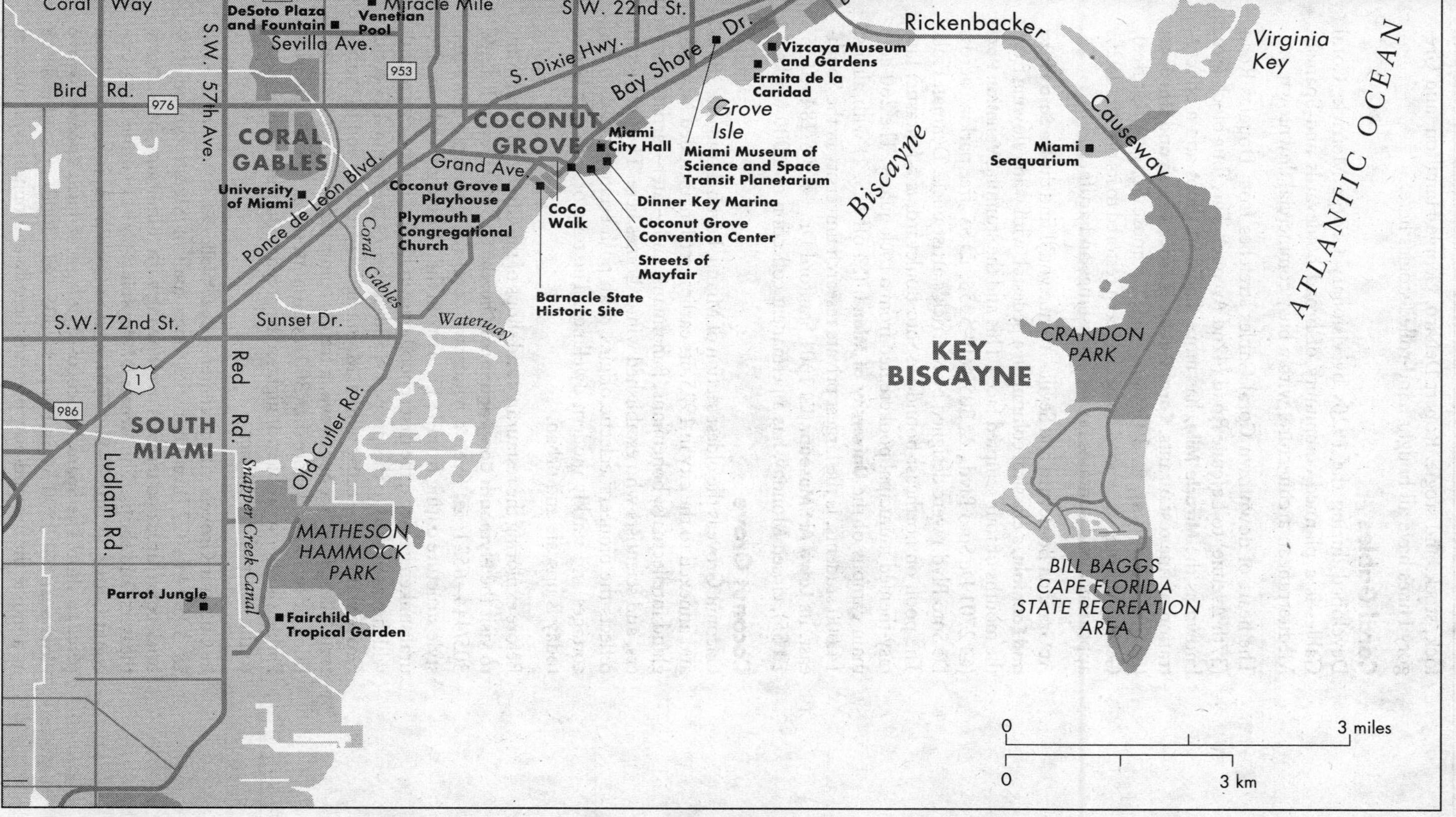
Coral Way
Miracle Mile
S.W. 22nd St.
DeSoto Plaza and Fountain
Venetian Pool
Sevilla Ave.
953
S. Dixie Hwy.
Bay Shore Dr.
Rickenbacker
Virginia Key
ATLANTIC OCEAN
Vizcaya Museum and Gardens
Ermita de la Caridad
Bird Rd.
976
S.W. 57th Ave.
CORAL GABLES
COCONUT GROVE
Grove Isle
Causeway
Miami City Hall
Miami Museum of Science and Space Transit Planetarium
Miami Seaquarium
Grand Ave.
University of Miami
Coconut Grove Playhouse
Ponce de León Blvd.
Plymouth Congregational Church
CoCo Walk
Dinner Key Marina
Coconut Grove Convention Center
Streets of Mayfair
Biscayne
Coral Gables
Barnacle State Historic Site
Waterway
S.W. 72nd St.
Sunset Dr.
CRANDON PARK
KEY BISCAYNE
1
Red Rd.
986
SOUTH MIAMI
Old Cutler Rd.
Ludlam Rd.
Snapper Creek Canal
MATHESON HAMMOCK PARK
Parrot Jungle
Fairchild Tropical Garden
BILL BAGGS CAPE FLORIDA STATE RECREATION AREA
0
3 miles
0
3 km

lock, stock, and stogie. Robert DeNiro, George Hamilton, and Gregory Hines have all bought hand-rolled stogies here.

Coral Gables

Developed during the 1920s by visionary George Merrick, Coral Gables is a planned community of broad boulevards and Spanish-Mediterranean architecture, with a busy commercial downtown.

The heart of downtown Coral Gables stretches from Douglas Road (37th Avenue) to LeJeune Road (42nd Avenue). This four-block area, known as the **Miracle Mile,** has more than 150 shops and a concentration of fine restaurants. **Coral Gables Merrick House and Gardens,** (✉ 907 Coral Way, ☎ 305/460–5361; 🎫 house $2, grounds free), George Merrick's boyhood home, has been restored to its original 1920s appearance and contains family furnishings and artifacts.

At Granada Boulevard and Sevilla Avenue you'll find the **De Soto Plaza and Fountain,** a classical column on a pedestal, with water flowing from the mouths of four sculpted faces. This and the stunning **Venetian Pool** (✉ 2701 De Soto Blvd., ☎ 305/460–5356; 🎫 $5, free parking across De Soto Blvd.) were designed by Merrick's artist-uncle, Denman Fink. The pool, on northeast-bound De Soto Boulevard, is a fantastic, fantasy-themed municipal pool created from a rock quarry. The 260-acre main campus of the **University of Miami,** (✉ off U.S. 1) with almost 14,000 students, is the largest private research university in the Southeast. Its **Lowe Art Museum** (✉ 1301 Stanford Dr., ☎ 305/284–3535; 🎫 $5), closed Monday, has a permanent collection of 8,000 works.

Coconut Grove

Coconut Grove is the oldest section of Miami, begun during the 1870s and annexed to the city in 1925. Its earliest settlers included New England intellectuals, bohemians, Bahamians, and—later—artists, writers, and scientists who established winter homes here. The Grove still reflects the pioneers' eclectic origins, with posh estates next to rustic cottages and starkly modern dwellings. The tone of Coconut Grove today is upscale and urban.

Before exploring the restaurants and shops of the Grove, you may want to visit the **Plymouth Congregational Church** (✉ 3400 Devon Rd., ☎ 305/444–6521; 🎫 free), a handsome coral-rock Mexican mission–style structure dating from 1917. Also on the 11-acre grounds are natural sunken gardens; the first schoolhouse in Dade County (one room), which was moved to this property; and the site of the original Coconut Grove water and electric works. Main Highway returns you to the historic ★ **Village of Coconut Grove,** a trendy commercial district with red-brick sidewalks and more than 300 restaurants, stores, and art galleries. Parking is often a problem at night, so be prepared to walk several blocks to the heart of the district.

In Coconut Grove's village center is **CocoWalk** (✉ 3015 Grand Ave., ☎ 305/444–0777), a multilevel open mall of Mediterranean-style brick courtyards and terraces overflowing with restaurants, bars, movie theaters, and shops. The **Streets Of Mayfair** (✉ 2911 Grand Ave., Coconut Grove, ☎ 305/448–1700), next to CocoWalk, is another good place to shop.The Spanish rococo–style apricot-hued **Coconut Grove Playhouse** (✉ 3500 Main Hwy., ☎ 305/442–4000) opened in 1926 as a movie theater and now presents Broadway-bound plays, musical revues, and experimental productions. The **Barnacle State Historical Site** (✉ 3485 Main Hwy., ☎ 305/448–9445; 🎫 $1), a 19th-century pioneer residence, was built by Commodore Ralph Munroe in 1891. The house, which is open Fridays and weekends, has a broad, sloping roof and deeply recessed verandas to channel sea breezes inside; many furnishings are original.

North on Bayshore Drive is **Dinner Key Marina** (✉ 3400 Pan American Dr., ☎ 305/579–6980), Greater Miami's largest marina. Antiques, boat, and home furnishings shows are held annually at the 105,000-square-ft **Coconut Grove Convention Center** (✉ 2700 S. Bayshore Dr., ☎ 305/579–3310). **Miami City Hall** (✉ 3500 Pan American Dr., ☎ 305/250–5400; 🎟 free) is known for its nautical-motif Art Deco trim. It was built in 1934 as the terminal for the Pan American Airways seaplane base at Dinner Key.

Past St. Kieran's Church on South Miami Avenue (drive north on South Bayshore Drive from Coconut Drive) is **Ermita de La Caridad** (Our Lady of Charity Shrine; ✉ 3609 S. Miami Ave., ☎ 305/854–2404; 🎟 free), a 90-ft-high conical shrine built to overlook the bay so that worshipers face Cuba.You can manipulate and marvel at the many hands-on sound, gravity, and electricity exhibits at the **Miami Museum of Science and Space Transit Planetarium** (✉ 3280 S. Miami Ave., ☎ 305/854–4247; 🎟 $10; $6 laser concerts), which also features traveling exhibits and virtual reality, life science demonstrations, and Internet technology.Overlooking Biscayne Bay on South Miami Avenue ★ is **Vizcaya Museum and Gardens** (✉ 3251 S. Miami Ave., ☎ 305/250–9133; 🎟 $10), an estate with an Italian Renaissance–style villa that was built in the early 20th century as the winter residence of Chicago industrialist James Deering. Today the house is a showplace of antiquities. At **Simpson Park** (✉ 55 S.W. 17th Rd. off South Miami Ave., ☎ 305/856–6801), you can enjoy a fragment of the dense jungle—marlberry, banyans, and black calabash—that once covered the entire 5 mi from downtown Miami to Coconut Grove.

South Miami

South Miami was a pioneer farming community that has managed to retain its small-town charm, even while growing into a major suburb. Contrary to what its name implies, South Miami is a city, not just a geographical moniker.

Fine old homes and mature trees line **Sunset Drive,** the city-designated "historic and scenic road" to and through downtown South Miami. You can watch a trained-bird show, stroll among exotic plants and trees, and see a cactus garden at **Parrot Jungle** (✉ 11000 S.W. 57th Ave., ☎ 305/666–7834; 🎟 $12.95), one of Miami's oldest and most popular attractions. Many of the 1,100 parrots, macaws, cockatoos, and other exotic birds fly free, but they'll come to you for seeds, sold from old-fashioned gum-ball machines.

Not far from Parrot Jungle is the 83-acre **Fairchild Tropical Garden** (✉ 10901 Old Cutler Rd., ☎ 305/667–1651; 🎟 $8), the largest tropical botanical garden in the continental United States. Old Cutler Road traverses Miami–Dade County's oldest and most scenic park, **Matheson Hammock Park** (✉ 9610 Old Cutler Rd., ☎ 305/665–5475; 🎟 free, $3.50 parking), which dates from the days of the Civilian Conservation Corps in the 1930s. The tide flushes a saltwater "atoll" pool through four gates at the park's bathing beach.

Virginia Key and Key Biscayne

The waters of Government Cut and the Port of Miami separate densely populated Miami Beach from two of Greater Miami's playground islands, Virginia Key and Key Biscayne—the latter no longer the laid-back village where Richard Nixon set up his presidential vacation compound. Parks and stretches of dense mangrove swamp occupy much of both keys.To reach the keys, take the **Rickenbacker Cause-**

way across Biscayne Bay at Brickell Avenue and Southwest 26th Road, about 2 mi south of downtown Miami. The causeway links several islands in the bay.

★ On Virginia Key, the **Miami Seaquarium** (✉ 4400 Rickenbacker Causeway, ☎ 305/361–5705; 🎫 $19.95, parking $3) features sea lion, dolphin, and killer whale performances and a 235,000-gallon tropical-reef aquarium.

Many educated beach enthusiasts rate **Crandon Park** (✉ 4000 Crandon Blvd., ☎ 305/361–5421; 🎫 $3.50 per vehicle) among the top 10 beaches in North America. Families flock here for the soft sand and good swimming.

The commercial center of Key Biscayne is a mix of shops and stores catering to neighborhood needs. At the key's south end is the **Bill Baggs Cape Florida State Recreation Area** (✉ 1200 S. Crandon Blvd., ☎ 305/361–5811; 🎫 $4 per vehicle; $1 per person on foot, bicycle, or bus), a 1¼-mi expanse of palm-topped white-sand beach with several boardwalks and fishing piers. Here you'll find the **Cape Florida Lighthouse,** South Florida's oldest structure.

Dining

With its fusion of tropical ingredients and classical techniques, Miami has become one of the undisputed capitals of so-called "New World Cuisine." The gourmet centers of the city are downtown Coral Gables and the Art Deco District of Miami Beach, with pockets of fine dining also in ethnic neighborhoods, such as Little Havana, and in major nightlife districts, such as Coconut Grove and Bayside downtown. For price ranges *see* Chart 1 (A) *in* On the Road with Fodor's.

$$$–$$$$ **Blue Door at Delano.** Chef Claude Troisgros has combined the decor and recipes of classic French cuisine with South American influences to create dishes like the *big raviol,* filled with taro-root mousseline and white-truffle oil. The *boeuf au manioc* is a beef tenderloin with a yuca biscuit. You'll be dining among the *crème de la crème* of Miami (and New York and Paris) society. Bon appetit! ✉ *1685 Collins Ave., Miami Beach,* ☎ *305/674–6400. Reservations essential. AE, D, DC, MC, V.*

$$$–$$$$ ✕ **Chef Allen's.** In an Art Deco setting of glass and neon, diners' gazes are drawn to the kitchen, visible through a large picture window, where chef Allen Susser creates "New World" masterpieces from a menu that changes nightly. Dishes such as honey-chilled roasted duck with stir-fried wild rice and green-apple chutney are almost too pretty to eat. Take home a bottle of Chef Allen's mango ketchup as a tasty souvenir. ✉ *19088 N.E. 29th Ave., North Miami Beach,* ☎ *305/935–2900. AE, DC, MC, V. No lunch Sat.–Thurs.*

$$$–$$$$ ✕ **Norman's.** This elegantly casual restaurant has won as many awards as it has customers. Chef Norman Van Aken has created a buzz by perfecting the art of "New World" cuisine—a combination rooted in Latin, American, Caribbean, and Asian influences. Norman's has captured the essence of Miami dining, delivering bold tastes in every dish. ✉ *21 Almeria Ave., Coral Gables,* ☎ *305/446–6767. AE, DC, MC, V. Closed Sun. No lunch Sat.*

$$–$$$$ ✕ **Astor Place.** Diners at this trendy hotel restaurant are wowed by creative spins on such appetizers as yellowtail snapper soft tacos and entrées like ancho-cinnamon pork tenderloin and skillet-steamed sea bass. Service is fast and friendly. ✉ *956 Washington Ave., Miami Beach,* ☎ *305/672–7217. AE, DC, MC, V.*

$$–$$$$ ★ ✕ **Yuca.** This high-style Cuban eatery, decorated with striking modern art prints and blond wood, attracts chic young Cubans and other fashionable types. Dazzling nouvelle tropical dishes include a traditional corn tamale filled with conch and plantain-coated dolphin with a tamarind-tartar sauce. ✉ *501 Lincoln Rd., Miami Beach,* ☎ *305/532–9822. AE, DC, MC, V.*

$–$$$$ ★ ✕ **Tony Chan's Water Club.** This beautiful dining room just off the lobby of the high-rise Doubletree Grand Hotel looks onto a bayside marina. The menu has more than 200 appetizers and entrées, including minced quail tossed with bamboo shoots, mushrooms wrapped in lettuce leaves, and pork chops sprinkled with green peppercorns in a black-bean-and-garlic sauce. ✉ *1717 N. Bayshore Dr., Downtown Miami,* ☎ *305/374–8888. AE, D, DC, MC, V. No lunch weekends.*

$$$ ✕ **Grand Cafe.** Inside the Grand Bay Hotel, this bi-level dining room has pink tablecloths and floral bouquets. International cuisine here means everything from pan-seared Florida crab cake to the cherry wood–smoked Chilean salmon. ✉ *2669 S. Bayshore Dr., Coconut Grove,* ☎ *305/858–9600. AE, DC, MC, V.*

$$–$$$ ★ ✕ **Two Sisters.** Stiff competition among Coral Gables restaurants helps keep the Hyatt Regency's dining room first-rate. The mood is understated, but the Pacific Rim–inspired dishes add pizzazz. Entrées such as stir-fried "tangled shrimp with jungle curry, rice ribbons, and coconut glaze," or jerk-marinated snapper with red-onion confit and ginger butter might make you consider a vacation in Polynesia. ✉ *Hyatt Regency, 50 Alhambra Plaza, Coral Gables,* ☎ *305/441–1234. AE, MC, V.*

$–$$$ ✕ **Los Ranchos.** Carlos Somoza, owner of this beautiful bay-side establishment, is a nephew of Nicaragua's deposed dictator Anastasio Somoza. Here he sustains a tradition begun more than 30 years ago in Managua, when the original Los Ranchos instilled in Nicaraguan palates a love of Argentine-style beef—lean, grass-fed tenderloin with *chimichurri,* a green sauce of chopped parsley, garlic, oil, vinegar, and other spices. Specialties include chorizo, *cuajada con maduro* (skim cheese with fried bananas), and shrimp sautéed in butter and topped with a creamy jalapeño sauce. There are several other locations throughout the city. ✉ *Bayside Marketplace, 401 Biscayne Blvd., Downtown Miami,* ☎ *305/375–8188 or 305/375–0666. AE, DC, MC, V.*

$–$$ ✕ **11th Street Diner.** The sights, sounds, and smells from the '50s are captured here without the artificial ambience of James Dean cutouts and poodle skirts. Low-priced, unpretentious diner meals are served 24 hours a day. ✉ *11th St. and Washington Ave., Miami Beach,* ☎ *305/534–6373. AE, MC, V .*

$–$$ ★ ✕ **Hy-Vong Vietnamese Cuisine.** Come to this tiny hole-in-the-wall for Vietnamese specialties like barbecued pork with sesame seeds and fish sauce, and imported brews. Expect a wait after 7 PM. ✉ *3458 S.W. 8th St., Little Havana,* ☎ *305/446–3674. No credit cards. Closed Mon. and 2 wks in Aug. No lunch.*

$–$$ **Joe's Stone Crab Restaurant.** "Before SoBe, Joe Be," touts this fourth-generation family restaurant. About a ton of stone-crab claws is served daily (except in summer, when they aren't available), with drawn butter, lemon wedges, and piquant mustard sauce. Save room for dessert—key lime pie or apple pie with a crumb-pecan topping. ✉ *227 Biscayne St., Miami Beach,* ☎ *305/673–0365. AE, D, DC, MC, V. Closed Sept. 1–Oct. 15. No lunch Sun.–Mon.*

$–$$ ✕ **Las Tapas.** Appetizer-size portions of Spanish-style foods are served along with full-size meals at this Bayside Marketplace restaurant, typically packed at all hours. ✉ *Bayside Marketplace, 401 Biscayne Blvd., Downtown Miami,* ☎ *305/372–2737. AE, D, DC, MC, V.*

$–$$ ★ ✕ **News Cafe.** This hip spot on Ocean Drive (open 24 hours) is always packed with people-watchers and those who enjoy such eclectic dishes as huge fresh-fruit bowls, burgers, bagels, pâtés, and chocolate fondue. The newer branch in Coconut Grove is twice as big. ✉ *800*

Ocean Dr., Miami Beach, ☎ *305/538–6397;* ✉ *2901 Florida Ave., Coconut Grove,* ☎ *305/774–6397. AE, DC, MC, V.*

$–$$ ★ ✕ **Shorty's Bar-B-Q.** Miami's choice for barbecue and all the trimmings since the 1950s, Shorty's serves meals family style at long picnic tables. ✉ *9200 S. Dixie Hwy., Kendall, Miami,* ☎ *305/670–7732;* ✉ *11575 S.W. 40th St., W. Kendall, Miami,* ☎ *305/227–3196. Reservations not accepted. D, MC, V.*

Lodging

Lodgings are concentrated in Miami Beach and downtown Miami, around the airport, and in Coral Gables, Coconut Grove, and Key Biscayne. For bed-and-breakfast accommodations contact **Bed & Breakfast Company, Tropical Florida** (✉ Box 262, Miami 33243, ☎ 305/661–3270).Winter is peak season; summer is also busy but rates are lower. For price ranges (which reflect high-season rates), *see* Chart 2 (A) *in* On the Road with Fodor's.

$$$$ ★ 🏨 **Alexander Hotel.** Every room is a large suite with two baths and a kitchen, ocean or bay view, and antique or reproduction furnishings. The hotel is renowned for service. ✉ *5225 Collins Ave., Miami Beach 33140,* ☎ *305/865–6500 or 800/327–6121,* FAX *305/864–8525. 150 suites. 2 restaurants, pools. AE, D, DC, MC, V.*

$$$$ ★ 🏨 **Biltmore Hotel.** The 1926 Biltmore was the centerpiece of Merrick's City Beautiful, and rises like a sienna-color wedding cake in the heart of a residential district. The vaulted lobby has hand-painted rafters on a twinkling sky-blue background. Large guest rooms are done in a restrained Moorish style. For $1,800 you can book the Everglades (a.k.a. Al Capone) Suite—President Clinton's room when he's in town. ✉ *1200 Anastasia Ave., Coral Gables 33134,* ☎ *305/445–1926 or 800/727–1926,* FAX *305/913–3159. 275 rooms. Restaurant, pool, tennis, health club. AE, DC, MC, V.*

$$$$ 🏨 **Delano Hotel.** If Calvin Klein had teamed with Salvador Dali to build a hotel, this weird, wonderful, slightly snooty property would be it. Miami's hotel du jour, owned by New Yorker Ian Schrager, appeals to female fashion models and men of independent means. Tourists enjoy the surreal atmosphere, stark white guest rooms, and fantasy pool. ✉ *1685 Collins Ave., Miami Beach 33139,* ☎ *305/672–2000 or 800/555–5001,* FAX *305/532–0099. 208 rooms. Restaurant, pool, health club. AE, D, DC, MC, V.*

$$$$ ★ 🏨 **Grand Bay Hotel.** Artwork and fresh flowers enhance the elegant lobby of this modern high-rise whose easterly views take in Biscayne Bay. Whoopi Goldberg, Arnold Schwarzenegger, and Bruce Willis have all stayed here, perhaps enjoying the hotel's pyramid-like stepped profile that gives each room facing the bay a private terrace. ✉ *2669 S. Bayshore Dr., Coconut Grove 33133,* ☎ *305/858–9600 or 800/327–2788,* FAX *305/858–1532. 181 rooms. Restaurant, pool, health club. AE, DC, MC, V.*

$$$$ ★ 🏨 **Sonesta Beach Resort Key Biscayne.** With its 750-ft beach, this hotel has always been one of Miami's best. Some rooms are in villas with full kitchens and screened-in pools. Facilities include parasailing, catamaran rental, and children's programs. Don't miss the Andy Warhol drawings of Mick Jagger. ✉ *350 Ocean Dr., Key Biscayne 33149,* ☎ *305/361–2021 or 800/766–3782,* FAX *305/361–3096. 300 rooms. 3 restaurants, pool, tennis, health club. AE, DC, MC, V.*

$$$$ ★ 🏨 **Turnberry Isle Resort & Club.** Guests can choose from the Mediterranean-style annex, the intimate Marina Hotel, the Yacht Club on the Intracoastal Waterway, or the Country Club Hotel beside the golf course at this 300-acre resort and condominium complex in North Dade County. The marina has moorings for 117 boats up to 150 ft, and there's

a free shuttle to the beach club and the Aventura Mall. ✉ *19999 W. Country Club Dr., Aventura 33180,* ☎ *305/932–6200 or 800/327–7028,* FAX *305/933–6560. 340 rooms. 7 restaurants, pools, tennis, health club. AE, D, DC, MC, V.*

$$$–$$$$ ★ **Indian Creek Hotel.** This 1936 Pueblo-inspired deco jewel may just be Miami's most charming accommodation. Owner Marc Levin rescued the inn and was fortunate enough to find original deco furniture in the basement (which no doubt helped him win the Miami Design Preservation League's award for outstanding restoration). The backyard pool is heavenly. ✉ *2727 Indian Creek Dr., Miami Beach 33140,* ☎ *305/531–2727,* FAX *305/531–5651. 61 rooms. Pool. AE, D, DC, MC, V.*

$$$–$$$$ ★ **Omni Colonnade Hotel.** The twin 13-story towers of this swank, $65 million hotel, office, and shopping complex dominate downtown Coral Gables. Oversize rooms have sitting areas and built-in armoires. ✉ *180 Aragon Ave., Coral Gables 33134,* ☎ *305/441–2600,* FAX *305/445–3929. 157 rooms. Restaurant, pool, exercise room. AE, D, DC, MC, V.*

$$$–$$$$ **Park Central.** Across the street from a glorious stretch of beach, this seven-story Art Deco hotel is a favorite of visiting fashion models and other trendsetters. There is an espresso bar on site and a restaurant, Casablanca. ✉ *640 Ocean Dr., Miami Beach 33139,* ☎ *305/538–1611 or 800/727–5236,* FAX *305/534–7520. 121 rooms. Restaurant, pool, exercise room. AE, DC, MC, V.*

$$$ ★ **Hotel Place St. Michel.** The finest boutique hotel in metropolitan Miami is in the heart of downtown Coral Gables. Art nouveau chandeliers are suspended from vaulted lobby ceilings, and the scent of fresh flowers is circulated through the public spaces by paddle fans. Each room is unique, but count on English, French, and Scottish antiques. ✉ *162 Alcazar Ave., Coral Gables 33134,* ☎ *305/444–1666 or 800/848–4683,* FAX *305/529–0074. 27 rooms. Restaurant. CP. AE, DC, MC, V.*

$$–$$$ ★ **Miami River Inn.** Ten minutes by foot from the heart of downtown, this turn-of-the-century inn consists of five clapboard buildings on a grassy, palm-studded compound. Don't be put off by the neighborhood—the setting is lovely, rooms are filled with antiques, and guests are treated to Continental breakfast. ✉ *118 S.W. South River Dr., Miami 33130,* ☎ *305/325–0045,* FAX *305/325–9227. 40 rooms. Pool. CP. AE, D, DC, MC, V.*

$$–$$$ **Nassau Suite Hotel.** The sister property of the nearby Beachcomber, this renovated 1937 hotel consists of 22 spacious and smart-looking suites. King beds, fully equipped kitchens, hardwood floors, white-wood blinds, free local calls, and privileges at the Beachcomber's bistro beg one to wonder how the rates remain so reasonable. ✉ *1414 Collins Ave., Miami Beach 33139,* ☎ *305/531–3755 or 888/305-4683,* FAX *305/673–8609. 22 suites. AE, D, DC, MC, V.*

$$ **The Beachcomber.** One of the best finds in SoBe, this small hotel may get lost in the shuffle, but it should stand out from the crowd. Note the ample space, hardwood floors, and clean bathrooms—were this property a block east on the ocean, you'd be paying three times as much. Save your money and enjoy the short walk. ✉ *1340 Collins Ave., Miami Beach 33139,* ☎ *305/531-3755 or 888/305-4683,* FAX *305/673–8609. 28 rooms. Restaurant. AE, D, DC, MC, V.*

$–$$ **Banana Bungalow.** This may seem like a university dormitory—indeed, some rooms have dorm-style bunk beds for about $14 a night—but the cleanliness, friendliness, and number of activities make this lodge worth checking into, especially for student travelers. A large pool, the bungalow's social center, is surrounded by a patio bar, Ping-Pong table, game room, outdoor grills, a café, and an activity board announcing Wave Runner rentals, scenic flights, and beach volleyball games held across the street. ✉ *2360 Collins Ave., 33139,* ☎ *305/538–1951 or 800/746–7835,* FAX *305/531–3217. 60 rooms. Restaurant, pool. MC, V.*

Nightlife and the Arts

The best sources for events are the widely distributed free weeklies *Miami Today* and *New Times;* the *Miami Herald* publishes a Weekend section on Friday and a Lively Arts section on Sunday. If you read Spanish, rely on *El Nuevo Herald* (the Spanish version of the *Miami Herald*).

Nightlife

The liveliest scenes are in SoBe (Miami Beach's Art Deco District—especially on Washington Avenue) and Coconut Grove, but clubs can be found in the suburbs, downtown, Little Havana, and Little Haiti.

BARS WITH MUSIC

Tobacco Road (⊠ 626 S. Miami Ave., Miami, ☎ 305/374–1198) holds Miami's oldest liquor license (Number 0001!) and is one of the city's oldest bars, with excellent blues nightly. **Mac's Club Deuce** (⊠ 222 14th St., Miami Beach, ☎ 305/673–9537) is a funky, working-class—some might say weird—SoBe spot, where top international models come to shoot pool.

DANCE CLUBS

Amnesia (⊠ 136 Collins Ave., Miami Beach, ☎ 305/531–5535) feels like a luxurious amphitheater in the tropics—with a rain forest, what used to be called go-go dancers, and dancing in the rain when showers pass over the open-air club. It's open Thursday–Sunday. **Bash** (⊠ 655 Washington Ave., Miami Beach, ☎ 305/538–2274) is a grotto-like bar with dance floors that reverberate to different sounds—sometimes reggae, sometimes Latin, but mostly loud disco. Many SoBe clubs fall out of favor quickly, but some that have hung on for more than a year include: **Liquid** (⊠ 1439–37 Washington Ave., ☎ 305/532–9154) , **Groove Jet** (⊠ 323 23rd St., ☎ 305/532–2002), and **Warsaw Ballroom** (⊠ 1450 Collins Ave., ☎ 305/531-4555). Most of these clubs draw a mix of gays and straights.

NIGHTCLUBS

Club Tropigala (⊠ Fontainebleau Hilton, 4441 Collins Ave., Miami Beach, ☎ 305/672–7469) is set in a four-tier round room decorated with orchids, banana leaves, and philodendrons to resemble a tropical jungle. The Vegas-style show features American standards as well as Latin music for dancing. Reservations are suggested, and men should wear jackets.

The Arts

BALLET

Miami City Ballet (⊠ 905 Lincoln Rd., Miami Beach, ☎ 305/532–7713 or 305/532–4880) is an acclaimed troupe under the direction of Edward Villella. You can watch rehearsals through a massive window or catch a performance between September and March at the **Jackie Gleason Theater of the Performing Arts** (☞ *below*).

MUSIC

New World Symphony (⊠ 541 Lincoln Rd., Miami Beach, ☎ 305/673–3331), conducted by Michael Tilson Thomas, is also a national orchestral academy for young music-school graduates. **Concert Association of Florida** (⊠ 555 Hank Meyer Blvd., at 17th St., Miami Beach , ☎ 305/532–3491) is the Southeast's largest presenter of classical artists, dance, and music—concerts are held at a variety of venues.

OPERA

Florida Grand Opera (⊠ 1200 Coral Way, Miami, ☎ 305/854–1643) presents five operas a year at the Dade County Auditorium.

THEATER

The **Coconut Grove Playhouse** (✉ 3500 Main Hwy., ☎ 305/442–4000) stages Broadway-bound plays and musical revues as well as experimental productions. **Colony Theater** (✉ 1040 Lincoln Rd., Miami Beach, ☎ 305/674–1026), once a movie theater, is now a city-owned 465-seat performing arts center featuring dance, drama, music, and experimental cinema. **Jackie Gleason Theater of the Performing Arts** (✉ 1700 Washington Ave., Miami Beach, ☎ 305/673–7300) is home of the Broadway Series and other stage events. **Teatro de Bellas Artes** (✉ 2173 S.W. 8th St., Miami, ☎ 305/325–0515), a 255-seat theater on Little Havana's Calle Ocho, presents Spanish plays and musicals year-round.

Outdoor Activities and Sports

Diving

Summer diving conditions in Greater Miami have been compared with those in the Caribbean. Winter can bring rough, cold waters. Fowey, Triumph, Long, and Emerald reefs are good for snorkelers and beginning divers. For charters, rentals, and instruction, try **Divers Paradise of Key Biscayne** (✉ 4000 Crandon Blvd., Key Biscayne, ☎ 305/361–3483) or the **Diving Locker** (✉ 223 Sunny Isles Blvd., N. Miami Beach, ☎ 305/947–6025). **Bubbles Dive Center** (✉ 2671 S.W. 27th Ave., Miami, ☎ 305/856–0565) is an all-purpose dive shop.

Golf

Dade County has more than 30 private and public golf courses; for county information, call 305/857–6868; for Miami Beach information, call 305/673–7730. A few of Miami's more notable courses include: the **Biltmore Golf Course** (✉ 1210 Anastasia Ave., Coral Gables, ☎ 305/460–5364); the "Blue Monster" at the **Doral Golf Resort and Spa** (✉ 4400 N.W. 87th Ave., Doral, ☎ 305/592–2000 or 800/713–6725); and **Turnberry Isle Resort & Club** (✉ 19999 W. Country Club Dr., Aventura, ☎ 305/933–6929) with 36 holes designed by Robert Trent Jones. The **Granada Golf Course** (✉ 2001 Granada Blvd., ☎ 305/460–5367) is one of two public courses amid Coral Gables's largest historic district.

Sailing

The center of sailing in Greater Miami remains at the **Dinner Key** and the **Coconut Grove** waterfronts, although moorings and rentals are found elsewhere up the bay and up the Miami River.

Tennis

Greater Miami has more than 60 private and public tennis centers. All public courts charge nonresidents an hourly fee. **Biltmore Tennis Center** (✉ 1150 Anastasia Ave., Coral Gables, ☎ 305/460–5360) has 10 hard courts. **Flamingo Tennis Center** (✉ 1000 12th St., Miami Beach, ☎ 305/673–7761) has 19 clay courts. **Tennis Center at Crandon Park** (✉ 7300 Crandon Blvd., Key Biscayne, ☎ 305/365–2300), which hosts the annual Lipton Championships in March, has 2 grass, 8 clay, and 17 hard courts.

Windsurfing

You can rent windsurfing equipment and take lessons at **Sailboards Miami** (✉ Key Biscayne, ☎ 305/361–7245), on Hobie Island just past the tollbooth for the Rickenbacker Causeway to Key Biscayne.

Spectator Sports

In addition to the usual spectator sports, in Miami you can watch the game known as *jai alai,* known as the fastest game on earth. Pelotas (hard balls) are thrown from handheld baskets called cestas, traveling at speeds of more than 170 mph. Locals place bets on the winning team or on the order in which teams will finish.

Baseball: The 1997 World Series champion **Florida Marlins** play at Pro Player Stadium (✉ 2269 N.W. 199th St., Miami, ☎ 305/626–7400). **Basketball: Miami Heat,** Miami Arena (✉ 1 S.E. 3rd Ave., Miami, ☎ 305/577–4328). **Football:** Miami's favorite team, the **Miami Dolphins** play at Pro Player Stadium (✉ 2269 N.W. 199th St., Miami, ☎ 305/620–2578). **Hockey: Florida Panthers** (✉ 13611 Green Toad Rd., Sunrise, ☎ 954/845–9292). **Miami Jai Alai** (✉ 3500 N.W. 37th Ave., Miami, ☎ 305/633–6400).

Beaches

Millions visit the beaches in Miami-Dade County each year. **Miami Beach** extends continuously for 10 mi. A boardwalk runs from 23rd to 44th streets, and along this stretch various groups congregate in specific areas. **Lummus Park,** the stretch of beach opposite the Art Deco District, between 5th and 15th streets, attracts all ages, with volleyball courts, in-line skating along an paved upland path, and children's playgrounds. Gays frequent the beach between 11th and 13th streets. Sidewalk cafés parallel the entire beach area. **North Beach,** along Ocean Terrace between 72nd and 75th streets, is more serene.

Two of metropolitan Miami's best beaches are on Key Biscayne. Nearest the causeway is the 3½-mi county beach in **Crandon Park** (✉ 4000 Crandon Blvd., ☎ 305/361–5421). **Bill Baggs Cape Florida State Recreation Area** (✉ 1200 S. Crandon Blvd., ☎ 305/361–5811) has beaches, boardwalks, and nature trails.

Shopping

Malls, an international free zone, and specialty shopping districts are the attractions in Miami. Many shopping areas have an ethnic flavor.

Shopping Districts

More than 500 garment manufacturers sell their clothing in more than 30 factory outlets and discount fashion stores in the **Fashion District,** east of I–95 along 5th Avenue from 25th to 29th streets. Most stores in the district are open from Monday through Saturday 9–5. The **Miami Free Zone** (✉ 2305 N.W. 107th Ave., ☎ 305/591–4300) is a vast international wholesale trade center where you can buy goods duty-free for export, or pay duty on goods released for domestic use. More than 140 companies sell products from more than 100 countries, including clothing, computers, cosmetics, electronics, liquor, and perfumes. At **Cauley Square** (✉ 22400 Old Dixie Hwy., Goulds, ☎ 305/258–3543)—a complex of clapboard, coral-rock, and stucco buildings that housed railroad workers at the turn of the century—shops primarily sell antiques and crafts. To get there, exit U.S. 1 at S.W. 224th Street; it's usually closed on Sunday.

WALT DISNEY WORLD® AND THE ORLANDO AREA

Once upon a time about the only things to see in Orlando were Walt Disney World and Mickey Mouse. Today, however, cosmopolitan Orlando is an international business center and tourist mecca. Many other attractions, interesting shopping areas, and a varied nightlife make the area an exciting, if sometimes frenetic and crowded, vacation destination. Away from the tourist areas, hundreds of spring-fed lakes surrounded by oak trees recall Orlando's bucolic past. About an hour's drive from the city, on the Atlantic coast, are the Cocoa Beach area and the Kennedy Space Center, Spaceport USA.

Visitor Information

Kissimmee/St. Cloud: Convention and Visitors Bureau (✉ 1925 E. Irlo Bronson Memorial Hwy., Kissimmee 34744, ☎ 407/363–5800, 407/847–5000, or 800/327–9159). **Orlando/Orange County:** Convention and Visitors Bureau (✉ 8445 International Dr., Orlando 32819, ☎ 407/363–5871).

Arriving and Departing

By Bus

Greyhound Lines (☎ 800/231–2222) provides service from major Florida cities and from outside the state.

By Car

From Jacksonville take I–95 south, then I–4 from Port Orange. From Tampa/St. Petersburg take I–4 east. From Miami take I–95 north and connect with Florida's Turnpike going northbound at White City. From Atlanta take I–75 south and connect with Florida's Turnpike.

By Plane

Orlando International Airport (✉ 6086 McCoy Rd., off the Bee Line Expressway, ☎ 407/825–2000) is served by major U.S. airlines as well as many foreign airlines.

By Train

Amtrak (☎ 800/872–7245) operates the *Silver Star* and the *Silver Meteor* to Florida. Both stop at Winter Park, Orlando, and Kissimmee.

Exploring Walt Disney World and the Orlando Area

Walt Disney World

★ The focal point of an Orlando vacation is **Walt Disney World** (✉ Box 10040, Lake Buena Vista 32830, ☎ 407/824–4321), a collection of theme parks and attractions connected by extensive bus, monorail, motor-launch, and ferry systems (free if you stay at an on-site resort or if you hold a four-park ticket). Admission is not cheap: A one-day adult ticket costs $44.52; a child's ticket is $36.04 (at press time, fall 1998) and admits you to only one of the parks: Magic Kingdom, Epcot, Disney-MGM, or Disney's Animal Kingdom. Your best bet, even if you plan to stay only two or three days, may be to purchase a Four-Day Value Pass ($157.94 adults, $126.14 children) or a Five-Day Park Hopper ($200.34 adults, $160.06 children); both admit you to all four major parks and include unlimited use of Disney transport. For longer stays, there are also a Six-Day All-in-One Hopper ($263.94 adults, $210.94 children) and a seven-day pass ($290.44 adults, $232.14 children).

THE MAGIC KINGDOM

The Magic Kingdom is divided into seven lands. To do the Kingdom justice, try to visit all (or at least most of) the lands. For a great overview, hop aboard the **Walt Disney World Railroad** and take a 1½-mi ride around the perimeter of the park. You can board at the Victorian-style station by the park entrance. Other stations are in Frontierland and at Mickey's Toontown Fair, on the border between Tomorrowland and Fantasyland.

Sprawling before you when you enter the Magic Kingdom is **Main Street**—a shop-filled boulevard with Victorian-style stores and restaurants. Stop at City Hall (on your left as you enter) to get information or to snap a picture with the Disney characters who make their rounds.

A cinema that runs vintage Disney cartoons is another attraction here. If you walk two blocks along Main Street, you'll enter Central Plaza, with Cinderella Castle rising directly in front of you. This is the hub of the Kingdom; all the lands radiate from it.

Adventureland is a mishmash of tropical and swashbuckling attractions that are among the most crowded in the Magic Kingdom. Visit as late in the afternoon as possible or, better yet, in the evening. The **Swiss Family Robinson Treehouse** is a good way to get both exercise and a panoramic view of the park. Visitors walk single file up the many-staired tree, a trip that can take up to a half hour. The **Jungle Cruise** takes visitors along the Nile, the Mekong, the Congo, and the Amazon rivers. The tour guide's narration is corny but worth a laugh. **Pirates of the Caribbean** is a journey through a world of pirate strongholds and treasure-filled dungeons. The audio-animatronic pirates are first-rate.

Frontierland's major draw is **Big Thunder Mountain Railroad**, a scream-inducing roller coaster. Children must be at least 3 ft, 4 inches. Try to go in the evening when the mountain is lighted up and lines are relatively short. **Splash Mountain**, an elaborate water-flume ride, is based on Disney's 1946 film *Song of the South*. The ride includes characters from the movie, and you'll hear some of the songs as well. An eight-person hollowed-out log takes you on a half-mile journey that passes through Brer Rabbit's habitat. The final plunge is down Chickapin Hill—the world's longest and sharpest flume drop—at speeds of up to 40 mph.

Liberty Square is a journey back to Colonial America. The **Hall of Presidents** is a 30-minute multimedia tribute to the Constitution and the nation's 42 presidents. The star attraction here is Disney's special-effects extravaganza, the **Haunted Mansion**. Scary but not terrifying, this ride on a "doom buggie" takes you past a plethora of dust, cobwebs, tombstones, and creepy characters.

Fantasyland is, as the map says, "where storybook dreams come true." Fanciful gingerbread houses, gleaming gold turrets, and streams sparkling with shiny pennies dot the landscape, and its rides are based on Disney's animated movies. The first attraction on the left as you enter Fantasyland is **Legend of the Lion King.** Unlike many other stage shows in the Magic Kingdom, this one showcases not humans but "humanimals," Disneyspeak for bigger-than-life-size figures manipulated by human "animateers" hidden from audience view (the adult Simba, for example, is nearly 8 ft tall). The preshow consists of the "Circle of Life" overture from the film. Other attractions include the rides **Dumbo the Flying Elephant, Peter Pan's Flight,** a much-improved **Snow White's Adventures,** and the **Mad Tea Party.** Kids of all ages love the antique **Cinderella's Golden Carousel.** Small children adore **It's a Small World,** a boat ride accompanied by its now-famous theme song of international brotherhood.

Mickey's Toontown Fair was built in 1988 in a quiet niche of Fantasyland to celebrate Mickey Mouse's 60th birthday. Now an official Magic Kingdom land, it is filled with all manner of things child size. Kids can visit **Mickey and Minnie's country houses, Goofy's Wiseacres Farm,** and **Toon Park,** a spongy green meadow filled with foam topiary in the shapes of goats, cows, pigs, and horses. This is a good opportunity for weary parents to rest their feet while children run around.

The new **Tomorrowland** made its long-awaited debut in 1995. **Space Mountain** is still here, and the needlelike spires of this space-age roller coaster are a Magic Kingdom landmark. Although the ride's speed never exceeds 28 mph, the experience in the dark, with everyone screaming, is thrilling, even for hard-core roller coaster fans. To see the interior without taking the ride, hop aboard the **Tomorrowland Transit Authority (TTA).** Despite a disappointing lack of truly special effects, **Alien Encounters** provides an eerie experience with another world.

EPCOT

Visitors familiar with the Magic Kingdom find something entirely different at Epcot, which, paradoxically, is an educational theme park, and a very successful one at that.

Future World consists of two concentric circles of pavilions. In the inner core are the **Spaceship Earth** geosphere—the giant, golf-ball-shape Epcot icon whose ride explores the development of human communication—and just beyond it, the Innoventions exhibit and Innoventions Plaza. Making up the circle's outer ring are seven corporate-sponsored pavilions containing rides and interactive displays on topics such as technology, motion, the seas, the land, and imagination.

The 40-acre **World Showcase Lagoon** is 1⅓ mi around, but in that space you can circumnavigate the globe—or at least explore it. Eleven pavilions present a Disney version of life in various countries with food, entertainment, and wares. Models of some of the world's best-known monuments, such as the Eiffel Tower, a Mayan temple, and a majestic Japanese pagoda, are painstakingly re-created. During the day these structures are impressive enough, but at night when the darkness inhibits one's ability to judge their size, you feel as though you are seeing the real thing.

Except for the boat rides in Mexico and Norway, the Showcase has no amusement-park-type rides. Instead, it has breathtaking films, ethnic art, cultural entertainment, audio-animatronic presentations, and dozens of fine shops and restaurants featuring national specialties. The most enjoyable diversions in World Showcase are not inside the national pavilions but in front of them: Throughout the day each pavilion offers some sort of live street show featuring comedy, song, or dance routines and demonstrations of folk arts and crafts.

DISNEY-MGM STUDIOS THEME PARK

The **Studios Backlot Tour,** a combination tram ride and walking tour, takes you on a 60-minute tour of the back-lot building blocks of movies: set design, costumes, props, lighting, and special effects—at the Catastrophe Canyon, in which your tram starts bouncing up and down in a simulated earthquake, an oil tanker explodes in gobs of smoke and flame, and a water tower crashes to the ground, touching off a flash flood.

One of the funniest attractions at the theme park is the **Magic of Disney Animation,** a 30-minute self-guided tour that takes visitors step by step through the Disney animation process by looking over the artists' shoulders from a raised, glass-enclosed walkway. The **Walt Disney Theater** usually runs *The Making of . . .*, a behind-the-scenes look at Disney's latest smash hit. Produced for the Disney Channel, programs have included *The Lion King, Toy Story,* and *The Hunchback of Notre Dame.*

The **Indiana Jones Epic Stunt Spectacular,** presented in a 2,200-seat amphitheater, is a 30-minute show featuring the stunt choreography of veteran coordinator Glenn Randall (*Raiders of the Lost Ark, Indiana Jones and the Temple of Doom, E.T.,* and *Jewel of the Nile* are among his credits).

Star Tours is a flight-simulator thrill ride. Created under the direction of George Lucas, the five 40-seat theaters become spaceships, and you're off to the moon of Endor. At the 13-story **Twilight Zone Tower of Terror,** reputedly the now-abandoned Hollywood Tower Hotel, you board a giant elevator and head upward past seemingly deserted hallways. Suddenly, the creaking vehicle plunges in a terrifying 130-ft free-fall drop, and then it does it all over again! The ride is for older children and adults.

ANIMAL KINGDOM

Walt Disney World's fourth major theme park opened in April 1998. Here, lifelike experiences with fictional animals and dinosaurs combine with high-adventure encounters with real exotic animals. Sprawling over 500 acres, the park resembles the animal reserves of Africa and Asia and serves as a habitat for more than 1,000 animals, including rare and endangered species.

Enter the Animal Kingdom and buy tickets at **The Oasis,** a cool green grotto filled with waterfalls and gardens alive with exotic birds, reptiles, and animals. **Safari Village,** the centerpoint of the park, and home of the **Tree of Life,** which serves as the park's great icon, like the Castle does in the Magic Kingdom. Its trunk is carved with a tapestry of more than 300 animal forms, and demonstrates mankind's respect for nature. Beneath the tree roots is a theater for **"It's Tough to be a Bug!"**, a humorous 3-D film and special effects show starring various insects. Bridges lead across **Discovery Row** to the other lands. Along the way, visitors can preview what's ahead: perhaps a hungry dinosaur at feeding time, or a fire-breathing dragon's lair.

The largest of Disney's Animal Kingdom is **Africa.** It starts in the village of **Harambe,** featuring the architecture of an East African port city on the northern banks of the Discovery River. At the giant baobab tree guests board their Jeeps for the exciting **Kilmanjaro Safaris,** where herds of wild animals roam freely among the trees, lakes, and grasslands of Africa. Passengers bounce over rutted roads, fording through pools of hippos and past great herds of wild animals. At the end of the 2-mi trip, visitors can follow **Gorilla Falls Exploration Trail** into a world of streams and waterfalls. Gorilla Falls is home to a troop of endangered lowland gorillas. Guests also see hippos, meerkats, and warthogs along the shady walking trail.

By **Wildlife Express** steam train, guests journey to **Conservation Station** to investigate the worldwide efforts to save endangered animals and preserve wild habitats. Here you can experience interactive displays and take a backstage look at how the park's animals are kept happy and healthy. At the **Affection Station,** you can observe and touch small animals; Disney educators are on hand to help you find information on ways to connect with conservation efforts in their own communities.

Another major land of animal wonders, **Asia,** was scheduled to open by early 1999. This area is devoted to the wild creatures and rain forests of southern Asia. The main attraction is a thrilling white-water rafting journey, **Tiger Rapids Run:** a hike through dense jungles past the ancient villages of Southeast Asia.

Between Africa and Asia is the Caravan Stage, where an outdoor show area presents **Wonders of Flight,** spectacular demonstrations by falcons, hawks, and other rare and fascinating birds.

In **DinoLand U.S.A.,** guests explore a simulated paleontological dig, complete with scaffolding, excavations, dinosaur skeletons, and fascinating "fossils." Enormous "bones" serve as a play space for youngsters who can climb, crawl, and slide among the well-preserved skeletons of Triceratops and Tyrannosaurus Rex. Nearby is a primeval forest, **Cretaceous Trail,** which gives walkers a visit with some of the survivors of the dinosaur age. Dinosaurs are brought back to life in the most thrilling of all the new adventures, **Countdown to Extinction.** Aboard time-traveling vehicles, passengers are whisked back 65 million years on a journey to save the last dinosaur from extinction when the crash of a fiery asteroid threatens everything in sight. At the 1,500-seat outdoor Theater in the Wild, a live musical performance of **Journey into the Jungle Book,** featuring Baloo, King Louie, and other stars from the film classic, is shown daily.

Across the river from Safari Village is **Camp Minnie-Mickey,** a meet-and-greet character location. Stars from many Disney favorites such as *The Jungle Book* and *Winnie the Pooh* sign autographs and pose for pictures. An outdoor theater-in-the-round hosts daily performances of *The Festival of the Lion King* and *Colors of the Wind,* in which Pocahontas introduces live animal performers.

OTHER ATTRACTIONS

Blizzard Beach (🎫 $27.51) promises the seemingly impossible—a seaside playground with an alpine theme. **Discovery Island** (🎫 $12.67) is a nature sanctuary with bird shows; admission is **River Country** (🎫 $16.91), the first of Walt Disney World's water parks, is a rustic and rugged swimming hole. **Typhoon Lagoon** (🎫 $26.45), four times the size of River Country, contains everything from an artificial coral reef with tropical fish (closed in winter) to a lazy river that circles the entire park.

The Orlando Area

Universal Studios Florida is the largest working film studio outside Hollywood. Visitors view live shows, participate in movie-themed attractions, and tour back-lot sets. The tour showcases the special-effects magic of creative consultant Steven Spielberg and the animation wizardry of Hanna-Barbera. Universal Studio's Islands of Adventure, set to open in summer 1999, will be a fun place for the young and young-at-heart. It will be the permanent home to the world's most beloved characters, including *The Cat In The Hat, Spider-Man, Popeye, The Incredible Hulk, Sinbad,* and the dinosaurs of *Jurassic Park.* ✉ *1000 Universal Studios Plaza (Exit 30A off I–4), Orlando,* ☎ *407/363–8000.* 🎫 *$39.75 adults, $32 children 3–9.*

Performing dolphins, killer whales, and a walk-through Plexiglas tunnel that lets you view sharks and barracudas capture your attention at **Sea World.** The park also has penguins, tropical fish, manatees, seals and sea lions, and other educational diversions. Take Exit 28 off I–4 and follow signs. ✉ *7007 Sea Harbor Dr., Orlando,* ☎ *407/351–3600.* 🎫 *$40.95 adults, $33.90 children 3–9.*

The **Orlando Science Center** moved in 1997 to a new 193,000-square-ft building with themed display halls and interactive exhibits. ✉ *777 E. Princeton St.,* ☎ *407/514–2000.* 🎫 *$9.50–$14.25, depending on programs selected.*

Cypress Gardens is a land of exotic gardens, with bird shows and a famous waterskiing revue. Take I–4 to the U.S. 27S exit and follow signs. ✉ *Off Rte. 540 east of Winter Haven,* ☎ *941/324–2111 or 800/237–4826.* 🎫 *$29.95.*

A big hit with children is **Gatorland,** where visitors can see thousands of alligators, crocodiles, and other Florida wildlife. ✉ *14501 S. Orange Blossom Trail, between Orlando and Kissimmee,* ☎ *407/855–5496 or 800/393–5297.* 🎫 *$16.95.*

Splendid China—12 mi southwest of Orlando—is a theme park with more than 60 scaled-down replicas of China's greatest landmarks.

Orlando Area

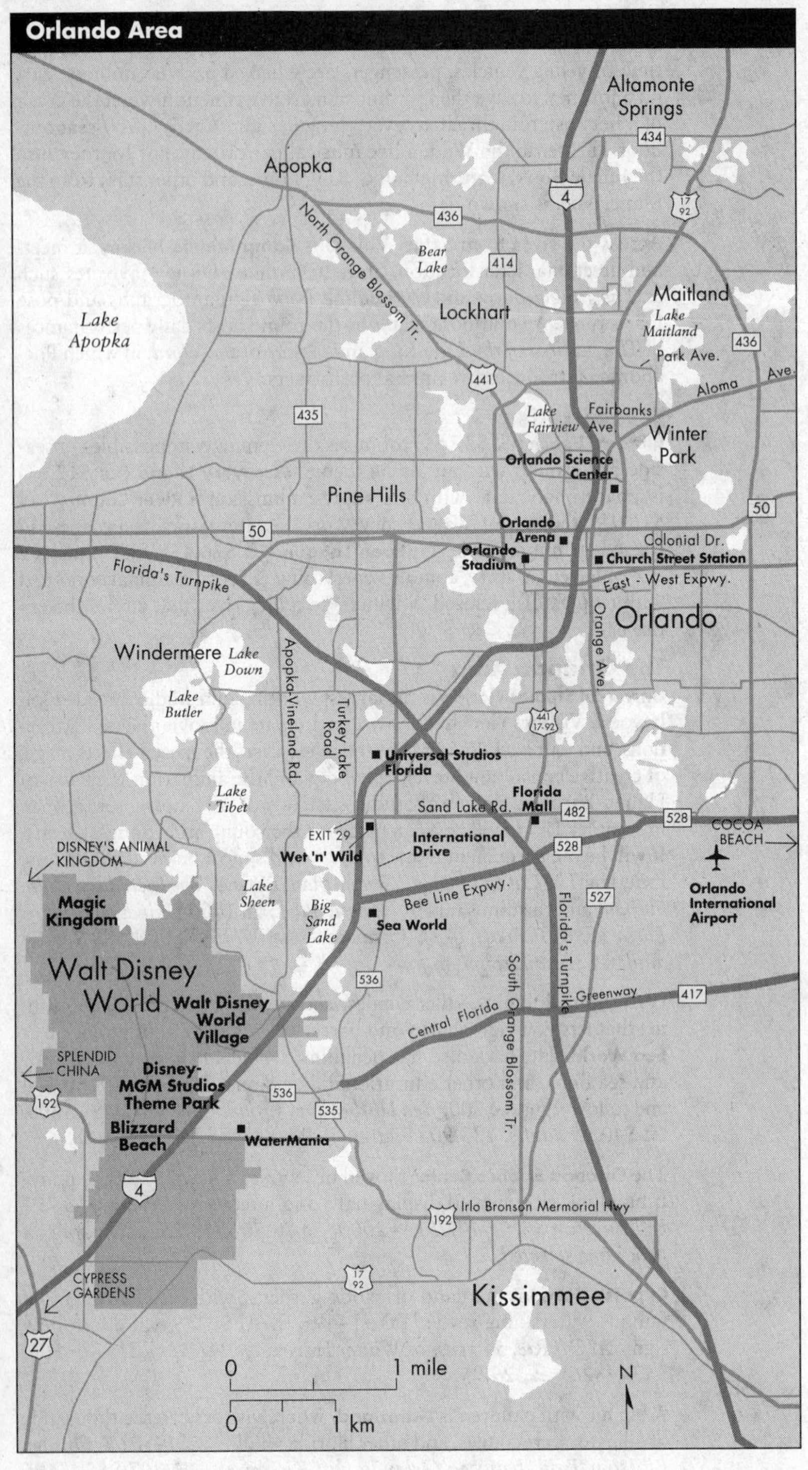
Altamonte Springs
434
Apopka
4
17 92
436
North Orange Blossom Tr.
Bear Lake
414
Maitland
Lake Maitland
436
Lake Apopka
Lockhart
Park Ave.
441
Aloma Ave.
435
Lake Fairview
Fairbanks Ave.
Winter Park
Orlando Science Center
Pine Hills
50
50
Orlando Arena
Colonial Dr.
Orlando Stadium
Church Street Station
Florida's Turnpike
East - West Expwy.
Orlando
Orange Ave.
Windermere
Lake Down
Lake Butler
Apopka-Vineland Rd.
Turkey Lake Road
441 17-92
Universal Studios Florida
Lake Tibet
Florida Mall
Sand Lake Rd.
482
528
COCOA BEACH
DISNEY'S ANIMAL KINGDOM
EXIT 29
Wet 'n' Wild
International Drive
528
Orlando International Airport
Lake Sheen
Magic Kingdom
Bee Line Expwy.
Big Sand Lake
Sea World
527
Florida's Turnpike
Walt Disney World
Walt Disney World Village
536
South Orange Blossom Tr.
Greenway
417
Central Florida
SPLENDID CHINA
Disney-MGM Studios Theme Park
192
536
535
Blizzard Beach
WaterMania
4
Irlo Bronson Memorial Hwy
192
CYPRESS GARDENS
17 92
Kissimmee
27
0
1 mile
0
1 km
N

Among the painstakingly crafted models are the Great Wall, the Imperial Palace of Beijing's Forbidden City, and Suzhou Gardens, a re-creation of a 14th-century Chinese village. ✉ *3000 Splendid China Blvd., Kissimmee,* ☎ *407/397–8800 or 800/244–6226.* *$28.88.*

★ In the Cocoa Beach area, 47 mi east of Orlando via Route 50 or the Bee Line Expressway, is the **Kennedy Space Center Visitor Complex.** You can see it on two narrated bus tours: One passes by some of NASA's office and assembly buildings, including current launch facilities and the space shuttle launching and landing sites. The other goes to Cape Canaveral Air Force Station, where early launch pads and unmanned rockets that were later adapted for manned use illuminate the history of the early space program. Even more dramatic is the IMAX film *The Dream Is Alive,* shown hourly in the Galaxy Theater. ✉ *Rte. 405, Kennedy Space Center,* ☎ *407/452–2121 or 800/572–4636.* *Free, bus tours $8, IMAX film $5.* ⏲ *Daily 9–sunset, last tour 2 hrs before dark; closed certain launch dates (call ahead).*

Dining and Lodging

Even dining is an adventure in the Orlando area, where international cuisines, fresh fish and seafood, and such exotic local dishes as grilled alligator tail are all on hand. Besides hotels in Walt Disney World, you'll find accommodations in Orlando; Kissimmee, just east of Walt Disney World; and other outlying towns. Lodging options include luxury hotels and resorts, family resorts, and motel chains. For price ranges *see* Charts 1 (B) and 2 (A) *in* On the Road with Fodor's.

Cocoa Beach

$$$$ ✕ **Mango Tree Restaurant.** Dine in elegance amid orchid gardens, with piano music playing in the background. Broiled grouper topped with scallops, shrimp, and hollandaise sauce is a favorite. ✉ *118 N. Atlantic Ave.,* ☎ *407/799–0513. AE, MC, V. Closed Mon. No lunch.*

$$–$$$ **Inn at Cocoa Beach.** The spacious rooms in this charming oceanfront inn are each unique, but all have some combination of reproduction 18th- and 19th-century armoires, and four-poster beds, plus balconies or patios with ocean views. Wine and cheese are served every evening. ✉ *4300 Ocean Beach Blvd., 32931,* ☎ *407/799–3460 or 800/343–5307 outside FL,* FAX *407/784–8632. 50 rooms. Pool. CP. AE, D, DC, MC, V.*

Kissimmee

$ **Sevilla Inn.** One of the best buys in the Orlando area, this motel has stucco and wood on the outside and up-to-date rooms inside. The tropically landscaped pool area looks like something you'd find at a much fancier resort. ✉ *4640 W. Irlo Bronson Memorial Hwy., 34746,* ☎ *407/396–4135 or 800/367–1363,* FAX *407/396–4942. 46 rooms. Pool. AE, D, MC, V.*

Lake Wales

$$$$ ✕ **Chalet Suzanne.** Expanded bit by quirky bit since it opened in the 1930s, this unlikely inn looks like a small Swiss village smack in the middle of orange groves. The menu is equally anachronistic: shrimp curry, broiled grapefruit, and crepes Suzanne. This makes a good place to stop after a visit to Cypress Gardens. ✉ *3800 Chalet Suzanne Dr.,* ☎ *941/676–6011. AE, DC, MC, V. Closed Mon. in summer.*

Orlando

$$$–$$$$ ★ ✕ **Chatham's Place.** The office exterior belies what's inside—a small, unpretentious restaurant that is one of Orlando's finest. You might find black grouper with pecan butter and grilled duck breast on the menu. ✉ *7575 Dr. Phillips Blvd.,* ☎ *407/345–2992. AE, D, DC, MC, V.*

$$$$ ★ **Peabody Orlando.** The bland facade gives no hint of this 27-story hotel's beautifully decorated interior, with marble floors, fountains, and modern art. Many rooms have views of Walt Disney World, but the real show is watching the Peabody's ducks waddle their way to the marble fountain, where they pass the day. ✉ *9801 International Dr., 32819,* ☎ *407/352–4000 or 800/732–2639,* FAX *407/351–9177. 891 rooms. 3 restaurants, pool, tennis, health club. AE, D, DC, MC, V.*

$$$ **Grosvenor Resort.** This colonial-style hotel, with comfortable rooms, plentiful amenities and recreational facilities, and spacious public areas, is one of the best deals in the area. ✉ *1850 Hotel Plaza Blvd., Lake Buena Vista 32830,* ☎ *407/828–4444 or 800/624–4109,* FAX *407/828–8192. 633 rooms. 2 restaurants, pools, tennis. AE, DC, MC, V.*

Walt Disney World

For restaurants within Walt Disney World, reservations are especially easy to make, thanks to the park's central reservations lines, 407/939–3463 and 407/560–7277. In addition, Epcot's WorldKey Information Center, a helpful reservations kiosk (you must show up in person), can be used for the very popular restaurants of Epcot. Reserve early in the day before beginning your sightseeing.

World Showcase, in Epcot, offers some of the best dining in the Orlando area, with specialties from various nations that will appeal to every taste. **L'Originale Alfredo di Roma Ristorante** ($$$$) in Italy of course, is known for its namesake dish, fettuccine Alfredo, served by singing waiters. **Marrakesh** ($$$–$$$$) delights the palate with fare that's more exotic to most American palates, such as Moroccan couscous.The **Rose and Crown** pub ($$$–$$$$), in the United Kingdom, serves hearty portions of fish-and-chips with a Guinness stout.

Although hotels and resorts on Disney property cost more than comparable facilities elsewhere, there are many perks to staying at one of them, including unlimited free transportation to all of Walt Disney World parks. Book all Disney hotels—including the following—through **Walt Disney World Central Reservations** (☎ 407/934–7639).

$$$$ ★ **Grand Floridian.** With its brick chimneys, gabled roof, sweeping verandas, and stained-glass domes, this resort exudes Victorian charm but has all the conveniences of a modern hotel. Water sports are a focal point at the marina. ☎ *407/824–3000,* FAX *407/824–3186. 990 rooms. 6 restaurants, pool, tennis, health club. AE, MC, V.*

$$ **Caribbean Beach Resort.** On a 42-acre tropical lake, this resort has several villages named after Caribbean islands, each with its own pool, but all share a white-sand beach. Facilities include a food court, a tropical lounge, and an island in the lagoon with bike paths, trails, and play areas. ☎ *407/934–3400,* FAX *407/934–3288. 2,112 rooms. Restaurant, pools. AE, MC, V.*

Motels

U.S. 192 is crammed with motels convenient to Walt Disney World. Rates range from inexpensive to moderate, and most have a pool but few other extras. Among these are **Best Western, Quality Suites,** and **Residence Inn** (☞ Toll-Free Numbers *in* the Gold Guide).

Campgrounds

Fort Wilderness Campground Resort (✉ Walt Disney World Central Reservations; ☞ Walt Disney World, *above*) encompasses 700 acres of forests, streams, and small lakes within Walt Disney World. You can rent a trailer or bring your own to campsites equipped with electrical outlets, outdoor grills, running water, and waste disposal. Tent sites with water and electricity are also available.

Nightlife and the Arts

Nightlife

Inside Walt Disney World every hotel has its quota of bars and lounges. Nightly shows include the laser show **IllumiNations** at Epcot and the **Polynesian Luau** at the Polynesian Resort (☎ 407/934–7639). **Pleasure Island** has seven clubs, a few restaurants, shops, and a 10-screen AMC cinema. In Orlando **Church Street Station** (✉ 129 W. Church St., ☎ 407/422–2434) is an entertainment complex in an authentic 19th-century setting. **Medieval Times** (✉ 4510 W. Irlo Bronson Memorial Hwy., Kissimmee, ☎ 407/239–0214 or 800/229–8300) has a dinner show with knights, nobles, and maidens.

The Arts

Carr Performing Arts Centre (✉ 401 W. Livingston St., Orlando, ☎ 407/849–2020) routinely features dance, music, and theater performances. **Orange County Convention and Civic Center** (✉ South end of International Dr., Orlando, ☎ 407/345–9800) presents big-name performers. The **Civic Theater of Central Florida** (✉ 1001 E. Princeton St., Orlando, ☎ 407/896–7365) presents a variety of shows.

Outdoor Activities and Sports

Biking

City-constructed bike paths traverse the Orlando area; there are also a few places suitable for cycling in the Winter Park area. Serious cyclists head to the rolling hills of nearby Lake County.

Golf

Cypress Creek Country Club (✉ 5353 Vineland Rd., Orlando, ☎ 407/351–2187) is a demanding 18-hole course with 16 water holes and lots of trees. **Grenelefe Golf & Tennis Resort** (✉ 3200 Rte. 546, Haines City, ☎ 941/422–7511 or 800/237–9549) has three excellent 18-hole courses, of which the toughest is the 7,325-yard West Course. **Timacuan Golf & Country Club** (✉ 550 Timacuan Blvd., Lake Mary, ☎ 407/321–0010) has a front nine that's open, with lots of sand, and a back nine that's heavily wooded. There are five championship courses within **Walt Disney World.**

Horseback Riding

Fort Wilderness Campground (✉ Walt Disney World, ☎ 407/824–2832) offers tame trail rides through backwoods.

Spectator Sports

Basketball: The NBA **Orlando Magic** (☎ 407/839–3900) play in Orlando Arena (✉ 600 W. Amelia St., 2 blocks west of I–4 Amelia St. exit, Orlando).

Beaches and Water Sports

A plethora of water sports is available in the Orlando area. Marinas at resorts in **Walt Disney World** rent all types of boats, from canoes and catamarans to pedal boats. Just north of the Kennedy Space Center, the **Canaveral National Seashore** (✉ 7611 S. Atlantic Ave, between New Smyrna Beach and Titusville, ☎ 904/428–3384) has 24 mi of unspoiled, uncrowded beaches with facilities for swimming and boating.

Shopping

Florida Mall (✉ 8001 S. Orange Blossom Trail, 4½ mi east of I–4 and International Dr., Orlando) is the largest mall in central Florida, with department stores, 200 specialty shops, seven theaters, and one of the area's better food courts. The festive **Mercado Mediterranean Village**

(✉ 8445 International Dr., Orlando) has specialty shops and a large food court with cuisines from around the world. **Renninger's Twin Markets,** near the charming village of Mount Dora (30 mi northwest of Orlando on U.S. 441) hosts hundreds of flea market and antiques dealers every weekend. The really big shows takes place the third weekends of November, January, and February, when some 1,400 antiques dealers converge. **Belz Factory Outlet World** (✉ 5401 W. Oak Ridge Rd., northern tip of International Dr., ☎ 406/354–0126) is the area's largest collection of outlet stores—more than 180, in two malls and four nearby annexes. **Pointe Orlando** (✉ 9101 International Dr., Orlando, ☎ 407/248–2838) is the latest arrival to the I-Drive, as International Drive is known to locals, and is home to 70 specialty shops.

THE FLORIDA KEYS

The string of 31 islands—or keys—placed like a comma between the Atlantic Ocean and the Gulf of Mexico, at the southern tip of Florida, presents a paradox to the visitor. On the one hand, the Keys are natural wonders of lush vegetation, tropical birds, and wildlife, washed by waters teeming with more than 600 kinds of fish; a place where swimming, fishing, and boating are a way of life. On the other hand, the Keys are a highly commercialized tourist attraction that has brought a clutter of unsightly billboards, motels, and shopping malls to U.S. 1 (also known as the Overseas Highway), which links the islands to the mainland. Although the 110-mi drive from Key Largo to Key West is often clogged with traffic on weekends and holidays, it is still a mesmerizing journey into expanses of blue water and blue sky, especially where the road is the only thing separating the ocean from the Gulf. A note about addresses, which are listed by island or mile marker (MM) number: Residents use the abbreviation BS for the Bay Side of the Overseas Highway (U.S. 1) and OS for the Atlantic Ocean side of the highway.

Visitor Information

Florida Keys & Key West: Visitors Bureau (✉ 402 Wall St., 33040, ☎ 800/352–5397). **Greater Key West:** Chamber of Commerce (✉ 402 Wall St., 33040, ☎ 305/294–2587 or 800/527–8539, FAX 305/294–7806). **Islamorada:** Chamber of Commerce (✉ MM 82.5, BS, Box 915, 33036, ☎ 305/664–4503 or 800/322–5397). **Key Largo:** Chamber of Commerce (✉ MM 106, BS, 106000 Overseas Hwy., 33037, ☎ 305/451–1414 or 800/822–1088). **Key West:** Business Guild (oriented toward gays and lesbians) (✉ Box 1208, 33041, ☎ 305/294–4603 or 800/535–7797). **Lower Keys:** Chamber of Commerce (✉ MM 31, OS, Box 430511, Big Pine Key 33043, ☎ 305/872–2411 or 800/872–3722, FAX 305/872–0752). **Marathon:** Chamber of Commerce & Visitor Center (✉ MM 53.5, BS, 12222 Overseas Hwy., 33050, ☎ 305/743–5417 or 800/842–9580).

Arriving and Departing

By Boat

You can travel to Key West via the Intracoastal Waterway through Florida Bay or in Hawk Channel along the Atlantic coast. Marinas abound in the Keys, but be sure to make docking reservations in advance. For more information contact the **Florida Marine Patrol** (✉ MM 48, BS, 2796 Overseas Hwy., Suite 100, State Regional Service Center, Marathon 33050, ☎ 305/289–2320).

By Bus

Greyhound Lines (☎ 800/231–2222) departs Miami International Airport (from Concourse E, Lower Level) for the Keys four times a day, stopping at Key Largo, Tavernier Islamorada, Layton, Marathon, Big Pine Key, Ramrod Key, Cudjoe Key, Sugarloaf Shores, and Key West.

By Car

From Miami take Florida's Turnpike (toll road) or State Highway 826/874 to the Homestead Extension of Florida's Turnpike south until it links with U.S. 1 in Florida City. Just south of here U.S. 1 becomes the Overseas Highway.

By Plane

Continuous improvements in service now link airports in Miami, Fort Lauderdale/Hollywood, Naples, Orlando, and Tampa directly with **Key West International Airport** (✉ S. Roosevelt Blvd., ☎ 305/296–5439). Service is provided by **American Eagle** (☎ 800/433–7300), **Cape Air** (☎ 800/352–0714), **Comair/Delta Connection** (☎ 800/354–9822), **Gulfstream International Airlines** (☎ 800/992–8532), and **US Airways/US Airways Express** (☎ 800/428–4322). Direct service between Miami and **Marathon** (✉ MM 52, BS, 9000 Overseas Hwy., ☎ 305/743–2155) is provided by American Eagle. US Airways Express connects Marathon with Tampa.

Exploring the Florida Keys

The Keys are divided into the Upper Keys (from Key Largo to Long Key Channel), the Middle Keys (from Long Key Channel to Seven Mile Bridge), and the Lower Keys (from Seven Mile Bridge to Key West). Pause to explore the flora and fauna of the backcountry and the fragile reefs and aquatic life of the surrounding waters as you weave your way south to historically rich Key West.

Upper Keys

The Upper Keys are dominated by **Key Largo,** with its wildlife refuges and nature parks. The 2,005-acre **Key Largo Hammocks State Botanical Site** (✉ 1 mi north of U.S. 1 on Rte. 905, OS, ☎ 305/451–1202; 🎫 free) is the largest remaining stand of West Indian tropical hardwood hammock and mangrove wetland in the Keys. **John Pennekamp Coral Reef State Park** (✉ MM 102.5, OS, Box 487, 102601 Overseas Hwy., ☎ 305/451–1202; 🎫 $3 per vehicle; $2 for walk-ins and cyclists) encompasses 78 square mi of coral reefs, which contain 40 species of coral and more than 650 varieties of fish. Diving and snorkeling here are exceptional. A concessionaire rents canoes and sailboats and offers boat trips to the reef.

The small **Maritime Museum of the Florida Keys** (✉ MM 102.5, BS, Key Largo, ☎ 305/451–6444; 🎫 $5) has exhibits depicting the history of shipwrecks and salvage efforts along the Keys, including retrieved treasures, reconstructed wreck sites, and artifacts in various stages of preservation.

Get a close-up look at bird life at the **Florida Keys Wild Bird Rehabilitation Center** (✉ MM 93.6, BS, 93600 Overseas Hwy., Tavernier, ☎ 305/852–4486; 🎫 free), where at any time the resident population can include ospreys, hawks, pelicans, cormorants, terns, and herons. **Theater of the Sea** (✉ MM 84.5, OS, Islamorada, ☎ 305/664–2431; 🎫 $15.75) has dolphin and sea lion shows, a touch tank, a pool where sharks are fed by a trainer, and several small aquariums. For $85, you can swim with the dolphins (reservations required). At **Robbie's Marina** (✉ MM 77.5, BS, Islamorada, ☎ 305/664–9814; 🎫 dock access $1), 50 or so tarpon—some as long as 5 ft—gather below the docks, waiting to be fed. The following two sites are available only by boat; you can take a ferry (🎫 $15 for one site, $25 for both) or rent a boat or kayak from the official state concessionaire, **Robbie's Marina** (☞

above). **Indian Key State Historic Site** (✉ MM 78.5, OS, Islamorada 33036, ☎ 305/664–4815; 🎫 tour $1, free if you arrive by ferry), inhabited by Indians for several thousand years before Europeans arrived, was also a base for early 19th-century shipwreck salvagers until an Indian attack wiped out the settlement in 1840. A virgin hardwood forest still cloaks **Lignumvitae Key State Botanical Site,** punctuated only by the house and gardens built by chemical magnate William Matheson in 1919 (🎫 tour $1, free if you arrive by ferry). For information and reservations (suggested for both sites) contact **Long Key State Recreation Area** (✉ MM 67.5, OS, Box 776, Long Key 33001, ☎ 305/664–4815; 🎫 $3.25 for 1 person, plus 50¢ per each additional person; canoe rental $4 per hour).

The Middle Keys

Once you cross **Long Key Viaduct** (MM 65), one of 42 bridges in the island chain, the Keys become more rustic. The second-longest bridge on the former rail line (known informally as the Overseas Railroad), this 2-mi-long structure has 222 reinforced-concrete arches. The nonprofit **Dolphin Research Center** (✉ MM 59, BS, ☎ 305/289–1121; 🎫 $12.50, DolphInsight $75, Dolphin Encounter $90) runs educational programs.

★ The Florida Keys Land Trust owns the **Museums of Tropical Crane Point Hammock,** in Marathon. Dioramas and displays in the **Museum of Natural History of the Florida Keys** explain the Keys' geology, wildlife, and cultural history. The **Florida Keys Children's Museum** has a 1-mi loop trail, the remnants of a Bahamian village, and the **George Adderly House,** the oldest surviving example of Conch-style architecture outside Key West. From November to Easter, weekly docent-led hammock tours may be available; bring good walking shoes and bug repellent. *✉ MM 50, BS, 5550 Overseas Hwy., Marathon, ☎ 305/743–9100. 🎫 $7.50.*

The Lower Keys

The **Seven Mile Bridge,** believed to be the world's longest segmented bridge, is the gateway to the Lower Keys. The delicate Key deer can be viewed at **National Key Deer Refuge** (✉ Headquarters, MM 30.5, BS, Big Pine Shopping Center, ☎ 305/872–2239; 🎫 free), on Big Pine Key.

The final key is **Key West,** famous for its climate, laid-back lifestyle, sizable gay population, colorful heritage, and 19th-century architecture. Key West's rich ethnic past comes alive in the **Bahama Village** area (✉ Thomas and Petronia Sts.), with the peach, yellow, and pink homes of early Bahamian settlers. The **San Carlos Institute** (✉ 516 Duval St., ☎ 305/294–3887; 🎫 $3) is a Cuban-American heritage center, with a museum and research library focusing on the history of Key West and 19th- and 20th-century Cuban exiles. **Fort Zachary Taylor State Historic Site** (✉ Southard St., ☎ 305/292–6713; 🎫 $2.50 per vehicle, $1.50 per pedestrian or bicyclist) was an important fort during the Civil and Spanish-American wars. It's 88 steps to the top of the 92-ft lighthouse at the **Lighthouse Museum** (✉ 938 Whitehead St., ☎ 305/294–0012; 🎫 $5). The adjacent keeper's cottage displays ship models and lighthouse artifacts. The **Audubon House and Gardens** (✉ 205 Whitehead St., ☎ 305/294–2116; 🎫 $7.50) has beautiful tropical gardens and a large collection of Audubon engravings. ★ The **Hemingway House** (✉ 907 Whitehead St., ☎ 305/294–1575; 🎫 $6.50) is dedicated to the life and work of the author who wrote 70% of his works in Key West, including *For Whom the Bell Tolls.*

The prettiest spot on the island is **Nancy Forrester's Secret Garden** (✉ 1 Free School La., ☎ 305/294–0015; 🎫 $6), where you can wind your way under the canopy of rare palms and cycads, along trails lined with ferns, bromeliads, bright gingers, and heliconias, and past towering native gumbo-limbos strewn with hanging orchids and twining vines. Many brides and grooms have exchanged vows here.

At the **Key West Aquarium** (✉ 1 Whitehead St., ☎ 305/296–2051; 🎫 $7) kids learn about the marine life found around the Keys in an up-close-and-personal experience with turtles, rays, sharks, parrot fish, eels, and tarpon swimming in glass tanks, coral pools, a pond, and touch tanks.

Sharon Wells, who conducts **Island City Strolls** (☎ 305/294–8380 or 305/294–KEYS) walking tours, was the state historian in Key West for nearly 20 years and has authored numerous books about Key West, including the *Walking and Biking Guide to Historic Key West,* available free at Key West bookstores. The Key West Literary Seminar (☎ 305/293–9291) sponsors **Writers' Walk,** a one-hour guided tour of the residences of prominent authors who have lived in Key West (Elizabeth Bishop, Robert Frost, Ernest Hemingway, Wallace Stevens, Tennessee Williams, among others).

Dining and Lodging

Many dishes served in the Keys have a Caribbean accent, mixing tropical fruits, vegetables, and spices with local fish and citrus. Local specialties include conch chowder, Florida lobster, and key lime pie. Accommodations, from historic hotels and guest houses to large resorts and run-of-the-mill motels, are more expensive here than elsewhere in southern Florida. For price ranges *see* Charts 1 (A) and 2 (A) *in* On the Road with Fodor's.

Islamorada

$$–$$$ ★ ✕ **Morada Bay.** The owners of the tony Moorings resort opened this new restaurant, which has a bayfront location perfect for sunset watching, and a contemporary menu featuring a died-and-gone-to-heaven shrimp bisque, portobello-mushroom burger, and cumin-seared snapper with roasted red peppers. ✉ *MM 81, BS, 81590 Overseas Hwy.,* ☎ *305/664–0604. AE, MC, V*

$–$$$ ★ ✕ **Grove Park Cafe.** You can nibble on triangles of freshly baked focaccia set in a pool of olive oil and balsamic vinegar as you peruse the menu, which includes specialties like Caribbean conch chowder and crab cakes served either as a salad on mixed greens or as a sandwich on focaccia. The herbs and some of the fruits used in the cooking are grown on the property. ✉ *MM 81.7, OS, 81701 Old Hwy.,* ☎ *305/664–0116. AE, D, MC, V. Closed Wed.*

$–$$$ ★ ✕ **Squid Row.** This affable roadside seafood eatery serves the freshest fish, courtesy of the seafood wholesalers who own it. The nightly special bouillabaisse is a favorite. If you finish it by yourself they'll serve you a free piece of key lime pie. ✉ *MM 81.9 , OS, Overseas Hwy.,* ☎ *305/664–9865. AE, D, DC, MC, V.*

$$–$$$ ✕ **Manny & Isa's.** What this restaurant lacks in ambience, it makes up for in always-perfect Cuban and Spanish dishes and local seafood selections, like succulent fish fingers served with black beans and rice. There are several fish, chicken, and pork chop selections. Manny's key lime pie is legendary. ✉ *MM 81.6, OS, 81610 Old Hwy., Islamorada,* ☎ *305/664–5019. AE, D, MC, V. Closed Tues. and mid-Oct.–mid.-Nov.*

$$$$ 🏨 **Cheeca Lodge.** This 27-acre, low-rise resort is set among tranquil, fish-filled lagoons and gardens. Suites have kitchens and screened balconies; fourth-floor rooms in the main lodge have ocean or bay views. The resort is the local leader in green activism with everything from recycling to ecotours. ✉ *MM 82, OS, Box 527, 33036,* ☎ *305/664–*

4651 or 800/327–2888, FAX 305/664–2893. 203 rooms. 2 restaurants, pools, tennis. AE, D, DC, MC, V.

Key Largo

$$–$$$$ ★ ✕ **Fish House.** Behind the screened, diner-style facade are display cases filled with the freshest catches, which are baked, blackened, broiled, fried, sautéed, steamed, or stewed as if every night were the finals of a seafood competition. (In fact, the Fish House wins many such competitions). Generous portions come with corn on the cob, new potatoes or rice, and coleslaw. ✉ *MM 102.4, OS, Overseas Hwy.,* ☎ *305/451–4665. AE, D, MC, V. Closed mid-Sept.–mid-Oct.*

$$–$$$ ★ ✕ **Cafe Largo.** Soothing jazz plays in this intimate bistro-style Italian restaurant. The chicken garlic—two thin breast cutlets lightly coated and sautéed, then covered in a light sauce of garlic and rosemary—is divine. The penne with shrimp and broccoli has tender shrimp, al dente broccoli, and a hint of garlic. There's a more-than-ample wine list, and the dessert list is short but sweet. ✉ *MM 99.5, BS, Overseas Hwy.,* ☎ *305/451–4885. AE, MC, V. No lunch.*

$–$$$ ★ ✕ **Mrs. Mac's Kitchen.** A local favorite, this open-air restaurant has nightly dinner specials and a tasty bowl of chili anytime in an informal room decked out with beer cans, bottles, and license plates from around the world. ✉ *MM 99.4, BS, 99336 Overseas Hwy.,* ☎ *305/451–3722. No credit cards. Closed Sun.*

$ ✕ **Chad's Deli & Bakery.** Each morning the namesake owner bakes eight kinds of fresh breads, which he uses to make sandwiches ($5–$6) large enough to feed two hungry adults. The menu also features salads, sides, soft drinks and a choice of two cookies. Residents have voted it #1 for best sandwiches in the Upper Keys. ✉ *MM 92.3, BS, Overseas Hwy.,* ☎ *305/853–5566. No credit cards. Closed Sun.*

$$$$ ★ **Westin Beach Resort, Key Largo.** This pink and turquoise resort is tucked away in a hardwood hammock. A $7 million upgrade is evident from the lush landscaping to the waterfront restaurant, Tree Tops. Fourth-floor bay-side rooms afford marvelous water views. All rooms are spacious and comfortable, with tropical decor. Lighted nature trails and boardwalks wind through the woods to a beach. Two pools, one for adults only, are separated by a coral rock wall and waterfall. ✉ *MM 96.9, BS, 97000 Overseas Hwy., 33037,* ☎ *305/852–5553 or 800/826–1006, FAX 305/852–8669. 200 rooms. 2 restaurants, pools. AE, D, DC, MC, V.*

$$$–$$$$ ★ **Kona Kai Resort.** Beautifully landscaped cottages, a sandy beach and marina, tropical furnishings, toiletries made from fruits and flowers, and a garden of fruits and rare and native plants make this one of the best places to stay in the Keys. It's upscale but laid-back. Guests help themselves to fresh towels and take their kitchen trash to the office. Studios and one- and two-bedroom suites have full kitchens and are spacious and light-filled. Beachfront hammocks and a pool make it easy to while away the day, but there are paddleboats, kayaks, tennis, basketball, and an art gallery for those who want more. ✉ *MM 97.8, BS, 97802 Overseas Hwy., 33037,* ☎ *305/852–7200 or 800/365–7829. 11 units. Pool. AE, D, MC, V.*

$$ ★ **Largo Lodge.** No two rooms are the same in this 1950s-vintage resort, but all are cozy and fully equipped with kitchens, rattan furniture, and screened porches but no phones. The prettiest palm alley you've ever seen sets the mood, and a tropical garden surrounds the guest cottages. With 200 ft of bay frontage, it's a top-value tropical hideaway. ✉ *MM 101.5, BS, 101740 Overseas Hwy., 33037,* ☎ *305/451–0424 or 800/468–4378. 7 units. MC, V.*

Key West

$$$$ ★ ✕ **Louie's Backyard.** Key West paintings and pastels adorn this oceanfront institution, where you dine outside under the mahoe tree. The

menu changes regularly but might include roasted rack of Australian lamb with huckleberry port, whipped sweet potatoes, and fried root vegetable strips. Top off the meal with Louie's lime tart or the irresistible chocolate terrine Grand Marnier with crème anglaise. ✉ *700 Waddell Ave.,* ☎ *305/294–1061. AE, DC, MC, V.*

$$–$$$ ✕ **Awful Arthur's Seafood Company.** This casual seafood eatery with outdoor tables, a friendly staff, and a motto of "Big Mussels, Great Legs and Fantastic Tails" has the best raw bar in town. The cooked fare is equally impressive with just about every form of shellfish imaginable. The lunch and dinner menus feature a few dishes that don't come from the sea, including a terrific portobello sandwich. ✉ *628 Duval St.,* ☎ *305/295–0888. AE, D, DC, MC, V.*

$$–$$$ ★ ✕ **Mangia Mangia.** Fresh homemade pasta comes Alfredo, marinara, meaty, or with pesto, either in the brick garden or in the nicely dressed-up old-house dining room. It's one of the best restaurants in Key West, and one of its best values. The wine list of more than 350 selections contains many under $20. ✉ *900 Southard St.,* ☎ *305/294–2469. AE, MC, V. No lunch.*

$$$$ ★ 🏨 **La Concha Holiday Inn.** This seven-story Art Deco hotel in the heart of downtown is Key West's tallest building and dates from 1926. The lobby's polished floor of pink, mauve, and green marble and a conversation pit with comfortable chairs are among the details beloved by La Concha's guests. Large rooms are furnished with 1920s-era antiques, lace curtains, and big closets. ✉ *430 Duval St., 33040,* ☎ *305/296–2991 or 800/745–2191,* FAX *305/294–3283. 160 rooms. Restaurant, pool. AE, D, DC, MC, V.*

$$$$ ★ 🏨 **Marquesa Hotel.** This coolly elegant restored 1884 home is Key West's finest lodging. Guests relax among richly landscaped pools and gardens against a backdrop of brick steps rising to the villalike suites on the property's perimeter. Elegant rooms contain eclectic antique and reproduction furnishings and botanical print fabrics. Although the clientele is mostly straight, the hotel is very gay-friendly. ✉ *600 Fleming St., 33040,* ☎ *305/292–1919 or 800/869–4631,* FAX *305/294–2121. 27 rooms. Restaurant, pools. AE, DC, MC, V.*

$$$$ ★ 🏨 **Paradise Inn.** Renovated cigar makers' cottages and authentically reproduced Bahamian-style houses with sundecks and balconies stand in the midst of a lush tropical garden with a heated pool and lily pond light years away from the bustle of Key West. Inside, French doors allow light to stream in on the earth-tone fine fabrics and upholstering. Gracious appointments include phones and whirlpools in marble bathrooms, polished oak floors, and armoires. Complimentary breakfast pastries are from Louie's Backyard. ✉ *819 Simonton St., 33040,* ☎ *305/293–8007 or 800/888–9648,* FAX *305/293–0807. 18 units. Pool. CP. AE, D, DC, MC, V.*

$$$–$$$$ 🏨 **Cuban Club Suites.** Originally built as a social club for cigar makers, the "club" was rebuilt as a luxury hotel. Eight fully equipped town-house units have either two bedrooms and two baths or one bedroom and 1½ baths. Grouped in two buildings that feel like an exclusive apartment complex, their wide balconies overlook the excitement of Duval Street. Guests have pool and beach privileges at the Marriott Reach, and pets are allowed. ✉ *1108 Duval St. , 33040,* ☎ *305/296–0465 or 800/432–4849,* FAX *305/293–7669. 8 suites. AE, MC, V.*

$$–$$$$ ★ 🏨 **Popular House/Key West Bed & Breakfast.** Jody Carlson brings the spirit of Key West inside her establishment. Doors stay open all day. Local art—large splashy canvases, a mural in the style of Gauguin—hangs on the walls, and tropical gardens and music set the mood. Jody offers both luxury rooms and inexpensive rooms (whose rates haven't been raised in 10 years) with shared bath. The Continental breakfast

is lavish. ✉ *415 William St., 33040,* ☎ *305/296–7274 or 800/438–6155,* FAX *305/293–0306. 9 rooms. AE, D, DC, MC, V.*

Marathon

$$ ★ ✕ **7 Mile Grill.** The walls of this open-air diner built in 1954 at the Marathon end of Seven Mile Bridge are lined with beer cans, mounted fish, sponges, and signs describing individual menu items. The prompt, friendly service rivals the great food at breakfast, lunch, and dinner. Favorites on the mostly seafood menu include creamy shrimp bisque and fresh grouper and dolphin grilled, broiled, or fried. Don't pass up the authentic key lime pie, which has won the local paper's "Best in the Keys" award three years in a row. ✉ *MM 47, BS, 1240 Overseas Hwy.,* ☎ *305/743–4481. No credit cards. Closed Wed. and at owner's discretion Aug.–Sept.*

$$–$$$ **Banana Bay Resort & Marina.** Situated among fruit trees and native and tropical plants, this 10-acre resort has the largest freshwater pool in the Keys, plus a marina, small sandy beach, and a protected snorkeling area. Rooms, done in a Caribbean plantation style, have either one king or two double beds and are loaded with amenities. Continental breakfast is served poolside. ✉ *MM 49.5, BS, 4590 Overseas Hwy., Marathon 33050,* ☎ *305/743–3500 or 800/226–2621,* FAX *305/743–2670. 60 rooms. Pool. CP. AE, D, DC, MC, V.*

$$ **Coral Lagoon.** Surrounded by lush landscaping on a short deep-water canal, each pastel-color duplex cottage has a hammock on a private sundeck. Units have king or twin beds and a sofa bed, central air, ceiling fans, video players ($1 tape rental), wall safes, hair dryers, free dockage, barbecues, a library, and complimentary morning coffee. ✉ *MM 53.5, OS, 12399, Marathon 33050,* ☎ *305/289–0121,* FAX *305/289–0195. 18 cottages. Pool. AE, D, MC, V.*

Nightlife and the Arts

Key West is the Keys' hub for artistic performances and nightlife. This city alone claims among its current residents 55 full-time writers and 500 painters and craftspeople. The most popular entertainment is the nightly gathering of street vendors, performers, and visitors on **Mallory Square Dock** to celebrate the sunset. The **Tennessee Williams Fine Arts Center** (✉ Florida Keys Community College, 5901 College Rd., ☎ 305/296–9081, ext. 5) offers dance, music, plays, and star performers from November to April. **Capt. Tony's Saloon** (✉ 428 Greene St., ☎ 305/294–1838) is a landmark bar noted for its connection with Ernest Hemingway. Hemingway liked to gamble in the club room at **Sloppy Joe's** (✉ 201 Duval St., ☎ 305/294–5717), a noisy bar.

Outdoor Activities and Sports

Biking

Cyclists are now able to ride all but a tiny portion of the bike path that runs along the Overseas Highway from Mile Marker 106 south to Mile Marker 73, then picks up again at Mile Marker 70 to Mile Marker 66, then again from Mile Marker 53 to the Seven Mile Bridge. Trails crisscross the Marathon area; most popular is the 2-mi section of the old **Seven Mile Bridge** leading to Pigeon Key. For rentals in Key Largo and Marathon, contact **Equipment Locker Sport & Cycle** (✉ Tradewinds Plaza, MM 101, OS, 101487 Overseas Hwy., Key Largo, ☎ 305/453–0140; ✉ MM 53, BS, 11518 Overseas Hwy., Marathon, ☎ 305/289–1670). In Islamorada, try **Pete's Bike Shop** (✉ MM 82.9, BS, 82229 Overseas Hwy., Islamorada, ☎ 305/664–1910). For mopeds rentals, contact **Keys Moped & Scooter** (✉ 523 Truman Ave., Key West, ☎ 305/294–0399) or **Moped Hospital** (✉ 601 Truman Ave., Key West, ☎ 305/296–3344).

Diving and Snorkeling

Divers will find miles of living coral reefs populated with 650 species of rainbow-hued tropical fish, as well as four centuries of explorable shipwrecks. Outstanding diving areas include **John Pennekamp Coral Reef State Park** (✉ MM 102.5, OS, Key Largo, ☎ 305/451–1202) and **Looe Key Reef,** 5 mi off Ramrod Key (✉ MM 27.5). **American Diving Headquarters** (✉ MM 105.5, BS, 10550 Overseas Hwy., Key Largo, ☎ 305/451–0037) and **Looe Key Dive Center** (✉ MM 27.5, OS, Ramrod Key, ☎ 305/872–2215 or 800/942–5397) lead dives in the area.

Fishing and Boating

Deep-sea fishing on the ocean or Gulf and flat-water fishing in the backcountry shallows are big activities here. Numerous marinas rent all types of boats and water-sports equipment. Particularly popular are the various glass-bottom-boat tours to the coral reefs. Check with local chambers of commerce for information on charter- and party-boat operators. In the Upper Keys try **Tag 'Em** for light tackle, fly or deep-sea game fishing (✉ c/o Holiday Isle, MM 84, OS, Islamorada, ☎ 305/852–8797 or 305/664–2321, ext. 642) or **Hubba Hubba** for backcountry fishing (✉ c/o Bud 'n' Mary's Fishing Marina, MM 79.8, OS, Islamorada, ☎ 305/664–9281). **Adventure Charters** (✉ 6810 Front St., Stock Island, ☎ 305/296–0362) charters out of Key West.

Golf

Key Colony Beach Par 3 (✉ MM 53.5, OS, 8th St., Key Colony Beach near Marathon, ☎ 305/289–1533) is a nine-hole public course. **Key West Resort Golf Club** (✉ 6450 E. College Rd., Stock Island, ☎ 305/294–5232) is an 18-hole public course.

Beaches

Since the natural shorelines of the Keys are a combination of marshes, rocky outcroppings, and grassy wetlands, most beaches for sunbathing and swimming are man-made from imported sand. The exception is **Bahia Honda State Park** (✉ MM 37, OS, Bahia Honda Key, ☎ 305/872–2353), which has a naturally sandy beach, plus a nature trail, campground and waterfront cabins (call for reservations up to 11 months in advance), marina, and dive shop. **Anne's Beach** (✉ MM 73.5, OS, Islamorada, ☎ 305/852–7161 or 888/227–8136) has a half-mile elevated wooden boardwalk that crosses a wetlands hammock at the edge of the shore. **Sombrero Beach** (✉ MM 50, OS, Sombrero Rd., Marathon, ☎ 305/289–6077 or 888/227–8136) has areas for swimmers, jet boats, and windsurfers. Behind the narrow, sandy beach is a large, grassy park with grills, picnic kiosks, showers, and a playground. Of the several Key West beaches, **Smathers Beach** (✉ S. Roosevelt Blvd.) has 2 mi of sandy beach and good windsurfing. **Higgs Memorial Beach** (✉ End of White St.) is good for sunbathing. Many hotels and motels also have their own small, shallow-water beach areas. Among those open to the public is **Plantation Yacht Harbor Resort & Marina** (✉ MM 87, BS, Plantation Key, ☎ 305/852–2381); there's a tiki bar just behind the crescent beach.

Shopping

The Keys are a thriving artists' community, so art is in good supply here. **Kona Kai Resort Gallery** (✉ MM 97.8, BS, Key Largo, ☎ 305/852–7200) showcases works by South Florida artists, including Everglades photographer Clyde Butcher. **Rain Barrel** (✉ MM 86.7, BS, 86700 Overseas Hwy., Islamorada, ☎ 305/852–3084) is a 3-acre crafts village with eight resident artists and works by scores of others.

Across the street, an enormous fabricated lobster by artist Richard Blaes stands in front of **Treasure Village** (✉ MM 86.7, OS, 86729 Old Hwy., Islamorada, ☏ 305/852–0511), which has a dozen crafts and specialty shops, plus the excellent Made to Order eat-in and carryout restaurant. **Redbone Gallery** (✉ MM 81, OS, 200 Industrial Dr., Islamorada, ☏ 305/664–2002) specializes in art with a fishing and marine theme. The **Gallery at Morada Bay** (✉ MM 81.6, BS, Overseas Hwy., Islamorada, ☏ 305/664–3650) carries fine arts and crafts, including blown glass and handpainted scarves by top South Florida artists. The new **World Wide Sportsman** (✉ MM 82.5, BS, Overseas Hwy., Islamorada, ☏ 305/664–4615) is a two-level attraction- retail center-lounge, selling upscale fishing equipment. Key West's unique specialty shops, such as **Fast Buck Freddie's** (✉ 500 Duval St., Key West, ☏ 305/294–2007), which sells banana-leaf-shape furniture, have gained an international reputation. In a town with a gazillion T-shirt shops, **Last Flight Out** (✉ 706A Duval St., ☏ 305/294–8008) stands out for its selection of classic namesake T's, collectibles, and specialty clothing and gifts that appeal to aviation types and those reaching for the stars.

SOUTHWEST FLORIDA

Swimming, sunbathing, sailing, and shelling draw increasing numbers of visitors to the 200-mi coastal stretch between the Tampa Bay area and the Everglades. Venturing inland from the miles of sun-splashed beaches along the Gulf of Mexico, many visitors discover the culturally rich and ethnically diverse towns, interesting historical sites, and stellar attractions, such as Busch Gardens. This area tends to be more affordable than other parts of Florida. The region is divided into three areas: Tampa Bay (including Tampa, St. Petersburg, Clearwater, and Tarpon Springs), Sarasota (including Bradenton and Venice), and Fort Myers/Naples.

Visitor Information

Greater Tampa: Chamber of Commerce (✉ Box 420, 33601, ☏ 813/228–7777). **Lee County:** Visitor and Convention Bureau (✉ 2180 W. 1st St., Fort Myers 33950, ☏ 941/338–3500 or 800/533–4753). **Naples Area:** Chamber of Commerce (✉ 3620 N. Tamiami Trail, 33940, ☏ 941/262–6141). **St. Petersburg:** Chamber of Commerce (✉ 100 2nd Ave. N, 33701, ☏ 813/821–4069). **Sanibel-Captiva:** Chamber of Commerce (✉ Causeway Rd., Sanibel 33957, ☏ 941/472–1080). **Sarasota:** Convention and Visitors Bureau (✉ 655 N. Tamiami Trail, 34236, ☏ 941/957–1877 or 800/522–9799). **Tampa/Hillsborough:** Convention and Visitors Association (✉ 111 Madison St., Suite 1010, Tampa 33601, ☏ 800/826–8358).

Arriving and Departing

By Bus

Greyhound Lines (☏ 800/231–2222) provides statewide service, including stops at Tampa, St. Petersburg, Sarasota, Fort Myers, and Naples. For local bus service contact **Hillsborough Area Regional Transit** (☏ 813/254–4278) for the Tampa area, **Sarasota County Area Transit** (☏ 941/951–5850) for Sarasota, and **Lee County Transit System** (☏ 941/275–8726) for the Fort Myers area.

By Car

From the Georgia-Florida border, it's a three-hour drive via I–75 south to Tampa, four hours to Sarasota, five to Fort Myers, and six to Naples. U.S. 41 (the Tamiami Trail) also traverses the region, but because it pierces many towns' business districts, traffic can be extremely heavy, particularly from Tampa south. Naples is linked to Fort Lauderdale, on the eastern side of the state, via Alligator Alley (Route 84).

By Plane

Most major U.S. airlines serve at least one of the region's airports. **Tampa International** (☎ 813/870–8700), 6 mi from downtown, is also served by international airlines. **Sarasota-Bradenton Airport** (☎ 941/359–5200) is 5 mi north of downtown Sarasota off U.S. 41. **Southwest Florida International Airport** (☎ 941/768–1000) is about 12 mi south of Fort Myers and 25 mi north of Naples.

By Train

Amtrak (☎ 800/872–7245) connects most of the country with Tampa's station.

Exploring Southwest Florida

The Tampa Bay Area

Tampa is the commercial center of southwestern Florida, with a bustling international port and the largest shrimp fleet in the state. Known as the City by the Bay, Tampa pays homage to its coastal setting with the ★ **Florida Aquarium** (✉ 701 Channelside Dr., ☎ 813/273–4000), whose 83-ft-high glass dome is already a landmark. More than 4,300 specimens of fish, other animals, and plants represent 550 species native to Florida. The 35,000-square-ft **Tampa Museum of Art** (✉ 600 N. Ashley Dr., ☎ 813/274–8130; 🎟 $5) has a permanent collection of more than 7,000 works, including the most comprehensive collection of Greek, Roman, and Etruscan antiquities in the southeastern United States and an excellent collection of 20th-century American art. Reserve a day in Tampa for a journey through **Busch Gardens,** a 335-acre African-inspired theme park with rides, live shows, and a monorail "safari." *✉ 3000 E. Busch Blvd., ☎ 813/987–5082. 🎟 $36.15.*

Busch Gardens' water-park cousin, 35-acre **Adventure Island** (✉ 10001 Malcolm McKinley Dr., ☎ 813/987–5660; 🎟 $21.95.) has water slides and man-made waves; it's closed late Oct. through mid-March.

★ With cobblestone streets and wrought-iron balconies, Tampa's **Ybor City** (pronounced *Ee*-bor) is one of only three National Historic Landmark districts in Florida. Cubans expanded their cigar-making industry to this city in 1866. The ornately tiled **Columbia Restaurant** and the stores lining 7th Avenue are representative of this enclave's ethnic history and vitality. Today once-empty cigar factories, like the one at **Ybor Square** (✉ 1901 13th St.), house boutiques, shops, restaurants, and nightclubs. To get here, take I–4 west to Exit 1 (22nd Street) and go south five blocks to 7th Avenue.

On the Gulf about 25 mi north of Tampa is colorful **Tarpon Springs.** Famous for its sponge divers, the town reflects the heritage of its predominantly Greek population. At **Weeki Wachee Spring** (✉ 45 mi north of Tampa on U.S. 19 and Rte. 50, Weeki Wachee, ☎ 352/596–2062; 🎟 $16.95), 27 mi north of Tarpon Springs, "mermaids" present shows in an underwater theater.

You can watch manatees up close at **Homosassa Springs State Wildlife Park** (✉ 1 mi west of U.S. 19 on Fish Bowl Dr., Homosassa Springs, ☎ 352/628–2311; 🎟 $7.95). Here you can also see reptile and alligator shows, cruise the Homosassa River, and view sea life in a floating observatory.

Head south from Tampa and cross Old Tampa Bay on I–275 to get to the heart of **St. Petersburg;** set on a peninsula with three sides bordered by bays and the Gulf of Mexico, this city has beautiful beaches. With more than 1,500 pieces, the **Salvador Dali Museum** (✉ 1000 3rd St. S, ☎ 813/823–3767; 🎟 $8) has the world's largest collection of originals by the Spanish surrealist. **Great Explorations!** (✉ 1120 4th St. S, ☎ 813/821–8885; 🎟 $6) is a hands-on museum with mind-stretching puzzles and games and a 90-ft-long pitch-black maze you crawl through.

The Sarasota Area

Known for its plentiful, clean beaches and profusion of golf courses, the Sarasota area, south of Tampa Bay via U.S. 41 or U.S. 301, is also a growing cultural center and winter home of the Ringling Brothers Barnum & Bailey Circus. Midway between Tampa and Sarasota, the low-key beach city of Brandenton is site of **De Soto National Memorial** (✉ 75th St. NW, ☎ 941/792–0458; 🎟 free), where costumed guides recount Spanish conquistador Hernando de Soto's 16th-century landing and expedition. Near Bradenton is **Gamble Plantation State Historical Site** (✉ 3708 Patten Ave., Ellenton, ☎ 941/723–4536; 🎟 $3), the only surviving pre–Civil War plantation house in South Florida.

★ In the smart resort city of Sarasota you'll find the **Ringling Museums** (✉ ½ mi south of Sarasota-Bradenton Airport on U.S. 41, ☎ 941/355–5700; 🎟 $8.50), which include the Venetian-style mansion of circus magnate John Ringling, his art museum with its collection of Rubens paintings, and a circus museum. The **Marie Selby Botanical Gardens** (✉ 811 S. Palm Ave., ☎ 941/366–5731; 🎟 $7) has world-class orchid displays as well as a small museum of botany and art, all contained in a restored mansion on the grounds. Kids enjoy the bird and reptile shows at **Sarasota Jungle Gardens** (✉ 3701 Bayshore Rd., ☎ 941/355–5305; 🎟 $9); also on site are a petting zoo and a museum displaying seashells and butterflies. For a good beach escape head for the barrier island of **Siesta Key,** across the water from Sarasota. To reach Siesta Key, take U.S. 41 south from southern Sarasota to either Siesta Drive or Stickney Point Road, which both lead west to the island.

The Fort Myers/Naples Area

The bustle of commercially oriented Fort Myers gives way to the relaxed atmosphere of the Gulf communities elsewhere in growing Lee County. Beach lovers head for the resort islands of Estero (popular with young singles) and Captiva and Sanibel, which are both known for superb shelling and fishing. Most of the beautiful residences here are hidden by Australian pines, but the beaches and tranquil Gulf waters are readily accessible.

Fort Myers is a small inland city; although it's a half hour from the nearest beach, it's downtown business district overlooks the broad, flat Caloosahatchee River. One of the most scenic stretches of highway in southeastern Florida, **McGregor Boulevard** is framed by hundreds of towering palms. Fort Myers's premier attraction, **Thomas A. Edison's Winter Home** (✉ 2350 McGregor Blvd., ☎ 941/334–3614; 🎟 $10, including access to Mangoes), on a 14-acre estate, houses Edison's laboratory and a museum devoted to his inventions. Next door is **Mangoes,** the winter house of the inventor's longtime friend, automaker Henry Ford.

The refined city of **Naples** is fast becoming Florida's west-coast version of Palm Beach, with excellent beaches and golf courses, luxury high-rise condos, and an upscale shopping and dining district. About 30 mi northeast of Naples you can return to Florida's unspoiled past at the **Corkscrew Swamp Sanctuary** (✉ 16 mi east of I–75 on Rte. 846, ☎ 941/348–9151; 🎟 $6.50), an 11,000-acre tract that the National Audubon Society set aside to protect 500-year-old trees and endangered birds.

Dining and Lodging

Around **Tampa** the ethnic diversity of the region makes for some adventurous dining, from honey-soaked Greek baklava to Cuban saffron rice casserole. A generous mix of roadside motels, historic hotels, and sprawling resorts can be found here.

Raw bars and seafood restaurants are everywhere in and around **Sarasota**; there are also many Continental restaurants and several family-style places run by members of the Amish community. Tamiami Trail (U.S. 41), which traverses the region, is lined with inexpensive motels, while the islands have more expensive resort complexes and high-rise hotels.

In **Fort Myers** and **Naples,** seafood reigns supreme. A particular treat is a succulent claw of the native stone crab, usually served with drawn butter or a tangy mustard sauce; stone crabs are in season from mid-October through mid-May. It's hard to find restaurants on Sanibel and Captiva islands that aren't expensive; for budget options (both dining and lodging) you'll have better luck in Fort Myers and Naples. For price ranges *see* Charts 1 (B) and 2 (A) *in* On the Road with Fodor's.

Bradenton

$$–$$$ 🏨 **Holiday Inn Riverfront.** Suites overlook a courtyard at this Spanish-style motor inn near the Manatee River. Rooms, with burgundy carpeting and mahogany furnishings, are a bit dark, but a third have river views. ✉ *100 Riverfront Dr. W, 34205,* ☎ *941/747–3727,* FAX *941/746–4289. 153 rooms. Restaurant, pool. AE, DC, MC, V.*

Captiva

$$$$ ★ 🏨 **South Seas Plantation Resort and Yacht Harbor.** More neighborhood than resort, this busy 330-acre property has many styles of accommodations, among them harborside villas, gulf cottages, and private homes. Activities include sailing, shelling, and strolling on the 2½ mi of beach and landscaped grounds covered with exotic vegetation. There are 18 swimming pools on the grounds. ✉ *South Seas Plantation Rd., 33924,* ☎ *941/472–5111 or 800/227–8482,* FAX *941/472–7541. 620 units. 4 restaurants, pools, tennis, exercise room. AE, DC, MC, V.*

Fort Myers and Fort Myers Beach

$$$$ ★ ✕ **Peter's La Cuisine.** Smack in the middle of downtown Fort Myers, two blocks off the river, is this charming restaurant in a restored brick building. The dining room's extra-high ceiling gives a spacious feel, and exposed brick walls, dim lighting, and a refined atmosphere provide a pleasant background for Continental cuisine with a twist. After dinner wander upstairs for a cordial and some great blues. ✉ *2224 Bay St.,* ☎ *941/332–2228. AE, MC, V. No lunch weekends.*

$$$–$$$$ ★ ✕ **Prawnbroker Restaurant and Fish Market.** This popular restaurant has an abundance of seafood seemingly just plucked from Gulf waters. plus some selections for culinary landlubbers. It's almost always crowded—and for good reason. ✉ *13451 McGregor Blvd.,* ☎ *941/489–2226. AE, MC, V. No lunch.*

$$–$$$$ ✕ **Snug Harbor.** This harbor-front restaurant serves absolutely fresh seafood—courtesy of the restaurant's private fishing fleet—in a casual, rustic atmosphere. ✉ *645 San Carlos Blvd., Fort Myers Beach,* ☎ *941/463–4343. Reservations not accepted. AE, MC, V.*

$$–$$$ 🏨 **Outrigger Beach Resort.** This informal, family-oriented resort is set on a wide beach overlooking the Gulf of Mexico. There's a broad deck for sunning, plus tiki huts to sit under when you want to escape from the heat, and a beachfront pool. ✉ *6200 Estero Blvd., Fort Myers Beach 33931,* ☎ *941/463–3131 or 800/749–3131,* FAX *941/463–6577. 144 units. Pool. MC, V.*

$$–$$$ 🏨 **Sheraton Harbor Place.** This modern, 25-story high-rise has a commanding position in the downtown skyline, rising above the river and yacht basin. Rooms have panoramic views of the water and the city. ✉ *2500 Edwards Dr., Fort Myers 33901,* ☎ *941/337–0300 or 800/325–3535,* FAX *941/337–1530. 417 rooms. Restaurant, pool, tennis, exercise room. AE, DC, MC, V.*

Naples

$$$–$$$$ ✕ **Bistro 821.** The decor for this trendy restaurant is spare and sophisticated. Entrées include marinated leg of lamb with basil mashed potatoes, snapper baked in parchment, wild mushroom pasta, vodka penne, risotto, and a seasonal vegetable plate. ✉ *821 5th Ave. S,* ☎ *941/261–5821. Reservations essential. AE, DC, MC, V. No lunch.*

Palmetto

$$–$$$ ✕ **Crab Trap.** Try the wild pig or seafood dishes at this rustic eatery near Bradenton. ✉ *U.S. 19 at Terra Ceia Bridge,* ☎ *941/722–6255. D, MC, V.*

St. Petersburg Beach

$$$$ ★ 🏨 **Don CeSar Beach Resort.** Still echoing with the ghosts of Scott and Zelda Fitzgerald, this sprawling beachfront "Pink Palace" has long been a Gulf Coast landmark. Turn-of-the-century elegance abounds, and service is first-rate. You can indulge in various treatments and sea scrubs at the beach spa. ✉ *3400 Gulf Blvd., 33706,* ☎ *813/360–1881,* FAX *813/367–3609. 295 rooms. 3 restaurants, pools, tennis, exercise room. AE, DC, MC, V.*

Sarasota

$$$$ ★ ✕ **Cafe L'Europe.** This art-filled café is on fashionable St. Armand's Circle, on Lido Key. The menu may include such dishes as Wiener schnitzel sautéed in butter and topped with anchovies, olives, and capers, or Dover sole served with fruit. ✉ *431 St. Armand's Circle,* ☎ *941/388–4415. AE, DC, MC, V.*

$$$ 🏨 **Hyatt Sarasota.** This contemporary hotel is ideally located, near the city center and the major art and entertainment venues. The spacious rooms overlook Sarasota Bay or the marina. ✉ *1000 Blvd. of the Arts, 34236,* ☎ *941/953–1234,* FAX *941/952–1987. 297 rooms. Restaurant, pool, health club. AE, DC, MC, V.*

Siesta Key

$$$–$$$$ ✕ **Ophelia's on the Bay.** Sample mussel soup, eggplant crepes, chicken potpie, seafood linguine, or cioppino, among other eclectic dishes, at this waterfront restaurant. ✉ *9105 Midnight Pass Rd.,* ☎ *941/349–2212. AE, D, DC, MC, V. No lunch.*

Tampa

$$$$ ★ ✕ **Bern's Steak House.** This nationally known steak house has more than just steak. Organically grown vegetables from the owner's farm are the specialty here, and scrumptious desserts are served upstairs in intimate glass-enclosed rooms. ✉ *1208 S. Howard Ave.,* ☎ *813/251–2421. AE, DC, MC, V. No lunch.*

$$$–$$$$ ✕ **Columbia.** An institution in Ybor City since 1905, this light and spacious Spanish restaurant serves excellent paella, with some flamenco dancing on the side. ✉ *2117 E. 7th Ave.,* ☎ *813/248–4961. AE, DC, MC, V.*

$$ 🏨 **Holiday Inn Busch Gardens.** This well-maintained motor lodge is just 1 mi west of Busch Gardens. Rooms are bright and spacious; some look out on a central courtyard with garden and pool. ✉ *2701 E. Fowler Ave., 33612,* ☎ *813/971–4710,* FAX *813/977–0155. 395 rooms. Restaurant, pool, exercise room. AE, DC, MC, V.*

Tarpon Springs

$$–$$$$ ✕ **Louis Pappas' Riverside Restaurant.** This waterfront landmark is always crowded with diners savoring the fine Greek fare, including a Greek salad made with feta cheese, onions, and olive oil. ✉ *10 W. Dodecanese Blvd., ☎ 813/937–5101. AE, DC, MC, V. No lunch Sun.*

Nightlife and the Arts

The region between Tampa and Sarasota hums with cultural activities. Professional theater, dance, and music events are presented at **Tampa Bay Performing Arts Center** (✉ 1010 W. C. MacInnes Pl., Tampa, ☎ 813/229–7827 or 800/955–1045) and **Ruth Eckerd Hall** (✉ 1111 McMullen Booth Rd., Clearwater, ☎ 813/791–7400). Broadway touring companies of plays, concerts, dance, ice-skating, and other shows are held at Sarasota's **Van Wezel Performing Arts Hall** (✉ 777 N. Tamiami Trail, Sarasota, ☎ 941/953–3366). Other major venues in the city are the **Florida West Coast Symphony Center** (✉ 709 N. Tamiami Trail, ☎ 941/953–4252), the **Sarasota Opera** (✉ Opera House, 61 N. Pineapple Ave., ☎ 941/953–7030), and the **Asolo Center for the Performing Arts** (✉ 5555 N. Tamiami Trail, ☎ 941/351–8000).

The **Naples Philharmonic Center for the Arts** (✉ 5833 Pelican Bay Blvd., ☎ 941/597–1111) presents plays, concerts, and art exhibits.

Outdoor Activities and Sports

Biking

Sanibel Island has the best biking in the region, with extensive paths along the waterways and through wildlife refuges. On Sanibel you can rent bicycles by the hour at **Bike Route** (✉ 2330 Palm Ridge Rd., ☎ 941/472–1955).

Boating and Sailing

Sailing is popular on the calm bays and Gulf waters. Sailing schools include **Fort Myers Yacht Charters** (✉ Port Sanibel Yacht Club, South Fort Myers, ☎ 941/540–8050). For powerboat rentals contact **Boat House of Sanibel** (✉ Sanibel Marina, 634 N. Yachtman Dr., ☎ 941/472–2531). **Jensen's Marina** (✉ Captiva, ☎ 941/472–5800) rents little powerboats perfect for fishing and shelling.

Canoeing

Canoeists can explore many waterways here, including those at **Myakka River State Park** (✉ Rte. 72, 15 mi south of Sarasota, ☎ 941/365–0100). **Tarpon Bay Marina** (✉ 900 Tarpon Bay Rd., Sanibel, ☎ 941/472–8900) has canoes and equipment for exploring the waters of the J. N. "Ding" Darling National Wildlife Refuge. With several locations throughout Florida, **Canoe Outpost** offers canoe and camping trips on the Little Manatee River (✉ 18001 U.S. 301S, Wimauma, 20 mi southeast of Tampa, ☎ 941/634–2228) and the Peace River (✉ Rte. 7, Arcadia, ☎ 941/494–1215).

Fishing

The Tampa Bay area and Fort Myers are major fishing centers. Speckled trout and kingfish are often caught in the Tampa Bay inlets. Deep-sea fishing enthusiasts can charter boats or join a party boat to catch tarpon, marlin, grouper, redfish, and shark. Charter outfitters include **Florida Deep Sea Fishing** (✉ 1 Corey Ave., St. Petersburg Beach, ☎ 813/360–2082). Fishing is popular in Sanibel. Call **Captain Pat Lovetro** (✉ Sanibel Marina, 634 N. Yachtman Dr., ☎ 941/472–2723) for half-day, six-hour, and full-day trips.

Golf

Championship and other courses abound here; all those listed have 18 holes. **Babe Zaharias Golf Course** (✉ 11412 Forest Hills Dr., Tampa, ☎ 813/932–8932); **Lely Flamingo Island Club** (✉ 8004 Lely Resort Blvd., Naples, ☎ 941/793–2223); the **Bay Beach Club Executive Golf Course** (✉ 7401 Estero Blvd., Fort Myers, ☎ 941/463–2064) offers lessons; **Resort at Longboat Key Club** (✉ 301 Gulf of Mexico Dr., Longboat Key, ☎ 941/383–8821); **Pelican's Nest Golf Course** (✉ 4450 Pelican's Nest Dr. SW Bonita Springs, ☎ 941/947–4600); the **Dunes** (✉ 949 Sandcastle Rd., Sanibel, ☎ 941/472–2535) rents golf clubs and offers lessons.

Spectator Sports

Baseball: Tampa Bay Devil Rays (✉ 1 Tropicana Dr., ☎ 813/825–3120) **Football: Tampa Bay Buccaneers** (✉ Tampa Stadium, 4201 N. Dale Mabry Hwy., ☎ 813/870–2700 or 800/282–0683), August–December. **Hockey: Tampa Bay Lightning** (✉ 401 Channelside Dr., ☎ 813/229–2658). **Horse Racing: Tampa Bay Downs** (✉ Race Track Rd., off Rte. 580, Oldsmar, ☎ 813/855–4401), Thoroughbred races from mid-December to early May.

Beaches

The waters of the Gulf of Mexico tend to be cloudy, so snorkeling and diving are best on the Atlantic side. The southwestern beaches are good for shelling and sunbathing on quiet stretches of sand. Sunsets are spectacular here.

In the Bradenton area the **Manatee County Beach,** on Anna Maria Island, has picnic facilities, a snack bar, showers, lifeguards, and rest rooms. **Estero Island (Fort Myers Beach),** 18 mi from downtown Fort Myers, attracts families and young singles; hotels, restaurants, and condominiums run its length. The island's shores slope gradually into the usually tranquil and warm Gulf waters. Along Gulf Shore Boulevard in Naples, **Lowdermilk Park** has 1,000 ft of beach, picnic tables, showers, rest rooms, and a pavilion with vending machines.

In the St. Petersburg area the 900-acre **Fort De Soto Park** encompasses six islands. Its 7 mi of beaches include two fishing piers, picnic sites, and a waterskiing and boating area. **Old Lighthouse Beach,** at the southern end of Sanibel Island, attracts a mix of singles, families, and shellers. Beautiful **Siesta Beach,** on Siesta Key near Sarasota, features a concession stand, picnic areas, nature trails, and facilities for soccer, softball, volleyball, and tennis. **Caspersen Beach,** on Beach Drive in South Venice, is one of the county's largest parks. Beachcombers find lots of shells and sharks' teeth here.

Shopping

Seven blocks of fine shops and restaurants line Tampa's Swan Avenue in **Old Hyde Park Village** (☎ 813/251–3500). If you're looking for Cuban cigars, try **Ybor City** on Tampa's east side. In Pinellas Park **Wagonwheel** (✉ 7801 Park Blvd., ☎ 813/544–5319) is a weekend flea market with about 2,000 vendors. For unique gifts, shop for natural sponges on **Dodecanese Boulevard** in Tarpon Springs.

Art lovers can browse through the art galleries on **Main Street and Palm Avenue** in downtown Sarasota. A British telephone booth or an Australian boomerang is available for a price at the unique shops of Harding Circle on fashionable **St. Armand's Circle,** west of downtown Sarasota across the Ringling Causeway.

For a great display of shells, coral, and jewelry, visit the **Shell Factory** (✉ 2787 N. Tamiami Trail, North Fort Myers, ☎ 888/743–5571). For boutiques selling resort wear, designer fashions, and jewelry, try the **Royal Palm Square** area (✉ Colonial Blvd., between McGregor Blvd. and U.S. 41) in Fort Myers. The largest shopping area in Naples is **Olde Naples,** an eight-block area bordered by Broad Avenue on the north and 4th Street South on the east. The **Waterside Shops** (✉ Seagate Dr. and U.S. 41), known by locals as Bell Tower because of its landmark, are anchored by a Saks Fifth Avenue and a Jacobson's department store and house 50 shops and several noteworthy eating spots.

THE GOLD AND TREASURE COASTS

The Gold Coast exudes wealth and opulence, but it's also steeped in natural beauty. Once famous as a spring-break haven for the college crowd, Fort Lauderdale now attracts families by offering a variety of recreational, sports, cultural, and historical activities. Farther north is the international high-society resort of Palm Beach, with its elegant mansions and world-class shopping. Following downtown Fort Lauderdale's lead, West Palm Beach is trying to renew itself through a combination of governmental efforts and the arts to become the hub of Palm Beach County and the Treasure Coast. Inland about 50 mi is 448,000-acre Lake Okeechobee, noted for catfish, bass, and perch fishing. Heading north from West Palm Beach to Sebastian Inlet, the Treasure Coast offers barrier islands, beaches, and sea-turtle havens to the east and citrus groves and cattle ranches to the west.

Visitor Information

Greater Fort Lauderdale: Convention & Visitors Bureau (✉ 1850 Eller Dr., Suite 303, 33301, ☎ 954/765–4466). **Palm Beach County:** Convention & Visitors Bureau (✉ 1555 Palm Beach Lakes Blvd., Suite 204, West Palm Beach 33401, ☎ 561/471–3995 or 800/833–5733); Chamber of Commerce of the Palm Beaches (✉ 401 N. Flagler Dr., West Palm Beach 33401, ☎ 561/833–3711).

Arriving and Departing

By Bus

Greyhound Lines (☎ 800/231–2222) stops in Fort Lauderdale and West Palm Beach, and **Broward Transit** (☎ 954/357–8400) serves the surrounding county. **CoTran** buses (☎ 561/233–1111) ply the Greater Palm Beach area.

By Car

Two major north–south routes, I–95 and U.S. 1, connect the region with Miami to the south and Jacksonville to the north. Alligator Alley (I–75) runs east–west from Fort Lauderdale to Naples. Florida's Turnpike is a less congested and less direct route from Orlando to the Gold and Treasure Coasts.

The four-lane route Okeechobee Boulevard (Route 704) carries traffic from west of downtown West Palm Beach, near the Amtrak station in the airport district, directly into Palm Beach. Flagler Drive will be given over exclusively to pedestrian use by the end of the decade.

By Plane

Major foreign and domestic carriers serve the **Fort Lauderdale–Hollywood International Airport** (✉ 4 mi south of downtown Fort Lauderdale off U.S. 1, ☎ 954/359–6100) and **Palm Beach International Airport** (✉ Congress Ave. and Belvedere Rd., West Palm Beach, ☎ 561/471–7400).

By Train

Amtrak (☎ 800/872–7245) provides daily service to Fort Lauderdale, Hollywood, and Deerfield Beach in Broward County and to West Palm Beach.

Exploring the Gold and Treasure Coasts

Fort Lauderdale and Palm Beach dazzle with their fabulous homes and pricey shops, shimmering beaches, plentiful sports activities, first-class museums, and cultural events. North of Palm Beach are the Treasure Coast's 70 mi of soothing sand, sea, and nature refuges.

Don't miss a visit to the splendidly redesigned **Fort Lauderdale beachfront,** along Route A1A. The beach side remains open and uncluttered, and trendy shops and restaurants (plus a mix of new and dated hotels) line the opposite side of the street. From the beach, picturesque **Las Olas Boulevard** takes you inland through the Isles, where expensive homes line canals dotted with yachts. After this the boulevard becomes an upscale shopping street, with Spanish colonial buildings housing boutiques and galleries. The **Museum of Art** (✉ 1 E. Las Olas Blvd., ☎ 954/763–6464; 🎫 $6), closed Monday, has an extensive early 20th-century European and American art collection.

Palm-lined **Riverwalk,** which begins around U.S. 1 south of Broward Boulevard, is a paved promenade that's being extended on both banks of the New River. Riverwalk leads into the city's newly burgeoning **Arts and Science District,** which has spawned a slew of new shops, restaurants, and entertainment venues in the heart of downtown.The top attraction ★ 👶 in the Arts and Science District is the **Museum of Discovery and Science** (✉ 401 S.W. 2nd St., ☎ 954/467–6637 for museum or 954/463–4629 for IMAX; 🎫 museum $6, IMAX $9, both $12.50), with an IMAX theater, and interactive exhibits on ecology, health, and outer space. For an interesting side trip, head south a few miles to the **Seminole Native Village** (✉ 4150 N. Rte. 7, Hollywood, ☎ 954/961–4519; 🎫 $5) to observe Native American lifestyles and arts or to take part in the action at the high-stakes bingo parlor and low-stakes poker tables.

As you travel north from Fort Lauderdale along U.S. 1, pause to admire the 1920s Spanish-style architecture in affluent **Boca Raton.** In the posh island community of **Palm Beach,** you can rub shoulders with the rich and famous as you stroll along the 12-mi-long-island's **Worth Avenue,** one of the world's premier shopping streets. To recapture the glitter and flamboyance of Florida's boom years, when railroad magnate Henry M. Flagler first established Palm Beach as a playground for the wealthy, visit his ornate hotel, the **Breakers,** a legendary bastion of wealth and privilege (☞ Dining and Lodging, *below*). Henry Flagler's palatial 73-room Whitehall Mansion, known as the **Flagler Museum** (✉ 1 Whitehall Way, ☎ 561/655–2833; 🎫 $7), which is closed Monday, contains original furnishings and an art collection.

After visiting Palm Beach, take a drive past the secluded mansions along **County Road** and around the northern tip of the island. Directly across the Fort Worth inlet from Palm Beach is the rapidly gentrifying mainland city of **West Palm Beach.** Long considered Palm Beach's impoverished cousin, West Palm is now economically vibrant in its own right—it's become the cultural, entertainment, and business center of the county and of the region to the north. The **Norton Gallery of Art** (✉ 1451 S. Olive St., ☎ 561/832–5194; 🎫 $5) has a fine collection of French Impressionist works. Southwest of West Palm Beach, at **Lion Country Safari** (✉ Southern Blvd. W [U.S. 98], ☎ 561/793–1084; 🎫 $14.95, car rental $6 per hr), you can drive (with car windows closed)

The Gold and Treasure Coasts

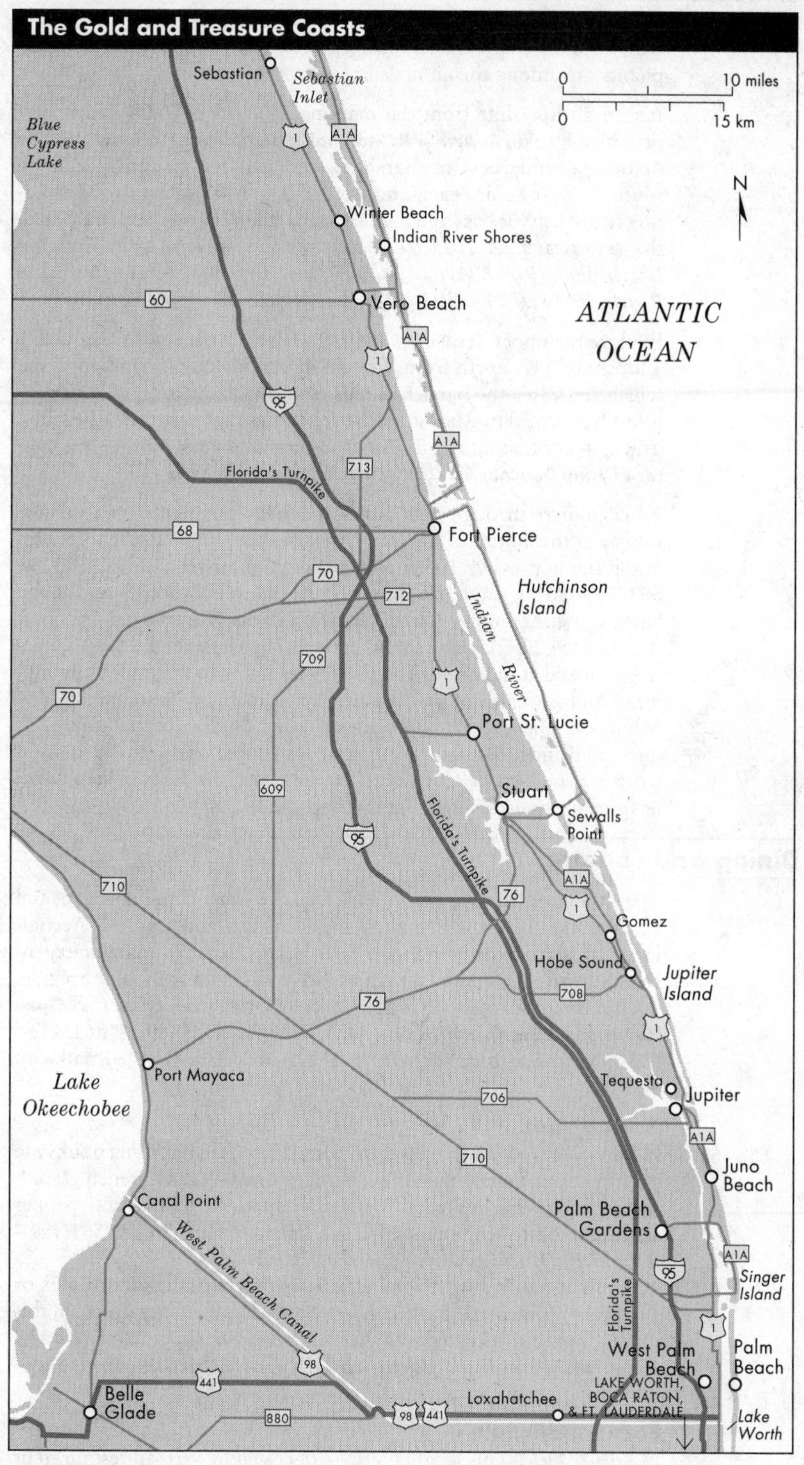

Sebastian
Sebastian Inlet
0 10 miles
0 15 km
N
Blue Cypress Lake
1
A1A
Winter Beach
Indian River Shores
60
Vero Beach
ATLANTIC OCEAN
A1A
1
95
A1A
713
Florida's Turnpike
68
Fort Pierce
70
712
Hutchinson Island
Indian River
709
70
1
Port St. Lucie
609
Stuart
Sewalls Point
95
Florida's Turnpike
710
A1A
76
1
Gomez
Hobe Sound
Jupiter Island
708
76
1
Port Mayaca
Lake Okeechobee
Tequesta
Jupiter
706
A1A
710
Juno Beach
Canal Point
Palm Beach Gardens
West Palm Beach Canal
A1A
95
Singer Island
Florida's Turnpike
1
West Palm Beach
Palm Beach
98
441
Belle Glade
LAKE WORTH, BOCA RATON, & FT. LAUDERDALE
Loxahatchee
880
98
441
Lake Worth

on 8 mi of paved roads through a 500-acre cageless zoo where 1,000 wild animals roam free. Lions, giraffes, zebras, ostriches, and elephants are among the animals in residence.

It's an abrupt shift from the man-made world of Palm Beach into primitive Florida at **Arthur R. Marshall Loxahatchee National Wildlife Refuge,** a wilderness of marshes, wetlands, and bountiful wildlife south of West Palm Beach and west of Boynton Beach. Stroll the nature trails, fish for bass and panfish, or paddle your own canoe through the waterways. ✉ *10119 Lee Rd., off U.S. 441 between Boynton Beach Blvd. (Rte. 804) and Atlantic Ave. (Rte. 806), west of Boynton Beach,* ☎ *561/734–8303;* 🎟 *$5 per vehicle, $1 per pedestrian.*

Explore the upper Treasure Coast at a leisurely pace by taking U.S. 1 and Route A1A north from West Palm Beach along the Indian River, which separates the barrier islands from the mainland. Of major interest from April to August are the sea turtles that nest on the beaches. You can learn about the turtles at **Loggerhead Park Marine Life Center of Juno Beach.** ✉ *1200 U.S. 1,* ☎ *561/627–8280. Closed Mon.*

You can drive through sand dunes at **Jupiter,** on the Intracoastal Waterway at the mouth of the scenic Loxahatchee River. Pause to photograph the impressive 105-ft **Jupiter Inlet Lighthouse** (✉ Rte. 707, ☎ 561/747–8380; 🎟 tour $5), one of the oldest lighthouses on the Atlantic coast. At Jupiter Island's **Blowing Rocks Preserve** (✉ Rte. 707, ☎ 561/575–2297), water sprays burst through holes in the shore's limestone facade at high tide. The preserve is home to large bird communities and a wealth of plants native to beachfront dune, marsh, and hammock. The revival of historic downtown **Stuart** is transforming this onetime fishing village into a magnet for people who want to live and work in a small-town atmosphere. The affluent community of **Vero Beach** has elegant houses, many dating from the 1920s.

Dining and Lodging

The Gold and Treasure coasts have a mix of American, European, and Caribbean cuisines, all emphasizing local fish and seafood. Accommodations are expensive in the Palm Beach area, but many inexpensive motels line U.S. 1 and the major exits of I–95 throughout the region. B&B accommodations are popular in Palm Beach County; contact **Open House Bed & Breakfast** (✉ Box 3025, Palm Beach 33480, ☎ 561/842–5190). For price ranges *see* Charts 1 (B) and 2 (A) *in* On the Road with Fodor's.

Boca Raton

$$$–$$$$ ★ ✕ **La Vieille Maison.** Closets transformed into private dining nooks are part of the charm of this 1920s home turned elegant French restaurant serving such dishes as venison chop with red currant–pepper sauce and roasted chestnuts. ✉ *770 E. Palmetto Park Rd.,* ☎ *561/391–6701. AE, D, DC, MC, V. Closed early July–Aug.*

$$ ✕ **Tom's Place.** It's worth the wait in line for mouthwatering ribs or chicken in homemade barbecue sauce and the sweet-potato pie in this casual, family-run eatery. ✉ *7251 N. Federal Hwy.,* ☎ *561/997–0920. Reservations not accepted. MC, V. Closed Sun., also Mon. May–mid-Nov.*

Fort Lauderdale

$$$$ ✕ **Burt & Jack's**This local favorite—operated by veteran restaurateur Jack Jackson and actor Burt Reynolds since 1984—offers seafood, steaks and chops, and scenic views of Port Everglades. ✉ *Berth 23, Port Everglades,* ☎ *954/522–2878. AE, D, DC, MC, V. No lunch.*

$$–$$$ ✕ **Shirttail Charlie's.** After dining on crab balls or coconut shrimp with piña colada sauce on the outdoor deck or in the upstairs dining room of this 1920s-style restaurant, enjoy a free cruise on the New River. ✉ *400 S.W. 3rd Ave., ☎ 954/463–3474. AE, D, MC, V.*

$$$ 🏨 **Riverside Hotel.** This 1936 hotel amid the upscale shops on Las Olas Boulevard has an attentive staff, murals by well-known artist Bob Jenny (one of which stretches across 725 square ft of the building's facade), and antique oak furnishings in the guest rooms. ✉ *620 E. Las Olas Blvd., 33301, ☎ 954/467–0671 or 800/325–3280, FAX 954/462–2148. 110 rooms. 2 restaurants, bar, pool. AE, DC, MC, V.*

Hutchinson Island

$$$$ ★ ✕🏨 **Indian River Plantation Marriott Beach Resort.** This luxury resort on 200 island acres evokes a Victorian seaside ambience with its latticework trim, tin roofs, and cool verandas. Feast on steak Diane or fresh snapper at the intimate Inlet Restaurant, or try the Sunday champagne brunch at Scalawags. ✉ *555 N.E. Ocean Blvd., Stuart 34996, ☎ 561/225–3700 or 800/775–5936, FAX 561/225–0003. 476 units. 5 restaurants, pools, tennis. AE, DC, MC, V.*

Palm Beach

$$$–$$$$ ★ ✕ **Ta-boo.** Dressed in gorgeous pinks, greens, and florals, the spaces of this Worth Avenue landmark are divided into discreet salons: One resembles a courtyard, another an elegant living room with a fireplace, and a third a skylighted gazebo. Expect eclectic fare including chicken and arugula from the grill, prime rib, steaks, frogs' legs, main course salads, and pizzas. ✉ *221 Worth Ave., ☎ 561/835–3500. AE, MC, V.*

$$$$ ★ ✕🏨 **The Breakers.** Dating from 1926 and enlarged in 1969, this opulent Italian Renaissance–style resort sprawls over 140 splendidly manicured acres. Cupids frolic in the Florentine fountain at the main entrance, while majestic ceiling vaults and frescoes grace the lobby. A $75 million renovation modernized the resort and enhanced its elegance without sacrificing old-world luxury. Many rooms have been enlarged, and all have been redecorated. You can dine on Continental specialties such as herb-crusted rack of lamb in the hotel's tapestry-filled Florentine Dining Room. ✉ *1 S. County Rd., 33480, ☎ 561/655–6611 or 800/833–3141, FAX 561/659–8403. 620 rooms. 5 restaurants, pool, tennis, health club. AE, D, DC, MC, V.*

$$–$$$$ 🏨 **Palm Beach Sea Lord Hotel.** This off-the-beaten-track motel in a garden setting has rooms overlooking the pool, the ocean, or Lake Worth. The reasonably priced café adds to the at-home, comfy feeling and attracts repeat customers. ✉ *2315 Ocean Blvd., 33480, ☎ FAX 561/582–1461. 40 units. Restaurant, pool. D, MC, V.*

Spas

Fort Lauderdale

$$$$ 🏨 **Wyndham Resort & Spa Fort Lauderdale.** The resort's spacious rooms have tropical decor and balconies overlooking a lake or a golf course. Menus follow the nutritional guidelines of the American Heart Association and the American Cancer Society. Fitness programs are available, and the resort offers combination spa-tennis and spa-golf packages. ✉ *250 Racquet Club Rd., 33326, ☎ 954/389–3300 or 800/327–8090, FAX 954/384–0563. 493 rooms. 4 restaurants, pools, tennis, health club. AE, D, MC, V.*

$$$–$$$$ 🏨 **Palm-Aire Spa Resort.** This 750-acre resort has both a luxurious resort hotel and a spa complex that promotes physical fitness and stress reduction. Large guest rooms have separate dressing rooms and private terraces. Guests can play 94 holes of golf. ✉ *2601 Palm-Aire Dr.*

N, Pompano Beach 33069, ☎ 954/972–3300 or 800/272–5624. 184 units. Restaurant, 2 pools, spa, tennis, exercise room. AE, D, MC, V.

Palm Beach

$$$$ **PGA National Resort & Spa.** At this sybaritic getaway where golf and tennis pros exercise during tournaments, the spa facilities include the signature mineral pools with salts from around the world. Choose from large guest rooms with tropical decor or cottage units with two bedrooms and a kitchen. The resort hosts a Senior PGA golf tournament each year. ✉ *400 Ave. of the Champions, Palm Beach Gardens 33418,* ☎ *561/627–2000 or 800/633–9150,* FAX *561/622–0261. 420 units. 4 restaurants, pools, tennis, exercise room. AE, D, DC, MC, V.*

Nightlife and the Arts

Fort Lauderdale and the Palm Beach area offer a full roster of performing arts events. Major venues include **Broward Center for the Performing Arts** (✉ 201 S.W. 5th Ave., Fort Lauderdale, ☎ 954/462–0222) and **Raymond F. Kravis Center for the Performing Arts** (✉ 701 Okeechobee Blvd., ☎ 561/832–7469), the cultural center of Palm Beach. Many of the cultural events in Vero Beach take place at the **Riverside Theatre** (✉ 3250 Riverside Park Dr., ☎ 561/231–6990). Fort Lauderdale has the liveliest nightlife, with comedy clubs, discos, and clubs featuring music for all ages and tastes; popular ones include **Baja Beach Club** (✉ Coral Ridge Mall, 3200 N. Federal Hwy., ☎ 954/561–2432), with karaoke and performing bartenders, and **O'Hara's Pub & Sidewalk Cafe** (✉ 722 E. Las Olas Blvd., ☎ 954/524–1764), which has nightly live jazz and blues.

Outdoor Activities and Sports

Biking

The beautiful **Palm Beach Bicycle Trail** runs for 10 mi along the shoreline of Lake Worth. For bike rentals try **Palm Beach Bicycle Trail Shop** (✉ 223 Sunrise Ave., ☎ 561/659–4583). In Fort Lauderdale, some of the most popular routes are along A1A—the beach road. For a free bicycle map, contact **County Bicycle Coordinator** (✉ 115 S. Andrews Ave., ☎ 954/357-6661).

Diving

A popular place to dive is the 23-mi-long, 2-mi-wide **Fort Lauderdale Reef,** one of 80 dive sites in Broward County. Palm Beach County offers excellent drift diving and anchor diving off the Atlantic coast. Try **Pro Dive** (✉ Radisson Bahia Mar Beach Resort, 801 Seabreeze Blvd., Fort Lauderdale, ☎ 954/761–3413 or 800/772–3483) for diving equipment and packages.

Fishing

Anglers can deep-sea or freshwater fish year-round. Pompano, amberjack, and snapper are caught off the numerous piers and bridges, while Lake Okeechobee yields bass and perch. Sailfish are a popular catch on deep-sea charters, offered at **Hillsboro Inlet Marina** (✉ 2629 N. Riverside Dr., Pompano Beach, ☎ 954/943–8222) and **B-Love Fleet** (✉ 314 E. Ocean Ave., Lantana, ☎ 561/588–7612).

Golf

Among the 50-plus golf courses in Greater Fort Lauderdale is **Colony West Country Club** (✉ 6800 N.W. 88th Ave., Tamarac, ☎ 954/726–8430). The **Breakers Hotel Golf Club** (✉ 1 S. County Rd., ☎ 561/655–6611 or 800/833–3141) has 36 holes. **Palm Beach Par 3** (✉ 2345 S. Ocean Blvd., ☎ 561/547–0598) has 18 holes, including four on the Atlantic and three on the inland waterway.

Spectator Sports

Horse Racing: Gulfstream Park Race Track (✉ 901 S. Federal Hwy., Hallandale, ☎ 954/454–7000), January–mid-March. **Pompano Harness Track** (✉ 1800 S.W. 3rd St., Pompano Beach, ☎ 954/972–2000), Monday, Wednesday–Saturday, October–August.

Polo: Palm Beach Polo and Country Club (✉ 13420 South Shore Blvd., West Palm Beach, ☎ 561/793–1440) has games on Sunday, January–April.

Beaches

Crystal-clear warm waters are the main draw of the miles of beaches along the Atlantic coast. Each coastal town has a public beach area; many, like **Pompano Beach** and **Deerfield Beach,** have fishing piers. The area is popular with snorkelers and divers.

The **beachfront,** along Route A1A between Las Olas Boulevard and Sunrise Boulevard in Fort Lauderdale, is a very popular beach; shops, restaurants, and hotels line the road. In Dania the **John U. Lloyd Beach State Recreation Area** (✉ 6503 N. Ocean Dr., ☎ 954/923–2833), the locals' favorite, is a fine beach with picnicking, fishing, and canoeing facilities and 251 acres of mangroves to explore. **Bathtub Beach,** on Hutchinson Island north of Jupiter, has placid waters and a gentle sea slope, making it ideal for children.

Shopping

Both Palm Beach and Fort Lauderdale have shopping districts that cater to an upscale clientele. In Fort Lauderdale expensive boutiques are clustered along tree-lined **Las Olas Boulevard.** In Palm Beach more than 250 specialty shops and pricey boutiques, with such famous names as Gucci and Cartier, beckon to well-heeled shoppers along **Worth Avenue.** A few miles west of Fort Lauderdale, bargain shoppers flock to **Sawgrass Mills Mall** (✉ 12801 W. Sunrise Blvd., Sunrise), which has 270 stores.

ELSEWHERE IN FLORIDA

Everglades and Biscayne National Parks

Arriving and Departing

Miami International Airport (☞ Miami, *above*) is about 35 mi from Homestead and Florida City, gateways to the national parks.Traveling south by car, use Florida's Turnpike or Rtes. 826/874 and the Florida's Turnpike Extension to reach the gateway towns.

What to See and Do

★ **Everglades National Park,** the country's largest remaining subtropical wilderness, contains more than 1.4 million acres—half land, half water—that can be explored by boat, by bike, on foot, and partly by car. This slow-moving "river of grass" is a maze of saw-grass marshes, mangrove swamps, salt prairies, and pinelands that shelter a variety of plants and animals, even though increased pollution by pesticide runoff from local farms has reduced the number of birds and brought the Florida panther to near extinction. The visitor center is superb; the three park entrances are in Homestead, along U.S. 41 (Tamiami Trail), and on the west coast of Florida, in Everglades City. ✉ *Main Visitor Center, 40001 Rte. 9336, Homestead 33034,* ☎ *305/242–7700.*

Biscayne National Park is the nation's largest marine park and the largest national park with a living coral reef in the continental United States.

It covers about 274 square mi, mostly underwater, and has several ecosystems. Shallow Biscayne Bay is home to the manatee, the upper Florida Keys harbor moray eels, and brilliantly colored parrot fish in a 150-mi coral reef, and bald eagles and other large birds inhabit the mainland mangrove forests. A visitor center with interactive exhibits, a glass-bottom-boat tour, canoeing, snorkeling, and scuba diving are popular ways to experience the park. ✉ *9700 S.W. 328th St., Box 1369, Homestead 33090,* ☎ *305/230–7275.*

The Panhandle: Northwestern Florida

Visitor Information

Pensacola: Visitor Information Center (✉ 1401 E. Gregory St., 32501, ☎ 850/434–1234 or 800/874–1234).

Arriving and Departing

Pensacola Regional Airport (☎ 850/435–1746) serves the region. I-10 and U.S. 90 are the main east–west highways across the top of the state, U.S. 98 runs along the coast, and U.S. 231, 331, and 29 and Route 85 traverse the Panhandle north–south.

What to See and Do

The Panhandle has been dubbed the Emerald Coast for its profusion of pine forests, magnolias, live oaks dripping with Spanish moss, lush bayous and swamps, and white-sand beaches lapped by blue-green waters. Historical and archaeological sites vie for attention with beautiful beaches, golf, hunting, hiking, water sports, and outstanding fishing.

Stroll through the historic districts of **Pensacola** and absorb some of the city's colorful Spanish, French, British, and Civil War past. **Fort Walton Beach** is a family vacation playground famous for its beaches and spectacular sand dunes. **Eglin Air Force Base** (✉ Rte. 85, ☎ 850/882–3931), in Fort Walton Beach, includes 10 auxiliary fields and a total of 21 runways; visitors can tour the base and the Airforce Armament Museum, which contains vintage aircraft, guns, and other weapons. Kids especially enjoy the **Indian Temple Mound Museum** (✉ 139 Miracle Strip Pkwy. [U.S. 98], Fort Walton Beach, ☎ 850/833–9595), where they can learn all about the prehistoric peoples who lived in the region during the past ★ 10,000 years. **Grayton Beach State Recreation Area** (Rte. 30A) near the quaint, Victorian-style community of Seaside, has one of the most scenic beaches along the Gulf Coast, if not the country.

Destin, Fort Walton Beach's neighbor, a once-quiet fishing village, has developed into a bustling seaside vacation spot popular with anglers, sun worshipers, and gourmets, and offers some of the area's finest restaurants. For sun-up 'til sun-down action, head for the snow-white beaches, miles of waterways, and amusement parks of **Panama City Beach,** a prime vacation area and the new *in* spot for students on spring break.

Northeastern Florida

Visitor Information

Amelia Island–Fernandina Beach: Chamber of Commerce (✉ 102 Centre St., Fernandina Beach 32034, ☎ 904/261–3248). **Daytona:** Destination Daytona! (✉ 126 E. Orange Ave., Daytona 32120, ☎ 904/255–0415 or 800/854–1234). **Jacksonville and its beaches:** Convention and Visitors Bureau (✉ 6 E. Bay St., Suite 200, 32202, ☎ 904/798–9111). **St. Augustine:** Visitor Information Center (✉ 10 Castillo Dr., 32084, ☎ 800/653–2489).

Arriving and Departing

Jacksonville International Airport (☎ 904/741–4902) and **Daytona Beach International Airport** (☎ 904/248–8069) serve the region. I–10 is the major east–west artery through the north, and I–4 from Tampa and Orlando enters the region to the south, near Daytona Beach. The primary north–south routes are I–95 along the east coast and I–75 through the center of the state.

What to See and Do

Variety is the key word for northeastern Florida: You can see live-oak-framed roads and plantations that recall the Old South all along St. Johns River; Thoroughbred horse farms in Ocala; impressive savannas in Gainesville; and the cosmopolitan city of Jacksonville. The beaches range from rocky shorelines to the glistening sand beaches of Jacksonville and the famous hard-packed, drivable beach at Daytona. The **Daytona 500** auto race is held annually at Daytona International Speedway (⊠ U.S. 92, ☎ 904/254–2700). Jacksonville is the host of collegiate football's **Gator Bowl** (☎ 904/396–1800).

St. Augustine, the oldest permanent settlement in the United States, dates to 1565. Explore the 300-year-old Spanish fortress of **Castillo de San Marcos National Monument** (⊠ 1 Castillo Dr., ☎ 904/829–6506; 🎟 $4), which guards Matanzas Bay. Stroll down St. George Street through St. Augustine's restored **Spanish Quarter** for a glimpse of life in the 1700s. Drink from the spring reputed to be the fountain of youth discovered by Ponce de León in 1513 at the **Fountain of Youth Archaeological Park** (⊠ 155 Magnolia Ave., ☎ 904/829–3168; 🎟 $4.75).

Silver Springs, the state's oldest attraction and the world's largest formation of clear artesian springs, offers glass-bottom-boat tours and a jungle cruise. ⊠ *Rte. 40, 1 mi east of Ocala,* ☎ *352/236–2121.* 🎟 *$26.95.*

Amelia Island, just north of Jacksonville, contains the historic town of Fernandina Beach, with its 19th-century mansions and many posh resorts. North of Fernandina Beach lies 1,086-acre **Fort Clinch State Park** (⊠ N. 14th St., ☎ 904/277–7274; 🎟 $3.25 per vehicle), with a brick fort, nature trails, swimming, and living history reenactments.

GEORGIA

Updated by
Jane F. Garvey

Capital	Atlanta
Population	7,200,882
Motto	Wisdom, Justice, and Moderation
State Bird	Brown thrasher
State Flower	Cherokee rose
Postal Abbreviation	GA

Statewide Visitor Information

Georgia Department of Industry, Trade and Tourism (✉ Box 1776, Atlanta 30301, ☎ 404/656–3590 or 800/847–4842). There are 11 **visitor centers** at various border points and 45 locally operated **welcome centers** in Atlanta, Savannah, and throughout the state.

Scenic Drives

Along the coast Jekyll Island's **North Riverview Drive** passes scenery ranging from historic homes in the Jekyll Island Historic District to glimpses of marshland. **Route 157** north from Cloudland Canyon State Park to the Tennessee border at Lookout Mountain has views of northwestern Georgia's mountains. **U.S. 76** east from Dalton to the Chattooga River traverses the North Georgia Mountains and beautiful sections of the Chattahoochee National Forest.

National and State Parks

National Parks

The **Andersonville National Historic Site** (✉ Rte. 1, Box 800, Andersonville 31711, ☎ 912/924–0343; free), which served as a Confederate prison camp, is the official site of the National Prisoner of War Museum for all POWs from the Civil War through Desert Storm. **Chattahoochee River National Recreation Area** (✉ 1978 Island Ford Pkwy., Dunwoody 30350, ☎ 770/399–8070, ext. 8070; $2 parking fee) has picnic areas, hiking trails and rivers with swimming areas. **Kennesaw Mountain National Battlefield** (✉ 900 Kennesaw Mountain Dr., Kennesaw 30152, ☎ 770/427–4686; free), a 2,884-acre park outside Atlanta, commemorates one of the Civil War's most decisive battles and has 16 mi of hiking trails.

State Parks

Georgia's state parks charge $2 per day per vehicle for all-day parking passes. **Cloudland Canyon State Park** (✉ 122 Cloudland Canyon Park Rd., Rising Fawn 30738, ☎ 706/657–4050), on the west side of Lookout Mountain in the state's northwest corner, has cabin facilities, camping, and dramatic scenery. **Vogel State Park** (✉ 7485 Vogel State Park Rd., Blairsville 30512, ☎ 706/745–2628), a 221-acre park surrounded by the Chattahoochee National Forest, includes a 17-acre lake. The park has cottages and campsites. **Providence Canyon** (✉ Rte. 1, Box 158, Lumpkin 31815, ☎ 912/838–6202), known as Georgia's Grand Canyon, is a day park for picnicking, exploring, and hiking.

ATLANTA

Atlanta is one of the fastest-growing cities in the United States, with a skyline that is constantly changing. Initially founded as a railroad center, the city has blossomed into a major metropolis with more than 3 million people. It is an aviation hub and a regional leader in commerce and industry; perhaps these are some of the reasons it was selected as host of the 1996 Summer Olympic Games. But for all its modernity, the city's winning character is still defined by its southern hospitality and its near-picture-perfect residential neighborhoods.

Visitor Information

Atlanta Chamber of Commerce (✉ 235 International Blvd., 30303, ☎ 404/880–9000). **Convention and Visitors Bureau information centers** (✉ Peachtree Center Mall, 233 Peachtree St., 30303, ☎ 404/222–6688 or 800/285–2682; also ✉ Underground Atlanta, 65 Upper Alabama St.; ✉ Georgia World Congress Center, 285 International Blvd.; ✉ Hartsfield International Airport, North Terminal at West Crossover; and ✉ Lenox Square Mall, 3393 Peachtree Rd.).

Arriving and Departing

By Bus

Greyhound Lines (✉ 232 Forsyth St., ☎ 404/584–1728 or 800/231–2222) provides transportation to downtown Atlanta, Decatur, Hapeville, Marietta, Conyers, Douglasville, and Norcross.

By Car

Atlanta is called the Crossroads of the South for good reason. Between South Carolina and Alabama, I–85 runs northeast–southwest through Atlanta and I–20 runs east–west; I–75 runs north–south through the state. I–285 makes a 65-mi loop around the metro area.

By Plane

Hartsfield Atlanta International Airport (☎ 404/530–6600) has scheduled flights by most major domestic and foreign carriers. Cab fare to downtown Atlanta, 13 mi north of the airport via I–75 and I–85N, is about $18 for one person, $20 for two people, and $8 each additional for three or more. The **Metropolitan Atlanta Rapid Transit Authority** (MARTA; ☎ 404/848–4711) rapid-rail subway system is one of the quickest and easiest ways to reach the downtown, Buckhead, Midtown, and the Lenox Square and Perimeter Mall districts; the fare is $1.50. MARTA also goes directly to the airport.

By Train

Amtrak (☎ 404/881–3060 or 800/872–7245) serves Brookwood Station (✉ 1688 Peachtree St.).

Getting Around Atlanta

By Car

Major public parking lots downtown are at the **CNN Center** (✉ Entrance off Techwood Dr.), the **Georgia World Congress Center** (✉ Off International Blvd.), **Peachtree Center** (☞ Exploring Atlanta, *below*), **Macy's** (✉ Carnegie Way, 1 block off Peachtree St.), and **Underground Atlanta** (✉ 65 Upper Alabama St.). Buckhead and Midtown have on-street parking and more lots.

By Public Transportation

MARTA (☎ 404/848–4711) operates buses and a modern rapid-rail subway system. Fare for either is $1.50; exact change or a token is required. The rapid-rail trains operate from 5:30 AM to 1:17 AM; bus schedules depend on the route.

By Taxi

You can hail a cab fairly easily at hotels in the downtown or Buckhead district. **Buckhead Safety Cab** (☎ 404/233–1152 or 404/233–

1153) and **Checker Cab** (☏ 404/351–1111) have 24-hour service. With advance reservations, **Carey Executive Limousine** (☏ 404/223–2000) also provides 24-hour service.

Orientation Tours

Bus and Van Tours

Atlanta Discovery Tours (☏ 770/667–1414) and **American Sightseeing Atlanta** (☏ 404/233–9140 or 800/572–3050) pick you up at area hotels for customized sightseeing tours. **Gray Line of Atlanta** (✉ 705 Lively Ave., Norcross 30071, ☏ 770/449–1806 or 800/593–1818, FAX 770/249–9397) offers tours of downtown, Midtown, Buckhead, and the King Center.

Walking Tours

Atlanta Preservation Center (✉ Suite 3, 156 7th St., 30303, ☏ 404/876–2041 or 404/876–2040 for tour hot line) has guided tours on selected days, including 10 historic neighborhoods, available from March through November, and a tour of the Fox Theatre that's available year-round.

Exploring Atlanta

Because Atlanta is a sprawling city, a car is a necessity, though there are in fact a number of walkable neighborhoods and districts with interesting architecture and attractions. Beginning downtown, you can move north past an eclectic mix of Renaissance Revival towers and contemporary glass-and-steel skyscrapers; through Midtown's genteel, garden-filled neighborhoods punctuated by parks and museums; and into upscale Buckhead, lined with mansions and glitzy shopping centers full of designer-name boutiques.

Downtown

Atlanta had its inauspicious beginning as a 19th-century settlement and later became a railway hub; a few sites from the earliest days are preserved downtown. A three-level, six-block entertainment and shopping center called **Underground Atlanta** (✉ 50 Upper Alabama St., ☏ 404/523–2311) encompasses some of the original city center's storefronts and streets. The **World of Coca-Cola** (✉ 55 Martin Luther King Jr. Dr., ☏ 404/676–5151; 🎟 $6) gives free samples and has three floors of memorabilia from the century-old soft drink company.

At the corner of Marietta Street and Techwood Drive is the **CNN Center** (✉ 1 CNN Center, ☏ 404/827–2300; 🎟 $7), headquarters of Cable News Network. There are daily guided behind-the-scenes tours, including newscasters in action. Children under six are not admitted to the tours.

Thrusting into the sky a block north of Woodruff Park are the striking angles of the red-marble **Georgia-Pacific Building** (✉ 133 Peachtree St., at John Wesley Dobbs Ave.). Built on the site of Loew's Grand Theatre, where *Gone With the Wind* premiered in 1939, the corporate flagship building houses the **High Museum of Art, Folk Art and Photography Galleries** (✉ 30 John Wesley Dobbs Ave., ☏ 404/577–6940; 🎟 free), a branch of the High Museum of Art (☞ Midtown, *below*).

★ Walking tours of the **Martin Luther King, Jr., National Historic District** start from the **King Center** (✉ 449 Auburn Ave., ☏ 404/524–1956; 🎟 free), established by King's widow, Coretta Scott King. Inside the center are a museum, a library, and a gift shop; in front is King's tomb, where a flame burns for eternity.

The Queen Anne–style clapboard house that was **Dr. King's Birth Home** (✉ 501 Auburn Ave., ☏ 404/331–3920; 🎟 free) is open for

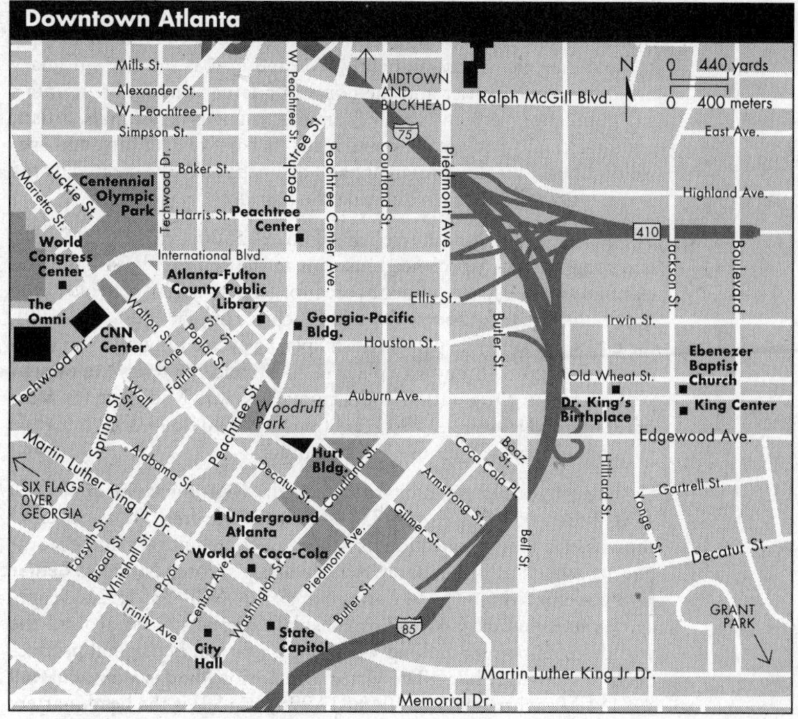

tours. Three generations of the King family have preached at **Ebenezer Baptist Church** (✉ 407 Auburn Ave., ☎ 404/688–7263; 🎟 free).

The **Georgia State Capitol** (✉ 206 Washington St., ☎ 404/656–2844; 🎟 free) houses government offices and a museum. Built in 1889, it has a dome gilded with gold leaf from ore mined in nearby Dahlonega, the site of the nation's first gold rush. The **Georgia Capitol Museum** completed a multiyear renovation in 1998 and has exhibits that examine Georgia wildlife, geology, agriculture, and industry and tell the story of the capitol building. The **Capitol Education Center,** which will provide visitor information, is due to open January 1999 across the street in Plaza Park.

Peachtree Center (☎ 404/524–3787), a climate-controlled complex filled with shops, restaurants, hotels, and offices, is on the city's main thoroughfare, **Peachtree Street.** In the lobby of the center's Marriott Marquis Two Tower is the **Atlanta International Museum** (✉ 285 Peachtree Center Ave., ☎ 404/688–2467; 🎟 free), which specializes in international art and design, as well as cultural exhibitions.

★ In Grant Park, 2 mi southeast of downtown, is the unique **Atlanta Cyclorama** (✉ Grant Park, 800 Cherokee Ave., ☎ 404/624–1071 for tickets, 404/658–7625 for information; 🎟 $5), a huge circular painting depicting the Battle of Atlanta (1864), when the city was burned by General William T. Sherman. It is closed on weekends.

Six Flags over Georgia (✉ I–20W at 7561 Six Flags Rd., Austell, ☎ 770/739–3400; 🎟 $32 adults, $21 children 3–9, a large theme park 10 mi west of downtown, has dozens of rides (including roller coasters and water rides), musical revues, and concerts by top-name artists. It is closed from November through February.

Midtown

Midtown, just north of downtown, was the heart of Atlanta's hippie scene during the 1960s and early '70s and now is the city's primary art and theater district and the home of a large segment of Atlanta's gay population, as well as young families, young professionals, artists, and musicians. The area is popular for its bars, restaurants, and specialty shops. Like downtown, it has a distinctive skyline created by the many office towers erected during the past decade.

SciTrek (✉ 395 Piedmont Ave., ☎ 404/522–5500, ext. 249; $7.50) is among the top 10 science museums in the country, with hands-on exhibits and Kidspace, a special area for two- to seven-year-olds. The Egyptian-style **Fox Theatre** (✉ 660 Peachtree St., ☎ 404/881–2100), the city's oldest movie palace, hosts splashy events ranging from touring companies of Broadway plays to rock concerts; tours are offered year-round (☞ Orientation Tours, *above*). New in Midtown, the **Margaret Mitchell House** (✉ 990 Peachtree St., ☎ 404/249–7012; $6) pays tribute to the famous Georgia author.

Designed by architect Richard Meier, the **High Museum of Art** (✉ 1280 Peachtree St., ☎ 404/733–4444; $6; free Thurs. after 1) showcases a major collection of American contemporary and decorative art as well as sub-Saharan African art. It's closed Monday. **Center for Puppetry Arts** (✉ 1404 Spring St., ☎ 404/873–3391; $5; special exhibitions may cost extra) displays puppets from around the world, holds puppet-making workshops, and stages original productions. It's closed Sunday. The Victorian mansion **Rhodes Memorial Hall** (✉ 1516 Peachtree St., ☎ 404/881–9980; $3) is the headquarters for the **Georgia Trust for Historic Preservation,** which presents exhibits on Georgia architecture. The **Fernbank Science Center** (✉ 156 Heaton Park Dr., ☎ 404/378–4311; free; planetarium shows $2), in Druid Hills, has an *Apollo* spacecraft and a planetarium.

Buckhead

A large portion of Buckhead, 5 mi north of Midtown on Peachtree Street, is to Atlanta what Beverly Hills is to Los Angeles. This residential and shopping area is home to fine dining, designer boutiques, and expensive homes. To see the manicured lawns and mansions of Atlanta's elite, take a scenic drive along Tuxedo, Valley, and Habersham roads.

The white-columned, neoclassical **Georgia Governor's Mansion** (✉ 391 W. Paces Ferry Rd., ☎ 404/261–1858; free) has many Federal-period antiques; it's open for tours Tuesday through Thursday. The **Atlanta History Center** (✉ 130 W. Paces Ferry Rd., ☎ 404/814–4000; $7)—comprising the **Atlanta History Museum,** the **Tullie Smith Farm** ($1), the symmetrical **Palladian Swan House** mansion ($2), and **McElreath Hall**—is a 32-acre site where city history is preserved.

Parks, Gardens, and Zoos

Zoo Atlanta (✉ 800 Cherokee Ave., ☎ 404/624–5600; $9) is in Grant Park, just southeast of downtown. Nearly 1,000 animals live in naturalistic habitats, such as the Ford African Rain Forest, Flamingo Lagoon, Masai Mara (re-created plains of Kenya), and Sumatran Tiger Exhibit.

Woodruff Park, at the corner of Peachtree Street and Park Place, is named for Robert W. Woodruff, the late Coca-Cola magnate. In warm weather the park is a favorite alfresco lunch spot. Near the CNN Center, **Centennial Olympic Park** (✉ Marietta St. and Techwood Dr.), a legacy of the 1996 Centennial Olympic Games, enhances the streetscape with green space and sculpture. It is the setting for special events such as the Arts Festival of Atlanta (☞ Festivals and Seasonal Events *in* The Southeast introduction). **Piedmont Park,** in Midtown between 10th Street and The Prado, is the city's premier urban green space, with a children's playground, tennis courts, a swimming pool, and paved paths for biking, running, and roller skating. You can rent bikes and in-line skates from Skate Escape (✉ 1086 Piedmont Ave., ☎ 404/892–1292), across the street. The park was designed for the 1895 Cotton States and International Exposition by Frederick Law Olmsted.

Adjoining Piedmont Park is the 30-acre **Atlanta Botanical Garden** (✉ 1345 Piedmont Ave., ½ mi north of 14th St., ☎ 404/876–5859; $6, free Thurs. after 3), with landscaped gardens and the climate-controlled Fuqua Conservatory. All exhibits are closed Monday. A new garden especially for kids is slated for completion in 1999.

Stone Mountain Park (✉ U.S. 78E, ☎ 770/498–5690; $6 parking, additional fees for individual attractions and special events) 7 mi northeast of the city, features the world's largest sculpture, a memorial to Confederate war heroes Jefferson Davis, Robert E. Lee, and Stonewall Jackson (a cable car takes you 825 ft up the mountain face for a closer look). The 3,200-acre park also contains an antebellum plantation and museums, plus a railroad, a riverboat, and nightly laser shows in summer. Many popular special events here showcase southern history and culture and include food and entertainment.

Dining

Atlanta prides itself on a wide selection of international restaurants. Various cuisines tempt the palates of Atlanta's dining public, but there is also plenty of opportunity to sample both the traditional and new-style fare of the Deep South. For price ranges *see* Chart 1 (A) *in* On the Road with Fodor's.

$$$$ ★ ✕ **The Dining Room, the Ritz-Carlton, Buckhead.** International acclaim praises this restaurant for its imaginative haute cuisine, which is basically French with Asian garnishes and flavors. The menus change daily, but the best deal is the tasting menu matching preselected wines with each dish. ✉ *3434 Peachtree Rd.,* ☎ *404/237–2700. Reservations essential. Jacket and tie. AE, D, DC, MC, V. Closed Sun. No lunch.*

$$$$ ★ ✕ **Seeger's.** When stellar chef Guenter Seeger left his helm at The Dining Room, at the Ritz-Carlton, Buckhead, (☞ *above*), he opened this sophisticated establishment. Such dishes as a roulade of foie gras with red wine/apple purée and quince gelée are quintessential Seeger. Local ingredients also appear, as in grilled lamb chops with Vidalia onions. The wine list is exceptional. Fixed-price menus (including a vegetable menu) may be paired with selected wines for an additional charge. ✉ *111 W. Paces Ferry Rd.,* ☎ *404/846–9779. Reservations essential. Jacket and tie. AE, D, DC, MC, V. Closed Sun. No lunch*

$$$–$$$$ ★ ✕ **Bacchanalia.** Having won many accolades since opening in 1993, this restaurant never disappoints. The influence is largely Mediterranean with an Asian flare; both four- and six-course meals are offered. The imaginative vegetable tasting ($40) menu is outstanding. ✉ *3125 Piedmont Rd.,* ☎ *404/365–0410. Reservations essential. AE, DC, MC, V. Closed Sun.–Mon. No lunch.*

$$$–$$$$ ★ ✕ **Ciboulette.** The warmly lit, contemporary dining space serves excellent Continental cuisine that has Atlantans lining up outside. The fish dishes bear innovative touches, and game dishes are frequent specials in season. ✉ *1529 Piedmont Ave.,* ☎ *404/874–7600. AE, D, DC, MC, V. Closed Sun. No lunch.*

$$$–$$$$ ✕ **Hedgerose.** Quiet and relaxed, this restaurant is perfect for business or romance. Lump crab hash or ravioli with scallops and caviar are tempting appetizers; grilled squab with foie gras and loin of lamb with oven-dried tomatoes are appealing entrées. The wine list is extensive. ✉ *490 E. Paces Ferry Rd.,* ☎ *404/233–7673. Reservations essential. Jacket and tie. AE, D, DC, MC, V. No lunch.*

$$–$$$ ✕ **City Grill.** The grand setting of this downtown restaurant in the historic Hurt Building includes high ceilings, bucolic murals, and romantic table lamps. The menu is American with a southern flair as seen in such dishes as Creole barbecued shrimp, cider-glazed quail, and hickory-grilled pork fillet with Tennessee whiskey sauce. Save room for the chocolate pecan souflée. ✉ *50 Hurt Plaza,* ☎ *404/524–2489. AE, D, DC, MC, V. Closed Sun. No lunch Sat.*

$$–$$$ ✕ **Luna Sí.** Funky meets uptown chic at this delightfully relaxed loft restaurant, where Latin music blares and customers are encouraged to write on the walls. The menu, which changes weekly, is dominated by seafood. Signature dishes include salmon with a ginger crust, and Cornish game hen and mashed potatoes. The heavenly homemade biscotti is a lovely way to finish. ✉ *1931 Peachtree Rd.,* ☎ *404/355–5993. AE, DC, MC, V. Reservations essential.*

$$–$$$ ★ ✕ **South City Kitchen.** The cuisine at this bright, popular restaurant is the traditional Low Country style of coastal South Carolina; the catfish is superb, and the desserts are delicious. ✉ *1144 Crescent Ave.,* ☎ *404/873–7358. AE, DC, MC, V.*

$–$$ ★ ✕ **Colonnade Restaurant.** For traditional southern cuisine, such as ham steak, turkey and dressing, and southern-style vegetables, insiders head for the Colonnade, an Atlanta institution since 1927. ✉ *1879 Cheshire Bridge Rd.,* ☎ *404/874–5642. Reservations not accepted. No credit cards.*

$ ✕ **Thelma's Kitchen.** After losing her location to the Centennial Olympic Park, Thelma Grundy moved down the road to the street level of a somewhat renovated Roxy Hotel. Brighter, spiffier, and more cheerful than the earlier spot, it still has some of the best southern food in town. Unique okra pancakes should not be missed. Fried catfish, "cold" slaw, macaroni and cheese, homemade cakes, and to-die-for pecan pie are all special. ✉ *768 Marietta St., NW,* ☎ *404/688–5855. Reservations not accepted. No credit cards. Closed weekends.*

Lodging

The city's booming convention business means hotel and motel options in all price ranges. The downtown, Buckhead, and north I–285 areas have the greatest concentration of accommodations. For price ranges *see* Chart 2 (A) *in* On the Road with Fodor's.

$$$$ ★ 🏨 **Ritz-Carlton, Buckhead.** The elegant lobby with fine art, a fireplace, and comfortable, authentic antique furniture is perfect for lingering over afternoon tea before returning to rooms containing luxury linens, marble baths, and reproduction period furnishings. ✉ *3434 Peachtree Rd., 30326,* ☎ *404/237–2700,* FAX *404/239–0078. 553 rooms. 2 restaurants, pool, health club. AE, D, DC, MC, V.*

$$$–$$$$ 🏨 **Atlanta Marriott Marquis.** The lobby of this convention hotel stretches to the skylighted roof 50 stories above. Traditionally furnished guest rooms open onto this central atrium. A skywalk connects the hotel to the Peachtree Center and its shops. ✉ *265 Peachtree Center Ave., 30303,* ☎ *404/521–0000,* FAX *404/586–6299. 1,731 rooms. 5 restaurants, pool, health club. AE, D, DC, MC, V.*

$$$–$$$$ 🏨 **JW Marriott.** Handsome Chippendale-style furniture graces both the lobby and the guest rooms of this elegant 25-story hotel, which connects with Lenox Square Mall. Rooms also have spacious marble baths with separate shower stalls. ✉ *3300 Lenox Rd., 30326,* ☎ *404/262–3344,* FAX *404/262–8689. 371 rooms. Restaurant, pool, health club. AE, D, DC, MC, V.*

$$$–$$$$ **Swissôtel.** An international clientele frequents this European-style luxury hotel, with its chic, modern glass exterior, sophisticated Biedermeier-style interiors, and fabulous art on view in the public spaces. Palm, an outpost of the popular Manhattan restaurant of the same name, is famous for its steaks. ✉ *3391 Peachtree Rd., 30326,* ☎ *404/365–0065 or 800/253–1397,* FAX *404/365–8787. 380 rooms. Restaurant, pool, health club . AE, D, DC, MC, V.*

$$$ **Embassy Suites.** This Buckhead high-rise is just blocks from two of the city's top shopping centers, Phipps Plaza and Lenox Square. Suites range from basic bedroom and sitting-room combinations to luxurious rooms with wet bars; a few standard rooms are available. All units have microwaves and refrigerators. ✉ *3285 Peachtree Rd., 30305,* ☎ *404/261–7733,* FAX *404/261–6857. 317 suites. Restaurant, pools. Full breakfast. AE, D, DC, MC, V.*

$$$ **Quality Hotel Downtown.** Rooms in this quiet downtown hotel have views of downtown; some have balconies. The marble lobby is lit by crystal chandeliers and modest-size rooms are done in teal and navy. ✉ *89 Luckie St., 30303,* ☎ *404/524–7991,* FAX *404/525–0672. 75 rooms. Pool. Full breakfast. AE, DC, MC, V.*

$$ **Buckhead Bed & Breakfast Inn.** Built in 1996, the inn sits on a busy corner but provides the intimacy and coziness lacking in large hotels. Though rooms are not especially spacious, the hotel is handy to the cluster of cathedrals that forms the hub of Buckhead. ✉ *70 Lenox Pointe, 30324,* ☎ *404/261–8284 or 888/224–8797,* FAX *404/237–9224. 18 rooms. Full breakfast. AE, MC, V.*

$–$$ **Sierra Suites Atlanta Brookhaven.** Studio-style suites with kitchens are decorated in earth tones and forest green. Light wood modern-style furniture with an oak finish is standard. *3967 Peachtree Rd.,* ☎ *404/237–9100 or 800/474–3772,* FAX *404/237–0055, 92 suites. Pool. CP. AE, CB, D, DC, MC, V.*

Nightlife and the Arts

Arts and nightlife events (and special events throughout the city) are listed in the *Atlanta Journal and Constitution* and *Creative Loafing* newspapers, both available at newsstands, and in *Peachtree, Presenting the Season,* and *KNOW ATLANTA* magazines, available at visitor information centers and in hotels. The **Arts Hotline** (☎ 404/853–3278) also gives daily arts and nightlife information. Ticket brokers include **TicketMaster** (☎ 404/249–6400 or 800/326–4000) and **Ticket-X-Press** (☎ 404/231–5888).

Nightlife

Underground Atlanta (☞ Shopping, *below*) and the **Buckhead, Virginia-Highland,** and **Little Five Points** neighborhoods are Atlanta's nightlife centers. Virginia-Highland's **Atkins Park Bar & Grill** (✉ 794 N. Highland Ave., ☎ 404/876–7249), one of the city's oldest neighborhood bars, attracts a 30-something crowd. **Blind Willie's** (✉ 828 N. Highland Ave., ☎ 404/873–2583) offers New Orleans– and Chicago-style blues. **Eddie's Attic** (✉ 515B N. McDonough St., ☎ 404/377–4976), next to the MARTA station in nearby Decatur, is the best venue for local acoustic acts. For contemporary rock try **The Point** (✉ 420 Moreland Ave., ☎ 404/659–3522).

In Buckhead, Latin music invites dancing at **Sanctuary** (✉ 128 E. Andrews Dr., ☎ 404/262–1377). At **Churchill Arms** (✉ 3223 Cain Hill Pl., ☎ 404/233–5633) folks of all ages gather to shoot pool and to listen to live piano music. **Tongue & Groove** (☒ 3055 Peachtree Rd., ☎ 404/261–2325) is Buckhead's see-and-be-seen nightspot.

The Arts

Most touring **Broadway productions** make their way to Atlanta's Fox Theatre (☞ Midtown *in* Exploring Atlanta, *above*), Center Stage (☒ 1374 W. Peachtree St., ☎ 404/874–1511), or the Civic Center (☒ 395 Piedmont Ave., ☎ 404/523–6275). The **Alliance Theater Company** (☒ 1280 Peachtree St., ☎ 404/733–5000) is one of the city's leading theatrical groups. Woodruff Arts Center's Symphony Hall (☒ 1280 Peachtree St., ☎ 404/733–5000) is the home of the acclaimed **Atlanta Symphony Orchestra.** The **Atlanta Ballet Company** (☎ 404/873–5811) performs at the Fox Theatre. In summer the **Atlanta Opera** (☎ 404/355–3311) usually presents four operas at the Fox Theatre.

Outdoor Activities and Sports

Golf

The only public course near downtown, **Bobby Jones Golf Course** (☒ 384 Woodward Way, ☎ 404/355–1009) has some of the city's worst fairways and greens; still, the 18-hole, par-71 course is always crowded. The **Alfred Tup Holmes Club** (☒ 2300 Wilson Dr., ☎ 404/753–6158) is known for doglegs and blind shots. **North Fulton Golf Course** (☒ 216 W. Wieuca Rd., ☎ 404/255–0723) has one of the best layouts in the city. Outside I–285, in the suburbs, Stone Mountain Park's (☒ U.S. 78, ☎ 770/498–5715) **Stonemont,** an 18-hole course, is the best.

Tennis

Bitsy Grant Tennis Center (☒ 2125 Northside Dr., ☎ 404/351–2774), in Chastain Park, has 13 clay courts, six of which are lighted, and 10 lighted hard courts; it's the area's best public facility. **Piedmont Park** (☒ Piedmont Ave. between 10th St. and the Prado, ☎ 404/872–1507) has 12 hard courts with lights. Access the tennis center from Park Drive off Monroe Drive; even though the sign reads DO NOT ENTER, the security guard will show you the parking lot.

Spectator Sports

Tickets for the teams listed below are available through **TicketMaster** (☎ 404/249–7630 or 800/326–4000).

Baseball: Atlanta Braves (☒ Atlanta-Turner Field, I–75/85 Exit 91, Fulton St.; I–20 westbound Exit 24, Capitol Ave.; or eastbound Exit 22, Windsor St./Spring St., ☎ 404/522–7630). **Basketball: Atlanta Hawks** (☒ Omni, 1 CNN Center, Suite 405, ☎ 404/827–3865). **Football: Atlanta Falcons** (☒ 1 Georgia Dome Dr., ☎ 404/223–9200).

Shopping

Antiques Stores

Shops selling antique pine pieces, collectibles, and crafts line **Bennett Street** in Buckhead. European furnishings and fine art are offered in more than 25 shops in Buckhead's **2300 Peachtree Road** complex. **Miami Circle,** a street on the northern edge of Buckhead off Piedmont Road, is a hot spot for lovers of antiques, with such stores as Gables Antiques (☒ 711 Miami Circle, ☎ 404/231–0734) and Williams Antiques (☒ 631 Miami Circle, ☎ 404/264–1142). **Chamblee Antique Row** (☒ Intersection of Broad St. and Peachtree Industrial Blvd., Chamblee, ☎ 770/458–1814) has antiques stores and malls.

Shopping Districts

Atlanta's shopping centers are generally open Monday through Saturday 10 to 6 and Sunday noon to 5; many stay open until 9 or 9:30

several weeknights and most weekends. The primary downtown shopping areas are **Underground Atlanta,** where specialty boutiques, chain stores, and pushcarts mix with restaurants and nightclubs; and the stretch of Peachtree between **Macy's** and **Peachtree Center Mall.** North of downtown in Buckhead, **Lenox Square** (✉ 3393 Peachtree St.) and **Phipps Plaza** (✉ 3500 Peachtree Rd.) attract shoppers from throughout the Southeast. Lenox's second level has more than 250 stores, while Phipps's now has more than 100 stores. **Perimeter Mall** (✉ 400 Ashford-Dunwoody Rd., Dunwoody) serves the Dunwoody area, and **Cumberland Mall** (✉ I–285 at Cobb Pkwy.) and **Galleria** (✉ 1 Galleria Pkwy.) are the most convenient to I–75/I–285.

SAVANNAH

Four hours southeast of Atlanta, but a world away from the bustling, modern metropolis, lies Savannah, wrapped in a mantle of Old World grace. Established in 1733, the city preserves its heritage in a 2½-square-mi historic district, the nation's largest urban landmark. Here 1,000 structures have been restored, and families still live in the 19th-century mansions and town houses. Known as the City of Festivals, Savannah rarely lets a weekend pass without some sort of celebration, from the St. Patrick's Day bash in March to the Riverfront Seafood Festival in April, from the spring azalea and dogwood festivals to the house tours and concerts at Christmas.

Visitor Information

Convention and Visitors Bureau (✉ 222 W. Oglethorpe Ave., 31401, ☎ 912/944–0456 or 800/444–2427). **Visitors Center** (✉ 301 Martin Luther King Jr. Blvd., 31499, ☎ 912/944–0455).

Arriving and Departing

By Bus

Greyhound Lines (✉ 610 W. Oglethorpe Ave., ☎ 800/231–2222).

By Car

I–95, running north–south along the coast, and I–16, leading east from Macon, intersect west of Savannah; I–16 dead-ends in downtown. The Coastal Highway (U.S. 17) runs north–south through town, and U.S. 80 runs east–west.

By Plane

Savannah International Airport, served by major airlines, is 18 mi west of town on I–16. There is no bus service into town, but **McCall's Limousine Service** (☎ 912/966–5364 or 800/673–9365) runs a van between the airport and the city for $15 per person one-way.

By Train

The **Amtrak** station (✉ 2611 Seaboard Coastline Dr., ☎ 912/234–2611 or 800/872–7245) is 4 mi southwest of downtown.

Getting Around Savannah

Savannah's historic district is best seen on foot so you can better observe the intricate architectural details. It's laid out in a grid pattern, and strategically placed benches allow for frequent rests. If you bring a car, park it in one of the metered and off-street pay lots here.

Exploring Savannah

A good way to start a tour is by picking up information at the **Visitors Center** (☞ Visitor Information, *above*) in the old Central Georgia railway station. For entertainment of every sort, visit the restored **City Market** (✉ W. St. Julian St. between Ellis and Franklin Sqs.), a four-block area of shops, art galleries, restaurants, and blues clubs.

Near the riverfront narrow cobblestone streets wind from Bay Street down to Factors Walk and below it, to River Street and the revitalized **River Front** district, a nine-block marketplace with boutiques, restaurants, and taverns. The **Ships of the Sea Museum** (✉ 41 Martin Luther King Jr. Blvd., ☎ 912/232–1511; 🎫 $5) displays memorabilia ranging from models of the earliest ships and nuclear submarines to nautical folk art.

★ The **Isaiah Davenport House** (✉ 324 E. State St., ☎ 912/236–8097; 🎫 $5), one of the city's finest examples of Federal architecture, is furnished with Chippendale, Hepplewhite, and Sheraton antiques. Within the graceful **Telfair Mansion and Art Museum** (✉ 121 Barnard St., ☎ 912/232–1177; 🎫 $6), designed by William Jay, is the South's oldest public art museum, displaying American, French, and German paintings from the 18th and 19th centuries along with classical sculptures. The **Juliette Gordon Low Birthplace/Girl Scout National Center** (✉ 142 Bull St., ☎ 912/233–4501; 🎫 $5), in a Regency town house that was the city's first National Historic Landmark, displays memorabilia and family furnishings of the founder of the Girl Scouts of America.

At the corner of Oglethorpe Avenue and McDonough Street, **Colonial Park Cemetery** is the burial ground for some of the city's earliest and most notable residents, such as Button Gwinnett, a signatory of the Declaration of Independence. **Cathedral of St. John the Baptist** (✉ 222 E. Harris St., ☎ 912/233–4709; 🎫 free), a late-19th-century structure, contains Austrian stained-glass windows, an Italian marble altar, and German-made stations of the cross. Tours are by appointment only.

★ The **Andrew Low House** (✉ 329 Abercorn St., ☎ 912/233–6854; 🎫 $6) was built in 1848 for Andrew Low, investor in the SS *Savannah,* the first steamship to cross the Atlantic Ocean in 1819. The home later belonged to his son, William, who married Juliette Gordon, founder of the Girl Scouts. Some of the city's most impressive ironwork decorates the exterior; inside is a fine collection of 19th-century antiques.

★ The **Green-Meldrim House** (✉ 14 W. Macon St., ☎ 912/233–3845; 🎫 $5) is a splendid Gothic Revival mansion built in 1852 for cotton merchant Charles Green. Now a parish house for St. John's Episcopal Church, it is furnished with 16th- through 18th-century antiques; one piece is original to the house.

Midnight in the Garden of Good and Evil

In his 1994 best-seller, *Midnight in the Garden of Good and Evil,* John Berendt focuses on the action surrounding the mysterious death of one Savannahian and the ensuing trials of Jim Williams (who was acquitted). Read the book before you visit the city. *Note: Unless otherwise indicated, the sites mentioned in the book are not open to the public.*

Songwriter Johnny Mercer's great-grandfather began building **Mercer House** (✉ 429 Bull St., on Monterey Sq.) in 1860. The redbrick Italianate mansion became the home of Jim Williams, the book's main character. Here his sometime house partner Danny Hansford was shot and died, and Williams himself died in the house in 1990. Today, Williams's sister lives here quietly. Jim Williams lived and worked in **Armstrong House** (✉ 447 Bull St.) before purchasing the Mercer House. **Lee**

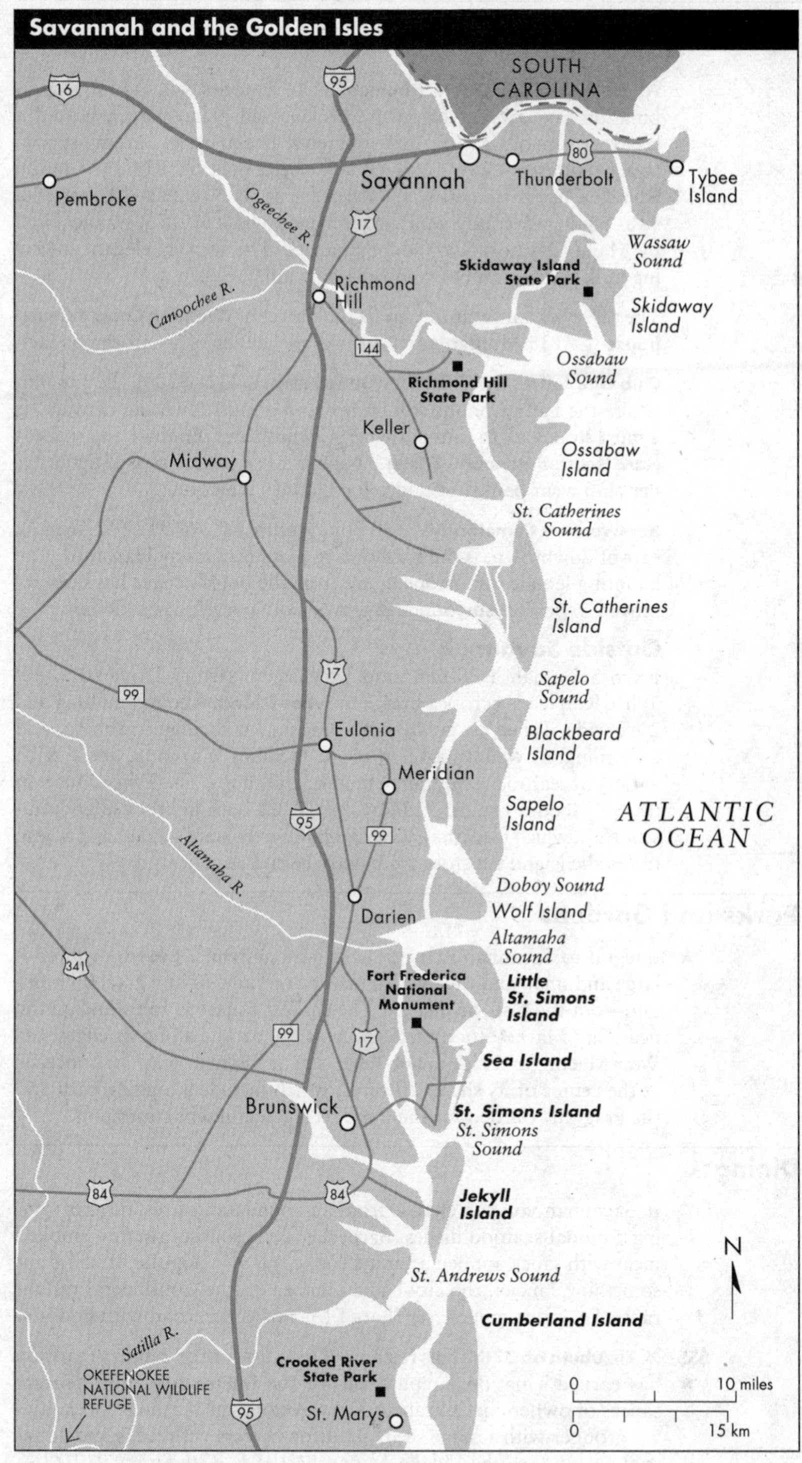
Savannah and the Golden Isles
SOUTH CAROLINA
16
95
80
Savannah
Thunderbolt
Tybee Island
Pembroke
Ogeechee R.
17
Wassaw Sound
Skidaway Island State Park
Richmond Hill
Canoochee R.
Skidaway Island
144
Ossabaw Sound
Richmond Hill State Park
Keller
Ossabaw Island
Midway
St. Catherines Sound
St. Catherines Island
17
Sapelo Sound
99
Blackbeard Island
Eulonia
Meridian
Sapelo Island
ATLANTIC OCEAN
95
99
Altamaha R.
Doboy Sound
Darien
Wolf Island
Altamaha Sound
341
Fort Frederica National Monument
Little St. Simons Island
99
17
Sea Island
Brunswick
St. Simons Island
St. Simons Sound
84
84
Jekyll Island
N
St. Andrews Sound
Cumberland Island
Satilla R.
OKEFENOKEE NATIONAL WILDLIFE REFUGE
Crooked River State Park
0
10 miles
95
St. Marys
0
15 km

Adler's home (✉ 425 Bull St.), residence of one of Williams's biggest adversaries, is half of the double town house facing West Wayne Street.

At **the first of Joe Odom's homes** (✉ 16 E. Jones St.), Odom, a combination tax lawyer, real estate broker, and piano player, hosted a steady stream of visitors. Author Berendt loaded up on a greasy-spoon-style breakfast at **Clary's Café** (✉ 404 Abercorn St., ☎ 912/233–0402). **Hamilton-Turner House** (✉ 330 Abercorn St., ☎ 912/233–1833 or 888/448–8849), a Second Empire–style mansion built in 1873, was acquired by Mandy Nichols, Joe Odom's fiancée. The sturdily elegant towering hulk is now is a bed-and-breakfast inn.

The three Williams murder trials took place at **Chatham County Courthouse** (✉ 133 Montgomery St.) over the course of about eight years.

Club One Jefferson (✉ 1 Jefferson St., ☎ 912/232–0200), the gay club where the Lady Chablis still bumps and grinds down the catwalk, is a must stop. Call to find out when Chablis sings. Emma Kelly sings at **Hard Hearted Hannah's East** (☞ Nightlife, *below*). She moved here after her club went bankrupt under Joe Odom's direction.

Bonaventure Cemetery (✉ 330 Bonaventure Rd., ☎ 912/651–6843), east of downtown, is the final resting place for Danny Hansford. The haunting female tombstone figure from the book's cover has been removed to protect surrounding graves from overenthusiastic fans.

Outside Savannah

From Savannah a 30-minute drive east on Victory Drive (U.S. 80/Tybee Rd.) leads across a bridge to **Tybee Island.** About 5 mi long and 2 mi wide, Tybee has white-sand beaches for shelling, crabbing, and swimming, as well as covered picnic facilities, a marina, and a wide variety of seafood restaurants, motels, and shops. The **Tybee Museum** (✉ 30 Meddin Dr., ☎ 912/786–4077; 🎫 both lighthouse and museum $3), which faces the **Tybee Lighthouse,** the state's oldest and tallest, traces the island's history from early Native American days.

Parks and Gardens

★ Integral to Savannah's design is its park system: 24 **town squares**—large and small and each with a historic monument or a graceful fountain—dot the historic district. The earliest square is Johnson Square, near City Market; food carts are typically parked along its edges. On West Macon Street is **Forsyth Park,** site of frequent outdoor concerts; at the center of its shady 20 acres, which include a jogging path and the Fragrant Garden for the Blind, is a graceful white fountain.

Dining

In Savannah you can choose from an abundance of restaurants serving regional seafood dishes. Barbecue (done southern-style—smoked meat with sauce applied after it's cooked) is also popular. If you want something fancier, the city has a number of fine Continental restaurants. For price ranges *see* Chart 1 (A) *in* On the Road with Fodor's.

$$$ ★ ✕ **Elizabeth on 37th.** This restaurant in a turn-of-the-century mansion has earned a national reputation for the fine seafood and delicate sauces of owner-chef Elizabeth Terry. Among the seasonal specialities are grouper with sesame seeds, Bluffton oysters with leeks and country ham, and stuffed Vidalia onions. ✉ *105 E. 37th St.,* ☎ *912/236–5547. Reservations essential. AE, D, DC, MC, V. Closed Sun. No lunch.*

$$–$$$ ★ ✕ **Bistro Savannah.** This establishment, housed in a circa 1878 building, specializes in fresh regional fare that uses both farmed and wild ingredients. Crab cakes with lemon-caper aioli and chowchow, shrimp

and tasso ham with stone ground grits, and crispy roasted duck confit with caramelized pear duck jus are among the highlights. ✉ *309 W. Congress St.,* ☎ *912/233–6266. AE, MC, V. No lunch.*

$$–$$$ ★ ✕ **Sapphire Grill.** New in 1998, this popular bistro has been packed every night with Savannah's young. Chef Chris Nason deftly uses squab, grits, and fried green tomatoes in his repertoire of classic Low Country dishes. The chocolate flan is sinful. ✉ *110 W. Congress St.,* ☎ *912/443–9962. Reservations essential. AE, D, DC, MC, V. No lunch.*

$$ ✕ **Johnny Harris.** What started as a small roadside stand in 1924 is now one of the city's culinary mainstays. The menu includes steaks, fried chicken, seafood, and barbecued meats smothered in the restaurant's famous sauce. There's live piano or guitar music on Friday night and dancing on Saturday night. ✉ *1651 E. Victory Dr.,* ☎ *912/354–7810. AE, DC, MC, V. Closed Sun.*

$$ **Seasons in Savannah.** In the heart of City Market, Seasons is a bright, refreshing place, especially useful for Sunday brunch, when so many of the downtown venues are closed. The lunch and dinner menus feature lots of seafood, including Low Country shrimp and grits, quail and corn bread, and Georgia pecan grouper. ✉ *315 W. Saint Julian St.* ☎ *912/233–6741. AE, D, DC, MC, V.*

$ ★ ✕ **Mrs. Wilkes Dining Room.** Come to this unassuming basement restaurant for comfort food served family style. Folks line up at breakfast and lunch for such quintessentially southern dishes as biscuits, grits, collard greens, mashed potatoes, and fried chicken. ✉ *107 W. Jones St.,* ☎ *912/232–5997. Reservations not accepted. No credit cards. Closed weekends. No dinner.*

$ ★ ✕ **Nita's Place.** Just a half block from the Colonial Cemetery, this little steam-table operation offers nothing in decor. But Juanita Dixon has established a reputation for down-home southern cooking with her salmon patties, baked chicken, perfectly cooked okra, outstanding squash casserole, and homemade desserts. ✉ *140 Abercorn St.,* ☎ *912/238–8233. Reservations not accepted. D, MC, V. Closed Sun. No dinner.*

$ **Wall's Bar-B-Q.** It's tricky to find this little hole in the wall, but the barbecue (get the tangy hot but not too hot mustard/tomato sauce), deviled crab, greens, sour cream pound cake, and layered Red Velvet cake are worth all the search. ✉ *515 E. York La., between Houston and York Sts..* ☎ *912/232–9754. Reservations not accepted. No credit cards. Closed Sun.–Tues.*

Lodging

For price ranges *see* Chart 2 (A) *in* On the Road with Fodor's.

$$$$ ★ 🏨 **Ballastone Inn.** This sumptuous inn occupies a mansion dating from 1838 that once served as a bordello. Each room is decorated differently. On the garden level, rooms are small and cozy, with exposed brick walls and beamed ceilings. Most rooms have working gas fireplaces, and three have whirlpool tubs. ✉ *14 E. Oglethorpe Ave., 31401,* ☎ *912/236–1484 or 800/822–4553,* FAX *912/236–4626. 18 rooms. Full breakfast. AE, MC, V.*

$$$–$$$$ ★ 🏨 **Gastonian.** The city's most deluxe accommodations are found at this 1868 inn two blocks from Forsyth Park. All rooms have working fireplaces and antiques from the Georgian and Regency periods; most have whirlpool or soak tubs. There's also an outdoor hot tub. Breakfast might include ginger pancakes, and pralines await you at turndown. ✉ *220 E. Gaston St., 31401,* ☎ *912/232–2869 or 800/322–6603,* FAX *912/232–0710. 16 rooms. Full breakfast. AE, MC, V.*

$$$–$$$$ ★ 🏨 **Kehoe House.** A fabulously appointed bed-and-breakfast inn, the Victorian Kehoe House has brass-and-marble chandeliers, a courtyard garden, a music room, and a sense of the luxurious that defines opulence. On the main floor, a double parlor with a 14-ft ceiling holds two fireplaces. Here, guests enjoy sumptuous breakfasts. Turndown service includes chocolates, wine, and bottled water. Complimentary visits to the Downtown Athletic Club are included. ✉ *123 Habersham St., 31401,* ☎ *912/232–1020 or 800/820–1020,* FAX *912/231–0208. 15 rooms, including 3 at adjacent town house. AE, D, DC, MC, V.*

$$$ **Hyatt Regency Savannah.** When this riverfront hotel was built in 1981, preservationists opposed a seven-story modern structure in the historic district. The main architectural features are the towering atrium and a pleasant central lounge, as well as glass elevators. Rooms have modern furnishings, marble baths, and balconies overlooking the atrium and the Savannah River. MD's Lounge is the ideal spot to have a drink and watch the river traffic drift by. Windows, the hotel's restaurant, is a great spot for Sunday buffet. ✉ *2 W. Bay St., 31401,* ☎ *912/238–1234 or 800/233–1234,* FAX *912/944–3678. 346 rooms. Restaurant, pool. AE, D, MC, V.*

$$$ ★ **President's Quarters.** Each room in this classic Savannah inn is named for an American president. Guests are greeted with wine and fruit, and complimentary afternoon tea comes with sumptuous cakes. Turndown service includes a glass of port or sherry. ✉ *225 E. President St., 31401,* ☎ *912/233–1600 or 800/233–1776,* FAX *912/238–0849. 16 rooms. CP. D, DC, MC, V.*

Nightlife

Savannah's nightlife is a reflection of the city's laid-back, easygoing personality. Some clubs have live reggae, hard rock, and other contemporary music, but most stay with traditional blues, jazz, and piano-bar vocalists. At **Hard Hearted Hannah's East** (✉ Pirate's House, 20 E. Broad St., ☎ 912/233–2225) Emma Kelly, the famed Lady of 6,000 Songs, performs Tuesday through Saturday. For authentic blues and sometimes rock, check out **Crossroads** (✉ 219 W. St. Julian St., ☎ 912/234–5438), which stages local and national talent Monday through Saturday. Irish music fills the air Wednesday through Saturday at **Kevin Barry's Irish Pub** (✉ 117 W. River St., ☎ 912/233–9626). If you're in the mood for a low-key evening, drop in for coffee at **Savannah Coffee House** (✉ 102 W. Congress St., ☎ 912/233–5311).

Shopping

Savannah's many specialty shops sell such merchandise as English antiques, antiquarian books, and Low Country handmade quilts. Stores in the historic district are housed in ground floors of mansions and town houses or in renovated warehouses along the waterfront. The **River Front** and **City Market** areas have a variety of shops.

THE GOLDEN ISLES

An hour south of Savannah lie the Golden Isles, a chain of barrier islands stretching along Georgia's coast to the Florida state line. The three most developed—Jekyll Island, Sea Island, and St. Simons Island—are the only ones accessible by car; they are connected to the mainland near Brunswick by a network of causeways. A ferry from St. Marys connects Cumberland Island National Seashore with the mainland, and a launch transports visitors from St. Simons to Little St. Simons, a private vacation retreat. Spring, when temperatures are mild, is the ideal time for a visit; the superb beaches attract large crowds in summer.

Visitor Information

Cumberland Island National Seashore (✉ National Park Service, Box 806, St. Marys 31558, ☎ 912/882–4335). **Jekyll Island:** Welcome Center (✉ 901 Jekyll Island Causeway, 31527, ☎ 912/635–3636 or 800/841–6586, FAX 912/634–4004). **Little St. Simons Island** (✉ Little St. Simons Island Retreat, 31522, ☎ 912/638–7472). **St. Simons Island:** Chamber of Commerce and Visitors Center (✉ Neptune Park, 530B Beachview Dr., 31522, ☎ 912/638–9014). **Sea Island** (✉ The Cloister resort, 31561, ☎ 912/638–3611 or 800/732–4752).

Arriving and Departing

By Bus

Greyhound Lines (☎ 800/231–2222) connects Brunswick with surrounding towns and cities, including Savannah and Jacksonville, Florida.

By Boat

To reach Cumberland Island, you must reserve passage on the **Cumberland Queen** ferry, which leaves from St. Marys for the 45-minute journey. For a schedule, reservations, and fare information, contact Cumberland Island National Seashore (☞ Visitor Information, *above*).

By Car

From Brunswick take the **Jekyll Island Causeway** ($2 per car) to Jekyll Island or the **F. J. Torras Causeway** (35¢) to St. Simons. From St. Simons you can reach Sea Island via the **Sea Island Causeway.** Only residents and park service personnel are allowed to drive cars on Cumberland Island.

By Plane

Glynco Jetport (☎ 912/265–2070), on the mainland 6 mi outside Brunswick, is served by Delta affiliate Atlantic Southeast Airlines (☎ 800/282–3424). International airports are in Savannah, an hour's drive north, and in Jacksonville, Florida, an hour's drive south, but there are no scheduled international flights operating at either airport. Jekyll and St. Simons islands maintain small airstrips for private planes.

Exploring the Golden Isles

Little St. Simons Island

Accessible by private boat, Little St. Simons is a Robinson Crusoe–style getaway just 6 mi long and less than 3 mi wide. The island's only development is a rustic but comfortable guest compound (☞ Dining and Lodging, *below*). The island's forests and marshes are inhabited by deer, armadillos, horses, raccoons, alligators, otters, and more than 200 species of birds. There's a 7-mi stretch of beach for swimming and water sports; other activities include horseback riding, nature walks, fishing, and shrimping and crabbing expeditions.

Sea Island

Five-mile-long Sea Island's main attraction is The Cloister (☞ Dining and Lodging, *below*), a Spanish Mediterranean–style resort. This luxurious, low-key property has a beach club with a health spa, formal and casual restaurants, and many outdoor activities. Outside the resort, beautiful mansions line Sea Island Drive.

St. Simons Island

St. Simons, north of Jekyll and Cumberland islands, offers the contrasting beauties of white-sand beaches and salt marshes. As large as Manhattan and with more than 14,000 residents, it's the Golden Isles' most complete and commercial resort destination: As far as lodging goes, you can choose from numerous hotels, beachfront cottages, and condominiums, as well as four golf-course developments.

At the island's south end, the **Village** is dotted with T-shirt and souvenir shops, boutiques, restaurants, and a public pier for fishing and crabbing. Overlooking the ocean is **Neptune Park,** with a playground, a miniature golf course, and picnic tables shaded by live oaks. Also in the park is the **St. Simons Lighthouse,** built in 1872; climb to the top for a view of the beachfront or visit the **Museum of Coastal History** (✉ 101 12th St., ☎ 912/638–4666; 🎫 both lighthouse and museum $3) in the former light keeper's cottage.

Fort Frederica National Monument, on the island's north end, contains the foundation ruins of a fort and buildings inhabited by English soldiers and civilians in the mid-18th century. Tours begin at the **National Park Service visitor center** (✉ Off Frederica Rd., ☎ 912/638–3639; 🎫 $4 per vehicle). Visit the Gothic-style, cruciform **Christ Church** (✉ Frederica Rd., ☎ 912/638–8683) and read a pictorial story of its history on three stained-glass windows. The church was rebuilt in 1886 after having been destroyed by Union troops during the Civil War.

Jekyll Island

The golf courses and system of bike paths here can be enjoyed year-round. Jekyll Island was once the favored retreat of the Vanderbilts, Rockefellers, Morgans, and other American aristocrats. Many of these millionaires' mansions are part of the **Jekyll Island Historic District** (✉ Exit 6 off I–95, ☎ 800/841–6586) and are open for tours. An 11-acre water park, **Summer Waves** (✉ 210 S. Riverview Dr., ☎ 912/635–2074; 🎫 $12.50), ranks as a top summer attraction.

Cumberland Island National Seashore

★ The largest and most remote of the Golden Isles, **Cumberland Island,** $4 day use fee, is a 200-square-mi sanctuary of marshes, dunes, beaches, forests, ponds, estuaries, and inlets. You can tour the unspoiled terrain and the ruins of Thomas Carnegie's **Dungeness** estate on your own or join history and nature walks led by park rangers (☞ Visitor Information, *above*). You must bring along whatever food, beverages, sunscreen, and insect repellent you may need; the island has no shops.

Dining and Lodging

For price ranges *see* Charts 1 (A) and 2 (A) *in* On the Road with Fodor's.

Cumberland Island

$$$$ ✕🏨 **Greyfield Inn.** This turn-of-the-century house, built by the Carnegie family, is the island's only lodging and stands by itself in the primitive landscape; its wide, colonnaded porches beckon invitingly. The inn is furnished with its original Asian and English antiques; burnished hardwood floors are warmed by antique Persian rugs. Rates include all meals, which are delightful: hearty breakfasts, box lunches, and festive dinners. ✉ *Box 900, Fernandina Beach, FL 32035,* ☎ *904/261–6408. 15 rooms. Restaurant. FAP. MC, V.*

Jekyll Island

$$–$$$ ★ ✕🏨 **Jekyll Island Club Hotel.** Built in 1886, the four-story clubhouse with wraparound verandas and Queen Anne–style towers and turrets once served as the winter hunting retreat for wealthy financiers. Rooms are custom-decorated with mahogany beds, armoires, and plush sofas and chairs. Some have views of the Intracoastal Waterway, Jekyll River, and the hotel's croquet lawn. The nearby Sans Souci Apartments, built in 1896 by William Rockefeller, have been converted into spacious guest rooms. The Grand Dining Room serves gourmet cuisine; meal-plan rates are available. ✉ *371 Riverview Dr., 31527,* ☎ *912/635–2600 or 800/535–9547,* FAX *912/635–2818. 134 rooms. 2 restaurants, pool, tennis. AE, D, DC, MC, V.*

Little St. Simons Island

$$$$ ★ **Lodge on Little St. Simons Island.** Guests stay in spacious, airy rooms with private baths in one of four buildings: a two-bedroom cottage; the 1917 Hunting Lodge, with two antiques-filled guest rooms; or one of two houses with four guest rooms each. All buildings have screened porches or decks. Meals, included in the rate, are served family-style in the main dining room; platters are heaped with fresh fish, home-baked breads, and pies. ✉ *Box 21078, 31522,* ☎ *912/638–7472,* FAX *912/634–1811. 15 rooms. Pool. FAP. D, MC, V.*

St. Simons Island

$$ ✕ **Blanche's Courtyard.** Seafood, such as blue crab soup, and simple but delicious steak and chicken dinners are among the local favorites. The apple fritters, renamed "sweet puppies" on the menu, are unforgettable. A ragtime band accompanies dancers on Saturday. ✉ *440 Kings Way,* ☎ *912/638–3030. AE, DC, MC, V. Closed Mon. Jan.–Mar. No lunch.*

$$$ **King and Prince Beach and Golf Resort.** This beachfront hotel-and-condominium complex has spacious guest rooms and two- and three-bedroom villas. Villas are privately owned, so the total number available for rent varies from time to time. ✉ *201 Arnold Rd. (Box 20798), 31522,* ☎ *912/638–3631 or 800/342–0212,* FAX *912/634–1720. 139 rooms, 44 villas. 2 restaurants, pools, golf, tennis. AE, D, DC, MC, V.*

$$–$$$ **Sea Palms Golf and Tennis Resort.** A contemporary resort complex with fully furnished villas, most with kitchens, nestles on an 800-acre site. ✉ *5445 Frederica Rd., St. Simons Island 31522,* ☎ *912/638–3351 or 800/841–6268,* FAX *912/634–8029. 154 rooms. 2 restaurants, pools, golf, tennis, health club. AE, DC, MC, V.*

Sea Island

$$–$$$$ ✕ **The Cloister.** At this classic resort, contemporary ocean-side villas, condominiums, and rental homes have grown up around a 1920s Spanish Mediterranean–style hotel with large guest rooms. Formal dining, casual grill lunches, and seafood and breakfast buffets are included in the rate. A spa offers a fitness room, daily aerobics classes, facials, massages, and other beauty treatments. ✉ *The Cloister, Sea Island 31561,* ☎ *912/638–3611 or 800/732–4752,* FAX *912/638–5823. 262 rooms. 4 restaurants, pools, golf, tennis. FAP. No credit cards.*

Campgrounds

Cumberland Island National Seashore (☞ Visitor Information, *above*) maintains two tent campgrounds, one with rest rooms and showers, the other with cold-water spigots only. Reserve well in advance.

Outdoor Activities and Sports

Biking

Sea Island, Jekyll Island, and St. Simons have paved bike paths. You can rent bikes from the **The Cloister** (☎ 912/638–3611), on Sea Island, or **Barry's Beach Service** (✉ 420 Arnold Rd., ☎ 912/638–8053), which also deals with other recreational equipment and **Benjy's Bike Shop** (✉ 130 Retreat Pl., ☎ 912/638–6766), both on St. Simons.

Fishing

The Intracoastal Waterway and the Atlantic Ocean are teeming with trout, barracuda, snapper, amberjack, and other fish. On St. Simons, **Ducky II Charter Boat Service** (✉ 402 Kelsall Ave., ☎ 912/634–0312) organizes deep-sea and inshore fishing. **Capt. Martin Noble Charter Fishing** (✉ Rte. 9, ☎ 912/634–1219) handles both offshore and inshore fishing for St. Simons. **St. Simons Transit Company** (✉ 105 Marina Dr., ☎ 912/638–5678) organizes river and deep-sea fishing expeditions and operates a water taxi service between the coastal islands. **Taylor Fish Camp** (✉ Lawrence Rd., ☎ 912/638–7690) offers guided fishing trips.

Golf

St. Simons Island has four courses: **Hampton Club** (✉ 100 Tabbystone, ☎ 912/634–0255), with 18 holes; **St. Simons Island Club** (✉ 100 Kings Way, ☎ 912/638–5131), with 18 holes; and **Sea Palms Golf and Tennis Resort** (✉ 5445 Frederica Rd., ☎ 912/638–3351), with 27 holes. Though it has several courses, Jekyll Island is known for two in particular: **Oceanside** (✉ Beachview Dr., ☎ 912/635–2170), with nine holes, and **Jekyll Island Golf Club** (✉ 322 Captain Wylly Rd., ☎ 912/635–2368 or 912/635–3464), with three 18-hole courses—Indian Mound, Oleander, and Pine Lake.

Tennis

Jekyll Island Tennis Courts (✉ 400 Captain Wylly Rd., ☎ 912/635–3154) offers 13 clay courts, seven of which are lighted. The center hosts USTA-sanctioned tournaments. **Sea Palms Golf and Tennis Resort** (✉ 5445 Frederica Rd., ☎ 912/638–3351) offers 12 Rubico courts, three of which are lighted.

Beaches

Wide expanses of clean, sandy beaches skirt all the islands. St. Simons' **East Beach** attracts large groups and families and has sailboat rentals. The beaches rimming **Jekyll Island** are usually not too busy during the week but become crowded on weekends. On **Sea Island** you can rent sailboats, sea kayaks, and boogie boards. The dunes and beaches of **Cumberland Island National Seashore** offer peaceful isolation.

ELSEWHERE IN GEORGIA

Okefenokee National Wildlife Refuge

Arriving and Departing

The refuge is near the Georgia-Florida border, 40 minutes northwest of Jacksonville, Florida, and 40 minutes southwest of the Golden Isles. From Atlanta take I–75 south to U.S. 82 into Waycross. From the Golden Isles take U.S. 84W to U.S. 301S.

What to See and Do

★ **Okefenokee National Wildlife Refuge** (✉ Folkston, ☎ 912/496–3331; 🎫 $5 per vehicle), covering about 730 square mi, is a vast peat bog once part of the ocean floor and now 100 ft above sea level. Its thick vegetation is inhabited by at least 54 reptile species (including alligators), 49 mammal species, and 234 types of birds.

The **Okefenokee Swamp Park** (✉ 8 mi south of Waycross, ☎ 912/283–0583; 🎫 $8) offers guided tours of the refuge. Boardwalks lead to an observation tower; guided boat tours are available, or you can rent a canoe ($14 per person). There's an eastern entrance at the Suwanee Canal Recreation Area (✉ Near Folkston, ☎ 912/496–7156 or 800/792–6796); the 11-mi waterway was built more than a century ago. Wilderness canoeing and camping in the Okefenokee's interior are by reserved fee permit only. Permits are tough to get, especially in cool weather. Call refuge headquarters (☎ 912/496–3331) *exactly 60 days* in advance of the desired starting date. There's also a western entrance at Stephen C. Foster State Park (✉ Rte. 1, Fargo, ☎ 912/637–

5274), an 80-acre park with boat rides through a swamp, a half-mile nature trail, restored homesteads, and cypress and black gum trees.

Lodging

$$$–$$$$ **Inn at Folkston.** Genna and Roger Wangsness restored this 1920s arts-and-crafts bungalow, right in the center of town, in 1998. There's a huge front veranda and four working gas-log fireplaces, two in guest rooms. All rooms are individually decorated. The "Garden Room" has a king-size bed and whirlpool tub. The inn is just 7 mi from the refuge. ✉ *509 W. Main St., Folkston 31537,* ☎ *912/496–6256 or 888/509–6246. 4 rooms. Full breakfast. AE, MC, V.*

Andersonville

Arriving and Departing

Take I–75 south from Macon to Route 49 and follow the signs that read THE ANDERSONVILLE TRAIL to Andersonville.

What to See and Do

The tiny town of Andersonville itself grew up around a railway stop. The depot is the **Andersonville Welcome Center** (✉ 114 Church St., ☎ 912/924–2558). Antiques and memorabilia fill the restored storefront shops that form its center. The first weekend in October is the Andersonville Historic Fair, which fills the town with thousands of visitors. The Memorial Day weekend fair is not quite as big as the fall event but still worth attending. The theme of both festivals is the Civil War. Both offer opportunities to buy collectibles.

★ **Andersonville National Historic Site** (☞ National and State Parks, *above*) marks the Civil War's most notorious prisoner-of-war camp, which opened in 1864: 13,000 Union prisoners died here. Today it is the site of a prisoner-of-war memorial and serves as a final resting place for U.S. veterans and their spouses. A small museum in the visitor center has exhibits on prison life. The site's living history event (called Andersonville Revisited) takes place the last weekend in February. People dressed as guards and prisoners reenact the Andersonville experience.

Dining and Lodging

$$$–$$$$ **Windsor Hotel.** Americus, only 10 mi from Andersonville, has one of America's most intriguing historic hotels. A monument to Victorian architecture, this Romanesque structure dominates downtown and is the symbol of the city. The entrance lobby, rich in Moorish detail, is breathtaking. Chef Michael Keller delivers fine Continental dishes, including poached salmon with hollandaise sauce and tournedos of beef with Merlot sauce. ✉ *125 W. Lamar St., Americus 31709,* ☎ *912/924–1555 or 888/297–9567, FAX 912/928–0533. 53 rooms. Restaurant. AE, D, MC, V. No dinner Sun.*

Callaway Gardens

Arriving and Departing

Callaway Gardens is on U.S. 27 in Pine Mountain, 70 mi southwest of Atlanta. From Atlanta drive south on I–85, I–185, and U.S. 27.

What to See and Do

★ **Callaway Gardens** is a 14,000-acre, year-round horticultural fantasyland and family-style golf and tennis resort, best known for its impressive gardens developed in the 1930s by a couple determined to breathe new life into the area's dormant cotton fields. On the grounds are four nationally recognized golf courses, 17 tennis courts, bicycling trails, and a lakefront beach.

The **Cecil B. Day Butterfly Center,** the largest glass-enclosed tropical conservatory of living butterflies in North America, and the **John A. Sibley Horticultural Center,** one of the most advanced garden greenhouse complexes in the world, are part of the gardens. Trails and paved paths traverse the world's largest collection of hollies and more than 700 varieties of azaleas and wildflowers. ✉ *Hwy. 27, Pine Mountain,* ☎ *706/663–2281 or 800/282–8181. FAX 706/663–5068.* *$10.*

Dining and Lodging

$$–$$$$ ✕ **Oak Tree Victorian Dinner Restaurant.** In the charming town of Hamilton, 5 mi from Callaway Gardens, this dramatic Victorian house-turned-restaurant serves plenty of pasta dishes, excellent homemade dressings, steak, and great coffee. There's a small but well-selected wine list. ✉ *U.S. 27, Hamilton,* ☎ *706/628–4218. Reservations recommended. AE, D, DC, MC, V. Closed Sun.*

$$$–$$$$ **Magnolia Hall.** Painted magnolia-leaf green with taupe shutters, this handsome Victorian cottage has all the gingerbread trim, including a wraparound porch. Each room has its own thermostat, and extra care was taken to make rooms soundproof. Breakfast is served in the formal dining room. ✉ *127 Barnes Mill Rd. Hamilton 31811,* ☎ *706/628–4566. 5 rooms. Full breakfast. No credit cards.*

Historic Sites Along I–75

Arriving and Departing

Take I–75 north to the Tennessee state line and look for the brown state historic markers that indicate a historic site.

What to See and Do

New Echota State Historic Site (✉ Rte. 225, 1 mi east of I–75N [exit 131], near Calhoun, ☎ 706/624–1321; $2.50) is the location of the 1825–38 capital of the Cherokee Nation, whose constitution was patterned after that of the United States. Some buildings have been reconstructed. Native Americans frequently hold special events at the site.

The **Chief Vann House** (✉ 82 Rte. 225, Chatsworth, ☎ 706/695–2598; $2.50), a three-story brick edifice, was built in 1804 by Moravian artisans hired by Chief James Vann, a leader of the Cherokee Nation. To get there, take Exit 131 from I–75 to Route 52A going west.

The **Chickamauga and Chattanooga National Military Park** (✉ U.S. 27 off I–75, Exit 141, south of Chattanooga, TN, ☎ 706/866–9241; free), established in 1890, was the nation's first military park. It stands on the site of one of the Civil War's bloodiest battles, with casualties that totaled more than 30,000. Monuments, battlements, and weapons adorn the road that traverses the 8,000-acre park, with markers explaining the action. An excellent visitor center offers reproduction memorabilia, superb books, and a film on the battle.

Dining and Lodging

$ ✕ **J. J.'s.** Locals enjoy the "day-old" ribs for their crispy tenderness, but the standout is the smoked catfish. Collard greens and fruit cobblers are good, too. The posted menu only notes the specials (stew, for example), so ask for details. ✉ *1517 Dean St., Rome,* ☎ *706/234–7895. Reservations not accepted. No credit cards. Closed Sun.*

$$$ **Claremont House.** A beautifully restored 1890s Victorian residence, the inn has huge rooms furnished with period antiques. Breakfast is sumptuous, with stuffed French toast and the like. Claremont House is about 30 minutes from New Echota State Historic Site and the Chief Vann House. ✉ *906 E. 2nd Ave., Rome 30161,* ☎ *706/291–0900 or 800/254–4797. FAX 706/802–0551. 5 rooms. AE, D, MC, V.*

NORTH CAROLINA

Updated by
Lisa H. Towle

Capital	Raleigh
Population	7,425,000
Motto	To Be Rather Than to Seem
State Bird	Cardinal
State Flower	Dogwood
Postal Abbreviation	NC

Statewide Visitor Information

North Carolina Division of Travel and Tourism (✉ 430 N. Salisbury St., Raleigh 27603, ☎ 919/733–4171 or 800/847–4862). **Welcome centers:** I–77S near Charlotte, I–77N near Dobson, I–85S near Kings Mountain, I–85N near Norlina, I–95S near Rowland, I–95N near Roanoke Rapids, I–26 near Columbus, and I–40W near Waynesville.

Scenic Drives

The **Blue Ridge Parkway,** with more than 250 mi of mountain views, nature exhibits, historic sites, parks, and hiking trails, extends from the Virginia state line to the Great Smoky Mountains National Park entrance near Cherokee. **U.S. 441** from Cherokee to Gatlinburg, Tennessee, cuts through the middle of the national park for about 35 mi, climbing to a crest of 6,643 ft at Clingmans Dome, a short distance from Newfound Gap. Portions of **U.S. 64** travel through the Hickory Nut Gorge between Lake Lure and Chimney Rock and the Cullasaja Gorge between Lake Toxaway and Franklin, affording spectacular views of mountain peaks and cascading waterfalls. **Route 12,** which connects the Outer Banks, offers great views of the ocean and a landscape dotted with lighthouses and weathered beach cottages.

National and State Parks

The state tourism division's travel guide (☞ Statewide Visitor Information, *above*) includes a complete listing of state and national parks and recreation areas as well as state forests.

National Parks

Cape Hatteras National Seashore (✉ Rte. 1, Box 675, Manteo 27954, ☎ 252/473–2111; 🖃 free), a natural habitat for hundreds of species of birds, wild animals, and aquatic life, stretches 75 mi from Nags Head to Ocracoke and encompasses 30,318 acres of marshland and sandy beaches. **Cape Lookout National Seashore** (✉ 131 Charles St., Harkers Island 28531, ☎ 252/728–2250; 🖃 free) extends 55 mi from Portsmouth Island to Shackleford Banks and includes 28,400 acres of uninhabited land and marsh, accessible only by boat or ferry. Portsmouth, a deserted village that was inhabited from 1753 until 1971, is being restored and is open to the public from April through November. **Great Smoky Mountains National Park** (✉ 107 Park Headquarters Rd., Gatlinburg, TN 37738, ☎ 423/436–1200; 🖃 free), with 8.5 million visitors a year, is the most visited national park in the country. Its 521,000 acres straddle the North Carolina–Tennessee border with opportunities for camping, hiking, fishing, plus historic sites and nature lore (☞ Tennessee). To enter the park from North Carolina, take U.S. 441 north from Cherokee.

State Parks

On the Intracoastal Waterway south of Wilmington, 712-acre **Carolina Beach State Park** (✉ Box 475, Carolina Beach 28428, ☎ 910/458–

8206, 910/458–7770 for marina) offers camping, fishing, boating, picnicking, and hiking. **Fort Macon** (✉ Box 127, Atlantic Beach 28512, ☎ 252/726–3775) centers on the fort built in 1834 to guard Beaufort Inlet. **Hanging Rock State Park** (✉ Box 278, Danbury 27016, ☎ 336/593–8480) has opportunities for rock climbing and rappelling, hiking, camping, picnicking, and swimming. **Jockey's Ridge State Park** (✉ Box 592, Nags Head 27959, ☎ 252/441–7132) offers hang-gliding instruction and flights from a 110-ft sand dune, the tallest in the East. **Kerr Lake State Recreation Area** (✉ 269 Glass House Rd., Henderson 27536, ☎ 252/438–7791) encompasses 106,860 acres and includes seven designated recreation sites around a huge man-made lake. **Merchant's Millpond** (✉ Rte. 1, Box 141-A, Gatesville 27938, ☎ 252/357–1191) can be explored by canoe and on foot. **Mt. Mitchell State Park** (✉ Rte. 5, Box 700, Burnsville 28714, ☎ 828/675–4611) organizes guided nature walks on the highest mountain in the East (6,684 ft).

THE PIEDMONT

The Piedmont is the heartland of North Carolina, a vast area of rolling hills that extends from the coastal plain, which is east of the Triangle area (Raleigh, Durham, and Chapel Hill), to the foothills of the Blue Ridge Mountains, which are west of Charlotte and the Triad area (Greensboro, Winston-Salem, and High Point). Scattered along I–40, I–77, and I–85, the major arteries of the region, are the state's largest towns, cities, and industries. Here also are large rivers and woodlands; historic villages dating from the mid-1700s; crafts, antiques, and outlet shops; world-renowned colleges and universities; and one of the largest concentrations of golf courses in the world.

Visitor Information

Charlotte: Charlotte Convention and Visitors Bureau (✉ 330 S. Tryon St., 28202, ☎ 704/331–2700 or 800/231–4636). **Durham:** Convention & Visitors Bureau (✉ 101 E. Morgan St., 27701, ☎ 919/687–0288 or 800/446–8604). **Greensboro:** Convention & Visitors Bureau (✉ 317 S. Greene St., 27401, ☎ 336/274–2282 or 800/344–2282). **Raleigh:** Capital Area Visitor Center (✉ 301 N. Blount St., 27611, ☎ 919/733–3456); Convention and Visitors Bureau (✉ 225 Hillsborough St., Suite 400, 27602, ☎ 919/834–5900 or 800/849–8499). **Winston-Salem:** Convention & Visitors Bureau (✉ 601 N. Cherry St., Suite 100, 27101, ☎ 910/725–2361 or 800/331–7018).

Arriving and Departing

By Bus

Greyhound (☎ 800/231–2222) provides service to Charlotte, Raleigh, Durham, Chapel Hill, Greensboro, and Winston-Salem.

By Car

I–40, U.S. 64, and U.S. 74 run east–west through the Piedmont; I–77 runs north from Charlotte; I–85 runs from Charlotte northeast through Greensboro and the Raleigh area.

By Plane

Major carriers serve **Charlotte-Douglas International Airport** (✉ Charlotte, ☎ 704/359–4013), **Raleigh-Durham International Airport** (✉ 10 mi northwest of Raleigh, ☎ 919/840–2123), and **Piedmont Triad International Airport** (✉ Greensboro, ☎ 910/665–5666). Taxi and limousine services are available at all airports.

By Train

Amtrak's (☎ 800/872–7245) *Carolinian* provides daily service to stations in 12 Piedmont cities, while the *Piedmont* connects nine cities daily. The *Crescent* services five cities and the *Silver Service* trains make local stops.

Exploring the Piedmont

Charlotte, the region's largest city, is known as a financial center and prides itself on its cosmopolitan flair. At **Discovery Place** (✉ 301 N. Tryon St., ☎ 704/372–6261 or 800/935–0553; 🎟 $6.50), an award-winning hands-on science museum, there's a touch tank, aquariums, an indoor rain forest, an Omnimax theater, a planetarium, and special exhibits.

The **Hezekiah Alexander Homesite and Charlotte History Museum,** built in 1774, is the city's oldest dwelling. Named for the settler who built it, the site includes a log kitchen; costumed docents give guided tours. *✉ 3500 Shamrock Dr., ☎ 704/568–1774. 🎟 Museum and grounds free, tour $4. ⏲ Tues.–Sun.*

Though it has served as a home for art since 1936, the **Mint Museum of Art** was built in 1837 as a U.S. mint. In recent years it has hosted internationally acclaimed exhibits. *✉ 2730 Randolph Rd., ☎ 704/337–2000. 🎟 $4. ⏲ Tues.–Sun.*

Straddling the North Carolina–South Carolina border near Charlotte is **Paramount's Carowinds** (✉ 15423 Carowinds Blvd., off I–77, ☎ 704/588–2600 or 800/888–4386; 🎟 $30), a 100-acre amusement park with water rides.

Greensboro, an hour and a half north of Charlotte on I–85, is the largest city in the Triad. **Guilford Courthouse National Military Park** (✉ 2332 New Garden Rd., ☎ 336/288–1776; 🎟 free) has over 200 acres of wooded hiking trails, monuments, and military memorabilia dating back to the Revolutionary War.

There's a dinosaur gallery, dozens of gems and minerals, and lemurs, snakes, and amphibians at the **Natural Science Center of Greensboro** (✉ 4301 Lawndale Dr., ☎ 336/288–3769; 🎟 $3.50). Smaller children enjoy the petting zoo.

Forty minutes south of Greensboro on U.S. 220, the **North Carolina Zoological Park** (✉ 4401 Zoo Pkwy., ☎ 336/879–7000 or 800/488–0444; 🎟 $8), in Asheboro, is home to more than 1,100 animals and 60,000 exotic and tropical plants.

A half hour west of Greensboro on I–40 is **Winston-Salem,** whose residents are known for their support of the arts and the city's museums. ★ **Old Salem,** a restored 18th-century village, re-creates the life of the Moravians, a Protestant sect that settled in the area in 1766. Also in the village is the **Museum of Early Southern Decorative Arts,** displaying period furnishings. *✉ 600 S. Main St., ☎ 336/721–7350. 🎟 $15 to enter Old Salem; $20 for Old Salem and Museum of Early Southern Decorative Arts.*

An hour's drive east from Greensboro on I–85 will bring you to **Durham,** a city once known for its tobacco production, but better known today for Duke University and its eclectic arts scene. **Duke University Chapel** (✉ West Campus, ☎ 919/681–1704; 🎟 free), an ornate neo-Gothic cathedral, is open for tours and free organ demonstrations.

The 55-acre **Sarah P. Duke Gardens** (✉ Anderson St., west of Duke University, ☎ 919/684–3698; 🎟 free) has a wisteria-draped gazebo and a Japanese garden with a lily pond teeming with goldfish.

The **North Carolina Museum of Life and Science** (✉ 433 Murray Ave., ☎ 919/220–5429; 🎟 $5.50) has exhibits ranging from life-size dinosaur models and NASA artifacts to Carolina wildlife and a butterfly house.

In Chapel Hill, 15 minutes south of Durham on U.S. 15/501, children can stargaze at the University of North Carolina's **Morehead Planetarium** (✉ 250 E. Franklin St., ☎ 919/962–1247; 🎟 $3.50), one of the largest planetariums in the country.

Raleigh, the state's capital, is a 30-minute drive from Chapel Hill on I–40. Its downtown is easily explored on foot. The Greek Revival–style **state capitol** (✉ Capitol Square, ☎ 919/733–4994; 🎟 free), completed in 1840, commands the highest point in Capitol Square.The **North Carolina Museum of History** (✉ 5 E. Edenton St., ☎ 919/715–0200; 🎟 free) combines artifacts, audiovisual programs, and interactive exhibits to bring the state's history to life. The **Executive Mansion** (✉ 200 N. Blount St., ☎ 919/733–3456; 🎟 free), a turn-of-the-century Queen Anne–style structure in brick with gingerbread trim, is the governor's home.

In September 1999, the **North Carolina Museum of Natural Sciences** (✉ 102 N. Salisbury St., ☎ 919/733–7450; 🎟 free) is scheduled to open its new facility next door (✉ 11 W. Jones St.) to its current location. The new museum will have four times the exhibit space of the old one—enough room for 10 major exhibits, a two-story waterfall, and dinosaur and whale skeletons.

The **North Carolina Museum of Art,** on Raleigh's western edge, exhibits art ranging from ancient Egyptian to contemporary. The Museum Cafe is a favorite place for lunch or Friday-night entertainment. ✉ *2110 Blue Ridge Rd.,* ☎ *919/839–6262.* 🎟 *Free.* ⏲ *Tues.–Sun.*

Dining and Lodging

The Piedmont has a growing number of upscale restaurants and ethnic eateries, as well as restaurants that specialize in the more traditional barbecue, fresh seafood, fried chicken, and country ham. Lodging, available at economy motels, upscale convention hotels, bed-and-breakfasts, and resorts, will be harder to come by during the first half of the summer of 1999, so book well in advance. The U.S. Open will take place June 17 through 20 in Pinehurst, and the Triangle hosts the Special Olympics World Games June 26 through July 4. Many city hotels offer weekend packages with discounted rates and extra amenities. For price ranges *see* Charts 1 (B) and 2 (B) *in* On the Road with Fodor's.

Chapel Hill

$$$$ ★ ✕🏨 **Fearrington House.** Set on a 200-year-old farm, this elegant French-style country inn anchors a bustling village center and is a member of Relais & Châteaux. Rooms are decorated with chintz, antiques, and original art, and the cuisine is a deft blend of regional and French. ✉ *Fearrington Village Center, Pittsboro 27312,* ☎ *919/542–2121,* FAX *919/542–4202. 29 rooms, 2 suites. 2 restaurants. AE, MC, V.*

Charlotte

$$$–$$$$ ★ ✕ **Bravo!** This hotel restaurant is known not only for its Northern Italian cuisine but also for its singing waitstaff. Sunday brunch is available. Men might feel more comfortable in a jacket. ✉ *Adams Mark Hotel, 555 S. McDowell St.,* ☎ *704/372–5440. AE, D, DC, MC, V.*

$$–$$$$ ✕ **Atlantic Beer & Ice Co.** Uptown, this eatery has a restaurant and bar on the main floor, a cigar and Scotch bar with billiards upstairs, and a jazz club on the lower level. The menu is Floribbean—a combination of foods from southern Florida and the Caribbean. ✉ *330 N. Tryon St.,* ☎ *704/339–0566. AE, DC, MC, V.*

$$$$ ✕🏨 **The Dunhill.** Built in 1929, the hotel has reproduction 18th-century furnishings. Its restaurant, Monticello's, gets rave reviews for beautifully presented California cuisine. ✉ *237 N. Tryon St., 28202,* ☎ *704/332–4141 or 800/354–4141,* FAX *704/376–4117. 59 rooms, 1 suite. Restaurant. AE, D, DC, MC, V.*

$$$$ ✕🏨 **Hyatt Charlotte at Southpark.** Rooms ring a four-story atrium lobby at this modern hotel, popular with business travelers. The restaurant serves Northern Italian cuisine. ✉ *5501 Carnegie Blvd., 28209-3462,* ☎ *704/554–1234 or 800/233–1234,* FAX *704/554–8319. 258 rooms, 4 suites. Restaurant, pool, health club. AE, D, DC, MC, V.*

$$$ 🏨 **Comfort Inn–Lake Norman.** North of Charlotte on I–77 near Lake Norman and Davidson College, this motel offers rooms with refrigerators and coffeemakers. Some rooms have VCRs, microwaves, and whirlpool baths. Jogging trails are nearby. ✉ *20740 Torrence Chapel Rd., Cornelius 28031,* ☎ *704/892–3500 or 800/484–9751,* FAX *704/892–6473. 84 rooms, 6 suites. Pool. CP. AE, D, DC, MC, V.*

Durham

$$$ ★ ✕ **Magnolia Grill.** This award-winning bistro is consistently one of the finest, most innovative places to dine in the state. The Gulf Stream grouper in a lobster bordelaise sauce and the Vidalia onion stuffed with portobello mushrooms, ruby chard, and Gorgonzola cheese are among the creative menu options. ✉ *1002 9th St.,* ☎ *919/286–3609. MC, V. Closed Sun. No lunch.*

$$$–$$$$ ★ ✕🏨 **Washington Duke Inn & Golf Club.** Part of the Duke University campus, this luxurious inn overlooks a Robert Trent Jones golf course. The business center has faxing and photocopying facilities plus computer assistance, while every guest room and meeting room has fast Internet access. Among the entrees at the elegant Fairview restaurant are Muscovy duck with mashed white beans, roasted garlic, and sweet and sour cranberry sauce and homemade fettuccine tossed with New Zealand mussels, littleneck clams, jumbo shrimp, and sea scallops in a tomato cream sauce; the bar is called the Bull Durham. ✉ *3001 Cameron Blvd., 27706,* ☎ *919/490–0999 or 800/443–3853,* FAX *919/688–0105. 164 rooms, 7 suites. Restaurant, pool. AE, DC, MC, V.*

Greensboro

$$$$ ✕ **Paisley Pineapple.** The dining is formal in this romantic Old Greensborough restaurant in a restored 1920s building. The menu, heavy on hearty fare such as rack of lamb, grilled veal tenderloin, and sautéed beef tenderloin, is tempered by light soups. Upstairs there's a sofa bar with live jazz. ✉ *345 S. Elm St.,* ☎ *336/279–8488. AE, MC, V.*

$$$ 🏨 **Holiday Inn Four Seasons/Joseph S. Koury Convention Center.** For the most part the accommodations here are standard fare. But if it's convenience you want, you've got it, as this hotel is close to major thoroughfares and shopping areas. Business travelers are the mainstay. ✉ *3121 High Point Rd., 27407,* ☎ *336/292–9161 or 800/242–6556,* FAX *336/294–3516. 986 rooms, 39 suites. 4 restaurants, pools, exercise room. AE, D, DC, MC, V.*

Raleigh

$$$–$$$$ ★ ✕ **Angus Barn, Ltd.** Housed in a huge rustic barn, this Raleigh fixture is known for its steaks, seafood, prime rib, homemade desserts, and extensive wine list. Its Wild Turkey lounge is a favorite gathering spot

among locals. ✉ *U.S. 70W at Aviation Pkwy.,* ☎ *919/781–2444. Reservations not accepted Sat. AE, D, DC, MC, V.*

$$$ ★ ✕ **WickedSmile.** Everything in this renovated 1920s building in downtown's warehouse district screams chic: sconces of twisted iron and fiberglass, menus in rustic folders of anodized aluminum. The food is influenced by French and Italian menus. Recent menus (they change monthly) have included seared foie gras and Atlantic salmon. You can sip single malts and martinis at the bar while you listen to the live jazz. ✉ *511 W. Hargett St.,* ☎ *919/828–2223. AE, MC, V.*

$$$–$$$$ ★ **Oakwood Inn.** This 1871 B&B in the Oakwood Historic District downtown is furnished with Victorian period pieces. Each room has a working fireplace. ✉ *411 N. Bloodworth St., 27604,* ☎ *919/832–9712 or 800/267–9712,* FAX *919/836–9263. 6 rooms. Full breakfast. AE, D, DC, MC, V.*

$$$–$$$$ **Raleigh Marriott Crabtree Valley.** Fresh floral arrangements adorn the elegantly decorated public rooms. Standard guest rooms are done in soft colors and have Asian floral prints and dark cherry-wood furnishings. There is dining at J. W.'s Steakhouse and Quinn's, which serves light fare and drinks daily. ✉ *4500 Marriott Dr., 27612,* ☎ *919/781–7000 or 800/228–9290,* FAX *919/571–7445. 375 rooms, 4 suites. Restaurant, pool, exercise room. AE, D, DC, MC, V.*

Winston-Salem

$$$ ✕ **Old Salem Tavern Dining Room.** Here you can dine on Moravian dishes, such as chicken potpie and sauerbraten, in a Moravian setting. In warm months drinks are served outside on the patio under the arbor. ✉ *736 S. Main St.,* ☎ *336/748–8585. AE, D, MC, V.*

$$$–$$$$ ★ **Henry F. Shaffner House.** This majestic Queen Anne, built around 1907 with tiger oak paneling and the finest materials, offers luxurious accommodations and lots of personal attention in a wonderfully convenient setting near Old Salem and the many downtown attractions. ✉ *150 S. Marshall St., 27101,* ☎ *336/777–0052 or 800/952–2256,* FAX *336/777–1188. 9 rooms. Full breakfast. AE, MC, V.*

Nightlife and the Arts

In Winston-Salem, the **Stevens Center at the North Carolina School for the Arts** (✉ 405 W. Fourth St., ☎ 336/721–1945) stages events and performances. The **Eastern Music Festival,** which takes place in summer in Greensboro, is six weeks of classical music. High Point's **North Carolina Shakespeare Festival** mounts several productions in late summer and early autumn and *A Christmas Carol* in December. **North Carolina Blumenthal Center for the Performing Arts** (✉ 130 N. Tryon St., ☎ 704/333–4686), in Charlotte, hosts operas, concerts, plays, and other cultural events. The **North Carolina Symphony Orchestra** (✉ 2 E. South St., ☎ 919/733–2750) performs in Raleigh's Memorial Auditorium, also home to the **North Carolina Theatre** (☎ 919/831–6941).

Outdoor Activities and Sports

Golf

The Sandhills area, in the southern part of the Piedmont, has more than three dozen courses, including Pinehurst's famous Number 2. For details contact the **Pinehurst Area Convention and Visitors Bureau** (✉ Box 2270, Southern Pines 28388, ☎ 910/692–3330 or 800/346–5362).

Spectator Sports

Basketball: Charlotte Hornets (✉ Charlotte Coliseum, 100 Hive Dr., Tyvola Rd. off Billy Graham Pkwy., ☎ 704/357–0252) is the state's NBA team. From November through March, the Piedmont is a college basketball fan's dream, with Atlantic Coast Conference rivals

Duke University (☎ 919/681–2583 or 800/672–2583) in Durham, **North Carolina State** (☎ 919/515–2106 or 800/310–7225) in Raleigh, the **University of North Carolina** (☎ 919/962–2296 or 800/722–4335) in Chapel Hill, and **Wake Forest University** (☎ 336/758–3322 or 888/758–3322) in Winston-Salem. **Football: Carolina Panthers** (✉ Ericsson Stadium, 800–1 S. Mint St., Charlotte, ☎ 704/358–7800), one of the National Football League's youngest franchises, plays in a 72,000-seat stadium in uptown Charlotte. **Ice Hockey:** The National Hockey League's **Carolina Hurricanes** (☎ 919/467–7825 or 888/645–8491) are headquartered in Raleigh but are playing in Greensboro at the Coliseum while waiting for the 21,000-seat Raleigh Entertainment & Sports Arena to open in the fall of 1999. **NASCAR Racing:** The Coca-Cola 600 and UAW-GM 500 races draw huge crowds to the **Charlotte Motor Speedway** (☎ 704/455–3200), off I–85 near Concord.

Shopping

The Piedmont is ideal for lovers of **antiques and crafts**; towns such as Waxhaw, Cameron, Pineville, and Matthews are devoted almost entirely to antiques. For more information, call Charlotte's visitor center (☞ Visitor Information, *above*). One of the country's largest antiques centers is **Metrolina Expo** (✉ 7100 N. Statesville Rd., ☎ 704/596–4643 or 800/824–3770), near Charlotte. **High Point,** 20 minutes southwest of Greensboro, is known as the furniture capital of the world.

The **N.C. Pottery Center** (✉ 235 E. Main St., ☎ 336/873–7887) in Seagrove, between Greensboro and Pinehurst, distributes information about and samples of work by potters from around the state. Burlington, between Greensboro and Durham, is a hub for **outlet stores.** Charlotte and Raleigh are major retail centers; the latter is home to one of the largest **farmers' markets** in the Southeast.

THE COAST

A chain of barrier islands flanks the North Carolina coast. The Outer Banks stretch some 130 mi from the Virginia state line south to Cape Lookout; the Crystal Coast includes the stretch from Cape Lookout to the Bogue Banks; the southern coast, to the South Carolina line, includes the Cape Fear River region and Wilmington, the state's primary port. English settlers came to these shores more than 400 years ago to establish a colony on Roanoke Island and mysteriously disappeared. Called the Graveyard of the Atlantic because of the hundreds of ships that met their demise here, the Outer Banks proved a safe hiding place for marauding pirates in the 1700s. For many years the region remained isolated, home only to a few fishermen and their families, but now, linked by bridges and ferries, the islands are a popular vacation spot. Nearby, the Albemarle region comprises charming towns full of early architecture. Hundreds of films have been shot in Wilmington, which has a restored historic district and waterfront. On the surrounding coast visitors can tour old plantation houses and azalea gardens, study sea life, and bask in the sun at nearby beaches.

Visitor Information

Cape Fear Coast: Convention and Visitors Bureau (✉ 24 N. 3rd St., Wilmington 28401, ☎ 910/341–4030 or 800/222–4757). **Carteret County:** Tourism Development Bureau (✉ 3409 Arendell St., Morehead City 28557, ☎ 252/726–8148 or 800/786–6962). **Craven County:** Convention and Visitors Bureau (✉ 314 S. Front St., New Bern 28563, ☎ 252/637–9400 or 800/437–5767). **Dare County:** Tourist Bureau (✉

U.S. 64/264, Manteo 27954, ☎ 252/473–2138). **Historic Albemarle Tour, Inc.** (✉ 1 Harding Sq., Washington 27858, ☎ 252/974–2950). **Ocracoke:** Visitor Center (✉ Cape Hatteras National Seashore, NC12 Hwy., Ocracoke 27960-0340, ☎ 252/928–4531).

Arriving and Departing

By Boat

There are nearly 150 marinas along the Intracoastal Waterway, including **Manteo Waterfront Docks** (☎ 252/473–3320) and the National Park Service's **Silver Lake Marina** (☎ 252/928–5111) in Ocracoke. Beaufort is a popular stopover. The Wilmington area has public marinas at **Carolina Beach State Park** (☎ 910/458–7770) and **Wrightsville Beach** (☎ 910/256–6666). The ***North Carolina Coastal Boating Guide,*** compiled by the North Carolina Department of Transportation (☎ 919/733–7600), lists marinas and other facilities for boaters.

By Bus

Greyhound (☎ 800/231–2222) serves Elizabeth City, on the Albemarle Sound; Wilmington; and Norfolk, Virginia.

By Car

Roads link the mainland to the Outer Banks at their northern end: U.S. 158 enters from the north, near Kill Devil Hills, and U.S. 64/264 enters Manteo on Roanoke Island, from the west. These connect with Route 12, the main route in the region, running south from Corolla to Ocracoke Island. Toll ferries (☎ 800/293–3779) connect Ocracoke with Cedar Island, to the south, and with Swan Quarter on the mainland; a free ferry travels between Hatteras Island and Ocracoke Island. From I–95 near Raleigh, U.S. 70 leads to Cedar Island via New Bern and Morehead City, and I–40 serves Wilmington.

By Plane

The closest airports are **Raleigh-Durham International** (☞ Arriving and Departing *in* the Piedmont, *above*); **Wilmington International,** in Wilmington (☎ 910/341–4125); and Virginia's **Norfolk International** (☎ 757/857–3351). SouthEast Air (☎ 252/473–3222 or 800/289–8202) and Outer Banks Airways (☎ 252/473–2227) provide charter service from **Dare County Regional Airport** (✉ Airport Rd., ☎ 252/473–2600), at the north end of Roanoke Island in Manteo.

Exploring the Coast

Start your tour of the Outer Banks at Nags Head and Kill Devil Hills, where the Cape Hatteras National Seashore begins (☞ National and State Parks, *above*). You can drive from Nags Head to Ocracoke in a day, but allow plenty of time in summer, when ferries are crowded. During major storms and hurricanes, follow the evacuation signs to safety.

Kill Devil Hills is the site of the first flight in history. The **Wright Brothers National Memorial** (✉ U.S. 158 Bypass, ☎ 252/441–7430; 🎟 $2 per adult, $4 per car) is a tribute to Wilbur and Orville's feat of December 17, 1903. A replica of the *Flyer* is housed in the visitor center. You can fly a kite from the tallest sand dune in the East (about 110 ft) in **Jockey's Ridge State Park** (☞ National and State Parks, *above*), just a few miles south of the Wright Brothers National Memorial.

Roanoke Island, accessible from U.S. 158 Bypass via U.S. 64/264, is the site of several attractions. From mid-June to late August, the outdoor drama ***Lost Colony*** (☎ 252/473–3414 or 800/488–5012; 🎟 $14) reenacts the story of the first colonists, who settled on Roanoke Island in 1587 and then disappeared. The **Elizabethan Gardens** (✉ 1411 U.S. 64,

North Carolina's Outer Banks

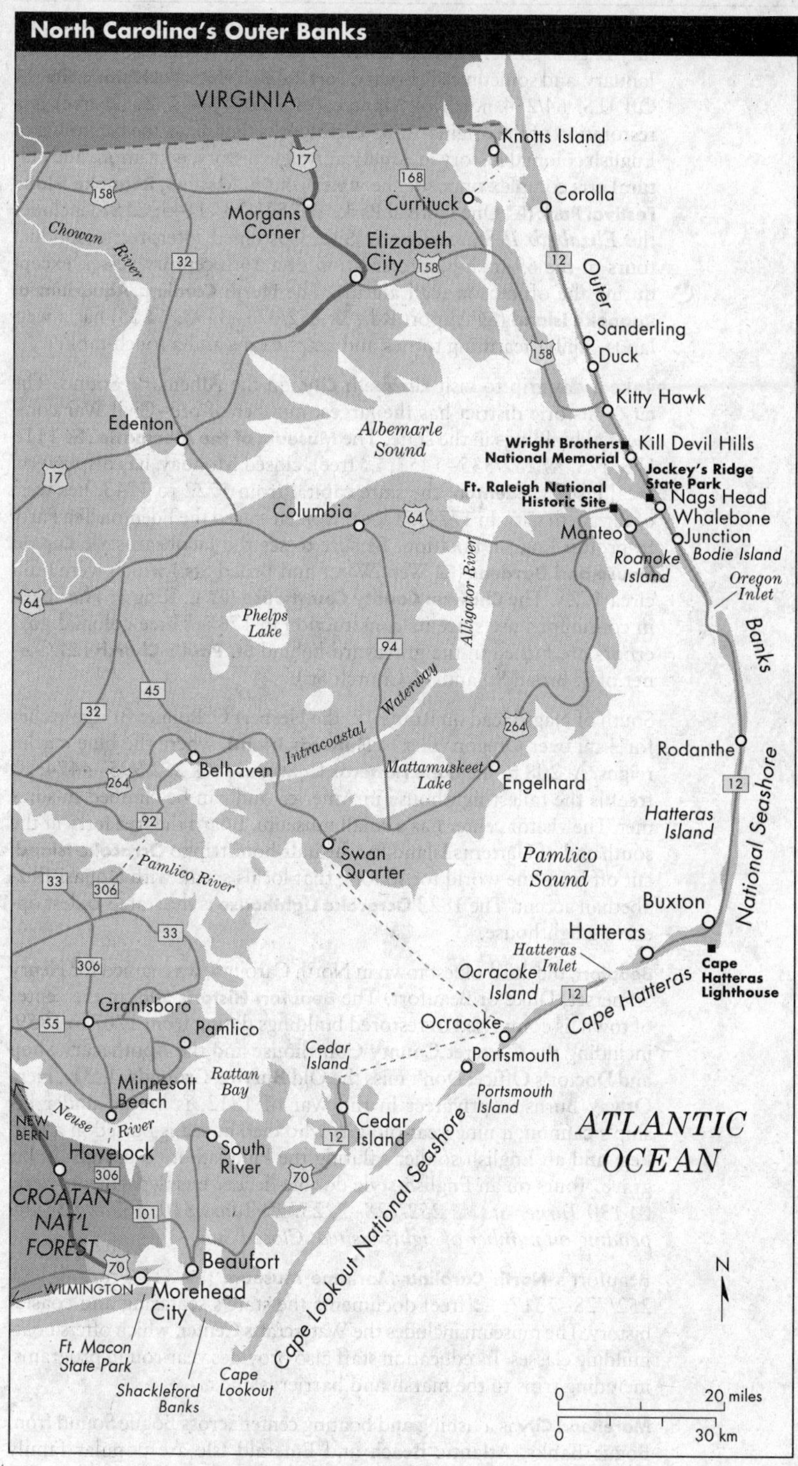
VIRGINIA
Knotts Island
Currituck
Corolla
Morgans Corner
Elizabeth City
Chowan River
Outer
Sanderling
Duck
Kitty Hawk
Edenton
Albemarle Sound
Wright Brothers National Memorial
Kill Devil Hills
Jockey's Ridge State Park
Ft. Raleigh National Historic Site
Nags Head
Columbia
Whalebone
Manteo
Junction
Bodie Island
Roanoke Island
Oregon Inlet
Phelps Lake
Alligator River
Banks
Intracoastal Waterway
Rodanthe
Belhaven
Mattamuskeet Lake
Engelhard
Hatteras Island
Swan Quarter
Pamlico Sound
National Seashore
Pamlico River
Buxton
Hatteras
Hatteras Inlet
Cape Hatteras Lighthouse
Ocracoke Island
Cape Hatteras
Grantsboro
Ocracoke
Pamlico
Cedar Island
Portsmouth
Rattan Bay
Minnesott Beach
Portsmouth Island
NEW BERN
Neuse River
Cedar Island
ATLANTIC OCEAN
Havelock
South River
CROATAN NAT'L FOREST
Cape Lookout National Seashore
Beaufort
WILMINGTON
Morehead City
Ft. Macon State Park
Shackleford Banks
Cape Lookout
N
0
20 miles
0
30 km

Manteo, ☎ 252/473–3234; $3) are a lush re-creation of a 16th-century English garden. The gardens are closed on weekends in December, January, and sometimes February. **Fort Raleigh National Historic Site** (✉ Off U.S. 64/264 north of Manteo, ☎ 252/473–5772; free) is a restoration of the original 1585 earthworks that mark the beginning of English colonial history in America. A new history, education, and cultural arts complex opposite the waterfront in Manteo, **Roanoke Island Festival Park** (✉ One Festival Park, ☎ 252/473–1144; $8) includes the *Elizabeth II* State Historic Site. Costumed interpreters conduct tours of the 69-ft ship, a re-creation of a 16th century vessel, except during the off-season (call ahead). The **North Carolina Aquarium at Roanoke Island** (✉ Airport Rd., ☎ 252/473–3493; $3) has a wetlands exhibit featuring turtles and amphibians and a touch-tank.

Take a day trip to visit **Elizabeth City,** on the Albemarle Sound. The city's historic district has the largest number of pre–Civil War commercial buildings in the state. The **Museum of the Albemarle** (✉ 1116 U.S. 17S, ☎ 252/335–1453; free), closed Monday, has displays on local history. **Edenton,** the state capital from 1722 to 1743, lies west of Elizabeth City. In 1774, 51 local women staged the Edenton Tea Party to protest English taxation. Be sure to see the Jacobean-style **Cupola House and Gardens** (✉ West Water and Broad Sts.) which were built circa 1725. The **Chowan County Courthouse** (✉ E. King St.) has been in continuous use since its construction in 1767. Three colonial governors are buried in the graveyard behind **St. Paul's Church** (✉ Corner of S. Broad St. and W. Church St.).

South of Nags Head on Route 12, the Herbert C. Bonner Bridge arches for 3 mi over Oregon Inlet to **Hatteras Island,** where the blue marlin reigns. At 208 ft, the **Cape Hatteras Lighthouse** (☎ 252/995–4474; free) is the tallest lighthouse in America and can be climbed in summer. The visitor center has a small museum. Board the free ferry at the south end of Hatteras Island for the half-hour trip to **Ocracoke Island,** cut off from the world for so long that locals speak with a quasi-Elizabethan accent. The 1823 **Ocracoke Lighthouse** is the state's oldest operating lighthouse.

Beaufort, the third-oldest town in North Carolina, was named for Henry Somerset, Duke of Beaufort. The **Beaufort Historic Site,** in the center of town, is comprised of restored buildings dating from 1767 to 1859, including the Carteret County Courthouse and the Apothecary Shop and Doctor's Office. Don't miss the Old Burying Grounds (1731). Here Otway Burns, a privateer in the War of 1812, is buried under his ship's cannon; a nine-year-old girl who died at sea is buried in a rum keg; and an English soldier saluting the king is buried upright in his grave. Tours on an English-style double-decker bus depart from here. *✉ 130 Turner St., ☎ 252/728–5225. Tours $10, $6, and $5 depending on number of sights visited. Closed Sun.*

Beaufort's **North Carolina Maritime Museum** (✉ 315 Front St., ☎ 252/728–7317; free) documents the state's seafaring and coastal history. The museum includes the Watercrafts Center, which offers boatbuilding classes. Its education staff also provides year-round programs, including trips to the marsh and barrier islands.

Morehead City is a fishing and boating center across Bogue Sound from Bogue Banks. Atlantic Beach and Emerald Isle are popular family beaches. The **North Carolina Aquarium at Pine Knoll Shores** on Bogue Banks (✉ Salter Path Rd., Milepost 7, ☎ 252/247–4004; $3) features a 2,000-gallon salt marsh tank with live alligators and a loggerhead turtle nursery.

New Bern, northwest of Morehead City, was the state capital during English rule until immediately after the Revolution. The reconstructed **Tryon Palace** (✉ 610 Pollock St., ☎ 252/514–4900; 🎫 $12), an elegant Georgian building, was the Colonial capitol and the home of Royal Governor William Tryon in the 1770s. An audiovisual orientation is given, costumed interpreters conduct tours of the house and gardens, and (in summer) actors deliver monologues describing a day in the life of the governor. The stately **John Wright Stanly House** (circa 1783), the **Dixon-Stevenson House** (circa 1826), and **New Bern Academy** (circa 1809) are within the 13-acre Tryon Palace complex.

U.S. 17S leads to **Wilmington,** a bustling harbor town and filmmaking center. The ***USS North Carolina*** Battleship Memorial (☎ 910/251–5797; 🎫 $8) is permanently docked off U.S. 421. You can park next to the site or take the river taxi from Riverfront Park (in summer only) for a self-guided tour.

Wilmington's restored waterfront and historic district, with its 18th-century churches, can be explored with the aid of a self-guided walking-tour map from the Cape Fear Coast Convention and Visitors Bureau (☞ Visitor Information, *above*). The 1770 **Burgwin-Wright House,** on Market Street, is built on the foundation of a jail. Downtown's Italianate **Zebulon Latimer House** was built in 1852 and can be seen from Third Street.

The **St. John's Museum of Art** (✉ 114 Orange St., ☎ 910/763–0281; 🎫 $2) houses a permanent collection of prints by Mary Cassatt ; it's closed on Monday. Open from Tuesday through Sunday, the **Cape Fear Museum** (✉ 814 Market St., ☎ 910/341–7413; 🎫 $2) traces the natural and cultural history of Cape Fear River country.

U.S. 421 leads south from Wilmington to the **Fort Fisher State Historic Site** (✉ Kure Beach, ☎ 910/458–5538; 🎫 free), the largest Confederate earthwork fortification of the Civil War. War relics and artifacts from sunken Confederate blockade runners are on display. The site is closed Monday from November through March. Not far from Kure Beach is the **North Carolina Aquarium at Fort Fisher** (✉ 2201 Fort Fisher Blvd., ☎ 910/458–8257; 🎫 $3), with its 20,000-gallon shark tank.

On the west side of the Cape Fear River, south of Wilmington on Route 133, a passenger ferry links Southport and **Bald Head Island** (☎ 910/457–5003). On a day trip to the island you can take a historic tour (reservations required) to see the 109-ft Old Baldy Lighthouse, dating from 1817; have a picnic or lunch at one of the restaurants; play golf; swim; or fish.

Dining and Lodging

Fresh seafood is in abundant supply, prepared almost any way. Hearty southern cooking, with chicken, ham, and fresh vegetables, is also widespread. Cottages, condominiums, motels, resorts, B&Bs, and country inns abound all along the coast. Most places offer lower rates from September through May. Condos and beach cottages may be rented through local realtors by the week or month. For price ranges *see* Charts 1 (B) and 2 (B) *in* On the Road with Fodor's.

Beaufort

$$–$$$ ✕ **Clawson's 1905 Restaurant.** Housed in what was a general store in the early 1900s, Clawson's offers hearty food such as zesty ribs, burgers, steaks, and pasta. It gets crowded in the summer, so arrive early for both lunch and dinner. There's also a coffee bar open 7 AM to closing. ✉ *429 Front St.,* ☎ *252/728–2133. D, MC, V.*

$$$ ★ **Langdon House.** You'll sleep surrounded by antiques at this B&B built in 1733. The host provides everything from sumptuous southern breakfasts and full beach baskets for picnics, to sightseeing suggestions. ✉ *135 Craven St., 28516,* ☎ *252/728–5499. 4 rooms. Full breakfast. No credit cards.*

Duck

$$$–$$$$ ★ ✕ **Sanderling Inn Resort & Conference Center.** For special pampering, come to this remote beachside resort built in 1985. Ceiling fans, wicker, and neutral tones give rooms a cool and casual feel. The restaurant, housed in an old lifesaving station, offers such delicacies as crab cakes, roast Carolina duckling with black-cherry sauce, and fricassee of shrimp. ✉ *1461 Duck Rd., 27949,* ☎ *252/261–4111 or 800/701–4111,* FAX *252/261–1638. 88 rooms, 29 efficiencies. Restaurant, pool, health club. AE, D, MC, V.*

$$$$ **Advice 5¢.** The name may be quirky, but this contemporary B&B in Duck's North Beach area is very serious about guest care. Just a short walk from downtown shops and restaurants, Advice also offers the use of Sea Pines tennis courts and swimming pool. Beds in each room are dressed with crisp, colorful linens. All rooms have ceiling fans and shuttered windows. ✉ *111 Scarborough La., 27949,* ☎ *252/255–1050 or 800/238–4235. 4 rooms, 1 suite. CP. MC, V.*

Kill Devil Hills

$$–$$$$ ✕ **Chardo's.** The pastas and homemade desserts at this casual Italian eatery are sure to satisfy any appetite. The entire menu is half price for half portions. ✉ *U.S. 158 Bypass, Milepost 9,* ☎ *252/441–0276. AE, D, DC, MC, V.*

$$$$ **Ramada Inn.** Guest rooms in this convention-style hotel have private balconies, some with ocean views. All rooms are equipped with refrigerators, microwave ovens, and coffeemakers. The hotel restaurant, Peppercorns, which overlooks the ocean, serves breakfast and dinner; lunch is available on the sundeck next to the pool. ✉ *1701 S. Virginia Dare Trail, off U.S. 158, Milepost 9.5 (Box 2716), 27948,* ☎ *252/441–2151 or 800/635–1824,* FAX *252/441–1830. 172 rooms. Restaurant, pool. AE, D, DC, MC, V.*

Manteo

$$–$$$ ✕ **Weeping Radish Brewery and Restaurant.** This Bavarian-style restaurant and microbrewery is known for its German cuisine and annual Octoberfest weekend held after Labor Day, featuring German and blues bands. Free tours of the brewery are given on request. ✉ *U.S. 64,* ☎ *252/473–1157. D, MC, V.*

$$$–$$$$ ✕ **Tranquil House Inn.** This waterfront B&B is only a few steps from shops and restaurants, and bikes are provided for adventures beyond. The restaurant, named 1587, serves inventive entrées such as sesame-crusted tuna with wasabi vinagrette; it's closed from December through February. ✉ *405 Queen Elizabeth Ave., 27954,* ☎ *252/473–1404 or 800/458–7069,* FAX *252/473–1526. 25 rooms. Restaurant. CP. AE, D, MC, V.*

Morehead City

$$$ ✕ **West Side Cafe.** A favorite among locals, this upscale café takes pride in offering fresh seafood any way you can eat it. Dinner is a delight here; live entertainment is often provided. ✉ *4370–A Arendell St.,* ☎ *252/240–0588. MC, V.*

Nags Head

$$$ ✕ **Windmill Point.** The menu changes frequently but you can always count on the signature dish, the seafood trio. Dinner promises stunning views of the sound at sunset. Those with nautical interests will

enjoy the fun memorabilia from the SS *United States.* ✉ *U.S. 158 Bypass, Milepost 16.5,* ☎ *252/441–1535. AE, D, DC, MC, V.*

$$$$ ★ **First Colony Inn.** This historic B&B with ocean views was built in 1932. Some rooms have Jacuzzis, others have four-poster or canopy beds and armoires. The entire property is smoke-free. ✉ *6720 S. Virginia Dare Trail, 27959,* ☎ *252/441–2343 or 800/368–9390,* FAX *252/441–9234. 26 rooms. Pool. Full breakfast. AE, D, MC, V.*

New Bern

$$$–$$$$ ★ ✕ **Harvey Mansion Historic Inn.** Beat and Carolyn Zuttel have opened an inn to go with their award-winning restaurant. Its all under one roof in a striking 1797 house near the confluence of the Trent and Neuse rivers. The mansion also functions as an art gallery and the cellar, with its exposed beams, has been turned into a low-key pub. ✉ *221 S. Front St.,* ☎ *252/638–3205. 3 rooms. Restaurant. CP. AE, D, DC, MC, V.*

$$$ ★ **Harmony House Inn.** At this historic B&B convenient to all the attractions, you can sleep in spacious rooms where Yankee soldiers stayed during the Civil War. Today they are furnished with a mixture of antiques and reproductions. The inn serves a hot breakfast buffet and complimentary white and dessert wines in the evening. ✉ *215 Pollock St., 28560,* ☎ *252/636–3810 or 800/636–3113,* FAX *252/636–3810. 10 rooms. Full breakfast. AE, D, DC, MC, V.*

Ocracoke

$$–$$$ ✕ **Island Inn.** This well-worn turn-of-the-century inn has third-floor rooms with cathedral ceilings and lovely views. The dining room is known for oyster omelets, crab cakes, and hush puppies. ✉ *Rte. 12 (Box 9), 27960,* ☎ *252/928–4351,* FAX *252/928–4352. 35 rooms. Restaurant, pool. D, MC, V.*

Southport

$$–$$$$ ✕ **Bald Head Island Resort.** Reached by ferry from Southport, this self-contained, carless community complete with grocery store, restaurants, and golf course has bleached-wood villas and shingled cottages that have won architectural design awards. Guests travel the island on foot, bicycles, or in golf carts. Historic day tours (with lunch) are available for $35. There are five restaurants on the resort with everything from steaks and steamed seafood to hot dogs and pizza on the menu. ✉ *Box 3069, Bald Head Island 28461,* ☎ *919/457–5000 or 800/234–1666,* FAX *919/457–9232. 195 homes/condos/villas, 2 B&Bs. 3 restaurants, pool. AE, DC, MC, V.*

Wilmington

$$–$$$$ ★ ✕ **Pilot House.** This Chandler's Wharf restaurant is known for its Sunday brunch, award-winning cream-based Carolina bisque, and shrimp and grits—a lunch favorite. You can dine indoors on linen tablecloths secured by vases of fresh flowers or on a riverside deck. ✉ *2 Ann St.,* ☎ *910/343–0200. AE, D, MC, V.*

$$$$ **Blockade Runner Resort Hotel.** This two-story, ocean-side complex is widely known for its service and its supervised childrens' programs. Guest rooms, which open off the exterior balcony, overlook either the inlet or the ocean (ocean views command higher prices). The Ocean Terrace Restaurant serves an especially popular Saturday seafood buffet and Sunday brunch. ✉ *275 Waynick Blvd., Wrightsville Beach 28480,* ☎ *910/256–2251 or 800/541–1161,* FAX *910/256–5502. 147 rooms, 3 suites. Restaurant, pool, health club. AE, D, DC, MC, V.*

$$$$ ★ **Inn at St. Thomas Court.** In the heart of the historic district, four former commercial buildings (including a convent) have been transformed into luxurious suites, each decorated in a different theme. ✉ *101 S. 2nd St., 28401,* ☎ *910/343–1800 or 800/525–0909,* FAX *910/251–1149. 34 suites. AE, D, DC, MC, V.*

Campgrounds

Camping is permitted in designated areas of the **Cape Hatteras** and **Cape Lookout national seashores** from mid-April through mid-October and at most state parks (☞ National and State Parks, *above*). Private campgrounds are scattered all along the coast. For more information contact the state's division of tourism (☞ Statewide Visitor Information, *above*).

Nightlife and the Arts

A favorite haunt on the Wilmington waterfront is the **Ice House Beer Garden** (⊠ 115 S. Water St., ☎ 910/763–2084), an indoor-outdoor bar with live rhythm and blues. In Wrightsville Beach at the **Blockade Runner Resort** (⊠ 275 Waynick Blvd., ☎ 910/256–2251), there's a lounge, live jazz, a weekly comedy show, and during summer, weekly dinner theater. In Wilmington, the **Thalian Hall Center for the Performing Arts** (⊠ 310 Chestnut St., ☎ 910/343–3664 or 800/523–2820), built between 1855 and 58 and restored to its former grandeur, hosts more than 250 theater, dance, and musical performances each year.

Outdoor Activities and Sports

Boating

You can travel hundreds of miles over the sounds and inlets of this vast region along the Intracoastal Waterway. For marina and docking information, pick up a copy of the ***North Carolina Coastal Boating Guide*** (☞ Arriving and Departing, *above*) or contact the appropriate county chamber of commerce (☞ Visitor Information, *above*).

Fishing

The region teems with bass, billfish, flounder, mullet, spot, trout, and other fish. Fishing is permitted from piers all along the coast and from certain bridges and causeways. Charter boats for deep-sea fishing are available at the **Oregon Inlet Fishing Center** (☎ 252/441–6301 or 800/272–5199) on the Outer Banks; **Flapjack & Gung Ho Charters** (☎ 910/458–4362 or 800/288–3474) at Carolina Beach Municipal Marina; and the ***Carolina Princess*** (☎ 252/726–5479 or 800/682–3456) in Morehead City. Licenses for freshwater fishing are available by calling the **North Carolina Wildlife Commission** (☎ 919/662–4370). No license is needed for saltwater fishing.

Golf

Among the public and semiprivate courses in the Greater Wilmington area is the breathtaking **Bald Head Island Golf Course** (☎ 910/457–7310), designed by George Cobb. Ocean Isle, near the South Carolina state line, also has a number of outstanding courses. Contact the **Cape Fear Coast Convention and Visitors Bureau** (☞ Visitor Information, *above*) or the **South Brunswick Islands Chamber of Commerce** (⊠ Box 1380, Shallotte 28459, ☎ 910/754–6644).

Scuba Diving

With more than 1,500 known shipwrecks off the coast of the Outer Banks, diving opportunities are legion. Dive shops include **Nags Head Pro Dive Shop** (⊠ Surfside Plaza, U.S. 158, Nags Head, ☎ 252/441–7594), **Aquatic Safaris** (⊠ 5751-4 Oleander Dr., Wilmington, ☎ 910/392–4386), and **Olympus Dive Center** (⊠ 713 Shepard St., Morehead City, ☎ 252/726–9432).

Surfing and Windsurfing

Kitty Hawk Kites (☞ Shopping, *below*), the oldest hang-gliding school on the East Coast, provides gear and instruction. Rentals are also available at shops in Wilmington, Wrightsville Beach, and Carolina Beach.

Beaches

Cape Hatteras and **Cape Lookout national seashores** offer more than 100 mi of beaches. **Atlantic Beach** and **Emerald Isle,** on Bogue Banks near Morehead City; **Wrightsville, Carolina,** and **Kure beaches,** near Wilmington; and **Ocean Isle,** farther south, are other top spots.

Shopping

You can find **nautical items** at antiques shops and **hand-carved wooden ducks and birds** at local crafts shops in Duck, a few miles north of Nags Head, and in Wanchese, at the south end of Roanoke Island. In Nags Head **Kitty Hawk Kites** (☎ 252/441–4124 or 800/334–4777), the largest kite store on the East Coast, offers every type of kite and windsock known to humanity as well as toys and outdoor clothing. New Bern and Wilmington are centers for **antiques**; in Wilmington many shops are at Chandler's Wharf, the Cotton Exchange, and the Water Street Market on the waterfront.

THE MOUNTAINS

The majestic peaks, meadows, and valleys of the Appalachian, Blue Ridge, and Smoky mountains characterize the west end of the state, which is divided into three distinct regions: the southern mountains (home to the Eastern Band of the Cherokee Nation); the northern mountains, known as the High Country (Boone, Blowing Rock, Banner Elk); and the central mountains, anchored by Asheville, for decades a retreat for the wealthy and famous. National parks, national forests, centers for handmade crafts, and the Blue Ridge Parkway are the area's main attractions, providing prime opportunities for shopping, skiing, hiking, bicycling, camping, fishing, canoeing, or just taking in the breathtaking views.

Visitor Information

Appalachian Trail Conference (✉ 160–A Zillicoa St., Asheville 28802, ☎ 828/254–3708). **Asheville:** Convention and Visitors Bureau (✉ Box 1010, 28802, ☎ 828/258–6111 or 800/257–1300). **Blowing Rock:** Chamber of Commerce (✉ Box 406, 28605, ☎ 828/295–7851). **Blue Ridge Parkway:** Superintendent (✉ 400 BB&T Bldg., 1 Pack Sq., Asheville 28801, ☎ 828/298–0398). **Boone:** Chamber of Commerce (✉ 208 W. Howard St., 28607, ☎ 828/262–3516 or 800/852–9506). **Cherokee:** Cherokee Visitor Center (✉ U.S. 441 Business, ☎ 828/497–9195 or 800/438–1601). **NC High Country Host** (✉ 1700 Blowing Rock Rd., Boone 28607, ☎ 828/264–1299 or 800/438–7500). **Smoky Mountain Host of NC** (✉ 4437 Georgia Rd., Franklin 28734, ☎ 828/369–9606 or 800/432–4678).

Arriving and Departing

By Bus

Greyhound (☎ 800/231–2222) serves Asheville.

By Car

You can reach Asheville from the east or the west via I–40. I–26 begins in Asheville and heads south, connecting with I–240, which circles the city. U.S. 23/19A also runs through Asheville.

The High Country is reached off I–40 via U.S. 321 at Hickory, Route 181 at Morganton, and U.S. 221 at Marion. U.S. 421 is a major east–west artery. The Blue Ridge Parkway bisects the region, traveling over mountain crests in the High Country.

By Plane

Asheville Regional Airport (✉ Rte. 280, Fletcher, ☎ 828/684–2226) is 15 mi south of Asheville.

Exploring the Mountains

The town of **Cherokee** is the capital of Qualla Boundary, a 56,000-acre Cherokee Indian Reservation. Displays and artifacts at the **Museum of the Cherokee Indian** (✉ U.S. 441 at Drama Rd., ☎ 828/497–3481; 🎟 $4) cover 10,000 years of Cherokee history. There's also an art gallery and an outdoor living exhibit of Cherokee life as it was in the 15th century. The **Qualla Arts and Crafts Mutual** (✉ U.S. 441 at Drama Rd., ☎ 828/497–3103; 🎟 free), across the street from the Museum of the Cherokee Indian, is a cooperative that displays and sells baskets, masks, and wood carvings handcrafted by 300 Cherokee artisans. At **Oconaluftee Indian Village** (✉ U.S. 441 at Drama Rd., ☎ 828/497–2315; 🎟 $10), guides in Native American costumes will lead you through the village while others demonstrate skills such as weaving, pottery, canoe construction, and hunting techniques. You're guaranteed a find at **Smoky Mountain Gold and Ruby Mine** (✉ U.S. 441 north, ☎ 828/497–6574; 🎟 free), on the Qualla Boundary, where gems such as aquamarines are plentiful. You can purchase the treasures you dig up and pan for: Gold ore costs $5 per bag.

The largest and most cosmopolitan city in the mountains, **Asheville** has been rated America's favorite place to live of cities of its size. The city's downtown is a pedestrian-friendly place, with upscale shopping, art galleries, museums, restaurants, and nightlife.

The 92,000-square-ft **Pack Place Education, Arts & Science Center,** in downtown Asheville, houses the **Asheville Art Museum, Colburn Gem & Mineral Museum, Health Adventure,** and **Diana Wortham Theatre.** The **YMI Cultural Center,** also maintained by Pack Place, is directly across the street. ✉ *2 Pack Sq.,* ☎ *828/257–4500.* 🎟 *$6.50. Closed Mon. June–Oct. and Sun.–Mon. Nov.–May.*

★ East of Asheville is the astonishing **Biltmore Estate,** built in the 1890s as the home of George Vanderbilt. The 250-room French Renaissance–style château is filled with priceless antiques and art treasures. The grounds, landscaped by Frederick Law Olmsted, include 75 acres of elaborate gardens, 72 acres of vineyards, and a state-of-the-art winery. ✉ *Exit 50 off I–40E,* ☎ *828/255–1700 or 800/624–1575.* 🎟 *$29.95.*

The **North Carolina Arboretum,** 426 acres that were part of the original Biltmore Estate, completes the dream of Frederick Law Olmsted and features southern Appalachian flora in a stunning number of settings, including the Quilt Garden, with bedding plants that are arranged in patterns reminiscent of Appalachian quilts. There is also the formal Stream Garden, which capitalizes on the Bent Creek trout stream that runs through the grounds. ✉ *10 mi southwest of downtown Asheville, adjacent to the Blue Ridge Pkwy.,* ☎ *828/665–2492.* 🎟 *Free.*

A 45-minute drive from Asheville is Madison County, home to the picturesque village of Hot Springs, a way station for hikers on the Appalachian Trail, and the **Hot Springs Spa.** These mineral springs maintain a natural 100°F temperature year-round, and since the turn of the century, they have provided relief for visitors suffering a variety of ailments, including rheumatism and arthritis. ✉ *1 Bridge St.,* ☎ *828/622–7676 or 800/462–0933.* 🎟 *$7.50–$25 per hr, depending on time of day and number of guests.*

The **Great Smoky Mountains Railway,** just 45 minutes west of Asheville, is one of the most popular attractions in western North Carolina. Choose from four excursions on diesel-electric and steam locomotives (fares vary). Open-sided cars or cabooses are ideal for picture taking as the spectacular scenery glides by. ✉ *119 Front St., Dillsboro 28725,* ☎ *828/586–8811 or 800/872–4681.* 🎫 *Fares start at $19.95. Closed Jan.–Mar.*

The most scenic route from Asheville to the Boone–Blowing Rock area is via the **Blue Ridge Parkway** (☎ 828/271–4779), a stunningly beautiful 469-mi road that gently winds through mountains and meadows and crosses mountain streams on its way from Waynesboro, Virginia, to Cherokee, North Carolina. The parkway is generally open year-round but often closes during heavy snows and icy conditions. Maps and information are available at visitor centers along the highway.

At Milepost 316.3 on the Blue Ridge Parkway is the **Linville Falls Visitor Center** (✉ Rte. 1, Box 789, Spruce Pine 28777, ☎ 828/765–1045; 🎫 free). From here it's an easy half-mile hike to one of North Carolina's most photographed waterfalls.

Just off the parkway, on U.S. 221 at Milepost 305, is **Grandfather Mountain,** which soars 6,000 ft and is famous for its mile-high swinging bridge. Sweaty-palmed visitors cross the 228-ft bridge, which sways over a 1,000 ft drop into Linville Valley. The **Natural History Museum** has exhibits on native minerals, flora and fauna, and pioneer life. The United Nations has designated Grandfather Mountain a Biosphere Reserve. ☎ *828/733–4337 or 800/468–7325.* 🎫 *$10. Closed in inclement weather.*

Blowing Rock refers to both a quiet mountain village and the nearby 4,000-ft rock for which it was named. Visitors to this looming outcrop can enjoy views from its **observation tower** (☎ 828/295–7111; 🎫 $4) and its gardens of mountain laurel and other native plants. The tower is closed weekdays in January and February.

The **Tweetsie Railroad** is a popular Wild West theme park where you can pan for gold and ride a train beset by train robbers. ✉ *U.S. 321, Blowing Rock 28605,* ☎ *828/264–9061 or 800/526–5740.* 🎫 *$16. Closed Nov.–Mid-May.*

Blue Ridge Gemstone Mine, midway between Asheville and Boone on the Blue Ridge Parkway, is in a region with one of the richest mineral deposits in the country. Though you can't enter the mine, you can purchase a gem bucket for anywhere from $5 to $100, take it to the flume line, and sort through it for rubies, emeralds, sapphires, and more. ✉ *Box 327, Little Switzerland 28749,* ☎ *828/765–5264.* 🎫 *Free. Closed Jan.–Mar.*

Boone, named for frontiersman Daniel Boone, lies at the convergence of three major highways—U.S. 321, U.S. 421, and Rte. 105. ***Horn in the West*** (✉ Amphitheater off U.S. 321, ☎ 828/264–2120; 🎫 $12), a project of the Southern Appalachian Historical Association, is an outdoor drama that traces the story of Daniel Boone. Show runs Tuesday through Sunday from mid-June to mid-August. Boone's **Appalachian Cultural Museum** (✉ University Hall near Greene's Motel, U.S. 321, ☎ 828/262–3117; 🎫 $2) is dedicated to the history and culture of the region from the geographic origins of the mountains to the beginnings of stock car racing. Also showcased are the many other aspects of mountain life—from antiques to quilts to the development of the tourism industry. The museum is closed Mondays.

Dining and Lodging

The spirit of the pioneers who settled the mountains has always been present in the area's food and shelter—basic, hardy, and family-oriented. Be sure to make reservations early for visits in the fall, when every nook and cranny is crammed with leaf peepers. For price ranges *see* Charts 1 (B) and 2 (B) *in* On the Road with Fodor's.

Asheville

$$–$$$ ✕ **Cafe on the Square.** When owners Bill and Shelagh Byrne moved to Asheville from San Francisco, they brought California-style cuisine with them. The menu is heavy on fresh seafood and pastas cooked with various salsas, chutneys, and simple marinades. The local business crowd frequents the restaurant during lunch, but theatergoers come for dinner. ✉ *1 Biltmore Ave.,* ☎ *828/251–5565. AE, D, MC, V.*

$$–$$$ ✕ **Mountain Smoke House.** Mountain barbecue and pig-pickin' buffets combined with bluegrass music and clogging add up to a lively experience for those who want more than food when they go out. The aroma will lead you to this dinner-only family-style restaurant, which serves as a showcase for local musicians. Vegetarians can be accommodated, too. ✉ *20 S. Spruce St.,* ☎ *828/253–4871. AE, D, DC, MC, V.*

$$$–$$$$ ★ ✕🏨 **Grove Park Inn.** With its supervised children's programs, racquetball and tennis courts, special weekend packages, and views of the Blue Ridge Mountains, this is Asheville's premier resort. Since its opening in 1913, the guest list has included Henry Ford, Thomas Edison, Harvey Firestone, Warren G. Harding, and F. Scott Fitzgerald. The inn, whose two newer wings are in keeping with the original design, is furnished with oak antiques in the Arts and Crafts style. The restaurants offer plenty of choices: Horizons specializes in game dishes from ostrich to boar; you can also order free-range chicken. ✉ *290 Macon Ave., 28804,* ☎ *828/252–2711 or 800/438–5800,* FAX *828/253–7053 for guests, 828/252–6102 for reservations. 498 rooms, 12 suites. 4 restaurants, pools, health club. AE, D, DC, MC, V.*

$$$–$$$$ ★ ✕🏨 **Richmond Hill Inn.** Once a private residence, this elegant Victorian mansion is on the National Register of Historic Places. Many of the rooms in the mansion are furnished with canopy beds, Victorian sofas, and other antiques, while the more modern cottages have contemporary pine poster beds. The restaurant, Gabrielle's, is known for its innovative cuisine, its rich cherry-wood paneling, and three-tiered chandelier. Reservations are necessary here but not at the Arbor Grille, a glass-enclosed sunporch. Gabrielle's is only open to the public for dinner and Sunday brunch; jacket and tie are required. ✉ *87 Richmond Hill Dr., 28806,* ☎ *828/252–7313 or 800/545–9238,* FAX *828/252–8726. 24 rooms, 3 suites, 9 cottages. 2 restaurants. Full breakfast. AE, MC, V.*

$$$ 🏨 **Comfort Inn.** Off I–240 near the River Ridge Outlet Mall, this hotel has standard but comfortable guest rooms and suites with garden tub Jacuzzis, private balconies, and dinette areas. Breakfast is served in front of the fireplace in the large sitting room. ✉ *800 Fairview Rd., 28805,* ☎ *828/298–9141,* FAX *828/298–6629. 149 rooms, 28 suites. Pool. CP. AE, D, DC, MC, V.*

$$ 🏨 **Mountaineer Inn.** A fixture along Tunnel Road for nearly 40 years, this motel has recently been remodeled. It's ever-popular with families and others who care less about fancy than they do about affordable, comfortable surroundings. Refrigerators and coffeemakers are in each uniquely decorated room. ✉ *155 Tunnel Rd., 28805,* ☎ *828/254–5331 or 800/255–4080,* FAX *828/254–5331. 79 rooms. CP. AE, D, MC, V.*

Blowing Rock

$$–$$$ 🏨 **Alpine Village Inn.** In the heart of Blowing Rock, this motel harks back to a simpler time. Its rooms are neat as a pin and attractive in a

homey way. Owners Rudy and Lynn Cutrera have decorated them with antiques, quilts, and even flowers on holidays. Room refrigerators are available. ✉ *297 Sunset Dr., 28605,* ☎ *828/295–7206. 15 rooms. AE, D, MC, V.*

Boone

$$–$$$ ✕🏨 **High Country Inn.** A popular honeymoon choice that also draws skiers, golfers, and other groups interested in the discount packages, the inn, made of native stone and surrounded by ponds, has rooms that range from luxurious to comfortable. Geno's, a popular sports bar, and the Waterwheel, with its Continental menu, are the dining options. ✉ *1785 Rte. 105S (Box 1339), 28607,* ☎ *828/264–1000 or 800/334–5605,* FAX *828/262–0073. 118 rooms, 2 suites, 1 log cabin. Restaurant, pool, exercise room. AE, D, MC, V.*

Cherokee

$$ ✕ **Nantahala Village Restaurant.** This roomy restaurant about 10 mi southwest of Cherokee is a favorite of folks in Swain County. The food isn't fancy, but it's good and it's filling. Trout, chicken, and country ham are some of the choices. Sunday brunch consists of old reliables like eggs Benedict. ✉ *9400 U.S. 19 West, Bryson City,* ☎ *828/488–9616 or 800/438–1507. D, MC, V. Closed late Nov.–early Mar.*

$$–$$$ 🏨 **Holiday Inn Cherokee.** Guest rooms are standard chain fare, but the staff at this well-equipped motel is very friendly. The in-house Chestnut Tree restaurant has dinner buffets that are veritable groaning boards, and the on-site native crafts shop, The Hunting Ground, with works by local artists, is a nice touch. ✉ *U.S. 19 S, 28719,* ☎ *828/497–9181 or 800/465–4329,* FAX *828/497–5973. 150 rooms, 4 suites. Restaurant, pools. AE, D, DC, MC, V.*

Hot Springs

$–$$$ ✕🏨 **Bridge Street Cafe & Inn.** This renovated storefront, circa 1922, is right on the Appalachian Trail and overlooks Spring Creek. Upstairs are brightly decorated rooms and two shared baths filled with antiques. One of the bathrooms has a claw-foot tub. The café downstairs has a hand-built wood-fired oven and grill from which emerge gourmet pizzas. ✉ *Bridge St. (Box 502), 28743,* ☎ *828/622–0002,* FAX *828/622–7282. 4 rooms. Restaurant. AE, D, MC, V. Closed Nov.–mid-Mar.*

Nightlife

With 1,800 gaming machines, video poker, video blackjack, and video craps, **Harrah's Cherokee Casino** (✉ Hwy. 19 off U.S. 441 N, Cherokee, ☎ 828/497–7777) is the largest casino in a 500-mi radius. The complex also has a 1,500-seat concert hall, three restaurants, and a child care area. An intimate, smoke-free listening room, **Be Here Now** (✉ 5 Biltmore Ave., Asheville, ☎ 828/258–2071) offers dancing and concerts. The **Hearthside Cafe** (✉ N. Main St. off NC 321 Bypass, Blowing Rock, ☎ 828/295–5500) at Chetola Resort is just the number for those in a mellow mood. Pianist Charles Ellis is a tradition.

Outdoor Activities and Sports

Canoeing and White-Water Rafting

Near Boone and Blowing Rock, the New River, a federally designated Wild and Scenic River (Classes I and II), provides hours of excitement for canoeists, as do the Watauga River, Wilson Creek, and the Toe River. The Toe becomes the Nolichucky River as it goes into Tennessee. As the Nolichucky traverses the deepest, most spectacular canyon east of the Grand Canyon, its rapids offer heart-pounding excitement for the adrenaline deprived. **Carolina Wilderness** (☎ 800/872–7437), **Edge of**

the World Outfitters (☎ 828/898–9550 or 800/789–EDGE), and **High Mountain Expeditions** (☎ 828/295–4200 or 800/262–9036) provide trips down the Nolichucky via raft.

Ski Areas

Downhill skiing is available at **Appalachian Ski Mountain,** at Blowing Rock (☎ 828/295–7828 or 800/322–2373); **Hawksnest Golf & Ski Resort** (☎ 828/963–6561 or 800/822–4295), at Banner Elk; **Ski Beech** (☎ 828/387–2011 or 800/438–2093), at Beech Mountain; and **Sugar Mountain** (☎ 828/898–4521 or 800/784–2768), at Banner Elk.

Shopping

The **Folk Art Center** (☎ 828/298–7928), at Milepost 382 on the Blue Ridge Parkway, sells mountain arts and crafts made by the 700 artisans of the Southern Highland Handicraft Guild. **Biltmore Village,** on the Biltmore Estate, has specialty shops, restaurants, and galleries built along cobbled sidewalks. There's a turn-of-the-century English hamlet feel, and everything from children's books to music, antiques, and wearable art can be found. **Malaprops** (✉ 55 Haywood St., ☎ 828/254–6734) bookstore and café is a mainstay in Asheville. Its two stories are filled with books about the region.

SOUTH CAROLINA

Updated by Mary Sue Lawrence

Capital	Columbia
Population	3,684,000
Mottoes	While I Breathe, I Hope; Prepared in Mind and Resources
State Bird	Carolina wren
State Flower	Yellow jessamine
Postal Abbreviation	SC

Statewide Visitor Information

South Carolina Department of Parks, Recreation and Tourism (⊠ 1205 Pendleton St., Box 71, Columbia 29202, ☎ 803/734–0235 or 800/872–3505). **Welcome centers:** U.S. 17 near Little River; I–95 near Dillon, Santee and Lake Marion, and Hardeeville; I–77 near Fort Mill; I–85 near Blacksburg and Fair Play; I–26 near Landrum; I–20 at North Augusta; and U.S. 301 near Allendale.

Scenic Drives

The **Cherokee Foothills Scenic Highway** (Route 11), passing small towns, peach orchards, and historical sites, traverses 130 mi of Blue Ridge foothills in the northwest corner of the state. The **Ashley River Road** (Route 61), which runs parallel to the river for about 11 mi north of Charleston, leads to famous plantations and gardens. The **Savannah River Scenic Highway** (follow signs from Route 28 near North Augusta to Route 24 near Westminster) follows the Savannah River for 100 mi along the Georgia border, winding past three lakes.

National and State Parks

National Parks

At **Cowpens National Battlefield** (⊠ Rte. 11, Box 308, Chesnee 29323, ☎ 864/461–2828; 🎫 free) the American patriots defeated the British in 1781; exhibits in the visitor center explain the battle. **Kings Mountain National Military Park** (⊠ I–85 near Blacksburg; Box 40, Kings Mountain, NC 28086, ☎ 864/936–7921; 🎫 free), where patriot forces whipped the redcoats in 1780, has exhibits depicting the famous battle and a self-guided trail. For white-water enthusiasts, the **Chattooga National Wild and Scenic River** (⊠ U.S. Forest Service, 4931 Broad River Rd., Columbia 29210-4021, ☎ 803/561–4000; 🎫 free) forms the border between South Carolina and Georgia for 40 mi. **Congaree Swamp National Monument** (⊠ Old Bluff Rd., Hopkins 29061, ☎ 803/776–4396; 🎫 free) contains the oldest and largest trees east of the Mississippi River.

State Parks

Several of South Carolina's 48 state parks operate like resort communities, with everything from deluxe accommodations to golf. **Hickory Knob State Resort Park** (⊠ Rte. 1, Box 199-B, McCormick 29835, ☎ 864/391–2450 or 800/491–1764), on Strom Thurmond Lake, has opportunities for fishing, golfing, and skeet shooting. **Devil's Fork State Park** (⊠ 161 Holcombe Circle, Salem 29676, ☎ 864/944–2639) has luxurious accommodations overlooking beautiful Lake Jocassee. **Calhoun Falls State Park** (⊠ Rte. 81, Calhoun Falls 29628, ☎ 803/447–8267) has a full-service marina, a campground, nature trails, and a picnic area.

The state's **coastal parks**—known for broad beaches, camping facilities, and nature preserves—draw the most visitors and are often booked months in advance. **Huntington Beach State Park** (✉ Murrells Inlet 29576, ☎ 803/237–4440) has a splendid beach, surf fishing, and a salt-marsh boardwalk, as well as Atalaya, a Moorish-style mansion. **Myrtle Beach State Park** (✉ U.S. 17, Myrtle Beach 29577, ☎ 803/238–5325) has cabins and year-round nature programs. **Hunting Island State Park** (✉ St. Helena Island 29920, ☎ 843/838–2011), a secluded domain of beach, has beachfront cottages, nature trails and varied fishing. **Edisto Beach State Park** (✉ S.C.174, Edisto Island 294TK, ☎ 843/869–2156) has cabins by the marsh and campsites by the ocean. For more information contact the **South Carolina Division of State Parks** (✉ 1205 Pendleton St., Columbia 29201, ☎ 803/734–0159).

CHARLESTON

The port city of Charleston has withstood three centuries of epidemics, earthquakes, fires, and hurricanes to become one of the South's best-preserved and most beloved cities. Residents have lovingly restored old downtown homes and commercial buildings, as well as more than 180 historic churches—so many that Charlestonians call their home the "Holy City." Each spring the city—festooned with dogwood and azaleas—celebrates its heritage with symphony galas, plantation oyster roasts, candlelight tours of historic homes and churches, and the renowned Spoleto Festival USA, a celebration of the arts staged in streets and performance halls throughout the city.

Visitor Information

Charleston Area Convention and Visitors Bureau (✉ Box 975, 375 Meeting St., 29402, ☎ 843/853–8000 or 800/868–8118).

Arriving and Departing

By Boat

Boaters arriving at Charleston Harbor via the Intracoastal Waterway may dock at **City Marina** (✉ Lockwood Blvd., ☎ 843/723–5098), **Ashley Marina** (✉ Lockwood Blvd., ☎ 843/722–1996), and at the Isle of Palms's **Wild Dunes Yacht Harbor** (☎ 843/886–5100).

By Bus

Greyhound Lines (✉ 3610 Dorchester Rd., North Charleston, ☎ 800/231–2222).

By Car

I–26 crosses the state from northwest to southeast and ends at Charleston. U.S. 17, a north–south coastal route, passes through the city.

By Plane

Charleston International Airport (☎ 843/767–1100), 12 mi west of downtown Charleston along I–26, is served by Continental, Delta, Midway Express, United Express, and US Airways. **Low Country Limousine Service** (☎ 843/767–7111 or 800/222–4771) charges $15 per person (or $10 per person for two or more) to downtown; make reservations in advance. Some hotels also provide shuttle service.

By Train

Amtrak (✉ 4565 Gaynor Ave., North Charleston, ☎ 843/744–8264 or 800/872–7245).

Getting Around Charleston

You can park your car and walk in the city's historic district, but you'll need a car to see attractions in outlying areas. **Charleston Transit** (☎ 843/747–0922) provides bus service within the city and to James Island, Isle of Palms, Sullivan's Island, Mount Pleasant, and North Charleston. It also operates the trolley-style Downtown Area Shuttle buses, called DASH (☎ 843/747–0922). Fare for either is 75¢, exact change, or $2 for a one-day DASH pass. **Taxi companies** include Yellow Cab (☎ 843/577–6565), Safety Cab (☎ 843/722–4066), and Low Country Limousine (☞ Arriving and Departing *above*).

A popular option is a **guided tour.** Guides are generally knowledgeable and often provide snippets of history and humor. **Charleston Carriage Co.** (☎ 843/577–0042), the city's oldest horse-drawn-carriage tour company, conducts one-hour tours of the historic district. **Charleston Tea Party Walking Tour** (☎ 843/577–5896 or 843/722–1779) offers city walking tours. **Gullah Tours** (☎ 843/763–7551) focuses on African-American influences on Charleston architecture, history, and culture.

Exploring Charleston

You can get a quick orientation to the city by viewing ***Forever Charleston,*** a 24-minute multimedia presentation shown by the Charleston Area Convention and Visitors Bureau (☞ Visitor Information, *above*).

★ The **Charleston Museum,** founded in 1773, has 500,000 items in its collection, including Charleston silver, fashions, toys, and snuffboxes, as well as exhibits on natural history, archaeology, and ornithology. Also part of the museum are two historic homes. The **Joseph Manigault House** (✉ 350 Meeting St.; 🎫 (☞ *below*)) was designed in 1803 and is noted for its carved-wood mantels and elaborate plasterwork. Furnishings are British, French, and American antiques, including rare tricolor Wedgwood pieces.The **Heyward-Washington House** (✉ 87 Church St.; 🎫 (☞ *below*)) was the residence of President George Washington during his 1791 visit and the setting for DuBose Heyward's ***Porgy.*** The mansion is notable for fine period furnishings by local craftspeople and includes a restored 18th-century kitchen. You can purchase a combined ticket for admission to the museum and both houses. The museum is across from the Charleston Area Convention and Visitor Bureau's visitor information center (where there's parking for 65¢ per hour). ✉ *360 Meeting St.,* ☎ *843/722–2996.* 🎫 *$6; combination ticket for museum and houses $15; for 2 sites $10.*

The stately 1819 **Aiken–Rhett House** mansion, with original wallpaper, paint colors, and some furnishings, was the headquarters of Confederate general P. G. T. Beauregard during his 1864 Civil War defense of Charleston. The house, kitchen, slave quarters, and work yard are much as they were when the original occupants lived here, making this one of the most complete examples of African-American urban life of the period. ✉ *48 Elizabeth St.,* ☎ *843/723–1159.* 🎫 *$7; combination ticket with Nathaniel Russell House (☞ below) $12; with Nathaniel Russell House and the Old Powder Magazine (☞ below) $14 .*

The heart of Charleston is the **Old City Market,** between Meeting and East Bay streets, with restaurants, shops, and produce stands. Here you can buy vegetables, fruits, benne-seed (sesame) wafers, sweet-grass baskets, jewelry, seashells, and other craft items.

The **Old Powder Magazine,** on one of Charleston's few remaining cobblestone thoroughfares, was built in 1713 and used during the Revolutionary War. It is now a museum with costumes, armor, and other

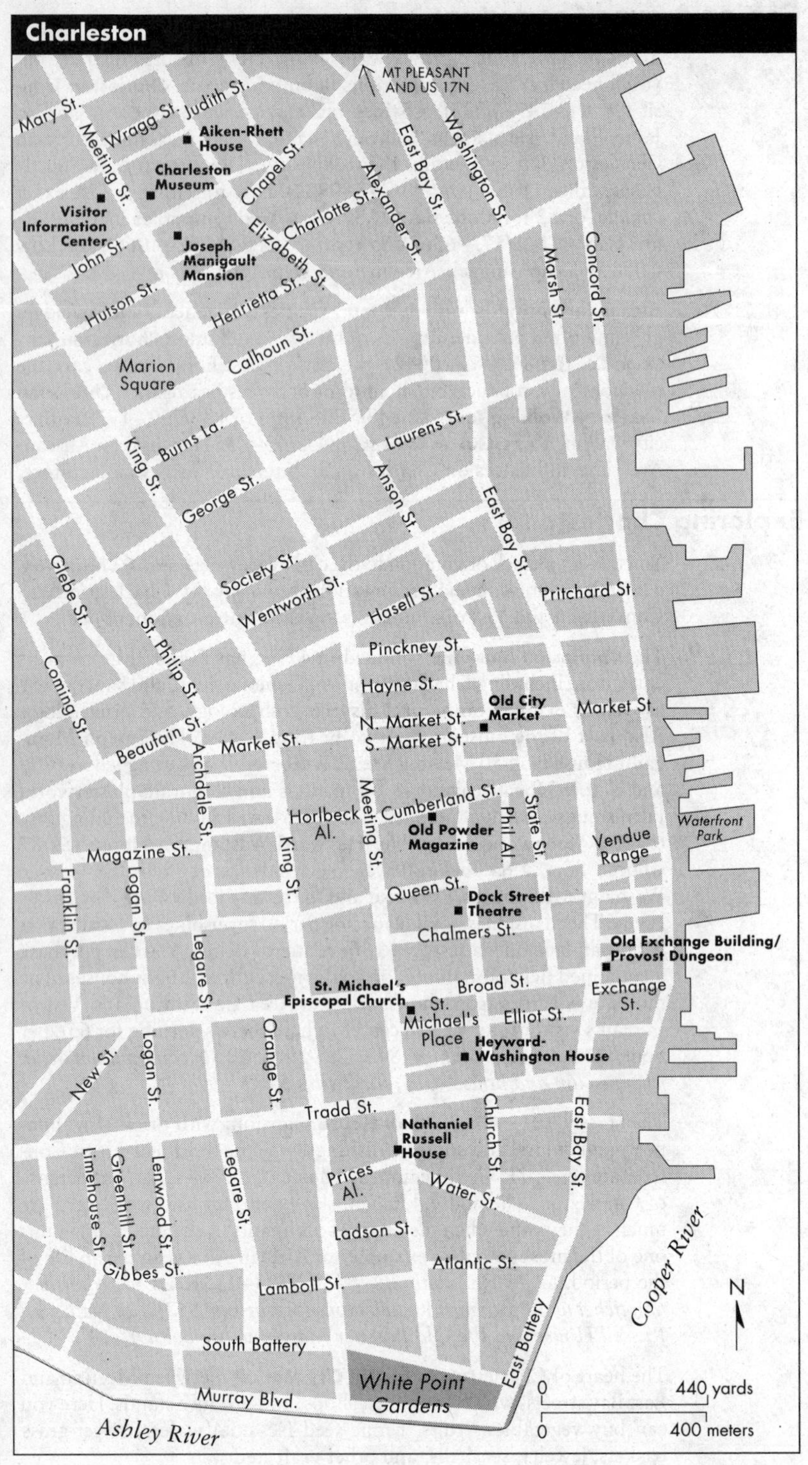
Charleston
MT PLEASANT AND US 17N
Mary St.
Meeting St.
Wragg St.
Judith St.
Aiken-Rhett House
Charleston Museum
Visitor Information Center
Chapel St.
Alexander St.
East Bay St.
Washington St.
Charlotte St.
Elizabeth St.
John St.
Joseph Manigault Mansion
Hutson St.
Henrietta St.
Concord St.
Marsh St.
Calhoun St.
Marion Square
Laurens St.
King St.
Burns La.
George St.
Anson St.
East Bay St.
Glebe St.
Society St.
Wentworth St.
Hasell St.
Pritchard St.
St. Philip St.
Coming St.
Pinckney St.
Hayne St.
Old City Market
Market St.
N. Market St.
S. Market St.
Beaufain St.
Market St.
Archdale St.
Horlbeck Al.
Cumberland St.
Old Powder Magazine
Meeting St.
Phil Al.
State St.
Waterfront Park
Vendue Range
Magazine St.
King St.
Logan St.
Franklin St.
Queen St.
Dock Street Theatre
Chalmers St.
Old Exchange Building/ Provost Dungeon
Legare St.
St. Michael's Episcopal Church
St. Michael's Place
Broad St.
Exchange St.
Elliot St.
Heyward-Washington House
New St.
Logan St.
Orange St.
Tradd St.
Nathaniel Russell House
Church St.
East Bay St.
Limehouse St.
Greenhill St.
Lenwood St.
Legare St.
Prices Al.
Water St.
Ladson St.
Atlantic St.
Gibbes St.
Lamboll St.
Cooper River
East Battery
N
South Battery
White Point Gardens
Murray Blvd.
0
440 yards
0
400 meters
Ashley River

artifacts from 18th-century Charleston. Newly restored, it offers a fascinating audiovisual tour. ✉ *79 Cumberland St.,* ☎ *843/805–6730.* 🎫 *$7; combination ticket with Aiken–Rhett House (☞ above) $12; with Aiken–Rhett House and Nathaniel Russell House (☞ below) $14.*

Dock Street Theatre (✉ 135 Church St., ☎ 843/720–3968; 🎫 free) combines the reconstructed early Georgian playhouse that originally stood on the site with the 1809 Planter's Hotel; call for tour information.

St. Michael's Episcopal Church (☎ 843/723–0603; 🎫 free), modeled on London's St. Martin's-in-the-Fields, stands at the corner of Meeting and Broad streets. Completed in 1761, this beautiful structure is Charleston's oldest surviving church. Its steeple clock and bells were imported from England in 1764.

Originally a customs house, the British used the **Old Exchange Building/Provost Dungeon** (✉ 122 E. Bay St., ☎ 843/727–2165; 🎫 $4) for prisoners during the Revolutionary War. Today a tableau of lifelike mannequins recalls this era.

★ The **Nathaniel Russell House,** one of the nation's finest examples of Adams-style architecture, was built in 1808. The interior is notable for its ornate detailing, its lavish period furnishings, and a "flying" circular staircase that spirals three stories with no apparent support. ✉ *51 Meeting St.,* ☎ *843/724–8481.* 🎫 *$7; combination ticket with Aiken–Rhett House (☞ above) $12 ; with Aiken–Rhett House and Old Powder Magazine (☞ above) $14 .*

Across the Cooper River bridges, via U.S. 17N, is the town of **Mount Pleasant,** named not for a mountain or a hill, but for a plantation in England from which some of the area's settlers hailed. In its Old Village neighborhood are antebellum homes and a sleepy, old-time town center with shops and cafés. **Patriots Point** (✉ Foot of Cooper River bridges, ☎ 843/884–2727; 🎫 $9) is the world's largest naval and maritime museum and home to the Medal of Honor Society. Berthed here are the aircraft carrier *Yorktown,* the nuclear ship *Savannah,* the World War II submarine *Clamagore,* the cutter *Ingham,* and the destroyer *Laffey.* Tours are offered on all vessels.

★ **Fort Sumter National Monument** (☎ 843/722–1691; 🎫 ferry fare $10.50), which can be reached from either Charleston's Municipal Marina or Patriot's Point, is on a man-made island in Charleston Harbor. It was here that the first shot of the Civil War was fired, on April 12, 1861, by Confederate forces. National Park Service rangers conduct free tours of the restored structure, which includes a historical museum.

Plantations, Parks, and Gardens

Charleston is famous for public parks, magnificent plantations, and secret gardens that lie behind the walls of private homes. **White Point Gardens,** on the point of the narrow Battery Peninsula bounded by the Ashley and Cooper rivers, is a popular gathering spot. **Waterfront Park,** along Concord Street on the Cooper River, has a fishing pier, unique interactive fountains, a picnic area, and landscaped gardens.

★ **Drayton Hall** (☎ 843/766–0188; 🎫 $8), built between 1738 and 1742, is the only plantation on the Ashley River that survived the Civil War. It is unfurnished, which serves to highlight the original plaster moldings, opulent hand-carved woodwork, and other ornamental details. This is considered one of the nation's finest examples of Georgian Palladian architecture. Drayton Hall is 9 mi northwest of downtown via Ashley River Road (Route 61).

★ **Magnolia Plantation and Gardens** (☎ 843/571–1266; 🎫 $10; house tour $6 extra; tram tour $5 extra; swamp tour $5 extra), 2 mi beyond Drayton Hall on Route 61, was begun in 1865. Its gardens hold one of the largest collections of azaleas and camellias in North America. Nature lovers can canoe through the 125-acre Waterfowl Refuge, see the 60-acre Audubon Swamp Garden along boardwalks and bridges, explore 500 acres of wildlife trails, and visit the petting zoo.

Middleton Place (☎ 843/556–6020 or 800/782–3608; 🎫 $14; house tour $7 extra), 4 mi north of Magnolia Plantation on Route 61, is the site of the nation's oldest landscaped gardens, dating from 1741. Much of the mansion was destroyed during the Civil War, but a restored wing houses impressive collections of silver, furniture, paintings, and historical documents. Children will enjoy the working plantation.

An avenue of oaks leads to **Boone Hall Plantation** (☎ 843/884–4371; 🎫 $12.50), 8 mi north of Charleston on U.S. 17, which is said to have inspired the painting MGM filmed to represent Tara in *Gone With the Wind.* You can explore the gardens, the first floor of the mansion, and the original slave quarters. Lunch is served in the old cotton gin.

Charles Towne Landing State Park (✉ Hwy. 171, ☎ 843/556–4450; 🎫 $5), across the Ashley River Bridge, is built on the site of a 1670 settlement. It includes a reconstructed village and fortifications, a replica of a 17th-century sailing vessel, gardens with bike trails and walking paths, and an animal park.

Cypress Gardens (✉ 24 mi north of Charleston via U.S. 52, ☎ 843/553–0515; 🎫 $5) was created from a swamp that was once the freshwater reserve of a vast rice plantation. You can explore the inky waters by boat or walk along paths lined with moss-draped cypress trees and flowering bushes.

Dining

Best known for Low Country specialties like she-crab soup, sautéed shrimp, red rice, grits, and pecan pie, Charleston is also famous for contemporary cookery blending down-home cooking with haute cuisine. For price ranges *see* Chart 1 (A) *in* On the Road with Fodor's.

$$–$$$ ✕ **Carolina's.** Always bustling, Carolina's draws Charlestonians and visitors alike. Its black-and-white bistro decor includes terra-cotta tiles and 1920s French posters. Fans return for the black-eyed-pea cakes, pasta with crawfish and *tasso* (spiced ham) in a spicy cream sauce, crab wontons, and pecan brittle basket with fruit and ice cream. ✉ *10 Exchange St.,* ☎ *843/724–3800. AE, MC, V. No lunch.*

$$–$$$ ★ ✕ **Magnolias.** Housed in an 1823 warehouse and decorated in a magnolia theme, this self-designated "uptown/down South" restaurant is prized for its Low Country fare, including shrimp and sausage over creamy grits with tasso gravy. Many entrées come with collard greens, buttermilk mashed potatoes, or succotash. ✉ *185 E. Bay St.,* ☎ *843/577–7771. AE, MC, V.*

$$–$$$ ★ ✕ **Peninsula Grill.** Surrounded by olive green wall coverings, black iron chandeliers, and 18th-century-style portraits, diners at this sophisticated restaurant in the Planters Inn can feast on such delights as lobster martini, wild mushroom grits with oysters, and New Zealand benne-seed-encrusted rack of lamb. For dessert, try the divine lemon tart with lemon sorbet, lemon crisps, and candied lemon. ✉ *112 N. Market St.,* ☎ *803/723–0700. AE, D, DC, MC, V.*

$$–$$$ ✕ **Union Hall.** The softly lit dining room creates a romantic ambience for Mediterranean-style cuisine with a distinctly southern touch. For starters, try the steak tartare with horseradish cream. Entrées include

pan-seared salmon with oven-cured tomatoes, pancetta, and a basil-cream crayfish sauce, and roast roulade of veal rib eye braised in vermouth with coriander corn pudding. ✉ *16 N. Market St.,* ☎ *843/853–4777. AE, D, DC, MC, V.*

$$ ✕ **Slightly North of Broad.** This whimsical eatery has several seats that overlook the action-packed kitchen. Low Country cuisine is given trendy treatment here: Try the corn fritters with caviar and crème fraîche or the grilled, barbecued tuna. You can order almost every item as either an appetizer or entrée. ✉ *192 E. Bay St.,* ☎ *843/723–3424. Reservations not accepted. AE, D, DC, MC, V.*

$$ ✕ **The Wreck.** Full of wacky character, this dockside spot serves up traditional dishes like boiled peanuts, fried shrimp, shrimp pilaf, deviled crab, and oyster platters in a shabby, candlelit, screened-in porch and small dining area. ✉ *106 Haddrell St., Mount Pleasant,* ☎ *803/884–0052. Reservations not accepted. No credit cards.*

$–$$ ★ ✕ **Alice's Fine Foods.** The food Southerners crave is here in its original, beloved form: Baked or fried chicken, ribs, fried fish, or other entrées come with a choice of three vegetables, including green beans, collard greens, okra and tomatoes, lima beans, yams, and squash. ✉ *468–470 King St.,* ☎ *803/853–9366. MC, V.*

$–$$ ★ ✕ **Gaulart and Maliclet French Cafe.** Chic and upbeat, the café serves ethnic and bistro French food. The menu of soups, salads, and sandwiches is enlivened by such evening specials as seafood Normandy and chicken sesame. ✉ *98 Broad St.,* ☎ *843/577–9797. AE, DC, MC, V.*

$–$$ ✕ **Pinkney Cafe & Espresso.** The best seats are outside on the porch of this historic Charleston single house, where you can enjoy super-fresh soups, pastas, seafood dishes, and the popular black bean burrito. The half-order of pasta is a great deal. A casual, artsy spot, Pinckney is popular with locals. ✉ *18 Pinkney St.,* ☎ *843/577–0961. Reservations not accepted. No credit cards.*

Lodging

Hotels and inns on the peninsula are generally more expensive than those in outlying areas of the city. Rates tend to increase during festivals, when reservations are essential, and on weekends. From December 1 to March 1 some rates drop by as much as 50%. Nearby world-class accommodations include the Kiawah Island, Wild Dunes, and Seabrook Island resorts. For price ranges *see* Chart 2 (A) *in* On the Road with Fodor's.

$$$$ ★ **Charleston Place.** This graceful, luxurious low-rise hotel has rooms with period reproductions, French bed linens, and fax machines. It's near upscale shops in the historic district. The Charleston Grill, with its mahogany-paneled walls and wrought-iron chandeliers, provides an elegant dining experience. ✉ *130 Market St., 29401,* ☎ *843/722–4900 or 800/611–5545,* FAX *843/724–7215. 440 rooms. 2 restaurants, pool, exercise room. AE, D, DC, MC, V.*

$$$$ ★ **John Rutledge House Inn.** The 1763 main house, built by a signatory of the U.S. Constitution, has ornate ironwork on its facade. Two carriage houses (each with four rooms) complete this luxury bed-and-breakfast. Rooms have plaster molding and wood floors and are decorated with antiques and four-poster beds. ✉ *116 Broad St., 29401,* ☎ *843/723–7999 or 800/476–9741,* FAX *843/720–2615. 19 rooms. CP. AE, D, DC, MC, V.*

$$$–$$$$ **Kiawah Island Resort.** Choose from inn rooms and completely equipped one- to five-bedroom villas and private homes in two luxurious resort villages on 10,000 mostly undeveloped acres. Inn rooms are decorated in pastel shades, and most have an ocean or wooded view. There are 10 mi of fine broad beaches and an array of recreational op-

portunities. ✉ *21 mi south of Charleston via U.S. 17; 12 Kiawah Beach Dr., Kiawah Island 29455,* ☎ *843/768–2121 or 800/654–2924,* FAX *843/768–6099. 150 rooms, 430 villas and homes. 8 restaurants, golf, tennis. AE, D, DC, MC, V.*

$$$–$$$$ **Mills House Hotel.** This luxurious property in the historic district is a reconstruction of a 19th-century hotel that once stood on the site. Antique furnishings and period decor lend charm to public areas; guest rooms are small and a bit standard. The elegant Barbadoes Room serves excellent seafood. ✉ *115 Meeting St., 29401,* ☎ *843/577–2400 or 800/874–9600,* FAX *843/722–2112. 215 rooms. Restaurant. AE, D, DC, MC, V.*

$$$ **Hawthorn Suites Hotel.** This deluxe hotel at the Old City Market has a restored entrance portico from an 1874 bank, a refurbished 1866 firehouse, and three lush gardens. The spacious suites, decorated with 18th-century reproductions and canopy beds, include full kitchens or wet bars. ✉ *181 Church St., 29401,* ☎ *843/577–2644 or 800/527–1133,* FAX *843/577–2697. 182 rooms. Exercise room. Full breakfast. AE, D, DC, MC, V.*

$$$ **Heart of Charleston Quality Inn.** With its ample parking and its proximity to the Gaillard Municipal Auditorium and many other must-see spots, this modest inn draws loyal repeat visitors. Rooms are modern motel style. ✉ *125 Calhoun St., 29401,* ☎ *843/722–3391 or 800/845–2504,* FAX *843/577–0361. 126 rooms. Restaurant, pool. AE, D, DC, MC, V.*

$$–$$$ **1837 Bed and Breakfast and Tea Room.** Though not as fancy as some of the B&Bs in town, this inn is long on hospitality; you'll get a sense of what it's really like to live in one of Charleston's beloved homes. Rooms are filled with antiques, including romantic canopied beds. A breakfast of homemade breads and hot entrées such as sausage pie or ham frittata is included, as is afternoon tea (open to the public for a nominal price). ✉ *126 Wentworth St., 29401,* ☎ *803/723–7166. 8 rooms. Full breakfast. AE, MC, V.*

$$–$$$ ★ **Hampton Inn–Historic District.** This downtown property has hardwood floors and a fireplace in the lobby, spacious guest rooms furnished in period reproductions, and a courtyard garden. ✉ *345 Meeting St., 29403,* ☎ *843/723–4000 or 800/426–7866,* FAX *843/722–3725. 171 rooms. Pool. AE, D, DC, MC, V.*

Motel

Red Roof Inn (✉ 301 Johnnie Dodds Blvd., 29464, ☎ 843/884–1411 or 800/843–7663, FAX 843/884–1411, ext. 160), 126 rooms, pool; *$–$$.*

Nightlife and the Arts

Nightlife

Charlie's Little Bar, above Saracen's Restaurant (✉ 141 E. Bay St., ☎ 843/723–6242), has live jazz or blues most weekends. **Chef & Clef Restaurant** (✉ 102 N. Market St., ☎ 843/722–7032) has jazz on the first floor and blues on the third. Try the **Jukebox** (✉ 4 Vendue Range, ☎ 843/723–3431), across the street from Waterfront Park, for beach music and dancing. **Lowcountry Legends Music Hall** (✉ 30 Cumberland St., ☎ 843/722–1829 or 800/348–7270) is Charleston's Preservation Hall, serving up music, legends, and folktales unique to the region. **Serenade** (✉ 37 John St., ☎ 843/973–3333) is a musical revue of jazz and Broadway tunes. **Southend Brewery** (✉ 161 E. Bay St., ☎ 803/853–4677) has a lively bar with beer brewed on the premises. You can dine and dance on the yacht ***Spirit of Carolina*** (☎ 843/722–2628).

Vickery's Bar & Grill (✉ 139 Calhoun St., ☎ 803/723–1558) is a festive nightspot with a spacious outdoor patio. **Windjammer** (✉ 1000 Ocean Blvd., ☎ 843/886–8596), on the Isle of Palms, is an oceanfront spot with live rock music.

The Arts

Spoleto Festival USA (☞ Festivals and Seasonal Events *in* The Southeast introduction), a world-class annual celebration, showcases opera, dance, theater, symphonic and chamber music, jazz, and the visual arts from late May through early June. **Piccolo Spoleto Festival** is the spirited companion festival of Spoleto Festival USA, showcasing the best in local and regional talent from every artistic discipline. Most performances are free. The **Charleston Symphony Orchestra** (☎ 843/723–7528) presents a variety of series at Gaillard Municipal Auditorium (✉ 77 Calhoun St., ☎ 843/577–4500), and chamber and pops series elsewhere.

Outdoor Activities and Sports

Golf

For a listing of area golf packages, contact the Charleston Area Convention and Visitors Bureau (☞ Visitor Information, *above*). Nonguests may play on a space-availability basis at **private island resorts** such as **Kiawah Island** (☎ 803/768–2121), **Seabrook Island** (☎ 803/768–2529), and **Wild Dunes** (☎ 803/886–2180) on the Isle of Palms. The prestigious Pete Dye–designed **Ocean Course at Kiawah Island** (☎ 803/768–7272) was the site of the 1991 Ryder Cup.

Top **public courses** in the area include **Charleston Municipal** (☎ 803/795–6517), **Charleston National Country Club** (☎ 803/884–7799), the **Dunes West Golf Club** (✉ Mount Pleasant, ☎ 803/856–9000), **Links at Stono Ferry** (✉ Hollywood, ☎ 803/763–1817), **Oak Point Golf Course** (✉ Johns Island, ☎ 803/768–7431), **Patriots Point** (✉ Mount Pleasant, ☎ 803/881–0042), and **Shadowmoss Golf Club** (✉ Charleston, ☎ 803/556–8251).

Beaches

South Carolina's climate allows swimming from April through October. There are public beaches at Beachwalker Park on Kiawah Island; Folly Beach County Park and Folly Beach on Folly Island; the Isle of Palms; and Sullivan's Island. Resorts with private beaches include Fairfield Ocean Ridge on Edisto Island; Kiawah Island Resort (☞ Lodging, *above*); Seabrook Island; and Wild Dunes Resort on the Isle of Palms. For more information contact the Charleston Area Convention and Visitors Bureau (☞ Visitor Information, *above*).

Shopping

The three-block **Old City Market** (☞ Exploring Charleston, *above*) yields colorful produce and varied gifts, including the sweet-grass baskets unique to this area. The craft, originally introduced by West Africans brought here as slaves, is now practiced by only a handful of their descendants. The baskets are priced from $15 to more than $200. (They are also sold at stands along U.S. 17 north of town, near Mount Pleasant; if you have the heart to bargain, you *may* be able to get a better price here than in Charleston.) The **Shops at Charleston Place** (✉ 130 Market St., ☎ 803/722–4900), in the historic district, includes Gucci, Brookstone, and Banana Republic. A small but pleasant **Saks Fifth Avenue** (✉ 211 King St., ☎ 803/853–9888) is across the street from the Shops at Charleston Place. **The Rainbow Market** (✉ 40 N. Market St.,

☎ 803/577–0380) is in two interconnected 150-year-old buildings. **Olde Colony Bakery** (✉ 280 King St., ☎ 803/722–2147) sells Charleston's famed benne wafer cookies.

Elegant antiques shops line King Street, among them **Geo. C. Birlant & Co.** (✉ 191 King St., ☎ 843/722–3842), with 18th- and 19th-century English selections and the famous Charleston Battery bench. **Livingston and Sons Antiques** (✉ 163 King St., ☎ 843/723–9697; ✉ 2137 Savannah Hwy., ☎ 843/556–6162) sells period furniture, clocks, and other items.

Among the town's chic art galleries are the **Historic Charleston Reproductions** (✉ 105 Broad St., ☎ 843/723–8292), with superb replicas of Charleston furniture and accessories approved by the Historic Charleston Foundation. The **Marty Whaley Adams Gallery** (✉ 120 Meeting St., ☎ 843/853–8512) carries original watercolors and monotypes plus prints and posters by this Charleston artist. **Virginia Fouché Bolton Art Gallery** (✉ 127 Meeting St., ☎ 843/577–9351) sells original paintings and limited-edition lithographs of Charleston scenes.

THE COAST

The South Carolina coast is a land of extremes, from glitzy to gracious. The Grand Strand, from the state's northeastern border to historic Georgetown, is one of the East Coast's family-vacation megacenters and the state's top tourist area. Here you'll find 60 mi of white-sand beaches, championship golf courses, campgrounds, seafood restaurants, malls and factory outlets, and, at last count, nearly a dozen live-entertainment theaters with everything from country-and-western music to magic acts. The Low Country is the area between Georgetown and the state's southeastern boundary, including Beaufort, as well as the barrier islands of Hilton Head, Edisto, and Fripp. Beaufort is a charming antebellum town with a compact historic district of lavish 18th- and 19th-century homes. Hilton Head's exclusive resorts and genteel good life make it one of the coast's most popular vacation getaways.

Visitor Information

Beaufort: Chamber of Commerce (✉ 1006 Bay St., Box 910, 29901-0910, ☎ 803/524–3163). **Georgetown:** Chamber of Commerce and Information Center (✉ 102 Broad St., Box 1776, 29442, ☎ 803/546–8436 or 800/777–7705). **Hilton Head Island:** Chamber of Commerce (✉ Box 5647, 29938, ☎ 803/785–3673). **Myrtle Beach:** Area Chamber of Commerce and Information Center (✉ 1200 N. Oak St., Box 2115, 29578-2115, ☎ 803/626–7444 or 800/356–3016, ext. 136, for brochures). **Pawleys Island:** Pawleys Island Chamber of Commerce (✉ U.S. 17, Box 569, 29585, ☎ 803/237–1921).

Arriving and Departing

By Boat

The South Carolina coast is accessible by boat via the Intracoastal Waterway. At **Myrtle Beach** you may dock at Hague Marina (☎ 803/293–2141), Harbor Gate (☎ 803/249–8888), and Marlin Quay (☎ 803/651–4444). **Hilton Head** has several marinas, including Shelter Cove Marina (☎ 803/842–7002), Harbour Town Marina (☎ 803/671–2704), and Schilling Boathouse (☎ 803/681–2628).

By Bus

Greyhound Lines (☎ 800/231–2222) serves Myrtle Beach and Beaufort.

By Car

Major interstates connect with U.S. 17, the principal north–south coastal route. Hilton Head Island has a new, 6-mi-long toll bridge, the Cross Island Parkway, that leads to the south end of the island, where most of the resorts and attractions are located (toll $1).

By Plane

The **Myrtle Beach International Airport** (☎ 803/448–1589) is served by US Airways, Air Canada, American Eagle, Conair, Delta's Atlantic Southeast Airlines, G. P. Express, Jet Xpress, Midway, and Spirit. **Hilton Head Island Airport** (☎ 803/689–5400) is served by US Air Express and Colgan Air. **Savannah International Airport** (☞ Savannah *in* Georgia) is about an hour's drive from Hilton Head.

By Train

Amtrak (☎ 800/872–7245) does not make stops in this area, although several of its stops are within driving distance: Florence is about 70 mi northwest of the Grand Strand; Yemassee, about 22 mi northwest of Beaufort; and Savannah, about 40 mi southwest of Hilton Head.

Exploring the Coast

With its high-rise beachfront hotels, nightlife, and amusement parks, **Myrtle Beach** is the hub of the Grand Strand. Downtown has a festive look, with its T-shirt shops, ice-cream parlors, and amusement parks, including the **Myrtle Beach Pavilion and Amusement Park** (✉ 9th Ave. N and Ocean Blvd., ☎ 803/448–6456; 🎫 fees for individual attractions; $18.50 1-day pass for unlimited access to most rides), **Ripleys Believe It or Not Museum** (✉ 901 N. Ocean Blvd., ☎ 803/448–2331; 🎫 $7.95), and the **Myrtle Beach National Wax Museum** (✉ 1000 N. Ocean Blvd., ☎ 803/448–9921; 🎫 $5). Attractions are open daily from mid-March through early October, but the schedule varies the rest of the year.

Ripley's Aquarium (✉ 9th Ave. N and U.S. 17N Bypass, ☎ 803/916–0888 or 800/734–8888; 🎫 $12.95) has an underwater tunnel exhibit longer than a football field and exotic marine creatures from poisonous lionfish to moray eels and an octopus. Children can examine horseshoe crabs and eels in touch tanks.

Myrtle Beach is the minigolf capital of the world, with courses that mimic Jurassic Park and Never-Never Land, and **Hawaiian Rumble** (✉ 3210 Rte. 17S, ☎ 803/272–7812; 🎫 $5 all day (9–5), $5 per round after 5 PM) is the crown jewel. The best part of the course is the volcano that erupts fire and rumbles at timed intervals. South of Myrtle Beach, **Wild Water** (✉ 910 Hwy. 17S, Surfside, ☎ 803/238–9453; 🎫 $17; $9.95 after 3 PM) provides splashy family fun for all ages.

Murrells Inlet, south of Myrtle Beach via U.S. 17, is a picturesque fishing village where you'll find fishing charters and some of the most popular seafood restaurants on the Strand. ★ **Brookgreen Gardens** (☎ 803/237–4218 or 800/849–1931; 🎫 $7.50), a few miles south of Murells Inlet off U.S. 17, is set on four former Colonial rice plantations. Begun in 1931, the gardens contain more than 2,000 plant species as well as more than 500 sculptures, including works by Frederic Remington and Daniel Chester French. Several miles down U.S. 17 from Brookgreen Gardens, **Pawleys Island** has weathered old summer cottages nestled in groves of oleander and oak. The famed Pawleys Island hammocks have been made by hand here since 1880.

Georgetown, on the shores of Winyah Bay at the end of the Grand Strand, was founded in 1729 and soon became the center of America's Colonial rice empire. Today you can enjoy its quaint waterfront and historic homes and churches. The **Rice Museum** (✉ Front and Screven Sts., ☎ 803/546–7423; 🎫 $2) traces the history of rice cultivation through maps, tools, and dioramas. It is housed in a graceful structure topped by an 1842 clock and tower.

Beaufort, about 18 mi east of U.S. 17 on U.S. 21 (about 70 mi southeast of Charleston) is a handsome waterfront town. Established in 1710, it achieved prosperity at the end of the 18th century, when Sea Island cotton became a major cash crop. A few lavish houses built by landowners and merchants have been converted into bed-and-breakfast inns or museums; others are open for tours part of the year.The **Arsenal/Beaufort Museum,** housed in a Gothic-style arsenal built in 1795 and remodeled in 1852, has exhibits on prehistoric relics, Native American pottery, the Revolutionary and Civil wars, and decorative arts. ✉ *713 Craven St.,* ☎ *803/525–7077.* 🎫 *$2. Closed Wed., Sun.*

St. Helena Island, 9 mi southeast of Beaufort via U.S. 21, is the site of the **Penn Center Historic District** and **York W. Bailey Museum.** Penn Center, established in the middle of the Civil War as the South's first school for freed slaves, is now an educational and cultural resource center.The **York W. Bailey Museum** (✉ Land's End Rd., ☎ 803/838–2432; 🎫 donation suggested) has photos and artifacts reflecting the heritage and lifestyles of sea island blacks. These islands are where Gullah, a musical language that combines English and African, developed.

Hilton Head Island, a 42-square-mi semitropical barrier island settled by cotton planters in the 1700s, has developed as a resort destination. Oak and pine woods, lagoons, and a temperate climate provide an incomparable environment for tennis, water sports, and golf. Choice stretches of the island are occupied by resorts, many of which have shops, restaurants, marinas, and several recreational facilities.

Hilton Head is blessed with vast nature preserves, including the **Sea Pines Forest Preserve** (✉ At southwest tip of island, via U.S. 278 , ☎ 803/842–1449; 🎫 $3 per car for nonguests), a 605-acre wilderness tract within the Sea Pines Plantation resort. The preserve's most interesting site is the 3,400-year-old Native American shell ring. On 4,000 acres of salt marsh and small islands, **Pinckney Island National Wildlife Refuge** (✉ Coastal Discovery Museum, 100 William Hilton Pkwy., ☎ 843/689–6767; 🎫 free) is laced with walking and bike trails.

Dining and Lodging

Freshwater and ocean fish and shellfish reign supreme throughout the region, from family-style restaurants—where they're served with hush puppies and coleslaw—to elegant resorts and upscale restaurants featuring haute cuisine. You can have your choice of hotels, cottages, villas, or high-rise condominiums. Attractive package plans are available between Labor Day and spring break. For price ranges *see* Charts 1 (A) and 2 (A) *in* On the Road with Fodor's.

Beaufort

$$–$$$ ✕ **Backstreet Cafe.** Dinners are also offered in appetizer portions at this high-ceiling, open café with navy blue walls. Blackened shrimp and scallops come with homemade apple chutney; other choices are beer-batter catfish with garlic mashed potatoes, fried chicken with red rice, or roast pork with collard greens. ✉ *812 Port Republic St.,* ☎ *803/524–2100. AE, MC, V. Closed Sun. No lunch Sat.*

$$ ✕ **11th Street Dockside Restaurant.** Succulent fried oysters, shrimp and fish, plus other seafood specialties such as a steamed seafood pot and seafood pasta, are available at this classic wharfside spot with a

screened porch and water views from nearly every table. ✉ *11th St. W.,* ☎ *803/524–7433. AE, D, DC, MC, V. No lunch.*

$$$–$$$$ ✕🏨 **Beaufort Inn.** Guest rooms in this peach-color 1897 Victorian have pine floors, tasteful floral and plaid fabrics, and comfortable chairs. The inn's superb restaurant serves guests sumptuous complimentary breakfasts and afternoon tea (reservations required); it's open to the public for unique Low Country dinners. ✉ *809 Port Republic St., 29902,* ☎ *843/521–9000,* FAX *843/521–9500. 11 rooms. Restaurant. Full breakfast. AE, MC, V.*

$$$$ 🏨 **Cuthbert House Inn.** Overlooking the bay, this pillared 1790 home has original Federal fireplaces and crown and rope molding. Owners and hosts Sharon and Gary Groves have filled it with 18th- and 19th-century heirlooms; rooms are elegant but cozy, with Oriental rugs on pine floors, and handmade quilts on the beds. ✉ *1203 Bay St., 29902,* ☎ *843/521–1315 or 800/327–9275,* FAX *843/521–1314. 8 rooms. Full breakfast. AE, D, MC, V.*

$$$$ ★ 🏨 **Rhett House Inn.** This stately 1820 Greek Revival mansion in the center of town is popular with visiting celebrities, who have included Barbra Streisand, Jeff Bridges, and Dennis Quaid. Completely refurbished by the owners, the inn is filled with antiques and original art. A new addition, a newly remodeled house across the street, expands the inn by six more rooms, each with gas fireplace, whirlpool tub, and private entrance and porch. ✉ *1009 Craven St., 29902,* ☎ *843/524–9030,* FAX *843/524–1310. 16 rooms. CP. AE, MC, V.*

$–$$ 🏨 **Howard Johnson.** This clean and cheerfully staffed hotel sits on the edge of the marsh a few miles from the historic district. Rooms are spacious and have desks; many have views of the river and marsh. ✉ *3651 Trask Pkwy. (U.S. 21), 29902,* ☎ *803/524–6020 or 800/528–1234,* FAX *803/521–4858. 43 rooms. Pool. CP. AE, D, DC, MC, V.*

Georgetown

$ ✕ **Kudzu Bakery.** Here you have a choice of a few sandwiches on homemade breads and the best desserts in town. Besides pies and pastries, you can purchase fresh breads, cheeses, and local specialty items. ✉ *714 Front St.,* ☎ *803/546–1847. MC, V. Closed Wed., Sun. No dinner.*

$$ 🏨 **1790 House.** Built in the center of town after the Revolution, at the peak of Georgetown's rice culture, this restored white Georgian house with a wraparound porch contains Colonial antique and reproduction furnishings. ✉ *630 Highmarket St., 29440,* ☎ *803/546–4821 or 800/890–7432. 6 rooms. Full breakfast. AE, D, MC, V.*

Hilton Head Island

$$–$$$ ✕ **Old Fort Pub.** Tucked away on a quiet site overlooking the marshlands of the Intracoastal Waterway and beside the Civil War ruins of Fort Mitchell, this restaurant specializes in oyster stew, corn-crusted pork chops, and mesquite-smoked filet mignon with mushroom cabernet sauce. The ambience is publike casual but the service is not. There's a Sunday brunch. ✉ *65 Skull Creek Dr.,* ☎ *803/681–2386. AE, D, DC, MC, V.*

$$–$$$ ★ ✕ **Starfire Contemporary Bistro.** Ultrafresh ingredients are served in a pleasingly unique way at this small, hip eatery. Try the wild mushroom soup with roasted rosemary, salmon with spiced seed crust atop a crunchy cucumber salad, and chocolate sorbet with homemade biscotti. Next door, the more casual Starfire Winebar and Grill offers many wines by the glass, great burgers, and pizza. ✉ *37 New Orleans Rd.,* ☎ *803/785–3434. AE, DC, MC, V. No lunch.*

$$$$ 🏨 **Main Street Inn.** Outside it resembles an Italianate villa; luxury abounds inside, too. Rooms have velvet and silk brocade linens, feather duvets, and porcelain and brass sinks. Included in the rate are a European breakfast of cheeses, quiche, breads, and pastries; afternoon tea;

and cookies at turndown. ✉ *2200 Main St., 29926,* ☎ *803/681–3001 or 800/471–3001,* FAX *803/681–5541. 34 rooms. Pool. AE, MC, V.*

$$$–$$$$ ★ **Disney's Hilton Head Island Resort.** The island's newest resort option has Adirondack lodge–country themes carried out in fun detail. More than 100 villas (from studios to three bedrooms/four baths with sleeping accommodations for up to 12) have fully furnished kitchen, dining, living, sleeping and porch areas; all have marsh or marina views. About a mile away, the resort's 13,000-square-ft beach house has a fireplace in the living room, a heated pool, and an arcade. ✉ *22 Harbourside La., 29928,* ☎ *803/341–4100 or 800/453–4911,* FAX *803/341–4130. 102 units. Restaurant, pool. AE, MC, V.*

$$$–$$$$ **Hilton Resort.** On the huge complex Palmetto Dunes Resort, the Hilton has spacious oceanfront rooms with kitchenettes and a colorful Caribbean motif. ✉ *23 Ocean La., 29928,* ☎ *803/842–8000 or 800/845–8001,* FAX *803/842–4988. 323 rooms. Restaurant, pool. AE, D, DC, MC, V.*

$$$–$$$$ ★ **Westin Resort, Hilton Head Island.** One of the island's most luxurious properties, this sprawling horseshoe-shape hotel has a lushly landscaped oceanfront setting. Guest rooms have down pillows, warm colors, and comfortable wicker and contemporary furniture. Public areas display fine Asian porcelain, screens, and paintings. For dinner, try the resort's Barony Grill Restaurant. ✉ 2 *Grass Lawn Ave., 29928,* ☎ *803/681–4000 or 800/228–3000,* FAX *803/681–1087. 450 rooms. 3 restaurants, pool, health club. AE, D, DC, MC, V.*

MOTEL

Red Roof Inn (✉ 5 Regency Pkwy., 29928, ☎ 803/686–6808 or 800/843–7663, FAX 803/842–3352); 112 rooms, pool; *$–$$.*

Myrtle Beach

$$–$$$ ★ **Collectors Cafe.** A successful restaurant, art gallery, and coffeehouse rolled into one, this unpretentiously arty spot has bright, funky paintings and tile work covering its walls and tabletops. You can shop for a painting while enjoying the veal-stuffed ravioli or barbecued duck over polenta cake with goat cheese cream. ✉ *7726 N. Kings Hwy.,* ☎ *803/449–9370. AE, D, DC, MC, V. Closed Sun.*

$$ **Sea Captain's House.** This picturesque restaurant with nautical decor and a fireplace has sweeping ocean views. Home-baked breads and desserts accompany Low Country fare. ✉ *3002 N. Ocean Blvd.,* ☎ *803/448–8082. AE, D, MC, V.*

$–$$ **Latif's Cafe and Bar.** The lunch crowd loves this hot spot, which has pastry cases full of homemade breads, cakes, and cookies. The soups are garden fresh, and there are yummy shrimp and black-bean cakes, as well as traditional and Asian chicken salads. ✉ *503 61st Ave. N,* ☎ *803/449–1716. AE, D, DC, MC, V. No dinner Sun.–Mon.*

$$$–$$$$ **Kingston Plantation.** Set amid 145 acres of ocean-side woodlands, this 20-story glass-sheathed tower is part of the Kingston Plantation complex of shops, restaurants, hotels, and one- and three-bedroom condos; refurbished in 1998, it's easily the nicest resort in town. Guest rooms have Carribean colors and kitchenettes. ✉ *9800 Lake Dr., 29572,* ☎ *803/449–0006 or 800/876–0010,* FAX *803/497–1110. 255 suites, 510 condos. 2 restaurants, pools, tennis, health club. AE, D, DC, MC, V.*

$$$ **Breakers Resort Hotel.** The Breakers is one of the better values along the Grand Strand. There are 24 types of rooms—the suites with kitchenettes are ideal for families. All the major attractions are within walking distance. ✉ *2006 N. Ocean Blvd. (Box 485), 29578-0485,* ☎ *803/444–4444 or 800/845–0688,* FAX *803/626–5001. 390 rooms. Restaurant, pools, exercise room. AE, D, DC, MC, V.*

MOTELS

Red Roof Inn (✉ 2801 S. Kings Hwy., 29577, ☎ 803/626–4444 or 800/843–7663, FAX 803/626–0753), 166 rooms, pool; *$$*. **Days Inn at Waccamaw** (✉ 3650 Hwy. 501, 29577, ☎ 803/236–1950 or 800/325–2525, FAX 803/236–9415), 160 rooms, restaurant, pool; *$–$$*.

Pawleys Island

$ ✕ **Island Country Store.** Despite its lackluster setting, this little store has terrific crab cakes plus hickory-smoked barbecue, roast chicken, and pizza (and they deliver). ✉ *The Island Shops, U.S. 17,* ☎ *803/237–8465. AE, MC, V.*

$$–$$$ ✕ **Pelican Inn.** This unusual inn, with the beach out back and creek out front, gives you a look at how families have idled away the summer at Pawleys for years. Rooms are no-fuss beachy (some share baths) with hardwood floors and throw rugs. There's no air-conditioning, but with the breezes and ceiling fans you'll barely miss it. Rates include two big family-style meals: full breakfast and a midday "dinner." ✉ *500 Myrtle Ave., P.O. Box 154, 29585,* ☎ *803/237–2295 or 803/288–8255. 6 rooms. Restaurant. Closed Nov.–March. 2-night minimum. Full breakfast. No credit cards.*

$$$$ **Litchfield Beach and Golf Resort.** The inn's contemporary gray-blue wood units on stilts, as well as a diverse range of other rentals from condos to villas, are within the expansive grounds, which include three private golf clubs. The beach is a short walk away. ✉ *U.S. 17, 2 mi north of Pawleys Island; Drawer 320, 29585,* ☎ *803/237–3000 or 800/845–1897,* FAX *803/237–4282. 96 suites, 254 condominiums, cottages, and villas. Restaurant, pools, golf, tennis, health club. AE, D, DC, MC, V.*

Nightlife and the Arts

Nightlife

Country-and-western shows are popular along the Grand Strand, which is fast emerging as the eastern focus of country music culture. Music lovers have several shows to choose from, including the 2,250-seat **Alabama Theater** (✉ At Barefoot Landing, 4750 U.S. 17, North Myrtle Beach, ☎ 803/272–1111 or 800/342–2262); **Carolina Opry** (✉ 82nd Ave. N, Myrtle Beach, ☎ 803/238–8888 or 800/843–6779); **Dolly Parton's Dixie Stampede** (✉ 8901-B U.S. 17 Business, next door to Carolina Opry, Myrtle Beach, ☎ 803/497–9700 or 800/433–4401); **Eddie Miles Theater: Salute to Elvis** (✉ 701 Main St., North Myrtle Beach, ☎ 803/238–8888 or 800/843–6779); and **Legends in Concert** (✉ 301 U.S. 17 Business, Surfside Beach, ☎ 803/238–7827 or 800/843–6779). The **House of Blues** (✉ 4640 U.S. 17S, N. Myrtle Beach, ☎ 803/272–3000), adjacent to Barefoot Landing, presents blues, rock, jazz, and country on stages in its restaurant and in its concert hall.

Shagging (the state dance) is popular at **Duck's** (✉ 229 Main St., North Myrtle Beach, ☎ 803/249–3858). You can also try the shag at **Studebaker's** (✉ U.S. 17 at 21st Ave. N, Myrtle Beach, ☎ 803/626–3855 or 803/448–9747). At **Broadway at the Beach** (✉ U.S. 17 Bypass between 21st and 24th Sts., North Myrtle Beach, ☎ 803/444–3200) you'll find an assortment of bars and nightclubs, including Hard Rock Cafe, Planet Hollywood, and the NASCAR cafe.

Hilton Head's hotels and resorts stage a variety of musical entertainment. **Monkey Business** (✉ Park Plaza, ☎ 803/686–3545) is a dance nightclub in Hilton Head. In Beaufort, **Bananas** (✉ 910 Bay St., ☎ 843/522–0910) has live bands on weekends. **Plum's** (✉ 904½ Bay St., ☎ 843/525–1946), in Beaufort, has a late-night bar and live bands during the weekends.

The Arts

Area **festivals** include the Canadian/American Days Festival in March, the Sun Fun Festival (☞ Festivals and Seasonal Events *in* The Southeast introduction) in early July, and the Atalaya Arts Festival in fall. At Art in the Park, held in Myrtle Beach's Chapin Park three times each summer, you can buy handmade crafts and original artwork by local artists. Hilton Head's **Self Family Arts Center** (✉ Shelter Cove La., ☎ 803/842–2787) has a theater, an art gallery, and a theater program for kids. During the warmer months there are free **outdoor concerts** at Harbour Town and Shelter Cove in Hilton Head.

Outdoor Activities and Sports

Biking

Pedaling is popular along the firmly packed beaches and pathways of **Hilton Head Island.** Rentals are available at most hotels and resorts and at such shops as **Harbour Town Bicycles** (✉ Heritage Plaza, ☎ 803/785–3546) and **South Beach Cycles** (✉ Sea Pines Plantation, ☎ 803/671–2453).

Fishing

Fishing is usually good from early spring through December. Licenses, required for fresh- and saltwater fishing from a private boat, can be purchased at local tackle shops. The **Grand Strand** has several piers and jetties, and fishing and sightseeing excursions depart from Murrells Inlet, North Myrtle Beach, Little River, and the Intracoastal Waterway at Route 544. Fishing tournaments are popular. On **Hilton Head** you can fish, pick oysters, dig for clams, or cast for shrimp.

Golf

The Grand Strand has 100 courses, most of them public and many of championship quality. **Myrtle Beach Golf Holiday** (☎ 803/448–5942 or 800/845–4653) offers package plans throughout the year; most area hotels have golf packages, too. Some of **Hilton Head**'s 29 courses are among the world's best; several are open to the public, including Palmetto Dunes (☎ 803/785–1138), Sea Pines (☎ 803/842–8484), Port Royal (☎ 803/689–5600), and Shipyard Golf and Racquet Clubs (☎ 803/785–5353). Sea Pines' Harbour Town Golf Links (☎ 803/671–2448) hosts the annual MCI Classic.

Horseback Riding

On Hilton Head trails wind through woods; horses can be rented at Sea Pines' **Lawton Stables** (☎ 803/671–2586).

Tennis

There are more than 200 courts throughout the **Grand Strand,** including free municipal courts in Myrtle Beach, North Myrtle Beach, and Surfside Beach. **Hilton Head** has more than 300 courts; four resorts on the island—Sea Pines, Shipyard Plantation, Palmetto Dunes, and Port Royal—are rated among the top 50 tennis destinations in the United States. Each April top women professionals participate in the Family Circle Magazine Cup Tennis Tournament at Sea Pines Racquet Club.

Water Sports

In Myrtle Beach surfboards, Hobie Cats, Jet Skis, Windsurfers, and sailboats are for rent at **Downwind Sails** (✉ Ocean Blvd. at 29th Ave. S, ☎ 803/448–7245). On Hilton Head you can take windsurfing or kayaking lessons and rent equipment from Outside Hilton Head, at either **Sea Pines Resort's South Beach Marina** (☎ 803/671–2643) or **Shelter Cove Plaza** (☎ 803/686–6996).

Beaches

Almost all **Grand Strand** beaches are open to the public. The widest expanses are in North Myrtle Beach. The ocean side of **Hilton Head Island** is a 12-mi stretch of gently sloping white sand. Although resort beaches on Hilton Head are reserved for guests and residents, there are about 35 public-beach entrances, from Folly Field to South Forest Beach near Sea Pines.

Shopping

The Grand Strand is a great place to find bargains. **Waccamaw Pottery and Factory Shoppes** (✉ U.S. 501 at the Waterway, Myrtle Beach, ☎ 803/236–1100) is one of the nation's largest outlet centers, with 3 mi of shops. In North Myrtle Beach shoppers head for the **Barefoot Landing** shopping center (✉ 4898 S. Kings Hwy., ☎ 803/272–8349). The **Hammock Shops at Pawleys Island** (✉ U.S. 17, ☎ 803/237–8448) sell the famous handmade hammocks; there are about a dozen boutiques and restaurants, too. Hilton Head specialty shops include **Red Piano Art Gallery** (✉ 220 Cordillo Pkwy., ☎ 803/785–2318) and, for shell and sand-dollar jewelry, the **Bird's Nest** (✉ Coligny Plaza, off Coligny Circle, ☎ 803/785–3737). On St. Helena Island near Beaufort, the **Red Piano Too Art Gallery** (✉ 853 Sea Island Pkwy., ☎ 843/838–2241) is filled with quirky folk and southern art, beads, and pottery.

ELSEWHERE IN SOUTH CAROLINA

Columbia

Visitor Information

Columbia Metropolitan Convention and Visitors Bureau (✉ 1012 Gervais St., Box 15, 29202, ☎ 803/254–0479 or 800/264–4884)

Arriving and Departing

I–20 leads northeast from Georgia to Columbia. I–77 runs south to Columbia, where it terminates. I–26 runs north–south through town.

What to See and Do

Columbia, in the middle of the state, was founded in 1786 as the capital city. The capitol, the **State House** (✉ Main and Gervais Sts., ☎ 803/734–2430; 🎟 free), built in 1855 from local granite, contains marble and mahogany accents and a replica of Houdon's statue of George Washington. You can still see where Sherman shelled the State House, each hit marked by a bronze star.

The **South Carolina State Museum** (✉ 301 Gervais St., ☎ 803/737–4595; 🎟 $4), set in a refurbished textile mill, interprets state history through exhibits on archaeology, fine arts, and scientific and technological accomplishments.

★ Two miles from the capitol area is **Riverbanks Zoological Park and Botanical Garden** (✉ I–26 at Greystone Blvd., ☎ 803/779–8717; 🎟 $5.75), with more than 450 species of birds and animals cared for in their natural habitats. The park also has a reptile house, an aquarium, and a cage-free aviary.

Dining and Lodging

$$$–$$$$ ✕ **Motor Supply Co. Bistro.** Dine on cuisine from around the world at this restaurant in the heart of town. Fresh seafood and homemade desserts are among the many offerings. On Sunday there's brunch and dinner. *✉ 920 Gervais St., ☎ 803/256–6687. AE, DC, MC, V.*

$-$$ ★ ✕ **Maurice Gourmet Barbecue–Piggie Park.** One of the South's best-known barbecue chefs, Maurice Bessinger has a fervent national following for his mustard sauce–based, pit-cooked ham barbecue. He also serves barbecued chicken, ribs, and baked beans. ✉ *1600 Charleston Hwy.,* ☎ *803/796–0220. D, MC, V.*

$$$$ **Claussen's Inn.** This small hotel, in a converted bakery warehouse in the attractive Five Points neighborhood, is near nightlife and specialty shops. It has an airy lobby with a Mexican tile floor; the rooms, some two stories, are arranged around it. There are eight loft suites with downstairs sitting rooms. ✉ *2003 Greene St., 29205,* ☎ *803/765–0440 or 800/622–3382,* FAX *803/799–7924. 29 rooms. AE, MC, V.*

$$$–$$$$ **Adam's Mark.** This upscale downtown hotel is near state offices and the University of South Carolina. Public areas have leather armchairs, suspended lights, and brass accents. Guest rooms are contemporary, with period reproduction armoires and desks. Finlay's Restaurant, in a spectacular atrium, serves American fare. ✉ *1200 Hampton St., 29201,* ☎ *803/771–7000 or 800/444–2326,* FAX *803/254–2911. 300 rooms. Restaurant, pool, health club. AE, D, DC, MC, V.*

$$$–$$$$ ★ **Richland Street B&B.** Relax on the front porch or in the spacious common area of this no-smoking inn in the heart of Columbia's historic district. Each antiques-furnished room has its own personality; the suite includes a whirlpool tub. The complimentary breakfast consists of fresh fruit and Belgian waffles or French toast; there are also afternoon refreshments. ✉ *1425 Richland St., 29201,* ☎ *803/779–700,* FAX *803/765–0370. 8 rooms. Full breakfast. AE, MC, V.*

$ **La Quinta Motor Inn.** At this three-story inn on a quiet street near the zoo, the rooms are spacious and well lit, with large working areas. ✉ *1335 Garner La., 29210,* ☎ *803/798–9590 or 800/531–5900,* FAX *803/731–5574. 122 rooms. Pool. AE, D, DC, MC, V.*

6 The Mississippi Valley

Arkansas, Kentucky, Louisiana, Mississippi, Tennessee

By Craig Seligman

Updated by Honey Naylor

STAND ON A SHORE of the Mississippi River, and you're swept with large emotions: Here are the waters that have sweetened the delta and fed the imagination of the South. The five states that constitute the Mississippi Valley all sweat history; each has Civil War battlefields and citizens with long, long memories. You can find the New South here, of course, but the Old South—of Cotton Is King, of Christ Is Coming, of aristocracy and its flip side, poverty—is never far away.

The soil is rich: No sight in the world affects a southerner like the fields of cotton ready for harvest. The region isn't only farmland, though; Tennessee, Kentucky, and Arkansas are blessed with some of the most beautiful mountain scenery in America. The metropolises, from Louisville to Shreveport to Jackson, have their big-city grandeur and decay. Outside them you'll see the regal old plantation houses, but you'll also pass along godforsaken stretches of state road with tumbledown shanties that can look more desolate than any city slum.

Yet the folk culture that sprouted among the poor people of these states took root and spread its branches far out into the world. Nashville calls itself the capital of country music; Memphis will always mean rhythm and blues; New Orleans is the cradle of jazz. And all three cities—all three musics—had a hand in delivering rock and roll. Graceland, the Memphis mansion where Elvis lived and died in tacky majesty, stands now as an unofficial monument to the best American art and the worst American taste.

The region gave the world not only music beloved the world over but also its own revered cuisine. A visitor can find ambrosial ribs in the barbecue palaces of Memphis or at hole-in-the-wall luncheonettes on Arkansas roadsides. Those lucky enough to have tasted fried chicken or fried catfish down here have been known to lose their taste for chicken and catfish anywhere else. Forget low fat. Forget nouvelle. The scent of collard greens stewing in pork fat, of sweet potatoes glistening with sugar and butter, emanates from some deep place as central to the culture as the one that produced the Mississippi blues of Muddy Waters and the long, hypnotic pauses of Faulkner.

Farther downriver the spirit changes. The sauces become more complex; the music turns airier, and so does the mood. The fundamentalism of the Bible Belt loosens into a kind of good-time Catholicism whose

The Mississippi Valley

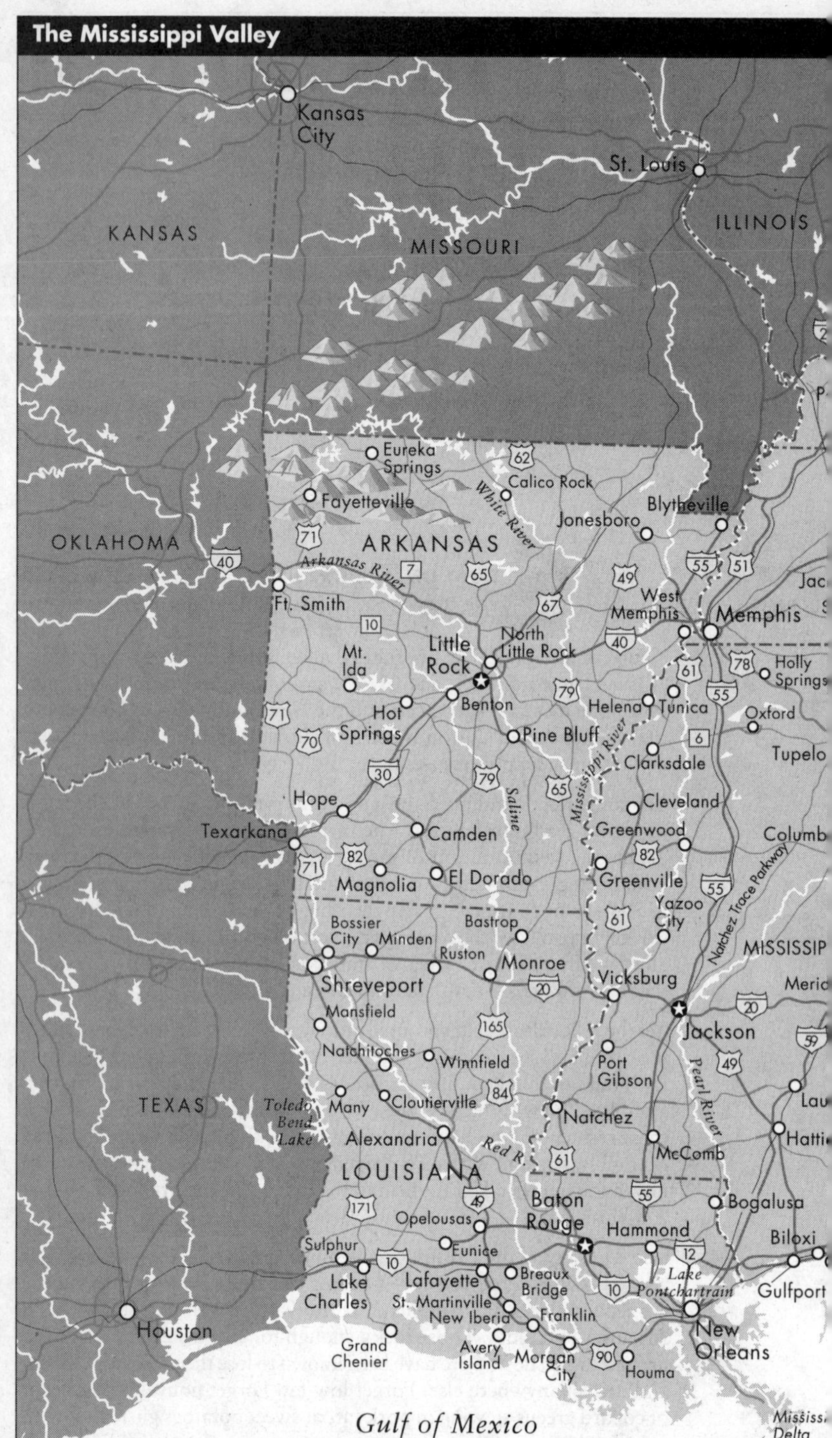

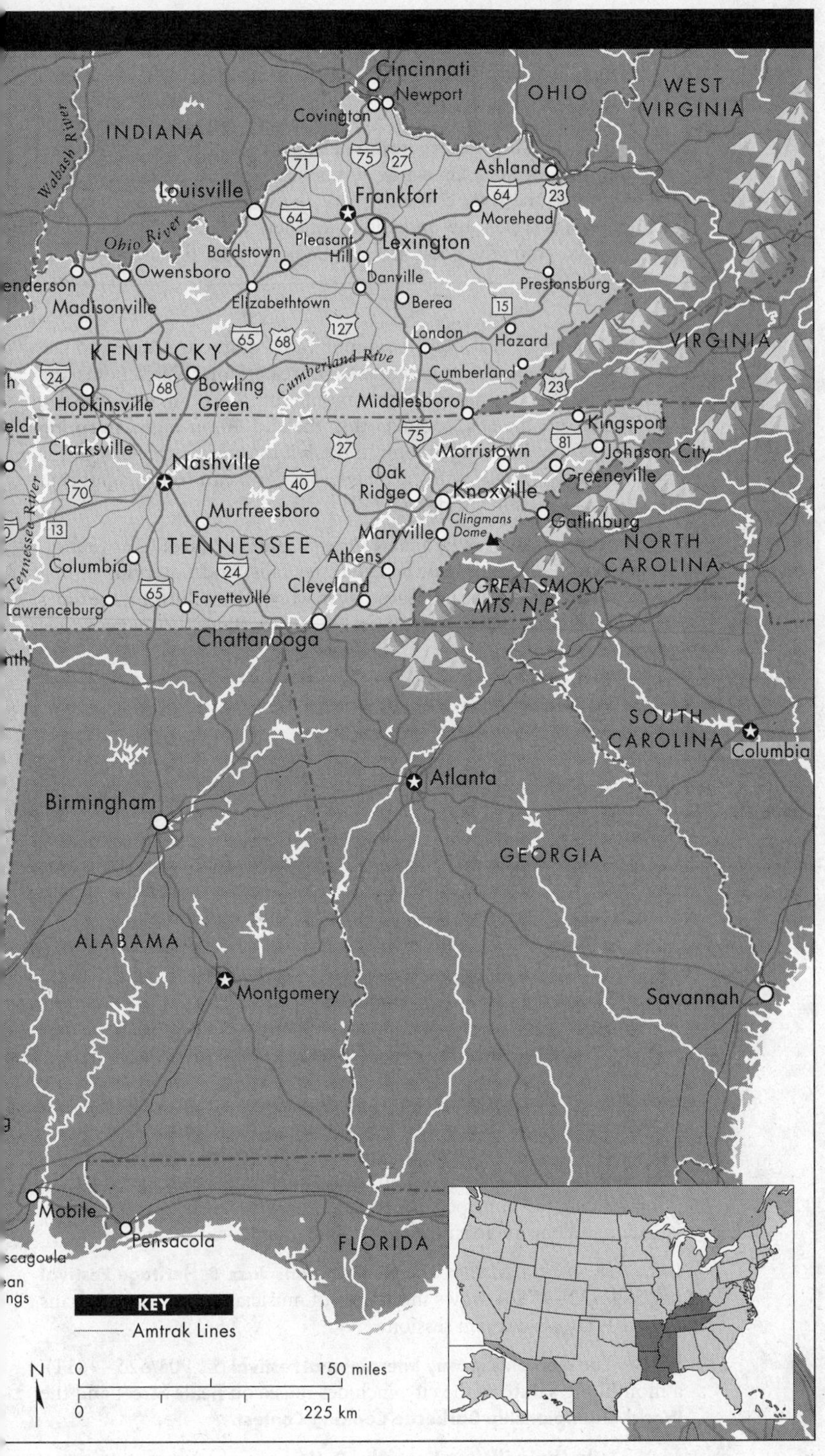

Cincinnati
Newport
Covington
OHIO
WEST VIRGINIA
INDIANA
Wabash River
Louisville
Frankfort
Ashland
Morehead
Lexington
Ohio River
Bardstown
Pleasant Hill
Owensboro
Danville
Prestonsburg
Elizabethtown
Berea
Madisonville
London
Hazard
VIRGINIA
KENTUCKY
Cumberland River
Cumberland
Bowling Green
Hopkinsville
Middlesboro
Kingsport
Clarksville
Morristown
Johnson City
Nashville
Greeneville
Oak Ridge
Knoxville
Murfreesboro
Gatlinburg
Tennessee River
Maryville
Clingmans Dome
NORTH CAROLINA
TENNESSEE
Athens
Columbia
GREAT SMOKY MTS. N.P.
Cleveland
Fayetteville
Lawrenceburg
Chattanooga
SOUTH CAROLINA
Columbia
Atlanta
Birmingham
GEORGIA
ALABAMA
Montgomery
Savannah
Mobile
Pensacola
FLORIDA
KEY
Amtrak Lines
N
0
150 miles
0
225 km

motto is *Laissez les bons temps rouler*—Let the good times roll. Cajun festivals, for everything from gumbo to petroleum, are just about always happening—any excuse for a party. The biggest excuse, of course, is Mardi Gras (Fat Tuesday), the day before Lent begins, which is celebrated throughout southern Louisiana and all along the Gulf Coast. By the time the Mississippi gets this close to the Gulf, its width is monumental, but the water is warm, unhurried. And so is New Orleans. It's as though the river chose this city as the place to deposit all the richness it has picked up on its long journey. You come here to slow down, relax, enjoy the good life, and dedicate your days to pleasure.

When to Go

The best times to visit the Mississippi Valley states are **April** and **October,** when temperatures and humidity are comfortable: in Louisiana and Mississippi, the mid-70s; in the mountains of Arkansas, Kentucky, and Tennessee, the 60s, cooling off to the mid-40s at night. In **spring** everything is in glorious bloom; in the **fall** the trees, especially in the mountains, are bright with turning leaves. You can tour magnificent historic mansions in spring and fall.

If you dislike crowds, avoid New Orleans during Mardi Gras (February or March, depending on when Easter falls) and Louisville during the Kentucky Derby (the first Saturday in May). Visits during these times require flight and hotel reservations long in advance; also, expect hotel prices to jump.

Festivals and Seasonal Events

Winter

JAN.–FEB.➢ The **Dixie National Rodeo/Western Festival/Livestock Show** (☏ 601/961–4000 or 800/354–7695) in **Jackson, Mississippi,** features rodeos and other events.

FEB. 16➢ **Mardi Gras** (☏ 504/566–5031) in **New Orleans, Louisiana,** caps two or more weeks of madness: street festivals, parades with fantastic floats, marching bands, and eye-popping costumes.

Spring

MAR.–APR.➢ In **Mississippi, spring pilgrimages** to elegant antebellum mansions are held throughout the state, with Natchez (☏ 800/647–6724 or 800/647–6742) claiming grande-dame status, followed by Columbus (☏ 800/327–2686) and Vicksburg (☏ 800/221–3536).

LATE APR.➢ The **Annual Arkansas Folk Festival** (☏ 501/269–8068), in **Mountain View,** salutes the folk culture of the Ozarks with music, dance, crafts, a parade, and a rodeo. The **Festival International de Louisiane** (☏ 318/232–3737), in **Lafayette,** brings together more than 600 local and far-flung performers in music, visual arts, theater, dance, cinema, and cuisine for a dizzying globe-grazing extravaganza.

LATE APR.–EARLY MAY➢ The **New Orleans Jazz & Heritage Festival** (☏ 504/522–4786) draws thousands of musicians, fans, and artisans for a 10-day all-out jam session.

MAY➢ The **Memphis in May International Festival** (☏ 901/525–4611), a monthlong salute to the city, includes music on Beale Street and the **World Championship Barbecue Cooking Contest.**

MAY 3➢ In **Louisville** the **Kentucky Derby,** one of horse racing's premier events, is preceded by a 10-day festival (☏ 502/584– 6383) with parades, riverboat races, and many a mint julep. For racing information, call Churchill Downs (☏ 502/636–4402).

Summer

EARLY JUNE➢ The **Great French Market Tomato Festival** (☏ 504/522–2621), in **New Orleans,** is one of many food festivals held throughout the state this month.

MID-JUNE➢ The **International Country Music Fan Fair** (☏ 615/889–7503), in **Nashville, Tennessee,** lets country music fans mix with their favorite stars in a weeklong celebration featuring live shows, exhibits, autograph sessions, and special concerts.

AUG.➢ **Memphis, Tennessee,** pulls out all the stops for the **Elvis International Tribute Week** (☏ 901/543–5333 or 901/332–3322).

LATE AUG.➢ **Louisville's Kentucky State Fair** (☏ 502/367–5000) draws some half-million people, with rooster-crowing contests, top-name concerts, a horse show, and an amusement park.

Autumn

EARLY SEPT.➢ The **Zydeco Music Festival** (☏ 318/942–2392), in **Plaisance, Louisiana,** is the original festival devoted to the state's indigenous musical genre.

LATE SEPT.➢ The **Festivals Acadiens** (☏ 318/232–3737) attract more than 100,000 annually to see, hear, taste, and experience Cajun life in **Lafayette,** the capital of French Louisiana.

EARLY OCT.➢ The first full weekend of the month, **Allart, Tennessee,** hosts the two-day **Great Pumpkin Festival** (☏ 615/879–9948), with contests, crafts, and gospel singing.

EARLY OCT.➢ Held on the weekend preceding Columbus Day, the **King Biscuit Blues Festival** (☏ 870/338–9144), named after a revered local blues radio-program broadcast since the 1940s, draws national and regional blues and gospel acts to **Helena, Arkansas.**

LATE OCT.➢ The **Canton Flea Market Arts and Crafts Festival** (☏ 601/859–1307 or 800/844–3369), the largest one-day crafts show in the Southeast, takes place on Courthouse Square in **Canton, Mississippi.**

Getting Around the Mississippi Valley

By Boat

In Louisiana ferries cross the Mississippi River in New Orleans, Carville, and St. Francisville. In Tennessee, ferries cross the Cumberland River near Nashville, Cumberland City, and at Dixon Springs; they also cross the Tennessee River at Dayton, Clifton, Saltillo, and near Decatur.

The **Delta Queen Steamboat Company** (✉ Robin St. Wharf, New Orleans, LA 70130, ☏ 800/543–1949), the nation's only overnight riverboat, offers paddle-wheeler cruises on the Mississippi, Ohio, Tennessee, Arkansas, Atchafalaya, and Cumberland rivers as far east as Chattanooga, as far west as Tulsa, Oklahoma, and as far north as Minneapolis.

By Bus

Greyhound Lines (☏ 800/231–2222) provides service to cities and towns throughout the region.

By Car

I–30 cuts diagonally across southern and central Arkansas. I–40 goes east–west through central Arkansas and central Tennessee. I–24 cuts diagonally across western Kentucky. I–64 runs east–west through Louisville. I–65 is a north–south route through Tennessee and central Kentucky. I–75 runs north–south through eastern Kentucky and Tennessee. I–55 runs from southern Louisiana north through Mississippi and Arkansas. I–49 cuts a diagonal swath north–south between Lafayette and Shreveport. I–10 runs east–west through southern Mississippi and New Orleans. I–20 is the major east–west road through northern Louisiana and Mississippi. There are bridges over the Mississippi River in New Orleans, Destrehan, Lutcher, Donaldsonville, and Baton Rouge, Louisiana, and in Vicksburg, in Natchez, and near Greenville, Mississippi. The river is bridged in Arkansas at Lake Village and Helena; in Tennessee at Memphis and east of Dyerburg; and in Kentucky at Hickman, Columbus, and Cairo.

By Plane

New Orleans International Airport (☎ 504/464–0831), **Cincinnati/Northern Kentucky International Airport** (☎ 606/283–3151), **Nashville International Airport** (☎ 615/275–1600), and **Standiford Field** (✉ Louisville, ☎ 502/367–4636) are served by most domestic carriers.

By Train

Amtrak (☎ 800/872–7245) serves all states of the Mississippi Valley.

ARKANSAS

By Marcia Schnedler

Capital	Little Rock
Population	2,523,000
Motto	The People Rule
State Bird	Mockingbird
State Flower	Apple blossom
Postal Abbreviation	AR

Statewide Visitor Information

Arkansas Department of Parks and Tourism (✉ 1 Capitol Mall, Little Rock 72201, ☎ 501/682–7777 or 800/628–8725). There are 12 state tourist information centers on major highways near the borders with other states and one in Little Rock.

Scenic Drives

Arkansas's billing as the Natural State is appropriate: The state has more than 17 million acres of public and private forests, 600,000 acres of lakes, and 9,700 mi of rivers and streams. Its **Ozark** and **Ouachita mountains** rival New England's for scenic vistas and fall colors, which can be seen along meandering roadways, including eight State and National Forest Scenic byways. **Route 7** between Arkadelphia and Harrison winds over both ranges and through two national forests. The **Talimena Scenic Byway** stretches across mountain crests from Mena to Talihina, Oklahoma, passing through **Queen Wilhelmina State Park.** The **St. Francis Scenic Byway**—part of the **Great River Road** that follows the Mississippi River—leads through wild terrain between Marianna and Helena/West Helena.

National and State Parks

Arkansas boasts 340 public and private campgrounds with some 9,800 campsites and has more than 300 trails stretching over 1,622 mi. The *Camper's and Hiker's Guide* and *Arkansas State Parks* booklet, both available from the state tourism department (☞ Statewide Visitor Information, *above*), provide locations, fees, and other useful information. Arkansas also is a mecca for fly-fishing and warm-water angling, as well as for hunting duck, deer, wild turkey, and small game. Contact the **Arkansas Game and Fish Commission** (☎ 501/223–6378 or 800/364–4263).

National Parks

★ The **Buffalo National River** (✉ 402 N. Walnut St., Suite 136, Harrison 72601, ☎ 870/741–5443), backed by limestone bluffs, became the first federally protected river in 1972. Its 132 mi are noted for canoeing, white-water rafting, hiking, fishing, wilderness areas, and historic sites. The **Ouachita National Forest** (✉ USFS, Box 1270, Hot Springs 71902, ☎ 501/321–5202), dotted by crystal lakes, is the oldest and largest in the South. The **Ozark National Forest** (✉ 605 W. Main St., Russellville 72801, ☎ 501/968–2354) encompasses wild hills, hollows, rivers, and streams, as well as Arkansas's highest peak—the 2,753-ft Mt. Magazine. **Hot Springs National Park** (✉ Box 1860, Hot Springs 71902, ☎ 501/624–3383, ext. 640) features Bathhouse Row—eight turn-of-the-century spa facilities—plus campgrounds and hiking in mountains and gorges surrounding the town. **Felsenthal National Wildlife Refuge** (✉ Box 1157, Crossett 71635, ☎ 870/364–3167) is a mosaic of wetlands, lakes, and rivers that draw fishers, boaters, and wildlife watchers.

State Parks

Arkansas has 50 state parks, museums, and monuments; 27 have campgrounds, 12 have lodges and cabins. **Devil's Den** (✉ 11333 W. Ark. 74, West Fork 72774, ☎ 501/761–3325) is set in an Ozark valley that has caves, crevices, bluffs, and Civilian Conservation Corps structures from the 1930s. **Village Creek** (✉ 201 CR 754, Wynne 72396, ☎ 870/238–9406) lies atop Crowley's Ridge, a forested highland, unusual in this area, which slices through the Mississippi Delta. Volunteers participate in seasonal excavations in **Parkin Archaeological State Park** (✉ Box 1110, Parkin 72373-1110, ☎ 870/755–2500) to uncover the remains of a Native American village chronicled by Hernando de Soto's Spanish expedition of 1541. **Petit Jean** (✉ 1285 Petit Jean Mountain Rd., Morrilton 72110, ☎ 501/727–5441), perched on a mountaintop, comprises canyons, waterfalls, a lake, a lodge, and cabins, plus the Museum of Automobiles. **Lake Chicot** (✉ 2542 Ark. 257, Lake Village 71653, ☎ 870/265–5480) sits on a 20-mi-long oxbow lake edged by cypress and noted for fishing and bird-watching.

LITTLE ROCK

Little Rock, on the south bank of the Arkansas River, is the state's geographical, governmental, and financial center, as well as a major convention hub. Spanish and French explorers passed the site in the 16th and 17th centuries, naming it La Petite Roche because of a small outcrop that marked the transition from the flat Mississippi Delta region to the Ouachita Mountain foothills. A simple translation turned the town into Little Rock when it became the territorial capital in 1821—the capital had been at Arkansas Post, the first European settlement in the lower Mississippi River valley. Within an hour of Little Rock's downtown are world-renowned duck hunting in rice-growing regions to the southeast and wild scenic vistas, streams, and trails in forested mountains to the north and west.

Visitor Information

Little Rock Convention & Visitors Bureau (✉ Box 3232, Little Rock 72203, ☎ 501/376–4781 or 800/844–4781). At press time (spring 1998), the historic home and gardens of **Curran Hall** (✉ 615 E. Capitol Ave.) are scheduled to open as a visitor information center in 1999.

Arriving and Departing

By Car

I–40 and I–30 lead to Little Rock, as do U.S. 65 and U.S. 67.

By Plane

Most major airlines fly into **Little Rock National Airport** (☎ 501/372–3439), 5 mi east of downtown off I–440. Major Little Rock hotels provide airport shuttles. Cab fare to downtown is about $8. For taxis, call **Black & White/Yellow Cabs** (☎ 501/374–0333) or **Capitol Cab** (☎ 501/568–0462).

Getting Around Little Rock

By Bus

Central Arkansas Transit (☎ 501/375–1163) serves Little Rock and North Little Rock.

By Car

Little Rock is easily negotiated by interstate highways and major streets. Plenty of parking facilities and taxis are available.

Exploring Little Rock

A series of free walking/driving tours lead through several historic areas in and near downtown. The **MacArthur Park Historic District** takes in some remaining antebellum buildings, including the 1843 **Trapnall Hall** (☒ 423 E. Capitol Ave., ☎ 501/324–9716; ☑ free), as well as fine Victorian-era architecture. The birthplace of General Douglas MacArthur, in the eponymous park, is part of an 1838 arsenal. MacArthur Park also includes the modern **Arkansas Arts Center** (☒ 9th and Commerce Sts., ☎ 501/372–4000; ☑ free), with an outstanding children's theater, a museum school, a gift shop, and a restaurant. The **Decorative Arts Museum** (☒ 7th and Rock Sts., ☎ 501/372–4000; ☑ free) is set in an 1840 mansion.

The area surrounding the **governor's mansion** (☒ 1800 Center St., ☎ 501/376–6884; ☑ free) encompasses elegant post–Civil War and turn-of-the-century churches and homes; tours of the mansion are by appointment. The 1881 Italianate **Villa Marre,** whose facade was featured in the TV series *Designing Women,* is now a museum. ☒ *1321 S. Scott St.,* ☎ *501/374–9979.* ☑ *$3. Closed Sat.*

★ Historic public buildings in the riverfront district include the **Old State House** (☒ 300 W. Markham St., ☎ 501/324–9685; ☑ free), constructed between 1833 and 1842; after a restoration it will reopen (in March 1999) as a museum devoted to Arkansas history. The **Arkansas Territorial Restoration** (☒ 200 E. 3rd St., ☎ 501/324–9351; ☑ $2) shows off restored and furnished frontier buildings with living-history tours. Its museum store sells the work of more than 200 Arkansas crafts artists.

The neoclassic **state capitol** (☒ Capitol Ave. and Woodlane, ☎ 501/682–5080), built between 1899 and 1915 on a hilltop west of downtown, has an imposing rotunda, grand marble staircases and columns, stained-glass skylights, murals, and six intricately crafted 4-inch-thick brass doors from Tiffany & Co.

The **Central High School Museum Visitor Center** (☒ 2125 W. 14th St., ☎ 501/374-1957; ☑ free), with exhibits and audiovisual presentations, marks the 40th aniversary of the school's integration, when nine black students were enrolled under the protection of federal troops. In historic Union Train Station, the interactive **Children's Museum of Arkansas** (☒ 1400 W. Markham St., ☎ 501/374–6655; ☑ $4) lets kids make stationery in the post office, shop at the farmers' market, or contribute to the Kids Gallery of collectibles.

The **Aerospace Education Center** (☒ 3301 E. Roosevelt Rd., ☎ 501/376–4629) has an IMAX theater (☑ $6), a small free museum, and a library. The **Museum of Discovery** (☒ 500 E. Markham St., ☎ 501/396–7050 or 800/880–6475; ☑ $5) explores science and culture with hands-on exhibits.

Outside Little Rock

Just 15 mi west of downtown is **Pinnacle Mountain State Park** (☒ 11901 Pinnacle Valley Rd., Roland 72135, ☎ 501/868–5806; ☑ free), whose habitats range from high upland peaks to river bottomlands lined with hardwoods and ancient cypress.

Less than 30 minutes east of downtown on U.S. 165 is the state park–operated **Plantation Agriculture Museum,** whose exhibits interpret the history of cotton agriculture. ✉ *4815 Hwy. 161, Scott,* ☎ *501/961–1409.* 🎟 *$2. Closed Mon. except holidays.*

Several miles beyond Scott off U.S. 165 sits **Toltec Mounds Archaeological State Park,** the remains of a large Native American ceremonial and governmental complex inhabited from AD 600 to AD 950. ✉ *490 Toltec Mounds Rd., Scott,* ☎ *501/961–9442.* 🎟 *$2. Closed Mon.*

Parks, Gardens, and Zoos

War Memorial Park (✉ North off I–630 at Fair Park Ave. and W. Markham St., ☎ 501/371–4770), one of the city's oldest and most popular parks, contains a public golf course, tennis courts, a football stadium, and the baseball park of the minor-league Arkansas Travelers. It also has a fitness center, a small amusement park, and a zoo.

Riverfront Park edges both sides of the Arkansas River. On the Little Rock side it lies behind the Old State House and Convention Center, with playgrounds, a history pavilion, and an amphitheater. The site of the **Bill Clinton Presidential Library** is east of I–30 adjacent to the park. On the North Little Rock side of the park is the dock for the ***Spirit*** (☎ 501/376–4150), a paddlewheel riverboat that has both excursion and dining cruises. The **Little Rock Zoo** (✉ 1 Jonesboro Dr., ☎ 501/663–4733; 🎟 $5) has gorillas, giant anteaters, and 175 other species.

Dining and Lodging

Note: Some of the counties outside the city are dry. For price ranges *see* Charts 1(B) *and* 2(B) *in* On the Road with Fodor's.

$$–$$$ ★ ✕ **Alouette's.** This prestigious French Continental restaurant provides formal and café-style settings in its richly decorated Venetian Room and somewhat more casual Salons Napoleon and Bastille. Its innovative menu changes biannually. An extensive wine list includes older vintages, and there is a full bar. ✉ *11401 N. Rodney Parham Rd.,* ☎ *501/225–4152. AE, D, DC, MC, V. Closed Sun.–Mon.*

$$–$$$ ✕ **Spaule.** This casually elegant spot has won numerous national and regional awards for its new American cuisine since its 1995 debut. Its menu and wine list change monthly and feature dishes such as cornmeal-crusted fried oysters and roasted veal. ✉ *5713 Kavanaugh Blvd.,* ☎ *501/664–3663. Reservations not accepted. AE, MC, V. Closed Sun.*

$$–$$$ ✕ **Trio's.** Intriguing lunch and dinner menus combine Caribbean, Italian, and southwestern elements plus its trademark pasta dishes. ✉ *8201 Cantrell Rd.,* ☎ *501/221–3330. AE, D, DC, MC, V. Closed Sun.*

$ ✕ **Franke's Cafeteria.** This family-owned local institution serves simple, good food for lunch or for an early dinner at its Rodney Parham and University restaurants. ✉ *11121 N. Rodney Parham Rd.,* ☎ *501/225–4487;* ✉ *300 S. University Ave.,* ☎ *501/663–4461;* ✉ *400 W. Capitol St.,* ☎ *501/372–1919. D, MC, V. Capitol location closed weekends.*

$$$$ 🏨 **Arkansas Excelsior Hotel.** Atop the Statehouse Convention Center on the banks of the Arkansas River, the Excelsior features concierge as well as standard floors. Among its three stylish dining spots is the award-winning Josephine's Library Restaurant. Business facilities and an airport shuttle are pluses. ✉ *3 Statehouse Plaza, 72201,* ☎ *501/375–5000 or 800/527–1745,* FAX *501/375–4721. 417 rooms. 3 restaurants, exercise room. AE, D, DC, MC, V.*

$$$$ 🏨 **Capital Hotel.** A careful restoration of this 1872 National Historic Landmark calls attention to the classic cast-iron facade, the atrium lobby's mosaic floors, lead-glass skylight, handsome columns, and high-ceiling rooms. Its restaurant, Ashley's, offers fine dining, with casual lunches and dinners served in the lounge. ✉ *111 W. Markham St., 72201,* ☎ *501/374–7474 or 800/766–7666,* FAX *501/370–7091. 122 rooms. 2 restaurants, exercise room. AE, D, DC, MC, V.*

$$$$ **Embassy Suites.** Opened in the fall of 1997, this all-suite hotel lies in west Little Rock, 10–15 minutes from downtown. The two-room suites include sofa beds and kitchenettes. It offers child care 5–10 PM Friday and Saturday and complimentary receptions 5–7 PM nightly. ✉ *11301 Financial Centre Pkwy., 72211,* ☎ *501/312–9000,* FAX *501/312–9455. 251 suites. Restaurant, pool, health club. Full breakfast. AE, D, DC, MC, V.*

$$$ **Holiday Inn–Select.** This award-winning west Little Rock hotel is convenient to downtown as well as nearby restaurants and businesses. Business facilities and an airport shuttle are provided. ✉ *201 S. Shackleford Rd., 72211,* ☎ *501/223–3000,* FAX *501/223–2833. 261 rooms. 2 restaurants, pool, health club. AE, D, DC, MC, V.*

Motels

Hampton Inn I–30 (✉ 6100 Mitchell Dr., 72209, ☎ 501/562–6667, FAX 501/568–6832), 122 rooms, pool; CP; *$$*. **La Quinta–North** (✉ 4100 McCain Blvd., North Little Rock 27117, ☎ 501/945–0808, FAX 501/945–0393), 122 rooms, pool; *$$*. **Motel 6** (✉ 10524 W. Markham St. [at I–430], 72205, ☎ 501/225–7366, FAX 501/227–7426), 146 rooms, pool; *$*.

Nightlife and the Arts

The Weekend section of Friday's *Arkansas Democrat-Gazette* and the weekly *Arkansas Times* list nightlife and arts events, and you can call a recorded "What's Happening" line (☎ 501/372–3399).

Nightlife

Juanita's (✉ 1300 S. Main St., ☎ 501/372–1228) serves up Mexican fare daily along with an eclectic mix of evening entertainment—from rock to jazz, bluegrass, folk, Latin, reggae, and more. **Vino's** (✉ 923 W. 7th, ☎ 501/375–8466) presents avant-garde Red Octopus theater productions and is home to the Little Rock Folk Club and other concert-giving organizations. It also has a microbrewery and tasty pizzas. At the **After Thought** (✉ 2721 Kavanaugh Blvd., ☎ 501/663–1196) the piano bar serves as a background for conversation, though the Monday Jazz Project is for listeners. The **Bobbisox Lounge,** at the Holiday Inn Airport (✉ I–440 Airport Exit, ☎ 501/490–1000), is a popular spot for DJ dancing.

The Arts

The **Arkansas Repertory Theater** (✉ 601 Main St., ☎ 501/378–0405) produces popular and avant-garde theater fare. The **Arkansas Symphony Orchestra** (☎ 501/666–1761), at various locations, plays classical and pops music. **Wildwood Park for the Performing Arts** (✉ 20919 Denny Rd., ☎ 501/821–7275) offers opera, jazz, cabaret, chamber performances, and festivals. The **Broadway Theater Series** (✉ Box 131, 72203, ☎ 501/376–1500) brings in national touring companies of Broadway shows. At **Murry's Dinner Playhouse** (✉ 6323 Asher Ave., ☎ 501/562–3131) a buffet combines with Broadway comedies and musicals or solo performances. The **UALR Fine Arts Galleries & Theatre** (✉ 2801 S. University, ☎ 501/569–3291) stages concerts and theatrical productions as well as exhibitions. The **Robinson Center** (✉ Markham St. and Broadway, ☎ 501/569–3182 for galleries; 501/569–3291 for theater) is the city's major theater for the performing arts.

Shopping

Major department stores are at **Park Plaza** and **University Mall,** on either side of Markham Street at University Avenue in Little Rock, and at **McCain Mall** at Arkansas 67/U.S. 167 and McCain Boulevard in North Little Rock. In a restored warehouse alongside Riverfront Park, the **River Market** (✉ 400 E. Markham St., ☎ 501/375–2552) has blossomed into a lively center of gourmet shops, boutiques, cafés, and ethnic-food stalls, with an outdoor farmers' market spring through late fall. It has become the anchor for a revitalized neighborhood, which now has the Museum of Discovery (☞ Exploring Little Rock, *above*), galleries, restaurants, and year-round special events. Galleries, specialty shops, and boutiques lie along winding **Kavanaugh Boulevard** and **Rodney Parham Road.**

THE ARKANSAS OZARKS

The forested mountains and hollows, sparkling waters, and calcite caverns of the Arkansas highlands provide a breathtaking backdrop for self-taught folk musicians getting together on a town square, for the display of handicrafts from pioneer days, and for tiny towns barely changed from a century ago. Yet the Ozarks also encompass upscale shopping malls, fine arts centers, and sophisticated restaurants. Its rivers offer superb fishing and canoeing; its lakes offer boating and water sports. Networks of trails lace the mountains, from easygoing, accessible paths to the rugged 178-mi-long Ozark Highlands trail. Dozens of scenic byways lead past exquisite vistas. Civil War battlefields at Pea Ridge and Prairie Grove, ecotours exploring natural and human history, railway excursions, antiques, outdoor theater, great golfing, and lively festivals and fairs round out the appeal of this scenic playground.

Visitor Information

Northwest Arkansas Tourism Association (✉ Box 5176, Bella Vista 72714, ☎ 888/398–3444). **Ozark Mountain Region** (✉ Box 137, Yellville 72687, ☎ 800/544–6867) covers the central Ozarks. **Ozark Gateway Tourist Council** (✉ Box 4049, Batesville 72503, ☎ 870/793–9316 or 800/264–0316) handles the eastern Ozarks.

Arriving and Departing

By Car

To reach northwest Arkansas from Little Rock, take I–40 west, then turn north on U.S. 71. The fastest route to other parts of the Ozarks from Little Rock is U.S. 65 north from I–40 at Conway and then the appropriate highway to your destination. At Harrison, U.S. 62 leads from U.S. 65 to Eureka Springs, Pea Ridge National Military Park, and U.S. 71 at Rogers.

By Plane

American Eagle, US Airways Express, Northwest Airlink, Trans World Express, and **Atlantic Southeast Airlines** have scheduled flights into Fayetteville's **Drake Field** (☎ 501/521–4750). A Northwest Arkansas regional airport west of Lowell is scheduled to open in late 1998.

Exploring the Arkansas Ozarks

Fayetteville, Springdale, Rogers, and Bentonville—together Arkansas's fastest-growing metropolitan area—feature walking/driving tours of ★ each of their fascinating historic districts. The **Shiloh Museum of Ozark History,** in Springdale (✉ 118 W. Johnson St., ☎ 501/750–8165; 📠

free; closed Sun.), and the **Rogers Historical Museum** (✉ 322 S. 2nd St., Rogers, ☎ 501/621–1154; 🎟 free; closed Sun.–Mon.) lead you through the history and culture of the region. **Headquarters House,** in Fayetteville (✉ 118 E. Dickson St., ☎ 501/521–2970; 🎟 $3 for living history tours of house and historic neighborhood; closed Sun., Tues., Fri.), served as both Union and Confederate headquarters during the Civil War. Bentonville's **Peel Mansion & Gardens** belonged to a pioneer businessman and U.S. Congressman. ✉ *400 S. Walton Blvd.,* ☎ *501/273–9664.* 🎟 *$3. Closed Sun.–Mon.*

Pea Ridge National Military Park (☎ 501/451–8122; 🎟 $2), 10 mi northeast of Rogers on U.S. 62, and **Prairie Grove Battlefield Park** (☎ 501/846–2990; 🎟 $2 for museum and guided tours), 10 mi southwest of Fayetteville on Arkansas on the same highway, preserve the sites of decisive Civil War battles. The **University of Arkansas** (☎ 501/575–2000) in Fayetteville, home of the hallowed Razorback teams and where President Bill and Hillary Rodham Clinton taught law, has museums and a lively arts calendar. Vintage cars on the **Arkansas and Missouri Railroad** in Springdale make daylong round-trips through the Ozarks to Van Buren, and two-hour excursions from Van Buren. ✉ *306 E. Emma St.,* ☎ *501/751–8600 or 800/687–8600.* 🎟 *Round trips $29–44, Van Buren excursions $17–$25, depending on day of wk and season. Closed Dec.–Mar.*

Eureka Springs, with more than 50 B&Bs and 60 motels and hotels plus cabins and campsites, has greeted visitors since its early days as a Victorian-era spa. Now it's as much a scene for family holidays as romantic weddings and honeymoons and serves as a base for scenic mountain drives, visits to colorful caverns, and outdoor activities. The town and its attractions host a packed schedule of music, crafts and other shows, festivals, and events.

Victorian homes and shops, including fine arts and crafts galleries that sponsor monthly evening events, line Main and Spring streets as they wind uphill from a narrow valley. The tall, airy **Thorncrown Chapel** (✉ U.S. 62W, ☎ 501/253–7401; 🎟 free) takes advantage of its woodland setting. The 33-acre **Eureka Springs Gardens** sprawl up the hillsides from a spring (✉ U.S. 62W, ☎ 501/253–9256; 🎟 $6). The ***Belle of the Ozarks*** floats along 60 mi of Beaver Lake shoreline (✉ Starkey Marina off U.S. 62W, ☎ 501/253–6200; 🎟 $12). Vintage steam locomotives of the **Eureka Springs & North Arkansas Railway** chug into the Ozarks from a historic depot. ✉ *299 N. Main St.,* ☎ *501/253–9623.* 🎟 *$8. Closed Nov.–Mar.*

★ The **Ozark Folk Center** (✉ Box 500, Mountain View 72560, ☎ 870/269–3851; 🎟 $7.50 each for crafts area and evening show or $13.25 for combination ticket) is a unique state park devoted to the perpetuation and lively demonstration of traditional Ozark Mountain crafts, acoustic music, and dance. The park has a lodge, a gift shop, and the **Iron Skillet Restaurant.** In neighboring **Mountain View** the music continues in informal sessions on the **courthouse square,** surrounded by crafts, antiques, and other shops in old stone buildings.

★ The U.S. Forest Service leads year-round tours of **Blanchard Springs Caverns** (✉ Box 1279, Mountain View 72560, ☎ 870/757–2211; 🎟 $9), 15 mi northwest of Mountain View off Arkansas 14, providing the state's premier underground experience.

At **Ozark Ecotours** (✉ Box 513, Jasper 72641, ☎ 870/46–5898; 🎟 $50 and up) local residents/guides take small groups on one-day trips into the rugged Buffalo River landscape to learn about Native American, pioneer, Civil War, and outlaw history and lore in the areas where events actually happened, as well as to explore its bountiful natural history. Some trips involve only easygoing hikes; others require canoeing, caving, and horseback riding.

Dining and Lodging

For price ranges *see* Charts 1(B) *and* 2(B) *in* On the Road with Fodor's.

Eureka Springs

$$$–$$$$ ★ ✕ **Chez Charles.** This fine dining spot in the Grand Hotel presents such American staples as steaks, chicken, pork, and seafood with high style, using imaginative spices and sauces. It also serves Sunday brunch. ✉ *37 N. Main St., ☎ 501/253–9509. Reservations essential. D, MC, V. Closed Tues.–Wed.*

$$–$$$ ✕ **Cottage Inn.** The fresh-made Mediterranean cuisine at this highly regarded establishment includes spanakopita. The wine list is extensive. ✉ *U.S. 62W, ☎ 501/253–5282. MC, V. Closed Mon.*

$$–$$$ ✕ **Ermilio's.** This cozy spot serves creative Italian-American fare. ✉ *26 White St., ☎ 501/253–8806. Reservations not accepted. MC, V. Closed Thurs. No lunch Sun.*

$$–$$$$ 🏨 **Heartstone Inn and Cottages.** Eureka Springs's largest B&B has accommodations graced with antiques in a Victorian home and in cottages with refrigerators and kitchenettes. A massage therapist is available. ✉ *35 Kingshighway, 72632, ☎ 501/253–8916. 11 rooms, 2 cottages. Full breakfast. AE, D, MC, V. Closed Jan.–Feb.*

$–$$$ 🏨 **Comfort Inn.** This modern Victorian-style motel has a massage therapist on call. ✉ *Rte. 6 (Box 7), 72632, ☎ 501/253–5241 or 800/828–0109, FAX 501/253–6502. 57 rooms. Pool. CP. AE, D, DC, MC, V.*

Fayetteville

$–$$ ✕ **AQ Chicken House.** Since 1947 it's been serving chicken as fresh as it gets. The menu has a full range of other entrées. ✉ *1925 N. College Ave., Fayetteville, ☎ 501/443–7555;* ✉ *U.S. 71B, Springdale, ☎ 501/751–4633. AE, D, DC, MC, V.*

$$ 🏨 **Fayetteville Clarion.** This hotel is near the University of Arkansas and historic districts. ✉ *1255 S. Shiloh Dr., Fayetteville 72701, ☎ 501/521–1166 or 800/223–7275, FAX 501/521–1204. 2 restaurants, pool, exercise room. AE, D, DC, MC, V.*

Johnson

$$–$$$ ★ ✕ **James at the Mill.** One of Arkansas's finest dining spots, this award-winning restaurant serves seasonally changing variations of what chef-owner Miles James has christened Ozark Plateau cuisine—traditional southern dishes updated with a nouvelle American twist, with lots of fresh local produce, game, and dry-aged rib-eye steaks in inventive combinations. ✉ *3906 Greathouse Springs Rd., Johnson, ☎ 501/443–1400. AE, D, DC, MC, V. Closed Sun. No lunch Sat.*

$$$–$$$$ 🏨 **Inn at the Mill.** Next to James at the Mill, this inn in a rural setting is built around a restored 1835 mill and pond. ✉ *3906 Greathouse Springs Rd., Johnson 72741, ☎ 501/443–1800, FAX 501/443–3879. 48 rooms. CP. AE, D, DC, MC, V.*

Lakeview

$$–$$$$ ★ ✕🏨 **Gaston's White River Resort.** This lodge draws serious anglers as well as families with first-class cottages, pool, tennis courts, private airstrip, a marina, fishing guides, and an outstanding restaurant. ✉ *1777 River Rd., Lakeview 72642, ☎ 870/431–5202, FAX 870/431–5216. 74 rooms. Restaurant. MC, V.*

Ponca and Silver Hill

$$$–$$$$ 🏨 **Buffalo Outdoor Center.** Log cabins with fully furnished kitchens and fireplaces are at two sites on the Buffalo River. The extensive array of

outdoor activities includes hiking trails, canoe and raft floats, kayaking, fishing, guided fishing trips, mountain biking, horseback trail rides, and hot air ballooning. ✉ *Box 1, Ponca 72670,* ☎ FAX *870/861–5514 or 800/221–5514;* ✉ *Rte. 1, Box 56, St. Joe 72675,* ☎ *870/439–2244,* FAX *870/439–2200. 15 cabins at Ponca, 10 cabins at Silver Hill. D, MC, V.*

Rogers

$$$–$$$$ ✕ **Tale of the Trout.** This country spot has raised its own trout for 50 years and also serves steak, quail, and seafood. ✉ *94 New Hope Rd., Rogers,* ☎ *501/636–0508. AE, D, DC, MC, V. Closed Sun.*

Springdale

$$$–$$$$ **Holiday Inn Northwest Arkansas.** Convenient to interstates, this hotel has a five-story atrium and waterfall along with a nightclub and meeting rooms. ✉ *1500 S. 48th St., Springdale 72762,* ☎ *501/751–8300,* FAX *501/751–4640. 206 rooms. Restaurant, pool, exercise room. AE, D, DC, MC, V.*

Nightlife and the Arts

Friday's Northwest Arkansas Weekend section in the *Arkansas Democrat-Gazette* lists nightlife and arts events.

The **Walton Arts Center** in Fayetteville (✉ 495 Dickson St., ☎ 501/443–9216) presents a wide range of performing and fine arts events. The **Arts Center of the Ozarks,** in Springdale (✉ 214 S. Main St., ☎ 501/751–5441), has an active schedule of visual and performing arts. Northwest Arkansas's major club and café scene is along Fayetteville's **Dickson Street,** between the University of Arkansas campus and Walton Arts Center.

WESTERN ARKANSAS

Western Arkansas reaches south from Fort Smith and Van Buren—which preserve the region's wild and woolly frontier heritage as well as its Victorian era—through the ancient forests and rivers of the Ouachita (pronounced *Wash*-i-taw) Mountains. The quartz-rich mountains cradle Hot Springs, nicknamed the Spa City, which was the boyhood home of President Bill Clinton. Five crystal-clear Diamond Lakes also lure vacationers who love water and beautiful scenery. The region's rivers offer white-water trips and scenic canoeing and fishing. The Ouachitas are laced with top-notch trail systems and campsites.

Visitor Information

Fort Smith Convention and Visitors Bureau (✉ 2 N. B St., 72901, ☎ 501/783–8888 or 800/637–1477). The **Hot Springs Convention & Visitors Bureau** (✉ mailing: Box K, Hot Springs 71902; walk-in center: 629 Central Ave., ☎ 800/772–2489) provides information for the city and surrounding five-county region.

Arriving and Departing

By Car

The easiest way to arrive and get around is by car. From Little Rock, I–30 and U.S. 70 lead to Hot Springs. I–40 reaches Fort Smith and Van Buren.

By Plane

Lone Star/Aspen Mountain Air (☎ 800/643–1505) flies from Dallas–Fort Worth to Hot Springs's municipal airport, and there is shuttle service between Hot Springs and Little Rock National Airport. **American Eagle, ASA, Trans World Express,** and **Northwest** fly into Fort Smith Regional Airport.

Exploring Western Arkansas

Native Americans called today's Hot Springs the Valley of the Vapors, whose 47 thermal springs were first encountered by Spanish explorer Hernando de Soto in 1541. In 1832 the U.S. Congress created the first federal reserve around the springs, which in 1921 became a national park. In the 1920s Hot Springs was a gambling town famed for its therapeutic bathhouses. Get a feel for this opulent era on Bathhouse Row ★ at the **Fordyce Bathhouse,** now the Hot Springs National Park Visitor Center (✉ 369 Central Ave., Box 1860, 71902, ☎ 501/624–3383). Only a handful of spas providing mineral baths remain, including the old-fashioned **Buckstaff** (✉ 509 Central Ave., ☎ 501/623–2308; 🎫 $14–$32), a 1912 National Historic Landmark, and five hotels and health spas.

Hot Springs offers a host of tourist activities and events, among them a wax museum, magic and illusion, country music and comedy shows, a Christian musical drama, and land-and-lake tours on amphibious "ducks." The 400-passenger ***Belle of Hot Springs*** sails Lake Hamilton daily on sightseeing, lunch, and dinner-dance cruises (✉ 5200 Central Ave./Ark. 7S, ☎ 501/525–4438; 🎫 $8.99 excursion only, $18–$25 for dinner cruise). At the restored headquarters of **Mountain Valley Spring Company** (✉ 150 Central Ave., ☎ 501/623–6671) you can enjoy free samples of natural spring water. The **Museum of Hot Springs** (✉ 201 Central Ave., ☎ 501/624–5545; 🎫 $3) includes the stories of the city's gambling-era and famous sports heroes. The **Mid-America Science Museum** explores science and nature in interactive exhibits. ✉ *400 Mid-America Blvd., off U.S. 270W,* ☎ *501/767–3461 or 800/632–0583.* 🎫 *$5. Closed Mon.*

A great view awaits atop the 216-ft **Hot Springs Mountain Tower** (✉ Hot Springs Mountain Dr. off Fountain St., ☎ 501/623–6035; 🎫 $3). **Window to the World** lets visitors get up close to thousands of exquisite handicrafts, from elaborate hats worn by Thailand's Hmong tribe to an Egyptian food cart. ✉ *120 Ouachita Ave.,* ☎ *501/623–4615.* 🎫 *$5. Closed Mon.*

President Bill Clinton's boyhood homes at 1011 Park Avenue and 213 Scully Street, along with his schools, church, and favorite teenage hangouts are detailed in a brochure and map available at the Hot Springs Visitor Center (☞ Visitor Information, *above*).

Dig for crystals or browse among those already cleaned and polished at **Ron Coleman Mining** (☎ 501/984–5443), 14 mi north of Hot Springs on Arkansas 7.

Fort Smith was established in 1817 on the Indian frontier. The Fort Smith visitor center is in **Miss Laura's** (✉ 2 N. B St., ☎ 501/783–8888 or 800/637–1477), the only former brothel on the National Register of Historic Places. From there a trolley carries visitors to museums, historic homes, and other sights. The **Fort Smith National Historic Site** (✉ 3rd St. and Rogers Ave., ☎ 501/783–3961; 🎫 free) includes the remains of two successive frontier forts and Hanging Judge Isaac Parker's gallows. The **Old Fort Museum** traces regional history (✉ 320 Rogers Ave., ☎ 501/783–7841; 🎫 $3). The **Fort Smith Trolley Museum** (✉ 100 S. 4th St., ☎ 501/783–0205; 🎫 free) contains a 1926 streetcar and other early transportation memorabilia. The **Patent Model Museum** demonstrates American inventiveness (✉ 400 N. 8th St., ☎ 501/782–

Hot Springs and the Ozarks

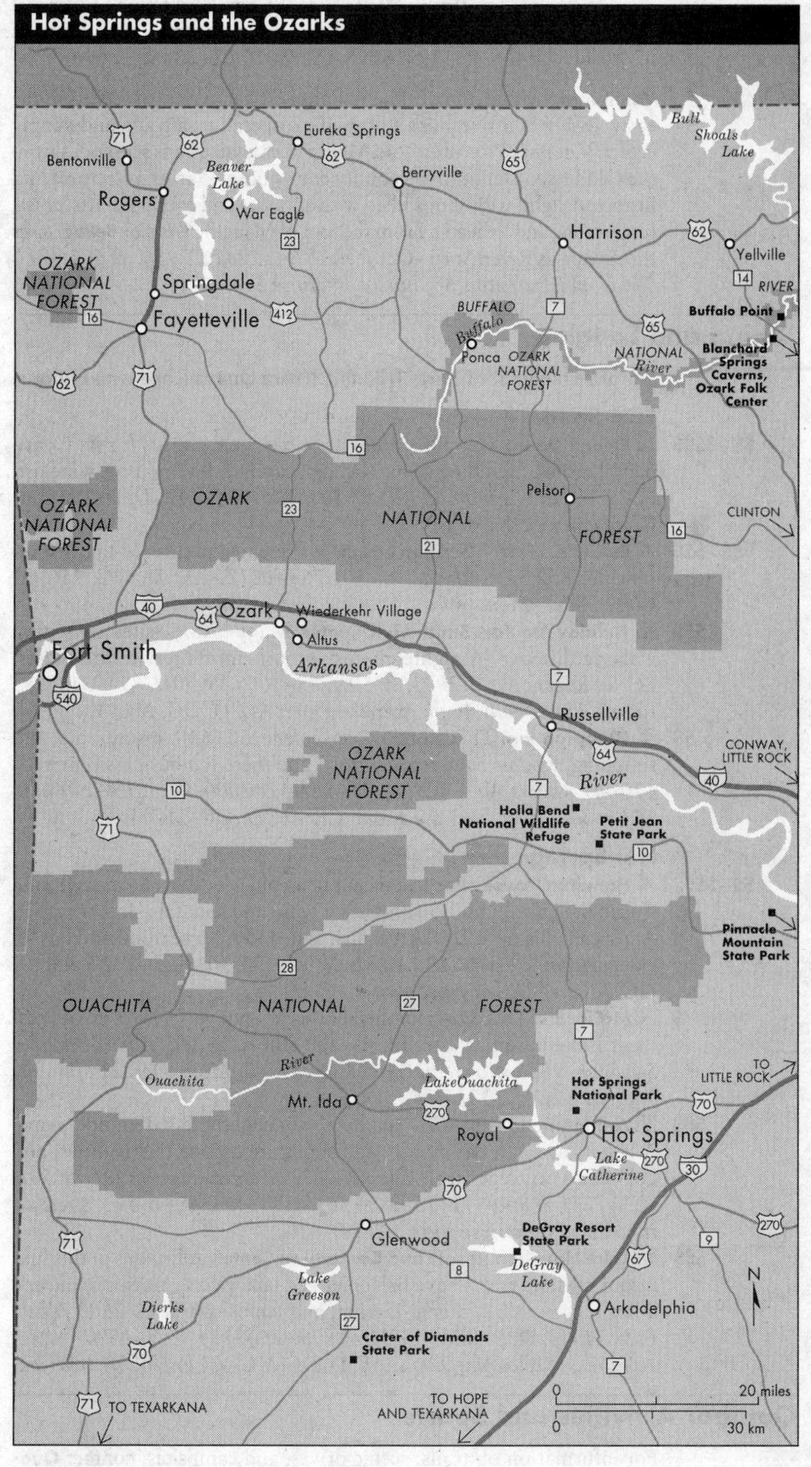

9014; 🎫 free). The **Darby House** was the boyhood home of General William O. Darby, who organized and commanded Darby's Rangers in World War II (✉ 311 N. 8th St., ☎ 501/782–3388; 🎫 free).

Van Buren, just north over the Arkansas River, was also settled in the early 1800s as a riverboat stop and prospered as a trade and supply center. Van Buren's century-old **Main Street,** which runs six blocks from the Old Frisco Depot to the county courthouse, is an architectural and historic delight, with shops filled with antiques and country crafts, cafés, restaurants, and a theater. From the foot of Main the ***Frontier Belle*** cruises the Arkansas River April–October. ✉ *Box 1241, 72956,* ☎ *501/471–5441.* 🎫 *Excursions $8; luncheon cruise $14.*

Dining and Lodging

For price ranges *see* Charts 1(B) *and* 2(B) *in* On the Road with Fodor's.

Fort Smith

$$–$$$$ ✕ **Folie à Deux.** This fine-dining spot has won awards for its Continental dishes, including steak Nicholas, and for its extensive wine list. ✉ *2909 Old Greenwood Rd.,* ☎ *501/648–0041. AE, D, DC, MC, V. Closed Sun.*

$$–$$$ ✕ **Emmy's.** Hearty German cuisine is presented in this old-line restaurant. ✉ *602 N. 16th St.,* ☎ *501/783–0012. AE, D, DC, MC, V. Closed Sun.–Mon.*

$$$ 🏨 **Holiday Inn Fort Smith Civic Center.** Many historic sites are within walking distance. A nightclub and airport shuttle service are pluses. ✉ *700 Rogers Ave., 72901,* ☎ *501/783–1000,* FAX *501/783–0312. 255 rooms. Restaurant, pool, exercise room. AE, D, DC, MC, V.*

$$ 🏨 **Hampton Inn.** This motel is convenient to I–540, restaurants, and shopping. Rooms have refrigerators, and there is a business center. ✉ *6201-D Rogers Ave., 72901,* ☎ *501/452–2000,* FAX *501/452–6668. 143 rooms. Pool, exercise room. CP. AE, D, DC, MC, V.*

Hot Springs

$$–$$$$ ✕ **Hamilton House.** The restaurant in an old Mediterranean-style villa overlooks Lake Hamilton and has a patio and fountain. It serves such American cuisine as steaks, cornish hen, and fresh seafood and has an extensive wine list. ✉ *130 Van Lyell Terr.,* ☎ *501/525–2727. AE, D, DC, MC, V. Closed most Sun.*

$ ✕ **McClard's.** This old-fashioned barbecue spot was a favorite of President Bill Clinton as a teenager—and still is. ✉ *505 Albert Pike,* ☎ *501/624–9586. No credit cards. Closed Sun.–Mon., Dec. 21–Jan. 21, 1 wk in July.*

$$$ 🏨 **Arlington.** This historic spa hotel is a slightly faded grande dame. A beauty salon, a bathhouse, and shops are among the facilities, and golf/tennis privileges are available. ✉ *239 Central Ave., 71901,* ☎ *501/623–7771 or 800/643–1502,* FAX *501/623–6191. 484 rooms. 3 restaurants, pools, exercise room. AE, D, MC, V.*

$$$ 🏨 **Lake Hamilton Resort and Conference Center.** All rooms in this luxurious all-suite resort have balconies and lake views. Amenities include a hot tub, massage, sauna, marina, and tennis courts. ✉ *2803 Albert Pike, 71913,* ☎ *501/767–5511 or 800/426–3184,* FAX *501/767–8576. 104 suites. Restaurant, pools. AE, D, DC, MC, V. Closed Christmas wk.*

Outdoor Activities and Sports

For information on trails, scenic drives, and campsites, contact **Ouachita National Forest** (✉ USFS Box 1270, Hot Springs 71902, ☎ 501/321–5202). Nearby Arkansas state parks include **DeGray Lake Resort** (✉ Rte. 3, Box 490, Bismarck 71929–8194, ☎ 501/865–2851 or 800/

606–2426), with a lodge, golf course, marina, campsites, horseback riding, and activities.

Spectator Sports

Thoroughbred racing: At Hot Springs's **Oaklawn Jockey Club** (✉ 2705 Central Ave., ☎ 800/625–5296) from late January through mid-April, with simulcasting the rest of year.

Shopping

Dozens of artists and gallery owners have transformed Hot Springs's Victorian downtown into a vibrant, cosmopolitan arts district. A **Gallery Walk** takes place the first Friday of each month. The **Hot Springs Mall** lies about 4 mi south of downtown on Arkansas 7/Central Avenue.

ELSEWHERE IN ARKANSAS

Texarkana

Visitor Information

Texarkana Chamber of Commerce (✉ Box 1468, Texarkana, TX 75504, ☎ 903/792–7191).

Arriving and Departing

From Little Rock take I–30 to Texarkana, which straddles the Arkansas-Texas border.

What to See and Do

The **Post Office** and **Photographer's Island** (✉ 500 State Line Ave.) are half in Arkansas, half in Texas. Winnings from a poker game made possible the 1885 **Ace of Clubs House** (✉ 5th and Pine Sts., ☎ 903/793–4831; 🎟 $5), which was built, fittingly, in the shape of the playing card. The **Texarkana Historical Museum** (✉ 219 State Line Ave., ☎ 903/793–4831; 🎟 $3) is in the city's oldest brick building. Opened in 1924, the elaborate **Perot Theater** (✉ 219 Main St., ☎ 903/792–4992) was restored by native son and presidential hopeful H. Ross Perot. Across the street, a mural pays tribute to another native son, ragtime composer Scott Joplin.

Dining and Lodging

$$$–$$$$ ✕ **Lake Country.** In an historic building, Lake Country presents market-fresh Continental specialties with Mediterranean touches. The wine list is expansive. ✉ *217 Walnut,* ☎ *870/773–1550. AE, D, MC, V. Closed Sun.*

$–$$$ ✕ **Cattleman's Steak House.** T-bones, ribeyes, and other choice cuts will have you believing you're deep in the heart of Texas. The menu also includes shrimp, fish, and sandwiches. ✉ *4081 N. State Line Ave.,* ☎ *870/774–4481. AE, D, MC, V. Closed Sun.*

$$$ 🏨 **Four Points Hotel.** This conveniently located and service-oriented hotel has a concierge floor with business services. Airport shuttle service is available. ✉ *5301 N. State Line Ave., 71854,* ☎ *903/792–3222,* FAX *903/793–3930. 139 rooms. Restaurant, pool, exercise room. A, D, DC, MC, V.*

$$ 🏨 **Hampton Inn.** Convenient to the interstate as well as the downtown historic district, this hotel offers guests free access to a nearby health club. ✉ *300 N. State Line Ave. at I–30, 71854,* ☎ *870/774–4444,* FAX *870/779–1303. 60 rooms. Pool. CP. AE, D, DC, MC, V.*

Hope

Visitor Information

The **Hope Visitor Center** (✉ S. Main and Division Sts., ☎ 870/722–2580) is in the restored 1912 railroad depot; it has a map showing Clinton sites.

Arriving and Departing

I–30 leads from Little Rock to Hope.

What to See and Do

Hope is Arkansas's watermelon capital, growing some of the world's largest and tastiest melons. It's also the birthplace of President Bill Clinton, who lived here until he was six. **The Clinton Birthplace** and gardens, where he lived with his grandparents until age four, has been restored. ✉ *117 S. Hervey at 2nd St.,* ☎ *870/777–4455.* *$5; purchase tickets at the Clinton Center on 2nd St. Closed Mon.; Sun. in winter.*

★ Near Hope is **Old Washington Historic State Park**(✉ Box 98, Washington, ☎ 870/983–268), established in 1824 on the Southwest Trail; it was the Confederate state capital after Little Rock's capture. Some 40 buildings remain from the 1820s–70s. Tours and museum admissions range from $1.75 to $12. **Crater of Diamonds State Park** (✉ Rte. 1, Box 364, Murfreesboro, ☎ 870/285–3113; $4.50), near Murfreesboro, is North America's only public diamond mine; you can keep what you find.

Dining and Lodging

$–$$ ✕ **Little B's.** This casual steak house serves all the usual cuts as well as Mexican dishes. ✉ *2406 N. Hervey St. (Hwy. 4),* ☎ *870/777–3377. A, D, MC, V.*

$ ✕ **Williams Tavern.** Within Old Washington Historic State Park, this tavern was built in 1832 as a residence, post office, and stagecoach stop at a plantation northeast of town. It serves simple, Southern-style lunches, and dinners during special events or by reservation for 25 or more. ✉ *Morrison and Carroll Sts., Washington,* ☎ *870/983–2890. AE, D, MC, V.*

$$ **Best Western of Hope.** This chain property is convenient to interstates and restaurants. Rooms all have refrigerators. ✉ *I–30 and Hwy. 4 (Box 6611), 71801,* ☎ *870/777–9222,* FAX *870/777–9077. 75 rooms. Pool. A, D, DC, MC, V.*

$$ **Holiday Inn Express.** Opened in late 1997, this hotel is convenient to highways and Clinton sites. All rooms have refrigerators. ✉ *2600 N. Hervey St., 71801,* ☎ *870/722–6262,* FAX *870/722–1922. 67 rooms. Pool. CP. A, D, DC, MC, V.*

Helena

Visitor Information

Helena Tourism Commission (✉ 226 Perry St., 72342, ☎ 870/338–9831).

Arriving and Departing

From Little Rock take I–40, turning south on U.S. 49.

What to See and Do

One of the oldest Mississippi River settlements and a Civil War battle site, Helena is home to the **Delta Cultural Center** (✉ 95 Missouri St., ☎ 870/338–4350; free), which documents the roots of the Delta blues, pioneer days, and the river life described by Mark Twain. Helena shows off numerous antebellum and postwar mansions, several of which are now B&Bs. The 1896 **Pillow-Thompson House** is one of the South's finest examples of Queen Anne architecture. ✉ *718 Perry St.,* ☎ *870/338–8535.* *Free. Closed Mon.*

Each October Helena hosts the **King Biscuit Blues Festival** (✉ Box 247, 72342, ☎ 870/338–9144), which has gained international acclaim.

Dining and Lodging

$$–$$$$ ✕ **Bell's Ducks by the River.** Its eclectic menu ranges from fresh Gulf Coast seafood to 30-ounce Angus steaks. Inventive attention is given to vegetables (especially potatoes), homemade rolls, and desserts. ✉ *115 Cherry St.,* ☎ *870/338–6655, AE, D, V, MC. Closed Sun.*

$ ✕ **Pasquale's Tamales.** This casual eatery is attached to Pasquale's tamale factory, which turns out dynamite tamales that share the menu with sandwiches, red beans and rice, muffalettas, and even spaghetti and meatballs. ✉ *211 Missouri St.,* ☎ *870/338–6722 or 800/390–3992. MC, V. Closed weekends.*

$ **Lady Luck Riverbluff Hotel.** Situated above the Mississippi River bridge leading to a riverboat casino, this hotel is also near Helena's historic district. ✉ *1007 Martin Luther King Dr. , 72342,* ☎ *870/338–6431 or 800/543–5362,* FAX *870/338–7927. 120 rooms. Pool. AE, D, V, MC.*

KENTUCKY

Updated by Susan Reigler

Capital	Frankfort
Population	3,908,000
Motto	United We Stand, Divided We Fall
State Bird	Cardinal
State Flower	Goldenrod
Postal Abbreviation	KY

Statewide Visitor Information

Kentucky Department of Travel Development (✉ 2200 Capital Plaza Tower, Frankfort 40601, ☎ 502/564–4930 or 800/225–8747). **Welcome centers:** I–75S at Florence, I–65N at Franklin, I–64W at Grayson, I–24E at Paducah, I–75N at Williamsburg, and U.S. 68 at Maysville.

Scenic Drives

A loop drive of rugged **Red River Gorge** in the eastern Kentucky mountains starts near Natural Bridge State Park, on **Route 77** near Slade. **Forest Development Road 918** is a 9-mi National Scenic Byway in the Daniel Boone National Forest, near Morehead. The 35-mi stretch of **Little Shepherd Trail** (U.S. 119) between Harlan and Whitesburg is breathtaking in fall. **Old Frankfort Pike** between Lexington and Frankfort passes through classic bluegrass countryside.

National and State Parks

National Parks

Daniel Boone National Forest (✉ U.S. 27, Whitley City; ✉ 100 Vaught Rd., Winchester 40391, ☎ 606/745–3100) offers spectacular mountain scenery, especially in the Red River Gorge Geological Area, known for its natural arches, native plants, and 300-ft cliffs. **Land Between the Lakes** (✉ 100 Van Morgan Dr., Golden Pond 42211, ☎ 502/924–2000) is an uninhabited 40-mi-long peninsula between Kentucky and Barkley lakes that is run as a demonstration project in environmental education and resource management. ★ **Mammoth Cave National Park** (✉ Entrances on Rte. 70, 10 mi west of Cave City, and on Rte. 255, 8 mi northwest of Park City; Mammoth Cave 42259, ☎ 502/758–2328) is a 350-mi-long complex of twisting underground passages full of colorful mineral formations.

State Parks

Kentucky's 50 state parks are ideal for hiking or simply taking in the beauty of the countryside; most also offer facilities for picnicking, camping, water sports, and horseback riding. Sixteen resort parks have rustic but comfortable lodges and/or cottages; 16 have tent and trailer sites, available April–October; 14 have year-round campgrounds. For information contact **Kentucky Department of Parks** (✉ Capital Plaza Tower, Frankfort 40601, ☎ 502/564–2172 or 800/255–7275).

LOUISVILLE

Louisville (locally pronounced *loo*-uh-vul) was founded in 1778 by a Revolutionary War hero, General George Rogers Clark, and named for King Louis XVI as gratitude for France's help during the war. The city's charter was signed in 1780 by Thomas Jefferson, then the governor of Virginia, of which Kentucky was the westernmost district. Louisville's culture and history have been greatly influenced by its location inside a bend in the mighty Ohio River and smack in the center of the eastern half of the nation. During the first half of the 19th century the city was a bustling river port. With the railroad's advent, it became a hub of train traffic. Waves of European immigrants settled into colorful neighborhoods that retain much of their character today. Louisville attracts crowds of visitors every May for the nation's premier horse race: the Kentucky Derby. Today, the city is an international air hub for United Parcel Service.

Visitor Information

Area Chamber of Commerce (✉ 600 W. Main St., 40202, ☎ 502/625–0060). **Convention & Visitors Bureau** (✉ 400 S. 1st St., 40202, ☎ 502/584–2121 or 800/792–5595).

Arriving and Departing

By Bus

Greyhound Lines (✉ 720 W. Muhammad Ali Blvd., ☎ 800/231–2222).

By Car

Louisville is well endowed with interstates: I–64 runs east–west, I–71 northeast, and I–65 north–south. I–264, also known as the Henry Watterson Expressway, rings the city. These converge downtown in a ramp-ridden area known as Spaghetti Junction; confusion here can result in a quick trip to Indiana.

By Plane

Louisville International Airport (☎ 502/367–4636) is 15 minutes south of downtown on I–65. It has a modern, spacious, comfortable terminal and is served by most major carriers. Cab fare from the airport to downtown Louisville runs about $15.

Getting Around Louisville

The downtown area is defined north–south by Broadway and the Ohio River, east–west by Preston and 18th streets. The **Transit Authority of River City** (✉ 1000 W. Broadway, ☎ 502/585–1234) operates local buses ($1 at peak times, 75¢ other times), as well as a free trolley along 4th Avenue between Broadway and the river. A car is needed for explorations beyond downtown.

Exploring Louisville

Downtown

The heart of Louisville is thick with historic sites. **West Main Street** has more examples of 19th-century cast-iron architecture than anyplace else in the country except New York City's SoHo. The **Hart Block** (✉ 728 W. Main St.), a five-story building designed in 1884 at the height of Louisville's Victorian era, has a facade that is a jigsaw puzzle of cast-iron pieces bolted together. Other historic attractions include the tiny **St. Charles Hotel** (✉ 634 W. Main St.), constructed before 1832. The Roman Catholic **Cathedral of the Assumption** (✉ 443 S. 5th St.), a Gothic Revival structure built between 1849 and 1852, was restored between 1985 and 1994. The **Jefferson County Courthouse** (✉ 531 W. Jefferson St.), a Greek Revival landmark designed by Gideon Shyrock, was built in 1835 with the intent of luring the state government to Louisville.

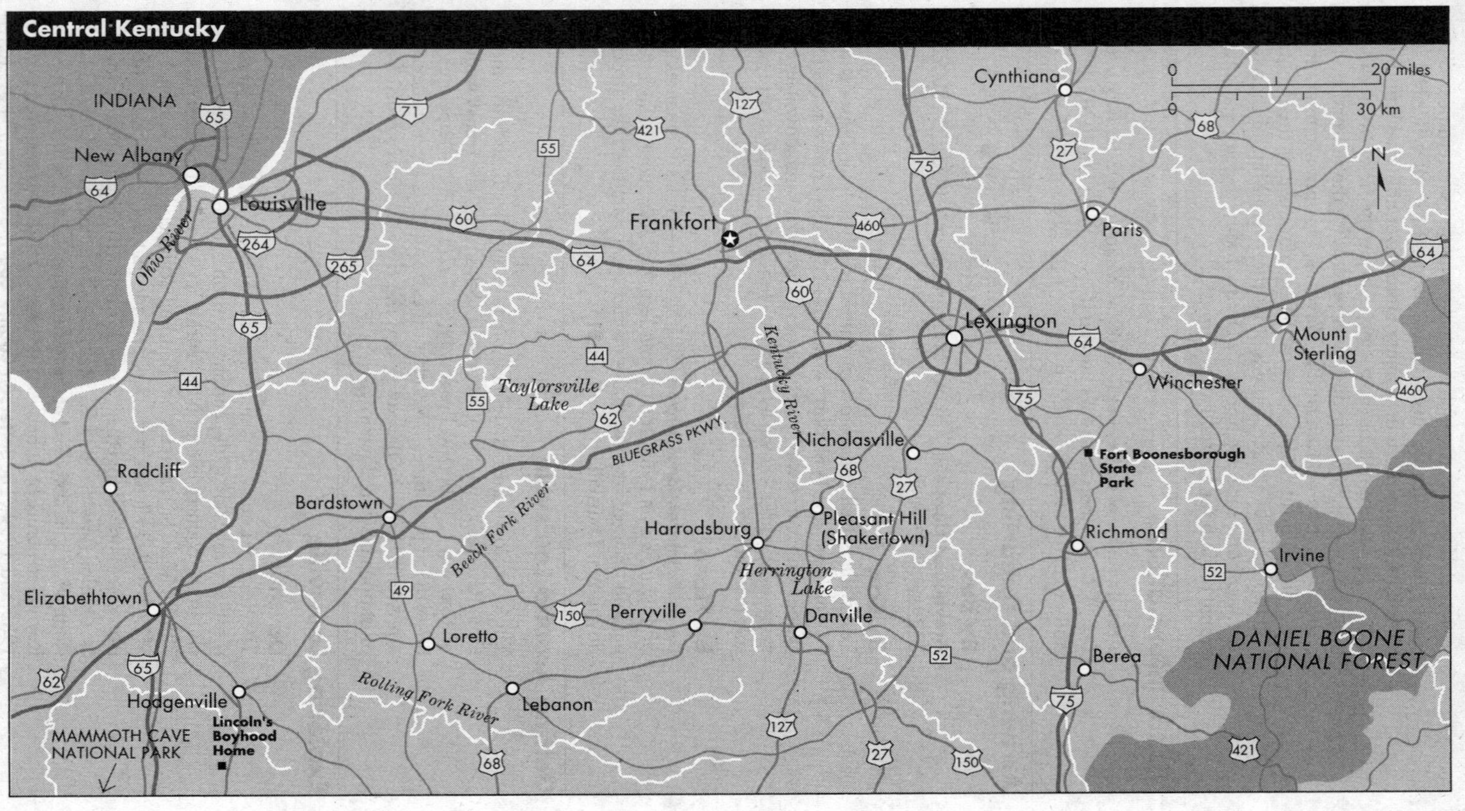

Central Kentucky
0
20 miles
0
30 km
N
INDIANA
New Albany
Louisville
Ohio River
Cynthiana
Paris
Frankfort
Lexington
Mount Sterling
Winchester
Taylorsville Lake
Kentucky River
BLUEGRASS PKWY
Nicholasville
Fort Boonesborough State Park
Radcliff
Bardstown
Beech Fork River
Harrodsburg
Pleasant Hill (Shakertown)
Herrington Lake
Richmond
Irvine
Elizabethtown
Perryville
Danville
Loretto
Berea
DANIEL BOONE NATIONAL FOREST
Rolling Fork River
Lebanon
Hodgenville
Lincoln's Boyhood Home
MAMMOTH CAVE NATIONAL PARK
65
71
127
421
55
75
27
68
64
60
460
264
265
44
62
49
150
52

The skyline is dominated by the 35-story **Aegon Center** (✉ 400 W. Market St.), the tallest building in Kentucky. A dramatic geodesic dome tops the 1992 art deco structure, designed by New York architect John Burgee. Also on the contemporary side, the grand **Humana Building** (✉ 500 W. Main St.) of 1985 is the eclectic work of architect Michael Graves. The **American Life and Accident Building** (✉ 3 Riverfront Plaza), designed by Mies van der Rohe and completed in 1973, is known as the Rusty Building because of its covering of oxidized Cor-Ten steel. Just off the riverfront Belvedere Promenade, the 1988 **Louisville Falls Fountain** spews water in the form of a 375-ft-tall fleur-de-lis, the city's symbol.

The **Kentucky Center for the Arts** (☞ Nightlife and the Arts, *below*), on Riverfront Plaza, is home to a distinguished collection of 20th-century sculpture by such artists as Louise Nevelson, Alexander Calder, and Jean Dubuffet. The **Louisville Science Center/IMAX Theatre** (✉ 727 W. Main St., ☎ 502/561–6103; 🎫 $7), a 19th-century warehouse full of science arcades and demonstrations, includes an Egyptian mummy's tomb, a Foucault pendulum, and lots of hands-on exhibits.

★ Look for the giant baseball bat in front of the **Louisville Slugger Museum** (✉ 800 W. Main St., ☎ 502/588–7228; 🎫 $5), and the giant baseball seemingly lodged in a pane of the plate glass factory next door. Visitors can enjoy interactive exhibits such as a "virtual pitch," in which a computerized baseball comes hurtling at you at 90 mph. A tour of the adjoining Hillerich & Bradsby factory, where the famous baseball bats are made, is included.

Scenic 6.9-mi **RiverWalk** stretches from downtown's 4th Street Wharf westward to Chickasaw Park. The path parallels the Ohio shore and offers a variety of vistas, from the locks and dam on the shipping channel to quiet, wooded portions where it's possible to spot deer. Parking is available at 4th Street, 8th Street, 10th Street, 31st Street, and at Lannan, Shawnee Park, and Chickasaw Parks. One-quarter mile east of RiverWalk, **Linear Park** (✉ 3rd St. and River Rd.; 🎫 free) has a playground with attractions for all age groups.

While near the river, check out the ***Belle of Louisville*** (☎ 502/574–2355; 🎫 $9), usually moored at City Wharf at 4th and River streets. Built in 1914, the gingerbread-trim steamboat is the oldest Mississippi-style stern-wheeler still afloat. Should you grow tired, you can hire a horse-drawn carriage from River City Horse Carriage (☎ 502/895–7268) or Louisville Horse Trams (☎ 502/581–0100).

Other Attractions

Butchertown was settled in the 1830s, largely by Germans who worked in meatpacking plants in the vicinity and lived in "shotgun" and "camelback" houses built in the shadow of the still-in-business (as your nose will tell you) Bourbon Stock Yards. In 1814 French immigrants settled in **Portland,** where goods came ashore to be portaged past the falls of the Ohio River. Today barges carry 5 million tons of cargo per month through the **McAlpine Locks and Dam** (✉ 27th St.).

The **Cherokee Triangle,** a classic Victorian village of grand homes on broad tree-lined streets, was built between 1870 and 1910. A few miles out Bardstown Road from the triangle is **Farmington** (✉ 3033 Bardstown Rd., ☎ 502/452–9920; 🎫 $4), a Federal-style mansion built in 1810 from a design by Thomas Jefferson, whose special touches include two octagonal rooms and an adventurously steep hidden staircase.

★ **Old Louisville** is the most elegant of Louisville's neighborhoods. Its architectural styles include Victorian Gothic, Richardsonian Romanesque,

Queen Anne, Italianate, Châteauesque, and Beaux Arts. Lead- and stained-glass windows, turrets, and gargoyles are much in evidence. The **Conrad-Caldwell House** (☒ 1402 St. James Ct., ☎ 502/636–5023; $3), an outstanding example of Victorian Romanesque Revival architecture with a carved-stone ornamental exterior and elaborate interior woodwork, is open for tours Sunday and Tuesday–Thursday 1–5 PM and by appointment. The southern edge of Old Louisville harbors the **University of Louisville** campus. Its ★ **J. B. Speed Art Museum** innovatively displays masterworks by Rembrandt, Rubens, Picasso, Caravaggio, and many others, as well as frequent contemporary exhibits. *☒ 2035 S. 3rd St., ☎ 502/636–2893. Free. Closed Mon.*

South of the university is **Churchill Downs,** world famous as the home of the Kentucky Derby. Since the track's opening in 1875, scores of heroic three-year-old Thoroughbreds have thundered past its famous twin spires into legend. During the regular racing season check out **"Dawn at the Downs"** (☎ 502/636–3351; $10.95), a program that allows fans to visit the track shortly after daybreak on Saturday, when the horses are out for exercise and the infield grass and flower beds are bejeweled with dew. It's magical. The **Kentucky Derby Museum** (☎ 502/637–1111; $6) documents the careers of the champions. During the annual Kentucky Derby Festival—the two weeks leading up to and including Derby Day (the first Saturday in May)—be prepared to pay more for everything in Louisville, from lodging to transportation. *☒ 700 Central Ave., ☎ 502/636–4400. Closed Dec.–Mar. and July–Sept.*

South of the city, near Louisville International Airport, **Kentucky Kingdom—The Thrill Park** has rides and games, including three roller coasters, a water park, and a playground for young children. *☒ 937 Phillips La., ☎ 502/366–2231; $25; $14.80 children under 54 ; free children 3 or younger. Closed Nov. –Mar.* East of downtown is pastoral **Locust Grove** (☒ 561 Blankenbaker La., ☎ 502/897–9845; $4), once the home of Louisville's founder. Three presidents—James Monroe, Andrew Jackson, and Zachary Taylor—slept here.

Outside Louisville

In bourbon country, about 25 mi south of the city, is **Bernheim Forest** (☒ Rte. 245 just off I–65, Clermont, ☎ 502/543–2451). This 14,000-acre preserve features 1,800 species of plants, a nature center, a museum, picnic areas, hiking trails, and lakes; in spring it has the state's best show of rhododendrons and azaleas. The forest is free on weekdays; weekends and holidays it's $5 per vehicle. Also in Clermont, a half mile southeast of Bernheim Forest on scenic Route 245, the **Jim Beam American Outpost Museum** (☎ 502/543–9877; free), which has a collection of the famous Jim Beam bourbon decanters and a film about making bourbon.

Farther southeast on Route 245 is **Bardstown,** a historic city in a bucolic setting, best known as the site of **My Old Kentucky Home State Park** (☒ 501 E. Stephen Foster Ave., ☎ 502/348–3502); it is closed January–February. **Federal Hill** ($4), its Georgian Colonial mansion, was visited by Stephen Foster in 1852, shortly before he wrote "My Old Kentucky Home," sung on Kentucky Derby Day.

Southeast of Bardstown, near Loretto, is **Maker's Mark Distillery** (☒ 3350 Burks Spring Rd., ☎ 502/865–2881; free), a National Historic Landmark and a working distillery. Southwest of Bardstown is the **Abraham Lincoln Birthplace National Historic Site** (☒ 3 mi south of Hodgenville on U.S. 31E/Rte. 61, ☎ 502/358–3137; free), where

Lincoln was born February 12, 1809. About 110 acres of the original Thomas Lincoln farm are included in the 116-acre park.

Parks, Gardens, and Zoos

In 1891 Louisville's Board of Parks hired Frederick Law Olmsted, designer of New York's Central Park, to design a system of public lands that would be "free to all forever." Among the results were **Shawnee Park** in the west, a plain of river bottomland; **Cherokee Park** in the east, where Beargrass Creek wanders among woods and meadows; and **Iroquois Park** in the south, a tall, rugged escarpment offering vistas of the city. Another Olmsted-designed jewel, little **Tyler Park,** on Baxter Avenue, is an envelope of solitude in the midst of city bustle. The **Louisville Zoo** (⊠ 1100 Trevilian Way, ☎ 502/459–2181; $7) houses more than 1,600 animals in naturalistic environments.

Dining

Louisville has eating options to suit any taste or pocketbook: from sophisticated gourmet restaurants with adventurous menus and tuxedoed waiters to no-frills family-style eateries where a server might know everyone's name. For price ranges *see* Chart 1 (A) *in* On the Road with Fodor's.

$$–$$$ ★ ✕ **English Grill.** The oak-paneled dining room evokes a 19th-century London gentlemen's club. The menu, a marvelous blend of Continental and Kentucky specialties, changes with the seasons; recent choices include breast of duck with terrine of foie gras and corn, grilled loin of lamb marinated with lemon and mint, and a bourbon *anglaise* dessert soufflé. ⊠ *335 W. Broadway, in the Camberly Brown Hotel,* ☎ *502/583–1234. AE, D, DC, MC, V.*

$$–$$$ ★ ✕ **Lilly's.** Owner-chef Kathy Cary's innovative "haute Kentucky" fare makes the most of farm-fresh produce and meats. Her seasonal menus include such dishes as sweetbreads and morels cooked with country ham and hard-boiled eggs or slow-roasted rabbit with lamb sausage. The stylish dining room, in green, black, and purple, is as eye catching as the food is palate pleasing. ⊠ *1147 Bardstown Rd.,* ☎ *502/451–0447. AE, MC, V. Closed Sun.*

$$–$$$ ★ ✕ **The Oakroom.** Chef Jim Gerhardt's bourbon-laced menu is a cross between Kentucky and Continental cuisines. Bluegrass free-range chicken with country ham-pesto stuffing and Kentucky beef Wellington for two are among the specialities. The beautiful formal dining room radiates Southern hospitality, the wine list is the best in the Ohio Valley. ⊠ *500 S. 4th St. in the Seelbach Hotel,* ☎ *502/585–3200. AE, D, DC, MC, V.*

$$–$$$ ✕ **Vincenzo's.** Deep leather chairs, 17th-century paintings, and crisp tablecloths provide the setting for just-so service. For the main course consider *vitello alla Sinatra* (spinach-stuffed veal scallopini with wine sauce). The award-winning wine list has many excellent Italian and California vintages. ⊠ *Humana Bldg., 150 S. 5th St.,* ☎ *502/580–1350. AE, D, DC, MC, V. Closed Sun.*

$$ ✕ **Asiatique.** Euro-Asian preparations are the order of the day in this casual suburban eatery decorated with modern art. Try the smoked salmon quesadilla with goat cheese and Asian-style salsa, lemongrass-scented beef medallions, or roasted quail on a noodle pancake. Order any dessert made with ginger ice cream. ⊠ *106 Sears Ave.,* ☎ *502/899–3578. AE, DC, MC, V.*

$$ ✕ **Cafe Metro.** Art deco ambience and creative Continental cuisine are hallmarks. All entrées have a set price and range from baked quail stuffed with veal, currants, and pine nuts to seafood in puff pastry. Decadent

desserts are de rigueur. ✉ *1700 Bardstown Rd.,* ☏ *502/458–4830. AE, DC, MC, V. Closed Sun.*

$$ ✕ **Indigo Bistro and Bar.** Warm yellow walls and hardwood trim distinguish the dining rooms, while yellow Veuve Clicquot labels shine out from a shelf behind the dark, European bar. *Pommes frites* are served with entrées like bistro chicken, rib-eye steak, or pecan-dusted trout fillets. Ginger crème brûlée is fabulous. There's outdoor patio seating in summer. ✉ *3930 Chenoweth Sq.,* ☏ *502/893–0106. AE, D, DC, MC, V. Closed Sun.*

$$ ★ ✕ **Lynn's Paradise Cafe.** Look for the giant red coffeepot and cup-and-saucer fountain out front. The funky decor owes much to Bakelite and Formica. Portions at breakfast, lunch, and dinner are enormous; in the morning have the breakfast burrito, for lunch try the Dagwood-size sandwiches. Dinner (Thursday through Saturday only) features famous meat loaf and a bourbon-teriyaki salmon. ✉ *984 Barret Ave.,* ☏ *502/583–3447. MC, V. Closed Mon.*

$$ ★ ✕ **Uptown Café.** Down the road from its sister bistro, the upscale Cafe Metro, the Uptown serves imaginative appetizers (including a luscious shrimp bisque), one of the best Caesar salads anywhere, and entrées like duck ravioli and salmon croquettes, making this a local favorite for fine food at a moderate price. Ask for a booth in the cozy back room. All wines are available by the glass. ✉ *1624 Bardstown Rd.,* ☏ *502/458–4212. AE, DC, MC, V. Closed Sun.*

$–$$ ✕ **Baxter Station Bar and Grill.** Just east of downtown, this former neighborhood bar serves up pub grub with flair: crab cakes, calamari, burgers, and a fine fried-fish sandwich. An excellent selection of imported and microbrewed beers are on tap. In good weather there's outdoor seating. ✉ *1201 Payne St.,* ☏ *502/584–1635. AE, MC, V. Closed Sun.*

$–$$ ✕ **Bobby J's Club Cafe.** A cool experience awaits at this art deco bistro with a menu that emphasizes Italian fare. Mussels steamed in white wine, gourmet pizzas, and sea bass with sun-dried tomato sauce are all favorites. Cigar smokers crowd the balcony, which has a good vantage of the Flying Martinis, the in-house jazz band. ✉ *1314 Bardstown Rd.,* ☏ *502/452–2665. AE, D, DC, MC, V. Closed Mon.*

$–$$ ✕ **Pat's Steak House.** Traditional southern cooking reigns in this cozy old-fashioned restaurant with a bar that smells evocatively of bourbon and tobacco. The waiters wear white coats and know most customers by name. Marvelous fried chicken livers share the menu with country ham, fried chicken, and tender aged steaks. ✉ *2437 Brownsboro Rd.,* ☏ *502/893–2062. No credit cards. Closed Sun.*

$ ✕ **Check's Cafe.** The fare in this Germantown eatery, like the atmosphere and the service, is decidedly down-home. Among menu favorites are chili, fish, and bratwurst sandwiches. ✉ *1101 E. Burnett Ave.,* ☏ *502/637–9515. No credit cards.*

$ ✕ **Come Back Inn.** This unprepossessing neighborhood hangout serves South Side Chicago Italian cuisine. Beef sandwiches, pastas with homemade marinara, and traditional pizzas are menu highlights. Formica tables and regulars at the bar add to the no-nonsense atmosphere. ✉ *909 Swan St.,* ☏ *502/627–1777. AE, MC, V. No dinner Mon.*

$ ✕ **El Mundo.** This tiny hole-in-the-wall Mexican cantina serves up some of the city's most authentic south-of-the-border fare. The chile *rellenos* (stuffed green peppers) and enchiladas are highly recommended. Take advantage of the self-serve hot sauces. ✉ *2345 Frankfort Ave.,* ☏ *502/899–9930. No credit cards. Closed Sun.*

$ ✕ **Mazzoni's Oyster Cafe.** This diner is the place to try deep-fried oysters rolled in cornmeal batter, a Louisville invention. A rich oyster stew and real panfried oyster dinner are also served. ✉ *2804 Taylorsville Rd.,* ☏ *502/451–4436. No credit cards. Closed Sun.*

Lodging

Like any port city, Louisville has a long tradition of hospitality to visitors. You can choose either a lovingly restored, pricey downtown hotel or a budget room in a place that promises to leave the light on for you. Bed-and-breakfast accommodations can be found through **Kentucky Homes B&B** (✉ 1219 S. 4th Ave., Louisville 40203, ☎ 502/635–7341). For price ranges *see* Chart 2 (A) *in* On the Road with Fodor's.

$$$–$$$$ **Hyatt Regency Louisville.** Hyatt's familiar plant-filled atrium and glass-and-brass lobby are the focus of this 18-story hotel. The rooms have been done in a back-to-nature theme, with redwood and soft pastels. ✉ *320 W. Jefferson St., 40202,* ☎ *502/587–3434,* FAX *502/581–0133. 388 rooms. 2 restaurants, pool, tennis, exercise room. AE, D, DC, MC, V.*

$$$–$$$$ ★ **The Seelbach.** The refurbished guest rooms in this 11-story landmark (built in 1905), now part of the Medallion chain, have four-poster beds, armoires, and marble baths with gold fixtures. ✉ *500 4th Ave., 40202,* ☎ *502/585–3200 or 800/333–3399,* FAX *502/585–9239. 322 rooms. Restaurant. AE, D, DC, MC, V.*

$$–$$$$ **Camberly Brown Hotel.** This 16-story historic hotel, built in 1923, has been fully restored, with Old English–style furnishings. The artwork, atmosphere, and service are impeccable. The English Grill (☞ Dining, *above*) is one of the city's finest restaurants. ✉ *335 W. Broadway, 40202,* ☎ *502/583–1234 or 800/866–7666,* FAX *502/587–7006. 294 rooms. Restaurant, exercise room. AE, D, DC, MC, V.*

$$–$$$ **Galt House East.** Overlooking the river, this downtown hotel has an elaborately landscaped, modern 18-story atrium, but the room furnishings are of the grandpa's-overstuffed-chair variety, emphasizing old-fashioned comfort. ✉ *141 N. 4th Ave., 40202,* ☎ *502/589–3300 or 800/843–4258,* FAX *502/585–4266. 600 rooms. Restaurant, pool. AE, D, DC, MC, V.*

$$–$$$ **Old Louisville Inn Bed & Breakfast.** The guest rooms in this 1901 brick house have elaborately carved mahogany woodwork and are furnished with antiques. The atmosphere and service have a pleasant taken-back-in-time quality. ✉ *1359 S. 3rd St., 40208,* ☎ *502/635–1574,* FAX *502/637–5892. 10 rooms. Full breakfast. AE, D, MC, V.*

$–$$$ **Breckinridge Inn.** This two-story motor hotel is clean, plain, and comfortable. The predominant style in the guest rooms is art deco. ✉ *2800 Breckinridge La. (at I–264), 40220,* ☎ *502/456–5050,* FAX *502/451–1577. 123 rooms. Restaurant, pool, tennis. AE, D, DC, MC, V.*

$$ **Executive Inn.** The English Tudor style of this six-story hotel near the airport is carried through from the public areas to the rooms, which may seem snug or gloomy, according to your taste. Some have private patios or balconies. ✉ *978 Phillips La. (off I–64), 40209,* ☎ *502/367–6161 or 800/626–2706; 800/222–8284 in KY,* FAX *502/367–6161. 465 rooms. Restaurant, pools, exercise room. AE, D, DC, MC, V.*

$ **Travelodge.** The unprepossessing cinder-block exterior disguises this inexpensive downtown motel. Rooms are spacious and clean; the location is central. ✉ *401 S. Second St., 40202,* ☎ *502/583–2841 or 800/255–3050,* FAX *502/583–2629. 98 rooms. Restaurant. AE, D, DC, MC, V.*

$ **Wilson Inn.** Far from downtown and painted a horrid salmon color outside, this five-story motor hotel has a pleasant, tree-filled lobby. Milder pastels and earth tones predominate in the plain, contemporary rooms. ✉ *9802 Bunsen Pkwy. (I–64 at Hurstbourne La.), 40299,* ☎ *502/499–0000 or 800/333–9457,* FAX *502/493–2905. 108 rooms. AE, D, DC, MC, V.*

Nightlife and the Arts

For news of arts and entertainment events, look for *Louisville* magazine on newsstands and for the Friday and Saturday editions of the *Courier-Journal* newspaper.

Nightlife

The **Comedy Caravan Nightclub** (✉ 1250 Bardstown Rd., in the Mid-City Mall, ☎ 502/459–0022) and the **Legends Comedy Club** (✉ 9700 Bluegrass Pkwy., in the Hurstbourne Hotel & Conference Center, ☎ 502/459–0022) present circuit comics of the stand-up variety. **Coyote's** (✉ 116 W. Jefferson St., ☎ 502/589–3866) has live country music, a raucous but friendly clientele, and free instruction in two-step and line dancing. **Country Palace Jamboree** (✉ 421 N. Main St., Mount Washington, about 20 minutes south of Louisville, ☎ 502/955–8452) is a fun place for families that like country music and dancing. The **Connection** (✉ 130 S. Floyd St., ☎ 502/585–5752) is a giant entertainment complex consisting of a restaurant, a bar with a Thursday-night talent show and the best and biggest dance floor in town, and a theater with female impersonator revues on the weekends.

The Arts

Actors Theatre of Louisville (✉ 316 W. Main St., ☎ 502/585–1210) is a Tony Award–winning repertory theater in a bank building (circa 1837) designated a National Historic Landmark. Each February, the Actors Theatre sponsors the **Humana Festival of New American Plays,** which has premiered several plays that have gone on to New York and London. The **Broadway Series** (✉ 611 W. Main St., ☎ 502/584–7469) hosts touring productions of Broadway's best. **Shakespeare in the Park** (✉ Central Park at S. 4th St., ☎ 502/634–8237) transforms Louisville into the bard's town on summer weekends. **Stage One: The Louisville Children's Theatre** (✉ 425 W. Market St., ☎ 502/584–7777 or 800/283–7777) offers professional productions on weekends from October to May.

The three stages at the **Kentucky Center for the Arts** (✉ 5 Riverfront Plaza, ☎ 502/562–0100 or 800/283–7777) are alive with entertainment ranging from Broadway to Bach, bagpipes to bluegrass. The **Louisville Orchestra** (✉ 609 W. Main St., ☎ 502/584–7777 or 800/283–7777) has received international attention for its recordings of contemporary works. The **Louisville Ballet** and **Kentucky Opera** (☎ 502/584–7777 or 800/283–7777) also perform at the arts center.

Spectator Sports

Horse racing: The Kentucky Derby at **Churchill Downs** (☞ Exploring Louisville, *above*) is a *very* tough ticket—unless you're willing to join tens of thousands of seatless young revelers in the infield, where you're unlikely to get even a glimpse of a horse.

Shopping

Shopping Districts

The Galleria (✉ 4th Ave. between Liberty St. and Muhammad Ali Blvd., ☎ 502/584–7170), a glass-enclosed mall with 80 stores and 11 fast-food restaurants, is a city melting pot and the best place to shop downtown. **Bardstown Road,** southeast of downtown, is a 2-mi strip for strolling and browsing in antiques shops, bookstores, and boutiques. The **Jefferson Mall** (☎ 502/968–4101), 10 mi south of downtown on Outer Loop, is a huge enclosed mall with more than 100 stores. **The Mall St. Matthews,** ☎ 502/893–0311 and **Oxmoor Center,** ☎ (502/426–3000) are both located at the intersection of the Watterson Expressway with Shelbyville Road. Together they house over 300 stores, including outlets of such upscale national retailers as Brooks Brothers, the Nature Company, and Eddie Bauer.

Department Stores

Louisville has several department stores: **Lazarus** (✉ Jefferson Mall, ☎ 502/966–1800; ✉ Oxmoor Center, ☎ 502/423–3000); **Jacobson's** (✉ Oxmoor Center, ☎ 502/327–0200); and **Dillard's** (✉ The Mall St. Matthews, ☎ 502/895–5032; ✉ Jefferson Mall, ☎ 502/968–6080). **Bigg's** "hypermarket" (✉ 12975 Shelbyville Rd., Middletown, ☎ 502/244–4760) is what its name suggests. It has everything from pastries to chain saws at bargain prices.

Specialty Stores

The **Kentucky Art & Craft Gallery** (✉ 609 W. Main St., ☎ 502/589–0102) sells top-quality crafts. **Baer Fabrics** (✉ 515 E. Market St., ☎ 502/583–5521) has been amassing its world-renowned collection of buttons since 1905. **Joe Ley Antiques** (✉ 615 E. Market St., ☎ 502/583–4014) has an outstanding 2-acre litter of hardware, fixtures, and doodads.

LEXINGTON AND THE BLUEGRASS

Lexington, the world capital of racehorse breeding and burley tobacco (a thin-bodied, air-cured variety), was named by patriotic hunters who camped here in 1775 shortly after hearing news of the first battle of the Revolutionary War at Lexington, Massachusetts. A log structure built by a member of that historic hunting party is preserved on the campus of Transylvania University. The Bluegrass is a lush region of rolling hills, meandering streams, and manicured horse farms.

Visitor Information

Frankfort/Franklin County: Tourist and Convention Commission (✉ 100 Capital Ave., Frankfort 40601, ☎ 502/875–8687 or 800/960–7200). **Lexington:** Greater Lexington Convention & Visitors Bureau (✉ Suite 363, 430 W. Vine St., 40507, ☎ 606/233–1221 or 800/845–3959). **Richmond:** Tourism Commission (✉ Box 250, City Hall, 40476, ☎ 606/623–1000).

Arriving and Departing

By Car

The Lexington area and the Bluegrass are well served by I–64 east–west, I–75 north–south, and the state parkway system, a toll network that bisects the state east–west.

By Plane

Lexington Bluegrass Airport (✉ 4000 Versailles Rd., ☎ 606/254–9336), 4 mi west of downtown Lexington, is served by Delta, US Airways, and regional lines.

Exploring Lexington and the Bluegrass

Lexington

Lexington Livery Company (☎ 606/259–0000) offers horse-drawn carriage rides ($25 for a 30-minute tour). In the **Gratz Park Historic District,** near 2nd Street and Broadway, are two fine houses from 1814: the lavish, privately owned Gratz House (✉ 231 N. Mill St., ☎ no phone), built by a rich hemp manufacturer, and the John Hunt Morgan House (✉ 201 N. Mill St., ☎ 606/233–3290; 🎫 $4), the home first of a swashbuckling Confederate general and then his great-grand-son, Thomas Hunt Morgan, who won a Nobel Prize in 1933 for proving the existence of the gene; the Morgan house is closed December 15–February and Mondays the rest of year. A statue of General Morgan stands on the lawn of the **Fayette County Courthouse** (⊠ 215 W. Main St.). When it was unveiled in 1911, it caused quite a stir because it portrays the Rebel raider astride a stallion, though his best-known mount was a mare, Black Bess.

The Greek Revival campus of **Transylvania University** (⊠ 300 N. Broadway, ☎ 606/233–8120), the first college west of the Alleghenies (established in 1780), has left its mark on two U.S. vice presidents, 50 senators, 34 ambassadors, and 36 Kentucky governors. The 1832 **Mary Todd Lincoln House** (⊠ 578 W. Main St., ☎ 606/233–9999; 🎫 $4) belonged to the parents of Abraham Lincoln's wife and displays Lincoln and Todd family memorabilia. The museum is closed Sunday and Monday and December through mid-March. U.S. Senator Henry Clay, the Great Compromiser, was a green 20-year-old lawyer when he came to Lexington in 1797 and opened his **law office** (⊠ 176–178 N. Mill St., ☎ no phone).

Two attractions at the **University of Kentucky** (⊠ Euclid Ave. and S. Limestone St., ☎ 606/257–3595) are an **anthropology museum** (⊠ 201 Lafferty Hall, ☎ 606/257–7112; 🎫 free), with exhibits on evolution and Kentucky culture, and an **art museum** (⊠ 121 Singletary Center for the Arts, ☎ 606/257–5716; 🎫 free), which has a fine permanent collection and frequent special exhibits; both are closed on Monday.

The interactive exhibits at the **Lexington Children's Museum** (⊠ 401 W. Main St., ☎ 606/258–3256; 🎫 $3) include an archaeology dig. A Lexington curiosity is the huge **castle** (⊠ just west of the city on Versailles Rd.), with eight turrets and 70-ft-tall corner towers. A Fayette County developer began, but never finished, construction in 1969 on what was to be his private residence. The **Headley-Whitney Museum** houses an eclectic, personal three-building collection of Asian porcelains, masks, paintings, shells, and jeweled bibelots. ⊠ *Old Frankfort Pike,* ☎ *606/255–6653.* 🎫 *Free. Closed Mon.*

The Bluegrass

Kentucky's **Bluegrass** area has more than 400 horse farms, some with Thoroughbred barns as elegant as French villas. Among the famous breeding farms is **Calumet** (⊠ just west of the city on Versailles Rd./U.S. 60, ☎ no phone), which has produced a record eight Kentucky Derby winners. The antebellum mansion at **Manchester Farm** (⊠ Van Meter Rd., ☎ no phone) is said to have been the inspiration for Tara in *Gone With the Wind.* **Spendthrift** (⊠ Ironworks Pike, ☎ 606/299–5271) is one of the few farms that routinely welcome visitors. Famous horses from the **C. V. Whitney Farm,** on Paris Pike, have included Regret, the first filly to win the Kentucky Derby, and the appropriately named Upset, the only horse ever to finish ahead of the legendary Man o' War. **Normandy** (⊠ Paris Pike, ☎ no phone) has a famous L-shape barn, built in 1927, with a clock tower and roof ornaments in animal shapes. A note about the plank fencing used by these farms to separate their paddocks: It is sometimes painted white, sometimes black. Some farm operators claim the traditional white provides better visibility for the horses and is more attractive. Others note that black requires less frequent repainting—a serious economic factor for farms that must maintain miles of such fences, which cost about $18,000 per mile to install (painting extra).

A number of Lexington-based companies conduct tours that take in several farms and the Keeneland Racecourse (☞ Spectator Sports, *below*). They include **Bluegrass Tours** (✉ Box 1176, 40589, ☎ 606/252–5744; 🎟 $18) and **Historic and Horse Farm Tours** (✉ Box 22593, 40522,☎ 606/268–2906, FAX 606/266–8603; 🎟 $23). A showcase for Thoroughbreds and other horses, **Kentucky Horse Park** encompasses a museum, an art gallery, and campgrounds. It also offers films, a breeds show, and farm tours. ✉ *4089 Iron Works Pike, off I–75, Lexington,* ☎ *606/233–4303.* 🎟 *$6.50.* ⏲ *Closed Mon.–Tues.*

The most historic bourbon distillery in Kentucky, **Labrot & Graham** is surrounded on all sides by horse farms. The whiskey is made in copper-pot stills housed in a limestone building dating from the early 1800s. ✉ *7855 McCracken Pike off U.S. 60,* ☎ *606/879–1812.* 🎟 *Free. Closed Sun.–Mon.*

Southward on scenic U.S. 25 is **Fort Boonesborough State Park** (☎ 606/527–3131 or 800/255–7275; 🎟 $4.50), a reconstruction of one of Daniel Boone's early forts, with a museum and demonstrations of pioneer crafts. In Richmond is the **White Hall State Historic Site** (☎ 606/623–9178; 🎟 $4), home of the abolitionist Cassius Marcellus Clay, a cousin of Henry Clay and an ambassador to Russia. The elegant mansion combines two houses and two styles, Georgian and Italianate.

In Berea, where the Bluegrass meets the mountains, charming, tuition-free **Berea College** (☎ 606/986–9341), founded in 1855, has 1,500 students—most from Appalachia—who work for their education. On the campus is the **Appalachian Museum** (✉ Jackson St., ☎ 606/986–9341, ext. 6078; 🎟 free), which charts regional history through arts and crafts.

★ The **Shaker Village of Pleasant Hill** (✉ Hwy. 68, ☎ 606/734–5411; 🎟 $6.50), 25 mi southwest of Lexington, has 27 restored buildings of frame, brick, or stone erected between 1805 and 1859 by members of a religious sect noted for industry, architecture, and furniture making. In Harrodsburg, the first permanent settlement in Kentucky, **Old Fort Harrod State Park** (☎ 606/734–3314; 🎟 $3.50) has a full-scale reproduction of the old fort, built on its original 1774 site.

About 15 mi south of Lexington the beautiful, deep blue-green **Kentucky River** flows gently but relentlessly through the Bluegrass. The combination of rolling river and rugged rock faces makes for dramatic landscapes. Take Jacks Creek Pike from Lexington through one of the most enchanting parts of Kentucky to **Raven Run Nature Sanctuary** (☎ 606/272–6105), a place of rugged, forested hills and untouched wildlife along the Kentucky River.

In lovely Danville, 30 mi southwest of Lexington, the **McDowell House and Apothecary Shop** (✉ 125 S. 2nd St., ☎ 606/236–2804; 🎟 free), the residence and shop of Dr. Ephraim McDowell (a noted surgeon of the early 19th century), is refurnished with period pieces. The house is closed November–March.West of Danville on U.S. 150 and north on U.S. 68 is **Perryville Battlefield** (☎ 606/332–8631), the site of Kentucky's most important (and bloodiest) Civil War battle, where 4,241 Union soldiers and 1,822 Confederates were killed or wounded.

Frankfort, between Louisville and Lexington on I–64, was chosen as the state capital in 1792 as a compromise between those cities' rival claims and has been caught in the middle ever since. The **state capitol** (☎ 502/564–3449), overlooking the Kentucky River at the south end of Capitol Avenue, is notable for its Ionic columns, high central dome, and lantern cupola; guided tours are given. Outside the capitol is the famous **Floral Clock,** a working outdoor timepiece whose face—made of thousands of plants—is swept by a 530-pound minute hand and a 420-pound hour hand.

In Frankfort Cemetery, on East Main Street, you can visit **Daniel Boone's grave** (he died in Missouri, but his remains were returned to Kentucky in 1845). The restored Georgian-style **Old Governor's Mansion** (✉ 420 High St., ☎ 502/564–5500; 🎫 free), built in 1798, served as the residence of 33 governors until a new mansion was built in 1914. The later **governor's mansion** (☎ 502/564–3449; 🎫 free) is styled on the Petit Trianon, Marie Antoinette's villa at Versailles. Both mansions are open for tours Tuesday and Thursday.

Dining and Lodging

Although Lexington offers varied dining options, including Continental and ethnic cuisines, most restaurants outside the city are decidedly down-home. Menus tend toward country-fried steak, country ham, and fried chicken. Many of the best places to dine are so out of the way and unimpressive looking that you probably won't discover them on your own. Don't be bashful about asking the locals for guidance. For price ranges *see* Chart 1 (B) *in* On the Road with Fodor's.

Restored historic properties, often modestly priced, are short on amenities but long on charm. State park lodges and cottages are bargains, rustic but comfortable. In many rural areas you'll have to settle for bare-bones accommodations. In Lexington **Dial Accommodations** (✉ 430 W. Vine St., ☎ 606/233–7299) can help with reservations. For price ranges *see* Chart 2 (B) *in* On the Road with Fodor's.

Berea

$$–$$$ ★ ✕🏨 **Boone Tavern.** This grand old Colonial-style hotel (1909) is operated by Berea College and outfitted with furniture handmade by students. The restaurant (jacket and tie for dinner) is famous for its spoon bread, chicken flakes in bird's nest, and Jefferson Davis pie. ✉ *Main and Prospect Sts. (Box 2345), 40403,* ☎ *606/986–9358 or 606/986–9359. 57 rooms. Restaurant. AE, D, DC, MC, V.*

Frankfort

$–$$ ✕ **Smile of Siam.** A few travel posters of Thailand are the only decoration, but the food is elegant. Coconut milk, lemon grass, lime leaves, peanuts, and cilantro flavor dishes including Thai beef stick, chicken red curry and *pad Thai* (stir-fried rice noodles). ✉ *19 Century Plaza, 502/227–9934. MC, V. Closed Sun.*

Harrodsburg

$$$ ✕🏨 **Beaumont Inn.** Guest rooms at this exemplar of southern hospitality are scattered among four timeworn (but polished) buildings furnished with antiques. The restaurant specializes in corn pudding and cured Kentucky country ham. ✉ *638 Beaumont Dr., 40330,* ☎ *606/734–3381,* FAX *606/734–6897. 33 rooms. Restaurant, pool, tennis. CP. AE, D, DC, MC, V. Closed mid-Dec.–mid-Mar.*

$$–$$$ ✕🏨 **Inn at Pleasant Hill.** Rooms in 27 restored buildings (circa 1800)—some with four stories and no elevators—are furnished with Shaker reproductions and handwoven rugs and curtains. The restaurant, Trustees' House at Pleasant Hill, serves hearty family-style meals and specializes in a tangy Shaker lemon pie for which people have been known to drive a hundred miles; reservations are essential. ✉ *3500 Lexington Rd., 40330,* ☎ FAX *606/734–5411. 80 rooms. Restaurant. MC, V.*

Lexington

$$$–$$$$ ✕ **A la Lucie.** This chef-owned eatery has a Parisian Left Bank ambience, with a tin roof, terrazzo floors, hot colors, green plants, and eclectic art. French, German, and American dishes appear on the menu, but the specialty is whatever seafood is at its seasonal best. ✉ *150 N. Limestone St.,* ☎ *606/252–5277. AE, DC, MC, V. Closed Sun.*

$$–$$$ ✕ **Dudley's Restaurant.** Huge tulip trees shade the courtyard of this chic, unpretentious, restaurant in a 100-year-old schoolhouse. A favorite on the Continental menu is pasta with chicken, sun-dried tomatoes, and vegetables. ✉ *380 S. Mill St.,* ☎ *606/252–1010. AE, MC, V.*

$$–$$$ ✕ **Lexington City Brewery.** This microbrewery and brew pub in a shopping center on the edge of the tobacco warehouse district serves up excellent wood-oven pizzas and German sausage platters to go with the topflight beer. Winner's Gold Ale and Smiley Pete's stout are must-sips. ✉ *1050 S. Broadway,* ☎ *606/259–2739. AE, MC, V.*

$$–$$$ ✕ **Merrick Inn.** A spacious, comfortable, not-too-formal restaurant occupies a sprawling, white-columned building that was formerly a horse farm (circa 1890), decorated in the Williamsburg style. The extensive menu offers steak, lamb, and a variety of pastas, but the specialty is fresh seasonal seafood. ✉ *3380 Tates Creek Rd.,* ☎ *606/269–5417. AE, DC, MC, V. Closed Sun.*

$$ ★ ✕ **Alfalfa Restaurant.** In this small, woody, old-fashioned restaurant, the fare is home-cooked organically grown vegetarian and ethnic dishes. The menu, written on a chalkboard, may include ham-and-apple quiche; the house salad is lavish. Each Wednesday a different cuisine—Greek, Italian, Indian, etc.—is served. ✉ *557 S. Limestone St.,* ☎ *606/253–0014. MC, V. No dinner Mon.*

$$ ✕ **Atomic Cafe.** The Bluegrass region may not seem like the place for Caribbean cuisine, but the conch fritters taste fresh off the boat. Jerk chicken and pork dishes are fiery. Shrimp lovers should check out the coconut-battered variety served here. Decor is suitably tropical, with evocative murals. ✉ *265 N. Limestone St.,* ☎ *606/254–1969. MC, V. Closed Sun.–Mon.*

$–$$ ★ ✕ **Joe Bologna's.** This longtime college hangout occupies a church built in 1890; the original stained-glass windows are still in place. You can feast on small or large servings of an assortment of pastas, as well as pizza. ✉ *120 W. Maxwell St.,* ☎ *606/252–4933. MC, V.*

$–$$ ✕ **Phil Dunn's CookShop.** The quilt made from jockey silks hanging on one wall identifies the bluegrass roots of this sophisticated bistro. The huge wooden counter in the middle of the room is a great place to sample an appetizer or enjoy dessert and coffee. Continental entrées include oven-roasted lamb chops, grilled Long Island duck, and spinach fettuccine with grilled vegetables. ✉ *431 Old E. Vine St.,* ☎ *606/231–0099. AE, MC, V. No dinner Sun.*

$–$$ ✕ **Roy & Nadine's.** An overstuffed sofa in the bar, fringed lamp shades, and Erté prints set the jazz age tone in this suburban restaurant famous for its 25-drink "shaken not stirred" martini list. The food is eclectic and international: pepper-seared carpaccio, a black bean ancho-Caesar salad, cumin-spiced chicken, and grilled rack of lamb. ✉ *3775 Harrodsburg Rd., in the Palomar Shopping Center,* ☎ *606/223–0797. AE, MC, V.*

$$$$ 🏨 **Camberly Club Hotel at Gratz Park.** In an elegantly refurbished three-story medical building dating from 1887, the guest rooms are furnished with antiques. Continental breakfast, afternoon tea, and evening cordials are features. ✉ *120 2nd St., 40507,* ☎ *606/231–1777 or 800/227–4362,* FAX *606/233–7593. 52 rooms. Restaurant. CP. AE, D, DC, MC, V.*

$$$$ ★ 🏨 **Marriott's Griffin Gate Resort.** This gleaming, contemporary seven-story resort hotel caters to a youngish crowd that likes physical activities and physical comforts. The rooms have private patios or balconies. ✉ *1800 Newtown Pike, 40511,* ☎ *606/231–5100,* FAX *606/231–*

5100, ext. 7580. 409 rooms. Restaurant, pool, health club, tennis. AE, D, DC, MC, V.

$$–$$$$ **Campbell House Inn.** Striving for a B&B ambience, this three-story motel has modern but homey rooms, with traditional furnishings. ✉ *1375 Harrodsburg Rd., 40504,* ☎ *606/255–4281 or 800/354–9235; 800/432–9254 in KY;* FAX *606/254–4368. 370 rooms. Restaurant, pool, tennis. AE, D, DC, MC, V.*

$$$ **Courtyard by Marriott.** The trademark of this three-story motel is a sunny, gardenlike central courtyard. The green, brown, and mauve rooms are modern, with light woodwork and oversize desks. ✉ *775 Newtown Ct., 40511,* ☎ *606/253–4646,* FAX *606/253–9118. 146 rooms. Restaurant, pool, exercise room. AE, D, DC, MC, V.*

$–$$ **Wilson Inn.** This five-story motor hotel resembles its Louisville counterpart: well away from downtown, contemporary in style with a tree-filled lobby, and colored a garish salmon outside but with pleasant pastels and earth tones inside. ✉ *2400 Buena Vista Dr., 40505,* ☎ *606/293–6113 or 800/945–7667,* FAX *606/293–6113, ext. 157. 110 rooms. AE, D, DC, MC, V.*

Nightlife and the Arts

Nightlife

After-dark offerings in Lexington are pretty sparse and pretty tame. From Thursday through Sunday you might check out the **Brewery** (✉ 509 W. Main St., ☎ 606/255–2822), a friendly Texas-roadhouse-style bar where the tunes are classic rock and classic country. Or you can visit **Comedy Off Broadway** (✉ 3199 Nicholasville Rd., ☎ 606/271–5653), where stand-up comics crack wise.

The Arts

Lexington's performing arts scene is vigorous. For information on performances contact the **Actors' Guild** (☎ 606/233–0663), **Lexington Ballet** (☎ 606/233–3925), **Lexington Philharmonic** (☎ 606/233–4226), and **Opera of Central Kentucky** (☎ 606/231–6994). Concerts, plays, and lectures are also presented at **Transylvania University** and the **University of Kentucky.** (☞ Exploring Lexington, *above*). The **Lexington Children's Theatre** (☎ 606/254–4546) offers performances for young audiences.

Outdoor Activities and Sports

Kentucky's lakes and streams provide great fishing for more than 200 species. You're seldom more than a 30-minute drive away from a public golf course. The state parks and national forests are full of hiking trails. Eastern Kentucky has several rivers that offer mild to moderate white-water rafting opportunities. For information contact the **Department of Parks** (☞ National and State Parks, *above*), tourism offices (☞ Visitor Information, *above*), or the state **Department of Fish and Wildlife Resources** (✉ 1 Game Farm Rd., Frankfort 40601, ☎ 502/564–4336).

Spectator Sports

Horse racing: Keeneland Race Course (✉ 4201 Versailles Rd., Lexington, ☎ 606/254–3412 or 800/456–3412); April and October.

Shopping

In Lexington **Fayette Mall** (✉ 3473 Nicholasville Rd., ☎ 606/272–3493) has more than 100 stores and a dozen places to eat. For something out of the ordinary, try **Dudley Square** (✉ 380 S. Mill St., ☎ no phone), in a restored 1881 school building; its shops purvey antiques, prints, quilts, and the like. **Victorian Square** (✉ 401 W. Main St., ☎ 606/252–7575) is an entire downtown block of renovated Victorian buildings that now contain tony retail and dining establishments. Lexington also has a plethora of ***antiques shops;*** the Convention & Visitors Bureau (☞ Visitor Information, *above*) maintains a list.

LOUISIANA

By Honey Naylor

Capital	Baton Rouge
Population	4,352,000
Motto	Union, Justice, and Confidence
State Bird	Pelican
State Flower	Magnolia
Postal Abbreviation	LA

Statewide Visitor Information

Louisiana Office of Tourism (✉ Box 94291, Baton Rouge 70804-9291, ☎ 800/334–8626). The office has information about FrancoFête, a yearlong, statewide celebration of 300 years of French culture and influence.

Scenic Drives

Gators laze along the exotic **Creole Nature Trail,** a circular drive out of Lake Charles designated a National Scenic Byway. **Routes 56 and 57** also form a circular drive south of Houma, where shrimp boats dock along the bayous from May to December. **Route 82** runs through the coastal marshes and wildlife refuges along the Gulf of Mexico. The **Longleaf Trail Scenic Byway,** south of Natchitoches, is a 17-mi highway through the Kisatchie National Forest linking Routes 117 and 119. **Route 182** runs alongside Bayou Teche in southern Louisiana.

National and State Parks

National Parks

The **Jean Lafitte National Historical Park and Preserve** (✉ 365 Canal St., New Orleans 70130, ☎ 504/589–3882) maintains coastal wetlands south of New Orleans and offers nature trails and canoeing through exotic swampland. The 100,000-acre Kisatchie Ranger District of the **Kisatchie National Forest** (✉ Box 2128, Natchitoches 71457, ☎ 318/352–2568) has hiking and equestrian trails through hardwood and pine forests.

State Parks

A prehistoric Native American site dating from between 1800 BC and 500 BC, the 400-acre **Poverty Point State Commemorative Area,** in the extreme northeast corner of Louisiana (✉ Rte. 577, Box 276, Epps 71237, ☎ 318/926–5492 or 888/926–5492), is one of the country's most important excavations, with hiking trails and an interpretive center in addition to the ancient Native American mounds. The 600-acre **Louisiana State Arboretum** (✉ Rte. 3, Box 494, Ville Platte 70586, ☎ 318/363–6289), lush with trees and plants native to the state, has 2½ mi of nature trails. Fishing, boating, and camping (cabins are available) are all possibilities in the 6,500-acre **Chicot State Park** (✉ Rte. 3, Box 494, Ville Platte 70586, ☎ 318/363–2403) and at **Bayou Segnette,** near New Orleans (✉ 7777 Westbank Expressway, Westwego 70094, ☎ 504/436–1107), **Lake Bistineau State Park** (✉ Box 589, Doyline 71023, ☎ 318/745–3503), **Lake Fausse Point State Park** (✉ Rte. 5, Box 5648, St. Martinville 70582, ☎ 318/229–4764), **North Toledo Bend State Park** (✉ Box 56, Zwolle 71486, ☎ 318/645–4715), and **Sam Houston Jones State Park** (✉ Rte. 4, Box 294, Lake Charles 70601, ☎ 318/855–2665).

NEW ORLEANS

Strategically situated on the Mississippi River, New Orleans is Louisiana's largest and most important city. From its beginnings in 1718 the city has played a vital role in the nation's history. To wrest control of the port city from the French in 1803, President Thomas Jefferson paid Napoléon $15 million and got the entire Louisiana Territory in the bargain. The Big Easy is the home of the splashiest festival in all North America: Mardi Gras, which is held each February or March, depending on when Lent falls. New Orleans is a fun-loving city with an insouciant spirit reminiscent of the Caribbean. As Jelly Roll Morton said, New Orleans is "the place where the birth of jazz originated." And local chefs gave the world exotic Creole cuisine. The French Quarter (also known as the Vieux Carré), with its honky-tonk Bourbon Street, is one of the nation's favorite partying places.

Visitor Information

New Orleans Metropolitan Convention & Visitors Bureau (☒ 1520 Sugar Bowl Dr., 70112, ☎ 504/566–5031 or 800/672–6124, FAX 504/566–5021). **New Orleans Welcome Center** (☒ 529 St. Ann St., in the French Quarter, ☎ 504/568–5661).

Arriving and Departing

By Boat

You can arrive from northern ports in grand 19th-century style aboard one of the authentic overnight steamboats that home-port in New Orleans—the *Delta Queen,* the *Mississippi Queen,* or the *American Queen*—all run by the **Delta Queen Steamboat Company** (☒ 30 Robin St. Wharf, 70130, ☎ 800/543–1949, FAX 504/585–0630).

By Bus and Train

Union Passenger Terminal (☒ 1001 Loyola Ave., ☎ 504/528–1610).

By Car

I–10 is the major east–west artery through the city; I–55, which runs north–south, connects with I–10 west of town. I–59 heads for the northeast. U.S. 61 and U.S. 90 also run through the city.

By Plane

New Orleans International Airport (also known as Moisant Field, ☎ 504/464–0831), 15 mi west of New Orleans, is served by many carriers. Cab fare for the 20- to 30-minute trip to downtown is $21 for one or two passengers, $8 for each additional passenger, plus tip. The 24-hour **Airport Shuttle** (☎ 504/522–3500; 🎫 $10 one-way) drops passengers off at all hotels. Buses operated by **Louisiana Transit** (☎ 504/737–9611) run between the airport and the Central Business District; the fare is $1.50 (exact change in coins).

Getting Around New Orleans

The French Quarter is best savored on leisurely strolls; the Central Business District (CBD) is also easily walkable.

By Car

Driving in New Orleans can be maddening. French Quarter streets are often clogged with traffic, street signs are indecipherable, and tow trucks operate with lightning speed. Leave your car in a secured garage until it's needed for excursions.

By Ferry

A ferry (***Crescent City Connection,*** ☎ 504/364–8100) crosses the Mississippi from the Canal Street Wharf to Algiers, leaving the pier every 25 minutes. It's free outgoing and $1 returning.

By Public Transportation

The **Regional Transit Authority,** or RTA (☎ 504/248–3900, TTY 504/248–2838), operates the bus and streetcar system and staffs a 24-hour information line.

Bus and **St. Charles Streetcar** fare is $1 (exact change); the **Riverfront Streetcar** ($1.25 exact change) links attractions along the Mississippi. The **Vieux Carré Shuttle** runs through the French Quarter to the foot of Canal Street. VisiTour passes, good on all RTA buses and streetcars, cost $4 (one day) and $8 (three days).

By Taxi

Cabs cruise the French Quarter and the CBD but not beyond. Reliable companies with 24-hour service are **United Cabs** (☎ 504/522–9771) and **Yellow-Checker Cabs** (☎ 504/943–2411). The fare is $1.70 at the flag drop, 20¢ for each additional ⅕ mi, and 50¢ for each additional passenger.

Orientation Tours

Bus and Van Tours

Two-hour city tours (🎫 $19), full- and half-day tours to plantation country (🎫 $23–$40)), a hop-on/hop-off trolley tour that stops at 10 attractions (🎫 $19), and combination bus–paddle wheeler tours (🎫 $31) are available from **Gray Line** (☎ 504/587–0861 or 800/535–7788). **Le 'Ob's Tours** (☎ 504/288–3478) runs a daily city tour that focuses on the heritage of African Americans (🎫 $30), as well as a plantation tour (🎫 $50–$65). **New Orleans Tours** (☎ 504/592–0560, 504/592–1991, or 800/543–6332) offers city tours (🎫 $19), combination city–paddle wheeler outings (🎫 $30), swamp tours 🎫 $38), and plantation tours ($26–$39). **Tours by Isabelle** (☎ 504/391–3544 or 888/223–2093) does a three-hour city tour (🎫 $30), town-and-country tours (🎫 $40), swamp tours (🎫 $45), and plantation tours that include lunch at Madewood Plantation (🎫 $80).

Cruises

Riverboat sightseeing and dinner-jazz cruises are offered by the **New Orleans Steamboat Company** (☎ 504/586–8777; 🎫 $42.50) and **New Orleans Paddle Wheels** (☎ 594/524–0814; 🎫 $39). Bayou tours are offered by **Honey Island Swamp Tours** (☎ 504/641–1769; 🎫 $30) and **Cypress Swamp Tours** (☎ 504/581–4501; 🎫 $30–$40).

Walking Tours

Special-Interest. Heritage Tours (☎ 504/949–9805; 🎫 $20) conducts literary and historical walking tours of the French Quarter. **Pat Bernard's Classic Tours** (☎ 504/899–1862; 🎫 $10) is operated by a native New Orleanian who is in love with the city; her chatty tours cover art, antiques, architecture, and history. **Save Our Cemeteries** (☎ 504/525–3377) conducts lively guided tours of St. Louis Cemetery No. 1 (🎫 $12) and Lafayette Cemetery (🎫 $6). Statistics for the **Superdome** (☎ 504/587–3810; 🎫 $6) are staggering and you can learn all about the huge facility during daily tours. **Voodoo haunts** and such are covered by both Magic Walking Tours (☎ 504/588–9693; 🎫 $13) and the New Orleans Historic Voodoo Museum (☎ 504/523–7685; 🎫 $15).

Exploring New Orleans

The French Quarter and the CBD

★ The **French Quarter** is the original colony founded in 1718 by French Creoles. A carefully preserved historic district that's also a residential district, the Quarter is home to some famous French Creole restaurants and many a jazz club. An eclectic crowd ambles in and out of small two- and three-story frame, old-brick, and pastel-stucco buildings, most of which date from the mid-19th century. Baskets of splashy subtropical plants dangle from the eaves of buildings with filigreed galleries, dollops of gingerbread, and dormer windows. Secluded courtyards are awash in greenery and brilliant blossoms.

The heart of the Quarter is **Jackson Square,** a pretty green park surrounded by a flagstone pedestrian mall and centered by an equestrian statue of Andrew Jackson. Originally known to Creoles as Place d'Armes, the square was renamed in the mid-19th century for the man who defeated the British in the Battle of New Orleans. The mall is alive with sidewalk artists, food vendors, Dixieland bands, and clowns.

St. Louis Cathedral is a quiet reminder of the city's spiritual life. The present church dates from 1794 and was restored in 1849. Tours are conducted daily except during services. **Pirate's Alley** and **Père Antoine's Alley,** two ancient flagstone passageways redolent of bygone days, run alongside St. Louis Cathedral.

St. Louis Cathedral is flanked by two 18th-century buildings of the **Louisiana State Museum** (✉ 751 Chartres St., ☎ 504/568–6968; 🎫 $4 to each state museum property, $10 combination ticket), which is closed Monday. As you face the church, the **Cabildo** is on the left, the **Presbytère** on the right. Transfer papers for the Louisiana Purchase of 1803 were signed on the second floor of the Cabildo. New Orleans's rich multicultural history is explored through historic documents and artifacts, among them a death mask of Napoléon—one of only three in the world. The Presbytère, originally built as a home for priests of the church, today houses changing exhibits.

You can see what life was like for wealthy 19th-century Creole apartment dwellers in the state museum's **1850s House** (✉ 523 St. Ann St., ☎ 504/568–6968; 🎫 $4), which contains period furnishings, antique dolls, and a quaint kitchen and is closed Monday.

The **Pontalba Buildings,** which line Jackson Square on St. Ann and St. Peter streets, are among the oldest apartment houses in the country. Built between 1849 and 1851, they have some of the city's loveliest ironwork galleries. The promenade of **Washington Artillery Park,** across Decatur Street from Jackson Square, affords a splendid perspective on the square and Ol' Man River.

★ Northeast of Jackson Square is the **French Market**—a complex of shops, offices, and eating places in a row of renovated buildings that once housed markets during Spanish and French rule. Here **Café du Monde** provides a 24-hour haven for café au lait and beignets (a unique New Orleans concoction: squares of fried dough dusted with powdered sugar).

The **Old U.S. Mint** (✉ 400 Esplanade Ave., ☎ 504/568–6968; 🎫 $4), which lies downriver of Jackson Square and is closed Monday, houses exhibits on jazz and Mardi Gras. This was the first branch of the U.S. Mint, in operation from 1838 until 1861. It's now part of the Louisiana State Museum.

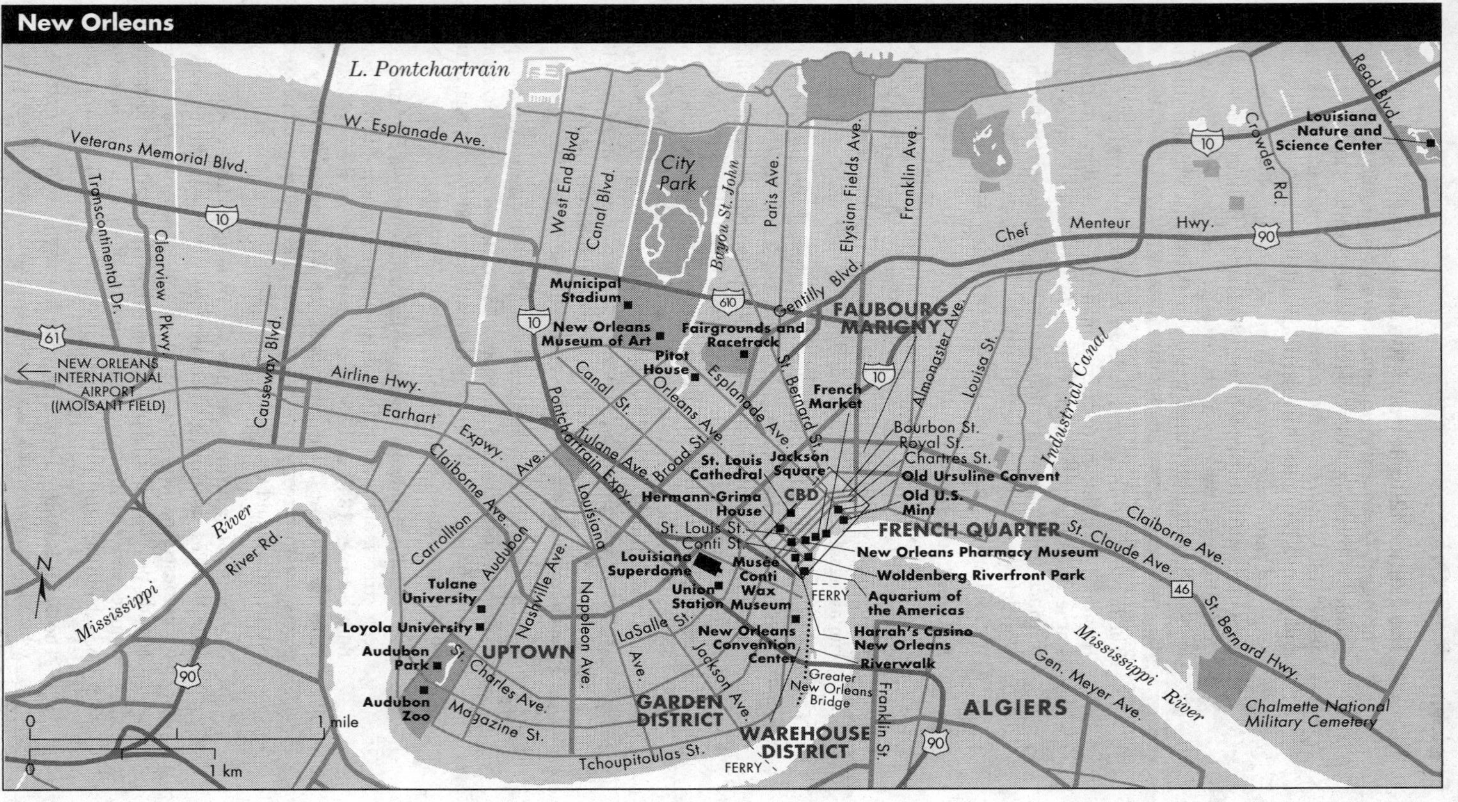
New Orleans
L. Pontchartrain
W. Esplanade Ave.
Veterans Memorial Blvd.
Transcontinental Dr.
Clearview Pkwy.
Causeway Blvd.
10
61
NEW ORLEANS INTERNATIONAL AIRPORT (MOISANT FIELD)
Airline Hwy.
Earhart Expwy.
Claiborne Ave.
West End Blvd.
Canal Blvd.
City Park
Bayou St. John
Paris Ave.
Elysian Fields Ave.
Franklin Ave.
Chef Menteur Hwy.
90
Crowder Rd.
Read Blvd.
Louisiana Nature and Science Center
Municipal Stadium
610
Gentilly Blvd.
FAUBOURG MARIGNY
Almonaster Ave.
Louisa St.
Industrial Canal
New Orleans Museum of Art
Fairgrounds and Racetrack
Pitot House
Canal St.
Orleans Ave.
Esplanade Ave.
St. Bernard St.
French Market
Pontchartrain Expy.
Tulane Ave.
Broad St.
St. Louis Cathedral
Jackson Square
Bourbon St.
Royal St.
Chartres St.
Old Ursuline Convent
Old U.S. Mint
CBD
Hermann-Grima House
St. Louis St.
Conti St.
FRENCH QUARTER
St. Claude Ave.
Claiborne Ave.
New Orleans Pharmacy Museum
Woldenberg Riverfront Park
Louisiana Superdome
Musée Conti Wax Museum
Union Station
FERRY
Aquarium of the Americas
46
St. Bernard Hwy.
Harrah's Casino New Orleans
New Orleans Convention Center
Riverwalk
Mississippi River
Gen. Meyer Ave.
Chalmette National Military Cemetery
Greater New Orleans Bridge
Franklin St.
ALGIERS
WAREHOUSE DISTRICT
GARDEN DISTRICT
Jackson Ave.
LaSalle St.
Louisiana Ave.
Napoleon Ave.
Nashville Ave.
Audubon
Carrollton
Tulane University
Loyola University
UPTOWN
Audubon Park
St. Charles Ave.
Audubon Zoo
Magazine St.
Tchoupitoulas St.
River Rd.
Mississippi River
N
0
1 mile
1 km

★ The **Old Ursuline Convent** (✉ 1100 Chartres St., ☎ 504/529–3040; 🎫 tours $5) erected in 1749 by order of Louis XV, is the only building remaining from the original colony. The Sisters of Ursula, who arrived here in 1727, occupied the building from 1749 to 1824. Guided tours of the complex take in the splendid **St. Mary's Church.** The convent is closed Monday.

The **Gallier House** (✉ 1118–32 Royal St., ☎ 504/525–5661; 🎫 $5), was built about 1857 by famed architect James Gallier, Jr., as his family home. This is one of the best-researched house-museums in the city and a fine example of how well-heeled Creoles lived. It's closed Sunday.

The tattered cottage at 941 Bourbon Street—dating from the late 18th century and typical of houses of the period—is **Lafitte's Blacksmith Shop,** a popular neighborhood bar. According to legend the cottage was once a front for pirate Jean Laffite's smuggling and slave trade. The **LaBranche House** (✉ 740 Royal St.), dating from about 1840, wraps around the corner of Royal and St. Peter streets. Its filigreed double galleries are the most photographed in the city.

The **New Orleans Pharmacy Museum** (✉ 514 Chartres St., ☎ 504/565–8027. 🎫 $3), closed Monday, is a musty old place where the nation's first licensed pharmacist lived and worked. It's full of ancient and mysterious medicinal things.

★ At the **Hermann-Grima House** (✉ 820 St. Louis St., ☎ 504/525–5661; 🎫 $5) guides take you through the Georgian-style town house, built in 1831, and its picturesque outbuildings. On Thursday in winter you can watch Creole cooking demonstrations—sorry, no tastings! The house is closed on Sunday.

Not to be missed are the tableaux in the **Musée Conti Wax Museum** (✉ 917 Conti St., ☎ 504/525–2605; 🎫 $6), which wax lifelike on such Louisiana legends as Andrew Jackson, Jean Laffite, and Marie Laveau, the 19th-century voodoo queen.

Canal Street, the upriver border of the French Quarter, is a main thoroughfare of the CBD as well as the dividing line between Uptown and Downtown. Nerve center of the nation's second-largest port, the CBD has the city's newest high-tech convention hotels, along with ritzy shopping malls, fast-food chains, stores, foreign agencies, and the mammoth Superdome.

The city's first land-based casino is very much on-again-off-again. At the foot of Canal Street, construction of **Harrah's Casino New Orleans,** began—and ended—in 1995. Harrah's eventually filed for bankruptcy and continues to try to sort out its financial problems. At press time (April 1998) the possibility seemed to exist that a casino might lumber to its feet some time in 1999. But don't bet on it.

At the foot of Canal Street, by the Mississippi River, is the **Aquarium of the Americas** (☎ 504/565–3033; 🎫 aquarium $10.95, IMAX $7, combination ticket $15), which offers close encounters with aquatic creatures in 60 displays in four major environments. A multimillion-dollar wing includes an IMAX theater. The 16-acre ★ **Woldenberg Riverfront Park,** surrounding the aquarium, affords excellent river views.

The ferry landing is across from the aquarium, adjacent to which is **Riverwalk.** This busy area comprises Spanish Plaza, a broad, open expanse of mosaic tile with a magnificent fountain; the Riverwalk shopping mall; and docks for sightseeing riverboats. Amazingly, a freighter that crashed into Riverwalk in 1996 left no long-term scars.

In the Warehouse District, near the New Orleans Convention Center, is the **Louisiana Children's Museum** (✉ 420 Julia St., ☎ 504/523–1357; 🎫 $5) with hands-on activities that are both educational and fun.

The Garden District and Uptown

Nestled between St. Charles, Louisiana, and Jackson avenues and Magazine Street, the **Garden District** is aptly named. Shunned by the French Creoles when they arrived in the early 19th century, American settlers built palatial estates upriver and surrounded them with lavish lawns. Many of the elegant Garden District houses were built during New Orleans's Golden Age, from 1830 until the Civil War. Some of these private homes are open to the public during Spring Fiesta tours.

Uptown is the area just upriver of the Garden District. Across from **Audubon Park** (☞ Parks, Gardens, and Zoos, *below*), **Tulane** and Loyola universities stand side by side on St. Charles Avenue.

Mid-City

Mid-City is between the Quarter and Lake Pontchartrain. One of Mid-City's major draws is the **Fair Grounds Race Track** (☞ Spectator Sports, *below*), the third-oldest racetrack in the nation. In lush City Park (☞ Parks, Gardens, and Zoos, *below*), the **New Orleans Museum of Art** (✉ 1 Collins-Diboll Dr., ☎ 504/488–2631; 🎫 $6) displays Italian paintings from the 13th to the 18th centuries, 20th-century European and American paintings and sculptures, Chinese jade, and the *Imperial Treasures,* by Peter Carl Fabergé. It's closed on Monday.

The **Pitot House** (✉ 1440 Moss St., ☎ 504/482–0312; 🎫 $3), across Bayou St. John from City Park, is a West Indies–style house built in the late 18th century. Inside are many antiques from 19th-century Louisiana. The house is closed Sunday through Tuesday.

North of town, **Lake Pontchartrain** is a boating and fishing destination with marinas, picnic grounds, and seafood restaurants.

Parks, Gardens, and Zoos

City Park (✉ City Park Ave., ☎ 504/482–4888), in Mid-City, is a 1,500-acre urban oasis shaded by majestic live oak trees. Its offerings include golf courses and tennis courts; lagoons for boating, canoeing, and fishing; botanical gardens; and a children's amusement park with a carousel and pony rides.

The lush 400-acre **Audubon Park** (✉ 6500–6800 blocks of St. Charles Ave.) features a 2-mi jogging trail with exercise stations, a riding stable, a swimming pool, tennis courts, a golf course, and a zoo.

The **Audubon Zoo** (✉ 6500 Magazine St., ☎ 504/861–2537; 🎫 $8.50) covers 58 acres of Audubon Park. Wooden walkways afford an up-close look at more than 1,800 animals in natural-habitat settings, including a Louisiana swamp and an African savanna. There's also a petting zoo and elephant and camel rides.

Dining

New Orleans is renowned for Creole and Cajun cuisine. The essence of Creole is in its classic French-style sauces and distinctive seasonings; Cajun cooking, with its hearty ingredients, tends to be more rustic in style. For price ranges *see* Chart 1 (A) *in* On the Road with Fodor's.

$$$–$$$$ ★ ✕ **Grill Room.** At this top-rated spot new American cuisine with strong Continental overtones is served in an opulent setting highlighted by original artwork. As the name suggests, there's a grill, over which much good fish is prepared. ✉ *Windsor Court Hotel, 2nd level, 300 Gravier*

St., CBD, ☎ 504/522–1992. *Reservations essential. Jacket required. AE, D, DC, MC, V.*

$$$ ✕ **Arnaud's.** Beveled glass, ceiling fans, and tile floors create an aura of traditional southern dining. The big, ambitious menu includes classic dishes such as rich shrimp bisque and beef Wellington. Cigar aficianados will feel at home in Arnaud's Bar, and the Richelieu Room is open for late-night live music, supping, and dancing. ✉ *813 Bienville St., French Quarter,* ☎ *504/523–5433. Reservations essential. Jacket required in main dining room. AE, D, DC, MC, V.*

$$$ ★ ✕ **Commander's Palace.** Housed in a renovated Victorian mansion, this elegant restaurant offers the best sampling in New Orleans of old Creole cooking, prepared with a combination of American and French touches. Chef Jamie Shannon's classics include trout with roasted pecans and poached oysters in a seasoned cream sauce with Oregon caviar. ✉ *1403 Washington Ave., Garden District,* ☎ *504/899–8221. Reservations essential. Jacket required. AE, D, DC, MC, V.*

$$–$$$ ★ ✕ **Bayona.** In an early 19th-century Creole cottage on a quiet street, chef Susan Spicer skillfully prepares such dishes as turnovers filled with spicy crawfish tails; a bisque of corn, leeks, and chicken; and fresh salmon fillet in white-wine sauce with sauerkraut. In good weather drinks and meals are served on a patio overflowing with tropical greenery. ✉ *430 Dauphine St.,* ☎ *504/525–4455. Reservations essential. AE, DC, MC, V. Closed Sun.*

$$–$$$ ✕ **Galatoire's.** Operated by the fourth generation of the family owners, Galatoire's is a tradition in New Orleans. Every imaginable Creole dish is served in a large, narrow dining room lit with brass chandeliers. Avoid the long lines by eating early. ✉ *209 Bourbon St., French Quarter,* ☎ *504/525–2021. Reservations accepted only Tues.–Thurs. for groups of 8 or more. Jacket required. AE, MC, V. Closed Mon.*

$$–$$$ ★ ✕ **K-Paul's Louisiana Kitchen.** National celebrity chef Paul Prudhomme's restaurant is a shrine to New Orleans Cajun cooking. Inventive gumbos, fried crawfish tails, blackened tuna, and sweet-potato–pecan pie are just a few of the jewels on the menu. Prices are steep at dinner but moderate at lunch; servings are generous. ✉ *416 Chartres St., French Quarter,* ☎ *504/524–7394. AE, DC, MC, V. Closed Sun.*

$$–$$$ ★ ✕ **Nola.** Fans of chef and TV personality Emeril Lagasse will appreciate this spin-off of the pricier and plusher Emeril's. Down-to-earth southern Louisiana dishes are served in energetic and colorful surroundings. The trout swathed in a horseradish-citrus crust and plank-roasted in a wood oven is unforgettable, as is the coconut cream pie with cinnamon ice cream. ✉ *534 St. Louis St., French Quarter,* ☎ *504/522–6652. Reservations essential. AE, D, DC, MC, V. No lunch Sun.*

$$–$$$ ✕ **Palace Cafe.** Just a few blocks from the Mississippi riverfront, the Palace, with its drugstore-tile floors and stained-cherry booths, is a convivial spot to try some of the more imaginative contemporary Creole dishes like crab chops, rabbit ravioli in piquant sauce, and seafood Napoléon. Wait till you see the menu of chocolate desserts. ✉ *605 Canal St., CBD,* ☎ *504/523–1661. Reservations essential. AE, DC, MC, V.*

$$ ✕ **Ralph & Kacoo's.** Getting past the door to the vast dining spaces usually means first taking a ticket and waiting your turn in a crowded bar decorated in a bayou theme. Freshness and consistency are trademarks here. You'll find them in the boiled shrimp, raw oysters, shrimp rémoulade, trout meunière, and fried seafood platter. This restaurant is popular with families. ✉ *519 Toulouse St., French Quarter,* ☎ *504/522–5226. Reservations not accepted. AE, D, MC, V.*

$–$$ ✕ **Praline Connection.** Down-home cooking in the southern Creole style is the forte of these laid-back restaurants. The fried or stewed chicken, smothered pork chops, barbecued ribs, and collard greens are definitively done. ✉ *542 Frenchmen St., Faubourg Marigny,* ☎ *504/943–*

3934; ✉ *901 S. Peters St., Warehouse District,* ☎ *504/523–3973. Reservations not accepted. AE, D, DC, MC, V.*

$ ★ ✕ **Camellia Grill.** This classy lunch counter with linen napkins and a maître d' serves the best omelets in town all day long, as well as great hamburgers, pecan pie, cheesecake, and banana cream pie. Expect long lines on weekends for breakfast. ✉ *626 S. Carrollton Ave., Uptown,* ☎ *504/866–9573. No credit cards.*

Lodging

Reserve well in advance of your New Orleans stay, especially during Mardi Gras or other seasonal events. Hotels frequently offer special packages at reduced rates, but never during Mardi Gras, when rates are much higher. For price ranges *see* Chart 2 (A) *in* On the Road with Fodor's.

$$$$ ★ **Fairmont Hotel.** The Fairmont is one of the oldest grand hotels in America. Its lobby is decked out in blue-and-gold Victorian splendor. Special touches in every room include down pillows and terry-cloth robes. ✉ *123 Baronne St., CBD, 70140,* ☎ *504/529–7111 or 800/527–4727,* FAX *504/529–4764. 700 rooms. 3 restaurants, pool, tennis, exercise room. AE, D, DC, MC, V.*

$$$$ ★ **Windsor Court Hotel.** Four blocks from the French Quarter, the Windsor Court has plush carpeting, canopy and four-poster beds, stocked wet bars, marble vanities, oversize mirrors, and dressing areas. Phones have voice mail and dataports. ✉ *300 Gravier St., CBD, 70130,* ☎ *504/523–6000 or 800/262–2662,* FAX *504/596–4513. 326 rooms. 2 restaurants, pool, health club. AE, D, DC, MC, V.*

$$$–$$$$ ★ **Royal Orleans Hotel (Omni).** An elegant white-marble hotel, the Royal O is reminiscent of a bygone era. Rooms, though not exceptionally large, are well appointed, with marble baths (telephone in each) and marble-top dressers and tables. ✉ *621 St. Louis St., French Quarter, 70140,* ☎ *504/529–5333,* FAX *504/529–7089. 362 rooms. Restaurant, pool, exercise room. AE, D, DC, MC, V.*

$$–$$$$ **Chateau Le Moyne Holiday Inn.** Old-world atmosphere and decor can be found just one block off Bourbon Street. Eight suites are in Creole cottages off a tropical courtyard; all rooms are furnished with antiques and reproductions, and have coffeemakers, hair dryers, and irons and ironing boards. ✉ *301 Dauphine St., French Quarter, 70112,* ☎ *504/581–1303,* FAX *504/523–5709. 171 rooms. Restaurant, pool. AE, D, DC, MC, V.*

$$–$$$ **Josephine Guest House.** European antiques fill the rooms of this restored Italianate mansion built in 1870. The bathrooms are impressive in both size and decor. A complimentary Continental breakfast, served on Wedgwood china from a silver tray, can be brought to your room. ✉ *1450 Josephine St., Garden District, 70130,* ☎ *504/524–6361 or 800/779–6361,* FAX *504/523–6484. 6 rooms. CP. AE, D, DC, MC, V.*

$$–$$$ ★ **Le Richelieu.** This small, friendly hotel offers many amenities usually found in luxury high-rises. Some rooms have mirrored walls, walk-in closets, and refrigerators; all have hair dryers. Luxury suites are available. ✉ *1234 Chartres St., French Quarter, 70116,* ☎ *504/529–2492 or 800/535–9653,* FAX *504/524–8179. 86 rooms. Pool. AE, D, DC, MC, V.*

$$–$$$ **Pontchartrain Hotel.** Maintaining the grand tradition is the hallmark of this quiet, elegant European-style hotel, which has which has reigned on St. Charles Avenue since it was built in 1927. Accommodations range from lavish sun-filled suites to small pension-style rooms with shower-baths. ✉ *2031 St. Charles Ave., Garden District, 70140,* ☎ *504/524–*

0581 or 800/777–6193, FAX 504/524–7828. 102 rooms. 2 restaurants. AE, D, DC, MC, V.

$$–$$$ **Rue Royal Inn.** This circa-1850 home has balcony rooms overlooking a courtyard and Royal Street; two suites have Jacuzzis. Each room has a coffeemaker and a small refrigerator. ✉ *1006 Royal St., French Quarter, 70116,* ☎ *504/524–3900 or 800/776–3901,* FAX *504/558–0566. 17 rooms. CP. AE, D, DC, MC, V.*

$–$$ **St. Charles Guest House.** Simple and affordable, this European-style pension is in four buildings one block from St. Charles Avenue. Rooms in the A and B buildings are larger. The small "backpacker" rooms share a bath and do not have air-conditioning. ✉ *1748 Prytania St., Garden District, 70130,* ☎ *504/523–6556,* FAX *504/522–6340. 36 rooms, 8 with shared bath. Pool. CP. AE, MC, V.*

Nightlife and the Arts

The Friday edition of the *Times-Picayune* and the weekly *Gambit* (free) carry comprehensive calendars of arts and entertainment events. *New Orleans* magazine (on newsstands) and *This Week in New Orleans* and *Where: New Orleans* (both available free in hotels) also publish calendars of events. Credit-card purchases of tickets for events at the Saenger Performing Arts Center and UNO Lakefront Arena can be made through **TicketMaster** (☎ 504/522–5555 or 800/488–5252).

Nightlife

New Orleans is a 24-hour town, meaning there are no legal closing times, and it ain't over till it's over. Bourbon Street in the French Quarter is lined with clubs; many local hangouts are Uptown.

BARS

Pat O'Brien's (✉ 718 St. Peter St., French Quarter, ☎ 504/525–4823) has three lively bars. At **Lafitte's Blacksmith Shop** (✉ 941 Bourbon St., French Quarter, ☎ 504/523–0066) drinks are served in a rustic 18th-century cottage. **Napoleon House** (✉ 500 Chartres St., French Quarter, ☎ 504/524–9752) is a longtime favorite hangout.

CASINOS

Riverboat gambling in Louisiana is indeed a movable feast. As of press time (summer 1998), the following casinos were still afloat. Some actually cruise, but others, contrary to state law, offer dockside gambling. Bally's ***Belle of Orleans*** (✉ Lake Pontchartrain, ☎ 504/568–9376) joins the ***Boomtown Belle*** (✉ Harvey Canal on the West bank, ☎ 504/366–7711) and the ***Treasure Chest*** (✉ Lake Pontchartrain in Kenner, ☎ 504/443–8000 or 800/298–0711).

JAZZ

Aboard the ***Creole Queen*** (✉ Poydras St. Wharf, CBD, ☎ 504/529–4567; 🎟 $39 dinner cruise) you'll cruise with jazz and a buffet. Live traditional jazz is also on land at the **Palm Court Jazz Cafe** (✉ 1204 Decatur St., French Quarter, ☎ 504/525–0200; 🎟 $4 cover at tables), **Pete Fountain's** (✉ 2 Poydras St., CBD, ☎ 504/523–4374; 🎟 $19), and **Preservation Hall** (✉ 726 St. Peter St., French Quarter, ☎ 504/523–8939; 🎟 $4).

R&B, CAJUN, ROCK, NEW WAVE

Top-notch local and nationally known musicians perform at **House of Blues** (✉ 225 Decatur St., French Quarter, ☎ 504/529–2583) and **Margaritaville Café** (✉ 1104 Decatur St., French Quarter, ☎ 504/592–2565). An institution, **Tipitina's** (✉ 501 Napoleon Ave., Uptown; ✉ 310 Howard Ave., Warehouse District; ✉ 233 N. Peters St., French Quarter, ☎ 504/897–3943) is a laid-back place with a mixed bag of music. **Jimmy's Music Club** (✉ 8200 Willow St., Uptown, ☎ 504/861–

8200) is popular with the college crowd. Industrial-strength rock rolls out of the sound system at the **Hard Rock Cafe** (✉ 440 N. Peters St., French Quarter, ☎ 504/529–8617). Two-step to a Cajun band at the **Maple Leaf Bar** (✉ 8316 Oak St., Uptown, ☎ 504/866–9359), **Mulate's** (✉ 201 Julia St., Warehouse District, ☎ 504/522–1492), and **Michaul's** (✉ 840 St. Charles Ave., CBD, ☎ 504/522–5517).

The Arts

CONCERTS

Free jazz concerts are held on weekends in **Dutch Alley** (French Market at St. Philip St., ☎ 504/596–3424).

THEATER

The avant-garde and the satirical are among the offerings at **Contemporary Arts Center** (✉ 900 Camp St., ☎ 504/523–1216). **Le Petit Théâtre du Vieux Carré** (✉ 616 St. Peter St., ☎ 504/522–2081) presents more traditional fare as well as children's theater. Touring Broadway shows and top-name talent appear at the **Saenger Performing Arts Center** (✉ 143 N. Rampart St., ☎ 504/524–2490). Nationally known artists perform at **Kiefer UNO Lakefront Arena** (✉ 6801 Franklin Ave., ☎ 504/286–7222).

Outdoor Activities and Sports

Biking

Bikes can be rented at **Bicycle Michael's** (✉ 618 Frenchmen St., ☎ 504/945–9505) and **French Quarter Bicycles** (✉ 522 Dumaine St., ☎ 504/529–3136).

Boating

Canoes, rowboats, and pedal boats can be rented for lazing along **City Park's lagoons** (✉ Dreyfous Dr., ☎ 504/483–9371).

Golf

There are four 18-hole courses at **City Park,** as well as a 100-tee double-decker driving range (✉ 1040 Fillmore Dr., ☎ 504/483–9396), and an 18-hole course at **Audubon Park** (✉ 473 Walnut St., ☎ 504/865–8260).

Tennis

There are 39 courts at **City Park's Wisner Tennis Center** (✉ Dreyfous Dr., ☎ 504/482–4888) and 10 courts in **Audubon Park** (✉ Rear of park off Tchoupitoulas St., ☎ 504/895–1042).

Spectator Sports

Baseball: The **New Orleans Zephyrs** (✉ 6000 Airline Hwy., Metairie, ☎ 504/734–5155), the Class AAA minor-league team of the Houston Astros, play their home games at Zephyr Stadium in Jefferson Parish. **Football:** The **New Orleans Saints** play in the Superdome (✉ 1 Sugar Bowl Dr., ☎ 504/522–2600). The **Sugar Bowl Classic** (☎ 504/525–8573) is played annually in the Dome around New Year's. The **Super Bowl,** hosted by New Orleans in 1997, has been played more times in this city than in any other. **Horse Racing:** There is Thoroughbred racing from Thanksgiving Day to April at the **Fair Grounds** (✉ 1751 Gentilly Blvd., ☎ 504/944–5515). A spiffy new clubhouse opened in 1997, replacing the one razed by fire in 1993. **Ice Hockey:**The **New Orleans Brass,** of the East Coast Ice Hockey League, play home games in Municipal Auditorium (✉ 1201 St. Peter St., ☎ 504/522–7825).

Shopping

Louisiana's **tax-free shopping** program grants shoppers from other countries a sales-tax rebate. Retailers who display the tax-free sign issue vouch-

In case you want to be welcomed there.

We're here to see that you're always welcomed at establishments everywhere. That's why millions of people carry the American Express® Card – for peace of mind, confidence, and security, around the world or just around the corner.

do more®

Cards

ers for the 9% sales tax, which can be redeemed on departure. Present the vouchers with your passport and international plane ticket at the tax-rebate office at New Orleans International Airport and receive up to $500 in cash back. If the amount redeemable exceeds $500, a check for the difference will be mailed to you. Store hours are generally Monday through Saturday from 10 to 5:30 or 6, Sunday from noon to 5. Many stores in the French Quarter and in malls stay open till 9. Sales are advertised in the daily *Times-Picayune*.

Shopping Districts

Most of the **French Quarter**'s ritzy antiques stores, musty bazaars, art galleries, and boutiques are housed in quaint 19th-century structures. The sleek indoor malls of the **CBD** include **Riverwalk** (✉ 1 Poydras St.), with more than 200 specialty shops and restaurants; **Canal Place** (✉ 1 Canal Pl.), with more than 40 tony shops, a food court, and cinemas; and **New Orleans Centre** (✉ 1400 Poydras St.), connected by a walkway to the Superdome and a hotel. The **Warehouse District** neighborhood of the CBD, especially Julia Street off St. Charles Avenue, is a major center for art galleries. Upriver from the CBD, **Magazine Street** has 6 mi of antiques stores and boutiques, many in once-grand Victorian houses, and **Riverbend** has specialty shops and restaurants, many cradled in small Creole cottages.

Department Stores

Maison Blanche (✉ 901 Canal St., CBD, ☎ 504/566–1000) is the local department store, with branches in suburban shopping centers.

Specialty Stores

ANTIQUES

Royal Street in the Quarter is lined with elegant antiques stores; **Magazine Street** has everything from Depression glass to Persian rugs. The Royal Street Guild and the Magazine Street Merchants' Association publish pamphlets that are available free at the New Orleans Welcome Center (☞ Visitor Information, *above*).

FLEA MARKET

Locals as well as tourists turn out for the **Community Flea Market** held daily from 7 to 7 in the French Market (☞ Exploring, *above*).

FOOD

Louisiana Products (✉ 507 St. Ann St., on Jackson Sq., ☎ 504/524–7331) has packaged Louisiana food products. **Old Town Praline Shop** (✉ 627 Royal St., ☎ 504/525–1413) has the best pralines in town.

JAZZ RECORDS

For hard-to-find vintage items, go to **Record Ron's** (✉ 239 Chartres St., ☎ 504/522–2239).

MASKS

Handmade Mardi Gras masks are available at **Little Shop of Fantasy** (✉ 523 Dumaine St., ☎ 504/529–4243) and **Rumors** (✉ 513 Royal St., ☎ 504/525–0292).

Side Trip to Plantation Country

Arriving and Departing

By car take I–10 or U.S. 61 west from New Orleans and follow the signs to the various plantations. Plantation Country maps are available at the New Orleans Welcome Center (☞ Visitor Information, *above*). Many local tour operators include visits to plantations in their itineraries (☞ Orientation Tours, *above*).

What to See and Do

Plantation Country lies upriver from New Orleans. You can see what went with the wind and hear tales of Yankee invaders and ghosts in some of the fine restored antebellum plantations sprinkled around the Great River Road between New Orleans and Baton Rouge, the state capital. The drive is marred by industrial plants, but elegant mansions such as **Nottoway** (✉ 2 mi north of White Castle, ☎ 504/545–2730) and **Houmas House** (✉ Rte. 942, ½ mi off Rte. 44, near Burnside, ☎ 504/473–7841) make the trip worthwhile.

CAJUN COUNTRY

Cajun Country, or Acadiana, comprises 22 parishes (counties) of southern Louisiana to the west of New Orleans. Cajuns are descendants of 17th-century French settlers who established a colony they called l'Acadie (*Cajun* is a corruption of *Acadian*) in the present-day Canadian provinces of Nova Scotia and New Brunswick. After the British expelled the Acadians in the mid-18th century (their exile is described in Longfellow's epic poem *Evangeline*), many eventually found a home in southern Louisiana. They have been here since 1762, sharing their unique cuisine and culture with the nation and imbuing the region with a distinctive flavor summed up in the Cajun phrase "Laissez les bons temps rouler!" ("Let the good times roll!")

Visitor Information

Southwest Louisiana Convention & Visitors Bureau (✉ 1211 N. Lakeshore Dr., Lake Charles 70601, ☎ 318/436–9588 or 800/456–7952, FAX 318/494–7952). **Lafayette Convention & Visitors Bureau** (✉ 1400 N.W. Evangeline Thruway, Box 52066, Lafayette 70505, ☎ 318/232–3808, 800/346–1958; 800/543–5340 in Canada, FAX 318/232–0161).

Arriving and Departing

By Bus

Greyhound (☎ 800/231–2222) has frequent daily service to Lafayette, Lake Charles, and environs.

By Car

The fastest route from New Orleans through Cajun Country is west on I–10. U.S. 90 is a slower but more scenic drive. If you have time, take the back roads for exploring this area. A ferry across the Mississippi costs $1 per car; most bridges are free.

By Plane

Lafayette Regional Airport (☎ 318/232–2808) is served by American Eagle, Atlantic Southeast (Delta), Continental, and Northwest Airlink. **Lake Charles Regional Airport** (☎ 318/477–6051) is served by American Eagle and Continental.

By Train

Amtrak (☎ 800/872–7245) serves Franklin, Schriever, Lafayette, New Iberia, and Thibodaux.

Exploring Cajun Country

U.S. 90 dips down south of New Orleans into Terrebonne Parish, a major center for shrimp and oyster fisheries (the blessing of the shrimp fleets in Chauvin and Dulac is a colorful April event). A slew of swamp tours are based here, including **Annie Miller's Terrebonne Swamp & Marsh Tours** (☎ 504/879–3934). **Hammond's Cajun Air Tours** (☎

504/876–0584) takes passengers up for a gull's-eye view of the alligators and other critters that inhabit the coastal wetlands.

Morgan City, on the Atchafalaya River, struck it rich when the first producing offshore oil well was completed on November 14, 1947, and the Kerr-McGee Rig No. 16 ushered in the black-gold rush. In 1917 the original *Tarzan of the Apes* was filmed in Morgan City; at the town Information Center (✉ 725 Myrtle St., ☎ 504/384–3343) you can see a video of the film.

Route 182 west of Morgan City branches off U.S. 90 and ambles northwest toward Lafayette, traveling for much of the way along ★ **Bayou Teche,** the largest of the state's many bayous. (*Teche* is an Indian word meaning "snake." According to an ancient legend, the death throes of a giant snake carved the bayou.) The road runs by rice paddies and canebrakes, and on the bayous you can see Cajun pirogues (canoelike boats) and cypress cabins built on stilts.

Franklin is an official Main Street U.S.A. town (a title bestowed by the National Trust for Historic Preservation). The street, lined with old-fashioned street lamps, rolls out beneath an arcade of live oaks. Six antebellum homes are open for tours in and around town. One of them, Oak Lawn Manor, is the home of Louisiana governor Mike Foster. Franklin is nestled on Route 182, along a bend in Bayou Teche, and there is a splendid view of it from Parc sur le Teche.

New Iberia is northwest of Franklin. Called the "Queen City of the Teche," it was founded in 1779 by Spanish settlers who named it for their homeland. **Shadows-on-the-Teche** (✉ 317 E. Main St., ☎ 318/369–6446; 🎟 $6), one of the South's best-known plantation homes, was built in 1834 for sugar planter David Weeks. The big brick house is virtually enveloped in moss-draped live oak trees.

★ Red-hot Tabasco sauce is a 19th-century Louisiana creation; on **Avery Island** at McIlhenny's Tabasco Company (✉ Rte. 329, ☎ 318/373–6129; 🎟 free), southwest of New Iberia, you can tour the factory where it's still being manufactured by descendants of its creator. Here also are the 200-acre Jungle Garden, lush with tropical plants, and Bird City (☎ 318/369–6243; 🎟 $5.50), a sanctuary with flurries of snow-white egrets.

★ Like Avery Island, **Rip Van Winkle Gardens,** formerly known as Live Oak Gardens (✉ 284 Rip Van Winkle Rd., off Rte. 14, ☎ 318/365–3332; 🎟 house and gardens $9, combination house, gardens, and boat tour $16), is actually a salt dome, capped by lush vegetation. The 19th-century American actor Joseph Jefferson, who toured the country portraying Rip Van Winkle, built a winter home here. His three-story house is surrounded by lovely formal and informal gardens. Boat tours on adjacent Lake Peigneur are also available.

Along Route 31, a pretty country road that hugs the banks of the Teche between New Iberia and St. Martinville to the north, you'll find **St. Martinville,** a little town awash with legends. Now a sleepy village, it was known in the 18th century as Petit Paris, a refuge for aristocrats fleeing the French Revolution. It was also a major debarkation point for exiled Acadians. Longfellow's poem *Evangeline* was based on the true story of two young lovers who were separated for years during the Acadian exile. The Evangeline Oak (✉ Evangeline Blvd. at Bayou Teche) is said to be the place where the ill-starred lovers met again—albeit briefly. On the town square is **St. Martin de Tours,** mother church of the Acadians, and the **Petit Paris Museum** (✉ 103 S. Main St., ☎ 318/394–7334; 🎟 $3), which has a Mardi Gras collection. Be sure to visit the small cemetery behind the church, where a bronze statue depicts the real-life Evangeline.

Tiny **Breaux Bridge,** just north of St. Martinville, calls itself the "crawfish capital of the world." The **Crawfish Festival,** held each May, draws more than 100,000 people. The town's other claim to fame is the Cajun food and music spot **Mulate's** (☞ Dining and Lodging, *below*).

Lafayette, 15 minutes west of Breaux Bridge, proudly proclaims itself the capital of French Louisiana. In this part of the state some 40% of the residents speak Cajun French, a 17th-century dialect. As most Cajuns also speak standard French as well as English, this is a superb place to test your language skills. **Cajun Mardi Gras** rivals its sister celebration in New Orleans. Lafayette, though it's short on the charm that typifies this region, has a few noteworthy attractions and is a good base for exploring the region.

The **Lafayette Natural History Museum** (✉ 637 Girard Park Dr., ☎ 318/291–5544; 🎟 free), within luxuriant **Girard Park,** offers workshops, movies, concerts, laser-light shows, and a planetarium. It's also the venue for the annual **Louisiana Native and Contemporary Crafts Festival,** held each September.

The **Acadiana Park Nature Station** (✉ E. Alexandre St., ☎ 318/291–6181; 🎟 free) is a three-story cypress-pole structure with an interpretive center, discovery boxes for children, a nature trail, and guided ★ tours (for a fee).The **Acadian Cultural Center** (✉ 501 Fisher Rd., ☎ 318/232–0789 or 318/232–0961; 🎟 Free), a unit of the **Jean Lafitte National Historical Park and Preserve,** traces the history of the Acadians through numerous audiovisual exhibits, including an excellent introductory film dramatizing the Acadian exile. The **Children's Museum of Acadiana,** has hands-on exhibits (✉ 201 E. Congress St., ☎ 318/232–8500; 🎟 $5).

Among the small towns that dot the flatlands west of Lafayette and whose residents are called Prairie Cajuns is **Eunice,** a tiny speck of a town home to Rendez-Vous des Cajuns (☞ Nightlife and the Arts, *below*) and the **Prairie Acadian Cultural Center** (✉ Corner of S. 3rd St. and Park Ave., ☎ 318/457–8499; 🎟 free). In a former railroad depot, the **Eunice Museum** (✉ 220 S. C. C. Duson Dr., ☎ 318/457–6540; 🎟 free) contains displays on Cajun culture, including its music and Mardi Gras. Eunice and the surrounding villages of Mamou, Church Point, and Iota are the major stomping grounds for the annual **Courir de Mardi Gras,** which features a band of masked and costumed horseback riders on a mad dash through the countryside.

North of Lafayette, **Grand Coteau** is a religious and educational center, and the entire peaceful little village is on the National Register of Historic Places. Of particular note in Grand Coteau is the **Church of St. Charles Borromeo,** a simple wooden structure with an ornate high-Baroque-style interior. A splendid antebellum mansion, **Chretien Point Plantation** (✉ 665 Chretien Point Rd., 12 mi north of Lafayette, ☎ 318/662–5876; 🎟 $6.50) is now a B&B. The staircase in Tara, Scarlett O'Hara's home in *Gone With the Wind,* was modeled on the one in this house.

Opelousas, the third-oldest town in the state, is a short drive from Grand Coteau on I–49. Founded by the French in 1720, the town was named for the Appalousa Indians, who lived here centuries before the French and Spanish arrived. For a brief period during the Civil War, Opelousas served as the state capital. At the intersection of I–49 and U.S. 190, the **Opelousas Tourist Information Center** (☎ 318/948–6263) houses memorabilia of Jim Bowie, the Alamo hero who spent his boyhood here. The **Opelousas Museum and Interpretive Center** (⊠ 329 N. Main St., ☎ 318/948–2589; Free) traces the history of this region.

Tucked away in the far southwest corner of the state, **Lake Charles** is a straight shot (71 mi) from Lafayette on I–10. Though the city has more than 50 mi of rivers, lakes, canals, and bayous, it's primarily industrial, but with a fleet of gambling riverboats that have turned it into a boomtown. The **Imperial Calcasieu Museum** (⊠ 204 W. Sallier St., ☎ 318/439–3797; $1) has an extensive collection on Lake Charles and Imperial Calcasieu Parish, including an old-fashioned pharmacy, an Audubon collection, a Gay '90s barbershop, and a fine-arts gallery. The **Children's Museum** (⊠ 925 Enterprise Blvd., ☎ 318/433–9420; $3) has innovative hands-on exhibits, including a miniature courtroom and grocery store and interactive computer games.

The **Creole Nature Trail** (☞ Scenic Drives, *above*), designated a National Scenic Byway by the Federal Highway Administration, begins on Route 27 in Sulphur and continues on Route 82. Beautiful in spring, this drive goes to the **Sabine Wildlife Refuge,** where a paved trail meanders into the wilds. There is an interpretive center and a tower at the end of the trail, which gives you an excellent view of the wilderness. (Take along insect repellent!)

You can make a detour off the Creole Nature Trail and continue east on Route 82 (Hug-the-Coast Highway), which whips along the windswept coastal marshes to the **Rockefeller Wildlife Refuge,** in **Grand Chenier.** At this 84,000-acre preserve, thousands of ducks, geese, gators, wading birds, and otters while away the winter months.

Dining and Lodging

With the state's wealth of waterways, it is no surprise that Louisiana tables are laden with seafood in every variety. In southern Louisiana sea creatures are prepared with a Cajun flair. Sleeping accommodations run from homey B&Bs to chain motels to luxury hotels to elegant antebellum mansions open for overnighters. For price ranges *see* Charts 1 (B) and 2 (B) *in* On the Road with Fodor's.

Breaux Bridge

$$–$$$ ★ ✕ **Mulate's.** This renowned roadhouse with tables covered in checkered plastic features Cajun seafood and dancing to live Cajun music noon and night. ⊠ *325 W. Mills Ave.,* ☎ *318/332–4648 or 800/422–2586; 800/634–9880 in LA. AE, MC, V.*

Carencro

$$–$$$$ ★ ✕ **Prudhomme's Cajun Café.** In a suburb of Lafayette, celebrity chef Paul Prudhomme's sister Enola has a country-kitchen café with outstanding Cajun fare. ⊠ *4676 N.E. Evangeline Thruway,* ☎ *318/896–7964. AE, MC, V. Closed Sun.*

Lafayette

$$–$$$$ ★ ✕ **Prejean's.** Housed in a cypress cottage, this local favorite has a cozy oyster bar, red-checked cloths, and live music nightly. Platters of traditional and new Cajun seafood are the specialties. ⊠ *3480 U.S. 167N, next to Evangeline Downs,* ☎ *318/896–3247. AE, DC, MC, V.*

$$$ ★ **Best Western Hotel Acadiana.** Near Bayou Vermilion, this is a plush hotel whose rooms have thick carpeting, marble-top dressers, and wet bars. Even-numbered rooms face the pool. ⊠ *1801 W. Pinhook Rd., 70508,* ☎ *318/233–8120 or 800/826–8386; 800/874–4664 in LA,* FAX *318/234–9667. 304 rooms. Restaurant, pool. AE, D, DC, MC, V.*

$$–$$$ **Holiday Inn Central–Holidome.** Built around an atrium that's banked with greenery, this modern motel has rooms done in contemporary decor and 17 acres within which you can find almost every diversion you'd ever need for a long life. ✉ *2032 N.E. Evangeline Thruway (Box 91807), 70509,* ☎ *318/233–6815 or 800/942–4868,* FAX *318/235–1954. 250 rooms. Restaurant, pool, 2 tennis courts. AE, D, DC, MC, V.*

Lake Charles

$$–$$$$ ★ **Café Margaux.** You might feel more comfortable in a jacket and tie at this restaurant, where candlelight, tuxedoed waiters, and a 5,000-bottle mahogany wine cellar provide the setting for specialties that include rack of lamb *en croûte* and fillet of flounder with lump crabmeat and brown meunière sauce. ✉ *765 Bayou Pines,* ☎ *318/433–2902. Reservations essential. AE, MC, V. Closed Sun.*

$$$ **Players East Hotel & Casino.** Perched between the lake and the interstate, this hotel has traditional furnishings in rooms done in soothing earth tones. Hotel guests can stroll the Casino Walk to board the Players Island Casino (☞ Nightlife and the Arts, *below*), which docks next door. ✉ *505 N. Lakeshore Dr., 70601,* ☎ *318/433–7121 or 800/367–1814,* FAX *318/436–8459. 270 rooms. Restaurant, pool. AE, D, DC, MC, V.*

$$ **Chateau Charles Hotel & Conference Center.** Set on 25 acres, the hotel includes two-bedroom suites with wet bars, microwaves, and minirefrigerators. ✉ *Box 1269, 70602,* ☎ *318/882–6130 or 800/935–6130,* FAX *318/882–6601. 248 rooms. Restaurant. AE, D, DC, MC, V.*

Napoleonville

$$$$ ★ **Madewood.** Expect gracious southern hospitality in this antiques-filled Greek Revival plantation mansion, which is both elegant and cozy. There are rooms in the main mansion and suites in a restored outbuilding. ✉ *4250 Rte. 308, 70390,* ☎ *504/369–7151 or 800/375–7151. 8 rooms. MAP. AE, D, MC, V.*

New Iberia

$$$ **leRosier.** Across the street from Shadows-on-the-Teche, leRosier is a four-room B&B whose shining star is the restaurant, presided over by chef Hallman Woods III. Among other accomplishments, Hall has prepared a five-course crawfish degustation for the James Beard Foundation. Expect fresh ingredients and succulent seafood in his small white-cloth dining room. ✉ *314 E. Main St., 70563,* ☎ *318/367–5306. 4 rooms. Restaurant. Reservations essential for dinner. Full breakfast. AE, MC, V.*

Opelousas

$–$$ **Palace Café.** This down-home coffee shop on the town square, operated by the same family since 1927, serves steak, fried chicken, sandwiches, burgers, and seafood. Locals flock here for the homemade baklava. ✉ *167 W. Landry St.,* ☎ *318/942–2142. MC, V.*

St. Martinville

$$–$$$ **La Place d'Evangeline.** Rooms are spacious at this B&B on the banks of the Bayou Teche. The restaurant serves hearty portions of seafood and Cajun dishes; the homemade bread is superb. ✉ *220 Evangeline Blvd., 70582,* ☎ *318/394–4010. 5 rooms. Restaurant. Full breakfast. AE, MC, V.*

Nightlife and the Arts

Nightlife

CAJUN MUSIC

Mulate's in Breaux Bridge and **Prejean's** in Lafayette (☞ Dining and Lodging, *above*) and **Randol's** (✉ 2320 Kaliste Saloom Rd., Lafayette,

☎ 318/981–7080) regularly feature Cajun music and dancing. **Slim's Y-Ki-Ki** (✉ Rte. 167, Washington Rd., Opelousas, ☎ 318/942–9980), a rural club, is one of the best Cajun dance venues in the state. **Fred's Lounge** (✉ 420 6th St., Mamou, ☎ 318/468–5411) is a bar with live Saturday-morning radio broadcasts (8–1) and plenty of dancing. ***Rendez-Vous des Cajuns*** (✉ Liberty Theatre, Park Ave. at 2nd St., Eunice, ☎ 318/457–7389; 🎟 $3) is a live Saturday-night radio show, mostly in French, that's been described as a combination of the *Grand Ole Opry,* the *Louisiana Hayride,* and the *Prairie Home Companion.*

GAMBLING

In Lake Charles gamblers find action on the two riverboats at **Players Island Casino** (☎ 800/977–7529) and on the ***Isle of Capri*** riverboat casino (☎ 800/843–4753), with a slew of slots and gaming tables.

The Arts

CONCERTS

Major concert attractions are booked into Lafayette's **Cajundome** (✉ 444 Cajundome Blvd., ☎ 318/265–2100) and **Heymann Performing Arts & Convention Center** (✉ 1373 S. College Rd., ☎ 318/268–5540), as well as in Lake Charles at the **Civic Center** (✉ 900 Lakeshore Dr., ☎ 318/491–1256).

THEATER

The **Lake Charles Little Theater** (✉ 813 Enterprise Blvd., Lake Charles, ☎ 318/433–7988) puts on plays and musicals. The **Théâtre 'Cadien** (✉ Lafayette, ☎ 318/893–5655 or 318/262–5810) performs plays in French at various venues. **Lafayette Community Theater** (✉ 529 Jefferson St., ☎ 318/235–1532) offers contemporary plays with a Cajun flair.

Outdoor Activities and Sports

Biking

These flatlands and lush parks make for easy riding. Bikes can be rented at **Pack & Paddle** (✉ 601 E. Pinhook Rd., Lafayette, ☎ 318/232–5854).

Canoeing

Paddling is almost a breeze on the easygoing Whisky Chitto Creek. Canoes can be rented at **Arrowhead Canoe Rentals** (✉ 9 mi west of Oberlin on Rte. 26, ☎ 318/639–2086 or 800/637–2086).

Fishing

Trips to fish, sightsee, bird-watch, or hunt can be arranged at **Cajun Fishing Tours** (✉ 1925 E. Main St., New Iberia, ☎ 318/364–7141). **Sportsman's Paradise** (☎ 504/594–2414) is a charter-fishing facility 20 mi south of Houma. **Salt, Inc. Charter Fishing Service** (☎ 504/594–6626 or 504/594–7581), on Route 56 south of Houma at Coco Marina, offers fishing trips in the bays and barrier islands of lower Terrebonne Parish as well as into the Gulf of Mexico. **Hackberry Rod & Gun** (☎ 318/762–3391), in Cameron (in the far southwest corner of the state), is a charter saltwater-fishing service.

Golf

City Park Golf Course (✉ Mudd Ave. and 8th St., Lafayette, ☎ 318/268–5557), **Pine Shadows Golf Center** (✉ 750 Goodman Rd., Lake Charles, ☎ 318/433–8681), and **Vieux Chêne Golf Course** (✉ Youngsville Hwy., Broussard, ☎ 318/837–1159) all have 18 holes.

Hiking and Nature Trails

The Old Stagecoach Road in Lake Charles's **Sam Houston Jones State Park** is a favorite for hikers who want to explore the park and the various tributaries of the Calcasieu River; the **Louisiana State Arboretum** in Ville Platte is a 600-acre facility with 4 mi of nature trails; for both (☞ National and State Parks, *above*). There are 7 mi of hiking trails in the **Port Hudson State Commemorative Area,** near Baton Rouge (✉ 756 W. Plains–Port Hudson Rd. [Hwy. 61], Zachary, ☎ 504/654–3775).

Spectator Sports

Home games of the **Ice Gators,** of the East Coast Hockey League, as well as NBA exhibition and collegiate basketball, professional soccer exhibition games, wrestling, and other sports events take place at the **Cajundome** (✉ 444 Cajundome Blvd., Lafayette, ☎ 318/265–2100). **Thoroughbred racing:** April through Labor Day at **Evangeline Downs** (✉ I–10 at I–49, Lafayette, ☎ 318/896–7266).

Shopping

For Cajun food to go, try the **Cajun Country Store** (✉ 401 E. Cypress St., Lafayette, ☎ 318/233–7977) and **B. F. Trappey's & Sons** (✉ 900 E. Main St., New Iberia, ☎ 318/365–8281).

Antiques seeking is a favorite pastime here. In Lafayette you can root around **Ruins & Relics** (✉ 802 Jefferson, at Taft St., ☎ 318/233–9163) and **Solomon's Splendor Antique Mall** (✉ 731 Rue de Belier, ☎ 318/984–5776).

ELSEWHERE IN LOUISIANA

Natchitoches and North-Central Louisiana

Visitor Information

Natchitoches Parish Tourist Commission (✉ 781 Front St., Box 411, 71458, ☎ 318/352–8072).

Arriving and Departing

I–49 cuts diagonally from southeast to northwest, connecting Lafayette with Shreveport. Route 1 runs diagonally from the northwest corner all the way to Grand Isle on the Gulf of Mexico.

What to See and Do

Nestled in the piney hills of north-central Louisiana, **Natchitoches** (pronounced *nak*-a-tish) is the oldest permanent European settlement of the Louisiana Purchase, four years older than New Orleans. The town has a quaint 33-block Historic Landmark District, with brick-paved streets and buildings garbed in lacy ironwork. In the center of the downtown area is pretty Cane River Lake, edged with live oak trees and rolling green lawns. Natchitoches appeared in the film version of *Steel Magnolias.* You can take trolley tours of town and cruises on the water. Popular events include the **Christmas Festival of Lights,** which draws about 150,000 people annually, and the **October Pilgrimage,** when several historic houses are open for tours. Near Natchitoches backpackers and hikers explore the 8,700-acre **Kisatchie Hills Wilderness** with its Backbone Trail, part of the Kisatchie National Forest (☞ National and State Parks, *above*).

Route 494 follows the Cane River Lake southward from Natchitoches, bordered by arching trees and dotted with handsome plantation houses. Famed primitive artist Clementine Hunter lived and worked at **Melrose Plantation** (✉ Rte. 119, Melrose, ☎ 318/379–0055; 🎟 $5), where nine quaint buildings can be toured. Twenty miles south of
★ Natchitoches, the **Kate Chopin House** (✉ Rte. 495, Cloutierville, ☎ 318/379–2233; 🎟 $5) was home in the 19th century to Kate Chopin, author of *The Awakening.* It now houses the **Bayou Folk Museum.**

To the west of Natchitoches, 15 mi south of the town of Many, lies **Hodges Gardens** (✉ U.S. 171, ☎ 318/586–3523; 🎟 $10), 4,700 acres of rolling pine forests with streams, waterfalls, and multilevel formal botanical gardens, where flowers and shrubs bloom year-round. Just to the west is the huge **Toledo Bend Lake,** a camping, boating, and bass-fishing delight, which lies along the Texas border.

Dining and Lodging

NATCHITOCHES

$$–$$$ ✕ **The Landing.** This popular white-cloth bistro offers pasta, chicken, veal, and seafood dishes; the spicy country-fried steak is a specialty. *✉ 530 Front St., ☎ 318/352–1579. AE, MC, V.*

$$ ✕ **Lasyone's Meat Pie Kitchen.** Natchitoches meat pies are known throughout the state, and this casual little spot does them better than anybody. *✉ 622 2nd St., ☎ 318/352–3353. No credit cards.*

$$ 🏨 **Fleur-de-lis.** The town's oldest B&B is a fine turn-of-the-century house painted in rich Victorian colors of rose and blue. The hosts will make you feel right at home. *✉ 336 2nd St., 71457, ☎ 318/352–6621 or 800/489–6621. 5 rooms. Full breakfast. AE, MC, V.*

$$ 🏨 **Ryders Inn.** Comfortable and predictable rooms can be found in this former Holiday Inn. *✉ Hwy. 1 South Bypass, 71457, ☎ 318/357–8281 or 888/252–8281, FAX 318/352–9907. 145 rooms. Restaurant, lobby lounge, pool. AE, D, DC, MC, V.*

Shreveport and Northern Louisiana

Visitor Information

Shreveport-Bossier Convention & Tourist Bureau (✉ 629 Spring St., Shreveport 71166, ☎ 318/222–9391 or 800/551–8682, FAX 318/222–0056) There are four **visitor centers** (✉ Southpark Mall, Jewella Rd., Shreveport; ✉ 100 John Wesley Blvd., Bossier City; ✉ Pierre Bossier Mall, Airline Dr., Bossier City; and ✉ Mall St. Vincent, St. Vincent and Southern Aves., Shreveport, ☎ 318/227–9880).

Arriving and Departing

Shreveport Regional Airport is served by American Eagle, Continental Express, Delta, Northwest, TWA, and US Airways. I–20 and U.S. 80 run east–west through the northern part of the state; Route 1 cuts diagonally from the northwest corner to the Gulf of Mexico; I–49 connects Shreveport with southern Louisiana. Other north–south routes are U.S. 171, 71, 165, and 167.

What to See and Do

While southern Louisiana dances to Cajun tunes and dines on Creole and Cajun fare, most of northern Louisiana has more in common with Mississippi, Georgia, and other southern states; Shreveport's ties are largely to neighboring Texas. North of Alexandria the flat marshlands and gray earth give way to stands of pine trees and bluffs of rich, red clay. It is not for naught that Louisiana is known as Sportsman's Paradise. Both the northern and southern regions of the state are laced with rivers and lakes, with ample places for camping and fishing.

Shreveport and Bossier City, joined by the Red River, constitute the largest metropolitan area in northern Louisiana. A cultural center, **Shreveport** has a symphony orchestra, resident opera and ballet companies, and excellent community-theater productions. The prestigious ★ **R. W. Norton Art Gallery** (✉ 4747 Creswell Ave., ☎ 318/865–4201; 🎟 free) has superb European and American art, including the area's largest permanent collection of works by Frederic Remington and Charles M. Russell. The **Louisiana State Exhibit Museum** (✉ Fairgrounds, ☎ 318/632–2020; 🎟 $3) has extensive displays and dioramas depicting the state's history, including a large collection of Native American artifacts from Poverty Point and other important excavations in Louisiana. The **Ark-La-Tex Antique and Classic Vehicle Museum** (✉ 601 Spring St., ☎ 318/222–0227; 🎫 $4) traces automotive history in both classic and vintage models. The **Sci-Port Discovery Center** (✉ 528 Commerce St., ☎ 318/424–3466; 🎫 $4) is a hands-on interactive science museum, with exhibits for all ages as well as national traveling exhibitions. The **American Rose Center** (✉ Jefferson-Paige Rd., ☎ 318/938–5402; 🎫 $4), headquarters of the American Rose Society, is a 118-acre piney-woods park with more than 20,000 rosebushes in more than 60 individual gardens. The place lights up like a Christmas tree during the Christmas in Roseland show, which runs from the day after Thanksgiving through New Year's Eve.

In **Bossier City** the **Eighth Air Force Museum** (✉ Barksdale Air Force Base, ☎ 318/456–3067; 🎫 free) has World War II aircraft, dioramas, uniforms, and barracks of the Second Bomb Wing and the Eighth Air Force, which are headquartered at Barksdale Air Force Base. Four **riverboat casinos** float on the water here: *Harrah's Casino, Shreveport* (✉ Shreveport, ☎ 800/427–7247), *Isle of Capri Casino & Hotel* (✉ Bossier City, ☎ 318/678–7777 or 800/843–4753), the *Horseshoe Riverboat Casino & Hotel* (✉ Bossier City, ☎ 800/895–0711), and *Casino Magic* (✉ I–20, Exit 19B, ☎ 318/746–0711). **Louisiana Downs** (✉ I–20, Bossier City, ☎ 318/747–7223), one of the South's largest racetracks, has Thoroughbred racing April through October.

South of Shreveport, the **Mansfield Battle Park** (✉ Rte. 2, 4 mi south of Mansfield, ☎ 318/872–1474; 🎫 free) is the site of the last major Confederate victory of the Civil War. More than 30,000 men were involved in the bitter battle. The site contains monuments and an interpretive center with audiovisual displays.

Dining and Lodging

SHREVEPORT

$$$$ ✕ **Monsieur Patout.** An enchanting jewel box of a restaurant, this small, prix fixe, *très intime* restaurant serves classic French cuisine. ✉ *855 Pierremont Rd.,* ☎ *318/868–9822. Reservations essential. AE, D, DC, MC, V.*

$$–$$$ ✕ **Superior Bar & Grill.** Even with a reservation you may have to hang out in the bar to wait for a table, but the fine mesquite-grilled steaks and Mexican food are worth the wait. ✉ *6123 Line Ave.,* ☎ *318/869–3243. AE, D, MC, V.*

$$$–$$$$ 🏨 **Sheraton Pierremont Hotel.** In this luxury property near the convention center, every guest room has a wet bar, a refrigerator, three phones, and a modem line. ✉ *1419 E. 70th St., 71105,* ☎ *318/797–9900 or 800/321–4182,* FAX *318/798–2923. 270 rooms. Restaurant, pool, health club.*

$$ 🏨 **Holiday Inn/Downtown Riverfront.** The Holiday Inn is just two blocks from Harrah's riverboat casino. It has remote-control TVs and VCRs; movie rentals are available. ✉ *102 Lake St., 71101,* ☎ *318/222–7717 or 800/284–8209. 185 rooms. Restaurant, health club.*

MISSISSIPPI

Updated by Charlotte Durham

Capital	Jackson
Population	2,731,000
Motto	By Virtue and Arms
State Bird	Mockingbird
State Flower	Magnolia
Postal Abbreviation	MS

Statewide Visitor Information

Mississippi Division of Tourism Development (✉ Box 22825, Jackson 39205, ☎ 601/359–3297 or 800/927–6378).

Scenic Drives

The **Natchez Trace Parkway** cuts a 313-mi swath across Mississippi from northeast of Tupelo to Natchez in the southwest, passing through Jackson at the center of the state. **U.S. 90** runs along the Mississippi Sound from Alabama to Louisiana, offering views of Gulf Coast beaches, ancient live oaks, and historic homes. Along the Mississippi River, **U.S. 61**—also known as Blues Alley and the birthplace of that musical form—runs through flat Delta cotton land to the hills of Vicksburg, then through Natchez to Louisiana.

National and State Parks

National Parks

Gulf Islands National Seashore (☞ The Gulf Coast *in* Elsewhere in Mississippi, *below*) includes Ship, Horn, and Petit Bois islands and has nature trails and expeditions into the marsh. Vicksburg's **National Military Park** (☞ Vicksburg *in* Elsewhere in Mississippi, *below*) rivals Gettysburg in historic appeal and scenic beauty.

State Parks

Just north of Port Gibson is **Grand Gulf Military Monument** (☞ Exploring the Natchez Trace, *below*). **J. P. Coleman State Park** (✉ 13 mi north of Iuka off Rte. 25 ; Rte. 5, Box 504, Iuka 38852, ☎ 601/423–6515) includes scenic Pickwick Lake, which has cabins, camping, hiking, and swimming. **Tishomingo State Park** (✉ 15 mi south of Iuka and 3 mi north of Dennis off Rte. 25; Rte. 1, Box 880, Tishomingo 38873, ☎ 601/438–6914), which vies with J. P. Coleman for the title of most spectacular Mississippi park, lies in the Appalachian foothills, making its terrain unique in Mississippi. Bring your own provisions to enjoy hiking and water sports.

THE NATCHEZ TRACE

The Natchez Trace Parkway, a long, thin park running for almost 450 mi from Nashville to Natchez, crosses early paths worn by the Choctaw and Chickasaw, flatboatmen, outlaws, itinerant preachers, post riders, soldiers, and settlers. The parkway extends for more than 300 mi in Mississippi, with other sections in Alabama and Tennessee. Meticulously manicured by the National Park Service, it is unmarred by billboards, and commercial traffic is prohibited.

Visitor Information

Natchez–Adams County: Convention & Visitors Bureau (✉ 422 Main St., Natchez 39120, ☎ 601/446–6345 or 800/647–6724). **Natchez Trace Parkway:** Visitor Center (✉ 2680 Natchez Trace Pkwy., Tupelo 38801, ☎ 601/680–4025 or 800/305–7417). **Jackson:** Metro Jackson Convention and Visitors Bureau (✉ Box 1450, 39215, ☎ 601/960–1891 or 800/354–7695).

Arriving and Departing

By Car

The Natchez Trace is interrupted at Jackson; I–55, I–220, and I–20, which run through the city, connect the two segments. Natchez, at the southwestern end of the Natchez Trace Parkway, is also bisected by U.S. 61.

By Plane

Jackson's **International Airport** (☎ 601/939–5631), east of the city off I–20, 10 minutes from downtown, is served by American, Continental Express, Delta, Northwest Airlink, Southwest Airlines, and US Airways.

By Train

Amtrak (☎ 800/872–7245) stops in Jackson on its way south from Memphis to New Orleans.

Exploring the Natchez Trace

The Mississippi segment of the Natchez Trace begins near Tupelo, in the northeast corner of the state in a hilly area of dense forests and sparkling streams. Enjoy this natural beauty at **J. P. Coleman State Park** or at **Tishomingo State Park** (☞ National and State Parks, *above*).

Tupelo

Tupelo (named after the gum tree), the largest city in northern Mississippi, sits in scenic hill country. It's the site of the 1864 Civil War battle of the same name.

At post 266 in Tupelo is the **Natchez Trace Parkway Visitor Center** (☞ Visitor Information, *above*), offering exhibits and the *Official Map and Guide,* with detailed mile-by-mile information on places from Nashville to Natchez.

Tupelo is probably best-known for **Elvis Presley's birthplace** (✉ 306 Elvis Presley Dr., ☎ 601/841–1245; 🎟 $5); the singer was born in a tiny, two-room shotgun house on January 8, 1935. The surrounding **Elvis Presley Park** includes a museum, a gift shop, and the **Elvis Presley Memorial Chapel.**

From Tupelo to Jackson

The three-hour trip from Tupelo to Jackson can easily take an entire day if you stop to read the brown wooden markers describing historic sites, explore nature trails, and admire the neat fields, trees, and wildflower meadows along the way. At Ridgeland the **Mississippi Crafts Center** (✉ Trace Milepost 102.4, ☎ 601/856–7546) sells high-quality crafts in a dogtrot log cabin created by members of the Craftsman's Guild of Mississippi. Rest rooms and picnic tables are present.

Jackson

Jackson, the state capital, has an interesting downtown, with many small museums and most of the city's notable architecture. The **Jim Buck Ross Mississippi Agriculture and Forestry Museum** (✉ 1150 Lakeland Dr., ☎ 601/354–6113; 🎟 $4) includes 10 old Mississippi farm buildings, as well as a working farm and a 1920s crossroads town. The general

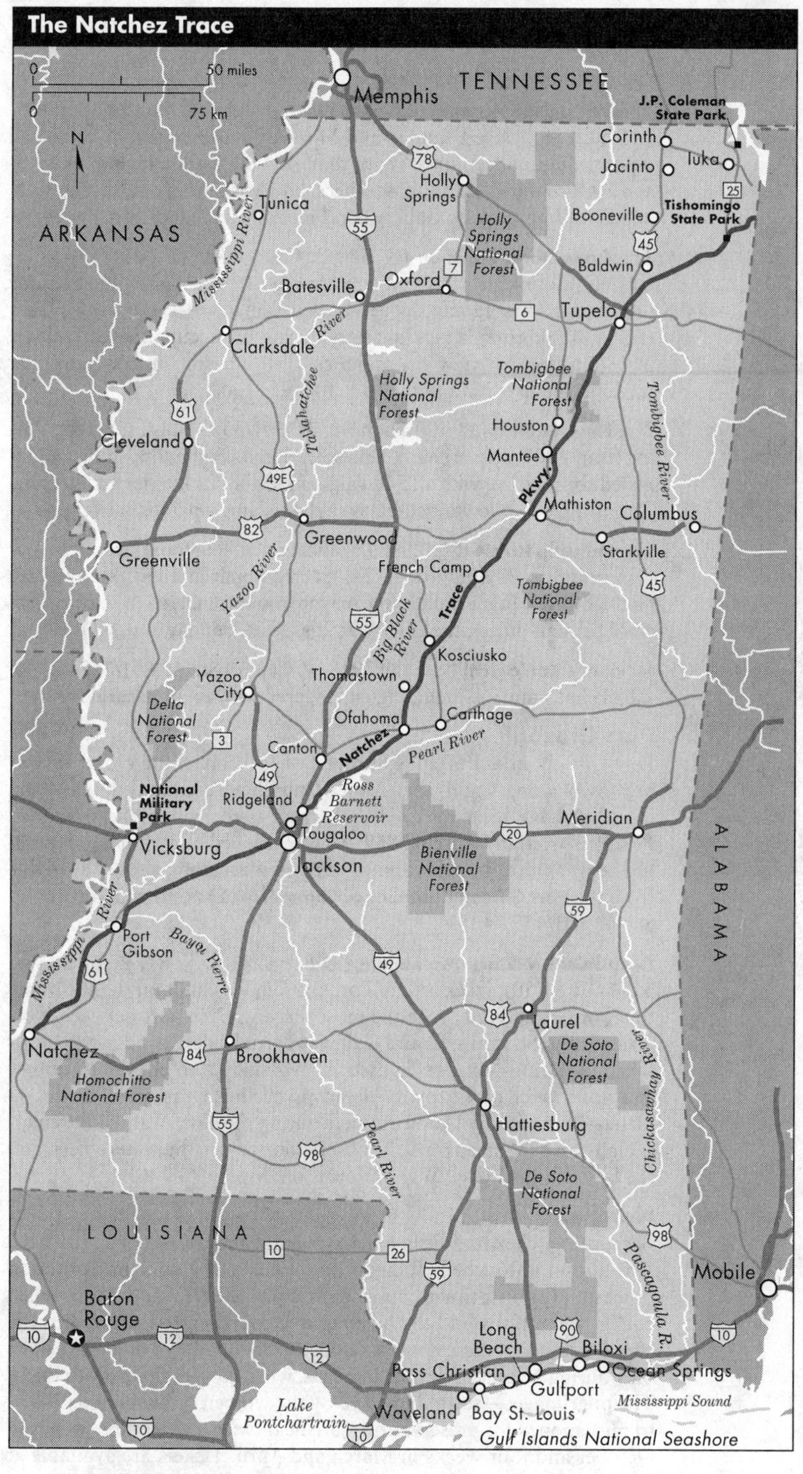
The Natchez Trace
0
50 miles
0
75 km
N
TENNESSEE
ARKANSAS
LOUISIANA
ALABAMA
Memphis
J.P. Coleman State Park
Corinth
Iuka
Jacinto
Holly Springs
Tunica
Booneville
Tishomingo State Park
Holly Springs National Forest
Baldwin
Batesville
Oxford
Tupelo
Mississippi River
Tallahatchee River
Clarksdale
Holly Springs National Forest
Tombigbee National Forest
Tombigbee River
Houston
Cleveland
Mantee
Pkwy.
Mathiston
Columbus
Greenwood
Greenville
Starkville
French Camp
Yazoo River
Tombigbee National Forest
Trace
Big Black River
Kosciusko
Thomastown
Yazoo City
Delta National Forest
Ofahoma
Carthage
Canton
Natchez
Pearl River
Ross Barnett Reservoir
National Military Park
Ridgeland
Meridian
Tougaloo
Vicksburg
Jackson
Bienville National Forest
Mississippi River
Port Gibson
Bayou Pierre
Laurel
Natchez
Brookhaven
De Soto National Forest
Chickasawhay River
Homochitto National Forest
Hattiesburg
Pearl River
De Soto National Forest
Pascagoula R.
Mobile
Baton Rouge
Long Beach
Biloxi
Pass Christian
Ocean Springs
Gulfport
Lake Pontchartrain
Waveland
Bay St. Louis
Mississippi Sound
Gulf Islands National Seashore
78
55
25
45
7
6
61
49E
82
45
55
3
49
20
59
49
61
84
84
55
98
98
10
26
59
90
10
10
12
12
10
10

store sells snacks and souvenirs; just outside the gates a shop sells Mississippi crafts, and a down-home restaurant serves blue-plate lunches (veggies, crisp fried catfish).

The **Mississippi Museum of Art** (✉ 201 E. Pascagoula St., ☎ 601/960–1515; 🎟 $3), closed Sunday and Monday, has changing exhibits and a permanent collection of more than 40,000 works, including 19th- and 20th-century American, southern, and Mississippi art. Its high-tech, hands-on Impressions Gallery combines art and education.

The **Governor's Mansion** (✉ 300 E. Capitol St., ☎ 601/359–3175; 🎟 free), closed Saturday through Monday, has been the official home of the state's first family since its completion in 1841. It was also General W. T. Sherman's headquarters during his occupation of Jackson in 1863. You can view the antiques-filled interior on free tours that leave on the half-hour between 9:30 and 11 AM.

The **New Capitol** (✉ 400 High St., ☎ 601/359–3114; 🎟 free), dating from 1903, sits in Beaux Arts splendor, its dome topped by a gold-plated copper eagle with a 15-ft wingspan. Elaborate interior architectural details include two stained-glass skylights and a painted ceiling.

The **Manship House** (✉ 420 E. Fortification St. [enter parking area from Congress St.], ☎ 601/961–4724; 🎟 free), built in 1857, is a restored Gothic Revival home built by the mayor who surrendered the city to General Sherman during the Civil War. It's closed Sunday and Monday.

Jackson's **Zoological Park** (✉ 2918 W. Capitol St., ☎ 601/352–2580; 🎟 $4) has animals, including endangered species, in natural settings.

Port Gibson

Port Gibson, about 60 mi southwest of Jackson, is the oldest surviving town along the Trace. Along **Church Street** many houses and churches have been restored; here, too, is the much-photographed **First Presbyterian Church** (1859), its spire topped by a 10-ft hand pointing heavenward. Information on the town's historic sites is available from the **Port Gibson Chamber of Commerce** (✉ South end of Church St., ☎ 601/437–4351).

Grand Gulf Military Monument (✉ Rte. 2 off U.S. 61, ☎ 601/437–5911; 🎟 $1.50), just north of Port Gibson, was built on the site of the town of Grand Gulf, once the most thriving river port between New Orleans and St. Louis. Grand Gulf was partially destroyed in the 1850s when capricious currents caused the Mississippi to change its course and flood much of the town. Already in decline, Grand Gulf was completely destroyed by Union gunners during the Civil War. Children especially love the steep trail, the observation tower, the waterwheel, and the bloodstained Civil War uniforms on display.

Natchez

Because Natchez had little military significance, it survived the Civil War almost untouched. Today it is famous for the opulent plantation homes and stylish town houses built between 1819 and 1860, when cotton plantations and the bustling river port poured riches into the city. A number of these houses are open year-round, but others are open only during Natchez Pilgrimage weeks, when crowds flock to see them. The pilgrimages—started in 1932 by the women of Natchez as a way to raise money for preservation—are held twice a year: three weeks in October and four weeks in March and April. Tickets are available at **Pilgrimage Tour Headquarters** (✉ 220 State St., 39121, ☎ 601/446–6631 or 800/647–6742; 🎟 four-house pass $20, pageants $10–$12), where all tours originate. **Carriage tours** of downtown Natchez begin at Pilgrimage Tour Headquarters.

★ **Rosalie** (✉ 100 Orleans St., ☎ 601/445–4555; $5), built in 1823, established the ideal form of the southern mansion, with its white columns, hipped roof, and red bricks. Furnishings purchased for the house in 1858 include a rare parlor set. A trip down south is not complete without a visit to the grand and gracious **Stanton Hall** (✉ 400 High St., ☎ 601/442–6282; $5), one of the most photographed houses in the country. Built around 1857 for cotton broker Frederick Stanton, the palatial former residence is now run as a house-museum by the Pilgrimage Garden Club.

Longwood (✉ 140 Lower Woodville Rd., ☎ 601/442–5193; $5) is the largest octagonal house in the United States. Construction began in 1860, but the outbreak of the Civil War prevented its completion; unfinished and mysterious, it will interest both adults and children.

Dining and Lodging

For price ranges *see* Charts 1 (B) and 2 (B) *in* On the Road with Fodor's.

Jackson

$$$–$$$$ ✕ **Nick's.** Large and elegant, this restaurant serves nouvelle versions of regional dishes. Lunch specialties are pasta salad and fish; for dinner another choice is beef tenderloin. ✉ *1501 Lakeland Dr.,* ☎ *601/981–8017. Jacket and tie required. AE, MC, V.*

$$–$$$ ✕ **The Mayflower.** A perfect 1930s period piece with black-and-white tile floors, booths, and Formica counters, this café specializes in Greek salads, fresh fish sautéed in lemon butter, and people-watching until all hours. ✉ *123 W. Capitol St.,* ☎ *601/355–4122. MC, V.*

$$–$$$ ✕ **Ralph & Kacoo's.** Here you'll dine on authentic hot-and-spicy Cajun food while listening to recorded music from southern Louisiana. The crawfish étouffée is superb. ✉ *100 Dyess Rd., just off I–55 and County Line Rd.,* ☎ *601/957–0702. AE, MC, V.*

$$ ✕ **The Palette.** A light-filled gallery in the Mississippi Museum of Art holds one of the state's finest lunch spots. Try the Wine Country pie, eight layers of meats, cheeses, and vegetables under a flaky crust. ✉ *201 E. Pascagoula St.,* ☎ *601/960–2003. MC, V. Closed Mon. No dinner.*

$$$$ **Millsaps-Buie House.** This 1888 Queen Anne Victorian, restored as a bed-and-breakfast in 1987, is listed on the National Register of Historic Places. Guest rooms are individually decorated with antiques, and the staff is attentive. ✉ *628 N. State St., 39202,* ☎ *601/352–0221 or 800/784–0221,* FAX *601/352–0221. 11 rooms. Full breakfast. AE, DC, MC, V.*

$$$ **Edison Walthall Hotel.** The cornerstone and huge brass mailbox are about all that remain of the original 1920s Walthall Hotel, but the marble floors and paneled library–cum–writing room almost fool you into thinking this is a restoration. The rooms have standard hotel decor, with some wicker furniture. ✉ *225 E. Capitol St., 39201,* ☎ *601/948–6161 or 800/932–6161,* FAX *601/948–0088. 208 rooms. Restaurant, pool. AE, DC, MC, V.*

$$$ **Jackson Hilton and Convention Center.** This high-rise convention hotel in the north end of town is sleekly contemporary. It reopened in August 1998 after a total renovation. ✉ *1001 County Line Rd., 39211,* ☎ *601/957–2800,* FAX *601/957–3191. 300 rooms. 2 restaurants, pool. AE, DC, MC, V.*

Natchez

$$–$$$ ✕ **Cock of the Walk.** The famous original of a regional franchise, this restaurant, in an old train depot overlooking the Mississippi River, specializes in fried catfish fillets, fried dill pickles, hush puppies, mustard greens, and coleslaw. ✉ *200 N. Broadway, on the Bluff,* ☎ *601/446–8920. AE, D, DC, MC, V.*

$$–$$$ ✕ **Natchez Landing.** The view of the Mississippi River from the porch tables is enthralling, especially when the *Delta Queen* and the *Mississippi Queen* steamboats dock. Specialties of the house include barbecue (pork ribs, chicken, and beef) and catfish, fried or grilled. ✉ *35 Silver St., Under-the-Hill,* ☎ *601/442–6639. AE, MC, V.*

$$–$$$ ✕ **Pearl Street Pasta.** The fresh pasta dishes at this intimate restaurant, including pasta primavera and breast of chicken with *tasso* (spiced ham), onions, and mushrooms over angel-hair pasta, suggest a taste of Italy in the Mississippi heartland. ✉ *105 S. Pearl St.,* ☎ *601/442–9284. AE, MC, V.*

$$$$ 🏨 **Dunleith.** At stately, colonnaded Dunleith a wing for overnight guests has rooms with antiques, fireplaces, and wonderful views of the landscaped grounds. Guests receive a complimentary tour of the house. ✉ *84 Homochitto St., 39120,* ☎ *601/446–8500 or 800/433–2445. 11 rooms. Full breakfast. AE, MC, V.*

$$$$ 🏨 **Monmouth.** This plantation mansion (circa 1818) was owned by Mississippi governor John A. Quitman from 1826 until his death in 1858. Guest rooms—in the main house, in servants' quarters, and in garden cottages—are furnished with tester beds and antiques. ✉ *36 Melrose Ave., 39120,* ☎ *601/442–5852 or 800/828–4531,* FAX *601/446–7762. 27 rooms. Full breakfast. AE, MC, V.*

$$ 🏨 **Ramada Hilltop Motel.** Remodeled in 1998, this motel sits on a bluff overlooking the Mississippi River to the north and Louisiana to the west. ✉ *130 John R. Junkin Dr., 39120,* ☎ *601/446–6311,* FAX *601/446–6321. 162 rooms. Restaurant, pool. AE, DC, MC, V.*

Tupelo

$$–$$$ ✕ **Harvey's.** A local favorite, Harvey's serves consistently good chow. Specialties are prime rib and pasta. ✉ *424 S. Gloster St.,* ☎ *601/842–6763. AE, MC, V. Closed Sun.*

$$–$$$ ✕ **Jefferson Place.** This rambling late-Victorian house is lively inside, with red-check tablecloths and bric-a-brac. It's popular with the college crowd and specializes in short orders and steaks. ✉ *823 Jefferson St.,* ☎ *601/844–8696. AE, MC, V. Closed Sun.*

$$–$$$ ✕ **Vanelli's.** Family pictures and scenes of Greece decorate this comfortably nondescript restaurant. Specialties (all homemade) include pizza with a choice of 10 toppings, lasagna, moussaka, and Greek salad. ✉ *1302 N. Gloster St.,* ☎ *601/844–4410. AE, D, DC, MC, V.*

$$ 🏨 **Ramada Inn.** This modern hotel caters to business travelers and conventioneers, as well as families. Breakfast and lunch buffets are served. ✉ *854 N. Gloster St., 38801,* ☎ FAX *601/844–4111. 232 rooms. Restaurant, pools. AE, DC, MC, V.*

$–$$ 🏨 **Trace Inn.** This old, rustic inn on 15 acres near the Natchez Trace offers neat rooms and friendly service. ✉ *3400 W. Main St., 38801,* ☎ *601/842–5555,* FAX *601/844–3105. 95 rooms. Restaurant, pool. AE, D, MC, V.*

Nightlife

Jackson

For live entertainment, from bluegrass to Celtic, try **Hal and Mal's** (✉ 200 S. Commerce St., ☎ 601/948–0888) on weekends. At the **Dock** (✉ Main Harbor Marina at Ross Barnett Reservoir, ☎ 601/856–7765), the mood is set by people who step off their boats to dine, drink, and listen to rock or rhythm and blues. **Stockyard Steaks** (✉ 6107 Ridgewood Rd., ☎ 601/957–9300) is a spot where patrons line up outside to line-dance inside.

Natchez

Under-the-Hill is a busy strip of restaurants, gift shops, and bars on the river. Gambling is offered at the permanently docked riverboat casino the ***Lady Luck*** (☎ 601/445–0605), and there's live music on weekends at **Under-the-Hill Saloon** (✉ 25 Silver St., ☎ 601/446–8023).

Shopping

In Jackson, **Everyday Gourmet** (✉ 2905 Old Canton Rd., ☎ 601/362–0723; ✉ 1625 E. County Line Rd., ☎ 601/977–9258) stocks state products including pecan pie, muscadine jelly, jams, cookbooks, fine ceramic tableware, and bread and biscuit mixes.

OXFORD AND HOLLY SPRINGS

Holly Springs and Oxford, in northern Mississippi, are sophisticated versions of the Mississippi small town. In these courthouse towns incorporated in 1837, you'll find historic architecture, arts and crafts, literary associations, and those unhurried pleasures of southern life that remain constant from generation to generation: entertaining conversation, good food, and nostalgic walks at twilight. Oxford and Lafayette counties were immortalized as "Jefferson County" and "Yoknapatawpha County" in the novels of Oxford native William Faulkner.

Visitor Information

Holly Springs: Chamber of Commerce (✉ 154 S. Memphis St., 38365, ☎ 601/252–2943). **Oxford:** Chamber of Commerce (✉ Jackson Ave., across from the fire station, Box 147, 38655, ☎ 601/234–4651).

Arriving and Departing

By Bus

Greyhound Lines has a station in Holly Springs (✉ 490 Craft St., ☎ 800/231–2222).

By Car

Oxford is accessible from I–55; it is 23 mi east of Batesville on Route 6. **Holly Springs,** near the Tennessee state line, is reached via U.S. 78 and Routes 4, 7, and 311.

By Train

Amtrak (☎ 800/872–7245) stops in Batesville.

Exploring Oxford and Holly Springs

Oxford

Even if you're not a Faulkner fan, this is a great place to experience small-town living. You won't be bored; the kinds of characters who fascinated Faulkner still live here, and the University of Mississippi keeps things lively. Oxford's **Courthouse Square** is a National Historic Landmark. At its center is the white-sandstone **Lafayette** (pronounced Luh-*fay*-it) **County Courthouse,** rebuilt in 1873 after Union troops burned it; the courtroom on the second floor is original. There's an information center at the nearby city hall.

University Avenue, from South Lamar Boulevard to the university, is one of the state's most beautiful sights when the trees flame orange and gold in the fall or when the dogwoods blossom in spring. The **University of Mississippi,** the state's beloved Ole Miss, opened in 1848. Its tree-shaded campus centers on the **Grove,** surrounded by historic buildings. Facing it is the beautifully restored antebellum **Barnard Observatory**

(☎ 601/232–5993; 🎫 free), which houses the **Center for the Study of Southern Culture,** with exhibits on southern music, folklore, and literature and the world's largest blues archive (40,000 records). The **Mississippi Room** (☎ 601/232–7408), in the John Davis Williams Library, contains a permanent exhibit on Faulkner, including the Nobel Prize for literature he won in 1949, as well as first editions of works by other Mississippi authors. The room is closed on weekends.

★ **Rowan Oak,** built in 1848, was William Faulkner's home from 1930 until his death in 1962. The two-story white-frame house with square columns is now a National Historic Landmark owned by the university. The writer's typewriter, desk, and other personal items still evoke his presence. ✉ *Old Taylor Rd.,* ☎ *601/234–3284.* 🎫 *Free.* 🕓 *Tues.–Sun.*

Faulkner's funeral was held at Rowan Oak, and he was buried in the family plot in **St. Peter's Cemetery** (✉ Jefferson and N. 16th Sts.; 🎫 free). Another Faulkner pilgrimage site is **College Hill Presbyterian Church** (✉ 8 mi northwest of Oxford on College Hill Rd., ☎ 601/234–5020; 🎫 free), where he and Estelle Oldham Franklin were married June 20, 1929.

Holly Springs

Holly Springs, 29 mi north of Oxford on Route 7, contains more than 200 structures (61 of which are antebellum homes) listed on the National Register of Historic Places. These include the 1858 **Montrose** (✉ 307 E. Salem Ave., ☎ 601/252–2943; 🎫 $5), open by appointment only, and the privately owned Salem Avenue mansions **Oakleigh, Cedarhurst,** and **Airliewood.**

Dining and Lodging

For price ranges *see* Charts 1 (B) and 2 (B) *in* On the Road with Fodor's.

Holly Springs

$ ✕ **City Cafe.** Breakfast and lunch specials pack them in at this meat-and-three eatery serving homemade soups, roast beef, and fried chicken livers. ✉ *135E Van Dorn Ave.,* ☎ *601/252–9895. No credit cards.*

$ ✕ **Phillips Grocery.** Constructed in 1882 as a saloon for railroad workers, it's decorated today with antiques and crafts and serves big, old-fashioned hamburgers. ✉ *541-A Van Dorn Ave.,* ☎ *601/252–4671. No credit cards. Closed Sun.*

$ 🏨 **Heritage Inn.** Rooms are comfortable if nondescript, with either a king-size bed or two doubles, and the lunch buffet has home-style southern cooking. The motel is on U.S. 78 where it meets Routes 7 and 4. ✉ *U.S. 78 (Box 476), 38635,* ☎ FAX *601/252–1120. 48 rooms. Restaurant, pool . AE, DC, MC, V.*

Oxford

$$–$$$ ✕ **Downtown Grill.** The Grill could be a club in Oxford, England, but the balcony overlooking the square is pure Oxford, Mississippi. Specialties include shrimp étouffée and Cajun-style spicy catfish Lafitte. ✉ *110 Courthouse Sq.,* ☎ *601/234–2659. AE, D, MC, V.*

$$ ✕ **Smitty's.** Look for home-style cooking here: red-eye gravy and grits, biscuits with blackberry preserves, fried catfish, chicken and dumplings, corn bread, and black-eyed peas. The atmosphere is down-home. ✉ *208 S. Lamar Blvd.,* ☎ *601/234–9111. No credit cards.*

$$ 🏨 **Holiday Inn.** These functional rooms are typical of the genre. The restaurant, however, prepares a surprisingly good breakfast and a noon buffet. ✉ *400 N. Lamar Blvd., 38655,* ☎ *601/234–3031,* FAX *601/234–2834. 123 rooms. Restaurant, pool. AE, DC, MC, V.*

$-$$ **Oliver-Britt House.** In a restored house built about 1900, this conveniently located B&B has pleasant rooms and is run in a casual fashion. ✉ *512 Van Buren Ave., 38655,* ☎ *601/234-8043. 5 rooms. Full breakfast weekends. AE, MC, V.*

Nightlife

In Oxford the **Gin** (✉ E. Harrison St. and S. 14th St., ☎ 601/234-0024) offers live dance music.

Shopping

At Oxford's well-stocked **Square Books** (✉ 160 Courthouse Sq., ☎ 601/236-2262), you can chat with the knowledgeable staff about local writers and savor cappuccino or dessert.

ELSEWHERE IN MISSISSIPPI

The Delta

Visitor Information

Mississippi Welcome Center (✉ 4210 Washington St., Vicksburg 39180, ☎ 601/638-4269). **Greenville/Washington County Convention and Visitors Bureau** (✉ 410 Washington Ave., Greenville 38701, ☎ 601/334-2711 or 800/467-3582).

Arriving and Departing

U.S. 61 runs from Memphis through the Delta to Vicksburg, Natchez, and Baton Rouge, Louisiana.

What to See and Do

Between Memphis and Vicksburg (☞ Vicksburg, *below*) is the **Delta,** a vast agricultural plain created by the Mississippi River. Drive through the Delta on U.S. 61, which will take you past **Tunica**'s gambling halls and their towering new hotels, or down Route 1 (the Great River Road) or Route 8 for good views of the Mississippi.

Stop for lunch in **Clarksdale,** where a renovated Carnegie Library houses a music museum. The exhibits and programs of the **Delta Blues Museum** (✉ 114 Delta Ave., ☎ 601/627-6820; free), closed Sunday, trace the history of the blues and its influence on other music.

The historic port city of **Greenville** has produced an extraordinary number of writers, including William Alexander Percy, Ellen Douglas, Hodding Carter, and Shelby Foote. The area was also home to the late Jim Henson, creator of Kermit the Frog. It's also noted as the home of Doe's (☞ Dining and Lodging, *below*).

Dining

CLARKSDALE

$-$$$ ✕ **Rest Haven.** The Delta's large Lebanese community influences the food, making Middle Eastern cuisine a regional specialty. Among the favorites are *kibbe* (seasoned lean ground steak with cracked wheat), spinach and meat pies, and cabbage rolls. Daily plate-lunch specials include chicken and dumplings. ✉ *419 State St. (U.S. 61),* ☎ *601/624-8601. No credit cards. Closed Sun.*

CLEVELAND

$$-$$$$ ✕ **KC's Restaurant.** The eclectic, sophisticated menu at this funky but fabulous restaurant changes every two weeks, but it always has French, Italian, Asian, and southwestern influences. Count on sampling wild game, fresh fish, free-range meats, and organic vegetables. ✉ *U.S. 61N at 1st St.,* ☎ *601/843-5301. AE, MC, V. No lunch Sat., no dinner Sun.*

GREENVILLE

$$–$$$$ ✕ **Doe's.** This tumbledown building is visually uninspiring. But when you see that huge steak hanging off your plate, you'll know why this place is famous. Hot tamales (a popular takeout item) are a specialty. ✉ *502 Nelson St.,* ☎ *601/334–3315. MC, V. No lunch.*

The Gulf Coast

Visitor Information

Mississippi Beach Convention and Visitors Bureau (✉ Box 6128, Gulfport 38506, ☎ 228/896–6699 or 800/237–9493). **Ocean Springs Chamber of Commerce** (✉ Box 187, 39566, ☎ 228/875–4424).

Arriving and Departing

U.S. 90 runs through the heart of Ocean Springs, Biloxi, and Gulfport.

What to See and Do

Oak-shaded **Ocean Springs** originated in 1699 as a French fort. It is now known as the former home of artist Walter Anderson. The **Walter Anderson Museum of Art** (✉ 510 Washington Ave., ☎ 228/872–3164; 🎟 $4) displays Anderson's work, including his cottage studio with intricately painted walls. The artist (1903–65) revealed his ecstatic communion with nature in thousands of drawings and watercolors, most kept secret until his death.

★ Ocean Springs is the headquarters of the **Gulf Islands National Seashore** (✉ 3500 Park Rd., Ocean Springs 39564, ☎ 228/875–9057). On the mainland there are nature trails and ranger programs. Out in the Gulf, pristine Ship, Horn, and Petit Bois islands, for which the park is named, have beaches as white and soft as sugar—some of the country's best. Excursion boats to Ship, rimmed by about 7 mi of this remarkable sand, leave from Biloxi in summer and from Gulfport from May through October. Charter operators regularly take wilderness-lovers to Horn and Petit Bois, both nationally designated wilderness areas, where camping is permitted.

A string of casino openings has turned **Biloxi** and its quiet beach into a mini–Las Vegas. Along with the neon lights and traffic jams have come big-name entertainment and more dining choices. In **Gulfport,** two casinos share the waterfront with the shrimp boats and banana warehouses vital to the area's economy.

Dining and Lodging

BILOXI

$$$–$$$$ 🏨 **Treasure Bay.** Formerly the Royal D'Iberville, this hotel has spacious rooms brightened with chintz, along with a casino. Furniture is hotel-functional; the large public areas are comfortably contemporary. ✉ *1980 W. Beach Blvd., 39530,* ☎ *228/385–6000 or 800/747–2839. 268 rooms. Restaurant, pools. AE, D, DC, MC, V.*

$$ 🏨 **President Casino Broadwater Resort.** This sprawling property comes complete with an 18-hole golf course, 10 tennis courts, a casino, and a marina, from which charter boats can be rented. Many rooms were renovated in 1998, and rates vary according to room size and location. ✉ *2110 Beach Blvd., 39533,* ☎ *228/388–2211 or 800/647–3964,* FAX *228/385–1801. 520 rooms. 4 restaurants, pools, 10 tennis courts, exercise room. AE, D, DC, MC, V.*

GULFPORT

$$$ ✕ **Vrazel's.** Dining nooks with windows facing the beach add charm here. Special attractions include the red snapper, Gulf trout, flounder, and shrimp prepared every which way. ✉ *3206 W. Beach Blvd. (U.S. 90),* ☎ *228/863–2229. AE, D, DC, MC, V. Closed Sun. No lunch Sat.*

OCEAN SPRINGS

$$$–$$$$ ✕ **Germaine's.** Formerly Trilby's, this little house surrounded by live oaks has served many a great meal to its faithful clientele. The atmosphere is reminiscent of New Orleans, with unadorned wooden floors, fireplaces, and attentive service. Specialties include crabmeat au gratin, broiled trout served with mushrooms and sautéed crabmeat, and sautéed veal in a creamy port sauce. ✉ *1203 Bienville Blvd. (U.S. 90E),* ☎ *228/875–4426. AE, DC, MC, V. Closed Mon. No dinner Sun.*

$$–$$$ ★ ✕ **Jocelyn's Restaurant.** The coast seafood served in this old frame house is as good as it gets. Crab, trout, flounder, and, when available, snapper are subtly seasoned and presented with garnishes as bright and original as modern art. ✉ *U.S. 90E, opposite Sunburst Bank,* ☎ *228/875–1925. Reservations not accepted. No credit cards.*

Vicksburg

Visitor Information

Vicksburg Convention and Visitors Bureau (✉ Box 110, Vicksburg 39181, ☎ 601/636–9421 or 800/221–3536).

Arriving and Departing

I–20 runs east–west and U.S. 61 north–south through Vicksburg.

What to See and Do

During the Civil War the Confederacy and the Union vied for control of this strategic location on the Mississippi Delta across the river from Louisiana. After a 47-day siege the city surrendered to Ulysses S. Grant on July 4, 1863, giving the Union control of the river and sounding the death knell for the Confederacy. Vicksburg's **National Military Park** (✉ Visitor Center, 3201 Clay St. [U.S. 80], I–20 Exit 4B, Vicksburg 39180, ☎ 601/636–0583) details the events of these turbulent times. Battle positions are marked, and monuments line the 16-mi drive through the park.Tours of grand antebellum homes and 24-hour riverfront gambling are other draws.

Dining and Lodging

$ ✕ **Walnut Hills.** If you're yearning for authentic regional cooking, this restaurant is a must. Diners eat round-table style, sampling two or three meats, seven vegetables, and desserts such as blackberry cobbler. Don't pass up the outstanding fried chicken, fresh snap beans, or purple-hull peas. ✉ *1214 Adams St.,* ☎ *601/638–4910. AE, DC, MC, V. Closed Sat. No dinner Sun.*

$$$–$$$$ ★ 🏨 **Cedar Grove.** This 1840s mansion and its grounds cover a full city block. The entire house is furnished with period antiques. You can hear nearby river traffic from the quiet, gaslighted grounds or survey the scene from the rooftop garden. A house tour and hearty breakfast are included. Croquet and bicycles are available. ✉ *2200 Oak St., 39180,* ☎ *601/636–1000 or 800/862–1300,* FAX *601/634–6126. 29 rooms. Restaurant, pool, tennis. Full breakfast. AE, D, DC, MC, V.*

$$$–$$$$ ★ 🏨 **Duff Green Mansion.** This 1856 mansion was used as a hospital during the Civil War. Each guest room is decorated with antiques, including half-tester beds. A large southern breakfast and a tour of the home are included. ✉ *1114 1st East St., 39180,* ☎ *601/636–6968 or 800/992–0037. 7 rooms, 2 suites. Pool. Full breakfast. AE, MC, V.*

TENNESSEE

Updated by Charlotte Durham

Capital	Nashville
Population	5,368,000
Motto	Agriculture and Commerce
State Bird	Mockingbird
State Flower	Iris
Postal Abbreviation	TN

Statewide Visitor Information

Tennessee Department of Tourist Development (✉ Box 23170, Nashville 37202, ☎ 615/741–2158).

Scenic Drives

U.S. 421 from Bristol to Trade passes through the Cherokee National Forest and crosses the Appalachian Trail. **Route 73** south from Townsend leads through a high valley ringed by the Great Smoky Mountains to the pioneer village of Cades Cove in Great Smoky Mountains National Park. **Route 25** from Gallatin to Springfield travels through an area of Thoroughbred farms and antebellum houses. Between Monteagle and Chattanooga **I–24** winds through the Cumberland Mountains.

National and State Parks

National Parks

Great Smoky Mountains National Park (✉ Gatlinburg 37738, ☎ 423/436–1200) encompasses tall peaks and lush valleys, with camping and fishing sites and more than 900 mi of horse and hiking trails.

State Parks

The State Parks Division of the **Tennessee Department of Environment and Conservation** (✉ 401 Church St., L&C Tower, 7th floor, Nashville 37243, ☎ 615/532–0001 or 800/421–6683) provides information on Tennessee's 50-plus state parks. The 16,000-acre **Fall Creek Falls State Resort Park** (✉ Rte. 3, Pikeville 37367, ☎ 423/881–5241 or 423/881–3297) has the highest waterfall east of the Rockies. Thick stands of cypress trees make **Reelfoot Lake State Resort Park** (✉ Rte. 1, Box 296, Tiptonville 38079, ☎ 901/253–7756), in northwestern Tennessee, a favorite wintering ground for the American bald eagle. **Roan Mountain State Resort Park** (✉ Rte. 1, Box 236, Roan Mountain 37687, ☎ 423/772–3303), in northeastern Tennessee, has a 600-acre natural rhododendron garden that blooms in late June.

MEMPHIS

On the bluffs overlooking the Mississippi River, Memphis is Tennessee's largest city and the commercial and cultural center of the western part of the state. It is a blend of southern tradition and modern efficiency, where aging cotton warehouses stand near sleek new office buildings and old-fashioned paddle wheelers steam upriver past the city's newest landmark, the gleaming stainless-steel Pyramid Arena. Memphis is perhaps best known for its music and for the two extraordinary men who introduced that music to the world: W. C. Handy, the Father of the Blues, and Elvis Presley, the King of Rock and Roll.

Visitor Information

Convention & Visitors Bureau (✉ 47 Union Ave., 38103, ☎ 901/543–5300). **Tennessee Welcome Center** (✉ 119 N. Riverside Dr., ☎ 901/543–5333).

Arriving and Departing

By Boat

Memphis is one stop on the paddle-wheeler cruises of the **Delta Queen Steamboat Co.** (✉ Robin Street Wharf, New Orleans, LA 70130, ☎ 800/543–1949). The *Delta Queen,* the *Mississippi Queen,* and the *American Queen* travel between St. Louis and New Orleans.

By Bus

Greyhound Lines (✉ 203 Union Ave., ☎ 800/231–2222).

By Car

Memphis is reached via the north–south I–55 or the east–west I–40. I–240 loops around the city.

By Plane

Memphis International Airport (☎ 901/922–8000), 9 mi southeast of downtown, is served by most major airlines and is a hub for Northwest Airlines. Driving time to downtown is about 15 minutes on I–240. Cab fare (**Yellow Cab** ☎ 901/577–7700) runs about $20 plus tip.

By Train

Amtrak (✉ 545 S. Main St., ☎ 800/872–7245).

Getting Around Memphis

Memphis's streets are well marked, and there's plenty of parking, so the city is best explored by car. The **Memphis Area Transit Authority** (☎ 901/274–6282) operates buses ($1.10) throughout downtown and the suburbs (additional fare for zones outside the city limits); a trolley (50¢) runs a 5-mi route linking the north and south ends of downtown via a riverfront loop.

Exploring Memphis

Downtown

Memphis begins at the Mississippi River, which is celebrated in a 52-acre river park (☎ 901/576–6595; 🎫 $8) on **Mud Island.** A footbridge and monorail at 125 Front Street get you to the island, where a five-block River Walk replicates the Mississippi's every twist, turn, and sandbar from Cairo, Illinois, to New Orleans. Also in the park are the Mississippi River Museum, the famed World War II B-17 bomber *Memphis Belle,* an amphitheater, shops, and a pool.

The 32-story, 22,000-seat stainless-steel **Pyramid Arena** (✉ 1 Auction Ave., ☎ 901/521–9675; 🎫 tours $4), opposite the north end of Mud Island, opened in 1991. **Magevney House,** built in the 1830s by a pioneer schoolteacher, is Memphis's oldest dwelling. It's a 20-minute walk from the Pyramid Arena. ✉ *198 Adams Ave.,* ☎ *901/526–4464.* 🎫 *Free. Closed Mon.*

The beautifully restored **Peabody Hotel** stands at the corner of Union Avenue and 2nd Street. **Beale Street** is where W. C. Handy played the blues in the early decades of the 20th century and where clubs and restaurants are thriving again. The **W. C. Handy Memphis Home and Museum** recalls the influential blues musician through a variety of memorabilia. ✉ *352 Beale St.,* ☎ *901/522–1556.* 🎫 *$2.*

Memphis

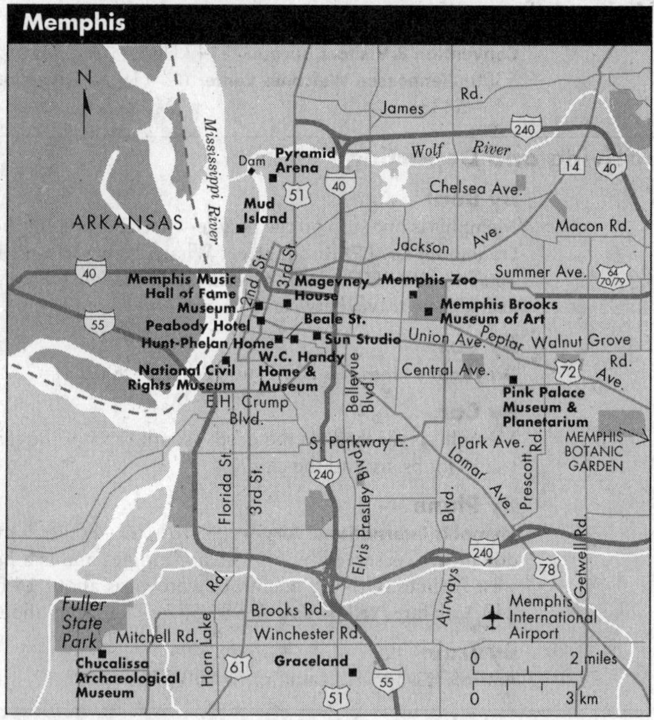

The **Hunt-Phelan Home,** with costumed docents, transports visitors to the mid-1800s. Ulysses S. Grant and Jefferson Davis were among the home's historic visitors (at different times, of course). ✉ *533 Beale St.,* ☎ *901/344–3166 or 800/350–9009.* 🎫 *$10.*

Exhibits in the **Memphis Music Hall of Fame Museum**—rare photographs, film footage, audiotapes, and memorabilia—trace the development of blues, country, and rock and roll, as well as the city's role in it all. ✉ *97 S. 2nd St.,* ☎ *901/525–4007.* 🎫 *$7.50.*

Sun Studio (✉ 706 Union Ave., ☎ 901/521–0664, 🎫 $8.50), the birthplace of rock and roll, is where Elvis Presley, Jerry Lee Lewis, B. B. King, and Roy Orbison launched their careers. Tours are given daily; the studio is seven blocks east of downtown.

South of downtown, the motel where Dr. Martin Luther King Jr., was assassinated in 1968 has been transformed into the **National Civil Rights Museum,** an outstanding facility which documents the movement through exhibits and clever audiovisual displays. ✉ *406 Mulberry St.,* ☎ *901/521–9699,* 🎫 *$6, free Mon. 3–5. Closed Tues.*

Other Attractions

★ **Graceland,** the estate once owned by Elvis Presley, is 12 mi south of downtown. A guided tour of the mansion, automobile museum, and burial site reveals the spoils of stardom. ✉ *3717 Elvis Presley Blvd.,* ☎ *901/332–3322 or 800/238–2000.* 🎫 *Mansion only $10, all attractions $18.50. Reservations essential. Closed Tues. Nov.–Feb.*

The **Memphis Brooks Museum of Art,** east of downtown in Overton Park, houses a collection of fine and decorative arts from antiquity to the present. ✉ *2080 Poplar Ave.,* ☎ *901/722–3500.* 🎫 *$5. Closed Mon.*

At the **Children's Museum of Memphis** (✉ 2525 Central Ave., ☎ 901/458–2678; 🎫 $5) youngsters can touch, climb, and explore their way through a child-size city. The **Memphis Pink Palace Museum and Planetarium** (✉ 3050 Central Ave., ☎ 901/320–6320; 🎫 museum $6, planetarium $3.50) has a mix of natural history and cultural history exhibits plus planetarium laser shows and an IMAX theater. **Chucalissa Archaeological Museum** (✉ 1987 Indian Village Dr., ☎ 901/785–3160; 🎫 $2) is a reconstruction of a Native American village that existed from AD 1000 to AD 1500. Skilled Choctaw craftspeople fashion jewelry, weapons, and pottery outside the **C. H. Nash Museum,** which houses historic originals of the same articles.

Parks, Gardens, and Zoos

Overton Park, a few miles east of downtown on Poplar Avenue, offers picnic areas, sports fields, hiking and biking trails, a nine-hole golf course, an art museum (☞ Other Attractions, *above*), and the popular 70-acre **Memphis Zoo** (✉ 2000 Galloway Ave., ☎ 901/725–3400; 🎫 $7), which includes 9-acre Cat Country and Primate Canyon. In East Memphis the 96-acre **Memphis Botanic Garden** (✉ 750 Cherry Rd., ☎ 901/685–1566; 🎫 $2) has scores of species, from camellias to cacti.

Dining

Although Memphis restaurants have a pleasing array of cuisines, the local passion remains barbecue; the city has 70-odd barbecue restaurants. For price ranges *see* Chart 1 (A) *in* On the Road with Fodor's.

$$$–$$$$ ★ ✕ **Chez Philippe.** Chef José Gutierrez serves sophisticated dishes in ornate surroundings. Nightly creations may include beef tenderloin, roasted wild boar, or Chilean snapper with Portobello mushrooms on a horseradish reduction. ✉ *Peabody Hotel, 149 Union Ave.,* ☎ *901/529–4188. Jacket required. AE, DC, MC, V. Closed Sun. No lunch.*

$$$–$$$$ ✕ **Erling Jensen.** Jensen earned a loyal following as the chef at La Tourelle but opened his eponymous restaurant in 1996. The Dane's cuisine is global; most noteworthy is his rack of lamb. ✉ *1004 S. Yates Rd.,* ☎ *901/763–3700. Reservations essential. AE, D, DC, MC, V. No lunch.*

$$–$$$$ ✕ **Landry's Seafood House.** A converted riverfront warehouse, this place packs 'em in for such seafood dishes as fried shrimp and stuffed flounder. ✉ *263 Wagner Pl.,* ☎ *901/526–1966. AE, DC, MC, V.*

$$–$$$$ ✕ **La Tourelle.** This turn-of-the-century bungalow in Overton Square has the romantic ambience of a French country inn. Five-course prix-fixe meals with an emphasis on fresh seafood supplement the à la carte menu. Men will feel most comfortable in a jacket and tie. ✉ *2146 Monroe Ave.,* ☎ *901/726–5771. MC, V.*

$$$ ✕ **Raji.** Chef Raji Jallepalli blends nouvelle styles and Indian seasonings in subtle fusion dishes. She serves a prix fixe four-course meal at 7 PM and occasional special theme dinners. ✉ *712 W. Brookhaven Circle,* ☎ *901/685–8723. Reservations essential. AE, MC, V. Closed Sun.–Mon. No lunch.*

$$–$$$ ✕ **Cafe Max.** The atmosphere is lively at this bistro in East Memphis, where selections include pasta, seafood, and grilled meats. ✉ *6161 Poplar Ave.,* ☎ *901/767–3633. AE, D, MC, V. No lunch.*

$$–$$$ ★ ✕ **Paulette's.** This Overton Square classic serves delicious crepes and salads and excellent grilled chicken, salmon, and swordfish in the atmosphere of a European inn. Save room for the hot chocolate crepes. ✉ *2110 Madison Ave.,* ☎ *901/726–5128. AE, D, DC, MC, V.*

$–$$ ✕ **Cafe Olé.** This popular midtown hangout offers a healthy version of Mexican cuisine (no animal fats are used), including spinach enchiladas and chili *rellenos* (cheese-stuffed fried green chilies). ✉ *959 S. Cooper St.,* ☎ *901/274–1504. AE, D, DC, MC, V.*

$–$$ ✕ **Charlie Vergos' Rendezvous.** Tourists and locals alike flock to this downtown basement restaurant to savor Vergos's "dry" barbecued pork ribs and other barbecue specialties. ✉ *52 S. 2nd St.,* ☎ *901/523–2746. AE, DC, MC, V. Closed Sun.–Mon. No lunch Tues.–Thurs.*

$–$$ ★ ✕ **Corky's.** There's always a line at this no-frills East Memphis barbecue restaurant. Once you taste the ribs (or sandwiches, or beef or pork platters), you'll understand why. ✉ *5259 Poplar Ave.,* ☎ *901/685–9744. AE, D, DC, MC, V.*

$ ✕ **The Cupboard.** Owner Charles Cavallo knows fresh produce, and his cooks turn out masterful "meat-and-three" plates. Lucky is the soul who visits when both macaroni and cheese and fried green tomatoes are offered. ✉ *1495 Union Ave.,* ☎ *901/276–8015. MC, V.*

Lodging

Memphis hotels are especially busy during the monthlong Memphis-in-May International Festival and in mid-August, during Elvis Tribute Week; book well ahead at these times. For bed-and-breakfasts contact the **Bed & Breakfast Reservation Service** (✉ Box 41621, Memphis 38174, ☎ 901/327–6129 or 800/336–2087, FAX 901/725–0194). For price ranges *see* Chart 2 (A) *in* On the Road with Fodor's.

$$$–$$$$ 🏨 **Adam's Mark Memphis.** Set in the flourishing eastern suburbs near I–240, this 27-story glass tower has views of the sprawling metropolis and its outskirts. ✉ *939 Ridge Lake Blvd., 38120,* ☎ *901/684–6664 or 800/444–2326,* FAX *901/762–7411. 408 rooms. Restaurant, pool, health club. AE, D, DC, MC, V.*

$$$–$$$$ ★ 🏨 **Peabody Hotel.** Even if you're not staying here, it's worth a stop to see this 12-story downtown landmark, built in 1925. The lobby preserves its original stained-glass skylights and the travertine-marble fountain that is home to the hotel's resident ducks. The rooms are decorated in a variety of period styles. ✉ *149 Union Ave., 38103,* ☎ *901/529–4000 or 800/732–2639,* FAX *901/529–3600. 468 rooms. 4 restaurants, indoor pool, health club. AE, DC, MC, V.*

$$–$$$ 🏨 **French Quarter Suites.** This pleasant Overton Square hotel is reminiscent of a New Orleans–style inn. All suites have oversize whirlpool tubs, and some have balconies. ✉ *2144 Madison Ave., 38104,* ☎ *901/728–4000 or 800/843–0353,* FAX *901/278–1262. 105 suites. Restaurant, pool, health club. AE, D, DC, MC, V.*

$$ 🏨 **Country Suites by Carlson.** This three-story hotel in East Memphis provides many of the comforts of home, such as kitchenettes. The decor includes teal carpeting and Aztec-pattern draperies. ✉ *4300 American Way, 38118,* ☎ *901/366–9333 or 800/456–4000,* FAX *901/366–7835. 120 suites. Pool, health club. CP. AE, D, DC, MC, V.*

$$ ★ 🏨 **Holiday Inn East.** Close to I–240 and the bustling Poplar/Ridgeway office complex, this sleek 10-story hotel is popular with business travelers. ✉ *5795 Poplar Ave., 38119,* ☎ *901/682–7881 or 800/465–4329,* FAX *901/682–7881, ext. 7760. 246 rooms. Restaurant, pool, health club. AE, D, DC, MC, V.*

$$ 🏨 **Radisson Hotel.** Across the street from the Peabody, this downtown hotel has its own lobby fountain and waterfall. Glass-walled elevators whisk guests to rooms around a 10-story atrium. ✉ *185 Union Ave., 38103,* ☎ *901/528–1800,* FAX *901/526–3226. 283 rooms. Restaurant, pool. AE, D, DC, MC, V.*

$–$$ 🏨 **Howard Johnson Lodge East.** All units have private patios or balconies; many have refrigerators and microwave ovens, and four have kitchens. There's also a coin laundry on site. ✉ *1541 Sycamore View, 38134,* ☎ *901/388–1300,* FAX *901/388–1300, ext. 247. 96 rooms. Pool. CP. AE, D, DC, MC, V.*

$–$$ **La Quinta Inn–Medical Center.** Convenient to midtown, this two-story inn has spacious, well-maintained rooms. ✉ *42 S. Camilla St., 38104,* ☎ *901/526–1050,* FAX *901/525–3219. 130 rooms. Pool. CP. AE, D, DC, MC, V.*

$ **Executive Inn.** This four-story motor lodge near Graceland has spacious, well-appointed rooms with tasteful touches of country decor. ✉ *3222 Airways Blvd., 38116,* ☎ *901/332–3800 or 800/221–2222,* FAX *901/345–2448. 118 rooms. Pool, exercise room. CP. DC, MC, V.*

Nightlife and the Arts

Call the Memphis **events hot line** (☎ 901/753–5847) for information about performances in the city.

Nightlife

To hear the blues as they were meant to be played, head for the clubs on Beale Street. Among the most popular clubs is **B. B. King's Blues Club** (✉ 147 Beale St., ☎ 901/524–5464), where B. B. himself occasionally performs. **Blues Hall/Rum Boogie Cafe** (✉ 182 Beale St., ☎ 901/528–0150) is also a good spot for the blues.

The Arts

The **Orpheum Theatre** (✉ 203 S. Main St., ☎ 901/525–3000) hosts touring Broadway shows, as well as performances by Opera Memphis (☎ 901/678–2706) and Ballet Memphis (☎ 901/763–0139). The **Memphis Symphony Orchestra** (☎ 901/324–3627) performs at various locations from September through May.

Spectator Sports

Baseball: The **Memphis Redbirds,** the St. Louis Cardinals AAA farm team, plays at Tim McCarver Stadium (✉ 800 Home Run La., ☎ 901/721–6050), while AutoZone Park, a new stadium downtown at Third and Madison, is under construction. Completion is targeted for the 1999 season.

Golf: Southwind Tournament Players Club (✉ 3325 Club Rd., at Southwind, ☎ 901/748–0534) hosts the **St. Jude Federal Express Golf Tournament** each summer, drawing the PGA tour's top pros. **Tennis:** The **International Indoor Tennis Tournament** (☎ 901/765–4400) is played in February at the Racquet Club (✉ 5111 Sanderlin Ave., East Memphis).

Shopping

The **Main Street Mall,** on Main Street between Beale and Poplar, is one of the nation's longest pedestrian-and-trolley malls. **Oak Court Mall** (✉ 4465 Poplar Ave., ☎ 901/682–8928), in the busy Poplar/Perkins area of East Memphis, has 70 specialty stores and two department stores. **Overton Square** (✉ 24 S. Cooper St., ☎ 901/278–6300)—a three-block midtown shopping, restaurant, and entertainment complex in vintage buildings and newer structures—has upscale boutiques and specialty shops. **Wolfchase Galleria** (✉ 2760 N. Germantown Pkwy., at U.S. 64, about 18 mi east of downtown Memphis, ☎ 901/381–2769), the county's newest and largest mall, opened in 1997. **Belz Factory Outlet Mall** (✉ 3536 Canada Rd., Exit 20 off I–40, 20 mi east of downtown Memphis, Lakeland, ☎ 901/386–3180) includes 50 stores, from Bugle Boy to Van Heusen.

NASHVILLE

Hailed as Music City, U.S.A. (country music, that is), and the birthplace of the Nashville Sound, Tennessee's capital city is also a leading center of higher education, appropriately known as the Athens of the South. The city has spawned such dissimilar institutions as the Grand Ole Opry and Vanderbilt University and has prospered from them both, becoming one of the mid-South's most vibrant communities.

Visitor Information

Nashville Convention & Visitors Bureau (✉ 161 4th Ave. N, 37219, ☎ 615/259–4700). **Visitor information center** (✉ 501 Broadway, 37219, ☎ 615/259–4747).

Arriving and Departing

By Bus

Greyhound Lines (✉ 200 8th Ave. S, ☎ 800/231–2222).

By Car

I–65 leads into Nashville from the north and south; I–24, from the northwest and southeast; I–40, from the east and west. I–440 loops around the city.

By Plane

Nashville International Airport (☎ 615/275–1675), about 8 mi east of downtown, is served by major airlines. To reach downtown by car, take I–40 west. Cab fare runs about $16–$18 plus tip. **Downtown Airport Express** (☎ 615/275–1180) has service to downtown hotels for $9.

Getting Around Nashville

The central city is bisected by the Cumberland River; numbered avenues are west of and parallel to it, and numbered streets east of and parallel to it.

By Bus

Metropolitan Transit Authority (MTA) buses (☎ 615/862–5950) serve the county; fare is $1.35 in exact change.

By Trolley

Nashville Trolley Company (☎ 615/862–5969) trolleys cover downtown and Music Row in summer months; the fare is 90¢.

Exploring Nashville

Downtown

Downtown attractions can be covered rather easily on foot. Overlooking the river is **Fort Nashborough** (✉ 170 1st Ave. N; 🎟 free), a replica of the crude log fort built in 1779 by Nashville's first settlers. In the **District,** the historic 2nd Avenue area south of Church Street, 19th-century buildings have been handsomely restored to house restaurants, clubs, boutiques, offices, and residences.

The **Downtown Presbyterian Church** (✉ 5th Ave. and Church St., ☎ 615/254–7584; 🎟 free), an Egyptian Revival tabernacle (circa 1851), was designed by noted Philadelphia architect William Strickland. **Ryman Auditorium and Museum** (✉ 116 5th Ave. N, ☎ 615/254–1445, 615/889–6611 for tickets to events; 🎟 tours $5.50), the home of the Grand Ole Opry from 1943 to 1974, is a shrine for die-hard fans. The renovated Ryman once again hosts performances.

Downtown Nashville

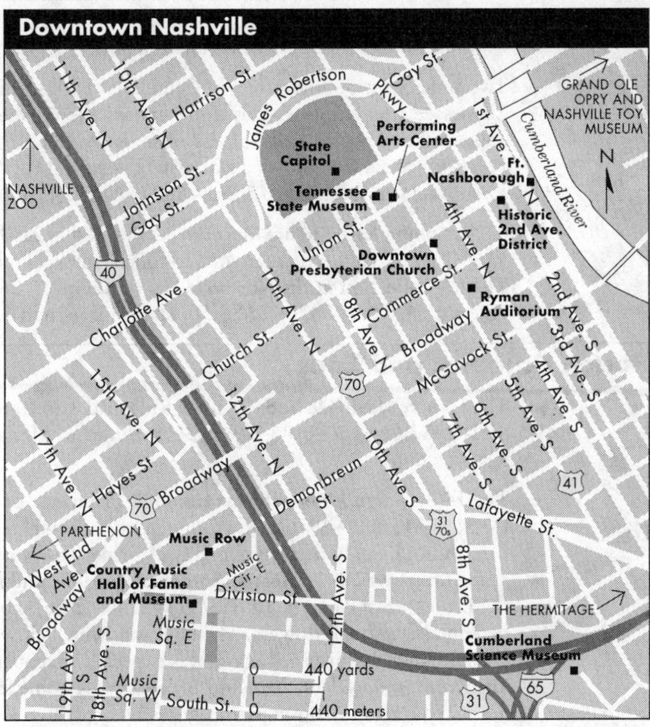

The James K. Polk Office Building is home to the **Tennessee State Museum,** where more than 6,000 artifacts trace the history of life in Tennessee. ✉ *505 Deaderick St.,* ☎ *615/741–2692.* 🎫 *Free. Closed Mon.*

In a park along Charlotte Avenue is the Greek Revival **state capitol** (☎ 615/741–2692; 🎫 free), designed by William Strickland, who is interred here along with the 11th U.S. president, James Polk, and his wife.

Other Attractions

Music Row (✉ Demonbreun St. exit off I–40) is the heart of Nashville's recording industry and the center of numerous country music attractions. A ticket to the **Country Music Hall of Fame and Museum** (✉ 4 Music Sq. E, ☎ 615/255–5333; 🎫 $10.75) includes admission to the legendary **RCA Studio B**, a few blocks away, where Elvis, Dolly Parton, and other greats once recorded. In 2000, the country shrine will move across from Nashville Arena downtown.

★ Since 1974, the **Grand Ole Opry** has been staged at the complex that housed Opryland U.S.A. theme park, which closed in 1997. The Opry survives and thrives, even as the former theme park's grounds are being converted into Opry Mills, a 200-store shopping, dining, and entertainment complex scheduled to open in 2000. Each weekend top stars perform at the Opry, which is the nation's oldest continuous radio show, first airing in 1925. The Opry is broadcast from the world's largest broadcast studio (it seats 4,424); advance ticket purchase is advised. The musical lineup for the Friday and Saturday night shows is announced on Wednesday evenings. ✉ *2804 Opryland Dr.,* ☎ *615/889–3060.* 🎫 *$17 for shows.*

The **Hermitage,** 12 mi east of downtown (Exit 221 off I–40), was built by Andrew Jackson, the seventh U.S. president, for his wife, Rachel. Their life and times are reflected with great care in the mansion, visitor center, and grounds. Both Jackson and his wife are entombed here. ✉ *4580 Rachel's La., Hermitage,* ☎ *615/889–2941.* 🎫 *$8.*

Two miles west of downtown in Centennial Park—built for the 1897 Tennessee Centennial Exposition—stands the **Parthenon,** an exact copy of the Athenian original and now used as an art gallery. *Athena Parthenos* is a 42-ft copy of a statue in the original Parthenon. ✉ *West End and 25th Aves.,* ☎ *615/862–8431.* 🎫 *$2.50. Closed Mon.*

At the **Cumberland Science Museum** (✉ 800 Ridley Blvd., ☎ 615/862–5160; 🎫 $6), children are invited to touch, smell, climb, and explore.

The toy collection at the **Nashville Toy Museum** (✉ 2613 McGavock Pike, ☎ 615/883–8870; 🎫 $3.50) spans more than 150 years.

Parks, Gardens, and Zoos

The 50-acre **Nashville Zoo** (✉ 1710 Ridge Rd. Circle, Joelton, Exit 31 off I–24W, ☎ 615/746–3449; 🎫 $6) includes an African savanna and a reptile house.

The 14,200-acre **J. Percy Priest Lake** (✉ 11 mi east of downtown off I–40, ☎ 615/889–1975) is surrounded by parks where you can swim, fish, camp, hike, bike, picnic, paddle, or ride. Thirty acres of gardens ★ at the **Cheekwood–Tennessee Botanical Gardens and Museum of Art** (✉ 1200 Forrest Park Dr., ☎ 615/353–2140; 🎫 $6) showcase annuals, perennials, and wildflowers. The museum, which closed at the end of 1997 for an 18-month renovation, is expected to reopen in mid-1999. **Riverfront Park** (✉ 1st Ave. and Broadway) is home to the new Tennessee Fox Trot Carousel, with figures by artist Red Grooms.

Dining

If you expect Nashville dining to be all corn bread, turnip greens, and grits, you're in for a surprise. Here you will find some of Tennessee's most sophisticated restaurants alongside the popular "meat-and-threes" (diners serving meat with three vegetable side dishes). For price ranges *see* Chart 1 (A) *in* On the Road with Fodor's.

$$$–$$$$ ✕ **Wild Boar.** This restaurant serves excellent contemporary French cuisine, with game, trout, duck, and beef on the menu; it also has an outstanding wine cellar. ✉ *2014 Broadway,* ☎ *615/329–1313. AE, D, DC, MC, V. No lunch weekends.*

$$–$$$$ ✕ **Mère Bulles.** This intimate District restaurant has river-view dining, a Continental menu, and an extensive wine list. Live entertainment—often jazz or folk music—is served up nightly. ✉ *152 2nd Ave. N,* ☎ *615/256–1946. AE, D, MC, V.*

$$$ ★ ✕ **Mario's.** Country music stars, visiting celebrities, and local society come here to see and be seen—and to savor the memorable osso buco and saltimbocca created by chef Ricardo Bacilieri. ✉ *2005 Broadway,* ☎ *615/327–3232. Reservations essential. Jacket and tie. AE, D, DC, MC, V. Closed Sun. No lunch.*

$$–$$$ ★ ✕ **F. Scott's.** This elegant café and wine bar has one of the largest wine selections in town. Try the roasted half-duck with root vegetables ragout and cranberries. ✉ *2210 Crestmoor,* ☎ *615/269–5861. AE, D, DC, MC, V.*

$$–$$$ ✕ **The Merchants.** An outdoor patio is an extra feature at this opulent three-level restaurant. Specialties include fresh seafood, grilled meats, and key lime pie. ✉ *401 Broadway,* ☎ *615/254–1892. AE, DC, MC, V. No lunch weekends.*

$$–$$$ ✕ **Sunset Grill.** Don't be surprised to see your favorite country stars at this hip, postmodern hangout. The hickory-smoked Tennessee trout is terrific. In summer, the outdoor courtyard is the place to be seen. ✉

2001A Belcourt Ave., ☎ 615/386–3663. AE, D, DC, MC, V. Closed Sun. No lunch Sat.

$–$$ ✕ **Elliston Place Soda Shop.** The burgers are tasty and the ice-cream sodas are frothy at this old-fashioned soda shop, where the 1950s atmosphere has been preserved. The chocolate shake is Nashville's best. ✉ *2111 Elliston Pl., ☎ 615/327–1090. No credit cards. Closed Sun.*

$–$$ ✕ **Loveless Cafe.** The appeal here is true down-home southern cooking: featherlight homemade biscuits and preserves, country ham and red-eye gravy, and fried chicken. ✉ *8400 Rte. 100, ☎ 615/646–9700. AE, MC, V. Closed Mon.*

$ ✕ **Hermitage House Smorgasbord.** No need to be shy about helping yourself to the bountiful spread of salads, meats, vegetables, and desserts here. Don't miss the apple fritters. ✉ *4144 Lebanon Rd., Hermitage, ☎ 615/883–9525. MC, V.*

$ ✕ **Old Spaghetti Factory.** This 2nd Avenue District spot offers a wide range of pasta dishes in a lively atmosphere that's great for families. ✉ *160 2nd Ave. N, ☎ 615/254–9010. D, MC, V.*

$ ✕ **Sylvan Park Restaurant.** The original location is a beacon for meat-and-three fans; purists say the three spin-off eateries aren't quite as good. ✉ *4502 Murphy Rd., ☎ 615/292–9275. No credit cards.*

Lodging

Nashville hotels are especially busy during the second week of June, when the **International Country Music Fan Fair** brings country music stars and their fans face to face at the Tennessee State Fairgrounds. Many tour companies offer packages, but plan ahead; this is country music's premier event and it sells out months in advance.

For information on B&Bs in the area, contact **Bed & Breakfast About Tennessee** (✉ Box 110227, Nashville 37222, ☎ 615/331–5244 or 800/458–2421) or **Tennessee Bed & Breakfast Innkeepers' Association** (✉ Box 120428, Nashville 37212, ☎ 800/820–8144).

For price ranges *see* Chart 2 (A) *in* On the Road with Fodor's.

$$$$ 🏨 **Loews Vanderbilt Plaza.** This beautiful hotel near Vanderbilt University has a well-deserved reputation for attentive service. ✉ *2100 West End Ave., 37203, ☎ 615/320–1700 or 800/235–6397, FAX 615/320–5019. 351 rooms. 2 restaurants. AE, D, MC, V.*

$$$$ ★ 🏨 **Opryland Hotel.** This massive plantation-style hotel adjacent to Opryland has a 2-acre glass-walled conservatory filled with 10,000 tropical plants and a skylighted indoor area replete with water cascades and a half-acre lake. A golf course is among the amenities. ✉ *2800 Opryland Dr., 37214, ☎ 615/889–1000, FAX 615/871–7741. 2,883 rooms. 7 restaurants, pools, tennis, exercise room. AE, D, MC, V.*

$$$–$$$$ 🏨 **Renaissance Nashville Hotel.** This ultracontemporary high-rise adjoins the Nashville Convention Center. The spacious rooms have period reproduction furnishings. ✉ *611 Commerce St., 37203, ☎ 615/255–8400 or 800/468–3571, FAX 615/255–8163. 673 rooms. 2 restaurants, pool, health club. AE, D, DC, MC, V.*

$$ ★ 🏨 **Courtyard by Marriott–Airport.** This handsome low-rise motor inn offers some amenities found in higher-price hotels: spacious rooms, king-size beds, and oversize desks. ✉ *2508 Elm Hill Pike, 37214, ☎ 615/883–9500 or 800/321–2211, FAX 615/883–0172. 145 rooms. Restaurant, pool, exercise room. AE, D, DC, MC, V.*

$$ 🏨 **Hampton Inn Vanderbilt.** The rooms at this contemporary inn near Vanderbilt University are colorful and spacious. There's a hospitality suite for social or business use. ✉ *1919 West End Ave., 37203, ☎ 615/329–1144 or 800/426–7866, FAX 615/320–7112. 171 rooms. Pool. CP. AE, D, DC, MC, V.*

$ **Comfort Inn Hermitage.** Near the Hermitage, this inn offers comfortable accommodations, some with water beds or whirlpool baths. ✉ *5768 Old Hickory Blvd., 37076,* ☎ *615/889–5060,* FAX *615/871–4137. 106 rooms. Pool. CP. AE, D, DC, MC, V.*

$ **La Quinta Inn–Metro Center.** Guest rooms are spacious and well lighted, with a large working area and an oversize bed. ✉ *2001 Metrocenter Blvd., 37228,* ☎ *615/259–2130 or 800/531–5900,* FAX *615/242–2650. 121 rooms. Pool. CP. AE, DC, MC, V.*

$ **Wilson Inn.** Three miles from the Grand Ole Opry, this five-story hotel is clean and convenient. Many rooms have kitchens. ✉ *600 Ermac Dr. (Elm Hill Pike exit from Briley Pkwy.), 37214,* ☎ *615/889–4466 or 800/333–9457,* FAX *615/889–0484. 110 rooms. Pool. CP. AE, D, MC, V.*

Nightlife and the Arts

Nightlife

The **Grand Ole Opry** (☞ Exploring, *above*) has packed in the crowds on Friday and Saturday nights since 1925. At the famous **Bluebird Cafe** (✉ 4104 Hillsboro Rd., Green Hills, ☎ 615/383–1461), country singers try out their latest material. The **Stock Yard Bull Pen Lounge** (✉ 901 2nd Ave. N, ☎ 615/255–6464) is a restaurant-lounge with nightly live country entertainment and dancing. There's a variety of live music downtown at **Mère Bulles** (☞ Dining, *above*). **Exit/In** (✉ 2208 Elliston Pl., ☎ 615/321–4400) showcases blues and rock. **Blue Sky Court** (✉ 412 4th Ave. S, ☎ 615/777–2583), convenient to downtown and Vanderbilt University, focuses on rock and blues. In the **District** (☞ Exploring, *above*), check out the **Wildflower Saloon** (✉ 120 2nd Ave. N, ☎ 615/251–1000) and local versions of **Planet Hollywood** (✉ 322 Broadway, ☎ 615/313–7827) and the **Hard Rock Cafe** (✉ 100 Broadway, ☎ 615/742–9900).

The Arts

The **Tennessee Performing Arts Center** (✉ 505 Deaderick St., ☎ 615/782–4000) is the venue for performances by the Nashville Ballet (☎ 615/244–7233), Nashville Opera (☎ 615/292–5710), Nashville Symphony Orchestra (☎ 615/255–5600), and Tennessee Repertory Theatre (☎ 615/244–4878). The center's Andrew Jackson Hall also hosts touring Broadway shows. Call **Ticketmaster** (☎ 615/737–4849) for tickets and information about arts events.

Spectator Sports

Football: The 1999 season is scheduled to be the first in Nashville's downtown stadium (☎ 615/733–3000 or 888/313–8326) for the NFL's former **Houston Oilers.** The team, which moved to Tennessee in 1997, played in Memphis while the stadium was being built on the east bank of the Cumberland River. **Hockey:** Nashville Arena (✉ 501 Broadway, ☎ 615/770–2309) hosts the NHL's **Nashville Predators,** an expansion team that began play here in 1998. **Baseball:** The **Nashville Sounds,** an AAA farm club of the Chicago White Sox, play at Herschel Greer Stadium (✉ 534 Chestnut St., ☎ 615/242–4371) just south of downtown, off I–65.

Shopping

The huge **Bellevue Center** mall, in southwest Nashville (✉ Bellevue exit from I–40, ☎ 615/646–8690), has more than 120 stores. Antiques lovers may want to browse through the shops along **8th Avenue South.** For the latest look in country-and-western wear, two-step over to the **District** (☞ Exploring Nashville, *above*).

EAST TENNESSEE

From the Great Smoky Mountains to the rippling waters of the Holston, French Broad, Nolichucky, and Tennessee rivers, East Tennessee offers a cornucopia of scenic grandeur and recreational opportunities. Mountain folkways may persist in certain smaller communities, but cities such as Knoxville and Chattanooga are modern and quite diverse.

Visitor Information

Chattanooga: Area Convention and Visitors Bureau (✉ 1001 Market St., 37402, ☎ 423/756–8687 or 800/322–3344). **Knoxville:** Area Convention and Visitors Bureau (✉ 810 Clinch Ave., 37902, ☎ 423/523–7263 or 800/727–8045).

Arriving and Departing

By Bus

Greyhound (☎ 800/231–2222) has stops in Chattanooga and in Knoxville.

By Car

I–75 runs north–south from Kentucky through Knoxville, then to Chattanooga. I–81 heads southwest from the Virginia border at Bristol, ending at I–40 northeast of Knoxville. I–40 enters from North Carolina and continues west to Knoxville, Nashville, and Memphis.

By Plane

Knoxville Airport (☎ 423/970–2773), served by American Eagle, ComAir, Delta, Northwest, Trans World Express, United, and US Airways, is about 12 mi from town. The **Chattanooga Airport** (☎ 615/855–2200), served by American Eagle, ASA, ComAir, Delta, Northwest Airlink, and US Airways, is about 8 mi from town.

Exploring East Tennessee

Founded in 1786, **Knoxville** became the first state capital when Tennessee was admitted to the Union in 1796. This scenic city at the foothills of the Great Smoky Mountains continues to grow with **Volunteer Landing**, a development along the Tennessee River with shops, restaurants, and residential space. Knoxville is home to the main campus of the **University of Tennessee**, as well as the headquarters of the **Tennessee Valley Authority** (TVA), with its vast complex of hydroelectric dams and recreational lakes.

Among the historic sites in Knoxville is the 1792 **Governor William Blount Mansion,** where the governor and his associates planned the admission of Tennessee as the 16th state in the Union. ✉ *200 W. Hill Ave.,* ☎ *423/525–2375.* 🎫 *$4. Closed Mon.*

The **Armstrong-Lockett House,** an 1834 farm mansion, is a showcase of American and English furniture and English silver. ✉ *2728 Kingston Pike,* ☎ *423/637–3163.* 🎫 *$4.50. Closed Mon. and Jan.–Feb.*

Housed in the 1874 U.S. Customs House, the **East Tennessee Historical Center** displays books and artifacts relating to the history of the state. ✉ *800 Market St.,* ☎ *423/544–5744.* 🎫 *Free. Closed Mon.*

The **Knoxville Museum of Art,** opened in 1992, has four exhibition galleries with contemporary prints, drawings, and paintings. ✉ *410 10th St., in World's Fair Park,* ☎ *423/525–6101.* 🎫 *Free except during special exhibits. Closed Mon.*

The **Knoxville Zoological Gardens** (✉ Rutledge Pike S, Exit 392 off I–40, ☎ 423/637–5331; 🎟 zoo $7, park $2) is famous for its reptile complex and for its breeding of large cats and African elephants.

Youngsters like the hands-on displays and audiovisual exhibits at the **East Tennessee Discovery Center and Akima Planetarium** (✉ 516 N. Beaman St., ☎ 423/594–1480; 🎟 $3).

Gatlinburg, the busy, tourist-oriented northern gateway to **Great Smoky Mountains National Park** (☞ National and State Parks, *above*) is southeast of Knoxville via U.S. 441/321. Set in the narrow valley of the Little Pigeon River (actually a turbulent mountain stream), Gatlinburg has an abundance of family attractions, including the **Gatlinburg Sky Lift** (☎ 423/436–4307; 🎟 $7) to the top of Crockett Mountain. The **Ober Gatlinburg Tramway** (☎ 423/436–5423; 🎟 $7) goes to a mountaintop amusement park, ski center, and shopping mall/crafts market. The tramway is closed the first two weeks of March.

Pigeon Forge, about 6 mi north of Gatlinburg on U.S. 441, has factory outlet malls and family attractions. One Pigeon Forge highlight is **Dollywood,** Dolly Parton's popular theme park, with rides, live music, and a re-created mountain village. Dolly performs annually, usually when the season opens. Other concerts between May and October are apt to include such stars as Kathy Mattea or the Statlers. Daredevil Falls, a waterfall ride, opened in 1998. ✉ *700 Dollywood La.,* ☎ *423/428–9488 or 800/365–5996.* 🎟 *$27.99. Closed Jan.–mid-Apr.*

The **Gatlinburg/Pigeon Forge area** is home to many amusement parks and offbeat museums, such as Gatlinburg's **Guinness World Records Museum** (☎ 423/436–9100; 🎟 $7.95). **Newfound Gap,** south from Gatlinburg on scenic U.S. 441, provides a haunting view of the Tennessee–North Carolina border. From here a 7-mi spur road leads to **Clingmans Dome**—at 6,643 ft, the highest point in Tennessee.

Chattanooga, a city of Civil War battlefields, museums of all kinds (art, antiques, history, even knives and tow trucks), and a famous choo-choo, is southwest of Knoxville off I–75. Begin your meandering here with a stop at the **Chattanooga Visitors Center** (✉ 2 Broad St., ☎ 423/266–7111). Dominating Chattanooga's skyline is 2,215-ft **Lookout Mountain,** 6 mi away, with panoramic views and the world's steepest **Incline Railway** (✉ 827 E. Brow Rd., ☎ 423/821–4224; 🎟 $8). From Lookout Mountain Scenic Highway, tours depart every 15 minutes to the 145-ft **Ruby Falls** (✉ 1550 Scenic Hwy., ☎ 423/821–2544; 🎟 $9), 1,120 ft underground and reached by elevator.

★ The **Tennessee Aquarium** (✉ 1 Broad St., ☎ 423/265–0695; 🎟 aquarium $10.25, IMAX theater $6.75), opened in 1992, is the world's largest freshwater aquarium, with 350 species of fish, mammals, birds, reptiles, and amphibians; an IMAX theater is nearby. Surrounding the aquarium is **Ross's Landing Park and Plaza,** commemorating Chattanooga's Civil War history as well as its role as a major railroad town.

The **Creative Discovery Children's Museum** (✉ 321 Chestnut St., ☎ 423/757–0510🎟 ; $7.75), has exhibits in four areas: invention, art, music, and science.

Oak Ridge, about 100 mi northeast of Chattanooga (take U.S. 27 to I–40E or I–75 to I–40W), is where atomic energy was secretly developed during World War II. The **American Museum of Science and Energy** (✉ 300 S. Tulane Ave., ☎ 423/576–3200; 🎟 free) focuses on the uses of nuclear, solar, and geothermal energy.

Dining and Lodging

Expect hearty food in the mountains: barbecued ribs, thick pork chops, and country ham with red-eye gravy. For reservations in hotels, motels, chalets, and condominiums in Gatlinburg, contact **Smoky Mountain Accommodations Reservation Service** (✉ 526 E. Pkwy., Suite 1, Gatlinburg 37738, ☎ 423/436–9700 or 800/231–2230). For price ranges *see* Charts 1 (B) and 2 (B) *in* On the Road with Fodor's.

Chattanooga

$$$–$$$$ ✕ **The Loft.** Locals and visitors alike flock to this cozy, candlelit restaurant for its clublike ambience, extensive wine list, and hearty specialties. The varied entrées include king crab legs, seafood fettuccine, and steak—all served with soup, salad, home-baked bread, fresh vegetables, and a baked potato or wild rice pilaf. ✉ *328 Cherokee Blvd.,* ☎ *423/266–3601. AE, D, DC, MC, V.*

$$–$$$$ ★ ✕ **212 Market.** Creative American cuisine is served at this hip spot directly across from the Tennessee Aquarium. The fish entrées are especially good, the homemade breads scrumptious, and the wine list impressive. ✉ *212 Market St.,* ☎ *423/265–1212. AE, MC, V.*

$$–$$$ ✕ **Big River Grille Brewing & Works.** This restored trolley-warehouse is handsomely appointed, with high ceilings, exposed-brick walls, and hardwood floors. You can watch the inner workings of the microbrewery through a soaring glass wall by the bar. The sandwiches and salads are large; wash them down with the sampler of six brews. ✉ *222 Broad St.,* ☎ *423/267–2739. AE, D, DC, MC, V.*

$$–$$$ ✕ **Town & Country.** Even though this meat-and-three fixture across the bridge from the Tennessee Aquarium seats more than 425, expect to wait a bit for the mouthwatering southern cuisine, from vegetable plates to steaks. ✉ *110 N. Market St.,* ☎ *423/267–8544. AE, D, DC, MC, V.*

$$$$ 🏨 **Bluff View Inn.** Chattanooga's best B&B, this 1928 Colonial Revival mansion hugs a bluff high above the Tennessee River and is part of the Bluff View Art District, which comprises five houses, three restaurants, and a sculpture garden. Tastefully decorated bedrooms in the main inn and two other houses have whirlpool baths and fireplaces. ✉ *412 E. 2nd St., 37403,* ☎ *423/265–5033,* FAX *423/757–0124. 16 rooms. 3 restaurants. Full breakfast. DC, MC, V.*

$$$$ 🏨 **Chattanooga Marriott.** The city's largest hotel is convenient to town attractions. ✉ *2 Carter Plaza, 37402,* ☎ *423/756–0002 or 800/841–1674,* FAX *423/266–2254. 343 rooms. Restaurant, pools, health club. AE, DC, MC, V.*

$$$$ ★ 🏨 **Radisson Read House.** The Georgian-style Read House, on the National Register of Historic Places, dates from the 1920s and has been impeccably restored to its original grandeur. Guest rooms in the main hotel continue the Georgian motif; rooms in the annex are more contemporary. ✉ *827 Broad St., 37402,* ☎ *423/266–4121,* FAX *423/267–6447. 238 rooms. 2 restaurants, pool. AE, D, DC, MC, V.*

$$$–$$$$ 🏨 **Chattanooga Choo-Choo Holiday Inn.** The hotel adjoins the 1905 Southern Railway Terminal, now a 30-acre complex with restaurants, shops, gardens, tennis courts, and an operating trolley. Rooms are comfortably appointed, and you can also stay in one of the 48 parlor cars. ✉ *1400 Market St., 37402,* ☎ *423/266–5000 or 800/872–2529,* FAX *423/265–4635. 351 rooms. 3 restaurants, pools. AE, DC, MC, V.*

Gatlinburg

$$–$$$$ ✕ **Burning Bush Restaurant.** Reproduction furnishings evoke a Colonial atmosphere, but the menu leans toward Continental. Specialties include broiled Tennessee quail. ✉ *1151 Parkway,* ☎ *423/436–4669. AE, D, MC, V.*

$$–$$$ ✕ **Smoky Mountain Trout House.** Trout is prepared eight ways, or you can have prime rib, country ham, or fried chicken. This restaurant is a truly rustic mountain cottage. ✉ *410 N. Parkway,* ☎ *423/436–5416. AE, DC, MC, V. Closed Dec.–Mar.*

$$$$ ★ 🏨 **Buckhorn Inn.** This country inn about 6 mi outside town has welcomed guests to its rustic rooms and cottages since 1938. The mountain views are spectacular. Breakfast and dinner are available for an extra charge. ✉ *2140 Tudor Mountain Rd., 37738,* ☎ *423/436–4668. 6 rooms, 4 1-bedroom cottages, 2 2-bedroom guest houses. Restaurant. Full breakfast, dinner. MC, V.*

$$$–$$$$ ★ 🏨 **Holiday Inn Resort Complex.** Near the Convention Center and the Ober Gatlinburg aerial tramway, this hotel offers the Holidome Indoor Recreation Center, with a pool and other attractions. ✉ *520 Airport Rd., 37738,* ☎ *423/436–9201 or 800/435–9201,* FAX *423/436–7974. 402 rooms. 2 restaurants, pools, exercise room. AE, D, DC, MC, V.*

$$–$$$ 🏨 **Best Western Twin Islands Motel.** Even though it's in busy downtown Gatlingburg, this motel has a peaceful air, thanks to the Little Pigeon River, which flows past each room. ✉ *539 Parkway , 37738,* ☎ *423/436–5121,* FAX *423/436–6208. 97 rooms, 10 suites. Restaurant, pool. AE, DC, MC, V.*

Knoxville

$$–$$$$ ★ ✕ **Regas Restaurant.** This cozy Knoxville classic, with fireplaces and original art, has been around for 70 years. The specialty, prime rib, is sliced to order and served with horseradish sauce. ✉ *318 Gay St.,* ☎ *423/637–9805. AE, D, DC, MC, V. No lunch Sat., no dinner Sun.*

$$–$$$ ✕ **Copper Cellar/Cumberland Grill.** A favorite of the college crowd and young professionals, the original downstairs Copper Cellar has an intimate atmosphere. Upstairs, the Cumberland Grill serves salads and sandwiches. Both serve outstanding desserts. ✉ *1807 Cumberland Ave.,* ☎ *423/673–3411. AE, DC, MC, V.*

$$$$ ★ 🏨 **Hyatt Regency Knoxville.** This handsome, contemporary adaptation of an Aztec pyramid sits atop a hill overlooking the city and nearby mountains. The nine-story atrium lobby blends modern furnishings with artwork in Central American motifs. ✉ *500 Hill Ave. SE, 37901,* ☎ *423/637–1234 or 800/233–1234,* FAX *423/522–5911. 387 rooms. Restaurant, pool, exercise room. AE, D, DC, MC, V.*

$$ 🏨 **Best Western Luxbury Hotel.** Midway between downtown Knoxville and Oak Ridge, this affordable hotel has oversize rooms with spacious work areas. ✉ *420 Peters Rd. N, 37922,* ☎ *423/539–0058 or 800/252–7748,* FAX *423/539–4887. 98 rooms. Pool. CP. AE, D, DC, MC, V.*

Nightlife and the Arts

Chattanooga

The **Tivoli Theater** (✉ 399 McCaulley Ave., ☎ 423/757–5050) presents concerts and operas. The **Chattanooga Little Theatre** (✉ 400 River St., ☎ 423/267–8534) stages productions year-round. For rock or blues head to **Sandbar** (✉ 1011 Riverside Dr., ☎ 423/622–4432).

Gatlinburg

Sweet Fanny Adams Theatre and Music Hall (✉ 461 Parkway, ☎ 423/436–4038) stages original musical comedies and Gay '90s revues, and hotel lounges offer DJs and live entertainment. At Ober Gatlinburg, the **Heidelberg Restaurant** (✉ 148 Parkway, ☎ 423/430–3094) has dancing and a show starring international entertainers, mostly German, from 5:30 to 11.

Knoxville

The **Bijou Theater** (✉ 803 S. Gay St., ☎ 423/522–0832) offers seasonal ballet, concerts, and plays. **Clarence Brown/Carousel Theatre,** on the

University of Tennessee campus (☎ 423/974–5161), is a theater-in-the-round with student and professional actors. **Old City,** on the north side of downtown, has lively restaurants, clubs, and shops. Try **Lucille's** (✉ 106 N. Central St., ☎ 423/546–3742), in Old City, for jazz. For dancing, there's **The Underground** (✉ 214 E. Jackson St., ☎ 423/525–3675), in Old City. **Patrick Sullivan's** (✉ 100 N. Central St., ☎ 423/694–9696) has saloon-style food and live rock and roll on weekends.

Outdoor Activities and Sports

Fishing

East Tennessee's lakes offer seasonal angling for striped bass, walleye, white bass, and muskie. **Gatlinburg**'s streams and rivers are stocked with trout from April to November. There are boat-launch ramps at **Norris Dam State Resort Park** (☎ 423/426–7461), north of Knoxville, and **Booker T. Washington State Park** (☎ 423/894–4955), near Chattanooga.

Golf

East Tennessee courses open to the public include 18-hole par 72 **Brainerd Golf Course** (☎ 423/855–2692), in Chattanooga, 18-hole par 70 **Whittle Springs Municipal Golf Course** (☎ 423/525–1022), in Knoxville, and 18-hole par 72 **Bent Creek Mountain Inn and Country Club** (☎ 423/436–2875), in Gatlinburg.

Hiking

A scenic portion of the **Appalachian Trail** runs along high ridges in the Great Smoky Mountains National Park (✉ Gatlinburg, ☎ 423/436–1200). The trail can be reached at Newfound Gap, off U.S. 441.

Horseback Riding

McCarter's Riding Stables (✉ U.S. 441 south of Gatlinburg, ☎ 423/436–5354) is open mid-March–October.

Rafting and Canoeing

East Tennessee has five white-water rivers: Ocoee, Hiwassee, French Broad, Tellico, and Nolichucky. The rafting season runs from April to early November; for canoe rentals and guided raft trips contact **Outdoor Adventure Rafting** (✉ Ocoee, ☎ 800/627–7636), **Wildwater, Ltd.** (✉ Ducktown, ☎ 800/451–9972), and **Rafting in the Smokies** (✉ Gatlinburg, ☎ 423/436–5008).

Ski Area

Ober Gatlinburg Ski Resort (✉ 1001 Parkway, ☎ 423/436–5423) has three lifts and 10 downhill slopes.

Shopping

At the **Great Smoky Arts and Crafts Community** (✉ Glades and Buckhorn Rds. off U.S. 321, 3 mi east of Gatlinburg, ☎ 423/671–3600, ext. 3504), a collection of 80 shops and crafts studios along 8 mi of country road, you can watch crafters at work and buy their wood carvings, dulcimers, quilts, and other Appalachian folk crafts. Pigeon Forge is famous for its **factory outlet malls** on U.S. 441. Chattanooga's **Warehouse Row** (✉ 12th and Market Sts., ☎ 423/267–1111) contains factory outlets for such top designers as Ellen Tracy, Ralph Lauren, Tommy Hilfiger, and Perry Ellis.

7 The Midwest and Great Lakes

Illinois, Indiana, Michigan, Minnesota, Ohio, Wisconsin

Updated by Peggy Ammerman, Eve Becker, Miriam Carey, Joanne Demski, Alicia Fedorczak, and Khristi Zimmeth

THE MIDWEST IS AMERICA, that prototypical vision of neat farmland, affluent suburbs, and compact, skyscrapered downtowns strung together along purposefully straight silver highways. Sauk Centre, Minnesota, was the setting for Sinclair Lewis's *Main Street*; Muncie, Indiana, was the subject of the sociological study called *Middletown, USA*. It is no accident that standup comedians use midwestern town names—Peoria, Sheboygan, Kokomo, Kalamazoo—to mean "the heart of the country." Transplanted midwesterners spend the rest of their lives longing for broad, clear horizons; thick, shady stands of beech and maple trees; and hazy summer afternoons when kids sell lemonade from sidewalk stands. People seem genuinely friendlier and more down-to-earth here.

Six states—Ohio, Indiana, Michigan, Illinois, Wisconsin, and Minnesota—occupy what was originally the Northwest Territory, a vast tract of forest and meadow awarded to the United States in the 1783 Treaty of Paris. Unlike the stark Great Plains to the west, this is gently rolling landscape, punctuated by rivers, woods, and trees. It is defined by great geological features: to the east, the Appalachian Mountains; to the north, the Great Lakes; to the south, the Ohio River; to the west, the majestic Mississippi River.

Smarting from years of being labeled "the sticks," midwestern cities are always trying to prove themselves, cheerfully rehabilitating their downtowns, rooting for their major league ball teams, and building gleaming convention centers and festival malls. Ohio has no fewer than five important cities (Cleveland, Cincinnati, Columbus, Dayton, and Toledo). Minnesota's major population center comprises two cities, Minneapolis and St. Paul, which means that there are twice as many parks and museums as you'd expect. Indiana's capital, Indianapolis, is a beautifully laid-out city that's also the amateur-sports capital of the country. In Michigan, Detroit is the home of America's auto industry. Surprisingly, it also has the greatest number of theater seats outside of New York City. Milwaukee, Wisconsin, poised on the western shore of Lake Michigan, is a rich melting pot of immigrant cultures, as is vibrant and powerful Chicago, Illinois, the region's one great metropolis.

But it's never more than an hour's drive from these cities to northern lake resorts, historic villages along sleepy back roads, utopian colonies, and pleasant university towns. Big swatches of forest and lakeshore are protected as parkland, and gorgeous scenic drives edge the Great Lakes and the dramatic bluffs of the Mississippi and Ohio river valleys.

When to Go

Summer is the most popular time to visit the Midwest and the Great Lakes. Generally, the farther north you go, the fewer people you'll find. Prices in most places peak in July and August. Daily temperatures average in the 80s in Illinois, Indiana, and Ohio, though July and August heat waves can push them high into the 90s. In Michigan, Wisconsin, and Minnesota, temperatures run 10° cooler. These three states have the best **fall** foliage, though you can see good color in all six. Depending on the weather, the leaves usually begin to turn in mid-September and reach their most colorful by mid-October. In **winter** Michigan has the only significant downhill skiing in the region, but cross-country is all the rage in Wisconsin and Minnesota. The Midwest usually gets at least one subzero cold snap every year. For the rest of winter expect temperatures in the 20s and 30s and about 10° colder in northern Michigan, Wisconsin, and Minnesota. Sudden snowstorms can make winter driving unpredictable and treacherous. **Spring** is damp and clammy, with erratic weather and temperatures ranging from the 30s to the 60s.

Festivals and Seasonal Events

Winter

JAN.➢ **International Falls, Minnesota,** hosts **Ice Box Days** (☏ 218/283–9400), a long-weekend festival of snow sculpture, skating, cross-country skiing, and the Freeze Your Gizzard Blizzard Run. The six-day **Plymouth International Ice Sculpture Spectacular** (☏ 734/459–6969), in **Plymouth, Michigan,** features 150 carvers from around the world, in addition to nightly light shows and a life-size ice carousel. The best snowmobile racers in the country gather in **Eagle River, Wisconsin,** to compete on a half-mile banked ice track at the **World's Championship Snowmobile Derby** (☏ 715/479–4424).

LATE JAN.–EARLY FEB.➢ Minnesota's 10-day **St. Paul Winter Carnival** (☏ 612/223–4700 or 800/488–4023) celebrates winter with a sleigh and cutter parade, an ice palace, car races on the ice, and ice sculptures by artists from around the world.

Spring

MARCH➢ During **Eagle Watch Weekend** (☏ 800/657–4972) the spring migration of bald eagles can be viewed along the Mississippi River in the vicinity of **Winona, Minnesota.**

MAY➢ The monthlong **Indianapolis 500 Festival** (☏ 317/636–4556) culminates in the most famous car race in the United States. The **Holland Tulip Time Festival** (☏ 800/822–2770), in **Holland, Michigan,** showcases flowers and Dutch traditions.

Summer

EARLY JUNE➢ The **Detroit Grand Prix** (☏ 313/393–7749), held on scenic Belle Isle, in Detroit, is the cornerstone of a three-day downtown event featuring parties and several support races.

LATE JUNE–EARLY JULY➢ **Milwaukee, Wisconsin,** holds **Summerfest** (☏ 414/273–2680 or 800/837–3378), a lakefront festival with rock, jazz, and popular music.

JULY➢ The **Minneapolis Aquatennial** (☏ 612/331–8371) celebrates the lakes of Minnesota with sailing regattas, waterskiing competitions, and other events on and around the city lakes. The 330-mi **Chicago-to-Mack-**

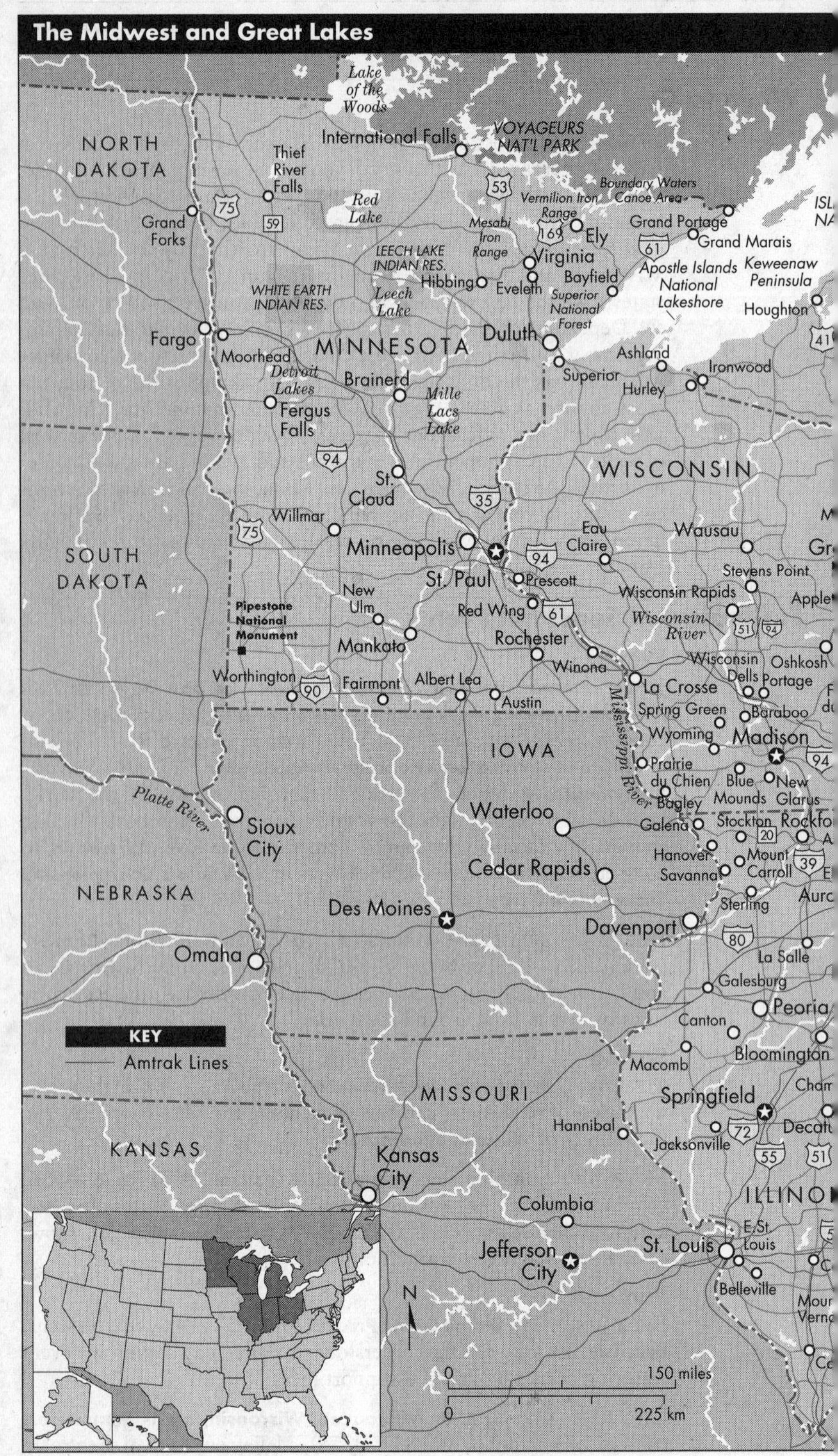
The Midwest and Great Lakes
NORTH DAKOTA
SOUTH DAKOTA
NEBRASKA
KANSAS
MINNESOTA
WISCONSIN
IOWA
MISSOURI
Lake of the Woods
International Falls
VOYAGEURS NAT'L PARK
Boundary Waters Canoe Area
Thief River Falls
Red Lake
Grand Forks
Vermilion Iron Range
Mesabi Iron Range
Ely
Grand Portage
Grand Marais
LEECH LAKE INDIAN RES.
Virginia
Bayfield
Apostle Islands National Lakeshore
Keweenaw Peninsula
Hibbing
Eveleth
Superior National Forest
Houghton
WHITE EARTH INDIAN RES.
Leech Lake
Duluth
Fargo
Moorhead
Ashland
Ironwood
Superior
Hurley
Detroit Lakes
Brainerd
Mille Lacs Lake
Fergus Falls
St. Cloud
Willmar
Wausau
Eau Claire
Minneapolis
St. Paul
Prescott
Stevens Point
Wisconsin Rapids
New Ulm
Red Wing
Pipestone National Monument
Mankato
Rochester
Wisconsin River
Winona
Wisconsin Dells
Oshkosh
Portage
Worthington
Fairmont
Albert Lea
Austin
La Crosse
Spring Green
Baraboo
Mississippi River
Wyoming
Madison
Prairie du Chien
Blue Mounds
New Glarus
Platte River
Bagley
Sioux City
Waterloo
Galena
Stockton
Hanover
Mount Carroll
Savanna
Cedar Rapids
Sterling
Des Moines
Davenport
Omaha
La Salle
Galesburg
Peoria
Canton
Bloomington
Macomb
Springfield
Hannibal
Jacksonville
Kansas City
ILLINOIS
Columbia
St. Louis
E. St. Louis
Jefferson City
Belleville
N
0
150 miles
0
225 km
KEY
Amtrak Lines

CANADA
Lake Superior
Copper Harbor
PICTURED ROCKS NAT'L LAKESHORE
Sudbury
Marquette
Sault Sainte Marie
MICHIGAN
Iron Mountain
Mackinac Island
Beaver Island
Mackinaw City
Manitoulin Island
Georgian Bay
Escanaba
Petoskey
Alpena
Northport
Grand Traverse Bay
Lake Huron
SLEEPING BEAR DUNES NAT'L LAKESHORE
Traverse City
Sturgeon Bay
MICHIGAN
Toronto
Lake Ontario
Manitowoc
Cadillac
Bay City
Lake Michigan
Sheboygan
Saginaw
Buffalo
NEW YORK
Cedarburg
Grand Rapids
Flint
Port Huron
Muskegon
Lansing
Milwaukee
Battle Creek
Lake Erie
Kenosha
Jackson
Detroit
Ashtabula
Waukegan
Kalamazoo
Ann Arbor
South Bass Island
Kelleys Island
PENNSYLVANIA
Woodstock
Marblehead
Evanston
Toledo
Catawba Point
Chicago
Cleveland
Angola
Port Clinton
Gary
South Bend
Sandusky
Youngstown
Michigan City
La Porte
Auburn
Akron
Mansfield
Ft. Wayne
Huntington
Lima
Canton
Marion
OHIO
Logansport
INDIANA
Wapakoneta
Muncie
Zanesville
Wheeling
Danville
Lafayette
Anderson
Noblesville
Columbus
Centerville
Zionsville
Crawfordsville
Richmond
Dayton
Marietta
Rockville
Indianapolis
Chillicothe
Terre Haute
Columbus
Dills-boro
Cincinnati
Bloomington
Madison
Aurora
WEST VIRGINIA
Wabash River
Vincennes
New Albany
Corydon
Gentryville
Louisville
KENTUCKY
New Harmony
Ohio R.
Evansville
VIRGINIA

inac Boat Race (☎ 312/861–7777) is one of the most challenging sailboat races in the country. Some 350,000 people flock to **Traverse City, Michigan,** during the **National Cherry Festival** (☎ 616/947–4230) to sample the best of the local orchards. During the **Great Circus Parade** (☎ 414/273–7877) antique circus wagons from Baraboo's famous Circus World Museum ride through the streets of **Milwaukee, Wisconsin.**

LATE JULY➢ The **Pro Football Hall of Fame Game** (☎ 330/456–8207) and induction ceremonies, in **Canton, Ohio,** kick off the football season. The **Cincinnati Riverfront Stadium Festival** (☎ 513/871–3900) is the largest festival in the country devoted to rhythm and blues.

LATE JULY–EARLY AUG.➢ The **Experimental Aircraft Association Fly-In** (☎ 920/426–4800), in **Oshkosh, Wisconsin,** gathers close to a million people and 30,000 aircraft from around the world.

AUG.➢ The **Wisconsin State Fair** (☎ 414/266–7000) attracts crowds to **Milwaukee** for livestock and crop shows, midway attractions, and stage shows. The **Illinois State Fair** (☎ 217/782–6661), in **Springfield,** has livestock shows, car and horse races, food, and entertainment. The citizens of **Young America, Minnesota,** recall their German roots with **Stiftungsfest** (☎ 612/467–3365), which features a parade, an arts fair, and ethnic food and music.

LATE AUG.–EARLY SEPT.➢ The **Michigan State Fair** (☎ 313/369–8250), in **Detroit,** is the nation's oldest state fair, with an animal birthing center and top musical acts performing inside the band shell.

Autumn

EARLY SEPT.➢ On Labor Day weekend, the **Montreux Detroit Jazz Festival** (☎ 313/963–7622) attracts more than 700,000 jazz fans.

OCT.➢ On the third weekend of the month, the **Chicago Marathon** (☎ 312/243–3274 or 888/243–3344) draws runners from all over the world. The **Circleville Pumpkin Show** (☎ 614/474–7000) is **Ohio**'s oldest, with a huge harvest party afterwards.

Getting Around the Midwest and Great Lakes

By Bus

The major intercity carrier is **Greyhound Lines** (☎ 800/231–2222). **Indian Trails** (☎ 800/292–3831) operates between Chicago and many cities in Michigan. In southern Wisconsin **United Limo** (☎ 800/833–5555) runs from Milwaukee to Chicago's O'Hare Airport and the Amtrak station downtown.

By Boat

From mid-May to October passenger and automobile **ferry** service operates between Ludington, Michigan, and Manitowoc, Wisconsin (☎ 616/845–5555).

By Car

I–80 and I–90 converge near Cleveland and run along the northern borders of Ohio and Indiana until they split at Chicago. I–80 then cuts across Illinois into Iowa, while I–90 curves up through Wisconsin and goes across southern Minnesota. Other major arteries are I–70, crossing the southern parts of Ohio, Indiana, and Illinois; I–94, which goes from Detroit across Michigan, hugs Lake Michigan through Indiana and Illinois, then crosses Wisconsin and Minnesota; and I–75, which stretches from Sault Sainte Marie, Michigan, to Cincinnati, Ohio. State routes and county roads provide a closer look at rural areas and are in good repair throughout the region.

By Plane

The region is served by all major airlines: American, Delta, Northwest, United, and US Airways. The largest airports are **Cleveland Hopkins International Airport** (☎ 216/265–6000), in Ohio; **Detroit Metropolitan Wayne County Airport** (☎ 313/942–3550), in Michigan; **General Mitchell Field** (☎ 414/747–5300), in Milwaukee, Wisconsin; **Indianapolis International Airport** (☎ 317/487–7243), in Indiana; **Minneapolis/St. Paul International Airport** (☎ 612/726–5555), in Minnesota; and **O'Hare International Airport** (☎ 773/686–2200), in Chicago, Illinois.

By Train

Amtrak (☎ 800/872–7245) is the primary passenger railroad serving the entire region. All routes go through Chicago. Among cities with commuter train service between the central city and the suburbs are Chicago (☎ 312/836–7000), Cleveland (☎ 216/621–9500), and Indianapolis (☎ 317/267–3000).

ILLINOIS

Updated by Eve Becker

Capital	Springfield
Population	11,896,000
Motto	State Sovereignty—National Union
State Bird	Cardinal
State Flower	Wood violet
Postal Abbreviation	IL

Statewide Visitor Information

Illinois Bureau of Tourism (✉ James R. Thompson Center, 100 W. Randolph St., Suite 3-400, Chicago 60601, ☎ 800/223–0121).

Scenic Drives

The Illinois part of the **Lake Michigan Circle Tour** follows the shoreline along Lake Shore Drive through Chicago and passes through the elegant suburbs of the North Shore: Evanston, Winnetka, Glencoe, Highland Park, and Lake Forest. **Great River Road** follows the Mississippi River, stretching the length of Illinois (more than 500 mi) from East Dubuque to Cairo (pronounced *kay*-ro).

National and State Parks

National Park

Shawnee National Forest (✉ 50 Rte. 145S, Harrisburg 62946, ☎ 618/253–7114 or 800/699–6637) blankets the southern tip of Illinois with 275,000 acres; it is here that glaciers stopped flattening the state during the last Ice Age.

State Parks

Illinois has more than 260 state parks, conservation areas, fish and wildlife areas, and recreation areas. For a magazine on state parks, contact the **Illinois Department of Natural Resources** (✉ 524 S. 2nd St., Springfield 62701-1787, ☎ 217/782–7454). **Illinois Beach State Park** (✉ Lake Front, Zion 60099, ☎ 847/662–4811), on Lake Michigan near the Wisconsin border, has sandy beaches along 6½ mi of shoreline. **Rend Lake/Wayne Fitzgerrell State Park** (✉ 11094 Ranger Rd., Whittington 62897, ☎ 618/629–2320) has the state's second-largest inland lake, where you can fish, sail, and swim. **Starved Rock State Park** (✉ Box 509, Utica 61373, ☎ 815/667–4726), on the Illinois River between LaSalle and Ottawa, has 18 canyons formed during the melting of the glaciers.

CHICAGO

From the elegance of Michigan Avenue's shops to the stunning sweep of the lakefront skyline, Chicago has much to offer. The Loop, the city's central business district, is a living museum of skyscraper architecture, while many outlying neighborhoods retain the grace and homey quality of pre–World War II America. Chicago's arts community is world class, and strong ethnic communities embrace immigrants from countries as disparate as Croatia and Cambodia, all of whom leave their cultural stamp on the city.

Visitor Information

Chicago Office of Tourism: Visitor Information Center (✉ Chicago Cultural Center, 77 E. Randolph St., 60602, ☎ 312/744–2400 or 800/

226–6632) and walk-in centers (✉ historic Water Tower, 806 N. Michigan Ave.; ✉ Navy Pier's Illinois Marketplace, 600 E. Grand Ave.). **Mayor's Office of Special Events:** General Information and Activities (✉ 121 N. La Salle St., Room 703, 60602, ☎ 312/744–3315 or 312/744–3370 for recordings).

Arriving and Departing

By Bus

Greyhound Lines (✉ 630 W. Harrison St., ☎ 312/408–5980 or 800/231–2222).

By Car

From the east the Indiana Toll Road (I–80/90) leads to the Chicago Skyway (also a toll road), which runs into the Dan Ryan Expressway (I–90/94); take the Dan Ryan west to any downtown exit. From the south, take I–57 to the Dan Ryan. From the west follow I–80 to I–55, which is the major artery from the southwest and leads into Lake Shore Drive. From the north I–94 and I–90 eastbound merge about 10 mi north of downtown to form the John F. Kennedy Expressway (I–90/94).

By Plane

Every national airline, most international airlines, and a number of regional carriers fly into **O'Hare International Airport,** some 20 mi northwest of downtown Chicago. One of the world's busiest airports, it is a hub for United and American airlines. The **Chicago Transit Authority** (☎ 312/836–7000) subway station is in the underground concourse between terminals; for $1.50, trains will take you into the Loop. **Airport Express** (☎ 312/454–7799 or 800/654–7871) provides express coach service from O'Hare to major downtown and Near North hotels for a fare of $15.50 one-way. Metered taxicab service is available at O'Hare; expect to pay $25–$30 (plus tip) to Near North and downtown locations.

Many major carriers also use **Midway Airport,** on the city's southwest side, close to downtown. The **Chicago Transit Authority**'s Orange Line train runs from Midway to the Loop, where you can transfer to other lines. Or for $11 you can take an **Airport Express** bus from Midway to hotels in the Loop and Near North. Cabs from Midway cost $17–$22, plus tip.

By Train

Amtrak serves Chicago's Union Station (✉ 225 S. Canal St., at Jackson St., ☎ 800/872–7245).

Getting Around Chicago

The best way to see Chicago is on foot, supplemented by public transportation or taxi. Streets are laid out in a grid, the center of which is the intersection of Madison Street, which runs east–west, and State Street, which runs north–south.

By Car

Leave your car behind if you're seeing the Loop, the Near North Side, or Lincoln Park. You'll need a car to go to the suburbs or outlying city neighborhoods. Downtown parking lots charge $7–$15 a day.

By Public Transportation

The **Chicago Transit Authority** and the **RTA** (☎ 312/836–7000 for both) provide information on how to get around on city rapid-transit and bus lines, suburban bus lines, and commuter trains; the base fare is $1.50. On the subway and the El, you must use a fare card, which can be purchased at the station. Buses accept either cash (exact change only) or fare cards.

By Taxi

Taxis are metered. The base fare is $1.60, plus $1.40 for each additional mile or minute of waiting time. Taxi drivers expect a 15% tip. Major companies are **American United Cab** (☎ 773/248–7600), **Checker Taxi Association** (☎ 312/243–2537), and **Yellow Cab** (☎ 312/829–4222).

Orientation Tours

The **Chicago Architecture Foundation** (✉ 224 S. Michigan Ave., ☎ 312/922–3432) operates downtown walking tours; bus tours; a river cruise; neighborhood tours; and, during summer, tours of two Prairie Avenue house museums—the Glessner House and the Henry B. Clarke House. **Chicago Motor Coach Co.** (☎ 312/666–1000) runs narrated tours of Chicago landmarks in double-decker buses. Tours depart from the Sears Tower (✉ Franklin and Jackson Sts.), the bridge at Michigan and Wacker streets, and the Water Tower (✉ Pearson and Michigan Sts.), among other locations. **Wendella Sightseeing Boats** (✉ Lower Michigan Ave. at the Wrigley Bldg., ☎ 312/337–1446), and **Mercury Chicago Skyline Cruiseline** (✉ Michigan Ave. at Wacker Dr., ☎ 312/332–1353) run guided tours of the Chicago River and Lake Michigan throughout the spring, summer, and early fall.

Exploring Chicago

Outside downtown and the Loop, Chicago is a city of neighborhoods whose rich ethnic diversity gives the city its special air.

The Loop

Walking through Chicago's central business district (defined by and named for the loop of the elevated train that circles it) is like taking a course in the history of American commercial architecture. From the Monadnock Building, the tallest load-bearing masonry structure in the world, to the Sears Tower, technically the tallest building of any kind in North America, Chicago's skyscrapers have unique personalities. Adorning the plazas of many buildings are sculptures by Picasso, Calder, Miró, and other artists.

The **Chicago Cultural Center** (✉ 78 E. Washington St., at Michigan Ave., ☎ 312/346–3278; free) used to be the city's main library; now it's used primarily for free exhibits, lectures, and performances. Two splendid Tiffany-glass domes are among its treasures.

The terra-cotta **Reliance Building** (✉ 32 N. State St. at Washington St.), designed by John Root and Charles Atwood in 1894, has the distinctive Chicago window, an innovation in early skyscrapers: two small panes of glass, which open to catch the Lake Michigan breezes, flanking a large center panel. The **Richard J. Daley Center** (✉ Dearborn and Washington Sts.), named for the late mayor, father of the current mayor Richard Daley, is headquarters for the Cook County court system; in the plaza is a 52-ft Cor-Ten steel sculpture by Picasso.

Spacious halls, high ceilings, and plenty of marble define the handsome neoclassical **Chicago City Hall/Cook County Building** (✉ 121 N. La Salle St.), designed by Holabird & Roche in 1911. If you're lucky, you may catch the city council in session—usually a good show, with plenty of hot air. Helmut Jahn's 1985 **James R. Thompson Center** (✉ Clark and Randolph Sts.), which houses state offices, has a jarring futuristic design in striking contrast to the city's classically styled civic structures.

A softly curving building emphasizing the bend in the Chicago River, **333 West Wacker Drive** was constructed in an irregular shape dictated by the triangular parcel on which it sits. The building, designed by Kohn

Pedersen Fox in 1983 and set in a spacious plaza, has forest-green marble columns and a shimmering green-glass skin resembling the color of the river.

The graceful 1969 **First National Bank** (✉ Dearborn and Madison Sts.) was one of the first skyscrapers to slope upward from its base like the capital letter *A*. The adjoining plaza is a summer lunchtime hangout. A Chagall mosaic, *The Four Seasons,* is at the northeast corner.

Chicago has some handsome examples of very early skyscrapers. The 1894 **Marquette Building** (✉ 140 S. Dearborn St.), by Holabird & Roche, features an exterior terra-cotta bas-relief and interior reliefs and mosaics depicting scenes from early Chicago history. The darkly handsome **Monadnock Building** (✉ 53 W. Jackson Blvd., at Dearborn St.) has walls 6 ft thick at the base; the north half was built by Burnham & Root in 1891, the south half by Holabird & Roche in 1893.

The Gothic-style **Fisher Building** (✉ 343 S. Dearborn St.), designed by D. H. Burnham & Co. in 1895, is exquisitely ornamented with carved terra-cotta cherubs and fish. The **Chicago Board of Trade** (✉ 141 W. Jackson Blvd., at La Salle St.), a 1930 design by Holabird & Root, is one of the few important Art Deco buildings in Chicago. At the top is a gilded statue of Ceres, the Roman goddess of agriculture—an apt overseer of the frenetic commodities trading within.

★ The **Sears Tower** (✉ 233 S. Wacker Dr., at Jackson Blvd., ☎ 312/875–9696, 🎟 $7) has 110 stories and reaches to 1,454 ft. A Skidmore, Owings & Merrill design of 1974, the tower affords unbeatable views from the sky deck, but there are long lines on weekends. The Wacker Drive lobby has a jolly mobile by Alexander Calder. The imposing red-stone **Rookery Building** (✉ 209 S. La Salle St., ☎ 312/553–6150), east of the Sears Tower, was designed in 1888 by Burnham &Root; Frank Lloyd Wright remodeled the magnificent lobby in 1905.

The Chicago Symphony Orchestra performs in Orchestra Hall, part of **Symphony Center** (✉ 220 S. Michigan Ave.), known for its excellent acoustics and elegant 1904 design.

★ The **Art Institute of Chicago** (✉ 111 S. Michigan Ave., ☎ 312/443–3600; 🎟 $7), across the street from the Symphony Center, is one of the finest museums in the world. In addition to its renowned collections of Impressionist and Postimpressionist paintings and medieval and Renaissance works, the museum contains the Thorne Miniature Rooms, illustrating interior decoration in every historical style; a renowned collection of Chinese, Japanese, and Korean art spanning five millennia; and a meticulous reconstruction of the trading room of the old Chicago Stock Exchange.

Largely unchanged since 1898, the **Fine Arts Building** (✉ 410 S. Michigan Ave.) contains movie theaters showing foreign and art films. The handsome detailing on the exterior previews the marble and woodwork in the lobby. Around the corner from the Fine Arts Building, the 4,000-seat **Auditorium Theatre** (✉ 50 E. Congress Pkwy., ☎ 312/922–2110), built in 1889 by Adler and Sullivan, has unobstructed sight lines and near-perfect acoustics. From May to September the mammoth **Buckingham Fountain** bubbles and gushes in **Grant Park,** two blocks east of the Auditorium Theatre. It's worth a detour to see the profusion of nymphs, cherubs, and fish. A light show takes place from 9 to 11 PM between May and September.

The **Harold Washington Library Center** (✉ 400 S. State St., ☎ 312/747–4999), a postmodern homage to classical-style public buildings, was completed in 1991. Said to be the largest municipal library in the

Chicago

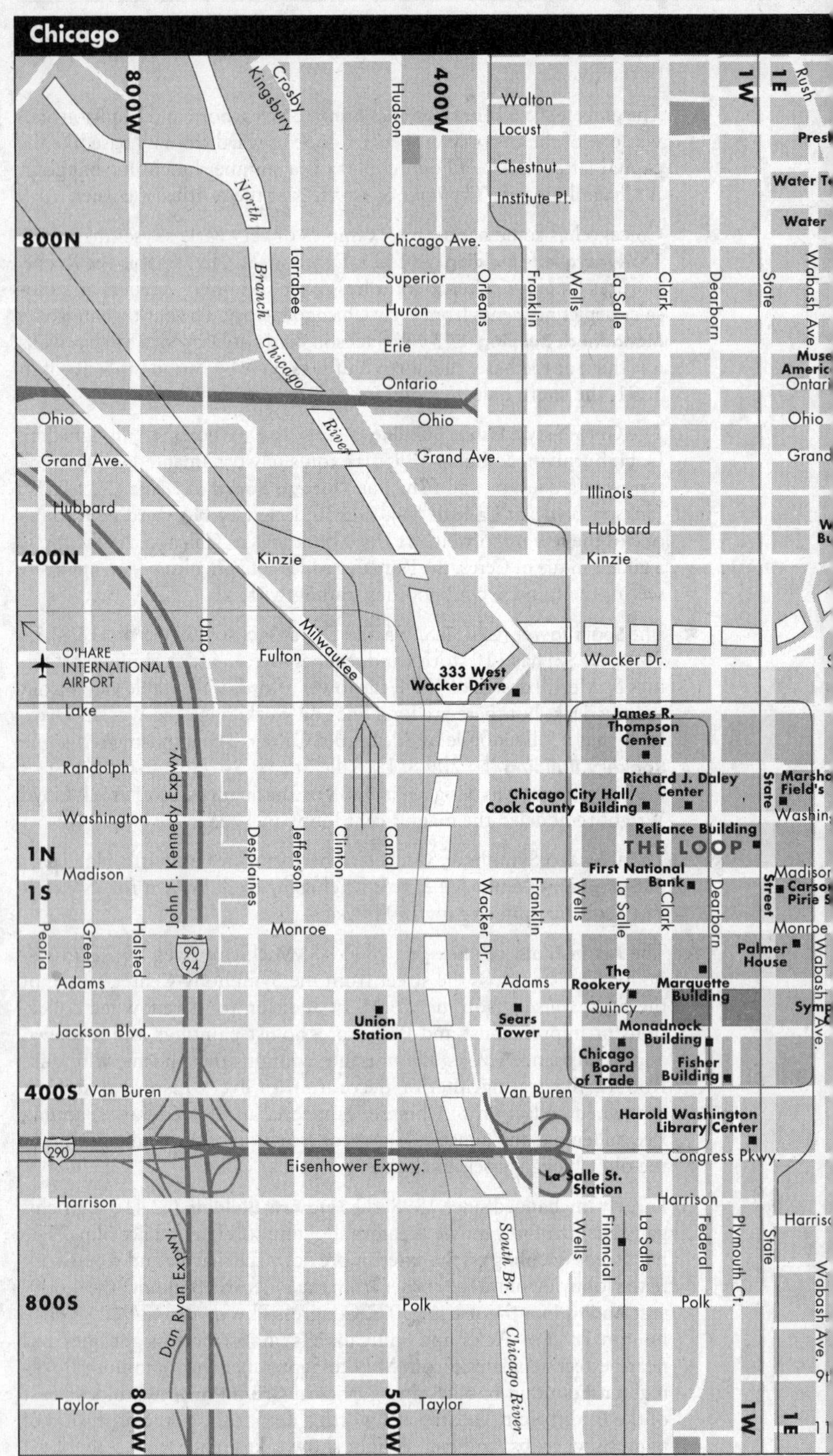

800W
Crosby
Kingsbury
Hudson
400W
Walton
Locust
Chestnut
Institute Pl.
1W
1E
Rush
North
Branch
Chicago
River
800N
Chicago Ave.
Superior
Huron
Erie
Ontario
Ohio
Grand Ave.
Larrabee
Orleans
Franklin
Wells
La Salle
Clark
Dearborn
State
Wabash Ave.
Ohio
Grand Ave.
Hubbard
400N
Kinzie
Illinois
Hubbard
Kinzie
Milwaukee
O'HARE INTERNATIONAL AIRPORT
Fulton
Wacker Dr.
333 West Wacker Drive
Lake
James R. Thompson Center
Randolph
Richard J. Daley Center
Chicago City Hall/ Cook County Building
Washington
Reliance Building
THE LOOP
1N
Madison
1S
First National Bank
State Street
John F. Kennedy Expwy.
Desplaines
Jefferson
Clinton
Canal
Wacker Dr.
Monroe
Peoria
Green
Halsted
90 94
Adams
Palmer House
The Rookery
Marquette Building
Quincy
Jackson Blvd.
Union Station
Sears Tower
Monadnock Building
Chicago Board of Trade
Fisher Building
400S
Van Buren
Harold Washington Library Center
290
Eisenhower Expwy.
Congress Pkwy.
La Salle St. Station
Harrison
Financial
Federal
Plymouth Ct.
South Br.
Chicago River
Dan Ryan Expwy.
800S
Polk
Taylor
500W

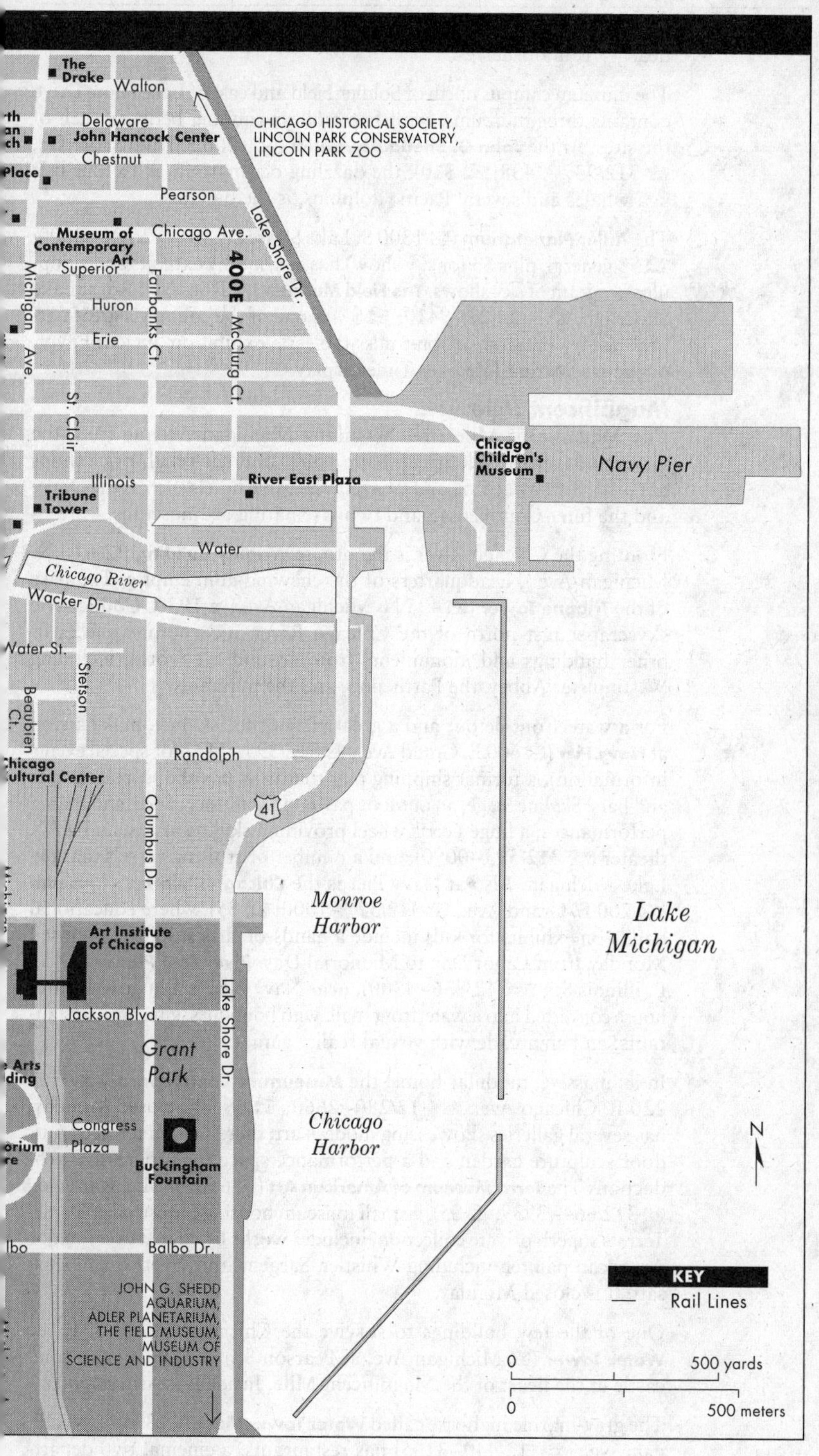
The Drake
Walton
Delaware
John Hancock Center
CHICAGO HISTORICAL SOCIETY,
LINCOLN PARK CONSERVATORY,
LINCOLN PARK ZOO
Chestnut
Pearson
Lake Shore Dr.
Museum of Contemporary Art
Chicago Ave.
400E
Superior
Huron
Erie
Michigan Ave.
Fairbanks Ct.
McClurg Ct.
St. Clair
Illinois
River East Plaza
Chicago Children's Museum
Navy Pier
Tribune Tower
Water
Chicago River
Wacker Dr.
Water St.
Stetson
Beaubien Ct.
Randolph
Chicago Cultural Center
41
Columbus Dr.
Monroe Harbor
Lake Michigan
Art Institute of Chicago
Jackson Blvd.
Grant Park
Lake Shore Dr.
Congress Plaza
Chicago Harbor
N
Buckingham Fountain
Balbo Dr.
JOHN G. SHEDD AQUARIUM,
ADLER PLANETARIUM,
THE FIELD MUSEUM,
MUSEUM OF
SCIENCE AND INDUSTRY
KEY
Rail Lines
0
500 yards
0
500 meters

nation, it includes a performing arts auditorium, winter garden, and nearly 71 mi of shelves.

The museum campus north of Soldier Field and east of Lake Shore Drive contains three museums, with free trolleys running between each of the sites. At the **John G. Shedd Aquarium** (✉ 1200 S. Lake Shore Dr., ☎ 312/939–2438; $10), the dazzling oceanarium, with four beluga whales and several Pacific dolphins, is the big draw.

The **Adler Planetarium** (✉ 1300 S. Lake Shore Dr., ☎ 312/322–0300; $3 general, plus $3 for sky show) has astronomy exhibits and a popular program of sky shows. ★ **The Field Museum** (✉ Roosevelt Rd. at Lake Shore Dr., ☎ 312/922–9410; $7) is one of the country's great natural history museums. Don't miss the eerie exhibit on ancient Egypt, or the fascinating Life over Time display.

Magnificent Mile

The Magnificent Mile stretches along Michigan Avenue from the Chicago River to Oak Street. Here you'll find such high-price shops as Gucci, Tiffany & Co., and Chanel; venerable hotels such as the Drake and the Inter-Continental; and two fascinating art museums.

Fronting the Chicago River is the ornate **Wrigley Building** (✉ 410 N. Michigan Ave.), headquarters of the chewing-gum empire. The base of the **Tribune Tower** (✉ 435 N. Michigan Ave.), a 1930s Gothic-style skyscraper just north of the Chicago River, incorporates pieces of other buildings and monuments from around the world, including Westminster Abbey, the Parthenon, and the pyramids.

For a waterfront detour and a great view of the skyline, make a stop at ★ **Navy Pier** (✉ 600 E. Grand Ave., ☎ 312/595–7437 for special events information), a former shipping pier that now has shops; restaurants and bars; Skyline Stage, an outdoor pavilion for music, dance, and drama performances; a huge Ferris wheel providing skyline vistas; an IMAX theater (☎ 312/595–0090); and a number of cruising vessels that ply Lake Michigan. Also at Navy Pier is the **Chicago Children's Museum** (✉ 700 E. Grand Ave., ☎ 312/527–1000; $5), where educational hands-on exhibits for kids include a hands-on arts studio. It is closed Monday from Labor Day to Memorial Day. **River East Plaza** (✉ 435 E. Illinois St., ☎ 312/836–4300), near Navy Pier, is a huge old warehouse converted into a waterfront mall, with boutiques, gift shops, restaurants, and an arcade with virtual reality games.

In its massive, modular home, the **Museum of Contemporary Art** (✉ 220 E. Chicago Ave., ☎ 312/280–2660; $6.50), closed Monday, has several galleries showcasing modern art; there's also a terraced outdoor sculpture garden and a performance space for progressive productions.The **Terra Museum of American Art** (✉ 666 N. Michigan Ave., ☎ 312/664–3939; $5), a small museum housing industrialist Daniel Terra's superb private collection, includes works by almost every major American painter, including Whistler, Sargent, the Wyeths, and Cassatt; it is closed Monday.

One of the few buildings to survive the Chicago fire of 1871, the **Water Tower** (✉ Michigan Ave. at Pearson St.) sits like a giant sand castle at the heart of the Magnificent Mile. Inside is a visitor center.

The gray-marble high-rise called **Water Tower Place** (✉ 835 N. Michigan Ave., ☎ 312/440–3165) has restaurants, a cinema, two department stores, and boutiques. You can view the city from a height of 1,000 ft at the observatory on the 94th floor of the 100-story **John Hancock Center** (✉ 875 N. Michigan Ave., ☎ 312/751–3681; $7); or have a drink in the bar on the 96th floor and save yourself the observatory fee. A change of pace from the North Michigan Avenue shops, the **Fourth Presbyterian Church** (✉ 126 E. Chestnut St., ☎ 312/787–4570) is a small, Gothic-style jewel with a quiet courtyard. On Fridays, the sanctuary often holds organ recitals and concerts.

Lincoln Park

Lincoln Park is the area that stretches from North Avenue to Diversey Parkway and from the lakefront on the east to about Racine Avenue on the west. The adjoining lakefront park is also called Lincoln Park (causing visitors occasional confusion), though it stretches several miles farther north than the neighborhood.

The **Chicago Historical Society** (✉ 1601 N. Clark St., ☎ 312/642–4600; 🎫 $5) contains a costumes alcove, as well as history galleries where you can view Lincoln's deathbed and the Bible of abolitionist John Brown. Children enjoy climbing aboard the Pioneer locomotive, Chicago's first train and the largest artifact in the museum's collection.

You'll find elegant town houses and small apartment buildings from ★ the late 1800s and early 1900s in the **Lincoln Park neighborhood,** the heart of which is the intersection of Fullerton Avenue, Lincoln Avenue, and Halsted Street. The area declined after World War II as residents moved to the suburbs, but it was rediscovered in the 1970s; now it's full of million-dollar homes. The **Biograph Theater** (✉ 2433 N. Lincoln Ave., ☎ 773/348–4123), where the gangster John Dillinger met his end at the hands of the FBI, is on the National Register of Historic Places and still shows first-run movies.

Other Attractions

River North—a former warehouse neighborhood west of Michigan Avenue, bounded roughly by Clark Street, Chicago Avenue, Orleans Street, and the Chicago River—bloomed during the mid-1980s gentrification craze and now is home to a number of art galleries and trendy restaurants. The Visitor Welcome Center in the historic Water Tower (✉ Michigan Ave. at Pearson St.) carries the *Chicago Gallery News,* which lists addresses, hours, and current exhibits.

The **Museum of Science and Industry** (✉ E. 57th St. and S. Lake Shore Dr., ☎ 773/684–1414; 🎫 $6), on the lake in Hyde Park about 7 mi south of the Loop, is a treasure trove of gadgetry, applied science, and hands-on exhibits. There's a genuine German U-boat, a reproduction coal mine, Colleen Moore's Fairy Castle (a dollhouse to end all dollhouses), actual spacecraft from early NASA missions, and a giant-screen Omnimax theater.

Parks, Gardens, and Zoos

Most of Chicago's more than 20 mi of shoreline is parkland or beach reserved for public use. A 19-mi path stretches along the lakefront, snaking through **Lincoln Park, Grant Park** (just east of the Loop), and **Jackson Park** (just south of the Museum of Science and Industry, with a wooded island and the Osaka Japanese garden) and winding past half a dozen harbors, two golf courses, Navy Pier, Buckingham Fountain, the lakefront museum campus, McCormick Place, and all the city's popular beaches. Bikes are the best way to cover maximum territory; they can be rented in summer at the concession near the Lincoln Park entrance at Fullerton Avenue and Cannon Drive. Beware of bicycle thieves along the comparatively deserted stretch south of McCormick Place, especially on weekdays and at night.

★ The 35-acre **Lincoln Park Zoo** (✉ 2200 N. Cannon Dr., ☎ 312/742–2000; 🎫 free), the nation's oldest, is home to all the requisite zoo denizens, including koalas, reptiles, great apes, and lowland gorillas. Youngsters especially enjoy the **Children's Zoo** and the **Farm-in-the-Zoo**, which features farm animals plus a learning center with films and demonstrations. In Lincoln Park's **South Pond,** just south of the Lincoln Park Zoo, you can rent paddleboats May–October. The **Lincoln Park Conservatory** (⊠ 2400 N. Stockton Dr., ☎ 312/742–7736; free), which borders the Lincoln Park Zoo, has a palm house, a fernery, special exhibits, and large outdoor gardens.

There are hundreds of parks in neighborhoods throughout the city and suburbs. Charging no admission, the **Garfield Park Conservatory** (⊠ 300 N. Central Park Blvd., ☎ 312/746–5100; free) maintains 5 acres of plants and flowers under glass and holds four shows a year. The **Chicago Botanic Garden** (⊠ 1000 Lake Cook Rd., Glencoe, ☎ 847/835–5440; $6 per car), north of the city in Glencoe, covers 385 acres and has 15 separate gardens and three greenhouses. The **Morton Arboretum** (⊠ Rte. 53 north of I–88, Lisle, ☎ 630/719–2465; $7 per car), in the western suburbs, has 1,700 acres of woody plants, woodlands, and outdoor gardens, plus 13 mi of walking trails.

Dining

Most eating places listed below are in the Near North, River North, and Loop areas, within walking distance of the major hotel districts. A few are a bit farther out, in the city's residential neighborhoods and ethnic enclaves. For clusters of ethnic restaurants too numerous to mention here, try Greektown, at Halsted and Madison streets; Chinatown, at Wentworth Avenue and 23rd Street; Little Italy, on Taylor Street between Racine and Ashland avenues; Argyle Street between Broadway and Sheridan Road (for Chinese and Vietnamese); Devon Avenue between Leavitt Street and Sacramento Avenue (Indian); and Clark Street from Belmont Avenue to Addison Street (Thai, Japanese, Chinese, Korean, Ethiopian, Italian, and Mexican).

Restaurant listings appear in the monthly *Chicago* magazine and in the Friday editions of the *Chicago Tribune* and the *Chicago Sun-Times* (Weekend section). For price ranges *see* Chart 1 (A) *in* On the Road with Fodor's.

$$$$ ✕ **Ambria.** Set in an art nouveau building in Lincoln Park, Ambria has a seasonally changing, contemporary French menu that emphasizes natural juices and vegetable reductions to accompany the entrées. Finish with the sensational dessert soufflé. ⊠ *2300 N. Lincoln Park West,* ☎ *773/472–5959. Reservations essential. Jacket required. AE, D, DC, MC, V. Closed Sun. No lunch.*

$$$$ ★ ✕ **Charlie Trotter's.** This top-of-the-line Lincoln Park town house accommodates 28 tables. Chef-owner Charlie Trotter prepares stellar new American cuisine, incorporating flavors from around the globe into classic French dishes. Dishes are presented in a multicourse degustation format; there's even a nightly vegetable-based (but not vegetarian) tasting menu. ⊠ *816 W. Armitage Ave.,* ☎ *773/248–6228. Reservations essential. AE, D, DC, MC, V. Closed Sun.–Mon. No lunch.*

$$$$ ★ ✕ **Everest.** On the 40th floor of a postmodern skyscraper in the heart of the financial district, Everest continues to scale heights by reinventing classic French cuisine with a contemporary twist. ⊠ *440 S. La Salle St.,* ☎ *312/663–8920. Reservations essential. AE, D, DC, MC, V. Closed Sun.–Mon. No lunch.*

$$$$ ✕ **Le Français.** In a country-French setting, this restaurant in the northwestern suburbs turns out contemporary French creations that are visual masterpieces. Portions are substantial for cuisine this fine, and the desserts are unparalleled. ⊠ *269 S. Milwaukee Ave., Wheeling,* ☎ *847/*

541–7470. *Reservations essential. Jacket required. AE, D, DC, MC, V. Closed Sun. No lunch Mon. and Sat.*

$$$$ ★ ✕ **Spiaggia.** In elegant pink-and-teal quarters overlooking the lake, Spiaggia is the most opulent Italian restaurant in town, with elaborate stuffed pastas, veal chops in a vodka-cream sauce, and other inventive dishes. Sample the kitchen's talents next door at Café Spiaggia, with lower prices but equally excellent meals. ✉ *980 N. Michigan Ave.,* ☎ *312/280–2750. Reservations essential. Jacket required. AE, D, DC, MC, V. No lunch Sun.*

$$$$ ★ ✕ **Trio.** Creative touches distinguish Trio's elaborate contemporary cuisine; dishes may be served on such unique objects as painters' palettes. An eight-course degustation menu, priced at $85, includes the chef's choice of specialties. ✉ *1625 Hinman, Evanston,* ☎ *847/733–8746. Reservations essential. AE, D, DC, MC, V. Closed Mon. No lunch.*

$$$ ✕ **Morton's of Chicago.** Chicago's best steak house serves beautiful, hefty steaks cooked to perfection. Excellent service, a classy ambience, and a very good wine list add to the appeal. Vegetarians and budget watchers should look elsewhere. ✉ *1050 N. State St.,* ☎ *312/266–4820. AE, D, DC, MC, V. No lunch.*

$$$ ✕ **Signature Room at the 95th.** The main draw here is the view—it's at the top of the John Hancock Center—though the elegant restaurant also has good food. At $8.95, the weekday lunch buffet is a good bargain. Dinner is a very formal affair; the expensive Sunday brunch is splendid. ✉ *John Hancock Center, 875 N. Michigan Ave.,* ☎ *312/787–9596. AE, D, DC, MC, V.*

$$$ ✕ **Spago.** There are two dining options at Wolfgang Puck's California spin-off: the casual grill, open for lunch and dinner daily, featuring such Puck signature dishes as his outstanding meat loaf and gourmet pizzas; and the main dining room, where the menu and setting are more refined. ✉ *520 N. Dearborn St.,* ☎ *312/527–3700. Reservations essential in main dining room. AE, D, DC, MC, V. No lunch weekends in main dining room; no lunch Sun. in grill.*

$$–$$$ ✕ **Arun's.** Long considered the city's best—and most expensive—Thai restaurant, Arun's is known for its congenial staff, its elegant dining room showcasing Thai art, and, last but not least, superbly presented dishes made with the freshest ingredients. ✉ *4156 N. Kedzie Ave.,* ☎ *773/539–1909. AE, D, DC, MC, V. Closed Mon. No lunch.*

$$–$$$ ★ ✕ **Brasserie Jo.** Discerning diners come here to sample Everest chef Jean Joho's food at relatively moderate prices. Don't miss the shrimp in a phyllo-dough bag or classic coq au vin. ✉ *59 W. Hubbard St.,* ☎ *312/595–0800. AE, D, DC, MC, V. No lunch weekends.*

$$–$$$ ★ ✕ **Frontera Grill/Topolobampo.** In Frontera Grill's cozy, colorful storefront, genuine regional Mexican cooking goes way beyond burritos and chips: from charbroiled catfish with jicama salad to garlicky skewered tenderloin with *poblano* peppers and bacon. At Topolobampo, next door, slightly higher prices give the chef an opportunity to experiment with more expensive ingredients. ✉ *445 N. Clark St.,* ☎ *312/661–1434. Reservations essential at Topolobampo. AE, D, DC, MC, V. Closed Sun.–Mon. No lunch Sat. at Topolobampo.*

$$–$$$ ✕ **Heaven on Seven.** Enter at Rush and Ontario streets to sample authentic Cajun and Creole specialties—shrimp étouffée, jambalaya, gumbo, and the like—served in lively surroundings. ✉ *600 N. Michigan Ave.,* ☎ *312/280–7774. AE, D, DC, MC, V.*

$$–$$$ ✕ **Maggiano's Little Italy.** This convivial restaurant serves up enormous portions of red-sauce Italian food in a wide-open dining room. Lunchtime sandwiches are especially good. ✉ *516 N. Clark St.,* ☎ *312/644–7700. AE, D, DC, MC, V.*

$$–$$$ ✕ **Marché.** This hip restaurant west of the Loop draws a see-and-be-seen crowd that includes many celebs. Standouts on the bistro menu

are spit-roasted chicken and tempting desserts such as crème brûlée and chocolate torte. ✉ *833 W. Randolph St.,* ☎ *312/226–8399. AE, D, DC, MC, V. No lunch Sat. or Sun.*

$$–$$$ ✕ **Philander's.** One of Oak Park's few fine restaurants, Philander's is also a prime place to hear live jazz every night. The hotel dining room feels like a classy tavern and serves reliable seafood, pastas, and vegetarian dishes, in addition to Peterson's ice cream—a local institution. ✉ *Carleton Hotel, 1120 Pleasant St., Oak Park,* ☎ *708/848–4250. AE, D, DC, MC, V. Closed Sun. No lunch.*

$$–$$$ ✕ **Printer's Row.** Named after its chic loft neighborhood in the South Loop, this warm and attractive restaurant specializes in game meats and seafood, with notable venison preparations. ✉ *550 S. Dearborn St.,* ☎ *312/461–0780. AE, D, DC, MC, V. Closed Sun. No lunch Sat.*

$$–$$$ ✕ **Rosebud Cafe.** Specializing in good, old-fashioned southern Italian cuisine, Rosebud serves a superior red sauce, and the roasted peppers, homemade sausage, chicken Vesuvio, and exquisitely prepared pastas are not to be missed. The wait for a table can stretch to an hour despite reservations. ✉ *1500 W. Taylor St.,* ☎ *312/942–1117. AE, D, DC, MC, V. No lunch weekends.*

$$ ✕ **The Berghoff.** This Loop institution has two huge, oak-paneled dining rooms and a splendid bar with Berghoff beer on tap. Expect a wait of 15 minutes or so at midday. American favorites augment the menu of German classics (Wiener schnitzel, sauerbraten). ✉ *17 W. Adams St.,* ☎ *312/427–3170. AE, MC, V. Closed Sun.*

$$ ✕ **Le Bouchon.** Chef-owner Jean-Claude Poilevey serves reasonably priced bistro fare at this intimate 45-seat French restaurant in Bucktown. The onion tart is a signature appetizer. Typical entrées include duck for two and sautéed rabbit with shallots and mustard. ✉ *1958 N. Damen Ave.,* ☎ *773/862–6600. AE, D, DC, MC, V. Closed Sun. No lunch.*

$$ ✕ **Mia Francesca.** Why is this tiny restaurant so insanely popular? Principally because of its very good, authentic Italian cooking; its moderate prices don't hurt. Try the classic bruschetta or full-flavored pasta and chicken dishes. ✉ *3311 N. Clark St.,* ☎ *773/281–3310. Reservations not accepted. AE, MC, V. No lunch.*

$$ ✕ **Yoshi's Cafe.** Chef Yoshi Katsumura's restaurant specializes in Asian-influenced French bistro cuisine. Dishes are gorgeously presented; try the fresh seafood, such as tuna tartare with homemade guacamole. ✉ *3257 N. Halsted St.,* ☎ *773/248–6160. AE, DC, MC, V. Closed Mon. No lunch.*

$ ✕ **Ann Sather.** The line often stretches down the street for hearty breakfasts at this large Swedish restaurant, emphasizing home-style food and service. Specialties include omelets, Swedish pancakes, homemade cinnamon rolls, potato sausage, chicken croquettes, and sandwiches. ✉ *929 W. Belmont Ave.,* ☎ *773/348–2378. AE, DC, MC, V.*

$ ✕ **Peterson's Old-Fashioned Ice Cream Parlor.** As its name implies, this place has ice cream sodas, malts, and sundaes that will make you nostalgic for the good old soda-fountain days. Peterson's also serves light meals. ✉ *1100 Chicago Ave., Oak Park,* ☎ *708/386–6130. No credit cards.*

$ ★ ✕ **Pizzeria Uno/Pizzeria Due.** This is where Chicago deep-dish pizza got its start. There's usually a shorter wait for a table at Pizzeria Due (same ownership and menu, different decor and longer hours), a block away. ✉ *Uno: 29 E. Ohio St.,* ☎ *312/321–1000;* ✉ *Due: 619 N. Wabash Ave.,* ☎ *312/943–2400. Reservations not accepted. AE, D, DC, MC, V.*

Lodging

Chicago is the country's biggest convention town, and accommodations can be tight when major events are scheduled. Most hotels run weekend specials when no big shows are on. Accommodations are concentrated in the Loop and the Near North Side. **Bed and Breakfast Chicago** (✉ Box 14088, 60614, ☎ 312/951–0085) handles more than 50 B&Bs in the downtown area. For price ranges *see* Chart 2(A) *in* On the Road with Fodor's.

$$$$ ★ **The Drake.** The grandest of Chicago's traditional hotels was built in 1920 in the style of an Italian Renaissance palace. The Palm Court, with its fountain and harpist, is a lovely setting for afternoon tea. Asian art and lamps bring a touch of class to the rooms, many of which have splendid lake views. *✉ 140 E. Walton Pl., 60611, ☎ 312/787–2200 or 800/553–7253, FAX 312/787–1431. 535 rooms. 3 restaurants, exercise room. AE, D, DC, MC, V.*

$$$$ **The Fairmont.** This 37-story neoclassical structure of Spanish pink granite is next to the Illinois Center complex (where guests have access to a huge athletic facility). Many of the sizable rooms have views of the lake and Grant Park. *✉ 200 N. Columbus Dr., 60601, ☎ 312/565–8000, FAX 312/856–1032. 692 rooms. 2 restaurants. AE, D, DC, MC, V.*

$$$$ ★ **Four Seasons.** Though it feels more like a grand English manor house than an urban skyscraper, the Four Seasons enjoys spectacular lake and city views. Rooms have handcrafted armoires and beds piled with throw pillows. *✉ 120 E. Delaware Pl., 60611, ☎ 312/280–8800, FAX 312/280–1748. 343 rooms. 2 restaurants, pool, health club. AE, D, DC, MC, V.*

$$$$ ★ **Renaissance Chicago Hotel.** The modern stone-and-glass exterior houses a tidy '90s interpretation of turn-of-the-century splendor. Lavish floral carpets, crystal-beaded chandeliers, and French provincial furniture create rich-looking public areas. Rooms have separate sitting areas. *✉ 1 W. Wacker Dr., 60601, ☎ 312/372–7200 or 800/468–3571, FAX 312/372–0093. 553 rooms. 2 restaurants, pool, exercise room. AE, D, DC, MC, V.*

$$$$ ★ **Ritz-Carlton.** The Ritz-Carlton, run by Four Seasons Hotels and Resorts, sits atop the Water Tower Place shopping mall. Magnificent flower arrangements adorn the public areas, and the two-story greenhouse lobby serves afternoon tea. The luxurious, spacious rooms are a tasteful blend of European styles. *✉ 160 E. Pearson St., 60611, ☎ 312/266–1000 or 800/621–6906, FAX 312/266–1194. 430 rooms. 3 restaurants, pool, health club. AE, D, DC, MC, V.*

$$$$ **Sutton Place Hotel.** This ultramodern hotel has a sleek, art deco lobby and similarly stylish guest rooms, with black leather headboards and photographs by Robert Mapplethorpe (not to worry, the subjects are floral). *✉ 21 E. Bellevue Pl., 60611, ☎ 312/266–2100 or 800/606–8188, FAX 312/266–2103. 246 rooms. Restaurant, exercise room. AE, D, DC, MC, V.*

$$$–$$$$ **Chicago Hilton and Towers.** Built in 1927, this huge grand hotel in the South Loop has a lavishly restored lobby filled with gilt and crystal. The large ballroom is worthy of Marie Antoinette. *✉ 720 S. Michigan Ave., 60605, ☎ 312/922–4400, FAX 312/922–5240. 1,543 rooms. 3 restaurants, pool, health club. AE, D, DC, MC, V.*

$$$–$$$$ **Hotel Inter-Continental Chicago.** A grand architectural gem, the Inter-Continental has a dramatic lobby, ornately painted ceilings, marble steps, and a second-floor terra-cotta fountain. The Italianate junior-Olympic-size pool helped earn the hotel a spot on the National Register of Historic Places. Its North Tower is less inspiring. *✉ 505 N. Michigan Ave., 60611, ☎ 312/944–4100 or 800/628–2112, FAX 312/944–3050. 844 rooms. 2 restaurants, pool, health club. AE, D, DC, MC, V.*

$$$–$$$$ **Lenox Suites.** Conveniently located near North Michigan Avenue, the hotel has one-room "suites" with a Murphy bed, sofa bed, and kitchenette, in addition to one-bedroom suites with a separate living room and kitchen. ✉ *616 N. Rush St., 60611,* ☎ *312/337–1000 or 800/445–3669,* FAX *312/337–7217. 324 suites. 2 restaurants, exercise room. AE, D, DC, MC, V.*

$$$–$$$$ **Palmer House Hilton.** Built in 1871 by the Chicago merchant Potter Palmer, this hotel has public areas that reflect the opulence of that era, including a frescoed rococo lobby. Its modern guest rooms are more ordinary. ✉ *17 E. Monroe St., 60603,* ☎ *312/726–7500,* FAX *312/917–1707. 1,639 rooms. 4 restaurants, pool, exercise room. AE, D, DC, MC, V.*

$$$–$$$$ **Sheraton Chicago Hotel and Towers.** This hotel attracts business travelers with its handsomely modern appointments and lighthouse-like location on the Chicago River, which guarantees unobstructed views. Standard rooms, however, are uninspiring, with gray carpet and gray bedspreads, though the marble bathrooms are full of amenities. Although the hotel is quite vast, you won't feel in danger of getting lost. ✉ *301 E. North Water St., 60611,* ☎ *312/464–1000 or 800/233–4100,* FAX *312/464–9140. 1,152 rooms. 5 restaurants, pool, exercise room. AE, D, DC, MC, V.*

$$$ **Best Western River North.** This former warehouse in the thriving River North entertainment district has an undistinguished exterior, but inside are large, reasonably priced guest rooms with pinstriped duvets, buffalo-plaid blankets, and black-and-white tiled bathrooms. Sofa sleepers in the suites and an indoor pool make it a family favorite. Parking is free. ✉ *125 W. Ohio St., 60610,* ☎ *312/467–8088 or 800/727–0800,* FAX *312/467–1665. 148 rooms. Pool, exercise room. AE, D, DC, MC, V.*

$$$ **Claridge Hotel.** Nestled among Victorian houses on a tree-lined Near North street, this simply outfitted 1930s building is intimate and homey. ✉ *1244 N. Dearborn Pkwy., 60610,* ☎ *312/787–4980 or 800/245–1258,* FAX *312/266–0978. 158 rooms. Restaurant. AE, D, DC, MC, V.*

$$–$$$ **The Raphael.** On a quiet, pretty street just off the Magnificent Mile, this hotel has Old World charm. Some of the guest rooms have quirky touches such as chaise longues and arched entries. ✉ *201 E. Delaware Pl., 60611,* ☎ *312/943–5000,* FAX *312/943–9483. 172 rooms. Restaurant. AE, D, DC, MC, V.*

$$ **City Suites Hotel.** Ten minutes north of the Loop in the Lakeview neighborhood, this small, European-style hotel has a fireplace in the lobby and cozy guest rooms with chic black-and-white tile baths. The location is unbeatable. ✉ *933 W. Belmont Ave., 60657,* ☎ *773/404–3400 or 800/248–9108,* FAX *773/404–3405. 45 rooms. AE, D, DC, MC, V.*

$ **Chicago International Hostel.** Near Loyola University in the Rogers Park neighborhood, this hostel has dormitory-style rooms with six or eight beds, each costing $13 a night. Guests have use of a kitchen. ✉ *6318 N. Winthrop Ave., 60660,* ☎ *773/262–1011. 100 beds, 6 private rooms. No credit cards.*

Motels

Comfort Inn of Lincoln Park (✉ 601 W. Diversey Pkwy., 60614, ☎ 773/348–2810, FAX 773/348–1912), 74 rooms; *$$.* **Hojo Inn** (✉ 720 N. La Salle St., 60610, ☎ 312/664–8100, FAX 312/664–2365), 71 rooms, restaurant; *$$.* **Ohio House** (✉ 600 N. La Salle St., 60610, ☎ 312/943–6000, FAX 312/943–6063), 50 rooms, restaurant; *$$.*

Nightlife and the Arts

For listings of arts and entertainment events, check the monthly *Chicago* magazine (on newsstands) or the Friday editions of the *Chicago Tri-*

bune or the *Chicago Sun-Times*. Two free weeklies, the *Reader* (available Thursday) and *New City* (available Wednesday), which can be found at bookstores, restaurants, and bars, are the best sources for what's happening in clubs and small theaters and for showings of noncommercial films.

Nightlife

Chicago comes alive at night. Shows usually begin at 9 PM; cover charges generally range from $3 to $10, depending on the day of the week. Most bars are open until 2 AM, and some larger dance clubs don't close until 4 AM.

BLUES CLUBS

In the years following World War II, Chicago-style blues grew into its own musical form. After fading in the '60s, Chicago blues is coming back, although more strongly on the trendy North Side than on the South Side, where it all began. **Kingston Mines** (✉ 2548 N. Halsted St., ☎ 773/477–4646) has been king of Chicago blues clubs for more than 30 years, with bands on two stages weekends. The intimate **B.L.U.E.S.** (✉ 2519 N. Halsted St., ☎ 773/528–1012) pulses with music in a rather small space. The elaborate **House of Blues** (✉ 329 N. Dearborn Ave., ☎ 312/527–2583) features top-notch groups playing in an ornate, theater-like setting with unconventional art adorning the walls. **Buddy Guy's Legends** (✉ 754 S. Wabash Ave., ☎ 312/427–0333), owned by the famous blues man, sits in a spacious former storefront. The **Checkerboard Lounge** (✉ 423 E. 43rd St., ☎ 773/624–3240) is in a rough neighborhood but has a long pedigree.

COMEDY CLUBS

Many comedy clubs have a drink minimum instead of or in addition to a cover charge. The granddaddy of all comedy clubs is **Second City** (✉ 1616 N. Wells St., ☎ 312/337–3992), which usually has two different revues playing at once. The best stand-up comedy in town is found at **Zanies** (✉ 1548 N. Wells St., ☎ 312/337–4027). **Improv Olympic** (✉ 3541 N. Clark St., ☎ 773/880–0199) presents improv troupes as well as staged shows.

DANCE CLUBS

Drink, eat, and dance at **Drink** (✉ 762 W. Fulton St., ☎ 312/733–7800), a trendy spot west of the Loop with five crowded rooms. **Polly Esther's** (✉ 213 W. Institute Pl., ☎ 312/664–0777) plays '70s and '80s dance music. **Liquid** (✉ 1997 N. Clybourn Ave., ☎ 773/528–3400) hosts popular swing nights on Sunday, Tuesday, and Thursday; other nights range from rock to salsa. **Mad Bar** (✉ 1640 N. Damen Ave., ☎ 773/227–2277), a see-and-be-seen Bucktown bar, has bands, DJs, and dancing.

FOLK CLUBS

No Exit Cafe/Gallery (✉ 6970 N. Glenwood Ave., ☎ 773/743–3355), a coffeehouse right out of the 1960s, has folk, jazz, and poetry readings. **Old Town School of Folk Music** (✉ 909 W. Armitage Ave., ☎ 773/525–7793) mixes local talent and outstanding nationally known performers.

JAZZ CLUBS

Jazz Showcase (✉ 59 W. Grand Ave., ☎ 312/670–2473) books nationally known groups in its classy River North home. **Pops for Champagne** (✉ 2934 N. Sheffield Ave., ☎ 773/472–1000) has jazz combos and a champagne bar. The **Green Mill** (✉ 4802 N. Broadway, ☎ 773/878–5552), a Chicago institution off the beaten track, books solid, sizzling local acts in an ornate '40s space. **Green Dolphin Street** (✉ 2200 N. Ashland Ave., ☎ 773/395–0066) plays bossa, bebop, Latin, and world jazz in a large, open club.

ROCK CLUBS

Metro (✉ 3730 N. Clark St., ☎ 773/549–0203) presents progressive nationally known and local artists. Downstairs from Metro, **Smart Bar** throbs with punk and funk dance tunes. The **Cubby Bear** (✉ 1059 W. Addison St., ☎ 773/327–1662), across from Wrigley Field, plays rock, fusion, and country-tinged acts. In the hip Wicker Park neighborhood, the **Double Door** (✉ 1572 N. Milwaukee Ave., ☎ 773/489–3160) books top and up-and-coming local artists. **Wild Hare** (✉ 3530 N. Clark St., ☎ 773/327–4273) is the city's premier reggae club.

FOR SINGLES

Chicago's legendary Rush Street singles scene is actually on **Division Street** between Clark and State; here you'll find such bars as **Original Mother's** (✉ 26 W. Division St., ☎ 312/642–7251), featured in the movie . . . *About Last Night.* **Butch McGuire's** (✉ 20 W. Division St., ☎ 312/337–9080) is jammed with out-of-towners on the make. River East Plaza (✉ 435 E. Illinois St.) has several popular singles spots, including the **Baja Beach Club** (☎ 312/222–1993) and **Dick's Last Resort** (☎ 312/836–7870). There's a cluster of bar life in the neighborhood around **Halsted and Armitage streets** in Lincoln Park.

GAY BARS

The area around Halsted Street approximately between Belmont and Waveland avenues has the city's highest concentration of gay bars, including the yuppified **Roscoe's Tavern & Cafe** (✉ 3356 N. Halsted St., ☎ 773/281–3355). **Berlin** (✉ 954 W. Belmont Ave., ☎ 773/348–4975) attracts a mixed crowd to its dance floor, video bar, and theme nights. **Gentry** (✉ 440 N. State St., ☎ 312/836–0933), a prime meeting spot downtown, has a piano bar and video bar.

The Arts

Chicago is a splendid city for the arts, with more than 50 theater groups, world-class orchestra and opera companies, and dozens of smaller musical ensembles.

THEATER

Half-price theater tickets are available for many productions on the day of performance at **Hot Tix** booths (✉ 108 N. State St. and historic Water Tower, 806 N. Michigan Ave., ☎ 312/977–1755 for both). With excellent acoustics, the **Auditorium Theatre** (✉ 50 E. Congress Pkwy., ☎ 312/922–2110) shows popular Broadway musicals. The grand **Shubert Theatre** (✉ 22 W. Monroe St., ☎ 312/977–1700), built in 1906, is home to touring Broadway plays, musicals, and dance companies. The **Chicago Theatre** (✉ 175 N. State St., ☎ 312/443–1130), a restored former movie palace, presents musicals, concerts, and special events. The **Athenaeum Theatre** (✉ 2936 N. Southport Ave., ☎ 773/935–6860) hosts provoking music, opera, dance, and drama performances.

Several local ensembles have made the big jump into national prominence, most notably the successful **Steppenwolf** (✉ 1650 N. Halsted St., ☎ 312/335–1650). **Victory Gardens** (✉ 2257 N. Lincoln Ave., ☎ 773/871–3000) showcases local playwrights on its four stages. The city's oldest repertory theater, the **Goodman Theatre** (✉ 200 S. Columbus Dr., ☎ 312/443–3800) presents contemporary works and classics.

MUSIC

The **Chicago Symphony Orchestra** performs from September to May at the Orchestra Hall (✉ 220 S. Michigan Ave., ☎ 312/294–3000 or 800/223–7114) under the direction of Daniel Barenboim. In summer the Chicago Symphony moves outdoors to take part in the **Ravinia Festival** (☎ 847/266–5100), in suburban Highland Park.

OPERA

From September to March the **Lyric Opera of Chicago** (✉ 20 N. Wacker Dr., ☎ 312/332–2244) performs grand opera with international stars; tickets are difficult to come by. The **Chicago Opera Theater** (☎ 773/292–7578) presents innovative versions of traditional favorites and contemporary American pieces, all sung in English.

DANCE

Ballet Chicago (☎ 312/251–8838) is the city's oldest resident classical ballet company. The **Joffrey Ballet of Chicago** (☎ 312/739–0120) moved to the city from New York four years ago. **Hubbard Street Dance Chicago** (☎ 312/663–0853) is known for its contemporary, jazzy vitality.

FILM

In addition to the usual commercial theaters, Chicago has several venues for the avant-garde, vintage, or merely offbeat. The **Film Center of the Art Institute** (✉ Columbus Dr. at Jackson Blvd., ☎ 312/443–3737) sometimes presents lectures in conjunction with its films. The **Fine Arts Theatre** (✉ 418 S. Michigan Ave., ☎ 312/939–3700) shows first-run avant-garde and foreign flicks. The ornate **Music Box Theatre** (✉ 3733 N. Southport Ave., ☎ 773/871–6604), a 1920s movie palace, shows many independent films.

Spectator Sports

Baseball: Chicago Cubs (✉ Wrigley Field, 1060 W. Addison St., ☎ 773/404–2827); **Chicago White Sox** (✉ Comiskey Park, 333 W. 35th St., ☎ 312/674–1000). **Basketball: Chicago Bulls** (✉ United Center, 1901 W. Madison St., ☎ 312/455–4000). **Football: Chicago Bears** (✉ Soldier Field, 425 E. McFetridge Dr., ☎ 847/295–6600). **Hockey: Chicago Blackhawks** (✉ United Center, 1901 W. Madison St., ☎ 312/455–7000). **Horse racing: Hawthorne Race Course** (✉ 3501 S. Laramie Ave., Stickney, ☎ 708/780–3700) has Thoroughbred racing July–November. **Sportsman's Park** (✉ 3301 S. Laramie Ave., Cicero, ☎ 708/652–2812) has Thoroughbred racing March–June. **Maywood Park** (✉ North and 5th Aves., Maywood, ☎ 708/343–4800) has harness racing year-round.

Shopping

Shopping Districts

The **Loop** and the **Magnificent Mile** (☞ Exploring Chicago, *above,* for both) are filled with major department and upscale specialty stores. **Oak Street** between Michigan Avenue and State Street has such top-of-the-line stores as Barneys New York (✉ 25 E. Oak St., ☎ 312/587–1700), Ultimo (✉ 114 E. Oak St., ☎ 312/787–0906), and Giorgio Armani (✉ 113 E. Oak St., ☎ 312/751–2244). Three vertical (multiple-story) malls combine department stores and specialty shops: **Water Tower Place** (☞ Exploring Chicago, *above*); the **900 North Michigan Shops** (☎ 312/915–3916); and **Chicago Place** (✉ 700 N. Michigan Ave., ☎ 312/642–4811). The **Lincoln Park neighborhood** has several worthwhile shopping strips. Clark Street between Armitage and Diversey avenues is home to clothing boutiques and specialty stores. From Diversey north to Addison Street are several large antiques stores, more boutiques, and some bookstores.

Department Stores

Marshall Field's (✉ 111 N. State St., at Randolph St., ☎ 312/781–1000), the city's biggest department store, takes up an entire city block. With 500 departments, it's the second-largest retail store in the country. **Carson Pirie Scott** (✉ 1 S. State St., ☎ 312/641–7000) doesn't have the grandeur or style of its North Michigan Avenue competitors, but it does have spectacular ornamental ironwork around the main entrance. To keep up with the latest fashion trends, visit **Bloomingdale's** (✉ 900 N. Michigan Ave., ☎ 312/440–4460). For couture clothing don't miss the tony **Neiman Marcus** (✉ 737 N. Michigan Ave., ☎ 312/642–5900). **Saks Fifth Avenue** (✉ Chicago Place, 700 N. Michigan Ave., ☎ 312/944–6500) is a must for those in search of high style.

Specialty Stores

Crate & Barrel (✉ 646 N. Michigan Ave., ☎ 312/787–5900) sells stylish and affordable home accessories and cookware. **NikeTown** (✉ 669 N. Michigan Ave., ☎ 312/642–6363) draws tourists with its displays of sports memorabilia and merchandise. **Viacom Entertainment Store** (✉ 600 N. Michigan Ave., ☎ 312/867–3500) takes retailing to a new dimension with merchandise that ties into *Star Trek*, MTV, and Nick at Nite. **Illinois Artisans Shop** (✉ James R. Thompson Center, 100 W. Randolph St., ☎ 312/814–5321) culls the best work from artists and craftspeople around the state.

Side Trip to Oak Park

Arriving and Departing

Take I–290 west to Harlem Avenue and exit from the left lane. Turn right at the top of the ramp, head north on Harlem Avenue to Lake Street, turn right, and proceed to Oak Park Avenue.

What to See and Do

Founded in the 1850s, just west of the Chicago border, Oak Park is one of Chicago's oldest suburbs and a living museum of Prairie School residential architecture. The **Frank Lloyd Wright Home and Studio** (✉ 951 Chicago Ave., corner of Forest Ave., ☎ 708/848–1976; 🎟 $8) looks just as it did in 1889, when it was built for Wright, who lived and worked there until 1909. The poured-concrete **Unity Temple** (✉ 875 Lake St., ☎ 708/383–8873; 🎟 $4–$6), which Frank Lloyd Wright designed in 1905, was the architect's first public building. Learn about Ernest Hemingway's first 20 years at the **Ernest Hemingway Museum** (✉ 200 N. Oak Park Ave., ☎ 708/848–2222), closed Monday through Thursday. The **Ernest Hemingway Birthplace** (✉ 339 N. Oak Park Ave., ☎ 708/848–2222), closed Monday, Tuesday, and Thursday, is the Victorian home where the Nobel Prize–winning author was born in 1899. Combined admission to the Hemingway museum and birthplace costs $6. The **Oak Park Visitors Center** (✉ 158 N. Forest Ave., ☎ 708/848–1500 or 888/625–7275) sells tour tickets and provides information.

Side Trip to Baha'i House of Worship

Arriving and Departing

Take Lake Shore Drive north until it ends at Hollywood, then turn right onto Sheridan Road and follow it about 10 mi.

What to See and Do

Baha'i House of Worship (✉ 100 Linden Ave., Wilmette, ☎ 847/853–2300; 🎟 free) is a lovely nine-sided building whose architectural styles and icons from the world's religions symbolize unity. The symmetry and harmony of the building are paralleled in the surrounding formal gardens.

Side Trip to Woodstock

Arriving and Departing

Take I–90 West and exit on Route 47 going north. Make a left on Calhoun Street and then a right on Dean Street.

What to See and Do

Woodstock, 65 mi north of Chicago, is a Victorian oasis set in rolling countryside. The city square, lined with antiques stores and restaurants, is home to summer band concerts and ice-cream socials. Most of *Groundhog Day,* starring Bill Murray, was filmed here. Orson Welles and Paul Newman cut their teeth at the **Woodstock Opera House** (✉ 121 Van Buren St., ☎ 815/338–5300), which was built in 1890 and still houses musical and theatrical productions. The **Old Court House Arts Center** (✉ 101 N. Johnson St., ☎ 815/338–4525; 🎫 free), built in 1857, showcases area artists' works. In the basement is the former jail, now the Tavern on the Square restaurant (☎ 815/334–9540), where meals are served from Tuesday through Sunday in the old cell blocks. The center is closed from Monday through Wednesday. The **Chester Gould–Dick Tracy Museum** (☎ 815/338–8281; 🎫 $1), in the Old Court House Arts Center (☞ *above*), displays the artwork of Chester Gould, the creator of the Dick Tracy comic strip, who lived and worked in Woodstock. It, too, is closed from Monday through Wednesday. Contact the **Woodstock Chamber of Commerce** (✉ 136 Cass St., 60098, ☎ 815/338–2436) for more information.

Side Trip to Naperville

Arriving and Departing

Naperville is about 35 mi west of the Loop. Take I–290 West to I–88 West, and exit south on Naperville Road. Proceed south to Diehl Street, take Diehl west to Washington Street, and Washington south to downtown Naperville.

What to See and Do

A living history museum, **Naper Settlement** (✉ 523 S. Webster St., Naperville, ☎ 630/420–6010;🎫 $6) is a bricks-and-sticks time line of the evolution of a 19th-century prairie town. Many of its buildings have hands-on activities and demonstrations. Start at the visitor center, then visit the 1864 American Gothic Revival chapel, the Victorian Martin-Mitchell House, and the Greek Revival Murray House. Children enjoy the re-created log-picket Fort Payne, and the rough-hewn, one-room Paw Paw house.

Just a block north of Naper Settlement, **downtown Naperville** is a charming area bordered to the west by the DuPage River. Stroll along the river walk, stopping to enjoy its shrubbery-shaded nooks, playgrounds, and even a covered bridge. Specialty clothing stores, home accessory shops, and antiques stores abound here. For more information on the area, call the **Naperville Chamber of Commerce** (✉ 131 N. Jefferson St., 60540, ☎ 630/355–4141).

GALENA AND NORTHWESTERN ILLINOIS

The tiny town of Galena (population: 3,600) has beautifully preserved pre–Civil War architecture, with houses in Federal, Italianate, and Gothic Revival styles; a large concentration of specialty shops; and (rare in the Midwest) hilly terrain. There's good biking, cross-country skiing, fishing, hunting, and camping in the region.

Lead mining took off here in the 1820s, and Galena had a near-monopoly on the shipping of ore down the Mississippi until the railroad came through in 1854. A depression later that decade and then the Civil War disrupted the lead trade and sent the city into an economic decline from which it never recovered. As a result, Galena today looks much as it did in the 1850s. This was once the home of Ulysses S. Grant, commander of the Union Army in the Civil War and later the 18th president of the United States.

The region surrounding Galena is dotted with tiny towns that have been similarly bypassed by the 20th century. Among their offbeat charms are an antique-tractor museum (in Stockton) and the world's largest mallard hatchery (in Hanover). Stockton is also a time capsule of turn-of-the-century architecture, and much of Mount Carroll is registered as a National Historic District.

Visitor Information

Galena/Jo Daviess County: Call the Galena/Jo Daviess County Convention and Visitors Bureau (☎ 815/777–3557 or 800/747–9377), or visit the Galena Area Chamber of Commerce's Visitor Information Center (✉ 101 Bouthillier St., Galena 61036)

Arriving and Departing

By Car

From Chicago take I–90 86 mi to Rockford, then Route 20 West 81 mi to Galena. From Iowa pick up Route 20 at Dubuque and continue 16 mi east across the Mississippi.

Exploring Galena and Northwestern Illinois

In Galena the **Ulysses S. Grant Home** (✉ 500 Bouthillier St., ☎ 815/777–0248; 🎫 $2), built in 1860 in the Italianate bracketed style, was presented to Grant in 1865 by Galena residents in honor of his service to the Union. The family lived there until Grant's victory in the 1868 presidential election. In 1904 Grant's children gave the house to the city of Galena. Now a state historic site, the house has been meticulously restored to its 1868 appearance.

The heart of the **Belvedere Mansion and Gardens** (✉ 1008 Park Ave., ☎ 815/777–0747; 🎫 $5) is the 1857 Italianate mansion built for a steamboat magnate. Some might consider its lavishness gaudy; accoutrements include the famous green drapes from the movie *Gone with the Wind* and furnishings from Liberace's estate. The mansion is closed from November through May.

The **Galena/Jo Daviess County History Museum** (✉ 211 S. Bench St., ☎ 815/777–9129; 🎫 $3.50) provides interesting background on the area. A large Civil War exhibit shows the effect of the war on Galena's development. Display cases house period dolls, toys, clothing, and household artifacts.

Galena's oldest house is the 1826 **Dowling House** (✉ 220 Diagonal St., ☎ 815/777–1250; 🎫 $3.50), which is open daily in summer and only on weekends in winter. The **Toy Soldier Collection** (✉ 245 N. Main St., ☎ 815/777–0383) has two floors of antique toy soldiers and military miniatures for sale. **Galena Trolley Tours** (✉ 314 S. Main St., ☎ 815/777–1248; 🎫 $8) offers tours of the town.

A huge swath of rolling countryside east of town, the **Galena Territory** started as a vacation-home development in the early 1980s but has taken on a life of its own as a recreation area with hunting, fishing, and golf. Watch out for deer and turkey on the back roads; they're everywhere.

Mallards outnumber people 200 to 1 in **Hanover,** southeast of Galena, off Route 20 on Route 84. The **Whistling Wings Hatchery** (✉ 113 Washington St., Hanover, ☎ 815/591–3512) hatches 200,000 mallards a year; a viewing window lets you see the baby ducks in incubators. **Savanna,** on Route 84 along the Mississippi, has many large, well-preserved 19th-century houses. In **Mount Carroll,** east of Savanna on Route 52, rolling hills and gracious 19th-century frame and masonry buildings recall a small New England town, complete with a town square.

Stockton, about 30 mi east of Galena on Route 20, is Illinois's highest town, at 1,000 ft; the business district preserves many lacy, cupola-topped Victorian structures. **Arlo's Tractor Collection and Museum** (⊠ 7871 S. Ridge Rd., Stockton, ☎ 815/947–2593; free) contains 60 restored antique tractors, all in working order. The museum is closed from November through April; tours are by appointment only.

Dining and Lodging

Galena-area restaurant fare runs to hearty steaks, burgers, and ribs. Several bakeries along Galena's Main Street sell tempting cookies and pastries. A stay in one of the area's 40-plus B&Bs is almost de rigueur; some are right in town; others are in the Galena Territory or other rustic outlying areas. The Convention and Visitors Bureau (☞ Visitor Information, *above*) has a complete list of B&Bs and other types of lodging. For price ranges *see* Charts 1 (B) and 2 (A) *in* On the Road with Fodor's.

East Dubuque

$$$ ✕ **Timmerman's Supper Club.** This swanky restaurant across the parking lot from Timmerman's Motor Lodge (but under separate ownership), has spectacular views, rib-eye steaks, and DJs on weekends. ⊠ *7777 Timmerman Dr.,* ☎ *815/747–3316. AE, D, MC, V.*

$$ **Timmerman's Motor Lodge.** Perched on a bluff near the Mississippi River, this modern complex is frequented by riverboat gamblers in neighboring Dubuque, Iowa. Most of the rooms are 1980s Holiday Inn style. ⊠ *7777 Timmerman Dr., 61025,* ☎ *815/747–3181 or 800/336–3181,* FAX *815/747–6556. 74 rooms. Restaurant, pool. AE, D, MC, V.*

Galena

$$$–$$$$ ★ ✕ **El Dorado.** Wild game specials include a mixed grill of locally raised venison, Texas antelope, and wild boar sausage. A Southwest motif prevails in the lofted space with exposed brick walls. ⊠ *219 N. Main St.,* ☎ *815/777–1224. AE, D, MC, V. Closed Tues. No lunch.*

$$–$$$ ✕ **Café Italia and Twisted Taco Café.** Featured in the movie *Field of Dreams,* this cozy wood-and tile restaurant serves minestrone, lasagna, veal parmigiana, and other Italian standards, in addition to a full Mexican menu. ⊠ *301 N. Main St.,* ☎ *815/777–0033. AE, D, DC, MC, V.*

$$$$ ✕ **DeSoto House Hotel.** Opened in 1855, the DeSoto House served as presidential campaign headquarters for Ulysses S. Grant, and Lincoln really did sleep here. The spacious rooms recall the 1860s. The stately Generals' Restaurant serves straightforward steaks, chops, and seafood; the Courtyard Restaurant is open for breakfast and lunch. ⊠ *230 S. Main St., 61036,* ☎ *815/777–0090 or 800/343–6562,* FAX *815/777–9529. 55 rooms. 2 restaurants. AE, D, DC, MC, V.*

$$$–$$$$ **Chestnut Mountain Resort.** Looking like a Swiss chalet, the resort sits atop a bluff that overlooks the Mississippi, 8 mi southeast of downtown Galena; bedrooms overlook the ski slopes. There are tennis courts, mountain bikes for rent, and ski packages that include lodging and meals. ⊠ *8700 W. Chestnut Rd., 61036,* ☎ *815/777–1320 or 800/397–1320,* FAX *815/777–1068. 119 rooms. Restaurant, pool. AE, D, DC, MC, V.*

Galena Territory

$$$$ ✕ **Eagle Ridge Inn and Resort.** This rustic yet elegant "inn resort for golf" is set on 6,800 acres; horseback riding, boating, and cross-country skiing opportunities abound. Guest rooms have views of lake or woodland. The formal Woodlands restaurant serves excellent American cuisine. ✉ *444 Eagle Ridge Dr., Galena 61036,* ☎ *815/777–2444 or 800/892–2269,* FAX *815/777–4502. 80 rooms; 320 condominiums, town houses, and homes. 2 restaurants, pool, exercise room. AE, D, DC, MC, V.*

Motels

Best Western Quiet House Suites (✉ 9915 Rte. 20E, Galena 61036, ☎ 815/777–2577, FAX 815/777–0584), 42 suites, pool, exercise room; *$$$$.* **Palace Motel** (✉ 11383 Rte. 20W, Galena 61036, ☎ 815/777–2043, FAX 815/777–2625), 64 rooms; *$$.* **Grant Hills Motel** (✉ Rte. 20E, Galena 61036, ☎ 815/777–2116), 35 rooms, pool; *$–$$.*

Nightlife

The **Depot Theater** (✉ 314 S. Main St., ☎ 815/777–1248), at the Galena Trolley Depot, presents cabaret-style theater in a candlelighted space. Shows tend to be historical in nature, such as Jim Post's *Mark Twain and the Laughing River.*

Outdoor Activities and Sports

Biking

Bicyclists will find plenty of hilly back roads around Galena. The **Old Stagecoach Trail** runs parallel to Route 20, winding from Lena through Apple River and Warren to Galena. **Chestnut Mountain Resort**(☞ Dining and Lodging, *above*) rents mountain bikes, or try Dubuque, Iowa. The Visitor Information Center (☞ Visitor Information, *above*) has maps.

Fishing

Licenses can be purchased at marinas, bait shops, hardware stores, and other outlets, or contact the **Illinois Bureau of Tourism** (☞ Statewide Visitor Information, *above*) or the **Illinois Department of Natural Resources** (✉ 2612 Locust St., Sterling 61081, ☎ 815/625–2968).

Golf

Eagle Ridge Inn and Resort, in Galena Territory (☞ Dining and Lodging, *above*) has three championship 18-hole courses, one 9-hole course. **Galena Golf Club** (✉ Rte. 20W, Galena, ☎ 815/777–3599) has one 18-hole course and a driving range. **Lacoma Golf Course** (✉ 8080 Timmerman Dr., East Dubuque, ☎ 815/747–3874) has one 18-hole course, two regulation 9-hole courses, and one 9-hole par-three course.

Hiking and Backpacking

Mississippi Palisades State Park (✉ 16327A Rte. 84N, Savanna, ☎ 815/273–2731), about 30 mi south of Galena, has hiking trails with river views and nature preserves with accessible lookouts. More cliffs and canyons, in addition to camping, fishing, and five 1-mi-long hiking trails can be found at **Apple River Canyon State Park** (✉ 8763 E. Canyon Rd., north of Rte. 20 between Stockton and Warren, ☎ 815/745–3302).

Horseback Riding

Shenandoah Riding Center (✉ Galena Territory, 200 N. Brodrecht Rd., off Rte. 20E, Galena, ☎ 815/777–2373) offers riding lessons and hay and sleigh rides.

Ski Areas

Cross-Country

Eagle Ridge Inn and Resort (☞ Dining and Lodging, *above*) maintains more than 35 mi of groomed trails. **Lacoma Golf Course** (☞ Golf *in* Outdoor Activities and Sports, *above*) opens its 260-acre course to skiers, but you have to break your own trails. **Mississippi Palisades State Park** (☞ Hiking and Backpacking, *in* Outdoor Activities and Sports, *above*) also has marked trails.

Downhill

It's not the Alps, or even the Catskills, but if you want downhill skiing in Illinois, try **Chestnut Mountain Resort** (☞ Dining and Lodging, *above*), with 19 runs that overlook the Mississippi, plus a 7-acre snowboard park and a children's learn-to-ski program.

Shopping

Galena's Main Street is lined with more than 20 antiques stores and art galleries, plus boutiques, crafts shops, restaurants, and bakeries. **Stockton, Warren,** and **Elizabeth** have antiques stores and artists' studios.

ELSEWHERE IN ILLINOIS

Springfield

Visitor Information

Springfield Convention and Visitors Bureau (✉ 109 N. 7th St., 62701, ☎ 217/789–2360 or 800/545–7300).

Arriving and Departing

Loop I–55 runs north–south through the city. I–72 comes from Champaign and Decatur to the east. The Amtrak route from Chicago to St. Louis stops in Springfield.

What to See and Do

Illinois's capital, Springfield has perhaps the highest concentration anywhere of sites dedicated to Abraham Lincoln, among them the **Lincoln Home National Historic Site** (✉ 426 S. 7th St., ☎ 217/492–4150), the only home Lincoln ever owned, now at the center of a restored four-square-block historic area. Pick up a free admission ticket at the site's visitor center. Springfield's Oak Ridge Cemetery is home to the free **Lincoln Tomb State Historic Site** (✉ 1500 N. Monument Ave., ☎ 217/782–2717; 🎫 free), the final resting place for Lincoln, Mary Todd, and three of their four sons. On Tuesday nights in summer, catch the Civil War Retreat Ceremony held at the tomb. The **Illinois Vietnam Veterans Memorial** (☎ 217/782–2717; 🎫 free), dedicated in 1988, is also at Oak Ridge Cemetery.

The **Lincoln-Herndon Law Offices** (✉ 6th and Adams Sts., ☎ 217/785–7960; 🎫 $2) provide glimpses into Lincoln's life and career before he became president. The **Old State Capitol** (✉ 5th and Adams Sts., ☎ 217/785–7960; 🎫 $2), where Lincoln delivered his "House Divided" speech and where he lay in state before burial, has been restored to the way it looked during Lincoln's legislative years. **Lincoln's New Salem State Historic Site** (✉ Rte. 97 near Petersburg, ☎ 217/632–4000; 🎫 free), which lies about 20 mi northwest of Springfield, is a reconstructed village where Lincoln spent his early adulthood; in summer volunteers in period dress re-create village life.

Aside from Lincolniana, Springfield is also home to the **Dana-Thomas House** (✉ 301 E. Lawrence Ave., ☎ 217/782–6776; 🎫 $3), built by

Frank Lloyd Wright from 1902 to 1904 for a local socialite and now a state historic site. Elaborately restored in the late 1980s, it's among the most perfectly preserved examples of early Wright architecture, art glass, and furniture. It's closed Monday and Tuesday.

Dining and Lodging

$$$ ✕ **Café Brio.** Colorful and lively, Brio serves tasty Mexican, Caribbean, and Mediterranean cuisine. Margaritas are made with fresh lime juice. *✉ 524 E. Monroe St., ☎ 217/544–0574. AE, MC, V. No dinner Sun.*

$$$ ✕ **Gumbo Ya Ya's.** This Creole and Cajun restaurant has live entertainment along with thick, spicy gumbo, hearty jambalaya, shrimp étouffée, and blackened steak and seafood. The view from the 30th floor is the best in town. *✉ Springfield Hilton, 700 E. Adams St., ☎ 217/789–1530. AE, D, DC, MC, V. No dinner Sun. No lunch.*

$$$$ **Springfield Hilton.** The 30-story hotel has good city views and spacious rooms. In the heart of downtown, it's within walking distance of Lincoln historical sites. *✉ 700 E. Adams St., 62701, ☎ 217/789–1530, FAX 217/789–0709. 367 rooms. 3 restaurants, pool, health club. AE, D, DC, MC, V.*

$$ **Mansion View Inn & Suites.** Across the street from the historic Governor's Mansion, the hotel has small but pleasant rooms with motel-like outdoor entrances. Some rooms have whirlpool tubs. *✉ 529 S. 4th St., 62701, ☎ 217/544–7411 or 800/252–1083, FAX 217/544–6211. 93 rooms. Restaurant, exercise room. AE, D, DC, MC, V.*

INDIANA

Updated by Peggy Ammerman Bowman

Capital	Indianapolis
Population	5,864,000
Motto	The Crossroads of America
State Bird	Cardinal
State Flower	Peony
Postal Abbreviation	IN

Statewide Visitor Information

Indiana Department of Commerce, Division of Tourism (✉ 1 N. Capitol Ave., Suite 700, Indianapolis 46204, ☎ 317/232–8860 or 800/289–6646).

Scenic Drives

Charming 19th-century river towns front the **Ohio River Scenic Route** from Madison to Aurora on Routes 56 and 156. Trace Indiana's early frontier history along the **Chief White Eyes Trail** from Madison to Dillsboro on Route 62. The 50-mi **Lincoln Heritage Trail–George Rogers Clark Trail,** on Routes 462, 62, and 162 from Corydon to Gentryville, takes a gentle ride across southern hill country. From Newburgh to Sulphur the **Hoosier Heritage Trail Scenic Route** follows the Ohio River's squiggly course, then cuts north through state forests on Route 66. Indiana's 40-mi portion of the 1,100-mi **Lake Michigan Circle Tour** around the second largest of the Great Lakes follows U.S. 12 from Illinois to Michigan.

National and State Parks

National Parks

A columned, circular stone building at **George Rogers Clark National Historical Park** (✉ 401 S. 2nd St., Vincennes 47591, ☎ 812/882–1776) pays tribute to Clark's campaign to wrest Fort Sackville from the British during the Revolutionary War. ★ At **Indiana Dunes National Lakeshore** (✉ 1100 N. Mineral Springs Rd., Porter 46304, ☎ 219/926–7561) dune grasses, arctic bearberries, and prickly pear cacti mingle along more than 20 mi of Lake Michigan shoreline and inland marshes. Walk in the footsteps of young Abraham Lincoln at the **Lincoln Boyhood National Memorial** (✉ Box 1816, Lincoln City 47552, ☎ 812/937–4541). Ridge-topped trails at the 194,000-acre **Hoosier National Forest** (✉ 811 Constitution Ave., Bedford 47421, ☎ 812/275–5987) afford glimpses of quiet lakes and pass through dense woodlands in the state's south-central corridor, which stretches to the banks of the Ohio River.

State Parks

Indiana's 21 state parks are operated by the **Department of Natural Resources** (✉ 402 W. Washington St., Room W298, Indianapolis 46204, ☎ 317/232–4124 or 800/622–4931 in IN) and are open daily year-round. **Falls of the Ohio** (✉ 201 W. Riverside Dr., Clarksville 47129, ☎ 812/280–9970) showcases 220 acres of the world's largest naturally exposed Devonian fossil beds. At **Spring Mill** (✉ Rte. 60, Box 376, Mitchell 47446, ☎ 812/849–4129) you can tour a reconstructed 1800s pioneer village and gristmill on its original site, hike an 80-acre tract of virgin hardwood forest, then explore two caves on foot or by boat. Just 15 mi apart, **Turkey Run** (✉ Rte. 1, Box 164, Marshall 47859, ☎ 765/597–2635) and **Shades** (✉ Rte. 1, Box 72, Waveland 47989,

(☎ 765/435–2810) both skirt Sugar Creek and are crisscrossed by steep, glacially scoured sandstone ravines blanketed in moss and ferns. A bird's-eye view of **Chain O' Lakes** (✉ 2355 E. 75 S. Albion 46701, ☎ 219/636–2654) glimpses eight kettle lakes resembling dark blue ink squirts linked by narrow channels. There are more than 212 acres of water, along with 7 mi of shoreline and woodlands.

INDIANAPOLIS

Indianapolis is a prime example of a city that has pulled itself up by the bootstraps—most notably in 1970, when the city merged with surrounding Marion County to create a consolidated governmental organization. Called Unigov, this city-county dynamo pioneered a strategic partnership of public- and private-sector interests that has enabled Indianapolis to effect major improvements over the years. One such improvement is the ongoing construction of an internationally recognized collection of topflight sports facilities that has earned Indianapolis the moniker Amateur Sports Capital of the World. For a city of its size, Indianapolis also has a surprising assortment of museums and performance halls, plus plenty of green space—most recently the Monon Trail, a greenbelt that will extend 10 mi from downtown to the county line upon its expected completion in the year 2000 (at press time, spring 1998, 7.2 mi had been completed). Finally, there's Circle Centre, a swanky, villagelike enclosed complex of shops and entertainment attractions that has transformed a formerly sleepy downtown into a revitalized urban center.

Visitor Information

City Center (✉ 201 S. Capitol Ave., 46225, ☎ 317/237–5200 or 800/468–4639). **Convention & Visitors Association** (✉ 1 RCA Dome, Suite 110, 46225, ☎ 317/639–4282 or 800/556–4639).

Arriving and Departing

By Bus

Greyhound Bus Terminal (✉ 127 N. Illinois St., ☎ 317/267–3071 or 800/231–2222).

By Car

With more segments of interstate highway (I–65, I–69, I–70, I–74, and I–465) intersecting here than anywhere else in the country, Indianapolis is indisputably a driving city. Car rentals are available at major hotels and at the airport.

By Plane

The **Indianapolis International Airport** (☎ 317/487–7243) is served by major and commuter airlines. The trip from the airport to downtown or to the west side of town is about 20–25 minutes. To the other sides of town it's a 30- to 45-minute drive. By taxi or limo, the cost is $8–$20 to downtown, and $23–$26 to most other destinations. **Indy Connection** (☎ 317/241–7100) charges $8 per passenger from the airport to downtown.

By Train

Union Station (✉ 350 S. Illinois St., ☎ 317/263–0550 or 800/872–7245) has Amtrak service.

Getting Around Indianapolis

It's easy to get around, and the center is comfortable for walking. Address numbering is logical, based on a rectangular coordinate system, with each block roughly equal to 100. The intersection of Washington and Meridian streets, just south of Monument Circle, is the zero point for numbering in all directions. **Indy Go** buses (☎ 317/635–3344) run from 4:45 AM to 11:45 PM on heavily traveled routes, with shorter schedules in the suburbs. Fares (75¢, $1 during rush hour) are payable upon boarding. **Yellow Cab** (☎ 317/487–7777) taxis are radio dispatched; call ahead to be sure of getting a cab, unless you're at the airport or downtown. The fare is $1.25 for the first ⅕ mi and 36¢ for each additional ⅕ mi or minute of waiting time.

Exploring Indianapolis

Attractions extend into a wider metropolitan area than the original square-mile downtown area. Many of the museums, arts and entertainment venues, and shopping areas, all generally within a 45-minute drive, are scattered around, both downtown and beyond in the contiguous counties.

Downtown

Monument Circle is Indianapolis's centerpiece. Avenues radiate from it across the grid of streets, as in Washington, D.C. (Indianapolis architect Alexander Ralston was a protégé of Pierre L'Enfant). At the center is the **Soldiers' and Sailors' Monument,** a 284-ft spire crowned by the 30-ft bronze statue *Victory,* better known as *Miss Indiana.* There's also an **observation area** with a panoramic view (☎ 317/262–7615; 🎫 free). Overlooking the monument is the **Hilbert Circle Theatre,** a vintage-1916 movie palace that is now the home of the **Indianapolis Symphony Orchestra** (☎ 317/262–1100, ext. 235), with tours by appointment; 🎫 $1). Also on Monument Circle is the city's oldest church, **Christ Church Cathedral** (☎ 317/636–4577), an 1857 English Gothic country–style masterpiece, with a spire, steep gables, bell tower, and arched Tiffany windows; tours are also available here by appointment.

The **Indiana State Museum** (✉ 202 N. Alabama St., ☎ 317/232–1637; 🎫 free), in the Old City Hall, showcases the state's history and culture. The massive limestone-and-marble **Indiana World War Memorial** (✉ 431 N. Meridian, ☎ 317/232–7615; free) pays tribute to fallen Hoosier veterans of World War I, World War II, the Korean War, and the Vietnam War. The circa-1929 Gothic Tudor–style Masonic **Scottish Rite Cathedral** (✉ 650 N. Meridian St., ☎ 317/262–3100), closed weekends, contains a 54-bell carillon and a 7,000-pipe organ.

There's lunchtime entertainment most Fridays at the vintage-1886 **Indianapolis City Market** (✉ 222 E. Market St., ☎ 317/634–9266), where shops sell ethnic and deli fare every day but Sunday.

Housed in a contemporary adobe building, the **Eiteljorg Museum of American Indians and Western Art** (✉ 500 W. Washington St., ☎ 317/636–9378; 🎫 $5), displays works by Frederic Remington and Georgia O'Keeffe, among others. It's closed on Monday from September through May. Next door is an **IMAX 3D** theater (☎ 317/262–8080).

The **Indiana Convention Center & RCA Dome** (✉ 100 S. Capitol Ave. ☎ 317/237–3663; 🎫 $5), reaching 19 stories and one of just six major air-supported domed stadiums in the world, is the home of the NFL's Indianapolis Colts. The Romanesque **Union Station** (✉ 39 W. Jackson Pl., ☎ 317/267–0701; 🎫 free) is a restored 1888 landmark with magnificent stained glass in a vaulted, skylighted ceiling.

Ornate Victorian furnishings, political mementos, and period ball gowns of the nation's 23rd president and first lady fill the 1875 **Pres-**

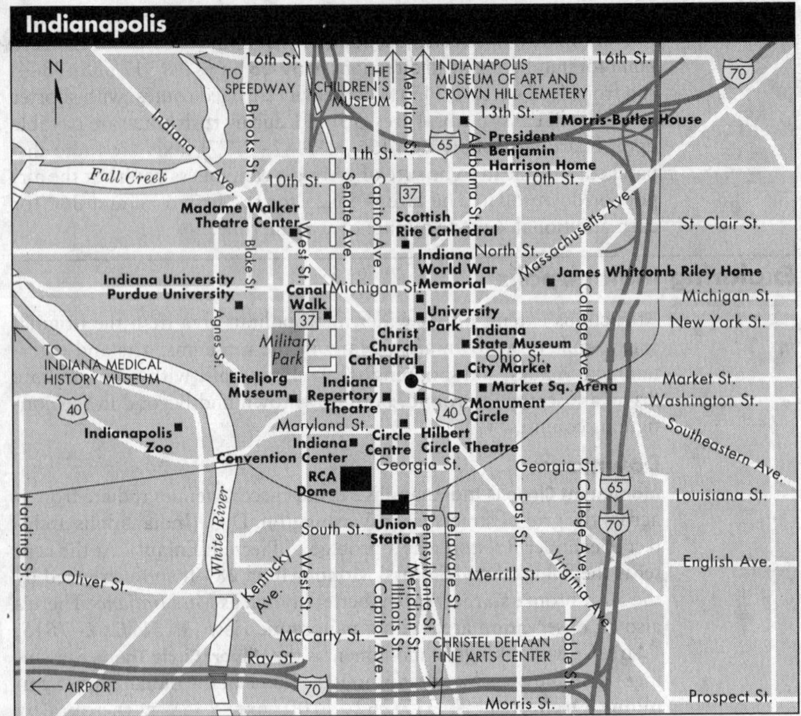

ident Benjamin Harrison Home (✉ 1230 N. Delaware St., ☎ 317/631–1898; 🎫 $5). The **Morris-Butler House** (✉ 1204 N. Park Ave., ☎ 317/636–5409; 🎫 $3), a beautifully restored 1865 Second Empire–style gem, is filled with fancy furnishings, dazzling chandeliers, and rich woodwork. It is closed on Monday.

In the historic Lockerbie Square neighborhood, the **James Whitcomb Riley Museum Home** (✉ 528 Lockerbie St., ☎ 317/631–5885; 🎫 $2), acclaimed as one of nation's finest examples of Victoriana, remains almost as the noted poet left it.

Midtown/Crosstown

Presenting "Jazz on the Avenue" Friday nights and once frequented by jazz legends Ella Fitzgerald and Wes Montgomery, the 1927 **Madame Walker Theatre Center** (✉ 617 Indiana Ave., ☎ 317/236–2099; 🎫 free) was named for the country's first black female self-made millionaire. Tours are by appointment.

Playscape, the world's largest water clock, a planetarium, IWERKS Cine-Dome Theater, a science center, and nine other major galleries make up **The Children's Museum of Indianapolis** (✉ 3000 N. Meridian St., ☎ 317/924–5431; 🎫 $6), which is closed from Labor Day through May 1. Be sure to take a spin on a turn-of-the-century carousel and explore a limestone cave.

The **Indianapolis Museum of Art** (✉ 1200 W. 38th St., ☎ 317/923–1331; 🎫 free), a five-pavilion complex and botanical gardens on 152 acres of manicured lawns, houses works by J. M. W. Turner, the old masters, and the neoimpressionists, along with major Asian, African, and decorative arts collections. It is closed on weekends. At century-old **Crown**

Hill Cemetery (✉ 3402 Boulevard Pl., ☎ 317/925–8231; 🎫 free), the nation's third largest, notorious criminal John Dillinger cozies up to President Benjamin Harrison and a host of American authors.

South Side

The stunning **Christel DeHaan Fine Arts Center** (✉ 1400 E. Hanna Ave., ☎ 317/788–3566; 🎫 free) at the University of Indianapolis contains exhibition space and a 500-seat concert hall renowned for its acoustics.

West Side

The **Indianapolis Motor Speedway Hall of Fame Museum** (✉ 4790 W. 16th St., ☎ 317/484–6747; 🎫 $2) displays 30 Indy 500–winning cars, as well as classic and antique autos. At the **Indiana Medical History Museum** (✉ 3045 W. Vermont St., ☎ 317/635–7329; 🎫 $3), a turn-of-the-century pathology laboratory, exhibits 15,000 medical treatment and health-care artifacts. It's closed from Sunday through Tuesday.

Parks and Gardens

There are jogging, biking, hiking, golfing, and swimming facilities at the rustic 4,200-acre **Eagle Creek Park** (✉ 7840 W. 56th St., ☎ 317/293–4828; 🎫 $3 per car). An exceptionally well-planned network of woodland trails and riverfront boardwalks traverses hilly terrain at **Holliday Park** (✉ 6349 Springmill Rd., ☎ 317/327–7180; 🎫 free).

Straddling White River, the **White River State Park** (✉ 801 W. Washington St., ☎ 317/634–4567) is a 250-acre greenbelt. Within the park, 3,000 animals and a whale and dolphin pavilion comprise the **Indianapolis Zoo** (✉ 1200 W. Washington St., ☎ 317/630–2001; 🎫 $9), near White River State Park.

The downtown **Canal Walk,** a 10½-block vestige of the historic 400-mi canal system linking the Great Lakes and the Ohio River, is an urban haven, with benches, fountains, and wide walkways lining both sides of the canal. The new 10 1/2-mi paved **Monon Rail-Trail** (☎ 317/327–7431) connects Broad Ripple Village (☞ Shopping, *below*) to the county line; further construction is expected to run to downtown Indianapolis.

Dining

For price ranges *see* Chart 1 (B) *in* On the Road with Fodor's.

$$$$ ✕ **Peter's Restaurant & Bar.** The seasonal menu here may include pomegranate-glazed Indiana duckling accompanied by sweet-potato custard and mustard greens. Chilean sea bass is seared and basted with a spicy orange-chili marinade. ✉ *8505 Keystone Crossing,* ☎ *317/465–1155. AE, D, MC, V. Closed Sun.*

$$–$$$ ✕ **Kona Jack's.** Of the three Jack's restaurants in a shopping center about 9 mi north of downtown, Kona Jack's is the best. More than a dozen creatively prepared fish dishes include champagne-marinated swordfish and seared red snapper with a Thai-style coconut-milk glaze. Nearby, Daddy Jack's serves classic American fare, and Deli Jack's makes giant specialty subs, interesting salads, and fresh-baked cookies. ✉ *9413 N. Meridian St.,* ☎ *317/843–1609. AE, DC, D, MC, V. Closed Sun.*

$$–$$$ ✕ **The Restaurant at the Canterbury.** Inside the Canterbury hotel, this is one of the city's best restaurants. The clubby dining room has wood paneling and crisp white linens. The traditional dishes—Dover sole, pepper-crusted rack of lamb—are expertly prepared. ✉ *123 S. Illinois St.,* ☎ *317/634–3000. AE, D, DC, MC, V.*

$$–$$$ ✕ **Snax/Something Different.** Tapas at Snax are just enough to whet an appetite for dinner, which is served next door at Something Different. The setting is industrial-chic, the menu innovative American: grilled halibut might be paired with wilted spinach and fried lily root. ✉ *2411 E. 65th St.,* ☎ *317/257–7973. AE, D, MC, V. Closed Sun.*

$ ✕ **Shapiro's Delicatessen & Cafeteria.** The strawberry cheesecake and corned-beef sandwiches piled high on rye are signature items at this nationally known deli, an Indianapolis institution since 1904. ✉ *808 S. Meridian St.,* ☎ *317/631–4041;* ✉ *2370 W. 86th St.,* ☎ *317/872–7255. Reservations not accepted. No credit cards.*

Lodging

For price ranges *see* Chart 2 (A) *in* On the Road with Fodor's.

$$$ ★ **Canterbury Hotel.** The luxurious guest rooms at this 60-year-old hostelry are equipped with armoires, queen-size four-poster beds, and elegant baths. A covered skywalk leads to Circle Centre. ✉ *123 S. Illinois St., 46225,* ☎ *317/634–3000 or 800/538–8186,* FAX *317/685–2519. 99 rooms. Restaurant. AE, D, DC, MC, V.*

$$$ **Omni Severin Hotel.** Across from historic Union Station, this hotel has crystal chandeliers, a marble staircase, and cast-iron balustrades recalling its 1913 origins. Guest rooms are a blend of traditional and Mediterranean styles. ✉ *40 W. Jackson Pl., 46225,* ☎ *317/634–6664 or 800/843–6664,* FAX *317/687–3619. 423 rooms. Restaurant, pool. AE, D, DC, MC, V.*

$$–$$$ **Radisson Plaza & Suite Hotel Indianapolis.** This upscale high-rise hotel is smack in the middle of the north-side Keystone at the Crossing shopping and entertainment complex (☞ Shopping, *below*), a 40-minute drive from downtown or the airport. A covered skywalk connects to 100 shops and restaurants. ✉ *8787 Keystone Crossing, 46240,* ☎ *317/846–2700 or 800/333–3333,* FAX *317/574–6780. 552 rooms. Restaurant. AE, D, DC, MC, V.*

$$ **University Place Conference Center & Hotel.** Rooms in this hotel on the shared campus of Indiana and Purdue universities are handsomely appointed, with desks, easy chairs, and 18th-century reproduction furnishings. ✉ *850 W. Michigan St., 46202,* ☎ *317/269–9000 or 800/222–8733,* FAX *317/231–5168. 276 rooms. 2 restaurants. AE, D, DC, MC, V.*

Nightlife and the Arts

Nightlife

Pub crawling is best in out-of-the-way neighborhoods such as **Broad Ripple Village**(☞ Shopping, *below*). Cruise the offbeat **Massachusetts Avenue Arts District** scene for interesting art galleries, unusual shops, and neighborhood eateries and taverns. There are Christmas lights and checkered flags year-round at **The Chatterbox** (✉ 435 Massachusetts Ave., ☎ 317/636–0584), where a varied clientele stops by for late-night jazz. On Level 4 of **Circle Centre** (☞ Shopping, *below*), there are nightclubs, nine cinemas, and virtual reality and arcade games.

The Arts

NUVO Newsweekly, Indianapolis Monthly magazine, Friday's edition of the *Indianapolis News,* and the Sunday edition of the *Indianapolis Star* list arts and events. Tickets for plays and concerts can be obtained through **Court Side Tickets , Inc.** (✉ 6100 N. Keystone Ave., ☎ 317/254–9500 or 800/627–1334), **TicketMaster** (✉ 2 W. Washington St., ☎ 317/239–5151), **Tickets Up Front & Travel** (✉ 1099 N. Meridian St., ☎ 317/633–6400), or **Premium Tickets & Tours** (✉ 2113 Broad Ripple Ave., ☎ 317/251–0163 or 800/768–0898).

MUSIC

Indianapolis Symphony Orchestra (✉ 45 Monument Circle, ☎ 317/639–4300) performs at the Hilbert Circle Theatre from September through May and outdoors at Conner Prairie in summer (☞ Hamilton County *in* Side Trips from Indianapolis, *below*). The **Indianapolis Opera** (✉ 250 E. 38th St., ☎ 317/940–6444) stages productions from its grand opera repertoire along with new works each season.

About 20 mi northeast of downtown Indianapolis, **Deer Creek Music Center** (✉ 12880 E. 146th St., Noblesville, ☎ 317/776–3337 or 317/841–8900) brings top-name pop, jazz, and rock performers to an outdoor facility.

THEATER

Indiana's only resident professional theater, the **Indiana Repertory Theatre** (✉ 140 W. Washington St., ☎ 317/635–5227 or 317/635–5252) presents major works in a restored 1927 movie palace downtown. **Beef & Boards Dinner Theatre** (✉ 9301 N. Michigan Rd., ☎ 317/872–9664) stages Broadway shows along with a dinner buffet on the northwest side. Original musical revues are presented at **American Cabaret Theatre** (✉ 401 E. Michigan, ☎ 317/631–0334).

Spectator Sports

Baseball: Indianapolis Indians (✉ Victory Field, 501 W. Maryland St., ☎ 317/269–3545). **Basketball: Indiana Pacers** (✉ Market Square Arena, 300 E. Market St., ☎ 317/239–5151). **Football: Indianapolis Colts** (✉ RCA Dome, 100 S. Capitol Ave., Box 535000, ☎ 317/297–7000). **Ice hockey: Indianapolis Ice** (✉ 222 E. Ohio St., Suite 810, ☎ 317/239–5151). **Soccer: Indiana Twisters** (✉ 11 S. Meridian St., Suite 402, ☎ 317/951–1811).

Shopping

Downtown, the Nordstrom (☎ 317/636–2121) and Parisian (☎ 317/971–6200) department stores headline the roster of more than 120 shops at **Circle Centre** (✉ 49 W. Maryland St., ☎ 317/681–8000). On the north side of town, the **Fashion Mall,** at Keystone at the Crossing (✉ 9000 Keystone Crossing, ☎ 317/574–4000), is anchored by the upscale Jacobson's (☎ 317/574–0088) and Parisian (☎ 317/581–8200) department stores. About 6 mi north of downtown, **Broad Ripple Village** (✉ 62nd St. at Broad Ripple and College Aves., ☎ 317/251–2782) has art galleries, gift shops, and boutiques.

Side Trips from Indianapolis

Bloomington, Brown County, and Columbus

About an hour's drive south of the capital city on Route 46, the flat expanse of farmland dominating the upper two-thirds of the state gives way to hilly terrain. In **Bloomington,** home of Indiana University, ethnic restaurants, boutiques, galleries, and shops surround the courthouse square and fill the block-long Fountain Square Mall (☎ 812/336–3681), distinguished by its historic storefront facades. For information contact the **Bloomington/Monroe Convention and Visitors Bureau** (✉ 2855 N. Walnut St., 47404, ☎ 812/334–8900 or 800/800–0037).

Columbus is a forward-thinking city with more than 50 contemporary-style structures by world-renowned architects. Contact the **Columbus Area Visitors Center** (✉ Box 1589, 5th and Franklin Sts., 47202, ☎ 812/378–2622 or 800/468–6564) for information.

In picturesque Brown County, the quaint village of **Nashville** was a gathering place for artists in the early 1900s. Today, country-cooking eateries and shops nestle in alongside artists' studios and galleries throughout town. Contact the **Nashville/Brown County Convention and Visitors Bureau** (✉ Box 840, 47448, ☎ 812/988-7303 or 800/753-3255).

Centerville and Richmond

Beginning in the 1820s, historic **Centerville** and **Richmond,** on the Ohio state line, saw as many as 200 wagons pass daily on the National Road, a western immigration trail (now U.S. Highway 40). Today this stretch of road is known as Antique Alley, with more than 550 dealers. The **Richmond-Wayne County Convention and Tourism Bureau** (✉ 701 National Rd. E, 47374, ☎ 317/935-8687 or 800/828-8414) has information on the area. Three forks of the Whitewater River converge in a gorge with scenic vistas, trails, and the stunning **Thistlethwaite Falls** (✉ Richmond Parks & Recreation, ☎ 317/983-7275).

Hamilton County

Towns in this county northeast of downtown were once simply bedroom communities for Indianapolis. But restoration of the stately, mansard-roofed county courthouse in Noblesville coincided with a renaissance of museums, shops, and restaurants. You can relive the past at **Conner Prairie** (☎ 317/776-6000 or 800/966-1836), a re-created 1830s pioneer village complex in Fishers. Contact the **Hamilton County Convention & Visitors Bureau** (✉ 11601 Municipal Dr., Fishers 46038, ☎ 317/598-4444 or 800/776-8687) for information.

Parke County

Dubbed the Covered-Bridge Capital of the World, Parke County has some 30 bridges scattered about within an hour's drive west of Indianapolis (take Route 136). Every October Rockville and nearby towns take part in the 10-day **covered-bridge festival,** with crafts fairs, quilts and antiques shows, and barbecue beef and bean soup dinners. During the **maple syrup festival** in early spring, sugar shacks open their doors for a peek inside. The **Parke County Convention and Visitors Bureau** (✉ Box 165, Rockville 47872, ☎ 765/569-5226) provides details about the area.

Zionsville

Brick streets and Stick-style, early 19th-century wood cottages create a fairy-tale setting. Though just a 30-minute drive from downtown's domed stadiums and shiny new high-rises, Zionsville seems to be perfectly preserved. The state's only officially recognized hunt club is here, along with quaint shops and restaurants. Contact **The Greater Zionsville Chamber of Commerce** (✉ 135 S. Elm St., ☎ 317/873-3836).

SOUTHERN INDIANA

Dense stands of oak, hickory, and maple crown the rolling terrain that dominates southern Indiana. Tucked among the hills and valleys are 19th-century riverfront towns, caves that beg to be explored, and vast stretches of clear blue water.

Visitor Information

Southern Indiana: Clark/Floyd Counties Convention and Tourism Bureau (✉ Lousville Municipal Bridge Bldg., Jeffersonville 47130, ☎ 812/282-6654). **Lincoln Hills Area:** Lincoln Hills/Patoka Lake Recreation Region (✉ Courthouse Annex, Cannelton 47520, ☎ 812/547-7028). **Madison Area:** Madison Area Convention and Visitors Bureau (✉ 301 E. Main St., Madison 47250, ☎ 812/265-2956 or 800/559-2956). **Vincennes Area:** Vincennes/Knox County Convention and Visitors Bureau (✉ Box 602, Vincennes 47591, ☎ 812/882-6440 or 800/886-6443). **Evansville and New Harmony:** Evansville Convention and Visitors Bureau (✉ 401 S.E. Riverside Dr., Evansville 47713, ☎ 812/425-5402 or 800/433-3025).

Arriving and Departing

By Bus

Service between Indianapolis, Evansville, and Vincennes is available on **Greyhound Lines** (☎ 317/267-3071 or 800/231-2222)

By Car

The major road through this region is I-64. From Indianapolis take I-70 and U.S. 41 to Vincennes and Evansville, I-65 and Route 7 to Madison, and I-65 to Clarksville and Jeffersonville. From Louisville, Kentucky, take I-65; from Cincinnati, Ohio, take I-74.

By Plane

Evansville Regional Airport (☎ 812/421-4400) is served by commuter and regional airlines.

Exploring Southern Indiana

Three-hundred-year-old **Vincennes** brims with history. **Grouseland** (✉ 3 W. Scott St., ☎ 812/882-2096) was the home of Indiana Territory governor William Henry Harrison. The log-and-mud **Old French House and Indian Museum** (✉ 509 N. 1st St., ☎ 800/886-6443) dates to 1806. In the southwesternmost corner of Indiana, quaint **New Harmony** was the site of two 19th-century utopian communities; contact Historic New Harmony, Inc. (✉ Box 579, New Harmony 47631, ☎ 812/682-4488 or 800/231-2168) for information.

In the historic Riverside District of **Evansville,** columned mansions such as the **Reitz Home Museum** (✉ 224 S.E. 1st St., ☎ 812/426-1871) overlook the Ohio River. The **Evansville Museum of Arts and Science** (✉ 411 S.E. Riverside Dr., ☎ 812/425-2406) has American and European art from 1700 to the present, a planetarium, and a reconstructed turn-of-the-century village.

In **Corydon,** Indiana's first capital, you can browse through 10,000 square ft of antiques in two downtown malls. Corydon's Federal-style **Corydon Capitol State Historic Site** (✉ 202 E. Walnut St., ☎ 812/738-4890) is where the state's first constitution was drafted. The **Corydon 1883 Scenic Railroad** (✉ Walnut and Water Sts., ☎ 812/738-8000) makes a 90-minute trip through the countryside. A pioneer village and caverns with waterfalls beg to be explored at **Squire Boone Caverns and Village** (✉ Box 411, Corydon 47112, ☎ 812/732-4381).

Dubbed the Williamsburg of the Midwest, **Madison** is an antebellum-era town whose entire main street and 100 additional blocks are listed on the National Register of Historic Places. See the gleaming white Greek Revival **Lanier Mansion State Historic Site** (✉ 511 W. 1st St., ☎ 812/265-3526), whose portico overlooks the Ohio River. Exhibits trace the heydays of steamboating and trains in southeastern Indiana at the **Jefferson County Historical Society Museum and 1895 Madison Railroad Station** (✉ 615 W. 1st St., ☎ 812/265-2335).

Dining and Lodging

Contact the **Indiana Bed & Breakfast Association** (✉ Box 1127, Goshen 46526, ☎ no phone) for information on the area's coziest accommodations. For price ranges see Charts 1 (B) and 2 (B) in On the Road with Fodor's.

Santa Claus

$$$ ✕🏨 **Santa's Lodge.** This two-story hostelry resembles a huge barn, with century-old hand-hewn barn timbers supporting the spacious lobby. Christmas decorations and antiques deck the halls. ✉ *Rte 162, Box 193, Santa Claus 47579,* ☎ *812/937–1902 or 800/640–7895,* FAX *812/937–1902. 46 rooms. Restaurant. AE, MC, V.*

Corydon

$$–$$$ 🏨 **Kintner House Inn.** Once the headquarters of Confederate general John Hunt Morgan, the inn dates from the mid-1800s. ✉ *101 S. Capitol St., at Chestnut St., 47112,* ☎ *812/738–2020. 14 rooms. Full breakfast. MC, V.*

New Harmony

$$ ✕🏨 **New Harmony Inn.** Set on spacious grounds overlooking a small lake, this inn has a fine restaurant that draws diners from the tristate area. ✉ *506 North St. (Box 581), 47631,* ☎ *812/682–4491 or 800/782–8605,* FAX *812/682–4491, ext. 329. 90 rooms. 2 restaurants, pool, tennis, health club. AE, D, MC, V.*

Outdoor Activities and Sports

Biking

Six routes on the **Hoosier Bikeway System** (✉ Dept. of Natural Resources, 402 W. Washington St., Room W271, Indianapolis 46204, ☎ 317/232–4070) run through this area.

Fishing

At **Patoka Lake** (✉ R.R. 1, Birdseye, ☎ 812/685–2464) and **Markland Dam,** on the Ohio River off Route 156, each season brings record catches of bass, carp, and catfish. Contact the **Division of Fish and Wildlife** (✉ Dept. of Natural Resources, Room W273, 402 W. Washington St., 46204, ☎ 317/232–4080) for permits and information.

NORTHERN INDIANA

Stretches of shifting dunes and inviting beaches along Lake Michigan give way to a neat grid of lush farmland dotted with Amish communities in northeastern Indiana. The state's second-largest city, Fort Wayne, has lake country to the west and charming Amish towns like Grabill to the northwest and east.

Visitor Information

Amish Country: Elkhart Convention and Visitors Bureau (✉ 219 Caravan Dr., Elkhart 46514, ☎ 219/262–8161 or 800/860–5957). **Fort Wayne:** Convention and Visitors Bureau (✉ 1021 S. Calhoun St., 46802, ☎ 219/424–3700 or 800/767–7752). **Lake Country:** Kosciusko County Convention and Visitors Bureau (✉ 313 S. Buffalo St., Warsaw 46580, ☎ 219/269–6090 or 800/800–6090). **North Coast:** Lake County Convention and Visitors Bureau (✉ 5800 Broadway, Suite S, Merrillville 46410, ☎ 219/980–1617 or 800/255–5253); Porter County Convention and Visitors Bureau (✉ 528 Indian Boundary Rd., Chesterton 46304, ☎ 219/926–2255 or 800/283–8687). **South Bend/Mishawaka:** Convention and Visitors Bureau (✉ 401 E. Colfax Ave., South Bend 46634, ☎ 219/234–0051 or 800/282–7881).

Arriving and Departing

By Bus

United Limo, in Osceola (☎ 219/674–6993), provides daily service to and from Chicago. Other service is available on **Greyhound Lines** (✉ 4671 Terminal Dr., South Bend, ☎ 800/231–2222).

By Car

Major east–west roads are I–80/90 and U.S. 12 and 20. Traversing the region north–south are I–65, I–69, and U.S. 31 and 41.

By Plane

The **Michiana Regional Transportation Center** (✉ 4477 Terminal Dr., ☎ 219/282–4590) is served by national and regional carriers.

By Train

Connecting South Bend, northwestern Indiana, and Chicago is the **South Shore Line** (✉ 2702 W. Washington St., South Bend, ☎ 219/233–3111 or 800/356–2079). **Amtrak** (☎ 800/872–7245).

Exploring Northern Indiana

Among the many outdoor areas are the **Indiana Dunes National Lakeshore** (☞ National and State Parks, *above*) and **Gibson Woods Nature Preserve** (✉ Gibson Woods County Park, 6201 Parish Ave., Hammond, ☎ 219/844–3188), a fine specimen of dune and swale topography.

In **Michigan City,** the turn-of-the-century gem copied after an English manor house, **Barker Mansion and Civic Center** (✉ 631 Washington St., 46360, ☎ 219/873–1520) is filled with opulent Baroque-style furnishings. One of the few remaining lighthouses along Lake Michigan is now **The Old Lighthouse Museum** (✉ Old Heisman Harbor Rd., 46360, ☎ 219/872–6133).

Fans flock to **South Bend** each year to see the **University of Notre Dame**'s Fighting Irish. Be sure to stop by the landmark Golden Dome (☎ 219/239–7367) and the College Football Hall of Fame (✉ 110 S. St. Joseph St., ☎ 219/235–9999 or 800/440–3263), a mammoth sports shrine with exhibits. On the university campus, the **Snite Museum of Art** (☎ 219/631–5466) contains works by Rembrandt, Chagall, and Picasso. Downtown South Bend's **East Race Waterway** (☎ 219/235–9328) attracts kayakers, tubers, and rafters.

The 75-mi corridor from South Bend southeast to Fort Wayne goes through Indiana's **Amish Country. Amish Acres** (✉ Rte. 19, 1600 W. Market St., Nappanee, ☎ 219/773–4188 or 800/800–4942) is a working farm with a restaurant and an inn. The **Borkhholder Dutch Village** (✉ County Rd. 101, Nappanee, ☎ 219/773–2828) has more than 500 arts, crafts, and antiques booths. More than 1,000 vendors crowd the open-air **Shipshewana Auction & Flea Market** (✉ Box 185, Rte. 5S, Shipshewana 46565, ☎ 219/768–4129) every Tuesday and Wednesday from May through October. The **Old Bag Factory** (✉ 1100 Chicago Ave., Goshen 46526, ☎ 219/534–0560), a massive redbrick structure dating from 1895, houses 18 shops, including a custom hardwood-furniture maker and a potter. Just outside Fort Wayne, **Grabill** seems caught in a time warp, with Amish buggies hitched up all around town. West of Fort Wayne, hundreds of kettle lakes, as well as **Lake Wawasee** and **Lake Maxinkuckee,** attract summer vacationers.

Dining and Lodging

For inn bookings contact the **Indiana Bed & Breakfast Association** (✉ Box 1127, Goshen 46526, ☎ no phone). For price ranges *see* Charts 1 (B) and 2 (B) *in* On the Road with Fodor's.

Amish Country

$$$–$$$$ **Checkerberry Inn.** Set on 100 acres, this elegant hostelry has the state's only professional croquet course, a walking lane, and woodlands. ✉ *62644 County Rd. 37, Goshen 46526, ☎ FAX 219/642–4445. 14 rooms. Restaurant, tennis. AE, MC, V.*

$$$–$$$$ **Essenhaus Country Inn.** A three-story softly lighted atrium with a potbellied stove is the centerpiece of this simple but modern inn. ✉ *240 U.S. 20, Middlebury 46540, ☎ FAX 219/825–9471. 40 rooms. Restaurant. AE, MC, V.*

Indiana's North Coast

$$–$$$$ ✕ **Miller Bakery Cafe.** This cozy bakery turned eatery has received rave reviews for its inventive fare. Start dinner with corn-bread custard, a savory bread pudding with cilantro pesto, or try the wild mushroom ragout. Then move on to New Zealand rack of lamb with coarse whole-grain mustard sauce, or sautéed veal medallions with caramelized mushrooms. ✉ *555 S. Lake St., Gary, ☎ 219/938–2229. MC, V. Closed Sun.*

$$$–$$$$ **Hutchinson Mansion Inn.** This 1876 mansion spanning almost one city block is filled with stained-glass windows and marble fireplaces. ✉ *220 W. 10th St., Michigan City 46360, ☎ 219/879–1700. 10 rooms. Full breakfast. AE, MC, V.*

South Bend/Mishawaka

$$$$ **Varsity Clubs of America.** Resembling a jumbo redbrick, white-pillared fraternity house, this all-suite hotel has a collection of Notre Dame memorabilia. ✉ *3800 N. Main St., Mishawaka 46545, ☎ 219/277–0500 or 800/946–4822. 60 suites. Exercise room. AE, DC, MC, V.*

MICHIGAN

Updated by Khristi Zimmeth

Capital	Lansing
Population	9,774,000
Motto	If You Seek a Pleasant Peninsula, Look About You
State Bird	Robin
State Flower	Apple blossom
Postal Abbreviation	MI

Statewide Visitor Information

Travel Michigan(✉ Box 30226, Lansing 48909, ☎ 800/543–2937). **Information centers:** I–94 at New Buffalo and Port Huron; I–69 at Coldwater; U.S. 23 at Dundee; U.S. 2 at Ironwood and Iron Mountain; U.S. 41 at Marquette and Menominee; I–75 at St. Ignace, Sault Sainte Marie, and Monroe; U.S. 27 in a rest area 1 mi north of Clare; and Route 108 in Mackinaw City.

Scenic Drives

Route BR–15 between Pentwater and Montague follows the Lake Michigan shoreline for about 25 mi. **Route M–23** between Tawas City and Mackinaw City follows the Lake Huron shoreline for more than 160 mi. In the Upper Peninsula **Route M–28** follows the Lake Superior shoreline between Marquette and Munising.

National and State Parks

National Parks

Isle Royale National Park (✉ 800 E. Lakeshore Dr., Houghton 49940, ☎ 906/482–0984), 48 mi off the Michigan coast in Lake Superior, is a wilderness park and can be reached by ferry from Houghton or Copper Harbor or by seaplane from Houghton. ★ **Pictured Rocks National Lakeshore** (✉ Box 40, Munising 49862, ☎ 906/387–2607), in the Upper Peninsula, extends 40 mi along Lake Superior between Munising and Grand Marais. **Sleeping Bear Dunes National Lakeshore** (✉ 9922 Front St., Box 277, Empire 49630, ☎ 616/326–5134) encompasses 35 mi of lower Michigan's Lake Michigan shore and includes the Manitou Islands. The 71,000-acre preserve has the highest sand dunes outside the Sahara.

State Parks

Michigan has 94 state parks, including 23 in the Upper Peninsula, many with spectacular waterfalls. Admission to all state parks is $4 per car, per day or $20 for an annual pass with unlimited usage. Most parks allow camping. A motor-vehicle permit, available at each park entrance, is required for admission. The *Michigan Travel Ideas and State Park Guide,* available from Travel Michigan (☞ Statewide Visitor Information, *above*), details park facilities.

Brimley State Park (✉ Rte. 2, Box 202, Brimley 49715, ☎ 906/248–3422), overlooking Lake Superior's Whitefish Bay, is one of 14 parks where you can rent a tent already set up and equipped with two cots and two sleeping pads. **Porcupine Mountains State Park** (✉ 412 S. Boundary Rd., Ontanogon 49953, ☎ 906/885–5275), on the rugged western edge of the Upper Peninsula, is one of 13 parks with cabins to rent. At **J. W. Wells State Park** (✉ Hwy. M–35, Cedar River 49813, ☎ 906/863–9747), some cabins are mere yards from the softly lapping Lake Michigan shoreline.

DETROIT

Founded seven decades before the American Revolution, the Midwest's oldest city is a busy industrial center, producing roughly a quarter of the nation's autos, trucks, and tractors. The riverfront harbor is one of the busiest ports on the Great Lakes. Downtown, a constant flow of traffic moves in and out of the Detroit–Windsor Tunnel and across the Ambassador Bridge, both of which connect Detroit with Windsor, Ontario, in Canada, directly across the Detroit River.

Though the city nicknamed itself the "Renaissance City" in the 1970s, until recently it did little to deserve the title. The 1990s have brought major changes, including a new mayor, plans for new sports stadiums, and a number of revitalized downtown areas, including the glitzy theater district, now second only to the Great White Way in its number of seats.

Visitor Information

Detroit Visitor Information Center (✉ 2 E. Jefferson Ave., in Hart Plaza just west of the Renaissance Center, 48226, ☎ 800/338-7648).

Arriving and Departing

By Bus

Greyhound Lines (✉ 1000 W. Lafayette St., ☎ 800/231–2222).

By Car

I–75 enters Detroit from the north and south, U.S. 10 from the north. Approaching from the west and northeast is I–94; from the west, I–96 and I–696. From the east Canadian Route 401 becomes Route 3 when entering Detroit from Windsor via the Ambassador Bridge and Route 3B when entering via the Detroit–Windsor Tunnel.

By Plane

Detroit Metropolitan Wayne County Airport (☎ 313/942–3550) in Romulus, about 26 mi west of downtown Detroit, is served by most major airlines, with nearly 1,000 arrivals and departures daily.

Commuter Transportation Company (☎ 800/488–7433) operates buses from the metropolitan airport to major downtown hotels from 6:45 AM to midnight; the fare is $13 one-way, $24 round-trip. Taxis to and from the airport take about 45 minutes; the fare is about $33 one-way.

By Train

Amtrak (✉ 16121 Michigan Ave., Dearborn, ☎ 800/872–7245).

Getting Around Detroit

By Car

Detroit is the Motor City; everyone drives. Many downtown streets are one-way; a detailed map is a necessity. The main streets into downtown are Woodward Avenue (north–south) and Jefferson Avenue (east–west). Rush hours should be avoided.

By Public Transportation

The **Department of Transportation** (☎ 313/933–1300) operates bus service throughout Detroit; the fare is $1.25. **Suburban Mobility Authority Regional Transportation** (☎ 313/962–5515) provides suburban bus service. The **People Mover** (☎ 313/224–2160) is an elevated, automated monorail that makes a 14-minute, 3-mi circuit of 13 downtown stations. Trains run about every three minutes; the fare is 50¢ (tokens are sold at each station).

By Taxi

The taxi fare is $1.40 at the flag drop, plus $1.40 per mile. Taxis can be ordered by phone or hired at stands at most major hotels. The two largest companies are **Checker Cab** (☎ 313/963–7000) and **City Cab** (☎ 313/833–7060).

Exploring Detroit

Starting from the Renaissance Center, on the banks of the river downtown, you can move outward to east Detroit, then on to the near northwest side, the cultural heart of Detroit.

Downtown

Detroit's most prominent landmark, the big, brassy **Renaissance Center,** known as the Ren Cen, dominates the city's skyline with six office towers and the spectacular 73-story Westin Hotel, one of the tallest hotels in the world. A city within a city, the waterfront complex has retail stores, services, and popular restaurants. The building was purchased in 1997 by General Motors, which plans to make the Ren Cen its world headquarters, so watch for renovations and major changes. There's a People Mover stop right at the Center.

Old Mariners' Church (✉ 170 E. Jefferson Ave., ☎ 313/259–2206) was made famous in Gordon Lightfoot's song "The Wreck of the *Edmund Fitzgerald.*" The 75-acre **Civic Center,** next to Old Mariners' Church, is a riverfront center for entertainment, festivals, and sports. At the heart of the Civic Center is **Philip A. Hart Plaza,** designed by Isamu Noguchi. In warm weather lunchtime crowds come here to enjoy the open spaces, sculptures, and the computer-controlled **Dodge Fountain.**

Randolph Rogers, who created the bronze doors of the U.S. Capitol, also designed **Cadillac Square,** site of many presidential speeches and the 1872 **Civil War Soldiers' and Sailors' Monument.** The blinking red light atop the 47-story **Penobscot Building** (✉ 645 Griswold, ☎ 313/961–8800), the state's tallest office tower, has been part of the Detroit skyline since 1928. A statue of Steven T. Mason, the first governor, stands over his grave in **Capitol Park,** site of Michigan's first capitol.

Grand Circus Park was envisioned as a full circus, as architectural circles were referred to then, when Detroit was rebuilt after a disastrous fire in 1805; only half was completed. A fountain in the west park honors Thomas A. Edison. Nearby is the opulent **Fox Theatre** (✉ 2211 Woodward Ave., ☎ 313/983–6611), which opened in 1928 as America's largest movie palace. Today it's an Art Deco showcase for big-name musical acts and large-screen movies.

Greektown, one of Detroit's most popular entertainment districts, is centered on Monroe Street. It percolates day and night with markets, bars, coffeehouses, shops, boutiques, and restaurants serving authentic Greek fare with an American flair.

Second Baptist Church (✉ 441 Monroe, ☎ 313/961–0920), organized in 1836, is Detroit's oldest black congregation. It was here that African-Americans gathered to celebrate the Emancipation Proclamation. **Old St. Mary's Catholic Church** (✉ 646 Monroe Ave., ☎ 313/961–8711), built in 1885, began as a parish of German and Irish immigrants in 1833.

Bricktown is a refurbished industrial corner of downtown filled with dining spots and bars. Characterized by a multitude of brick facades, it's a good place for a leisurely lunch, a shopping spree, or cocktails.

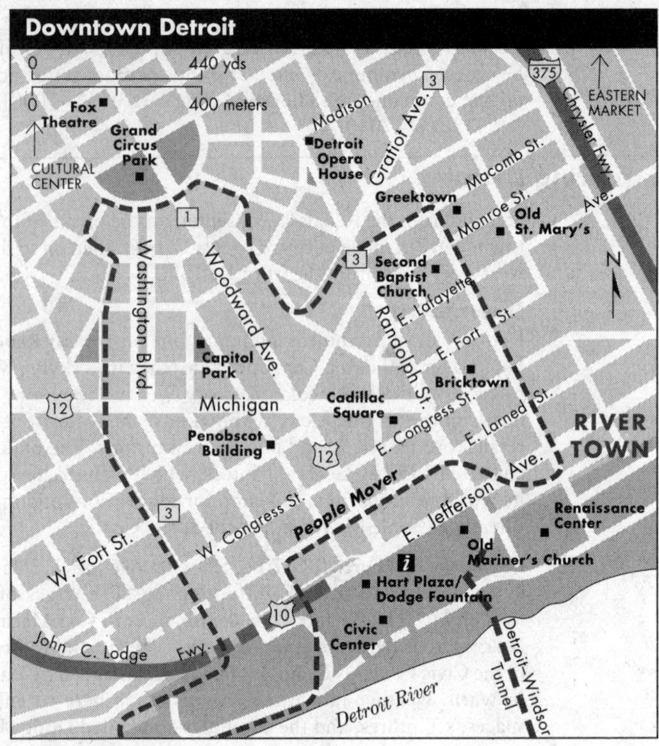

Detroit East

In the 1880s the section east of the Renaissance Center, between the river and Jefferson Avenue, blossomed with lumberyards, shipyards, and railroads. Known as **Rivertown,** the area is seeing new life today, with parks, shops, restaurants, and nightspots set in rejuvenated warehouses and carriage houses. **Stroh River Place,** opened in 1988, has attracted businesses, restaurants, and shops to a 21-acre site that stood empty for years.

Rivertown is the home of **Pewabic Pottery** (✉ 10125 E. Jefferson Ave., ☎ 313/822–0954; 🎟 free), founded in 1907, which produced the brilliantly glazed ceramic Pewabic tiles found in buildings throughout the nation. The pottery houses a ceramics museum, a workshop, and a learning center.

Farmers and city slickers have gathered in the historic open-air **Eastern Market** (✉ 2934 Russell St., ☎ 313/833–1560) since 1892 to barter and bargain over fresh produce, meats, fish, and plants. Public shopping hours start Saturday at 5 AM. Stores stay open til 5 PM; open-air markets shut down about 2 PM, when the stock runs out.

Near Northwest Detroit

Two and a half miles from downtown via Woodward Avenue is the **University Cultural Center,** a collection of art, history, and science museums and institutions clustered throughout some 40 city blocks.

The main exhibit at the **Detroit Historical Museum** (✉ 5401 Woodward Ave., ☎ 313/833–1805; 🎟 $3, free Wed.) explores the city's ties to the automobile. Other worthwhile exhibits are the Lawrence Scripps Wilkinson toy collection, and the Streets of Old Detroit—a walk through the city's long history.

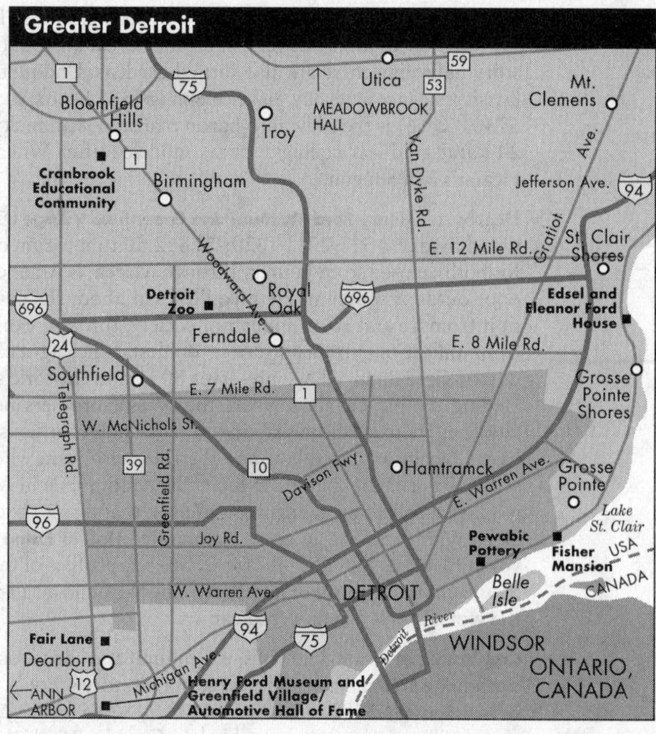

With more than 100 galleries, the **Detroit Institute of Arts** (✉ 5200 Woodward Ave., ☎ 313/833–7900; 🎫 $4) displays 5,000 years of world-famous art treasures, including works by van Gogh, Rembrandt, and Renoir. Diego Rivera's *Detroit Industry,* four immense frescoes, is a must-see. The institute is closed Monday and Tuesday.

Home to 1.3 million books, the Cultural Center branch of the **Detroit Public Library** (5201 Woodward Ave., ☎ 313/833–1000 or 313/833–1722 for recorded information) is the system's largest. Its Burton Historical Collection is the state's most comprehensive on city, state, and Great Lakes lore. The library is closed Sunday and Monday.

The **International Institute of Metropolitan Detroit** (✉ 111 E. Kirby St., ☎ 313/871–8600; 🎫 free) is a museum, a working social agency for foreigners, and a lunchtime café. Its Gallery of Nations displays the arts and crafts of 43 countries. The **Museum of African-American History** (✉ 315 E. Warren Ave., ☎ 313/494-5800; 🎫 $3), the largest museum of its kind in the world, tells the story of the black experience in America through exhibits and audiovisual presentations.

Other Attractions

Scattered around Detroit are the lavish homes of four of the city's famed auto barons. Henry Ford's **Fair Lane** (4901 Evergreen Rd., Dearborn, ☎ 313/593–5590; 🎫 $7) blends a Scottish Baronial style with a simple, Arts-and-Crafts design. Here you'll get a look at the bowling alley where Ford used to shoot pins with his friends Thomas Edison and naturalist John Burroughs. Ford's son Edsel built the **Eleanor and Edsel Ford Estate** (110 Lakeshore Rd., Grosse Pointe Shores, ☎ 313/884–4222; 🎫 $5), a 1929 Cotswold–style residence with beautiful artwork and gardens. The largest of the auto baron's homes, the opulent **Meadowbrook Hall** (Oakland University, Rochester, ☎ 248/

370–3140; 🎫 $6), was built in the late 1920s for Matilda Dodge, widow of auto pioneer John Dodge. Among its more than 100 rooms is a two-story ballroom; there are also formal gardens. Undoubtedly the most lavish residence in its day, **Fisher Mansion** (383 Lenox St., ☎ 313/331–6740; 🎫 $6) is the only auto baron mansion within city limits. With 24-karat-gold-leaf ceilings, it was modeled after William Randolph Hearst's San Simeon.

Dearborn's **Henry Ford Museum and Greenfield Village** (✉ 20900 Oakwood Blvd., ☎ 313/271–1620; 🎫 $12.50 to museum or village; $22 for both), closed from January through March, is America's largest indoor-outdoor museum. Here you'll learn about the country's evolution from a rural to an industrial society, through exhibits covering communications, transportation, domestic life, agriculture, and industry. Greenfield Village preserves 80 famous historic structures, including the bicycle shop where the Wright brothers built their first airplane, Thomas Edison's laboratory, an Illinois courthouse where Abraham Lincoln practiced law, and the Dearborn farm where Ford himself was born. An ongoing exhibit, the Automobile in American Life, is a lavish collection of chrome and neon that traces the country's love affair with cars. The adjacent **Automotive Hall of Fame** (21400 Oakwood Blvd., ☎ 888/298–4748; 🎫 $6) has profiles of the men behind the machines, a mural of automotive history, and a full-size replica of the world's first gas-powered car.

Cranbrook, in Bloomfield Hills, is a cultural and educational center with a graduate art academy and college preparatory schools. **Historic Cranbrook House** (✉ 380 Lone Pine Rd., ☎ 248/645–3149; 🎫 $6), a mansion built for newspaper publisher George Booth, has lead-glass windows, art objects, and formal gardens with fountains and sculpture. The **Cranbrook Academy of Art Museum** (✉ 1221 N. Woodward Ave., ☎ 248/645–3312; 🎫 $3) has major exhibitions of contemporary art and a permanent collection that includes works by Eliel and Eero Saarinen and Charles Eames. **Cranbrook Institute of Science** (✉ 1221 N. Woodward Ave., ☎ 248/645–3200; 🎫 $7) has intriguing hands-on physics experiments, geology displays, and dinosaur excavation exhibits.

Parks, Gardens, and Zoos

More than 1,200 animals from 300 species live uncaged in natural habitats at the **Detroit Zoo** (✉ 8450 W. Ten Mile Rd., Royal Oak, ☎ 248/398–0903; 🎫 $5.50). Highlights include the world's largest "penguinarium," a walk-through aviary with tropical birds and plants, and a wildlife interpretive gallery with a butterfly house.

Belle Isle (☎ 313/852–4075), a 1,000-acre island park in the Detroit River 3 mi southeast of the city center, is reached by way of East Jefferson Avenue and East Grand Boulevard. Here are woods, walking trails, sports facilities, a nine-hole golf course, and a ½-mi-long beach.

Among Belle Isle's other attractions is the **Whitcomb Conservatory** (☎ no phone; 🎫 $2), with one of the largest orchid collections in the country. **Belle Isle Aquarium** (☎ 313/852–4141; 🎫 $2), the nation's oldest freshwater aquarium, exhibits more than 200 species of fish, reptiles, and amphibians. The **Belle Isle Nature Center** (☎ no phone; 🎫 donations accepted) has changing exhibits and presentations on local natural history. The **Belle Isle Zoo** (☎ 313/852–4083; 🎫 $3), closed from November through April, has an elevated walkway that gives you a bird's-eye view of animals roaming in natural settings.

Also on Belle Isle, the **Dossin Great Lakes Museum** (☒ 100 Strand Dr., ☎ 313/267–6440; $2) has displays about Great Lakes shipping, the prohibition era in Detroit, and an ongoing exhibition—the Storm of 1913—recalling the Great Lakes' worst-ever storm. Visitors can listen to ship-to-shore radio messages and view the river and city through a periscope. The museum is closed Monday and Tuesday.

Dining

Each wave of immigrants to Detroit has made its culinary mark: You'll find soul food restaurants in the inner city, a vibrant Mexican community on the west side, and Greek restaurants in Greektown. Detroiters often dine across the river in Windsor, Ontario, where a favorable rate of exchange makes for excellent values. For price ranges *see* Chart 1 (A) *in* On the Road with Fodor's.

$$$–$$$$ ✕ **The Summit.** This revolving restaurant on the 71st floor of the Westin Hotel has a superb view of Detroit. Charbroiled steaks and swordfish à la Louisiana are staples on the menu. ☒ *Renaissance Center,* ☎ *313/568–8600. Jacket and tie. AE, D, DC, MC, V.*

$$$–$$$$ ★ ✕ **Van Dyke Place.** The evening ritual at this restored turn-of-the-century mansion includes dinner in the opulent main-floor dining room. The French-inspired menu includes such dishes as rack of lamb with chickpea crust. ☒ *649 Van Dyke Ave.,* ☎ *313/821–2620. Reservations essential. Jacket and tie. AE, MC, V. Closed Sun.–Mon.*

$$$–$$$$ ★ ✕ **The Whitney.** One of Detroit's poshest restaurants was once the mansion of lumber baron David Whitney. Chef Paul Grosz turns out creative American dishes, snappy pastas, and very fresh seafood. Brunch is served on Sunday. ☒ *4421 Woodward Ave.,* ☎ *313/832–5700. Reservations essential. Jacket and tie. AE, D, MC, V. No lunch.*

$$–$$$$ ✕ **Caucus Club.** This venerable Detroit institution recalls the era when elegant restaurants had boardroom decor, with lots of oil paintings and wood. The menu is of similar vintage: corned-beef hash, steaks, chops, Dover sole, and its famous baby-back ribs. ☒ *150 W. Congress St.,* ☎ *313/965–4970. AE, D, DC, MC, V. Closed weekends.*

$$–$$$$ ★ ✕ **Lelli's Inn.** When Detroiters think Italian, Lelli's comes to mind. Exceptional veal, minestrone, red sauce, and homemade ice creams are served in a cavernous 650-seat dining room. ☒ *7618 Woodward Ave.,* ☎ *313/871–1590. Jacket and tie. AE, DC, MC, V. Closed Mon.*

$$–$$$$ ✕ **Rattlesnake Club.** Superchef Jimmy Schmidt has an innovative hand with pickerel, salmon, and veal—but his signature dish is the rack of lamb. The dining room is all marble and rosewood, with terrific views of the Detroit River and Windsor skyline. ☒ *300 River Pl.,* ☎ *313/567–4400. AE, D, DC, MC, V.*

$$–$$$ ★ ✕ **Blue Nile.** Detroit's only Ethiopian restaurant is, surprisingly, in the heart of Greektown. Richly seasoned meats and vegetables are served on communal trays covered with *injera,* a pancakelike flat bread that used to scoop up other foods. ☒ *Trappers Alley, 508 Monroe Ave.,* ☎ *313/964–6699. AE, D, DC, MC, V.*

$$–$$$ ★ ✕ **Fishbone's Rhythm Kitchen Cafe.** This authentic New Orleans–style restaurant in the heart of Greektown is loud, brash, funky, and fun. Spicy Creole fare on the seasonal menu includes gator, gumbo, crawfish, and gulf oysters on the half shell. The whiskey ribs are tops year-round. ☒ *400 Monroe Ave.,* ☎ *313/965–4600. AE, D, DC, MC, V.*

$$–$$$ ✕ **Pegasus Taverna.** Specialties such as *pastitsio* (Greek-style lasagna) and *avgolemono* (chicken-lemon soup) are prepared in a huge open kitchen in at this upscale Greek taverna. You'll also find American favorites such as Caesar salad and sandwiches. ☒ *558 Monroe Ave.,* ☎ *313/964–6800. AE, D, DC, MC, V.*

$$–$$$ ✕ **Traffic Jam & Snug.** The menu changes often, but you can count on wheatberry and other interesting breads, inventive salads, and daily entrées that range from spinach lasagna to a piled-high Caesar salad. Desserts are the speciality—if you dare, try the "death by chocolate," a hot-fudge-covered sundae. ✉ *511 W. Canfield St.,* ☎ *313/831–9470. Reservations not accepted. D, DC, MC, V. No dinner Mon.; no lunch weekends.*

$–$$ ✕ **Under the Eagle.** As is typical of Detroit's modestly priced Polish cafés, the Eagle's food is first-rate, with generous portions of stick-to-your-ribs roast duckling and kielbasa. For the adventuresome there's *czarnina* (duck-blood soup). ✉ *9000 Joseph Campau St.,* ☎ *313/875–5905. No credit cards. Closed Wed.*

$–$$ ★ ✕ **Wah Court.** Across the river in Windsor, Ontario, near the Ambassador Bridge, this no-frills Cantonese restaurant is known for its abundant menu of nearly 200 items. Dim sum is served daily, with the biggest selection on Sunday. ✉ *2037 Wyandotte Ave. W, Windsor,* ☎ *519/254–1388. MC, V.*

$ ✕ **Lafayette Coney Island.** Detroit's contribution to the world of gastronomy is the so-called coney island: a loose beef burger in a hot-dog bun, smothered with cheese, onions, and chili. At 3 AM, suburbanites and visiting celebrities in stretch limos share counter stools with workers getting off the night shift at this area institution. *118 Lafayette St.,* ☎ *313/964–8198. Reservations not accepted. No credit cards.*

Lodging

In addition to downtown Detroit, accommodations are available in suburban Troy, with its high concentration of corporate headquarters, and in Dearborn, where the Ford Motor Company has its headquarters. Most hotels, motels, and inns also offer reduced-price weekend packages. For price ranges *see* Chart 2 (A) *in* On the Road with Fodor's.

$$$–$$$$ 🏨 **Atheneum Suites Hotel.** Business travelers and visiting celebrities favor this downtown newcomer. Spacious, individually decorated suites have Greek overtones. The lobby bar bustles with activity. ✉ *1000 Brush Ave., 48226,* ☎ *313/962–2323 or 800/772–2323,* FAX *313/962–2424. 174 suites. Restaurant, pool, health club. AE, MC, DC, V.*

$$–$$$$ ★ 🏨 **Ritz-Carlton, Dearborn.** Like other Ritz-Carlton hotels around the world, Dearborn's has a reputation for impeccable taste and service. Its mahogany-paneled walls, overstuffed settees, and antique art suggest a clubby, British elegance. Reinforcing that image is a traditional afternoon tea and hors d'oeuvres served in the lobby lounge. ✉ *300 Town Center Dr., Dearborn 48126,* ☎ *313/441–2000 or 800/241–3333,* FAX *313/441–2051. 308 rooms. Restaurant, pool, exercise room. AE, D, DC, MC, V.*

$$$ 🏨 **Crowne Plaza Hotel Pontchartrain.** The Pontch, as it is familiarly known, has light, airy rooms done in neutral shades accented by green-and-rose fabrics. Most rooms have wonderful views of the city and the river; do not, however, accept a room at the back of the hotel—which is across the street from a fire station—unless you are a heavy sleeper. ✉ *2 Washington Blvd., 48226,* ☎ *313/965–0200 or 800/537–6624,* FAX *313/965–9464. 416 rooms. Restaurant, pool, health club. AE, DC, MC, V.*

$$$ 🏨 **Doubletree Guest Suites.** This all-suites hotel is a feast for the eyes, with an eight-story atrium full of trees, flowers, ivy, a small fountain, and a miniwaterfall. The rooftop running track gives an eagle-eye view of the city. ✉ *850 Tower Dr., Troy 48098,* ☎ *810/879–7500 or 800/424–2900,* FAX *810/879–9139. 251 suites. Restaurant, pool, health club. Full breakfast. AE, D, DC, MC, V.*

$$$ ★ **Westin Hotel.** At 73 stories, this hotel is known for its size more than anything else. Guest rooms are neither large nor special, but each commands a waterfront view of the city and of neighboring Windsor, Ontario. ✉ *Renaissance Center, Jefferson Ave. at Randolph St., 48243,* ☎ *313/568–8000 or 800/228–3000,* FAX *313/568–8146. 1,400 rooms. Restaurant, pool, health club. AE, D, DC, MC, V.*

$$–$$$ **Dearborn Inn and Marriott Hotel.** Henry Ford built this hotel in 1931 to house foreign dignitaries and inventors such as Thomas Edison and Charles Lindbergh. The Colonial-inspired property is across from the Henry Ford Museum and Greenfield Village. Adjacent to the main building are five historic homes associated with such famous Americans as Patrick Henry, Edgar Allan Poe, and Walt Whitman. ✉ *20301 Oakwood Blvd., Dearborn 48124,* ☎ *313/271–2700 or 800/228–9290,* FAX *313/271–7464. 220 rooms, 5 cottages. 2 restaurants, pool, tennis, exercise room. AE, D, DC, MC, V.*

$$–$$$ **Hyatt Regency Dearborn.** Opposite Ford's world headquarters, this large, modern hotel with a trademark Hyatt atrium is five minutes from the Henry Ford Museum and Greenfield Village. ✉ *Fairlane Town Center, Dearborn 48126,* ☎ *313/593–1234,* FAX *313/593–3366. 771 rooms. 2 restaurants, pool. AE, D, DC, MC, V.*

$$–$$$ **Somerset Inn.** In the heart of Troy's corporate district, 25 mi north of Detroit, this is a favorite with the business set. Guest rooms are small and standard, but the entry level is lovely, with marble floors, greenery, and several small sitting rooms tucked around the perimeter. ✉ *2601 W. Big Beaver Rd., Troy 48084,* ☎ *810/643–7800 or 800/228–8769,* FAX *810/643–2296. 250 rooms. Restaurant, pools, health club. AE, D, DC, MC, V.*

$$ ★ **Doubletree Hotel Detroit.** One of Detroit's most modern hotels, the Doubletree is connected by skywalk to the Renaissance Center and by People Mover to the rest of downtown. Rooms are bright and large. ✉ *333 E. Jefferson Ave., 48226,* ☎ *313/222–7700,* FAX *313/222–6509. 254 rooms. Restaurant, pool, tennis, health club. AE, D, DC, MC, V.*

$–$$ **Shorecrest Motor Inn.** This pleasant, no-frills two-story hotel is two blocks east of the Renaissance Center and within walking distance of downtown attractions. ✉ *1316 E. Jefferson Ave., 48207,* ☎ *313/568–3000 or 800/992–9616,* FAX *313/568–3002. 54 rooms. Restaurant. AE, D, DC, MC, V.*

Nightlife and the Arts

Nightlife

Much of Detroit's nightlife is centered downtown and in suburban Royal Oak, home to cutting-edge restaurants and smoky coffeehouses. In Greektown, tourists crowd the **Bouzouki Lounge** (✉ 432 E. Lafayette St., ☎ 313/964–5744) to see and hear traditional Greek music, folksingers, and belly dancers. On the west side of the city is **Baker's Keyboard Lounge** (✉ 20510 Livernois Ave., ☎ 313/345–6300), a dimly lighted, smoke-filled jazz club.

In Rivertown, the **Soup Kitchen Saloon** (✉ 1585 Franklin St., ☎ 313/259–2643) is the home of the Detroit blues. The **Rhinoceros Restaurant** (✉ 265 Riopelle St., ☎ 313/259–2208) and **Woodbridge Tavern** (✉ 289 St. Aubin, ☎ 313/259–0578) are former speakeasies where downtown professionals loosen their ties and stomp their feet. Poetry readings, art exhibitions, and no-nonsense live acts give **Alvin's** (✉ 5756 Cass St., ☎ 313/832–2355) a bohemian appeal, especially among students at nearby Wayne State University.

The Arts

Metro Times, a free weekly tabloid available throughout the metropolitan area, has a comprehensive calendar of events. Also check the arts sections of the *Detroit News* and *Detroit Free Press,* and the calendar section of *Hour Detroit.*

The **Detroit Repertory Theater** (✉ 13103 Woodrow Wilson Ave., ☎ 313/868–1347) is one of the city's oldest resident theater companies. Touring Broadway shows and nationally known entertainers appear at the **Fisher Theater** (✉ 3011 W. Grand Blvd., ☎ 313/872–1000) and the **Masonic Temple** (✉ 500 Temple St., ☎ 313/832–2232). **Detroit Symphony Orchestra Hall** (✉ 3177 Woodward Ave., ☎ 313/576–5111) is home to the **Chamber Music Society of Detroit** and the **Detroit Symphony.** The **Detroit Opera House** (1526 Broadway, ☎ 313/961–3500) is the newly restored home of the acclaimed Michigan Opera Theatre; it also hosts visiting ballet and musical troupes from across the country.

Spectator Sports

Baseball: Detroit Tigers (✉ Tiger Stadium, 2121 Trumbull at Michigan Ave., ☎ 313/962–4000). **Basketball: Detroit Pistons** (✉ The Palace of Auburn Hills, 2 Championship Dr., 30 mi north of Detroit, Auburn Hills, ☎ 248/377–0100). **Football: Detroit Lions** (✉ Pontiac Silverdome, 30 mi north of Detroit, Pontiac, ☎ 248/335–4131). **Hockey: Detroit Red Wings** (✉ Joe Louis Arena, downtown on the riverfront, ☎ 313/983–6606).

Shopping

Shopping is scarce downtown, where once-fashionable Woodward Avenue is now a forlorn and mostly abandoned strip; these days, most shopping is concentrated in the suburbs. Near the University Cultural Center, **New Center One** attracts office workers during lunchtime. In suburban Troy, the **Somerset Collection and Somerset North** has tony boutiques and well-known upscale chains such as Neiman Marcus, Saks Fifth Avenue, and Nordstrom. **Suburban Birmingham** is home to some of the Midwest's finest art galleries as well as exclusive boutiques. In funky **Royal Oak,** you'll find small stores stocking everything from leather clothing and paraphernalia to fine antiques.

Crowley's, whose major store is at New Center One Mall, is well known for fashions for men, women, and children. The area leader in fashion and home furnishings is **J. L. Hudson's,** whose onetime downtown flagship has been replaced by a suburban headquarters at Northland Mall in Southfield.

ELSEWHERE IN MICHIGAN

Ann Arbor

Visitor Information

Ann Arbor Convention and Visitors Bureau (120 W. Huron St., 48104, ☎ 800/888–9487).

Arriving and Departing

Ann Arbor, 50 mi west of downtown Detroit, is intersected by U.S. 23 and I–94.

What to See and Do

Leafy, liberal, and young (thanks to the student population of the University of Michigan), Ann Arbor is consistently rated among the country's most desirable communities. The downtown shopping district, which extends along **Main Street,** is known for its specialty stores run by knowledgeable, independent owners. The State Street area, closer to campus, has one of the finest concentrations of book and music stores in the country. Among them is the original **Borders Books and Music** (✉ 612 E. Liberty, ☎ 313/668–7100), started in 1971 by two University of Michigan graduates. On campus are three exceptional free museums. The natural-history exhibits at the **University of Michigan Exhibit Museum** (✉ 1109 Geddes Ave., ☎ 313/763–6085) range from miniature dioramas to towering dinosaur skeletons. The **Kelsey Museum of Archaeology** (✉ 434 S. State St., ☎ 313/764–9304) houses ancient Greek, Egyptian, Roman, and Near Eastern artifacts. The **University of Michigan Museum of Art** (✉ 525 S. State St., ☎ 313/764–0395) has a permanent collection of 13,000 pieces, including works by Rodin, Picasso, and Monet. Try your hands at the 250 working-science exhibits at the **Ann Arbor Hands-On Museum** (✉ 219 E. Huron St., ☎ 313/995–5439; 🎟 $4), housed inside an 1882 firehouse downtown.

Dining and Lodging

$$–$$$$ ✕ **Gandy Dancer.** Housed in a 19th-century railroad depot on the edge of town, this flagship of the popular Joe Muer seafood chain specializes in fresh seafood and tasty pastas. The Sunday brunch is a lavish, diet-busting spread. ✉ *401 Depot St.,* ☎ *313/769–0592. AE, DC, MC, V.*

$$$$ ✕🏨 **Bell Tower.** The only hotel in the heart of campus has a traditional, European style. The elegant restaurant, Escoffier, serves old-style French cuisine such as baked rainbow trout stuffed with scallop mousse, or sauteed sweetbreads with grapes and Madeira. ✉ *300 S. Thayer St., 48104.* ☎ *313/769–3010 or 800/562–3559,* FAX *313/769–4339. 56 rooms, 10 suites. Restaurant. D, DC, MC, V.*

Mackinac Island

Visitor Information

Mackinac Island Chamber of Commerce (✉ Box 451, Mackinac Island 49757, ☎ 906/847–3783).

Arriving and Departing

By car, take I–75 north from Detroit to Mackinaw City. Island ferries depart from Mackinaw City and St. Ignace, at the northern end of the Mackinac Bridge.

What to See and Do

No autos are allowed on **Mackinac Island** (island, town, and straits are all pronounced *Mack*-i-naw), but the quaint Victorian village begs to be explored on foot. A small park at the eastern end of the village, along the boardwalk, affords terrific views of the Mackinac Bridge and ships passing through the straits. Farther afield, 8 mi of paved roads circle the island; bicycles rent by the hour or day at concessions near the ferry docks on Huron Street. **Mackinac Island Carriage Tours** (✉ Main St., ☎ 906/847–3573) conducts horse-drawn tours covering historic points of interest, including Fort Mackinac, Arch Rock, Skull Cave, Surrey Hill, and the Grand Hotel.

On a bluff above the harbor, **Fort Mackinac** (☎ 906/847–3328) was a British stronghold during the American Revolution and the War of 1812. Fourteen original buildings are preserved as a museum; costumed guides conduct tours and reenactments. **Marquette Park,** directly below the fort along Main Street, commemorates the work of French missionary Jacques Marquette with a bark chapel patterned after those built on the island in the 1600s. The venerable **Grand Hotel** (☎ 906/847–3331), now more than a century old, charges visitors $6 just to look, but the Victorian opulence of the public rooms and the view from the world's longest porch are worth it.

Dining and Lodging

$$$$ ✕🅿 **Island House.** If the Grand Hotel is out of your price range, opt instead for the Island House, the island's oldest hotel and a registered historic site. This is also the home of Governor's Dining Room, one of the island's most acclaimed restaurants, serving fish and steak in a formal dining room with views of the lake and nearby islands. ✉ *1 Lakeshore Dr.,* ☎ *906/847–3347,* FAX *906/847–3819. 94 rooms, 3 suites. Restaurant, pool. MC, V.*

Keweenaw Peninsula

Visitor Information

Keweenaw Tourism Council (✉ 326 Shelden Ave., Houghton 49931, ☎ 906/482–2388 or 800/338–7982).

Arriving and Departing

The Keweenaw, in the northwestern section of the Upper Peninsula, is reached by U.S. 41.

What to See and Do

Curving into Lake Superior like a crooked finger, the Keweenaw (*Key-wa-naw*) was the site of extensive copper mining from the 1840s to the 1960s. In **Hancock,** you can take a guided tour of now-defunct mine workings. Quincy Mine Hoist (☎ 906/482–5569; 🎫 $10). **Houghton** is home to Michigan Technical University, whose Seaman Mineral Museum (☎ 906/487–2572; 🎫 $4) has displays of minerals native to the Upper Peninsula.

North on U.S. 41, the Victorian stone architecture in **Calumet** gives just a hint of the wealth in the copper towns during the boom days. At the circa-1900 **Calumet Theater** (☎ 906/337–2610), stars such as Lillian Russell, Sarah Bernhardt, and Douglas Fairbanks Sr. performed. At **Coppertown, U.S.A.** (☎ 906/337–4354; 🎫 $3), a visitor center tells the story of the mines, towns, and people of the Keweenaw. North of Coppertown, in the old mining town of Delaware, **Delaware Copper Mine Tours** (☎ 906/289–4688; 🎫 $7) provides guided walking tours through the first level of a mid-1800s mine.

At the tip of the Keweenaw Peninsula, **Copper Harbor,** Michigan's northernmost community, is an always uncrowded biking and camping destination. **Fort Wilkins State Park** (☎ 906/289–4215) contains the restored buildings of an Army post established in 1844 and abandoned in 1870. The complex also has copper-mine shafts, hiking trails, and campgrounds. **Brockway Mountain Drive** climbs 900 ft above Copper Harbor to provide magnificent views of the peninsula and Lake Superior.

Lake Michigan Shore

Visitor Information

The **West Michigan Tourist Association** (✉ 1253 Front St., Grand Rapids 49504, ☎ 616/456–8557) provides information on the Lake Michigan Shore area.

Arriving and Departing

U.S. 31 edges Lake Michigan from St. Joseph to Mackinaw City.

What to See and Do

The Lake Michigan shoreline, which extends from the southwestern corner of the state up to the Mackinac Bridge, is one of Michigan's greatest natural resources. Its placid waters, cool breezes, and sugary beaches (including some of the largest sand dunes in the world) have attracted generations of tourists, including such regulars as Al Capone, Ernest Hemingway, and L. Frank Baum (who wrote many of his books about Oz over the course of several summer vacations here).

Resort towns, some of which triple in population between Memorial Day and Labor Day, dot the shoreline. **St. Joseph** is a picturesque community whose turn-of-the-century downtown and two 1,000-ft-long piers make it ideal for walkers. The artists' colony of **Saugatuck** has many fine restaurants and shops, an active gay and lesbian community, and enough B&Bs to qualify it as bed-and-breakfast capital of the state. Saugatuck Dune Rides (☎ 616/857–2253) offers freewheeling dune-buggy rides along Lake Michigan. In **Douglas,** the S. S. *Keewatin* (☎ 616/857–2151), one of the Great Lakes' last passenger steamboats, is permanently docked as a maritime museum.

Near Douglas is **Holland,** home of the Tulip Time Festival in May (☞ Festivals and Seasonal Events *in* the Midwest introduction). The **De Klomp Wooden Shoe and Delftware Factory** (✉ 12755 Quincy St., ☎ 616/399–1900; 🎫 free) is the only place outside the Netherlands where earthenware is hand-painted and fired using Delft blue glaze.

North of Holland is the eastern shore's largest city, **Muskegon,** an industrial town known mainly as the home of the Muskegon Winter Sports Complex (☎ 616/744–9629), with the Midwest's only luge run. The **Frauenthal Center for the Performing Arts** (✉ 425 W. Western St., ☎ 616/722–4538) is a gaudy Art Deco theater that is home to traveling Broadway-quality plays, silent films, and the West Shore Symphony Orchestra. Eight miles north of Muskegon is **Michigan's Adventure Amusement Park** (✉ Russell Rd. exit off U.S. 31, ☎ 616/766–3377; 🎫 $15), with more than 20 thrill rides, 10 water slides, a wave pool, shows, games, food, and the only two roller coasters in Michigan.

A two-hour drive north of Muskegon is **Traverse City,** the state's premier sports-vacation destination. Much to the chagrin of longtime residents, the area south of Grand Traverse Bay was "discovered" by sportsmen—and developers—about 25 years ago. Unfortunately, the roads have not kept pace with the boom in sailors, golfers, and skiers. The two-lane highways can resemble parking lots, particularly during the popular National Cherry Festival (☞ Festivals and Seasonal Events *in* the Midwest introduction). For a pleasant diversion follow Route 37 around the **Old Mission Peninsula,** filled with the cherry orchards and vineyards that are the area's main industry next to tourism. A good time to visit is in the spring, when crowds are small.

Some of the finest views of Lake Michigan are found on the **Leelanau Peninsula,** the finger that juts into Little Traverse Bay. Follow Route 119 to **Harbor Springs,** a resort village overlooking Little Traverse Bay.

MINNESOTA

By Don Davenport and Karin Winegar

Updated by Alicia Fedorczak

Capital	St. Paul
Population	4,686,000
Motto	Star of the North
State Bird	Common loon
State Flower	Pink lady's slipper
Postal Abbreviation	MN

Statewide Visitor Information

Minnesota Office of Tourism (✉ 500 Metro Sq., 121 7th Pl. E, St. Paul 55101, ☎ 612/296–5029 or 800/657–3700). There are 12 visitor centers around the state.

Scenic Drives

U.S. 61, along the Mississippi River between Red Wing and Winona, is often compared with the Rhine Valley in beauty; between Duluth and the Canadian border (☞ Duluth and the North Shore, *below*), it hugs the edge of Lake Superior for 160 mi, providing spectacular views of the lake and its rocky shoreline. **Route 59,** between Fergus Falls and Detroit Lakes, traverses some of central Minnesota's prime lake country.

National and State Parks

National Parks

Voyageurs National Park (☞ The Iron Range and Boundary Waters, *below*), in far northern Minnesota, has 30 major lakes and is part of the watery highway that makes up the state's northern border with Canada.

Pipestone National Monument, in southwestern Minnesota, protects the red stone quarry mined for centuries by Native Americans for material to carve their ceremonial pipes. The quarry is still in use, and traditional stone craft is still practiced at the **cultural center** in the Monument Headquarters (✉ Hwy. 75, Pipestone 56164, ☎ 507/825–5464).

State Parks

Minnesota has 68 state parks, 62 with camping facilities. For information contact the **Department of Natural Resources** (✉ DNR Information Center, 500 Lafayette Rd., Box 40, St. Paul 55155-4040, ☎ 612/296–6157).

Fort Snelling State Park, just south of downtown St. Paul (✉ Rte. 5 and Post Rd., St. Paul 55111, ☎ 612/725–2389), preserves the historic fort built at the junction of the Mississippi and Minnesota rivers in 1819. **Itasca State Park** (✉ HC05, Box 4, Lake Itasca 56460, ☎ 218/266–2114) is Minnesota's oldest state park, established in 1891 to protect the headwaters of the Mississippi River, which rises from Lake Itasca. **Soudan Underground Mine State Park** (✉ 1379 Stuntz Bay Rd., Soudan 55782, ☎ 218/753–2245) has hiking trails and tours of the Soudan Mine, Minnesota's oldest and largest iron mine, which operated until 1962. **Gooseberry Falls State Park** (✉ 1300 Hwy. 61 E, Two Harbors 55616, ☎ 218/834–3855) and **Temperance River State Park** (✉ Hwy. 61, Box 33, Schroeder 55613, ☎ 218/663–7476), with roaring waterfalls and scenic vistas, are typical of parks found along Lake Superior's shore.

MINNEAPOLIS AND ST. PAUL

Drawing comparisons between Minneapolis and St. Paul is much like comparing two favorite aunts—a difficult task. St. Paul has a slightly reserved, antique feel about it; Minneapolis is hipper, noisier, and busier. Both cities have tall, gleaming glass skylines; St. Paul's is designed to blend with the city's Art Deco and Victorian architecture, while Minneapolis's is more eclectic. St. Paul has preserved much of its architectural heritage, while most of downtown Minneapolis is new. Both cities straddle the Mississippi River, and riverboat traffic calls at the Twin Cities from as far away as New Orleans.

There are 2.4 million people in the Greater Minneapolis/St. Paul metropolitan area, but Minneapolis wins the population race with 368,400. The strong Scandinavian strain in the cities' ancestry has not prevented them from constructing miles-long skyway systems. Residents can drive downtown, park, walk to work, go to lunch, shop, see a show, and return to their cars without once setting foot outdoors—a blessing in the blustery Minnesota winters.

Visitor Information

Minneapolis: Convention and Visitors Association (✉ 4000 Multifoods Tower, 33 S. 6th St., 55402, ☎ 612/661–4700). **St. Paul:** Convention and Visitors Bureau (✉ 55 E. 5th St., Suite 102, 55101, ☎ 612/297–6985 or 800/627–6101).

Arriving and Departing

By Bus

Greyhound Lines has stations in St. Paul (✉ 25 W. 7th St., ☎ 612/222–0509) and in Minneapolis (✉ 29 N. 9th St., ☎ 612/371–3323).

By Car

The major north–south route through the area is I–35, which divides into I–35W bisecting Minneapolis and I–35E through St. Paul. I–94 goes east–west through both cities. A beltway circles the Twin Cities, with I–494 looping through the southern suburbs and I–694 cutting through the north.

By Plane

Minneapolis/St. Paul International Airport (☎ 612/726–5555) lies between the cities on I–494, 8 mi south of downtown St. Paul and 10 mi south of downtown Minneapolis. It is served by most major domestic airlines and several foreign carriers. From the airport to either city, **Metropolitan Transit Commission** (☎ 612/349–7000) buses cost $1 ($1.50 during rush hour); taxis take about 30 minutes and charge $17–$20 to both downtown Minneapolis and St. Paul.

By Train

St. Paul's **Amtrak** station (✉ 730 Transfer Rd., ☎ 612/644–1127) serves both cities.

Getting Around Minneapolis and St. Paul

Both cities are laid out on a grid, with streets running north–south and east–west. However, many downtown streets parallel the Mississippi River and run on a diagonal, and not all streets cross the river. Both downtowns have extensive skyway systems. Many St. Paul attractions can be reached on foot, but most of those in Minneapolis require wheels. Express fare on **Metropolitan Transit Commission** (☎ 612/349–7000) buses between Minneapolis and St. Paul during rush hour is $2. Within each city's central business district the fare is 50¢. Outside the downtown area the fare is $1, $1.50 during peak hours (6–9 AM and 3:30–6:30 PM).

Taxi fare is $3.20 for the first mile and $1.30 for each additional mile. The largest taxi firms in St. Paul are **Yellow** (☎ 612/222–4433) and **City Wide** (☎ 612/489–1111); in Minneapolis, **Blue and White** (☎ 612/333–3333) and **Yellow** (☎ 612/824–4444). **Town Taxi** (☎ 612/331–8294) serves all suburbs.

Exploring Minneapolis and St. Paul

Minneapolis

Downtown Minneapolis is easily walkable in any season. The climate-controlled skyway system connects hundreds of shops and restaurants. In general, skyways remain open during the business hours of the buildings they connect.

The Mississippi River's **Falls of St. Anthony,** discovered by Father Louis Hennepin three centuries ago, drop 16 ft at the eastern edge of downtown. Harnessed by dams and diminished in grandeur, the historic falls are today bypassed by the **Upper St. Anthony Lock** (✉ Foot of Portland Ave.), which allows river traffic to reach industrial sections of Minneapolis. An observation deck provides views of lock operations.

The **Stone Arch Bridge,** a railroad bridge over the Mississippi River near the Upper St. Anthony Lock, was built in the late 19th century by railroad baron James J. Hill, and later restored and open to foot and bicycle traffic. Guided walking tours of the **St. Anthony Falls Historic District** are available from April through October (☎ 612/627–5433).

The **University of Minnesota,** with an enrollment of close to 60,000, is one of the largest campuses in the country. **Dinkytown,** on the east bank, and **Seven Corners,** on the west bank, are good places to find campus bars, nightspots, university shops, record emporiums, and bookstores.

The University of Minnesota's **James Ford Bell Museum of Natural History** (✉ University Ave. SE at 17th Ave., ☎ 612/624–7083; 🎫 $3) has dioramas of Minnesota wildlife, an art gallery of wildlife paintings, and a touch-and-see room for kids. The most talked-about building on campus is the **Weisman Art Museum** (✉ 333 E. River Rd., ☎ 612/625–9494; 🎫 free), a wild-looking metallic structure designed by famed avant-garde architect Frank Gehry. Inside are student and faculty works as well as a permanent collection of 1900–1950 American art.

Downtown Minneapolis, much of it built in the past 25 years, towers skyward several blocks west of the university. Two of the downtown's more recent additions are the 57-story **Norwest Center** (✉ 77 S. 7th St.), designed by Cesar Pelli, and its smaller companion, **Gaviidae Common** (✉ 651 Nicollet Mall), the latest downtown shopping hub. The mirrored, 51-story **IDS Building** (✉ 80 S. 8th St.) contains **Crystal Court,** a focal point of the skyway system, with shops, restaurants, and offices. The 42-story **Piper Jaffray Tower** (✉ 222 S. 9th St.), sheathed in aqua glass, and the 17-story **Lutheran Brotherhood Building** (✉ 625 4th Ave. SE), in copper-color glass, are sparkling members of the skyline. At the **Foshay Tower** (✉ 821 Marquette Ave., ☎ 612/341–2522)—Minneapolis's first skyscraper, constructed in 1929—a 31st-floor observation deck provides spectacular views of the city.

Nicollet Mall, a mile-long pedestrian mall, runs from 2nd Street to Grant Avenue, with an extensive system of skyways connecting many shops and a public library. Inside the library, the **Minneapolis Planetarium**

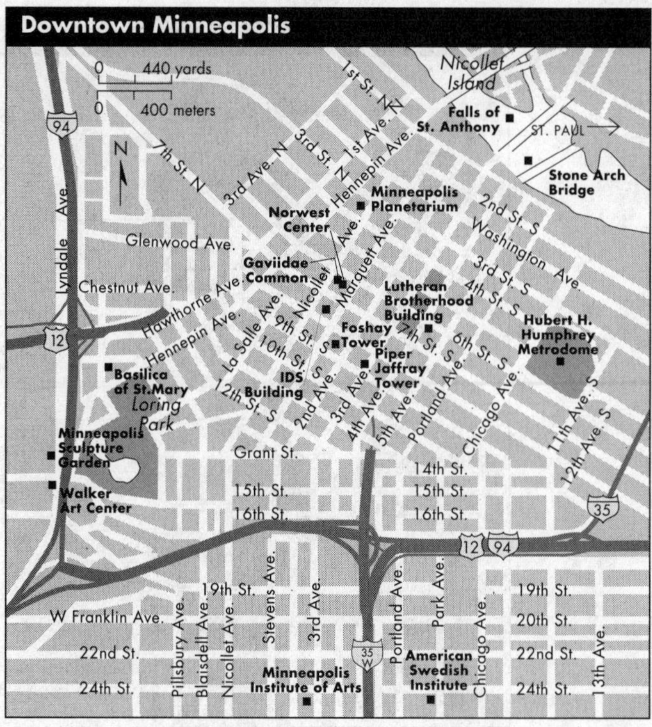

(✉ 300 Nicollet Mall, ☎ 612/630–6150; 🎟 $2.50–$4) offers sky shows that tour the night sky and investigate the latest discoveries in space science.

Another downtown landmark, the inflated **Hubert H. Humphrey Metrodome** (✉ 900 S. 5th St., ☎ 612/332–0386), is home to the Minnesota Twins baseball team and the Minnesota Vikings and University of Minnesota football teams. Behind-the-scenes tours of locker rooms, the playing field, and the press box are available.

The **Minneapolis Institute of Arts** (✉ 2400 3rd Ave. S, ☎ 612/870–3131; 🎟 free, except during special exhibits), 1 mi south of downtown and west of I–35W, displays more than 80,000 works of art from every age and culture, including works by the French Impressionists, rare Chinese jade, and a photography collection ranging from 1863 to the present. The building also houses the **Children's Theatre Company**, which puts on adventurous plays for all ages. The institute and theater company are both closed on Monday.

The **American Swedish Institute** (✉ 2600 Park Ave., ☎ 612/871–4907; 🎟 $3) is set in a 33-room Romanesque château filled with decorative woodwork. The museum, five blocks east of the Minneapolis Institute of Arts, displays art, pioneer items, Swedish glass, ceramics, and furniture relating to the area's Swedish heritage, including temporary exhibits.

★ The **Walker Art Center** (✉ Vineland Pl., adjoining Guthrie Theater, ☎ 612/375–7600; 🎟 $4, free Thurs. and 1st Sat. of the month), closed Monday, houses an outstanding collection of 20th-century American and European sculpture, prints, and photography, as well as traveling exhibits. The center also brings national and international acts to Min-

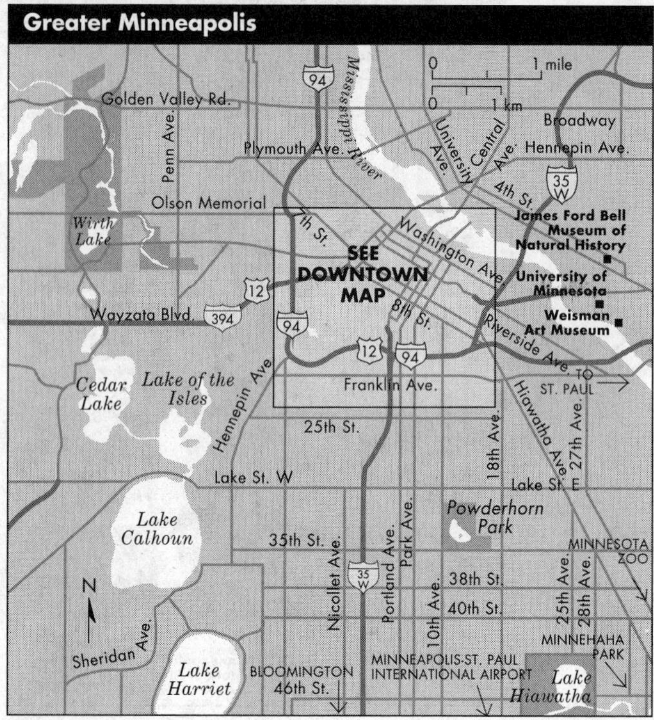

neapolis. Adjacent to the museum is the **Minneapolis Sculpture Garden,** the nation's largest outdoor urban sculpture garden. The **Irene Hixon Whitney Footbridge,** designed by sculptor Siah Armajani, connects the arts complex to Loring Park, across I–94. From the footbridge, the **Basilica of Saint Mary** (✉ 88 N. 17th St.) is easily viewed. The basilica was the first in the United States, celebrating its first mass in 1914.

St. Paul

Like its twin, downtown St. Paul is easily explored on foot thanks to its all-weather, climate-controlled skyway system. The Mississippi River runs east–west through the city.

City Hall and the **Ramsey County Courthouse** (✉ 15 W. Kellogg Blvd., ☎ 612/266–8000) look out across the Mississippi River from a 20-story building of a design known as American Perpendicular. Here, Memorial Hall (4th Street entrance) features Swedish sculptor Carl Milles's towering ***Vision of Peace*** statue, the largest carved-onyx figure in the world, standing 36 ft high and weighing 60 tons.

Rice Park, at the corner of West 5th and Washington streets, is St. Paul's oldest urban park, dating from 1849. It's a favorite with downtowners. Facing Rice Park on the north is the **Landmark Center** (✉ 75 W. 5th St., ☎ 612/292–3225), which is the restored Federal Courthouse, constructed in 1902. This towering Romanesque Revival structure has a six-story indoor courtyard, stained-glass skylights, and a marble-tile foyer. Of particular interest within are a branch of the **Minnesota Museum of American Art** (☎ 612/292–4355; 🎟 donation requested), which has strong holdings in Asian and 19th- and 20th-century American art, as well as changing exhibits of contemporary sculpture, paintings, and photography; and the **Schubert Club Musi-**

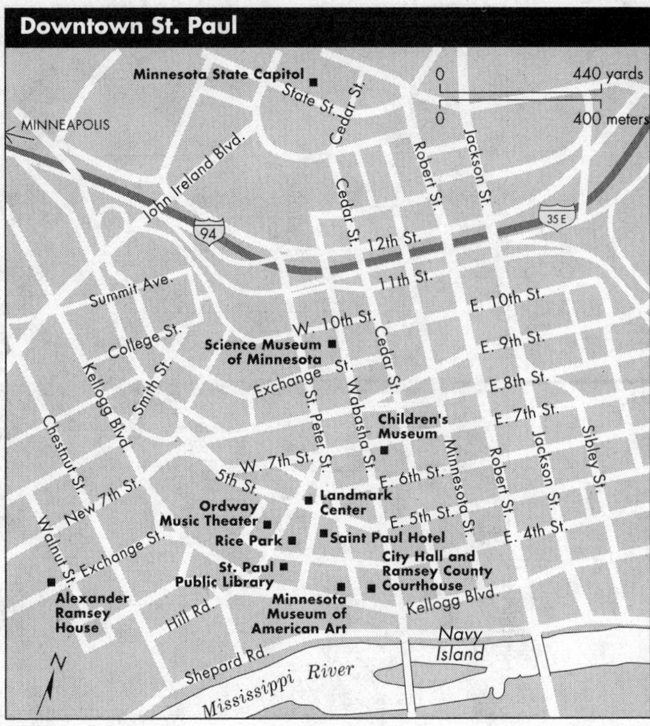

cal Instrument Museum (☎ 612/292–3268), with an outstanding collection of keyboard instruments dating from the 1700s.

On the south side of Rice Park is the block-long Italian Renaissance Revival **St. Paul Public Library.** On the west side of Rice Park is the **Ordway Music Theater** (☞ Nightlife and the Arts, *below*), a state-of-the-art auditorium with faceted-glass walls set in a facade of brick and copper.

West of Rice Park is the **Alexander Ramsey House** (✉ 265 S. Exchange St., ☎ 612/296–8760; 🎫 $4), home to the first governor of the Minnesota Territory. Built in 1872, the restored French Second Empire mansion has 15 rooms containing marble fireplaces, period furnishings, and rich collections of china and silver. It's open May through December.

The **Minnesota Children's Museum** (✉ 10 W. 7th St. , ☎ 612/225–6000; 🎫 $4–$6), closed Monday, has educational, hands-on exhibits, plus storytimes and sing-alongs.

The **Science Museum of Minnesota** (✉ 30 E. 10th St., ☎ 612/221–9488; 🎫 $5, films extra) has exhibits on archaeology, technology, and biology, with many exciting hands-on exhibits for kids. In the **McKnight Omnitheater** 70mm films are projected overhead on a massive tilted screen. Between Labor Day and late December the theater and museum are closed Monday.

Constructed of more than 25 varieties of marble, sandstone, and granite, the **Minnesota State Capitol** (✉ Aurora and Cedar Sts., ☎ 612/296–2881) is just northwest of downtown St. Paul. Its 223-ft-high marble dome is the world's largest.

The Cathedral of St. Paul (✉ 239 Selby Ave., ☎ 612/228–1766), a classic Renaissance-style domed church echoing St. Peter's in Rome, lies a half mile southwest of the capitol. Inside are beautiful stained-glass

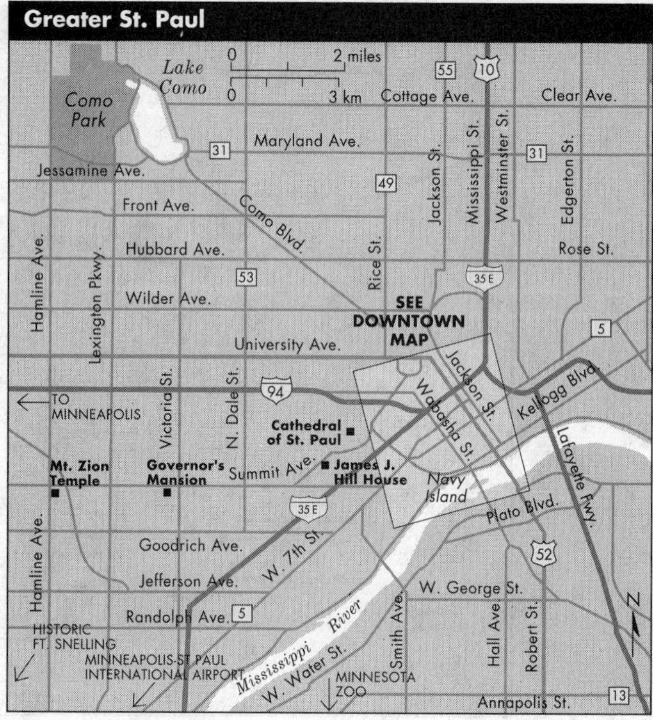

windows, statues, paintings, and other works of art, as well as a small historical museum on the lower level.

★ **Summit Avenue,** which runs 4½ mi from the cathedral to the Mississippi River, has the nation's longest stretch of intact residential Victorian architecture. F. Scott Fitzgerald was living at 599 Summit in 1918 when he wrote *This Side of Paradise.* The **James J. Hill House** (✉ 240 Summit Ave., ☎ 612/297–2555; 🎫 $4), once home of the transportation pioneer and builder of the Great Northern Railroad, is a Richardsonian Romanesque mansion, with carved woodwork, tiled fireplaces, and a skylighted art gallery hosting changing exhibits. The **governor's mansion** (✉ 1006 Summit Ave., ☎ 612/297–8177; 🎫 free) offers infrequent tours. **Mt. Zion Temple** (✉ 1300 Summit Ave., ☎ 612/698–3881) is the home of the oldest (1856) Jewish congregation in Minnesota.

At the confluence of the Mississippi and Minnesota rivers is **Historic Fort Snelling** (✉ Rtes. 5 and 55, near the International Airport south of St. Paul, ☎ 612/725–2389; 🎫 $4 per vehicle). The northernmost outpost in the old Northwest Territories, it remained an active military post until after World War II. Seventeen buildings have been restored, and costumed guides portray 1820s fort life with demonstrations of blacksmithing, carpentry, and military ceremonies. Exhibits and short films on the fort are shown in the **History Center,** which is closed weekends from November through April. (The fort is closed every day from November through April.)

Parks, Gardens, and Zoos

Minneapolis

Minnehaha Park, on the Mississippi near the airport, is the site of Minnehaha Falls, which was made famous by Longfellow's *Song of Hi-*

awatha. Above the waterfall is a statue of Hiawatha and Minnehaha. Minnehaha Parkway follows Minnehaha Creek, providing miles of jogging, biking, and roller-blading trails that run west to Lake Harriet, one of the many lakes in Minneapolis.

Wirth Park (✉ Plymouth Ave. and Theodore Wirth Pkwy., just west of downtown) has not only bicycling and walking paths through wooded areas but also the **Eloise Butler Wildflower Garden**—a little Eden of local forest and prairie flora. Wirth also has a moderately challenging 18-hole public golf course, which doubles as a cross-country ski area in winter.

In Minneapolis's Apple Valley suburb, the **Minnesota Zoo** (✉ 13000 Zoo Blvd. Apple Valley, ☎ 612/431–9200; 🎫 $8) houses some 1,700 animals in natural settings along six year-round trails. There's also a monorail, the Zoo Lab, a seasonal children's zoo, bird and animal shows, and daily films and slide shows.

St. Paul

Como Park (✉ N. Lexington Ave. at Como Ave.) has picnic areas, walking trails, playgrounds, and tennis and swimming facilities. **Como Park Zoo** (☎ 612/478–8200) is home to large cats, land and water birds, primates, and aquatic animals. The adjacent **Como Park Conservatory**, in a domed greenhouse, has sunken gardens, a fern room, biblical plantings, and seasonal flower shows.

Dining

Although Minnesotans are chided for the bland gastronomic traditions of their Scandinavian and German ancestry, the growing immigrant population is helping to spice up Twin Cities cuisine. For price ranges *see* Chart 1 (A) *in* On the Road with Fodor's.

Minneapolis

$$$–$$$$ ✕ **D'Amico Cucina.** From the faux *marbre* plates and gleaming white linens to the marble floors and leather chairs, this is haute cuisine with a modern Italian accent. The seasonal menu includes artistically presented pastas. ✉ *Butler Sq., 100 N. 6th St.,* ☎ *612/338–2401. AE, D, DC, MC, V.*

$$$–$$$$ ✕ **Goodfellow's.** The changing menu at this plush restaurant includes regional game such as venison, pheasant, and trout in season, as well as excellent presentations of lamb, veal, and pork dishes. ✉ *City Center, 40 S. 7th St.,* ☎ *612/332–4800. AE, D, MC, V. Closed Sun.*

$$$–$$$$ ✕ **Whitney Grille.** In the lavish Whitney Hotel, the Grille has a flower-filled garden plaza and a hushed main room with rich woods and muted floral fabrics. The regional American specialties change seasonally, and have included beef tenderloin with goose-liver pâté and port wine demi-glacé, and crisp whole red snapper. ✉ *150 Portland Ave.,* ☎ *612/372–6405. AE, D, DC, MC, V.*

$$–$$$$ ✕ **Kincaid's Steak, Chop and Fish House.** Kincaid's imposing interior of marble, brass, glass, and wood sets the mood for all-American standards such as filet mignon, mesquite-grilled salmon, grilled-rosemary lamb, and roasted chicken Dijon. ✉ *8400 Normandale Lake Blvd. Bloomington,* ☎ *612/921–2255. AE, D, DC, MC, V.*

$$–$$$$ ✕ **Murray's.** A Minneapolis institution, Murray's has been serving steak since 1946. Silver Butter Knife steaks, hickory-smoked shrimp, and their signature garlic toast are served in a plush atmosphere with piano and violin accompaniment. ✉ *26 S. 6th St.* ☎ *612/339–0909. AE, D, DC, MC, V.*

$$$ ✕ **New French Cafe & Bar.** In Minneapolis' Warehouse District, the New French Cafe is not so new; in fact, it's been a favorite for the past 20 years. The open kitchen turns out French and Mediterranean specialties, including beef tenderloin and tuna; French bread and pastries are baked in the adjoining bakery. ✉ *128 N. 4th St.,* ☎ *612/338–3790. AE, D, MC, V.*

$$–$$$ ✕ **Loring Cafe.** There's a terrific view of Loring Park from this bohemian-chic café. The menu changes nightly, including pasta, vegetarian, and meat dishes; artichoke ramekin is a standout appetizer. ✉ *1624 Harmon Pl.,* ☎ *612/332–1617. AE, MC, V.*

$–$$ ✕ **Chez Bananas.** Inflatable toys set the tone for Caribbean food served in a warehouse storefront. Try coconut-curry chicken with black beans and rice, or peppered sirloin with garlic-mashed potatoes. ✉ *129 N. 4th St.* ☎ *612/340–0032. AE, DC, MC, V.*

$ ✕ **Bryant-Lake Bowl.** This 1930s-era eight-lane bowling alley contains one of the Twin Cities' hippest restaurants. Impressive wine and beer lists complement such specials as soft-shell tacos and fresh ravioli with four cheeses—and after your meal you can bowl a few frames or catch a performance in the attached 99-seat theater. Breakfast is a bargain. ✉ *810 W. Lake St.,*☎ *612/825–3737. AE, D, DC, MC, V.*

St. Paul

$$–$$$$ ✕ **St. Paul Grill.** The Saint Paul Hotel's stylish, contemporary bistro has a view of Rice Park. The menu is American: dry-aged steaks, fresh fish, pastas, chicken potpie, homemade roast beef hash, and weekly specials. ✉ *350 Market St.,* ☎ *612/224–7455. AE, D, DC, MC, V.*

$$–$$$ ✕ **Dakota Bar and Grill.** The Twin Cities' best jazz club also serves inventive midwestern fare, including grilled rainbow trout and salmon-walleye croquettes. Like the music, the atmosphere is contemporary and cool. There's also a Sunday brunch. ✉ *Bandana Sq., 1021 E. Bandana Blvd.,* ☎ *612/642–1442. AE, D, DC, MC, V. No lunch.*

$$ ✕ **Ristorante Luci.** This intimate, neighborhood trattoria serves regional Italian dishes, including pasta and fresh fish. ✉ *470 Cleveland Ave. S.,* ☎ *612/699–8258. MC, V.*

$ ✕ **Cafe Latte.** This café doubles as a furiously successful and almost-always-jammed wine bar. Soups, salads, breads, stews, and several varieties of chocolate cake are dished out in the cafeteria; the smoke-free wine bar specializes in individual pizzas and salads. ✉ *850 Grand Ave.,* ☎ *612/224–5687. AE, DC, MC, V.*

$ ✕ **Mickey's Diner.** This quintessential 1930s diner, with lots of chrome and vinyl, a lunch counter, and a few tiny booths, is listed on the National Register of Historic Places. The stick-to-the-ribs fare and great breakfasts make it a local institution. ✉ *36 W. 7th St., at St. Peter St.,* ☎ *612/222–5633. D, MC, V.*

Lodging

There is no shortage of lodging in the Twin Cities. Accommodations are available in the downtowns, along I–494 in the suburbs and industrial parks of Bloomington and Richfield (known as the Strip), and near the Minneapolis/St. Paul International Airport and the Mall of America. A number of hotels are attached to shopping centers, the better to ignore Minnesota's fierce winters and summer heat. For price ranges *see* Chart 2 (A) *in* On the Road with Fodor's.

Minneapolis

$$$$ 🏨 **Hyatt Regency Hotel.** A wide, sweeping lobby with a fountain and potted trees is the focal point of this hotel. It's in the heart of downtown Minneapolis, connected by skyways to many restaurants and shopping areas. Many rooms have a skyline view of the city. ✉ *1300*

Nicollet Mall, 55403, ☎ 612/370–1234, FAX 612/370–1463. 554 rooms. Restaurant. AE, D, DC, MC, V.

$$$$ ★ **Hyatt Whitney Hotel.** An 1880s flour mill converted into a small European-style hotel, the Whitney has suites only; half of them overlook the Mississippi. The lobby is warm with rich woods, brass, and marble. ✉ *150 Portland Ave., 55401, ☎ 612/339–9300 or 800/233–1234, FAX 612/339–1333. 96 suites. Restaurant. AE, D, DC, MC, V.*

$$$ **Marriott City Center Hotel.** At this sleek, 31-story hotel within the City Center shopping mall, contemporary rooms are done in peach and jade. In the restaurant you may be entertained by members of the waitstaff, most of whom are professional singers. ✉ *30 S. 7th St., 55402, ☎ 612/349–4000, FAX 612/332–7165. 626 rooms. 2 restaurants, health club. AE, D, DC, MC, V.*

$$–$$$ **Nicollet Island Inn.** This charming 1893 limestone inn is on Nicollet Island in the middle of the Mississippi River, with downtown Minneapolis on one shore and the Riverplace and St. Anthony Main on the other. There's early American reproduction furniture in the rooms, some of which have river views. ✉ *95 Merriam St., 55401, ☎ 612/331–1800, FAX 612/331–6528. 24 rooms. Restaurant. AE, D, DC, MC, V.*

$$–$$$ **Regal Minneapolis Hotel.** The desk staff at this 14-story hotel is cheery enough, but the public areas feel a bit somber. Rooms are contemporary, with sweeping views of downtown. ✉ *1313 Nicollet Mall, 55403, ☎ 612/332–0371 or 800/522–8856, FAX 612/359–2160. 325 rooms. Restaurant, pool, exercise room. AE, DC, MC, V.*

$$ **Holiday Inn Metrodome.** A 10-minute bus ride from downtown, this hotel is in the heart of the theater and entertainment district and is close to both the Metrodome and the University of Minnesota. ✉ *1500 Washington Ave. S, 55454, ☎ 612/333–4646 or 800/448–3663, FAX 612/333–7910. 265 rooms. Restaurant, pool. AE, D, DC, MC, V.*

St. Paul

$$$ **Embassy Suites–St. Paul.** With terra-cotta, brickwork, tropical plants, and a courtyard fountain, this hotel has a neo–New Orleans Garden District style. It is close to I–35E and within walking distance of major downtown businesses. ✉ *175 E. 10th St., 55101, ☎ 612/224–5400, FAX 612/224–0957. 210 suites. Restaurant, pool. Full breakfast. AE, D, DC, MC, V.*

$$–$$$ **Holiday Inn Express.** In what was once a paint shop for the Pacific Northern Railroad, this hotel is connected by skyway to the Bandana Square shopping center. Rooms are contemporary. ✉ *1010 W. Bandana Blvd., 55108, ☎ 612/647–1637. FAX 612/647–0244 109 rooms. Indoor pool. CP. AE, D, DC, MC, V.*

$$–$$$ **Saint Paul Hotel.** Built in 1910, this stately stone hotel overlooks Rice Park and is within walking distance of St. Paul's shopping and entertainment district. Rooms are traditional in style. ✉ *350 Market St., 55102, ☎ 612/292–9292 or 800/292–9292, FAX 612/228–9506. 255 rooms. 2 restaurants. AE, D, DC, MC, V.*

$$ **Best Western Kelly Inn.** Visiting state legislators have frequented this clean, efficient hotel within walking distance of the state capitol for the past 30 years. ✉ *161 St. Anthony St., 55103, ☎ 612/227–8711, FAX 612/227–1698. 126 rooms. Restaurant, pool. AE, DC, MC, V.*

$$ **Radisson Hotel Saint Paul.** This 22-story riverside tower has a lobby with Asian touches and traditional American–style rooms, many with river views. ✉ *11 E. Kellogg Blvd., 55101, ☎ 612/292–1900, FAX 612/224–8999. 494 rooms. Restaurant, pool, exercise room. Full breakfast. AE, D, DC, MC, V.*

$–$$ **Sheraton Midway–St. Paul.** This contemporary four-story hotel is in the busy district centered on Snelling and University avenues. Hallways painted in shades of pink lead to bright, comfortable rooms with contemporary oak woodwork. ✉ *400 Hamline Ave. N, 55104,* ☎ *612/642–1234 or 800/535–2339,* FAX *612/642–1126. 211 rooms. Restaurant, pool, exercise room. AE, D, DC, MC, V.*

Nightlife and the Arts

Nightlife

With closings at 1 AM, "the wee small hours" does not apply to the Twin Cities. Most bars and clubs attract a youngish crowd. Plenty of nightspots serve the The Twin Cities' sizable gay and lesbian community.

MINNEAPOLIS

Clubs and bars are generally clustered in three areas—downtown Minneapolis, Uptown, and Seven Corners. Downtown, the intimate **Fine Line Music Café** (✉ 318 1st Ave. N, ☎ 612/338–8100) showcases locally and nationally known jazz and rock musicians. In a former bus station, **First Avenue** (✉ 29 N. 7th St., ☎ 612/332–1775) attracts top rock groups and is a great place for dancing; the club was featured in the movie *Purple Rain.* Blues, rock, and alternative bands take the stage six nights a week at the **Cabooze** (✉ 917 Cedar Ave. S, ☎ 612/338–6425). The best gay bar in downtown Minneapolis is the **Gay Nineties** (✉ 408 S. Hennepin Ave., ☎ 612/333–7755).

ST. PAUL

St. Paul is said to close down with the end of the business day, but several good nightspots can be found on Grand Avenue and downtown. The **Dakota Bar and Grill** (✉ Bandana Sq., 1021 E. Bandana Blvd., ☎ 612/642–1442) is one of the best jazz bars in the Midwest, with some of the Twin Cities' finest performers. The **Artist's Quarter** (✉ 366 Jackson St., ☎ 612/292–1359) showcases local and national jazz performers in a dark, jazz-minimalist space. For blues check out the **Blue Saloon** (✉ 601 Western Ave. N, ☎ 612/228–9959).

The Arts

The "About Town" section of the monthly *Minneapolis St. Paul* magazine has extensive listings of events, as does the free monthly *Twin Cities Directory.* Check out the *St. Paul Pioneer Press,* the Minneapolis-based *Star Tribune,* and the free newsweekly *City Pages* for events. **Ticketmaster** (☎ 612/989–5151) sells tickets for sporting events, concerts, theater, attractions, and special events.

MINNEAPOLIS

The Hennepin Avenue Theatre District, between 8th and 10th Streets in downtown Minneapolis, is home to the city's hottest entertainment. The Twin Cities Broadway Theatre season brings national touring productions to the historic **State** (✉ 805 Hennepin Ave., ☎ 612/339–7007) and **Orpheum Theatres** (✉ 910 Hennepin Ave., ☎ same phone). The **Hey City Theater** hosts almost nightly performances of the smash hit, *Tony n' Tina's Wedding* (✉ 824 Hennepin Ave., ☎ 612/333–9202).

The award-winning **Guthrie Theater** (✉ 725 Vineland Pl., ☎ 612/377–2224) has a repertory company known for its balance of classics and avant-garde productions. High-caliber national acts show up at the **Walker Art Center** (✉ Vineland Pl., ☎ 612/375–7622). The **Brave New Workshop** (✉ 2605 Hennepin Ave. S., ☎ 612/332–6620) will keep you laughing with original sketch comedy. The acclaimed Minnesota Orchestra performs in **Orchestra Hall** (✉ 1111 Nicollet Mall, ☎ 612/371–5656).

ST. PAUL

The **Great American History Theater** (✉ 30 E. 10th St., ☎ 612/292–4323) presents plays about Minnesota and midwestern history. The **Penumbra Theater Company** (✉ 270 N. Kent St., ☎ 612/224–3180) is Minnesota's only black professional theater company. The **Ordway Music Theater** (✉ 345 Washington St., ☎ 612/224–4222) is home to the St. Paul Chamber Orchestra, the Minnesota Opera, and other performing-arts groups.

Outdoor Activities and Sports

Beaches

With its hundreds of lakes, greater Minneapolis is beach country. **Thomas Beach,** at the south end of Lake Calhoun, is one of the best. Further information is available from the Minneapolis Parks and Recreation Board (☎ 612/661–4875).

Spectator Sports

Baseball: Minnesota Twins (✉ Hubert H. Humphrey Metrodome, 501 Chicago Ave. S, Minneapolis, ☎ 612/375–1116). **St. Paul Saints** (✉ 1771 Energy Park Dr., St. Paul, ☎ 612/644–6659). **Basketball: Minnesota Timberwolves** (✉ Target Center, 600 1st Ave. N, Minneapolis, ☎ 612/337–3865). **Football: Minnesota Vikings** (✉ Hubert H. Humphrey Metrodome, 501 Chicago Ave. S, Minneapolis, ☎ 612/333–8828).

Shopping

The skyway systems in each of the Twin Cities connect hundreds of stores, shops, and enclosed shopping malls.

Minneapolis

Among the many shops along **Nicollet Mall** (☞ Exploring Minneapolis and St. Paul, *above*) are Dayton's (✉ 700 Nicollet Mall), the city's largest department store, and **Gaviidae Common** (✉ 651 Nicollet Mall), with three levels of upscale shops, including branches of Saks Fifth Avenue and Neiman Marcus. **City Center** (✉ 7th St. and Hennepin Ave.) has 60 shops and 19 restaurants. There are more than 40 mostly one-of-a-kind, hip, urban shops and several restaurants at **Uptown,** a smaller shopping center on Calhoun Square (✉ Lake and Hennepin Aves.).

St. Paul

The World Trade Center (✉ 30 E. 7th St.), downtown, has more than 100 specialty shops and restaurants, including Dayton's. **Victoria Crossing** (✉ 850 Grand Ave.) is a collection of small shops and specialty stores anchoring the 100-plus other stores along Grand Avenue's 26 blocks.

Bloomington

Bloomington, south of Minneapolis, is Minnesota's third-largest city and home to the **Mall of America** (✉ 24th Ave. S and Killebrew Dr., ☎ 612/883–8800), the world's largest enclosed mall. Appropriately nicknamed the Megamall, it has more than 500 stores and shops, including Macy's, Bloomingdale's, Sears, and Nordstrom. Beneath its central dome is Camp Snoopy, a large amusement park.

ELSEWHERE IN MINNESOTA

Southeastern Minnesota

Visitor Information

Red Wing Chamber of Commerce (✉ 420 Levee St., Box 133, 55066, ☎ 612/385–5934 or 800/498–3444).

Winona Chamber and Convention Bureau (✉ 67 Main St., Box 870, 55987, ☎ 507/452–2272 or 800/657–4972).

Arriving and Departing

From the Twin Cities follow U.S. 61 southeast along the Mississippi River.

What to See and Do

This picturesque corner of the state has high, wooded bluffs that provide vast panoramas of the Mississippi River. The river towns and villages are noted for their charming 19th-century architecture. **Red Wing** is famous for boots and pottery bearing its name. Levee Park, Bay Point Park, and Covill Park have stunning views of the Mississippi, which widens into Lake Pepin here. The Victorian **St. James Hotel** (☞ *below*), built in 1875, has boutiques, shops, and an art gallery as well as grand public spaces recalling the heyday of riverboats.

Frontenac State Park (☎ 612/345–3401), 10 mi south of Red Wing on U.S. 61, has a picnic area with a 400-ft-high bluff and great views of Lake Pepin, as well as a bird sanctuary. Just outside the park is **Old Frontenac**, a Civil War–era village with a charming 1865 Craftsman-style bed-and-breakfast inn.

Winona is an early lumbering town settled by New Englanders and Germans. Here **Garvin Heights Scenic Lookout** (✉ Huff St. past U.S. 14 and U.S. 61) has picnic facilities, hiking trails, and scenic views from atop a 575-ft bluff. The **Julius C. Wilkie Steamboat Center** (✉ Foot of Main St. in Levee Park, ☎ 507/454–1254; 🎫 $9.95–$26.95), open from Memorial Day through Labor Day, is a steamboat replica with exhibits on steamboating and river life. Exhibits of the local Polish heritage found at the **Polish Cultural Institute** (✉ 102 N. Liberty St., ☎ 507/454–3431; 🎫 free) include family heirlooms and many religious artifacts. The museum is open from May through November.

Dining and Lodging

$$ ✕ **Staghead Coffeehouse.** At this casual eatery with pressed-tin ceilings, oak tables, and brick walls, the menu usually includes pork, chicken, and pasta, as well as scones, muffins, and specialty coffees for breakfast. ✉ *219 Bush St.,* ☎ *612/388–6581. MC, V. Closed Sun. No dinner Mon.*

$$–$$$ ✕🏨 **St. James Hotel.** This 1875 hotel is the area's most atmospheric lodging, with a view of the Mississippi River. In the elegant, lower-level Port of Red Wing resaurant, limestone walls and no windows set a romantic mood, enhanced by sophisticated meals such as smoked, roasted duckling and lobster-stuffed chicken. ✉ *406 Main St.,* ☎ *612/388–2846,* FAX *612/388–5226. 61 rooms. 3 restaurants. AE, D, DC, MC, V.*

Duluth and the North Shore

Visitor Information

Duluth Convention and Visitors Bureau (✉ 100 Lake Place Dr., 55802, ☎ 218/722–4011 or 800/438–5884).

Arriving and Departing

From the Twin Cities head north on I–35.

What to See and Do

Set at the edge of the north-woods wilderness and the western end of Lake Superior is **Duluth,** a city of gracious old homes with one of the largest ports on the Great Lakes. **Skyline Parkway,** a 16-mi scenic boulevard above the city, has views of Lake Superior and the Duluth-Superior Harbor, with its 50 mi of dock line. Vista Fleet Excursions (✉ 5th Ave. W and the waterfront, ☎ 218/722–6218) operates narrated boat tours of the harbor. The **Aerial Lift Bridge** (✉ Canal Dr.), an unusual 386-ft elevator bridge, spans the canal entrance to the harbor. Not far from the harbor, the **Depot** (✉ 506 W. Michigan St., ☎ 218/727–8025), an 1892 landmark train station, houses the **Lake Superior Museum of Transportation** (🎫 $6), with an extensive collection of locomotives and rolling stock. **Lake Superior Zoological Gardens** (✉ 72nd Ave. W and Grand Ave., ☎ 218/723–3747) has a children's zoo and animals from all over the world.

Lake Superior's rugged **North Shore** is best viewed from U.S. 61 north of Duluth. **Gooseberry Falls State Park** (✉ 1300 Hwy. 61, Two Harbors 55616, ☎ 218/834–3855) and **Temperance River State Park** (✉ Hwy. 61, Box 33, Schroeder 55613, ☎ 218/663–7476) are typical of parks found along Lake Superior's shore, with roaring waterfalls and scenic vistas.

North of Grand Marais, the **Gunflint Trail** attracts cross-country skiers with 60 mi of groomed trails leading deep into Superior National Forest. **Gunflint Lodge** (✉ 143 S. Gunflint Lake, ☎ 218/388–2294 or 800/328–3325) was once a much-used highway traveled by voyageurs such as Justine Kerfoot, author of *Woman of the Boundary Waters.* Kerfoot's daughter and her husband now run the famous lodge and its restaurant.

Dining and Lodging

$$–$$$ ✕ **Grandma's Saloon & Deli.** Duluth's famous Grandma's Marathon is sponsored by this lively restaurant on the waterfront. The hands-down favorite dish is *chicken tetrazzini,* fettuccine and sautéed chicken in a mozzarrella-Mornay sauce. ✉ *522 S. Lake Ave.,* ☎ *218/727–4192. AE, D, DC, MC, V.*

$$ 🏨 **Fitger's Inn** Built in the 1850s in the old Fitger's Brewery, the inn has cozy rooms with lake views, some with fireplaces and skylights. Newer suites have double whirlpools. The inn is part of the Fitger's Brewery Complex, a cluster of nightclubs and retail shops four blocks from downtown. ✉ *600 E. Superior St.,* ☎ *218/722–8826 or 888/348–4377,* FAX *218/722–8826. 60 rooms. Restaurant. CP. AE, D, DC, MC, V.*

The Iron Range and Boundary Waters

Visitor Information

The **Ely Chamber of Commerce** (✉ 1600 Sheridan St., 55731, ☎ 218/365–6123 or 800/777–7281) provides information on canoe outfitters and trips. The **Rainy Lake Visitor Center** (✉ 11 mi east of International Falls on Rte. 11, ☎ 218/286–5258) is at Voyageurs National Park.

Arriving and Departing

From Duluth take U.S. 53 north.

What to See and Do

The discovery of iron ore in the north woods brought an influx of immigrants who wove a rich and varied cultural heritage. Known as the Range because it encompasses the huge Mesabi and Vermilion iron ranges, the region is ringed by deep forests and many lakes.

Eveleth, which produces taconite, a form of processed iron ore, is home to the **United States Hockey Hall of Fame** (✉ 801 Hat Trick Ave., ☎ 218/744–5167; 🎫 $3), where pictures, films, and artifacts tell the story of hockey in America. In Virginia, 2 mi north of Eveleth, rimmed with open-pit mines and reserves of iron ore, the **Mine View in the Sky observation platform,** at the southern edge of town, overlooks part of the vast Rochleau Mine works. The **Virginia Historical Society Heritage Museum** (✉ 800 Olcott Park, 9th Ave. N, ☎ 218/741–1136; 🎫 donations accepted) has exhibits on iron mining and other local history.

West of Virginia on U.S. 169 is **Hibbing,** the largest town in the Mesabi Range and the place where the Greyhound bus system began in 1914. The **Greyhound Origin Center** (✉ Hibbing Memorial Center Bldg., 5th Ave. and 23rd St., ☎ 612/263–5814; 🎫 $2) has displays and artifacts on the history of the company. Tours of the **Hull-Rust Mahoning Mine,** the world's largest open-pit iron ore mine, may be arranged during the summer at the Hibbing Area Chamber of Commerce (✉ 211 E. Howard St., Box 727, 55746, ☎ 218/262–3895; 🎫 free). The **Paulucci Space Theater** (✉ U.S. 169 and 23rd St., ☎ 218/262–6720; 🎫 $4) has programs on astronomy and space exploration.

Ely, east of Virginia on U.S. 169, lies in the heart of the Superior National Forest. ★ It is the gateway to the western portion of the **Boundary Waters Canoe Area Wilderness,** a federally protected area of more than 1,000 pristine lakes surrounded by dense forests. Area outfitters rent canoes and camping equipment and provide assistance in planning canoe trips. The **Vermilion Interpretive Center** (✉ 1900 E. Camp St., ☎ 218/365–3226), closed in winter, has exhibits on the Vermilion iron range, the fur trade, and Native Americans.

International Falls, at the northern terminus of U.S. 53 on the Canadian border, is known as the "icebox of the nation" because of its severe winters. The town lies at the western edge of **Voyageurs National Park** (☞ National and State Parks, *above*), where the Rainy Lake Visitor Center (☞ *above*) has a slide show, exhibits, maps, and information, as well as guided boat tours of the lake and other points in the park. In town is the **Koochiching County Historical Museum** (✉ 214 6th Ave., Box 1147, ☎ 218/283–4316), with exhibits on early settlement, gold mining, and Native Americans. The **International Falls Chamber of Commerce** (✉ 301 2nd Ave., 56649, ☎ 218/283–9400 or 800/325–5766) has brochures and information on area outfitters, camping, and attractions.

Dining and Lodging

$$ ✕🏨 **Kahler Park Hotel.** The best hotel in the Range has a lovely lobby with a marble fireplace, and an excellent restaurant, Reflections. Sunday brunch is an institution, complete with an omelet buffet. ✉ *1402 Howard St., Hibbing 55746,* ☎ *218/262–3481 or 800/262–3481,* FAX *218/262–1906. 125 rooms. Restaurant, pool. AE, D, DC, MC, V.*

OHIO

Updated by Miriam Carey

Capital	Columbus
Population	11,186,000
Motto	With God, All Things Are Possible
State Bird	Cardinal
State Flower	Scarlet carnation
Postal Abbreviation	OH

Statewide Visitor Information

Ohio Division of Travel and Tourism (✉ Box 1001, Columbus 43266, ☎ 800/282–5393). **Ohio Historical Society** (✉ 1982 Velma Ave., Columbus 43211, ☎ 614/297–2300).

Scenic Drives

The **Lake Erie Circle Tour** consists of nearly 200 mi of state routes and U.S. highways along the Lake Erie shoreline from Toledo to Conneaut (☞ Northwest Ohio and the Lake Erie Islands, *below*). **Route 7,** which runs parallel to the Ohio River along the state's southeastern border, cuts through the French-settled village of Gallipolis; the site of Ohio's only significant Civil War battle, near Pomeroy; and Marietta, the historic first city of the Northwest Territory.

National and State Parks

National Parks

National monuments include the **Hopewell Culture National Historic Park** (☞ Columbus, *below*) and **Perry's Victory and International Peace Memorial,** in Put-in-Bay (☞ Northwest Ohio and the Lake Erie Islands, *below*). **William Howard Taft's boyhood home** (✉ 2038 Auburn Ave., Cincinnati, ☎ 513/684–3262) is a national historic site. The **Cuyahoga Valley National Recreation Area** (✉ 15610 Vaughn Rd., Brecksville 44141, ☎ 440/526–5256) occupies 22 mi of forested valley between Cleveland and Akron along the Cuyahoga River.

State Parks

Of the 72 state parks, eight are classified as Ohio State Park Resorts (☎ 800/282–7275), which have cabins for rent, along with facilities for swimming, boating, golf, tennis, and dining. For more information contact the **Ohio Department of Natural Resources.** ✉ *Ohio State Parks Information Center, Fountain Sq., Bldg. C–1, Columbus 43224,* ☎ *614/265–7000.*

COLUMBUS

Ohio's largest city and the state capital, Columbus is known for its entrepreneurial spirit and economic vitality. The state's largest university, Ohio State, is here, as are the headquarters of a number of Fortune 500 companies, many of whose executives claim they would not leave the city—even if they were promoted.

Visitor Information

Greater Columbus Convention and Visitors Bureau (✉ 10 W. Broad St., Suite 1300, 43215, ☎ 614/221–6623 or 800/354–2657).

Arriving and Departing

By Bus

Greyhound Lines (✉ E. Town St. at 3rd St., ☎ 800/231–2222) serves Columbus.

By Car

Columbus is in the center of the state, at the intersection of I–70 and I–71.

By Plane

Port Columbus International Airport, 10 mi east of downtown Columbus, is served by major airlines and by **ComAir** (☎ 800/354–9822), **Midwest Express,** and **Skyway** (☎ 614/238–7750). A cab from the airport to downtown costs about $18; the airport shuttle costs $8.50.

Getting Around Columbus

Downtown is fairly compact and easily walkable. Some government buildings are connected to each other and to nearby buildings through underground walkways. The **Central Ohio Transit Authority** (☎ 614/228–1776), or COTA, operates buses within Columbus.

Exploring Columbus

At the heart of downtown is the domeless Greek Revival **state capitol** (✉ Corner of High and Broad Sts., ☎ 614/752–9777), distinguished by its skylights, stained glass, and period details.The lively **Riffe Gallery** (✉ 77 S. High St., ☎ 614/644–9624), in the Vern Riffe Center for Government and the Arts, has works by Ohio artists. COSI (pronounced co-*sigh*), the **Center of Science and Industry** (✉ 280 E. Broad St., Columbus, ☎ 614/228–2674; 🎫 $16), has colorful hands-on exhibits including a planetarium and an animal lab with basketball-playing rats.

The **Short North** (☎ 614/421–1030), a strip of trendy shops, clubs, vintage clothing and antiques stores, restaurants, and art galleries north of downtown, holds a Gallery Hop the first Saturday of every month. ★ The **Wexner Center for the Arts** (✉ N. High St. at 15th Ave., ☎ 614/292–0330 or 614/292–3535), on the Ohio State University campus, houses contemporary art in a dramatic building designed by Peter Eisenmann.

★ **German Village** (☎ 614/221–8888), a neighborhood of tightly packed brick homes built by immigrants in the 19th century, lies just south of downtown. In the **Brewery District** (☎ 614/621–2222), next to German Village, old breweries have been turned into restaurants and bars.

South of Columbus is the **Hopewell Culture National Historical Park** (✉ Rte. 104, 2 mi. north of Chillicothe, ☎ 614/774–1125). Here burial and ceremonial earth mounds rise from the ground in mysterious formations, the legacy of the Hopewell nation and other Native Americans.

World-renowned zookeeper "Jungle" Jack Hanna presides over three generations of gorillas and other creatures of the wild at the **Columbus Zoo** (✉ 9990 Riverside Dr., ☎ 614/645–3550), about 18 mi northwest of downtown off I–270.

Dining

Restaurants in Columbus range from trendy to down-home. Fine restaurants can be found in the Short North, tucked away in German Village, and in suburban neighborhoods. For price ranges *see* Chart 1 (B) *in* On the Road with Fodor's.

$$$–$$$$ ✕ **Rigsby's Cuisine Volatile.** As the name suggests, this café is purposely unpredictable: Each day brings a new selection of American twists on world cuisine—all part of a menu devised by Kent Rigsby, who studied at the San Francisco Culinary Academy. Everything is as fresh as it gets. ✉ *698 N. High St.,* ☎ *614/461–7888. AE, D, DC, MC, V. Closed Sun.*

$$–$$$$ ✕ **Lindey's.** This German Village favorite has enough out-of-the-way rooms to get lost in—and a menu to match, including a Sunday blues brunch with a gumbo du jour. ✉ *169 E. Beck St.,* ☎ *614/228–4343. AE, D, DC, MC, V.*

$$–$$$$ ✕ **Spagio.** The name says it all: *spa* signifies healthful cuisine, and *gio*, short for geography, refers to its far-reaching menu. Next door to the copper-, glass-, and oak-clad restaurant is Spagio Cellars, a lively place with wine tastings, light tapas, and jazz. ✉ *1295 Grandview Ave.,* ☎ *614/486–1114. AE, DC, MC, V.*

$–$$$ ✕ **Schmidt's Sausage Haus.** Homemade German sausage is the specialty in this rustic, converted 18th-century barn. ✉ *240 E. Kossuth St.,* ☎ *614/444–6808. AE, D, DC, MC, V.*

$–$$ ✕ **Katzinger's Deli.** An enormous menu and a serve-yourself pickle barrel make this New York–style deli in German Village a favorite. ✉ *475 S. 3rd St.,* ☎ *614/228–3354. MC, V.*

Lodging

Lodging is mostly in downtown Columbus and nearby German Village. For price ranges *see* Chart 2 (B) *in* On the Road with Fodor's.

$$$$ **Courtyard by Marriott.** Formerly a warehouse, this unusual hotel has a bi-level, contemporary lobby and luxurious suites with kitchens. The location is convenient to everything. ✉ *35 W. Spring St., 43215,* ☎ *614/228–3200,* FAX *614/228–6752. 149 rooms. Restaurant. AE, D, DC, MC, V.*

$$$$ **Hyatt Regency, Columbus.** Adjacent to the convention center, this ultramodern high-rise hotel caters mainly to business travelers. (The Hyatt on Capitol Square is more for the political crowd.) ✉ *350 N. High St., 43215,* ☎ *614/463–1234,* FAX *614/280–3034. 632 rooms. Restaurant, pool, exercise room. AE, D, DC, MC, V.*

$$$$ ★ **Westin Hotel, Columbus.** High ceilings, marble floors, and stone columns give this turn-of-the-century hotel a grand air. Rooms are done in a Queen Anne style, with marble baths. ✉ *310 S. High St., 43215,* ☎ *614/228–3800,* FAX *614/228–7666. 196 rooms. Restaurant. AE, D, DC, MC, V.*

$$ **German Village Inn.** Friendly service and low rates are the advantages of this no-frills German Village hotel close to downtown. ✉ *920 S. High St., 43206,* ☎ *614/443–6506,* FAX *614/443–5663. 43 rooms. AE, D, DC, MC, V.*

Nightlife and the Arts

Three free weekly newspapers—the *Columbus Guardian*, the *Other Paper*, and *Columbus Alive!*—have complete listings of goings-on in the city.

Nightlife

Columbus's hot spots are near the Ohio State University campus (expect crowds on nights the OSU Buckeyes football team plays) and in the Short North. Almost every bar in town broadcasts the locally beloved Ohio State University Buckeyes' football games. Live music is available on weekends at the **Short North Tavern** (✉ 674 N. High St., ☎ 614/221–2432). You can catch the latest music videos on the large screen of the **Union Station Video Cafe** (✉ 630 N. High St., ☎ 614/

228–3740). **Little Brother's** (✉ 1100 N. Peyster, ☎ 614/421–2025), in the Short North, showcases breakthrough rock artists, some traditional blues acts, and timeless eclectic music.

The Arts

The **Columbus Association for the Performing Arts** (☎ 614/469–0939) operates the **Capitol Theatre,** in the Riffe Center (✉ 77 S. High St., ☎ 614/460–7214), and the **Ohio Theater** (✉ 55 E. State St., ☎ 614/469–1045 or 614/469–0939 for tickets), home to the **Columbus Symphony Orchestra** (☎ 614/228–8600) and the **BalletMet** (☎ 614/229–4860 or 614/229–4848 for tickets). **Opera/Columbus** and touring Broadway shows take the stage at the **Palace Theatre** (✉ 34 W. Broad St., ☎ 614/469–9850 or 614/431–3600 for tickets).

Shopping

Columbus is the world headquarters of Leslie Wexner's empire of clothing stores, which include the Limited, Express, Structure, Henri Bendel, Victoria's Secret, and Abercrombie & Fitch, all of which are represented downtown in **Columbus City Center** (✉ 111 S. 3rd St., ☎ 614/221–4900). You can't miss **Lazarus** (✉ 141 S. High St., ☎ 614/463–2121), the granddaddy of Columbus department stores; its old-fashioned water tower sticks up out of the skyline like a Tootsie Roll Pop. **Ohio Factory Shops** (✉ 8000 Factory Shops Blvd., Jeffersonville, ☎ 614/948–9090 or 800/746–7644), 35 minutes south of Columbus, has more than 80 outlets. The **Wexner Center for the Arts** (☞ Exploring Columbus, *above*) has a gift shop with intriguing items, some handcrafted.

CINCINNATI

Cincinnati is a well-regulated city with a proud history, an active riverfront, and a busy downtown. A river's width from the South, in many respects it resembles a southern city: Its summers are hot and humid, a result of being in a basin along the Ohio River, and its politics tend toward the conservative.

Visitor Information

Greater Cincinnati Convention and Visitors Bureau (✉ 300 W. 6th St., at Plum St., 45202, ☎ 513/621–6994 or 800/246–2987).

Arriving and Departing

By Bus

Greyhound Lines (✉ 1005 Gilbert Ave., ☎ 800/231–2222).

By Car

I–71, I–75, and I–74 all converge on downtown Cincinnati.

By Plane

Cincinnati/Northern Kentucky International Airport is 12 mi south of downtown, off I–275, in Kentucky. It is served by major airlines and by **ComAir** (☎ 800/354–9822). **Jetport Express** (☎ 606/767–3702) makes regular trips from the airport to downtown hotels ($12 one-way, $16 round-trip). Taxis downtown cost about $25 plus tip.

By Train

Amtrak (✉ Union Terminal, 1301 Western Ave., ☎ 800/872–7245).

Getting Around Cincinnati

Downtown Cincinnati is entirely walkable. Skywalks connect hotels, convention centers, stores, and garages. **Metro** (☎ 513/621–4455) runs buses out of Government Square (✉ 5th St. between Walnut and Main Sts.); there is also a downtown loop bus (Bus 79).

Exploring Cincinnati

Fountain Square (✉ 5th and Vine Sts.) is the center of downtown Cincinnati. The city is laid out along the river, with numbered streets running east–west (2nd Street is Pete Rose Way); north–south streets have names. Vine Street divides the city into east and west.

If you have only an hour in Cincinnati, spend it at **Carew Tower** (✉ 5th and Race Sts.) looking at the gorgeous Rookwood pottery in the arcade. Also don't miss the **Omni Netherland Plaza Hotel,** whose marble-and-rosewood interior is filled with mirrors and murals.

You can cross the Ohio River from Cincinnati into Covington, Kentucky, on the **Roebling Suspension Bridge,** built by John A. Roebling, who would later design the Brooklyn Bridge. **Covington Landing,** a floating entertainment complex in the form of a side-wheeler and a wharf, is west of Roebling Bridge. Beyond the Covington wharf is **BB Riverboats** (☎ 606/261–8500), running river tours year-round. **Covington** itself, east of Roebling Bridge, is a neighborhood of fine antebellum mansions, with wonderful views from Riverside Drive.

On the Ohio side of the river, the narrow streets and funky houses of **Mount Adams,** the first hill east of downtown, are reminiscent of San Francisco. The yard of the **Immaculata Church** (✉ Pavillion and Guido Sts., ☎ 513/721–6544) provides a sterling view of the city.

Eden Park, on Mt. Adams, is the site of the Krohn Conservatory (☞ Parks, Gardens, and Zoos, *below*) and the **Cincinnati Art Museum** (☎ 513/721–5204; 🎟 $5, free on Sat.), which has an outstanding collection of Near Eastern and ancient art. Downtown, the **Contemporary Arts Center** (✉ 115 E. 5th St., ☎ 513/345–8400 or 513/721–0390; 🎟 $3.50) presents some of today's most cutting-edge artists. The **Taft Museum** (✉ 316 Pike St., ☎ 513/241–0343; 🎟 $4) is famous for its Chinese porcelains.

You could spend a full day in the magnificently restored **Museum Center at Union Terminal,** which looks like a huge Art Deco cabinet radio. This historic former train station houses the Museum of Natural History, which has a cave with real bats; the Cincinnati Historical Society; and the Robert D. Lindner Family OmniMax Theater. ✉ *1301 Western Ave. (off I–75 at Ezzard Charles Dr.),* ☎ *513/287–7000 or 800/733–2077.*

Paramount's **Kings Island Theme Park,** 24 mi north of Cincinnati in Kings Mills, has eight theme areas, including a water park and the world's longest wooden roller coaster. ✉ *I–71 Exit 24,* ☎ *800/288–0808.* 🎟 *$32.95; $18.95 seniors, children under 4. Closed Labor Day–mid-Apr. and weekdays mid-Apr.–Memorial Day.*

Parks, Gardens, and Zoos

Krohn Conservatory (☎ 513/421–4086; 🎟 free), in Eden Park, has a greenhouse and gardens with more than 5,000 species of plants.

The **Cincinnati Zoo and Botanical Garden** (✉ 3400 Vine St., ☎ 513/281–4700; 🎟 $8), famous for its white Bengal tigers, is the second-oldest zoo in the country. Follow the paw-print signs off I–75 Exit 6 or I–71 Exit 7.

Bicentennial Commons, an outdoor recreation center at Sawyer Point on the Ohio River, uses monuments to tell the story of Cincinnati's ori-

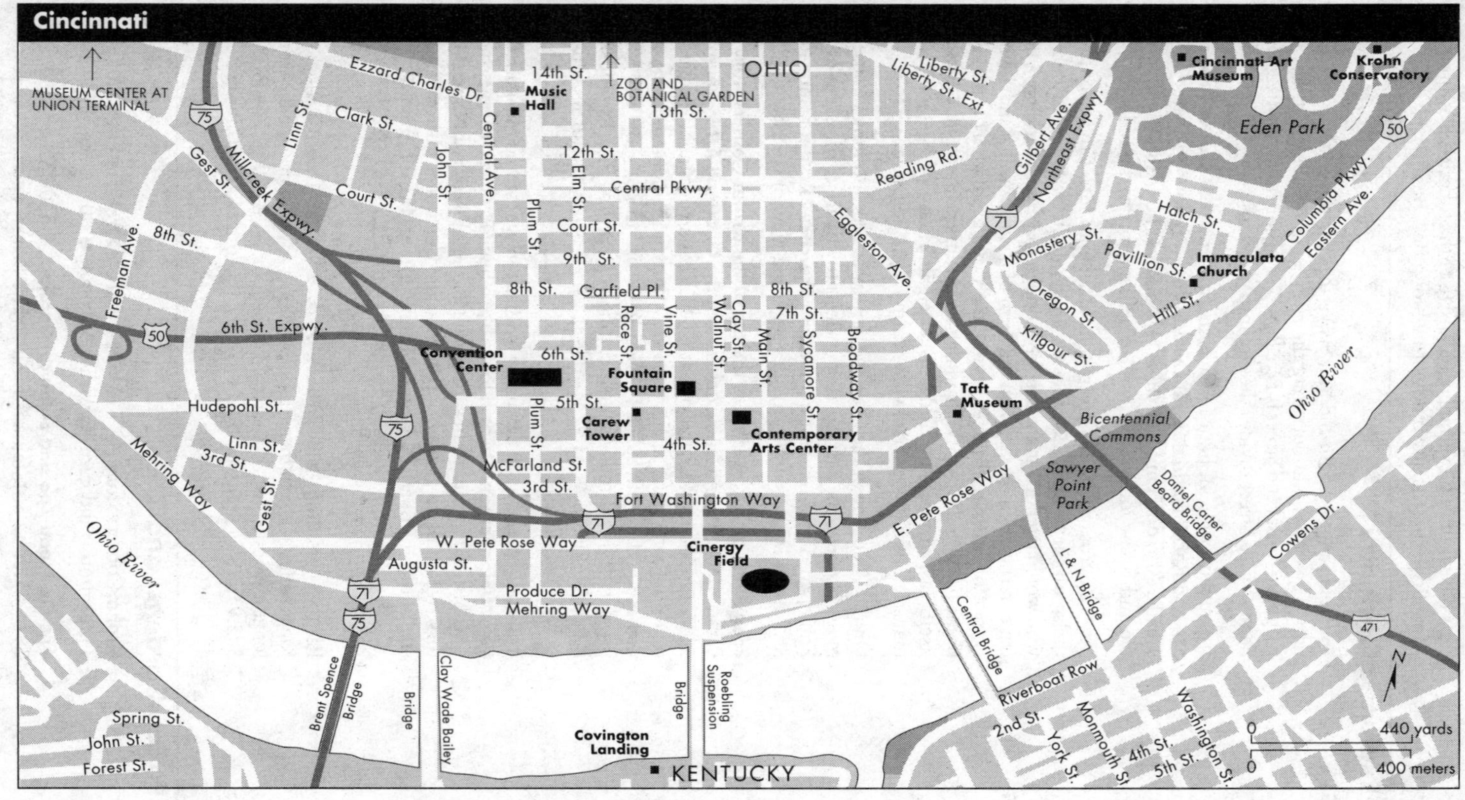
Cincinnati
MUSEUM CENTER AT UNION TERMINAL
ZOO AND BOTANICAL GARDEN
OHIO
KENTUCKY
Music Hall
Cincinnati Art Museum
Krohn Conservatory
Eden Park
Immaculata Church
Convention Center
Fountain Square
Carew Tower
Contemporary Arts Center
Taft Museum
Bicentennial Commons
Sawyer Point Park
Cinergy Field
Covington Landing
Ohio River
Ohio River
14th St.
13th St.
12th St.
Ezzard Charles Dr.
Clark St.
Linn St.
John St.
Central Ave.
Gest St.
Millcreek Expwy.
Court St.
8th St.
Freeman Ave.
6th St. Expwy.
Hudepohl St.
Linn St.
3rd St.
Gest St.
Mehring Way
Elm St.
Plum St.
Central Pkwy.
Court St.
9th St.
8th St.
Garfield Pl.
Race St.
Vine St.
Walnut St.
Clay St.
Main St.
Sycamore St.
Broadway St.
8th St.
7th St.
6th St.
5th St.
Plum St.
4th St.
McFarland St.
3rd St.
Fort Washington Way
W. Pete Rose Way
Augusta St.
Produce Dr.
Mehring Way
E. Pete Rose Way
Liberty St.
Liberty St. Ext.
Reading Rd.
Eggleston Ave.
Gilbert Ave.
Northeast Expwy.
Monastery St.
Pavillion St.
Hatch St.
Hill St.
Oregon St.
Kilgour St.
Columbia Pkwy.
Eastern Ave.
Daniel Carter Beard Bridge
L & N Bridge
Central Bridge
Roebling Suspension Bridge
Clay Wade Bailey Bridge
Brent Spence Bridge
Cowens Dr.
Riverboat Row
2nd St.
York St.
Monmouth St.
4th St.
5th St.
Washington St.
Spring St.
John St.
Forest St.
75
71
50
471
N
0
440 yards
0
400 meters

gins as a river town. Look for the famous flying pigs, a playful reminder of the city's prominence as a meatpacking center.

Dining

Famous for its chili, Cincinnati has more good restaurants than the most ravenous traveler could sample in any one visit, including high-rise revolving restaurants, riverboat restaurants, and rathskellers. For price ranges *see* Chart 1 (B) *in* On the Road with Fodor's.

$$$$ ★ ✕ **The Celestial.** The views from the top of Mt. Adams are as much of a draw as the French and American cuisine. ✉ *1071 Celestial St.,* ☎ *513/241–4455. Jacket required. AE, DC, MC, V. Closed Sun.*

$$$$ ✕ **The Maisonette.** Since 1964 the Maisonette has been ranked among the foremost restaurants in the United States. The food is fresh and French, the atmosphere formal. ✉ *114 E. 6th St.,* ☎ *513/721–2260. Reservations essential. Jacket required. AE, D, DC, MC, V. Closed Sun.*

$$ ✕ **Montgomery Inn at the Boathouse.** The barbecued ribs are famous, and you can't get any closer to the river without jumping in for a swim. Lunchtime and happy hour both draw crowds. ✉ *925 Eastern Ave.,* ☎ *513/721–7427. AE, D, DC, MC, V. No lunch weekends.*

$–$$ ✕ **Lenhardt's.** Schnitzel, Viennese and Hungarian goulash, sauerbraten, and potato pancakes are served at this casual restaurant. The outdoor beer garden is a great summer escape. ✉ *151 W. McMillan St.,* ☎ *513/281–3600. AE, D, MC, V. Closed Sun.–Mon., 1st 2 wks in Aug., 2 wks at Christmas.*

$–$$ ✕ **Rookwood Pottery.** The wood-and-brick dining rooms contain what were once the kilns of the famous Mt. Adams pottery. Families come here for giant burgers and other simple fare. ✉ *1077 Celestial St.,* ☎ *513/721–5456. AE, DC, MC, V.*

Dining and Lodging

$$$$ ★ ✕ **Cincinnatian Hotel.** A sedate French Second Empire–style hotel with an unusual contemporary interior, this showplace has a new wedding suite and a luxury whirlpool room. Reservations are essential at the Palace (☎ 513/381–6006), where the chef delights diners with his regional American cuisine—and his crème brûlée. ✉ *601 Vine St., 45202,* ☎ *513/381–3000 or 800/942–9000 in OH,* FAX *513/651–0256. 147 rooms. 2 restaurants, health club. AE, D, DC, MC, V.*

Lodging

Downtown Cincinnati has several choice hotels. Many offer weekend packages including tickets to Reds or Bengals games. Staying in the suburbs is less expensive. For price ranges *see* Chart 2 (B) *in* On the Road with Fodor's.

$$$$ ★ **Omni Netherland Plaza.** Downtown's grand Art Deco hotel is in the Carew Tower (☞ Exploring Cincinnati, *above*). The two-story lobby has bas-relief sculptures and dramatic fountains and light fixtures; guest rooms have 10-ft ceilings and soft pastel colors. The restaurant, Orchids, serves American cuisine in the exquisite Palm Court Café. ✉ *35 W. 5th St., 45202,* ☎ *513/421–9100,* FAX *513/421–4291. 621 rooms. 2 restaurants, health club. AE, D, DC, MC, V.*

$$$–$$$$ **Amos Shinkle Townhouse B&B.** The master bedroom in this antebellum mansion, once home to the man who hired John A. Roebling to build a suspension bridge across the Ohio River, has a whirlpool and a crystal chandelier in the bathroom. ✉ *215 Garrard St., Covington, KY 41011,* ☎ *606/431–2118. 7 rooms. AE, D, DC, MC, V.*

$$ **Best Western Mariemont Inn.** Even the cash machine is in the Tudor style at this charming inn on the National Register of Historic Places. Amenities include a pub and free parking. ✉ *6880 Wooster Pike (U.S. 50), Mariemont 45227, ☎ 513/271–2100, FAX 513/271–1057. 60 rooms. Restaurant. AE, D, DC, MC, V.*

Nightlife and the Arts

Nightlife

At Covington Landing, **Howl at the Moon Saloon** (✉ Foot of Madison Ave., Covington, KY 41011, ☎ 606/491–7733) features dueling piano players and sing-alongs. In Mt. Adams, **Longworth's** (✉ 1108 St. Gregory St., ☎ 513/579–0900) has a DJ, a garden, and live music on weekends. The **Incline** (✉ 1071 Celestial St., ☎ 513/241–4455), a sophisticated bar at the Celestial Restaurant, spotlights vocalists.

The Arts

The **Music Hall** (✉ 1241 Elm St., ☎ 513/721–8222), built in the 18th century in a style since dubbed "sauerbraten Gothic," is home to the Cincinnati Symphony Orchestra as well as the Cincinnati Pops Orchestra (☎ 513/381–3300), which performs from September through May at the Music Hall and June and July at Riverbend; the Cincinnati Opera (☎ 513/241–2742), with performances in June and July; and the Cincinnati Ballet (☎ 513/621–5219), with performances from October through May.

Spectator Sports

Baseball: Cincinnati Reds (✉ 100 Cinergy Field, ☎ 513/421–4510). **Football: Cincinnati Bengals** (✉ 1 Bengals Dr., ☎ 513/621–3550).

Shopping

Upscale shopping is available in the new **Fountain Place Lazarus** (✉ 5th and Race Sts.) **Tower Place** (✉ at 4th and Race Sts.), an atrium shopping mall. Skywalks connect Tower Place with **McAlpin's** and **Saks Fifth Avenue** (via Carew Tower). Over the Roebling Bridge in Covington, Kentucky, **Mainstrasse Village** has gift and antiques shops and vintage clothing boutiques.

NORTHWEST OHIO AND THE LAKE ERIE ISLANDS

Between Toledo and Cleveland lie a stretch of the Lake Erie shore and a group of islands that constitute the Riviera and Madeira of Ohio. Families rent cottages at Catawba Point or Put-in-Bay (the port village on South Bass Island) and swim, fish, and boat, topping the week off with a trip to Cedar Point Amusement Park in Sandusky.

Visitor Information

Erie County: Visitors Bureau (✉ 231 W. Washington Row, Sandusky 44870, ☎ 419/625–2984 or 800/255–3743) covers Cedar Point, Kelleys Island, and Sandusky. **Ottawa County:** Visitors Bureau (✉ 109 Madison St., Port Clinton 43452, ☎ 419/734–4386 or 800/441–1271) covers Catawba, Lakeside, Marblehead, Port Clinton, Oak Harbor, and Put-in-Bay. **Greater Toledo:** Convention and Visitors Bureau (✉ SeaGate Convention Center, 401 Jefferson Ave., 2nd floor, 43604, ☎ 419/321–6404 or 800/243–4667). **Kelleys Island:** Chamber of Commerce (✉ Box 783F, 43438, ☎ 419/746–2360). **Put-in-Bay:** Chamber of Commerce (✉ Box 250-BN, 43456, ☎ 419/285–2832).

Arriving and Departing

By Boat

Ferries serve the Lake Erie islands from May through October. **Put-in-Bay Jet Express** (☎ 800/245–1538), from Port Clinton to Put-in-Bay, takes passengers and bicycles only and has late-night service. Starting in March, **Miller Boat Line** (☎ 419/285–2421) takes passengers and cars (reservations required) from Catawba to Lime Kiln Dock (on the opposite side of South Bass Island from Put-in-Bay) and to Middle Bass Island. **Neumann Boat Line** (☎ 419/798–5800) takes passengers from Marblehead to Kelleys Island.

By Bus

Greyhound Lines has national service from Toledo (✉ 811 Jefferson Ave., ☎ 800/231–2222). **Toledo Area Regional Transit Authority** (TARTA; ☎ 419/243–7433) covers Toledo and its suburbs.

By Car

The Ohio Turnpike (I–80/90) runs between 5 and 10 mi south of the Lake Erie shoreline. For Toledo take Exit 4 (I–75) or Exit 5 (U.S. 280); for Port Clinton, Exit 6 (Route 53); for Sandusky, Exit 7 (U.S. 250). Toledo is on I–75. Route 2 hugs the lake between Toledo and Sandusky; Route 269 loops out to Marblehead.

By Plane

Toledo Express Airport is served by six airlines. For **Cleveland Hopkins Airport** *see* Arriving and Departing *in* Cleveland, *below.* Griffing Island Airlines (☎ 419/734–3149), out of **Port Clinton Airport** (✉ 3255 E. State Rd.), and Griffing Flying Service (☎ 419/626–5161) fly to the Lake Erie Islands out of **Griffing–Sandusky Airport** (✉ 3115 Cleveland Rd., east of Sandusky).

By Train

Amtrak (☎ 800/872–7245) stops in Toledo and Sandusky.

Exploring Northwest Ohio and the Lake Erie Islands

A true lakefront town, **Toledo** combines natural beauty with colloquial artistry such as glassblowing. Its multicultural mix supports great ethnic eats, interesting architecture, and a host of unusual storefront shops. Just down the coastline the shores of Lake Erie teem with wildlife. The Toledo Mud Hens, a Detroit Tigers farm team, play in **Ned Skeldon Stadium,** at Lucas County Recreation Center (✉ 2901 Key St., off U.S. 24, Maumee, ☎ 419/893–9481). The **Toledo Museum of Art** (✉ 2445 Monroe St., at Scottwood Ave., off I–75, ☎ 419/255–8000) has a fine collection of European and American paintings, ancient Greek and Egyptian statues, and regionally produced and internationally recognized blown glass.

Vacationland begins at **Port Clinton,** a center for fishing excursions, at the northern base of the Marblehead Peninsula, some 30 mi east of Toledo on Route 2 (☞ Outdoor Activities and Sports, *below*). Port Clinton is also the base for a ferry to South Bass Island's **Put-in-Bay** (☞ Arriving and Departing, *above*), a port village consisting of a marina, a grassy lakefront park dotted with small cannons, and a strip of shops, bars, and restaurants, with a vintage wooden merry-go-round. Now a town of wild parties, Put-in-Bay was the site of Commodore Oliver Hazard Perry's naval victory over the British in the War of 1812. From the top of **Perry's Victory and International Peace Memorial,** a single massive Doric column east of downtown, you can see all the way to Canada. From May through September you can hop on a ferry to

Middle Bass Island to sample the wares of the Lonz Winery (☎ 419/285–5411), which looks like a European monastery.

Back on the mainland, at the eastern tip of the peninsula, is **Marblehead,** site of the oldest continuously working lighthouse on Lake Erie. From Marblehead it's a short ferry ride to **Kelleys Island,** which has two remarkable geologic features: Glacial grooves (waves in the rock) carved during the Ice Age can be seen on the north shore, and the south shore has prehistoric Native American pictographs.

Sandusky, a small port city with lush gardens enlivening its town square, makes a good touring base. It's near the highways and ferries and has thousands of motel rooms as well as a few romantic Victorian hideaways.

Cedar Point Amusement Park (✉ Off U.S. 250N, ☎ 419/627–2350; 🎫 $29.95) is in the *Guinness Book of Records* because it has the most roller coasters in the world (12, and counting), among them the fastest one and the highest wooden one. It also has Snake River Falls, the tallest, deepest, and fastest water ride in the world; a water park; and a mile-long sandy beach. The park is open daily in summer and on weekends in September.

Dining and Lodging

The chambers of commerce in Put-in-Bay and on Kelleys Island (☞ Visitor Information, *above*) give advice on lodging, which should be arranged well in advance. For price ranges *see* Charts 1 (B) and 2 (B) *in* On the Road with Fodor's.

Catawba Point

$$$ ★ ✕ **Mon Ami.** This well-established winery and restaurant has a chalet-style dining room with 4-ft-thick stone walls and a patio surrounded by wooden casks. Pasta and fresh fish are the specialties. ✉ *3845 E. Wine Cellar Rd., off N.E. Catawba Rd. (Rte. 53),* ☎ *419/797–4445 or 800/777–4266. AE, MC, V.*

Grand Rapids

$$$–$$$$ 🏨 **Mill House.** This country-Victorian house on the Maumee River 40 minutes from downtown Toledo was built in 1900 as a working gristmill. One of the four French Country–style guest rooms has its own private entrance and whirlpool tub. ✉ *24070 Front St., 43522,* ☎ *419/832–6455. 4 rooms. CP. AE, D, MC, V.*

Marblehead

$$$–$$$$ 🏨 **Old Stone House Bed & Breakfast.** This Federal-style mansion is full of Victorian antiques. ✉ *133 Clemons St., 43440,* ☎ *419/798–5922. 13 rooms. CP. D, MC, V.*

Port Clinton

$$–$$$ ✕ **Garden at the Lighthouse.** Dinner is served in a terraced garden at this Victorian house originally built for the lighthouse keeper. ✉ *226 E. Perry St.,* ☎ *419/732–2151. AE, D, DC, MC, V. Closed Sun., Mon. Sept.–May.*

$$$–$$$$ ✕🏨 **Island House Hotel.** This 110-year-old redbrick hotel with tall windows has a casual dining room serving fresh fish. ✉ *102 Madison St., 43452,* ☎ *419/734–2166 or 800/233–7307. 39 rooms. Restaurant. AE, D, DC, MC, V.*

$$$$ 🏨 **Beach Cliff Lodge.** Close to the ferry and the state park, this unpretentious place has freezers and fish-cleaning services. ✉ *4189 N.W. Catawba Rd., 43452,* ☎ *419/797–4553. 8 rooms, 19 cottages. No credit cards.*

Put-in-Bay

$$$ ✕ **Crescent Tavern.** If you're going to eat only one meal in Put-in-Bay, this seafood, steak, and pasta restaurant inside a gracious Victorian house is the place. ✉ *Delaware Ave.,* ☎ *419/285–4211. D, MC, V. Closed Oct.–Mar.*

$–$$ ✕ **Frosty's.** With a bar and a pool table on one side, and Formica tables on the other, this noisy hangout caters to rowdies and families. ✉ *Delaware Ave.,* ☎ *419/285–4741. D, MC, V. Closed Oct.–Mar.*

$–$$ **Park Hotel.** This white-frame hotel, dating from the 1870s, has etched glass and a gracious Victorian lobby, but it's also smack in the middle of the island revelry. Bring earplugs. ✉ *234 Delaware Ave., Box 60, 43456,* ☎ *419/285–3581. 26 rooms. CP. MC, V. Closed Oct.–Mar.*

Sandusky

$$$$ ★ **Hotel Breakers.** Built in 1905 to resemble a French château, with a five-story rotunda, stained glass, and vintage wicker furniture, this is *the* place to stay on the beach at Cedar Point, especially if you can get a turret room. ✉ *Cedar Point Amusement Park, Box 5006, 44871,* ☎ *419/627–2106. 400 rooms. 4 restaurants, pool. D, MC, V. Closed Oct.–Apr.*

$$$$ ✕ **Radisson Harbour Inn.** This big hotel is successfully disguised as a rambling, weathered beach house. It's on the property of Cedar Point Amusement Park, connected via a walkway to many restaurants and shops. ✉ *2001 Cleveland Rd., at Cedar Point Causeway, 44870,* ☎ *419/627–2500. 237 rooms. Restaurant, pool, exercise room. AE, D, DC, MC, V.*

$$$ **Wagner's 1844 Inn.** Each of the three guest rooms at this inn a block from downtown has a private bath, canopy beds, and globe lamps. Guests have use of a pool table, TV, and travel library. ✉ *230 E. Washington St., 44870,* ☎ *419/626–1726. 3 rooms. CP. D, MC, V.*

Toledo

$–$$ ✕ **Tony Packo's Cafe.** Before Max Klinger ever mentioned it on *M*A*S*H,* Tony Packo's was famous for its Tiffany lamps and Hungarian hot dogs. (The buns are imprinted with the restaurant's logo, lest you forget where you are.) ✉ *1902 Front St.,* ☎ *419/691–6054. AE, D, MC, V.*

$$–$$$$ **Crowne Plaza.** This is the only downtown hotel right on the Maumee River, connected by walkways to office buildings and the convention center.✉ *2 SeaGate/Summit St., 43604,* ☎ *419/241–1411,* FAX *419/241–8161. 241 rooms. Restaurant, exercise room. AE, D, DC, MC, V.*

Motels

The majority of area motels are in and around Sandusky, on the roads to Cedar Point. **Best Western Resort Inn** (✉ 1530 Cleveland Rd., Sandusky 44870, ☎ 419/625–9234), 106 rooms, restaurant, pool; *$$–$$$.* **Comfort Inn** (✉ 11020 U.S. 250, Milan Rd., Milan 44846, ☎ 419/499–4681), 103 rooms, pool; *$$–$$$.*

Campground

St. Hazard's Village on the Beach has tent and RV sites, hot showers, a beach, bike rentals, boat rentals, and charter-fishing packages. ✉ *Fox Rd. (Box 69), Middle Bass Island 43446,* ☎ *419/285–6121. Closed Oct.–Mar.*

Outdoor Activities and Sports

Beaches and Water Sports

The best Lake Erie beach is at **East Harbor State Park,** off Route 163 on Marblehead Peninsula. **Cedar Point Amusement Park** also has good swimming. You can rent sailboats and take sailing lessons from **Ad-**

venture Plus Yacht Charters and Sailing at the Sandusky Harbor Marina (☎ 419/625–5000).

Fishing

The western Lake Erie Basin is known as the "walleye capital of the world"; Toledo even has a **Walleye Hot Line** (☎ 419/893–9740), which operates from March through May. Smallmouth bass and Lake Erie perch are also plentiful. Nonresident fishing licenses are sold at bait shops, or contact the **Division of Wildlife** (☎ 419/625–8062). There's ice fishing when the lake freezes.

The breakwater in Port Clinton and the pier at Catawba Point are both good fishing areas. Per-head fishing boats leave from **Fisherman's Wharf** in Port Clinton (☎ 419/734–6388) and from **Battery Park Marina** in Sandusky (☎ 419/625–6142), among other places.

CLEVELAND

In recent years Cleveland has emerged with a new cultural identity. Major attractions such as the Rock and Roll Hall of Fame and Museum and the Great Lakes Science Center have been the main catalysts, in addition to a world-class orchestra, a stunning art museum, and blooming gardens on the east side of town. Sports fans rejoice in the city's newest sports venues at Gateway, and theater lovers enjoy a rejuvenated theater district. Neighborhoods such as the Flats, the Warehouse District, and Northcoast Harbor buzz with restaurants, shops, and nightclubs. Friendly Clevelanders welcome their first crop of tourists and indulge in providing gratuitous sightseeing tips to those who ask for directions.

Visitor Information

Cleveland Convention and Visitors Bureau, Visitor Information Center (✉ 3100 Terminal Tower, 50 Public Sq., ☎ 216/621–4110 or 800/321–1001).

Arriving and Departing

By Bus

Greyhound Lines (✉ E. 15th St. and Chester Ave., ☎ 800/231–2222).

By Car

I–90 runs east–west through downtown Cleveland. I–71 and I–77 come up from the south. Driving from the east on the Ohio Turnpike (I–80), take Exit 10 to I–71N.

By Plane

Cleveland Hopkins International Airport, 10 mi southwest of downtown, is served by major airlines and several commuter lines. From here the **Rapid Transit Authority** rail system (☎ 216/621–9500) takes 20 minutes to Public Square and costs $1.50. A taxi takes twice as long and costs about $20.

By Train

Amtrak (✉ 200 Memorial Shoreway NE, ☎ 800/872–7245).

Getting Around Cleveland

The RTA rapid-transit system (☎ 216/621–9500), though not extensive, efficiently bridges east and west, with Tower City as its hub. RTA buses travel from Public Square on five downtown loop routes. A light-rail system, the **Waterfront Line,** links Tower City with the Flats entertainment district, the Rock and Roll Hall of Fame and Museum and the Great Lakes Science Center (both at North Coast Harbor), and municipal parking lots.

Exploring Cleveland

Begin your tour of Cleveland at **Terminal Tower,** the city's central landmark. **Tower City Center,** an office and shopping complex, includes the shops of the Avenue (☞ Shopping, *below*). Pick up a copy of "Walks," a brochure outlining some popular Cleveland walking tours, at the **visitor center** just inside the entrance to Tower City Center. The specialty-shop-filled **Old Arcade** runs between Superior and Euclid avenues, a short block east of Public Square. Built in 1890, this is still downtown's most architecturally significant building. Like a nave without a cathedral, it rises five stories, with brass railings, ironwork, walkways, and a skylight.

South of Public Square on Ontario Street you'll find **Gund Arena** (⊠ 1 Center Court, ☎ 216/420–2000), a sports venue that hosts basketball, hockey, indoor football, concerts, and other events. Next to the arena is **Jacobs Field** (⊠ 2401 Ontario St., ☎ 216/420–4200), a trapezoid-shape baseball park that looks brand new and old-fashioned at the same time.

For a fabulous view of the lake, take East 9th Street to North Coast ★ Harbor, formerly the East 9th Street Pier. The **Rock and Roll Hall of Fame and Museum** (⊠ 1 Key Plaza, ☎ 216/781–7625 or 800/282–5393 for a brochure; 🎫 $14.95) has 55 high- and low-tech exhibits—from interactive kiosks exploring performer influences to the Sun recording studio, where Elvis Presley, Carl Perkins, and Roy Orbison made their first records. Stage costumes that once belonged to Chuck Berry and Iggy Pop, handwritten lyrics by Jimi Hendrix, Janis Joplin's Porsche, and a number of thought-provoking films are among the museum's holdings. **The Great Lakes Science Center** (⊠ 601 Erieside, ☎ 216/694–2000; 🎫 $6.75) focuses on the environment and technology, particularly in relation to the Great Lakes. The 165,000-square-ft museum has dozens of hands-on exhibits and a 324-seat Omnimax Theater. From June through September, the ***Goodtime III*** (☎ 216/861–5110) gives sightseeing tours on the Cuyahoga River and short lake cruises.

University Circle, reached by rapid transit or a 15-minute drive from downtown, contains more than 50 cultural institutions. The centerpiece of University Circle is the **Cleveland Museum of Art** (⊠ 11150 E. Blvd., ☎ 216/421–7340; 🎫 free), a white-marble temple set among spring-flowering trees and reflected in a lagoon. The museum (closed Monday) is world renowned for its medieval European collection, Egyptian art, and European and American paintings. The **Museum of Natural History** (⊠ 1 Wade Oval Dr., ☎ 216/231–4600) has an observatory and planetarium. The **Children's Museum** (⊠ 10730 Euclid Ave., ☎ 216/791–5437; 🎫 $5) has interactive exhibits on topics such as geography, bridge-building, climate, and weather. Juno, the see-through woman, and a newly remodeled, 18-ft-high tooth are among the favorite permanant exhibits at the **Health Museum** (⊠ 8911 Euclid Ave., ☎ 216/231–5710; 🎫 $4.50); traveling exhibits focus on current health issues and are designed to be fun and educational for kids. The **Western Reserve Historical Society** (⊠ 10825 East Blvd., ☎ 216/721–5722; 🎫 $6), closed Monday, has an extensive Napoleonic collection and, in the **Crawford Auto-Aviation Museum,** just about every old car you'd want to see. Also in University Circle is **Severance Hall,** home of the Cleveland Orchestra (☞ Nightlife and the Arts, *below*), with the city's most beautiful Art Deco interior.

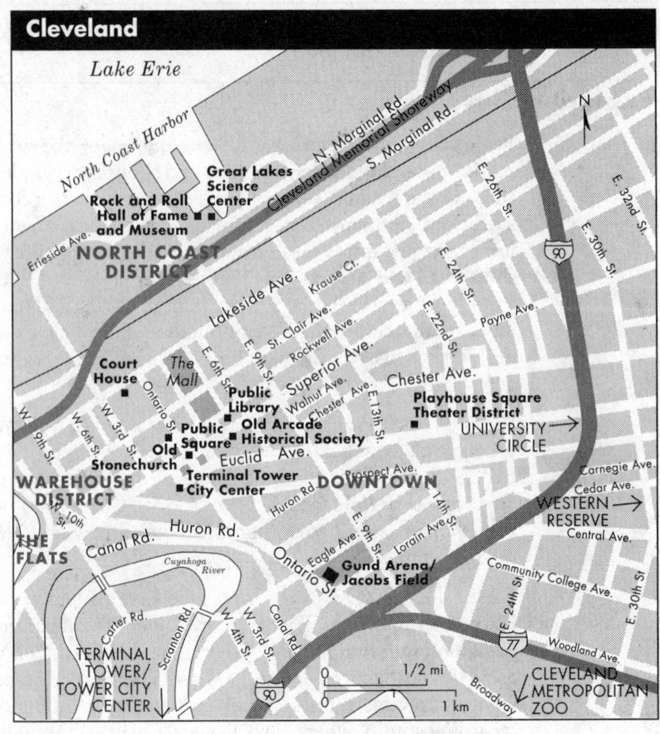

Parks, Gardens, and Zoos

Cleveland Metroparks Zoo and Rainforest (✉ Brookside Park Dr. off W. 25th St., ☎ 216/661–6500; 🎟 $7) has tropical plants and animals in a simulated rain-forest environment, in addition to an excellent outdoor zoo. At **Edgewater Park,** just west of downtown, you can swim while enjoying a startlingly close-up view of downtown. The park also has a fishing pier, bait shop, fitness course, playgrounds, and picnic facilities. The stiff wind off the lake attracts kite flyers, boomerang enthusiasts, windsurfers, and the occasional hang glider. Drive through the **Cleveland Cultural Gardens** (✉ Martin Luther King Blvd. in University Circle, north of Chester Ave. and south of I–90, ☎ 216/664–2517) to see gardens representing more than 20 nationalities. The **Rockefeller Park Greenhouse** (✉ 750 E. 88th St., ☎ 216/664–3103), the oldest civic horticultural center in the country, houses seasonal flower and plant exhibits indoors; outside you'll find a Japanese garden, a formal English garden, and a talking garden for people with vision impairments. In Aurora, 30 mi southeast of Cleveland, **Sea World** (✉ Rtes. 43 and 82, ☎ 330/995–2121; 330/562–8101 or 800/637–4268 for recording) is a kid-friendly summertime destination (it's open only from June through August).

Dining

Ethnic food predominates in Cleveland, whether it's a Polish kielbasa smothered with Cleveland's famous Stadium Mustard, an open-pit barbecued sparerib, or a spicy burrito. There are restaurant rows in the Flats, the Warehouse District, the area around Gund Arena and Jacobs Field, Little Italy, and on Coventry Road in Cleveland Heights. For price ranges *see* Chart 1 (B) *in* On the Road with Fodor's.

$$$–$$$$ ★ ✕ **Moxie.** In the lively town of Beachwood, 20 min southeast of downtown Cleveland by car, this trendy newcomer is a must. It's unassuming from the outside, but once you step into the large, bright room and taste the creatively prepared pastas and game with bold sauces, you'll understand why they named it Moxie. ✉ *3355 Richmond Rd., off I-271, Beachwood,* ☎ *216/831–5599. AE, D, DC, MC, V.*

$$$–$$$$ ✕ **Sans Souci.** Sophisticated seafood dishes and contemporary cuisine are served in a comfortably elegant dining room overlooking Public Square. ✉ *24 Public Sq.,* ☎ *216/696–5600. Reservations essential. AE, D, DC, MC, V.*

$$–$$$$ ✕ **La Dolce Vita.** Strolling mariachi musicians on the weekends and live opera give this relatively upscale Little Italy restaurant a festive mood. On Monday nights there's an eight-course meal; on other days, specials include veal, seafood, and risotto dishes. ✉ *12112 Mayfield Rd.,* ☎ *216/721–8155. Reservations essential Mon. MC, V.*

$$–$$$ **Lola.** Chef-owner Michael Simon describes this hot spot in the Tremont neighborhood as "an American bistro specializing in urban comfort food." Translation: homey classics with nouvelle twists. Bestsellers on the winter menu are shrimp–escargot pot pie; wild-mushroom shepherd's pie; and macaroni-and-cheese with fresh rosemary, goat cheese, and roasted chicken. Fish and game are also first-rate, and desserts are out of this world. ✉ *900 Literary Rd.,* ☎ *216/771–5652. AE, D, DC, MC, V. Reservations essential.*

$$–$$$ ✕ **The Palazzo.** The two granddaughters of the original owner prepare and serve northern Italian cuisine in this romantic hideaway. Whether turning out updated versions of her recipes or new dishes inspired by annual trips back to Italy, they do their grandma proud. ✉ *10031 Detroit Ave.,* ☎ *216/651–3900. AE, MC, V. Closed Sun.–Wed.*

$–$$$ ✕ **Keka.** An adventurous tapas menu features inexpensive crowd-pleasers like roasted redskin potatoes with cumin and mustard seeds, served with garlic mayonnaise. Simple Spanish wine comes in plain glasses, adding to the rustic mood. ✉ *2523 Market St.,* ☎ *216/241–5352. AE, MC, V. Closed Mon.*

$$ ✕ **Luchita's.** The menu changes every three months at this basic Mexican restaurant. It's jammed on the weekends—and with good reason: great authentic Mexican fare in generous portions, along with good margaritas and friendly service. What more could you need? ✉ *3456 W. 117th St.,* ☎ *216/252–1169. AE, MC, V. Closed Mon.*

$–$$ ✕ **Nate's Deli and Restaurant.** This breakfast and lunch spot on the near West Side serves traditional deli fare as well as Middle Eastern specialties. The creamy hummus may be the best in town. ✉ *1923 W. 25th St.,* ☎ *216/696–7529. No credit cards. Closed Sun. No dinner.*

$–$$ ✕ **Tommy's.** An institution on hippie-tinged Coventry Road, Tommy's serves hefty salads and sandwiches, many of them vegetarian, and embarrassingly large but delicious milk shakes made with Cleveland's own Pierre's ice cream. ✉ *1824 Coventry Rd., Cleveland Heights,* ☎ *216/321–7757. MC, V.*

Lodging

Many downtown hotels have weekend packages; those in the suburbs have lower weekday rates. For price ranges *see* Chart 2 (A) *in* On the Road with Fodor's.

$$$$ ✕▣ **Baricelli Inn.** Every room is different in this simple, European-style brownstone mansion, now a bed-and-breakfast, convenient to University Circle. Contemporary European and American dinners are served in the dining room (closed Sunday). ✉ *2203 Cornell Rd., 44106,* ☎ *216/791–6500,* FAX *216/791–9131. 7 rooms. Restaurant. CP. AE, DC, MC, V.*

$$$$ 🏨 **Cleveland Marriott Key Center.** Attached to Key Tower, the tallest building in Cleveland, this hotel faces the historic Mall "C" and abuts Public Square. Plush accommodations have fantastic views of Lake Erie and the downtown skyline. ✉ *127 Public Sq., 44114,* ☎ *216/696–9200,* FAX *216/696–0966. 400 rooms. Restaurant, exercise room. AE, D, DC, MC, V.*

$$$$ 🏨 **Embassy Suites Hotel.** The cherry-wood lobby of this all-suite hotel feels like an old-style ocean liner or a private club. Some rooms have in-suite kitchens. ✉ *1701 E. 12th St., 44114,* ☎ *216/523–8000,* FAX *216/523–1698. 268 suites. Restaurant, health club. AE, D, DC, MC, V.*

$$$$ 🏨 **Holiday Inn–Lakeside.** Across from Burke Lakefront Airport and convenient to the train station, the Rock and Roll Hall of Fame and Museum, and the Great Lakes Science Center, this hotel has lake views and an unbeatable location. ✉ *1111 Lakeside, 44114,* ☎ *216/241–5100,* FAX *216/241–5437. 370 rooms. Restaurant, pool, exercise room. AE, D, DC, MC, V.*

$$$$ 🏨 **Omni International Hotel.** On the grounds of the renowned Cleveland Clinic (there are special rates for clinic patients), there's nothing clinical about this luxurious international hotel. The Classics Restaurant (no lunch Saturday and closed Sunday) serves French and Continental cuisine, and is open to the public. ✉ *2065 E. 96th St. (at Carnegie Ave.), 44106,* ☎ *216/791–1900,* FAX *216/231–3329. 300 rooms. 3 restaurants, exercise room. AE, D, DC, MC, V.*

$$$$ 🏨 **Renaissance Cleveland Hotel.** The city's original grand hotel has a lobby with an ornate Carrara marble fountain. Guest rooms have period furniture, spacious marble bathrooms, and fine views. ✉ *24 Public Sq., 44113,* ☎ *216/696–5600,* FAX *216/696–0432. 491 rooms. 2 restaurants, pool, health club. AE, D, DC, MC, V.*

$$$$ ★ 🏨 **Ritz-Carlton.** The city's only four-star hotel is filled with antiques and original 18th-century art. The Riverview Room restaurant has excellent views of the Flats. ✉ *1515 W. 3rd St., 44113,* ☎ *216/623–1300,* FAX *216/623–0515. 208 rooms. Restaurant, pool, exercise room. AE, D, DC, MC, V.*

$$$$ 🏨 **Sheraton Cleveland City Center Hotel.** This hotel is geared to business travelers, with upgraded communications systems and plenty of phones and work space in all rooms. ✉ *777 St. Clair Ave., 44114,* ☎ *216/771–7600 or 800/321–1090 in OH,* FAX *216/566–0736. 475 rooms. Restaurant, health club. AE, D, DC, MC, V.*

$$$–$$$$ 🏨 **Ramada Inn–Southeast.** This seven-story suburban hotel, with a restful, blue-and-gray lobby, provides easy access to Sea World and Geauga Lake. ✉ *24801 Rockside Rd. (at I–271), Bedford Heights 44146,* ☎ FAX *330/439–2500. 130 rooms. Restaurant, pool. AE, D, DC, MC, V.*

$$$ 🏨 **Mario's International Spa and Hotel.** A charming country getaway full of antiques and Victorian draperies, the spa started out as a hair salon. The restaurant, which is open to the public, has a private area for robe-clad spa diners. Meals are wholesome but tasty, ranging from Roman pizza to six-course northern Italian dinners. ✉ *35 E. Garfield Rd. (Rtes. 82 and 306), Aurora 44202,* ☎ *330/562–9171,* FAX *330/562–2386. 14 rooms. Restaurant, health club. AE, D, DC, MC, V.*

$ 🏨 **Brooklyn YMCA.** Bare-bones single rooms for men are available on a first-come, first-served basis. ✉ *3881 Pearl Rd., 44109,* ☎ *216/749–2355. 69 rooms. Pool, exercise room. D, MC, V.*

Motels

Motels are concentrated around the Berea–Middleburg Heights exit off I–71 (near the airport), the Rockside Road/Brecksville exit off I–77, and the Chagrin Boulevard/Beachwood exit off I–271. Closer to Aurora, rates are higher in summer. 🏨 **Aurora Woodlands Best West-**

ern Inn (✉ 800 N. Aurora Rd., Aurora 44202, ☎ 330/562–9151), 140 rooms, restaurant, pool, exercise room; $$$$. **Radisson Inn Beachwood** (✉ 26300 Chagrin Blvd., Beachwood 44122, ☎ 330/831–5150 or 800/221–2222), 203 rooms, restaurant, pool, exercise room; $$$$. **La Siesta Motel** (✉ 8300 Pearl Rd., Strongsville 44136, ☎ 440/234–4488), 38 rooms; $$$–$$$$. **Quality Inn Airport** (✉ 16161 Brook Park Rd., Cleveland 44142, ☎ 440/267–5100 or 800/228–5151, FAX 440/267–2428), 153 rooms, pools; $$.

Nightlife and the Arts

Nightlife

Nightlife is concentrated on both banks of the Flats—where the crowd is young and into everything from oldies rock to punk rock—as well as in the more mature Warehouse District. At the south end of the Flats, the **Powerhouse** is a beautifully restored building that was originally a power station for Cleveland's trolley cars; today it houses the Improv Comedy Club (☎ 216/696–4677) and other shops and restaurants. For a look at the Flats the way it used to be—a blue-collar haven—stop in at the **Harbor Inn** bar (✉ 1219 Main Ave., ☎ 216/241–3232). **Wilbert's** (✉ 1360 W. 9th St., ☎ 216/771–2583), between the Warehouse District and the Flats, specializes in roots rock and roll. At **Liquid Café & Bar** (✉ 1212 W. 6th St., ☎ 216/479–7717), in the Warehouse District, patrons sit in comfy chairs playing Scrabble and other board games. Across the river in Ohio City, Market Avenue is lined with sidewalk cafés. In the center of the action here is the **Great Lakes Brewing Company** (✉ 2516 Market Ave., ☎ 216/771–4404). **Market Avenue Wine Bar** (✉ 2526 Main Ave., ☎ 216/696–9463) has a brilliant wine list, and live piano jazz on weekends.

The Arts

Playhouse Square Center (✉ 1501 Euclid Ave., at E. 17th St., ☎ 216/771–8403) is home to the Cleveland Ballet, Cleveland Opera, and the Great Lakes Theater Festival. The **Cleveland Play House** (✉ 8500 Euclid Ave., ☎ 216/795–7000) and **Karamu House** (✉ 2355 E. 89th St., ☎ 216/795–7070) are near University Circle. **Severance Hall** (✉ 11001 Euclid Ave., ☎ 216/231–1111) is home to the Cleveland Orchestra, except during summer, when the orchestra moves to a pastoral outdoor shed, **Blossom Music Center** (☎ 330/566–8184 or 888/225–6776), between Cleveland and Akron. Tickets to many events are sold through **TicketMaster** (☎ 216/241–5555) and **Advantix** (☎ 216/241–6000).

Spectator Sports

Baseball: Cleveland Indians (✉ Jacobs Field, 2401 Ontario St., at Carnegie Ave., ☎ 216/420–4200). **Basketball: Cavaliers** (✉ Gund Arena, Ontario St. at Huron Rd., ☎ 216/420–2000). **Football: Cleveland Browns** (✉ W. 3rd. and Lakeside., ☎ 216/891–5000).

Shopping

Cleveland has two glitzy downtown malls, the **Galleria** (✉ 1301 E. 9th St., ☎ 216/861–4343) and the **Avenue** (✉ Tower City Center, ☎ 216/241–8550), with views of the river. The **West Side Market** (✉ Corner of W. 25th St. and Lorain Rd.), the world's largest indoor/outdoor farmers' market, sells freshly baked breads, fruit picked that morning, and perhaps the sharpest cheddar cheese you've ever eaten.

ELSEWHERE IN OHIO

Neil Armstrong Air and Space Museum

Arriving and Departing

The museum is off I–75, halfway between Cincinnati and Toledo (about an hour from either), in Wapakoneta, Neil Armstrong's hometown.

What to See and Do

Ohio is a leading producer of astronauts. At the **Neil Armstrong Air and Space Museum** (✉ I–75 Exit 111, ☎ 419/738–8811; 🎫 $5), you can begin to identify with these explorers. The museum is closed from December through February.

Dayton

Arriving and Departing

Dayton is 54 mi north of Cincinnati on I–75, just below the interchange with I–70. **Dayton International Airport** is served by several major carriers and commuter lines.

What to See and Do

Aviation is central to the history of Dayton. The **Dayton/Montgomery County Convention and Visitors Bureau** (✉ 1 Chamber Plaza, Suite A, 5th and Main Sts., 45402, ☎ 937/226–8211 or 800/221–8235) publishes a helpful visitors' guide and operates an information center at the United States Air Force Museum (☞ *below*).

The **Dayton Aviation Heritage National Historical Park** (☎ 937/225–7705) includes the field where Dayton natives Orville and Wilbur Wright first practiced flying, as well as the **Wright Brothers Bicycle Shop** (✉ 22 S. Williams St.), the **Wright Memorial,** and the home of a Wright Brothers associate, noted African-American poet Paul Laurence Dunbar.

The **United States Air Force Museum** (✉ Wright-Patterson Air Force Base, Springfield Pike, ☎ 937/255–3284; 🎫 free), an internationally known attraction, explains the story of flight, from Icarus to the Space Age. The **IMAX theater** shows flight-related films several times daily (☎ 937/253–4629; 🎫 $5). Also here are museum shops, a café, and picnic tables. Take I–75 to the Route 4/Harshman Road Exit.

South of Dayton, the **National Afro-American Museum and Cultural Center** (✉ 1350 Brush Row Rd., Wilberforce 45384, ☎ 937/376–4944; 🎫 $4) is one of the largest African-American museums in the United States. Among the many exhibits exploring history and art is the permanent From Victory to Freedom, which examines black politics from the '40s through the '60s. To get here, take Route 72 to Route 42. The museum is closed Monday.

Dining and Lodging

$$$ ✕ **Pine Club** Fresh, panfried trout, extra-thick lamb chops, and stewed tomatoes are the house specialties in this aptly named restaurant with pine-paneled walls and a large bar in the center. ✉ *1926 Brown St.,* ☎ *937/228–7463. AE, D, DC, MC, V. No lunch, closed Sun.*

$$ ✕ **Clifton Mill.** Among America's oldest gristmills, this historic site lies along the scenic Little Miami River. Southern-style breakfasts and lunches are served; just follow the scent of freshly baked breads. ✉ *75 Water St., Clifton,* ☎ *937/767–5501. AE, MC, V. No dinner.*

$$$$ ✕🏨 **Crowne Plaza.** Big plush chairs will make you feel right at home in the rooms. From the rooftop restaurant you can often see military jets cruising to and from the nearby Air Force.✉ *5th and Jefferson Sts.,*

45402, ☎ 937/224–0800, FAX 937/224–1231. 284 rooms. 2 restaurants, pool. AE, D, DC, MC, V.

$$ **Signature Inn.** Guests receive discounts at local eateries, shops, and fitness centers. Some rooms are equipped with Jacuzzis for rest and relaxation. ✉ *250 Byers Rd., Miamisburg, 45342, ☎ 937/865–0077, FAX 937/865–0077. 125 rooms. Pool. CP. AE, D, DC, MC, V.*

Akron

Arriving and Departing

Akron is about 25 mi south of Cleveland, off I–77.

What to See and Do

The **Akron/Summit Convention and Visitors Bureau** (☎ 330/374–7560 or 800/245–4254) has information on attractions and events around the Rubber City, where you just might catch the Goodyear blimp landing across from Goodyear Park. **Inventure Place and National Inventors Hall of Fame** honors famous inventors and inventions in a striking museum in downtown Akron. In the spirit of encouraging future inventors, the museum has one room full of computers, which you're invited to play with and even disassemble. ✉ *221 S. Broadway, at University Ave., ☎ 330/762–4463 or 800/968–4332.*

Dining and Lodging

$$$–$$$$ ✕ **Inn at Turner's Mill.** Just outside of Akron, this country cove is cozy and inviting, with a fireplace and a straightforward menu of Midwestern game and fresh vegetables. There's live jazz on weekends. ✉ *36 E. Streetsborough Rd., Hudson, ☎ 330/656–2949. MC, V.*

$–$$ ✕ **Luigi's.** Come here for crisp-crust pizza, piping-hot pasta, and red wine served in carafes. A miniature big band plays above the entranceway when you put a nickel in the jukebox. ✉ *105 N. Main St., ☎ 330/253–2999. No credit cards.*

$$$$ **Sheraton Suites–Akron/Cuyahoga Falls.** In a lovely wooded area near downtown Cuyahoga Falls, this all-suites hotel has kitchenettes and ironing boards. ✉ *1989 Front St., Cuyahoga Falls 44221, ☎ 330/929–3000, FAX 330/929–3031. 209 rooms. Restaurant, pool. AE, D, DC, MC, V.*

$$–$$$ **Comfort Inn–Akron West.** Some rooms in this no-frills hotel have whirlpool tubs. ✉ *130 Montrose Ave. 44321, ☎ 330/666–5050, FAX 330/668–2550. 133 rooms. Pool. AE, D, DC, MC, V.*

Canton

Arriving and Departing

Canton is about 50 mi south of Cleveland, off I–77.

What to See and Do

The **Canton/Stark County Convention & Visitors Bureau** (✉ 229 Wells Ave. NW, Canton 44703, ☎ 330/452–0243 or 800/533–4302) maintains an information center along the approach road to the Hall of Fame. The **Pro Football Hall of Fame** (✉ 2121 George Halas Dr. NW, Fulton Rd. Exit off I–77 and U.S. 62, ☎ 330/456–8207) has a dome shaped like a football in kickoff position. Two enshrinement halls are the serious purpose, but displays include a chronology of the game, mementos of the great players, and video replays showing great moments in football.

Dining and Lodging

$$$ ✕ **Bender's Tavern.** Jerry Jacob has fresh ingredients flown in for his top-quality preparations. The turn-of-the-century barn and livery has been in the Jacob family for more than 60 years and is still going strong. ✉ *132 Court Ave., SW, Canton, ☎ 330/656–2949. MC, V.*

$$$ ✕ **Cité Grille.** The friendly, trendy waitstaff sets a clipping pace for an evening of brisk fun and smart contemporary cuisine. ✉ *6041 Whipple Ave.,* ☎ *330/494–6758. AE, MC, V.*

$$$$ 🏨 **Canton Hilton.** Rooms are bright and sunny at this hotel near the Pro Football Hall of Fame and shopping centers. ✉ *320 Market Ave. S, 44703,* ☎ *330/454–5000,* FAX *330/454–5494. 170 rooms. Restaurant, pool. AE, D, DC, MC, V.*

$$ 🏨 **Sheraton at Belden Village.** You can try your hand at a golf simulator at this hotel in Canton's shopping district. A free shuttle takes guests to the Hall of Fame. ✉ *44718,* ☎ *330/494–6494,* FAX *330/494–7129. 152 rooms. Restaurant, pool. AE, D, DC, MC, V.*

WISCONSIN

By Don Davenport

Updated by Joanne Kempinger Demski

Capital	Madison
Population	5,169,700
Motto	Forward
State Bird	Robin
State Flower	Wood violet
Postal Abbreviation	WI

Statewide Visitor Information

Wisconsin Department of Tourism (✉ Box 7976, Madison 53707, ☎ 608/266–2161 or 800/432–8747).

Information centers: I–90N at Rest Area 22, near Beloit; I–94E at Rest Area 25, near Hudson; I–94N at Rest Area 26, near Kenosha; I–90E at Rest Area 31, near La Crosse; Route 12N at Rest Area 24, near Genoa City; Prairie du Chien, at the Route 18 bridge; 201 W. Washington Ave., Madison; Highways 2 and 53 in Superior; Highways 151 and 61 near Dickeyville; Highways 51 and 2 in Hurley; and at 342 N. Michigan Ave., in Chicago, Illinois.

Scenic Drives

As part of the **Great River Road,** scenic Route 35 follows the Mississippi River between Prairie du Chien and Prescott. Route 107, between Merrill and Tomahawk, travels along the 400-mi-long **Wisconsin River valley.** In northeastern Wisconsin Routes 57 and 42 circle the **Door County Peninsula,** providing 250 mi of spectacular Lake Michigan scenery.

National and State Parks

National Park

Apostle Islands National Lakeshore(☞ Elsewhere in Wisconsin, *below*).

State Parks

Wisconsin's state park system includes 48 parks and recreation areas, nine forests, and numerous trails. Camping is allowed in 36 state parks and seven state forests. The **Wisconsin Department of Natural Resources** (✉ Bureau of Parks and Recreation, Box 7921, Madison 53707, ☎ 608/266–2181) provides information.

Devil's Lake State Park (✉ S5975 Park Rd., Baraboo 53913, ☎ 608/356–8301) is one of the state's most popular, with hiking, camping, and 500-ft-high bluffs overlooking Devil's Lake. **Pattison State Park** (✉ 6294 S. State Rd. 35, Superior 54880, ☎ 715/399–3111) is distinctive for the 165-ft Big Manitou Falls, Wisconsin's highest waterfall and the fourth highest east of the Rocky Mountains. **Peninsula State Park** (✉ Hwy. 42, Fish Creek 54212, ☎ 920/868–3258) covers nearly 4,000 acres on the shores of Green Bay. With golf, hiking, bicycling, and lakeshore camping facilities, it is one of the state's most heavily used parks. **Wyalusing State Park** (✉ 13342 County Rte. C, Bagley 53801, ☎ 608/996–2261) stands at the confluence of the Wisconsin and Mississippi rivers, providing sweeping vistas of the river valleys.

MILWAUKEE

On the shores of Lake Michigan, Wisconsin's largest city is an international seaport and the state's primary commercial and manufacturing center. A small-town atmosphere prevails in Milwaukee, which is not so much a city as a large collection of neighborhoods. Modern steel-and-glass high-rises occupy much of the downtown area, but its early heritage persists in the restored and well-kept 19th-century buildings that share the city skyline. First settled by Potawatomi and later by French fur traders in the late 18th century, the city boomed in the 1840s with the arrival of German brewers, whose influence is still present. Milwaukee has also become known as a city of festivals, the biggest being Summerfest and the Great Circus Parade (☞ Festivals and Seasonal Events *in* the Midwest and Great Lakes introduction).

Visitor Information

Greater Milwaukee: Convention and Visitors Bureau (✉ 510 W. Kilbourn Ave., 53203, ☎ 414/273–7222 or 800/231–0903).

Arriving and Departing

By Bus

Greyhound Lines (✉ 606 N. 7th St., ☎ 800/231–2222).

By Car

From the north, I–43 provides controlled access into downtown Milwaukee. I–94 leads to downtown from Chicago and other points south and west of the city. If you are traveling to sites in the wider metropolitan area, from I–94 you can connect to I–894, which bypasses central Milwaukee.

By Plane

General Mitchell International Airport (✉ 5300 S. Howell Ave., ☎ 414/747–5300), 6 mi south of downtown via I–94, is served by several domestic and international carriers. **Milwaukee County Transit System** (☎ 414/344–6711) operates buses to and from the airport; fare is $1.35, and exact change is required. Taxis between the airport and downtown take about 20 minutes; fare runs from $16 to $18.

By Train

Amtrak (✉ 433 W. St. Paul Ave., ☎ 800/872–7245).

Getting Around Milwaukee

Lake Michigan is the city's eastern boundary; Wisconsin Avenue is the main east–west thoroughfare. The Milwaukee River divides the downtown area east and west. The East–West Expressway (I–94/I–794) is the dividing line between north and south. Streets are numbered in ascending order from the Milwaukee River west well into the suburbs. Many downtown attractions are near the Milwaukee River and can be reached on foot. **Milwaukee County Transit System** (☞ Arriving and Departing by Plane, *above*) provides bus service. **Taxis** can be ordered by phone; try **Yellow Cab** (☎ 414/271–1800) or **City Veterans** (☎ 414/291–8080).

Exploring Milwaukee

Downtown

Milwaukee's central business district is 1 mi long and only a few blocks wide and is divided by the Milwaukee River. On the east side the **Iron Block Building** (✉ N. Water St. and E. Wisconsin Ave.) is one of the few remaining ironclad buildings in the United States. Its metal facade was brought in by ship from an eastern foundry and installed during the Civil War. In the 1860s Milwaukee exported more wheat than any other port in the world; the mass exportation gave impetus to the building of the **Grain Exchange Room** in the Mackie Building (✉ 225 E. Michigan St.). The 10,000-square-ft trading room has three-story-high columns and painted ceiling panels depicting Wisconsin wildflowers.

★ The **Milwaukee Art Museum**(✉ 750 N. Lincoln Memorial Dr., ☎ 414/224–3200; 🎟 $5), in the lakefront War Memorial Center, houses notable collections of paintings, drawings, sculpture, photography, and decorative arts. Its permanent collection is strong in European and American art of the 19th and 20th centuries. The museum is closed on Monday.

En route from the lakefront to the river, stop a moment at **Cathedral Square.** This quiet park (✉ E. Kilbourn Ave. and Jefferson St.) was built on the site of Milwaukee's first courthouse. Across the street from Cathedral Square, **St. John's Cathedral** dedicated in 1853, was the first Roman Catholic cathedral built in Wisconsin.

The **Milwaukee County Historical Center** (✉ 910 N. Old World 3rd St., ☎ 414/273–8288; 🎟 free), a museum housed in a former bank building, displays early firefighting equipment, military artifacts, toys, and women's fashions. It also contains a research library with naturalization records and genealogical resources.

The banks of the Milwaukee River are busy in summer, especially at noon, when downtown workers lunch in the nearby parks and public areas such as **Père Marquette Park** (✉ Old World 3rd St. and W. Kilbourn Ave.), on the river.

There are also **river cruises** of Milwaukee's harbor and lakefront during warm weather; call the Convention and Visitors Bureau (☞ *above*) for details on cruise companies.

As you cross the river to the west side, notice that the east-side streets are not directly opposite the west-side streets and that the bridges across the river are built at an angle. This layout dates from the 1840s, when the area east of the river was called Juneautown and the region to the west was known as Kilbourntown. The rival communities had a fierce argument over which would pay for the bridges that connected them; so intense was the antagonism that citizens venturing into rival territory carried white flags. The Great Bridge War, as it was called, was finally settled by the state legislature in 1845, but the streets on either side of the river were never aligned.

★ Considered among the best natural history museums in the country, the **Milwaukee Public Museum** (✉ 800 W. Wells St., ☎ 414/278–2702; 🎟 $5.50; $9.75 for museum and IMAX) is known for its collection of more than 6 million specimens and artifacts. Its award-winning walk-through exhibits include the "Streets of Old Milwaukee," depicting the city in the 1890s; a two-story rain forest; and the "Third Planet" (complete with full-size dinosaurs), where visitors walk into the interior of the Earth to learn about its history. Within the museum, the **Humphrey IMAX Dome Theater** (🎟 $6.50) is run in cooperation with Discovery World.

Discovery World, as the **James Lovell Museum of Science, Economics, and Technology** (✉ 712 W. Wells St., ☎ 414/765–9966; 🎟 $5) in the Milwaukee Public Museum is called, has more than 140 interactive exhibits on magnets, motors, electricity, health, and computers. It also puts on the "Great Electric Show" and the "Light Wave–Laser Beam Show" on weekends and some weekdays.

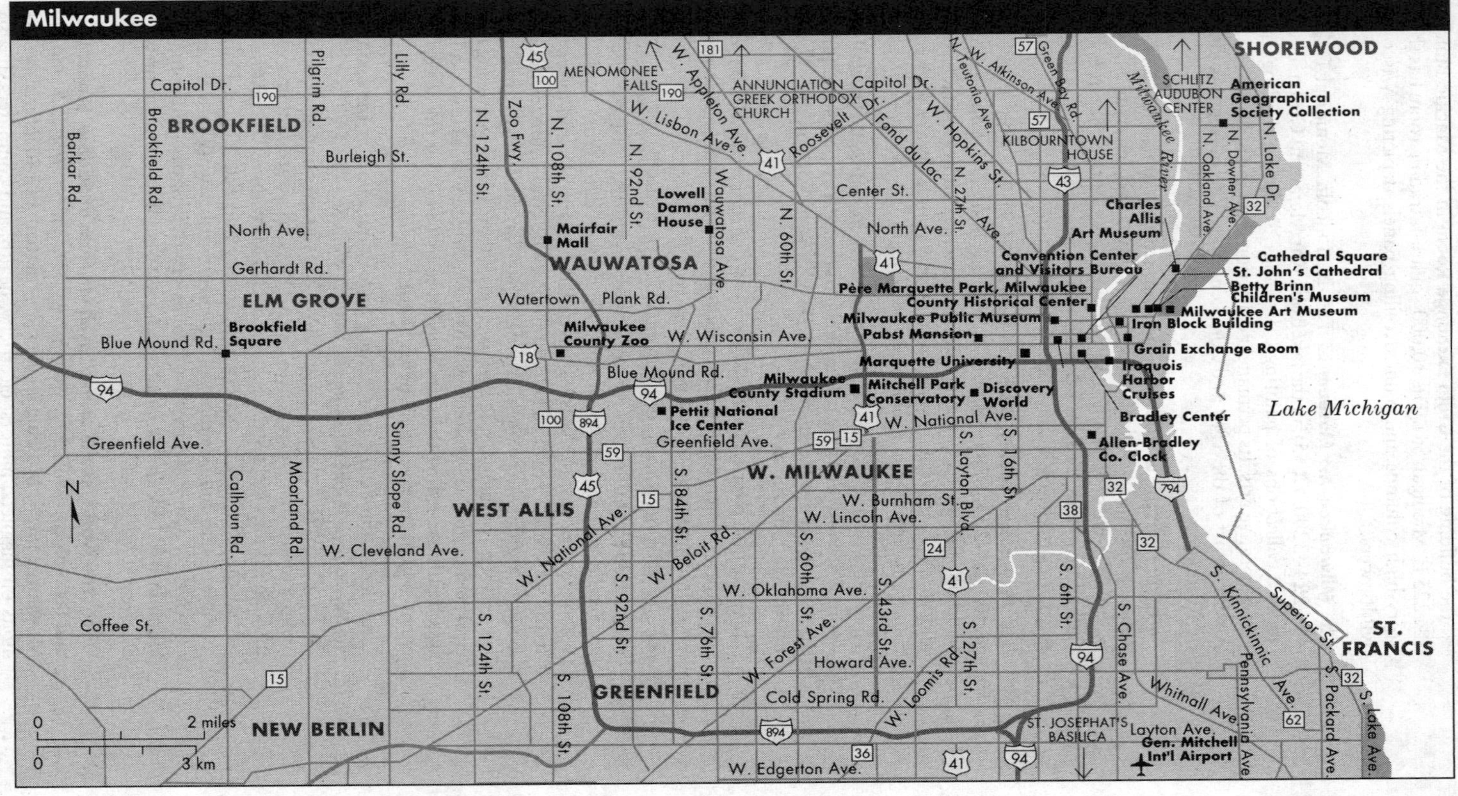
Milwaukee
SHOREWOOD
SCHLITZ AUDUBON CENTER
American Geographical Society Collection
N. Lake Dr.
N. Downer Ave.
N. Oakland Ave.
Milwaukee River
Charles Allis Art Museum
Convention Center and Visitors Bureau
Cathedral Square
St. John's Cathedral
Betty Brinn Children's Museum
Milwaukee Art Museum
Iron Block Building
Grain Exchange Room
Iroquois Harbor Cruises
Bradley Center
Allen-Bradley Co. Clock
Lake Michigan
Père Marquette Park, Milwaukee County Historical Center
Milwaukee Public Museum
Pabst Mansion
Marquette University
Mitchell Park Conservatory
Discovery World
Milwaukee County Stadium
Pettit National Ice Center
Milwaukee County Zoo
Brookfield Square
Mairfair Mall
Lowell Damon House
KILBOURNTOWN HOUSE
ANNUNCIATION GREEK ORTHODOX CHURCH
MENOMONEE FALLS
Capitol Dr.
W. Appleton Ave.
W. Lisbon Ave.
Roosevelt Dr.
Fond du Lac Ave.
W. Hopkins St.
N. Teutonia Ave.
W. Atkinson Ave.
Green Bay Rd.
Center St.
North Ave.
N. 27th St.
N. 60th St.
N. 92nd St.
N. 108th St.
N. 124th St.
Wauwatosa Ave.
Zoo Fwy.
Watertown Plank Rd.
W. Wisconsin Ave.
Blue Mound Rd.
Greenfield Ave.
W. National Ave.
BROOKFIELD
ELM GROVE
WAUWATOSA
W. MILWAUKEE
WEST ALLIS
GREENFIELD
NEW BERLIN
ST. FRANCIS
Barkar Rd.
Brookfield Rd.
Pilgrim Rd.
Lilly Rd.
Burleigh St.
Gerhardt Rd.
Calhoun Rd.
Moorland Rd.
Sunny Slope Rd.
W. Cleveland Ave.
Coffee St.
W. Burnham St.
W. Lincoln Ave.
W. Beloit Rd.
W. Oklahoma Ave.
W. Forest Ave.
Howard Ave.
Cold Spring Rd.
W. Loomis Rd.
W. Edgerton Ave.
S. 124th St.
S. 108th St.
S. 92nd St.
S. 84th St.
S. 76th St.
S. 60th St.
S. 43rd St.
S. 27th St.
S. Layton Blvd.
S. 16th St.
S. 6th St.
S. Chase Ave.
Whitnall Ave.
Layton Ave.
Pennsylvania Ave.
S. Kinnickinnic Ave.
Superior St.
S. Packard Ave.
S. Lake Ave.
ST. JOSEPHAT'S BASILICA
Gen. Mitchell Int'l Airport
N
0
2 miles
0
3 km

St. Joan of Arc Chapel (☎ 414/288–6873; 🎫 free), a small, stone 15th-century chapel, was moved from its original site near Lyon, France, in 1964 and reconstructed on the central mall of the Marquette University campus. One of the stones was reputedly kissed by Joan before she was sent to her death and is discernibly colder than the others.

The **Patrick and Beatrice Haggerty Museum of Art** (✉ 13th and Clybourn Sts., ☎ 414/288–7290; 🎫 free) houses Marquette University's collection of more than 6,000 works of art, including Renaissance, Baroque, and modern paintings, sculpture, prints, photography, and decorative arts; it also has changing exhibitions.

★ The **Pabst Mansion** (✉ 2000 W. Wisconsin Ave., ☎ 414/931–0808; 🎫 $7), completed in 1892 for the beer baron Captain Frederick Pabst, is one of Milwaukee's treasured landmarks. The 37-room Flemish Renaissance–style mansion has a tan pressed-brick exterior with carved-stone and terra-cotta ornamentation. Inside are woodwork, ironwork, marble, tile, and stained glass.

★ Milwaukee's **Mitchell Park Conservatory** (✉ 524 S. Layton Blvd., ☎ 414/649–9800; 🎫 $3.25) consists of three 85-ft-high glass domes housing tropical, arid, and seasonal plants and flowers; its lilies and poinsettias are spectacular at Easter and Christmas.

Other Attractions

The **Allen-Bradley Co. Clock** (✉ 1201 S. 2nd St.) is a Milwaukee landmark and, according to the *Guinness Book of Records,* "the largest four-faced clock in the world." Great Lakes ships often use the clock as a navigational reference point.

The **American Geographical Society Collection** (✉ 2311 E. Hartford Ave., ☎ 414/229–6282; 🎫 free), in the Golda Meir Library on the University of Wisconsin–Milwaukee campus, has an exceptional assemblage of maps, old globes, atlases, and charts, plus about 200,000 books and journals. It's closed on weekends.

The **University of Wisconsin** (☎ 414/229–5070) has three worthwhile art venues: the **Institute of Visual Arts** (✉ 3253 N. Downer Ave.), **Gallery Three** (✉ 2400 E. Kenwood Blvd.), and **Gallery Two** (✉ 3203 N. Downer Ave.). All three venues show avant-garde exhibits by regional, national, and international artists, and all three are closed Monday and Tuesday. Admission is free.

The **Charles Allis Art Museum** (✉ 1801 N. Prospect Ave., ☎ 414/278–8295; 🎫 $2), closed Monday and Tuesday, occupies an elegant Tudor-style house built in 1911 for the first president of the Allis-Chalmers Manufacturing Company. The home has stained-glass windows by Louis Comfort Tiffany and a stunning worldwide collection of paintings and objets d'art, including works by major 19th- and 20th-century French and American painters.

The **Lowell Damon House** (✉ Wauwatosa Ave. and Rogers St., ☎ 414/273–8288; 🎫 free), completed in 1847, is a classic example of Colonial-style architecture. It is open Wednesday and Sunday only.

The **Annunciation Greek Orthodox Church** (✉ 9400 W. Congress St., ☎ 414/461–9400; 🎫 $2) was Frank Lloyd Wright's last major work; the famed Wisconsin architect called it his "little jewel." Since it opened in 1961, the blue-domed Byzantine-style church has drawn visitors from all over the world. It can only be seen on Tuesday and Friday by prearranged group tour.

Built by immigrant parishioners and local craftsmen at the turn of the century, **St. Josephat's Basilica** (✉ 601 W. Lincoln Ave., ☎ 414/645–

5623; 🎫 $2) has a copper dome modeled after the one atop St. Peter's in Rome. Inside is a remarkable collection of relics.

The **Pettit National Ice Center** (✉ 500 S. 84th St., ☎ 414/266–0100; 🎫 $4) has an Olympic-size skating rink, two hockey rinks, and plenty of space for jogging. Visitors can spend time on the ice or watch local Olympic speed skaters practice.

Betty Brinn Children's Museum (✉ 929 E. Wisconsin Ave., ☎ 414/291–0888; 🎫 $3), closed Monday, is a hands-on museum for children ages 10 and under.

Outside Milwaukee

★ **Old World Wisconsin** (✉ S103 W37890 Hwy. 67, ☎ 414/594–6300; 🎫 $10.25), the State Historical Society's living history museum near Eagle, celebrates the state's ethnic heritage in architecture, with more than 65 historic buildings on 576 acres in the Southern Kettle Moraine State Forest. The restored farm and village buildings gathered from across the state depict 19th- and 20th-century rural Wisconsin. All were originally built and inhabited by European immigrants; they are grouped in German, Norwegian, Danish, and Finnish farmsteads. Costumed interpreters representing each ethnic group relate the story of immigration to Wisconsin and perform chores, such as making soap, that were intrinsic to rural life a century ago. The museum is open from May through October. From January through March, the forest is open for cross-country skiing (🎫 $4 per person).

Kohler is a planned, landscaped village surrounding the factories of the plumbing-fixtures manufacturer Kohler Company. The **Kohler Design Center** (✉ 101 Upper Rd., ☎ 920/457–3699; 🎫 free) houses the company's ceramic art collection, archives, and artifacts from an earlier factory and village, plus a showroom of model bathrooms. There are daily guided tours of **Waelderhaus** (✉ W. Riverside Dr., ☎ 920/452–4079; 🎫 free), a reproduction of founder John M. Kohler's ancestral home in Austria.The **Woodlake Kohler Complex**, in nearby Sheboygan, comprises more than 25 shops, galleries, and restaurants. The **American Club** (✉ Highland Dr., ☎ 920/457–8000 or 800/344–2838; 🎫 free), built as a company-owned hotel for workers, is now a posh resort hotel on the National Register of Historic Places. The compound has two 18-hole golf courses, an indoor sports complex, a 500-acre wilderness preserve, and several restaurants.

Parks, Gardens, and Zoos

★ The 660-acre **Whitnall Park** (✉ 5879 S. 92nd St., in suburban Hales Corners), one of the largest municipal parks in the nation, has an 18-hole golf course, recreational facilities, picnic areas, and nature and cross-country skiing trails. Within the park is the internationally famous **Alfred L. Boerner Botanical Gardens** (☎ 414/425–1130;🎫 free), with trees, shrubs, and flowers in formal and informal gardens. The park's **Wehr Nature Center** (☎ 414/425–8550; 🎫 free) has wildlife exhibits, woodlands and wetlands, a lake, nature trails, and wild gardens.

Forests, ponds, marshland, and nature trails attract nature lovers to the **Schlitz Audubon Center** (✉ 1111 E. Brown Deer Rd., ☎ 414/352–2880; 🎫 $4), a 225-acre wildlife area with an environmental research and education center. It's closed on Monday.

★ 👶 The **Milwaukee County Zoo** (✉ 10001 W. Bluemound Rd., ☎ 414/771–3040; 🎫 $6) has more than 3,000 wild animals and birds, including endangered species. Educational programs, a petting zoo, narrated tram tours, miniature-train rides, and cross-country skiing trails are additional draws.

Dining

A German culinary influence is much in evidence here; Milwaukee restaurants are also noted for their decadent desserts. For price ranges *see* Chart 1 (A) *in* On the Road with Fodor's.

$$$ ★ ✕ **Grenadier's.** Imaginative dishes such as tenderloin of veal with raspberry sauce combine classical French influences with Asian or Indian flavors and are served in the dining room and the handsome, darkly furnished piano bar. ✉ *747 N. Broadway St.,* ☏ *414/276–0747. Jacket required. AE, D, DC, MC, V. Closed Sun. No lunch Sat.*

$$$ ✕ **Harold's.** Velvet-back booths, low lighting, etched glass, and rich greenery set a romantic, if slightly generic, mood at this restaurant in the Grand Milwaukee Hotel. Oysters Rockefeller and rack of lamb Provençal are typical of the traditional fare. ✉ *4747 S. Howell Ave.,* ☏ *414/481–8000. AE, D, DC, MC, V. Closed Sun. No lunch Sat.*

$$$ ★ ✕ **Sanford.** Nationally acclaimed chef Sanford D'Amato serves contemporary American cuisine in this elegant restaurant in a remodeled grocery store. ✉ *1547 N. Jackson St.,* ☏ *414/276–9608. AE, D, DC, MC, V. Closed Sun. No lunch.*

$$$ ★ ✕ **Steven Wade's Cafe.** Creative dishes distinguish Steven Wade's: Try marinated duck breasts pan-roasted with cranberry-pecan Chambord sauce, or seared steer tenderloin and coffee-cognac demi-glace with garlic-mashed potatoes. Once a residence, the café has a casual, intimate atmosphere with a small bar. ✉ *17001 W. Greenfield Ave., New Berlin,* ☏ *414/784–0774. AE, D, DC, MC, V. Closed Sun. No lunch Sat. and Mon.*

$$–$$$ ✕ **Bartolotta.** On a quaint street in the village of Wauwatosa, Bartolotta is known for its rustic Italian cuisine, especially fresh fish. ✉ *812 N. 68th St.,* ☏ *414/771–7910. AE, D, DC MC, V. Closed Sun., no lunch Sat.*

$$–$$$ ✕ **Boder's on the River.** With tieback curtains, fireplaces, and antiques, this family-owned and -operated restaurant in the suburbs has a cheerful country look. Roast duckling and baked whitefish are a few of the Wisconsin specialties. Come for Sunday brunch or the Friday-night seafood buffet. ✉ *11919 N. River Rd. 43W, Mequon,* ☏ *414/242–0335. AE, D, DC, MC, V. Closed Mon.*

$$–$$$ ✕ **Boulevard Inn.** Continental cuisine is served at this elegant restaurant overlooking Lake Michigan. Diners can enjoy Caesar salad and honey duck served at their table while listening to contemporary piano music. Sit-down brunch is served on Sundays. Reservations are recommended. ✉ *925 E. Wells St.,* ☏ *414/765–1166. AE, D, DC, MC, V.*

$$–$$$ ★ ✕ **English Room.** In the Pfister Hotel, Milwaukee's premier hotel restaurant has a formal atmosphere and plenty of original 19th-century paintings. Recommended dishes are rack of lamb, seared crab cakes, and lobster-and-shrimp bisque. ✉ *424 E. Wisconsin Ave.,* ☏ *414/390–3832. AE, D, DC, MC, V. No lunch.*

$$–$$$ ✕ **Giovanni's.** This bright Sicilian eatery serves large portions of rich Italian food. Veal steak Giovanni is excellent, and pasta is a sure bet. ✉ *1683 N. Van Buren St.,* ☏ *414/291–5600. AE, D, DC, MC, V. No lunch weekends.*

$$–$$$ ✕ **Jake's.** There are two locations for this longtime Milwaukee favorite that earned its reputation with perfectly prepared steaks and heaps of french-fried onion rings. Not to be missed are the fresh fish selections, escargot, roast duckling, and Bailey's chocolate-chip cheesecake. ✉ *6030 W. North Ave., Wauwatosa,* ☏ *414/771–0550;* ✉ *21445 W. Capitol Dr., Brookfield,* ☏ *414/781–7995. AE, DC, MC, V. No lunch.*

$$–$$$ ★ ✕ **Karl Ratzsch's Old World Restaurant.** In the authentic German atmosphere of this family-owned restaurant, dirndl-skirted waitresses serve schnitzel, roast duckling, and sauerbraten. The main dining room is decked out with murals, chandeliers made from antlers, and antique beer steins. Piano music on Friday and Saturday nights adds to the fun. ✉ *320 E. Mason St.,* ☎ *414/276–2720. AE, D, DC, MC, V. No lunch.*

$$ ✕ **Chip and Py's.** In the northern suburbs, this stylish restaurant has light gray dual-level dining rooms, a huge fireplace, and contemporary art. There's an eclectic menu and live jazz on weekends and Wednesday evenings. ✉ *1340 W. Town Square Rd., Mequon,* ☎ *414/241–9589. AE, D, DC, MC, V. Closed Mon. No lunch Sun.*

$$ ✕ **Elsa's on the Park.** Across from Cathedral Square Park, this chic but casual restaurant has frequently changing art exhibits and serves big, juicy hamburgers and pork-chop sandwiches. ✉ *833 N. Jefferson St.,* ☎ *414/765–0615. AE, MC, V. No lunch weekends.*

$–$$ ✕ **Three Brothers.** Set in an 1887 tavern, one of Milwaukee's revered ethnic restaurants serves chicken *paprikash* (a stewed chicken dish with paprika), roast goose and duck, boneless leg of lamb stuffed with spinach and cheese, Serbian salad, and homemade desserts at old-style kitchen tables. It's about 10 minutes from downtown, on the near south side. ✉ *2414 S. St. Clair St.,* ☎ *414/481–7530. No credit cards. Closed Mon. No lunch.*

$ ✕ **De Marinis.** These popular Italian-American restaurants have excellent pizza and pasta. The pesto-and-artichoke-packed Garden Pizza is one of the best. ✉ *N88 W15229 Main St., Menomonee Falls,* ☎ *414/253–1568;* ✉ *1211 E. Conway St.,* ☎ *414/481–2348. AE, D, MC, V.*

$ ✕ **Watts Tea Shop.** This genteel spot for breakfast, lunch, or tea with scones is above George Watts & Sons, Milwaukee's premier store for china, crystal, and silver. Indulge in fresh-squeezed juice and a custard-filled sunshine cake. ✉ *761 N. Jefferson St.,* ☎ *414/291–5120. AE, D, MC, V. Closed Sun. No dinner.*

Lodging

In summer accommodations should be booked well ahead, especially for weekends. For price ranges *see* Chart 2 (A) *in* On the Road with Fodor's.

$$$–$$$$ ★ **Pfister Hotel.** Milwaukee's grandest old hotel dates from 1893. Rooms in the tower, which was added in 1975, are bright and contemporary with a Victorian accent in keeping with the original hotel. A collection of 19th-century art hangs in the elegant Victorian lobby. ✉ *424 E. Wisconsin Ave., 53202,* ☎ *414/273–8222 or 800/558–8222,* FAX *414/273–0747. 307 rooms. 3 restaurants, pool. AE, D, DC, MC, V.*

$$$ ★ **Wyndham Milwaukee Center.** In the center of the city's growing theater district by the river, the Wyndham has an opulent lobby tiled with Italian marble. Guest rooms are contemporary, with mahogany furnishings. The hotel has an excellent Sunday brunch as well as a pasta bar. ✉ *139 E. Kilbourn Ave., 53202,* ☎ *414/276–8686 or 800/996–3426,* FAX *414/276–8007. 221 rooms. Restaurant, health club. AE, D, DC, MC, V.*

$$–$$$ ★ **Embassy Suites–Milwaukee West.** The sweeping atrium lobby, with fountains, potted plants, and glass elevators, is the focal point of this hotel in the western suburbs. The two-bedroom suites are a medley of pastels and earth tones. ✉ *1200 S. Moorland Rd., Brookfield 53005,* ☎ *414/782–2900 or 800/444–6404,* FAX *414/796–9159. 203 suites. Restaurant, pool, exercise room. AE, D, DC, MC, V.*

$$–$$$ **Grand Milwaukee Hotel.** Across from the airport, the Grand is the largest hotel in the state, with a cinema and nightclub as well as extensive sports and recreation facilities. The marble-walled lobby is il-

luminated with chandeliers. ✉ *4747 S. Howell Ave., 53207,* ☎ *414/481–8000 or 800/558–3862,* FAX *414/481–8065. 510 rooms. 2 restaurants, pools, tennis, health club. AE, D, DC, MC, V.*

$$–$$$ **Hyatt Regency.** This centrally located high-rise hotel has an 18-story open atrium and a revolving rooftop restaurant. ✉ *333 W. Kilbourn Ave., 53203,* ☎ *414/276–1234 or 800/233–1234,* FAX *414/276–6338. 484 rooms. 2 restaurants, exercise room. AE, D, DC, MC, V.*

$$ **Astor Hotel.** Close to Lake Michigan, the Astor has the air of a grand old hotel. Most of the rooms have been remodeled and furnished with antiques and period reproductions. Even the bathrooms are equipped with antique fixtures. ✉ *924 E. Juneau Ave., 53202,* ☎ *414/271–4220 or 800/558–0200,* FAX *414/271–6370. 97 rooms. Restaurant. AE, D, DC, MC, V.*

Motels

Best Western Midway Hotel–Airport (✉ 5105 S. Howell Ave., 53207, ☎ 414/769–2100 or 800/528–1234, FAX 414/769–0064), 139 rooms, restaurant, pool; *$$.* **Holiday Inn South–Airport** (✉ 6331 S. 13th St., 53221, ☎ 414/764–1500 or 800/465–4329, FAX 414/764–6531), 159 rooms, restaurant, pool; *$$.* **Holiday Inn Express** (✉ 11111 W. North Ave., Wauwatosa 53226, ☎ 414/778–0333 or 800/465–4329, FAX 414/778–0331), 122 rooms; *$–$$.*

Nightlife and the Arts

Milwaukee Magazine (on newsstands) lists arts and entertainment events. Also check the daily entertainment sections of the *Milwaukee Journal Sentinel.*

Nightlife

You'll find clubs, bars, and a slew of friendly saloons. The **Safe House** (✉ 779 N. Front St., ☎ 414/271–2007), with a James Bond spy-hideout decor, is a favorite hangout for young people and out-of-towners. **Major Goolsby's** (✉ 340 W. Kilbourn Ave., ☎ 414/271–3414) is regarded as one of the country's top-10 sports bars. Jazz fans go to the **Estate** (✉ 2423 N. Murray Ave., ☎ 414/964–9923).

The Arts

Milwaukee's theater district is in a two-block downtown area bounded by the Milwaukee River, East Wells Street, North Water Street, and East State Street. Most tickets are sold at box offices.

The **Riverside Theater** (✉ 116 W. Wisconsin Ave., ☎ 414/224–3000) hosts touring theater companies, Broadway shows, and other entertainment. The **Pabst Theater** (✉ 144 E. Wells St., ☎ 414/286–3663) presents live entertainment. The Milwaukee Center (✉ 108 E. Wells St., ☎ 414/224–9490) is home to the **Milwaukee Repertory Theater.** The **Marcus Center for the Performing Arts** (✉ 929 N. Water St., ☎ 414/273–7206) comprises the **Milwaukee Symphony Orchestra, Milwaukee Ballet Company, Florentine Opera Company,** and **First Stage Milwaukee.**

Spectator Sports

Baseball: Milwaukee Brewers (✉ Milwaukee County Stadium, 201 S. 46th St., ☎ 414/933–9000). **Basketball: Milwaukee Bucks** (✉ Bradley Center, 1001 N. 4th St., ☎ 414/227–0500). **Hockey: Milwaukee Admirals** (✉ Bradley Center, 1001 N. 4th St., ☎ 414/227–0550).

Beaches

Lake Michigan is the place to swim, but be prepared: Mid-summer water temperatures linger in the 50s and 60s. Among the most popular of the narrow sandy beaches are **Bradford Beach** (✉ 2400 N. Lincoln Memorial Dr.), **Doctors Beach** (✉ 1870 E. Fox La., Fox Point), **Grant Beach** (✉ 100 Hawthorne Ave., South Milwaukee), and **McKinley Beach** (✉ 1750 N. Lincoln Memorial Dr.). The **Milwaukee County Aquatic Department** (☎ 414/645–4095) has information.

Shopping

Using the downtown skywalk system, it's possible to browse in hundreds of stores over several blocks without once setting foot outside. Downtown Milwaukee's major shopping area is on Wisconsin Avenue west of the Milwaukee River. The major downtown retail center, the **Grand Avenue Mall** (✉ 275 W. Wisconsin Ave.), spans four city blocks and has 130 specialty shops and kiosks and 17 eateries. **Historic Third Ward,** a turn-of-the-century wholesale and manufacturing district listed on the National Register of Historic Places, borders the harbor, the river, and downtown. Two Milwaukee landmarks, **Usinger's Sausage** and **Mader's Restaurant**, are near the Historic Third Ward, on Old World 3rd Street, where several interesting stores and markets can also be found. **Jefferson Street,** stretching four blocks from Wisconsin to Kilbourn, is lined with upscale stores and shops. **George Watts and Son, Inc.** (✉ 761 N. Jefferson St., ☎ 414/291–5120) has more than a thousand patterns of china, silver, and crystal.

In the metropolitan area, near the Milwaukee County Zoo, **Mayfair Mall** (✉ 2500 N. Mayfair Rd., Wauwatosa) has more than 160 shops that surround a multistory atrium complete with swaying bamboo. Some 145 stores at **Northridge Shopping Center** (✉ 7700 W. Brown Deer Rd.) include a Younkers department store, Boston Store, Sears, and JC Penney. Wisconsin's largest shopping center, **Southridge Mall** (✉ 5300 S. 76th St., Greendale) has more than 145 specialty stores and five major department stores. **Brookfield Square** (✉ 95 N. Moorland Rd., Brookfield) is a sprawling suburban complex with about 100 stores. **Bayshore** (✉ 5900 N. Port Washington Rd., Glendale) has about 70 stores, including Sears and the Boston Store.

About 40 minutes south of downtown Milwaukee, on I–94E, you'll find two large discount shopping malls. The **Factory Outlet Centre,** just off Highway 50, has more than 100 stores with brand-name merchandise. Two miles south of the Factory Outlet Centre, off Highway 165, is **Lakeside Market Place** with more than 75 designer outlet stores.

Side Trip to Cedarburg

Visitor Information

Cedarburg Chamber of Commerce (✉ W63 N645 Washington Ave., Box 104, Cedarburg, 53012, ☎ 414/377–9620).

Arriving and Departing

Take I–94 West to I–43 North, then get off at the Cedarburg Exit (County C). Drive west to Washington Avenue, Cedarburg's main street.

What to See and Do

The entire downtown district of Cedarburg, most of it built of Niagara limestone by 19th-century pioneers, is on the National Register of Historic Places. Victorian "Painted Ladies" with beautifully landscaped yards are abundant. Throughout a nine-block area you'll find antiques shops, crafts shops, candy stores, and restaurants. Weekend flea markets take place in May, July, September, and October.Within the Wittenberg Woolen Mill, which was first built in 1864, **Cedar Creek Settlement** (✉ N70 W6340 Bridge Rd., ☎ 800/827–8020) is a collection of crafts and antiques shops. Also within the mill is a winery (🎫 $2). Wisconsin's last remaining **covered bridge** (✉ off Hwy. 143) crosses Cedar Creek 3 mi north of town. The 120-ft white-pine bridge was built in 1876 and retired in 1962. A small park beside the bridge invites picnicking.

ELSEWHERE IN WISCONSIN

Madison and Southern Wisconsin

Visitor Information

Greater Madison Convention and Visitors Bureau (✉ 615 E. Washington Ave., 53703, ☎ 608/255–2537 or 800/373–6376).

Arriving and Departing

Take I–94 west from Milwaukee to Madison.

What to See and Do

Madison, named after President James Madison, is the state capital and home to the University of Wisconsin. The center of the city lies on an eight-block-wide isthmus between lakes Mendota and Monona. The Roman Renaissance–style **Wisconsin State Capitol** (☎ 608/266–0382; 🎫 free), built between 1906 and 1917, dominates the downtown skyline; there are tours daily. A **farmers' market** is held on Capitol Square every Saturday from May through October. The **State Historical Society Museum** (✉ 30 N. Carroll St., Capitol Sq., ☎ 608/264–6555; 🎫 free) has permanent and changing exhibits on Wisconsin history, from prehistoric Native American cultures to contemporary social issues. The museum is closed Mondays.

Capitol Square is connected to the university's campus by State Street, a mile-long tree-lined shopping district of imports shops, ethnic restaurants, and artisans' studios. The **Madison Art Center,** in the lobby of the **Civic Center** (✉ 211 State St., ☎ 608/257–0158; 🎫 free), has a large permanent collection and frequent temporary exhibitions. It's closed on Mondays.

The **University of Wisconsin,** which opened in 1849 with 20 students, now has an enrollment of about 40,000. The university's **Elvehjem Museum of Art** (✉ 800 University Ave., ☎ 608/263–2246; 🎫 free) is one of the state's best, with a permanent collection of paintings, sculpture, and decorative arts dating from 2300 BC to the present. Away from downtown, the **University Arboretum** (✉ 1207 Seminole Hwy., ☎ 608/263–7888; 🎫 free) has more than 1,200 acres of natural plant and animal communities, such as prairie and forest landscapes, and horticultural collections of upper Midwest specimens.

On the shore of Lake Monona, **Monona Terrace Community and Convention Center** (✉ 1 John Nolen Dr., ☎ 608/261–4000; 🎫 $2), Madison's newest downtown showpiece, includes a rooftop garden, café, sports hall of fame room, gift shop, and a memorial to singer Otis Redding, who died in a plane crash not far from the center. Designed by Frank Lloyd Wright in 1937 but not completed until 1997, the 250,000 sq-ft structure is open to the public for guided tours.

The **Henry Vilas Zoo** (✉ 702 S. Randall Ave., ☎ 608/266–4732; 🎫 free) has exhibits of nearly 200 animal species, plus a petting zoo. On Madison's south side, **Olbrich Botanical Gardens** (✉ 3330 Atwood Ave., ☎ 608/246–4550; 🎫 gardens free, conservatory $1) has 14 acres of outdoor rose, herb, and rock gardens and a glass-pyramid conservatory with tropical plants and flowers.

Blue Mounds is at the eastern edge of Wisconsin's lead-mining region. At **Blue Mound State Park** (✉ 2 mi northwest of Blue Mounds, ☎ 608/437–5711), towers on one of the hill's summits provide glorious vistas. **Cave of the Mounds** (✉ Cave of the Mounds Rd., ☎ 608/437–3038; 🎟 $9) is small, but filled with diverse and colorful mineral formations. It's closed weekdays from mid-November to mid-March.

Nestled in a picturesque valley near Blue Mounds is **Little Norway** (✉ 3576 Hwy. JG North, Blue Mounds, ☎ 608/437–8211; 🎟 $7), a restored 1856 Norwegian homestead with its original log buildings and an outstanding collection of Norwegian antiques and pioneer arts and crafts. It's open from May through October.

Founded in 1845 by Swiss settlers from the canton of Glarus, the village of **New Glarus** retains its Swiss character in language, food, architecture, and festivities. The **Swiss Historical Village** (✉ 612 7th Ave., ☎ 608/527–2317) contains original buildings and reconstructions from early New Glarus, as well as displays that trace Swiss immigration to America.

Frank Lloyd Wright chose the farming community of **Spring Green,** on the Wisconsin River, for his home Taliesin and for his architectural school. Wright's influence is evident in a number of buildings in the village; notice the use of geometric shapes, low flat-roofed profiles, cantilevered projections, and steeplelike spires. There are summertime walking tours of the Wright-designed buildings at **Taliesin** (✉ 3 mi south of Spring Green on Hwy. 23, ☎ 608/588–7900), including his home and office for nearly 50 years, the 1903 Hillside Home School, galleries, a drafting studio, and a theater. Walking tours range from $8 to $60; the more expensive ones include admission to buildings along the way. Between November and April, tours are by shuttle bus ($10).

The extraordinary multilevel, stone **House on the Rock** (✉ 5754 Hwy. 23, ☎ 608/935–3639; 🎟 $15.50), closed from January through mid-March, stands atop a 60-ft chimney of rock overlooking the Wyoming Valley. Begun by artist Alex Jordan in the early 1940s and opened to the public in 1961, the complex now contains re-creations of historic village streets complete with shops, as well as extensive collections of dolls, cannons, and musical machines. Here you'll also find the world's largest carousel.

The renowned **American Players Theater** (✉ County Rte. C and Golf Course Rd., Box 819, Spring Green, ☎ 608/588–7401. 🎟 $19–$35) presents Shakespeare and other classics in a beautiful, wooded outdoor amphitheater near the Wisconsin River, every evening but Monday from mid-June through mid-October.

On the western edge of the state, **Prairie du Chien** dates from 1673, when explorers Marquette and Joliet reached the confluence of the Wisconsin and Mississippi rivers 6 mi to the south. It became a flourishing fur market in the late 17th century. Now a bustling river community, it's a summertime destination of the steamers *Delta Queen* and *Mississippi Queen.* The family of the fur trader Hercules Dousman (Wisconsin's first millionaire) built the **Villa Louis Mansion** (✉ 521 Villa Louis Rd., ☎ 608/326–2721; 🎟 $7.75) in 1870. Open to the public from May through October, it contains one of the finest collections of Victorian decorative arts in the country. The **Astor Fur Warehouse,** on the villa grounds, has exhibits on the fur trade of the upper Mississippi. Near the fur warehouse is **Wyalusing State Park** (☞ National and State Parks, *above*).

Dining

For price ranges *see* Chart 1 (B) *in* On the Road with Fodor's.

$$$$ ★ ✕ **White Horse Inn.** Behind the civic center, this local favorite serves a dynamite chicken Mafalda, a mélange of grilled chicken, sausage, leeks, and pasta in cream sauce. Sunday brunch draws a crowd. ✉ *202 N. Henry St., behind the Civic Center*, ☎ *608/255–9933. AE, MC, V. No lunch Sat.*

$$$ ★ ✕ **Pasta Per Tutti.** Fresh pasta and seafood and homemade breads and desserts make this contemporary Italian restaurant a local favorite. ✉ *2009 Atwood Ave.,* ☎ *608/242–1800. MC, V. No lunch.*

Lodging

Hotels in Madison should be booked well in advance. For price ranges *see* Chart 2 (A) *in* On the Road with Fodor's.

$$$$ **Sheraton Madison.** Across from the Dane County Expo Center and minutes from the State Capitol and campus, the Sheraton has modern, comfortable rooms. ✉ *706 John Nolen Dr., 53713,* ☎ *608/251–2300 or 800/325–3535,* FAX *608/251–1189. 279 rooms. 2 restaurants, pool, exercise room. AE, D, DC, MC, V.*

$$$–$$$$ **Madison Concourse Hotel.** A marble lobby greets visitors. ✉ *1 West Dayton St., 53703,* ☎ *608/257–6000 or 800/356–8293,* FAX *608/257–5280. 360 rooms. 2 restaurants, pool, exercise room. AE, D, DC, MC, V.*

Wisconsin Dells and Baraboo

Visitor Information

Baraboo Chamber of Commerce (✉ 124 2nd St., 53913, ☎ 608/356–8333 or 800/227–2266).

Wisconsin Dells Visitor and Convention Bureau (✉ 701 Superior St., Wisconsin Dells *53965,* ☎ 608/254–4636 or 800/223–3557).

Arriving and Departing

Take I–90 West from Milwaukee to Madison, then I–90/94 northwest to the Dells. Baraboo is off U.S. 12 to the south of I–90/94.

What to See and Do

One of the state's foremost natural attractions is the **Wisconsin Dells,** nearly 15 mi of soaring, eroded rock formations created over thousands of years as the Wisconsin River cut into soft limestone. The two small communities encompassed by the Dells—Wisconsin Dells and Lake Delton, with a combined population of fewer than 4,000—draw nearly 3 million visitors annually to frolic in the water parks, play miniature golf, and enjoy the rides, shows, and other planned attractions that today nearly overshadow the area's scenic wonders.

During the summer and fall tourist seasons you can view the river and its spectacular rock formations on cruise boats or aboard World War II amphibious vehicles that travel on both land and water. Several water parks have slides, wave pools, and inner-tube and raft rides. The notorious Confederate spy Belle Boyd, who died here while on a speaking tour in 1910, is buried in **Spring Grove Cemetery.**

When you need a break from the nonstop action, scenic **Mirror Lake State Park** (✉ just south of the Dells off U.S. 12, ☎ 608/254–2333) has campgrounds, hiking trails, and 20 mi of cross-country ski trails. **Rocky Arbor State Park** (✉ 1 mi north off U.S. 12, ☎ 608/254–8001 in summer, 608/254–2333 off-season) is another good choice for downtime, with camping, hiking, and great scenery.

South of Wisconsin Dells is **Baraboo,** former site of an early 19th-century fur-trading post run by a Frenchman named Baribault. It is best known as the place where the five Ringling brothers began their circus careers in 1882, and as the winter headquarters of their Ringling Brothers Circus from 1884 to 1918. The **Circus World Museum** (✉ 426 Water St., ☎ 608/356–8341; 🎫 $3.25), a State Historical Society site, preserves the history of the more than 100 circuses that began in Wisconsin. Along with an outstanding collection of antique circus wagons, the museum presents big-top performances (🎫 $11.95) from mid-May through mid-September, featuring circus stars of today.

Dining and Lodging

$$$ ✕ **Dell-Bar Steak House.** This 55-year old restaurant built in the Frank Lloyd Wright style serves seafood and meat dishes such as Killer Shrimp, pan-fried Walleye, osso buco, lamb chops, and prime rib. Expect a crackling fire in winter, and live piano music year-round. ✉ *800 Wisconsin Dells Pkwy., Lake Delton,* ☎ *608/253–1861. AE D, DC, MC, V.*

$$$$ 🏨 **Black Wolf Lodge.** This Northwoods–themed hotel and recreation facility has huge indoor and outdoor water activity centers including water slides and seven indoor and outdoor pools. Of the seven different styles of rooms, some have lofts, whirlpools, fireplaces, big-screen televisions, and/or patios. ✉ *I–90/94 and Hwy. 12, Wisconsin Dells, 53965,* ☎ *800/559–9653,* FAX *608/253–2224. 204 rooms. Restaurant, pools, exercise room. AE, D, DC, MC, V.*

Door County

Arriving and Departing

Take I–43 north from Milwaukee to Green Bay, then Route 57 north.

What to See and Do

Jutting out from the Wisconsin mainland like the thumb on a mitten, 70-mi-long **Door County Peninsula** is bordered by the waters of Lake Michigan and Green Bay. It was named for the Porte des Morts (Door of Death), a treacherous strait separating the peninsula from nearby offshore islands. Scores of ships have come to grief in Door County waters, but today large Great Lakes freighters often slip through the Door to seek shelter in the lee of the islands during Lake Michigan's autumn storms. Soil conditions and climate make the peninsula ideal for cherry and apple production, and its orchards produce more than 20 million pounds of fruit each year. The peninsula is carpeted in blossoms when the trees bloom in late May.

A visit to the peninsula can include stops at a half dozen quaint lakeshore towns, each filled with charming restaurants, shops, and inns. First-time visitors often make a circle tour via Routes 57 and 42. The Lake Michigan side of the peninsula is somewhat less settled and the landscape rougher. The peninsula's rugged beauty attracts large numbers of artists, whose works are shown in studios, galleries, and shops in all the villages.

Sturgeon Bay, the peninsula's chief community and a busy shipbuilding port, sits on a partially man-made ship canal connecting the waters of Lake Michigan and Green Bay. Here the **Door County Maritime Museum** (✉ 120 N. Madison Ave, at the foot of the bridge leading into town, ☎ 920/743–5958; 🎫 $4.50) has displays on local shipbuilding and commercial fishing.

Beside Route 57, along the peninsula's Lake Michigan side, you can see the rocky shoreline and sea caves at **Cave Point County Park,** near Valmy. Just north of **Jacksonport** you'll cross the 45th parallel, halfway between the equator and the north pole.

Northport, at the tip of the Door County Peninsula, is the port of departure for the daily car ferries to **Washington Island,** 6 mi offshore; passenger ferries leave from nearby Gills Rock. The island's 600 inhabitants celebrate their heritage with an annual **Scandinavian festival,** in August. Narrated tram tours aboard the Washington Island *Cherry Train* (☎ 920/847–2039; 🎫 $6) or the *VikingTour Train* (☎ 920/854–2972; 🎫 $6, or $13 for tour-and-ferry package) leave from the ferry dock between late May and mid-October. The island has nearly 100 mi of roads that are great for cycling. You may take your own bicycle on the ferry or rent one on the island. To get away from it all, take the ferry from Washington Island to remote **Rock Island State Park,** a wilderness area permitting only hiking and backpack camping.

Back on the mainland, villages on the **Green Bay** side of the peninsula evoke New England in atmosphere and charm and provide exceptional views of Green Bay, where sunsets can be breathtaking. **Fish Creek** is home to the **Peninsula Players Theater** (☎ 847/864–6104; 🎫 $19.50–$26), allegedly America's oldest professional resident summer theater. Here, too, is beautiful **Peninsula State Park,** where hiking and bicycling trails abound.

Complete your visit to Door County by sampling the region's famed **fish boil,** which originated more than 100 years ago. It's a simple but delicious meal that has reached legendary status in the region. A huge caldron of water is brought to a boil over a wood fire. A basket of red potatoes is cooked in the caldron, followed by a basket of fresh local whitefish steaks. At the moment the fish is cooked to perfection, kerosene is dumped on the fire, and the flames shoot high in the air, causing the caldron to boil over, expelling most of the fish oils and fat. The steaming whitefish is then served with melted butter, potatoes, coleslaw, and another favorite, Door County cherry pie. The **Door County Chamber of Commerce** (✉ Box 406, Sturgeon Bay 54235-0406, ☎ 920/743–4456 or 800/527–3529) provides information on county attractions.

Dining and Lodging

$$–$$$ ✕ **Al Johnsons Swedish Restaurant and Butik.** Goats graze on the grass roof of this locally famous restaurant, a breakfast hot spot. Specialties include Swedish limpa bread, fruit soups, and wafer-thin pancakes topped with fresh fruit and whipped cream. ✉ *702 N. Bay Shore Dr., Sister Bay,* ☎ *920/854–2626. AE, D, MC, V.*

$$–$$$ ✕ **Paulson's.** This airy, Victorian cottage–like restaurant serves Swedish meatballs, whitefish, prime rib, and pastas. Be sure to visit the Victorian gift shop and bakery, where cherry muffins are sold. No liquor is served. ✉ *10341 Hwy. 42, Ephraim,* ☎ *920/854–5717. D, MC, V. Closed Dec. and Jan. and weekdays Nov.–mid-May.*

$$ ✕ **The Cookery.** Door County products—mostly cherries—are used in many of the dishes on this restaurant's breakfast, lunch, and dinner menus. Don't miss the cherry muffins and cherry-chocolate-chip coffee cake. The pantry offers goodies to go. ✉ *Main St. and Hwy. 42, Fish Creek,* ☎ *414/868–3634. Closed weekdays Nov., Jan.–Feb., first 2 weeks of Apr. Closed Mar. and first 3 weeks of Dec.*

$$ ✕ **Sister Bay Café.** This quaint café on Sister Bay's main street serves Scandinavian-American specials such as Norwegian farmer's stew, heart-shape waffles topped with strawberries and whipped cream, and *risegrot*—a hot, creamy rice pudding–like dish that's a breakfast favorite. ✉ *611 Bay Shore Dr., Sister Bay,* ☎ *920/854–2429. DC, MC, V. Closed Jan.–Mar., and some weekends off-season.*

$$$$ ★ ✕🏨 **White Gull Inn.** Since 1896 the White Gull has provided intimate lodging and excellent food. Cottages and rooms are rustic and old-fashioned, with hardwood floors, canopy beds, braided rugs, and porches.

Lamb, beef, and seafood dishes with unusual sauces are served in the candlelit, antiques-filled restaurant. ✉ *4225 Main St., Fish Creek 54212,* ☎ *920/868–3517,* FAX *920/868–2367. 9 rooms, 5 cottages. Restaurant. AE, D, DC, MC, V.*

$$$–$$$$ ★ **Inn at Cedar Crossing.** At this inn in Sturgeon Bay's historic district you can sample some of the area's best cuisine before retiring upstairs in a room with a four-poster bed, fireplace, whirlpool, and sitting area. ✉ *336 Louisiana St., Sturgeon Bay 54235,* ☎ *920/743–4200,* FAX *920/743–4422. 9 rooms. D, MC, V.*

$$$$ ★ **Baileys Harbor Yacht Club Resort.** A 1,000-acre wildlife sanctuary and nature preserve near the waterfront provide the backdrop for the rooms, suites, villas, and cottages of this resort. Some suites have gas fireplaces and large whirlpool baths. ✉ *8150 Ridges Rd., Baileys Harbor 54202,* ☎ *920/839–2336 or 800/927–2492,* FAX *920/839–2093. 83 rooms. Pools, tennis. D, MC, V.*

$$$$ **Landmark Resort and Conference Center.** The largest resort in Door County, the Landmark is in a wooded area overlooking a golf course and rolling farmland. Many of its traditionally styled suites have spectacular views. ✉ *7643 Hillside Rd., Egg Harbor 54209,* ☎ *920/868–3205 or 800/273–7877,* FAX *920/868–2569. 293 suites. Restaurant, pools, exercise room, tennis. AE, D, DC, MC, V.*

$$ **High Point Inn.** This modern facility overlooks the town of Ephraim. Clean and comfortable one-, two-, and three-bedroom condominium suites are available. ✉ *10386 Water St., Ephraim 54211,* ☎ *920/854–9773 or 800/595–6894.,* FAX *920/854–9738. 42 rooms. Pools, exercise room. D, MC, V.*

$$ **White Lace Inn.** Guest rooms at this inn have plenty of white lace, as well as antiques, fireplaces, and whirlpools. Gardens surround the four houses, which are connected by a gazebo. There's also a cozy lobby with Victorian furniture and original hardwood floors, walls, and ceilings. ✉ *16 N. 5th Ave., Sturgeon Bay, 54235,* ☎ *920/743–1105. 19 rooms. AE, D, MC, V.*

Bayfield and the Apostle Islands

Visitor Information

Bayfield Chamber of Commerce (✉ Box 138, 54814, ☎ 715/779–3335 or 800/447–4094).

Madeline Island Chamber of Commerce (✉ Box 274, La Pointe 54850, ☎ 715/747–2801, FAX 715/747–2800).

Arriving and Departing

Take I–94 west from Milwaukee to Portage, U.S. 51 north to Hurley, U.S. 2 west to Ashland, and then Route 13 north to Bayfield.

What to See and Do

Known as the gateway to the Apostle Islands National Lakeshore, the commercial fishing village of **Bayfield,** population 700, also has some worthwhile attractions of its own. At the **Cooperage Museum** (✉ 1 Washington Ave., ☎ 715/747–2051; $3), Wisconsin's only working barrel factory and museum, you can learn about the art of barrel making from summer through fall. From fall through spring, **Lake Superior Big Top Chautauqua** (✉ 3 mi south of Bayfield off Hwy. 13, ☎ 715/373–5552; $12–$14) hosts concerts, plays, lectures, and original historical musicals under canvas in the spirit of old-time summer tent shows.

★ Accessible from Bayfield, the **Apostle Islands National Lakeshore** comprises 21 of Lake Superior's 22 Apostle Islands and a segment of mainland near Bayfield. Named by French missionaries who mistakenly thought the islands numbered 12, the Apostles encompass 42,000 acres spread over 600 sq mi of Lake Superior. Primitive camping and hiking are allowed on most of the islands. Sailing is a favorite pastime here, as is charter-boat fishing for lake trout or whitefish. At **Lakeshore headquarters** (⊠ Washington Ave. and 4th St., Box 4, Bayfield 54814, ☎ 715/779–3397) you'll find publications, exhibits, and a movie about the Apostle Islands. In summer the **Little Sand Bay Visitor Center** (⊠ 13 mi north of Bayfield on Rte. 13, ☎ 715/779–3459) has exhibits and daily guided tours of a former commercial fishing operation. **Stockton Island,** the largest island in the national lakeshore, has a visitor center (☎ 715/779–3397) with natural and cultural history exhibits and a park naturalist on duty. The island is closed from Labor Day to Memorial Day. There are guided tours of the **Raspberry Island Lighthouse** buildings and gardens as well as historic **Manitou Island Fish Camp,** on Manitou Island (closed Labor Day to Memorial Day).

From April to December the car- and passenger-carrying **Madeline Island Ferry** (⊠ Washington Ave., Bayfield, ☎ 715/747–2051) connects Bayfield to **Madeline Island.** Here the village of **La Pointe** was established in the early 17th century as a French trading post. The **Madeline Island Historical Museum** (⊠ Ferry Dock, La Pointe, ☎ 715/747–2415), on the site of a former fur-trading post, houses exhibits on island history. Narrated island tours are given by **Madeline Island Bus Tours** (⊠ Ferry Dock, La Pointe, ☎ 715/747–2051) from mid-June through Labor Day. **Big Bay State Park** (☎ 715/747–6425) has camping, a long sandy beach, picnic areas, and hiking and nature trails; sea kayaking and biking are especially popular.

Dining and Lodging

$$ ✕ **Maggie's Restaurant.** "Real food, real drinks, real fun, and fake flamingos" is the slogan at this casual, wood-paneled eatery, where flamingos and flamingo memorabilia are ubiquitous. Great burgers share the menu with more sophisticated fare. ⊠ *257 Manypenny Ave., Bayfield,* ☎ *715/779–5641. MC, V.*

$$ 🏨 **Winfield Inn.** Flower gardens and a large deck overlooking the bay and Madeline Island set this inn apart. The six apartments have kitchens. ⊠ *Rte. 1, Box 33, Bayfield, 54814,* ☎ *715/779–3252,* FAX *715/779–5180. 31 rooms, 6 apartments. AE, D, MC, V.*

8 The Great Plains

Iowa, Kansas, Missouri, Nebraska, North Dakota, Oklahoma, South Dakota

By Suzanne De Galan

THE NAME GREAT PLAINS EVOKES AN IMAGE of flat farmland stretching to the horizon, unbroken save for the occasional cluster of buildings marking a town or farmstead. Those who go there, however, know this limitless terrain destroys as many preconceived images as it confirms. The seemingly uniform landscape actually encompasses geography as diverse as the towering buttes that loom over the horizons of western South Dakota and the fertile river valleys that crisscross the eastern boundaries of Missouri and Kansas.

The cultural legacy of the Great Plains owes as much to such artists as Louis Sullivan and Grant Wood as to the cowboy and Native American artifacts that stud the region. And although European settlement came later here, St. Louis existed more than a decade before the signing of the Declaration of Independence; and Coronado had already explored Kansas two centuries before that.

Much is owed to the 1804–1806 expedition led by explorers Lewis and Clark who followed the Missouri River from St. Louis through the Dakotas, and then crossed the mountains to the Pacific coast. After fur traders came the railroad companies that lured thousands of immigrants with large, inexpensive parcels of land; towns sprang up along rail lines and pioneer trails; and Native Americans were inexorably forced into smaller and smaller territories. The sod-breaking plow and hardy winter wheat helped transform the long- and short-grass prairies of the high plains into America's breadbasket. In the remaining grasslands cattle fed where bison once reigned.

Life on the Great Plains in the 19th century was harsh and sometimes violent, yet it's a life that today's residents love to re-create. Countless historical theme parks and Old West towns dot the region, along with abundant archaeological and Civil War battle sites, U.S. Army forts, pioneer trail markers, and museums of Native American and pioneer lore. Great Plains folk think nothing of journeying 100 mi to see a building covered with thousands of bushels of corn (the Corn Palace in Mitchell, South Dakota) or wrecked cars arranged to resemble the monoliths of Stonehenge. This tendency achieves its ultimate expression in Mt. Rushmore, where the 60-ft faces of four U.S. presidents have been carved into a wall of South Dakota granite.

But alongside these landmarks and oddities lies another Great Plains. To know it, you must drive its hundreds of miles of roads bisecting fields of grain or leave the highway for one of its small towns, just to walk the Main Street and see the serene, mellow old houses. Here, somewhere between myth and reality, the true spirit of this region is revealed.

When to Go

The traditional tourist season for most of the Great Plains is **summer,** despite the soaring temperatures and high humidity. Many tourist attractions are open only during June, July, and August. Northern states, such as the Dakotas and Nebraska, are generally cooler, but you should be prepared for anything in this variable region. **Winter** weather is equally extreme, especially in Nebraska and the Dakotas, where subzero temperatures and snowy conditions are common. South Dakota offers cross-country skiing and snowmobiling, but again, make sure hotels and restaurants are open. **Spring** and **fall** can be excellent times to visit, with moderate temperatures and crowds at a minimum. Fall in the Ozarks or in such places as the eastern border of Iowa has the added attraction of colorful foliage.

Festivals and Seasonal Events

Winter

EARLY DEC.➢ **Christmas on the River** (☎ 816/741–2000), in **Parkville, Missouri,** has a 1,000-voice children's choir, Santa's arrival by riverboat, and performances of Dickens's *A Christmas Carol.*

Spring

APRIL➢ Nearly one million people enjoy fine art, food, and performances during **Oklahoma City's Festival of the Arts** (☎ 405/270–4848), a 32-year-old springtime tradition, held in Myriad Gardens.

MAY➢ **Oklahoma Cattlemen's Association Range Round-up** (☎ 405/282–3004) in **Guthrie** cowhands compete in saddle bronco riding, wild cow roping, and other contests.

JUNE➢ **Oklahoma Mozart International Festival** (☎ 918/336–9900) in **Bartlesville** holds concerts, barbecues, and powwows celebrating the composer and local culture. **Nebraskaland Days** (☎ 308/532–7939) is a Western hootenanny in **North Platte** that's highlighted by the Buffalo Bill Rodeo. The **Red Earth Native American Cultural Festival** (☎ 405/427–5228), in **Oklahoma City,** attracts hundreds of Native American dancers from the United States and Canada for competitions and performances.

LATE JUNE–EARLY JULY➢ **DeSmet, South Dakota** hosts the annual **Laura Ingalls Wilder Pageant** (☎ 605/854–3383 or 605/854–3181).

LATE JULY➢ The annual **Bix Beiderbeck Jazz Festival** (☎ 319/324–7170) is held in **Davenport, Iowa**'s riverfront park.

Summer

JULY➢ **Kansas City Blues & Jazz Festival** (☎ 816/753–3378 or 800/530–5266) features performances by nationally known blues and jazz artists on three stages. On Independence Day weekend, **National Tom Sawyer Days** (☎ 573/221–2477) features Americana-oriented activities such as fence painting in Mark Twain's hometown of **Hannibal, Missouri. Black Hills and Northern Plains Indian Powwow and Exposition** (☎ 605/394–4115) is the best known of many powwows held annually across South Dakota.

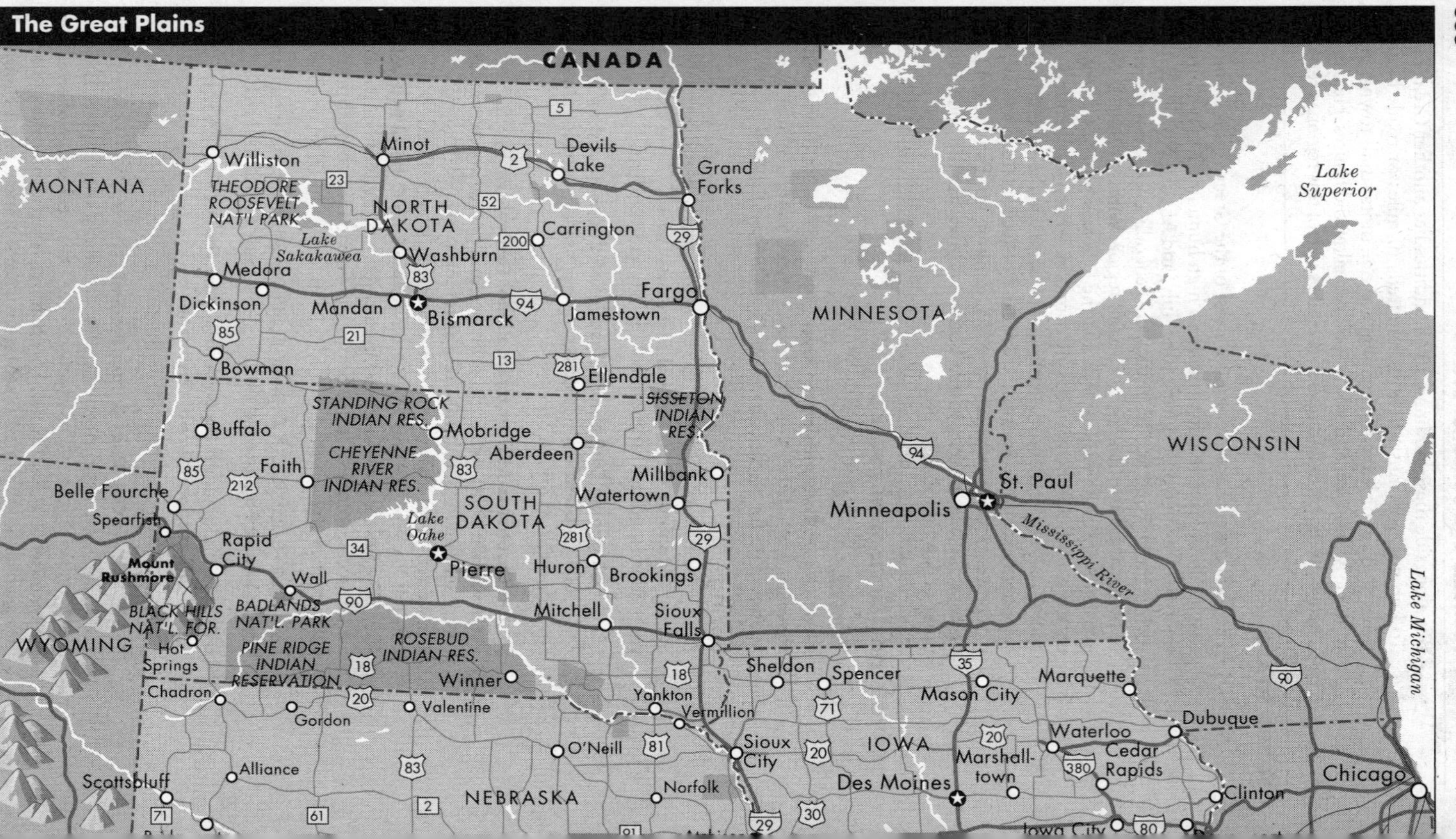
The Great Plains
CANADA
MONTANA
NORTH DAKOTA
SOUTH DAKOTA
MINNESOTA
WISCONSIN
IOWA
NEBRASKA
WYOMING
Lake Superior
Lake Michigan
Williston
Minot
Devils Lake
Grand Forks
THEODORE ROOSEVELT NAT'L PARK
Lake Sakakawea
Carrington
Washburn
Medora
Dickinson
Mandan
Bismarck
Jamestown
Fargo
Bowman
Ellendale
SISSETON INDIAN RES.
STANDING ROCK INDIAN RES.
Buffalo
Mobridge
Aberdeen
CHEYENNE RIVER INDIAN RES.
Faith
Millbank
Belle Fourche
Watertown
Spearfish
Lake Oahe
Rapid City
Mount Rushmore
Pierre
Huron
Brookings
Wall
BLACK HILLS NAT'L. FOR.
BADLANDS NAT'L PARK
Mitchell
Sioux Falls
ROSEBUD INDIAN RES.
Hot Springs
PINE RIDGE INDIAN RESERVATION
Winner
Chadron
Gordon
Valentine
Yankton
Vermillion
O'Neill
Alliance
Scottsbluff
Norfolk
Sioux City
Sheldon
Spencer
Mason City
Marquette
Dubuque
Waterloo
Cedar Rapids
Marshall-town
Des Moines
Clinton
Chicago
St. Paul
Minneapolis
Mississippi River

ILLINOIS
MISSOURI
KANSAS
OKLAHOMA
ARKANSAS
TENNESSEE
COLORADO
NEW MEXICO
TEXAS
Burlington
Keokuk
Hannibal
Alton
St. Louis
St. Genevieve
Cape Girardeau
Poplar Bluff
St. Charles
Ottumwa
Macon
Columbia
Jefferson City
Van Buren
West Plains
Kirksville
Lake of the Ozarks
Waynesville
Springfield
THE OZARKS
Osceola
Sedalia
Independence
Kansas City
Clinton
Joplin
Branson
Table Rock Lake
Council Bluffs
Omaha
Rock Port
St. Joseph
Atchison
Manhattan
Topeka
Lawrence
Emporia
Fort Scott
Coffeyville
Bartlesville
OSAGE INDIAN RES.
Muskogee
Tulsa
McAllister
Hugo
Atoka
Lincoln
Nebraska City
Auburn
Beatrice
El Dorado
Florence
Abilene
Wichita
Ponca City
Shawnee
Ardmore
Marietta
Grand Island
Hastings
Mankato
Hutchinson
Enid
Guthrie
Oklahoma City
Duncan
Kearney
Red Cloud
Waconda Lake
Russell
Great Bend
Medicine Lodge
Clinton
Elk City
Lawton
Altus
North Platte
Platte River
McCook
Oakley
Goodland
Scott City
Garden City
Dodge City
Liberal
Woodward
Guymon
Ogallala
McConaughy
Amarillo
Denver
150 miles
225 km
KEY
Amtrak Lines

JULY–AUG.➤ In **Kansas,** the **Dodge City Roundup Rodeo** (☎ 316/225–2244) is a five-day rodeo during the city's Dodge City Days festival.

AUG.➤ The **Iowa State Fair** (☎ 515/262–3111), in **Des Moines,** is a short course in farm machinery, animals, crops, and crafts; less bucolically minded visitors can enjoy carnival rides and musical entertainment. **Days of '76** (☎ 605/578–1876), in **Deadwood, South Dakota,** celebrates the town's wild and woolly gold rush days with a parade, a rodeo, and other activities. **Pioneer Days at Bonanzaville USA** (☎ 701/282–2822) transforms the pioneer village near **West Fargo, North Dakota,** into a living museum for two days, with costumed shopkeepers, tradespeople, and townspeople.

MID-AUG.➤ **Sturgis, South Dakota**'s **Black Hills Motor Classic** (a.k.a. **Sturgis Rally and Races**; ☎ 605/347–6570) draws more than 200,000 bike buffs from around the country each year. During the weeklong event many businesses turn their buildings over to sellers of leather goods, rally T-shirts, and other biker-related paraphernalia.

Autumn

SEPT.➤ **Santa-Cali-Gon Days** (☎ 816/252–4745), in **Independence, Missouri,** celebrates the opening of the West through the Santa Fe, California, and Oregon trails, all of which originated in this gateway town. The **United Tribes International Powwow** (☎ 701/255–3285) brings Native Americans from around the country to **Bismarck, North Dakota,** to hold dance competitions and celebrate cultural ties.

OCT.➤ **Octoberfest** (☎ 573/486–2744) in **Hermann, Missouri,** draws thousands of people each weekend to celebrate this Missouri River town's German and wine-making heritage. **Norsk Hostfest** (☎ 701/852–2368), in **Minot, North Dakota,** brings international crowds to sample Scandinavian culture through food, dancing, and costumes. The **Covered Bridge Festival** (☎ 515/462–1185) in **Winterset, Iowa,** includes tours of Madison County's six restored covered bridges as well as visits to sights made famous by the eponymous book and movie.

NOV.➤ The **American Royal** (☎ 816/221–5242 or 800/767–7700) is an annual celebration of **Kansas City**'s heritage, featuring rodeos, horse shows, livestock shows, and a no-holds-barred barbecue.

Getting Around the Great Plains

By Bus

The major intercity carrier is **Greyhound Lines** (☎ 800/231–2222). In addition, **Jefferson Lines** (☎ 612/332–8745 or 800/767–5333) serves some cities in Kansas, Missouri, Iowa, and Oklahoma. **Jackrabbit Lines** (☎ 605/348–3300) serves all of South Dakota and a few destinations in neighboring states. Many Greyhound stops in this region are small towns that have no ticket booth; call to check whether you must purchase your ticket in advance.

By Car

Three interstates converge at Oklahoma City: I–40, running east–west through Oklahoma; I–44, which proceeds northeast from Oklahoma City to Tulsa, Oklahoma, and through Missouri to St. Louis; and I–35, one of two major north–south arteries in the Great Plains. From Oklahoma City I–35 proceeds north through Wichita and Kansas City, Kansas, and Des Moines, Iowa. Another north–south route is I–29, which begins in Kansas City and runs along the eastern borders of Nebraska, South Dakota, and North Dakota, passing through Omaha, Sioux Falls, Fargo, and Grand Forks. Major east–west arteries are I–94 in North Dakota, which passes through Medora, the Bismarck-Mandan area, and Fargo; I–90 in South Dakota, running from Rapid City to Sioux Falls; I–80 through Nebraska and Iowa, which links North Platte, Lincoln, and Omaha with Des Moines and Iowa City; and I–70, which bisects Missouri and Kansas and links St. Louis with Kansas City and points west. Roads are generally in good condition throughout the region. However, these main arteries are often closed for short periods because of winter blizzard conditions.

By Plane

Major domestic carriers serve the region, including American, Continental, Delta, Northwest, United, and US Airways. The largest airports are in Missouri, **Lambert–St. Louis International Airport** (☎ 314/890–1333) and **Kansas City International Airport** (☎ 816/243–5237); in Iowa, **Des Moines International Airport** (☎ 515/256–5050 or 800/993–2556); in Oklahoma, **Will Rogers World Airport** (☎ 405/681–0050) and **Tulsa International Airport** (☎ 918/838–5000); and in South Dakota, **Sioux Falls Regional Airport** (☎ 605/336–0762).

By Train

Amtrak (☎ 800/872–7245) provides some service through the Great Plains but not necessarily to the major cities, and South Dakota and Oklahoma are not served at all.

IOWA

Updated by Diana Lambdin Meyer

Capital	Des Moines
Population	2,852,000
Motto	Our Liberties We Prize and Our Rights We Will Maintain
State Bird	Eastern goldfinch
State Flower	Wild rose
Postal Abbreviation	IA

Statewide Visitor Information

The **Division of Tourism** (✉ Iowa Department of Economic Development, 200 E. Grand Ave., Des Moines 50309, ☎ 515/242–4705 or 800/345–4692) has 21 welcome centers along I–35 and I–80 and in towns throughout the state. For regional visitor information call or write **Eastern Iowa Tourism Association** (✉ 116 E. 4th St., Box 485, Vinton 52349, ☎ 319/472–5135 or 800/891–3482), **Central Iowa Tourism Region** (✉ Box 454, Webster City 50595, ☎ 515/832–4808 or 800/285–5842), and **Western Iowa Tourism Region** (✉ 502 Coolbaugh St., Red Oak 51566, ☎ 712/623–4232 or 888/632–4232).

Scenic Drives

Iowa's most beautiful scenic drive is perhaps the series of roads that take you south along the high bluffs and verdant banks of the Mississippi River on the state's eastern border (☞ Dubuque and the Great River Road, *below*). In southeast Iowa **Route 5** from Des Moines to Lake Rathbun, near Centerville, makes a nice detour from I–35; to return to the interstate, take **Route 2W** from Centerville for about 50 mi.

National and State Parks

National Parks

Effigy Mounds National Monument (☞ Exploring Dubuque and the Great River Road, *below*) has scenic hiking trails along prehistoric burial mounds. Iowa has four federal reservoir areas around large man-made lakes: **Coralville Lake** (✉ 2850 Prairie du Chien Rd. NE, Iowa City 52240, ☎ 319/338–3543), **Rathbun Lake** (✉ Rte. 3, Centerville 52544, ☎ 515/647–2464), **Lake Red Rock** (✉ R.R. 3, Box 149A, Knoxville 50138-9522, ☎ 515/828–7522), and **Saylorville Lake** (✉ 5600 N.W. 78th Ave., Johnston 50131, ☎ 515/276–4656).

The **Walnut Creek National Wildlife Refuge** (✉ 9981 Pacific St., Prairie City 50228, ☎ 515/994–2415), 20 mi east of Des Moines on I–80, has 8,600 acres of reconstructed tallgrass prairie, 5 mi of hiking trails accessible to travelers with disabilities, a prairie education center, and an elk and bison viewing area.

State Parks

Iowa's 76 state parks include 5,700 campsites, many with shower facilities and electrical hookups. Some well-developed parks with modern campsites, cabins, lodge rentals, and boat rentals are **Clear Lake** (☎ 515/357–4212), near Mason City; **George Wyth Memorial** (☎ 319/232–5505), near Waterloo; **Lacey-Keosauqua** (☎ 319/293–3502), near Keosauqua; and **Lake of Three Fires** (☎ 712/523–2700), near Bedford. Virgin prairie areas, part of the state park system but lacking facilities, include **Cayler Prairie,** near the Great Lakes area in northwestern Iowa; **Hayden Prairie,** near the Minnesota border in the northeastern corner of the state;

Kalsow Prairie, about 90 mi northwest of Des Moines; and **Sheeder Prairie,** about 50 mi west of Des Moines. Contact the **Iowa Department of Natural Resources** (☎ 515/281–5145) for more information.

DES MOINES

Viewed from an airplane or a car topping a hill, the capital of Iowa is a cluster of office towers that seem to pop out of a green corduroy landscape. Downtown straddles the vee of two rivers—the Raccoon and the Des Moines; the '80s-built skyline faces granite government buildings and a classic gold-domed capitol across four bridges. Major businesses in this relatively hassle-free city of more than 400,000 residents include insurance, finance, publishing, and agribusiness. Although hardly a glittering metropolis, Des Moines has a number of museums, historic districts, and parks, as well as Drake University. The U.S. presidential race starts here with the Iowa caucuses, and every cultural wave breaks on Des Moines's shores—eventually.

Visitor Information

Des Moines visitor centers are in the **airport** lobby (☎ 515/287–4396) and in the **skywalk** above the corner of 6th and Locust streets downtown (☎ 515/286–4960).

Arriving and Departing

By Bus

Greyhound Lines (☎ 800/231–2222) and **Jefferson** (☎ 515/283–0074) share a terminal at Keosauqua Way and 12th Street.

By Car

I–80, the major east–west thoroughfare through the state, and I–35, Iowa's main north–south route, intersect northwest of Des Moines and link with I–235, which runs across the northern part of the city.

By Plane

Des Moines International Airport (☎ 515/256–5100), about 3 mi south of downtown, has scheduled service by major domestic airlines. The drive into town takes about 10 minutes in normal traffic. Cab fare, including tip, is less than $10. Hotel shuttles serve the route, and major car-rental companies are in the airport.

Getting Around Des Moines

Streets both in the city and in suburban Urbandale and West Des Moines are laid out in a grid, which makes getting around fairly easy. However, a car is essential, as attractions are scattered about the city and suburbs. Downtown is compact enough to explore in comfortable shoes.

Exploring Des Moines

Downtown

Start a walking tour of downtown Des Moines at the **capitol complex** (✉ E. 9th St. and Grand Ave., ☎ 515/281–5591 or 800/451–2625; 🎫 free), on the east bank of the Des Moines River. There you can see the elaborate murals in the rotunda of the capitol and climb into the dome, covered in 22-karat gold leaf. Near the capitol, the **Botanical Center** (✉ 909 E. River Dr., ☎ 515/242–2934; 🎫 $1.50) has flower displays and a three-story, dome-topped jungle. The **Iowa Historical Building** (✉ 600 E. Locust St., ☎ 515/281–5111; 🎫 free), one block west of the capitol, shakes off any dusty-old-stuff image with its postmodern design, abstract sculpture of neon and glass, and striking fountain display. The building houses the state archives, library, and museum.

Just west of downtown in Greenwood-Ashworth Park, the **Des Moines Art Center**(✉ 4700 Grand Ave., ☎ 515/277–4405; 🎫 $4; free until 1 PM) houses a permanent collection of contemporary art. The **Science Center of Iowa** (✉ 4500 Grand Ave., ☎ 515/274–6868 or 800/472–1014; 🎫 $5.50) in Greenwood-Ashworth Park, has interactive programs that include laser shows, a planetarium, and a space shuttle simulator appropriate for all ages.

Terrace Hill, an 1866 Victorian mansion known as the "palace of the prairie," is the Iowa governor's mansion. ✉ *2300 Grand Ave.,* ☎ *515/281–3604.* 🎫 *$5. Closed Sat.–Mon. and Jan.–Feb.*

Some of the city's most interesting historic buildings can be found on the west side of the Des Moines River (follow Locust Street from the east side). Self-guided walking tours are detailed in brochures from **Downtown Des Moines, Inc.** (✉ Suite 255, 400 Locust St., ☎ 515/243–6625). The **Sherman Hill Historic District** has impressive Victorian houses. The **Court Avenue District** contains a number of restored 19th-century warehouses and other commercial buildings, many of which now house shops, restaurants, and entertainment venues.

Outside the City

Living History Farms, a 600-acre open-air museum a few miles northwest of Des Moines, is well worth a half-day's exploration. The farms are a trip back in time through the sights, sounds, and smells of an 18th-century Native American village, two working farms of 1850 and 1900, and an 1875 town. ✉ *2600 N.W. 111th St., Urbandale 50322,* ☎ *515/278–2400.* 🎫 *$5. Closed Nov.–Apr. Call for special events in winter.*

Dining

Des Moines's staple fare is Italian, followed closely by Chinese food, although lately there has been a trend toward more exotic cuisines, such as Thai, Indian, and Middle Eastern. Downtown, sample Court Avenue's lineup of pubs and Italian, Tex-Mex, and Cajun places. For price ranges *see* Chart 1 (A) *in* On the Road with Fodor's.

$$$ ★ ✕ **Anna's.** Large chandeliers, an elevated bar, and a wall of wine bottles are distinctive features of this restaurant in the Savery Hotel downtown. The menu includes prime rib and lighter versions of Continental dishes. ✉ *401 Locust St.,* ☎ *515/244–2151. AE, D, MC, V. No lunch.*

$$ ✕ **Cafe Su.** Dim sum appetizers are the specialty at this chic restaurant in the Valley Junction shopping area in West Des Moines. Contemporary decor complements the traditional Chinese cuisine. ✉ *225 5th St.,* ☎ *515/274–5102. AE, D, DC, MC, V. Closed Sun. and Mon.*

$$ ✕ **Jesse's Embers.** Just west of downtown, Jesse's is prized for grilled prime steaks cooked over an open pit in the main dining room. The room is small, plain, and crowded with neighborhood people waiting in the bar, but service is swift. ✉ *3301 Ingersoll Ave.,* ☎ *515/255–6011. AE, MC, V. Closed Sun.*

$$ ✕ **Tursi's Latin King.** This family-owned restaurant has served traditional midwestern and Italian-American food downtown since 1947. ✉ *2200 Hubble St.,* ☎ *515/266–4466. AE, D, MC, V. Closed Sun. and Mon.*

$$ ✕ **Waterfront Seafood Market.** Saltwater and freshwater fish are flown in daily from around the world to this seafood market and restaurant where dress is super casual. ✉ *2900 University Ave., West Des Moines,* ☎ *515/223–5106. AE, D, MC, V. Closed Sun.*

$–$$ ✕ **The Greenbrier.** The large menu of this restaurant in the northern suburb of Johnston mixes elegant and basic fare, with choices like Iowa pork chops, rack of lamb, and fish. Frosted glass and dark wood accent the three dining rooms and bar. ✉ *5810 Merle Hay Rd., Johnston,* ☎ *515/253–0124. Reservations not accepted. AE, D, MC, V. Closed Sun.*

$ ★ ✗ **Drake Diner.** Students from nearby Drake University mix with older patrons at this chrome-and-neon spot, with a traditional soup, salad, and sandwich menu. ✉ *1111 25th St.,* ☎ *515/277–1111. AE, D, DC, MC, V.*

$ ✗ **El Patio.** Southwestern artifacts fill this converted bungalow just west of downtown, which seats diners in colorful rooms and on a covered patio. More Tex than Mex, the food is still a cut above the fare found at chains. ✉ *611 37th St.,* ☎ *515/274–2303. AE, MC, V. No lunch.*

$ ★ ✗ **India Cafe.** Classic aromatic dishes range from zingy lamb vindaloo to mild tandoori chicken. The restaurant's peach-color walls are hung with Indian paintings, and seating is at booths and tables with armchairs. ✉ *Parkwood Plaza, 86th and Douglas Sts., Urbandale,* ☎ *515/278–2929. AE, MC, V.*

Lodging

Most establishments cater to business travelers and have modern amenities and convenient locations. Downtown renovations or newer suburban hotels dominate, with low-cost motels clustered near interstate exits and the occasional suburban bed-and-breakfast (**Iowa Bed and Breakfast Innkeepers' Association,** ✉ 9001 Hickman Rd., Suite 2B, Des Moines 50322, ☎ 800/888–4667) for variety. For price ranges *see* Chart 2 (A) *in* On the Road with Fodor's.

$$$ 🏨 **Des Moines Marriott.** The downtown location on the skywalk, which connects several downtown buildings, is a plus. Rooms are plush contemporary, with unobstructed views of the city from the higher floors. The restaurant, Quenelle's, serves rich Continental fare. ✉ *700 Grand Ave., 50309,* ☎ *515/245–5500,* FAX *515/245–5567. 415 rooms. 2 restaurants, pool, health club. AE, D, MC, V.*

$$–$$$ ★ 🏨 **Embassy Suites Hotel on the River.** This hotel across the bridge from the Court Avenue District has seven balconies ringing an atrium with a waterfall. Beyond this, the Embassy Suites lacks flash, which it makes up for with lots of attentive service. ✉ *101 E. Locust St., 50309,* ☎ *515/244–1700,* FAX *515/244–2537. 234 suites. Restaurant, pool, health club. Full breakfast. AE, D, DC, MC, V.*

$$ 🏨 **Holiday Inn Downtown.** Expect fresh but ordinary rooms and a few suites with whirlpool baths at this chain motel north of downtown. ✉ *1050 6th Ave., 50314,* ☎ *515/283–0151,* FAX *515/283–0151. 253 rooms. Restaurant, pool. AE, D, MC, V.*

$–$$ ★ 🏨 **Holiday Inn Express.** This attractive low-rise hotel next to Drake University has airy guest rooms and a meeting room. ✉ *1140 24th St., 50311,* ☎ *515/255–4000 or 800/252–7838,* FAX *515/255–1192. 52 rooms. CP. AE, D, MC, V.*

$–$$ 🏨 **Valley West Inn.** The three-story inn next to West Des Moines's big mall has simply furnished rooms decorated in rosy fabrics and blond woods. ✉ *3535 Westown Pkwy., West Des Moines 50266,* ☎ *515/225–2524 or 800/833–6755,* FAX *515/225–9058. 136 rooms. Restaurant, pool. AE, D, DC, MC, V.*

$ 🏨 **Airport Comfort Inn.** Free 24-hour airport shuttle service is offered by this three-story hotel two blocks from the airport . Meeting rooms are available. ✉ *5231 Fleur Dr., 50321,* ☎ *515/287–3434. 55 rooms. Pool. CP. AE, D, DC, MC, V.*

$ ★ 🏨 **Heartland Inn.** The inn, a rustic three-story building on the northeastern edge of Des Moines, is next to an amusement complex. Airport shuttle service is provided ✉ *5000 N.E. 56th St., Altoona 50009,*

☎ *515/967–2400 or 800/334–3277,* FAX *515/967–0150. 87 rooms. Pool. CP. AE, D, DC, MC, V.*

The Arts

The **Des Moines Art Center** (✉ 4700 Grand Ave., ☎ 515/277–4405), just west of downtown in Greenwood-Ashworth Park, hosts poetry readings, lectures, and film presentations. It also houses a permanent collection of contemporary art (☞ Exploring Des Moines, *above*). The **Des Moines Symphony** (✉ 221 Walnut St. , ☎ 515/243–1160) presents impressive local musical talents along with guest performers throughout the year.

Spectator Sports

Track and Field: The Drake Relays (✉ Drake University, Forest and 27th Sts., ☎ 515/271–3791) in late April draw track and field athletes from 744 colleges, universities, and high schools, as well as some big-name Olympians and professional athletes. Call for ticket packages.

Shopping

Valley Junction (☎ 515/222–3642), six square blocks 5 mi west of downtown on 5th Street in West Des Moines, has a mix of antiques stores and contemporary shops selling country furnishings, collectibles, and Iowa souvenirs.

EAST-CENTRAL IOWA

This region east of Des Moines is a mix of historic towns, trim farmsteads, and forested river valleys. Cedar Rapids is the largest town in the area; Iowa City, about 25 mi south, is the home of the University of Iowa. The Amana Colonies, a cluster of seven villages west of Iowa City that were founded in the 19th century as a utopian religious community, are the major attraction.

Visitor Information

Amana Colonies: Welcome Center (✉ 39 38th Ave., near U.S. 151 and Rte. 220, Amana 52203, ☎ 319/622–7622 or 800/245–5465), with information and a lodging reservation service. **Cedar Rapids area:** Convention and Visitors Bureau (✉ 119 1st Ave. SE, 52401, ☎ 319/622–3828 or 800/735–5557). **Iowa City/Coralville:** Visitors Bureau (✉ 408 1st Ave., Coralville 52241, ☎ 319/337–6592 or 800/283–6592).

Arriving and Departing

By Car

I–80, the state's major east–west thoroughfare, runs from Des Moines east to Iowa City. From Iowa City I–380 passes Lake MacBride on the way north to Cedar Rapids. From Cedar Rapids U.S. 151 meanders southwest for about 25 mi through a rural farmscape to Middle Amana, the start of the cluster of Amana colonies.

By Plane

The **Cedar Rapids/Iowa City Municipal Airport** (☎ 319/362–8336), 7 mi south of Cedar Rapids and just off I–380, is served by American Eagle, Delta Connection, US Airways, TWA, Northwest/Northwest Airlink, and United.

Exploring East-Central Iowa

★ Begin at the **Amana Colonies,** as the seven villages of Amana are known (☞ Visitor Information, *above*): Amana itself (site of the welcome center), West Amana, South Amana, High Amana, East Amana, Middle Amana, and Homestead. Although descendants of the German/Swiss immigrants who founded the community voted to end its communal way of life in 1932, little has changed visibly.

A 25-mi circuit of the Amana Colonies takes in nearly 500 restored buildings, including barns and kitchens now housing museums, and a schoolhouse, together designated a National Historic Landmark. Members of the Amana community still manufacture prized woolen goods, furniture, wine, cheese, baskets, and more. The original **Amana Appliance Store** (✉ 836 48th Ave., ☏ 319/622–7655), founded after residents voted to abandon their communal life, is still in business. The **Museum of Amana History** is filled with historical artifacts and documents relating to the settlement of the area. ✉ *4310 220th Trail,* ☏ *319/622–3567.* 🎫 *$4. Closed Jan.–Feb., limited hours until late spring.*

Cedar Rapids is on U.S. 151 in east-central Iowa, just north of the Amana Colonies. In the 19th and early 20th centuries, waves of Czechoslovakian immigrants settled in this manufacturing town. A sampling of Czech heritage is on view at the **National Czech & Slovak Museum & Library.** ✉ *30 16th Ave. SW,* ☏ *319/362–8500.* 🎫 *$6. Closed Mon.*

Cedar Rapids has the world's largest permanent collection of paintings by renowned native son Grant Wood, at its **Museum of Art.** ✉ *410 3rd Ave. SE,* ☏ *319/366–7503.* 🎫 *$4. Closed Mon.*

Iowa City, in east-central Iowa, served as the seat of state government until the capital was moved to Des Moines in the mid-19th century. The golden dome of the **Old Capitol** (✉ 24 Old Capitol Dr., ☏ 319/335–0548) is now the focal point of the beautiful but hilly campus of the **University of Iowa** on the banks of the Iowa River.

West Branch, a community of 2,000 with more than two dozen buildings listed on the National Register of Historic Places, is just west of Iowa City on I–80. The **Herbert Hoover Presidential Library and Birthplace** (✉ Parkside Dr. and Main St., ☏ 319/643–5301; 🎫 $2), the cottage where the future president was born to Quaker parents in 1874, contains period furnishings, many of them original.

Dining and Lodging

Amana kitchens are bountiful in rich German meals, often served family style. Try the locally made rhubarb wine. Hotels in Cedar Rapids tend to cater to business travelers, but the Amanas, like many Iowa towns, are home to a burgeoning number of B&Bs (**Iowa Bed and Breakfast Innkeepers' Association,** ✉ 9001 Hickman Rd., Suite 220, Des Moines 50322, ☏ 800/888–4667). Decent chain hotels and motels dominate in Iowa City. For price ranges *see* Charts 1 (B) and 2 (B) *in* On the Road with Fodor's.

Amana Colonies

$–$$ ✕ **Bill Zuber's Restaurant.** The comfortable surroundings haven't changed much since the 1950s, nor has the menu, which is a primer on German cuisine: lots of baked or fried meat, plus salad, vegetables, and dessert, all for a reasonable price. ✉ *Main St., Homestead,* ☏ *319/622–3911. AE, D, MC, V.*

$–$$ ★ ✕ **Brick Haus Restaurant.** This restaurant, in the middle of prime Amana shopping, has long tables covered in checkered cloths. Large

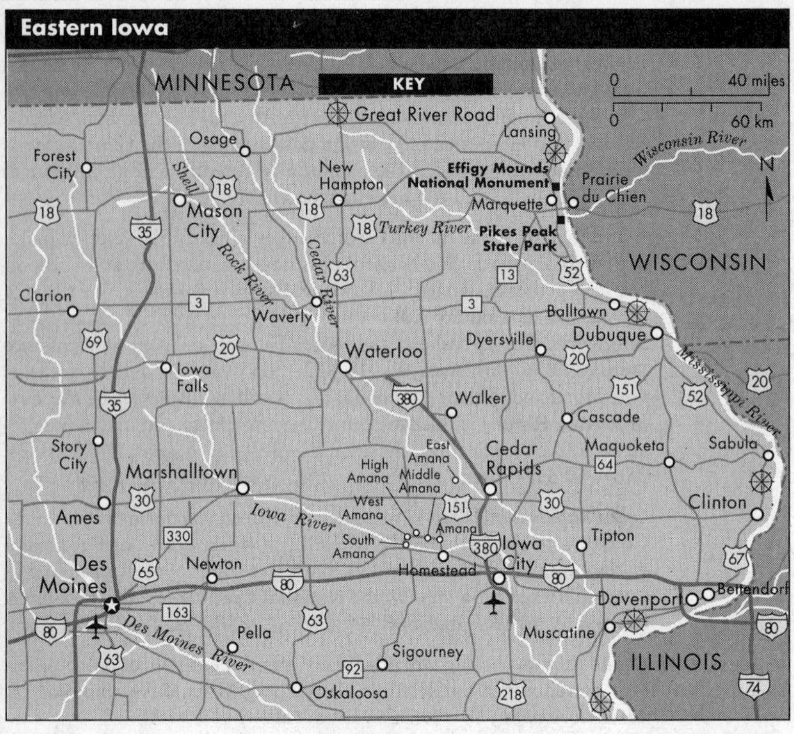

portions of Wiener schnitzel *mit* spaetzle are a specialty. ✉ *728 47th Ave., Amana,* ☎ *319/622–3278. AE, D, MC, V.*

$–$$ ✕ **Ox Yoke Inn.** Traditional German-American food is served in an Old Country–inspired setting, including walls lined with beer steins. ✉ *Main St., Amana,* ☎ *319/622–3441. AE, D, MC, V.*

$$$–$$$$ **Amana Holiday Inn.** Rustic touches such as a pool and sauna in a barn-like setting enliven this otherwise standard hotel. ✉ *Exit 225 off I–80; Box 187, Little Amana 52203,* ☎ *319/668–1175 or 800/633–9244,* FAX *319/668–2853. 156 rooms. Restaurant, pool. AE, D, MC, V.*

$$ **Die Heimat Country Inn.** This two-story B&B is the oldest in the colonies and has small rooms decorated with locally made, traditional furnishings and deluxe rooms with canopy beds. Meeting rooms are available. ✉ *4430 V St., Box 160, Homestead 52236,* ☎ *319/622–3937. 19 rooms. Full breakfast. D, MC, V.*

$$ ★ **Rawson's Bed & Breakfast.** Once a kitchen workers' dormitory when Homestead still practiced communal living, this unique B & B has two large, distinctive rooms, with exposed beams and brick walls, and one suite. All three have period furnishings and fabrics and lavish baths. ✉ *4424 V St., Box 118, Homestead 52235,* ☎ *319/622–6035. 3 rooms. Full breakfast. D, MC, V.*

Cedar Rapids

$$–$$$ **Collins Plaza.** In this hotel north of downtown, rooms are large, with traditional furnishings and pastel colors. There's an airport shuttle. ✉ *1200 Collins Rd. NE, 52402,* ☎ *319/393–6600 or 800/541–1067,* FAX *319/393–2308. 221 rooms. Restaurant, pool, exercise room. AE, DC, D, MC, V.*

Iowa City

$$ ✕ **Givanni's.** Neon lights enhance the exposed-brick walls at this Italian/American/vegetarian restaurant in the downtown pedestrian mall. ✉ *109 E. College St.,* ☎ *319/338–5967. AE, D, DC, MC, V.*

$–$$ ✕ **Iowa River Power Company.** The former power station for much of eastern Iowa, set on the banks of the Iowa River, was remodeled into a unique restaurant serving classic American cuisine. ✉ *501 1st Ave., Coralville,* ☏ *319/351–1904. AE, DC, MC, V.*

Motel

Heartland Inn (✉ 3315 Southgate Ct. SW, Cedar Rapids 52304, ☏ 319/362–9012 or 800/334–3277, FAX 319/362–9694), 87 rooms, pool. $.

Walcott

$ ✕ **Iowa-80 Kitchen.** With a native stone fireplace, beamed ceiling, and spacious dining room, this is one of the most elegantly furnished truck stops in the country. A 48-ft salad bar, an in-house bakery, laundry facilities, and a warehouse store answer all a traveler's needs. Walcott is about 55 mi east of Iowa City. ✉ *395 W. Iowa 80 Rd.,* ☏ *319/284–6965. D, MC, V.*

Shopping

The commercial hub of Amana shopping is the eight-block center of Amana, just east of the visitor center. The **Woolen Mill Salesroom** (✉ 800 48th Ave., ☏ 319/622–3432) sells all manner of woolens, from clothing for men, women, and kids to blankets; you can take a self-guided tour of the mill. On weekdays at the **Furniture and Clock Shop** (✉ 724 48th Ave., ☏ 319/622–3291), you can watch craftspeople making the products sold here. The fragrant, creaky **Old Fashioned High Amana Store** (✉ 1308 G St.,☏ 319/622–3797), 2 mi west of the visitor center, stocks old-time-type gifts. The **Amana Arts Guild Center** (✉ 1210 G St., ☏ 319/622–3678) sells high-quality quilts and crafts. **Little Amana,** at I–80 and U.S. 151, is more of a quick-stop outlet for woolens, gifts, and souvenirs than a typical Amana village. The **Tanger Factory Outlet Center** (✉ Exit 220 off I–80, Williamsburg, ☏ 800/552–1151) has 70 stores mainly selling women's designer clothing.

DUBUQUE AND THE GREAT RIVER ROAD

The mighty Mississippi River forms the eastern border of Iowa, and the top third of this border, from the Minnesota line to Dubuque, has the oldest settlements, highest bluffs, and closest river access of the entire stretch. The **Great River Road** is a network of federal, state, and county roads that wind along this magnificent stretch of riverbank.

Visitor Information

Tourist Information Center (✉ Port of Dubuque Welcome Center, 3rd St. and Ice Harbor, Dubuque 52001, ☏ 319/556–4372 or 800/798–8844).

Arriving and Departing

By Bus

Greyhound Lines (☏ 800/231–2222) links Dubuque to most major cities; its local bus station is in the lower level of the Julien Inn (✉ 200 Main St.). **Prairie Trailways** (☏ 800/877–2457) provides direct, daily service between Dubuque and the Chicago area Amtrak stations.

By Car

You can link up with Iowa's **Great River Road** from the north on U.S. 18 at Prairie du Chien, Wisconsin, or pick up the scenic route anywhere along Iowa's eastern border. For its entire length the Great River Road is marked with signs that have a 12-spoke pilot's wheel symbol.

Exploring Dubuque and the Great River Road

Just 11 mi south of the Minnesota border, the **Municipal Park,** in Lansing, Iowa, provides spectacular views of the Mississippi River. The **Effigy Mounds National Monument**(✉ Rte. 76, , ☎ 319/873–3491; 🎟 $2 per person, up to $4 per car), 3 mi north of McGregor along the Great River Road, has hiking trails that run alongside eerie, animal-shape prehistoric Native American burial mounds. One-, four-, and six-hour walks lead to cliff-top views of the upper Mississippi River valley.

Pikes Peak State Park (☎ 319/873–2341), 3 mi south of McGregor, affords a view of the Wisconsin River as it links up with the Mississippi. The stretch of road approaching **Balltown,** 7 mi north of Dubuque, reveals green hills rolling down to the river.

Dubuque is full of river merchants' homes, some of them lavish Victorian houses turned B&Bs, snuggled against the limestone cliffs that back this small harbor town. Here you can get out of your car and explore Cable Car Square (☎ 319/583–5000), at 4th and Bluff streets, site of two dozen shops and restaurants. From April through November you can ride the **Fenelon Place Elevator** (☎ 319/582–6496; 🎟 $1.50) to the top of a 200-ft bluff for a sweeping view of the city.

Dyersville, 25 mi west of Dubuque on U.S. 20, found fame as a setting for the 1989 movie *Field of Dreams.* The **Field of Dreams Movie Site** (✉ 28963 Lansing Rd., ☎ 319/875–8404 or 888/875–8404; 🎟 free), about 3 mi north of town, has been preserved as a tourist attraction. Bring your own equipment to play in the continual pickup game (the field is closed November–March). Dyersville has several interesting museums, including the **National Farm Toy Museum** (✉ 1110 16th Ave. SE, ☎ 319/875–2727; 🎟 $4).

Dining and Lodging

Ethnic and family-style restaurants line Dubuque's 4th Street at Cable Car Square. As in the rest of the state, B&Bs are abundant (**Iowa Bed and Breakfast Innkeepers' Association,** ✉ 9001 Hickman Rd., Suite 2B, Des Moines 50322, ☎ 800/888–4667). For price ranges *see* Charts 1 (B) and 2 (B) *in* On the Road with Fodor's.

Balltown

$–$$ ★ ✕ **Breitbach's Country Dining.** This funky, rambling piece of folk architecture has a good home-style kitchen. ✉ *563 Balltown Rd.,* ☎ *319/552–2220. No credit cards.*

Dubuque

$$–$$$ ✕ **Yen Ching.** This café offers predictable Chinese food, with a few spicy Hunan dishes for variety. ✉ *926 Main St.,* ☎ *319/556–2574. AE, MC, V. Closed Sun.*

$$$–$$$$ ★ **Hancock House.** This meticulously restored Victorian perched halfway up a bluff has four-poster beds, lace-covered windows, ornate fireplaces, and a rare Tiffany lamp collection. Four rooms have whirlpool baths. ✉ *1105 Grove Terr., 52001,* ☎ *319/557–8989,* FAX *319/583–0813. 9 rooms. Full breakfast. D, MC, V.*

$$$ **Redstone Inn.** Bedrooms are grand and baths lavish at this British manor–like establishment on the prairie. ✉ *504 Bluff St., 52001,* ☎ *319/582–1894,* FAX *319/582–1893. 15 rooms. Full breakfast. AE, D, MC, V.*

ELSEWHERE IN IOWA

Iowa's Great Lakes

Arriving and Departing

Take I–80 west from Des Moines and U.S. 71 north to Spirit Lake or take I–35 north from Des Moines to U.S. 18, which leads west to the Great Lakes area.

Visitor Information

Iowa Great Lakes Chamber of Commerce (✉ 56 N. Okoboji Grove Rd., Box 9, Arnolds Park 51331, ☎ 712/332–2107).

What to See and Do

The Iowa Great Lakes lie in the northwest corner of the state. The region has six lakes (including West Okoboji—one of only three true blue-water lakes in the world) and a dozen vacation resorts. You can climb aboard the ***Queen II*** excursion boat (✉ Arnolds Park, ☎ 712/332–5159) for a tour of West Okoboji.

Dining and Lodging

Lodging rates may drop substantially in this area between late fall and spring.

$$ ✕ **Lighthouse Bar & Grill.** Guests come by boat, bike, or car and dine inside or out in a nautical atmosphere. Steak and seafood get top billing on the menu, which has everything from sandwiches to full dinners. ✉ *U.S. 71 at East Oak Mall,Okoboji,* ☎ *712/332–5995. AE, MC, V.*

$$ ✕ **Maxwell's on the Lake.** A lovely view, elegant dining, fine service, and unique hors d'oeuvres and entrées from an extensive menu (with lots of seafood and steak) make dining a memorable experience. ✉ *144 Lakeshore Dr., Arnold's Park,* ☎ *712/332–7578. AE, MC, V.*

$$$$ **Beaches Resort.** On the quiet north end of West Lake Okoboji, these clapboard cottages offer simple but comfortable furnishings at a family-oriented resort. At day's end, you can gather around the fire pit on the sandy beach for complimentary s'mores. ✉ *15109 215th Ave., Spirit Lake 51360,* ☎ *712/336–2230. 6 cottages, 5 apartments, 1 house. Restaurant. D, MC, V.*

$$$$ **Village East Resort.** Overlooking Brooks Golf Course and East Lake Okoboji, this resort has indoor and outdoor pools. Additional draws are a pro shop and weight room. ✉ *Box 499, Okoboji 51355-0499,* ☎ *712/332–2161 or 800/727–4561. 101 rooms. Restaurant, pools, tennis, health club. AE, D, DC, MC, V.*

Riverboat Gambling on the Mississippi River

Arriving and Departing

From Des Moines take I–80 east to Davenport and follow signs to the riverfront.

What to See and Do

Davenport, the largest of the Quad Cities (the other three are Bettendorf in Iowa and Rock Island and Moline in Illinois), introduced casino riverboat gambling to the nation and continues to be a popular place for this activity. The **President Riverboat Casino** (✉ 130 West River Dr., ☎ 800/262–8711), a National Historic Landmark, is as big as a football field and has five decks decorated in Victorian splendor; hotels, restaurants, and antiques shops are within walking distance. The **Bix Beiderbeck Jazz Festival** (☎ 319/324–7170) is held each July in Davenport's riverfront park.

Dining and Lodging

$ ✕ **Rudy's.** A Mexican-American restaurant chain, Rudy's has five locations around the Quad Cities and is always packed with locals. This location in the East Village of Davenport is the original and most charming. ✉ *2214 E. 11th St., Davenport,* ☎ *319/322–0668. No credit cards.*

$$$–$$$$ 🏨 **Jumer's Castle Lodge.** Impressive both inside and out, this lodge is furnished with heavy walnut carvings, rich carpets, and elegant accessories. ✉ *900 Spruce Hill Dr., Bettendorf 52722,* ☎ FAX *800/285–8635. 210 rooms. Restaurant, pool, exercise room. AE, D, MC, V.*

The Covered Bridges Region

Arriving and Departing

Take I–35 south from Des Moines to U.S. 92, which leads west into Madison County.

What to See and Do

Made famous by Robert James Waller's novel *The Bridges of Madison County* and the eponymous 1995 movie, **Madison County,** 50 mi southwest of Des Moines, is home to six covered bridges that date from the 1880s. Bus tours (☎ 515/462–1185) of the bridges take place all day, or you can take a self-guided one. Tours are also available at Francesca's Farmhouse and other buildings used as sites for the movie. The Covered Bridge Festival is held here each October. In Winterset, the **birthplace of John Wayne** (✉ 224 S. 2nd St., ☎ 515/462–1044; 🎫 $3) is furnished with family memorabilia and authentic turn-of-the-century pieces; you can watch Wayne's films in the gift shop.

Dining and Lodging

$$–$$$ ✕ **Summerset House.** An Italianate Victorian mansion just two blocks from the courthouse square now serves as a tearoom. Lunch fare includes elegant sandwiches and quiche; some choices for the five-course dinner are salmon steaks, apricot-glazed game hens, or prime rib. ✉ *204 W. Washington St., Winterset,* ☎ *515/462–9099. Reservations essential. MC, V.*

$ ✕ **Northside Cafe.** You'll find typical café fare—meat loaf, fried chicken, mashed potatoes, and homemade pie—at this spot, where Clint Eastwood ate in the movie *The Bridges of Madison County.* ✉ *61 W. Jefferson St., Winterset,* ☎ *515/462–1523. No credit cards.*

$$$ 🏨 **Hutchings-Wintrode Bed and Breakfast.** This 1886 brick home, just four blocks from the courthouse, has been refurbished with antiques and period decor. ✉ *503 E. Jefferson St., Winterset 50273,* ☎ *515/462–3095. 3 rooms. Full breakfast. MC, V.*

KANSAS

By Janet Majure

Updated by Diana Lambdin Meyer

Capital	Topeka
Population	2,595,000
Motto	To the Stars Through Difficulties
State Bird	Western meadowlark
State Flower	Wild native sunflower
Postal Abbreviation	KS

Statewide Visitor Information

Kansas Department of Commerce, Travel & Tourism Division (✉ 700 S.W. Harrison St., Suite 1300, Topeka 66603-3712, ☎ 785/296–2009 or 800/252–6727). There are visitor information centers on I–70W in Kansas City (☎ 785/299–2253), on I–70E in Goodland (☎ 785/899–6695), on I–35N at South Haven (☎ 316/892–5283), and in Topeka (☎ 785/296–3966).

Scenic Drives

Route 177 south from I–70 to historic Council Grove provides lovely views—especially in late afternoon or early morning—of the undulating Flint Hills.

National and State Parks

National Parks

Federal sites include the **Fort Larned National Historic Site** (☞ The Santa Fe Trail Region, *below*); the **Fort Scott National Historic Site** (✉ Old Fort Blvd., Fort Scott 66701, ☎ 316/223–0310 or 800/245–3678; 🎫 $2), which centers on a fort built in 1842 to keep the peace in Native American territory; and the **Cimarron National Grassland** (✉ Box J, 242 E. Hwy. 56, Elkhart 67950, ☎ 316/697–4621; 🎫 free), less than a mile from central Elkhart, which offers a self-guided auto tour of key Santa Fe Trail sites.

State Parks

Kansas has 24 state parks, most associated with recreational lakes, run by the **Department of Wildlife and Parks** (✉ 512 S.E. 25th Ave., Pratt 67124, ☎ 316/672–5911). Two of the best are **Scott County State Park** (✉ 520 W. Scott Lake Dr., Scott City 67871, ☎ 316/872–2061), containing archaeological evidence of the northernmost Native American pueblo and the first white settlement in Kansas, and **Milford State Park** (✉ 8811 State Park Rd., Milford 66514, ☎ 785/238–3014), with a 37,000-acre reservoir, a nature center, and a fish hatchery.

EAST-CENTRAL KANSAS

Heading west from Kansas City across east-central Kansas, you'll follow in the footsteps of pioneers who traveled the Oregon, Santa Fe, Smoky Hill, and Chisholm trails. Native American history, Civil War sites, and the Old West loom large along this 150-mi stretch of prairie.

Visitor Information

Abilene: Convention & Visitors Bureau (✉ 201 N.W. 2nd St., 67410, ☎ 785/263–2231 or 800/569–5915). **Atchison:** Visitor Center (✉ 200 S. 10th St., 66002, ☎ 913/367–2427 or 800/234–1854). **Kansas City, Kansas:** Convention & Visitors Bureau (✉ 727 Minnesota Ave., 66117,

☎ 913/321–5800 or 800/264–1563); **Overland Park** Convention & Visitors Bureau (✉ 10975 Benson Dr., Suite 360, 66210, ☎ 913/491–0123 or 800/262–7275). **Lawrence:** Convention & Visitors Bureau (✉ 734 Vermont St., 66044, ☎ 785/865–4411 or 800/318–8995). **Topeka:** Convention & Visitors Bureau (✉ 1275 S.W. Topeka Blvd., 66612, ☎ 785/234–1030 or 800/235–1030).

Arriving and Departing

By Bus

Greyhound Lines (☎ 800/231–2222) connects Kansas City, Lawrence, Topeka, and Abilene en route to Denver. **Jefferson Lines** (☎ 800/735–7433) serves Kansas City, Overland Park, and Lawrence.

By Car

I–70W enters Kansas from Kansas City, Missouri; I–70E, from Colorado. Most attractions are just off the interstate. Note: Kansas weather is extremely variable. Listen to the radio for forecasts, as ice storms, heavy snowfalls, flash floods, and high winds can make driving treacherous. Road conditions are also posted at toll booths along I–70.

By Plane

The biggest airport serving east-central Kansas is **Kansas City International Airport** (☞ Missouri). US Airways Express serves Topeka's **Forbes Field** (☎ 785/862–6515).

By Train

Amtrak (☎ 800/872–7245) serves Lawrence, Topeka, and Kansas City.

Exploring East-Central Kansas

Along I–70 you'll encounter an array of historic sites. Kansas City, which straddles the border between Kansas and Missouri, was a major provisioning point for frontier travelers in the 19th century.

The Mahaffie Farmstead & Stagecoach Stop (✉ 1100 Kansas City Rd., Olathe 66061, ☎ 913/782–6972; 🎫 $3) once served the Santa Fe Trail, one of the routes established in the 19th century for trade and later for westward expansion. There are guided tours of the stone house, one of three farmstead buildings here listed on the National Register of Historic Places. The farmstead is closed in January and on weekends from February through April.

In Fairway, a Kansas City suburb, the **Shawnee Indian Mission** (✉ 3403 W. 53rd St., ☎ 913/262–0867; 🎫 free) was begun in 1839 as a school to teach English and trade skills to Native Americans. Two of its three buildings can be toured. It's closed Mondays.

About 40 mi west of Kansas City on I–70 is **Lawrence.** The town was rebuilt after being raided and burned by William Quantrill and a band of Confederate sympathizers for the antislavery stance of its citizens during the Civil War; many structures from this time remain. Stroll along Massachusetts Street through the lovely downtown area, where turn-of-the-century buildings and retail shops retain a small-town flavor.

A few blocks away from Massachusetts Street is the scenic main campus of the 29,000-student **University of Kansas.** Lining Jayhawk Boulevard is an assortment of university buildings, including the Romanesque structure of native limestone that houses the **University of Kansas Natural History Museum** (✉ Dyche Hall, ☎ 785/864–4540), one of the school's four museums. The Natural History Museum displays fossils, mounted animals, and rotating exhibits. Children will enjoy the dinosaur bones and live snakes. Also in Lawrence is **Haskell Indian Nations University** (✉ 155 Indian Ave., ☎ 785/749–8450), which has provided higher education for Native Americans since 1884.

Fifty miles northwest of Kansas City on Route 7 and overlooking the Missouri River is **Atchison,** the birthplace of famed aviator Amelia Earhart. The **Amelia Earhart Birthplace Museum,** (✉ 223 N. Terrace St., 66002, ☎ 913/367–4217; 🎫 $2) owned by Ninety-Nines, Inc., an international group of women pilots, displays flying memorabilia.

Trees from 50 states and 38 countries grow in harmony at the **International Forest of Friendship** (✉ 1.5 mi southwest of Atchison at Warnock Lake, ☎ 913/367–1419; 🎫 free), a gift to the United States for its bicentennial from the city and Ninety-Nines, Inc. The forest is accessed through Memory Lane, which is paved with plaques that list the names of more than 600 pilots, astronauts, and manufacturers who have contributed to aviation. About 70 mi west of Kansas City on I–70 is **Topeka,** with its outstanding classical state **capitol** (✉ 300 W. 10th St., ☎ 785/296–3966), begun in 1866 and completed nearly 40 years later. Lobby murals include a striking depiction of abolitionist John Brown by John Steuart Curry. Be sure to visit the ornate senate chambers, which have magnificent bronze columns and variegated-marble accents. West of downtown Topeka, the **Kansas Museum of History** (✉ 6425 S.W. 6th St., ☎ 785/272–8681; 🎫 free), perversely situated in a modernist box of a building, traces Kansas's history from the Native American era to the present. Kids like **Discovery Place,** a hands-on exhibit involving 19th-century clothes, tools, and household items. Just outside Topeka, the **Combat Air Museum** (✉ Hangars 602 and 604, Forbes Field, ☎ 785/862–3303; 🎫 $4) has two hangars full of military aircraft dating from World War I. **Historic Ward-Meade Park** (✉ 124 N. Fillmore St., ☎ 785/295–3888) is as lovely as it is historic, with a restored mansion, a cabin, a train depot, a one-room schoolhouse, and botanical gardens. **Gage Park** (✉ 635 Gage Blvd., ☎ 785/368–3838) has a carousel and is home to the **Topeka Zoo** (☎ 785/272–5821; 🎫 $3.50).

Tallgrass Prairie National Preserve (✉ Rte. 1, Box 14, Strong City 66869, ☎ 316/273–8494; 🎫 donations accepted), contains the last large vestiges of the bluestem, or tallgrass, prairie that once covered much of the Great Plains.The historic **Grand Central Hotel** (✉ 215 Broadway St., ☎ 316/273–6763) in Cottonwood Falls has been welcoming guests since 1884.

The small town of **Abilene,** about 85 mi west of Topeka, is famous for cattle drives and for Dwight D. Eisenhower. The **Eisenhower Center complex** (✉ 200 S.E. 4th St., ☎ 785/263–4751; 🎫 $3) includes the late president's **boyhood home,** as well as the **Eisenhower Museum,** the **Eisenhower Presidential Library,** and the **Place of Meditation,** a chapel where the president, his wife Mamie, and their son, Doud Dwight, are interred. The museum displays memorabilia of Eisenhower's life, from his youth in Abilene and his success as a general during World War II through his popular presidency.

Also in Abilene is the **Dickinson County Historical Museum** (✉ 412 S. Campbell St., ☎ 785/263–2681; 🎫 $2.50), with exhibits on the life of the Plains Indians. **The Greyhound Hall of Fame** (✉ 407 S. Buckeye St., ☎ 785/263–3000; 🎫 donations accepted) documents the history of this illustrious canine breed.

Dining and Lodging

Typical Kansas roadhouse fare is chicken-fried steak and fried chicken. In addition, good barbecue and Mexican food can be found in the area's cities and towns. Accommodations range from business-class hotels in the Kansas City suburb of Overland Park to basic roadside motels in the western part of the region to bed-and-breakfasts (contact **Kansas Bed & Breakfast Association,** ✉ Rte. 1, Box 93, WaKeeney 67672). For price ranges *see* Charts 1 (B) and 2 (B) *in* On the Road with Fodor's.

Abilene

$$ ✕ **Kirby House.** The traditional midwestern fare is nothing special, but the modestly elegant setting, in a restored Victorian mansion, makes this place worthwhile. ✉ *205 N.E. 3rd St.,* ☎ *785/263–7336. AE, D, MC, V.*

$ ✕ **Mr. K's Farmhouse.** Once a favorite of Dwight and Mamie Eisenhower, the "house on the hill" serves fried chicken and homemade desserts. ✉ *407 S. Van Buren,* ☎ *785/263–7995. D, MC, V. Closed Mon.*

Kansas City

$$ ✕ **Dick Clark's American Bandstand Grill.** Rock 'n' roll history comes alive in this diner owned by America's perpetual teenager. Vintage posters, gold albums, and artists' contracts on the walls complement a varied menu. Clark and other music celebrities often stop in. ✉ *10975 Metcalf Ave., Overland Park,* ☎ *913/451–1600. AE, D, MC, V.*

$$ ★ ✕ **Tatsu's French Restaurant.** French cuisine with an Asian flair is found in the unexpected setting of a suburban shopping strip. ✉ *4603 W. 90th St., Prairie Village,* ☎ *913/383–9801. AE, D, DC, MC, V. Closed Sun. No lunch Sat.*

$ ★ ✕ **Hayward's Pit Bar-B-Que.** Locals flock to this hillside restaurant for piles of succulent smoked beef, ribs, chicken, pork, and sausage. ✉ *11051 Antioch Rd., Overland Park,* ☎ *913/451–8080. AE, MC, V.*

$$$$ 🏨 **Doubletree Hotel.** Adjacent to two major highways, a business park, and a scenic public jogging trail, this 18-story hotel is convenient to shopping, restaurants, and a bowling alley. ✉ *10100 College Blvd., Overland Park 66210,* ☎ *913/451–6100,* FAX *913/451–3873. 357 rooms. Restaurant, pool, health club. AE, D, DC, MC, V.*

$$$ ★ 🏨 **Overland Park Marriott Hotel.** This upscale hotel in a suburban business area has a marble-floor lobby and traditionally styled rooms. The concierge level has slightly larger rooms. ✉ *10800 Metcalf Ave., Overland Park 66210,* ☎ *913/451–8000,* FAX *913/451–5914. 390 rooms. 2 restaurants, pool, health club. AE, D, DC, MC, V.*

Lawrence

$$ ★ ✕ **Free State Brewing Co.** Kansas's first legal brew pub, opened in 1989, serves dishes like fish-and-chips and a Burgundy beef sandwich (shredded beef brisket on a baguette, smothered with gravy) to complement the selection of beers. Brewery tours are offered on Saturday. ✉ *636 Massachusetts St.,* ☎ *785/843–4555. Reservations not accepted. AE, D, DC, MC, V.*

$$$$ ★ 🏨 **Eldridge Hotel.** Listed on the National Register of Historic Places, this downtown hotel has attractive suites with parlors and wet bars; rooms on the top (fifth) floor have great views. The downtown location means some traffic noise but great convenience. ✉ *701 Massachusetts St., 66044,* ☎ *785/749–5011 or 800/527–0909,* FAX *785/749–4512. 48 suites. Restaurant, exercise room. AE, D, MC, V.*

Topeka

$$ ✕🏨 **Heritage House.** Rooms range from dramatic to cozy at this turn-of-the-century clapboard home. The intimate restaurant serves a frequently changing Continental menu for lunch and dinner. ✉ *3535 S.W. 6th St., 66606,* ☎ *785/233–3800,* FAX *785/233–9793. 11 rooms. Restaurant. Jacket and tie. AE, D, DC, MC, V.*

$$$ Club House Inn. In western Topeka near the Kansas Museum of History, this modern white-stucco B&B inn has spacious rooms, many overlooking a landscaped courtyard, and suites with kitchenettes. *⊠ 924 S.W. Henderson St., 66615, ☎ 785/273–8888, FAX 785/273–5809. 121 rooms. Pool. AE, D, DC, MC, V.*

Motels

I–70 is lined with chain hotels(☞ Lodging *in* Chapter 1). **Best Western Inn** (⊠ 2210 N. Buckeye St., Abilene 67410, ☎ 785/263–2050, FAX 785/263–7230), 62 rooms, restaurant, pool; *$.*

Campgrounds

Four Seasons RV Acres (⊠ 6 mi east of Abilene off I–70; 2502 Mink Rd., Abilene 67410, ☎ 785/598–2221 or 800/658–4667). **KOA Campgrounds of Lawrence** (⊠ 1473 Hwy. 40, Lawrence 66044, ☎ 785/842–3877). **KOA Campground** (⊠ Rte. 1, Grantville 66429, ☎ 913/246–3419). Camping is also available in state parks at reservoirs.

Nightlife

The New Theatre Restaurant (⊠ 9229 Foster St., Overland Park 66212, ☎ 913/649–7469), an Equity theater and restaurant, stages first-run and recent musicals and comedies.

Outdoor Activities and Sports

Fishing

Most of east-central Kansas follows the Kansas River, called the Kaw River locally, where a series of large-scale flood-control reservoirs yield good fishing for walleye, bass, and crappie. Good sites include **Clinton State Park** (⊠ 798 N. 1415 Rd., Lawrence 66049); **Perry State Park** (⊠ 5441 West Lake Rd., Ozawkie 66070), near Topeka; **Tuttle Creek State Park** (⊠ 5020-B Tuttle Creek Blvd., Manhattan 66502); and **Milford State Park**(☞ National and State Parks, *above*). Licenses are required and can be purchased at county clerks' offices, state parks offices, and some retail outlets. **The Kansas Department of Fish and Game** (☎ 316/672–5911) has further information.

Hiking

Kansas's reservoirs are bordered by state parks with marked nature trails. The **Konza Prairie** (⊠ 5 mi off I–70 at Exit 307, McDowell Creek Rd., ☎ 913/587–0441), an 8,600-acre section of tallgrass prairie set aside for research and preservation, has a self-guided nature trail.

Spectator Sports

Basketball: Jayhawks (⊠ Memorial Stadium, 11th and Mississippi Sts., ☎ 785/864–3141 or 800/344–2957). **Horse and dog racing: Woodlands** (⊠ 99th St. and Leavenworth Rd., Kansas City, ☎ 913/299–9797) puts on greyhound races year-round and horse races in late summer.

Shopping

Lawrence Riverfront Factory Outlets (⊠ 1 Riverfront Plaza, ☎ 785/842–5511), at the north end of downtown, has nearly 50 stores. The mall's north-side picture windows provide excellent views of the nearly 20 bald eagles that live in the cottonwood trees on the banks of the Kansas River, which rushes past the front of the mall. **The Tanger Center** (⊠ 1035 N. 3rd St., Lawrence, ☎ 800/406–4215), about a mile north of downtown, has 25 factory outlet stores from major-name manufacturers of clothing, shoes, and other goods.

THE SANTA FE TRAIL REGION

Although the Santa Fe Trail spans the entire state, the towns in western Kansas are most closely associated with its lore and history. This is the Kansas we know from film and myth: remote, flat, treeless, littered with tumbleweeds, windy, but imbued with a romance identified with such names as Wyatt Earp and Dodge City. Towns sprang up here first along the trail, then near the railroad lines that followed. Today agriculture is the mainstay. Tourism is growing, but don't expect resorts.

Visitor Information

Dodge City: Convention & Visitors Bureau (☒ Box 1474, 4th and Spruce Sts., 67801, ☎ 316/225–8186). **Hutchinson:** Convention & Visitors Bureau (☒ 117 N. Walnut St., 67501, ☎ 316/662–3391). **Larned:** Chamber of Commerce (☒ 502 Broadway, 67550, ☎ 316/285–6916 or 800/747–6919).

Arriving and Departing

By Bus

Greyhound Lines (☎ 800/231–2222) connects with **TNM&O Coaches** (☎ 316/276–3731) to provide service to Dodge City from Wichita. The **Hutchinson Shuttle Service** (☎ 316/662–5205) connects with Great Bend, Newton, Wichita, and other cities in central Kansas.

By Car

From Kansas City or Topeka take I–70 west and I–135 south, then Route 61 to Hutchinson. Eastbound travelers enter Dodge City via U.S. 50 or U.S. 56.

By Plane

Dodge City Regional Airport (☎ 316/227–8679), about 2 mi east of downtown, is served by US Airways Express.

By Train

Amtrak (☎ 800/872–7245) serves Hutchinson, Newton, Garden City, and Dodge City.

Exploring the Santa Fe Trail Region

Hutchinson is home to the state fairgrounds and some of the world's largest grain elevators, but what really makes this small town worth a visit is the **Kansas Cosmosphere & Space Center** (☒ 1100 N. Plum St., ☎ 316/662–2305 or 800/397–0330; $4). Housing more than $100 million worth of space exhibits, the center's museum has the largest collection outside the Smithsonian Institution. Various displays—including interactive exhibits—trace the history of space exploration and solutions to the many challenges of human flight. Exhibits include the *Apollo 13 Odyssey* command module and the world's largest display of Soviet space artifacts. The center also has a planetarium and an Omnimax theater.

Travel west out of Hutchison on 4th Street (which becomes County Road 636) for about 30 mi, and you will see signs to the **Quivira National Wildlife Refuge** (☒ Rte. 3, Box 48A, Stafford 67578, ☎ 316/486–2393; free). More than 250 bird species have been spotted on its 21,000 acres, including bald eagles, pelicans, and whooping cranes.

Drive north through the Quivira refuge, then turn west on County Road 484, which becomes Route 19, to **Larned,** a well-preserved Old West town. Two miles west of Larned on Route 156, the **Santa Fe Trail Cen-**

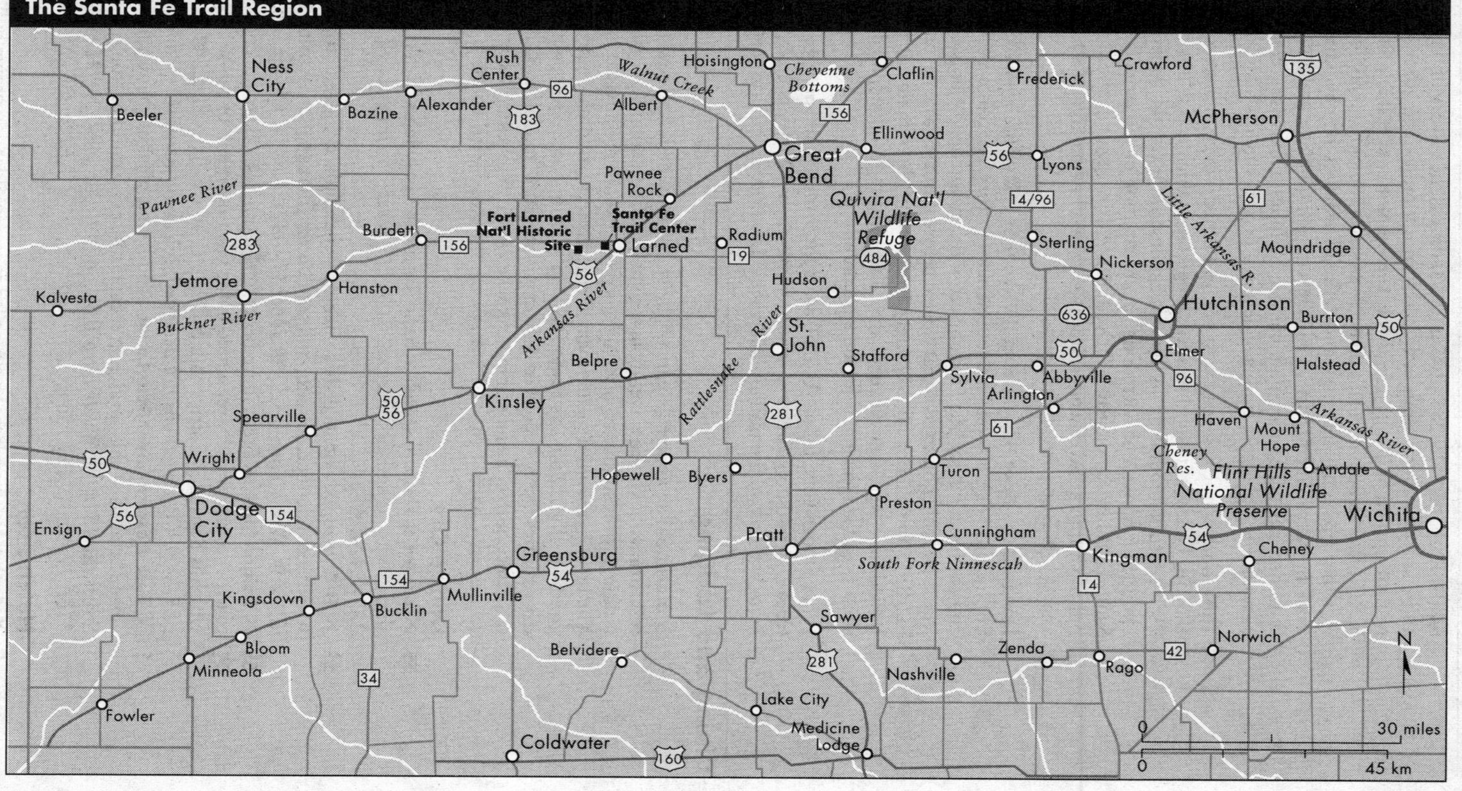
The Santa Fe Trail Region
Ness City
Beeler
Bazine
Alexander
Rush Center
Walnut Creek
Albert
Hoisington
Cheyenne Bottoms
Claflin
Frederick
Crawford
McPherson
Great Bend
Ellinwood
Lyons
Pawnee Rock
Pawnee River
Burdett
Fort Larned Nat'l Historic Site
Santa Fe Trail Center
Larned
Radium
Quivira Nat'l Wildlife Refuge
Sterling
Nickerson
Little Arkansas R.
Moundridge
Jetmore
Hanston
Kalvesta
Hudson
Buckner River
Arkansas River
St. John
Rattlesnake River
Belpre
Stafford
Hutchinson
Burrton
Elmer
Halstead
Sylvia
Abbyville
Arlington
Kinsley
Spearville
Wright
Haven
Mount Hope
Arkansas River
Hopewell
Byers
Turon
Cheney Res.
Flint Hills National Wildlife Preserve
Andale
Dodge City
Ensign
Preston
Wichita
Pratt
Cunningham
Kingman
Cheney
Greensburg
South Fork Ninnescah
Mullinville
Kingsdown
Bucklin
Sawyer
Bloom
Belvidere
Zenda
Rago
Norwich
Minneola
Nashville
Lake City
Fowler
Medicine Lodge
Coldwater
N
0
30 miles
0
45 km
96
183
156
135
56
14/96
61
283
156
19
484
56
636
50
50
96
50 56
281
61
50
56
154
54
154
54
14
281
42
34
160

ter (✉ Rte. 3, ☎ 316/285–2054; 🎟 $3) details the history of the trail and displays artifacts from early 20th-century prairie life. About 6 mi west of Larned on Route 156 is **Fort Larned National Historic Site** (✉ R.R. 3, ☎ 316/285–6911), a meticulous restoration of an 1868 prairie fort that protected travelers and railroad workers on the Santa Fe Trail. Buffalo Soldiers (post–Civil War regiments of black soldiers) were stationed here. The nine-building site includes a museum, restored barracks, and a nature trail; a slide show depicts the fort's history.

Turn south on the first road west of Fort Larned, which intersects with U.S. 56. Follow this southwest to **Dodge City,** which capitalizes on its 19th-century reputation as the "wickedest little city in America." Founded 5 mi west of Fort Dodge in anticipation of the arrival of the Santa Fe Railroad, the town thrived on the drinking and gambling of buffalo hunters and cowboys. It was here that lawmen Bat Masterson and Wyatt Earp earned their fame.

Dodge City's **Boot Hill Museum** (✉ Front St., ☎ 316/227–8188; 🎟 $6) includes exhibits on Native American history, the Santa Fe Trail, and the town's early life; Front Street, a reconstruction of houses, saloons, and other businesses that existed before the original town burned in 1885; and a Boot Hill cemetery re-creation (the remains of those buried here were moved years ago). In summer, gunfights, medicine shows, and stagecoach rides are staged daily.

From Dodge City, follow U.S. 50 west for 9 mi to the **Santa Fe Trail tracks,** a 140-acre preserve where, more than 125 years later, ruts from wagons on the trail are still visible in the sandy prairie earth.

Dining and Lodging

Motels hold sway in this part of the state, and you'll find few fancy restaurants. If you're traveling in summer, make reservations early for lodging; for restaurants, reservations on weekends are advised. Note: The term *red beer* on menus means beer mixed with tomato juice (it's good—really!). Kansas's liquor laws vary from county to county; in dry counties alcohol is served only in private clubs, to which many hotels offer courtesy memberships (ask when you call to reserve). For price ranges *see* Charts 1 (B) and 2 (B) *in* On the Road with Fodor's.

Dodge City

$$ ✕ **Big Art's.** Those in search of basic American sandwiches, steaks, and shakes will be satisfied here. ✉ *1005 W. Wyatt Earp Blvd.,* ☎ *316/227–2424. AE, MC, V.*

$$ ✕ **El Charro.** Mexican dishes such as "enchilada delights," topped with cheese, lettuce, tomato, and sour cream, make this a favorite. ✉ *1209 W. Wyatt Earp Blvd.,* ☎ *316/225–0371. MC, V. Closed Sun.*

$$ ★ ✕ **Saigon Market.** Fresh ingredients for Vietnamese dishes are cooked to order and colorfully presented in the restaurant half of this market, which is housed in a strip mall. ✉ *1202 E. Wyatt Earp Blvd.,* ☎ *316/225–9099. Reservations not accepted. No credit cards. Closed Mon.*

$ 🏨 **Best Western Silver Spur Lodge.** You'll find pleasant but undistinguished rooms at this sprawling complex just five minutes from Front Street. ✉ *1510 W. Wyatt Earp Blvd., 67801,* ☎ *316/227–2125,* FAX *316/227–2030. 121 rooms. 2 restaurants, pool. AE, D, DC, MC, V.*

Hutchinson

$ ★ ✕ **Anchor Inn.** Two large brick-walled rooms in older downtown buildings are the setting for Mexican dishes that use the restaurant's distinctive homemade flour tortillas. Portions are bounteous. ✉ *126–128 S. Main St.,* ☎ *316/669–0311. Reservations not accepted weekend evenings. MC, V. Closed Sun. May–Sept.*

$ ✕ **Roy's Hickory Pit BBQ.** This tiny restaurant seating 36 serves barbecued pork spareribs, beef brisket, sausage, ham, and turkey. There's nothing else on the menu besides beans, salad, and bread—but who needs more? ✉ *1018 W. 5th St.,* ☎ *316/663–7421. Reservations not accepted. No credit cards. Closed Sun.–Mon.*

$$ ★ **Ramada Inn Hutchinson.** Rooms in the "minidome" section of this busy convention hotel look onto a quiet, landscaped courtyard. "Maindome" rooms open onto a recreation area with a putting green and swimming pool. ✉ *1400 N. Lorraine St., 67501,* ☎ *316/669–9311 or 800/362–5018,* FAX *316/669–9830. 220 rooms. Restaurant, pool, exercise room. AE, D, DC, MC, V.*

Larned

$ ✕ **Harvest Inn.** Chicken, steaks, and seafood are on the menu at this family restaurant; food is also served in the accompanying bar, the Grain Club. ✉ *718 Ft. Larned Ave.,* ☎ *316/285–3870. Reservations not accepted. D, MC, V.*

Motels

EconoLodge and **Super 8**(☞ Lodging *in* Chapter 1) are in Dodge City. **Best Western Townsman Inn** (✉ 123 E. 14th St., Larned 67550, ☎ 316/285–3114, FAX 316/285–7139), 44 rooms, pool; *$.* **Quality Inn City Center** (✉ 15 W. 4th St., Hutchinson 67501, ☎ 316/663–1211, FAX 316/663–6636), 98 rooms, restaurant, pool; *$$$.* **Scotsman Inn** (✉ 322 E. 4th St., Hutchinson 67501, ☎ 316/669–8281, FAX 316/669–8282), 48 rooms; *$.*

Campgrounds

Gunsmoke Campground (✉ R.R. 2, W. Hwy. 50, Dodge City 67801, ☎ 316/227–8247). **Melody Acres RV Park** (✉ 1009 E. Blanchard St., Hutchinson 67501, ☎ 316/665–5048). **Watersports Campground** (✉ 500 E. Cherry St., Dodge City 67801, ☎ 316/225–9003 or 888/441–0941).

Nightlife

In Dodge City, the **Boot Hill Museum Repertory Co.** (☞ Boot Hill Museum *in* Exploring the Santa Fe Trail Region, *above*) puts on the 19th-century–style Long Branch Variety Show. Also in Dodge City, the **Longhorn Saloon** (✉ 706 N. 2nd St., ☎ 316/225–3546) has a restaurant and a 1,350-square-ft wooden dance floor for western stomping.

Outdoor Activities and Sports

Hiking

At **Dillon Nature Center,** in Hutchinson (✉ 3002 E. 30th St., ☎ 316/663–7411), a 2-mi-long National Recreation Trail takes in woods, prairie, and wetlands.

Spectator Sports

Rodeo: The Professional Rodeo Cowboys Association's biggest Kansas rodeo is the **Dodge City Roundup Rodeo** (☎ 316/225–2244), held for five days each summer during the Dodge City Days festival.

ELSEWHERE IN KANSAS

Wichita

Visitor Information

Convention and Visitors Bureau (✉ 100 S. Main St., Suite 100, 67202, ☎ 316/265–2800 or 800/288–9424).

Arriving and Departing

Wichita lies about 190 mi southwest of Kansas City on the Kansas Turnpike (I–35). Most visitors arrive by car or fly into **Wichita Mid-Continent Airport** (☎ 316/946–4700), served by most major domestic carriers.

What to See and Do

Originally a frontier town, **Wichita** is known today as one of the airplane-production capitals of the world—Beech, Cessna, and Learjet are based here, and Boeing has a major installation. The city is also home to such corporate giants as Coleman, which manufactures camping equipment, and Pizza Hut.

The **Indian Center Museum** (✉ 650 N. Seneca St., ☎ 316/262–5221; 🎫 $2) displays artifacts from numerous tribes, including the Crow and the Sioux. The **Old Cowtown Museum** (✉ 1871 Sim Park Dr., ☎ 316/264–0671; 🎫 $6) is a re-created 19th-century town. At **Botanica, the Wichita Gardens** (✉ 701 N. Amidon, ☎ 316/264–0448; 🎫 $4.50 Apr.–Dec., free Jan.–Mar.), more than 9 acres of perennials and woody plants are displayed among dozens of fountains and pools. The **Wichita Greyhound Park** (✉ 10 mi north of downtown Wichita on I–135, ☎ 316/755–4000 or 800/872–2894) offers live horse- and greyhound racing, as well as simulcast races from around the country.

Dining and Lodging

$$ ✕ **Scotch & Sirloin.** Hearty comfort food is served amidst red carpets and brass candelabras. Though prime rib is the specialty, you'll also find seafood and poultry on the menu. ✉ *5325 Kellogg, 67218,* ☎ *316/685–8701. AE, D, MC, V.*

$ ✕ **River City Brewery.** This rustic pub lives up to its slogan of fresh ales, flavorful food, and fair prices. Venison is a regular favorite. ✉ *150 N. Mosely,* ☎ *316/263–2739. AE, D, MC, V.*

$$$$ 🏨 **Hyatt Regency.** On the east bank of the Arkansas River, the Hyatt is connected to the Century II Convention Center. ✉ *400 W. Waterman St.,* ☎ *316/293–1923 or 800/233–1234,* FAX *316/293–1200. 303 rooms. Restaurant, pool, health club. CP. AE, D, DC, MC, V.*

Fort Scott

Visitor Information

The **Fort Scott Visitor Center** (✉ 231 E. Wall St., ☎ 800/245–3678) has an hourly trolley tour (from April through December only) of town highlights.

Arriving and Departing

Fort Scott is an easy 100-mi drive south of Kansas City on Route 69. Designated a National Military Highway, the route is sparsely populated but dotted with several historical markers describing the Indian and Civil War battles that took place in the region.

What to See and Do

The violence and bloodshed in this area during the period leading up to the Civil War are considered by many historians to have had a greater impact on the start of the war than the shots fired at Fort Sumter. Today ★ nine of the original buildings at the **Fort Scott National Historic Site** (✉ Old Fort Blvd., ☎ 316/223–0310; 🎫 $2 Mar.–Nov., free Dec.–Feb.) are fully restored, and daily reenactments demonstrate life in this frontier post. Fort Scott offers numerous summer and fall festivals and activities.

Dining and Lodging

$ ✕ **Papa Don's.** Feast on excellent pizza and pasta, then finish up with ice cream and cookies at this charming stop on historic Main Street. ✉ *22 N. Main,* ☎ *316/223–4171. D, MC, V.*

$$ **The Lyons House Bed and Breakfast.** One of two identical homes built side-by-side in the 1860s for daughters of a wealthy banker, this three-story Victorian home is completely restored in rich velvets, tapestries, and detailed walnut carvings. ✉ *742 S. National,* ☎ *316/223–0779 or 800/784–8378. 4 rooms.*

MISSOURI

Updated by Diana Lambdin Meyer

Capital	Jefferson City
Population	5,402,000
Motto	Let the Welfare of the People Be the Supreme Law
State Bird	Eastern bluebird
State Flower	Hawthorn
Postal Abbreviation	MO

Statewide Visitor Information

The **Missouri Division of Tourism** (✉ Truman State Office Bldg., Box 1055, Jefferson City 65102, ☎ 573/751–4133 or 800/877–1234 in MO) operates six visitor centers.

Scenic Drives

Route 21 from St. Louis to Doniphan in extreme southern Missouri passes through national forests and rugged hill country. Scenic routes in the Ozark Mountains of southwestern Missouri include **Route 76, Route 248,** and **U.S. 65** south of Springfield.

National and State Parks

National Parks

The **Ozark National Scenic Riverways** (✉ National Park Service, Box 490, Van Buren 63965, ☎ 573/323–4236) includes the Current and Jacks Fork rivers, two south-central Missouri rivers that were the first to be federally protected. Both offer good canoeing. The **Mark Twain National Forest** (✉ 401 Fairgrounds Rd., Rolla 65401, ☎ 573/364–4621) is in southern Missouri.

State Parks

Lake of the Ozarks State Park (✉ U.S. 54, ☎ 573/348–2694) is the largest state park in Missouri. The popular **Missouri River State Trail,** known to locals as the Katy Trail, is a walking-and-cycling path, much of it along the Missouri River between Sedalia and St. Charles. Other significant parks include **Elephant Rocks** (✉ Belleview 63623, ☎ 573/546–3454), **Johnson's Shut-Ins** (✉ Middle Brook 63656, ☎ 573/546–2450), **Mastodon State Park** (✉ Imperial 63052, ☎ 314/464–3079), and **Onondaga Cave State Park** (✉ Leasburg 65535, ☎ 573/245–6576). For more information contact the **Missouri Department of Natural Resources** (Division of State Parks, ✉ Box 176, Jefferson City 65101, ☎ 573/751–2479 or 800/334–6946).

ST. LOUIS

Founded by the French in 1764 as a fur-trading settlement on the west bank of the Mississippi River, St. Louis is best known for the soaring silver arch so impressive to travelers entering the city from the east. In its early days the city thrived as a river port, then as a rail hub, and today it's the world headquarters for such diverse corporations as Anheuser-Busch. The building of the Gateway Arch nearly 30 years ago did more than commemorate the city's role in westward expansion—it helped spark the rebirth of a downtown that had been abandoned in the rush for the suburbs.

Visitor Information

Convention and Visitors Commission (✉ One Metropolitan Square, Suite 1100, 63102, ☎ 314/421–1023 or 800/888–3861) is open weekdays from 8:30 to 5. **Visitor centers** are at the airport and downtown (✉ 308 Washington Ave., ☎ 314/241–1764). The **Missouri Tourist Information Center** (✉ I–270 at the Riverview exit, ☎ 314/869–7100) is just west of the Missouri-Illinois border.

Arriving and Departing

By Bus

Greyhound Lines (✉ 1450 N. 13th St., ☎ 800/231–2222).

By Car

From I–70, I–55, and I–44 follow the exits for downtown St. Louis. From U.S. 40 (I–64), exit at Broadway.

By Plane

Lambert–St. Louis International Airport (☎ 314/426–8000), 10 mi northwest of downtown on I–70, has scheduled flights by most major domestic and foreign carriers. It's about 20 minutes by car from the airport to downtown St. Louis; taxis cost about $20. Transportation is also provided to downtown stops by the **Bi-State** bus (☎ 314/231–2345) and to downtown hotels by **Airport Express** shuttle vans (☎ 314/429–4950).

By Train

Amtrak (✉ 550 S. 16th St., ☎ 314/331–3300 or 800/872–7245).

Getting Around St. Louis

Downtown sights can be explored on foot; elsewhere you'll need a car. **MetroLink**(☎ 314/231–2345), the city's light-rail system, stops near major attractions downtown. The price of a one-way ticket is $1. Rides are free between Laclede's Landing and Union Station weekdays from 10 to 3.

Exploring St. Louis

Downtown

A ride to the top of the 630-ft **Gateway Arch** is a must. The centerpiece of the 91-acre **Jefferson National Expansion Memorial Park**, the arch was built in 1966 to commemorate the city where thousands of 19th-century pioneers stopped for provisions before traveling west. A tram takes visitors up through one of the arch's legs to an observation room with a terrific view of the city and the Mississippi. Below it is the underground visitor center and the **Museum of Westward Expansion.** ✉ *On the riverfront at Market St.,* ☎ *314/425–4465.* 🎫 *$6.*

Just down the steps from the Gateway Arch is the Mississippi riverfront and its cobblestone levee, where permanently moored **riverboats** house a handful of mostly fast-food restaurants. The ***Tom Sawyer*** and ***Becky Thatcher*** (☎ 314/621–4040), replicas of 19th-century steamboats, offer one-hour sightseeing trips and two-hour dinner cruises. Nearby is the ***President Casino on the Admiral*** (☎ 314/622–1111), a noncruising riverboat that offers casino gambling in a Las Vegas–style environment. Northwest of the Gateway Arch is **Laclede's Landing,** nine square blocks of cobblestone streets and restored 19th-century warehouses, now filled with shops, galleries, restaurants, and nightspots.

West of the Gateway Arch is St. Louis's oldest church, the **Old Cathedral Basilica of St. Louis, the King** (✉ 209 Walnut St., ☎ 314/231–

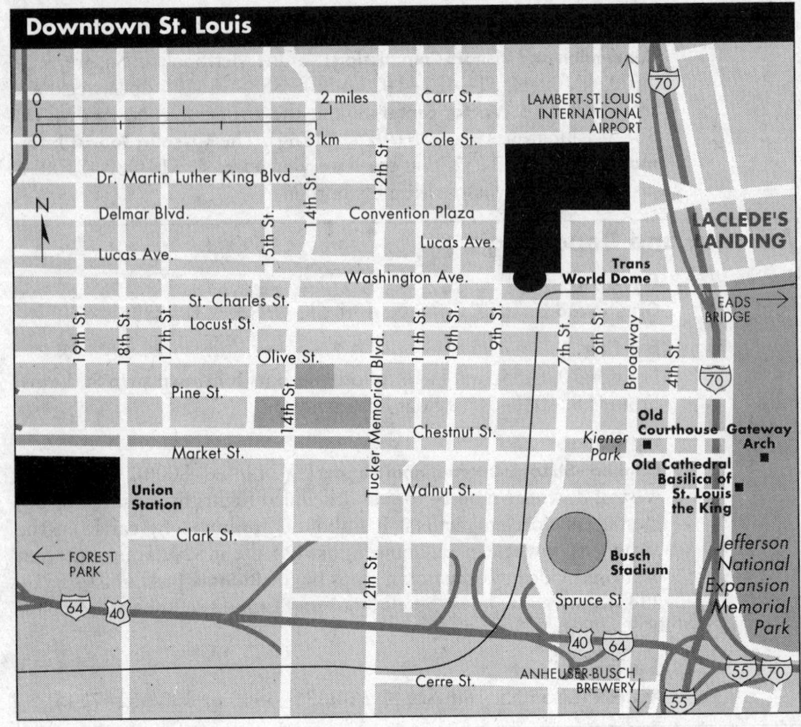

3250), a simple Greek Revival structure built in 1834. On Market Street, the **Old Courthouse** (✉ 11 N. 4th St., ☎ 314/425–4465; 🎫 $4) houses displays and photographs of early St. Louis.

South of the Old Courthouse is **Busch Stadium,** home of the St. Louis Cardinals (☞ Spectator Sports, *below*). Just across the street is the **National Bowling Hall of Fame** (☎ 314/231–6340; 🎫 $5), where you can bowl in a 1930s alley and learn more about the history of the sport. On the northeast side of the stadium is the **St. Louis Cardinals Hall of Fame,** displaying sports memorabilia and audio and video highlights of the city's baseball history. ✉ *Off I–40 (exit at 9th St.),* ☎ *314/421–3263.* 🎫 *$5. Closed weekends Jan.–Mar.*

Other Attractions

St. Louis is home to the world's largest brewer, **Anheuser-Busch,** maker of Budweiser beer. Tours of the company's world headquarters, in south St. Louis, include the stables where the famous Clydesdale horses are kept. ✉ *12th and Lynch Sts.,* ☎ *314/577–2626.* 🎫 *Free. Closed Sun.*

On the western edge of town is **Forest Park** (✉ North of U.S. 40 between Kingshighway and Skinker Blvds.), whose grounds include a variety of attractions. Within the park, the **St. Louis Zoo** (✉ 1 Government Dr., ☎ 314/781–0900; 🎫 free) has a high-tech education center. The **St. Louis Art Museum** (✉ 1 Fine Arts Dr., ☎ 314/721–0072; 🎫 free), next to the St. Louis Zoo, has outstanding pre-Columbian and German expressionist collections. The **St. Louis Science Center** (✉ 5050 Oakland Ave., ☎ 314/289–4444; 🎫 free), in the southeast part of Forest Park, contains more than 600 hands-on exhibits on ecology, space, and humanity. **The Magic House** (✉ 516 Kirkwood Blvd., ☎ 314/822–8900; 🎫 $4.50) is a restored Victorian house with interactive learning experiences.

A mind-boggling collection of mosaics covers the walls, ceilings, and three domes of the **Cathedral of St. Louis** (✉ Lindell Blvd. and Newstead Ave., ☎ 314/533–2824), also known as the New Cathedral.

The **Missouri Botanical Garden** (✉ 4344 Shaw Ave., ☎ 314/577–5100; 🎟 $3), known locally as Shaw's Garden for founder Henry Shaw, is a 15-minute drive southwest of downtown. Highlights include an impressive Japanese garden and a tropical rain forest housed in a geodesic dome.

St. Louisans love **Ted Drewes'** frozen custard (✉ 6726 Chippewa St., ☎ 314/481–2652) so much they'll stand in lines that spill into the street, but don't worry—the lines move fast. You'll label yourself a tourist if you have to ask what a concrete is (it's frozen custard so thick it won't budge even when you flip the cup upside down).

Six Flags over Mid-America–St. Louis (✉ I–44 and Allenton Rd., Eureka, ☎ 314/938–4800; 🎟 $29.95, $24.95 children 4–10), about 30 mi southwest of St. Louis, has amusement rides and shows. **Grant's Farm** (✉ 10501 Gravois, ☎ 314/843–1700; 🎟 $6), closed from November through March, is a favorite of St. Louis children for its petting zoo, animal preserve, and train ride to visit the Clydesdales; reservations are essential.

Dining

St. Louis's Hill neighborhood has an Italian restaurant on nearly every corner; other ethnic restaurants are found throughout the city. Even the abundant steak houses carry an Italian dish or two. The Central West End and Laclede's Landing have a number of restaurants, as does Clayton, the St. Louis County seat, about 7 mi west of downtown. For price ranges *see* Chart 1 (A) *in* On the Road with Fodor's.

$$$ ✕ **Tony's.** St. Louis's only five-star restaurant since the 1950s, Tony's has been run by the Bommarito family for three generations. Superb Italian dishes and prime steaks make it a favorite. ✉ *410 Market St.,* ☎ *314/231–7007. Reservations essential. Jacket and tie. AE, D, DC, MC, V. Closed Sun. No lunch.*

$$–$$$ ✕ **Sidney Street Cafe.** Tables for two in the atrium and a candlelighted dining room lend romance to this former storefront in the Benton Park neighborhood. The eclectic cuisine includes raspberry or tequila-lime chicken. ✉ *2000 Sidney St.,* ☎ *314/771–5777. AE, D, DC, MC, V. Closed Sun.–Mon.*

$$ ✕ **Blue Water Grill.** Grilled seafood with a southwestern flair is the specialty at this small, festive restaurant near the Hill. On Monday night diners can mix and match "Flying Saucers," an assortment of miniature entrées. ✉ *2607 Hampton Ave.,* ☎ *314/645–0707. AE, MC, V. Closed Sun.*

$$ ✕ **Cardwell's.** At this sophisticated Clayton establishment, diners can eat in the airy café with marble-top tables and French doors or in the more formal, elegant dining room. The frequently changing menu may include salmon with a sesame-seed crust or perhaps even wild boar. ✉ *8100 Maryland St.,* ☎ *314/726–5055. AE, MC, V. Closed Sun.*

$–$$ ★ ✕ **Cunetto's House of Pasta.** There's usually a wait at this popular restaurant on the Hill, but relaxing in the cocktail lounge is part of the experience. Once seated, you'll find plenty of veal and beef dishes from which to choose, as well as more than 30 different pastas. ✉ *5453 Magnolia Ave.,* ☎ *314/781–1135. Reservations not accepted for dinner. AE, DC, MC, V. Closed Sun.*

$ ★ ✕ **Big Sky Café.** Owned and operated by the same family as the Blue Water Grill (☞ *above*), this casual café is popular with the business lunch crowd in Webster Groves. Try the pungent garlic mashed potatoes. ✉ *45 S. Old Orchard,* ☎ *314/962–5757. AE, MC, V.*

$ ✕ **Blueberry Hill.** At this St. Louis original, in the hip University City
★ neighborhood, you can order a burger and a Rock 'n Roll beer, plunk a quarter into the famous 2,000-tune jukebox, and let the good times roll. ✉ *6504 Delmar Blvd.,* ☎ *314/727–0880. Reservations not accepted. AE, D, DC, MC, V.*

$ ✕ **Rigazzi's.** Generous, inexpensive servings of pasta keep locals coming back to this no-frills pasta house on the Hill. ✉ *4945 Daggett St.,* ☎ *314/772–4900. AE, MC, V. Closed Sun.*

Lodging

Most of St. Louis's big hotels are downtown or in Clayton, about 7 mi west. For bed-and-breakfasts in town, call or write **Bed and Breakfasts of St. Louis, River Country of Missouri and Illinois** (✉ 1900 Wyoming St., St. Louis 63118, ☎ 314/771–1993). For price ranges *see* Chart 2 (A) *in* On the Road with Fodor's.

$$$–$$$$ **Hyatt Regency St. Louis at Union Station.** Most of the rooms are in a contemporary garden setting beneath the arched trusses of Union Station's original train station. The Regency Club offers deluxe rooms and suites. ✉ *1 St. Louis Union Station, 63103,* ☎ *314/231–1234,* FAX *314/436–6827. 536 rooms. 2 restaurants, pool, exercise room. AE, D, DC, MC, V.*

$$$ **Omni Majestic.** This small European-style hotel downtown is often the choice of visiting celebrities. The building, more than 85 years old, is filled with reproduction antiques. ✉ *1019 Pine St., 63101,* ☎ *314/436–2355 or 800/451–2355,* FAX *314/436–0223. 94 rooms. Restaurant. AE, D, DC, MC, V.*

$$$ **Ritz-Carlton, St. Louis.** Chandeliers and museum-quality oil paintings fill this luxury hotel in Clayton. Some rooms on the top floors have views of the downtown St. Louis skyline. ✉ *100 Carondelet Plaza, Clayton 63105,* ☎ *314/863–6300 or 800/241–3333,* FAX *314/863–3525. 301 rooms. 2 restaurants, pool, exercise room. AE, D, DC, MC, V.*

$$ **Drury Inn–Union Station.** Lead-glass windows and marble columns
★ give historic charm to this former YMCA. Among its assets are its complimentary breakfasts and its excellent location next door to Union Station. ✉ *201 S. 20th St., 63103,* ☎ *314/231–3900,* FAX *314/231–3900. 176 rooms. Restaurant, pool. CP. AE, D, DC, MC, V.*

Motels

Red Roof Inn (✉ 5823 Wilson St., ☎ 314/645–0101, FAX 314/645–0101, ext. 444), 110 rooms; *$$.* **Budgetel Inn West Port** (✉ 12330 Dorsett Rd., 63043, ☎ 314/878–1212, FAX 314/878–3409), 145 rooms, breakfast room; *$.* **Fairfield Inn by Marriott** (✉ 9079 Dunn Rd., 63042, ☎ 314/731–7700, FAX 314/731–7700, ext. 709), 135 rooms, pool; *$.*

Nightlife and the Arts

Nightlife

Much of St. Louis's nightlife can be found in the jazz and blues clubs in the redeveloped areas of **Laclede's Landing,** on the riverfront, and in **Soulard,** on the southern edge of downtown. For gambling head to the **President Riverboat Casino** (✉ 800 N. 1st St., ☎ 314/622–3000 or 800/772–3647), **Casino St. Charles** (✉ S. 5th St., ☎ 314/949–7777), or upriver to the ***Alton Belle* Riverboat Casino** (✉ 219 Piasa St., Alton, IL, ☎ 618/474–7500 or 800/336–7568). To find out who's playing where, consult the *St. Louis Post-Dispatch*'s Thursday calendar section or the free weekly paper the *Riverfront Times.*

The Arts

The **Fabulous Fox Theatre** (✉ 527 N. Grand Blvd., ☎ 314/534–1678) hosts major shows and concerts. The **Riverport Amphitheatre** (✉ 14141 Riverport Dr., ☎ 314/298–9944) stages big-name concerts. The St. Louis Symphony Orchestra presents programs at **Powell Symphony Hall** (✉ 718 N. Grand Blvd., ☎ 314/534–1700). For tickets to major events call **Dialtix** (☎ 314/291–7600).

Spectator Sports

Baseball: St. Louis Cardinals (✉ Busch Stadium, 250 Stadium Plaza, ☎ 314/421–3060). **Football: St. Louis Rams** (✉ Trans World Dome, 801 Convention Plaza, ☎ 800/847–7267). **Ice hockey: St. Louis Blues** (✉ Kiel Center, 1401 Clark Ave., ☎ 314/291–7600). **Incline roller hockey: St. Louis Vipers** (✉ 1819 Clarkson Blvd., ☎ 314/530–1967). **Soccer: St. Louis Ambush** (✉ 7547 Ravensridge, ☎ 314/962–4625).

Shopping

For browsing in boutiques and specialty shops, try **Union Station** (✉ 1820 Market St.), an impressive former train station, and **Laclede's Landing** (☞ Exploring St. Louis, *above*). The **Central West End,** along Euclid Avenue east of Forest Park, is an area of hip boutiques and restaurants. The city's most sophisticated shoppers head for **Plaza Frontenac** (✉ Clayton Rd. and Lindbergh Blvd., ☎ 314/432–0604), home to nearly 50 upscale stores. Antiques and crafts lovers should visit historic downtown **St. Charles** (✉ I–70 and First Capital Dr.), seven cobblestoned blocks of shops and restaurants on the banks of the Missouri River.

KANSAS CITY

With upwards of 200 fountains, more than any city except Rome, and more boulevard miles (155) than Paris, Kansas City is attractive and cosmopolitan. This spread-out metropolitan area, which straddles the Missouri-Kansas line, has a rich history as a frontier river port and trade center, where wagon trains were outfitted before heading west on the Santa Fe and Oregon trails. Through the years it has been home to the nation's second-largest stockyards, to saxophone player Charlie "Bird" Parker and his Kansas City–style bebop, and to some of the best barbecue in the world.

Visitor Information

Greater Kansas City: The Convention and Visitors Bureau (✉ 1100 Main St., Suite 2550, 64105, ☎ 816/221–5242 or 800/767–7700) is in City Center Square in downtown Kansas City. Its visitor information (☎ 816/691–3800) offers a weekly recording of activities. The **Missouri Information Center** (✉ I–70 and Blue Ridge Cutoff; 4010 Blue Ridge Cutoff, 64133, ☎ 816/889–3330) overlooks the Truman Sports Complex.

Arriving and Departing

By Bus

Greyhound Lines (✉ 11th St. and Troost Ave., ☎ 800/231–2222).

By Car

From I–70 or I–35 exit at Broadway for downtown. From the airport, I–29 from the north merges with I–35 north of the city.

By Plane

Kansas City International Airport (☎ 816/243–5237), 20 minutes northwest of downtown on I–29, is served by major domestic airlines.

Taxi service is zoned; the maximum fare from the airport to downtown Kansas City is $26. For $11 **KCI Shuttle** buses (☎ 816/243–5950) will take you to major downtown hotels.

By Train

Amtrak (✉ 2200 Main St., ☎ 816/421–3622 or 800/872–7245).

Getting Around Kansas City

Attractions are scattered throughout the metropolitan region, making cars important for visitors. However, **Kansas City Trolley Co.**'s replica trolleys (☎ 816/221–3399; 🎫 $5, exact change required) offers a fun mode of transportation between the sites downtown and the River Market area, as well as Crown Center, Westport, and the Country Club Plaza; the drivers are usually entertaining and well versed in local history.

Exploring Kansas City

Plaza, Midtown, Downtown

Kansas City's **Country Club Plaza** (✉ 47th and Main Sts., ☎ 816/753–0100) is known for its more than 180 fine shops and restaurants, its Spanish-style architecture, and its annual display of holiday lights from Thanksgiving to January, when hundreds of thousands of gaily colored bulbs outline the plaza's buildings. Here you'll also find many of the city's ★ fountains and statues. Several blocks east of the plaza is the **Nelson-Atkins Museum of Art** (✉ 4525 Oak St., ☎ 816/561–4000; 🎫 $5, free on Sat.), known principally for its outstanding Asian art collection and the Henry Moore Sculpture Garden on the south grounds.

The **Kemper Museum of Contemporary Art and Design** (✉ 4420 Warwick Blvd., ☎ 816/753–5784; 🎫 free) has a permanent collection of 400 works of art encompassing a broad range of media. Next to the Kemper Museum is the **Kansas City Art Institute** (✉ 4415 Warwick Blvd., ☎ 816/561–4852; 🎫 free), a four-year college of art and design spread across 4 acres dotted with sculptures. A tour of the campus includes a visit to the institute's student-run student gallery, which exhibits two- to three-dimensional contemporary artwork.

Before there was a Kansas City, there was a **Westport** (✉ North of the Plaza at Broadway and Westport Rd., ☎ 816/756–2789), built along the Santa Fe Trail as an outfitting center for wagon trains heading west. Today this area is filled with renovated and new buildings housing trendy shops, restaurants, and nightspots.

On the crest of a hill at the northern edge of Penn Valley Park, north ★ of Westport, is the **Liberty Memorial** (✉ 100 W. 26th St., ☎ 816/221–1918), dedicated to those who served in World War I. Extensive structural renovation has temporarily closed the tower's 217-ft observation deck and the museum. However, museum items are on display in the **Town Pavilion** (✉ 12th and Main Sts.).

Just across Main Street from the Liberty Memorial is **Crown Center** (✉ 2450 Grand Ave., ☎ 816/274–8444), an 85-acre shopping mall and entertainment, office, and hotel complex. In summer free Friday night concerts are held on the terrace; a covered outdoor ice-skating rink is open in winter. Kansas City–based Hallmark Cards, the largest maker of greeting cards in the world, built Crown Center and has its headquarters here. Monday through Saturday you can stop by the **Hallmark Visitors Center** (✉ 2501 McGee St., ☎ 816/274–3613), which features a display about the history of the greeting card industry and a bow-making machine (you get to keep the bow). **Kaleidoscope,** (✉ 2501 McGee St., ☎ 816/274–8300; 🎫 free; reservations required),

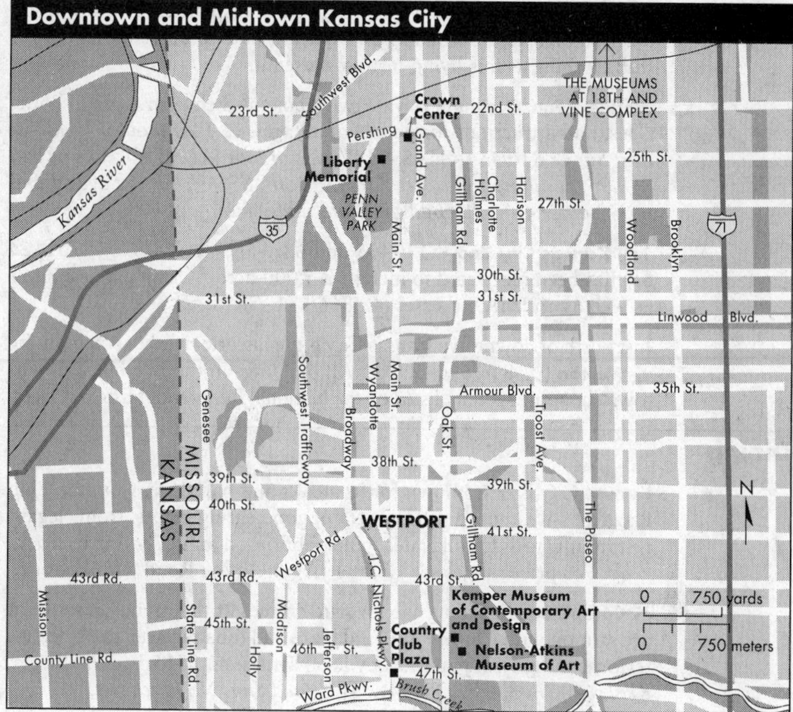

Downtown and Midtown Kansas City

is a hands-on creative arts center for children offered as a public service by Hallmark employees.

In the River Market area, north of downtown, the ***Arabia* Steamboat Museum** (✉ 400 Grand Ave., ☎ 816/471–4030; 🎫 $6.50) houses goods—from French perfume to buttons to coffeepots—all salvaged from the *Arabia*'s muddy grave 132 years after it sank in the Missouri River in 1856.

In the Museums at 18th and Vine complex, the cornerstone of the historic 18th and Vine district, the **Negro Leagues Baseball Museum** (✉ 1616 E. 18th St., ☎ 816/221–1920; 🎫 $6, $8 joint ticket with Kansas City Jazz Museum) documents the history of African-Americans in baseball with exhibit films and a multimedia gallery. The **Kansas City Jazz Museum** ✉ (1616 E. 18th St., ☎ 816/474–8463; 🎫 $6, $8 joint ticket with Negro Leagues Baseball Museum), which shares the Museums at 18th and Vine complex with the Negro Leagues Baseball Museum, honors Louis Armstrong, Duke Ellington, Ella Fitzgerald, and Charlie Parker. You can listen to hundreds of jazz CDs in the interactive studio and sound library.

Other Attractions

Just east of Kansas City is **Independence,** once the home of President Harry S. Truman. Truman's life and career are the focus at the **Harry S. Truman Library and Museum** (✉ U.S. 24 and Delaware St., ☎ 816/833–1225; 🎫 $5). The **Truman Home** (✉ 219 N. Delaware St., ☎ 816/254–9929; 🎫 $2; ✉ 223 Main St., for ticket center), which is closed Sunday, was the Trumans's summer White House.

Fleming Park (✉ 22807 Woods Chapel Rd., ☎ 816/795–8200), in Blue Springs south of Independence, contains the 970-acre Lake Jacomo. Also in Fleming Park is **Missouri Town 1855** (🎫 $3), a reproduction

1800s town created from more than 30 transplanted period houses, barns, stores, and outbuildings. The staff and volunteers dress in period clothing at this living-history museum.

★ **Worlds of Fun/Oceans of Fun** are two adjoining theme parks, with shows, rides, and attractions for people of all ages. ✉ *East loop of I–435 at Exit 54,* ☎ *816/454–4545;* *Worlds of Fun $26.95, Oceans of Fun $18.95, combination ticket $36.95. Both: $5.95 children ages 4 and up or under 48" tall, children 3 and under free.*

The **Kansas City Zoo** (✉ I–435 and 63rd St., ☎ 816/871–5701; $5) has been renovated to include a 5,000-acre African plains exhibit as well as an **IMAX theater** (☎ 816/871–5858; $6).

Just north of downtown Kansas City is the historic riverboat community of **Weston** (☎ 816/640–2909). All buildings in the five-block downtown shopping area are listed on the National Register of Historic Places.

Dining

Kansas City is best known for its steaks and barbecue. Country Club Plaza and Westport have a variety of good eating places, from elegant restaurants to sidewalk cafés to neighborhood joints serving barroom grub. For price ranges *see* Chart 1 (A) *in* On the Road with Fodor's.

$$ ✕ **Cafe Allegro.** Among the favorite entrées at this trendy restaurant are salmon with Chinese mustard glaze and tuna tartare. The brick interior is hung with paintings by local artists. ✉ *1815 W. 39th St.,* ☎ *816/561–3663. AE, DC, MC, V. Closed Sun. No lunch Sat.*

$$ ✕ **Golden Ox.** Just down the street from Kemper Arena, this popular steak house serves prime rib in a comfortable western atmosphere. ✉ *1600 Gennessee St.,* ☎ *816/842–2866. AE, D, DC, MC, V. No lunch Sun.*

$$ ★ ✕ **Plaza III–The Steakhouse.** This handsome, nationally known restaurant at Country Club Plaza serves excellent steaks, prime rib, and seafood; its steak soup is legendary. ✉ *4749 Pennsylvania Ave.,* ☎ *816/753–0000. AE, D, DC, MC, V. No lunch Sun.*

$$ ✕ **Savoy Grill.** Locals often choose this historic, turn-of-the-century beauty when celebrating a special occasion. Maine lobster and a T-bone steak from the restaurant's own herd are good choices here. ✉ *219 W. 9th St.,* ☎ *816/842–3890. AE, D, DC, MC, V. No lunch Sun.*

$$ ★ ✕ **Stroud's.** This sprawling building on Kansas City's north side was once the first stagecoach stop for travelers on their way to St. Joseph. After feasting on fried chicken and homemade pies, take a stroll around the grounds, complete with ponds, geese, and swans. ✉ *5410 N.E. Oak Ridge Dr.,* ☎ *816/454–9600. AE, DC, MC, V.*

$ ★ ✕ **Arthur Bryant's.** Although there are reportedly more than 70 barbecue joints in Kansas City, Bryant's—low on decor but high on taste—tops the list for locals, who don't mind standing in line to order from the counter. ✉ *1727 Brooklyn Ave.,* ☎ *816/231–1123. AE, MC, V.*

Lodging

Kansas City offers a core of major hotels within walking distance of Country Club Plaza and Westport or in the Crown Center complex. For a listing of B&Bs contact **Bed & Breakfast Kansas City** (✉ Box 14781, Lenexa 66285, ☎ 913/888–3636). For price ranges *see* Chart 2 (A) *in* On the Road with Fodor's.

$$$–$$$$ ★ **Ritz-Carlton.** Crystal chandeliers, imported marble, and fine art fill this luxury hotel. Some rooms have balconies and views of the plaza.

✉ *401 Ward Pkwy., 64112,* ☎ *816/756–1500,* FAX *816/756–1635. 366 rooms. 2 restaurants, pool, health club. AE, D, DC, MC, V.*

$$$ 🏨 **Westin Crown Center.** Part of the Crown Center complex, the Westin has a bustling lobby complete with a five-story waterfall and a natural limestone cliff. All rooms have views; the best ones face Crown Center Square to the east. ✉ *1 Pershing Rd., 64108,* ☎ *816/474–4400 or 800/228–3000,* FAX *816/391–4490. 774 rooms. 3 restaurants, pool, health club. AE, D, DC, MC, V.*

$$–$$$ ★ 🏨 **The Raphael.** Built in 1927 as an apartment house, the Raphael today is the only intimate, European-style hotel in the city. Despite its small size, many rooms are large and have excellent views of the plaza. ✉ *325 Ward Pkwy., 64112,* ☎ *816/756–3800 or 800/821–5343,* FAX *816/756–3800. 123 rooms. Restaurant. AE, D, DC, MC, V.*

$$ 🏨 **Quarterage Hotel.** This intimate brick hotel in the Westport area is central to many activities in the metropolitan area. ✉ *560 Westport Rd., 64111,* ☎ *816/931–0001 or 800/942–4233,* FAX *816/931–8891. 123 rooms. Health club. Full breakfast. AE, D, DC, MC, V.*

$–$$ 🏨 **Drury Inn–Stadium.** Across from the sports complex, this chain hotel offers clean, comfortable rooms. Make reservations well ahead of time during sporting events—rooms fill up fast. ✉ *3830 Blue Ridge Cutoff, 64133,* ☎ FAX *816/923–3000. 133 rooms. Pool. Complimentary breakfast. AE, D, DC, MC, V.*

Nightlife and the Arts

Nightlife

Much of Kansas City's nightlife can be found in the Westport and Plaza areas. The **Grand Emporium** (✉ 3832 Main St., ☎ 816/531–1504) is *the* place in town for blues. The city is justly proud of its jazz heritage, and live performances are featured at several establishments; for information call the **Jazz Hotline** (☎ 816/763–1052). The **Blue Room** (☎ 816/474–8463, ext. 215 or 216), in the Kansas City Jazz Museum (☞ Exploring Kansas City, *above*), reels jazz fans in on Monday, Thursday, Friday, and Saturday nights with live bands.

Standford's Comedy House (✉ 504 Westport Rd., ☎ 816/756–1450; 🎟 $10) features local and national comedians. **Riverboat gambling** is popular along the banks of this Missouri River town. Three noncruising boats in the Kansas City area are the Argosy (✉ Hwy. 9 and I–635, Riverside, ☎ 816/741–7568), Harrah's Casino (✉ Armour Rd., North Kansas City, ☎ 816/471–3364), and Sam's Town (✉ E. 18th St., North Kansas City, ☎ 816/764–4757).

The Arts

The **Folly Theater** (✉ 12th and Central Sts., ☎ 816/842–5500) stages comedy acts, ballet, operas, and theater. The **Midland Center for the Performing Arts** (✉ 1228 Main St., ☎ 816/471–8600) has shows and concerts. The Lyric Opera of Kansas City and the Kansas City Symphony perform at the **Lyric Theatre** (✉ 11th and Central Sts., ☎ 816/471–7344). For information on upcoming events check the Friday and Sunday editions of the *Kansas City Star.* Call **TicketMaster** (☎ 816/931–3330) for tickets to main events.

Spectator Sports

Baseball: Kansas City Royals (✉ Kauffman Stadium, Truman Sports Complex, I–70 and Blue Ridge Cutoff, ☎ 816/921–8000). **Football: Kansas City Chiefs** (✉ Arrowhead Stadium, Truman Sports Complex, ☎ 816/924–9400). **Indoor soccer: Kansas City Attack** (✉ Kemper Arena, 1800 Gennessee, ☎ 816/474–2255). **Outdoor soccer: Kansas City Wizards** (✉ 706 Broadway, Suite 100, 64105, ☎ 816/472–4625).

Shopping

Kansas City's finest shopping is at **Country Club Plaza,** and a number of specialty shops and boutiques are concentrated in **Westport** and at **Crown Center** (for all, ☞ Exploring Kansas City, *above*).

THE OZARKS

The Ozark hill region of southern Missouri is famed for its wooded mountaintops; clear, spring-fed streams; and its water playgrounds of Lake of the Ozarks and Table Rock Lake. Branson, the nation's second country music capital after Nashville, attracts 5 million visitors a year to its star-studded theaters.

Visitor Information

Greater Lake of the Ozarks: Convention and Visitors Bureau (✉ Box 827, Osage Beach 65065, ☎ 573/348–1599 or 800/386–5253). **Table Rock Lake/Kimberling City Area:** Chamber of Commerce (✉ Box 495, Kimberling City 65686, ☎ 417/739–2564). **Branson:** Branson Lakes Area Chamber of Commerce (✉ Box 220, 65616, ☎ 417/334–4136). **Springfield:** Convention and Visitors Bureau and Tourist Information Center (✉ 3315 E. Battlefield Rd., 65804-4048, ☎ 417/881–5300 or 800/678–8766).

Arriving and Departing

By Car

Many of the towns and attractions in this wide-ranging region can be reached from I–44, which cuts diagonally across the state from St. Louis to Springfield. Branson lies about 40 mi south of Springfield on U.S. 65. The Lake of the Ozarks is centrally located between St. Louis and Kansas City.

Exploring the Ozarks

Central Missouri's **Lake of the Ozarks,** formed by the damming of the Osage River in 1931, is the state's largest lake, with 1,300 mi of shoreline sprawling over 58,000 acres. In summer crowds of vacationing families descend on the numerous resorts, motels, and tourist attractions; better times to visit may be spring, when the dogwoods are abloom, and fall, when the wooded hills come alive with color.

Lake of the Ozarks State Park, (☞ National and State Parks, *above*) just south of Osage Beach, encompasses 90 mi of shoreline and offers hiking trails, other recreational activities, and tours of Ozark Caverns (☎ 314/346–2500; 🎫 $4).

You're deep in the country's Bible Belt when you reach **Springfield** (off I–44), home to two Bible colleges and a theological seminary and near several sights and cultural events with religious themes. For many people the first stop in Springfield has little to do with religion. The enormous **Bass Pro Shops Outdoor World** (✉ 1935 S. Campbell Ave., ☎ 417/887–1915), dubbed the "Sportsman's Disney World," has cascading waterfalls, a wildlife trophy collection, a boat showroom, sporting goods shops.

The visitor center at **Wilson's Creek National Battlefield** (✉ Rte. ZZ and Farm Rd. 182, ☎ 417/732–2662; 🎫 $2), southwest of Springfield, documents the first major Civil War battle fought west of the Mississippi. In Mansfield, roughly 40 mi east of Springfield on U.S. 60, is the **Laura Ingalls Wilder Home** (✉ Rte. A, ☎ 417/924–3626; 🎫 $6), a National Historic Landmark, where the much-loved children's author wrote her *Little House* books; it's closed November through ★ February. About 70 mi west of Springfield is the **George Washington Carver National Monument** (✉ Off Rte. V, ☎ 417/325–4151), honoring the birthplace of the famous black botanist and agronomist. North of the Carver Monument, in Carthage, you can tour the **Precious Moments Chapel,** which features 30 stained-glass windows and 52 colorful murals designed by Sam Butcher, creator of the Precious Moments dolls and figurines. A gift shop on premises sells Precious Moments items. (✉ 4321 Chapel Rd., ☎ 800/543–7975; donations accepted).

About 40 mi south of Springfield on U.S. 65 is **Lake Taneycomo,** the first of Missouri's man-made lakes. Lake Taneycomo's larger, more developed neighbor, **Table Rock State Park** (✉ Branson, ☎ 417/334–4704), has boating, picnicking, and plenty of motels, resorts, and commercial campgrounds. **Kimberling City** is the main resort town serving Lake Taneycomo and Table Rock.

With more than 60,000 seats in such star-studded venues as the Roy Clark Celebrity Theatre (☞ Nightlife and the Arts, *below*), **Branson** rivals Nashville as a country music mecca. Most growth has occurred along Route 76, already crowded with miniature golf courses, bumper-car concessions, souvenir and hillbilly crafts shops, motels, and resorts. **White Water** (✉ Rte. 76, Branson, ☎ 417/334–7488; $20.35) is the place for water-soaked rides and activities.

★ **Silver Dollar City** (✉ Rte. 76, ☎ 417/338–8100), just west of Branson, features Ozark artisans demonstrating traditional crafts, along with rides and music shows. Also west of Branson is the **Shepherd of the Hills Homestead and Outdoor Theatre,** a working pioneer homestead, with a gristmill, a sawmill, and smith and wheelwright shops. The *Shepherd of the Hills* inspirational drama is performed here. ✉ *Rte. 76,* ☎ *417/334–4191. $5. Closed Jan.–Apr..*

Dining and Lodging

To find out about B&Bs in the area, contact the **Ozark Mountain Country Bed and Breakfast** reservation service (✉ Box 295, Branson 65616, ☎ 417/334–4720 or 800/695–1546). For price ranges *see* Charts 1 (B) and 2 (B) *in* On the Road with Fodor's.

Branson Area

$$$ ★ ✕ **Candlestick Inn.** Prime rib rubbed in garlic and seared on the grill and fresh seafood are the specialties at this restaurant overlooking Lake Taneycomo. The two elegant dining rooms have floor-to-ceiling glass. ✉ *Rte. 76E, Branson,* ☎ *417/334–3633. AE, D, MC, V.*

$$–$$$ **Holiday Inn Branson.** Although this modern hotel is not right on Lake Taneycomo, you can view the lake from some rooms. Service is friendly and the location is convenient to area attractions. ✉ *1420 Rte. 76W (Box 340), Branson 65616,* ☎ *417/334–5101, FAX 417/334–0789. 220 rooms. Restaurant, pool. AE, D, DC, MC, V.*

$ **Kimberling Inn Resort and Conference Center.** This small resort motel on Table Rock Lake is within walking distance of Kimberling City Shopping Village's crafts shops, restaurants, and bowling. ✉ *Box 159B, Kimberling City 65686,* ☎ *417/739–4311 or 800/833–5551. 120 rooms. 3 restaurants, pools. AE, D, DC, MC, V.*

Lake of the Ozarks

$$$ ✕ **Blue Heron.** Enjoy cocktails poolside before moving to the dining room overlooking the lake at this seasonal restaurant serving steak and seafood. ✉ *Bus. Rte. 54 and Rte. HH, Osage Beach,* ☎ *573/365–4646.*

Reservations not accepted. AE, D, MC, V. Closed Sun.–Mon. and Dec.–Mar. No lunch.

$$$$ ★ **Lodge of the Four Seasons.** Golf is the primary draw here (45 holes). There's also fine dining in the Toledo Room. In winter, the rates drop dramatically but you can still expect the pampering of a first-class resort. ✉ *Box 215, Lake Ozark 65049,* ☎ *573/365–3000 or 800/843–5253,* FAX *573/865–8525. 311 rooms. 3 restaurants, pools, tennis. AE, D, DC, MC, V.*

$$$$ ★ **Marriott's Tan-Tar-A Resort and Golf Club.** One of the top choices in the region for vacations and business meetings, the resort offers two golf courses and fine dining at its Windrose Restaurant. ✉ *Rte. KK, Osage Beach 65065,* ☎ *573/348–3131 or 800/826–8272,* FAX *573/348–3206. 938 rooms. 5 restaurants, pools, tennis, exercise room. AE, D, DC, MC, V.*

$$$ **Holiday Inn Resort and Conference Center.** The hotel does not have lake access, but for a slightly higher rate you can have a view of it. ✉ *Bus. Rte. 54 (Box 1930), Lake Ozark 65049,* ☎ *573/365–2334 or 800/532–3575,* FAX *314/365–6887. 217 rooms. Restaurant, pools, exercise room. AE, D, DC, MC, V.*

Springfield

$$–$$$ **Hemingway's Blue Water Cafe.** In the Bass Pro Shops Outdoor World (☞ Exploring the Ozarks, *above*), this restaurant offers seafood, steak, pasta, and poultry. ✉ *1935 S. Campbell Ave.,* ☎ *417/887–3388. AE, D, MC, V.*

$$$ **Clarion Inn.** The rooms at this hotel in the southern end of town are clean and comfortable; the lobby is more ornate with a deep-green-and-burgundy color scheme and marble-top desks. ✉ *3333 S. Glenstone Ave., 65804,* ☎ *417/883–6550,* FAX *417/883–5720. 200 rooms. Restaurant, pool. AE, D, DC, MC, V.*

$$$ **University Plaza Holiday Inn.** Boasting the largest conference center in Missouri, this hotel has guest rooms arranged around a nine-story atrium. ✉ *333 John Q. Hammons Pkwy., 65806,* ☎ *417/864–7333,* FAX *417/831–5893, ext. 7177. 271 rooms. 2 restaurants, pools, tennis, exercise room. AE, D, DC, MC, V.*

Motels

EconoLodge (✉ 2808 N. Kansas Expressway, Springfield 65803, ☎ 417/869–5600), 83 rooms; *$*. **Red Roof Inn** (✉ 2655 N. Glenstone Ave., Springfield 65803, ☎ 417/831–2100), 112 rooms; *$*.

Campgrounds

Missouri Association of RV Parks and Campgrounds (✉ 3020 S. National Ave., No. D149, Springfield 63102-2121, ☎ 573/564–7993). **In the Lake of the Ozarks area: Deer Valley Park and Campground** (✉ Sunrise Beach, ☎ 573/374–5277), closed mid-October–mid-April; **Lake of the Ozarks State Park** (☞ Exploring the Ozarks, *above*). **In the Branson area: Blue Mountain Campground** (✉ Branson, 800/779–2114); **Port of Kimberling Marina and Campground** (✉ Kimberling City, ☎ 417/739–5377); **Silver Dollar City Campground** (✉ Branson, ☎ 417/338–8189 or 800/477–5164), closed November–March.

Nightlife and the Arts

Among the music shows in the Lake of the Ozarks region is the **Kin-Fokes Country Music Show** (✉ 28 Camden Sq., Camdenton, ☎ 573/346–6797). Music theaters in Branson include **Andy Williams Moon River Theater** (✉ 2500 W. Hwy. 76, ☎ 417/334–1800), **Baldknobbers Hillbilly Jamboree Show** (✉ 2635 W. Hwy. 76, ☎ 417/334–4528), **Grand Palace** (✉ 2700 W. Hwy. 76, ☎ 417/336–1220), **Jim Stafford**

Theater (✉ 1340 W. Hwy. 76, ☎ 417/335–8080), **Mel Tillis Theater** (✉ 2527 State Hwy. 248, ☎ 417/335–6635), **Mickey Gilley's Family Theater** (✉ 3455 W. Hwy. 76, ☎ 417/334–3210), **Presley's Mountain Music Jubilee** (✉ 2920 76 Country Blvd., ☎ 417/334–4874), **Roy Clark Celebrity Theater** (✉ 3425 W. Hwy. 76, ☎ 417/334–0076), and the **Shoji Tabuchi Show** (✉ 3260 Shepherd of the Hills Expressway, ☎ 417/334–3734). Contact the Branson Lakes Area Chamber of Commerce (☞ Visitor Information, *above*) for a complete listing.

Outdoor Activities and Sports

Canoeing

The Ozarks have some of the finest streams in the country, such as the **Current** and **Jacks Fork rivers,** two waterways protected as the **Ozark National Scenic Riverways** (☞ National and State Parks, *above*). For a list of outfitters contact the Missouri Division of Tourism (☞ Statewide Visitor Information, *above*).

Fishing

Bull Shoals Lake, Lake Taneycomo, and **Table Rock Lake** all offer excellent fishing for bass, catfish, trout, and other fish. Other good spots include **Lake of the Ozarks** and **Truman Lake.** Contact the **Missouri Department of Conservation** (✉ Box 180, Jefferson City 65102, ☎ 573/751–4115) for information on permits, costs, and seasons.

Hiking and Backpacking

The partially completed **Ozark Trail** passes through national and state forest and parkland as well as private property. For information and maps contact the **Missouri Department of Natural Resources** (✉ Division of State Parks, 101 Adams St., Jefferson City 65101, ☎ 573/751–2479 or 800/334–6946) or individual state parks (☞ National and State Parks, *above*).

Shopping

Osage Village (✉ U.S. 54, Osage Beach, ☎ 573/348–2065) is a major factory-outlet mall with about 115 stores, restaurants, and theaters.

ELSEWHERE IN MISSOURI

Hannibal

Visitor Information

Hannibal Visitors and Convention Bureau (✉ 320 Broadway, Box 624, 63401, ☎ 573/221–2477).

Arriving and Departing

Hannibal is about two hours north of St. Louis on U.S. 61.

What to See and Do

Hannibal is Mark Twain country. His boyhood home is preserved at ★ the **Mark Twain Home and Museum** (✉ 208 Hill St., ☎ 573/221–9010; 🎟 $5). The **Mark Twain Cave** (✉ Rte. 79, ☎ 573/221–1656; 🎟 $9) is where Tom Sawyer and Becky Thatcher got lost in Twain's classic *Adventures of Tom Sawyer.*

Dining and Lodging

$$ ✕ **Lula Bell's Cafe and Bed & Breakfast.** Listed on the National Register of Historic Places, this former bordello attracts a more family-oriented clientele today for a wide selection of soups and salads for lunch, shrimp and prime rib for dinner. ✉ *111 Bird St.,* ☎ *573/221–6662 or 800/882–4890. AE, D, MC, V. Closed Sun.*

$ ✕ **Riverman's Inn.** Located in the National Historic District on Hannibal's main drag, this restaurant serves homestyle cooking from breakfast 'til dinner in a casual setting. ✉ *105 S. Main,* ☏ *573/248–3077. No credit cards. Closed Mon.*

Ste. Genevieve

Arriving and Departing

Ste. Genevieve is about one hour south of St. Louis on I–55.

What to See and Do

Numerous historic homes in this small river town, the oldest permanent settlement in Missouri, include examples of 18th-century French creole architecture, characterized by vertical log construction. The **Great River Road Interpretive Center** (✉ 66 S. Main St., 63670, ☏ 573/883–7097 or 800/373–7007) houses the visitor center and sells tickets for the ferryboat ride across the Mississippi River to Illinois.

Lodging

$$$–$$$$ **Main Street Inn.** One of the many inns and restaurants in the National Historic District, this home built in 1883 is fully furnished in period antiques and offers a pleasant view of the Mississippi River. Complimentary wine is served in the evening. ✉ *221 N. Main St.,* ☏ *573/883–9199 or 800/918–9199. 7 rooms. Full breakfast. AE, D, MC, V.*

$$$–$$$$ **The Southern Hotel.** At this 1790 Federal-style brick building inn, guests can relax in historic gardens or over a game of pool on the 1870 pool table in the common room. Some bedrooms have fireplaces. ✉ *146 S. 3rd St.,* ☏ *573/883–3493 or 800/275–1412. 8 rooms. D, MC, V.*

St. Joseph

Visitor Information

St. Joseph Convention and Visitors Bureau (✉ Box 445, 109 S. 4th St., 64502, ☏ 816/233–6688 or 800/785–0360).

Arriving and Departing

St. Joseph is about one hour north of Kansas City on I–29.

What to See and Do

During the short experiment called the Pony Express, riders set out on the 2,000-mi trip to Sacramento, California, from what is now St. Joseph's **Pony Express National Memorial** (✉ 914 Penn St., ☏ 816/279–5059). The **Jesse James Home** (✉ 12th and Penn Sts., ☏ 816/232–8206) is where a reward money–seeking member of James's own gang shot and killed the notorious outlaw. You can still see a bullet hole in the wall.

$$ ✕ **The Hoof and Horn.** Open since 1898, next to the St. Joseph stockyards, this is the oldest restaurant in St. Joseph; it serves some of the best prime rib and steak in the Midwest. The atmosphere in the rustic building is authentic to the days cattle drivers would walk in fresh from the trail and Pony Express riders filled their bellies before their journeys. ✉ *429 Illinois Ave.,* ☏ *816/238–0742. AE, DC, MC, V. Closed Sun.*

$ ✕ **Jerre Anne's Cafeteria and Bakery.** Although this restaurant is small and often crowded, locals say it's worth the wait for the heaping portions of meat loaf, and mashed potatoes, and homemade pie. ✉ *2640 Mitchell St.,* ☏ *816/232–6585. No credit cards. Closed Sun. and Mon.*

NEBRASKA

Updated by Kathy Lutz Dusenbery

Capital	Lincoln
Population	1,657,000
Motto	Equality Before the Law
State Bird	Western meadowlark
State Flower	Goldenrod
Postal Abbreviation	NE

Statewide Visitor Information

The **Nebraska Department of Economic Development, Division of Travel and Tourism** (✉ Box 98913, Lincoln 68509-8913, ☎ 402/471–3791 or 800/228–4307) staffs 24 rest and information areas along I–80.

Scenic Drives

Route 2, from Grand Island west to Crawford, is a long, lonesome road through the Sandhills, traversing 332 mi of delicate wildflowers, tranquil rivers, and grazing cattle. The 130-mi drive north on **U.S. 83** from North Platte to Valentine affords fine views of the Sandhills' native shortgrass prairie. **U.S. 26** from Ogallala to Scottsbluff is a 128-mi historic segment of the Oregon Trail, passing such natural landmarks as Ash Hollow; Courthouse, Jail, and Chimney rocks; and Scotts Bluff National Monument.

National and State Parks

National Parks

Homestead National Monument (✉ Rte. 3, Box 47, 68310, ☎ 402/223–3514; 🎫 free), near Beatrice, commemorates the Homestead Act of 1862 and the pioneers who settled the prairies between 1863 and 1936. **Nebraska National Forest** (✉ Box 39, 69142, ☎ 308/533–2257; 🎫 free), at Halsey, is the largest planted forest in the country.

State Parks

The **Nebraska Game and Parks Commission** (✉ Box 30370, Lincoln 68503, ☎ 402/471–0641) manages and provides information on all eight state parks. Among them are **Fort Robinson State Park** (☞ Exploring Northwest Nebraska, *below*); **Eugene T. Mahoney State Park** and **Platte River State Park**(☞ Exploring Southeast Nebraska, *below*); and **Indian Cave State Park** (✉ 2 mi north and 5 mi east of Shubert; Box 30, 68437, ☎ 402/883–2575) in the state's southeast corner. A day pass ($2.50) or an annual one ($14) may be purchased at any state park and is good for admission to all of them.

SOUTHEAST NEBRASKA

This is a land of city sophistication and country charm. Visitors can tour museums and historic buildings, shop in restored warehouses, and ride riverboats.

Visitor Information

Beatrice: Chamber of Commerce (✉ 226 S 6th St., 68310, ☎ 816/223–2338). **Lincoln:** Convention and Visitors Bureau (✉ 1221 N St., 68508, ☎ 402/434–5335 or 800/423–8212). **Nebraska City:** Convention and Visitors Bureau (✉ 806 1st Ave., 68410, ☎ 402/873–6654).

Omaha: Greater Omaha Convention and Visitors Bureau (✉ 6800 Mercy Rd., Suite 202, 68106, ☎ 402/444–4660 or 800/332–1819).

Arriving and Departing

By Bus

Omaha and Lincoln are served by **Greyhound Lines** (☎ 800/231–2222). Local bus service is provided in Lincoln by **StarTran** (☎ 402/476–1234) and in Omaha by **Metro Area Transit** (☎ 402/341–0800).

By Car

I–80 links Des Moines with Omaha (I–480 serves downtown Omaha) and Lincoln. U.S. 75S from Omaha leads to Nebraska City. From Lincoln, Route 2 goes to Nebraska City. To get to Beatrice, take U.S. 77 south from Lincoln.

By Plane

Eppley Airfield, about 3 mi from downtown Omaha, is served by most domestic carriers as well as **United Express** (☎ 800/554–5111). Cab fare from the airport to downtown is about $8. **Lincoln Municipal Airport,** about 3 mi from downtown Lincoln, is served by several major airlines. Taxis to downtown cost about $10. **Eppley Express** (☎ 308/234–6066 or 800/888–9793) runs an airport van from Lincoln Municipal Airport to Eppley Airfield ($18 fare).

By Train

Amtrak's (☎ 800/872–7245) *Desert Wind, Pioneer,* and *California Zephyr* stop in Lincoln and Omaha.

Exploring Southeast Nebraska

Nebraska's multistory state capitol dominates the Lincoln skyline; the river city of Omaha is the region's center of commerce and industry. Minutes away from both downtowns are expansive prairies, state parks, and attractions that chronicle the opening of the West to settlement.

Omaha is a quintessentially friendly midwestern city with a refurbished 12-block market area by the river. The **Henry Doorly Zoo** (✉ 3701 S. 10th St., ☎ 402/733–8401; 🎫 $7.25) has the world's largest indoor rain forest—the Lied Jungle—and a saltwater aquarium. "Ride the rails" at the **Western Heritage Museum** (✉ 801 S. 10th St., ☎ 402/444–5071; 🎫 $3), where you're invited to climb aboard at Nebraska's largest restored Art Deco railroad station. Formerly Omaha's Union Station, the museum highlights the history of the Omaha and Union Pacific railroads through interactive exhibits. Lifelike sculptures of soldiers, salesmen, and other rail travelers of the 1930s and '40s sit in restored train cars and "talk" about the politics, music, and the society of the time.

Father Flanagan's **Boys Town** (✉ 138th St. and W. Dodge Rd., 68010, ☎ 402/498–1140; 🎫 free) lies just outside Omaha, about 2 mi west of I–680. It remains the only official village in the nation created just for children. Founded in 1917 and made famous by the 1938 movie starring Spencer Tracy and Mickey Rooney, the town includes schools, churches, and farmland.

In Fremont, about 50 mi northwest of Bellevue, you can board the historic **Fremont and Elkhorn Valley Railroad** (✉ 1835 N. Somers Ave., ☎ 402/727–0615; 🎫 $11) for a tour through the lush Elkhorn River valley. Hop the **Fremont Dinner Train** (✉ 650 N. H St., ☎ 800/942–7245; 🎫 $42.95) for a dining experience reminiscent of rail travel in the 1940s. It offers dinner and mystery trips during its scenic 30-mi round-trip run.

About 60 mi south of Fremont on I–80W halfway between Lincoln and Omaha are the **Eugene T. Mahoney State Park** (✉ 28500 W. Park Hwy., Ashland 68003, ☎ 402/944–2523; 🎟 $2.50) and the **Platte River State Park** (✉ Hwy. 50, then 2 mi west on Hwy. 66 near Louisville, ☎ 402/234–2217; 🎟 $2.50). You'll find campsites at Mahoney and cabins and teepees at Platte River. In both areas you can go horseback riding, swimming, hiking, and canoeing; both areas also provide spectacular vistas of the Platte River valley. Platte River has buffalo stew cookouts in summer on Friday and Saturday nights.

The **Strategic Air Command Museum** (✉ I–80, exit 426, Ashland, ☎ 402/944–3100 or 800/358–5029; 🎟 $6) provides a glimpse of aviation wonders and includes a children's interactive gallery. Stroll beneath the wings of aircraft that changed the course of history, see missiles huge and small, view rare film footage, and browse through an extensive collection of military artifacts.

Lincoln, home of the University of Nebraska and the state government, rises to meet you as you drive along I–80W. You can scan the city's skyline from atop the **Nebraska State Capitol Building** (✉ 1445 K St., ☎ 402/471–0448), with its 400-ft spire that towers over the surrounding plains. Free tours of the capitol take place daily from 9 to 4.

A five-minute drive north from the capitol will take you to the **University of Nebraska,** at 14th and U streets. There you'll find the **State Museum of Natural History** (☎ 402/472–2642; 🎟 $2), nicknamed Elephant Hall due to its huge collection of extinct animals that once roamed the Great Plains. Within the State Museum is the **Ralph Mueller Planetarium** (☎ 402/472–2641), with regularly scheduled laser light shows and astronomy shows. Call for ticket information. At **Nine-Mile Prairie** (✉ 1 mi west of N.W. 48th St. and Fletcher Ave.; 🎟 free) you can park your car and get out to hike the natural prairies.

From Lincoln you can take Route 2 southeast to U.S. 75, then U.S. 136 southeast to Brownville. At the **Brownville State Recreation Area,** the *Spirit of Brownville* riverboat (☎ 402/825–6001) coordinates sightseeing, dining, and dancing cruises on the mighty Missouri River.

U.S. 75N brings you to **Nebraska City,** a tidy town rimmed with historic sites and apple orchards, including the **Arbor Day Farm** (✉ 100 Arbor Ave., ☎ 402/873–8710), where you can buy apple cider and visit the gift shop year-round. Apples are available in season, and lip-smacking desserts are served in the Pie Garden from May through October.

Hop the **Nebraska City Trolley** (☎ 402/873–3000; 🎟 $3) at stops throughout town. It links historic sites to 11 downtown factory outlets clustered around 8th and 1st Corso streets and to the **Factory Stores of America Mall** (✉ 1001 Rte. 2, ☎ 402/873–7727), which sells merchandise ranging from toy trucks to sweaters. The trolley also stops at **John Brown's Cave and Historical Village** (✉ 1908 4th Corso St., ☎ 402/873–3115; 🎟 $5), where you can visit a cave and a passageway that were once part of the Underground Railroad; it is closed from December through April.

★ While in Nebraska City peek into the past with a visit to the **Arbor Lodge State Historical Park and Arboretum** (✉ 2nd and Centennial Aves., ☎ 402/873–7222; 🎟 $2.50). On the grounds are the 52-room mansion and carriage house of J. Sterling Morton, the 19th-century politician and lover of trees who inaugurated the first Arbor Day, now observed nationwide as a day for planting trees. The mansion was later inhabited by his son, Morton Salt baron Joy Morton.

Dining and Lodging

Dining choices in this varied region range from international cuisine to pizza. Lodging runs from full-service hotels to comfortable B&Bs (contact the **Nebraska Association of Bed and Breakfast,** ✉ Rte. 2, Box 17, Elgin 68636, ☎ 402/843–2287). For price ranges *see* Charts 1 (B) and 2 (B) *in* On the Road with Fodor's.

Brownville

$$$ **Thompson House Bed and Breakfast.** Rooms in this Victorian three-story house have antiques and kerosene lamps. There's also a game room and parlor. ✉ *5th and College Sts., Box 162, 68321,* ☎ *402/825–6551. 5 rooms. Full breakfast. MC, V.*

Lincoln

$$$–$$$$ ★ ✕ **Billy's.** A fascinating collection of political memorabilia and antiques captures the elegance of a bygone era in this upscale restaurant. The menu covers all the classics: rib-eye steak, chicken cordon bleu, and the like. ✉ *1301 H St.,* ☎ *402/474–0084. AE, D, DC, MC, V.*

$–$$$$ ★ ✕ **Valentino's Restaurant.** Besides pizza with original or home-style crust, the restaurant also serves Italian specials and dessert pizzas with such toppings as cherries and cream cheese. ✉ *3457 Holdrege St.,* ☎ *402/467–3611. AE, D, MC, V.*

$$ ✕ **Misty's Restaurant.** Adorned with Cornhusker football paraphernalia, this is, by locals' accounts, the prime-rib palace of the Plains. ✉ *6235 Havelock Ave.,* ☎ *402/466–8424. AE, D, MC, V.*

$$ ✕ **Rock 'n' Roll Runza.** Waitresses on roller skates serve Runzas—a hamburger-cabbage sandwich—at this '50s-style restaurant. ✉ *210 N. 14th St.,* ☎ *402/474–2030. D, MC, V.*

$ ✕ **Arturo's Restaurant & Cantina.** At Lincoln's first Mexican restaurant you'll find a wide variety of traditional Mexican dishes all made with fresh ingredients. This is the only place in the world where you can order a Tasha, a simple but delicious family recipe made with refried beans and cheese and wrapped in a corn tortilla. ✉ *40th & Van-Dorn St.,* ☎ *402/488–8201. D, MC, V.*

$$$$ **The Cornhusker.** The lobby of this elegant hotel has a grand curving staircase, hand-painted murals, and an Italian-marble floor. East- and south-wing rooms have good views of downtown Lincoln. ✉ *333 S. 13th St., 68508,* ☎ *402/474–7474 or 800/793–7474,* FAX *402/474–1847. 290 rooms. 2 restaurants, pool, exercise room. AE, D, DC, MC, V.*

$$$ ★ **Rogers House Bed and Breakfast.** Built in 1914, this ivy-covered brick mansion was converted into a B&B by the current owners in 1984. The antiques-filled public areas, with oak floors, include a living room with a fireplace and a sunroom where guests eat breakfast. ✉ *2145 B St., 68502,* ☎ *402/476–6961,* FAX *402/476–6473. 12 rooms. Full breakfast. AE, D, MC, V.*

Nebraska City

$$ ★ ✕ **Teresa's Family Restaurant.** Booths line the walls of this casual country kitchen, where old-fashioned food such as meat loaf and homemade lemon pie is served at yesterday's prices. ✉ *812 Central Ave.,* ☎ *402/873–9100. MC, V.*

$ ★ ✕ **Ulbrick's.** This converted gas station and café is nothing fancy, but the made-from-scratch family-style dinners of fried chicken, creamed corn and cabbage, and homemade egg noodles are exceptional. ✉ *1513 S. 11th St.,* ☎ *402/873–5458. No credit cards.*

$$$ **Arbor Day Farm Lied Conference Center.** Set amid a 260-acre educational complex devoted to environmental programs, Arbor Day Farm is surrounded by arboretums and interpretive nature trails. Ideal for conventions, the complex also has meeting rooms that can ac-

commodate up to 400 people. Guest rooms are spacious and modern. ✉ *2700 Sylvan Rd.,* ☎ *402/873–8733 or 800–546–5433,* FAX *402/873–4999. 96 rooms. Pool. MC, V.*

$$ **Whispering Pines.** Nestled among pines on 6½ quiet acres, this 118-year-old two-story brick house has been completely refurbished as a B&B and filled with antiques. Take a dip in the six-person hot tub before retiring at night. ✉ *21st St. and 6th Ave., 68410,* ☎ *402/873–5850. 5 rooms. Full breakfast. D, MC, V.*

Omaha

$$ ✕ **Austins.** Throw your peanut shells on the floor at this casual eatery where the atmosphere is western and the food pure country. Chicken-fried steak, prime rib, and barbecued ribs are the specialties. ✉ *12020 Anne St.,* ☎ *402/896–5373. Reservations not accepted. AE, MC, V.*

$$ ✕ **Garden Café.** Home-style cooking with everything made from scratch is what this café in the historic Old Market is known for. Noteworthy are the potato casseroles, soups, salads, and desserts. ✉ *12th and Harvey Sts.,* ☎ *402/422–1574. AE, DC, MC, V.*

$$ ✕ **Johnny's Café.** Since 1922 this has been *the* place for mouthwatering steaks, seafood, and midwestern dishes. ✉ *4702 S. 27th St.,* ☎ *402/731–4774. AE, D, DC, MC, V.*

$$ ★ ✕ **Mr. C's.** Christmas lights surround you at this Italian steak house, where the lasagna and manicotti are as good as the sirloin. ✉ *5319 N. 30th St.,* ☎ *402/451–1998. AE, DC, MC, V.*

$$ ✕ **Neon Goose.** Dine under a chandelier or on the fresh-air veranda at this lively restaurant with piano bar. Good menu choices are unusual quiches, melt-in-your-mouth omelets, and fresh seafood. ✉ *1012 S. 10th St.,* ☎ *402/341–2063. AE, DC, MC, V.*

$ ✕ **Bohemian Cafe.** Gaily painted Czech plates hang on the walls of this family-style restaurant, where you can try such Czechoslovakian favorites as goulash. ✉ *1406 S. 13th St.,* ☎ *402/342–9838. D, MC, V.*

$$$$ ★ **Double Tree Hotel.** In the heart of the downtown business and entertainment district, the Double Tree is close to the Old Market and Henry Doorly Zoo and only 10 minutes from Eppley Air Field. Rooms on all of its 19 stories are spacious. ✉ *1616 Dodge St., 68102,* ☎ *402/346–7600,* FAX *402/346–5722. 413 rooms. Restaurant, pool. AE, D, DC, MC, V.*

$$$ **Marriott Hotel.** This six-story hotel in suburban Omaha is near the upscale Regency Fashion Court shopping area. ✉ *10220 Regency Circle, 68114,* ☎ *402/399–9000,* FAX *402/399–0223. 301 rooms. 2 restaurants, pool, exercise room. AE, D, DC, MC, V.*

Motels

Oak Creek Inn (✉ 2808 S. 72nd St., Omaha 68124, ☎ 402/397–7137), 102 rooms, pool, exercise room; *$$.*

Campgrounds

Indian Cave State Park(☞ National and State Parks, *above*) and **Eugene T. Mahoney State Park** (☞ Exploring Southeast Nebraska, *above*) have excellent tent and RV camping.

Outdoor Activities and Sports

Fishing

The 13 Salt Valley lakes surrounding Lincoln, especially **Branched Oak** (✉ N.W. 140th St. and W. Raymond Rd.) and **Pawnee** (✉ N.W. 98th and W. Adams Sts.), contain a variety of fish, including largemouth bass, northern pike, walleye, and channel catfish. For more information about fishing in Nebraska, contact the **Game and Parks Commission** (☎ 402/471–0641).

Spectator Sports

Football: University of Nebraska Cornhuskers (✉ 117 S. Stadium St., ☎ 402/472–3111).

Shopping

Nebraska Furniture Mart (✉ 700 S. 72nd St., Omaha, ☎ 402/397–6100 or 800/359–1200) is reputed to be the largest furniture store west of the Mississippi. Omaha's **Old Market** (✉ Between 10th and 13th Sts., ☎ 402/346–4445) is a collection of boutiques, galleries, and restaurants in the oldest part of town. Lincoln's charming, restored warehouse shopping district, **Historic Haymarket** (✉ Between 7th and 9th Sts. and between O and S Sts., ☎ 402/435–7496), has quaint antiques stores, novelty gift shops, and some fine restaurants.

NORTHWEST NEBRASKA

Rugged and beautiful, this is true Old West territory, with dramatic buttes and bluffs, Ponderosa pines, craggy ridges, and canyons.

Visitor Information

Alliance: Box Butte Visitors Committee (✉ Alliance Chamber of Commerce, Box 571, 69301, ☎ 308/762–1520). **Chadron:** Chamber of Commerce (✉ Box 646, 69337, ☎ 308/432–4401). **Scottsbluff:** Scotts Bluff County Visitors Promotion Committee (✉ 1517 Broadway, 69361, ☎ 308/632–2133 or 800/788–9475). **Valentine:** Visitor Center (✉ Box 201, 69201, ☎ 402/376–2969 or 800/658–4024).

Arriving and Departing

By Car

From Omaha and Lincoln take I–80 west about 275 mi to U.S. 26, which closely follows the Oregon and Mormon trails as it takes you to Scottsbluff. To bypass Kearney and North Platte, take I–80 to Grand Island, then scenic Route 2 to the north, which runs parallel to I–80 through Nebraska's Sandhills.

Exploring Northwest Nebraska

You can retrace the route of the wagon trains by exiting I–80 near Ogallala and heading west on U.S. 26. Four miles south of Bridgeport on Route 88, you can see **Courthouse** and **Jail rocks,** sandstone outcroppings that pioneers used as landmarks on the trail west. One mile south of the junction of U.S. 26 and Route 92 and 4 mi south of Bayard, the **Chimney Rock National Historic Site** (☎ 308/586–2581) is an impressive outcropping that pioneers described as "towering to the heavens." The visitor center, open year-round, commemorates those who traveled the Oregon Trail. Oregon Trail wagon traces are still visible at the **Scotts Bluff National Monument** (✉ 3 mi west of Gering on Rte. 92, ☎ 308/436–4340), an enormous bluff that rises out of the rocky plains. Once described as the "Lighthouse of the Plains," it now has a museum at its base.

About 35 mi north of Mitchell on Route 29, the **Agate Fossil Beds National Monument** has fossil deposits dating back 20 million years. A museum (☎ 308/668–2211; 🎟 free) preserves and displays fossils and Native American artifacts, including personal items that belonged to Chief Red Cloud and to Captain James H. Cook, the frontiersman, cattle driver, and Army scout who discovered the fossils on his land.

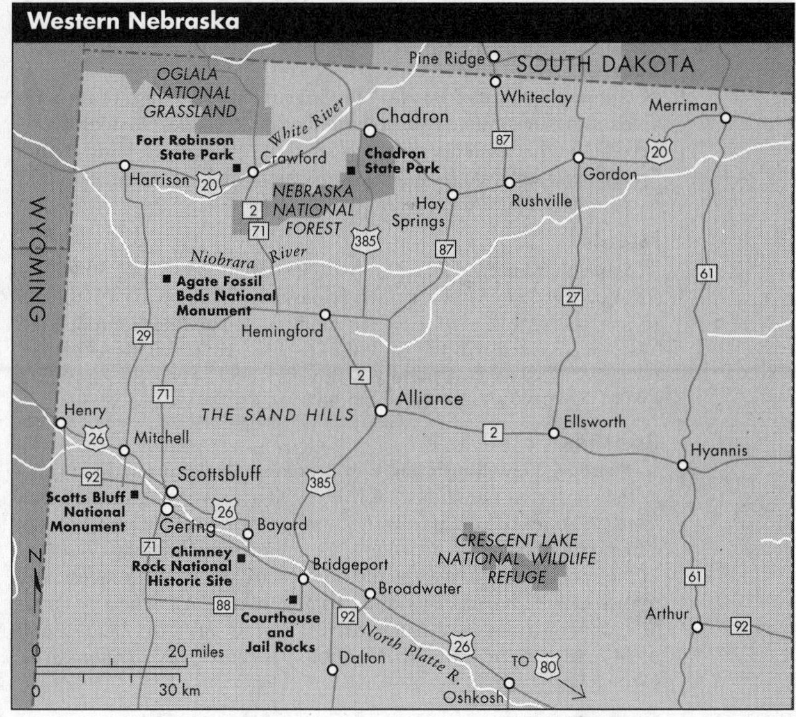

North on Route 29 to Harrison, then east on U.S. 20 is **Fort Robinson State Park** (☎ 308/665–2900; free), where activities include trail rides, historic tours, cookouts, swimming, trout fishing, hiking, and stagecoach rides. From late May to late August the park has a summer theater program. Tent sites and electrical hookups are available.

Dining and Lodging

Travelers to the northwest Nebraska chow down at casual, out-of-the-way restaurants, wagon train–style cookouts, and ranches. Inexpensive cattle ranches and B&Bs (contact the **Nebraska Association of Bed and Breakfast,** ✉ Rte. 2, Box 17, Elgin 68636, ☎ 402/843–2287) provide charming alternatives to chain motels. For price ranges *see* Charts 1 (B) and 2 (B) *in* On the Road with Fodor's.

Bayard

$–$$ ★ **Oregon Trail Wagon Train.** You can sleep under the stars and eat cookouts of fire-grilled rib eyes, stew, spoon bread, and vinegar pudding on covered-wagon tours through some of Nebraska's remaining short-grass prairies. One- to four-day treks are available. ✉ *Rte. 2, Box 502, 69334,* ☎ *308/586–1850,* FAX *308/586–1848. 3 cabins (each sleeps 6). Reservations essential. MC, V.*

Crawford

$ **Fort Robinson State Park Lodge.** Dating from the 1800s, this historic fort in Fort Robinson State Park includes a two-story lodge with large verandas and tall columns. Built in 1909 as an enlisted men's barracks, the lodge now has 22 modern rooms with private baths but no telephones or TVs. Cabins, which can sleep up to 12 people, are also available, and there's also the officers' quarters, a group facility that can sleep up to 60 people. ✉ *3 mi west of Crawford; Box 392, Craw-*

ford 69339, ☎ 308/665–2900, FAX 308/665–2906. 22 rooms, 31 cabins. Restaurant. MC, V.

Scottsbluff

$ ✕ **Grampy's Pancake House.** This large family-style restaurant is divided into three dining rooms with booths and tables. Besides strawberry and other varieties of pancakes, there are omelets, blintzes, and other breakfast treats, as well as simple lunch and dinner fare. ✉ *1802 E. 20th Pl., ☎ 308/632–6906. AE, D, MC, V.*

Motels

Scottsbluff Inn (✉ 1901 21st Ave., Scottsbluff 69361, ☎ 308/635–3111 or 800/597–3111 for reservations only, FAX 308/635–7646), 138 rooms, restaurant, pool, exercise room; *$*. **Landmark Inn** (✉ 246 Main St., Bayard 69334, ☎ 308/586–1375 or 800/658–4424), 10 rooms; *$*. **Town Line Motel** (✉ Box 423, 3591 Hwy. 20, Crawford 69339, ☎ 308/665–1450 or 800/903–1450), 24 rooms; *$*.

Ranches

$$ **Meadow View Ranch Bed and Breakfast Bunkhouse.** Guests stay in the converted bunkhouse of this 5,000-acre working ranch 18 mi from the South Dakota border. Accommodations include a kitchenette, a living room, and two bedrooms. Complimentary breakfast is served in the ranch kitchen, and picnic lunches are packed on request. Activities include horseback riding, fishing, hiking in the nearby Sandhills, wagon rides, and cattle drives. ✉ *HC 91, Box 29, Gordon 69343, ☎ 308/282–0679. Bunkhouse (sleeps 7). No credit cards. Closed Nov.–Apr.*

Campgrounds

Chadron State Park(☞ Hiking and Backpacking *in* Outdoor Activities and Sports, *below*) is a favorite. **Fort Robinson State Park** (☞ Exploring Northwest Nebraska, *above*) have tent and RV camping.

Outdoor Activities and Sports

Hiking and Backpacking

Fort Robinson State Park (☞ Exploring Northwest Nebraska, *above*) and **Chadron State Park** (✉ 8 mi south of Chadron on U.S. 385, ☎ 308/432–6167) has several hiking trails, jeep rides, paddleboats, fishing, a swimming pool, and tennis courts.

ELSEWHERE IN NEBRASKA

Lake McConaughy and Ogallala

Arriving and Departing

From Lincoln and Omaha take I–80 west to Ogallala.

What to See and Do

★ The white-sand beaches of **Lake McConaughy State Recreation Area and the Kingsley Dam** (✉ 9 mi north of Ogallala on Rte. 61, ☎ 308/284–3542; $2.50) annually attract thousands of visitors. In Ogallala, **Front Street** (☎ 308/284–6000) depicts an 1880s Main Street, complete with a wooden boardwalk, jail, barbershop, and cowboy museum. The restaurant proudly serves Nebraska steaks and puts on nightly western shows from Memorial Day through Labor Day. The **Mansion on the Hill** (✉ W. 10th and Spruce, ☎ 308/284–4066; free) is a museum with exhibits on 19th-century cattle drives. Ogallala is also home to the infamous **Boot Hill Cemetery** (✉ W. 10th and Parkhill Dr.).

Red Cloud

Arriving and Departing

From Lincoln and Omaha take I–80 west to Grand Island, then U.S. 34 south to U.S. 281, and continue south.

What to See and Do

Red Cloud was the home of Pulitzer Prize–winning author Willa Cather. The **Willa Cather Historical Center** (☒ 326 N. Webster St., ☏ 402/746–2653; 🎫 $1) is dedicated to the author, who loved the Plains, 610 acres of which are preserved as the **Cather Memorial Prairie** (☒ 5 mi south of Red Cloud).

On the National Register of Historic Places is the **Starke Round Barn,** 4 mi east of Red Cloud on Highway 136. Built in 1902, this three-story barn is held together by balanced tension and stress rather than nails or pegs.

The Great Platte River Road

Arriving and Departing

From Omaha and Lincoln take I–80 west.

What to See and Do

Westward-bound pioneers on the Mormon and Oregon trails once hugged the shores of the Platte River, a verdant natural pathway. Today I–80 follows the same route, cutting through the state's heartland and affording glimpses of this pioneer past. **Sculpture gardens** dot the landscape along the highway for 500 mi across the Nebraska plains. At nine rest areas large stone-and-metal artworks constitute what some critics have called a "museum without walls."

The **Stuhr Museum of the Prairie Pioneer** (☒ Junction of U.S. 34 and U.S. 281, ☏ 308/385–5316; 🎫 $6.50), in Grand Island, houses Native American and Old West artifacts and features the 60-building Railroad Town, which includes the birthplace of actor Henry Fonda, antique farm machinery, a restored 19th-century farmhouse, and people in period costumes. The Railroad Town is closed from mid-October through April.

From early March to mid-April visitors flock to an area near Grand Island and Kearney to witness the migration of thousands of Sandhill cranes as they pause here before resuming their flight north. The **Crane Meadows Nature Center** (☒ ½ mi south of I–80 at the Alda exit, ☏ 308/382–1820; 🎫 tours $15) and the **Lillian Rowe Audubon Sanctuary** (☏ 308/468–5282; 🎫 tours $15) offer tours. The Crane Meadows Nature Center also has a visitor center with wildlife displays.

Fort Kearny State Historical Park (☒ 2 mi south of I–80 on Rte. 44 and then 4 mi east on L–50A, ☏ 308/865–5305; 🎫 $2.50) has a re-created stockade and interpretive exhibits detailing the role of the outpost on the frontier.

★ **Harold Warp's Pioneer Village** (☒ Junction of U.S. 6, U.S. 34, and Hwy. 10 in Minden, ☏ 308/832–1181; 🎫 $6) has an extensive collection of pioneer memorabilia; horse-drawn covered-wagon rides; and crafts demonstrations.The Old West comes alive in **North Platte,** where Buffalo Bill Cody and his famous Wild West show began. You can tour his ranch house, enjoy trail rides, or chow down on buffalo stew in the **Buffalo Bill Ranch State Historical Park** (☏ 308/535–8035; 🎫 $2.50), 6 mi northwest of I–80. In Hastings, which lies near the junction of U.S. 34 and Highway 281, you'll find the **Hastings Museum** (☒ 1330 N. Burlington Ave., ☏ 402/461–4629 or 800-508–4629; 🎫 $5), which has exhibits on natural history and frontier days; related films are shown in its IMAX theater.

Two-hour tours of **The Dancing Leaf Earth Lodge Cultural Learning Center** (☒ 6100 E. Opal Springs Rd., Wellfleet, ☎ 308/963–4233; $8) give modern travelers the opportunity to experience primitive Native American life. Earth lodges, a natural trail, spiritual bonding points, and archaeological sites are among the attractions.

Lodging

$–$$ **Home Comfort B&B.** On 15 acres of Nebraska farmland, this comfortable bed-and-breakfast is within walking distance of Harold Warp's Pioneer Village (☞ *above*). *☒ 1523 N. Brown, Minden 68959, ☎ 308/832–0533. No credit cards.*

Sandhills/Valentine Region

Arriving and Departing

From Lincoln and Omaha take I–80 west to Grand Island. Go north on U.S. 281 to Route 22; then follow it west 9 mi and go north on Route 11. At Burwell follow Route 91 west, U.S. 183 north, and U.S. 20 west to Valentine.

What to See and Do

Fort Hartsuff State Historical Park (☒ 3 mi north of Elyria off Hwy. 11, ☎ 308/346–4715; $2.50) is a restored 1870s infantry post with guides in period uniforms and costumes. It is closed from November through April.

For a view of the Great Plains as it once was, you can take a drive through hundreds of miles of mixed-grass prairie, where outdoor attractions beckon. The **Niobrara River** draws canoeists from throughout the state. Outfitters include **Dryland Aquatics** (☒ Box 33C, Sparks 69220, ☎ 800/337–3119), **A&C Canoe Rentals** (☒ 518 N. Ray St., Valentine 69201, ☎ 402/376–2839), **Brewers Canoers** (☒ 433 E. U.S. 20, Valentine 69201, ☎ 402/376–2046), **Graham Canoe Outfitters** (☒ HC 13, Box 16A, Valentine 69201, ☎ 402/376–3708), and **Little Outlaw Canoe & Tube Rentals** (☒ Box 15, Valentine 69201, ☎ 402/376–1822). Native wildlife is abundant at the **Valentine National Wildlife Refuge** (☒ HC 14, Box 67, Valentine 69201, ☎ 402/376–1889), south of Valentine on U.S. 83. Its 70,000 acres of prairie and wetlands shelter ducks, geese, hawks, eagles, deer, coyotes, beavers, and other species. There are trails for driving or hiking through this open country; information kiosks are at entrances to the refuge.

The **Fort Niobrara National Wildlife Refuge** (☒ HC 14, Box 67, Valentine 69201, ☎ 402/376–3789), 5 mi east of Valentine on Route 12, rewards you with a forested terrain and large species, such as bison, elk, and longhorn cattle. A visitor center and picnic facilities are available.

NORTH DAKOTA

Updated by Sue Berg

Capital	Bismarck
Population	641,000
Motto	Liberty and Union, Now and Forever, One and Inseparable
State Bird	Western meadowlark
State Flower	Wild prairie rose
Postal Abbreviation	ND

Statewide Visitor Information

North Dakota Tourism Department (✉ Liberty Memorial Bldg., 604 E. Blvd., Bismarck 58505, ☎ 701/328–2525 or 800/435–5663. **Welcome centers:** along I–94E, 1 mi west of Beach; off I–94 at the Oriska Rest Area, 12 mi east of Valley City; off I–29N at the Lake Agassiz Rest Area, 8 mi south of Hankinson interchange; along I–29S, 1 mi north of the Pembina interchange; one block west of the junction of U.S. 2 and U.S. 85 in Williston; at the junction of U.S. 12 and U.S. 85 in Bowman; at the 45th Street interchange off I–94W in Fargo; and on U.S. 2, 10 mi east of Grand Forks at Fisher's Landing.

Scenic Drives

The **Pembina Gorge** in northeastern North Dakota is a beautiful forested valley created by glaciers and the winding Pembina River; from I–29 at the Joliette exit near the northern boundary of the state, drive west on Route 5, then north on Route 32 to Walhalla. **Theodore Roosevelt National Park's South Unit loop road** begins near park headquarters in Medora and winds 36 mi through an eerie world of lonesome pinnacles and spires, steep gorges, and ravaged buttes. The 26-mi **North Unit Road** begins at the park entrance along U.S. 85, 15 mi south of Watford City; the high ground above the Little Missouri River has dramatic overlooks, and a lower area near the visitor center features a series of slump rocks, huge sections of bluff that gradually slid intact to the valley floor.

National and State Parks

National Park

Theodore Roosevelt National Park (☞ Exploring the Badlands, *below*).

State Parks

North Dakota's state parks are open year-round. Among the most scenic are **Cross Ranch State Park,** 40 mi north of Mandan, off Highway 25 (✉ HC 2, Box 152, Sanger 58567, ☎ 701/794–3731); **Fort Abraham Lincoln State Park** (☞ Exploring the Missouri River Corridor, *below*); two parks on U.S. 2 and Highway 19 that are part of **Devils Lake State Parks** (✉ Rte. 1, Box 165, Devils Lake 58301, ☎ 701/766–4015); **Lake Sakakawea State Park,** 1 mi north of Pick City, off Garrison Lake (✉ Box 732, Riverdale 58565, ☎ 701/487–3315); and **Icelandic State Park,** on Route 5, 5 mi west of Cavalier (✉ 13571 Hwy. 5, Cavalier 58220, ☎ 701/265–4561). All parks listed offer camping facilities; for camping reservations during the summer season, contact the **North Dakota Parks and Recreation Department** (✉ 1835 E. Bismarck Expressway, Bismarck 58554, ☎ 701/328–5357 or 800/807–4723).

MISSOURI RIVER CORRIDOR

The Missouri River is both a geographic and a symbolic barrier between the two North Dakotas—the east and the west. Bismarck, the state capital, is on the east bank of the river and is a busy political hub, while at sprawling Lake Sakakawea, a short drive to the northwest, urban life seems a world away. Meriwether Lewis and William Clark followed the Missouri River through North Dakota during their famous exploration of the Louisiana Purchase. On their way west, Lewis and Clark spent the winter of 1804–05 near present-day Washburn, where they were joined by the guide Sakakawea, her husband, and her infant son. Lewis and Clark returned through North Dakota in 1806. Today's routes 1804 and 1806 mark parts of the Lewis and Clark Trail in North Dakota. Bicentennial celebrations in honor of the expedition are now being planned.

Visitor Information

Bismarck-Mandan: Convention and Visitors Bureau (☒ Box 2274, 107 W. Main, Bismarck 58501, ☎ 701/222–4308 or 800/767–3555). **Minot:** Convention and Visitors Bureau (☒ 1020 S. Broadway, 58701, ☎ 701/857–8206 or 800/264–2626).

Arriving and Departing

By Bus

Greyhound Lines (☎ 800/231–2222) and **Minot-Bismarck Bus Service** (☎ 701/223–6576) serve Bismarck and Minot (☎ 701/852–2477).

By Car

I–94, the state's major east–west thoroughfare, runs through the Bismarck–Mandan area. U.S. 83 runs north–south from Bismarck to Minot, the state's second- and fourth-largest cities, respectively. U.S. 2 runs east–west along the top half of the state, including Minot.

By Plane

Bismarck Municipal Airport (☎ 701/222–6502) and **Minot International Airport** (☎ 701/857–4724) are served by Northwest and United Express. Both are about 5 mi from downtown; cab fare is about $5.

By Train

Amtrak (☎ 800/872–7245) stops in Minot and Williston.

Exploring the Missouri River Corridor

As with the rest of North Dakota, most of the attractions described here are open in the summer only (often Memorial Day–Labor Day); be sure to call ahead before you visit. The 19-story **state capitol** (☒ 600 E. Boulevard Ave., 58505, ☎ 701/328–2480), in north Bismarck, is visible for miles across the Dakota prairie; free tours of the limestone-and-marble Art Deco structure, built in the 1930s, are offered weekdays year-round and also on weekends Memorial Day–Labor Day. The **North Dakota Heritage Center** (☒ 612 E. Boulevard Ave., ☎ 701/328–2666; 🎫 free) is the state's largest museum and archive. Exhibits include Native American and pioneer artifacts and natural history displays. The facility is across the street from the capitol. The **Former Governors' Mansion State Historic Site** (☒ 4th St. and Ave. B, ☎ 701/328–2666; 🎫 free) is an elegant Victorian structure containing political memorabilia and period furnishings. The ***Lewis and Clark* Riverboat,** departing from the Port of Bismarck (☒ N. River Rd., ☎ 701/255–4233; 🎫 $10.95), offers summer cruises on the Missouri River, plying the same route taken by the traders, trappers, and settlers of the last century.

Custer buffs often visit **Fort Abraham Lincoln State Park** (✉ Hwy. 1806, Mandan, ☎ 701/663–9571; 🎫 $3 per vehicle for park only, $5 per person for park, fort, and sites). You can also reach the park from Bismarck by crossing the river on I–94 to Mandan, then either traveling 4 mi south on Route 1806 or taking the 9-mi **Fort Lincoln Trolley** (☎ 701/663–9018; 🎫 $4) from south Mandan. Among the reconstructed buildings at the fort are the barracks (where you can stay overnight for $15) and the **Custer House,** a replica of the 1870s house where General George Armstrong Custer lived with his wife, Libby, before his fateful expedition to the Little Big Horn. Nearby is the reconstructed **On-A-Slant Indian Village,** once home to the Mandan tribe.

From Bismarck take U.S. 83 north to Washburn, where the new **Lewis & Clark Interpretive Center** (✉ ¼ mi off U.S. 83, ☎ 701/462–8535; 🎫 $2) will be the hub of bicentennial celebrations in 2004. The center is one of only four in the nation to have a complete set of reproduction prints by Karl Bodmer, the artist/explorer who followed Lewis & Clark's trail some 25 years later along the Missouri River. From Washburn, take Route 200A west to the **Knife River Indian Villages National Historic Site** (✉ ¼ mi north of Stanton, ☎ 701/745–3309; 🎫 free). The area preserves depressions formed by the Hidatsa and Mandan tribes' earth lodges, circular earth-and-timber structures. Pottery shards and other artifacts are displayed at the museum and interpretive center. There's also a full-scale furnished replica of an earth lodge.

Twenty miles north of Stanton is the 600-square-mi **Lake Sakakawea,** affording countless recreational opportunities, including swimming and boating. State parks and small resort communities are sprinkled along its shores. Free tours of the **Garrison Dam power plant** are conducted by the U.S. Army Corps of Engineers (☎ 701/654–7441). For more information on the lake, contact the tourism department (☞ Statewide Visitor Information, *above*).

Dining and Lodging

For a listing of area bed-and-breakfasts, contact the tourism department (☞ Statewide Visitor Information, *above*). For price ranges *see* Charts 1 (B) and 2 (B) *in* On the Road with Fodor's.

Bismarck

$$$–$$$$ ★ ✗ **Peacock Alley Bar and Grill.** In what was once the historic Patterson Hotel, this restaurant enjoys local fame as the scene of countless political deals, captured in period photographs. The menu features seafood specials such as Cajun firecracker shrimp and regional dishes such as pheasant in white-wine sauce. ✉ *422 E. Main St.,* ☎ *701/255–7917. AE, D, DC, MC, V.*

$$ ✗ **Fiesta Villa.** This family-run Mexican restaurant is suitably housed in a mission-style building. Beef or chicken fajitas are a good choice here, and they go well with the excellent margaritas. ✉ *4th and Main Sts.,* ☎ *701/222–8075. AE, D, MC, V.*

$$$ 🏨 **Radisson Inn.** Rooms are spacious and comfortable, with overstuffed chairs and soothing color schemes. The hotel is across from Kirkwood Mall (☞ Shopping, *below*), Bismarck's largest shopping venue. ✉ *800 S. 3rd St., 58504,* ☎ *701/258–7700,* FAX *701/224–8212. 306 rooms. Restaurant, pool, health club. AE, D, DC, MC, V.*

Mandan

$ ★ ✗ **Mandan Drug.** For a fun lunch (it's open 9–6), follow a sandwich or homemade soup with an old-fashioned cherry soda or a brown cow—that's a root beer float with chocolate syrup. The homemade candy is hard to resist. ✉ *316 W. Main St.,* ☎ *701/663–5900. MC, V. Closed Sun.*

$$ **Best Western Seven Seas Inn and Conference Center.** Nautical decor fills the public areas, from scrimshaw displays to 200-year-old anchors to carpeting made to resemble ship's planking. Rooms continue the theme with maritime art. ✉ *I–94, Exit 152; 2611 Old Red Trail, 58554,* ☎ *701/663–7401 or 800/597–7327,* FAX *701/663–0025. 103 rooms. Restaurant, pool. AE, D, DC, MC, V.*

Minot

$$ ★ **Best Western International Inn.** Larger-than-average rooms have contemporary furnishings at this five-story hotel on a hill above downtown. ✉ *1505 N. Broadway, 58703,* ☎ *701/852–3161 or 800/735–4493,* FAX *701/838–5538. 270 rooms. Restaurant, pool. AE, D, DC, MC, V.*

Motel

Expressway Inn (✉ 200 E. Bismarck Expressway, Bismarck 58504, ☎ FAX 701/222–2900; ☎ 800/456–6388), 163 rooms, pool; CP; *$.*

Campgrounds

There are campgrounds at **Fort Abraham Lincoln State Park** (☞ Exploring the Missouri River Corridor, *above*) and **Lake Sakakawea State Park** (☞ National and State Parks, *above*).

Nightlife

Gambling

Prairie Knights Casino, on Standing Rock Reservation, 44 mi south of Mandan on Route 1806, is the fanciest of the five reservation casinos in North Dakota, with murals by Native American artists and first-class dining. The games (slots, blackjack, poker), two bars, and two restaurants are open 24 hours a day. The Lodge at Prairie Knights is an adjacent hotel ($$) with a gift shop that sells Native American items. ✉ *HC 1, Box 26A, Fort Yates 58538,* ☎ *701/854–7777 or 800/425–8277,* FAX *701/854–3795. 69 rooms. AE, D, DC, MC, V.*

Outdoor Activities and Sports

Biking

The 246-mi **Lewis and Clark Bike Tour** follows the Missouri River along Routes 1804, 200, and 22, from the South Dakota border to the Montana border. Contact the tourism department (☞ Statewide Visitor Information, *above*) for details. **Dakota Cyclery** (✉ 1606 E. Main Ave., Bismarck, ☎ 701/222–1218) rents bicycles and can provide information about area biking.

Fishing

Walleye, salmon, and northern pike are the big catches on Lake Sakakawea. The **North Dakota Game and Fish Department** (✉ 100 N. Bismarck Expressway, Bismarck 58501, ☎ 701/328–6300) provides a list of area fishing guides. The *North Dakota Hunting and Fishing Guide* outlines seasons and regulations and is available through the tourism department (☞ Statewide Visitor Information, *above*).

Hiking

The 17-mi **Roughrider Trail,** along Missouri River bottomland, is a treasure. For details contact the Parks and Recreation Department (☞ National and State Parks, *above*).

Shopping

Kirkwood Mall, between South 3rd and South 7th streets in Bismarck, has five major department stores and 100 specialty shops, including locally owned **Maxwell's** (☎ 701/222–4332), a cozy bookstore with a special section for regional reading materials.

Across the river in Mandan, the **Five Nations Arts** (✉ 401 W. Main, ☎ 701/663–4663) sells handmade Native American star quilts, beadwork, sculptures, and more.

THE BADLANDS

Theodore Roosevelt, who ranched in western North Dakota in the late 1800s, once said, "I would never have been president if it had not been for my experiences in North Dakota." He was referring to the **Badlands,** where a national park that bears his name is now the heart of this wide-open country, largely unchanged since the president's time.

Visitor Information

Medora: Theodore Roosevelt Medora Foundation (✉ c/o Rough Riders, 1 Main St., Box 198, 58645, ☎ 800/633–6721 or 701/623–4444). **Williston:** Convention and Visitors Bureau (✉ 10 Main St., 58801, ☎ 701/774–9041 or 800/615–9041). **Dickinson:** Convention and Visitors Bureau (✉ 24 2nd St. W, 58601, ☎ 701/225–4988 or 800/279–7391).

Arriving and Departing

By Bus

Greyhound Lines (☎ 800/231–2222) stops in Dickinson and Medora.

By Car

I–94 crosses the Badlands, with an exit at Medora for the South Unit of Theodore Roosevelt National Park. U.S. 85 links the park's North and South units.

By Plane

Bismarck Municipal Airport (☞ Missouri River Corridor, *above*) is the nearest large airport. The commuter airline United Express serves **Williston Airport** (☎ 701/774–8594) and **Dickinson Airport** (☎ 701/225–5856).

Exploring the Badlands

★ **Theodore Roosevelt National Park** (✉ Box 7, Medora 58645, ☎ 701/623–4466; 🎫 $5 per person, $10 per vehicle) is divided into three units, separated by about 50 mi of Badlands and the **Little Missouri National Grasslands.** Scenic loops through the **South Unit** (☞ Scenic Drives, *above*) are marked with low speed limits to protect the bison, wild horses, mule deer, pronghorn antelope, and bighorn sheep that roam here. You can get a panoramic view of the Badlands from the park's **Painted Canyon Overlook and Visitors Center** (☎ 701/623–4466; 🎫 free), on I–94, 7 mi east of Medora, a good place to start a tour. The center provides picnic tables from which to enjoy the sweeping vista.

If you're up for an hour-long horseback ride in the **South Unit** of the park, contact **Peaceful Valley Ranch** (☎ 701/623–4496), 7 mi north of the park entrance. They'll take you on some of the park's 80 mi of marked horse trails. The visitor center will provide you with maps if you prefer to hike.

The **North Unit,** off U.S. 85 south of Watford City, offers the same scenic driving and hiking opportunities but in a less crowded setting. This is a good place to spot the wildlife you may have missed in the South Unit.

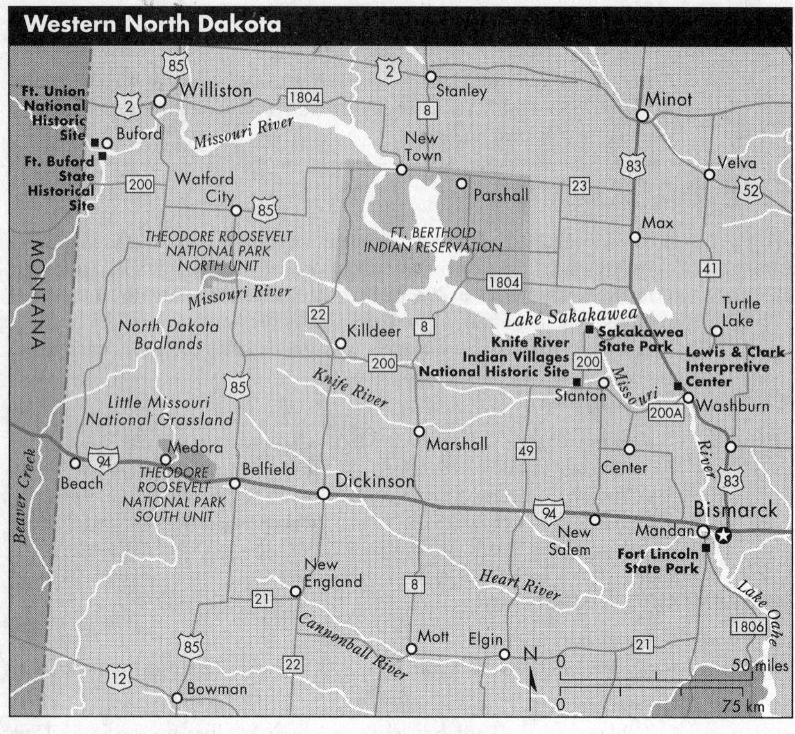

Outside the park, historic **Medora** is a walkable small town with a number of tiny shops, museums, and other attractions. The **Château de Mores** (✉ ½ mi southwest of Medora on Hwy. 10, ☎ 701/623–4355; 🎟 $5), an elegant 26-room mansion on a bluff overlooking the town, was built in the mid-1880s by the Marquis de Mores, a French nobleman who ran a short-lived cattle and meatpacking enterprise from here. You can see a collection of antique dolls in the **Medora Doll House** (🎟 $3).The **Museum of the Badlands** (🎟 $3) displays Native American artifacts, wildlife exhibits, and wax figures depicting frontier days. The **Schafer Heritage Center** (🎟 free) is an art gallery with an exhibit about Harold Schafer, who since the early 1960s has been investing his Mr. Bubble fortune in rebuilding Medora. The Theodore Roosevelt Medora Foundation (☞ Visitor Information, *above*) oversees these three sights, which are open June through August only; call ahead for more information.

Dickinson, an oil-boom-and-bust community on I–94, is now renowned for its dinosaur deposits. You can see 10 full-scale dinosaurs and other fossil, mineral, and animal collections at the **Dakota Dinosaur Museum.** *✉ 200 Museum Dr., off I–94, Exit 61, ☎ 701/225–3466. 🎟 $5. Closed Nov.–Feb.*

Fort Buford State Historic Site (☎ 701/572–9034; 🎟 $4), 22 mi southwest of Williston via Route 1804, is built around the 1866 fort that once imprisoned famous Native American leaders, including Sioux leader Sitting Bull and Nez Percé chief Joseph. It is closed mid-September through mid-May. Two miles west of Fort Buford on Route 1804 is the **Fort Union Trading Post** (☎ 701/572–9083; 🎟 free). This national historic site is a reconstructed fur trading post of John Jacob Astor's American Fur Company. Fort Union dominated the fur trade along the upper Missouri River from 1828 to 1867 and hosted such notable visitors as Prince Maximilian of Germany and John James Audubon.

Dining and Lodging

For price ranges *see* Charts 1 (B) and 2 (B) *in* On the Road with Fodor's.

Medora

$$–$$$ ★ ✕ **Rough Rider Hotel Dining Room.** Housed in a two-story wood-frame building, this rustic restaurant serves barbecued buffalo ribs, prime rib, and other beef specialties. ✉ *Main St.,* ☎ *701/623–4444. AE, D, MC, V. Operates as a B&B Oct.–Apr.*

$$ ✕ **Trapper's Kettle Restaurant.** Be prepared for reminders of the fur trade at this restaurant's two locations—traps, furs, stuffed and mounted animals, and a canoe, which holds the salad bar. Go for chili topped with melted cheese. ✉ *I–94 and U.S. 85, Belfield,* ☎ *701/575–8585;* ✉ *3901 2nd Ave. W, Williston,* ☎ *701/774–2831. AE, MC, V.*

Williston

$$–$$$ ✕ **El Rancho Restaurant.** The Old West atmosphere here was replaced by the earthy colors and art of the Southwest, but beef—especially prime rib—remains the specialty. Seafood and chicken are also on the menu. ✉ *1623 2nd Ave. W,* ☎ *701/572–6321. AE, D, DC, MC, V.*

Motels

AmericInn Motel & Suites (✉ 75 E. River Road S, Medora 58645, ☎ 701/623–4422 or 800/634–3444), 56 rooms, pool; CP; *$$$* . **Badlands Motel** (✉ Box 198, Medora 58645, ☎ 701/623–4422), 116 rooms, pool; closed Oct.–Apr.; *$$*. **El Rancho Motor Hotel** (✉ 1623 2nd Ave. W, Williston 58801, ☎ FAX 701/572–6321 or 800/433–8529), 92 rooms, restaurant; *$*. **Hospitality Inn** (✉ I–94 and Rte. 22, Dickinson 58601, ☎ 701/227–1853 or 800/422–0949, FAX 701/225–0090), 149 rooms, restaurant, pool; *$$*.

Campgrounds

Cottonwood Campground (✉ 5 mi inside Theodore Roosevelt National Park, ☎ 701/623–4466). **Medora Campground** (✉ Medora, ☎ 701/623–4435). **Red Trail Campground** (✉ Box 367, Medora, ☎ 701/623–4317 or 800/621–4317).

Nightlife

The ***Medora Musical*** (✉ 1 mi west of Medora, ☎ 701/623–4444; $15–$17), in the outdoor Burning Hills Amphitheater, is a theater tribute to western Americana, featuring everything from singing to history to fireworks. Prior to the show, you can dine at the **Pitchfork Fondue,** ($10–$17), a cowboy name for a steak dinner picnic held right outside the theater on the prairie bluff.

Outdoor Activities and Sports

Biking

The roads in the north and south units of Theodore Roosevelt National Park are challenging and scenic.

Hiking and Backpacking

All units of Theodore Roosevelt National Park offer spectacular hiking and backpacking opportunities. The Little Missouri National Grasslands (☞ Exploring the Badlands, *above*), which stretches between the main park units, is also a popular spot.

Shopping

Specialty shops lining Medora's Main Street include **Chateau Nuts** (☏ 701/623–4825), which stocks every nut imaginable in quantities large enough to make a squirrel's heart race.

ELSEWHERE IN NORTH DAKOTA

The Lakes Region

Visitor Information

Devils Lake Tourism & Promotion (✉ Box 87, Devils Lake 58301, ☏ 701/662–4903 or 800/233–8048).

Arriving and Departing

U.S. 2 is the principal east–west route through the region, connecting with I–29 at Grand Forks. U.S. 281 runs north–south through the region, with secondary roads leading to lakes and area attractions. Devils Lake is served by **United Express. Amtrak** stops in Devils Lake and Rugby.

What to See and Do

Jamestown, at U.S. 281 and I–94, marks the southern end of this region. The world's largest buffalo sculpture and a live bison herd are both clearly visible from I–94.

Devils Lake, the heart of the lakes region, is surrounded by hundreds of smaller lakes and prairie potholes filled with marsh water. A major breeding ground for North America's migratory waterfowl, the area offers fine birding. Devils Lake itself has excellent jumbo perch and walleye fishing. Check ahead, however, for fishing and camping plans. Rising lake levels have eroded rural roadways. For more information on fishing in the area, contact the Game and Fish Department (✉ 100 N. Bismarck Expressway, Bismarck 58501, ☏ 701/328–6300). On the Devils Lake Sioux Indian Reservation is the **Fort Totten State Historic Site** (✉ Rte. 57, ☏ 701/766–4441; 🎟 $4), the best-preserved military fort west of the Mississippi River. Built in 1867, it later served as one of the nation's largest government-run schools for Native Americans. It is closed mid-September through mid-May.

At **Rugby,** west of Devils Lake on U.S. 2, is the geographical center of North America. Marked by a stone monument, the landmark includes a spacious **Geographical Center Historical Museum** (☏ 701/776–6414; 🎟 $4) containing thousands of objects, such as 19th-century farming equipment and antique cars. It is closed mid-September through mid-May. ★ The **International Peace Garden** (✉ 13 mi north of Dunseith on U.S. 281, ☏ 701/263–4390; 🎟 $7 per vehicle, free in winter) is a 2,300-acre garden straddling the border between Canada and the United States and planted as a symbol of peace between the two nations. In addition to the 100,000 flowers planted annually, the garden includes an 18-ft floral clock, the Peace Tower, and the Peace Chapel.

Dining and Lodging

$$–$$$ ✕ **Birchwood Steakhouse and Northern Lights Lounge.** Delicious prime rib is a staple at this beautiful lakeside restaurant bordering Canada. ✉ *North of Rte. 43, Lake Metígoshe,* ☏ *701/263–4283. MC, V.*

$$ ✕ **Mr. & Mrs. J's.** The "Pig-out Omelette" is the specialty; a huge salad bar complements traditional fare. ✉ *U.S. 2E, Devils Lake,* ☏ *701/662–8815. AE, D, MC, V.*

MOTEL

Dakota Motor Inn (✉ Hwy. 2E, Devils Lake 58301, ☎ FAX 701/662–4001 or ☎ 800/280–4001), 80 rooms, restaurant, pool; $.

CAMPGROUND

Grahams Island State Park (✉ Rte. 1, Box 165, Devils Lake 58301, ☎ 701/766–4015) is 15 mi southwest of Devils Lake, off Route 19. Check before visiting for updates on lake flooding.

The Red River Valley

Visitor Information

Fargo/Moorhead Convention and Visitors Bureau (✉ 2001 44th St. SW, Fargo 58103, ☎ 701/282–3653 or 800/235–7654). **Grand Forks Convention and Visitors Bureau** (✉ 4251 Gateway Dr., 58203, ☎ 701/746–0444 or 800/866–4566). **Wahpeton Visitors Center** (✉ 120 N. 4th St., 58075, ☎ 701/642–8559 or 800/892–6673).

Arriving and Departing

I–94 links Fargo with Minneapolis–St. Paul to the east and with Billings, Montana, to the west. I–29 connects Fargo with Grand Forks, 75 mi north, and with Sioux Falls, South Dakota, to the south. **Hector International Airport** (☎ 701/241–1501), in Fargo, and **Grand Forks International Airport** (☎ 701/795–6981) are served by Northwest and Mesaba; Fargo is also served by United Express. **Amtrak** (☎ 800/872–7245) serves both cities. **Greyhound Lines** (☎ 800/231–2222) provides service to Fargo and Grand Forks.

What to See and Do

The **Red River of the North** forms the eastern boundary of North Dakota with Minnesota. The fertile valley formed by the river was the destination of northern European immigrants in the late 19th century and still contains more than a third of the state's population. The region is an enormous shopping hub, drawing bargain hunters from Minnesota, Canada, and the rest of North Dakota. In April 1997, awesomely devastating floods rolled through the Red River Valley. Flood recovery has moved quickly, but you may still encounter lingering effects, especially in Grand Forks, the hardest-hit city.

In the southeast corner of the state, off I–29, is **Wahpeton.** You can ride on the restored 1926 **Prairie Rose Carousel** (✉ 10 mi east of I–29); rides cost $1. Nearby is the **Ehnstrom Nature Center and Chahinkapa Park Zoo** (☎ 701/642–8709; 🎟 $3), with such native species as eagles, bison, and elk; they are closed from mid-September through April. Ten miles west of I–29 is Mooreton's **Bagg Bonanza Farm** (☎ 701/274–8989; 🎟 $3.50), a national historic site that re-creates the *Bonanza*-like farm life of the late 1800s and early 1900s. Nine of the 21 buildings have been restored. The farm is open Friday and weekends June through September. Head north 50 mi on I–29 to **Fargo,** the state's largest city and the setting for the Coen brothers' acclaimed 1996 film of the same name. **Bonanzaville USA** (✉ Exit 65, I–29, West Fargo, ☎ 701/282–2822 or 800/700–5317; 🎟 $6) is a pioneer village and museum with 40 original and re-created buildings that show life in 1880s Dakota Territory. **Roger Maris Baseball Museum** (✉ West Acres Shopping Center, I–29 and 13th Ave. S, ☎ 701/282–2222; 🎟 free) honors baseball's all-time best single-season home-run hitter. Hands-on learning is the theme at the **Children's Museum at Yunker Farm** (✉ 1201 28th Ave. N, 58102, ☎ 701/232–6102; 🎟 $3).

Seventy-five miles north of Fargo on I–29 is **Grand Forks,** the state's cultural and technological center. Grand Forks is home to the **North Dakota Museum of Art** (✉ Centennial Dr., ☎ 701/777–4195; 🎟 free) and the Center for Aerospace Sciences (✉ 4125 University Ave., ☎ 701/777–2791; 🎟 free, by appointment only), both at the **University of North Dakota.** Seventy miles north of Grand Forks via I–29, the **Pembina State Museum** (✉ 375 Hwy. 59, ☎ 701/825–6840; 🎟 free; $2 for elevator to top of tower) has exhibits on North Dakota history and an observation tower. Just west, in **Icelandic State Park** (☞ National and State Parks, *above*), the Pioneer Heritage Interpretive Center (☎ 701/265–4561; 🎟 $3 per vehicle) uses artifacts and exhibits to showcase the ethnic diversity of the region.

Dining and Lodging

$$–$$$ ✕ **Old Broadway Food and Brewing Co.** Featuring Gay '90s decor under 18-ft ceilings, with a plethora of antiques, the restaurant and microbrewery are in the circa 1900 Stern's clothing store. Ribs, smoked on the premises, are a mainstay on the menu. ✉ *22 N. Broadway, Fargo,* ☎ *701/237–6161. AE, D, DC, MC, V.*

MOTELS

🏨 **Best Western Doublewood Inn and Conference Center** (✉ 3333 13th Ave. S, Fargo 58103, ☎ 701/235–3333 or 800/433–3235), 173 rooms, restaurant, pool ; *$$$.* 🏨 **Road King Inn** (✉ 3300 30th Ave. S, Grand Forks 58201, ☎ 701/746–1391 or 800/707–1391), 85 rooms, pool; *$$.*

OKLAHOMA

Updated by Anne Defrange

Capital	Oklahoma City
Population	3,317,000
Motto	Labor Conquers All Things
State Bird	Scissor-tailed flycatcher
State Flower	Mistletoe
Postal Abbreviation	OK

Statewide Visitor Information

Oklahoma Tourism and Recreation Department (✉ 15 N. Robinson Ave., Oklahoma City 73102, ☎ 405/521–2409 or 800/652–6552). **State Historical Society** (✉ 2100 N. Lincoln Blvd., Oklahoma City 73105, ☎ 405/521–2491).

Scenic Drives

Route 49 traverses the prairies and granite peaks of the Wichita Mountains Wildlife Refuge (☞ Exploring Southwestern Oklahoma, *below*). **Route 10,** which follows the Spring, Neosho, and Illinois rivers from Wyandotte through Grove to Gore, is a winding drive through the Cherokee Nation. **Route 1** through the northern section of the Ouachita National Forest (☞ National and State Parks, *below*), from Talihina east about 50 mi to the state border, makes a beautiful drive in autumn, when the forest foliage is most colorful.

National and State Parks

National Park

Natural hot springs are the main attraction at the **Chickasaw National Recreation Area** (✉ Box 201, off I–35, Sulphur 73086, ☎ 580/622–3165), in southern Oklahoma.

The **Ouachita National Forest** (✉ HC 64, Box 3467, Heavener 74937, ☎ 918/653–2991), in southeastern Oklahoma, is a scenic region of small mountain ranges.

State Parks

Oklahoma has 52 state parks, and all but two have camping facilities. Some of the best are **Alabaster Caverns State Park** (✉ Rte. 1, Box 32, Freedom 73842, ☎ 580/621–3381), **Beavers Bend Resort Park** (☞ Exploring Southeastern Oklahoma, *below*), **Roman Nose Resort Park** (✉ Rte. 1, Watonga 73772, ☎ 580/623–4215), **Quartz Mountain State Park** (☞ Exploring Southwestern Oklahoma, *below*), and **Red Rock Canyon State Park** (✉ Box 502, Hinton 73047, ☎ 405/542–6344).

CENTRAL OKLAHOMA

Oklahoma's image as a western state was largely forged in central Oklahoma, where pickup trucks, cowboy boots, and oil wells are still the ultimate status symbols. The Chisholm Trail, the most famous of the cattle trails that moved Texas cattle north through Indian Territory after the end of the Civil War, came through here 130 years ago, and the country's largest live cattle auction still gets under way in Oklahoma City's Stockyards City every Monday morning. Many towns in central Oklahoma, including Guthrie, Oklahoma City, and Norman, share a common heritage: They were born in one day, following the April 22, 1889, land run, which opened a parcel of land in central Oklahoma to non-Indian settlement. Would-be homesteaders lined up on the borders and literally raced for claims.

Visitor Information

The *Daily Oklahoman*'s Friday weekend section and the *Gazette* (a free weekly distributed in Oklahoma City and Norman restaurants and hotels) list events. **Guthrie:** Convention and Visitors Bureau (⊠ 212 W. Oklahoma St., Box 995, 73044, ☎ 405/282–1947 or 800/299–1889). **Oklahoma City:** Convention and Visitors Bureau (⊠ 189 W. Sheridan St., 73102, ☎ 405/297–8912 or 800/225–5652). **Norman:** Convention and Visitors Bureau (⊠ 200 S. Jones, 73069, ☎ 405/366–8095 or 800/767–7260).

Arriving and Departing

By Bus

Greyhound Lines (⊠ 427 W. Sheridan St., Oklahoma City, ☎ 800/231–2222).

By Car

Interstate 35 takes travelers north and south through central Oklahoma; I–40 crosses east and west. Interstate 44, which runs diagonally from the northeast to the southwest, intersects both I–35 and I–40 in Oklahoma City.

By Plane

The **Will Rogers World Airport** (☎ 405/680–3200), in southwestern Oklahoma City, is served by major domestic airlines.

Getting Around Central Oklahoma

A car is a necessity here since public transportation is limited.

Exploring Central Oklahoma

A fitting place to begin a tour is **Guthrie,** where Oklahoma began in 1889. From territorial days until 1910, Guthrie was the state capital. After a bitter political fight, the capital was moved to Oklahoma City, and Guthrie was forgotten. Two decades ago the town's architectural treasures were rediscovered: More than 400 city blocks of turn-the-century commercial and residential properties remained, with most of their stained-glass windows and stamped-tin ceilings intact. The Guthrie Chamber of Commerce (☞ Visitor Information, *above*) conducts guided walking tours. Gift shops, antiques malls, and restaurants abound in the downtown district, the largest urban area listed on the National Register of Historic Places. **First Capital Trolley** (☎ 405/282–6000) makes regular tours of downtown Guthrie, admission $2, beginning from the corner of Second Street and Harrison Avenue. For a more in-depth look at the town's history, stop by the **State Capital Publishing Museum** (⊠ 301 W. Harrison Ave., ☎ 405/282–4123; 🎫 free), where vintage printing presses are on display along with exhibits about territorial life. On weekdays you can take a walk through history at the **Scottish Rite Temple** (⊠ 900 E. Oklahoma Ave., ☎ 405/282–1281; 🎫 free), one of the world's largest Masonic lodges, with an ancient Egyptian room, a Roman atrium, a Pompeiian room, a Gothic library, and an Italian Renaissance lounge.

Oklahoma City, 20 mi south of Guthrie, is in the midst of a massive downtown renewal project. Most of the activity is in Bricktown, a renovated warehouse district east of the commercial area. Among the urban renewal projects are the newly constructed Bricktown Ballpark, home of the the RedHawks baseball team; and a number of new restaurants and entertainment venues housed in Bricktown's industrial buildings. Efforts to repair damages from the Murrah Building bombing are still underway: The ground has been cleared for a future memorial, but in the meantime a chain-link fence holds mementoes from thousands of visitors.

Most Oklahoma City attractions are found east and north of downtown, including the limestone-and-granite **Oklahoma State Capitol** (✉ N.E. 23rd St. and Lincoln Blvd., ☎ 405/521–3356). The oil wells on the grounds aren't just for show; although the earliest well dried up in 1986, the remainder actually do pump oil.

An extensive collection of Western fine art and artifacts is on display at the **National Cowboy Hall of Fame and Western Heritage Center** (✉ 1700 N.E. 63rd St., ☎ 405/478–2250; 🎫 $6.50), north of the capitol off I–44. A **Rodeo Hall of Fame** and tributes to Western performers complement the artwork. The **Children's Corral** gives hands-on experience with bedrolls, saddles, lariats, and the like.

Five roller coasters, faux saloons and livery stables, and staged gunfights entertain visitors at **Frontier City Theme Park** (✉ 11501 N.E. Expressway, ☎ 405/478–2412; 🎫 $20) a 70-acre western-style amusement park. Musical and entertainment revues play daily from Memorial Day to Labor Day and fireworks displays are frequent throughout the summer. The park is closed on weekdays from September through May.

Parks, Gardens, and Zoos

A walk through the **Crystal Bridge Tropical Conservatory**, a glass botanical tube at the **Myriad Botanical Gardens** (✉ 301 W. Reno Ave., ☎ 405/297–3995; 🎫 $2), takes visitors through habitats ranging from desert to rain forest, complete with a 35-ft waterfall.

The **Oklahoma City Zoological Park** (✉ 2101 N.E. 50th St., ☎ 405/424–3344; 🎫 $4) has natural habitats for primates, wildcats, and other species. Dolphin shows are scheduled throughout the summer.

Thoroughbred and quarter-horse pari-mutuel races are scheduled at **Remington Park** (✉ 1 Remington Pl., ☎ 405/424–9000 or 800/456–9000; 🎫 $1.50) in fall, spring, and summer. It's closed Tuesday; call ahead for race dates and reservations.

Dining and Lodging

Century-old brick warehouses in downtown Oklahoma City have turned Bricktown into a favorite dining district for locals. Western Avenue north of 50th Street is known as Restaurant Row; the trendiest new places debut there. For price ranges *see* Chart 1 (B) *in* On the Road with Fodor's.

The more expensive hotels in Oklahoma City have restaurants, clubs, and lounges, but rooms generally differ little from those in moderately priced establishments. If you don't plan to spend a lot of time at the hotel, you may be better off stopping at one of the chain motels along the highways. For price ranges *see* Chart 2 (B) *in* On the Road with Fodor's.

Ames

$$$ ★ 🏨 **Island Guest Ranch.** At this 2,800-acre working ranch 90 mi north of Oklahoma City, guests help herd cattle, ride horses, fish, hike, and attend staged powwows and team roping and penning in the ranch's own rodeo arena. Rooms, each with private bath, are in two rustic

bunkhouses; hearty meals are served in the main log lodge. Rates include all meals and activities; reservations should be made at least several weeks in advance. The owners will meet you at the airport on request. ✉ *Ames 73718,* ☎ *580/753–4574 or 800/928–4574,* FAX *405/753–4574. 10 rooms. MC, V. Closed Oct.–Mar.*

Guthrie

$$ ✕ **Granny Had One.** Though this is both an antiques store and tearoom, the menu is the main draw: It includes everything from peanut-butter-and-jelly sandwiches to smoked salmon to steak, with especially tasty homemade soups and breads. ✉ *113 W. Harrison St.,* ☎ *405/282–4482. AE, D, DC, MC, V.*

$–$$ ✕ **Stables Café** Huge platters of steak, ribs, sandwiches, and burgers are doled out at this typically rustic barbecue joint in the heart of downtown. ✉ *223 N. Division St.,* ☎ *405/282–0893. D, MC, V.*

Norman

$$$–$$$$ ★ **Montford Inn Bed & Breakfast.** Native American collectibles and football memorabilia (the University of Oklahoma is nearby) blend seamlessly with antiques in this supremely comfortable inn. Rooms have fireplaces, whirpool tubs, writing desks, king-size beds, televisions tucked inside armoires, and coffeemakers. Two cottages and a detached house have kitchenettes. ✉ *322 W. Tonhawa, Norman 73069,* ☎ *405/321–2200 or 800/321–8969,* FAX *405/321–8347. 15 rooms, 2 cottages, 1 house. AE, D, MC, V.*

Oklahoma City

$$$$ ★ ✕ **Coach House.** The dark-wood-paneled walls of this small, cozy restaurant are covered with images of the hunt, a theme reflected in the menu, which features pheasant, quail, and venison. Other specialties are scallops with roasted corn cakes, and, for dessert, individual chocolate cakes. ✉ *6437 Avondale Dr.,* ☎ *405/842–1000. AE, MC, V.*

$$ ✕ **Bricktown Brewery.** Even the shrimp are steamed in beer in this airy brew pub, where blowups of historical photographs are displayed against exposed brick. Land Run Lager and Copperhead Ale complement the chicken potpie, fish-and-chips, and bratwurst. ✉ *1 Oklahoma Ave.,* ☎ *405/232–2739. AE, DC, MC, V.*

$$ ★ ✕ **Cattlemen's Steakhouse.** Beef is the star attraction at this classic steak house in the heart of Stockyards City. Cowboys clad in spurs look right at home among the western murals, cattle-branding irons, and other western paraphernalia. ✉ *1309 S. Agnew Ave.,* ☎ *405/236–0416. AE, D, DC, MC, V.*

$$$$ **Waterford Marriott.** This elegant hotel in northwest Oklahoma City has a popular restaurant with summertime jazz concerts. ✉ *6300 Waterford Blvd.* ☎ *405/848–4782. 197 rooms. Restaurants, pool, health club. AE, D, DC, MC, V.*

$$$$ **Westin Oklahoma City.** This 15-story glass-and-stone building in the heart of downtown has extensive business facilities and access to the Myriad Convention Center by underground tunnel. ✉ *1 N. Broadway, 73102,* ☎ *405/235–2780,* FAX *405/272–0369. 395 rooms. Restaurant, pool. AE, D, DC, MC, V.*

$$$ **Clarion Hotel and Conference Center.** The Clarion is conveniently close to museums and the capitol. Unlike most other hotels in the area, the Clarion has several concierge floors. ✉ *4345 N. Lincoln Blvd., 73105,* ☎ *405/528–2741 or 800/741–2741,* FAX *405/525–8185. 307 rooms. 2 restaurants, pool, tennis. AE, D, DC, MC, V.*

Motels

Holiday Inn Airport (✉ 2101 S. Meridian, 73108, ☎ 405/685–4000 or 800/622–7666, FAX 405/681–1674), 245 rooms, restaurant, pool, exercise room; *$$$.* **Motel 6 Oklahoma City Airport** (✉ 820 S.

Meridian, 73108, ☎ 405/946–6662, FAX 405/946–4058), 128 rooms, pool; $. **Motel 6 Oklahoma City North** (✉ 11900 N.E. Expressway, 73131, ☎ 405/478–8666, FAX 405/478–7442), 101 rooms, pool; $.

Shopping

Malls in the area contain locally owned shops and boutiques as well as familiar chains. Prominent malls include **Crossroads** (✉ Intersection of I–40 and I–35), **Penn Square** (✉ 1901 N.W. Expressway), and **Quail Springs** (✉ Memorial Rd and May Ave.). The **Route 66** gallery and gift shop (✉ 50 Penn Pl., 5000 N. Pennsylvania Ave., ☎ 405/848–6166) sells jewelry and sculpture by regional artists, plus T-shirts, caps, and calendars commemorating the old highway's neon glory days.

NORTHEASTERN OKLAHOMA

The Ozark Mountains lap over from Arkansas into northeastern Oklahoma to form the Grand Lake O' the Cherokees region. The infamous Cherokee Trail of Tears—along which thousands of Cherokee traveled in the 1830s when they were forcibly resettled from their Georgia homes—ended here. And with a dozen more Native American tribes headquartered here, powwows and tribal museums are plentiful. Today tribal governments are vital once again, and Native American art, language, and customs are actively being preserved.

Visitor Information

Tahlequah: Chamber of Commerce (✉ 123 E. Delaware St., 74464, ☎ 918/456–3742). **Tulsa:** Visitor Information Center and Chamber of Commerce (✉ 616 S. Boston St., 74119, ☎ 918/585–1201).

Arriving and Departing

By Bus

Greyhound Lines (✉ 317 S. Detroit St., ☎ 800/231–2222) serves Tulsa.

By Car

In Tulsa I–44 and I–244 form a downtown loop. The Keystone, Cherokee, and Broken Arrow expressways also lead downtown. From Tulsa U.S. 75 leads north to the Bartlesville area. I–44 is the main route northeast from Tulsa and connects with many smaller, more scenic highways. A 400-mi segment of the old Route 66 travels through Oklahoma; the 100-mi leg that connects with I–35 north of Oklahoma City and I–44 just west of Tulsa is the easiest to follow. Look for old gas stations, shady city parks, and tiny grocery stores in towns such as Chandler and Sapulpa. Route 66 parallels I–44 northeast of Tulsa, where classic landmarks include **Arrowood Trading Post** (✉ 2700 N. Old Highway 66, Catoosa, ☎ 918/266–3663). The **Buffalo Ranch** (✉ 1 mi north of Afton on Rte. 66, ☎ 918/257–4544) is classic Route 66 kitsch, with a bison herd out back and a huge selection of souvenirs.

By Plane

Tulsa International Airport (☎ 918/838–5000), 10 mi northeast of downtown Tulsa, is served by major domestic airlines. Average cab fare to the downtown area is about $12. Major hotels have shuttle bus service.

Exploring Northeastern Oklahoma

The oil money with which Tulsa was built in the 1920s left the city with a legacy of culture, art, and Art Deco architecture second only to that of Miami, Florida; stop by the chamber of commerce (☞ Visitor Information, *above*) for a walking-tour map that includes more than a dozen downtown buildings. About 3 mi from the downtown area is the **Gilcrease Museum** (✉ 1400 Gilcrease Museum Rd., ☎ 918/596–2700; 🎟 $5 suggested donation). Its collection, dedicated to western art and Americana, includes paintings by such artists as Frederic Remington and Charles Russell, as well as a wide-ranging selection of Native American art and artifacts. A few miles southeast of downtown is the **Philbrook Museum of Art** (✉ 2727 S. Rockford Rd., ☎ 918/749–7941; 🎟 $4), where a wide-ranging collection is housed inside the Italianate villa of former oil baron Waite Phillips.

Northwest of Tulsa and 8 mi north of Pawhuska on the Tallgrass Prairie Drive is the **Tallgrass Prairie Reserve** (☎ 918/287–4803), a 52,000-acre swath of unbroken tallgrass prairie with a bison herd, a cowboy bunkhouse, and hiking and driving trails.

From Pawhuska take Route 60 east to Route 123 through the **Prairie Wild Horse Refuge** (☎ 918/336–1564), where 1,200 horses can be spotted on either side of the highway.

★ Also on Route 123, about 20 mi south of Bartlesville, is **Woolaroc** (☎ 918/336–0307; 🎟 $4), whose name is derived from the words *wood, land,* and *rock*. Once a ranch, Woolaroc is now a drive-through wildlife preserve that's home to bison and 40 other species (visitors must remain in their vehicles). The preserve surrounds a museum packed with western lore: gun and rifle exhibits; Native American artifacts; western art, including works by Remington and Russell; and such memorabilia as Theodore Roosevelt's saddle. The historic **Woolaroc Lodge,** formerly used by oilman Frank Phillips, is filled with every animal trophy imaginable. The preserve is closed Monday from September through May.

Southeast of Woolaroc by way of Nowata lies the Dog Iron Ranch and **Will Rogers Birthplace** (✉ 2 mi east of Oologah, ☎ 918/275–4201; 🎟 free). The great humorist's childhood home, built in 1875, is a two-story log-and-clapboard structure containing period furnishings; you'll also find longhorn cattle and barnyard animals on the grounds of the working ranch. On Route 88 in Claremore is the sandstone **Will Rogers Memorial** (☎ 800/324–9455; 🎟 free), where Rogers and members of his family are buried; it also has memorabilia, a theater that shows Rogers's movies and newsreels, and a hands-on children's museum.

Take I–44 and U.S. 59 to **Grove** and the **Grand Lake O' the Cherokees.** Numerous recreational options here include a dinner cruise or sightseeing tour aboard the *Cherokee Queen* riverboat (☎ 918/786–4272; 🎟 $7.50 for sightseeing tour).

About 50 mi south of Grove on Route 10 is **Tahlequah,** capital of the Cherokee Nation. The **Cherokee Heritage Center** (✉ Willis Rd., ☎ 918/456–6007; 🎟 free), 3 mi south of Tahlequah off U.S. 62, chronicles the history of the Cherokee Nation, from the time of the Trail of Tears to the present. Within the Heritage Center are the **Cherokee National Museum** (🎟 $2.75), where a new exhibit focuses on the oral traditon of the elders; the **Ancient Village at Tsa-La-Gi** (🎟 $4), where costumed tribal members demonstrate basketweaving, pottery, stickball games, and other Cherokee traditions; and **Adams Corner,** a re-created pioneer village from the 1800s. The center is open weekdays only from September through May; in summer it's open from Monday through Saturday.

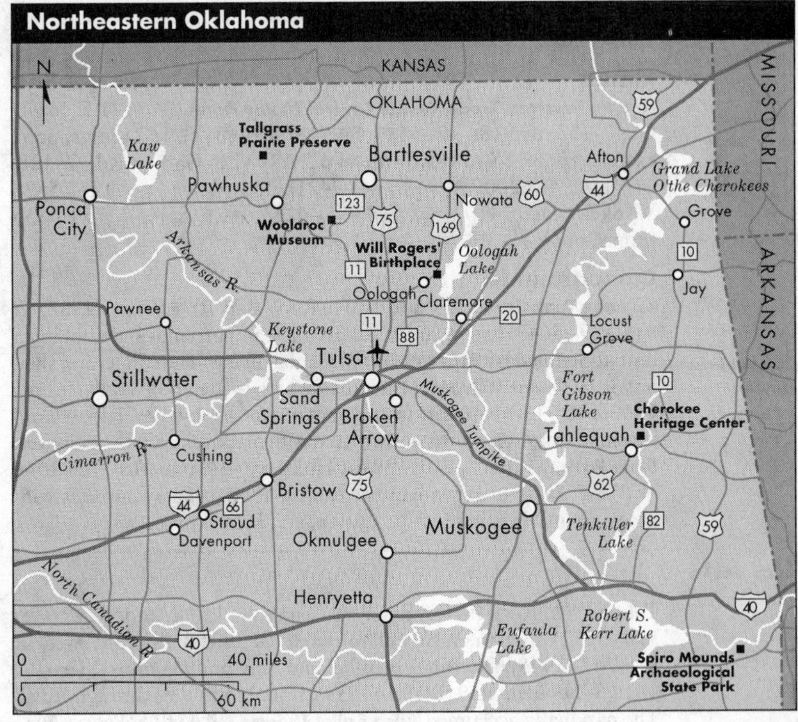

Southwest of Tahlequah on U.S. 62 is **Okmulgee,** whose sandstone **Creek Council House** (✉ 106 W. 6th St., ☎ 918/756–2324; free), on a shady square, has been meticulously restored. The two-story structure was the center of Creek political life from 1878 until the turn of the century, when tribal governments were liquidated. It's now a museum, library, and center for the preservation of the Creek language.

Dining and Lodging

Tulsa probably has the best dining in the state, and you'll be hard pressed to find any restaurants that qualify as expensive. Lodging choices are more humdrum. For price ranges *see* Charts 1 (B) and 2 (B) *in* On the Road with Fodor's.

$ ★ ✕ **Nelson's Buffeteria.** This lively, old-fashioned lunchroom is known for its 1940s decor and the best chicken-fried steak in town. Food is served cafeteria style. ✉ *514 S. Boston St.,* ☎ *918/584–9969. MC, V. Closed weekends. No dinner.*

$$$$ ✕🏨 **Adam's Mark Hotel.** Next door to the Performing Arts Center and connected to a shopping mall with an indoor ice-skating rink, the Adam's Mark has the most highly regarded staff in Tulsa. Rooms have minibars and tiny balconies. At Bravo Ristorante, the hotel's dining room, traditional Italian cuisine is served by a waitstaff of both professional and student vocalists who deliver arias with your meal. ✉ *100 E. 2nd St., 74103,* ☎ *918/582–9000 or 800/444–2326,* FAX *918/560–2261. 468 rooms. 2 restaurants, pools, exercise room. AE, D, DC, MC, V.*

$$$$ ✕🏨 **Doubletree Inn Downtown.** Visitors are welcomed with chocolate chip cookies in this modern high-rise, connected by skywalk to the Tulsa Convention Center. The Grille draws a crowd with its innovative southwestern cuisine. ✉ *616 W. 7th St., 74127,* ☎ *918/587–8000,*

℻ *918/587–1642. 449 rooms. 2 restaurants, pool, excercise room. AE, D, DC, MC, V.*

Motels

Best Western Trade Winds Central Motor Hotel (✉ 3141 E. Skelly Dr., 74135, ☎ 918/749–5561, ℻ 918/749–6312), 167 rooms, pool, exercise room; *$$–$$$$*. **Motel 6** (✉ 1011 S. Garnett Rd., 74128, ☎ 918/234–6200, ℻ 918/234–9421), 153 rooms , pool; (✉ 5828 W. Skelly Dr., 74107, ☎ 918/445–0223, ℻ 918/445–2750), 155 rooms, pool; *$*.

Campgrounds

Lake Tenkiller State Park (✉ HCR 68, Box 1095, Vian 74962, ☎ 918/489–5643) has secluded cabins and campgrounds overlooking a limestone-lined lake that's great for scuba diving. The cabins and shelters at **Osage Hills State Park** (✉ Red Eagle Rte., Box 84, Pawhuska 74056, ☎ 918/336–4141) were built in the '30s by the Civilian Conservation Corps on rolling hills covered with blackjack oak. **Sequoyah State Park** (✉ Rte. 1, Box 198–3, Hulbert 74441, ☎ 918/772–2046 or 918/772–2545 for lodge) has cabins, a lodge, and campsites with access to a swimming beach, marina, and heated pool.

The Arts

Tulsa's downtown Performing Arts Center (✉ 110 E. 2nd St., ☎ 918/596–7122) hosts the **Tulsa Philharmonic** (✉ 2901 S. Harvard Ave., ☎ 918/747–7445) between September and May, and the **Tulsa Opera** (✉ 1610 S. Boulder, ☎ 918/582–4035), from November through April. The nationally acclaimed **Tulsa Ballet Theatre** (✉ 4512 S. Peoria Ave., ☎ 918/749–6006) performs from September through April.

Outdoor Activities and Sports

Fishing

Tulsa World's sports section has up-to-date fishing information, or check with the **Department of Wildlife and Conservation** (☎ 405/521–2221). Fishing licenses can be purchased in most tackle shops.

Hiking

Every park in the area has hiking trails. For general information call the **Tourism and Recreation Department** (☞ Statewide Visitor Information, *above*).

Shopping

Cherry Street, a six-block stretch between Utica and Peoria avenues along 15th Street in Tulsa, is lined with antiques stores, bars, bakeries, and sandwich shops.

SOUTHWESTERN OKLAHOMA

The frontier doesn't seem far away in this rugged, sparsely populated region; oceans of grass are broken by blue-granite mountains, and almost every small town has a saddle shop. During the 19th century this was the domain of the buffalo and the Kiowa and Comanche tribes; travelers may still spot Native American tepees and brush arbors in rural areas during the summer.

Visitor Information

Lawton: Chamber of Commerce (✉ Box 1376, 73502, ☎ 405/355–3541).

Arriving and Departing

By Bus

Greyhound Lines (✉ 15 N.E. 20th St., ☎ 800/231–2222) serves Lawton.

By Car

As with the rest of the state, you'll need a car to tour this region. Most of the area lies between I–44 and I–40 southwest of Oklahoma City; U.S. and state highways connect with these interstates.

By Plane

The **Will Rogers World Airport** (☞ Central Oklahoma, *above*) gives the best access to the region.

Exploring Southwestern Oklahoma

At the foot of the Wichita Mountains, **Lawton** makes a good base for exploring the region. The **Museum of the Great Plains** (✉ 601 Ferris Ave., ☎ 405/581–3460; 🎟 $2) has a reproduction trading post and an outdoor fort recalling the pre–Louisiana Purchase days when the Red River was the international border with Spain.

A short drive north of Lawton on I–44 brings you to the **Fort Sill Military Reservation** (✉ Key Gate off Sheridan Rd., ☎ 405/442–8111 or 405/351–5123; 🎟 free), built in 1869 for the Native Americans of the southern plains. Seven original buildings contain exhibits on the fort's history. Geronimo's Guardhouse is named for the famous Chiricahua Apache warrior, who died at the fort in 1909 as a prisoner of war. The Fort Sill Apache Tribe dances the Apache fire dance here in September.

Just north of Lawton I–44 crosses U.S. 49, which runs along the ★ northern border of Fort Sill and westward to the **Wichita Mountains Wildlife Refuge** (✉ Rte. 1, Indiahoma, ☎ 405/429–3222), one of the most beautiful areas in the state. Here the wildlife is thick and the scenery—boulder-topped mountains overlooking clear, still lakes—often breathtaking. The refuge is home to bison, longhorn cattle, and other species. It's also the best place in the state for rock climbing and mountain biking. Hiking trails are abundant and camping is allowed, but backcountry camping and biking are by permit only. Rangers conduct specialized guided tours, by reservation only.

From the western end of the Wichita Mountains Wildlife Refuge, U.S. 54 and 62 lead southwest to Altus. From here travel north on U.S. 283/Route 44 to **Quartz Mountain State Park** (✉ Lone Wolf, ☎ 405/563–2238). A state-run lodge is being rebuilt following a fire, but the scenery alone is worth the trip—bare rock outcroppings reflected in pristine Altus Lake and abundant wildflowers in spring. You can also explore caves, visit the park's nature center, or take advantage of guided tours and special programs throughout the year.

★ You can relive travel on the Mother Road at the **Oklahoma Route 66 Museum** (✉ 2229 Gary Blvd., off I–40, Clinton, ☎ 580/323–7866; 🎟 $3). Exhibits are organized by decade, beginning with the road's construction in the 1920s, continuing through the Dust Bowl in the 30s, the military highway days of the 40s, and the vacation-oriented 50s (complete with a re-created diner and drive-in movie theater). Operated by the Oklahoma Historical Society, the museum provides historical background as well as on-the-road nostalgia.

Dining and Lodging

When possible, pack lunches for park picnics; at night you'll probably have to content yourself with chain restaurants. Unless you plan to camp, your hotel will probably be little more than a convenient base for exploring. For price ranges *see* Charts 1 (B) and 2 (B) *in* On the Road with Fodor's.

Altus

$$ **Best Western.** This business-oriented hotel has refrigerators and two phones in many of its rooms. ✉ *2804 N. Main St., 73521,* ☎ *580/482–9300,* FAX *580/482–2245. 104 rooms. Pool. AE, D, DC, MC, V.*

Lawton

$ ★ ✕ **Woody's BBQ.** Seated under a ceiling fan in one of two rustic dining rooms, you'll be treated to pork ribs or beef brisket with unusual side dishes such as okra, fried mushrooms, and "wood chips" (fried potatoes with melted cheese and bacon). ✉ *1107 W. Lee Blvd.,* ☎ *580/355–4950. MC, V.*

$$ **Howard Johnson Lodge and Convention Center.** The public areas of this low-rise stucco hotel just off I–44 are a hodgepodge of decorative themes, from Victorian-style frosted glass to a rustic chandelier of antlers. Whirlpool suites are done up with high-tech glass and chrome. ✉ *1125 E. Gore St., 73501,* ☎ *580/353–0200,* FAX *580/353–6801. 144 rooms. Restaurant, pool, tennis. AE, D, DC, MC, V.*

Meers

$ ✕ **Meers Store.** All that's left of a boomtown that grew up during a brief gold rush in 1901 are this eatery and a federal seismographic station by the cash register. The restaurant's claim to fame is not gold but the Meersburger—a 7-inch burger made of 100% longhorn beef. ✉ *Rte. 115, 4 mi east of the Wichita Mountains Wildlife Refuge,* ☎ *580/429–8051. No credit cards.*

Motels

Ramada Inn (✉ 601 N. 2nd St., Lawton 73507, ☎ 580/355–7155, FAX 580/353–6162), 98 rooms, restaurant, pool; *$*

Campgrounds

Quartz Mountain State Park (☞ Exploring Southwestern Oklahoma, *above*) has camping facilities. For camping information on other state parks in the area, contact the state tourism department (☞ Statewide Visitor Information, *above*).

Outdoor Activities and Sports

Fishing

The best bets are Altus Lake or any of the lakes at the Wichita Mountains Wildlife Refuge (☞ Exploring Southwestern Oklahoma, *above*). The sports section in the *Daily Oklahoman* has fishing reports for the lakes in the area, or contact the **Department of Wildlife and Conservation** (☎ 405/521–3855).

Hiking

Check specific parks (☞ National and State Parks, *above*) or contact the **Tourism and Recreation Department** (☞ Statewide Visitor Information, *above*).

SOUTHEASTERN OKLAHOMA

Home to the Choctaw Tribe since the 1830s, the green and hilly southeastern corner of the state seems a world apart from the rest of Oklahoma. Here are pine and hardwood forests, populated by plentiful game and traversed by fast-running mountain streams. Outdoor enthusiasts favor this part of the state, where food, lodging, and entertainment tend toward the rustic.

Visitor Information

Kiamichi Country: Regional Tourism Association (✉ Box 638, Wilburton 74578, ☎ 918/465–2367 or 800/722–8180).

Arriving and Departing

By Bus

Greyhound Lines provides bus service to Wilburton and Idabel (☎ 800/231–2222).

By Car

Much of southeastern Oklahoma is accessible only by two-lane roads. From I–40E near Sallisaw U.S. 259 leads south. From I–35S take U.S. 70 west.

By Plane

The **Will Rogers World Airport** (☎ 405/681–5311) in southwest Oklahoma City provides the best access to the northern Ouachita National Forest area. Extreme southeastern Oklahoma is closer to Dallas and the **Dallas–Fort Worth International Airport** (☎ 214/574–6720).

Getting Around Southeastern Oklahoma

This sprawling, mountainous region requires a car. Highways are generally well marked, but navigating along winding mountain roads can require patience and a little extra time.

Exploring Southeastern Oklahoma

Spectacular views can be seen from the **Talimena Scenic Byway,** marked SH–1 and running east–west through the heart of the Ouachita National Forest. The highway extends west into the Sans Bois Mountain area and intersects with southbound U.S. 259, which continues into the Kiamichi Mountains.

U.S. 59, south from I–40E, leads to the **Overstreet-Kerr Living History Farm** (✉ Rte. 2, Box 693, Keota 74941, ☎ 918/966–3396; 🎫 $3), where century-old strains of livestock and crops are being preserved. A three-story farmhouse, the former home of a prosperous farmer and his Choctaw wife, is also open for tours.

U.S. 59 intersects with SH–9, the road to Spiro and **Spiro Mounds Archaeological State Park** (✉ Rte. 2, Box 339AA, 74959, ☎ 918/962–2062). Once the headquarters of a confederation of 60 tribes, the park—which is closed Monday and Tuesday—contains remains of 11 earthen mounds used as dwellings by the Spiro, an ancient people who lived here from about AD 600 to 1450. A 1½-mi trail runs alongside the mounds, and a visitor center contains artifacts.

Southwest of Spiro is Wilburton and **Robbers Cave State Park** (✉ Hwy. 2, 5 mi north of Wilburton, Box 9, 74578, ☎ 918/465–2562), where a cave hidden in 100-ft sandstone bluffs is said to have been a hideout for such notorious outlaws as the Daltons and the James Gang. Steps have been carved into the rock, and guided tours, complete with colorful tales, are conducted by a park naturalist.

No development has been allowed in the 26,445-acre **Winding Stair National Recreation Area** (✉ HC 64, Box 3467, Heavener 74937, ☎ 918/653–2991), but there are plenty of picnic areas and easy trails within a short distance of the Talimena Scenic Byway. The scenic byway intersects with U.S. 259, which takes travelers south to **Beavers Bend Resort Park** (✉ Hwy. 259A, 7 mi north of Broken Bow, Box 10, Broken Bow 74728, ☎ 580/494–6300). Built on the Mountain Fork River at the edge of the Ouachita National Forest, the park is so secluded that wild turkeys have been spotted strolling on the resort's golf fairways. The history and culture of the forest from prehistoric times to the present are interpreted at the park's **Forest Heritage Center** (☎ 580/494–6497; free)

Dining and Lodging

Lodging is rustic in southeast Oklahoma, and room service is virtually nonexistent. Many restaurants close by 9 PM. For price ranges *see* Chart 1 (B) *in* On the Road with Fodor's.

Hochatown

$$ ✕ **Stevens Gap Restaurant.** Here you can sample regional specialties like catfish fillets served with hush puppies and baked sweet potatoes or southern-fried chicken, fried okra, and brown beans. You can also get breakfast (biscuits, gravy, and the works) all day long. ✉ *U.S. 259 and Stevens Gap Rd.,* ☎ *580/494–6350. No credit cards.*

$$$ ★ **Lakeview Lodge.** Every room at this state-operated lodge has a balcony view of Broken Bow Lake and the pristine wilderness. Breakfast is served in the lodge's Great Room, where a fire roars in a native stone fireplace when weather warrants. ✉ *U.S. 259, Box 10, Broken Bow 74728,* ☎ *580/494–6179,* FAX *580/494–6179. 40 rooms. Golf. CP. AE, D, DC, MC, V.*

Krebs

$$ ★ ✕ **Pete's Place.** Pete Prichard started selling sandwiches and illicit "Choc" beer—named for the Choctaws who lived in the area—out of his house in 1925; now his grandchildren operate a sprawling restaurant with a (legal) microbrewery and 15 private dining rooms clustered around three main dining areas. ✉ *120 S.W. 8th St.,* ☎ *918/423–2042. No lunch Mon.–Sat.; no dinner Sun. AE, D, DC, MC, V.*

Octavia

$$$–$$$$ **Eagle Creek Guest Cottages.** Seven cottages are spread out over 40 acres on the backside of a mountain; some are on the banks of Big Eagle Creek or on a private lake. Some of the pine-and-calico cabins have native stone fireplaces, whirlpools, and big back porches. All have full kitchens, VCRs, microwave ovens, televisions, and great views. ✉ *U.S. 259, HC 15, Box 250, Smithville 74957,* ☎ *580/244–7597. 7 cottages. AE, D, DC, MC, V.*

Wilburton

$$ **Belle Starr View Lodge.** Overlooking a valley in Robbers Cave State Park, the lodge has comfortable rooms with color TVs but no phones. Breakfast (not included in the rates) requires a bit of a hike to the park restaurant. ✉ *Rte. 2, Box 9, Wilburton,* ☎ *918/465–2562,* FAX *918/465–5763. 20 rooms. AE, D, DC, MC, V.*

Outdoor Activities and Sports

Boating and Fishing

Mountain Fork River is stocked with rainbow trout; there are brown trout in the Lower Mountain Fork. The required trout-fishing stamp is obtainable at park offices and bait shops. The Mountain Fork River is also popular with canoeists. **Beavers Bend River Floats** (✉ Rte. 4, 11–7, Broken Bow, ☎ 580/494–6070) rents canoes and provides transportation.

WW Trading Post and Canoes (✉ R.R. 1, Box 532, ☎ 580/584–6856) rents fly-fishing equipment and supplies, along with canoes.

Hiking

The **Ouachita Trail,** a 46-mi hiking and horse trail through the Ouachita National Forest, was pieced together from bison paths, military roads, and centuries-old footpaths. Backcountry camping is allowed all along the trail; numerous campgrounds have also been established. For more and information contact the Choctaw Ranger District (✉ HC 64, Box 3467, Heavener 74937, ☎ 918/653–2991).

SOUTH DAKOTA

Updated by Tom Griffith

Capital	Pierre
Population	738,000
Motto	Great Faces, Great Places
State Bird	Chinese ring-necked pheasant
State Flower	Pasqueflower
Postal Abbreviation	SD

Statewide Visitor Information

South Dakota Department of Tourism (✉ 711 E. Wells Ave., Pierre 57501, ☎ 800/732–5682) makes available state highway maps and the annual *South Dakota Vacation Guide* free of charge. Call the **Department of Transportation** for maps of summer road construction (☎ 605/773–3571) and winter road-condition reports (☎ 605/773–3536).

Scenic Drives

The beautiful **Needles Highway** (Route 87) offers views of spectacular needle-sharp granite spires. **Iron Mountain Road** (U.S. 16A) has views of Mt. Rushmore over pigtail bridges and through tunnels. Both highways run through Custer State Park (☞ National and State Parks, *below*). U.S. 14A follows scenic **Spearfish Canyon.**

National and State Parks

National Parks

For **Badlands National Park** and **Black Hills National Forest,** *see* The Black Hills, Deadwood, and the Badlands, *below.* **Jewel Cave National Monument,** 53 mi southwest of Rapid City on U.S. 16 (✉ R.R. 1, Box 60AA, Custer 57730, ☎ 605/673–2288), gets its name from the calcite crystals lining the walls of one of the world's longest caves. Scenic, historic, and spelunking tours are offered June–August. **Wind Cave National Park,** 50 mi south of Rapid City on U.S. 385 (✉ R.R. 1, Box 190, Hot Springs 57747, ☎ 605/745–4600), is 28,000 acres of prairie and forest above one of the world's longest caves with perhaps the world's best collection of box work—a honeycomb-like calcite formation. Five different guided tours are offered daily June–August.

State Parks

South Dakota's state park system encompasses 13 parks. The crown ★ jewel is **Custer State Park** (✉ HC 83, Box 70, Custer 57730, ☎ 605/255–4515 or 800/710–2267 for campground reservations), which has 73,000 spectacular acres of grasslands and pine-covered hills that are home to bison, deer, bighorn sheep, prairie dogs, and pronghorn.

THE BLACK HILLS, DEADWOOD, AND THE BADLANDS

Unlike the agricultural eastern half of the state, this is a land of prairies, pine forests, and desolate, rocky landscapes. It's also where most of the state's tourists go—to visit such places as Deadwood, the 19th-century mining town turned gambling mecca, and Mt. Rushmore, where the stern grandeur of those giant carvings of four presidents on its face remains after more than 50 years.

Affordable Adventures (✉ Box 546, Rapid City 57709, ☎ 605/342–7691, FAX 605/341–4614) specializes in individual and group tours to many of western South Dakota's most scenic and historic locations, including Rapid City, Mt. Rushmore, Custer State Park, Crazy Horse Memorial, Badlands National Park, Wounded Knee, and Pine Ridge.

Visitor Information

Black Hills, Badlands and Lakes Association (✉ 1861 Discovery Circle, Rapid City 57701, ☎ 605/355–3600, FAX 605/355–3601). **Deadwood Area Chamber of Commerce & Visitor Bureau** (✉ 735 Main St., 57732, ☎ 605/578–1876 or 800/999–1876). **Rapid City Chamber of Commerce and Convention & Visitors Bureau** (✉ Civic Center, Box 747, 444 N. Mt. Rushmore Rd., 57709, ☎ 605/343–1744 or 800/487–3223, FAX 605/348–9217). **Wall:** USDA Forest Service Buffalo Gap National Grasslands Visitor Center (✉ Box 425, 57790, ☎ 605/279–2125) has 24 exhibits informing travelers on local history, flora and fauna, and activities in the national grasslands, including rockhounding.

Arriving and Departing

By Bus

Gray Line of the Black Hills (✉ Box 1106, Rapid City 57709, ☎ 605/342–4461) offers bus tours of the region, including trips to Mt. Rushmore and Black Hills National Forest. **Jack Rabbit Lines** (✉ 301 N. Dakota, Sioux Falls 57102, ☎ 800/444–6287) serves Wall, Rapid City, Mitchell, and Pierre, the capital.

By Car

Unless you are traveling with a package tour, a car is essential here. Make rental reservations early; Rapid City has many business travelers, and rental agencies are often booked. I–90 bisects the state slightly south of its center; it leads to Wall and Rapid City. From Rapid City U.S. 14 leads to towns and attractions in the northern part of the Black Hills, while U.S. 16 winds through its southern half. Route 44 is an alternate route between the Black Hills and the Badlands. The Black Hills have seven tunnels with limited clearance; they are marked on state maps and in the state's tourism booklet.

By Plane

Rapid City Regional Airport (☎ 605/393–9924), 10 mi southeast of downtown via Route 44, is served by Northwest Airlines, Skywest (a Delta connection), and United Express.

Exploring the Black Hills, Deadwood, and the Badlands

The Black Hills

As with the rest of the state, many of the region's attractions are open only in the summer; be sure to call ahead before you visit. To the locals **Rapid City** is West River, meaning west of the Missouri. South Dakota's second-largest city, this cross between western town and progressive community is a good base from which to explore the Black Hills. Cowboy boots are common here, and business leaders often travel by pickup truck or four-wheel-drive vehicle. Yet the city supports a convention center and a modern, acoustically advanced performance hall and has more than its share of bookstores downtown, along with a modern shopping mall on the outskirts.

The **Journey** (✉ 222 New York St., near the Rushmore Plaza Civic Center, ☎ 605/394–6923; 🎟 $6.50) combines the collections of the **Sioux Indian Museum**, the **Minnilusa Pioneer Museum**, the **Museum** of Geology, the State Archaeological Research Center, and a private collection of American Indian artifacts into a sweeping pageant of the history and evolution of the Black Hills. In Box Elder, just outside Rapid City, is the **South Dakota Air & Space Museum** (✉ 2890 Davis Dr., ¾ mi north of I–90 Exit 66, ☎ 605/385–5188; 🎫 free). Outside the Ellsworth Air Force Base (base tours offered in summer), it displays a model of a Stealth bomber that's 60% actual size, General Dwight D. Eisenhower's Mitchell B-25 bomber, and numerous other planes, as well as a once-operational missile silo.

In Rapid City **Storybook Island** (✉ Near intersection of Jackson Blvd. and Sheridan Lake Rd., ☎ 605/342–6357; 🎫 free) lets children romp through scenes from fairy tales and nursery rhymes. **Reptile Gardens** (✉ 6 mi south on U.S. 16, ☎ 605/342–5873; 🎫 $9) features the Bewitched Village, where a variety of animal shows are staged. Children may ride miniature horses and see giant tortoises outside in the floral gardens. **Bear Country U.S.A.** (✉ 8 mi south of Rapid City on U.S. 16, ☎ 605/343–2290; 🎫 $8.50) is a drive-through wildlife park featuring black bears, wolves, and most other North American wildlife, as well as a walk-through wildlife center with bear cubs, wolf pups, and other offspring.

The vast **Black Hills National Forest** (✉ R.R. 2, Box 200, Custer 57730, ☎ 605/673–2251; 🎫 free) covers 1.3 million acres on the state's western edge. Its most famous attraction is Keystone's ★ **Mt. Rushmore National Memorial** (✉ 21 mi southwest of Rapid City on U.S. 16, ☎ 605/574–2523; 🎫 free), the granite cliff where the faces of Presidents Washington, Jefferson, Lincoln, and Theodore Roosevelt are carved. Sculptor Gutzon Borglum labored at this monumental task for more than 14 years; it was finally finished by his son, Lincoln, in 1941. The memorial is spectacular in the morning light and at night, when a special lighting ceremony (June–mid-September) dramatically illuminates the carving.

Also in Keystone, the **Rushmore-Borglum Story** museum (✉ 342 Winter St., ☎ 605/666–4448) contains newsreel footage of the original blasting of the rock face, as well as exhibits and drawings about the project and its artist; the museum is open May through September.

Nineteen miles southwest of Keystone on U.S.16/385, another monumental likeness is emerging; when finished, the ★ **Crazy Horse Memorial** (☎ 605/673–4681; 🎫 $7 per person or $17 per carload) will depict the Lakota warrior who defeated General Custer at Little Bighorn. The site includes a visitor center and the **Indian Museum of North America.** Expect frequent blasting at this work-in-progress, which will be the world's largest sculpture when completed.

Flintstones, Bedrock City (✉ Intersection of U.S. 16 and 385, Custer, ☎ 605/673–4079; 🎫 $5.50) is a full-scale tribute to the enduring cartoon characters, complete with a curio shop, a train ride, a drive-in restaurant serving brontoburgers, and camping.

Southeast of Custer is **Wind Cave National Park** (☞ National and State Parks, *above*). In Lakota tradition it was from Wind Cave that the first Lakota people were tricked by *Iktomi* (spider person) into leaving their ancestral home.

★ The fossilized remains of ancient mammoths at the **Mammoth Site** (✉ 1 block north of the U.S. 18 Bypass, Hot Springs, ☎ 605/745–6017; 🎫 $5) should prove fascinating to children and adults alike. The site, discovered in 1974, is believed to contain up to 100 mammoths (51 have been unearthed so far) and 29 other species in the sinkhole where

The Black Hills

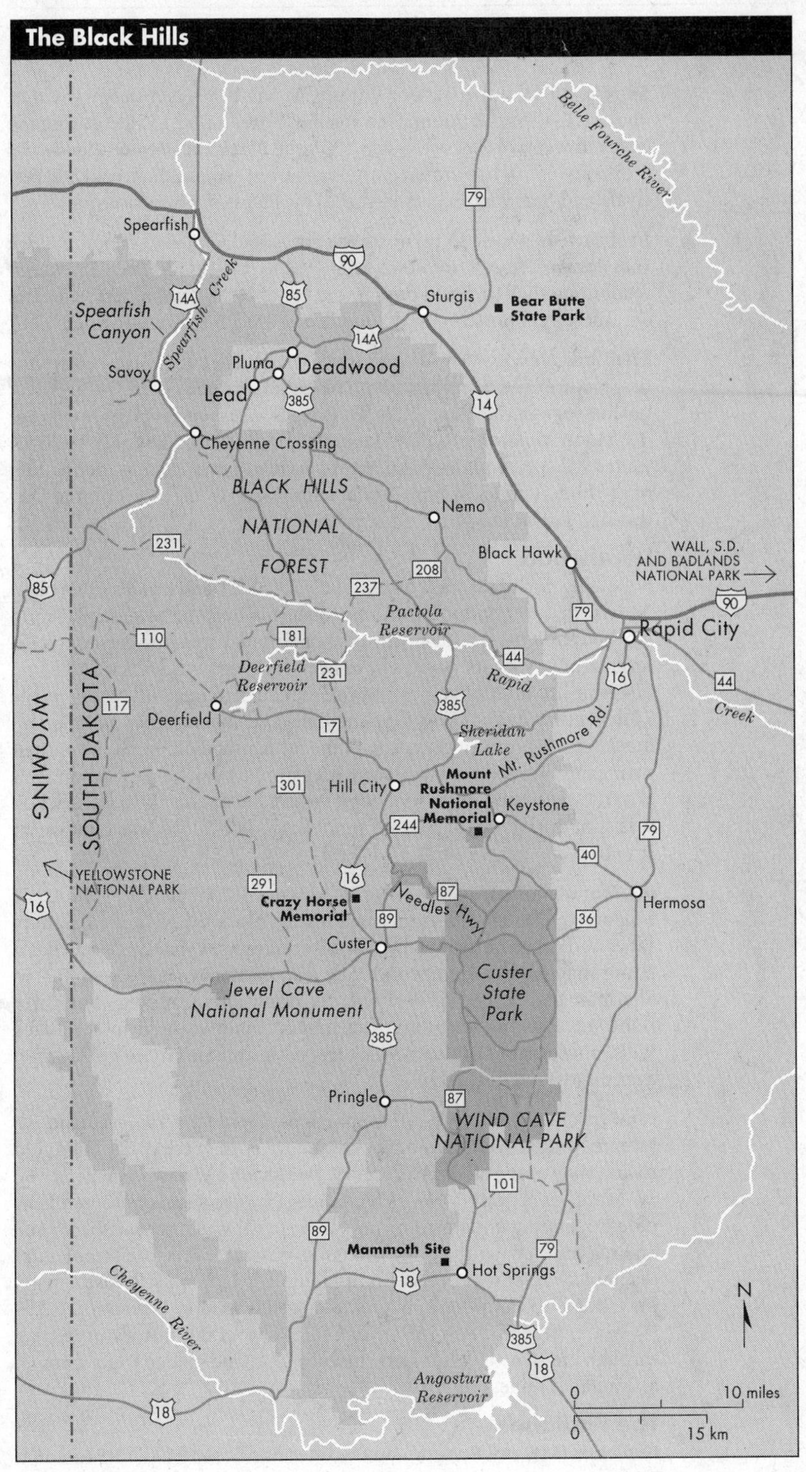

they came to drink some 26,000 years ago. A visitor center is built over the area; excavation is in progress.

Sturgis, 29 mi northwest of Rapid City via I–90, is a sleepy town of about 5,600 whose population swells to 200,000–215,000 during the first full week of August. Since 1938 the **Black Hills Motor Classic** (☎ 605/347–6570) has drawn enthusiasts from around the world (☞ Festivals and Seasonal Events in the Great Plains introduction).

In Spearfish, about 45 mi northwest of Rapid City via I–90, the ***Black Hills Passion Play*** (☎ 605/642–2646; 🎫 $10–$16) has since 1939 been recounting the last seven days in the life of Jesus Christ; performances are Tuesday, Thursday, and Sunday at 8 PM June through August.

The films *Dances with Wolves* (the 1990 Academy Award winner for best picture) and *Thunderheart* have generated new interest—and new businesses—in the Black Hills. **Ft. Hays *Dances with Wolves* Movie Set** (✉ Moon Meadows Rd. and Hwy. 16, Rapid City, ☎ 605/394–9653; 🎫 free) displays photos and shows a video taken during the making of the film. A chuck wagon dinner show ($12) is served Memorial Day through Labor Day.

Deadwood

Following the legalization of gambling in 1989, **Deadwood**'s town planners rushed to revitalize and refurbish this once-infamous gold-mining boomtown—41 mi northwest of Rapid City—for the projected onslaught of visitors. Streets have been repaved with bricks, and Main Street utility lines have been buried in order to keep all traces of the 20th century out of view. Gaming halls and casinos now make up almost every storefront downtown; the refurbished old hotels have their own gambling rooms. If a place with gambling can be wholesome, this is it (the maximum bet is $5), but it wasn't always so: Wild Bill Hickok was shot during a poker game and Poker Alice Tubbs was famous for smoking big cigars in this Old West town.

Mt. Moriah Cemetery (✉ At top of Lincoln St., ☎ 605/578–2600; 🎫 $1), above Deadwood, is the final resting place for Hickok, Calamity Jane, and other notorious Deadwood residents. From there one has a panoramic view of Deadwood. The **Adams Memorial Museum** (✉ 54 Sherman St., ☎ 605/578–1714; 🎫 donations accepted) has three floors of displays, including the first locomotive used in the Black Hills, photographs of the town's early days, and the largest gold nugget ever discovered in the Hills.

Lead (pronounced Leed), 50 mi north of Rapid City via I–90 and Alternate Route 14A, is a mining community born in the Black Hills gold rush frenzy of the late 19th century. **Homestake Visitor Center** (✉ 160 W. Main St., ☎ 605/584–3110; 🎫 $4.25) offers surface tours of the oldest operating underground gold mine in the western hemisphere and an area for viewing the mine's massive open cut. Free ore samples are available. The town itself contains a number of historic houses, many once home to immigrant miners. **Black Hills Mining Museum** (✉ 323 W. Main, ☎ 605/584–1605; 🎫 $4.25) shows the history of mining through life-size models, video presentations, and guided tours through a simulated mine.

The Badlands

Badlands National Park (✉ Box 6, Interior 57750, ☎ 605/433–5361; 🎫 $5 per person, $10 per car), 80 mi east of Rapid City off I–90, can seem like another planet. Millions of years of erosion have left these 244,000 acres with desolate gorges, buttes, and ridges colored in rust, pink, and gold. Scenic overlooks are marked. The Ben Reifel Visitor

Center, 2 mi north of Interior via Route 377 or from I–90 off Exit 131 or 110, offers information and maps.

South of the park, on the Pine Ridge Indian Reservation, is the **Wounded Knee Massacre Monument,** a commemoration on the site where more than 300 Sioux, mostly women and children, were killed when soldiers opened fire after a brief skirmish in 1890.

If you're traveling on I–90, you'll see the signs every few miles for **Wall Drug** (✉ 510 Main St., ☎ 605/279–2175), the pharmacy turned tourist mecca that enticed depression-era travelers with offers of free ice water. The store has nearly every tourist trinket imaginable plus a restaurant seating more than 500, the Hole-in-the-Wall Bookstore—which has an excellent selection of western literature—a chapel, a selection of knives and boots, and western art. **Wall** itself, a sleepy community on the edge of the Badlands, has several motels and restaurants.

Dining and Lodging

During the summer reservations are helpful and often required to ensure lodging; calling two or three days ahead is usually adequate. For price ranges *see* Charts 1 (B) and 2 (B) *in* On the Road with Fodor's.

Deadwood

$$–$$$ ★ ✕ **Deadwood Social Club.** On the second floor of historic Saloon No. 10, this warm restaurant wraps you in wood and old-time photos of Deadwood's past. Its menu stretches from free-range chicken and angel-hair pasta with exquisite sauces to melt-in-your-mouth rib eyes. Downstairs is the saloon, billed as "the only museum in the world with a bar." ✉ *657 Main St.,* ☎ *605/578–3346. MC, V.*

$$–$$$ ✕ **Jake's.** This fine-dining restaurant takes up the fourth floor of the Midnight Star Casino, a renovated former clothing store owned by actor Kevin Costner. (The rest of the building contains a bar and grill and a gaming hall.) Entrées are prepared by a world-class chef. ✉ *677 Main St.,* ☎ *605/578–1555. AE, D, DC, MC, V.*

$$$ ★ 🏨 **Bullock Hotel.** This 1895 hotel has been meticulously restored to its ornate Victorian origins. The first floor, containing the gaming hall, has high ceilings and brass-and-crystal chandeliers. Guest rooms are furnished with Victorian reproductions and have large windows. The hotel has also opened the nearby Branch House, which offers four suites and four rooms decorated in mission-style furnishings. ✉ *633 Main St., 57732,* ☎ *605/578–1745 or 888/428–5562,* FAX *605/578–1382. 36 rooms. Restaurant, lounge, beauty salon, massage, spa, exercise room. AE, D, MC, V.*

$$$ 🏨 **Deadwood Gulch Resort.** The Black Hills's most complete resort includes a 100-room hotel, casinos, creek-side restaurant, lounges, convention center, amusement park, giant arcade, and first-class RV park and campground. There is a trolley service to Main Street. ✉ *Hwy. 85 S (Box 643), 57732,* ☎ *605/578–2036 or 800/847–2522,* FAX *605/578–2037. 100 rooms. Restaurant, pool. AE, D, MC, V.*

Interior

$ ★ ✕🏨 **Cedar Pass Lodge.** In Badlands National Park, the lodge's wood-frame cabins with knotty pine interiors have a 1950s look. Each cabin has a private bath. The restaurant specializes in American Indian tacos (fried bread covered with traditional taco fixings). It also serves hearty meat-and-potatoes fare. ✉ *1 Cedar St. (Box 5), Interior 57750,* ☎ *605/433–5460,* FAX *605/433–5560. 24 cabins. Restaurant. AE, D, MC, V. Closed Nov.–mid-Mar.*

Rapid City

$$$–$$$$ ✕ **American Pie Bistro.** Here you get an unusual combination of city sophistication and home-cooked meals, including fancied-up meat-and-potato dishes such as apricot roast chicken and rack of lamb, as well as tomato-basil shrimp. ✉ *710 St. Joseph St., Rapid City,* ☏ *605/343–3773. AE, MC, V.*

$$$–$$$$ ✕ **Landmark Restaurant and Lounge.** This hotel restaurant is popular for its lunch buffet and for specialties that include prime rib, beef Wellington, freshwater fish, and wild game. ✉ *Alex Johnson Hotel, 523 6th St., Rapid City,* ☏ *605/342–1210. AE, D, DC, MC, V.*

$$–$$$$ ✕ **Fireside Inn Restaurant & Lounge.** Seating in one of the two dining rooms here is around a huge slate fireplace. The large menu includes prime rib, seafood, and Italian dishes. ✉ *6½ mi west of Rapid City on Rte. 44,* ☏ *605/342–3900. Reservations not accepted. MC, V.*

$$ ✕ **Firehouse Brewing Co.** This former firehouse serves up hearty fare such as marinated buffalo steak, rancher's (beef) pie, and rosemary chicken. A wide variety of beers, from light to stout, are brewed on the premises. ✉ *610 Main St., Rapid City,* ☏ *605/348–1915. AE, D, DC, MC, V.*

$$ ✕ **Flying T Chuckwagon.** At this converted barn, ranch-style meals of barbecued beef, potatoes, and baked beans are served on tin plates. A western show featuring music and cowboy comedy follows dinner. ✉ *6 mi south of Rapid City on U.S. 16,* ☏ *605/342–1905. Reservations essential. No credit cards. Closed mid-Sept.–late May. No lunch.*

$ ✕ **Circle B Ranch Chuck Wagon Supper & Music Show.** Chuck-wagon suppers include tender roast beef and chicken, biscuits, and all the trimmings. The ranch also offers western music shows, miniature golf, gold panning, and trail and wagon rides. A show and dinner is $14. ✉ *15 mi west of Rapid City on U.S. 385, 1 mi north of Rte. 44,* ☏ *605/348–7358 or 800/403–7358. MC, V. Closed Oct.–Apr. No lunch.*

$$$$ 🏨 **Holiday Inn Rushmore Plaza.** This eight-story hotel has a lobby with an atrium, glass elevators, and a 60-ft waterfall. Rooms have mauve and gray tones. ✉ *505 N. 5th St., Rapid City 57701,* ☏ *605/348–4000,* FAX *605/348–9777. 205 rooms, 46 suites. Restaurant, lounge, pool, sauna, exercise room. AE, D, DC, MC, V.*

$$$–$$$$ ★ 🏨 **Alex Johnson Hotel.** Western elegance pervades this nine-story hotel in a historic landmark. The lobby has leather wing chairs, a soaring beamed ceiling, and a torch chandelier made of Lakota war lances. The rooms are furnished with replicas of the original furniture when the hotel opened in 1928. The hotel was officially dedicated to the Lakota Indians, so Native American patterns and artwork predominate. ✉ *523 6th St., Rapid City 57701,* ☏ *605/342–1210 or 800/888–2539. 144 rooms. Restaurant, lounge, pub. AE, D, DC, MC, V.*

Sturgis

$–$$ ✕ **World Famous Roadkill Cafe.** Started by two bike-rally enthusiasts, the café promises on its Day-Glo menu to bring food "from your grill to ours!" including the "Chicken That Didn't Quite Cross the Road," "Smidgen of Pigeon," and the daily special "Guess That Mess!" These clever menu titles hide the fact that the café actually offers standard fare, from breakfast to tuna melt and buffalo and beef burgers, as well as a car-filling collection of roadkill cookbooks and novelty items. ✉ *1333 Main St., Sturgis,* ☏ *605/347–4502. Reservations not accepted. MC, V. Closed Sept.–May.*

Wall

$–$$ ✕ **Cactus Family Restaurant and Lounge.** This full-menu restaurant in downtown Wall specializes in delicious hotcakes and pies. A giant roast beef buffet is offered in summer. ✉ *519 Main St., Wall,* ☏ *605/279–2561. D, MC, V.*

$-$$ ★ ✕ **Elkton House Restaurant.** This comfortable restaurant with sunroom and wood paneling has fast service and a terrific hot roast beef sandwich, served on white bread with gravy and mashed potatoes. ✉ *South Blvd., Wall,* ☏ *605/279–2152. D, MC, V.*

Motel

Super 8 Motel (✉ 1–90 at Exit 100, Box 426, Wall 57790, ☏ 605/279–2688), 29 rooms; *$$.*

Campgrounds

For information on state campgrounds contact the **Department of Game, Fish, and Parks** (✉ 523 E. Capitol Ave., Pierre 57501, ☏ 605/773–3485 or 800/710–2267 for camping reservations).

Around Deadwood: **Custer Crossing Campground and Store** (✉ HCR 73, Box 1527, Deadwood 57732, ☏ 605/584–1009), 15 mi south of town; **Deadwood Gulch Resort** (✉ Hwy. 85S, Box 643, Deadwood 57732, ☏ 605/578–1294 or 800/695–1876) on the southern edge of town; **Deadwood KOA** (✉ Box 451, Deadwood 57732, ☏ 605/578–3830), 1 mi west of town; and **Wild Bill's Campground** (✉ HCR 73, Box 1101, Deadwood 57732, ☏ 605/578–2800), on U.S. 385.

Around the Badlands: **Circle 10 Campground** (✉ Rte. 1, Box 51½, Philip 57567, ☏ 605/433–5451).

Outdoor Activities and Sports

Fishing

Some of the best fishing in the state lies east of the Badlands in the large lakes along the Missouri River, but mountain streams throughout the Black Hills offer good trout fishing. Custer State Park has trout fishing in several lakes. For more information contact the state Department of Tourism's **fishing division** (☏ 800/445–3474).

Hiking

The **Centennial Trail,** 111 mi long, runs through the Black Hills National Forest, from the Plains Indians' sacred site at Bear Butte in the north to Wind Cave National Park, passing from grasslands into the hills in the high country. For more information contact the state Department of Tourism (☞ Statewide Visitor Information, *above*).

Snowmobiling

With 310 mi of marked and groomed trails, the Black Hills is a premier spot in the country for snowmobiling. A map of the trail network is available from the Department of Tourism (☞ Statewide Visitor Information, *above*). For trail conditions, updated three times weekly, call 800/445–3474.

Ski Areas

The Black Hills' winter-sports magazine, *Romancing the Snow,* has information on cross-country and downhill skiing and is available from the Black Hills, Badlands, and Lakes Association (☞ Visitor Information, *above*). For ski reports call 800/445–3474.

Cross-Country Skiing

The Black Hills offer skiing on 600 mi of abandoned logging roads, railroad beds, and fire trails, as well as several trail networks, including the **Big Hill** (16 mi of trails on the rim of Spearfish Canyon). Information is available from **Ski Cross Country** (✉ 701 3rd St., Spearfish 57783, ☏ 605/642–3851), a ski equipment sales and rental shop.

Downhill Skiing

Deer Mountain Ski Area (☒ Box 622, Deadwood 57732, ☎ 605/584–3230) has 25 trails, a 700-ft vertical drop, and one triple chair- and two Poma lifts. Lessons, rentals, and cross-country trails are available. **Terry Peak Ski Area** (☒ Box 774, Lead 57754, ☎ 605/584–2165 or 800/456–0524 for ski conditions) offers a 1,052-ft vertical drop, five chairlifts, and state-of-the-art snowmaking. A rental shop, lessons, and a lodge are available.

Shopping

Rapid City stores carry western souvenirs, crafts, and clothing. Nearly every gift shop carries the locally famous "Black Hills Gold," a combination of metals that produce distinctive green and red tints; you can watch jewelry being made at **Landstrom's Original Black Hills Gold Creations** (☒ 405 Canal St., Rapid City, ☎ 800/770–5000). **Prairie Edge Trading Co. & Galleries** (☒ 606 Main St., Rapid City, ☎ 605/342–3086) displays fine art and crafts of the Plains Indians, as well as works by various other Great Plains artists, in a restored 1886 three-story building. A turn-of-the-century-style trading company in the same building has books, regional crafts, and a world-class collection of Italian glass beads. **Prince & Pauper Bookshop** (☒ 612 St. Joseph St., Rapid City, ☎ 605/342–7964 or 800/354–0988) has a large selection of books by regional and Native American authors, as well as rare and out-of-print local-history books. **Alex Johnson's Mercantile** (☒ 608 St. Joseph St., Rapid City, ☎ 605/343–2383) sells books, wood carvings, jewelry, and unique gifts.

Rushmore Mall (☒ Just off I–90 north of Rapid City, ☎ 605/348–3378) contains such specialty shops as Leather Unlimited (for coats and jackets) (☎ 605/348–0011) as well as department and western stores. Among the latter is RCC-Western Stores (☎ 605/341–6633), which has one of the largest selections of boots in the area and can outfit you from head to toe in the latest western fashions.

For Native American art, jewelry, baskets, and other goods, check out the gift shop of the **Indian Museum of North America** (☞ The Black Hills *in* Exploring the Black Hills, Deadlands, and the Badlands, *above*).

ELSEWHERE IN SOUTH DAKOTA

Sioux Falls

Visitor Information

Sioux Falls Convention and Visitors Bureau (☒ Box 1425, Sioux Falls 57101-1425, ☎ 605/336–1620, FAX 605/336–6499).

Arriving and Departing

Sioux Falls is in the southeastern corner of the state, at the intersection of I–90 and I–29. **Sioux Falls Regional Airport** (☎ 605/336–0762) is served by Northwest, TWA, and United airlines.

What to See and Do

Sioux Falls, the state's largest city, is an ideal starting point for most attractions in the eastern part of the state. The city is a commercial hub; restaurants, hotels, and shops are numerous. The **Great Plains Zoo and Delbridge Museum of Natural History** (☒ 805 S. Kiwanis Ave., ☎ 605/367–7059; $6) contains, besides its live-animal displays, one of the world's largest collections of mounted animals. The **Old Courthouse Museum** (☒ 200 W. 6th St., ☎ 605/367–4210; free) is a massive Romanesque structure made of a native red stone called Sioux quartzite. It houses exhibits on the history of the area, including Native American artifacts. The **Pettigrew Home and Museum** (✉ 131 N. Duluth Ave., ☎ 605/367–7097; 🎫 free) was built in 1889 and was later the home of South Dakota's first full-term senator, Richard F. Pettigrew. The Queen Anne–style home contains period furnishings and Native American and natural history exhibits.

Dining

$$–$$$$ ✕ **Minerva's.** Wooden floors, a salad bar, and a strong wine list complement a menu that focuses on pasta, fresh seafood, and aged steak. *✉ 301 S. Phillips, ☎ 605/334–0386. AE, D, DC, MC, V. Closed Sun.*

$–$$$ ✕ **Champps Sports Cafe.** A lively atmosphere and great pub fare—pastas, sandwiches, hamburgers, fries, onion rings—make this a fun, reliable spot. *✉ 2101 W. 41st St., in Western Mall, ☎ 605/331–4386. AE, D, DC, MC, V.*

Mitchell

Visitor Information

Mitchell Department of Tourism (✉ Box 776, 57301, ☎ 605/996–7311 or 800/257–2676, FAX 605/996–8273).

Arriving and Departing

Mitchell is 70 mi west of Sioux Falls on I–90.

What to See and Do

The city of Mitchell trumpets the "world's only" **Corn Palace** (✉ 604 N. Main St., ☎ 605/996–7311 or 800/257–2676; 🎫 free). This fanciful structure, built in 1892, is topped by gaily painted Moorish domes, with a facade covered with multicolored corn, grain, and grasses in various designs and murals. Inside is an exhibition hall built to showcase the state's agricultural production. The exterior designs are changed annually. Across the street from the Corn Palace is the **Enchanted World Doll Museum** (✉ 615 N. Main St., ☎ 605/996–9896; 🎫 $3), with 4,000 antique and modern dolls displayed in 400 scenes.

Dining

$–$$$$ ✕ **Chef Louie's Steakhouse.** Steaks, barbecued ribs, and seafood are served in a casual setting. Pheasant is a seasonal specialty in the summer and fall. *✉ 601 E. Havens, ☎ 605/996–7565. AE, D, DC, MC, V. Closed Sun.*

DeSmet

Visitor Information

Glacial Lakes and Prairies Association (✉ Box 244, Watertown 57201, ☎ 605/886–7305, FAX 605/886–7935).

Arriving and Departing

From Sioux Falls follow I–29 north for 49 mi, then U.S. 14 west for about 37 mi.

What to See and Do

Fans of the *Little House* children's books may want to visit the town where author Laura Ingalls Wilder lived for 15 years. The Ingalls family moved to DeSmet in 1879 and lived first in a shanty, next in a farmhouse, and then in town in a home that Pa Ingalls built in 1887. The first and last are open to the public and contain period furnishings and memorabilia. The community also hosts the annual **Laura Ingalls Wilder Pageant** (✉ Laura Ingalls Wilder Memorial Society, Box 426, DeSmet 57231, ☎ 605/854–3383 or 605/854–3181), held late June–early July.

Dining and Lodging

$–$$ ✕ **The Oxbow Restaurant.** A little of everything—burgers, steaks, fish—are on the menu at this family-style restaurant run by the Myers family. ✉ *Hwy. 14,* ☎ *605/854–9988. No credit cards.*

$ 🏨 **Cottage Inn Motel.** Across the street from the Oxbow restaurant, and also run by the Myers family, this motel has clean, spacious rooms. ✉ *Hwy. 14, 57231,* ☎ *605/854–3396 or 800/848–0215. 37 rooms. AE, D, DC, MC, V.*

Pierre

Visitor Information

Pierre Convention and Visitors Bureau (✉ Box 548, Pierre 57501-0548, ☎ 605/224–7361, FAX 605/224–6485).

Arriving and Departing

Pierre (pronounced "Peer") is on U.S. 83, about 225 mi west of Sioux Falls.

What to See and Do

The **state capitol** (✉ 500 E. Capitol Ave., ☎ 605/773–3765; 🎟 free), a magnificent Greek Revival building completed in 1910, has a rich interior decorated with mosaic floors, stained-glass skylights, allegorical murals, and an impressive columned staircase. The state historical society has a museum and archives at the **Cultural Heritage Center** (✉ 900 Governors Dr., ☎ 605/773–3458; 🎟 $3). Exhibits focus on the history of the state with emphasis on the city of Pierre, which evolved from a French trading post in the early 1800s. The first of three phases for a permanent exhibit (South Dakota Experience) was completed in 1992. It offers a taste of the state from 1743, the year European trappers first arrived, through the beginning of the 20th century. The second phase, completed in the fall of 1994, focuses on the life of the Plains Indians prior to 1743. The third phase, not scheduled for completion until 2000, will cover 20th-century events.

Dining

$$ ✕🏨 **Best Western Ramkota Inn.** The largest hotel in Pierre is also one of the capital's social hubs. Hearty breakfasts and buffets are hallmarks at the restaurant. ✉ *920 W. Sioux St.,* ☎ *605/224–6877,* FAX *605/224–1042. 151 rooms. Restaurant, pool, exercise room. AE, D, DC, MC, V.*

9 The Southwest

Arizona, Nevada, New Mexico, Texas

By Edie Jarolim

Updated by Deke Castleman, Kimberly Harwell, Stuart Wade, Kay Winzenried, and Nancy Zimmerman

A **REGION THAT DEMANDS** superlatives, the Southwest is the ruggedly beautiful, wide-open land out of which America's myths continue to emerge. Cowboys and Indians, Old World conquistadors and new religions, rising and falling fortunes in gold, copper, and oil—all feed into the vision of an untamed territory with limitless horizons.

Of course, Phoenix and Dallas are sophisticated metropolises, and Santa Fe is becoming a rival Los Angeles in wealth and number of art galleries per square foot. Las Vegas is sui generis, an unbridled, peculiarly American phenomenon. Foodies all over the country sing the praises of the delicately spiced southwestern cuisine, an outgrowth of Asian immigration into the area, now duplicated in cosmopolitan restaurants nationwide. Nor is there a region that has better Mexican food, whether you like it Tex-Mex, Sonoran, or New Mexican style. Southwestern furnishings—an eclectic blend that might include mission chests, Navajo blankets, Mexican tinwork mirrors, *yristras* (strings of red chili peppers), and even bleached cow skulls à la Georgia O'Keeffe—have become so popular in upscale homes that they're a bit of a cliché.

But other, more ancient cultures vie here with contemporary ones. The country's largest Native American reservation, that of the Navajo Nation, occupies millions of acres and traverses state boundaries, and dozens of other tribes—among them Hopi, Zuni, and Apache—live in the region as well. It is their vanishing civilization and, above all, the area's natural phenomena—spectacular canyons, eerily towering rock formations, and clear, lambent light—that continue to capture the imagination of all who visit or live in the area. The southwestern landscape is a glorious lesson in geologic upheaval to be learned at such sites as Carlsbad Caverns in New Mexico, the Grand Canyon in Arizona, and the Rio Grand in Texas.

Clearly anything is possible in such an unrestrained place. The heyday of the western movie may be over, but when 1990s screen heroines Thelma and Louise light out for freedom, they find it in the Southwest, still the most natural setting for outlandish deeds and grand gestures.

When to Go

In the semiarid climate of most of the Southwest, **spring** is the season of choice, with cool, fresh, clear weather. In March and April, when

The Southwest

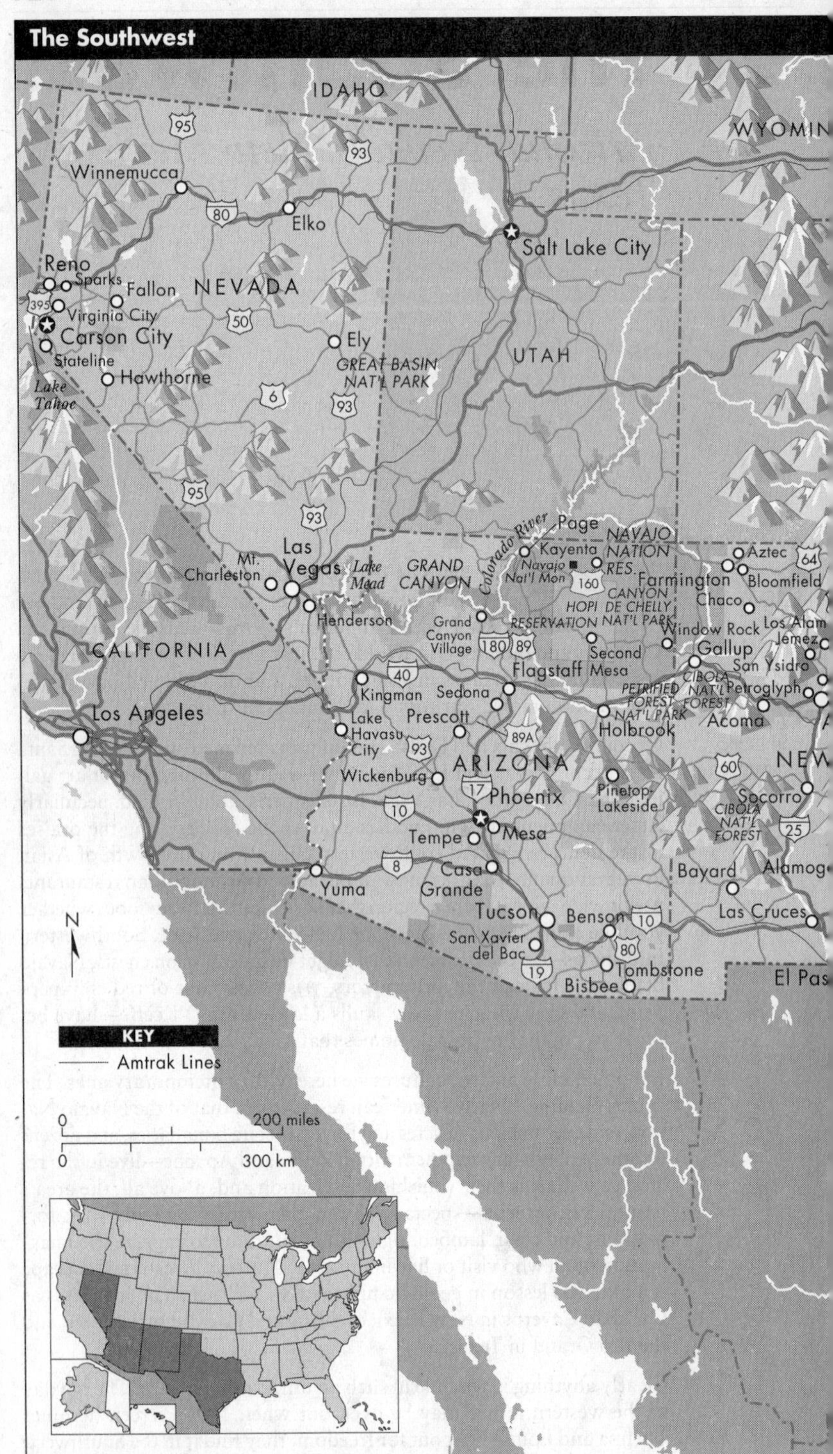

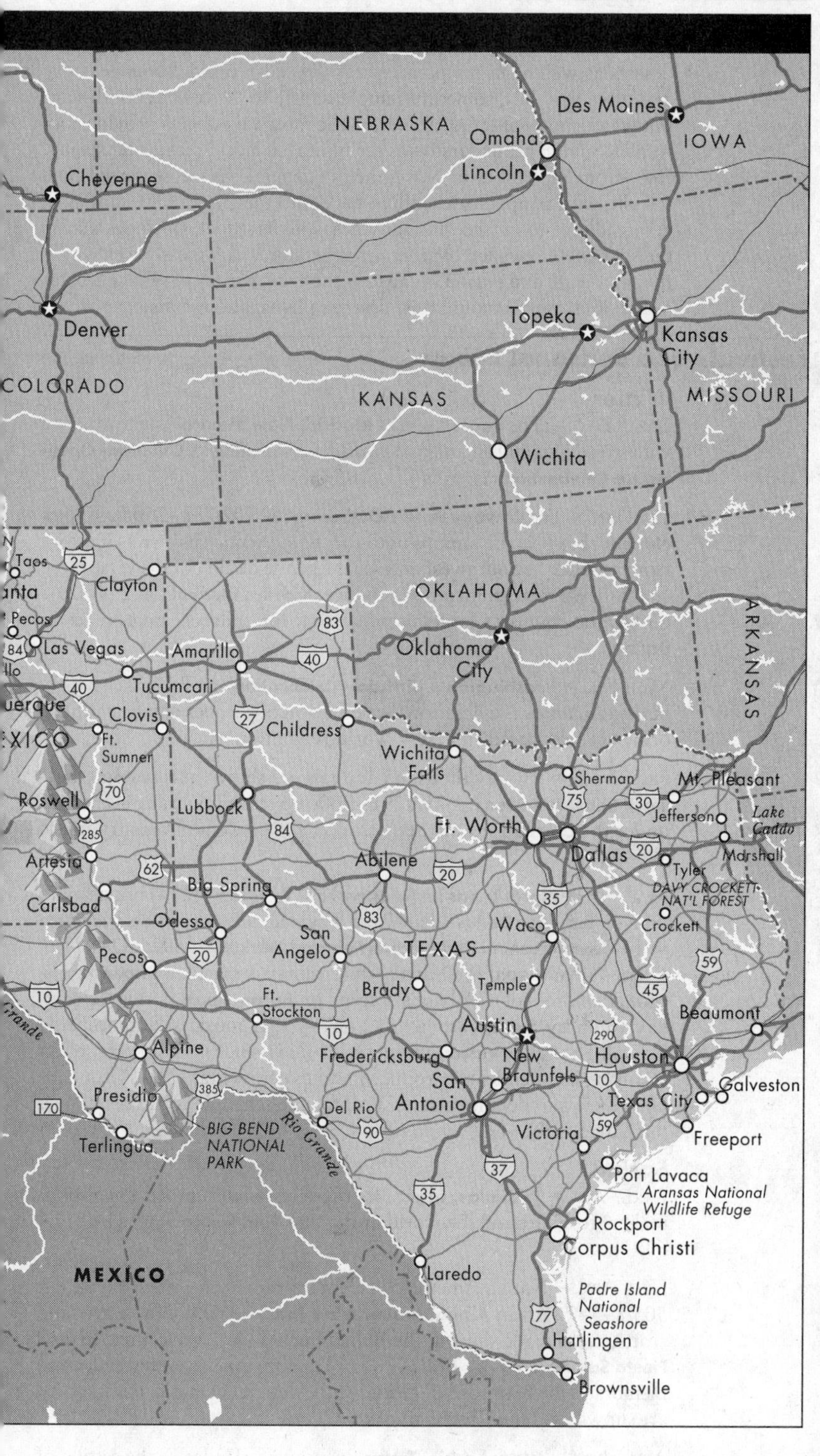
NEBRASKA
Des Moines
Omaha
IOWA
Lincoln
Cheyenne
Topeka
Kansas City
Denver
COLORADO
KANSAS
MISSOURI
Wichita
Taos
25
Clayton
OKLAHOMA
Pecos
83
ARKANSAS
Las Vegas
Amarillo
40
Oklahoma City
84
Tucumcari
40
Clovis
27
Childress
Ft. Sumner
Wichita Falls
Sherman
Mt. Pleasant
70
Roswell
Lubbock
75
30
Jefferson
Lake Caddo
285
84
Ft. Worth
Dallas
20
Marshall
Artesia
Abilene
62
20
Tyler
Big Spring
DAVY CROCKETT NAT'L FOREST
Carlsbad
35
83
Crockett
Odessa
Waco
San Angelo
TEXAS
Pecos
20
59
Brady
Temple
45
10
Ft. Stockton
Beaumont
Austin
10
290
Alpine
Fredericksburg
Houston
New Braunfels
San Antonio
10
Galveston
Presidio
385
Texas City
170
Del Rio
BIG BEND NATIONAL PARK
Rio Grande
90
Victoria
59
Freeport
Terlingua
37
Port Lavaca
Aransas National Wildlife Refuge
35
Rockport
Corpus Christi
MEXICO
Laredo
Padre Island National Seashore
77
Harlingen
Brownsville

temperatures average in the 70s, short-lived wildflowers produce carpets of extravagant color in many parts of the region, including some deserts as well as in temperate areas like East Texas. **Summer** is dry and often very hot, sometimes unpleasantly so, across the Southwest; but water sports abound, and dramatic mountain chains provide cool respite. Summer thunderstorms are typical in most areas. After spring, **fall**—from September to November, in general—is the preferred time to visit, with temperatures falling back into the 70s and 80s, and gorgeous foliage to be seen in many areas. Skiers flock to slopes across the Southwest in **winter.** In general, temperatures vary greatly even within the same state and season because of the great variety of microclimates in the Southwest's mountains, deserts, plains, and forests.

Festivals and Seasonal Events

Winter

EARLY DEC.➢ The ghost town of **Madrid, New Mexico,** is reawakened with streetlights and an arts-and-crafts festival during its **Christmas Open-House Celebration** (☏ 505/471–1054).

LATE JAN.➢ The **Cowboy Poetry Gathering** (☏ 702/738–7508), in **Elko, Nevada,** has become famous both for the authentic characters it draws from around the Southwest and for the gentle quality of the verse these rough-hewn men and women produce. **KidFilm Festival** (☏ 214/821–6397), the country's largest media event for children, takes place in **Dallas.**

MID.-FEB.➢ **Washington's Birthday Celebration** (☏ 956/722–0589), in **Laredo, Texas** is a binational celebration of parades and fiestas honoring the first successful New World revolutionary.

FEB.–MAR.➢ Twenty thousand animals are shown at **Houston**'s **Livestock Show & Rodeo** (☏ 713/791–9000), a truly Texas-size event held under the curved roof of the Astrodome. Rodeos and country music abound.

MAR.➢ The **North Texas Irish Festival** (☏ 214/821–4174) brings more than 47 bands to **Dallas**'s Fair Park. High-quality artwork is the norm at the **Heard Museum Guild Indian Fair and Market** (☏ 602/252–8840), a juried invitational for Native American artists held in **Phoenix, Arizona.** Hundreds of rock bands descend on **Austin, Texas** during the four-day **South by Southwest** (☏ 512/467–7979) music and multimedia festival. The **Dallas Video Festival** (☏ 214/651–8600) is a four-day event featuring independently produced and experimental videos, from animated clips to documentaries. Call for the schedule, since it's subject to change.

Spring

EARLY APR.➢ In **Dallas,** film buffs rub elbows with professional filmmakers from around the world at the **USA Film Festival** (☏ 214/821–6397).

LATE APR.➢ Native Americans celebrate **American Indian Week** (☏ 505/843–7270) in **Albuquerque, New Mexico,** with dance, arts and crafts, and a trade show at the Indian Pueblo Cultural Center. Texas's **Fiesta San Antonio** (☏ 210/227–5191), more than a century old, commemorates the Battle of San Jacinto with a festival of music, food, sports, art shows, and the River Parade.

APR.–JUNE➢ **Waxahachie, Texas,** just outside Dallas, is the setting of **Scarborough Faire** (☏ 972/938–1888), an English Renaissance festival with games, period foods, and performances.

MAY 5➢ **Cinco de Mayo,** a fiesta celebrating Mexican history and heritage, is held in many cities and towns across the Southwest.

Summer

LATE JUNE➢ New Mexico's craftspeople are world famous, and some of the best display and sell their work at the **New Mexico Arts & Crafts Fair** (☎ 505/884–9043) in **Albuquerque, New Mexico.**

EARLY JULY➢ The **National Basque Festival** (☎ 702/738–7138), in **Elko, Nevada,** celebrates the heritage of the Basque people (recruited to the area from northern Spain because of their remarkable shepherding abilities) in the American West.

LATE JULY➢ The **Fiesta de Santiago y Santa Ana** (☎ 505/758–3873 or 800/732–8267), a colorful street party and fair, began as a trade fair nearly 300 years ago; today it's a the major annual event in **Taos, New Mexico.**

LATE AUG.➢ The weeklong **Nevada State Fair** (☎ 702/688–5767), in **Reno, Nevada,** features rides, farm animal competitions, livestock shows, fast food, and all the other accoutrements of a real state fair.

Autumn

MID-SEPT.➢ On the first weekend after Labor Day, Zozobra, or "Old Man Gloom," is burned to open the annual **Fiestas de Santa Fe** (☎ 505/984–6760 or 800/777–2489), in **Santa Fe, New Mexico.** During the celebration, Santa Fe Plaza is filled with music, dancing, and food vendors.

LATE SEPT.–LATE OCT.➢ The **State Fair of Texas** (☎ 214/421–8716), the nation's largest state fair, holds its three-week annual run at **Dallas**'s Fair Park, declared a National Historic Landmark in 1986 for its Art Deco architecture.

MID-OCT.➢ The **Albuquerque International Balloon Fiesta** (☎ 505/821–1000), in which more than 850 colorful hot-air balloons rise in spectacular unison with the dawn, is probably **New Mexico**'s best-known event.

Getting Around the Southwest

By Bus

Greyhound Lines (☎ 800/231–2222) provides service to towns and cities throughout the region.

By Car

The Southwest is traversed by two of the country's major east–west highways: I–80, the northern route, which passes through Reno, Nevada; and I–40, which enters Texas at the Oklahoma border, heading to Los Angeles by way of Amarillo, Texas; Albuquerque, New Mexico; and Flagstaff, Arizona. Other east–west arteries include I–10, which links New Orleans and Los Angeles via Houston, San Antonio and El Paso, Texas, and Tucson and Phoenix, Arizona; and I–20, which connects Dallas and El Paso. The major north–south routes of the region are I–15, which heads south from Salt Lake City to Las Vegas; I–25, from Denver to El Paso by way of Albuquerque; and I–35, from Oklahoma to the Mexican border by way of Dallas and Fort Worth.

By Plane

America West, American, Delta, and Southwest all provide extensive service to and among the southwestern states; Continental, TWA, and United offer more limited service. The region's major airports include, in Texas, **Dallas–Fort Worth International Airport** (☎ 214/574–8888) and **Houston Intercontinental Airport** (☎ 713/230–3100); in Nevada,

Reno-Tahoe International Airport (☎ 702/328–6400) and **McCarran International Airport** (☎ 702/261–5743), in Las Vegas; in New Mexico, **Albuquerque International Airport** (☎ 505/842–4366); and in Phoenix, Arizona, **Sky Harbor International Airport** (☎ 602/273–3300).

By Train

Amtrak (☎ 800/872–7245) serves all the states of the region, with one major line between New Orleans and Los Angeles, and another passing through southeastern Colorado to Albuquerque and Flagstaff.

ARIZONA

By Edie Jarolim

Updated by Andrea Ibañez, Kim Westerman, and Rich Rubin

Capital Phoenix
Population 4,555,000
Motto God Enriches
State Bird Cactus wren
State Flower Saguaro cactus
Postal Abbreviation AZ

Statewide Visitor Information

Arizona Office of Tourism (✉ 2702 N. 3rd St., Suite 4015, Phoenix 85004, ☎ 602/230–7733 or 800/842–8257, FAX 602/240–5475).

Scenic Drives

The drive from the South Rim to the North Rim of the Grand Canyon follows U.S. 89 through the **Arizona Strip,** a starkly beautiful, largely uninhabited part of the state. Almost all the Grand Canyon drives are breathtaking, especially West Rim Drive on the South Rim and the dirt road to Point Sublime on the North Rim. Fall foliage is spectacular on U.S. 89A from Flagstaff to Sedona via **Oak Creek Canyon.** From Tucson, I–10 east of Benson passes through the startling rock formations of **Texas Canyon.**

National and State Parks

National Parks

Among the state's national parks are **Grand Canyon National Park** (☞ Grand Canyon National Park, *below*), **Petrified Forest National Park** (☞ Northeast Arizona, *below*), and **Saguaro National Park** (☞ Tucson, *below*); **Canyon de Chelly** (☞ Northeast Arizona, *below*) is a national monument. For Native American ruins in scenic settings, visit **Walnut Canyon National Monument** and **Wupatki National Monument** (☞ Flagstaff, *below*), in the Flagstaff area, **Tuzigoot National Monument** (✉ Broadway Rd., Clarkdale 86324, ☎ 520/634–5564; 🎫 $2 per person), south of Sedona, and **Navajo National Monument** (☞ Northeast Arizona, *below*). Little-visited spots of unusual beauty include **Sunset Crater Volcano National Monument** (☞ Flagstaff, *below*), west of Flagstaff, and **Chiricahua National Monument** (✉ Hwy. 191 to Hwy. 181, 58 mi northeast of Douglas, 85643, ☎ 520/824–3560; 🎫 $4 per car), in the southeastern part of the state.

State Parks

Arizona's 24 state parks run a wide spectrum, from the relatively tiny 54-acre **Slide Rock,** near Sedona (✉ 6871 N. Hwy. 89A, Box 10358, Sedona 86339, ☎ 520/282–3034; 🎫 $5 per vehicle, $1 per pedestrian or bicycle) to 13,000-acre **Lake Havasu** (✉ 1801 Hwy. 95, Lake Havasu, 86406, ☎ 520/855–9394; 🎫 $4–$7 per vehicle; $1 per pedestrian or biycle), notable for **London Bridge,** a transplanted 18th-century bridge. Boating and water-sports enthusiasts congregate at **Alamo Lake State Park** (✉ U.S. 60, 37 mi north of Wenden, Box 38, Wenden 85357, ☎ 520/669–2088; 🎫 $4 per vehicle; $1 per pedestrian or bicycle), and **Roper Lake State Historic Park** (✉ 101 E. Roper Lake Rd., Rte. 2, Box 712, Safford 85546, ☎ 520/428–6760; 🎫 $4 per vehicle; $1 per pedestrian or bicycle). Desert rats will like **Catalina State Park** (✉ 11570 N. Oracle Rd., Box 36986, Tucson 85740, ☎ 520/628–5798; 🎫 $4 per vehicle; $1 per pedestrian or bicycle), and the **Boyce Thompson Southwestern Arboretum,** an hour east of Phoenix (✉ 37615 E. Hwy. 60, Superior 85273, ☎ 520/689–2723; 🎟 $5 per person). Head to **Red Rock State Park** (✉ 4050 Red Rock Loop Rd., Sedona 86336, ☎ 520/282–6907; 🎟 $5 per vehicle; $1 per pedestrian or bicycle), and **Tonto Natural Bridge State Historic Park** (✉ Hwy. 87, 10 mi north of Payson, Box 1245, Payson 85547, ☎ 520/476–4202; 🎟 $5 per vehicle; $1 per pedestrian or bicycle), for dramatic scenery. For a taste of the state's lively frontier history, visit **Riordan Mansion State Park** (✉ 1300 Riordan Ranch St., Riordan 86001, ☎ 520/779–4395; 🎟 $4); **Jerome State Historic Park** (✉ Douglas Rd., Box D, Jerome 86331, ☎ 520/634–5381), in north-central Arizona; **Tombstone Courthouse State Historic Park** (✉ 219 Toughnut St., Tombstone 85638, ☎ 520/457–3311) and **Tubac Presidio Historic Park** (✉ 1 Burruel St., Box 1296, Tubac 85646, ☎ 520/398–2252; 🎟 $5 per vehicle; $1 per pedestrian or bicycle), in the southeast; and **Yuma Territorial Prison State Historic Park** (✉ 100 N. Prison Hill Rd., Yuma 85364, ☎ 520/343–2500), in the southwest. The **Arizona State Parks Department** (✉ 1300 W. Washington St., Phoenix 85007, ☎ 602/542–4174) provides information on all the above parks.

GRAND CANYON NATIONAL PARK

Not even the finest photographs pack a fraction of the impact of a personal experience of the Grand Canyon. This awesome, vastly silent ancient erosion of the surface of our planet is 277 mi long, 17 mi across at its widest spot, and more than 1 mi deep at its lowest point. Its twisted and contorted layers of rock reveal a fascinating geological profile of the earth. All around you, otherworldly stone monuments change colors with the hours.

Visitor Information

Before you go, write to **Grand Canyon National Park** (✉ Box 129, Grand Canyon 86023, ☎ 520/638–7888) for a complimentary *Trip Planner.* Accommodations: **Amfac Parks and Resorts** (✉ 14001 E. Iliff, Suite 600, Aurora, CO 80014, ☎ 303/297–2757, 520/638–2631 for same-day reservations). North and South Rim camping: **Destinet** (✉ Box 85705, San Diego, CA 92186-5705, ☎ 800/365–2267). A free newspaper, the *Guide,* which contains a detailed area map, is available at both rims.

Arriving and Departing

By Bus

Greyhound Lines (☎ 800/231–2222) stops at Flagstaff and Williams. **Nava-Hopi Tours** (☎ 800/892–8687, 520/774–5003 in Flagstaff) provides bus service to the canyon's South Rim from Flagstaff and Williams.

By Car

From the east, west, or south, the best access to the Grand Canyon is from Flagstaff, either northwest on U.S. 180 (81 mi) to Grand Canyon Village on the South Rim or for a scenic route, north on U.S. 89 to Route 64W; from Utah, take U.S. 89S. To visit the North Rim, some 210 mi from Flagstaff, follow U.S. 89 north to Bitter Springs, and then take U.S. 89A to the junction of Route 67. From the west on I–40, the most direct route to the South Rim is via Route 64 to U.S. 180. Summer traffic approaching the South Rim is very congested around Grand Canyon Village. Facilities at the more remote North Rim open May 15. From October 15 through December 1 or until heavy snows close the road, the park remains open for day use only.

The quickest route from Los Angeles is U.S. 93, which intersects with I–40 in Kingman, Arizona.

By Plane

McCarran International Airport (☎ 702/261–5743), in Las Vegas, Nevada, is the primary hub for flights to **Grand Canyon National Park Airport** (☎ 520/638–2446). Carriers include Eagle Canyon Airlines (☎ 800/634–6377), **Air Vegas** (☎ 702/736–3599), and Scenic Airlines (☎ 800/535–4448). You can make connections from **Sky Harbor International Airport** (☎ 520/273–3300), in Phoenix, with two commuter lines, Sky Cab (☎ 800/999–1778) and West Wind (☎ 602/991–5557). The **Tusayan Grand Canyon Shuttle** (☎ 520/638–0871) operates between Grand Canyon airport and the nearby towns of Tusayan and Grand Canyon Village. The **Fred Harvey Transportation Company** (☎ 520/638–2822 or 520/638–2631) provides taxi service.

By Train

The town closest to the Grand Canyon served directly by **Amtrak** (☎ 520/774–8679 or 800/872–7245) is Flagstaff. From Williams you can take the historic **Grand Canyon Railway** (☎ 800/843–8724) to the South Rim.

Exploring Grand Canyon National Park

Access to both the South Rim and North Rim areas of the Grand Canyon is carefully managed by the National Park Service. Large crowds converge on the South Rim every summer, and there is talk of limiting auto access to the area. The most trafficked spots are popular for good reason, but a walk into the canyon itself opens up extraordinary perspectives.

South Rim

From **Mather Point,** at the outskirts of Grand Canyon Village, you'll get your first glimpse of the canyon from one of the most impressive and accessible vistas on the rim.

Scenic overlooks on the 25-mi-long East Rim Drive include **Yaki Point,** where the much-traveled Kaibab Trail starts the canyon descent to the inner gorge; **Grandview Point,** which supports large stands of ponderosa and piñon pine, oak, and juniper; and **Moran Point,** a favorite of photographers. At the **Tusayan Ruins and Museum** (☎ 520/638–2305), 3 mi east of Moran Point, partially intact rock dwellings are evidence of early habitation in the gorge. **Lipan Point** is the widest part of the canyon. The highest points along the tour are **Desert View** and the **Watchtower,** site of a lookout tower with a panoramic view of the Grand Canyon (☎ 520/638–2736) and a trading post with Native American art (☞ Shopping, *below*).

Back in Grand Canyon Village, the paved Village Rim Trail (about a mile round-trip) starts at **Hopi House,** one of the canyon's first curio stores (☞ Shopping, *below*). Stops along the way include the historic **El Tovar Hotel,** the jewel in the crown of the country's national park system (☞ Dining and Lodging, *below*); **Lookout Studio,** a combination lookout point, museum, and gift shop; **Bright Angel Trailhead,** the starting point for the best-known trail to the bottom of the canyon; and **Bright Angel Lodge,** with a fireplace made of regional rocks arranged in layers that match those of the canyon.

On West Rim Drive you can get an unobstructed view from **Trailview Overlook** of the distant San Francisco Peaks, Arizona's highest mountains. At **Maricopa Point** you'll see the remnants of an early Grand Canyon mining operation. The **Abyss** reveals a sheer canyon drop of 3,000 ft. **Pima Point** provides a bird's-eye view of the Tonto Plateau

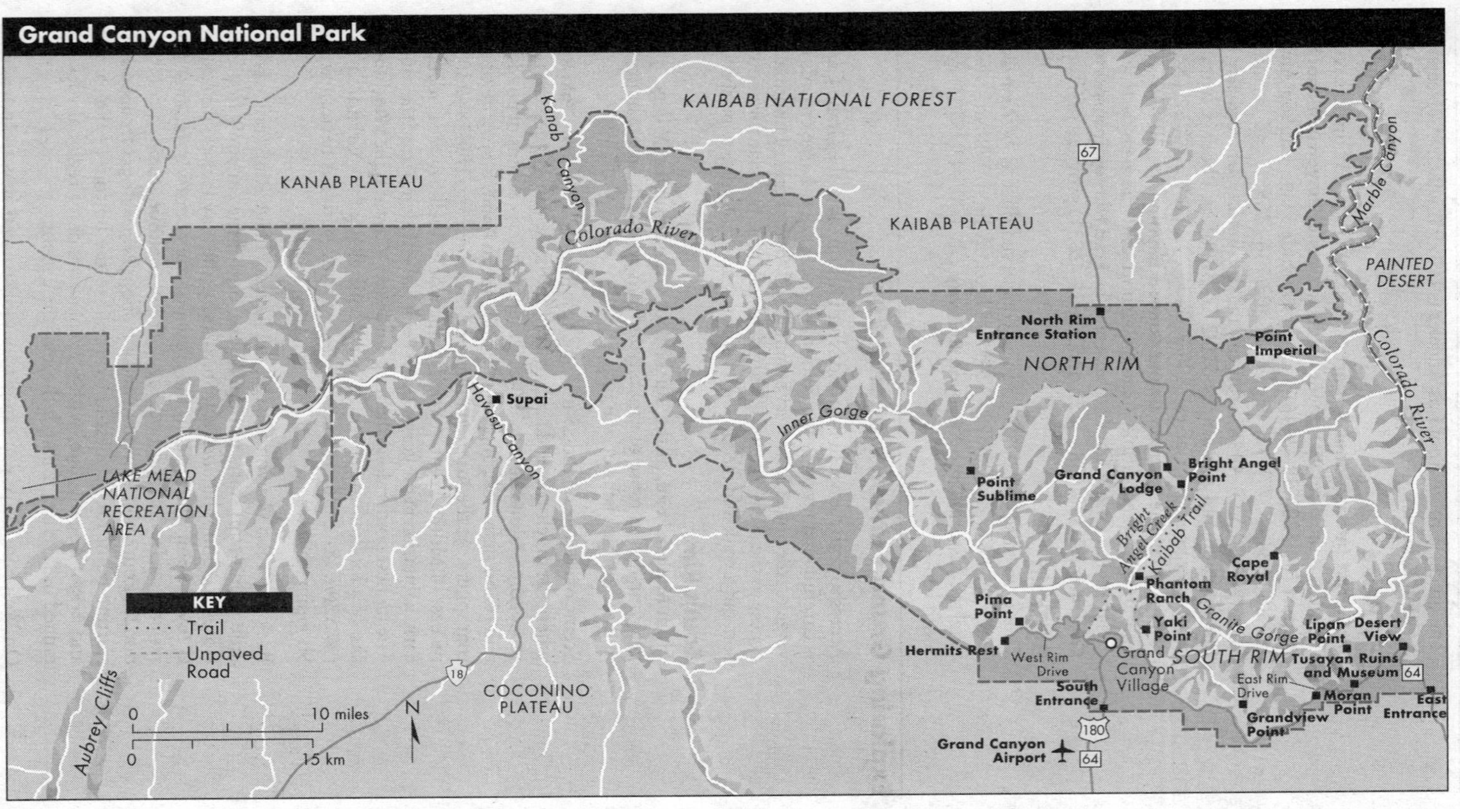
Grand Canyon National Park
KAIBAB NATIONAL FOREST
KANAB PLATEAU
Kanab Canyon
Colorado River
KAIBAB PLATEAU
67
Marble Canyon
PAINTED DESERT
North Rim Entrance Station
NORTH RIM
Point Imperial
Colorado River
Supai
Havasu Canyon
Inner Gorge
LAKE MEAD NATIONAL RECREATION AREA
Point Sublime
Grand Canyon Lodge
Bright Angel Point
Bright Angel Creek
Kaibab Trail
Cape Royal
Phantom Ranch
Pima Point
Yaki Point
Granite Gorge
Lipan Point
Desert View
Hermits Rest
West Rim Drive
Grand Canyon Village
SOUTH RIM
Tusayan Ruins and Museum
64
East Rim Drive
Moran Point
East Entrance
South Entrance
Grandview Point
KEY
Trail
Unpaved Road
18
COCONINO PLATEAU
N
0
10 miles
0
15 km
Aubrey Cliffs
180
Grand Canyon Airport
64

and the Tonto Trail, which winds for more than 90 mi through the canyon. **Hermits Rest,** the westernmost viewpoint, and **Hermit Trail,** (☞ Outdoor Activities and Sports, *below*), which descends from it, were named for Louis Boucher, a 19th-century prospector who had a roughly built home down in the canyon. The West Rim Drive is closed to auto traffic in summer; from early May through September free shuttle buses leave daily from Grand Canyon Village for Hermits Rest.

North Rim

The relative solitude of the North Rim, set in deep forest near the 9,000-ft crest of Kaibab Plateau in the isolated Arizona Strip, is well worth the extra miles. From central Arizona, the only route into this area is more than 200 mi of lonely road to the northwest of Flagstaff. From late fall through early spring the North Rim and its facilities are closed because heavy snows cut off highway access to the area.

The trail to **Bright Angel Point,** one of the most awe-inspiring overlooks on either rim, starts on the grounds of the Grand Canyon Lodge (☞ Dining and Lodging, *below*), a massive stone structure built in 1928 by the Union Pacific Railroad. At 8,803 ft, **Point Imperial** is the canyon's highest viewpoint. **Cape Royal** is the southernmost viewpoint on the North Rim.

Dining and Lodging

It's difficult to find rooms in the South Rim area in summer. The North Rim is less crowded but has limited lodging facilities. Make reservations as much as six months in advance. If you can't find accommodations in the immediate South Rim area, try the nearby communities of Williams, an hour away by car, or Flagstaff. Camping inside the park is permitted only in designated areas. For information on park camping and reservations, contact Destinet (☞ Visitor Information, *above*). The Arizona Office of Tourism (☞ Statewide Visitor Information, *above*) can provide a campground directory. For price ranges *see* Charts 1 (B) and 2 (B) *in* On the Road with Fodor's.

South Rim

$$$$ ★ ✕🏨 **El Tovar Hotel.** Built in 1905 of native stone and heavy pine logs, El Tovar has maintained its reputation for excellence ever since, though at a time when indoor plumbing is no longer a luxury, rooms don't seem as posh as they might have in the past. Some are small but well appointed, and many have canyon views. For decades the hotel's restaurant has served fine seasonal southwestern cuisine in a hunting-lodge-style dining room of hand-hewn logs and beamed ceilings. ✉ *Amfac Parks and Resorts, 14001 E. Iliff Ave., Suite 600, Aurora, CO 80014,* ☎ *303/297–2757;* FAX *520/638–2631, 303/297–3175 for reservations. 80 rooms. Restaurant. AE, D, DC, MC, V.*

$–$$$$ ★ ✕🏨 **Bright Angel Lodge.** Built in 1935, this log-and-stone structure a few yards from the canyon rim has rooms in the main lodge or in quaint cabins (some with fireplaces) scattered among the pines. The informal steak house overlooks the abyss. ✉ *Amfac Parks and Resorts, 14001 E. Iliff Ave., Suite 600, Aurora, CO 80014,* ☎ *303/297–2757;* FAX *520/638–2631, 303/297–3175 for reservations. 30 rooms, 11 with bath; 47 cabins. Restaurant. AE, D, DC, MC, V.*

$–$$$$ 🏨 **Grand Canyon National Park Lodges.** The seven Fred Harvey Company lodges on the South Rim—Bright Angel Lodge, El Tovar, Maswik Lodge, Yavapai Lodge, Moqui Lodge, Kachina Lodge, and Thunderbird Lodge—are all comfortable, if not luxurious; come for the setting, not for the amenities. Moqui is on U.S. 180, just outside the park; the others are in Grand Canyon Village. ✉ *Amfac Parks and Resorts, 14001*

E. Iliff Ave., Suite 600, Aurora, CO 80014, ☎ 303/297–2757, FAX 303/297–3175. 1,000 rooms. 5 restaurants. AE, D, DC, MC, V.

CAMPGROUNDS

In Grand Canyon Village, ⛺ **Mather Campground** (☞ Destinet *in* Visitor Information, *above*) has RV and tent sites. ⛺ **Trailer Village** (✉ Amfac Parks and Resorts, 14001 E. Iliff Ave., Suite 600, Aurora, CO 80014, ☎ 303/297–2757) has RV sites. Commercial and Forest Service campgrounds outside the park include ⛺ **Flintstone Bedrock City** (✉ Grand Canyon Hwy., HCR 34, Box A, Williams 86046, ☎ 520/635–2600), with tent and RV sites; ⛺ **Grand Canyon Camper Village** (✉ Hwy. 64, 1 mi south of park entrance, Box 490, Tusayan 86023, ☎ 520/638–2887), with RV and tent sites; and ⛺ **Ten X Campground** (✉ Kaibab National Forest, Tusayan Ranger District, Box 3088, Grand Canyon 86023, ☎ 520/638–2443), with larger sites (closed in winter).

Bottom of the Canyon

$ ✕🏨 **Phantom Ranch.** Dormitory accommodations (with shared bath) for hikers and cabins (with outside shower) for hikers and mule riders nestle in a grove of cottonwood trees at the bottom of the canyon. The restaurant has a limited menu, with meals served family style. Arrangements—and payment—for both food and lodging should be made 9–11 months in advance. ✉ *Amfac Parks and Resorts, 14001 E. Iliff Ave., Suite 600, Aurora, CO 80014, ☎ 303/297–2757; FAX 520/638–2631, 303/297–3175 for reservations. 4 dorms, 11 cabins. AE, D, DC, MC, V.*

CAMPGROUNDS

For information about the campgrounds at **Indian Gardens,** about halfway down the canyon, and **Bright Angel,** near the bottom, contact the Backcountry Reservations Office (☞ Hiking *in* Outdoor Activities and Sports, *below*).

North Rim

$$–$$$ 🏨 **Grand Canyon Lodge.** This historic stone structure, built in 1928, has comfortable though not luxurious rooms. The lounge area, with hardwood floors and high beamed ceilings, has a spectacular view of the canyon through massive plate-glass windows. ✉ *Amfac Parks and Resorts, 14001 E. Iliff, Suite 600, Aurora, CO 80014, ☎ 303/297–2757; FAX 520/638–2611, 303/297–3175 for reservations. 44 rooms, 157 cabins. Restaurant. AE, D, DC, MC, V.*

CAMPGROUNDS

⛺ **North Rim Campground** (☞ Destinet *in* Visitor Information, *above*), inside the park, has RV and tent sites. Outside the park, ⛺ **Demotte Campground** (✉ Kaibab National Forest, North Kaibab Ranger District, Box 248, Fredonia 86022, ☎ 520/643–7395), is run by the Forest Service.

Outdoor Activities and Sports

Hiking

Detailed area maps of the many canyon trails are available at ranger stations and visitor centers. Overnight hikes require a permit; write **Backcountry Reservations Office** (✉ Box 129, Grand Canyon 86023, ☎ no phone). Send away for one in advance if possible; otherwise, pick one up at the Backcountry Reservations Office, either near the entrance to Maswik Lodge, on the South Rim, or at the North Rim's ranger station. Allow five days to hike the gorge from rim to rim.

Bright Angel Trail, a steep (4,460-ft), demanding ascent, connects the bottom of the canyon to the South Rim (8 mi). The 9-mi **Hermit Trail**

provides inspiring views of Hermit Gorge and the Redwall and Supai formations. The steep, 7-mi **South Kaibab Trail** begins near Yaki Point, on East Rim Drive near Grand Canyon Village. The 14-mi **North Kaibab Trail,** the only maintained trail into the canyon from the North Rim, connects at the bottom of the canyon with the South Kaibab Trail.

Mule Trips

Mule trips down the precipitous trails to the inner gorge are nearly as well known as the canyon itself. Inquire via **Amfac** (✉ 14001 E. Iliff, Suite 600, Aurora, CO 80014, ☎ 303/297–2757) about prices and restrictions for riders. Book months in advance.

Rafting

Reservations for white-water rafting trips, which last from three to 18 days, must often be made more than six months ahead of time. For a complete list of park-service-approved concessionaires, contact the **River Permits Office** (✉ Grand Canyon National Park, Box 129, Grand Canyon 86023, ☎ 520/638–7888). **Fred Harvey Transportation Company** (☎ 520/638–2822) specializes in smooth-water rafting day trips.

Shopping

Native American items sold at most of the lodges and at major gift shops are authentic. The **Desert View Trading Post** (✉ East Rim Dr., ☎ 520/638–2360) sells Southwest souvenirs and Native American crafts. The **El Tovar Hotel Gift Shop** (✉ Near the rim in Grand Canyon Village, ☎ 520/638–2631) features silver jewelry. **Hopi House** (✉ East of El Tovar Hotel, ☎ 520/638–2631) has some museum-quality Native American artifacts.

NORTHEAST ARIZONA

A vast and magnificent landscape of lofty buttes and towering cliffs, northeast Arizona is the home of the Navajo and Hopi peoples, who call the area "the rez." The mysterious ruins of ancient tribes can be found within the stunning landscapes of Navajo National Monument, Monument Valley, and Canyon de Chelly. All of these monuments lie within the northeastern portion of the Navajo reservation. Just below the southeastern boundary of the Navajo reservation, straddling I–40, the Petrified Forest National Park is an intriguing geologic open book of the Earth's distant past. Above the far northwest corner of the Navajo reservation on U.S. 80 lies Glen Canyon Dam. Behind it more than 120 mi of Lake Powell's emerald waters are held in precipitous canyons of erosion-carved stone.

Throughout both reservations, excellent Native American arts and crafts may be found for sale in shops, galleries, and trading posts. Visitors are sometimes invited to watch ancient cultural traditions such as Hopi ceremonial dances; however, the privacy, customs, and laws of the tribes should be respected.

Visitor Information

Glen Canyon National Recreation Area (✉ Box 1507, Page 86040-1507, ☎ 520/608–6404). **Hopi Tribe Office of Public Relations** (✉ Box 123, Kykotsmovi 86039, ☎ 520/734–2441). **Navajo Tourism Department** (✉ Box 663, Window Rock 86515, ☎ 520/871–6436). **Page/Lake Powell:** Chamber of Commerce & Visitor Bureau (✉ 644 N. Navajo, Box 727, Page 86040, ☎ 520/645–2741).

Arriving and Departing

By Bus

Greyhound Lines (☎ 800/231–2222) goes to Phoenix and Flagstaff. **Navajo Transit System** (☎ 520/729–4002) provides the only bus travel on the reservation. Service is inexpensive but slow.

By Car

From the east or west I–40 passes through Flagstaff, a good entry point to the region. From the north or northwest U.S. 89 brings you to Page. From the northeast U.S. 64 leads west from Farmington, New Mexico. Touring Navajo and Hopi country involves driving long distances among widely scattered communities, so a detailed road map is essential. In this sparsely populated area, service stations are rare, so fuel up wherever you can. Never drive into dips or low-lying road areas during a heavy rainstorm; dangerous flash floods are common.

By Plane

No major airlines fly directly to this area. You'll need to make flight connections in Phoenix (☞ Arriving and Departing *in* Metropolitan Phoenix, *below*) to travel on to either **Flagstaff Pullium Airport** (☎ 520/556–1234) or to **Page Municipal Airport** (☎ 520/645–2494), near Lake Powell. **Scenic Airlines** (☎ 800/634–6801) flies from Phoenix and Las Vegas to Page and Monument Valley.

By Train

Amtrak (☎ 520/774–8679 or 800/872–7245) stops in Flagstaff, a good jumping-off point for a car trip into the area.

Exploring Northeast Arizona

Some 115 mi east of Flagstaff off I–40, **Petrified Forest National Park** (✉ Box 2217, Petrified Forest, 86028, ☎ 520/524–6228; 🎫 $10 per vehicle) is strewn with ancient ruins and fossilized tree trunks whose wood cells were replaced over the centuries by brightly hued mineral deposits. The park's 94,000 acres include portions of the **Painted Desert**, a colorful but essentially barren and waterless series of windswept plains, hills, and mesas. Also look for Native American petroglyphs.

Window Rock, northeast of Petrified Forest, is the capital of the Navajo Nation and the business and social center for families from the surrounding rural areas. The **Navajo Nation Museum,** next to the Navajo Nation Inn on Route 264 (✉ Box 4950, Window Rock, 86515, ☎ 520/871–6673; 🎫 $1), has exhibits on Navajo art, culture, and history. It is closed weekends in winter. The adjoining **Navajo Arts and Crafts Enterprise**(☞ Shopping, *below*) displays local works.

Northwest of Window Rock and occupying nearly 84,000 acres, **Canyon de Chelly** (✉ Box 588, Chinle 86503–0588, ☎ 520/674–5500; 🎫 donations accepted) is one of the Southwest's most extraordinary national monuments. Gigantic sandstone cliffs rise hundreds of feet above small streams, hogans, tilled fields, peach orchards, and grazing lands; and thousand-year-old cliff dwellings, petroglyphs, and pictographs made by precursors of the Pueblo people are carved into some of its sheer cliff walls. Paved rim drives afford marvelous views. There are also horseback and Jeep tours of the canyon.

At the approximate center of the Navajo reservation lies the 4,000-square-mi **Hopi reservation,** a series of stone-and-adobe villages built on high mesas. On First Mesa is the town of **Walpi,** built on solid rock and surrounded by steep cliffs. Its 30 residents defy modernity and live without electricity and running water. In Second Mesa's oldest and largest village, **Shungopavi,** the famous Hopi snake dances—no longer open to the public—are held in August of even-number years. Also on Second Mesa is the **Hopi Cultural Center** (☎ 520/734–6650) with a pueblo-style museum, shops, and a good restaurant and motel (☞ Dining and Lodging, *below*). The center is closed weekends. **Kykotsmovi,** at the eastern base of Third Mesa, is known for its greenery and peach orchards. It is the site of the Hopi Tribal headquarters. Atop Third Mesa, **Oraibi,** established around AD 1150, is widely believed to be the oldest continuously inhabited community in the United States. The Hopi people are much more strict about privacy rules than the Navajo; avoid taking pictures or notes.

Monument Valley (✉ Visitor center, 3½ mi off U.S. 163, 24 mi north of Kayenta, ☎ 801/727–3353), near the Utah border north of Kayenta, may look familiar to those who have seen it in westerns and commercials. This sprawling expanse of soaring red buttes, eroded mesas, deep canyons, and naturally sculpted rock formations was populated by the ancestors of the Pueblo people and has been home to generations of Navajo. Within this vast area lies the 30,000-acre **Monument Valley Navajo Tribal Park** and its 17-mi self-guided tour.

At **Navajo National Monument** (✉ HC 71, Box 3, Tonalea 86044, ☎ 520/672–2366; 🎫 free), southwest of Monument Valley off U.S. 160, two unoccupied 13th-century cliff pueblos, **Keet Seel** and **Betatakin,** stand under the overhang of soaring orange and ocher cliffs. The largest Native American ruins in Arizona, these pueblos, too, were built by the ancestors of the Pueblo people, whose reasons for suddenly abandoning them prior to AD 1300 are still disputed by scholars.

For information on the construction of **Glen Canyon Dam and Lake Powell,** 136 mi north of Flagstaff on U.S. 89, stop at the **Carl Hayden Visitor Center** (✉ Glen Canyon Dam, ☎ 520/608–6404). The best way to see eerie, man-made Lake Powell as it twists through rugged canyon country is by boat (☞ Outdoor Activities and Sports, *below*). Take a half-day excursion to **Rainbow Bridge National Monument** (🎫 free), a 290-ft red-sandstone arch that straddles one of the lake's coves.

Dining and Lodging

Northeast Arizona is vast, and few communities have places to eat and sleep. Among them are Page, Window Rock, Fort Defiance, Ganado, Chinle, Holbrook, Hopi Second Mesa, Keams Canyon, Tuba City, Kayenta, Goulding's Trading Post/Monument Valley, and Cameron. No alcoholic beverages are sold on the Navajo and Hopi reservations, and possession or consumption of alcohol is against the law in these areas. In summer, lodging reservations are highly advised. For price ranges *see* Charts 1 (B) and 2 (B) *in* On the Road with Fodor's.

Cameron

$$$ ✕🏨 **Cameron Trading Post and Motel.** This is a good place to fuel up along the drive from the Hopi mesas to the Grand Canyon. Motel rooms and RV sites are available; there's also a wood-beamed dining room serving hearty Navajo fare, and a curio shop and art gallery. ✉ *54 mi north of Flagstaff on U.S. 89, Box 339, Cameron 86020,* ☎ *520/679–2231,* FAX *520/679–2350. 62 units. Restaurant. AE, DC, MC, V.*

Chinle/Canyon de Chelly

$$$$ ✕🏨 **Best Western Canyon de Chelly.** This rustic motel about 2 mi south of Canyon de Chelly has cheerful, modern rooms, each with a coffeemaker and cable TV. There's also an indoor pool. ✉ *Rte. 7 off U.S. 191, Box 295, Chinle 86503,* ☎ *520/674–5875. 99 rooms. Restaurant, pool. AE, D, DC, MC, V.*

$$$$ ✕🏨 **Holiday Inn Canyon de Chelly.** This Navajo-staffed complex stands on the site of a former trading post and incorporates part of the historic structure. Rooms are predictably pastel, but the lobby restaurant serves Navajo specialties like fresh mountain trout dusted in blue cornmeal. ✉ *Indian Rte. 7, Box 1889, Chinle 86503,* ☎ *520/674–5000,* FAX *520/674–8264. 108 rooms. Restaurant. AE, D, DC, MC, V.*

$$$$ ✕🏨 **Thunderbird Lodge.** At the mouth of Canyon de Chelly, the lodge has stone and adobe units spread over manicured lawns among cottonwood trees. Some rooms have hewn beam ceilings and rustic furniture. An all-Navajo staff prepares inexpensive meals in the cafeteria. ✉ *½ mi south of canyon visitor center, Box 548, Chinle 86503,* ☎ *520/674–5841 or 800/679–2473. 72 rooms. Restaurant. AE, D, DC, MC, V.*

CAMPGROUNDS

⛺ **Cottonwood Campground** (✉ Near visitor center, Canyon de Chelly National Monument, Box 588, Chinle 86503, ☎ 520/674–5500) has free individual campsites and group sites that you can reserve for a fee. There are flush toilets but no showers.

Hopi Reservation–Second Mesa

$$$ ★ ✕🏨 **Hopi Cultural Center Motel.** High atop Second Mesa, this pueblo-style lodging has immaculate rooms. A comfortable, inexpensive restaurant serves traditional dishes such as Hopi blue-corn pancakes and *nok qui vi* (lamb stew). ✉ *Rte. 264, Box 67, 86043,* ☎ *520/734–2401,* FAX *520/734–6651. 33 units. Restaurant. AE, D, DC, MC, V.*

Kayenta

$$$–$$$$ 🏨 **Best Western Wetherill Inn.** This clean, cheerful, two-story motel was named for frontier explorer and trader John Wetherill. There's a well-stocked gift shop on site. ✉ *U.S. 163, Box 175, 86033,* ☎ *520/697–3231. 54 rooms. Pool. AE, D, DC, MC, V.*

$$$ 🏨 **Holiday Inn.** This typical Holiday inn near Monument Valley has one of the few swimming pools in the area. ✉ *South of junction of U.S. 160 and 163, Box 307, 86033,* ☎ *520/697–3221,* FAX *520/697–3349. 160 rooms. Restaurant, pool. AE, D, DC, MC, V.*

Keams Canyon

$ ✕ **Keams Canyon Restaurant.** At this typical rural roadside café you'll find a few American dishes and Native American standards such as Navajo tacos. Closing time on weekends is 6 PM. ✉ *Keams Canyon Shopping Center (off Rte. 264),* ☎ *520/738–2296. MC, V.*

Lake Powell/Page

$$$$ ★ ✕🏨 **Wahweap Lodge.** On a promontory above Lake Powell, the rustic Wahweap Lodge serves as a base for boating, fishing, and other outdoor pursuits. Rooms have balconies or patios, and many have lake views. The Rainbow Room, with a panoramic lake view, has a seasonal menu of southwestern and Continental fare. ✉ *U.S. 89, 5 mi north of Page, Box 1597, Page 86040,* ☎ *520/645–2433 or 800/528–6154. 350 rooms. Restaurant, pool. AE, D, DC, MC, V.*

$$$–$$$$ 🏨 **Best Western at Lake Powell.** On the main street of Page, overlooking Glen Canyon Dam, this friendly motel has a pool and hot tub, and a breakfast café. Many good restaurants are nearby. ✉ *208 N. Lake Powell Blvd., Box 4899, 86040,* ☎ *520/645–5988 or 800/528–1234,* FAX *520/645–2578. 132 rooms. Pool, exercise room. AE, D, DC, MC, V.*

Monument Valley, Utah

$$$$ ✕🏨 **Goulding's Lodge.** Built near the base of an immense red sandstone butte, Goulding's has spectacular views of Monument Valley from all of its rooms. The on-premises Stagecoach Restaurant, decorated with memorabilia from movies shot in the area, serves tasty American fare.

A landing strip for Scenic Airlines out of Phoenix and Las Vegas is just across the street. ✉ *2 mi west of U.S. 163, just north of UT border, Box 360001, Monument Valley, UT 84536,* ☎ *435/727–3231 or 801/727–3231,* FAX *435/727–3344. 62 rooms. Restaurant, pool. AE, D, DC, MC, V.*

CAMPGROUNDS

⛺ **Mitten View Campground** (✉ Monument Valley Navajo Tribal Park, near visitor center, off U.S. 163, 86003, ☎ 801/727–3287) and ⛺ **Good Sam Campground** (✉ Off U.S. 163 near Goulding's Lodge , 86003, ☎ 801/727–3232, ext. 425) are both open year-round. Registration for Good Sam Campground is at Goulding's Lodge.

Navajo National Monument

CAMPGROUNDS

⛺ **Navajo National Monument** (☞ Exploring Northeast Arizona, *above*) has single and group sites. RVs longer than 25 ft are discouraged.

Outdoor Activities and Sports

Boating

Rental boats, water-sports equipment, and excursion boats are available at **Wahweap Marina** (✉ U.S. 89, 5 mi north of Page, ☎ 520/645–2433 or 800/528–6154). Rentals are also available at **Hall's Crossing Marina**(✉ ☎ 801/684–7000, **Hite Marina**(✉ ☎ 801/648–2278, and **Bullfrog Marina & Resort**(✉ ☎ 801/684–3000.

Hiking

There's excellent hiking in **Canyon de Chelly.** Guides are required for all but the White House Ruin Trail; contact the visitor center. In addition to casual hikes along the rim areas, you can sign up for guided hikes to Betatakin at **Navajo National Monument** (☎ 520/672–2367) from early May to mid-October. A permit is needed for the unsupervised longer hike to Keet Seel (open only from Memorial Day to Labor Day). **Monument Valley** also has superb hiking trails. Permits are available at the Visitors Center (☎ 801/727–3287).

Horseback Riding

Edward Black (☎ 800/551–4039) gives long and short trail rides from his stable in Mexican Hat, near the Monument Valley area. Year-round guided trail rides are offered at **Bigman's** (☎ 520/677–3219).

Shopping

You may find exactly what you want at a good price from one of the many roadside vendors in the area, but the following have dependable selections of Native American wares. **Cameron Trading Post** (✉ 54 mi north of Flagstaff on U.S. 89, ☎ 520/679–2231 or 800/338–7385) sells Navajo, Hopi, Zuni, and New Mexico Pueblo jewelry, rugs, baskets, and pottery. **Navajo Arts and Crafts Enterprise** (✉ Off Rte. 264, next to Navajo Nation Inn, ☎ 520/871–4108 or 800/662–6189), in Window Rock, stocks fine authentic Navajo products. **Hubbell Trading Post** (✉ Rte. 264, 1 mi west of Ganado, ☎ 520/755–3254) is famous for its "Ganado red" Navajo rugs; it also has a good collection of Native American pottery.

FLAGSTAFF

Few visitors slow down long enough to explore Flagstaff, a town of 54,000. Still, set against a backdrop of pine forests and the snowcapped San Francisco Peaks, "Flag" (as it's known locally) makes a good base for exploring the Grand Canyon and Navajo-Hopi country. Downtown retains a frontier flavor, and motels and restaurants abound.

Visitor Information

The **Flagstaff Visitors Center** (✉ 1 E. Rte. 66, 86001, ☎ 520/774–9541 or 800/842–7293) has information on the area.

Arriving and Departing

Flagstaff is 138 mi north of Phoenix and 80 mi south of the Grand Canyon, at the junction of I–40 and I–17.

Exploring Flagstaff

The **Historic Railroad District,** where many interesting shops and buildings are concentrated, is near the Santa Fe railroad station. To view an architectural masterpiece built by two lumber-baron brothers, visit the **Riordan Mansion State Historic Park** (✉ 1300 Riordan Ranch St., ☎ 520/779–4395; 🎫 $4). The **Lowell Observatory** (✉ 1400 W. Mars Hill, ☎ 520/774–2096; 🎫 $3) has educational displays on astronomy and allows visitors to peer through its 24-inch telescope on some evenings (schedules vary seasonally). Set in a striking native-stone building, the **Museum of Northern Arizona** (✉ 3101 N. Fort Valley Rd., ☎ 520/774–5213; 🎫 $5) traces the natural and cultural history of the Colorado Plateau.

Head to the **Arizona Snowbowl & Flagstaff Nordic Center** (☎ 520/779–1951; 🎫 $33 per day) for fine downhill and cross-country skiing in winter and excellent views and good hiking trails in summer; you'll see the exit 5 mi north of town on U.S. 180. In a pine forest about 10 mi southeast of Flagstaff, off I–40, is **Walnut Canyon National Monument** (✉ Walnut Canyon Rd., ☎ 520/526–3367; 🎫 $4 per vehicle, $2 per pedestrian), the site of 14th-century cliff dwellings. The 2,000-square-mi San Francisco Volcanic Field, about 20 mi north of Flagstaff on U.S. 89, is home to **Sunset Crater Volcano National Monument** (☎ 520/556–7042; 🎫 $4 per vehicle, $2 per pedestrian, includes admission to Wupatki National Monument). You can take a 20-mi loop road from Sunset Crater to **Wupatki National Monument** (☎ 520/556–7040), rich in Native American history.

Dining and Lodging

For price ranges *see* Charts 1 (B) and 2 (B) *in* On the Road with Fodor's.

$$$–$$$$ ✕ **Cottage Place.** Unexpectedly elegant in a town known for hearty food and drive-through service, this restaurant in a 50-year-old cottage serves Continental cuisine in a series of intimate dining rooms. Try the artichoke chicken breast or chateaubriand for two, carved table-side. *✉ 126 W. Cottage Ave., ☎ 520/774–8431. AE, MC, V. Closed Mon. No lunch.*

$$ ✕ **Café Espress.** The menu is largely vegetarian at this wholesome all-day (Sunday–Thursday 7 AM–9 PM, Friday–Saturday 7 AM–10 PM) natural-food restaurant, whose walls are covered with works by local artists. The baked goods are heavenly. *✉ 16 N. San Francisco St., ☎ 520/774–0541. MC, V. Closed Sun.*

$$$$ 🏨 **Inn at Four Ten.** This quiet but convenient downtown bed-and-breakfast, in a beautifully restored 1907 building, has spacious two-room suites. Fresh-baked cookies are served in the afternoon. *✉ 410 N. Leroux St., 86001, ☎ 520/774–0088 or 800/774–2008. 8 suites. Full breakfast. AE, MC, V.*

$$$$ 🏨 **Little America of Flagstaff.** The biggest motel in town is deservedly popular: It's surrounded by evergreen forest, and it's one of the few places in Flagstaff with room service. Plush rooms have brass chandeliers and French provincial–style furniture. A courtesy van gives complimentary rides to the airport and bus and train stations. ✉ *2515 E. Butler Ave. (Box 3900), 86004,* ☎ *520/779–2741 or 800/352–4386,* FAX *520/779–7983. 248 rooms. Restaurant, pool, exercise room. AE, D, DC, MC, V.*

Nightlife and the Arts

Nightlife

There's usually a country-and-western band at the **Museum Club** (✉ 3404 E. Rte. 66, ☎ 520/526–9434), a lively cowboy honky-tonk. **Main Street Bar and Grill** (✉ 14 S. San Francisco St., ☎ 520/774–1519) features bluegrass, jazz, and rock. **Charly's** (✉ 23 N. Leroux St., ☎ 520/779–1919) attracts a loyal local following to its late-night jazz and blues bands. **Monsoon's** (✉ 22 E. Rte. 66, ☎ 520/774–7929) books an eclectic array of live music, from alternative to world beat.

The Arts

Between the **Flagstaff Symphony Orchestra** (✉ Ardrey Auditorium, on campus of Northern Arizona University, corner of Riordan Rd. and Knowles Dr., ☎ 520/774–5107), **Theatrikos Community Theater** (✉ 11 W. Cherry Ave., ☎ 520/774–1662), and Northern Arizona University's **School of Performing Arts** (☎ 520/523–5661), you're bound to find entertainment. In August the **Flagstaff Festival of the Arts** (☎ 520/774–7750 or 800/266–7740) fills the town with music.

The **Coconino Center for the Arts** (✉ 2300 N. Fort Valley Rd., ☎ 520/779–6921) hosts a Festival of Native American Arts each July and August. The center also sponsors the Trappings of the American West from mid-May to early June, with a focus on cowboy art. From May through September the **Museum of Northern Arizona** (☞ Exploring, *above*) celebrates Native American art.

SEDONA AND ENVIRONS

Sedona is perhaps the most attractive stopover en route north from Phoenix to the Grand Canyon. Startling formations of deep red rocks reach up into an almost always clear blue sky, both colors intensified by dark-green pine forests. Filmmakers in the 1940s and '50s saw this as a quintessential Wild West landscape and shot more than 80 films in the area. Now an upscale art colony, Sedona is also a center of interest to New Age enthusiasts, who believe the area contains important vortices (energy centers).

Visitor Information

For information on the area contact **Sedona–Oak Creek Canyon Chamber of Commerce** (✉ U.S. 89A and Forest Rd., Box 478, Sedona 86339, ☎ 520/282–7722 or 800/288–7336).

Arriving and Departing

By Car

Sedona is 125 mi north of downtown Phoenix and 27 mi south of Flagstaff, at the south end of Oak Creek Canyon on U.S. 89A.

By Plane

There are no commercial flights into Sedona.

Exploring Sedona and Environs

Tlaquepaque Mall (✉ Rte. 179, ☎ 520/282–4838) has the largest concentration of shops. The **Chapel of the Holy Cross** (✉ Chapel Rd., ☎ 520/282–4069) is worth a visit for its striking architecture and stunning vistas.

Scenic hiking areas close to town include Long Canyon, Devil's Kitchen, and Boynton Canyon, and there are almost limitless other opportunities for hikes and walks; stop at the **Sedona Ranger District** office (✉ 250 Brewer Rd., ☎ 520/282–4119) between Monday and Saturday for more information. Five miles southwest of Sedona, **Red Rock State Park** (☎ 520/282–6907; 🎫 $5 per car, $1 per pedestrian) has incredible rock formations. Visit **Slide Rock State Park** (☎ 520/282–3034; 🎫 $5 for up to 4 people, $1 for each additional person), 8 mi north of Sedona in Oak Creek Canyon, for a picnic and a plunge into a natural swimming hole.

On Cleopatra Hill, **Jerome** is about 37 mi southwest of Sedona on U.S. 89A. This town was once known as the Billion Dollar Copper Camp, but after the last mines closed in 1953, the booming population of 15,000 dwindled to 50 determined souls, earning Jerome the "ghost town" designation it still holds, even though the population has risen to almost 450. Today, with many artsy boutiques, Jerome is a shopper's haven. The town's mining history is chronicled at the **Mine Museum** (✉ 200 Main St., ☎ 520/634–5477; 🎫 $1) and **Jerome State Historic Park** (✉ State Park Rd., ☎ 520/634–5381; 🎫 $2).

Dining and Lodging

For price ranges *see* Charts 1 (A) and 2 (A) *in* On the Road with Fodor's.

$$$–$$$$ ★ ✕ **Heartline Café.** This plant-filled café west of Sedona serves tasty southwestern-style food, such as grilled salmon marinated in tequila and lime. On nice days you can eat on the rose-planted terrace. ✉ *1610 W. U.S. 89A,* ☎ *520/282–0785. AE, D, DC, MC, V. No lunch Sun.*

$$$–$$$$ ✕ **Pietro's.** Good northern Italian cuisine is served by a friendly, attentive staff in a lively (often noisy) room. Creative pastas might include fettuccine with duck, cabbage, and figs; the veal *piccata* is excellent. ✉ *2445 W. Hwy. 89A,* ☎ *520/282–2525. AE, D, DC, MC, V. No lunch.*

$$$$ ★ 🏨 **Enchantment Resort.** Designed as a tennis resort, Enchantment has excellent sports facilities (including a putting green), but it's the setting of Boynton Canyon that makes it unique. Rooms are in pueblo-style casitas, many with beehive fireplaces and kitchenettes, and all have dazzling views. ✉ *525 Boynton Canyon Rd., 86336,* ☎ *520/282–2900 or 800/826–4180,* FAX *520/282–9249. 162 rooms. Restaurant, pools, tennis, health club. AE, D, MC, V.*

$$$–$$$$ 🏨 **Sky Ranch Lodge.** An excellent value in an expensive town, the lodge has simply furnished rooms with southwestern touches, such as Mexican tiles surrounding the dressers. Some rooms have fireplaces and kitchenettes; others, balconies with views of Sedona's red-rock canyons. ✉ *Airport Rd. (Box 2579), 86339,* ☎ *520/282–6400,* FAX *520/282–7682. 92 rooms, 2 cottages. Pool. MC, V.*

PRESCOTT

In a forested bowl among the Mingus Mountains, Prescott was Arizona's first territorial capital and remains the Southwest's richest repository of late-19th-century New England–style architecture. Because of its temperate climate, in summer the town draws escapees from the Phoenix heat—as well as retirees year-round. The town's two institutions of higher learning, Yavapai and Prescott colleges, ensure a younger scene, too. Many visitors come to buy reasonably priced antiques and collectibles on the stretch of Cortez Street east of Courthouse Plaza.

Visitor Information

Prescott Chamber of Commerce (✉ 117 W. Goodwin St., 86303, ☎ 520/445–2000 or 800/266–7534).

Arriving and Departing

By Bus

Greyhound Lines (✉ 820 E. Sheldon St., ☎ 520/445–5470 or 800/231–2222).

By Car

Prescott is 34 mi southwest of Jerome via U.S. 89A. From Phoenix take I–17 north for 60 mi to Cordes Junction, and then drive northwest on Hwy. 69 for 36 mi into town.

By Plane

There are daily flights from Phoenix into **Prescott Municipal Airport** (☎ 520/445–7860), 10 mi north of town.

Exploring Prescott

Courthouse Plaza, bounded by Gurley and Goodwin streets to the north and south and Cortez and Montezuma streets to the west and east, is the heart of the city. **Whiskey Row,** named for a string of brawling pioneer taverns, runs along Montequma Street, flanking the plaza's west side; it was once lined with 20 saloons and houses of pleasure.

Two blocks west of Courthouse Plaza, the **Sharlot Hall Museum** (✉ 415 W. Gurley St., ☎ 520/445–3122; 🎫 $5 donation requested per family), devoted to the area's history, includes the log cabin that housed the territorial governor and three restored late-19th-century houses. The **Phippen Museum of Western Art** (✉ 4701 Hwy. 89 N, ☎ 520/778–1385; 🎫 $3), about 5 mi north of downtown, hosts work by many prominent artists of the West, along with the painting and bronze sculpture of George Phippen. The **Prescott Resort Conference Center and Casino** (✉ 1500 Hwy. 69, Prescott 86201, ☎ 520/776–1666 or 800/967–4637) is nearby.

Dining and Lodging

For price ranges *see* Charts 1 (B) and 2 (B) *in* On the Road with Fodor's.

$$–$$$ ✕ **Nolaz.** Come here for New Orleans–style fare—jambalaya, Creole shrimp, blackened salmon—and friendly service. ✉ *216 W. Gurley St.,* ☎ *520/445–3765. AE, MC, V. Closed Sun. No lunch Sat.*

$–$$ ✕ **Prescott Brewing Company.** In addition to the pub fare you'd expect, including fish-and-chips, you'll also find a surprising range of vegetarian selections. Four good beers are brewed on the premises. ✉ *130 W. Gurley St.,* ☎ *520/771–2795. AE, D, DC, MC, V.*

$$$$ ★ ✕🏨 **Hassayampa Inn.** Built in 1927 for early automobile travelers, the Hassayampa Inn oozes character. Rooms are individually decorated, some with original furnishings such as oak headboards inset with tiles. A cocktail in the elegant lounge and a full breakfast are included in the reasonable rates. The Peacock Room, the hotel's art-nouveau-style dining room, serves impressive Continental cuisine. ✉ *122 Gurley St.,*

Prescott 86301, ☎ 520/778–9434, 800/322–1927 in AZ. 68 rooms. Restaurant. Full breakfast. AE, D, DC, MC, V.

METROPOLITAN PHOENIX

One of America's newest, fastest-growing major urban centers, metropolitan Phoenix lies at the northern tip of the Sonoran Desert, in the Valley of the Sun, named for its 330-plus days of sunshine each year. Now-chic Scottsdale began in 1901 as less than a dozen adobe houses and 30-odd tents put up by seekers of healthful desert air. Glendale and Peoria on the west side and Tempe, Mesa, Gilbert, and Chandler on the east constitute the nation's third-largest Silicon Valley. Excellent hiking, golf, shopping, and dining and some of the best luxury resorts in the country make the Valley one of the country's leading business and vacation destinations.

Visitor Information

Arizona Office of Tourism (✉ 2702 N. 3rd St., Phoenix 85004, ☎ 602/230–7733 or 888/520–3444). **Phoenix Chamber of Commerce** (✉ Bank One Plaza, 201 N. Central Ave., Suite 2700, Phoenix 85073, ☎ 602/254–5521). **Phoenix and Valley of the Sun Convention and Visitors Bureau** (✉ Arizona Center, 400 E. Van Buren St., Suite 600, Phoenix 85004).

Arriving and Departing

By Bus

Greyhound Lines (✉ 2115 W. Buckeye Rd., ☎ 602/389–4207 or 800/231–2222).

By Car

From the west you'll probably come to Phoenix on I–10. I–40 enters Arizona in the northwest; U.S. 93 continues to Phoenix. From the east I–10 brings you from El Paso into Tucson, then north to Phoenix. The northeastern route, I–40 from Albuquerque, leads to Flagstaff, where I–17 goes south to Phoenix.

By Plane

Sky Harbor International Airport (☎ 602/273–3300), 3 mi east of downtown Phoenix, is home base for America West and a hub for Southwest. It is also served by other major airlines. By car, Tempe is 10 minutes from the airport; Scottsdale about 30 minutes; Glendale and Mesa, 25 minutes; and Sun City, 30–45 minutes. **Valley Metro** (☎ 602/253–5000) buses connect with downtown Phoenix or Tempe for $1.25. A **taxi** trip into downtown Phoenix costs $6.50–$12 plus tip and $1 airport surcharge. **Supershuttle** (☎ 800/258–3826) can run 25% less than a taxi for longer trips.

By Train

Amtrak (✉ 401 W. Harrison St., ☎ 602/253–0121 or 800/872–7245).

Getting Around Metropolitan Phoenix

If you plan to see anything beyond the pedestrian-friendly downtowns of Phoenix, Scottsdale, or Tempe, you will need a car.

Exploring Metropolitan Phoenix

★ The **Heard Museum** (✉ 22 E. Monte Vista Rd., ☎ 602/252–8848 or 602/252–8840; 🎫 $6) has an exceptional collection of fine art, basketry, pottery, and kachina dolls that makes it the world's foremost showcase of Native American art and artifacts, primarily southwestern. Interactive exhibits, a multimedia show, and live demonstrations by artisans and performers add to the experience. Western painting is the focus of the galleries at the **Phoenix Art Museum** (✉ 1625 N. Central Ave., ☎ 602/257–1222; 🎫 $4).

A piece of the city as it was at the turn of the century still stands in parklike **Heritage Square** (✉ 7th and Monroe Sts., ☎ 602/262–5071), at the east end of downtown. Within Heritage Square is the **Arizona Science Center** (✉ 147 E. Adams St., ☎ 602/256–9388; 🎫 $6.50, $11 combined admission to science center, planetarium, and theater) where lively hands-on exhibits let kids discover the science of making gigantic soap bubbles, the technology of satellite weather systems, and more. Within the science center are the **Dorrance Planetarium** and the **Irene P. Flinn Theater,** with a 50-ft screen.

Chock-full of amusing oddities, the **Mystery Castle** (✉ 800 E. Mineral Rd., at the foot of South Mountain Park, ☎ 602/268–1581; 🎫 $4) was constructed out of native stone, railroad refuse, kitchen appliances, and anything else its builder could get his hands on. At the **Hall of Flame** (✉ 6101 E. Van Buren St., ☎ 602/275–3473; 🎫 $4), retired firefighters lead tours through more than 100 restored fire engines and tell harrowing tales of the "world's most dangerous profession." Kids can climb on a 1916 engine, operate alarm systems, and learn lessons on fire safety from the pros.

Scottsdale, a nearby suburb, has a downtown rich in historic sites, nationally known art galleries, and smart boutiques. Historic **Old Town,** with its rustic storefronts and wooden sidewalks, has the look of the Old West and souvenirs galore; **Main Street and Marshall Way** are the places to go for the area's leading fine art galleries. Tour **Taliesen West** (✉ Cactus Rd. and Frank Lloyd Wright Blvd., ☎ 602/860–8810; 🎫 $10 in winter, $8 summer) for a look at the western studio, school, and home of master architect Frank Lloyd Wright.

An hour's drive south of Phoenix, **Casa Grande Ruins National Monument** (✉ north of Coolidge on Rte. 87, ☎ 520/723–3172; 🎫 $2 per person or $4 per car) is the site of the 35-ft-tall Casa Grande (Big House), built in the early 13th century by the Hohokam Indians. These early inhabitants farmed the area from more than 1,500 years ago until they vanished around 1450. A small museum displays artifacts and archaelogical exhibits.

Parks, Gardens, and Zoos

The **Desert Botanical Garden** (✉ 1201 N. Galvin Pkwy., ☎ 602/941–1217; 🎫 $7) is an urban oasis with the world's largest collection of desert plants in a natural setting.

Five designated trails wind through the 125-acre **Phoenix Zoo** (✉ 455 N. Galvin Pkwy., ☎ 602/273–7771; 🎫 $8.50), where the habitats of an African savanna and a tropical rain forest are expertly replicated. Ruby, an Asian elephant, puts her brush to canvas to rival the best of abstract expressionists. Children can help groom goats and sheep at the zoo's big red barn.

Dining

For price ranges *see* Chart 1 (A) *in* On the Road with Fodor's.

$$$–$$$$ ★ ✕ **Marquesa.** Catalonia, the region around Barcelona, is the inspiration for this Valley jewel. Among the extraordinary appetizers are *pebrots del piquillo* (crab and fontina cheese baked into sweet red peppers). For dinner, there's a first-class paella. ✉ *Scottsdale Princess Resort, 7575 E. Princess Dr., Scottsdale,* ☎ *602/585–4848. Reservations essential. AE, D, DC, MC, V. No lunch.*

$$$ ✕ **Restaurant Oceana.** The daily-changing menu may include fresh-caught diver-harvested scallops the size of hockey pucks, Casco Bay cod, or Belon oysters from Washington, all caught the same day. Desserts are homemade and spectacular—try the gingerbread cake with an apple-cider sabayon or chocolate cake with a molten chocolate center. ✉ *8900 E. Pinnacle Peak Rd., Scottsdale,* ☎ *602/515–2277. AE, D, DC, MC, V. No lunch.*

$$–$$$ ★ ✕ **Franco's Trattoria.** Florence-born Franco puts together meals that sing with the flavors of Tuscany. Start with focaccia and hunks of imported Italian cheeses sliced off huge wheels. Veal is a specialty: One standout dish is *orecchie d'elefante,* pounded, breaded, fried veal that's splayed across the plate and coated with tomatoes, shallots, and basil. ✉ *8120 N. Hayden Rd., Scottsdale,* ☎ *602/948–6655. AE, MC, V. Closed Sun. and July. No lunch.*

$$–$$$ ✕ **Michael's at the Citadel.** A brick-lined waterfall greets you at the entrance to Michael's. Entrées are the real stars here: sesame-crusted swordfish with green-coconut curry; venison with a dried-cherry demi-glaze; grilled lamb with a goat-cheese potato tart. ✉ *8700 E. Pinnacle Peak Rd., Scottsdale,* ☎ *602/515–2575. AE, DC, MC, V. No lunch.*

$$–$$$ ★ ✕ **Rancho Pinot Grill.** The attention to quality paid by the husband-and-wife proprietors—he manages, she cooks—has made this one of the town's top restaurants. The inventive menu changes daily; look for *posole,* a mouthwatering broth with hominy, salt pork, and cabbage; or quail with soba noodles. ✉ *6208 N. Scottsdale Rd., Scottsdale,* ☎ *602/468-9463. Reservations essential. AE, D, MC, V. Closed Sun. and Mon. and mid-Aug.–mid-Sept. No lunch.*

$$–$$$ ✕ **Restaurant Hapa.** "Hapa" is Hawaiian slang for "half," which describes the half-Japanese, half-American background of the chef. But there's nothing halfway about Hapa's flavorful, Asian-inspired cuisine. Appetizers like skillet-roasted mussels coated in a Thai-inspired broth let you know you're in for a big-time experience. The signature entrée is beef tenderloin, lined with hot Chinese mustard and caramelized brown sugar. ✉ *6204 N. Scottsdale Rd., Scottsdale,* ☎ *602/998–8220. MC, V. No dinner Sun. No lunch.*

$$–$$$ ★ ✕ **RoxSand.** Chef RoxSand Scocos doesn't follow trends; she sets them. Who else would think to stuff tamales with curried lamb moistened in a Thai-style peanut sauce? The heavenly *b'stilla* is a Moroccan-inspired appetizer of braised chicken wrapped in phyllo dough, covered with almonds and powdered sugar. The air-dried duck entrée is a house specialty. ✉ *2594 E. Camelback Rd. (Biltmore Fashion Park), Phoenix,* ☎ *602/381–0444. AE, DC, MC, V.*

$$–$$$ ✕ **Roy's.** Roy is Roy Yamaguchi, a James Beard award-winning chef and one of the pioneers of Pacific Rim cooking. This is his 13th restaurant; other branches are scattered all over the globe. Look for inventive dishes like steamed pork and crab buns with a spicy Maui onion black-bean sauce; or nori-crusted ono fish with a hot-and-sour red-pepper sauce. ✉ *7001 N. Scottsdale Rd. (Scottsdale Seville), Scottsdale,* ☎ *602/905–1155. AE, MC, V. No lunch Sun.*

$$–$$$ ★ ✕ **Vincent Guerithault on Camelback.** No one can say whether chef Guerithault prepares French food with a southwestern flair, or southwestern fare with a French touch. Whatever it is, it's amazing. You may want to make a meal of the famous appetizers: duck tamale, smoked-salmon quesadilla, or chipotle-lobster ravioli. The duck confit, baked salmon, and grilled wild boar loin make choosing an entrée difficult. ✉ *3930 E. Camelback Rd., Phoenix,* ☎ *602/224–0225. Reservations essential. AE, D, DC, MC, V. No lunch weekends.*

$$ ★ ✕ **Pizzeria Bianco.** Bronx-native Chris Bianco is a craftsman of pizza. His wood-fired crust is a work of art, not too bready, not too light. Toppings include imported cheeses, homemade fennel sausage, wood-roasted cremini mushrooms, and the freshest herbs and spices. ✉ *623 E. Adams St., Phoenix,* ☎ *602/258–8300. MC, V. Closed Mon. No lunch weekends.*

$$ ★ ✕ **Such Is Life.** Authentic, Yucatan-inspired Mexican fare keeps this place packed. For starters, try the *nopal polanco,* a prickly pear cactus pad topped with cheese and chorizo. The lusty, lemon-tinged chicken soup is thick with poultry, avocado, and hard-boiled egg. Entrées include chicken mole and adobo pork, simmered in a fragrant ancho-chili sauce. ✉ *3602 N. 24th St., Phoenix,* ☎ *602/955–7822. Reservations essential. AE, D, DC, MC, V. Closed Sun. No lunch Sat.*

Lodging

Phoenix is famous for its world-class resorts. For price ranges *see* Chart 2 (A) *in* On the Road with Fodor's.

$$$$ ★ **Arizona Biltmore.** The world's only resort with a direct design link to Frank Lloyd Wright, the Biltmore has set the standard in central Phoenix since it opened in 1929. Every president since Herbert Hoover has stayed here: The vast lobby and landscaped grounds might explain why. ✉ *24th St. and Missouri Ave., Phoenix 85016,* ☎ *602/955–6600 or 800/950–0086,* FAX *602/381–7600. 600 rooms, 50 villas. 3 restaurants, pools, golf, tennis, health club. AE, D, DC, MC, V.*

$$$$ ★ **The Boulders.** The desert setting of the valley's most serene luxury resort is its most spectacular feature; buildings nestle among hill-size granite boulders in Carefree (just over the border from Scottsdale). Accommodations have wood-beam ceilings, kiva fireplaces, and huge bath-dressing areas. The golf course is one of the Valley's most famous. ✉ *34631 N. Tom Darlington Dr., Carefree 85377,* ☎ *602/488–9009 or 800/553–1717,* FAX *602/488–4118. 160 casitas, 33 patio homes. 4 restaurants, pools, golf, tennis, health club. AE, D, DC, MC, V.*

$$$$ ★ **Hermosa Inn.** Once the home and studio of cowboy artist Lon Megargee, the Hermosa lives up to its name (Spanish for "beautiful"), providing a restful alternative to the megaresorts. Individually decorated casitas and villas as big as private homes boast an enviable collection of museum-quality art. ✉ *5532 N. Palo Cristi Rd., Paradise Valley, 85253,* ☎ *602/955–8614 or 800/241–1210,* FAX *602/955–8299. 4 villas, 3 haciendas, 22 casitas, 17 ranchos. Restaurant, tennis. AE, D, DC, MC, V.*

$$$$ ★ **Marriott's Camelback Inn.** Desert landscaping, large rooms (some with private swimming pools), and a world-class spa make this a perennial favorite for those wanting to be pampered in a dramatic setting between the Camelback and Mummy mountains. ✉ *5402 E. Lincoln Dr., Scottsdale 85253,* ☎ *602/948–1700 or 800/242–2635,* FAX *602/951–8469. 447 rooms. 5 restaurants, pools, golf, tennis, health club. AE, D, DC, MC, V.*

$$$$ ★ **The Phoenician.** With its crystal chandeliers, marble floors, and cascading series of swimming pools (one tiled in mother-of-pearl), this swanky resort makes you forget you're in the middle of the desert. The Centre for Well-Being is among the best spas in the state. Rooms are spacious; ask for one facing south to enjoy views of the resort's pools and the city. ✉ *6000 E. Camelback Rd., Scottsdale 85251,* ☎ *602/941–8200 or 800/888–8234. 654 rooms. 4 restaurants, pools, golf, tennis, health club. AE, D, DC, MC, V.*

$$$$ **Royal Palms.** A luxurious Mediterranean look prevails, from the titular palms at the entrance to the manicured gardens dotted with antique fountains. Casitas are given individually themed treatment by

well-known designers; they're among the most alluring lodgings in the area. ✉ *5200 E. Camelback Rd., Phoenix, 85018,* ☎ *602/840–3610 or 800/672–6011,* FAX *602/840–6927. 112 rooms and casitas, 4 suites. Restaurant, pool, tennis, health club. AE, D, DC, MC, V.*

$$ **Hotel San Carlos.** Built in 1927, this downtown landmark retains historic touches such as pedestal sinks in the rooms and crystal chandeliers in the lobby. The 3-inch concrete walls in the rooms ensure quiet, and though the rooms aren't huge, the staff is among the Valley's friendliest. ✉ *202 N. Central Ave., 85004,* ☎ *602/253–4121 or 800/528–5446,* FAX *602/253–6668. 132 rooms. Restaurant, pool, exercise room. AE, D, DC, MC, V.*

$$ **Quality Hotel & Resort.** With a 1.5-acre Getaway Lagoon complete with rock waterfalls pouring into a free-form pool, and plenty of facilities (a putting green, playground, and business center), the Quality is central Phoenix's best bargain oasis. Cabana suites on the VIP floor have private rooftop pools with great views of the Phoenix skyline. ✉ *3600 N. Second Ave., 85013,* ☎ *602/248–0222 or 800/256–1237,* FAX *602/265–6331. 280 rooms. Restaurant, pools, exercise room. AE, D, DC, MC, V.*

Nightlife and the Arts

Cultural and entertainment events are listed in the free weekly *New Times* newspaper, distributed Wednesday. The *Rep Entertainment Guide* and Sunday "Arts" section of the *Arizona Republic* also detail the current goings-on.

Nightlife

There are plenty of nightclubs, restaurants, and bars in downtown's **Arizona Center,** but there's no lack of nightlife elsewhere, particularly in Scottsdale and Tempe. On Camelback Road, restaurants abound in the **Biltmore Fashion Park.** Scottsdale's Main Street comes alive for **Art Walk,** held Thursday evenings from 7 to 9. **Mill Avenue,** near the ASU campus, is the center of action in Tempe.

The Arts

Downtown Phoenix's **Symphony Hall** (✉ 225 E. Adams St., ☎ 602/262–7272) and **Herberger Theater Center** (✉ 222 E. Monroe St., ☎ 602/252–8497) are home to many performing arts groups.

Outdoor Activities and Sports

Golf

The Valley of the Sun has more than 100 courses, from par-3 to PGA-championship links. For a detailed listing contact the **Arizona Golf Association** (✉ 7226 N. 16th St., Suite 200, Phoenix 85020, ☎ 602/944–3035, 800/458–8484 in AZ).

Hiking

Phoenix has some of the best-trod hiking trails in the world, and the area favorite is in **Squaw Peak Park** (✉ 2701 Squaw Peak Dr., north of Lincoln Dr., east of South Peak Pkwy., ☎ 602/262–7901). The 1¼-mi trail to the top is steep; plan for an hour each direction. **Camelback Mountain** (✉ E. McDonald Dr. and Tatum Blvd., ☎ 602/256–3220), the city's most prominent landmark, presents a challenging climb that will take anywhere from one to three hours. The mountains of **South Mountain Park** (✉ 10919 S. Central Ave., south of Baseline Rd., ☎ 602/495–0222), the world's largest city park, contain more than 40 mi of multiuse trails. Rangers can help you plan hikes to see some of the 200 Native American petroglyph sites in the park.

Spectator Sports

Baseball: Arizona Diamondbacks (✉ Box 2095, Phoenix, 85001, ☎ 602/514–8383), Phoenix's major-league baseball team, play at the Bank One Ballpark, next to the America West Arena. Several major-league baseball teams train in the Phoenix area during March. Contact the **Cactus League Baseball Association** at the Mesa Convention and Visitor's Bureau (✉ 120 N. Center St., Mesa 85201, ☎ 602/827–4700 or 800/283–6372) for information. **Basketball: Phoenix Suns** (✉ 201 E. Jefferson St., ☎ 602/379–7867). **Football: Arizona Cardinals** (✉ Sun Devil Stadium, 5th St. and College Ave., Tempe, ☎ 602/379–0102). **Golf:** The **Phoenix Open** (✉ 17020 N. Hayden Rd., Scottsdale, ☎ 602/870–4431) is held each January at the Tournament Players Club of Scottsdale. **Rodeo: Parada del Sol** (☎ 602/990–3179) festivities begin in January; the rodeo is held the first week in February. **Rodeo of Rodeos** (✉ 4133 N. 7th St., Phoenix, ☎ 602/263–8671), one of the Southwest's oldest and best, is held every March.

Shopping

The valley is a shopper's delight, with everything from glitzy malls in Phoenix and Mesa to charming boutiques and galleries on downtown Scottsdale's 5th Avenue.

Arizona Center (✉ 400 E. Van Buren St., Phoenix, ☎ 602/271–4000) is a modern, open-air center with two tiers of shops and restaurants. Anchored by Saks Fifth Avenue and Macy's, **Biltmore Fashion Park** (✉ 24th St. and Camelback Rd., Phoenix) has posh shops as well as some of the city's most popular restaurants and cafés.

Souvenir shops and stores selling Native American jewelry and crafts are found along Scottsdale's **5th Avenue,** between Goldwater Boulevard and Scottsdale Road, and in **Old Town,** bordered by Brown Avenue, Scottsdale Road, Indian School Road, and 2nd Street. Head to **Main Street,** just west of Scottsdale Road, or to **Marshall Way** for the fine art for which Scottsdale is known. Retractable skylights open to reveal sunny skies at the **Scottsdale Fashion Square** (✉ Scottsdale and Camelback Rds.), which includes Neiman Marcus, Robinson-May, and Dillard's department stores, among others. The ritzy **Borgata** (✉ 6166 N. Scottsdale Rd.) has more than 50 boutiques in an Italian village–style complex.

On the west side are the double-decker **Metrocenter** (✉ I–17 and Peoria Ave., Phoenix) mall and **Arizona Mills** (✉ 1500 W. Baseline Rd., Tempe, ☎ 602/491–9700), a mammoth center with almost 200 outlet stores, a food court, cinemas, and a faux rain forest. Thirty miles east of Phoenix, **Superstition Springs Center** (✉ U.S. 60 and Superstition Springs Rd., Mesa) has the usual assortment of shops and eateries, a botanical garden, and a 15-ft Gila monster slide for the kids. The town of Casa Grande, some 45 minutes to the south via I–10, is home to two huge outlet malls, **Factory Stores of America** (✉ Exit 194 off I–10), and **Tanger Factory Outlet Center** (✉ Exit 198 off I–10).

TUCSON

Tucson, Arizona's second-largest city, has a small-town atmosphere enriched by its deep Hispanic and Old West roots. Because of its large university, myriad resorts, and desirable climate—the sun shines more than 320 days a year, on the average—Tucson hosts all kinds of recreational and cultural activities, including historical tours, year-round.

Visitor Information

Convention and Visitors Bureau (✉ 130 S. Scott Ave., 85701, ☎ 520/624–1817 or 800/638–8350).

Arriving and Departing

By Bus

Greyhound Lines (✉ 2 S. 4th Ave., ☎ 520/792–3475 or 800/231–2222). **Arizona Shuttle Service** (☎ 520/795–6771) runs express buses from Phoenix's Sky Harbor Airport to Tucson.

By Car

From Phoenix, 111 mi to the northwest, or from the east, take I–10 to Tucson. From the south take I–19.

By Plane

Tucson International Airport (☎ 520/573–8000), 8½ mi south of downtown, is served by 12 carriers, some of which serve Mexico as well as domestic destinations.

By Train

Amtrak (✉ 400 E. Toole Ave., ☎ 520/623–4442 or 800/872–7245).

Exploring Tucson

Tuscon covers more than 500 square mi in a valley ringed by mountains, so a car is necessary. The downtown area, just east of I–10 off the Broadway-Congress exit, is easy to navigate on foot.

In the El Presidio neighborhood, the **Tucson Museum of Art** (✉ 140 N. Main Ave., ☎ 520/624–2333; 🎫 $2) houses a permanent collection of pre-Columbian art and hosts traveling shows, mostly of contemporary art. The museum lies within Tucson's **Historic Block**—a neighborhood that takes visitors back to a time when the city was a fortress and Arizona was still part of New Spain. The historic buildings on this block are listed in the National Register of Historic Buildings. You can enter **La Casa Cordova** (✉ 175 N. Meyer Ave.), the **Stevens House** (✉ 150 N. Main Ave.), and the **J. Knox Corbett House** (✉ 180 N. Main Ave.). The **Edward Nye Fish House** houses the art museum's western collection.

The city divides **Saguaro National Park** (☎ 520/733–5158 for west, 520/733–5153 for east; 🎫 $4 per vehicle or $2 per pedestrian for Saguaro East; free Saguaro West) into two sections; the one west of town is the most heavily visited, in part because of its new **Red Hills Visitor Center**. Both parks are forested by the huge saguaro cactus, a native of the Sonoran Desert that is known for its towering height (often 50 ft) and for arms that reach out in strange configurations.

★ Near Saguaro National Park West is the **Arizona–Sonora Desert Museum** (✉ 2021 N. Kinney Rd., ☎ 520/883–2702; 🎫 $8.95), where birds and animals busy themselves in a desert microcosm. **Old Tucson Studios** (✉ 201 S. Kinney Rd., in Tucson Mountain Park, ☎ 520/883–0100; 🎫 $14.95) is a western theme park that's been used as a location for 250 westerns over the past 50 years.

Among the museums on the **University of Arizona** campus (✉ Corner of Park Ave. and Speedway Blvd.) are the **Center for Creative Photography** (☎ 520/621–7968), the **Arizona Historical Society's Museum** (☎ 520/628–5774), the **Arizona State Museum** (☎ 520/621–6302), and the **Grace H. Flandrau Science Center and Planetarium** (☎ 520/621–4515). Entrance to all of these museums is free.

Tucson

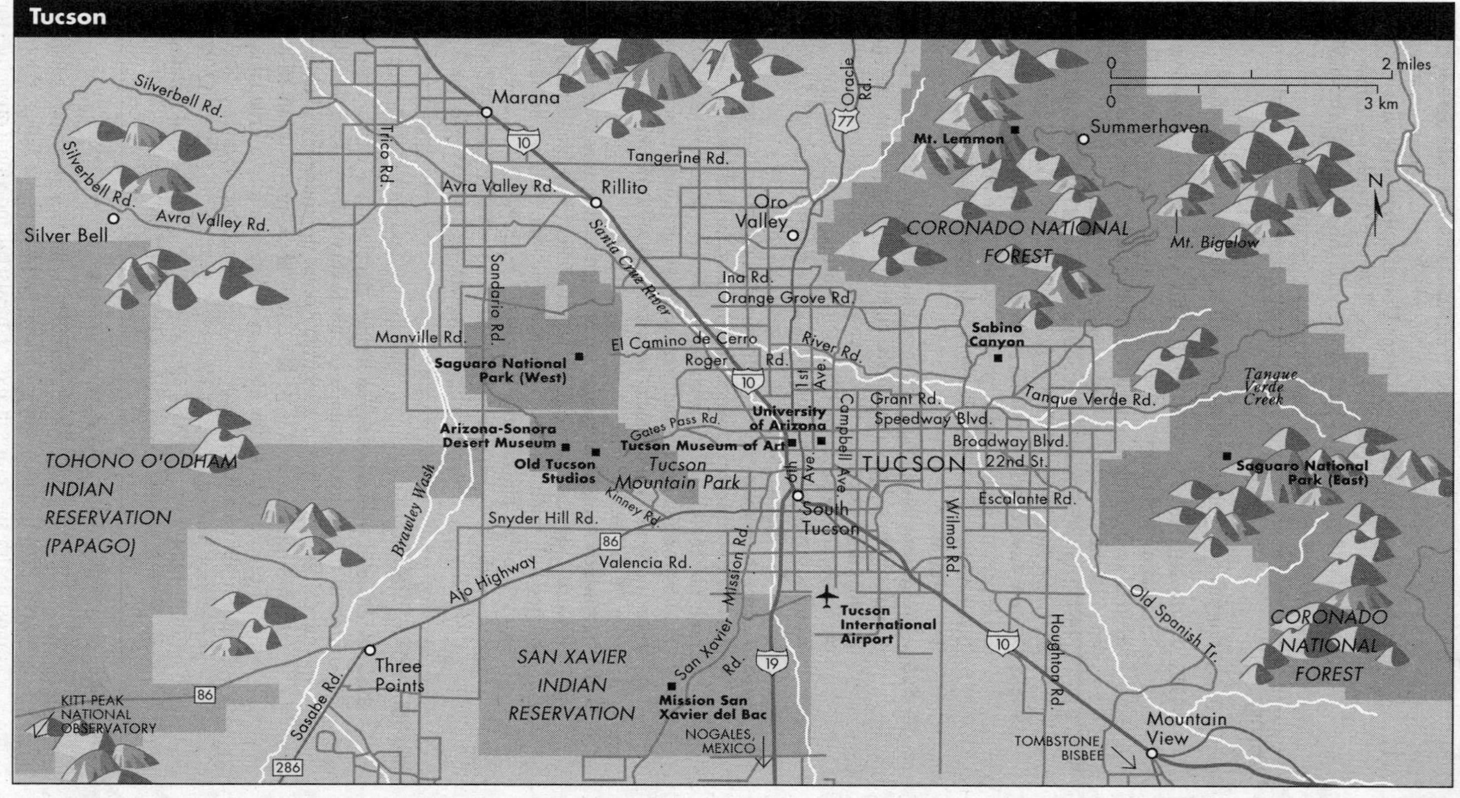

Tucson
0 2 miles
0 3 km
N
Marana
Rillito
Silver Bell
Silverbell Rd.
Avra Valley Rd.
Trico Rd.
Tangerine Rd.
Oro Valley
Oracle Rd.
77
10
Summerhaven
Mt. Lemmon
Mt. Bigelow
CORONADO NATIONAL FOREST
Santa Cruz River
Ina Rd.
Orange Grove Rd.
Sandario Rd.
Manville Rd.
El Camino de Cerro
Roger Rd.
River Rd.
Sabino Canyon
Tanque Verde Rd.
Tanque Verde Creek
Saguaro National Park (West)
Saguaro National Park (East)
1st Ave.
Campbell Ave.
Grant Rd.
Speedway Blvd.
Broadway Blvd.
22nd St.
University of Arizona
Gates Pass Rd.
Arizona-Sonora Desert Museum
Old Tucson Studios
Tucson Museum of Art
Tucson Mountain Park
TUCSON
6th Ave.
South Tucson
Escalante Rd.
Wilmot Rd.
Kinney Rd.
Snyder Hill Rd.
86
Valencia Rd.
Mission Rd.
TOHONO O'ODHAM INDIAN RESERVATION (PAPAGO)
Brawley Wash
Ajo Highway
Tucson International Airport
Old Spanish Tr.
Houghton Rd.
CORONADO NATIONAL FOREST
Three Points
SAN XAVIER INDIAN RESERVATION
San Xavier Rd.
19
Mission San Xavier del Bac
KITT PEAK NATIONAL OBSERVATORY
Sasabe Rd.
286
NOGALES, MEXICO
TOMBSTONE, BISBEE
Mountain View

Just southwest of Tucson, the 1692 **Mission San Xavier del Bac** (✉ I-19 Exit 92, San Xavier Rd., ☎ 520/294–2624; donations accepted) is the oldest Catholic church in the United States still serving the community for which it was built: the Tohonó O'odham Indian tribe. Painted statues, carvings, and frescoes make this beautiful Spanish-Moorish-style structure a sight to behold.

Dining

For price ranges *see* Chart 1 (A) *in* On the Road with Fodor's.

$$$$ ✕ **Vivace.** Daniel Scordato has had his hand in some of the best Italian restaurants in town, and his latest venture is no exception. The industrial-chic dining room has gray columns, black iron chairs, and an open kitchen. Appetizers are a bit pricey, but the grilled shrimp in a phyllo cup with tomato, basil, and garlic sauce is hard to resist. ✉ *4811 E. Grant Rd., Suite 155,* ☎ *520/795–7221. MC, V. No lunch Sun.*

$$–$$$ ✕ **Café Terra Cotta.** Specialties at this very southwestern restaurant include prawns stuffed with herbed goat cheese and pork tenderloin with black beans. ✉ *4310 N. Campbell Ave.,* ☎ *520/577–8100. AE, D, DC, MC, V.*

$$–$$$ ✕ **Kingfisher Grill.** Brick walls and black banquettes create a chic setting for Kingfisher's innovative cuisine. You might find mesquite-grilled pork chops or crayfish étouffée on the seasonally changing menu. Added bonuses: an extensive bourbon selection and late hours (food is served until midnight). ✉ *2564 E. Grant Rd.,* ☎ *520/323–7739. AE, D, DC, MC, V. No lunch weekends.*

$–$$ ★ ✕ **Café Poca Cosa.** Chef-owner Susan Davila pays homage to different regions of her native Mexico in what is arguably Tucson's best restaurant. The chalkboard menu changes daily; ingredients are always fresh. The tiny original restaurant across the street (✉ 20 S. Scott Ave.) is open for breakfast and lunch during the week. ✉ *Park Inn, 88 E. Broadway,* ☎ *520/622–6400. MC, V. Closed Sun.*

$–$$ ✕ **Pinnacle Peak Steakhouse.** No nouvelle-cuisine fans welcome here: It's a cowboy steak house all the way. Excellent mesquite-broiled steak comes with salad and pinto beans; for dessert, there's a heavenly hot apple cobbler. The restaurant is part of Trail Dust Town, a re-created turn-of-the-century town. ✉ *6541 E. Tanque Verde Rd.,* ☎ *520/296–0911. Reservations not accepted. AE, D, DC, MC, V. No lunch.*

Dining and Lodging

$$$$ ✕🏨 **Loews Ventana Canyon Resort.** Expect to see desert cottontails around the 93-acre grounds of this luxury resort, along with hummingbirds, quail, and other birds. Rooms are modern and chic; each bath has a miniature TV. At the center of the property, an 80-ft waterfall cascades down the Catalina Mountains into a little lake. The elegant Ventana Room serves seasonal specialties such as grilled loin of venison with pecans. ✉ *7000 N. Resort Dr. 85750,* ☎ *520/299–2020 or 800/234–5117,* FAX *520/299–6832. 398 rooms. 4 restaurants, pools, golf, tennis, health club. AE, D, DC, MC, V.*

Lodging

Resorts in the area are known for their outdoor-recreation facilities, which often include trails for hiking and horseback riding. Prices for most health-spa resorts include all meals; call individual properties for details. For price ranges *see* Chart 2 (A) *in* On the Road with Fodor's.

$$$$ ★ 🏨 **Arizona Inn.** Though it's close to the university and downtown, this landmark 1930s-era inn is secluded on 14 acres of lushly landscaped grounds. The spacious rooms are spread out in pink stucco houses; all have patios and some have fireplaces. Large groups may rent a guest house. ✉ *2200 E. Elm St., 85719,* ☎ *520/325–1541 or 800/933–1093,* FAX *520/881–5830. 86 rooms, 2 5-bedroom guest houses, 1 2-bedroom guest house. 2 restaurants, pool, tennis. AE, MC, V.*

$$$$ ★ **Canyon Ranch.** Since 1979, this world-class health spa has drawn an international crowd of glitterati. Set on 70 acres in the desert foothills northeast of Tucson, the resort has a full-time staff of dieticians, exercise physiologists, and medical professionals who attend to body and soul. There's a four-night minimum stay. ✉ *8600 E. Rockcliff Rd., 85715,* ☎ *520/749–9000 or 800/742–9000,* FAX *520/749–1646. 153 rooms. Restaurant, pools, tennis, health club. AE, D, MC, V.*

$$$$ **Miraval.** Some 20 mi north of Tucson, Miraval is known for its secluded desert setting, beautiful southwestern rooms, and progressive mind-body programs, many based on Eastern philosophy. ✉ *5000 E. Via Estancia Miraval, Catalina 85739,* ☎ *520/825–4000 or 800/825–4000,* FAX *520/792–5870. 106 rooms. 2 restaurants, pools, tennis, exercise room. FAP. AE, D, DC, MC, V.*

$$$$ ★ **Sheraton Tucson El Conquistador.** In the rugged Santa Catalina Mountains, this golf and tennis resort has a truly southwestern feel. A mural in the cathedral-celing lobby illustrates cowboys and cacti; rooms, either in private casitas or the main hotel building, have balconies or patios, and some suites have kiva-shape fireplaces. ✉ *10000 N. Oracle Rd., 85737,* ☎ *520/544–5000 or 800/325–7832,* FAX *520/544–1224. 428 rooms. 4 restaurants, pools, golf, tennis, exercise rooms. AE, D, DC, MC, V.*

$$$$ **Tanque Verde Ranch.** One of the oldest guest ranches in the country, Tanque Verde sits on more than 600 acres in the Rincon Mountains between Coronado National Forest and Saguaro National Park. Rooms are in the main ranch house or in private casitas; many have patios and fireplaces. ✉ *14301 E. Speedway Blvd., 85748,* ☎ *520/296–6275 or 800/234–3833,* FAX *520/721–9426. 74 rooms. Restaurant, pools, tennis, exercise room. FAP. AE, D, MC, V.*

$$$$ **Westin La Paloma.** Vying with the Sheraton for convention business, this sprawling pink resort has top-notch golf, fitness, and beauty centers; there's also a huge pool with Tucson's only swim-up bar and Arizona's longest resort water slide. Child-care programs help parents relax. ✉ *3800 E. Sunrise Dr., 85718,* ☎ *520/742–6000,* FAX *520/577–5878. 487 rooms. 5 restaurants, pools, golf, tennis, exercise room. AE, D, DC, MC, V.*

$$$$ **White Stallion Ranch.** Many scenes from the television show *High Chaparral* were shot on this family-run ranch, set on 3,000 desert mountain acres. Activities include horseback rides, a weekend rodeo, cookouts, and hikes and along mountain trails. Longhorn cattle roam the grounds; there's also a children's petting zoo. Rooms are spare (no phones or TVs) but comfortable. ✉ *9251 W. Twin Peaks Rd., 85743,* ☎ *520/297–0252 or 888/977–2624,* FAX *520/744–2786. 32 rooms. Pool, tennis. FAP. No credit cards. Closed May–Sept.*

$$$ **Windmill Inn.** In a shopping plaza, this modern inn has 122 suites, each with a microwave, wet bar, two TVs, and three phones. Complimentary coffee, muffins, and a newspaper are delivered to your door. ✉ *4250 N. Campbell Ave., 85718,* ☎ *520/577–0007 or 800/547–4747,* FAX *520/577–0045. 122 suites. Pool. CP. AE, D, DC, MC, V.*

$$ ★ **Best Western Ghost Ranch Lodge.** The logo of this hotel was designed by Georgia O'Keeffe, a friend of the original owner. The Spanish tile–roof units are spread out over 8 acres encompassing an orange grove and garden with 400 types of cacti. The cottages are a bargain, with separate kitchens and carports. ✉ *801 W. Miracle Mile, 85705,* ☎ *520/*

791–7565 or 800/456–7565, FAX 520/791–3898. 82 rooms, 10 cottages sleeping up to 4 people. Restaurant, pool. CP. AE, D, DC, MC, V.

$$ **Hotel Congress.** This downtown hotel, built in 1919 in art deco style, has a convenient location, low rates, and a hip young crowd that frequents the popular Club Congress. Rooms have original iron beds. ✉ *311 E. Congress St., 85701,* ☎ *520/622–8848 or 800/722–8848,* FAX *520/792–6366. 40 rooms. Restaurant. AE, MC, V.*

Campgrounds

The public campground closest to Tucson is at **Catalina State Park** (✉ 11570 N. Oracle Rd., ☎ 520/628–5798). Recreational vehicles can park in any number of facilities around town; the Convention and Visitors Bureau (☞ Visitor Information, *above*) can provide information about specific locations.

Nightlife and the Arts

Nightlife

Cactus Moon (✉ 5470 E. Broadway, ☎ 520/748–0049), **Maverick** (✉ 4702 E. 22nd St., ☎ 520/748–0456), and the **Stampede** (✉ 4385 W. Ina Rd., ☎ 520/744–7744) are lively country-and-western nightclubs.

The Arts

The Tucson Symphony Orchestra (☎ 520/882–8585) and the Arizona Opera Company (☎ 520/293–4336) perform in the **Tucson Convention Center's Music Hall** (✉ 260 S. Church St., ☎ 520/791–4226). The **Arizona Theatre Company** (☎ 520/884–8210) comes to Tucson's Temple of Music and Art (✉ 330 S. Scott Ave., ☎ 520/622–2823) from September through May.

Outdoor Activities and Sports

Golf

Tucson has five **municipal golf courses** (✉ Tucson Parks and Recreation Dept., ☎ 520/791–4336), as well as many excellent resort courses, such as those at the **Lodge at Ventana Canyon** (✉ 6200 N. Club House La., off Kold Rd., ☎ 520/577–4061), **OmniTucson National Golf Resort and Spa** (✉ 2727 W. Club Dr., ☎ 520/297–2271), **Westin La Paloma** and **Sheraton Tucson El Conquistador** (for the last two, *see* Lodging, *above*). For information about other courses in the area, send $5 for the *Tucson and Southern Arizona Golf Guide* (✉ Madden Publishing, Box 42915, Tucson 85733, ☎ 520/322–0895).

Hiking

For great hiking opportunities around Tucson, head for **Tucson Mountain Park, Mt. Lemmon, Sabino Canyon,** or **Kitt Peak.** A little-visited treasure, **Chiricahua National Monument,** about two hours east of Tucson off I–10, south of Bowie, has spectacular rugged rock vistas. Directly south of Tucson, the Huachuca Mountains, home of **Ramsey Canyon,** are a bird-watcher's paradise. The Santa Ritas, just south of Tucson, host another bird lover's haven, **Madera Canyon.** The local chapter of the **Sierra Club** (☎ 520/620–6401) welcomes out-of-town visitors on its weekend hikes.

Horseback Riding

Tucson stables include **Desert-High Country Stables** (✉ 6501 W. Ina Rd., ☎ 520/744–3789) and **Pusch Ridge Stables** (✉ 13700 N. Oracle Rd., ☎ 520/825–1664). Many resorts also have horseback riding.

Shopping

In Tucson, **Old Town Artisans** (✉ 186 N. Meyer Ave., ☎ 520/622–0351) and the **Kaibab Shops** (✉ 2841–43 N. Campbell Ave., ☎ 520/795–6905) both carry a broad selection of fine southwestern crafts and clothing. Hard-core bargain hunters head for **Nogales,** the Mexican border town 63 mi south of Tucson on I–19. For work by regional artists, try the **Tubac** artists' community, 45 mi south of Tucson, just off I–19 at Exit 34.

SOUTHERN ARIZONA

Southeastern Arizona is a relatively undiscovered treasure of mountains, deserts, canyons, and dusty little cowboy towns. Of particular interest are Bisbee and Tombstone, which recall Arizona during its Wild West heyday.

Visitor Information

Bisbee: Chamber of Commerce (✉ 7 Main St., Box BA, 85603, ☎ 520/432–5421). **Tombstone:** Office of Tourism (✉ Box 917, 85638, ☎ 520/457–3421 or 800/457–3423).

Arriving and Departing

By Car

East of Tucson, U.S. 80 cuts south from I–10 to Tombstone and Bisbee.

Exploring Southern Arizona

Tombstone

Born on the site of a wildly successful silver mine, this town 67 mi southeast of Tucson on U.S. 80 was headquarters of many of the West's rowdies in the late 1800s. The famous shoot-out at the OK Corral and other gunfights are replayed on Sunday on the town's main drag, **Allen Street.** As you enter Tombstone from the northwest, you'll pass **Boot Hill Graveyard** (✉ Hwy. 80), where the victims of the OK Corral shoot-out are buried. The **Tombstone Courthouse State Historic Park** (✉ Toughnut and 3rd Sts., ☎ 520/457–3311; 🎫 $2.50) has a reconstruction of the town's original 1882 courthouse, plus area artifacts and old photographs.

Bisbee

Once a mining boomtown, Bisbee, set on a mountainside 24 mi south of Tombstone, is now an artists' colony. Arizona's largest pit mine yielded some 94 million tons of copper ore before mining activity halted in the early 1970s; at the **Lavender Pit Mine** you can still see the huge crater left by the process. The **Mining and Historical Museum** (✉ 5 Copper Queen Plaza, ☎ 520/432–7071; 🎫 $3) is filled with old photos and artifacts from the town's heyday. Behind the museum is the venerable **Copper Queen Hotel** (☞ Dining and Lodging, *below*), home away from home to such guests as "Black Jack" Pershing, John Wayne, and Teddy Roosevelt. The **Copper Queen mine tour** (✉ 478 N. Dart Rd., ☎ 520/432–2071), led by retired miners, is an entertaining way to learn about the town's history.

Dining and Lodging

For price ranges *see* Charts 1 (B) and 2 (B) *in* On the Road with Fodor's.

Bisbee

$$ ★ ✕ **Café Roka.** One of the best bargains in southern Arizona, this chic northern Italian restaurant is in a historic building with exposed brick walls and an original 1906 tinwork ceiling. Generous portions of pasta are served with soup, salad, and sorbet. ✉ *35 Main St.,* ☎ *520/432–5153. MC, V. Closed Sun.–Tues. No lunch.*

$$–$$$$ ★ **Copper Queen Hotel.** This turn-of-the-century hotel in the heart of downtown has thin walls but a lot of Victorian charm. The boom-days memorabilia throughout is fascinating. ✉ *11 Howell Ave., Drawer CQ, 85603,* ☎ *520/432–2216 or 800/247–5829,* FAX *520/432–4298. 45 rooms. Pool. AE, D, DC, MC, V.*

Tombstone

$$ ✕ **Nellie Cashman's.** Named for the Tombstone pioneer who opened it in 1882, Nellie Cashman's is known for its juicy pork chops, chicken-fried steaks, and country breakfasts complete with biscuits and gravy. ✉ *5th and Toughnut Sts.,* ☎ *520/457–2212. AE, D, MC, V.*

$$–$$$ ✕ **Tombstone Boarding House & Country Inn.** Two meticulously restored 1880s adobes sit side by side in a quiet residential neighborhood. In one of the buildings, a dining room serves a limited but daily-changing menu of Continental cuisine to guests and the public. ✉ *108 N. 4th St., Box 906, 85638,* ☎ *520/457–3716,* FAX *520/457–3038. 8 rooms. Restaurant. Full breakfast. No credit cards.*

$$–$$$ **Best Western Look-Out Lodge.** Western-print bedspreads and wood-hewn clocks give this motel off U.S. 80 a lot of character. Rooms have views of the Dragoon Mountains and desert valley. ✉ *U.S. 80W, Box 787, 85638,* ☎ *520/457–2223 or 800/652–6772,* FAX *520/457–3870. 40 rooms. Pool. CP. AE, D, DC, MC, V.*

NEVADA

Updated by
Deke
Castleman

Capital	Carson City
Population	1,677,000
Motto	Battle Born
State Bird	Mountain bluebird
State Flower	Sagebrush
Postal Abbreviation	NV

Statewide Visitor Information

Nevada Commission on Tourism (✉ Capitol Complex, Carson City 89710, ☎ 702/687–4322 or 800/638–2328).

Scenic Drives

The **"Loneliest Road in America"** is U.S. 50 in Nevada, which winds across the central part of the state from Carson City to Ely. **U.S. 93** runs from north of Las Vegas through more than 500 mi of long desert valleys and passes 13,061-ft **Wheeler Peak,** the second-highest point in the state. For a good look at the Southwest's desert, particularly in the spring, take **U.S. 93/95** southeast from Las Vegas, turning east onto Route 147 in Henderson, which takes you through Lake Mead National Recreation Area to Valley of Fire State Park (☞ Las Vegas, *below*).

National and State Parks

National Park

Great Basin National Park (✉ Off U.S. 50 at the Nevada–Utah border, Baker 89311, ☎ 702/234–7331; admission free) is 77,092 acres of dramatic mountains, lush meadows, alpine lakes, limestone caves, and a stand of bristlecone pines (the oldest living trees in the world), with many areas for camping, hiking, and picnicking.

State Parks

For information on Nevada's 23 state parks, contact the state tourism office (☞ Statewide Visitor Information, *above*). **Washoe Lake State Recreation Area** (✉ Off U.S. 395; 4855 E. Lake Blvd., Carson City 89704, ☎ 702/687–4319), with views of the majestic Sierra Nevada, is popular for fishing and horseback riding.

LAS VEGAS

Las Vegas is known around the world as a fantasy land for adults. It was given its name, which means "the meadows," in the 1820s by a Spanish scouting party who found a spring in the area. Mormons settled the valley briefly in 1855, but until the turn of the century it was little more than a handful of ranches and homesteads. The San Pedro, Los Angeles, and Salt Lake Railroad founded the town of Las Vegas in 1905 as a watering stop for its steam trains. The construction of Hoover Dam in the 1930s brought a large wave of settlers seeking jobs.

The Las Vegas that we know today began shortly after World War II when mobster Benjamin "Bugsy" Siegel decided to build a gambling resort in the desert (gambling had been legalized in the state in 1931). Bugsy built his Flamingo with money borrowed from fellow mobsters, who rubbed him out when the casino flopped. The resort eventually recovered and casino-hotels on the Las Vegas Strip caught on. Now the city is home to 15 of the 16 largest hotels in the world.

Visitor Information

Las Vegas Chamber of Commerce (✉ 711 E. Desert Inn Rd., 89109, ☎ 702/735–1616). **Las Vegas Convention and Visitors Authority** (✉ 3150 Paradise Rd., 89109, ☎ 702/892–0711).

Arriving and Departing

By Bus

Greyhound Lines (✉ 200 S. Main St., ☎ 800/231–2222).

By Car

Major highways leading into Las Vegas are I–15 from Los Angeles and Salt Lake City, U.S. 95 from Reno, and U.S. 93 from Arizona.

By Plane

McCarran International Airport (☎ 702/261–5743), about 2 mi from the southern end of the Strip, is served by major airlines. Taxi fare from the airport to Strip hotels is about $9–$12; to the downtown hotels, about $15–$18; but the least-expensive way to reach your hotel ($4–$6 per person) is by **Bell Trans Limousine** (☎ 702/739–7990), which you will find near the taxis.

By Train

Amtrak passenger service to Las Vegas was discontinued in March 1997.

Getting Around Las Vegas

Taxis, easily found in front of every hotel, are the most convenient way to get around. The **Strip bus** (Citizens Area Transit, or CAT, ☎ 702/228–7433) costs $1.50 and links the Strip and the downtown with stops near major hotels. You can rent a car to drive out of town or explore the desert, but be sure to gas up before you go; you won't find many stations out there.

Exploring Las Vegas

Las Vegas is a relatively small city; downtown and small sections of the Strip are easy to explore on foot. But beware the extremely hot months of June, July, and August, when walking outside for an extended length of time is not recommended. The massive casino hotels along the Strip make distances deceptive; a stroll "next door" may take 10 minutes because properties are so large. Take taxis or buses between the Strip and downtown and for longer distances along the Strip.

The downtown casino center may be only four blocks long, but it is the most brightly lighted four blocks in the world thanks to the $70 million **Fremont Street Experience,** a four-block pedestrian mall covered by an arched 100-ft-high awning that's illuminated by 2 *million* lightbulbs. A kaleidoscopic light-and-sound show is presented here on the hour after dark until midnight. A focal point of downtown is **Jackie Gaughan's Plaza Hotel and Casino** (✉ 1 N. Main St., ☎ 702/386–2110), built on the site of the old Union Pacific train station—freight trains still rumble right past the back door at all hours.

Among the downtown hotel-casinos, the **Golden Nugget** (✉ 129 E. Fremont St., ☎ 702/385–7111) has a particularly attractive lobby, where you can see an enormous, 61-pound gold nugget. **Binion's Horseshoe** (✉ 128 E. Fremont St., ☎ 702/382–1600) is an old-fashioned gambling joint with $1 million in cash on display.

Lied Discovery Children's Museum (✉ 833 Las Vegas Blvd. N, ☎ 702/382–5473; 🎟 $5) has hands-on science exhibits. **Southern Nevada Zo-**

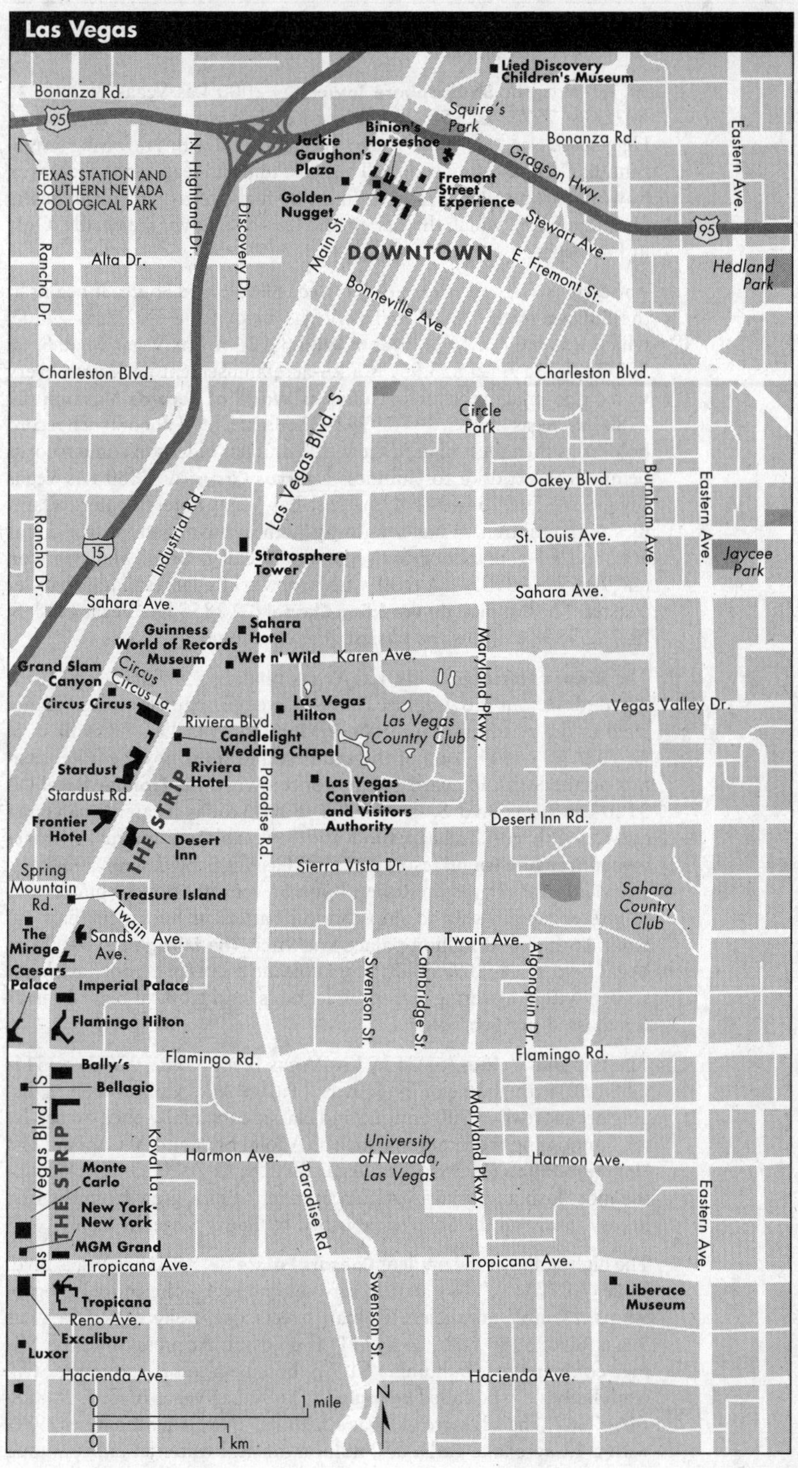
Las Vegas
Lied Discovery Children's Museum
Bonanza Rd.
Squire's Park
Binion's Horseshoe
Jackie Gaughon's Plaza
Bonanza Rd.
Gragson Hwy.
Eastern Ave.
Fremont Street Experience
Golden Nugget
TEXAS STATION AND SOUTHERN NEVADA ZOOLOGICAL PARK
N. Highland Dr.
Discovery Dr.
Main St.
Stewart Ave.
DOWNTOWN
E. Fremont St.
Alta Dr.
Rancho Dr.
Bonneville Ave.
Hedland Park
Charleston Blvd.
Charleston Blvd.
Circle Park
Las Vegas Blvd. S
Oakey Blvd.
Burnham Ave.
Eastern Ave.
Industrial Rd.
St. Louis Ave.
Stratosphere Tower
Jaycee Park
Rancho Dr.
Sahara Ave.
Sahara Ave.
Guinness World of Records Museum
Sahara Hotel
Wet n' Wild
Karen Ave.
Grand Slam Canyon
Circus Circus La.
Circus Circus
Las Vegas Hilton
Vegas Valley Dr.
Riviera Blvd.
Las Vegas Country Club
Candlelight Wedding Chapel
Maryland Pkwy.
Stardust
Riviera Hotel
THE STRIP
Las Vegas Convention and Visitors Authority
Stardust Rd.
Paradise Rd.
Frontier Hotel
Desert Inn Rd.
Desert Inn
Sierra Vista Dr.
Spring Mountain Rd.
Treasure Island
Sahara Country Club
Twain Ave.
The Mirage
Sands Ave.
Twain Ave.
Caesars Palace
Imperial Palace
Swenson St.
Cambridge St.
Algonquin Dr.
Flamingo Hilton
Flamingo Rd.
Flamingo Rd.
Bally's
Bellagio
Las Vegas Blvd. S
Koval La.
Maryland Pkwy.
University of Nevada, Las Vegas
Harmon Ave.
Harmon Ave.
Paradise Rd.
Monte Carlo
New York-New York
MGM Grand
Eastern Ave.
Tropicana Ave.
Tropicana Ave.
Liberace Museum
Tropicana
Reno Ave.
Swenson St.
Excalibur
Luxor
Hacienda Ave.
Hacienda Ave.
0
1 mile
0
1 km
N
95
15

ological Park (✉ 1775 N. Rancho Dr., ☎ 702/648–5955; 🎫 $5) is a small but enjoyable zoo.

At 1,149 ft, the **Stratosphere Tower** (✉ 2000 Las Vegas Blvd. S, ☎ 702/380–7777; 🎫 $5) is the tallest building west of the Mississippi. High-speed elevators whisk you to a 12-story pod with a revolving restaurant, bar, and meeting rooms. The most unusual features of the tower, however, are a roller coaster (it runs 900 ft above ground!) and the Big Shot thrill ride, which thrusts up and free-falls down the needle. Only in Las Vegas.

The **Strip** is a 3½-mi stretch of Las Vegas Boulevard South. It begins at the **Sahara Hotel** (✉ 2535 Las Vegas Blvd. S, ☎ 702/737–2111), which was built in 1952. **Wet n' Wild** (✉ 2600 Las Vegas Blvd. S, ☎ 702/737–3819; 🎫 $23.95) is a 26-acre amusement park with every water ride imaginable. The **Guinness World of Records Museum** (✉ 2780 Las Vegas Blvd. S, ☎ 702/792–3766; 🎫 $4.95) honors such record holders as the tallest man in the world and has videos of some records being set. Next door to Guinness is **Circus Circus** (✉ 2880 Las Vegas Blvd. S, ☎ 702/734–0410), the first Las Vegas hotel to cater to families with children. It has a midway with carnival games, free circus acts, and a 5-acre indoor amusement park called **Grand Slam Canyon** (☎ 702/794–3939; 🎫 free) with the world's largest indoor roller coaster. The **Candlelight Wedding Chapel** (✉ 2855 Las Vegas Blvd. S, ☎ 702/735–4179) is the busiest chapel in town.

The **Riviera Hotel** (✉ 2901 Las Vegas Blvd. S, ☎ 702/734–5110) is noted for its four showrooms. The reclusive billionaire Howard Hughes lived in the penthouse of the **Desert Inn** (✉ 3145 Las Vegas Blvd. S, ☎ 702/733–4444), one of the smallest and most upscale hotel-casinos on the Strip. Howard Hughes once owned the **Frontier Hotel** (✉ 3120 Las Vegas Blvd. S, ☎ 702/794–8200); today it caters to a young crowd, with good, cheap food and low table minimums. Mirage-owned **Treasure Island** resort (✉ 3300 Las Vegas Blvd. S, ☎ 702/894–7111) is loosely based on Robert Louis Stevenson's novel—pirates and sailors engage in ship-to-ship cannon battles in Buccaneer Bay out front.At the $670 million palace known as **The Mirage** (✉ 3400 Las Vegas Blvd. S, ☎ 702/791–7111), a volcano erupts in a front yard landscaped with a towering waterfall, lagoons, and tropical plants; inside is a glassed-in tigers' den.

The **Imperial Palace** (✉ 3535 Las Vegas Blvd. S; ☎ 702/731–3311; 🎫 $6.50) is the home of the Imperial Palace Auto Collection. On display are more than 300 antique and classic cars, many once owned by the famous and the infamous, such as Adolf Hitler and Al Capone. The **Flamingo Hilton** (✉ 3555 Las Vegas Blvd. S, ☎ 702/733–3111), with the most lush and luxurious pool area in the city, grew from the first luxury resort on the Strip, established by Bugsy Siegel in 1946.

The high stakes at the opulent **Caesars Palace** (✉ 3570 Las Vegas Blvd. S, ☎ 702/731–7110) attract serious gamblers; the indoor Forum Shops resemble an ancient Roman streetscape. **Bally's** (✉ 3645 Las Vegas Blvd. S, ☎ 702/739–4111) is colossal. At press time, the Mirage company was building a $1.7 billion megaresort across the Strip from Bally's. To be called **Bellagio** (✉ 3600 Las Vegas Blvd. S, ☎ 888/744–7687), the 122-acre site was scheduled to open in September 1998, with a 12-acre lake and a $30 million musical water-jet ballet among its major features.

The emerald-green **MGM Grand** (✉ 3799 Las Vegas Blvd. S, ☎ 702/891–1111) houses the second-largest casino in the world—so large it's divided into four parts, each delineated by different types of carpet. The sprawling grounds of the **Tropicana** (✉ 3801 Las Vegas Blvd. S, ☎ 702/739–2222) are attractively landscaped—some of the plantings are more than 40 years old. The blue-and-pink castlelike **Excalibur** (✉ 3850 Las Vegas Blvd. S, ☎ 702/597–7777) was built with a medieval theme. Victorian-themed **Monte Carlo** (✉ 3770 Las Vegas Blvd. S, ☎ 702/730–7777) has 3,000 rooms and the largest microbrewery in town. Megaresort **New York–New York** (✉ 3790 Las Vegas Blvd. S, ☎ 702/740–6969) has 2,035 rooms, a replica of the New York City skyline, a Greenwich Village–like food court, a Central Park casino, and a roller coaster. **Luxor** (✉ 3900 Las Vegas Blvd. S, ☎ 702/262–4000) is a 30-story Egyptian-style pyramid with an ultra-high-tech arcade and similarly advanced entertainment options. The **Liberace Museum** (✉ 1775 E. Tropicana Ave., ☎ 702/798–5595; $6.95), 2 mi east of the Strip, occupies three buildings: one for the entertainer's pianos and cars, one for his costumes, and the third for general memorabilia.

Outside Vegas

The awe-inspiring **Hoover Dam** (✉ Rte. 93, east of Boulder City, ☎ 702/293–8321; tour $6), about 35 mi east of Las Vegas, was constructed in the 1930s to tame the destructive waters of the Colorado River and produce electricity. Tours into the 727-ft-high, 660-ft-thick dam are conducted daily.

Construction of Hoover Dam created **Lake Mead** (✉ Alan Bible Visitor Center, U.S. 93 and Lakeshore Dr., ☎ 702/293–8906), the largest man-made lake in the western hemisphere, with more than 500 mi of shoreline. It is popular for boating, fishing, and swimming. For water tours of the lake and Hoover Dam, contact **Lake Mead Cruises** (☎ 702/293–6180).

Dramatic **Valley of Fire State Park** (✉ Rte. 169, Overton, ☎ 702/397–2088), 55 mi northeast of Lake Mead, contains distinctive polychrome sandstone formations and mysterious Anasazi petroglyphs.

Red Rock Canyon (✉ Rte. 159, ☎ 702/363–1921; $5), though closer to Las Vegas (only 20 mi west) than Valley of Fire, is slightly less spectacular. Still, the sheer sandstone cliffs and twisting ravines are an internationally known rock-climbing destination. A 13-mi loop drive begins at the canyon visitor center.

For a respite from the noise and excitement of Las Vegas and the heat of the desert, travel 35 mi northwest of the city on U.S. 95 and Route 157 to **Mt. Charleston,** with its forest, canyons, and 12,000-ft peak. The skiing in winter (Lee Canyon) and hiking, camping, and picnicking the rest of the year are excellent.

Though it isn't exactly in the vicinity (it's a five-hour drive; one hour by small plane and 40 minutes by jet), Las Vegas does consider itself a gateway to the awesome, vastly silent **Grand Canyon National Park** (✉ Box 129, Grand Canyon, AZ 86023, ☎ 520/638–7888; ☞ Arizona). One of the world's greatest wonders, the canyon is stunning in depth and size, and its layers of rock reveal a fascinating geological profile of Earth. **South Rim Travel** (☎ 520/638–2748 or 800/682–4393), through its sister company, TriStar Vacations, has the only jet service from Las Vegas to the Grand Canyon; it is a full-service travel agency that can also arrange rooms, cars, and Colorado River trips. For longer flights in smaller planes at lower elevations, try **Eagle Canyon Airlines** (☎ 702/736–3333).

Casino Gambling

Most major hotels in Las Vegas (as well as in Reno and Lake Tahoe) are centered on large casinos. The three largest casinos in Las Vegas are at MGM Grand, Riviera, and Excalibur. The games played in the casinos are slots, blackjack, baccarat, craps, roulette, keno, video poker, Let It Ride, Caribbean Stud, wheel of fortune, and race and sports betting. Admission to the casinos is free, but plan to spend, spend, spend once you enter. Most larger casinos give free gaming lessons, usually during the slower weekday morning hours. Slot machines are by far the favorite game; thanks to progressive computer-linked slot jackpots, such as Megabucks and Quartermania, wins have gone into the millions.

With more than 60 major hotel-casinos competing for visitors and their dollars, most try to separate themselves from the pack with some distinguishing characteristic. Those with the most imaginative themes or attractive particulars are listed below.

Binion's Horseshoe (✉ 128 E. Fremont St., ☎ 702/382–1600) is home of the World Series of Poker, the world's highest-paying gambling tournament, and attracts some of the world's largest wagers with its no-limit gambling.

Caesars Palace (✉ 3570 Las Vegas Blvd. S, ☎ 702/731–7110), a sprawling ersatz temple for serious gamblers with money to burn, lays on the ancient-Rome theme, complete with toga-clad cocktail waitresses and Cleopatra's Barge lounge.

Circus Circus (✉ 2880 Las Vegas Blvd. S, ☎ 702/734–0410) casino is under a pink-and-white big top and takes on the hurly-burly atmosphere of a three-ring circus. For such a huge hotel, it has surprisingly low minimums, and its slot club is the only one in town that gives a cash rebate for blackjack play.

Desert Inn (✉ 3145 Las Vegas Blvd. S, ☎ 702/733–4444) is small, relaxed, elegant, and—best of all—quiet, appealing to the most exclusive clientele in town.

Excalibur (✉ 3850 Las Vegas Blvd. S, ☎ 702/597–7777) recalls the days of King Arthur. The casino is cavernous and cacophonous—with 2,630 slot machines, what else could it be?

Flamingo Hilton (✉ 3555 Las Vegas Blvd. S, ☎ 702/733–3111) bears no resemblance to the "classy little joint" built by Bugsy Siegel in 1946. The splendiferous pink-flamingo theme is rampant in the huge casino, which is typical of a center-Strip megaresort: sprawling, raucous, and all the $5 minimum tables jammed with players. Video poker payouts are good, and the Flamingo is known for offering its slot club members free rooms throughout the year.

Golden Nugget (✉ 129 E. Fremont St., ☎ 702/385–7111) is more Hollywood than Vegas, with white marble, gold leaf, and gold-plated elevators. The casino combines high Strip class with low downtown minimums.

Jackie Gaughan's Plaza (✉ 1 N. Main St., ☎ 702/386–2110) is low-roller heaven, with penny slots, full-pay nickel video poker, 25¢ craps, and $2 blackjack galore.

Las Vegas Hilton (✉ 3000 W. Paradise Rd., ☎ 702/732–5111) has a NASA-esque sports book, with 46 video screens, and the imaginative new Space Quest casino.

Luxor (✉ 3900 Las Vegas Blvd. S, ☎ 702/262–4000) re-creates ancient Egypt with its 29-million-cubic-ft pyramid. The casino is roomy, regal, and round, with surprisingly fresh air throughout.

MGM Grand (✉ 3805 Las Vegas Blvd. S, ☎ 702/891–1111) is the world's second-largest casino, with 3,500 slot machines, more than 100 gaming tables, and a Hollywood entertainment theme.

The Mirage (✉ 3400 Las Vegas Blvd. S, ☎ 702/791–7111) transports you to the South Seas, with thatch-roof gaming areas and tropical plants and flowers flanking an indoor stream and pond. The high-roller slot area has machines that take $500 tokens.

Tropicana (✉ 3801 Las Vegas Blvd. S, ☎ 702/739–2222) is lush and tropical, with a stunning pool area complete with swim-up blackjack in summer.

Getting Married in Las Vegas

Nevada is one of the easiest—and least-expensive—states in which to get married. There is no blood test or waiting period; all you need is a license ($35) from the **Marriage License Bureau** (✉ 200 S. 3rd St., ☎ 702/455–4415), and you're ready to go. In Las Vegas there are about 25 chapels along the Strip, not including the numerous chapels in the hotel-casinos. (☞ Exploring Las Vegas, *above*). Services start at around $50.

Dining

Las Vegas has become the USA's hottest restaurant market. On average, a new dining establishment opens here every week. Dining options range from elegant gourmet and exotic ethnic meals to all-you-can-eat buffets, for which the city is justly famous. Most hotels have buffets at breakfast ($4–$5), lunch ($6–$8), and dinner ($8–$12). The cheapest buffet is at Circus Circus; the two best are at the Rio and Texas Station. Bally's has the best Sunday champagne brunch (the Sterling). For price ranges *see* Chart 1 (A) *in* On the Road with Fodor's.

$$$–$$$$ ★ ✕ **Palace Court.** The flagship restaurant of Caesars Palace is under a beautiful dome in a round room with greenery and floor-to-ceiling picture windows. The fare is classic French; chateaubriand is a specialty. ✉ *3570 Las Vegas Blvd. S,* ☎ *702/731–7547. Jacket and tie. AE, D, DC, MC, V.*

$$$ ✕ **Pamplemousse.** The loving creation of Georges LaForges, a former Las Vegas maître d', this restaurant looks like a little French country inn. Classic French food is served *sans* menu; the waiter recites the daily specials and their method of preparation. ✉ *400 E. Sahara Ave.,* ☎ *702/733–2066. Jacket required. AE, D, DC, MC, V. No lunch.*

$$–$$$ ✕ **The Broiler.** This is a good, popular, and fairly inexpensive steak house, with an excellent salad bar (including soups and desserts), as well as mesquite-grilled steaks, veal, and chicken. ✉ *Boulder Station, 4111 Boulder Hwy.,* ☎ *702/432–7777. AE, D, DC, MC, V. No lunch.*

$$–$$$ ★ ✕ **Mayflower Cuisinier.** Head to this off-Strip restaurant for creative Chinese dishes with Californian and Pan-Asian accents and an occasional French flair: pan-seared ostrich with brandy sauce, coconut-milk curry-chicken pasta, and Asian portobello mushroom burrito. ✉ *4750 W. Sahara Ave.,* ☎ *702/870–8432. AE, D, DC, MC, V.*

$$–$$$ ✕ **Second Street Grill.** Although you'll find steaks, lamb chops, and veal on the menu, seafood is the specialty; it's flown in fresh daily from Hawai'i. This restaurant has been around for years, but it's fairly unknown in the Las Vegas fine-dining firmament, so you can almost al-

ways get a reservation. ✉ *Fremont Hotel, 200 E. Fremont St.*, ☎ *702/385–3232. AE, D, DC, MC, V. No lunch.*

$$–$$$ ✕ **Top of the World.** Floor-to-ceiling windows at this airy eatery near the top of the 1,149-ft-tall Stratosphere Tower afford 360-degree views of the valley as the restaurant rotates. Continental fare is spiced up with a few twists: tequila and lime shrimp, spinach and wild mushroom salad, and the like. ✉ *Stratosphere Tower, 2000 Las Vegas Blvd. S,* ☎ *702/380–7731. AE, D, DC, MC, V. No lunch.*

$$ ✕ **Battista's Hole in the Wall.** Battista Locatelli, a former opera singer, roams his domain, which is a short walk from the Strip. Decorated with wine bottles, garlic, and celebrity photos, this Italian restaurant has lots of specials, with all the free wine you can drink. ✉ *4041 Audrie St.,* ☎ *702/732–1424. AE, D, DC, MC, V. No lunch.*

$$ ★ ✕ **Bertolini's.** This sidewalk café inside the Forum Shops at Caesars can be noisy, but the northern Italian fare is first rate. Order individual pizzas, soups, salads, and luscious gelato and sorbet. ✉ *3570 Las Vegas Blvd. S,* ☎ *702/735–4663. AE, DC, MC, V.*

$–$$ ✕ **Roberta's.** This is Las Vegas's most venerable "bargain gourmet" room, at the historic El Cortez downtown. You won't believe the prices, especially for a 16-ounce prime rib or a pound of king crab legs. ✉ *El Cortez, 600 E. Fremont St.,* ☎ *702/386–0692. AE, MC, V. No lunch.*

$–$$ ✕ **Viva Mercado's.** Don't let the shopping center location fool you: This is one of the most popular Mexican restaurants in town—and for good reason. The room is cozy, and the food is low-fat and creative, especially the house specials. ✉ *6182 W. Flamingo Rd.,* ☎ *702/871–8826. Reservations not accepted. AE, MC, V.*

$ ★ ✕ **Ralph's Diner.** The linoleum is black-and-white checkerboard; jukes on the tables play 1950s music; and daily blue-plate specials start at $3.95. The cooking is all-American and the soda fountain serves up old-fashioned malts, shakes, and splits. ✉ *Stardust Hotel, 3000 Las Vegas Blvd. S.,* ☎ *702/732–6580. Reservations not accepted. AE, D, DC, MC, V.*

Lodging

Las Vegas lodging ranges from virtual palaces to simple motels. The hotels tend to be a better bet for cleanliness and convenience; the motels, while a little frayed around the edges, can be great bargains. In general, lodging in Vegas is far less expensive than that at other major American resorts, though rates fluctuate widely according to supply and demand. The largest and most lavish hotels are on the Strip; downtown hotels are generally less expensive. The range we're quoting, generally, is from a standard room (during a regular weekday) to deluxe suites (on a busy weekend). For price ranges *see* Chart 2 (A) *in* On the Road with Fodor's.

$$–$$$$ ★ **Caesars Palace.** Caesars caters to an upscale clientele, with world-class service, lavish restaurants, and superstar entertainers like Diana Ross and David Copperfield. Its casino is full of fancy people making sizable wagers, but there are plenty of nickel slots too. Most guest rooms are opulent, even by Las Vegas standards, and many have Roman-style tubs. ✉ *3570 Las Vegas Blvd. S, 89109,* ☎ *702/731–7110 or 800/634–6661,* FAX *702/731–6636. 2,512 rooms. 9 restaurants, pools. AE, D, DC, MC, V.*

$$–$$$$ **Desert Inn.** Surrounded by a private golf course and offering suites, town houses, and even villas, this hotel is one of the town's classiest. The elegant rooms have a southwestern theme. ✉ *3145 Las Vegas Blvd. S, 89109,* ☎ *702/733–4444 or 800/634–6906,* FAX *702/733–4774. 715 rooms. 5 restaurants, health club. AE, D, DC, MC, V.*

$$–$$$$ **Las Vegas Hilton.** With 29 floors and three wings, this megasize hotel seems even larger because it sits next to the low-rise Convention Center; it's one of the most recognizable hotels in town. The rooms are large, and those on the higher floors have great views. A high-tech Star Trek simulator show opened in January 1998. *3000 Paradise Rd., 89109,* *702/732–5111 or 800/732–7117,* FAX *702/794–3611. 3,174 rooms. 11 restaurants, pool. AE, D, DC, MC, V.*

$$–$$$$ ★ **The Mirage.** This extravagant hotel, opened in 1989, launched the current building boom in Las Vegas—a boom that has lasted for 10 years and counting. It's the centerpiece of the Strip, still the standard by which all other new megaresorts are measured. With its lush tropical landscaping, minimal neon, efficient use of recycled water, rainforest dome, and exemplary service, the Mirage symbolizes the new Las Vegas. *3400 Las Vegas Blvd. S, 89109,* *702/791–7111 or 800/627–6667,* FAX *702/791–7446. 3,049 rooms. 8 restaurants, pool, exercise room. AE, D, DC, MC, V.*

$–$$$$ **Flamingo Hilton.** The first luxury hotel in Las Vegas, once surrounded only by desert, the Flamingo has been completely rebuilt over the years and is now the fifth-largest hotel in Las Vegas. With a timeshare tower, a lush 15-acre pool area and wildlife park (yes, there are flamingos), and very reasonable rates, it would still make Bugsy proud. *3555 Las Vegas Blvd. S, 89109,* *702/733–3111 or 800/732–2111,* FAX *702/733–3528. 3,530 rooms. 8 restaurants, pools. AE, D, DC, MC, V.*

$–$$$$ **Golden Nugget.** The largest and classiest joint in Glitter Gulch, the Nugget runs the gamut from traditional downtown bargains (dollar draft beer) to Strip-style fanciness (a segregated baccarat pit for high rollers). The lobby is all marble and etched glass; guest rooms reflect the same elegance. *129 E. Fremont St., 89101,* *702/385–7111 or 800/634–3454,* FAX *702/386–8362. 1,909 rooms. 5 restaurants, pool, health club. AE, D, DC, MC, V.*

$–$$$$ **MGM Grand.** This movie-theme megaresort is the largest in the world. Four emerald-green hotel towers bring to mind the *Wizard of Oz*; a 33-acre theme park re-creates Hollywood back lots with rides and performances. *3799 Las Vegas Blvd. S, 89119,* *702/891–1111 or 800/929–1111,* FAX *702/891–1030. 5,005 rooms. 10 restaurants, pool, health club. AE, D, DC, MC, V.*

$–$$$$ ★ **Rio Suite.** These four red-and-blue towers contain only suites. Ask for a unit on one of the top floors and on the east side, facing the Strip. In February 1997, the fourth expansion in six years added a 41-story tower that contains the most festive casino in town—singers, dancers, and jugglers all in Mardi Gras costumes perform in a Masquerade Show that features parade floats inching along a 950-ft track suspended from the high ceiling. *3700 W. Flamingo Rd. (at Valley View), 89109,* *702/252–7777 or 800/888–1808,* FAX *702/253–6090. 2,569 suites. 13 restaurants, pool, health club. AE, D, DC, MC, V.*

$$–$$$ **Bally's.** This is the only hotel in the city with two full-size showrooms: one for headliners and one for the long-running production show *Jubilee!* Many of the attractive guest rooms are suites, and some have round beds under mirrored ceilings. A $25 million elevated monorail links the MGM Grand and Bally's. *3645 Las Vegas Blvd. S, 89109,* *702/739–4111 or 800/634–3434,* FAX *702/739–4405. 2,832 rooms. 5 restaurants, pool, health club. AE, D, DC, MC, V.*

$–$$$ **Excalibur.** This pink-and-blue turreted castle is the third-largest resort hotel in Las Vegas. Many families come to experience its Renaissance theme, complete with a King Arthur's jousting tournament, medieval midway, and strolling minstrels, mimes, and musicians. *3850 Las Vegas Blvd. S,* *702/597–7777 or 800/937–7777,* FAX *702/597–7009. 4,032 rooms. 7 restaurants, pool. AE, D, DC, MC, V.*

$–$$$ **Harrah's Las Vegas.** In 1997 Harrah's replaced its signature riverboat facade with a more tasteful though nondescript design, as part of a $200 million expansion and renovation. However, it's still the flagship of Harrah's extensive national gambling fleet. The rooms are modest by Strip standards. ✉ *3475 Las Vegas Blvd. S, 89109,* ☎ *702/369–5000 or 800/634–6765,* FAX *702/369–5008. 2,700 rooms. 6 restaurants, pool, exercise room. AE, D, DC, MC, V.*

$–$$$ **Luxor.** This bronze-color pyramid-shape building recalls ancient Egypt with a sphinx out front and a replica of King Tut's tomb inside. "Inclinators" rise to the top floor at a 39-degree angle; the Egyptian theme continues in the large guest rooms. ✉ *3900 Las Vegas Blvd. S, 89119,* ☎ *702/262–4000 or 800/288–1000,* FAX *702/262–4454. 4,476 rooms. 7 restaurants, pool. AE, D, DC, MC, V.*

$–$$$ **Riviera.** One of the city's most famous and venerable hotels, the Riviera has one of the largest casinos in the world. The location is convenient to the upper Strip and the convention center. ✉ *2901 Las Vegas Blvd. S, 89109,* ☎ *702/734–5110 or 800/634–6753,* FAX *702/794–9663. 2,220 rooms. 5 restaurants, pool, health club. AE, D, DC, MC, V.*

$–$$$ **Sam's Town.** This friendly hotel outside town has an Old West theme that feels authentic because the place is so close to the desert. Some rooms have views of the desert and mountains; the inside-facing rooms overlook an 18-story courtyard complete with trees, creeks, and a waterfall. ✉ *5111 Boulder Hwy., 89122,* ☎ *702/456–7777 or 800/634–6371,* FAX *702/454–8014. 650 rooms. 5 restaurants, pool. AE, D, DC, MC, V.*

$–$$$ **Stardust.** From its first incarnation as a motor hotel to its more recent 32-story tower, the Stardust has been one of the best-known hotels on the Strip. The tower rooms—large and attractive—are almost always a bargain. ✉ *3000 Las Vegas Blvd. S, 89109,* ☎ *702/732–6111 or 800/634–6757,* FAX *702/732–6296. 2,500 rooms. 6 restaurants, pool, health club. AE, D, DC, MC, V.*

$–$$$ **Treasure Island.** The hotel's theme is loosely based on Robert Louis Stevenson's novel, and the landscaping and decor are ersatz South Seas. There's a re-created 18th-century pirate village and a monorail to the Mirage. ✉ *3300 Las Vegas Blvd. S, 89109,* ☎ *702/894–7111 or 800/944–7444,* FAX *702/894–7446. 2,912 rooms. 5 restaurants, pool, health club. AE, D, DC, MC, V.*

$–$$$ **Tropicana.** Two high-rise towers loom above beautiful grounds, complete with waterfalls and swans. Rooms have a tropical theme, with bamboo and pastels. ✉ *3801 Las Vegas Blvd. S, 89109,* ☎ *702/739–2222 or 800/634–4000,* FAX *702/739–2469. 1,912 rooms. 6 restaurants, pools, health club. AE, D, DC, MC, V.*

$–$$ **Sahara.** Like many of its neighbors, the Sahara began as a small motor hotel and built itself up by adding towers. It finally expanded its casino in 1997, though it will still serve as a business hotel for the convention center down the street. Tower rooms are large, and those that face south overlook the Strip. ✉ *2535 Las Vegas Blvd. S, 89109,* ☎ *702/737–2111 or 800/634–6666,* FAX *702/791–2027. 1,710 rooms. 5 restaurants, health club. AE, D, DC, MC, V.*

$ **Jackie Gaughan's Plaza.** This casino-hotel was built on the original site of the Union Pacific train station; the front-facing rooms look down at Glitter Gulch, the back at the railroad yards. Rooms are done in light mauve tones. ✉ *1 Main St., 89101,* ☎ *702/386–2110 or 800/634–6575,* FAX *702/382–8281. 1,037 rooms. 3 restaurants, pool. AE, D, DC, MC, V.*

$ **Circus Circus.** Catering primarily to families with children, the hotel has painted circus tents in the hallways and a generally chaotic atmosphere. The brightly colored rooms (red carpets and chairs; red-, pink-, and blue-striped wallpaper) are small but clean. ✉ *2880 Las Vegas Blvd. S, 89109,* ☎ *702/734–0410 or 800/634–3450,* FAX *702/734–2268. 3,774 rooms. 7 restaurants, pools. AE, D, DC, MC, V.*

Motels

Days Inn–Town Hall (✉ 4155 Koval La., 89109, ☎ 702/731–2111 or 800/634–6541, FAX 702/731–1113), 360 rooms, restaurant, pool; *$.* **Motel 6** (✉ 195 E. Tropicana Ave., 89109, ☎ 702/798–0728, FAX 702/798–5657), 877 rooms, pools; *$.* **Westward Ho** (✉ 2900 Las Vegas Blvd. S, 89109, ☎ 702/731–2900 or 800/634–6651, FAX 702/731–6154), 1,000 rooms, restaurant, pools; *$.*

Nightlife and the Arts

Nightlife

Perhaps no other city in America—or even the world—has more to do at night than Las Vegas.

SHOW

Hotel showrooms seat from several hundred to 2,000. Most are luxurious and intimate, with few, if any, bad seats. The old-style seating system involves arriving early and tipping the maître d' or captain. The new trend is reserved seating, which eliminates the waiting and "survival of the tippest." When a show is expected to sell out, hotel guests are given ticket preference.

Showrooms present four main types of entertainment: headliner shows, such as David Copperfield, Tom Jones, and Liza Minnelli; big production shows, such as Bally's *Jubilee!* or the Tropicana's *Folies Bergères,* which include elaborate song-and-dance numbers, smaller specialty acts, and topless showgirls; small production shows, with song and dance on a smaller scale, such as *Forever Plaid* at the Flamingo Hilton; and the ubiquitous lounge shows, where pop bands play dance music and the only admission is the purchase of a drink or two.

The major hotels' entertainment venues are as follows: **Bally's,** headliners and large production show; **Caesars Palace,** headliners; **Excalibur,** large production show; **Flamingo Hilton,** large and small production shows; **Harrah's Las Vegas,** small production show; **Imperial Palace,** small production show; **MGM Grand,** headliners and large production shows; **Mirage,** large production show; **Rio Suite,** small production show; **Riviera,** large and small production shows; **Stardust,** large production show; **Desert Inn,** headliners; **Treasure Island,** Cirque du Soleil; **Tropicana,** large production show. *See* Exploring Las Vegas *and* Lodging (both *above*) for addresses and phone numbers.

COMEDY CLUBS

MGM Grand has **Catch a Rising Star.** Harrah's has the **Improv.** The Tropicana has the **Comedy Stop.** The Riviera has the **Comedy Club.**

The Arts

Most arts events in Las Vegas are associated with the **University of Nevada, Las Vegas** (☎ 702/895–3011). For additional information call the **Allied Arts Council** (☎ 702/731–5419).

Outdoor Activities and Sports

Spectator Sports

Boxing: Caesars Palace and **MGM Grand** present championship bouts.**Golf: PGA Las Vegas Invitational** (✉ Desert Inn, ☎ 702/382–6616); October. **Rodeo: National Finals Rodeo** (✉ Thomas Mack Center, University of Nevada, ☎ 702/731–2115).

Shopping

Las Vegas's best shopping is on the Strip at the **Fashion Show Mall** (✉ 3200 Las Vegas Blvd. S, ☎ 702/369–8382), a collection of 150 shops and department stores, including Saks Fifth Avenue and Neiman Marcus. **Forum Shops at Caesars** (✉ 3570 Las Vegas Blvd. S, ☎ 702/893–4800), a complex of 135 specialty stores adjoining Caesars Palace, dazzles shoppers with two replicated Roman markets, complete with columns, piazzas, fountains, and a simulated-sky ceiling. You'll find the likes of Gucci, Ann Taylor, the Museum Company, and the Warner Bros. Studio Store alongside several popular restaurants. **Boulevard Mall** (✉ 3528 S. Maryland Pkwy., ☎ 702/735–8268), about 3 mi from the Strip, is the largest shopping mall in Nevada. **Meadows Mall** (✉ 4300 Meadows La., ☎ 702/878–4849) is on the northwest side of town and has a big merry-go-round for kids. **Gamblers General Store** (✉ 800 S. Main St., ☎ 702/382–9903) carries all manner of gambling paraphernalia.

RENO

Reno, once the gambling and divorce capital of the country, is smaller, less crowded, friendlier, and prettier than Las Vegas. Established in 1859 as a trading station at a bridge over the Truckee River, Reno grew along with the silver mines of nearby Virginia City (starting in 1860), the railroad (which gave Reno its name in 1868), and gambling (legalized in 1931). Today Reno is getting a boost from the National Bowling Stadium—the only one of its kind in the country—as well as the 1,700-room Silver Legacy downtown.

Visitor Information

Reno-Sparks Convention and Visitors Authority (✉ 4590 S. Virginia St., Reno 89502, ☎ 702/827–7600 or 800/367–7366).

Arriving and Departing

By Bus

Greyhound Lines (✉ 155 Stevenson St., ☎ 702/322–2970 or 800/231–2222).

By Car

The major highways leading to Reno are I–80 (east–west) and U.S. 395 (north–south).

By Plane

Reno-Tahoe International Airport (☎ 702/328–6400), served by national and regional airlines, is on the east side of the city, just minutes from downtown.

By Train

Amtrak (✉ 135 E. Commercial Row, ☎ 702/329–8638 or 800/872–7245).

Getting Around Reno

Reno is such a small city that the best way to get around is on foot or by taxi. Taxis are easily hired at the airport and in front of the major hotels; the main taxi firms are **Reno-Sparks Cab Co.** (☎ 702/333–3333), **Whittlesea Checker** (☎ 702/322–2222), and **Yellow** (☎ 702/355–5555). Rental-car agencies are at the airport. **Reno Citifare** (☎ 702/348–7433) provides local bus service. Many large hotels have courtesy buses on call.

Exploring Reno

One advantage Reno has over Las Vegas is weather: Its summer temperatures are much more agreeable and therefore much more pleasant for strolling. The city's focal point is the famous Reno Arch, a sign over the upper end of Virginia Street proclaiming it "The Biggest Little City in the World."

As in Las Vegas, gambling is a favorite pastime. Although not as garish as their Vegas counterparts, Reno's casinos still offer plenty of glitter and glitz. With the exception of the Reno Hilton, Peppermill, Atlantis, and John Ascuaga's Nugget, they are crowded into five square blocks downtown. Some of the better casinos are listed below.

Circus Circus (✉ 500 N. Sierra St., ☎ 702/329–0711 or 800/648–5010), marked by a neon clown sucking a lollipop, is the best stop for families with children. Complete with clowns, games, fun-house mirrors, and circus acts, the midway on the mezzanine above the casino floor is open from 10 AM to midnight.

Club Cal-Neva (✉ 38 E. 2nd St., ☎ 702/323–1046) is the best place in town to gamble, with low limits and optimal rules.

Eldorado (✉ 345 N. Virginia St., ☎ 702/786–5700) is an action-packed casino, with tons of slots and good bar-top video poker, and one of the largest roulette tables around.

Flamingo Hilton (✉ 255 N. Sierra St., ☎ 702/322–1111 or 800/648–4882) reproduces its Vegas counterpart, complete with a gigantic, neon pink-feathered flamingo.

Harrah's (✉ 219 N. Center St., ☎ 702/786–3232 or 800/648–3773) debuted in 1937 as the Tango Club and now occupies two city blocks, with a sprawling casino, race and sports book, and arcade; it also has a 29-story Hampton Inn annex. Minimums are low and service is friendly.

Silver Legacy (✉ 407 N. Virginia St., ☎ 702/329–4777) is a classy Victorian–themed casino with a 120-ft-tall mining rig that mints silver dollar tokens.

Four casinos lie outside the downtown area. **Reno Hilton** (✉ 2500 E. 2nd St., ☎ 702/789–2000 or 800/648–5080), with 100,000 square ft, is the largest casino in Reno. **Peppermill** (✉ 2707 S. Virginia St., ☎ 702/826–2121 or 800/648–6992) is the gaudiest, glitziest, and noisiest. **Atlantis** (✉ 3800 S. Virginia St., ☎ 702/825–4700 or 800/723–6500) has the best buffet in Reno. And **John Ascuaga's Nugget** (✉ 1100 Nugget Ave., Sparks, ☎ 702/356–3300 or 800/648–1177) doubled its room count in 1997 by adding a 1,000-room tower; a new, small casino and a restaurant were part of the package.

Besides the hotel-casinos, Reno has a number of cultural and family-friendly attractions.On the University of Nevada campus, the sleekly designed **Fleischmann Planetarium** (✉ 1600 N. Virginia St., ☎ 702/784–4811; 🎟 free) has films and astronomy presentations. Mining exhibits and Native American artifacts are on display at the **Nevada Historical Society** (✉ 1650 N. Virginia St., ☎ 702/688–1190; 🎟 free). The **Nevada Museum of Art** (✉ 160 W. Liberty St., ☎ 702/329–3333; 🎟 $3), the state's largest art museum, has changing exhibits. More than 220 antique and classic automobiles, including an Elvis Presley Cadillac, are on display at the **National Automobile Museum** (✉ Mill and Lake Sts., ☎ 702/333–9300; 🎟 $7.50).

Wilbur D. May Great Basin Adventure (✉ 1502 Washington St., ☎ 702/785–4153; 🎫 $2.50), in Rancho San Rafael Park, has a mining exhibit that traces the evolution of the Great Basin; also here are a petting zoo, flume ride, and a touch-and-feel discovery room. In Sparks, the family amusement park **Wild Island** (✉ 250 Wild Island Ct., ☎ 702/331–9453; 🎫 call for prices) includes a water park; a 36-hole minigolf course; Indy, sprint, and bumper cars; and a state-of-the-art video arcade.

The always-festive **Downtown River Walk** (✉ S. Virginia St. and the river, ☎ 702/334–2077) is often the location for special events featuring street performers, musicians, dancers, food, art displays, and games. **Victorian Square** (✉ Victorian Ave. between Rock and Pyramid) is fringed by restored turn-of-the-century houses and Victorian-dressed casinos and storefronts; a bandstand-gazebo is the focal point for the many festivals held here.

Outside Reno

Only 25 mi from Reno (U.S. 395 south to Rte. 341), **Virginia City** was once the largest population center in Nevada, with more than 20,000 residents, 110 saloons, and one church. The Comstock Lode, one of the largest gold and silver deposits ever discovered, was responsible for Virginia City's boom (1860–80). Today it's one of the liveliest and most authentically maintained historic mining towns in the West. Little has changed here in more than 100 years.

Visitor Information

For information contact the **Virginia City Chamber of Commerce** (✉ C St. across from the post office; Box 464, 89440, ☎ 702/847–0311).

You can still belly up to the grand mahogany bar and hear honky-tonk piano music at the **Bucket of Blood** (☎ 702/847–0322) saloon on C Street. The lavish interiors of **Mackay Mansion** (✉ 129 D St., ☎ 702/847–0173; 🎫 $3) and the **Castle** (✉ B St. just south of Taylor, ☎ no phone; 🎫 $3) offer a glimpse into the past, with such adornments as Oriental rugs, Italian marble, and Brussels lace, as well as table settings made from the silver mined beneath these houses. **Virginia & Truckee Railroad** (✉ Washington and F Sts., ☎ 702/847–0380; 🎫 $5) takes visitors on historic steam-powered locomotives through the Comstock mining region. Virginia City's most famous resident was Mark Twain, who lived here from 1861 to 1864 while working as a reporter for the *Territorial Enterprise;* the **Mark Twain Museum** (✉ 47 S. C St., ☎ 702/847–0525; 🎫 $1) occupies the newspaper's pressroom and exhibits 19th-century printing equipment.

South of Virginia City is **Carson City,** the state capital. The **Carson City Chamber of Commerce** (✉ 1900 S. Carson St., ☎ 702/882–1565) has information on the town's attractions.

The **Nevada State Museum** (✉ 600 N. Carson St., ☎ 702/687–4811; 🎫 $3), once a U.S. mint, is packed with exhibits on subjects like Nevada natural history, the early mining days, antique gaming devices, and willow baskets woven by Washoe artists. The **Nevada State Railroad Museum** (✉ 2180 S. Carson St., ☎ 702/687–6953; 🎫 $2) has an extensive collection of historical passenger and freight cars and two restored Virginia & Truckee trains.

Genoa, the oldest settlement in Nevada, is a quaint Victorian town about 20 mi south of Carson City, just west of U.S. 395. **Mormon Station State Historic Park** (✉ Foothill Rd. and Genoa La., ☎ 702/687–4379; 🎫 free) contains an early log cabin and Mormon artifacts. **Walley's Hot**

Springs Resort (✉ 2001 Foothill Rd., ☎ 702/782–8155) has hot mineral pools dating from 1862.

Dining

Reno dining options range from plush gourmet restaurants and extensive hotel buffets to interesting little eateries scattered around the city. As in Las Vegas, the best-value dining options are the hotel-casino breakfast, lunch, and dinner buffets. Favorite buffets are at the **Atlantis, John Ascuaga's Nugget** (☞ Exploring Reno, *above*), and the **Eldorado** (☞ Lodging, *below*). For price ranges *see* Chart 1 (B) *in* On the Road with Fodor's.

$$$$ ✕ **19th Hole.** This ritzy restaurant on the Lakeridge Golf Course has a great view of the city and nearby mountains and serves well-prepared American and Continental food. ✉ *1200 Razorback Rd.,* ☎ *702/825–1250. D, MC, V.*

$$$–$$$$ ✕ **Pimparel's La Table Francaise.** In a converted house off the beaten track, Pimparel's specializes in award-winning French provincial cuisine. It's a locals' favorite for special occasions. ✉ *3065 W. 4th St.,* ☎ *702/323–3200. AE, D, DC, MC, V. No lunch.*

$$$–$$$$ ✕ **Harrah's Steak House.** The hotel-casino's dark and romantic restaurant has been serving prime beef and fresh seafood since 1967. ✉ *219 N. Center St.,* ☎ *702/786–3232. AE, D, DC, MC, V.*

$$$–$$$$ ✕ **La Strada.** This excellent northern Italian restaurant is upstairs from the Eldorado Casino. The pastas and sauces are homemade, and the gourmet pizzas bake in a wood-fired oven. ✉ *345 N. Virginia St.,* ☎ *702/786–5700. AE, D, DC, MC, V. No lunch.*

$$–$$$ ✕ **Café de Thai.** The soups, salads, stir-fry dishes, and satay are all divine, concocted by a Thai chef trained at the Culinary Institute of America. ✉ *3314 S. McCarran,* ☎ *702/829–8424. MC, V.*

$$–$$$ ✕ **John A's Oyster Bar.** This nautically themed restaurant and bar serves the best steamers, pan roasts, cioppino, chowder, shrimp Louie, and cocktails this side of Fisherman's Wharf. ✉ *1100 Nugget Ave., Sparks,* ☎ *702/356–3300. AE, D, DC, MC, V.*

$$ ✕ **Bertha Miranda's Mexican Restaurant.** Begun as a hole-in-the-wall, this has grown into a highly successful establishment. The food is made fresh by Bertha's family. Be sure to try the salsa. ✉ *336 Mill St.,* ☎ *702/786–9697. MC, V.*

$$ ✕ **Louis' Basque Corner.** Basque shepherds once populated northern Nevada. You can sample the Basque legacy at this family-style restaurant, which specializes in oxtail, lamb, and tongue. ✉ *301 E. 4th St.,* ☎ *702/323–7203. AE, DC, MC, V.*

$–$$ ✕ **Blue Heron.** You won't find many natural-foods restaurants in this meat-and-potatoes state, but here is one. You can choose among grains, veggies, tofu and tempeh dishes, and even macrobiotic meals. ✉ *1091 S. Virginia St.,* ☎ *702/786–4110. DC, MC, V.*

$–$$ ✕ **Nugget Diner.** Think classic Americana diner: Seating is on stools at front and back counters. The Awful Awful Burger is renowned, as is the prime rib. ✉ *Nugget Casino, 233 N. Virginia St.,* ☎ *702/323–0716. MC, V.*

Lodging

Most of Reno's hotels are downtown. For price ranges *see* Chart 2 (B) *in* On the Road with Fodor's.

$$$–$$$$ 🏨 **Harrah's.** This is one of the most luxurious hotels in downtown Reno. Large guest rooms decorated in blues and mauves overlook downtown and the entire mountain-ringed valley. ✉ *219 N. Center St., 89501,*

☎ 702/786–3232 or 800/648–3773, FAX 702/788–2815. 565 rooms. 6 restaurants, pool, health club. AE, MC, V.

$$–$$$$ 🏨 **Flamingo Hilton.** This sister hotel of the Las Vegas and Laughlin Flamingos sports a million-dollar sign and a 21-story tower. The guest rooms facing west have a nice view of the mountains. ✉ *255 N. Sierra St., 89501,* ☎ *702/322–1111 or 800/648–4822,* FAX *702/322–1111. 604 rooms. 4 restaurants. AE, D, DC, MC, V.*

$$–$$$$ 🏨 **Reno Hilton.** Formerly Bally's, this 27-story hotel near the airport is Nevada's largest hotel north of Las Vegas. In fact, almost everything here is the area's largest: the buffet, race and sports books, showroom, convention facilities, bowling alley, arcade, wedding chapel, driving range, and RV park. ✉ *2500 E. 2nd St., 89595,* ☎ *702/789–2000 or 800/648–5080,* FAX *702/789–2418. 2,001 rooms. 5 restaurants, pool, health club. AE, D, DC, MC, V.*

$–$$$$ 🏨 **Eldorado.** Known for its fine food and attention to detail, the Eldorado recently completed an all-suites tower. Rooms overlook the mountains. ✉ *345 N. Virginia St., 89501,* ☎ *702/786–5700 or 800/648–5966,* FAX *702/322–7124. 836 rooms. 8 restaurants, pool, spa. AE, D, DC, MC, V.*

$–$$$$ 🏨 **Peppermill.** Three miles from downtown, this is the home of Reno's most colorful casino, but its rooms are plush and sedate. ✉ *2707 S. Virginia St., 89502,* ☎ *702/826–2121 or 800/648–6992,* FAX *702/826–5205. 1,070 rooms. 5 restaurants, pool, health club. AE, D, DC, MC, V.*

$–$$$$ 🏨 **Silver Legacy.** Opened in 1995, this two-tower Las Vegas–style megaresort centers on a 120-ft-tall mining machine that coins dollar tokens. Skywalks connect to Circus Circus and Eldorado. ✉ *407 N. Virginia St., 89501,* ☎ *702/329–4777 or 800/687–8733. 1,700 rooms. 5 restaurants. AE, D, DC, MC, V.*

$–$$$ 🏨 **John Ascuaga's Nugget.** This casino-hotel in neighboring Sparks offers some of the largest and most luxurious rooms around—as well as a rare indoor pool. A 1,000-room tower was completed in early 1997. ✉ *1100 Nugget Ave., Sparks 89431,* ☎ *702/356–3300 or 800/648–1177,* FAX *702/356–3434. 1,983 rooms. 7 restaurants, pool. AE, D, DC, MC, V.*

$–$$ 🏨 **Circus Circus.** This smaller version of the giant Las Vegas hotel has the same family-oriented atmosphere. The rooms, though small and garish, are good value—when you can get one. ✉ *500 N. Sierra St., 89503,* ☎ *702/329–0711 or 800/648–5010,* FAX *702/329–0599. 1,625 rooms. 3 restaurants. AE, DC, MC, V.*

$–$$ 🏨 **Comstock.** The lobby and casino have an Old West theme; spectacular neon lights simulate fireworks exploding across the exterior tower walls. The Victorian-style rooms are small, with city or mountain views. ✉ *200 W. 2nd St., 89501,* ☎ *702/329–1880 or 800/648–4866,* FAX *702/348–0539. 310 rooms. 3 restaurants, pool, health club. MC, V.*

Nightlife and the Arts

Nightlife

As in Las Vegas, Reno area nightlife breaks down into four categories: headliners, big production shows, small production shows, and lounge acts. Options at the major Reno hotels follow; for addresses and phone numbers, *see* Lodging, *above.* **Circus Circus** has continual circus acts. **Harrah's Reno** has headliners and small production shows. Mostly country-and-western headliners play at **John Ascuaga's Nugget. Reno Hilton** has headliners, a large production show, and a comedy club.

The Arts

Most of the arts in Reno—such as the **Nevada Festival Ballet** (☎ 702/785–7915), the **Nevada Opera Association** (☎ 702/786–4046), the

Reno Philharmonic (☏ 702/323–6393), and the **Performing Arts Series** (☏ 702/348–9413)—center on the **University of Nevada, Reno** (☏ 702/784–1110).

Shopping

The **Park Lane Mall** (✉ 310 E. Plumb La., ☏ 702/825–9452) is the cozier of Reno's two indoor shopping centers; check out the Made in Nevada store. The **Meadowood Mall** (✉ Virginia St. at McCarran Blvd., ☏ 702/827–8450) is the newer, more spacious, and upscale Reno mall. **AAA Slots of Fun** (✉ 11 E. Plaza, ☏ 702/324–7711) has a large selection of new and used slot and video poker machines for sale.

LAKE TAHOE

Southwest of Reno, Lake Tahoe's vast expanse of crystal-blue water surrounded by rugged peaks is a playground for residents and visitors. Half in Nevada and half in California, it is the largest alpine lake in North America, 22 mi long and 12 mi wide. The region is known for outstanding skiing in winter; boating, fishing, and mountain sports in summer; and casino entertainment year-round.

Visitor Information

Tahoe-Douglas Chamber of Commerce (✉ U.S. 50 at the Round Hill Shopping Center, Box 7139, Stateline 89449, ☏ 702/588–4591). **Incline Village/Crystal Bay Visitors and Convention Bureau** (✉ 969 Tahoe Blvd., Incline Village 89451-9508, ☏ 702/832–1606 or 800/468–2463).

Arriving and Departing

By Car

From Reno take U.S. 395S through Carson City to U.S. 50, which leads to South Lake Tahoe; U.S. 395S to Route 431 leads to North Lake Tahoe.

By Plane

The closest major airport to Lake Tahoe is **Reno-Tahoe International Airport** (☞ Reno, *above*). No regularly scheduled commercial flights serve the **Lake Tahoe Airport** (☏ 916/542–6180), near Stateline.

Exploring Lake Tahoe

A scenic drive circling Lake Tahoe (Routes 28 and 89) affords stunning lake, forest, and mountain vistas. You also can explore the lake aboard the **MS *Dixie II*** (✉ Zephyr Cove, ☏ 702/588–3508; 🎫 $14–$38). **Crystal Bay,** the northernmost community on the Nevada side, has a small-town, outdoorsy feel, along with several casinos.

Affluent **Incline Village,** 2 mi east of Crystal Bay, has lakeshore residences, weekend condos, and inviting shopping areas. South of Incline Village, the **Ponderosa Ranch** (✉ Rte. 28, ☏ 702/831–0691; 🎫 $6.50–$8.50) is a Hollywood-style western "town" based on the TV series *Bonanza*. The entire attraction is open from early May through October, but there's scaled-back access (they open the ranch house, where the gift shop is) through the winter.

At the south end of the lake are the neon signs of **Stateline,** where four towering and two low-rise casinos cluster in two blocks. Across the border in California is **South Lake Tahoe,** the most populous town on the lake. Ski Run Boulevard takes you southeast to the **Heavenly Ski**

Area (☎ 702/586–7000; $12), where the tram lifts you to fantastic skiing in winter and unbeatable views over the water year-round.

Dining and Lodging

For price ranges *see* Charts 1 (B) and 2 (B) *in* On the Road with Fodor's.

Incline Village

$$$$ ✕ **Sage Room Steak House.** A historic landmark in Lake Tahoe, this romantic restaurant is a descendant of the Wagon Wheel Saloon and Gambling Hall, the beginning of what was to become Harvey's Resort. Sautéed prawns Mediterranean are excellent. ✉ *Harvey's Resort Hotel/Casino, U.S. 50,* ☎ *702/588–2411. AE, D, DC, MC, V.*

$$$$ ✕ **The Summit.** The view is specatular from this 16th-floor restaurant. The creative menu includes artfully presented salads, seafood entrées, and decadent desserts. ✉ *Harrah's Casino/Hotel Lake Tahoe, U.S. 50,* ☎ *702/588–6611. AE, D, DC, MC, V.*

$$$–$$$$ ✕ **Lone Eagle Grille.** This restaurant in the Hyatt Regency Hotel has a fantastic view of the lake. Specialties include duck, fish, and steak; there's a salad-and-dessert buffet. ✉ *Country Club Dr. at Lakeshore,* ☎ *702/831–1111. AE, D, DC, MC, V.*

$$–$$$ ✕ **Azzara's.** This typical trattoria serves excellent food—a dozen different pasta dishes, along with pizza, chicken, lamb, veal, and shrimp—with understated elegance. ✉ *930 Tahoe Blvd.,* ☎ *702/831–0346. AE, MC, V. No lunch.*

Stateline

$$–$$$$ ✕ **El Vaquero.** Wrought iron, a fountain, and tiles give this restaurant an authentic Old Mexico feel. Fare is traditional Mexican. ✉ *Harvey's Resort Hotel/Casino, U.S. 50,* ☎ *702/588–2411. AE, D, DC, MC, V.*

$$–$$$$ ✕ **Empress Court.** Plush velvet booths and etched-glass partitions provide the setting for traditional Chinese cuisine. The grilled-squab salad is a standout dish. ✉ *Caesars Tahoe, U.S. 50,* ☎ *702/588–3515. AE, DC, MC, V. No lunch.*

$ ✕ **The Forest.** On the 18th floor of Harrah's, this has the best view of any buffet in Nevada. The interior simulates a forest. ✉ *Harrah's Casino/Hotel Lake Tahoe, U.S. 50,* ☎ *702/588–6611. Reservations not accepted. AE, DC, MC, V.*

$$$$ 🏨 **Caesars Tahoe.** Once you negotiate the lobby stairs and casino areas, you'll find hallways with faux Corinthian columns and plush rooms in fantasyland color schemes, such as hot pink with mint green. The indoor pool has a waterfall and swim tunnel. ✉ *U.S. 50 (Box 5800), 89449,* ☎ *702/588–3515 or 800/648–3353,* FAX *702/586–2050. 440 rooms. 5 restaurants, pool, health club. AE, D, DC, MC, V.*

$$$$ ★ 🏨 **Harrah's Casino/Hotel Lake Tahoe.** The rooms are large and comfortable, and all have two full bathrooms, each complete with telephone and TV. Most rooms also have excellent views of the lake and the mountains. ✉ *U.S. 50 (Box 8), 89449,* ☎ *702/588–6606 or 800/648–3773,* FAX *702/586–6607. 533 rooms. 7 restaurants, indoor pool, health club. AE, DC, MC, V.*

$$$$ 🏨 **Harvey's Resort Hotel/Casino.** This family-owned hotel is Lake Tahoe's largest resort. Rooms have a traditional American style. Most have a view of the lake and the mountains. ✉ *U.S. 50 (Box 128), 89449,* ☎ *702/588–2411 or 800/648–3361,* FAX *702/588–6643. 740 rooms. 8 restaurants. AE, D, DC, MC, V.*

$$$–$$$$ 🏨 **Hyatt Regency Lake Tahoe.** Rooms are large and attractive, with warm color schemes and lake views. Amenities include a private beach, water sports, Camp Hyatt for kids, and a forest-theme casino. ✉ *Country Club Dr. at Lakeshore, Incline Village 89450,* ☎ *702/832–1234 or*

800/233–1234, FAX 702/831–7508. 460 rooms. 3 restaurants, pool, health club. AE, DC, MC, V.

Nightlife

Lake Tahoe nightlife centers on the top-name entertainment and production shows at the casino-hotels. **Caesars Tahoe** and **Harrah's** (☞ Dining and Lodging, *above*) both present headliners.

Outdoor Activities and Sports

Fishing

The lake is renowned for mighty Macinkaw and rainbow trout. Nonresident fishing permits are available at most sporting goods stores. For more information call the **Department of Wildlife** (☎ 702/688–1500).

Golf

Edgewood at Tahoe (✉ Stateline, ☎ 702/588–3566) has 18 holes. **Glenbrook Golf Course** (✉ Glenbrook, ☎ 702/749–5201) has nine holes. **Incline Village Championship Golf Course** (✉ 955 Fairway Blvd., ☎ 702/832–1144) has 18 holes. **Incline Village Executive Course** (✉ 690 Wilson Way, ☎ 702/832–1150) has 18 holes.

Hiking

More than 250 mi of hiking trails traverse the area, many through high mountain passes and along streams and meadows with sweeping views. Contact the **U.S. Forest Service** (☎ 916/573–2600) for information.

Ski Areas

Lake Tahoe has more than 15 world-class downhill resorts and nearly a dozen cross-country skiing centers—all within an hour of one another. Elevations range from 6,000 to 10,000 ft, with vertical drops up to nearly 4,000 ft. More than 150 lifts operate during the season, which usually lasts from November through May.

Cross-Country

Diamond Peak (✉ 1210 Ski Way, Incline Village 89450, ☎ 702/832–1177) has 22 mi of groomed high-elevation track with skating lanes.

Downhill

Diamond Peak (☞ *above*) has seven lifts, 29 runs, and a 1,840-ft vertical drop. **Heavenly Ski Area** (✉ Box 2180, Stateline 89449, ☎ 702/586–7000 or 800/243–2836), straddling the Nevada-California border, has 25 lifts, 71 trails (including the longest run in Tahoe), and a 3,600-ft drop. **Mt. Rose** (✉ 22222 Mt. Rose Hwy., Reno 89511, ☎ 702/849–0704) has one of the highest base elevations in the area, with unequaled powder skiing, five lifts, 41 runs, and a 1,440-ft drop.

NEW MEXICO

Updated by Nancy Zimmerman

Capital	Santa Fe
Population	1,730,000
Motto	It Grows as It Goes
State Bird	Roadrunner
State Flower	Yucca
Postal Abbreviation	NM

Statewide Visitor Information

Visitor information to New Mexico can be obtained from the **New Mexico Department of Tourism** (✉ Lamy Bldg., 491 Old Santa Fe Trail, Santa Fe 87503, ☎ 505/827–7400 or 800/733–6396, FAX 505/827–7402). For outdoor activity information, contact the **USDA Forest Service, Southwestern Region** (✉ Public Affairs Office, 517 Gold Ave. SW, Albuquerque 87102, ☎ 505/842–3292). For information about New Mexico's Native American reservations, contact the **Indian Pueblo Cultural Center** (✉ 2401 12th St. NW, Albuquerque 87102, ☎ 505/843–7270).

Scenic Drives

The old **High Road** is not the most direct route from Santa Fe to Taos, but it takes you through rolling hillsides studded with orchards and tiny picturesque villages set against a rugged mountain backdrop. No visit to northern New Mexico is complete without the 100-mi trip along the **Enchanted Circle,** a breathtaking panorama of deep canyons, passes, alpine valleys, and towering mountains of the verdant Carson National Forest. **Route 66,** America's most nostalgic highway, includes a colorful stretch that now constitutes Albuquerque's Central Avenue. A scenic route between Albuquerque and Santa Fe, the **Turquoise Trail** (Route 14) snakes up through a portion of Cibola National Forest and several mining semi–ghost towns.

National and State Parks

National Park

Carlsbad Caverns National Park (☞ Elsewhere in New Mexico, *below*) is a spectacular system of caves and rock formations.

State Parks

New Mexico's 33 state parks range from the high mountain lakes and pine forests of the north to the Chihuahuan Desert lowlands in the south. Pristine and unspoiled, they have every conceivable outdoor recreational facility. For maps and brochures contact the **State Parks and Recreation Division** (✉ Energy, Minerals, and Natural Resources Dept., 2040 S. Pacheco St., Box 1147, Santa Fe 87504-1147, ☎ 505/827–7173 or 888/667–2757, FAX 505/827–1376).

Native American Reservations

Two general classifications of Native Americans live in New Mexico: the Pueblos, who established an agricultural civilization here many centuries ago, and the descendants of the nomadic tribes who came into the area much later—the Navajo, Mescalero Apache, and Jicarilla Apache. The settlements of various **Pueblo** tribes are described in the Albuquerque and Santa Fe sections. Note: When visiting Indian lands, it's important to respect all rules and requests regarding photography, videotaping, recording, and sketching. Some pueblos charge a fee for these activities; others ban them outright. The pueblos welcome visitors, but expect their sovereignty to be respected.

The Jicarilla Apache live on a 750,000-acre reservation in north-central New Mexico. The tribe has a well-defined tourist program promoting big-game hunting, fishing, and camping on a 15,000-acre game preserve; for details contact the **Jicarilla Apache Tribe** (✉ Box 507, Dulce 87528, ☎ 505/759–3242, FAX 505/759–3005).

A reservation of a half-million acres of timbered mountains and green valleys in southeastern New Mexico is home to the Mescalero Apache. The tribe owns and operates one of the most elegant luxury resorts in the state, Inn of the Mountain Gods, as well as Ski Apache, 16 mi from Ruidoso. Contact the **Mescalero Apache Tribe** (✉ Tribal Office, Hwy. 70, Box 227, Mescalero 88340, ☎ 505/671–4494).

The Navajo Reservation, home to the largest Native American group in the United States, covers 17.6 million acres in New Mexico, Arizona, and Utah. There are a few towns on the reservation; for the most part it is a vast area of stark pinnacles, colorful rock formations, high desert, and mountains. The tribe encourages tourism; write or call the **Navajo Nation Tourism Office** (✉ Box 663, Window Rock, AZ 86515, ☎ 520/871–6436 or 520/871–7371, FAX 520/871–7381).

ALBUQUERQUE

A large city—its population is nearing the half-million mark—Albuquerque spreads out in all directions with no apparent ground rules. The hot-air balloons that take part in the annual October International Balloon Fiesta are an apt simile for the city's free spirit. As in the rest of New Mexico, Albuquerque's Native American, Spanish, and Anglo cultures are well blended.

Albuquerque began as an important trade and transportation station on the Camino Real–Chihuahua Trail, which wound down into Mexico and remains a travel crossroads today. The original four-block core, known as Old Town, is the city's tourist hub, with unique shops, galleries, museums, and restaurants.

Visitor Information

Convention and Visitors Bureau (✉ 20 First Plaza NW, Box 26866, 87125, ☎ 505/842–9918 or 800/284–2282).

Arriving and Departing

By Bus

Albuquerque is served by **Greyhound Lines** and **TNMO Coaches Transportation Center** (✉ 300 2nd St. SW, ☎ 505/243–4435 or 800/231–2222).

By Car

I–25 enters Albuquerque from points north and south; I–40, from points east and west.

By Plane

Albuquerque International Airport (☎ 505/842–4366) is 5 mi south of downtown; the trip takes 10–15 minutes. Taxis charge $10–$12 plus tip. In Albuquerque, **Sun Tran** buses (☎ 505/843–9200) pick up on the baggage claim level about every 20 minutes; the fee is 75¢.

By Train

Amtrak (☎ 800/872–7245) serves the Albuquerque station (✉ 214 1st St. SW, ☎ 505/842–9650).

Exploring Albuquerque

Albuquerque sprawls in all directions, so it's best to see the city by car. Historic and colorful Route 66 is Albuquerque's Central Avenue, unifying as nothing else can the diverse areas of the city: Old Town, to the west, cradled at the bend of the Rio Grande; the downtown business and government centers; the University of New Mexico, to the east; and, farther east, Nob Hill, a lively strip of restaurants, boutiques, galleries, and shops. The railroad tracks, running north and south, and east–west Central Avenue divide the city into quadrants: southwest (SW), northwest (NW), southeast (SE), and northeast (NE).

The city began in 1706 in what is now Old Town, and tree-shaded **Old Town Plaza** remains the heart of Albuquerque's heritage. The **San Felipe de Neri Church** (✉ 2005 North Plaza NW, ☎ 505/243–4628), facing the plaza, has been enlarged and expanded several times over the years, but its massive adobe walls and other original sections remain intact. Most of the old adobe houses surrounding the plaza have been converted into charming shops, galleries, and restaurants.

The striking glass-and-sandstone **New Mexico Museum of Natural History and Science** (✉ 1801 Mountain Rd. NW, ☎ 505/841–2802; 🎫 $5.25) presents a simulated active volcano and frigid Ice Age cave, dinosaurs, and an Evolator (short for Evolution Elevator)—a six-minute high-tech ride through 35 million years of New Mexico's geologic history.

The spectacular two-story **Indian Pueblo Cultural Center** (✉ 2401 12th St. NW, ☎ 505/843–7270; 🎫 free, museum $4) holds one of the largest collections of Native American arts and crafts in the Southwest, a valuable resource for the study of the region's first inhabitants. The 19 Pueblo tribes of New Mexico each operate separate alcoves devoted to their own arts and crafts. Free performances of ceremonial dances are given on most weekends and on special holidays.

Sandia Peak Aerial Tramway (✉ 10 Tramway Loop NE, ☎ 505/856–7325; 🎫 $14), among the world's longest aerial tramways, makes an awesome 2¾-mi climb from the edge of the city to a point near 10,678-ft Sandia Crest for an overview of Albuquerque—and half of New Mexico. At sunset the sky is a kaleidoscope of colors over the desert. The tram closes for servicing during two weeks of fall and spring; call ahead.

On the city's western fringe lies **Petroglyph National Monument** (✉ 4735 Unser Blvd. NW, 87120, ☎ 505/899–0205; 🎫 weekdays $1 per car, weekends $2 per car), which contains more than 15,000 ancient rock drawings inscribed as early as AD 1300 in the volcanic rocks and cliffs.

Spend an afternoon at the **Albuquerque Biological Park** (✉ 903 10th St. SW, ☎ 505/764–6200; 🎫 $4.25), an environmental museum that includes the **Albuquerque Aquarium, Rio Grande Zoo,** and **Rio Grande Botanic Garden.** The Eel Cave and Shark Tank are real kid pleasers, and the Zoo is home to more than 1,000 animals, including elephants, bison, koalas, and Mexican wolves. Wander through the beautiful gardens, which showcase plants from the Southwest and other climates. At the **Albuquerque Children's Museum** (✉ 800 Rio Grande Blvd. NW, ☎ 505/842–1537; 🎫 $4), arts and cultural exhibits, a computer lab, and the Make-It-Take-It art room keep youngsters entertained for hours. Don't miss the Bubble Room, where kids can enclose themselves in a giant bubble. Within the Children's Museum is **Explora!**, a hands-on science center where changing exhibits allow kids to conduct their own experiments such as using wind to make sand dunes and mini-tornadoes.

Outside Albuquerque

Coronado State Monument and Park (✉ Off I–25 on Rte. 44 (Box 853), Bernalillo 87004, ☎ 505/867–5589), a prehistoric Native American pueblo once known as Kuaua, sits on a bluff overlooking the Rio Grande near Bernalillo, 20 mi north of Albuquerque; it is believed to have been the headquarters of Coronado's army of 1,200, who came seeking the legendary Seven Cities of Gold in 1540.

Fort Sumner State Monument (✉ Off I–40 and U.S. 84, Box 356, Fort Sumner 88119, ☎ 505/355–2573; 🎫 $1) is about 170 mi southeast of Albuquerque, near the Billy the Kid Museum and the cemetery where he is buried, just off Billy the Kid Road. Artifacts and photographs relating to the fort and to the Bosque Redondo Reservation nearby are on display. Nine thousand Navajo and Mescalero Apache were forcibly relocated to the reservation from 1863 to 1868, brought there by Kit Carson after the infamous "Long Walk" from their original homelands in the Four Corners Area.

Bosque Del Apache National Wildlife Refuge (✉ Off I–25, Socorro, ☎ 505/835–1828; 🎫 $3) is known to bird-watchers around the world as a place to see more than 329 species, including migratory birds. In winter you'll find more than 30,000 cranes, eagles, and snow geese; spring and fall, look for migrant warblers, flycatchers, and shorebirds; in summer nesting songbirds, waders, and ducks make this their home. The reserve is 90 mi south of Albuquerque off I–25.

Pueblos near Albuquerque

Made up of a series of terraced adobe structures and dominated by the massive mission church of San Estevan del Rey, **Acoma Pueblo** (✉ Box 309, Acoma 87034, ☎ 505/470–4966 or 800/747–0181; 🎫 $7, including guided tour) sits atop a 367-ft mesa that rises abruptly from the valley floor 64 mi west of Albuquerque. Most of its residents now live on the valley floor but retain traditional residences without electricity or running water on the mesa. Also known as Sky City, the pueblo may be visited only on paid, guided tours. Pueblo artists sell their prized thin-walled pottery.

Santo Domingo Pueblo (✉ Box 99, Santo Domingo 87052, ☎ 505/465–2214; 🎫 free), off I–25 at the Santo Domingo exit between Albuquerque and Santa Fe, operates a Tribal Cultural Center, where its outstanding *heishi* (shell) jewelry is sold. The August 4 Corn Dance is one of the most colorful and dramatic of all the Pueblo ceremonial dances.

The sun symbol appearing on New Mexico's flag was adopted from the **Zia Pueblo** (✉ 135 Capital Square Dr., Zia Pueblo 87053, ☎ 505/867–3304; 🎫 free), which has been at its present site (40 mi northwest of Albuquerque) since the early 1300s. Skillful Zia potters make polychrome wares, and painters produce highly prized watercolors.

Jemez Pueblo (✉ Box 100, Jemez 87024, ☎ 505/834–7359; 🎫 free), 51 mi northwest of Albuquerque, is the state's sole Towa-speaking pueblo. It is noted for its polychrome pottery and fine yucca-frond baskets. The beautiful **San Jose de los Jemez Mission,** a stone structure built in 1622, is at the Jemez State Monument (✉ Box 143, Jemez Springs 87025, ☎ 505/829–3530; 🎫 $2), 13 mi north of Jemez Pueblo.

Dining

Many of Albuquerque's best restaurants specialize in northern New Mexico cooking, but you'll also find French, Continental, Mediterranean, Italian, and standard American fare. For price ranges *see* Chart 1 (B) *in* On the Road with Fodor's.

$$$–$$$$ ★ ✕ **Artichoke Café.** Grilled duck, pumpkin ravioli with fresh spinach and butternut squash, and free-range chicken with fresh wild mushrooms are a few specialties served in this turn-of-the-century brick building just east of downtown. The large, modern, bilivel dining room spills onto a small courtyard. ✉ *424 Central Ave. SE,* ☎ *505/243–0200. AE, D, DC, MC, V. Closed Sun. No lunch Sat.*

$$$–$$$$ ✕ **Maria Teresa.** This nationally preserved landmark in Old Town, next to the Sheraton, is a restored 1840s adobe with 32-inch-thick brick adobe walls, fireplaces, early Spanish-American furnishings, and walled gardens. Aged beef, seafood, chicken, and New Mexican specialties, such as *carne adovada* (cubed pork marinated and baked in red chili), are served. ✉ *618 Rio Grande Blvd. NW,* ☎ *505/242–3900. AE, DC, MC, V.*

$$–$$$$ ✕ **High Finance Restaurant and Tavern.** To get to this restaurant in the center of Cibola National Park, you must either take the Sandia Peak Tram, hike 3 mi into the park, or ski through the Sandia Ski Area. On the edge of Sandia Peak more than 10,000 ft above sea level, it's a sublime place to watch a New Mexico sunset; every seat in the house has a view that spans 11,000 square mi. Sesame-fried calamari is one of their better-known starters; entrées run along the steak, seafood, and pasta lines. ✉ *40 Tramway Rd. NE,* ☎ *505/243–9742. Reservations essential. AE, D, DC, MC, V. Closed Apr. and Nov.; call ahead.*

$$$ ✕ **Monte Vista Fire Station.** Now a national historic landmark, this spacious, airy restaurant was once a working firehouse. The American menu includes a wide variety of seafood, beef, and pasta dishes; highlights are crab ravioli and duck with raspberry coulis. ✉ *3201 Central Ave. NE,* ☎ *505/255–2424. AE, D, DC, MC, V. No lunch weekends.*

$$–$$$ ★ ✕ **Scalo Northern Italian Grill.** Bankers and bikers gather at this lively, informal restaurant with an open kitchen and full-service bar to enjoy such wonders as *quaglia arrosta con polenta* (quail stuffed with fontina cheese, figs, and prosciutto, served atop creamy polenta), in addition to excellent pastas and pizzas. ✉ *3500 Central Ave. SE, in the Nob Hill Business Center,* ☎ *505/255–8781. AE, D, MC, V. No lunch Sun.*

Lodging

For price ranges *see* Chart 2 (B) *in* On the Road with Fodor's.

$$$$ **Albuquerque Marriott.** The region's natural colors and southwestern touches, such as kachina dolls and Native American pottery and art, are combined elegantly at this 17-story luxury uptown property near the city's largest malls. Fifty-six Concierge Service rooms are loaded with business amenities. ✉ *2101 Louisiana Blvd. NE, 87110,* ☎ *505/881–6800 or 800/334–2086,* FAX *505/888–2982. 411 rooms. Restaurant, pool, health club. AE, D, DC, MC, V.*

$$$$ ★ **Casas de Sueños.** Long a gathering spot for artists and now a bed-and-breakfast on a 2-acre compound adjacent to Old Town, Houses of Dreams has attractive casitas, many with fireplaces or hot tubs on private patios. ✉ *310 Rio Grande Blvd. SW, 87104,* ☎ *505/247–4560 or 800/242–8987,* FAX *505/842–8493. 19 casitas. AE, D, DC, MC, V.*

$$$$ **Hyatt Regency Albuquerque.** Adjacent to the convention center in the heart of downtown are the two soaring desert-color towers of this modern luxury hotel. The spacious, contemporary rooms in mauve, burgundy, and tan combine southwestern style with standard Hyatt amenities. ✉ *330 Tijeras Ave. NW, 87102,* ☎ *505/842–1234,* FAX

505/766–6710. 395 rooms. Restaurant, pool, health club. AE, D, DC, MC, V.

$$$–$$$$ **La Posada de Albuquerque.** A tiled lobby fountain, an encircling balcony, massive vigas, and Native American war-dance murals are a few of the atmospheric touches that set this historic hotel apart—thanks to New Mexico native Conrad Hilton, who opened the hotel in 1939. Hopi pottery and R. C. Gorman prints lend character to the rooms. ✉ *125 2nd St. NW, 87102,* ☎ *505/242–9090 or 800/777–5732,* FAX *505/242–8664. 114 rooms. Restaurant. AE, D, DC, MC, V.*

$$$ **Barcelona Suites.** This colorful hotel just off I-40 has the feel of Old Mexico, with tiles and wrought iron—though rooms have more of a Southwest feel. Complimentary breakfast and evening cocktails are served around the atrium fountain. Each two-room suite has a galley kitchen with a wet bar and microwave oven; three rooms have hot tubs. ✉ *900 Louisiana Blvd. NE, 87110,* ☎ *505/255–5566 or 800/878–9258,* FAX *505/266–6644. 64 suites. Kitchenettes, pools. AE, D, DC, MC, V.*

$$$ **Radisson Albuquerque Airport.** Arched balconies, desert colors, a courtyard pool, and indoor and outdoor dining add to the Spanish/southwestern flavor of this two-story motor hotel near the airport. Rooms are reliably comfortable. ✉ *1901 University Blvd. SE, 87106,* ☎ *505/247–0512,* FAX *505/843–7148. 148 rooms. Restaurant, pool. AE, D, DC, MC, V.*

Campgrounds

Fifteen minutes south of Albuquerque on I–25, the **Isleta Lakes and Recreation Area** (✉ Box 383, Isleta 87022, ☎ 505/877–0370) has complete campground facilities with tent sites and RV hookups. Within Albuquerque, there are tent sites and RV facilities at the **Albuquerque KOA Central** (✉ 12400 Skyline Rd. NE, 87123, ☎ 505/296–2729). Just north of town is the **Albuquerque North KOA** (✉ 555 S. Hill Rd., Box 758, Bernalillo 87004, ☎ 505/867–5227).

Nightlife and the Arts

To find out what's on in town, check the *Albuquerque Journal* on Friday and Sunday or the *Albuquerque Tribune* on Thursday.

Nightlife

Dingo Bar (✉ 313 Gold Ave. SW, ☎ 505/243–0663) is a small downtown nightclub drawing big crowds with its mix of jazz, blues, punk, pop, and world-beat dance music.

The Arts

The **New Mexico Symphony Orchestra** (✉ 3301 Menaul Blvd. NE, Suite 4, ☎ 505/881–8999) is among the state's largest performing arts organizations.

Outdoor Activities and Sports

Contact the **Albuquerque Cultural and Recreational Services Department** (✉ 400 Marquette NW, Box 1293, 87103, ☎ 505/768–3550) for information on its network of parks and recreational programs, including golf courses, paved tracks for biking and jogging, pools, tennis courts, playing fields, playgrounds, and even a shooting range.

Hot-Air Ballooning

The **Albuquerque International Balloon Fiesta** (☞ Festivals and Seasonal Events *in* the Southwest introduction) is the world's largest gathering of balloonists. You can also hire a pilot and balloon for your own ride. **Braden's Balloons** (✉ 3900 2nd St. NW, ☎ 505/345–6199) is a reliable firm. **World Balloon Corporation** (✉ 4800 Eubank NE, ☎ 505/293–6800) can safely take you up and away.

Shopping

Albuquerque residents mainly shop at malls and outlet stores. **Winrock Center** (✉ Louisiana Blvd. exit off I–40, ☎ 505/883–6132) and **Coronado Center** (✉ Louisiana and Menaul Blvds., ☎ 505/881–2700) are two of the area's main malls. **Cottonwood Mall** (✉ Coors Blvd. at Coors Bypass, ☎ 505/899–7467) has 147 shops. **Nob Hill,** a seven-block strip of shops stretching along Central Avenue from Girard to Washington streets, is the city's newest and trendiest shopping district. Neon-lighted boutiques, restaurants, galleries, and performing-arts spaces encourage strolling and people-watching.

Meander down tiny lanes and through small plazas in **Old Town** Albuquerque, whose dozens of one-of-a-kind shops include **V. Whipple's Old Mexico Shop** (✉ 400 E. San Felipe NW, ☎ 505/243–6070).

SANTA FE

With its crisp, clear air and bright, sunny weather, New Mexico's capital couldn't be more welcoming. Perched on a 7,000-ft plateau at the base of the Sangre de Cristo Mountains, Santa Fe is surrounded by the remnants of a 2,000-year-old Pueblo civilization and filled with evidence of the Spanish, who founded the city as early as 1607. Rows of chic art galleries (Santa Fe claims to be the country's third most important arts center, after New York and Los Angeles), smart restaurants, and shops selling southwestern furnishings and apparel combine to give the city an unusual cosmopolitan flair. Its population, an estimated 60,000, swells to nearly double that during the peak summer season and to a lesser degree in the winter, with the arrival of skiers lured by the challenging slopes of the Santa Fe Ski Area and nearby Taos Ski Valley.

Visitor Information

Chamber of Commerce (✉ 510 N. Guadalupe St., Suite L, De Vargas Center N, 87504, ☎ 505/983–7317). **Convention and Visitors Bureau** (✉ 201 W. Marcy St., Box 909, 87504, ☎ 505/984–6760 or 800/777–2489, FAX 505/984–6679).

Arriving and Departing

By Bus

Santa Fe can be reached via **Texas New Mexico & Oklahoma Greyhound** (✉ 858 St. Michael's Dr., ☎ 505/471–0008 or 800/231–2222).

By Car

Santa Fe is accessible from points north and south on I–25 or U.S. 84/285.

By Plane

Albuquerque International Airport (☎ 505/842–4366) serves both cities. **Shuttle bus** service is available from Greyhound (☎ 800/231–2222) and Shuttlejack (☎ 505/982–4311). For charter flights between Albuquerque and Santa Fe, contact the Albuquerque airport or the **Santa Fe Municipal Airport** (☎ 505/473–7243).

By Train

Amtrak's (☎ 800/872–7245) nearest station to Santa Fe is in Lamy (☎ 505/466–4511), which is linked over the 17 mi to Santa Fe by an Amtrak shuttle-bus service (☎ 505/982–8829 in Santa Fe).

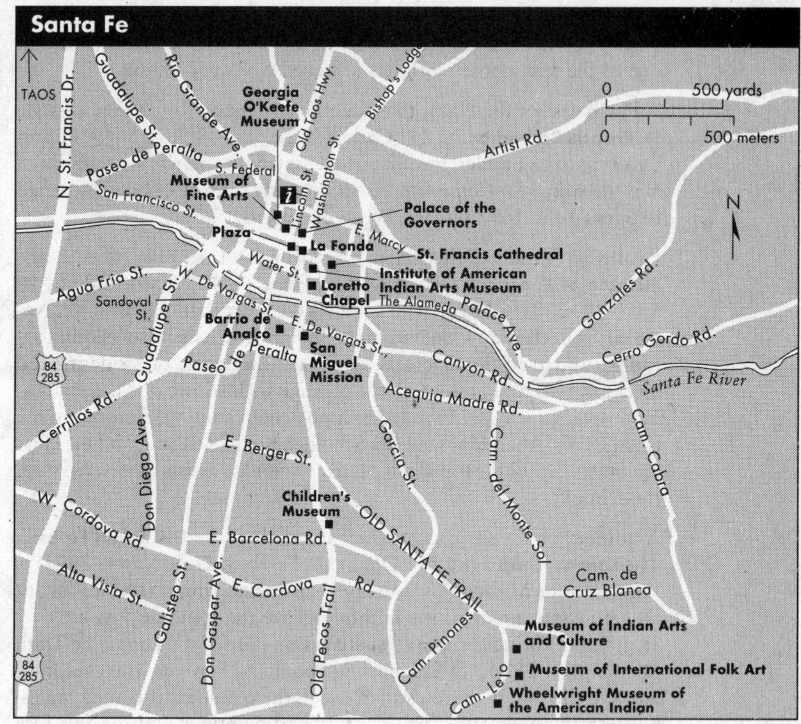

Getting Around Santa Fe

Santa Fe's downtown core is easily maneuvered on foot. The city's public bus system is limited in scale, so you'll need a car to visit attractions in the outer reaches. Otherwise, public transportation in town is monopolized by **Capital City Cab Company** (☎ 505/438–0000).

Exploring Santa Fe

★ The heart of Santa Fe is its historic **Plaza.** Established as early as 1607 as the city's social and political hub, it was later the terminus of the Santa Fe Trail, where freight wagons unloaded after completing their arduous journeys. Today the Plaza is lined with shops, art galleries, and restaurants. Fronting the Plaza is the oldest public building in the ★ United States: the Pueblo-style **Palace of the Governors,** which houses the **State History Museum** (✉ N. Plaza, ☎ 505/827–6483; 🎫 $5; 4-day pass to all 4 state museums and Georgia O'Keeffe Museum, $10), closed Monday between January and June. Under the portal of the Palace of the Governors, Native American artisans from area pueblos display and sell their wares. Across the street from the southeast corner of the Plaza is Santa Fe's landmark hotel, **La Fonda.**

The building that began Santa Fe's Pueblo Revival style is the **Museum of Fine Arts** (✉ 107 W. Palace Ave., ☎ 505/827–4455; 🎫 $5; 4-day pass to all 4 state museums and Georgia O'Keeffe Museum, $10), also closed Monday between January and June. On display are the works of regional artists, including Georgia O'Keeffe, as well as the early painters of the Santa Fe and Taos art colonies.

The **Georgia O'Keeffe Museum** (✉ 217 Johnson St., ☎ 505/995–0785; 🎫 $5; 4-day pass good at all 4 state museums, $10) opened in July 1997. Its founders plan eventually to house the world's largest collection of art by O'Keeffe, one of the many artists who have drawn their inspiration from the unique beauty of the New Mexico landscape, but one of the few whose work has achieved worldwide fame.

A block east of the Plaza, the magnificent French Romanesque–style **St. Francis Cathedral** (✉ 231 Cathedral Pl., ☎ 505/982–5619) houses the crypt of its builder, Jean Baptiste Lamy, Santa Fe's first archbishop, and the statue *La Conquistadora* (Our Lady of the Conquest), carried to Santa Fe in 1692 by Don Diego de Vargas.

Facing St. Francis Cathedral, in a renovated former post office, is the **Institute of American Indian Arts Museum** (✉ 108 Cathedral Pl., ☎ 505/988–6281; 🎫 free), which houses the more than 8,000-object **National Collection of Contemporary Indian Art.** Its paintings, photography, and traditional crafts showcase the work of students and teachers, past and present, of the prestigious **Institute of American Indian Arts,** which was founded as a one-room studio classroom in the early 1930s. Allan Houser, Fritz Scholder, Kevin Red Star, and Earl Biss are only a few of the top-flight Native American artists associated with the school.

A number of the city's sights trace the path of the **Old Santa Fe Trail.** The **Loretto Chapel** (✉ 211 Old Santa Fe Trail, ☎ 505/984–7971) is known for its Miraculous Staircase—an engineering marvel leading to the choir loft; many of the faithful believe the staircase was built by St. Joseph. The adobe **San Miguel Mission** (✉ 401 Old Santa Fe Trail, ☎ 505/983–3974; 🎫 $1), built in about 1625 by the Tlaxcala Indians and the oldest church still in use in the continental United States, houses a number of priceless statues and paintings and the San Jose Bell, said to have been cast in Spain in 1356. **Barrio De Analco** (now called East De Vargas Street), lined with historic houses, is believed to be one of the oldest continuously inhabited streets in the United States.

★ 🐤 The fascinating **Museum of International Folk Art** (✉ 706 Camino Lejo, ☎ 505/827–6350; 🎫 $5; 4-day pass to all 4 state state museums and Georgia O'Keeffe Museum, $10)—closed Monday from January through June—contains textiles, dolls, jewelry, ornaments, and other folk art objects from many countries and is among the premier museums of its kind in the world.

Rearing up from a piñon-and-juniper forest behind the Museum of International Folk Art is the privately owned **Wheelwright Museum of the American Indian** (✉ 704 Camino Lejo, ☎ 505/982–4636; 🎫 free), housed in a building shaped like a traditional Navajo hogan; works of many Native American cultures are on display.

The **Museum of Indian Arts and Culture** (✉ 708 Camino Lejo, ☎ 505/827–6344; 🎫 $5; 4-day pass to all 4 state museums and Georgia O'Keeffe Museum, $10) focuses on the history and contemporary culture of New Mexico's Pueblo, Navajo, and Apache tribes.

🐤 The **Santa Fe Children's Museum** (✉ 1050 Old Pecos Trail, ☎ 505/989–8359; 🎫 $3) has hands-on exhibits on the arts and sciences. Older kids enjoy the climbing wall.

Outside Santa Fe

Just under 200 mi northwest of Santa Fe, **Chaco Culture National Historical Park** (🎫 $8, good for 7 days) contains the remains of close to a dozen major ruins and about 400 smaller settlements. The most spectacular is **Pueblo Bonito,** the largest prehistoric Southwest Indian–dwelling complex ever excavated. Chaco's magnificent kivas, as well as a 400-mi network of paved road and a solstice marker, testify that the site was the climax of the Anasazi culture, which peaked in about AD 1150. ✉ *Star Rte. 4, Box 6500, Bloomfield 87413,* ☎ *505/786–7014.*

Forty-five minutes northwest of Santa Fe, **Los Alamos,** birthplace of the atomic bomb, spreads over fingerlike mesas at an altitude of 7,300 ft. Though research continues at the Los Alamos National Laboratory on off-limits nuclear weaponry, visitors can drop in on the interesting **Bradbury Science Museum** (✉ 15th St. at Central Ave., ☎ 505/667–4444; 🎫 free). The area also abounds with interesting archaeological sites, including **Bandelier National Monument** (✉ HCR1, Box 1, Suite 15, Los Alamos 87544, ☎ 505/672–3861; 🎫 $10 per car, good for 7 days), which contains the remains of one of the largest Anasazi centers.

A kind of Williamsburg of the Southwest, **El Rancho de las Golondrinas,** 15 mi south of Santa Fe off I–25, is a reconstruction of a small, traditional New Mexico farming village, complete with grinding mills, a blacksmith shop, animals, working fields, homes, and a *morada* (meeting place) of the Penitente order. ✉ *La Cienega,* ☎ *505/471–2261.* 🎫 *$3.50, $5 during festivals. Closed Nov.–Mar.*

About 25 mi southeast of Santa Fe, **Pecos National Historical Park** is the site of a once-flourishing Native American pueblo. An early trading center, Pecos was the largest and easternmost pueblo reached by the Spanish conquistadors in 1541. Franciscan priests built a mission church here in the 1620s, but the pueblo was abandoned in 1838 because of disease and raiding nomadic tribes. ✉ *Box 418, Pecos 87552,* ☎ *505/757–6032.* 🎫 *Free.*

Pueblos near Santa Fe

The Native American pueblos near Santa Fe vary in their craft specialties and in the recreational facilities they offer tourists. Most have ceremonial dances on feast days that are open to the public, but call ahead for regulations.

Pojoaque Pueblo (✉ Rte. 11, Box 71, Santa Fe 87501, ☎ 505/455–2278) features the **Poeh Museum** (🎫 free), a cultural center focusing on the Tewa-speaking Native Americans. The pueblo also operates an official **state tourist center** on U.S. 285, with an extensive selection of northern New Mexican arts and crafts.

San Ildefonso Pueblo (✉ Rte. 5, Box 315-A, Santa Fe 87501, ☎ 505/455–3549; 🎫 $3 per car), just off the road to Los Alamos, was the home of the most famous of all pueblo potters, Maria Martinez, whose exquisite polished black-on-black pottery is revered among collectors. The pueblo still boasts a number of highly acclaimed potters, as well as other artists and craftspeople.

San Juan Pueblo (✉ Box 1099, San Juan 87566, ☎ 505/852–4400) is headquarters of the Eight Northern Indian Pueblos Council. In its beautiful arts center, the **Oke Oweenge Crafts Cooperative,** the pueblo's distinctive redware and micaceous clay pottery can be purchased. Two handsome kivas, a New England–style church, and the **Tewa Indian Restaurant** are other attractions.

Santa Clara Pueblo (✉ Box 580, Española 87532, ☎ 505/753–7326) is home of the beautiful 740-room **Puyé Cliff Dwellings** (🎫 $5), a national landmark. It is also famous for its shiny red-and-black engraved pottery and for its many well-known painters and sculptors. Tours are conducted on weekdays.

Dining

For price ranges *see* Chart 1 (A) *in* On the Road with Fodor's.

$$$ ★ ✕ **Café Pasqual's.** Only a block southwest of the Plaza, this cheerful, informal café decked out with piñatas and *ristras* (strings of red chile peppers) serves regional specialties and possibly the best southwestern-style breakfast in town. Expect a line outside. ✉ *121 Don Gaspar Ave.,* ☎ *505/983–9340. AE, MC, V.*

$$$ ✕ **The Compound.** This restaurant shimmers with Old World elegance. The American-Continental menu includes chicken in champagne, roast loin of lamb, Russian caviar, and New Zealand raspberries. ✉ *653 Canyon Rd.,* ☎ *505/982–4353. Reservations essential. Jacket and tie. AE. Closed Jan.–Feb. and Sun.–Mon. No lunch.*

$$$ ★ ✕ **Coyote Cafe.** Owner-chef Mark Miller has quite a following, thanks to his famed "Cowboy"—a 22-ounce rib-eye steak served with barbecued black beans and red-chile-dusted onion rings; other favorites are the squash-blossom and corn-cake appetizers. In summer the restaurant opens its less-expensive Rooftop Cantina. ✉ *132 W. Water St.,* ☎ *505/983–1615. AE, D, DC, MC, V.*

$$–$$$ ★ ✕ **El Nido.** Since 1920, Santa Feans have made the 6-mi drive to the tiny village of Tesuque to eat at this former dance hall and trading post, now known for its cozy, firelit rooms and solid menu of choice aged beef, seafood, and local specialties such as green chile stew. ✉ *U.S. 285, 6 mi north of Santa Fe to Tesuque exit, then 1½ mi farther to restaurant,* ☎ *505/988–4340. AE, MC, V. Closed Mon.*

$$–$$$ ✕ **Ore House on the Plaza.** Here seafood and steaks are artfully prepared, and margaritas come in more than 80 variations. You can eat on the balcony overlooking the Plaza. ✉ *50 Lincoln Ave.,* ☎ *505/983–8687. AE, MC, V.*

$$–$$$ ✕ **Pink Adobe.** Operating for more than 50 years, this local institution occupies a three-century-old adobe full of fireplaces and artwork. Perennial specials on the eclectic menu are Steak Dunnigan, smothered in green chile and mushrooms; and savory Shrimp Louisianne—fat and crispy deep-fried shrimp. ✉ *406 Old Santa Fe Trail,* ☎ *505/983–7712. AE, D, DC, MC, V. No lunch weekends.*

$$ ✕ **La Tertulia.** This lovely restaurant in a converted 19th-century convent is almost as well known for its splendid Spanish colonial art collection as for its fine New Mexican cuisine and extraordinary house sangria. ✉ *416 Agua Fria St.,* ☎ *505/988–2769. AE, D, DC, MC, V. Closed Mon.*

$–$$ ✕ **Guadalupe Café.** A local favorite, this informal café features New Mexican dishes, including sizable sopaipillas (fluffy fried bread). The seasonal raspberry pancakes are one of many breakfast favorites that keep the place crowded every morning. ✉ *422 Old Santa Fe Trail,* ☎ *505/982–9762. Reservations not accepted. D, DC, MC, V.*

$–$$ ✕ **Plaza Café.** The red-leather banquettes, black Formica tables, tile floors, vintage Santa Fe photos, and coffered tin ceiling haven't changed since 1918. Standard American fare is served along with an interesting mix of southwestern and Greek specialties. ✉ *54 Lincoln Ave.,* ☎ *505/982–1664. Reservations not accepted. AE, D, MC, V.*

$–$$ ✕ **The Shed.** The Shed is housed in a rambling adobe hacienda dating from 1692. Try the red-chili enchiladas or *posole* (hominy stew). Expect a line at lunchtime. ✉ *113½ E. Palace Ave.,* ☎ *505/982–9030. Reservations not accepted for lunch. AE, DC, MC, V. No dinner Sun.–Tues.*

Lodging

Hotel rates fluctuate considerably from place to place, but are generally lower from November through April (excluding the Thanksgiving and Christmas holidays)—after which they soar. Bed-and-breakfasts are a less expensive alternative; contact **Bed & Breakfast of New Mexico** (✉ Box 2805, Santa Fe 87504, ☎ 505/982–3332). For price ranges *see* Chart 2 (A) *in* On the Road with Fodor's.

$$$$ **Bishop's Lodge.** Three miles north of downtown Santa Fe, in the rolling foothills of the Sangre de Cristo Mountains, this 1,000-acre resort was the retreat of Jean Baptiste Lamy, the first archbishop of Santa Fe. Rooms are in 11 one- and three-story lodges. The restaurant is one of the area's best. Organized outdoor activities abound, and there's also a children's program. ✉ *Bishop's Lodge Rd., Santa Fe 87504,* ☎ *505/983–6377 or 800/732–2240,* FAX *505/989–8739. 88 rooms. Restaurant, pool, tennis. AE, D, MC, V.*

$$$$ **Eldorado Hotel.** One of the city's most luxurious hotels, in the heart of downtown, the Eldorado has southwestern-style rooms in desert colors; many have balconies with mountain views. The Old House restaurant is outstanding. Evenings, there's live music in the lounge. ✉ *309 W. San Francisco St., 87501,* ☎ *505/988–4455 or 800/955–4455,* FAX *505/995–4455. 219 rooms, 19 casitas. 2 restaurants, pool. AE, D, DC, MC, V.*

$$$$ ★ **Inn of the Anasazi.** One of Santa Fe's finer hotels, the inn has rooms with beamed ceilings, kiva fireplaces, and handcrafted furnishings. The excellent restaurant serves a mix of North American and North American cowboy cuisine. ✉ *113 Washington Ave., 87501,* ☎ *505/988–3030 or 800/688–8100,* FAX *505/988–3277. 59 rooms. Restaurant. AE, D, DC, MC, V.*

$$$$ ★ **Rancho Encantado.** Robert Redford, Johnny Cash, and the Dalai Lama have all been guests at this 168-acre resort in the piñon-covered hills above the distant Rio Grande Valley. Guest rooms have fine Spanish and western antiques; some have fireplaces and/or private patios. Call for directions to Tesuque. ✉ *1 State Rd. 592, Tesuque; Mailing address:* ✉ *Rte. 4, Box 57C, Santa Fe 87501,* ☎ *505/982–3537 or 800/722–9339,* FAX *505/983–8269. 29 rooms, 29 villas. Restaurant, pools, tennis. AE, D, DC, MC, V.*

$$$–$$$$ **Hotel Santa Fe.** The largest off-reservation Native American–owned hotel in the country, this comfortable hotel has rooms with locally handmade furniture and Pueblo paintings. Its gift shop sells works by Picurís and other Pueblo Indian artists at prices lower than those of most nearby retail stores; guests get an additional 25% discount. ✉ *1501 Paseo de Peralta, 87505,* ☎ *505/982–1200 or 800/825–9876,* FAX *505/984–2211. 131 rooms. Restaurant. AE, D, DC, MC, V.*

$$$ **Inn of the Governors.** This unpretentious inn, one of the nicest in town, is two blocks from the Plaza. Rooms have a Mexican theme, with bright colors, hand-painted folk art, southwestern fabrics, and handmade furnishings. ✉ *234 Don Gaspar Ave. at Alameda St., 87501,* ☎ *505/982–4333 or 800/234–4534,* FAX *505/989–9149. 100 rooms. Restaurant, pool. AE, DC, MC, V.*

$$$ ★ **La Fonda.** The oldest hotel in Santa Fe may be the only one that can boast having had both Kit Carson and John F. Kennedy as guests. Each room is unique, with hand-carved and -painted Spanish colonial–style furniture and motifs painted by local artists. ✉ *100 E. San Francisco St., 87501,* ☎ *505/982–5511 or 800/523–5002,* FAX *505/988–2952. 153 rooms. Restaurant, pool. AE, D, DC, MC, V.*

$$$ **La Posada de Santa Fe.** This Victorian-era inn near the Plaza is on 6 acres of beautifully landscaped gardens and expansive green lawns. Most rooms have fireplaces, beamed ceilings, and Native American rugs; the five in the main building are drenched in Victoriana. ✉ *330 E. Palace Ave., 87501,* ☎ *505/986–0000 or 800/727–5276,* FAX *505/982–6850. 119 rooms, 20 casitas. Restaurant, pool. AE, DC, MC, V.*

$$–$$$ **Territorial Inn.** This elegant, 100-year-old Victorian home is just two blocks from the Plaza. Some rooms have their own fireplaces. There's a hot tub on the back patio. ✉ *215 Washington Ave., 87501,* ☎ *505/989–7737,* FAX *505/986–9212. 10 rooms. AE, D, MC, V.*

Campgrounds

La Bajada Welcome Center (✉ La Bajada Hill, 13 mi southwest of Santa Fe on I–25, ☎ 505/471–5242) provides information on private campgrounds near Santa Fe. **Babbitt's Los Campos RV Park** (✉ 3574 Cerrillos Rd., 87505, ☎ 505/473–1949) is the only full-service RV park within city limits. The **Santa Fe National Forest** (✉ 1220 S. St. Francis Dr., Box 1689, 87504, ☎ 505/988–6940), right in Santa Fe's backyard, has public sites open from May through October. Operated by the Tesuque Pueblo Indians, **Tesuque Pueblo RV Campground** (✉ U.S. 285/Rte. 5, Box 360-H, 87501, ☎ 505/455–2661), just outside Santa Fe, has RV hookups and tent sites.

Nightlife and the Arts

Check the entertainment listings in Santa Fe's daily newspaper, the *New Mexican,* or the weekly *Santa Fe Reporter,* published on Wednesday, for special performances and events.

Nightlife

The lounges, hotels, and nightspots of Santa Fe present many entertainment options. **Evangelo's,** downtown (✉ 200 W. San Francisco St., ☎ 505/982–9014), has Hawai'i à la New Mexico decor, 200 imported beers, and pool tables in a funky basement; bands play upstairs on weekends. **El Farol** (✉ 808 Canyon Rd., ☎ 505/983–9912) features live blues, jazz, and folk music in a rustic centuries-old adobe. **Rodeo Nites** (✉ 2911 Cerrillos Rd., ☎ 505/473–4138) attracts a country-and-western crowd.

The Arts

Artistically and visually the city's crown jewel, the famed **Santa Fe Opera** (✉ U.S. 285, ☎ 505/986–5900) is housed every summer in a modern open-air amphitheater carved into a hillside 7 mi north of the city. The **Santa Fe Symphony** (☎ 505/983–1414) performs from September through May at Sweeney Center (✉ 201 W. Marcy St.). The **Santa Fe Pro Musica** plays at the Lensic Theater (✉ 211 W. San Francisco St., ☎ 505/988–4640) from September through May. The **Santa Fe Chamber Music Festival** (☎ 505/983–2075) brings internationally known musicians to the St. Francis Auditorium at the Museum of Fine Arts (✉ 107 W. Palace Ave.) from July to August.

Outdoor Activities and Sports

Horseback Riding

Bishop's Lodge (✉ Bishop's Lodge Rd., ☎ 505/983–6377) rents horses to guests and nonguests from April through November. **Santa Fe Detours** (✉ 100 E. San Francisco St., ☎ 505/983–6565 or 800/338–6877) leads excursions.

Hot-Air Ballooning

Santa Fe Detours (☞ *above*) arranges excursions.

River Rafting

New Wave Rafting Company (✉ 103 E. Water St., Suite F, ☎ 505/984–1444 or 800/984–1444). **Los Rios River Runners** (✉ Box 2734, Taos, ☎ 505/776–8854 or 800/544–1181, FAX 505/776–1842). **Santa Fe Rafting Company and Outfitters** (✉ 1000 Cerrillos Rd., ☎ 505/988–4914 or 800/467–7238). **Kokopelli Rafting Adventures** (✉ 541 Cordova Rd., ☎ 505/983–3734 or 800/879–9035).

Ski Areas

Ski New Mexico (✉ 1210 Luisa St., Suite 8, Santa Fe 87505, ☎ 505/982–5300) and **Santa Fe Central Reservations** (✉ 320 Artist Rd., Suite 10, Santa Fe 87501, ☎ 505/983–8200 or 800/776–7669) are good sources for information on skiing near Santa Fe.

Cross-Country

Santa Fe National Forest (✉ 1220 S. St. Francis Dr., Box 1689, 87504, ☎ 505/988–6940) has hundreds of miles of trails of varying difficulty, some leading to natural hot springs.

Downhill

The small but excellent **Santa Fe Ski Area** (✉ 1210 Luisa St., Suite 5, Santa Fe 87505, ☎ 505/982–4429 or 505/983–9155) has a 1,650-ft vertical drop, 38 trails, and seven lifts.

TAOS

At the base of the rugged Sangre de Cristo Mountains about 60 mi northeast of Santa Fe, Taos is a small, old frontier town steeped in the history of New Mexico. Stately elms and cottonwood trees, narrow streets, and a profusion of adobe all cast a lingering spell on the memory; the charming old **Plaza,** surrounded by art galleries and boutiques, adds to the allure. Georgia O'Keeffe, Ansel Adams, and D. H. Lawrence are among Taos's former residents; so are such Wild West figures as Kit Carson and New Mexico's first governor, Charles Bent. Taos is a famed ski resort in winter and a hiking and mountain-biking venue in the summer.

Visitor Information

Taos County Chamber of Commerce (✉ 1139 Paseo del Pueblo Sur, Drawer 1, Taos 87571, ☎ 505/758–3873 or 800/732–8267).

Arriving and Departing

By Bus

Texas, New Mexico & Oklahoma Coaches, a subsidiary of Greyhound/Trailways, runs buses once a day from Albuquerque to the Taos Bus Station (✉ Corner of Paseo del Pueblo Sur and Paseo del Cañon, ☎ 505/758–1144).

By Car

The main route from Santa Fe to Taos is U.S. 68. From points north, take NM 522; from points east or west, take I–64.

By Plane

The **Taos Municipal Airport** (✉ U.S. 64, ☎ 505/758–4995), 12 mi west of the city, services only private planes and air charters. For air-charter information, call 505/758–4995. **Pride of Taos** (☎ 505/758–8340) runs daily shuttle service to the Albuquerque Airport ($35 one-way, $65 round-trip) and between Taos and Santa Fe ($25 one-way, $50 round-trip); reserve in advance. **Faust's Transportation** (✉ In nearby El Prado, ☎ 505/758–3410 or 505/758–7359) provides radio-dispatched taxis between the Taos airport and town ($12) and between the Albuquerque airport and Taos ($35 one-way, $65 round-trip).

By Train

Amtrak (☏ 800/872–7245) provides service into Lamy Station (✉ County Rd. 41, Lamy 87500) a half hour outside Santa Fe, the closest train station to Taos. **Faust's Transportation** (✉ In nearby El Prado, ☏ 505/758–3410 or 505/758–7359) dispatches taxis to the train station.

Getting Around

Taos radiates around its famous central Plaza and is easily maneuvered on foot. The main street through town is Paseo del Pueblo Norte, coming down from Colorado; the route then becomes Paseo del Pueblo Sur and heads out toward Santa Fe. **Faust's Transportation** (☏ 505/758–3410 or 505/758–7359), in nearby El Prado, has a fleet of radio-dispatched cabs.

Orientation Tours

Pride of Taos Tours (✉ Box 1192, Taos 87571, ☏ 505/758–8340) provides 70-minute narrated trolley tours of Taos highlights. The departure point for tours, shuttles, and pickups is next to the Taos County Chamber of Commerce (☞ Visitor Information, *above*) and the Plaza.

Exploring Taos

The **Taos Pueblo** (☏ 505/758–9593; 🎫 $5 per car plus $2 per person), 2 mi north of the Plaza, at the base of the 12,282-ft Taos Mountains, is the home of the Taos Tiwa-speaking Indians, whose apartment-house-style pueblo dwelling is one of the oldest continuously inhabited communities in the United States. Life here predates Marco Polo's 13th-century travels in China and the arrival of the Spanish in America in 1540. Unlike many nomadic Native American tribes forced to relocate to government-designated reservations, the Taos Pueblos have resided at the base of the Taos Mountain for centuries; this continuity has made possible the link between pre-Columbian inhabitants who originally lived in the Taos Valley and their descendants who reside there now.

Four miles south of town is the farming and ranching community **Ranchos de Taos** (✉ Ranchos de Taos, ☏ 505/758–2754), site of the beautiful **San Francisco de Asís Church.** Its massive, buttressed adobe walls and graceful towers are a prime example of early Mission architecture. Generations of painters and photographers, including Georgia O'Keeffe and Ansel Adams, have been inspired by the earthy, clean lines of the exterior walls and supporting bulwarks, which cast eerie shapes and shadows.

Dining and Lodging

For price ranges *see* Chart 2 (A) *in* On the Road with Fodor's.

$$$ ★ ✕ **Villa Fontana.** Warm coral walls, intimate dining rooms, and crisp linen tablecloths give this first-class restaurant the rich charm of an Italian country inn. Northern Italian classics—polenta with chicken livers, venison casserole with blueberries—are presented with finesse. ✉ *5 mi north of Taos along Rte. 68N,* ☏ *505/758–5800. AE, D, MC, V. Closed Sun.*

$$–$$$ ✕ **Doc Martin's.** Patrick Lambert brings snap and imagination to this pleasant, casual restaurant in the historic Taos Inn (☞ *below*). Warm duck salad and seared salmon in roasted-garlic cream sauce are among the tasty, well-presented dishes on the menu. Don't skip the superb desserts: Aztec chocolate mousse with roasted-banana sauce, or coconut-milk crème brûlée. ✉ *125 Paseo del Pueblo Norte,* ☎ *505/758–1977. AE, D, MC, V.*

$$–$$$ ✕ **Trading Post Cafe.** Perfectly marinated salmon gravlax, first-rate paella, and homemade raspberry sorbet are just a few of the reasons this chic-looking restaurant attracts a crowd. ✉ *4179 U.S. 68, at NM 518, Rancho de Taos,* ☎ *505/758–5089. MC, V. Closed Sun.*

$$ ✕ **Jacquelina's.** The beautifully presented southwestern food here is tops: Try the grilled salmon with tomatillo salsa, or barbecued shrimp with *poblano* (rich, dark-green chile) corn salsa. The Sunday brunch is superb. ✉ *1541 Paseo del Pueblo Sur,* ☎ *505/751–0399. AE, D, DC, MC, V. Closed Mon. No lunch Sat.*

$–$$ ✕ **Fred's Place.** A friendly young waitstaff delivers Fred's northern New Mexican specialties—*carne adovada* (a spicy marinated meat dish), blue-corn enchiladas—to a devoted group of regulars. Expect to wait for a table—you'll be glad you did. ✉ *332 Paseo del Pueblo Sur,* ☎ *505/758–0514. Reservations not accepted. MC, V. Closed Sun. No lunch.*

$ ★ ✕ **Casa Fresen Bakery.** A jewel in the tiny village of Arroyo Seco on the way to the Taos Ski Valley(☞ Ski Areas, *below*), this café, bakery, and gourmet market has the most delicious deli food in the area. Its freshly baked breads are reason enough to stop in. ✉ *8 mi northwest of Taos on Rte. 150,* ☎ *505/776–2969. MC, V.*

$$$ 🏨 **Taos Inn.** Only steps from Taos Plaza, this local landmark is listed on the National Register of Historic Places. The lobby, which also serves as seating for the Adobe Bar, is built around an old town well, from which a fountain now bubbles forth. Rooms have Native American–style wood-burning fireplaces and furniture built by local artists. ✉ *125 Paseo del Pueblo Norte, 87571,* ☎ *505/758–2233 or 800/826–7466,* FAX *505/758–5776. 36 rooms. Restaurant. AE, DC, MC, V.*

$$–$$$ 🏨 **Casa Europa.** Pastures and mountains surround this spacious 17th-century pueblo-style adobe B&B outside town. The delightful rooms have kiva fireplaces and marble bathrooms; there's also a five-room suite with a hot tub. Owners Rudi and Marcia Zwicker serve gourmet breakfasts every morning and European-style homemade pastries every afternoon—except during ski season, when they serve fireside hors d'oeuvres in the evenings instead. A hot tub and sauna soothe ski-weary muscles. ✉ *840 Upper Ranchitos Rd., HC 68 Box 3F, 87571,* ☎ *505/758–9798 or 888/758–9798. 7 rooms. Full breakfast. MC, V.*

$$–$$$ ★ 🏨 **Mabel Dodge Luhan House.** D. H. and Freida Lawrence, Georgia O'Keeffe, and Willa Cather have all been guests at this National Historic Landmark hotel, once the home of heiress and Taos socialite Mabel Dodge Luhan. The nine guest rooms in the main house are simple but tasteful; there's also a two-bedroom gatehouse cottage. ✉ *242 Morada La., 87571,* ☎ *505/758–9456 or 800/846–2235,* FAX *505/737–0365. 18 rooms, 13 with bath, 1 cottage. Full breakfast. AE, MC, V.*

$$–$$$ 🏨 **Touchstone Inn.** Nestled against the Taos Pueblo land, this elegant B&B enjoys magnificent views of the mountains. Each luxury suite has a kiva fireplace, a whirlpool bath, and eclectic antiques. The owner, Bren Price, is an artist, and her work is displayed throughout the inn. ✉ *110 Mabel Dodge La., 87571,* ☎ *800/758–0192. 8 suites. MC, V.*

$$ ★ 🏨 **Austing Haus.** The Taos Ski Valley forms a stunning backdrop to this soaring timber-frame building—especially when viewed through the glass-paneled front of the hotel. Many of the spotless rooms have four-poster beds; there are also three hot tubs. The restaurant calls to mind a grand alpine resort, with huge etched-glass windows and fine Continental cuisine. ✉ *Taos Ski Valley Rd., Rte. 150, Box 8, Taos 87525,* ☎ *505/776–2649 or 800/748–2932,* FAX *505/776–8751. 44 rooms, 3 chalets. Restaurant. AE, DC, MC, V.*

$$ 🏨 **San Geronimo Lodge.** Set on 2½ acres just outside of Carson National Forest, the lodge was originally constructed in 1925 by an Oklahoma socialite wanting to accommodate her friends. Rooms have handcrafted furniture, and most have kiva fireplaces. A hot tub and massage services are added bonuses. ✉ *1101 Witt Rd., Taos 87571,* ☎ *505/751–3776 or 800/894–4119. 18 rooms. Pool. Full breakfast. MC, V.*

Campgrounds

Carson National Forest Service (✉ Box 558, Taos 87571, ☎ 505/758–6200) provides information about the many camping sites in the forest. **Taos RV Park** (✉ Hwy. 68, Box 729TCVG, Ranchos de Taos 87557, ☎ 505/758–1667 or 800/323–6009), with 29 spaces, is open year-round.

Ski Areas

Within a 90-mi radius of Taos are plenty of winter ski resorts with beginning, intermediate, and advanced slopes, as well as snowmobile and cross-country skiing trails. All provide excellent lodging accommodations and child-care programs at reasonable prices.

Cross-Country

Carson National Forest (✉ Box 558, Taos 87571, ☎ 505/758–6200) has 440 mi of trails. **Enchanted Forest Cross-Country Ski Area** (✉ Box 219, Red River 87558, ☎ 505/754–2374), near Taos, has 20 mi of trails.

Downhill

Angel Fire Resort (✉ Drawer B, Angel Fire 87710, ☎ 505/377–6401 or 800/633–7463) has a 2,180-ft drop, 59 trails, and 6 lifts. **Red River Ski Area** (✉ Box 900, Red River 87558, ☎ 505/754–2223, FAX 505/754–6184) has a 600-ft drop, 44 trails, and 7 lifts. **Sipapu Lodge and Ski Area** (✉ Box 29, Vadito 87579, ☎ 505/587–2240) has a 865-ft drop, 19 trails, and 3 lifts. **Taos Ski Valley** (✉ Box 90, Taos Ski Valley 87525, ☎ 505/776–2291, FAX 505/776–8596) has a whopping 2,612-ft drop, 72 trails, and 11 lifts.

ELSEWHERE IN NEW MEXICO

Carlsbad Caverns National Park

Arriving and Departing

The park is in the southeastern part of the state, 320 mi from Albuquerque via I–25, U.S. 380, and U.S. 285, and 167 mi west of El Paso, Texas, via U.S. 180. **Mesa Airlines** (☎ 800/637–2247 or 505/885–0245 in Carlsbad) provides air-shuttle service between the Albuquerque airport and **Cavern City Air Terminal** in Carlsbad.

What to See and Do

★ **Carlsbad Caverns National Park** (✉ 3225 National Parks Hwy., Carlsbad 88220, ☎ 505/785–2232; 🎟 $6) contains one of the world's largest and most spectacular cave systems: 83 caves, with huge subterranean chambers, fantastic rock formations, and delicate mineral sculptures. Only two caves are open to the public for regular tours, with some off-trail viewing options available during special trips. At **Carlsbad Cavern** the descent to the 750-ft level is made by foot or elevator; either way, you can see the Big Room, large enough to hold 14 football fields. Reservations are essential a day in advance for the much less accessible **Slaughter Canyon Cave** (☎ 505/785–2232), 25 mi from the main cavern. The last few miles of the road are gravel, and you must plan on a half-mile trek up a 500-ft rise to reach the cave's entrance.

The park is the area's main lure, but the town of **Carlsbad** is an interesting place to see as well. For information contact the Chamber of Commerce (⊠ 302 S. Canal St., 88220, ☎ 505/887–6516). The **Living Desert State Park** (⊠ 1504 Miehls Dr., Carlsbad 88220, ☎ 505/887–5516; 🎫 $3) is also worth a visit while you're in the area.

Dining and Lodging

For price ranges *see* Charts 1 (B) and 2 (B) *in* On the Road with Fodor's.

$–$$ ✕ **Lucy's.** At this family-owned oasis of great Mexican food, the motto is: "the best margaritas and hottest chile in the world." All the New Mexican standards are available, including chicken fajita burritos smothered with chef Adam's special *queso* (cheese); there's also an unusual line of low-fat Mexican cuisine. ⊠ *701 S. Canal St.,* ☎ *505/887–7714. AE, D, DC, MC, V.*

$ ✕ **Cortez Cafe.** Established in 1937, this family-owned restaurant is known for traditional Mexican dishes such as sour-cream enchiladas. ⊠ *506 S. Canal St.,* ☎ *505/885–4747. AE, D, DC, MC, V.*

$–$$ 🏨 **Holiday Inn Carlsbad Downtown.** Ideal for families, the hotel has a playground, laundry room, and exercise equipment—and there's no extra charge for children under 19 who stay with their parents. Tasteful rugs and paintings in soft southwestern colors enliven the spacious rooms. The restaurant, Ventanas (Windows), serves fine Continental cuisine.⊠ *601 S. Canal St., Carlsbad 88220,* ☎ *505/885–8500 or 800/742–9586,* FAX *505/887–5999. 100 rooms. 2 restaurants, pool, exercise room. Full breakfast. AE, D, DC, MC, V.*

$ 🏨 **Best Western Stevens Inn.** Classy accommodations and reliable service make this reasonably priced inn a steal. Local scenes of cavern formations and Carlsbad's historic courthouse are etched in mirrored-glass murals and carved into wooden doors. Rooms have mirrored vanities and prints of Western scenes; some have kitchenettes. If you like country-and-western music, there are shows nightly in the Silver Spur bar. The Flume restaurant has a very good prime rib special. ⊠ *1829 S. Canal St., Carlsbad 88220,* ☎ *505/887–2851 or 800/730–2851,* FAX *505/887–6338. 202 rooms. Restaurant, pool. AE, D, DC, MC, V.*

TEXAS

Updated by Kim Harwell, Stuart Wade, and Kay Winzenried

Capital	Austin
Population	19,439,300
Motto	Friendship
State Bird	Mockingbird
State Flower	Bluebonnet
Postal Abbreviation	TX

Statewide Visitor Information

Texas Department of Tourism (✉ Box 12728, Austin 78711, ☎ 800/888–8839).

Scenic Drives

In far southwest Texas, **Route 170** from Lajitas through Presidio and into the Chinati Mountains is one of the most spectacular drives in the state, plunging over mountains and through canyons along the Rio Grande (thus its name: El Camino del Rio, or River Road). **U.S. 83** from Leakey to Uvalde is a roller coaster of a ride through the lush western edges of Hill Country, in central Texas. In the northern panhandle, **I–27** from Lubbock to Amarillo carries you through the buffalo grass and sheer cliffs of the Llano Estacado (Staked Plain, so named because its lack of trees forced pioneers to tie their horses to stakes). From Center, a small town near the Louisiana border, south into the Sabine National Forest, **Route 87** takes you over several dramatic lakes and through one of the huge pine forests for which east Texas is famous.

National and State Parks

National Parks

★ **Big Bend National Park** (✉ U.S. 385 from Marathon; Superintendent, Big Bend National Park, 79834, ☎ 915/477–2251), the state's premier natural attraction, is an 801,163-acre landscape laid bare by millions of years of erosion, with spectacular canyons, a junglelike floodplain, the sprawling Chihuahuan Desert, and the cool woodlands of the Chisos Mountains. Though the park has hundreds of campsites, the only hotel is the Chisos Mountain Lodge (☎ 915/477–2291), which is often booked months in advance.

Canoeing and camping are top draws to **Davy Crockett National Forest** (✉ Ratcliff Lake, 1240 E. Loop 304, Crockett 75835, ☎ 409/544–2046), a 161,500-acre park in the "piney woods" of east Texas, about 20 mi east of the historic town of Crockett on Route 7.

Aransas National Wildlife Refuge (✉ Rte. 2040, Tivoli, ☎ 512/286–3559), on a peninsula jutting 12 mi into the Gulf of Mexico near Rockport, is the principal wintering ground of the endangered whooping crane; the best time to spot them and some 300 other species of birds is between November and March.

State Parks

You can call a central reservations number (☎ 512/389–8900) to book any campsite in the Texas state park system. **Caddo Lake State Park** (✉ Rte. 43, ☎ 903/679–3351), 8,017 acres on the southern shore of the lake near Karnack, has campgrounds and cabins, and facilities for fishing, swimming, and boating.

Named after the local term for "high plains," **Caprock Canyons State Park** (✉ Rte. 1065, Quitaque, ☎ 806/455–1492), in the panhandle, is marked by canyons, striking geologic formations, and an abundance of wildlife, including African aoudad (a kind of sheep), mule deer, buffalo, antelope, and golden eagles.

Enchanted Rock State Natural Area (✉ Rte. 965, Llano, ☎ 915/247–3903), near Fredericksburg in the Hill Country, is so named because of the noises emitted by the underground heating and cooling of its massive, 425-ft-high dome of solid pink granite. The rock is the reputed site of ancient human sacrifices and is the second-largest batholith (underground rock formation uncovered by erosion) in the United States.

Fishing is king at **Inks Lake State Park** (✉ Rte. 29, Park Rd. 4, Barnet, ☎ 512/793–2223), northwest of Austin at the edge of the Hill Country.

★ On the high plains east of the panhandle town of Canyon is **Palo Duro Canyon State Park** (✉ Rte. 217, Park Rd. 5, ☎ 806/488–2227), site of the last great battle with the Comanche. Among its rock spires and precipitous cliffs is an outdoor amphitheater where the historical drama *Texas* is presented each year.

HOUSTON AND GALVESTON

Unbridled energy has always been **Houston**'s trademark. The forceful, wildcatter temperament that transformed what was once a swamp near the junction of the Buffalo and White Oak bayous into the nation's fourth-largest city also made the city a world energy center and pushed exploration into outer space—indeed, the first words spoken from the moon broadcast its name throughout the universe: "Houston, Tranquility Base here. The Eagle has landed." This same wild spirit explains much about the unrestricted growth that resulted in the city's patchwork layout: It's not unusual to find a luxury apartment complex next to a muffler repair shop, or a palm reader's storefront adjacent to a church. Magnificent glass and metal towers dominate the downtown corridor, but for the most part Houston's cityscape is characterized by random upcroppings of impressive architecture interspersed with groomed greenbelts and lively neighborhoods.

Houston is nevertheless an international business hub and the energy capital of the United States, evidenced by the Texas-size conventions that periodically fill its major hotels to bursting points. Medical institutions spawned from the discoveries of the famous heart transplant team of Cooley and DeBakey and research conducted at M.D. Anderson Cancer Center have earned Houston the title of "healing center." Top-notch museums, galleries, and performance halls affirm the city's commitment to creativity and expression, and its many ethnic restaurants add to the cosmopolitan flavor.

One of Texas's most popular year-round coastal destinations, **Galveston** is an island in the Gulf of Mexico 50 mi southeast of Houston, connected to the mainland by a causeway and bridge. Though its Victorian revival homes, beachfront cottages, and resort businesses have a slightly Coney Island feel, especially on the north end of the island, miles of private and rental residences on the southern end make this an appealing vacation destination.

Once one of the world's great port cities, Galveston was nearly devastated by a hurricane in 1900 that swept over the entire island, leaving the city in a state of decline. In the 1950s, preservationists launched

Galveston's renaissance by restoring stately homes and building up commercial districts with modern facilities. The result: a resort-like town with a southern flair.

Visitor Information

Greater Houston: Convention & Visitors Bureau (✉ 801 Congress Ave., 77002, ☎ 713/227–3100 or 800/365–7575).

Galveston Island: Convention & Visitors Bureau (✉ 2106 Seawall Blvd., in the Moody Center, 77550, ☎ 409/763–6564 or 888/425–4753), Strand Visitors Center (✉ 2016 Strand, ☎ 713/280–3907).

Arriving and Departing

By Bus

Greyhound Lines (✉ 2121 Main St., Houston, ☎ 800/231–2222). **Texas Bus Lines** (✉ 714 25th St., Galveston, ☎ 409/765–7731).

By Car

Houston is ringed by I–610 and Beltway 8. A tighter loop, comprising several expressways, circles the downtown and provides remarkable views of the city, especially at dawn and dusk. Radiating out from these rings like spokes of a wheel are I–10, heading east to Louisiana and west to San Antonio; U.S. 59, northeast to Longview or southwest to Victoria; and I–45, southeast to Galveston (about an hour away) or north to Dallas. HOV lanes, tollways, and crosstown connectors have reduced traffic congestion, but all these highways can be extremely heavy during rush hours.

By Plane

Houston's two major airports are served by about 22 airlines between them. (Be sure to check which airport you will be using, as many airlines serve both.) **Southwest Airlines** (☎ 281/922–4180 or 800/435–9792) has particularly extensive, frequent, and inexpensive service among nine Texas cities and other U.S. destinations. The airport more convenient to downtown is **W. P. Hobby Airport** (☎ 713/643–4597), 9 mi to the southeast. During rush hour, the trip into the city will take about 45 minutes; taxi fare runs about $20. **George Bush Intercontinental Airport** (☎ 281/230–3100), 15 mi north of downtown, but closer to the Galleria area, is the city's international airport. The trip downtown during peak hours takes up to an hour; cab fare is about $32; confirm the fee with your driver before leaving the airport or your hotel. **Airport Express** (☎ 713/523–8888) van service connects several Houston to both Hobby ($12) and the George Bush ($17). **METRO city express bus service** (☎ 713/635–4000) to the George Bush costs $1.50. **Galveston Limousine Service** (☎ 409/740–5466 in Galveston, 800/640–4826 elsewhere in TX) has regularly scheduled service to island locations from both Houston airports for $21–$26.

By Train

In Houston, **Amtrak** (☎ 713/224–1577 or 800/872–7245) trains run out of the old **Southern Pacific Station** (✉ 902 Washington Ave.).

Getting Around Houston and Galveston

Both Houston and Galveston demand cars, as attractions are spread out. Public transportation, though available, is not easy to figure out and may require multiple transfers. Houston's city bus system, **Metro** (☎ 713/635–4000), is most useful for straight-line routes. Galveston has island bus service, but of far more interest is the **Galveston Island Trolley** (✉ 2100 Seawall Blvd. or 2016 Strand, ☎ 409/762–2950; 📠

60¢), or **Treasure Island Tour Train** (✉ 2106 Seawall Blvd., ☎ 409/765–9564; 🎫 $4.50), which departs regularly from just outside the Convention & Visitors Bureau (☞ Visitor Information, *above*) for tours of local sights.

Exploring Houston and Galveston

Houston

Houston can be divided neatly into three major areas. One is its very modern downtown (including the theater district), which spurred one architecture critic to declare the city "America's future." Another is the area a couple of miles south of downtown, where some of the Southwest's leading museums are found along with Rice University and the internationally renowned Texas Medical Center. Finally, there are the thriving shopping and business centers west of downtown, centered around the Galleria.

DOWNTOWN

You may want to start by taking in the entire urban panorama from the observation deck (weekdays only) of I. M. Pei's 75-story **Chase Tower,** formerly known as Texas Commerce Tower (✉ 600 Travis St.). **Texas Street,** visible from the tower, is 100 ft wide, precisely the width needed to accommodate 14 Texas longhorns tip to tip in the days when cattle were driven to market along this route. **Tranquility Park** (✉ between Walker and Rusk Sts. east of Smith St.), a cool, human-scale oasis of fountains and diagonal walkways among the skyscrapers, was built to commemorate the first landing on the moon by the Apollo 11 mission.

The major buildings of the theater district are a few steps from Tranquility Park. The **Jesse H. Jones Hall for the Performing Arts** (✉ 615 Louisiana St., ☎ 713/227–1910 or 800/828–2787), home to the Houston Symphony Orchestra and the Society for the Performing Arts, is a huge hall that appears almost encased by a second, colonnaded building; its teak auditorium is more attractive than the exterior. The **Alley Theatre** (✉ 615 Texas Ave., ☎ 713/228–8421 or 800/259–2553), a fortresslike but innovative low-lying structure, is the venue of the city's resident professional theater company. At the **Gus S. Wortham Theater Center** (✉ 500 Texas St., ☎ 713/237–1439 or 800/828–2787), the Houston Grand Opera and the Houston Ballet perform in two side-by-side theaters. A new addition to the cultural neighborhood is **The Aerial Theater at Bayou Place** (✉ 520 Texas Ave., ☎ 713/693–1600), with live performances from jazz to comedy. **City hall** (✉ 901 Bagby St.), just northwest of Tranquility Park, is an unremarkable building whose chief interest lies in its allegorical interior murals.

Architectural additions to the skyline have spread out from the **Smith–Louisiana corridor,** a daunting canyon formed by towers of glass and steel, running south from Tranquility Park on the west side of downtown. A walk down these streets may be the truest measure of the city's modernism, intensified by the **outdoor sculptures** of Joan Miró, Claes Oldenburg, Louise Nevelson, and Jean Dubuffet. (Dubuffet's *Monument au Fantôme,* on Louisiana Street between Lamar and Dallas streets, is a particular delight to children.) The downtown area may leave you with an eerie sense of emptiness, but there's a good reason for that beyond the universal depopulation of America's urban centers: More than 70 of the major business and government buildings downtown are connected by a 6¾-mi labyrinth of **underground tunnels and skywalks,** used by those in the know as a welcome escape from the humidity for which Houston is justly infamous.

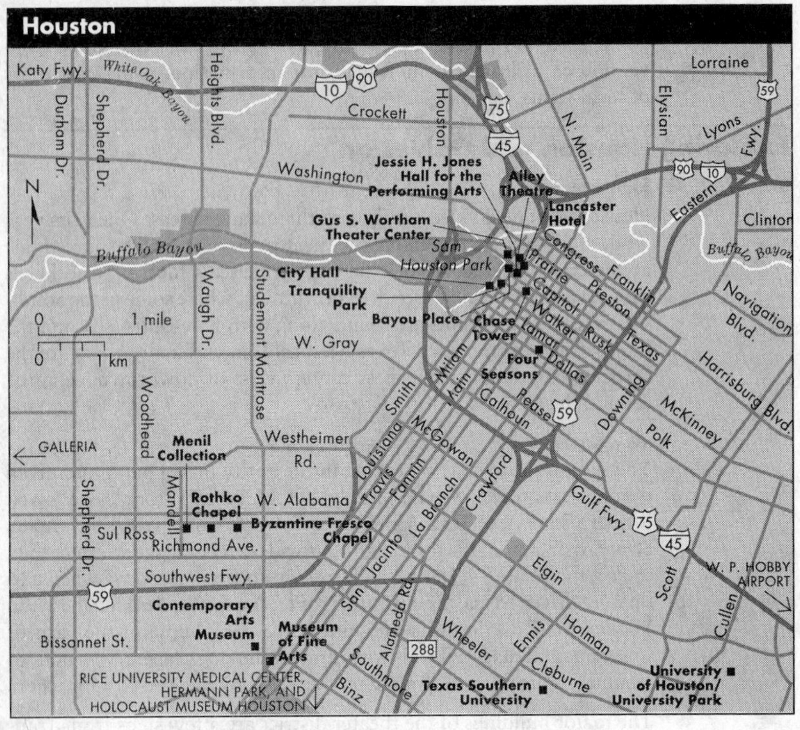

THE MUSEUM DISTRICT

Most museums are clustered within an area bordering the verdant campus of **Rice University,** one of Texas's finest educational institutions, and **Hermann Park,** the city's playground. Walking from one institution to the other is possible, but the expanse can be taxing; it's best to segment your visit.

The **Museum of Fine Arts** (✉ 1001 Bissonnet, north of Rice University, between Montrose and Main Sts., ☎ 713/639–7300; 🎫 $3, free Thurs.) is remarkable for the completeness of its enormous collection; it is housed in a complicated series of wings and galleries, many designed by Ludwig Mies van der Rohe. Renaissance and 18th-century art, and Impressionist and Postimpressionist works are particularly well represented. The **Lillie and Hugh Roy Cullen Sculpture Garden** across the street displays 19th- and 20th-century sculptures by Rodin, Matisse, Giacometti, and Stella in a setting designed by Isamu Noguchi. The museum is closed on Monday.

Housed in a stark, cylindrical edifice, the **Holocaust Museum Houston** (✉ 5401 Caroline St., ☎ 713/942–8000; 🎫 free) is an education center as well as a memorial. The main exhibit, "Bearing Witness: A Community Remembers," can be viewed individually or by guided tour. The 30-minute film *Voices* presents a moving oral history by local survivors.

The **Contemporary Arts Museum** (✉ 5216 Montrose Blvd., ☎ 713/526–0773; 🎫 free), housed in an aluminum-sheathed trapezoid, is the home of avant-garde art in Houston, with many traveling exhibitions. The museum is closed on Monday.

★ The **Menil Collection** (✉ 1515 Sul Ross St., ☎ 713/525–9400; 🎫 free), closed Monday and Tuesday, is the one of the city's premier cultural treasures. Italian architect Renzo Piano designed the spacious building, with its airy galleries. John and Dominique de Menil collected the eclectic art, which ranges from tribal African sculptures to Andy Warhol's paintings of Campbell's soup cans. A separate gallery across the street houses the paintings of American artist Cy Twombly. Adjacent to the lawns surrounding the Menil complex, the moody **Rothko Chapel** (✉ 3900 Yupon St., at Sul Ross St., ☎ 713/524–9839; 🎫 free), is an octagonal sanctuary designed by Philip Johnson. Fourteen Mark Rothko paintings panel the chapel's walls, which at first look like simple black canvases; only when you come close can you see the subtle coloring. Outside the ecumenical chapel is Barnett Newman's sculpture *Broken Obelisk,* which symbolizes the life and assassination of Martin Luther King Jr.

Frescoes from a 13th-century votive chapel have been preserved in the **Byzantine Fresco Chapel Museum,** just a block from the Rothko (✉ 4011 Yupon St., ☎ 713/521–3990; 🎫 free). The dome and apse were rescued from thieves and restored under a unique arrangement with the Greek Orthodox Church and the Republic of Cyprus. Suspended in a black reliquary box are frosted-glass panels replicating the tiny chapel structure.

Across town in the River Oaks neighborhood, the **Bayou Bend Collection and Gardens** (✉ 1 Westcott St., ☎ 713/639–7750; 🎫 home $10, gardens $3 or $7 for guided tour) lets you step back in time to witness the elegant lifestyle of the first half of this century. Noted Houston philanthropist and collector Ima Hogg donated the 28-room mansion, complete with period pieces dating back to the 1600s, to the Fine Arts Museum. The home is surrounded by gardens and natural woods that make this a peaceful retreat from the city. Guided and self-guided tours must be scheduled in advance.

THE GALLERIA AREA

The **Galleria,** one of the country's most upscale commercial zones, is on the west side of Houston, near the intersection of Westheimer Road and I–610. Shopping complexes, office towers, hotels, and other businesses have sprung up around this regional mall, making this one of the most important business districts in the city. Many of Houston's best restaurants are here; and the River Oaks neighborhood, with its multimillion dollar mansions and garden parkways, is nearby.

OTHER NEIGHBORHOODS

Kids and adults can learn about space exploration at **Space Center Houston** (✉ 1601 NASA Rd. 1 off I–45, ☎ 281/244–2100; 🎫 $12.95), 25 mi south of the city. Life on the deck of a space shuttle is simulated in the **Space Center Plaza.** In the **Kids Space Place,** children can ride on the lunar rover and try out tasks in the Apollo command module. The adjacent **Johnson Space Center** tour includes a visit to Mission Control and laboratories that simulate weightlessness and other space-related concepts.

Galveston

History and the waterfront are the main draws to Galveston, once the largest city in Texas. Its wealthy classes built the Victorian homes that give the island its vacation-resort appearance. These homes as well as some beautifully restored iron-front commercial buildings are concentrated on the northern, or bay, side of the island—especially along a street known as the Strand—and on Broadway, a boulevard that runs east–west through Galveston's midsection. Also hugging the north rim of the island, from 9th to 51st streets, is the harbor, port to small fishing boats and shrimp trawlers and to the *Elissa,* the tall ship that is Galveston's pride and joy. The southern, or ocean, side of the island is lined with beaches (☞ Beaches, *below*), hotels, parks, and restaurants.

THE STRAND AND BROADWAY

The **Strand,** especially the five blocks from 20th to 25th streets, is the heart of historic Galveston (it's now on the National Register of Historic Places). When Galveston was still a powerful port city—before the Houston Ship Channel was dug, diverting most boat traffic inland—this stretch, formerly the site of stores, offices, and warehouses, was known as the Wall Street of the South.

As you stroll up the Strand, you'll pass dozens of shops, outlet stores, and restaurants. The **Center for Transportation and Commerce** (✉ 2500 Strand, ☎ 409/765–5700), which also houses the **Railroad Museum,** is an Art Deco building that was once the Santa Fe Railroad terminal. The **Tremont House,** a block from the Center for Transportation and Commerce, is a onetime dry-goods warehouse converted into a hotel; full of Victorian elegance, it's considered the top hotel on the island. Two blocks south of the Strand is the newly revitalized arts area, **Gallery Row,** on Post Office Street, with art galleries, antique stores, and **The Grand 1894 Opera House** (☞ Nightlife and the Arts, *below*).

Broadway, a major thoroughfare just five minutes by car (or 20 minutes by foot) south of the Tremont House, is home to the "Broadway Beauties," three of the finest examples of historic restoration in Texas. The Victorian **Bishop's Palace** (✉ 1402 Broadway, ☎ 409/762–2475; 🎫 $5), a limestone-and-granite castle built in 1886 for Colonel Walter Gresham, has 11 rare stone and wood mantels—a testament to the colonel's fondness for fireplaces—and a wooden staircase that took 61 craftsmen seven years to carve.

Ashton Villa (✉ 2328 Broadway, ☎ 409/762–3933; 🎫 $4), a formal Italianate villa, was built in 1859 of brick—appropriately so, as owner James Moreau Brown started out as a humble mason. A freethinking man, Brown had to install curtains to shield daintier guests from the naked Cupids painted on one wall. The **Moody Mansion** (✉ 2618 Broadway, ☎ 409/762–7668; 🎫 $6), built in 1894, is brick, with interiors of exotic woods and gilded trim. The ballroom looks just like it did when Mary Moody made her debut here in December 1911.

THE ELISSA

In 1961 a marine archaeologist and naval historian named Peter Throckmorton spotted a rotting iron hulk in the shipyards outside Athens, Greece, and realized the 150-ft wreck was what remained of a beautiful square-rigger constructed in 1877. After almost 20 years, the Scottish-built ***Elissa***—the oldest ship on the Lloyd's Register—has been restored by the Galveston Historical Foundation and hundreds of volunteers. The ship, which in the last century carried cargoes to Galveston Harbor, may be toured above and below decks and is the centerpiece of the **Texas Seaport Museum** (✉ Pier 21, ☎ 409/763–1877; 🎫 $5).

Moody Gardens' Discovery Museum and IMAX Ridefilm Theater (✉ 1 Hope Blvd., ☎ 800/582–4673; 🎫 $6 per venue, discount combination tickets available) includes the Rainforest Pyramid, a 40,000 sq-ft tropical habitat for exotic flora and fauna; a 3D IMAX theater; and IMAX Ridefilm, an adventure ride synchronized with NASA space footage. Another family favorite is the free, 15-minute ride on the **Port Bolivar Ferry** (✉ North of Stewart Beach on Ferry Rd.; parking available adjacent to ferry landing), which crosses Galveston Bay.

Oil and gas production are explained aboard the offshore rig **Ocean Star** (✉ Pier 19, ☎ 409/766–7827; 💳 $5).

Parks, Gardens, and Zoos

Houston

Hermann Park, with its 545 acres of luxuriant trees, lawns, duck-filled reflecting pools, picnic areas, and 18-hole golf course, is only a short drive south of downtown on Main Street. Sitting on the northern perimeter of the Texas Medical Center, the park is also home to the **Houston Zoological Gardens** (✉ 1513 N. MacGregor St., ☎ 713/523–5888; 💳 $2.50), which includes a primate rain forest, petting zoo, and aquarium. The excellent **Museum of Natural Science** (✉ 1 Hermann Circle Dr., ☎ 713/639–4600 ; 💳 $4 entry fee, plus additional charges for each venue; combination discount tickets available), also on park grounds, includes the **Baker Planetarium, Cockrell Butterfly Center,** and **Wortham IMAX Theatre,** with a six-story-high projection screen.

Memorial Park, several miles west of downtown between the 610 Loop and South Shepherd Drive, has 1,500 acres of mostly virgin woodland—prime territory for walking, jogging, and biking. An **Arboretum and Nature Center** creates a sanctuary for native species.

The small downtown **Sam Houston Park,** bounded by Bagby, McKinney, and Dallas streets, preserves some of the city's 19th-century buildings. Tickets for daily guided tours are available at the Heritage Society (☎ 713/655–1912; 💳 $4), on the Bagby side.

Galveston

Stewart Beach Park (✉ 6th St. and Seawall Blvd., ☎ 409/765–5023; 💳 $5 parking) has a bathhouse, amusement park, bumper boats, miniature golf course, and watercoaster.

Galveston Island State Park, toward the western, unpopulated end of the island (✉ 3 Mile Rd., ☎ 409/737–1222; 💳 $3), is a 2,000-acre natural habitat ideal for birding and walking.

Dining

For price ranges *see* Chart 1 (A) *in* On the Road with Fodor's.

Houston

$$$–$$$$ ✕ **Cafe Annie.** Chef Robert Del Grande, one of the founders of Southwestern cuisine, serves up the best of his innovative, fiery cookery at this acclaimed restaurant. Start any meal with the layered gulf crabmeat tostada. ✉ *1728 Post Oak Blvd.,* ☎ *713/840–1111. Reservations essential. AE, DC, MC, V.*

$$$–$$$$ ★ ✕ **Tony's.** Houston's culinary icon, Tony Vallone introduced European cuisine to the city when he opened his namesake restaurant, a favorite among royalty, film stars, foreign dignitaries, and corporate titans. An exceptional wine list complements artfully prepared dishes such as Sweetwater Hen Nancy (roasted hen served atop a wild-mushroom risotto with a morel-and-sherry sauce) and seared red snapper with lobster medallions, baby golden beets, and blood-orange sauce. ✉ *1801 Post Oak Blvd.,* ☎ *713/622–6778. AE, DC, MC, V. Reservations essential.*

$$–$$$ ✕ **Grotto.** Part of the award-winning family of Vallone restaurants, this trendy bistro has a more casual menu than its siblings, Tony's and Anthony's. Rich Italian heritage goes into every item on the menu. The risotto *frutti di mare* is a medley of fresh shellfish. ✉ *3920 Westheimer Blvd.,* ☎ *713/622–3663. AE, DC, MC, V.*

$$ ✕ **Solero.** After-work professionals and arts patrons gather at this chic downtown restaurant for Spanish and South American tapas—assorted hot and cold small plates. The menu accommodates vegetarians. ✉ *910 Prairie Ave.* , ☎ *713/227–2665. AE, D, MC, V.*

$–$$ ✕ **Ouisie's Table.** Here you'll find American cuisine with southern and Asian influences. Enjoy favorites like Ousie's Spud (smoked salmon, caviar, and sour cream on a baked potato) or creations such as sautéed-sesame salmon with Chinese vegetables over linguine. Garden and veranda seating enhances a fabulous Sunday brunch. ✉ *3939 San Felipe,* ☎ *713/528–2264. AE, D, DC, MC, V. Closed Mon.*

$ ✕ **Cafe Express.** Each of the sporty, gourmet cafés in this local chain developed by Robert Del Grande (of Cafe Annie) serves flavorful pasta, salads, and burgers. The Post Oak branch is in the heart of the busy Galleria area. ✉ *1800 Post Oak Blvd.,* ☎ *713/963–9222; call for additional locations. AE, D, DC, MC, V.*

$ ✕ **Goode Company.** Down-home Texas barbecue is prepared ranch-style—smoked, and served with tasty red sauce. Patrons line up on the sidewalk to eat at picnic tables on the covered patio. A standard order is the chopped-beef brisket sandwich on jalapeño-cheese bread. ✉ *5109 Kirby Dr.* , ☎ *713/522–2530. AE, DC, MC, V.*

Galveston

$$–$$$ ✕ **Fisherman's Wharf.** You can tell by the mix of cops, businesspeople, and students that this waterfront institution, with indoor and outdoor dining and a harbor view, is a great deal for fresh seafood. ✉ *3901 Ave. O,* ☎ *409/765–5708. AE, D, DC, MC, V.*

$$–$$$ ✕ **Gaido's.** Since 1911 this local institution has been serving some of the best seafood in town. Try the famous gulf shrimp, sea scallops, or bay oysters as you gaze at the Gulf through picture windows. ✉ *39th St. and Seawall Blvd.,* ☎ *409/762–9625. AE, DC, MC, V.*

$–$$ ✕ **Benno's on the Beach.** There's a Coney Island feel to this little red, white, and blue joint, cited by some as the best place in Galveston for deep-fried and Cajun-style seafood. Dine in or take out. ✉ *1200 Seawall Blvd.,* ☎ *409/762–4621. AE, D, MC, V.*

Lodging

For price ranges *see* Chart 2 (A) *in* On the Road with Fodor's.

Houston

$$$$ **Four Seasons Hotel.** This elegant, highly touted newcomer is convenient to the Convention Center and all central business addresses. Deluxe amenities and top-notch service make it a discriminating traveler's choice. ✉ *1300 Lamar St., 77010,* ☎ *713/650–1300,* FAX *713/650–8169. 399 rooms. 2 restaurants, pool, spa. Full breakfast. AE, D, DC, MC, V.*

$$$$ **Houstonian Hotel, Club and Spa.** Spread over 18 acres in a heavily wooded area near Memorial Park, just west of downtown and near the Galleria, the Houstonian has luxurious rooms and sports and fitness facilities galore—golf, tennis, a climbing wall, and indoor racket games. ✉ *111 N. Post Oak La., 77024,* ☎ *713/680–2626,* FAX *713/686–3701. 290 rooms. 4 restaurants, 2 bars, pools, golf, tennis, health club. Full breakfast. AE, D, DC, MC, V.*

$$$$ **Lancaster.** This small luxury hotel with the feel of a European manor house is in the heart of the theater district. The intimate setting and classical theme contrasts with the steel and glass surroundings. ✉ *701 Texas Ave., 77002,* ☎ *713/228–9500,* FAX *713/223–4528. 94 rooms. Restaurant, health club. Full breakfast. AE, D, DC, MC, V.*

$$$ **The Wyndham Warwick.** With lovely views of Hermann Park and Rice University, the Wyndham Warwick is adjacent to the museum and medical districts. ✉ *5701 Main St., 77005,* ☎ *713/526–1991,* FAX *713/639–4545. 310 rooms. 2 restaurants, pool, exercise room. Full breakfast. AE, D, DC, MC, V.*

$$–$$$ **Westin Galleria.** Shoppers are in prime position at this tower flanking Galleria shopping—one of two Westin hotels in the Galleria area (the two hotels share facilities). The Westin Galleria is on the quieter side of the center. ✉ *5060 W. Alabama, 77056,* ☎ *713/960–8100,* FAX *713/960–6553. 495 rooms. Restaurant, pool, health club. Full breakfast. AE, DC, MC, V.*

Galveston

$$$–$$$$ **San Luis Resort and Condominiums.** Balconied rooms overlook the gulf at this spiffy high-rise resort complex, with hotel rooms in one wing and more-expensive condominiums in another. The hotel's steakhouse restaurant is widely touted as best on the Gulf. ✉ *5222 Seawall Blvd., 77551,* ☎ *409/744–1500 or 800/392–5937,* FAX *409/744–8452. 244 rooms, 150 condominiums. 2 restaurants, pool, health club. Full breakfast. AE, D, DC, MC, V.*

$$$–$$$$ **Tremont House.** Just steps off the Strand in the heart of old Galveston, this hotel recalls the grandeur of Victorian days. Rooms have soaring ceilings and 11-ft windows, and the four-story atrium lobby has a hand-carved 1888 mahogany bar. A rooftop terrace is a great place to watch the sunset and harbor activity. ✉ *2300 Ship's Mechanic Row, 77550,* ☎ *409/763–0300 or 800/874–2300,* FAX *409/763–1539. 117 rooms. Restaurant, bar. Full breakfast. AE, DC, MC, V.*

$$$ **Hotel Galvez.** This seaside grand dame was once called "Queen of the Gulf." A music hall, parlors, a loggia, and veranda evoke a bygone era. ✉ *2024 Seawall Blvd., 77550,* ☎ *409/765–7721 or 800/392–4285,* FAX *409/765–5780. 228 rooms. Restaurant, pool, health club. Full breakfast. AE, DC, MC, V.*

$$ **Commodore.** Right on the beach, this functional hotel has a large pool and ocean views from many room balconies. ✉ *3618 Seawall Blvd., 77552,* ☎ *409/763–2375 or 800/231–9921,* FAX *409/763–2379. 92 rooms. Restaurant, pool. CP. AE, D, DC, MC, V.*

Nightlife and the Arts

Nightlife

Bayou Place (✉ 500 Texas Ave.), Houston's newest entertainment complex, is a hub of evening activity, with restaurants, clubs, and the Angelika Film Center (✉ 510 Texas Ave., ☎ 713/255–1470), a sophisticated SoHo spin-off with independent and foreign films and before- or after-theater gourmet dining. For jazz, head to **Cody's** (✉ 2450 University Blvd., ☎ 713/520–5660); for blues, **Silky's** (✉ 4219 Washington Ave., ☎ 713/880–2990) is hard to beat. The **Swank Lounge,** upstairs at Solero's (✉ 910 Prairie Ave., ☎ 713/227–2665) is a popular late-night hangout with live music.

The Arts

HOUSTON

Houston is one of the few cities in the United States with four resident performance companies (☞ Downtown *in* Exploring Houston and Galveston, *above*). Ticket information on the city's **symphony orchestra, opera, ballet,** and **theater** may be obtained by calling 713/227–2787 or 800/828–2787. The largest professional African-American theater company, the **Black Ensemble** (✉ 3535 Main St., ☎ 713/520–0055) appears in gripping performances on its own stage in the theater district. Complete listings of events are carried in the *Houston Chronicle (Friday Weekend Preview), Houston Press,* and *Key* magazine.

GALVESTON

The **Grand 1894 Opera House** (✉ 2020 Post Office St., ☎ 409/765–1894 or 800/821–1894), where performances of various kinds are held year-round, is worth visiting for the architecture alone. Sarah Bernhardt and Anna Pavlova both performed on this storied stage. The **Strand Street Theater** (✉ 2317 Ship's Mechanic Row, ☎ 409/763–4591) is another venue for variety theater.

Spectator Sports

Baseball: Houston Astros (✉ Astrodome, 8400 Kirby Dr., at Loop 610 and Fannin St., ☎ 713/799–9500). **Basketball: Houston Rockets** (✉ The Compaq Arena [formerly the Summit], 10 Greenway Plaza, ☎ 713/627–3865). **Hockey: Houston Aeros** (✉ The Compaq Arena, 10 Greenway Plaza, ☎ 713/627–2376). **Soccer: Houston Hotshots** (✉ The Compaq Arena, 10 Greenway Plaza, ☎ 713/468–5100).

Beaches

Galveston's ocean beaches are all open to the public. The eastern end of the island, especially around Stewart Beach Park, has amenities of all kinds, including rentals of surfboards, windsurfers, sailboats, chairs, and umbrellas. To the west are quieter, less crowded beaches. The seawall along the waterfront attracts runners, cyclists, and rollerbladers.

Shopping

Houston

The city's premier shopping area is the **Galleria** (✉ Post Oak Blvd. and Westheimer Rd.), famous for high-quality stores like Neiman Marcus, Saks Fifth Avenue, and Tiffany & Co. The **Pavilion on Post Oak,** north of the Galleria, and **Westheimer Road,** on the east side of the 1–610 Freeway, are both lined with galleries, bookstores, and boutiques. The headquarters for boots and other western gear is **Stelzig's Western Wear** (✉ 3123 Post Oak Blvd.). Gift packs of sauces, cooking equipment, and stylish western wear are found at **Goode Company BBQ Hall of Flame** (✉ 5015 Kirby Ave.). The **Village** (✉ University Blvd. and Kirby Dr.), next to Rice University, was Houston's first mall; it still has many small shops as well as some national names. For antiques, vintage clothing, and folk art, try the stores in **The Heights,** a re-gentrified neighborhood north of I–10 (19th Street between Heights Blvd. and Yale St.). The **Parks Shops in Houston Center** (✉ 1200 McKinney St.), with 70 stores, is a downtown mall that provides a convenient entrance to the city's tunnel system. Tunnel maps are free at hotel concierge desks and banks.

Galleries are scattered throughout the museum district. Two notables are **Gremillion & Co.** (✉ 2501 Sunset Blvd., ☎ 713/522–2701), for contemporary art, and **Nolan-Rankin** (✉ 4621 Montrose Ave., ☎ 713/528–0664), for the European masters.

Galveston

The historic stretches along the Strand and Gallery Row are the best places to shop in Galveston. The **Old Strand Emporium** (✉ 2112 Strand, ☎ 409/763–9445) is a charming deli and gourmet grocery. Antiques, collectibles, and peanut products are found at the **Old Peanut Butter Warehouse** (✉ 100 20th St., ☎ 409/762–8358).

SAN ANTONIO AND THE HILL COUNTRY

The Alamo—symbol either of Texan heroism or Anglo arrogance—is by no means the only reason to visit **San Antonio.** A mélange of easily mingling ethnic groups, it is in many ways Texas's most beautiful and atmospheric city. Northwest of San Antonio is the **Hill Country,** an anomaly in generally flat Texas, rich with pretty landscapes, early American history, and echoes of the linen-to-silk story of Lyndon Baines Johnson, the nation's 36th president.

Visitor Information

Hill Country: Tourism Association (✉ 1700 Sidney Baker St., Kerrville 78028, ☎ 830/895–5505). **Bandera:** Convention & Visitors Bureau (✉ 1808 Hwy. 16 S; Box 171, 78003, ☎ 830/796–3045 or 800/364–3833). **Fredericksburg:** Convention & Visitors Bureau (✉ 106 N. Adams St., 78624, ☎ 830/997–6523). **Kerrville:** Convention & Visitors Bureau (✉ 1700 Sidney Baker St., 78028, ☎ 830/792–3535 or 800/221–7958). **San Antonio:** Alamo Visitor Center (✉ 216 E. Crockett St.; Box 845, 78293, ☎ 210/225–8587); Convention & Visitors Bureau (✉ 317 Alamo Plaza, 78205, ☎ 210/270–8700 or 800/447–3372) also has booths at the airport).

Arriving and Departing

By Bus

Buses run out of San Antonio's **Greyhound station** (✉ 500 N. St. Mary's St., ☎ 800/231–2222) to all major cities and most local towns.

By Car

Good highways serve most directions, including I–35 from Dallas and I–10 from Houston. I–410 rings the city, and several highways take you downtown.

By Plane

More than a dozen airlines serve **San Antonio International Airport** (☎ 210/341–9443), about a 15-minute drive north of downtown. Inexpensive shuttle services (☎ 210/366–3183) operate 24 hours a day. **Southwest Airlines** (☎ 210/617–1221 or 800/435–9792) provides regional service.

By Train

Amtrak serves San Antonio's station (✉ 224 Hoefgen St., ☎ 210/223–3226 or 800/872–7245), with thrice weekly trains north to Fort Worth, Dallas, east Texas, and Chicago and east to New Orleans and beyond; and Monday, Thursday, and Saturday west to Los Angeles.

Exploring San Antonio and the Hill Country

Much of San Antonio can be explored on foot, although some of its attractions will require transportation. For the Hill Country, a car is a must; you can visit several towns in a day, catching some of the landscapes in between as you drive.

San Antonio

At the heart of San Antonio, the **Alamo** (✉ Alamo Plaza, ☎ 210/225–1391; 🎟 free) stands as a repository of Texas history, a monument to the 189 volunteers who died there in 1836 during a 13-day siege by the Mexican dictator and general Santa Anna. They fought not for Texas's independence but for adherence to the liberal 1824 constitution of Mexico, of which Texas was then a part. When the Alamo was

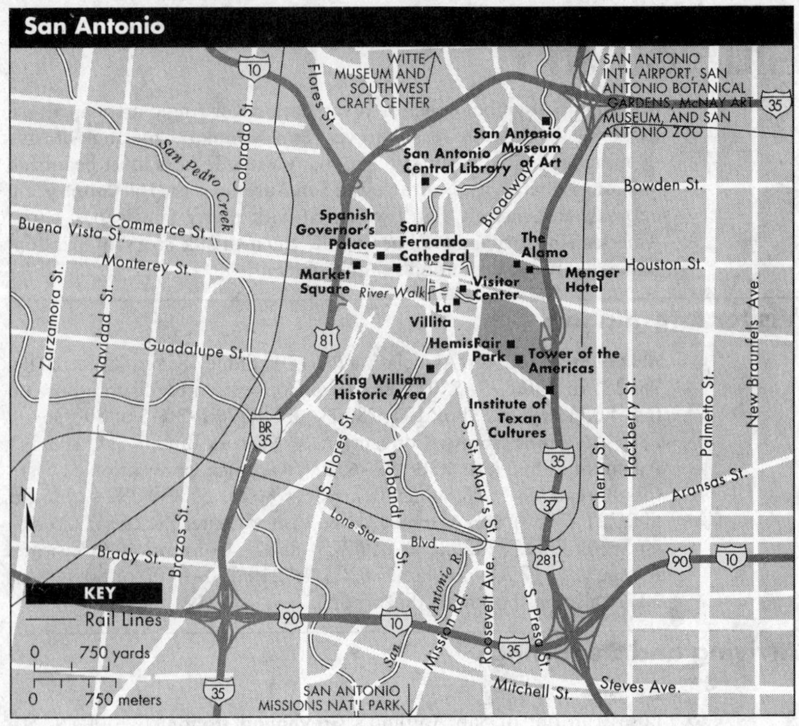

finally breached on March 6, at dreadful cost to the Mexican army, the slaughter that followed would be remembered in history as the major turning point of the Texas revolution. Santa Anna claimed victory, but as a liberal aide wrote privately, "One more such 'glorious victory' and we are finished." Indeed, three weeks later, Santa Anna was captured and the revolution completed, as Sam Houston led his sharpshooting volunteers—crying, "Remember the Alamo! Remember Goliad!"—to victory at San Jacinto. Today the historic chapel and barracks contain the guns and other paraphernalia used by William Travis, Davy Crockett, James Bowie, and other Texas heroes. Outside in the peaceful courtyard, a history wall elucidates the history of the Alamo and of the Mission San Antonio de Valero, as this mission—San Antonio's first—was originally called. In the Rivercenter mall, the **Alamo IMAX Theatre** (✉ 849 E. Commerce St., ☎ 210/225–4629 or 800/354–4629; 🎫 $6.95) shows a 45-minute film, *Alamo . . . The Price of Freedom,* on a giant screen five times a day.

On Alamo Plaza is the 1859 **Menger Hotel,** San Antonio's most historic lodging. Its longevity attests to Texas's age-old appreciation of good beer and revelry: As legend has it, William Menger built the hotel to accommodate the many carousers who frequented his brewery, which stood on the same site. Step inside the hotel to see its moody, mahogany bar, a precise replica of the pub in London's House of Lords; here Teddy Roosevelt supposedly recruited his Rough Riders, cowboys fresh from the Chisholm Trail drank to excess and fought, and cattlemen closed deals with a handshake over three fingers of rye.

The **Texas Star Trail,** which begins and ends at the Alamo, is a 2½-mi walking tour designated by blue disks in the sidewalks. Information on the trail, which takes you past 80 historic sites and landmarks, is available at the Alamo Visitor Center at Alamo Plaza.

★ **River Walk,** or Paseo del Rio, is the city's leading tourist attraction. Built a full story below street level, it comprises about 3 mi of scenic stone pathways lining both banks of the San Antonio River as it flows through downtown. In some places the walk is peaceful and quiet; in others it is a mad conglomeration of restaurants, bars, hotels, and strolling mariachi bands, all of which can also be seen from river taxis and charter boats. Near La Mansion del Rio hotel (☞ Dining and Lodging, *below*), at the Navarro Street Bridge, is the huge retail-and-entertainment complex known as **South Bank.** Each January parts of the river are drained to clear the bottom of debris, and locals revel in the River Walk Mud Festival and Mud Parade. During the annual Fiesta River Parade (April) and Holiday River Parade (November), colorfully festooned floats create a spectacle.

HemisFair Park, onetime the site of a World's Fair and currently home to the 750-ft **Tower of the Americas** (⊠ 222 S. Alamo, ☎ 210/207–8615), is southeast of River Walk. An **observation deck** (🎫 $3) and a rotating restaurant atop the tower affords bird's-eye views of the city.

The University of Texas's **Institute of Texan Cultures** (⊠ HemisFair Plaza, ☎ 210/458–2300; 🎫 $4), just beyond the Tower of the Americas, is an interactive museum focusing on the 30 ethnic groups who made Texas what it is today. Here you can walk through a re-created sharecropper's house; observe and listen to an animated, recorded conversation that might have taken place between a Spanish governor and a Comanche chief in the 1790s; or learn how and when your ancestors settled in Texas.

Leading German merchants settled the **King William Historic Area** in the late 19th century. The elegant Victorian mansions, set in a quiet, leafy neighborhood, are a pleasure to behold; Madison, Guenther, and King William streets are particularly pretty for a stroll or drive. Stop in for a guided tour of the 1876 Victorian **Steves Homestead** (⊠ 509 King William St., ☎ 210/225–5924; 🎫 $2) or the 1860 **Guenther House** (⊠ 205 E. Guenther St., ☎ 210/227–1061; 🎫 free), home of the family that founded the adjacent Pioneer Flour Mills. At the latter you'll find a small museum of mill memorabilia, a gift shop, and a cheerful restaurant serving fine German pastries and full breakfasts and lunches.

Except for the Alamo, all of San Antonio's historic missions constitute **San Antonio Missions National Park** (🎫 free). Established along the San Antonio River in the 18th century, the missions stand as reminders of Spain's most successful attempt to extend its New World dominion northward from Mexico. All of the missions are active parish churches, and all are beautiful, in their way. Start your tour at the **Misión San José** (⊠ 6539 San José Dr., ☎ 210/932–1001), the "Queen of Missions," where a visitor center illuminates the history of the missions; here you can pick up a map of the **Mission Trail** that connects San José with the others. San José has had its outer wall, Native American dwellings, granary, water mill, and workshops restored. **Misión Concepción** (⊠ 807 Mission Rd., ☎ 210/534–1540) is known for its frescoes; **San Juan** (⊠ 9102 Graf, ☎ 210/532–3914) with its Romanesque arches, has a serene chapel; and **Espada** (⊠ 10040 Espada Rd., ☎ 210/627–2021), the southernmost mission, includes an Arab-inspired aqueduct that was part of the missions' famous *acequia* water management system.

The **Buckhorn Hall of Horns, Fins, and Feathers** (⊠ 318 E. Houston St., ☎ 210/270–9467; 🎫 $5) is said to contain the world's largest collection of animal horns. The **San Fernando Cathedral** (⊠ Commerce and Flores Sts., ☎ 210/227–1297), in town just west of the river, is where Santa Anna raised his flag—an ominous message of no mercy—

to intimidate the Alamo defenders. The seat of a bishopric, it was visited by Pope John Paul II in 1987. The beautiful 18th-century **Spanish Governor's Palace** (✉ 105 Plaza de Armas, ☎ 210/224–0601; 🎫 $1), seat of Spanish power in Texas, is an ideal picnic site.

San Antonio's arts scene is marked by a strong southwestern flavor. The **San Antonio Museum of Art** (✉ 200 W. Jones Ave., ☎ 210/829–7262; 🎫 $4) houses choice collections of pre-Columbian, Native American, and Spanish colonial art, as well as the Nelson A. Rockefeller Center for Latin American Art, the nation's largest such facility, with more than 2,500 folk art objects donated from the Rockefeller collection. The **Southwest Craft Center** (✉ 300 Augusta St., ☎ 210/224–1848; 🎫 free) is filled with local crafts, many made by artists-in-residence, but may be most remarkable for its building, once an Ursuline school for girls—a fine example of San Antonio's adaptive use of historic structures.

You can't miss the 240,000-square-ft **San Antonio Central Library** (✉ 600 Soledad St., ☎ 210/207–2500): Its burnt-orange color, locally known as enchilada-red, and its modern design by the Mexican architect Ricardo Legoretta have been a source of contention among traditionalists. Inside, the library is fully computerized, providing access to videos, CDs, and laser discs, including a comprehensive Spanish-language interface.

At the **Witte Museum** (✉ 3801 Broadway, Brackenridge Park, ☎ 210/357–1900; 🎫 $5.95), a four-level "science tree house" is filled with interactive exhibits that let kids lift themselves with pulleys and ropes, play music with laser beams, and launch tennis balls 30 ft in the air.

The **San Antonio Zoo** (✉ 3903 N. St. Mary's St., ☎ 210/734–7183; 🎫 $6) has the nation's third-largest animal collection, most in outdoor habitats.

On the outskirts of the city, the **McNay Art Museum** (✉ 6000 N. New Braunfels Ave., Box 6069, ☎ 210/824–5368; 🎫 donation requested), in a private mansion with handsome tile floors and a splendid, Moorish-style courtyard, has an impressive collection of Postimpressionist and modern paintings and sculpture, along with a theater arts library. Not far from the McNay Art Museum are the **San Antonio Botanical Gardens** (✉ 555 Funston Pl., ☎ 210/207–3250; 🎫 $4), 33 acres containing formal gardens, wildflower-spangled meadows, native Texas vegetation, and a "touch and smell" garden specially designed for blind people.

The Hill Country

A drive through the Hill Country from San Antonio makes a pleasant excursion. Starting toward the northwest, it's less than an hour's trip on I–10 to the Kerrville area. However, you may want to take the far prettier Route 16, a hilly road that leads to **Bandera** (population: 877), one of the nation's oldest Polish communities (dating from 1855) and site of an 1854 Mormon colony. **Boerne** (population: 5,200), on I–10, was founded by Germans and named after a German writer. One of its fine early buildings is the **Kuhlmann-King House,** which can be toured by appointment with the local historical society (✉ 402 E. Blanco St., ☎ 830/249–2030 or 830/249–8000; 🎫 donations accepted). **Cascade Caverns** (✉ Exit 543 off I–10, ☎ 830/755–8080; 🎫 $7.95) has a 90-ft underground waterfall and visitor facilities, including RV campsites and a pool.

Kerrville, a town of little obvious interest, is said to have the best climate in the nation. This has led to a proliferation of hotels, children's summer camps, guest ranches, and religious centers. **Kerrville State Park** (☎ 830/257–5392; 🎫 $4), 500 acres along the cypress-edged Guadalupe River, is a good place to spot the white-tail deer that abound in the area. **Fredericksburg,** probably the Hill Country's prettiest town and the heart of its predominantly German-American population, is just 24 mi north of Kerrville, on Route 16. Its main street (bilingually signposted as HAUPTSTRASSE) is a sort of German version of a classic western movie scene except that it's lined with chic stores, antiques shops, small German eateries, and "Sunday Houses" built by German farmers as hostelries to use on the nights before church. One of Fredericksburg's famous sons was Chester W. Nimitz, commander in chief of the U.S. Pacific fleet in World War II. The restored Nimitz Steamboat Hotel now forms part of the **Admiral Nimitz Museum** (✉ 340 E. Main St., ☎ 830/997–4379; 🎫 $3), which displays restored hotel rooms, exhibits on the war in the Pacific, and the Garden of Peace, donated by the Japanese government.

Luckenbach—made famous by the Waylon Jennings and Willie Nelson duet "Let's Go to Luckenbach, Texas"—is actually only a speck (population: 25) on the map. A little east of Fredericksburg on Route 1376, Luckenbach was founded in 1850 and remains largely unchanged, with one unpainted general store and tavern, a rural dance hall, and a blacksmith's shop. Although the rustic little complex is open daily except Wednesday, you may want to stop by on Sunday afternoon, when informal groups of fiddlers, guitarists, and banjo pickers gather under the live oaks.

The **LBJ National Historical Park** is separated into two districts: one in Johnson City and the other near Stonewall, 14 mi away. At the center of **Johnson City** (Rte. 281 60 mi north of San Antonio; Rte. 290 50 mi west of Austin)—the poor, dusty town where our 36th President was born and raised—is a brand-new **visitor center** (✉ Ave. G and Lady Bird La., ☎ 830/868–7128) with films and exhibits on the area. Nearby are LBJ's small, white-frame **boyhood home**, where rangers give free guided tours daily, and the **Johnson Settlement** (☎ 830/868–7283; 🎫 free), a ranch complex once owned by LBJ's family. On certain weekends, costumed interpreters demonstrate the skills and trades of frontier Texas; call for a schedule. A worthwhile bus tour (🎫 $3) departs daily from the **LBJ Ranch District** (✉ east of Stonewall on U.S. 290, ☎ 830/644–2420), with stops at Johnson's birthplace, the one-room school he attended, and his grave; along the way you'll also pass the **White House**, where Lady Bird Johnson still lives.

Blanco (just south of Johnson City on Route 281), the onetime county seat, is ornamented by a fine bit of classic Texas: the Second Empire–style **Old Blanco County Courthouse.**

The drive back to San Antonio on U.S. 281 is pretty, but if you have time, go by way of **San Marcos** on Route 32. This road, which skips along parts of a ridge called the **Devil's Backbone,** leads through classic Hill Country landscapes. If time permits, make a short detour to **Natural Bridge Caverns** (✉ follow signs from Rte. 1863 between San Antonio and New Braunfels, ☎ 210/651–6101; 🎫 $9), a mile-long series of multicolored subterranean rooms and corridors. "Thunder lizard" tracks dating from 100 million years ago can be found at **Dinosaur Flats** (Rte. 306, 2 mi southwest of Sattler).

Dining and Lodging

The Bandera and Kerrville visitor centers (☞ Visitor Information, *above*) have information on guest ranches. The Hill Country is chock-full of bed-and-breakfasts, particularly in tourist towns like Fredericksburg. Ask for listings at local convention and visitor centers or try the reservation services **Be My Guest** (✉ 402 W. Main St., Fredericksburg 78624, ☎ 830/997–7227 or 830/997–8555) and **Gastehaus Schmidt** (✉ 231 W. Main St., Fredericksburg 78624, ☎ 830/997–5612). For price ranges *see* Charts 1 (A) and 2 (A) *in* On the Road with Fodor's.

San Antonio

$$$$ ✕ **Polo's.** Inside the elegant Fairmount Hotel is the equally classic Polo's. With its artfully blended contemporary southwestern and Asian cuisine—black pasta stuffed with lobster and crab, for example—Polo's has been featured on the cover of *Texas Monthly* magazine. ✉ *401 S. Alamo St., ☎ 210/224–8800. AE, DC, MC, V. Closed Sun.*

$$$–$$$$ ★ ✕ **Biga.** Chef Bruce Auden's inventive Southwest and American menu might include beer-battered onion rings or artichoke Brie, followed by oak-fired pheasant—all served inside a gracious, century-old manse. ✉ *206 E. Locust, ☎ 210/225–0722. AE, DC, MC, V. Closed Sun.*

$$$ ✕ **Boudro's.** Among the better River Walk options, this cavelike southwestern original serves seafood, steak, and extras such as guacamole prepared tableside. The wine list is commendable. ✉ *421 E. Commerce St., ☎ 210/224–8484. AE, D, DC, MC, V.*

$$–$$$ ✕ **Liberty Bar.** Built in 1890 and leaning conspicuously at its foundation (attributed to a 1921 flood), the former Liberty Schooner Saloon serves old-time favorites like pot roast and excellent pies. The rustic bar is a comfortable place to sip a beer. ✉ *328 E. Josephine St., ☎ 210/227–1187. AE, D, DC, MC, V.*

$$ ★ ✕ **Zuni Grill.** With a bright industrial-warehouse brick interior along the River Walk, and outdoor seating with an idyllic river view, this predominantly southwestern restaurant is known for its fajitas and its Zuni Burger (served with white cheddar). Try a cactus margarita, made with cactus juice and aged tequila. ✉ *511 River Walk, ☎ 210/227–0864. AE, D, DC, MC, V.*

$–$$ ✕ **County Line Barbecue.** Texas is famous for its barbecued ribs, smoked brisket, and related fare. In San Antonio there's only one contender. ✉ *On Rte. 1604, ½ mi west of U.S. 281, ☎ 210/496–0011. AE, D, DC, MC, V.*

$$$$ 🏨 **Fairmount.** This historic luxury hotel made the *Guinness Book of Records* when its 3.2-million-pound brick bulk was moved six blocks in 1985 to its present location. Canopy beds, overstuffed chairs, and marble baths create a superrefined atmosphere. ✉ *401 S. Alamo St., 78205, ☎ 210/224–8800 or 800/642–3363, FAX 210/224–2767. 37 rooms. Restaurant. AE, D, DC, MC, V.*

$$$$ ★ 🏨 **Havana Riverwalk Inn.** San Antonio's most bohemian boutique hotel occupies a once-dilapidated Mediterannean Revival structure built in 1914. Every room is an experience: You'll find carved teak and wicker chairs from India, beds fashioned from the grillwork of old buildings, and vintage chairs from French hotels and bistros. Don't miss Club Cohiba, the riverside martini bar. ✉ *1015 Navarro, 78205, ☎ 210/222–2008, FAX 210/222–2717. 27 rooms. Restaurant. AE, D, DC, MC, V.*

$$$$ 🏨 **Hyatt Regency Hill Country Resort.** On the west side of the city near Sea World, this sophisticated Texas country resort occupies a vast stretch of former ranch land. On the grounds is a 4-acre water park with a man-made river where you can go tubing; there are also basketball and volleyball courts and an 18-hole golf course. ✉ *9800 Hyatt Dr., 78251, ☎ 210/647–1234 or 210/233–1234, FAX 210/681–9681. 500 rooms. 2 restaurants, pools, tennis, health club. AE, D, DC, MC, V.*

$$$–$$$$ 🏨 **La Mansion del Rio.** A Spanish motif marks this large hotel on a quiet portion of River Walk. Inside and out it's replete with Mediterranean tiles, archways, and soft wood tones. Rooms are very modern. ✉ 112

College St., 78205, ☎ 210/225–2581 or 800/292–7300, FAX 210/226–1365. 322 rooms. 2 restaurants, pool. AE, D, DC, MC, V.

$$$ **The Camberly Gunter.** Since 1909 this downtown hotel has been a favorite of cattlemen and business travelers. The marble lobby has a beautiful coffered ceiling supported by massive columns. Rooms have antique reproduction furniture and modern conveniences such as large desks with dataports. ✉ *205 E. Houston St., 78205, ☎ 210/227–3241, FAX 210/227–9305. 312 rooms. Restaurant, pool, exercise room. AE, D, DC, MC, V.*

$$$ ★ **Menger Hotel.** Since its 1859 opening, the Menger has lodged, among others, Robert E. Lee, Ulysses S. Grant, Teddy Roosevelt, Oscar Wilde, Sarah Bernhardt, Roy Rogers, and Dale Evans, all of whom must have appreciated the charming, three-story Victorian lobby, sunny dining room, flowered courtyard, and four-poster beds (in the oldest part of the hotel only). ✉ *204 Alamo Plaza, 78205, ☎ 210/223–4361 or 800/345–9285, FAX 210/228–0022. 320 rooms. Restaurant, pool, health club. AE, D, DC, MC, V.*

$ **Bullis House.** The rooms in this historic mansion are spacious and well restored—and a good deal in a town where lodging is surprisingly expensive. Next door in a separate building is a modern youth hostel; there's also a newer 1920s-style bungalow with two rooms. ✉ *621 Pierce St., 78208, ☎ 210/223–9426. 10 rooms; hostel with 40 beds; 2-room bungalow. Pool. CP. AE, D, MC, V.*

The Hill Country

$ ✕ **Friedhelm's.** This Bavarian restaurant is known as the best in town, no small feat in an area full of such eateries. Try the Bavarian schnitzel, a breaded cutlet topped with Emmentaler cheese and jalapeño sauce. ✉ *905 W. Main St., Fredericksburg, ☎ 830/997–6300. AE, D, MC, V. Closed Mon.*

$$ **Holiday Inn Y.O. Ranch.** This sprawling ranch-theme hotel is named after a well-known 50,000-acre dude ranch to which regular excursions are arranged. The large rooms—sporting cattle horns and the like—carry out the western theme. ✉ *2033 Sidney Baker St., Kerrville 78028, ☎ 830/257–4440, 800/465–4329 outside TX, FAX 830/896–8189. 200 rooms. Restaurant, pool, tennis. AE, D, DC, MC, V.*

Nightlife and the Arts

Nightlife

Around the 3000 block of San Antonio's **North St. Mary's Street,** you'll find a colorful assortment of bars and restaurants in converted commercial buildings, many with live entertainment. **River Walk** favorites include **Durty Nellie's Pub** (✉ Hilton Palacio del Rio, 200 S. Alamo St., ☎ 210/222–1400), where sing-alongs are popular. World-class Jim Cullum's Jazz Band plays superb Dixieland at the **Landing** (✉ Hyatt Regency Hotel, 123 Losoya St., ☎ 210/223–7266). Don't miss the **Menger Hotel bar** (☞ Dining and Lodging, *above*).

The Arts

At San Antonio's **Mexican Cultural Institute** (✉ 600 HemisFair Plaza, ☎ 210/227–0123), Mexican culture is depicted in film, dance, art, and other media. A 1929 movie/vaudeville theater has been restored to its Baroque splendor as the **Majestic Performing Arts Center** (✉ 224 E. Houston St., ☎ 210/226–5700), a venue for touring Broadway shows and home to the San Antonio Symphony Orchestra. **Kerrville** annually hosts one of the country's largest folk music festivals, usually held the last weekend in May and the first two weekends in June.

Outdoor Activities and Sports

Water Sports

Rafting, tubing, and canoeing are popular on the **Guadalupe River** between Canyon Lake, north of San Antonio, and New Braunfels. Try **Jerry's Rentals** (✉ River Rd. north of New Braunfels, ☎ 830/625–2036), **Rockin' R River Rides** (☎ 830/629–9999), or **Gruene River Co.** (☎ 830/625–2800), on the river in New Braunfels. With its surrounding steep evergreen hills, **Canyon Lake** is one of the most scenic lakes in Texas and has two yacht clubs, two marinas, a water-skiing club, and excellent fishing (an 86-pound flathead catfish is just one local record).

Spectator Sports

Baseball: San Antonio Missions (✉ 5757 Hwy. 90 W, ☎ 210/675–7275). **Basketball: San Antonio Spurs** (✉ Alamodome, 100 Montana St., ☎ 210/554–7787 or 800/688–7787). **Horse Racing: Retama Park** (✉ I-35, exit 174A, San Antonio, ☎ 210/651–7000); June–November, Wednesday–Sunday; simulcasts daily, year-round.

Shopping

San Antonio

With its rich ethnic heritage, this city is a wonderful place to buy Mexican imports, most of them inexpensive and many of high quality. **El Mercado** is the Mexican market building that is part of **Market Square** (✉ 514 W. Commerce St., ☎ 210/207–8600). The building contains about 35 shops, including stores selling blankets, Mexican dresses, men's guayabera shirts, and strings of brightly painted papier-mâché vegetables. The lively Farmer's Market is another area of Market Square worth visiting. **La Villita** (✉ 418 Villita St.), a restored village a few blocks south of downtown, is now a conglomeration of crafts shops and small restaurants, some in adobe buildings dating from the 1820s. It's noteworthy for its Latin American importers and demonstrations by its resident glassblower. **Rivercenter** (✉ 849 E. Commerce St., ☎ 210/225–0000) is a fairly standard, if very ritzy, shopping mall right on the river. **Paris Hatters** (✉ 119 Broadway, ☎ 210/223–3453) is an atmospheric place to buy western hats.

The Hill Country

Fredericksburg's main street is lined with antiques shops, imaginative stores, fragrant German bakeries, and western saloons.

AUSTIN

Created as the capital of the then-new Republic of Texas in 1839, **Austin** is a liberal enclave in a generally conservative state and a heavily treed, hilly town in a land commonly known for its monotonous flatness. For many years a quiet university town, within the past two decades Austin has grown rapidly, developing into another Silicon Valley, home to many semiconductor and computer companies. The growth of high-tech industry, combined with the state government and the university, has made for a vital and culturally diverse community; indeed, Austin now has the country's second-fastest-growing job market (the first is Las Vegas).

With numerous clubs and music venues, Austin draws many top musicians. Billing itself as the "live music capital of the world," the city has been on the national music map since 1984 when *Austin City Limits,* a showcase for bands that taped at the University of Texas campus, began airing nationwide. Austin then cemented its music reputation by putting on the annual music industry conference called South by Southwest, which draws bands and record company executives from around the world every March. Because of its natural beauty and the economic incentives provided to film there, Austin also hosts many TV and film crews.

Visitor Information

Austin Convention and Visitors Bureau (✉ 201 E. 2nd St., 78701, ☎ 512/478–0098). **Chamber of Commerce** (✉ 111 Congress Ave., 78701, ☎ 512/478–9383).

Arriving and Departing

Between Dallas–Fort Worth and San Antonio on I–35, Austin is accessible from Houston via U.S. 290. **Robert Mueller Municipal Airport** (☎ 512/472–3321) handles local flights. **Bergstrom,** a new airport still under construction at press time (spring 1998), was scheduled to open in 1999. **Amtrak** (✉ 250 N. Lamar Blvd., 78703, ☎ 512/476–5684 or 800/872–7245) serves the city with three trains weekly west to Los Angeles and the same number north to Chicago. **Greyhound Lines** has a station in Austin (✉ 916 E. Koenig La., 78751, ☎ 512/454–9686 or 800/231–2222).

Exploring Austin

Austin's downtown is dominated by its impressive **capitol,** constructed in 1888 of Texas pink granite. Tours of the capitol and the adjacent **governor's mansion** (☎ 512/463–5518; 🎫 free) start from the Capitol Complex Visitors Center (✉ 112 E. 11th St., 78701, ☎ 512/305–8400 or 512/463–0063 for tour information).

The sprawling **University of Texas** campus flanks the capitol's north end. The campus is home to the **Lyndon Baines Johnson Presidential Library and Museum** (✉ 2313 Red River Rd., ☎ 512/916–5136; 🎫 free). Also of interest on the UT campus is the **Archer M. Huntingdon Art Gallery** (✉ 23rd and San Jacinto Sts., ☎ 512/471–7324; 🎫 free). Austin's **Lyric Opera** (☎ 512/472–5927), the **Austin Symphony** (☎ 512/476–6064), and **Ballet Austin** (☎ 512/476–2163) all perform at the Performing Arts Center and Bass Concert Hall, adjacent to the Huntingdon Art Gallery. **Guadalupe Street,** which borders the west side of the UT campus, is lined with trendy boutiques and restaurants.

With the stately capitol seated at its north end, **Congress Avenue**—specifically, the bridge at its southern downtown end—is also home to a colony of hundreds of thousands of Mexican bats. Attracted to the small space between the arches of the bridge and the road above, the nocturnal critters swarm into town every evening at dusk, creating a creepy but memorable cocktail-hour spectacle for hundreds of spectators. The grassy expanse on the bridge's northeastern end is a good vantage point.

Parks, Gardens, and Zoos

Many people and companies have moved to Austin to enjoy a quality of life enhanced by pristine waterways and extensive greenbelts for hiking, biking, and running. **Zilker Park** (✉ 2100 Barton Springs Rd., ☎ 512/499–6700), the city's largest public park, connects to **Town Lake's hike and bike trail. Barton Springs** (☎ 512/476–9044), a huge natural-spring pool, is Zilker Park's main attraction. Built in the early 1900s when the city dammed Barton Creek, the pool is more than ¼ mi long and a constant 68°F. It is considered one of the nation's premier swimming holes, and Austinites cherish it as the jewel of their city. Little ones love swimming in the pool and also enjoy riding on the **miniature Amtrak train** that circles the park's perimeter between the months of April and October.

The **Zilker Botanical Gardens** (✉ 2220 Barton Springs Rd., ☎ 512/477–8672; admission free), across from Zilker Park, has more than 26 acres of horticultural delights, including butterfly trails and xeriscape gardens with native plants that thrive in an arid southwestern climate. The **Austin Nature and Science Center** (✉ 301 Nature Center Dr., ☎ 512/327–8180; admission free), adjacent to the botanical gardens, has 80 acres of trails, interactive exhibits teaching about the environment, and animal exhibits. The **National Wildflower Research Center** (✉ 4801 LaCrosse Ave., 78739, ☎ 512/292–4100; admission $3.50), in a 43-acre complex sponsored by Lady Bird Johnson, has extensive plantings of wildflowers that bloom all year round. The center is closed on Monday.

A bit farther afield, the **Wild Basin Wilderness Preserve** (✉ 805 N. Capital of Texas Hwy., 78746, ☎ 512/327–7622; admission free) has 227 acres of walking trails with beautiful contrasting views of the Hill Country and downtown Austin; there are guided tours on weekends.

Dining

Austin's restaurant selection is one of the most varied and sophisticated in Texas. For price ranges *see* Chart 1 (A) *in* On the Road with Fodor's.

$$$ ✕ **Hudson's on the Bend.** A bit outside town, overlooking a bend in beautiful Lake Austin, Hudson's serves exotic southwestern novelties as grilled tenderloin of ostrich with porcini sauce. ✉ *3509 Ranch Rd. 620,* ☎ *512/266–1369. Reservations essential. AE, DC, MC, V. No lunch.*

$$–$$$ ✕ **Castle Hill Café.** Here you'll find irresistible tortilla soup, imaginative salads, and eclectic entrées such as marinated beef medallions. The café is consistently voted among Austin's finest. ✉ *1101 W. 5th St.,* ☎ *512/476–0728. AE, D, MC, V.*

$$ ✕ **Bitter End.** A sleek, slightly industrial interior sets the scene for the see-and-be-seen crowd at this cozy brew pub. Duck liver pâté, wood-fired pizzas, and an ever-updated Italian-tinged menu are all enhanced by outstanding home-brewed ales. ✉ *311 Colorado St.,* ☎ *512/478–2337. AE, D, DC, MC, V.*

$$ ✕ **Güeros.** The ceiling is high, the floorboards worn, and the windows long and tall in this former feed store, now a favorite Tex-Mex restaurant with live music and a spacious, rustic bar. After President Clinton ordered the Numero Dos during a visit to Austin in 1996, the dish was renamed El Presidente. ✉ *1412 S. Congress Ave.,* ☎ *512/447–7688. AE, D, DC, MC, V.*

$ ✕ **Threadgill's.** Southern-style food and a friendly atmosphere make Threadgill's a local legend, drawing the likes of Janis Joplin to sample its massive chicken-fried steak. Homemade cobbler and live music add to the appeal. ✉ *6416 N. Lamar Blvd.,* ☎ *512/451–5440;* ✉ *301 W. Riverside,* ☎ *512/472–9304. MC, V.*

Lodging

For price ranges *see* Chart 2 (A) *in* On the Road with Fodor's.

$$$$ 🏨 **Four Seasons.** Built along the banks of Town Lake in downtown Austin, this luxury hotel has beautiful views of sunsets over the water and the loveliest lakeside Sunday brunch in town. It is also a prime location in summer for watching the bat exodus from under the Congress Avenue Bridge (☞ Exploring Austin, *above*). ✉ *98 San Jacinto*

Blvd., 78701, ☎ *512/478–4500 or 800/332–3442,* FAX *512/478–3117. 292 rooms. Restaurant, pool. AE, DC, MC, V.*

$$$ **Driskill Hotel.** Fronting Congress Avenue, Austin's main downtown street, this historic Renaissance Revival edifice was built in 1886. Step inside to see its elegant lobby, which has vaulted ceilings. ✉ *604 Brazos St., 78701,* ☎ *512/474–5911 or 800/252–9367,* FAX *512/474–2188. 177 rooms. Restaurant. AE, D, DC, MC, V.*

$$–$$$ **Doubletree Guest Suites.** Conveniently located between downtown and the university, this all-suite hotel is only a block away from the capitol, which is visible from many of the rooms. ✉ *30 W. 15th St., 78701,* ☎ *512/478–7000 or 800/424–2900,* FAX *512/478–5103. 189 suites. Restaurant, pool, exercise room. AE, D, DC, MC, V.*

Nightlife

Numerous traveling and homegrown bands play nightly in the city's many music venues, most of which are clustered around downtown's **Sixth Street,** between Red River Drive and Congress Avenue. To find out who's playing where, pick up a free *Austin Chronicle* or Thursday's *Austin American Statesman.* Some of the town's most distinctive clubs are a little farther afield: If country-western and line dancing are your thing, do the two-step at the **Broken Spoke** (✉ 3201 S. Lamar Blvd., 78704, ☎ 512/442–6189). Rustic, quirky, and no bigger than your parents' basement, the smoky, no-frills **Continental Club** (✉ 1315 S. Congress Ave., ☎ 512/441–2444) plays country-tinged rock. **Liberty Lunch** (✉ 405 W. 2nd St., ☎ 512/477–0461) is another local musical institution. A restored downtown movie palace, the **Paramount** (✉ 713 Congress Ave., ☎ 512/472–5470) is home to both musical acts and touring theater companies. Local theater thrives at the **Zachary Scott Theatre** (✉ 1510 Toomey Rd., ☎ 512/476–0541), named for an Austin native son who was successful in 1930s Hollywood.

DALLAS AND FORT WORTH

These twin cities, separated by 30 mi of suburbs, may be the oddest couple in a state of odd couples. **Dallas** is glitzy and ritzy, a swelling, modernistic business metropolis where style takes precedence over substance and image is everything. **Fort Worth,** sneered at as "Cowtown" by its neighbors, lives in the shadow of its wild history as a rip-roaring cowboy town, a place of gunfights and cattle drives—even though its cultural establishment is superior to Dallas's. In Fort Worth, that fellow in the faded jeans and cowboy hat could well be the president of the bank. In Dallas, people tend to be a bit more formal.

Visitor Information

Dallas: Convention & Visitors Bureau (✉ 1201 Elm St., Ste. 2000, 75270, ☎ 214/746–6677 or 800/232–5527, 214/746–6679 for recorded schedule of events); information booths are downtown (✉ 1303 Commerce St.), in NorthPark Center (✉ Northwest Hwy. at Central Expressway), and at the West End Market Place 9 (✉ 603 Munger, Suite 124). **Fort Worth:** Convention & Visitors Bureau (✉ 415 Throckmorton St., 76102, ☎ 817/336–8791 or 800/433–5747); information booths are downtown (✉ Fourth St. at Throckmorton St.) and at the Stockyards (✉ 130 E. Exchange Ave.). **Dallas–Fort Worth International Airport** (☎ 972/574–3694) also has information booths.

Arriving and Departing

By Bus

Greyhound Lines (☎ 214/655–7082 or 800/231–2222) has stations in Dallas (✉ 205 S. Lamar St.) and Fort Worth (✉ 901 Commerce St.).

By Car

The **Metroplex,** as the Greater Dallas–Fort Worth area is known, is well served by interstates. The main approaches include I–35 from Oklahoma to the north and Waco to the south; I–30 from Arkansas; I–20 from Louisiana or New Mexico; and I–45 from Houston. The twin cities are linked by I–20, which is the southern route, and I–30, generally the more useful road. There are two tollways in the Dallas area, the Dallas North Tollway, running from I–35E north of downtown into Collin County to the north, and Mountain Creek Bridge, in southwestern Dallas County. Two major expressways, I–30 and I–635, have High Occupancy Vehicle (HOV) lanes for vehicles with two or more occupants. Though the highway number designations are easy to find on a map, many of these thoroughfares are also known and referred to locally by name, which can make getting directions somewhat confusing. For example, State Highway 183, which leads to the south entrance of DFW Airport, is often referred to as Airport Freeway. U.S. Highway 75 is known to locals as Central Expressway (since it is perpetually in a state of construction, it is a good route to avoid). Dallas is circled by the I–635 ring road, known as the LBJ Freeway; Fort Worth is looped by I–820.

By Plane

Dallas–Fort Worth International Airport (☎ 214/574–8888), midway between Dallas and Fort Worth, is the main airport for both cities and is currently the second-largest and second-busiest airport in the world. Taxi service to either downtown Dallas or downtown Fort Worth generally runs $25–$30. Cheaper van service is provided by the 24-hour **Supershuttle** (☎ 817/329–2000). Fort Worth's public transportation system, **The T** (☎ 817/215–8600) runs an $8 shuttle between the airport and downtown Fort Worth. Ritzier service is provided by **Advantage Limousine** (☎ 972/618–7313).

Love Field (✉ Cedar Springs at Mockingbird La., Dallas, ☎ 214/670–6073), a $10–$15 taxi ride from downtown Dallas, is the hub of Southwest Airlines (☎ 972/263–1717 or 800/435–9792).

By Train

Amtrak (☎ 214/653–1101 or 800/872–7245) service connects Dallas–Fort Worth to San Antonio, Houston, and Chicago; from these cities other connections are possible. Dallas service originates at **Union Station** (✉ 400 Houston St., ☎ 214/653–1101). In Fort Worth, service originates from the old **Santa Fe Depot** (✉ 1501 Jones St., ☎ 817/332–2931), across from the convention center.

Getting Around Dallas and Fort Worth

A car is the best way to see Dallas and Forth Worth, though both cities have bus systems. Public transportation in Dallas is run by **Dallas Area Rapid Transit** (DART) (☎ 214/979–1111) and consists of buses that service Dallas and 12 suburban cities along with a light-rail system with a limited route.

Exploring Dallas and Fort Worth

Dallas

Many thousands visit Dallas, in spite of—or perhaps because of—the city's unhappy legacy as the assassination site of President John F. Kennedy, which occurred downtown. Also downtown is one of the most remarkable flowerings of skyscraping architecture anywhere—that same skyline familiar to the world from the television show *Dallas*—accompanied by the restaurants and shops of the **West End,** a former warehouse district. Near the West End are several major cultural institutions, and only a little farther away is ★ **Deep Ellum,** the lively center of the city's alternative scene. A short car trip from downtown are several historic areas that give a sense of the old Dallas. To the north, where the city's establishment has long been entrenched, there's shopping galore.

DOWNTOWN

On November 22, 1963, shots rang out on **Dealey Plaza,** at the west end of downtown, as the presidential motorcade rounded the corner from Houston Street onto the Elm Street approach to the Triple Underpass. Eventually the Warren Commission would conclude—to the continuing disbelief of many Americans—that President Kennedy was gunned down by Lee Harvey Oswald, acting alone and firing from the sixth floor of the **Texas School Book Depository.** Today, the Sixth Floor exhibit reveals the details of the assassination, along with an account of the conspiracy theories that continue to emerge. ✉ *411 Elm St.,* ☎ *214/747–6660.* 🎫 *$7.*

The grassy knoll from which many believe a second gunman fired is just to the right of the Book Depository, on the Elm Street side. **Dealey Plaza,** where visitors inevitably congregate to look up at the so-called sniper's perch, is directly across the street. The stark **cenotaph,** designed like an empty house by architect Philip Johnson as a personal tribute to his friend Kennedy, is a short walk from Dealey Plaza, at Main and Market streets.

Those with more of an *X-Files* view of life can check out the **Conspiracy Museum** (✉ 110 S. Market, ☎ 214/741–3040; 🎫 $7), where the history of presidential assassinations and cover-ups from 1835 to the present is meticulously examined.

The **West End Historic District** is an area of brick warehouses built between 1900 and 1930 and brought back to life in 1976. Now filled with restaurants and shops, it is one of the city's biggest draws both day and night. Within the historic district is the **West End Market Place** (✉ 603 Munger Ave., ☎ 214/748–4801), once a candy-and-cracker factory and now a lively, five-story shopping-and-eating center built around an atrium.

The **Old Red Courthouse** (✉ Main St. at Houston St.) faces Philip Johnson's cenotaph. This 1892 Romanesque building of red sandstone is one of the city's oldest surviving structures and a familiar landmark. The **John Neely Bryan Cabin,** a reconstructed 1841 log cabin and trading post that was the city's first building, is adjacent to the courthouse on the Dallas County Historical Plaza.

Almost all the major skyscrapers that make up the famous Dallas skyline were completed in the 1980s, many by renowned architect I. M. Pei. The **Dallas City Hall** (✉ 1500 Marilla St.), a striking Pei creation, is notable for the stunning bronze Henry Moore sculpture on the broad plaza outside. Next to City Hall in **Pioneer Plaza** stands Robert Summer's interpretation of life on the old Shawnee Trail: 70 longhorn

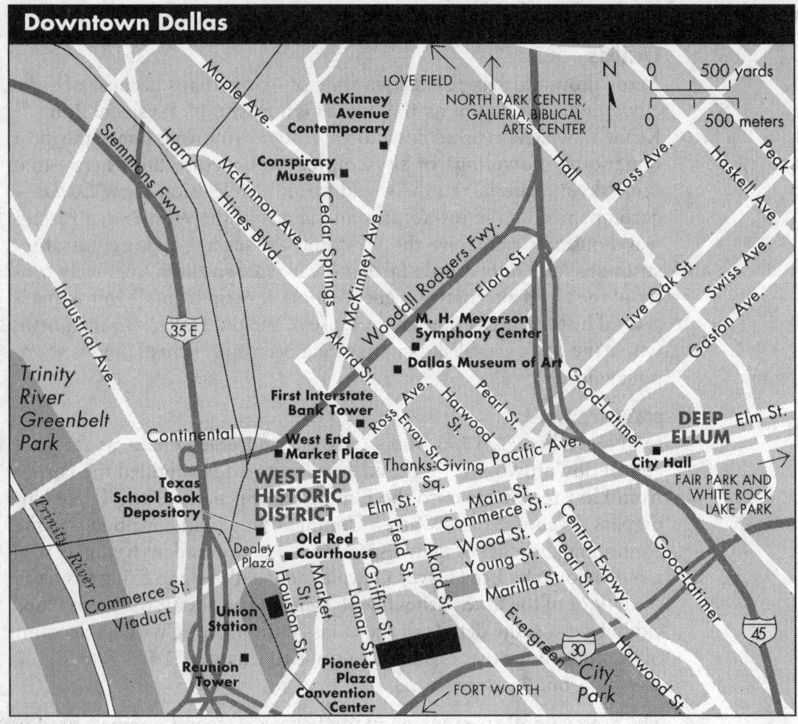

steer and three cowboys. It is said to be the largest bronze sculpture in the world.

The **NationsBank Tower** (✉ 901 Main St.) is visible for miles, thanks to its 72 stepped stories outlined in green lights. Lending a peculiar, science-fiction twist to the skyline is **Reunion Tower** (✉ 300 Reunion Blvd.), with an **observation deck** (🎫 $2) and a revolving rooftop restaurant and bar. In **Thanks-Giving Square** (✉ Pacific Ave. and Ervay St., ☎ 214/969–1977), a small triangular plaza designed by Philip Johnson contains quiet gardens and a chapel with stained glass by Gabriel Loire.

Housed in a series of low, white limestone galleries built off a central barrel vault, the **Dallas Museum of Art** (✉ 1717 N. Harwood St., ☎ 214/922–1200; 🎫 free) is in the Arts District, on the north edge of downtown. Standout exhibits are Claes Oldenburg's *Stake Hitch,* a huge stake and rope sculpture, and Frederic Church's chilling painting *The Icebergs.*

The I. M. Pei–designed **Morton H. Meyerson Symphony Center** (✉ 2301 Flora St., ☎ 214/670–3600) is a place of sweeping, dramatic curves, ever-changing vanishing points, and surprising views. Inside is the **Herman W. Lay Family Organ**, a hand-built and installed Fisk organ with 4,535 pipes. **De Musica,** a solid iron sculpture by the great Basque sculptor Eduardo Chillida, rests in front of the Symphony Center.

OTHER ATTRACTIONS

Deep Ellum, a 20-minute walk east from downtown, was born as the city's first black neighborhood. Today it is the throbbing center of Dallas' avant-garde, with trend-setting art galleries, bars, clubs, and restaurants. The area centers on Commerce, Main, and Elm streets; its name is a phonetic rendering of *deep elm* pronounced with a southern drawl.

Fair Park (☒ 1300 Robert B. Cullum Blvd., ☎ 214/670–8400), just southeast of Deep Ellum, is a 277-acre National Historic Landmark comprising the largest collection of 1930s Art Deco architecture in the United States. Most of the grounds date from the 1936 Texas Centennial Exhibition, although the park has hosted the State Fair of Texas since 1886. In the **Hall of State** (☒ 3939 Grand Ave., ☎ 214/421–4500; 🎟 free) murals tell the story of Texas in heroic terms. Fair Park also contains six major exhibit spaces: the **African-American Museum** (☒ 3536 Grand Ave., ☎ 214/565–9026; 🎟 free); the **Age of Steam Railroad Museum** (☎ 214/428–0101; 🎟 free); the **Dallas Aquarium** (☎ 214/670–8443; 🎟 $2); the **Dallas Horticultural Center** (☎ 214/428–7476; 🎟 free); the **Dallas Museum of Natural History** (☒ 3535 E. Grand Ave., ☎ 214/421–3466; 🎟 $4); and the **Science Place** (☒ 1318 Second Ave., ☎ 214/428–5555; 🎟 $6), which also houses Dallas' **IMAX Theater** (🎟 $6; or $10 for Science Place and IMAX Theater).

In east Dallas, **Swiss Avenue** has the city's best representations of two distinct periods. On lower Swiss Avenue (2900 block), nearer to downtown, the **Wilson Block Historic District** is an unaltered block of turn-of-the-century frame houses restored as offices for nonprofit groups. Set-back Prairie-style and other mansions are common in the **Swiss Avenue Historic District** (particularly the 5000–5500 blocks).

McKinney Avenue, just north of downtown in the city's burgeoning "Uptown" neighborhood, is lined with bustling bars and trendy restaurants. Authentic, restored **trolleys** (☎ 214/855–5267; 🎟 $1.50) run up McKinney from outside the Dallas Museum of Art. The **McKinney Avenue Contemporary** (☒ 3120 McKinney Ave., ☎ 214/953–1622; free), locally know as "the MAC," consists of a theater, gallery space, and video installation space.

In the **Biblical Arts Center,** (☒ 7500 Park La., ☎ 214/691–4661; 🎟 $4), a bit north of McKinney Avenue, sound and light bring a 124-by-20-ft biblical mural to life. Here you'll also find a replica of Christ's tomb at Calvary.

Anyone interested in the entertainment industry will be star-struck by **The Movie Studios at Las Colinas** (☒ 6301 N. O'Connor Rd., Irving, ☎ 972/869–0700; 🎟 $12.95), about 25 minutes northwest of downtown. Tours include a visit to the soundstage facilities used in the filming of such movies as *JFK, Silkwood,* and *Robocop.*

Just minutes north of Dallas lies one of the city's most enduring landmarks, **Southfork Ranch** (☒ 3700 Hogge Rd., Parker, ☎ 972/442–7800; 🎟 $6.50). Built in 1970, the ranch became one of the city's best-known symbols when the TV show *Dallas* premiered in 1978. Visitors can still tour the mansion, have lunch at Miss Ellie's Deli, and try to remember who shot J. R.

Fort Worth

Downtown Fort Worth is where you'll find the city's financial core, most of its historic buildings, and Sundance Square, the restored turn-of-the-century neighborhood that is one of the city's main attractions. The Stockyards and adjacent western-theme stores, restaurants, and hotels are a few miles north of downtown, clustered around Main Street and Exchange Avenue. The cultural district, west of downtown on Lancaster Avenue, is home to four well-known museums, a coliseum complex, and several parks.

DOWNTOWN

In Fort Worth's underrated downtown, modern glass-and-steel towers stand face-to-face with human-scale century-old Victorian buildings. The billionaire Bass brothers of Fort Worth are to be thanked for what may be the most eye-pleasing juxtaposition of scale: Rather than tear down several blocks of brick buildings to accommodate the twin towers of their giant City Center development, they created **Sundance Square** (bounded by Houston, Commerce, Second, and Third streets) by restoring the area as a center of tall-windowed restaurants, shops, nightclubs, and offices. Sundance Square's name recalls the Sundance Kid (Harry Longbaugh), who with Butch Cassidy (Robert Leroy Parker) hid out around 1898 in the nearby neighborhood, south and east of the present square, known as Hell's Half-Acre. This was a violent quarter of dank saloons, drunken cowboys, and dirty brothels. The **Sid Richardson Collection of Western Art** (✉ 309 Main St., ☎ 817/332–6554; 🎫 free) conjures up parts of this dark world in the idealized oils of Frederic Remington and Charles Russell.

In Sundance Square, the **Fire Station Museum** (✉ 215 Commerce St., ☎ 817/732–1631; 🎫 free) houses an exhibit on 150 years of city history. The 1907 building fronts on the street where cattle headed for the Chisholm Trail used to pass.

The wedge-shape **Flatiron Building** (✉ 1000 Houston St.), also downtown, is topped by gargoyles and panthers. Built in 1907 as medical offices, it was patterned on similar Renaissance Revival structures in New York and Philadelphia. Near the Flatiron Building, the former **Texas Hotel,** now the Radisson Plaza (✉ 815 N. Main St., ☎ 817/870–2100), is where President Kennedy slept the night before he was assassinated.

The **Tarrant County Courthouse** (✉ 100 E. Weatherford St.), on the northern edge of downtown, is an 1895 Beaux Arts building of native red granite. A sad reminder of American history, the building that now houses the Ellis Pecan Company was once the **Ku Klux Klan Building** (✉ 1012 N. Main St.).

THE STOCKYARDS

The **Fort Worth Stockyards Historic District** recalls the prosperity brought to the city in 1902 when two major Chicago meat packers, Armour and Swift, set up plants here to ship meat across the country in refrigerator cars. In the **Livestock Exchange Building** (✉ 131 E. Exchange Ave.), where cattle agents kept their offices, you'll find the **Stockyards Museum** (☎ 817/625–5082; 🎫 free). Across the street from the Livestock Exchange Building, **Stockyard Station** (✉ 130 E. Exchange Ave., ☎ 817/625–9715) is a fast-growing marketplace of shops and restaurants, all housed in former sheep and hog pens. **Cowtown Coliseum** (✉ 121 E. Exchange Ave., ☎ 817/625–1025) was constructed in 1908 to house what became the Southwestern Exposition and Fat Stock Show; today it is the site of Saturday-night rodeos. The **Tarantula Train** (✉ 2318 8th Ave., ☎ 817/625–7245; 🎫 $19.95), a restored historic 1896 steam locomotive, links the Stockyards with nearby **Grapevine** (☎ 817/481–0454 or 800/457–6338), home to three of Texas' 27 wineries. Information on the Stockyards area is available at the **Stockyards Visitors Center** (✉ 130 E. Exchange Ave., ☎ 817/624–4741).

THE CULTURAL DISTRICT

★ Architect Louis Kahn's last and finest building was the **Kimbell Art Museum,** six long concrete vaults with skylights running the length of each. Here are top-notch collections of both early 20th-century European art and old masters, including Munch's *Girls on a Jetty* and Goya's *The Matador Pedro Romero,* depicting the great bullfighter who killed 5,600 of the animals. *✉ 3333 Camp Bowie Blvd., ☎ 817/332–8451. 🎫 Free. Closed Mon.*

The **Amon Carter Museum** (✉ 3501 Camp Bowie Blvd., ☎ 817/738–1933; 🎟 free), along with the city's two other major museums, is a short walk from the Kimbell. Designed by Philip Johnson, the Amon Carter has a collection of American art centered on Remingtons and Russells. Texas' oldest art museum, the **Modern Art Museum of Fort Worth** (✉ 1309 Montgomery St., ☎ 817/738–9215; 🎟 free) focuses on such painters as Picasso, Rauschenberg, and Warhol. Biology, geology, computer science, and astronomy are the order of the day at the **Fort Worth Museum of Science and History** (✉ 1501 Montgomery St., ☎ 817/732–1631; 🎟 $5), which also incorporates the **Noble Planetarium** (🎟 $3) and the **Omni Theater** (🎟 $6).

The **Will Rogers Memorial Center** (✉ 1 Amon Carter Sq., ☎ 817/871–8150), near Fort Worth's museums, is a partially restored coliseum-and-stock-pen complex named after the humorist and Fort Worth booster, who described the city as "where the West begins" (and Dallas as "where the East peters out"). The center includes an equestrian arena that's used for horse and livestock shows.

Parks, Gardens, and Zoos

Dallas

Fair Park (☞ Exploring Dallas and Fort Worth, *above*), with its many museums and formal gardens, is one of the city's most visited parks; every fall it hosts Texas' largest State Fair (☞ Festivals and Seasonal Events *in* the Southwest introduction). At **White Rock Lake Park** (✉ 8300 Garland Rd., ☎ 214/670–8283), a 9⅓-mi jogging and bicycling path circles the sailboat-dotted lake. White Rock Lake Park is also home to the **Dallas Arboretum and Botanical Garden** (✉ 8617 Garland Rd., ☎ 214/327–8263; 🎟 $6), 66 acres of gardens and lawns. **Old City Park,** just south of downtown (✉ 1717 Gano St., ☎ 214/421–5141; 🎟 $5), is an outdoor museum consisting of more than 33 historic buildings, including log cabins, antebellum mansions, and a Victorian bandstand. At the **Dallas Zoo** (✉ 621 E. Clarendon St., ☎ 214/670–5656; 🎟 $6), a monorail brings you past lowland gorillas in a natural habitat.

Fort Worth

★ **Water Gardens Park** (✉ 15th and Commerce Sts.) is a dramatic blend of modern sculpture and cascading fountains designed by Philip Johnson and John Burgee. In one area, visitors can stand 38 ft below street level and view 1,000 gallons of water tumbling down a 710-ft wall. Just south of the cultural district, the **Fort Worth Botanic Garden** (✉ 3220 Botanic Garden Dr., at University Dr., ☎ 817/871–7686; 🎟 free, Japanese garden $2) has a 10,000-square-ft conservatory. In Forest Park ★ is the **Fort Worth Zoo** (✉ 1989 Colonial Pkwy., ☎ 817/871–7050; 🎟 $7) has more than 5,000 exotic and native animals as exotic as a Komodo dragon and a rare white tiger.

Dining

For price ranges *see* Chart 1 (A) *in* On the Road with Fodor's.

Dallas

$$$$ ★ ✕ **Mansion on Turtle Creek.** Chef Dean Fearing helped pioneer Southwestern cuisine, and he continues to wow his customers with amazing renditions of tortilla soup, warm lobster tacos, or perhaps halibut with cashews in basil sauce. Count on finding Dallas/Fort Worth's most beautiful, celebrated, and powerful crowd inside this opulent room. ✉ *Mansion Hotel, 2821 Turtle Creek Blvd.,* ☎ *214/559–2100. Reservations essential. Jacket required. AE, DC, MC, V.*

$$$–$$$$ ✕ **Enigma.** Noted as much for its peculiarities (the restaurant has no freezer and there are 26 different menus) as for its food, Enigma consists of a tiny dining room more reminiscent of a gallery than a top-notch eatery. Look for unusual delicacies such as Scottish partridge and rack of kangaroo. ✉ *3005 Routh St.,* ☏ *214/953–1111. Reservations essential. AE, DC, MC, V. Closed Sun. No lunch.*

$$$–$$$$ ★ ✕ **Star Canyon.** Stephan Pyles' trendy Oak Lawn restaurant is the hottest ticket in town—which means reservations are nearly impossible to get in less than weeks in advance. Prepare to be dazzled by Southwestern-inspired inventions such as tamale tart with roast-garlic custard or red-chile- and Shiner-Bock-braised *osso buco*. The dining room has a branded ceiling, and a barbed-wire motif is etched into the bar area's glass panels. ✉ *3102 Oak Lawn Ave.,* ☏ *214/520–7827. Reservations essential. AE, DC, MC. V. No lunch.*

$$–$$$ ✕ **Del Frisco's.** Even in Dallas, cattle is king, and you can't get a better piece of beef than in this legendary steak house. ✉ *5251 Spring Valley Rd.,* ☏ *972/490–9000. AE, DC, MC, V. Closed Sun. No lunch.*

$–$$$ ✕ **Routh Street Brewery.** Routh Street is among the best of Dallas' brew pubs, with tasty Texas Hill Country cuisine—sausages, sauerkraut, and the like—to go with the brews. ✉ *3011 Routh St.,* ☏ *214/922–8835. AE, DC, MC, V.*

$$ ★ ✕ **Barclay's.** In a charming old house, chef Nick Barclay reinvents British classics. A reasonable fixed-price menu have earned this relative newcomer a key position on the Dallas dining scene. ✉ *2917 Fairmount St.,* ☏ *214/855–0700. AE, MC, V. Closed Tues., Wed. No lunch.*

$$ ✕ **Deep Ellum Café.** Multiethnic specialties such as Portobello mushroom burritos and Vietnamese grilled-chicken salad are served in this funky eatery in the heart of trendy Deep Ellum. ✉ *2706 Elm St.,* ☏ *214/741–9012. AE, MC, V.*

$–$$ ✕ **Mariano's.** Owner Mariano Martinez invented the frozen margarita in Dallas in 1971. Today folks flock in to enjoy his original icy masterpieces along with credible Tex-Mex fare. ✉ *5500 Greenville Ave.,* ☏ *214/691–3888. AE, DC, MC, V. Closed Mon.*

Fort Worth

$$–$$$ ✕ **Angeluna.** A see-and-be-seen crowd and a sometimes-raucous atmosphere make this newcomer on Sundance Square an exciting place to dine. Chef Clark McDaniel serves eclectic winners such as chipotle-dusted rare tuna steak and key lime tart. ✉ *215 E. Fourth St.,* ☏ *817/334–0080. AE, DC, MC, V.*

$$–$$$ ★ ✕ **Bistro Louise.** People drive 30 mi from Dallas to dine on tea-smoked duck, macadamia-crusted shrimp, and the like. ✉ *2900 S. Hulen St.,* ☏ *817/922–9244. AE, DC, D, MC, V. Closed Sun.*

$$–$$$ ✕ **Reata.** This is about as Texan as restaurants get in the Metroplex, with leather-trimmed menus, cow-covered chairs, and beef straight from the owner's ranch. Other selling points include a great view, good food, and friendly service. ✉ *500 Throckmorton St., Bank One Tower, 35th floor,* ☏ *817/336–1009. AE, MC, V.*

$$–$$$ ★ ✕ **Saint-Emilion.** Though it doesn't look like much from the outside, this is one of Tarrant County's best restaurants, with a legendary crispy-roast duck and excellent daily specials. The wine list is so extensive that it has its own table of contents. ✉ *3617 W. 7th St.,* ☏ *817/737–2781. Reservations essential. AE, MC, V. Closed Mon. No lunch.*

$–$$ ✕ **Angelo's Barbecue.** Angelo's is famous for its succulent smoked ribs, so tender that the meat falls off the bone. Arrive early, as they've been known to run out of ribs well before closing. ✉ *2533 White Settlement Rd.,* ☏ *817/332–0357. Reservations not accepted. No credit cards. Closed Sun.*

$ ✕ **Joe T. Garcia's.** This is the ultimate Tex-Mex joint, where cowboy-boot-clad customers drink Mexican beer and the bartenders mix potent margaritas. There's usually a wait for tables, which on Saturday nights can stretch to an hour. It's worth it. ✉ *2201 N. Commerce St.,* ☎ *817/626–4356. Reservations not accepted. No credit cards.*

Dining and Lodging

For price ranges *see* Charts 1 and 2 (A) *in* On the Road with Fodor's.

$$$$ ★ ✕🏨 **Hotel St. Germain.** Built as a private residence in 1906, this tiny boutique hotel with white-glove service is one of the most intimate and romantic in the city. The dining room (closed Sunday and Monday, no lunch) is known for its stellar $75-per-person prix fixe menu, which might include French Riviera bouillon, classic *terrine de foie gras,* or rack of lamb. ✉ *2516 Maple Ave., 75201,* ☎ *214/871–2516,* FAX *214/871–0740. 7 suites. Restaurant. AE, D, DC, MC, V.*

Lodging

For price ranges *see* Chart 2 (A) *in* On the Road with Fodor's.

Dallas

$$$$ 🏨 **Adolphus.** Beer baron Adolphus Busch created this Beaux Arts building, Dallas' finest old hotel, in 1912, sparing nothing in the way of rich ornamentation inside and out. Within is the celebrated French Room restaurant (closed Sunday, no lunch), with classics such as roasted duck breast in port sauce. ✉ *1321 Commerce St., 75202,* ☎ *214/742–8200 or 800/221–9083,* FAX *214/651–3561. 432 rooms. 3 restaurants, exercise room. AE, D, DC, MC, V.*

$$$$ ★ 🏨 **Four Seasons Resort and Club.** Looking like a Frank Lloyd Wright–designed country club, this hotel is quite possibly the city's best. Every room has a balcony that overlooks the TPC (Tournament Players Course) golf course, site of the Professional Golfers' Association's GTE Byron Nelson Classic. ✉ *4150 N. MacArthur Blvd., Irving, 75038,* ☎ *972/717–0700 or 800/332–3442,* FAX *972/717–2550. 357 rooms. 3 restaurants, pools, golf, tennis, health club. AE, DC, MC, V.*

$$$$ 🏨 **Mansion on Turtle Creek.** The Mansion is the only five-star, five-diamond hotel in the Southwest. The service is legendary, as is the food in the dining room (☞ *above*). ✉ *2821 Turtle Creek Blvd., 75219,* ☎ *214/559–2100,* FAX *214/528–4187. 142 rooms. 2 restaurants, bar, pool, health club. AE, D, DC, MC, V.*

$$$ 🏨 **Wyndham Anatole.** Political bigwigs such as George Bush and Colin Powell have made this huge glass-and-chrome complex their home away from home. ✉ *2201 Stemmons Fwy., 75207,* ☎ *214/748–1200 or 800/996–3426,* FAX *214/761–7242. 1,620 rooms. 7 restaurants, pools, tennis, health club. AE, D, DC, MC, V.*

$$–$$$ 🏨 **Dallas Parkway Hilton.** Though it looks like a standard chain, this is one of the few hotels in North Dallas with reasonable room rates. Guests can work out at the International Athletic Club, a few blocks north, for $7. ✉ *4801 LBJ Fwy., 75244,* ☎ *972/661–3600 or 800/445–8667,* FAX *972/385–3156. 310 rooms. Restaurant, pool. AE, D, DC, MC, V.*

$$–$$$ 🏨 **Stoneleigh.** Just north of downtown, this elegant, old brick hotel has long been favored by celebrities—including Oliver Stone while filming his movie on the Kennedy assassination. It's in the tony Turtle Creek neighborhood, just blocks away from the McKinney Avenue shopping and restaurant district. ✉ *2927 Maple Ave., 75201,* ☎ *214/871–7111 or 800/255–9299,* FAX *214/871–9379. 153 rooms. 2 restaurants, pool, exercise room. AE, D, DC, MC, V.*

Fort Worth

$$$–$$$$ ★ **The Worthington.** This 12-story ultramodern, white-concrete structure stretches along two city blocks, forming a dramatic glassed-in bridge (where lunch, brunch, and tea are served) over Houston Street. There's a spacious austerity to the rooms and lobby. ✉ *200 Main St., 76102,* ☎ *817/870–1000 or 800/433–5677, FAX 817/338–9176. 504 rooms. 3 restaurants, pool, tennis, health club. AE, D, DC, MC, V.*

$$–$$$ **Miss Molly's.** Once a prim little inn, then a raucous bordello, this place above the Star Café, just outside the Stockyards, has been reincarnated as an attractive B&B. ✉ *109½ W. Exchange Ave., 76106,* ☎ *817/626–1522 or 800/996–6559, FAX 817/625–2723. 8 rooms. Full breakfast. AE, D, DC, MC, V.*

$$–$$$ **Stockyards Hotel.** A storybook place that's seen more than its share of cowboys, rustlers, gangsters, and oil barons, the hotel has been used in many a movie. In the Booger Red Saloon, the bar stools are saddles. ✉ *109 E. Exchange Ave., 76106,* ☎ *817/625–6427 or 800/423–8471, FAX 817/624–2571. 46 rooms. Restaurant. AE, D, DC, MC, V.*

$–$$ **Green Oaks Park Hotel.** From the outside, it's certainly unimpressive, but the interior is clean, the staff is efficient, and it's one of the few places in the Metroplex where you can get a decent room for under $100. ✉ *6901 West Fwy., 76116,* ☎ *817/738–7311 or 800/433–2174, FAX 817/377–1308. 282 rooms. Restaurant, tennis, exercise room. AE, D, DC, MC, V.*

Nightlife and the Arts

Nightlife

DALLAS

Bars and Nightclubs. Much of Dallas bar life swirls around lower and upper **Greenville Avenue,** north of downtown. Siblings **Mick's** (✉ 2827 Greenville Ave., ☎ 214/827–3993) and **Terilli's** (✉ 2815 Greenville Ave., ☎ 214/827–3993) are known for live jazz, Italian food, and trendy surroundings. For country music and two-stepping, try **Country 2000** (✉ 10707 Finnell St., ☎ 214/654–9595).

Poor David's Pub (✉ 1924 Greenville Ave., ☎ 214/821–9891) is one of Dallas's better-known music venues.

Dance Clubs. At **Red Jacket** (✉ 3603 Greenville Ave., ☎ 214/823–8333) you can dance to everything from lounge to swing to 1970s disco. The scene is young and avant-garde in Deep Ellum, where **Club Dada** (✉ 2720 Elm St., ☎ 214/744–3232) is one of several trend-setting music spots. The **Club Clearview** complex (✉ 2806 Elm St., ☎ 214/283–5358) offers scenesters four distinct connected clubs, and **Trees** (✉ 2707 Elm St., ☎ 214/748–5009) serves up loud local and touring bands in a warehouselike setting. West End partygoers make **Dallas Alley** (✉ Market at Munger, ☎ 214/880–7420) their one-stop shop; one cover provides admission to several clubs. The notorious **Starck** club (✉ 703 McKinney Ave., ☎ 214/522–5665 or 214/922–9677), Dallas' answer to Studio 54, pumps dance music to the masses in its stylish, sleek environs. In Oak Lawn, **Village Station** (✉ 3911 Cedar Springs, ☎ 214/380–3808) caters to a predominately gay crowd, with disco on Sunday nights.

FORT WORTH

The area around the Stockyards is crammed with distinctly western-style saloons. The best may be the **White Elephant Saloon** (✉ 106 E. Exchange Ave., ☎ 817/624–1887), a legendary 100-year-old Wild West bar with live country music seven nights a week. The most famous saloon is **Billy Bob's Texas** (✉ 2520 Rodeo Plaza, ☎ 817/624–7117 or 817/589–1711), built in an old cattle-pen building, with big-name country music performers. Downtown, **Caravan of Dreams** (✉ 312 Houston St., ☎ 817/877–3000) is a world-class music venue specializing in jazz and blues greats, including top performers like Lyle Lovett. Don't miss the rooftop cactus garden. Fort Worth's beautiful people flock to downtown's **8.0** (✉ 111 E. Third,☎ 817/979–0880), one of the trendiest bars in a decidedly untrendy city.

The Arts

DALLAS

The top performing-arts attraction in Dallas is whatever's on at the **Morton H. Meyerson Symphony Center** (☞ Exploring Dallas and Fort Worth, *above*), home to the **Dallas Symphony Orchestra** (☎ 214/692–0203). The **Dallas Theater Center** performs at the **Kalita Humphreys Theatre** (✉ 3636 Turtle Creek Blvd., ☎ 214/522–8199), the only theater ever designed by Frank Lloyd Wright, and the **Arts District Theater** (✉ 2401 Flora, ☎ 214/522–8199). The **Majestic Theatre** (✉ 1925 Elm St., ☎ 214/880–0137), a beautifully restored 1920s vaudeville house and movie palace, hosts various performance groups. In Fair Park, **Starplex** (✉ 1818 1st Ave., ☎ 214/421–1111) hosts most of the big-name bands that come to town; the **Music Hall at Fair Park** is the site of performances by the **Dallas Opera** (☎ 214/443–1043) and the **Dallas Summer Musicals** (☎ 214/421–5678).

FORT WORTH

Casa Mañana Theater (✉ 3101 W. Lancaster Ave., ☎ 817/332–9319), a theater-in-the-round under one of Buckminster Fuller's first geodesic domes, hosts the city's summer series of musicals. Other local theaters include the **Jubilee Theatre** (✉ 506 Main St., ☎ 817/338–4411), **Circle Theatre** (✉ 230 W. Fourth St., ☎ 817/877–3040), and **Stage West** (✉ 3055 S. University Dr., ☎ 817/784–9378).

As of 1998, Sundance Square's brand-new **Nancy Lee and Perry R. Bass Performance Hall** is the home of the Fort Worth-Dallas Ballet (☎ 817/763–0207), the Fort Worth Opera (☎ 817/731–0833), and the Fort Worth Symphony Orchestra (☎ 817/926–8831).

Spectator Sports

Auto racing: Texas Motor Speedway (✉ I–35W and Hwy. 114, Fort Worth, ☎ 817/215–8500). **Texas Motorplex** (✉ 7500 W. Hwy. 287, Ennis, ☎ 972/878–0634). **Baseball: Texas Rangers** (✉ The Ballpark at Arlington, 1000 Ballpark Way, Arlington, ☎ 817/273–5100). **Basketball: Dallas Mavericks** (✉ Reunion Arena, 777 Sports St., Dallas, ☎ 972/988–3865). **Football: Dallas Cowboys** (✉ Texas Stadium, 2401 E. Airport Fwy., Irving, ☎ 972/579–5000). **Hockey: Dallas Stars** (✉ Reunion Arena, 777 Sports St., ☎ 214/467–8277). **Fort Worth Brahmas** (✉ Tarrant County Convention Center, 1111 Houston St., Fort Worth, ☎ 817/335–7825 or 817/884–2222). **Fort Worth Fire** (✉ Will Rogers Coliseum, 1 Amon Carter Sq., ☎ 817/336–1992). **Horse racing: Lone Star Park** (✉ 1001 Meyers Rd., Grand Prairie, ☎ 972/263–7223). **Soccer: Dallas Sidekicks** (✉ Reunion Arena, 777 Sports St., ☎ 972/988–3865). The **Burn** (✉ Cotton Bowl, Fair Park, Dallas, ☎ 214/979–0303).

Shopping

Dallas

Ever since 1873, when Dallas ensured its future by successfully finagling to become the site of the intersection of two intercontinental rail lines (by sneaking in an amendment to the railroads' enabling law), the city has been the southwestern hub of American commerce. The **Galleria**

(✉ LBJ Fwy. at the Dallas North Tollway, ☎ 972/702–7100), with more than 200 retailers, is one of Dallas' best-known malls. Also well known for its collection of high-end retailers, **Highland Park Village** (✉ Mockingbird La. at Preston Rd., ☎ 214/559–2740) is touted as the first planned shopping center in America. **NorthPark Center** (✉ Central Expressway at Northwest Hwy., ☎ 214/363–7441), developed as the nation's first indoor mall by art collector Ray Nasher, has rotating exhibits of world-class art on its walls. In downtown Dallas, the original **Neiman Marcus** (✉ 1618 Main St., ☎ 214/741–6911) is a huge draw.

The **West End Market Place** (✉ 603 Munger Ave., ☎ 214/748–4801) contains more than 50 specialty shops and many eateries. If you're in the mood for the fresh fruit and vegetables that have made the Rio Grande Valley famous, stop by the **Dallas Farmer's Market** (✉ 1010 S. Pearl St., ☎ 214/939–2808), on the southeastern edge of downtown. There are some fine clothing stores on trendy **McKinney Avenue** , and the elegant **Crescent** (✉ 500 Crescent Ct., off McKinney Ave.) has *very* ritzy shops.

Fort Worth

Both Fort Worth's attitude and its economy have always pointed west, and that's reflected in the shopping here. Most visitors head right to the **Stockyards,** where there are several good western-wear outlets. Check out **Fincher's** (✉ 115 E. Exchange Ave., ☎ 817/624–7302), a western store since 1902 in a building that began life as a bank; you can still walk into the old vaults. A great place for boots is **M. L. Leddy's Boot and Saddlery** (✉ 2455 N. Main St., ☎ 817/624–3149).

Downtown's **Sundance Square** is a perennial draw, with several small stores. **Fort Worth Outlet Square** (✉ 150 Throckmorton St., ☎ 817/390–3720 or 800/414–2817), a large, modern indoor mall with its own privately operated subway, is attached to Sundance Square and is a better choice for shopping. **Barber's Book Store** (✉ 215 W. 8th St., ☎ 817/335–5469), specializing in Texana and rare and fine books, is the oldest bookstore in Texas.

ELSEWHERE IN TEXAS

East Texas

Arriving and Departing

Between Dallas and Shreveport, Louisiana, lies east Texas, whose main east–west artery is I–20. Marshall, the heart of the region, is about a three-hour drive from Dallas or a half hour from the Louisiana line. **Amtrak** trains serve Marshall three times a week.

What to See and Do

Heading into east Texas from the Dallas–Fort Worth area, you'll pass two great boundaries: a natural line, marking the start of a piney, hilly region totally unlike the Great Plains; and a man-made one, the beginning of what was the slaveholding part of the United States. In every way, east Texas—a region once dependent on cotton—feels more southern than western. After Texas seceded from the union in 1861, **Marshall** became the seat of civil authority west of the Mississippi and the wartime capital of Missouri; five Confederate generals are buried in its cemetery. Marshall is full of historic homes, some of which—like the **Starr Family Home** (✉ 407 W. Travis St., ☎ 903/935–3044; 🎫 $3)—can be toured; others are small hostelries. One of Marshall's charms is beautiful **Stagecoach Road** (take Poplar Street, which heads east from U.S. 59, and follow markers); in places you can see the results of the stages cutting some 20 ft into the ground on this undisturbed section of the old main road to Shreveport. Off U.S. 59 signs lead to **Marshall Pottery** (✉ 4901 Elysian Field Rd., ☎ 903/938–9201; free), a huge working pottery factory.

Jefferson, a 20-minute drive north of Marshall, is one of Texas's most historic towns, a charming place on Big Cypress Bayou that once served hundreds of steamboats coming up from New Orleans. When his offer to run track through the town was rebuffed, railroad baron Jay Gould is said to have angrily scrawled in the hotel register of the Excelsior House the prophetic words "The End of Jefferson." Today the superb **Excelsior House** (✉ 211 W. Austin St., ☎ 903/665–2513), built in the 1850s, is a tribute to the restorer's art (reservations are required months in advance). **Gould's private railroad car** is across the street from the Excelsior House.

Caddo Lake, overhung with Spanish moss and edged with bald cypresses, is a major fishing destination straddling the Texas-Louisiana border. At various times it has been home to the beleaguered Caddo Indians, to bootleggers hiding out in its dense shore growth, to the great singer of spirituals Leadbelly (reared at Swanson's Landing), to thriving steamboat traffic from New Orleans, and to all manner of legend. **Caddo Lake State Park** (☞ National and State Parks, *above*) is on the south shore.

Dining and Lodging

$$$ **Pride House.** Ornate woodwork and original stained glass distinguish this old Victorian mansion, one of Jefferson's finest B&Bs. ✉ *409 E. Broadway, Jefferson 75657,* ☎ *903/665–2675. 10 rooms. Full breakfast. AE, D, MC, V.*

$$–$$$ **Caddo Cottage.** This is the ideal place for a family looking for a quiet time along one of the most beautiful parts of Caddo Lake. The two-story lake house sleeps four. ✉ *Rte. 2, Box 66, Uncertain 75661,* ☎ *903/789–3988. No credit cards.*

El Paso

Arriving and Departing

At Texas' far southwestern corner, El Paso is an 11-hour drive from San Antonio; about 12 from Dallas–Fort Worth; 6 from Santa Fe, New Mexico; and 5 from Phoenix, Arizona. **El Paso International Airport** (the major local carrier is Southwest Airlines, ☎ 800/435–9792) and **Amtrak** (✉ Union Station, 700 San Francisco St., ☎ 800/872–7245) serve the city.

What to See and Do

Dramatically situated a few miles between the southern end of the Rockies and the northern terminus of Mexico's Sierra Madre range, **El Paso** (established by the Spanish in 1598) was a major stopping point on the way west during the California gold rush. Outside the city, in El Paso's lower valley, are several important historic sites. ★ **Mission Ysleta** (✉ Old Pueblo Rd., Zaragosa exit off I–10 east of El Paso, ☎ 915/859–9848), circa 1681, is the oldest Spanish mission in the Southwest. Adjacent to Mission Ysleta is the **Tigua Indian Reservation** (✉ 119 S. Old Pueblo Rd., ☎ 915/859–7913), home of the oldest ethnic group in Texas, with Tigua pottery, jewelry, art, and replicas of ancient Native American homes for sale. **Soccoro Mission** (✉ 328 S. Nevares, ☎ 915/859–7718), to the south of the Tigua Indian Reservation, is famed for its fine vigas—the carved ceiling beams that mark local architecture. **San Elizario Presidio** (✉ 1556 San Elizario Rd., ☎ 915/851–2333), a fort built to protect the missions, is also near the Soccoro Mission.

Across the Rio Grande from El Paso is the Mexican city of **Juarez,** where the shopping is often sensational; try the **El Paso–Juarez International Trolley** (✉ Santa Fe and San Francisco Sts., ☎ 915/544–0061; 💳 $11). Panoramic views of El Paso can be seen from **Scenic Drive,** which you'll find by driving north on Mesa Street and then right on Rim Road. **Transmountain Road,** off I–10 west of downtown, takes you through Smuggler's Gap, a dramatic cut across the Franklin Mountains. For information on Juarez and El Paso contact the **El Paso Convention & Visitors Bureau** (✉ 1 Civic Center Plaza, 79901, ☎ 915/534–0696 or 800/351–6024).

Dining and Lodging

For price ranges *see* Charts 1 (B) and 2 (B) *in* On the Road with Fodor's.

$$ **Camino Royal Paso del Norte.** This elegant, brick downtown hotel is listed on the National Register of Historic Places. The jewel of the lobby is the dark-wood circular Dome Bar, which sits under a superb 1912 Tiffany skylight. Guest rooms are functional and large. ✉ *101 S. El Paso St., 79901,* ☎ *915/534–3000 or 800/722–6466,* FAX *915/534–3024. 359 rooms. 2 restaurants, pool, exercise room. AE, D, DC, MC, V.*

South Padre Island

Visitor Information

South Padre Island Convention & Visitors Bureau (✉ 600 Padre Island Blvd.; Box 3500, 78597, ☎ 956/761–6433 or 800/767–2373).

Arriving and Departing

South Padre Island, with Texas's most beautiful beaches, is in the southeastern corner of the state, near the Mexican border town of Matamoros. The island is reached by a bridge across the Intracoastal Waterway from Port Isabel, which, in turn, is accessible from Routes 48 and 100.

What to See and Do

At the southern tip of one of the largest barrier islands in the world—113-mi-long Padre Island—the resort town and white-sand beaches of **South Padre Island** (population: 1,677) attract college students at spring break but delight nature seekers, beach- and sun-lovers, and fishermen the rest of the year. North of South Padre Island, the 80½-mi

★ **Padre Island National Seashore** (✉ 9405 South Padre Island Dr., Corpus Christi 78418, ☎ 512/949–8173) is entirely natural, unchanged from the days when scavenging Karankawa Indians roamed among its sand dunes, sea oats, and morning glories.

10 The Rockies

Colorado, Idaho, Montana, Wyoming, Utah

Updated by Peggy Ammerman, Stacey Clark, Jane McConnell, Candy Moulton, and Kristin Rodine

TO MANY MINDS, THE TERM ROCKY MOUNTAINS conjures up images of wolves and outlaws, the click of cowboy spurs and the rustling of leather chaps. Indeed, it's hard to forget the broken treaties and betrayals to Native Americans, the energy and innocence of wide-open spaces, boomtowns, and the search for precious metals that have figured so heavily in the making of Idaho, Colorado, Montana, Wyoming, and Utah. The unpredictable charms and crimes of nature and human action that thrived in the Old West have marked the Rocky Mountains with a crude but poetic beauty.

But most enduring of all are the mountains—a 4,000-mi-long chain that stretches from Alaska to northern New Mexico. Begun about 70 million years ago, when sandstone, shale, granite, marble, and volcanic rock surged and split and gave under the plow of glacial ice, the Rockies emerged to run intermittently along what is now the Idaho–Montana boundary down to a central section sloping through western Wyoming's Yellowstone and Grand Teton national parks and into northern Colorado and Utah.

This mountain backdrop still inspires the kind of fear and wonder it once did from mountain folk and Native Americans. What you'll see from atop these summits is a landscape of breathtaking beauty and variety. The westernmost state, Idaho, has terrain encompassing everything from fruit orchards to the tallest sand dunes in the United States. Utah has 84,990 sq mi of mind-bogglingly varied topography—a vast salt lake, mountain peaks and lush evergreen forests, and improbable red-rock canyons in the southern reaches. Montana claims 25 million acres of public land, most of it aloft in the northern Rockies. Its Glacier National Park is home to the grizzly bear, wolf, mountain goat, and moose. Wyoming, the ninth-largest and least populated state in the Union, is dotted with thermal pools, bubbling hot springs, and, within a square-mile area in Yellowstone National Park, a quarter of the earth's geysers. In Colorado, the ski capital of the United States, high-country lakes, meadows frosted with blue columbine, and treeless alpine tundra assemble in one sweeping vista, while Denver—the Mile-High City—and the university town of Boulder attract visitors and settlers from all corners of the globe.

CANADA
MONTANA
IDAHO
WYOMING
NORTH DAKOTA
SOUTH DAKOTA
WATERTON-GLACIER INT'L PEACE PARK
BLACKFEET INDIAN RES.
St. Mary
GLACIER NAT'L PARK
Sand Point
Libby
Kalispell
Cut Bank
Shelby
Havre
FORT BELKNAP INDIAN RES.
Malta
Scobey
Westby
FORT PECK INDIAN RES.
Wolf Point
Sidney
Conrad
Bigfork
Flathead Lake
Coeur d'Alene
Hot Springs
Kellogg
Polson
Fort Benton
Missouri River
Fort Peck Lake
COEUR D'ALENE INDIAN RES.
Wallace
FLATHEAD INDIAN RES.
Fairfield
Great Falls
Circle
Avery
Moiese
Jordan
Lincoln
Lewistown
Glendive
Moscow
Dworshak Res.
Missoula
Helena
Lewiston
NEZ PERCE INDIAN RES.
Stevensville
Deer Lodge
Harlowton
Roundup
Ingomar
Yellowstone R.
Baker
BITTERROOT NAT'L FOREST
Anaconda
Miles City
Butte
Forsyth
Elk City
Billings
Hardin
Riggins
Wisdom
Bozeman
Livingston
CROW INDIAN RES.
N. CHEYENNE INDIAN RES.
Broadus
Snake River
New Meadows
Salmon
Dillon
Red Lodge
BIGHORN CANYON NAT'L REC. AREA
McCall
Devils Tower
Lima
YELLOWSTONE NAT'L PARK
Sheridan
Weiser
Challis
Sundance
Rapid City
Payette
Stanley
Cody
Buffalo
Emmett
Dubois
Gilette
SAWTOOTH NAT'L REC AREA
Worland
Caldwell
Butte City
GRAND TETON NAT'L
Newcastle
Nampa
Boise

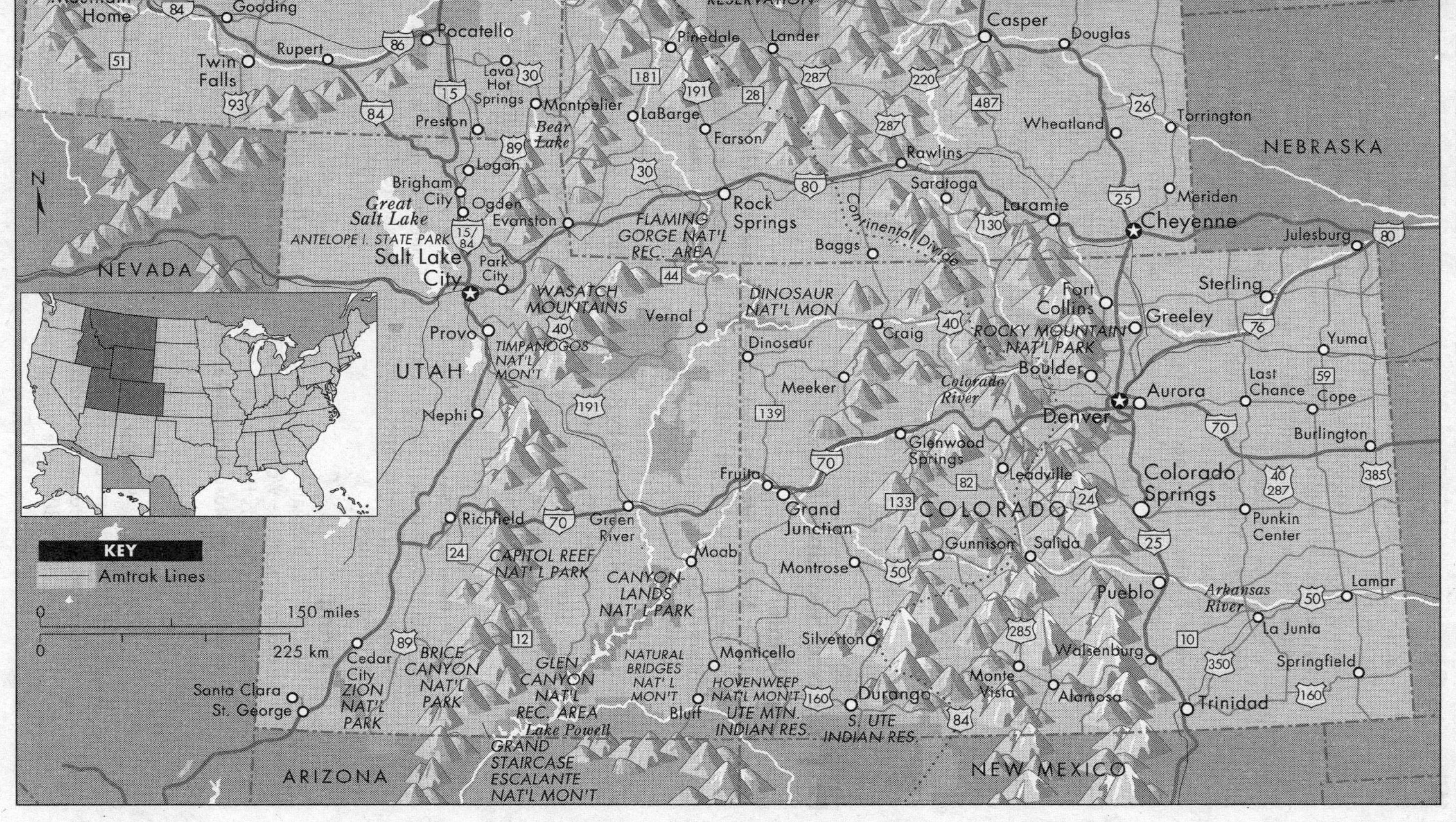
Home
Gooding
Pocatello
Rupert
Twin Falls
Lava Hot Springs
Montpelier
Preston
Bear Lake
LaBarge
Farson
Pinedale
Lander
Casper
Douglas
Wheatland
Torrington
NEBRASKA
Logan
Brigham City
Ogden
Great Salt Lake
ANTELOPE I. STATE PARK
Evanston
Salt Lake City
Park City
NEVADA
FLAMING GORGE NAT'L REC. AREA
Rock Springs
Rawlins
Saratoga
Continental Divide
Baggs
Laramie
Cheyenne
Meriden
Julesburg
WASATCH MOUNTAINS
Vernal
DINOSAUR NAT'L MON
Dinosaur
Craig
Fort Collins
ROCKY MOUNTAIN NAT'L PARK
Greeley
Sterling
Yuma
Provo
TIMPANOGOS NAT'L MON'T
UTAH
Meeker
Colorado River
Boulder
Denver
Aurora
Last Chance
Cope
Burlington
Nephi
Glenwood Springs
Leadville
Fruita
Grand Junction
COLORADO
Colorado Springs
Punkin Center
Richfield
Green River
CAPITOL REEF NAT' L PARK
CANYONLANDS NAT' L PARK
Moab
Montrose
Gunnison
Salida
Pueblo
Arkansas River
Lamar
La Junta
KEY
Amtrak Lines
0
150 miles
0
225 km
Cedar City
ZION NAT'L PARK
BRICE CANYON NAT'L PARK
GLEN CANYON NAT'L REC. AREA
NATURAL BRIDGES NAT' L MON'T
Monticello
HOVENWEEP NAT'L MON'T
Bluff
UTE MTN. INDIAN RES.
Silverton
Durango
S. UTE INDIAN RES.
Monte Vista
Alamosa
Walsenburg
Springfield
Trinidad
Santa Clara
St. George
Lake Powell
GRAND STAIRCASE ESCALANTE NAT'L MON'T
ARIZONA
NEW MEXICO

When to Go

Many visitors think the Rockies have only two seasons: skiing and hiking. But for those willing to risk sometimes capricious weather, fall and spring are the Rockies' best-kept secrets. **Spring** is a good time for fishing, rafting the runoff, or birding and viewing wildlife. **Fall** may be the prettiest season of all, with golden splashes of aspen on the mountainsides, more wildlife at lower elevations, and excellent fishing during spawning. You will also pay less during these shoulder seasons, and you may have a corner of Yellowstone all to yourself. Driving in the **winter** can be chancy, and although the interstates are kept open even in fearsome weather, highway passes like the Going-to-the-Sun Highway in Glacier National Park and the Mirror Lake Highway between Park City and the Utah/Wyoming border can be blocked from late October to June. High altitude (over 7,000 ft above sea level) and high latitude (the nearer you get to Canada) result in longer winters. Winter visitors should prepare for the possibility of temperatures below zero—but the climate is dry, so the cold is less cruel. Wilderness snowbanks can linger through June, so backcountry hikers generally crowd in from July through Labor Day. **Summer** temperatures rarely rise into the 90s (except in southern Utah, where the barometer may top 100°), but the thinner atmosphere at high altitudes makes it necessary for visitors to shield themselves from ultraviolet rays.

Festivals and Seasonal Events

Winter

JAN.➢ **National Western Stock Show and Rodeo** (☎ 303/295–1660), in **Denver,** is the biggest indoor rodeo in the world, attracting all the stars of the rodeo circuit for two weeks. The **Western Montana Wine Festival** (☎ 406/728–3100) in **Missoula** features tastings of regional wines, accompanied by superb food. Utah's **Sundance Film Festival** (☎ 801/328–3456), founded by Robert Redford, brings independent filmmakers to **Park City** and **Salt Lake City** for one of the country's premier film screening events. During **Ullr Fest** (☎ 970/453–6018), the town of **Breckenridge, Colorado** declares itself an independent kingdom and pays homage to the Norse God of snow in a weeklong wild revel.

FEB.➢ **Race to the Sky** (☎ 406/442–4008), near **Helena, Montana,** is a 500-mi dogsled race that crisscrosses the Continental Divide at elevations up to 7,000 ft. Spectators can watch a shorter (300-mi) race at check-in sites.

Spring

MAR.➢ The Irish and other wearers of the green flock to **Butte, Montana** for one of the West's largest and most rollicking **St. Patrick's Day** parades. Collectors from around the world gather in **Great Falls, Montana** for the **C.M. Russell Auction of Original Western Art** (☎ 800/803–3351).

LATE MAY➢ Memorial Day brings the annual **Bolder Boulder** run (☎ 303/444–7223) to **Boulder, Colorado,** where a top international field and 40,000 ordinary citizens race through the closed streets of town. In **Missoula, Montana,** the annual **International Wildlife Film Festival** (☎ 406/728–9380) is the longest running such festival in the world (since 1978).

Summer

LATE JUNE➢ In Colorado, the **Telluride Bluegrass & Country Music Festival** (☎ 800/624–2422) has become so popular the organizers have had to limit the number of spectators to 10,000.

JULY➢ The popular **Mormon Miracle Pageant** (☎ 435/835–3000) is a musical drama of American and Mormon history set against the backdrop of the temple in **Manti, Utah.** Wyoming's **Cheyenne Frontier Days** (☎ 307/778–7222 or 800/227–6336), the rodeo daddy of 'em all since 1897, includes evening shows featuring the biggest names in country music, as well as parades, Native American dancing, and very popular pancake breakfasts. The Grant-Kohrs Ranch in **Deer Lodge, Montana** celebrates cowboy lore and skills during **Western Heritage Days** (☎ 406/846–2070) with roping, branding, chuck-wagon cooking, and traditional cowboy music.

JUNE–AUG.➢ **Colorado Shakespeare Festival** (☎ 303/492–0554), in **Boulder,** presents one full-scale traditional and three nontraditional Shakespeare productions and one non-Shakespearean play Tuesday–Sunday nights. The actors are recruited from around the country. At the **Aspen Music Festival and School** (☎ 970/925–3254) students from around the world perform with faculty, and world-class soloists and conductors are also featured. **Grand Teton Music Festival** (☎ 307/733–1128), the most important classical music concert series in the northern Rockies, attracts musicians from the nation's finest orchestras.

LATE JULY–EARLY AUG.➢ The **Festival of the American West** (☎ 800/225–3378), near **Logan, Utah,** includes a Great West Fair and a multimedia pageant, "The West: America's Odyssey."

AUG.➢ During the first week of August, **Bear Lake Raspberry Days** celebrates the harvest of the legendary raspberries of **Bear Lake, Idaho.** At the **Cowboy Poetry Gathering** (☎ 406/538–5436) in **Lewiston, Montana,** U.S. and Canadian performers share verses about a man and a horse following a cow. In **Vail, Colorado,** the **International Festival of Dance** (☎ 970/949–1999) is set amid wildflowers in the outdoor Ford Amphitheater. The **Crow Fair and Rodeo** (☎ 406/638–2601) celebrates native culture and customs in **Crow Agency, Montana,** tepee capital of the world.

LATE JULY–AUG.➢ In **Sandpoint, Idaho,** the **Festival at Sandpoint** (☎ 208/265–4554) presents classical, jazz, and pop concerts.

LATE JUN.–EARLY SEPT.➢ **Cedar City** is the setting of the **Utah Shakespearean Festival** (☎ 435/586–7878 or 800/752–9849)), with feasts, bawdy Elizabethan skits, and performances in an open-air replica of the Globe Theatre.

Autumn

SEPT.➢ **Libby, Montana**'s four-day **Nordicfest** (☎ 800/785–6541) celebrates Scandinavian food, costumes, music, dance, and crafts.

EARLY OCT.➢ In **Denver,** the **Great American Beer Festival** (☎ 303/447–0126) is the country's largest beer fest, with samples of nearly 2,000 brews.

OCT.–LATE DEC.➢ Join the **Eagle Watch** (☎ 406/475–3128) to see hundreds of bald eagles gather annually in Canyon Ferry State Park, near **Helena, Montana,** during freshwater salmon spawning.

Getting Around the Rockies

By Bus

Greyhound Lines (☎ 800/231–2222) has extensive service throughout Colorado and connects major cities throughout the region, including Salt Lake City, Cheyenne, Boise, Pocatello, and Missoula. Various smaller bus lines connect with Greyhound to provide service to smaller communities as well as to the parks.

By Car

Major interstates crisscross the region, winding their way through accessible mountain passes. The busiest but least scenic east–west thoroughfare is I–80, which crosses southern Wyoming, then jogs south through Utah, skirting past Salt Lake City before heading west across the Great Salt Lake Desert to Nevada. To reach Yellowstone National Park, you must either make the long drive north from Rock Springs or come south from I–90, which crosses southern Montana. In Colorado, I–70 runs east–west, passing through Denver and Grand Junction to southeastern Utah. I–15 traverses Utah north–south, passing through all major cities before connecting to Las Vegas to the south, and to I–84 in Idaho, to the north. I–84 heads west to Boise and on to Portland. I–90 passes through Sheridan in northeastern Wyoming before crossing Montana and northern Idaho; it comes within 100 mi of Glacier National Park, which can be reached by going north from Missoula on U.S. 93 and east on U.S. 2. I–15 goes along the east side of the park; you can reach Glacier by driving west on U.S. 89. I–25 comes up from New Mexico and passes through Colorado Springs and Denver in Colorado and Cheyenne and Casper in Wyoming and then joins I–90 in Montana. Throughout the Rockies drivers should be extremely cautious about winter travel, when whiteouts and ice are not uncommon. Because major airports are few and far between, the most popular mode of travel is by car or camper, and by far the busiest driving season is summer. Major attractions such as Glacier and Yellowstone National Park are well away from the interstates, requiring visitors to drive dozens or even hundreds of miles on scenic two-lane highways to the entrances.

By Plane

The **Denver International Airport** (☎ 303/342–2000) is the primary airline hub in the Rockies. In Utah, commercial airlines serve **Salt Lake International Airport** (☎ 801/575–2400). Several domestic airlines fly from Denver and Salt Lake into **Jackson Hole Airport** (☎ 307/733–4767), in Wyoming, with additional service during the ski season. The **BoiseAir Terminal** (☎ 208/383–3110), in Idaho, is served by Delta, Sky West, United, and other airlines. In Montana the **Missoula Airport** (☎ 406/728–4381) and **Glacier Park International Airport** (☎ 406/257–5994), in Kalispell, are served by major domestic airlines. **Salt Lake City Airport** (☎ 801/575–2400) also provides an access point to Wyoming and Idaho.

By Train

Amtrak (☎ 800/872–7245) connects the Rockies to both coasts and all major American cities; trains run through Boise, Salt Lake City, and Denver, with other stops in between. Amtrak trains also run through northern Montana, with stops in Essex and Whitefish, along the border of Glacier National Park. Connecting motor-coach services are provided in the summer from Pocatello, Idaho, to Yellowstone National Park.

COLORADO

By Sandra Widener
Updated by Jane McConnell

Capital	Denver
Population	3,893,000
Motto	Nothing Without Providence
State Bird	Lark bunting
State Flower	Columbine
Postal Abbreviation	CO

Statewide Visitor Information

Colorado Travel and Tourism Authority (⊠ 1625 Broadway, Suite 1700, Denver 80202, ☏ 800/433–2656).

Scenic Drives

Colorado has 17 designated scenic routes, which are marked by signs that have blue columbines. The 232-mi **San Juan Skyway** traverses historic ranching and mining towns such as Durango, Silverton, Ouray, Telluride, and Cortez. The **Peak-to-Peak Highway** follows Routes 119, 72, and 7 through gold-mining towns to Rocky Mountain National Park.

National and State Parks

National Parks

Great Sand Dunes National Monument (⊠ 35 mi northeast of Alamosa off Rte. 150; Mosca 81146, ☏ 719/378–2312), with sand dunes almost 700 ft high, has a year-round campground and a nature trail. **Mesa Verde National Park** (⊠ U.S. 160, 8 mi east of Cortez; Mesa Verde National Park 81330, ☏ 970/529–4465) has well-preserved cliff dwellings of the ancient Anasazi Indians. **Rocky Mountain National Park** (⊠ Hwy. 36, Estes Park 80517, ☏ 970/586–1206) presents a 265,000-acre picture-book vision of craggy mountains, abundant wildlife, and deep-blue mountain lakes, with camping, hiking, and scenic drives.

State Parks

In the state's 40 parks you can hike, fish, sail, and take in idyllic views. Contact the **Colorado Division of Parks** (⊠ Dept. of Natural Resources, 1313 Sherman St., Denver 80203, ☏ 303/866–3437) for information.

DENVER

In Denver winter weather reports frequently begin with skiing conditions. After the lifts shut down for the summer, weekends are often occupied with trips to the mountains to hike, camp, and fish. The sharp-edged skyscrapers, clean streets, and dozens of well-used parks evoke the image of a young, progressive city, but much of the essence of Denver lies in its western past. Areas like LoDo, a historic part of lower downtown, buzz with jazz clubs, restaurants, and art galleries housed in century-old buildings.

Visitor Information

Denver Metro Convention and Visitors Bureau (⊠ 155 California St., Suite 300, 80202, ☏ 303/892–1112).

Arriving and Departing

By Bus

Greyhound Lines (⊠ 1055 19th St., ☎ 800/231–2222).

By Car

I–70 (east–west) and I–25 (north–south) intersect near downtown.

By Plane

Denver International Airport (☎ 303/342–2000), 23 mi from downtown Denver, is served by most major carriers. Cab fare downtown should average about $35; **RTD,** the local bus service (☞ Getting Around Denver, *below*), can also get you there. The **Airporter** (☎ 303/227–0000) provides express bus service from the airport to locations in Denver and surrounding areas; a trip to downtown Denver costs about $20 depending on your destination. Reservations are essential.

By Train

Amtrak (☎ 800/872–7245) serves **Union Station** (⊠ 17th St. at Wynkoop St.).

Getting Around Denver

By Car

Despite many one-way streets, driving in Denver is not difficult, and finding a spot in a parking lot is usually easy. Traffic on I–25 and I–70 can be congested during rush hours.

By Public Transportation

A free shuttle bus operates frequently down the length of the 16th Street Mall. The region's public bus service, **RTD** (☎ 303/299–6000 or 303/299–6700), has routes throughout Denver and to outlying towns such as Boulder, Longmont, and Nederland. RTD's **light-rail system** serves the downtown and southwestern regions. Buy bus tokens (75¢ or $1.25, depending on time of day) at grocery stores or pay on board; rail tickets are available from machines in the train stations.

By Taxi

Yellow Cab (☎ 303/777–7777) and **Metro Taxi** (☎ 303/333–3333) are two 24-hour taxi services.

Orientation Tours

Gray Line (☎ 303/289–2841) conducts a 2½-hour city tour and a mountain-parks tour.

Exploring Denver

At the **Civic Center,** a three-block park, lawns, gardens, and a Greek amphitheater present Denver's official face to the world. The backdrop for the Civic Center is the **state capitol** (⊠ 1475 Sherman St., ☎ 303/866–2604). As a reminder of the state's mining heritage, the dome of the 1886 building is periodically recovered with hammered gold leaf. The balcony affords a panoramic view of the Rockies. The capitol is closed weekends. Just off the Civic Center park is the **Colorado History Museum** (⊠ 1300 Broadway, ☎ 303/866–3682; 🎟 $3), with Colorado and western memorabilia and dioramas, plus special exhibits. ★ The **Denver Art Museum** (⊠ 100 W. 14th Ave., ☎ 303/640–2793; 🎟 $4.50) has an excellent collection of Native American art, as well as superlative holdings in pre-Columbian and Spanish colonial art. The museum is closed Monday. Connected to the art museum by an underground walkway is the new **Denver Public Library** (⊠ 10 W. 14th Ave., ☎ 303/640–6200). This Michael Graves–designed building

Denver

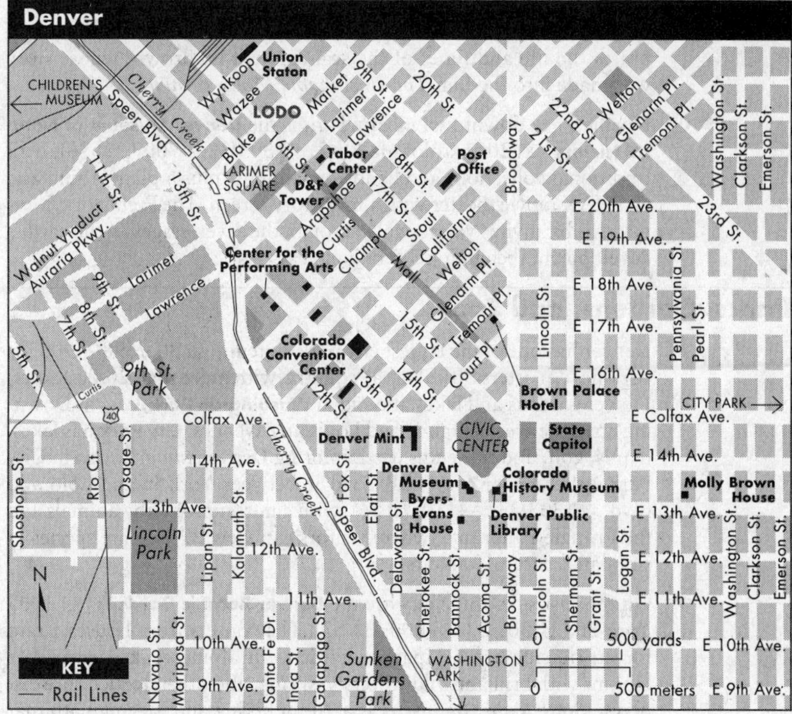

houses a world-renowned collection of books, photographs, and newspapers that chronicle the American West.

Behind the Denver Art Museum, the elaborate redbrick Victorian **Byers-Evans House,** built in 1883, now houses the **Denver History Museum** (✉ 1310 Bannock St., ☎ 303/620–4933; 🎫 $3).

Near the Civic Center is the **Denver Mint** (✉ W. Colfax Ave. and Cherokee St., ☎ 303/405–4761; 🎫 free)—officially known as the United States Mint—where more than 10 billion coins are stamped yearly. Free tours take place on weekdays; the mint is closed on weekends.

Free shuttle buses are the only vehicles allowed on the **16th Street Mall,** which has shade trees, outdoor cafés, historic buildings, and shops. Be ★ sure to peek inside the **Brown Palace** (✉ 321 17th St., ☎ 303/297–3111), the grande dame of Denver hotels, built in 1892 and still proud of her antique charms.

The 330-ft **D&F Tower** (✉ 16th St. at Arapahoe St.) emulates the campanile of St. Mark's Cathedral in Venice. **Denver Center for the Performing Arts** (✉ Curtis and 14th Sts.) is a huge space-age complex of theaters and a symphony hall.

Denver's most charming shopping area is historic **Larimer Square** (✉ Larimer and 15th Sts.), which showcases some of the city's oldest retail buildings and finest specialty shops. **LoDo,** north of Larimer Street between Speer Boulevard and 22nd Street, is a quirky historic area filled with art galleries, nightclubs, brew pubs, and restaurants.

West of LoDo is **Denver Children's Museum** (✉ 2121 Crescent Dr., ☎ 303/433–7444; 🎫 $5), where interactive exhibits include a working TV station, a child-size grocery store, and an outdoor ski hill.

East of downtown, the **Molly Brown House Museum** (✉ 1340 Pennsylvania St., ☎ 303/832–4092; 🎫 $5), a Victorian confection, celebrates the life and times of the scandalous Ms. Brown, whose story was made into the film *The Unsinkable Molly Brown.*

★ ☺ Northeast of downtown in City Park is the **Denver Museum of Natural History** (✉ 2001 Colorado Blvd., ☎ 303/322–7009; 🎫 $6), with traditional collections and hands-on exhibits, plus a planetarium and an IMAX movie theater with a four-story screen. The Prehistoric Journey exhibit invites you to walk through the seven stages of the earth's development, beginning 3.5 billion years ago.

Parks, Gardens, and Zoos

Denver has one of the largest city park systems (☎ 303/698–4900 for park headquarters office) in the country, with more than 20,000 acres. Flower gardens and lakes abound in **Washington Park,** east of Downing Street between Virginia and Louisiana avenues. **City Park** has lakes, tennis, golf, and museums (☞ Exploring Denver, *above*). Also in City Park is the **Denver Zoo,** (✉ E. 23rd St. between York St. and Colorado Blvd., ☎ 303/331–4110; 🎫 $6), with a nursery for baby animals and the Primate Panorama, where visitors can view 29 primate species in simulated natural habitats.

★ On the east side of the city are the **Denver Botanic Gardens** (✉ 1005 York St., ☎ 303/331–4000; 🎫 $3). The conservatory houses a rain forest; outside are a Japanese garden, an alpine rock garden that blooms with brilliant wildflowers in spring, and other horticulture displays. **Platte River Greenway** is a 20-mi biking and jogging path that follows Cherry Creek and the Platte River, much of it through downtown Denver.

Dining

Beef, buffalo, and burritos are prominent in Denver's culinary history, but more sophisticated fare can also be found. Cruise LoDo or 17th Avenue east for inventive kitchens, and check out Federal Street for cheap ethnic eats. For price ranges *see* Chart 1(A) *in* On the Road with Fodor's.

$$$–$$$$ ✕ **Buckhorn Exchange.** The neighborhood has deteriorated, but this Denver landmark with handsome men's-club decor is still a great place to eat elk, buffalo, and beef and to gawk at the deer and other trophies mounted on the walls. ✉ *1000 Osage St.,* ☎ *303/534–9505. AE, D, DC, MC, V. No lunch weekends.*

$$$–$$$$ ★ ✕ **Cliff Young's.** The maroon chairs, dark banquettes, crisp white napery, and dancing to piano and violin music make this elegant Art Deco restaurant seem frozen in the 1950s. The menu relies on American fare such as free-range veal and Colorado rack of lamb. ✉ *700 E. 17th Ave.,* ☎ *303/831–8900. Reservations essential. AE, D, DC, MC, V. No lunch. Closed Sun.*

$$$–$$$$ ★ ✕ **The Fort.** This adobe structure, complete with flickering *luminarias* and a piñon bonfire in the courtyard, is a perfect replica of Bent's Fort, a Colorado fur trade center. Buffalo meat and game are the specialties; elk with huckleberry sauce and mesquite-grilled guinea hen are especially good. Costumed characters from the fur trade wander the restaurant, playing mandolins and telling tall tales. ✉ *U.S. 285 and Hwy. 8,* ☎ *303/697–4771. AE, D, DC, MC, V.*

$$–$$$ ✕ **Barolo Grill.** This restaurant looks like a chichi farmhouse—dried flowers in brass urns, straw baskets, and hand-painted porcelain. Choose from wild boar stewed with apricots, risotto croquettes flavored with minced shrimp, or smoked-salmon pizza. ✉ *3030 E. 6th Ave., ☏ 303/393–1040. Reservations essential. AE, D, DC, MC, V. Closed Sun.–Mon. No lunch.*

$$–$$$ ★ ✕ **Brasserie Z.** Chef Kevin Taylor of Zenith American Grill fame has created a simple, sublime menu of such brasserie classics as Marseille seafood stew and *steak-frites*. The soaring space, in the former Guarantee National Bank building, has become a favorite hangout of Denver's movers and shakers. ✉ *815 17th St., ☏ 303/293–2322. AE, DC, MC, V. No lunch weekends.*

$$–$$$ ✕ **Denver Chophouse & Brewery.** The best of the many LoDo brew pubs and restaurants surrounding the ballpark, the Chophouse, all dark wood and exposed brick, is housed in the old Union Pacific Railroad warehouse. The food is basic American and plenty of it: steak, seafood, and chicken served with hot cornbread and honey-butter and "bottomless" salad tossed at the table. ✉ *1735 19th St., ☏ 303/296–0800. AE, DC, MC, V.*

$$–$$$ ✕ **European Café.** In a space gleaming with polished brass and crystal, this mainstay of fine dining in Denver serves beautifully presented dishes that pay homage to French master chefs such as Paul Bocuse. Try lamb chops with shiitake mushrooms and Madeira glaze. ✉ *1040 15th St., ☏ 303/825–6555. Reservations essential. AE, D, DC, MC, V. No lunch weekends.*

$$–$$$ ★ ✕ **Strings.** This light, airy spot with its wide-open kitchen is a preferred hangout for visiting celebs, whose autographs are mounted. The food is casual-contemporary; one specialty is spaghetti with caviar and asparagus in champagne-cream sauce. ✉ *1700 Humboldt St., ☏ 303/831–7310. Reservations essential. AE, D, DC, MC, V. No lunch Sun.*

$$ ✕ **La Coupole.** Brass railings, black-leather banquettes and exposed-brick walls team up with a heavenly coq au vin, bouillabaisse, and *tarte Tatin* (apple upside-down tart) to transport happy diners to the Left Bank. ✉ *2191 Arapahoe St., ☏ 303/297–2288. AE, D, DC, MC, V. Closed Mon.*

$–$$ ✕ **T-WA Inn.** This South Asian hole-in-the-wall serves great food, including delicate Vietnamese spring rolls and daily specials. ✉ *555 S. Federal Blvd., ☏ 303/922–4584. AE, MC, V.*

$–$$ ★ ✕ **Wynkoop Brewing Company.** The beer is brewed on the premises, and the pub fare is hearty. Try the shepherd's pie or grilled marlin sandwich; then check out the pool hall and cabaret for a full night's entertainment. ✉ *1634 18th St., ☏ 303/297–2700. AE, D, DC, MC, V.*

$ ✕ **Bluebonnet Café and Lounge.** Its location in a fairly seedy neighborhood southeast of downtown doesn't stop the crowds from lining up early. The western decor, Naugahyde, and jukebox set an upbeat mood for killer margaritas and great burritos. ✉ *457 S. Broadway, ☏ 303/778–0147. Reservations not accepted. MC, V.*

Lodging

Denver's lodging choices range from the stately Brown Palace to the YMCA, with bed-and-breakfasts and other options in between. **Bed & Breakfast Innkeepers of Colorado** (✉ Box 38416, Dept. S-95, Colorado Springs 80937-8416, ☏ 800/265–7696) handles B&Bs throughout the state. **Hostelling International–Rocky Mountain Council** (✉ Box 2370, Boulder 80306, ☏ 303/442–1166) provides information about hostels in 10 Colorado locations. For price ranges *see* Chart 2(A) *in* On the Road with Fodor's.

$$$$ ★ 🏨 **Brown Palace Hotel.** This downtown grande-dame hotel has hosted President Eisenhower, the Beatles, and other illustrious guests. The eight-story lobby is topped by a glorious stained-glass ceiling. Rooms are Victorian in style. ✉ *321 17th St., 80202, ☏ 303/297–3111 or 800/*

321–2599, FAX *303/312–5900. 230 rooms. 4 restaurants, exercise room. AE, D, DC, MC, V.*

$$$–$$$$ ★ **Oxford.** The city's most charming small hotel was a Denver fixture in the Victorian era. Guest rooms have exquisite antiques and reproductions. ✉ *1600 17th St., 80202,* ☎ *303/628–5400 or 800/228–5838,* FAX *303/628–5413. 81 rooms. Restaurant, health club. AE, D, DC, MC, V.*

$$$–$$$$ **Westin Tabor Center.** Oversize rooms at this high-rise overlooking the 16th Street Mall are done in gray and taupe and have paisley duvets. A mountain vista from the indoor-pool room makes swimming laps a pleasure. The hotel restaurant is a branch of The Palm, the Manhattan-based steakhouse. ✉ *1672 Lawrence St., 80202,* ☎ *303/572–9100,* FAX *303/572–7288. 420 rooms. 2 restaurants, pool, health club. AE, D, DC, MC, V.*

$$$ **Adam's Mark.** In the mid-1990s the I. M. Pei–designed Radisson and the old May D&F Department Store across the street from it were converted into a convention-oriented property—one of the 25 largest hotels in the country. The location, at the south end of the 16th Street Mall, is ideal. ✉ *1550 Court Place, 80202,* ☎ *303/893–3333 or 800/444–2326,* FAX *303/623–0303. 1,225 rooms. 3 restaurants, pool, exercise room. AE, D, DC, MC, V.*

$$$ ★ **Loews Giorgio.** A 12-story steel-and-black glass facade conceals the delightful Italian baroque motif within. Rooms are spacious and elegant, with Continental touches. It's halfway between downtown and the Denver Tech Center, a residential and shopping outpost. ✉ *4150 E. Mississippi Ave.,* ☎ *303/782–9300 or 800/235–6397,* FAX *303/758–6542. 183 rooms. Restaurant. AE, D, DC, MC, V.*

$$–$$$ **Castle Marne.** This B&B with balconies, a four-story turret, and intricate stone- and woodwork is east of downtown and near several fine restaurants. Rooms are full of antiques and art. ✉ *1572 Race St., 80206,* ☎ *303/331–0621 or 800/926–2763,* FAX *303/331–0623. 9 rooms. Full breakfast. AE, D, DC, MC, V.*

$$–$$$ ★ **Queen Anne Inn.** North of downtown in a reclaimed historic area, this B&B (composed of two adjacent Victorian houses) makes a romantic getaway, with fresh flowers and antiques. An afternoon Colorado-wine tasting is free. ✉ *2147 Tremont Pl., 80205,* ☎ *303/296–6666 or 800/432–4667,* FAX *303/296–2151. 14 rooms. Full breakfast. AE, D, DC, MC, V.*

$$ **Comfort Inn/Downtown.** The advantages to this hotel are its reasonable rates and its location, right across from—and connected to—the Brown Palace in the heart of downtown. Rooms higher up have panoramic views. ✉ *401 17th St., 80202,* ☎ *303/296–0400 or 800/221–2222,* FAX *303/297–0774. 229 rooms. Restaurant. AE, D, DC, MC, V.*

$$ **Holiday Chalet.** This turn-of-the-century house turned hotel is in the heart of Capitol Hill, immediately east of downtown. It's full of charm, with stained-glass windows and family heirlooms, and each room has a full kitchen. ✉ *1820 E. Colfax St., 80218,* ☎ *303/321–9975 or 800/626–4497,* FAX *303/377–6556. 10 rooms. CP. AE, D, DC, MC, V.*

Nightlife and the Arts

Friday's *Denver Post* and *Rocky Mountain News* list entertainment events, as does the weekly *Westword.* **TicketMan** (☎ 303/430–1111) sells tickets to major events. The **Ticket Bus** (✉ 16th St. Mall at Curtis St.) is open weekdays from 10 to 6 and sells same-day half-price tickets.

Nightlife

Downtown and **LoDo** host most of Denver's nightlife. Downtown is where you'll find mainstream entertainment; LoDo is home to rock clubs and small theaters. Remember that Denver's altitude makes you react more quickly to alcohol.

COMEDY

Comedy Works (✉ 1226 15th St., ☏ 303/595–3637) features local and nationally known stand-up comics.

COUNTRY AND WESTERN

The **Grizzly Rose** (✉ I–25 Exit 215, ☏ 303/295–1330), with its miles of dance floor, hosts national bands.

JAZZ

El Chapultepec (✉ 20th St. at Market St., ☏ 303/295–9126) is a smoky dive where visiting jazz musicians often jam after hours.

ROCK

Herman's Hideaway (✉ 1578 S. Broadway, ☏ 303/777–5840) is a favorite for both hot local bands and national acts; there's some blues and reggae, too. **Rock Island** (✉ Wazee and 15th Sts., ☏ 303/572–7625) caters to the young, restless, and hip. The **Mercury Café** (✉ 2199 California St., ☏ 303/294–9281) triples as a health-food restaurant, fringe theater, and rock club specializing in progressive and newer-wave music. The **I-Beam** (✉ 1427 Larimer St., ☏ 303/534–2326) is LoDo's only dance club, with a mix of DJs and live music and an occasional disco night.

The Arts

The modern **Denver Center for the Performing Arts** (✉ 14th and Curtis Sts., ☏ 303/893–3272) houses most of the city's large concert halls and theaters.

DANCE

The **Colorado Ballet** (☏ 303/837–8888) presents classics in the performing arts center.

MUSIC

The **Colorado Symphony Orchestra** (✉ 13th and Curtis Sts., ☏ 303/986–8742) performs at Boettcher Concert Hall.

THEATER

The **Denver Center Theater Company** (☏ 303/893–4100) presents fine repertory theater. **Robert Garner Attractions** (☏ 303/893–4100) brings Broadway-caliber plays to the city.

Spectator Sports

Baseball: Colorado Rockies (✉ Coors Stadium, 22nd and Wazee Sts., downtown, ☏ 303/762–5437). **Basketball: Denver Nuggets** (✉ McNichols Sports Arena, west of downtown across I–25, ☏ 303/893–3865). **Football: Denver Broncos** (✉ Mile High Stadium, 1900 Eliot St., ☏ 303/433–7466). **Hockey: Colorado Avalanche** (✉ McNichols Arena, west of downtown across I–25, ☏ 303/893–6700).

Shopping

Denver is one of the top places to buy recreational equipment and clothing. Pick up a pair of cowboy boots and other western apparel at any western store.

Shopping Districts

The Cherry Creek shopping district, 2 mi from downtown, is Denver's best. On one side of 1st Avenue at Milwaukee Street is the **Cherry Creek Shopping Mall,** a granite-and-glass behemoth containing some of the nation's finest retailers. On the other side is **Cherry Creek North,** with art galleries and specialty shops. On the **16th Street Mall** are Tabor Center and other large downtown retailers. **South Broadway** between 1st Avenue and Evans Street has blocks of antiques stores; prices are sometimes lower than those elsewhere. **LoDo** has the trendiest galleries, many in restored warehouses.

Books

Tattered Cover (⊠ 1st Ave. at Milwaukee St., ☎ 303/322–7727) has overstuffed armchairs, four floors of books (more than 400,000 titles), afternoon lectures and musical presentations, and a knowledgeable staff.

Sporting Goods

Gart Brothers Sports Castle (⊠ 1000 Broadway, ☎ 303/861–1122) is a huge, multistory shrine to the Colorado sporting lifestyle.

Western Wear

Denver Buffalo Company Trading Post (⊠ 1109 Lincoln St., ☎ 303/832–0884) has top-of-the-line western clothing and souvenirs. **Miller Stockman** (⊠ 16th St. Mall, at California St., ☎ 303/825–5339) is an old-line Denver retailer.

Side Trip to Boulder

Arriving and Departing

From Denver take I–25 north to the Boulder Turnpike (Highway 36). Denver's RTD buses make the 27-mi commute regularly.

What to See and Do

Home of the University of Colorado, Boulder is a quintessential college town, but it's also the headquarters of a hard-core group of professional athletes who live to bike and run. The atmosphere is peaceful, new age, and cultural, with a gorgeous backdrop of mountains. One of the city's main attractions is the **Pearl Street Mall,** a see-and-be-seen pedestrian street with benches, grassy spots, great shopping, and outdoor cafés. Weekdays from 10 to 3, the **Celestial Seasonings Plant** (⊠ 4600 Sleepytime Dr., ☎ 303/581–1202) conducts free tours; you'll see raw tea ingredients (the Mint Room is off-limits because of its potent scent), then watch them being blended. Rich in lectures, theater, and music year-round, Boulder celebrates classical music each summer at its **Colorado Music Festival** (⊠ Chautauqua Park, ☎ 303/449–1397).

Side Trip to Central City and Blackhawk

Arriving and Departing

From I–70 take Highway 58 to Golden, then Highway 6 up Clear Creek Canyon, and finally Highway 119 northwest 1 mi past Blackhawk to Central City. The town is 35 mi from Denver.

What to See and Do

Abandoned mines along the scenic road that leads to these historic towns testify to the silver- and gold-mining heritage of the area. Now that low-stakes gambling has arrived, the jingle of slot machines is a constant. The narrow, winding streets are edged with brick storefronts from the last century. The **Central City Opera House** (☎ 303/292–6700), a small Victorian jewel in the center of town, stages opera in summer.

Side Trip to Georgetown

Arriving and Departing

Take I–70 west to the Georgetown exit, 46 mi from Denver.

What to See and Do

With gingerbread Victorian houses on quiet streets, Georgetown provides a tantalizing glimpse of Colorado's heady mining past. This National Historic District has restaurants, small shops, and the **Georgetown Loop Railroad** (☎ 303/569–2403), a 3-mi narrow-gauge line that travels into the mountains and back.

Side Trip to Golden

Arriving and Departing

From I–70 take Highway 58 to Golden, 12 mi west of Denver.

What to See and Do

Coors (✉ 13th and Ford Sts., ☎ 303/277–2337) operates the world's largest brewery; daily tours cover the basics of brewing beer and end with a trip to the tasting rooms. The drive up Lookout Mountain to the **Buffalo Bill Grave and Museum** (✉ Rte. 5 off I–70 Exit 256, or 19th Ave. out of Golden, ☎ 303/526–0747) affords a sensational panoramic view of Denver. Contrary to popular belief, Bill Cody never expressed a burning desire to be buried here: The *Denver Post* bought the corpse from Bill's sister and bribed her to concoct a teary story about his dying wish. Apparently, rival towns were so outraged that the National Guard had to be called in to protect the grave from robbers.

COLORADO SPRINGS AND ENVIRONS

At the center of the state, 65 mi south of Denver, is Colorado Springs, Colorado's second-largest city. In addition to its natural wonders such as Pike's Peak, the region has such man-made attractions as the Air Force Academy and the Broadmoor resort.

Visitor Information

Colorado Springs: Convention and Visitors Bureau (✉ 104 S. Cascade Ave., 80903, ☎ 719/635–7506 or 800/368–4748).

Arriving and Departing

By Bus

Greyhound Lines (✉ 120 S. Weber St., ☎ 800/231–2222) serves national routes and **Springs Transit Management** (✉ 127 E. Kiowa St., ☎ 719/475–9733) serves local ones.

By Car

From Denver take I–25 south.

By Plane

Colorado Springs Airport (✉ 7770 Drennan Rd., ☎ 719/550–1900), 14 mi from the city, is served by domestic airlines.

Exploring Colorado Springs and Environs

A mix of attractions surrounding **Colorado Springs** complements the city's Victorian houses and wide tree-lined streets. **U.S. Olympic Training Center** (✉ 1 Olympic Plaza, ☎ 719/578–4500; free) conducts tours of the sprawling complex where hundreds of athletes train. The **Broadmoor** (✉ 1 Lake Ave.) is a rambling ensemble of pink-stucco Italian Renaissance–style hotel buildings combined with gardens and a picture-perfect lake skimmed by black swans. The **Carriage House Museum** (✉ Lake Circle, ☎ 719/634–7711, ext. 5353; 🎫 free), on the Broadmoor's grounds, displays an old stagecoach, vintage cars, and carriages used at presidential inaugurals.

The **Cheyenne Mountain Zoo** (✉ 4250 Cheyenne Mountain Zoo Rd., ☎ 719/633–9925; 🎫 $6.75), set on a mountainside, is a haven for more than 100 endangered species and other animals. You can hike 224 steep steps or take an elevator to the top of **Seven Falls** (✉ Cheyenne Blvd., ☎ 719/632–0765; 🎫 $6), a series of falls plunging into a tiny pool, set in a breathtaking red-rock canyon.

Two routes—a cog railway (✉ 515 Ruxton Ave., Manitou Springs, ☎ 719/685–5401) and a toll road (✉ 10 mi west on Highway 24, left at marked exit at Cascade)—lead to breathtaking views atop **Pike's Peak,** the summit Zebulon Pike claimed could never be scaled. The railway is $23 round-trip; the toll road, $6. The **Air Force Academy** (✉ 10 mi north on I–25, Exits 156B and 150B, ☎ 719/472–0102) has a futuristic **Cadet Chapel,** with 17 spires, each rising 150 ft. The academy gives guided tours in summer. The **Garden of the Gods** (✉ Off Ridge Rd., north of U.S. 24, ☎ 719/634–6666) has picnic spots and hikes among 1,350 acres of weird, windswept red-rock formations and unusual plant life.

Cripple Creek—24 mi west from Colorado Springs to Divide, then 20 mi south on Highway 67—was once known for vast deposits of gold and has gone upscale with the legalization of low-stakes gambling. The **Cripple Creek and Victor Narrow Gauge Railroad** (☎ 719/689–2640; 🎫 $7.50 round-trip), on the north end of town, runs a 4-mi route (May–October) past old mines and older mountains.

Southwest of Colorado Springs on U.S. 50 is **Cañon City,** gateway to one of the Rockies' most powerful sights. The 1,053-ft-deep **Royal Gorge** (☎ 719/275–7507; 🎫 $12 toll, including aerial tram), often called the Grand Canyon of Colorado, was carved by the Arkansas River more than 3 million years ago. It's spanned by the world's highest **suspension bridge.** Other activities include riding the aerial tram (2,200 ft long and 1,178 ft above the canyon floor) and traveling aboard the **Scenic Railway,** the world's steepest incline rail. A theater presents a 25-minute multimedia show, and there's outdoor musical entertainment in summer.

Famous films such as *True Grit* and *Cat Ballou* were shot in **Buckskin Joe Park and Railway** (✉ Off Hwy. 50, Cañon City, ☎ 719/275–5149; 🎫 $13), which vividly evokes the Old West. Children love the horse-drawn trolley rides, horseback rides, and gold-panning. Adults enjoy the live entertainment in the Crystal Palace and Saloon.

Dining and Lodging

Steak and other basic western foods, along with Mexican dishes, are the mainstays hereabouts. The Colorado Springs Convention and Visitors Bureau (☞ Visitor Information, *above*) provides lodging assistance. For price ranges *see* Charts 1(B) and 2(B) *in* On the Road with Fodor's.

Colorado Springs

$$$–$$$$ ★ ✕ **Corbett's.** The halogen lamps and modern art are matched by a contemporary menu that's light and health conscious. One good appetizer is house-smoked trout in tangy horseradish sauce, set off by sweet pears and chèvre. ✉ *817 W. Colorado Ave.,* ☎ *719/471–0004. Reservations essential. AE, D, DC, MC, V. No lunch.*

Central Colorado

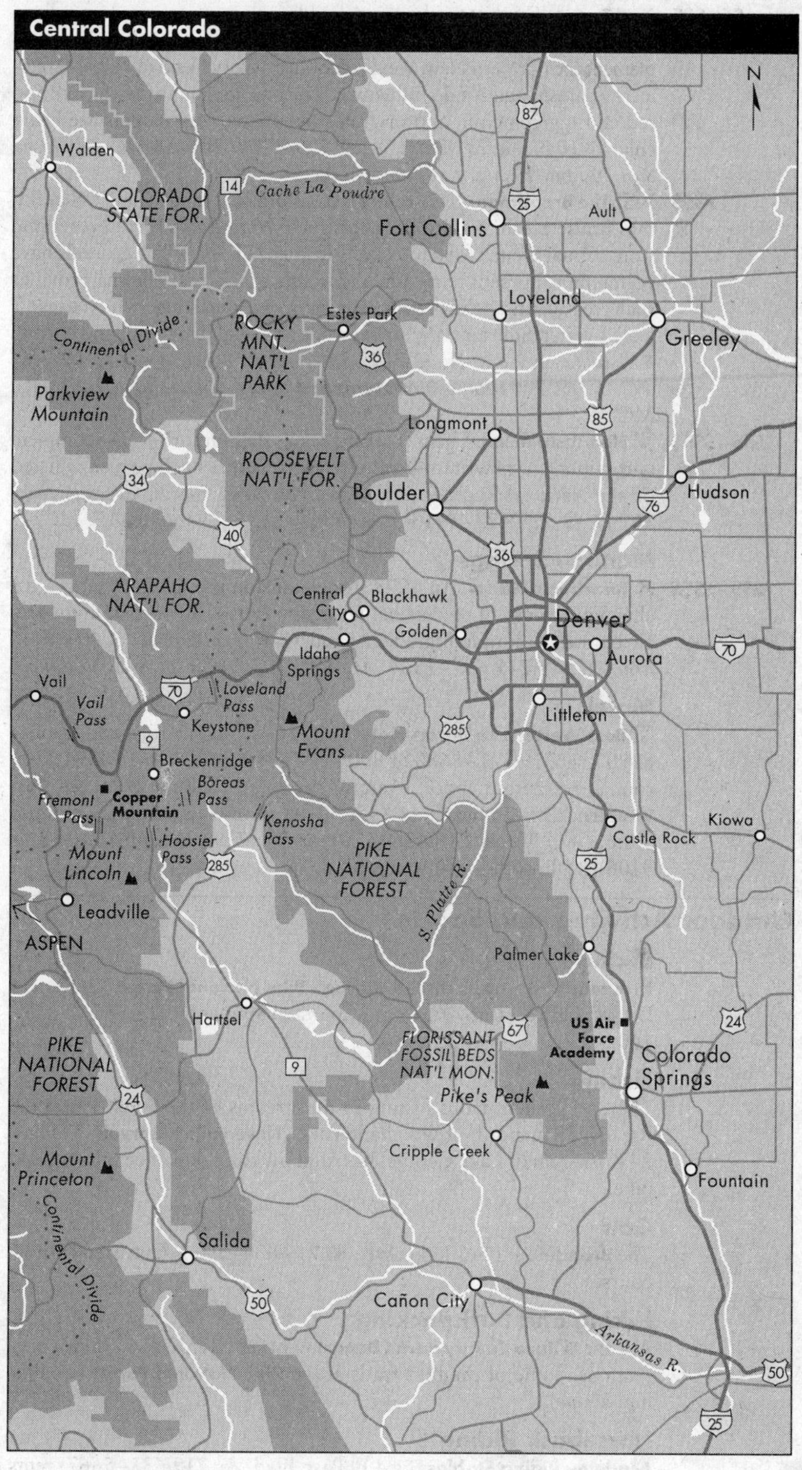
N
Walden
COLORADO STATE FOR.
14
Cache La Poudre
87
25
Fort Collins
Ault
Loveland
Greeley
Estes Park
ROCKY MNT. NAT'L PARK
36
Continental Divide
Parkview Mountain
Longmont
85
ROOSEVELT NAT'L FOR.
34
Boulder
Hudson
76
40
36
ARAPAHO NAT'L FOR.
Central City
Blackhawk
Golden
Denver
Aurora
70
Idaho Springs
Vail
Vail Pass
70
Loveland Pass
Keystone
Mount Evans
285
Littleton
9
Breckenridge
Fremont Pass
Copper Mountain
Boreas Pass
Kenosha Pass
Hoosier Pass
Mount Lincoln
285
PIKE NATIONAL FOREST
S. Platte R.
Castle Rock
Kiowa
25
Leadville
ASPEN
Palmer Lake
Hartsel
US Air Force Academy
24
67
FLORISSANT FOSSIL BEDS NAT'L MON.
9
Colorado Springs
PIKE NATIONAL FOREST
24
Pike's Peak
Cripple Creek
Mount Princeton
Fountain
Continental Divide
Salida
Cañon City
50
Arkansas R.
50
25

$$–$$$ ★ ✕ **El Tesoro.** This historic building doubles as a restaurant and art gallery; exposed brick walls, colorful rugs, and *ristras* (strings) of chilies complement the northern New Mexican food, a savory blend of Native American, Spanish, and Anglo influences. The *posole* (hominy with pork and red chili), green chili, and originals like mango quesadillas are heavenly. ✉ *10 N. Sierra Madre St.,* ☎ *719/471–0106. D, MC, V. Closed Sun. No lunch Sat., no dinner Mon.*

$$$$ ★ ✕🏨 **The Broadmoor.** This resort is a Colorado legend. The 1918 buildings house plush, traditional rooms; the restaurants serve everything from formal French food to Sunday brunch. The park-like grounds have golf, tennis, horseback riding, and boating facilities. The spa provides such treatments as the Broadmoor Falls water massage, which uses 17 jets of water. Substantially lower rates are available in fall and spring. ✉ *1 Lake Ave., 80901,* ☎ *719/634–7711 or 800/634–7711,* FAX *719/577–5779. 700 rooms. 9 restaurants, 3 pools, health club. AE, D, DC, MC, V.*

$$$–$$$$ ★ 🏨 **Hearthstone Inn.** Theme rooms such as the Author's Den—complete with vintage typewriter—lend character to this B&B, which is listed on the National Register of Historic Places. ✉ *506 N. Cascade Ave., 80903,* ☎ *719/473–4413 or 800/521–1885. 25 rooms. AE, MC, V.*

Manitou Springs

$$$–$$$$ ✕ **Briarhurst Manor.** An 1878 stone mansion provides the setting for chef Sigi Krauss's fine cuisine. Dishes such as chateaubriand are prepared with Colorado ingredients and a European touch. ✉ *404 Manitou Ave.,* ☎ *719/685–1864. AE, DC, MC, V. Closed Sun. No lunch.*

Motels

🏨 **Best Western Le Baron Hotel** (✉ 314 W. Bijou, Colorado Springs 80905, ☎ 719/471–8680 or 800/477–8610, FAX 719/471–0894), 206 rooms, restaurant, pool, exercise room; *$$.* 🏨 **Palmer House Best Western** (✉ I–25 near Exit 145, 3010 North Chestnut St., Colorado Springs 80907, ☎ 719/636–5201 or 800/223–9127, FAX 719/636–3108), 150 rooms, restaurant, pool; *$$.*

Outdoor Activities and Sports

Biking

Mountain-bike trails thread through **Pike National Forest** (✉ Ranger District Office, 601 S. Weber St., Colorado Springs 80903, ☎ 719/636–1602).

Fishing

There's excellent trout fishing in the streams of the **South Platte** (✉ Rte. 67, 28 mi north of Woodland Park). **Elevenmile Reservoir** (✉ Hwy. 24W to town of Lake George) has rainbow trout, kokanee salmon, and pike.

Golf

The **Broadmoor** (✉ 1 Lake Ave., ☎ 719/634–7711) has three 18-hole courses.

Hiking and Backpacking

Ask the **El Paso County Parks Department** (☎ 719/520–6375) for suggestions. Some of the best trails are in **Pike National Forest** (☞ Biking, *above*).

Horseback Riding

Academy Riding Stables (✉ 4 El Paso Blvd., ☎ 719/633–5667) rents horses for guided tours through Garden of the Gods park (☞ Exploring Colorado Springs and Environs, *above*). Reservations are essential.

NORTHWESTERN COLORADO

As you climb west from Denver, the mountains rear up, pine forests line the road, and the legendary Colorado of powder skiing, alpine scenery, and the great outdoors begins. As once-primitive mining towns have attracted skiers and scenery buffs, sophisticated dining and lodging have followed.

Visitor Information

Aspen Chamber Resort Association (✉ 328 E. Hyman Ave., 81611, ☎ 970/925–5656; ✉ 425 Rio Grande Pl., 81611, ☎ 970/925–1940). **Glenwood Springs Chamber Resort Association** (✉ 1102 Grand Ave., 81601, ☎ 970/945–6589 or 800/221–0098). **Steamboat Springs Chamber Resort Association** (✉ 1255 S. Lincoln Ave., ☎ 970/879–0880 or 800/922–2722). **Summit County Chamber of Commerce** (✉ Main St., Frisco 80443, ☎ 800/530–3099). **Vail Valley Tourism and Convention Bureau** (✉ 100 E. Meadow Dr., 81657, ☎ 970/476–1000 or 800/525–3236).

Arriving and Departing

By Bus

Greyhound Lines (☎ 800/231–2222).

By Car

I–70 is the main route to the Summit County resorts, Vail, and Glenwood Springs. From Glenwood Springs, Highway 82 heads to Aspen. Highway 36 leads to Rocky Mountain National Park and Estes Park; Highway 40 heads to Steamboat Springs.

By Plane

Aspen Airport (☎ 970/920–5385) is 7 mi east of town; most flights connect from Denver. **Steamboat Springs Airport** (☎ 970/879–1204) is 3 mi northwest of town. **Eagle County Airport** (☎ 970/524–9490), 35 mi west of Vail, serves Vail Valley. Regional and national airlines fly to all three airports, but Vail has scheduled service only during ski season.

By Train

Amtrak (☎ 800/872–7245) stops in Glenwood Springs, Granby, and Winter Park.

Exploring Northwestern Colorado

Estes Park is the northern gateway to **Rocky Mountain National Park** (☞ National and State Parks, *above*), where Trail Ridge Road (closed in winter) provides a spectacular ride on one of the highest auto routes in the world. On the west side of Estes Park is **Grand Lake,** the largest natural lake in Colorado, with the world's highest yacht club. The turn-of-the-century town of the same name is also a snowmobiling mecca in winter.

The resort skiing closest to Denver is off I–70 at **Winter Park,** a family-oriented resort with more challenging terrain on the Mary Jane side. Denverites often come here via the Ski Train (☎ 303/296–4754) on weekends. The mountains of **Summit County,** 70 mi from Denver off I–70, attract climbers, hikers, and skiers. **Copper Mountain,** the first Club Med in North America, has terrain for most abilities, with an emphasis on intermediate and advanced skiers. **Keystone Resort** encompasses the peaks of Keystone, for beginning and intermediate skiers, and the Outback and North Peak for serious skiers. **Breckenridge** is an old mining town transformed into a resort. For a change from resort atmosphere and prices, head to **Lake Dillon,** a large reservoir popular with boaters. Up U.S. 40 from I–70, **Steamboat Springs** has great, uncrowded skiing for all abilities and a decidedly western feel.

West of Summit County is **Vail,** celebrated home of the largest ski mountain in North America. Constructed from the ground up to look like a European ski village, the town is huge, varied in its attractions, and pricey. It tends to be more conservative and family oriented than Aspen. **Beaver Creek** was created for those seeking an even more exclusive atmosphere than that of Vail; everything here lives up to its billing, from the billeting to the bill of fare. The ski area is geared to intermediate and advanced skiers.

At the turnoff for Aspen on I–70 is **Glenwood Springs,** where the main attraction besides scenery is **Yampah Hot Springs** (✉ Pine St., ☎ 970/945–0667; 🎫 $8.75), the world's largest outdoor mineral hot springs.

You know all about **Aspen,** the glitzy resort where actors and moguls vacation in ski season. It's expensive—and worth it if your passions are people-watching and great skiing. Many prefer the other seasons, though, for the beauty of the setting or for the summer **Aspen Music Festival** (☎ 970/925–3254).

Within Aspen's orbit are several **ski areas,** each geared to a different level of ability. Skiers can get a multiday ticket to all four mountains: **Buttermilk,** serving primarily beginners and low-intermediate skiers; **Aspen Highlands,** for intermediate skiers, with some of the highest vertical drops and best views; **Snowmass,** a perfect intermediate hill; and for experts, **Aspen Mountain,** which hosts international competitions.

Dining and Lodging

The celebrity atmosphere of towns like Aspen and Vail attracts celebrity chefs, and hot restaurants come and go here as quickly as in New York. If you don't want to spend the money to eat with stars, consider heading to nearby towns, where the atmosphere and prices are more down-home western. The ski resorts make getting accommodations easy. Calling the following numbers can hook you up with many different kinds of lodgings: **Aspen** (☎ 800/262–7736), **Beaver Creek** (☎ 800/622–3131), **Breckenridge** (☎ 800/221–1091), **Copper Mountain** (☎ 800/458–8386), **Keystone** (☎ 800/222–0188), **Steamboat Springs** (☎ 800/922–2722), **Vail** (☎ 800/525–3875), and **Winter Park** (☎ 800/729–5813). Condos are the most common and, because they have kitchens, can help cut down on food expenses. For price ranges *see* Charts 1(A) and 2(A) *in* On the Road with Fodor's.

Aspen

$$$–$$$$ ✕ **Renaissance.** In this abstract rendition of a sultan's tent, owner-chef Charles Dale artfully transforms ordinary ingredients into culinary gold. Opt for his menu degustation—six courses matched with the appropriate glass of wine. Upstairs, the R Bistro is more casual and less expensive. ✉ *304 E. Hopkins St., Aspen,* ☎ *970/925–2402. Reservations essential. AE, D, DC, MC, V. Closed May and Oct.–Thanksgiving. No lunch.*

$$$–$$$$ ★ ✕ **Syzygy.** Upstairs and unmarked, this restaurant is for those who like sleek modern design and sophisticated food that blends international flavors. ✉ *520 E. Hyman,* ☎ *970/925–3700. Reservations essential. AE, D, DC, MC, V. Closed May and Oct.–Thanksgiving. No lunch.*

$$$ ✕ **Ajax Tavern.** This is a bright, bustling restaurant with mahogany paneling, leather banquettes, and an open kitchen. The menu emphasizes Mediterranean flavors prepared with classic French techniques, using regional ingredients whenever possible. ✉ *685 E. Durant Ave., ☎ 970/920–9333. Reservations essential. AE, D, DC, MC, V.*

$$$$ ★ 🏨 **Hotel Jerome.** Rooms and suites in this century-old brick building have retained their Victorian charm with period furnishings such as carved cherry armoires; many bathrooms have Jacuzzis and separate showers. The J-Bar is a lively local's hangout; the Library Bar has more of a gentlemen's club atmosphere. ✉ *330 E. Main St., 81611, ☎ 970/920–1000 or 800/331–7213, FAX 970/925–2784. 93 rooms. 2 restaurants, pool. AE, DC, MC, V.*

$$$$ 🏨 **St. Regis Aspen.** Formerly the Ritz, this grand hotel was renamed after New York's prestigious St. Regis when it became part of the ITT Sheraton empire in early 1998. The imposing château-like facade surrounds a central courtyard; the lobby showcases a $5 million art collection. ✉ *315 E. Dean St., 81611, ☎ 970/920–3300 or 800/325–3535, FAX 970/925–8998. 257 rooms. 2 restaurants, pool, health club. AE, MC, V.*

$$–$$$$ 🏨 **Snowflake Inn.** The wide-ranging accommodations here are all quite comfortable. Most are decorated in tartans or bright colors. Afternoon tea is served in the wood-beamed lobby, around a stone fireplace. ✉ *221 E. Hyman Ave., 81611, ☎ 970/925–3221 or 800/247–2069, FAX 970/925–8740. 38 units. Pool. CP. AE, D, DC, MC, V.*

Beaver Creek

$$$$ ★ 🏨 **Hyatt Regency Beaver Creek.** An antler chandelier, huge stone fireplaces, and upholstered comfort characterize the public rooms here. Guests exiting the hotel step into their warmed and waiting ski boots and skis. Non-skiers can take advantage of the full spa and health club, as well as a top-notch children's program. Watch for much lower rates off-season. ✉ *136 E. Thomas Place, Beaver Creek or Box 1595, Avon 81620, ☎ 970/949–1234 or 800/233–1234, FAX 970/949–4164. 321 rooms. 3 restaurants, pool, health club. AE, D, DC, MC, V.*

Breckenridge

$$–$$$ ★ 🏨 **B&Bs on North Main. St.** Two picture-perfect five-room inns date from the 1880s; a rustic timber-frame barn is a more modern addition. ✉ *303 N. Main St., ☎ 970/453–2975 or 800/795–2975. 10 rooms, 1 3-bedroom cottage. Full breakfast. AE.*

Glenwood Springs

$$ 🏨 **Hotel Colorado.** Teddy Roosevelt stayed at this hotel, now listed in the National Historic Register, to take advantage of the adjacent hot springs. The imposing sandstone structure has an imposing marble lobby. Bedrooms are huge and sparsely furnished. ✉ *526 Pine St., 81601, ☎ 970/945–6511 or 800/544–3998, FAX 970/945–7030. 128 rooms. 2 restaurants, exercise room. AE, D, DC, MC, V.*

Grand Lake

$–$$ 🏨 **Grand Lake Lodge.** Set majestically above Grand Lake and bordering Rocky Mountain National Park, the lodge is actually a collection of rustic cabins. Some have wood-burning stoves for heat, and all are comfortable and well worn. ✉ *15500 U.S. Hwy. 34 (Box 569), 80447, ☎ 970/627–3967 in summer or 303/759–5848. 56 cabins. Restaurant, pool. AE, D, MC, V. Closed mid-Sept.–May.*

Keystone

$$–$$$ ★ ✕🏨 **Ski Tip Lodge.**This premium B&B reflects its 1880s origins with four-poster beds, handmade quilts, and log-cabin decor. In the main room, huge picture windows overlook a forest. The dining room's Amer-

ican regional cuisine is exceptional. The lodge is a half mile from the slopes. ✉ *Box 38, Keystone, 80435,* ☏ *970/496–4950 or 800/222–0188. 11 rooms. Restaurant, bar. AE, D, DC, MC, V.*

Steamboat Springs

$$–$$$ ★ ✕ **Antares.** In a splendid Victorian building with fieldstone walls, pressed-tin ceilings, and stained glass, you'll find exciting cuisine inspired by America's rich ethnic stew. Mussels in a citrus-chili-chardonnay broth, or pompano with a pineapple and Pommery mustard fondue, might be on the menu. ✉ *57½ 8th St.,* ☏ *970/879–9939. Reservations essential. AE, MC, V. No lunch.*

$$–$$$ ★ ✕ **La Montaña.** Among the standouts at this Mexican-Southwest establishment are red-chili pasta in a shrimp, garlic, and cilantro sauce; interwoven strands of mesquite-grilled elk, lamb, and chorizo sausage; and pecan-crusted elk loin with bourbon cream sauce. ✉ *Après Ski Way and Village Dr.,* ☏ *970/879–5800. AE, D, MC, V. No lunch.*

$$–$$$ **Sky Valley Lodge.** Glorious scenery surrounds this homey property a few miles from downtown. Rooms are English country style. ✉ *31490 E. Hwy. 40, 80477,* ☏ *970/879–7749 or 800/538–7519,* FAX *970/879–7752. 24 rooms. CP. AE, D, DC, MC, V.*

Vail

$$$ ★ ✕ **Sweet Basil.** A meal here will wake up your taste buds. The creative menu includes such preparations as a salmon paillard with bok choy, sesame purée, and tomato-cilantro sauce. ✉ *193 E. Gore Creek Dr.,* ☏ *970/476–0125. Reservations essential. AE, MC, V.*

$$–$$$ ★ ✕ **Terra Bistro.** Situated in the Vail Athletic Club, where a warm fireplace contrasts with black-iron chairs and black-and-white photographs, this soaring space has an innovative, seasonally changing menu that caters to both meat-and-potatoes diners and vegans. Everything is crisply textured and pungently seasoned. Organic produce and free-range meat and poultry are used whenever possible. ✉ *352 E. Meadow Dr.,* ☏ *970/476–6836. Reservations essential. AE, D, DC, MC, V. No lunch.*

$$$$ ★ **Sonnenalp.** A German family runs this centrally located Bavarian-style hotel, where small but luxurious rooms have an authentically German Alpine feeling. Accommodations are in two buildings: the pretty Swiss Chalet and the more contemporary Bavaria Haus. Both buildings have European-style spas. ✉ *20 Vail Rd., 81657,* ☏ *970/476–5656 or 800/654–8312,* FAX *970/476–1639. 150 rooms. 4 restaurants, 3 pools, health club. AE, DC, MC, V.*

Winter Park

$$–$$$ ★ ✕ **Gasthaus Eichler.** This is Winter Park's most romantic dining room, with quaint Bavarian decor, antler chandeliers, and stained-glass windows. Veal and grilled items round out the menu of German classics such as sauerbraten. The Eichler also has 15 cozy Old World rooms, with down comforters, lace curtains, armoires, cable TVs, and whirlpool tubs. ✉ *Winter Park Dr., 80482,* ☏ *970/726–5133 or 800/543–3899. 15 rooms. Restaurant. AE, MC, V.*

Ranches

$$$$ ★ **C Lazy U Ranch.** Near Rocky Mountain National Park, this rambling southwestern-style wooden lodge has fireplaces and Navajo rugs in its rooms and cabins. Activities include horseback riding, ice skating, and dogsledding. The fare ranges from old-fashioned ranch food (steak and barbecue) to contemporary cuisine. ✉ *3640 Colorado Hwy. 125 (Box 379), Granby 80446,* ☏ *970/887–3344,* FAX *970/887–3917. 19 rooms, 20 cabins. Restaurant, pool, exercise room. No credit cards. Closed Apr.–May and Oct.–Dec. 21.*

$$$$ ★ **Home Ranch.** This rustic yet luxurious western lodge in the Steamboat Springs area is a member of the prestigious Relais & Chateaux group. Each log cabin has a wood-burning stove and hot tub. Hiking, fishing, and horseback riding are the main summer activities; in winter, lift tickets to Steamboat Springs are included in the price. ✉ *54880 County Rd. 129 (Box 822), Clark 80428,* ☎ *970/879–1780,* FAX *970/879–1795. 8 cabins, 6 lodge rooms. Restaurant, pool. AE, MC, V. Closed Apr.–May and Oct.–Nov.*

Campgrounds

You can reserve camping spaces at many of the national forest campgrounds by phone (☎ 800/280–2267). **Tiger Run Resort** (✉ 3 mi north of Breckenridge on Hwy. 9, 80424, ☎ 970/453–9690) is a retreat for RVs, with tennis courts, a pool, and a recreation room. **Winding River Resort Village** (✉ 1447 County Rd. 491, Box 629, Grand Lake 80447, ☎ 970/627–3215) is a combination campground and low-cost dude ranch in a beautiful forest.

Outdoor Activities and Sports

Boating

Sailing regattas are common at Grand Lake. Rent fishing boats and motorboats at **Beacon Landing Marina** (✉ Grand County Rd. 64, 6 mi south of Grand Lake off Hwy. 34, ☎ 970/627–3671). **Lake Dillon Marina** (✉ Dillon, ☎ 970/468–5100) rents sailboats and motorboats.

Fishing

Grand Lake and the connected reservoirs Shadow Mountain Lake and Lake Granby are known for their trout fishing. Dillon Reservoir is stocked with salmon and trout. The Lower Blue River, below Dillon Reservoir, is a Gold Medal catch-and-release area, as is the Fryingpan River near Aspen.

Golf

Sheraton Steamboat Golf Club (✉ 2200 Village Inn Ct., ☎ 970/879–2220) was designed by Robert Trent Jones, Jr. Reservations are essential at the Jack Nicklaus–designed **Breckenridge Golf Club** (✉ 200 Clubhouse Dr., ☎ 970/453–9104). The difficult **Eagle/Vail Golf Course** (✉ 0431 Eagle Dr., Avon, ☎ 970/949–5267) has reduced fees in fall and spring.

Hiking and Backpacking

To find out about parks and wilderness areas with hiking and backpacking trails, contact the **Holy Cross Ranger District Office** (✉ 24747 Hwy. 24, Minturn, near Vail, ☎ 970/827–5715), the **Aspen Ranger District Office** (✉ 806 W. Hallam St., ☎ 970/925–3445), or the **Dillon Ranger District Office** (✉ Blue River Pkwy., Silverthorne, ☎ 970/468–5400).

Rafting

The Colorado River lures both white-water enthusiasts and beginners, as does the Arkansas River near Buena Vista. Contact rafting firms through the **Colorado River Outfitters Association** (✉ Box 440021, Aurora 80044, ☎ 303/369–4632).

Ski Areas

For **snow conditions** at Colorado resorts, call 303/825–7669.

Cross-Country

Aspen/Snowmass Nordic Trail System (☎ 970/925–1940) contains 48 mi of trails through the Roaring Fork Valley. **Breckenridge Nordic Ski Center** (☎ 970/453–6855) maintains 19 mi of trails. **Copper Moun-**

tain/Trak Cross-Country Center** (☏ 970/986–2882) has 16 mi of groomed track and skate lanes. **Devil's Thumb Ranch** (✉ Devil's Thumb, 10 mi north of Winter Park, ☏ 970/726–5632) is a full-service resort with 48 mi of groomed trails. **Frisco Nordic Center** (✉ 112 N. Summit Blvd., ☏ 970/668–0866) has nearly 25 mi of one-way loops. **Keystone Nordic Center** (☏ 970/468–4275) provides 11 mi of prepared trails and 35 mi of backcountry skiing through Arapahoe National Forest. **Steamboat Ski Touring Center** (☏ 970/879–8180) has trails emanating from the golf course. **Vail Cross-Country Ski Centers** (☏ 970/479–4391) has information on Vail Valley trails.

Downhill

Aspen Highlands (✉ 1600 Maroon Creek Rd., Aspen 81611, ☏ 970/925–1220) has 619 acres of runs, 8 lifts, and a 3,635-ft vertical drop. **Aspen Mountain** (✉ Box 1248, Aspen 81612, ☏ 970/925–1220) has 675 acres of runs, a gondola, 7 lifts, and a 3,267-ft drop. **Beaver Creek** (✉ Box 7, Vail 81658, ☏ 970/476–5601) has 1,625 acres of runs, 14 lifts, and a 4,040-ft drop. **Breckenridge** (✉ Box 1058, Breckenridge 80424, ☏ 970/453–5000) has 2,031 acres of runs, 19 lifts, and a 3,398-ft drop. **Copper Mountain** (✉ Box 3001, Copper Mountain 80443, ☏ 970/968–2882) has 2,433 acres of runs, 21 lifts, and a 2,601-ft drop. **Keystone** (✉ Box 38, Keystone 80435, ☏ 970/468–2316) has 1,755 acres of runs, 19 lifts, and a 2,900-ft drop. **Snowmass** (✉ Box 5566, Snowmass Village 80446, ☏ 970/925–1220) has 2,655 acres of runs, 18 lifts, and a 4,406-ft drop. **Steamboat** (✉ 2305 Mt. Werner Circle, Steamboat Springs 80487, ☏ 970/879–6111) has 2,939 acres of runs, a gondola, 20 lifts, and a 3,668-ft drop. **Buttermilk** (✉ Box 1248, Aspen 81612, ☏ 970/925–1220) has 410 acres of runs, 7 lifts, and a 2,030-ft drop. **Vail** (✉ Box 7, Vail 81658, ☏ 970/476–5601) has 4,644 acres of runs, a gondola, 29 lifts, and a 3,330-ft drop. **Winter Park** (✉ Box 36, Winter Park 80482, ☏ 970/726–5514) has 2,581 acres of runs, 20 lifts, and a 3,060-ft drop.

Shopping

The town of **Silverthorne** has an outlet shopping complex (✉ I–70 at Silverthorne, ☏ 970/468–9440) with nearly 80 stores.

SOUTHWESTERN COLORADO

Ski areas and red-rock deserts, cowboy hangouts and haunts of ancient cultures mark this region. The feeling is down-home—you may see a cowboy in the distance riding off after a stray or walk into a bar where ranchers discussing stock prices sit next to climbers enthusing over an ascent route.

Visitor Information

Southwest Colorado Travel Region (✉ Box 2102, Montrose 81402, ☏ 800/933–4340). **Durango:** Chamber of Commerce (✉ 111 S. Camino del Rio, Box 2587, 81302, ☏ 970/247–0312 or 800/525–8855). **Telluride:** Chamber of Commerce (✉ 666 W. Colorado Ave., Box 653, 81435, ☏ 970/728–3041 or 800/525–3455).

Arriving and Departing

By Bus

Greyhound Lines (☏ 800/231–2222) serves Durango and major mountain towns such as Purgatory, Silverton, Ouray, Ridgeway, and Montrose.

By Car

Highway 141 from Grand Junction to Highway 145 leads to Telluride; Highway 550 is the route from Durango to Silverton and Ouray.

By Plane

Durango–La Plata County Airport (☎ 970/247–8143) is 14 mi east of Durango, and **Montrose Regional Airport** (☎ 970/249–3203) is 1 mi from Montrose. **Gunnison County Airport** (☎ 970/641–2304) is 23 mi south of Crested Butte. **Telluride Regional Airport** (☎ 970/728–5313) is 2 mi from Telluride.

Exploring Southwestern Colorado

Telluride is another old mining town turned ski resort but with a difference: Its relative isolation in a box canyon makes it more laid-back than many other Colorado resorts, and its beauty is legendary. Skiers of all abilities will find suitable terrain.The summer brings nationally known **festivals** of film (☎ 970/728–4401), bluegrass (☎ 800/624–2422), and jazz (☎ 970/728–7009). South of Telluride is a complete change of scene: **Mesa Verde** (☞ National and State Parks, *above*), where the forests give way to dramatic red-rock cliff dwellings. The structures were fashioned more than 700 years ago by the Anasazi, believed to be the ancestors of the Pueblos.

East of Mesa Verde is **Durango,** a surprisingly large town with dramatic views of the San Juan Mountains, and strong frontier traditions. A trip on the **Durango and Silverton Narrow Gauge Railroad** (✉ 479 Main Ave., ☎ 970/247–2733; 🎟 $49.10 round-trip) is worth the trouble of reserving well in advance. The eight-hour round-trip takes you over tracks laid between the two towns in 1881, past unspoiled scenery, dramatic gorge crossings, and rails dug into the mountainside. **Silverton** is a smaller, more untouched frontier mining town.

Ouray, about 25 mi up the twisty, breathtaking Million-Dollar Highway, is a sleepy western town surrounded by the magnificent, red San Juan Mountains. Dive into the **Ouray Hot Springs Pool** (☎ 970/325–4638; 🎟 $6) or, for a more rustic dip, **Orvis Hot Springs** (☎ 970/626–5324; 🎟 $7). North of Ouray is **Crested Butte,** an old Victorian mining town tucked away in another gorgeous setting; the town serves as base for the excellent Crested Butte Mountain Resort ski area, 2 mi away and best suited for high-intermediate and expert skiers.

Dining and Lodging

For price ranges *see* Charts 1(B) and 2(B) *in* On the Road with Fodor's.

Crested Butte

$$$$ ★ ✕ **Soupçon.** Mac Bailey, the impish owner-chef of Soupçon ("soup's on," get it?) prepares innovative variations on classic bistro cuisine. The duck and fish are sublime, as are the two intimate dining rooms, which are inside a log cabin. ✉ *Just off 2nd St. behind the Forest Queen,* ☎ *970/349–5448. Reservations essential. AE, MC, V. Closed late Apr.–mid-June and Oct.–Thanksgiving. No lunch.*

$$ ★ ✕ **Slogar.** A soul-satisfying prix-fixe meal of plump fried chicken, flaky buttermilk biscuits, coleslaw, mashed potatoes, and homemade ice cream costs just $12.95 inside this Victorian tavern with a lace and stained-glass motif. ✉ *2nd and Whiterock Sts.,* ☎ *970/349–5765. AE, MC, V. Closed late Apr.–mid-June and Oct.–Thanksgiving. No lunch.*

$$$$ ★ 🏨 **Crested Butte Club.** This quaint, stylish inn has cherry-wood antiques and claw-foot brass tubs. The bar is a convivial gathering spot, and the full-scale health club is a great place to relax after skiing or biking. ✉ *512 2nd St., 81224,* ☎ *970/349–6655 or 800/815–2582,* FAX *970/349–6654. 7 rooms. Pool, health club. CP. D, MC, V.*

Durango

$$$–$$$$ ✕ **Ariano's.** Pasta made fresh daily and a sure touch with meats make this northern Italian restaurant one of Durango's most popular. Veal scallopini sautéed with fresh sage and garlic is among the best dishes. ✉ *150 E. 6th St.,* ☎ *970/247–8146. Reservations not accepted. AE, D, DC, MC, V.*

$$–$$$ ✕ **Cypress Café.** The Greek-influenced menu, with flavorful vegetarian, lamb, and chicken dishes, is a welcome respite from the region's standard meat-and-potatoes fare. The outdoor patio, shaded by fruit trees, is one of the nicest places to dine in Durango on a summer day. ✉ *725 E. 2nd Ave.,* ☎ *970/385–6884. AE, MC, V. No lunch winter weekends.*

$$$$ **New Rochester Hotel.** This former flophouse was built in 1892. Its spacious rooms are full of Western artifacts and are named for the many movies shot in the area, such as Butch Cassidy and the Sundance Kid. ✉ *726 E. 2nd Ave., 81301,* ☎ *970/385–1920 or 800/664–1920,* FAX *970/385–1967. 15 rooms. Full breakfast. AE, D, DC, MC, V.*

Ouray

$$$–$$$$ **China Clipper Inn.** A welcome relief from the area's typical Western- and Victorian-style inns, the China Clipper is tastefully decorated with Oriental and nautical antiques. Innkeepers Elaine and Earl Yarbrough are warm and interesting without being overly ingratiating. ✉ *525 2nd St., 81427,* ☎ *970/325–0565 or 800/315–0565,* FAX *970/325–4190. 11 rooms. Full breakfast. MC, V.*

Telluride

$$$$ ✕ **Campagna.** Oak and terra-cotta floors and vintage photos of the Italian countryside give this place the feel of a Tuscan farmhouse; its assured, classically simple cuisine comes as no surprise. Wild mushrooms (porcini or Portobello) and wild boar chops are among the enticing possibilities. Finish off your meal with a perfect tiramisu and a shot of fiery grappa. ✉ *435 W. Pacific Ave.,* ☎ *970/728–6190. Reservations essential. MC, V. No lunch.*

$$$$ ★ ✕ **La Marmotte.** At this rustic restaurant decorated like a French country cottage, the Gallic owners and chefs change the menu constantly, serving such dishes as duck confit or lamb with red-bell-pepper sauce and white beans. ✉ *150 W. San Juan Ave.,* ☎ *970/728–6232. Reservations essential. AE, MC, V. No lunch.*

$$$$ ★ **The Peaks at Telluride Resort and Spa.** The prisonlike, pastel exterior can be excused at this ski-in/ski-out luxury resort, thanks to its invigorating spa treatments, some of which purport to have their roots in indigenous Indian rites. But the biggest kick is the two-story water slide, which deposits you into the glorious outdoor pool, with Mt. Wilson looming in the background. ✉ *136 Country Club Dr., 81435,* ☎ *970/728–6800 or 800/223–6725,* FAX *970/728–6567. 177 rooms. 2 restaurants, pool, exercise room. AE, DC, MC, V.*

$$$$ ★ **San Sophia Inn.** If you eschew Victorian frills, this is the inn for you: There's no trace of Laura Ashley here, except for the brass beds and down comforters. Rooms, although smallish, are luxurious, done in handsome desert shades and with pine armoires. Exquisitely presented dishes on the menu might include beef tenderloin stuffed with spinach and fontina with brandy demiglace. ✉ *330 W. Pacific St., 81435,* ☎ *970/728–3001 or 800/537–4781. 16 rooms. Restaurant. Full breakfast. AE, MC, V.*

$$$–$$$$ **New Sheridan Hotel.** William Jennings Bryan delivered his rousing "Cross of Gold" speech here in 1896, garnering a presidential nomination in the process. Victoriana abounds, with exposed brick walls, old tintypes, brass beds, red-velour love seats, and wicker rocking chairs. Turndown service and complimentary breakfast and afternoon tea complete the experience of fin-de-siècle gracious living. The bar is a local institution. ✉ *231 W. Colorado Ave., 81435,* ☎ *970/728–4351. 26 rooms, 6 condominium suites. Restaurant, exercise room. Full breakfast. AE, D, MC, V.*

Ranch

$$$$ ★ **Skyline Ranch.** Burlap walls, pine furniture, and down comforters deck the rooms in the slab-wood buildings of this rustic western ranch, which has prime horseback riding and fly-fishing. In winter, guests cross-country ski or head to Telluride for downhill skiing. The cuisine is French-American, with a menu that changes daily. ✉ *Off Hwy. 145, 8 mi south of Telluride, Telluride 81435,* ☎ *970/728–3757 or 888/754–1126,* FAX *970/728–6728. 10 lodge rooms, 6 cabins. Restaurant. AE, MC, V.*

Campgrounds

Ranger district offices (☞ Hiking and Backpacking *in* Outdoor Activities and Sports, *below*) have information on campgrounds in the state and national forests. Near Durango is a **KOA** campground (✉ East on Hwy. 160, ☎ 970/247–0783), that's closed mid-October–April.

Outdoor Activities and Sports

Biking

Crested Butte is a mountain-biking destination; Durango is home to many world-class road cyclists because of its great riding terrain. Bike rental locations abound in both towns.

Fishing

The Dolores River, in the San Juan National Forest(☞ Hiking and Backpacking, *below*), and the Animas River, near Durango, are good for trout. The Vallecito Reservoir, also near Durango, has pike, trout, and salmon. At **Ridgway State Park** (☎ 970/626–5822), 15 mi north of Ouray, you can catch rainbow trout.

Golf

Some of the best 18-hole courses in the area are **Hillcrest Golf Course** (✉ 2300 Rim Dr., Durango, ☎ 970/247–1499), **Tamarron** (✉ 40292 Rte. 550, north of Durango, ☎ 970/259–2000), **Telluride Golf Club** (✉ Telluride Mountain Village, ☎ 970/728–3856), and **Crested Butte Country Club** (✉ 385 Country Club Dr., outside Crested Butte, ☎ 970/349–6127).

Hiking and Backpacking

The 500-mi **Colorado Trail,** from Durango to Denver, is a major route. The **San Juan National Forest District Office** (✉ 701 Camino del Rio, Room 101, Durango, ☎ 970/247–4874) has information on trails in the area.

Rafting

Rafting is popular on the San Miguel, Dolores, Gunnison, and Animas rivers. Arrange trips through the **Colorado River Outfitters Association** (✉ Box 440021, Aurora 80044, ☎ 303/369–4632).

Ski Areas

For **snow conditions** at Colorado resorts, call 303/825–7669.

Cross-Country

Trails abound; check with local tourist offices for details. **Purgatory Ski Touring Center** (✉ Purgatory Ski Area, 1 Skier Pl., Durango 81301, ☎ 970/247–9000) manages 26 mi of trails; **Telluride Nordic Center** (✉ Box 1784, Telluride 81435, ☎ 970/728–7570) has 48 mi of trails and a free shuttle from the alpine ski area.

Downhill

Crested Butte (✉ Off Rte. 135, Box A, 81225, ☎ 970/349–2333) has 1,162 acres of runs, 13 lifts, and a 2,787-ft vertical drop. **Purgatory** (✉ Hwy. 550, 81301, ☎ 970/247–9000) has 1,200 acres of runs, 11 lifts, and a 2,029-ft drop. **Telluride** (✉ Rte. 145, Box 11155, 81435, ☎ 970/728–3856) has 1,050 acres of runs, 12 lifts, and a 3,522-ft drop.

Shopping

Western Goods

Toh-Atin Gallery (✉ 145 W. 9th St., Durango, ☎ 970/247–8277) and the related **Toh-Atin's Art on Main** (✉ 865 Main Ave., ☎ 970/247–4540), around the corner, are perhaps the foremost western, Native American, and southwestern fine art and crafts galleries in Colorado. **North Moon** (✉ 133 W. Colorado Ave., Telluride, ☎ 970/728–4145) carries painted lodgepole-pine furnishings, contemporary Native American ceramics that depart from tribal traditions, metallic sculptures, and petroglyph-inspired jewelry.

ELSEWHERE IN COLORADO

South Central Colorado

Arriving and Departing

Buena Vista is 90 mi west of Colorado Springs on U.S. 24; the only way to get there is by car. Pueblo is a half hour south of Colorado Springs on I–25 south; Trinidad is just over an hour farther. **Pueblo Memorial Airport** (☎ 719/948–3355) is served by United Express.

What to See and Do

Hiking, biking, and climbing are king in **Buena Vista,** where the Collegiate Peaks Wilderness Area has 14,000-ft peaks. On the Arkansas River, Buena Vista also bills itself as "the white-water-rafting capital of the world." Contact **Dvorak Kayak & Rafting Expeditions** (✉ Nathrop, ☎ 800/824–3795) for trip information. After a full day of activities, head to the **Mt. Princeton Hot Springs** (✉ 5 mi west of Nathrop, CR 162, ☎ 719/395–2447; 🎫 $6) for a restorative soak. The **Buena Vista Heritage Museum** (✉ E. Main St., ☎ 719/395–8458; 🎫 $2) contains artifacts from the life and times of the regional pioneers.

Pueblo, a multiethnic working-class steel town in the shadow of Colorado Springs, nonetheless has some glorious historical neighborhoods, such as the **Union Avenue Historic District.** Walking-tour brochures are available at the Chamber of Commerce (✉ 210 N. Santa Fe Ave., 81003, ☎ 719/542–1704). The **Rosemount Victorian Museum** (✉ 419 W. 14th St., ☎ 719/545–5290; 🎫 $5) is an opulent mansion whose rooms are virtually intact. The **Sangre de Cristo Arts Center** (✉ 210 N. Santa Fe Ave., ☎ 719/543–0130; 🎫 free) celebrates regional arts and crafts.

U.S. 50 roughly follows the faded tracks of the **Santa Fe Trail** from the Kansas border through La Junta, where U.S. 350 picks up the scent, traveling southwest to Trinidad. If you detour onto the quiet county roads, you can still discern the faint outline of the trail. Here, amid the magpies and prairie dogs, it takes little imagination to conjure visions of the pioneers struggling to travel just 10 mi a day by oxcart over vast stretches of territory. Just east of La Junta, **Bent's Fort** (✉ 35110 Hwy. 194 E, ☎ 719/384–2596; 🎟 $2), now a living museum, was the most important stop along the route.

The **Trinidad History Museum** (✉ 300 E. Main St., ☎ 719/846–7217; 🎟 $5), housed inside two 19th-century mansions, has exhibits chronicling the effect of the Santa Fe Trail on the community.

Dining and Lodging

$–$$ ★ ✕ **Irish Brew Pub & Grill.** Pub grub is elevated to an art form here. The grilled smoked-duck sausage with goat cheese is a standout, as are beaver (yes, beaver) sandwiches. Nine varieties of beer are brewed on the premises. ✉ *108 W. 3rd St., Pueblo* ☎ *970/728–6232. Reservations essential. AE, D, DC, MC, V. Closed Sun.*

$$ ★ 🏨 **Abriendo Inn.** With original parquet floors, stained glass, and Minnequa oak wainscoting, this exquisite 1906 home is on the National Register of Historic Places. Fresh fruit and cookies are left out for guests, and cheese and crackers are served in the evening. ✉ *300 W. Abriendo Ave., Pueblo 81004,* ☎ *719/544–2703,* FAX *719/542–6544. 10 rooms. Full breakfast. AE, DC, MC, V.*

$ 🏨 **River Run Inn.** On the Arkansas River, this cozy Victorian home has breathtaking mountain prospects. For those who can't get a room, there's a coed dorm on the property. ✉ *8495 CR 160, east off Hwy. 285, Salida 81201,* ☎ *719/539–3818 or 800/385–6925. 7 rooms; 13-bed dorm room. Full breakfast. AE, MC, V.*

The San Luis Valley

Arriving and Departing

Alamosa is 150 mi east of Durango on U.S. 160 or 115 mi from Pueblo on U.S. 160E to I–25N. Great Sand Dunes National Monument is on Route 150 north of U.S. 160; San Luis is on Route 159 south of U.S. 160. The **Durango–La Plata Airport** (☎ 970/247–8143) receives daily flights from American, America West, Reno Air, and United Express.

What to See and Do

Nestled between the San Juan Mountains and the Sangre de Cristo range and watered by the mighty Rio Grande and its tributaries, the 8,000-square-mi **San Luis Valley** is the world's largest alpine valley. The **Alamosa National Vista Wildlife Refuge** (✉ 9383 El Rancho La., ☎ 719/589–4021) is an important sanctuary for the nearly extinct whooping crane and its cousin, the sandhill. The terrain of the San Luis Valley ranges from the stark moonscape of the Wheeler Geologic Area to the tawny, undulating **Great Sand Dunes National Monument** (✉ 35 mi from Alamosa, east on U.S. 160 and north on Rte. 150, ☎ 719/378–2312). Created by windswept grains from the Rio Grande floor, the sand dunes—which rise up to 700 ft and stretch for 55 square mi—are an improbable, unforgettable sight, as curvaceous as Rubens's nudes.

San Luis, founded in 1851, is the oldest incorporated town in Colorado. Its Hispanic heritage is celebrated in the **San Luis Museum and Cultural Center** (✉ 401 Church Pl., ☎ 719/672–3611; 🎟 $1). Murals depicting famous stories and legends of the area adorn the town's tree-lined streets.

Dining and Lodging

$–$$ ✕ **Ace Inn & Old Town Bar.** Arrive hungry, and expect to find heaping portions of sopaipillas—fried burritos stuffed with beans, rice, and beef and smothered in red and green chilies—among other Mexican specialties. Save room for the sopaipilla sundae drowned in cinnamon wine sauce. The smallest margarita here is 28 ounces! ✉ *326 Main St., Alamosa,* ☎ *719/589–9801. D, MC, V.*

$–$$ ★ **Cottonwood Inn B&B.** This pretty cranberry-and-azure house, built in 1908, features Stickley furniture and regional photographs and watercolors. Rooms are sunny, with country-French washed walls; some have claw-foot tubs. ✉ *123 San Juan Ave., Alamosa 81101,* ☎ *719/589–3882 or 800/955–2623. 9 rooms. Full breakfast. AE, D, MC, V.*

IDAHO

Updated by Peggy Ammerman

Capital	Boise
Population	1,210,200
Motto	It Is Perpetual
State Bird	Mountain bluebird
State Flower	Syringa
Postal Abbreviation	ID

Statewide Visitor Information

Idaho Travel Council (✉ Dept. of Commerce, 700 W. State St., Box 83720, Boise 83720-0093, ☎ 208/334–2470 or 800/635–7820).

Scenic Drives

Eighteen historic or scenic byways and segments of 10 historic trails are shown on the Official Idaho Highway Map, available from the Idaho Travel Council (☞ Statewide Visitor Information, *above*). The 35-mi **Lewis and Clark Back Country Byway,** 11 mi southeast of the town of Salmon off Route 28 at Tendoy, traces the passage of explorers Meriwether Lewis and George Rogers Clark through the Continental Divide, along the crest of the Bitterroot and Beaverhead Mountains near the Montana state line. The **Lake Coeur d'Alene Scenic Byway** cuts southwest on Route 3 through thick pine forests for 25 mi and then heads north on Route 97, shadowing the crooked eastern lakeshore for 35 mi.

National and State Parks

National Parks

With 40% of its acreage in trees, Idaho is the most heavily forested of the Rocky Mountain states. For information on all of Idaho's forests, contact the **Boise National Forest** (✉ 1750 Front St., Boise 83702, ☎ 208/354–4100). The Snake River Canyon plunges 1 mi at **Hells Canyon National Recreation Area** (✉ Rte. 1, Box 270A, Enterprise, OR, ☎ 503/426–4978), making it the deepest river gorge in the nation. Idaho has 3,000 mi of white-water river action, the most in the nation. Legend has it that the Main Salmon River was nicknamed the River of No Return by Lewis and Clark boatmen after they witnessed the waters churning "with great violence from one rock to another . . . foaming and roaring . . . so as to render the passage of anything impossible." Reconsidering, the expedition party backtracked to Montana and pursued an alternate route via the Lolo Pass over the Continental Divide. Today the Main Salmon and its Middle Fork, an acclaimed stretch of white water, are surrounded by the 2-million-acre **Frank Church–River of No Return Wilderness Area** (✉ Rte. 2, Grangeville 83530, ☎ 208/983–1950). Selected as a training site for U.S. astronauts because of its striking lunarlike appearance, the **Craters of the Moon National Monument** (✉ Box 29, Arco 83213, ☎ 208/527–3257) covers 83 square mi, with spatter cones, lava caves, and other eerie volcanic-formed features. Part of the **Sawtooth National Recreation Area** (✉ Star Rte., Ketchum 83340, ☎ 208/726–7672; 💳 $5 per vehicle), the jagged Sawtooth Mountains (often called America's Alps), with 42 peaks reaching at least 10,000 ft, join the Boulder and White Cloud ranges and march across 1,180 square mi, beginning just north of Ketchum on Route 75. Additional National Park Service properties include **Nez Percé National Historical Park** (✉ Hwy. 95, Box 93, Spalding 83551, ☎ 208/843–2261); **Hagerman Fossil Beds National Monument** (✉ Box 570,

Hagerman 83332, ☎ 208/837–4793); and **City of Rocks National Reserve** (✉ Box 169, Almo 83312, ☎ 208/824–5519). Other federal land in Idaho is under the jurisdiction of the **Bureau of Land Management Idaho State Office** (✉ 3380 Americana Terr., Boise 83706, ☎ 208/384–3000).

State Parks

The **Idaho Department of Parks & Recreation** (✉ Box 83720, Boise 83720, ☎ 208/334–4199 or 800/635–7820) maintains 24 state parks. **Heyburn State Park** (✉ Rte. 1, Box 139, Plummer 83851, ☎ 208/686–1308; 🎫 $2), at the southern tip of Lake Coeur d'Alene on Route 5, encompasses nearly 8,000 acres of land and water and is known for its migratory herons, eagles, and osprey as well as an annual fall harvest of wild rice. Rising 470 ft, North America's tallest single-structured sand dunes are the centerpiece of **Bruneau Dunes State Park** (✉ HC 85, Box 41, Mountain Home 83647, ☎ 208/366–7919; 🎫 $3), just a stone's throw from the Snake River and roughly 60 mi southeast of Boise on Route 78. Both fly fishers and a third of the Rocky Mountain trumpeter swan population flock to Henry's Fork of the Snake River, which winds through **Harriman State Park** (✉ HC 66, Box 500, Island Park 83429, ☎ 208/558–7368; 🎫 $3), on U.S. 20, 33 mi southwest of West Yellowstone, Montana.

Outdoor Activities and Sports

The **Idaho Travel Council** (☞ Statewide Visitor Information, *above*) has information about private campgrounds. For camping on federal and state lands, phone the national and state parks listed above. For information about hiking, backpacking, and rafting, contact the regional travel associations and local chambers of commerce (☞ Visitor Information, *below*) or **Idaho Outfitters and Guides Association** (✉ Box 95, Boise 83701, ☎ 208/342–1919 or 800/847–4843).

The fishing season generally runs from the Saturday before Memorial Day through November. The **Idaho Department of Fish & Game** (✉ Box 25, 600 S. Walnut Ave., Boise 83707, ☎ 208/334–3748 or 800/554–8685) provides information and licenses. The department also publishes a wildlife Viewing Guide that lists the best and most easily accessible viewing sites in the state.

SOUTHERN IDAHO

Idaho's longest river, the Snake, carves a steely blue course of nearly 1,000 mi through southern Idaho, linking together a diverse mix of terrain. Vast stretches of fertile farmland give way to desert plateaus blanketed in jet-black lava. Sweeps of sugary sand dunes anchor both the southwestern and eastern portions of the state. In between, waterfalls and springs spill into deep, rugged canyons. Pine-and-sage-clad mountains along the upper fringe of the Snake River plain hint of the taller Northern Rockies peaks that rise within the state's borders.

Visitor Information

Southwest Idaho Travel Association (✉ Box 2106, 168 N. 9th St., Suite 200, Boise 83702, ☎ 208/344–7777 or 800/635–5240). **South Central Idaho Travel Association** (✉ 858 Blue Lakes Blvd., Twin Falls 83301, ☎ 208/733–3974 or 800/255–8946). **Southeastern Idaho Travel Association** (✉ Box 498, Lava Hot Springs 83246, ☎ 208/776–5273 or 800/423–8597). **Yellowstone/Teton Territory Travel Association** (✉ 505 Lindsay Blvd., Idaho Falls 83402, ☎ 208/523–1010 or 800/634–3246).

Arriving and Departing

By Bus

Greyhound Lines (✉ 1212 W. Bannock St., Boise, ☎ 800/231–2222) serves Boise, Twin Falls, Pocatello, and Idaho Falls. **Sun Valley Express** runs several daily round-trip van shuttles between Boise and Sun Valley (✉ Boise Municipal Airport, ☎ 800/634–6539)). **Sun Valley Stages** (✉ Boise Municipal Airport, ☎ 800/821–9064) runs daily round-trip motor coaches between the airport, Sun Valley, and Twin Falls.

By Car

Boise is reached by I–84 from the south and the north.

By Plane

Boise Municipal Airport (☎ 208/383–3110), 3 mi from downtown, is served by national and regional airlines. The **Boise Urban Stages** (☎ 208/336–1010) shuttle bus to town costs $1; taxis cost $7–$10.

By Train

Amtrak (✉ 1701 Eastover Terr., Boise, ☎ 800/872–7245).

Orientation Tours

The **Boise Tour Train** (✉ Capitol Blvd., ☎ 208/342–4796 or 800/999–5993; 🎟 $6) provides a one-hour introduction to the city from June through September; tours depart from the depot across from the rose garden in Julia Davis Park.

Exploring Southern Idaho

Boise

The name Boise, French for "wooded," is traced to French-Canadian trappers, who found a tree-laced greenway on the Boise River, a sight for sore eyes after trekking across the area's semiarid plain. Boise and surrounding Ada County now form a modern center of government and business. A mean temperature of 51°F and annual rainfall averaging just under 12 inches create a hospitable setting for the headquarters of seven major corporations and a countywide population of 250,000.

Next to the Boise River, the grassy expanse of **Julia Davis Park** is home to two museums and the **Boise City Zoo** (✉ 355 N. Julia Davis Dr., ☎ 208/384–4260; 🎟 $3), where zebras and Bengal tigers roam. An Old West saloon and relics from Idaho's early history as an Oregon Trail outpost fill the **Idaho State Historical Museum** (✉ 610 N. Julia Davis Dr., ☎ 208/334–2120; 🎟 free).The **Boise Art Museum** (✉ 670 S. Julia Davis Dr., ☎ 208/345–8330;🎟 Free) displays works based on historical and contemporary themes.

Lady Bluebeard and Diamondfield Jack were among the more notorious felons who did time at the **Old Idaho Territorial Penitentiary** (✉ 2445 Old Penitentiary Rd., ☎ 208/368–6080; 🎟 $4). In operation from 1870 until 1973, today it welcomes visitors for shorter stays. You can also tour a garden of Idaho native plants, a garden for children, and other theme gardens within the penitentiary confines at the **Idaho Botanical Gardens** (✉ 2355 Penitentiary Rd., ☎ 208/343–8649; 🎟 $3), open from Tuesday to Sunday from April through October.

The **Discovery Center of Idaho** (✉ 131 W. Myrtle St., ☎ 208/343–9895; 🎟 $4), a hands-on science learning center open from Tuesday to Sunday, has more than 100 displays. The **Morrison-Knudsen Nature Center** (✉ 600 S. Walnut Ave., ☎ 208/334–2225; 🎟 $2.50, grounds free), open from Tuesday to Sunday, has ecosystem exhibits of wetlands, plains, high-desert terrain, and mountain streams.

Idaho

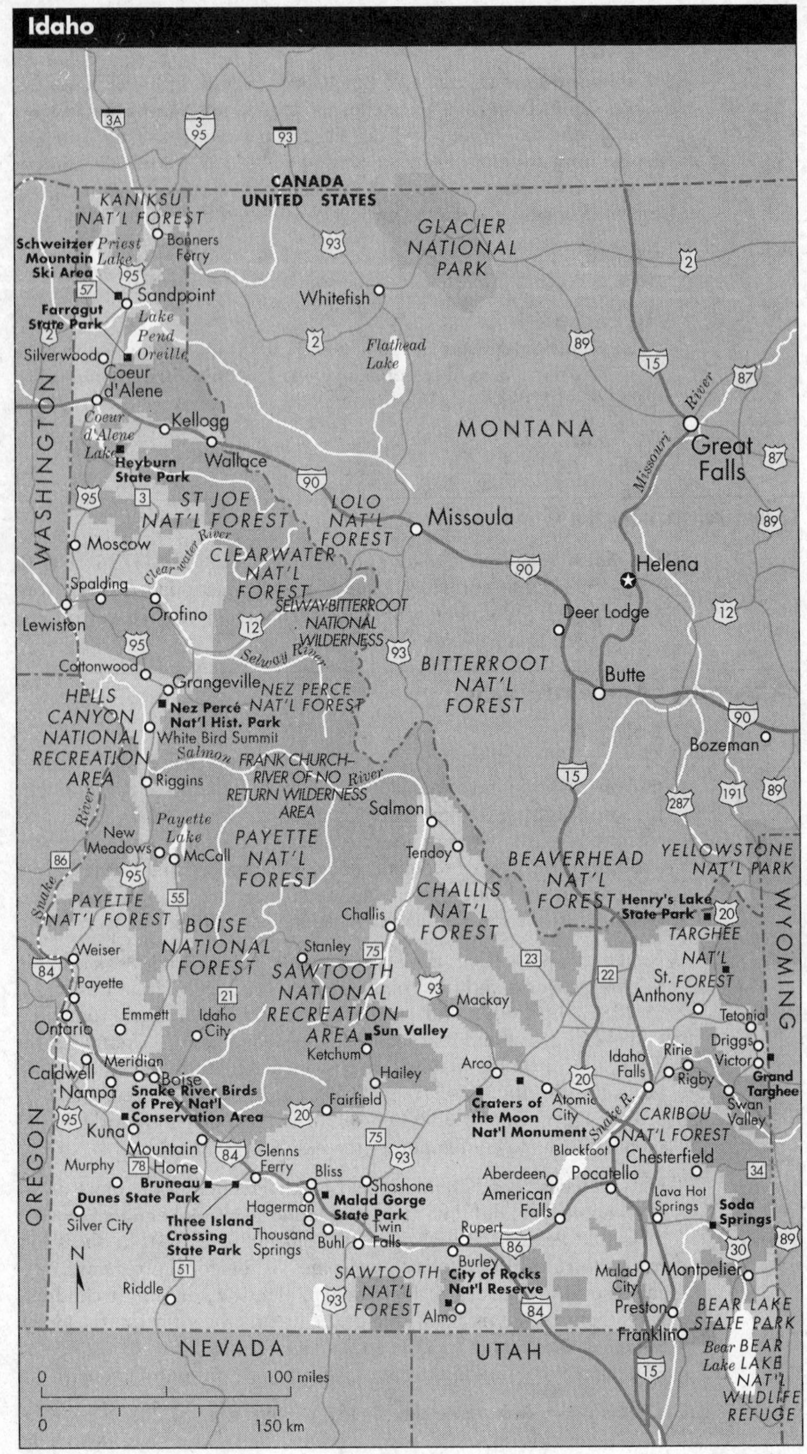
CANADA
UNITED STATES
KANIKSU NAT'L FOREST
Schweitzer Mountain Ski Area
Priest Lake
Bonners Ferry
Sandpoint
Farragut State Park
Lake Pend Oreille
Silverwood
Coeur d'Alene
Coeur d'Alene Lake
Kellogg
Wallace
Heyburn State Park
ST JOE NAT'L FOREST
GLACIER NATIONAL PARK
Whitefish
Flathead Lake
MONTANA
Great Falls
Missouri River
LOLO NAT'L FOREST
Missoula
Helena
Deer Lodge
Butte
Bozeman
WASHINGTON
Moscow
Clearwater River
CLEARWATER NAT'L FOREST
Spalding
Orofino
Lewiston
SELWAY-BITTERROOT NATIONAL WILDERNESS
Selway River
BITTERROOT NAT'L FOREST
Cottonwood
Grangeville
NEZ PERCE NAT'L FOREST
Nez Percé Nat'l Hist. Park
White Bird Summit
HELLS CANYON NATIONAL RECREATION AREA
Salmon River
FRANK CHURCH–RIVER OF NO RETURN WILDERNESS AREA
Riggins
Salmon
Tendoy
Payette Lake
New Meadows
McCall
PAYETTE NAT'L FOREST
BEAVERHEAD NAT'L FOREST
YELLOWSTONE NAT'L PARK
WYOMING
Henry's Lake State Park
TARGHEE NAT'L FOREST
CHALLIS NAT'L FOREST
Challis
Snake River
PAYETTE NAT'L FOREST
BOISE NATIONAL FOREST
Weiser
Stanley
SAWTOOTH NATIONAL RECREATION AREA
Payette
St. Anthony
Mackay
Tetonia
Emmett
Idaho City
Ontario
Sun Valley
Ketchum
Driggs
Victor
Grand Targhee
Meridian
Caldwell
Nampa
Boise
Snake River Birds of Prey Nat'l Conservation Area
Hailey
Arco
Idaho Falls
Ririe
Rigby
Swan Valley
Fairfield
Craters of the Moon Nat'l Monument
Atomic City
Snake R.
CARIBOU NAT'L FOREST
Kuna
Mountain Home
Glenns Ferry
Blackfoot
Chesterfield
Murphy
Bruneau Dunes State Park
Bliss
Shoshone
Aberdeen
Pocatello
Malad Gorge State Park
Hagerman
American Falls
Lava Hot Springs
Soda Springs
OREGON
Silver City
Three Island Crossing State Park
Thousand Springs
Buhl
Twin Falls
Rupert
Burley
City of Rocks Nat'l Reserve
Malad City
Montpelier
SAWTOOTH NAT'L FOREST
Almo
Riddle
Preston
Franklin
BEAR LAKE STATE PARK
Bear Lake
BEAR LAKE NAT'L WILDLIFE REFUGE
NEVADA
UTAH
N
0
100 miles
0
150 km

Eight miles south of downtown Boise (follow South Cole Road from I–84's Exit 50 and follow signs), the **World Center for Birds of Prey** (✉ 5666 Flying Hawk La., ☎ 208/362–8687; 🎫 $4), open from Tuesday to Sunday, has live falcons, California condors, and other birds of prey. Guided 1½ tours throughout the day leave from the visitor center. Thirty miles southwest of Nampa (from I–84's Exit 44 head south from the town of Meridian to Kuna, then take Swan Falls Road south into park), the **Snake River Birds of Prey National Conservation Area** (☎ 208/384–3056) encompasses 483,000 acres along 80 mi of the Snake River. In spring 15 species of migratory raptors head for the cliffs that tower 700 ft above the river.

The largest concentration of Basque people in the United States has called Idaho's Snake River plain home since the late 1800s. You can visit a restored 1864 former boardinghouse; then go next door to the **Basque Museum and Cultural Center** (611 Grove St., ☎ 208/343–2671; 🎫 $1) to see colorful costumes, relics, and exhibits on Basque culture. The center is closed Sunday and Monday.

The Owyhee Uplands and the South-Central Region

South of Boise, from the Owyhee Mountains and arid Uplands east along the verdant Snake River canyon to Twin Falls, you'll find Oregon Trail wagon ruts, rocky gorges, hushed waterfalls, and springs trickling from canyon walls behind a veil of moss and ferns. Just south of Murphy a 25-mi gravel road off Route 78 leads to the onetime queen ★ of Idaho's mining region, **Silver City** (☎ 208/495–2319), now a ghost town with 70 rustic buildings. **Three Island Crossing State Park** (✉ Rte. 78 off I–84 near Glenns Ferry, ☎ 208/366–2394; 🎫 $3) marks an important Oregon Trail wagon-train fording sight on the Snake River. At **Malad Gorge State Park** (✉ Off U.S. 30 north of Hagerman, ☎ 208/837–4505; 🎫 $2) a suspension footbridge spans a 250-ft chasm as a 60-ft waterfall gushes into the Devil's Washbowl below. Warmed by geothermal springs, Idaho's "banana belt," the **Hagerman Valley**—a patchwork of melon fields, orchards, and trout farms off U.S. 30—is the gateway to the **Thousand Springs Scenic Byway.** Five miles north of the town of Twin Falls (take Fells Avenue east from U.S. 30 and head north on 3300 East Road), the **Shoshone Falls** (☎ 800/255–8946 or 208/736–2240; 🎫 free) cascade 212 ft—52 ft farther than Niagara Falls. Spring is the best time to view them.

Blackfoot, Bear Lake, and Lava Hot Springs

Billionaire J. R. Simplot made Idaho famous for its potatoes beginning in the 1940s. Today much of southeastern Idaho's fertile Snake River crescent, stretching from Burley to Idaho Falls, is devoted to agriculture.

★ A must-see is the **World Potato Exposition** (✉ 130 N. Main St., ☎ 208/785–2517; 🎫 $2), open from Tuesday through Saturday between May and October in Blackfoot. Exhibits explain potato production and display spud oddities. The gift shop sells potato cookbooks and fudge and hands out "free 'taters for out-of-staters." **Bear Lake State Park** (☎ 208/945–2790; 🎫 $3), south of the town of Montpelier off U.S. 89 at St. Charles, is known for its dip-net fishing. Light reflecting off limestone particles suspended in the 80,000-acre lake (roughly half of which is in Utah) give it a stunning turquoise color that has earned it the moniker of Caribbean of the Rockies. **Bear Lake National Wildlife Refuge** (☎ 208/847–1757; 🎫 free), on the north shore of the lake, has one of the largest Canada geese populations in the western U.S. The new National Oregon Trail Visitors Center (☎ 208/847–0375) at the junction of U.S. 89 and 30 in Montpelier has maps and other visitor information about the Oregon Trail. A continuous flow of warm spring water at the base of lava cliffs has spawned the charming resort community of **Lava Hot Springs,** 21 mi west of Soda Springs on U.S. 30.

Yellowstone/Teton Territory

Sixty miles of interconnecting scenic byways yield breathtaking views of the back sides of the Grand Tetons and Yellowstone Park. The **Mesa Falls Scenic Byway** (Route 47) travels through a 23-mi-wide caldera (volcanic crater) before traversing the Idaho portions of the **Targhee National Forest** (☎ 208/624–3151), which shelters pristine Upper and Lower Mesa Falls. The **Teton Scenic Byway** (Routes 32, 33, and 31 as the byway heads south from Ashton) passes through the small farming communities of Tetonia, Driggs, and Victor, all dwarfed by the Tetons just to the east. In winter hundreds of inches of dry, powdery snow draws skiers to the resort of **Grand Targhee** (✉ Box SKI, Alta, WY 83422, ☎ 800/827–4433) just over the state line near Driggs.

Dining and Lodging

For price ranges *see* Chart 1 (B) *in* On the Road with Fodor's.

Boise

$$$–$$$$ ★ ✕ **Peter Schott's New American Cuisine.** Many regard this small restaurant run by a local cooking-show celebrity as Idaho's best. Inventive American cuisine with a Northern Italian flair is Schott's specialty; fresh fish dominates the menu, and the wine list is complete. ✉ *Idanha Hotel, 928 Main St.,* ☎ *208/336–9100. AE, D, DC, MC, V. Closed Sun. No lunch.*

$$$–$$$$ ✕ **Sandpiper.** High ceilings, oak tables, river views, and live music on weekends create a fun atmosphere for dining on steak, seafood, and prime rib. ✉ *1100 W. Jefferson St.,* ☎ *208/344–8911. AE, D, DC, MC, V. No lunch Sat., Sun.*

$–$$$ ✕ **Tablerock Brewpub & Grill.** Boise's first microbrewery, across from Julia Davis Park, has a southwestern motif, complete with cacti and prints by Native American artists. Huge burritos, spicy chili, and a half dozen varieties of burgers are served. ✉ *705 Fulton St.,* ☎ *208/342–0944. AE, D, DC, MC, V.*

$–$$ ✕ **Bar Gernika Basque Pub & Eatery.** This cozy downtown pub and restaurant is known for its marinated pork, sweet-red-pepper sandwiches, and other Basque specialties, as well as traditional American sandwich fare. Beef Tongue Saturdays are a local tradition. ✉ *202 S. Capitol Blvd.,* ☎ *208/244–2175. AE, MC, V. Closed Sun.*

$–$$ ✕ **Onati–The Basque Restaurant.** Photographs and memorabilia of Basque culture and history in Idaho line the walls of this roomy eatery set in the back of a casual bar. Savory lamb stew, chorizo sausage and rice, and squid in tomato sauce are standouts on the authentic Basque menu. ✉ *3544 Chinden Blvd.,* ☎ *208/343–6464. AE, DC, MC, V.*

$$$–$$$$ ★ 🏨 **Idanha Hotel.** Close to business and shopping areas, this French château–style bed-and-breakfast has distinctive turrets and antiques-filled rooms that bely its 1901 origins. ✉ *928 Main St., 83702,* ☎ *208/342–3611,* FAX *208/383–9690. 45 rooms. Restaurant. CP. AE, D, DC, MC, V.*

$$$–$$$$ 🏨 **Owyhee Plaza.** Giant light fixtures and rich oak paneling remain from 1910, when this three-story downtown hotel was built. Prices are lower at the adjacent motel. ✉ *1109 Main St., 83702,* ☎ *208/343–4611 or 800/233–4611,* FAX *208/381–0695. 100 rooms. 2 restaurants, pool. AE, D, DC, MC, V.*

$$–$$$ ★ 🏨 **Idaho Heritage Inn.** Rooms have names with political themes at this B&B in a former governor's mansion, about a mile east of downtown. Antiques, wallpaper, and old-style bed frames evoke an early 1900s mood. ✉ *109 W. Idaho St., 83702,* ☎ *208/342–8066. 6 rooms. Full breakfast. AE, D, DC, MC, V.*

Idaho Falls

$$–$$$ ✕ **Mama Inez.** Five homemade salsas head the menu at this friendly Mexican restaurant two blocks from the scenic Snake River Falls. Try the braised-pork burritos heaped with green-chile sauce. ✉ *346 Park Ave.,* ☎ *208/525–8968. MC, V. Closed Sun.*

$$ 🏨 **Best Western Driftwood.** Rooms in this low slung two-story motel have refrigerators or kitchenettes. Picture windows gaze across the lawn to the falls of the Snake River, just a short walk away. On the grounds are a rose garden and lush landscaped niches with benches and chairs. ✉ *575 Riverview Pkwy., 83402,* ☎ *800/528–1234 or 208/523–2242. 74 rooms. Pool. AE, D, DC, MC, V.*

Lava Hot Springs

$–$$ 🏨 **Riverside Inn and Hot Springs.** This restored 1914 inn by the Portneuf River has mineral hot tubs and an immaculate interior. Originally called the Honeymoon Hotel because it was so romantic, the inn has cozy rooms with antique quilts. President Truman once stayed here. ✉ *Box 127, 255 Portneuf Ave., 83246,* ☎ *208/776–5504 or 800/773–5504,* FAX *208/776–5504. 16 rooms, 12 with bath. Restaurant. CP. D, MC, V.*

Twin Falls

$$–$$$$ ✕ **Rock Creek.** There's a massive salad bar to accompany your steak, prime rib, and seafood—plus all kinds of wine, vintage ports, and single-malt whiskeys. ✉ *200 Addison Ave. W,* ☎ *208/734–4154. AE, MC, V. No lunch.*

$ ★ ✕ **Buffalo Café.** Ask anybody in town where to go for breakfast, and you'll get the same answer: this tiny café. The house specialty is the Buffalo Chip, a concoction of eggs, fried potatoes, cheese, bacon, peppers, and onion. ✉ *218 4th Ave. W,* ☎ *208/734–0271. No credit cards. No dinner.*

Nightlife and the Arts

The **Idaho Shakespeare Festival** holds performances in the open-air theater in Boise's Julia Davis Park (✉ 412 S. 9th St., ☎ 208/336–9221) from June through September. The **Boise River Festival** (☎ 800/635–5240 or 208/344–7777), held the last Thursday–Sunday in June, includes more than 300 events, a huge nighttime parade, and entertainment on six stages.

Outdoor Activities and Sports

Fishing

The **Silver Creek Preserve** (✉ Box 165, Sun Valley, 83353, ☎ 208/788–2203; 📠 free), northeast of Shoshone in south-central Idaho, has rainbow, brown, and brook trout catch-and-release fishing. Eastern Idaho's **Henry's Fork of the Snake River** and **Henry's Lake** in Henry's Lake State Park (☎ 208/558–7532) are renowned fly-fishing waters, with enormous rainbow and cutthroat trout. The **Targhee National Forest** (✉ 420 N. Bridge St., St. Anthony 83445, ☎ 208/624–3151) watershed is home to Big Springs, spawning grounds for rainbow trout, which can be viewed from a bridge. **Bear Lake** (☞ Blackfoot, Bear Lake, and Lava Hot Springs, *above*), in the southeast corner of the state, is the only place where fishing for ciscoes with dip nets is allowed. Fishing licenses are required.

Ski Areas

DOWNHILL

Bogus Basin (✉ 2405 Bogus Basin Rd., Boise 83702, ☎ 208/332–5151), 48 runs, 6 lifts, 1,800-ft drop. **Grand Targhee** (✉ Driggs 83422, ☎ 800/827–4433), 62 runs, 3 lifts, 2,200-ft drop. **Kelly Canyon** (✉ Box 367, Ririe 83443, ☎ 208/538–6261), 23 runs, 4 lifts, 1,000-ft drop. **Pebble Creek** (✉ Box 370, Inkom 83245, ☎ 208/775–4452), 24 runs, 3 lifts, 2,000-ft drop. **Pomerelle** (✉ Box 158, Albion, 83311, ☎ 208/673–5599), 17 runs, 2 lifts, 1,000-ft drop.

Shopping

The **8th Street Marketplace** (✉ Capitol Blvd. and Front St.), a brick warehouse converted into more than 30 stores, sits on the east side of 8th Street across from the convention center. Near the marketplace, **Capitol Terrace** (✉ Idaho and Main Sts., Boise) looks like a New Orleans French Quarter building, with a balcony level of shops.

CENTRAL IDAHO

Idaho's midsection is a dense mosaic of rugged wilderness terrain so impenetrable that even cartographers are hard-pressed to sketch roadways across much of the northern part of this region. A teeming waterway system fed by the **Snake** and **Salmon rivers** spins a lacy web across the bumpy landscape and has been the favored mode of transportation since the days of Lewis and Clark. The 420-mi Salmon is the longest undammed river in the lower 48 states.

Visitor Information

Hells Canyon and Lewiston-Clarkston: North Central Idaho Travel Association (✉ 2207 E. Main St., Suite G, Lewiston 83501, ☎ 208/743–3531 or 800/473–3543). **McCall:** Visitors Information (✉ Box D, McCall 83638, ☎ 208/634–7631). **Ketchum–Sun Valley:** Chamber of Commerce (✉ Box 2420, Sun Valley 83353, ☎ 208/726–3423 or 800/634–3347). **Sawtooth Mountains:** Stanley/Sawtooth Chamber of Commerce (✉ Box 8, Hwy. 75, Stanley 83278, ☎ 208/774–3411).

Arriving and Departing

From Montana, take U.S. 93. From Oregon, take U.S. 12 to U.S. 95. From Boise, take I–84 to U.S. 20/26.

Exploring Central Idaho

Sun Valley–Ketchum

At the precise point where alpine and desert climes converge, the legendary Sun Valley resort opened in 1935. Its signature pedestrian mall is patterned after an Austrian village. **Ketchum,** a mile from Sun Valley, is an old mining town with shops and restaurants. Just outside Ketchum, beside Trail Creek, the **Ernest Hemingway Memorial** commemorates the writer's last years there.

McCall

The 108-mi drive north from Boise on Route 55 to the resort town of McCall runs along the shore of the Payette River as it jumps down mountains, over boulders, and through alpine forests. The arid plains of the Snake River give way to higher and higher mountains covered by tremendous stands of pines.

Hells Canyon and Lewiston-Clarkston

The ragged Seven Devils Range stands at 9,000 ft, rimming the southeastern lip of the Snake River Canyon, a deep, dark basalt abyss within the **Hells Canyon National Recreation Area** (☞ National Parks, *above*). Route 71 traces a portion of the gorge, but the best way to take in the scenery is by jet boat or raft (☞ Rafting *in* Outdoor Activities and Sports, *below*). North of Hells Canyon, Lewiston and its sister city, Clarkston, Oregon, owe their lifeblood to the confluence of the Clearwater and Snake rivers. Ships ply the waters 470 mi from the ocean via the Columbia River to Lewiston's inland seaport. Route 12, among the few east–west motor routes in this part of the state, travels from Lewiston to **Lolo Pass** on the Montana border, following the route that Sacagawea, Lewis and Clark's Native American guide, traced through the rugged wilderness. The **Nez Percé National Historical Park** (☞ National Parks, *above*) displays Nez Percé artifacts and outlines the history of the Native American nation and its famous leader, Chief Joseph.

Dining and Lodging

For price ranges *see* Chart 1 (A) *in* On the Road with Fodor's.

McCall

$$$–$$$$ 🏨 **The Shore Lodge.** Thanks to its lakefront location, the lodge has become almost synonymous with McCall. Lakefront suites are large, with high ceilings and excellent views, but street-side units are like small motel rooms. The Narrows restaurant specializes in game. ✉ *501 W. Lake St., 83638,* ☎ *208/634–2244 or 800/657–6464,* FAX *208/634–7504. 116 rooms. 2 restaurants, exercise room. AE, D, MC, V.*

$–$$ 🏨 **Hotel McCall.** This hybrid between a hotel and a B&B is in the center of town. Rooms (and prices) vary widely; six are small, dark, and share a bath, while others are almost grand and have lots of light and antique furnishings. Some have views of Payette Lake. ✉ *3rd and Lake Sts., Box 1778, 83638,* ☎ *208/634–8105,* FAX *208/634–8755. 22 rooms, 16 with bath. CP. AE, MC, V.*

Sun Valley–Ketchum

$$–$$$ ✕ **Michel's Christiania Restaurant.** Among the highlights at this Sun Valley classic are roast lamb in a parsley crust, sautéed ruby Idaho trout with hazelnuts and cream, and savory tenderloin of venison. ✉ *Sun Valley Rd. and Walnut St., Ketchum,* ☎ *208/726–3388. AE, MC, V.*

$ ✕ **Desperado's.** Huge burritos, black beans, and four kinds of salsa headline the menu at this popular Mexican restaurant in the heart of Ketchum. ✉ *4th St. and Washington Ave.,* ☎ *208/726–3068. MC, V.*

$$–$$$$ ✕🏨 **Sun Valley Lodge and Inn.** Sun Valley's biggest resort is made up of a family-oriented inn, lodge-style accommodations, and condominiums. On the grounds are three pools, 18 tennis courts, and an ice-skating rink. Within the lodge complex, the Lodge Dining Room is the area's signature restaurant, known for its legendary Sunday brunch. The resort is surrounded by towering pines; some rooms on the back side overlook the ice rink and the ski-run carved face of Bald Mountain, a mile away. ✉ *Sun Valley Resort, Sun Valley 83353,* ☎ *208/622–4111 or 800/786–8259, 208/622–2150 for dining room,* FAX *208/622–3700. 146 lodge rooms, 114 inn rooms, 280 condos. 3 restaurants, pools, 18 tennis courts. AE, D, DC, MC, V.*

$$$–$$$$ 🏨 **Knob Hill Inn.** Rooms at this modern luxury hotel with an alpine motif have large tubs, wet bars, and balconies with mountain views. Intermediate rooms, suites, and penthouses have fireplaces. ✉ *960 N. Main St., Box 800, Ketchum 83340,* ☎ *208/726–8010 or 800/526–8010,* FAX *208/726–2712. 25 rooms. 2 restaurants, pool, exercise room. Full breakfast. AE, MC, V.*

$$$ **Idaho Country Inn.** Log beams and a river-rock fireplace in the roomy lounge and dining room lend a western feel to this quiet lodging in a residential neighborhood. Guest rooms are spacious and luxurious. ✉ *134 Latigo La., Box 2355, Sun Valley 83353,* ☎ *208/726–1019,* FAX *208/726–5718. 10 rooms. Full breakfast. AE, MC, V.*

$–$$ **Lift Tower Lodge.** Look for the lift tower and chair out front (Western-style lawn art) in front of this basic motel. Half of the rooms face the ski mountain; the rest front Route 75, Ketchum's heavily traveled main drag. Ketchum's ski lifts and restaurants are only about three blocks away. ✉ *703 Main St., Box 185, Ketchum 83340,* ☎ *208/726–5163 or 800/462–8646,* FAX *208/726–2614. 14 rooms. AE, D, DC, MC, V.*

Wilderness Camps and Lodges

$$$$ **The Lodge at Riggins Hot Springs.** About 10 mi north of Riggins next to the Salmon River, this massive wood A-frame is nestled among pine trees overlooking the banks of the Salmon River, which is visible from the 10 rooms. Rafting, jet boating, and fishing trips can be arranged, and the huge outdoor pool is fed by hot springs. Meals are outstanding. ✉ *Box 1247, Riggins, 83549,* ☎ FAX *208/628–3785. 10 rooms. Pool. FAP. MC, V.*

$$$$ **Twin Peaks Ranch.** Nestled in a mile-high valley between the Salmon River and the Frank Church–River of No Return Wilderness Area, Twin Peaks was one of America's first dude ranches; it was homesteaded in 1923 and later established as a dude ranch by the E. du Pont family. The 2,300-acre property, 2 mi off U.S. 93, contains cabins, the original ranch house, and an apple orchard set on several acres of lawn. Experienced wranglers teach horsemanship in the full-size rodeo arena; guided day rides and overnight pack trips are also available. Stocked trout ponds attract anglers, and guided fishing and white-water rafting trips can be arranged. ✉ *Box 774, Salmon 83467,* ☎ *800/659–4899, 208/894–2290, or 800/659–4899. 13 cabins. Pool. MC, V. Closed Jan.–Apr.*

$$ **Idaho Rocky Mountain Ranch.** The ranch's 8,000-square-ft lodgepole-pine lodge remains much the same as when it was constructed in the 1930s. Period photographs hang on the walls, and animal trophies, rustic artifacts, and a massive rock fireplace immediately catch the eye. Lodge rooms and most of the duplex cabins have Oakley stone showers and handcrafted log furniture. All kinds of activities are available, from hot-springs bathing to volleyball to horseback riding. ✉ *HC 64, off Rte. 75; Box 9934, Stanley 83278,* ☎ *208/774–3544. 2 lodge rooms, 8 duplex cabins. Pool. MAP. D, MC, V. Closed May, Oct.*

Outdoor Activities and Sports

Fishing

Steelhead fishing is a major attraction in the **Frank Church–River of No Return Wilderness Area** (☞ National Parks, *above*). The 20-pound fish swim 1,800 mi to the ocean and back again to spawn in the Salmon River.

Hiking and Backpacking

The **Sawtooth National Recreation Area** (☞ National Parks, *above*) draws hikers and backpackers from afar. In winter several yurts (tents made of skins) in the Boulder, Smoky, and Sawtooth mountains are accessible for day ski trips or backcountry multiday trips. Extensive trail systems run through the **Selway Bitterroot** and **Frank Church–River of No Return** wilderness areas.

Rafting

Salmon and Stanley are launching points for trips on the **Salmon River,** including the famous **Middle Fork,** which spans 100 mi with 100 rapids. Reserve well ahead for summer. Riggins and White Bird are the takeoff points for trips down the northern portion of the Salmon and **Snake** rivers. The **Selway** and **Clearwater** rivers are other choice rafting waterways.

Ski Areas

Cross-Country

The central Idaho mountain valleys and backcountry are ideal for Nordic skiing. The **Wood River Trails** (✉ Blaine County Recreation District, 308 N. Main, Hailey 83333, ☎ 208/788–2117) system in the Ketchum–Sun Valley area grooms more than 100 mi of trails. The **Sun Valley Nordic Center** (✉ Box 10, Sun Valley 83353, ☎ 208/622–2250 or 800/786–8259) includes almost 25 mi of groomed trails spread across the Sun Valley Golf Course, just north of the Sun Valley Lodge and Inn (☞ Dining and Lodging, *above*).

Downhill

Brundage (✉ Box 1062, McCall 83638, ☎ 208/634–4151 or 800/888–7544), 38 runs, 4 lifts, 1,800-ft drop. **Sun Valley** (✉ Sun Valley 83353, ☎ 800/635–8261 or 800/786–8259), 80 runs, 18 lifts, 3,400-ft drop. **Soldier Mountain** (✉ Box 465, Fairfield 83327, ☎ 208/764–2526), 42 runs, 3 lifts, 1,400-ft vertical drop.

NORTHERN IDAHO

Water reigns supreme in wooded northern Idaho, which claims more than 140 lakes (the highest concentration in the western United States) and 2,000 mi of streams and rivers. Six major lakes, including **Coeur d'Alene** and the state's largest, **Pend Oreille,** dominate the Panhandle.

Visitor Information

Coeur d'Alene: Convention & Visitors Bureau (✉ Box 1088, 83816, ☎ 208/664–0587). **North Idaho Travel Association:** Greater Sandpoint Chamber of Commerce (✉ Box 928, Sandpoint 83864, ☎ 208/263–2161 or 800/800–2106). **Silver Valley:** Wallace Visitor Information Center, Wallace Chamber of Commerce (✉ 10 River St., Wallace 83873, ☎ 208/753–7151).

Arriving and Departing

By Bus

Greyhound (✉ 1527 Northwest Blvd., Coeur d'Alene, ☎ 800/231–2222).

By Car

The major highways serving northern Idaho are I–90 (east–west) and U.S. 95 (north–south).

By Plane

The nearest airport is **Spokane International** (☎ 509/455–6455), 20 mi from Coeur d'Alene in eastern Washington.

By Train

Amtrak (☎ 800/872–7245) serves Sandpoint, about 40 mi north of Coeur d'Alene.

Exploring Northern Idaho

Coeur d'Alene and the Silver Valley

Nestled in a pine-green mantle beside a gem of a lake of the same name, the city of **Coeur d'Alene** has perhaps the most idyllic setting of any town in the state. Restaurants with waterfront dining, a 3,300-ft floating boardwalk, and resort hotels cluster along the water's edge. The American bald eagle and the largest population of osprey in the western United States make their homes here; the watery playground attracts sailors and water-skiers as well. With more than 29 golf courses within an hour's drive of Coeur d'Alene, it's a golfer's paradise; sightseeing cruises pass by the floating 14th hole of the golf course at the Coeur d'Alene Resort (☞ Dining and Lodging, *below*).

Silver Valley, the world's largest silver-mining district, is centered in the towns of Kellogg and Wallace along I–90. The entire town of **Wallace** is listed on the National Register of Historic Places. Throughout July and August, the **Sixth Street Melodrama** (☎ 208/752–8871; 🎫 $8) recalls Wallace's colorful past. The **Wallace District Mining Museum** (☎ 208/753–7151; 🎫 $3) contains a mother lode of mining history. From July to mid-October, the Sierra Silver Mine Tour (☎ 208/752–5151; 🎫 $6.50) provides a peek into an old mine.

The Northern Lakes

The resort town of **Sandpoint,** on the northwestern shores of Lake Pend Oreille, is completely surrounded by mountains; it has been a railroad depot and a mining town but now survives on tourism and lumber. Many buildings here date from the early 1900s. At the southern end of Lake Pend Oreille, the 4,000-acre **Farragut State Park** (☎ 208/683–2425; 🎫 $3) supports a diverse wildlife population.

Route 57 provides access to remote **Priest Lake,** with 70 mi of densely wooded shoreline, and the **Upper Priest Lake Scenic Area,** just a jump from the Canadian border. The **Grove of Ancient Cedars,** on the west side of Priest Lake, is a virgin forest with trees up to 12 ft across and 150 ft high.

Dining and Lodging

For price ranges *see* Chart 1 (B) *in* On the Road with Fodor's.

Coeur d'Alene

$$–$$$$ ✕ **Cedars Floating Restaurant.** This restaurant is actually *on* the lake, giving it wonderful views. Beer-marinated, charbroiled steak is a specialty. ✉ *U.S. 95, ¼ mi south of I–90,* ☎ *208/664–2922. AE, DC, MC, V. No lunch.*

$ ✕ **Hudson's Hamburgers.** These folks have been in business since 1907—even rivals admit that Hudson's serves the town's favorite burgers. ✉ *207 Sherman Ave.,* ☎ *208/664–5444. No credit cards. Closed Sun. No dinner.*

$$$–$$$$ ✕🏨 **Coeur d'Alene Resort.** The plush rooms at this lakeside resort have fireplaces or balconies with terrific views of the water. Beverly's, one of the hotel's two restaurants, is known for its fine Northwest cuisine and superb wine cellar and also delivers incomparable views of the lake and the mountains. ✉ *2nd and Front Sts., 83814,* ☎ *208/765–4000 or 800/688–5253,* FAX *208/667–2707. 337 rooms. 2 restaurants, pools, golf, exercise room. AE, D, DC, MC, V.*

$$$ 🏨 **Blackwell House.** This B&B in a Victorian jewel of a house is close to the lake and shopping. Its quaintly elegant rooms have wing chairs and antique beds, and the bathtubs are big and old-fashioned. ✉ *820 Sherman Ave., 83814,* ☎ *208/664–0656 or 800/899–0656. 8 rooms, 6 with bath. Full breakfast. AE, D, MC, V.*

Priest Lake

$$$–$$$$ 🏨 **Hill's Resort.** Cabins or condos all have kitchenettes, and some have fireplaces. The restaurant serves steaks and oysters, and there's dancing in the summer. Nearby are hiking trails, a golf course, and a boat launch. ✉ *HCR 5, Box 162A, 83856,* ☎ *208/443-2551,* FAX *208/443-2363. 52 units. Restaurant. D, MC, V.*

Outdoor Activities and Sports

Fishing

Lake Pend Oreille is famous for kamloops (large rainbow trout), Priest Lake for mackinaw, and Lake Coeur d'Alene for cutthroat trout and chinook salmon. The St. Joe and Coeur d'Alene rivers are good for stream angling.

Ski Areas

DOWNHILL

Schweitzer Mountain (✉ Box 815, Sandpoint 83864, ☎ 208/263-9555 or 800/831-8810), 55 runs, gondola, six lifts, 2,400-ft vertical drop.
Silver Mountain (✉ 610 Bunker Ave., Kellogg 83837, ☎ 208/783-1111), 52 runs, six lifts, 2,200-ft drop.

Shopping

Plaza Shops at the Coeur d'Alene (210 Sherman Ave., at 2nd St., Coeur d'Alene) is an enclosed minimall with 22 small shops, several selling merchandise with a Northwest feeling.

MONTANA

Updated by Kristin Rodine

Capital	Helena
Population	879,000
Motto	Oro y Plata (Gold and Silver)
State Bird	Western meadowlark
State Flower	Bitterroot
Postal Abbreviation	MT

Statewide Visitor Information

Travel Montana (✉ Dept. of Commerce, 1424 9th Ave., Helena 59620, ☎ 406/444–2654 or 800/847–4868).

Scenic Drives

Beartooth Highway, the stretch of U.S. 212 from Red Lodge to Yellowstone National Park, is a slow but spectacular 68-mi route over a 10,947-ft mountain pass; it's open from June to mid-October. For 187 mi between Helena and East Glacier, **I–15, U.S. 287** and **U.S. 89** parallel the Rocky Mountain Front as it rises from the eastern plains. The 50-mi-long **Going-to-the-Sun Road** runs through Glacier National Park (☞ Exploring the Flathead and Western Montana, *below*).

National and State Parks

Millions of acres of Big Sky Country—Montana's nickname for its vast wide-open spaces—are public reserves, including national parks, monuments, and recreation areas. There are eight national wildlife refuges, 10 national forests, and 15 wilderness areas. Yellowstone National Park is also a logical part of a Montana itinerary.

National Parks

Glacier National Park (☞ Exploring the Flathead and Western Montana, *below*) crowns the Continental Divide on the Montana-Canada border. **Little Bighorn Battlefield National Monument**(☞ Bighorn Country, *below*) preserves the battle site in southeastern Montana.

State Parks

The **Montana Department of Fish, Wildlife and Parks** (✉ 1420 E. 6th Ave., Helena 59620, ☎ 406/444–2535) manages 41 state parks, including **Bannack State Park,** west of Dillon, a ghost town of homes, saloons, and a gallows; **Missouri Headwaters State Park,** near Three Forks, where Lewis and Clark came upon the confluence of the three rivers that form the Missouri; and **Makoshika State Park,** northeast of Billings near Glendive, which contains dramatic badlands formations and dinosaur fossils.

THE FLATHEAD AND WESTERN MONTANA

The northwestern, or Flathead, region is a destination resort area, with such attractions as Flathead Lake and Glacier National Park. In western Montana south of the Flathead, forests, lakes, and meadows mix with ranch country and small valley towns.

Visitor Information

Glacier Country: Regional Tourism Commission (☒ Box 1396, Dept. 507–10–21, Kalispell 59903, ☎ 406/756–7128 or 800/338–5072).

Arriving and Departing

By Bus

Intermountain Bus Co. (☎ 406/755–4011) stops in Kalispell. **Greyhound Lines** (☎ 800/231–2222) serves Missoula.

By Car

I–90 and U.S. 93 pass through Missoula. U.S. 93 and Route 35 lead off I–90 to Kalispell, in the Flathead; from there U.S. 2 leads to Glacier National Park. From Great Falls take I–15 and then U.S. 89 to St. Mary, at the east entrance to Glacier's Going-to-the-Sun Road, which is open from June through September, depending on snowfall. In winter, skirt along the southern edge of the park by taking U.S. 2 west from U.S. 89 at Browning.

By Plane

Glacier Park International Airport (☎ 406/257–5994), northeast of Kalispell, and **Missoula International Airport** (☎ 406/728–4381) are served by major domestic airlines.

By Train

Amtrak (☎ 800/872–7245) stops in Essex, Whitefish, West Glacier, and East Glacier.

Exploring the Flathead and Western Montana

The Flathead

The relatively close proximity of Flathead's towns is atypical of Montana. Bigfork, Kalispell, and Whitefish make good touring bases.

★ **Glacier National Park** (☒ West Glacier 59936, ☎ 406/888–5441; 🎫 $5 per vehicle for 7 days) preserves more than a million spectacular acres of peaks, waterfalls, lakes, and wildlife best seen from a hiking trail (☞ Outdoor Activities and Sports, *below*) or on horseback. The 52-mi **Going-to-the-Sun Road,** the park's only through road, is a cliff-hanger and unsuitable for oversize vehicles. A shuttle service is available (☎ 406/862–2539), and guided bus tours (☎ 406/226–5551) leave from either end. Most of the park, including this road, is closed to vehicles in winter.

South of Kalispell is **Flathead Lake,** the largest freshwater lake west of the Mississippi. An 85-mi loop drive around it takes in cherry orchards, parks, sweeping views of the Mission and Swan ranges, and the arts community of **Bigfork,** which has a repertory theater company.

Western Montana

Missoula, 60 mi south of Kalispell via U.S. 93, is home to the **University of Montana** (☎ 406/243–5874 to arrange a free guided tour) and to a thriving community of writers and artists. The Clark Fork, Bitterroot, and Blackfoot rivers converge here—it's not unusual to see anglers casting just downstream of the movie theater. The **Missoula Museum of the Arts** (☒ 335 N. Pattee St., ☎ 406/728–0447; 🎫 $2; free on Tues.) exhibits contemporary works. Hand-carved steeds circle 'round **A Carousel for Missoula** (☎ 406/549–8382; 🎫 $1) in downtown Caras Park, along the Clark Fork River.

The **Rocky Mountain Elk Foundation Wildlife Visitor Center** (☒ 2291 W. Broadway, ☎ 406/523–4545 or 800/225–5355; 🎫 free) has natural history, art, and wildlife displays. At **Smokejumper Visitor Center**

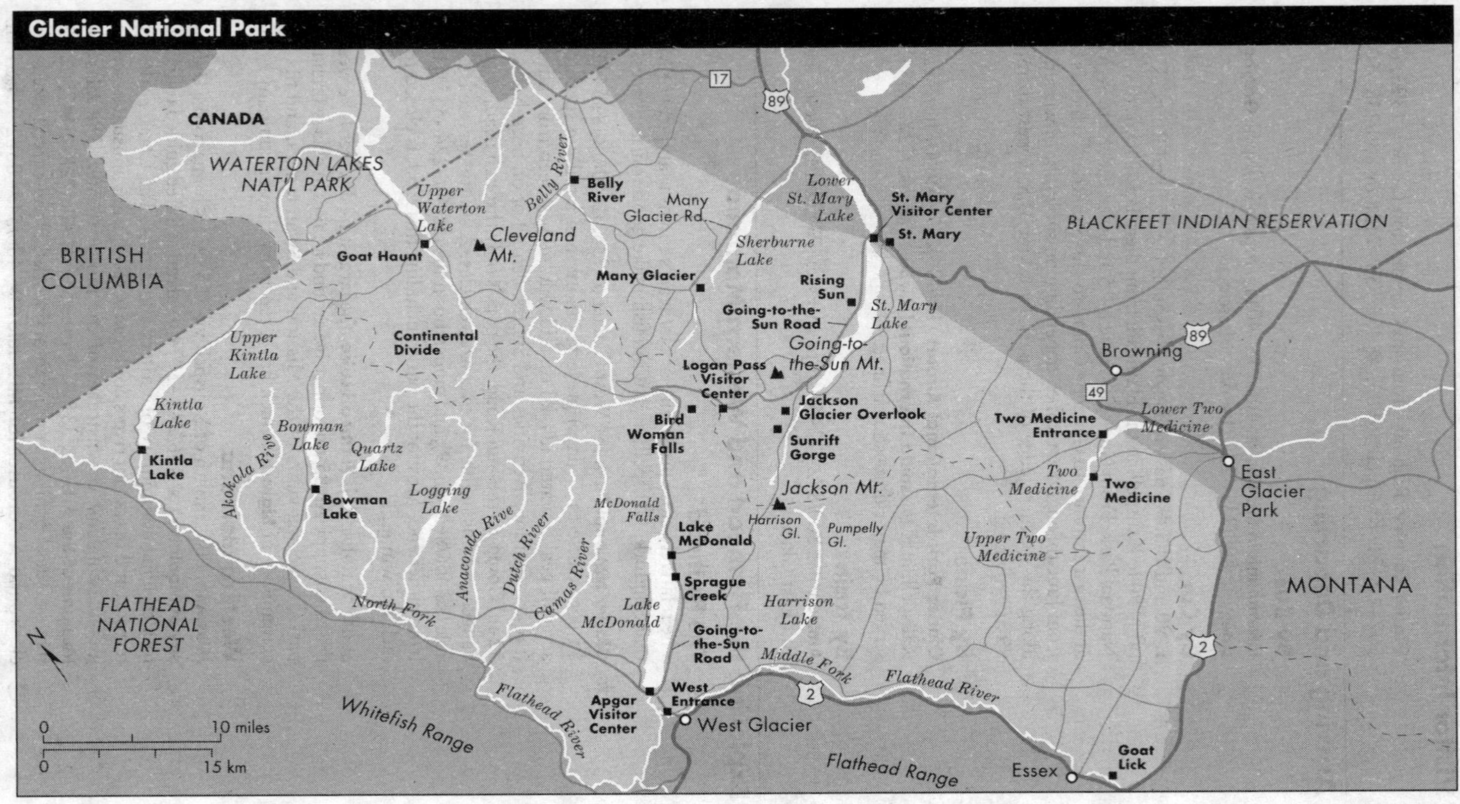
Glacier National Park
CANADA
WATERTON LAKES NAT'L PARK
BRITISH COLUMBIA
FLATHEAD NATIONAL FOREST
BLACKFEET INDIAN RESERVATION
MONTANA
Upper Waterton Lake
Goat Haunt
Cleveland Mt.
Belly River
Belly River
Many Glacier Rd.
Many Glacier
Lower St. Mary Lake
St. Mary Visitor Center
St. Mary
Sherburne Lake
Rising Sun
St. Mary Lake
Going-to-the-Sun Road
Going-to-the-Sun Mt.
Continental Divide
Upper Kintla Lake
Kintla Lake
Kintla Lake
Bowman Lake
Bowman Lake
Akokala River
Quartz Lake
Logging Lake
Logan Pass Visitor Center
Bird Woman Falls
Jackson Glacier Overlook
Sunrift Gorge
Jackson Mt.
Harrison Gl.
Pumpelly Gl.
McDonald Falls
Lake McDonald
Sprague Creek
Lake McDonald
Anaconda River
Dutch River
Camas River
North Fork
Harrison Lake
Going-to-the-Sun Road
Middle Fork
Flathead River
West Entrance
Apgar Visitor Center
West Glacier
Flathead River
Whitefish Range
Flathead Range
Essex
Goat Lick
Browning
Two Medicine Entrance
Lower Two Medicine
Two Medicine
Two Medicine
Upper Two Medicine
East Glacier Park
17
89
89
49
2
2
0
10 miles
0
15 km
N

(✉ W. Broadway/Old Hwy. 10, ☎ 406/329–4934; 🎫 free) guides conduct summer tours and provide firsthand accounts of forest fires and smoke jumping. View bison, elk, deer, antelope, and bighorn sheep ★ through your car window at the **National Bison Range** (🎫 $4 per vehicle) at Moiese, north of Missoula en route to the Flathead.

East of Missoula, Route 200 leads to **Seeley-Swan Valley,** densely forested and full of lakes. View loons and other waterfowl from turnouts along the scenic 18-mi **Clearwater Chain-of-Lakes** (✉ Rte. 83, from Salmon Lake to Rainy Lake).

South of Missoula on U.S. 93, **Bitterroot Valley** stretches between the Sapphire Mountains and the Bitterroots, one of the northern Rockies' most rugged ranges. Jesuit missionaries founded **St. Mary's Mission** (☎ 406/777–5734; 🎫 $3) in 1841 at Stevensville.

Dining and Lodging

Reserve well in advance for Glacier and for Flathead's summer and ski seasons. For price ranges *see* Charts 1 (B) and 2 (B) *in* On the Road with Fodor's.

Bigfork

$$$–$$$$ ★ 🏨 **O'Duach'ain Country Inn Bed & Breakfast.** In a quiet lodgepole-pine forest near Flathead Lake and the Swan River, this log house and cabin next door are full of Old West antiques and Navajo rugs; two stone fireplaces warm the main house. *✉ 675 Ferndale Dr., 59911, ☎ 406/837–6851, FAX 406/837–0778. 5 rooms, 4 with bath. Full breakfast. AE, D, MC, V.*

Glacier National Park

Glacier Park, Inc. runs Glacier's grand lodges, which were built by the Great Northern Railroad at the turn of the century. All three have facilities for outdoor activities such as horseback riding, hiking, and fishing. Rooms are rustic—no TVs—but comfortable. The hotels are open in summer only; make reservations far in advance by calling the central Glacier Park office. *✉ Greyhound Tower, Station 1210, Phoenix, AZ 85077, ☎ 602/207–6000.*

$$$$ ✕🏨 **Glacier Park Lodge.** On the east side of the park across from the Amtrak station, this beautiful hotel is constructed of giant timbers. There's a golf course on the grounds. *154 rooms. Restaurant, pool. D, MC, V. Closed mid-Sept.-mid-May.*

$$$$ ✕🏨 **Many Glacier Hotel.** On the east side of the park, 12 mi west of Babb, the park's largest lodge has commanding views of Swiftcurrent Lake and the mountains. *208 rooms. Restaurant. D, MC, V. Closed mid-Sept.–mid-May.*

$$–$$$$ ✕🏨 **Lake McDonald Lodge.** This former hunting refuge near West Glacier has four-person cabins, plus motel units and a lodge on the lake. Boating, fishing, and horseback riding are prime activities. *100 rooms. Restaurant. D, MC, V. Closed mid-Sept.–mid-May.*

Hot Springs

$$–$$$$ 🏨 **Lost Trail Hot Springs Resort.** Hot springs feed the swimming pool and a hot tub at this resort 90 mi south of Missoula in the Bitterroot National Forest. RV spaces are available. *✉ Off U.S. 93, Box 8321, Sula 59871, ☎ 406/821–3574, FAX 406/821–4012 or 800/825–3574. 8 rooms, 9 cabins. Restaurant, pools. AE, MC, V.*

$–$$$ 🏨 **Chico Hot Springs Lodge.** Built at the turn of the century, this resort is nestled against the Absarokee Mountains 29 mi north of Yellowstone. The dining room is famous, as are the mineral hot springs. Accommodations are in condominiums or the old lodge, as well as in cabins and two small motels. *Drawer D, Pray 59065,* ☎ *406/333–4933 or 800/468–9232,* FAX *406/333–4694. 78 rooms, 8 condominiums, 4 cabins. Restaurant, pools. AE, D, MC, V.*

Missoula

$$–$$$ ★ ✕ **Guy's Lolo Creek Steak House.** This quintessentially Montana restaurant in a massive log structure 8 mi south of Missoula feels like a hunting lodge, complete with stuffed wildlife on the walls. Guy's signature sirloins are cooked over an open-pit barbecue and come in three sizes. Plenty of other menu choices satisfy non-steak eaters. ✉ *6600 U.S. 12 W, Lolo,* ☎ *406/273–2622. AE, D, MC, V.*

$–$$ ✕ **The Shack.** Innovative omelets and hash browns with herb-scented gravy draw a crowd of locals to this humble eatery at breakfast-time; creative lunch and dinner specials are served throughout the rest of the day. ✉ *222 W. Main St.,* ☎ *406/549–9903. MC, V.*

$$$–$$$$ **Goldsmith's Inn.** Built in 1911 as the residence of the University of Montana's first president, this prairie-style B&B has big white eaves and a huge porch. It's on the shore of the Clark Fork River, near the university campus. Next door is Goldsmith's Premium Ice Cream, a great place for dessert or morning coffee. ✉ *809 E. Front St., 59801,* ☎ *406/721–6732. 7 units. Full breakfast. AE, D, MC, V.*

Ranches

Montana's guest ranches range from working ranches to deluxe spreads with nary a cow in sight; check Travel Montana's directory (☞ Statewide Visitor Information, *above*). Those listed throughout this chapter are categorized as either $$ (less than $1,000 per person per week) or $$$ ($1,000–$1,900 per person based on double occupancy). Meals and recreation are included.

$$$ **Flathead Lake Lodge.** Reserve at least a year in advance (one-week minimum) for this deluxe 2,000-acre dude ranch on the shores of Flathead Lake. Each of the rustic western lodges has a big stone fireplace. Horseback riding, boating, waterskiing, and fishing are among the activities. ✉ *Box 248, Bigfork 59911,* ☎ *406/837–4391,* FAX *406/837–6977. 18 rooms, 20 cottages. Tennis. AP. MC, V. Closed Oct.–Apr.*

Motels

Doubletree Hotel (✉ 100 Madison St., Missoula 59801, ☎ 406/728–3100 or 800/237–7445, FAX 406/728–2530), 172 rooms, 2 restaurants, pool; *$$$.* **Best Western Outlaw Inn** (✉ 1701 Hwy. 93 S, Kalispell 59901, ☎ 406/755–6100 or 800/237–7445, FAX 406/756–8994), 220 rooms, restaurant, pool; *$$–$$$.*

Campgrounds

Glacier National Park's 10 campgrounds are available on a first-come, first-served basis; they fill by noon. Other public campgrounds are in national forests and state parks. Look for private campgrounds with RV services near towns or check Travel Montana's directory (☞ Statewide Visitor Information, *above*).

Outdoor Activities and Sports

Biking

Glacier's Going-to-the-Sun Road is a challenging ride. **Backcountry Bicycle Tours** (✉ Box 4029, Bozeman 59772, ☎ 406/586–3556) organizes five- to seven-day trips in Glacier National Park as well as the rest of the state.

Fishing

In the Flathead Valley, fish for cutthroat and bull trout in the Flathead River or perch, whitefish, and lake trout in Flathead Lake. **Pointer Scenic**

Cruises (✉ Bigfork, ☎ 406/837–5617) operates custom charter tours on Flathead Lake. For western Montana waterways, fish the Clark Fork, Bitterroot, and Blackfoot rivers; Rock Creek, a blue-ribbon trout stream; or Seeley Lake. Local stores sell fishing licenses.

Golf

Eagle Bend Golf Club (✉ Box 960, Bigfork 59911, ☎ 406/837–7300 or 800/255–5641) is a 27-hole championship course with splendid views.

Hiking and Backpacking

Glacier National Park has 730 mi of trails. **Glacier Wilderness Guides** (✉ Box 535, West Glacier 59936, ☎ 406/888–5466 or 800/521–7238) leads backcountry trips. The **Great Bear, Bob Marshall,** and **Scapegoat wilderness areas** (✉ Flathead National Forest, 1935 3rd Ave. E, Kalispell 59901, ☎ 406/755–5401) constitute a million-acre refuge along the Continental Divide. The **Jewel Basin Hiking Area,** 13 mi east of Bigfork off Route 83, is a short, minimal-ascent trail to high-country lakes and superb views. For information on backcountry hiking, contact the **U.S. Forest Service Northern Region Office** (✉ 2000 E. Broadway Ave., Missoula 59807, ☎ 406/329–3511).

Rafting and Canoeing

Rafting outfitters include **Glacier Raft Co.** (✉ Box 218M, West Glacier 59936, ☎ 406/888–5454 or 800/332–9995). Canoes take the calmer waters of Glacier Park's Lake McDonald. For canoe rentals try **Glacier Park Boat Company** (✉ Box 5262, Kalispell 59903, ☎ 406/888–5727 May–Sept.; 406/752–5488 Oct.–Apr.).

Most stretches of the Clark Fork and Bitterroot can be run by raft or canoe; the Blackfoot is more difficult. A good outfitter is **Western Waters** (✉ 5455 Keil Loop, Missoula, ☎ 406/543–3203). Northeast of Missoula near Seeley Lake, the **Clearwater River Canoe Trail** follows an easy 4-mi stretch.

Water Sports

Flathead Lake supports a large sailing community, countless water-skiers and windsurfers, and cruises on the ***Port Polson Princess*** (✉ Polson, ☎ 406/883–2448 or 800/882–6363).

Ski Areas

For **ski reports** call 406/444–2654 or 800/847–4868.

Cross-Country

Trails are found at Glacier National Park, in the Flathead National Forest, and in Lolo National Forest near Missoula. On Glacier's southern border, the **Izaak Walton Inn** (✉ U.S. 2, Essex 59916, ☎ 406/888–5700, FAX 406/888–5200) has 18 mi of groomed trails.

Downhill

Big Mountain (✉ Box 1400, Whitefish 59937, ☎ 406/862–1900 or 800/858–5439) has 63 runs, 9 lifts, and a 2,300-ft vertical drop.

SOUTHWESTERN MONTANA

Montana's pioneer history began here, and evidence of the early mining frontier—from rough-and-tumble camps to the mansions of the magnates—is inescapable. In the high country north and west of Yellowstone National Park you'll find world-class fishing and some of the state's best ski terrain.

Visitor Information

Gold West Country: Regional Tourism Commission (✉ 1155 Main St., Deer Lodge 59722, ☎ 406/846–1943 or 800/879–1159). **Yellowstone Country:** Regional Tourism Commission (✉ Box 1107, Red Lodge 59068, ☎ 406/446–1005 or 800/736–5276).

Arriving and Departing

By Bus

Intermountain Bus Co. (☎ 406/442–5860) stops in Helena and Butte (☎ 406/723–3287). **Greyhound Lines** serves Bozeman (☎ 800/231–2222). In summer **Karst Stages** (☎ 800/332–0504) runs between Bozeman, Livingston, and Yellowstone.

By Car

I–15 passes through Helena. Use I–90 for Butte and Bozeman. U.S. 191, 89, 287, and 212 link the region with Yellowstone.

By Plane

Helena Regional Airport (☎ 406/442–2821), Bozeman's **Gallatin Field Airport** (☎ 406/388–6632), and Butte's **Bert Mooney Airport**(☎ 406/494–3771) are served by major domestic airlines.

Exploring Southwestern Montana

The humble mining origins of **Helena,** Montana's capital, are visible in its earliest commercial district, **Reeder's Alley.** By 1888, the "Queen City of the Rockies" had 50 resident millionaires and a legacy of major gold rushes. The mansions on the **West Side** and commercial buildings on the main street, **Last Chance Gulch,** preserve the era's opulence.

Helena's vibrant arts scene includes dramatic performances and movies in the two auditoriums within the **Myrna Loy Theater** (✉ 15 N. Ewing St., ☎ 406/443–0287). Free tours are conducted at the **Archie Bray Foundation** (✉ 2915 Country Club Ave., ☎ 406/443–3502; 🎟 free), a nationally known center for ceramic arts. The **Montana Historical Society Museum** (✉ 225 N. Roberts St., ☎ 406/444–2694; 🎟 donations accepted) showcases valuable collections of western paintings and historic memorabilia.

The millionaires may have resided in Helena, but the miners lived in **Butte,** a tough, wily town with a rich ethnic mix. The **Berkeley Pit,** a mile-wide open-pit copper mine, sits at the edge of the **Butte National Historic District,** a downtown area of ornate buildings with an Old West feel. On the northern edge of Deer Lodge, the **Grant-Kohrs Ranch National Historic Site** (✉ 316 Main St., ☎ 406/846–2070; 🎟 $2) preserves the home and outbuildings of a 19th-century ranch, still worked by cowboys and draft horses. The **Towe Ford Museum** (✉ 1106 Main St., ☎ 406/846–3111; 🎟 $7.95) is a car buff's delight, with more than 100 vintage Fords and Lincolns dating from 1903 to the 1970s.

★ Montana's oldest state park, **Lewis and Clark Caverns** (✉ Rte. 2, off I–90, ☎ 406/287–3032; 🎟 $3) lies 40 mi east of Butte. Two-hour tours lead through narrow passages and vaulted chambers past colorful, intriguingly varied limestone formations. The park is closed from mid-October through mid-April.

Bozeman, 50 mi east of Butte on I–90, is a regional trade center, a place crazy for food, art, and the outdoors. At Montana State University, ★ the **Museum of the Rockies** (✉ 600 W. Kagy Blvd., ☎ 406/994–3466; 🎟 $6) presents paleontology exhibits, a hands-on dinosaur playroom, planetarium shows, and western art and history exhibits.

South of town, U.S. 191 follows the Gallatin River to West Yellowstone, the gateway to **Yellowstone National Park** (☞ Wyoming chapter). On the U.S. 89 approach to Yellowstone, **Livingston**—former home of Calamity Jane and now a haven for hiking, fishing, and other outdoor activities—sits at the head of Paradise Valley, which is bisected by the Yellowstone River. U.S. 212, the most spectacular route to Yellowstone, passes through **Red Lodge.** The coal mines here drew immigrants from Great Britain, Italy, Finland, Yugoslavia, and other nations at the turn of the century. The town celebrates its diverse heritage each August with a weeklong celebration.

Dining and Lodging

For price ranges *see* Charts 1 (B) and 2 (B) *in* On the Road with Fodor's.

Big Sky

$$$$ ✕🏨 **Big Sky Ski and Summer Resort.** After enjoying a stint of golf, fishing, horseback riding, or skiing, come back to large, bright rooms in the ski lodge or condominiums of this resort in Gallatin Canyon, 43 mi south of Bozeman and 18 mi from Yellowstone National Park. ✉ *Box 160001, 59716,* ☎ *406/995–5000 or 800/548–4486,* FAX *406/995–5001. 298 rooms. 24 restaurants, pool, health club. AE, D, DC, MC, V. Closed mid-Apr.–late May, early Oct.–late Nov.*

Bozeman

$$ ✕ **Mackenzie River Pizza Co.** Zesty gourmet pizzas are baked in a brick oven. Eat in or take it to go. ✉ *232 E. Main St.,* ☎ *406/587–0055. Reservations not accepted. AE, MC, V.*

$$$ 🏨 **Voss Inn.** Afternoon tea is served in the parlor of this antiques-filled, 1883 Victorian B&B in Bozeman's historic district. The owners take guests on fishing trips to Yellowstone. ✉ *319 S. Willson Ave., 59715,* ☎ *406/587–0982,* FAX *406/585–2964. 6 rooms. Full breakfast. AE, MC, V.*

Butte

$–$$ ✕ **Uptown Cafe.** Fresh seafood, steaks, and pasta are served in this informal café. ✉ *47 E. Broadway,* ☎ *406/723–4735. AE, MC, V.*

Helena

$–$$ ✕ **The Windbag Saloon and Grill.** This historic, cherrywood-paneled saloon, once a sporting house called Big Dorothy's, was named in honor of the hot political debates you're likely to overhear while dining on burgers, quiche, salads, and sandwiches. ✉ *19 S. Last Chance Gulch,* ☎ *406/443–9669. AE, D, MC, V.*

$$–$$$ ★ 🏨 **The Sanders.** Wilbur Fisk Sanders, frontier politician and vigilante, once lived in this 1875 mansion, now a centrally located B&B on the National Register of Historic Places. The colonel's rock collection is still in the front hall. ✉ *328 N. Ewing St., 59601,* ☎ *406/442–3309,* FAX *406/443–2361. 7 rooms. Full breakfast. AE, MC, V.*

Motels

🏨 **War Bonnett Inn** (✉ 2100 Cornell Ave., Butte 59701, ☎ 406/494–7800), 134 rooms, restaurant, pool, exercise room; *$$–$$$.* 🏨 **Jorgenson's Holiday Motel** (✉ 1714 11th Ave., Helena 59601, ☎ 406/442–1770 or 800/272–1770 in MT, FAX 406/449–0155), 117 rooms, restaurant, pool; *$–$$$.* 🏨 **Bozeman Inn** (✉ 1235 N. 7th Ave., Bozeman 59715, ☎ 406/587–3176 or 800/648–7515, FAX 406/585–3591), 49 rooms, restaurant, pool; *$–$$.*

Ranch

For price ranges *see* Lodging *in* The Flathead and Western Montana, *above.*

$$–$$$ ⛺ **Lazy K Bar.** This working ranch, built in 1880, sits on 22,000 acres below the Crazy Mountains. Guests can do a lot of riding, including actual cattle moving and other ranch work, if they choose. Rates include everything except gratuities, with a one-week minimum stay. ✉ *Box 550M, Big Timber 59011,* ☎ *406/537–4404,* FAX *406/537–4593. FAP. No credit cards. Closed mid-Sept.–mid-June.*

Campgrounds

Public campgrounds are in national forests and state parks; private ones with RV services are near towns. Check Travel Montana's directory (☞ Statewide Visitor Information, *above*). In peak season campgrounds near Yellowstone fill early in the day.

The Arts

The String Orchestra of the Rockies performs at the **Big Sky Arts Festival** at the Big Sky Ski and Summer Resort (☞ Dining and Lodging, *above*) in July. Big Timber hosts August's **Montana Cowboy Poetry Gathering** (✉ Sweet Grass Chamber of Commerce, ☎ 406/932–5131).

Outdoor Activities and Sports

Fishing

Few trout streams rival the Missouri, Beaverhead, and Big Hole rivers; one outfitter is the **Complete Fly Fisher** (✉ Wise River, ☎ 406/832–3175). Livingston, Ennis, and West Yellowstone are base towns for the superb fly-fishing on the Yellowstone, Madison, and other local rivers; **Dan Bailey's Fly Shop** (✉ 209 W. Park St., Livingston, ☎ 406/222–1673 or 800/356–4052) is a Montana legend. Licenses are sold at local stores.

Golf

Big Sky Golf Course (✉ Rte. 64, Big Sky, ☎ 406/995–4706), 18 holes.

Hiking and Backpacking

Wilderness areas include the **Gates of the Mountains** (☎ 406/449–5201), near Helena; the **Anaconda-Pintler Wilderness** (☎ 406/496–3400), near Anaconda; the **Lee Metcalf Wilderness** (☎ 406/587–6701), near Bozeman; and **Absarokee-Beartooth Wilderness** (☎ 406/587–6701), near Livingston.

Rafting and Canoeing

The Missouri River north of Helena is easy for rafts and canoes. Bear Trap Canyon, on the Madison River near Ennis, and Yankee Jim, on the Yellowstone near Gardiner, require white-water experience or an outfitter, such as the **Yellowstone Raft Co.** (☎ 406/848–7777 or 800/858–7781).

Ski Areas

For **ski reports** call 406/444–2654 or 800/847–4868.

Cross-Country

In winter many national forest roads and trails become backcountry ski trails. **Lone Mountain Ranch** (✉ Box 160069, Big Sky 59716, ☎ 406/995–4644 or 800/514–4644, FAX 406/995–4670) has 45 mi of groomed and tracked trails, food, lodging, and even guided cross-country ski tours of nearby Yellowstone National Park.

Downhill

Big Sky Resort (☞ Dining and Lodging, *above*) has 75 runs, 15 lifts, and a 4,180-ft vertical drop.

BIGHORN COUNTRY

Despite the heavy influence of cowboy culture, southeastern Montana is Native American land. The Northern Cheyenne and the Crow still inhabit this stunning country of rimrock, badlands, wide-open grasslands, and rugged mountains. Billings is a convenient base for touring.

Visitor Information

Custer Country: Regional Tourism Commission (✉ Rte. 1, Box 1206A, Hardin 59034, ☎ 406/665–1671 or 800/346–1876).

Arriving and Departing

By Bus

Greyhound Lines (☎ 800/231–2222) and **Rimrock Stages** (☎ 406/549–2339 or 800/255–7655) serve Billings.

By Car

The main routes between Yellowstone and Broadus, in the southeastern corner of the state, are I–94, I–90, U.S. 212, and Route 59.

By Plane

Major domestic airlines fly to **Logan International Airport** (☎ 406/657–8495), in Billings.

Exploring Bighorn Country

Booms in coal, oil, and gas made **Billings** Montana's largest town. Sprawled between steep-face rimrocks and the Yellowstone River, it has big-city services and a stockman's heart. In summer the town puts on a nightly rodeo. The **Moss Mansion** (✉ 914 Division St., ☎ 406/256–5100; 🎫 $5) is an elegantly restored 1903 dwelling, with daily tours. A broader view of the social history of the Yellowstone Valley can be found in the varied exhibits of the **Western Heritage Center** (✉ 2822 Montana Ave., ☎ 406/256–6809; 🎫 free). The **Yellowstone Art Center** (✉ 401 N. 27th Ave., ☎ 406/256–6804; 🎫 donations accepted) showcases regional art in the original county jail.

Southeast of Billings on I–94 lie the Crow and Northern Cheyenne Indian reservations. **Crow Fair** (☎ 406/638–2601), held in Crow Agency for five days in August, draws visitors from all over the West for parades, rodeos, traditional dancing, and horse races.

★ Fifteen miles southeast of Hardin on I–90, **Little Bighorn Battlefield National Monument** (✉ National Park Service, Crow Agency 59022, ☎ 406/638–2621; 🎫 $4 per vehicle) preserves the site where in 1876 the Cheyenne and Sioux defended their lives and homeland in a bloody battle with General George Armstrong Custer. You can explore the windswept prairie on your own or with a guided tour.

Dining and Lodging

Billings

$–$$$ ✕ **CJ's Restaurant.** Mesquite-grilled ribs, steaks, chicken, and seafood dominate the fare, with barbecue sauces ranging from mild to three-alarm. ✉ *2456 Central Ave.,* ☎ *406/656–1400. AE, D, DC, MC, V.*

$$$–$$$$ ✕🏨 **Radisson Northern Hotel.** Though a fire destroyed the original 1905 building, this hotel still has an American West theme, with woven rugs, bedspreads, and a gaming table. A massive fireplace dominates the lobby, which has glorious views. The Golden Belle restaurant serves fine Continental cuisine. ✉ *Broadway at 1st Ave. N, Box 1296, 59101,* ☎ *406/245–5121 or 800/333–3333,* FAX *406/259–9862. 160 rooms. Restaurant. AE, D, DC, MC, V.*

Motel

Ponderosa Inn Best Western (✉ 2511 1st Ave. N, Billings 59101, ☎ 406/259–5511 or 800/628–9081, FAX 406/245–8004), 131 rooms, restaurant, pool, exercise room; *$$*.

Campgrounds

Public campgrounds are in **Custer National Forest** and **Bighorn Canyon National Recreation Area**; for private campgrounds check Travel Montana's listing (☞ Statewide Visitor Information, *above*).

Outdoor Activities and Sports

Fishing

Trout anglers fish the Yellowstone River above Columbus. Walleye, bass, and warmer-water fish are found downriver. The Bighorn River below Yellowtail Dam near Pryor is trout heaven; lake species inhabit the reservoir above the dam.

Hiking and Backpacking

The northern region of the arid Pryor Mountains, south of Billings, is on the Crow Reservation; permits for backcountry travel are issued by the **Crow Tribal Council** (✉ Crow Agency 59022, ☎ 406/638–2601). The southern Pryors are in **Custer National Forest** (✉ 2602 1st Ave. N, Billings 59103, ☎ 406/657–6361).

Rafting and Canoeing

Canoes, rafts, and drift boats ply the Yellowstone River and the Bighorn River below Yellowtail Dam.

Ski Area

Red Lodge Mountain (✉ Box 750, Red Lodge 59068, ☎ 406/446–2610 or 800/444–8977), an hour southwest of Billings, has 45 runs, 8 lifts, and a 2,350-ft vertical drop.

ELSEWHERE IN MONTANA

Central and Eastern Montana

Visitor Information

Russell Country Regional Tourism Commission (✉ Box 1366, Great Falls 59403, ☎ 406/761–5036 or 800/527–5348). **Custer Country Regional Tourism Commission** (✉ Rte. 1, Box 1206A, Hardin 59034, ☎ 406/665–1671).

Arriving and Departing

I–15 and U.S. 89 traverse the region north–south; U.S. 2 and I–94 run east–west.

What to See and Do

Montana's heartland is open grasslands and, rising abruptly from the plains, the sheer escarpment of the Rocky Mountain Front. In **Great**
★ **Falls,** the **C. M. Russell Museum** (✉ 400 13th St. N, ☎ 406/727–8787; $4) has a formidable collection of works by the cowboy artist, along with his original log-cabin studio. Cowboy life thrives in **Miles City,** which in May hosts the **Miles City Bucking Horse Sale,** three days of horse trading, rodeo, and street dances.

Dining and Lodging

$–$$$ ✕ **Jaker's.** Arrive hungry for heaping plates of ribs, steaks, and seafood. ✉ *1500 10th Ave. S., Great Falls,* ☎ *406/727–1033. AE, D, MC, V.*

UTAH

By Stacey Clark

Capital	Salt Lake City
Population	2,059,000
Motto	Industry
State Bird	California gull
State Flower	Sego lily
Postal Abbreviation	UT

Statewide Visitor Information

Utah Travel Council (✉ Council Hall, Capitol Hill, Salt Lake City 84114, ☎ 801/538–1030 or 800/200–1160). Ten **regional visitor information centers** supply brochures and travel advice (call the Utah Travel Council for locations), and **welcome centers** are near all major entrances to the state. The **Salt Lake Organizing Committee for the Olympic Winter Games of 2002** (✉ 257 E. 200 South St., Suite 600, Salt Lake City 84111, ☎ 801/212–2002) provides information on venues for the games, which will be hosted by Salt Lake City.

Scenic Drives

From Logan **U.S. 89** runs north through a limestone canyon with steep, striated walls, cresting above Bear Lake on the Utah–Idaho border. In northeastern Utah **U.S. 191** jogs north out of Vernal and past geologic formations that are up to a billion years old before meeting **Route 44,** which yields an elongated view of Flaming Gorge National Recreation Area. **Route 12,** in southwestern Utah, turns east from U.S. 89, skirting through Bryce Canyon National Park and Grand Staircase-Escalante National Monument, and then north over aspen-covered Boulder Mountain to Capitol Reef National Park. Utah has 27 officially designated scenic byways; visitor and welcome centers provide information on these.

National and State Parks

National Parks

Utah's five national parks are **Bryce Canyon,** filled with unusual geologic formations; **Capitol Reef,** distinguished by colorfully striped rock walls and ancient petroglyphs; **Zion,** with towering cliffs (for both, ☞ Exploring Southwestern Utah, *below*); **Canyonlands,** with drives through three geologically distinct districts; and **Arches,** known for its sandstone formations (for all three, ☞ Exploring Southeastern Utah, *below*).

Utah's seven national monuments include the excavations at **Dinosaur National Monument**(☞ Elsewhere in Utah, *below*); the limestone caverns of **Timpanogos Cave** (✉ Rte. 3, American Fork 84003, ☎ 801/756–5238 in summer, 801/756–5239 in winter); and the giant, stream-formed spans of **Natural Bridges National Monument**(☞ Exploring Southeastern Utah, *below*). You can fish or boat at **Glen Canyon National Recreation Area**(☞ Exploring Southeastern Utah, *below*) and **Flaming Gorge National Recreation Area**(☞ Elsewhere in Utah, *below*). **Grand Staircase–Escalante National Monument** achieved monument status in 1996. Though amenities and services remain few, it has stunning river canyons and geologic formations (✉ 176 E. D. L. Sargent Dr., Cedar City 84720, ☎ 435/865–5100).

State Parks

The **Division of State Parks** (✉ 1594 W. North Temple St., Salt Lake City 84114, ☎ 801/538–7220) publishes a directory of Utah's 45 state parks. **Goblin Valley State Park** (✉ Box 93, Green River 84525, ☎ 435/564–3633), off I–70 on Route 24 in eastern Utah, has acres of wind-eroded sandstone "goblins" around a desert campground. **This Is the Place State Park** (✉ 2601 Sunnyside Ave., Salt Lake City 84108, ☎ 801/584–8391), on the eastern bench of the Salt Lake Valley, details the trek of Mormon pioneers and re-creates an 1850s township, complete with cooking, crafts making, and blacksmithing demonstrations.

SALT LAKE CITY

On July 24, 1847, Mormon leader Brigham Young looked out over the Salt Lake Valley and announced to the ragged party behind him, "This is the right place." So began the religious settlement that would become Salt Lake City. The Church of Jesus Christ of Latter-Day Saints, as the Mormon Church is officially known, continues to shape the city, which has evolved into a winter-sports destination, a center for biomedical research, and the gateway to the natural wonders of southern Utah.

Visitor Information

Convention and Visitors Bureau (✉ Salt Palace Convention Center, 90 S. West Temple St., 84101, ☎ 801/521–2822).

Arriving and Departing

By Bus

Greyhound Lines (✉ 160 W. South Temple St., ☎ 800/231–2222).

By Car

I–15 runs north–south through Salt Lake, I–80 east–west. I–215 circles the valley.

By Plane

Salt Lake International Airport (☎ 801/575–2400) is 7 mi north of downtown. Major hotels provide shuttles, and **Utah Transit Authority** (☎ 801/287–4636) buses link the airport to regular city routes. Taxi fare to downtown averages $10–$15 including tip.

By Train

Amtrak (☎ 800/872–7245) serves the city's **Rio Grande Depot** (✉ 320 S. Rio Grande St., ☎ 801/532–3472).

Getting Around Salt Lake City

Salt Lake City streets are laid out geometrically and numbered in increments of 100 in each direction, with Temple Square as their root. Parking is inexpensive, and streets and highways are less crowded than those in comparable urban areas. **Utah Transit Authority** (☎ 801/287–4636) buses and trolleys serve the valley; the fare is $1, with a free-fare zone in downtown shopping areas.

Exploring Salt Lake City

City attractions fan out from Temple Square. To the north is the Capitol Hill District, to the south are shopping and arts locations, to the west is the Great Salt Lake, and to the east lie the ski resorts of the Wasatch Mountains.

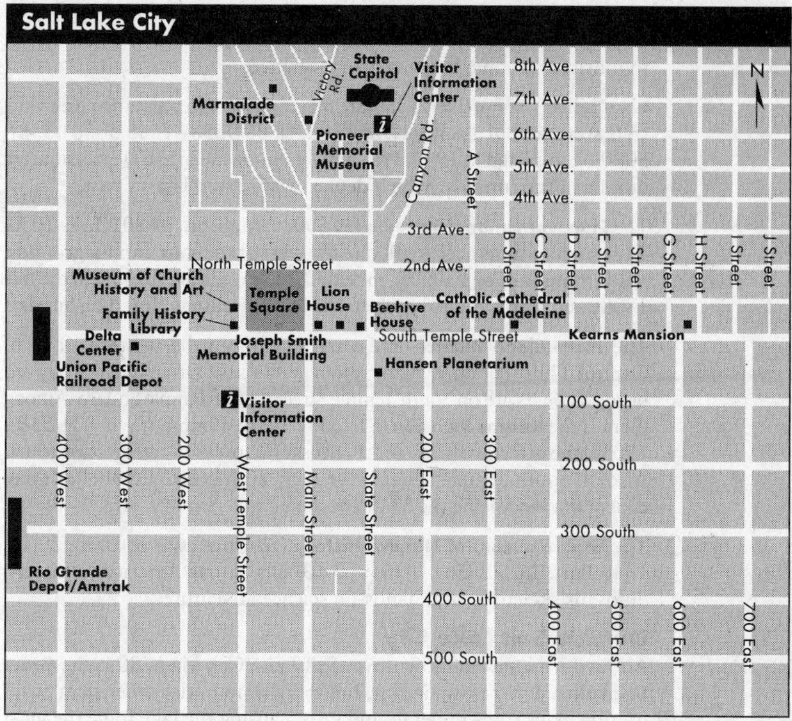

Historic **Temple Square** (✉ North Visitors' Center, 50 W. North Temple St., ☎ 801/240–2534) is the 10-acre center of sites important to Mormonism. Two visitor centers house exhibits and art with religious themes. The **Mormon Tabernacle Choir** performs on Thursday and Saturday in the squat, domed Salt Lake Tabernacle. The six-spired granite **Salt Lake Temple** is open only to church members, but the public may enter (free of charge) the other buildings and monuments on the beautifully landscaped grounds.

East of Temple Square and across Main Street, the **Joseph Smith Memorial Building** (☎ 801/240–1266 or 800/537–9703; 🎫 free) is a Mormon community center where visitors can learn how to do computerized genealogical research and can watch an hour-long film on early Mormon history and the emigration of Mormons to the Salt Lake Valley in the mid-19th century. The center, set in what was once the elegant Hotel Utah, also has two restaurants.

On West Temple Street directly west of Temple Square is the **Museum of Church History and Art** (☎ 801/240–3310; 🎫 free), displaying Mormon artifacts, paintings, fabric art, and sculptures. Also on West Temple Street, the **Family History Library** (☎ 801/240–2331) provides free public access to the Mormons' huge collection of genealogical records.

On the corner of South Temple and State streets, one block east of Temple Square, is the 1854 **Beehive House** (☎ 801/240–2671; 🎫 free), the home of Brigham Young while he served as territorial governor; free tours are conducted daily. The **Lion House** (☎ 801/363–5466) received the overflow of Young's large family; it is now a social center and restaurant.

Another impressive turn-of-the-century structure, half a block south of the Beehive House, houses the **Hansen Planetarium** (✉ 15 S. State

St., ☎ 801/538–2098; 🎫 free, shows $2–$5)), where a moon rock display is among the exhibits. A domed theater hosts laser shows set to music, and some live stage performances.

On a hill at the north end of State Street sits the Renaissance Revival–style **state capitol** (✉ 300 N. State St., ☎ 801/538–1563 or 801/538–3000), completed in 1915. Free hourly tours take in the Depression-era murals in the rotunda, which depict events from Utah's past.

The **Pioneer Memorial Museum** (✉ 300 N. Main St., ☎ 801/538–1050; 🎫 free; donations accepted), directly west of the state capitol grounds, holds thousands of artifacts, including tools and carriages from the late 1800s and a doll and toy collection. The museum is closed on Sunday.

The **Marmalade District**—the streets bisecting the western slope of Capitol Hill—contains many pioneer houses. Other well-preserved historic houses are on South Temple Street east of Temple Square. Among them is the **Kearns Mansion** (✉ 603 E. South Temple St., ☎ 801/538–1005), the governor's residence, accessible only by free guided tours. Also on South Temple Street is the early 20th-century **Catholic Cathedral of the Madeleine** (✉ 331 E. South Temple St., ☎ 801/328–8941).

The **Utah Museum of Natural History** (✉ University of Utah, 200 S. 1340 East, ☎ 801/581–4303; 🎫 $3) has Native American artifacts, dinosaur skeletons, and hands-on science adventures.

Outside Salt Lake City

About 17 mi west of downtown Salt Lake City via I–80 is the **Great Salt Lake.** Water flows into it, but there is no outlet other than evaporation. This traps minerals and salts, causing the lake to be the most saline body of water on earth except for the Dead Sea. There are two beaches here, each with showers. The south and west shores and neighboring wetlands are prime nesting grounds for many species of migratory, shore, and wading birds. A sunset dinner cruise departs from **Antelope Island State Park** (☎ 801/773–2941), which is accessed from I–15 via a 7.5-mile causeway ($6 per vehicle).

Rising to more than 11,000 ft east of the Salt Lake Valley, the **Wasatch Mountains** provide an impressive backdrop and recreational escape for city dwellers. Southeast of Salt Lake City are two scenic canyons, Big Cottonwood on Route 190 and Little Cottonwood on Route 210. Resorts here offer hiking, biking, arts festivals and concerts in summer, and skiing in winter (☞ Ski Areas, *below*).

Over the ridge line but merely 29 mi east of Salt Lake City via I–80 is **Park City,** Utah's premier ski destination. Park City's three ski areas will host several events during the 2002 Olympic Winter Games. Park City's historic Main Street has a museum, galleries, shops, and restaurants, several bed-and-breakfasts, three golf courses, and an outlet mall.

Parks, Gardens, and Zoos

Red Butte Gardens and Arboretum (☎ 801/581–5322; 🎫 $3), east of Salt Lake City's University of Utah campus and Research Park, has 150 acres of trees, shrubs, herbs, wildflowers, and stream-fed pools tucked into a private canyon in the Wasatch foothills. A concert series is held each summer.

In the city's eastern foothills, **Hogle Zoo** (✉ 2600 Sunnyside Ave., ☎ 801/582–1631; 🎫 $5) has more than 1,300 animals. Bring walking shoes and a hat—exhibits are spread out, and shade is at a premium.

Dining

Although liquor laws have some peculiarities, mixed drinks, wine, and beer are available at most restaurants; when in doubt, call ahead. For price ranges *see* Chart 1 (A) *in* On the Road with Fodor's.

$$$$ ★ ✕ **Glitretind.** Dishes such as New England lobster with saffron sauce and Caspian caviar make this restaurant worth the splurge. ✉ *Stein Eriksen Lodge, Deer Valley,* ☎ *435/649–3700. AE, DC, MC, V.*

$$–$$$ ✕ **Baci Trattoria.** Northern and southern Italian food is served in an elegant setting of marble and stained glass. ✉ *134 W. Pierpont Ave.,* ☎ *801/328–1500. AE, D, DC, MC, V. Closed Sun.*

$$–$$$ ✕ **Lamb's Restaurant.** Lamb's claims to be Utah's oldest restaurant; it opened in 1919 and still has a turn-of-the-century feel. On the menu are beef, chicken, and seafood dishes, plus sandwiches. ✉ *169 S. Main St.,* ☎ *801/364–7166. AE, D, DC, MC, V. Closed Sun.*

$$–$$$ ★ ✕ **Santa Fe Restaurant.** Inside a streamside lodge in scenic Emigration Canyon, 15 minutes east of downtown, Santa Fe Restaurant earns acclaim for its creative regional dishes such as buffalo steak and rainbow trout, all served with unusual sauces. ✉ *2100 Emigration Canyon Rd.,* ☎ *801/582–5888. MC, V.*

$$ ✕ **Market Street Grill.** The stylish black-and-white decor is catchy, but creative preparations of seafood, steaks, and chicken steal the show. ✉ *48 Market St.,* ☎ *801/322–4668. AE, D, DC, MC, V.*

$–$$ ✕ **Creekside Restaurant.** The seasonal colors of the Wasatch Mountains and views of ski runs add to the allure of this Mediterranean-style restaurant. Wood-oven-baked pizzas have gourmet toppings; pasta, grilled chicken, and steak round out the menu. ✉ *Solitude Resort, 12000 Big Cottonwood Canyon,* ☎ *801/536–5787. AE, D, MC, V.*

$–$$ ★ ✕ **Desert Edge Pub.** This tavern brews 15 beers and ales. Sizzling black-bean enchiladas, pasta-salad specials, and sandwiches comprise the menu. ✉ *600 S. 700 East,* ☎ *801/521–8917. AE, D, MC, V.*

Lodging

Contact the **Utah Hotel and Lodging Association** (✉ 9 Exchange Pl., Suite 812, Salt Lake City 84111, ☎ 801/359–0104 or 800/733–8824) for further suggestions and a statewide reservation service. Prices vary widely with the seasons. The ski resorts listed below are no more than 30 mi away from Salt Lake City. For price ranges *see* Chart 2 (A) *in* On the Road with Fodor's.

$$$–$$$$ ★ **Cliff Lodge at Snowbird Resort.** The large guest rooms in this angular gray building have wide glass walls providing spectacular views winter and summer. The redwood-and-brass lobby is sumptuous. On the grounds is a full-service day spa. ✉ *Snowbird Resort 84092,* ☎ *801/521–6040 or 800/453–3000,* FAX *801/742–3300. 348 rooms. 3 restaurants, pools, exercise room. AE, D, DC, MC, V.*

$$–$$$$ **Shadow Ridge Resort** This lodging is positioned so that guests can virtually ski straight into Park City Mountain Resort's lift lines from most of its rooms, which range from a single hotel room to a two-bedroom condominium suite with full kitchen. Guests have access to a hot tub and a sauna. ✉ *50 Shadow Ridge St., Box 1820, Park City 84060,* ☎ *435/655–3315 or 800/443-1045,* FAX *435/645–9132. 150 rooms. Restaurant, pool . AE, D, DC, MC, V.*

$$–$$$ **Anton Boxrud Bed & Breakfast.** This antiques-filled Victorian manor near the governor's mansion is a pleasant 15-minute walk from the city center. The complimentary evening snacks and beverages served near the parlor's bay window are as delicious as the bountiful breakfasts. ✉ *57 S. 600 East, 84102,* ☎ *801/363–8035 or 800/524–5511,* FAX *801/596–1316. 7 rooms. Full breakfast. AE, D, DC, MC, V.*

$$–$$$ ★ **Peery Hotel.** Most of the rooms in this four-story 1910 hotel have eclectic antique reproductions and fanciful linens. The plush lobby encourages loitering. *✉ 110 W. 300 South, 84102, ☎ 801/521–4300 or 800/331–0073, FAX 801/575–5014. 77 rooms. Restaurant, pool, exercise room.CP. AE, D, DC, MC, V.*

$–$$ **Little America Hotel & Towers.** Salt Lake's largest hotel has 17 floors of elegant rooms with textured fabrics, plush seating, and variable lighting. The lobby and mezzanine have enormous brick fireplaces. *✉ 500 S. Main St., 84101, ☎ 801/363–6781 or 800/453–9450, FAX 801/596–5911. 850 rooms. 2 restaurants, pool, exercise room. AE, D, DC, MC, V.*

Motels

Airport Inn (✉ 2333 W. North Temple St., 84116, ☎ 801/539–0438 or 800/835–9755, FAX 801/539–8852), 100 rooms, restaurant, pool; *$–$$*. **Skyline Inn** (✉ 2475 E. 1700 South, 84108, ☎ 801/582–5350, FAX 801/582–5350), 24 rooms, pool; *$*.

Nightlife and the Arts

A calendar of events is available at the **Salt Lake Convention and Visitors Bureau**(☞ Visitor Information, *above*). The free *This Week in Salt Lake* magazine is widely available at stores and visitor centers. The *Salt Lake Tribune* carries daily arts-and-entertainment listings.

Nightlife

Many nightspots are private clubs, meaning that membership is required (temporary memberships cost about $5). Weekends are wild at the **Dead Goat Saloon** (✉ 165 S. West Temple St., ☎ 801/328–4628), a subterranean hangout with live music and a busy dance floor. A good place to spot Utah Jazz basketball players is **Port O' Call** (✉ 78 W. 400 South, ☎ 801/521–0589), a sports bar with 14 satellite dishes and 26 TVs. The art deco–style **Zephyr Club** (✉ 301 S. West Temple St., ☎ 801/355–2582) has live blues, rock, reggae, and dancing. The **Bay** (✉ 404 S. West Temple St., ☎ 801/363–2623) is a smoke- and alcohol-free club with three dance floors.

The Arts

Salt Lake's best performing arts bets are **Ballet West** (✉ 50 W. 200 South, ☎ 801/355–2787), **Pioneer Theater Company** (✉ 300 S. 1340 East, ☎ 801/581–6961), **Salt Lake Acting Company** (✉ 168 W. 500 North, ☎ 801/363–7522), **Utah Opera Company** (✉ 50 W. 200 South, ☎ 801/355–2787), and **Utah Symphony** (✉ Abravanel Hall, 123 W. South Temple St., ☎ 801/533–6683). Concerts are presented at the **Delta Center** (✉ 300 W. South Temple St., ☎ 801/325–7328), and the **"E" Center** (✉ 3200 S. Decker Lake Dr., ☎ 801/988–4888).

Spectator Sports

Basketball: NBA Utah Jazz, and **WNBA Utah Starzz** (✉ Delta Center, 300 W. South Temple St., ☎ 801/355–3865).

Ski Areas

Cross-Country

Solitude Nordic Center (✉ Rte. 190, ☎ 801/536–5774 or 800/748–4754) and **White Pine Touring** (✉ Park City, ☎ 435/649–8701) offer cross-country skiing tours, rentals, lessons, and advice.

Downhill

Alta (✉ Rte. 210, ☎ 801/742–3333), 40 runs, 8 lifts, 2,020-ft vertical drop. **Brighton** (✉ Rte. 190, ☎ 801/532–4731 or 800/873–5512),

64 runs, 7 lifts, 1,745-ft drop. **The Canyons** (✉ Park West Rd., off Rte. 224, Park City , ☎ 435/649–5400 or 800/754–1636), 74 runs, 8 lifts, gondola, 2,400-ft drop. **Deer Valley** (✉ Rte. 224, Park City, ☎ 435/649–1000 or 800/424–3337), 67 runs, 14 lifts, 2,200-ft drop. **Park City Mountain Resort** (✉ Rte. 224 off I–80, Park City, ☎ 435/649–8111 or 800/222–7275), 93 runs, 14 lifts, 3,100-ft drop. **Solitude** (✉ Rte. 190, ☎ 801/534–1400 or 800/748–4754), 63 runs and bowls, 7 lifts, 2,047-ft drop, 12 mi of groomed cross-country track. **Snowbird** (✉ Rte. 210, ☎ 801/742–2222 or 800/453–3000), 66 runs, 8 lifts and a high-speed tram, 3,240-ft drop.

Shopping

Directly south of Temple Square, **Crossroads Plaza** (✉ 50 S. Main St., ☎ 801/531–1799) has four floors of stores, theaters, and restaurants. East across Main Street, **ZCMI Center** (✉ 36 S. State St., ☎ 801/321–8745) has 80 stores and restaurants. Just a few blocks south and east, **Trolley Square** (✉ 600 S. 700 East, ☎ 801/521–9877) once housed electric trolleys; today it has the city's most varied shopping, as well as restaurants and movie theaters. Clustered around a flour mill built in 1877 are the shops of **Gardner Village** (✉ 1100 W. 7800 South St., ☎ 801/566–8903). East of I–15 in the south end of the city, the **Factory Stores of America Mall** (✉ 12101 S. Factory Outlet Dr., ☎ 801/572–6440) has discount outlets with everything from cookware and coats to Doc Martens.

SOUTHWESTERN UTAH

Southwestern Utah is a panoply of natural wonders; heading the list are Zion, Capitol Reef, and Bryce Canyon national parks, where clear air and high elevations create spectacular 100-mi vistas. The picturesque towns of St. George, Cedar City, Springdale, and Torrey are full of historic sites. The weather here is mild year-round, though summers can be hot.

Visitor Information

Color Country Travel Bureau (✉ 906 N. 14th St. W, Box 1550, St. George 84771, ☎ 435/628–4171 or 800/233–8824). **Capitol Reef Country** (✉ Rte. 24, Box 7, Teasdale 84773, ☎ 800/858–7951).

Arriving and Departing

By Bus

Greyhound Lines (☎ 800/231–2222) stops in St. George and Cedar City.

By Car

I–15 and U.S. 89 pass north–south through the region.

By Plane

St. George and **Cedar City airports** are served by **Skywest Airlines** (☎ 800/453–9417).

Exploring Southwestern Utah

At **Bryce Canyon National Park** millions of years of geologic mayhem have created gigantic bowls filled with strange pinnacles and quilted drapes of stone. An 18-mi scenic drive skirts the western rim, providing views of the amphitheaters. ✉ *Rte. 12, Bryce Canyon 84717,* ☎ *435/834–5322.* 🎟 *$10 per vehicle. Some roads closed Nov.–Mar.*

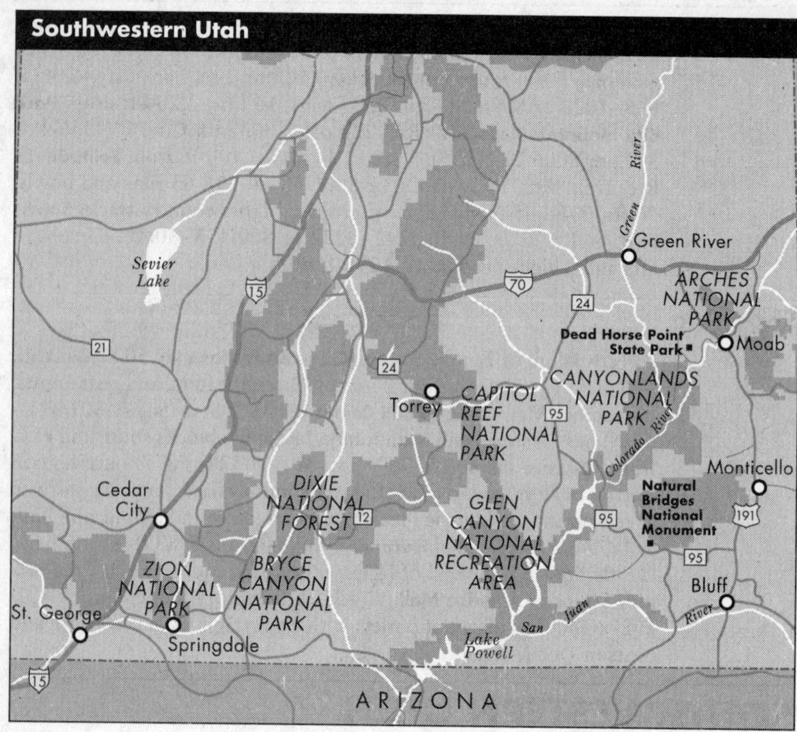

Once called "Land of the Sleeping Rainbow" because of its colorfully striped cliffs, **Capitol Reef National Park** is dominated by a 100-mi-long stone uplift called the Waterpocket Fold. At the base of this soaring "reef" are still-flourishing riverside orchards planted by early settlers. Hikes lead to petroglyphs and hidden formations. The park also has an impressive backcountry scenic route ($5 per vehicle). ✉ *Rte. 24, HC 70, Box 15, Torrey 84775,* ☎ *435/425–3791.*

The Virgin River carved the towering cliffs of Zion Canyon and still flows along its floor. Spring-fed hanging gardens sprout lush greens along the walls. The roads, tram tours, and horseback and hiking trails of **Zion National Park** (✉ Rte. 9, Box 1099, Springdale 84767, 🎫 $10 per vehicle, ☎ 435/772–3256) provide access to the beauties of this vividly hued canyon and its tributaries. The park can be very crowded in summer.

Southwest of Zion National Park, in St. George, you can tour the historic district and **Brigham Young's winter home** (✉ 89 W. 100 North St., ☎ 435/673–5181; 🎫 Free). In Santa Clara the **house of missionary Jacob Hamblin** (✉ 3386 Santa Clara Dr., ☎ 435/673–2161; 🎫 free) has cotton plants and a vineyard. Both sites are operated by the Mormon Church.

Dining and Lodging

Accommodations Referral Service (☎ 800/259–3343) provides area-wide lodging recommendations. For price ranges *see* Charts 1 (B) and 2 (B) *in* On the Road with Fodor's.

Bryce Canyon

$$$–$$$$ ✕🏨 **Bryce Canyon Lodge.** A huge limestone fireplace and a log and wrought-iron chandelier dominate the lobby of this National Historic

Landmark building inside the park. Guests have their choice of motel-style rooms with porches, or cozy lodgepole-pine cabins, some with cathedral fireplaces and gas fireplaces. Reserve far in advance, or call the day before your arrival—cancellations occasionally make last-minute reservations possible. ✉ *2 mi south of park entrance on Rte. 63, Box 400, Cedar City 84720,* ☎ *Advance Reservations: 303/297–2757. Same-day Availability: 435/834–5361,* FAX *435/586–3157. 74 rooms and 40 cabins. Restaurant. AE, D, DC, MC, V. Closed Nov.–Apr.*

$$–$$$ ✕ **Best Western Ruby's Inn.** Just north of the park entrance, this is Grand Central Station for visitors to Bryce. A nightly rodeo takes place nearby. Rooms vary in age, with sprawling wings added as the park gained popularity. The lobby is Southwestern chic, with rough-hewn log beams and poles. ✉ *Rte. 63, Box 1, 84717,* ☎ *435/834–5341 or 800/468–8660,* FAX *435/834–5265. 369 rooms. Restaurant, pool. AE, D, DC, MC, V.*

Cedar City

$$ ★ ✕ **Milt's Stage Stop.** Locals swear by the 12-ounce rib-eye steak, prime rib, and fresh seafood at this restaurant in scenic Cedar Canyon. In winter, deer feed in front of the restaurant as a fireplace blazes inside. The mountain views are splendid year-round. ✉ *5 mi east of town on Rte. 14,* ☎ *435/586–9344. AE, D, DC, MC, V.*

St. George

$$–$$$ ✕ **Basila's Cafe.** Greek and Italian specialties fill the menu here, along with artfully arranged salads. The surrounding red rock makes outdoor dining particularly captivating at sunset. ✉ *2 W. St. George Blvd.,* ☎ *435/673–7671. AE, D, MC, V.*

$$ ✕ **Pancho and Lefty's.** The Mexican cuisine ranges from authentic tamales wrapped in corn husks to avocado-laced taco salads, all further enlivened by spirited decor and tart margaritas. ✉ *1050 S. Bluff St.,* ☎ *435/628–4772. AE, MC, V.*

$$$ **Ramada Inn.** On St. George's major thoroughfare and close to restaurants, shopping, and the historic district, this is one of the city's most convenient and best-appointed properties, with a hot tub, business services, and meeting rooms. ✉ *1440 E. St. George Blvd., 84770,* ☎ *435/628–2828 or 800/713–9435,* FAX *435/628–0505. 136 rooms. Pool. AE, D, MC, V.*

Springdale

$$ ★ ✕ **Bit and Spur Restaurant and Saloon.** This low-slung eatery serves healthful southwestern-style Mexican food. Works by local artists fill the pine-paneled interior, and the patio is redolent of scents from the herb garden. ✉ *1212 Zion Park Blvd.,* ☎ *435/772–3498. MC, V.*

$$ ✕ **Flannigan's.** Named for one of Springdale's original settlement families, this intimate restaurant has wide windows with views of Zion Canyon, and a collection of Everett Ruess woodcut prints inside. Pastas, chicken, fish, and steaks comprise the menu. ✉ *428 Zion Park Blvd.,* ☎ *435/772–3244. AE, MC, V.*

$$$–$$$$ ★ **Snow Family Guest Ranch.** Just minutes from Zion National Park in the town of Virgin, this western-style B&B has inviting common areas—both indoors and out—and breakfasts worth lingering over. ✉ *533 E. Hwy. 9, Box 790190, Virgin 84779,* ☎ *435/635–2500 or 800/308–7669. 9 rooms. Pool. Full breakfast. AE, MC, V.*

$$ **Cliffrose Lodge and Gardens.** Acres of lawn, trees, and gardens surround this hotel on the banks of the Virgin River, ¼ mi from Zion. Rooms are warm with desert hues. ✉ *281 Zion Park Blvd., 84767,* ☎ *435/772–3234 or 800/243–8824,* FAX *435/772–3900. 36 rooms. Pool. AE, D, MC, V.*

Torrey

$$ ✕ **Café Diablo.** Come here for innovative Southwest cuisine—hearty *chipotle*-fried ribs, local trout crusted with pumpkin seeds, jicama salad with eggplant sopaipillas, and the like. ✉ *599 W. Main St.,* ☏ *435/425–3070. MC, V. Closed Nov.–Apr.*

$$–$$$ ★ **SkyRidge Bed & Breakfast.** This colorful three-story inn has comfortable guest rooms, two with private outdoor hot tubs. There are 75 windows in the building, and all have exceptional views of the desert and mountains surrounding Capitol Reef National Park. ✉ *950 E. Hwy. 24, Box 750220,* ☏ FAX *435/425–3222. 6 rooms. Full breakfast. MC, V.*

Campgrounds

You can choose from among more than 100 campgrounds in this region, both public and private; for more information contact the **Utah Travel Council**(☞ Statewide Visitor Information, *above*).

Outdoor Activities and Sports

Biking

A spin along Route 9 through Zion, Route 18 through Snow Canyon, or the Bryce Canyon Scenic Loop yields classic southwestern scenery. Route 24 through Capitol Reef accesses historic sites and off-road riding. **Bicycle Utah** (☏ 800/200–1160) provides a free directory of biking routes.

Golf

St. George attracts golfers year-round to more than a dozen courses, including **Dixie Red Hills** (✉ 1000 N. 700 West, ☏ 435/634–5852), with nine holes; **Entrada at Snow Canyon** (✉ 2511 W. Entrada Trail, ☏ 435/674–7500), with 18 holes; and **South Gate** (✉ 1975 Tonaquint Dr., ☏ 435/628–0000), with 18 holes. The **Washington County Travel Council** (☏ 435/634–5747 or 800/869–6635) has more golfing information.

Hiking and Backpacking

Bryce Canyon, Capitol Reef, and Zion national parks have many trails of varying difficulty. Zion's paved **Gateway to the Narrows Trail** follows the Virgin River. Bryce's moderately difficult **Navajo Loop Trail** yields views of towering Thor's Hammer. Capitol Reef's **Hickman Bridge Trail** is a short nature trail through a sheltered canyon to the base of a natural bridge.

SOUTHEASTERN UTAH

For years the canyon country of southeastern Utah has captured the imagination of filmmakers, serving as the site of such western and adventure films as *Stagecoach, Indiana Jones and the Last Crusade,* and *Thelma and Louise.* Rugged Arches and Canyonlands national parks invite exploration via scenic drives, four-wheeling, hiking, rock climbing, river running, and cycling.

Visitor Information

Grand County Travel Council and Visitor Center: (✉ Main and Center Sts., Box 550, Moab 84532, ☏ 435/259–8825 or 800/635–6622). **San Juan County Travel Council and Visitor Center**: (✉ 117 S. Main St., Box 490, Monticello 84535, ☏ 435/587–3235 or 800/574–4386).

Arriving and Departing

By Car

I–70 runs east–west through the region; U.S. 191 slices north–south.

By Plane

Alpine Air (☎ 801/575–2839) flies weekdays from Salt Lake City to **Canyonlands Field,** in Moab.

Exploring Southeastern Utah

The town of **Green River,** at the junction of I–70 and U.S. 6/191, is named for the river running through it and is the major "put-in" for raft trips on the Green River to its confluence with the Colorado.

A sweeping view of the Canyonlands' multicolor upside-down geography is found at **Dead Horse Point State Park** (✉ Rte. 313, ☎ 435/259–261; 🎟 $4 per vehicle), named for a band of wild horses once stranded on this isolated peninsula.

Arches National Park (✉ U.S. 191, Box 907, Moab 84532, ☎ 435/259–8161; 🎟 $10 per vehicle), just northwest of Moab, contains sandstone formations carved by wind and water. Trails and two scenic roads lead through towering pillars and arches.

Moab, below I–70 on U.S. 191, has become a major destination for mountain bikers, with bike shops, T-shirt stores, restaurants, and motels on virtually every corner. Just south of Moab, Utah's only commercial winery, **Arches Vineyard** (✉ 420 S. Kane Creek Blvd., ☎ 435/259–5397; 🎟 free), gives tours and has a tasting room.

The landscape of **Canyonlands National Park,** (✉ Rte. 313, Moab 84532, ☎ 435/259–716; 🎟 $10 per vehicle) southwest of Moab, is divided into three geologically distinct districts, each with its own visitor center. Scenic loops, trails, and four-wheel-drive roads lead to views of massive canyons or uplifts crowded with stone spires and other bizarre features.

The city of **Monticello** is 53 mi south of Moab on U.S. 191, but at a 7,000 ft elevation compared to Moab's 4,000, it has much cooler temperatures. South and west of Monticello, just north of Route 95, a 9-mi scenic drive takes in views of three river-carved bridges at **Natural Bridges National Monument** (✉ Rte. 275, ☎ 435/692–1234; 🎟 $5 per vehicle).

Southwest of Monticello—take U.S. 191 south and U.S. 95 west or U.S. 95 and Route 276 west—at Lake Powell, part of the **Glen Canyon National Recreation Area** (☎ 520/608–6404; 🎟 $10 per vehicle), is a stark meeting of water and stone, with nearly 2,000 mi of meandering shoreline resulting from the construction of Glen Canyon Dam on the Colorado River. Side canyons and coves hold Indian ruins, rock art, and natural wonders such as the **Rainbow Bridge National Monument.** Spring and fall are the best times to visit—summer temperatures are often over 100°F.

The town of **Bluff,** 48 mi south of Monticello on U.S. 191, rests on the bank of the San Juan River at the border of the vast Navajo Nation. Houses built in the 1880s of sandstone and red adobe are clustered at the town's center.

East of Bluff, **Hovenweep National Monument** (✉ Rte. 262, ☎ 970/749–0510; 🎟 $5 per vehicle) has several tower structures built by Pueblo Indians about 800 years ago.

Dining and Lodging

The cuisine in southeastern Utah tends toward fast food and hearty meals made from local produce. For price ranges *see* Charts 1 (B) and 2 (B) *in* On the Road with Fodor's.

Bluff

$$ ★ ✕ **Cow Canyon Trading Post.** This small restaurant adjacent to a funky trading post serves three dinner entrées daily—perhaps chicken-and-vegetable shish kebabs on a bed of wild rice, a phyllo pie stuffed with spinach and ham, or cold carrot soup with spring greens. ✉ *Rte. 163,* ☎ *435/672–2208. MC, V.*

$$ 🏨 **Recapture Lodge.** This locally owned property is unassuming, clean, and comfortable. Evening slide shows feature local geology, art, and history. ✉ *U.S. 191, Box 309, 84512,* ☎ *435/672–2281,* FAX *435/672–2284. 36 rooms. Pool. AE, D, MC, V.*

Green River

$ ✕ **Ray's Tavern.** Huge hamburgers topped with slabs of tomato and onion and served on a heap of steak fries are the main draw for a crowd of river runners, tourists, and locals looking for lunch and a game of pool. ✉ *25 S. Broadway,* ☎ *435/564–3511. No credit cards.*

Moab

$$–$$$ ✕ **Center Café.** This spare, modern café serves roast game hen, prawns and pasta baked in paper, and cioppino (fisherman's stew), among other things. ✉ *92 E. Center St.,* ☎ *435/259–4295. AE, MC, V.*

$$ ✕ **Rio Colorado.** The Rio has standard decor, but its varied menu includes Mexican entrées, steak, pasta, chicken, and salads. Sunday brunch gets a big turnout. ✉ *2 S. 100 West,* ☎ *435/259–6666. MC, V.*

$$$–$$$$ 🏨 **Pack Creek Ranch.** This guest ranch on a forested mountain loop has rustic log cabins and activities ranging from horseback riding—followed by a massage—to cross-country skiing and weekend entertainment. Meals are included in the rates in season; from November through March, guests cook for themselves in each cabin's full kitchen, and rates are reduced accordingly. ✉ *La Sal Mt. Loop Rd. (Box 1270), Moab 84532,* ☎ *435/259–5505,* FAX *435/259–8879. 11 cabins, 1 ranch house with 12 beds. Pool. AE, D, MC, V.*

$$–$$$$ ★ 🏨 **Sunflower Hill Bed and Breakfast.** Moab's best bed-and-breakfast consists of two separate buildings, the Garden Cottage and the Farmhouse, connected by perennial gardens. For breakfast, a hot entrée is served with yogurt and homemade bread or huge fruit muffins. ✉ *185 N. 3rd East, 84532,* ☎ *435/259–2974. 11 rooms. Full breakfast. MC, V.*

Monticello

$$$–$$$$ ★ ✕🏨 **Grist Mill Inn.** Housed in a three-story flour mill built in 1933, the Grist Mill is full of antiques and unique accessories like treadle sewing machines and vintage telephones. Lodgings are in suite-size rooms and a next-door cottage. A chef trained in Germany prepares gourmet meals for hotel guests and the public. ✉ *64 S. 300 East,* ☎ *435/587–2597 or 800/645–3762. 10 rooms. Full breakfast. AE, D, DC, MC, V.*

Campgrounds

Campground directories are provided by the **Grand County Travel Council** and the **San Juan County Travel Council** (☞ Visitor Information, *above*).

Outdoor Activities and Sports

Biking

Southeastern Utah has hundreds of charted mountain-biking trails, including the **Moab Slickrock Trail,** 4 mi east of Moab, a 10-mi roller-coaster route marked only by dashes of paint on raw rock. Bikes are ideal for exploring the landscape and roads of **Hovenweep National Monument** (☞ Exploring Southeastern Utah, *above*). The **Abajo Mountain Loop,** west of Monticello, winds through cool pine and aspen forests. For area-wide rentals and advice, try **Kaibab Tours** (✉ 391 S. Main St., Moab, ☎ 435/259–7423 or 800/451–1133, FAX 435/259–6135).

Hiking and Backpacking

Call the travel council of Grand County or San Juan (☞ Visitor Information, *above*) for advice on trails. Remember to bring water along on any hike in this region.

Rafting

Outfitters operate float trips and white-water treks on the Colorado River through black-granite-walled Westwater Canyon and the rapids of Cataract Canyon and also on the Green River through Desolation and Gray canyons, both of which shelter Anasazi Indian ruins. Float trips on the San Juan River wind through petroglyph-etched cliffs. Call 800/200–1160 for a free hiking directory.

ELSEWHERE IN UTAH

Northeastern Utah

Dinosaurs have left their remains in these mountains; centuries later, Butch Cassidy and other outlaws stashed caches of "loot" as they fled through the canyons. Sheep- and cattle-ranching remain the predominant industries today; some working ranches arrange horseback riding adventures and even full-fledged cattle drives. Call 800/200–1160 for a free Ranch Recreation directory.

Visitor Information

Vernal Information Center (✉ 25 E. Main St., ☎ 435/789–6932 or 800/477–5558).

Arriving and Departing

U.S. 40 runs east–west through the region. U.S. 191 runs north–south.

What to See and Do

The excavations at **Dinosaur National Monument** (✉ Quarry Visitor Center, Box 128, Jensen 84035, ☎ 435/789–2115; 🎫 $5 per vehicle) showcase the largest collection of Jurassic-period fossils ever unearthed. Some 2,000 dinosaur bones—discoveries began in 1909—lie exposed in a sandstone face inside the visitor center, 20 mi east of Vernal. A 6-mi scenic drive leads from the visitor center to the cabin of Josie Morris, a "cowgirl" who counted Butch Cassidy among her suitors.

Flaming Gorge National Recreation Area (✉ Box 279, Manila 84046, ☎ 435/784–3445; 🎫 $5 per vehicle) is north of Dinosaur National Monument via U.S. 191. Behind 500-ft-high Flaming Gorge Dam, Flaming Gorge Lake stretches north for 90 mi between twisting red-rock canyon walls. The lake is good for boating, camping, and trophy trout fishing. South of the dam, the Green River is known for excellent fishing and calm-water rafting.

Dining and Lodging

$$–$$$ ✕ **The Curry Manor.** The diverse menu includes entrées like Parmesan–pesto chicken, baked salmon stuffed with crab, and pork tenderloin with wild-berry sauce. ✉ *189 S. Vernal Ave., Vernal.,* ☎ *435/789–2289. MC, V.*

$–$$ ✕ **Skillet and Car 19 Restaurant.** "The Skillet", as it's locally known, serves big breakfasts, and mostly burgers at lunchtime. For dinner there are steaks, chicken, crispy fried catfish, and the like. ✉ *363 W. Main St., Vernal,* ☎ *435/789–3641. D, MC, V.*

$$$$ ★ **Falcon's Ledge Lodge.** Falconry, fly-fishing, and horseback riding are all part of the experience at this lodge in a pristine canyon. Vaulted ceilings, sweeping views, and Jacuzzi tubs in most guest rooms make it a luxurious getaway. Gourmet dinner specialties include fresh trout, "olive lover's" steak, and bread baked fresh daily. ✉ *Stillwater Canyon, Box 67, Altamont 84001,* ☎ *435/454–3737,* FAX *435/454–3392. 9 rooms. AE, MC, V.*

$$–$$$ **Flaming Gorge Lodge.** With a good restaurant, boat rentals, and guided fishing service, this is the best lodging choice near Flaming Gorge. ✉ *Greendale, U.S. 191, Dutch John 84023,* ☎ *435/889–3773,* FAX *435/889–3788. 45 rooms. Restaurant. AE, D, MC, V.*

$–$$ **Best Western Antlers Motel.** Locals favor this clean, comfortable motel with a wading pool and playground. ✉ *423 W. Main St., Vernal 84078,* ☎ *435/789–1202. 43 rooms. Restaurant, pool. AE, D, DC, MC, V.*

WYOMING

By Geoffrey O'Gara

Updated by Candy Moulton

Capital	Cheyenne
Population	481,000
Motto	Equal Rights
State Bird	Meadowlark
State Flower	Indian paintbrush
Postal Abbreviation	WY

Statewide Visitor Information

Wyoming Division of Tourism (✉ I–25 at College Dr., Cheyenne 82002, ☎ 307/777–7777 or 800/225–5996 for recorded ski reports). **Information centers** in Cheyenne, Evanston, Jackson, and Sheridan are open year-round; those in Pine Bluffs, Chugwater, and near Laramie close in winter.

Scenic Drives

North of Cody and east of Yellowstone is the 60-mi **Beartooth Highway,** U.S. 212. Switchbacking across Beartooth Pass at 10,947 ft, it's the state's highest highway and open only in summer. Add a few miles to your drive and take the **Chief Joseph Scenic Highway** (Route 296, south from Beartooth Highway toward Cody) to see the gorge carved by the Clarks Fork of the Yellowstone River. There is more scenery than service on these roads, so gas up in Cody or at the northeastern end of the route, in Red Lodge or in Cooke City, Montana.

National and State Parks

National Parks

Yellowstone National Park (☞ Exploring Yellowstone, Grand Teton, Jackson, and Cody, *below*) is widely considered the crown jewel of the national park system. **Grand Teton National Park** (☞ Exploring Yellowstone, Grand Teton, Jackson, and Cody, *below*) encompasses the jagged Teton Range, the Snake River, and, in between, a string of pristine lakes. **Devils Tower National Monument** (☞ Elsewhere in Wyoming, *below*) contains a site that is sacred to Native Americans.

State Parks

Wyoming's state parks are listed on the Division of Tourism's state road map. Historic sites include **South Pass City** (✉ 125 South Pass Main, ☎ 307/332–3684), a history-rich gold camp near the Oregon Trail, and **Fort Bridger State Historic Site** (✉ Fort Bridger, ☎ 307/782–3842), the pioneer trading post started by Jim Bridger and later used by the military. **Hot Springs State Park** (☎ 307/864–2176), in Thermopolis on U.S. 20, has the world's largest hot spring.

YELLOWSTONE, GRAND TETON, JACKSON, AND CODY

When John Colter's descriptions of **Yellowstone** were reported in St. Louis newspapers in 1810, most readers dismissed them as tall tales. Colter had left the Lewis and Clark expedition to trap and explore in a region virtually unknown to whites, and his reports of giant elk roaming among fuming mud pots, waterfalls, and geysers in a wilderness of evergreens and towering peaks were just too far-fetched to be taken seriously. Sixty years and several expeditions later, however, the nation

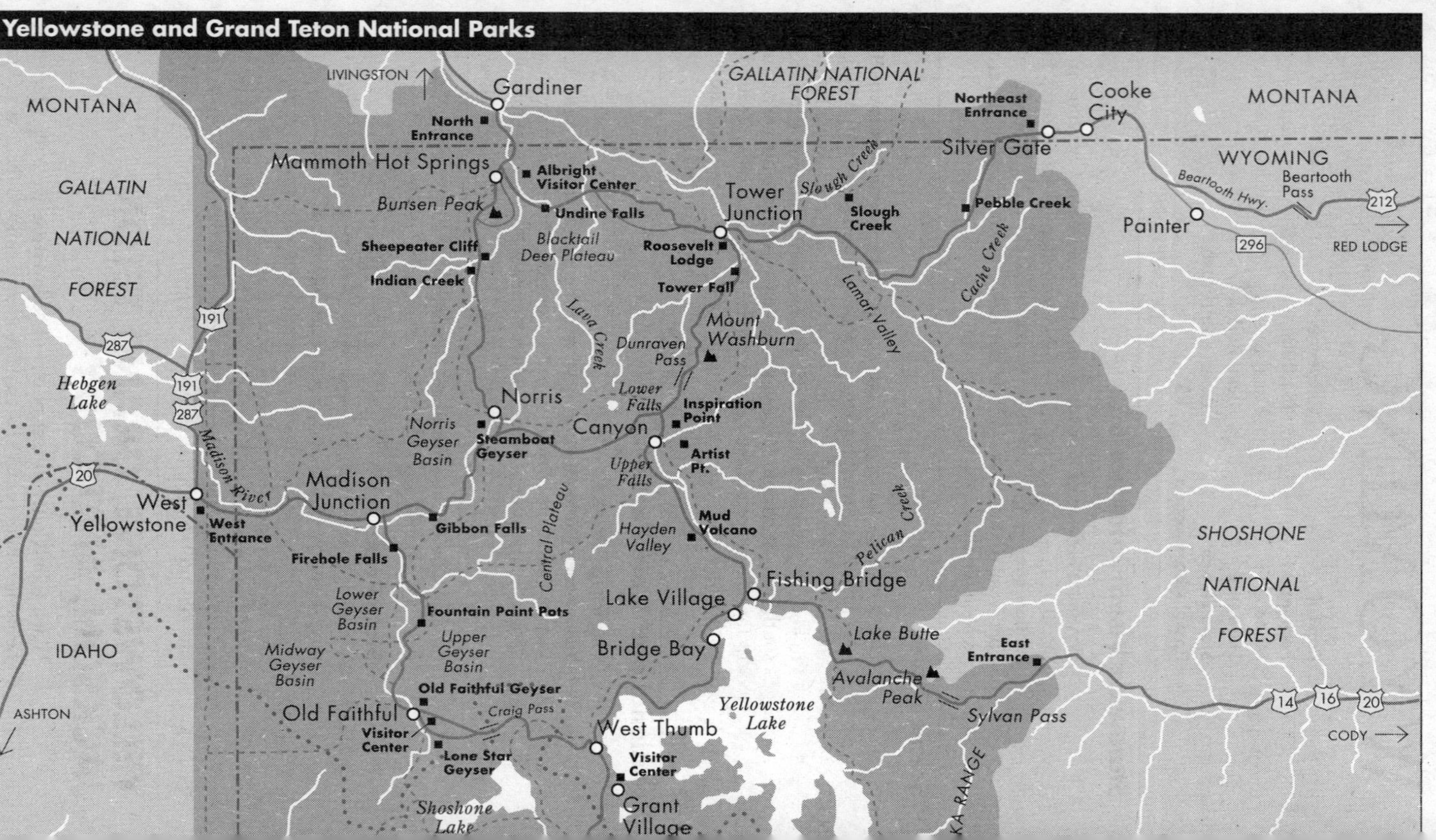
Yellowstone and Grand Teton National Parks
LIVINGSTON
Gardiner
North Entrance
GALLATIN NATIONAL FOREST
Northeast Entrance
Cooke City
MONTANA
MONTANA
Mammoth Hot Springs
Albright Visitor Center
Silver Gate
WYOMING
Beartooth Pass
Beartooth Hwy.
212
GALLATIN
Bunsen Peak
Undine Falls
Tower Junction
Slough Creek
Slough Creek
Pebble Creek
Painter
296
RED LODGE
NATIONAL
Sheepeater Cliff
Blacktail Deer Plateau
Roosevelt Lodge
Indian Creek
Tower Fall
Cache Creek
Lamar Valley
FOREST
191
287
Lava Creek
Mount Washburn
Dunraven Pass
Hebgen Lake
191
287
Norris
Lower Falls
Inspiration Point
Norris Geyser Basin
Steamboat Geyser
Canyon
Artist Pt.
Madison River
Upper Falls
20
West Yellowstone
Madison Junction
West Entrance
Gibbon Falls
Central Plateau
Hayden Valley
Mud Volcano
Pelican Creek
SHOSHONE
Firehole Falls
Fishing Bridge
NATIONAL
Lower Geyser Basin
Fountain Paint Pots
Lake Village
Upper Geyser Basin
Lake Butte
FOREST
IDAHO
Midway Geyser Basin
Bridge Bay
East Entrance
Avalanche Peak
Old Faithful Geyser
14
16
20
ASHTON
Old Faithful
Craig Pass
Yellowstone Lake
Sylvan Pass
CODY
Visitor Center
West Thumb
Lone Star Geyser
Visitor Center
Shoshone Lake
Grant Village
KA RANGE

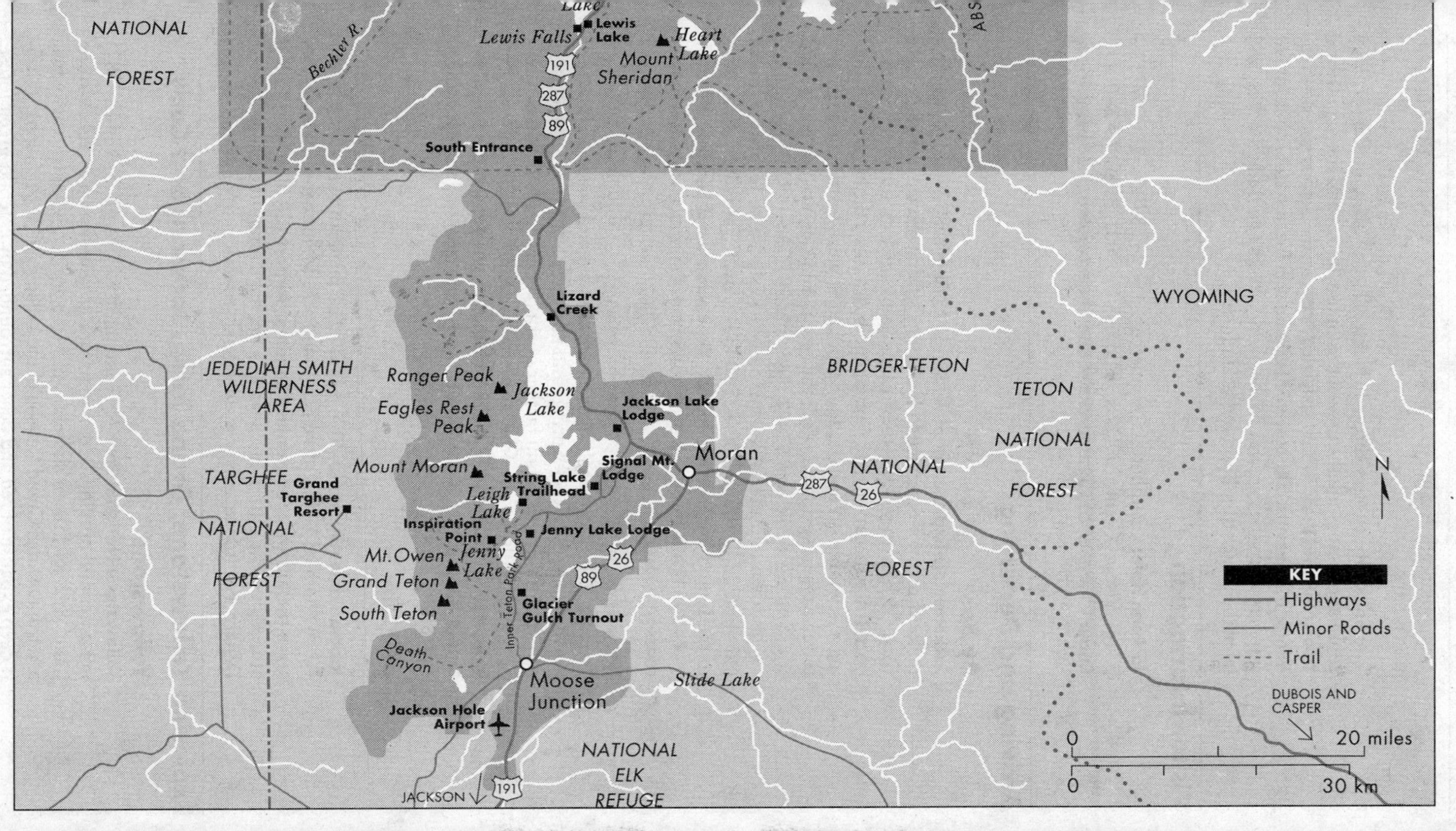
NATIONAL FOREST
Lewis Falls
Lewis Lake
Heart Lake
Mount Sheridan
Bechler R.
South Entrance
WYOMING
Lizard Creek
JEDEDIAH SMITH WILDERNESS AREA
Ranger Peak
Jackson Lake
Eagles Rest Peak
Jackson Lake Lodge
BRIDGER-TETON NATIONAL FOREST
TETON NATIONAL FOREST
Moran
Signal Mt. Lodge
Mount Moran
String Lake Trailhead
TARGHEE NATIONAL FOREST
Grand Targhee Resort
Leigh Lake
Inspiration Point
Jenny Lake Lodge
Mt. Owen
Jenny Lake
Grand Teton
South Teton
Inner Teton Park Road
Glacier Gulch Turnout
Death Canyon
Moose Junction
Slide Lake
Jackson Hole Airport
NATIONAL ELK REFUGE
JACKSON
191
287
89
26
N
KEY
Highways
Minor Roads
Trail
DUBOIS AND CASPER
0
20 miles
0
30 km

was convinced, and in 1872 Yellowstone became the country's first national park.

The Snake River runs through Jackson Hole Valley, making its way south and west along the foot of the Grand Tetons and through **Grand Teton National Park,** which is nestled between the Tetons and the Gros Ventre Mountains. The town of **Jackson** was first a rendezvous for fur trappers, then the gateway to the nearby parks and dude ranches, and later the center of a booming ski industry.

Visitor Information

Jackson Hole: Chamber of Commerce (✉ Box E, 83001, ☎ 307/733–3316); Visitors Council (✉ Box 982, Dept. 8, 83001, ☎ 800/782–0011). **Cody:** Chamber of Commerce (✉ 836 Sheridan Ave., 82414, ☎ 307/587–2297).

Arriving and Departing

By Bus

Jackson Hole Express (☎ 307/733–1719 or 800/652–9510) operates the only direct bus service to Jackson, a shuttle service from Salt Lake City, Utah, with pickups there at the Salt Lake City International Airport, Amtrak station, and Greyhound bus station. Buses run daily during the winter ski season, four times each week in the summer, and fewer days in spring and fall; the cost is $45 one-way, or $79 round trip. During ski season **START** buses (☎ 307/733–4521) operate between town and the Jackson Hole Ski Resort. The **Targhee Express** (☎ 307/733–3101 or 800/827–4433) crosses Teton Pass on its way to the Grand Targhee Ski Resort. **TW Recreational Services** (☎ 307/344–7901) has bus tours of Yellowstone in summer and snow-coach tours in winter.

By Car

To reach Yellowstone through the Teton Valley and Jackson Hole, turn north off I–80 at Rock Springs and take U.S. 191 the 177 mi to Jackson; Yellowstone is 60 mi farther north on U.S. 191/89. You can also approach Yellowstone from the east through Cody, 52 mi from Yellowstone on U.S. 14/16/20; for north and west entrances *see* Montana. Grand Teton National Park is 10 mi north of Jackson on U.S. 191/89.

By Plane

Several airlines have daily service from Denver and Salt Lake City into **Jackson Hole Airport** (☎ 307/733–7682), 9 mi north of town and about 40 mi south of Yellowstone National Park. Major car-rental agencies serve the airport. **Yellowstone Regional Airport** (☎ 307/587–5096), at Cody on the park's east side, is served by commuter airlines out of Denver. For information on additional services, *see* Montana.

Exploring Yellowstone, Grand Teton, Jackson, and Cody

Yellowstone

Yellowstone National Park (✉ Mammoth 82190, ☎ 307/344–7381) preserves and provides access to natural treasures such as **Yellowstone Lake**, with its 110-mi shoreline and lake cruises, wildlife, waterfowl, and trout fishing; **Grand Canyon of the Yellowstone**, a 24 mi-long, 1,200-ft deep expanse of red and ocher surrounded by emerald-green forest; the multicolored, steaming **Mammoth Hot Springs**; and 900 mi of horse trails, 1,000 mi of hiking trails, and 370 mi of public roads. Visitor centers throughout the park are the departure points for guided hikes and are the sites of evening talks and campfire programs (check the park newsletter *Discover Yellowstone* for details). Park service literature and warnings about interaction with the wildlife—grizzly bears and bison, especially—should be taken seriously.

Roads from all five Yellowstone entrances eventually join the figure-8 that is **Grand Loop Road,** which makes many areas accessible by vehicle. If you enter from the south, start in the Old Faithful area. The best-known geyser is, of course, **Old Faithful,** the crowd-pleaser that erupts every hour or so. Wooden walkways wind by other geysers, mud pots, and colorful springs and along nearby Firehole River. Stay on the walkways—geysers can be dangerous. Elk and bison frequent this area. Near the west park entrance is **Norris Geyser Basin;** among its hundreds of springs and geysers is the unpredictable Steamboat Geyser, which shoots water more than 300 ft into the air.

A short hike from **Canyon,** at the intersection of the loops, are Inspiration, Grandview, and Lookout points, where the vistas confirm Colter's accounts. The **North Rim Trail** leads to views of the 308-ft Upper Falls and 109-ft Lower Falls. In the northeast corner of the park is beautiful **Lamar Valley,** which attracts bison in the summer.

Grand Teton

Grand Teton National Park (✉ Moose 83012, ☎ 307/739–3300 or 307/739–3399) was established in 1929 and expanded to its present size when the Rockefeller family donated land it owned in Jackson Hole. The park is south of Yellowstone and linked to it by the John D. Rockefeller Memorial Parkway (U.S. 89).

Technical climbers rope up and drag themselves to the 13,770-ft summit of the **Grand,** but day hikers find many rewards, too—from a journey up Cascade Canyon to a lakeshore ramble. Jenny, Leigh, and Jackson lakes, strung along the base of the Tetons, attract fishers and canoeists; windsurfers and sailors favor Jackson Lake. The **Snake River** is great for rafting, with smooth and fast-moving water and occasional sightings of moose or bison. Willow Flats and Oxbow Bend are excellent places to see waterfowl, and Signal Mountain Road affords a top-of-the-park view of the Tetons.

Jackson

With its raised wooden sidewalks and old-fashioned storefronts, the town of **Jackson** may look like a western-movie set, but it's the real thing. Residents hotly debate whether and how much to control development, with most locals determined to avoid what they call Aspenization. For the time being the town remains compact and folksy, a place where genuine cowboys rub shoulders with the store-bought variety and where the antler-arched square, whoop-it-up nightlife, and surrounding wilderness are pretty much intact.

Jackson is walk-around size and easy to relax in after white-water rafting, hiking, or skiing. Whether your idea of relaxation is enjoying an epicurean meal, lolling in a hot tub, or two-stepping at the **Cowboy Bar** (✉ 25 N. Cache Dr., ☎ 307/733–2207), Jackson fills the bill.

Granite Hot Springs, south of Jackson off U.S. 191 and 10 mi into Bridger–Teton National Forest along a gravel road, has a creekside campground, a hot-springs pool, hiking trails, and scenery. Three miles north of Jackson at the **National Elk Refuge** (✉ Elk Refuge Visitor's Center, 2820 Rungius Rd., Jackson 83001, ☎ 307/733–3534) operates horse-drawn sleigh trips through the herd of more than 7,000 elk in their winter preserve. Trips run from December 15 through March; the cost is $8 per person.

Cody

Most people use Cody as a way station en route to or from Yellowstone's east entrance, but the town's museum is a must-see for anyone interested in the history of the American West. The **Buffalo Bill Historical Center** (✉ 720 Sheridan Ave., ☎ 307/587–4771) has a **Plains Indian Museum, the Cody Firearms Museum,** the **Buffalo Bill Museum,** and the **Whitney Gallery of Western Art.**

Dining and Lodging

You can make reservations for a stay in Jackson or Jackson Hole Ski Resort through **Central Reservations** (☎ 800/443–6931). **Bed & Breakfast Rocky Mountains** (✉ 906 S. Pearl St., Denver, CO 80209, ☎ 303/744–8415) handles B&Bs throughout the region. **Jackson Hole Bed & Breakfast Association** can make reservations at any of the 15 bed-and-breakfasts in the area (✉ Box 6396, Jackson 83002, ☎ 800/542–2632). For information about the many guest ranches between Cody and Yellowstone, contact the **East Yellowstone Valley Lodges** (✉ 1231 Yellowstone Hwy., Cody 82414, ☎ 307/587–9595).

For price ranges *see* Charts 1 (A) and 2 (A) *in* On the Road with Fodor's.

Grand Teton

Grand Teton Lodge Company operates three of the park's lodges—Jackson Lake, Jenny Lake, and Colter Bay Village (☞ *below*). ✉ *Box 240, Moran 83013,* ☎ *307/543–3100,* FAX *307/543–3143. AE, DC, MC, V.*

$$$$ ★ ✕🏨 **Jenny Lake Lodge.** Set amid pines and a wildflower meadow, this lodge has cabins and rooms that are rustic yet luxurious, with sturdy pine beds covered with handmade quilts and electric blankets. In the restaurant you can sample Rocky Mountain cuisine such as roast prime rib of buffalo or breast of pheasant. ✉ *Jenny Lake Rd. 37 cabins. Restaurant, bar. AP. Closed mid-Oct.–late May.*

$$–$$$$ ✕🏨 **Jackson Lake Lodge.** This brown stone edifice has huge windows overlooking Willow Flats. Guest rooms in the adjacent buildings are larger and more attractive than those in the main lodge. The Mural Room's menu sometimes features local game such as venison or antelope. The lodge has the park's only swimming pool. ✉ *Off U.S. 89 north of Jackson Lake Junction. 385 rooms. 2 restaurants, pool. Closed late-Oct.–early May.*

$$–$$$ ★ ✕🏨 **Signal Mountain Lodge.** On the shore of Jackson Lake, the lodge's main building is made of volcanic stone and pine shingle; inside is a cozy lounge with a fireplace, a piano, and Adirondack furniture. Guest rooms are in a separate cluster of cabinlike units, some with kitchenettes. The Aspens restaurant serves such dishes as shrimp linguine and medallions of elk. ✉ *Inner Teton Park Rd., Moran 83013,* ☎ *307/543–2831.* FAX *307/543–2569. 79 rooms. Restaurant. AE, DC, MC, V. Closed mid-Oct.–early May.*

$–$$ ✕🏨 **Colter Bay Village.** There are log cabins and less expensive tent cabins (canvas-covered wood frames) at this resort near the shore of Jackson Lake. The Chuckwagon restaurant serves lasagna, trout, and barbecued spareribs. ✉ *Off U.S. 89. 250 cabins, 66 tent cabins, 113 RV spaces. 2 restaurants. Closed late Sept.–early June.*

Jackson

$$ ★ ✕ **Nani's.** The ever-changing menu at this cozy Italian restaurant may include braised veal shanks with saffron risotto and other regional dishes. ✉ *240 N. Glenwood St.,* ☎ *307/733–3888. DC, MC, V.*

$$ ★ ✕ **Sweetwater Restaurant.** Mediterranean meals are served in a log-cabin atmosphere. Start with hummus or a Montrachet tart (a goat-cheese and caramelized-onion pastry); then go on to lamb dishes,

Chicken Bombay, or fresh fish. ✉ *King and Pearl Sts.,* ☎ *307/733–3553. AE, D, MC, V, DC.*

$ ✕ **The Bunnery.** This pine-paneled whole-grain bakery and restaurant serves irresistible breakfasts, from omelets with blue cheese and sautéed spinach to home-baked pastries. Sandwiches, burgers, and Mexican dishes are served for lunch and dinner. ✉ *130 N. Cache St.,* ☎ *307/733–5474. Reservations not accepted. MC, V.*

$$–$$$ ★ ✕🏨 **Spring Creek Ranch.** You can spend all day gazing at the Tetons from this luxury resort atop Gros Ventre Butte, near Jackson. Other activities include tennis, horseback riding, cross-country skiing, and sleigh rides. There are 36 hotel rooms, plus a changing mix of studios, suites, and condos with lofts and kitchenettes. Native American art decorates the fine Granary restaurant, where reservations are essential. ✉ *1800 Spirit Dance Rd., 83001,* ☎ *307/733–8833 or 800/443–6139,* FAX *307/733–1524. 117 units. Restaurant, pool. AE, D, DC, MC, V.*

$$$ 🏨 **Cowboy Village Resort.** Each of the pine-log cabins in this quiet complex has bunk beds and a kitchenette, making it a good choice for families and groups who don't mind close quarters. ✉ *120 S. Flat Creek Dr., 83001,* ☎ *307/733–3121,* FAX *307/739–1955. 82 cabins. AE, D, MC, V.*

$$–$$$ 🏨 **Painted Porch Bed & Breakfast.** This 1901 farmhouse 8 mi north of Jackson has antiques-filled rooms, some with Japanese soaking tubs. ✉ *Teton Village Rd., Box 3965, 83001,* ☎ *307/733–1981. 4 rooms. Full breakfast. MC, V.*

MOTELS

🏨 **Days Inn** (✉ 350 S. Hwy. 89, Jackson 83001, ☎ 307/739–9010, FAX 307/733–0044), 91 rooms, CP; *$$$.* 🏨 **Virginian Motel** (✉ 750 W. Broadway, Jackson 83001, ☎ 307/733–2792, FAX 307/733–4063), 170 rooms, restaurant, pool; *$$–$$$.* 🏨 **Antler Motel** (✉ 43 W. Pearl St., Jackson 83001, ☎ 307/733–2535 or 800/522–2406, FAX 307/733–4158). 107 rooms, exercise room; *$–$$.* 🏨 **Motel 6** (✉ 600 S. Highway 89, Jackson 83001, ☎ 307/733–1620, FAX 307/734–9175), 155 rooms, pool; *$.*

Teton Village

$$–$$$ ★ ✕ **Mangy Moose.** Folks pour in off the ski slopes for a lot of food and talk at this two-level restaurant plus bar with an outdoor deck. The place is full of antiques, including a biplane suspended from the ceiling. There's a high noise level but decent food at fair prices. ✉ *South end of Teton Village,* ☎ *307/733–4913. AE, MC, V.*

$$$–$$$$ ★ ✕🏨 **Alpenhof.** This European-style hotel is close to Jackson Hole Ski Area's lifts. The restaurant, which serves veal, wild game, and seafood, is small, quiet, and comfortable. ✉ *Teton Village Rd., Box 288, Teton Village, 83025,* ☎ *307/733–3242,* FAX *307/739–1516. 43 rooms. 2 restaurants, pool. AE, D, MC, DC, V.*

Yellowstone

The lodgings and restaurants within Yellowstone are operated by **AmFac Parks and Resorts.** There are gas stations, snack bars, and other services throughout the park. ✉ *Yellowstone National Park, 82190,* ☎ *307/344–7901,* FAX *307/344–2456. AE, D, DC, MC, V.*

$–$$$$ ★ ✕🏨 **Old Faithful Inn.** You can loll in front of the lobby's immense stone fireplace and look up six stories at wood balconies that seem to disappear into the night sky. Guest rooms are a mixed bag: In some you might find brass beds and Victorian cherry-wood furnishings; others have inexpensive motel-style furniture. The dining room (☎ 307/344–7901, ext. 4999), a huge hall centered on a fireplace of volcanic stone, serves shrimp scampi and other delights; dinner reservations are essential. ✉ *First left turn off Old Faithful Bypass Rd., Old Faithful. 325 rooms, 248 with bath. Restaurant. Closed late-Oct.–early May.*

$-$$$ ★ ✕☎ **Lake Yellowstone Hotel.** The park's oldest (late 1800s) and most elegant resort, at the north end of the lake, has a pale-yellow neoclassical facade. The lobby's tall windows overlook the water, and some rooms have brass beds and vintage fixtures. Cabins are much more rustic. The restaurant (☎ 307/242–3701) serves Thai curried shrimp, fettuccine with smoked salmon and snow peas, and other eclectic fare; reservations are essential. ✉ *Lake Village Rd., Lake Village. 194 rooms, 110 cabins. Restaurant. Closed late Sept.–mid-May.*

$-$$ ✕☎ **Old Faithful Snow Lodge.** This compact motel tucked off to one side in the Old Faithful complex is drab looking, but it's one of the only two park lodgings open in winter. The cozy lobby is warmed by a woodstove, and the small restaurant serves family fare. ✉ *Off Old Faithful Bypass Rd., next to visitor center, Old Faithful. 100 rooms. Restaurant. Closed mid-Oct.–mid-Dec., mid-Mar.–mid-May.*

$ ✕☎ **Mammoth Hot Springs Hotel.** The smallish cabins here are arranged around "auto courts"; four have hot tubs. The dining room (☎ 307/344–7901) serves regional American fare, including prime rib and chicken with Brie and raspberry sauce. The cafeteria-style Terrace Grill, across from the lodge, has large windows that take in the scenic outdoors. Horseback riding can be arranged. ✉ *North entrance to park, Mammoth. 126 cabins, 96 hotel rooms. 2 restaurants. Closed mid-Sept.–mid-Dec., early Mar.–late May.*

$ ★ ✕☎ **Roosevelt Lodge.** Near the Lamar Valley in the park's northeast corner, this simple, homey log lodge is more ranch house than resort. The dining room serves barbecued ribs, Roosevelt beans, and other western fare. Accommodations are in nearby cabins. ✉ *Tower–Roosevelt Junction on Grand Loop Rd., Tower-Roosevelt. 86 cabins, 17 with bath. Restaurant. Closed early Sept.–early June.*

Cody

$$-$$$ ✕ **Proud Cut Saloon.** Looking straight out of the Old West, with game mounts and vintage photos, this popular downtown eatery serves what it bills as "kick-ass cowboy cuisine": steak, prime rib, fish, and chicken. ✉ *1227 Sheridan Ave.,* ☎ *307/527–6905. AE, D, DC, MC, V.*

$$-$$$ ✕☎ **Irma Hotel.** An ornate cherry-wood bar is one of the highlights of this hostelry. Some rooms have a turn-of-the-century western style. ✉ *1192 Sheridan Ave., 82414,* ☎ FAX *307/587–4221. 40 rooms. Restaurant. AE, D, DC, MC, V.*

$$ ☎ **Pahaska Teepee Resort.** Buffalo Bill's original getaway in the high country is 2 mi east of Yellowstone's East Entrance. Horseback riding and snowmobiling are available on the grounds. ✉ *183 Yellowstone Hwy., 82414,* ☎ *307/527–7701 or 800/628–7791,* FAX *307/527–4019. 52 cabins. Restaurant. MC, V.*

Campgrounds

In Grand Teton the **National Park Service** (✉ Drawer 170, Moose 83012, ☎ 307/739–3300) has five campgrounds, none with RV hookups, but all with fire grates and rest rooms. The privately run **Colter Bay Trailer Village** (✉ Grand Teton Lodge Co., Box 240, Moran 83013, ☎ 307/543–3100) has 113 full RV hookups.

Among the 11 **Yellowstone National Park** (☎ 307/344–7381) campsite areas and one RV park, Bridge Bay (420 sites and a marina) is the largest, and Slough Creek (32 tent-trailer sites) is the smallest. There are also 300 backcountry campsites, for which you need a permit from park rangers.

Outdoor Activities and Sports

The **Jackson Hole Chamber of Commerce** (☞ Visitor Information, *above*) has lists of outfitters and news about winter and summer activities. For sports in the parks—including skiing, horseback riding, hiking, and climbing—contact the visitor centers.

Boating

You can rent boats on Jackson Lake through **Colter Bay Marina** (☎ 307/543–3100) or **Signal Mountain Marina** (☎ 307/543–2831).

Climbing

Two options for climbers are **Jackson Hole Mountain Guides** (☎ 307/733–4979) and **Exum Mountain Guides** (☎ 307/733–2297).

Fishing

Blue-ribbon trout streams thread through northwestern Wyoming, and Jackson Lake has set records for Mackinaw trout. The license for fishing in Yellowstone costs $10 for seven days or $20 for the season; in Grand Teton they cost $6 per day. You can buy licenses at entrance gates or park offices in both parks. For fishing elsewhere, buy licenses at sporting goods or general merchandise stores, or contact **Wyoming Game and Fish** (✉ 5400 Bishop Blvd., Cheyenne 82002, ☎ 307/777–4600). Fly shops in Jackson include **Jack Dennis Sporting Goods** (✉ 50 E. Broadway, ☎ 307/733–3270) and **High Country Flies** (✉ 165 N. Center St., ☎ 307/733–7210).

Golf

Jackson Hole Golf and Tennis Club (✉ Off U.S. 89, 8 mi north of Jackson, ☎ 307/733–3111) and **Teton Pines Golf Club** (✉ 3450 N. Clubhouse Dr., ☎ 307/733–1733) have 18 holes.

Rafting and Canoeing

Peaceful, scenic floats on the Upper Snake include the beautiful Oxbow, which you can navigate by canoe or kayak. Guided rafting trips are available from **Barker-Ewing Scenic Float Trips** (✉ Moose, ☎ 307/733–1000 or 800/365–1800), **Snake River Kayak & Canoe School** (✉ Jackson, ☎ 307/733–3127 or 800/824–5375), and **Triangle X** (✉ Moose, ☎ 307/733–5500). For guided white-water trips in Snake River Canyon, try **Dave Hansen Whitewater** (✉ Jackson, ☎ 307/733–6295), **Barker-Ewing Float Trips** (✉ Jackson, ☎ 800/448–4202), or **Lewis & Clark Expeditions** (✉ Jackson, ☎ 307/733–4022 or 800/824–5375). Rent canoes and kayaks in Jackson from **Leisure Sports** (✉ 1075 S. U.S. 89, ☎ 307/733–3040) and **Teton Aquatics** (✉ 155 W. Gill St., ☎ 307/733–3127).

Ski Areas

Cross-Country

Cross-country skiing and snowshoeing are permitted in parts of both Yellowstone and Grand Teton national parks and surrounding forests. **Cowboy Village Resort at Togwotee** (✉ Box 91, Moran 83013, ☎ 307/543–2847), at Togwotee Pass within Bridger–Teton and Shoshone national forests (U.S. 26/287), operates 13½ mi of trails. **Spring Creek Ranch Resort** (✉ 1800 Spirit Dance Rd., Box 3154, 83001, ☎ 307/733–8833 or 800/443–6139) has 8 mi of trails. **Jackson Hole Nordic Center** (✉ Box 290, Teton Village 83025, ☎ 307/733–2292) has 12 mi of trails.

Downhill

Grand Targhee Ski Resort (✉ Box SKI, Alta 83422, ☎ 307/353–2300 or 800/827–4433), 64 runs, 3 lifts, 1 rope tow, 2,200-ft vertical drop. **Jackson Hole Mountain Ski Resort** (✉ Box 290, Teton Village 83025, ☎ 307/733–2292 or 800/443–6931), 58 runs, 9 lifts including a high-speed quad, 4,139-ft drop (the longest of any U.S. ski area), some snowmaking. **Snow King** (✉ Box SKI, Jackson 83001, ☎ 307/733–5200 or 800/522–5464), 400 acres of slopes, 3 lifts, 1,571-ft drop.

Shopping

Shopping in Jackson is centered on the town square. Western wear and outdoor clothing, some of it locally made, dominate in such stores as **Cowboy Couture** (✉ 185 West Broadway, ☎ 307/734–8778), **Jackson Hole Clothiers** (✉ 45 E. Deloney St., ☎ 307/733–7211), and **Hide Out Leather** (✉ 40 Center St., ☎ 307/733–2422). Specialists in the latest outdoor equipment include **Teton Mountaineering** (✉ 170 N. Cache St., ☎ 307/733–3595) and **Skinny Skis** (✉ 65 W. Deloney St., ☎ 307/733–6094). **Trailside Gallery** (✉ 105 N. Center St., ☎ 307/733–3186) features western jewelry and art. For photographic art try **Tom Mangelsen Images of Nature Gallery** (✉ 170 N. Cache St., ☎ 307/733–9752).

ELSEWHERE IN WYOMING

Cheyenne

Visitor Information

Cheyenne: Chamber of Commerce (✉ Box 1147, 82003, ☎ 307/638–3388, FAX 307/778–1450).

Arriving and Departing

Both I–80 and I–25 pass through Cheyenne. Commuter airlines fly between Denver and **Cheyenne Municipal Airport** (☎ 307/634–7071). **Greyhound** (☎ 800/231–2222) provides bus service.

What to See and Do

The **Frontier Days** rodeo (☎ 307/778–7222 or 800/227–6336), held the last week of July, is a reminder that the state's capital city was once nicknamed Hell on Wheels. Outside the gold-domed **state capitol** is a statue of Esther Hobart Morris, who helped gain equal rights for Wyoming women, who got the vote in 1869, 51 years before the rest of the nation. Morris was the first woman to hold U.S. public office and was appointed a justice of the peace in 1870. (In 1924 Nellie Tayloe Ross became the nation's first elected female governor.)

The **Old West Museum** (✉ Frontier Park, 4610 N. Carey Ave., ☎ 307/778–7290 or 800/778–7290; $4) has 125 carriages among its vast collection of westernabilia. During Frontier Days, top Western wildlife and landscape artists from around the country exhibit their work here. Guided tours are tailored for children.

Dining and Lodging

$$$–$$$$ **Hitching Post Inn.** State legislators frequent this hotel near the capitol. The Hitch, as locals call it, books country-western performers in its lounge. *✉ 1700 W. Lincolnway, ☎ 307/638–3301 or 800/528–1234, FAX 307/638–3301. 5 restaurants, pools, health club. 166 rooms. AE, D, DC, MC, V.*

$$$ **Little America Hotel and Resort.** At the intersection of I–80 and I–25, the resort has an executive 9-hole golf course. The large pastel rooms have double vanities and comfy beds with plenty of pillows. *✉ 2800 W. Lincolnway, 82001, ☎ 307/775–8400 or 800/445–6945, FAX 307/775–8425. 188 rooms. Restaurant. AE, D, DC, MC, V.*

$$ **Rainsford Inn.** The inn is on historic Cattleman's Row, in the heart of downtown Cheyenne; its masculine "Cattle Baron Corner" overlooks 17th Street, where Cheyenne's cattle barons lived in the late 1800s. All rooms have whirlpool tubs, and one has a gas fireplace. *✉ 219 E. 18th St., ☎ 307/638–2337, FAX 307/634–4506. 7 suites, 2 with bath. Full breakfast. AE, D, DC, MC, V.*

Devils Tower Area

Arriving and Departing

Devils Tower is 6 mi off U.S. 15 on Route 24.

What to See and Do

Native American legend has it that the corrugated **Devils Tower** was formed when a tree stump turned into granite and grew taller to protect some stranded children from a clawing bear. Geologists say that the rock tower, rising 1,280 ft above the Belle Fourche River, is the core of a defunct volcano. It was a tourist magnet long before a spaceship landed on top of it in the movie *Close Encounters of the Third Kind,* and the tower is still a significant site for Native Americans. During the month of July a voluntary ban on rock climbing gives Native Americans an opportunity to conduct spiritual activities here. For information contact **Devils Tower National Monument** (✉ Devils Tower 82714, ☎ 307/467–5383).

Dining and Lodging

$–$$ ✕ **Log Cabin Café.** Locals crowd this small log-cabin restaurant full of country crafts, for burgers, steaks, and seafood. *✉ E. Hwy. 14, ☎ 307/283–3393. MC, V.*

$ ✕ **Country Cottage.** This one-stop shop sells gifts, flowers, and simple daytime meals such as submarine sandwiches. *✉ 423 Cleveland St., Sundance, ☎ 307/283–2450. MC, V. No dinner.*

$$–$$$ 🏨 **Best Western Inn at Sundance.** Built in 1997, this place has spacious, spanking-new rooms with dark-green carpet and plum-color drapes. Guests enjoy the indoor pool and hot tub. *✉ 2700 E. Cleveland St., Box 927, Sundance 82729, ☎ 307/283–2800 or 800/238–0965, FAX 307/283–2727. 44 rooms. Pool. CP. AE, D, DC, MC, V.*

$–$$$ 🏨 **Bear Lodge Motel.** This downtown motel has a cozy lobby with a stone fireplace and wildlife mounts on the walls. There's also an indoor hot tub. *✉ 218 Cleveland St., ☎ 307/283–1611, FAX 307/283–2537. 33 rooms. AE, D, DC, MC, V.*

Saratoga

Arriving and Departing

Saratoga is in south-central Wyoming, 20 mi south of I–80. It's also accessible via Wyoming 130 (the Snowy Range Road) in summer only, or via Wyoming 230 year-round.

Saratoga Platte Valley Chamber of Commerce (✉ Box 1095, 82331, ☎ 307/326–8855).

What to See and Do

Recreational opportunities abound in the **Medicine Bow National Forest;** and the North Platte and Encampment rivers are known for excellent white-water floating, kayaking, rafting, and fishing. The **Grand Encampment Museum** (✉ Box 43, Encampment 82325, ☎ 307/327–5308), 18 mi south of Saratoga, has a complete historic town and a modern interpretive center. For information on hunting and dude-ranch opportunities, contact the **Saratoga Platte Valley Chamber of Commerce** (✉ Box 1095, 82331, ☎ 307/326–8855).

Dining and Lodging

$ ✕🏨 **Hotel Wolf.** This Victorian downtown hotel on the National Register of Historic Places has smallish rooms on the second and third floors (there are no elevators). The restaurant, with antique oak tables, crystal chandeliers, and lacy drapes, serves the best prime rib and steak in town, and the Wolf Burger is hard to beat. *✉ 101 E. Bridge St., 82331, ☎ 307/326–5525. 7 rooms. Restaurant. AE, DC, MC, V.*

$$$$ **Saratoga Inn.** Pole-frame furniture gives a western flair to southern Wyoming's most elegant inn. The North Platte River runs through the inn's property, so fishing is literally right out the back door. In addition, there are tennis courts and a 9-hole golf course, a mineral hot springs nearby, and activities like horseback riding and, in winter, skiing. The inn brews all its own beers, which guests can sample during the daily social hour. ✉ *E. Pic-Pike Rd., Box 869, 82331,* ☎ *307/326–5261. 50 rooms. FAP. Restaurant, pool, golf, tennis. AE, DC, MC, V. Closed Apr. and Nov.*

Casper

Visitor Information

Casper Chamber of Commerce (✉ 500 N. Center St., 82601, ☎ 307/234–5311 or 800/852–1889.

Arriving and Departing

Commuter airlines, including United Express (☎ 800/241–6522) and Delta/Skywest (☎ 800/221–1212), fly from Denver and Salt Lake City to **Natrona County International Airport. Powder River Transportation** (☎ 800/237–7211) buses connect with national carriers. Casper is in central Wyoming, 140 mi south of Sheridan and 178 mi north of Cheyenne via I–25.

What to See and Do

Oil and gas exploration have contributed to Casper's growth as the state's largest city. Five major emigrant trails passed near or through Casper between 1843 and 1870, including the Oregon, California, and Mormon trails, which crossed the North Platte River near Casper. You can learn about these emigrant trails and central Wyoming's military history at **Fort Casper Historic Site** (✉ 4001 Fort Caspar Rd., ☎ 307/235–8462; admission free). The **Casper Planetarium** (✉ 904 S. Poplar St., ☎ 307/577–0310; admission $2) has multimedia programs on astronomy and space subjects. **Werner Wildlife Museum** (✉ 405 E. 15th St., ☎ 307/235–2108; admission free), closed on Sunday, has displays of birds and animals indigenous to Wyoming.

Dining and Lodging

$$–$$$ ✕ **Bootlegger's Brewery & Restaurant.** Children are welcome at this lively brew pub in the heart of downtown. Pasta, pizza, calzones, and steaks are all good accompaniments to the freshly brewed beers. ✉ *256 S. Center St.,* ☎ *307/473–2668. AE, D, DC, MC, V.*

$$–$$$ ✕ **Parkway Plaza.** Guest rooms are large and quiet, with double vanities, one inside the bathroom and one outside. Furnishings are contemporary in the rooms, but western in the public areas. Poor Boys Steakhouse is one of Casper's best, with western-style blue-and-white checked tablecloths and hearty portions of steak, seafood, and chicken. ✉ *123 W. "E" St., 82601,* ☎ *307/235–1777,* FAX *307/235–8068. 272 rooms. Restaurant, pool. AE, D, MC, V.*

$$ **Casper Hilton Inn.** The large, muted rooms are contemporary and comfortable. There's an indoor pool and a hot tub. ✉ *I–25 and N. Poplar St., 82601,* ☎ *307/266–6000,* FAX *307/473–1010. 226 rooms. Restaurant, pool. AE, D, DC, MC, V.*

Sheridan

Visitor Information

Sheridan Chamber of Commerce (✉ Box 707, 82801, ☎ 307/672–2485 or 800/453–3650, FAX 307/672–7321).

Arriving and Departing

Commuter airlines fly from Denver to **Sheridan County Airport** (☎ 307/674–4222). **Powder River Transportation** (☎ 800/237–7211) buses connect with national carriers. Sheridan is 130 mi south of Billings, Montana, via I–90 and 140 mi north of Casper via I–25.

What to See and Do

This is authentic cowboy country, with a touch of dudish sophistication. The **Equestrian Center** (☎ 307/674–5179) holds polo matches on summer weekends, as well as horse shows and a steeplechase. Mosey into **King's Saddlery and Ropes** (✉ 184 N. Main St., ☎ 307/672–2702 or 800/443–8919) to view hundreds of lariats, as well as hand-tooled leather saddles. Or see western collectibles, saddles, and tack in the store's museum.

Dining and Lodging

$$$–$$$$ ✕ **Ciao Bistro.** Nine tables are squeezed into this European-style cafe's cramped quarters, but the menu is full of tempting choices such as prawns in cognac cream. Their signature Ciao salad, with avocado and coconut-flavored chicken, is a winner. ✉ *120 N. Main St.,* ☎ *307/672–2838. MC, V.*

$$$–$$$$ ✕🏨 **Sheridan Holiday Inn.** This five-floor lodging with a four-story atrium is five minutes from downtown. Facilities include a pool, sauna, hot tub, putting green, exercise room, racquetball court, and beauty salon. ✉ *1809 Sugarland Dr., 82801,* ☎ *307/672–8931,* FAX *307/672–6388. 213 rooms. Restaurant, pool, exercise room. AE, D, DC, MC, V.*

$$$$ 🏨 **Eaton's Guest Ranch.** This is the place credited with creating the dude ranch, and it's still going strong after nearly a century as a working cattle ranch that takes guests. The price includes all meals and activities such as horseback riding, fishing, cookouts, and pack trips. The ranch is west of Sheridan on the edge of the Bighorn National Forest. Make summer reservations by March. ✉ *270 Eaton Ranch Rd., Wolf 82844,* ☎ *307/655–9285,* FAX *307/655–9269. 51 cabins. Pool. D, MC, V. Closed Oct.–May.*

11 The West Coast

California, Oregon, Washington

By Bonnie Engel

Updated by Julie Fay and Donald Olson

SOME VISITORS FROM THE EAST picture the West Coast as America's frontier, but the shoreline of California, Oregon, and Washington presents no barrier to the region's businesspeople, who carry the pioneering spirit to the Pacific Rim. West Coast entrepreneurs generate high-tech products and services the world will take for granted in the next millennium, while "fusion" chefs reinvent classic cooking techniques with Asian influences.

Throughout its history the West Coast has been a destination for trendsetters and fortune seekers. The gold-hungry Spanish built missions and huge ranchos in what is now California, long before modern empire builders headed for Silicon Valley in a race to lead the nation's communications, information, and technology revolution.

Others have migrated to the West Coast because of its magnificent natural beauty and (for the most part) temperate weather. Washington and Oregon are similar in topography and climate, cooler than California, and are bisected by the Cascade Mountains. Rain-soaked Seattle, Washington, is home to one of the world's busiest container ports as well as the legendary Bill Gates, chairman of Microsoft. Portland, a busy inland port in Oregon's lush Willamette River valley, is known for its curtain of fog, rain, and pine trees.

Despite development, nature continues to provide a critical perspective on human pursuits. The ragged edges of Washington's Olympic Peninsula and the Oregon coast illustrate the power of the ocean; the mountains surrounding Seattle evoke a sobering sense of scale, as does the view from Yosemite's valley floor; and tremors along the San Andreas Fault remind California residents that the earth is an unstable place. Every town along the West Coast sits amid some grand gesture of nature.

The great West Coast cities—Seattle, Portland, San Francisco, San Jose, Los Angeles, and San Diego—continue to attract a hopeful, worldly mix of immigrants in search of personal freedom and economic opportunity. In contrast to the urban areas, the extraordinary landscapes of these states feature wild climatic changes and altitudes—deserts, forests, a 1,500-mi seashore, mountains, and rich agricultural valleys. In addition to the athletic attractions of rock climbing, deep-sea fishing, wilderness camping, surfing, skiing, and snowboarding, tourists and residents enjoy five-star resorts, historic western towns, Disneyland, Hollywood studios, world-class museums, and top-notch art and entertainment from grunge to opera.

When to Go

You can take a West Coast vacation any time of the year. Weather in coastal areas is generally mild year-round, with the rainy season running from **late fall through early spring**—though rain may occur any time of year, especially in Washington. Ski season in the High Sierra and Cascades runs from October through March, occasionally into April and May. These same months are also ideal for those who want to enjoy the sun-drenched delights of the desert; wildflowers are at their peak in April. **Summer** is the busiest tourist season, when you can expect the most congestion and the highest prices. It's also a time of heavy fog in the coastal areas (Mark Twain once remarked that the coldest winter he ever spent was a summer in San Francisco). Inland areas such as Napa Valley, the Columbia Gorge, and the High Sierra can be hot in summer, with temperatures reaching up to 90°F in the plains and mountains; in California's Central Valley and desert regions, summer temperatures can soar to 110°F. Whenever you visit the West Coast, expect temperatures to vary widely from night to day, sometimes by as much as 40°F. Most West Coast attractions are open daily year-round.

Festivals and Seasonal Events

Winter

JAN. 1➢ The **Tournament of Roses** (☏ 626/449–4100), in **Pasadena, California,** features a parade of more than 50 floral floats, equestrian units, and marching bands and is followed by the Rose Bowl football game.

LATE JAN.–EARLY FEB.➢ California's **AT&T Pebble Beach National Pro-Am** (☏ 408/649–1533) pairs 180 top professional golfers with amateurs from the business, sports, and entertainment worlds.

FEB.➢ **Chinese New Year** celebrations are held in **San Francisco** (☏ 415/982–3000) and **Los Angeles** (☏ 213/617–0396), complete with dragon parades, fireworks, and feasts.

Spring

EARLY MAR.➢ The **Mendocino Whale Festival** (☏ 707/961–6300), in **Mendocino, California,** combines whale-watching with art viewing, wine tasting, lighthouse tours, music, and merriment.

LATE MAR.–EARLY APR.➢ **Washington**'s **Skagit Valley Tulip Festival** (☏ 360/428–8547) showcases millions of colorful tulips and daffodils in bloom.

MEMORIAL DAY WEEKEND➢ The **Sacramento Jazz Jubilee** (☏ 916/372–5277) brings more than 100 jazz bands to **Sacramento, California,** for four days of jamming.

LATE MAY➢ The **Northwest Folklife Festival** (☏ 206/684–7300) lures musicians and artists to **Seattle** for one of the largest folk festivals in the United States.

Summer

MID-FEB.–LATE OCT.➢ The **Oregon Shakespeare Festival** (☏ 541/482–4331), held in **Ashland,** presents four plays by Shakespeare—plus seven other plays by both classical and contemporary playwrights—plus tours, concerts, and lectures.

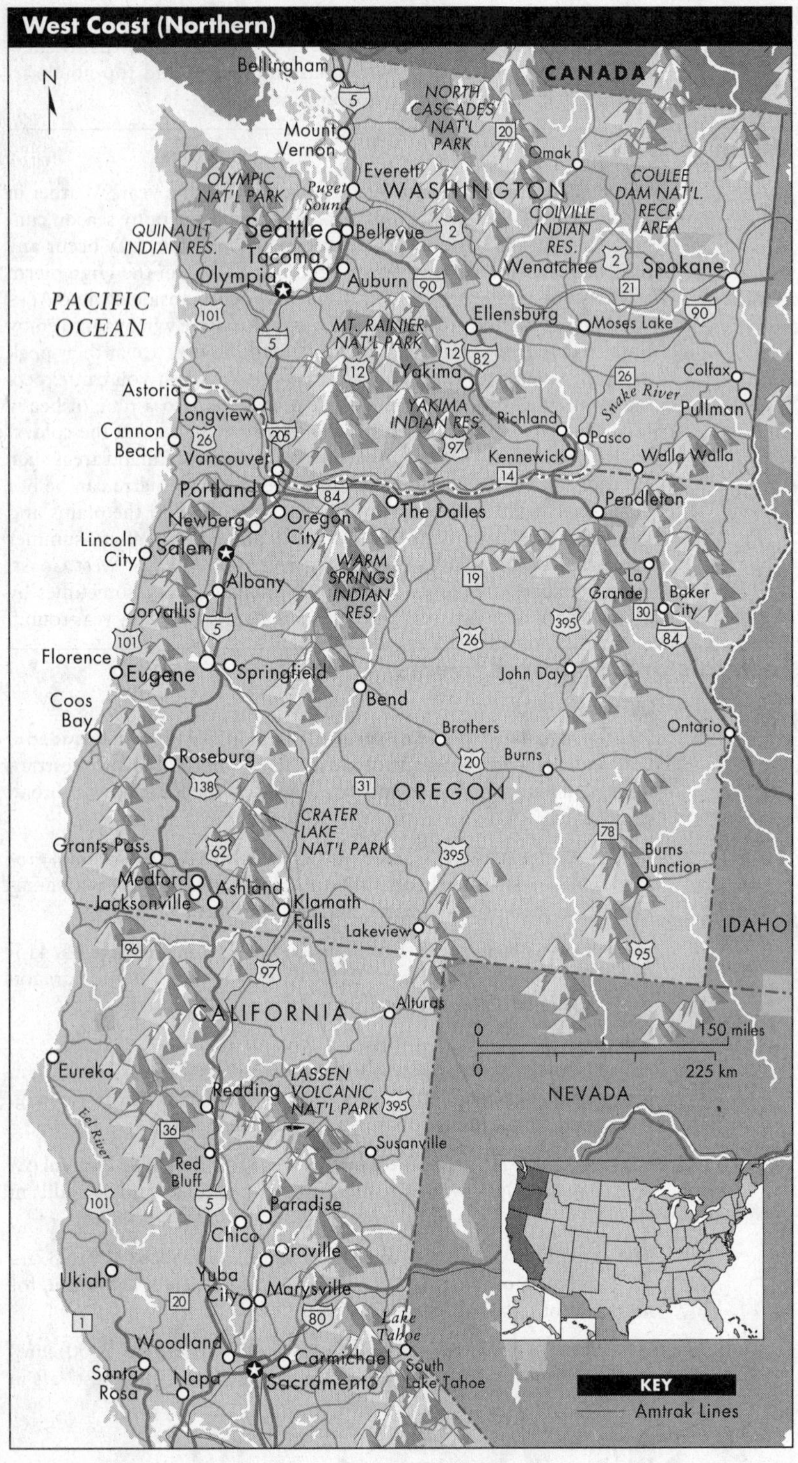
West Coast (Northern)
N
CANADA
Bellingham
NORTH CASCADES NAT'L PARK
Mount Vernon
Omak
Everett
OLYMPIC NAT'L PARK
Puget Sound
WASHINGTON
COULEE DAM NAT'L. RECR. AREA
COLVILLE INDIAN RES.
QUINAULT INDIAN RES.
Seattle
Bellevue
Tacoma
Olympia
Auburn
Wenatchee
Spokane
PACIFIC OCEAN
Ellensburg
Moses Lake
MT. RAINIER NAT'L PARK
Yakima
Colfax
Astoria
Snake River
Pullman
Longview
YAKIMA INDIAN RES.
Richland
Cannon Beach
Pasco
Vancouver
Kennewick
Walla Walla
Portland
The Dalles
Pendleton
Newberg
Oregon City
Lincoln City
Salem
WARM SPRINGS INDIAN RES.
La Grande
Albany
Baker City
Corvallis
Florence
Eugene
Springfield
John Day
Bend
Coos Bay
Brothers
Ontario
Burns
Roseburg
OREGON
CRATER LAKE NAT'L PARK
Grants Pass
Burns Junction
Medford
Ashland
Jacksonville
Klamath Falls
Lakeview
IDAHO
CALIFORNIA
Alturas
0 150 miles
0 225 km
Eureka
LASSEN VOLCANIC NAT'L PARK
NEVADA
Redding
Eel River
Susanville
Red Bluff
Paradise
Chico
Oroville
Ukiah
Yuba City
Marysville
Lake Tahoe
Woodland
Carmichael
South Lake Tahoe
Santa Rosa
Napa
Sacramento
KEY
Amtrak Lines

West Coast (Southern)

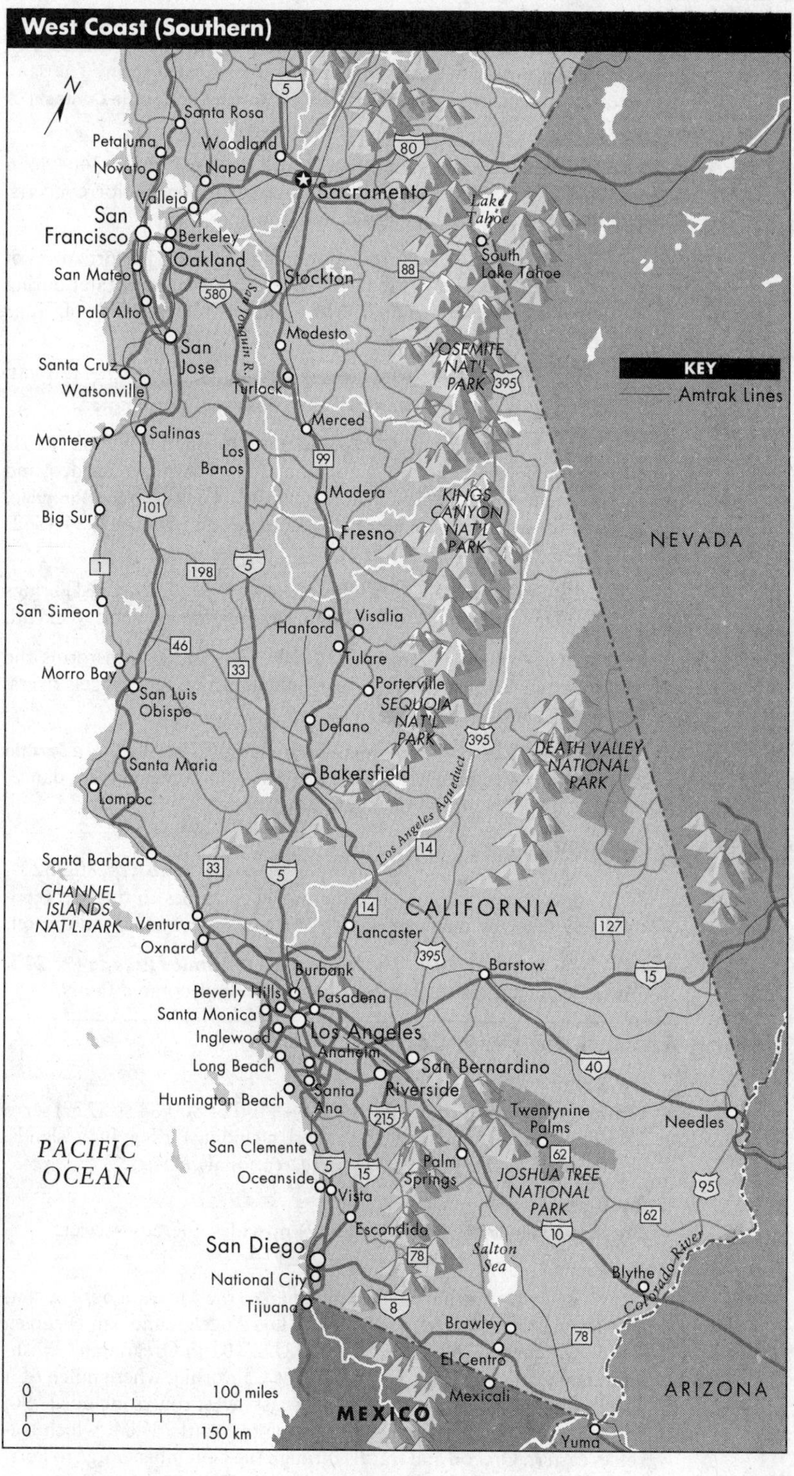

JUNE➢ The **Portland Rose Festival** (☎ 503/227–2681) includes a rose show, carnivals, celebrity entertainment, a hot-air balloon race, two parades, an air show, bands, and a world-class auto show. The sand becomes an art form at **Oregon**'s **Cannon Beach Sandcastle Contest** (☎ 503/436–2623), attended by thousands each year.

MID-JUNE–EARLY JULY➢ The **Oregon Bach Festival** (☎ 541/346–5666 or 800/457–1486) brings stellar musicians to **Eugene** for concerts, recitals, lectures, chamber music, and opera.

MID-JUNE–EARLY SEPT.➢ Contemporary and classical performances of music, dance, and theater are held in an outdoor amphitheater during **Jacksonville, Oregon**'s annual **Britt Festivals** (☎ 541/773–6077 or 800/882–7488).

LATE JULY➢ The **Pacific Northwest Arts & Crafts Fair** (☎ 206/454–4900) brings the work of Northwest artists to **Bellevue, Washington.**

EARLY AUG.➢ In California, **Old Spanish Days Fiesta** (☎ 805/962–8101) is **Santa Barbara**'s biggest event, with parades, a carnival, a rodeo, and dancers in the Spanish marketplace. At Linfield College in **McMannville, Oregon,** the **International Pinot Noir Celebration** (☎ 800/775–4762) features Oregon wines and foods.

EARLY AUG.➢ The **Mt. Hood Festival of Jazz** (☎ 503/231–0161) brings acclaimed jazz musicians to **Gresham, Oregon,** for a tuneful weekend.

EARLY AUG.➢ **Seattle**'s **Seafair** (☎ 206/728–0123) transforms the waterfront into a showplace of hydroplane racers, Blue Angels flyers, Navy ships, and fireboats.

LATE AUG.–EARLY SEPT.➢ **Bumbershoot** (☎ 206/281–8111), a **Seattle** festival of the arts, presents more than 450 performers in music, dance, theater, comedy, and the visual and literary arts.

Autumn

LATE AUG.–OCT.➢ The **Renaissance Pleasure Faire** (☎ 800/523–2473) draws revelers in Elizabethan-style costumes to the **San Francisco Bay Area** for many weekends of music, merriment, and theater.

LATE NOV.–EARLY DEC.➢ The **Hollywood Christmas Parade** (☎ 213/469–2337) features celebrities riding festively decorated floats.

Getting Around the West Coast

By Boat

Washington State Ferries (☎ 206/464–6400 or 800/843–3779) serve 20 destinations around the Puget Sound, including the San Juan Islands. Ferries can accommodate cars and recreational vehicles.

By Bus

Greyhound Lines (☎ 800/231–2222) provides intercity service.

By Car

I–5 runs north–south from the Canadian to the Mexican border, connecting Seattle, Portland, Sacramento, Los Angeles, and San Diego en route. The coastal route is designated U.S. 101 in Oregon and Washington; it's called Highway 1 in most of California, where much of it travels through coastal valleys. Major east–west routes include I–90, which bisects Washington from Spokane to Seattle; I–84, which traverses eastern Oregon and travels through the Columbia Gorge to Portland; I–80, the main highway crossing the High Sierra in California from Lake Tahoe to San Francisco; I–10, the historic route through southern California's desert to Los Angeles; and I–8, the southernmost route, hugging the Mexican border from El Centro to San Diego.

I–15 is the route between southern California and Las Vegas. The interstate highways are open all year, but you should expect temporary closures during severe winter storms. State highways crossing high mountain passes are normally closed in winter.

By Plane

The West Coast is served by all major domestic airlines and most international carriers. Major airports in California include **Los Angeles International Airport** (☎ 310/646–5252), plus John Wayne Orange County Airport and other regional airports at Burbank, Long Beach, and Ontario; **San Diego International Airport Lindbergh Field** (☎ 619/231–2100); and **San Francisco International Airport** (☎ 650/876–2377), plus regional airports at Oakland and San Jose. The region's other major airports are Oregon's **Portland International Airport** (☎ 503/335–1234) and Washington's **Seattle-Tacoma International Airport** (☎ 206/433–4645).

By Train

Amtrak (☎ 800/872–7245) serves rail passengers in the region. Trains run daily between Seattle and Los Angeles; the trip takes 35 hours. Commuter trains serve Los Angeles from San Diego and Santa Barbara. **CalTrain** (☎ 650/508–6200 or 800/660–4287) brings passengers to San Francisco from peninsula locations. Transcontinental trains serve Los Angeles, San Francisco/Oakland, Portland, and Seattle.

CALIFORNIA

Capital	Sacramento
Population	32,268,000
Motto	Eureka
State Bird	Valley quail
State Flower	Golden poppy
Postal Abbreviation	CA

Statewide Visitor Information

California Division of Tourism (✉ 801 K St., Suite 1600, Sacramento 95814, ☎ 916/322–2881 or 800/862–2543, FAX 916/322–3402 or 916/322–0501).

Scenic Drives

The land- and seascapes along the nearly 400 mi of coastline between San Francisco Bay and the Oregon border are beautiful and rugged; switchbacked **Highway 1** is punctuated by groves of giant redwood trees, tiny coastal towns, and secluded coves and beaches. **U.S. 395** north from San Bernardino rises in elevation gradually from the Mojave Desert to the Sierra foothills and on past the east entrance to Yosemite National Park. **Highway 49** winds 325 mi through northern California's historic Gold Country.

National and State Parks

National Parks

California has eight national parks: Death Valley, Joshua Tree, Lassen Volcanic, Redwood, Sequoia, Kings Canyon, Yosemite, and the Channel Islands. National monuments include Cabrillo, in San Diego, and Muir Woods, north of San Francisco. For information contact the western regional office of the **National Park Service** (✉ Fort Mason Center, Bldg. 201, San Francisco 94123, ☎ 415/556–0560).

State Parks

The **California State Park System** (✉ Dept. of Parks and Recreation, Box 942896, Sacramento 94296, ☎ 916/653–6995) includes more than 200 sites; many are recreational and scenic, others historic or scientific.

SAN FRANCISCO

San Francisco's slightly more than 750,000 residents nest on a 46.6-square-mi tip of land between San Francisco Bay and the Pacific Ocean. Experiencing San Francisco means visiting its neighborhoods: the colorful Mission District, gay-friendly Castro, countercultural Haight Street, serene Pacific Heights, bustling Chinatown, and still-bohemian North Beach.

Visitor Information

San Francisco Convention and Visitors Bureau (✉ Box 429097, San Francisco 94142, ☎ 415/974–6900); send $1 for booklet or pick one up at the lower level of Hallidie Plaza, at the corner of Market and Powell streets.

Arriving and Departing

By Bus

Greyhound Lines (☏ 800/231–2222) serves San Francisco's **Transbay Terminal** (✉ 1st and Mission Sts.).

By Car

I–80 comes into San Francisco from the east, crossing the Bay Bridge from Oakland. U.S. 101 runs north–south through the city and across the Golden Gate Bridge.

By Plane

San Francisco International Airport (SFO; ☏ 415/876–2377), 20 minutes south of the city off U.S. 101, is served by most major airlines. Several domestic airlines serve **Oakland Airport** (☏ 510/577–4000), across the bay. **SuperShuttle** (☏ 415/558–8500) will take you from SFO to anywhere within the city limits ($10–$28). **Taxis** between downtown and either airport take 20–30 minutes and cost about $30.

By Train

Amtrak (☏ 800/872–7245) trains stop in Oakland (✉ Jack London Sq., 245 2nd St.) and Emeryville (✉ 5885 Landregan St.); shuttle buses connect the Emeryville station and San Francisco's Ferry Building, on the Embarcadero. **CalTrain** (✉ 4th and Townsend Sts., ☏ 800/660–4287) connects the city with the region to the south.

Getting Around San Francisco

By Car

Watch out for one-way streets, curb your wheels when parking on hills, and check street signs for parking restrictions. Public parking garages (look for the city seal) tend to be less expensive than private lots. Hotel garages charge as much as $28 per day. Except at a few marked intersections, a right turn at a red light is legal.

By Public Transportation

Most of the light-rail and bus lines of the Municipal Railway System, called **Muni** (☏ 415/673–6864), operate continuously; standard fare is $1, and exact change (coins or a dollar bill) is required. If you'll be changing buses, get a transfer (good for 90 minutes) when you board. Three **cable car** lines crisscross downtown; information and tickets ($2)—and multiday tourist passes—can be obtained at the main turnaround, at Powell and Market streets. **BART** (Bay Area Rapid Transit; ☏ 800/817–1717) trains service the East Bay and beyond to Daly City, Concord, Dublin, and Richmond; wall maps list destinations and fares.

By Taxi

Rates are high—$1.70 to get in; it's difficult to hail a cab in most neighborhoods. Call **Yellow Cab Co.** (☏ 415/626–2345) for a taxi.

Orientation Tours

Gray Line (✉ 350 8th St., ☏ 415/558–9400 or 800/826–0202) offers tours on buses and double-deckers ranging in price from $16 to $39. The **Great Pacific Tour** (✉ 518 Octavia St., ☏ 415/626–4499) lasts 3½ hours at a cost of $29; multilingual guides are available, and the company will pick you up at most downtown hotels.

Walking Tours

The **Chinese Culture Center** (☏ 415/986–1822) offers a Heritage Walk and a Culinary Walk through Chinatown. Elaine Sosa's **Javawalk** (☏ 415/673–9255) visits some of the city's cafés.

San Francisco

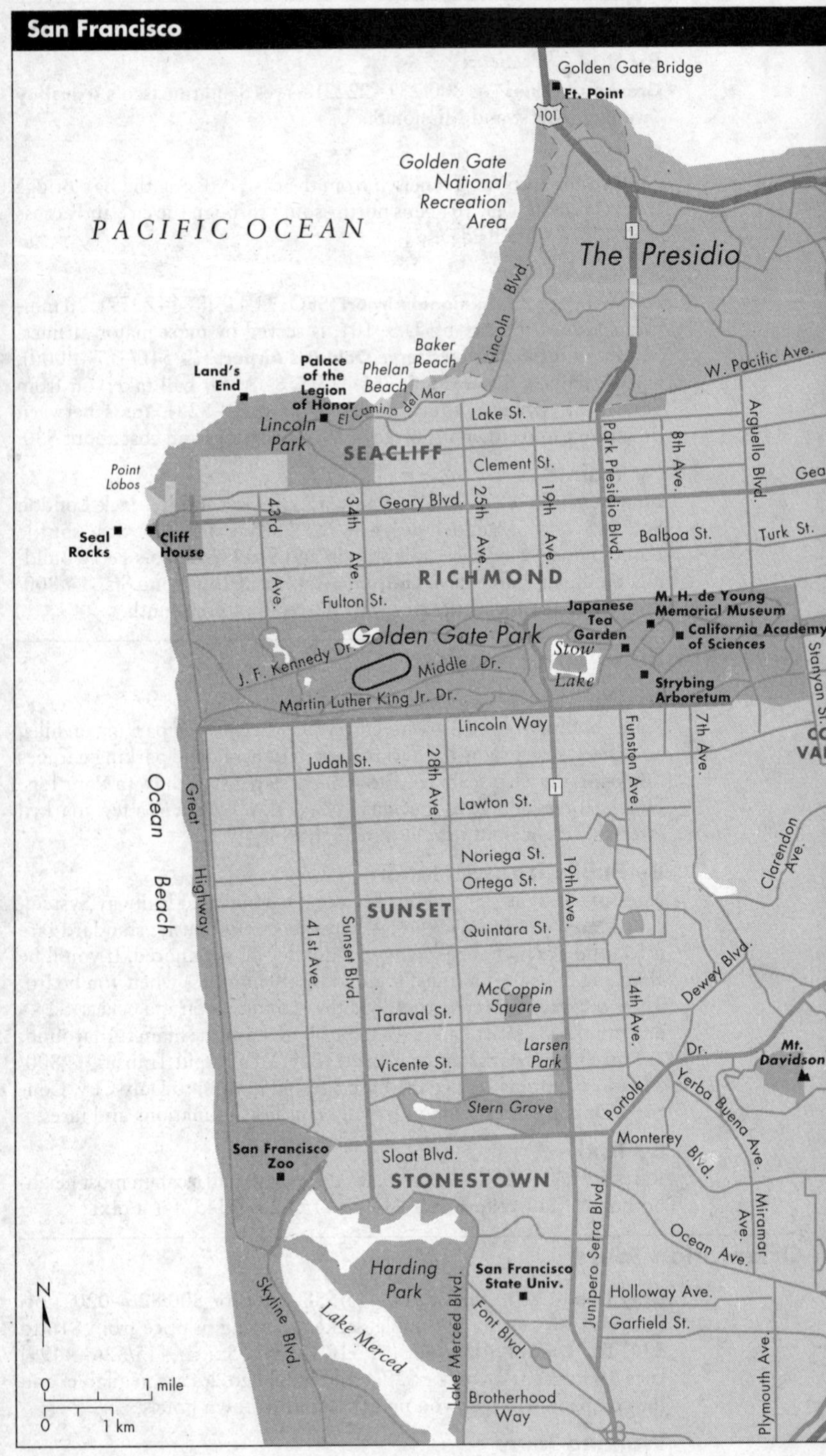

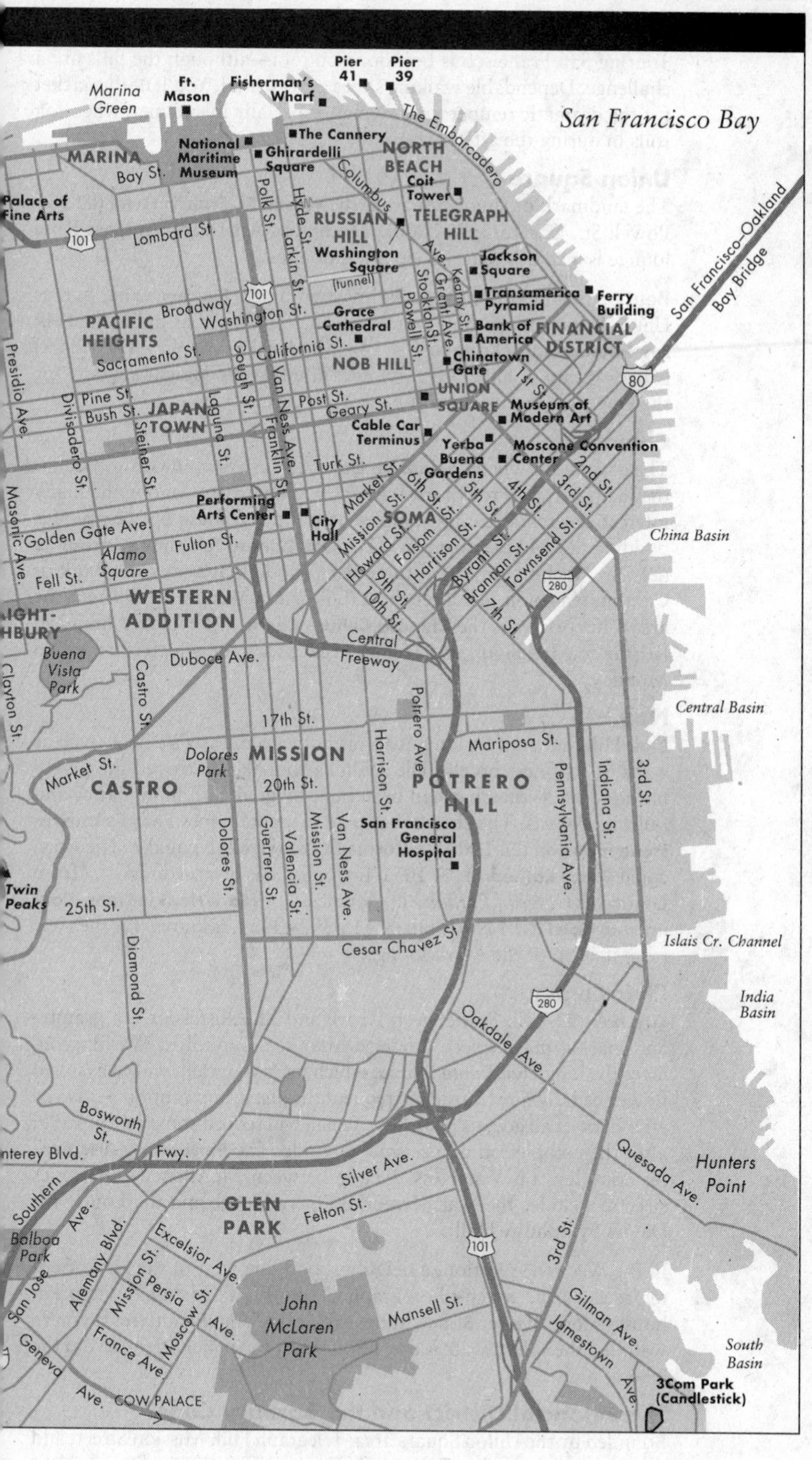

San Francisco Bay
Pier 41
Pier 39
Fisherman's Wharf
Ft. Mason
Marina Green
The Embarcadero
The Cannery
National Maritime Museum
Ghirardelli Square
MARINA
Bay St.
NORTH BEACH
Coit Tower
Palace of Fine Arts
RUSSIAN HILL
TELEGRAPH HILL
Lombard St.
Washington Square
(tunnel)
Jackson Square
Transamerica Pyramid
Ferry Building
San Francisco–Oakland Bay Bridge
PACIFIC HEIGHTS
Broadway
Washington St.
Grace Cathedral
Bank of America
FINANCIAL DISTRICT
Sacramento St.
California St.
NOB HILL
Chinatown Gate
Pine St.
Bush St.
JAPAN TOWN
Post St.
Geary St.
UNION SQUARE
Museum of Modern Art
Cable Car Terminus
Yerba Buena Gardens
Moscone Convention Center
Turk St.
Market St.
Performing Arts Center
City Hall
SOMA
Golden Gate Ave.
Fulton St.
Alamo Square
Fell St.
China Basin
WESTERN ADDITION
Central Freeway
Buena Vista Park
Duboce Ave.
Central Basin
17th St.
Mariposa St.
Dolores Park
MISSION
CASTRO
20th St.
POTRERO HILL
San Francisco General Hospital
Twin Peaks
25th St.
Cesar Chavez St.
Islais Cr. Channel
India Basin
Oakdale Ave.
Bosworth St.
Monterey Blvd.
Fwy.
Silver Ave.
Quesada Ave.
Hunters Point
GLEN PARK
Felton St.
Southern
Balboa Park
Excelsior Ave.
John McLaren Park
Mansell St.
Gilman Ave.
Jamestown Ave.
South Basin
Geneva Ave.
COW PALACE
3Com Park (Candlestick)

Exploring San Francisco

Touring San Francisco is best done on foot—although the hills are a challenge. Dependable walking shoes are essential. You'll need a jacket for the dramatic temperature swings, especially in summer, when fog rolls in during the afternoon.

Union Square

The landmark of Union Square is the **Westin St. Francis Hotel** (✉ 335 Powell St., ☎ 415/397–7000). The hotel's Art Deco Compass Rose lounge is a stylish place to sip afternoon tea.

Boutiques and sidewalk cafés line two-block **Maiden Lane,** across Union Square from the St. Francis. The building that holds the **Folk Art International/Xanadu** (✉ 140 Maiden La., ☎ 415/392–9999) gallery is said to have been architect Frank Lloyd Wright's model for the Guggenheim museum in New York City.

Chinatown

The dragon-crowned **Chinatown Gate** (✉ Bush St. and Grant Ave.), is the main entrance to colorful, fragrant Chinatown. Among the many interesting architectural examples here is the **Chinese Six Companies** building (✉ 843 Stockton St.). The **Old Chinese Telephone Exchange** (✉ 743 Washington St.), a three-tier pagoda that's now the Bank of Canton, was built just after the 1906 earthquake. To learn about the area's history, visit the **Chinese Culture Center** (✉ Holiday Inn, 750 Kearny St., 3rd Floor, ☎ 415/986–1822; 🎫 free), which is closed on Monday.

Nob Hill

Nob Hill, north of Union Square, is home to the city's elite as well as some of its finest hotels. The 1906 earthquake destroyed the neighborhood mansions that had been built by gold rush millionaires and railroad barons. The shell of railroad magnate James Flood's **brownstone mansion** (✉ 1000 California St.) survived the quake. The Episcopal **Grace Cathedral** (✉ 1051 Taylor St.) has bronze doors cast from Ghiberti's *Gates of Paradise* in Florence. The **Mark Hopkins Inter-Continental Hotel** (✉ 1 Nob Hill, ☎ 415/392–3434) is known for the view from its Top of the Mark lounge.

Civic Center

City hall (✉ Polk St. between Grove and McAllister Sts.), a granite-and-marble masterpiece modeled after the Capitol in Washington, faces the long **Civic Center Plaza,** which has a fountain, walkways, and flower beds. Many transients frequent the plaza, and caution is advised after dark. If all goes as planned, city hall will reopen sometime in 1999, after the completion of a seismic upgrade. The **Performing Arts Center** complex, on Van Ness Avenue between McAllister and Hayes streets, includes the War Memorial Opera House and the Louise M. Davies Symphony Hall.

In the Western Addition, a neighborhood due west of the Civic Center area, is the much-photographed row of six identical Victorian houses along **Steiner Street,** at the east end of Alamo Square. If you're walking, the safest route is up Fulton Street to Steiner Street; avoid the area at night.

The Financial District and the Barbary Coast

Bounded by the Union Square area, Telegraph Hill, Mission Street, and the Embarcadero, San Francisco's Financial District is distinguished from the rest of town by its steel-and-glass high-rises and older, more decorative architectural monuments to commerce. The city's signature high-rise is the 853-ft **Transamerica Pyramid** (✉ Clay and Montgomery Sts.). Dominating the Financial District skyline is the 52-story **Bank of America** (✉ California and Kearny Sts.).

Other notable structures in the Financial District include the **Pacific Stock Exchange** (✉ 301 Pine St.). The ceiling and entry are black marble in the **Stock Exchange Tower** (✉ 155 Sansome St.), an Art Deco gem. **Jackson Square** is at the heart of what used to be called the Barbary Coast, a late-19th-century haven for brawling and boozing. The brick buildings and narrow alleys in the area bordered by Pacific Avenue and Washington, Sansome, and Montgomery streets recall the romance and rowdiness of early San Francisco.

The Embarcadero and South of Market (SoMa)

The beacon of the port area is the **Ferry Building,** at the foot of Market Street on the Embarcadero. The clock tower is 230 ft high and was modeled after the campanile of Seville's cathedral. A **waterfront promenade** that extends from the piers north of the Ferry Building to the San Francisco–Oakland Bay Bridge is great for watching sailboats on the bay or enjoying a picnic.

Across the Embarcadero from the Ferry Building, the **Hyatt Regency Hotel** (✉ 5 Embarcadero, ☎ 415/788–1234) is noted for its lobby and 17-story hanging garden. On the waterfront side of the Hyatt Regency is **Justin Herman Plaza,** often the site of arts-and-crafts shows and political rallies.

The **Center for the Arts at Yerba Buena Gardens** (✉ 701 Mission St., ☎ 415/978–2787; 🎟 $5), in the SoMa (South of Market Street) area, presents dance, music, performance, theater, visual arts, film, video, ★ and installations. The **San Francisco Museum of Modern Art** (✉ 151 3rd St., ☎ 415/357–4000; 🎟 $8), which is closed on Wednesday, has a fine permanent collection.

The **Ansel Adams Center** (✉ 250 4th St., ☎ 415/495–7000; 🎟 $5), which is closed on Monday, exhibits photography. The **Cartoon Art Museum** (✉ 814 Mission St., Suite 200, ☎ 415/546–3922; 🎟 $4), which is closed Monday and Tuesday, is a worthwhile stop.

North Beach and Telegraph Hill

★ The streets of **North Beach** are packed with Italian delicatessens and bakeries, coffeehouses, and, increasingly, Chinese markets. Grant and Columbus avenues contain intriguing vintage clothing and other shops.

Telegraph Hill rises to the east of North Beach. From Filbert Street above Grant Avenue, the Greenwich Stairs climb to **Coit Tower,** a monument to the city's volunteer firemen. Inside are the works of 25 muralists, most notably the Mexican painter Diego Rivera. From the top there's a panoramic view of the bay, bridges, and islands.

The Northern Waterfront and Fisherman's Wharf

Fisherman's Wharf and the waterfront are at the end of the Powell-Hyde cable car line from Union Square. The **National Maritime Museum** (✉ Polk St. at Beach St., ☎ 415/556–3002; 🎟 donation suggested) and Ghirardelli Square are west of the Hyde Street cable car turnaround; Fisherman's Wharf and Pier 39 are east of it. The historic vessels at the **Hyde Street Pier** (✉ Hyde St. at Jefferson St., ☎ 415/556–3002; 🎟 $4) are a delight to explore. **Bay cruises** leave from Piers 39 and 41 (☎ 415/705–5555 or 415/546–2628).

The renovated factory buildings of **Ghirardelli Square** (✉ N. Point St. between Polk and Larkin Sts.) are filled with shops, restaurants, and galleries. East of the Hyde Street Pier is the **Cannery** (✉ Leavenworth and Beach Sts.), a former fruit and vegetable cannery that houses shops, restaurants, and the Museum of the City of San Francisco (☎ 415/928–0289; free).

Lombard Street, better known as "the crookedest street in the world," is south of the waterfront area between Hyde and Leavenworth streets.

The shopping and entertainment options at the popular **Pier 39** include Underwater World at Pier 39, which surveys Bay Area marine life. Above ground are a carousel, food stalls, and some noisy sea lions that bask on the pier's north side.

To the west of the waterfront area, at the edge of the Marina District, is the **Palace of Fine Arts** (✉ Baker and Beach Sts.), with massive columns, an imposing rotunda, and a swan-filled lagoon. Built for the 1915 Panama-Pacific International Exposition, the palace is a cherished ★ San Francisco landmark. The **Exploratorium** (✉ Palace of Fine Arts, ☎ 415/561–0360; $9) contains imaginative interactive exhibits.

To reach the **Golden Gate Bridge,** walk along the bay from the Marina District or take Muni Bus 28 to the toll plaza. Conditions are sometimes gusty and misty, but a walk across the nearly 2-mi-long bridge offers unparalleled views of the skyline, the bay, the Marin Headlands, and the Pacific Ocean.

Golden Gate Park and the Western Shore

★ **Golden Gate Park,** in the northwestern part of town, is ideal for strolling, especially on Sunday, when many of its streets are closed to car traffic. Several museums are in the park's eastern section. The strengths of the **M. H. de Young Memorial Museum** (☎ 415/863–3330; $7, good also for Asian Art Museum) include its collection of American art. Adjoining the de Young is the **Asian Art Museum** (☎ 415/668–8921; $7, good also for de Young Museum). The Asian and de Young are closed on Monday and Tuesday. Inside the **California Academy of Sciences** (☎ 415/750–7145; $8.50), a fine natural history museum, is the Steinhart Aquarium (☎ 415/750–7145). The **Strybing Arboretum and Botanical Gardens** (✉ 9th Ave. at Lincoln Way, ☎ 415/661–1316; free) shelters Californian, Australian, Mediterranean, and South African plants.

The **Beach Chalet,** at the park's west end, contains a visitor center and a brew-pub restaurant with views of Ocean Beach. At the north end of Ocean Beach is the **Cliff House** (✉ 1066 Point Lobos Ave., ☎ 415/386–3330), a restaurant where you can dine to the sound of crashing surf. The **San Francisco Zoo** (✉ Sloat Blvd. at Great Hwy., ☎ 415/753–7083; $7), at the south end of Ocean Beach, has a petting corral for children.

Dining

For price ranges *see* Chart 1 (A) *in* On the Road with Fodor's.

$$$–$$$$ ✕ **Aqua.** Talented chef-owner Michael Mina creates contemporary versions of French, Italian, and American seafood classics. ✉ *252 California St. (downtown),* ☎ *415/956–9662. Reservations essential. AE, DC, MC, V. Closed Sun. No lunch Sat.*

$$$–$$$$ ★ ✕ **Postrio.** In Wolfgang Puck's open kitchen and stunning three-level bar and dining area, the food is Californian with Mediterranean and Asian overtones, emphasizing pastas and grilled seafood. ✉ *545 Post St. (Union Sq.),* ☎ *415/776–7825. AE, D, DC, MC, V.*

$$$ ★ ✕ **Farallon.** Outfitted with kelp-covered columns and sea urchin chandeliers, this swanky restaurant is loaded with style. Chef Mark Franz cooks up exquisite seafood, such as spot prawns and lobster suspended in a pyramid of aspic. ✉ *450 Post St. (Union Sq.),* ☎ *415/956–6969. AE, DC, MC, V.*

$$$ ★ ✕ **Stars.** This huge dining room with a clublike ambience is the culinary temple of famed chef Jeremiah Tower. The menu ranges from grills to ragouts to sautés—some daringly creative and some classical. ✉ *150 Redwood Alley (Civic Center),* ☎ *415/861–7827. Reservations essential. AE, DC, MC, V. No lunch weekends.*

$$–$$$ ✕ **Harbor Village.** Classic Cantonese cooking, dim sum breakfasts and lunches, and fresh seafood from its own tanks are the hallmarks of this restaurant with great bay views. ✉ *4 Embarcadero Center,* ☎ *415/781–8833. Reservations not accepted for weekend lunch. AE, DC, MC, V.*

$$ ★ ✕ **Rose Pistola.** Chef-owner Reed Hearon celebrates North Beach's Liguran roots with a wide assortment of small antipasti plates, such as roasted peppers and house-cured fish, in addition to pizzas from a wood-burning oven and cioppino, the classic San Francisco Italian seafood stew. ✉ *532 Columbus Ave. (North Beach),* ☎ *415/399–0499. Reservations essential. AE, MC, V.*

$$ ✕ **Scala's Bistro.** Smart leather-and-wood booths, an extravagant mural along one wall, and an appealing menu of Italian plates make this one of downtown's most attractive destinations. ✉ *432 Powell St. (Union Sq.),* ☎ *415/395–8555. AE, D, DC, MC, V.*

$ ✕ **Café Claude.** Order a *croque monsieur, salade niçoise,* or simple daube from the French-speaking staff at this café in a Financial District alley, and you might forget what country you're in. Order a *pastis,* and you'll soon be whistling the "Marseillaise." ✉ *7 Claude La. (downtown),* ☎ *415/392–3505. AE, DC, MC, V. Closed Sun.*

$ ✕ **Helmand.** Authentic Afghani cooking, elegant surroundings, and amazingly low prices are Helmand hallmarks. Look for *aushak* (leek-filled ravioli served with yogurt and ground beef) and the exceptional lamb dishes. There's free validated parking at night at 468 Broadway. ✉ *430 Broadway (North Beach),* ☎ *415/362–0641. AE, MC, V. No lunch weekends.*

$ ✕ **Mifune.** Bowls of thin brown *soba* (buckwheat) and thick white *udon* (wheat) are the traditional Japanese specialties served at this outpost of an Osaka-based noodle empire. ✉ *Japan Center, Kintetsu Bldg., 1737 Post St. (Japantown),* ☎ *415/922–0337. Reservations not accepted. AE, D, DC, MC, V.*

Lodging

For assistance with hotel reservations try **San Francisco Reservations** (☎ 800/677–1500). For price ranges *see* Chart 2 (A) *in* On the Road with Fodor's.

$$$$ ★ **Campton Place.** Rooms here, though small, are supremely elegant, decorated with Asian touches in subtle earth tones. Highly attentive service begins the moment you step into the marble-floor lobby. ✉ *340 Stockton St. (Union Sq.), 94108,* ☎ *415/781–5555 or 800/235–4300,* FAX *415/955–5536. 117 rooms. Restaurant. AE, DC, MC, V.*

$$$$ **The Clift.** Dark paneling and enormous lobby chandeliers lend the Clift a note of grandeur. Rooms, some rich with dark woods and burgundies, others refreshingly pastel, all have large writing desks, plants, and flowers. ✉ *495 Geary St. (Union Sq.), 94102,* ☎ *415/775–4700 or 800/652–5438,* FAX *415/441–4621. 326 rooms. Restaurant. AE, DC, MC, V.*

$$$$ ★ **Ritz-Carlton, San Francisco.** The Ritz-Carlton is a stunning tribute to beauty, splendor, and warm, sincere service. Rooms are spacious, and every bath is appointed with double sinks and vanity tables. ✉ *600 Stockton St. (Nob Hill), 94108,* ☎ *415/296–7465 or 800/241–3333,* FAX *415/296–8261. 336 rooms. 2 restaurants. AE, D, DC, MC, V.*

$$$–$$$$ 🏨 **Hotel Rex.** The stylish Rex celebrates literary and artistic creativity. Rooms have writing desks and lamps with whimsically hand-painted shades. ✉ *562 Sutter St. (Union Sq.), 94102,* ☎ *415/433–4434,* FAX *415/433–3695. 94 rooms. AE, D, DC, MC, V.*

$$$ 🏨 **Petite Auberge.** Rooms are small at this B&B with a country-French flair, but each has an old-fashioned writing desk and armoire. Most rooms have working fireplaces; deluxe suites come equipped with whirlpool baths. ✉ *863 Bush St. (Union Sq.), 94108,* ☎ *415/928–6000 or 800/365–3004,* FAX *415/775–5717. 26 rooms. AE, DC, MC, V.*

$$ 🏨 **Bijou.** In the small, inexpensive rooms of this hotel hang black-and-white prints from classic films, many of them San Francisco–themed. ✉ *111 Mason St., at Eddy St., 94102,* ☎ *415/771–1200 or 800/771–1022,* FAX *415/346–3196. 65 rooms. AE, D, DC, MC, V.*

$–$$ ★ 🏨 **San Remo Hotel.** This Italianate Victorian near Fisherman's Wharf has a down-home, slightly tatty elegance. Rooms share six tiled shower rooms, one bathtub chamber, and six scrupulously clean toilets. ✉ *2237 Mason St., 94133,* ☎ *415/776–8688 or 800/352–7366,* FAX *415/776–2811. 62 rooms. AE, DC, MC, V.*

$ 🏨 **Adelaide Inn.** The bedspreads don't match the curtains, but the rooms are clean and cheap at this friendly small hotel popular with Europeans. ✉ *5 Isadora Duncan Ct., at Taylor between Geary and Post Sts. (Union Sq.), 94102,* ☎ *415/441–2474,* FAX *415/441–0161. 18 rooms. AE, MC, V.*

$ 🏨 **Marina Inn.** B&B accommodations in English country–style rooms are offered here at motel prices. ✉ *3110 Octavia St. (Marina), 94123,* ☎ *415/928–1000 or 800/274–1420,* FAX *415/928–5909. 40 rooms. CP. AE, MC, V.*

Nightlife and the Arts

For club and events listings, see the pink Datebook section of the Sunday *Examiner-Chronicle* or pick up the weekly *Bay Guardian* or *S.F. Weekly,* available throughout the city. You can charge tickets from **BASS** (☎ 415/776–1999) by phone. Half-price same-day tickets to many stage shows go on sale at 11 AM Tuesday–Saturday at the **TIX Bay Area** (☎ 415/433–7827) ticket booth, on the Stockton Street side of Union Square. Credit cards are not accepted.

Nightlife

COMEDY CLUBS

Cobb's Comedy Club (✉ 2801 Leavenworth St., at Beach St., ☎ 415/928–4320) books stand-up comedians. The **Punch Line** (✉ 444 Battery St., ☎ 415/397–7573) is another stand-up venue.

DANCE CLUBS

The **Sol y Luna** (✉ 475 Sacramento St., ☎ 415/296–8191) supper club, sizzles with live salsa, flamenco, merengue, and more, from Wednesday to Saturday. The **Metronome Ballroom** (✉ 1830 17th St., ☎ 415/252–9000) is a lively alcohol-free spot for ballroom dancing on the weekend.

MUSIC CLUBS

Bottom of the Hill (✉ 1233 17th St., ☎ 415/626–4455) showcases alternative rock and blues. **Cafe Du Nord** (✉ 2170 Market St., ☎ 415/861–5016) presents jazz, blues, and alternative music. The **Coconut Grove** (✉ 1415 Van Ness Ave., ☎ 415/776–1616), a '40s-style supper club, hosts big-band swing acts with an occasional dose of rockabilly, R&B, and Latin jazz. The **Great American Music Hall** (✉ 859 O'Farrell St., ☎ 415/885–0750) hosts top blues, folk, jazz, and rock entertainers. **Slim's** (✉ 333 11th St., ☎ 415/522–0333) specializes in basic rock, jazz, and blues.

SAN FRANCISCO'S FAVORITE BARS

The eccentric **Cypress Club** (✉ 500 Jackson St., ☏ 415/296–8555) restaurant hosts live jazz nightly. Combos at the famously kitschy **Tonga Room** (✉ Fairmont Hotel, 950 Mason St., ☏ 415/772–5278) play Top-40 pop on a floating barge. **Vesuvio Cafe** (✉ 255 Columbus Ave., ☏ 415/362–3370) recalls the heyday of the beat poets, with memorabilia from the era covering nearly every surface.

GAY AND LESBIAN NIGHTLIFE

The Stud (✉ 399 9th St., ☏ 415/252–7883) hosts a gender-bending mix of straight, lesbian, gay, and bisexual urbanites and suburbanites. The **CoCo Club** (✉ 139 8th St.; enter on Minna St., ☏ 415/626–2337) hosts theme nights, including a drag cabaret, a coed erotic cabaret, and a women's speakeasy.

The Arts

The **American Conservatory Theater** (✉ Geary Theater, 415 Geary St., ☏ 415/749–2228), a repertory company, specializes in classics and contemporary dramas. The **San Francisco Ballet** (✉ War Memorial Opera House, 301 Van Ness Ave., ☏ 415/865–2000) performs from February to May. The **San Francisco Opera** (✉ War Memorial Opera House, 301 Van Ness Ave., ☏ 415/864–3330) performs between September and December. The **San Francisco Symphony** (✉ Louise M. Davies Symphony Hall, 201 Van Ness Ave., ☏ 415/864–6000) plays from September to May.

Spectator Sports

Baseball: San Francisco Giants (✉ 3Com Park, off U.S. 101, ☏ 415/467–8000). **Oakland A's** (✉ Oakland Coliseum, off I–880 at 66th Ave., ☏ 510/638–0500). **Basketball: Golden State Warriors** (✉ Oakland Coliseum Arena, ☏ 510/762–2277). **Football: San Francisco 49ers** (✉ 3Com Park, ☏ 415/468–2249). **Oakland Raiders** (✉ Oakland Coliseum, ☏ 510/639–7700).

Shopping

Shopping Districts

Union Square is flanked by the Macy's, Saks Fifth Avenue, and Neiman Marcus department stores. On or near the square are Tiffany & Co., Disney, Border's Books and Music, Niketown, and Virgin Megastore. **Fisherman's Wharf,** the **Embarcadero Center,** and **Chinatown** are three shopping areas near tourist attractions. The **SoMa** area, between 2nd, 10th, Townsend, and Howard streets, contains many clothing, record, and other discount outlets. The **Haight-Ashbury District** contains some interesting shops, particularly on the 1500 block of Haight Street.

Antiques

Telegraph Hill Antiques (✉ 580 Union St., ☏ 415/982–7055) stocks fine china and porcelain, crystal, cut glass, Victoriana, and bronzes.

Books

City Lights (✉ 261 Columbus Ave., ☏ 415/362–8193), stomping ground of the 1950s beat poets, is well stocked with poetry, contemporary literature and music, and translations of Third World literature.

Clothing

Solo (✉ 1599 Haight St., ☏ 415/621–0342) sells women's clothes made of luxurious fabrics.

Gifts

Gordon Bennett (✉ 2102 Union St., ☎ 415/929–1172; ✉ Ghirardelli Sq., ☎ 415/351–1172) carries housewares, dried-flower arrangements, ceramics, and other creations, many by local artists.

Side Trip to Berkeley and Oakland

Arriving and Departing

By car, follow I–80 across the Bay Bridge; exit at University Avenue for Berkeley or pick up I–580 and exit at Grand Avenue for Oakland. By BART, Berkeley is 45 minutes to an hour from the city; exit at the downtown Berkeley stop, then take the shuttle to campus. Oakland is a 45-minute BART ride from San Francisco; exit at the Lake Merritt station for the museum.

What to See and Do

Berkeley is the home of the **University of California at Berkeley.** Along Telegraph Avenue south of the campus is a student-oriented business district with a dog-eared counterculture ambience.

Oakland has the second-largest port in California. **Jack London Square** (✉ Embarcadero at Broadway, ☎ 510/814–6000), along the waterfront, holds shops, restaurants, small museums, and historic sites. The **Oakland Museum** (✉ 1000 Oak St., ☎ 510/238–3401; $5) displays California art, history, and natural sciences through engaging exhibits and films.

Dining

$$–$$$$ ★ ✕ **Chez Panisse.** This culinary institution was one of the birthplaces of California cuisine. Meals at the formal downstairs restaurant are pricey; things are less expensive upstairs in the informal café. ✉ *1517 Shattuck Ave., north of University Ave.,* ☎ *510/548–5525 for restaurant, 510/548–5049 for café. Reservations essential for restaurant. AE, D, DC, MC, V. Closed Sun.*

Side Trip to Sausalito and Muir Woods

Arriving and Departing

To reach Sausalito by car, cross the Golden Gate Bridge and drive north a few miles to the Sausalito exit. **Golden Gate Ferry** (☎ 415/923–2000) crosses the bay to Sausalito from the south wing of the Ferry Building at Market Street and the Embarcadero; the trip takes 30 minutes. **Blue and Gold Fleet** (☎ 415/705–5555) ferries depart daily for Sausalito from Fisherman's Wharf. To drive to Muir Woods, continue north on U.S. 101 to the Highway 1–Stinson Beach exit and follow the signs.

What to See and Do

Sausalito, a hillside town on Richardson Bay, an inlet of San Francisco Bay in Marin County, has usually sunny weather and superb views. The main street, Bridgeway, has waterfront restaurants, shops, and hotels.

★ The 550-acre **Muir Woods National Monument** contains majestic redwoods, some nearly 250 ft tall and 1,000 years old. To avoid traffic congestion visit between 8 and 10 AM or after 4 PM. ✉ *Panoramic Hwy. off Hwy. 1,* ☎ *415/388–2595,* *Free.*

SAN JOSE

Visitor Information

San Jose Convention and Visitors Bureau (✉ 150 W. San Carlos St., 95110, ☎ 408/977–0900 or 408/295–2265)

Arriving and Departing

By Car

San Jose is 44 mi south of San Francisco; the easiest route to downtown is I–280 south to the Guadalupe Parkway (also known as Highway 87) north to the Santa Clara Street exit east.

By Plane

San Jose International Airport (✉ Airport Blvd. off Hwy. 87, ☎ 408/277–4759) is served by major airlines. **South & East Bay Airport Shuttle** (☎ 408/559–9477) transports visitors to and from the airport.

By Train

CalTrain (☎ 800/660–4287) runs from 4th and Townsend streets in San Francisco to San Jose's Rod Diridon station ($5 one-way). A **shuttle bus** (☎ 408/321–2300) links downtown San Jose to the CalTrain station during morning and evening commute hours.

Getting Around

By Bus or Train

Light-rail trains pass near most major attractions and historic sites downtown. Tickets cost $1.10 one-way or $2.50 for a day pass. The **Transit Information Center** (✉ 4 N. 2nd St., ☎ 408/321–2300) has information about local bus routes.

Exploring San Jose

In 1777, El Pueblo de San Jose de Guadalupe became California's first civil settlement under Spanish rule. Today, strikingly modern architecture contrasts with restored 19th-century and mission-style buildings.

Much of downtown San Jose can be toured on foot. The **Children's Discovery Museum** (✉ 180 Woz Way, at Auzerais St., ☎ 408/298–5437; $6) contains interactive installations on space, technology, the humanities, and the arts. At the northeast corner of the Plaza de Cesar Chavez is the **San Jose Museum of Art** (✉ 110 S. Market St., ☎ 408/294–2787; $7). The adjacent multidome **Cathedral Basilica of St. Joseph** (✉ 90 S. Market St., ☎ 408/283–8100), built in 1877, has extraordinary stained-glass windows and murals. On the square's western edge at Park Avenue is the dazzling ★ **Tech Museum of Innovation** (✉ 201 S. Market St., ☎ 408/279–7150; $6), which has many hands-on exhibits about technology.

Follow Market Street north from the plaza and turn left on Santa Clara Street. Turn right on San Pedro Street, and continue two blocks—past the sidewalk cafés and restaurants—to St. John Street and turn left. The **Fallon House** (✉ 175 W. St. John St., ☎ 408/993–8182; $6) was built in 1855 by San Jose's seventh mayor. Across the street is the circa-1797 **Peralta Adobe** (✉ 184 W. St. John St.), the last remaining structure from the pueblo that was once San Jose. For one admission fee you can visit both the Fallon House and the Peralta Adobe. The ★ **Egyptian Museum and Planetarium** (✉ 1600 Park Ave., ☎ 408/947–3636; $6.75 museum, $4 planetarium) exhibits Egyptian and Babylonian antiquities, including mummies.

Dining and Lodging

$$$ ★ ✕ **Emile's.** The cuisine of Swiss chef and owner Emile Mooser has classical and contemporary Californian influences. Specialties include house-cured gravlax, rack of lamb, fresh game, and a Grand Marnier soufflé. ✉ *545 S. 2nd St.,* ☎ *408/289–1960. AE, D, DC, MC, V. Closed Sun.–Mon. No lunch Tues.–Thurs. and Sat.*

$-$$ ✕ **Gordon Biersch Brewery Restaurant.** San Jose's younger set feasts on the kitchen's legendary garlic fries, lemon roast chicken, specialty pastas, and burgers. ✉ *33 E. San Fernando St.,* ☎ *408/294–6785. AE, MC, V.*

$$$-$$$$ 🏨 **Hotel De Anza.** This lushly appointed 1931 Art Deco hotel has hand-painted ceilings, a warm color scheme, and an enclosed terrace with towering palms and dramatic fountains. ✉ *233 W. Santa Clara St., 95113,* ☎ *408/286–1000 or 800/843–3700,* FAX *408/286–0500. 91 rooms, 9 suites. Restaurant, exercise room. AE, D, DC, MC, V.*

Nightlife and the Arts

San Jose Live! (Pavillion, ✉ 150 S. 1st St., ☎ 408/294–5483) consists of five clubs and a restaurant. The **Center for Performing Arts** (✉ 255 Almaden Blvd., ☎ 408/277–3900; 408/998–2277 for BASS tickets) is a venue for drama, musical-theater, symphony, opera, and ballet performances. **San Jose Repertory Theatre** (✉ 101 Paseo de San Antonio, ☎ 408/291–2255) is a well-regarded company.

Outdoor Activities and Sports

The 17,400-seat **San Jose Arena** (✉ Santa Clara St. at Autumn St., ☎ 408/287–9200 or 408/998–2277) hosts many events and is home to the San Jose Sharks of the National Hockey League.

THE WINE COUNTRY

California's **Napa and Sonoma counties** produce some of the world's finest wines. The Napa Valley becomes crowded on weekends, when visitors jam the gift shops and restaurants. In Sonoma County the pace is less frenetic. Along the coast in the city of **Mendocino,** things slow down even more. Admission is free to the wineries listed below, but most have nominal tasting fees, either by the glass or for a set number of wines.

Visitor Information

Fort Bragg–Mendocino Coast Chamber of Commerce (✉ Box 1141, Fort Bragg 95437, ☎ 800/726–2780). **Napa Valley Conference and Visitors Bureau** (✉ 1310 Napa Town Center, 94559, ☎ 707/226–7459). **Sonoma County Convention and Visitors Bureau** (✉ 5000 Roberts Lake Rd., Rohnert Park 94928, ☎ 707/586–8100 or 800/326–7666).

Arriving and Departing

By Bus

Greyhound Lines (☎ 800/231–2222) runs buses from San Francisco to the cities of Sonoma and Santa Rosa in Sonoma County; the line's buses stop along U.S. 101 in inland Mendocino County. **Sonoma County Area Transit** (☎ 707/585–7516) and **Napa Valley Transit** (☎ 707/255–7631) provide local transportation.

By Car

The best way to get around the Wine Country is by car. From San Francisco cross the Golden Gate Bridge and follow U.S. 101 north to Highway 37 east to Highway 121 north and east. Take Highway 12 north from Highway 121 for Sonoma wineries; continue east on Highway 121 to Highway 29 north for Napa wineries. From the East Bay take I–80 north to Highway 37 east to Highway 29 north for Napa; Highway 12 heads west from Highway 29 toward Sonoma. To get to Mendocino from San Francisco, take U.S. 101 north to Highway 128 west to Highway 1 north.

By Train

The **Napa Valley Wine Train** (☎ 707/253–2111 or 800/427–4124) serves lunch ($65–$75), dinner ($70–$82), and a weekend brunch ($57) on restored Pullman cars that run between Napa and St. Helena.

Exploring the Wine Country

The Napa Valley

Along Highway 29 north of the town of **Napa** and parallel to the highway on the Silverado Trail are some of California's most important wineries. **Domaine Chandon** (✉ California Dr., Yountville, ☎ 707/944–2280) is owned by Moët-Hennessey and Louis Vuitton. **Stag's Leap** (✉ 5766 Silverado Trail, Yountville, ☎ 707/944–2020) produces a superb chardonnay.

The largest wine caves in America are below **Rutherford Hill** (✉ 200 Rutherford Hill Rd., Rutherford, ☎ 707/963–7194). **Beaulieu Vineyard** (✉ 1960 St. Helena Hwy., Rutherford, ☎ 707/963–2411) utilizes the same wine-making process it did in the last century. At **Robert Mondavi** (✉ 7801 St. Helena Hwy., Oakville, ☎ 707/259–9463), the 60-minute tour is encouraged before imbibing. Visitors ride up the side of a hill in a gondola to reach **Sterling Vineyards** (✉ 1111 Dunaweal La., Calistoga, ☎ 707/942–3300).

Calistoga, at the Napa Valley's north end, was founded as a spa and remains notable for its mineral water, hot mineral springs, mud baths, steam baths, and massages. **Indian Springs** (✉ 1712 Lincoln Ave., ☎ 707/942–4913) has full spa amenities.

The Sonoma Valley

East of U.S. 101 and west of the Napa Valley, Highway 12 runs through the hills of Sonoma County. The historic central plaza in the town of Sonoma is the site of **Mission San Francisco Solano** (✉ 114 Spain St. E, ☎ 707/938–1519; 🎫 $2), now a museum with a fine collection of 19th-century watercolors.

California's wine-making industry got its start at the **Buena Vista Carneros Winery** (✉ 18000 Old Winery Rd., Sonoma, ☎ 707/938–1266) in 1857. The **Benziger Family Winery** (✉ 1883 London Ranch Rd., Glen Ellen, ☎ 707/935–3000) specializes in premium estate and Sonoma County wines. The rustic grounds at **Kenwood Vineyards** (✉ 9592 Sonoma Hwy., Kenwood, ☎ 707/833–5891) complement the attractive tasting room. The well-conceived tour at **Korbel Champagne Cellars** (✉ 13250 River Rd., west of U.S. 101, Guerneville, ☎ 707/887–2294) explains the process of making sparkling wine.

Mendocino

This coastal city on windswept headlands 153 mi north of San Francisco was a logging center in the late 1800s, but its chief industry these days is tourism. The town stood in for Cabot Cove, Maine, in the TV show *Murder, She Wrote.*

The **Mendocino Art Center** (✉ 45200 Little Lake St., ☎ 707/937–5818) contains a gallery and a theater. The restored 1854 **Ford House** (✉ Main St., west of Lansing St., ☎ 707/937–5397; 🎫 free) holds the visitor ★ center for Mendocino Headlands State Park. The **Mendocino Coast Botanical Gardens** (✉ 18220 N. Hwy. 1, ☎ 707/964–4352; 🎫 $5) contains a splendid array of flowers and other plant life within three separate microclimates.

Husch (✉ 4400 Hwy. 128, Philo, ☎ 707/895–3216) sells award-winning chardonnays and a superb gewürztraminer. At **Roederer Estate** (✉ 4501 Hwy. 128, Philo, ☎ 707/895–2288), you can taste sparkling wines produced by the American affiliate of the famous French champagne maker.

Dining and Lodging

For price ranges *see* Charts 1 (A) and 2 (A) *in* On the Road with Fodor's.

Calistoga

$$–$$$ ★ ✕ **Catahoula Restaurant and Saloon.** Chef Jan Birnbaum employs a large wood-burning oven to churn out such California-Cajun dishes as spicy gumbo with andouille sausage and oven-braised lamb shank with red beans. ✉ *Mount View Hotel, 1457 Lincoln Ave.,* ☎ *707/942–2275. Reservations essential. MC, V. Closed Tues. and Jan.*

$$$–$$$$ 🏨 **Mount View Hotel.** This full-service European spa offers state-of-the-art pampering. Three cottages here are equipped with private redwood decks, Jacuzzis, and wet bars. ✉ *1457 Lincoln Ave., 94515,* ☎ *707/942–6877,* FAX *707/942–6904. 33 rooms. Restaurant, pool. AE, MC, V.*

Mendocino

$$–$$$ ★ ✕ **Cafe Beaujolais.** All the rustic charm of peaceful, backwoods Mendocino is here, with great country cooking to boot. The ever-evolving, cross-cultural dinner menu includes delicacies like Yucatecan Thai crab cakes. ✉ *961 Ukiah St.,* ☎ *707/937–5614. No credit cards.*

$$$–$$$$ ★ 🏨 **Whitegate Inn.** With a white picket fence, a latticework gazebo, and a romantic garden, the Whitegate is a picturebook Victorian. Guest rooms and public spaces have high ceilings and floral fabrics. ✉ *499 Howard St., 95460,* ☎ *707/937–4892 or 800/531–7282,* FAX *707/937–1131. 7 rooms. Full breakfast. AE, D, DC, MC, V.*

Rutherford

$$$$ ★ ✕🏨 **Auberge du Soleil.** The dining terrace of this hilltop inn, looking down across groves of olive trees to the Napa Valley vineyards, is the closest you can get to the atmosphere, charm, and cuisine of southern France without a passport. The inn itself is a luxurious retreat with full spa facilities. ✉ *180 Rutherford Hill Rd., off Silverado Trail north of Rte. 128, 94573,* ☎ *707/963–1211 or 800/348–5406,* FAX *707/963–8764. 52 rooms. Restaurant, pool, exercise room. CP. AE, D, DC, MC, V.*

St. Helena

$$$$ 🏨 **Meadowood Resort.** Croquet lawns, a nine-hole golf course, and gorgeous hiking trails add to the glamour of this sprawling 256-acre resort with a rambling country lodge and 40 bungalow suites. ✉ *900 Meadowood La., 94574,* ☎ *707/963–3646 or 800/458–8080,* FAX *707/963–5863. 85 rooms. 2 restaurants, pools. AE, D, DC, MC, V.*

Santa Rosa

$$$ ★ ✕ **John Ash & Co.** The chef emphasizes presentation, innovation, and freshness and uses mainly seasonal foods grown in Sonoma County. This is a favorite spot for Sunday brunch. ✉ *4430 Barnes Rd.,* ☎ *707/527–7687. Weekend reservations essential. AE, MC, V. No lunch Mon.*

Sonoma

$$$–$$$$ 🏨 **Thistle Dew Inn.** Half a block from Sonoma Plaza, this Victorian inn has Arts and Crafts furnishings and antique quilts. Welcome bonuses include a hot tub and free use of the inn's bicycles. ✉ *171 W. Spain St., 95476,* ☎ *707/938–2909 or 800/382–7895 in CA. 6 rooms. Full breakfast. AE, MC, V.*

Yountville

$$$$ ★ ✕ **French Laundry.** This intimate, cottage-style restaurant, surrounded by lush gardens, offers exquisite prix-fixe French menus of four or five

courses. ✉ *6640 Washington St.,* ☎ *707/944–2380. Reservations essential. AE, MC, V. Closed 1st 2 wks in Jan.; lunch hrs and days vary.*

Outdoor Activities and Sports

Hot-Air Ballooning

Many hotels arrange excursions, or contact **Napa Valley Balloons** (☎ 707/944–0228 or 800/253–2224 in CA). For Sonoma trips try **Sonoma Thunder Wine Country Balloon Safaris** (☎ 707/538–7359 or 800/759–5638).

YOSEMITE NATIONAL PARK

Yosemite's U-shape valleys were formed by the action of glaciers during recent ice ages. A pass to the park, good for a week, costs $20 per car or $10 per person if you don't arrive in a car.

Visitor Information

Yosemite National Park (✉ Box 577, Yosemite National Park 95389, ☎ 209/372–0264; 209/372–0200 for 24-hr information).

Arriving and Departing

By Bus

Yosemite VIA (☎ 209/384–2576 or 800/369–7275) runs three daily buses from Merced to Yosemite Valley. **Greyhound** (☎ 800/231–2222) serves Merced from the California coast.

By Car

Yosemite is a four- to five-hour drive from San Francisco (take I–80 to I–580 to I–205 to Highway 120) and a six-hour drive from Los Angeles (take I–5 north to Highway 99 to Fresno, and Highway 41 north to Yosemite). Highways 41, 120, and 140 all intersect with Highway 99, which runs north–south through California's Central Valley.

By Plane

Fresno Air Terminal (✉ 5175 E. Clinton Ave., ☎ 209/498–4095), the nearest major airport, is served by national and regional carriers.

Exploring Yosemite National Park

★ The highlights of **Yosemite Valley** include Yosemite Fall, the highest waterfall in North America; the famous El Capitan and Half Dome granite peaks; misty Bridalveil Fall; and Glacier Point, which affords a phenomenal bird's-eye view of the entire valley. Near **Wawona** at the park's south entrance are the historic Wawona Hotel and the Mariposa Grove of Big Trees. A free **shuttle bus** runs around the east end of Yosemite Valley year-round. A summer shuttle runs from Wawona to the Mariposa Grove of Big Trees.

Dining and Lodging

Besides the Ahwahnee Hotel's classy restaurant, dining options in Yosemite Valley include fast food and picnic fixings from a grocery store. **Yosemite Concession Services Corporation** (☎ 209/252–4848) handles reservations for the park's fancy hotels, modest lodge rooms, and Yosemite Valley tent cabins and tent sites.

ELSEWHERE IN NORTHERN CALIFORNIA

The Gold Country

Arriving and Departing

Sacramento International Airport (✉ 6900 Airport Blvd., off I–5, ☎ 916/874–0700) is served by major domestic airlines.

Greyhound (☎ 800/231–2222) serves Sacramento, Auburn, Grass Valley, and Placerville from San Francisco.

The most convenient way to see the area is by car. I–80 intersects with Highway 49, the main route through the region, at Auburn; U.S. 50 intersects with Highway 49 at Placerville.

What to See and Do

When gold was discovered at **Coloma** in 1848, people came from all over the world to search for the treasure. Today, clustered along Highway 49 are restored villages and ghost towns, antiques shops, crafts stores, and vineyards. The heart of the Gold Country lies on Highway 49 between Nevada City and Mariposa.

★ **Empire Mine State Historic Park** (✉ 10791 E. Empire St., Grass Valley, ☎ 530/273–8522; $3) has exhibits on gold mining. ★ The **Marshall Gold Discovery State Historical Park** (✉ Hwy. 49, Coloma, ☎ 530/622–3470; $5) has a replica of Sutter's Mill, where the gold rush started. ★ In **Columbia State Historic Park** (✉ Hwy. 49, ☎ 209/532–4301; free) you can ride a stagecoach, pan for gold, or watch a blacksmith working at his anvil. At the **California State Mining and Mineral Museum** (✉ Mariposa County Fairgrounds, Hwy. 49, Mariposa, ☎ 209/742–7625; $3.50) a glittering 13-pound crystalized gold nugget vividly illustrates what the gold rush was all about. The museum is closed on Tuesday year-round and on Monday between October and April.

Sacramento, the California state capital, is also the largest Gold Country city. The **Visitor Information Center** (✉ 1101 2nd St., ☎ 916/442–7644) has the latest on key attractions, plus lodging, reservations, and other services. The **Discovery Museum** (✉ 101 I St., ☎ 916/264–7057; $4) presents a streamlined introduction to Sacramento's history. ★ The **California State Railroad Museum** (✉ 125 I St., ☎ 916/445–6645; $6) displays restored locomotives and railroad cars.

Dining and Lodging

SACRAMENTO

$$$ ★ ✕ **Biba.** The capitol crowd flocks here for delicate pasta dishes, baked spinach lasagna, and homemade tortelloni, as well as specialties from the Emilia-Romagna region of Italy. ✉ *2801 Capitol Ave.,* ☎ *916/455–2422. AE, MC, V. Closed Sun. No lunch Sat.*

$$ ✕ **Best Western Sutter House.** A great downtown value, this property has rooms that open onto a courtyard surrounding a pool. The restaurant, Scorpio's, is superb. ✉ *1100 H St., 95814,* ☎ *916/441–1314; 800/830–1314 in CA;* FAX *916/441–5961. 98 rooms. Restaurant, pool. CP. AE, D, DC, MC, V.*

Lake Tahoe

Arriving and Departing

Reno–Tahoe International Airport (✉ U.S. 395, Exit 65B, Reno, NV, ☎ 702/328–6400), about 40 mi from Lake Tahoe, is served by several domestic airlines. **Tahoe Casino Express** (☎ 702/785–2424 or 800/446–6128) provides shuttle service from Reno to Lake Tahoe.

Amtrak (☎ 800/872–7245) and **Greyhound Lines** (☎ 800/231–2222) also serve the Tahoe area. **South Tahoe Area Ground Express** (☎ 530/573–2080) and **Tahoe Area Regional Transit** (☎ 530/581–6365) are the local bus companies. Lake Tahoe is 198 mi northeast of San Francisco; to drive takes about four hours. The major route is I–80 through the Sierra Nevadas; U.S. 50 from Sacramento is the direct route to the south shore. Tire chains are sometimes necessary in winter.

What to See and Do

Visitors to Lake Tahoe's California side—where gambling isn't legal—come to ski, hike, fish, camp, and boat in the spectacular Sierra Nevada range, 6,000 ft to 10,000 ft above sea level. Ski resorts, such as Alpine Meadows and Squaw Valley, open at the end of November and operate as late as May. Tourist information is provided by the **Lake Tahoe Visitors Authority** (☎ 530/544–5050 or 800/288–2463). Ride the ★ **Heavenly Tram** (✉ North on Ski Run Blvd. off U.S. 50 and follow signs, ☎ 702/586–7000; 🎫 $12) for a view of the lake from 8,200 ft.

The 72-mi Lake Tahoe shoreline is best seen along a route through wooded flatlands and past beaches, climbing to vistas on the rugged west side of the lake. The drive should take about three hours but can be slow going in summer and on holiday weekends.

West of South Lake Tahoe on Highway 89 is the **Pope-Baldwin Recreation Area** (☎ 530/541–5227; 🎫 free), where three grand century-old mansions (fees to enter vary) are open to the public. The **Lake Tahoe Visitors Center** (☎ 530/573–2674), on Taylor Creek, is near the site of a onetime Washoe Indian settlement; there are trails through meadow, ★ marsh, and forest. Tahoe's **Emerald Bay** is famed for its shape and color.

The ***Hornblower's Tahoe Queen*** (✉ Ski Run Marina, off U.S. 50, South Lake Tahoe, ☎ 530/541–3364; 🎫 $16–$40), a glass-bottom stern-wheeler, cruises on the lake and swings by Emerald Bay year-round. Beyond Emerald Bay is **D. L. Bliss State Park** (☎ 530/525–7277; 🎫 $5), with 6 mi of shorefront and 168 family campsites. At Tahoe City Highway 89 turns north to **Squaw Valley,** site of the 1960 Winter Olympics.

Dining and Lodging

$$–$$$$ ★ ✕🏨 **Harvey's Resort Hotel/Casino.** Any description of Harvey's runs to superlatives. Rooms have custom furnishings, oversize marble baths, and minibars. The health club, spa, and pool are free to guests, a rarity for this area. Among the resort's restaurants, Llewellyn's is outstanding. ✉ *U.S. 50, Box 128, Stateline, NV 89449,* ☎ *702/588–2411 or 800/648–3361,* FAX *702/782–4889. 741 rooms. 8 restaurants, pool, health club. AE, D, DC, MC, V.*

$$–$$$$ 🏨 **Inn by the Lake.** Across the road from a beach, this luxury motel has spacious rooms, all with balconies. The inn provides a free shuttle bus to the casinos. ✉ *3300 Lake Tahoe Blvd., South Lake Tahoe 96150,* ☎ *530/542–0330 or 800/877–1466,* FAX *530/541–6596. 99 rooms. Pool. CP. AE, D, DC, MC, V.*

THE CENTRAL COAST

Raging surf, rugged rocks, hidden tidal pools, and wind-warped trees mark the coastline south from San Francisco. Several towns provide entertainment, but the Pacific Ocean dominates. Coast-hugging Highway 1, sometimes precariously narrow, is the route of choice; it's slow and winding, but the views are worth the extra time.

Visitor Information

Monterey Peninsula Visitors and Convention Bureau (✉ 380 Alvarado St., Monterey 93942, ☎ 831/649–1770). **Santa Barbara Conference and Visitors Bureau** (✉ 12 E. Carrillo St., 93101, ☎ 805/966–9222 or 800/927–4688).

Arriving and Departing

By Car

Highway 1 heads south from San Francisco through the region. The quickest (if less scenic) route to Monterey from San Francisco or San Jose is I–280 south to Highway 17 west to Highway 1 south. U.S. 101 is the quickest route to Santa Barbara from Los Angeles or San Francisco. To get to Monterey from Los Angeles, take U.S. 101 to Salinas and head west on Highway 68.

By Plane

Airlines serving **Monterey Peninsula Airport** (✉ 200 Fred Kane Dr., ☎ 831/648–7000) and **Santa Barbara Municipal Airport** (✉ 500 Fowler Rd., ☎ 805/683–4011) include America West, American Eagle, United, United Express, and Skywest/Delta.

By Train

Amtrak's *Coast Starlight* makes stops in Santa Barbara, San Luis Obispo, and Salinas on its run from San Diego to Seattle.

Exploring the Central Coast

About 125 mi south of San Francisco, the city of **Monterey** is rich in California history. The Path of History is a 2-mi self-guided tour ★ through **Monterey State Historic Park** (☎ 831/649–7118). Two highlights are the Custom House (✉ 1 Custom House Plaza, ☎ 831/649–2909; 🎫 free), built by the Mexican government in 1827, and the Pacific House (✉ 10 Custom House Plaza, ☎ 831/649–7118; 🎫 free), a former hotel and saloon that is now a museum of early California life.

Monterey's barking sea lions are best seen along **Fisherman's Wharf,** a touristy pier. A footpath leads from Fisherman's Wharf to **Cannery Row,** where the old tin-roof canneries made famous by John Steinbeck's eponymous book have been converted into restaurants, art galleries, ★ and minimalls. The outstanding **Monterey Bay Aquarium** (✉ 886 Cannery Row, ☎ 831/648–4888, 800/756–3737 in CA for tickets; 🎫 $14.75) is a window on the sea waters beyond.

Pacific Grove recalls its Victorian heritage in tiny board-and-batten cottages and in stately mansions. For years migrating monarch butterflies from Canada and the Pacific Northwest have made Pacific Grove their winter home. Monarch Grove Sanctuary (✉ 1073 Lighthouse Ave.) is a good viewing spot.

★ The celebrated **17-Mile Drive** offers a chance to explore an 8,400-acre microcosm of the Monterey Peninsula's coastal landscape. You'll find the weather-sculpted Lone Cypress tree here. At Seal Rock and Bird Rock, just offshore, you can watch the creatures sunning themselves en masse. Also along the drive is the famous Pebble Beach Golf Links.

Carmel was an important religious center for Spanish California. The stone buildings and tower dome of the 1770 **Carmel Mission** (✉ Rio Rd. and Lasuen Dr., ☎ 831/624–3600; 🎫 $2) have been beautifully restored. Another example of Carmel's architectural heritage is the late poet Robinson Jeffers's **Tor House** (✉ 26304 Ocean View Ave., ☎ 831/

624–1813 or 831/624–1840; 🎫 $7). The house is open only on Friday and Saturday; reservations are essential to view it.

Carmel's greatest beauty is in the rugged coastline and surrounding cypress forests, best seen at **Carmel River State Park,** off Scenic Road and south of Carmel Beach, and the larger **Point Lobos State Reserve** (☎ 831/24–4909 for both), a 1,250-acre headland south of Carmel. At the latter, the Sea Lion Point Trail is a good spot to observe sea lions, otters, harbor seals, and seasonally migrating whales.

You can catch the quintessential view of California's coast from the elegant concrete arc of **Bixby Creek Bridge,** 13 mi south of Carmel. **Big Sur** begins at the Point Sur Light Station, atop a sandstone cliff south of Bixby Creek. At **Pfeiffer Big Sur State Park** (☎ 831/667–2315) a trail leads up a small valley to a waterfall. One of the few places where you can actually reach the water is Pfeiffer Beach (follow the road just past the Big Sur Ranger Station for 2 mi).

★ **Hearst Castle** reigns in solitary splendor a few miles north of Cambria. William Randolph Hearst's grandiose mansion contains extravagant marble halls, ornate swimming pools, and an extensive European art and antiquities collection. A film ($6) at the giant-screen theater details Hearst's life and the castle's construction. Tour reservations are usually required and may be made up to eight weeks in advance. ☎ *805/927–2020 or 800/444–4445.* 🎫 *$14 day tours ($25 sunset).*

The coastal ribbon of Highway 1 ends at **Morro Bay.** Morro Rock, with the sheltered harbor on one side and the Pacific surf on the other, is a preserve for peregrine falcons. At **San Luis Obispo,** south of Morro Bay, halfway between San Francisco and Los Angeles, are such historic sites as the 1772 Mission San Luis Obispo de Tolosa (☎ 805/543–6850) downtown. Drop by the garish, goofy **Madonna Inn** (✉ 100 Madonna Rd., off U.S. 101, ☎ 805/543–3000 or 800/543–9666) if only for a drink and a look at the kitschy accoutrements.

Temperate **Santa Barbara** seems like the most relaxed place in the world. It retains its Spanish character with wide tree-shaded streets, red-tile-roof arcades downtown, and courtyards filled with upscale boutiques and restaurants. Scenic murals adorn the interior walls of the Spanish-Moorish-style ★ **Santa Barbara County Courthouse** (✉ 1100 Anacapa St., ☎ 805/962–6464), well worth a visit. The Spanish built what is now **El Presidio State Historic Park** (✉ 123 E. Cañon Perdido St., ☎ 805/966–9719) as a military stronghold in 1782. Along the Santa Barbara waterfront, not far from downtown, is **Stearns Wharf** (✉ Cabrillo Blvd. at State St.), a pier holding shops, eateries, and the Museum of Natural History's Sea Center. The landmark ★ **Mission Santa Barbara** (✉ 2201 Laguna St., ☎ 805/682–4713) lies a bit north of Stearns Wharf. In the Santa Ynez foothills, the **Santa Barbara Botanic Garden** (✉ 1212 Mission Canyon Rd., ☎ 805/682–4726; 🎫 $3) contains 65 acres of native plants.

Dining and Lodging

For price ranges *see* Charts 1 (A) and 2 (A) *in* On the Road with Fodor's.

Big Sur

$$$–$$$$ ✕ **Nepenthe.** On an 800-ft cliff overlooking lush meadows and the ocean, the house now occupied by this restaurant was once owned by Orson Welles. The food—from roast chicken to sandwiches and hamburgers—is only adequate; it's the location that warrants a stop. ✉ *Hwy. 1 at south end of town,* ☎ *831/667–2345. AE, MC, V.*

$$$$ ★ ✕🏨 **Post Ranch Inn.** Each unit at this cliff-top resort has its own spa tub, stereo, private deck, fireplace, and massage table. The inn's restaurant, serving cutting-edge American fare, is the best in the area. ✉ *Hwy. 1 (Box 219), 93920,* ☎ *831/667–2200 or 800/527–2200,* FAX *831/667–2512. 30 rooms. Restaurant, pools, exercise room. CP. AE, MC, V.*

$$$$ ★ ✕🏨 **Ventana.** The activities at this quintessential California getaway with lodge-style rooms are purposely limited to sunning at poolside—there is a clothing-optional deck—and walks in the hills nearby. The hotel's stone and wood restaurant serves California cuisine with Continental influences (weekend brunch on the terrace is a real event). ✉ *Hwy 1. 93920,* ☎ *831/667–2331 or 800/628–6500,* FAX *831/667–2419. 59 rooms, 3 houses. Restaurant, pools, exercise room. CP. AE, D, DC, MC, V.*

$$$ 🏨 **Big Sur Lodge.** Motel-style cottages at this lodge within Pfeiffer Big Sur State Park—some with fireplaces or kitchens—are set around a meadow surrounded by redwood and oak trees. ✉ *Hwy. 1 (Box 190), 93920,* ☎ *831/667–3100 or 800/424–4787,* FAX *831/667–3110. 61 rooms. Restaurant, pool. AE, MC, V.*

Cambria

$$–$$$ ★ ✕ **Sea Chest.** Perched on the sea's edge, the best seafood joint in Cambria has a very popular oyster bar. ✉ *6216 Moonstone Beach,* ☎ *805/927–4514. Reservations not accepted. No lunch. No credit cards.*

$–$$ ★ ✕ **Hamlet at Moonstone Gardens.** This patio in the middle of 3 acres of luxuriant gardens is perfect for lunch. An upstairs dining room overlooks the Pacific. Salmon comes poached in white wine; meat entrées range from hamburgers to rack of lamb. ✉ *Hwy. 1 on east side,* ☎ *805/927–3535. MC, V.*

$$–$$$ 🏨 **Cypress Cove Inn.** This romantic getaway was designed in the Welsh style, with outside walls made of old stone. Ask for a room facing the Pacific. ✉ *6348 Moonstone Beach Dr., 93428,* ☎ *805/927–2600 or 800/568–8517. 21 rooms, 1 suite. Hot tub. AE, MC ,V.*

$$ 🏨 **San Simeon Pines Resort.** The accommodations at this motel-style resort include cottages with landscaped backyards. Rooms in parts of the complex are for adults only; others are reserved for families. ✉ *7200 Moonstone Beach Dr. (mailing address: Box 117), San Simeon 93452,* ☎ *805/927–4648. 58 rooms. Pool. AE, MC, V.*

Carmel

$$$ ★ ✕ **Kincaid's Bistro.** The country-French cuisine at this atmospheric spot includes cassoulet made with white beans, duck confit, rabbit sausage, and garlic prawns. ✉ *Crossroads Center, 217 Crossroads Blvd.,* ☎ *831/624–9626. AE, D, MC, V. Closed Sun. No lunch Sat.*

$–$$ ✕ **Caffé Napoli.** Redolent of garlic and olive oil, this small Italian restaurant is a favorite of locals, who come for the crisp-crusted pizzas, house-made pastas, and fresh seafood. ✉ *Ocean Ave. at Lincoln,* ☎ *831/625–4033 . Reservations essential on weekends. MC, V.*

$$$$ ★ ✕🏨 **Highlands Inn.** On cliffs above the Pacific, the inn has plush spa suites and condominium-style units with wood-burning fireplaces and ocean-view decks. Some accommodations have full kitchens. ✉ *Hwy. 1 (Box 1700), 93921,* ☎ *831/624–3801 or 800/538–9525, 800/682–4811 in CA;* FAX *831/626–1574. 142 rooms. 2 restaurants, pool. AE, D, DC, MC, V.*

$–$$ 🏨 **Carmel River Inn.** This great value near area beaches is across the street from a supermarket (some rooms have kitchenettes). ✉ *Hwy. 1, at the Carmel River Bridge (Box 221609), 93922,* ☎ *831/624–1575 or 800/882–8142,* FAX *831/624–0290. 43 rooms. Pool. MC, V.*

Monterey

$$$–$$$$ ✕ **Fresh Cream.** The cuisine at this harborview restaurant is French, with imaginative Californian accents. Some favorites on the menu (which changes weekly) are the rack of lamb Dijonnaise and the blackened ahi tuna with pineapple rum-butter sauce. ✉ *99 Pacific St., Suite 100C,* ☎ *831/375–9798. AE, D, DC, MC, V. No lunch.*

$–$$$ ✕ **Paradiso Trattoria and Oyster Bar.** Mediterranean specialties and pizzas from a wood-burning oven are the luncheon fare at this Cannery Row eatery. Seafood is a good choice for dinner, served in a dining room overlooking a lighted beachfront or at the gleaming oyster bar. ✉ *654 Cannery Row,* ☎ *831/375–4155. AE, D, DC, MC, V.*

$–$$$ ✕ **Tarpy's Roadhouse.** Fun, dressed-down roadhouse lunch and dinner are served in a renovated farmhouse built in the early 1900s. The kitchen cooks everything Mom used to make, only better. ✉ *2999 Monterey–Salinas Hwy. (Hwy. 68), at Canyon Del Rey Rd.,* ☎ *831/647–1444. AE, D, MC, V.*

$$$–$$$$ ★ **Spindrift Inn.** This Cannery Row hotel has beach access and a rooftop garden. Rooms are spacious, with hardwood floors, featherbeds, fireplaces, canopied beds, down comforters, and other luxuries. ✉ *652 Cannery Row, 93940,* ☎ *831/646–8900 or 800/841–1879,* FAX *831/646–5342. 42 rooms. CP. AE, D, DC, MC, V.*

$–$$$ **Quality Inn.** Some of the rooms at this friendly property have fireplaces; in-room coffee is complimentary. ✉ *1058 Munras Ave., 93940,* ☎ *831/372–3381,* FAX *831/372–4687. 55 rooms. Hot tub. AE, D, DC, MC, V.*

Morro Bay

$$–$$$ **Embarcadero Inn.** A drab metallic exterior hides a more welcoming interior of sparkling clean rooms, all of them with old maritime photographs on the walls and balconies that face the sea. ✉ *456 Embarcadero, 93442,* ☎ *805/772–2700 or 800/292–7625,* FAX *805/772–1060. 26 rooms, 4 suites. 2 hot tubs. AE, D, DC, MC, V.*

Pacific Grove

$$$ ★ ✕ **Old Bath House.** This romantic converted bathhouse overlooks the water at Lovers Point. The menu makes the most of local seafood and produce. ✉ *620 Ocean View Blvd.,* ☎ *831/375–5195. AE, D, DC, MC, V. No lunch.*

Santa Barbara

$$$ ★ ✕ **Citronelle.** The accent at this offspring of Citron in Los Angeles is on French Riviera–style dishes: light and delicate but loaded with intriguing good tastes. Sweeping harbor views can be had from the dining room. ✉ *901 E. Cabrillo Blvd.,* ☎ *805/963–0111. AE, D, DC, MC, V.*

$$–$$$ ✕ **Brophy Bros.** The seafood salads at this boisterous harborfront restaurant are excellent, as are the daytime ocean views. Arrive hungry—the entrée portions—straightforward fish and seafood—are huge. ✉ *119 Harbor Way,* ☎ *805/966–4418. AE, MC, V.*

$ ★ ✕ **La Super-Rica.** Fans of this food stand with a patio drive for miles to fill up on soft tacos and incredible beans. ✉ *622 N. Milpas St., at Alphonse St.,* ☎ *805/963–4940. No credit cards.*

$ ✕ **Roy.** This downtown storefront is a real bargain. Owner-chef Leroy Gandy serves a $12.50 prix-fixe dinner that includes a small salad, fresh soup, and a tempting roster of Cal-Mediterranean main courses. Expect a wait on weekends. ✉ *7 W. Carrillo St.,* ☎ *805/966–5636. AE, D, DC, MC, V.*

$$$$ ★ **Four Seasons Biltmore.** This grande dame of Santa Barbara hostelries is more formal than other city accommodations, with lush gardens and palm trees galore. ✉ *1260 Channel Dr., Montecito 93108,* ☎ *805/*

969–2261 or 800/332–3442, FAX 805/969–5715. 234 rooms. 2 restaurants, pool, health club. AE, DC, MC, V.

$$–$$$$ ★ **Glenborough Inn.** One of the best B&Bs in Santa Barbara County, this inn is composed of four buildings constructed around the dawn of the 20th century. Several of the very private rooms retain an old, darkwood feel. ✉ *1327 Bath St., 93101,* ☎ *805/966–0589 or 800/962–0589,* FAX *805/564–8610. 6 rooms, 8 suites. Full breakfast. AE, MC, V.*

$$–$$$$ **Hotel Santa Barbara.** The central location of this hotel makes it one of the better bargains in town. The rooms are serviceable; from the top floors, guests can see the ocean. Rooms in the back are quieter. ✉ *533 State St. 93101,* ☎ *888/259–7700. 75 rooms. AE, D, MC, V.*

$ **Motel 6.** Low price and great location near the beach are the pluses for this no-frills motel. ✉ *443 Corona Del Mar Dr., 93103,* ☎ *805/564–1392,* FAX *805/963–4687. 51 rooms. Pool. AE, D, DC, MC, V.*

Nightlife and the Arts

The Carmel-Monterey area's top performing arts venue is the **Sunset Community Cultural Center** (✉ San Carlos St. between 8th and 10th Aves., Carmel, ☎ 831/624–3996), which presents concerts, lectures, and headline performers. The **Arlington Theater** (☎ 805/963–4408) is home to the Santa Barbara Symphony.

Outdoor Activities and Sports

Biking

The Monterey Peninsula is prime biking territory, with paths following parts of the shoreline. **Bay Sports** (✉ 640 Wave St., ☎ 831/646–9090) rents bikes. In Santa Barbara the **Cabrillo Bike Lane** passes the city zoo, a bird refuge, beaches, and the harbor. Rent bikes, quadricycles, and skates from **Beach Rentals** (✉ 22 State St., ☎ 805/966–6733).

Fishing

Charter boats leave from Monterey, Morro Bay, and Santa Barbara. Most trips—from such outfits as **Monterey Sport Fishing and Whale Watching** (✉ 96 Fisherman's Wharf, Monterey, ☎ 831/372–2203) or **Sea Landing Sportfishing** (✉ Cabrillo Blvd. at Bath, Santa Barbara, ☎ 805/963–3564)—include equipment rental, bait, fish cleaning, and a license.

Golf

Pebble Beach Golf Links (✉ 17-Mile Dr., ☎ 831/625–8518), with its sweeping ocean views, is one of the world's most famous courses; reservations are essential. At **Spyglass Hill** (✉ Spyglass Hill Rd., ☎ 831/624–3811), the holes are unforgiving, but the views offer consolation. The **Santa Barbara Golf Club** (✉ Las Positas Rd. and McCaw Ave., ☎ 805/687–7087) and **Sandpiper Golf Course** (✉ 7925 Hollister Ave., Goleta, ☎ 805/968–1541) are two options farther south.

Whale-Watching

On their annual migration between the Bering Sea and Baja California, 45-ft gray whales can be spotted at many points not far off the coast. The migration south takes place from December through February; the journey north, from March to mid-May. Other species of whales can be seen in the summer and autumn.

Beaches

In general, the shoreline north of San Luis Obispo is rocky and backed by cliffs, the water rough and often cold, and sunbathing limited to only the warmest hours of the early afternoon. Still, **Point Lobos State Reserve, Big Sur,** and **Morro Bay** provide unparalleled beach experiences. ★ **Pismo Beach** marks the first of the classic southern California beaches, with long, low stretches of sand. From Point Concepción down through Santa Barbara and into Ventura County are some fine beaches. Santa Barbara's **East Beach** has lifeguards, volleyball courts, a jogging-and-biking trail, a jungle-gym play area, and a bathhouse with a gym, showers, and changing rooms. **Arroyo Burro County Beach,** near Santa Barbara, is a state preserve, with a small grassy area that has picnic tables and with sandy beaches below the cliffs. **El Capitan, Refugio,** and **Gaviota state beaches** near Santa Barbara have campsites, picnic tables, and fire pits.

LOS ANGELES

Los Angeles is a wholly 20th-century city, created, defined, dependent on, and thrust into prominence by the advances of the modern age: automobiles, airplanes, and the movies. It is among the nation's most ethnically diverse cities, with thriving Hispanic, Korean, Chinese, Japanese, and Middle Eastern communities.

Visitor Information

Convention and Visitors Bureau (⊠ 633 W. 5th St., Suite 6000, 90071, ☎ 213/624–7300).

Arriving and Departing

By Bus

Greyhound Lines (⊠ 1716 E. 7th St., at Alameda St., ☎ 800/231–2222).

By Car

The main north–south route into Los Angeles is I–5 (called the Golden State or Santa Ana Freeway here). U.S. 101 (called the Hollywood Freeway) travels south through Los Angeles. I–10 (called the Santa Monica Freeway) runs east–west across the United States; its western terminus is Santa Monica. I–15 travels north from San Diego to Los Angeles, then heads northeast toward California's border with Nevada.

By Plane

Los Angeles International Airport (LAX; ☎ 310/646–5252), about 25 mi west of downtown and 10 mi from Beverly Hills, is served by more than 85 major airlines. Four smaller regional airports—in Burbank, Long Beach, Orange County, and Ontario—also serve the greater L.A. area. Taxis to downtown cost $24–$30 (request a flat fee—metered fares are more) and take 20–60 minutes, depending on traffic. **SuperShuttle** (☎ 310/782–6600) services downtown hotels for about $12 ($13 to Disneyland hotels); fares to private residences vary. **Airport Bus** (☎ 714/938–8900 or 800/772–5299) provides service from LAX to the Pasadena ($12 one-way, $20 round-trip) and Anaheim ($14 and $22) areas.

By Train

Amtrak (☎ 800/872–7245) serves Los Angeles's Union Station (⊠ 800 N. Alameda St.).

Getting Around Los Angeles

Freeways, whose names can change along the route, are the most efficient way to get from one end of the city to another.

By Public Transportation

The **Southern California Metropolitan Transit Authority** (MTA; ☎ 213/626–4455) provides bus and light-rail service. Bus fare is $1.35 plus 25¢ for a transfer. **DASH** (Downtown Area Short Hop; ☎ 213/626–

Los Angeles

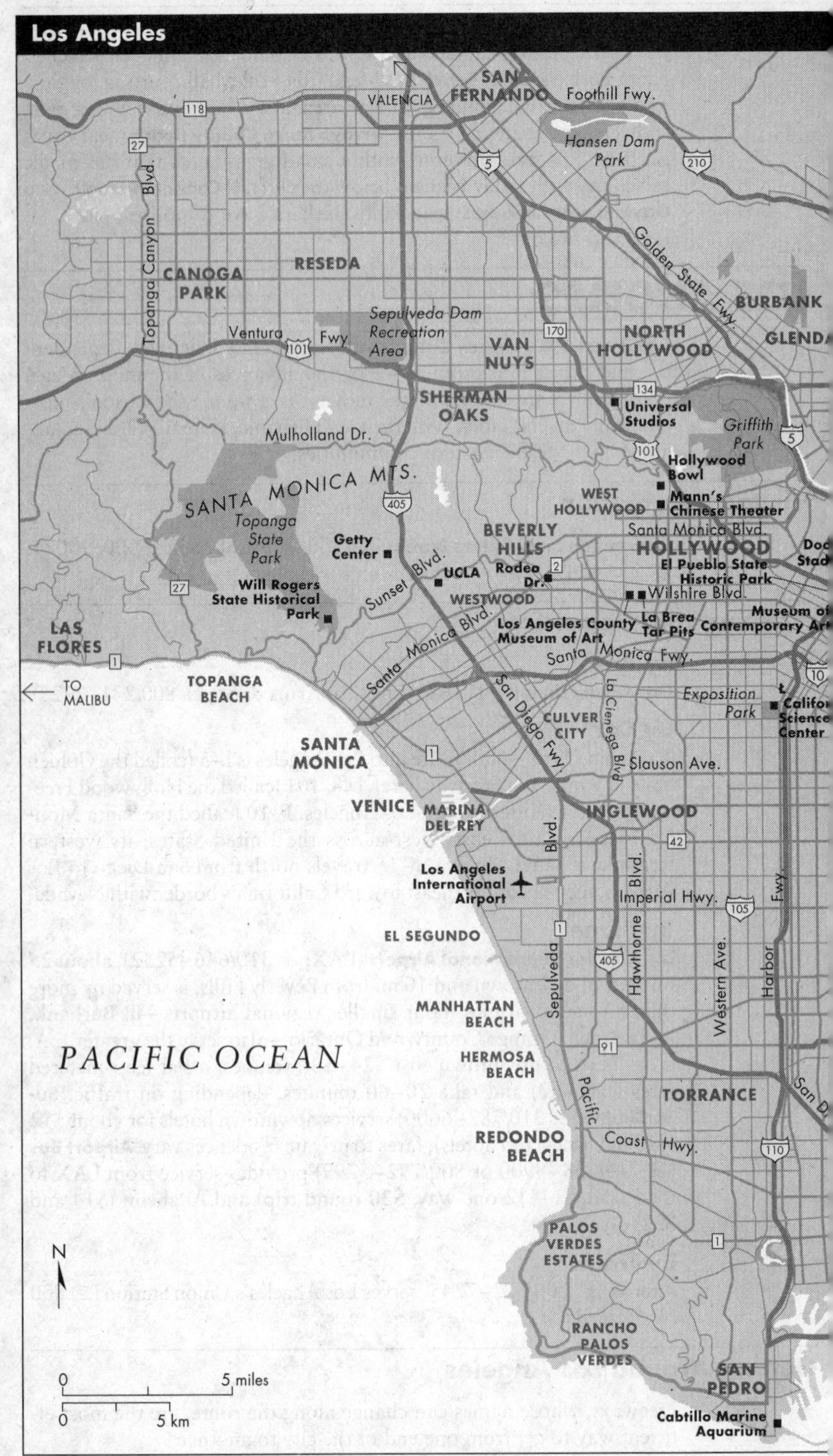

SAN FERNANDO
VALENCIA
Foothill Fwy.
Hansen Dam Park
118
27
5
210
Topanga Canyon Blvd.
Golden State Fwy.
CANOGA PARK
RESEDA
BURBANK
Sepulveda Dam Recreation Area
Ventura
101
Fwy
170
VAN NUYS
NORTH HOLLYWOOD
GLENDA
SHERMAN OAKS
134
Universal Studios
Griffith Park
Mulholland Dr.
101
Hollywood Bowl
SANTA MONICA MTS.
405
WEST HOLLYWOOD
Mann's Chinese Theater
Topanga State Park
BEVERLY HILLS
Santa Monica Blvd.
HOLLYWOOD
Getty Center
Rodeo Dr.
2
El Pueblo State Historic Park
Will Rogers State Historical Park
27
Sunset Blvd.
UCLA
WESTWOOD
Wilshire Blvd.
LAS FLORES
Los Angeles County Museum of Art
La Brea Tar Pits
Museum of Contemporary Art
Santa Monica Blvd.
1
Santa Monica Fwy.
TO MALIBU
TOPANGA BEACH
La Cienega Blvd.
Exposition Park
San Diego Fwy.
CULVER CITY
SANTA MONICA
1
Slauson Ave.
VENICE
MARINA DEL REY
INGLEWOOD
42
Los Angeles International Airport
Blvd.
Imperial Hwy.
105
Fwy.
EL SEGUNDO
1
405
Sepulveda
Hawthorne Blvd.
Western Ave.
Harbor
MANHATTAN BEACH
PACIFIC OCEAN
HERMOSA BEACH
91
Pacific
TORRANCE
REDONDO BEACH
Coast Hwy.
110
PALOS VERDES ESTATES
1
N
RANCHO PALOS VERDES
SAN PEDRO
0
5 miles
0
5 km
Cabtillo Marine Aquarium

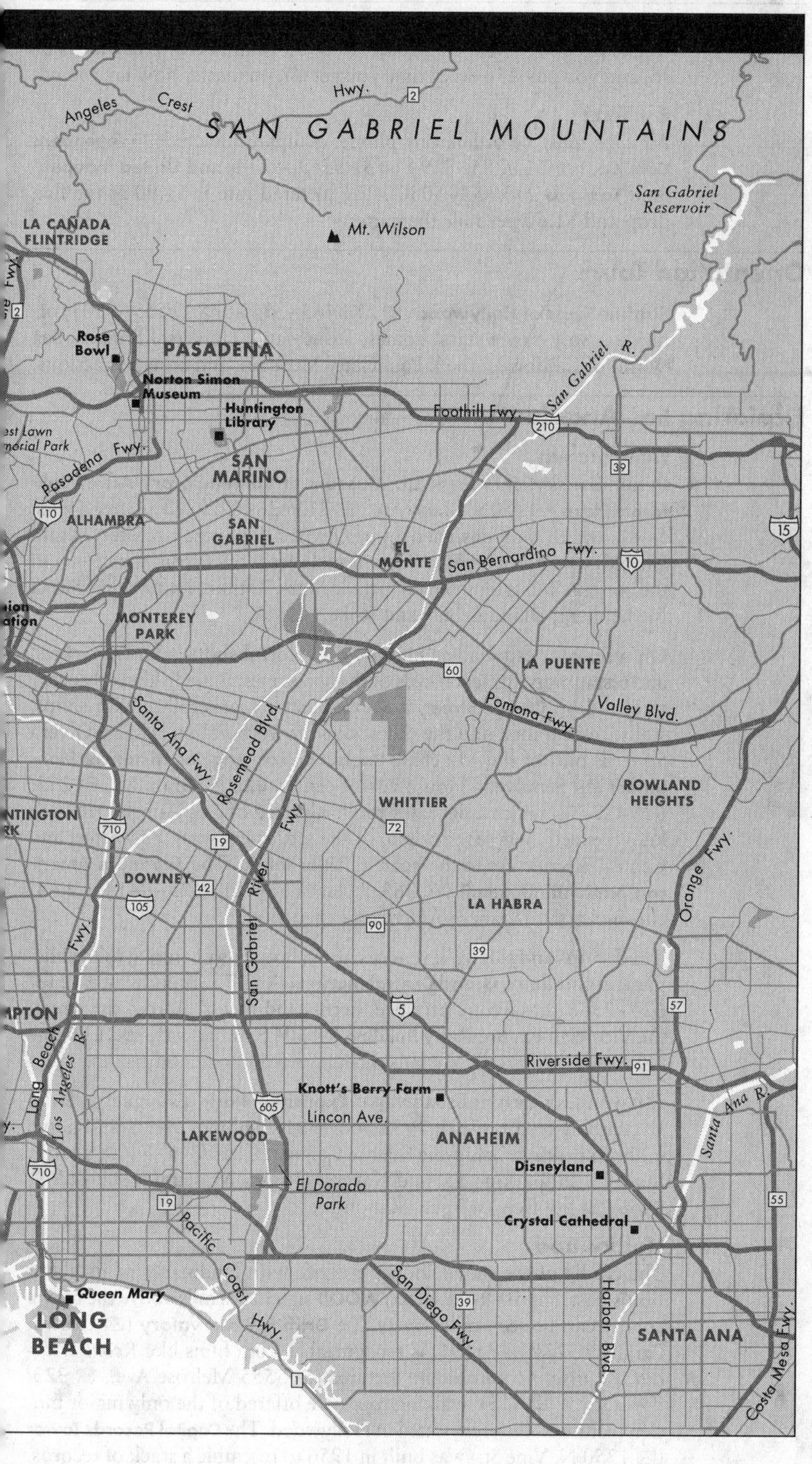

SAN GABRIEL MOUNTAINS
Angeles Crest Hwy.
2
San Gabriel Reservoir
Mt. Wilson
LA CAÑADA FLINTRIDGE
Rose Bowl
PASADENA
Norton Simon Museum
Huntington Library
SAN MARINO
Pasadena Fwy.
110
ALHAMBRA
SAN GABRIEL
Foothill Fwy.
210
San Gabriel R.
39
15
EL MONTE
San Bernardino Fwy.
10
MONTEREY PARK
60
LA PUENTE
Pomona Fwy.
Valley Blvd.
Santa Ana Fwy.
Rosemead Blvd.
San Gabriel River Fwy.
WHITTIER
72
ROWLAND HEIGHTS
710
19
DOWNEY
42
105
LA HABRA
90
39
Orange Fwy.
57
5
Long Beach Fwy.
Los Angeles R.
Riverside Fwy.
91
Knott's Berry Farm
Lincon Ave.
605
LAKEWOOD
ANAHEIM
Santa Ana R.
Disneyland
El Dorado Park
19
55
Pacific Coast Hwy.
Crystal Cathedral
San Diego Fwy.
39
Queen Mary
LONG BEACH
Harbor Blvd.
SANTA ANA
Costa Mesa Fwy.
1

4455) is a system of minibuses serving the downtown area. DASH runs weekdays 6 AM–7 PM, Saturday 10–5. Stops are every two blocks or so, and you pay 25¢ every time you get on, no matter how far you go.

By Taxi

All cabs must be ordered by phone; companies include **Independent Cab. Co.** (☎ 213/385–8294 or 310/569–8214) and **United Independent Taxi** (☎ 213/653–5050). The metered rate is $1.90 at the flag drop and $1.60 per mile thereafter.

Orientation Tours

Starline Tours of Hollywood (☎ 213/463–3333 or 800/959–3131) offers tours of movie stars' homes, Disneyland, Universal Studios, Sea World of California, the J. Paul Getty Museum, and other attractions.

Exploring Los Angeles

Downtown

★ Pyramidal skylights mark the **Museum of Contemporary Art at California Plaza** (✉ 250 S. Grand Ave., ☎ 213/626–6222; 🎫 $6; free Thurs. 5–8), which was designed by renowned Japanese architect Arata Isozaki. The permanent collection includes works from the 1940s to the present; artists represented include Mark Rothko, Franz Kline, Susan Rothenberg, Diane Arbus, and Robert Frank.

On weekends especially, **Chinatown**'s colorful shops, exotic markets, and restaurants attract crowds of shoppers. Fiestas are held nearly every weekend on **Olvera Street,** a Mexican-style marketplace with shops, stalls, restaurants, and the oldest downtown building (1818). Olvera Street is part of the 44-acre **El Pueblo de Los Angeles Historical Monument** (✉ Sepulveda House visitor center, 622 N. Main St., ☎ 213/628–1274), which celebrates the birthplace of Los Angeles (no one knows exactly where the original 1781 settlement was). First Street and
★ Central Avenue are in the heart of **Little Tokyo.** The **Japanese American National Museum** (✉ 369 E. 1st St., ☎ 213/625–0414; 🎫 $4) chronicles the Japanese-American experience.

Amid shops and sidewalk vendors along Broadway catering to the Hispanic community, **Grand Central Market** (✉ 317 S. Broadway, ☎ 213/624–2378) has exotic produce, herbs, and meats. Across the street, the Victorian-era **Bradbury Building** (✉ 304 S. Broadway, ☎ 213/626–1893) has a filigreed, glassed-in courtyard and open balconies.

A few miles south of Broadway is **Exposition Park** (✉ Figueroa St. at Exposition Blvd.), site of 1932 and 1984 Olympics events and home to the impressive **California Science Center** (☎ 213/744–7400; 🎫 free; Imax $7.25; parking $5) and **Natural History Museum** (☎ 213/763-3466; 🎫 $6; free 1st Tues. of month).

Hollywood

The cradle of the movie industry is rife with landmarks of its glamorous past.The 50-ft-tall **HOLLYWOOD** sign in the hills above the movie colony can be seen miles away.The **Griffith Observatory** (✉ Griffith Park, ☎ 323/664–1191) is recognizable from films like *Rebel Without a Cause.* At **Paramount Pictures** (✉ 5555 Melrose Ave., ☎ 323/956–5575; 🎫 $15), walking tours are offered of the only major motion picture studio still located in Hollywood. The **Capitol Records Tower** (✉ 1750 N. Vine St.) was built in 1956 to resemble a stack of records. Along Hollywood Boulevard, **Frederick's of Hollywood** (✉ 6608 Hollywood Blvd., ☎ 213/466–8506), the famous name in risqué lingerie,
★ has a bra museum. **Mann's Chinese Theatre** (✉ 6925 Hollywood Blvd.,

☎ 213/464–8111), originally Grauman's Chinese, invented the gala movie premiere; its famous courtyard holds the footprints and other bodily impressions of more than 160 celebrities. The **Hollywood Entertainment Museum** (✉ 7021 Hollywood Blvd., ☎ 323/485–7900; 🎟 $7.50) tracks the evolution of Hollywood through multimedia exhibits.

The **Hollywood Walk of Fame** immortalizes the names of movie and other entertainment greats on brass plaques embedded in pink stars along the city's sidewalks. Marlon Brando is at 1765 Vine Street, Clark Gable at 1608 Vine, John Wayne at 1541 Vine, and Marilyn Monroe at 6774 Hollywood Boulevard.

Museum Row and Farmers Market

Wilshire Boulevard begins its grand, 16-mi sweep to the sea in downtown Los Angeles. Along the way, it passes through formerly grand but now run-down neighborhoods near MacArthur Park, the elegant old-money enclave of Hancock Park, the showy city of Beverly Hills, and the high-priced high-rise condo corridor in Westwood before ending its march at the cliffs above the Pacific Ocean. For most visitors, the three-block stretch of Wilshire Boulevard east of Fairfax Avenue, with its four museums of widely varying themes and a prehistoric tar pit to boot, turns out to be the most entertaining portion to explore.

At **La Brea Tar Pits** more than 100 tons of fossils have been removed. Many fossils are on view next door at the **George C. Page Museum** (✉ 5801 Wilshire Blvd., ☎ 213/936–2230; 🎟 $6; free 1st Tues. of month). ★ Next door is the **Los Angeles County Museum of Art** (✉ 5905 Wilshire Blvd., ☎ 323/857–6000; 🎟 $6; free 2nd Tues. of month), containing fine collections of American and Asian art, and a small sculpture garden. The **Petersen Automotive Museum** (✉ 6060 Wilshire Blvd., ☎ 323/930–2277; 🎟 $7) traces the history of the automobile. North of Museum Row is **Farmers Market** (✉ 6333 W. 3rd St., ☎ 323/933–9211), a partly covered marketplace with food stalls, produce vendors, and a few boutiques located near CBS Television City.

Beverly Hills

Beverly Hills lures armies of visitors on the lookout for a famous face and a glimpse of opulence—especially along the ritzy **Rodeo Drive** shopping district. For years the "Pink Palace," the **Beverly Hills Hotel** (✉ 9641 Sunset Blvd., ☎ 310/276–2251), has been a landmark of the ★ Hollywood high life. The **Museum of Television and Radio** (✉ 465 N. Beverly Dr., ☎ 310/786–1000; 🎟 $6) has a collection of 90,000 radio and TV shows spanning 77 years.

The Westside

The Westside districts of Westwood, Brentwood, and Bel Air are among L.A.'s most exclusive, with palatial homes, chic shops, and fine restau- ★ rants. The **Museum of Tolerance** (✉ 9786 W. Pico Blvd., ☎ 310/553–8403; 🎟 $8) uses state-of-the-art technology to challenge bigotry and racism. **Westwood,** which straddles the hillsides between Wilshire and Sunset boulevards, is home to the **University of California at Los Angeles.** UCLA has sculpture and botanical gardens, the Fowler Museum of Cultural History (310/825–4361; 🎟 $5 [free Sun. and Thurs.]), and offers walking tours of the campus (☎ 310/206–0616). The university operates the nearby **Armand Hammer Museum of Art and Cultural Center** (✉ 10899 Wilshire Blvd., ☎ 310/443–7000; 🎟 $4.50, free Thurs. 6–9; parking $2.75). Northwest of Beverly Hills in the Santa ★ Monica Mountains is the Richard Meier–designed **Getty Center** (✉ 1200 Getty Center Dr., ☎ 310/440–7300; 🎟 free; $5 parking), the new home of most of oil billionaire J. Paul Getty's art collection.

Santa Monica and the Beach Cities

Wilshire Boulevard ends at Ocean Avenue in **Santa Monica.** The **Santa Monica Pier** (☎ 310/458–8900) has a 46-horse antique carousel, an amusement park, gift shops, arcade, cafés, and a psychic adviser. A sandy beach stretches north and south of the pier. Palm-shaded **Palisades Park** overlooks the beach from the cliffs above. North from Santa Monica along the Pacific Coast Highway is **Malibu,** site of the beachfront homes of many stars.

Venice, immediately south of Santa Monica, is known for its active scenes—street vendors, musicians, in-line skaters, guys and gals pumping iron, and folks simply tanning—on Ocean Front Walk and the Venice Boardwalk.

San Fernando Valley

★ **Universal Studios Hollywood,** 5 mi north of Hollywood in the San Fernando Valley via the Hollywood Freeway, is a tremendously popular theme park, with five- to seven-hour tram tours of its attractions, which feature plenty of special effects and stage shows. ✉ *100 Universal City Pl.,* ☎ *818/508–9600.* *$36 adults, $26 children. AE, MC, V.*

NBC studios (✉ 3000 W. Alameda, Burbank, ☎ 818/840–3537; $7) offers a walking tour of its facility.

Warner Bros. Studios provides a behind-the-scenes walking tour of its television and film operations. Reserve tickets at least one week in advance. ✉ *4000 Warner Blvd., Burbank,* ☎ *818/954–1744.* *$30. AE, MC, V. No children under 10.*

Pasadena

The communities northeast of downtown L.A. were the first suburbs of the city, established by wealthy Angelenos in the 1880s. In Highland Park the **Southwest Museum** (✉ 234 Museum Dr., ☎ 323/221–2163; $5), which is closed on Monday, houses a collection of ★ Native American art and artifacts. In San Marino the **Huntington Library, Art Collections, and Botanical Gardens** (✉ 1151 Oxford Rd., ☎ 626/405–2100; $8.50; free 1st Thurs. of month) is spread over 207 hilly acres. The complex's collections number more than 4 million items, including a Gutenberg Bible, the Ellesmere manuscript of Chaucer's *Canterbury Tales,* and first editions of Shakespeare.

In Pasadena the **Norton Simon Museum** (✉ 411 W. Colorado Blvd., ☎ 626/449–6840; $4) houses Impressionist paintings, as well as ★ masterpieces by Rembrandt, Goya, and Picasso. **Gamble House** (✉ 4 Westmoreland Pl., ☎ 626/793–3334), built by Charles and Henry Greene in 1908, is the ultimate in California Craftsman–style architecture. The restored historic buildings of **Old Town Pasadena** now house many popular cafes and shops.

Long Beach

To the south, in Long Beach, is the ***Queen Mary*** (✉ Pier H, ☎ 562/435–3511), the famous ocean liner that now houses a hotel, shops, and restaurants. Also in Long Beach are two aquariums: the new **Long Beach Aquarium of the Pacific** (✉ 100 Aquarium Dr., ☎ 562/590–3100; $13) and the smaller **Cabrillo Marine Aquarium** (✉ 3720 Stephen White Dr., San Pedro, ☎ 310/548–7562; $2 donation requested; parking $6.50), designed by Frank Gehry.

Outside Los Angeles

Santa Catalina Island, 26 mi offshore, is a good day trip or weekend getaway from Los Angeles. No private cars are permitted on the island (golf carts can be rented), but the main town of Avalon can be easily explored on foot. From San Pedro and Long Beach, **Catalina Express** (☎ 310/519–1212 or 800/995–4386) provides boat service. **Santa Catalina Island Co.** (☎ 310/510–8687) and **Catalina Adventure Tours** (☎ 310/510–2888) operate escorted bus tours of the interior, coastal cruises, and glass-bottom-boat rides.

Parks, Gardens, and Zoos

★ **Griffith Park** (✉ Ventura and Golden State Fwys., ☎ 213/665–5188) has acres of picnic areas, hiking and bridle trails, a carousel, and pony rides. Also in the park are the **Los Angeles Zoo** (☎ 213/666–4090; 🎫 $8.25); **Travel Town** (✉ 5200 Zoo Dr., ☎ 213/662–5874; 🎫 free), with railcars, planes, and classic cars; and the **Planetarium and Observatory** (✉ Enter at Los Feliz Blvd. and Vermont Ave., ☎ 213/664–1191; 🎫 $4).

Dining

Parking can be difficult; most restaurants listed here offer valet parking. For price ranges *see* Chart 1 (A) *in* On the Road with Fodor's.

$$$$ ★ ✕ **L'Orangerie.** French specialties at this elegant restaurant (jacket and tie advised) include duck with foie gras, John Dory with roasted figs, rack of lamb for two, and a sublime apple tart. ✉ *903 N. La Cienega Blvd., West Hollywood,* ☎ *310/652–9770. Reservations essential. AE, D, DC, MC, V. Closed Mon. No lunch.*

$$$–$$$$ ★ ✕ **Campanile.** The restaurant in Charlie Chaplin's former office complex serves dishes that include grilled sardine, rosemary charred rack of lamb, and crusty sourdough-base breads. ✉ *624 S. La Brea Ave., Hollywood,* ☎ *213/938–1447. Reservations essential. AE, D, DC, MC, V. Brunch Sat.–Sun. No dinner Sun.*

$$$–$$$$ ★ ✕ **Citrus.** One of L.A.'s most prominent chefs, Michel Richard, creates superb dishes by blending French and American cuisines. You can't miss with the delectable tuna burger, the impossibly thin angel-hair pasta, or the carpaccio salad. ✉ *6703 Melrose Ave., Hollywood,* ☎ *213/857–0034. AE, MC, V. Closed Sun. No lunch Sat.*

$$$–$$$$ ★ ✕ **Dining Room at the Regent Beverly Wilshire.** The classy California cuisine served here includes Santa Barbara blue prawns with sweet-potato agnolotti. Adjoining the Dining Room is a cocktail lounge, with romantic lighting and a pianist playing show tunes. ✉ *Regent Beverly Wilshire Hotel, 9500 Wilshire Blvd., Beverly Hills,* ☎ *310/274–8179. Jacket. AE, D, DC, MC, V.*

$$$–$$$$ ★ ✕ **Granita.** The menu at this Wolfgang Puck eatery favors seafood items. There's also a spicy shrimp pizza with sun-dried tomatoes and herb pesto and a roasted Chinese duck with dried fruit chutney. ✉ *23725 W. Malibu Rd. (Malibu),* ☎ *310/456–0488. Reservations essential. D, DC, MC, V. Brunch Sat., Sun. No lunch.*

$$$ ✕ **Spago Hollywood.** At this restaurant that propelled Wolfgang Puck into the culinary spotlight, the proof is in the tasting: grilled baby Sonoma lamb, pizza with Santa Barbara shrimp, and baby salmon. ✉ *1114 Horn Ave., West Hollywood,* ☎ *310/652–4025. Reservations essential. D, DC, MC, V. Closed Mon. No lunch.*

$$–$$$ ★ ✕ **Ca'Brea.** The modern Italian fare includes roast leg of lamb with black-truffle-and-mustard sauce and whole boneless chicken marinated and grilled with herbs. ✉ *346 S. La Brea Ave. (Hollywood),* ☎ *213/938–2863. AE, D, DC, MC, V. Closed Sun. No lunch weekends.*

$$–$$$ ★ ✕ **La Cachette.** Owner-chef Jean-François Meteigner's modern French cuisine manages to be both light and appealing. ✉ *10506 Little Santa Monica Blvd., West Los Angeles,* ☎ *310/470–4992. Reservations essential. AE, MC, V. No lunch weekends.*

$$–$$$ ★ ✕ **Cafe Pinot.** The Pinot menu is rooted in the traditional French bistro standards—steak *frites,* roast chicken encrusted with five mustards, lamb shank—but it also includes some superb light spa dishes and a few worthy pastas. ✉ *700 W. 5th St. (downtown),* ☎ *213/239–6500. Reservations essential. DC, MC, V. No lunch weekends.*

$$–$$$ ✕ **Chan Dara.** Try any of the Thai noodle dishes here, especially those with crab and shrimp. Also tops on the extensive menu are *satay* (skewered meat appetizers with peanut sauce) and barbecued chicken and catfish. ✉ *310 N. Larchmont Blvd., Hollywood,* ☎ *213/467–1052. AE, D, DC, MC, V. No lunch weekends.*

$$–$$$ ✕ **Dive!** Only Steven Spielberg could have created such a restaurant—it's as much a theme park as a place to eat. The specialty is submarine sandwiches; good ones include the Parisian chicken and the brick oven–baked Tuscan steak. ✉ *10250 Santa Monica Blvd., Century City,* ☎ *310/788–3483. Reservations not accepted. AE, D, DC, MC, V.*

$$–$$$ ★ ✕ **Restaurant Katsu.** This stylishly stark, beautifully designed sushi bar and restaurant is the stage for exquisite and delicious Japanese delicacies. ✉ *1972 N. Hillhurst Ave., Los Feliz,* ☎ *213/665–1891. Reservations essential. AE, DC, MC, V. Closed Sun. No lunch Sat.*

$$–$$$ ★ ✕ **Valentino.** The light, modern Italian dishes at this top-notch restaurant include calamari al pesto, seafood risotto, and pigeon in honey-fig sauce. Order from the lengthy list of daily specials. ✉ *3115 Pico Blvd., Santa Monica,* ☎ *310/829–4313. Reservations essential. AE, DC, MC, V. Closed Sun. No lunch Sat. and Mon.–Thurs.*

$$–$$$ ★ ✕ **Yujean Kang's Gourmet Chinese Cuisine.** Start with the tender slices of veal on a bed of enoki and black mushrooms and topped with a tangle of quick-fried shoestring yams or the sea bass with kumquats and a passion-fruit sauce; then finish with poached plums or with watermelon ice under a mantle of white chocolate. ✉ *67 N. Raymond Ave., Pasadena,* ☎ *818/585–0855. AE, D, DC, MC, V.*

$$ ★ ✕ **Border Grill.** The eclectic menu here ranges from grilled tandoori skirt steak marinated in garlic and cilantro to grilled fish tacos to vinegar-and-pepper-grilled turkey. ✉ *1445 4th St., Santa Monica,* ☎ *310/451–1655. AE, D, DC, MC, V.*

$$ ★ ✕ **Broadway Deli.** Whatever you feel like eating at this brasserie-cum-upscale-diner, you will probably find it on the menu, from a platter of assorted smoked fish or Caesar salad to shepherd's pie, carpaccio, steak, and grilled swordfish. ✉ *1457 3rd St. Promenade, Santa Monica,* ☎ *310/451–0616. Reservations not accepted. AE, MC, V.*

$$ ★ ✕ **El Cholo.** This restaurant serves zesty margaritas and tacos (including some you make yourself), along with L.A.-Mex versions of chicken enchiladas, *carnitas,* and other standards. ✉ *1121 S. Western Ave., Mid-Wilshire,* ☎ *213/734–2773. AE, DC, MC, V.*

Lodging

Because of L.A.'s sprawl, select a hotel that is close to where you'll be touring. For price ranges *see* Chart 2 (A) *in* On the Road with Fodor's.

$$$$ ★ **Mondrian.** Each apartment-size accommodation at this ultra-hip Ian Schrager–run property is done in white with industrial gray carpeting, floor-to-ceiling windows, slipcovered sofas, marble-top coffee tables, and a kitchen with sleek Philippe Starck–designed accessories. ✉ *8440 Sunset Blvd., 90069,* ☎ *213/650–8999 or 800/525–8029,* FAX *213/650–5215. 238 rooms. Restaurant, pool, health club. AE, D, DC, MC, V.*

$$$$ **Regal Biltmore Hotel.** Many historic details at this 1923 classic remain. Guest rooms have overstuffed beds, flowing draperies, and period furnishings. There's a concierge level, and rooms and services provided on the 11th floor cater to business travelers. ✉ *506 S. Grand*

Ave., 90071, ☎ 213/624–1011 or 800/245–8673, FAX 213/612–1545. 683 rooms. 3 restaurants, pool, health club. AE, D, DC, MC, V.

$$$$ ★ **Regent Beverly Wilshire.** Known of late as the Pretty Woman Hotel (its presidential suite was showcased in the film), the Regent is a long-time classic. Accommodations have appropriate period furnishings and glorious marble bathrooms with deep tubs. ✉ *9500 Wilshire Blvd., 90212, ☎ 310/275–5200; 800/427–4354 in CA; 800/421–4354 in the rest of the U.S.; FAX 310/274–2851. 344 rooms. 2 restaurants, pool, health club. AE, D, DC, MC, V.*

$$$$ ★ **Shutters On The Beach.** Locals looking to get away from it all often come to Los Angeles's only hotel sitting directly on the sand. Amenities include fluffy beds with Frette linens, lavish tubs, and complimentary classic movies for the VCR. ✉ *1 Pico Blvd., 90405, ☎ 310/458–0030 or 800/334–9000, FAX 310/458–4589. 198 rooms. 2 restaurants, pool, hot tub, health club. AE, D, DC, MC, V.*

$$$ ★ **Beverly Hills Inn.** This European-style inn is a nice alternative to the town's more mammoth (and more expensive) luxury hotels. The address is trendy, the service is excellent, and a complimentary breakfast is delivered to your door each morning. ✉ *125 S. Spalding Dr., 90212, ☎ 310/278–0303 or 800/463–4466, FAX 310/278–1728. 54 rooms. Pool, exercise room. CP. AE, DC, MC, V.*

$$$ **Clarion Hotel Hollywood Roosevelt.** A landmark hotel with a hip Art Deco lobby, the Hollywood Roosevelt hosted Tinseltown's golden-age elite. The room decor isn't as grand as in the old days, but the hotels is convenient to some attractions (Mann's Chinese Theater is across the street). ✉ *7000 Hollywood Blvd., 90028, ☎ 213/466–7000 or 800/950–7667, FAX 213/462–8056. 359 rooms. Restaurant, pool, hot tub, exercise room. AE, D, DC, MC, V.*

$$$ ★ **Westin LAX.** Here's a great place to stay if you want to be pampered but also need to be close to the airport. Many suites have private outdoor hot tubs. ✉ *5400 W. Century Blvd., 90045, ☎ 310/216–5858 or 800/937–8461, FAX 310/670–1948. 762 rooms. Restaurant, pool, exercise room. AE, D, DC, MC, V.*

$$ **Carlyle Inn.** The contemporary four-story hotel gives guests several extras such as a buffet breakfast in the morning and a glass of wine in the late afternoon. Modern rooms are done in peach with light-pine furniture; amenities include bathrobe, hair dryer, and turndown service. ✉ *1119 S. Robertson Blvd., 90035, ☎ 310/275–4445 or 800/322–7595, FAX 310/859–0496. 32 rooms. Restaurant, exercise room. Full breakfast. AE, D, DC, MC, V.*

$$ **Continental Plaza Los Angeles Airport.** Low prices and friendly service make the Continental Plaza a good value. The rooms are spacious and well equipped. Guests have health club privileges next door. ✉ *9750 Airport Blvd., 90045, ☎ 310/645–4600 or 800/529–4683, FAX 310/645–7489. 582 rooms. Restaurant, pool. AE, D, DC, MC, V.*

$$ **Figueroa Hotel and Convention Center.** The Spanish feel of this 12-story hotel built in 1926 is accented by terra-cotta-color rooms, hand-painted furniture, wrought-iron beds, and, in many rooms, ceiling fans. The hotel's Clay Pit restaurant serves aromatic and tasty Indian food. ✉ *939 S. Figueroa St., 90015, ☎ 213/627–8971 or 800/421–9092, FAX 213/689–0305. 287 rooms. 2 restaurants, pool. AE, DC, MC, V.*

$$ **Hotel Carmel.** Price and location (near the beach and shopping) make this hotel a popular choice. Basic rooms are spacious, some with ocean views. ✉ *201 Broadway, 90401, ☎ 310/451–2469 or 800/445–8695, FAX 310/393–4180. 104 rooms. CP. AE, D, DC, MC, V.*

$$ **Kawada Hotel.** Akin to a small European hotel, this property near the Music Center and local government buildings has good service, immaculate (if smallish) rooms, and an excellent restaurant. ✉ *200 S.*

Hill St., 90012, ☎ 213/621–4455 or 800/752–9232, FAX 213/687–4455. 117 rooms. Restaurant, deli. AE, DC, MC, V.

$$ **Sportsmen's Lodge.** An English country–style structure, this hotel has attractive grounds and rooms done in soft colors. Studio suites with private patios are available. ✉ *12825 Ventura Blvd., 91604, ☎ 818/769–4700 or 800/821–8511, FAX 213/877–3898. 191 rooms. 3 restaurants, pool, exercise room. AE, D, DC, MC, V.*

$–$$ **Crescent Hotel.** A rare value in its swank zip code, this small-European-style hotel is lean on services, but provides little extras such as complimentary snacks and fresh fruits. Standard rooms are on the spartan side, but the price is right. ✉ *403 N. Crescent Dr., 90210, ☎ 310/247–0505 or 800/451–1566, FAX 310/247–9053. 39 rooms. AE, D, DC, MC, V.*

$–$$ **The InnTowne.** This contemporary three-story hotel 1½ blocks from the convention center has large rooms with beige and white or gray and white color schemes. A bar and coffee shop are on site. ✉ *913 S. Figueroa St., 90015, ☎ 213/628–2222 or 800/457–8520, FAX 213/687–0566. 170 rooms. Pool. AE, D, DC, MC, V.*

$ **Banana Bungalow Hotel and International Hostel.** You'll get good value for your money at this friendly, no-smoking inn, which is popular with international backpackers and college students. ✉ *2775 Cahuenga Blvd. W, 90068, ☎ 213/851–1129 or 800/446–7835, FAX 213/851–1569. 45 rooms. Restaurant, pool, exercise room. MC, V.*

Nightlife and the Arts

The Calendar section of the *Los Angeles Times* and the listings in the alternative *LA Weekly* are the best sources for event information. Tickets can be purchased by phone from **TeleCharge** (☎ 800/762–7666), **Ticketmaster** (☎ 213/480–3232), or **Good Time Tickets** (☎ 213/464–7383).

Nightlife

COMEDY

The **Comedy Store** (✉ 8433 Sunset Blvd., Hollywood, ☎ 213/656–6225) showcases comedians, including top names. The **Improvisation** (✉ 8162 Melrose Ave., West Hollywood, ☎ 213/651–2583) features comedy and some music. The **Laugh Factory** (✉ 8001 Sunset Blvd., Hollywood, ☎ 213/656–8860) offers stand-up comedy and improvisation.

DANCE CLUBS

Coconut Teaszer (✉ 8117 Sunset Blvd., Hollywood, ☎ 213/654–4773) has dancing to live music, a great barbecue menu, and pool tables. The spacious **Love Lounge** (✉ 657 N. Robertson Blvd., West Hollywood, ☎ 310/659–0472) opens its doors Tuesday–Friday, with a different theme—from drag shows to retro new wave—each night. **The World** (✉ 7070 Hollywood Blvd., Hollywood, ☎ 213/467–7070) delivers the world in the form of a different dance theme every night.

LIVE MUSIC

Studio musicians often sit in at the **Baked Potato** (✉ 3787 Cahuenga Blvd. W, North Hollywood, ☎ 818/980–1615), a club near Universal Studios. At the **Atlas Bar and Grill** (✉ 3760 Wilshire Blvd, Los Angeles, ☎ 213/380–8400) you'll hear jazz and torch in a classy, historic Art Deco supper club. **Marla's Memory Lane Supper Club** (✉ 2323 W. Martin Luther King Jr. Blvd., Los Angeles, ☎ 213/294–8430) swings with blues and jazz.

The **Roxy** (✉ 9009 Sunset Blvd., West Hollywood, ☎ 310/276–2222), classy and comfortable, is L.A.'s premier rock club, though it presents stage productions as well. The **Viper Room** (✉ 8852 Sunset Blvd., West Hollywood, ☎ 310/358–1880) presents pop, rock, blues, and jazz/fusion performers.

For the most current alternative sounds, head to **Spaceland** (✉ 1717 Silverlake Blvd., Silverlake, ☎ 213/413–4442).

The Arts

MUSIC

The **Dorothy Chandler Pavilion** (✉ 135 N. Grand Ave., ☎ 213/972–7211) is home to the Los Angeles Philharmonic Orchestra and presents other large-scale productions. The **Hollywood Bowl** (✉ 2301 Highland Ave., Hollywood, ☎ 213/850–2000) offers an outdoor summer season of classical and popular music. The outdoor **Greek Theater** (✉ 2700 N. Vermont Ave., ☎ 213/665–1927) presents summer jazz, popular, and Pops concerts.

THEATER

Plays are presented at two of the three theaters at the **Music Center** (✉ 135 N. Grand Ave.): the Ahmanson Theatre (☎ 213/972–7211) and the Mark Taper Forum (☎ 213/972–7353). The **Center Theatre Group at Mark Taper Forum** is a resident company that also books its shows into other theaters. The **James A. Doolittle Theatre** (✉ 1615 N. Vine St., Hollywood, ☎ 213/462–6666) presents dramas. The **Geffen Playhouse** (✉ 10886 Le Conte Ave., Westwood, ☎ 310/208–6500 or 310/208–5454) presents musicals and comedies year-round.

Spectator Sports

Baseball: Los Angeles Dodgers (✉ Dodger Stadium, 1000 Elysian Park Ave., downtown, ☎ 213/224–1400). **Basketball: Los Angeles Lakers** (✉ The Forum, 3900 W. Manchester Ave., Inglewood, ☎ 310/419–3182). **Los Angeles Clippers** (✉ L.A. Sports Arena, 3939 S. Figueroa St., downtown, ☎ 213/748–8000). **Hockey: Los Angeles Kings** (✉ The Forum, 3900 W. Manchester Ave., Inglewood, ☎ 310/673–6003). **Horse Racing: Santa Anita Race Track** (✉ Huntington Dr. and Colorado Pl., Arcadia, ☎ 626/574–7223) late December–April, October–mid-November; **Hollywood Park** (✉ Century Blvd. and Avenue of Champions, Inglewood, ☎ 310/419–1500) April–mid-July, mid-November–December 24. **Soccer: Galaxy** (✉ Rose Bowl, Arroyo Blvd., Pasadena, ☎ 213/817–5425).

Beaches

Los Angeles County beaches (and state beaches operated by the county) have lifeguards. Public parking (for a fee) is widely available, most state beaches have picnic and rest-room facilities, and most city beaches (some local favorites are listed below from north to south) are lined with a boardwalk that has plenty of services.

Leo Carrillo State Beach (✉ 35000 Pacific Coast Hwy. [PCH], Malibu, ☎ 818/880–0350) is fun at low tide, when tide pools emerge. There are hiking trails, sea caves, and tunnels, and you can often see whales, dolphins, and sea lions.

Zuma Beach Park (✉ 30000 PCH, Malibu, ☎ 310/457–9891), Malibu's largest and sandiest beach, is a favorite surfing spot and teen hangout.

Westward Beach/Point Dume State Beach (✉ South end of Westward Beach Rd., Malibu, ☎ 310/457–9891) has tide pools and sandstone cliffs. It's a favorite surfing spot among older surfers because of its slow, long-breaking waves.

Surfrider Beach/Malibu Lagoon State Beach (✉ 23200 PCH, Malibu, ☎ 818/880–0350), north of Malibu Pier, has steady 3- to 5-ft waves that make it great for long-board surfing. The International Surfing Contest is held here each September. The lagoon is a sanctuary for many birds.

Topanga County Beach (✉ 18700 block of PCH, Malibu, ☎ 310/394–3266), rocky but a favorite with surfers, stretches from the mouth of Topanga Canyon down to Coastline Drive.

Will Rogers County Beach (✉ 15800 PCH, Pacific Palisades, ☎ 310/394–3266) is a wide, sandy beach with a steady, even surf. There's plenty of beach, volleyball, and bodysurfing action parallel to the pedestrian bridge. Parking is limited.

Santa Monica State Beach (✉ Santa Monica Blvd. and Ocean Ave., Santa Monica, ☎ 310/394–3266), the widest stretch of beach on the Pacific coast, is also one of the most popular, with bike paths, facilities for people with disabilities, playgrounds, and volleyball.

Manhattan State Beach (✉ West of the Strand, Manhattan Beach, ☎ 310/372–2166), 44 acres of sandy beach, offers swimming, diving, surfing, fishing, and picnic facilities.

Redondo Beach (✉ Foot of Torrance Blvd., Redondo Beach, ☎ 310/372–2166) is usually packed in summer, and parking is limited.

Shopping

Shopping Districts

Rodeo Drive in Beverly Hills is the world-famous street where pricey shops sell designer fashions for men and women. In downtown L.A., the **Citadel Factory Stores** (✉ 5675 E. Telegraph Rd., No. 50, ☎ 213/888–1220) has Benetton, Fila, and other outlets. For vintage styles or the just plain weird, go to **Melrose Avenue** between La Brea and Crescent Heights. The **Beverly Center** (✉ Beverly Blvd. at La Cienega Blvd.) holds more than 200 upscale stores and boutiques. The **Santa Monica Promenade** and **Montana Avenue** feature boutique after boutique of quality goods.

Department Stores

Los Angeles has branches of many national and regional chains, including Neiman Marcus, Saks Fifth Avenue, Sears, Macy's, Nordstrom, and Robinsons-May.

Gifts and More

Tesoro (✉ 401 N. Cañon Dr., ☎ 310/273–9890) stocks trendy ceramics, southwestern blankets, and contemporary art.

Star Wares on Main (✉ 2817 Main St., ☎ 310/399–0224) carries sample costumes from movies like *Independence Day* and celebrity memorabilia of stars from Loretta Swit to Liz Taylor.

Music

Aron's Records (✉ 1150 N. Highland Ave., Hollywood, ☎ 213/469–4700) carries new releases and an extensive selection of old records.

Vintage Clothing

Golyester (✉ 136 S. La Brea Ave., ☎ 213/931–1339) sells funky used clothing and home furnishings.

ORANGE COUNTY

Orange County sits between Los Angeles to the north and San Diego to the south. Though primarily suburban, it is one of the top tourist destinations in California, with attractions such as Disneyland, pro sports, and miles of beaches.

Visitor Information

Anaheim Area: Convention and Visitors Bureau (✉ Anaheim Convention Center, 800 W. Katella Ave., 92802, ☎ 714/999–8999); Visitor Information Hot Line (☎ 714/635–8900).

Arriving and Departing

By Bus

Greyhound Lines (☎ 800/231–2222) serves Santa Ana and Anaheim.

By Car

I–405 (San Diego Freeway) and I–5 (Santa Ana Freeway) run north–south through Orange County. I–405 merges into I–5 south of Laguna.

By Plane

John Wayne Orange County Airport (✉ MacArthur Blvd. and I–405, Santa Ana, ☎ 949/252–5252) is served by a number of major carriers.

By Train

Amtrak (☎ 800/872–7245) trains stop in Fullerton, Anaheim, Santa Ana, Irvine, San Juan Capistrano, and San Clemente.

Exploring Orange County

Inland Orange County

★ Anaheim is the home of **Disneyland.** Visitors enter the Magic Kingdom by way of Walt Disney's idealized turn-of-the-century Main Street. Along with the various thrill rides and high-tech wizardry are the strolling Disney characters, a daily parade on Main Street, a dazzling nighttime "Fantasmic" show, and fireworks nightly in summer. The rides in **Fantasyland** are based on children's stories. **Frontierland** depicts the Wild West. The highlight of **Adventureland** is the Indiana Jones thrill ride. New Orleans Square is the setting for **Pirates of the Caribbean**—a boat ride through a scene lavish with animated characters—and the Blue Bayou restaurant. The nearby **Haunted Mansion** is full of holographic ghosts. In Critter Country is **Splash Mountain,** a flume ride that drops 52 ft at 40 mph. **Mickey's Toontown** is a child-size interactive community that gives kids the feeling of being inside a cartoon with Mickey and other characters. The new **Tomorrowland** has a Buck Rogers-ish feel. The lures here are Space Mountain, Honey I Shrunk the Audience, and Innoventions. ✉ *1313 Harbor Blvd.,* ☎ *714/999–4565.* *$34 adults, $26 children.*

★ **Knott's Berry Farm,** a 150-acre complex of food, shops, rides, and other attractions, is near Disneyland, in Buena Park. **Ghost Town** re-creates an 1880s mining town; the **Gold Mine** ride descends into a replica of a working gold mine. **Camp Snoopy** is a kid-size High Sierra wonderland where Snoopy and the *Peanuts* gang hang out. At **Wild Water Wilderness** riders can brave white water in an inner tube in the **Big Foot Rapids** or commune with Native peoples of the northwest coast in the spooky **Mystery Lodge.** Thrill rides are placed throughout the park, including the **Wind Jammer, Boomerang, Jaguar!,** and **Montezooma's Revenge** roller coasters. **X-K-1** is a living version of a video game. The **Boardwalk** includes dolphin and sea lion shows at the Pacific Pavilion, along with the Good Time and 3-D Nu Wave theaters. And don't forget what made Knott's famous: the fried chicken dinners and boysenberry pies at **Mrs. Knott's Chicken Dinner Restaurant,** outside the park gates in

Knott's California MarketPlace. ✉ *8039 Beach Blvd., Buena Park,* ☎ *714/220–5200.* 🎫 *$35; $25 children.*

The **Movieland Wax Museum** (✉ 7711 Beach Blvd., Buena Park, ☎ 714/522–1155; 🎫 $12.95) re-creates the famous in wax.

Garden Grove is the site of the **Crystal Cathedral** (✉ 12141 Lewis St., Garden Grove, ☎ 714/971–4013), the domain of televangelist Robert Schuller.

The Coast

Pacific Coast Highway (Highway 1) is the main thoroughfare for all the beach towns along the Orange County coast. **Huntington Beach** is a popular surfer hangout; you can watch the action from the Huntington Pier. South of Huntington Beach is **Newport Beach,** a Beverly-Hills-by-the-sea. Nearly 10,000 boats bob in the U-shape Newport Harbor, which arcs around eight small islands. **Balboa Peninsula,** with its Victorian Balboa Pavilion and active Fun Zone, is a popular visitor area. The **Orange County Museum of Art** (✉ 850 San Clemente Dr., ☎ 949/759–1122; 🎫 $5) emphasizes works by California artists.

★ Farther south is **Corona del Mar,** a small jewel of a town with exceptional beaches. You can walk clear out onto the bay on a rough-and-tumble rock jetty, or you can wander about tide pools and hidden caves. Protected by small cliffs, the beaches here resemble those of northern California's coastline. In **Laguna Beach** art galleries in town coexist with volleyball games and sun worship on nearby Main Beach; in July and August the Pageant of the Masters (☎ 949/494–1145) features living models re-creating famous paintings. Below Laguna the small harbor town of **Dana Point** is reminiscent of northern California's beaches. In March migrating swallows and spectacle-loving tourists flock to **Mission San Juan Capistrano** (✉ Camino Capistrano and Ortega Hwy., ☎ 949/248–2049).

Dining and Lodging

For price ranges *see* Charts 1 (A) and 2 (A) *in* On the Road with Fodor's.

Anaheim

$$–$$$ ✕ **JW's.** This upscale steak house specializes in aged beef but serves seafood along with lamb chops and chicken. The dining areas are quiet places where you can talk serious business or romance. ✉ *Anaheim Marriott, 700 W. Convention Way,* ☎ *714/750–8000. AE, D, DC, MC, V. No lunch.*

$$–$$$ ✕ **Mr. Stox.** Prime rib, mesquite-grilled rack of lamb, and fresh fish specials are popular at this cozy family-owned restaurant. The pastas, breads, and pastries are made on the premises, and the wine list has won awards. ✉ *1105 E. Katella Ave.,* ☎ *714/634–2994. AE, D, DC, MC, V. No lunch weekends.*

$–$$$ ✕ **Luigi's D'Italia.** Though the surroundings are simple, the Italian cuisine, from spaghetti marinara to cioppino, is excellent. ✉ *801 S. State College Blvd.,* ☎ *714/490–0990. AE, MC, V.*

$$$$ ★ 🏨 **Disneyland Hotel.** There's a 1950s charm to the buildings at this Disney-owned resort. A stay here can be on the expensive side, but is worth it for the true Disney vacation experience. You can save a few dollars with combined room/ticket packages. ✉ *1150 W. Cerritos Ave., 92802,* ☎ *714/778–6600,* FAX *714/956–6510. 1,136 rooms. 6 restaurants, pools, health club. AE, D, DC, MC, V.*

$$$ 🏨 **Radisson Maingate.** Some of the handsomely decorated rooms in the two eight-story buildings here have pull-out sofas as well as beds. Regular shuttles can zip you over to Disneyland or Knotts Berry Farm, and parking is free. ✉ *1850 S. Harbor Blvd., 92802,* ☎ *714/750–2801*

or 800/333-3333, FAX *714/971-4754. 502 rooms. Restaurant, pool. AE, D, DC, MC, V.*

$$ ★ **Candy Cane Inn.** The name of this motel speaks volumes about the fanciful, family-friendly feel inside. Rooms are spacious, a few with microwaves. Free Disneyland shuttles run every 30 minutes. ✉ *1747 S. Harbor Blvd., 92802,* ☎ *714/774-5284 or 800/345-7057,* FAX *714/772-5462 or 714/772-1305. 172 rooms. Pool. AE, D, DC, MC, V.*

$$ **Quality Hotel Maingate.** Studio suites at this property near Disneyland and the convention center include two double beds, a sofa with a pull-out bed, and a refrigerator. They're ideal for families on a budget, as is the complimentary hourly shuttle to Disneyland. ✉ *616 Convention Way, 92802,* ☎ *714/750-3131 or 800/231-6215,* FAX *714/750-9027. 283 rooms. 2 restaurants, pool. AE, D, DC, MC, V.*

$-$$ **Best Western Stovall's Inn.** Nice touches at this well-kept motel include a topiary garden, room decor in soft desert colors, and a friendly staff. A free shuttle makes frequent trips to Disneyland. ✉ *1110 W. Katella Ave., 92802,* ☎ *714/778-1880 or 800/854-8175,* FAX *714/778-3805. 290 rooms. Pools. AE, D, DC, MC, V.*

Brea

$$$-$$$$ ★ ✕ **La Vie en Rose.** In this reproduction Norman farmhouse complete with a large turret, traditional French cuisine is served. The menu includes seafood, lamb, and veal. For dessert try the silky creme brûlée or a Grand Marnier soufflé. ✉ *240 S. State College Blvd., across from the Brea Mall,* ☎ *714/529-8333. AE, DC, MC, V. Closed Sun.*

Costa Mesa

$-$$ ✕ **Memphis Soul Cafe and Bar.** The gumbo is the best in the county, bar none. The turkey sandwich with pesto is addicting, and the pork chops are superb. ✉ *2920 Bristol St.,* ☎ *714/432-7685. Reservations recommended at lunch. AE, DC, MC, V.*

Dana Point

$$-$$$ ✕ **Luciana's.** This intimate Italian restaurant is a real find. The well-prepared food—linguine with clams, prawns, calamari, and green-lip mussels in a light tomato sauce; veal medallions with haricot verts and oven-dried tomatoes—is served with care. ✉ *24312 Del Prado Ave.,* ☎ *949/661-6500. AE, DC, MC, V. No lunch.*

$$$$ ★ ✕ **Ritz-Carlton–Laguna Niguel.** One of California's most highly respected hotels, the Ritz has beach access, a spectacular ocean view, the Dining Room restaurant, a lavishly decorated lobby, and spacious rooms. ✉ *1 Ritz-Carlton Dr., 92677,* ☎ *949/240-2000 or 800/241-3333,* FAX *949/240-0829. 362 rooms. 3 restaurants, pools, tennis, health club. AE, D, DC, MC, V.*

Irvine

$$-$$$ ★ ✕ **Prego.** Reminiscent of a Tuscan villa, this restaurant with an outdoor patio glows with soft lighting and golden walls. Try the spit-roasted meats and chicken, the charcoal-grilled fresh fish, or pizzas from the oak-burning oven. ✉ *18420 Von Karman Ave.,* ☎ *949/553-1333. AE, DC, MC, V. No lunch weekends.*

$-$$ ✕ **Kitima Thai Cuisine.** Orange County's best Thai restaurant is tucked away in an office building. The names may be gimmicky—"rock and roll shrimp salad," "Rambo chicken" (sautéed with green chilies and sweet basil)—but fresh ingredients are used in every dish. ✉ *2010 Main St., Suite 170,* ☎ *949/261-2929. AE, D, DC, MC, V.*

$$$-$$$$ **Irvine Marriott.** Towering over Koll Business Center, the Marriott is convenient for business travelers. Despite its size, the hotel has an intimate feel. Weekend discounts and packages are usually available, and there's a courtesy van to the South Coast Plaza mall and the airport. ✉ *1800 Von Karman Ave., 92612,* ☎ *949/553-0100,* FAX *949/*

261–7059. 492 rooms. 2 restaurants, pool, hot tub, tennis, health club. AE, D, DC, MC, V.

Laguna Beach

$$$–$$$$ ★ ✕ **Five Feet.** Delicate pot stickers, goat-cheese wontons with raspberry coulis, fish in garlic–black-bean sauce, and rabbit with foie gras and wild mushrooms are a few of the scrumptious dishes here. The setting is pure Laguna: exposed ceiling, open kitchen, high noise level, and brick walls hung with works by local artists. ✉ *328 Gleneyre St.,* ☎ *949/497–4955. AE, D, DC, MC, V. No lunch.*

$$–$$$ ✕ **Ti Amo.** Justifiably acclaimed for the refinement of its pastas and creativity of its main courses, this Italian eatery has charming nooks and crannies. To maximize the romance, request a table in the lush garden in back. ✉ *31727 S. Pacific Coast Hwy.,* ☎ *949/499–5350. AE, D, DC, MC, V. No lunch.*

$$$$ ★ 🏨 **Inn at Laguna Beach.** This oceanfront Mediterranean-style inn on a bluff has luxurious amenities and many rooms with views. ✉ *211 N. Pacific Coast Hwy., 92651,* ☎ *949/497–9722 or 800/544–4479,* FAX *949/497–9972. 70 rooms. Pool. AE, D, DC, MC, V.*

Newport Beach

$$$–$$$$ ★ ✕ **Aubergine.** A husband-and-wife team runs this restaurant inside a homey cottage. He heads up the kitchen and she handles the dining room. A few Californian touches influence the otherwise modern French menu. ✉ *508 29th St.,* ☎ *949/723–4150. AE, MC, V. Closed Sun.–Mon. No lunch.*

$$ ★ ✕ **El Torito Grill.** The tortillas, turkey mole enchilada, and miniature blue-corn duck tamales are good choices here. The bar serves hand-shaken margaritas and 80 brands of tequila. ✉ *Fashion Island, 941 Newport Center Dr.,* ☎ *949/640–2875. AE, D, DC, MC, V.*

$–$$ ✕ **Crab Cooker.** This shanty serves fresh fish grilled over mesquite at low, low prices. ✉ *2200 Newport Blvd.,* ☎ *949/673–0100. Reservations not accepted. No credit cards.*

$$$$ ★ 🏨 **Four Seasons Hotel.** A suitably stylish hotel in an ultrachic neighborhood (it's across the street from the Fashion Island mall), the 20-story Four Seasons caters to luxury seekers by offering weekend golf packages (in conjunction with the nearby Pelican Hill golf course) and fitness weekend packages. Guest rooms have spectacular views, private bars, and original artwork on the walls. ✉ *690 Newport Center Dr., 92660,* ☎ *949/759–0808 or 800/332–3442,* FAX *949/759–0568. 285 rooms. 2 restaurants, pool, tennis, health club. AE, D, DC, MC, V.*

$$$–$$$$ 🏨 **Sutton Place Hotel.** This ultramodern hotel has an eye-catching ziggurat design. The luxuriously appointed rooms all have minibars. ✉ *4500 MacArthur Blvd., 92660,* ☎ *949/476–2001 or 800/810–6888,* FAX *949/476–0153. 435 rooms. 2 restaurants, pool, 2 tennis courts, health club. AE, D, DC, MC, V.*

Nightlife and the Arts

The **Orange County Performing Arts Center** (✉ 600 Town Center Dr., Costa Mesa, ☎ 714/556–2787) presents symphony orchestras, opera companies, and musicals. Next door to the center is the **South Coast Repertory Theater** (✉ 655 Town Center Dr., Costa Mesa, ☎ 714/957–4033), which presents traditional and contemporary works. The **Irvine Meadows Amphitheater** (✉ 8800 Irvine Center Dr., ☎ 949/855–4515) presents summer concerts.

Outdoor Activities and Sports

Biking

A **bike path** runs from Marina del Rey down to San Diego with only minor breaks. For rentals try **Rainbow Bicycles** (✉ Laguna, ☎ 949/494–5806) or **Team Bicycle Rentals** (✉ Huntington Beach, ☎ 714/969–5480).

Water Sports

Water-sports equipment rentals are near most piers, including **Hobie Sports** (✉ Dana Point, ☎ 949/496–2366; ✉ Laguna, ☎ 949/497–3304). **Balboa Boat Rentals** (☎ 949/673–7200), in Newport Harbor, and **Embarcadero Marina** (☎ 949/496–6177), at Dana Point, rent sail and powerboats.

Spectator Sports

Baseball: Anaheim Angels (✉ Edison Field, 2000 Gene Autry Way, ☎ 714/634–2000). **Hockey: Mighty Ducks of Anaheim** (✉ The Arrowhead Pond of Anaheim, 2695 E. Katella, ☎ 714/740–2000).

Beaches

The beaches along Highway 1 in Orange County are among the finest and most varied in southern California, with fine swimming, great surfing, and many services. Take posted warnings about undertow seriously.

Huntington Beach State Beach is a long stretch of flat, sandy beach with changing rooms, concessions, fire pits, and lifeguards. **Lower Newport Bay** is a sheltered 740-acre preserve for ducks and geese. **Newport Dunes Resort** offers picnic facilities, changing rooms, and a boat launch. **Corona del Mar State Beach** has sandy beaches backed by rocky bluffs and tide pools and caves. **Laguna** has the county's best spot for scuba diving—the Marine Life Refuge, which runs from Seal Rock to Diver's Cove. **Main Beach,** a sandy arc steps from downtown Laguna, is a popular picnic and volleyball venue. In South Laguna **Aliso County Park** has recreational facilities and a fishing pier. **Doheny State Park,** near Dana Point Harbor, has food stands, camping, and a fishing pier. **San Clemente State Beach** has camping facilities and food stands and is renowned for its surf.

SAN DIEGO

San Diego is the birthplace of Spanish California. Its combination of history, pleasing climate, outdoor recreation and sports, and cultural life makes it a popular destination.

Visitor Information

International Visitor Information Center (✉ 11 Horton Plaza, 92101, ☎ 619/236–1212). **Mission Bay Visitor Information Center** (✉ 2688 E. Mission Bay Dr., off I–5, 92109, ☎ 619/276–8200).

Arriving and Departing

By Bus

Greyhound Lines (✉ 120 W. Broadway, ☎ 800/231–2222).

By Car

I–5 runs north–south. I–8 comes into San Diego from the east, I–15 from the northeast.

By Plane

San Diego International Airport (✉ N. Harbor Dr., ☎ 619/231–2100) is 3 mi northwest of downtown and is served by most domestic and many international air carriers. The **Cloud 9 Shuttle** (☎ 619/278–8877 or 800/974–8885) has door-to-door service to anywhere in San Diego County, often for less than a taxi. **San Diego Transit** (☎ 619/233–3004) Bus 2 leaves the airport every 10–15 minutes and costs $1.50. Taxi fare is $7–$9 (plus tip) to most center-city hotels.

By Train

Amtrak (☎ 800/872–7245) trains arrive at **Santa Fe Depot** (✉ Kettner Blvd. and Broadway, ☎ 619/239–9021).

Getting Around San Diego

It's best to have a car, but avoid the freeways during rush hours. The **San Diego Trolley** (☎ 619/233–3004) travels the 20 mi from downtown to within 100 ft of the Mexican border; other trolleys on the line serve Seaport Village, the Convention Center, and inland areas. **San Diego Harbor Excursion** (☎ 619/234–4111) provides water-taxi service from Seaport Village to Coronado.

Exploring San Diego

Central San Diego

★ **Balboa Park** encompasses 1,200 acres of cultural, recreational, and environmental delights, including a theater complex and public gardens. Among the park's several museums are the Mingei International Museum of World Folk Art (☎ 619/239–0003; 🎫 $5), devoted to folk art; the San Diego Museum of Art (☎ 619/232–7931; 🎫 $7 Tues.–Thurs., $8 Fri.–Sun.), which hosts major traveling shows; and the San Diego Aerospace Museum and International Aerospace Hall of Fame (☎ 619/234–8291; 🎫 $6). Wide-format films are shown on the Omnimax screen of the **Reuben H. Fleet Space Theater and Science Center** (☎ 619/238–1233; 🎫 $4). Across from the Museum of Man, the **Alcazar Garden** is an impressive horticultural display.

★ Balboa Park's most famous attraction is the **San Diego Zoo** (✉ 2920 Zoo Dr., ☎ 619/234–3153; 🎫 $15), where more than 4,000 animals of 800 species roam in habitats built around natural canyons. The zoo is also an enormous botanical garden with one of the world's largest collections of subtropical plants.

Coronado is a city of numerous Victorian houses whose most prominent landmark is the historic Hotel Del Coronado, all turrets and gingerbread. Silver Strand State Beach is one of San Diego's nicest. You can reach Coronado via the 2¼-mi San Diego–Coronado Bridge, which yields a stunning view of the San Diego skyline, or by ferry (☎ 619/234–411) or water taxi (☎ 619/235–8294).

The **Embarcadero** is a waterfront walkway lined with restaurants and cruise-ship piers. The **Maritime Museum** (✉ 1306 N. Harbor Dr., ☎ 619/234–9153; 🎫 $5) has a collection of restored ships, including the windjammer ***Star of India.*** **Seaport Village,** a bustling array of specialty shops, snack bars, and restaurants, spreads out across 14 acres and connects the harbor with the San Diego Convention Center.

The **Gaslamp Quarter** is a 16-block National Historic District containing most of San Diego's Victorian-era commercial buildings. At the fringe of the redeveloped quarter, the **William Heath Davis House** (✉ 410 Island Ave., at 4th Ave., ☎ 619/233–4692), one of the first residences in town, serves as the information center.

San Diego

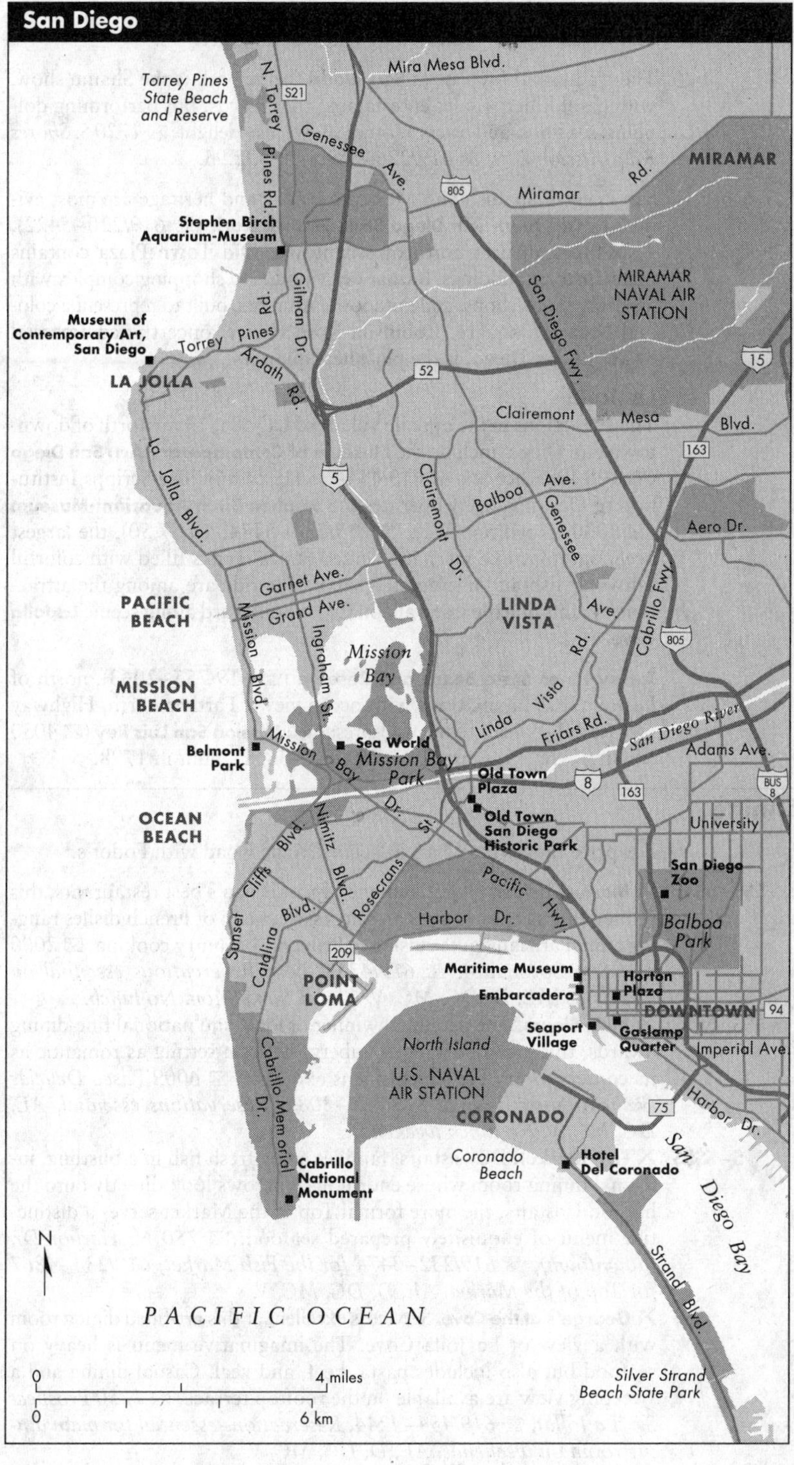
Torrey Pines State Beach and Reserve
N. Torrey Pines Rd.
S21
Mira Mesa Blvd.
Genessee Ave.
805
Miramar Rd.
MIRAMAR
Stephen Birch Aquarium-Museum
Gilman Dr.
San Diego Fwy.
MIRAMAR NAVAL AIR STATION
Museum of Contemporary Art, San Diego
Torrey Pines Rd.
Ardath Rd.
52
15
LA JOLLA
Clairemont Mesa Blvd.
163
La Jolla Blvd.
5
Clairemont Dr.
Balboa Ave.
Genessee Ave.
Aero Dr.
Cabrillo Fwy
Garnet Ave.
Grand Ave.
PACIFIC BEACH
LINDA VISTA
Mission Blvd.
Ingraham St.
Mission Bay
Linda Vista Rd.
MISSION BEACH
Friars Rd.
San Diego River
Adams Ave.
Belmont Park
Sea World
Mission Bay Park
Mission Bay Dr.
Old Town Plaza
8
BUS 8
Old Town San Diego Historic Park
University
OCEAN BEACH
Nimitz Blvd.
Rosecrans St.
Pacific Hwy.
San Diego Zoo
Sunset Cliffs Blvd.
Harbor Dr.
Balboa Park
Catalina Blvd.
209
POINT LOMA
Maritime Museum
Embarcadero
Horton Plaza
DOWNTOWN
94
Seaport Village
Gaslamp Quarter
Imperial Ave.
North Island
U.S. NAVAL AIR STATION
Cabrillo Memorial Dr.
CORONADO
75
Harbor Dr.
Coronado Beach
Hotel Del Coronado
Cabrillo National Monument
San Diego Bay
Strand Blvd.
N
PACIFIC OCEAN
0
4 miles
0
6 km
Silver Strand Beach State Park

Mission Bay, San Diego's monument to sports and fitness, is a 4,600-acre aquatic park dedicated to action and leisure.

The traditional favorite at **Sea World** theme park is the Shamu show, with giant killer whales entertaining the crowds, but performing dolphins, sea lions, and otters at other shows also delight. ✉ *1720 S. Shores Rd., Mission Bay,* ☎ *619/226–3815.* *$32.95.*

San Diego's Spanish and Mexican history and heritage are most evident in **Old Town San Diego State Historic Park** (☎ 619/220–5422), a six-block district north of downtown. **Old Town Plaza** contains many historic buildings. **Bazaar del Mundo** is a shopping complex with gardens, exotic shops, and outdoor restaurants, built to represent a colonial Mexican square. **Robinson-Rose House,** once the commercial center of San Diego, is the park headquarters.

La Jolla

The attractions in the upscale village of La Jolla, 13 mi north of downtown San Diego, include the **Museum of Contemporary Art, San Diego** (✉ 700 Prospect St., ☎ 619/454–3541; $4). The Scripps Institution of Oceanography operates the **Stephen Birch Aquarium-Museum** (✉ 2300 Expedition Way, ☎ 619/534–3474; $7.50), the largest oceanographic exhibit in the United States. Tanks filled with colorful saltwater fish and a simulated submarine ride are among the attractions. ★ Palms line the sidewalk on Coast Boulevard along scenic **La Jolla Cove.**

Torrey Pines State Beach and Reserve (☎ 619/755–2063), north of La Jolla, has hiking trails with ocean views. Farther north, Highway 76 east of I–5 leads to the well-preserved **Mission San Luis Rey** (✉ 4050 Mission Ave., Oceanside, ☎ 760/757–3651), built in 1798.

Dining

For price ranges *see* Chart 1 (A) *in* On the Road with Fodor's.

$$$–$$$$ ✕ **Marius.** Invariably ranked one of San Diego's best restaurants, this refined dining room serves an impressive menu of French dishes ranging from Parisian haute cuisine to Provençal country cooking. ✉ *2000 2nd St. (Coronado),* ☎ *619/435–3000. Reservations essential on weekends. AE, D, DC, MC, V. Closed Sun.–Mon. No lunch.*

$$$–$$$$ ✕ **Mille Fleurs.** The perennial winner of local and national fine-dining awards, this gem of a French auberge offers a setting as romantic as its contemporary French cuisine is exquisite. ✉ *6009 Paseo Delicias (Rancho Santa Fe),* ☎ *619/756–3085. Reservations essential. AE, DC, MC, V. No lunch weekends.*

$–$$$$ ✕ **Fish Market.** Downstairs, families enjoy fresh fish in a bustling, informal dining room whose enormous windows look directly onto the harbor. Upstairs, the more formal Top of the Market serves a distinctive menu of exquisitely prepared seafood. ✉ *750 N. Harbor Dr. (downtown),* ☎ *619/232–3474 for the Fish Market; 619/234–4867 for Top of the Market. AE, D, DC, MC, V.*

$$$ ★ ✕ **George's at the Cove.** Service is excellent at this art-filled dining room with a view of La Jolla Cove. The imaginative menu is heavy on seafood but also includes pasta, beef, and veal. Casual dining and a sweeping view are available on the rooftop terrace. ✉ *1250 Prospect St. (La Jolla),* ☎ *619/454–4244. Reservations essential for main dining room on weekends. AE, D, DC, MC, V.*

$$–$$$ ✕ **Café Pacifica.** This charming café serves eclectic contemporary cuisine with an emphasis on seafood. Light, interesting sauces and imaginative garnishes are teamed with perfectly cooked, very fresh fish. ✉

2414 *San Diego Ave. (Old Town),* ☎ *619/291–6666. AE, D, DC, MC, V. No lunch.*

$$–$$$ ★ ✕ **Dobson's.** The perennial favorite here is mussel bisque. Fish, veal, fowl, and beef entrées are menu highlights. ✉ *956 Broadway Circle (downtown),* ☎ *619/231–6771. Reservations essential on weekends. AE, MC, V. Closed Sun. No lunch Sat.*

$$–$$$ ✕ **Fio's.** Contemporary variations on traditional Italian cuisine are served in a high-ceiling, brick-and-wood dining room overlooking the 5th Avenue street scene. The menu includes a range of imaginative pizzas baked in the wood-burning oven and classic Italian dishes. ✉ *801 5th Ave. (downtown),* ☎ *619/234–3467. Reservations essential on weekends. AE, D, DC, MC, V. No lunch weekends.*

$$–$$$ ★ ✕ **Laurel.** The stylish restaurant of San Diego culinary star Douglas Organ spotlights the cooking of southern France and the Mediterranean. The ambience is sophisticated yet casual: Guinea hen confit, risotto, and roast fish are among the best dishes. ✉ *505 Laurel St. (uptown),* ☎ *619/239–2222. AE, D, DC, MC, V. No lunch.*

$–$$ ★ ✕ **Bayou Bar and Grill.** Seafood gumbo and fresh Louisiana Gulf seafood dishes are among the Cajun and creole specialties served here. Desserts include praline cheesecake and an award-winning bread pudding. ✉ *329 Market St. (downtown),* ☎ *619/696–8747. AE, D, DC, MC, V.*

$–$$ ★ ✕ **Palenque.** This Pacific Beach restaurant serves a wonderful selection of regional Mexican dishes, including chicken with mole and *camarones con chipotle,* large shrimp cooked in a chili-tequila cream sauce (an old family recipe of the proprietor). ✉ *1653 Garnet Ave. (Pacific Beach),* ☎ *619/272–7816. AE, D, DC, MC, V. No lunch Mon.*

$ ✕ **Hob Nob Hill.** The French toast, pot roast, and fried chicken taste truly homemade at this restaurant whose dark-wood booths lend the place a vintage feel. ✉ *2271 1st Ave. (uptown),* ☎ *619/239–8176. AE, D, MC, V.*

$ ✕ **Mission Coffee Cup Cafe.** This colorful coffeehouse serves a menu of eclectic cuisine at breakfast and lunch. Try the cinnamon-bread French toast with berries, the tamales with eggs and green chili salsa, or the Asian quesadilla. The original Mission Cafe serves a similar menu in a funkier setting and stays open for dinner. *Coffee Cup Cafe:* ✉ *1109 Wall St. (La Jolla),* ☎ *619/454–2819. Original Mission Cafe:* ✉ *3795 Mission Blvd. (Mission Beach),* ☎ *619/488–9060. AE, MC, V.*

Lodging

For price ranges *see* Chart 2 (A) *in* On the Road with Fodor's.

$$$–$$$$ 🏨 **Hotel Del Coronado.** Rooms and suites in the 1888 original Victorian building are charmingly quirky. A newer high-rise has more standard accommodations. ✉ *1500 Orange Ave. (Coronado), 92118,* ☎ *619/435–6611 or 800/468–3533,* FAX *619/522–8262. 692 rooms. 3 restaurants, pool. AE, D, DC, MC, V.*

$$$–$$$$ ★ 🏨 **Hyatt Regency La Jolla.** The warm and fluffy down comforters and cushy chairs and couches at this postmodern complex will make you feel right at home. Rates are lower on weekends at this business-oriented hotel. ✉ *Aventine Center, 3777 La Jolla Village Dr. (La Jolla), 92122,* ☎ *619/552–1234 or 800/233–1234 (central reservations),* FAX *619/552–6066. 425 rooms. 4 restaurants, pool, health club. AE, D, DC, MC, V.*

$$$–$$$$ ★ 🏨 **La Valencia.** This centrally located pink-stucco hotel is a La Jolla landmark. It has a courtyard for patio dining and an elegant lobby where guests congregate to enjoy the ocean view. Rooms have a romantic European style. ✉ *1132 Prospect St. (La Jolla), 92037,* ☎ *619/454–0771*

or 800/451–0772, FAX 619/456–3921. 107 rooms. 3 restaurants, pool, exercise room. AE, D, DC, MC, V.

$$–$$$$ **Heritage Park Bed & Breakfast Inn.** This romantic 1889 Queen Anne mansion is full of 19th-century antiques. ✉ *2470 Heritage Park Row (Old Town), 92110,* ☎ *619/299–6832 or 800/995–2470. 12 rooms. CP. AE, MC, V.*

$$$ ★ **Westgate Hotel.** Antiques, Italian marble counters, and bath fixtures with 24-karat-gold overlays typify the opulent furnishings here. High tea, breathtaking views, and nearby Horton Plaza are other highlights. ✉ *1055 2nd Ave. (downtown), 92101,* ☎ *619/238–1818 or 800/221–3802; 800/522–1564 in CA; FAX 619/557–3737. 223 rooms. 2 restaurants, exercise room. AE, D, DC, MC, V.*

$$–$$$ **Lodge at Torrey Pines.** This easygoing resort on a bluff between La Jolla and Del Mar commands an expansive coastline view. ✉ *11480 Torrey Pines Rd. (La Jolla), 92037,* ☎ *619/453–4420 or 800/995–4507, FAX 619/453–0691. 74 rooms. 2 restaurants, pool. AE, D, DC, MC, V.*

$$ ★ **Vacation Inn.** At this cheerful property rustic colors and reproduction furnishings lend rooms an old-country-inn feel. ✉ *3900 Old Town Ave. (Old Town),* ☎ *619/299–7400 or 800/451–9846, FAX 619/299–1619. 125 rooms. Pool. AE, D, DC, MC, V.*

$ **Super 8 Bayview.** This motel's location is less noisy than those of other low-cost establishments. The accommodations are nondescript but clean, and some have refrigerators. ✉ *1835 Columbia St., 92101,* ☎ *619/544–0164 or 800/537–9902, FAX 619/237–9940. 101 rooms. Pool. CP. AE, DC, MC, V.*

$ **Travelodge Point Loma.** For far less money, you'll get the same view here as at the higher-price hotels. The rooms are adequate and clean. ✉ *5102 N. Harbor Dr. (Point Loma), 92106,* ☎ *619/223–8171 or 800/578–7878, FAX 619/222–7330. 45 rooms. Pool. AE, D, DC, MC, V.*

Nightlife and the Arts

The daily *San Diego Union-Tribune* and weekly *Reader* have nightlife and cultural-event listings. Half-price tickets to most theater, music, and dance events can be bought on the day of performance at the **TIMES ARTS TIX Ticket Center** (✉ Horton Plaza, ☎ 619/497–5000). Only cash is accepted. **TicketMaster** (☎ 619/220–8497) sells tickets to many San Diego cultural and entertainment events.

Nightlife

San Diego's nightlife ranges from quiet piano bars to cutting-edge rock. The **Casbah** (✉ 2501 Kettner Blvd., ☎ 619/232–4355) showcases rock, reggae, and funk bands every night. **Humphrey's** (✉ 2241 Shelter Island Dr., ☎ 619/523–1010) presents outdoor concerts in the summer. **Leo's Little Bit O' Country** (✉ 680 W. San Marcos Blvd., San Marcos, ☎ 619/744–4120) hosts country-and-western dancing. The **Comedy Store** (✉ 916 Pearl St., La Jolla, ☎ 619/454–9176) books local and national talent. The best local Latin, jazz, and blues bands alternate appearances during the week at the classy bar at the **U. S. Grant Hotel** (✉ 326 Broadway, downtown, ☎ 619/232–3121).

The Arts

The **Old Globe Theatre** (✉ Simon Edison Centre, Balboa Park, ☎ 619/239–2255) presents classics, experimental works, and a summer Shakespeare festival. The **San Diego Opera** (☎ 619/232–7636) performs at the Civic Theatre (✉ 202 C St., ☎ 619/236–6510) from January to April.

Outdoor Activities and Sports

Baseball: San Diego Padres (✉ Qualcomm Stadium, 9449 Friars Rd., ☏ 619/283–4494). **Football: San Diego Chargers** (✉ Qualcomm Stadium, ☏ 619/280–2111). **Horse Racing: Del Mar Thoroughbred Club** (✉ 2260 Jimmy Durante Blvd.; take I–5 to the Via de la Valle exit, ☏ 619/755–1141); July–September.

Beaches

The following beaches are listed geographically from north to south.

La Jolla Cove is a favorite of rough-water swimmers, but Children's Pool, a shallow lagoon at the south end, is a safer haven. Follow Coast Boulevard north to the signs; or take the La Jolla Village Drive exit from I–5, head west to Torrey Pines Road, turn left and drive down the hill to Girard Avenue, then turn right and follow the signs.

Mission Beach/Pacific Beach has a boardwalk that's popular with strollers, roller skaters, and cyclists. The south end is full of surfers, swimmers, and volleyball players. Pacific Beach is a teen hangout; it's crowded in summer, and parking is a challenge. Exit I–5 at Garnet Avenue and head west to Mission Boulevard.

Ocean Beach is a haven for volleyball players, sunbathers, and swimmers. You'll find food vendors and fire rings; limited parking is available. The municipal pier at the south end is open to the public for fishing and walking and has a restaurant at the end. Take I–8 west to Sunset Cliffs Boulevard and head south; turn right on Santa Monica Avenue.

Coronado Beach is perfect for sunbathing or Frisbee throwing. There are rest rooms and fire rings; parking can be difficult on busy days. From the bridge turn left on Orange Avenue; then follow signs.

Silver Strand State Beach, Coronado, has relatively calm water, an RV campground ($12–$16 per night), and other facilities. Parking is $4 per car, but collection is lax from Labor Day through February. Take the Palm Avenue exit off I–5 west to Highway 75; turn right and follow signs.

Shopping

Horton Plaza (✉ Broadway and G St. from 1st to 4th Aves., ☏ 619/238–1596), occupying several square blocks downtown, is a multilevel, postmodern mall. The Robinsons-May, Saks, Nordstrom, and Neiman Marcus department stores anchor the also huge **Fashion Valley** mall (✉ 452 Fashion Valley Dr., ☏ 619/297–3386).

The **Gaslamp Quarter** is home to art galleries, antiques shops, and other specialty stores. Trendy boutiques and galleries line **Girard Avenue** and **Prospect Street** in La Jolla. Old Town has the **Bazaar del Mundo, La Esplanade,** and the **Old Town Mercado,** with international goods, toys, souvenirs, and arts and crafts. Gay and funky **Hillcrest** is home to many gift, book, and music stores.

ELSEWHERE IN SOUTHERN CALIFORNIA

Palm Springs

A desert playground for Hollywood celebrities since the 1930s, Palm Springs has plenty of attractions: luxurious resorts, nearly year-round golf and tennis, and fine upscale and outlet shopping.

Visitor Information

Palm Springs Desert Resorts Bureau (✉ 69–930 Hwy. 111, Suite 201, Rancho Mirage 92270, ☎ 760/770–9000 or 800/967–3767). **Palm Springs Visitor Information Center** (✉ 2781 N. Palm Canyon, Palm Springs 92262, ☎ 800/347–7746). Both can make reservations for accommodations in the area and have lists of golf courses that are open to the public.

Arriving and Departing

Palm Springs is about a two-hour drive east of Los Angeles and a three-hour drive northeast of San Diego. From L.A. take I–10 east to Highway 111. From San Diego take I–15 north to Highway 60, then I–10 east to Highway 111. **Palm Springs Regional Airport** is served by national and regional airlines.

What to See and Do

★ For an overview of the area, ride up the **Palm Springs Aerial Tramway** (✉ 1 Tramway Rd., ☎ 760/325–1391; $17.65). The region's natural attractions include **Joshua Tree National Park** (✉ Hwy. 62 northeast from Hwy. 111, ☎ 760/367–7511). Its oddly shaped trees, with their branches raised like arms, and its weather-sculpted rocks are entrancing. Come eyeball to eyeball with coyotes, mountain lions, cheetahs, and golden eagles at the **Living Desert Wildlife and Botanical Park** (✉ 47-900 Portola Ave., Palm Desert, ☎ 760/346–5694; $7.50). Easy to challenging trails traverse desert gardens populated with plants of the Mojave, Colorado, and Sonoran deserts.

The **Palm Springs Desert Museum** (✉ 101 Museum Dr., ☎ 760/325–0189; $7.50) has a fine collection that emphasizes natural science and 20th-century art. The museum's Annenberg Theater presents plays, concerts, lectures, operas, and other cultural events. The hottest ★ ticket in the desert is the **Fabulous Palm Springs Follies** (✉ Plaza Theater, 128 S. Palm Canyon Dr., ☎ 760/327–0225; $27–$65), a vaudeville-style revue that stars extravagantly costumed retired (but very much in shape) showgirls, singers, and dancers.

Dining and Lodging

$$$–$$$$ ★ ✕ **Cuistot.** Signature dishes at chef-owner Bernard Dervieux's French restaurant include grilled shrimp with spinach linguine, Chinese-style duck in a mango-Madeira-ginger sauce, and rack of lamb with rosemary. ✉ *73-111 El Paseo, Palm Desert,* ☎ *760/340–1000. Reservations essential. AE, DC, MC, V. Closed Mon. No lunch Sun.*

$$ ✕ **Palomino Euro Bistro.** The cuisine at this ultrapopular restaurant ranges from pizza and snacking items to grilled and roasted entrées with Mediterranean influences. ✉ *73–101 Hwy. 111, Palm Desert,* ☎ *760/773–9091. Reservations essential. AE, D, MC, V. No lunch.*

$$ ✕ **Shame on the Moon.** The kitchen here turns out consistently delicious Continental fare like roasted salmon with horseradish crust and calves' liver and onions with a bourbon glaze. The desserts are alluringly decadent. ✉ *69-950 Frank Sinatra Dr.,* ☎ *760/324–5515. Reservations essential. AE, MC, V. No lunch.*

$$$$ **Givenchy Hotel and Spa.** Indulgence is the word for this French-style resort with opulent rooms, perfectly manicured gardens, and fine restaurants. Personalized spa services include everything from facials to marine mud wraps to aromatherapy. ✉ *4200 E. Palm Canyon Dr., 92264,* ☎ *760/770–5000 or 800/276–5000,* FAX *760/324–6104. 98 rooms. 3 restaurants, pool, health club. AE, D, DC, MC, V.*

$$–$$$$ **Ingleside Inn.** Many rooms at this 1920s hacienda-style inn have antiques, fireplaces, and private patios; all have two-person whirlpool tubs and steam showers. ✉ *200 W. Ramon Rd., 92264,* ☎ *760/325–*

0046 or 800/772–6655, FAX 760/325–0710. 30 rooms. Restaurant, pool. CP. AE, D, DC, MC, V.

$–$$ **Hampton Inn.** Appointments here are basic but clean. There are barbecues available for guest use. ✉ *200 N. Palm Canyon Dr., 92262,* ☎ *760/320–0555 or 800/732–7755,* FAX *760/320–2261. 96 rooms. Pool. CP. AE, D, DC, MC, V.*

Death Valley

Arriving and Departing

To reach Death Valley from the west (about 300 mi from Los Angeles), exit U.S. 395 at either Highway 190 or 178. From the southeast (about 140 mi from Las Vegas), take Highway 127 north from I–15 and Highway 178 past Badwater and Artists Palette to Highway 190 at Furnace Creek. Zabriskie Point and Dante's View are off Highway 190 heading back southeast to Highway 127. Reliable maps are a must.

What to See and Do

★ **Death Valley National Park** (visitor center: ✉ Furnace Creek, Hwy. 190, ☎ 760/786–2331) is a desert wonderland of sand dunes, crusty salt flats, 11,000-ft mountains, and hills and canyons of many hues. In the northwestern section is **Scotty's Castle** (✉ Hwy. 190, north from Furnace Creek, ☎ 760/786–2392; $8), a Moorish-style mansion built by a onetime performer in Buffalo Bill's Wild West Show. **Harmony Borax Works** (✉ Hwy. 190, near Furnace Creek) illustrates the mining history of the valley, from which the 20-mule teams hauled borax to the railroad at Mojave. **Dante's View** (✉ Hwy. 190, south of Furnace Creek), 5,000 ft up in the Black Mountains, has views of the lowest (Badwater) and highest (Mt. Whitney) points in the contiguous United States.

OREGON

By Donald S. Olson

Capital	Salem
Population	3,243,000
Motto	She Flies with Her Own Wings
State Bird	Western meadowlark
State Flower	Oregon grape
Postal Abbreviation	OR

Statewide Visitor Information

Oregon State Welcome Center (✉ 12348 N. Center St., Portland 97217, ☎ 503/285–1631). **Oregon Tourism Commission** (✉ 775 Summer St. NE, Salem 97310, ☎ 800/547–7842).

Scenic Drives

The **Columbia Gorge Scenic Highway** (Route 30) twists and turns its way above I–84 through the heavily wooded, waterfall-laced Columbia Gorge east of Portland. **U.S. 101** hugs the largely unspoiled Oregon coastline. **Highway 138** from Roseburg to Crater Lake is a National Scenic Byway through rugged canyons past waterfalls, mountain lakes, and camping areas.

National and State Parks

National Parks

Crater Lake National Park (✉ Box 7, Crater Lake 97604, ☎ 541/594–2211, ext. 402; 🎟 $10 per vehicle) has guided boat trips of the pristine lake, and many nature trails (☞ Ashland/The Rogue Valley in Elsewhere in Oregon, *below*). In the high-desert country of eastern Oregon, **John Day Fossil Beds National Monument** (✉ HCR 82, Box 126, Kimberly 97848–9701, ☎ 541/987–2333; 🎟 free) contains the richest concentration of prehistoric plant and animal fossils in the world. **Newberry National Volcanic Monument,** administered by the Deschutes National Forest (✉ 1645 Hwy. 20E, Bend 97701, ☎ 541/388–2715; 🎟 $5 per vehicle), provides recreation for campers, cross-country skiers, snowmobilers, fishers, and hikers. **Oregon Caves National Monument** (✉ 19000 Caves Hwy., Cave Junction 97523, ☎ 541/592–3400; 🎟 $6) conducts guided tours of the Marble Halls of Oregon. **Oregon Dunes National Recreation Area** (✉ 855 Highway Ave., Reedsport 97467, ☎ 541/271–3611; 🎟 $3 per vehicle) covers 40 mi of undulating camel-color sand and freshwater lakes (☞ Exploring the Oregon Coast, *below*).

State Parks

Oregon's 225 state parks run the gamut from sage-scented desert to mountains to sea. The **Oregon State Parks and Recreation Department** (✉ 1115 Commercial St. NE, Salem 97310, ☎ 800/551–6949) has information on the parks, campsite availability, and facilities.

PORTLAND

Portland, one of America's most important gateways to the Pacific Rim, has earned a reputation as a well-planned, relaxing city. Straddling the banks of the wide Willamette River, this is one of the largest inland ports on the West Coast. It also boasts flower-filled parks, efficient mass transit, excellent hotels and restaurants, and restored historic buildings.

Visitor Information

Portland/Oregon Visitors Association (✉ 2 World Trade Center, 26 S.W. Salmon St., 97204, ☎ 503/222–2223 or 800/962–3700). Portland Guides in green jackets walk the sidewalks downtown; they can assist with directions and answer questions about the city.

Arriving and Departing

By Bus

Greyhound Lines (✉ 550 N.W. 6th Ave., ☎ 800/231–2222).

By Car

I–84 (Banfield Freeway) and Highway 26 (the Sunset) run east–west; I–5 and I–205 run north–south.

By Plane

Portland International Airport (☎ 503/335–1234), in northeast Portland about 10 mi from the city center, is served by major domestic carriers. Transportation to and from the airport is available through **Portland Taxi** (☎ 503/256–5400) and **Broadway Cab** (☎ 503/227–1234), as well as **Raz Transportation** buses (☎ 503/246–3301) and hotel shuttle services. A taxi ride downtown costs about $25; the bus is $9.

By Train

Amtrak serves Union Station (✉ 800 N.W. 6th Ave., ☎ 503/273–4865 or 800/872–7245).

Getting Around Portland

The metropolitan area is laid out in a grid system, with numbered avenues running north–south and named streets running east–west. The **MAX light-rail line** links eastern and western Portland suburbs to the downtown core, the Lloyd Center District, the Convention Center, and the Rose Quarter, which includes Memorial Coliseum and a sports arena. A western extension to Beaverton–Hillsboro includes a stop at the Washington Park Zoo. At 260 ft below ground, the transit station is the deepest in the nation. The **Tri-Met bus system** covers the metro area extensively. Call 503/238–7433 for schedules and routes for both Tri-Met and MAX.

Exploring Portland

Downtown

Pioneer Courthouse Square (✉ S.W. Broadway and S.W. Morrison St.), the downtown area's main gathering place and people-watching venue, sits across from the classically sedate **Pioneer Courthouse,** the oldest public building in the Northwest, built in 1869.

The 1930s-era **Portland Art Museum** is one of several interesting buildings that line the South Park Blocks, a tree-lined boulevard of statues and fountains with Portland State University at its southern end. The museum contains 35 centuries of Asian, European, and Native American art and is a regional venue for large traveling exhibitions. ✉ *1219 S.W. Park Ave.,* ☎ *503/226–2811. Closed Mon.* 🎫 *$6.*

Across from the art museum, towering murals of Lewis and Clark and the Oregon Trail frame the entrance to the **Oregon History Center** (✉ 1200 S.W. Park Ave., ☎ 503/222–1741; 🎫 $6), where the state's history from prehistoric times to the present is documented in dramatic galleries and hands-on exhibits.

The **Old Church,** built in 1882, is a prime example of Carpenter Gothic architecture, complete with rough-cut lumber, tall spires, and the origi-

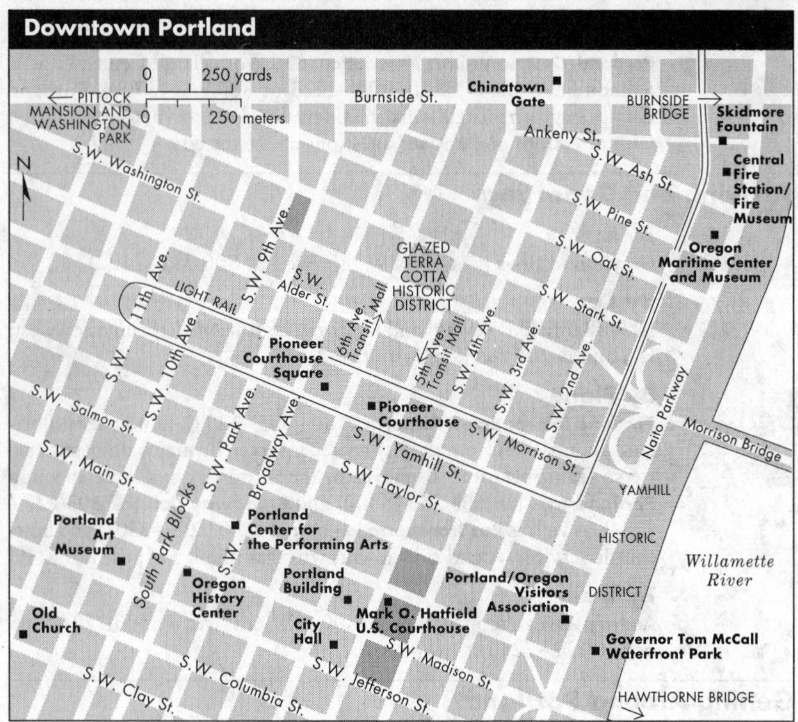

nal stained-glass windows. Free concerts are presented on Wednesday at noon. ✉ *1422 S.W. 11th Ave.,* ☎ *503/222–2031. Closed Sun.* 🎫 *Free.*

Architect Michael Graves's **Portland Building** (✉ 1120 S.W. 5th Ave.) was one of the country's first postmodern designs. **Portlandia,** the second-largest hammered-copper sculpture in the world (after the Statue of Liberty), kneels on the second-story balcony. Across Madison Street from the Portland Building is the classically styled and newly restored **city hall,** built in 1895, with high ceilings, marble hallways, a glass-roofed atrium, and pillars inside. The **Mark O. Hatfield U.S. Courthouse** (✉ S.W. 2nd Ave. between Main and Madison), completed in 1997, has rooftop terraces with sweeping vistas of the city and the Willamette River.

Across Naito Parkway along the Willamette River you'll find **Governor Tom McCall Waterfront Park,** a grassy 2-mi expanse (a former expressway) used as a venue for festivals and concerts as well as picnics, jogging, and biking. From the park you can see some of the many distinctive bridges that have earned Portland the name Bridgetown. The **Japanese-American Historical Plaza** (✉ Waterfront Park and N.W. Couch) commemorates with evocative words and art the Japanese Americans interned by the U.S. government during World War II.

Many fine examples of 19th-century cast-iron architecture are preserved in the **Yamhill and Skidmore National Historic districts,** which begin on Naito Parkway across from the waterfront park. The former commercial waterfront of Portland is now a district of galleries, fountains, and shops that is particularly lively on weekends.

The main mast of the battleship ***Oregon***, which served in three wars, stands at the foot of Oak Street. The exterior of the **Oregon Maritime Center and Museum** (✉ 113 S.W. Naito Pkwy., ☎ 503/224–7724; 🎫 $4) incorporates fine street-level examples of cast-iron architecture. Inside are models of ships that once plied the Columbia River. The admission fee allows you to board the last operating stern-wheeler tug in the United States, docked across the street. The north side of the Central Fire Station houses the **Jeff Morris Memorial Fire Museum** (✉ 111 S.W. Naito Pkwy.), a collection of antique pumps and other equipment that can be viewed from outside the building.

The **Portland Saturday Market** (☎ 503/222–6072), underneath the west end of the Burnside Bridge and open weekends from March through Christmas, has live entertainment and 300 merchants selling ethnic foods, arts, and crafts. Graceful **Skidmore Fountain,** built in 1888, is the splashing centerpiece of Ankeny Square, the Saturday Market's western boundary.

The official entrance to Portland's **Chinatown** is the ornate **Chinatown Gate** (✉ N.W. 4th Ave. and W. Burnside St.). In the 1890s Portland's Chinese community was the second largest in the United States. Today it is compressed into several blocks in the northwestern part of town, with many restaurants, shops, and grocery stores.

The **Children's Museum** (✉ 3037 S.W. 2nd Ave., ☎ 503/823–2227; 🎫 $4), just south of downtown, has hands-on, interactive exhibits.

Pittock Mansion (✉ 3229 N.W. Pittock Dr., ☎ 503/823–3624; 🎫 $4.50), 1,000 ft above the city about 2 mi west of downtown, yields superb views of the skyline, rivers, and Cascade Mountains. The 1914 mansion was built for Henry Pittock, former editor of *The Oregonian.* Set in its own scenic park, the opulent manor is filled with art and antiques of the 1880s.

Other Neighborhoods

In an attempt to ward off suburban sprawl, fast-growing Portland has put a new emphasis on "urban density" and revitalization of its inner-city neighborhoods. As a result, several areas have been transformed. Many of the storefronts and warehouses in the formerly industrial **Pearl District,** bordered by Burnside and Marshall streets and N.W. 8th and N.W. 15th avenues, have been converted over the past 10 years into lofts, art galleries, furniture and design stores, and restaurants. A few blocks west of the Pearl District, grand old Portland houses, some dating back 100 years, line the streets of **Nob Hill,** one of the city's oldest neighborhoods. At the heart of Nob Hill are the 20 fashion-conscious blocks of **N.W. 23rd Avenue between Burnside and Vaughn streets**—now a citywide destination for dining, café hopping. Several of the avenue's old homes have been turned into upscale boutiques, with everything from women's clothing to antique linens. Across the Willamette River, **S.E. Hawthorne Boulevard between 30th and 39th avenues** has become the east side's most popular stomping ground. More down-to-earth than N.W. 23rd and still countercultural around the edges, S.E. Hawthorne is lined with bookstores, coffeehouses, taverns, restaurants, antiques stores, and unusual boutiques. The **Oregon Museum of Science and Industry** (✉ 1945 S.E. Water Ave., ☎ 503/797–4000; 🎫 $6.50–$13), in a restored steam plant on the Willamette's east bank, has touring exhibits, permanent displays, a planetarium, a submarine, laser shows, and an Omnimax theater.

Parks, Gardens, and Zoos

★ **Washington Park** (✉ 611 S.W. Kingston Ave., ☎ 503/223–5055), covering 322 acres in the west hills, is the site of the renowned **International Rose Test Garden** and, directly above it, the serene **Japanese Gardens,** considered one of the most authentic outside Japan. The **Metro Washington Park Zoo** (✉ 4001 S.W. Canyon Rd., ☎ 503/226–

7627; $5.50) has Asian elephants, an African section, and animals indigenous to the Northwest.

Dining

Bounteous local produce from land and sea receives star billing at many Portland dining establishments, and recent Pacific Rim immigrants have added depth and spice to the restaurant scene. For price ranges see Chart 1 (A) in On the Road with Fodor's.

$$–$$$ ✕ **Heathman Restaurant and Bar.** Master chef Philippe Boulot assembles Pacific Northwest products and ingredients in a classical style. Salmon, specialty seafood dishes, and local free-range game—venison, veal, rabbit—appear on the seasonally changing menu. ✉ *1001 S.W. Broadway,* ☎ *503/790–7752. Reservations essential. AE, DC, MC, V.*

$$–$$$ ✕ **Jake's Famous Crawfish.** White-coated waiters at this revered, century-old restaurant serve up fresh seafood, selected from a lengthy sheet of daily specials, in a warren of old-fashioned wood-paneled dining rooms. Alder-smoked salmon and crab-crawfish-salmon cakes are consistent standouts. ✉ *401 S.W. 12th Ave.,* ☎ *503/226–1419. Reservations essential. AE, D, DC, MC, V. No lunch weekends.*

$$–$$$ ★ ✕ **Zefiro.** The sophisticated menu at this chic and popular neighborhood eatery applies Southeast Asian and Mediterranean cooking principles to local ingredients such as wild mushrooms and salmon. ✉ *500 N.W. 21st Ave.,* ☎ *503/226–3394. Reservations essential. AE, DC, MC, V. Closed Sun.*

$$ ✕ **Assaggio.** This small, stylish Italian restaurant in the Sellwood district evokes Italy, and the food is perhaps the most authentically Italian in the city. Farfalle, penne, fusilli, and spaghetti are cooked al dente and not overly sauced; many dishes are available as family-style samplers. ✉ *7742 S.E. 13th Ave.,* ☎ *503/232–6151. No reservations. MC, V. No lunch. Closed Sun.–Mon.*

$$ ✕ **Bima Restaurant and Bar.** Housed in a restored warehouse in Portland's arts-filled Pearl District, Bima takes its cues from the cuisines of the Gulf of Mexico coast. Pecan-crusted catfish, assorted fish and meat skewers, fish tacos, and luscious ribs are some of the specialties. There's a bar menu as well. ✉ *1338 N.W. Hoyt,* ☎ *503/241–3465. AE, MC, V. Closed Sun.*

$–$$ ✕ **Misohapi.** The vibrant flavors of Vietnam and Thailand find full expression in this snappy Nob Hill eatery. Hot and sour seafood soup, lemongrass seafood, and peanutty pad Thai noodles with shrimp are among the star attractions. ✉ *1123 N.W. 23rd Ave.,* ☎ *503/796–2012. MC, V. Closed Sun.*

$$ ✕ **Montage.** Spicy Cajun is the jumping-off point for the menu at this sassy bistro under the Morrison Bridge, on Portland's east side. Jambalaya, blackened pork and catfish, Hoppin' Jon, rabbit tenders, and macaroni dishes are some of the specialties served from 11:30 AM until the wee hours in an atmosphere that's loud, crowded, and casually hip. ✉ *301 S.E. Morrison,* ☎ *503/234–1324. No credit cards. No lunch weekends.*

$$ ★ ✕ **Tapeo.** The best of Portland's Spanish restaurants serves hot and cold tapas on hand-painted plates in an intimate, inviting atmosphere. Grilled prawns with red cabbage, duck breast with lentils, braised rabbit with sherry, and quail with a warm chocolate sauce are some of the best. ✉ *2764 N.W. Thurman,* ☎ *503/226–0409. D, MC, V. No lunch. Closed Mon.*

Brew Pubs

Portland has one of the largest microbrewery scenes of North America. Its dozens of small breweries and affiliated pubs offer both satisfying dining and good value. Among the standouts is the **Pilsner Room**

(✉ 0309 S.W. Montgomery St., ☎ 503/220–1865), which showcase local brews and inexpensive nouvelle pub cuisine. The **Bridgeport Brew Pub** (✉ 1318 N.W. Marshall St., ☎ 503/241–7179) serves thick hand-thrown pizzas; wash them down with creamy pints of Bridgeport real ale. **McMenamins Edgefield** (✉ 2126 S.W. Halsey St., Troutdale, ☎ 503/492–4686) is the showpiece of the vast microbrewing empire of the McMenamin brothers; the 12-acre estate has its own pub, restaurant, movie theater, 105-room inn, winery, and brewery. The McMenamin brothers' newest venture, **Ringlers** (✉ 1332 W. Burnside St., ☎ 503/225–0543), occupies the first floor of a historic Portland building that houses the Crystal Ballroom (☞ Nightlife, *below*).

Lodging

You'll find many national and regional chains near the airport. The city center and waterfront support both elegant new and historic hotels. Bed-and-breakfasts cluster in the West Hills and across the river in the Lloyd Center/Convention Center area. Northwest Bed & Breakfast (☎ 503/243–7616 or 503/370–9033) is a good source for information and reservations in Portland and the entire coastal region. For price ranges see Chart 2 (A) in On the Road with Fodor's.

$$$$ ★ **The Heathman.** Superior service, an award-winning restaurant, an elegant tea court, and a library of signed first editions by authors who have been guests here have earned the Heathman a reputation for quality. The guest rooms have original artwork by Northwest artists. ✉ *1001 S.W. Broadway, 97205,* ☎ *503/241–4100 or 800/551–0011,* FAX *503/790–7110. 150 rooms. Restaurant, exercise room. AE, D, DC, MC, V.*

$$$–$$$$ **The Benson.** Portland's grandest hotel, built in 1912, has maintained its turn-of-the-century splendor, with Russian-walnut–paneled walls in the guest rooms and a piano in the lobby. ✉ *309 S.W. Broadway, 97205,* ☎ *503/228–2000 or 800/426–0670,* FAX *503/226–4603. 287 rooms. 2 restaurants, exercise room. AE, D, DC, MC, V.*

$$$–$$$$ **Doubletree Hotel Portland–Lloyd Center.** At Portland's second-largest hotel, service runs like a well-oiled machine. Many of the large rooms with balconies have views of the mountains or the city center. Lloyd Center shopping and MAX light-rail are across the street. ✉ *1000 N.E. Multnomah St., 97232,* ☎ *503/281–6111,* FAX *503/284–8553. 476 rooms. 3 restaurants, pool, exercise room. AE, D, DC, MC, V.*

$$$–$$$$ **The Governor.** Portland's most distinctive old hotel has a clubby lobby with mahogany walls and a mural of Northwest Indians fishing in Celilo Falls. Guest rooms, painted in soothing earth tones, have large windows and whirlpool tubs; some also have fireplaces and balconies. ✉ *611 S.W. 10th Ave., 97205,* ☎ *503/224–3400 or 800/554–3456,* FAX *503/241–2122. 100 rooms. Restaurant. AE, D, DC, MC, V.*

$$$–$$$$ **Hotel Vintage Plaza.** As the hotel's name might suggest, the names of the rooms take their theme from Oregon's wine country, and there's also a complimentary wine hour each evening. Top-floor rooms have skylights and wall-to-wall conservatory-style windows. ✉ *422 S.W. Broadway, 97205,* ☎ *503/228–1212 or 800/243–0555,* FAX *503/228–3598. 107 rooms. 2 restaurants, exercise room. AE, D, DC, MC, V.*

$$–$$$ **Shilo Inn Suites Hotel.** Each suite has three TVs, a VCR, a microwave, four phones, a refrigerator, a wet bar, and two oversize beds. The hotel is close to the airport and offers a full range of business services. ✉ *11707 N.E. Airport Way, 97220,* ☎ *503/252–7500 or 800/222–2244,* FAX *503/254–0794. 200 rooms. Restaurant, pool, exercise room. CP. AE, D, DC, MC, V.*

$$ **MacMaster House.** Built in 1886, this 17-room Colonial Revival mansion is comfortable and funky. Fashionable Northwest 23rd Avenue is less than 10 minutes away by foot. ✉ *1041 S.W. Vista Ave., 97205,* ☎ *503/223–7362 or 800/774–9523. 7 rooms, 2 with bath. Full breakfast. AE, D, MC, V.*

$$ 🏨 **Mallory Hotel.** The rooms in this Portland stalwart, eight blocks from the city center, are on the small side and about half haven't been refurbished since the 1970s—but it's clean and friendly, and the city center is only eight blocks away. Pets are allowed for $10 extra. ✉ *729 S.W. 15th Ave., 97205,* ☎ *503/223–6311 or 800/228–8657,* FAX *503/223–0522. 136 rooms. Restaurant. AE, D, DC, MC, V.*

$–$$ 🏨 **Best Western Inn at the Convention Center.** Rooms are done in pleasing creams and rusts at this property across the street from the convention center. ✉ *420 N.E. Holladay St., 97232,* ☎ *503/233–6331,* FAX *503/233–2677. 97 rooms. Restaurant. AE, D, DC, MC, V.*

$–$$ 🏨 **Portland Guest House.** This northeast Portland 1890s B&B has mocha-colored exterior paint and original hardwood floors. Rooms are done in white on white with Victorian walnut furniture and original Pacific Northwest art. ✉ *1720 N.E. 15th Ave., 97212,* ☎ *503/282–1402. 7 rooms, 5 with bath. Full breakfast. MC, V.*

Nightlife and the Arts

The Oregonian (on newsstands) and *Willamette Week* (available free in the metro area) list arts and entertainment events. *Just Out* (available free in the metro area) is the city's gay newspaper.

Nightlife

Rock 'n' Rodeo (✉ 220 S.E. Spokane St., ☎ 503/235–2417) remains a hot spot for country-and-western music and line dancing. **The Crystal Ballroom** (✉ S.W. 14th and Burnside St., ☎ 503/225–0047), dating from 1914 and completely restored in 1997, hosts dancing to live bands on its huge "elastic" floor, built on ball bearings. The top jazz spots in Portland are **Brasserie Montmartre** (✉ 626 S.W. Park Ave., ☎ 503/224–5552) and **Jazz De Opus** (✉ 33 N.W. 2nd Ave., ☎ 503/222–6077). For comedy try **Harvey's Comedy Club** (✉ 436 N.W. 6th Ave., ☎ 503/241–0338), which presents headliners with a national reputation. **Embers** (✉ 110 N.W. Broadway, ☎ 503/222–3082), a full-throttle disco, is popular with both straights and gays. Several gay bars line S.W. Stark Street downtown, including **C.C. Slaughters** (✉ 1014 S.W. Stark, ☎ 503/248–9135).

The **Portland Center for the Performing Arts** (✉ S.W. Broadway and S.W. Main St., ☎ 503/796–9293), which includes the 2,776-seat Arlene Schnitzer Concert Hall and (across the street) the Performing Arts Building, presents rock concerts, symphony orchestra performances, theater, dance, lectures, and touring Broadway musicals. Portland Center Stage performs from November to April at the Performing Art Building's **Intermediate Theater** (✉ 1111 S.W. Broadway, ☎ 503/274–6588). The **Oregon Symphony** (☎ 503/228–1353) performs more than 40 concerts each season at the Arlene Schnitzer Concert Hall. The **Portland Opera** (☎ 503/241–1802) and the **Oregon Ballet Theater** (☎ 503/222–5538) perform at the **Civic Auditorium** (✉ S.W. 3rd Ave. and Clay St. downtown). **Portland Repertory Theatre** (✉ 25 S.W. Salmon, ☎ 503/224–4491) presents a full season of plays in the city's World Trade Center.

Spectator Sports

Basketball: Portland Trail Blazers (✉ Rose Garden Arena, 1 Center Ct., east end of Broadway Bridge, ☎ 503/797–9619).

Shopping

For local products try the **Made In Oregon** shops, with locations at Portland International Airport, Lloyd Center, the Galleria, Old Town, Washington Square, and Clackamas Town Center. Merchandise ranges from books to smoked salmon, hazelnuts, honey, dried fruits, local wines, and Pendleton woolen products.

Pioneer Place (✉ 700 S.W. 5th Ave., ☎ 503/228–5800) is the jewel in the city's shopping crown. More than 80 specialty shops are anchored by a gleaming Saks Fifth Avenue store. The original **Meier & Frank** (✉ 621 S.W. 5th Ave., ☎ 503/223–0512) department store, a Portland landmark since 1857, sits across the street from Pioneer Place. **Nordstrom** (✉ 701 S.W. Broadway, ☎ 503/224–6666), across from Pioneer Courthouse Square, has quality apparel and accessories and a large shoe department. High-tech **Niketown** (✉ 930 S.W. 6th Ave., ☎ 503/221–6453), the original branch of a now-national chain, is part sports shrine, part sales outlet.

With more than 1 million new and used volumes, **Powell's City of Books** (✉ 1005 W. Burnside St., ☎ 503/228–4651) is one of the largest bookstores in the world. The **Portland Pendleton Shop** (✉ 900 S.W. 4th Ave., ☎ 503/242–0037) carries men's and women's wear, including the Oregon mill's famous Pendleton shirts and blankets.

THE OREGON COAST

Oregon has 400 mi of white-sand beaches, not a grain of which is privately owned. U.S. 101 parallels the coast from Astoria south to California, past monoliths of sea-tortured rock, brooding headlands, hidden beaches, historic lighthouses, tiny ports, and, of course, the tumultuous Pacific.

Visitor Information

Astoria–Warrenton area: Chamber of Commerce (✉ 111 W. Marine Dr., 97103, ☎ 503/325–6311 or 800/875–6807). **Coos Bay/North Bend area:** Chamber of Commerce (✉ 50 E. Central St., Coos Bay 97420, ☎ 541/269–0215 or 800/824–8486). **Cannon Beach:** Chamber of Commerce (✉ 2nd and Spruce Sts., 97110, ☎ 503/436–2623). **Florence area:** Chamber of Commerce (✉ 270 Hwy. 101, 97439, ☎ 541/997–3128). **Lincoln City:** Visitors Center (✉ 801 S.W. Hwy. 101, Suite 1, 97367, ☎ 541/994–8378 or 800/452–2151).

Arriving and Departing

By Bus

Greyhound Lines (☎ 800/231–2222) serves coastal communities such as Coos Bay, Florence, and Lincoln City.

By Car

The best way to see the coast is by car, following twisting, slow-paced, two-lane U.S. 101. Highway 26 (the Sunset) is the main link to Portland.

Exploring the Oregon Coast

Astoria, founded in 1811 at the site where the mighty Columbia River meets the Pacific Ocean, is believed to be the first official settlement established by the United States on the West Coast. Here Lewis and Clark wept with joy when they first saw the Pacific. The Victorian houses once owned by fur, timber, and fishing magnates still dot the flanks of

Western Oregon

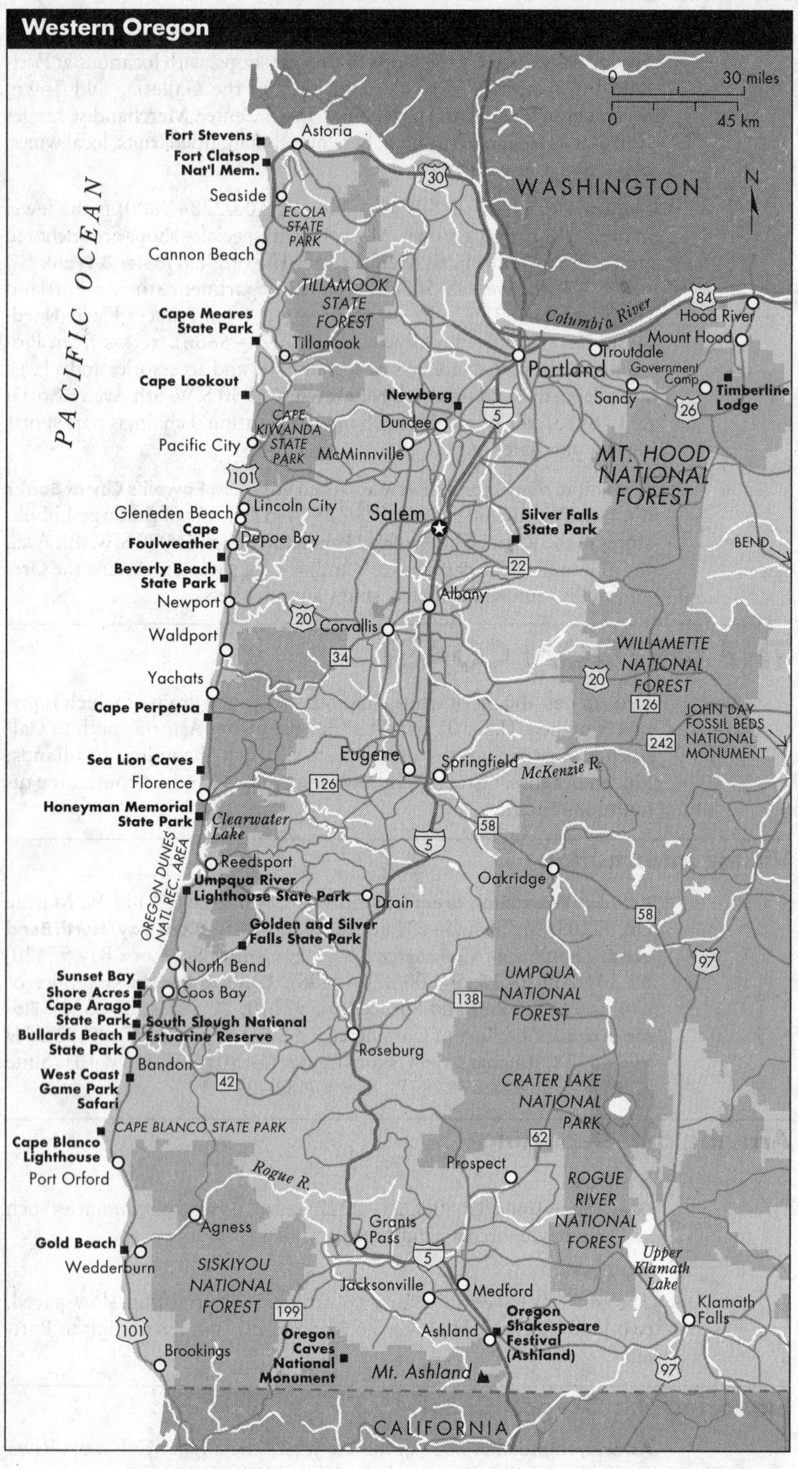

0 30 miles
0 45 km
N
WASHINGTON
PACIFIC OCEAN
Fort Stevens
Astoria
Fort Clatsop Nat'l Mem.
30
Seaside
ECOLA STATE PARK
Cannon Beach
TILLAMOOK STATE FOREST
84
Columbia River
Hood River
Cape Meares State Park
Mount Hood
Tillamook
Troutdale
Portland
Government Camp
Cape Lookout
Sandy
Timberline Lodge
Newberg
26
5
CAPE KIWANDA STATE PARK
Dundee
Pacific City
McMinnville
MT. HOOD NATIONAL FOREST
101
Lincoln City
Gleneden Beach
Salem
Silver Falls State Park
Cape Foulweather
Depoe Bay
BEND
22
Beverly Beach State Park
Newport
Albany
20
Corvallis
Waldport
34
WILLAMETTE NATIONAL FOREST
Yachats
20
126
Cape Perpetua
JOHN DAY FOSSIL BEDS NATIONAL MONUMENT
242
Sea Lion Caves
Eugene
Springfield
McKenzie R.
Florence
126
Honeyman Memorial State Park
Clearwater Lake
58
5
OREGON DUNES NAT'L REC. AREA
Reedsport
Umpqua River Lighthouse State Park
Oakridge
Drain
58
Golden and Silver Falls State Park
North Bend
97
UMPQUA NATIONAL FOREST
Sunset Bay
Shore Acres
Coos Bay
138
Cape Arago State Park
South Slough National Estuarine Reserve
Bullards Beach State Park
Roseburg
Bandon
West Coast Game Park Safari
42
CRATER LAKE NATIONAL PARK
CAPE BLANCO STATE PARK
62
Cape Blanco Lighthouse
Port Orford
Prospect
Rogue R.
ROGUE RIVER NATIONAL FOREST
Agness
Grants Pass
Gold Beach
Wedderburn
5
Upper Klamath Lake
SISKIYOU NATIONAL FOREST
Jacksonville
Medford
199
Oregon Shakespeare Festival (Ashland)
Klamath Falls
101
Ashland
Brookings
Oregon Caves National Monument
Mt. Ashland
97
CALIFORNIA

Coxcomb Hill; some are now inviting B&Bs. Patterned after Trajan's Column in Rome, the 125-ft **Astor Column** atop Coxcomb Hill rewards a climb up 164 spiral stairs with breathtaking views over Astoria, the Columbia, the Coast Range, and the ocean.

The **Columbia River Maritime Museum** (✉ 1792 Marine Dr., ☎ 503/325–2323; 🎫 $5) has exhibits ranging from the fully operational lightship Columbia to poignant personal belongings from some of the 2,000 ships that have been wrecked at the mouth of the river since 1811.

★ Five and a half miles southeast of Astoria is the **Fort Clatsop National Memorial** (✉ Fort Clatsop Loop Rd., ☎ 503/861–2471; 🎫 $2), a replica of the log stockade depicted in Clark's journal, commemorating the achievement of Lewis and Clark.

Thirty miles south of Astoria and close enough to Portland to make it ★ a popular weekend getaway, **Cannon Beach** draws visitors to its long, sandy beach, restaurants, and weathered-cedar shopping district, especially in June, when the Cannon Beach Sandcastle Contest takes place ☞ Festivals and Seasonal Events *in* West Coast introduction. **Haystack Rock,** a 235-ft offshore sea stack with tide pools at its base, is one of the most photographed sites on the coast. At the north end of Cannon Beach, **Ecola State Park** (☎ 503/436–2844; 🎫 $3 per vehicle) is a playground of sea-sculpted rock, sandy beach, tide pools, green headlands, and panoramic views.

South of Tillamook Bay, on the lush coastal plain that is Oregon's dairy country, **Tillamook** is famous for its cheese and ice cream. Both can be tasted at the **Tillamook County Creamery** (✉ 4175 Hwy. 101, ☎ 503/842–4481). The **Three Capes Scenic Loop,** west of Tillamook, encompasses magnificent coastal scenery, a lighthouse, offshore wildlife refuges, sand dunes, camping areas, and hiking trails.

Bustling **Lincoln City,** 43 mi south of Tillamook on U.S. 101, is known for its excellent seafood restaurants, lodgings, and proximity to some of the Oregon coast's most scenic landscapes.

Twenty-five miles south of Lincoln City, **Newport,** with its fishing fleet, art galleries, and seafood markets along a charming old bay front, is a fine place for an afternoon stroll. Across Yaquina Bay, the ★ **Oregon Coast Aquarium** (✉ 2820 S.E. Ferry Slip Rd., ☎ 541/867–3474; 🎫 $8) has more than 4 acres of outdoor pools, cliffs, and caves for frolicking sea otters, sea lions, and even Keiko, the orca whale featured in the *Free Willy* movies. Indoor galleries are devoted to Oregon's coastal habitats and native marine life.

South of Newport, the coast takes on a very different character—slower paced, less touristy, far less crowded, but just as rich in scenery and out- ★ door sporting activities. **Cape Perpetua** (✉ 9 mi south of Yachats, off U.S. 101, ☎ 541/747–3289; 🎫 free), the highest lookout point on the Oregon coast, towers 800 ft above the rocky shoreline and has hiking trails and an informative visitors center. The **Sea Lion Caves** (✉ 91560 U.S. 101, 12 mi south of Cape Perpetua, ☎ 541/547–3111; 🎫 $6.50) is a huge vaulted chamber where kids can get a close view of hundreds of sea lions, the largest of which weigh a ton or more. The peaceful village of Florence is the northern gateway to the **Oregon Dunes National Recreation Area** (☞ National and State Parks, *above*), a remarkable 40-mi swath of tawny sand. The dunes, some more than 500 ft high, are popular with campers, hikers, mountain bikers, dune-buggy enthusiasts, and even dogsledders. Children particularly enjoy the sandy slopes surrounding cool Cleawox Lake. **Umpqua River Lighthouse State Park** (✉ 460 Lighthouse Rd., 1 mi west of U.S. 101, ☎ 541/271–4118) adjoins an operating lighthouse and encompasses a small freshwater lake and campground. Also in the park are a whale-watching station, 500-ft-high sand dunes, and the **Douglas County Coastal Visitors Center** (☎ 541/271–4631; 🎫 free), which has local history exhibits.

Coos Bay is the Oregon coast's largest metropolitan area. At the end of a gravel road in **Golden and Silver Falls State Park** (✉ 24 mi northeast of Coos Bay off U.S. 101, ☎ 541/888–3778; 🎫 free), Glenn Creek pours over a high rock ledge deep in the old-growth forest. West of Coos Bay, the Cape Arago Highway presents spectacular scenery at three state parks (☎ 541/888–4902). **Sunset Bay** (🎫 free) has a white-sand beach, picnicking, and campgrounds. **Shore Acres** (🎫 $3 per vehicle), once the estate of a timber baron, has a 7.5-acre formal garden and a glass-enclosed storm-watch viewpoint. **Cape Arago** (🎫 free), overlooking the **Oregon Islands National Wildlife Refuge** is a prime site for viewing sea lions and seabirds. Four miles south of the small fishing village of Charleston, the rich tidal estuaries of **South Slough National Estuarine Reserve** (✉ Seven Devils Rd., ☎ 541/888–5558; 🎫 free) support life ranging from algae to bald eagles and black bears.

Bullards Beach State Park (☎ 541/347–2209, 🎫 free), 2 mi north of Bandon, spreads over miles of shoreline and sand dunes. It has a campground as well as the restored Coquille River Lighthouse. **West Coast Game Park Safari** (✉ U.S. 101, 7 mi south of Bandon, ☎ 541/347–3106; 🎫 $7), closed weekdays in January and February, keeps animals of more than 75 exotic species, some of which children can pet. **Cape Blanco Lighthouse,** west of the community of Sixes, was built in 1870 and is still operating. It is the most westerly lighthouse in the contiguous 48 states. Adjacent **Cape Blanco State Park** (☎ 541/332–6774, 🎫 free) has sweeping views of rocks and beaches plus a campground.

Many knowledgeable coastal travelers consider the 63-mi stretch of U.S. 101 between Port Orford and Gold Beach to be Oregon's most beautiful. The highway soars up green headlands, some hundreds of feet high, past awesome scenery: caves, towering arches, natural and man-made bridges. Take time to admire the views by making use of the many turnouts along the way.

Gold Beach, about 30 mi north of the California border, is notable mainly as the place where the wild Rogue River meets the ocean. Daily jet-boat excursions roar up the scenic, rapids-filled Rogue from Wedderburn, Gold Beach's sister city across the bay, from late spring to late fall. Gold Beach also marks the entrance to Oregon's banana belt, where milder temperatures encourage a blossoming trade in lilies and daffodils. You'll even see a few palm trees here.

Dining and Lodging

For price ranges see Charts 1 (B) and 2 (B) in On the Road with Fodor's.

Astoria

$$–$$$ ✕ **Cannery Café.** Housed in a 100-year-old renovated cannery on a pier, this bright, contemporary restaurant has windows that look onto the Columbia River. Fresh salads, large sandwiches, clam chowder, and crab cakes are lunch staples. ✉ *16th St.,* ☎ *503/325–8642. MC, V. Closed Tues.–Wed. in winter.*

$$–$$$$ 🏨 **Franklin Street Station Bed & Breakfast.** The ticking of a grandfather clock and the mellow marine light shining through leaded-glass windows set a relaxed tone at this B&B, built in 1900. Breakfasts are huge, hot, and satisfying. ✉ *1140 Franklin Ave., 97103,* ☎ *503/325–4314 or 800/448–1098. 5 rooms. Full breakfast. AE, D, MC, V.*

Brookings

$$$–$$$$ ✕ **Starboard Tack.** Fishing vessels docked in the adjacent boat basin and picture windows looking out to the sea lend a salty ambience to this pleasant, low-key restaurant. The fresh daily seafood specials—usually halibut and salmon—are the best choices, along with the prime rib. ✉ *16011 Boat Basin Rd.,* ☎ *541/469–6006. AE, MC, V.*

$$$$ ★ **Chetco River Inn.** Acres of private forest surround this modern fishing lodge 17½ mi up the Chetco River from Brookings. Fishing guides are available on request, as are eclectic dinners cooked by the B&B's owner, Sandra Burgger; she's also a font of information on the many hiking trails in the area. Quilts and fishing gear decorate the comfortable bedrooms. ✉ *21202 High Prairie Rd., 97415,* ☎ *541/670–1645 or 800/327–2688. 4 rooms. Full breakfast. MC, V.*

Cannon Beach

$$–$$$$ ✕ **Dooger's.** This comfortable family-style eatery's fresh, well-prepared seafood, exquisite clam chowder, and low prices keep 'em coming back for more. ✉ *1371 S. Hemlock St.,* ☎ *503/436–2225. AE, D, MC, V.*

$$$ ✕ **The Bistro.** Cannon Beach's most romantic restaurant is candlelit and intimate. The three-course prix-fixe menu features imaginatively prepared fresh seafood. ✉ *263 N. Hemlock St.,* ☎ *503/436–2661. MC, V. Closed most of Jan. and Tues.–Wed. in winter.*

$$$$ ★ ✕ **Stephanie Inn.** Sophisticated country-style furnishings, fireplaces, large bathrooms with Jacuzzi bathtubs, and balconies commanding outstanding oceanfront views of Haystack Rock make this oceanfront hotel a treat. The inn also serves four-course prix-fixe dinners of Pacific Northwest cuisine; reservations are essential. Room rates include generous country breakfasts and evening wine and hors d'oeuvres. ✉ *2740 S. Pacific, 97110,* ☎ *503/436–2221 or 800/633–3466,* FAX *503/436–9711. 46 rooms. Restaurant. Full breakfast. AE, D, DC, MC, V.*

Coos Bay

$$–$$$$ ✕ **Portside Restaurant.** At this unpretentious spot with picture windows overlooking the busy Charleston boat basin, you'll be treated to seafood straight off the local fishing boats. Try the steamed Dungeness crab with drawn butter, a local specialty, or the all-you-can-eat seafood buffet on Friday night. ✉ *8001 Kingfisher Rd. (follow Cape Arago Hwy. from Coos Bay),* ☎ *541/888–5544. AE, DC, MC, V.*

$$–$$$ ✕ **Blue Heron Bistro.** You'll get subtle preparations of local seafood, chicken, and homemade pasta with an international flair at this busy bistro. There are no flat spots on the far-ranging menu; the innovative soups and desserts are also excellent. ✉ *100 Commercial St.,* ☎ *541/267–3933. AE, D, MC, V. Closed Sun. in winter.*

$$$ **Coos Bay Manor.** Built in 1912 on a quiet residential street in Coos Bay, this 15-room Colonial Revival manor is listed on the National Register of Historic Places. An unusual open balcony on the second floor leads to the five large, comfortable guest rooms. Breakfast is served in the wainscoted dining room or, weather permitting, outside on the second-floor porch. ✉ *955 S. 5th St., 97420,* ☎ *541/269–1224 or 800/269–1224. 5 rooms, 3 with bath. Full breakfast. D, MC, V.*

Florence

$$–$$$ ✕ **Bridgewater Seafood Restaurant.** The salty ambience of Florence's photogenic Old Town permeates this spacious, creaky-floored fish house. Steaks, salads, and, of course, plenty of fresh seafood are the mainstays. ✉ *1297 Bay St.,* ☎ *541/997–9405. MC, V.*

Gleneden Beach

$$$$ ✕ **Salishan Lodge.** Nestled into a 350-acre hillside forest preserve, Salishan embodies a uniquely Northwestern elegance—from the soothing

silvered-cedar tone of its guest rooms (all with fireplaces) to its collections of original art. The dining room is famous for its seasonal Northwest cuisine and wine list. Guests have use of an 18-hole championship golf course, tennis courts, hiking trails, and a business center. ✉ *7760 N. Hwy. 101, 97388,* ☎ *541/764–3600 or 888/452–2300. 205 rooms. 2 restaurants, indoor pool, exercise room. AE, D, DC, MC, V.*

Gold Beach

$$$$ ★ ✕🏨 **Tu Tu Tun Lodge.** Private decks at this lavishly appointed fishing resort overlook the clear blue Rogue River. All units have an upscale rustic charm. Four-course prix-fixe gourmet dinners are served at one sitting each night. ✉ *96550 North Bank Rogue, 97444,* ☎ *541/247–6664 or 800/864–6357,* FAX *541/247–0672. 18 rooms, 1 2-bedroom house, 1 3-bedroom house. Restaurant, pool. D, MC, V. Dining room closed Nov.–Apr.*

$–$$ 🏨 **Ireland's Rustic Lodges.** Original one- and two-bedroom cabins filled with rough-and-tumble charm plus newer motel rooms and three houses are set amid landscaped grounds. Most units have a fireplace and a deck overlooking the sea. ✉ *29330 Ellensburg Ave. (U.S. 101), 97444,* ☎ *541/247–7718,* FAX *541/247–0229. 7 cabins, 30 motel rooms, 2-, 3- and 4-bedroom houses. MC, V.*

Lincoln City

$$$–$$$$ ★ ✕ **Bay House.** This bungalow serves meals to linger over while you enjoy views across sunset-gilded Siletz Bay. The seasonal Northwest cuisine includes shellfish linguine, fresh halibut Parmesan, and roast duckling with dried cherries and Pinot Noir sauce. The wine list is extensive, the service impeccable. ✉ *5911 S.W. Hwy. 101,* ☎ *541/996–3222. AE, D, MC, V. Closed Mon.–Tues., Nov.–Apr. No lunch.*

$$–$$$$ ✕ **Kyllos.** Perched on stilts beside the world's shortest river (the D) and bestowing views of Pacific surf and sand, Kyllos is a spacious, light-filled aerie. It's also one of the best places in Lincoln City to enjoy simple but satisfying seafood, meat, and pasta dishes. ✉ *1110 N.W. 1st Ct.,* ☎ *541/994–3179. AE, D, MC, V.*

$$–$$$$ 🏨 **Ester Lee Motel.** This small whitewashed motel on a seaside bluff attracts repeat guests. Amenities include wood-burning fireplaces, full kitchens, and cable TV in all rooms. ✉ *3803 S.W. Hwy. 101, 97367,* ☎ *541/996–3606 or 888/996–3606. 53 rooms. D, MC, V.*

Newport

$$$–$$$$ ✕ **Canyon Way Restaurant and Bookstore.** The best dining (and bookstore) in Newport is just up the hill from the center of the Bay Front. Cod, Dungeness crab cakes, bouillabaisse, and Yaquina Bay oysters are among the specialties served inside or on the outdoor patio. There's also a deli counter for takeout. ✉ *S.W. Canyon Way,* ☎ *541/265–8319. AE, MC, V. No dinner Mon.*

$$$–$$$$ ✕ **Whale's Tale.** Fresh local seafood, thick clam chowder, burgers, and hearty sandwiches are all on the lunch and dinner menu of this casual, family-oriented Bay Front eatery; the breakfasts are considered the best in Newport. ✉ *452 S.W. Bay Blvd.,* ☎ *541/265–8660. AE, D, DC, MC, V. Closed Wed. Nov.–Apr.*

$$–$$$$ ★ ✕🏨 **Sylvia Beach Hotel.** Each of the phoneless, TV-less, antiques-filled guest rooms at this restored 1912 B&B is named for a famous writer and decorated accordingly. (A pendulum swings over the bed in the Poe Room.) Upstairs is a well-stocked library with a fireplace, a slumbering cat, and too-comfortable chairs. Tables of Content, the hotel's restaurant, serves a filling, multicourse fixe-prix dinner; reservations are essential. ✉ *267 N.W. Cliff St., 97365,* ☎ *541/265–5428. 20 rooms. Restaurant. Full breakfast. AE, MC, V. No lunch.*

Waldport

$$–$$$ ★ ✕ **La Serre.** Perhaps the best restaurant on the Oregon coast, La Serre serves fresh seafood dishes including razor clams lightly breaded and flash-fried in lemon-garlic butter, fishermen's stew, and a famous Seafood Extravaganza with grilled salmon, blackened cod, and Dungeness crab cakes. Reservations are essential. ✉ *2nd and Beach Sts.,* ☎ *541/547–3420. AE, MC, V. Closed Tues. and all of Jan. No lunch.*

Yachats

$$$$ **Ziggurat.** It's hard to miss this terraced, pyramid-shape B&B just south of Yachats, one of the most charming small communities on the coast. Two large suites opening onto a grassy cliff are on the first floor; a third guest room, with two balconies and outstanding views, is on the fourth level. ✉ *95330 Hwy. 101,* ☎ *541/547–3925. 3 rooms. Full breakfast. No credit cards.*

Campgrounds

Seventeen state parks along the coast have campgrounds, most with trailer hookups and tent sites. Many are near the shore, and some have group facilities and hiker/biker or horse camps. The Oregon State Parks and Recreation Department (☞ National and State Parks, *above*) has details. **Honeyman State Park** (✉ 84505 Hwy. 101, Florence 97439, ☎ 541/997–3641; $3 per vehicle day use) adjoins the Oregon Dunes National Recreation Area. Reserve well ahead.

Outdoor Activities and Sports

Biking

The **Oregon Coast Bike Route** parallels U.S. 101 and the coast from Astoria south to Brookings.

Fishing

Salmon, delectable Dungeness crab, and dozens of species of bottom fish are the quarry here, accessible from jetties, docks, and riverbanks from Astoria to Brookings. Charter boats and guides are plentiful; contact local chambers of commerce (☞ Visitor Information, *above*) for information on fishing permits, seasons, rates, and schedules.

Golf

The Oregon coast has about 20 public and private courses, including **Salishan Golf Links** (✉ 7760 N. Hwy. 101, Gleneden Beach, ☎ 541/764–3632), the coast's most challenging course, with 18 holes. Newport has the nine-hole **Agate Beach Golf Course** (☎ 541/265–7331). In Florence the 18-hole **Ocean Dunes Golf Links** (☎ 541/997–3232) draws amateurs and professionals. Gold Beach's **Cedar Bend Golf Course** (☎ 541/247–6911) has nine holes.

Beaches

Virtually the entire 400-mi coastline of Oregon consists of clean white-sand beaches, accessible to all. Thanks to its sea-sculpted stone, **Face Rock Wayside,** in Bandon, is thought by many to have the most beautiful walking beach in the state. The placid semicircular lagoon at **Sunset Bay State Park,** on Cape Arago, is Oregon's safest swimming beach. Fossils, clams, mussels, and other eons-old marine creatures embedded in soft sandstone cliffs make **Beverly Beach State Park,** 5 mi north of Newport, a favorite with young beachcombers.

Shopping

Hemlock Street, the main drag of Cannon Beach, is the best place on the coast to browse for unusual clothing, souvenirs, picnic supplies, books, and gifts. Newport's **Bay Boulevard** is a good place to find local artwork, gifts, and fresh seafood. There are bargains galore at the **Lincoln City Factory Stores** (✉ 1510 E. Devils Lake Rd., ☎ 541/996–5000). Particularly good deals on vintage items can be found in the antiques malls in Astoria, Seaside, and Lincoln City.

ELSEWHERE IN OREGON

Mt. Hood and Bend

Arriving and Departing

Mt. Hood lies about an hour east of Portland on U.S. 26; the only way to get there is by car. Continue east on U.S. 26, then south on U.S. 97 for the resort town of Bend, two hours beyond Mt. Hood. **Redmond Municipal Airport** (☎ 541/548–6059), about 14 mi north of Bend, is served by Horizon Airlines (☎ 800/547–9308) and United Express (☎ 800/241–6522).

What to See and Do

★ Mt. Hood, 11,245 ft and surrounded by the 1.1-million-acre **Mt. Hood National Forest** (✉ 16400 Champion Way, Sandy 97055, ☎ 503/668–1700), is an all-season playground that attracts more than 7 million visitors annually for skiing, snowboarding, camping, hiking, and fishing. Historic **Timberline Lodge,** off U.S. 26 a few miles east of Government Camp (✉ Timberline 97028, ☎ 503/272–3311 or 800/547–1406), has withstood howling winter storms on the mountain's flank for more than 60 years; it's hard to beat for romantic getaways.

Hood River, a town 60 mi east of Portland on I–84 in the spectacular Columbia Gorge, is the self-proclaimed sailboarding capital of the world. Columbia Gorge Sailpark (✉ Port Marina, ☎ 541/386–2000), on the river downtown, has a boat basin, a swimming beach, jogging trails, and picnic tables.

The skiing is excellent in **Bend,** which occupies a tawny high-desert plateau in the very center of Oregon, framed on the west by three 10,000-ft Cascade peaks. With its plentiful dining and lodging options, Bend makes a fine base camp for skiing at nearby Mt. Bachelor, whitewater rafting on the Deschutes River, world-class rock climbing at Smith Rocks State Park, and other outdoor activities. Don't miss the archaeological and wildlife displays at the High Desert Museum (✉ 59800 S. Hwy. 97, 3½ mi south of Bend, ☎ 541/382–4754; $5.50). **Newberry National Volcanic Monument** (☞ National and State Parks, *above*), 25 mi southeast of Bend, contains more than 50,000 acres of lakes, lava flows, and spectacular geological features.

Willamette Valley/Wine Country

Arriving and Departing

I–5, the state's main north–south freeway, runs straight down the center of the Willamette Valley from Portland. **Eugene Airport** (☎ 541/687–5430) is served by Horizon and United Express.

What to See and Do

Oregon's **wine country** occupies the wet, temperate trough between the Coast Range to the west and the Cascades to the east. More than 60 wineries dot the hills between Portland and Salem, and dozens more are scattered from Newport to as far south as Ashland, on the California border. Although tiny in comparison with California's, Oregon's wine industry is booming. Cool-climate varietals such as pinot noir, chardonnay, and Johannesberg Riesling have gained the esteem of international connoisseurs.

Most vineyards welcome visitors. The best way to tour is by car. *Discover Oregon Wineries,* an indispensable map and guide to the wine country, is available free at wine shops and wineries or by calling the Oregon Wine Winegrowers Association (☎ 800/242–2363).

Salem, the state capital, makes a good base for exploring; in addition to its hotels, B&Bs, and restaurants, there are some fine gardens and museums. A gilded 23-ft-high bronze statue of the Oregon Pioneer atop the 106-ft capitol dome is the centerpiece of Salem's **capitol** (✉ 900 Court St., ☎ 503/986–1388), where Oregon's legislators convene every two years. Across from the capitol are the tradition-steeped brick buildings of **Willamette University,** the oldest college in the West, founded in 1842. Just south of downtown Salem, **Bush's Pasture Park** (✉ 600 Mission St. SE) includes Bush House (☎ 503/363–4714; 🎫 $1.50), a Victorian mansion with 10 fireplaces and original furnishings, and Bush Barn, an art center with two exhibition rooms and a sales gallery. **Deepwood Estate** (✉ 1116 Mission St. SE, ☎ 503/363–1825; 🎫 $3), on the National Register of Historic Places, encompasses 5½ acres of lawns, formal English gardens, and a fanciful 1894 Queen Anne mansion with splendid interior woodwork and original stained glass. **Mission Mill Village** (✉ 1313 Mill St. SE, ☎ 503/585–701; 🎫 $5) offers tours of its historic circa 1889 woolen mill and collection of pioneer homes. **Silver Falls State Park** (✉ Hwy. 214, 26 mi east of Salem, ☎ 503/873–8681; 🎫 $3 per vehicle) covers 8,700 acres and includes 10 waterfalls accessible to hikers.

Liberal-minded **Eugene** is Oregon's second-largest city and the home of the University of Oregon. In town the **Willamette Science and Technology Center** (✉ 2300 Leo Harris Pkwy., ☎ 541/682–3020; 🎫 $3) has imaginative hands-on scientific exhibits and a planetarium.

South of Eugene, the sleepy farming community of **Roseburg** is on the Umpqua River, famous among fishers. West of town are a dozen of the region's wineries. The **Douglas County Museum** (✉ Douglas County Fairgrounds, I–5 Exit 123, ☎ 541/440–4507; 🎫 free) has an exceptional fossil collection.

Dining and Lodging

Northwest Bed & Breakfast (☎ 503/243–7616 or 503/370–9033) can help you with reservations for the Willamette Valley's extensive B&B network.

$$–$$$$ ★ ✕ **Excelsior Inn.** This small, stylish hotel across from the University of Oregon campus is quietly sophisticated, with cherry-wood doors and moldings, marble-and-tile baths, and in-room VCRs and modem lines. A full breakfast is served in the appealing Excelsior Café, which also has a seasonal menu for lunch and dinner. *✉ 754 E. 13th St., Eugene, 97401, ☎ 541/342–6963 or 800/321–6963, FAX 541/342–1417. 14 rooms. Restaurant. Full breakfast. AE, D, DC, MC.*

Ashland/The Rogue Valley

Arriving and Departing

Ashland is midway between Portland and San Francisco on I–5, about 15 mi north of the California border. **Rogue Valley Airport** (☎ 541/772–8068), in nearby Medford, is served by Horizon Airlines and United Express.

What to See and Do

Ashland is home to the Tony Award–winning **Oregon Shakespeare Festival** (✉ 15 S. Pioneer St., 97520, ☎ 541/482–4331), which annually attracts more than 100,000 visitors to this relaxing Rogue Valley town. The local arts scene, a warm climate, and opulent B&Bs and sumptuous restaurants make this a pleasant place for a holiday. A few miles south of Ashland you'll find excellent downhill and Nordic skiing atop 7,523-ft **Mt. Ashland.** West of Ashland, the famous Rogue River boils and churns through the rugged, remote Kalmiopsis Wilderness in **Siskiyou National Forest** (☎ 541/471–6516). The local wineries are also worth a visit.

Jacksonville, in the eastern part of the state, preserves the look and feel of an Old West pioneer settlement; the entire town is a National Historic Landmark. Each summer from mid-June to Labor Day Jacksonville hosts the Britt Festivals (☎ 541/773–6077 or 800/882–7488), a concert series featuring some of the world's best jazz and classical musicians ★ performing in an outdoor amphitheatre. The main attraction at **Crater Lake National Park** (☞ National and State Parks, *above*) began 6,800 years ago, when Mt. Mazama decapitated itself in a huge explosion. Rain and snowmelt eventually filled the caldera, creating a sapphire-blue lake so clear that sunlight penetrates to a depth of 400 ft. Visitors can drive or hike the park's 25-mi **Rim Drive,** explore nature trails, and (in summer) take guided boat trips around the lake itself. The park is about 80 mi northeast of Jacksonville along Highway 62.

Dining and Lodging

$$$$ 🏨 **Mt. Ashland Inn.** Built from hand-hewn cedar logs close to the summit ski area on Mt. Ashland, this modern, 5,500-square-ft lodge provides magnificent views of Mt. Shasta and the Siskiyou range. Antiques and hand-stitched quilts lend character to the guest rooms; a sauna and outdoor hot tub overlooking the mountains add to the alpine splendor. Best of all, it's only 15 mi from Ashland's world-famous Shakespeare Festival theatres. *550 Mt. Ashland Rd., 97520,* ☎ *541/482–8707 or 800/830–8707,* FAX *541/484–8707. 5 rooms. Full breakfast. AE, D, MC, V.*

WASHINGTON

By Tom Gauntt

Updated by Julie Fay

Capital	Olympia
Population	5,447,720
Motto	By-and-by
State Bird	American goldfinch
State Flower	Rhododendron
Postal Abbreviation	WA

Statewide Visitor Information

Washington Tourism Development Division (✉ Box 42500, Olympia 98504-2500, ☎ 360/586–2088 or 800/544–1800).

Scenic Drives

About 90 mi north of Seattle, starting from just south of Bellingham on I–5, Highway 11 loops 25 mi around **Chuckanut Bay.** On one side of Highway 11 is the steep, heavily wooded Chuckanut Mountain and on the other are sweeping views of Puget Sound and the San Juan Islands. The area is also dotted with fine restaurants. Near the Oregon border, Highway 14 winds east from Vancouver into the **Columbia River National Scenic Area.** The road clings to the steep slopes of the gorge and traverses several tunnels and picturesque towns such as Carson, known for its hot springs, and White Salmon, renowned for windsurfing.

National and State Parks

National Parks

Mt. Rainier National Park (✉ Tahoma Woods, Star Rte., Ashford 98304, ☎ 360/569–2211), about 85 mi southeast of Seattle, comprises 14,411-ft Mt. Rainier—the fifth-highest mountain in the lower 48 states—and nearly 400 square mi of surrounding wilderness. The Jackson Memorial Visitor Center at Paradise has exhibits, films, and a 360-degree view of the summit and surrounding peaks. Call for off-season hours. For a vision of the apocalypse, head for the **Mount St. Helens National Volcanic Monument** (✉ 42218 N.E. Yale Bridge Rd., Amboy 98601). The visitor center (☎ 360/247–3900) is on Highway 504, 5 mi east of the Castle Rock exit off I–5, and the monument is 45 mi east of Castle Rock. Although the crater still steams and small earthquakes are common, excellent views are available within 5 mi of the mountain. **Olympic National Park** (✉ 600 E. Park Ave., Port Angeles 98362, ☎ 360/452–4501) is one of the most outstanding pieces of natural beauty in the United States, with such diverse areas as its jagged wilderness coastline; a lush, temperate rain forest; 60-odd active glaciers; and Hurricane Ridge, with its alpine contours. **North Cascades National Park** (✉ 2105 State Rte. 20, Sedro-Woolley 98284, ☎ 360/856–5700), a little-known park about 120 mi northeast of Seattle, holds some of the state's most rugged mountains, craggy peaks, and jewel-like lakes. Heavy snows in the Cascades close State Route 20 through the park most winters from October through April.

State Park

Leadbetter Point State Park (✉ Robert Gray Dr., 2 mi south of Ilwaco, Box 488, 98624, ☎ 360/642–3078), at the northernmost tip of the Long Beach Peninsula, is a wildlife refuge that's good for bird-watching. The dunes at the very tip are closed from April to August to protect the nesting snowy plover. Black brant, sandpipers, turnstones, yellowlegs, sanderlings, knots, and plovers are among the 100 species known to inhabit the point.

SEATTLE

Seattle is growing by leaps and bounds. Constant traffic on all the main highways and thoroughfares is the first and most obvious indication that city planning has not been sufficient to meet the needs of this Pacific Rim metropolis. Certain high-profile businesses in the region (e.g., Boeing, Microsoft, Starbucks) have brought a great deal of wealth to the city, resulting in a burst of construction and renovation, including a world-class symphony hall and new Nordstrom flagship store in the downtown retail core. These developments follow on the heels of the recently rebuilt Key Arena (a basketball venue). In the works are a new baseball park and a regional transit authority that will construct light-rail lines from the city to the suburbs. Though it is plain to see that the area's growing pains show no sign of ending anytime soon, there are already countless wonderful restaurants, full-service hotels, and entertainment venues springing up everywhere. Add that to the natural beauty of the city and its environs and you'll probably be too enthralled to notice the gray skies.

Visitor Information

Seattle/King County: Stop by Convention and Visitors Bureau (⊠ 800 Convention Pl., at Pike St., 98101, ☎ 206/461–5840) or the street-level visitor center (☎ 206/467–1600) at the Westlake Center (⊠ 5th Ave. and Pine St.). Or write to the Visitor Information Center (⊠ 520 Pike St., Suite 1300, 98101).

Arriving and Departing

By Bus

Greyhound Lines (⊠ 8th Ave. and Stewart St., ☎ 800/231–2222).

By Car

I–5 enters Seattle from the north and south, I–90 from the east.

By Plane

Seattle-Tacoma International Airport (Sea-Tac) is 20 mi south of downtown and is served by major American and some foreign airlines. A cab ride between the airport and downtown takes about 30 to 45 minutes and costs about $25. **Gray Line Airport Express** (☎ 206/626–6088) buses run to and from major downtown hotels; fare is $7.50 one-way, $13 round-trip.

By Train

Amtrak (⊠ 303 S. Jackson St., ☎ 800/872–7245).

Getting Around Seattle

A car is the handiest way to cover metropolitan Seattle, but bus service is convenient and efficient, too. Despite occasional steep hills, downtown is good for walking.

By Car

Hills, tunnels, reversible express lanes, and frustrating rush hours can make driving a chore. Main thoroughfares into downtown are Aurora Avenue (called the Alaskan Way Viaduct along the waterfront) and I–5.

By Public Transportation

Metropolitan Transit (☎ 206/553–3000) provides free rides in the downtown-waterfront area until 7 PM; fares to other destinations range from 85¢ to about $1.60, depending on the zone and time of day. The elevated **monorail** (☎ 206/441–6038) runs the 2 mi from the Seattle Center to Westlake Center; the fare is $1.

By Taxi

Either pick up a cab at any hotel taxi stand or call the cab company directly. Fare is $1.80 at the flag drop and then $1.80 per mi. Major companies are **Farwest** (☎ 206/622–1717) and **Yellow Cab** (☎ 206/622–6500).

Orientation Tours

Bus Tour

Gray Line Tour (✉ Washington State Convention and Trade Center, 800 Convention Pl., ☎ 206/626–5208; 🎫 $24–$33) provides guided bus tours of the city and environs ranging from a daily 2½-hour spin to the six-hour Grand City Tour, which runs in spring, summer, and fall.

Boat Tour

Argosy Cruises (✉ Pier 55, ☎ 206/623–1445; 🎫 $13–$21) operates one-hour tours of Elliott Bay, the Port of Seattle, Lake Union, Hiram M. Chittenden Locks, and Lake Washington.

Train Tour

Spirit of Washington Dinner Train (✉ 625 South 4th St., Renton, ☎ 206/227–7245; 🎫 $47–$69) Seven vintage rail cars transport diners on a four-hour round-trip excursion from Renton to Woodinville, along the eastern shore of Lake Washington, passing through Mercer Island, Bellevue, Kirkland, and the Sammamish River Valley. During the 45-minute stop in Woodinville, guests are invited to tour the Columbia Winery and visit the tasting room.

Exploring Seattle

Downtown

Downtown Seattle is bounded by the Kingdome to the south, the Seattle Center to the north, I–5 to the east, and the waterfront to the west. You can reach most points of interest by foot, bus, or monorail. But remember that Seattle is a city of hills, so wear your walking shoes.

★ The five-story **Seattle Art Museum** (✉ 100 University St., ☎ 206/654–3100; 🎫 $6), by postmodern theorist Robert Venturi, is a work of art in itself, with a limestone exterior and vertical fluting accented by terra-cotta, cut granite, and marble. Inside are extensive collections of Asian, Native American, African, Oceanic, and pre-Columbian art, a café, and a gift shop.

Pike Place Market (✉ 1st Ave. at Pike St., ☎ 206/682–7453) got its start in 1907, when the city issued permits allowing farmers to sell produce from their wagons parked at Pike Place. Urban renewal almost closed the market, but citizens rallied and voted it a historical asset. Sold here are fresh seafood (which can be packed in dry ice for your flight home), produce, cheese, Northwest wines, bulk spices, teas, coffees, and arts and crafts.

At the base of the Pike Street Hillclimb at Pier 59 is the **Seattle Aquarium** (☎ 206/386–4320; 🎫 $7.50), showcasing Northwest marine life. Sea otters and seals swim and dive in their pools, and the State of the Sound exhibit shows aquatic life and the ecology of Puget Sound.

An 1889 fire destroyed many of the wood-frame buildings in the area ★ now known as **Pioneer Square,** but the residents rebuilt them with brick

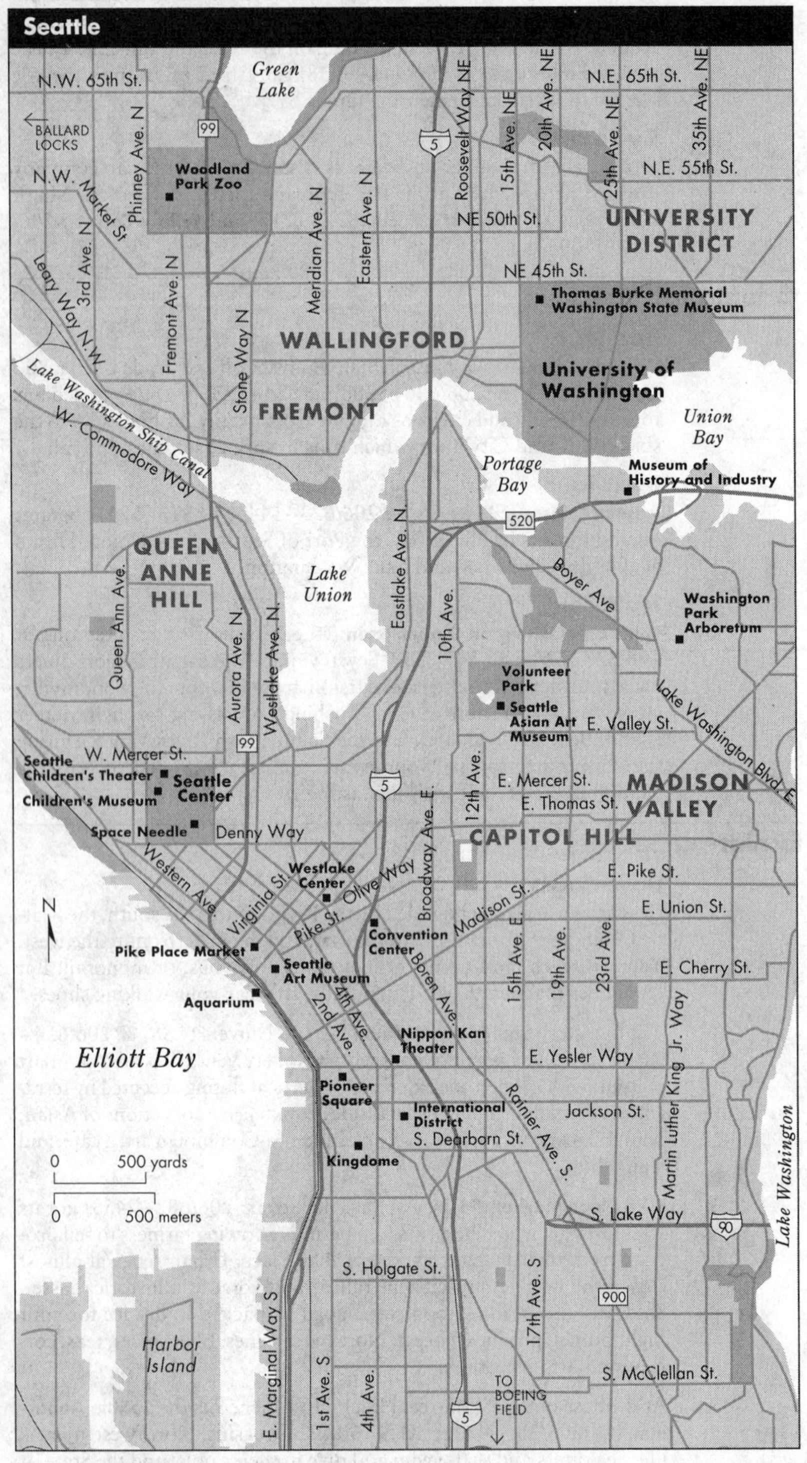
Seattle
Green Lake
N.W. 65th St.
BALLARD LOCKS
N.W. Market St
Phinney Ave. N
Woodland Park Zoo
99
5
Roosevelt Way NE
15th Ave. NE
20th Ave. NE
N.E. 65th St.
25th Ave. NE
35th Ave. NE
N.E. 55th St.
NE 50th St.
UNIVERSITY DISTRICT
3rd Ave. N
Leary Way N.W.
Fremont Ave. N
Meridian Ave. N
Eastern Ave. N
NE 45th St.
Thomas Burke Memorial Washington State Museum
Stone Way N
WALLINGFORD
University of Washington
Lake Washington Ship Canal
W. Commodore Way
FREMONT
Union Bay
Portage Bay
Museum of History and Industry
520
QUEEN ANNE HILL
Lake Union
Eastlake Ave. N.
Boyer Ave
Washington Park Arboretum
Queen Ann Ave.
Aurora Ave. N.
Westlake Ave. N.
10th Ave.
Volunteer Park
Seattle Asian Art Museum
E. Valley St.
Lake Washington Blvd. E.
Seattle Children's Theater
W. Mercer St.
Seattle Center
Children's Museum
12th Ave.
E. Mercer St.
MADISON VALLEY
E. Thomas St.
Space Needle
Denny Way
Broadway Ave. E.
CAPITOL HILL
Western Ave.
Westlake Center
Olive Way
E. Pike St.
Virginia St.
Madison St.
E. Union St.
N
Pike St.
Convention Center
Pike Place Market
Boren Ave.
15th Ave. E
19th Ave.
23rd Ave.
E. Cherry St.
Seattle Art Museum
Aquarium
4th Ave.
2nd Ave.
Nippon Kan Theater
Martin Luther King Jr. Way
Elliott Bay
E. Yesler Way
Pioneer Square
International District
Jackson St.
Rainier Ave. S.
S. Dearborn St.
0 500 yards
Kingdome
0 500 meters
S. Lake Way
90
Lake Washington
S. Holgate St.
17th Ave. S
900
Harbor Island
E. Marginal Way S
1st Ave. S
4th Ave.
TO BOEING FIELD
S. McClellan St.
5

and mortar. This area was in a state of decline from the Depression until the 1970s, when buildings were restored and stores and cafés moved in. Some older saloons remain, giving the area a historical flavor. College kids party hearty here at night; during the day you can browse through the art galleries and the several dozen stalls and shops at the Downtown Antique Market (✉ 2218 Western Ave., ☎ 206/448-6307). **Gallery Walk** (☎ 206/587-0260) is a free open house hosted the first Thursday of every month by Seattle's art galleries, most of them in Pioneer Square.

Southeast of Pioneer Square is the **International District** (known locally as the ID), where a third of the residents are ethnic Chinese, a third Filipino, and a third from elsewhere in Asia. The ID began as a haven for Chinese workers after they'd finished building the transcontinental railroad. Today the district is full of Chinese, Japanese, and Korean restaurants, as well as herbalists, massage parlors, and acupuncturists. The **Nippon Kan Theater** (✉ 628 S. Washington St., ☎ 206/224-0181) was historically the focal point for Japanese-American activities. It includes the Kabuki theater, now a national historic site, which hosts many Asian-oriented productions.

North of Downtown

From Westlake Center (☞ Shopping, *below*), a shopping complex completed in 1989, you can catch the monorail to **Seattle Center,** a 74-acre complex built for the 1962 Seattle World's Fair. It includes an amusement park, theaters, a renovated coliseum, exhibition halls, museums, and shops. Look for the **Pacific Science Center** (☎ 206/443-2001; $7.50) with its planetarium and IMAX Theater. Also within Seattle Center is **The Children's Museum** (☎ 206/441-1768; $5.50), with hands-on exhibits replicating home life around the globe, as well as intergenerational programs, special exhibits, and workshops. The museum is on the first level of the Center House. Also within the Seattle Center is the **Space Needle** (☎ 206/443-2111), a Seattle landmark that is visible from almost anywhere in the downtown area and looks like something from *The Jetsons.* Take the glass elevator to the observation deck for a sweeping view of the city.

On the northwest corner of the campus of the **University of Washington** is the Thomas Burke Memorial Washington State Museum (✉ 17th Ave. NE and N.E. 45th St., ☎ 206/543-5590; $5.50), Washington's natural history and anthropological museum. South of the University of Washington's Husky Stadium, across the Montlake Cut, is the **Museum of History and Industry** (✉ 2700 24th Ave. E, ☎ 206/324-1125; $5.50).

Parks, Gardens, and Zoos

Near the university at the **Washington Park Arboretum** (✉ 2300 Arboretum Dr. E, ☎ 206/543-8800), Rhododendron Glen and Azalea Way are in bloom from March through June. The Hiram M. Chittenden Locks, better known as the **Ballard Locks** (✉ 3015 N.W. 54th St., west of the Ballard Bridge, ☎ 206/783-7059), control the 8-mi-long Lake Washington Ship Canal, which connects freshwater Lake Washington to Puget Sound. Animals at the 92-acre **Woodland Park Zoo** (✉ N. 50th St. and Fremont Ave., ☎ 206/684-4800; $8) roam freely within "bioclimatic" zones that re-create their native habitats. From downtown or the Seattle Center head north on Highway 99 (Aurora Avenue North), across the Aurora Bridge to the 45th Street exit.

Dining

For price ranges *see* Chart 1 (A) *in* On the Road with Fodor's.

$$$$ ★ ✕ **Rover's.** Chef-owner Thierry Rautureau brings a personal touch to this intimate Madison Valley restaurant. Dishes of particular note are the diver's sea scallops with foie gras, served over chestnut purée, and the duck breast with wild mushrooms and huckleberry sauce, all available as part of the five- and eight-course prix fixe menus. ✉ *2808 E. Madison,* ☎ *206/325–7442. Reservations essential. AE, DC, MC, V. Closed Sun. and Mon. No lunch.*

$$$–$$$$ ✕ **Campagne.** Overlooking Pike Place Market and Elliott Bay, Campagne is intimate and urbane with its white walls, picture windows, and colorful modern prints. The flavors of Provence pervade the menu in dishes such as striped bass filet grilled with fennel and served with lemon-thyme sabayon. Downstairs is a more casual café. ✉ *Inn at the Market, 86 Pine St.,* ☎ *206/728–2800. Reservations essential. Jacket required. AE, MC, V.*

$$ ✕ **Cactus.** In a charming neighborhood shopping district on the shores of Lake Washington, Cactus is a casual outpost of Southwestern and Mexican cuisines. Of particular note are the extensive tapas menu and specialty drinks such as the spicy Saguaro Martini. Try the Navajo fry bread and the grilled ancho-cinnamon chicken served with plaintain cakes and sautéed greens. ✉ *4220 E. Madison,* ☎ *206/324–4140. D, DC, MC, V. No lunch Sun.*

$$ ★ ✕ **Wild Ginger.** The specialty is Pacific Rim cookery, including tasty southern Chinese, Vietnamese, Thai, and Korean dishes served in a warm, clubby dining room. Daily specials are based on seasonally available products. ✉ *1400 Western Ave.,* ☎ *206/623–4450. AE, D, DC, MC, V. No lunch Sun.*

$–$$ ✕ **Anthony's Bell Street Diner.** In addition to one of the best views of Elliott Bay, this waterfront diner has become known for its Manila Clam Chili, Mahi Mahi tacos, and wild blackberry cobbler. It's also convenient to the Market and the waterfront. ✉ *2201 Alaskan Way,* ☎ *206/448–6688. AE, D, DC, MC, V.*

Lodging

Seattle has an abundance of lodgings, from deluxe downtown hotels to less expensive digs in the University District. For information on bed-and-breakfasts, contact the **Pacific Bed & Breakfast Agency** (✉ P.O. Box 46894, Seattle 98146, ☎ 206/439–7677, FAX 206/431–0932). For price ranges *see* Chart 2 (A) *in* On the Road with Fodor's.

$$$$ ★ 🏨 **Alexis.** At this intimate hotel in a restored 1901 building near the waterfront, guest rooms are done in subdued colors. Some suites have whirlpool baths; others have wood-burning fireplaces. Pets are welcome. ✉ *1007 1st Ave., 98104,* ☎ *206/624–4844 or 800/426–7033,* FAX *206/621–9009. 109 rooms. Restaurant, bar, café, exercise room. AE, D, DC, MC, V.*

$$$$ ★ 🏨 **Four Seasons Olympic Hotel.** Restored to its 1920s grandeur, the Olympic is Seattle's most elegant hotel. Public rooms are furnished with marble, thick rugs, wood paneling, and potted plants. The less luxurious guest rooms are homey, with comfortable reading chairs and floral-print fabrics. ✉ *411 University St., 98101,* ☎ *206/621–1700 or 800/223–8772,* FAX *206/682–9633. 450 rooms. 3 restaurants, pool, health club. AE, D, DC, MC, V.*

$$$$ 🏨 **Hotel Monaco.** Goldfish in your room (upon request) is just one of the eclectic touches you'll find at this new luxury hotel in the heart of Seattle's financial district. Spacious guest rooms with bold colors and patterns all come with CD players and fax machines. Join the other

hotel guests around the fireplace in the lobby for complimentary evening wine. ✉ *1101 4th Avenue, 98101,* ☎ *206/621–1770 or 800/945–2240,* FAX *206/621–7779. 189 rooms. Restaurant, exercise room. AE, D, DC, MC, V.*

$$$–$$$$ **Edgewater.** The only hotel on Elliott Bay has comfortably rustic rooms with unfinished wood furnishings and plaid fabric in red, green, and blue. ✉ *Pier 67, 2411 Alaskan Way, 98121,* ☎ *206/728–7000 or 800/624–0670,* FAX *206/441–4119. 236 rooms. Restaurant, bar. AE, D, DC, MC, V.*

$$$–$$$$ ★ **Inn at the Market.** Adjacent to the Pike Place Market, this hotel combines the best aspects of a small, deluxe hotel with the informality of the Pacific Northwest. Rooms are spacious, with contemporary furnishings and ceramic sculptures, and views of either the city, Elliott Bay, and Pike Place Market, or the hotel courtyard. ✉ *86 Pine St., 98101,* ☎ *206/443–3600,* FAX *206/448–0631. 65 rooms. AE, D, DC, MC, V.*

$$$ **Edmond Meany Tower Hotel.** At this pleasant hotel a few blocks from the University of Washington campus, nearly all the rooms have views of the Cascades or the Olympic Mountains, the University of Washington, or Lake Union. ✉ *4507 Brooklyn Ave. NE, 98105,* ☎ *206/634–2000,* FAX *206/547–6029. 155 rooms. 2 restaurants. AE, DC, MC, V.*

$ **Seattle YMCA.** A member of the American Youth Hostels Association, this Y has single and double rooms that are clean and plainly furnished with bed, phone, desk, and lamp. Ten dollars extra gets you a room with a private bath; for another $3 or $4 you'll have a view of Elliott Bay. ✉ *909 4th Ave., 98104,* ☎ *206/382–5000. 198 beds, 3 rooms with baths. Pool, health club. D, MC, V.*

Motels

Doubletree Inn (✉ 205 Strander Blvd., Tukwila 98188, ☎ 206/246–8220, FAX 206/575–4749), 200 rooms, 2 restaurants, pool; *$$$.* **University Plaza Hotel** (✉ 400 N.E. 45th St., 98105, ☎ 206/634–0100, FAX 206/633–2743), 135 rooms, restaurant, pool, exercise room; *$$–$$$.*

Nightlife and the Arts

Nightlife

For a relatively small city, Seattle has a strong and diverse music scene.

BARS AND NIGHTCLUBS

Palace Kitchen (✉ 2030 5th Ave., ☎ 206/448–2001), is a happening bar with great food. **Entros** (✉ 823 Yale Ave. N., ☎ 206/624–0057), bills itself as an "intelligent amusement park," where patrons play socially interactive games such as "interface, the high-tech trust walk." **Arnie's Northshore Restaurant** (✉ 1900 N. Northlake Way, ☎ 206/547–3242) has a lounge with giant windows overlooking Gas Works Park and Lake Union. A Seattle favorite, **Ray's Boathouse** (✉ 6049 Seaview Ave. NW, ☎ 206/789–3770) is on the shore of Shilshole Bay, a perfect spot for watching the sun set behind the Olympic Mountains.

BREW PUBS

The **Elysian Brewing Company** (✉ 1221 E. Pike St., ☎ 206/860–1920) serves lunch and dinner in a remodeled furniture warehouse on Capitol Hill. Near the Kingdome and the waterfront is the bigger, more mainstream **Pyramid Alehouse** (✉ 1201 1st Ave., ☎ 206/682–3377), serving lunch and dinner, with daily tours. The **Trolleyman Pub** (✉ 3400 Phinney Ave. N., ☎ 206/548–8000), in the eclectic Fremont neighborhood, is the smaller of the two Red Hook Breweries; the other is in Woodinville. The emphasis is on beer rather than food, but some sandwiches are available.

BLUES/R&B CLUB

The **Ballard Firehouse** (✉ 5429 Russell St. NW, ☎ 206/784–3516) is a mostly blues mecca in Ballard. The **Central Tavern** (✉ 207 1st Avenue S., ☎ 206/622–0209), an often crowded club in Pioneer Square, presents local and national blues and reggae acts.

COMEDY CLUB

Comedy Underground (✉ 222 Main St., ☎ 206/628–0303), a Pioneer Square club that's literally underground, beneath Swannie's, presents stand-up comedy and open-mike nights.

DANCE CLUBS

Fenix Underground (✉ 323 2nd Ave. S, ☎ 206/467–1111) is one of several popular clubs in Pioneer Square. **Fenix** (✉ 315 2nd Ave. S, ☎ 206/467–1111) pulsates with recorded dance music. On Capitol Hill **Neighbours** (✉ 1509 Broadway E, ☎ 206/324–5358) attracts a good mix of gay men and everyone else.

JAZZ CLUB

Downtown, **Dimitriou's Jazz Alley** (✉ 2037 6th Ave., ☎ 206/441–9729) books nationally known performers every night except Monday, when local talent is showcased. Dinner is served before the first show.

ROCK CLUBS

Alibi Room (✉ 85 Pike St., ☎ 206/623–3180), in the Pike Place Market, is a restaurant and bar with live music, disco dancing, and independent film screenings in conjunction with the Seattle Film Festival. **Crocodile Cafe** (✉ 2200 2nd Ave., ☎ 206/448–2114) rocks with live local groups from Tuesday through Saturday. At the **OK Hotel** (✉ 212 Alaskan Way S, ☎ 206/621–7903), closed Monday, you'll find grunge, acoustic, and jazz, plus occasional poetry readings.

The Arts

Friday's editions of the *Seattle Times* and the *Post-Intelligencer* list the coming week's events. Seattle's free weekly papers, the *Seattle Weekly*, (Wednesdays) and *The Stranger* (Thursdays) cover the arts.

To charge tickets, call **TicketMaster** (☎ 206/628–0888). **Ticket/Ticket,** with two locations (✉ 401 Broadway E and ✉ 1st Ave. and Pike St., ☎ 206/324–2744), sells half-price same-day tickets for cash only.

DANCE

The **Pacific Northwest Ballet** (✉ Opera House, Seattle Center, ☎ 206/441–2424) is a resident company and school that presents 60–70 performances annually. **On The Boards** (✉ 100 W. Roy, ☎ 206/325–7902) is the foremost center in the region for contemporary dance, theater, music, and multimedia presentation.

MUSIC

The **Seattle Symphony** (✉ Benaroya Music Hall, Second Ave. and University St., ☎ 206/215–4747), which presents some 160 concerts between July and June in and around town, opened a brand-new symphony hall for the 1998–99 season. **Northwest Chamber Orchestra** (☎ 206/343–0445), the Northwest's only professional chamber orchestra, presents a full spectrum of music, from Baroque to modern, at various venues.

OPERA

The **Seattle Opera** (✉ Opera House, Seattle Center, ☎ 206/389–7600), considered one of the top companies in America, presents five productions during its August–May season.

THEATER

The **Seattle Repertory Theater** (✉ Bagley Wright Theater, Seattle Center, 155 Mercer St., ☎ 206/443–2222) presents high-quality programming in nine productions during its October–May season. The **Seattle Children's Theater** (✉ 2nd Ave. N. and Thomas St., at the Seattle Center, ☎ 206/441–3322) has a strong reputation. The **New City Arts Center** (✉ 1703 13th Ave., ☎ 206/323–6800) is home to experimental performances by the resident company Theatre Zero, in conjunction with national and international artists. The **Group Theatre** (✉ Seattle Center, Center House, lower level, ☎ 206/441–1299) presents socially provocative works by artists of varied cultures and ethnic backgrounds. **A Contemporary Theater** (ACT; ✉ 7th Ave. and Union St., ☎ 206/292–7676) develops works by new playwrights.

Spectator Sports

Baseball: Seattle Mariners (✉ Kingdome, 201 S. King St., ☎ 206/628–3555). **Basketball: Seattle SuperSonics** (✉ Key Arena, 1st Ave. N, ☎ 206/281–5850). **Football: Seattle Seahawks** (✉ Kingdome, 201 S. King St., ☎ 206/827–9777).

Shopping

Shopping Centers

City Centre (✉ 1420 5th Ave., ☎ 206/467–9670), a gleaming marble tower, houses upscale shops such as Ann Taylor and Barneys of New York. **Westlake Center** (✉ 1601 5th Ave., ☎ 206/467–1600) is a three-story steel-and-glass building with 80 shops and covered walkways that connect it to branches of Seattle's major department stores, Nordstrom and the Bon.

Food Market

Vendors at the partially open-air **Pike Place Market** (☞ Exploring Seattle, *above*) sell fresh meat, seafood, produce, flowers, and crafts.

Specialty Stores

CLOTHING

Mario's (✉ 1513 6th Ave., ☎ 206/223–1461) has trendy and designer fashions for men. **Boutique Europa** (✉ 1420 5th Ave., ☎ 206/587–6292) carries sophisticated European clothing. On the edge of the Pike Place Market, **Local Brilliance** (✉ 1535 1st Ave., ☎ 206/343–5864) showcases fashions by local designers. **Nubia's** (✉ 1507 6th Ave., ☎ 206/622–0297) sells unconstructed knits for women's business and casual wear as well as belts, beads, and other accessories.

OUTDOOR WEAR AND EQUIPMENT

★ With its 65-ft climbing wall, the 8,000-sq-ft flagship branch of **REI** (✉ 222 Yale Ave. N, ☎ 206/223–1944) has become Seattle's second most visited landmark (after the Space Needle). **Eddie Bauer** (✉ 5th Ave. and Union St., ☎ 206/622–2766) specializes in classic sports and outdoor apparel.

TOYS

Children will love **Magic Mouse Toys** (✉ 603 1st Ave., ☎ 206/682–8097) with its two floors of toys, from small windups to giant plush animals.

Side Trip to Whidbey Island

On a nice day there's no better short excursion from Seattle than a ferry trip across Puget Sound to Whidbey Island. It's a great way to watch the seagulls, sailboats, and massive container vessels in the sound—

not to mention the surrounding scenery, including the Kitsap Peninsula and Olympic Mountains, Mt. Rainier, the Cascade Range, and the Seattle skyline.

Arriving and Departing

BY PLANE

From Seattle-Tacoma International Airport, **Harbor Airlines** (☎ 800/359–3220) flies to Oak Harbor. Kenmore Air (☎ 425/486–1257 or 800/543–9595), on Lake Union, provides sea plane charter service.

BY CAR

Whidbey Island can be reached by ferry from Mukilteo, or you can drive from Seattle along I–5, then head west on Highway 20 and cross the dramatic Deception Pass via the bridge at the north end of the island.

BY FERRY

The **Washington State Ferry System** (☎ 206/464–6400 or 800/843–3779) provides car and passenger service from Mukilteo, on Highway 525 30 mi north of Seattle, to Clinton, on Whidbey Island.

What to See and Do

Whidbey Island is mostly rural, with undulating hills, gentle beaches, and little coves. **Langley,** a quaint town with inviting inns and a handful of good restaurants, shops, and galleries, sits atop a 50-ft bluff overlooking the southeastern shore. A little over halfway up 50-mi-long Whidbey Island is **Coupeville,** site of many restored Victorian houses and one of the largest National Historic Districts in the state. The town was founded in 1852 by Captain Thomas Coupe, whose house, built the next year, is one of the state's oldest.

Ebey's Landing National Historic Reserve (☎ 360/678–4636), headquartered in Coupeville, is a 17,000-acre area including Keystone, Coupeville, and Penn Cove. Established by Congress in 1978, the reserve is the first and largest of its kind, dotted with 91 nationally registered historic structures along with farmland, parks, and trails. At **Deception Pass State Park** (☎ 360/675–2417), at the north end of Whidbey Island, you can take in the spectacular view while strolling among the madrona trees, with their peeling reddish-brown bark.

Dining

For price ranges *see* Chart 1 (B) *in* On the Road with Fodor's.

$$$$ ✕ **Country Kitchen.** Tables for two line the walls of this intimate restaurant. The prix-fixe, five course menu might include locally gathered mussels in a black bean sauce, breast of duck in a loganberry sauce, or Columbia River salmon. ✉ *Inn at Langley, 400 1st St., Langley,* ☎ *360/221–3033, MC, V. Reservations essential.*

$$$ ✕ **Garibyan Brothers Café Langley.** Mediterranean fare is served at this casual café. ✉ *113 1st St., Langley,* ☎ *360/221–3090. AE, MC, V. Closed Tues. in winter.*

$$$ ★ ✕ **Rosi's.** Inside the Victorian home of its chef-owners, Rosi's specializes in outstanding Italian and Pacific Northwest cuisine. Chicken mascarpone, osso bucco, scallops pesto, prime rib, and Penn Cove mussels are among the entrées. ✉ *606 N. Main St., Coupeville,* ☎ *360/678–3989. AE, MC, V. No lunch.*

Side Trip to Tacoma

Seattleites often make fun of the industrial aromas emanating from Tacoma, but the city has a strong cultural scene, restored residential neighborhoods and historic theaters, fine bay views, and a world-class zoo.

Visitor Information

Tacoma–Pierce County Visitors and Convention Bureau (✉ 906 Broadway, Tacoma 98402, ☎ 253/627–2836).

Arriving and Departing

Tacoma is about 35 mi south of Seattle via I–5. Sea-Tac Airport is about a 30-minute drive away. The city is served by major bus, train, and air carriers.

What to See and Do

Union Station (✉ 1717 Pacific Ave., ☎ 253/593–6313) is an heirloom from the golden age of railroads, when Tacoma was the western terminus for the transcontinental Northern Pacific Railroad. Built by Reed and Stem, the architects of New York City's Grand Central Station, the massive copper-domed Beaux Arts depot was opened in 1911. It now houses federal district courts. The rotunda is open to the public and displays a large exhibit of Dale Chihuly art glass. Across the street is the **University of Washington, Tacoma campus,** housed in beautifully restored 19th Century warehouses. The **Washington State Historical Society Museum** (✉ 1911 Pacific Ave., ☎ 253/272–3500; 🎫 $7) near Union Station houses exhibits on the natural, Native American, pioneer, maritime, and industrial history of the state.

Downtown on Broadway is **Antique Row,** with antiques shops, two restored theaters, and funky boutiques. The **Tacoma Art Museum** (✉ 1123 Pacific Ave., ☎ 253/272–4258; 🎫 $4) contains a rich collection of American and French paintings, as well as Chinese jades and imperial robes. **Wright Park** (✉ 6th and Division Sts., I and J Sts.) is a 30-acre park just north of downtown. Within the park is the W. W. Seymour Botanical Conservatory (✉ 316 S. G St., ☎ 253/591–5330), a Victorian-style greenhouse with an extensive collection of exotic flora.

Northeast of Tacoma, the 700-acre **Point Defiance Park** is one of the largest urban parks in the country. The **Point Defiance Zoo and Aquarium,** founded in 1888, is now one of the top zoos in America. (✉ *5400 N. Pearl St.,* ☎ *253/591–5337;* 🎫 *$7).*

Dining

For price ranges *see* Chart 1(B) *in* On the Road with Fodor's.

$–$$ ✕ **Swiss.** You'll find good pub fare and Northwest microbrews at this restaurant in a distinctive 1913 building that was once Tacoma's Swiss Hall. ✉ *1904 S. Jefferson Ave.,* ☎ *253/572–2821. No credit cards.*

Side Trip to Olympia

Arriving and Departing

Olympia is on I–5, about 60 mi southwest of Seattle and 25 mi southwest of Tacoma.

What to See and Do

Olympia, Washington's state capital, is fairly quiet except when the legislature is in session. You can tour the **Legislative Building** (✉ Capitol Way between 10th and 14th Aves.), a handsome Romanesque structure with a 287-ft dome that closely resembles the capitol in that *other* Washington.

Dining

For price ranges *see* Chart 1(B) *in* On the Road with Fodor's.

$$$–$$$$ ✕ **Louisa.** Ten minutes south of downtown Olympia is Louisa, an elegant setting for sophisticated Northwest cuisine. Housemade butternut squash ravioli, served with sage pesto and goat cheese and accompanied by a glass of David Lake Syrah, is the perfect treat on a rainy day on the Sound. ✉ *211 Cleveland Ave., Tumwater,* ☎ *360/352–3732. Reservations accepted. MC, V. Closed Sun. and Mon., no lunch Sat.*

THE OLYMPIC PENINSULA

The rugged Olympic Peninsula forms the northwest corner of the continental United States. Much of it is wilderness, with the Olympic National Park and National Forest at its heart. The peninsula has tremendous variety: the wild Pacific shore, the sheltered waters along the Hood Canal and the Strait of Juan de Fuca, the rivers of the Olympic's rain forests, and the towering Olympic Mountains.

Visitor Information

North Olympic Peninsula Visitor & Convention Bureau (✉ Box 670, Port Angeles 98362, ☎ 360/452–8552 or 800/942–4042). **Port Angeles:** Visitor center (✉ 121 E. Railroad Ave., 98362, ☎ 360/452–2363).

Arriving and Departing

By Bus

Olympic Van Tours and Bus Lines (☎ 360/452–3858) serves the Olympic Peninsula.

By Car

U.S. 101 loops around the Olympic Peninsula, which can be reached from Olympia via Routes 8 and 101 and from Tacoma, 50 mi away, via Highway 16.

By Ferry

The **Washington State Ferry System** (☎ 206/464–6400 or 800/843–3779) provides car and passenger service from downtown Seattle to Bremerton. The **Black Ball Ferry Line** (☎ 360/457–4491) operates between Port Angeles, on the Olympic Peninsula, and Victoria, British Columbia.

By Plane

Horizon Air (☎ 800/547–9308) flies into Port Angeles from the Seattle-Tacoma airport. Private charter airlines fly into Port Angeles, Forks, and Hoquiam.

Exploring the Olympic Peninsula

From Olympia go west along Highway 101 and Routes 8 and 12 to **Gray's Harbor** and the twin seaports of **Hoquiam** and **Aberdeen.** From Hoquiam you can drive north on **Route 109,** which sticks to the coast and passes through resorts and ample beach areas such as Copalis Beach, Pacific Beach, and Moclips. Route 109 eventually leads to the Quinault Indian Reservation and the tribal center of **Taholah,** whose main draw is pristine, expansive scenery.

Route 109 dead-ends at Taholah, and you must backtrack to return to U.S. 101. About 20 mi north of Aberdeen on U.S. 101, 1½ mi north of the Hoh River Bridge, is Hoh River Rainforest Road, which goes ★ east to the **Hoh Rain Forest** (☎ 360/452–4501), part of the Olympic National Park. This complex ecosystem of conifers, hardwoods, grasses, mosses, and other flora shelters such wildlife as elks, otters, beavers, salmon, and flying squirrels. The average annual rainfall here is 145 inches. The Hoh Visitor Center (often unstaffed September–May) at

Western Washington

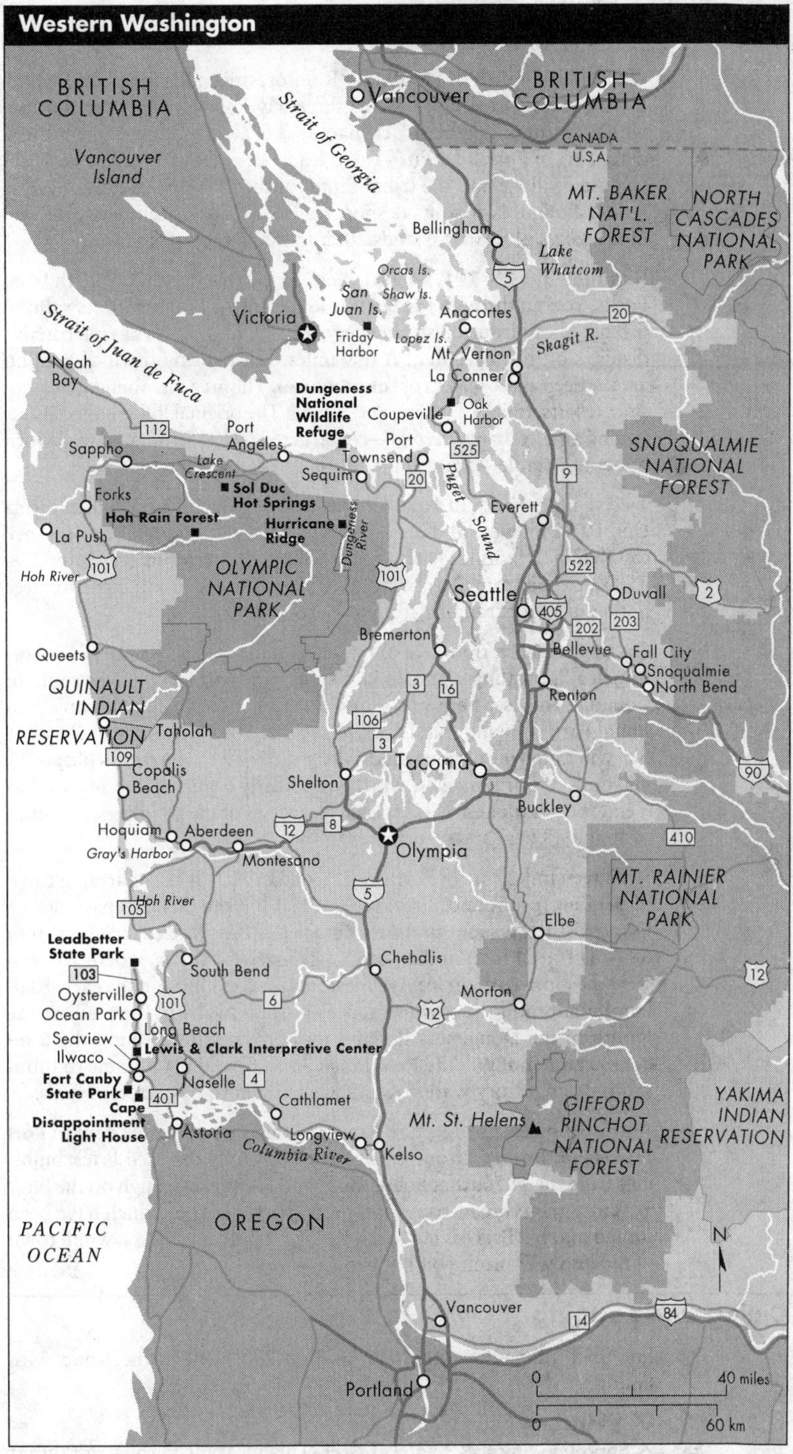

the campground and the ranger station at road's end (18 mi east of U.S. 101) have interpretative displays and information on nature trails.

On U.S. 101 north of Hoh River Rainforest Road is the small logging town of **Forks,** renowned for its three-day Fourth of July celebration, which features logging-truck parades, fireworks, and a demolition derby. From Forks, La Push Road leads west about 15 mi to **La Push,** a coastal village and the tribal center of the Quileute Indians. Several points along this road have short trails with access to the ocean, fabulous views of nearby islands, and dramatic rock formations.

Returning to U.S. 101, which swings to the east as you go north from Forks, you go through the **Sol Duc River Valley,** famous for its salmon fishing. The Soleduck Fish Hatchery (☎ 360/327–3246) has interpretive displays on fish breeding. A few miles past the tiny town of Sappho are the deep azure waters of **Lake Crescent.** The area has abundant campsites, resorts, trails, canoeing, and fishing. The original lodge buildings(☞ Dining and Lodging, *below*)—constructed in 1915 and now well worn but comfortable—are still in use.

Twelve miles south of Lake Crescent on Soleduck Road (which meets U.S. 101 1 mi west of the western tip of Lake Crescent) is an entrance to Olympic National Park and to **Sol Duc Hot Springs** (☎ 360/327–3583), closed from October to mid-May, where you can dip into three hot sulfur pools ranging from 98°F to 104°F.

On the northern tip of the Olympic Peninsula, on U.S. 101E, is **Port Angeles,** a bustling commercial fishing port and ferry access route to Canada. This is where you'll find the visitor center for Olympic National Park (☞ National Parks, *above*), at 3002 Mt. Angeles Road. A bus will take you or you can drive up the road to **Hurricane Ridge,** 17 mi south of Port Angeles, which rises nearly a mile above sea level as it enters the park and yields spectacular views of the Olympics, the Strait of Juan de Fuca, and Vancouver Island.

Seventeen miles east of Port Angeles on U.S. 101 is the charming town of **Sequim** (pronounced *squim*). Animal life present and past can be found at the **Museum and Arts Center** (✉ 175 W. Cedar St., ☎ 360/683–8110; 🎫 free) in the Sequim–Dungeness Valley, where you can view the remains of an Ice Age mastodon and exhibits on the early Klallam Indians and the town's pioneer history. In the fertile plain at the mouth of the Dungeness River, 4 mi northwest of Sequim, the **Dungeness National Wildlife Refuge** (☎ 360/457–8451) is home to thousands of migratory waterfowl, as well as clams, oysters, and seals.

About 10 mi east of Sequim, Route 20 turns northward 12 mi to **Port Townsend.** Its waterfront is lined with carefully restored brick buildings from the 1870s that house shops and restaurants. High on the bluff are large gingerbread-trim Victorian homes, many of which have been turned into B&Bs. Driving south on U.S. 101 through the sawmill town of **Shelton** will bring you back to Olympia.

Dining and Lodging

For price ranges *see* Charts 1 (B) and 2 (B) *in* On the Road with Fodor's.

Gig Harbor

$$$ ✕ **Shoreline Steak & Seafood Grill.** This pleasant marina restaurant specializes in seafood and serves Sunday brunch. ✉ *8827 N. Harborview Dr.,* ☎ *253/853–6353. AE, D, DC, MC, V.*

$–$$$$ ★ **Sandpiper Beach Resort.** Within the four-story Sandpiper complex are 30 suites, most with a sitting room, dining area, fireplace, small kitchen, and porch. With no in-room phones, no pool, no TVs, and no restaurant, this is the place to get away from it all. ✉ *4159 Rte. 109, 1½ mi south of Pacific Beach, Box A, 98571,* ☎ *360/276–4580 or 800/567–4737,* FAX *360/276–4464. 30 suites. MC, V.*

Port Angeles

$$$–$$$$ ✕ **C'est Si Bon.** This locally famous spot run by a French couple is probably the most elegant restaurant on the informal Olympic Peninsula. Fine art on the walls competes with views of the flower-laden terrace and the Olympic Mountains beyond. The cuisine, of course, is French. ✉ *23 Cedar Park Dr. (4 mi east of town),* ☎ *360/452–8888. Reservations essential. AE, D, MC, V. Closed Mon. No lunch.*

$$–$$$$ **Lake Crescent Lodge.** This old but comfortable accommodation with a big main lodge and small cabins overlooks Lake Crescent. Units in the lodge are minimal—some are dimly lighted, with bathrooms down the hall—but the setting makes up for sparse amenities. ✉ *416 Lake Crescent Rd., Port Angeles 98363,* ☎ *360/928–3211. 52 rooms, 47 with bath. Restaurant, boating, fishing. AE, DC, MC, V. Closed mid-Nov.–Apr.*

$$$ **Sol Duc Hot Springs Resort.** This casual resort dates from the turn of the century. Some of the minimally outfitted cabins are rustic; others are more modern. Guests have access to three hot springs, and there are plenty of hiking trails nearby. ✉ *12 mi south of U.S. 101 on Soleduck Rd., Box 2169, 98362,* ☎ *360/327–3593,* FAX *360/327–3398. 32 units, camping and RV facilities. Restaurant, pool. AE, D, MC, V. Closed mid-Oct.–mid-May.*

Port Townsend

$$–$$$ ★ ✕ **Fountain Café.** This small café off the main tourist drag is one of the best restaurants in town. Count on seafood and pasta specialties with imaginative twists, such as oysters in anchovy-wine sauce. ✉ *920 Washington St.,* ☎ *360/385–1364. MC, V. Closed Tues. No lunch.*

$$–$$$ ✕ **Salal Café.** Featuring home-style cooking and daily specials, this cooperatively run restaurant stands out for its ample breakfasts—try one of many variations on the potato-egg scramble—and regionally inspired seafood dishes such as mussels in miso broth and oyster-mushroom risotto. Prices are reasonable. ✉ *634 Water St.,* ☎ *360/385–6532. Reservations not accepted. MC. No dinner Sun.–Wed.*

$$$–$$$$ **James House.** Commanding a spot on the bluff overlooking downtown and the waterfront, this antiques-filled Victorian B&B is a great place to see how the well-heeled lived in the late 1800s. ✉ *1238 Washington St., 98368,* ☎ *360/385–1238 or 800/385–1238. 12 rooms. Full breakfast. AE, MC, V.*

$$–$$$$ **Palace Hotel.** This friendly hotel in the historic section of downtown is pleasingly decorated to reflect its 1889 construction date and its one-time history as a bordello. Rooms have no phones, but they do have cable TV. ✉ *1004 Water St., 98368,* ☎ *360/385–0773 or 800/962–0741,* FAX *360/385–0780. 15 units. AE, D, MC, V.*

Quinault

$$$$ **Lake Quinault Lodge.** Built in 1926 of cedar shingles, this deluxe lodge is set on a perfect glacial lake in the midst of the Olympic National Forest. The lobby has antique reproductions and a fireplace. ✉ *S. Shore Rd., Box 7, 98575,* ☎ *360/288–2571,* FAX *360/288–2901. 92 rooms. Restaurant, pool. AE, MC, V.*

Campgrounds

Some of the best campgrounds within the Olympic National Park are **Hoh River** (☎ 360/374–6925), **Mora** (☎ 360/374–5460), and **Fairholm**

(☎ 360/928–3380). Elsewhere on the peninsula are **Bogachiel State Park** (☎ 360/374–6356), near Forks, closed after dusk in winter; **Fort Flagler State Park** (☎ 360/385–1259), near Port Townsend, closed for overnight camping November–February; **Ocean City State Park** (⊠ 148 Rte. 115, Hoquiam 98550, ☎ 360/289–3553); and **Pacific Beach State Park** (☎ 360/276–4297). There is also camping at **Sol Duc Hot Springs Resort** (☞ Port Angeles, *above*).

Outdoor Activities and Sports

Biking

Biking is popular in the flatter parts of Port Townsend and within Olympic National Park. There are bike-rental shops in Port Townsend and other resort areas on the peninsula.

Fishing

Trout and salmon are abundant in rivers throughout the peninsula. Contact the area tourist office (☞ Visitor Information, *above*) for details.

Hiking

Ocean and mountain areas contain hiking trails for all levels. Contact the **Olympic National Forest** (☎ 360/288–2525) or **Olympic National Park Visitor Center** (⊠ 3002 Mt. Angeles Rd., Port Angeles 98362, ☎ 360/452–0330).

Skiing

Hurricane Ridge (☞ Exploring the Olympic Peninsula, *above*) has 25 mi of cross-country ski trails.

Beaches

Beaches abound on the Olympic Peninsula, though the ones on tribal or private lands are not generally accessible. Remember that the North Pacific is not for swimming—unless you wear a wet suit. For walking and exploring, the main beaches are Copalis and Pacific, north of Hoquiam; a series of scenic, unnamed beaches north of Kalaloch; and Rialto Beach, near La Push.

Shopping

Confirmed shoppers head for the waterfront boutiques and stores of **Port Townsend,** all of which showcase Northwest arts and crafts.

LONG BEACH PENINSULA

If the waters of the Pacific and the Columbia River met in a less turbulent manner, a huge seaport might sit at the river's mouth. Instead, the entrance to the Columbia is sparsely populated, dotted with fishing villages and cranberry bogs. Although only a 3½-hour drive southwest of Seattle and two hours northwest of Portland, Long Beach Peninsula is worlds away from either city. Just north of the river's mouth, the peninsula separates the Pacific Ocean and Willapa Bay and is known for excellent bird-watching, beachcombing, hiking, and a handful of gourmet restaurants.

Visitor Information

Visitors Bureau (⊠ Intersection of Hwys. 101 and 103, Seaview 98631, ☎ 360/642–2400 or 800/451–2542).

Arriving and Departing

By Car

Long Beach is accessible from the east via Highway 4, which connects with I–5 near Longview, and from the north and south via U.S. 101.

Exploring Long Beach Peninsula

U.S. 101 crosses the broad Columbia River between Astoria, Oregon, and Megler, Washington, in a high, graceful span. Just beyond, on Highway 103, is **Ilwaco,** a small fishing community of about 600. The **Ilwaco Heritage Museum** (✉ 115 S.E. Lake St., ☎ 360/642–3446; free) uses dioramas to present the history of southwestern Washington.

A couple miles south of Ilwaco is the **Cape Disappointment Lighthouse,** first used in 1856 and one of the oldest lighthouses on the West Coast. The cape was named by an English fur trader in 1788 in honor of his unsuccessful attempt to find the Northwest Passage.

Fort Canby State Park (✉ 3 mi west of Ilwaco, off U.S. 101, ☎ 360/642–3078) was an active military installation until 1957, when it was turned over to the Washington State Parks and Recreation Commission. Now it is best known for great views of the Columbia River Bar during winter storms. The **Lewis & Clark Interpretive Center** (✉ Robert Gray Dr., ☎ 360/642–3029 or 360/642–3078; free) documents the 8,000-mi round-trip journey of the famous pair, from Wood River, Illinois, to the mouth of the Columbia.

The town of **Long Beach** has beach activities and an old-fashioned amusement park with go-carts and bumper cars. About halfway up the peninsula is **Ocean Park,** the area's commercial center. A few miles north of Ocean Park is **Oysterville,** established as an oystering town in 1854. When the native shellfish were fished to extinction, a Japanese oyster was introduced, but the town never made a comeback. Tides have washed away homes, businesses, and a Methodist church, but the village still exists. Maps inside the vestibule of the restored **Oysterville Church** direct you through town, which is now on the National Register of Historic Places. At the northern tip of the peninsula is **Leadbetter State Park**(☞ National and State Parks, *above*).

Dining and Lodging

For price ranges *see* Charts 1 (B) and 2 (B) *in* On the Road with Fodor's.

Ilwaco

$$$–$$$$ **Chickadee Inn.** This B&B is set in a renovated New England–style church. The cozy guest accommodations—most of them upstairs in the old Sunday-school rooms—have eyelet or printed chintz curtains and coverlets. ✉ *120 Williams St. NE, 98624,* ☎ *360/642–8686 or 888/244–2523. 9 rooms. AE, D, MC, V.*

Seaview

$$$–$$$$ ★ ✕ **Shoalwater Restaurant.** The dining room at the Shelburne Inn (☞ *below*) has been acclaimed by *Gourmet* and *Bon Appétit.* Seafood brought from the fishing boats to the restaurant's back door is always fresh; mushrooms and salad greens are gathered from the peninsula's woods and gardens. ✉ *Pacific Hwy. and N. 45th St.,* ☎ *360/642–4142. AE, D, MC, V.*

$$–$$$ ✕ **42nd Street Cafe.** The daily-changing fare runs the gamut from deep-fried seafood to expensive gourmet dishes—the iron-skillet-fried chicken is a hit. ✉ *Hwy. 103 and 42nd St.,* ☎ *360/642–2323. MC, V.*

$ ✕ **My Mom's Pie Kitchen.** Fresh blackberry, banana-cream, chocolate-almond, and sour-cream-raisin are among the pie varieties you'll find in this cozy restaurant inside a Victorian house. Also on the menu are clam chowder and quiche. Call ahead, as hours are erratic. ✉ *4316 S. Pacific Hwy., ☎ 360/642–2342. MC, V. No dinner.*

$$$$ **Shelburne Inn.** This bright and cheerful, antiques-filled inn built in 1896, complete with a pub, is on the National Register of Historic Places. It is also right on the highway; the quietest rooms are on the west side. ✉ *4415 Pacific Way, Box 250, Seaview 98644, ☎ 360/642–2442 or 800/466–1896, FAX 360/642–8904. 15 rooms. Restaurant. AE, MC, V.*

$–$$$$ **Sou'wester.** Choose from rooms and apartments in a historic lodge, in cabins, or in classic mobile-home units on the surrounding property just behind the beach. The lodge was built in 1892 as the summer retreat of a wealthy businessman and politician from Portland. ✉ *Beach Access Rd., 39th Place, Box 102, 98644, ☎ 360/642–2542. 9 rooms, 6 with bath; 4 cabins, 10 trailers. D, MC, V.*

Campgrounds

You can camp at **Fort Canby State Park** (☞ Exploring Long Beach Peninsula, *above*).

Outdoor Activities and Sports

Biking

Good areas for bicycling on the peninsula include Fort Canby and North Head roads, Sandridge Road to Ocean Park and Oysterville, U.S. 101 from Naselle to Seaview, and Route 103 along Willapa Bay. There are rentals available in virtually every town.

Fishing

Salmon, rock cod, lingcod, flounder, perch, sea bass, and sturgeon are plentiful. A guide is available from the **Port of Ilwaco** (✉ Box 307, 98624, ☎ 360/642–3145). The clamming season varies depending on the supply; for details call the **Washington Department of Fisheries** (☎ 360/902–2200) or the **fisheries' shellfish lab** (☎ 360/665–4166). There are tackle shops all over Long Beach Peninsula, and most sell fishing licenses.

Golf

Peninsula Golf Course (☎ 360/642–2828) has nine holes at the north end of Long Beach. **Surfside Golf Course** (☎ 360/665–4148), 2 mi north of Ocean Park, has nine holes.

Hiking

There are hiking trails at **Fort Canby State Park** (☞ Exploring Long Beach Peninsula, *above*) and **Leadbetter State Park** (☞ National and State Parks, *above*).

Shopping

The **Bookvendor** (✉ 101 Pacific Ave., Long Beach, ☎ 360/642–2702) stocks children's books, classics, and travel books. **North Head Gallery** (✉ 600 S. Pacific Ave., Long Beach, ☎ 360/642–8884) has the largest selection of Elton Bennett originals, plus Bennett reproductions and works from other Northwest artists.

ELSEWHERE IN WASHINGTON

The San Juan Islands

The San Juan Islands beckon to those who long for quiet, whether it be kayaking in a cove, walking a deserted beach, or nestling by the fire in an old farmhouse. Come summertime, however, solitude becomes a precious commodity; not surprisingly, tourism and development are hotly debated issues among locals.

Visitor Information

The San Juan Islands Visitor Information Service (✉ Box 65, Lopez Island 98261, ☎ 360/468–3663).

Arriving and Departing

BY PLANE

From Seattle-Tacoma International Airport, **Harbor Airlines** (☎ 800/359–3220) flies to San Juan Island. **Kenmore Air** (☎ 206/486–1257 or 800/543–9595) flies sea planes from Lake Union in Seattle to the San Juan Islands. **West Isle Air** (☎ 360/293–4691 or 800/874–4434) flies to San Juan Island from Anacortes and Bellingham.

BY CAR

By car from Seattle, drive north on I–5 to La Conner; go west on Route 534 to Route 20 and follow signs to Anacortes; then pick up the ferry for the San Juan Islands.

BY FERRY

The **Washington State Ferry System** (☎ 206/464–6400 or 800/843–3779) provides car and passenger service from Anacortes, about 90 mi north of Seattle, to the San Juan Islands. The **San Juan Islands Shuttle Express** (✉ Alaska Ferry Terminal, 355 Harris Ave., No. 105, Bellingham 98225, ☎ 888/373–8522 or 360/671–1137) provides daily passenger service from Bellingham to Orcas Island and San Juan Island's Friday Harbor along with a lecture on the wildlife and natural history of the area. You can also take a three-hour whale-watching trip out of Friday Harbor.

What to See and Do

The major islands are **Lopez Island,** with old orchards, weathered barns, and sheep and cow pastures; **Shaw Island,** where Franciscan nuns in traditional habits run the ferry dock; **Orcas,** a large, mountainous horseshoe-shape island with marvelous hilltop views and several good restaurants; and **San Juan Island,** with the colorful, active waterfront town of Friday Harbor. Lopez, Orcas, and San Juan all have excellent bed-and-breakfast accommodations.

Dining

$$$$ ★ ✕ **Christina's.** Some of the best salmon entrées in Washington compete for diners' attention with romantic water views at this Orcas Island favorite. *✉ N. Beach Rd. and Horseshoe Hwy., Eastsound, ☎ 360/376–4904. AE, D, DC, MC, V. Closed Tues. and Wed. Oct.–Apr.*

$$$–$$$$ ✕ **Springtree Café.** Chef James Boyle devises his daily menu around fresh seafood and Waldron Island organic produce and herbs. Try the Caesar salad—made with tofu instead of eggs, followed by king salmon in pesto sauce or ginger shrimp with mango and rum. *✉ 310 Spring St., Friday Harbor, ☎ 360/378–4848. AE, MC, V. Closed Sun. and Mon. Oct.–Apr.*

Lodging

$$$$ **Edenwild.** This large gray Victorian-style farmhouse is surrounded by gardens and framed by Fisherman's Bay. The boldly painted rooms are airy; some have fireplaces. *✉ Eades La. at Lopez Village Rd., Lopez Island 98261, ☎ 360/468–3238, FAX 360/468–4080. 8 rooms. Full breakfast. AE, D, MC.*

$$$$ **Mariella Inn and Cottages** An 8-acre cove just outside Friday Harbor is the site of this antiques-filled 100-year-old country house. Rooms look out on either the water or the exquisite gardens. *✉ 630 Turn Point*

Rd, Friday Harbor 98250, ☎ 360/378–6868 or 800/700–7668, FAX 360/378–6822. 8 rooms, 3 suites, 12 cottages. Restaurant. AE, MC, V.

The North Cascades

Visitor Information

Leavenworth Chamber of Commerce (✉ 894 Hwy. 2, 98826, ☎ 509/548–5807).

Arriving and Departing

Three highways pierce the Cascade Range in northern Washington, and one—the North Cascades Highway (Highway 20) through the North Cascades National Park—is closed in winter. Highway 2 from Everett crosses Stevens Pass before Leavenworth and continues east to Spokane. There is no passenger train or air service to the North Cascades, but the area is served by Greyhound buses, which stop at Leavenworth.

What to See and Do

Cross-country skiers flock to the eastern slopes of the North Cascades for high dry-powder snow from early November until May. The small Bavarian-theme town of Leavenworth is especially popular; trails on the local golf course are groomed for skiers. Mission Ridge downhill ski area is nearby.

In summer rafters can run the rapids of the Wenatchee River, or there's hiking above the tree line in the nearby **Wenatchee National Forest** to Enchantment Lakes; an advance permit is required from the Leavenworth Ranger Station (☎ 509/548–6977).

Dining

$$$–$$$$ ✕ **Restaurant Osterreich.** Chef Leopold Haas's Austrian background shows up in his sophisticated menu. Try the appetizer of marinated duck breast in a dumpling coating, or the elk stew entrée. The atmosphere is infinitely more casual than the food. ✉ *Tyrolean Ritz Hotel, 633A Front St., Leavenworth,* ☎ *509/548–4031. MC, V. Closed Mon.*

Lodging

$$$–$$$$ **Pension Anna.** This family-run Austrian-style pension in the heart of the village has a homey mood, with antique pine furniture, fresh flowers, and comforters on the beds. A hearty European-style breakfast (cold cuts, cheeses, and soft-boiled eggs) is included. ✉ *926 Commercial, 98826,* ☎ *509/548–6273,* FAX *509/548–4656. 15 rooms. Full breakfast. AE, D, MC, V.*

Yakima Valley

Visitor Information

Yakima Valley Visitor and Convention Bureau (✉ 10 N. 8th St., Yakima 98901-2515, ☎ 509/575–1300).

Arriving and Departing

The valley is along I–82 between Yakima and the tri-city area of Richland, Kennewick, and Pasco. From Seattle drive east on I–90 to Ellensburg and south on Highway 97 (about 180 mi). Yakima has a small airport with limited service from Seattle, Spokane, and Portland on United Airlines. There is no passenger train service, but the area is served by Greyhound buses, which stop in Yakima, Toppenish, Sunnyside, Wapato, and Prosser.

What to See and Do

Aside from the views of 12,688-ft Mt. Adams and 14,411-ft Mt. Rainier to the west, the main attractions are the dozens of small wineries that dot this fertile area. Some of the best-known vineyards are **Hogue Cel-**

lars, Château Ste. Michelle, and **Covey Run Winery.** The **Yakima Valley Wine Growers Association** (☎ 509/786–1304) publishes maps of the region and a brochure that lists local wineries with tasting-room tours.

Dining

$ ✕ **Grant's Brewery Pub.** America's oldest brew pub is a Yakima institution. Burgers, salads, and sandwiches complement the suds daily, and there's live jazz on weekends. ✉ *32 N. Front St., Yakima,* ☎ *509/575–2922. MC, V.*

Lodging

$$$–$$$$ ★ **Birchfield Manor.** The only true luxury accommodation in the valley sits on a perfectly flat plateau, surrounded by fields and grazing cattle. The Old Manor House contains an award-winning restaurant and four upstairs rooms. A recently constructed cottage house has a country ambience and modern conveniences such as TVs, whirlpool tubs, steam-sauna showers, and gas fireplaces. ✉ *2018 Birchfield Rd, Moxee City, 98901,* ☎ *509/452–2334,* FAX *509/452–2334. 11 rooms. AE, DC, MC, V.*

Spokane

Spokane (pronounced Spo-*can*) is a bit of the Midwest dropped into the Northwest. Its 400,000 residents don't necessarily embrace Seattle as the state's cultural capital or Olympia as the seat of government. Wedged against the Idaho border (which locals cross regularly in search of outdoor recreation), Spokane is separated from Seattle by a good 300 mi and the formidable Cascade Range.

Visitor Information

Spokane Visitors Bureau. (✉ 201 W. Main, 99201, ☎ 509/747–3230).

Arriving and Departing

Spokane International Airport is served by Horizon, Northwest, Alaska, Delta, and United airlines. Amtrak and Greyhound both serve Spokane. By car Spokane can be reached by I–90 (east–west) and Highway 195 (north–south).

What to See and Do

In town the main attraction is **Riverfront Park** (✉ 507 N. Howard St., ☎ 509/625–6600), 100 acres covering several islands in the Spokane River, including a spectacular falls that's especially magnificent during spring runoff in March. Developed from old downtown railroad yards to be the site of the Expo '74 world's fair, Riverfront Park retains one of the ultramodernist buildings from that exposition; it houses an IMAX theater, a skating rink (winters only), and exhibition space. At the southern edge of the park, the 1909 carousel hand-carved by master builder Charles Looff is a local landmark. In sharp architectural contrast to Riverfront Park's Expo '74 building is the 1902 **Great Northern Railroad Station,** nearly at the center of the park near Washington Street, with its tall stone clock tower.

Two miles south on Grand Boulevard at 18th Avenue, **Manito Park** has a formal English garden, a conservatory, rose and perennial gardens, a Japanese garden complete with ponds stocked with koi, and a duck pond. It's a pleasant place to stroll in summer; in winter bring ice skates for a turn or two on the frozen duck pond.

Cheney Cowles Museum (✉ 2316 W. 1st Ave., ☎ 509/456–3931) displays pioneer and mining relics. Open for viewing next door is the museum-run Campbell House, a mining-era residence.

Dining

$$$$ ★ ✕ **Patsy Clark's.** One of Spokane's finest mansions—complete with Italian marble, wood carvings and clocks, and a Tiffany stained-glass window—is a suitably elegant place to dine on Continental cuisine. Entrés might include veal medallions stuffed with wild mushrooms, prosciutto, and spinach, doused with blackberry-port demi-glace. ✉ *2208 W. 2nd Ave.,* ☎ *509/838–8300. AE, D, DC, MC, V.*

$$–$$$$ ✕ **Clinkerdagger's.** In a building that housed a flour mill in Spokane's early days, Clinks, as it's known locally, has a fine view of the Spokane River and Riverfront Park to the south. There might be four or five specials when fresh seafood is available. ✉ *621 W. Mallon Ave.,* ☎ *509/328–5965. AE, D, DC, MC, V.*

$$$ ✕ **Luna.** Luna's seasonal cuisine has strong southwestern and Californian influences. The focus on fruits and vegetables is natural, as the building was once a produce market. ✉ *5620 S. Perry St.,* ☎ *509/448–2383. AE, D, MC, V.*

Lodging

$$$ **Cavanaugh's Inn at the Park.** This hotel's greatest asset is its location, adjacent to Riverfront Park and a two-block walk from the downtown shopping district. All five stories in the main building open onto the spacious central-atrium lobby; more guest rooms are in two newer wings. ✉ *303 W. North River Dr., 99201,* ☎ *509/326–8000 or 800/843–4667,* FAX *509/325–7329. 402 rooms. 2 restaurants. AE, D, DC, MC, V.*

The Arts

The **Spokane Symphony,** under the direction of Brazilian-born conductor Fabio Mechetti, plays a season of classical and pops concerts from September to April in the Opera House (✉ 601 W. Riverside Dr., ☎ 509/624–1200). **Interplayers Ensemble** (✉ 174 S. Howard St., ☎ 509/455–7529) is a professional theater company with productions from October through June.

Outdoor Activities and Sports

Just 30 mi east of Spokane on I–90 is Idaho's **Lake Coeur d'Alene** (☞ Idaho), which has fishing, camping, hiking, water sports, and resort accommodations. A walking path named the Centennial Trail flanks the Spokane River continuously from west of downtown Spokane to east of Coeur d'Alene.

GOLF

The most challenging Spokane golf course is the 18-hole **Creek at Qualchan** (✉ 301 E. Meadow La., ☎ 509/448–9317).

SKIING

Skiers flock to **Mt. Spokane** (✉ Hwy. 206, 31 mi north of Spokane, ☎ 509/238–6281 or 509/238–6845 for cross-country ski area), which holds the modest 49 Degrees North (✉ Hwy. 395, 58 mi north of Spokane near Chewelah, ☎ 509/935–6649) downhill resort and 11 mi of groomed cross-country ski trails. A state Sno-Park pass, available at the resort and numerous outlets throughout the state, is required at the cross-country ski areas.

SPECTATOR SPORTS

Baseball: Spokane Indians (✉ Seafirst Stadium, Broadway and Havana St., ☎ 509/535–2922) play in the Class A Northwest League.

Hockey: Spokane Chiefs (✉ Spokane Arena, 701 Mallon Ave., at N. Howard St., ☎ 509/328–0450) play in the Western Hockey League.

The Palouse

Visitor Information

Walla Walla: Chamber of Commerce (✉ 29 E. Sumach St., 99362, ☏ 509/525–0850). **Pullman:** Chamber of Commerce (✉ 415 N. Grande Ave., 99163, ☏ 509/334–3565).

Arriving and Departing

From Spokane drive south on Highway 195 to Pullman or at Colfax take Highways 26, 127, and then 12 to Walla Walla. Pullman has a small airport that it shares with Moscow, Idaho, 8 mi to the east, with limited service from Lewiston, Idaho. There is no passenger-train service, but the area is served by Greyhound buses, which stop in Pullman and Walla Walla.

What to See and Do

The Palouse is rich in Northwest history. The Lewis and Clark expedition passed through in 1805, and in 1836 missionary Marcus Whitman built a medical mission 7 mi west of present-day Walla Walla. A band of Cayuse Indians massacred Whitman and more than a dozen other settlers in 1847; a **visitor center** (✉ Off U.S. 12, 7 mi west of Walla Walla, ☏ 509/529–2761) now marks the site. Nearby **Fort Walla Walla Park** ✉ (755 Myra Rd., ☏ 509/525–7703) has 14 historic buildings and a pioneer museum.

The U.S. Calvary lost an important battle to the Indians on the site of the **Steptoe Battlefield,** north of Pullman on Highway 195 near Rosalia. On Highway 12 between Colfax and Walla Walla, **Dayton** is worth a stop just to see the impressive 88 Victorian buildings listed on the National Register of Historic Places. A brochure with two self-guided walking tours of Dayton is available from the Dayton Chamber of Commerce (✉ 166 E. Main St., ☏ 509/382–4825).

History buffs can take a walking or bicycle tour of Walla Walla, one of the earliest settlements in the Inland Northwest. Maps are available from the Chamber of Commerce (☞ Visitor Information, *above*). **Pioneer Park** (✉ E. Alder St.), which has a fine aviary, was landscaped by sons of Frederick Law Olmsted, who designed New York City's Central Park.

In winter skiers head southeast of Walla Walla to the Blue Mountains, to **Ski Bluewood** (✉ Touchet River Rd., 21 mi south of Dayton, ☏ 509/382–4725), for downhill and cross-country skiing.

Just north of the confluence with the Snake River, the Palouse River gushes over a basalt cliff higher than Niagara Falls and drops 198 ft into a steep-walled basin. Sure-footed hikers venture to the overlook above the falls, which are at their fastest during spring runoff in March. Just downstream from the falls is the **Marmes Rock Shelter,** where remains of the earliest-known inhabitants of North America, dating back 10,000 years, were discovered by archaeologists.

Dining and Lodging

$$$ ✕ **Paisano's.** This Italian mainstay has the largest wine inventory in Walla Walla, with local vineyards well represented. Breads and desserts are baked fresh daily. ✉ *26 E. Main St., Suite 1, Walla Walla,* ☏ *509/527–3511. MC, V. Closed Sun.*

$$$–$$$$ **Green Gables Inn.** A 1909 Craftsman-style mansion houses this lovely Walla Walla B&B, whose rooms are equipped with terry-cloth robes, bath amenities, and cable TV. A full breakfast is served by candlelight on antique china. ✉ *922 Bonsella, Walla Walla, 99362,* ☏ *509/525–5501 or 888/525–5501. 5 rooms. Full breakfast. AE, D, MC, V.*

12 Alaska and Hawai'i

Updated by
Steve Crohn
and Bill
Sherwonit

THE TWO YOUNGEST STATES IN THE UNION, Alaska and Hawai'i, have more in common than their images might suggest. Both are thousands of miles from the U.S. mainland, both have dramatic landscapes, and both are populated largely by indigenous people. The two states also share a reliance on water—rivers, lakes, and the Pacific Ocean—which supplies a means of transportation, a source of food, and countless recreational possibilities. Humpback whales also forge a link, summering in Alaska's Inside Passage and Prince William Sound, then swimming the 4,000 mi to Hawai'i to mate, calve, and nurse their young in the warm waters off Maui, the Big Island, and O'ahu. Although Alaskan and Hawaiian stores are stocked with the same goods found on the mainland, each state retains its unique exotic flavor.

Alaska, with its vast, austere wilderness and extreme weather, is demanding, but it rewards exploration with temperate summers, a frontier atmosphere, and flora and fauna rarely accessible elsewhere. From the nation's highest mountain, Mt. McKinley, to the islands, glaciers, and fjords of the southeast, the state provides superb hiking, boating, and fishing—and scenery as majestic and unspoiled as any in North America.

Hawai'i's gentle climate and tremendous diversity make it welcoming and endlessly fascinating. Each of the eight major volcanic islands has its own character—from lush tropical scenery and stunning white beaches to towering dramatic cliffs and rugged volcanic terrain. If you enjoy rampant commercialism in a spotlessly clean environment, O'ahu's Waikīkī is the place for you, but for pineapple plantations and active volcanoes, cheerful towns, and remote natural refuges, head for Maui and the Big Island. Kaua'i is worthwhile for its Nā Pali Coast and gorgeous Waimea Canyon; Moloka'i and Lānai'i are more tranquil getaways.

When to Go

Alaska

Most visitors come to Alaska in **summer,** when milder temperatures and the midnight sun prevail. Predictably, hotels and campgrounds are crowded, and prices are often higher than in the off-season: Advance planning is essential. The farther north you go in summer, the longer the days; Fairbanks in June is never really dark, although the sun does set for a couple of hours. In the interior temperatures can easily reach the 80s and 90s in June and July. The rest of the state is cooler, and rain is common in coastal areas. Mosquitoes are fierce in summer, especially in wilderness areas; never travel without repellent. **Fall** in Alaska is an abbreviated three weeks, when trees and bushes blaze with color and daytime temperatures are still pleasant. It comes as early as late August in the interior and in September farther south. **Winters** are extremely cold in the interior (daytime temperatures of 0°F or lower), but many Alaskans prefer that season, because it opens up most of the state for travel by snowmobile and dogsled. In the southeast's temperate maritime climate, though, temperatures rarely dip below freezing. **Spring** is often a monthlong soggy period of thawing and freezing, starting at the beginning of April.

Hawai'i

Hawai'i's long days of sunshine and fairly mild year-round temperatures allow for 12 months of pleasurable island travel. In resort areas near sea level the average afternoon temperature during the coldest months of December and January is 80°F; during the hottest months of August through October, temperatures can reach the low 90s. The northern shores of each island usually receive more rain than those in the south. Mid-December through mid-April and July through August are peak travel times, which means accommodation rates can be 10%–15% higher than those in other seasons.

Festivals and Seasonal Events

Alaska

MID-FEB.➢ The **Anchorage Fur Rendezvous** (☎ 907/277–8615) brings a three-day world-championship sled-dog race through city streets, plus hundreds of other winter activities.

EARLY MAR.➢ The **Iditarod Trail Sled Dog Race** (☎ 907/376–5155) officially covers 1,049 mi from **Anchorage to Nome** and can take up to two weeks to complete, though the record is less than 10 days.

EARLY MAY➢ **Kachemak Bay Shorebird Festival** (☎ 907/235–7740) celebrates the return of migrating shorebirds to **South Central Alaska.**

JUNE➢ Enjoy chamber music by world-renowned musicians in a beautiful setting at the **Sitka Summer Music Festival** (☎ 907/277–4852).

EARLY JULY➢ The **July 4th Mount Marathon Race and Celebration** in **Seward** (☎ 907/224–8051) is a grueling race up a 3,022-ft mountain, followed by a parade and festival of crafts, games, and food booths.

LATE AUG.–EARLY SEPT.➢ **Alaska State Fair** (☎ 907/745–4827) in **Palmer,** north of Anchorage, is a traditional celebration complete with cooking, handicrafts, livestock, and brewing competitions.

EARLY NOV.➢ Dancing, guitar playing, and fiddling are all part of the **Athabascan Fiddling Festival** (☎ 800/327–5774) in **Fairbanks.**

Hawai'i

LATE MAR.–EARLY APR.➢ Reserve tickets months in advance for the **Merrie Monarch Festival** (☎ 808/935–9168) in **Hilo** on the Big Island—a full week of hula competitions beginning Easter Sunday.

MAY 1➢ The statewide **Lei Day** (☎ 808/547–7393) is an annual flower-filled celebration with lei-making competitions and exquisite leis for sale.

JUNE➢ On **King Kamehameha Day** (☎ 808/586–0333), twin statues of the king who united Hawai'i's various islands are draped in giant leis in **Honolulu, O'ahu,** and **Hāwī** on the Big Island.

Alaska and Hawai'i

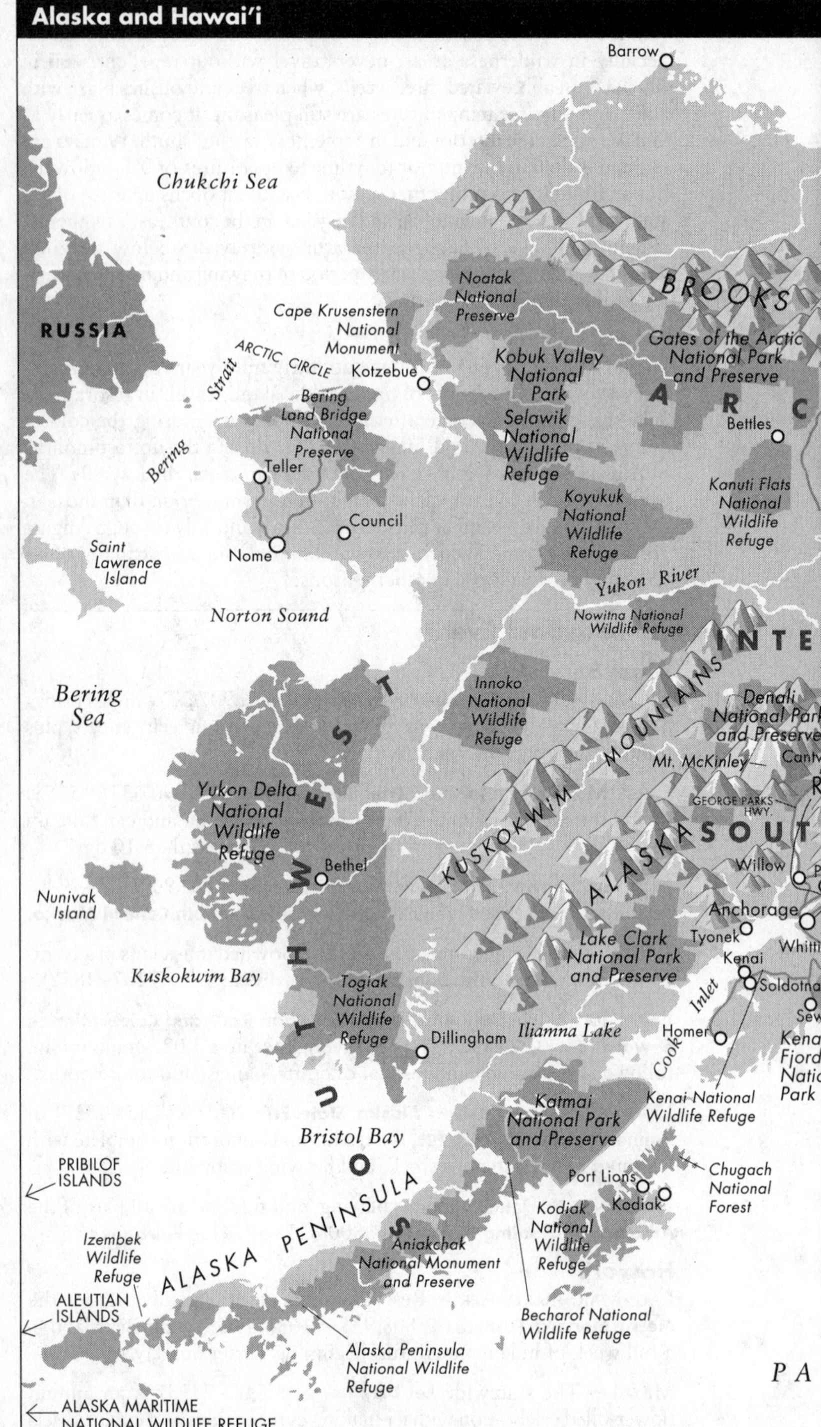
Barrow
Chukchi Sea
RUSSIA
Noatak National Preserve
BROOKS
Cape Krusenstern National Monument
ARCTIC CIRCLE
Bering Strait
Kotzebue
Kobuk Valley National Park
Gates of the Arctic National Park and Preserve
A R C
Bering Land Bridge National Preserve
Selawik National Wildlife Refuge
Bettles
Teller
Kanuti Flats National Wildlife Refuge
Koyukuk National Wildlife Refuge
Council
Saint Lawrence Island
Nome
Yukon River
Norton Sound
Nowitna National Wildlife Refuge
INTE
Innoko National Wildlife Refuge
Bering Sea
WEST
Denali National Park and Preserve
MOUNTAINS
Mt. McKinley
GEORGE PARKS HWY.
Yukon Delta National Wildlife Refuge
KUSKOKWIM
ALASKA
SOUT
Bethel
Willow
Nunivak Island
Anchorage
Tyonek
Lake Clark National Park and Preserve
Kenai
Kuskokwim Bay
Soldotna
Cook Inlet
Togiak National Wildlife Refuge
Iliamna Lake
Homer
Dillingham
Kenai National Wildlife Refuge
SOUTHWEST
Katmai National Park and Preserve
Bristol Bay
Chugach National Forest
PRIBILOF ISLANDS
Port Lions
Kodiak
ALASKA PENINSULA
Kodiak National Wildlife Refuge
Izembek Wildlife Refuge
Aniakchak National Monument and Preserve
ALEUTIAN ISLANDS
Becharof National Wildlife Refuge
Alaska Peninsula National Wildlife Refuge
PA
ALASKA MARITIME NATIONAL WILDLIFE REFUGE

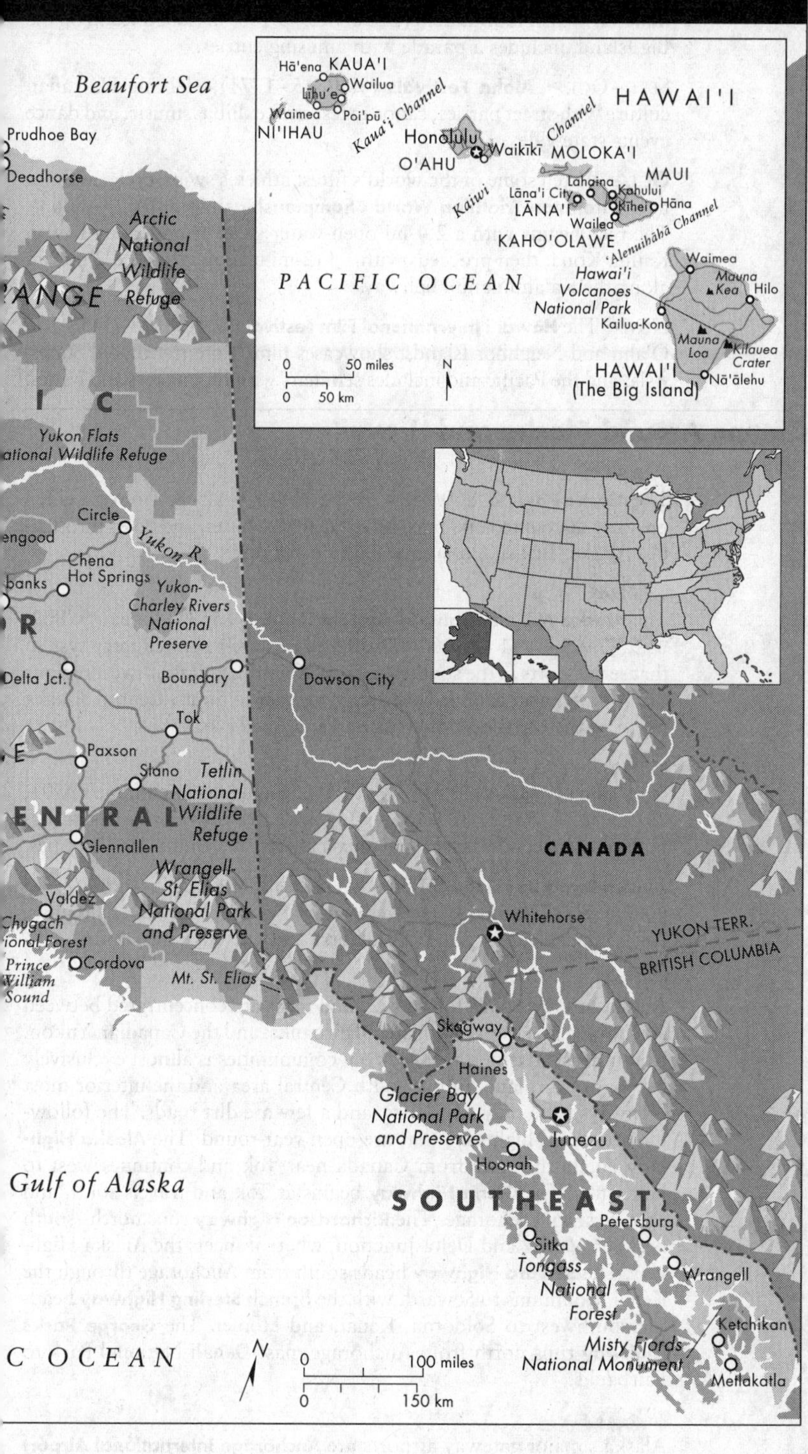

Beaufort Sea
Prudhoe Bay
Deadhorse
Arctic National Wildlife Refuge
Yukon Flats National Wildlife Refuge
Circle
Chena Hot Springs
Yukon R.
Yukon-Charley Rivers National Preserve
Delta Jct.
Boundary
Dawson City
Tok
Paxson
Slano
Tetlin National Wildlife Refuge
Glennallen
Wrangell-St. Elias National Park and Preserve
Valdez
Cordova
Mt. St. Elias
CANADA
Whitehorse
YUKON TERR.
BRITISH COLUMBIA
Skagway
Haines
Glacier Bay National Park and Preserve
Juneau
Hoonah
Gulf of Alaska
SOUTHEAST
Petersburg
Sitka
Tongass National Forest
Wrangell
Ketchikan
Misty Fjords National Monument
Metlakatla
0 100 miles
0 150 km
N
Hā'ena
KAUA'I
Wailua
Līhu'e
Waimea
Poi'pū
NI'IHAU
Kaua'i Channel
HAWAI'I
Honolulu
Waikīkī
O'AHU
Channel
MOLOKA'I
MAUI
Lahaina
Lāna'i City
Kahului
Kīhei
Hāna
LĀNA'I
Wailea
Kaiwi
KAHO'OLAWE
'Alenuihāhā Channel
PACIFIC OCEAN
Waimea
Mauna Kea
Hilo
Hawai'i Volcanoes National Park
Kailua-Kona
Mauna Loa
Kilauea Crater
HAWAI'I (The Big Island)
Nā'ālehu
0 50 miles
0 50 km
N

AUG.➢ A world-class marlin-fishing competition, the **Hawaiian International Billfish Tournament** (☎ 808/329–6155) in **Kailua-Kona** on the Big Island, includes a parade with amusing entries.

SEPT.–OCT.➢ **Aloha Festivals** (808/545–1771) celebrate Hawaiian culture with street parties, canoe races, craft exhibits, music, and dance events statewide.

OCT.➢ Watch some of the world's fittest athletes swim, cycle, and run in the **Ironman Triathlon World Championships** (☎ 808/329–0063). The race begins with a 2.4-mi open-water swim from Kailua Pier in Kailua-Kona, then proceeds with a 112-mi bike race and 26.2 mi run along the Ka'ahumanu Highway.

NOV.➢ The **Hawai'i International Film Festival** (☎ 808/528–3456), on O'ahu and Neighbor Islands, showcases films from the United States, Asia, and the Pacific and includes seminars with filmmakers and critics.

Getting Around Alaska and Hawai'i

Alaska

The **Alaska Pass** (☎ 800/248–7598 or 800/89–82–85 from the U.K.) provides discounted one-price travel on trains, buses, and boats throughout Alaska, British Columbia, and the Yukon.

BY BOAT

The **Alaska Marine Highway System** (✉ Box 25535, Juneau 99802, ☎ 907/465–3941 or 800/642–0066) is a state-operated ferry system that serves ports in the southeast, South Central, and southwest regions of the state. You cannot get from southeast to South Central Alaska by ferry; the boats do not cross the Gulf of Alaska.

BY BUS

Gray Line of Alaska (✉ 745 W. 4th Ave., Suite 200 Anchorage 99501, ☎ 907/277–5581, 907/456–7741 in Fairbanks) provides transportation and conducts seasonal tours between and within Alaskan cities.

Alaska Direct Bus Lines (✉ Box 501, Anchorage 99510, ☎ 907/277–6652 or 800/770–6652) operates year-round service between Fairbanks, Anchorage, Skagway, and Whitehorse and will customize tours.

BY CAR

Alaska has few roads for its size, and most are concentrated between Anchorage, the Kenai Peninsula, Fairbanks, and the Canadian Yukon. In southeast Alaska travel between communities is almost exclusively by boat or airplane. In the South Central area and the interior most highways have only two lanes, and a few are dirt roads. The following are paved highways that are open year-round: The **Alaska Highway** enters the state from Canada near Tok and continues west to Fairbanks. The **Glenn Highway** begins at Tok and travels south and then west to Anchorage. The **Richardson Highway** runs north–south between Valdez and Delta Junction, where it meets the Alaska Highway. The **Seward Highway** heads south from Anchorage through the Kenai Mountains to Seward, with the branch **Sterling Highway** heading southwest to Soldotna, Kenai, and Homer. The **George Parks Highway** runs north from Anchorage, past Denali National Park to Fairbanks.

BY PLANE

Alaska's major gateway airports are **Anchorage International Airport** (☎ 907/266–2437), **Fairbanks International Airport** (☎ 907/474–2500), and **Juneau International Airport** (☎ 907/789–7821). Carriers include Alaska Airlines, Northwest, Delta, Reno Air, and United.

BY TRAIN

The **Alaska Railroad** (☎ 907/265–2494 in Anchorage, 907/456–4155 in Fairbanks, 800/544–0552 for individual reservations, 800/895–7245 for group reservations) runs mainline service from Seward through Anchorage to Fairbanks. A secondary line links Portage, southeast of Anchorage, and Whittier on Prince William Sound. Travel to Seward is in summer only; the rest of the route operates year-round, with reduced services September–May.

The **White Pass and Yukon Route** (☎ 907/983–2217 or 800/343–7373) operates between Skagway and Carcross, Yukon Territory, following the route that gold seekers took into the Yukon.

Hawai'i

BY BOAT

An alternative way to tour the Islands is with **American Hawaii Cruises** (✉ 2 North Riverside Plaza, Chicago, IL 60606, ☎ 312/466–6000 or 800/765–7000). Its 800-passenger ship, the S.S. *Independence,* leaves Honolulu year-round on seven-day cruises that visit O'ahu, the Big Island, Maui, and Kaua'i.

BY BUS

Honolulu is the only city with a municipal service, **The Bus** (☎ 808/848–5555). The county-run **Hele-On Bus** (☎ 808/935–8241) operates between Hilo and Kailua-Kona, and to other points on the Big Island. The other islands have no public bus system, although shuttles run between the airports and major shopping centers and hotels.

BY CAR

No Hawaiian island can be circumnavigated by car. The Big Island's roads are well maintained, although lava has closed the road from Kalapana to just east of Kamoamoa in Hawai'i Volcanoes National Park. On Maui, highways are in fairly good shape—though often crowded—and a four-wheel-drive vehicle may be necessary for the road south of Hāna. Kaua'i's main route runs south from Līhu'e and west to Polihale Beach; a narrower northern route runs to Hā'ena, the beginning of the roadless Nā Pali Coast. Moloka'i's main route becomes narrow and potholed as it nears Hālawa Valley in the east. Lāna'i's few paved roads are fine, but a four-wheel-drive vehicle is essential for exploring. On O'ahu's Wai'anae Coast the paved road ends just before Ka'ena Point.

BY PLANE

Honolulu International Airport (☎ 808/836–6411), on O'ahu, is served by American, Continental, Delta, Northwest, TWA, United, and Hawaiian Airlines. Aloha and Hawaiian airlines fly interisland between Honolulu and the four major Neighbor Island airports: **Kona International Airport** (✉ The Big Island, ☎ 808/329–2484), also served by United with direct flights from the mainland; **Hilo International Airport** (✉ The Big Island, ☎ 808/934–5801); **Kahului Airport** (✉ Maui, ☎ 808/872–3803); and **Līhu'e Airport** (✉ Kaua'i, ☎ 808/246–1400).

ALASKA

Updated by
Bill Sherwonit

Capital	Juneau
Population	609,300
Motto	North to the Future
State Bird	Willow ptarmigan
State Flower	Forget-me-not
Postal Abbreviation	AK

Statewide Visitor Information

The **Alaska Division of Tourism** (✉ Box 110801, Juneau 99811, ☎ 907/465–2010, FAX 907/465–2287) provides general visitor information. The **Alaska Public Lands Information Center** (✉ 605 W. 4th Ave., Suite 105, Anchorage 99501, ☎ 907/271–2737) is a clearinghouse of information on state and federal lands, including hiking trails, cabins, and campgrounds. The **Department of Fish and Game** (✉ Box 25526, Juneau 99802, ☎ 907/465–4180 for seasons and regulations, 907/465–2376 for licenses) can answer questions about sportfishing. The **Alaska Native Tourism Council** (✉ 1577 C St., Suite 304, Anchorage 99501, ☎ 907/274–5400, FAX 907/263–9971) represents the state's Native-run attractions. **Alaska Bed & Breakfast Association Reservation Service** (✉ Box 22800, Juneau 99802, ☎ 907/586–2959) can set you up at a B&B.

Cruising

More than a third of Alaska's visitors arrive by cruise ship. Most cruises leave from Vancouver, British Columbia, on a weeklong itinerary up the Inside Passage of Alaska's Southeast Panhandle, visiting Ketchikan, Sitka, Juneau, and Skagway. Many include a day in Glacier Bay National Park, but call ahead to be sure. Some cruises also continue across the Gulf of Alaska, to the South Central towns of Seward and Valdez. The major cruise tour operators serving Alaska are **Princess Cruises and Tours** (✉ 2815 2nd Ave., Suite 400, Seattle, WA 98121, ☎ 206/728–4202 or 800/426–0442) and **Holland America Line/Westours** (✉ 300 Elliott Ave. W, Seattle, WA 98119, ☎ 206/281–3535 or 800/426–0327). For a small-ship cruise tour, contact **Alaska Sightseeing/Cruise West** (✉ 2401 4th Ave., Suite 700, Seattle, WA 98121, ☎ 206/441–8687 or 800/426–7702). State ferries provide year-round budget service for passengers and vehicles (☞ Arriving and Departing *in* Southeast, *below*) on similar routes.

National and State Parks

Alaska has more land in national parks, wilderness areas, and national wildlife refuges than all the other states combined.

National Parks

Denali National Park and Preserve (☞ The Interior, *below*) is home to North America's tallest peak, Mt. McKinley; admission to the park is $5 per person, or $10 per family. **Glacier Bay National Park and Preserve** (☞ Southeast, *below*) is a marine preserve where 17 spectacular glaciers meet tidewater and seals float on icebergs. **Katmai National Park and Preserve** (☞ Southwest, *below*), a mixture of volcanic moonscape, rugged coast, large lake systems, mountains, and forested lowlands on the Alaska Peninsula, is home to huge coastal brown bears that fish for salmon in the Brooks River. On the Kenai Peninsula south of Anchorage is **Kenai Fjords National Park** (☞ South Central, *below*), known for its tidewater glaciers, rugged fjords, and abundant marine wildlife. The country's largest national park, **Wrangell–St. Elias** (☞ South Central, *below*), east of Anchorage along the Canadian border, is six times the size of Yellowstone.

The nation's largest national forest, the **Tongass** (☞ Southeast, *below*), stretches the length of the Panhandle. **Chugach National Forest** (☞ South Central, *below*) encompasses much of the Kenai Peninsula and Prince William Sound.

State Parks

Chugach State Park (✉ HC 52, Box 8999, Indian 99540, ☎ 907/345–5014), near Anchorage, has more than 100 mi of hiking trails, excellent wildlife viewing, and easily accessible wilderness. **Denali State Park** (✉ HC 32, Box 6706, Wasilla 99654, ☎ 907/745–3975) has a ridge-top trail and public-use cabins.

SOUTHEAST

Southeast Alaska is a maritime region of thousands of islands blanketed by old-growth spruce forest. The waters abound in Pacific salmon (five species) and sea mammals. The shore is home to deer, bears, and coastal communities that cling to the mountainsides. The wet climate inspires locals to call galoshes "Juneau tennis shoes," although summer does bring some breathtakingly beautiful sunny days. The villages of Tlingit, Haida, and Tsimshian Indians, as well as museums and cultural centers in the region's larger communities, give insights into Native American cultures.

Visitor Information

Southeast: Tourism Council (✉ Box 20710, Juneau 99802, ☎ 907/586–4777, FAX 907/463–4961). **Ketchikan:** Visitors Bureau (✉ 131 Front St., 99901, ☎ 907/225–6166 or 800/770–3300, 800/770–2200 for brochures; FAX 907/225–4250). **Sitka:** Visitors Bureau (✉ Centennial Bldg., Box 1226, 99835, ☎ 907/747–5940, FAX 907/747–3739) provides brochures and advice. **Juneau:** Log Cabin Information Center (✉ 134 3rd St., 99801, ☎ 907/586–2201 or 888/581–2201, FAX 907/586–6304).

Arriving and Departing

Southeast Alaska is accessible mainly by air or water. The mainland road system (from Anchorage, through the Canadian Yukon) connects only with tiny northern communities after hundreds of miles of wilderness road. Cruise ships (☞ Cruising, *above*) and state ferries are the most common means of visitor transportation.

By Car

Ferries to Southeast Alaska leave from Bellingham, Washington, and from Prince Rupert, British Columbia. From the north, the Alaska and Haines or Klondike highways lead to Skagway and Haines, and ferries continue south through the region.

By Ferry

The **Alaska Marine Highway System** (✉ Box 25535, Juneau 99802, ☎ 907/465–3941 or 800/642–0066, FAX 907/465–2476) is an extensive network of large and small vessels that link most Southeast communities. All ferries take cars (reservations necessary in summer) and have cafeterias or restaurants; most also have staterooms, but many Alaskans camp on deck in tents or on the lounges' floors. The system makes connections with BC Ferries in Prince Rupert, British Columbia.

By Plane

Regular jet service is available from Pacific Coast and southwestern U.S. cities to Ketchikan, Wrangell, Petersburg, Sitka, and **Juneau International Airport,** ☎ 907/789–7821). The Southeast is served year-round by **Alaska Airlines** (☎ 800/426–0333). In summer **Delta Airlines** (☎ 800/221–1212) also provides service. Flight service to the villages is available from the region's larger communities.

Exploring the Southeast

Ketchikan

Ketchikan is a fishing and logging town at the southern end of the Panhandle. Its centerpiece is **Creek Street,** the historic red-light district, now home to quaint shops built on stilts over Ketchikan Creek. Ten miles north ★ of town, **Totem Bight State Historical Park** (✉ N. Tongass Hwy., ☎ 907/247–8574) displays beautiful totem poles—many date only from the 1930s but replicate much older totem poles. The village of **Saxman** (☎ 907/225–5163), 2½ mi south of Ketchikan, also has many totem poles. Original totem poles, some 200 years old, can be seen at the **Totem Heritage Center** (✉ 601 Deermont St., ☎ 907/225–5900; 🎟 $3). The city, in fact, contains the largest collection of totem poles in the world.

Sitka

This historic town was the capital of Russian America before Alaska was sold to the United States in 1867. Russian cannons still crown **Castle Hill,** and the flagpole where the Stars and Stripes replaced the czarist Russian standard still stands. **St. Michael's Cathedral** (✉ Lincoln St., ☎ 907/747–8120; 🎟 $1) is a 1976 replica of the 1848 church. During the 1966 fire that destroyed the original, townspeople entered the burning building to rescue precious icons and other religious objects, which are now on display.

Open in summer only, the **Russian Bishop's House** (✉ Lincoln St.; 🎟 $2) is a log structure built in 1842 that's been restored by the National Park Service. The **Sheldon Jackson Museum** (✉ 104 College Dr., ☎ 907/747–8981; 🎟 $3) has a fine collection of priceless Tlingit, Haida, Tsimshian, Athabascan, Aleut, and Eskimo items. In **Sitka National Historical Park** (✉ Box 738, 106 Metlakatla St., 99835, ☎ 907/747–6281), Tlingit carvers still work at the venerable craft of carving totems; a forest trail winds among 15 totems, both old and new.

Juneau

The state capital clings to the mountainside along a narrow saltwater channel. It was born as a gold rush town in 1880 and remained an active gold-mining center until World War II. Today its number one employer is the state government, with transportation and tourism important runners-up.

Although Juneau's hills are steep, most visitors can explore the charming town on foot. Houses downtown date from the gold rush. On South Franklin Street, the **Red Dog Saloon** (☎ 907/463–3777) preserves the rough-and-tumble spirit of '98. The Victorian **Alaskan Hotel** (☞ Dining and Lodging, below) is a more genteel relic of the gold rush era. The tiny, onion-domed **St. Nicholas Russian Orthodox Church** (✉ 5th and Gold Sts., ☎ 907/586–1023), constructed in 1894, is the oldest original Russian church in Alaska. The **Alaska State Museum** (✉ 395 Whittier St., ☎ 907/465–2901; 🎟 $3), near the waterfront, highlights the state's rich cultural heritage, with Native American artifacts, gold rush memorabilia, and natural history displays.

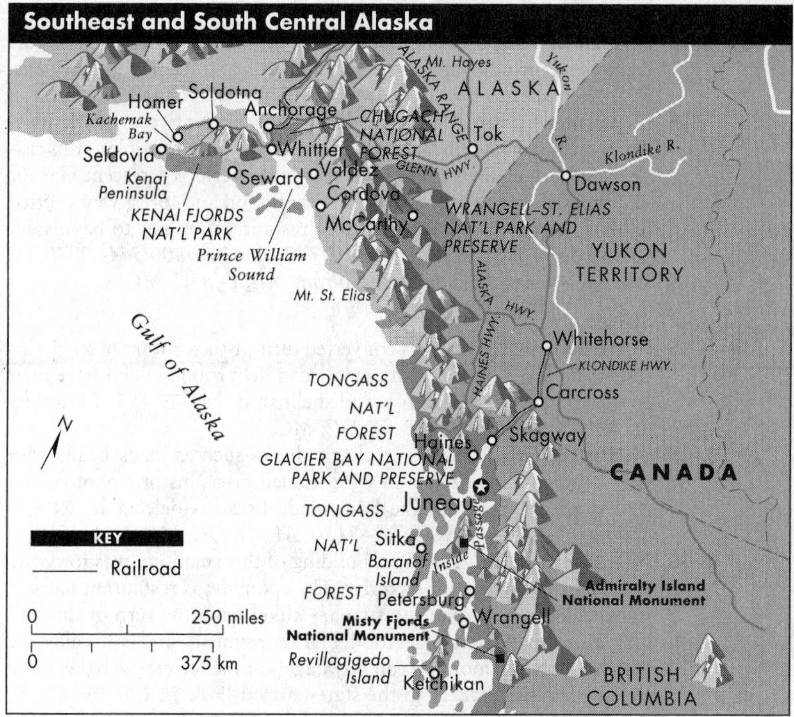

Glacier Bay National Park and Preserve

Whales, porpoises, sea otters, sea lions, seals, and seabirds inhabit the ★ 62-mi-long **Glacier Bay** (✉ Box 140, Gustavus 99826, ☎ 907/697–2230), a remote and wild marine park wilderness accessible only by boat. In addition to wildlife, the bay has 17 tidewater glaciers and about a dozen inlets or arms to explore, making it a favorite destination for sea kayaking as well as wildlife viewing from charter boats and cruise ships; contact Glacier Bay Tours and Cruises (☎ 800/622–2042) for details. Visitor services are available in the nearby community of Gustavus, 30 minutes by plane from Juneau.

Tongass National Forest

The largest of the nation's forests, the **Tongass** (✉ Centennial Hall, 101 Egan Dr., Juneau 99801, ☎ 907/586–8751) encompasses 16.8 million acres, or nearly three-fourths of Southeast Alaska. Mostly covered by old-growth temperate rain forest, the Tongass is a breeding ground for black and brown bears, bald eagles, Sitka black-tailed deer, mountain goats, and wolves. **Misty Fjords** (☎ 907/225–2148) and **Admiralty Island** (☎ 907/586–8790), two national monuments, have rugged shorelines and breathtaking vistas.

Dining and Lodging

For price ranges *see* Charts 1 (B) and 2 (B) *in* On the Road with Fodor's.

Ketchikan

$$$$ ★ ✕ **Salmon Falls Resort.** It's a half-hour drive from town, but the fresh seafood and steaks served in the huge, octagonal dining room make the trip more than worthwhile. Built of pine logs, the restaurant overlooks the waters of Clover Passage, where sunsets can be vivid red and remarkable. This is a convenient stop after a visit to Totem Bight Park. ✉ *Mile 17, N. Tongass Hwy.,* ☎ *907/225–2752. AE, MC, V.*

Sitka

$$$–$$$$ ✕ **Channel Club.** Fine steaks and seafood are served in nautical surroundings, including glass and fishnet floats and whalebone carvings. ✉ *2906 Halibut Point Rd.,* ☏ *907/747–9916. AE, DC, MC, V.*

$$$ 🏨 **Westmark Shee Atika.** Southeast Alaskan Native artwork illustrates the history, legends, and exploits of the Tlingit people at this rustic Westmark chain outpost. Many rooms overlook Crescent Harbor and the islands beyond; others have mountain and forest views. Fried halibut nuggets in the Raven Room restaurant are not to be missed. ✉ *330 Seward St., 99835,* ☏ *907/747–6241 or 800/544–0970,* FAX *907/747–5486. 98 rooms. Restaurant. AE, D, DC, MC, V.*

Juneau

$$$–$$$$ ✕ **The Summit.** Housed in a converted turn-of-the-century brothel, this restaurant serves its meals in a small, candlelit room. Diners have their choice of nearly 15 local fish and shellfish dishes. ✉ *455 S. Franklin St.,* ☏ *907/586–2050. AE, D, DC, MC, V.*

$–$$ ★ ✕ **The Fiddlehead.** Healthy, eclectic dishes such as black beans with rice is served in a cozy room with stained glass, historic photos, and a view of Mt. Juneau. The homemade bread is delectable. ✉ *429 Willoughby Ave.,* ☏ *907/586–3150. AE, D, DC, MC, V.*

$–$$ ✕🏨 **Silverbow Inn.** The main building of this small inn was for years one of the town's major bakeries. The eponymous restaurant has settings, chairs, and tables (no two are alike) from the turn of the century. Homemade pastas, seafood, blackened meats, and crab cakes are top-notch. Next door you can buy bagels at the Silverbow bakery, the oldest operating bakery in the state (circa 1890). ✉ *120 2nd St.,* ☏ *907/586–9866. CP. MC, V. No lunch (restaurant).*

$$$$ 🏨 **Baranof Hotel.** This grande dame of Juneau hotels still reflects its 1930s origins. The lobby is art-deco style, but guest rooms are contemporary. There's a travel agency on site. ✉ *127 N. Franklin St., 99801,* ☏ *907/586–2660 or 800/544–0970,* FAX *907/586–8315. 194 rooms. Restaurant. AE, D, DC, MC, V.*

$$$–$$$$ ★ 🏨 **The Prospector.** A short walk west of downtown, this small, modern hotel has very large rooms with bright watercolors and views of the channel, mountains, or city. Outstanding prime rib is served in the McGuires' dining room and lounge. ✉ *375 Whittier St., 99801,* ☏ *907/586–3737 or 800/331–2711,* FAX *907/586–1204. 60 rooms. Restaurant. AE, D, DC, MC, V.*

$$ ★ 🏨 **Alaskan Hotel.** This historic 1913 hotel is 15 mi from the ferry terminal and 9 mi from the airport (city bus service is available). Rooms are on three floors and have turn-of-the-century antiques and iron beds. ✉ *167 S. Franklin St.,* ☏ *907/586–1000 or 800/327–9347,* FAX *907/463–3775. 42 rooms. D, DC, MC, V.*

Wilderness Camps and Lodges

Accommodations range from spartan bunkhouses to luxury lodges serving candlelight dinners. One agency that books area sportfishing lodges is **Alaska Sportfishing Packages** (✉ Box 9170, Seattle, WA 98109, ☏ 206/216–2920 or 800/426–0603, FAX 206/216–2973 or 800/323–2231).

Campgrounds

State and national forest campgrounds are available near all Southeast communities (☞ Alaska Public Lands Information Center *in* Statewide Visitor Information, *above*). *The Milepost,* available in most Alaska and Washington bookstores, lists campgrounds throughout the state.

Outdoor Activities and Sports

Fishing

Southeast Alaskans are blessed with great salmon fishing off city docks and on beaches where creeks meet saltwater. Another option is to take an air taxi to a remote spot for a day's fishing or an extended stay (☞ Wilderness Camps and Lodges, *above*). Fishing licenses are available in most grocery and sporting-goods stores.

Kayaking and Rafting

You can bring your own kayak aboard state ferries or hire a local outfitter—such as **Alaska Discovery Wilderness Adventures** (✉ 5449 Shaune Dr., Suite 4, Juneau 99801, ☎ 907/780–6226 or 800/586–1911)—for a guided Inside Passage or Glacier Bay excursion. The company also guides kayak trips on Admiralty Island and at Icy Bay, near Yakutat, and float trips on the Tatshenshini and Alsek rivers. For rafting on the Mendenhall River as well as glacial travel, canoe and kayak trips, and hiking, contact **Alaska Travel Adventures** (✉ 9085 Glacier Hwy., Suite 301, Juneau 99801, ☎ 907/789–0052, 800/478–0052 in AK). Guided sea-kayaking tours of nearby Misty Fjords National Monument in Tongass National Forest are available from **Southeast Exposure** (✉ Box 9143, Ketchikan 99901, ☎ 907/225–8829).

Wildlife Viewing

Southeast Alaska is renowned for its whales, eagles, and brown bears (the coastal cousins of grizzlies). **Glacier Bay National Park** is a prime viewing area for several species of whales, including humpbacks and orcas. **Alaska Discovery Wilderness Adventures** (☞ Kayaking and Rafting, *above*) also leads whale-watching tours at Icy Strait, near Chichagof Island. Popular bear-viewing areas are **Pack Creek,** within Admiralty Island National Monument (☞ Tongass National Forest, *above*) and **Anan Creek,** in the Tongass Forest near Wrangell (☎ 907/874–2323). The **Alaska Chilkat Bald Eagle Preserve** (☎ 907/766–2292), near Haines, hosts the world's largest gathering of bald eagles: Between 1,000 and 4,000 eagles gather here each November and December.

Ski Areas

The **Eaglecrest** ski area, across the channel from Juneau on Douglas Island, has 31 trails, three lifts, a ski school, and equipment rental. ✉ *155 S. Seward St., Juneau 99801,* ☎ *907/586–5284, 907/586–5330 for recorded ski conditions. Closed May–Nov.*

Check with local visitor centers for **cross-country ski trails** groomed for either diagonal or skate skiing.

Shopping

Silver Lining Seafoods (✉ 1705 Tongass Ave., ☎ 907/225–9865), north of Ketchikan's city dock, has excellent locally smoked seafood and fish-motif postcards and T-shirts by local artist Ray Troll.

In Juneau the **Alaska Steam Laundry Building,** on South Franklin Street, has shops and a good coffeehouse downstairs. The **Senate Building Mall,** also on South Franklin, houses a Christmas store and other import shops. In the Senate Building Mall, **Taku Smokeries** has two retail outlets selling locally smoked seafood.

SOUTH CENTRAL

South Central Alaska is home to most of the state's population and many of its most sought-out attractions. Many visitors start their trips in Anchorage, then continue south to the fishing and artists' communities of the Kenai Peninsula.

Visitor Information

Anchorage: Convention and Visitors Bureau (✉ 524 W. 4th Ave., 99501, ☎ 907/276–4118, 907/276–3200 for events hot line; FAX 907/278–5559), Log Cabin and Downtown Visitor Information Center (✉ W. 4th Ave. and F St., ☎ 907/274–3531). **Kenai Peninsula:** Tourism Marketing Council (✉ 150 N. Willow, Kenai 99611, ☎ 907/283–3850 or 800/535–3624 to order a vacation planner, FAX 907/283–2838). **Soldotna:** Visitor Information Center (✉ 44790 Sterling Hwy., 99669, ☎ 907/262–1337, FAX 907/262–3566). **Homer:** Visitor Center (✉ Box 541, 99603, ☎ 907/235–7740, FAX 907/235–8766). **Seward:** Visitor Information Center (✉ Mile 2, Seward Hwy., Box 749, 99664, ☎ 907/224–8051, FAX 907/224–5353).

Arriving and Departing

By Bus

Gray Line of Alaska (☎ 907/277–5581 in Anchorage, 907/456–7741 in Fairbanks) serves Anchorage, Denali, and Fairbanks.

By Car

To get to Anchorage from Tok, on the Alaska Highway near the Canadian border, head southwest on the Glenn Highway. From Fairbanks travel south on the George Parks Highway. From Anchorage, the Seward and Sterling highways lead south to the Kenai Peninsula.

By Ferry

The South Central section of the **Alaska Marine Highway** ferry system (☞ Southeast, *above*) links communities on Prince William Sound, the Gulf of Alaska, and Cook Inlet. Road connections to and from Anchorage can be made in Whittier and Seward. There is no ferry service between the South Central and Southeast regions.

By Plane

Anchorage International Airport (☎ 907/266–2437), about 6 mi from downtown, is served by Alaska Airlines, American West, Continental, Northwest, Delta Airlines, Reno Air, and United. Commuter plane service is available to Denali National Park, Homer, Kenai, and other destinations within the region. A cab from the Anchorage airport to downtown costs about $15 plus tip. Some hotels have shuttles.

By Train

The **Alaska Railroad** (☎ 800/544–0552, 907/265–2494 in Anchorage, 907/456–4155 in Fairbanks; FAX 907/265–2323) has mainline service between Seward, Anchorage, Denali National Park, and Fairbanks, and secondary service between Portage and Whittier.

Exploring South Central

Anchorage

Anchorage is a young, spirited city in a spectacular setting between mountains and sea. Nearly half the state's population resides here, which may explain why you can find everything from oil industry high-rises to backwoods cabins with resident sled-dog teams.

The **Anchorage Museum of History and Art** (✉ W. 7th Ave. and A St., ☎ 907/343–6173; 🎫 $5) has an outstanding exhibit on Native Alaskan life and a permanent display of artwork depicting Alaska as seen by explorers, resident painters, and latter-day visitors. The **Imaginarium** (✉ 737 W. 5th Ave., ☎ 907/276–3179; 🎫 $5) is an interactive science museum with a shop that sells educational toys. At **Ship Creek,** just north of downtown, you can see salmon jump in summer as they head upstream to spawn; there's a platform for easy viewing.

Earthquake Park, at the west end of Northern Lights Boulevard, shows the damage wrought by the 1964 quake, when houses tumbled into the ocean. Trees have claimed the earth mounds and ponds created by the quake's force. The **floatplane base at Lake Hood,** near the Anchorage International Airport, is the world's largest and busiest. Plan a sunset stroll by the scenic **Coastal Trail,** which runs along Cook Inlet, with several trailhead access points in mid- and downtown.

The Kenai Peninsula

Thrusting into the Gulf of Alaska south of Anchorage, the Kenai Peninsula is a glacier-hewn landscape with magnificent wildlife viewing and fishing from its spectacular coastline. In summer the Alaska Railroad runs a passenger train daily to **Seward,** a small fishing and timber town on Resurrection Bay, but most people drive the three hours from Anchorage. Tour boats leave Seward's busy downtown harbor for excursions that include visits to sea lion and bird rookeries and close-up views of tidewater glaciers.

Seward is the jumping-off point for **Kenai Fjords National Park** (☞ *below*). **Mariah Tours** (☎ 800/270–1238) has wildlife and glacier tours of the park.

At the southern terminus of the Seward Highway, 225 mi from Anchorage, lies **Homer,** in a breathtaking setting that includes a sand spit jutting into Kachemak Bay. The town's buildings are picturesque, and you can comb the beach, fish off the docks, or charter a boat for halibut fishing (☞ Outdoor Activities and Sports, *below*). Wildlife abounds in the bay, and fishing charters may give you a close-up view of seals, porpoises, birds, and, more rarely, whales. If you walk along the docks at the end of the day, you can see fishermen unloading their catch. Across from the end of the Homer spit is **Halibut Cove,** one of the prettiest spots in South Central Alaska and reachable by water taxi. **Seldovia,** on the other side of Kachemak Bay from Homer, has an onion-domed Russian church and excellent fishing.

Kenai Fjords National Park

One of only three national parks connected to Alaska's highway system, the 670,000-acre **Kenai Fjords** (✉ Box 1727, Seward 99664, ☎ 907/224–3175) is known for its abundant marine wildlife, deep-blue tidewater glaciers, waterfalls, and coastal fjords (long and steep-sided glacially carved valleys now filled with seawater). People come here by boat to see whales, porpoises, seals, and seabirds, fish for salmon, and hear the booming echoes of calving tidewater glaciers. Yet the park's most popular visitor attraction is on land: **Exit Glacier** is a short walk from the one gravel road that leads into the park.

Wrangell–St. Elias National Park and Preserve

Bridging the Canadian border, 13-million-acre **Wrangell–St. Elias** (✉ Box 29, Glennallen 99588, ☎ 907/822–5234) could fit six Yellowstones within its borders. Known to some as Alaska's Mountain Kingdom, the park encompasses four major mountain ranges and six of the continent's 10 highest peaks, including the 18,008-ft **Mt. St. Elias.**

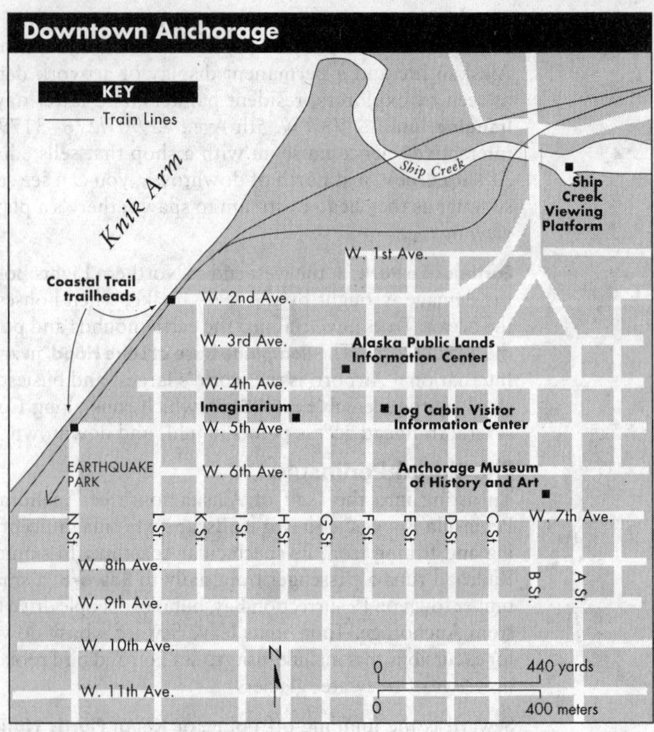

Here, too, is North America's largest subpolar ice field, the Bagley, which calved several gigantic glaciers; one of them, the **Malaspina,** is larger than Rhode Island. The park has two main entryways: On the north side is Nabesna Road; on the east is 60-mi-long McCarthy Road, which leads to the historic town of **McCarthy** and neighboring **Kennecott Mine** (now closed), two of the park's key attractions for those who don't want to venture far from the road system.

Chugach National Forest

Second only to the Tongass in size, **Chugach National Forest** (⊠ 3301 C St., Anchorage 99503, ☏ 907/271–2500) encompasses much of Prince William Sound, the Kenai Peninsula, and the Copper River Delta region. Its 5.8 million acres include forested hills and valleys, rugged coastal mountains, one of the world's largest tidewater glaciers, and wetlands that support migrating waterfowl and shorebirds. About an hour's drive south of Anchorage, **Portage Glacier** and the **Begich-Boggs Visitor Center** are two of Alaska's premier visitor attractions.

Dining

For price ranges *see* Charts 1 (B) and 2 (B) *in* On the Road with Fodor's. For information on wilderness camps and lodges, *see* Southeast, *above*.

For bed-and-breakfast reservations, call **Alaska Private Lodging: Stay with a Friend** (⊠ Box 200047, Anchorage 99520, ☏ 907/258–1717, FAX 907/258–6613).

Anchorage

$$$$ ★ ✕ **Marx Brothers Cafe.** The second-oldest house in Anchorage was originally constructed for the engineers who built the Alaska Railroad; now it's a restaurant serving sophisticated fare such as macadamia-crusted

halibut, and, for dessert, wild-berry crisp with Alaskan birch syrup. There are more than 500 selections on the wine list. ✉ *627 W. 3rd Ave.,* ☎ *907/278–2133. AE, DC, MC, V. No lunch.*

$$$$ ✕ **Seven Glaciers Restaurant.** A high-speed tram transports you to this restaurant at the top of a 2,300-ft mountain. You're assured a culinary adventure as well: Meat, fish, and fowl dishes are served "architecturally." Translation: Your steak may arrive standing on its side. ✉ *Westin Alyeska Prince Hotel, 1000 Arlberg, Girdwood,* ☎ *907/754–2237. Reservations essential. AE, D, MC, V. Closed Sun.–Thurs. in winter. No lunch.*

$$$–$$$$ ★ ✕ **Double Musky.** It's worth the 40-mi trip south of town and the wait once you arrive. The little building set among spruce trees is casually decorated with Mardi Gras memorabilia, the better to prepare you for the fine Cajun dishes and huge, tender steaks to come. ✉ *Crow Creek Rd., Girdwood,* ☎ *907/783–2822. Reservations not accepted. AE, D, DC, MC, V. Closed Mon. No lunch.*

$$$–$$$$ ✕ **Simon and Seafort's Saloon and Grill.** Waitresses in long black dresses and frilly white aprons create a Gay Nineties mood at this long-time Anchorage restaurant, whose large windows look out across Cook Inlet. Fresh local seafood and salt-rock-roasted prime rib are the specialties. Expect a crowd in summer. ✉ *420 L St.,* ☎ *907/274–3502. AE, MC, V. No lunch Sun.*

$$$ ✕ **Sacks Cafe.** A favorite before- or after-show dining option for those attending concerts and plays at Anchorage's Performing Arts Center, this downtown restaurant serves fresh seafood, pasta, and dinner salads. It also has takeout service for sandwiches, salads, and espresso. Sunday brunch is served until 2:30. ✉ *625 W. 5th Ave.,* ☎ *907/276–3546. Reservations not accepted (except some holidays). AE, MC, V.*

$–$$ ✕ **Downtown Deli.** Alaska's governor owns this classic delicatessen, where you can get anything from deli classics like chopped-liver sandwiches to local specialties such as reindeer stew. Nestle into a wooden booth inside, or watch the street action from a sidewalk table outside. ✉ *525 W. 4th Ave.,* ☎ *907/276–7116. AE, D, DC, MC, V.*

$$$$ **Anchorage Hotel.** Built in 1961, this charming hotel has its original sinks and tubs, and the hallways upstairs are lined with old photos of the city. There's a fireplace in the lobby. ✉ *330 E St., 99501,* ☎ *907/272–4553 or 800/544–0988,* FAX *907/277–4483. 26 rooms. CP. AE, D, DC, MC, V.*

$$$$ ★ **Hotel Captain Cook.** This three-tower hotel takes up a full city block. Teak paneling lines most public walls, recalling Captain Cook's voyages in the South Pacific. ✉ *W. 5th Ave. and K St., 99501 (Box 102280),* ☎ *907/276–6000 or 800/843–1950, 800/478–3100 in AK;* FAX *907/343–2298. 643 rooms. 3 restaurants, pool, health club. AE, D, DC, MC, V.*

$$$$ **Voyager Hotel.** All the rooms in this small four-story hotel have full kitchens and bathrooms with pedestal sinks and wainscoting. Upstairs, west-side rooms look out on the Cook Inlet. ✉ *501 K St., 99501,* ☎ *907/277–9501 or 800/247–9070,* FAX *907/274–0333. 38 rooms. Restaurant. AE, D, DC, MC, V.*

$$$$ **Westin Alyeska Prince Hotel.** Seven glaciers and lush forests surround this luxury hotel at the base of Mt. Alyeska. Rooms have refrigerators, safes, heated towel racks, ski-boot storage, bathrobes, and slippers, and all have views of the Chugach Mountains. A tram taking guests to Seven Glaciers restaurant (☞ *above*) leaves from the hotel. ✉ *1000 Arlberg, Box 249, Girdwood, 99587,* ☎ *907/754–1111 or 800/880–3880,* FAX *907/754–2200. 307 rooms. 4 restaurants, pool, exercise room. AE, D, DC, MC, V.*

$$ **Alaskan Samovar Inn.** This well-worn but clean motel is east of downtown on one of the city's main thoroughfares. Victorian-style rooms are small and dark, but each has a whirlpool tub, cable TV, and refrigerator. ✉ *720 Gambell St., 99501,* ☎ *907/277–1511 or 800/478–1511,* FAX *907/272–5192. 68 rooms. Restaurant. AE, D, MC, V.*

$ **Anchorage International Hostel.** At this cinder-block building downtown, most guests share dorm-style rooms, though there's a limited number of private rooms (with shared bathrooms). There's a 1 AM curfew and a four-night minimum stay in summer. ✉ *700 H St., 99501,* ☎ *907/276–3635,* FAX *907/276–7772. Dorm rooms (95 beds), 4 private rooms, none with bath. MC, V.*

The Kenai Peninsula

$$–$$$ ✕ **Harbor Dinner Club.** Run by the same family since 1958, this eatery serves local halibut and salmon in a plain dining room with a view of Resurrection Bay and the mountains. There's dancing in the lounge. ✉ *220 5th Ave., Seward,* ☎ *907/224–3012. AE, D, DC, MC, V.*

$$ ★ ✕ **The Saltry.** A half-hour ride from Homer Harbor on the Kachemak Bay Ferry takes you to this restaurant with a deck over the water. Once there, sample some of South Central Alaska's best seafood dishes, including fine sushi. Arrange for boat and dining reservations through the Central Charter Booking Agency. ✉ *Halibut Cove,* ☎ *907/235–7847 or 800/478–7847 in AK. MC, V. Closed winter.*

$$$$ **Land's End.** The three wings of this hotel have a contemporary nautical theme. All rooms facing the bay have small balconies for watching the sunset. ✉ *4786 Homer Spit Rd., Homer 99603,* ☎ *907/235–2500, 800/478–0400 in AK (reservations only);* FAX *907/235–0420. 61 rooms. Restaurant. AE, D, DC, MC, V.*

$$$$ **Best Western Hotel Seward.** Gold-rush–style rooms in this downtown hotel have VCRs and refrigerators, and some have views of Resurrection Bay. The hotel runs a shuttle to the harbor (summer only) and is close to the ferry. ✉ *221 Fifth Ave., Seward 99664,* ☎ *907/224–2378 or 800/528–1234,* FAX *907/224–3112. 38 rooms. AE, D, DC, MC, V.*

Campgrounds

In Anchorage, the city-operated **Centennial and Lions Campground** (✉ Box 196650, 99519, ☎ 907/333–9711) has 88 spaces and showers; it's closed from mid-October through April. Near Anchorage, **Chugach State Park** (✉ HC52 Box 8999, Indian 99540, ☎ 907/345–5014) has three public campgrounds. For **Kenai Peninsula** and other area campgrounds, contact the Alaska Public Lands Information Center (☞ Statewide Visitor Information, *above*).

Nightlife and the Arts

The **Alaska Center for the Performing Arts** (✉ 621 W. 6th Ave., ☎ 907/263–2900) is home to a local symphony orchestra and theater companies and also presents operas, symphonies, and performances by national and international touring companies. The **Fly-by-Night Club** (✉ 3300 Spenard Rd., ☎ 907/279–7726) features everything from pop rock to stage revues with tacky jokes. The *Anchorage Daily News* publishes a weekend activity guide every Friday.

Outdoor Activities and Sports

Biking

Most South Central highways are suitable for biking on the shoulder. Anchorage has more than 125 mi of bike trails. The **Matanuska Valley** is an increasingly popular place for farm-road rides. Bikes are available for rent at many hotels and at **Downtown Bicycle Rental** (✉

5th Ave. and C St., Anchorage, ☎ 907/279–5293) and **Anchorage Coastal Bicycle Rentals** at the **Adventure Café** (✉ 414 K St., Anchorage, ☎ 907/276–8282).

Fishing

All South Central coastal communities have fishing charters, outfitters, and guides. Although Anchorage does not have good saltwater fishing—glacial runoff makes the water too murky—the freshwater lakes are stocked, and a hatchery-enhanced run of salmon returns to Ship Creek, in the city's downtown area, each summer. In Homer, **Central Charter Booking Agency** (✉ 4241 Homer Spit, 99603, ☎ 907/235–7847, 800/478–7847 in AK) arranges salmon and halibut charters. **Alaska Wildland Adventures** (✉ Box 389, Girdwood 99587, ☎ 800/334–8730, 800/478–4100 in AK) sells float and fish packages on the Kenai River, world famous for its huge salmon runs. Licenses are sold in most grocery and other retail stores.

Hiking and Backpacking

There are public cabins for rent along many hiking trails in South Central Alaska (☞ Alaska Public Lands Information Center *in* Statewide Visitor Information, *above*). **Chugach State Park** (☎ 907/345–5014), just east of Anchorage, has nearly 30 trails totaling more than 150 mi. Trails are also maintained within **Chugach National Forest** (☞ *above*), on the Kenai Peninsula.

Kayaking and Rafting

Floating is available on hundreds of rivers within a small area. **Nova River Runners** (✉ Box 1129, Chickaloon 99674, ☎ 907/745–5753, 800/746–5753 in AK) leads guided day trips on the Chickaloon, Matanuska, and Six-Mile rivers and overnighters on the Talkeetna and Copper rivers. **Ketchum Air Service** (✉ Box 190588, Anchorage 99519, ☎ 907/243–5525 or 800/433–9114) provides drop-off and pickup service and gear for wilderness float trips.

Sled-Dog Racing

On winter weekends the **Alaska Sled Dog and Racing Association** (☎ 907/562–2235) hosts races. The three-day **Fur Rendezvous World-Championship Sled Dog Race** is staged in downtown Anchorage in mid-February. March brings the famous, 1,049-mi **Iditarod,** which begins in Anchorage and ends in Nome.

Wildlife Viewing

Some of Alaska's best wildlife viewing is possible right outside Anchorage in **Chugach State Park:** Look for moose, Dall sheep, bears, and many smaller mammals and bird life in this accessible wilderness. Along the coastline of the **Kenai Peninsula,** you'll often see whales, sea lions, sea otters, seals, and seabirds.

Ski Areas

The **Alyeska Resort** (✉ Box 249, Girdwood 99587, ☎ 907/754–1111 or 800/880–3880, 907/754–7669 for recorded ski conditions), about 40 mi south of Anchorage, is the largest in the state, with 786 acres of skiable terrain, a 3,125-ft vertical drop, 68 trails, seven lifts, and a 60-passenger tram. It also has a 307-room hotel, a ski school, and two mountaintop restaurants (☞ Seven Glaciers *in* Dining, *above*). **Hilltop Ski Area** (✉ 7015 Abbott Rd., Anchorage 99516, ☎ 907/346–1446, 907/346–2167 for recorded ski conditions), 10 mi from downtown Anchorage, has one lift, one surface lift, and one rope tow, nine trails, a vertical drop of 300 ft, ski instruction, cross-country trails, and a national-grade half-pipe for snowboarders. **Alpenglow at Arctic Valley** (☎ 907/428–1208, 907/249–9292 for recorded ski conditions) is in the Chugach Mountains about 15 mi northeast of downtown Anchorage. It has three double-chairs, a T-bar, a pony tow, open-bowl skiing with a 1,300-ft vertical drop, two day lodges, a rental shop, and a ski school.

Anchorage also has a vast and diverse Nordic ski-trail system, with more than 70 mi of groomed trails. The **Nordic Ski Club of Anchorage** (☏ 907/276–7609) has a ski hot line (☏ 907/248–6667) that gives grooming and trail condition updates.

Shopping

The shops along 4th and 5th avenues sell T-shirts, trinkets, and Alaskan arts and crafts. At the **Alaska Native Arts and Crafts Association** (✉ 333 W. 4th Ave., ☏ 907/274–2932) you'll find genuine, if pricey, local baskets, carvings, and beadwork.

THE INTERIOR

The Alaska and George Parks highways give access to this diverse area, a vast wilderness of birch and spruce forest, high mountains, tundra valleys, and abundant wildlife. Its crown jewel is Denali National Park, 240 highway mi north of Anchorage. En route here from Anchorage, you'll travel through green Matanuska Valley farm country. North of Fairbanks, two hot springs retreats are open year-round.

Visitor Information

Denali National Park and Preserve (✉ Superintendent, Box 9, Denali National Park 99755, ☏ 907/683–2294 year-round, 907/683–1266 in summer; FAX 907/683–9612 year-round). **Fairbanks:** Convention and Visitors Bureau Information Cabin (✉ 550 1st Ave., 99701, ☏ 907/456–5774 or 800/327–5774, 907/456–4636 for events hot line; FAX 907/452–2867).

Arriving and Departing

By Car

Much of the Interior is inaccessible by road, but some major roadways do pass through the region. Fairbanks is connected to Anchorage in South Central Alaska by the George Parks Highway; the Steese, Elliot, and Dalton highways provide access north of Fairbanks. Hardy RVers and campers drive the Alaska Highway through British Columbia and the Yukon to Fairbanks; the drive takes at least a week.

By Plane

Year-round, Alaska Airlines and Delta have daily nonstop jet service between Anchorage and the **Fairbanks International Airport** (☏ 907/474–2500). In summer Alaska Airlines flies nonstop between Seattle and Fairbanks. Also in summer Northwest flies to Fairbanks from Minneapolis. A number of bush carriers originate in Fairbanks and will take you to otherwise inaccessible destinations in the region.

By Train

The **Alaska Railroad** (☏ 800/544–0552, 907/265–2494 in Anchorage, 907/465–4155 in Fairbanks; FAX 907/265–2323) runs between Anchorage and Fairbanks via Denali.

Exploring the Interior

Denali National Park

Denali encompasses 6 million acres of wilderness, including the majestic **Mt. McKinley**—at 20,320 ft, the highest peak in North America. Along with panoramic vistas of unspoiled taiga and tundra, the park is the natural habitat of bears, wolves, moose, Dall sheep, and caribou. The only road through the park is closed to private vehicles beyond Mile 12. You can, however, take a shuttle bus (☎ 800/622–7275), which costs $12–$30 depending on turnaround point, on an 11-hour round-trip excursion to **Wonder Lake,** famous for its views of wading moose and Mt. McKinley. If you tire of the ride, you can get out and walk, then catch another bus (they leave from the park entrance every half hour starting at 5 AM) in either direction. Check with the **visitor center,** near the park entrance, for the day's schedule of naturalist walks and sled-dog demonstrations. Denali is open year-round, but services and accommodations are limited from September to May. For information on camping *see* Campgrounds *in* Dining and Lodging, *below.*

Fairbanks

Built on the banks of the Chena River, Fairbanks was founded by gold miners early in the century and later became a transportation hub for all the Interior. Today it's the state's second-largest city, although its atmosphere is more that of a frontier town. Its residents cope with incredible winter temperatures (lows reach –50°F) and darkness or twilight almost around the clock in the dead of winter.

One of Fairbanks's main attractions is the **University of Alaska** (✉ 501 Yukon Dr., ☎ 907/474–7211). On its grounds are the **Large Animal Research Station** (☎ 907/474–7207), home to live musk ox and caribou, and the **University of Alaska Museum** (☎ 907/474–7505; 🎫 $5), whose collection includes a 36,000-year-old mummified steppe bison, a whale skull, dinosaur fossils, and ivory carvings. In summer, daily programs focus on Alaska's northern Native peoples and the aurora borealis; visitors are welcome to explore and touch such items as Native masks and tools, wolf pelts, and historic artifacts. The **Geophysical Institute** (☎ 907/474–7558) shows a free video on the aurora borealis on Thursday afternoon from June through August. The west ridge of the campus has an excellent view of the Alaska Range to the south.

Another big draw in Fairbanks is **Alaskaland Park** (✉ Airport Way and Peger Rd., ☎ 907/459–1087), on the Chena River near downtown. Among its numerous free attractions are museums, a theater, an art gallery, a native village, and a reconstructed gold rush town. The park is closed between Labor Day and Memorial Day.

Hot Springs Retreats

The discovery of natural hot springs in the frozen wilderness just north of Fairbanks sent early miners scrambling to build communities around this heaven-sent phenomenon. Today, Fairbanks residents come to soak in pools filled with hot spring water and to enjoy excellent fishing, hiking, and cross-country skiing. The springs are also a favorite viewing point for the famed northern lights.

Dining and Lodging

For price ranges *see* Charts 1 (B) and 2 (B) *in* On the Road with Fodor's.

Denali

$–$$ ✕ **Lynx Creek Pizza & Pub.** Young park workers enjoy after-work beer and pizza in this funky frame building just outside Denali. Try the reindeer-sausage pizza topping. ✉ *Parks Hwy., 1½ mi north of park entrance,* ☎ *907/683–2548. Reservations not accepted. AE, D, MC, V. Closed Sept.–May.*

$$$$ **Denali National Park Hotel.** The park's only official hotel is 1½ mi inside the park entrance. Naturalists present nightly programs in summer. ✉ *241 W. Ship Creek Ave., Anchorage 99501,* ☎ *907/276–7234 or 800/276-7234;* FAX *907/258–3668. 100 rooms. Restaurant. AE, D, MC, V. Closed mid-Sept.–May.*

$$$$ **Denali Princess Lodge.** This large log complex above the Nenana River, just 1 mi north of Denali, is the park's most luxurious hotel. Suites have whirlpools, and the lounge has a fireplace. ✉ *Parks Hwy., 1 mi north of park entrance. Reservations: 2815 2nd Ave., Suite 400, Seattle, WA 98121,* ☎ *907/683–2282 in summer, 800/426–0500 for reservations;* FAX *907/683–2545 in summer, 206/443–1979 for reservations. 280 rooms. 2 restaurants. AE, DC, MC, V. Closed mid-Sept.–mid-May.*

$ **Denali Hostel.** A log building with two dormitory-style bunkhouses, this independent hostel offers bus service to and from the park. It's 10 mi north of the park entrance, near Healy. ✉ *Box 801, Denali National Park 99755,* ☎ *907/683–1295,* FAX *907/683–2106. 25 beds. No credit cards. Closed mid-Sept.–mid-May.*

WILDERNESS CAMPS AND LODGES

$$$$ ★ **Camp Denali.** This rustic compound in the heart of the park has cabins lighted by gaslight. Its authentic charm, delicious home cooking, and views of Mt. McKinley make it a favorite place to stay in Denali. A knowledgeable staff and naturalist programs will acquaint you with the surrounding wilderness. Visits are arranged according to a fixed schedule, with a three-night minimum stay. ✉ *Wonder Lake, Box 67, Denali National Park 99755,* ☎ *907/683–2290,* FAX *907/683–1568. 17 cabins. FAP. No credit cards. Closed early Sept.–early June.*

$$$$ **Denali Wilderness Lodge.** Built as a hunting camp to supply gold rush–era miners, this complex of more than two dozen log buildings is reachable only by bush plane. Activities include horseback riding, hiking, bird-watching, and nature walks. There's a two-night minimum stay. ✉ *30 mi east of Denali Park entrance; Mailing address: Box 71784, Fairbanks 99707,* ☎ *907/683–1287 in summer, 800/541–9779 year-round;* FAX *907/479–4410 in winter, 907/683–1286 in summer. 13 cabins. FAP. Closed Sept.–late May.*

CAMPGROUNDS

There are seven campgrounds in Denali. Three are open to private vehicles for tent and RV camping, three others are reached by shuttle bus and are restricted to tent camping, and one is for backpackers only. For reservations call **Denali Park Resorts** (☎ 907/272–7275 or 800/622–7275). For more information contact the park superintendent (☞ Visitor Information, *above*). Several private campgrounds are outside the park along the highway; try **Grizzly Bear Cabins and Campground** (✉ Box 7, Denali National Park 99755, ☎ 907/683–2696 in summer, 907/683–1337 in winter). For general campsite information and availability, contact the **Alaska Public Lands Information Center** (☞ Statewide Visitor Information, *above*).

Fairbanks

$$$–$$$$ ✕ **Two Rivers Lodge.** Once a wilderness homestead, this rustic log building is now a full-service restaurant with award-winning cuisine. In summer guests may sit on a deck that overlooks a pond and sample tapas, appetizer-size portions of Spanish dishes cooked in a wood-fired oven. The wine list is one of Alaska's largest. ✉ *Mile 16, Chena Hot Springs Rd., Fairbanks,* ☎ *907/488–6815. AE, D, MC, V. No lunch.*

$$$$ ★ **Sophie Station.** Every room has a full-size kitchen and refrigerator at this all-suite hotel near Fairbanks International Airport. ✉ *1717 University Ave., Fairbanks 99709,* ☎ *907/479–3650 or 800/528–4916,* FAX *907/479–7951. 147 rooms. Restaurant. AE, D, DC, MC, V.*

$$$$ **Westmark Fairbanks.** This full-service member of Alaska's biggest chain is built around a courtyard on a quiet street in downtown Fairbanks. Some rooms have exercise equipment. ✉ *813 Noble St., Fairbanks 99701,* ☎ *907/456–7722, 800/544–0970 for central reservations;* FAX *907/451–7478. 238 rooms. Restaurant. AE, D, DC, MC, V.*

Hot Springs

$$$$ ✕ **Chena Hot Springs Resort.** This resort, just 60 mi from Fairbanks on Chena Hot Springs Road, is the local favorite. There's a campground with RV hookups, as well as antiques-filled hotel rooms and rustic cabins with electricity but no water. Nonguests can pay to use the heated pool and eat in the restaurant. ✉ *Box 73440, Fairbanks 99707,* ☎ *907/452–7867, 800/478–4681 in AK;* FAX *907/456–3122. 47 rooms, 8 cabins. Restaurant, pool, health club. AE, D, DC, MC, V.*

$$$–$$$$ ✕ **Arctic Circle Hot Springs Resort.** A 2½-hour drive from Fairbanks on the Steese Highway, this four-story spa-hotel dates from 1930. There are also one- and two-bedroom cabins with whirlpool baths and kitchenettes. The entire complex is naturally heated by hot springs. ✉ *Box 254, Central 99730,* ☎ *907/520–5113,* FAX *907/520–5116. 24 rooms, 10 cabins. Restaurant, pool. MC, V.*

Outdoor Activities and Sports

Canoeing

The Chena River attracts canoeists, both in Fairbanks and out in the wilderness. Entry points are marked along Chena Hot Springs Road. Avoid the Tanana River, with its hidden sandbars and swift current.

Fishing

Char, grayling, and pike are abundant in the lakes and rivers of the Interior. The Chena River between Fairbanks and Chena Hot Springs is known for its grayling fishing.

Hiking and Backpacking

Skilled outdoorspeople can hike virtually anywhere in Denali National Park. There are well-marked beginner trails near the park entrance.

Rafting

Several companies run white-water trips on the thrilling Nenana River, which parallels the George Parks Highway near the Denali entrance. Try **Denali Raft Adventures** (✉ Drawer 190, Denali National Park 99755, ☎ 907/683–2234) or **McKinley Raft Tours** (✉ Box 138, Denali National Park 99755, ☎ 907/683–2392).

Sled-Dog Racing

The **North American Open Sled Dog Championship** is held in downtown Fairbanks in March. Check with the visitor center (☞ Visitor Information, *above*) for details.

Wildlife Viewing

Few places in North America can equal the wildlife-viewing opportunities at Denali National Park, where most visitors see grizzly bears, caribou, moose, and Dall sheep. Wolves and golden eagles can also sometimes be spied.

Spectator Sports

The **University of Alaska Nanooks** (☎ 907/474–7205) draw big crowds of ice hockey fans.

SOUTHWEST

Visitor Information

Southwest Alaska Municipal Conference (✉ 3300 Arctic Blvd., Suite 203, Anchorage 99503, ☎ 907/562–7380, FAX 907/562–0438).

Arriving and Departing

Alaska Airlines (☎ 800/426–0333) runs daily nonstop jet service to Kodiak Island from Anchorage. For packages to Kodiak contact **Alaska Airlines Vacations** (✉ SEARV, Box 68900, Seattle, WA 98168, ☎ 800/468–2248).

Commuter planes serve the town of King Salmon, which is just a short floatplane ride from Katmai National Park and Preserve, 290 mi southwest of Anchorage. Airlines serving King Salmon include **Alaska Airlines** (☞ *above*), **PenAir** (☎ 907/243–2323 or 800/448–4226), and Reeve Aleutian Airways (☞ *below*).

Contact **Reeve Aleutian Airways** (✉ 4700 W. International Airport Rd., Anchorage 99502, ☎ 907/243–4700 or 800/544–2248) for flight and package-tour information on the Aleutian and Pribilof islands, in the remote Bering Sea region.

Getting Around

The **Alaska Marine Highway System** (☞ Southeast, *above*) serves some Alaska Peninsula and Aleutian Islands communities in summer.

Exploring the Southwest

Kodiak

The largest island in the United States, Kodiak is home to the brown bear, North America's largest land mammal. Before the seat of colonial government was moved to Sitka, Kodiak was the original capital of Russian Alaska. Today the town is a commercial fishing center: Visitors can go halibut fishing, sea kayaking, or flightseeing for bears. Much of the rain-forest-covered island lies within 1.6-million-acre **Kodiak Island National Refuge** (☎ 907/487–2600).

Katmai National Park and Preserve

Katmai National Park and Preserve (✉ Box 7, King Salmon 99613, ☎ 907/246–3305) is a more remote and less developed park than Denali, but therein lies its charm. A lush valley within what is now the park became a land of steaming fumaroles after the 1912 eruption of Mt. Novarupta and the collapse of nearby Mt. Katmai's peak. Residents fled the area, which is now dubbed the Valley of Ten Thousand Smokes. These days the area is known for its trophy rainbow trout and salmon, as well as brown bears, which congregate near **Brooks River.** Hiking, boat tours, and coastal kayaking are other Katmai attractions. **Katmailand Inc.** (✉ 4550 Aircraft Dr., Suite 2, Anchorage, 99502, ☎ 907/243–5448 or 800/544–0551) offers tours and backcountry lodging.

The Aleutian and Pribilof Islands

For most people package tours are the only practical way to see these areas. Schedules are changeable, depending on the weather.

The **Aleutian Islands,** a volcanic, treeless archipelago of 20 large and several hundred smaller islands, stretch 1,000 mi from the Alaska Peninsula toward Japan. The Aleuts who live in the tiny settlements here work in canneries or as commercial fishermen and guides; many continue to lead subsistence lifestyles. Out here, where the wind blows constantly and fog is common, bird-watching opportunities are limitless: Look for terns, guillemots, murres, and puffins. The Japanese invaded the Aleutian Islands during World War II, and at Dutch Harbor on Unalaska Island you can still see concrete bunkers, gun batteries, and a partially sunken ship. **The Grand Aleutian Hotel** (✉ Box 9221169, Dutch Harbor 99692, ☎ 800/891–1194, FAX 907/581–7157), in Dutch Harbor, offers guided activities and tours as well as lodging.

Every spring the largest herd of northern fur seals in the world—nearly 1 million seals—comes to the tiny, volcanic **Pribilof Islands,** in the Bering Sea about 200 mi northwest of Cold Bay. Most tours fly to **St. Paul Island,** largest of the Pribilofs and home to the world's largest Aleut community (about 600 of the island's 750 year-round residents are Aleuts). The island is also the summer home of legions of birds. Contact **Reeve Aleutian Airways** (☞ Arriving and Departing, *above*) for tour information.

Next to St. Paul Island, **St. George Island** is the only other island in the Pribilof chain to be inhabited by humans. It is also a birder's paradise; more than 1.5 million seabirds nest here each summer.

THE ARCTIC

Visitor Information

Barrow and **Kotzebue:** Alaska Native Tourism Council (☞ Statewide Visitor Information, *above*). **Nome:** Convention and Visitors Bureau (✉ Box 240, Nome 99762, ☎ 907/443–5535, FAX 907/443–5832).

Arriving and Departing

Nearly all destinations in the Arctic are accessible only by plane. The only public highway that leads to the Arctic—the Dalton Highway—is open to traffic all the way to Deadhorse, on the North Slope, but is impassable in winter due to snow conditions. **Alaska Airlines Vacations** (✉ SEARV, Box 68900, Seattle, WA 98168, ☎ 800/468–2248) runs air tours of the Arctic from Anchorage and Fairbanks.

Exploring the Arctic

Gold was discovered in 1898 in **Nome,** just below the Arctic Circle. Colorful saloons and low-slung, ramshackle buildings help perpetuate its vintage gold-camp aura. **Kotzebue** is a proud Eskimo community north of Nome where salmon dries on wooden racks and Eskimo boats rest in yards. The **Living Museum of the Arctic** (☎ 907/442–3301; 🎫 free) preserves Nome's Eskimo heritage, as does a cultural camp where elders pass on traditions to the next generation. At the top of the state, tours of the **Prudhoe Bay** area explore the oil industry life there, as well as the wildlife and tundra surrounding it. Fees range from $20 for a one-hour tour to $50 for a four-hour tour; call Tour Arctic (☎ 907/659–2368) for information. In **Barrow,** the northernmost community in the United States, the sun rises on May 10 and doesn't set for nearly three months.

In the northernmost portion of the Brooks Range, the 18-million-acre ★ **Arctic National Wildlife Refuge** (☎ 907/456–0250) contains the United States' only protected Arctic coastal lands as well as millions of acres of mountains and alpine tundra. The refuge is home to one of the world's largest groups of caribou, the 160,000-member Porcupine Caribou Herd. Other residents are grizzly and polar bears, Dall sheep, wolves, musk ox, and myriad bird species. Accessible only by boat, plane, or foot, the refuge can be explored by backpacking or river running.

HAWAI'I

Updated by Steve Crohn

Capital	Honolulu
Population	1,186,600
Motto	The Life of the Land Is Perpetuated in Righteousness
State Bird	Nēnē (Hawaiian goose)
State Flower	Hibiscus
Postal Abbreviation	HI

Statewide Visitor Information

Hawai'i Visitors and Convention Bureau (✉ Royal Hawaiian Shopping Center, 2201 Kalākaua Ave., Suite A 401-A, Honolulu 96815, ☎ 808/923–1811, 800/464–2924 for brochures). **Surf Report:** ☎ 808/596–7873. **Weather:** ☎ 808/973–4381 for O'ahu weather.

Scenic Drives

On the eastern tip of O'ahu the 10-mi stretch of **Kalaniana'ole Highway** from Hanauma Bay to Waimānalo is a cliff-side road resembling U.S. 1 up the California coast. On the Big Island **Highway 19** north out of Hilo runs along the lush and rugged Hāmākua Coast to Waipi'o Valley, past sugarcane fields and spectacular ocean views. From Pā'ia to Hāna, Maui's **Hāna Highway** (Highway 36) is a winding 55-mi coastal route that spans rivers and passes tropical waterfalls. From the town of Waimea, Kaua'i's **Waimea Canyon Drive** meanders upward past panoramas of Waimea Canyon, culminating at the 4,120-ft Kalalau Lookout.

National and State Parks

National Parks

Some of Hawai'i's best National Park Service attractions are **Hawai'i Volcanoes National Park** (🎫 $10 per car; $5 on foot or by bike) **Pu'uhonua o Hōnaunau National Historic Park** (🎫 $2) and **Pu'ukoholā National Historic Site** (✉ Hwy. 270, Kawaihae, ☎ 808/882–7218; 🎫 free). **Haleakalā National Park** (☞ Maui, *below*); **Kalaupapa** (☞ Elsewhere in Hawai'i, *below*); and the **USS *Arizona*** Memorial (✉ 1 Arizona Memorial Pl., Honolulu 96818-3145, ☎ 808/422–0561; 🎫 free). A 20-minute drive west from downtown Honolulu, the memorial bridges the hulk of the USS *Arizona,* which sank with 1,102 men aboard during the attack on Pearl Harbor on December 7, 1941.

State Parks

Popular state parks include **Hāpuna State Recreation Area** (☞ The Big Island of Hawai'i, *below*), **Kōke'e State Park** (☞ Kaua'i, *below*), and **Wailua River State Park** (✉ Wailua Marina, Kapa'a, Kaua'i 96746, ☎ 808/822–5065), where you can see the sites of ancient villages and an enormous fern-laced lava tube. For information write to the **District Office of the Hawai'i Department of Land and Natural Resources,** Division of State Parks (✉ Box 621, Honolulu 96809, ☎ 808/587–0300).

HONOLULU AND WAIKĪKĪ

Honolulu, on the island of O'ahu, is the urban metropolis of the Aloha State. Here the salad of cultures is artfully tossed in a blend that is harmonious yet allows each culture to retain its distinct flavor and texture. Its downtown sector contrasts royal history with the modern-day action of a major government and business capital. Just 3½ mi from downtown is the tourist mecca of Waikīkī. Set on the sunny, dry side of O'ahu, Waikīkī provides a stunning physical setting along with the buzz of international hotel and shopping destinations.

Arriving and Departing

By Plane

Honolulu International Airport (☎ 808/836–6411) is only 20 minutes from Waikīkī. U.S. carriers serving Honolulu include American, Continental, Delta, Hawaiian, Northwest, TWA, and United. A cab from the airport to downtown costs about $20 plus tip. **TransHawaiian Services** (☎ 808/566–7333) runs a shuttle service to Waikīkī (💵 $8 one-way, $14 round-trip). Some hotels also provide pickup and shuttle service; ask when you make reservations.

Getting Around Honolulu and Waikīkī

By Car

Don't bother renting a car unless you're planning to travel outside Waikīkī. When making hotel or plane reservations, ask if there's a car tie-in. Driving in rush hour (6:30 AM–8:30 AM and 3:30 PM–5:30 PM) is frustrating because of traffic, parking limitations, and numerous one-way streets. At peak times—summer, Christmas vacation, and February—reservations are a must. **Avis** (☎ 800/831–8000), **Hertz** (☎ 800/654–3131), and **Budget** (☎ 800/527–7000) are among the many national agencies with locations in Honolulu.

By Public Transportation

You can go anywhere on the island for $1 on Honolulu's municipal transportation system, affectionately known as **The Bus** (☎ 808/848–5555); *and* you'll receive a free transfer if you ask for it when boarding. Exact change is required, and dollar bills are accepted. A four-day pass for visitors costs $10 and is sold at the more than 30 ABC Stores in Waikīkī. Monthly passes are available for $25.

By Taxi

You can usually get a cab outside your hotel. Meter rates are $1.50–$2 at the drop of the flag, plus $1.95 for each additional mile. The two biggest cab companies are **Charley's** (☎ 808/531–1333) and **SIDA of Hawai'i** (☎ 808/836–0011).

Orientation Tours

The **Pearl Harbor and Punchbowl Tour** offered by Polynesian Adventure Tours (☎ 808/833–3000) includes a Navy launch out to the *Arizona* Memorial. In downtown Honolulu the **Chinatown Walking Tour** (☎ 808/533–3181) provides a look at O'ahu's oldest neighborhood.

Exploring Honolulu and Waikīkī

In Hawai'i directions are often given as *mauka* (toward the mountains) and *makai* (toward the ocean), or they may refer to Diamond Head (east, toward the famous volcanic landmark) and *ewa* (west).

Downtown Honolulu

Aloha Tower Marketplace (✉ 101 Ala Moana Blvd., at Piers 8, 9, and 10, ☎ 808/528–5700 or 800/378–6937) has two stories of shops, kiosks, and indoor and outdoor restaurants—some with live entertainment—right next to Honolulu Harbor. The landmark 10-story Aloha Tower is its anchor; to view the harbor take the free ride up to the observation deck. A trolley runs regularly between the marketplace and Waikīkī.

Honolulu and Waikīkī

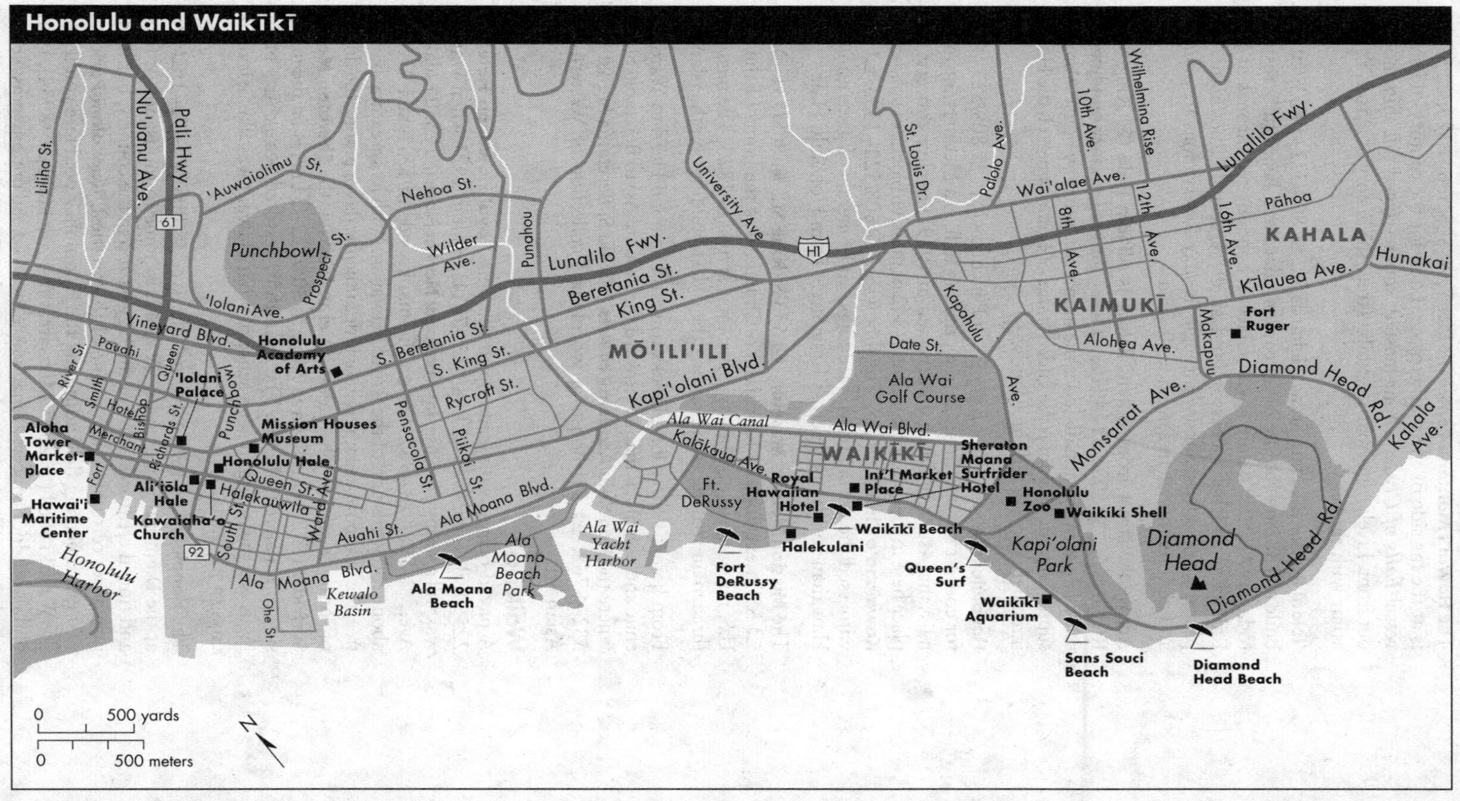

The **Hawai'i Maritime Center** (✉ Pier 7, ☎ 808/536–6373; 🎟 $7.50) is at the far side of the marketplace. Look for the century-old sailing vessel *Falls of Clyde,* a four-masted, square-rigged tall ship moored out front. Lively, informative exhibits trace the history of Hawai'i's love affair with the sea.

'Iolani Palace (✉ King St. at Richards St., ☎ 808/522–0832; 🎟 $8), built in 1882 on the site of an earlier palace and beautifully restored today, is America's only royal palace. It contains the thrones of King Kalākaua and his successor (and sister) Queen Lili'uokalani. The palace is closed from Sunday through Tuesday. Reservations are essential, and children under five are not allowed.

Across the street from 'Iolani Palace is **Ali'iōla Hale** (✉ King St. at Richards St., ☎ 808/539–4919; 🎟 free), the old judiciary building that served as parliament hall under the monarchy and now houses the state supreme court. In front is the gilded statue of Kamehameha I, the Hawaiian chief who unified the islands.

Honolulu Hale (✉ 530 S. King St., at Punchbowl St., ☎ 808/527–6666 for concert information; 🎟 free), the city hall, is a Mediterranean Renaissance–style building constructed in 1929. Free live concerts take place here in the evenings. Built in 1842 of massive blocks of solid coral, **Kawaiaha'o Church** (✉ 957 Punchbowl St., ☎ 808/522–1333; 🎟 free) witnessed the coronations, weddings, and funerals of generations of Hawaiian royalty; it's across King Street from Honolulu Hale.

The **Mission Houses Museum** (✉ 553 S. King St., ☎ 808/531–0481; 🎟 $5), next door to Kawaiaha'o Church, was the home of the first U.S. missionaries to Hawai'i after their arrival in 1820. The mission's three main structures are among the oldest buildings on the islands.

From here it's three long blocks toward Diamond Head to Ward Avenue and one block mauka (toward the mountains) to Beretania Street, where the **Honolulu Academy of Arts** (✉ 900 S. Beretania St., ☎ 808/532–8768; 🎟 $4) houses a world-class collection of Western and Asian art.

Waikīkī

A paved ocean walk leads up to the pink **Royal Hawaiian Hotel** (✉ 2259 Kalākaua Ave., ☎ 808/923–7311), built in 1921 when Waikīkī was still a sleepy paradise. **International Market Place** (✉ 2330 Kalākaua Ave., ☎ 808/923–9871) is on the mauka side of Kalākaua Avenue, about 100 yards east of the Royal Hawaiian. With its spreading banyan tree, the outdoor bazaar retains a little authentic flavor among the dozens of souvenir stands. The oldest hotel in Waikīkī, the **Sheraton Moana Surfrider** (✉ 2365 Kalākaua Ave., ☎ 808/922–3111) is on the makai side of Kalākaua Avenue. The beautifully restored Beaux Arts building is worth visiting to get a sense of what Hawai'i was like before the days of jet travel.

The **Honolulu Zoo** (✉ 151 Kapahulu Ave., ☎ 808/971–7171;🎟 $6), at the Diamond Head end of Waikīkī, is home to thousands of furry and finned creatures. It's not the biggest zoo in the country, but its 40 lush acres certainly make it one of the prettiest. **Kapi'olani Park** is a vast green playing field adjoining the Honolulu Zoo. Here you'll find the Waikīkī Shell (✉ 2805 Monsarrat Ave., ☎ 808/924–8934), Honolulu's outdoor concert arena, where locals spread out on "grass seats" (the lawn) with picnics, to hear some of Hawai'i's best musicians and visiting pop stars. Most concerts are held between May 1 and Labor Day. Check the newspapers to see what's playing. Next door to the Waikīkī Shell, the **Kodak Hula Show** (☎ 808/833–1661; 🎟 free) has been wowing crowds for more than 50 years. It takes place on Tuesday, Wednesday, and Thursday mornings at 10.

The **Waikīkī Aquarium** (✉ 2777 Kalākaua Ave., ☎ 808/923–9741; 🎫 $6) harbors more than 300 species of marine life.

The steep hike to the summit of **Diamond Head** (✉ Monsarrat Ave. near 18th Ave., ☎ 808/971–2525) gives you a marvelous view of O'ahu's southern coastline. The entrance is about 1 mi above Kapi'olani Park. Drive through the tunnel to the inside of the crater, and then park and start walking.

Dining

The Aloha State is known for fine ethnic food—especially Chinese, Japanese, and Thai—and the culinarily spectacular Hawai'i Regional cuisine, based on fresh local produce and seafood. For price ranges *see* Chart 1 (A) *in* On the Road with Fodor's.

$$$$ ★ ✕ **La Mer.** This exotic, oceanfront Mandalay mansion serves some of Hawai'i's best contemporary cuisine. A standout entrée is *onaga* (red snapper) fillet accompanied by a confit of tomato, truffle juice, and fried basil. ✉ *Halekūlani, 2199 Kālia Rd., Waikīki,* ☎ *808/923–2311. Reservations essential. Jacket required. AE, MC, V. No lunch.*

$$$–$$$$ ★ ✕ **Bali by the Sea.** The glorious ocean-side views of Waikīkī Beach might be upstaged here by entrées such as roast duck with black-currant-and-litchi glaze or *kiawe 'ōpakapaka* (mesquite-grilled snapper). The pastry chef and sommelier are both well recognized far and wide. ✉ *Hilton Hawaiian Village, 2005 Kālia Rd., Waikīki,* ☎ *808/941–2254. Reservations essential. AE, D, DC, MC, V. No dinner Sun.*

$$$–$$$$ ★ ✕ **Sam Choy's.** His motto is "Never trust a skinny chef," and indeed, Choy's broad girth and even broader smile let you know you'll be well taken care of. The theme is upscale local, as the Hawai'i–born chef contemporizes the foods he grew up with. The result? Brie–stuffed wontons with pineapple marmalade, seared ahi seasoned with ginger, and roasted duck with orange sauce. Portions are huge. ✉ *449 Kapahulu Ave., 2nd level,* ☎ *808/732–8645. AE, MC, V. No lunch.*

$$$ ✕ **Hau Tree Lāna'i.** Right beside the sand at Kaimana Beach you can dine under graceful hau trees, listening to the waves. For breakfast try the Belgian waffle or salmon omelet. Two standout dinner entrées are the jumbo shrimp fettuccine and a bleu-cheese-and-herb-crusted New York steak. ✉ *New Otani Kaimana Beach Hotel, 2863 Kalākaua Ave., Waikīki,* ☎ *808/921–7066. Reservations essential. AE, D, DC, MC, V.*

$$–$$$ ★ ✕ **Alan Wong's.** In his fabulous, low-key restaurant, Wong focuses heavily on Hawaiian-grown products to keep the flavors super-fresh, and he's utterly creative, turning local "grinds" into gourmet treats. Garlic-mashed potatoes come with a black bean salsa, grilled pork chops with a coconut-ginger sweet potato puree. Don't miss the coconut sorbet served in a chocolate and macadamia nut shell, surrounded by exotic fruits. Finding the restaurant can be difficult: Look for a white apartment building and a small sign after a parking garage, where your car can be valet parked. ✉ *McCully Court, 1857 S. King St., 3rd floor,* ☎ *808/949–2526. AE, MC, V. No lunch.*

$$–$$$ ★ ✕ **Golden Dragon.** Chef Steve Chiang is known for his unconventional Cantonese and nouvelle-Chinese cuisine; signature dishes include stir-fried lobster with *haupia* (coconut pudding), and Szechuan beef. ✉ *Hilton Hawaiian Village, 2005 Kālia Rd., Waikīki,* ☎ *808/946–5336. Reservations essential. AE, D, DC, MC, V. No lunch.*

$$–$$$ ★ ✕ **Keo's Thai Cuisine.** Hollywood celebrities have discovered this orchid-filled nook, where the Evil Jungle Prince (chicken, shrimp, or vegetables in a sauce of fresh basil, coconut milk, and red chili) is tops. ✉ *625 Kapahulu Ave., Honolulu,* ☎ *808/737–8240. Reservations essential. AE, D, DC, MC, V. No lunch.*

$$–$$$ ✕ **Roy's.** Two walls of windows allow you to gaze out at Maunalua Bay and Diamond Head in the distance. The noisy two-story restaurant has a devoted following, thanks to its Euro–Asian–Hawai'an cuisine. It's hard to find a better blackened ahi in a hot, soy-mustard sauce. Of the individual pizzas, the best is topped with vine-ripened tomatoes, goat cheese, and roasted garlic. ✉ *Hawai'i Kai Corporate Plaza, 6600 Kalaniana'ole Hwy.,* ☎ *808/396–7697. AE, D, DC, MC, V.*

$$–$$$ ★ ✕ **3660 On The Rise.** Ten minutes from Waikīkī, in the up-and-coming culinary center of Kaimukī, this stellar restaurant is known for homegrown ingredients combined with European flavors: Dungeness crab cakes served atop angel-hair pasta with a ginger-cilantro aioli; fettuccine laced with sautéed shellfish and grilled shiitake mushrooms. Light hardwoods, frosted glass, green marble, and black granite create a casual yet high-style ambience. ✉ *3660 Wai'alae Ave.,* ☎ *808/737–1177. AE, DC, MC, V.*

$–$$ ✕ **California Pizza Kitchen.** This pair of dining and watering holes for young fast-trackers is worth the more-than-likely wait for a table. At the Kāhala site, a glass atrium with tiled and mirrored walls and one side open to the shopping mall creates a sidewalk-café effect. Pizzas have unusual toppings: Thai chicken, Peking duck, Caribbean shrimp. Pasta is made fresh daily on the premises.✉ *Kāhala Mall, 4211 Wai'alae Ave., Honolulu,* ☎ *808/737–9446;* ✉ *1910 Ala Moana Blvd., Honolulu,* ☎ *808/955–5161. Reservations not accepted. AE, D, DC, MC, V.*

$ ✕ **'Ono Hawaiian Foods.** There's usually a line outside after about 5 PM at this no-frills storefront restaurant. Locals come for Island innovations such as poi, *lomilomi* salmon (salmon massaged until tender and served with minced onions and tomatoes), and *laulau* (steamed bundle of ti leaves containing pork, butterfish, and taro tops). ✉ *726 Kapahulu Ave., Honolulu,* ☎ *808/737–2275. Reservations not accepted. No credit cards. Closed Sun.*

Lodging

O'ahu's best accommodations are in or near Waikīkī, with a few places of note in Honolulu. Except for the peak months of January, February, and August, you'll have no trouble getting a room if you call first. For bed-and-breakfasts contact **Bed and Breakfast Hawai'i** (✉ Box 449, Kapa'a 96746, ☎ 808/822–7771 or 800/733–1632, FAX 808/822–2723). For price ranges *see* Chart 2 (A) *in* On the Road with Fodor's.

$$$$ ★ 🏨 **Halekūlani.** This serene and elegantly modern hotel has beautifully detailed marble-and-wood rooms, some with breathtaking ocean views, plus two of the finest restaurants in Honolulu. It's right on Waikīkī beach, with lovely views of Diamond Head. ✉ *2199 Kālia Rd., Waikīkī96815,* ☎ *808/923–2311 or 800/367–2343,* FAX *808/926–8004. 456 rooms. 3 restaurants, pool, exercise room. AE, DC, MC, V.*

$$$$ 🏨 **Hilton Hawaiian Village.** Waikīkī's largest resort includes four towers, a botanical garden, and a pond with penguins. Rooms are done in raspberry or aqua, with rattan and bamboo furnishings. ✉ *2005 Kālia Rd., Waikīkī, 96815,* ☎ *808/949–4321 or 800/445–8667,* FAX *808/947–7898. 2,542 rooms. 6 restaurants, pools, exercise room, beach. AE, D, DC, MC, V.*

$$$$ ★ 🏨 **'Ihilani Resort & Spa.** On O'ahu's western shore, 'Ihilani is a 25-minute drive from Honolulu International Airport. A glass-dome atrium is the centerpiece of the sleek, 15-story hotel. Guest rooms have

marble bathrooms with deep soaking tubs, and private lānai, many with ocean views. The 35,000-square-ft 'Ihilani Spa presents everything from seaweed baths to stair-climbers. ✉ *92–1001 'Ōlani St., Kapolei 96707,* ☎ *808/679–0079 or 800/626–4446,* FAX *808/679–0295. 387 rooms. 4 restaurants, pools, spa, golf, tennis. AE, DC, MC, V.*

$$$$ **Kahala Mandarin Oriental Hawai'i.** Minutes away from Waikīkī, on the quiet side of Diamond Head, this elegant oceanfront hotel is an oasis of peace and comfort. Guest rooms are in off-white hues, with touches of Asia and old Hawai'i in the art and furnishings. Banquet rooms look out over a koi-filled fishpond and rock lagoon. ✉ *5000 Kahala Ave., Honolulu 96816,* ☎ *808/734–2211 or 800/367–2525,* FAX *808/737–2478. 370 rooms. 2 restaurants, pool, exercise room, beach. AE, D, DC, MC, V.*

$$$$ **Waikīkī Parc.** Though its main entrance is down a narrow side street, this hotel is just one block from Waikīkī's beach. Guest rooms are done in cool blues and whites, with lots of rattan and plush carpeting. Added draws are the fine Japanese restaurant, Kacho; and the lovely Parc Café, known for its reasonably priced all-you-can-eat buffets. ✉ *2233 Helumoa Rd., Waikīkī 96815,* ☎ *808/921–7272 or 800/422–0450,* FAX *808/923–1336. 298 rooms. 2 restaurants, pool. AE, D, DC, MC, V.*

$$$–$$$$ ★ **New Otani Kaimana Beach Hotel.** Polished to a shine, this hotel is open to the trade winds—right on the beach at the quiet end of Waikīkī, practically at the foot of Diamond Head. Get a room with an ocean view, if possible, and dine at least once at the Hau Tree Lānai. ✉ *2863 Kalākaua Ave., Honolulu 96815,* ☎ *808/923–1555 or 800/356–8264,* FAX *808/922–9404. 125 rooms. 2 restaurants. AE, D, DC, MC, V.*

$$$ **Aston at the Waikīkī Banyan.** Families enjoy this high-rise condominium resort near Diamond Head, one block from Waikīkī Beach and two blocks from the Honolulu Zoo. One-bedroom suites have daily maid service and private lānai. Look for the fishpond in the lobby area. ✉ *201 'Ōhua Ave., Honolulu 96815,* ☎ *808/922–0555 or 800/922–7866,* FAX *808/922–8785. 876 suites, Pool, tennis. AE, D, DC, MC, V.*

$$$ **Outrigger Waikīkī Hotel.** At this beachfront property in the heart of the best shopping and dining action, rooms have a Polynesian motif, and each has a lānai. ✉ *2335 Kalākaua Ave., Waikīkī 96815,* ☎ *808/923–0711 or 800/688–7444,* FAX *800/622–4852. 530 rooms. 6 restaurants, pool. AE, D, DC, MC, V.*

$$–$$$ **Mānoa Valley Inn.** Tucked away in Mānoa Valley, just 2 mi from Waikīkī, this stately hotel built in 1919 features a complimentary Continental breakfast buffet on a shady lānai, and fresh tropical fruit and cheese in the afternoon. The country-style rooms have antique four-poster beds. ✉ *2001 Vancouver Dr., Honolulu 96822,* ☎ *808/947–6019 or 800/535–0085,* FAX *800/633–5085. 8 guest rooms, 4 with private bath; 1 cottage. CP. AE, DC, MC, V.*

$$ **Outrigger Royal Islander.** This inexpensive link in the Outrigger hotel chain is just a two-minute walk from a very nice section of Waikīkī Beach. Some rooms have ocean or park views and a few suites have kitchenettes; all accommodations have private lānai. Guests have access to pools at other Outrigger hotels. ✉ *2164 Kālia Rd., Honolulu 96815,* ☎ *808/922–1961 or 800/688–7444,* FAX *808/923–4632. 101 rooms. AE, D, DC, MC, V.*

$–$$ **Waikīkī.** One block from the beach in Waikīkī, this eight-story hotel is convenient and clean; many rooms have private lānai. For a little extra you can rent a refrigerator for your room. ✉ *2424 Koa Ave., Honolulu 96815,* ☎ *808/926–8841 or 800/367–5004,* FAX *808/924–3770. 72 rooms. Restaurant. AE, DC, MC, V.*

$ **Royal Grove Hotel.** This small flamingo-pink hotel has rooms with kitchenettes. ✉ *15 Uluniu Ave., Waikīkī 96815,* ☎ *808/923–7691,* FAX *808/922–7508. 85 rooms. Pool. AE, D, DC, MC, V.*

Nightlife and the Arts

Cocktail and Dinner Shows

Don Ho (✉ Waikīkī Beachcomber Hotel, 2300 Kalākaua Ave., ☎ 808/931–3009). Waikīkī's old pro still packs them in to his Polynesian revue with its cast of attractive Hawaiian performers. There's a candlelight dinner show Tuesday–Friday and Sunday at 7 and a cocktail show at 9. Magician John Hirokawa displays mystifying sleight-of-hand in **Magic of Polynesia** (✉ Hilton Hawaiian Village Dome, 2005 Kālia Rd., ☎ 808/949–4321), with hula dancers and island music. Shows are nightly at 6:30 and 8:45.

Dinner Cruises

Patterned after an ancient Polynesian vessel, ***Ali'i Kai* Catamaran** (✉ Pier 8, Honolulu, ☎ 808/524–6694) takes passengers on a deluxe dinner cruise, complete with two open bars and a Polynesian show. **Windjammer Cruises** (✉ Pier 7, Honolulu, ☎ 808/537–1122) ferries you along O'ahu's south shores on the 1,000-passenger *Kulamanu,* done up like a clipper ship.

Lū'au

Royal Hawaiian Lū'au (✉ 2259 Kalākaua Ave., Waikīkī, ☎ 808/923–7311) takes place at the venerable Royal Hawaiian and is a notch above many other commercial lū'au presentations on the island.

Nightclubs

At **Lewers Lounge** (✉ Halekūlani, 2199 Kālia Rd., ☎ 808/923–2311), Loretta Ables sings contemporary jazz and standards Tuesday–Saturday 9 PM–12:30 AM. A vocalist-pianist sits in Sunday and Monday 9 PM–12:30 AM. The **Paradise Lounge,** at Hilton Hawaiian Village (✉ 2005 Kālia Rd., ☎ 808/949–4321), has all kinds of acts (Friday–Saturday 8–midnight). **Nick's Fishmarket** (✉ Waikīkī Gateway Hotel, 2070 Kalākaua Ave., ☎ 808/955–6333) is probably the most comfortable of Waikīkī's upscale dance lounges, with an elegant crowd, smooth music, and an intimate, dark atmosphere. At **Rumours** (✉ Ala Moana Hotel, 410 Atkinson St., ☎ 808/955–4811), there's disco dancing with high-tech lights.

Theater

The **Diamond Head Theater** (✉ 520 Makapu'u Ave., ☎ 808/734–0274) is five minutes away from Waikīkī, right next to Diamond Head. Its repertoire includes a little of everything: musical comedies as well as experimental, contemporary, and classical dramas.The **John F. Kennedy Theater** (✉ 1770 East–West Rd., ☎ 808/956–7655) at the University of Hawai'i's Manoa campus is the setting for eclectic dramatic offerings—everything from Kabuki, Noh, and Chinese opera to contemporary musical comedy.

Outdoor Activities and Sports

Golf

Ala Wai Golf Course (✉ 404 Kapahulu Ave., ☎ 808/733–7387), on Waikīkī's mauka end, is quite popular; call ahead. Advance reservations are also recommended at the 6,350-yard **Hawai'i Kai Championship Course** and the neighboring 2,386-yard **Hawai'i Kai Executive Course** (✉ 8902 Kalaniana'ole Hwy., Honolulu, ☎ 808/395–2358 for either).

Tennis

In the Waikīkī area there are four free public courts at **Kapi'olani Tennis Courts** (✉ 2748 Kalākaua Ave., ☎ 808/971–2525); nine at the **Diamond Head Tennis Center** (✉ 3908 Pākī Ave., ☎ 808/971–7150);

and 10 at **Ala Moana Park** (✉ Makai side of Ala Moana Blvd., ☎ 808/522–7031).

Water Sports

Seemingly endless ocean options—from sailing to surfing—can be arranged through any hotel travel desk or beach concession. Try the **Waikīkī Beach Center,** next to the Sheraton Moana Surfrider, or the **C & K Beach Service,** by the Hilton Hawaiian Village (☎ no phones).

Sailing lessons may be arranged through **Tradewind Charters** (☎ 808/973–0311). For scuba diving, **South Seas Aquatics** (☎ 808/922–0852) offers two-tank boat dives for $75. **Ocean Works, Inc.** (☎ 808/926–3483) has a four-day scuba-diving course.

Hanauma Bay is famous for snorkeling. **Hanauma Bay Snorkeling Excursions** (☎ 808/941–5555) runs to and from Waikīkī. **Hanauma Bay Snorkeling Tours & Rentals** (☎ 808/944–8828) has a half-day Hanauma Bay excursion.

Beaches

Honolulu

Ala Moana Beach Park, across from Ala Moana Shopping Center, has a protective reef that keeps waters calm. Facilities include bathhouses, indoor and outdoor showers, lifeguards, concession stands, and tennis courts. **Hanauma Bay,** a 30-minute drive (or a $1 bus ride) east of Waikīkī, is a designated marine preserve with coral reefs and turquoise waters. Food and snorkel-equipment rental concessions, changing rooms, and showers are among the facilities.

Waikīkī

Fort DeRussy Beach, the widest part of Waikīkī Beach, has volleyball courts, picnic tables, showers, dressing rooms, and food stands. **Queen's Surf,** across from the Honolulu Zoo, is named for Queen Lili'uokalani's beach house, which once stood here. The sand is soft, and there are plenty of shade trees and picnic tables; there's also a changing house with showers. The beach attracts a mixture of families and gays.

Shopping

Just outside Waikīkī is the **Ala Moana Shopping Center** (✉ 1450 Ala Moana Blvd., ☎ 808/946–2811), a 50-acre open-air mall with a host of major department stores, including Liberty House, Hawai'i's homegrown department store chain. **Ward Centre** (✉ 1200 Ala Moana Blvd., ☎ 808/591–8451) has upscale boutiques and eateries. **Ward Warehouse** (✉ 1050 Ala Moana Blvd.) is a two-story mall with 65 shops and restaurants. **Aloha Tower Marketplace** (☞ Exploring Honolulu and Waikīkī, *above*) bills itself as a festival marketplace. Along with food and entertainment, it has shops and kiosks selling mostly visitor-oriented merchandise, from expensive sunglasses to refrigerator magnets.

In Waikīkī shopping options include the **International Market Place** (☞ Exploring Honolulu and Waikīkī, *above*). The **Royal Hawaiian Shopping Center** (✉ 2201 Kalākaua Ave., ☎ 808/922–0588) is three stories high and three blocks long, with 120 stores.

Side Trip to the North Shore

Arriving and Departing

From the Diamond Head end of Waikīkī go toward the mountains on Kapahulu Avenue and follow the signs to the Lunalilo Freeway (H–1). Take H–1 northwest to H–2 through Wahiawa. Then follow the signs to Hale'iwa, which marks the official beginning of the north shore.

What to See and Do

The **North Shore** of O'ahu is the flip side of Honolulu. Instead of high-rises there are old homes and stores, some converted into businesses catering to tourists, surfers, and beach bums. The area's wide, uncrowded beaches, rural countryside, and slower pace are reminiscent of Hawai'i's other islands.

Hale'iwa is a sleepy plantation town that has come of age with contemporary boutiques and galleries. Northeast of Hale'iwa the road continues past such beaches as Waimea Bay, where winter waves can crest at 30 ft. Waimea Valley, home of **Waimea Valley Park** (✉ 59-864 Kamehameha Hwy., Hale'iwa, ☎ 808/638–8511) and once an ancient Hawaiian community, is a lush garden setting with wildlife, walks, and cliff-diving shows. You can have a free hula lesson here.

East of Hale'iwa is the **Polynesian Cultural Center** (✉ 55–370 Kamehameha Hwy., Laie, ☎ 808/293–3333 or 808/923–1861; 🎫 $55, includes dinner), 40 acres containing lagoons and seven re-created South Pacific villages, with a spectacular evening lū'au and revue. The center is closed on Sunday.

THE BIG ISLAND OF HAWAI'I

Nearly twice as large as all the other Hawaiian Islands combined, this youngest of the chain is still growing: Since 1983 lava flowing from Kīlauea, the world's most active volcano, has added more than 70 acres to the island. In a land of South Seas superlatives, the Big Island is also the Aloha State's most diverse region. You can hike into volcanic craters, catch marlin, visit *paniolo* (cowboy) country, tour orchid farms and waterfalls, or simply sunbathe along 266 mi of coastline.

Visitor Information

Information and brochures are dispensed at the **Hawai'i Visitors and Convention Bureau** (HVCB) booths at Big Island airports and at HVCB offices in Hilo and Kailua-Kona. ✉ *250 Keawe St., Hilo,* ☎ *808/961–5797,* FAX *808/961–2126;* ✉ *75-5719 Ali'i Dr., Kailua-Kona,* ☎ *808/329–7787,* FAX *808/326–7563.*

Arriving and Departing

Visitors to the west side of the island fly into **Kona International Airport** (☎ 808/329–2484). Those staying on the east side fly into **Hilo International Airport** (☎ 808/934–5801). Both airports are served by Aloha and Hawaiian airlines; United has direct flights from the mainland to Kona International.

Exploring the Big Island

The Big Island is so large and varied that it's best to split up your exploring itinerary. You might spend a night in the county seat of Hilo, visit the paniolo town of Waimea, head to Volcanoes National Park for some hiking, then wind up on the west coast, home of the best beaches, weather, and nightlife.

Hilo and the Hamakua Coast

Hilo is nicknamed the City of Rainbows because of its frequent showers, but rain or shine, this east coast town is truly beautiful. You can take a self-guided walking tour of downtown Hilo and its historic buildings with the help of a "Discover Downtown Hilo" map from the **Lyman House Memorial Museum** (✉ 276 Haili St., Hilo, ☎ 808/935–5021; 🎫 $4.50 with guided tour, map $1.50).

Banyan Drive, in Hilo, is lined with huge, leafy banyan trees with dangling aerial roots. They were planted along here in the '30s by visiting luminaries such as Amelia Earhart and Franklin Delano Roosevelt; look for their names on plaques on the trees.

'Akaka Falls State Park, where two waterfalls provide dramatic photo opportunities, is about 10 mi north of Hilo and 5 mi inland off Highway 19. **Honoka'a,** one of the sleepy little towns along Highway 19 north of Hilo, is where the first macadamia trees were planted in Hawai'i in 1881. **Waipi'o** lies 8 mi west of Honoka'a on Highway 240. Arrange here for a four-wheel-drive tour of **Waipi'o Valley** (☎ 808/775–7121)—the least strenuous way to visit the valley's dramatic 2,000-ft cliffs and 1,200-ft waterfalls. The view from an overlook at the end of the highway is spectacular.

If you drive cross-island over to the west coast from here, stop at **Waimea** (also known by its older name, Kamuela), home to the **Parker Ranch Visitor Center and Museum** (✉ Off Hwy. 19, ☎ 808/885–7655). Several residences are open on the property and a prestigious art collection is on display. It's a 90-minute drive from Hilo.

Hawai'i Volcanoes National Park

Hawai'i Volcanoes National Park, a 344-square-mi park established in 1916, features an abundance of attractions inspired by Kīlauea. Just beyond the park entrance, 30 mi southwest of Hilo on Highway 11, is **Kīlauea Visitor Center** (☎ 808/967–7184), open daily 7:45–5, where displays and a movie focus on past eruptions. **Volcano House** (☎ 808/967–7321), dating from 1941, is a charming lodge with a huge stone fireplace. Windows in the restaurant and bar provide picture-perfect views of Kīlauea Caldera and its steaming fire pit, Halema'uma'u Crater. Drive around the caldera to see the **Thomas A. Jaggar Museum** (☎ 808/967–7643), with seismographs and filmstrips of current and previous eruptions. *Park Headquarters:* ✉ *Highway Belt Rd. (Hwy. 11), Box 52, Hawai'i Volcanoes National Park 96718,* ☎ *808/985–6000;* 🎫 *$10 per car, $5 on foot or bike, $20 annual pass.*

Kailua-Kona

Kailua Pier is the center of much of the action in this seaside village on the west coast. During the sportfishing tournaments each summer, daily catches are weighed in here. In October it's the jumping-off point for the **Ironman Triathlon** (☞ Festivals and Seasonal Events *in* the Alaska and Hawai'i introduction). A short walk from the pier, **Hulihe'e Palace** (✉ 75-5718 Ali'i Dr., ☎ 808/329–1877; 🎫 $5) is one of only three royal palaces in America. Tour guides can fill you in on the royal lifestyle here, but the oversize doors and koa-wood furniture will more graphically illustrate how huge some of the early Hawaiian people were. During weekday afternoons hula *hālau* (schools) rehearse on the grounds.

A boat shuttles passengers from Kailua Pier to the 65-ft ***Atlantis IV* submarine** (✉ 75–5669 Ali'i Dr., ☎ 808/329–6626; 🎫 $79), which feels more like an amusement park ride than the real thing. A large glass dome in the bow and 13 viewing ports on the sides give up to 48 passengers clear views of the watery world outside.

Kohala Coast

Tour the Kohala Coast by driving north from Kailua-Kona on Highway 19 along the base of Mt. Hualālai, past sweeping stretches of old lava flows. When you get to the split in the road 33 mi from Kailua-Kona, turn left on Highway 270 toward Kawaihae and stop at the **Pu'ukōhola National Historic Site** (☎ 808/882–7218). The visitor center tells the story of the three stone *heiau* (temples), one of them submerged just offshore, built here by King Kamehameha's men in 1791.

Dining and Lodging

With so many good restaurants on the scene, choosing a place to eat in the western part of the Big Island is difficult. The Kohala Coast is somewhat pricey, although Hilo dining has remained fairly inexpensive and family oriented. The same is true of accommodations. You can find good deals on charming accommodations by contacting **Hawai'i's Best Bed and Breakfasts** (✉ Box 563, Kamuela 96743, ☎ 808/885–4550 or 800/262–9912). For price ranges *see* Charts 1 (A) and 2 (A) *in* On the Road with Fodor's.

Hilo

$$–$$$ ✕ **Café Pesto.** Even folks who don't like pizza like the kind made here. Sample pizza *al pesto,* with sun-dried tomatoes, eggplant, and fresh basil pesto, or order seafood risotto made with sweet Thai chili, Hawaiian spiny lobster, jumbo scallops, and tiger prawns. ✉ *308 Kamehameha Ave.,* ☎ *808/969–6640. AE, D, DC, MC, V.*

$$–$$$ ★ ✕ **Harrington's.** A popular and reliable steak-and-seafood restaurant, Harrington's has a dining lānai that extends out over the water. The mahimahi meunière and the Slavic steak (thinly sliced and slathered with garlic butter) are outstanding. ✉ *135 Kalaniana'ole St.,* ☎ *808/961–4966. MC, V.*

$$–$$$$ 🏨 **Hawai'i Naniloa Hotel.** Ask for a room with an ocean or bay view when you book at this attractively modern hotel. The glass-walled exercise room has wraparound oceanfront views. ✉ *93 Banyan Dr., 96720,* ☎ *808/969–3333 or 800/367–5360,* FAX *808/969–6622. 325 rooms. 2 restaurants, pools, golf, health club. AE, DC, MC, V.*

$–$$ 🏨 **Dolphin Bay Hotel.** All units have kitchens in this clean, homey hotel in a lovely, green Hawaiian garden setting four blocks from Hilo Bay. ✉ *333 'Iliahi St., Hilo 96720,* ☎ *808/935–1466,* FAX *808/935–1523. 13 rooms, 4 1-bedroom units, 1 2-bedroom unit. MC, V.*

Kailua-Kona

$$–$$$$ ✕ **Jameson's by the Sea.** Sit outside next to the ocean or inside by the picture windows for glorious sunset views over Magic Sands Beach. The co-owner and chef serves three or four island fish specials daily plus a tasty baked shrimp stuffed with crab and garnished with hollandaise sauce. ✉ *77–6452 Ali'i Dr.,* ☎ *808/329–3195. AE, D, DC, MC, V. No lunch weekends.*

$$–$$$ ★ 🏨 **King Kamehameha's Kona Beach Hotel.** Although its rooms are not particularly special, this is the only centrally located Kailua-Kona hotel—right next to the pier—with a white-sand beach. ✉ *75–5660 Palani Rd., Kailua-Kona 96740,* ☎ *808/329–2911 or 800/367–6060,* FAX *808/329–4602. 460 rooms. 2 restaurants, pool, tennis, beach. AE, D, DC, MC, V.*

$$ 🏨 **Kona Islander Inn.** Turn-of-the-century plantation-style architecture in a setting of palms and torch-lit paths make this apartment-style hotel, across the street from Waterfront Row, a good value. Of the 145 condominiums that make up the property, 40 are available for rent. Weekly rates are available.✉ *75-5776 Kuakini Hwy., Kailua-Kona 96740,* ☎ *808/329–3181 or 800/535–0085,* FAX *808/326–4137. 40 condominiums for rent. Pool. AE, D, DC, MC, V.*

Kohala Coast and Waimea

$$$–$$$$ ★ ✕ **CanoeHouse.** In this open-air beachfront restaurant surrounded by fishponds, you can sample pesto-seared scallops with roasted taro and guava sauce, or grilled Korean-style chicken with red Thai curry-coconut sauce and pineapple salsa. ✉ *Mauna Lani Bay Hotel, 68–1400 Mauna Lani Dr., Kohala Coast,* ☎ *808/885–6622. AE, D, DC, MC, V.*

$$–$$$ ★ ✕ **Merriman's.** Peter Merriman earns rave reviews for his imaginative use of fresh, local ingredients, including vegetarian selections. Wok-

charred *ahi* fish is a favorite entrée. ✉ *Opelo Plaza II corner of Rte. 19 and Opelo Rd., Kamuela,* ☎ *808/885–6822. AE, MC, V.*

$$$$ ★ **Kona Village Resort.** Accommodations at this resort 15 mi north of Kailua-Kona are in thatched-roof bungalows by the sea or around fishponds. The extra-large rooms have no telephones, TVs, or radios but do come with ceiling fans and bright tropical prints. ✉ *Box 1299, Kailua-Kona 96745,* ☎ *808/325–5555 or 800/367–5290,* FAX *808/325–5124. 125 units. 2 restaurants, pools, tennis, health club, beach. FAP. AE, DC, MC, V. Closed 1 wk in Dec.*

$$$$ ★ **Orchid at Mauna Lani Resort.** This ITT Sheraton hotel sits on 32 beachfront acres. Rooms are handsome and traditional, with massive highboys and marble bathrooms. Sailing, snorkeling, and scuba are available, and there's a protected swimming lagoon. The hotel hosts the annual Big Island Bounty, a festival of food and wine. ✉ *1 N. Kanikū Dr., Kohala Coast 96743,* ☎ *808/885–2000 or 800/845–9905,* FAX *808/885–1064. 593 rooms. 3 restaurants, pool, golf, tennis, health club, beach. AE, D, DC, MC, V.*

$$ **Waimea Country Lodge.** Rooms, all with kitchenettes, look out on the green pastures of the island's cool upcountry. ✉ *Box 2559, Kamuela 96743,* ☎ *808/885–4100,* FAX *808/885–6711. 21 rooms. AE, D, DC, MC, V.*

Nightlife

The hottest place on the island is the **Second Floor,** a disco at the Hilton Waikoloa Village, about half an hour from Kailua-Kona (✉ 425 Waikoloa Beach Dr., off Queen Ka'ahumanu Hwy., ☎ 808/886–1234). From Tuesday through Saturday you might be able to find some easy-listening jazz at the **Honu Bar,** in the Mauna Lani Bay Hotel and Bungalows (✉ 68-1400 Mauna Lani Dr., Kohala Coast, ☎ 808/885–6622).

In Hilo **Fiascos** (✉ 200 Kanoelehua Ave., Hilo, ☎ 808/935–7666) sometimes has live music. **D'Angoras Restaurant and Nightclub** (✉ Hilo Lagoon Center, 101 Aupuni St., ☎ 808/934–7888) serves reasonably priced dinners until the music starts at about 10 PM. There's swing music Sunday afternoons from 3 to 6.

Outdoor Activities and Sports

Camping and Hiking

Popular areas are the 13,796-ft **Mauna Kea,** in the northeast, and **Hawai'i Volcanoes National Park.** For more information contact the **Department of Parks and Recreation** (✉ 25 Aupuni St., Hilo 96740, ☎ 808/961–8311).

Fishing

More than 50 charter boats are available for hire, most of them out of Honokohau Harbor, just north of Kailua. For bookings call the **Kona Activities Center** (☎ 808/329–3171 or 800/367–5288).

Golf

On the Kohala Coast the **Mauna Kea Beach Resort** (✉ 1 Mauna Kea Beach Dr., ☎ 808/882–7222) has a well-regarded 18-hole course. The North and South courses of the **Francis I'i Brown Golf Course** (✉ Mauna Lani Resort, ☎ 808/885–6655) have 36 holes.

Sailing/Snorkeling

Captain Zodiac Raft Expedition (☎ 808/329–3199) offers a four-hour snorkel cruise off the Kona Coast. From January through April you may see humpback whales.

Scuba Diving

The Kona Coast has calm waters for diving. Outfitters include **Big Island Divers** (☎ 808/329–6068 or 800/488–6068). Many Kohala Coast resorts, such as Waikoloa Resort, hold scuba diving classes for guests.

Beaches

Onekahakaha Beach Park, a protected white-sand beach 3 mi south of Hilo, is a favorite of local families. Close to Kailua-Kona the most popular beach is **Kahalu'u Beach Park,** where the swimming, snorkeling, and fine facilities attract weekend crowds. Currents can pull swimmers away from the beach when the surf is high. On the Kohala Coast **Anaeho'omalu Beach** (☒ Royal Waikoloan Resort) is an expanse perfect for water sports. Instruction and equipment rentals are available at the north end. The long, white **Kauna'oa Beach** (☒ Mauna Kea Beach Resort) is one of the most beautiful on the island, but beware of the high surf that pounds the shore in winter. Amenities here are hotel owned. Between the Mauna Kea Beach and Mauna Lani resorts, **Hāpuna State Recreation Area** is a half-mile crescent of sand flanked by rocky points. The surf can be hazardous in winter, but calmer summer water makes it ideal for swimming, snorkeling, and scuba diving.

Shopping

Many talented artists seek out the solitude and beauty of the Big Island. Consequently, galleries abound in Kailua-Kona, Waimea, Holualoa, Volcano, Hilo and even in such-out-of the way bergs as Kukuihaele, where you can purchase original artwork, fine woodwork, or other handmade crafts. Kailua-Kona has souvenirs from far-flung corners of the globe. In general, major stores and shopping centers on the Big Island open at 9 or 9:30 AM and close by 4:30 or 5 PM. Hilo's **Prince Kūhiō Shopping Plaza** (☒ 111 E. Puainako, Hilo, ☎ 808/959–8451) has specialty boutiques and larger stores; it stays open until 9 on Thursday and Friday. In Kona, most of the stores at the **Kona Coast Shopping Center** (☒ Palani Rd.) are open daily 9–9, though the KTA Super Stores (☒ 74-5594 Palani Rd., ☎ 808/329–1677) outlet (a supermarket) is open from 6 AM to midnight. **Ali'i Drive** is lined with small shopping malls. On the makai side, extending an entire block, is **Kona Inn Shopping Village** (☒ 75-5744 Ali'i Dr., ☎ 808/329–6573.) Much of this shopping arcade was once Kona Inn, a hotel built in 1929 that was a longtime landmark. Broad lawns on the ocean side are lovely for afternoon picnics.

MAUI

Maui is known for its perfect beaches, lively nightlife, and sophisticated resorts. Presiding over everything—from the sunny active western Maui Gold Coast to laid-back Hāna, on the east side—is Haleakalā, the 10,023-ft dormant volcano whose peak is among the finest sunrise-viewing vantage points in the world.

Visitor Information

Maui Visitors Bureau (☒ 1727 Wili Pa Loop, Wailuku 96793, ☎ 808/244–3530).

Arriving and Departing

Maui's major airport, **Kahului Airport** (☎ 808/872–3800 or 808/372–3830), at the center of the island, is served by United, American, Delta, Hawaiian, and Aloha airlines. If you're staying in West Maui, you might be better off flying into **Kapalua–West Maui Airport** (☎ 808/669–0623), served by Aloha Airlines. The landing strip at **Hāna Airport** (☎ 808/248–8208) is served by Aloha Airlines.

Exploring Maui

West Maui

The road that follows the island's northwest coast passes through the beach towns of **Nāpili, Kahana,** and **Honokōwai,** which are all packed with condos and have a few restaurants. To the south is **Lahaina,** former capital of the islands and a 19th-century whaling town, where many old buildings have been renovated. On the ocean side of Lahaina's **Front Street** is a **banyan tree** planted in 1873 and the largest of its kind in Hawai'i. Docked at Lahaina Harbor is the brig ***Carthaginian II*** (☎ 808/661–3262; 🎫 $3), built in Germany in the 1920s and now open as a museum. Also worth a visit is the **Baldwin Home** (✉ 696 Front St., ☎ 808/661–3262; 🎫 $3), where missionary doctor Dwight Baldwin lived in the 1830s. The **Seamen's Hospital** (✉ 1024 Front St., ☎ 808/661–3262) was built in the 1830s for King Kamehameha III and later turned into a hospital.

Central Maui

Kahului is an industrial town that most tourists pass through on their way to the airport. The **Alexander & Baldwin Sugar Museum** (✉ 3957 Hansen Rd., Pu'unēnē, ☎ 808/871–8058; 🎫 $4), which details the rise of sugarcane in the Islands, is about 2 mi from Ka'ahumanu Avenue (Highway 32), Kahului's main street. A right onto Pu'unēnē Avenue (Hwy. 350) from Highway 32 will take you there. The museum is closed on Sunday.

Wailuku's Historical District centers on Main Street—drive out of Kahului on Kahumanu Avenue. **'Īao Valley State Park** is the home of 'Īao **Needle,** a 1,200-ft rock spire rising from the valley floor. Drive toward the mountains on Wailuku's Main Street to reach the park.

Haleakalā and Upcountry

Haleakalā, a 10,023-ft dormant volcano, is the font from which all of East Maui flowed and the centerpiece of a 27,284-acre national park—the terrain and views are unmatched anywhere else in the world. Bring a sweater or jacket since it's chilly at the top. From Kahului, drive on Haleakalā Highway (Highway 37) toward the volcano's slopes. Veer to the left at the fork of Highway 377. After about 6 mi make a left onto Haleakalā Crater Road, where the switchback ascent begins. You can stop and learn something of the volcano's origins and eruption history at the **Park Headquarters/Visitor Center,** at 7,000-ft elevation on Haleakalā Highway. Maps, posters, and other memorabilia are available at the gift shop here. **Haleakalā Visitor Center,** at 9,740-ft elevation, has exhibits inside and a trail that leads to a small crater nearby. The road ends at **Pu'u 'Ula'ula Overlook,** the highest point on Maui, where you'll find a glass-enclosed lookout. On a clear day you can see the islands of Moloka'i, Lāna'i, Kaho'olawe, and Hawai'i. Before you head up Haleakalā, call (☎ 808/871–5054) for the latest park weather conditions. ✉ *Haleakala Crater Rd. (Hwy. 378), Makawao,* ☎ *808/572–9306.* 🎫 *$10 per car.* ⏲ *Park headquarters and visitor center daily 7:30–4; Haleakalā visitor center daily sunrise–3.*

Upcountry, as the western slopes of Haleakalā are known, encompasses the fertile land responsible for much of Hawai'i's produce and flowers. Heading down from the volcano's summit on Highway 377, stop at **Kula Botanical Gardens** (✉ RR 2, Upper Kula Rd., Kula, ☎ 808/878–1715; 🎫 $4) to admire the tropical flora.

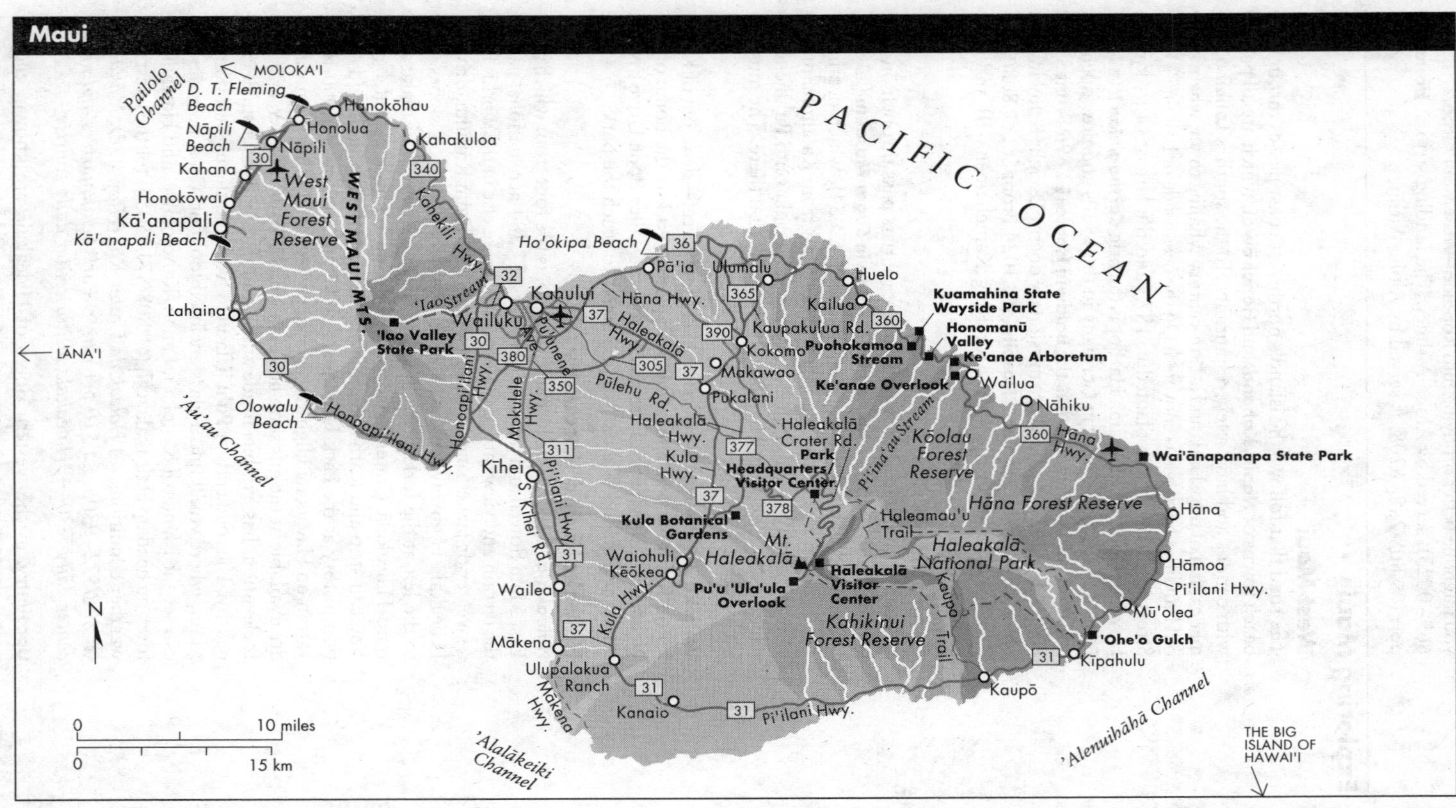

Maui
PACIFIC OCEAN
MOLOKA'I
LĀNA'I
THE BIG ISLAND OF HAWAI'I
Pailolo Channel
'Au'au Channel
'Alalākeiki Channel
'Alenuihāhā Channel
D. T. Fleming Beach
Hanokōhau
Honolua
Nāpili Beach
Nāpili
Kahana
Kahakuloa
Honokōwai
Kā'anapali
Kā'anapali Beach
West Maui Forest Reserve
WEST MAUI MTS.
Kahekili Hwy.
Lahaina
'Iao Valley State Park
'Iao Stream
Olowalu Beach
Honoapi'ilani Hwy.
Wailuku
Kahului
Pu'unene Ave.
Mokulele Hwy.
Kīhei
S. Kīhei Rd.
Pi'ilani Hwy
Wailea
Mākena
Ulupalakua Ranch
Mākena Hwy.
Kanaio
Ho'okipa Beach
Pā'ia
Ulumalu
Hāna Hwy.
Haleakalā Hwy.
Pūlehu Rd.
Haleakalā Hwy.
Kula Hwy.
Kaupakulua Rd.
Kokomo
Makawao
Pukalani
Haleakalā Crater Rd.
Park Headquarters/ Visitor Center
Kula Botanical Gardens
Waiohuli
Kēōkea
Kula Hwy.
Mt. Haleakalā
Pu'u 'Ula'ula Overlook
Haleakalā Visitor Center
Kahikinui Forest Reserve
Huelo
Kailua
Kuamahina State Wayside Park
Honomanū Valley
Puohokamoa Stream
Ke'anae Arboretum
Ke'anae Overlook
Wailua
Pi'ina'au Stream
Kōolau Forest Reserve
Nāhiku
Hāna Hwy.
Wai'ānapanapa State Park
Hāna Forest Reserve
Haleamau'u Trail
Haleakalā National Park
Kaupo Trail
Hāna
Hāmoa
Pi'ilani Hwy.
Mū'olea
'Ohe'o Gulch
Kīpahulu
Kaupō
Pi'ilani Hwy.
36
32
30
340
37
365
390
360
380
350
305
311
377
378
31
N
0
10 miles
0
15 km

East Maui

The **Road to Hāna** is 55 mi of hairpin turns and spectacular scenery. It begins in **Pā'ia** on the north coast and passes **Ho'okipa Beach.** At Mile Marker 11 stop at the bridge over **Puahokamoa Stream,** where there are pools, waterfalls, and picnic tables. Another mile takes you to **Kaumahina State Wayside Park,** which has a picnic area and a lovely overlook to the Keanae Peninsula. Past **Honomanū Valley,** with its 3,000-ft cliffs and a 1,000-ft waterfall, is the **Ke'anae Arboretum** (✉ Hāna Hwy., Mile Marker 17, Ke'anae; 🎫 free) devoted to native plants and trees. Nearby is the **Ke'anae Overlook,** with views of taro farms and the ocean; it's an excellent spot for photos. As you continue on toward Hāna, you'll pass **Wai'ānapanapa State Park** (✉ Hāna Hwy. near Mile Marker 32, Hāna, ☎ 808/248–8061; 🎫 free), which has state-run cabins and picnic areas.

Hāna is just down the road from Wai'ānapanapa State Park. **'Ohe'o Gulch** and its famous pools are about 10 mi past Hāna on a bumpy stretch of road called Pi'ilani Highway; swimming is hazardous here, but it's great for sunning and picture taking.

Dining and Lodging

Some of Maui's best restaurants are at resort hotels, which are mainly in West Maui.

For B&B accommodations contact **Bed & Breakfast Maui-Style** (✉ Box 98, Kīhei 96784, ☎ 808/879–7865 or 800/848–5567). For price ranges *see* Charts 1(A) and 2(A) *in* On the Road with Fodor's.

East Maui

$$$–$$$$ ★ ✕ **Hali'imaile General Store.** It was a camp store in the 1920s, and now its painted tin exterior looks a little out of place in an Upcountry pineapple field, but the classic cuisine here has become a Maui institution. Sample fine smoked duck with pineapple chutney or dynamite barbecued ribs. ✉ *900 Hali'imaile Rd., 2 mi north of Pukalani,* ☎ *808/572–2666. MC, V.*

$$$ ★ ✕ **A Pacific Cafe.** Kaua'i's superstar chef, Jean-Marie Josselin, serves up foods from lands bordering the Pacific: smoked and grilled island chicken with Thai black rice, pineapple, lemon-jalapeño marmalade, and green curry is one example. ✉ *Azeka Place II, Kīhei,* ☎ *808/879–0069. AE, DC, MC, V. No lunch.*

$$–$$$ ✕ **Makawao Steak House.** This Upcountry steak joint is arguably one of the best on the island—a tender New York strip goes for less than $25. The fresh fish and fresh-baked bread are just as good. ✉ *3612 Baldwin Ave.,* ☎ *808/572–8711. AE, D, DC, MC, V. No lunch.*

$$$$ ★ 🏨 **Four Seasons Resort.** Low-key elegance defines this stunning property with open-air public areas and access to one of Maui's best beaches. Nearly all rooms have ocean views and elegant marble bathrooms with high ceilings. ✉ *3900 Wailea Alanui, Wailea 96753,* ☎ *808/874–8000 or 800/334–6284,* FAX *808/874–6449. 380 rooms. 3 restaurants, pool, health club, beach. AE, D, DC, MC, V.*

$$$$ ★ 🏨 **Hotel Hāna-Maui.** One of the best places to stay in Hawai'i is this small, secluded Hāna hotel surrounded by a 7,000-acre ranch. Rooms have bleached-wood floors, overstuffed furniture in natural fabrics, and local art. ✉ *Box 9, Hāna 96713,* ☎ *808/248–8211 or 800/321–4262,* FAX *808/248–7264. 96 rooms. Restaurant, bar, pools, spa, tennis. AE, D, DC, MC, V.*

$$ 🏨 **Aloha Cottages.** Clean, two-bedroom units and one studio have kitchens and a view of papaya, banana, and avocado trees on the neighboring property. ✉ *Hāna 96713,* ☎ *808/248–8420. 4 cottages. No credit cards.*

West Maui

$$$–$$$$ ★ ✕ **Gerard's.** One of Hawai'i's most talented chefs, owner Gerard Reversade changes the French menu daily: You might find confit of duck or shiitake and oyster mushrooms in puff pastry. Prepare to do some stargazing, as this is a celebrity favorite. ✉ *Plantation Inn, 174 Lahainaluna Rd., Lahaina,* ☎ *808/661–8939. AE, D, DC, MC, V. No lunch.*

$$$ ★ ✕ **Avalon.** Signature items at this trendy locale include shrimp with shiitake mushrooms and sun-dried tomatoes; and whole *'ōpakapaka* (snapper) in garlic and black bean sauce—not to mention its "new wave" sushi bar. ✉ *Mariner's Alley, 844 Front St., Lahaina,* ☎ *808/667–5559. AE, D, DC, MC, V.*

$$–$$$ ★ ✕ **Lahaina Coolers.** This breezy little café with a surfboard hanging from its ceiling serves up such tantalizing fare as shrimp-pesto linguine with prawns, basil, garlic, and cream, plus pizzas, steaks, and burgers. For dessert, try a chocolate taco filled with tropical fruit and berry "salsa." ✉ *180 Dickenson St., Lahaina,* ☎ *808/661–7082. AE, MC, V.*

$$ ✕🏨 **Lahaina Hotel.** The 12 rooms here have antique beds and wardrobes, and country-print curtains and spreads. Downstairs is the trendy David Paul's Lahaina Grill. ✉ *127 Lahainaluna Rd., Lahaina 96761,* ☎ *808/661–0577 or 800/669–3444,* FAX *808/667–9480. 12 rooms. Restaurant. AE, D, MC, V.*

$$$$ ★ 🏨 **Kapalua Bay Hotel.** Flowering vanda and dendrobium orchids fill the lobby of this resort hotel, with a fine view of the ocean beyond. Rooms are spacious and appealing. ✉ *1 Bay Dr., Kapalua 96761,* ☎ *808/669–5656 or 800/367–8000,* FAX *808/669–4694. 194 rooms, 135 condo units. 3 restaurants, pools, tennis, beach. AE, D, DC, MC, V.*

$$$$ ★ 🏨 **Ritz-Carlton.** This quietly luxurious Kapula resort has spacious, comfortable rooms with oversize marble bathrooms and individual lānai, most with panoramic ocean views. Service and business facilities are first rate.✉ *1 Ritz-Carlton Dr., Kapalua,* ☎ *808/669–6200 or 800/262–8440,* FAX *808/669–3908. 550 rooms. 4 restaurants, pool, golf, tennis, health club. AE, D, DC, MC, V.*

Nightlife

The best options are in resort areas and Lahaina. **Moose McGillycuddy's** (✉ 844 Front St., Lahaina, ☎ 808/667–7758) has live music Tuesday and Thursday evenings. **Molokini Lounge** (✉ Maui Prince Hotel, Mākena Resort, ☎ 808/874–1111) is a pleasant bar with live Hawaiian music, a dance floor, and an ocean view. The best lū'au on Maui is the **Old Lahaina Lū'au** (✉ 1251 Front St., Lahaina, ☎ 808/667–1998), performed daily from 5:30 to 8:30.

Outdoor Activities and Sports

Golf

Maui's major resorts all have golf courses, and all are open to the public. Most lower their greens fees after 2:30 on weekday afternoons. **Kapalua Golf Club** (✉ 300 Kapalua Dr., Kapalua, ☎ 808/669–8044) has three 18-holers. **Kā'anapali Golf Courses** (✉ Kā'anapali Beach Resort, Kā'anapali, ☎ 808/661–3691) are two of Maui's most famous.The **Wailea Golf Club** (✉ 100 Wailea Golf Club Dr., Wailea, ☎ 808/875–5111) has three courses.

Fees are lower at Maui's municipal courses such as **Waiehu Municipal Golf Course** (✉ Off Hwy. 340 in West Maui, ☎ 808/244–5934), on the northeast coast, a few miles past Wailuku.

Tennis

The finest facilities are at the **Wailea Tennis Club** (✉ 131 Wailea Ike Pl., Kīhei, ☎ 808/879–1958), often called Wimbledon West because of its grass courts.

Water Sports

Fishing. You can fish year-round in Maui for such catch as Pacific blue marlin and wahoo. Plenty of fishing boats run out of Lahaina and Mā'alaea harbors, including those from **Lucky Strike Charters** (✉ Box 1502, Lahaina 96767, ☎ 808/661–4606).

Sailing, Snorkeling, and Scuba Diving. Many outfitters provide combination sailing and snorkeling cruises or scuba expeditions; some also have whale-watching expeditions and sunset cruises. Call **Ocean Activities Center** (✉ 1325 S. Kīhei Rd., Kīhei, ☎ 808/879–4485); **Trilogy Excursions** (✉ 180 Lahainaluna Rd., Lahaina, ☎ 808/661–4743 or 800/874–2666); or **Maui–Moloka'i Sea Cruises** (✉ 831 Eha St., Wailuku , ☎ 808/242–8777).

Surfing. Although on land it may not look as if there are seasons on Maui, the tides tell another story. In winter the surf is up on the northern shores of the Hawaiian Islands, while summer brings big swells to the southern side. You can rent surfboards and boogie boards at many surf shops, such as **Second Wind** (✉ 111 Hāna Hwy., Kahului, ☎ 808/877–7467), **Lightning Bolt Maui** (✉ 55 Ka'ahumanu Ave., Kahului, ☎ 808/877–3484), and **Ole Surfboards** (✉ 277 Wili Ko Pl., Lahaina, ☎ 808/661–3459).

Whale-Watching. Quite a few operations run whale-watching excursions off the coast of Maui, with many boats departing from the wharves at Lahaina and Ma'alaea each day. **Pacific Whale Foundation** (✉ Kealia Beach Plaza, 101 N. Kīhei Rd., Kīhei 96753, ☎ 808/879–8811) pioneered whale-watching back in 1979 and now runs four boats, plus sea kayaks and special trips to encounter turtles and dolphins.

Windsurfing. Ho'okipa Bay, 10 mi east of Kahului, is the windsurfing capital of the world. Rent a board or take lessons from **Kā'anapali Windsurfing School** (✉ 104 Wahikuli Rd., Lahaina, ☎ 808/667–1964).

Beaches

If you start at the northern end of West Maui and work your way down the coast, you'll find many beaches. **D. T. Fleming Beach,** 1 mi north of Kapalua, is a sandy cove better for sunbathing than swimming. **Nāpili Beach,** a secluded crescent, is right outside the Nāpili Kai Beach Club. **Kā'anapali Beach** is best for people-watching; cruises, windsurfers, and parasails launch from here. Farther south of Kā'anapali are **Wailea**'s five crescent-shape beaches, which stretch for nearly 2 mi with little interruption. South of Wailea are **Big Beach,** a 3,000-ft-long, 100-ft-wide strand, and **Little Beach,** popular for nude sunbathing (officially illegal here).

Shopping

You can have fun browsing through the stores of Front Street in Lahaina or the boutiques in the major hotels. Maui also has several major shopping malls. **Ka'ahumanu Center** (✉ 275 Ka'ahumanu Ave., Kahului, ☎ 808/877–3369) has nearly 100 shops and restaurants. Also in Kahului is the **Maui Mall Shopping Center** (✉ Corner of Ka'ahumanu and Pu'unēnē Aves., ☎ 808/877–7559), with 33 stores. **Whalers Village** (✉ 2435 Kā'anapali Pkwy., Kā'anapali, ☎ 808/661–4567) in the Kā'anapali resort area has good restaurants and upscale boutiques such as Tiffany & Co. and Prada.

KAUA'I

Kaua'i's natural beauty is amazingly diverse. The cooler, damper north shore has lush landscaping, mist-shrouded peaks, and world-class golf courses; the southern shore has the sunshine; and the west coast is home to two geologic wonders: Waimea Canyon—the Grand Canyon of the Pacific—and the Nā Pali Coast.

Visitor Information

Hawai'i Visitors and Convention Bureau (✉ 3016 Umi St., Suite 207, Līhu'e 96766, ☎ 808/245–3971). **Kaua'i Visitor Center** (✉ Coconut Plantation Marketplace, Kapa'a 96746, ☎ 808/822–5113; ✉ Kaua'i Village, Kapa'a 96746, ☎ 808/822–7727).

Arriving and Departing

Līhu'e Airport (☎ 808/246–1400), 3 mi east of the county seat of Līhu'e, handles most of Kaua'i's air traffic; it is served by Aloha and Hawaiian.

Exploring Kaua'i

A coastal road runs around the rim of Kaua'i and dead-ends on either side of the rugged Nā Pali Coast. If you're looking for sunshine, head to the southern resort of Po'ipū; for greener scenery and a wetter climate, try Hanalei and Princeville to the north. For a bird's-eye view of the whole island, consider a helicopter excursion.

The Road North

Kīlauea Lighthouse (☎ 808/828–1413), built in 1913, is now part of a wildlife refuge near the former plantation town of Kīlauea, north of Wailua on Highway 56. The **Hanalei Valley Overlook** encompasses a view of more than a half mile of taro, the staple plant of the Hawaiian diet, plus a 900-acre endangered-waterfowl refuge. **Hanalei** is the site of the **Waioli Mission** (✉ Kūhiō Hwy., ☎ 808/245–3202), founded by Christian missionaries in 1837.

Smith's Tropical Paradise (✉ 174 Wailua Rd., Kapa'a, ☎ 808/822–4654) is a 30-acre expanse of jungle, exotic foliage, tropical birds, and lagoons. From Wailua Marina, on the east coast, boats cruise up Wailua River to **Fern Grotto** (✉ Smith's Motor Boat Service, 174 Wailua Rd., Kapa'a, ☎ 808/821–6892; 🎟 $15), a yawning lava tube with enormous fishtail ferns.

To the South and West

Kaua'i Museum (✉ 4428 Rice St., Līhu'e, ☎ 808/245–6931; 🎟 $5) is chock-full of exhibits about the island's history. **Kilohana** (✉ 3–2087 Kaumuali'i Hwy., ☎ 808/245–5608; 🎟 free), a historic sugar plantation, is now a 35-acre visitor attraction. **Po'ipū** is the premiere resort town of Kaua'i's south shore and a mecca for body surfers. **Spouting Horn,** a waterspout that shoots up through an ancient lava tube, lies just west of Po'ipū along Highway 52.

Waimea, a sleepy little town, marks the first landfall of British captain James Cook to the Sandwich Islands in 1778. **Waimea Canyon,** created by an ancient fault in the earth's crust, stretches inland from Waimea. The canyon, 3,600 ft deep, 2 mi wide, and 10 mi long, is known as the Grand Canyon of the Pacific. Waimea Canyon Drive passes through **Kōke'e State Park** (☎ 808/335–5871), a 4,345-acre wilderness. The drive ends 4 mi above the park at the 4,120-ft **Kalalau Lookout,** the best viewpoint in Kaua'i.

For a flightseeing adventure you won't easily forget—the rugged splendor of the Nā Pali Coast or the hidden waterfalls of Waimea Canyon—call the **South Sea Tour Company** (✉ Main Terminal, Līhu'e Airport, ☎ 808/245–2222 or 800/367–9214). The spectacular Nā Pali Coast is not accessible by land, so this may be your best way to have a good look.

Dining and Lodging

For an insider's look at Kaua'i, book with **Bed & Breakfast Hawai'i** (✉ Box 449, Kapa'a 96746, ☎ 808/822–7771 or 800/733–1632). For price ranges *see* Charts 1(A) and 2(A) *in* On the Road with Fodor's.

East and North Kaua'i

$$$–$$$$ ✕ **La Cascata.** Terra-cotta floors and trompe l'oeil paintings give the restaurant the feel of an Italian villa, an influence that shows up in the cuisine as well: Grilled Hawaiian swordfish with balsamic vinegar and pancetta has a southern Italian flair. ✉ *Princeville Hotel, Princeville,* ☎ *808/826–9644. Reservations essential. Jacket required. AE, D, DC, MC, V. No lunch.*

$$$ ★ ✕ **A Pacific Cafe.** With its cutting-edge cuisine, chef Jean-Marie Josselin's restaurant has won many awards. The daily-changing menu might include grilled moonfish with black-olive polenta, sundried tomatoes, pancetta, and shiitake mushrooms; or lamb with a cabernet-hoisin sauce and fried, grated potatoes. The macadamia-nut torte is topped with toasted coconut; and the crème brûlée, a huge portion served in a pastry shell, is tops. ✉ *Kaua'i Village Shopping Center, Hwy. 56, Kapa'a,* ☎ *808/822–0013. AE, D, DC, MC, V. No lunch.*

$$–$$$ ★ ✕ **Roy's Po'ipū Bar & Grill.** Hawai'i's culinary superstar Roy Yamaguchi serves first-rate Euro-Asian-Pacific cuisine. Who but Roy could team fresh seared 'ōpakapaka with orange shrimp butter and Chinese black-bean sauce? ✉ *Po'ipū Shopping Village, 2360 Kiahuna Plantation Dr., Po'ipū Beach,* ☎ *808/742–5000. AE, D, DC, MC, V.*

$$ ✕ **Bull Shed.** This A-frame restaurant is rustic, with exposed wood, ocean views, and family-style tables. Alaskan king crab and prime rib are on the menu. ✉ *796 Kūhiō Ave., Kapa'a,* ☎ *808/822–3791. AE, D, DC, MC, V. No lunch.*

$$$$ ★ 🏨 **Princeville Hotel.** This splendid cliff-side property has breathtaking views of Hanalei Bay. Bathrooms have gold-plated fixtures and picture windows that cloud up for privacy at the flick of a switch. The setting and service are unmatched. ✉ *Box 3069, Princeville 96722,* ☎ *808/826–9644 or 800/826–4400,* FAX *808/826–1166. 252 rooms. 3 restaurants, pool, golf courses, tennis. AE, D, DC, MC, V.*

$$ 🏨 **Kapa'a Sands.** Furnishings in this intimate condominium are bungalow style, with rustic wood and ceiling fans. Ask for an oceanfront room with open-air lānai and Pacific views. ✉ *380 Papaloa Rd., Kapa'a 96746,* ☎ *808/822–4901 or 800/222–4901. 21 units. Kitchenettes, pool. AE, D, DC, MC, V.*

South and West

$$$ ★ ✕ **Beach House.** This may be the best ocean view from any restaurant on the south shore. The cuisine is equally superlative: The menu changes often, but you might find grilled salmon with spinach won-ton and shrimp-tomato broth; or grilled Black Angus fillet with tumbleweed shrimp and port-Gorgonzola sauce. ✉ *5022 Lawai Rd., Kōloa,* ☎ *808/742–1424. AE, D, DC, MC, V. No lunch.*

$$–$$$ ✕ **Brennecke's Beach Broiler.** At this veteran restaurant with picture windows overlooking the ocean, the chef specializes in mesquite-broiled foods and homemade desserts. ✉ *Hoone Rd., Po'ipū,* ☎ *808/742–7588. AE, MC, V.*

$-$$$ ★ ✕ **Green Garden.** In business since 1948, this family-run no-frills restaurant is brightened by an assortment of hanging and standing plants. Local fare includes breaded mahimahi fillet and passion-fruit chiffon pie. ✉ *Hwy. 50, Hanapēpē,* ☎ *808/335–5422. AE, D, DC, MC, V. Closed Tues.*

$$$$ ★ 🏨 **Hyatt Regency Kaua'i.** Low-rise, plantation-style architecture with dramatic open-air courtyards, lush tropical landscaping, and spectacular rock-enclosed swimming lagoons make this the most Hawaiian of Hyatts—and one of the most striking hotel resorts anywhere. Two-thirds of the rooms have ocean views. The 25,000-square-ft spa is first-rate. ✉ *1571 Po'ipū Rd., Koloa 96756,* ☎ *808/742–1234 or 800/233–1234,* FAX *808/742–6229. 600 rooms. 4 restaurants, pools, spa, golf, tennis, beach. AE, D, DC, MC, V.*

$$$ 🏨 **Garden Isle Cottages.** Tropical flower gardens surround these spacious oceanside cottages five minutes from the restaurants of Po'ipū. There are no telephones, but some have kitchens. One of the cottages, Hale Waipahu, sits on the highest point in Po'ipū, with a 360-degree ocean vista that takes in Brennecke's Beach. Six units have kitchens with microwaves, ceiling fans, and a washer and dryer. There's also a barbecue area. ✉ *2666 Pu'uholo Rd., Kōloa 96756,* ☎ *808/742–6717 or 800/742–6711. 9 cottages. No credit cards.*

$ ★ 🏨 **Kōke'e Lodge.** Twelve mountaintop cabins are surrounded by pine trees and hiking trails. Furnishings are rustic (prices vary according to quality), but each is cozy, with a fireplace and fully equipped kitchen. ✉ *Box 819, Waimea 96796,* ☎ *808/335–6061. 12 cabins. Restaurant. AE, MC, V.*

Nightlife

Locals enjoy **Kūhiō's Nightclub** (✉ Hyatt Regency Kaua'i, ☎ 808/742–1234), a south-shore hot spot. **Legends Nightclub** (✉ Pacific Ocean Plaza, 3501 Rice St., 2nd floor, Nawiliwili, ☎ 808/245–5775) delivers Top-40 tunes in a garden setting. Of Kaua'i's lū'au options, **Kaua'i Coconut Beach Resort Lū'au** (✉ Coconut Plantation, Kapa'a, ☎ 808/822–3455, ext. 651) is regarded by many as the best on the island.

Outdoor Activities and Sports

Fishing

For deep-sea fishing, **Sportfishing Kaua'i** (✉ Box 1195, Koloa, ☎ 808/742–7013) has a 28-ft, six-passenger custom sportfisher.

Golf

Best known are the Makai and Prince courses at **Princeville Resort** (✉ Princeville, ☎ 808/826–3580).

Hiking

Kōke'e State Park has 45 mi of hiking trails. The **Department of Land and Natural Resources** (✉ Līhu'e, ☎ 808/241–3444) provides hiking information.

Snorkeling and Scuba Diving

Explore spectacular underwater reefs with **Dive Kaua'i** (✉ 4–976 Kūhiō Hwy., Suite 4, Kapa'a, ☎ 808/822–0452). **Hanalei Sea Tours** (✉ Box 1437, Hanalei, ☎ 808/826–7254) has a four-hour snorkeling cruise off the Nā Pali coast.

Tennis

Princeville Tennis Center (✉ Box 3040, Princeville 96722, ☎ 808/826–9823) has six courts.

Beaches

The waters that hug Kaua'i are clean, clear, and inviting, but be careful where you go in: The south shore sees higher surf in the summer, and north-shore waters are treacherous in winter.

North Shore

On the winding section of Highway 56 west of Hanalei is **Lumahai Beach,** flanked by high mountains and lava rocks. There are no lifeguards here, so swim only in summer. **Hanalei Beach Park** has views of the Nā Pali coast and shaded picnic tables, but swimming here can be treacherous. Near the end of Highway 56, **Ha'ēna State Park** is good for swimming when the surf is down in summer. Highway 56 dead-ends at **Kē'ē Beach,** a fine swimming beach in summer.

South and West Shores

Kalapak Beach, a sheltered bay ideal for water sports, fronts the Marriott in Līhu'e. Small- to medium-size waves make **Brennecke's Beach** in Po'ipū a bodysurfer's heaven, and there are showers, rest rooms, and lifeguards. At the end of Highway 50W is **Polihale Beach Park,** a long, wide strand flanked by huge cliffs. Swim here only when the surf is small; there are no lifeguards.

Shopping

In Līhu'e is **Kukui Grove Center** (✉ 3–2600 Kaumuali'i Hwy., ☎ 808/245–7784), Kaua'i's largest mall. **Coconut Plantation Marketplace** (✉ 4–484 Kūhiō Hwy., Kapa'a, ☎ 808/822–3641) is a standout among east-coast malls. **Kaua'i Village** (✉ 4–831 Kūhiō Hwy., Kapa'a, ☎ 808/822–4904) has 19th-century plantation-style architecture and 25 shops. **Princeville Center** (✉ 5–4280 Kūhiō Hwy., Kapa'a, ☎ 808/826–3040), in the north end of the island, has interesting shops.

ELSEWHERE IN HAWAI'I

Moloka'i

With its slow pace and emphasis on Hawaiiana, Moloka'i drowses in another era. There are no high-rises, no traffic jams, and no stoplights on the 10-by-38-mi island. The fanciest hotels are bungalow style, and there's plenty of undeveloped countryside.

Visitor Information

Moloka'i Visitors Association (✉ Box 960, Kaunakakai 96748, ☎ 808/553–3876 or 800/800–6367). **Maui Visitors Bureau** (✉ 1727 Wili Pa Loop, Wailuku, Maui 96793, ☎ 808/244–3530).

Arriving and Departing

Ho'olehua Airport (☎ 808/567–6140), a tiny strip just west of central Moloka'i, is served by Hawaiian, Aloha, and Moloka'i airlines.

What to See and Do

The **Meyer Sugar Mill** (✉ Rte. 470, 2 mi southwest of Pālā'au State Park, Kala'e, ☎ 808/567–6436; 🎫 $3.50) was built in 1878 and reconstructed to teach visitors about sugar's importance to the local economy. It's closed on Sunday.

Kalaupapa National Historic Park (✉ Box 222, Moloka'i 96742, ☎ 808/567–6102) was a leper colony until 1888. The pretty little town is now a National Historic Landmark. It's most accessible via **Damien Tours** (☎ 808/567–6171) or **Moloka'i Mule Ride** (✉ 100 Kala'e Hwy., Kualapu'u 96757, ☎ 808/567–6088).

Lāna'i

Visitor Information

For visitor information contact **Destination Lāna'i** (✉ Box 700, Lāna'i City 96763, ☏ 808/565–7600).

Arriving and Departing

Hawaiian and **Aloha** airlines serve this tiny island, whose airport (☏ 808/565–6757) is a 10-minute drive from Lāna'i City.

What to See and Do

For decades Lāna'i was known as the Pineapple Island, with hundreds of acres devoted to growing the golden fruit. Today this 140-square-mi island has been dubbed Hawai'i's Private Island, as developers replace pineapples with people. There are now two upscale hotels and two championship golf courses, but despite these additions, Lāna'i—the third smallest of the islands—remains remote.

Lāna'i is for those who love the outdoors, because the island has no commercial attractions other than those offered at the two resorts. You can visit such sights as the **Garden of the Gods,** where rocks and boulders are scattered across a crimson landscape; spend a leisurely day at **Hulopo'e Beach,** where the waters are brilliantly blue and clear; or hike or drive to the top of **Lāna'ihale,** a 3,370-ft perch with a view of every inhabited Hawaiian island except Kaua'i and Ni'ihau.

INDEX

A

B

G

I

J

K

NOTES

NOTES

NOTES

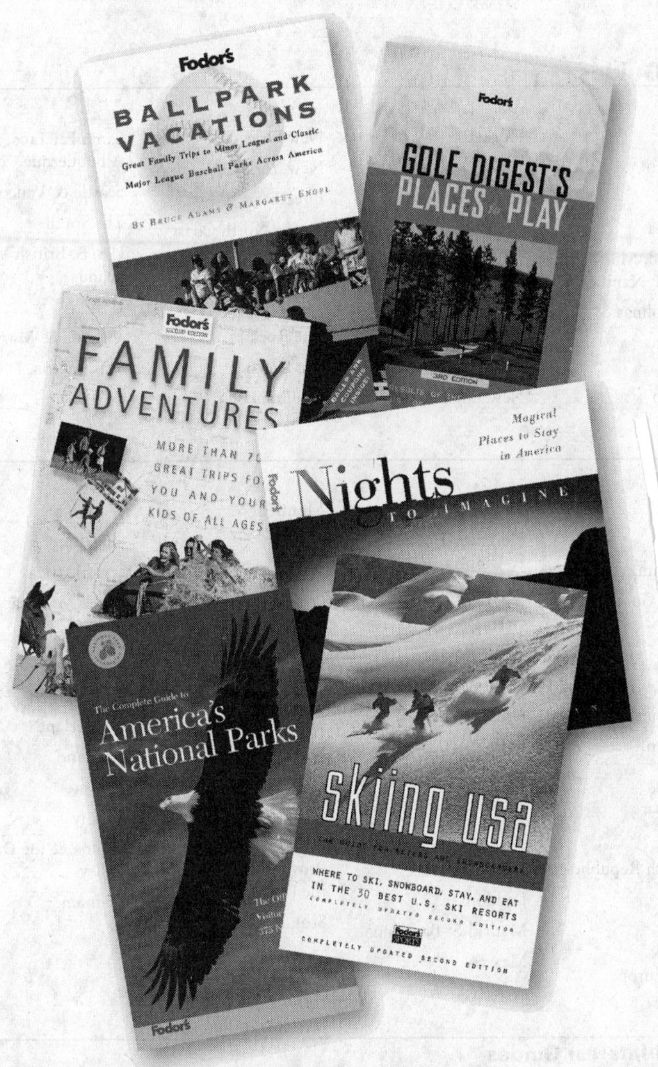
Fodor's
BALLPARK VACATIONS
Great Family Trips to Minor League and Classic Major League Baseball Parks Across America
By Bruce Adams & Margaret Engel
Fodor's
GOLF DIGEST'S PLACES to PLAY
3RD EDITION
Fodor's
FAMILY ADVENTURES
MORE THAN 70 GREAT TRIPS FOR YOU AND YOUR KIDS OF ALL AGES
Magical Places to Stay in America
Nights TO IMAGINE
The Complete Guide to America's National Parks
Fodor's
Skiing USA
WHERE TO SKI, SNOWBOARD, STAY, AND EAT IN THE 30 BEST U.S. SKI RESORTS
COMPLETELY UPDATED SECOND EDITION

Fodor's Travel Publications

Available at bookstores everywhere. For descriptions of all our titles, a key to Fodor's guidebook series, and on-line ordering, visit http://www.fodors.com/books/

Gold Guides

U.S.

Alaska
Arizona
Boston
California
Cape Cod, Martha's Vineyard, Nantucket
The Carolinas & Georgia
Chicago
Colorado
Florida
Hawai'i
Las Vegas, Reno, Tahoe
Los Angeles
Maine, Vermont, New Hampshire
Maui & Lāna'i
Miami & the Keys
New England
New Orleans
New York City
Oregon
Pacific North Coast
Philadelphia & the Pennsylvania Dutch Country
The Rockies
San Diego
San Francisco
Santa Fe, Taos, Albuquerque
Seattle & Vancouver
The South
U.S. & British Virgin Islands
USA
Virginia & Maryland
Washington, D.C.

Foreign

Australia
Austria
The Bahamas
Belize & Guatemala
Bermuda
Canada
Cancún, Cozumel, Yucatán Peninsula
Caribbean
China
Costa Rica
Cuba
The Czech Republic & Slovakia
Denmark
Eastern & Central Europe
Europe
Florence, Tuscany & Umbria
France
Germany
Great Britain
Greece
Hong Kong
India
Ireland
Israel
Italy
Japan
London
Madrid & Barcelona
Mexico
Montréal & Québec City
Moscow, St. Petersburg, Kiev
The Netherlands, Belgium & Luxembourg
New Zealand
Norway
Nova Scotia, New Brunswick, Prince Edward Island
Paris
Portugal
Provence & the Riviera
Scandinavia
Scotland
Singapore
South Africa
South America
Southeast Asia
Spain
Sweden
Switzerland
Thailand
Toronto
Turkey
Vienna & the Danube Valley
Vietnam

Special-Interest Guides

Adventures to Imagine
Alaska Ports of Call
Ballpark Vacations
The Best Cruises
Caribbean Ports of Call
The Complete Guide to America's National Parks
Europe Ports of Call
Family Adventures
Fodor's Gay Guide to the USA
Fodor's How to Pack
Great American Learning Vacations
Great American Sports & Adventure Vacations
Great American Vacations
Great American Vacations for Travelers with Disabilities
Halliday's New Orleans Food Explorer
Healthy Escapes
Kodak Guide to Shooting Great Travel Pictures
National Parks and Seashores of the East
National Parks of the West
Nights to Imagine
Orlando Like a Pro
Rock & Roll Traveler Great Britain and Ireland
Rock & Roll Traveler USA
Sunday in San Francisco
Walt Disney World for Adults
Weekends in New York
Wendy Perrin's Secrets Every Smart Traveler Should Know
Worlds to Imagine

Fodor's Special Series

Fodor's Best Bed & Breakfasts

America
California
The Mid-Atlantic
New England
The Pacific Northwest
The South
The Southwest
The Upper Great Lakes

Compass American Guides

Alaska
Arizona
Boston
Chicago
Coastal California
Colorado
Florida
Hawai'i
Hollywood
Idaho
Las Vegas
Maine
Manhattan
Minnesota
Montana
New Mexico
New Orleans
Oregon
Pacific Northwest
San Francisco
Santa Fe
South Carolina
South Dakota
Southwest
Texas
Underwater Wonders of the National Parks
Utah
Virginia
Washington
Wine Country
Wisconsin
Wyoming

Citypacks

Amsterdam
Atlanta
Berlin
Boston
Chicago
Florence
Hong Kong
London
Los Angeles
Miami
Montréal
New York City
Paris
Prague
Rome
San Francisco
Sydney
Tokyo
Toronto
Venice
Washington, D.C.

Exploring Guides

Australia
Boston & New England
Britain
California
Canada
Caribbean
China
Costa Rica
Cuba
Egypt
Florence & Tuscany
Florida
France
Germany
Greek Islands
Hawai'i
India
Ireland
Israel
Italy
Japan
London
Mexico
Moscow & St. Petersburg
New York City
Paris
Portugal
Prague
Provence
Rome
San Francisco
Scotland
Singapore & Malaysia
South Africa
Spain
Thailand
Turkey
Venice
Vietnam

Flashmaps

Boston
New York
San Francisco
Washington, D.C.

Fodor's Cityguides

Boston
New York
San Francisco

Fodor's Gay Guides

Amsterdam
Los Angeles & Southern California
New York City
Pacific Northwest
San Francisco and the Bay Area
South Florida
USA

Karen Brown Guides

Austria
California
England B&Bs
England, Wales & Scotland
France B&Bs
France Inns
Germany
Ireland
Italy B&Bs
Italy Inns
Portugal
Spain
Switzerland

Pocket Guides

Acapulco
Aruba
Atlanta
Barbados
Beijing
Berlin
Budapest
Dublin
Honolulu
Jamaica
London
Mexico City
New York City
Paris
Prague
Puerto Rico
Rome
San Francisco
Savannah & Charleston
Shanghai
Sydney
Washington, D.C.

Languages for Travelers (Cassette & Phrasebook)

French
German
Italian
Spanish

Mobil Travel Guides

America's Best Hotels & Restaurants
Arizona
California and the West
Florida
Great Lakes
Major Cities
Mid-Atlantic
Northeast
Northwest and Great Plains
Southeast
Southern California
Southwest and South Central

Rivages Guides

Bed and Breakfasts of Character and Charm in France
Hotels and Country Inns of Character and Charm in France
Hotels and Country Inns of Character and Charm in Italy
Hotels and Country Inns of Character and Charm in Paris
Hotels and Country Inns of Character and Charm in Portugal
Hotels and Country Inns of Character and Charm in Spain
Wines & Vineyards of Character and Charm in France

Short Escapes

Britain
France
Near New York City
New England

Fodor's Sports

Golf Digest's Places to Play (USA)
Golf Digest's Places to Play in the Southeast
Golf Digest's Places to Play in the Southwest
Skiing USA
USA Today The Complete Four Sport Stadium Guide

Fodor's upCLOSE Guides

California
Europe
France
Great Britain
Ireland
Italy
London
Los Angeles
Mexico
New York City
Paris
San Francisco